CURRENT LAW STATUTES ANNOTATED

1979

AUSTRALIA
The Law Book Co. Ltd.
Sydney : Melbourne : Brisbane

CANADA AND U.S.A.
The Carswell Company Ltd.
Agincourt, Ontario

INDIA
N. M. Tripathi Private Ltd.
Bombay

ISRAEL
Steimatzky's Agency Ltd.
Jerusalem : Tel Aviv : Haifa

MALAYSIA : SINGAPORE : BRUNEI
Malayan Law Journal (Pte.) Ltd.
Singapore

NEW ZEALAND
Sweet & Maxwell (N.Z.) Ltd.
Wellington

PAKISTAN
Pakistan Law House
Karachi

CURRENT LAW
STATUTES
ANNOTATED
1979

GENERAL EDITOR

PETER ALLSOP, M.A.
Barrister

ASSISTANT GENERAL EDITOR

KATHRYN FITZHENRY, B.A., LL.B.

LONDON

SWEET & MAXWELL STEVENS & SONS

EDINBURGH

W. GREEN & SON

1979

Published by
SWEET & MAXWELL LIMITED
and STEVENS & SONS LIMITED
of 11 New Fetter Lane, London,
and W. GREEN & SON LIMITED
of St. Giles Street, Edinburgh,
and printed in Great Britain by
The Eastern Press Limited
London and Reading

ISBN 0 421 26900 6

CONTENTS

CHRONOLOGICAL TABLE

STATUTES

c. 1. Price Commission (Amendment) Act 1979.
2. Customs and Excise Management Act 1979.
3. Customs and Excise Duties (General Reliefs) Act 1979.
4. Alcoholic Liquor Duties Act 1979.
5. Hydrocarbon Oil Duties Act 1979.
6. Matches and Mechanical Lighters Duties Act 1979.
7. Tobacco Products Duty Act 1979.
8. Excise Duties (Surcharges or Rebates) Act 1979.
9. Films Act 1979.
10. Public Lending Right Act 1979.
11. Electricity (Scotland) Act 1979.
12. Wages Councils Act 1979.
13. Agricultural Statistics Act 1979.
14. Capital Gains Tax Act 1979.
15. House of Commons (Redistribution of Seats) Act 1979.
16. Criminal Evidence Act 1979.
17. Vaccine Damage Payments Act 1979.
18. Social Security Act 1979.
19. Administration of Justice (Emergency Provisions) (Scotland) Act 1979.
20. Consolidated Fund Act 1979.
21. Forestry Act 1979.
22. Confirmation to Small Estates (Scotland) Act 1979.
23. Public Health Laboratory Service Act 1979.
24. Appropriation Act 1979.
25. Finance Act 1979.
26. Legal Aid Act 1979.
27. Kiribati Act 1979.
28. Carriage by Air and Road Act 1979.
29. International Monetary Fund Act 1979.
30. Exchange Equalisation Account Act 1979.
31. Prosecution of Offences Act 1979.
32. Industry Act 1979.

Contents

INDEX OF SHORT TITLES

References are to chapter numbers of 1979

"CURRENT LAW"
STATUTE CITATOR 1979

This edition of the "Current Law" Statute Citator 1979 is a Noter-up to the Statute Book for the period January to December 31, 1979. It comprises in a single table:

(i) Statutes passed;
(ii) Statutory Instruments issued under rule-making powers;
(iii) Cases on the construction of statutes; and
(iv) Statutes repealed and amended.
(S.) Amendments relating to Scotland only.
(*) Duplication.

Acts of the Parliaments of England, Great Britain and the United Kingdom

CAP.

25 Edw. 3 St. 5 (1351)

5. repealed: order 79/1575.

35 Edw. 3 (1361)

1. Justices of the Peace Act 1361.
see *Goodlad* v. *Chief Constable of South Yorkshire* [1979] Crim.L.R. 51, Sheffield Crown Ct.

10 Eliz. 1 (1567)

14. Incest Act 1567.
see *Vaughan* v. *H.M. Advocate*, 1979 S.L.T. 49.

19 Jac. (1621)

18. Bankruptcy Act 1621.
see *McManus's Trustee* v. *McManus* (O.H.), 1979 S.L.T.(Notes) 71.

5 Will. & Mar. (1693)

22. Real Rights Act 1693.
repealed in pt.: 1979,c.33,sch.4.

23. Register of Sasines Act 1693.
repealed in pt.: 1979,c.33,sch.4.

7 & 8 Will. 3 (1695)

12. Statute of Frauds (Ireland) 1695 (Eire).
see *Kelly* v. *Park Hall Schools* (1978) 111 I.L.T.R. 9, Eire Sup.Ct.

16 Geo. 2 (1742)

18. Justices Jurisdiction Act 1742.
repealed: 1979,c.55,sch.3.

54 Geo. 3 (1814)

123. Hop Trade Act 1814.
repealed: regs. 79/1095.

55 Geo. 3 (1815)

94. Herring Fishery (Scotland) Act 1815.
s. 13, repealed: 1979,c.45,sch.7.

CAP.

2 & 3 Will. 4 (1832)

71. Prescription Act 1832.
s. 3, see *Allen* v. *Greenwood* [1979] 2 W.L.R. 187, C.A.

3 & 4 Will. 4 (1833)

41. Judicial Committee Act 1833.
s. 3, see *Thomas* v. *The Queen* [1978] 3 W.L.R. 927, P.C.
s. 24, order 79/720.

7 Will. 4 & 1 Vict. (1837)

26. Wills Act 1837.
ss. 14, 15, see *In the Estate of Crannis (decd.), Mansell* v. *Crannis* (1978) 122 S.J. 489, Browne-Wilkinson J.
s. 15, see *Ross* v. *Caunters* [1979] 3 W.L.R. 605, Megarry V.-C.

1 & 2 Vict. (1838)

110. Judgments Act 1838.
s. 17, amended: order 79/1382.

114. Debtors (Scotland) Act 1838.
s. 26, see *City Bakeries* v. *S. & S. Snack Bars & Restaurants*, 1979 S.L.T. (Sh.Ct.) 28.

4 & 5 Vict. (1841)

38. School Sites Act 1841.
s. 2, see *Re Clayton's Deed Poll* [1979] 2 All E.R. 1133, Whitford J.

5 & 6 Vict. (1842)

45. Literary Copyright Act 1842.
see *Redwood Music* v. *B. Feldman & Co.* [1979] R.P.C. 385, C.A.

7 & 8 Vict. (1844)

32. Bank Charter Act 1844.
s. 21, repealed: 1979,c.37,s.46,sch.7.

CAP.

8 & 9 Vict. (*1845*)

18. Land Clauses Consolidation Act 1845.
s. 92, see *London Transport Executive* v. *Congregational Union of England and Wales* (*Inc.*) (1979) 37 P. & C.R. 155, Goulding J.

33. Railway Clauses Consolidation (Scotland) Act 1845.
s. 60, see *Sudjic* v. *British Railways Board*, 1979 S.L.T.(Sh.Ct.) 64.

38. Bank Notes (Scotland) Act 1845.
s. 13, repealed: 1979,c.37,s.46,sch.7.

11 & 12 Vict. (*1848*)

44. Justices Protection Act 1848.
repealed: 1979,c.55,sch.3.

12 & 13 Vict. (*1849*)

16. Justices Protection (Ireland) Act 1849.
s. 4, repealed in pt.: order 79/297.

14 & 15 Vict. (*1851*)

92. Summary Jurisdiction (Ireland) Act 1851.
s. 15, repealed: order 78/1050.

15 & 16 Vict. (*1852*)

xxvii. Sunderland and South Shields Waterworks Act 1852.
s. LV, repealed: order 79/1457.

17 & 18 Vict. (*1854*)

91. Lands Valuation (Scotland) Act 1854.
s. 42, see *Forth Yacht Marina* v. *Assessor for Fife*, 1976 S.C. 201.

19 & 20 Vict. (*1856*)

60. Mercantile Law Amendment (Scotland) Act 1856.
s. 17, see *Graham* v. *The Shore Porters Society* (O.H.), 1979 S.L.T. 119.

63. Grand Jury (Ireland) Act 1856.
repealed: order 78/1051.

20 & 21 Vict. (*1857*)

60. Irish Bankrupt and Insolvent Act 1857.
s. 267, see *Re Keaney* [1977] N.I. 67, Murray J.

79. Probates and Letters of Administration Act (Ireland) 1857.
ss. 2 (in pt.) 31, 50–57, 59, 61, 63, 65 (in pt.), 66 (in pt.), 71, 72, 74, 80, 81, 84, 92, 93, 98, 99A, 100, repealed: order 79/1575.

21 & 22 Vict. (*1858*)

27. Chancery Amendment Act 1858.
s. 2, see *Johnson* v. *Agnew* [1979] 2 W.L.R. 487, H.L.

73. Stipendiary Magistrates Act 1858.
repealed, except ss. 7, 15.

CAP.

22 Vict. (*1859*)

12. Defence Act 1859.
s. 6, repealed in pt.: order 78/1050.

22 & 23 Vict. (*1859*)

31. Court of Probate Act (Ireland) 1859.
ss. 12, 16, 17 (in pt.), 18 (in pt.), 19, 21, 22, 24, repealed: order 79/1575.

vi. Sunderland and South Shields Waterworks Amendment Act 1859.
ss. VII, XIV, orders 79/1457.

23 & 24 Vict. (*1860*)

115. Crown Debts and Judgments Act 1860.
s. 1, amended: 1979,c.2,sch.4.

154. Landlord and Tenant Law Amendment Act, Ireland, 1860.
s. 65, amended: order 79/296.

24 & 25 Vict. (*1861*)

100. Offences against the Person Act 1861.
s. 20, see *Flack* v. *Hunt* (1979) 123 S.J. 751, D.C.

27 & 28 Vict. (*1864*)

25. Naval Prize Act 1864.
s. 47, amended: 1979,c.2,sch.4.
s. 48, amended: *ibid.*
s. 48A, amended: *ibid.*
s. 49, amended: *ibid.*

28 & 29 Vict. (*1865*)

18. Criminal Procedure Act 1865.
s. 8, see *R.* v. *Angeli* [1978] 3 All E.R. 950, C.A.

125. Dockyard Ports Regulation Act 1865.
ss. 3, 5, orders 78/1880, 1881.
s. 6, order 78/1880.
s. 7, order 78/1881.

29 & 30 Vict. (*1866*)

37. Hop (Prevention of Frauds) Act 1866.
repealed: regs. 79/1095.

30 & 31 Vict. (*1867*)

17. Lyon King of Arms Act 1867.
sch. B, order 79/443.

31 & 32 Vict. (*1868*)

64. Land Registers (Scotland) Act 1868.
s. 6, amended: 1979,c.33,sch.2; repealed in pt.: *ibid.*,sch.4.
s. 25, order 79/1127; substituted: 1979, c.33,s.23.

101. Titles to Land Consolidation (Scotland) Act 1868.
s. 142, amended: 1979,c.33,sch.2; repealed in pt.: *ibid.*,sch.4.
s. 158, see *McInally* v. *Kildonan Homes* (O.H.), 1979 S.L.T.(Notes) 89.

CAP.

31 & 32 Vict. (1868)—cont.

123. Salmon Fisheries (Scotland) Act 1868.
sch. G, amended: 1979,c.11,sch.11.

lxxii. Sunderland and South Shields Water Act 1868.
ss. 15, 16, 22, repealed: order 79/1457.

32 & 33 Vict. (1869)

115. Metropolitan Public Carriage Act 1869.
s. 9, order 79/706.

33 & 34 Vict. (1870)

52. Extradition Act 1870.
see *Re Budlong*; *Re Kember*, *The Times*, December 7, 1979, D.C.
s. 1, order 78/1889.
s. 2, orders 78/1887, 1888; 79/453, 913, 1311.
s. 17, orders 78/1887–1889; 79/453, 913, 1311.
s. 21, orders 78/1886–1889; 79/913, 1311.

34 & 35 Vict. (1871)

36. Pensions Commutation Act 1871.
ss. 4, 7, regs. 78/1257.

35 & 36 Vict. (1872)

58. Bankruptcy (Ireland) Amendment Act 1872.
s. 62, amended: order 79/296.

61. Steam Whistles Act 1872.
repealed: order 78/1049.

37 & 38 Vict. (1874)

94. Conveyancing (Scotland) Act 1874.
s. 10, see *McKenzie, Petitioner*, 1979 S.L.T.(Sh.Ct.) 68.

38 & 39 Vict. (1875)

17. Explosives Act 1875.
s. 3, see *R.* v. *Wheatley* [1979] 1 W.L.R. 144, C.A.
s. 40, amended: 1979,c.2,sch.4.
s. 43, amended: *ibid.*
ss. 43, 83, 104, S.R. 1979 No. 290.

41. Intestates' Widows and Children (Scotland) Act 1875.
ss. 3, 5, amended: 1979,c.22,s.1
s. 7, repealed in pt.: *ibid.*,s.1,,sch.
schs. A, B, amended: *ibid.*,s.1.
sch. C, repealed: *ibid.*,s.1,sch.

39 & 40 Vict. (1876)

24. Small Testate Estates (Scotland) Act 1876.
ss. 3, 5, amended: 1979,c.22,s.1.
s. 7, repealed in pt.: *ibid.*,s.1,,sch.
sch. A, amended: *ibid.*,s.1.
sch. C, repealed: *ibid.*,s.1,sch.

36. Customs Consolidation Act 1876.
s. 283, repealed: 1979,c.58,sch.2.

70. Sheriff Courts (Scotland) Act 1876.
s. 54, Act of Sederunt 79/1405.

CAP.

40 & 41 Vict. (1877)

43. Justices' Clerks Act 1877.
repealed: 1979,c.55,sch.3.

59. Colonial Stock Act 1877.
s. 20, amended: 1979,c.27,sch.

41 & 42 Vict. (1878)

49. Weights and Measures Act 1878.
s. 86, sch. 6, repealed: 1979,c.45,sch.7.

52. Public Health (Ireland) Act 1878.
ss. 2, 50, 51, amended: order 79/1049.
ss. 52, 53. repealed: *ibid.*
s. 54, amended and repealed in pt.: *ibid.*
ss. 55, 59, 60, repealed: *ibid.*
ss. 79, 107, 112, 114, sch. C., amended: *ibid.*

76. Telegraph Act 1878.
s. 8, see *Post Office* v. *Hampshire County Council* [1979] 2 W.L.R. 907, C.A.; *Post Office* v. *Mears Construction* [1979] 2 All E.R. 814, Willis J.

xiv. Sevenoaks Waterworks Act 1878.
repealed: order 79/1079.

42 & 43 Vict. (1879)

11. Bankers' Books Evidence Act 1879.
s. 9, substituted: 1979,c.37,sch.6.

21. Customs and Inland Revenue Act 1879.
s. 5, amended: 1979,c.2,sch.4.

22. Prosecution of Offences Act 1879.
repealed: 1979,c.31,sch.2.
s. 2, see *Turner* v. *D.P.P.* (1978) 68 Cr.App.R. 70, Mars Jones J.
ss. 2, 5, 8, regs. 78/1846.
*s. 5, repealed in pt.: 1979,c.31,sch.2.
*s. 7, repealed: *ibid.*

58. Public Offices Fees Act 1879.
s. 2, orders 79/779, 780, 966–968, 1149; S.Rs. 1979 Nos. 160, 161.
s. 3, orders 79/779, 780, 966, 968; S.Rs. 1979 Nos. 160, 161.

43 & 44 Vict. (1880)

20. Inland Revenue Act 1880.
s. 57, repealed: 1979,c.37,sch.7.
sch. 3, repealed: *ibid.*

44 & 45 Vict. (1881)

12. Customs and Inland Revenue Act 1881.
s. 34, repealed: 1979, c. 22, sch.

41. Conveyancing Act 1881.
s. 46, see *Industrial Development Authority* v. *Moran* [1978] I.R. 159, Sup.Ct. of Ireland.

45 & 46 Vict. (1882)

37. Corn Returns Act 1882.
ss. 4, 5, 14, regs. 79/607, 614.

44. Pensions Commutation Act 1882.
s. 3, regs. 78/1257.

CAP.

45 & 46 Vict. (1882)—cont.

61. Bills of Exchange Act 1882.
s. 11, see *Korea Exchange Bank* v. *Debenhams (Central Buying)* (1979) 123 S.J. 163, C.A.
s. 26, see *Rolfe, Lubell & Co.* v. *Keith* [1979] 1 All E.R. 860, Kilner Brown J.
s. 50, see *Barclays Bank* v. *W. J. Simms Son and Cooke (Southern)* [1979] 3 All E.R. 522, Robert Goff J.

73. Ancient Monuments Protection Act 1882.
sch., repealed: 1979,c.46,sch.5.

75. Married Women's Property Act 1882.
s. 17, see *Chambers* v. *Chambers* (1979) 123 S.J. 689, Wood J.
s. 17, amended: order 78/1045.

77. Citation Amendment (Scotland) Act 1882.
s. 3, see *Smith* v. *Conner & Co.*, 1979 S.L.T.(Sh.Ct.) 25.

46 & 47 Vict. (1883)

3. Explosive Substances Act 1883.
s. 4, see *R.* v. *Wheatley* [1979] 1 W.L.R. 144, C.A.

47 & 48 Vict. (1884)

58. Prosecution of Offences Act 1884.
repealed: 1979,c.31,sch.2.

71. Intestates' Estates Act 1884.
s. 5, repealed: order 79/1575.
s. 9, repealed in pt.: *ibid.*

48 & 49 Vict. (1885)

72. Housing of the Working Classes Act 1885.
s. 9, amended: order 78/1049.

49 & 50 Vict. (1886)

29. Crofters Holdings (Scotland) Act 1886.
ss. 8, 34, see *Gilmour* v. *Master of Lovat*, 1979 S.L.T.(Land Ct.) 2.
s. 29, rules 79/379.

50 & 51 Vict. (1887)

35. Criminal Procedure (Scotland) Act 1887.
s. 59, see *Christie* v. *Barclay*, 1974 J.C. 68.

55. Sheriffs Act 1887.
s. 20, order 79/1442.

51 & 52 Vict. (1888)

21. Law of Distress Amendment Act 1888.
s. 8, rules 79/711.

41. Local Government Act 1888.
s. 42, repealed in pt.: 1979,c.55,sch.3.

52 & 53 Vict. (1889)

23. Herring Fishery (Scotland) Act 1889.
s. 4, repealed: 1979,c.45,sch.7.

63. Interpretation Act 1889.
s. 26, see *Migwain* v. *Transport and General Workers' Union* [1979] I.C.R. 597, E.A.T.

CAP.

53 & 54 Vict. (1890)

8. Customs and Inland Revenue Act 1890.
s. 31, repealed in pt.: 1979,c.4,sch.4.

39. Partnership Act 1890.
ss. 4, 6, 9, see *Highland Engineering* v. *Anderson* (O.H.), 1979 S.L.T. 122.
s. 24, see *Hutcheon and Partners* v. *Hutcheon*, 1979 S.L.T.(Sh.Ct.) 62.

59. Public Health Acts Amendment Act 1890.
s. 11, amended: order 78/1049.
s. 26, repealed in pt.: *ibid.*
s. 38, repealed: *ibid.*

54 & 55 Vict. (1891)

36. Consular Fees and Salaries Act 1891.
s. 2, regs. 79/875.

38. Stamp Duties Management Act 1891.
s. 23, amended: 1979,c.2,sch.4.

xxxiii. Sunderland and South Shields Water Act 1891.
ss. 23, 24, 33, repealed: order 79/1457.

56 & 57 Vict. (1894)

30. Finance Act 1894.
s. 2, see *Trustees of the Late Sir James Douglas Wishart Thomson* v. *I.R.C.* [1978] T.R. 171, Ct. of Session.

60. Merchant Shipping Act 1894.
Pt. VIII, repealed: 1979,c.39,sch.7.
ss. 7, 10, 15, 18, 20, 21, 44, 47, 48, 49, amended: 1979,c.39,sch.6.
s. 66, amended (S.): *ibid.*,sch.6.
s. 73, amended: *ibid.*,sch.6; repealed in pt.: *ibid.*,schs.6,7.
s. 74, amended: *ibid.*,sch.6.
s. 84, order 79/306.
s. 85, amended: 1979,c.39,s.31.
ss. 111, 112, amended: *ibid.*,sch.6
s. 238, order 79/293.
ss. 271, 280, 281, 285–287, amended: 1979,c.39,sch.6.
s. 360, repealed in pt.: *ibid.*,schs.6,7.
s. 369, repealed in pt.: *ibid*,s.28,sch.7.
ss. 373, 385, amended: *ibid.*,sch.6.
s. 386, amended: *ibid.*,s.28.
ss. 413, 417, amended: *ibid.*,sch.6.
s. 418, order 79/462.
s. 420, repealed in pt.: 1979,c.39,s.28, sch.7.
s. 421, order 78/1914.
s. 422, amended: 1979,c.39,sch.6.
s. 424, order 79/462.
s. 427, rules 78/1873, 1874.
s. 430, amended: 1979,c.39,sch.6.
s. 431, repealed in pt.: *ibid.*,s.28,sch.7.
ss. 432, 433, 436, amended: *ibid.*,sch.6.
s. 446, amended: *ibid.*,sch.6; repealed in pt.: *ibid.*,schs.6,7.
s. 447, amended: *ibid.*, sch. 6.
s. 457, repealed: *ibid.*,s.44,sch.7.
ss. 459, 463, amended: *ibid.*,s.28.
s. 464, amended: *ibid.*,s.32.
s. 465, amended: *ibid.*,s.28.
s. 468, repealed: *ibid.*,sch.7.
s. 471, amended: *ibid.*,s.28.
s. 488, amended: *ibid.*,s.28,sch.6.
s. 492, amended: 1979,c.2,sch.4.

CAP.

56 & 57 Vict. (1894)—cont.

60. *Merchant Shipping Act 1894—cont.*
s. 517, amended: 1979,c.39,s.28.
ss. 518, 519, 536, 543, amended: *ibid.*, sch.6.
s. 637, repealed: *ibid.*,s.33,sch.7.
s. 638, repealed in pt.: *ibid.*,sch.7.
ss. 640, 641, repealed: *ibid.*,s.33,sch.7.
ss. 666, 667, amended: *ibid.*,sch.6.
s. 668, amended: *ibid.*,s.33.
ss. 670–672, 675, repealed: *ibid.*,s.34, sch.7.
s. 677, repealed in pt.: *ibid.*
s. 680, amended: *ibid.*,sch.6.
s. 683, amended: *ibid.*,s.42.
ss. 689, 692, 696, amended: *ibid.*,sch.6.
s. 702, amended (S.): *ibid.*,sch.6.
s. 703, substituted (S.): *ibid.*,sch.6.
ss. 722, 723, amended: *ibid.*,sch.6.
s. 724, repealed in pt.: *ibid.*,schs.6,7.
s. 726, amended: *ibid.*,sch.6.
s. 728, amended: *ibid.*,s.26.
ss. 729, 730, repealed: *ibid.*,s.28,sch.7.
s. 735, order 79/110.
s. 738, orders 79/293, 462.

71. Sale of Goods Act 1893.
repealed, except s. 26: 1979,c.54,sch.3.
s. 25, see *Dawber Williamson Roofing* v. *Humberside County Council*, October 22, Mais J.

57 & 58 Vict. (1895)

14. Courts of Law Fees (Scotland) Act 1895.
s. 2, Acts of Sederunt 79/347, 348.

30. Finance Act 1894.
s. 2, see *Thomson's Trs.* v. *Inland Revenue* (H.L.), 1979 S.L.T. 166.
s. 8, orders 79/1689, 1690.

60. Merchant Shipping Act 1894.
s. 373, order 79/1455.
s. 427, amended: 1979,c.27,sch.
ss. 503, 504, see *Afromar Inc.* v. *Greek Atlantic Cod Fishing Co.*; *The Penelope II*, *The Times*, November 21, 1979, C.A.
s. 735, order 79/1448.

73. Local Government Act 1894.
s. 16, repealed: order 79/1123.
s. 19, repealed in pt.: *ibid.*
s. 63, repealed: *ibid.*

58 & 59 Vict. (1896)

25. Friendly Societies Act 1896.
s. 49, see *Re Bucks Constabulary Widows' and Orphans' Fund Friendly Society; Thompson* v. *Holdsworth (No. 2)* [1979] 1 All E.R. 623, Walton J.

45. Stanneries Court (Abolition) Act 1896.
s. 1, see *R.* v. *East Powder JJ., ex p. Lampshire* [1979] 2 W.L.R. 479, D.C.

48. Light Railways Act 1896.
s. 7, 9, orders 78/1937; 79/317, 1091, 1270, 1421.
s. 10, orders 79/317, 1091, 1270, 1421.
s. 11, orders 79/317, 1421.

CAP.

58 & 59 Vict. (1896)—cont.

48. *Light Railways Act 1896—cont.*
s. 12, order 78/1937.
s. 18, orders 78/1937; 79/317, 1270.
s. 24, order 79/1091.

60 & 61 Vict. (1897)

26. Metropolitan Police Courts Act 1897.
ss. 1, 8, repealed: 1979,c.55,sch.3.

63. Foreign Prison-Made Goods Act 1897.
s. 1, amended: 1979,c.2,sch.4.

61 & 62 Vict. (1898)

36. Criminal Evidence Act 1898.
s. 1, see *Knowles* v. *H.M. Advocate*, 1975 J.C. 6; *R.* v. *France* [1979] Crim.L.R. 48, C.A.; *R.* v. *Nelson* (1978) 68 Cr.App.R. 12, C.A.; *R.* v. *Coltress* (1978) 68 Cr.App.R. 193, C.A.; amended: 1979,c.16,s.1.

44. Merchant Shipping (Mercantile Marine Fund) Act 1898.
s. 2, amended: 1979,c.39,s.36; repealed in pt.: *ibid.*,s.36,sch.7.
s. 3, regs. 79/631.
s. 5, amended: 1979,c.39,s.36; repealed in pt.: *ibid.*,sch.7.
s. 7, repealed in pt.: *ibid.*,sch.7.
sch. 2, repealed: *ibid.*,sch.7.
sch. 3, repealed in pt.: *ibid.*,s.36,sch.7.

46. Revenue Act 1898.
s. 1, amended: 1979,c.2,sch.4.

63 & 64 Vict. (1900)

32. Merchant Shipping (Liability of Shipowners and Others) Act 1900.
s. 2, amended: 1979,c.39,sch.5; repealed in pt.: *ibid.*,sch.7.

1 Edw. 7 (1901)

7. Finance Act 1901.
s. 10, amended: 1979,c.2,sch.4.

22. Factory and Workshop Act 1901.
s. 149, see *Occidental Inc.* v. *Assessor for Orkney*, 1979 S.L.T. 60.

2 Edw. 7 (1902)

8. Cremation Act 1902.
s. 7, regs. 79/1138.

6 Edw. 7 (1906)

14. Alkali, etc. Works Regulation Act 1906.
ss. 3–5, 8, 9 (in pt.), 11 (in pt.), repealed: order 78/1049.
s. 12, amended and repealed in pt.: *ibid.*
s. 16A, amended: *ibid.*
ss. 18 (in pt.), 19, 20 (in pt.), 22 (in pt.), repealed: *ibid.*
sch. 1, amended: *ibid.*

31. Local Government (Ireland) Act (1898) (Amendment) Act 1906.
repealed: order 78/1051.

CAP.

6 Edw. 7 (1906)—cont.

34. Prevention of Corruption Act 1906.
s. 1, see *R.* v. *Mills* (1978) 68 Cr.App.R. 154, C.A.

48. Merchant Shipping Act 1906.
s. 16, amended: 1979,c.39,sch.6.
s. 50, regs. 79/341.
s. 69, repealed: 1979,c.39,sch.7.
ss. 76, 77, amended: *ibid.*
s. 82, repealed in pt.: *ibid.*,sch.7.

55. Public Trustee Act 1906.
s. 9, order 79/189.

7 Edw. 7 (1907)

24. Limited Partnerships Act 1907.
s. 4, repealed in pt.: 1979,c.37,sch.7.

51. Sheriff Courts (Scotland) Act 1907.
s. 27(B), see *Thomson* v. *Thomson*, 1979 S.L.T.(Sh.Ct.) 11.
s. 34, sch. 1, see *Austin* v. *Gibson*, 1979 S.L.T.(Land Ct.) 12.
s. 40, Acts of Sederunt 79/347, 1034.
sch. 1, see *Wailes Dove Bitumatic* v. *Plastic Sealant Services*, 1979 S.L.T. (Sh.Ct.) 41; *Ellis* v. *MacDonald*, 1980 S.L.T. 11.

53. Public Health Acts Amendment Act 1907.
ss. 34, 35, 45, 94, amended: order 78/1049.

55. London Cab and Stage Carriage Act 1907.
s. 1, order 79/706.

8 Edw. 7 (1908)

3. Prosecution of Offences Act 1908.
repealed: 1979,c.31,sch.2.
ss. 1, 2, see *Turner* v. *D.P.P.* (1978) 68 Cr.App.R. 70, Mars Jones J.
*s. 2, repealed in pt.: 1979,c.31,sch.2.

17. Cran Measures Act 1908.
repealed: 1979,c.45,sch.7.

1 & 2 Geo. 5 (1911)

42. Merchant Shipping Act 1911.
s. 1, repealed in pt.: 1979,c.39,sch.7.

46. Copyright Act 1911.
ss. 5, 16, 24, 35, see *Redwood Music* v. *B. Feldman & Co.* [1979] R.P.C. 385, C.A.

49. Small Landholders (Scotland) Act 1911.
s. 26, see *Gilmour* v. *Master of Lovat*, 1979 S.L.T.(Land Ct.) 2.
s. 28, rules 79/379.

2 & 3 Geo. 5 (1912–13)

10. Seal Fisheries (North Pacific) Act 1912.
s. 4, amended: 1979,c.2,sch.4.

30. Trade Union Act 1913.
s. 3, see *McCarthy* v. *Association of Professional Executive, Clerical and Computer Staff* [1979] I.R.L.R. 255, Certification Officer; *Reeves* v. *Tranport and General Workers' Union* [1979] I.R.L.R. 290, Certification Officer.

31. Pilotage Act 1913.
ss. 1, 2, 6, repealed: 1979,c.39,sch.7.
s. 7, orders 79/712, 1340; amended: 1979, c.39,sch.2; repealed in pt.: *ibid.*,sch.7.
s. 8, repealed in pt.: *ibid.*,schs.2,7.
s. 9, repealed: *ibid.*,schs.2,7.
s. 10, repealed in pt.: *ibid.*,schs.2,7.
s. 11, amended and substituted: *ibid.*, s. 8; repealed in pt.: *ibid.*,sch.7.
ss. 13, 14, repealed: *ibid.*,s.8,sch.7.
s. 17, amended: *ibid.*,ss.9,13,sch.2; repealed in pt.: *ibid.*,s.9,sch.7.
s. 18, amended: *ibid.*,sch.2.
s. 20, amended: *ibid.*,s.13,sch.2.
s. 22, repealed in pt.: *ibid.*,sch.7.
s. 23, amended: *ibid.*,sch.2.
s. 24, repealed: *ibid.*,schs.2,7.
s. 27, amended: *ibid.*,sch.2.
s. 30, amended: *ibid.*,s.13,sch.2; repealed in pt.: *ibid.*,schs.2,7.
s. 31, amended: *ibid.*,sch.2.
s. 32, amended: *ibid.*,sch.2; repealed in pt.: *ibid.*,schs.2,7.
s. 33, repealed in pt.: *ibid.*,schs.2,7.
s. 34, amended: *ibid.*,sch.2; repealed in pt.: *ibid.*,sch.7.
s. 35, amended: *ibid.*,sch.2; repealed in pt.: *ibid.*,schs.2,7.
s. 36, amended: *ibid.*,s.13,sch.2.
s. 37, amended: *ibid.*,s.13.
s. 39, repealed in pt.: *ibid.*,schs.2,7.
s. 41, amended: *ibid.*,s.13.
ss. 42, 43, amended: *ibid.*,s.13,sch.2.
s. 44, amended: *ibid.*,sch.2.
s. 45, amended: *ibid.*,s.13,sch.2.
s. 46, amended: *ibid.*,sch.2.
s. 47, amended: *ibid.*,s.13.
s. 48, amended: 1979,c.2,sch.4; c.39, s.13,sch.2; repealed in pt.: *ibid.*,schs. 2,7.
s. 50, amended: *ibid.*,s.13,sch.2.
s. 51, amended: *ibid.*,sch.2.
ss. 56, 58, 59, repealed: *ibid.*,schs.2,7.
s. 61, amended: *ibid.*,sch.2.
sch. 1, repealed in pt.: *ibid.*,sch.7.

3 & 4 Geo. 5 (1913)

20. Bankruptcy (Scotland) Act 1913.
s. 30, see *Murdoch* v. *Newman Industrial Control* (O.H.), 1980 S.L.T. 13.

27. Forgery Act 1913.
ss. 1, 6, see *R.* v. *Hiscox* (1978) 68 Cr.App.R. 411, C.A.
s. 7, see *R.* v. *Macer* [1979] Crim.L.R. 659, Courts-Martial Appeal Ct.

32. Ancient Monuments Consolidation and Amendment Act 1913.
repealed: 1979,c.46,sch.5.

xvii. South Staffordshire Waterworks Act 1913.
s. 21, amended: order 79/1369.

CAP.

4 & 5 Geo. 5 (1914)

59. Bankruptcy Act 1914.
ss. 4, 41, see *Re A Debtor (No. 2 of 1977), ex p. The Debtor* v. *Goacher* [1979] 1 All E.R. 870, D.C.
s. 31, see *Re Cushla* [1979] 3 All E.R. 415, Vinelott J.
s. 40, amended: 1979,c.53,s.4.
s. 45, see *Re Green (A Bankrupt), ex p. Official Receiver* v. *Cutting* [1979] 1 All E.R. 832, Walton J.
s. 108, see *Re a Debtor (No. 13 of 1964), ex p. Official Receiver and Trustee* v. *The Debtor* [1979] 3 All E.R. 15, D.C.
s. 133, order 79/780.
ss. 155, 164, see *Browne* v. *Phillips* [1979] Crim.L.R. 381, D.C.

61. Special Constables Act 1914.
s. 4, S.R. 1978 No. 359.

5 & 6 Geo. 5 (1914–15)

18. Injuries in War Compensation Act 1914 (Session 2).
s. 1, scheme 79/1506.

90. Indictments Act 1915.
s. 5, see *R.* v. *Walters*; *R.* v. *Tovey*; *R.* v. *Padfield* [1979] R.T.R. 220, C.A.

6 & 7 Geo. 5 (1916)

31. Police, Factories etc. (Miscellaneous Provisions) Act 1916.
s. 5, regs. 79/1230.

58. Registration of Business Names Act 1916.
s. 8, see *Thomas Montgomery & Sons* v. *W. B. Anderson & Sons* (O.H.), February 7, 1979.

64. Prevention of Corruption Act 1916.
s. 2, see *R.* v. *Mills* (1978) 68 Cr.App.R. 154, C.A.

9 & 10 Geo. 5 (1919)

45. Housing (Ireland) Act 1919.
s. 6, S.R. 1979 No. 379.

92. Aliens Restriction (Amendment) Act 1919.
s. 4, repealed: 1979,c.39,sch.7.

10 & 11 Geo. 5 (1920)

17. Increase of Rent and Mortgage Interest (Restrictions) Act 1920.
repealed: order 78/1050.

33. Maintenance Orders (Facilities for Enforcement) Act 1920.
s. 3, amended: 1979,c.55,sch.2.

75. Official Secrets Act 1920.
s. 8, see *Att.-Gen.* v. *Leveller Magazine* [1979] 2 W.L.R. 247, H.L.

11 & 12 Geo. 5 (1921)

28. Merchant Shipping Act 1921.
s. 1, repealed in pt.: 1979,c.39,sch.7.
s. 2, amended: *ibid.*,sch.6.

CAP.

11 & 12 Geo. 5 (1921)—cont.

35. Corn Sales Act 1921.
s. 5, amended: regs. 79/357.

xlvii. Sunderland and South Shields Water Act 1921.
ss. 55, 58, 59, repealed: order 79/1457.

12 & 13 Geo. 5 (1922)

xxvi. Sunderland and South Shields Water Act 1922.
ss. 19, 20, 22, repealed: order 79/1457.

13 & 14 Geo. 5 (1923)

4. Fees (Increase) Act 1923.
s. 7, order 79/1258.
s. 8, regs. 79/875.

15 & 16 Geo. 5 (1925)

19. Trustee Act 1925.
s. 15, see *Re Earl of Strafford (decd.)*; *Royal Bank of Scotland* v. *Byng* [1979] 1 All E.R. 513, C.A.

20. Law of Property Act 1925.
s. 40, see *Ram Narayan S/O Shanker* v. *Rishad Hussain Shah S/O Tasaduq Hussain Shah* [1979] 1 W.L.R. 1349, P.C.
s. 41, see *Raineri* v. *Miles*; *Wiejski (Third Party)* [1979] 3 All E.R. 763, C.A.
s. 49, see *Universal Corp.* v. *Five Ways Properties* [1979] 1 All E.R. 552, C.A.
s. 53, see *Roban Jig & Tool Co. and Elkadart* v. *Taylor* [1979] F.S.R. 130, C.A.
s. 62, see *Nickerson* v. *Barraclough* [1979] 3 All E.R. 312, Megarry V.-C.
s. 63, see *Cedar Holdings* v. *Green* [1979] 3 W.L.R. 31, C.A.
s. 109, see *Re John Willment (Ashford)* [1979] 2 All E.R. 615, Brightman J.
s. 146, see *Clifford* v. *Personal Representatives of Johnson decd.* (1979) 251 E.G. 571, C.A.; *Old Grovebury Manor Farm* v. *W. Seymour Plant Sales and Hire* [1979] 1 W.L.R. 263; 3 All E.R. 504, C.A.
s. 172, see *Re Shilena Hosiery Co.* [1979] 2 All E.R. 6, Brightman J.

21. Land Registration Act 1925.
ss. 3, 20, 70, 74, see *Williams & Glyn's Bank* v. *Boland* [1979] 2 W.L.R. 550, C.A.
s. 13, see *M.E.P.C.* v. *Christian-Edwards* [1979] 3 W.L.R. 713, H.L.
s. 49, amended: 1979,c.53,s.3.
s. 70, see *Bird* v. *Syme Thomson* [1978] 3 All E.R. 1027, Templeman J.
ss. 132, 133, order 79/1019.

22. Land Charges Act 1925.
s. 13, see *Midland Bank Trust Co.* v. *Green* [1979] 3 W.L.R. 167, C.A.

23. Administration of Estates Act 1925.
s. 41, see *Re Phelps (decd.)*; *Wells* v. *Phelps* [1979] 3 All E.R. 373, C.A.

CAP.

15 & 16 Geo. 5 (1925)—cont.

42. Merchant Shipping (International Labour Conventions) Act 1925.
s. 4, amended: 1979,c.39,sch.6.

49. Supreme Court of Judicature (Consolidation) Act 1925.
s. 31, see *R.* v. *Board of Visitors of Hull Prison, ex p. St. Germain* [1978] 2 W.L.R. 42, C.A.
s. 41, see *Jefferson* v. *Bhetcha* [1979] 1 W.L.R. 898, C.A.
s. 99, rules 79/35, 402, 522, 1542.
s. 213, order 79/968.

86. Criminal Justice Act 1925.
s. 34, repealed: 1979,c.31,sch.2.

xvii. Imperial Institute Act 1925.
s. 8, amended: 1979,c.27,sch.
sch. 2, repealed in pt.: 1979,c.60,sch.3.

16 & 17 Geo. 5 (1926)

40. Indian and Colonial Divorce Jurisdiction Act 1926.
s. 2, repealed in pt.: 1979,c.60,sch.3.

42. Merchant Shipping (International Labour Conventions) Act 1925.
s. 6, order 79/1449.

51. Electricity (Supply) Act 1926.
s. 44, amended: 1979,c.46,sch.4.

59. Coroners (Amendment) Act 1926.
s. 13, see *R.* v. *H.M. Coroner at Hammersmith, ex p. Peach, The Times*, November 16, 1979, D.C.

17 & 18 Geo. 5 (1927)

36. Landlord and Tenant Act 1927.
s. 19, see *Bocardo S.A.* v. *S. & M. Hotels* [1979] 3 All E.R. 737, C.A.

39. Medical and Dentists Acts Amendment Act 1927.
s. 1, repealed: order 79/289.
sch., repealed in pt.: *ibid.*

18 & 19 Geo. 5 (1928)

24. Northern Ireland (Miscellaneous Provisions) Act 1928.
s. 3, repealed: order 79/1575.

35. Easter Act 1928.
sch., repealed in pt.: 1979,c.60,sch.3.

43. Agricultural Credits Act 1928.
s. 5, amended: 1979,c.37,sch.6.

44. Rating and Valuation (Apportionment) Act 1928.
s. 3, see *Occidental Inc.* v. *Assessor for Orkney*, 1979 S.L.T. 60.

19 & 20 Geo. 5 (1929)

13. Agricultural Credits (Scotland) Act 1929.
s. 9, amended: 1979,c.37,sch.6.

29. Government Annuities Act 1929.
ss. 43, 52, regs. 79/552.

CAP.

21 & 22 Geo. 5 (1931)

16. Ancient Monuments Act 1931.
repealed: 1979,c.46,sch.5.

22 & 23 Geo. 5 (1931–32)

9. Merchant Shipping (Safety and Load Line Conventions) Act 1932.
ss. 12, 24, 27, 29–31, amended: 1979, c.39,sch.6.
s. 36, order 79/1707.

25. Finance Act 1932.
s. 24, repealed: 1979,c.30,sch.
s. 25, repealed in pt.: *ibid.*

xiv. York Waterworks Act 1932.
s. 77, substituted: order 79/1527.

23 & 24 Geo. 5 (1932–33)

6. Visiting Forces (British Commonwealth) Act 1933.
s. 4, applied: 1979,c.27,sch.

12. Children and Young Persons Act 1933.
s. 21, see *Portsea Island Mutual Co-operative Society* v. *Leyland* [1978] I.C.R. 1195, D.C.
s. 56, see *R.* v. *Billericay JJ., ex p. Johnson* [1979] Crim.L.R. 315, D.C.
s. 107, amended: 1979,c.55,sch.2.

14. London Passenger Transport Act 1933.
s. 106, regs. 78/1791.

21. Solicitors (Scotland) Act 1933.
s. 18, Act of Sederunt 79/1410.

36. Administration of Justice (Miscellaneous Provisions) Act 1933.
s. 2, see *R.* v. *Walters*; *R.* v. *Tovey*; *R.* v. *Padfield* [1979] R.T.R. 220, C.A.

41. Administration of Justice (Scotland) Act 1933.
s. 4, Acts of Sederunt 79/190, 723.
s. 16, Acts of Sederunt 78/1804; 79/226, 348, 516, 613, 670, 1033, 1438.

24 & 25 Geo. 5 (1933–34)

41. Law Reform (Miscellaneous Provisions) Act 1934.
s. 1, see *Kandalla* v. *British Airways Corp.* (1979) 123 S.J. 769, Griffiths J.
s. 3, see *B.P. Exploration Co. (Libya)* v. *Hunt (No. 2)* [1979] 1 W.L.R. 783, Goff J.

49. Whaling Industry (Regulation) Act 1934.
amended: 1979,c.27,sch.

25 & 26 Geo. 5 (1935)

Supreme Court Act 1935 (South Australia).
s. 30, see *Thompson* v. *Faraonio* (1979) 123 S.J. 301, P.C.

26 Geo. 5 & 1 Edw. 8 (1935–36)

36. Pilotage Authorities (Limitation of Liability) Act 1936.
ss. 1, 4, amended: 1979,c.39,sch.5.

CAP.

26 Geo. 5 & 1 Edw. 8 (1935–36)—cont.

49. Public Health Act 1936.
s. 2, amended: 1979,c.2,sch.4.
ss. 2, 3, 9, order 79/134.
s. 61, regs. 79/601.
s. 143, orders 79/1315, 1316, 1434, 1435.
s. 278, see *George Whitehouse* v. *Anglian Water Authority* (Ref./157/1977) 247 E.G. 223; *Leonidis* v. *Thames Water Authority* (1979) 25 E.G. 669, Parker J.
s. 343, see *Cook* v. *Minion* (1978) 37 P. & C.R. 58, Goulding J.

1 Edw. 8 & 1 Geo. 6 (1936–37)

6. Public Order Act 1936.
s. 1, amended: 1979,c.31,sch.1.
s. 5, see *R.* v. *Edwards; R.* v. *Roberts* (1978) 67 Cr.App.R. 228, C.A.; *R.* v. *Gedge* [1979] Crim.L.R. 167, C.A.
s. 9, see *R.* v. *Edwards; R.* v. *Roberts* (1978) 67 Cr.App.R. 228, C.A.

33. Diseases of Fish Act 1937.
s. 1, amended: 1979,c.2,sch.4.
s. 2, order 79/186.
ss. 2, 11, orders 79/1366, 1367.

40. Public Health (Drainage of Trade Premises) Act 1937.
s. 14, see *Thames Water Authority* v. *Blue and White Launderettes, The Times*, December 21, 1979, C.A.

43. Public Records (Scotland) Act 1937.
s. 10, Act of Sederunt 79/804.

1 & 2 Geo. 6 (1937–38)

22. Trade Marks Act 1938.
ss. 3, 11, 12, see *Tornado Trade Mark* [1979] R.P.C. 155, Trade Marks Registry.
s. 4, see *Rolls-Royce Motors* v. *Zanelli* [1979] R.P.C. 148, Browne-Wilkinson J.
ss. 9, 10, 11, see *The Chef Trade Mark* [1979] R.P.C. 143, Board of Trade.
ss. 9, 10, 11, 12, see *Golden Jet Trade Mark* [1979] R.P.C. 19, Trade Marks Registry.
ss. 9, 10, 17, 26, 28, see *Update Trade Mark* [1979] R.P.C. 165, Board of Trade.
ss. 11, 12, see *Semigres Trade Mark* [1979] R.P.C. 330, Trade Marks Registry.
ss. 11, 12, 23, see *Fif Trade Mark* [1979] R.P.C. 355, Whitford J.
ss. 11–13, 17, 26, 32, see *Oscar Trade Mark* [1979] R.P.C. 197, Trade Marks Registry.
ss. 12, 14, 18, see *Granada Trade Mark* [1979] R.P.C. 303, Trade Marks Registry.
ss. 12, 23, 26, 27, 30, 32, see *Atlas Trade Mark* [1979] R.P.C. 59, Trade Marks Registry.

CAP.

1 & 2 Geo. 6 (1937–38)—cont.

22. *Trade Marks Act 1938—cont.*
ss. 12, 26, 32, 68, see *Revue Trade Mark* [1979] R.P.C. 27, Trade Marks Registry.
s. 64A, amended: 1979,c.2,sch.4.

24. Conveyancing Amendment (Scotland) Act 1938.
s. 6, amended: 1979,c.33,sch.2.

44. Road Haulage Wages Act 1938.
ss. 4, 5, see *R.* v. *C.A.C., ex p. R.H.M. Foods* [1979] I.C.R. 657, Mocatta J.

63. Administration of Justice (Miscellaneous Provisions) Act 1938.
sch. 2, repealed in pt.: 1979,c.55,sch.3.

72. Nursing Homes Registration (Scotland) Act 1938.
ss. 1, 5, amended: 1979,c.36,sch.7.
s. 10, amended: *ibid.*,sch.7; repealed in pt.: *ibid.*,schs.7,8.

22. Trade Marks Act 1938 (N.Z.)
s. 16, see *Pioneer Hi-Bred Corn Co.* v. *Hy-Line Chicks Pty.* [1979] R.P.C. 410, N.Z.C.A.

2 & 3 Geo. 6 (1938–39)

21. Limitation Act 1939.
s. 2D, see *Deeming* v. *British Steel Corp.* (1978) S.J. 303, C.A.; *Walkley* v. *Precision Forgings* [1979] 1 W.L.R. 606, H.L.; *Browes* v. *Jones & Middleton (A Firm)* (1979) 123 S.J. 489, C.A.; *Mead* v. *Mead*, September 18, 1979, Milmo J. Cardiff Crown Ct.; *Stannard* v. *Stonar School*, August 13, 1979, Judge Hawser.
s. 22, see *Tolley* v. *Morris* [1979] 1 W.L.R. 592, H.L.
s. 23, see *Kamouh* v. *Associated Electrical Industries International* [1979] 2 W.L.R. 795, Parker J.
s. 26, see *Lewisham London Borough* v. *Leslie & Co.* (1979) 250 E.G. 1289, C.A.

49. House of Commons Members' Fund Act 1939.
sch. 1, amended: resolution 79/1667.

57. War Risks Insurance Act 1939.
s. 15, amended: 1979,c.54,sch.2.

69. Import, Export and Customs Powers (Defence) Act 1939.
s. 1, orders 78/1812; 79/164, 276, 1437; amended: 1979,c.2,sch.4.
s. 3, amended: *ibid.*
s. 9, amended: *ibid.*

82. Personal Injuries (Emergency Provisions) Act 1939.
s. 2, schemes 79/270, 1232.

xcvii. London Building Acts (Amendment) Act 1939.
s. 82, see *Marsh* v. *Betstyle Construction Co. and the Greater London Council*, August 6, 1979, Judge Lewis Hawser, Q.C.

CAP.

3 & 4 Geo. 6 (1939–40)

29. Finance Act 1940.
ss. 46, 47, 58, see *I.R.C.* v. *Standard Industrial Trust* [1979] S.T.C. 372, C.A.

6 & 7 Geo. 6 (1942–43)

32. Hydro-Electric Development (Scotland) Act 1943.
repealed, except ss. 2 in pt., 16 in pt., 17, 27 in pt., 28, sch. 4: 1979,c.11, sch.12.

39. Pensions Appeal Tribunals Act 1943.
sch., rules 78/1780; 79/94(S.); S.R. 1979 No. 397.

40. Law Reform (Frustrated Contracts) Act 1943.
ss. 1, 2, see *B.P. Exploration Co. (Libya)* v. *Hunt (No. 2)* [1979] 1 W.L.R. 783, Goff J.
s. 2, amended: 1979,c.54,sch.2.

7 & 8 Geo. 6 (1943–44)

31. Education Act 1944.
s. 8, see *Meade* v. *Haringey London Borough Council* [1979] 1 W.L.R. 637, C.A.
ss. 8, 36, 76, see *Winward* v. *Cheshire County Council* (1978) 77 L.G.R. 172, Judge Mervyn Davies.
s. 13, see *North Yorkshire County Council* v. *Department of Education and Science* (1978) 77 L.G.R. 457, Browne-Wilkinson J.
ss. 17, 24, see *Jones* v. *Lee*, *The Times*, November 21, 1979, C.A.
s. 49, regs. 79/695.
s. 81, regs. 79/542.
s. 99, see *Meade* v. *Haringey London Borough Council* [1979] 1 W.L.R 637, C.A.

8 & 9 Geo. 6 (1944–45)

21. Wages Councils (Northern Ireland) Act 1945.
s. 10, S.Rs. 1979 Nos. 347, 359, 360.

42. Water Act 1945.
s. 19, orders, 78/1849, 1940, 1955; 79/7, 8, 28, 39, 48, 57, 101, 128, 147, 161, 199, 248, 335, 343, 344, 479, 502, 505, 536, 537, 557, 561, 593, 596, 684, 1329, 1330.
s. 23, orders 78/1782, 1932; 79/175, 176, 509, 512, 513, 562, 679, 801, 831, 901, 1065, 1078, 1168, 1361, 1369, 1457, 1498, 1527, 1560.
s. 32, orders 79/801, 1079, 1528.
s. 33, orders 78/1823; 79/1079, 1527.
s. 37, see *Royco Homes* v. *Southern Water Authority* [1979] 1 W.L.R. 1366, H.L.
s. 50, orders 78/1923; 79/48, 801, 1079, 1168, 1369, 1528.
sch. 3, see *George Whitehouse* v. *Anglian Water Authority* (Ref./157/1977) 247 E.G. 223.

CAP.

9 & 10 Geo. 6 (1945–46)

19. Bretton Woods Agreements Act 1945.
preamble, ss. 2, 3, repealed in pt.: 1979, c.29,sch.

36. Statutory Instruments Act 1946.
s. 5, orders 79/459, 1375.

42. Water (Scotland) Act 1946.
ss. 21, 44, orders 78/1607; 79/455, 973, 1471, 1513.

45. United Nations Act 1946.
s. 1, order 78/1894–1898; repealed in pt.: 1979,c.60,sch.3.

49. Acquisition of Land (Authorisation Procedure) Act 1946.
ss. 1, 8, repealed in pt.: 1979,c.46,sch.5.
sch. 1, see *George* v. *Secretary of State for the Environment* (1979) 259 E.G. 339, C.A.; repealed in pt.: 1979,c.46, sch.5; order 79/571.

58. Borrowing (Control and Guarantees) Act 1946.
ss. 1, 3, order 79/794.

64. Finance Act 1946.
s. 63, repealed: 1979, c. 30, sch.

10 & 11 Geo. 6 (1946–47)

14. Exchange Control Act 1947.
s. 1, 2, order 79/1331.
s. 7, see *Shelley* v. *Paddock* (1979) 123 S.J. 706, C.A.
s. 8, see *Re Transatlantic Life Assurance Co.* [1979] 3 All E.R. 352, Slade J.
s. 15, order 79/1333.
ss. 16, 17, see *Swiss Bank Corp.* v. *Lloyds Bank* [1979] 2 All E.R. 853, Browne-Wilkinson J.
s. 23, order 79/1335.
s. 31, orders 79/647, 648, 1331–1334, 1336, 1337.
s. 36, orders 78/1942; 79/321, 647, 648, 740, 1331–1334, 1338; directions 79/1194.
s. 37, directions 79/1339.
s. 42, orders 78/1942, 79/321, 740, 1194; directions 79/1335.
sch. 5, see *A.* v. *H.M. Treasury*; *B.* v. *H.M. Treasury* [1979] 2 All E.R. 586, T. P. Russell Q.C., amended: 1979, c.2,sch.4.

27. National Health Service (Scotland) Act 1947.
s. 34, regs. 78/1762.

39. Statistics of Trade Act 1947.
ss. 2, 11, order 79/1484.

40. Industrial Organisation and Development Act 1947.
s. 9, order 79/748.

41. Fire Services Act 1947.
s. 17, see *R.* v. *Leicestershire Fire Authority, ex p. Thompson* (1978) 77 L.G.R. 373, D.C.
s. 18, regs. 78/1727.
s. 26, orders 79/407, 855, 1286, 1360.

42. Acquisition of Land (Authorisation Procedure) (Scotland) Act 1947.
ss. 1, 7, sch. 1, repealed in pt.: 1979, c.46,sch.5.

CAP.

10 & 11 Geo. 6 (1946–47)—cont.

43. Local Government (Scotland) Act 1947.
s. 238, see *British Railways Board* v. *Glasgow Corporation*, 1976 S.C. 224.

44. Crown Proceedings Act 1947.
s. 5, substituted: 1979,c.39,sch.5.
s. 40, see *Mutasa* v. *Att.-Gen.* [1979] 3 All E.R. 257, Boreham J.

48. Agriculture Act 1947.
ss. 78–81, repealed: 1979,c.13,sch.2.

54. Electricity Act 1947.
repealed, except ss. 1 in pt., 2 in pt., 4 in pt., 11 in pt., 13, 19 in pt., 22, 54 in pt., 57 in pt., 60, 67, 68 in pt., 69, sch. 2, sch. 4 in pt.: 1979,c.11,sch.12.

Malaysian Income Tax Ordinance 1947.
s. 10, see *International Investment* v. *The Comptroller-General of Inland Revenue* [1978] T.R. 247, P.C.

11 & 12 Geo. 6 (1947–48)

10. Administration of Justice (Scotland) Act 1948.
s. 2, Act of Sederunt 79/190.

29. National Assistance Act 1948.
s. 22, regs. 79/823, 1084.
s. 29, see *Wyatt* v. *Hillingdon London Borough Council* (1978) 76 L.G.R. 727, C.A.
s. 43, amended: 1979,c.55,sch.2.

36. House of Commons Members' Fund Act 1948.
s. 3, resolution 79/1667.

37. Radioactive Substances Act 1948.
s. 2, amended: 1979,c.2,sch.4.

38. Companies Act 1948.
see *British Airways Board* v. ***Parish*** (1979) 123 S.J. 139, C.A.
s. 95, see *Re Bond Worth* [1979] 3 W.L.R. 629, Slade J.; *Borden (U.K.)* v. *Scottish Timber Products* [1979] 3 W.L.R. 672, C.A.
s. 116, see *Re Transatlantic Life Assurance Co.* [1979] 3 All E.R. 352, Slade J.
s. 141, see *Re Moorgate Mercantile Holdings* (1979) 123 S.J. 551, Slade J.
s. 155, repealed in pt.: 1979,c.37,s.46, sch.7.
ss. 191, 194, see *Gibson's Exr.* v. *Gibson* (O.H.), 1980 S.L.T. 2.
s. 196, see *Parsons* v. *Albert J. Parsons and Sons* [1979] I.C.R. 271, C.A.
s. 222, see *Re Southard & Co.* [1979] 1 W.L.R. 1198, C.A.
s. 225, see *Re Camburn Petroleum Products* [1979] 3 All E.R. 297, Slade J.
s. 231, see *Re Aro Co.*, *The Times*, November 30, 1979, C.A.
s. 268, see *Re Castle New Homes* [1979] 2 All E.R. 775, Slade J.; *Re Spiraflite (1974)* [1979] 2 All E.R. 766, Megarry J.
s. 319, see *Re Piccadilly Estate Hotels* (1978) 77 L.G.R. 79, Slade J.
s. 325, amended: 1979,c.53,s.4.

CAP.

11 & 12 Geo. 6 (1947–48)—cont.

38. *Companies Act 1948—cont.*
s. 332, see *Re Sarflax* [1979] 2 W.L.R. 202, Oliver J.
s. 333, see *Gibson's Exr.* v. *Gibson* (O.H.), 1980 S.L.T. 2.
s. 346, see *Re Camburn Petroleum Products* [1979] 3 All E.R. 297, Slade J.; *Re Southard & Co.* [1979] 1 W.L.R. 1198, C.A.
s. 365, rules 79/209; orders 79/968, 1149.
ss. 429–431, repealed: 1979,c.37,s.46,sch. 7.
s. 432, repealed: *ibid.*,sch.7.
s. 433, repealed in pt.: *ibid.*,s.46,sch.7.
s. 434, repealed in pt.: *ibid.*,sch.7.
s. 441, see *Re A Company* [1979] Crim.L.R. 650, C.A.
s. 454, regs. 79/54, 1618.
sch. 1, see *Re Emmadart* [1979] 1 All E.R. 599, Brightman J.
sch. 8, amended: regs. 79/1618.

41. Law Reform (Personal Injuries Act) 1948.
s. 2, see *Lim Poh Choo* v. *Camden and Islington Area Health Authority* [1979] 3 W.L.R. 44, H.L.

43. Children Act 1948.
ss. 1, 2, see *Lewisham London Borough Council* v. *Lewisham Juvenile Court JJ.* [1979] 2 W.L.R. 513, H.L.; *Wheatley* v. *Waltham Forest London Borough Council* (*Note*) [1979] 2 W.L.R. 543, D.C.
s. 2, see *Re M. (Minors)* (1979) 123 S.J. 284, D.C.; *M.* v. *Wigan Metropolitan Borough Council* [1979] 2 All E.R. 958, D.C.; *Re M.* (*Review of Care Order*) (1979) 9 Fam.Law 186, D.C.
s. 26, amended: 1979, c. 55, sch. 2.

44. Merchant Shipping Act 1948.
ss. 1, 3, 5, regs. 79/798.

45. Agriculture (Scotland) Act 1948.
sch. 6, see *Austin* v. *Gibson*, 1979 S.L.T.(Land Ct.) 12.

56. British Nationality Act 1948.
s. 1, repealed in pt.: 1979,c.60,s.2.
s. 7, see *R.* v. *Secretary of State for Home Affairs, ex p. Akhtar*, *The Times*, December 27, 1979, D.C.
s. 29, regs. 79/240, 1072.

58. Criminal Justice Act 1948.
s. 52, rules 78/1919.

63. Agricultural Holdings Act 1948.
s. 2, see *Luton* v. *Tinsey* (1978) 249 E.G. 239, C.A.; *Short Bros. (Plant)* v. *Edwards* (1978) 249 E.G. 539, C.A.
s. 8, see *Tummon* v. *Barclays Bank Trust Co.* (1979) 250 E.G. 980, Judge Goodall, Bodmin County Ct.
s. 24, see *Beevers* v. *Mason* (1978) 37 P. & C.R. 452, C.A.
s. 25, see *R.* v. *Agricultural Land Tribunal for the South Eastern Area, ex p. Parslow* (1979) 251 E.G. 667, D.C.

CAP.

12, 13 & 14 Geo. 6 (1948–49)

10. House of Commons (Redistribution of Seats) Act 1949.
s. 3, order 78/1911.

42. Lands Tribunal Act 1949.
s. 1, see *Cupar Trading Estate* v. *Fife Regional Council*, 1979 S.L.T. (Lands Tr.) 2.

43. Merchant Shipping (Safety Convention) Act 1949.
ss. 3, 5, 6, 12, amended: 1979,c.39,sch.6.
s. 14, repealed in pt.: *ibid.*,s.28.
ss. 19, 21, amended: *ibid.*,sch.6.
s. 23, rules 79/976; amended: 1979,c.39, sch.6.
s. 24, amended: 1979,c.2,sch.4; c.39,sch. 6; repealed in pt.: *ibid.*,sch.7.
s. 33, regs. 79/798.

44. Patents Act 1949.
s. 9, see *Xerox Corp.* (*Chatterji's*) *Application* [1979] R.P.C. 375, Whitford J.

54. Wireless Telegraphy Act 1949.
s. 1, see *Monks* v. *Pilgrim* [1979] Crim.L.R. 595, D.C.
s. 2, regs. 79/841, 1490.

66. House of Commons (Redistribution of Seats) Act 1949.
sch. 2, amended: 1979,c.15,s.1.

67. Civil Aviation Act 1949.
s. 8, orders 79/929, 930, 1318; amended: 1979,c.2,sch.4.
s. 41, order 79/929.
s. 57, order 79/1318.
ss. 57, 58, orders 79/929, 930.
ss. 59, 61, order 79/930.
s. 66, repealed in pt.: 1979,c.60,sch.3.

68. Representation of the People Act 1949.
modified: regs. 79/338.
s. 9, see *Marshall* v. *B.B.C.* (1979) 123 S.J. 336, C.A.
s. 20, regs. 79/429–431, 588, 589.
s. 42, regs. 79/434.
s. 159, amended: 1979,c.31,sch.1.
s. 160, Act of Sederunt 79/516, 521, 543; S.R. 1979 No. 179.
s. 171, regs. 79/434.

74. Coast Protection Act 1949.
s. 47, amended: 1979,c.46,sch.4.

75. Agricultural Holdings (Scotland) Act 1949.
s. 2, see *Maclean* v. *Galloway*, 1979 S.L.T.(Sh.Ct.) 32.
s. 17, regs. 79/799.
ss. 24–26, 28, 93, see *Austin* v. *Gibson*, 1979 S.L.T.(Land Ct.) 12.
sch. 6, instrument 79/800.

76. Marriage Act 1949.
s. 3, amended: 1979,c.55,sch.2.

87. Patents Act 1949.
s. 4, see *Garcock Inc.'s Application* [1979] F.S.R. 604, Whitford J.
ss. 4, 6, 30, 31, 32, 69, see *American Cyanamid Co.* v. *Ethicon* [1979] R.P.C. 215, Graham J.
ss. 4, 30, 31, see *Holtite* v. *Jost (Great Britain)* [1979] R.P.C. 81, H.L.

CAP.

12, 13 & 14 Geo. 6 (1948–49)—cont.

87. *Patents Act 1949—cont.*
s. 14, see *Bristol-Myers Co.* v. *Beecham Group* [1978] F.S.R. 553, Sup.Ct. of Israel; *General Tyre and Rubber Co. (Hofelt & Corl's) Application* [1977] F.S.R. 402, Whitford J.
s. 23, see *Hovercraft Development's Patent Extension* [1979] F.S.R. 481, Whitford J.
ss. 29, 31, see *S.C.M. Corp's Application* [1979] R.P.C. 341, C.A.
ss. 32, 85, see *Bristol-Myers Co.* v. *Beecham Group* [1978] F.S.R. 553, Sup.Ct. of Israel.
s. 66, see *Plasticisers* v. *Pixdane* [1978] F.S.R. 595, D. W. Falconer, Q.C.
s. 101, see *I.T.S. Rubber's Application* [1979] R.P.C. 318, Whitford J.

88. Registered Designs Act 1949.
s. 1, see *Cook & Hurst's Design Application* [1979] R.P.C. 197, Whitford J.

97. National Parks and Access to the Countryside Act 1949.
see *R.* v. *Secretary of State for the Environment, ex p. Pearson* [1979] J.P.L. 765, D.C.
ss. 27, 32, see *Suffolk County Council* v. *Mason* [1979] 2 W.L.R. 571, H.L.
ss. 32, 33, sch. 1, see *R.* v. *Secretary of State for the Environment, ex p. Stewart* (1979) 37 P. & C.R. 279, D.C.

101. Justices of the Peace Act 1949.
ss. 1, 3, 5, 13, repealed: 1979,c.55, sch.3.
s. 15, rules 79/170, 570, 757, 758, 952, 953, 1220–1222; repealed in pt.: 1979, c.55,sch.3.
ss. 16, 17, repealed: *ibid.*
s. 18, orders, 78/1952; 79/1284; repealed: 1979,c.55,sch.3.
ss. 19, 20 (in pt.), 21, 23, 25–27, 42, 44, sch. 4, repealed: *ibid.*

14 Geo. 6 (1950)

12. Foreign Compensation Act 1950.
s. 7, order 79/109.

27. Arbitration Act 1950.
see *Japan Line* v. *Aggeliki Charis Compania Maritima S.A.* (1979) 123 S.J. 487, C.A.
s. 4, see *Paczy* v. *Haendler & Natermann GmbH* [1979] F.S.R. 420, Whitford J.
s. 8, amended: 1979,c.42,s.6.
ss. 8, 9, see *Termarea S.R.L.* v. *Rederiaktiebolaget Sally* [1979] 2 All E.R. 989, Mocatta J.
s. 9, substituted: 1979,c.42,s.6.
s. 10, amended: *ibid.*,s.6; repealed in pt.: *ibid.*,ss.6,8.
s. 14, amended: *ibid.*,s.7.
s. 21, repealed: 1979,c.42,ss.1,8.
ss. 21, 28, see *Antco Shipping* v. *Seabridge Shipping* [1979] 1 W.L.R. 1103, C.A.

CAP.

14 Geo. 6 (1950)—cont.

27. *Arbitration Act 1950—cont.*
ss. 21, 32, see ***Imperial Metal Industries (Kynoch)* v. *Amalgamated Union of*** *Engineering Workers (Technical, Ad-* ***ministrative and Supervisory Section)*** **[1979] I.C.R. 23, C.A.**
s. 24, see *Paczy* v. *Haendler & Natermann GmbH* [1979] F.S.R. 420, Whitford J.
s. 26, see *Leonidis* v. *Thames Water Authority* (1979) 251 E.G. 669, Parker J.
s. 27, see *Sioux Inc.* v. *China Salvage Co., Kwangchow Branch*, *The Times*, December 13, 1979, C.A.
ss. 28, 30–32, amended: 1979,c.42,s.7.
s. 35, order 79/304.

28. **Shops Act 1950.**
ss. 47, 58, see *Newark District Council* v. *E. & A. Market Promotions* (1978) 77 L.G.R. 6, C.A.
s. 69, regs. 79/1294.

36. **Diseases of Animals Act 1950.**
s. 1, orders 78/1875 (S.); 79/37, 773, 815, 1013, 1701.
s. 5, orders 78/1875 (S.); 79/789 (S.), 1288.
s. 11, orders 78/1875 (S.); 79/773, 815.
ss. 17, 19, order 78/1875 (S.).
s. 20, orders 79/773, 1013.
s. 24, order 79/1701; amended: 1979, c.2,sch.4.
s. 50, orders 79/37; 773.
s. 73, amended: 1979,c.2,sch.4.
s. 84, orders 79/815, 1701.
s. 85, orders 78/1875 (S.): 79/37, 773, 789 (S.), 1013, 1288, 1365, 1701.

37. **Maintenance Orders Act 1950.**
s. 3, amended: 1979,c.55,sch.2.

28. **Registration of Deeds Ordinance (Revised Ordinance 1950, No. 2) (Trinidad).**
s. 16, see *Mahabir* v. *Payne* [1979] 1 W.L.R. 507, P.C.

14 & 15 Geo. 6 (1950–51)

11. **Administration of Justice (Pensions) Act 1950.**
s. 6, order 79/1275; amended: order 79/680.

53. **Midwives Act 1951.**
repealed: 1979,c.36,sch.8.

54. **Midwives (Scotland) Act 1951.**
repealed: 1979,c.36,sch.8.

55. **Nurses (Scotland) Act 1951.**
Pts. I, II, repealed: 1979,c.36,sch.8.
ss. 27, 29, amended: *ibid.*,sch.7.
s. 32, repealed in pt.: *ibid.*,schs.7,8.
Pt. IV (except s. 36 in pt.), repealed: *ibid.*,sch.8.
schs. 1, 4, repealed: *ibid.*

60. **Mineral Workings Act 1951.**
s. 19, repealed in pt.: order 79/1123.

65. **Reserve and Auxiliary Forces (Protection of Civil Interests) Act 1951.**
ss. 5, 29, 57, sch. 2, amended: order 79/1573.
s. 65, order 79/291.

CAP.

15 & 16 Geo. 6 & 1 Eliz. 2 (1951–52)

10. **Income Tax Act 1952.**
s. 175, see *T. & E. Homes Ltd.* v. *Robinson* [1979] 1 W.L.R. 452, C.A.
s. 412, see *Vestey* v. *I.C.R. The Times*, November 24, 1979, H.L.

41. **Finance Act 1952.**
s. 71, see *Barty-King* v. *Ministry of* *Defence* [1979] 2 All E.R. 80, May J.

44. **Customs and Excise Act 1952.**
Pts. I–III, repealed, except ss. 35–37, 41–43.
ss. 35–37, repealed: 1979,c.3,sch.3.
ss. 41–43, repealed: *ibid.*
s. 44, see *Allgemeine Gold-und-Silberscheideanstalg* v. *Customs and Excise Comrs. The Times*, December 11, 1979, C.A.
P. IV, repealed: 1979,c.4,sch.4.
s. 140, regs. 78/1786.
ss. 219–222, repealed: 1979,c.6,sch.
ss. 226–228, repealed: 1979,c.4,sch.4.
Pt. IX, repealed, except ss. 237, 241–243: 1979,c.2,sch.6.
ss. 237, 241–243, repealed: 1979,c.4,sch. 4.
Pt. X, repealed, except ss. 263 in pt., 271 in pt., 272: 1979,c.2,sch.6.
s. 263, repealed in pt.: 1979,c.4,sch.4.
s. 271, repealed in pt.: 1979,c.7,sch.2.
s. 272, repealed: 1979,c.3,sch.3.
Pts. XI, XII, repealed, except ss. 307 in pt., 309 in pt., 310, 315 in pt.: 1979, c.2,sch.6.
s. 307, repealed in pt.: 1979,c.4,sch.4.
s. 309, repealed in pt.: 1979,c.3,sch.3.
s. 310, repealed: *ibid.*
s. 315, repealed in pt.: 1979,c.4,sch.4.
sch. 7, repealed in pt.: 1979,c.2,sch.6.
sch. 10, repealed in pt.: 1979,c.2,sch.6; c.4,sch.4.

47. **Rating and Valuation (Scotland) Act 1952.**
s. 6, Acts of Sederunt 79/1408, 1409.

52. **Prison Act 1952.**
s. 47, see *R.* v. *Hull Prison Board of Visitors, ex p. St. Germain (No. 2)* [1979] 3 All E.R. 545, D.C.

55. **Magistrates' Courts Act 1952.**
see *R.* v. *Colchester Stipendiary Magistrate, ex p. Beck* [1979] Crim.L.R. 250, D.C.
s. 1, see *R.* v. *West London Justices, ex p. Klahn* [1979] 2 All E.R. 221, D.C.
s. 2, see *R.* v. *East Powder JJ., ex p. Lampshire* [1979] 2 W.L.R. 479, D.C.
s. 4, see *R.* v. *Colchester Stipendiary Magistrate, ex p. Beck* [1979] 2 W.L.R. 637, P.C.
s. 28, see *R.* v. *T. (A Juvenile)* [1979] Crim.L.R. 588, Snaresbrook Crown Ct.
s. 29, see *R.* v. *Brentwood JJ., ex p. Jones* [1979] Crim.L.R. 115, D.C.
s. 38, see *R.* v. *Houghton*; *R.* v. *Franciosy* **(1978) 68 Cr.App.R. 197, C.A.**

CAP.

15 & 16 Geo. 6 & 1 Eliz. 2 (1951–52)—cont.

55. *Magistrates' Courts Act 1952—cont.*
ss. 44, 56, amended: 1979,c.55,sch.2.
s. 76, see *R.* v. *Halifax JJ., ex p. Woolverton* (1978) 123 S.J. 123, D.C.
s. 100, see *R.* v. *Sandwell JJ., ex p. West Midlands Passenger Transport Board* [1979] R.T.R. 17, D.C.; *Lee* v. *Wiltshire Chief Constable* [1979] R.T.R. 349, D.C.
s. 102, see *De Costa Small* v. *Kirkpatrick* (1978) 68 Cr.App.R. 186, D.C.
s. 104, see *R.* v. *Eastbourne JJ., ex p. Barsoum*, January 26, 1979; *R.* v. *Sandwell JJ., ex p. West Midlands Passenger Transport Board* [1979] R.T.R. 17, D.C.; *R.* v. *Coventry JJ., ex p. Sayers* [1979] R.T.R. 22, D.C.
s. 114, amended: 1979,c.55,sch.2.
ss. 116, 118, 121, repealed in pt.: 1979, c.55,sch.3.
sch. 2, see *Re Phelps (decd.); Wells* v. *Phelps* [1979] 3 All E.R. 373, C.A.

67. Visiting Forces Act 1952.
ss. 1, 10, amended: 1979,c.27,sch.
sch., amended: order 78/1407.

xli. Clifton Suspension Bridge Act 1952.
s. 3, amended: order 79/1123.
s. 26, repealed in pt.: *ibid.*
ss. 46, 61, amended: *ibid.*
s. 65, repealed in pt.: *ibid.*
s. 67, amended: *ibid.*

1 & 2 Eliz. 2 (1952–53)

14. Prevention of Crime Act 1953.
s. 1, see *Bates* v. *Bulman* (1978) 68 Cr. App.R. 21, D.C.; *R.* v. *Ambrose*, January 31, 1979, London Crown Court, Judge Layton.
ss. 1, 4, see *Harrison* v. *Thornton (Note)* (1966) 68 Cr.App.R. 28, D.C.

20. Births and Deaths Registration Act 1953.
s. 11, amended: 1979,c.36,sch.7.

34. Finance Act 1953.
s. 2, repealed: 1979,c.4,sch.4.
s. 3, repealed in pt.: 1979,c.6,sch.
ss. 33, 35, repealed in pt., 1979,c.2,sch.6.

36. Post Office Act 1953.
ss. 16, 17, amended: 1979,c.9,sch.4.

47. Emergency Laws (Miscellaneous Provisions) Act 1953.
s. 6, repealed: 1979,c.36,sch.8.

49. Historic Buildings and Ancient Monuments Act 1953.
Pts. II, III, repealed: 1979,c.46,sch.5.
s. 4A, added: *ibid.*,s.48.
ss. 5, 8, amended: *ibid.*,sch.4.
s. 20, repealed: *ibid.*,sch.5.
s. 22, repealed in pt.: *ibid.*
sch., repealed: *ibid.*

Trade Marks Act 1952–53 (Canada).
ss. 2, 6, 7, 18, 20, 49, see *Off! Trade Mark* [1979] F.S.R. 243, Fed.Ct. of Canada.

CAP.

2 & 3 Eliz. 2 (1953–54)

17. Royal Irish Constabulary (Widows' Pensions) Act 1954.
s. 1, regs. 79/1401.

30. Protection of Birds Act 1954.
s. 7, order 79/1007; amended: 1979,c.2, sch.4.
s. 9, orders 78/1872; 79/423, 437, 438.
s. 13, orders 79/70, 99 (S.), 141 (S.), 423, 437, 438.
s. 14, amended: 1979,c.2,sch.4.
sch. 1, amended: order 79/423.
sch. 2, amended: order 79/437.
sch. 4, amended: order 79/438.

39. Agriculture (Miscellaneous Provisions) Act 1954.
s. 10, order 79/587.

48. Summary Procedure (Scotland) Act 1954.
ss. 71, 73, see *Christie* v. *Barclay*, 1974 J.C. 68.

56. Landlord and Tenant Act 1954.
s. 3, see *Baron* v. *Phillips* (1979) 38 P. & C.R. 91, C.A.
s. 23, see *Land Reclamation Co.* v. *Basildon District Council* (1979) 250 E.G. 549, C.A.; *Hillil Property & Investment Co.* v. *Naraine Pharmacy* (1979) 123 S.J. 437, C.A.; *Land Reclamation Co.* v. *Basildon District Council* [1979] 1 W.L.R. 767, C.A.; *Ross Auto Wash* v. *Herbert* (1979) 250 E.G. 971, Fox J.; *Bell* v. *Franks (Alfred) & Bartlett Co.* (1979) 123 S.J. 804, C.A.
s. 24A, see *Michael Kramer & Co.* v. *Airways Pension Fund Trustees* (1976) 246 E.G. 911, C.A.; *Fawke* v. *Viscount Chelsea* [1979] 3 W.L.R. 508, C.A.; *Victor Blake (Menswear)* v. *Westminster City Council* (1979) 38 P. & C.R. 448, Deputy Judge Michael Wheeler, Q.C.
s. 25, see *Germax Securities* v. *Spiegal* (1978) 123 S.J. 164, C.A.
s. 26, see *Bristol Cars* v. *R. K. H. Hotels (In Liquidation)* (1979) 38 P. & C.R. 411, C.A.
s. 29, see *Polyviou* v. *Seeley* (1979) 252 E.G. 375, C.A.
s. 30, see *Harvey Textiles* v. *Hillel* (1979) 249 E.G. 1063, Whitford J.
ss. 30, 31A, see *Redfern* v. *Reeves* (1978) 37 P. & C.R. 364, C.A.
s. 32, see *Kirkwood* v. *Johnson* (1979) 38 P. & C.R. 392, C.A.
s. 34, see *Fawke* v. *Viscount Chelsea* [1979] 3 W.L.R. 508, C.A.
s. 35, see *O'May* v. *City of London Real Property Co.* (1979) 249 E.G. 1065, Goulding J.; *Kirkwood* v. *Johnson* (1979) 38 P. & C.R. 392, C.A.
s. 38, see *Stevenson and Rush (Holdings) Ltd.* v. *Langdon* (1979) 38 P. & C.R. 208, C.A.
s. 41, see *Carshalton Beeches Bowling Club* v. *Cameron* (1979) 249 E.G. 1279, C.A.
s. 43, see *Grant* v. *Gresham* (1979) 252 E.G. 55, C.A.

CAP.

2 & 3 Eliz. 2 (1953–54)—cont.

56. *Landlord and Tenant Act 1954—cont.*
s. 64, see *Bristol Cars* v. *R. K. H. Hotels (In Liquidation)* (1979) 251 E.G. 1279, C.A.

60. Electricity Reorganisation (Scotland) Act 1954.
repealed, except ss. 1 in pt., 15 in pt., 16, 17, sch. 1 in pt.: 1979,c.11,sch.12.

70. Mines and Quarries Act 1954.
s. 34, see *Connolly* v. *National Coal Board* (O.H.), 1979 S.L.T. 51.
ss. 75–77, repealed: regs. 79/318.

3 & 4 Eliz. 2 (1954–55)

8. Northern Ireland Act 1955.
repealed: order 79/1573.

18. Army Act 1955.
ss. 119, 122–124, 126, 127, 129, rules 79/1456.
s. 134, see *R.* v. *Bisset* (1979) 123 S.J. 718, Court Martial Appeal Ct.
s. 225, amended: 1979,c.27,sch.

19. Air Force Act 1955.
s. 223, amended: 1979,c.27,sch.

21. Crofters (Scotland) Act 1955.
s. 12, see *Foljambe* v. *Crofters of Melness*, 1979 S.L.T.(Land Ct.) 9.
s. 14, schs. 2, 5, see *Gilmour* v. *Master of Lovat*, 1979 S.L.T.(Land Ct.) 2.

4 & 5 Eliz. 2 (1955–56)

16. Food and Drugs Act 1955.
s. 2, see *Greater Manchester Council* v. *Lockwood Foods* [1979] Crim.L.R. 593, D.C.
s. 3, amended: 1979,c.4,sch.3.
s. 4, regs. 79/1254.
ss. 4, 7, regs. 78/1787; 79/752.
s. 13, regs. 79/693, 1426, 1427.
s. 82, regs. 79/1427.
s. 123, regs. 78/1787; 79/693, 752, 1254, 1426, 1427.
s. 123A, regs. 79/752.
s. 134, regs. 79/1427.
s. 135, amended: 1979,c.2,sch.4.
sch. 10, regs. 79/1427.

30. Food and Drugs (Scotland) Act 1956.
s. 2, see *Skinner* v. *MacLean*, 1979 S.L.T.(Notes) 35.
s. 3, amended: 1979,c.4,sch.3.
ss. 4, 7, regs. 79/107, 383, 1073.
s. 13, regs. 79/768.
s. 26, regs. 79/383, 1073.
s. 56, regs. 79/107, 383, 768, 1073.
s. 56A, regs. 79/1073.
s. 58, amended: 1979,c.2,sch.4.

46. Administration of Justice Act 1956.
s. 35, repealed: 1979,c.53,s.7.
s. 36, amended: 1979,c.53,s.7.

48. Sugar Act 1956.
s. 18, order 79/222.

54. Finance Act 1956.
sch. 2, see *Tyrer* v. *Smart* [1979] 1 W.L.R. 113, H.L.

CAP.

4 & 5 Eliz. 2 (1955–56)—cont.

69. Sexual Offences Act 1956.
s. 30, see *R.* v. *Farrugia, Borg, Agius and Gauchi* (1979) 69 Cr.App.R. 108, C.A.

74. Copyright Act 1956.
see *Lady Anne Tennant* v. *Associated Newspapers Group* [1979] F.S.R. 298, Megarry V.-C.
ss. 1, 2, see *Performing Right Society* v. *Harlequin Record Shops* [1979] 1 W.L.R. 851, Browne-Wilkinson J.
ss. 1, 3, 9, 17, 18, 48, see *Nichols Advanced Vehicle System Inc.* v. *Rees, Oliver* [1979] R.P.C. 128, Templeman J.
ss. 1, 13, 32, 48, 49, see *Spelling Goldberg Productions Inc.* v. *B.P.C. Publishing* [1979] F.S.R. 494, Judge Mervyn Davies, Q.C.
s. 3, see *Oscar Trade Mark* [1979] R.P.C. 197, Trade Marks Registry.
ss. 3, 9, 48, 49, see *L. B. (Plastics)* v. *Swish Products* [1979] F.S.R. 145, H.L.
ss. 4, 20, 36, see *Roban Jig & Tool Co. and Elkadart* v. *Taylor* [1979] F.S.R. 130, C.A.
ss. 5, 8, see *Carlin Music Corp.* v. *Collins* [1979] F.S.R. 548, C.A.
s. 17, see *Hunter* v. *Fitzroy Robinson and Partners* [1978] F.S.R. 167, Oliver J.
s. 22, amended: 1979,c.2,sch.4.
s. 31, order 79/577, 910.
ss. 32, 47, order 79/910.
sch. 7, see *Redwood Music* v. *B. Feldman & Co.* [1979] R.P.C. 1, Goff J.

76. Medical Act 1956.
ss. 3, 4, 7, 10–13, 15–17, 23, repealed in pt.: order 79/289.
s. 28, see *Tarnesby* v. *Kensington, Chelsea and Westminster Area Health Authority (Teaching)* (1978) 123 S.J. 49, Neill J.
s. 33, repealed in pt.: order 79/289.
s. 37, order 78/1796.
s. 39, repealed: order 79/289.
ss. 49, 54, repealed in pt.: *ibid.*
sch. 3, amended and repealed in pt.: *ibid.*

5 & 6 Eliz. 2 (1957)

11. Homicide Act 1957.
s. 2, see *R.* v. *Kiszko* (1978) 68 Cr.App.R. 62, C.A.; *R.* v. *Vinagre* (1979) 69 Cr.App.R. 104, C.A.

15. Nurses Act 1957.
repealed: 1979,c.36,sch.8.
s. 32, instrument 79/49.

16. Nurses Agencies Act 1957.
ss. 1, 3, amended: 1979,c.36,sch.7.
s. 8, repealed in pt.: *ibid.*,schs.7,8.

21. Cinematograph Films Act 1957.
s. 2, amended: order 79/395.
s. 4, amended: 1979,c.2,sch.4.

CAP.

5 & 6 Eliz. 2 (1957)—cont.

28. Dentists Act 1957.
s. 2, amended: order 79/289.
s. 25, see *McEniff* v. *General Dental Council*, *The Times*, December 1, 1979, P.C.

40. Thermal Insulation (Industrial Buildings) Act 1957.
repealed (S.): order 79/594.
s. 2, repealed: regs. 79/601.
s. 10, amended: *ibid.*

48. Electricity Act 1957.
s. 28, repealed: 1979,c.11,sch.12.
s. 29, repealed in pt.: *ibid.*
s. 35, repealed: *ibid.*
sch. 4, repealed: *ibid.*

49. Finance Act 1957.
s. 5, repealed: 1979,c.2,sch.6.
s. 42, repealed in pt.: *ibid.*
sch. 2, repealed: *ibid.*

53. Naval Discipline Act 1957.
s. 135, amended: 1979,c.27,sch.

55. Affiliation Proceedings Act 1957.
s. 3, amended: 1979,c.55,sch.2.

56. Housing Act 1957.
s. 5, see *Chorley Borough Council* v. *Barratt Developments (North West)* [1979] 3 All E.R. 634, Blackett-Ord V.-C.
ss. 9–11, see *Elliott* v. *Brighton Borough Council*, June 16, 1979, Judge Grant, Brighton County Ct.
ss. 16, 20, 39, see *Dudlow Estates* v. *Sefton Metropolitan Borough Council* (1979) 249 E.G. 1271, C.A.

57. Agriculture Act 1957.
ss. 5, 35, order 79/1541.

59. Coal Mining (Subsidence) Act 1957.
s. 9, amended: 1979,c.46,sch.6.

6 & 7 Eliz. 2 (1957–58)

6. Import Duties Act 1958.
s. 4, repealed: 1979,c.3,sch.3.
s. 5, orders 78/1866, 1933; 79/121, 153; repealed: 1979,c.3,sch.3.
s. 6, repealed: *ibid.*
ss. 10, 12, repealed in pt.: *ibid.*
s. 13, order 79/153, repealed: 1979,c.3, sch.3.
ss. 15, 16, repealed: *ibid.*
sch. 3, orders 78/1866, 1933; 79/121, 153; repealed in pt.: 1979,c.3,sch.3.
sch. 4, repealed in pt.: *ibid.*

11. Isle of Man Act 1958.
repealed: 1979,c.58,sch.2.

30. Land Powers (Defence) Act 1958.
s. 6, amended: 1979,c.46,sch.4; repealed in pt.: *ibid.*,schs.4,5.

34. Litter Act 1958.
s. 1, see *Witney* v. *Cattanach* [1979] Crim.L.R. 461, D.C.

39. Maintenance Orders Act 1958.
s. 19, order 79/116.

CAP.

6 & 7 Eliz. 2 (1957–58)—cont.

40. Matrimonial Proceedings (Children) Act 1958.
s. 8, see *Hunter* v. *Hunter* (O.H.), 1976 S.L.T.(Notes) 2.

45. Prevention of Fraud (Investments) Act 1958.
s. 13, amended: 1979,c.37,sch.6.
s. 26, amended: 1979,c.60,s.6.

47. Agricultural Marketing Act 1958.
s. 5, amended: 1979,c.13,sch.1.

51. Public Records Act 1958.
sch. 1, amended: 1979,c.43,sch.6.
sch. 2, amended: 1979,c.13,sch.1; repealed in pt.: *ibid.*,sch.2.

56. Finance Act 1958.
s. 6, repealed: 1979,c.4,sch.4.
s. 40, repealed in pt.: 1979,c.2,sch.6.

61. Interest on Damages (Scotland) Act 1958.
s. 1, see *Mouland* v. *Ferguson* (O.H.), 1979 S.L.T.(Notes) 85.

62. Merchant Shipping (Liability of Shipowners and Others) Act 1958.
see *The Penelope II*, *The Times*, November 21, 1979, C.A.
repealed (except s. 11 in pt.): 1979,c.39, sch.7.
s. 1, order 79/790.

66. Tribunals and Inquiries Act 1958.
s. 11, see *Watt* v. *Lord Advocate*, 1979 S.L.T. 137.

69. Opencast Coal Act 1958.
s. 7, sch. 1, see *Wigan Borough Council* v. *Secretary of State for Energy and the National Coal Board* [1979] J.P.L. 610, Deputy Judge Michael Kempster, Q.C.
ss. 35, 49, orders 78/1802; 79/942.

7 & 8 Eliz. 2 (1958–59)

5. Adoption Act 1958.
ss. 4, 5, see *A. and B.* v. *C.*, 1977 S.C. 27.
s. 9, rules 79/978.

11. European Monetary Agreement Act 1959.
repealed: 1979, c. 29, sch.

17. International Bank and Monetary Fund Act 1959.
preamble, repealed in pt.: 1979,c.29,sch.

22. County Courts Act 1959.
s. 94, see *Harmsworth* v. *London Transport Executive* (1979) 123 S.J. 825, C.A.
s. 102, rules 79/1045.
s. 141, repealed: 1979,c.53,s.7.
s. 142, amended: 1979,c.53,s.7.
s. 168, rules 79/105.
s. 177, orders 79/967, 1149.
s. 192, amended: 1979,c.53,s.7.

24. Building (Scotland) Act 1959.
s. 3, regs. 79/310; order 79/594.
s. 16, see *Waddell* v. *Dumfries and Galloway Regional Council*, 1979 S.L.T.(Sh.Ct.) 45.
s. 17, amended: 1979,c.46,sch.4; repealed in pt.: *ibid.*,schs.4,5.

CAP.

7 & 8 Eliz. 2 (1958–59)—cont.

25. Highways Act 1959.
ss. 7, 9, 13, see *Lovelock* v. *Secretary for Transport* [1979] R.T.R. 250, C.A.
s. 34, see *R.* v. *Secretary of State for the Environment, ex p. Stewart* (1979) 37 P. & C.R. 279, D.C.
s. 116, see *R.* v. *Surrey County Council, ex p. Send Parish Council* [1979] J.P.L. 613, D.C.
sch. 1, see *Lovelock* v. *Secretary of State for Transport* [1979] R.T.R. 250, C.A.; repealed in pt.: order 79/571.
sch. 2, see *Bushell* v. *Secretary of State for the Environment* (1979) 123 S.J. 605, C.A.

40. Deer (Scotland) Act 1959.
ss. 22, 23, 24, 25, see *Miln* v. *Maher*, 1979 S.L.T.(Notes) 10.

45. Metropolitan Magistrates' Courts Act 1959.
s. 2, repealed: 1979,c.55,sch.3.

55. Dog Licences Act 1959.
ss. 15, 16, amended: 1979,c.2,sch.4.

58. Finance Act 1959.
ss. 2, 3, repealed in pt.: 1979,c.4,sch.4.
s. 37, repealed in pt.: 1979,c.2,sch.6.

66. Obscene Publications Act 1959.
s. 1, see *R.* v. *Wells Street Stipendiary Magistrates, ex p. Golding* [1979] Crim.L.R. 254, D.C.
ss. 2, 3, see *R.* v. *Metropolitan Police Commissioner, ex p. Blackburn, The Times*, December 1, 1979, D.C.
s. 3, see *Roandale* v. *Metropolitan Police Commissioner*, December 15, 1978, Park J.

69. Wages Councils Act 1959.
repealed: 1979,c.12,sch.7.
s. 4, sch. 1, orders 79/862, 863.

72. Mental Health Act 1959.
s. 52, see *B.* v. *B.* (*Mental Health Patient*) [1979] 3 All E.R. 494, C.A.
s. 126, see *R.* v. *Holmes* [1979] Crim. L.R. 52, Bodmin Crown Ct.
sch. 7, repealed in pt.: 1979,c.36,sch.8.

8 & 9 Eliz. 2 (1960)

34. Radioactive Substances Act 1960.
s. 13, amended: order 78/1049.
ss. 117, 118, 127, 129, see *Middlemas* v. *McAleer* [1979] R.T.R. 245, D.C.
s. 160, regs. 79/654.
sch. 1, repealed in pt.: *ibid.*

44. Finance Act 1960.
s. 3, repealed: 1979,c.4,sch.4.
s. 7, repealed in pt.: 1979,c.6,sch.
s. 10, repealed in pt.: 1979,c.3,sch.3.
s. 79, repealed in pt.: 1979,c.2,sch.6.
sch. 1, repealed: 1979,c.4,sch.4.

57. Films Act 1960.
s. 6, amended: 1979,c.9,s.1.

58. Charities Act 1960.
s. 4, see *I.R.C.* v. *McMullen* [1979] 1 W.L.R. 130, C.A.
s. 19, order 79/284.
ss. 29, 43, 45, regs. 78/1386.

CAP.

8 & 9 Eliz. 2 (1960)—cont.

61. Mental Health (Scotland) Act 1960.
s. 90, order 79/508.
sch. 4, repealed in pt.: 1979,c.36,sch.8.

65. Administration of Justice Act 1960.
s. 14, see *Re Tarling* [1979] 1 All E.R. 981, Gibson J.

66. Professions Supplementary to Medicine Act 1960.
s. 2, order 79/365.

iii. Glasgow Corporation Consolidation (General Powers) Order Confirmation Act 1960.
s. 96, order 79/825; amended: *ibid.*

Internal Security Act 1960 (Laws of Malaysia Act 82) (Malaysia).
ss. 47, 57, see *Teh Cheng Poh alias Char Meh* v. *Public Prosecutor, Malaysia* [1979] 2 W.L.R. 623, P.C.

21. Arms Act 1960 (Malaysia).
s. 9, see *Teh Cheng Poh alias Char Meh* v. *Public Prosecutor, Malaysia* [1979] 2 W.L.R. 623, P.C.

9 & 10 Eliz. 2 (1961)

11. Diplomatic Immunities (Conferences with Commonwealth Countries and Republic of Ireland) Act 1961.
s. 1, amended: 1979,c.27,sch.
s. 1, repealed in pt.: 1979,c.60,sch.3.

14. Nurses (Amendment) Act 1961.
repealed: 1979,c.36,sch.8.

27. Carriage by Air Act 1961.
ss. 1–3, amended: 1979,c.28,sch.2.
s. 4, order 79/765; amended: 1979,c.28, sch.2; repealed in pt.: *ibid.*,s.6.sch.2.
s. 4A, added: *ibid.*,s.2.
s. 8A, added: *ibid.*,s.3.
s. 10, order 79/931.
sch. 1, see *Fothergill* v. *Monarch Airlines* [1979] 3 W.L.R. 491, C.A.; amended: 1979,c.28,s.4; substituted: *ibid.*,s.1,sch.1.

33. Land Compensation Act 1961.
ss. 4, 5, 31, see *Trustees for Methodist Church Purposes* v. *North Tyneside Metropolitan Borough Council* (1979) 250 E.G. 647, Browne-Wilkinson J.
s. 5, see *Stoke on Trent City Council* v. *Wood Mitchell & Co.* [1979] 2 All E.R 65, C.A.; *Service Welding* v. *Tyne and Wear County Council* (1979) 250 E.G. 1291, C.A.
ss. 17, 18, 22, see *Robert Hitchins Builders* v. *Secretary of State for the Environment; Wakeley Brothers (Rainham, Kent)* v. *Secretary of State for the Environment* (1979) 37 P. & C.R. 140, Sir Douglas Frank Q.C.
s. 32, regs. 78/1741; 79/616, 1166.

34. Factories Act 1961.
ss. 6, 28, see *Gay* v. *St. Cuthberts Co-operative Association*, 1977 S.C. 212.
s. 28, see *Devine* v. *Costain Concrete Co.* (O.H.), 1979 S.L.T.(Notes) 97.
s. 29, see *Ball* v. *Vaughan Bros.* (*Drop Forgings*), June 26, 1979, Hodgson J., Birmingham Crown Ct.

CAP.

9 & 10 Eliz. 2 (1961)—cont.

34. *Factories Act 1961—cont.*
ss. 124, 175, see *MacDonald* v. *Secretary of State for Scotland*, 1979 S.L.T. (Sh.Ct.) 8.

35. Police Pensions Act 1961.
s. 1, regs. 79/76.

36. Finance Act 1961.
s. 5, repealed in pt.: 1979,c.58,sch.2.
s. 9, repealed: 1979,c.8,sch.2.
s. 11, repealed: 1979,c.2,sch.6.
s. 37, amended: *ibid.*,sch.4; repealed in pt.: *ibid.*,sch.6.
schs. 3, 4, repealed: 1979,c.8,sch.2.

37. Small Estates (Representation) Act 1961.
repealed: 1979,c.22,sch.

40. Consumer Protection Act 1961.
ss. 1, 2, sch., regs. 79/1125.

41. Flood Prevention (Scotland) Act 1961.
s. 3, amended: 1979,c.46,sch.4.

57. Trusts (Scotland) Act 1961.
s. 5, see *Baird* v. *Lord Advocate* [1979] 2 W.L.R. 369, H.L.; *Thomson's Trs.* v. *Inland Revenue* (H.L.), 1979 S.L.T. 166.

63. Highways (Miscellaneous Provisions) Act 1961.
s. 1, see *Tarrant* v. *Rowlands* [1979] R.T.R. 144, Cantley J.
s. 3, instruments 79/606, 1260.

64. Public Health Act 1961.
s. 4, regs. 79/601.

65. Housing Act 1961.
s. 32, see *Newham London Borough* v. *Patel* [1979] J.P.L. 303, C.A.

Crimes Act 1961 (N.Z.)
s. 406, see *Thomas* v. *The Queen* [1978] 3 W.L.R. 927, P.C.

2. Southern Rhodesia (Constitution) Act 1961.
repealed: 1979,c.60,sch.3.

10 & 11 Eliz. 2 (1962)

8. Civil Aviation (Eurocontrol) Act 1962.
ss. 4, 7, regs. 78/1799; 79/154, 237, 267, 1274

12. Education Act 1962.
ss. 1, 4, sch. 1, regs. 79/889.
ss. 3, 4, regs. 79/333.

19. West Indies Act 1962.
s. 5, order 79/919.

20. International Monetary Fund Act 1962.
repealed: 1979,c.29,sch.

30. Northern Ireland Act 1962.
sch. 1, repealed in pt.: order 78/1045.

33. Health Visiting and Social Work (Training) Act 1962.
s. 3, repealed in pt.: 1979,c.36,sch.8.
sch. 1, amended: *ibid.*,sch.7.

37. Building Societies Act 1962.
s. 32, see *Nash* v. *Halifax Building Society* [1979] 2 W.L.R. 184, Browne-Wilkinson, J.
s. 58, order 79/1301.
s. 59, amended: 1979,c.37,sch.6.

CAP.

10 & 11 Eliz. 2 (1962)—cont.

43. Carriage by Air (Supplementary Provisions) Act 1962.
s. 4, amended: 1979,c.28,sch.2.
s. 4A, added: *ibid.*,s.3.
sch. amended: *ibid.*,sch.2.

44. Finance Act 1962.
s. 34, repealed in pt.: 1979,c.2,sch.6.

47. Education (Scotland) Act 1962.
trust schemes: 79/81, 82, 173, 451, 496, 760, 1227.
s. 19, regs. 79/1185, 1186.
s. 49, regs. 79/840.
s. 53, regs. 79/824.
s. 75, regs. 79/766.
s. 144, regs. 79/824, 840.

58. Pipe-lines Act 1962.
s. 56, repealed: 1979,c.2,sch.6

No. 1. Ecclesiastical Fees Measure 1962.
s. 2, order 79/194.

11 Eliz. 2 (1962)

4. Foreign Compensation Act 1962.
s. 3, order 79/109.

1963

9. Purchase Tax Act 1963.
s. 1, amended: 1979,c.2,sch.5.
s. 25, amended and repealed in pt.: *ibid.*
s. 34, sch. 2, amended: *ibid.*

11. Agriculture (Miscellaneous Provisions) Act 1963.
s. 16, orders 79/751, 1281.

12. Local Government (Financial Provisions) (Scotland) Act 1963.
s. 9, regs. 79/227, 235.
s. 13, see *Occidental Inc.* v. *Assessor for Orkney*, 1979 S.L.T. 60.

16. Protection of Depositors Act 1963.
repealed: 1979,c.37,sch.7.
s. 1, amended: *ibid.*,s.39.

18. Stock Transfer Act 1963.
s. 3, order 79/277.
sch. 1, amended: *ibid.*

24. British Museum Act 1963.
s. 10, order 79/1086.
sch. 3, amended: *ibid.*

25. Finance Act 1963.
s. 4, repealed in pt.: 1979,c.6,sch.
s. 6, repealed: 1979,c.4,sch.4.
s. 7, repealed: 1979,c.2,sch.6.
s. 73, repealed in pt.: 1979,c.2,sch.6.
sch. 2, repealed: 1979,c.4,sch.4.

31. Weights and Measures Act 1963.
s. 2, repealed in pt.: 1979,c.45,sch.7.
s. 4, regs. 79/1436; amended: 1979,c.45, sch.7.
s. 5, amended: *ibid.*
s. 6, amended: *ibid.*,sch.5; repealed in pt.: *ibid.*,schs.5,7.
ss. 7, 8, repealed: *ibid.*,schs.5,7.
s. 9A, repealed in pt.: *ibid.*,sch.7.
s. 11, regs. 78/1362; 79/41, 729, 1359. amended: 1979,c.45,s.16,sch.4; repealed in pt.: *ibid.*,s.16,sch.7.

CAP.

1963—cont.

31. *Weights and Measures Act 1963—cont.*
s. 12, amended: *ibid.*,s.17,sch.4; repealed in pt.: *ibid.*,s.17,sch.7.
s. 12A, added: *ibid.*,s.17.
s. 13, repealed in pt.: *ibid.*,sch.7.
s. 14, regs. 78/1362; 79/41, 729; amended: 1979,c.45,s.16.
s. 15, amended: *ibid.*,sch.5.
s. 21, order 79/1752; amended: 1979,c.2, sch.4.
s. 24, repealed in pt.: 1979,c.45,schs.5,7.
s. 26, amended: *ibid.*,sch.5; repealed in in pt.: *ibid.*,sch.7.
s. 27, substituted: *ibid.*,sch.5.
s. 28, repealed: *ibid.*,schs.5,7.
s. 29, repealed in pt.: *ibid.*,sch.7.
ss. 42, 44, 48, 51, amended: *ibid.*,sch.5.
ss. 43, 48, regs. 79/1359.
s. 52, amended: *ibid.*,ss.17,18; repealed in pt.: *ibid.*,s.18,sch.7.
s. 54, orders 79/955, 1752; repealed in pt.: 1979,c.45,sch.7.
s. 58, regs. 78/1362; 79/41, 729, 1436; amended: 1979,c.4,sch.3; c.45,sch.5.
s. 59, repealed: 1979,c.4,sch.4.
s. 60, repealed: 1979,c.45,schs.5,7.
schs. 1, 1A, amended: *ibid.*,sch.5.
sch. 4, amended: 1979,c.4,sch.3; c.45, sch.5; order 79/1752; repealed in pt.: 1979,c.45,schs.5,7; order 79/1752.
sch. 6, amended: order 79/1753.
sch. 10, repealed in pt.: 1979,c.4,sch.4.

37. Children and Young Persons Act 1963.
s. 1, see *R.* v. *Local Commissioner for Administration for the North and East Area of England, ex p. Bradford Metropolitan City Council* [1979] 2 W.L.R. 1, C.A.

38. Water Resources Act 1963.
s. 67, orders 78/1945; 79/1499.
s. 82, order 79/1196.

49. Contracts of Employment Act 1963.
sch. 1, see *Smith* v. *Lord Advocate*, 1979 S.L.T. 233.

51. Land Compensation (Scotland) Act 1963.
s. 12, see *Cupar Trading Estate* v. *Fife Regional Council*, 1979 S.L.T. (Lands Tr.) 2; *Murray Bookmakers* v. *Glasgow District Council*, 1979 S.L.T. (Lands Tr.) 8.
ss. 25, 26, see *London & Clydeside Estates* v. *Aberdeen District Council*, 1979 S.L.T. 221.
s. 40, regs. 78/1742; 79/615, 1165.

59. Electricity and Gas Act 1963.
ss. 2, 3, 4, repealed in pt.: 1979,c.11, sch.12.
sch. 1, repealed in pt.: *ibid.*
sch. 3, repealed: *ibid.*

Trade Marks Act 1963 (Eire).
ss. 17, 18, see *Dent Trade Mark* [1979] F.S.R. 205, High Ct. of Ireland.

1964

14. Plant Varieties and Seeds Act 1964.
s. 16, regs. 79/133, 366, 774, 888, 1003–1005.

CAP.

1964—cont.

14. *Plant Varieties and Seeds Act 1964—cont.*
ss. 17, 24, regs. 79/774, 1004, 1005.
s. 26, regs. 79/774, 1003–1005.
s. 33, order 79/882.
s. 36, regs. 79/774, 1003–1005.

16. Industrial Training Act 1964.
s. 2B, amended: 1979,c.13,sch.1.
s. 9A, order 79/793.

24. Trade Union (Amalgamations etc.) Act 1964.
s. 7, regs. 79/1385.

26. Licensing Act 1964.
see *Martin* v. *Spalding* (1979) 123 S.J. 456, D.C.
s. 59, see *Taylor* v. *Speed* [1979] Crim. L.R. 114, D.C.
s. 74, see *Martin* v. *Spalding* [1979] 2 All E.R. 1193, D.C.; *Knole Park Golf Club* v. *Chief Superintendent, Kent County Constabulary* [1979] 3 All E.R. 829, D.C.
s. 87, amended: 1979,c.2,sch.4.
ss. 102, 104–107, repealed: order 79/1977.
ss. 160, 180, see *Southall* v. *Haime* [1979] Crim.L.R. 249, D.C.
s. 167, amended: regs. 79/1476.
s. 181, amended: 1979,c.4,sch.3.
s. 201, amended: 1979,c.4,sch.3; c.55, sch.2.
sch. 9, repealed: order 79/1977.

28. Agriculture and Horticulture Act 1964.
s. 1, amended: 1979,c.2,sch.4; repealed in pt.: 1979,c.58,sch.2.
sch., amended: 1979,c.2,sch.4; c.3,sch.2.

29. Continental Shelf Act 1964.
s. 1, order 79/1447.
s. 2, orders 79/641, 1083, 1136, 1273.
s. 21, order 79/1058.

40. Harbours Act 1964.
s. 14, order 79/1656.

42. Administration of Justice Act 1964.
ss. 2, 3, 9, 10, 13–17, 27, 28, 30, 32, 36, repealed: 1979,c.55,sch.3.
s. 37, repealed in pt.: *ibid.*
s. 38, amended: *ibid.*,sch.2.
sch. 3, repealed in pt.: *ibid.*,sch.3.

44. Nurses Act 1964.
repealed: 1979,c.36,sch.8.

47. Merchant Shipping Act 1964.
s. 5, amended: 1979,c.39,sch.6.
s. 7, amended: *ibid.*,sch.6; repealed in pt.: *ibid.*,s.28,sch.7.

48. Police Act 1964.
s. 5, see *R.* v. *Knightsbridge Crown Court, ex p. Umeh* [1979] Crim.L.R. 727, D.C.
s. 33, see *Crosby* v. *Sandford* [1979] Crim.L.R. 668, C.A.; regs. 79/694, 991, 1216, 1470.
s. 34, regs. 79/76.
s. 35, regs. 79/75.
s. 46, regs. 79/1470.
s. 51, see *Hickman* v. *O'Dwyer* [1979] Crim.L.R. 309, D.C.; *Wershof* v. *Metropolitan Police Commissioner* (1978) 68 Cr.App.R. 82; *Grant* v. *Gorman* [1979] Crim.L.R. 669, D.C.

CAP.

1964—cont.

49. Finance Act 1964.
s. 1, 2, repealed in pt.: 1979,c.4,sch.4.
s. 8, repealed: 1979,c.8,sch.2.
s. 10, amended: 1979,c.2,sch.5; repealed in pt.: *ibid.*,sch.6.
s. 26, repealed in pt.: *ibid.*

53. Hire-Purchase Act 1964.
s. 27, amended: 1979,c.54,sch.2.

60. Emergency Laws (Re-enactments and Repeals) Act 1964.
s. 1, order 79/1223.
s. 4, order 78/1876.
s. 6, orders 79/604, 700, 1289, 1290.
s. 7, orders 78/1876; 79/604, 700, 1289, 1290.
s. 22, orders 79/604, 1289.

81. Diplomatic Privileges Act 1964.
s. 2, amended: 1979,c.2,sch.4.
s. 7, amended: *ibid.*
s. 8, repealed in pt.: 1979,c.60,sch.3.
sch. 1, see *Shaw* v. *Shaw* [1979] 3 W.L.R. 24, Balcombe J.

92. Finance (No. 2) Act 1964.
s. 7, amended: 1979,c.2,sch.4.
s. 9, amended: *ibid.*
s. 10, amended: *ibid.*

No. 5. Faculty Jurisdiction Measure 1964.
s. 2, amended: 1979,c.46,sch.4.

Patents Act 1964 (Eire).
ss. 2, 6, 9, 18, 19, see *Rank Hovis McDougall* v. *The Controller of Patents, Designs and Trade Marks* [1978] F.S.R. 588, High Ct. of Ireland.

No. 30. Emergency (Essential Powers) Act 1964 (Malaysia).
s. 2, see *Teh Cheng Poh alias Char Meh* v. *Public Prosecutor, Malaysia* [1979] 2 W.L.R. 623, P.C.

1965

2. Administration of Justice Act 1965.
s. 27, repealed: 1979,c.31,sch.2.

3. Remuneration of Teachers Act 1965.
s. 1, orders 78/1773; 79/339.
ss. 1, 2, see *Lewis* v. *Dyfed County Council* (1978) 77 L.G.R. 339, C.A.
ss. 1, 2, order 79/1193.
ss. 2, 7, orders 78/1773; 79/428.

10. Superannuation (Amendment) Act 1965.
sch. 2, orders 79/680, 1275.

12. Industrial and Provident Societies Act 1965.
s. 2, amended: 1979,c.34,ss.2,6.
s. 10, amended: *ibid.*,s.4.
s. 16, amended: *ibid.*,s.6.
s. 53, amended: *ibid.*,ss.6,23.
ss. 61–66, 68, amended: *ibid.*,s.28.
s. 70, regs. 78/1729; 79/937.

14. Cereals Marketing Act 1965.
s. 1, order 79/782.
ss. 13, 15, 16, amended: regs. 79/26.

15. Dangerous Drugs Act 1965.
s. 5, see *Christison* v. *Hogg*, 1974 J.C. 55, Ct. of Justiciary.

CAP.

1965—cont.

24. Severn Bridge Tolls Act 1965.
s. 2, order 79/883.

25. Finance Act 1965.
Pt. III, except s. 45 in pt., repealed: 1979,c.14,sch.8.
s. 19, see *Aberdeen Construction Group* v. *I.R.C.* [1978] A.C. 885, H.L.
ss. 20, 25, 42, see *Chinn* v. *Hochstrasser*; *Chinn* v. *Collins* [1979] 2 W.L.R. 411, C.A.
s. 22, see *Marren* v. *Ingles* [1979] 1 W.L.R. 1131, C.A.
s. 25, see *Roome* v. *Edwards*, *The Times*, December 5, 1979, C.A.
s. 35, see *I.R.C.* v. *Helen Slater Charitable Trust*, *The Times*, December 1, 1979, Slade J.
s. 39, orders 79/117, 300–302.
s. 92, amended: 1979,c.5,sch.6; c.8,sch.1.
s. 94, repealed: 1979,c.14,sch.8.
sch. 2, see *Tyrer* v. *Smart* [1979] S.T.C. 34, H.L.
sch. 5, see *Esslemont* v. *Estill* [1979] S.T.C. 624, Oliver J.
sch. 6, see *Eilbeck* v. *Rawling* [1979] S.T.C. 16, Slade J.; *Watkins* v. *Kidson* [1979] 1 W.L.R. 876, H.L.; *Marson* v. *Marriage*, *The Times*, December 22, 1979, Fox J.; *I.R.C.* v. *Beveridge*, First Division, July 19, 1979.
schs. 6, 7, see *Aberdeen Construction Co.* v. *I.R.C.* [1978] A.C. 885, H.L.
schs. 6–9, repealed: 1979,c.14,sch.8.
sch. 7, see *Floor* v. *Davis* [1979] 2 W.L.R. 830, H.L.; *W. T. Ramsay* v. *I.R.C.* [1979] 1 W.L.R. 974 C.A.; *Marren* v. *Ingles* [1979] 1 W.L.R. 1131, C.A.; *Rank Xerox* v. *Lane* (1979) 123 S.J. 736, H.L.
sch. 10, see *Roome* v. *Edwards*, *The Times*, December 5, 1979, C.A.
sch. 10, repealed in pt.: 1979,c.14,sch.8.

28. Justices of the Peace Act 1965.
repealed: 1979,c.55,sch.3.

33. Control of Office and Industrial Development Act 1965.
ss. 6, 8, see *R.K.T. Investments* v. *Hackney London Borough Council* (1978) 36 P. & C.R. 442, Sir Douglas Frank, Q.C.

37. Carriage of Goods by Road Act 1965.
s. 8A, added: 1979,c.28,s.3.
sch., amended: *ibid.*, s. 4.

45. Backing of Warrants (Republic of Ireland) Act 1965.
see *R.* v. *Durham Prison Governor, ex p. Carlisle* [1979] Crim.L.R. 175, D.C.
sch., amended: 1979,c.55,sch.2.

46. Highlands and Islands Development (Scotland) Act 1965.
s. 1, order 79/1461.

47. Merchant Shipping Act 1965.
s. 1, regs. 79/1519; order 79/306; amended: 1979,c.39,s.31,sch.6; repealed in pt.: *ibid.*,sch.7.
s. 5, sch. 1, repealed in pt.: *ibid.*

CAP.

1965—cont.

49. Registration of Births and Marriages (Scotland) Act 1965.
s. 21, amended: 1979,c.36,sch.7; repealed in pt.: *ibid.*,schs.7,8.
s. 54, regs. 79/143.

51. National Insurance Act 1965.
ss. 22, 75, see *Watt* v. *Lord Advocate*, 1979 S.L.T. 137.
s. 66, see *Gara, Appellant*, 1979 S.L.T. (Notes) 29.

56. Compulsory Purchase Act 1965.
s. 36, orders 78/1945; 79/1499.

57. Nuclear Installations Act 1965.
s. 14, repealed in pt.: 1979,c.39,sch.7.
s. 26, regs. 78/1779.

59. New Towns Act 1965.
ss. 43, 53, order 79/204.

62. Redundancy Payments Act 1965.
s. 1, see *Nottinghamshire County Council* v. *Lee* [1979] I.C.R. 818, E.A.T.; *Secretary of State for Employment* v. *Globe Elastic Thread Co.* [1979] 3 W.L.R. 143, H.L.; *Smith* v. *Lord Advocate*, 1979 S.L.T. 233; *Pillinger* v. *Manchester Area Health Authority* [1979] I.R.L.R. 430, E.A.T.
s. 2, see *Paton Calvert & Co.* v. *Westerside* [1979] I.R.L.R. 108, E.A.T.; *Hindes* v. *Supersine* [1979] I.C.R. 517, E.A.T.
s. 3, see *Turvey* v. *C. W. Cheyney & Son* [1979] I.C.R. 341, E.A.T.; *Air Canada* v. *Lee* [1978] I.C.R. 1202; *Glencross* v. *Dymoke* [1979] I.C.R. 536, E.A.T.; *Smith* v. *Lord Advocate*, 1979 S.L.T. 233.
ss. 4, 21, see *Pritchard-Rhodes* v. *Boon and Milton* [1979] I.R.L.R. 19, E.A.T.
s. 6, see *Fabar Construction* v. *Race* [1979] I.C.R. 529, E.A.T.
s. 8, see *Smith* v. *Lord Advocate*, 1979 S.L.T. 233.
ss. 9, 30, see *Secretary of State for Employment* v. *Globe Elastic Thread Co.* [1979] 3 W.L.R. 143, H.L.
s. 10, see *Lignacite Products* v. *Krollman* [1979] I.R.L.R. 22, E.A.T.
s. 13, see *Smith* v. *Lord Advocate*, 1979 S.L.T. 233.
s. 32, see *Smith* v. *Lord Advocate*, 1979 S.L.T. 233.
s. 53, see *Fabar Construction* v. *Race* [1979] I.C.R. 529, E.A.T.

64. Commons Registration Act 1965.
ss. 1, 22, see *Re Box Hill Common* [1979] 2 W.L.R. 177, C.A.

66. Hire-Purchase Act 1965.
*ss. 20, 54, 58, amended: 1979,c.54, sch.2.

67. Hire-Purchase (Scotland) Act 1965.
ss. 20, 50, 54, amended: 1979,c.54,sch.2.

74. Superannuation Act 1965.
s. 39, repealed in pt.: 1979,c.43,sch.7.
s. 39A, rules 79/668.

CAP.

1965—cont.

75. Rent Act 1965.
s. 30, see *R.* v. *Blankley* [1979] Crim. L.R. 166, Knightsbridge Crown Ct.

76. Southern Rhodesia Act 1965.
s. 1, see *Mutasa* v. *Att.Gen.* [1979] 3 All E.R. 257, Boreham J.
s. 2, orders 79/820, 1374.

82. Coal Industry Act 1965.
s. 1, order 79/1012.

xxiv. Gulf Oil Refining Act 1965.
s. 5, see *Allen* v. *Gulf Oil Refining* [1979] 3 W.L.R. 523, C.A.

1966

4. Mines (Working Facilities and Support) Act 1966.
s. 7, amended: 1979,c.46,sch.4; repealed in pt.: *ibid.*,schs.4,5.

5. Local Government (Scotland) Act 1966.
s. 18, see *British Railways Board* v. *Glasgow Corporation*, 1976 S.C. 224.

18. Finance Act 1966.
s. 2, amended: 1979,c.2,sch.4; c.8,sch.1.
ss. 10, 11, repealed: 1979,c.2,sch.6.
s. 43, repealed: 1979,c.14,sch.8.
s. 53, amended: 1979,c.2,sch.4.
sch. 1, amended: *ibid.*
sch. 2, repealed in pt.: 1979,c.2,sch.6; c.4,sch.4.
sch. 10, repealed: 1979,c.14,sch.8.

19. Law Reform (Miscellaneous Provisions) (Scotland) Act 1966.
see *Trustees of the Late Sir James Douglas Wishart Thomson* v. *I.R.C.* [1978] T.R. 171, Ct. of Session.

36. Veterinary Surgeons Act 1966.
ss. 11, 25, order 78/1809.

38. Sea Fisheries Regulation Act 1966.
s. 11, see *Alexander* v. *Tonkin* [1979] 1 W.L.R. 629, D.C.

41. Arbitration (International Investment) Disputes Act 1966.
s. 6, order 79/572.

45. Armed Forces Act 1966.
s. 2, regs. 79/192, 215.

1967

1. Land Commission Act 1967.
ss. 27, 32, 36, 38, 44, 46, 47, 100, see *Secretary of State for Scotland* v. *Ravenstoke Securities*, 1976 S.C. 171.

3. Income Tax Act 1967.
s. 3, see *Hock Heng Co. Sdn. Bhd.* v. *Director-General of Revenue* (1979) 123 S.J. 284, P.C.

4. West Indies Act 1967.
s. 5, orders 78/1901; 79/916.
s. 10, order 79/918.
ss. 13, 14, orders 78/1899; 79/917.
s. 17, orders 78/1900; 79/918.

7. Misrepresentation Act 1967.
s. 4, repealed: 1979,c.54,sch.3.
s. 6, repealed in pt.: *ibid.*

CAP.

1967—cont.

8. Plant Health Act 1967.
s. 2, amended: 1979,c.2,sch.4.
s. 3, orders 79/638, 639.
s. 5, order 79/638.

9. General Rate Act 1967.
ss. 2, 6, see *B. Kettle* v. *Newcastle-under-Lyme Borough Council* (1979) 251 E.G. 59, C.A.
s. 17, see *Brent London Borough Council* v. *Ladbroke Rentals* (1979) 252 E.G. 702, Kilner-Brown J.; *Bar Hill Development* v. *South Cambridgeshire District Council* (1979) 252 E.G. 915, D.C.
ss. 17, 17A, 53, see *Windsor Securities* v. *Liverpool City Council* (1978) 77 L.G.R. 502, C.A.
s. 17A, see *Post Office* v. *Oxford City Council* (1979) 77 L.G.R. 534, D.C.
ss. 17A, 17B, see *Westminster City Council* v. *Haymarket Publishing* (1979) 123 S.J. 804, Dillon J.
s. 33, order 79/1373.
s. 40, see *Forces Help Society and Lord Roberts Workshops* v. *Canterbury City Council* (1978) 77 L.G.R. 541, Slade J.
s. 48, regs. 79/1514.
s. 79, see *Re Piccadilly Estate Hotels* (1978) 77 L.G.R. 79, Slade J.
s. 101, order 79/1038.
ss. 99, 103, see *R.* v. *Liverpool City JJ, ex p. Greaves*; *Greaves* v. *Liverpool City Council* (1979) 77 L.G.R. 440, D.C.
s. 114, order 79/1516.
sch. 1, see *Graylaw Investments* v. *Ipswich Borough Council* (1978) 77 L.G.R. 297, C.A.; *Windsor Securities* v. *Liverpool City Council* (1978) 77 L.G.R. 502, C.A.; *Brent London Borough Council* v. *Ladbroke Rentals* (1979) 252 E.G. 702, Kilner-Brown J.; *Bar Hill Development* v. *South Cambridgeshire District Council* (1979) 252 E.G. 915, D.C.
sch. 1, amended: 1979,c.46,sch.4; repealed in pt.: *ibid.*,schs.4,5.
sch. 6, order 79/1373.

10. Forestry Act 1967.
s. 4, repealed: 1979,c.21,sch.2.
s. 9, amended: 1979,c.21,sch.1; repealed in pt.: *ibid.*,sch.2.
ss. 10, 11, 14–16, 19–21, 23–26, regs. 79/791.
s. 32, regs. 79/791, 792.
s. 43, amended: 1979,c.21,sch.1.

13. Parliamentary Commissioner Act 1967.
s. 5, order 79/915.
sch. 2, repealed in pt.: orders 79/578, 1451.
sch. 3, amended: order 79/915.

16. Teachers of Nursing Act 1967.
repealed: 1979,c.36,sch.8.

22. Agriculture Act 1967.
s. 9, amended: order 79/578.
s. 13, order 79/393.
s. 64, order 79/323.

CAP.

1967—cont.

27. Merchant Shipping (Load Lines) Act 1967.
s. 2, rules 79/1267.
s. 3, amended: 1979,c.39,sch.6.
s. 4, amended: *ibid.*,sch.6; repealed in pt.: *ibid.*,schs.6,7.
ss. 5, 9, amended: *ibid.*,sch.6.
s. 11, repealed in pt.: *ibid.*,s.28,sch.7.
s. 13, amended: *ibid.*,sch.6.
s. 17, repealed in pt.: 1979,c.39,s.28,sch. 7.
s. 24, amended: *ibid.*,sch.6; repealed in pt.: *ibid.*,sch.7.
s. 27, sch. 1, repealed in pt.: *ibid.*

29. Housing Subsidies Act 1967.
s. 28, order 79/894.

36. Remuneration of Teachers (Scotland) Act 1967.
ss. 2, 8, order 78/1747.

43. Legal Aid (Scotland) Act 1967.
s. 1, regs. 79/1522; amended: 1979,c.26, s.6,sch.2; regs. 79/1522; repealed in pt.: 1979,c.26,sch.2.
s. 2, regs. 78/1817; 79/409, 1521, 1522; amended: 1979,c.26,sch.1.
s. 3, regs. 78/1817; 79/409, 1521; amended: 1979,c.26,ss.9,10.
s. 4, regs. 79/324, 325, 1390; amended: 1979,c.26,sch.1; regs. 79/1390; repealed in pt.: 1979,c.26,schs.1,2.
s. 11, regs. 79/1390, 1522.
s. 13, amended: 1979,c.26,s.6.
s. 15, regs. 78/1817, 1818; 79/156, 409, 410, 1390, 1521, 1522.
s. 16, Acts of Adjournal 78/1686; 79/95.
s. 18, amended: 1979,c.26,sch.1.
s. 20, amended: *ibid.*,s.6,sch.1.
sch. 1, amended: regs. 79/1390.

45. Uniform Laws on International Sales 1967.
s. 1, amended: 1979,c.54,sch.2.
sch. 2, see *Butler Machine Tool Co.* v. *Ex-Cell-O Corp.* [1979] 1 W.L.R. 401, C.A.

46. Protection of Birds Act 1967.
s. 7, orders 79/70, 99 (S.), 141 (S.).

52. Tokyo Convention Act 1967.
s. 2, order 78/1889.

54. Finance Act 1967.
s. 1, repealed in pt.: 1979,c.4,sch.4.
s. 2, repealed: 1979,c.3,sch.3.
s. 3, repealed: 1979,c.2,sch.6.
s. 4, repealed in pt.: 1979,c.2,sch.6; c. 4,sch.4.
s. 5, repealed in pt.: 1979,c.2,sch.6.
s. 6, repealed: 1979,c.4,sch.4.
s. 7, amended: 1979,c.2,sch.4.
s. 9, amended: 1979,c.2,sch.5.
ss. 32, 35, 37, repealed: 1979,c.14,sch.8.
s. 40, order 79/1687.
s. 45, amended: 1979,c.2,sch.4; repealed in pt.: 1979,c.14,sch.8.
sch. 5, repealed in pt.: 1979,c.4,sch.4.
sch. 6, repealed in pt.: 1979,c.2,sch.6; c.4,sch.4.
sch. 9, repealed in pt.: 1979,c.2,sch.6; c.4,sch.4.
sch. 13, repealed: 1979,c.14,sch.8.

CAP.

1968—cont.

60. *Theft Act 1968—cont.*
s. 10, see *R.* v. *Jones*, November 30, 1979, Solomon J., Middlesex Crown Ct.
s. 12, see *R.* v. *Mulroy* [1979] R.T.R. 214, C.A.; *R.* v. *Ambler* [1979] R.T.R. 217, C.A.; *A. C. (A Minor)* v. *Hume* [1979] R.T.R. 424, D.C.
s. 15, see *R.* v. *Hircock* (1978) 67 Cr.App.R. 278, C.A.; *R.* v. *Banaster* [1979] R.T.R. 113, C.A.
s. 16, see *Smith* v. *Koumourou* [1979] R.T.R. 355, D.C.
s. 22, see *R.* v. *Reeves* (1978) 68 Cr. App.R. 331, C.A.
s. 27, see *R.* v. *Bradley*, *The Times*, November 20, 1979, C.A.
s. 28, see *Malone* v. *Met. Police Commissioner* [1979] 1 All E.R. 256, C.A.
s. 30, amended: 1979,c.31,sch.1.

61. **Civil Aviation Act 1968.**
s. 14, amended: 1979,c.2,sch.4.
s. 15, regs. 79/154, 267, 1274.
s. 19, order 79/930.

64. **Civil Evidence Act 1968.**
sch., repealed in pt.: 1979,c.12,sch.7.

65. **Gaming Act 1968.**
s. 48, orders 78/1847; 79/380; amended: *ibid.*
s. 51, orders 78/1847; 79/380.
sch. 2, see *Mecca* v. *Glasgow District Licensing Court*, 1979 S.L.T.(Sh.Ct.) 42.

67. **Medicines Act 1968.**
s. 11, amended: 1979,c.36,sch.7; repealed in pt.: *ibid.*,schs.7,8.
s. 15, order 79/1114.
s. 51, order 79/315.
s. 57, orders 79/45, 1008.
s. 58, orders 79/36, 1040.
s. 62, orders 79/382, 1181.
s. 116, amended: 1979,c.2,sch.4.
s. 129, orders 79/36, 45, 315, 1008, 1040.
sch. 4, amended: order 79/1573.

69. **Justices of the Peace Act 1968.**
s. 1, repealed in pt.: 1979,c.55,sch.3.
ss. 3, 5, sch. 2, repealed: *ibid.*
sch. 3, repealed in pt.: *ibid.*

72. **Town and Country Plannning Act 1968.**
s. 59, repealed: 1979,c.46,sch.5.

73. **Transport Act 1968.**
s. 42, order 79/944.
s. 69, amended: 1979,c.5,sch.6.
ss. 86, 103, see *Green* v. *Harrison* [1979] R.T.R. 483, D.C.
s. 96, see *Green* v. *Harrison* [1979] Crim.L.R. 395, D.C.
s. 101, regs. 78/1938.
s. 135, see *Tuck* v. *National Freight Corporation* [1978] 1 W.L.R. 37, H.L.
sch. 11, repealed in pt.: 1979,c.12,sch.7.

xxxiii. **Medway Water (Bewl Bridge Reservoir) Act 1968.**
s. 44, repealed: order 79/1196.
s. 53, amended and repealed in pt.: *ibid.*
s. 105, repealed in pt.: *ibid.*

CAP.

1968—cont.

No. 1. **Pastoral Measure 1968.**
s. 53, order 79/195.

Copyright Act (Com.) (Australia).
s. 103, see *R.C.A. Corp.* v. *Custom Cleared Sales Pty.* [1978] F.S.R. 576, Sup.Ct. of N.S.W.

Indemnity Act 1968 (St. Christopher, Nevis and Anguilla).
see *Att.Gen. of the State of St. Christopher, Nevis and Anguilla* v. *Reynolds* (1979) 123 S.J. 488, P.C.

1969

1. **Electricity (Scotland) Act 1969.**
repealed: 1979,c.11,sch.12.

15. **Representation of the People Act 1969.**
modified: regs. 79/338.
s. 9, see *Marshall* v. *British Broadcasting Corp.* [1979] 1 W.L.R. 1071, C.A.

16. **Customs Duties (Dumping and Subsidies) Act 1969.**
ss. 1, 2, 10, 15, order 79/104.
ss. 1, 10, 15, orders 79/842, 1182.
s. 9, amended: 1979,c.2,sch.4.
s. 10, amended: *ibid.*
s. 17. amended: *ibid.*

19. **Decimal Currency Act 1969.**
s. 6, amended: order 79/1574.
s. 7, repealed in pt.: order 79/1573.

22. **Redundant Churches and Other Religious Buildings Act 1969.**
s. 1, order 79/478.

30. **Town and Country Planning (Scotland) Act 1969.**
s. 59, repealed: 1979,c.64,sch.5.

32. **Finance Act 1969.**
s. 1, repealed in pt.: 1979,c.4,sch.4.
s. 36, see *Thomson's Trs.* v. *Inland Revenue* (H.L.), 1979 S.L.T. 166.
s. 41, order 78/1838.
ss. 41, 42, repealed: 1979,c.14,sch.8.
s. 54, repealed: 1979,c.3,sch.3.
s. 61, amended: 1979,c.2,sch.4; repealed in pt.: 1979,c.14,sch.8.
sch. 7, amended: order 79/241; repealed in pt.: 1979,c.4,sch.4.
schs. 18, 19, repealed: 1979,c.14,sch.8.
sch. 19, see *Stoke on Trent City Council* v. *Wood Mitchell & Co.* [1979] 2 All E.R. 65, C.A.

34. **Housing (Scotland) Act 1969.**
s. 59, order 79/253.

39. **Age of Majority (Scotland) Act 1996.**
sch. 1, repealed in pt.: 1979,c.2,sch.6.

40. **Medical Act 1969.**
s. 4, order of council 79/844.
ss. 4, 6, 13, sch. 3, repealed in pt.: order 79/289.

46. **Family Law Reform Act 1969.**
s. 22, regs. 79/1226.
sch. 1, repealed in pt.: 1979,c.2,sch.6.

47. **Nurses Act 1969.**
repealed: 1979,c.36,sch.8.

CAP.

1969—cont.

48. Post Office Act 1969.
s. 40, repealed in pt.: 1979,c.37,sch.7.
s. 74, amended: 1979,c.14,sch.7.
s. 81, amended: 1979,c.12,sch.6.
sch. 4, amended: 1979,c.2,sch.4.
sch. 6, repealed in pt.: 1979,c.37,sch.7.

49. Education (Scotland) Act 1969.
trust schemes: 79/81, 82, 173, 451, 496, 760, 1227.

50. Trustee Savings Banks Act 1969.
ss. 28, 86, regs. 79/259.
s. 88, warrant 79/258.

54. Children and Young Persons Act 1969.
see *E.* v. *E. and Cheshire County Council (Intervener)* (1978) 9 Fam.Law 185, C.A.
s. 1, see *Essex County Council* v. *T.L.R. and K.B.R. (Minors)* (1979) 9 Fam. Law 15, D.C.; *R.* v. *Milton Keynes JJ., ex p. R.* (1979) 123 S.J. 321, D.C.; *Re W. (Minors) (Wardship: Jurisdiction)* [1979] 3 W.L.R. 252, C.A.
s. 7, see *R.* v. *Billericay JJ., ex p. Johnson* [1979] Crim.L.R. 315, D.C.
s. 34, order 79/125.
s. 47, order 79/285.
s. 69, order 79/125.

58. Administration of Justice Act 1969.
s. 16, amended: order 78/1045.
s. 27, repealed in pt.: order 79/1575.

63. Police Act 1969.
s. 4, regs. 79/75, 694, 1216, 1470.

No. 1. Emergency (Essential Powers) Ordinance 1969.
s. 2, see *Teh Cheng Poh alias Char Meh* v. *Public Prosecutor, Malaysia* [1979] 2 W.L.R. 623, P.C.

1970

9. Taxes Management Act 1970.
s. 8, see *Napier* v. *I.R.C.* [1978] T.R. 403, C.A.
ss. 11, 12, 25, 27, 28, amended: 1979, c.14,sch.7.
s. 20C, see *R.* v. *I.R.C., ex p. Rossminster, The Times*, December 14, 1979, H.L.
ss. 31, 50, 55, see *Hallamshire Industrial Finance Trust* v. *I.R.C.* [1979] 1 W.L.R. 620, Browne-Wilkinson J.
s. 47, amended: 1979,c.14,sch.7; repealed in pt.: *ibid.*,sch.8.
s. 50, see *Slater* v. *Richardson and Bottoms* [1974] S.T.C. 630, Oliver J.; *R. & D. McKerron* v. *I.R.C.* [1978] T.R. 489, Ct. of Session.
s. 51, see *Galleri* v. *Wirral General Comrs.* [1979] S.T.C. 216, Walton J.
s. 53, repealed in pt.: 1979,c.14,sch.8.
s. 56, see *Thomas* v. *Ingram* [1979] S.T.C. 1, Fox J.
s. 57, amended: 1979,c.14,sch.7.
s. 89, order 79/1687.
s. 99, see *Lord Advocate* v. *Ruffle (O. H)*, March 16, 1979.
ss. 111, 118, 119, amended: 1979,c.14, sch.7.

CAP.

1970—cont.

10. Income and Corporation Taxes Act 1970.
s. 8, amended: 1979,c.25,s.1; c.47,s.8, sch.2.
s. 10, see *Aspden* v. *Baxi* [1979] S.T.C. 566, Brightman J.
s. 13, repealed: 1979,c.47,schs.1,5.
s. 14, amended: 1979,c.25,s.1; c.47,s.8, sch.1.
s. 14A, added: *ibid.*,sch.1.
s. 15, repealed in pt.: *ibid.*,sch.5.
s. 16, amended: 1979,c.47,sch.2.
s. 34, see *Vaughan-Neil* v. *I.R.C.* [1979] 1 W.L.R. 1283, Oliver J.
ss. 52, 109, see *I.R.C.* v. *Plummer* (1979) 123 S.J. 769, H.L.
s. 108, see *Alloway* v. *Phillips* [1979] 1 W.L.R. 564, Brightman J.
s. 122, amended: 1979,c.47,s.10.
s. 130, see *Tucker* v. *Granada Motorway Services* [1979] 1 W.L.R. 683, H.L.
s. 168, see *Salt* v. *Chamberlain* (1979) 123 S.J. 490, Oliver J.
s. 181, see *Edwards* v. *Clinch* [1979] 1 W.L.R. 338, Walton J.
s. 183, see *Jenkins* v. *Horn* [1979] 2 All E.R. 1141, Browne-Wilkinson J.
s. 186, amended: 1979,c.14,sch.7.
s. 189, see *Ward* v. *Dunn* [1979] S.T.C. 178, Walton J.
s. 204, see *Garforth* v. *Newsmith Stainless* [1979] 1 W.L.R. 409; [1979] S.T.C. 129, Walton J.; regs. 79/747.
s. 219, amended: 1979,c.47,schs.1,2; repealed in pt.: *ibid.*,schs.1,5.
s. 246, amended: 1979,c.14,sch.7.
ss. 265–270, amended: 1979,c.14,sch.7.
ss. 272, 273, see *Burman* v. *Hedges & Butler* [1979] 1 W.L.R. 160, Walton J.
ss. 296, 298, see *Lothbury Investment Corp.* v. *I.R.C.* (1979) 123 S.J. 720, Goulding J.
ss. 273–276, 278–280, amended: 1979,c. 14,sch.7.
ss. 305, 321, 352, 359, 360, amended: 1979,c.14,sch.7.
ss. 334, 337, amended: order 79/1576.
s. 360, see *I.R.C.* v. *Helen Slater Charitable Trust, The Times*, December 1, 1979, Slade J.
s. 365, repealed in pt.: 1979,c.47,sch.5.
ss. 434, 457, see *I.R.C.* v. *Plummer* (1979) 123 S.J. 769, H.L.
s. 460, see *Clark* v. *I.R.C.* [1978] S.T.C. 614; [1979] 1 All E.R. 385, Fox J.
ss. 460–468, see *I.R.C.* v. *Wiggins* [1979] 1 W.L.R. 325, Walton J.; *Williams* v. *I.R.C.* [1979] T.R. 39, C.A.
s. 474, amended: 1979,c.14,sch.7.
ss. 488, 489, see *Yuill* v. *Wilson* [1979] 1 W.L.R. 987, C.A.; amended: 1979, c.14,sch.7.
s. 490, see *Essex* v. *I.R.C.* [1979] S.T.C. 525, Slade J.
s. 497, orders 79/117, 300–303.
s. 525, amended: 1979,c.14,sch.7.
s. 526, see *Burman* v. *Hedges & Butler* [1979] 1 W.L.R. 160, Walton J.; amended: 1979,c.14,sch.7; c.47,sch.2.

CAP.

1970—cont.

10. *Income and Corporation Taxes Act 1970 —cont.*
s. 540, amended: 1979,c.14,sch.7.
sch. 12, amended: 1979,c.47,s.10.

11. Sea Fish Industry Act 1970.
s. 1, order 78/1822.
ss. 22–24, 35–37, amended: order 79/1691.
s. 23, order 78/1821.
ss. 44, 45, 57, scheme 78/1820.
s. 49, scheme 79/421.

24. Finance Act 1970.
s. 5, repealed: 1979,c.2,sch.6.
s. 6, repealed in pt.: 1979,c.4,sch.4.
s. 7, repealed in pt.: 1979,c.2,sch6; c.4,sch.4.
s. 28, repealed in pt.: 1979,c.14,sch.8.
s. 29, amended: 1979,c.14,sch.7.
s. 30, order 79/1690.
s. 36, repealed in pt.: 1979,c.2,sch.6.
sch. 2, repealed in pt.: *ibid.*
schs. 3, 6, amended: 1979,c.14,sch.7.
sch. 15, repealed in pt.: *ibid.*,sch.8.

26. Films Act 1970.
s. 5, order 79/395.

27. Fishing Vessels (Safety Provisions) Act 1970.
s. 1, amended: 1979,c.39,sch.6; repealed in pt.: *ibid.*,s.28,sch.7.
s. 4, amended: *ibid.*,sch.6.
s. 6, regs. 79/631.
s. 7, rules 78/1873.

31. Administration of Justice Act 1970.
s. 36, see *Centrax Trustees* v. *Ross* [1979] 2 All E.R. 952, Goulding J.
s. 44, order 79/1382.
sch. 3, repealed in pt.: 1979,c.42,s.8.

35. Conveyancing and Feudal Reform (Scotland) Act 1970.
s. 1, see *Reid* v. *Stafford*, 1979 S.L.T. (Lands Tr.) 16.
s. 28, amended: 1979,c.33,sch.2.

36. Merchant Shipping Act 1970.
ss. 1–3, amended: 1979,c.39,sch.6.
ss. 2, 3, regs. 79/1519.
s. 6, amended: 1979,c.39,sch.6; repealed in pt.: *ibid.*,schs.6,7.
s. 8, amended: *ibid.*,sch.6.
s. 9, regs. 79/97.
s. 11, amended: 1979,c.39,s.39.
s. 15, amended: *ibid.*,s.37; repealed in pt.: *ibid.*,sch.7.
ss. 19–24, amended: 1979,c.39,sch.6.
s. 20, regs. 79/491.
ss. 27, 28, amended: 1979,c.39,s.45,sch. 6.
s. 30, amended: *ibid.*,sch.6.
ss. 34–38, repealed: *ibid.*,sch.7.
s. 43, regs. 79/599; amended: 1979, c.39,s.37,sch.6.
ss. 45–48, 50, 51, amended: *ibid.*,sch.6.
ss. 52, 54, amended: *ibid.*,s.37.
s. 55, amended: *ibid.*,ss.28,32.
s. 56, amended: *ibid.*,s.32.
s. 59, amended: *ibid.*,sch.6.
s. 61, amended: *ibid.*,ss.28,29.

CAP.

1970—cont.

36. *Merchant Shipping Act 1970—cont.*
s. 62, regs. 79/97, 1519; amended: 1979,c.39,sch.6.
s. 65, regs. 79/1519; amended: 1979, c.39,sch.6.
s. 68, regs. 79/97, 1519; amended: 1979,c.39,sch.6.
ss. 69–71, regs. 79/1519; amended: 1979,c.39,sch.6.
s. 72, amended: *ibid.*,s.30,sch.6.
ss. 73, 74, amended: *ibid.*,sch.6.
s. 76, amended: *ibid.*,s.37,sch.6.
ss. 77, 78, 86, amended: *ibid.*,sch.6.
s. 84, regs. 79/631.
s. 89, order 79/120; amended: 1979,c. 39,sch.6.
s. 92, amended: *ibid.*,s.37.
s. 95, amended: *ibid.*,s.45; order 79/296; repealed in pt.: 1979,c.39,sch.7; order 79/296.
s. 97, amended: 1979,c.39,s.29.
s. 99, regs. 79/97, 491, 599, 1519; repealed: 1979,c.39,sch.7.
s. 101, order 79/809; amended: 1979, c.39,s.37.
sch. 2, amended: *ibid.*,s.28,sch.6; repealed in pt.: *ibid.*,sch.7.
sch. 5, repealed in pt.: *ibid.*,sch.7.

39. Local Authorities (Goods and Services) Act 1970.
s. 1, order 78/1761.
s. 29, schemes 79/876, 877.

41. Equal Pay Act 1970.
see *Pointon* v. *The University of Sussex* [1979] I.R.L.R. 119, C.A.
s. 1, see *Handley* v. *H. Mono* [1979] I.C.R. 147, E.A.T.; *O'Brien* v. *Sim Chem* [1979] I.C.R. 13, E.A.T.; *Maidment* v. *Cooper & Co. (Birmingham)* [1978] I.C.R. 1094, E.A.T.; *Clay Cross (Quarry Service)* v. *Fletcher* [1979] 1 All E.R. 474, C.A.; *Methven v. Cow Industrial Polymers* [1979] I.C.R. 613, E.A.T.; *Jenkins* v. *Kingsgate (Clothing Productions)*, *The Times*, November 15, 1979, E.A.T.; *Durrant* v. *North Yorkshire Area Authority and Secretary of State for Social Services* [1979] I.R.L.R. 401, E.A.T.
s. 4, amended: 1979,c.12,sch.6.
s. 6, see *Worringham* v. *Lloyds Bank* [1979] I.R.L.R. 440, C.A.

49. International Monetary Fund Act 1970.
repealed: 1979,c.29,sch.

55. Family Income Supplements Act 1970.
ss. 2, 3, regs. 79/939, 1430.
ss. 4, 6, regs. 79/1504.
s. 7, amended: 1979,c.18,sch.3.
s. 10, regs. 79/160, 939, 1430, 1504, 1505; amended: 1979,c.18,sch.3.

Unemployment Levy Act 1970 (Trinidad and Tobago).
ss. 2, 7, 14, 17, 19, see *Mootoo* v. *Att.-Gen. of Trinidad and Tobago* [1979] 1 W.L.R. 1334, P.C.

CAP.

1971

3. Guardianship of Minors Act 1971.
see *Faulkner* v. *Faulkner* (1979) 123 S.J. 751, D.C.
s. 9, see *C.* v. *H.* (1979) 123 S.J. 537, D.C.
s. 15, amended: 1979,c.55,sch.2.

10. Vehicles (Excise) Act 1971.
ss. 1, 8, see *Smith* v. *Koumourou* [1979] R.T.R. 355, D.C.
s. 3, amended: 1979,c.2,sch.4.
s. 28, amended: *ibid.*
s. 35, amended: *ibid.*

12. Hydrocarbon Oil (Customs and Excise) Act 1971.
repealed, except s. 22, sch. 6 in pt.: 1979, c.5,sch.7.
s. 22, repealed: 1979,c.2,sch.6.
sch. 6, repealed in pt.: 1979,c.2,sch.6; c.8,sch.2.

19. Carriage of Goods by Sea Act 1971.
s. 1, order 79/790.
s. 2, order 78/1885.
s. 6, amended: 1979,c.39,sch.5.

23. Courts Act 1971.
s. 3, repealed in pt.: 1979,c.55,sch.3.
s. 9, see *Killington* v. *Butcher* [1979] Crim.L.R. 458, D.C.; *R.* v. *Inner London Crown Court, ex p. Obajuwana* (1979) 69 Cr.App.R. 125, D.C.
ss. 11, 57, see *R.* v. *Menocal* [1979] 2 W.L.R. 876, H.L.
s. 53, repealed in pt.: 1979,c.55,sch.3.
s. 56, sch. 4, see *R.* v. *Midgley* [1979] R.T.R. 1, C.A.
sch. 2, rules 79/668.
sch. 7, repealed in pt.: 1979,c.55,sch.3.
sch. 8, repealed in pt.: 1979,c.31,sch.2; c.55,sch.3.
sch. 9, repealed in pt.: 1979,c.2,sch.6; c.45,sch.7.

24. Coinage Act 1971.
s. 2, see *Jenkins* v. *Horn* [1979] 2 All E.R. 1141, Browne-Wilkinson J.

29. National Savings Bank Act 1971.
s. 22, order 78/1839.

31. Interest on Damages (Scotland) Act 1971.
s. 1, see *Mouland* v. *Ferguson* (O.H.), 1979 S.L.T.(Notes) 85.

32. Attachment of Earnings Act 1971.
s. 13, see *Re Green (A Bankrupt), ex p. Official Receiver* v. *Cutting* [1979] 1 All E.R. 832, Walton J.
s. 24, amended: 1979,c.39,s.39.
sch. 3, amended: 1979,c.12,sch.6.

34. Water Resources Act 1971.
s. 1, orders 79/994, 995, 1020.

38. Misuse of Drugs Act 1971.
see *R.* v. *Webb* [1979] Crim.L.R. 462, Canterbury Crown Ct.
s. 2, order 79/299.

CAP.

1971—cont.

38. *Misuse of Drugs Act 1971—cont.*
s. 4, see *R.* v. *Blake; R.* v. *O'Connor* (1978) 68 Cr.App.R. 1, C.A.; *R.* v. *Buckley* [1979] Crim.L.R. 665, C.A.; *R.* v. *Harris* (1979) 69 Cr.App.R. 122, C.A.; *R.* v. *Moore* [1979] Crim.L.R. 789, Surbiton Crown Ct.
s. 5, see *R.* v. *Peaston* (1978) 69 Cr.App.R. 203, C.A.; *R.* v. *Best* [1979] Crim.L.R. 787, C.A.; *R.* v. *Moore* [1979] Crim.L.R. 789, Surbiton Crown Ct.
ss. 7, 10, regs. 79/326.
ss. 7, 10, 31, 38, S.R. 1979 No. 258.
s. 12, amended: 1979,c.2,sch.4.
s. 22, amended: *ibid.*
ss. 23, 24, see *Wither* v. *Reed*, 1979 S.L.T. 192.
s. 26, repealed: 1979,c.2,sch.6.
s. 27, see *R.* v. *Menocal* [1979] 2 W.L.R. 876, H.L.
s. 30, regs. 79/218; S.R. 1979 No. 57.
s. 31, regs. 79/218, 326; S.R. 1979 No. 57.
s. 37, see *R.* v. *Buckley* [1979] Crim. L.R. 665, C.A.
s. 38, S.R. 1979 No. 57.
sch. 2, amended: order 79/299.

41. Highways Act 1971.
s. 4, see *Lovelock* v. *Secretary of State for Transport* [1979] R.T.R. 250, C.A.
ss. 14, 54, repealed in pt.: order 79/571.

48. Criminal Damage Act 1971.
s. 1, see *R.* v. *Stephenson* [1979] 3 W.L.R. 193, C.A.; *R.* v. *Orpin* [1979] Crim.L.R. 722, York Crown Ct.; *A.C. (A Minor)* v. *Hume* [1979] R.T.R. 424, D.C.

53. Recognition of Divorces and Legal Separations Act 1971.
see *Viswalingham* v. *Viswalingham* (1979) 123 S.J. 604, C.A.
s. 2, see *Quazi* v. *Quazi* [1979] 3 W.L.R. 833, H.L.
s. 8, see *Joyce* v. *Joyce and O'Hare* [1979] 2 All E.R. 156, Lane J.

56. Pensions (Increase) Act 1971.
s. 5, regs. 78/1808; 79/762, 771; repealed in pt.: order 79/1451.
s. 10, regs. 79/1276.
s. 11, regs. 79/1277.
s. 11A, regs. 79/1276, 1277.
s. 13, repealed in pt.: order 79/1451.
sch. 2, amended: 1979,c.50,s.4.

57. Pool Competitions Act 1971.
s. 8, order 79/763.

58. Sheriff Courts (Scotland) Act 1971.
s. 32, Acts of Sederunt 78/1979; 79/226, 613, 1520.

59. Merchant Shipping (Oil Pollution) Act 1971.
s. 4, order 79/790; amended: 1979,c.39, s.38; repealed in pt.: *ibid.*,s.38,sch.7.
s. 5, amended: *ibid.*,s.38,sch.5.
s. 7, amended: *ibid.*,sch.5.

CAP.

1971—cont.

59. *Merchant Shipping (Oil Pollution) Act 1971—cont.*
s. 8A, order 79/1450; repealed: 1979, c.39,sch.7.
s. 10, amended: *ibid.*,sch.6.
s. 14, amended: *ibid.*,s.38.
s. 15, amended: *ibid.*,sch.5.
s. 19, order 79/1450.

60. **Prevention of Oil Pollution Act 1971.**
ss. 9–11, 17, amended: 1979,c.39,sch.6.
s. 16, order 79/1453.
s. 18, amended: 1979,c.39,s.28,sch.6; repealed in pt.: *ibid.*,s.28,sch.7.
s. 21, order 79/721.
s. 25, order 79/1452.
s. 101, amended: 1979,c.39,s.37.

61. **Mineral Workings (Offshore Installations) Act 1971.**
s. 6, regs. 79/1023.
s. 10, amended: 1979,c.2,sch.4.

62. **Tribunals and Inquiries Act 1971.**
ss. 8, 19, amended: 1979,c.38,s.24.
s. 10, regs. 79/5, 514; rules 78/1780.
s. 15, order 79/659.
sch. 1, amended: rules 78/1780; 79/659.

64. **Diplomatic and Other Privileges Act 1971.**
s. 1, amended: 1979,c.2,sch.4.

65. **Licensing (Abolition of State Management) Act 1971.**
s. 5, order 79/977.

68. **Finance Act 1971.**
s. 3, repealed in pt.: 1979,c.5,sch.7; c.8, sch.2.
s. 6, repealed in pt.: 1979,c.5,sch.7.
s. 11, repealed: 1979,c.2,sch.6.
s. 18, repealed in pt.: 1979,c.47,sch.5.
ss. 29, 30, see *Slater* v. *Richardson and Bottoms* [1974] S.T.C. 630, Oliver J.
s. 41, see *Benson* v. *Yard Arm Club* [1979] 1 W.L.R. 347, C.A.
ss. 41, 42, see *Hampton* v. *Fortes Autogrill, The Times*, December 4, 1979, Fox J.
s. 43, amended: 1979,c.47,s.14.
s. 55, repealed in pt.: 1979,c.14,sch.8.
ss. 56, 58–60, repealed: *ibid.*
s. 69, repealed in pt.: 1979,c.2,sch.6; c.14,sch.8.
sch. 1, repealed: 1979,c.2,sch.6.
schs. 3, 6, 8, 9, repealed in pt.: 1979, c.14,sch.8.
sch. 4, amended: 1979,c.47,sch.2; repealed in pt.: *ibid.*,sch.5.
sch. 8, amended: 1979,c.47,s.14.
schs. 10, 12, repealed: 1979,c.14,sch.8.

69. **Medicines Act 1971.**
s. 1, regs. 79/899.

70. **Hijacking Act 1971.**
ss. 3, 6, order 78/1887.

71. **Mineral Workings Act 1971.**
ss. 3, 5, order 79/211.

72. **Industrial Relations Act 1971.**
s. 24, see *Carr* v. *Alexander Russell (Note)* [1979] I.C.R. 469, Ct. of Session.

CAP.

1971—cont.

75. **Civil Aviation Act 1971.**
ss. 5, 24, regs. 79/514.
ss. 21, 22, amended: 1979,c.27,sch.
s. 26, regs. 79/5.
s. 29, schemes 78/1797, 1798; 79/414.
s. 29A, schemes 78/1797, 1798.
sch. 10, regs. 79/154.

77. **Immigration Act 1971.**
s. 3, see *R.* v. *Secretary of State for the Home Department, ex p. Zamir* [1979] Crim.L.R. 391, D.C.
s. 4, see *R.* v. *Secretary of State for the Home Department, ex p. Ram* [1979] 1 W.L.R. 148, D.C.
ss. 9, 32, order 79/730.
ss. 14, 24, 28, see *Horne* v. *Gaygusuz* [1979] Crim.L.R. 594, D.C.
s. 24, see *R.* v. *Bello* (1978) 67 Cr.App. R. 288, C.A.
ss. 24, 28, see *R.* v. *Eastbourne JJ., ex p. Barsoum*, January 26, 1979, D.C.
s. 24, sch. 3, see *R.* v. *Inner London Crown Court, ex p. Obajuwana* (1979) 69 Cr.App.R. 125.
sch. 2, see *R.* v. *Secretary of State for the Home Department, ex p. Ram* [1979] 1 W.L.R. 148, D.C.: *Re Shahid Iqbal (Note)* [1979] 1 W.L.R. 425, C.A.; amended: 1979,c.55,sch.2.

78. **Town and Country Planning Act 1971.**
s. 21, orders 79/200–203, 328, 329, 890, 891, 1042, 1043, 1187, 1189, 1485, 1486.
s. 22, see *Wakelin* v. *Secretary of State for the Environment* (1978) 77 L.G.R. 101, C.A.
s. 23, see *Day* v. *Secretary of State for the Environment* (1979) 251 E.G. 163, D.C.
s. 28, see *Wain and L.D.R.S.* v. *Secretary of State for the Environment and Waltham Forest London Borough* [1979] J.P.L. 231, Stocker J.
s. 29, see *R.* v. *Sheffield City Council, ex p. Mansfield* (1978) 37 P. & C.R. 1, D.C.
s. 30, see *George Wimpey & Co.* v. *New Forest District Council* (1979) 250 E.G.249, Sir Douglas Frank, Q.C.
s. 53, see *Western Fish Products* v. *Penwith District Council* (1978) 77 L.G.R. 185, C.A.
ss. 56, 58, amended: 1979,c.46,sch.4.
ss. 67, 68, regs. 79/838.
s. 69, order 79/839.
ss. 73–75, see *B.L. Holdings* v. *Robert J. Wood and Partners* [1978] J.P.L. 833, Gibson J.
s. 74, see *B. L. Holdings* v. *Robert J. Wood and Partners* (1979) 123 S.J. 570, C.A.
s. 78, see *Richmond-upon-Thames London Borough Council* v. *Secretary of State for the Environment* (1979) 37 P. & C.R. 151, Sir Douglas Frank, Q.C.
s. 86, order 79/908.
s. 87, see *Bristol Stadium* v. *Brown* (1979) 252 E.G. 803, D.C.

CAP.

1971—cont.

78. *Town and Country Planning Act 1971—cont.*
s. 88, see *Skinner* v. *Secretary of State for the Environment* (1978) 247 E.G. 1179, D.C.; *Stanton* v. *Secretary of State for the Environment* (1978) 248 E.G. 227, D.C.
s. 90, see *Scott Markets* v. *Waltham* *Forest London Borough* (1979) 77 L.G.R. 565, C.A.; *Bristol Stadium* v. *Brown* (1979) 252 E.G. 803, D.C.
s. 94, see *Broxbourne Borough Council* v. *Secretary of State for the Environ-* *ment* [1979] 2 All E.R. 13, D.C.; *Western Fish Products* v. *Penwith District Council* (1978) 77 L.G.R. 185, C.A.
s. 109, see *Royal Borough of Kensington and Chelsea* v. *Elmton* (1978) 246 E.G. 1011, D.C.
ss. 209, 210, 217, 244, see *Ashby* v. *Secretary of State for the Environment* [1979] 37 P. & C.R. 197, Sir Douglas Frank, Q.C.
s. 245, see *Winchester City Council* v. *Secretary of State for the Environment* (1978) 36 P. & C.R. 455, Forbes J.; *Sheffield City Council* v. *Secretary of State for the Environment* (1979) 251 E.G. 165, Drake J.; *Charles Church* v. *Secretary of State for the Environment* (1979) 251 E.G. 674, Sir Douglas Frank, Q.C.
s. 246, see *Wain and L.D.R.S.* v. *Secretary of State for the Environment and Waltham Forest London Borough* [1979] J.P.L. 231, Stocker J.; *Day* v. *Secretary of State for the Environment* (1979) 251 E.G. 163, D.C.
s. 287, orders 79/200–203, 328, 329, 839, 890, 891, 1042, 1043, 1187, 1189, 1485, 1486.
sch. 23, repealed in pt.: 1979,c.46,sch.5.

Firearms (Increased Penalties) Act 1971 (Laws of Malaysia Act 37) (Malaysia).
s. 8, see *Teh Cheng Poh alias Char Meh* v. *Public Prosecutor, Malaysia* [1979] 2 W.L.R. 623, P.C.

17. West Indies Associated States Supreme Court (Grenada) Act 1971 (West Indies).
s. 41, see *Ferguson* v. *The Queen* [1979] 1 W.L.R. 94, P.C.

1972

5. Local Employment Act 1972.
ss. 1, 18, order 79/837.
ss. 8, 18, order 79/334.

11. Superannuation Act 1972.
s. 1, order 79/1540.
s. 7, regs. 78/1794 (S.), 1926 (S.); 79/2, 592.
s. 9, regs. 79/47, 1206.
s. 12, regs. 78/1794 (S.), 1926 (S.); 79/47, 592, 1206.
s. 24, regs. 79/785 (S.).
sch. 3, regs. 79/1206.

CAP.

1972—cont.

17. Electricity Act 1972.
repealed, except ss. 2, 4.

18. Maintenance Orders (Reciprocal Enforcement) Act 1972.
ss. 1, 24, 45, order 79/115.
s. 26, amended: order 79/1314.
s. 27, amended: 1979,c.55,sch.2.
s. 40, orders 79/1314, 1317.

20. Road Traffic Act 1972.
s. 1, see *R.* v. *Wheeler*, January 25, 1979, Judge ap Robert, Newport Crown Ct.; *R.* v. *Wright (Ernest)* [1979] R.T.R. 15, C.A.; *R.* v. *Midgley* [1979] R.T.R. 1, C.A.; *R.* v. *Yarnold* [1978] R.T.R. 526, C.A.; *R.* v. *Davis* [1979] R.T.R. 316, C.A.; *R.* v. *Clancy* [1979] R.T.R. 312, C.A.; *R.* v. *O'Connor* [1979] R.T.R. 467, C.A.
s. 2, see *R.* v. *Banks* [1978] R.T.R. 535, C.A.; *Killington* v. *Butcher* [1979] Crim.L.R. 458, D.C.
s. 3, see *Killington* v. *Butcher* [1979] Crim.L.R. 458, D.C.; *Lockhart* v. *Smith*, 1979 S.L.T.(Sh.Ct.) 52; *Jarvis* v. *Williams* [1979] R.T.R. 497, D.C.
s. 5, see *R.* v. *Wright (Ernest)* [1979] R.T.R. 15, C.A.
ss. 5, 6, see *Sharpe* v. *Perry* [1979] R.T.R. 235, D.C.
s. 6, see *Topping* v. *Scott*, 1979 S.L.T. (Notes) 21; *R.* v. *Midgley* [1979] R.T.R. 1, C.A.; *Shersby* v. *Klippel* [1979] R.T.R. 116, D.C.; *Sutherland* v. *Aitchison*, 1979 S.L.T.(Notes) 37; *Ferns* v. *Tudhope*, 1979 S.L.T.(Notes), 23; *R.* v. *Wedlake* [1978] R.T.R. 529, C.A.; *Park* v. *Hicks* [1979] Crim.L.R. 57, D.C.; *Griffiths* v. *Willett* [1979] Crim.L.R. 320, D.C.; *Beck* v. *Watson* [1979] Crim.L.R. 533, D.C.; *Sutherland* v. *Aitchison*, 1975 J.C. 1; *Grant* v. *Gorman* [1979] Crim.L.R. 669, D.C.; *Mulcaster* v. *Wheatstone* [1979] Crim.L.R. 728, D.C.; *R.* v. *Beardsley* [1979] R.T.R. 472, C.A.; *R.* v. *Salters* [1979] R.T.R. 470, C.A.
s. 7, see *R.* v. *Trump*, *The Times*, December 29, 1979, C.A.
s. 8, see *Manz* v. *Miln*, 1977 J.C. 78; *Blyth* v. *Macphail*, 1977 J.C. 74; *Topping* v. *Scott*, 1979 S.L.T.(Notes) 21; *Stewart* v. *Fekkes*, 1977 J.C. 85; *R.* v. *Wedlake* [1978] R.T.R. 529, C.A.; *Williams* v. *Critchley* [1979] R.T.R. 47, D.C.; *Shersby* v. *Klippel* [1979] R.T.R. 116, D.C.; *R.* v. *Moore (George)* [1979] R.T.R. 98, C.A.; *Mallows* v. *Harris* [1979] Crim.L.R. 320; *Knight* v. *Taylor* [1979] Crim. L.R. 319, D.C.; *Siddiqui* v. *Swain* [1979] R.T.R. 454, D.C.; ***Chief Constable of West Midlands Police* v. *Billingham* [1979] 2 All E.R. 182, D.C.; *Price* v. *Davies* [1979] R.T.R. 204,** D.C.; *Morris* v. *Beardmore* [1979] 3 W.L.R. 93, M.C.; ***Knight* v. *Taylor* [1979] R.T.R. 304, D.C.;**

CAP.

1972—cont.

20. *Road Traffic Act 1972—cont.*
Sharpe v. *Perry* [1979] R.T.R. 235, D.C.; *Lee* v. *Wiltshire Chief Constable* [1979] R.T.R. 349, D.C.; *Grant* v. *Gorman* [1979] Crim.L.R. 669, D.C.; *R.* v. *Miles* [1979] R.T.R. 509, C.A.

s. 9, see *R.* v. *Wedlake* [1978] R.T.R. 529, C.A.; *Williams* v. *Critchley* [1979] R.T.R. 47, D.C.; *Blyth* v. *Macphail*, 1977 J.C. 74; *Brown* v. *Ridge* [1979] R.T.R. 138, D.C.; *Beck* v. *Sager* [1979] R.T.R. 475, D.C.; *Mallows* v. *Harris* [1979] Crim.L.R. 320, D.C.; *Morris* v. *Beardmore* [1979] 3 W.L.R. 93, D.C.; *Griffiths* v. *Willett* [1979] R.T.R. 195, D.C.; *Price* v. *Davies* [1979] R.T.R. 204, D.C.; *Sharpe* v. *Perry* [1979] R.T.R. 235, D.C.; *Alcock* v. *Read* [1979] Crim.L.R. 534, D.C.; *Lee* v. *Wiltsthire Chief Constable* [1979] R.T.R. 349, D.C.; *Payne* v. *Diccox* [1979] Crim.L.R. 670, D.C.

s. 10, see *Ferns* v. *Tudhope*, 1979 S.L.T. (Notes) 23; *Sutherland* v. *Aitchison*, 1979 S.L.T.(Notes) 37.

s. 12, see *Brown* v. *Ridge* [1979] R.T.R. 138, D.C.; *Price* v. *Davies* [1979] R.T.R. 204, D.C.

s. 14, see *Hay* v. *Police*, January 2, 1979, Judge Bennett, Q.C., Wakefield Crown Ct.; *Ferrari* v. *McNaughton*, 1979 S.L.T.(Notes) 62.

s. 15, regs. 79/1101(S.).

s. 20, see *Sutherland* v. *Aitchison*, 1975 J.C. 1.

s. 20, regs. 79/233.

s. 22, see *R.* v. *Saunders* [1978] Crim. L.R. 98, Nottingham Crown Ct.; *Skeen* v. *Smith*, 1979 S.L.T. 295.

s. 25, see *Ward* v. *Rawson* [1978] R.T.R. 498, D.C.

s. 37, see *Hoadley* v. *Dartford District Council* [1979] R.T.R. 359, C.A.

s. 40, see *R.* v. *Sandwell JJ., ex p. West Midlands Passenger Transport Board* [1979] R.T.R. 17, D.C.; *Patterson* v. *Redpath Brothers* [1979] Crim.L.R. 187, D.C.; *Passmoor* v. *Gibbons* [1979] R.T.R. 53, D.C.; regs. 79/803, 843; *Lovett* v. *Payne* [1979] Crim.L.R. 729, D.C.

s. 40, regs. 79/803, 843, 1062, 1145.

s. 42, order 79/1198.

s. 43, regs. 79/439, 1215.

s. 47, regs. 78/1811; 79/1092.

ss. 49–52, regs. 79/1092.

s. 50, regs. 78/1810, 1811.

s. 63, regs. 78/1870; 79/1088.

ss. 75, 78, regs. 79/803.

s. 84, regs. 79/1412.

s. 93, see *R.* v. *Banks* [1978] R.T.R. 535, C.A.; *R.* v. *Yarnold* [1978] R.T.R. 526, C.A.; *Smith* v. *Peaston*, 1977 J.C. 81; *Urry* v. *Gibb*, 1979 S.L.T. (Notes) 19; *Smith* v. *Baker*, 1979 S.L.T.(Notes) 19; *Powell* v. *Gliha* [1979] R.T.R. 126, D.C.; *R.* v. *Mulroy* [1979] R.T.R. 214, C.A.; *Smith* v. *Craddock*, 1979 S.L.T. (Notes) 46; *Park* v. *Hicks* [1979] R.T.R. 259, D.C.; *R.* v. *O'Connor* [1979] R.T.R. 467, C.A.; *R.* v. *Fenwick* [1979] R.T.R. 506; C.A.; *R.* v. *Beardsley* [1979] R.T.R. 472, C.A.; *R.* v. *Salters* [1979] R.T.R. 470, C.A.; *R.* v. *Cunningham* [1979] R.T.R. 465, C.A.

s. 99, see *Mitchell* v. *Dean*, 1979 S.L.T. (Notes) 12; *Boustead* v. *MacLeod*, 1979 S.L.T.(Notes) 48.

ss. 99, 101, see *Graham* v. *Annan*, High Court of Justiciary, October 9, 1979.

s. 101, see *Smith* v. *Peaston*, 1977 J.C. 81; *Urry* v. *Gibb*, 1979 S.L.T.(Notes) 19; *Tudhope* v. *Birbeck*, 1979 S.L.T. (Notes) 47.

s. 107, regs. 79/1412.

s. 114, see *North West Traffic Area Licensing Authority* v. *Brady* [1979] R.T.R. 500, D.C.

s. 143, see *Mitchell* v. *Dean*, 1979 S.L.T.(Notes) 12; *Boustead* v. *MacLeod*, 1979 S.L.T.(Notes) 48; *Lockhart* v. *Smith*, 1979 S.L.T. (Sh.Ct.) 52; *Graham* v. *Annan*, High Court of Justiciary, October 9, 1979.

s. 159, see *Smith* v. *Peaston*, 1977 J.C. 81.

s. 162, see *Smith* v. *Peaston*, 1977 J.C. 81.

s. 169, see *Holloway* v. *Brown* [1978] R.T.R. 537, D.C.

s. 179, see *R.* v. *Okike* [1978] R.T.R. 489, C.A.; *Shield* v. *Crighton* (Note) [1978] R.T.R. 494, C.A.

s. 196, see *Lock* v. *Leatherdale* [1979] R.T.R. 201, D.C.

s. 199, regs. 78/1810, 1870; 79/439, 803, 843, 1215, 1412.

sch. 4, see *R.* v. *Yarnold* [1978] R.T.R. 526, C.A.; *R.* v. *Wedlake* [1978] R.T.R. 529, C.A.; *R.* v. *Okike* [1978] R.T.R. 489, C.A.; *R.* v. *Coventry JJ., ex p. Sayers* [1979] R.T.R. 22, D.C.; *Powell* v. *Gliha* [1979] R.T.R. 126, D.C.; *R.* v. *Mulroy* [1979] R.T.R. 214, C.A.; *Killington* v. *Butcher* [1979] Crim.L.R. 458, D.C.; *Park* v. *Hicks* [1979] R.T.R. 259, D.C.; *R.* v. *O'Connor* [1979] R.T.R. 467, C.A.; *R.* v. *Fenwick* [1979] R.T.R. 506, C.A.; *R.* v. *Cunningham* [1979] R.T.R. 465, C.A.

25. Betting and Gaming Duties Act 1972.

s. 15, amended: 1979, c. 2, sch. 4.

s. 20, amended: *ibid.*

s. 30, amended: *ibid.*

schs. 2, 4, repealed in pt.: 1979, c.2, sch.6.

35. Defective Premises Act 1972.

s. 1, see *Alexander* v. *Mercouris* [1979] 1 W.L.R. 1270, C.A.

s. 2, order 79/381.

CAP.

1972—cont.

38. Matrimonial Proceedings (Polygamous Marriages) Act 1972.
ss. 3, 5, repealed in pt.: order 78/1045.

41. Finance Act 1972.
s. 1, amended: 1979,c.2,sch.4.
s. 2, see *R.H.M. Bakeries (Northern)* v. *Customs and Excise Comrs.* [1979] S.T.C. 72, Neill J.; *Church of Scientology of California* v. *Customs and Excise Commissioners* [1979] S.T.C. 297, Neill J.
s. 3, order 79/819.
s. 4, see *Customs and Excise Comrs.* v. *C. & A. Modes* [1979] S.T.C. 433, Drake J.
s. 5, see *Customs and Excise Comrs.* v. *Oliver, The Times*, December 8, 1979. Griffiths J.
ss. 5, 10, see *Tynewydd Labour Working Men's Club and Institute* v. *Customs and Excise Commissioners* [1979] S.T.C. 570, Forbes J.; *Customs and Excise Commissioners* v. *Tilling Management Services* [1979] S.T.C. 365, Neill J.
s. 9, amended: 1979,c.47,s.1.
s. 12, see *Customs and Excise Comrs.* v. *Bushby* [1979] S.T.C. 8, Neill J.; orders 79/242, 244–246, 657, 1554; amended: 1979,c.2,sch.4.
s. 13, see *Customs and Excise Comrs.* v. *The Little Span Club* [1979] S.T.C. 170, Neill J.; *Tynewydd Labour Working Men's Club and Institute* v. *Customs and Excise Comrs.* [1979] S.T.C. 570, Forbes J.; orders 79/243, 246.
s. 17, amended: 1979,c.2,sch.4; c.6,s.9; c.58,sch.1; repealed in pt.: 1979,c.2. sch.6; c.58,sch.2.
s. 21, see *Customs and Excise Comrs.* v. *Save and Prosper Group* [1979] S.T.C. 205, Neill J.
s. 27, amended: 1979,c.2,sch.4.
s. 30, see *Customs and Excise Comrs.* v. *J. H. Corbitt (Numismatists)* [1979] 3 W.L.R. 300, C.A.
s. 30, regs. 79/224.
s. 31, see *S. J. Grange Ltd.* v. *Customs and Excise Comrs.* [1979] 1 W.L.R. 239, C.A.; *Customs and Excise Comrs.* v. *J. H. Corbitt (Numismatists)* (1979) 123 S.J. 306, C.A.; *Tynewydd Labour Working Men's Club and Institute* v. *Customs and Excise Comrs.* [1979] S.T.C. 570, Forbes J.; *Abedin* v. *Customs and Excise Comrs.* [1979] S.T.C. 426, Neill J.
s. 38, see *Grice* v. *Needs* [1979] 3 All E.R. 501, D.C.
s. 38, amended: 1979,c.2,sch.4.
s. 40, see *Tynewydd Labour Working Men's Club and Institute* v. *Customs and Excise Comrs.* [1979] S.T.C. 570, Forbes J.; *Customs and Excise Comrs.* v. *J. H. Corbitt (Numismatists)* [1979] 3 W.L.R. 300, C.A.; *Abedin* v. *Customs and Excise Comrs.* [1979] S.T.C. 426, Neill J.; *Shahbag Restaurant* v. *Customs and Excise Comrs.* [1978] T.R. 467, Neill J.; amended: 1979,c.2,sch.4.

CAP.

1972—cont.

41. *Finance Act 1972—cont.*
s. 43, orders 79/242–246, 657, 819, 1554; repealed in pt.: 1979,c.58,sch.2.
s. 47, amended: 1979,c.2,sch.4.
s. 50, repealed: 1979,c.58,sch.2.
s. 55, repealed in pt.: 1979,c.2,sch.6; c.3,sch.3.
s. 57, repealed in pt.: 1979,c.4,sch.4.
s. 79, amended: 1979,c.14,sch.7.
s. 95, amended: 1979,c.47,s.7.
s. 98, orders 79/117, 302.
ss. 112–119, repealed: 1979,c.14,sch.8.
s. 124, repealed in pt.: *ibid.*
s. 134, repealed in pt.: 1979,c.2,sch.6; c.14,sch.8.
sch. 4, see *Customs and Excise Comrs.* v. *Bushby* [1979] S.T.C. 8, Neill J.; *Customs and Excise Comrs.* v. *G. & B. Practical Management Development* [1979] S.T.C. 280, Q.B.D.; *A.C.T. Construction Co.* v. *Customs and Excise Comrs.* [1979] 2 All E.R. 691, Drake J.; *Customs and Excise Comrs.* v. *Morrison Dunbar and Mecca* [1978] T.R. 267, Neill J.
sch. 4, amended: 1979,c.2,sch.4; c.5, sch.6; orders 79/242–246, 657, 1554; repealed in pt.: 1979,c.5,sch.7.
sch. 5, see *Customs and Excise Comrs.* v. *The Little Span Club* [1979] S.T.C. 170, Neill J.; *Tynewydd Labour Working Men's Club and Institute* v. *Customs and Excise Comrs.* [1979] S.T.C. 570, Forbes J.; amended: orders 79/243, 246.
sch. 7, amended: 1979,c.2,sch.4; repealed in pt.: 1979,c.58,sch.2.
sch. 12, amended: 1979,c.14,sch.7.
sch. 24, repealed in pt.: *ibid.*,sch.8.
sch. 28, amended: 1979,c.2,s.177.

43. Field Monuments Act 1972.
repealed: 1979,c.46,sch.5.

46. Housing (Financial Provisions) Scotland Act 197.
s. 17, regs. 79/1308.
sch. 2, regs. 79/1041; amended: regs. 79/1308.
sch. 3, amended: *ibid.*

47. Housing Finance Act 1972.
s. 8, order 79/234.
s. 25, regs. 79/1014, 1319.
s. 90, see *Legal and General Assurance Society* v. *Keane* (1978) P. & C.R. 399, C.A.
sch. 3, amended and repealed in pt.: regs. 79/1319.

48. Parliamentary and other Pensions Act 1972.
ss. 4, 29, order 79/905.

50. Legal Advice and Assistance Act 1972.
s. 1, regs. 78/1818; amended: 1979, c.26,sch.1.
s. 2, amended and repealed in pt. (S.): *ibid.*,s.6; repealed in pt.: *ibid.*,sch.2.

CAP.

1972—cont.

50. *Legal Advice and Assistance Act 1972 —cont.*
s. 3, amended: *ibid.*,s.7(S.),sch.1.
s. 4, regs. 79/156 (S.); amended (S.): 1979,c.26,s.8; regs. 79/156; repealed in pt.: 1979,c.26,sch.2; *ibid.*,s.8(S.).
s. 11, regs. 78/1818; 79/156; amended: 1979,c.26,sch.1.
s. 14, amended: *ibid.*,sch.1.
sch. 1, amended (S.): order 79/156; repealed: 1979,c.26,s.8(S.),sch.2.
sch. 2, repealed in pt.: *ibid.*,sch.1.

52. Town and Country Planning (Scotland) Act 1972.
s. 21, order 79/198.
ss. 26, 27, 33, 211, 214, 233, see *British Airports Authority* v. *Secretary of State for Scotland*, First Division, November 22, 1978.
ss. 54, 56, amended: 1979,c.46,sch.4.
ss. 65, 66, regs. 79/838.
s. 278, sch. 24, see *Murray Bookmakers* v. *Glasgow District Council*, 1979 S.L.T.(Lands Tr.) 8.
sch. 21, repealed in pt.: 1979,c.46,sch.5.

53. Contracts of Employment Act 1972.
see *Active Elderly Housing Association* v. *Sparrow* (1978) 13 I.T.R. 395, E.A.T.
s. 11, see *Bullock* v. *Merseyside County Council* [1979] I.C.R. 79, C.A.
s. 35, see *Lloyds Bank* v. *Secretary of State for Employment* (1978) 123 S.J. 47, E.A.T.
sch. 1, see *Opie* v. *John Gubbins (Insurance Brokers)* [1978] I.R.L.R. 541, E.A.T.; *Lloyds Bank* v. *Secretary of State for Employment* (1978) 123 S.J. 47, E.A.T.; *Larkin* v. *Cambos Enterprises (Stretford)* [1978] I.C.R. 1247, E.A.T.; *Wessex National* v. *Long* (1978) 13 I.T.R. 413, E.A.T.; *Scarlett* v. *Godfrey Abbot Group* [1978] I.C.R. 1106, E.A.T.; *Bullock* v. *Merseyside County Council* [1979] I.C.R. 79, C.A.; *Cookson & Zinn* v. *Morgan* [1979] I.C.R. 425, E.A.T.; *Hillingdon Area Health Authority* v. *Kauders* [1979] I.C.R. 472, E.A.T.; *Southwood Hostel Management Committee* v. *Taylor* [1979] I.C.R. 813, E.A.T.; *Fisher* v. *York Trailer Co.* [1979] I.C.R. 834, E.A.T.; *Teesside Times* v. *Drury*, *The Times*, December 19, 1979, C.A.
sch. 16, see *Lloyds Bank* v. *Secretary of State for Environment* [1979] I.C.R. 258, E.A.T.

59. Administration of Justice (Scotland) Act 1972.
s. 1, see *Moore* v. *Greater Glasgow Health Board*, First Division, February 9, 1978.

60. Gas Act 1972.
sch. 4, order 78/1848.

61. Land Charges Act 1972.
s. 1, see *Allen* v. *Greehi Builders* [1978] 3 All E.R. 1163, Browne-Wilkinson J.

CAP.

1972—cont.

62. Agriculture (Miscellaneous Provisions) Act 1972.
s. 18, repealed: 1979,c.13,sch.1.
s. 20, order 79/638.

63. Industry Act 1972.
s. 1, orders 79/269, 837; amended: order 79/975.
s. 3, order 79/975.
s. 5, orders 79/837, 975.
s. 10, amended: 1979,c.59,s.10.
sch. 2, orders 79/837, 975.

65. National Debt Act 1972.
s. 3, regs, 79/553.
s. 11, regs. 78/1855; 79/1388.

68. European Communities Act 1972.
s. 1, order 79/1446; amended: 1979, c.57,s.1.
s. 2, regs. 78/1832, 1927, 1938; 79/80, 132, 221, 249, 319, 555, 586, 654, 693, 749, 768 (S.), 847, 941, 956; order 78/1910; 79/1089, 1094, 1095, 1175, 1205, 1224, 1379, 1426, 1427, 1459, 1476, 1748, 1755; S.Rs. 1978 Nos. 366, 393; 1979 Nos. 121, 261, 401.
s. 4, regs. 78/1938.
s. 5, orders 78/1941; 79/155; amended: 1979,c.3,sch.2; repealed in pt.: 1979, c.2,sch.6; c.3,sch.3.
s. 6, regs. 79/433; order 79/1541; amended: 1979,c.2,sch.4; c.3,sch.2.
s. 12, amended: 1979,c.13,sch.1.
sch. 2, amended: 1979,c.3,sch.2.
sch. 4, regs. 78/1938; repealed in pt.: 1979,c.2,sch.6; c.3,sch.3; c.12,sch.7.

70. Local Government Act 1972.
s. 5, order 79/710.
s. 47, see *Enfield London Borough Council* v. *Local Government Boundary Commission for England* [1979] 3 All E.R. 747, H.L.
ss. 47, 48, order 79/90.
s. 51, orders 78/1783, 1792, 1793, 1806, 1813, 1814, 1841–1843, 1859–1864; 79/90, 1015, 1016, 1027, 1028, 1071, 1107–1113, 1131, 1264–1266, 1295, 1320–1324, 1327, 1328, 1341, 1346–1349, 1368, 1411, 1472–1474, 1494–1496, 1523–1525.
s. 131, amended: 1979,c.46,sch.4.
ss. 173, 178, regs. 78/1795, 1917.
s. 177, regs. 79/1122.
s. 216, repealed in pt.: 1979,c.55,sch.3.
s. 217, amended: *ibid.*,sch.2; repealed in pt.: *ibid.*,sch.3.
s. 247, order 79/909.
s. 254, orders 79/228, 1123.
s. 262, order 79/969.
ss. 265, 266, orders 78/1844; 79/72.
sch. 11, see *Enfield London Borough Council* v. *Local Government Boundary Commission for England* [1979] 3 All E.R. 747, H.L.
sch. 16, see *Att.-Gen., ex rel. Co-operative Retail Services* v. *Taff-Ely Borough Council* (1979) 250 E.G. 757, C.A.
sch. 27, repealed in pt.: 1979,c.55,sch.3.

CAP.

1972—cont.

71. Criminal Justice Act 1972.
s. 1, see *R.* v. *Miller* (Note) (1976) 68 Cr.App.R. 56, C.A.
s. 51, amended: 1979,c.55,sch.2.
ss. 61, 62, repealed: *ibid.*,sch.3.

xiv. Thames Barrier and Flood Prevention Act 1972.
ss. 56, 59, order 79/696.

xxxi. Derby Corporation Act 1972.
ss. 29–39, 40 (in part), 41, 42 (in part) repealed: order 79/805.

xli. Liverpool Corporation Act 1972.
s. 4, amended: order 79/806.
ss. 5, 6, 7 (in part), 8–14, 15 (in part), 16–30, 31 (in part), 32–43, repealed in pt.: *ibid.*
s. 501, amended: *ibid.*

221. Criminal Procedure Ordinance (Laws of Hong Kong 1972, rev.) (Hong Kong).
s. 83, see *Kwan Ping Bong* v. *The Queen* [1979] 2 W.L.R. 433, P.C.
s. 83E, see *Au Pui-Kuen* v. *Att.Gen. of Hong Kong* [1979] 2 W.L.R. 274, P.C.

Matrimonial Proceedings and Property Ordinance 1972 (Hong Kong).
see *De Lasala* v. *De Lasala* (1979) 123 S.J. 301, J.C.

1973

3. Sea Fish Industry Act 1973.
s. 1, order 79/1691.

9. Counter-Inflation Act 1973.
s. 1, order 79/795.
ss. 5, 15, sch. 3, orders 79/60, 178, 568.

13. Supply of Goods (Implied Terms) Act 1973
ss. 1–7, repealed: 1979,c.54,sch.3.
ss. 14, 15, amended: *ibid.*,sch.2.

14. Costs in Criminal Cases Act 1973.
s. 4, see *R.* v. *Smith* (1978) 67 Cr.App.R. 332, C.A.; *R.* v. *Mountain*; *R.* v. *Kilminster* (1978) 68 Cr.App.R. 41, C.A.

15. Administration of Justice Act 1973.
s. 1, repealed in pt.: 1979,c.55,sch.3.
s. 2, amended: *ibid.*,sch.2; repealed in pt.: *ibid.*,sch.3.
s. 3, repealed: *ibid.*
s. 5, substituted: *ibid.*,sch.2.
s. 8, see *Centrax Trustees* v. *Ross* [1979] 2 All E.R. 952, Goulding J.
s. 9, amended: 1979,c.55,sch.2.
s. 10, regs. 79/210.
s. 20, repealed in pt.: 1979,c.55,sch.3.
sch. 1, amended: *ibid.*,sch.2; repealed in pt.: *ibid.*,sch.3.
sch. 3, S.R. 1979 No. 67.

16. Education Act 1973.
s. 3, regs. 79/900.

18. Matrimonial Causes Act 1973.
see *De Lasala* v. *De Lasala* (1979) 123 S.J. 301, J.C.

CAP.

1973—cont.

18. *Matrimonial Causes Act 1973—cont.*
s. 1, see *Day* v. *Day* [1979] 2 All E.R. 187, C.A.; *Stevens* v. *Stevens* [1979] 1 W.L.R. 885, Sheldon J.
s. 2, see *Piper* v. *Piper* (1978) 8 Fam. Law 243, C.A.
s. 3, see *C.* v. *C.* (*Divorce—Exceptional* *Hardship* [1979] 2 W.L.R. 95, C.A.; *Woolf* v. *Woolf* (1978) 9 Fam.Law 216, C.A.
s. 10, see *Bateman* v. *Bateman* [1979] 2 W.L.R. 377, Pinchas J.
s. 13, see *D.* v. *D.* [1979] 3 W.L.R. 185, Dunn J.
s. 23, see *Minton* v. *Minton* [1979] 2 W.L.R. 31, H.L.
ss. 24, 25, see *Lilford (Lord) Glynn* [1979] 1 W.L.R. 78, C.A.
s. 25, see *Bateman* v. *Bateman* [1979] 2 W.L.R. 377, Pinchas J.; *Wilkinson* v. *Wilkinson* (1979) 123 S.J. 752, Booth J.; *K.* v. *K.*, *The Times*, December 4, 1979, Wood J.
ss. 31, 34, see *Jessel* v. *Jessel* [1979] 1 W.L.R. 1148, C.A.
s. 41, see *Ashley* v. *Ashley* (1979) 9 Fam.Law 219, C.A.; *A.* v. *A.* (*Children: Arrangements*) [1979] 1 W.L.R. 533, C.A.
s. 42, see *Rowe* v. *Rowe* (1979) 123 S.J. 352, C.A.
s. 45, see *Puttick* v. *Att.-Gen. and* *Puttick* [1979] 3 W.L.R. 542, Sir George Baker P.
s. 50, rules 79/400.
s. 51, order 79/966.

19. Independent Broadcasting Authority Act 1973.
ss. 2, 22, see *Wilson* v. *Independent Broadcasting Authority* (O.H.), February 11, 1979.
ss. 39, 40, order 79/114.

26. Land Compensation Act 1973.
s. 48, see *Wakerley* v. *St. Edmundsbury Borough Council* (1979) 249 E.G. 639, C.A.

32. National Health Service Reorganisation Act 1973.
s. 15, order 79/51.
sch. 1, see *R.* v. *Central Arbitration Committee, ex p. North Western Regional Health Authority* [1978] I.C.R. 1228, D.C.

33. Protection of Wrecks Act 1973.
s. 1, orders 79/31, 56.
s. 3, orders 79/6, 56.

35. Employment Agencies Act 1973.
ss. 2, 12, regs. 79/770.
ss. 12, 13, regs. 79/342, 1741.

36. Northern Ireland Constitution Act 1973.
ss. 19, 23, see *Purvis* v. *Magherafelt District Council* [1978] N.I. 26, Murray J.
s. 28, amended: 1979,c.15,s.1.
s. 38, orders 79/927, 1576.

CAP.

1973—cont.

37. **Water Act 1973.**
ss. 2, 3, 36, orders 79/466–474.
s. 16, see *George Wimpey & Co.* v. *Secretary of State for the Environment and Maidstone District Council* [1978] J.P.L. 773, Forbes J.

38. **Social Security Act 1973.**
s. 66, regs. 78/1827.
s. 68, amended: 1979,c.18,sch.3.
sch. 27, repealed in pt.: 1978,c.12,sch.7.

41. **Fair Trading Act 1973.**
ss. 41, 42, see *Director-General of Fair Trading* v. *Boswell*, 1979 S.L.T. (Sh.Ct.) 9.
s. 131, amended: 1979,c.38,s.9.
s. 133, amended: *ibid.*,s.10.

45. **Domicile and Matrimonial Proceedings Act 1973.**
Pt. IV, repealed: order 78/1045.
s. 1, see *Puttick* v. *Att.-Gen.* [1979] 3 W.L.R. 542, Sir George Baker P.
s. 17, repealed in pt.: order 78/1045; 1979,c.60,sch.3.
sch. 5, repealed: order 78/1045.

47. **Protection of Aircraft Act 1973.**
ss. 5, 27, order 78/1888.

51. **Finance Act 1973.**
s. 2, repealed: 1979, c. 2,sch.6.
s. 12, repealed in pt.: 1979,c.47,sch.5.
s. 16, see *I.R.C.* v. *Regent Trust Co.*, *The Times*, November 30, 1979, Slade J.
s. 37, repealed: 1979,c.14,sch.8.
s. 38, amended: *ibid.*, sch. 7.
s. 51, repealed: 1979,c.14,sch.8.
s. 54, repealed in pt.: *ibid.*
s. 56, regs. 78/1831; 79/42, 1257, 1342, 1376.
s. 59, amended: 1979,c.14,sch.7; repealed in pt.: 1979,c.2,sch.6.
sch. 16, amended: 1979,c.14,sch.7; repealed in pt.: *ibid.*,sch.8.
sch. 20, repealed: 1979,c.14,sch.8.
sch. 21, repealed in pt.: *ibid.*

52. **Prescription and Limitation (Scotland) Act 1973.**
s. 1, amended: 1979,c.33,s.10.
ss. 6, 11, see *Highland Engineering* v. *Anderson* (O.H.), 1979 S.L.T. 122.
ss. 6, 11, 14, see *Dunlop* v. *McGowans*, 1979 S.L.T. 34.
s. 17, see *Wilson* v. *Morrington Quarries* (O.H.), 1979 S.L.T. 82; *Morrison* v. *Scotstoun Marine* (O.H.), 1979 S.L.T. (Notes) 76.
ss. 18, 22, see *Love* v. *Haran Sealant Services* (O.H.), 1979 S.L.T. 89; *McIntyre* v. *Armitage Shanks*, 1979 S.L.T. 110.

53. **Northern Ireland (Emergency Provisions) Act 1973.**
s. 6, see *R.* v. *Thomson* [1977] N.I. 74, C.C.A.; *R.* v. *McCormick* [1977] N.I. 105, McGonigal L.J.; *R.* v. *Milne* [1978] N.I. 110, McGonigal L.J.
s. 25, see *R.* (*McCreesh*) v. *County Court Judge for Armagh* [1978] N.I. 164, C.A.

CAP.

1973—cont.

56. **Land Compensation (Scotland) Act 1973.**
ss. 1–4, see *Inglis* v. *British Airports Authority* (*No.* 2), 1979 S.L.T.(Lands Tr.) 11.

57. **Badgers Act 1973.**
s. 6, order 79/1249.

62. **Powers of Criminal Courts Act 1973.**
s. 1, see *R.* v. *Harling* (1977) 65 Cr. App.R. 320, C.A.
s. 13, see *R.* v. *Robinson* [1979] Crim. L.R. 785, C.A.
s. 14, see *R.* v. *Carnwell* (1978) 68 Cr. App.R. 58, C.A.
s. 17, see *R.* v. *Adair* (1978) 123 S.J. 32, C.A.
s. 23, see *R.* v. *Tyson* (1979) 68 Cr. App.R. 314, C.A.; *R.* v. *Folan* (1979) 69 Cr.App.R. 93, C.A.
s. 28, see *R.* v. *Gooden*, *The Times*, December 5, 1979, C.A.
s. 30, see *R.* v. *Carnwell* (1978) 68 Cr. App.R. 58, C.A.
ss. 31, 32, amended: 1979,c.2,sch.4.
ss. 32, 51, amended: 1979,c.55,sch.2.
s. 35, see *R.* v. *Vivian* [1979] 1 All E.R. 48, C.A.
ss. 35, 43, see *Malone* v. *Met. Police Comr.* [1979] 1 All E.R. 256, C.A.
s. 43, see *R.* v. *Menocal* [1979] 2 W.L.R. 876, H.L.
s. 54, sch. 3, order 79/1285.

65. **Local Government (Scotland) Act 1973.**
orders 78/1607; 79/455.
s. 7, rules 79/656.
ss. 45, 50, regs. 78/1816, 1879.
s. 111, regs. 79/227, 235.
s. 112, regs. 79/1307.
s. 182, amended: 1979,c.46,sch.4.
s. 225, orders 78/1934; 79/92, 93, 672, 776.
s. 229, orders 79/239, 356, 671, 775, 878–880, 1195, 1391, 1564.
s. 233, orders 78/1934; 79/92, 93, 239, 356, 671, 672, 775, 776, 878–880; rules 79/656, 1195, 1391, 1564.
sch. 23, repealed in pt.: 1979,c.46,sch.4.

1974

4. **Legal Aid Act 1974.**
s. 1, regs. 79/350, 1395; amended: regs. 79/350, 1395; repealed in pt.: 1979, c.26,schs.1,2.
s. 2, amended: *ibid.*,s.1,sch.1; repealed in pt.: *ibid.*,s.1,sch.2.
s. 2A, added: *ibid.*,s.1.
s. 3, amended: *ibid.*,s.2.
s. 4, regs. 79/166, 1164; amended: 1979,c.26,s.3; regs. 79/166, 1164; repealed in pt.: *ibid.*,s.3,sch.2.
s. 5, repealed in pt.: *ibid.*,schs.1,2.
s. 6, regs. 79/351, 1394; amended: regs. 79/351, 1394; repealed in pt.: 1979, c.26,schs.1,2.
s. 7, amended: *ibid.*,s.1; repealed in pt.: *ibid.*,s.1,sch.2.
s. 8, see *Miller* v. *Littner* (1979) 123 S.J. 473, Oliver J.

CAP.

1974—cont.

4. *Legal Aid Act 1974—cont.*
s. 9, *Hanlon* v. *The Law Society*, *The Times*, December 5, 1979, C.A.;
s. 9, regs. 79/351, 1394; amended: 1979,c.26,ss.4,5; regs. 79/351, 1394; repealed in pt.: 1979,c.26,schs.1,2.
s. 11, regs. 79/280, 281; amended: 1979, c.26,sch.1; repealed in pt.: *ibid.*,schs. 1,2.
s. 13, see *Maynard* v. *Osmond* (*No.* 2) [1979] 1 W.L.R. 31, C.A.; *Miller* v. *Littner* (1979) 123 S.J. 473, Oliver J.; *Millican* v. *Tucker* (1979) 123 S.J. 860, Browne-Wilkinson J.; amended: 1979,c.26,s.1.
s. 20, regs. 79/166, 280, 281, 350, 351, 1164, 1394, 1395; amended: 1979, c. 26,s.4.
ss. 21–23, amended: *ibid.*,sch.1.
s. 24, repealed in pt.: *ibid.*,s.5,sch.2.
s. 25, amended: *ibid.*,s.1,sch.1.
s. 28, see *R.* v. ***Rogers* [1979] 1 All E.R. 693, Master Matthews.**
s. 34, regs. 79/61.
s. 35, amended: 1979,c.55,sch.2.
s. 39, regs. 79/360.
s. 43, amended: 1979,c.26,sch.1.
sch. 1, repealed in pt.: *ibid.*,schs.1,2.

7. **Local Government Act 1974.**
s. 1, amended: 1979,c.55,sch.2.
s. 2, regs. 79/1514.
s. 3, order 78/1867.
s. 4, orders 78/1868, 1869.
s. 10, regs. 79/337, 1514.
s. 11, regs. 79/417, 1303.
ss. 15, 16, see *Windsor Securities* v. *Liverpool City Council* (1979) 250 E.G. 57, C.A.
ss. 19, 22, order 79/1516.
ss. 26, 34, see *R.* v. ***Local Commissioner*** *for Administration for the North and* ***East Area of England, ex p. Bradford Metropolitan City Council* [1979] 2 W.L.R. 1, C.A.**
sch. 2, regs. 79/337, 1514.
sch. 3, order 79/1516.

9. **Pensions (Increase) Act 1974.**
s. 4, repealed in pt.: order 79/1451.

23. **Juries Act 1974.**
s. 12, see *R.* v. *Paling* (1978) 67 Cr. App.R. 299, C.A.
s. 16, see *R.* v. *Richardson* [1979] 3 All E.R. 247, C.A.

24. **Prices Act 1974.**
s. 2, orders 78/1790; 79/34, 384, 660.
s. 4, see *Warinco A.G.* v. *Samor S.p.A.* [1979] 1 Lloyd's Rep. 450, C.A.
s. 4, orders 79/4, 361, 364, 1124; S.Rs. 1979 Nos. 293, 294.

28. **Northern Ireland Act 1974.**
s. 1, order 79/816.
sch. 1, orders 78/1038, 1044, 1045, 1049–1051, 1406, 1906–1909; 79/294, 296, 297, 922–926, 1573, 1574, 1575; S.Rs. 1978 Nos. 348, 362, 406; 1979 Nos. 191, 213, 270, 292, 325, 334; amended: order 79/1573.

CAP.

1974—cont.

30. **Finance Act 1974.**
s. 1, repealed in pt.: 1979,c.2,sch.6.
s. 4, repealed: 1979,c.4,sch.4.
s. 8, repealed in pt.: 1979,c.14,sch.8.
s. 19, amended: 1979,c.47,s.10.
ss. 26, 30, amended: 1979,c.14,sch.8.
ss. 31–33, repealed: *ibid.*,sch.8.
ss. 38–45, amended: *ibid.*,sch.7.
s. 48, repealed: *ibid.*,sch.8.
s. 55, orders 79/722, 761 (S.).
s. 57, amended: 1979,c.14,sch.7; repealed in pt.: 1979,c.2,sch.6; c.14,sch.8.
sch. 3, amended: 1979,c.14,sch.7.
sch. 6, amended: *ibid.*
sch. 8, amended: *ibid.*; repealed in pt.; *ibid.*,sch.8.
schs. 9, 10, amended: *ibid.*,sch.7.

32. **Town and Country Amenities Act 1974.**
s. 13, repealed in pt.: 1979,c.46,sch.5.

35. **Carriage of Passengers by Road Act 1974.**
s. 8, amended: 1979,c.28,s.3; repealed in pt.: *ibid.*,ss.3,6.
sch., amended: *ibid.*,s.4.

37. **Health and Safety at Work Act 1974.**
ss. 3, 33, see *Aitchison* v. *Howard Doris*, 1979 S.L.T. (Notes) 22.
s. 11, regs. 79/318, 427, 1203, 1298, 1378.
s. 15, regs. 78/1951; 79/318, 427, 1203, 1298, 1378.
s. 18, regs. 79/427.
s. 24, see *British Airways Board* **v.** *Henderson* **[1979] I.C.R. 77, Industrial Tribunal.**
s. 50, regs. 79/1203, 1298, 1378.
s. 62, regs. 79/601.
sch. 3, regs. 79/318, 1203; amended: 1979,c.2,sch.4.

39. **Consumer Credit Act 1974.**
s. 16, order 79/1099.
s. 22, regs. 79/796.
s. 74, amended: 1979,c.37,s.38.
s. 82, regs. 79/661, 667.
s. 114, amended: 1979,c.37,s.38.
s. 146, amended: order 79/1576.
s. 147, regs. 79/796.
s. 174, amended: 1979,c.38,s.10.
s. 182, regs. 79/661, 667, 1099, 1685.
s. 185, amended: 1979,c.37,s.38.
s. 189, regs. 79/661, 667, 796; amended: 1979,c.54,sch.2.
s. 191, amended: order 79/1573.
s. 192, order 79/1685.
sch. 4, repealed: 1979,c.54,sch.3.

40. **Control of Pollution Act 1974.**
s. 5, see *R.* v. *Derbyshire County Council*, *ex p. North East Derbyshire District Council* (1979) 77 L.G.R. 389, D.C.
s. 75, regs. 79/1.
s. 108, sch. 3, order 79/1085.

43. **Merchant Shipping Act 1974.**
s. 1, repealed in pt.: 1979,c.39,s.38,sch.7.
s. 2, amended: 1979,c.2,sch.4; c.39,s.38.
s. 3, amended: *ibid.*,sch.6.
s. 4, amended: *ibid.*,s.38; repealed in pt.: *ibid.*,sch.7.

CAP.

1974—cont.

43. *Merchant Shipping Act 1974—cont.*
ss. 5, 6, amended: *ibid.*,s.38.
s. 6, Act of Sederunt 79/670.
s. 9, repealed: 1979,c.39,sch.7.
s. 14, amended: *ibid.*,s.40,sch.6.
s. 19, repealed in pt.: *ibid.*,sch.7.
s. 24, order 79/808.
sch. 1, amended: *ibid.*,s.38.
sch. 2, amended: *ibid.*,sch.6.
sch. 4, amended: 1979,c.2,sch.4; c.39,s. 40.
sch. 5, regs. 79/1519; amended: 1979, c.39,sch.6.

44. Housing Act 1974.
ss. 13, 15, see *Goodman* v. *Dolphin Square Trust* (1979) 38 P. & C.R. 257, C.A.
s. 119, regs. 79/1515.
s. 131, order 79/1214.

45. Housing (Scotland) Act 1974.
s. 9, amended: 1979,c.33,sch.2.
sch. 2, amended: *ibid.*

46. Friendly Societies Act 1974.
s. 104, regs. 78/1717.

47. Solicitors Act 1974.
s. 38, amended: 1979,c.55,sch.2.
s. 87, amended: 1979,c.37,sch.6.

48. Railways Act 1974.
ss. 5, 6, order 78/1763.

49. Insurance Companies Act 1974.
ss. 12, 85, see *Medical Defence Union* v. *Department of Trade* [1979] 2 W.L.R. 686, Megarry V.-C.

50. Road Traffic Act 1974.
s. 24, order 79/85 (S.).
s. 24, sch. 6, see *Ward* v. ***Rawson*** [1978] R.T.R. 498, D.C.

51. Rent Act 1974.
s. 5, see *Dominal Securities* v. *McLeod* (1978) 37 P. & C.R. 411, C.A.

52. Trade Union and Labour Relations Act 1974.
s. 2, see *NWL* v. *Nelson* (1979) 123 S.J. 488, C.A.; *Associated Newspapers Group* v. *Wade* [1979] 1 W.L.R. 697, C.A.
s. 8, regs. 79/1385; amended: *ibid.*
s. 13, see *United Biscuits (U.K.)* v. *Fall* [1979] I.R.L.R. 110, Ackner J.; *Associated Newspapers Group* v. *Wade* [1979] 1 W.L.R. 697, C.A.; *NWL* v. *Woods*; *NWL* v. *Nelson* [1979] 1 W.L.R. 1294, H.L.; *P.B.D.S. (National Carriers)* v. *Filkins* [1979] I.R.L.R. 356, C.A.; *Express Newspapers* v. *McShane*, *The Times*, December 13, 1979, H.L.
s. 17, see *Associated Newspapers Group* v. *Wade* [1979] 1 W.L.R. 697, C.A.; *NWL* v. *Woods*; *NWL* v. *Nelson* [1979] 1 W.L.R. 1294, H.L.
s. 28, see *NWL* v. *Woods; NWL* v. *Nelson* [1979] 1 W.L.R. 1294, H.L.
s. 29, see *NWL* v. *Woods; NWL* v. *Nelson* [1979] 1 W.L.R. 1294, H.L.

CAP.

1974—cont.

52. *Trade Union and Labour Relations Act 1974—cont.*
s. 30, see *Airfix Footwear* v. *Cope* [1978] I.C.R. 1210, E.A.T.; *Parsons* v. *Albert J. Parsons and Sons* [1979] I.C.R. 271, C.A.; *Squibb U.K. Staff Association* v. *Certification Officer* [1979] I.C.R. 235, C.A.
sch. 1, see *Adams* v. *Charles Zub Associates* [1978] I.R.L.R. 551, E.A.T.; *Nelson and Woollett* v. *The Post Office* [1978] I.R.L.R. 548, E.A.T.; *Sutton & Gates (Luton)* v. *Boxall* [1979] I.C.R. 67, E.A.T.; *Wall's Meat Co.* v. *Khan* [1979] I.C.R. 52, C.A.; *Harris (Ipswich)* v. *Harrison* [1978] I.C.R. 1256, E.A.T.; *Bentley Engineering Co.* v. *Mistry* [1979] I.C.R. 47, E.A.T.; *Larkin* v. *Cambos Enterprises (Stretford)* [1978] I.C.R. 1247, E.A.T.; *Khanum* v. *Mid-Glamorgan Area Health Authority* [1979] I.C.R. 40, E.A.T.; *Nothman* v. *Barnet London Borough Council* [1979] 1 W.L.R. 67, H.L.; *Beard* v. *St. Joseph's School Governors* [1978] I.C.R. 1234, E.A.T.; *Edwards* v. *Petbow* (1978) 13 I.T.R. 431, E.A.T.; *Saggers* v. *British Railways Board (No. 2)* [1978] I.C.R. 1111, E.A.T.; *Winnett* v. *Seamarks Brothers* [1978] I.C.R. 1240, E.A.T.; *Zucker* v. *Astrid Jewels* [1978] I.C.R. 1088, E.A.T.; *Land* v. *West Yorkshire Metropolitan County Council* (1979) 123 S.J. 283, E.A.T.; *Courtaulds Northern Textiles* v. *Andrew* [1979] I.R.L.R. 84, E.A.T.; *Bullock* v. *Merseyside County Council* [1979] I.C.R. 79, C.A.; *O'Brian* v. *Prudential Assurance Co.* [1979] I.R.L.R. 140, E.A.T.; *Dupont Furniture Products* v. *Moore* [1979] I.C.R. 165, E.A.T.; *Riley and Greater London Citizens' Advice Bureau* v. *Tesco Stores* [1979] I.C.R. 223, E.A.T.; *Marsden* v. *Fairey Stainless* [1979] I.R.L.R. 103, E.A.T.; *Thames Television* v. *Wallis* [1979] I.R.L.R. 136, E.A.T.; *Banerjee* v. *City and East London Area Health Authority* [1979] I.R.L.R. 147, E.A.T.; *J. Sainsbury* v. *Savage* [1979] I.C.R. 96, E.A.T.; *Crown Agents for Overseas Governments and Administration* v. *Lawal* [1979] I.C.R. 103, E.A.T.; *Leonard* v. *Fergus & Haynes Civil Engineering*, 1979 S.L.T.(Notes) 38; *Stepney Cast Stone Co.* v. *Macarthur* [1979] I.R.L.R. 181, E.A.T.; *Dixon* v. *British Broadcasting Corp.* [1979] 2 All E.R. 112, C.A.; *Land* v. *West Yorkshire Metropolitan County Council* [1979] I.C.R. 452, E.A.T.; *Presley* v. *Llanelli Borough Council* [1979] I.C.R. 419, E.A.T.; *International Paint Co.* v. *Cameron* [1979] I.C.R. 429, E.A.T.; *Lowson* v. *Percy Main & District Social Club & Institute* [1979] I.R.L.R. 227, E.A.T.; *Cookson & Zinn* v. *Morgan* [1979] I.C.R. 425, E.A.T.; *Parker* v. *Clifford Dunn* [1979] I.C.R. 463, E.A.T.; *Howard* v.

CAP.

1974—cont.

52. *Trade Union and Labour Relations Act 1974—cont.*
Department of National Savings [1979] I.C.R. 584, E.A.T.; *Lake* v. *Essex County Council* [1979] I.C.R. 577, C.A.; *Hollister* v. *National Farmers' Union* [1979] I.C.R. 542, C.A.; *Edwards* v. *Cardiff City Council* [1979] I.R.L.R. 303, E.A.T.; *Nelson* v. *British Broadcasting Corpn.* [1979] I.R.L.R. 346, C.A.; *A.E.I. Cables* v. *McLay*, 1979 S.L.T.(Notes) 66; *Derby City Council* v. *Marshall* [1979] I.C.R. 731, E.A.T.; *Winfield* v. *London Philharmonic Orchestra* [1979] I.C.R. 726, E.A.T.; *Duff* v. *Evan Thomas Radcliffe & Co.* [1979] I.C.R. 720, E.A.T.; *Marley Tile Co.* v. *Shaw*, *The Times*, November 21, 1979, C.A.; *Fisher* v. *York Trailer Co.* [1979] I.C.R. 834, E.A.T.; *Pillinger* v. *Manchester Area Health Authority* [1979] I.R.L.R. 430, E.A.T.; *W. Weddel & Co.* v. *Tepper*, *The Times*, December 22, 1979, C.A.
sch. 3, see *Nelson* v. *British Broadcasting Corp.* [1979] I.R.L.R. 346, C.A.
sch. 3, repealed in pt.: 1979,c.12,sch.7.

53. **Rehabilitation of Offenders Act 1974.**
s. 7, amended: 1979,c.37,s.43.

i. **Harwich Harbour Act 1974.**
s. 13, amended: order 79/1656.

Supreme Court Act 1935–1974 (South Australia).
s. 30C, see *Thompson* v. *Faraonio* [1979] 1 W.L.R. 1157, P.C.

Supreme Court Amendment Act 1974 (South Australia).
s. 3, see *Thompson* v. *Faraonio* [1979] 1 W.L.R. 1157, P.C.

134. **Dangerous Drugs Ordinance (Laws of Hong Kong 1974) (Hong Kong).**
s. 47, see *Kwan Ping Bong* v. *The Queen* [1979] 2 W.L.R. 433, P.C.

1975

3. **Arbitration Act 1975.**
s. 1, see *Paczy* v. *Haendler & Natermann GmbH* [1979] F.S.R. 420, Whitford J.
s. 7, order 79/304.

7. **Finance Act 1975.**
s. 1, repealed: 1979,c.47,sch.5.
s. 4, repealed: 1979,c.2,sch.6.
s. 8, amended: order 79/1576.
s. 51, amended: 1979,c.14,sch.7.
s. 53, repealed: *ibid.*,sch.8.
sch. 2, amended: order 79/1576.
sch. 4, order 79/1688; amended: 1979, c.46,sch.4; order 79/1688, repealed in pt.: order 79/1575.
sch. 5, see *Pearson* v. *I.R.C.* [1979] 3 W.L.R. 112, C.A.; *Von Ernst & Cie S.A.* v. *I.R.C.* [1979] S.T.C. 478, Browne-Wilkinson J.

CAP.

1975—cont.

7. *Finance Act 1975—cont.*
sch. 5, amended: 1979,c.47,s.23.
sch. 7, see *Von Ernst & Cie S.A.* v. *I.R.C.*, *The Times*, December 6, 1979, C.A.; orders 79/1454, 1979.
sch. 10, amended: 1979,c.14,sch.7.
sch. 12, repealed in pt.: *ibid.*,sch.8.; order 79/924.

14. **Social Security Act 1975.**
s. 1, regs. 79/591.
s. 3, regs. 78/1877; 79/359, 591.
s. 4, regs. 79/358, 591; amended: 1979, c.18,s.14,sch.3; orders 79/1694, 1736.
ss. 7, 8, regs. 79/591; amended: orders 78/1840; 79/1694.
s. 9, regs. 79/591; amended: orders 78/1840; 79/993, 1694.
s. 10, regs. 79/591; order 78/1840.
s. 11, regs. 79/591.
s. 12, see *Nabi* v. *British Leyland (U.K.)* *The Times*, December 1, 1979, C.A.
s. 13, regs. 79/591, 676; amended: 1979, c.18,sch.3.
s. 14, amended: *ibid.*
ss. 14, 17, see *Sun and Sand* v. *Fitzjohn* [1979] I.C.R. 268, E.A.T.
s. 15, amended: 1979,c.18,schs.1,3.
s. 16, amended: *ibid.*,sch.1.
s. 17, regs. 79/1278, 1299.
s. 19, see *R.* v. *National Insurance Commissioner, ex p. Thompson*, Appendix to Social Security Decision No. R.(U.) 5/77, D.C.
s. 20, regs. 79/934, 940, 1299.
s. 28, amended: order 79/993.
s. 29, regs. 79/642; amended: order 79/993.
s. 30, regs. 79/642; amended: 1979,c.18, c.4; order 79/993.
s. 33, regs. 79/642.
s. 35, regs. 79/375; amended: 1979,c.18, s.2.
s. 36, regs. 79/1278.
s. 37A, regs. 79/172; amended: 1979, c.18,s.3.
s. 39, regs. 79/642; amended: 1979, c.18,sch.1.
s. 40, regs. 79/642.
s. 45, regs. 79/628.
s. 57, amended: order 79/993.
s. 58, regs. 79/1278.
s. 59, amended: 1979,c.18,sch.1; order 79/993.
s. 66, regs. 79/359.
s. 67, order 79/394.
s. 76, regs. 79/265, 632, 992.
s. 77, regs. 79/632, 992.
s. 79, regs. 79/628, 781.
s. 80, regs. 79/628.
s. 81, regs. 79/223, 628, 1199.
s. 82, regs. 79/223.
s. 83, regs. 79/597.
s. 85, regs. 79/223, 359, 597, 642; amended: 1979,c.18,s.15.
s. 86, amended: *ibid.*,s.7.
ss. 88–90, regs. 79/628.
s. 97, amended: 1979,c.18,s.9.
s. 110, amended: 1979,c.18,sch.3.
s. 113, regs. 79/264.

CAP.

1975—cont.

14. *Social Security Act 1975—cont.*
s. 115, regs. 79/628, 676, 781.
s. 119, regs. 79/1067, 1163; amended: 1979,c.18,s.8,sch.3.
s. 120, orders 78/1840; 79/1694.
s. 121, order 79/1694.
s. 122, orders 79/1694, 1736.
s. 124, orders 79/993, 1429.
s. 125, repealed in pt.: 1979,c.48,s.8.
s. 126A, order 79/993; added: 1979,c.18, s.12.
s. 128, regs. 79/591.
s. 129, regs. 78/1877; 79/9, 591.
s. 130, regs. 75/591, 1431.
s. 131, regs. 79/463, 591, 1278, 1432.
s. 132, regs. 79/591.
s. 134, regs. 79/358, 591; amended: 1979,c.18,s.14; order 79/1736; modified: regs. 79/591.
s. 139, regs. 78/1877; 79/345, 375, 597, 628, 642, 1278.
s. 141, regs. 79/628.
s. 143, order 79/290, 921.
s. 146, regs. 79/591.
s. 162, regs. 79/642.
s. 167, amended: 1979,c.18,s.4.
sch. 1, regs. 78/1877; 79/591.
schs. 3, 4, amended: 1979,c.18,schs.1,3.
sch. 13, regs. 79/628, 676, 781.
sch. 14, regs. 79/1278.
sch. 15, regs. 79/375, 597, 628, 642, 1278; amended: 1979,c.18,ss.4,15.
sch. 16, regs. 79/628.

15. Social Security (Northern Ireland) Act 1975.
s. 1, S.R. 1979 No. 186.
s. 2, S.R. 1978 No. 401.
s. 3, S.Rs. 1978 Nos. 79, 369, 371, 400; 1979 No. 186.
s. 4, S.Rs. 1978 No. 401; 1979 No. 186.
ss. 7, 8, S.R. 1979 No. 186.
s. 9, S.Rs. 1978 No. 369; 1979 No. 186.
ss. 10, 11, S.R. 1979 No. 186.
s. 13, S.Rs. 1979 Nos. 186, 193.
s. 16, S.R. 1979 No. 211.
s. 17, S.Rs. 1979 Nos. 211, 371, 377.
s. 20, S.Rs. 1979 Nos. 211, 286, 377.
ss. 29, 30, S.R. 1979 No. 243.
s. 33, S.Rs. 1979 Nos. 211, 243.
s. 35, S.R. 1979 No. 102.
s. 36, S.Rs. 1978, No. 385; 1979 No. 371.
s. 37A, S.R. 1979 No. 47.
s. 39, 40, S.Rs. 1979 Nos. 243.
s. 58, S.R. 1979 No. 371.
s. 66, S.Rs. 1978 Nos. 97, 371.
ss. 76, 77, S.Rs. 1979 Nos. 78, 208, 275.
s. 79, S.Rs. 1979 Nos. 211, 259.
s. 81, S.R. 1979 No. 68.
s. 82, S.Rs. 1979 No. 371; 1979 No. 68.
s. 83, S.R. 1979 No. 242.
s. 85, S.Rs. 1979 Nos. 68, 97, 242, 243.
s. 97, amended: 1979,c.18,s.9.
s. 113, S.R. 1979 No. 77.
s. 115, S.R. 1979 No. 193.
s. 119, S.Rs. 1978 No. 371; 1979 Nos. 314, 354.
s. 120, S.Rs. 1978 No. 387; 1979 No. 273.

CAP.

1975—cont.

15. *Social Security (Northern Ireland) Act 1975—cont.*
s. 123, regs. 79/591.
s. 124, S.Rs. 1978 No. 400; 1979 No. 14.
s. 125, S.R. 1979 No. 394.
s. 126, S.Rs. 1978 Nos. 371; 1979 Nos. 131, 211, 371, 392.
s. 128, S.Rs. 1978 No. 400; 1979 No. 186.
ss. 129, 130–132, S.R. 1979 No. 186.
s. 134, S.Rs. 1979 Nos. 92, 186, 303.
s. 146, S.R. 1979 No. 186.
s. 152, S.R. 1979 No. 243.
s. 155, amended: order 79/1573.
sch. 1, S.Rs. 1978 Nos. 369, 400, 401; 1979 No. 186.
sch. 13, S.R. 1979 No. 193.
sch. 14, S.R. 1979 No. 371.
sch. 17, S.R. 1979 No. 243.

16. Industrial Injuries and Diseases (Old Cases) Act 1975.
s. 2, amended: order 79/993.
ss. 2, 4, scheme 79/1190.
s. 5, scheme 79/996.
s. 7, amended: order 79/993.

17. Industrial Injuries and Diseases (Northern Ireland Old Cases) Act 1975.
ss. 2, 4, S.R. 1979 No. 346.
s. 4, amended: order 79/1573.

18. Social Security (Consequential Provisions) Act 1975.
s. 2, regs. 79/643, 940; S.R. 1979 No. 244.
sch. 2, repealed in pt.: 1979,c.47,sch.5.
sch. 3, regs. 78/1877; 79/591, 628, 643, 940; S.Rs. 1978 No. 400; 1979 Nos. 186, 211, 242.

21. Criminal Procedure (Scotland) Act 1975.
s. 114, Act of Adjournal 79/1155.
s. 141, see *Burton* v. *H.M. Advocate*, 1979 S.L.T.(Notes) 59.
s. 141, amended: 1979,c.16,s.1.
s. 216, see *Vaughan* v. *H.M. Advocate*, 1979 S.L.T. 49.
s. 282, Acts of Adjournal 78/1686; 79/95, 232, 612.
s. 314, see *Skeen* v. *Evans*, 1979 S.L.T. (Notes) 55.
ss. 331, 334, see *Beattie* v. *McKinnon*. 1977 J.C. 64.
s. 346, amended: 1979,c.16,s.1.
s. 357, see *Mitchell* v. *Dean*, 1979 S.L.T. (Notes) 12; *Boustead* v. *MacLeod*, 1979 S.L.T.(Notes) 48.
ss. 416, 417, see *Mackay* v. *Tudhope*, 1979 S.L.T.(Notes) 43.
s. 457, Acts of Adjournal 78/1686; 79/95, 232, 612.
sch. 7C, repealed in pt.: 1979,c.39,sch.7.

22. Oil Taxation Act 1975.
s. 1, amended: 1979,c.47,ss.18,21.
s. 2, amended: *ibid.*,ss.19,22.
ss. 3, 4, amended: *ibid.*,s.20.
ss. 8, 10, amended: *ibid.*,s.21.

24. House of Commons Disqualification Act 1975.
sch. 1, amended: 1979,c.10,sch.; c.12,sch. 6; c.18,sch.3; c.39,s.1; c.43,sch.1; repealed in pt.; 1979,c.36,sch.8.

CAP.

1975—cont.

25. Northern Ireland Assembly Disqualification Act 1975.
sch. 1, amended: 1979,c.10,sch.; c.12,sch. 6; c.39,s.1; c.43,sch.1; order 79/294: repealed in pt.: 1979,c.36,sch.8.

26. Ministers of the Crown Act 1975.
s. 1, orders 79/571, 578, 907.
s. 2, order 79/578, 907.
s. 5, order 79/1451.
s. 7, sch. 2, regs. 79/1276, 1277; repealed: order 79/1451.

27. Ministerial and other Salaries Act 1975.
s. 1, order 79/905.

28. Housing Rents and Subsidies (Scotland) Act 1975.
s. 2, orders 79/378, 669.

30. Local Government (Scotland) Act 1975.
orders 78/1607; 79/455.
ss. 2, 3, 37, see *Assessor for Lothian Region* v. *Wilson*, 1979 S.L.T. 93.
s. 6, order 79/951.

34. Evidence (Proceedings in Other Jurisdictions) Act 1975.
see *Halcon International Inc.* v. *The Steel Transport and Trading Co.* [1979] R.P.C. 97, C.A.
s. 10, orders 78/1890–1892, 1920; 79/1711.

35. Farriers (Registration) Act 1975.
s. 19, order 78/1928.

37. Nursing Homes Act 1975.
s. 4, amended: 1979,c.36,sch.7.
s. 20, amended: *ibid.*; repealed in pt.: *ibid.*,schs.7,8.

45. Finance (No. 2) Act 1975.
s. 1, repealed in pt.: 1979,c.2,sch.6.
s. 8, repealed: *ibid.*
ss. 9, 10, repealed: 1979,c.4,sch.4.
s. 11, repealed: 1979,c.5,sch.7.
ss. 12, 13, repealed: 1979,c.6,sch.
ss. 14, 15, repealed: 1979,c.4,sch.4.
s. 16, repealed: 1979,c.2,sch.6.
s. 17, see *Customs and Excise Comrs.* v. *Mechanical Services (Trailer Engineers)* [1979] 1 All E.R. 501, C.A.
s. 17, repealed: 1979,c.47,s.1,sch.5.
s. 18, repealed in pt.: *ibid.*,sch.5.
s. 42, amended: 1979,c.14,sch.7.
s. 44, repealed in pt.: *ibid.*,sch.8.
ss. 47, 48, order 79/1687.
s. 57, repealed: 1979,c.14,sch.8.
s. 58, amended: *ibid.*,sch.7.
ss. 59–64, repealed: *ibid.*,sch.8.
s. 69, amended: 1979,c.47,s.15.
s. 70, see *Kirvell* v. *Guy* [1979] S.T.C. 312, Walton J.
s. 75, repealed in pt.: 1979,c.2,sch.6; c. 14,sch.8.
sch. 3, repealed in pt.: 1979,c.2,sch.6; c. 3,sch.3; c.4,sch.4; c.5,sch.7; c.6,sch.
schs. 4, 5, repealed: 1979,c.4,sch.4.
sch. 6, repealed in pt.: 1979,c.2,sch.6; c.4,sch.4.
sch. 7, see *Customs and Excise Comrs.* v. *Mechanical Services (Trailer Engineers)* [1979] 1 All E.R. 501, C.A.; repealed: 1979,c.47,s.1,sch.5.

CAP.

1975—cont.

45. *Finance (No. 2) Act 1975—cont.*
sch. 8, amended: 1979,c.14,sch.7; repealed in pt.: *ibid.*,sch.8.
sch. 12, see *Kirvell* v. *Guy* [1979] S.T.C. 312, Walton J.

46. International Road Haulage Permits Act 1975.
s. 3, see *Holloway* v. *Brown* [1978] R.T.R. 537, D.C.

48. Conservation of Wild Creatures and Wild Plants Act 1975.
sch. 1, order 79/353; amended: *ibid.*

51. Salmon and Freshwater Fisheries Act 1975.
sch. 4, amended: 1979,c.2,sch.4.

52. Safety of Sports Grounds Act 1975.
s. 1, orders 79/1022, 1026.

54. Limitation Act 1975.
s. 2, see *Casey* v. *J. Murphy & Sons*, December 13, 1979, C.A.

55. Statutory Corporations (Financial Provisions) Act 1975.
schs. 2, 3, 4, repealed in pt.: 1979,c.11, sch.12.

59. Criminal Jurisdiction Act 1975.
s. 12, repealed: 1979,c.31,sch.2.
s. 14, repealed in pt.: *ibid.*

60. Social Security Pensions Act 1975.
ss. 1, 3, 5, regs. 79/591.
s. 6, amended: 1979,c.18,sch.3; order 79/993; repealed in pt.: 1979,c.18, sch.3.
s. 8, amended: *ibid.*,sch.1.
s. 9, regs. 79/1428.
s. 11, amended: 1979,c.18,sch.3.
s. 17, repealed: 1979,c.18,sch.1.
s. 20, regs. 79/642; amended: 1979,c.18, sch.1.
s. 21, order 79/832; amended 1979,c.18, s.10.
s. 23, order 79/993; amended: 1979, c.18,sch.3.
s. 27, regs. 79/591.
s. 31, regs. 78/1827.
s. 34, amended: 1979,c.18,sch.3.
s. 35, regs. 79/676; amended: 1979, c.18,sch.3; order 79/993; repealed in pt.: 1979,c.18,sch.3.
s. 37, amended: *ibid.*
s. 59, order 79/1047; amended: 1979, c.18,s.11,sch.3.
s. 59A, added: *ibid.*,s.11.
s. 60A, added: *ibid.*,s.18.
s. 61, regs. 79/345; amended: 1979,c.18, sch.3.
s. 63, regs. 79/345, 591, 643.
s. 66, amended: 1979,c.18,sch.3.
s. 67, orders 79/171, 367, 1030.
s. 68, amended: 1979,c.18,sch.3.
sch. 1, regs. 79/642; amended: 1979, c.18,schs.1,3; order 79/993.
sch. 2, regs. 78/1827.
sch. 4, repealed in pt.: 1979,c.47,sch.5; c.55,sch.3.

CAP.

1975—cont.

61. Child Benefit Act 1975.
s. 3, see *Decision No. R.(F.)* 2/79.
s. 4A, added: 1979,c.18,s.15.
s. 5, regs. 79/998.
s. 15, order 79/921.
s. 24, see *Decision No. R.(F.)* 1/79.

63. Inheritance (Provision for Family and Dependants) Act 1975.
ss. 1–3, see *Re Coventry (decd.)*; *Coventry* v. *Coventry* [1979] 3 W.L.R. 802, C.A.
ss. 1, 2, see *Re McC.* (1979) 9 Fam. Law 26, Sir George Baker P.
ss. 1, 3, see *Re Christie (decd.)*; *Christie* v. *Keeble* [1979] 2 W.L.R. 105, Vivian Price Q.C.; *Re Beaumont (decd.)*; *Martin* v. *Midland Bank Trust Co.* [1979] 3 W.L.R. 818, Sir Robert Megarry V.-C.; *Malone* v. *Harrison* [1979] 1 W.L.R. 1353, Hollings J.

65. Sex Discrimination Act 1975.
s. 1, see *Roberts* v. *Cleveland Area Health Authority*; *Garland* v. *British Rail Engineering*; *MacGregor Wallcoverings* v. *Turton* [1979] 1 W.L.R. 754, C.A.; *Ministry of Defence* v. *Jeremiah* (1979) 123 S.J. 735, C.A.; *Durrant* v. *North Yorkshire Area Health Authority and Secretary of State for Social Services* [1979] I.R.L.R. 401, E.A.T.
s. 6, see *Knight* v. *Att.-Gen.* [1979] I.C.R. 194, E.A.T.; *Department of the Environment* v. *Fox* (1979) 123 S.J. 404, E.A.T.; *Roberts* v. *Cleveland Area Health Authority*; *Garland* v. *British Rail Engineering*; *MacGregor Wallcoverings* v. *Turton* [1979] 1 W.L.R. 754, C.A.; *Hugh-Jones* v. *St. John's College, Cambridge* (1979) 123 S.J. 603, E.A.T.; *Jeremiah* v. *Ministry of Defence* [1979] I.R.L.R. 436, C.A.
s. 20, repealed in pt.: 1979,c.36,sch.8.
ss. 43, 51, see *Hugh-Jones* v. *St. John's College, Cambridge* (1979) 123 S.J. 603, E.A.T.
s. 51, see *Greater London Council* v. *Farrar*, *The Times*, November 21, 1979, E.A.T.
s. 65, see *Nelson* v. *Tyne & Wear Passenger Transport Executive* [1978] I.C.R. 183, E.A.T.
s. 85, see *Department of the Environment* v. *Fox* [1979] I.C.R. 736, E.A.T.
s. 85, 86, see *Knight* v. *Att.-Gen.* [1979] I.C.R. 194, E.A.T.
sch. 4, amended: 1979,c.36,sch.7; repealed in pt.: *ibid.*,sch.8.
sch. 5, repealed in pt.: *ibid.*

68. Industry Act 1975.
s. 8, amended: 1979,c.32,s.1,sch.

69. Scottish Development Agency Act 1975.
s. 13, amended: 1979,c.32,s.1,sch.

70. Welsh Development Agency Act 1950.
s. 18, amended: 1979,c.32,s.1,sch.

CAP.

1975—cont.

71. Employment Protection Act 1975.
s. 1, see *U.K. Association of Professional Engineers* v. *A.C.A.S.* [1979] I.C.R. 303, C.A.
s. 8, regs. 79/1385; amended: *ibid.*
s. 11, see *National Union of Gold, Silver and Allied Trades* v. *Albury Brothers* [1979] I.C.R. 84, C.A.; *National Employers Life Assurance Co.* v. *A.C.A.S. and A.S.T.M.S.* [1979] I.R.L.R. 282, Browne-Wilkinson J.
ss. 12, 14, see *National Employers Life Assurance Co.* v. *A.C.A.S.* [1979] I.C.R. 620, Browne-Wilkinson J.; *Engineers' and Managers' Association* v. *A.C.A.S.* [1979] I.C.R. 637, C.A.
s. 14, see *National Employers Life Assurance Co.* v. *A.C.A.S. and A.S.T.M.S.* [1979] I.R.L.R. 282, Browne-Wilkinson J.; *Engineers' and Managers' Association* v. *A.C.A.S. and U.K. Association of Professional Engineers* [1979] I.R.L.R. 246, C.A.
s. 35, see *Nu-Swift International* v. *Mallinson* [1979] I.C.R. 157, E.A.T.; *Lloyds Bank* v. *Secretary of State for Employment* [1979] I.C.R. 258, E.A.T.
s. 36, see *Inner London Education Authority* v. *Nash* [1979] I.C.R. 229, E.A.T.
s. 53, see *Cheall* v. *Vauxhall Motors* [1979] I.R.L.R. 253.
s. 57, see *McCormack* v. *Shell Chemicals* *U.K.* [1979] I.R.L.R. 40; *Young* v. *Carr Fasteners* [1979] I.R.L.R. 420, E.A.T.; *Sood* v. *G.E.C. Elliott Process Automation* [1979] I.R.L.R. 416, E.A.T.
s. 64, see *Fox Brothers (Clothes) (In Liquidation)* v. *Bryant* [1979] I.C.R. 64, E.A.T.
s. 70, see *Lowson* v. *Percy Main & District Social Club & Institute* [1979] I.C.R. 568, E.A.T.; *Marchant* v. *Early Town Council* [1979] I.R.L.R. 311, E.A.T.
s. 76, see *Manning* v. *R. & H. Wale (Export)* [1979] I.C.R. 433, E.A.T.; *Gallear* v. *J. F. Watson & Son* [1979] I.R.L.R. 306, E.A.T.; *Peara* v. *Enderlin* [1979] I.C.R. 804, E.A.T.
ss. 81, 84, see *Scott* v. *Creager* [1979] I.C.R. 403, E.A.T.
s. 85, see *Barrett* v. *National Coal Board* [1978] I.C.R. 1101, E.A.T.
s. 88, see *Kumchyk* v. *Derby City* *Council* [1978] I.C.R. 1116, E.A.T.; *Squibb U.K. Staff Association* v. *Certification Officer* [1979] I.C.R. 235, C.A.
ss. 89–96, repealed: 1979,c.12,sch.7.
s. 99, see *Hamish Armour (Receiver of Barry Staines)* v. *A.S.T.M.S.* [1979] I.R.L.R. 24, E.A.T.; *Spillers-French (Holdings)* v. *Union of Shop, Distributive and Allied Workers* (1979) 123 S.J. 654, E.A.T.
ss. 99–101 amended: order 79/958.

CAP.

1975—cont.

71. *Employment Protection Act 1975—cont.*
ss. 99, 101, see ***National Union of Gold, Silver and Allied Trades* v. *Albury Brothers*** **[1979] I.C.R. 84, C.A.**
ss. 101, 102, see *Spillers-French (Holdings)* v. *Union of Shop, Distributive and Allied Workers* [1979] I.R.L.R. 339, E.A.T.
s. 106, order 79/958.
s. 119, see ***National Association of Teachers in Further and Higher Education* v. *Manchester City Council*** **[1978] I.C.R. 1190, E.A.T.**
s. 127, repealed in pt.: 1979,c.12,sch.7.
sch. 4, see ***Barrett* v. *National Coal Board*** **[1978] I.C.R. 1101, E.A.T.**
sch. 6, see *International Aviation Services (U.K.)* v. *Jones* [1979] I.C.R. 371, E.A.T.
schs. 7, 8, repealed: 1979,c.12,sch.7.
sch. 11, see ***R.* v. *Central Arbitration Committee, ex p. North Western Regional Health Authority*** **[1978] I.C.R. 1228, D.C.**
sch. 16, see ***Active Elderly Housing Association* v. *Sparrow*** **(1978) 13 I.T.R. 395, E.A.T.**
sch. 17, repealed in pt.: 1979,c.12,sch.7.

72. Children Act 1975.
s. 3, see *A. and B.* v. *C.*, 1977 S.C. 27.
s. 10, see *Re S.* (1978) 9 Fam.Law 88, C.A.
s. 85, see *C.* v. *H.* (1979) 123 S.J. 537, D.C.

74. Petroleum and Submarine Pipe-lines Act 1975.
s. 9, repealed in pt.: 1979,c.47,s.22, sch.5.
s. 15, repealed in pt.: *ibid.*,sch.5.

76. Local Land Charges Act 1975.
s. 14, rules 79/1404.

78. Airports Authority Act 1975.
ss. 1, 2, 9, see *Cinnamond* v. *British Airports Authority* [1979] R.T.R. 331, Forbes J.

81. Moneylenders (Crown Agents) Act 1975.
repealed: 1979,c.43,sch.7.

1976

1. National Coal Board (Finance) Act 1976.
s. 2, order 79/374.

2. Armed Forces Act 1976.
s. 1, continued in force: order 79/906.

3. Road Traffic (Drivers' Ages and Hours of Work) Act 1976.
s. 1, schs. 1, 2, see *North West Traffic Area Licensing Authority* v. *Brady* [1979] R.T.R. 500, D.C.
s. 2, regs. 78/1938; repealed in pt.: 1979,c.12,sch.7.

4. Trustee Savings Banks Act 1976.
s. 3, order 78/1718.
s. 16, orders 79/551, 1183.
s. 38, order 79/1475.
sch. 5, repealed in pt.: 1979, c.37,sch.7.

CAP.

1976—cont.

6. Solicitors (Scotland) Act 1976.
s. 5, amended: 1979,c.37,sch.6.

8. Prevention of Terrorism (Temporary Provisions) Act 1976.
s. 1, order 79/745.
ss. 10, 11, see *H.M. Advocate* v. *Von*, 1979 S.L.T.(Notes) 62.
ss. 12, 14, see ***R.* v. *Durham Prison Governor, ex p. Carlisle*** **[1979] Crim. L.R. 175, D.C.**
ss. 13, 14, sch. 3, orders 79/168, 169.
s. 17, order 79/352.
sch. 1, amended: order 79/745.

10. Post Office (Banking Services) Act 1976.
s. 1, repealed in pt.: 1979,c.37,sch.7.

13. Damages (Scotland) Act 1976.
s. 1, see *Finnie* v. *Cameron* (O.H.) 1979 S.L.T. 57; *McAllister* v. *Abram* (O.H.), 1979 S.L.T. (Notes) 6.

16. Statute Law (Repeals) Act 1976.
s. 3, order 79/111.

21. Crofting Reform (Scotland) Act 1976.
ss. 1, 3, 4, see ***Gilmour* v. *Master of Lovat***, 1979 S.L.T.(Land Ct.) 2.
s. 2, see ***Mackintosh* v. *Countess of Seafield's Trs.***, 1979 S.L.T.(Land Ct.) 6.

24. Development Land Tax Act 1976.
s. 1, amended: 1979,c.47,s.24; repealed in pt.: *ibid.*,s.24,sch.5.
s. 5, amended: 1979,c.14,sch.7.
s. 12, amended: 1979,c.14,sch.7; c.47, s.24.
s. 13, repealed: *ibid.*,sch.5.
s. 40, amended: *ibid.*,s.24.
s. 47, amended: 1979,c.14,sch.7.
sch. 6, amended: 1979,c.14,sch.7; repealed in pt.: 1979,c.47,sch.5.
sch. 7, amended: *ibid.*,sch.4; repealed in pt.: *ibid.*,schs.4,5.
sch. 8, amended: 1979,c.14,sch.7; c.47, sch.4.

25. Fair Employment (Northern Ireland) Act 1976.
s. 56, amended: order 79/1573.

32. Lotteries and Amusements Act 1976.
ss. 1, 14, see *Imperial Tobacco* v. *Att.-Gen.* [1979] 2 W.L.R. 805, C.A.

34. Restrictive Trade Practices Act 1976.
s. 41, amended: 1979,c.38,s.10.
sch. 1, amended: 1979,c.36,sch.7.

35. Police Pensions Act 1976.
s. 1, regs. 79/406.
s. 1, 3, regs. 79/1259, 1287, 1406.
s. 4, regs. 79/406, 1259, 1287, 1406.
s. 5, regs. 79/1287, 1406.

37. Food and Drugs (Control of Food Premises) Act 1976.
s. 7, regs. 79/27.

39. Divorce (Scotland) Act 1976.
s. 1, see *Craigie* v. *Craigie*, 1979 S.L.T. (Notes) 60; *Nolan* v. *Nolan* (O.H.), 1979 S.L.T. 293.
s. 5, see *Gray* v. *Gray* (O.H.), 1979 S.L.T.(Notes) 94.

CAP.

1976—cont.

40. Finance Act 1976.
s. 2, regs. 78/1786; repealed: 1979,c.4, sch.4.
s. 3, repealed: *ibid.*
ss. 4, 5, repealed: 1979,c.7,sch.2.
s. 6, repealed in pt.: 1979,c.7,sch.2; c. 8,sch.2.
ss. 9, 10, repealed: 1979,c.5,sch.7.
s. 15, repealed: 1979,c.2,sch.6.
s. 17, repealed: 1979,c.47,sch.5.
s. 29, repealed in pt.: *ibid.*
s. 31, repealed: *ibid.*
s. 36, repealed in pt.: *ibid.*
s. 43, repealed: *ibid.*
ss. 52, 53, repealed: 1979,c.14,sch.8.
s. 54, amended: *ibid.*,sch.7.
ss. 55, 56, repealed: *ibid.*,sch.8.
ss. 67, 82, amended: *ibid.*,sch.7.
s. 84, amended: order 79/1576.
s. 122, amended: order 79/927.
s. 127, order 79/370.
s. 132, amended: 1979,c.14,sch.7; repealed in pt.: 1979,c.2,sch.6.
sch. 3, repealed in pt.: 1979,c.2,sch.6; c. 4,sch.4; c.8,sch.2.
sch. 4, regs. 79/346; amended: order 79/1576.
sch. 5, amended: 1979,c.47,sch.3.
sch. 10, amended: 1979,c.14,sch.7.
sch. 11, repealed in pt.: *ibid.*,sch.8.
schs. 12, 13, amended: *ibid.*,sch.7.

47. Stock Exchange (Completion of Bargains) Act 1976.
s. 3, regs. 79/53.
s. 7, orders 79/55, 238.

50. Domestic Violence and Matrimonial Proceedings Act 1976.
see *Re V. (A Minor) (Wardship)* (1979) 123 S.J. 201, Sir George Baker P.
s. 1, see *McLean* v. *Nugent* (1979) 123 S.J. 521, C.A.
s. 2, see *Morgan* v. *Morgan* (1979) 9 Fam.Law 87, C.A.; *McLaren* v. *McLaren* (1978) 9 Fam.Law 153, C.A.

52. Armed Forces Act 1976.
s. 2, regs. 79/215.
sch. 3, rules 79/1456.

55. Agriculture (Miscellaneous Provisions) Act 1976.
s. 6, repealed: 1979,c.13,sch.2.
s. 7, regs. 79/25, 26, 357.
s. 18, see *Jackson* v. *Hall*; *Williamson* v. *Thompson*, *The Times*, December 20, 1979, H.L.
sch. 2, repealed: 1979,c.13,sch.2.

57. Local Government (Miscellaneous Provisions) Act 1976.
s. 81, orders 79/805, 806.
sch. 1, repealed in pt.: 1979,c.46,sch.5.

58. International Carriage of Perishable Foodstuffs Act 1976.
ss. 1–3, 4, 20, regs. 79/415.
ss. 3, 4, 20, regs. 79/416.
s. 21, order 79/413.

CAP.

1976—cont.

60. Insolvency Act 1976.
s. 7, see *Re Reed (A Debtor)* [1979] 2 All E.R. 22, D.C.; *Re A Debtor (No. 13 of 1964), ex p. Official Receiver* v. *The Debtor* [1979] 3 All E.R. 15, D.C.; *Re A Debtor (No. 1E of 1978)* (1979) 123 S.J. 602, D.C.
s. 10, rules 79/209.

61. Electricity (Financial Provisions) (Scotland) Act 1976.
s. 1, repealed: 1979,c.11,sch.12.
s. 2, orders 79/412, 960.

63. Bail Act 1976.
s. 6, see *R.* v. *Harbax Singh* [1979] 2 W.L.R. 100, C.A.; *R.* v. *Tyson* (1979) 68 Cr.App.R. 314, C.A.

66. Licensing (Scotland) Act 1976.
s. 16, see *Chief Constable of Grampian* v. *City of Aberdeen District Licensing Board*, 1979 S.L.T.(Sh.Ct.) 2.
s. 39, see *Kieran* v. *Adams*, 1979 S.L.T. (Sh.Ct.) 13; *Robertson* v. *Inverclyde Licensing Board*, 1979 S.L.T.(Sh.Ct.) 16.
s. 39, Act of Sederunt 79/1520.
s. 62, see *Wallace* v. *Kyle and Carrick Licensing Board*, 1979 S.L.T.(Sh.Ct.) 12.
s. 63, amended: 1979,c.2,sch.4.
s. 123, amended: regs. 79/1755.
s. 139, amended: 1979,c.4,sch.3; regs. 79/1755.
sch. 7, repealed in pt.: 1979,c.4,sch.4.

69. Companies Act 1976.
schs. 1, 2, repealed in pt.: 1979,c.37,sch. 7.

70. Land Drainage Act 1976.
s. 11, orders 78/1819; 79/266, 579, 1243.
s. 17, see *Strutts Kingston Estate Settlement Trustees* v. *Kingston Brook International Drainage Board* (Ref./138/1977) (1979) 251 E.G. 577.
s. 25, orders 78/1980; 79/511.
s. 109, orders 78/1980; 79/266.
s. 111, amended: 1979,c.46,sch.4.

71. Supplementary Benefits Act 1976.
s. 2, regs. 79/997; amended: 1979,c.18, sch.3.
s. 6, see *R.* v. *Manchester Supplementary Benefits Appeal Tribunal, ex p. Riley* [1979] 1 W.L.R. 426, Sheen J.
s. 7, see *Bloomfield* v. *Supplementary Benefits Commission* (1978) 123 S.J. 33, Sheen J.; *Sampson* v. *Supplementary Benefits Commission* (1979) 123 S.J. 284, Watkins J.
s. 14, amended: 1979,c.18,s.6,sch.3.
s. 15, amended: *ibid.*,sch.3; repealed in pt.: *ibid.*
s. 15A, added: *ibid.*,s.6.
s. 19, amended: 1979,c.55,sch.2.
s. 33, amended: 1979,c.18,sch.3.
sch. 1, see *R.* v. *Greater Birmingham Supplementary Benefit Appeal Tribunal, ex p. Khan* [1979] 3 All E.R. 759, D.C.

CAP.

1976—cont.

71. *Supplementary Benefits Act 1976—cont.*
sch. 1, amended: regs. 79/997.
sch. 2, amended: 1979,c.18,sch.3.
sch. 4, substituted: *ibid.*,s.6,sch.2.

72. Endangered Species (Import and Export) Act 1976.
s. 1, amended: 1979,c.2,sch.4.
s. 3, orders 78/1280, 1939; 79/1054.
ss. 4, 5, amended: 1979,c.2,sch.4.
s. 10, amended: *ibid.*
s. 11, orders 78/1939; 79/1054.
sch. 2, amended: order 79/1054.
sch. 3, amended: orders 78/1280; 79/1054.

74. Race Relations Act 1976.
s. 1, see *Singh* v. *Rowntree Mackintosh* [1979] I.C.R. 554, E.A.T.; *Panesar* v. *Nestlé Co.*, *The Times*, December 5, 1979, C.A.
ss. 1, 4, 30, 54, 63, see *Zarczynska* v. *Levy* [1979] 1 W.L.R. 125, E.A.T.
s. 68, see *Jalota* v. *Imperial Metal Industry* (*Kynoch*) [1979] I.R.L.R. 313, E.A.T.

75. Development of Rural Wales Act 1976.
sch. 4, repealed in pt.: 1979,c.46,sch.5.

76. Energy Act 1976.
s. 1, orders 79/193, 797, 1383.
s. 17, order 79/193.

77. Weights and Measures, etc. Act 1976.
ss. 2, 7, 10, repealed in pt.: 1979,c.45, sch.7.
s. 13, amended: order 79/1573.
sch. 5, repealed in pt.: order 79/1573.

80. Rent (Agriculture) Act 1976.
s. 1, see *Earl of Normanton* v. *Giles*, *The Times*, December 18, 1979, H.L.
ss. 2, 4, sch. 9, see *Skinner* v. *Cooper* [1979] 1 W.L.R. 666, C.A.

81. Education Act 1976.
ss. 1–3, repealed: 1979,c.49,s.1.
s. 2, see *North Yorkshire County Council* v. ***Secretary of State for Education and Science*, *The Times*, October 20, 1978, Browne-Wilkinson J.**

82. Sexual Offences (Amendment) Act 1976.
s. 2, see *R.* v. *Hinds and Butler* [1979] Crim.L.R. 111, Northampton Crown Ct.; *R.* v. *Mills* (1978) 68 Cr.App.R. 327, C.A.

86. Fishery Limits Act 1976.
ss. 2, 6, orders 78/1950; 79/504.
sch. 2, repealed in pt.: 1979,c.45,sch.7.

Courts of Judicature (Amendment) Act 1976 (Malaysia).
s. 13, see *Lee Chow Meng* v. *Public* *Prosecutor* (1979) 123 S.J. 353, P.C.

Constitution of the Republic of Trinidad and Tobago Act 1976 (No. 4 of 1976) (Trinidad and Tobago).
sch., see *Abbott* v. *Att.-Gen. of Trinidad and Tobago* [1979] 1 W.L.R. 1342, P.C.

CAP.

1977

3. Aircraft and Shipbuilding Industries Act 1977.
s. 11, order 79/961; amended: 1979,c.59, s.1.

5. Social Security (Miscellaneous Provisions) Act 1977.
s. 1, regs. 79/676.
s. 3, repealed in pt.: 1979,c.18,sch.3.
s. 4, amended: *ibid.*,sch.1.
s. 5, repealed in pt.: *ibid.*,sch.3.
s. 12, orders 78/1902; 79/113, 1312.
s. 13, repealed in pt.: 1979,c.18,sch.3.

6. International Finance, Trade and Aid Act 1977.
ss. 1, 2, repealed: 1979,c.29,sch.
s. 3, repealed: 1979,c.30,sch.

8. Job Release Act 1977.
s. 1, order 79/957.

15. Marriage (Scotland) Act 1977.
ss. 3, 19, 25, regs. 79/144.

16. New Towns (Scotland) Act 1977.
s. 3, regs. 79/98.

22. Redundancy Rebates Act 1977.
s. 2, amended: order 79/1573.

25. Minibus Act 1977.
s. 1, order 78/1930.
s. 3, regs. 78/1931.

29. Town and Country Planning (Amendment) Act 1977.
s. 1, see *Scott Markets* v. *Waltham Forest London Borough* [1979] J.P.L. 96, Mars-Jones J.

33. Price Commission Act 1977.
s. 4, amended: 1979,c.1,s.1; repealed in pt.: *ibid.*,s.1,sch.
s. 5, amended: *ibid.*,s.1.
s. 7, repealed in pt.: *ibid.*,s.1,sch.
s. 9, regs. 79/229; amended: 1979,c.1, s.1; repealed in pt.: *ibid.*,s.1,sch.
s. 11, order 78/1716.
s. 12, order 79/129.
s. 13, repealed in pt.: 1979,c.1,s.1,sch.
s. 22, regs. 79/229.

36. Finance Act 1977.
s. 1, repealed in pt.: 1979,c.4,sch.4.
s. 2, repealed in pt.: 1979,c.7,sch.2.
s. 3, amended: 1979,c.7,s.11; repealed in pt.: *ibid.*,sch.2.
s. 4, repealed: 1979,c.5,sch.7.
s. 7, orders 79/241, 1489.
ss. 8, 9, repealed: 1979,c.2,sch.6.
s. 10, amended: 1979,c.3,sch.2.
s. 12, repealed: *ibid.*,sch.3.
ss. 22, 23, repealed in pt.: 1979,c.47, sch.5.
s. 40, repealed: 1979,c.14,sch.8.
ss. 41, 42, amended: *ibid.*,sch.7.
s. 43, repealed: *ibid.*,sch.8.
ss. 45, 46, amended: *ibid.*,sch.7.
s. 59, amended: 1979,c.2,sch.4; repealed **in pt.: 1979,c.14,sch.8.**
schs. 1, 2, repealed: 1979,c.4,sch.4.
sch. 6, repealed in pt.: 1979,c.2,sch.6.

CAP.

1977—cont.

37. Patents Act 1977.
s. 60, see *Smith Kline & French Laboratories* v. *R. D. Harbottle (Mercantile)* [1979] F.S.R. 555, Oliver J.
s. 60, sch. 4, see *Belegging-en-Exploitatiemaatschappij Lavender B.V.* v. *Witten Industrial Diamonds* [1979] F.S.R. 59, C.A.

38. Administration of Justice Act 1977.
s. 21, repealed: 1979,c.55,sch.3.
s. 32, order 79/972.
sch. 2, repealed in pt.: 1979,c.55,sch.3.

39. Coal Industry Act 1977.
s. 5, order 79/1011.
s. 7, order 79/385.

41. Water Charges Equalisation Act 1977.
ss. 1–3, order 78/1921.

42. Rent Act 1977.
s. 1, see *St. Catherine's College* v. *Dorling* (1979) 251 E.G. 265, C.A.
ss. 1, 8, see *St. Catherine's College* v. *Dorling* [1979] 3 All E.R. 250, C.A.
s. 2, see *Atyeo* v. *Fardoe* (1978) 37 P. & C.R. 494, C.A.; *Heath Estates* v. *Burchell* (1979) 251 E.G. 1173, C.A.
s. 9, see *McHale* v. *Daneham* (1979) 249 E.G. 969, Judge Edwards.
s. 12, see *Guppy* v. *O'Donnell*, July 27, 1979, Judge Rowland, Westminster County Court.
s. 142, rules 78/1961.
sch. 1, see *Helby* v. *Rafferty* [1978] 3 All E.R. 1016, C.A.; *Atyeo* v. *Fardoe* (1978) 37 P. & C.R. 494, C.A.

45. Criminal Law Act 1977.
ss. 1, 5, see *R.* v. *Duncalf* [1979] 1 W.L.R. 918, C.A.
ss. 1, 5, see *R.* v. *Walters*; *R.* v. *Tovey*; *R.* v. *Padfield* [1979] R.T.R. 220, C.A.
s. 16, see *R.* v. *Brentwood JJ., ex p. Jones* [1979] R.T.R. 155, D.C.
s. 18, amended (S.): 1979,c.39,s.42.
s. 50, see *R.* v. *Midgley* [1979] R.T.R. 1, C.A.
s. 53, see *R.* v. *Wells Street Stipendiary Magistrates, ex p. Golding* [1979] Crim.L.R. 254, D.C.
s. 65, see *R.* v. *Adair* (1978) 123 S.J. 32, C.A.; *R.* v. *Brentwood JJ., ex p. Jones* [1979] R.T.R. 155, D.C.
sch. 5, repealed in pt.: 1979,c.2,sch.6.
sch. 6, repealed in pt.: 1979,c.36,sch.8; c.39,sch.7.
sch. 12, see *R.* v. *Adair* (1978) 123 S.J. 32, C.A.
schs. 12, 14, see *R.* v. *Brentwood JJ., ex p. Jones* [1979] Crim.L.R. 115, D.C.

46. Insurance Brokers (Registration) Act 1977.
ss. 27, 28, orders 79/408, 489, 490.

48. Housing (Homeless Persons) Act 1977.
see *R.* v. *Beverley Borough Council, ex p. McPhee* [1979] J.P.L. 94, D.C.

CAP.

1977—cont.

48. *Housing (Homeless Persons) Act 1977—cont.*
s. 3, see *Thornton* v. *Kirklees Metropolitan Borough Council* [1979] 2 All E.R. 349, C.A.; *De Falco* v. *Crawley Borough Council*; *Silvestri* v. *Same*, *The Times*, December 13, 1979, C.A.
ss. 5, 6, see *R.* v. *Bristol City Council, ex p. Browne* [1979] 3 All E.R. 344, D.C.

49. National Health Service Act 1977.
ss. 1, 3, see *R.* v. *Secretary of State for Social Services, ex p. Hincks* (1979) 123 S.J. 436, Wien J.
s. 5, amended: 1979,c.23,s.1.
s. 16, regs. 79/739, 897.
s. 77, regs. 79/681.
ss. 78, 79, regs. 79/677.
s. 83, regs. 79/681.
s. 128, amended: 1979,c.36,sch.7; repealed in pt.: *ibid.*,schs.7,8.
sch. 3, amended: 1979,c.23,s.2.
sch. 5, regs. 79/738, 739, 897.
sch. 12, regs. 79/677.
sch. 15, repealed in pt.: 1979,c.36,sch.8.

50. Unfair Contract Terms Act 1977.
ss. 6, 14, 20, 25, amended: 1979,c.54, sch.2.
sch. 3, repealed in pt.: 1979,c.54,sch.3.

1978

2. Commonwealth Development Corporation Act 1978.
s. 17, repealed in pt.: 1979,c.60,sch.3.
sch. 1, regs. 79/495.

5. Northern Ireland (Emergency Provisions) Act 1978.
s. 21, order 79/746.
s. 33, orders 78/1865; 79/817.
sch. 2, amended: order 79/746.

6. Employment Subsidies Act 1978.
s. 3, S.R. 1979 No. 382; amended: order 79/1573.

10. European Assembly Elections Act 1978.
s. 9, order 79/349 (S.).
sch. 1, orders 79/219, 220, 349 (S.); regs. 79/322, 338, 1021.
sch. 2, orders 78/1903, 1904.

11. Shipbuilding (Redundancy) Payments Act 1978.
ss. 1, 2, orders 79/881, 898.

12. Medical Act 1978.
s. 1, orders 79/112, 1358.
s. 2, repealed in pt.: order 79/289.
s. 4, order 79/289.
s. 27, order 79/29.
s. 32, order 79/920.
sch. 1, order 79/1358.
sch. 2, repealed: order 79/289.
sch. 6, repealed in pt.: *ibid.*

14. Housing (Financial Provisions) (Scotland) Act 1978.
ss. 1, 2, order 79/100.

CAP.

1978—cont.

17. Internationally Protected Persons Act 1978.
s. 3, order 79/453.
s. 4, orders 79/453, 456, 573–575.
s. 5, order 79/455.

18. Export Guarantees and Overseas Investment Act 1978.
s. 13, order 79/180.

22. Domestic Proceedings and Magistrates' Courts Act 1978.
s. 86, repealed: 1979,c.55,sch.3.
s. 88, amended: *ibid.*,sch.2.
s. 89, order 79/731.

23. Judicature (Northern Ireland) Act 1978.
s. 53, amended: order 79/1573.
s. 55, S.Rs. 1979 Nos. 86, 205, 206.
s. 56, amended and repealed in pt.: order 79/1573.
s. 69, S.R. 1979 No. 103.
s. 82, S.R. 1979 No. 105.
s. 84, amended: order 79/1576.
s. 104, S.R. 1979 No. 122.
s. 116, S.Rs. 1979 Nos. 59, 154, 158–161, 262.
s. 119, amended: order 79/1573.
s. 123, orders 79/124, 422.
sch. 5, repealed in pt.: order 79/1575.

26. Suppression of Terrorism Act 1978.
s. 8, order 79/497.

27. Home Purchase Assistance and Housing Corporation Guarantee Act 1978.
s. 2, order 78/1785.
sch., amended: 1979,c.37,sch.6; order 78/1785.

29. National Health Service (Scotland) Act 1978.
s. 69, regs. 79/704.
ss. 70, 71, regs. 79/705.
s. 75, regs. 79/704.
s. 106, regs. 79/705.
s. 108, regs. 79/704, 705; repealed in pt.: 1979,c.36,schs.7,8.
sch. 11, regs. 79/704, 705.
sch. 15, repealed in pt.: 1979,c.36,sch.8.

30. Interpretation Act 1978.
s. 24, amended: order 79/1573.

33. State Immunity Act 1978.
s. 4, repealed in pt.: 1979,c.60,sch.3.
ss. 13, 14, see *Hispano Americana Mercantile S.A.* v. *Central Bank of Nigeria* (1979) 123 S.J. 336, C.A.
s. 14, order 79/457.
s. 23, order 79/458.

38. Consumer Safety Act 1978.
s. 3, sch. 1, orders 78/1728; 79/44, 887.

42. Finance Act 1978.
s. 1, repealed: 1979,c.7,sch.2.
s. 2, regs. 78/1786; repealed: 1979,c.4, sch.4.
ss. 3, 5, repealed: 1979,c.2,sch.6.
s. 6, orders 79/104, 181, 191, 314, 492, 510, 566, 567, 627, 842, 1148, 1182; repealed in pt.: 1979,c.3,sch.3; c.8, sch.2.

CAP.

1978—cont.

42. *Finance Act 1978—cont.*
s. 10, repealed in pt.: 1979,c.8,sch.2.
s. 18, repealed: 1979,c.47,sch.5.
ss. 19, 20, repealed in pt.: *ibid.*
ss. 44, 45 in pt., 46–52, repealed: 1979, c.14,sch.8.
ss. 54, 57, 61, 64, amended: *ibid.*,sch.7.
s. 76, repealed: 1979,c.47,sch.5.
s. 79, repealed: 1979,c.2,sch.6.
s. 80, amended: 1979,c.2,sch.4; repealed in pt.: 1979,c.14,sch.8.
schs. 7, 8, repealed: 1979,c.14,sch.8.
sch. 11, repealed in pt.: *ibid.*
sch. 12, repealed in pt.: 1979,c.2,sch.6; c.3,sch.3; c.4,sch.4; c.5,sch.7; c.6,sch.; c.7,sch.2.

43. Independent Broadcasting Authority Act 1978.
s. 3, order 79/461.

44. Employment Protection (Consolidation) Act 1978.
s. 12, order 79/1403.
s. 15, order 78/1777.
s. 18, order 79/1403; amended: 1979,c. 12,sch.6.
s. 33, amended: 1979,c.36,sch.7.
s. 57, see *Hinckley and Bosworth Borough Council* v. *Ainscough* [1979] I.R.L.R. 224, E.A.T.; *Dixon* v. *Wilson Walton Engineering* [1979] I.C.R. 438, Industrial Tribunal.
s. 58, see *Curry* v. *Marlow District Council* [1979] I.C.R. 769, E.A.T.
s. 62, see *Dixon* v. *Wilson Walton Engineering* [1979] I.C.R. 438, Industrial Tribunal.
s. 64, amended: order 79/959.
s. 75, orders 78/1778; 79/1723.
s. 77, see *Bradley* v. *Edward Ryde & Sons* [1979] I.C.R. 488, E.A.T.
s. 81, see *O'Hare* v. *Rotaprint*, *The Times*, November 22, 1979, E.A.T.
s. 122, order 78/1777.
s. 132, amended: 1979,c.18,sch.3.
s. 148, order 78/1777.
s. 149, order 79/959.
s. 153, repealed in pt.: 1979,c.36,schs.7,8.
s. 154, order 78/1777.
schs. 1, 2, 3, order 79/1403.
sch. 11, see *International Aviation Services (U.K.) (Trading as I.A.S. Cargo Airlines)* v. *Jones* [1979] I.R.L.R. 155, E.A.T.
sch. 13, see *Allen & Son* v. *Coventry* [1979] I.R.L.R. 399, E.A.T.
sch. 14, order 78/1777.

49. Community Service by Offenders (Scotland) Act 1978.
s. 15, order 78/1944.

51. Scotland Act 1978.
repealed: order 79/928.
s. 85, order 79/928.
sch. 17, order 78/1912.

52. Wales Act 1978.
repealed: order 79/933.
s. 80, order 79/933.
sch. 12, order 78/1915.

CAP.

1978—cont.

53. Chronically Sick and Disabled Persons (Northern Ireland) Act 1978.
s. 14, S.R. 1979 No. 365.
s. 19, amended: order 79/1573.
s. 21, S.Rs. 1979 Nos. 364, 365.

55. Transport Act 1978.
s. 11, order 79/119.
ss. 19, 20, orders 78/1764; 79/1416.

56. Parliamentary Pensions Act 1978.
s. 11, order 78/1837.

1979

1. Price Commission (Amendment) Act 1979.
Royal Assent, February 12, 1979.

2. Customs and Excise Management Act 1979.
Royal Assent, February 22, 1979.
ss. 1, 17, 21, 34, amended: 1979,c.58, sch.1.
s. 35, regs. 79/564, 565; amended: 1979, c.58,sch.1.
s. 36, amended: *ibid.*
s. 42, regs. 79/564.
ss. 43, 53, 57, 61, 63, 64, 66, 69, 70, 74, 78, amended: 1979,c.58,sch.1.
s. 81, regs. 79/564.
ss. 83, 90, 92, amended: 1979,c.58,sch.1.
s. 93, regs. 79/207, 208, 1146.
s. 105, amended: order 79/241.
s. 140, repealed in pt.: *ibid.*
s. 159, amended: 1979,c.58,sch.1.
s. 174, repealed: *ibid.*,sch.2.
sch. 2, order 79/1393.
sch. 3, amended: 1979,c.58,sch.1.
schs. 4, 7, repealed in pt.: *ibid.*,sch.2.

3. Customs and Excise Duties (General Reliefs) Act 1979.
Royal Assent, February 22, 1979.
s. 1, order 79/1142.
s. 2, regs. 79/554, 555.
s. 4, order 79/737.
s. 6, repealed: 1979,c.58,sch.2.
ss. 7, 8, 10, 11, amended: *ibid.*,sch.1.
s. 13, order 79/655.
sch. 1, repealed: 1979,c.58,sch.2.

4. Alcoholic Liquor Duties Act 1979.
Royal Assent, February 22, 1979.
s. 1, amended: order 79/241.
s. 2, regs. 79/1146; substituted: order 79/241.
s. 3, regs. 79/1146; amended: order 79/241.
s. 4, amended and repealed in pt.: *ibid.*
s. 5, amended: *ibid.*
s. 8, regs. 79/1146.
s. 12, amended: order 79/241.
s. 13, regs. 79/1146.
s. 14, amended: order 79/241.
s. 15, regs. 79/1146.
s. 16, regs. 79/1146; amended: order 79/241.
s. 19, regs. 79/1146.
ss. 20, 21, amended: order 79/241.
s. 22, regs. 79/1146; amended: order 79/241; 1979,c.58,sch.1.
ss. 23, 26, 27, amended: order 79/241.
s. 28, regs. 79/1146.

CAP.

1979—cont.

4. *Alcoholic Liquor Duties Act 1979—cont.*
s. 30, amended: order 79/241.
ss. 31, 33, regs. 79/1146.
ss. 36, 37, amended: order 79/241.
s. 43, amended: 1979,c.58,sch.1.
s. 45, amended: order 79/241.
ss. 46, 49, regs. 79/1146.
s. 56, regs. 79/1146, 1240.
ss. 57, 58, amended: order 79/241; 1979,c.58,sch.1.
s. 59, amended: *ibid.*
s. 60, regs. 79/1146, amended: order 79/241.
s. 61, regs. 79/1240.
s. 62, regs. 79/1146, 1218, 1240; amended: order 79/241.
s. 63, regs. 79/1146; amended: order 79/241.
s. 68, substituted: *ibid.*
ss. 71, 74–76, amended: *ibid.*
s. 77, regs. 79/1146.
s. 78, amended: order 79/241.
s. 82, regs. 79/1146; amended: order 79/241.
schs. 1, 2, substituted: *ibid.*

5. Hydrocarbon Oil Duties Act 1979.
Royal Assent, February 22, 1979.
ss. 6, 11, 14, amended: 1979,c.47,s.2.

6. Matches and Mechanical Lighters Duties Act 1979.
Royal Assent, February 22, 1979.
ss. 3, 7, amended: 1979,c.58,sch.1.

7. Tobacco Products Duty Act 1979.
Royal Assent, February 22, 1979.
ss. 2, 7, regs. 79/904.
sch. 1, amended: 1979,c.47,s.3; order 79/1489.

8. Excise Duties (Surcharges or Rebates) Act 1979.
Royal Assent, February 22, 1979.
s. 2, amended: 1979,c.47,s.4.
s. 3, repealed in pt.: 1979,c.58,sch.2.

9. Films Act 1979.
Royal Assent, February 22, 1979.

10. Public Lending Right Act 1979.
Royal Assent, March 22, 1979.

11. Electricity (Scotland) Act 1979.
Royal Assent, March 22, 1979.

12. Wages Councils Act 1979.
Royal Assent, March 22, 1979.
s. 4, order 79/864, 865.

13. Agricultural Statistics Act 1979.
Royal Assent, March 22, 1979.

14. Capital Gains Tax Act 1979.
Royal Assent, March 22, 1979.
sch. 2, orders 79/1231, 1676.

15. House of Commons (Redistribution of Seats) Act 1979.
Royal Assent, March 22, 1979.

16. Criminal Evidence Act 1979.
Royal Assent, March 22, 1979.

17. Vaccine Damage Payments Act 1979.
Royal Assent, March 22, 1979.
s. 1, regs. 79/1441.
ss. 2–5, 7, 8, regs. 79/432.

CAP.

1979—cont.

18. Social Security Act 1979.
Royal Assent, March 22, 1979.
s. 21, orders 79/369, 1031.

19. Administration of Justice (Emergency Provisions) (Scotland) Act 1979.
Royal Assent, March 22, 1979.
s. 1, order 79/550.

20. Consolidated Fund Act 1979.
Royal Assent, March 22, 1979.

21. Forestry Act 1979.
Royal Assent, March 29, 1979.
s. 2, regs. 79/836.

22. Confirmation to Small Estates (Scotland) Act 1979.
Royal Assent, March 29, 1979.

23. Public Health Laboratory Service Act 1979.
Royal Assent, March 29, 1979.

24. Appropriation Act 1979.
Royal Assent, April 4, 1979.

25. Finance Act 1979.
Royal Assent, April 4, 1979.
ss. 1, 2, repealed in pt.: 1979,c.47,sch.5.

26. Legal Aid Act 1979.
Royal Assent, April 4, 1979.
s. 14, orders 79/756, 826.

27. Kiribati Act 1979.
Royal Assent, June 19, 1979.
s. 2, order 79/719.
s. 6, orders 79/719, 720.

28. Carriage by Air and Road Act 1979.
Royal Assent, April 4, 1979.
s. 2, see *Fothergill* v. *Monarch Airlines* [1979] 3 W.L.R. 491, C.A.

29. International Monetary Fund Act 1979.
Royal Assent, April 4, 1979.

30. Exchange Equalisation Account Act 1979.
Royal Assent, April 4, 1979.

31. Prosecution of Offences Act 1979.
Royal Assent, April 4, 1979.

32. Industry Act 1979.
Royal Assent, April 4, 1979.

33. Land Registration (Scotland) Act 1979.
Royal Assent, April 4, 1979.

34. Credit Unions Act 1979.
Royal Assent, April 4, 1979.
ss. 13, 29, orders 79/866.
s. 33, order 79/936.

35. Independent Broadcasting Authority Act 1979.
Royal Assent, April 4, 1979.

36. Nurses, Midwives and Health Visitors Act 1979.
Royal Assent, April 4, 1979.
s. 23, amended: order 79/1573.

37. Banking Act 1979.
Royal Assent, April 4, 1979.
s. 2, regs. 79/1204.
s. 52, order 79/938.

38. Estate Agents Act 1979.
Royal Assent, April 4, 1979.

CAP.

1979—cont.

39. Merchant Shipping Act 1979.
Royal Assent, April 4, 1979.
s. 43, sch. 6, regs. 79/1519.
s. 52, order 79/807.

40. Representation of the People Act 1979.
Royal Assent, April 4, 1979.

41. Pneumoconiosis etc. (Workers' Compensation) Act 1979.
Royal Assent, April 4, 1979.
ss. 4, 5, 7, regs. 79/727.

42. Arbitration Act 1979.
Royal Assent, April 4, 1979.
s. 1, see *Pioneer Shipping and Armada Marine S.A.* v. *B.T.P. Tioxide*, *The Times*, November 16, 1979, C.A.
s. 4, order 79/754.
s. 8, order 79/750.

43. Crown Agents Act 1979.
Royal Assent, April 4, 1979.

44. Leasehold Reform Act 1979.
Royal Assent, April 4, 1979.

45. Weights and Measures Act 1979.
Royal Assent, April 4, 1979.
s. 15, amended: order 79/1573.
s. 24, order 79/1228.

46. Ancient Monuments and Archaeological Areas Act 1979.
Royal Assent, April 4, 1979.
s. 65, order 79/786.

47. Finance (No. 2) Act 1979.
Royal Assent, July 26, 1979.

48. Pensioners' Payments and Social Security Act 1979.
Royal Assent, July 26, 1979.

49. Education Act 1979.
Royal Assent, July 26, 1979.

50. European Assembly (Pay and Pensions) Act 1979.
Royal Assent, July 26, 1979.

51. Appropriation (No. 2) Act 1979.
Royal Assent, July 27, 1979.

52. Southern Rhodesia Act 1979.
Royal Assent, November 14, 1979.
s. 3, order 79/1445; repealed in pt.: 1979,c.60,sch.3.

53. Charging Orders Act 1979.
Royal Assent, December 6, 1979.

54. Sale of Goods Act 1979.
Royal Assent, December 6, 1979.

55. Justices of the Peace Act 1979.
Royal Assent, December 6, 1979.

56. Consolidated Fund (No. 2) Act 1979.
Royal Assent, December 20, 1979.

57. European Communities (Greek Accession) Act 1979.
Royal Assent, December 20, 1979.

58. Isle of Man Act 1979.
Royal Assent, December 20, 1979.

59. Shipbuilding Act 1979.
Royal Assent, December 20, 1979.

60. Zimbabwe Act 1979.
Royal Assent, December 20, 1979.

STATUTES FOR 1979

Price Commission (Amendment) Act 1979 *

(1979 c. 1)

An Act to limit the application of section 9 of the Price Commission Act 1977. [12th February 1979]

General Note

Powers to control prices

The Price Commission Act 1977 (c. 33) introduced new powers to control prices. First, the Commission may select and investigate individual price increase applications notified under the Prices and Charges (Notification of Increases) Order 1978 (S.I. 1978 No. 1083) (s. 4), and also individual prices and distributors' margins (s. 5). Price increases are frozen during an investigation for a period of up to four months following the notification of increase (s. 4 (2) (*b*)) or, in the case of an increase of which no notification is required, for a period of up to three months following notification of an investigation (s. 5 (3) (*a*)). The Secretary of State for Prices and Consumer Protection may make an order after an investigation and on the recommendation of the Commission freezing price increases for up to 12 months (ss. 6 (6) and 7 (5) (6)). The provisions about prices also apply to charges for services. The Commission's power to enforce the universal cost and marginal controls of the Price Code which were established by the Counter-Inflation Act 1973 ended on July 31, 1978 (s. 17 of the 1977 Act, and see now the Counter-Inflation (Price Code) Order 1978 (S.I. 1978 No. 1082)).

Secondly, the Commission must examine, within a specified period, any question relating to prices within a sector of industry or commerce referred to the Commission by the Secretary of State, who may make orders regulating prices or accept undertakings in consequence of reports on examinations (ss. 10 to 13).

Safeguards

There are three principal protections in the 1977 Act for enterprises affected by the exercise of the price control powers. First, general and specific statutory criteria must be considered by the Commission when deciding whether to investigate a price increase, price or margin, or when considering whether to permit an interim price increase during an investigation (see below) and in carrying out investigations or examinations or preparing reports (s. 2 (3)). Generally, the Commission is obliged to ensure that any price restraint is consistent with the making of adequate profits by efficient suppliers of goods and services (s. 2 (1)). The Commission is therefore under a legal obligation to consider profitability in making decisions. More specifically, the criteria require the Commission to take account of a range of factors including the following: the need to recover costs; the desirability of making the best use of resources; the need to defray the cost of capital, including compensation for the risk element; the need to take into account changes in prices in determining the value of assets; and the need to finance innovation, improvement and expansion (s. 2 (2)). An increase in costs which can be met by greater efficiency may not, therefore, justify a price increase in the eyes of the Commission. The Secretary of State is also obliged to have regard to the statutory criteria when considering whether to veto examinations, to make orders, to accept undertakings and to initiate enforcement proceedings (s. 20 (1) and (2)).

* Annotations by John Tinnion, LL.B., Solicitor, University of Leeds.

Secondly, the Commission may order an interim price increase during an investigation by serving a "variation notice" (ss. 4 (5) (*a*) and (i) and 5 (4)). The Commission cannot then recommend a restriction in the price so as to make the amount of it less than is authorised in the variation notice (s. 6 (6) (*c*) (ii)) and the Secretary of State may not by subsequent order impose a more severe restriction than is contained in the Commission's recommendation (s. 7 (5) (*a*) (i)). The Commission has used the discretionary power to allow an interim price increase during an investigation on a number of occasions.

Thirdly, the Commission was compelled by the 1977 Act to apply an overriding safeguard for basic profits and to serve a variation notice allowing an interim increase where profits would have fallen below a prescribed minimum level as a result of a price freeze during an investigation (ss. 4 (5) (6) (ii) and 5 (4)). Any subsequent order by the Secretary of State could not restrict the price below that of the interim increase set by the notice (ss. 6 (6) (*c*) (ii) and 7 (5) (*a*) (i)). The Secretary of State was obliged and given power to make regulations, after consultation, setting the minimum level of safeguards for basic profits (ss. 9 and 22 (3) and the Prices and Charges (Safeguard for Basic Profits) Regulations 1977 (S.I. 1977 No. 1282)). Under the regulations, enterprises under investigation by the Commission could automatically claim price increases of an amount necessary to obtain a rate of return on capital of about 12½ per cent., or higher, after allowing for depreciation and valuation of stock under current cost accounting methods. Alternatively, enterprises could claim whatever price increase was necessary to provide 80 per cent. of the profit earned in 1977.

The present amendment Act is concerned with the overriding safeguards for basic profits, the existence of which is claimed to have distorted the purpose of the 1977 Act. Where profit safeguards have applied, the Commission has been obliged not to give precedence to the statutory criteria in considering whether a proposed increase was justified on merits. The profit safeguards have been invoked in 20 out of 31 major investigations completed by the Commission. In nine of those cases the notified price increases were fully safeguarded and in 11 other cases the increases were partially covered. The Commission has been critical of the way in which its work has been handicapped by the automatic profit safeguards (Quarterly Report, April 1978).

The new Act

The new Act limits the application of the mandatory safeguards for basic profits contained in regulations made under s. 9 of the Price Commission Act 1977. Firms which pre-notify price increases after January 16, 1979, the date upon which the new measures were announced by the Prime Minister (H.C. Vol. 960, col. 1558), will not automatically qualify for interim price increases to safeguard profits where the Commission decide to carry out an investigation. However, the Commission is placed under the new duty to award an interim increase to cover the costs of imported raw materials.

The basic profit safeguards will be maintained, in a form to be agreed, where the Government direct the Commission to examine the profit margins of whole sectors of industry since it will not be possible to assess how the general recommendations of the Commission for a whole sector will bear on the financial position and viability of individual enterprises. The Commission's discretion to grant interim price increases to enterprises under investigation in accordance with the guidelines in s. 2 of the 1977 Act remains unaffected.

The limits on the application of s. 9 are effective until February 12, 1980, after which s. 9 is automatically revived, in its original form, unless the limits are extended for a period up to 12 months by Order in Council laid in draft and approved by a resolution of each House of Parliament.

Parliamentary Debates

Price Commission (Amendment) Bill: H.L. Vol. 398, cols. 493, 637 and 832; H.C. Vol. 961, cols. 1058, 1501 and 1612.

Industrial situation (price controls): H.C. Vol. 960, col. 1558.

Amendment of Price Commission Act 1977

1.—(1) Section 9 of the Price Commission Act 1977 (safeguard for basic profits) shall cease to apply except as regards the profits which persons are not to be prevented from earning by virtue of any such notice as is mentioned in section 13 (1) of that Act (enforcement of orders made in consequence of reports on examinations); and accordingly that Act shall be amended as provided in the following provisions of this section.

(2) Section 4 (5) (*b*) and (ii) (duty of the Price Commission to give a variation notice to the relevant person in cases where it appears to them that, apart from section 4 (5), his profit would, in consequence of a notification under section 4 (1), be kept below the profit determined in his case in pursuance of the said section 9) shall cease to have effect.

(3) In section 4 (5)—

(*a*) after paragraph (*a*) there shall be inserted—

" (*aa*) that the whole or part of the increase ought not to be so restricted because of an increase in the costs of imported raw materials,";

(*b*) after paragraph (*i*) there shall be inserted—

" (*ia*) it shall be the duty of the Commission, in a case falling within paragraph (*aa*) of this subsection, to give to the relevant person a variation notice allowing so much of the increase as they consider ought not to be restricted for the reason mentioned in that paragraph.".

(4) In section 5 (4) (application of section 4 (5) in relation to notifications in respect of prices) for the words " and for any other reference to the increase there were substituted a reference to the price " there shall be substituted the words " and as if—

(i) in paragraph (*aa*), for the words from " the whole " to " restricted " there were substituted the words " a particular increase in the price ought not to be restricted by virtue of section 5 (3) of this Act ";

(ii) in paragraph (*ia*), for the words from " so " to " as " there were substituted the words " the increase in the price which "; and

(iii) for any reference to the increase (except those in paragraphs (*a*), (*aa*) and (*ia*)) there were substituted a reference to the price; ".

(5) In section 7 (restrictions, undertakings and orders in consequence of reports on investigations) there shall be omitted—

(*a*) in subsection (1), the words " and subject to section 9 of this Act ";

(*b*) in subsection (5) (*a*) (ii), the words " except by virtue of section 9 of this Act ";

(*c*) subsection (7) (*b*) and the word " and " preceding it; and

(*d*) in subsection (8), the words " apart from section 9 of this Act ".

(6) In section 9 (safeguard for basic profits)—

(*a*) subsection (1) (*a*) (which provides for the making of regulations as to the profits which are relevant for the purposes of section 4 (5) (*b*)) shall be omitted; and

(*b*) in subsection (1) (*b*), for the words " any provision of section 7 of this Act " there shall be substituted the words " any such notice as is mentioned in section 13 (1) of this Act ".

(7) In section 13 (enforcement of orders and supervision of undertakings in consequence of reports on examinations) there shall be omitted—

(*a*) in subsection (1) (*b*), the words " by virtue of subsection (6) of this section "; and

(*b*) in subsection (6), the words from " and section 9 (1) " onwards.

(8) The enactments mentioned in the Schedule to this Act are hereby repealed to the extent specified in the third column of that Schedule.

(9) The preceding provisions of this section shall not apply in relation to any increase of which notice was given to the Price Commission as mentioned in section 4 (1) of the Price Commission Act 1977 before 17th January 1979; but as from the passing of this Act the regulations then in force under section 9 of that Act shall apply in relation to any such increase only so far as they were made in pursuance of subsection (1) (*a*) of the said section 9.

GENERAL NOTE

Subs. (1)

This removes the obligation on, and the power of the Secretary of State for Prices and Consumer Protection to make regulations under s. 9 of the Price Commission Act 1977 relating to the minimum levels of profit safeguarded during and after an individual investigation by the Commission into proposed price increases, prices and distributors' margins and service charges. The present minimum levels of profit are set by the Prices and Charges (Safeguard for Basic Profits) Regulations 1977 (S.I. 1977 No. 1282).

For "variation of notice," see s. 4 (6) of the 1977 Act.

The safeguard for minimum profit provisions of s. 9 of the 1977 Act continue to apply to notices made under s. 13 (1) of that Act as a result of sectorial examinations made by the Commission at the request of the Secretary of State.

Subs. (2)

This removes the obligation on the Commission to serve a variation notice allowing an interim price increase to safeguard basic profits during an investigation which was imposed by ss. 4 (5) (*b*) (ii) and 5 (4) of the 1977 Act.

The effect of the service of a notification of an investigation under s. 4 (1) of the 1977 Act is to freeze the price increase for up to four months during which the investigation is carried out.

Subss. (3) *and* (4)

These impose on the Commission an obligation to serve a variation notice allowing an increase during an investigation where it appears to the Commission that the increase or part of the increase is due to an increase in the cost of imported raw materials.

Subs. (6)

S. 9 (1) of the 1977 Act now reads:

"(1) It shall be the duty of the Secretary of State to make regulations, by reference to such matters as he thinks fit, as to the profits as defined by the regulations and which persons are not to be prevented from earning by virtue of any such notice as is mentioned in section 13 (1) of this Act."

The duty and power remains to make regulations to safeguard basic profits when the Commission examines whole industrial sectors at the invitation of the Secretary of State and he serves notices controlling prices under s. 13 (1) of the 1977 Act as a result of a recommendation by the Commission that prices should be limited throughout the sector or that marginal controls should be applied to some or to all the enterprises within the sector. New regulations will be made after consultation as required by s. 9 (2) of the 1977 Act to safeguard profits in such cases. These regulations are likely to be based not on historic safeguards which guarantee past levels of profit but on current safeguards which maintain profitability irrespective of the recommendation the Commission makes for the industry as a whole (see H.C. Vol. 961, col. 1068).

Subs. (9)

This contains transitional provisions whereby regulations under s. 9 of the 1977 Act in force when the Act was passed are to continue to apply *during investigations* by the Commission into proposed price increases notified to it before January 17, 1979.

Subss. (5), (7) *and* (8)

These make consequential amendments and repeals.

Duration of Act

2.—(1) As from the end of the relevant period the Price Commission Act 1977 shall have effect as it would if the following provisions of this Act, namely section 1 and the Schedule, had not been enacted, but without prejudice to the operation of those provisions during that period.

(2) Subject to subsection (3), the relevant period for the purposes of this section is the period of one year beginning with the date on which this Act is passed.

(3) Her Majesty may by Order in Council extend or further extend the relevant period for the purposes of this section; but the extension effected by any particular Order under this subsection shall not exceed 12 months.

(4) An Order under subsection (3) shall not be made unless a draft of the Order has been laid before Parliament and approved by a resolution of each House of Parliament.

General Note

This section revives the provisions repealed by s. 1 and the Schedule on February 12, 1980, but makes provision for postponement of that revival for not more than 12 months at a time by Order in Council approved in draft by both Houses of Parliament.

Short title

3.—This Act may be cited as the Price Commission (Amendment) Act 1979.

Section 1 (8)

SCHEDULE

Repeals

Chapter	Short title	Extent of repeal
1977 c. 33.	Price Commission Act 1977.	Section 4 (5) (*b*) and (ii). In section 7— (*a*) in subsection (1), the words " and subject to section 9 of this Act "; (*b*) in subsection (5) (*a*) (ii), the words " except by virtue of section 9 of this Act "; (*c*) subsection (7) (*b*) and the word " and " preceding it; and (*d*) subsection (8), the words " apart from section 9 of this Act ". Section 9 (1) (*a*). In section 13— (*a*) in subsection (1) (*b*), the words " by virtue of subsection (6) of this section "; and (*b*) in subsection (6), the words from " and section 9 (1) " onwards.

Customs and Excise Management Act 1979

(1979 c. 2)

Arrangement of Sections

Part I

Preliminary

Part II

Administration

Appointment and duties of Commissioners, officers, etc.

Offences in connection with Commissioners, officers, etc.

Commissioners' receipts and expenses

Part III

Customs and Excise Control Areas

PART IV

CONTROL OF IMPORTATION

PART V

CONTROL OF EXPORTATION

PART VI

CONTROL OF COASTWISE TRAFFIC

PART VII

CUSTOMS AND EXCISE CONTROL: SUPPLEMENTARY PROVISIONS

PART VIII

WAREHOUSES AND QUEEN'S WAREHOUSES AND RELATED PROVISIONS ABOUT PIPE-LINES

PART IX

CONTROL OF EXCISE LICENCE TRADES AND REVENUE TRADERS

PART X

DUTIES AND DRAWBACKS—GENERAL PROVISIONS

General provisions relating to imported goods

General provisions relating to charge of duty on and delivery of goods

Drawback, allowances, duties, etc.—general

PART XI

DETENTION OF PERSONS, FORFEITURE AND LEGAL PROCEEDINGS

Detention of persons

Forfeiture

General provisions as to legal proceedings

Saving for outlying enactments of certain general provisions as to offences

An Act to consolidate the enactments relating to the collection and management of the revenues of cusoms and excise and in some cases to other matters in relation to which the Commissioners of Customs and Excise for the time being perform functions, with amendments to give effect to recommendations of the Law Commission and the Scottish Law Commission.

[22nd February 1979]

General Note

This Act consolidates the enactments relating to the collection and management of customs and excise revenues.

Pt. I (ss. 1–5) contains preliminary provisions: s. 1 is the interpretation section; s. 2 applies this Part to hovercraft; s. 3 relates to pipe-lines; s. 4 applies the Act to certain Crown aircraft; s. 5 relates to the time of importation and exportation.

Pt. II (ss. 6–18) provides for the administration of the Act: s. 6 relates to the appointment and duties of Commissioners; s. 7 sets out the privileges of Commissioners; s. 8 defines the exercise of powers and duties of Commissioners; s. 9 deals with EEC obligations; s. 10 concerns the disclosure by the Commissioners of information as to imports; s. 11 relates to police assistance; s. 12 gives the Commissioners power to hold inquiries; s. 13 sets out penalties for unlawfully assuming character of officer; s. 14 deals with the failure to surrender a commission; s. 15 concerns offences of bribery and collusion; s. 16 contains offences regarding the obstruction of officers; s. 17 provides for the disposal of customs duties; s. 18 relates to the remuneration and expenses of Commissioners.

Pt. III (ss. 19–34) sets out control areas: s. 19 confers power to appoint ports; s. 20 relates to wharves; s. 21 deals with control of aircraft into and out of the U.K.; s. 22 gives power to name examination stations; s. 23 refers to control of hovercraft; s. 24 controls the movement of goods by pipe-line; s. 25 relates to transit sheds; s. 26 concerns the movement of goods into and out of Northern Ireland by land; s. 27 gives officers powers of boarding; s. 28 confers powers of access; s. 29 gives officers powers of detention of ships, etc.; s. 30 deals with the control of movement of uncleared goods; s. 31 relates to movement of goods to and from inland clearance depot; s. 32 gives the penalty for carrying away officers; s. 33 confers power to inspect aircraft, aerodromes, records, etc.; s. 34 allows officers to prevent flight of aircraft.

Pt. IV (ss. 35–51) relates to the control of importation: s. 35 provides for reporting by inwards vehicles; s. 36 makes provision as to naval ships; s. 37 concerns the entry of goods on importation; s. 38 deals with entry by bill of sight; s. 39 relates to entry of surplus stores; s. 40 makes provision for removal of uncleared goods to Queen's warehouse; s. 41 states the penalty for failing to comply with entry provisions; s. 42 regulates unloading and removal of goods; s. 43 relates to the duty on imported goods; s. 44 excludes importers keeping standing deposits from the provisions of s. 43 (1); s. 45 concerns deferred payment of duty; s. 46 permits goods to be warehoused without payment of duty; s. 47 exempts from payment goods entered for transit; s. 48 exempts goods temporarily imported; s. 49 deals with forfeiture of goods improperly imported; s. 50 gives the penalty for improper importation of goods; s. 51 makes special provisions as to proof in Northern Ireland.

Pt. V (ss. 52–68) provides for the control of exportation: s. 52 defines "dutiable or restricted goods"; s. 53 concerns the entry outwards of such goods; s. 54 deals with the entry outwards of goods which are not dutiable or restricted; s. 55 provides for a register of exporters and assignment of identifying numbers; s. 56 makes alternative provisions to entry for registered exporters; s. 57 relates to the specification of certain goods; s. 58 relaxes the requirements of s. 57 where particulars of goods are recorded by computer; s. 59 makes restrictions on putting export goods alongside for loading; s. 60 makes additional restrictions as to certain goods; s. 61 sets out provisions as to stores; s. 62 gives the requirements as to information and documentation regarding export goods; s. 63 deals with entry outwards of exporting ships; s. 64 concerns the clearance outwards of ships and aircraft; s. 65 gives power to refuse or cancel clearance of ship or aircraft; s. 66 enables the Commissioners to make regulations as to exportation; s. 67 sets out offences in relation to exportation of goods; s. 68 deals with exporting prohibited or restricted goods.

Pt. VI (ss. 69–74) provides for control of coastwise traffic: s. 69 defines a coasting ship; s. 70 makes exceptional provisions for the coasting trade; s. 71 deals with the clearance of coasting ships and transire; s. 72 gives additional powers to officers in relation to coasting ships; s. 73 confers power to make regulations as to carriage of goods coastwise; s. 74 sets out offences in connection with carriage of goods coastwise.

Pt. VII (ss. 75–91) makes supplementary provisions as to customs and excise control; s. 75 relates to movement of explosives; s. 76 gives power to require pre-entry and clearance of goods; s. 77 makes further requirements as to information on goods; s. 78 deals with the customs and excise control of persons entering or leaving the U.K.; s. 79 confers power to require evidence in support of information; s. 80 relates to information and documents of goods evidenced under EEC law or practice; s. 81 gives power to regulate small craft to prevent smuggling; s. 82 confers power to haul up revenue vessels and patrol coasts; s. 83 states the penalty for removing seals or locks; s. 84 gives the penalty for signalling to smugglers; s. 85 states the penalty for interfering with revenue vessels; s. 86 makes special penalty provisions for armed or disguised offenders; s. 87 sets out the penalty for offering goods for sale as smuggled goods; s. 88 provides for the forfeiture of ship, aircraft or vehicle constructed for concealing goods; s. 89 concerns the forfeiture of a ship jettisoning or destroying cargo to prevent seizure;

s. 90 deals with forfeiture of ship or aircraft unable to account for missing cargo; s. 91 relates to ships failing to bring to.

Pt. VIII (ss. 92–100) makes provisions as to warehouses and pipe-lines: s. 92 gives Commissioners power to approve warehouses; s. 93 enables Commissioners to regulate warehouses and goods; s. 94 concerns deficiency in warehoused goods; s. 95 deals with deficiency in goods occurring during removal from warehouse without payment of duty; s. 96 relates to deficiency in certain goods moved by pipe-line; s. 97 restricts compensation for loss or damage to goods in warehouse or pipe-line; s. 98 sets out the procedure on warehouse ceasing to be approved; s. 99 makes provisions as to deposit in Queen's warehouse; s. 100 states general offences relating to warehouses and warehoused goods.

Pt. IX (ss. 101–118) provides for the control of excise licence trades and revenue traders; s. 101 deals with excise licences; s. 102 allows for payment of excise licences by cheque; s. 103 concerns renewal of excise licences; s. 104 regulates the transfer and removal of excise licence trades and licences; s. 105 permits certain sales without an excise licence; s. 106 specifies offences in connection with certain excise licences; s. 107 gives power to require persons carrying on excise licence trade to display sign; s. 108 concerns the making of entries; s. 109 relates to new or further entries of same premises; s. 110 sets out proof as to entries; s. 111 states offences in connection with entries; s. 112 gives officers power of entry upon premises of revenue traders; s. 113 enables officers to search for concealed pipes; s. 114 gives Commissioners power to prohibit use of certain substances in exciseable goods; s. 115 enables officers to keep a specimen on premises of revenue traders; s. 116 provides for payment of excise duty by revenue traders; s. 117 makes traders liable for execution and distress; s. 118 relates to the liability of ostensible owner or principal manager.

Pt. X (ss. 119–137) makes general provisions for duties and drawbacks; s. 119 allows the delivery of imported goods on giving security for duty; s. 120 empowers the Secretary of State to make regulations determining origin of goods; s. 121 gives power to impose restrictions where duty depends on certain matters other than use; s. 122 concerns regulations where customs duty depends on use; s. 123 provides for repayment of duty where goods returned or destroyed by importer; s. 124 concerns forfeiture for breach of certain conditions; s. 125 deals with valuation of goods for purpose of *ad valorem* duties; s. 126 imposes excise duty on manufactured or composite imported articles; s. 127 sets out the method of determining disputes as to duties on imported goods; s. 128 enables Commissioners to restrict delivery of goods; s. 129 gives power to remit duty on denatured goods; s. 130 provides for repayment of duty on goods lost or destroyed; s. 131 allows for enforcement of bond in respect of goods removed without payment of duty; s. 132 permits an extension of drawback; s. 133 makes general provisions as to claims for drawback; s. 134 deals with drawback and allowance on goods damaged or destroyed after shipment; s. 135 sets time limits on payment of drawback or allowance; s. 136 relates to offences in connection with claims for drawback; s. 137 provides for recovery and calculation of duties and drawbacks.

Pt. XI (ss. 138–156) makes provision for detention of persons, forfeiture and legal proceedings: s. 138 relates to detention; s. 139 concerns seizure and condemnation of goods; s. 140 provides for forfeiture of spirits; s. 141 deals with forfeiture of ships, etc., used in connection with goods liable to forfeiture; s. 142 makes special provision as to forfeiture of larger ships; s. 143 gives a penalty in lieu of forfeiture of larger ships where officer implicated in offence; s. 144 protects officers in relation to seizure and detention of goods; s. 145 deals with institution of proceedings; s. 146 is a service of process provision; s. 147 specifies the proceedings for offences; s. 148 determines the place of trial; s. 149 relates to non-payment of penalties and maximum terms of imprisonment; s. 150 makes incidental provisions as to legal proceedings; s. 151 provides for the application of penalties; s. 152 enables Commissioners to mitigate penalties; s. 153 sets out proof requirements for certain documents; s. 154 contains general provisions as to proof; s. 155 states the persons who may conduct proceedings; s. 156 is a saving provision for outlying enactments.

Pt. XII (ss. 157–178) contains general and miscellaneous provisions: s. 157 relates to bonds and security; s. 158 gives power to require provision of facilities; s. 159 enables officers to examine and take account of goods; s. 160 gives power to take samples; s. 161 empowers officers to search premises; s. 162 gives power to enter land in connection with access to pipe-lines; s. 163 enables officers to search vehicles or vessels; s. 164 gives power to search persons; s. 165 gives power to pay rewards; s. 166 deals with agents; s. 167 relates to untrue declarations; s. 168 concerns counterfeiting documents; s. 169 deals with false scales, etc.; s. 170 states the penalty for fraudulent evasion of duty; s. 171 contains general provisions as to offences and penalties; s. 172 concerns the making of regulations; s. 173 relates to the giving of directions; s. 174 deals with removal of goods to and from the Isle of Man; s. 175 has special provisions for Scotland; s. 176 concerns game licences; s. 177 contains consequential amendments, repeals and saving and transitional provisions; s. 178 deals with citation and commencement.

The Act received the Royal Assent on February 22, 1979, and came into force on April 1, 1979.

Parliamentary Debates

Hansard, H.L. Vol. 397, cols. 555, 1170; Vol. 398, col. 831.

Table of Derivations

Customs and Excise Act 1952

1952	1979
s. 1	s. 6
2 (1)	175 (2)
(2) (3)	7
3 (1)	6
4	8
5	11
6	12
7	13
8	14
9	15
10	16
11	17
12	18
13	19
14	20
15 (1)–(5)	21
(6)	4
16	22
17	25
18	26
19	27
20	28
21	29
22	30
23	32
24	33
25	34
26	35
27	36
28	37
29	38
30	39
31	40
32	41
33	42
34 (1)–(3)	43 (1) (3)
(4)	43 (5)
38	46
39	47
40	48
44	49
45	50
46	51
47 (1)	53 (1)
(1), proviso	53 (3)
(3)	53 (4) (5)
(4)	53 (8)
(5)	52
48 (1)	60 (1) (3)
s. 48 (2) (3)	s. 60 (5)–(7)
49 (1)	57 (1)–(3)
(2) (3)	57 (9) (10)
(4)	57 (7)
(5)	57 (5)
50 (1) (2)	61 (1)–(3)
(3)–(5)	61 (5) (8)
51	63
52	64
53	65
54	66
55	67
56	68
57	69
58	70
59	71
60	72
61	73
62	74
63	75
64	76
65	77
67	79 (1)
68	81
69	82
71	84
72	85
73	86
74	87
75	88
76	89
77	90
78	91
79	5 (1)–(5) (8)
80 (1)	92 (1)–(4)
(2)–(5)	92 (5)–(8)
82 (3)	97
85 (1) (2)	94
(3)	95
90	98
91	99
92	100
233	101
234	102
235	103
237	104
238	105
239	106
240	107
s. 244	s. 108
245	109
246	110
247	111
248 (1)	112 (1) (2)
(2)	112 (3) (4)
249	113
250	114
251	115
252	116
253 (1)	117 (1) (2) (8)
(2)	117 (3) (4)
(3)	117 (5) (6)
(4)	117 (7)
254	118
255	119
256	123
257	124
258 (3) (4)	125 (3) (4)
259 (1)	126 (1) (2) (4)
(3)	126 (5)
260	127
261	128
262	129
263 (1) (2)	130
264	131
266	132
267	133
268	134
270	135
271	136
273	137
274	138
275	139
276	140
277	141
278	142
279	143
280	144
281	145
282	146
283 (1)	147
(2)	ss. 12, 14, 15, 20–23, 24 (5) (6), 25–27, 30–36,

Customs and Excise Act 1952—*continued*

1952	1979
s. 283 (2) ..	ss. 41, 50, 53 (4)–(7), 54 (7)–(10), 56 (4), 57 (9)–(12), 59 (6), 60 (4)–(7), 61 (5)–(8), 62 (4), 63–68, 70–77, 78 (2)–(4), 80, 83–85, 87, 91, 92 (5)–(8), 93, 94, 96, 100–102, 106–108, 111, 114, 115, 125 (3) (4), 129, 133, 136, 139, 141, 156 (3), 158, 159, 163, 167–170
(3) (4)	s. 147
(5) ...	ss. 12, 14, 15, 20–23, 24 (5) (6), 25–27, 30–36,
s. 283 (5) ..	ss. 41, 50,53 (4)–(7), 54 (7)–(10), 56 (4),57 (9)–(12), 59 (6), 60 (4)–(7), 61 (5)–(8), 62 (4), 63–68, 70–77, 78 (2)–(4), 80, 83–85, 87, 91, 92 (5)–(8), 93, 94, 96, 100–102, 106–108, 111, 114, 115, 125 (3) (4), 129, 133, 136, 139, 141, 156 (4), 158, 159, 163, 167–170
proviso	Sch. 1
284	s. 148
285 (1) ...	149 (2)
(2) ...	149 (1)
(3) ...	149 (3)
286	150
287	151
288	152
289	153
290	154
291	155
s. 292	s. 157
293	158
294	159
295	160
296	161
297	163
298	164
299	165
300	166
301	167
302	168
303	169
304	170
305	171 (1) (3)–(5)
306	172
307 (1) ...	1 (1)
(2) ...	1 (6)
308 (3) ...	Sch. 7, para. 3
309 (1) (2) (5)	s. 174
313	176 (1)–(3) (6)
315 (*a*) (*b*)	175 (1)
(*e*) ...	117 (9)
(*f*) (*g*)	175 (1)
318 (1) ...	Sch. 4, para. 1
Sch. 7	Sch. 3
Sch. 10, Pt. I	Sch. 4, para. 1
Pt. II	Sch. 4, para. 12

Finance Act 1953

1953	1979
s. 33 (1)	s. 156 (2)

Copyright Act 1956

1956	1979
Sch. 7, para. 44 (*a*) .	s. 174

Finance Act 1957

1957	1979
s. 5	s. 126 (3)
Sch. 2	Sch. 2

County Courts Act (Northern Ireland) 1959

1959	1979
s. 152 (3) (*a*) .	s. 147, Sch. 3

Finance Act 1961

1961	1979
s. 11	s. 176 (4)–(6)

Recorded Delivery Service Act 1962

1962	1979
s. 1	s. 102

Pipe-lines Act 1962

1962	1979
s. 56 (1)	s. 162
70 (2)	162

Finance Act 1963

1963	1979
s. 7 (1) (2) ...	s. 1 (5)
(4)	112 (5)

Finance Act 1964

1964	1979
s. 10 (1)	s. 1 (4)

Finance Act 1966

1966	1979
s. 10 (1) ...	s. 2
(3) ...	23
(4) (*a*) .	2
(*b*) .	164
(*c*) .	23
(5) (6) .	2
(7) ...	60 (2)
(*a*) .	60 (4)
(*b*) .	60 (3)
s. 10 (7) (*a*) .	s. 1 (1)
11 (1) ...	24 (1) (2)
(2) ...	1 (1), 3, 37
(3) ...	5 (6) (7)
(4) ...	3
(5) ...	57 (6)
(6) ...	24 (3) (4)
(7) ...	24 (5 (6)
s. 11 (8) ...	s. 96
(9) ...	97
(10) ..	ss. 1 (1), 24 (2)
(11) ..	s. 24 (7)
Sch. 2, para. 1 ...	ss. 60 (2), 61 (4), 81, 141–143

Finance Act 1967

1967	1979
s. 3	s. 10
Sch. 6, para. 5 .	112 (5)
para. 7 .	117 (6)

Criminal Justice Act 1967

1967	1979
s. 12 (5) (*a*) .	s. 85
93 (4)	149 (2)

Finance Act 1968

1968	1979
s. 6 (1)	s. 78 (1)
(2) (3) ..	78 (2)–(4)
(4)	79 (1)

Hovercraft Act 1968

1968	1979
Sch., para. 4 ..	s. 1 (1)

Age of Majority (Northern Ireland) Act 1969

1969	1979
s. 1	ss. 108, 118, 157
Sch. 1, Pt. I.	s. 108

Age of Majority (Scotland) Act 1969

1969	1979
s. 1	ss. 108, 118, 157
Sch. 1, Pt. I .	s. 108

Family Law Reform Act 1969

1969	1979
s. 1	ss. 108, 118, 157
Sch. 1, Pt. I .	s. 108

Finance Act 1970

1970	1979
s. 7 (5)	s. 137
Sch. 2, para. 5 (1) .	44
Sch. 2, para. 5 (2) (*a*) .	43 (4)
Sch. 2, para. 5 (3) (4) .	58

Hydrocarbon Oil (Customs and Excise) Act 1971

1971	1979
s. 22	ss. 112 (6), 113

Courts Act 1971

1971	1979
Sch. 9	s. 147, Sch. 3

Misuse of Drugs Act 1971

1971	1979
s. 26 (1)–(3)	ss. 50, 68, 170, Sch. 1

Finance Act 1971

1971	1979
Sch. 1	
para.	
1 (2)–(6)	s. 54 (1)–(5)
para. 1 (7)	52
para. 2 ...	53 (2)
para. 3 ...	55 (1)
para. 4 ...	56 (1) (2)
para. 5 (1)	57 (1)–(3)
para. 5 (2)	57 (4)
para. 5 (3)	57 (8)
para. 5 (4) (*a*)	57 (1)–(3)
para. 5 (4) (*b*) (*c*)	57 (9) (10)
Sch. 1,	
para. 5 (5)	s. 57 (6)
para. 6 ...	59 (1) (2)
paras. 7, 8	62 (1) (2)
para. 9 ...	66
para. 11 (1) (2)	54 (7)–(10)
para. 11 (3)	ss. 53 (6), 54 (7)–(10), 57 (11) (12)
para. 11 (4)	s. 56 (4)
Sch. 1,	
para. 11 (5)	ss. 53 (7), 54 (7)–(10), 57 (11) (12), 59 (6), 62 (4)
para. 12 (1)	s. 59 (3)
para. 13 ..	ss. 53 (3), 54 (6), 55 (2), 56 (3), 57 (8), 59 (5), 62 (3)
para. 14 (2)	s. 59 (4)
para. 15 ..	ss. 53 (2), 59 (7), 62 (2)

Betting and Gaming Duties Act 1972

1972	1979
Sch. 2, para. 7 .	s. 102
Sch. 4, para. 10 .	102

Finance Act 1972

1972	1979
s. 55 (4)	s. 78 (1)

European Communities Act 1972

1972	1979
s. 5 (4)	s. 1 (7), Sch. 7, para. 5
(7)	9
(8)	80
Sch. 4, para. 2 (3) .	79 (2)
para. 2 (7) .	121
para. 2 (8) .	125 (1), (2), Sch. 7, para. 1

Northern Ireland Constitution Act 1973

1973	1979
Sch. 5, para. 1 .	s. 1 (1)

Finance Act 1973

1973	1979
s. 2	s. 120
2 (4)	172

Finance Act 1975

1975	1979
s. 4	Sch. 4, para. 12

Criminal Procedure (Scotland) Act 1975

1975	1979
s. 193 A	ss. 13, 16, 24 (5) (6), 50, 53 (4) (5), 63, 64, 68, 100, 129, 159, 167, 168, 170
289 B (1)	ss. 13, 16, 24 (5) (6), 50, 53 (4) (5), 63, 64, 68, 100, 129, 159, 167, 168, 170, Sch. 1
B (6)	s. 171 (2)
289 C (5)	ss. 12, 27, 30, 41, 60 (5)–(7), 61 (5)–(8), 64, 70–72, 85, 91, 101, 139

Finance (No. 2) Act 1975

1975	1979
s. 8 (4)	s. 7
16 (1)–(5)	93
(7) (8)	93
Sch. 3, para. 1 (1)	ss. 49, 51, 79 (2), 92 (1)–(4), 119–121, 123, 126 (4), 127, Sch. 4, paras. 3, 4, 6, 7, 12, Sch. 7, paras. 4, 8
Sch. 3, para. 1 (2)	ss. 114, 117 paras. 5, (5) (8), Sch. 4, paras. 5, 12
Sch. 3, para. 23	Sch. 4, para. 11
Sch. 6, para. 1	s. 43 (2)
para. 2	46
para. 3	92 (1)–(4)
para. 4	100
Sch. 14, Pt. I, para. 2	Sch. 7, para. 6

Finance Act 1976

1976	1979
s. 15 (1) (2)	s. 45
Sch. 3, para. 2	112 (3)
para. 3	113
para. 4	117 (6)
para. 6	160

Finance Act 1977

1977	1979
s. 8 (1) (2)	s. 122
(3)	121
9	124
Sch. 6, para. 21	Sch. 4, para. 9

Criminal Law Act 1977

1977	1979
s. 27	ss. 24 (5) (6), 50, 53 (4) (5), 63, 64, 68, 84, 100, 129, 159, 167, 168, 170, Sch. 1
28 (2)	13, 16, 24 (5), (6), 50, 53 (4) (5), 63, 64,
s. 28 (2)	ss. 68, 100, 129, 159, 167, 168, 170, Sch. 1
(7)	s. 171 (2)
31 (6)	ss. 12, 27, 30, 41, 60 (5)–(7), 61 (5)–(8), 64, 70–72, 85, 91, 101, 139
s. 32 (1)	ss. 13, 16, 24 (5) (6), 50, 53 (4) (5), 63, 64, 68, 100, 129, 159, 167, 168, 170
Sch. 5, para. 1 (1) (*a*)	Sch. 1
(2) (*c*)	Sch. 1
(3)	Sch. 1

FINANCE ACT 1978

1978	1979
s. 3	s. 93
4	31
5	83
Sch. 12, para. 7 (1) .	ss. 1 (5), 112 (5)
para. 11 ...	s. 92 (1)–(4)
para. 12 ...	94
para. 13 ...	126 (1) (2)
para. 13 (*a*)	126 (3)
para. 13 (*b*)	Sch. 2
para. 14 ...	s. 130
para. 16 ...	149 (1)
para. 17 ...	151
para. 18 ...	173
para. 19 (1)	1 (1)
para. 19 (2)	ss. 51, 61 (1)–(3), 21, 92 (1)–(4) 93, 117 (1) (2), 171 (1) (3)–(5)
Sch. 12, para. 19 (3)	ss. 108–111, 112 (1)
para. 19 (4)	s. 43 (1)(5)
para. 19 (5)	ss. 5 (1)–(5) (8), 86
para. 19 (6)	101, 104, 107, 112 (1) (6), 113, 115, 116, 117 (1) (2) (5), 140, 158, 160, Sch. 4, para. 12, Sch. 7, para. 9
para. 19 (7) (*a*) .	24 (2), 25, 30
para. 19 (7) (*b*) .	s. 34
Sch. 12, para. 19 (7) (*c*) .	s. 159
para. 19 (8)	ss. 5 (1)–(5) (8), 21–23, 26–28, 30, 34, 35, 42, 50, 53 (1), 60 (5)–(7), 61 (5)–(8), 64, 65, 67, 164, Sch. 4, para. 12, Sch. 7, para. 9
para. 21 ..	Sch. 4, para. 12
para. 22 ..	Sch. 4, para. 12
para. 23 ..	s. 124
para. 24 ..	Sch. 1

CUSTOMS AND EXCISE (ENTRY FOR INWARD PROCESSING) REGULATIONS 1977
(S.I. 1977 No. 1091)

1977	1979
Regs. 1–2 ...	s. 37

AMENDMENTS OF UNITS OF MEASUREMENT (NAUTICAL MILE) ORDER 1977
(S.I. 1977 No. 1936)

1977	1979
Arts. 1–4 ...	s. 1 (1)

CUSTOMS AND EXCISE (COMMUNITY TRANSIT GOODS) REGULATIONS
(S.I. 1978 No. 1602)

1978	1979
Regs. 1–3 ...	ss. 1 (1), 37, 53 (1), 57 (1)–(3)

CUSTOMS AND EXCISE (WAREHOUSE) REGULATIONS 1978 (S.I. 1978 No. 1603)

1978	1979
Regs. 1–4 ...	ss. 1 (1), 52, 92–94, 98

LAW COMMISSIONS' REPORT (CMND. 7418)

Recommendation No.	1979
1	s. 81
2	117 (8)
3	127
4	Sch. 4, para. 12

PART I

PRELIMINARY

Interpretation

1.—(1) In this Act, unless the context otherwise requires—

"aerodrome" means any area of land or water designed, equipped, set apart or commonly used for affording facilities for landing and departure of aircraft;

"approved route" has the meaning given by section 26 below;

"approved wharf" has the meaning given by section 20 below;

" armed forces " means the Royal Navy, the Royal Marines, the regular army and the regular air force, and any reserve or auxiliary force of any of those services which has been called out on permanent service, or called into actual service, or embodied;

" assigned matter " means any matter in relation to which the Commissioners are for the time being required in pursuance of any enactment to perform any duties;

" boarding station " means a boarding station for the time being appointed under section 19 below;

" boundary " means the land boundary of Northern Ireland;

" British ship " means a British ship within the meaning of the Merchant Shipping Act 1894, so, however, as not to include a ship registered in any country other than the United Kingdom, the Channel Islands, the Isle of Man or a colony within the meaning of the British Nationality Act 1948;

" claimant ", in relation to proceedings for the condemnation of any thing as being forfeited, means a person claiming that the thing is not liable to forfeiture;

" coasting ship " has the meaning given by section 69 below;

" commander ", in relation to an aircraft, includes any person having or taking the charge or command of the aircraft;

" the Commissioners " means the Commissioners of Customs and Excise;

" Community transit goods "—

(*a*) in relation to imported goods, means—

(i) goods which have been imported under the internal or external Community transit procedure for transit through the United Kingdom with a view to exportation where the importation was and the transit and exportation are to be part of one Community transit operation; or

(ii) goods which have, at the port or airport at which they were imported, been placed under the internal or external Community transit procedure for transit through the United Kingdom with a view to exportation where the transit and exportation are to be part of one Community transit operation;

(*b*) in relation to goods for exportation, means—

(i) goods which have been imported as mentioned in paragraph (*a*) (i) of this definition and are to be exported as part of the Community transit operation in the course of which they were imported; or

(iii) goods which have, under the internal or external Community transit procedure, transited the United Kingdom from the port or airport at which they were imported and are to be exported as part of the Community transit operation which commenced at that port or airport;

" container " includes any bundle or package and any box, cask or other receptacle whatsoever;

" the customs and excise Acts " means the Customs and Excise Acts 1979 and any other enactment for the time being in force relating to customs or excise;

" the Customs and Excise Acts 1979 " means—

this Act,

the Customs and Excise Duties (General Reliefs) Act 1979,
the Alcoholic Liquor Duties Act 1979,
the Hydrocarbon Oil Duties Act 1979,
the Matches and Mechanical Lighters Duties Act 1979, and
the Tobacco Products Duty Act 1979;

" customs warehouse " means a place of security approved by the Commissioners under subsection (2) (whether or not it is also approved under subsection (1)) of section 92 below;

" customs and excise airport " has the meaning given by section 21 (7) below;

" customs and excise station " has the meaning given by section 26 below;

" drawback goods " means goods in the case of which a claim for drawback has been or is to be made;

" dutiable goods ", except in the expression " dutiable or restricted goods ", means goods of a class or description subject to any duty of customs or excise, whether or not those goods are in fact chargeable with that duty, and whether or not that duty has been paid thereon;

" dutiable or restricted goods " has the meaning given by section 52 below;

" examination station " has the meaning given by section 22 below;

" excise licence trade " means, subject to subsection (5) below, a trade or business for the carrying on of which an excise licence is required;

" excise warehouse " means a place of security approved by the Commissioners under subsection (1) (whether or not it is also approved under subsection (2)) of section 92 below, and, except in that section, also includes a distiller's warehouse;

" exporter ", in relation to goods for exportation or for use as stores, includes the shipper of the goods and any person performing in relation to an aircraft functions corresponding with those of a shipper;

" goods " includes stores and baggage;

" holiday ", in relation to any part of the United Kingdom, means any day that is a bank holiday in that part of the United Kingdom under the Banking and Financial Dealings Act 1971, Christmas Day, Good Friday and the day appointed for the purposes of customs and excise for the celebration of Her Majesty's birthday;

" hovercraft " means a hovercraft within the meaning of the Hovercraft Act 1968;

" importer ", in relation to any goods at any time between their importation and the time when they are delivered out of charge, includes any owner or other person for the time being possessed of or beneficially interested in the goods and, in relation to goods imported by means of a pipe-line, includes the owner of the pipe-line;

" justice " and " justice of the peace " in Scotland includes a sheriff and in Northern Ireland, in relation to any powers and duties which can under any enactment for the time being in force be exercised and performed only by a resident magistrate, means a resident magistrate;

" land " and " landing ", in relation to aircraft, include alighting on water;

" law officer of the Crown " means the Attorney General or in Northern Ireland the Attorney General for Northern Ireland;

" licence year ", in relation to an excise licence issuable annually, means the period of 12 months ending on the date on which that licence expires in any year;

" master ", in relation to a ship, includes any person having or taking the charge or command of the ship;

" nautical mile " means a distance of 1,852 metres;

" night " means the period between 11 p.m. and 5 a.m.;

" occupier ", in relation to any bonded premises, means the person who has given security to the Crown in respect of those premises;

" officer " means, subject to section 8 (2) below, a person commissioned by the Commissioners;

" owner ", in relation to an aircraft, includes the operator of the aircraft;

" owner ", in relation to a pipe-line, means (except in the case of a pipe-line vested in the Crown which in pursuance of arrangements in that behalf is operated by another) the person in whom the line is vested and, in the said excepted case, means the person operating the line;

" perfect entry " means an entry made in accordance with section 37 below or warehousing regulations, as the case may require;

" pipe-line " has the meaning given by section 65 of the Pipe-lines Act 1962 (that Act being taken, for the purposes of this definition, to extend to Northern Ireland);

" port " means a port appointed by the Commissioners under section 19 below;

" prescribed area " means such an area in Northern Ireland adjoining the boundary as the Commissioners may by regulations prescribe;

" prescribed sum ", in relation to the penalty provided for an offence, has the meaning given by section 171 (2) below;

" prohibited or restricted goods " means goods of a class or description of which the importation, exportation or carriage coastwise is for the time being prohibited or restricted under or by virtue of any enactment;

" proper ", in relation to the person by, with or to whom, or the place at which, anything is to be done, means the person or place appointed or authorised in that behalf by the Commissioners;

" proprietor ", in relation to any goods, includes any owner, importer, exporter, shipping or other person for the time being possessed of or beneficially interested in those goods;

" Queen's warehouse " means any place provided by the Crown or appointed by the Commissioners for the deposit of goods for security thereof and of the duties chargeable thereon;

" the revenue trade provisions of the customs and excise Acts " means—

(*a*) the provisions of the customs and excise Acts relating to the protection, security, collection or management of the revenues derived from the duties of excise on goods produced or manufactured in the United Kingdom;

(*b*) the provisions of the customs and excise Acts relating to any activity or facility for the carrying on or provision of which an excise licence is required; and (*c*) the provisions of the Betting and Gaming Duties Act 1972 (so far as not included in paragraph (*b*) above);

" revenue trader " means any person carrying on a trade or business subject to any of the revenue trade provisions of the customs and excise Acts, whether or not that trade or business is an excise licence trade, and includes a registered club;

" ship " and " vessel " include any boat or other vessel whatsoever (and, to the extent provided in section 2 below, any hovercraft);

" shipment " includes loading into an aircraft, and " shipped " and cognate expressions shall be construed accordingly;

" stores " means, subject to subsection (4) below, goods for use in a ship or aircraft and includes fuel and spare parts and other articles of equipment, whether or not for immediate fitting;

" tons register " means the tons of a ship's net tonnage as ascertained and registered according to the tonnage regulations of the Merchant Shipping Act 1894 or, in the case of a ship which is not registered under that Act, ascertained in like manner as if it were to be so registered;

" transit goods ", except in the expression " Community transit goods ", means imported goods entered on importation for transit or transhipment;

" transit or transhipment ", in relation to the entry of goods, means transit through the United Kingdom or transhipment with a view to the re-exportation of the goods in question;

" transit shed " has the meaning given by section 25 below;

" vehicle " includes a railway vehicle;

" warehouse ", except in the expressions " Queen's warehouse " and " distiller's warehouse ", means a place of security approved by the Commissioners under subsection (1) or (2) or subsections (1) and (2) of section 92 below and, except in that section, also includes a distiller's warehouse; and " warehoused " and cognate expressions shall, subject to subsection (4) of that section, be construed accordingly;

" warehousing regulations " means regulations under section 93 below.

(2) This Act and the other Acts included in the Customs and Excise Acts 1979 shall be construed as one Act but where a provision of this Act refers to this Act that reference is not to be construed as including a reference to any of the others.

(3) Any expression used in this Act or in any instrument made under this Act to which a meaning is given by any other Act included in the Customs and Excise Acts 1979 has, except where the context otherwise requires, the same meaning in this Act or any such instrument as in that Act; and for ease of reference the Table below indicates the expressions used in this Act to which a meaning is given by any other such Act—

Alcoholic Liquor Duties Act 1979

" beer "
" brewer " and " brewer for sale "
" cider "
" compounder "
" distiller "
" distiller's warehouse "
" dutiable alcoholic liquor "

" licensed ", in relation to producers of wine or made-wine
" made-wine "
" producer of made-wine "
" producer of wine "
" proof "
" rectifier "
" registered club "
" spirits "
" wine "

Hydrocarbon Oil Duties Act 1979

" rebate "
" refinery "

Tobacco Products Duty Act 1979

" tobacco products "

(4) Subject to section 12 of the Customs and Excise Duties (General Reliefs) Act 1979 (by which goods for use in naval ships or establishments may be required to be treated as exported), any goods for use in a ship or aircraft as merchandise for sale by retail to persons carried therein shall be treated for the purposes of the customs and excise Acts as stores, and any reference in those Acts to the consumption of stores shall, in relation to goods so treated, be construed as referring to the sale thereof as aforesaid.

(5) A person who deals in or sells tobacco products in the course of a trade or business carried on by him shall be deemed for the purposes of this Act to be carrying on an excise licence trade (and to be a revenue trader) notwithstanding that no excise licence is required for carrying on that trade or business.

(6) In computing for the purposes of this Act any period expressed therein as a period of clear days no account shall be taken of the day of the event from which the period is computed or of any Sunday or holiday.

(7) The provisions of this Act in so far as they relate to customs duties apply, notwithstanding that any duties are imposed for the benefit of the Communities, as if the revenue from duties so imposed remained part of the revenues of the Crown.

Application to hovercraft

2.—(1) This Part, Parts III to VII and Parts X to XII of this Act shall apply as if references to ships or vessels included references to hovercraft, and the said Parts III to VII shall apply in relation to an approved wharf or transit shed which is not in a port as if it were in a port.

(2) All other provisions of the customs and excise Acts shall apply as if references (however expressed) to goods or passengers carried in or moved by ships or vessels included references to goods or passengers carried in or moved by hovercraft.

(3) In all the provisions of the customs and excise Acts " landed ", " loaded ", " master ", " shipped ", " shipped as stores ", " transhipment ", " voyage ", " waterborne " and cognate expressions shall be construed in accordance with subsections (1) and (2) above.

(4) References in the customs and excise Acts to goods imported or exported by land, or conveyed into or out of Northern Ireland by land, include references to goods imported, exported or conveyed across any

part of the boundary of Northern Ireland; and it is hereby declared that in those Acts references to vehicles include references to hovercraft proceeding over land or water or partly over land and partly over water.

(5) Any power of making regulations or other instruments relating to the importation or exportation of goods conferred by the customs and excise Acts may be exercised so as to make provision for the importation or exportation of goods by hovercraft which is different from the provision made for the importation or exportation of goods by other means.

Application to pipe-lines

3.—(1) In the customs and excise Acts " shipping " and " loading " and cognate expressions, where used in relation to importation or exportation, include, in relation to importation or exportation by means of a pipe-line, the conveyance of goods by means of the pipe-line and the charging and discharging of goods into and from the pipe-line, but subject to any necessary modifications.

(2) In the customs and excise Acts " importer ", in relation to goods imported by means of a pipe-line, includes the owner of the pipe-line.

(3) Any power of making regulations or other instruments relating to the importation or exportation of goods conferred by the customs and excise Acts may be exercised so as to make provision for the importation or exportation of goods by means of a pipe-line which is different from the provision made for the importation or exportation of goods by other means.

Application to certain Crown aircraft

4.—(1) The provisions of the Customs and Excise Acts 1979 relating to aircraft shall apply in relation to any aircraft belonging to or employed in the service of Her Majesty other than a military aircraft.

(2) In this section " military aircraft " includes naval and air force aircraft and any aircraft commanded by a person in naval, military or air force service detailed for the purpose of such command.

Time of importation, exportation, etc.

5.—(1) The provisions of this section shall have effect for the purposes of the customs and excise Acts.

(2) Subject to subsections (3) and (6) below, the time of importation of any goods shall be deemed to be—

(*a*) where the goods are brought by sea, the time when the ship carrying them comes within the limits of a port;

(*b*) where the goods are brought by air, the time when the aircraft carrying them lands in the United Kingdom or the time when the goods are unloaded in the United Kingdom, whichever is the earlier;

(*c*) where the goods are brought by land, the time when the goods are brought across the boundary into Northern Ireland.

(3) In the case of goods brought by sea of which entry is not required under section 37 below, the time of importation shall be deemed to be the time when the ship carrying them came within the limits of the port at which the goods are discharged.

(4) Subject to subsections (5) and (7) below, the time of exportation of any goods from the United Kingdom shall be deemed to be—

(*a*) where the goods are exported by sea or air, the time when the goods are shipped for exportation;

(*b*) where the goods are exported by land, the time when they are cleared by the proper officer at the last customs and excise station on their way to the boundary.

(5) In the case of goods of a class or description with respect to the exportation of which any prohibition or restriction is for the time being in force under or by virtue of any enactment which are exported by sea or air, the time of exportation shall be deemed to be the time when the exporting ship or aircraft departs from the last port or customs and excise airport at which it is cleared before departing for a destination outside the United Kingdom.

(6) Goods imported by means of a pipe-line shall be treated as imported at the time when they are brought within the limits of a port or brought across the boundary into Northern Ireland.

(7) Goods exported by means of a pipe-line shall be treated as exported at the time when they are charged into that pipe-line for exportation.

(8) A ship shall be deemed to have arrived at or departed from a port at the time when the ship comes within or, as the case may be, leaves the limits of that port.

PART II

ADMINISTRATION

Appointment and duties of Commissioners, officers, etc.

Appointment and general duties of Commissioners, etc.

6.—(1) Her Majesty may from time to time, under the Great Seal of the United Kingdom, appoint persons to be Commissioners of Customs and Excise, and any person so appointed shall hold office during Her Majesty's pleasure and may be paid such remuneration and allowances as the Minister for the Civil Service may determine.

(2) In addition to the duties conferred on them by or under any other enactment, the Commissioners shall, subject to the general control of the Treasury, be charged with the duty of collecting and accounting for, and otherwise managing, the revenues of customs and excise.

(3) The Commissioners may commission such officers and appoint or authorise such other persons to discharge any duties in relation to any assigned matter on such terms and conditions, and may pay to them such remuneration and allowances, as the Commissioners may with the sanction of the Minister for the Civil Service determine.

(4) The Commissioners may at their pleasure suspend, reduce, discharge or restore any officer or person so commissioned, appointed or authorised.

(5) The days on which and the hours between which offices of customs and excise are to be open or officers are to be available for the performance of particular duties shall be such as the Commissioners may direct.

Privileges of Commissioners, etc.

7.—(1) Save as expressly provided by or under any enactment, no sum granted by way of remuneration or superannuation allowance to any person as being or having been a Commissioner, officer or person appointed by the Commissioners to discharge any duty relating to customs or excise shall before payment thereof to or for the use of that person be capable of assignment or be liable to be taken under or by virtue of any legal process.

(2) The benefits and advantages arising from membership of the Customs Annuity and Benevolent Fund shall be available to and in respect of the Commissioners, all officers and all persons appointed by the Commissioners to discharge any duty relating to any assigned matter.

Exercise of powers and performance of duties

8.—(1) Any act or thing required or authorised by or under any enactment to be done by the Commissioners or any of them may be done—

(*a*) by any one or more of the Commissioners; or

(*b*) if the Commissioners so authorise, by a secretary or assistant secretary to the Commissioners; or

(*c*) by any other person authorised generally or specially in that behalf in writing by the Commissioners.

(2) Any person, whether an officer or not, engaged by the orders or with the concurrence of the Commissioners (whether previously or subsequently expressed) in the performance of any act or duty relating to an assigned matter which is by law required or authorised to be performed by or with an officer, shall be deemed to be the proper officer by or with whom that act or duty is to be performed.

(3) Any person deemed by virtue of subsection (2) above to be the proper officer shall have all the powers of an officer in relation to the act or duty performed or to be performed by him as mentioned in that subsection.

General duties of Commissioners in relation to customs matters concerning the European Communities

9. For the purpose of implementing Community obligations the Commissioners shall co-operate with other customs services on matters of mutual concern, and (without prejudice to the foregoing) may for that purpose—

(*a*) give effect, in accordance with such arrangements as they may direct or by regulations prescribe, to any Community requirement or practice as to the movement of goods between countries, including any rules requiring payment to be made in connection with the exportation of goods to compensate for any relief from customs duty allowed or to be allowed (and may recover any such payment as if it were an amount of customs duty unpaid); and

(*b*) give effect to any reciprocal arrangements made between member States (with or without other countries or territories) for securing, by the exchange of information or otherwise, the due administration of their customs laws and the prevention or detection of fraud or evasion.

Disclosure by Commissioners of certain information as to imported goods

10.—(1) On being notified at any time by the Treasury that they are satisfied that it is in the national interest that the information in question should be disclosed to persons other than the Commissioners, the Commissioners may disclose through such person as may be specified in the notification such information to which this section applies, in respect of imported goods of such descriptions, as may be so specified.

(2) The information to which this section applies is information

contained in any document with which the Commissioners have been provided in pursuance of the Customs and Excise Acts 1979 for the purpose of making entry of any goods on their importation, being information of the following descriptions only, namely—

(*a*) the description of the goods, including any maker's catalogue number;

(*b*) the quantities of the goods imported in a particular period, so, however, that if any quantity is given by value it shall not also be given in any other form;

(*c*) the name of the maker of the goods;

(*d*) the country of origin of the goods;

(*e*) the country from which the goods were consigned.

(3) Without prejudice to paragraph 10 of Schedule 7 to this Act, this section also applies to information of any of those descriptions contained in any document with which the Commissioners have been provided for that purpose after 7th March 1967 in pursuance of the Customs and Excise Act 1952.

(4) The Treasury may by order add to the descriptions of information to which this section applies any further description of information contained in any document such as is mentioned in subsection (2) or (3) above other than the price of the goods or the name of the importer of the goods.

(5) The power to make orders under subsection (4) above shall be exercisable by statutory instrument subject to annulment in pursuance of a resolution of either House of Parliament.

Assistance to be rendered by police, etc.

11. It shall be the duty of every constable and every member of Her Majesty's armed forces or coastguard to assist in the enforcement of the law relating to any assigned matter.

Power to hold inquiries

12.—(1) The Commissioners may hold or cause to be held such inquiries as they consider necessary or desirable for the purposes of any assigned matter, including inquiries into the conduct of any officer or of any person appointed by them.

(2) The person holding any such inquiry—

(*a*) may require any person, subject to the tender of the reasonable expenses of his attendance, to attend as a witness and give evidence or to produce any document in his possession or control which relates to any matter in question at the inquiry and is such as would be subject to production in a court of law; and

(*b*) may require evidence to be given on oath, and for that purpose shall have power to administer oaths.

(3) If any person fails without reasonable excuse to comply with any such requirement as aforesaid, he shall be liable on summary conviction to a penalty of £25.

(4) Subject to the foregoing provisions of this section, the procedure and conduct of any inquiry under this section shall be such as the Commissioners may direct.

Offences in connection with Commissioners, officers, etc.

Unlawful assumption of character of officer, etc.

13. If, for the purpose of obtaining admission to any house or other place, or of doing or procuring to be done any act which he would not be entitled to do or procure to be done of his own authority, or for any other unlawful purpose, any person falsely assumes the name, designation or character of a Commissioner or officer or of a person appointed by the Commissioners he may be detained and shall, in addition to any other punishment to which he may have rendered himself liable, be liable—

(*a*) on summary conviction, to a penalty of the prescribed sum, or to imprisonment for a term not exceeding 3 months, or to both; or

(*b*) on conviction on indictment, to a penalty of any amount, or to imprisonment for a term not exceeding 2 years, or to both.

Failure to surrender commission, etc.

14.—(1) If any person to whom a commission or other written authority has been issued by the Commissioners is required by the Commissioners to deliver up or account to their satisfaction for that commission or authority and fails to comply within such period as may be specified in the requirement, he shall be liable on summary conviction to a penalty of £20.

(2) If the failure continues after he is convicted thereof he shall be guilty of a further offence and be liable on summary conviction to a penalty of £5 for every day on which the failure has so continued.

Bribery and collusion

15.—(1) If any Commissioner or officer or any person appointed or authorised by the Commissioners to discharge any duty relating to an assigned matter—

(*a*) directly or indirectly asks for or takes in connection with any of his duties any payment or other reward whatsoever, whether pecuniary or other, or any promise or security for any such payment or reward, not being a payment or reward which he is lawfully entitled to claim or receive; or

(*b*) enters into or acquiesces in any agreement to do, abstain from doing, permit, conceal or connive at any act or thing whereby Her Majesty is or may be defrauded or which is otherwise unlawful, being an act or thing relating to an assigned matter,

he shall be guilty of an offence under this section.

(2) If any person—

(*a*) directly or indirectly offers or gives to any Commissioner or officer or to any person appointed or authorised by the Commissioners as aforesaid any payment or other reward whatsoever, whether pecuniary or other, or any promise or security for any such payment or reward; or

(*b*) proposes or enters into any agreement with any Commissioner, officer or person appointed or authorised as aforesaid,

in order to induce him to do, abstain from doing, permit, conceal or connive at any act or thing whereby Her Majesty is or may be defrauded or which is otherwise unlawful, being an act or thing relating to an assigned matter, or otherwise to take any course contrary to his duty, he shall be guilty of an offence under this section.

(3) Any person committing an offence under this section shall be liable on summary conviction to a penalty of £500 and may be detained.

Obstruction of officers, etc.

16.—(1) Any person who—

(*a*) obstructs, hinders, molests or assaults any person duly engaged in the performance of any duty or the exercise of any power imposed or conferred on him by or under any enactment relating to an assigned matter, or any person acting in his aid; or

(*b*) does anything which impedes or is calculated to impede the carrying out of any search for any thing liable to forfeiture under any such enactment or the detention, seizure or removal of any such thing; or

(*c*) rescues, damages or destroys any thing so liable to forfeiture or does anything calculated to prevent the procuring or giving of evidence as to whether or not any thing is so liable to forfeiture; or

(*d*) prevents the detention of any person by a person duly engaged or acting as aforesaid or rescues any person so detained,

or who attempts to do any of the aforementioned things, shall be guilty of an offence under this section.

(2) A person guilty of an offence under this section shall be liable—

(*a*) on summary conviction, to a penalty of the prescribed sum, or to imprisonment for a term not exceeding 3 months, or to both; or

(*b*) on conviction on indictment, to a penalty of any amount, or to imprisonment for a term not exceeding 2 years, or to both.

(3) Any person committing an offence under this section and any person aiding or abetting the commission of such an offence may be detained.

Commissioners' receipts and expenses

Disposal of duties, etc.

17.—(1) Save for such sums as may be required for any disbursements permitted by section 10 of the Exchequer and Audit Departments Act 1866, all money and securities for money collected or received in Great Britain for or on account of customs or excise shall be paid or remitted to and accounted for by the Bank of England in such manner as the Commissioners may with the approval of the Treasury direct, and shall be placed to the account in the books of the Bank entitled " the General Account of the Commissioners of Customs and Excise ".

(2) The Bank shall deliver to the Commissioners each day a statement in writing of the money or securities for money, if any, received on that day from or on account of the Commissioners, and every statement so delivered shall be deemed to be a sufficient acknowledgement by the Bank of the receipt of the money and securities specified therein.

(3) Any money and securities for money standing to the credit of the General Account shall be dealt with as provided in section 10 of the Exchequer and Audit Departments Act 1866 subject, however, to payment to the Government of the Isle of Man of the amounts mentioned in section 2 (1) of the Isle of Man Act 1958 (payments of Isle of Man share of equal duties).

(4) All money and securities for money collected or received in Northern Ireland for or on account of—

(*a*) duties of customs or excise on goods imported into or manufactured or produced in Northern Ireland; or

(*b*) any duties of excise specified in any order of the Treasury for the time being in force under section 37 (3) of the Northern Ireland Constitution Act 1973,

shall be dealt with as provided in section 10 of the Exchequer and Audit Departments Act 1866.

(5) Notwithstanding anything in section 10 of the Exchequer and Audit Departments Act 1866 or in subsection (1) above as to the disbursements which may be made out of money collected or received for or on account of customs or excise—

(*a*) any sum required for the purpose of such disbursements in the Port of London shall be paid out of the General Account; and

(*b*) no repayment of sums overpaid in error shall be made unless the claim thereto is made and evidence in support thereof is submitted to the Commissioners within 6 years of the date of the overpayment and the claim is established to the satisfaction of the Commissioners.

(6) Any reference in this section to money and securities for money collected or received for or on account of customs or excise or of any duties thereof includes a reference to any sums received under or by virtue of any enactment relating to customs or excise or to those duties by way of pecuniary penalties or the pecuniary proceeds of any forfeiture, costs, or otherwise howsoever.

Remuneration and expenses of Commissioners

18. Any remuneration and allowances payable to the Commissioners under this Act and any expenses of the Commissioners under the Customs and Excise Acts 1979 shall be defrayed out of money provided by Parliament.

PART III

CUSTOMS AND EXCISE CONTROL AREAS

Appointment of ports, etc.

19.—(1) The Commissioners may by order made by statutory instrument appoint and name as a port for the purposes of customs and excise any area in the United Kingdom specified in the order.

(2) The appointment of any port for those purposes made before 1st August 1952 may be revoked, and the name or limits of any such port may be altered, by an order under subsection (1) above as if the appointment had been made by an order under that subsection.

(3) The Commissioners may in any port from time to time appoint boarding stations for the purpose of the boarding of or disembarkation from ships by officers.

Approved wharves

20.—(1) The Commissioners may approve, for such periods and subject to such conditions and restrictions as they think fit, places for the loading or unloading of goods or of any class or description of goods; and any place so approved is referred to in this Act as an " approved wharf ".

(2) The Commissioners may at any time for reasonable cause revoke or vary the terms of any approval given under this section.

(3) Any person contravening or failing to comply with any condition or restriction imposed by the Commissioners under this section shall be liable on summary conviction to a penalty of £100.

Control of movement of aircraft, etc., into and out of the United Kingdom

21.—(1) Save as permitted by the Commissioners, the commander of an aircraft entering the United Kingdom from a place outside the United Kingdom shall not cause or permit the aircraft to land—

(*a*) for the first time after its arrival in the United Kingdom; or

(*b*) at any time while it is carrying passengers or goods brought in that aircraft from a place outside the United Kingdom and not yet cleared,

at any place other than a customs and excise airport.

(2) Save as permitted by the Commissioners, no person importing or concerned in importing any goods in any aircraft shall bring the goods into the United Kingdom at any place other than a customs and excise airport.

(3) Save as permitted by the Commissioners—

(*a*) no person shall depart on a flight to a place or area outside the United Kingdom from any place in the United Kingdom other than a customs and excise airport; and

(*b*) the commander of any aircraft engaged in a flight from a customs and excise airport to a place or area outside the United Kingdom shall not cause or permit it to land at any place in the United Kingdom other than a customs and excise airport specified in the application for clearance for that flight.

(4) Subsections (1) to (3) above shall not apply in relation to any aircraft flying from or to any place or area outside the United Kingdom to or from any place in the United Kingdom which is required by or under any enactment relating to air navigation, or is compelled by accident, stress of weather or other unavoidable cause, to land at a place other than a customs and excise airport; but, subject to subsection (5) below,—

(*a*) the commander of any such aircraft—

(i) shall immediately report the landing to an officer or constable and shall on demand produce to him the journey log book belonging to the aircraft,

(ii) shall not without the consent of an officer permit any goods carried in the aircraft to be unloaded from, or any of the crew or passengers to depart from the vicinity of, the aircraft, and

(iii) shall comply with any directions given by an officer with respect to any such goods; and

(*b*) no passenger or member of the crew shall without the consent of an officer or constable leave the immediate vicinity of any such aircraft.

(5) Nothing in subsection (4) above shall prohibit—

(*a*) the departure of passengers or crew from the vicinity of an aircraft; or

(*b*) the removal of goods from an aircraft,

where that departure or removal is necessary for reasons of health, safety or the preservation of life or property.

(6) Any person contravening or failing to comply with any provision of this section shall be liable on summary conviction to a penalty of £200, or to imprisonment for a term not exceeding 3 months, or to both.

(7) In this Act " customs and excise airport " means an aerodrome for the time being designated as a place for the landing or departure of aircraft for the purposes of the customs and excise Acts by an order made by the Secretary of State with the concurrence of the Commissioners

which is in force under an Order in Council made in pursuance of section 8 of the Civil Aviation Act 1949.

Approval of examination stations at customs and excise airports

22.—(1) The Commissioners may, in any customs and excise airport, approve for such periods and subject to such conditions and restrictions as they think fit a part of, or a place at, that airport for the loading and unloading of goods and the embarkation and disembarkation of passengers; and any such part or place so approved is referred to in this Act as an " examination station ".

(2) The Commissioners may at any time for reasonable cause revoke or vary the terms of any approval given under this section.

(3) Any person contravening or failing to comply with any condition or restriction imposed by the Commissioners under this section shall be liable on summary conviction to a penalty of £100.

Control of movement of hovercraft

23.—(1) The Commissioners may by regulations impose conditions and restrictions as respects the movement of hovercraft and the carriage of goods by hovercraft, and in particular—

(*a*) may prescribe the procedure to be followed by hovercraft proceeding to or from a port or any customs and excise airport or customs and excise station, and authorise the proper officer to give directions as to their routes; and

(*b*) may make provision for cases where by reason of accident, or in any other circumstance, it is impracticable to comply with any conditions or restrictions imposed or directions given as respects hovercraft.

(2) Subsection (1) above shall apply to hovercraft proceeding to or from any approved wharf or transit shed which is not in a port as if it were a port.

(3) If any person contravenes or fails to comply with any regulation made under subsection (1) above, or with any direction given by the Commissioners or the proper officer in pursuance of any such regulation, he shall be liable on summary conviction to a penalty of £100 and any goods in respect of which the offence was committed shall be liable to forfeiture.

Control of movement of goods by pipe-line

24.—(1) Goods shall not be imported or exported by means of a pipe-line that is not for the time being approved by the Commissioners for the purposes of this section.

(2) Uncleared goods, that is to say—

(*a*) imported goods, whether or not chargeable with duty, which have not been cleared out of charge, and in particular goods which are, or are to be, moved under section 30 below; or

(*b*) dutiable goods moved from warehouse without payment of duty,

shall not be moved by means of a pipe-line that is not for the time being approved by the Commissioners for the purposes of this section.

(3) The Commissioners may give their approval under this section for such period and subject to such conditions as they think fit, and may at any time for reasonable cause—

(*a*) vary the terms of their approval; and

(b) (if they have given to the owner of the pipe-line not less than 3 months' written notice of their intention so to do) revoke their approval.

(4) Section 49 of the Pipe-lines Act 1962 (procedure for service of documents under that Act) shall apply to a notice required by subsection (3) (b) above to be served on the owner of a pipe-line as it applies to a document required by that Act to be so served.

(5) A person who—

(a) contravenes subsection (1) or (2) above, or contravenes or fails to comply with a condition imposed by the Commissioners under subsection (3) above; or

(b) except with the authority of the proper officer or for just and sufficient cause, obtains access to goods which are in, or in course of conveyance by, a pipe-line approved under this section,

shall be guilty of an offence under this section and may be detained; and any goods in respect of which the offence was committed shall be liable to forfeiture.

(6) A person guilty of an offence under this section shall be liable—

(a) on summary conviction, to a penalty of the prescribed sum, or to imprisonment for a term not exceeding 6 months, or to both; or

(b) on conviction on indictment, to a penalty of any amount, or to imprisonment for a term not exceding 2 years, or to both.

(7) In the application of subsection (4) above to Northern Ireland, the reference to the Pipe-lines Act 1962 shall have effect as if that Act extended to Northern Ireland.

Approval of transit sheds

25.—(1) The Commissioners may approve, for such periods and subject to such conditions and restrictions as they see fit, places for the deposit of goods imported and not yet cleared out of charge, including goods not yet reported and entered under this Act; and any place so approved is referred to in this Act as a " transit shed ".

(2) Where, by any local Act, provision is made for the landing of goods without entry for deposit in transit sheds authorised thereunder, the provisions of this Act relating to goods deposited in transit sheds approved under this section shall have effect in relation to goods deposited in transit sheds authorised under that Act.

(3) The Commissioners may at any time for reasonable cause revoke or vary the terms of any approval given under subsection (1) above.

(4) Any person contravening or failing to comply with any condition or restriction imposed by the Commissioners under subsection (1) above shall be liable on summary conviction to a penalty of £100.

Power to regulate movements of goods into and out of Northern Ireland by land

26.—(1) The Commissioners may, for the purpose of safeguarding the revenue and for the better enforcement of any prohibition or restriction for the time being in force under or by virtue of any enactment with respect to the importation or exportation of any goods, make regulations—

(a) prohibiting the importation or exportation by land of all goods or of any class or description of goods except within such hours and by such routes within Northern Ireland (referred to in this

Act as " approved routes ") as may be prescribed by the regulations;

(*b*) appointing places for the examination and entry of and payment of any duty chargeable on any goods being imported or exported by land (referred to in this Act as " customs and excise stations ").

(2) If any person contravenes or fails to comply with any regulation made under subsection (1) above he shall be liable on summary conviction to a penalty of £100, and any goods in respect of which the offence was committed shall be liable to forfeiture.

Officers' powers of boarding

27.—(1) At any time while a ship is within the limits of a port, or an aircraft is at a customs and excise airport, or a vehicle is on an approved route, any officer and any other person duly engaged in the prevention of smuggling may board the ship, aircraft or vehicle and remain therein and rummage and search any part thereof.

(2) The Commissioners may station officers in any ship at any time while it is within the limits of a port, and if the master of any ship neglects or refuses to provide—

(*a*) reasonable accommodation below decks for any officer stationed therein; or

(*b*) means of safe access to and egress from the ship in accordance with the requirements of any such officer,

the master shall be liable on summary conviction to a penalty of £50.

Officers' powers of access, etc.

28.—(1) Without prejudice to section 27 above, the proper officer shall have free access to every part of any ship or aircraft at a port or customs and excise airport and of any vehicle brought to a customs and excise station, and may—

(*a*) cause any goods to be marked before they are unloaded from that ship, aircraft or vehicle;

(*b*) lock up, seal, mark or otherwise secure any goods carried in the ship, aircraft or vehicle or any place or container in which they are so carried; and

(*c*) break open any place or container which is locked and of which the keys are withheld.

(2) Any goods found concealed on board any such ship, aircraft or vehicle shall be liable to forfeiture.

Officers' powers of detention of ships, etc.

29.—(1) Where, in the case of a ship, aircraft or vehicle of which due report has been made under section 35 below, any goods are still on board that ship, aircraft or vehicle at the expiration of the relevant period, the proper officer may detain that ship, aircraft or vehicle until there have been repaid to the Commissioners—

(*a*) any expenses properly incurred in watching and guarding the goods beyond the relevant period, except, in the case of a ship or aircraft, in respect of the day of clearance inwards; and

(*b*) where the goods are removed by virtue of any provision of the Customs and Excise Acts 1979 from the ship, aircraft or vehicle to a Queen's warehouse, the expenses of that removal.

(2) In subsection (1) above, " the relevant period " means—

(*a*) in the case of a ship or vehicle, 21 clear days from the date of making due report of the ship or vehicle under section 35 below or such longer period as the Commissioners may in any case allow;

(*b*) in the case of an aircarft, 7 clear days from the date of making due report of the aircraft under that section or such longer period as the Commissioners may in any case allow.

(3) Where, in the case of—

(*a*) any derelict or other ship or aircraft coming, driven or brought into the United Kingdom under legal process, by stress of weather or for safety; or

(*b*) any vehicle in Northern Ireland which suffers any mishap,

it is necessary for the protection of the revenue to station any officer in charge thereof, whether on board or otherwise, the proper officer may detain that ship, aircraft or vehicle until any expenses thereby incurred by the Commissioners have been repaid.

Control of movement of uncleared goods within or between port or airport and other places

30.—(1) The Commissioners may from time to time give general or special directions as to the manner in which, and the conditions under which, goods to which this section applies, or any class or description of such goods, may be moved within the limits of any port or customs and excise airport or between any port or customs and excise airport and any other place.

(2) This section applies to goods chargeable with any duty which has not been paid, to drawback goods, and to any other goods which have not been cleared out of charge.

(3) Any directions under subsection (1) above may require that any goods to which this section applies shall be moved only—

(*a*) by persons licensed by the Commissioners for that purpose;

(*b*) in such ships, aircraft or vehicles or by such other means as may be approved by the Commissioners for that purpose;

and any such licence or approval may be granted for such period and subject to such conditions and restrictions as the Commissioners think fit and may be revoked at any time by the Commissioners.

(4) Any person contravening or failing to comply with any direction given or condition of restriction imposed, or the terms of any licence granted, by the Commissioners under this section shall be liable on summary conviction to a penalty of £50.

Control of movement of goods to and from inland clearance depot, etc.

31.—(1) The Commissioners may by regulations impose conditions and restrictions as respects—

(*a*) the movement of imported goods between the place of importation and a place approved by the Commissioners for the clearance out of charge of such goods; and

(*b*) the movement of goods intended for export between a place approved by the Commissioners for the examination of such goods and the place of exportation.

(2) Regulations under subsection (1) above may in particular—

(*a*) require the goods to be moved within such period and by such route as may be specified by or under the regulations;

(*b*) require the goods to be carried in a vehicle or container complying with such requirements and secured in such manner as may be so specified;

(*c*) prohibit, except in such circumstances as may be so specified, any unloading or loading of the vehicle or container or any interference with its security.

(3) If any person contravenes or fails to comply with any regulation under subsection (1) above or any requirement imposed by or under any such regulation, that person and the person then in charge of the goods shall each be liable on summary conviction to a penalty of £500 and any goods in respect of which the offence was committed shall be liable to forfeiture.

Penalty for carrying away officers

32.—(1) If any ship or aircraft departs from any place, or any vehicle crosses the boundary out of Northern Ireland, carrying on board without his consent any officer of customs and excise or other Government officer, including an officer of the Government of Northern Ireland, the master of the ship or commander of the aircraft or the person in charge of the vehicle shall be liable on summary conviction to a penalty of £100.

(2) Without prejudice to the liability of any person under subsection (1) above, the amount of any expenses incurred by the Commissioners or by any Government department, including a department of the Government of Northern Ireland, by reason of the carrying away of any officer may be recovered summarily as a civil debt from that person or from the owner of the ship, aircraft or vehicle concerned.

(3) For the purposes of this section, the guard of a railway train shall be deemed to be the person in charge of any vehicle forming part of that train.

Power to inspect aircraft, aerodromes, records, etc.

33.—(1) The commander of an aircraft shall permit an officer at any time to board the aircraft and inspect—

(*a*) the aircraft and any goods loaded therein; and

(*b*) all documents relating to the aircraft or to goods or persons carried therein;

and an officer shall have the right of access at any time to any place to which access is required for the purpose of any such inspection.

(2) The person in control of any aerodrome shall permit an officer at any time to enter upon and inspect the aerodrome and all buildings and goods thereon.

(3) The person in control of an aerodrome licensed under any enactment relating to air navigation and, if so required by the Commissioners, the person in control of any other aerodrome shall—

(*a*) keep a record in such form and manner as the Commissioners may approve of all aircraft arriving at or departing from the aerodrome;

(*b*) keep that record available and produce it on demand to any officer, together with all other documents kept on the aerodrome which relate to the movement of aircraft; and

(*c*) permit any officer to make copies of and take extracts from any such record or document.

(4) If any person contravenes or fails to comply with any of the provisions of this section he shall be liable on summary conviction to a penalty of £200 or to imprisonment for a term not exceeding 3 months, or to both.

Power to prevent flight of aircraft

34.—(1) If it appears to any officer or constable that an aircraft is intended or likely to depart for a destination outside the United Kingdom from—

(*a*) any place other than a customs and excise airport; or

(*b*) a customs and excise airport before clearance outwards is given,

he may give such instructions and take such steps by way of detention of the aircraft or otherwise as appear to him necessary in order to prevent the flight.

(2) Any person who contravenes any instructions given under subsection (1) above shall be liable on summary conviction to a penalty of £200, or to imprisonment for a term not exceeding 3 months, or to both.

(3) If an aircraft flies in contravention of any instruction given under subsection (1) above or notwithstanding any steps taken to prevent the flight, the owner and the commander thereof shall, without prejudice to the liability of any other person under subsection (2) above, each be liable on summary conviction to a penalty of £200, or to imprisonment for a term not exceeding 3 months, or to both, unless he proves that the flight took place without his consent or connivance.

Part IV

Control of Importation

Inward entry and clearance

Report inwards

35.—(1) Report shall be made in such form and manner and containing such particulars as the Commissioners may direct of every ship and aircraft to which this section applies, of every vehicle entering Northern Ireland by land, and of all goods otherwise conveyed into Northern Ireland by land.

(2) This section applies to every ship arriving at a port—

(*a*) from any place outside the United Kingdom; or

(*b*) carrying any goods brought in that ship from some place outside the United Kingdom and not yet cleared on importation.

(3) This section applies to every aircraft arriving at any place in the United Kingdom—

(*a*) from any place or area outside the United Kingdom; or

(*b*) carrying passengers or goods taken on board that aircraft at a place outside the United Kingdom, being passengers or goods either—

(i) bound for a destination in the United Kingdom and not already cleared at a customs and excise airport; or

(ii) bound for a destination outside the United Kingdom.

(4) The Commissioners may make regulations prescribing the procedure for making report under this section.

(5) If the person by whom the report should be made fails to make report as required by or under this section—

(*a*) he shall be liable on summary conviction to a penalty of £100; and

(*b*) any goods required to be reported which are not duly reported may be detained by any officer until so reported or until the omission is explained to the satisfaction of the Commissioners, and may in the meantime be deposited in a Queen's warehouse.

(6) The person making the report shall at the time of making it answer all such questions relating to the ship, aircraft or vehicle, to the goods carried therein, to the crew and to the voyage, flight or journey as may be put to him by the proper officer; and if he refuses to answer he shall be liable on summary conviction to a penalty of £100.

(7) If at any time after a ship or aircraft carrying goods brought therein from any place outside the United Kingdom arrives within 12 nautical miles of the coast of the United Kingdom, or after a vehicle crosses the boundary into Northern Ireland, and before report has been made in accordance with this section—

(*a*) bulk is broken; or

(*b*) any alteration is made in the stowage of any goods carried so as to facilitate the unloading of any part thereof before due report has been made; or

(*c*) any part of the goods is staved, destroyed or thrown overboard or any container is opened,

and the matter is not explained to the satisfaction of the Commissioners, the master of the ship or commander of the aircraft or the person in charge of the vehicle shall be liable on summary conviction to a penalty of £100.

(8) For the purposes of subsection (7) above, the guard of a railway train shall be deemed to be the person in charge of any vehicle forming part of that train.

Provisions as to Her Majesty's ships, etc.

36.—(1) The person in command of any ship having a commission from Her Majesty or any foreign State which has on board any goods loaded in any place outside the United Kingdom shall, before any such goods are unloaded, or at any time when called upon to do so by the proper officer, deliver to the proper officer an account of the goods in accordance with subsection (2) below, and if he fails so to do he shall be liable on summary conviction to a penalty of £100.

(2) An account of goods under subsection (1) above shall be in such form, and shall contain to the best of the knowledge of the person delivering the account such particulars, and shall be delivered in such manner, as the Commissioners may direct.

(3) The person delivering such an account shall when delivering it answer all such questions relating to the goods as may be put to him by the proper officer and if he refuses to answer he shall be liable on summary conviction to a penalty of £100.

(4) Subject in the case of ships having a commission from Her Majesty to any regulations made by the Treasury, the provisions of Parts III to VII of this Act as to the boarding and search of ships shall have effect in relation to such a ship as aforesaid as they have effect in relation to any other ship, and any officer may remove to a Queen's warehouse any goods loaded as aforesaid found on board the ship.

Entry of goods on importation

37.—(1) The importer of any goods, other than goods which are exempt from the requirements of this section, shall deliver to the proper officer an entry thereof in such form and manner and containing such particulars as the Commissioners may direct.

(2) The following goods are exempt from the requirements of this section—

(*a*) whales and fresh fish (including shell-fish) of British taking brought by British ships;

(*b*) passengers' baggage; and

(*c*) Community transit goods.

(3) Subject to subsections (4) and (5) below, goods may be entered under this section—

(*a*) for home use, if so eligible; or

(*b*) for warehousing; or

(*c*) for transit or transhipment; or

(*d*) for inward processing; or

(*e*) in such cases as the Commissioners may permit, for temporary retention with a view to subsequent re-exportation.

(4) All goods imported by means of a pipe-line and chargeable with duty shall be entered for warehousing.

(5) The Commissioners may—

(*a*) refuse to accept an entry of any goods if they are not satisfied that those goods were imported before the time of the delivery of the entry;

(*b*) subject to subsection (4) above, direct that goods of any class or description specified in the direction shall not be permitted to be entered for warehousing.

(6) If, in the case of any goods which are not dutiable goods, any such entry as aforesaid is inaccurate in any particular, the importer shall, within 14 clear days of the delivery of the entry or such longer period as the Commissioners may in any case allow, deliver to the proper officer a full and accurate account of the goods.

(7) If an account of the goods is delivered in accordance with subsection (6) above and the Commissioners are satisfied that the inaccuracy was inadvertent and immaterial except for statistical purposes, then notwithstanding anything in the Customs and Excise Acts 1979 or in any instrument made thereunder the goods shall not be liable to forfeiture, or the importer to any penalty, by reason only of the inaccuracy of the entry.

Entry by bill of sight

38.—(1) Without prejudice to section 37 above, where on the importation of any goods the importer is unable for want of full information to make immediately perfect entry thereof, he may, subject to subsection (2) below, on making a signed declaration to that effect before the proper officer, deliver to that officer an entry of the goods by bill of sight in such form and manner and containing such particulars as the Commissioners may direct.

(2) Notwithstanding subsection (1) above, the Commissioners may refuse to accept an entry by bill of sight of any goods if they are not satisfied that those goods were imported before the delivery of the entry.

(3) An entry of any goods by bill of sight under subsection (1) above when signed by the proper officer shall be the warrant for the examination of the goods by the importer in the presence of the proper officer with a view to making perfect entry thereof.

(4) If within such period from the date of the entry of any goods by bill of sight as the Commissioners may allow, no entry purporting to be a perfect entry has been made of those goods, the proper officer may cause the goods to be deposited in a Queen's warehouse; and, without prejudice to section 99 (3) below, if any goods so deposited are not cleared within one month from the date of deposit the Commissioners may sell them.

Entry of surplus stores

39.—(1) With the permission of the proper officer, surplus stores of any ship or aircraft—

(*a*) if intended for private use and in quantities which do not appear to him to be excessive, may be entered and otherwise treated as if they were goods imported in the ship or aircraft; or

(*b*) in any other case may, subject to subsection (2) below, be entered for warehousing notwithstanding that they could not lawfully be imported as merchandise.

(2) Goods entered for warehousing by virtue of subsection (1) (*b*) above shall not, except with the sanction of the Commissioners, be further entered, or be removed from the warehouse, otherwise than for use as stores.

Removal of uncleared goods to Queen's warehouse

40.—(1) Where in the case of any imported goods—

(*a*) entry has not been made thereof by the expiration of the relevant period; or

(*b*) at the expiration of 21 clear days from the relevant date; entry having been made of the goods, they have not been unloaded from the importing ship or aircraft or, in the case of goods which have been unloaded or which have been imported by land, have not been produced for examination and clearance; or

(*c*) being goods imported by sea and not being in large quantity, they are at any time after the arrival of the importing ship at the port at which they are to be unloaded the only goods remaining to be unloaded from that ship at that port,

the proper officer may cause the goods to be deposited in a Queen's warehouse.

(2) Where any small package or consignment of goods is imported, the proper officer may at any time after the relevant date cause that package or consignment to be deposited in a Queen's warehouse to await entry.

(3) Without prejudice to section 99 (3) below, if any goods deposited in a Queen's warehouse by the proper office under this section are not cleared by the importer thereof—

(*a*) in the case of goods which are in the opinion of the Commissioners of a perishable nature, forthwith; or

(*b*) in any other case, within 3 months after they have been so deposited or such longer time as the Commissioners may in any case allow,

the Commissioners may sell them.

(4) In this section—

(*a*) " the relevant period " means a period of, in the case of goods imported by air, 7 or, in any other case, 14 clear days from the relevant date; and

(*b*) " the relevant date " means, subject to subsection (5) below, the date when report was made of the importing ship, aircraft or vehicle or of the goods under section 35 above, or, where no such report was made, the date when it should properly have been made.

(5) Where any restriction is placed upon the unloading of goods from any ship or aircraft by virtue of any enactment relating to the prevention of epidemic and infectious diseases, then, in relation to that

ship or aircraft, " the relevant date " in this section means the date of the removal of the restriction.

Failure to comply with provisions as to entry

41. Without prejudice to any liability under any other provision of the Customs and Excise Acts 1979, any person making entry of goods on their importation who fails to comply with any of the requirements of this Part of this Act in connection with that entry shall be liable on summary conviction to a penalty of £50, and the goods in question shall be liable to forfeiture.

Power to regulate unloading, removal, etc. of imported goods

42.—(1) The Commissioners may make regulations—

(*a*) prescribing the procedure to be followed by a ship arriving at a port, an aircraft arriving at a customs and excise airport, or a person conveying goods into Northern Ireland by land;

(*b*) regulating the unloading, landing, movement and removal of goods on their importation;

and different regulations may be made with respect to importation by sea, air or land respectively.

(2) If any person contravenes or fails to comply with any regulation made under this section or with any direction given by the Commissioners or the proper officer in pursuance of any such regulation, he shall be liable on summary conviction to a penalty of £100 and any goods in respect of which the offence was committed shall be liable to forfeiture.

Provisions as to duty on imported goods

Duty on imported goods

43.—(1) Save as permitted by or under the customs and excise Acts or section 2 (2) of the European Communities Act 1972 or any Community regulation or other instrument having the force of law, no imported goods shall be delivered or removed on importation until the importer has paid to the proper officer any duty chargeable thereon, and that duty shall, in the case of goods of which entry is made, be paid on making the entry.

(2) The duties of customs or excise and the rates thereof chargeable on imported goods—

(*a*) if entry is made thereof, except where the entry or, in the case of an entry by bill of sight, the perfect entry is for warehousing, shall be those in force with respect to such goods at the time of the delivery of the entry;

(*b*) if entry or, in the case of goods entered by bill of sight, perfect entry is made thereof for warehousing, shall be ascertained in accordance with warehousing regulations;

(*c*) if no entry is made thereof, shall be those in force with respect to such goods at the time of their importation.

(3) Any goods brought or coming into the United Kingdom by sea otherwise than as cargo, stores or baggage carried in a ship shall be chargeable with the like duty, if any, as would be applicable to those goods if they had been imported as merchandise; and if any question arises as to the origin of the goods they shall, unless that question is determined under section 120 below, section 14 of the Customs and Excise Duties (General Reliefs) Act 1979 (produce of the sea or continental shelf) or under a Community regulation or other instrument

having the force of law, be deemed to be the produce of such country as the Commissioners may on investigation determine.

(4) Where, in accordance with approval given by the Commissioners, entry of goods is made by any method involving the use of a computer, subsection (2) above shall have effect as if the reference in paragraph (*a*) to the time of the delivery of the entry were a reference to the time when particulars contained in the entry are accepted by the computer.

(5) Subject to sections 10 and 11 of the Customs and Excise Duties (General Reliefs) Act 1979 (reliefs for re-imported goods) and save as provided by or under any such enactments or instruments as are mentioned in subsection (1) above, any goods which are re-imported into the United Kingdom after exportation therefrom, whether they were manufactured or produced in or outside the United Kingdom and whether or not any duty was paid thereon at a previous importation, shall be treated for the purpose of charging duty—

(*a*) as if they were being imported for the first time; and

(*b*) in the case of goods manufactured or produced in the United Kingdom, as if they had not been so manufactured or produced.

Exclusion of s. 43 (1) for importers etc. keeping standing deposits

44. Where the Commissioners so direct, section 43 (1) above shall not apply if and so long as the importer or his agent pays to, and keeps deposited with, the Commissioners a sum by way of standing deposit sufficient in their opinion to cover any duty which may become payable in respect of goods entered by that importer or agent, and if the importer or agent complies with such other conditions as the Commissioners may impose.

Deferred payment of customs duty

45.—(1) The Commissioners may by regulations provide for the payment of customs duty to be deferred in such cases as may be specified by the regulations and subject to such conditions as may be imposed by or under the regulations; and duty of which payment is deferred under the regulations shall be treated, for such purposes as may be specified thereby, as if it had been paid.

(2) Regulations under this section may make different provision for goods of different descriptions or for goods of the same description in different circumstances.

Goods to be warehoused without payment of duty

46. Any goods which are on their importation permitted to be entered for warehousing shall be allowed, subject to such conditions or restrictions as may be imposed by or under warehousing regulations, to be warehoused without payment of duty.

Relief from payment of duty of goods entered for transit or transhipment

47. Where any goods are entered for transit or transhipment, the Commissioners may allow the goods to be removed for that purpose, subject to such conditions and restrictions as they see fit, without payment of duty.

Relief from payment of duty of goods temporarily imported

48. In such cases as the Commissioners may by regulations prescribe, where the Commissioners are satisfied that goods are imported only temporarily with a view to subsequent re-exportation, they may permit the goods to be delivered on importation, subject to such conditions as they see fit to impose, without payment of duty.

Forfeiture, offences, etc. in connection with importation

Forfeiture of goods improperly imported

49.—(1) Where—

(*a*) except as provided by or under the Customs and Excise Acts 1979, any imported goods, being goods chargeable on their importation with customs or excise duty, are, without payment of that duty—

(i) unshipped in any port,

(ii) unloaded from any aircraft in the United Kingdom,

(iii) unloaded from any vehicle in, or otherwise brought across the boundary into, Northern Ireland, or

(iv) removed from their place of importation or from any approved wharf, examination station or transit shed; or

(*b*) any goods are imported, landed or unloaded contrary to any prohibition or restriction for the time being in force with respect thereto under or by virtue of any enactment; or

(*c*) any goods, being goods chargeable with any duty or goods the importation of which is for the time being prohibited or restricted by or under any enactment, are found, whether before or after the unloading thereof, to have been concealed in any manner on board any ship or aircraft or, while in Northern Ireland, in any vehicle; or

(*d*) any goods are imported concealed in a container holding goods of a different description; or

(*e*) any imported goods are found, whether before or after delivery, not to correspond with the entry made thereof; or

(*f*) any imported goods are concealed or packed in any manner appearing to be intended to deceive an officer,

those goods shall, subject to subsection (2) below, be liable to forfeiture.

(2) Where any goods, the importation of which is for the time being prohibited or restricted by or under any enactment, are on their importation either—

(*a*) reported as intended for exportation in the same ship, aircraft or vehicle; or

(*b*) entered for transit or transhipment; or

(*c*) entered to be warehoused for exportation or for use as stores,

the Commissioners may, if they see fit, permit the goods to be dealt with accordingly.

Penalty for improper importation of goods

50.—(1) Subsection (2) below applies to goods of the following descriptions, that is to say—

(*a*) goods chargeable with a duty which has not been paid; and

(*b*) goods the importation, landing or unloading of which is for the time being prohibited or restricted by or under any enactment.

(2) If any person with intent to defraud Her Majesty of any such duty or to evade any such prohibition or restriction as is mentioned in subsection (1) above—

(*a*) unships or lands in any port or unloads from any aircraft in the

United Kingdom or from any vehicle in Northern Ireland any goods to which this subsection applies, or assists or is otherwise concerned in such unshipping, landing or unloading; or

(*b*) removes from their place of importation or from any approved wharf, examination station, transit shed or customs and excise station any goods to which this subsection applies or assists or is otherwise concerned in such removal,

he shall be guilty of an offence under this subsection and may be detained.

(3) If any person imports or is concerned in importing any goods contrary to any prohibition or restriction for the time being in force under or by virtue of any enactment with respect to those goods, whether or not the goods are unloaded, and does so with intent to evade the prohibition or restriction, he shall be guilty of an offence under this subsection and may be detained.

(4) Subject to subsection (5) below, a person guilty of an offence under subsection (2) or (3) above shall be liable—

(*a*) on summary conviction, to a penalty of the prescribed sum or three times the value of the goods, whichever is the greater, or to imprisonment for a term not exceeding 6 months, or to both; or

(*b*) on conviction on indictment, to a penalty of any amount, or to imprisonment for a term not exceeding 2 years, or to both.

(5) In the case of an offence under subsection (2) or (3) above in connection with a prohibition or restriction on importation having effect by virtue of section 3 of the Misuse of Drugs Act 1971, subsection (4) above shall have effect subject to the modifications specified in Schedule 1 to this Act.

(6) If any person—

(*a*) imports or causes to be imported any goods concealed in a container holding goods of a different description; or

(*b*) directly or indirectly imports or causes to be imported or entered any goods found, whether before or after delivery, not to correspond with the entry made thereof,

he shall be liable on summary conviction to a penalty of three times the value of the goods or £100, whichever is the greater.

(7) In any case where a person would, apart from this subsection, be guilty of—

(*a*) an offence under this section in connection with the importation of goods contrary to a prohibition or restriction; and

(*b*) a corresponding offence under the enactment or other instrument imposing the prohibition or restriction, being an offence for which a fine or other penalty is expressly provided by that enactment or other instrument,

he shall not be guilty of the offences mentioned in paragraph (*a*) of this subsection.

Special provisions as to proof in Northern Ireland

51.—(1) If goods of any class or description chargeable with duty on their importation from the Republic of Ireland are found in the possession or control of any person within the prescribed area in Northern Ireland, any officer or any person having by law in Northern Ireland the powers of an officer may require that person to furnish proof that the goods have not been imported from the Republic of Ireland or that the duty chargeable on their importation has been paid.

(2) If proof of any matter is required to be furnished in relation to any

goods under subsection (1) above but is not furnished to the satisfaction of the Commissioners, the goods shall, for the purposes of proceedings under the customs and excise Acts, be deemed to have been unlawfully imported from the Republic of Ireland without payment of duty, unless the contrary is proved.

Part V

Control of Exportation

Outward entry and clearance of goods

Meaning for this Part of " dutiable or restricted goods "

52. For the purposes of this Part of this Act " dutiable or restricted goods " are goods of the following descriptions, that is to say—

(*a*) goods from warehouse, other than goods which have been kept, without being warehoused, in a warehouse by virtue of section 92 (4) below;

(*b*) transit goods;

(*c*) any other goods chargeable with any duty which has not been paid;

(*d*) drawback goods;

(*e*) goods with respect to the exportation of which any restriction is for the time being in force under or by virtue of any enactment;

(*f*) any goods required by or under any provision of this Act other than a provision of this Part or by or under a provision of any other Act to be entered before exportation or before shipment for exportation or as stores.

Entry outwards of dutiable or restricted goods

53.—(1) Where any dutiable or restricted goods, not being Community transit goods, are to be shipped for exportation or as stores for use on a voyage or flight to an eventual destination outside the United Kingdom or are brought to any customs and excise station for exportation, the exporter shall, subject to subsection (3) below and section 56 below—

(*a*) deliver to the proper officer an entry outwards of the goods under this section in such form and manner and containing such particulars as the Commissioners may direct; and

(*b*) give security to the satisfaction of the Commissioners that the goods will be duly shipped or exported and discharged at the destination for which they are entered outwards within such time as the Commissioners consider reasonable, or, in the case of goods for use as stores, will be duly so used, or that they will be otherwise accounted for to the satisfaction of the Commissioners.

(2) Directions under this section may, if the Commissioners think fit, contain provisions authorising the delivery in circumstances specified in the directions of provisional entries under this section, and imposing requirements on persons delivering such entries as to the subsequent delivery of perfected entries, and the obtaining and retention for a specified period of receipts for perfected entries.

This subsection shall not come into force until such day as the Commissioners may appoint by order made by statutory instrument.

(3) The Commissioners may relax all or any of the requirements imposed by or under subsection (1) or (2) above as they think fit in relation to any goods.

(4) If any goods of which entry is required under this section are shipped for exportation or as stores or are waterborne for such shipment before entry thereof has been duly made, the goods shall be liable to forfeiture and, where the shipping or making waterborne is done with fraudulent intent, any person concerned therein with knowledge of that intent shall be guilty of an offence under this subsection and may be detained.

(5) A person guilty of an offence under subsection (4) above shall be liable—

(*a*) on summary conviction, to a penalty of the prescribed sum or of three times the value of the good, whichever is the greater, or to imprisonment for a term not exceeding 6 months, or to both; or

(*b*) on conviction on indictment, to a penalty of any amount, or to imprisonment for a term not exceeding 2 years, or to both.

(6) Any person who, being required by directions given under subsection (2) above to obtain and retain for a specified period a receipt for any entry, fails to produce a receipt complying with the directions on demand made by the proper officer at any time during that period shall be liable on summary conviction to a penalty of £100.

(7) Any person who contravenes or fails to comply with any directions given under subsection (2) above be liable on summary conviction to a penalty of £100.

(8) If any goods are found not to correspond with any entry thereof made under this section, they shall be liable to forfeiture.

Entry outwards of goods which are not dutiable or restricted goods

54.—(1) Subject to subsection (6) below and to section 56 below, before any goods which are not dutiable or restricted goods are exported or shipped for exportation, the exporter shall, unless the goods are Community transit goods, deliver to the proper officer an entry outwards of the goods under this section.

(2) The form of entries under this section, the particulars to be contained therein and the manner of their delivery shall be such as the Commissioners may from time to time direct.

(3) Directions under this section may, if the Commissioners think fit, contain provisions authorising the delivery in circumstances specified in the directions of provisional entries under this section, and imposing requirements on persons delivering such entries as to the subsequent delivery of perfected entries, and the obtaining and retention for a specified period of receipts for perfected entries.

(4) Where the particulars contained in any entry delivered under this section are in any way incorrect or inaccurate, the person delivering it shall notify the proper officer of any necessary correction within a period of 14 days beginning with the day of delivery.

(5) The Commissioners may give directions under this section imposing on persons specified in the directions requirements as to the giving of information with respect to, and the furnishing of documents in connection with, goods which have been entered under this section but are not exported or shipped for exportation within a specified period beginning with the day of delivery of the entry.

(6) The Commissioners may relax any requirement imposed by or under this section as they think fit in relation to any goods.

(7) If any goods of which entry is required under this section are exported or shipped for exportation before delivery of an entry in respect thereof the exporter shall be liable on summary conviction to a penalty of £100.

(8) Any person who fails to comply with subsection (4) above in the case of any entry shall be liable on summary conviction to a penalty of £10.

(9) Any person who, being required by directions given under this section to obtain and retain for a specified period a receipt for any entry, fails to produce a receipt complying with the directions on demand made by the proper officer at any time during that period shall be liable on summary conviction to a penalty of £100.

(10) Any person who contravenes or fails to comply with any directions given under this section shall be liable on summary conviction to a penalty of £100.

Register of exporters and assignment of identifying numbers

55.—(1) The Commissioners shall have power—

(*a*) to maintain a register of exporters;

(*b*) to enter therein any person applying for registration and appearing to them to be concerned in the exportation of goods and to satisfy such requirements for registration as they may think fit to impose;

(*c*) to give directions imposing requirements on registered persons (and, in particular, requirements as to the keeping of records and accounts and the giving of access thereto) as a condition of their remaining on the register;

(*d*) to assign to registered persons numbers for use for export purposes; and

(*e*) to cancel the registration of any person if it appears to them that he has failed to comply with any direction under this section or that there is other reasonable cause for cancellation.

(2) The Commissioners may relax any requirement imposed under this section as they think fit in relation to any goods.

Alternative to entry for registered exporters

56.—(1) If the Commissioners think fit so to direct—

(*a*) dutiable or restricted goods falling within paragraph (*c*) or (*d*) of section 52 above may be shipped for exportation without entry under section 53 above; and

(*b*) goods which are not dutiable or restricted goods may be shipped for exportation without entry under section 54 above,

if, before shipment, a number assigned under section 55 above to a person concerned in the exportation of the goods, together with such particulars of the goods and other information relating thereto as the directions may require, is furnished in accordance with the directions to a person specified therein.

(2) Directions under this section may contain provision enabling the Commissioners to exclude shipments of goods from their operation in particular cases by giving notice to that effect in accordance with the directions.

(3) The Commissioners may relax any requirement imposed under this section as they think fit in relation to any goods.

(4) If any person, for the purpose of enabling any goods to be shipped without entry by virtue of directions given under this section,

furnishes a number other than one for the time being assigned to him under section 55 above, then, unless the number is one for the time being assigned to another person under that section and is furnished with that person's consent, he shall be liable on summary conviction to a penalty of £100.

Specification of certain goods

57.—(1) Subject to subsection (2) below and section 58 below, in any of the following events, that is to say—

(*a*) where any dutiable or restricted goods are, by virtue of section 53 (3) or 56 above, exported without entry under section 53 above, shipped for exportation without such an entry or shipped as stores for use on a voyage or flight to an eventual destination outside the United Kingdom without such an entry; or

(*b*) where any goods which are not dutiable or restricted goods are, by virtue of section 56 above, shipped for exportation without entry under section 54 above,

the exporter of the goods shall deliver to the proper officer a specification of the goods in accordance with this section.

(2) No specification need be delivered as required by subsection (1) above in the case of Community transit goods or in the case of goods shipped as stores where the shipment as stores is permitted by the Commissioners and such conditions as they see fit to impose are complied with.

(3) A specification of goods under this section shall—

(*a*) be in such form and contain such particulars as the Commissioners may direct; and

(*b*) be delivered in such manner as they may direct within a period of 14 days or such longer period as they may direct—

(i) after the clearance outwards of the ship or aircraft from the place of loading; or

(ii) in the case of goods exported by land, after the goods have been exported.

(4) Where any goods are shipped for exportation without entry by virtue of directions given under section 56 above, the person whose number was furnished in relation to the goods for the purpose of their shipment without entry shall, if it was so furnished with his consent, be the exporter of the goods for the purposes of this section.

(5) For the purposes of this section, any ship built, or aircraft manufactured, in the United Kingdom departing for the first time for a voyage or flight to a place outside the United Kingdom for the purpose of its delivery to a consignee outside the United Kingdom shall be treated both as goods shipped for exportation and as the exporting ship or aircraft, and the owner of the ship or aircraft or, where the owner is outside the United Kingdom, the builder of the ship or the manufacturer of the aircraft shall be deemed to be the exporter.

(6) For goods exported by means of a pipe-line the period for delivery of a specification of the goods under this section shall be 14 days from the time when the goods are charged into the pipe-line for exportation or such longer period as the Commissioners may direct.

(7) Where any goods in respect of which a specification is required under this section are shipped as stores on board any ship which has touched at a port for the purpose only of shipping those goods and then departing for a place outside the United Kingdom, and which is permitted by the Commissioners to depart without being cleared outwards from that port, this section shall have effect as if for the reference in subsection (3)

above to the clearance outwards of the ship there were substituted a reference to the shipping of the goods.

(8) The Commissioners may give a direction under this subsection requiring any person delivering a specification under this section in relation to goods shipped for exportation to obtain a receipt therefor in accordance with the direction and to retain it for a period specified therein.

The Commissioners may relax any requirement imposed under this subsection as they think fit in relation to any goods.

(9) If in the case of any such goods as are mentioned in subsection (1) above no specification is delivered in accordance with this section, the exporter of the goods shall be liable on summary conviction to a penalty of £100.

(10) If, when a specification has been delivered under this section, any goods to which it relates have not in fact been exported or shipped as stores or the particulars contained therein are in any other way incorrect or inaccurate, the person signing the specification and the exporter of the goods shall each be liable on summary conviction to a penalty of £10 unless one of them notifies the proper officer of any necessary correction within a period of 14 days beginning with the day of delivery.

(11) Any person who contravenes or fails to comply with any direction given under subsection (8) above shall be liable on summary conviction to a penalty of £100.

(12) Any person who, being required by a direction given under subsection (8) above to obtain and retain for a specified period a receipt for a specification under this section, fails to produce a receipt complying with the direction on demand made by the proper officer at any time during that period shall be liable on summary conviction to a penalty of £100.

Relaxation of requirements of s. 57 where particulars of goods recorded by computer

58.—(1) In connection with any arrangements approved by the Commissioners for recording particulars of exported goods by computer they may relax the requirements of section 57 above by suspending the obligation to deliver the specifications there mentioned on condition that—

(*a*) the particulars which should otherwise be contained in the specifications, or such of those particulars as the Commissioners may specify, are recorded by computer in accordance with the arrangements; and

(*b*) the particulars so recorded are subsequently delivered to the proper officer within such time as the Commissioners may specify;

and subject to such other conditions as they may impose.

(2) If under subsection (1) above particulars are recorded by computer, and any goods to which the particulars relate have not in fact been exported or shipped as stores, or the particulars are in any other way incorrect or inaccurate, the exporter of the goods and any other person who caused the incorrect or inaccurate particulars to be recorded shall each be liable on summary conviction to a penalty of £5 unless one of them, either himself or by an agent, corrects the particulars within the period mentioned in section 57 (3) above.

Restrictions on putting export goods alongside for loading

59.—(1) This section applies to all goods which are required to be entered outwards before shipment for exportation, whether under section 53 or section 54 above.

(2) The Commissioners may make regulations—

(*a*) prohibiting, as from such date as is specified in the regulations, the putting of any goods to which this section applies alongside any ship or aircraft for loading for exportation, except under a written authority in that behalf obtained in accordance with, and in such form as is specified in, the regulations; and

(*b*) requiring any person putting goods alongside a ship or aircraft under one or more such authorities to endorse the authority or each of the authorities with such particulars as are specified in the regulations, and to deliver the endorsed authority or authorities, together with a written statement of the number of authorities delivered, to the proper officer within such period as is so specified.

(3) Regulations under subsection (2) above may make different provision for different circumstances.

(4) Without prejudice to section 3 above, subsection (2) above shall apply to the charging of goods into a pipe-line for exportation as it applies to the putting of goods alongside a ship or aircraft for loading for exportation.

(5) The Commissioners may relax any requirement imposed under subsection (2) above as they think fit in relation to any goods.

(6) Any person who contravenes or fails to comply with any regulation under subsection (2) above shall be liable on summary conviction to a penalty of £100.

(7) This section shall not come into force until such day as the Commissioners may appoint by order made by statutory instrument.

Additional restrictions as to certain export goods

60.—(1) No person shall export any dutiable or restricted goods falling within paragraphs (*a*) to (*d*) of section 52 above, or enter any such goods for exportation, in any ship of less than 40 tons register.

(2) Subsection (1) above shall not apply to hovercraft, but dutiable or restricted goods shall only be exported in a hovercraft if it is of a class or description for the time being approved by the Commissioners and subject to such conditions and restrictions as they may impose.

(3) Any goods shipped or entered contrary to subsection (1) or (2) above shall be liable to forfeiture.

(4) A person contravening or failing to comply with subsection (2) above, or with any condition or restriction imposed thereunder, shall be liable on summary conviction to a penalty of three times the value of the goods or £100, whichever is the greater.

(5) If any goods which have been entered at any port, customs and excise airport or customs and excise station under section 53 above have not been duly shipped before the clearance from that port or airport of the ship or aircraft for which they were entered or, as the case may be, have not been duly exported by land, the goods shall be liable to forfeiture unless notice of the failure to ship or export is given to the proper officer immediately after that clearance has been given.

(6) Subject to subsection (7) below, if any goods entered but not shipped or exported as mentioned in subsection (5) above have not, at the expiration of a period of 14 days after the clearance of the ship or aircraft as mentioned in that subsection or, in the case of goods

entered for exportation by land, after the date of the entry, been either—

(*a*) warehoused; or

(*b*) again entered for exportation or for use as stores; or

(*c*) otherwise accounted for to the satisfaction of the Commissioners,

the person by whom the entry was made shall be liable on summary conviction to a penalty of £25.

(7) Subsection (6) above shall not apply where, before the expiration of the said period, the goods have been seized by virtue of subsection (5) above.

Provisions as to stores

61.—(1) The Commissioners may give directions—

(*a*) as to the quantity of any goods which may be carried in any ship or aircraft as stores for use on a voyage or flight to an eventual destination outside the United Kingdom;

(*b*) as to the authorisation to be obtained for the supply and carriage of, and the procedure to be followed in supplying, any goods as stores for use as mentioned in paragraph (*a*) above, whether or not any duty is chargeable or has been paid, or any drawback is payable, in respect of those goods.

(2) Save as provided in subsection (3) below and in section 18 of the Hydrocarbon Oil Duties Act 1979 (relief for fuel for ships in home waters) and notwithstanding anything in the customs and excise Acts, goods shall not be permitted to be shipped as stores without payment of duty or on drawback except in a ship of not less than 40 tons register or in an aircraft departing for a voyage or flight to some place outside the United Kingdom.

(3) The Commissioners may, in such cases and subject to such conditions and restrictions as they see fit, permit goods to be shipped as mentioned in subsection (2) above in any ship of less than 40 tons register which is departing for a place or area outside the United Kingdom.

(4) For the purposes of subsections (2) and (3) above, all hovercraft (of whatever size) shall be treated as ships of less than 40 tons register.

(5) If any goods shipped or carried as stores for use on a voyage or flight to an eventual destination outside the United Kingdom are without the authority of the proper officer landed or unloaded at any place in the United Kingdom—

(*a*) the goods shall be liable to forfeiture; and

(*b*) the master or commander and the owner of the ship or aircraft shall each be liable on summary conviction to a penalty of three times the value of the goods or £100, whichever is the greater.

(6) The proper officer may lock up, mark, seal or otherwise secure any goods entered, shipped or carried as stores for use as mentioned in subsection (5) above or any place or container in which such goods are kept or held.

(7) If any ship or aircraft which has departed from any port or customs and excise airport for a destination outside the United Kingdom carrying stores fails to reach the destination for which it was cleared outwards and returns to any place within the United Kingdom, then—

(*a*) if the failure was not due to stress of weather, mechanical defect or any other unavoidable cause and any deficiency is discovered in the said goods; or

(*b*) if the failure was due to any such cause as is mentioned in paragraph (*a*) above and any deficiency is discovered in the said goods which, in the opinion of the Commissioners, exceeds the quantity which might fairly have been consumed having regard to the length of time between the ship's or aircraft's departure and return as aforesaid,

the master of the ship or the commander of the aircraft shall be liable on summary conviction to a penalty of £50, and shall also pay on the deficiency or, as the case may be, on the excess deficiency any duty chargeable on the importation of such goods.

(8) Any duty payable under subsection (7) above shall be recoverable summarily as a civil debt.

Information, documentation, etc. as to export goods

62.—(1) The Commissioners may give directions under this subsection imposing on persons specified in the directions requirements as to the giving of information with respect to, or the furnishing of documents in connection with, goods exported, or intended to be exported, in any such vehicle or container as is specified in the directions, or by such other means, or in accordance with any such commercial procedure, as is so specified.

(2) The Commissioners may give directions under this subsection providing that, before any goods are shipped for exportation, a number identifying the goods in compliance with the directions is to be given in accordance with the directions by and to such persons as are specified in the directions.

This subsection shall not come into force until such day as the Commissioners may appoint by order made by statutory instrument.

(3) The Commissioners may relax any requirement imposed under subsection (1) or (2) above as they think fit in relation to any goods.

(4) Any person who contravenes or fails to comply with any direction given under subsection (1) or (2) above shall be liable on summary conviction to a penalty of £100.

Outward entry and clearance of ships, etc.

Entry outwards of exporting ships

63.—(1) Where a ship is to load any goods at a port for exportation or as stores for use on a voyage to an eventual destination outside the United Kingdom, the master of the ship shall, before any goods are taken on board that ship at that port, other than goods for exportation loaded in accordance with a stiffening order issued by the proper officer, deliver to the proper officer—

(*a*) an entry outwards of the ship in such form and manner and containing such particulars as the Commissioners may direct; and

(*b*) a certificate from the proper officer of the clearance inwards or coastwise of the ship of her last voyage with cargo; and

(*c*) if the ship has already loaded goods at some other port for exportation or as stores for use as aforesaid or has been cleared in ballast from some other port, the clearance outwards of the ship from that other port.

(2) If, on the arrival at any port of a ship carrying goods coastwise from one place in the United Kingdom to another such place, it is desired that the ship shall proceed with those goods or any of them to a place outside the United Kingdom, entry outwards shall be made of that ship (whether or not any other goods are to be loaded at that port) and of any

of those goods which are dutiable or restricted goods as if the goods were to be loaded for exportation at that port, but any such entry may, subject to such conditions as the Commissioners see fit to impose, be made without the goods being first discharged.

(3) A ship may, subject to subsection (4) below, be entered outwards from a port under this section notwithstanding that before departing for any place outside the United Kingdom the ship is to go to another port.

(4) A ship carrying cargo brought in that ship from some place outside the United Kingdom and intended to be discharged in the United Kingdom may only be entered outwards by virtue of subsection (3) above subject to such conditions as the Commissioners see fit to impose.

(5) If, when a ship is required by this section to be entered outwards from any port, any goods are taken on board that ship at that port, except in accordance with such a stiffening order as is mentioned in subsection (1) above, before the ship is so entered, the goods shall be liable to forfeiture and the master of the ship shall be liable on summary conviction to a penalty of £100.

(6) Where goods are taken on board a ship as mentioned in subsection (5) above or made waterborne for that purpose with fraudulent intent, any person concerned therein with knowledge of that intent may be detained and shall be liable—

(*a*) on summary conviction, to a penalty of the prescribed sum or of three times the value of the goods, whichever is the greater, or to imprisonment for a term not exceeding 6 months, or to both; or

(*b*) on conviction on indictment, to a penalty of any amount, or to imprisonment for a term not exceeding 2 years, or to both.

Clearance outwards of ships and aircraft

64.—(1) Save as permitted by the Commissioners, no ship or aircraft shall depart from any port or customs and excise airport from which it commences, or at which it touches during, a voyage or flight to an eventual destination outside the United Kingdom until clearance of the ship or aircraft for that departure has been obtained from the proper officer at that port or airport.

(2) The Commissioners may give directions—

(*a*) as to the procedure for obtaining clearance under this section;

(*b*) as to the documents to be produced and the information to be furnished by any person applying for such clearance.

(3) Where clearance is sought under this section for any ship which is in ballast or has on board no goods other than stores, the baggage of passengers carried in that ship, chalk, slate, or empty returned containers upon which no freight or profit is earned, the proper officer in granting clearance thereof shall, on the application of the master, clear the ship as in ballast.

(4) Any officer may board any ship which is cleared outwards from a port at any time while the ship is within the limits of a port or within 3 nautical miles of the coast of the United Kingdom and require the production of the ship's clearance, and if the master refuses to produce it or to answer such questions as the officer may put to him concerning the ship, cargo and intended voyage, he shall be liable on summary conviction to a penalty of £25.

(5) Every ship departing from a port shall, if so required for the purpose of disembarking an officer or of further examination, bring to

at the boarding station, and if any ship fails to comply with any such requirement the master shall be liable on summary conviction to a penalty of £50.

(6) If any ship or aircraft required to be cleared under this section departs from any port or customs and excise airport without a valid clearance, the master or commander shall be liable on summary conviction to a penalty of £100.

(7) If, where any aircraft is required to obtain clearance from any customs and excise airport under this section, any goods are loaded, or are waterborne for loading, into that aircraft at that airport before application for clearance has been made, the goods shall be liable to forfeiture and, where the loading or making waterborne is done with fraudulent intent, any person concerned therein with knowledge of that intent shall be guilty of an offence under this subsection and may be detained.

(8) A person guilty of an offence under subsection (7) above shall be liable—

(*a*) on summary conviction, to a penalty of the prescribed sum or of three times the value of the goods, whichever is the greater, or to imprisonment for a term not exceeding 6 months, or to both; or

(*b*) on conviction on indictment, to a penalty of any amount, or to imprisonment for a term not exceeding 2 years, or to both.

Power to refuse or cancel clearance of ship or aircraft

65.—(1) For the purpose of the detention thereof in pursuance of any power or duty conferred or imposed by or under any enactment, or for the purpose of securing compliance with any provision of the Customs and Excise Acts 1979 or of any other enactment or of any instrument made thereunder, being a provision relating to the importation or exportation of goods—

(*a*) the proper officer may at any time refuse clearance of any ship or aircraft; and

(*b*) where clearance has been granted to a ship or aircraft, any officer may at any time while the ship is within the limits of any port or the aircraft is at any customs and excise airport demand that the clearance shall be returned to him.

(2) Any such demand may be made either orally or in writing on the master of the ship or commander of the aircraft, and if made in writing may be served—

(*a*) by delivering it to him personally; or

(*b*) by leaving it at his last known place of abode; or

(*c*) by leaving it on board the ship or aircraft with the person appearing to be in charge or command thereof.

(3) Where a demand for the return of a clearance is made as aforesaid—

(*a*) the clearance shall forthwith become void; and

(*b*) if the demand is not complied with, the master of the ship or the commander of the aircraft shall be liable on summary to a penalty of £100.

General regulation of exportation, etc.

Power to make regulations as to exportation, etc.

66.—(1) The Commissioners may make regulations—

(a) regulating with respect to ships and aircraft respectively the loading and making waterborne for loading of goods for exportation or as stores and the embarking of passengers for a destination outside the United Kingdom;

(b) prescribing the procedure to be followed and the documents to be produced and information to be furnished by any person conveying goods out of Northern Ireland by land;

(c) requiring delivery of a certificate of the fuel shipped in any ship as the Commissioners may direct of all cargo carried in an exporting ship and, if the Commissioners so direct, such other documents relating to the cargo as are specified in the direction;

(d) requiring delivery of a certificate of the fuel shipped in any ship departing from a port for a place outside the United Kingdom.

(2) If any person contravenes or fails to comply with any regulation made under this section, he shall be liable on summary conviction to a penalty of £100 and any goods in respect of which the offence was committed shall be liable to forfeiture.

Offences in relation to exportation

Offences in relation to exportation of goods

67.—(1) If any goods which have been loaded or retained on board any ship or aircraft for exportation are not exported to and discharged at a place outside the United Kingdom but are unloaded in the United Kingdom, then, unless—

(a) the unloading was authorised by the proper officer; and

(b) except where that officer otherwise permits, any duty chargeable and unpaid on the goods is paid and any drawback or allowance paid in respect thereof is repaid,

the master of the ship or the commander of the aircraft and any person concerned in the unshipping, relanding, landing, unloading or carrying of the goods from the ship or aircraft without such authority, payment or repayment shall each be guilty of an offence under this section.

(2) The Commissioners may impose such conditions as they see fit with respect to any goods loaded or retained as mentioned in subsection (1) above which are permitted to be unloaded in the United Kingdom.

(3) If any person contravenes or fails to comply with, or is concerned in any contravention of or failure to comply with, any condition imposed under subsection (2) above shall be guilty of an offence under this section.

(4) Where any goods loaded or retained as mentioned in subsection (1) above or brought to a customs and excise station for exportation by land are—

(a) goods from warehouse, other than goods which have been kept, without being warehoused, in a warehouse by virtue of section 92 (4) below;

(b) transit goods;

(c) other goods chargeable with a duty which has not been paid; or

(d) drawback goods,

then if any container in which the goods are held is without the authority of the proper officer opened, or any mark, letter or device on any such container or on any lot of the goods is without that authority cancelled, obliterated or altered, every person concerned in the opening, cancellation, obliteration or alteration shall be guilty of an offence under this section.

(5) Any goods in respect of which an offence under this section is committed shall be liable to forfeiture and any person guilty of an offence under this section shall be liable on summary conviction to a penalty of three times the value of the goods or £100, whichever is the greater.

Offences in relation to exportation of prohibited or restricted goods

68.—(1) If any goods are—

(*a*) exported or shipped as stores; or

(*b*) brought to any place in the United Kingdom for the purpose of being exported or shipped as stores,

and the exportation or shipment is or would be contrary to any prohibition or restriction for the time being in force with respect to those goods under or by virtue of any enactment, the goods shall be liable to forfeiture and the exporter or intending exporter of the goods and any agent of his concerned in the exportation or shipment or intended exportation or shipment shall each be liable on summary conviction to a penalty of three times the value of the goods or £100, whichever is the greater.

(2) Any person knowingly concerned in the exportation or shipment as stores, or in the attempted exportation or shipment as stores, of any goods with intent to evade any such prohibition or restriction as is mentioned in subsection (1) above shall be guilty of an offence under this subsection and may be detained.

(3) Subject to subsection (4) below, a person guilty of an offence under subsection (2) above shall be liable—

(*a*) on summary conviction, to a penalty of the prescribed sum or of three times the value of the goods, whichever is the greater, or to imprisonment for a term not exceeding 6 months, or to both; or

(*b*) on conviction on indictment, to a penalty of any amount, or to imprisonment for a term not exceeding 2 years, or to both.

(4) In the case of an offence under subsection (2) above in connection with a prohibition or restriction on exportation having effect by virtue of section 3 of the Misuse of Drugs Act 1971, subsection (3) above shall have effect subject to the modifications specified in Schedule 1 to this Act.

(5) If by virtue of any such restriction as is mentioned in subsection (1) above any goods may be exported only when consigned to a particular place or person and any goods so consigned are delivered to some other place or person, the ship, aircraft or vehicle in which they were exported shall be liable to forfeiture unless it is proved to the satisfaction of the Commissioners that both the owner of the ship, aircraft or vehicle and the master of the ship, commander of the aircraft or person in charge of the vehicle—

(*a*) took all reasonable steps to secure that the goods were delivered to the particular place to which or person to whom they were consigned; and

(*b*) did not connive at or, except under duress, consent to the delivery of the goods to that other place or person.

(6) In any case where a person would, apart from this subsection, be guilty of—

(*a*) an offence under subsection (1) or (2) above; and

(*b*) a corresponding offence under the enactment or instrument imposing the prohibition or restriction in question, being an offence for which a fine or other penalty is expressly provided by that enactment or other instrument, he shall not be guilty of the offence mentioned in paragraph (*a*) of this subsection.

PART VI

CONTROL OF COASTWISE TRAFFIC

Coasting trade

69.—(1) Subject to section 70 below, any ship for the time being engaged in the trade of carrying goods coastwise between places in the United Kingdom shall for the purposes of the Customs and Excise Acts 1979 be a coasting ship.

(2) Subject to that section, no goods not yet entered on importation and no goods for exportation shall be carried in a ship engaged in the trade of carrying goods coastwise.

(3) The Commissioners may from time to time give directions as to what trade by water between places in the United Kingdom is or is not to be deemed to be carrying goods coastwise.

Coasting trade—exceptional provisions

70.—(1) The Commissioners may, subject to such conditions and restrictions as they see fit to impose, permit a ship to carry goods coastwise notwithstanding that the ship is carrying goods brought therein from some place outside the United Kingdom and not yet entered on importation; but a ship so permitted to carry goods coastwise shall not for the purposes of the Customs and Excise Acts 1979 be a coasting ship.

(2) The Commissioners may, subject to such conditions and restrictions as they see fit to impose, permit goods brought by an importing ship to some place in the United Kingdom but consigned to and intended to be delivered at some other such place to be transhipped before due entry of the goods has been made to another ship for carriage coastwise to that other place.

(3) Where any ship has begun to load goods at any place in the United Kingdom for exportation or as stores for use on a voyage to an eventual destination outside the United Kingdom and is to go to any other such place to complete loading, the Commissioners may, subject to such conditions as they see fit to impose, permit that ship to carry other goods coastwise until she has completed her loading.

(4) If, where any goods are permitted to be carried coastwise in any ship under this section, the goods are loaded, unloaded, carried or otherwise dealt with contrary to any condition or restriction imposed by the Commissioners, the goods shall be liable to forfeiture and the master of the ship shall be liable on summary conviction to a penalty of £50.

Clearance of coasting ship and transire

71.—(1) Subject to the provisions of this section and save as permitted by the Commissioners, before any coasting ship departs from any port the master thereof shall deliver to the proper officer an account in such form and manner and containing such particulars as the Commissioners may direct; and that account when signed by the proper officer shall be the transire, that is to say, the clearance of the ship from that port and the pass for any goods to which the account relates.

(2) The Commissioners may, subject to such conditions as they see

fit to impose, grant a general transire in respect of any coasting ship and any goods carried therein.

(3) Any such general transire may be revoked by the proper officer by notice in writing delivered to the master or the owner of the ship or to any member of the crew on board the ship.

(4) If a coasting ship departs from any port without a correct account having been delivered, except as permitted by the Commissioners or under and in compliance with any conditions imposed on the grant of a general transire, the master shall be liable on summary conviction to a penalty of £50.

Additional powers of officers in relation to coasting ships

72.—(1) The proper officer may examine any goods carried or to be carried in a coasting ship—

(*a*) at any time while they are on board the ship; or

(*b*) at any place in the United Kingdom to which the goods have been brought for shipment in, or at which they have been unloaded from, the ship.

(2) For the purpose of examining any goods in pursuance of subsection (1) above, the proper officer may require any container to be opened or unpacked; and any such opening or unpacking and any repacking shall be done by or at the expense of the proprietor of the goods.

(3) The proper officer—

(*a*) may board and search a coasting ship at any time during its voyage;

(*b*) may at any time require any document which should properly be on board a coasting ship to be produced or brought to him for examination;

and if the master of the ship fails to produce or bring any such document to the proper officer when required, he shall be liable on summary conviction to a penalty of £50.

Power to make regulations as to carriage of goods coastwise, etc.

73.—(1) The Commissioners may make regulations as to the carriage of goods coastwise—

(*a*) regulating the loading and unloading and the making waterborne for loading of the goods;

(*b*) requiring the keeping and production by the master of a coasting ship of such record of the cargo carried in that ship as may be prescribed by the regulations.

(2) If any person contravenes or fails to comply with any regulation made under this section, he shall be liable on summary conviction to a penalty of £50 and any goods in respect of which the offence was committed shall be liable to forfeiture.

Offences in connection with carriage of goods coastwise

74.—(1) If in the case of any coasting ship—

(*a*) any goods are taken on board or removed therefrom at sea or at any place outside the United Kingdom; or

(*b*) except for some unavoidable cause, the ship touches at any place outside the United Kingdom or deviates from her voyage; or

(*c*) the ship touches at any place outside the United Kingdom and the master does not report that fact in writing to the proper officer at the first port at which the ship arrives thereafter,

the master of the ship shall be liable on summary conviction to a penalty of £100.

(2) Any goods which are shipped and carried coastwise, or which, having been carried coastwise, are unloaded in any place in the United Kingdom, otherwise than in accordance with the provisions of sections 69 to 71 above or of any regulations made under section 73 above, or which are brought to any place for the purpose of being so shipped and carried coastwise, shall be liable to forfeiture.

(3) If any goods—

(*a*) are carried coastwise or shipped as stores in a coasting ship contrary to any prohibition or restriction for the time being in force with respect thereto under or by virtue of any enactment; or

(*b*) are brought to any place in the United Kingdom for the purpose of being so carried or shipped,

then those goods shall be liable to forfeiture and the shipper or intending shipper of the goods shall be liable on summary conviction to a penalty of £100.

(4) In any case where a person would, apart from this subsection, be guilty of—

(*a*) an offence under subsection (3) above; and

(*b*) a corresponding offence under the enactment or other instrument imposing the prohibition or restriction in question, being an offence for which a fine or other penalty is expressly provided by that enactment or other instrument,

he shall not be guilty of the offence mentioned in paragraph (*a*) of this subsection.

PART VII

CUSTOMS AND EXCISE CONTROL: SUPPLEMENTARY PROVISIONS

Special requirements as to movement of certain goods

Explosives

75.—(1) No goods which are explosives within the meaning of the Explosives Act 1875 shall be loaded into any ship or aircraft for exportation, exported by land or shipped for carriage coastwise as cargo, until due entry has been made of the goods in such form and manner and containing such particulars as the Commissioners may direct.

(2) Without prejudice to sections 53 and 60 above, any goods required to be entered under this section which are loaded, exported or shipped as mentioned in subsection (1) above without being entered under this section shall be liable to forfeiture, and the exporter or, as the case may be, shipper shall be liable on summary conviction to a penalty of £100.

Power to require pre-entry and clearance of goods

76.—(1) Without prejudice to any other requirement of this Act as to the entry or clearance of goods, the Commissioners may, where they are satisfied that it is expedient in the public interest, by order made by statutory instrument require with respect to any goods entry and clearance of the goods in such manner as the Commissioners may direct before their exportation or shipment for exportation, for carriage coastwise or as stores.

(2) Without prejudice to sections 53 and 60 above, if any person required by virtue of an order made under this section to make entry or obtain clearance of any goods, ships or exports, or attempts to ship or export, those goods without such entry or clearance or otherwise contrary to the order, he shall be liable on summary conviction to a penalty of £100.

Additional provisions as to information

Information in relation to goods imported or exported

77.—(1) An officer may require any person—

(*a*) concerned with the importation, exportation or shipment for carriage coastwise of goods of which an entry or specification is required for that purpose by or under this Act; or

(*b*) concerned in the carriage, unloading, landing or loading of goods which are being or have been imported or exported,

to furnish in such form as the officer may require any information relating to the goods and to produce and allow the officer to inspect and take extracts from or make copies of any invoice, bill of lading or other book or document whatsoever relating to the goods.

(2) If any person without reasonable cause fails to comply with a requirement imposed on him under subsection (1) above he shall be liable on summary conviction to a penalty of £50.

(3) Where any prohibition or restriction to which this subsection applies, that is to say, any prohibition or restriction under or by virtue of any enactment with respect to—

(*a*) the exportation of goods to any particular destination; or

(*b*) the exportation of goods of any particular class or description to any particular destination,

is for the time being in force, then, if any person about to ship for exportation or to export any goods or, as the case may be, any goods of that class or description, in the course of making entry thereof before shipment or exportation makes a declaration as to the ultimate destination thereof, and the Commissioners have reason to suspect that the declaration is untrue in any material particular, the goods may be detained until the Commissioners are satisfied as to the truth of the declaration, and if they are not so satisfied the goods shall be liable to forfeiture.

(4) Any person concerned in the exportation of any goods which are subject to any prohibition or restriction to which subsection (3) above applies shall, if so required by the Commissioners, satisfy the Commissioners that those goods have not reached any destination other than that mentioned in the entry delivered in respect of the goods.

(5) If any person required under subsection (4) above to satisfy the Commissioners as mentioned in that subsection fails to do so, then, unless he proves—

(*a*) that he did not consent to or connive at the goods reaching any destination other than that mentioned in the entry delivered in respect of the goods; and

(*b*) that he took all reasonable steps to secure that the ultimate destination of the goods was not other than that so mentioned,

he shall be liable on summary conviction to a penalty of three times the value of the goods or £100, whichever is the greater.

Customs and excise control of persons entering or leaving the United Kingdom

78.—(1) Any person entering the United Kingdom shall, at such place and in such manner as the Commissioners may direct, declare any thing contained in his baggage or carried with him which—

(*a*) he has obtained outside the United Kingdom; or

(*b*) being dutiable goods or chargeable goods, he has obtained in the United Kingdom without payment of duty or tax,

and in respect of which he is not entitled to exemption from duty and tax by virtue of any order under section 13 of the Customs and Excise Duties (General Reliefs) Act 1979 (personal reliefs).

In this subsection " chargeable goods " means goods on the importation of which value added tax is chargeable or goods obtained in the United Kingdom before 1st April 1973 which are chargeable goods within the meaning of the Purchase Tax Act 1963; and " tax " means value added tax or purchase tax.

(2) Any person entering or leaving the United Kingdom shall answer such questions as the proper officer may put to him with respect to his baggage and any thing contained therein or carried with him, and shall, if required by the proper officer, produce that baggage and any such thing for examination at such place as the Commissioners may direct.

(3) Any person failing to declare any thing or to produce any baggage or thing as required by this section shall be liable on summary conviction to a penalty of three times the value of the thing not declared or of the baggage or thing not produced, as the case may be, or £100, whichever is the greater.

(4) Any thing chargeable with any duty or tax which is found concealed, or is not declared, and any thing which is being taken into or out of the United Kingdom contrary to any prohibition or restriction for the time being in force with respect thereto under or by virtue of any enactment, shall be liable to forfeiture.

Power to require evidence in support of information

79.—(1) The Commissioners may, if they consider it necessary, require evidence to be produced to their satisfaction in support of any information required by or under Parts III to VII of this Act to be provided in respect of goods imported or exported.

(2) Without prejudice to subsection (1) above, where any question as to the duties chargeable on any imported goods, or the operation of any prohibition or restriction on importation, depends on any question as to the place from which the goods were consigned, or any question where they or other goods are to be treated as grown, manufactured or produced, or any question as to payments made or relief from duty allowed in any country or territory, then—

(*a*) the Commissioners may require the importer of the goods to furnish to them, in such form as they may prescribe, proof of—

(i) any statement made to them as to any fact necessary to determine that question, or

(ii) the accuracy of any certificate or other document furnished in connection with the importation of the goods and relating to the matter in issue,

and if such proof is not furnished to their satisfaction, the question may be determined without regard to that statement or to that certificate or document; and

(*b*) if in any proceedings relating to the goods or to the duty chargeable thereon the accuracy of any such certificate or document comes in question, it shall be for the person relying on it to furnish proof of its accuracy.

Power to require information or production of documents where origin of goods exported is evidenced under Community law or practice

80.—(1) Where on the exportation of any goods from the United Kingdom there has been furnished for the purpose of any Community requirement or practice any certificate or other evidence as to the origin of those goods, or as to payments made or relief from duty allowed in any country or territory, then, for the purpose of verifying or investigating that certificate or evidence, the Commissioners or an officer may require the exporter, or any other person appearing to the Commissioners or officer to have been concerned in any way with the goods, or with any goods from which, directly or indirectly, they have been produced or manufactured, or to have been concerned with the obtaining or furnishing of the certificate or evidence,—

(*a*) to furnish such information, in such form and within such time, as the Commissioners or officer may specify in the requirement; or

(*b*) to produce for inspection, and to allow the taking of copies or extracts from, such invoices, bills of lading, books or documents as may be so specified.

(2) Any person who, without reasonable cause, fails to comply with a requirement imposed on him under subsection (1) above shall be liable on summary conviction to a penalty of £50.

Prevention of smuggling

Power to regulate small craft

81.—(1) In this section " small ships " means—

(*a*) ships not exceeding 100 tons register; and

(*b*) hovercraft, of whatever size.

(2) The Commissioners may make general regulations with respect to small ships and any such regulations may in particular make provision as to the purposes for which and the limits within which such ships may be used.

(3) Different provision may be made by regulations under this section for different classes or descriptions of small ships.

(4) The Commissioners may, in respect of any small ship, grant a licence exempting that ship from all or any of the provisions of any regulations made under this section.

(5) Any such licence may be granted for such period, for such purposes and subject to such conditions and restrictions as the Commissioners see fit, and may be revoked at any time by the Commissioners.

(6) Any small ship which, except under and in accordance with the terms of a licence granted under this section, is used contrary to any regulation made under this section, and any ship granted such a licence which is found not to have that licence on board, shall be liable to forfeiture.

(7) Every boat belonging to a British ship and every other vessel not exceeding 100 tons register, not being a fishing boat entered in the fishing boat register under the Merchant Shipping Act 1894, and every hovercraft, shall be marked in such manner as the Commissioners may direct, and any such boat, vessel or hovercraft which is not so marked shall be liable to forfeiture.

Power to haul up revenue vessels, patrol coasts, etc.

82.—(1) The person in command or charge of any vessel in the service of Her Majesty which is engaged in the prevention of smuggling—

(*a*) may haul up and leave that vessel on any part of the coast or of the shore or bank of any river or creek; and

(*b*) may moor that vessel at any place below high water mark on any part of the coast or of any such shore or bank.

(2) Any officer and any person acting in aid of an officer or otherwise duly engaged in the prevention of smuggling may for that purpose patrol upon and pass freely along and over any part of the coast or of the shore or bank of any river or creek, over any railway or aerodrome or land adjoining any aerodrome, and over any land in Northern Ireland within the prescribed area.

(3) Nothing in this section shall authorise the use of or entry into any garden or pleasure ground.

Penalty for removing seals, etc.

83.—(1) Where, in pursuance of any power conferred by the customs and excise Acts or of any requirement imposed by or under those Acts, a seal, lock or mark is used to secure or identify any goods for any of the purposes of those Acts and—

(*a*) at any time while the goods are in the United Kingdom or within the limits of any port or on passage between ports in the United Kingdom, the seal, lock or mark is wilfully and prematurely removed or tampered with by any person; or

(*b*) at any time before the seal, lock or mark is lawfully removed, any of the goods are wilfully removed by any person,

that person and the person then in charge of the goods shall each be liable on summary conviction to a penalty of £500.

(2) For the purposes of subsection (1) above, goods in a ship or aircraft shall be deemed to be in the charge of the master of the ship or commander of the aircraft.

(3) Where, in pursuance of any Community requirement or practice which relates to the movement of goods between countries or of any international agreement to which the United Kingdom is a party and which so relates,—

(*a*) a seal, lock or mark is used (whether in the United Kingdom or elsewhere) to secure or identify any goods for customs and excise purposes; and

(*b*) at any time while the goods are in the United Kingdom, the seal, lock or mark is wilfully and prematurely removed or tampered with by any person,

that person and the person then in charge of the goods shall each be liable on summary conviction to a penalty of £500.

Penalty for signalling to smugglers

84.—(1) In this section references to a " prohibited signal " or a " prohibited message " are references to a signal or message connected with the smuggling or intended smuggling of goods into or out of the United Kingdom.

(2) Any person who by any means makes any prohibited signal or transmits any prohibited message from any part of the United Kingdom or from any ship or aircraft for the information of a person in any ship or aircraft or across the boundary shall be liable on summary conviction to a penalty of £100, or to imprisonment for a term not exceeding

6 months, or to both, and may be detained; and any equipment or apparatus used for sending the signal or message shall be liable to forfeiture.

(3) Subsection (2) above applies whether or not the person for whom the signal or message is intended is in a position to receive it or is actually engaged at the time in smuggling goods.

(4) If, in any proceedings under subsection (2) above, any question arises as to whether any signal or message was a prohibited signal or message, the burden of proof shall lie upon the defendant or claimant.

(5) If any officer or constable or any member of Her Majesty's armed forces or coastguard has reasonable grounds for suspecting that any prohibited signal or message is being or is about to be made or transmitted from any ship, aircraft, vehicle, house or place, he may board or enter that ship, aircraft, vehicle, house or place and take such steps as are reasonably necessary to stop or prevent the sending of the signal or message.

Penalty for interfering with revenue vessels, etc.

85.—(1) Any person who save for just and sufficient cause interferes in any way with any ship, aircraft, vehicle, buoy, anchor, chain, rope or mark which is being used for the purposes of any functions of the Commissioners under Parts III to VII of this Act shall be liable on summary conviction to a penalty of £25.

(2) Any person who fires upon any vessel aircraft or vehicle in the service of Her Majesty while that vessel, aircraft or vehicle is engaged in the prevention of smuggling shall be liable on conviction on indictment to imprisonment for a term not exceeding 5 years.

Special penalty where offender armed or disguised

86. Any person concerned in the movement, carriage or concealment of goods—

(*a*) contrary to or for the purpose of contravening any prohibition or restriction for the time being in force under or by virtue of any enactment with respect to the importation thereof; or

(*b*) without payment having been made of or security given for any duty payable thereon,

who, while so concerned, is armed with any offensive weapon or disguised in any way, and any person so armed or disguised found in the United Kingdom in possession of any goods liable to forfeiture under any provision of the customs and excise Acts relating to imported goods or prohibited or restricted goods, shall be liable on conviction on indictment to imprisonment for a term not exceeding 3 years and may be detained.

Penalty for offering goods for sale as smuggled goods

87. If any person offers any goods for sale as having been imported without payment of duty, or has having been otherwise unlawfully imported, then, whether or not the goods were so imported or were in fact chargeable with duty, the goods shall be liable to forfeiture and the person so offering them for sale shall be liable on summary conviction to a penalty of three times the value of the goods or £100, whichever is the greater, and may be detained.

Forfeiture of ships, etc. for certain offences

Forfeiture of ship, aircraft or vehicle constructed, etc. for concealing goods

88. Where—

(*a*) a ship is or has been within the limits of any port or within 3 or, being a British ship, 12 nautical miles of the coast of the United Kingdom; or

(*b*) an aircraft is or has been at any place, whether on land or on water, in the United Kingdom; or

(*c*) a vehicle is or has been within the limits of any port or at any aerodrome or, while in Northern Ireland, within the prescribed area,

while constructed, adapted, altered or fitted in any manner for the purpose of concealing goods, that ship, aircraft or vehicle shall be liable to forfeiture.

Forfeiture of ship jettisoning cargo, etc.

89.—(1) If any part of the cargo of a ship is thrown overboard or is staved or destroyed to prevent seizure—

(*a*) while the ship is within 3 nautical miles of the coast of the United Kingdom; or

(*b*) where the ship, having been properly summoned to bring to by any vessel in the service of Her Majesty, fails so to do and chase is given, at any time during the chase,

the ship shall be liable to forfeiture.

(2) For the purposes of this section a ship shall be deemed to have been properly summoned to bring to—

(*a*) if the vessel making the summons did so by means of an international signal code or other recognised means and while flying her proper ensign; and

(*b*) in the case of a ship which is not a British ship, if at the time when the summons was made the ship was within 3 nautical miles of the coast of the United Kingdom.

Forfeiture of ship or aircraft unable to account for missing cargo

90. Where a ship has been within the limits of any port, or an aircraft has been in the United Kingdom, with a cargo on board and a substantial part of that cargo is afterwards found to be missing, then, if the master of the ship or commander of the aircraft fails to account therefor to the satisfaction of the Commissioners, the ship or aircraft shall be liable to forfeiture.

Ships failing to bring to

91.—(1) If, save for just and sufficient cause, any ship which is liable to forfeiture or examination under or by virtue of any provision of the Customs and Excise Acts 1979 does not bring to when required to do so, the master of the ship shall be liable on summary conviction to a penalty of £50.

(2) Where any ship liable to forfeiture or examination as aforesaid has failed to bring to when required to do so and chase has been given thereto by any vessel in the service of Her Majesty and, after the commander of that vessel has hoisted the proper ensign and caused a gun to be fired as a signal, the ship still fails to bring to, the ship may be fired upon.

Part VIII

Warehouses and Queen's Warehouses and Related Provisions about Pipe-lines

Approval of warehouses

92.—(1) The Commissioners may approve, for such periods and subject to such conditions as they think fit, places of security for the deposit, keeping and securing—

(*a*) of imported goods chargeable as such with excise duty (whether or not also chargeable with customs duty) without payment of the excise duty;

(*b*) of goods for exportation or for use as stores, being goods not eligible for home use;

(*c*) of goods manufactured or produced in the United Kingdom and permitted by or under the customs and excise Acts to be warehoused without payment of any duty of excise chargeable thereon;

(*d*) of goods imported into or manufactured or produced in the United Kingdom and permitted by or under the customs and excise Acts to be warehoused on drawback,

subject to and in accordance with warehousing regulations; and any place of security so approved is referred to in this Act as an " excise warehouse ".

(2) The Commissioners may approve, for such periods and subject to such conditions as they think fit, places of security for the deposit, keeping and securing—

(*a*) of imported goods chargeable with customs duty or otherwise not for the time being in free circulation in member States (whether not also chargeable with excise duty) without payment of the customs duty;

(*b*) of such other goods as the Commissioners may allow to be warehoused for exportation or for use as stores in cases where relief from or repayment of any customs duty or other payment is conditional on their exportation or use as stores,

subject to and in accordance with warehousing regulations; and any place of security so approved is referred to in this Act as a " customs warehouse ".

(3) The same place may be approved under this section both as a customs and as an excise warehouse.

(4) Notwithstanding subsection (2) above and the terms of the approval of the warehouse but subject to directions under subsection (5) below, goods of the following descriptions, not being goods chargeable with excise duty which has not been paid, that is to say—

(*a*) goods originating in member States;

(*b*) goods which are in free circulation in member States; and

(*c*) goods placed on importation under a customs procedure (other than warehousing) involving the suspension of, or the giving of relief from, customs duties,

may be kept, without being warehoused, in a customs warehouse.

(5) The Commissioners may from time to time give directions—

(*a*) as to the goods which may or may not be deposited in any particular warehouse or class of warehouse;

(*b*) as to the part of any warehouse in which any class or description of goods may be kept or secured.

(6) If, after the approval of a warehouse as an excise warehouse, the occupier thereof makes without the previous consent of the Commissioners

any alteration therein or addition thereto, he shall be liable on summary conviction to a penalty of £200.

(7) The Commissioners may at any time for reasonable cause revoke or vary the terms of their approval of any warehouse under this section.

(8) Any person contravening or failing to comply with any condition imposed or direction given by the Commissioners under this section shall be liable on summary conviction to a penalty of £100.

Regulation of warehouses and warehoused goods

93.—(1) The Commissioners may by regulations under this section (referred to in this Act as " warehousing regulations ") regulate the deposit, keeping, securing and treatment of goods in and the removal of goods from warehouse.

(2) Warehousing regulations may, without prejudice to the generality of subsection (1) above, include provisions—

(*a*) imposing or providing for the imposition under the regulations of conditions and restrictions subject to which goods may be deposited in, kept in or removed from warehouse or made available there to their owner for any prescribed purpose;

(*b*) requiring goods deposited in warehouse to be produced to or made available for inspection by an officer on request by him;

(*c*) permitting the carrying out on warehoused goods of such operations (other than operations consisting of the mixing of spirits with wine or made-wine) as may be prescribed by or allowed under the regulations in such manner and subject to such conditions and restrictions as may be imposed by or under the regulations;

(*d*) for determining, for the purpose of charging or securing the payment of duty, the duties of customs or excise and the rates thereof to be applied to warehoused goods (other than goods falling within section 92 (2) (*b*) above) and in that connection—

(i) for determining the time by reference to which warehoused goods are to be classified;

(ii) for determining the time at which warehoused goods are to be treated as having been removed from warehouse;

(iii) for ascertaining the quantity which is to be taken as the quantity of warehoused goods;

(*e*) enabling the Commissioners to allow goods to be removed from warehouse without payment of duty in such circumstances and subject to such conditions as they may determine;

(*f*) permitting goods to be destroyed or abandoned to the Commissioners without payment of customs duty in such circumstances and subject to such conditions as they may determine,

and may contain such incidental or supplementary provisions as the Commissioners think necessary or expedient for the protection of the revenue.

(3) Warehousing regulations may make different provision for warehouses or parts of warehouses of different descriptions or for goods of different classes or descriptions or of the same class or description in different circumstances.

(4) Warehousing regulations may make provision about the removal of goods from one warehouse to another or from one part of a warehouse to another part or for treating goods remaining in a warehouse as if, for all or any prescribed purposes of the customs and excise Acts, they had been so removed; and regulations about the removal of goods may, for all or any prescribed purposes of those Acts, include provision for

treating the goods as having been warehoused or removed from warehouse (where they would not otherwise be so treated).

(5) Warehousing regulations made by virtue of paragraph (*a*) or (*c*) of subsection (2) above may also provide for the forfeiture of goods in the event of non-compliance with any condition or restriction imposed by virtue of that paragraph or in the event of the carrying out of any operation on warehoused goods which is not by virtue of the said paragraph (*c*) permitted to be carried out in warehouse.

(6) If any person fails to comply with any warehousing regulation or with any condition or restriction imposed under a warehousing regulation he shall be liable on summary conviction to a penalty of £100.

(7) In this section " prescribed " means prescribed by warehousing regulations.

Deficiency in warehoused goods

94.—(1) Subject to subsection (2) below, this section applies where goods have been warehoused and, before they are lawfully removed from warehouse in accordance with a proper clearance thereof, they are found to be missing or deficient.

(2) This section shall not apply in relation to a deficiency in goods entered and cleared from warehouse for exportation or shipment as stores unless the proper officer has reasonable grounds to suppose that the whole or part of the deficiency has arisen from unlawful abstraction.

(3) In any case where this section applies, unless it is shown to the satisfaction of the Commissioners that the absence of or deficiency in the good can be accounted for by natural waste or other legitimate cause, the Commissioners may require the occupier of the warehouse or the proprietor of the goods to pay immediately in respect of the missing goods or of the whole or any part of the deficiency, as they see fit, the duty chargeable or deemed under warehousing regulations to be chargeable on such goods or, in the case of goods warehoused on drawback which could not lawfully be entered for home use, an amount equal to the drawback and any allowance paid in respect of the goods.

(4) If, on the written demand of an officer, the occupier of the warehouse or the proprietor of the goods refuses to pay any sum which he is required to pay under subsection (3) above he shall in addition be liable on summary conviction to a penalty of double that sum.

(5) This section has effect without prejudice to any penalty or forfeiture incurred under any other provision of the customs and excise Acts.

Deficiency in goods occurring in course of removal from warehouse without payment of duty

95.—(1) Where any goods have been lawfully permitted to be taken from a warehouse without payment of duty for removal to another warehouse or to some other place, section 94 above shall, subject to subsection (2) below, have effect in relation to those goods in the course of that removal as if those goods were still in warehouse.

(2) In its application in relation to any goods by virtue of subsection (1) above, section 94 above shall have effect as if the following provisions were omitted, namely—

(*a*) subsection (2), and the reference to that subsection in subsection (1); and

(*b*) the references in subsections (3) and (4) to the occupier of the warehouse.

Deficiency in certain goods moved by pipe-line

96.—(1) This section applies where goods of any of the following descriptions, that is to say—

(*a*) goods which are chargeable with a duty which has not been paid;

(*b*) goods on which duty has been repaid or remitted in whole or in part; and

(*c*) goods on which drawback has been paid,

are moved by pipe-line, or notified to the proper officer as being goods to be moved by pipe-line, and are at any time thereafter found to be missing or deficient.

(2) In any case where this section applies, unless it is shown to the satisfaction of the Commissioners that the absence of or deficiency in the goods can be accounted for by natural waste or other legitimate cause, the Commissioners may require the owner of the pipe-line or the proprietor of the goods to pay immediately in respect of the missing goods, or in respect of the whole or any part of the deficiency, as they see fit, the amount of the duty unpaid or repaid thereon or, as the case may be, an amount equal to the drawback paid thereon.

(3) If, on the written demand of an officer, any person refuses to pay any sum which he is required to pay under subsection (2) above he shall in addition be liable on summary conviction to a penalty of double that sum.

(4) For the purposes of this section any absence or deficiency in the case of goods moved by a pipe-line used for the importation or exportation of goods shall be deemed to have taken place within the United Kingdom unless the contrary is shown.

(5) This section has effect without prejudice to any penalty or forfeiture incurred under any other provision of the customs and excise Acts.

Restriction on compensation for loss or damage to goods in, or for removal of goods from, warehouse or pipe-line

97.—(1) This section applies to—

(*a*) any loss or damage caused to goods while in a warehouse or pipe-line; and

(*b*) any unlawful removal of goods from a warehouse or pipe-line.

(2) Subject to subsection (3) below, no compensation shall be payable by, and no action shall lie against, the Commissioners or any officer acting in the execution of his duty for any loss or damage to which this section applies or for any unlawful removal to which this section applies.

(3) If any goods in a warehouse or pipe-line are destroyed, stolen or unlawfully removed by or with the assistance or connivance of an officer and that officer is convicted of the offence, then, except where the proprietor of the goods or the occupier of the warehouse or, as the case may be, the owner of the pipe-line was a party to the offence, the Commissioners shall pay compensation for any loss caused by any such destruction, theft or removal.

(4) Where compensation is payable by virtue of subsection (3) above then, notwithstanding any provision of the Customs and Excise Acts 1979, no duty shall be payable on the goods by the proprietor of the goods or by the occupier of the warehouse or, as the case may be, the owner of the pipe-line, and any sum paid by way of duty on those goods by any of those persons before the conviction shall be repaid.

Procedure on warehouse ceasing to be approved

98.—(1) Where the Commissioners intend to revoke or not to renew their approval of a warehouse, they shall, not later than the beginning of the prescribed period ending with the date when the revocation is to take effect or the approval is due to expire, as the case may be, give notice of their intention, specifying therein the said date.

(2) The notice shall be given in writing and shall be deemed to have been served on all persons interested in any goods then deposited in that warehouse, or permitted under the Customs and Excise Acts 1979 to be so deposited between the date of the giving of the notice and the date specified therein, if addressed to the occupier of, and left at, the warehouse.

(3) If, after the date specified in the notice or such later date as the Commissioners may in any case allow, any goods not duly cleared still remain in the warehouse they may be taken by an officer to a Queen's warehouse and, without prejudice to section 99 (3) below, if they are not cleared therefrom within one month may be sold.

(4) In this section " the prescribed period " means—

(*a*) in the case of a warehouse which is a customs warehouse but not also an excise warehouse, such period as may be prescribed by warehousing regulations;

(*b*) in the case of a warehouse which is or is also an excise warehouse, 3 months.

Provisions as to deposit in Queen's warehouse

99.—(1) The following provisions of this section shall have effect in relation to any goods which are deposited in a Queen's warehouse under or by virtue of any provision of the Customs and Excise Acts 1979.

(2) Such rent shall be payable while the goods are deposited as may be fixed by the Commissioners.

(3) If the goods are of a combustible or inflammable nature or otherwise of such a character as to require special care or treatment—

(*a*) they shall, in addition to any other charges payable thereon, be chargeable with such expenses for securing, watching and guarding them as the Commissioners see fit;

(*b*) neither the Commissioners nor any officer shall be liable to make good any damage which the goods may have sustained; and

(*c*) if the proprietor of the goods has not cleared them within a period of 14 days from the date of deposit, they may be sold by the Commissioners;

but, in the case of goods deposited by virtue of section 40 (2) above, paragraph (*c*) above shall only apply if the goods are of a combustible or inflammable nature.

(4) Save as permitted by or under the Customs and Excise Acts 1979, the goods shall not be removed from the warehouse until—

(*a*) any duty chargeable thereon; and

(*b*) any charges in respect thereof—

(i) for their removal to the warehouse, and

(ii) under subsections (2) and (3) above,

have been paid and, in the case of goods requiring entry and not yet entered, until entry has been made thereof.

(5) The officer having the custody of the goods may refuse to allow them to be removed until it is shown to his satisfaction that any freight charges due thereon have been paid.

(6) If the goods are sold under or by virtue of any provision of the Customs and Excise Acts 1979, the proceeds of sale shall be applied—

(a) first, in paying any duty chargeable on the goods;
(b) secondly, in defraying any such charges as are mentioned in subsection (4) above; and
(c) thirdly, in defraying any charges for freight;

and if the person who was immediately before the sale the proprietor of the goods makes application in that behalf the remainder, if any, shall be paid over to him.

(7) When the goods are authorised to be sold under or by virtue of any provision of the Customs and Excise Acts 1979 but cannot be sold—

(a) if the goods are to be exported, for a sum sufficient to make the payment mentioned in paragraph (b) of subsection (6) above; or
(b) in any other case, for a sum sufficient to make the payments mentioned in paragraphs (a) and (b) of that subsection,

General offences relating to warehouses and warehoused goods

100.—(1) Any person who, except with the authority of the proper officer or for just and sufficient cause, opens any of the doors or locks of a warehouse or Queen's warehouse or makes or obtains access to any such warehouse or to any goods warehoused therein shall be liable on summary conviction to a penalty of £500 and may be detained.

(2) Where—

(a) any goods which have been entered for warehousing are taken into the warehouse without the authority of, or otherwise than in accordance with any directions given by, the proper officer; or
(b) save as permitted by the Customs and Excise Acts 1979 or by or under warehousing regulations, any goods which have been entered for warehousing are removed without being duly warehoused or are otherwise not duly warehoused; or
(c) any goods which have been deposited in a warehouse or Queen's warehouse are unlawfully removed therefrom or are unlawfully loaded into any ship, aircraft or vehicle for removal or for exportation or use as stores; or
(d) any goods entered for warehousing are concealed either before or after they have been warehoused; or
(e) any goods which have been lawfully permitted to be removed from a warehouse or Queen's warehouse without payment of duty for any purpose are not duly delivered at the destination to which they should have been taken in accordance with that permission,

those goods shall be liable to forfeiture.

(3) If any person who took, removed, loaded or concealed any goods as mentioned in subsection (2) above did so with intent to defraud Her Majesty of any duty chargeable thereon or to evade any prohibition or restriction for the time being in force with respect thereto under or by virtue of any enactment, he shall be guilty of an offence under this subsection and may be detained.

(4) A person guilty of an offence under subsection (3) above shall be liable—

(a) on summary conviction, to a penalty of the prescribed sum or of three times the value of the goods, whichever is the greater, or to imprisonment for a term not exceeding 6 months, or to both; or (*b*) on conviction on indictment, to a penalty of any amount, or to imprisonment for a term not exceeding 2 years, or to both.

Part IX

Control of Excise Licence Trades and Revenue Traders

Excise licences—general provisions

Excise licences

101.—(1) An excise licence shall be in such form and contain such particulars as the Commissioners may direct and, subject to the provisions of any enactment relating to the licence or trade in question, may be granted by the proper officer on payment of the appropriate duty.

(2) An excise licence for the carrying on of a trade shall be granted in respect of one set of premises only, but a licence for the same trade may be granted to the same person in respect of each of two or more sets of premises.

(3) Where an excise licence trade is carried on at any set of premises by two or more persons in partnership, then, subject to the provisions of any enactment relating to the licence or trade in question, not more than one licence shall be required to be taken out by those persons in respect of those premises in any once licence year.

(4) Without prejudice to any other requirement as to the production of licences contained in the Customs and Excise Acts 1979, if any person who is the holder of an excise licence to carry on any trade or to manufacture or sell any goods fails to produce his licence for examination within a reasonable time after being so requested by an officer he shall be liable on summary conviction to a penalty of £50.

Payment for excise licences by cheque

102.—(1) Any government department or local authority having power to grant an excise licence may, if they think fit, grant the licence upon receipt of a cheque for the amount of the duty payable thereon.

(2) Where a licence is granted to any person on receipt of a cheque and the cheque is subsequently dishonoured, the licence shall be void as from the time when it was granted, and the department or authority who granted it shall send to that person, by letter sent by registered post or the recorded delivery service and addressed to him at the address given by him when applying for the licence, a notice requiring him to deliver up the licence within the period of 7 days from the date when the notice was posted.

(3) If a person who has been required under subsection (2) above to deliver up a licence fails to comply with the requirement within the period mentioned in that subsection he shall be liable on summary conviction to a penalty of the following amount, that is to say—

(*a*) where the licence is a gaming licence or a gaming machine licence, a penalty of £500;

(*b*) in any other case, a penalty of £50.

Renewal of excise licences

103.—(1) Subject to subsection (2) below, where a person who has taken out an excise licence issuable annually in respect of any trade takes out a fresh licence in respect of that trade for the next following licence year, then, subject to the provisions of any enactment relating to the licence or trade in question, the fresh licence shall bear the date of the day immediately following that on which the previous licence expires.

(2) Where an application for the fresh licence is made after the day on which the previous licence expires or such later day as the Commissioners may in any case allow, the licence shall bear the date of the day when the application is made.

Transfer and removal of excise licence trades and licences

104.—(1) Subject to any provision of the Customs and Excise Acts 1979 or of any other enactment relating to the licence or trade in question, where the holder of an excise licence to carry on any trade dies, or where the holder of such a licence in respect of premises specified therein leaves those premises, the proper officer may transfer that licence in such manner as the Commissioners may direct, without any additional payment, to some other person for the remainder of the period for which the licence was granted.

(2) Subject to any such provision as aforesaid, where any person who holds an excise licence in respect of any premises removes his trade to other premises on which it may be lawfully carried on, the proper officer may authorise in such manner as the Commissioners may direct the carrying on, without any additional payment other than any required to be paid by subsection (3) below, of that trade on those other premises for the remainder of the period for which the licence was granted.

(3) Where, in a case falling within subsection (2) above, the amount of the duty payable on the grant of the licence was determined by reference to the annual value of the premises in respect of which it was granted and would have been greater if the licence had originally been granted in respect of the premises to which the trade is removed, such additional sum shall be payable as bears the same proportion to the difference as the remainder of the period for which the licence was granted bears to a year.

(4) Notwithstanding anything in subsections (1) to (3) above, where by any other enactment relating to the licence or trade in question the authorisation of any court or other authority or the production of any certificate is required for such a transfer or removal of an excise licence trade as is mentioned in this section, no transfer or removal of an excise licence to carry on that trade shall be granted unless it is shown to the satisfaction of the proper officer that the authorisation or certificate has been granted.

Certain sales permitted without excise licence

105.—(1) Where any imported goods are on importation warehoused without payment of duty, then, notwithstanding that they are goods for the sale of which an excise licence is required, a licence shall not be required for a sale of those goods at any time before they are delivered for home use if the sale is made to one person or to persons carrying on trade or business in partnership and—

(*a*) is of not less than one complete container or lot of the goods; and

(*b*) if it is a sale of wine or a sale of spirits, is of not less than 100 gallons.

(2) Any person may sell by auction by sample in any place any goods

for the sale of which an excise licence is required without holding such a licence if the proprietor of the goods holds a licence for the sale of such goods granted in respect of premises in the same locality.

(3) The Commissioners may if they see fit authorise any person to sell by auction any goods for the sale of which an excise licence is required without holding such a licence where they are satisfied that the goods are the property of a private person and are not being sold for profit or by way of trade.

Offences in connection with certain excise licences

106.—(1) If any person holding an excise licence for the sale of any goods contravenes the terms of that licence, or sells otherwise than as he is authorised by the licence, or contravenes or fails to comply with any provision of the Customs and Excise Acts 1979 or any other Act applicable to the licence, then, if he does not thereby commit an offence under any other enactment, he shall be liable on summary conviction to a penalty of £50.

(2) Subject to subsection (3) below, if in the case of any goods for the sale of which an excise licence is required, any person solicits or takes any order for any such goods otherwise than under the authority of the appropriate licence for their sale granted in respect of the premises at which the order is solicited or taken, he shall be liable on summary conviction to the same penalty as a person selling those goods without that licence.

(3) Subsection (2) above shall not apply—

(*a*) in relation to a sale of goods in warehouse for which an excise licence is by virtue of section 105 above not required; or

(*b*) to a bona fide traveller taking orders for goods which his employer is duly licensed to sell.

Power to require person carrying on excise licence trade to display sign

107.—(1) The Commissioners may require any person holding an excise licence to carry on any trade to affix to and maintain on the premises in respect of which the licence is granted, in such form and manner and containing such particulars as they may direct, a notification of the person to whom and the purpose for which the licence is granted.

(2) If any person contravenes or fails to comply with any requirement made or direction given under this section he shall be liable on summary conviction to a penalty of £50.

(3) If any person not duly licensed to carry on an excise licence trade affixes to any premises any sign or notice purporting to show that he is so licensed he shall be liable on summary conviction to a penalty of £50.

General provisions as to entries of premises, etc.

Making of entries

108.—(1) Where by or under the revenue trade provisions of the customs and excise Acts any person is required to make entry of any premises or article—

(*a*) the entry shall be made in such form and manner and contain such particulars; and

(*b*) the premises or article shall be, and be kept, marked in such manner,

as the Commissioners may direct.

(2) No entry shall be valid unless the person by whom it was made—

(*a*) had at the time of its making attained the age of 18 years; and

(*b*) was at that time and is for the time being a true and real owner of the trade in respect of which the entry was made.

(3) Where any person required to make entry is a body corporate—

(*a*) the entry shall be signed by a director, general manager, secretary or other similar officer of the body and, except where authority for that person to sign has been given under the seal of the body, shall be made under that seal; and

(*b*) both the body corporate and the person by whom the entry is signed shall be liable for all duties charged in respect of the trade to which the entry relates.

(4) If any person making entry of any premises or article contravenes or fails to comply with any direction of the Commissioners given under this section with respect thereto, he shall be liable on summary conviction to a penalty of £100.

New or further entries of same premises

109.—(1) The Commissioners may at any time, by notice in writing to the person by whom any existing entry was signed addressed to him at any premises entered by him, require a new entry to be made of any premises or article to which the existing entry relates, and the existing entry shall, without prejudice to any liability incurred, becoming void at the expiration of 14 days from the delivery of the notice.

(2) Save as permitted by the Commissioners and subject to such conditions as they may impose, no premises or article of which entry has been made by any person shall, while that entry remains in force, be entered by any other person for any purpose of the revenue trade provisions of the customs and excise Acts, and any entry made in contravention of this subsection shall be void.

(3) Where the person by whom entry has been made of any premises absconds or quits possession of the premises and discontinues the trade in respect of which the entry was made, and the Commissioners permit a further entry to be made of the premises by some other person, the former entry shall be deemed to have been withdrawn and shall be void.

Proof as to entries

110. For the purpose of any proceedings before any court, if any question arises as to whether or not entry under the revenue trade provisions of the customs and excise Acts has been made by any person, or of any premises or article, or for any purpose, then—

(*a*) if a document purporting to be an original entry made by the person, or of the premises or article, or for the purpose, in question is produced to the court by an officer, that document shall, until the contrary is proved, be sufficient evidence that the entry was so made; and

(*b*) if the officer in whose custody any such entry, if made, would be gives evidence that the original entries produced by him to the court constitute all those in his custody and that no such entry as is in question is among them, it shall be deemed, until the contrary is proved, that no such entry has been made.

Offences in connection with entries

111.—(1) If any person uses for any purpose of his trade any premises or article required by or under the revenue trade provisions of the customs and excise Acts to be entered for that purpose without entry having been duly made thereof, he shall be liable on summary conviction to a penalty of £200, and any such article and any goods found on any such premises or in any such article shall be liable to forfeiture.

(2) If any person who has made entry of any premises or article fraudulently uses those premises or that article for any purpose other than that for which entry was made thereof he shall be liable on summary conviction to a penalty of £100.

General provisions as to revenue traders

Power of entry upon premises, etc. of revenue traders

112.—(1) An officer may, subject to subsection (2) below, at any time enter upon any premises of which entry is made, or is required by or under the revenue trade provisions of the customs and excise Acts to be made, or any other premises owned or used by a revenue trader for the purposes of his trade and may inspect the premises and search for, examine and take account of any machinery, vessels, utensils, goods or materials belonging to or in any way connected with that trade.

(2) Except in the case of such traders as are mentioned in subsection (3) below, no officer shall exercise the powers conferred on him by subsection (1) above by night unless he is accompanied by a constable.

(3) Where any such premises as are mentioned in subsection (1) above are those of a distiller, rectifier, compounder, brewer for sale, producer of wine, producer of made-wine or maker of cider, and an officer, after having demanded admission into the premises and declared his name and business at the entrance thereof, is not immediately admitted, that officer and any person acting in his aid may, subject to subsection (4) below, break open any door or window of the premises or break through any wall thereof for the purpose of obtaining admission.

(4) No officer or person acting in his aid shall exercise the powers conferred on him by subsection (3) above by night unless he is accompanied by a constable.

(5) Subsection (1) above applies to vehicles, vessels, aircraft, hovercraft or structures in or from which tobacco products are sold or dealt in or dutiable alcoholic liquors are sold by retail as it applies to premises.

(6) This section applies to the occupier of a refinery as it applies to a distiller, whether or not the occupier is a revenue trader.

Power to search for concealed pipes, etc.

113.—(1) If an officer has reasonable grounds to suspect that any secret pipe or other means of conveyance, cock, vessel or utensil is kept or used by a revenue trader to whom this section applies, that officer may, subject to subsection (2) below, at any time, break open any part of the premises of that trader and forcibly enter thereon and so far as is reasonably necessary break up the ground in or adjoining those premises or any wall thereof to search for that pipe or other means of conveyance, cock, vessel or utensil.

(2) No officer shall exercise the powers conferred on him by subsection (1) above by night unless he is accompanied by a constable.

(3) If the officer finds any such pipe or other form of conveyance leading to or from the trader's premises, he may enter any other premises from or into which it leads, and so far as is reasonably necessary break up any part of those other premises to trace its course, and may cut it

away and turn any cock thereon, and examine whether it conveys or conceals any goods chargeable with a duty of excise, or any materials used in the manufacture of such goods, in such manner as to prevent a true account thereof from being taken.

(4) Every such pipe or other means of conveyance, cock, vessel or utensil as aforesaid, and all goods chargeable with a duty of excise or materials for the manufacture of such goods found therein, shall be liable to forfeiture, and the trader shall be liable on summary conviction to a penalty of £100.

(5) If any damage is done in any such search as aforesaid and the search is unsuccessful, the Commissioners shall make good the damage.

(6) The revenue traders to whom this section applies are distillers, rectifiers, compounders, brewers for sale, producers of wine, producers of made made-wine and makers of cider.

(7) This section also applies to the occupier of a refinery as it applies to the traders mentioned in subsection (6) above, whether or not the occupier is a revenue trader.

Power to prohibit use of certain substances in exciseable goods

114.—(1) If it appears to the satisfaction of the Commissioners that any substance or liquor is used, or is capable of being used, in the manufacture or preparation for sale of any goods chargeable, as goods manufactured or produced in the United Kingdom, with a duty of excise, and that that substance or liquor is of a noxious or detrimental nature or, being a chemical or artificial extract or product, may affect prejudicially the interests of the revenue, the Commissioners may by regulations prohibit the use of that substance or liquor in the manufacture or preparation for sale of any goods specified in the regulations.

(2) If while any such regulations are in force any person knowingly uses a substance or liquor thereby prohibited in the manufacture or preparation for sale of any goods specified in the regulations he shall be liable on summary conviction to a penalty of £50.

(3) Any substance or liquor the use of which is for the time being prohibited by any such regulations found in the possession of any person licensed for the manufacture or sale of any goods specified in the regulations, and any goods in the manufacture or preparation of which any substance or liquid has been used contrary to any such prohibition, shall be liable to forfeiture.

Power to keep specimen on premises of revenue traders

115.—(1) The proper officer may place and leave on the premises of a revenue trader a specimen, that is to say, a document in which may be entered any particulars relating to the trader's trade from time to time recorded by that or any other officer.

(2) Any such specimen shall be deposited at some place on premises entered by the trader where convenient access may be had thereto at any time by the trader and by any officer, and any officer may at any time remove the specimen and deposit a new one in its place.

(3) Where any charge of duty made by an officer upon a trader is not recorded in a specimen, the officer shall, if so required in writing by the trader at the time when the officer takes his account for the purpose of charging duty, give to the trader a copy of the charge in writing under his hand.

(4) If any person other than an officer removes, conceals, withholds, damages or destroys a specimen, or alters, defaces, or obliterates any

entry therein, he shall be liable on summary conviction to a penalty of £200.

Payment of excise duty by revenue traders

116.—(1) Every revenue trader shall pay any duty of excise payable in respect of his trade at or within such time, at such place and to such person as the Commissioners may direct whether or not payment of that duty has been secured by bond or otherwise.

(2) If any duty payable is not paid in accordance with subsection (1) above, it shall be paid on demand made by the Commissioners either to the trader personally or by delivering the demand in writing at his place of abode or business.

(3) If any duty is not paid on demand made under subsection (2) above the trader shall in addition be liable on summary conviction to a penalty of double the amount due.

Execution and distress against revenue traders

117.—(1) Where any sum is owing by a revenue trader in respect of any relevant excise duty or of any relevant penalty, all the following things which are in the possession or custody of that trader or of any agent of his or of any other person on his behalf shall be liable to be taken in execution in default of the payment of that sum, that is to say—

(*a*) all goods liable to a relevant excise duty, whether or not that duty has been paid;

(*b*) all materials for manufacturing or producing any such goods; and

(*c*) all apparatus, equipment, machinery, tools, vessels and utensils for, or for preparing any such materials for, such manufacture or production, or by which the trade in respect of which the duty is imposed is carried on.

(2) Subsection (1) above shall also apply in relation to things falling within paragraph (*a*), (*b*) or (*c*) of that subsection which, although they are not still in the possession or custody of the trader, an agent of his or other person on his behalf, were in such possession or custody—

(*a*) at the time when the relevant excise duty was charged or became chargeable or at any time while it was owing; or

(*b*) at the time of the commission of the offence for which the penalty was incurred.

(3) Notwithstanding anything in subsection (1) or (2) above, but subject to subsection (4) below, where the proper officer has taken account of and charged any goods chargeable with a relevant excise duty and those goods are in the ordinary course of trade sold for full and valuable consideration to a bona fide purchaser and delivered into his possession before the issue of any warrant or process for distress or seizure of the goods, those goods shall not be liable to be seized under this section.

(4) Where any goods have been seized under this section, the burden of proof that the goods are by virtue of subsection (3) above not liable to be so seized shall lie upon the person claiming that they are not so liable.

(5) Where any relevant excise duty payable by a revenue trader remains unpaid after the time within which it is payable, the proper officer may by warrant signed by him empower any person to distrain any thing liable to be taken in execution under this section and, subject to subsection (6) below, to sell any thing so distrained by public auction after giving 6 days' notice of the sale.

(6) Where, under subsection (5) above, any thing has been distrained in respect of duty payable by a distiller, brewer, licensed producer of wine, licensed producer of made-wine or registered maker of cider he may, subject in the case of a distiller to the requirements of section 27 (3) and (4) of the Alcoholic Liquor Duties Act 1979 in connection with the sending out or other removal of spirits, at any time before the day appointed for the sale remove the whole or part of any products of or materials for his manufacture which have been so distrained upon paying to the proper officer in or towards payment of the duty the true value of those products or materials.

(7) The proceeds of any sale under subsection (5) above shall be applied in or towards payment of the costs and expenses of the distress and sale and in or towards payment of the duty due from the trader, and the surplus (if any) shall be paid to the trader.

(8) In this section—

" relevant excise duty " means excise duty other than duty chargeable on imported goods; and

" relevant penalty " means a penalty incurred under the revenue trade provisions of the customs and excise Acts.

(9) In the application of this section to Scotland any reference to distress or seizure shall be construed as a reference to poinding.

Liability of ostensible owner or principal manager

118. Any person who acts ostensibly as the owner or who is a principal manager of the business of a revenue trader in respect of which entry of any premises or article has been made or who occupies or uses any entered premises or article shall, notwithstanding that he is under full age, be liable in like manner as the real and true owner of the business for all duties charged and all penalties incurred in respect of that business.

PART X

DUTIES AND DRAWBACKS—GENERAL PROVISIONS

General provisions relating to imported goods

Delivery of imported goods on giving of security for duty

119.—(1) Where it is impracticable immediately to ascertain whether any or what duty is payable in respect of any imported goods which are entered for home use, whether on importation or from warehouse, the Commissioners may, if they think fit and notwithstanding any other provision of the Customs and Excise Acts 1979, allow those goods to be delivered upon the importer giving security by deposit of money or otherwise to their satisfaction for payment of any amount unpaid which may be payable by way of duty.

(2) The Commissioners may for the purposes of subsection (1) above treat goods as entered for home use notwithstanding that the entry does not contain all the particulars required for perfect entry if it contains as many of those particulars as are then known to the importer, and in that event the importer shall supply the remaining particulars as soon as may be to the Commissioners.

(3) Where goods are allowed to be delivered under this section, the Commissioners shall, when they have determined the amount of duty which in their opinion is payable, give to the importer a notice specifying that amount.

(4) On the giving of a notice under subsection (3) above the amount specified in the notice or, where any amount has been deposited under subsection (1) above, any difference between those amounts shall forthwith be paid or repaid as the case may require.

(5) Subject to subsection (6) below, if the importer disputes the correctness of the amount specified in a notice given to him under subsection (3) above he may at any time within 3 months of the date of the notice make such a requirement for reference to arbitration or such an application to the court as is provided for by section 127 below, and that section shall have effect accordingly.

(6) No requirement or application shall be made by virtue of subsection (5) above until any sum falling to be paid by the importer under subsection (4) above has been paid, and where any sum so falls to be paid no interest shall be paid under section 127 (2) below in respect of any period before that sum is paid.

Regulations for determining origin of goods

120.—(1) The Secretary of State may by regulations make provision for determining, for the purposes of any duty of customs or excise, the origin of any goods in cases where it does not fall to be determined under a Community regulation or any Act or other instrument having the force of law.

(2) Regulations under this section may—

(*a*) make provision as to the evidence which is to be required or is to be sufficient for the purpose of showing that goods are of a particular origin; and

(*b*) make different provision for different purposes and in relation to goods of different descriptions.

(3) Subject to the provisions of any regulations under this section, where in connection with a duty of customs or excise chargeable on any goods any question arises as to the origin of the goods, the Commissioners may require the importer of the goods to furnish to them, in such form as they may prescribe, proof of any statement made to them as to any fact necessary to determine that question; and if such proof is not furnished to their satisfaction, the question may be determined without regard to that statement.

Power to impose restrictions where duty depends on certain matters other than use

121. Where any question as to the duties of customs or excise chargeable on any imported goods depends on any matter (other than the use to be made of the goods) not reasonably ascertainable from an examination of the goods, and that question is not in law conclusively determined by the production of any certificate or other document, then, on the importation of those goods, the Commissioners may impose such conditions as they see fit for the prevention of abuse or the protection of the revenue (including conditions requiring security for the observance of any conditions so imposed).

Regulations where customs duty depends on use

122.—(1) The Commissioners may, in accordance with subsection (2) below, make regulations applying in cases where any question as to the duties of customs chargeable on any goods depends on the use to be made of them.

(2) In cases in which a Community instrument makes provision for the purpose of securing that the relevant use is made of the goods,

regulations under this section may make provision for any matter which under the instrument is required or authorised to be dealt with by the authorities of member States or which otherwise arises out of the instrument; and in other cases regulations under this section may make such provision for that purpose as appears to the Commissioners to be necessary or expedient.

Repayment of duty where goods returned or destroyed by importer

123.—(1) Subject to such conditions as the Commissioners see fit to impose, where it is shown to the satisfaction of the Commissioners—

(*a*) that goods were imported in pursuance of a contract of sale and that the description, quality, state or condition of the goods was not in accordance with the contract or that the goods were damaged in transit; and

(*b*) that the importer with the consent of the seller either—

(i) returned the goods unused to the seller and for that purpose complied with the provisions of section 53 above as to entry in like manner as if they had been dutiable or restricted goods for the purposes of Part V of this Act; or

(ii) destroyed the goods unused,

the importer shall be entitled to obtain from the Commissioners repayment of any duty of customs or excise paid on the importation of the goods.

(2) Nothing in this section shall apply to goods imported on approval, or on sale or return, or on other similar terms.

Forfeiture for breach of certain conditions

124.—(1) Where—

(*a*) any imported goods have been relieved from customs or excise duty chargeable on their importation or have been charged with duty at a reduced rate; and

(*b*) any condition or other obligation required to be complied with in connection with the relief or with the charge of duty at that rate is not complied with,

the goods shall be liable to forfeiture.

(2) The provisions of this section shall apply whether or not any undertaking or security has been given for compliance with the condition or obligation or for the payment of the duty payable apart therefrom, and the forfeiture of any goods under this section shall not affect any liability of any person who has given any such undertaking or security.

Valuation of goods for purpose of ad valorem duties

125.—(1) For the purposes of any duty for the time being chargeable on any imported goods by reference to their value (whether a Community customs duty or not), the value of the goods shall, subject to subsection (2) below, be taken according to the rules applicable in the case of Community customs duties, and duty shall be paid on that value.

(2) In relation to an importation in the course of trade within the Communities the value of any imported goods for the purposes mentioned in subsection (1) above shall be determined on the basis of a delivery to the buyer at the port or place of importation into the United Kingdom.

(3) The Commissioners may make regulations for the purpose of giving effect to the foregoing provisions of this section, and in particular for requiring any importer or other person concerned with the importation of goods—

(*a*) to furnish to the Commissioners in such form as they may require, such information as is in their opinion necessary for a proper valuation of the goods; and

(*b*) to produce any books of account or other documents of whatever nature relating to the purchase, importation or sale of the goods by that person.

(4) If any person contravenes or fails to comply with any regulation made under subsection (3) above he shall be liable on summary conviction to a penalty of £50.

Charge of excise duty on manufactured or composite imported articles

126.—(1) Subject to subsections (2) to (4) below, if any imported goods contain as a part or ingredient thereof any article chargeable with excise duty, excise duty shall be chargeable on the goods in respect of each such article according to the quantity thereof appearing to the Commissioners to be used in the manufacture or preparation of the goods.

(2) Where, in the opinion of the Treasury, it is necessary for the protection of the revenue, such imported goods shall be chargeable with the amount of excise duty with which they would be chargeable if they consisted wholly of the chargeable article or, if the goods contain more than one such article, of that one of the chargeable articles which will yield the highest amount of excise duty.

(3) Schedule 2 to this Act shall have effect with respect to the excise duties to be charged, and the excise drawbacks to be allowed, on imported composite goods containing a dutiable part or ingredient and with respect to rebates and drawbacks of excise duties charged in accordance with that Schedule.

(4) Subsections (1) and (2) above do not apply where other provision is made by any other enactment relating to excise duties on imported goods.

(5) Any rebate which can be allowed by law on any article when separately charged shall be allowed in charging goods under subsection (1) or (2) above in respect of any quantity of that article used in the manufacture or preparation of the goods.

Determination of disputes as to duties on imported goods

127.—(1) If, before the delivery of any imported goods out of charge, any dispute arises as to whether any or what duty is payable on those goods, the importer shall pay the amount demanded by the proper officer but may, not later than 3 months after the date of the payment—

(*a*) if the dispute is in relation to the value of the goods, require the question to be referred to the arbitration of a referee appointed by the Lord Chancellor (not being an official of any government department), whose decision shall be final and conclusive; or

(*b*) in any other case, apply to the High Court or, in Scotland, to the Court of Session for a declaration as to the amount of duty, if any, properly payable on the goods.

(2) If on any such reference or application the referee or court determines that a lesser or no amount was properly payable in respect of duty on the goods, the amount overpaid shall be repaid by the Commissioners, together with interest thereon from the date of the overpayment at such rate as the referee or court may determine; and any sum so repaid shall be accepted by the importer in satisfaction of all claims in respect of the importation of the goods in question and the duty payable thereon

and of all damages and expenses incidental to the dispute other than the costs of the proceedings.

(3) The procedure on any reference to a referee under this section shall be such as may be determined by the referee.

General provisions relating to charge of duty on and delivery of goods

Restriction of delivery of goods

128.—(1) During any period not exceeding 3 months specified at any time by order of the Commissioners for the purposes of this section, the Commissioners may refuse to allow the removal for home use on payment of duty, or the sending out for home use after the charging of duty, of goods of any class or description chargeable with a duty of customs or excise, notwithstanding payment of that duty, in quantities exceeding those which appear to the Commissioners to be reasonable in the circumstances.

(2) Where the Commissioners have during any such period exercised their powers under this section with respect to goods of any class or description, then, in the case of any such goods which are removed or sent out for home use after the end of that period, the duties of customs or excise and the rates thereof chargeable on those goods shall, notwithstanding any other provision of the customs and excise Acts relating to the determination of those duties and rates, be those in force at the date of the removal or sending out of the goods.

Power to remit or repay duty on denatured goods

129.—(1) Subject to subsection (2) below, where any goods—

(*a*) which have been imported but not yet cleared for any purpose for which they may be entered on importation; or

(*b*) which are warehoused,

have by reason of their state or condition ceased to be worth the full duty chargeable thereon and have been denatured in such manner as the Commissioners may direct and in accordance with such conditions as they see fit to impose, the Commissioners may remit or repay the whole or part of any duty chargeable or paid thereon, or waive repayment of the whole or part of any drawback paid on their warehousing, upon the delivery of the goods for use for such purposes as the Commissioners may allow.

(2) Subsection (1) above does not apply in relation to spirits.

(3) Where, whether under subsection (1) above or otherwise, any goods chargeable with duty have gone into home use after having been denatured by mixture with some other substance, any person who separates the goods from that other substance shall be guilty of an offence under this subsection and may be detained, and the goods shall be liable to forfeiture.

(4) A person guilty of an offence under subsection (3) above shall be liable—

(*a*) on summary conviction, to a penalty of the prescribed sum or of three times the value of the goods, whichever is the greater, or to imprisonment for a term not exceeding 6 months, or to both; or

(*b*) on conviction on indictment, to a penalty of any amount, or to imprisonment for a term not exceeding 2 years, or to both.

Power to remit or repay duty on goods lost or destroyed, etc.

130.—(1) Where it is shown to the satisfaction of the Commissioners that any goods chargeable with any duty have been lost or destroyed by unavoidable accident—

(*a*) after importation but before clearance for any purpose for which they might be entered on importation; or

(*b*) in the case of goods chargeable with a duty of excise on their manufacture or production or on their removal from the place of their manufacture or production, at any time before their removal from that place; or

(*c*) while in a warehouse or Queen's warehouse; or

(*d*) at any time while that duty is otherwise lawfully unpaid, except when payment of that duty has become due but has been allowed by the Commissioners to be deferred; or

(*e*) at any time after drawback of that duty has been paid,

the Commissioners may remit or repay any duty chargeable or paid thereon or waive repayment of any drawback paid on their warehousing.

(2) The Commissioners may, at the request of the proprietor of the goods in question and subject to compliance with such conditions as the Commissioners see fit to impose, permit the destruction of, and waive payment of duty or repayment of drawback on—

(*a*) any part of any warehoused goods which becomes damaged or surplus by reason of the carrying out of any permitted operation on those goods in warehouse, and any refuse resulting from any such operation; and

(*b*) any imported goods not yet cleared for any purpose for which they might be entered on importation or any warehoused goods, being in either case goods which have by reason of their state or condition ceased to be worth the full duty chargeable thereon.

Enforcement of bond in respect of goods removed without payment of duty

131. If any goods which have been lawfully permitted to be removed for any purposes without payment of duty are unlawfully taken from any ship, aircraft, vehicle or place before that purpose is accomplished, the Commissioners may if they see fit enforce any bond given in respect thereof notwithstanding that any time prescribed in the bond for accomplishing that purpose has not expired.

Drawback, allowances, duties, etc.—general

Extension of drawback

132.—(1) Without prejudice to any other provision of the Customs and Excise Acts 1979 or any other Act, where drawback is allowable on the shipment of any goods as stores, the like drawback shall, subject to such conditions and restrictions as the Commissioners see fit to impose, be allowed on the warehousing in an excise warehouse of those goods for use as stores.

(2) Without prejudice to any other provision of the Customs and Excise Acts 1979 or any other Act, where drawback would be payable on the exportation of any goods, or on the warehousing of any goods for exportation, then, subject to such conditions and restrictions as the Commissioners see fit, the like drawback shall be payable on the shipment of any such goods as stores or, as the case may be, on their warehousing in an excise warehouse for use as stores.

General provisions as to claims for drawback

133.—(1) Any claim for drawback shall be made in such form and manner and contain such particulars as the Commissioners may direct.

(2) Where drawback has been claimed in the case of any goods subsections (3) to (6) below shall apply in relation to the claim.

(3) No drawback shall be payable unless it is shown to the satisfaction of the Commissioners that duty in respect of the goods or of the article contained therein or used in the manufacture or preparation thereof in respect of which the claim is made has been duly paid and has not been drawn back.

(4) No drawback shall be paid until the person entitled thereto or his agent has made a declaration in such form and manner and containing such particulars as the Commissioners may direct that the conditions on which the drawback is payable have been fulfilled.

(5) The Commissioners may require any person who has been concerned at any stage with the goods or article—

(*a*) to furnish such information as may be reasonably necessary to enable the Commissioners to determine whether duty has been duly paid and not drawn back and for enabling a calculation to be made of the amount of drawback payable; and

(*b*) to produce any book of account or other document of whatever nature relating to the goods or article.

(6) If any person fails to comply with any requirement made under subsection (5) above, he shall be liable on summary conviction to a penalty of £50.

Drawback and allowance on goods damaged or destroyed after shipment

134.—(1) Where it is proved to the satisfaction of the Commissioners that any goods after being duly shipped for exportation have been destroyed by accident on board the exporting ship or aircraft, any amount payable in respect of the goods by way of drawback, allowance or repayment of duty shall be payable in the same manner as if the goods had been exported to their destination.

(2) Where it is proved to the satisfaction of the Commissioners that any goods, after being duly shipped for exportation, have been materially damaged by accident on board the exporting ship or aircraft, and the goods are with the consent of and in accordance with any conditions imposed by the Commissioners relanded or unloaded again in or brought back into the United Kingdom and either abandoned to the Commissioners or destroyed, any amount payable in respect of the goods by way of drawback, allowance or repayment of duty shall be paid as if they had been duly exported and not so relanded, unloaded or brought back.

(3) Notwithstanding any provision of the Customs and Excise Acts 1979 or any other Act relating to the reimportation of exported goods, the person to whom any amount is payable or has been paid under subsection (2) above shall not be required to pay any duty in respect of any goods relanded, unloaded or brought back under that subsection.

Time limit on payment of drawback or allowance

135. No payment shall be made in respect of any drawback or allowance unless the debenture or other document authorising payment is presented for payment within 2 years from the date of the event on the happening of which the drawback or allowance became payable.

Offences in connection with claims for drawback, etc.

136.—(1) If any person obtains or attempts to obtain, or does anything whereby there might be obtained by any person, any amount by way of drawback, allowance, remission or repayment of, or any rebate from, any duty in respect of any goods which is not lawfully payable or allowable in respect thereof or which is greater than the amount so payable or allowable, he shall be guilty of an offence under this subsection.

(2) A person guilty of an offence under subsection (1) above shall be liable on summary conviction—

(*a*) if the offence was committed with intent to defraud Her Majesty, to a penalty of three times the value of the goods or £200, whichever is the greater;

(*b*) in any other case, to a penalty of three times the amount improperly obtained or allowed or which might have been improperly obtained or allowed or £100, whichever is the greater.

(3) Any goods in respect of which an offence under subsection (1) above is committed shall be liable to forfeiture; but in the case of a claim for drawback, the Commissioners may, if they see fit, instead of seizing the goods either refuse to allow any drawback thereon or allow only such drawback as they consider proper.

(4) Without prejudice to the foregoing provisions of this section, if, in the case of any goods upon which a claim for drawback, allowance, remission or repayment of duty has been made, it is found that those goods do not correspond with any entry made thereof in connection with that claim, the goods shall be liable to forfeiture and any person by whom any such entry or claim was made shall be liable on summary conviction to a penalty of three times the amount claimed or £100, whichever is the greater.

(5) Subsection (4) above applies in the case of any goods upon which a claim for drawback, allowance, remission or repayment of duty has been made where it is found that the goods, if sold for home use, would realise less than the amount claimed as it applies where the finding specified in that subsection is made except that it does not apply by virtue of this subsection to any claim under—

(*a*) section 123 or 134 (2) above; or

(*b*) section 46, 61 or 64 of the Alcoholic Liquor Duties Act 1979 (remission or repayment of duty on certain spoilt liquors).

Recovery of duties and calculation of duties, drawbacks, etc.

137.—(1) Without prejudice to any other provision of the Customs and Excise Acts 1979, any amount due by way of customs or excise duty may be recovered as a debt due to the Crown.

(2) Any duty, drawback, allowance or rebate the rate of which is expressed by reference to a specified quantity or weight of any goods shall, subject to subsection (3) below, be chargeable or allowable on any fraction of that quantity or weight of the goods, and the amount payable or allowable on any such fraction shall be calculated proportionately.

(3) The Commissioners may for the purposes of subsection (2) above determine the fractions to be taken into account in the case of any weight or quantity.

(4) For the purpose of calculating any amount due from or to any person under the customs and excise Acts by way of duty, drawback, allowance, repayment or rebate any fraction of a penny in that amount shall be disregarded.

Part XI

Detention of Persons, Forfeiture and Legal Proceedings

Detention of persons

Provisions as to detention of persons

138.—(1) Any person who has committed, or whom there are reasonable grounds to suspect of having committed, any offence for which he is liable to be detained under the customs and excise Acts may be detained by any officer or constable or any member of Her Majesty's armed forces or coastguard at any time within 3 years from the date of the commission of the offence.

(2) Where it was not practicable to detain any person so liable at the time of the commission of the offence, or where any such person having been then or subsequently detained for that offence has escaped, he may be detained by any officer or constable or any member of Her Majesty's armed forces or coastguard at any time and may be proceeded against in like manner as if the offence had been committed at the date when he was finally detained.

(3) Where any person who is a member of the crew of any ship in Her Majesty's employment or service is detained by an officer for an offence under the customs and excise Acts, the commanding officer of the ship shall, if so required by the detaining officer, keep that person secured on board that ship until he can be brought before a court and shall then deliver him up to the proper officer.

(4) Where any person has been detained by virtue of this section otherwise than by an officer, the person detaining him shall give notice of the detention to an officer at the nearest convenient office of customs and excise.

Forfeiture

Provisions as to detention, seizure and condemnation of goods, etc.

139.—(1) Any thing liable to forfeiture under the customs and excise Acts may be seized or detained by any officer or constable or any member of Her Majesty's armed forces or coastguard.

(2) Where any thing is seized or detained as liable to forfeiture under the customs and excise Acts by a person other than an officer, that person shall, subject to subsection (3) below, either—

(*a*) deliver that thing to the nearest convenient office of customs and excise; or

(*b*) if such delivery is not practicable, give to the Commissioners at the nearest convenient office of customs and excise notice in writing of the seizure or detention with full particulars of the thing seized or detained.

(3) Where the person seizing or detaining any thing as liable to forfeiture under the customs and excise Acts is a constable and that thing is or may be required for use in connection with any proceedings to be brought otherwise than under those Acts it may, subject to subsection (4) below, be retained in the custody of the police until either those proceedings are completed or it is decided that no such proceedings shall be brought.

(4) The following provisions apply in relation to things retained in the custody of the police by virtue of subsection (3) above, that is to say—

(*a*) notice in writing of the seizure or detention and of the intention to retain the thing in question in the custody of the police, together with full particulars as to that thing, shall be given to the Commissioners at the nearest convenient office of customs and excise;

(*b*) any officer shall be permitted to examine that thing and take account thereof at any time while it remains in the custody of the police;

(*c*) nothing in the Police (Property) Act 1897 shall apply in relation to that thing.

(5) Subject to subsections (3) and (4) above and to Schedule 3 to this Act, any thing seized or detained under the customs and excise Acts shall, pending the determination as to its forfeiture or disposal, be dealt with, and, if condemned or deemed to have been condemned or forfeited, shall be disposed of in such manner as the Commissioners may direct.

(6) Schedule 3 to this Act shall have effect for the purpose of forfeitures, and of proceedings for the condemnation of any thing as being forfeited, under the customs and excise Acts.

(7) If any person, not being an officer, by whom any thing is seized or detained or who has custody thereof after its seizure or detention, fails to comply with any requirement of this section or with any direction of the Commissioners given thereunder, he shall be liable on summary conviction to a penalty of £50.

(8) Subsections (2) to (7) above shall apply in relation to any dutiable goods seized or detained by any person other than an officer notwithstanding that they were not so seized as liable to forfeiture under the customs and excise Acts.

Forfeiture of spirits

140. Where, by any provision of, or of any instrument made under, the Customs and Excise Acts 1979, any spirits become liable to forfeiture by reason of some offence committed by a revenue trader, then—

(*a*) where that provision specifies the quantity of those spirits but does not specify the spirits so liable, the Commissioners may seize the equivalent of that quantity computed at proof from any spirits in the stock of that trader; and

(*b*) where that provision specifies the spirits so liable the Commissioners may, if they think fit, seize instead of the spirits so specified an equivalent quantity computed at proof of any other spirits in the stock of that trader.

Forfeiture of ships, etc. used in connection with goods liable to forfeiture

141.—(1) Without prejudice to any other provision of the Customs and Excise Acts 1979, where any thing has become liable to forfeiture under the customs and excise Acts—

(*a*) any ship, aircraft, vehicle, animal, container (including any article of passengers' baggage) or other thing whatsoever which has been used for the carriage, handling, deposit or concealment of the thing so liable to forfeiture, either at a time when it was so liable or for the purpose of the commission of the offence for which it later became so liable; and

(*b*) any other thing mixed, packed or found with the thing so liable,

shall also be liable to forfeiture

(2) Where any ship, aircraft, vehicle or animal has become liable to forfeiture under the customs and excise Acts, whether by virtue of sub-

section (1) above or otherwise, all tackle, apparel or furniture thereof shall also be liable to forfeiture.

(3) Where any of the following, that is to say—

(*a*) any ship not exceeding 100 tons register;

(*b*) any aircraft; or

(*c*) any hovercraft,

becomes liable to forfeiture under this section by reason of having been used in the importation, exportation or carriage of goods contrary to or for the purpose of contravening any prohibition or restriction for the time being in force with respect to those goods, or without payment having been made of, or security given for, any duty payable thereon, the owner and the master or commander shall each be liable on summary conviction to a penalty equal to the value of the ship, aircraft or hovercraft or £500, whichever is the less.

Special provision as to forfeiture of larger ships

142.—(1) Notwithstanding any other provision of the Customs and Excise Acts 1979, a ship of 250 or more tons register shall not be liable to forfeiture under or by virtue of any provision of the Customs and Excise Acts 1979, except under section 88 above, unless the offence in respect of or in connection with which the forfeiture is claimed—

(*a*) was substantially the object of the voyage during which the offence was committed; or

(*b*) was committed while the ship was under chase by a vessel in the service of Her Majesty after failing to bring to when properly summoned to do so by that vessel.

(2) For the purposes of this section, a ship shall be deemed to have been properly summoned to bring to—

(*a*) if the vessel making the summons did so by means of an international signal code or other recognised means and while flying her proper ensign; and

(*b*) in the case of a ship which is not a British ship, if at the time when the summons was made the ship was within 3 nautical miles of the coast of the United Kingdom.

(3) For the purposes of this section, all hovercraft (of whatever size) shall be treated as ships of less than 250 tons register.

(4) The exemption from forfeiture of any ship under this section shall not affect any liability to forfeiture of goods carried therein.

Penalty in lieu of forfeiture of larger ship where responsible officer implicated in offence

143.—(1) Where any ship of 250 or more tons register would, but for section 142 above, be liable to forfeiture for or in connection with any offence under the customs and excise Acts and, in the opinion of the Commissioners, a responsible officer of the ship is implicated either by his own act or by neglect in that offence, the Commissioners may fine that ship such sum not exceeding £50 as they see fit.

(2) For the purposes of this section, all hovercraft (of whatever size) shall be treated as ships of less than 250 tons register.

(3) Where any ship is liable to a fine under subsection (1) above but the Commissioners consider that fine an inadequate penalty for the offence, they may take proceedings in accordance with Schedule 3 to this Act, in like manner as they might but for section 142 above have taken proceedings for the condemnation of the ship if notice of claim had been given in respect thereof, for the condemnation of the ship in such sum not exceeding £500 as the court may see fit.

(4) Where any fine is to be imposed or any proceedings are to be taken under this section, the Commissioners may require such sum as they see fit, not exceeding £50 or, as the case may be, £500, to be deposited with them to await their final decision or, as the case may be, the decision of the court, and may detain the ship until that sum has been so deposited.

(5) No claim shall lie against the Commissioners for damages in respect of the payment of any deposit or the detention of any ship under this section.

(6) For the purposes of this section—

(*a*) " responsible officer ", in relation to any ship, means the master, a mate or an engineer of the ship and, in the case of a ship carrying a passenger certificate, the purser or chief steward and, in the case of a ship manned wholly or partly by Asiatic seamen, the serang or other leading Asiatic officer of the ship;

(*b*) without prejudice to any other grounds upon which a responsible officer of any ship may be held to be implicated by neglect, he may be so held if goods not owned to by any member of the crew are discovered in a place under that officer's supervision in which they could not reasonably have been put if he had exercised proper care at the time of the loading of the ship or subsequently.

Protection of officers, etc. in relation to seizure and detention of goods, etc.

144.—(1) Where, in any proceedings for the condemnation of any thing seized as liable to forfeiture under the customs and excise Acts, judgment is given for the claimant, the court may, if it sees fit, certify that there were reasonable grounds for the seizure.

(2) Where any proceedings, whether civil or criminal, are brought against the Commissioners, a law officer of the Crown or any person authorised by or under the Customs and Excise Acts 1979 to seize or detain any thing liable to forfeiture under the customs and excise Acts on account of the seizure or detention of any thing, and judgment is given for the plaintiff or prosecutor, then if either—

(*a*) a certificate relating to the seizure has been granted under subsection (1) above; or

(*b*) the court is satisfied that there were reasonable grounds for seizing or detaining that thing under the customs and excise Acts,

the plaintiff or prosecutor shall not be entitled to recover any damages or costs and the defendant shall not be liable to any punishment.

(3) Nothing in subsection (2) above shall affect any right of any person to the return of the thing seized or detained or to compensation in respect of any damage to the thing or in respect of the destruction thereof.

(4) Any certificate under subsection (1) above may be proved by the production of either the original certificate or a certified copy thereof purporting to be signed by an officer of the court by which it was granted.

General provisions as to legal proceedings

Institution of proceedings

145.—(1) Subject to the following provisions of this section, no proceedings for an offence under the customs and excise Acts or for condemnation under Schedule 3 to this Act shall be instituted except by order of the Commissioners.

(2) Subject to the following provisions of this section, any proceedings under the customs and excise Acts instituted in a magistrates' court, and any such proceedings instituted in a court of summary jurisdiction in Northern Ireland, shall be commenced in the name of an officer.

(3) Subsections (1) and (2) above shall not apply to proceedings on indictment in Scotland.

(4) In the case of the death, removal, discharge or absence of the officer in whose name any proceedings were commenced under subsection (2) above, those proceedings may be continued by any officer authorised in that behalf by the Commissioners.

(5) Nothing in the foregoing provisions of this section shall prevent the institution of proceedings for an offence under the customs and excise Acts by order and in the name of a law officer of the Crown in any case in which he thinks it proper that proceedings should be so instituted.

(6) Notwithstanding anything in the foregoing provisions of this section, where any person has been detained for any offence for which he is liable to be detained under the customs and excise Acts, any court before which he is brought may proceed to deal with the case although the proceedings have not been instituted by order of the Commissioners or have not been commenced in the name of an officer.

Service of process

146.—(1) Any summons or other process issued anywhere in the United Kingdom for the purpose of any proceedings under the customs and excise Acts may be served on the person to whom it is addressed in any part of the United Kingdom without any further endorsement, and shall be deemed to have been duly served—

(*a*) if delivered to him personally; or

(*b*) if left at his last known place of abode or business or, in the case of a body corporate, at their registered or principal office; or

(*c*) if left on board any vessel or aircraft to which he may belong or have lately belonged.

(2) Any summons, notice, order or other document issued for the purposes of any proceedings under the customs and excise Acts, or of any appeal from the decision of the court in any such proceedings, may be served by an officer.

In this subsection " appeal " includes an appeal by way of case stated.

(3) This section shall not apply in relation to proceedings instituted in the High Court or Court of Session.

Proceedings for offences

147.—(1) Save as otherwise expressly provided in the customs and excise Acts and notwithstanding anything in any other enactment, any proceedings for an offence under those Acts—

(*a*) may be commenced at any time within 3 years from the date of the commission of the offence; and

(*b*) shall not be commenced later than 3 years from that date.

(2) Where, in England or Wales, a magistrates' court has begun to inquire into an information charging a person with an offence under the customs and excise Acts as examining justices the court shall not proceed under section 25 (3) of the Criminal Law Act 1977 to try the information summarily without the consent of—

(*a*) the Attorney-General, in a case where the proceedings were instituted by his order and in his name; or

(*b*) the Commissioners, in any other case.

(3) In the case of proceedings in England or Wales, without prejudice to any right to require the statement of a case for the opinion of the High Court, the prosecutor may appeal to the Crown Court against any decision of a magistrates' court in proceedings for an offence under the customs and excise Acts.

(4) In any case of proceedings in Northern Ireland, without prejudice to any right to require the statement of a case for the opinion of the High Court, the prosecutor may appeal to the county court against any decision of a court of summary jurisdiction in proceedings for an offence under the customs and excise Acts.

(5) In the application of the customs and excise Acts to Scotland, and subject to any express provision made by the enactment in question, any offence which is made punishable on summary conviction—

(*a*) shall if prosecuted summarily be prosecuted in the sheriff court;

(*b*) may be also prosecuted by any other method.

Place of trial for offences

148.—(1) Proceedings for an offence under the customs and excise Acts may be commenced—

(*a*) in any court having jurisdiction in the place where the person charged with the offence resides or is found; or

(*b*) if any thing was detained or seized in connection with the offence, in any court having jurisdiction in the place where that thing was so detained or seized or was found or condemned as forfeited; or

(*c*) in any court having jurisdiction anywhere in that part of the United Kingdom, namely—

(i) England and Wales,

(ii) Scotland, or

(iii) Northern Ireland,

in which the place where the offence was committed is situated.

(2) Where any such offence was committed at some place outside the area of any commission of the peace, the place of the commission of the offence shall, for the purposes of the jurisdiction of any court, be deemed to be any place in the United Kingdom where the offender is found or to which he is first brought after the commission of the offence.

(3) The jurisdiction under subsection (2) above shall be in addition to and not in derogation of any jurisdiction or power of any court under any other enactment.

Non-payment of penalties, etc.: maximum terms of imprisonment

149.—(1) Where, in any proceedings for an offence under the customs and excise Acts, a magistrates' court in England or Wales or a court of summary jurisdiction in Scotland, in addition to ordering the person convicted to pay a penalty for the offence—

(*a*) orders him to be imprisoned for a term in respect of the same offence; and

(*b*) further (whether at the same time or subsequently) orders him to be imprisoned for a term in respect of non-payment of that penalty or default of a sufficient distress to satisfy the amount of that penalty,

the aggregate of the terms for which he is so ordered to be imprisoned shall not exceed 15 months.

(2) Where the sum adjudged to be paid by the conviction of a court of summary jurisdiction in Scotland under the customs and excise Acts (including any expenses adjudged to be paid by the conviction whose amount is ascertained by the conviction) exceeds £50 the maximum period of imprisonment that may be imposed in respect of the non-payment of that sum shall, notwithstanding anything in section 199 of the Criminal Procedure (Scotland) Act 1975, be fixed in accordance with the following scale, that is to say—

Where the amount of the sum adjudged to be paid by the conviction—	The said period shall be a period not exceeding—
exceeds £50 but does not exceed £100	90 days
exceeds £100 but does not exceed £250	6 months
exceeds £250 but does not exceed £500	9 months
exceeds £500	12 months.

(3) Where, under any enactment for the time being in force in Northern Ireland, a court of summary jurisdiction has power to order a person to be imprisoned in respect of the non-payment of a penalty, or of the default of a sufficient distress to satisfy the amount of that penalty, for a term in addition and succession to a term of imprisonment imposed for the same offence as the penalty, then in relation to a sentence for an offence under the customs and excise Acts the aggregate of those terms of imprisonment may, notwithstanding anything in any such enactment, be any period not exceeding 15 months.

Incidental provisions as to legal proceedings

150.—(1) Where liability for any offence under the customs and excise Acts is incurred by two or more persons jointly, those persons shall each be liable for the full amount of any pecuniary penalty and may be proceeded against jointly or severally as the Commissioners may see fit.

(2) In any proceedings for an offence under the customs and excise Acts instituted in England, Wales or Northern Ireland, any court by whom the matter is considered may mitigate any pecuniary penalty as they see fit.

(3) In any proceedings for an offence or for the condemnation of any thing as being forfeited under the customs and excise Acts, the fact that security has been given by bond or otherwise for the payment of any duty or for compliance with any condition in respect of the non-payment of which or non-compliance with which the proceedings are instituted shall not be a defence.

Application of penalties

151. The balance of any sum paid or recovered on account of any penalty imposed under the customs and excise Acts, after paying any such compensation or costs as are mentioned in section 114 of the Magistrates' Courts Act 1952 to persons other than the Commissioners shall, notwithstanding any local or other special right or privilege of whatever origin, be accounted for and paid to the Commissioners or as they direct.

Power of Commissioners to mitigate penalties, etc.

152. The Commissioners may, as they see fit—

(*a*) stay, sist or compound any proceedings for an offence or for the condemnation of any thing as being forfeited under the customs and excise Acts; or

(*b*) restore, subject to such conditions (if any) as they think proper, any thing forfeited or seized under those Acts; or

(*c*) after judgment, mitigate or remit any pecuniary penalty imposed under those Acts; or

(*d*) order any person who has been imprisoned to be discharged before the expiration of his term of imprisonment, being a person imprisoned for any offence under those Acts or in respect of the non-payment of a penalty or other sum adjudged to be paid or awarded in relation to such an offence or in respect of the default of a sufficient distress to satisfy such a sum;

but paragraph (*a*) above shall not apply to proceedings on indictment in Scotland.

Proof of certain documents

153.—(1) Any document purporting to be signed either by one or more of the Commissioners, or by their order, or by any other person with their authority, shall, until the contrary is proved, be deemed to have been so signed and to be made and issued by the Commissioners, and may be proved by the production of a copy thereof purporting to be so signed.

(2) Without prejudice to subsection (1) above, the Documentary Evidence Act 1868 shall apply in relation to—

(*a*) any document issued by the Commissioners;

(*b*) any document issued before 1st April 1909, by the Commissioners of Customs or the Commissioners of Customs and the Commissioners of Inland Revenue jointly;

(*c*) any document issued before that date in relation to the revenue of excise by the Commissioners of Inland Revenue,

as it applies in relation to the documents mentioned in that Act.

(3) That Act shall, as applied by subsection (2) above, have effect as if the persons mentioned in paragraphs (*a*) to (*c*) of that subsection were included in the first column of the Schedule to that Act, and any of the Commissioners or any secretary or assistant secretary to the Commissioners were specified in the second column of that Schedule in connection with those persons.

Proof of certain other matters

154.—(1) An averment in any process in proceedings under the customs and excise Acts—

(*a*) that those proceedings were instituted by the order of the Commissioners; or

(*b*) that any person is or was a Commissioner, officer or constable, or a member of Her Majesty's armed forces or coastguard; or

(*c*) that any person is or was appointed or authorised by the Commissioners to discharge, or was engaged by the orders or with the concurrence of the Commissioners in the discharge of, any duty; or

(*d*) that the Commissioners have or have not been satisfied as to any matter as to which they are required by any provision of those Acts to be satisfied; or

(*e*) that any ship is a British ship; or

(*f*) that any goods thrown overboard, staved or destroyed were so dealt with in order to prevent or avoid the seizure of those goods,

shall, until the contrary is proved, be sufficient evidence of the matter in question.

(2) Where in any proceedings relating to customs or excise any question arises as to the place from which any goods have been brought or as to whether or not—

(*a*) any duty has been paid or secured in respect of any goods; or

(*b*) any goods or other things whatsoever are of the description or nature alleged in the information, writ or other process; or

(*c*) any goods have been lawfully imported or lawfully unloaded from any ship or aircraft; or

(*d*) any goods have been lawfully loaded into any ship or aircraft or lawfully exported or were lawfully waterborne; or

(*e*) any goods were lawfully brought to any place for the purpose of being loaded into any ship or aircraft or exported; or

(*f*) any goods are or were subject to any prohibition of or restriction on their importation or exportation,

then, where those proceedings are brought by or against the Commissioners, a law officer of the Crown or an officer, or against any other person in respect of anything purporting to have been done in pursuance of any power or duty conferred or imposed on him by or under the customs and excise Acts, the burden of proof shall lie upon the other party to the proceedings.

Persons who may conduct proceedings

155.—(1) Any officer or any other person authorised in that behalf by the Commissioners may, although he is not a barrister, advocate or solicitor, conduct any proceedings before any magistrates' court in England or Wales or court of summary jurisdiction in Scotland or Northern Ireland or before any examining justices, being proceedings under any enactment relating to an assigned matter or proceedings arising out of the same circumstances as any proceedings commenced under any such enactment, whether or not the last mentioned proceedings are persisted in.

(2) Any person who has been admitted as a solicitor and is employed by the Commissioners may act as a solicitor in any proceedings in England, Wales or Northern Ireland relating to any assigned matter notwithstanding that he does not hold a current practising certificate.

Saving for outlying enactments of certain general provisions as to offences

Saving for outlying enactments of certain general provisions as to offences

156.—(1) In subsections (2), (3) and (4) below (which reproduce certain enactments not required as general provisions for the purposes of the enactments re-enacted in the Customs and Excise Acts 1979) " the outlying provisions of the customs and excise Acts " means—

(*a*) the Betting and Gaming Duties Act 1972, as for the time being amended; and

(*b*) all other provisions of the customs and excise Acts, as for the time being amended, which were passed before the commencement of this Act and are not re-enacted in the Customs and Excise Acts 1979.

(2) It is hereby declared that any act or omission in respect of which

a pecuniary penalty (however described) is imposed by any of the outlying provisions of the customs and excise Acts is an offence under that provision; and accordingly in this Part of this Act any reference to an offence under the customs and excise Acts includes a reference to such an act or omission.

(3) Subject to any express provision made by the enactment in question, an offence under any of the outlying provisions of the customs and excise Acts—

(*a*) where it is punishable with imprisonment for a term of 2 years, with or without a pecuniary penalty, shall be punishable either on summary conviction or on conviction on indictment;

(*b*) in any other case, shall be punishable on summary conviction.

This subsection does not apply to Scotland.

(4) Without prejudice to any other method of prosecution and subject to any express provision made by the enactment in question, it shall be competent in Scotland to prosecute an offence under any of the outlying provisions of the customs and excise Acts summarily in the sheriff court; but no sentence of the sheriff court on summary conviction shall impose any term of imprisonment exceeding 6 months.

Part XII

General and Miscellaneous

General powers, etc.

Bonds and security

157.—(1) Without prejudice to any express requirement as to security contained in the customs and excise Acts, the Commissioners may, if they see fit, require any person to give security by bond or otherwise for the observance of any condition in connection with customs or excise.

(2) Any bond taken for the purposes of any assigned matter—

(*a*) shall be taken on behalf of Her Majesty; and

(*b*) shall be valid notwithstanding that it is entered into by a person under full age; and

(*c*) may be cancelled at any time by or by order of the Commissioners.

Power to require provision of facilities

158.—(1) A person to whom this section applies, that is to say, a revenue trader and any person required by the Commissioners under the Customs and Excise Acts 1979 to give security in respect of any premises or place to be used for the examination of goods by an officer, shall—

(*a*) provide and maintain such appliances and afford such other facilities reasonably necessary to enable an officer to take any account or make any examination or search or to perform any other of his duties on the premises of that trader or at the bonded premises or place as the Commissioners may direct;

(*b*) keep any appliances so provided in a convenient place approved by the proper officer for that purpose; and

(*c*) allow the proper officer at any time to use anything so provided and give him any assistance necessary for the performance of his duties.

(2) Any person who contravenes or fails to comply with any provision

of subsection (1) above shall be liable on summary conviction to a penalty of £100.

(3) A person to whom this section applies shall provide and maintain any fitting required for the purpose or affixing any lock which the proper officer may require to affix to the premises of that person or any part thereof or to any vessel, utensil or other apparatus whatsoever kept thereon, and in default—

(a) the fitting may be provided or any work necessary for its maintenance may be carried out by the proper officer, and any expenses so incurred shall be paid on demand by that person; and

(b) if that person fails to pay those expenses on demand, he shall in addition be liable on summary conviction to a penalty of £100.

(4) If any person to whom this section applies or any servant of his—

(a) wilfully destroys or damages any such fitting as is mentioned in subsection (3) above or any lock or key provided for use therewith, or any label or seal placed on any such lock; or

(b) improperly obtains access to any place or article secured by any such lock; or

(c) has any such fitting or any article intended to be secured by means thereof so constructed that that intention is defeated,

he shall be liable on summary conviction to a penalty of £500 and may be detained.

Power to examine and take account of goods

159.—(1) Without prejudice to any other power conferred by the Customs and Excise Acts 1979, an officer may examine and take account of any goods—

(a) which are imported; or

(b) which are in a warehouse or Queen's warehouse; or

(c) which have been loaded into any ship or aircraft at any place in the United Kingdom; or

(d) which are entered for exportation or for use as stores; or

(e) which are brought to any place in the United Kingdom for exportation or for shipment for exportation or as stores; or

(f) in the case of which any claim for drawback, allowance, rebate, remission or repayment of duty is made;

and may for that purpose require any container to be opened or unpacked.

(2) Any examination of goods by an officer under the Customs and Excise Acts 1979 shall be made at such place as the Commissioners appoint for the purpose.

(3) In the case of such goods as the Commissioners may direct, and subject to such conditions as they see fit to impose, an officer may permit goods to be skipped on the quay or bulked, sorted, lotted, packed or repacked before account is taken thereof.

(4) Any opening, unpacking, weighing, measuring, repacking, bulking, sorting, lotting, marking, numbering, loading, unloading, carrying or landing of goods or their containers for the purposes of, or incidental to, the examination by an officer, removal or warehousing thereof shall be done, and any facilities or assistance required for any such examination shall be provided, by or at the expense of the proprietor of the goods.

(5) If any imported goods which an officer has power under the Customs and Excise Acts 1979 to examine are without the authority

of the proper officer removed from customs and excise charge before they have been examined, those goods shall be liable to forfeiture.

(6) If any goods falling within subsection (5) above are removed by a person with intent to defraud Her Majesty of any duty chargeable thereon or to evade any prohibition or restriction for the time being in force with respect thereto under or by virtue of any enactment, that person shall be guilty of an offence under this subsection and may be detained.

(7) A person guilty of an offence under subsection (6) above shall be liable—

(*a*) on summary conviction, to a penalty of the prescribed sum or of three times the value of the goods, whichever is the greater, or to imprisonment for a term not exceeding 6 months, or to both; or

(*b*) on conviction on indictment, to a penalty of any amount, or to imprisonment for a term not exceeding 2 years, or to both.

(8) Without prejudice to the foregoing provisions of this section, where by this section or by or under any other provision of the Customs and Excise Acts 1979 an account is authorised or required to be taken of any goods for any purpose by an officer, the Commissioners may, with the consent of the proprietor of the goods, accept as the account of those goods for that purpose an account taken by such other person as may be approved in that behalf by both the Commissioners and the proprietor of the goods.

Power to take samples

160.—(1) An officer may at any time take samples of any goods—

(*a*) which he is empowered by the Customs and Excise Acts 1979 to examine; or

(*b*) which are on premises where goods chargeable with any duty are manufactured, prepared or subjected to any process; or

(*c*) which, being dutiable goods, are held by any person as stock for his business or as materials for manufacture or processing.

(2) Where an officer takes from any vessel, pipe or utensil on the premises of any of the following revenue traders, that is to say, a distiller, brewer for sale, producer of wine, producer of made-wine or maker of cider, a sample of any product of, or of any materials for, the manufacture of that trader—

(*a*) the trader may, if he wishes, stir up and mix together the contents of that vessel, pipe or utensil before the sample is taken; and

(*b*) the sample taken by the officer shall be deemed to be representative of the whole contents of that vessel, pipe or utensil.

(3) Any sample taken under this section shall be disposed of and accounted for in such manner as the Commissioners may direct.

(4) Where any sample is taken under this section from any goods chargeable with a duty of customs or excise after that duty has been paid, other than—

(*a*) a sample taken when goods are first entered on importation; or

(*b*) a sample taken from goods in respect of which a claim for drawback, allowance, rebate, remission or repayment of that duty is being made,

and the sample so taken is to be retained, the officer taking it shall, if so required by the person in possession of the goods, pay for the sample on behalf of the Commissioners such sum as reasonably represents the wholesale value thereof.

Power to search premises

161.—(1) Without prejudice to any other power conferred by the Customs and Excise Acts 1979 but subject to subsection (2) below, where there are reasonable grounds to suspect that any thing liable to forfeiture under the customs and excise Acts is kept or concealed in any building or place, any officer having a writ of assistance may—

(*a*) enter that building or place at any time, whether by day or night, on any day, and search for, seize, and detain or remove any such thing; and

(*b*) so far as is reasonably necessary for the purpose of such entry, search, seizure, detention or removal, break open any door, window or container and force and remove any other impediment or obstruction.

(2) No officer shall exercise the power of entry conferred on him by subsection (1) above by night unless he is accompanied by a constable.

(3) Without prejudice to subsection (1) above or to any other power conferred by the Customs and Excise Acts 1979, if a justice of the peace is satisfied by information upon oath given by an officer that there are reasonable grounds to suspect that any thing liable to forfeiture under the customs and excise Acts is kept or concealed in any building or place, he may by warrant under his hand given on any day authorise that officer or any other person named in the warrant to enter and search any building or place so named.

(4) An officer or person named in a warrant under subsection (3) above shall thereupon have the like powers in relation to the building or place named in the warrant, subject to the like conditions as to entry by night, as if he were an officer having a writ of assistance and acting upon reasonable grounds of suspicion.

(5) Where there are reasonable grounds to suspect that any still, vessel, utensil, spirits or materials for the manufacture of spirits is or are unlawfully kept or deposited in any building or place, subsections (3) and (4) above shall apply in relation to any constable as they would apply in relation to an officer.

(6) A writ of assistance shall continue in force during the reign in which it is issued and for 6 months thereafter.

Power to enter land for or in connection with access to pipe-lines

162. Where any thing conveyed by a pipe-line is chargeable with a duty of customs or excise which has not been paid, an officer may enter any land adjacent to the pipe-line in order to get to the pipe-line for the purpose of exercising in relation to that thing any power conferred by or under the Customs and Excise Acts 1979 or to get from the pipe-line after an exercise of any such power.

This section does not extend to Northern Ireland.

Power to search vehicles or vessels

163.—(1) Without prejudice to any other power conferred by the Customs and Excise Acts 1979, where there are reasonable grounds to suspect that any vehicle or vessel is or may be carrying any goods which are—

(*a*) chargeable with any duty which has not been paid or secured; or

(*b*) in the course of being unlawfully removed from or to any place; or

(*c*) otherwise liable to forfeiture under the customs and excise Acts, any officer or constable or member of Her Majesty's armed forces or coastguard may stop and search that vehicle or vessel.

(2) If when so required by any such officer, constable or member the person in charge of any such vehicle or vessel refuses to stop or to permit the vehicle or vessel to be searched, he shall be liable on summary conviction to a penalty of £100.

Power to search persons

164.—(1) Where there are reasonable grounds to suspect that any person to whom this section applies is carrying any article—

(*a*) which is chargeable with any duty which has not been paid or secured; or

(*b*) with respect to the importation or exportation of which any prohibition or restriction is for the time being in force under or by virtue of any enactment,

any officer or any person acting under the directions of an officer may, subject to subsections (2) and (3) below, search him and any article he has with him.

(2) A person who is to be searched in pursuance of this section may require to be taken before a justice of the peace or a superior of the officer or other person concerned, and the justice or superior shall consider the grounds for suspicion and direct accordingly whether or not the search is to take place.

(3) No woman or girl shall be searched in pursuance of this section except by a woman.

(4) This section applies to the following persons, namely—

(*a*) any person who is on board or has landed from any ship or aircraft;

(*b*) any person entering or about to leave the United Kingdom;

(*c*) any person within the dock area of a port;

(*d*) any person at a customs and excise airport;

(*e*) any person in, entering or leaving any approved wharf or transit shed which is not in a port;

(*f*) in Northern Ireland, any person travelling from or to any place which is on or beyond the boundary.

Power to pay rewards

165. Subject to any directions of the Treasury as to amount, the Commissioners may at their discretion pay rewards in respect of any service which appears to them to merit reward rendered to them by any person in relation to any assigned matter.

Agents

166.—(1) If any person requests an officer or a person appointed by the Commissioners to transact any business relating to an assigned matter with him on behalf of another person, the officer or person so appointed may refuse to transact that business with him unless written authority from that other person is produced in such form as the Commissioners may direct.

(2) Subject to subsection (1) above, anything required by the Customs and Excise Acts 1979 to be done by the importer or exporter of any goods may, except where the Commissioners otherwise require, be done on his behalf by an agent.

General offences

Untrue declarations, etc.

167.—(1) If any person either knowingly or recklessly—

(*a*) makes or signs, or causes to be made or signed, or delivers or causes to be delivered to the Commissioners or an officer, any declaration, notice, certificate or other document whatsoever; or

(*b*) makes any statement in answer to any question put to him by an officer which he is required by or under any enactment to answer,

being a document or statement produced or made for any purpose of any assigned matter, which is untrue in any material particular, he shall be guilty of an offence under this subsection and may be detained; and any goods in relation to which the document or statement was made shall be liable to forfeiture.

(2) Without prejudice to subsection (4) below, a person who commits an offence under subsection (1) above shall be liable—

(*a*) on summary conviction, to a penalty of the prescribed sum, or to imprisonment for a term not exceeding 6 months, or to both; or

(*b*) on conviction on indictment, to a penalty of any amount, or to imprisonment for a term not exceeding 2 years, or to both.

(3) If any person—

(*a*) makes or signs, or causes to be made or signed, or delivers or causes to be delivered to the Commissioners or an officer, any declaration, notice, certificate or other document whatsoever; or

(*b*) makes any statement in answer to any question put to him by an officer which he is required by or under any enactment to answer,

being a document or statement produced or made for any purpose of any assigned matter, which is untrue in any material particular, then, without prejudice to subsection (4) below, he shall be liable on summary conviction to a penalty of £300.

(4) Where by reason of any such document or statement as is mentioned in subsection (1) or (3) above the full amount of any duty payable is not paid or any overpayment is made in respect of any drawback, allowance, rebate or repayment of duty, the amount of the duty unpaid or of the overpayment shall be recoverable as a debt due to the Crown or may be summarily recovered as a civil debt.

Counterfeiting documents, etc.

168.—(1) If any person—

(*a*) counterfeits or falsifies any document which is required by or under any enactment relating to an assigned matter or which is used in the transaction of any business relating to an assigned matter; or

(*b*) knowingly accepts, receives or uses any such document so counterfeited or falsified; or

(*c*) alters any such document after it is officially issued; or

(*d*) counterfeits any seal, signature, initials or other mark of, or used by, any officer for the verification of such a document or for the security of goods or for any other purpose relating to an assigned matter,

he shall be guilty of an offence under this section and may be detained.

(2) A person guilty of an offence under this section shall be liable—

(*a*) on summary conviction, to a penalty of the prescribed sum, or to imprisonment for a term not exceeding 6 months, or to both; or

(*b*) on conviction on indictment, to a penalty of any amount, or to imprisonment for a term not exceeding 2 years, or to both.

False scales, etc.

169.—(1) If any person required by or under the customs and excise Acts to provide scales for any purpose of those Acts provides, uses or permits to be used any scales which are false or unjust he shall be guilty of an offence under this section.

(2) Where any article is or is to be weighed, counted, gauged or measured for the purposes of the taking of an account or the making of an examination by an officer, then if—

(*a*) any such person as is mentioned in subsection (1) above; or

(*b*) any person by whom or on whose behalf the article is weighed, counted, gauged or measured,

does anything whereby the officer is or might be prevented from, or hindered or deceived in, taking a true and just account or making a due examination, he shall be guilty of an offence under this section.

This subsection applies whether the thing is done before, during or after the weighing, counting, gauging or measuring of the article in question.

(3) Any person committing an offence under this section shall be liable on summary conviction to a penalty of £200 and any false or unjust scales, and any article in connection with which the offence was committed, shall be liable to forfeiture.

(4) In this section " scales " includes weights, measures and weighing or measuring machines or instruments.

Penalty for fraudulent evasion of duty, etc.

170.—(1) Without prejudice to any other provision of the Customs and Excise Acts 1979, if any person—

(*a*) knowingly acquires possession of any of the following goods, that is to say—

(i) goods which have been unlawfully removed from a warehouse or Queen's warehouse;

(ii) goods which are chargeable with a duty which has not been paid;

(iii) goods with respect to the importation or exportation of which any prohibition or restriction is for the time being in force under or by virtue of any enactment; or

(*b*) is in any way knowingly concerned in carrying, removing, depositing, harbouring, keeping or concealing or in any manner dealing with any such goods,

and does so with intent to defraud Her Majesty of any duty payable on the goods or to evade any such prohibition or restriction with respect to the goods he shall be guilty of an offence under this section and may be detained.

(2) Without prejudice to any other provision of the Customs and Excise Acts 1979, if any person is, in relation to any goods, in any way knowingly concerned in any fraudulent evasion or attempt at evasion—

(*a*) of any duty chargeable on the goods;

(*b*) of any prohibition or restriction for the time being in force with respect to the goods under or by virtue of any enactment; or

(*c*) of any provision of the Customs and Excise Acts 1979 applicable to the goods,

he shall be guilty of an offence under this section and may be detained.

(3) Subject to subsection (4) below, a person guilty of an offence under this section shall be liable—

(*a*) on summary conviction, to a penalty of the prescribed sum or of three times the value of the goods, whichever is the greater, or to imprisonment for a term not exceeding 6 months, or to both; or

(*b*) on conviction on indictment, to a penalty of any amount, or to imprisonment for a term not exceeding 2 years, or to both.

(4) In the case of an offence under this section in connection with a prohibition or restriction on importation or exportation having effect by virtue of section 3 of the Misuse of Drugs Act 1971, subsection (3) above shall have effect subject to the modifications specified in Schedule 1 to this Act.

(5) In any case where a person would, apart from this subsection, be guilty of—

(*a*) an offence under this section in connection with a prohibition or restriction; and

(*b*) a corresponding offence under the enactment or other instrument imposing the prohibition or restriction, being an offence for which a fine or other penalty is expressly provided by that enactment or other instrument,

he shall not be guilty of the offence mentioned in paragraph (*a*) of this subsection.

General provisions as to offences and penalties

171.—(1) Where—

(*a*) by any provision of any enactment relating to an assigned matter a punishment is prescribed for any offence thereunder or for any contravention of or failure to comply with any regulation, direction, condition or requirement made, given or imposed thereunder; and

(*b*) any person is convicted in the same proceedings of more than one such offence, contravention or failure,

that person shall be liable to that punishment for each such offence, contravention or failure of which he is so convicted.

(2) In this Act the " prescribed sum ", in relation to the penalty provided for an offence, means—

(*a*) if the offence was committed in England, Wales or Northern Ireland, the prescribed sum within the meaning of section 28 of the Criminal Law Act 1977 (£1,000 or other sum substituted by order under section 61 (1) of that Act);

(*b*) if the offence was committed in Scotland, the prescribed sum within the meaning of section 289B of the Criminal Procedure (Scotland) Act 1975 (£1,000 or other sum substituted by order under section 289D (1) of that Act);

and in subsection (1) (*a*) above, the reference to a provision by which a punishment is prescribed includes a reference to a provision which makes a person liable to a penalty of the prescribed sum within the meaning of this subsection.

(3) Where a penalty for an offence under any enactment relating to an assigned matter is required to be fixed by reference to the value of any goods, that value shall be taken as the price which those goods

might reasonably be expected to have fetched, after payment of any duty or tax chargeable thereon, if they had been sold in the open market at or about the date of the commission of the offence for which the penalty is imposed.

(4) Where an offence under any enactment relating to an assigned matter which has been committed by a body corporate is proved to have been committed with the consent or connivance of, or to be attributable to any neglect on the part of, any director, manager, secretary or other similar officer of the body corporate or any person purporting to act in any such capacity, he as well as the body corporate shall be guilty of that offence and shall be liable to be proceeded against and punished accordingly.

In this subsection " director ", in relation to any body corporate established by or under any enactment for the purpose of carrying on under national ownership an industry or part of an industry or undertaking, being a body corporate whose affairs are managed by the members thereof, means a member of that body corporate.

(5) Where in any proceedings for an offence under the customs and excise Acts any question arises as to the duty or the rate thereof chargeable on any imported goods, and it is not possible to ascertain the relevant time specified in section 43 above, that duty or rate shall be determined as if the goods had been imported without entry at the time when the proceedings were commenced.

Miscellaneous

Regulations

172.—(1) Any power to make regulations under this Act shall be exercisable by statutory instrument.

(2) Subject to subsection (3) below, a statutory instrument containing regulations made under this Act shall be subject to annulment in pursuance of a resolution of either House of Parliament.

(3) A statutory instrument containing regulations made under section 120 above shall be subject to annulment in pursuance of a resolution of the House of Commons.

Directions

173. Directions given under any provision of this Act may make different provision for different circumstances and may be varied or revoked by subsequent directions thereunder.

Removal from or to Isle of Man not to be importation or exportation

174.—(1) For the purposes of the customs and excise Acts, subject to section 6 (2) and (3) of the Customs and Excise Duties (General Reliefs) Act 1979 and subsection (2) below, goods removed into the United Kingdom from the Isle of Man shall be deemed not to be imported into the United Kingdom.

(2) Subsection (1) above shall not apply to the removal of—

(*a*) any explosives within the meaning of the Explosives Act 1875 on the unloading or landing of which any restriction is for the time being in force under or by virtue of that Act; or

(*b*) copies of copyright works to which section 22 of the Copyright Act 1956 applies.

(3) For the purposes of the customs and excise Acts, subject to

subsection (4) below, goods removed from the United Kingdom to the Isle of Man shall be deemed not to be exported from the United Kingdom.

(4) Any enactment relating to the allowance of drawback of any excise duty on the exportation from the United Kingdom of any goods shall have effect, subject to such conditions and modifications as the Commissioners may by regulations prescribe, as if the removal of such goods to the Isle of Man were the exportation of the goods.

Scotland—special provisions

175.—(1) In the application of this Act to Scotland—

(*a*) any reference to costs shall be construed as a reference to expenses;

(*b*) any provision that any amount shall be recoverable summarily as a civil debt shall be construed as if the word " summarily " were omitted;

(*c*) any reference to a plaintiff shall be construed as a reference to a pursuer;

(*d*) any reference to a magistrates' court shall be construed as a reference to the sheriff court.

(2) No Commissioner or officer and no person appointed by the Commissioners to discharge any duty relating to customs or excise shall be compelled to serve on any jury in Scotland whatsoever.

Game licences

176.—(1) Subject to the following provisions of this section, and save as expressly provided in section 102 above, the provisions of this Act relating to excise shall not apply in relation to the excise duties on licences to kill game and on licences to deal in game (which, by virtue of the Order in Council made under section 6 of the Finance Act 1908, are leviable by local authorities).

(2) The Treasury may by order provide that, subject to such modifications, if any, as may be specified in the order, any provision of this Act so specified which confers or imposes powers, duties or liabilities with respect to excise duties and to the issue and cancellation of excise licences on which those duties are imposed and to other matters relating to excise duties and licences shall have effect in relation to a local authority and their officers with respect to the duties and licences referred to in subsection (1) above as they have effect in relation to the Commissioners and officers with respect to other excise duties and licences; and those provisions and, subject as aforesaid, any provisions relating to punishments and penalties in connection therewith shall have effect accordingly.

(3) Any order under this section shall be made by statutory instrument and may amend the Order in Council made under section 6 of the Finance Act 1908.

(4) Notwithstanding anything in section 145 as applied under subsection (2) above, a local authority may authorise the bringing by any constable of procedings, or any particular proceedings, for an offence under this or any other Act relating to the duties referred to in subsection (1) above.

(5) A document purporting to be a copy of a resolution authorising the bringing of proceedings in accordance with subsection (4) above and to be signed by an officer of the local authority shall be evidence, until the contrary is shown, that the bringing of the proceedings was duly authorised.

(6) This section extends to England and Wales only.

Consequential amendments, repeals and saving and transitional provisions

177.—(1) The enactments specified in Schedule 4 to this Act shall be amended in accordance with the provisions of that Schedule.

(2) The enactments specified in Schedule 5 to this Act (which relate to purchase tax and whose repeal by virtue of section 54 (8) of and Part II of Schedule 28 to the Finance Act 1972 has not yet taken effect) shall be amended in accordance with the provisions of that Schedule; and accordingly the following entry shall be inserted at the end of Part II of the said Schedule 28—

" 1979 c. 2	The Customs and Excise Management Act 1979.	Schedule 5."

(3) The enactments specified in Schedule 6 to this Act are hereby repealed to the extent specified in the third column of that Schedule.

(4) The saving and transitional provisions contained in Schedule 7 to this Act shall have effect.

(5) The provisions of Schedules 4, 5 and 7 to this Act shall not be taken as prejudicing the operation of sections 15 to 17 of the Interpretation Act 1978 (which relate to the effect of repeals).

Citation and commencement

178.—(1) This Act may be cited as the Customs and Excise Management Act 1979.

(2) This Act, the Customs and Excise Duties (General Reliefs) Act 1979, the Alcoholic Liquors Duties Act 1979, the Hydrocarbon Oil Duties Act 1979, the Matches and Mechanical Lighters Duties Act 1979 and the Tobacco Products Duty Act 1979 may be cited together as the Customs and Excise Acts 1979.

(3) This Act shall come into operation on 1st April 1979.

SCHEDULES

Sections 50 (5), 68 (4) and 170 (4)

SCHEDULE 1

CONTROLLED DRUGS: VARIATION OF PUNISHMENTS FOR CERTAIN OFFENCES UNDER THIS ACT

1. Sections 50 (4), 68 (3) and 170 (3) of this Act shall have effect in a case where the goods in respect of which the offence referred to in that subsection was committed were a Class A drug or a Class B drug as if for the words from " shall be liable " onwards there were substituted the following words, that is to say—

" shall be liable—

(*a*) on summary conviction, to a penalty of the prescribed sum or of three times the value of the goods, whichever is the greater, or to imprisonment for a term not exceeding 6 months, or to both;

(*b*) on conviction on indictment, to a penalty of any amount, or to imprisonment for a term not exceeding 14 years, or to both.".

2. Sections 50 (4), 68 (3) and 170 (3) of this Act shall have effect in a case where the goods in respect of which the offence referred to in that subsection was committed were a Class C drug as if for the words from " shall be liable " onwards there were substituted the following words, that is to say—

" shall be liable—

(*a*) on summary conviction in Great Britain, to a penalty of three times the value of the goods or £500, whichever is the greater, or to imprisonment for a term not exceeding 3 months, or to both;

(*b*) on summary conviction in Northern Ireland, to a penalty of three times the value of the goods or £100, whichever is the greater, or to imprisonment for a term not exceeding 6 months, or to both;

(c) on conviction on indictment, to a penalty of any amount, or to imprisonment for a term not exceeding 5 years, or to both.".

3. In this Schedule "Class A drug", "Class B drug" and "Class C drug" have the same meanings as in the Misuse of Drugs Act 1971.

Section 126 (3)

SCHEDULE 2

Composite Goods: Supplementary Provisions as to Excise Duties and Drawbacks

Duties

1.—(1) Where under subsection (1) of the principal section imported goods of any class or description are chargeable with a duty of excise in respect of any article contained in the goods as a part or ingredient of them and it appears to the Treasury on the recommendation of the Commissioners that to charge the duty according to the quantity of the article used in the manufacture or preparation of the goods (as provided by the principal section) is inconvenient and of no material advantage to the revenue or to importers of goods of that class or description, then the Treasury may by order give a direction in relation to goods of that class or description under and in accordance with this paragraph.

(2) An order under this paragraph may direct that in the case of goods of the class or description to which it applies the duty chargeable shall be calculated in such of the following ways as may be provided by the order, that is to say—

(a) at a rate specified in the order by reference to the weight, quantity or value of the goods; or

(b) by reference to a quantity so specified of the article, and (where material) on the basis that the article is of such value, type or quality as may be so specified.

(3) If it appears to the Treasury on the recommendation of the Commissioners that, in the case of goods of any class or description, the net amounts payable in the absence of any direction under this paragraph are insignificant, the order may direct that any such goods shall be treated for the purpose of the duty as not containing the article in respect of which the duty is chargeable.

(4) If it appears to the Treasury on the recommendation of the Commissioners that goods of any class or description are substantially of the same nature and use as if they consisted wholly of the article in respect of which the duty is chargeable, the order may direct that any such goods shall be treated for the purpose of the duty as consisting wholly of that article.

(5) In making an order under this paragraph the Treasury shall have regard to the quantity and (where material) the type or quality of the article in question appearing to them, on the advice of the Commissioners, to be ordinarily used in the manufacture or preparation of goods of the class or description to which the order applies which are imported into the United Kingdom.

2. Where a direction given by virtue of paragraph 1 above is in force as regards goods of any class or description and any article contained in them, and goods of that class or description are imported into the United Kingdom containing a quantity of that article such as, in the opinion of the Commissioners, to suggest that advantage is being taken of the direction for the purpose of evading duty on the article, the Commissioners may, notwithstanding the direction, require that on those goods the duty in question shall be calculated as if they consisted wholly of that article or (if the Commissioners see fit) shall be calculated according to the quantity of the article actually contained in the goods.

3. Nothing in paragraphs 1 and 2 above shall affect the powers of the Treasury under subsection (2) of the principal section; and any goods as regards which a direction under that subsection is for the time being in force shall be deemed to be excepted from any order under paragraph 1 above.

Drawbacks

4. Where a direction is given by virtue of paragraph 1 above as regards imported goods of any class or description, the Treasury may by order provide

that for the purpose of allowing any drawback of excise duties there shall, in such cases and subject to such conditions (if any) as may be specified in the order, be treated as paid on imported goods of that class or description the same duties as would be chargeable apart from the direction.

5.—(1) Where, in the case of imported goods of any class or description which contain as a part or ingredient any article chargeable with a duty of excise, drawback of the duty may be allowed in respect of the article according to the quantity contained in the goods or the quantity used in their preparation or manufacture, and it appears to the Treasury on the recommendation of the Commissioners that to allow the drawback according to that quantity is inconvenient and of no material advantage to the revenue or to the persons entitled to the drawback, then the Treasury may by order give the like directions as to the manner in which the drawback is to be calculated, or in which the goods are to be treated for the purposes of the drawback, as by virtue of paragraph 1 above they may give in relation to charging duty.

(2) For the purposes of this paragraph, the reference in paragraph 1 (5) above to goods imported into the United Kingdom shall be taken as a reference to goods in the case of which the drawback may be allowed.

Supplementary

6. Where any order under paragraph 1 or 5 above directs that, for the purpose of any duty or of any drawback, goods are to be treated as not containing or as consisting wholly of a particular article, the goods shall be so treated also for the purpose of determining whether any other duty is chargeable or any other drawback may be allowed, as the case may be; but any duty or drawback which is charged or allowed shall, notwithstanding the direction, be calculated by reference to the actual quantity and value of the goods and, except for the duty or drawback to which the direction relates, by reference to their actual composition.

7. Where a resolution passed by the House of Commons has statutory effect under the Provisional Collection of Taxes Act 1968 in relation to any duty of excise charged on imported goods, and any provision about that duty contained in an order under paragraph 1 above is expressed to be made in view of the resolution, then that provision may be varied or revoked retrospectively by an order made not later than one month after the resolution ceases to have statutory effect, and that order may include provision for repayment of any duty overpaid or for other matters arising from its having retrospective effect; but no such order shall have retrospective effect for the purpose of increasing the duty chargeable on any goods.

8. The power to make orders under this Schedule shall be exerciseable by statutory instrument subject to annulment in pursuance of a resolution of the House of Commons.

Interpretation

9. In this Schedule "the principal section" means section 126 of this Act.

Sections 139, 143 and 145 SCHEDULE 3

PROVISIONS RELATING TO FORFEITURE

Notice of seizure

1.—(1) The Commissioners shall, except as provided in sub-paragraph (2) below, give notice of the seizure of any thing as liable to forfeiture and of the grounds therefor to any person who to their knowledge was at the time of the seizure the owner or one of the owners thereof.

(2) Notice need not be given under this paragraph if the seizure was made in the presence of—

(*a*) the person whose offence or suspected offence occasioned the seizure; or

(*b*) the owner or any of the owners of the thing seized or any servant or agent of his; or

(*c*) in the case of any thing seized in any ship or aircraft, the master or commander.

2. Notice under paragraph 1 above shall be given in writing and shall be deemed to have been duly served on the person concerned—

(a) if delivered to him personally; or

(b) if addressed to him and left or forwarded by post to him at his usual or last known place of abode or business or, in the case of a body corporate, at their registered or principal office; or

(c) where he has no address within the United Kingdom, or his address is unknown, by publication of notice of the seizure in the London, Edinburgh or Belfast Gazette.

Notice of claim

3. Any person claiming that any thing seized as liable to forfeiture is not so liable shall, within one month of the date of the notice of seizure or, where no such notice has been served on him, within one month of the date of the seizure, give notice of his claim in writing to the Commissioners at any office of customs and excise.

4.—(1) Any notice under paragraph 3 above shall specify the name and address of the claimant and, in the case of a claimant who is outside the United Kingdom, shall specify the name and address of a solicitor in the United Kingdom who is authorised to accept service of process and to act on behalf of the claimant.

(2) Service of process upon a solicitor so specified shall be deemed to be proper service upon the claimant.

Condemnation

5. If on the expiration of the relevant period under paragraph 3 above for the giving of notice of claim in respect of any thing no such notice has been given to the Commissioners, or if, in the case of any such notice given, any requirement of paragraph 4 above is not complied with, the thing in question shall be deemed to have been duly condemned as forfeited.

6. Where notice of claim in respect of any thing is duly given in accordance with paragraphs 3 and 4 above, the Commissioners shall take proceedings for the condemnation of that thing by the court, and if the court finds that the thing was at the time of seizure liable to forfeiture the court shall condemn it as forfeited.

7. Where any thing is in accordance with either of paragraphs 5 or 6 above condemned or deemed to have been condemned as forfeited, then, without prejudice to any delivery up or sale of the thing by the Commissioners under paragraph 16 below, the forfeiture shall have effect as from the date when the liability to forfeiture arose.

Proceedings for condemnation by court

8. Proceedings for condemnation shall be civil proceedings and may be instituted—

(a) in England or Wales either in the High Court or in a magistrates' court;

(b) in Scotland either in the Court of Session or in the sheriff court;

(c) in Northern Ireland either in the High Court or in a court of summary jurisdiction.

9. Proceedings for the condemnation of any thing instituted in a magistrates' court in England or Wales, in the sheriff court in Scotland or in a court of summary jurisdiction in Northern Ireland may be so instituted—

(a) in any such court having jurisdiction in the place where any offence in connection with that thing was committed or where any proceedings for such an offence are instituted; or

(b) in any such court having jurisdiction in the place where the claimant resides or, if the claimant has specified a solicitor under paragraph 4 above, in the place where that solicitor has his office; or

(c) in any such court having jurisdiction in the place where that thing was found, detained or seized or to which it is first brought after being found, detained or seized.

10.—(1) In any proceedings for condemnation instituted in England, Wales or Northen Ireland, the claimant or his solicitor shall make oath that the thing seized was, or was to the best of his knowledge and belief, the property of the claimant at the time of the seizure.

(2) In any such proceedings instituted in the High Court, the claimant shall give such security for the costs of the proceedings as may be determined by the Court.

(3) If any requirement of this paragraph is not complied with, the court shall give judgment for the Commissioners.

11.—(1) In the case of any proceedings for condemnation instituted in a magistrates' court in England or Wales, without prejudice to any right to require the statement of a case for the opinion of the High Court, either party may appeal against the decision of that court to the Crown Court.

(2) In the case of any proceedings for condemnation instituted in a court of summary jurisdiction in Northern Ireland, without prejudice to any right to require the statement of a case for the opinion of the High Court, either party may appeal against the decision of that court to the county court.

12. Where an appeal, including an appeal by way of case stated, has been made against the decision of the court in any proceedings for the condemnation of any thing, that thing shall, pending the final determination of the matter, be left with the Commissioners or at any convenient office of customs and excise.

Provisions as to proof

13. In any proceedings arising out of the seizure of any thing, the fact, form and manner of the seizure shall be taken to have been as set forth in the process without any further evidence thereof, unless the contrary is proved.

14. In any proceedings, the condemnation by a court of any thing as forfeited may be proved by the production either of the order or certificate of condemnation or of a certified copy thereof purporting to be signed by an officer of the court by which the order or certificate was made or granted.

Special provisions as to certain claimants

15. For the purposes of any claim to, or proceedings for the condemnation of, any thing, where that thing is at the time of seizure the property of a body corporate, of two or more partners or of any number of persons exceeding five, the oath required by paragraph 10 above to be taken and any other thing required by this Schedule or by any rules of the court to be done by, or by any person authorised by, the claimant or owner may be taken or done by, or by any other person authorised by, the following persons respectively, that is to say—

(*a*) where the owner is a body corporate, the secretary or some duly authorised officer of that body;

(*b*) where the owners are in partnership, any one of those owners;

(*c*) where the owners are any number of persons exceeding five not being in partnership, any two of those persons on behalf of themselves and their co-owners.

Power to deal with seizures before condemnation, etc.

16. Where any thing has been seized as liable to forfeiture the Commissioners may at any time if they see fit and notwithstanding that the thing has not yet been condemned, or is not yet deemed to have been condemned, as forfeited—

(*a*) deliver it up to any claimant upon his paying to the Commissioners such sum as they think proper, being a sum not exceeding that which in their opinion represents the value of the thing, including any duty or tax chargeable thereon which has not been paid;

(*b*) if the thing seized is a living creature or is in the opinion of the Commissioners of a perishable nature, sell or destroy it.

17.—(1) If, where any thing is delivered up, sold or destroyed under paragraph 16 above, it is held in proceedings taken under this Schedule that the thing was not liable to forfeiture at the time of its seizure, the Commissioners shall, subject to any deduction allowed under sub-paragraph (2) below, on demand by the claimant tender to him—

(*a*) an amount equal to any sum paid by him under sub-paragraph (*a*) of that paragraph; or

(*b*) where they have sold the thing, an amount equal to the proceeds of sale; or

(*c*) where they have destroyed the thing, an amount equal to the market value of the thing at the time of its seizure.

(2) Where the amount to be tendered under sub-paragraph (1) (*a*), (*b*) or (*c*)

above includes any sum on account of any duty or tax chargeable on the thing which had not been paid before its seizure the Commissioners may deduct so much of that amount as represents that duty or tax.

(3) If the claimant accepts any amount tendered to him under sub-paragraph (1) above, he shall not be entitled to maintain any action on account of the seizure, detention, sale or destruction of the thing.

(4) For the purposes of sub-paragraph (1) (*c*) above, the market value of any thing at the time of its seizure shall be taken to be such amount as the Commissioners and the claimant may agree or, in default of agreement, as may be determined by a referee appointed by the Lord Chancellor (not being an official of any government department), whose decision shall be final and conclusive; and the procedure on any reference to a referee shall be such as may be determined by the referee.

Section 177 (1)

SCHEDULE 4

Consequential Amendments

Construction of references in Acts passed before 1st April 1909 and in instruments made thereunder

1. Save where the context otherwise requires, any reference in, or in any instrument made under, any enactment relating to customs or excise passed before 1st April 1909 to any of the persons mentioned in column 1 of the following Table shall be construed as a reference to the persons respectively specified in relation thereto in column 2.

TABLE

Original reference	*To be construed as reference to—*
Commissioners of Customs ... ... Commissioners of Inland Revenue ... Commissioners of Excise	Commissioners of Customs and Excise.
Solicitor for the Customs ... ... Solicitor of Inland Revenue	Solicitor for the Customs and Excise.
Secretary for the Customs ... ... Secretary of the Commissioners of Inland Revenue	Secretary to the Commissioners of Customs and Excise.
Accountant and Comptroller General of Customs ... ... Accountant and Comptroller General of Inland Revenue	Accountant and Comptroller General of the Customs and Excise.
Collector of Customs ... ... Collector of Inland Revenue ... ... Collector of Excise	Collector of Customs and Excise.
Officer of Customs ... ... Officer of Inland Revenue ... ... Officer of Excise	Officer of Customs and Excise.

Isle of Man Act 1958

2. In section 2 (1) of the Isle of Man Act 1958 the words from " shall not be paid " to " but " shall be omitted.

Diplomatic Privileges Act 1964

3. In section 2 of the Diplomatic Privileges Act 1964, after subsection (5) there shall be inserted the following subsection—

" (5A) The reference in Article 36 to customs duties shall be construed as including a reference to excise duties chargeable on goods imported into the United Kingdom."

Provisional Collection of Taxes Act 1964

4. In section 3 of the Provisional Collection of Taxes Act 1968, after subsection (2) there shall be inserted the following subsection—

"(2A) Subsection (2) above shall apply for the purposes of a duty of excise imposed as mentioned in subsection (1) above to the extent that the duty is charged on goods imported into the United Kingdom, as it applies for the purposes of a duty of customs so imposed.".

5. In section 3 (3) of the Provisional Collection of Taxes Act 1968, after the words "duty of excise" there shall be inserted the words "then—

(*a*) where it is a duty of excise charged otherwise than on goods; or

(*b*) where it is a duty of excise charged on goods, to the extent that it is charged on goods produced or manufactured in the United Kingdom;".

Consular Relations Act 1968

6. In section 1 of the Consular Relations Act 1968, after subsection (8) there shall be inserted the following subsection—

"(8A) The references in Articles 50 and 62 to customs duties shall be construed as including references to excise duties chargeable on goods imported into the United Kingdom."

7. In section 5 of the Consular Relations Act 1968, after subsection (1) there shall be inserted the following subsection—

"(1A) In subsection (1) (*b*) of this section the expression "the law relating to customs", to the extent that it refers to the law relating to duties on goods, refers to the law relating to duties (whether of customs or excise) for the time being chargeable on goods imported into the United Kingdom."

Misuse of Drugs Act 1971

8. In section 12 (1) (*b*) of the Misuse of Drugs Act 1971, after the words "the Customs and Excise Act 1952" there shall be inserted the words "or under section 50, 68 or 170 of the Customs and Excise Management Act 1979".

Finance Act 1972

9. In section 17 of the Finance Act 1972, after subsection (1) there shall be inserted the following subsection—

"(1A) Section 125 (3) of the Customs and Excise Management Act 1979 shall have effect in its application by virtue of subsection (1) of this section as if the reference to subsections (1) and (2) of that section included a reference to section 11 of this Act."

10. In section 17 of the Finance Act 1972, for subsection (2) there shall be substituted the following subsection—

"(2) The following provisions of the Customs and Excise Management Act 1979 shall be excepted from the enactments which are to have effect as mentioned in subsection (1) of this section, that is to say—

(*a*) section 43 (5) (re-importation);

(*b*) section 125 (1) and (2) (valuation of goods imported);

(*c*) section 126 (charge of duty on manufactured or composite imported articles);

(*d*) section 127 (1) (*b*) (declaration as to duty payable); and

(*e*) section 174 (Isle of Man)."

11. In section 27 of the Finance Act 1972, for subsection (1) as originally enacted) there shall be substituted the following subsection—

"(1) Where imported goods subject to a duty of customs or excise or a duty of customs and a duty of excise are supplied while warehoused, the supply shall be disregarded for the purposes of this Part of this Act if the goods are supplied before payment of the duty to which they are subject or, where they are subject to a duty of customs and a duty of excise, of the duty of excise."

Table of textual amendments

12. In the enactments specified in the following Table, for so much of the provision in column 1 as is specified in column 2 there shall be substituted the words in column 3.

TABLE

PART I

ENACTMENTS OF THE PARLIAMENT OF THE UNITED KINGDOM

Section or Schedule	Words or provision replaced	Replacement
	CROWN DEBTS AND JUDGMENTS ACT 1860 c. 115	
Section 1 (as amended by the Customs and Excise Act 1952).	From "the Customs" to "1952".	"customs and excise contained in subsection (2) of section 157 of the Customs and Excise Management Act 1979".
	"sections".	"subsection".
	NAVAL PRIZE ACT 1864 c. 25	
Section 47.	"duties of Customs".	"duties chargeable on imported goods (whether of customs or excise)".
	"the Customs" (twice).	"customs or excise".
Sections 48 and 48A.	"relating to the Customs".	"relating to customs or excise".
Section 49.	"duties of Customs".	"duties (whether of customs or excise) chargeable on imported goods".
	EXPLOSIVES ACT 1875 c. 17	
Section 40 (9) (*e*).	"the Customs" (twice).	"customs or exeise".
Section 43.	"the Customs" (twice).	"customs or excise".
	CUSTOMS AND INLAND REVENUE ACT 1879 c. 21	
Section 5 (as originally enacted).	From the beginning to "following".	"The importation of the following goods is prohibited, that is to say".
	STAMP DUTIES MANAGEMENT ACT 1891 c. 38	
Section 23.	"duty of excise".	"duty of excise other than a duty of excise chargeable on goods imported into the United Kingdom".
	MERCHANT SHIPPING ACT 1894 c. 60	
Section 492.	"customs laws" (twice).	"customs or excise laws".
	FOREIGN PRISON-MADE GOODS ACT 1897 c. 63	
Section 1 (as originally enacted).	From the beginning to "following".	"The importation of the following goods is prohibited".
	REVENUE ACT 1898 c. 46	
Section 1 (as originally enacted).	From the beginning to "following".	"The importation of the following articles is prohibited".
	FINANCE ACT 1901 c. 7	
Section 10.	"customs import duty" (in three places).	"customs duty".

SCHEDULE 4—*continued*

Section or Schedule	Words or provision replaced	Replacement
	SEAL FISHERIES (NORTH PACIFIC) ACT 1912 c. 10	
Section 4 (as originally enacted).	From " shall " onwards.	" are hereby prohibited to be imported ".
	PILOTAGE ACT 1913 (2 & 3 Geo. 5) c. 31	
Section 48 (3).	" relating to Customs ".	" relating to customs or excise ".
	PUBLIC HEALTH ACT 1936 c. 49	
Section 2 (1).	" relating to the Customs ".	" for the time being in force relating to customs or excise ".
	DISEASES OF FISH ACT 1937 c. 33	
Section 1 (2).	" the Customs Acts ".	" the enactments for the time being in force relating to customs or excise ".
	TRADE MARKS ACT 1938 c. 22	
Section 64A (5).	" section 11 of the Customs and Excise Act 1952 ".	" section 17 of the Customs and Excise Management Act 1979 ".
	" customs ".	" duties (whether of customs or excise) charged on imported goods ".
	IMPORT, EXPORT AND CUSTOMS POWERS (DEFENCE) ACT 1939 c. 69	
Sections 1 (4) and 3 (1).	" enactments relating to customs ".	" enactments for the time being in force relating to customs or excise ".
Section 1 (5) (as originally enacted).	" section eleven of the Customs and Inland Revenue Act 1879 ".	" section 145 of the Customs and Excise Management Act 1979 ".
Section 9 (2).	" Customs Consolidation Act 1876, and the enactments amending that Act ".	" Customs and Excise Management Act 1979 ".
	EXCHANGE CONTROL ACT 1947, c. 14	
Schedule 5, Part III, paragraph 1 (1) and (2).	" enactments relating to customs ".	" enactments for the time being in force relating to customs or excise ".
Schedule 5, Part III, paragraph 2 (as originally enacted).	" section one hundred and sixty-eight of the Customs Consolidation Act 1876 ".	" section 167 of the Customs and Excise Management Act 1979 ".
	RADIOACTIVE SUBSTANCES ACT 1948 c. 37	
Section 2 (2).	" enactments relating to customs ".	" enactments for the time being in force relating to customs or excise ".
Section 2 (3).	" Customs Consolidation Act 1876, and the enactments amending that Act ".	" Customs and Excise Management Act 1979 ".
	MERCHANT SHIPPING (SAFETY CONVENTION) ACT 1949 c. 43	
Section 24 (5).	" the Customs Consolidation Act 1876 ".	" section 35 of the Customs and Excise Management Act 1979 ".

SCHEDULE 4—*continued*

Section or Schedule	Words or provision replaced	Replacement
	CIVIL AVIATION ACT 1949 c. 67	
Section 8 (2) (*m*).	" relating to customs ".	" for the time being in force relating to customs or excise ".
	DISEASES OF ANIMALS ACT 1950 c. 36	
Section 24 (6).	" section 79 (2) of the Customs and Excise Act 1952 ".	" section 5 (2) of the Customs and Excise Management Act 1979 ".
	" that Act ".	" the customs and excise Acts ".
Section 73 (4A) (*a*).	" the Customs and Excise Act 1952, or at a customs airport ".	" the Customs and Excise Management Act 1979, or at a customs and excise airport ".
	POST OFFICE ACT 1953 c. 36	
Section 16 (1).	" customs ".	" customs or excise ".
Section 17 (1).	" customs duty ".	" duty charged on imported goods (whether a customs or an excise duty) ".
	PROTECTION OF BIRDS ACT 1954 c. 30	
Section 7 (3).	" the Customs and Excise Act 1952, the Seventh Schedule ".	" the Customs and Excise Management Act 1979, Schedule 3 ".
Section 14 (1) (in the definition of " importation ").	" the Customs and Excise Act 1952 ".	" the Customs and Excise Management Act 1979 ".
	FOOD AND DRUGS ACT 1955 (4 Eliz. 2) c. 16	
Section 135 (1) (in the definition of " importation ").	" the Customs and Excise Act 1952 ".	" the Customs and Excise Management Act 1979 ".
	FOOD AND DRUGS (SCOTLAND) ACT 1956 c. 30	
Section 58 (1) (in the definition of " importation ").	" the Customs and Excise Act 1952 ".	" the Customs and Excise Management Act 1979 ".
	COPYRIGHT ACT 1956 c. 74	
Section 22 (6).	" section eleven of the Customs and Excise Act 1952 ".	" section 17 of the Customs and Excise Management Act 1979 ".
	" customs ".	" duties (whether of customs or excise) charged on imported goods ".
Section 22 (7).	" the Customs and Excise Act 1952 ".	" the Customs and Excise Management Act 1979 ".
	CINEMATOGRAPH FILMS ACT 1957 c. 21	
Section 4 (5).	" section three hundred and one of the Customs and Excise Act 1952 ".	" section 167 of the Customs and Excise Management Act 1979 ".
	ISLE OF MAN ACT 1958 c. 11	
Section 2 (4).	" duties of customs " (in four places).	" duties of customs or excise ".

SCHEDULE 4—*continued*

Section or Schedule	Words or provision replaced	Replacement
	DOG LICENCES ACT 1959 c. 55	
Section 15 (1).	From "section three hundred and thirteen" to "dog licences)".	"section 176 (2) of the Customs and Excise Management Act 1979 (which makes provision for the application of certain provisions of that Act to game licences and duties thereon and is applied by section 16 (5) below)".
Section 16 (5).	From the beginning to "the said section three hundred and thirteen".	"Subsections (1) to (3) of section 176 of the Customs and Excise Management Act 1979 (which make provision for the application of certain provisions of that Act to game licences and duties thereon), and any order made by the Treasury under that section,".
	From "duties transferred under section six" to "the said Act of 1908".	"duties on licences to kill and to deal in game and to local authorities and their officers with respect to those duties and licences, and the reference in the said subsection (3) to the Order in Council made under section 6 of the Finance Act 1908".
	FINANCE ACT 1961 c. 36	
Section 37 (3).	"the Customs and Excise Act 1952".	"the Customs and Excise Management Act 1979".
	WEIGHTS AND MEASURES ACT 1963 c. 31	
Section 21 (5) (*b*) (ii).	"the Customs and Excise Act 1952".	"the Customs and Excise Management Act 1979".
	LICENSING ACT 1964 c. 26	
Section 87 (1).	"section 16 of the Customs and Excise Act 1952".	"section 22 of the Customs and Excise Management Act 1979".
	AGRICULTURE AND HORTICULTURE ACT 1964 c. 28	
Section 1 (12).	"enactments relating to customs".	"enactments for the time being in force relating to customs or excise".
	"duties of customs".	"duties (whether of customs or excise) charged on imported goods".

SCHEDULE 4—*continued*

Section or Schedule	Words or provision replaced	Replacement
	AGRICULTURE AND HORTICULTURE ACT 1964 c. 28—*continued*	
Schedule, paragraph 1 (1).	From " the Customs and Excise Act 1952 " to " customs generally ".	" the Customs and Excise Management Act 1979 (as for the time being amended) and any other statutory provisions for the time being in force and relating to customs or excise generally ".
	" duties of customs ".	" duties (whether of customs or excise) charged on imported goods ".
Schedule, paragraph 1 (2).	" customs generally ".	" customs or excise generally ".
	From " section 259 " to " 1952 ".	" section 126 of the Customs and Excise Management Act 1979 ".
Schedule, paragraph 1 (3) (*a*).	" section 46 of the Customs and Excise Act 1952 ".	" section 51 of the Customs and Excise Management Act 1979 ".
	DIPLOMATIC PRIVILEGES ACT 1964 c. 81	
Section 7 (1) (*b*).	" customs duties ".	" duties (whether of customs or excise) chargeable on imported goods ".
	FINANCE (No. 2) ACT 1964 c. 92	
Section 7 (11).	" customs station ".	" customs and excise station ".
Section 9 (5).	" the Customs and Excise Act 1952 ".	" the Customs and Excise Management Act 1979 ".
	" that Act ".	" the Customs and Excise Acts 1979 ".
	" section 270 ".	" section 135 ".
	" section 271 (1) ".	" section 136 (1) and (2) ".
	" section 301 (2) ".	" section 167 (4) ".
Section 9 (6).	" section 11 of the Customs and Excise Act 1952 ".	" section 17 of the Customs and Excise Management Act 1979 ".
Section 10 (2).	" the Customs and Excise Act 1952 ".	" the Customs and Excise Management Act 1979 ".
	FINANCE ACT 1966 c. 18	
Section 2 (13) (*b*).	" section 11 of the Act of 1952 ".	" section 17 of the Customs and Excise Management Act 1979 ".
Section 53 (2).	From " Customs and Excise Act 1952 " to " that Act ".	" Customs and Excise Management Act 1979 ".
Schedule 1, paragraph 4.	" Act of 1952 ".	" Customs and Excise Management Act 1979 ".
	" that Act ".	" the Customs and Excise Acts 1979 ".
	" section 270 ".	" section 135 ".
	" section 271 (1) ".	" section 136 (1) and (2) ".
	" section 301 (2) ".	" section 167 (4) ".

SCHEDULE 4—*continued*

Section or Schedule	Words or provision replaced	Replacement
	PLANT HEALTH ACT 1967 c. 8	
Section 2 (2).	"the Customs and Excise Act 1952".	"the Customs and Excise Management Act 1979".
	FINANCE ACT 1967 c. 54	
Section 7 (8) (*b*).	"sections 281 and 287 of the Act of 1952".	"sections 145 and 151 of the Customs and Excise Management Act 1979".
	"the excise Acts" (twice).	"the customs and excise Acts".
Section 45 (3) (*a*).	From "Customs and Excise Act 1952" to "that Act".	"Customs and Excise Management Act 1979".
	WIRELESS TELEGRAPHY ACT 1967 c. 72	
Section 7 (5).	"the Customs and Excise Act 1952".	"the Customs and Excise Management Act 1979".
Section 7 (6).	"1952".	"1979".
	PROVISIONAL COLLECTION OF TAXES ACT 1968 c. 2	
Section 3 (3).	"the excise Acts".	"the revenue trade provisions of the customs and excise Acts".
Section 3 (5).	"the Customs and Excise Act 1952".	"the Customs and Excise Management Act 1979".
Section 4.	"duty of customs or excise".	"duty of excise".
	CONSULAR RELATIONS ACT 1968 c. 18	
Section 8 (1).	From "customs duty" to "which are".	"duty (whether of customs or excise) paid on imported hydrocarbon oil (within the meaning of the Hydrocarbon Oil Duties Act 1979) or value added tax paid on the importation of such oil which is".
Section 8 (1) (*b*).	"they".	"it".
	"customs duty"	"duty".
	FIREARMS ACT 1968 c. 27	
Section 45 (2) (*b*).	"enactments relating to customs".	"enactments for the time being in force relating to customs or excise".
	TRADE DESCRIPTIONS ACT 1968 c. 29	
Section 32 (*b*).	"Customs and Excise Act 1952".	"Customs and Excise Management Act 1979".

SCHEDULE 4—*continued*

Section or Schedule	Words or provision replaced	Replacement
	INTERNATIONAL ORGANISATIONS ACT 1968 c. 48	
Section 9.	" customs duty ".	" duty ".
Schedule 1, paragraphs 3 (1), 4, 9, 10, 16 and 17.	" customs duties ".	" duties (whether of customs or excise) ".
Schedule 1, paragraphs 6 and 12.	From " customs duty " to " which are ".	" duty (whether of customs or excise) paid on imported hydrocarbon oil (within the meaning of the Hydrocarbon Oil Duties Act 1979) or value added tax paid on the importation of such oil which is ".
	CIVIL AVIATION ACT 1968 c. 61	
Section 14 (5) (*a*).	" customs duty ".	" duty (whether of customs or excise) chargeable on imported goods ".
	MEDICINES ACT 1968 c. 67	
Section 116 (1).	" section 44 of the Customs and Excise Act 1952 ".	" section 49 of the Customs and Excise Management Act 1979 ".
Section 116 (2).	" section 56 of the Customs and Excise Act 1952 ".	" section 68 of the Customs and Excise Management Act 1979 ".
	CUSTOMS DUTIES (DUMPING AND SUBSIDIES) ACT 1969 c. 16	
Section 9 (2).	" the Customs and Excise Act 1952 ".	" the Customs and Excise Management Act 1979 ".
	" the customs Acts ".	" the enactments for the time being in force relating to customs or excise ".
	" section 255 of the Customs and Excise Act 1952 ".	" section 119 of the Customs and Excise Management Act 1978 ".
Section 10 (1).	" duty of customs " and " customs duty ".	" duty (whether of customs or excise) ".
Section 17 (in the definition of " importer ").	" customs charge ".	" charge ".
	FINANCE ACT 1969 c. 32	
Section 61 (3) (*a*).	" the Customs and Excise Act 1952 ".	" the Customs and Excise Acts 1979 ".
	POST OFFICE ACT 1969 c. 48	
Schedule 4, paragraph 2 (5).	" of customs ".	" (whether of customs or excise) charged on imported goods ".

SCHEDULE 4—*continued*

Section or Schedule	Words or provision replaced	Replacement
	VEHICLES (EXCISE) ACT 1971 c. 10	
Section 3 (2).	From " and to the issue " onwards.	" (other than duties on imported goods) and to the issue and cancellation of licences on which duties of excise are imposed and to other matters (not being matters relating only to duties on imported goods) under the Acts relating to duties of excise and excise licences; and, subject to those provisions and in particular to section 28 or 29 and to section 35 (3) of this Act, all enactments relating to those duties and to punishments and penalties in connection therewith (other than enactments relating only to duties on imported goods) shall apply accordingly ".
Section 28 (5).	" Section 281 of the Customs and Excise Act 1952 ".	" Section 145 of the Customs and Excise Management Act 1979 ".
	" section 283 (1)".	" section 147 (1)".
Section 35 (3).	" Section 287 of the Customs and Excise Act 1952 ".	" Section 151 of the Customs and Excise Management Act 1979 ".
	MISUSE OF DRUGS ACT 1971 c. 38	
Section 22 (*a*) (ii).	" the Customs and Excise Act 1952, that is to say sections 45 (1), 56 (2) and 304 ".	" the Customs and Excise Management Act 1979, that is to say, sections 50 (1) to (4), 68 (2) and (3) and 170 ".
	MINERAL WORKINGS (OFFSHORE INSTALLATIONS) ACT 1971 c. 61	
Section 10 (2).	Paragraph (*b*).	" (*b*) the Customs and Excise Acts 1979, or any enactment to be construed as one with those Acts or any of them;".
	DIPLOMATIC AND OTHER PRIVILEGES ACT 1971 c. 64	
Section 1 (1).	From " customs duty " to " 1971) ".	" duty (whether of customs or excise) paid on imported hydrocarbon oil (within the meaning of the Hydrocarbon Oil Duties Act 1979) or value added tax paid on the importation of such oil ".
Section 1 (1) (*b*).	" customs duty ".	" duty ".

SCHEDULE 4—*continued*

Section or Schedule	Words or provision replaced	Replacement
	BETTING AND GAMING DUTIES ACT 1972 c. 25	
Section 15 (4) and 20 (3).	"the excise Acts".	"the customs and excise Acts".
Section 30 (2).	"the Customs and Excise Act 1952".	"the Customs and Excise Management Act 1979".
	FINANCE ACT 1972 c. 41	
Section 1 (3) (*a*).	"section 11 of the Customs and Excise Act 1952".	"section 17 of the Customs and Excise Management Act 1979".
Section 12 (8).	"the Customs and Excise Act 1952".	"the Customs and Excise Management Act 1979".
Section 17 (1).	"the Customs and Excise Act 1952".	"the Customs and Excise Acts 1979".
	"to customs generally".	"generally to customs or excise duties on imported goods".
	"duties of customs".	"duties (whether of customs or excise)".
Section 27 (2).	From the beginning to "customs".	"Where goods produced or manufactured in the United Kingdom subject to a duty of excise or such goods mixed with imported goods subject to a duty (whether of customs or excise".
Section 38 (8).	"Sections 281 to 291 of the Customs and Excise Act 1952".	"Sections 145 to 155 of the Customs and Excise Management Act 1979".
	"section 290 (2)".	"section 154 (2)".
Section 40 (5).	"section 260 of the Customs and Excise Act 1952".	"section 127 of the Customs and Excise Management Act 1979".
Section 47 (2).	"section 79 of the Customs and Excise Act 1952".	"section 5 of the Customs and Excise Management Act 1979".
	"section 28 of the Customs and Excise Act 1952".	"section 37 of the Customs and Excise Management Act 1979".
Schedule 4, Group 10, Items 6 (*a*) and (*b*) and 12 (*a*).	"customs airport".	"customs and excise airport".
Schedule 4, Group 10, Note (1).	From "customs airport" onwards.	"'customs and excise airport' have the same meanings as in the Customs and Excise Management Act 1979.".
Schedule 4, Group 15, Item 1.	"section 28 of the Customs and Excise Act 1952".	"section 37 of the Customs and Excise Management Act 1979".
Schedule 7, paragraph 2 (2) (*a*).	"section 11 of the Customs and Excise Act 1952".	"section 17 of the Customs and Excise Management Act 1979".
Schedule 7, paragraph 22 (5).	"Sections 281 to 291 of the Customs and Excise Act 1952".	"Sections 145 to 155 of the Customs and Excise Management Act 1979".

SCHEDULE 4—*continued*

Section or Schedule	Words or provision replaced	Replacement
FINANCE ACT 1972 C. 41—*continued*		
Schedule 7, paragraph 22 (6).	"Section 290 (2) of the Customs and Excise Act 1952".	"Section 154 (2) of the Customs and Excise Management Act 1979".
Schedule 7, paragraph 23.	"the Customs and Excise Act 1952".	"the Customs and Excise Management Act 1979".
EUROPEAN COMMUNITIES ACT 1972 c. 68		
Section 6 (5).	Paragraph (*a*).	"(*a*) the Customs and Excise Management Act 1979 (as for the time being amended by any later Act) and any other statutory provisions for the time being in force relating generally to customs or excise duties on imported goods; and".
	From "section 267" to "customs duties".	"section 133 (except subsection (3) and the reference to that subsection in subsection (2)) and section 159 of the Customs and Excise Management Act 1979 shall apply as they apply in relation to a drawback of excise duties".
Section 6 (6).	"section 259 of the Customs and Excise Act 1952".	"section 126 of the Customs and Excise Management Act 1979".
POWERS OF CRIMINAL COURTS ACT 1973 c. 62		
Sections 31 (7) and 32 (2).	"section 285 of the Customs and Excise Act 1952".	"section 149 (1) of the Customs and Excise Management Act 1979".
HEALTH AND SAFETY AT WORK ETC. ACT 1974 c. 37		
Schedule 3, paragraph 2 (2).	"the Customs and Excise Act 1952".	"the Customs and Excise Acts 1979".
MERCHANT SHIPPING ACT 1974 c. 43		
Section 2 (9) (in the definition of "importer").	"customs purposes".	"customs or excise purposes".
Schedule 4, paragraph 1 (3).	"Section 53 of the Customs and Excise Act 1952".	"Section 65 of the Customs and Excise Management Act 1979".
Schedule 4, paragraph 2 (1) (*c*).	"customs Acts which relate to duties of customs".	"enactments for the time being in force relating to duties (whether of customs or excise) chargeable on goods imported into the United Kingdom".

SCHEDULE 4—*continued*

Section or Schedule	Words or provision replaced	Replacement
SALMON AND FRESHWATER FISHERIES ACT 1975 c. 51		
Schedule 4, paragraph 6.	"Schedule 7 to the Customs and Excise Act 1952".	"Schedule 3 to the Customs and Excise Management Act 1979".
	Paragraph (*a*).	"(*a*) paragraphs 1 (2) and 5 shall be omitted;".
LICENSING (SCOTLAND) ACT 1976 c. 66		
Section 63 (2).	"section 16 of the Customs and Excise Act 1952".	"section 22 of the Customs and Excise Management Act 1979".
ENDANGERED SPECIES (IMPORT AND EXPORT) ACT 1976 c. 72		
Section 1 (8).	"the Customs and Excise Act 1952".	"the Customs and Excise Management Act 1979".
Section 4 (8).	"section 45 or 304 of the Customs and Excise Act 1952".	"section 50 or 170 of the Customs and Excise Management Act 1979".
Section 5 (4) (in the definition of "airport").	From "customs airport" to "1952".	"customs and excise airport as mentioned in section 21 (7) of the Customs and Excise Management Act 1979".
Section 5 (4) (in the definition of "port").	"section 13 (1)".	"section 19 (1)".
FINANCE ACT 1977 c. 36		
Section 10 (5).	"made by the Commissioners".	"made by statutory instrument by the Commissioners which shall be subject to annulment in pursuance of a resolution of either House of Parliament".
Section 59 (3) (*a*).	"the Customs and Excise Act 1952".	"such of the Customs and Excise Acts 1979 as the provision in question requires".
FINANCE ACT 1978 c. 42		
Section 80 (3) (*a*).	"the Customs and Excise Act 1952".	"the Customs and Excise Management Act 1979".

PART II

ENACTMENTS OF THE PARLIAMENT OF NORTHERN IRELAND

Section or Schedule	Words or provision replaced	Replacement
CONTROL OF FERTILISERS ACT (NORTHERN IRELAND) 1953 c. 33		
Section 8 (2).	"section four of the Customs and Excise Act 1952".	"section 8 of the Customs and Excise Management Act 1979".
DISEASES OF ANIMALS ACT (NORTHERN IRELAND) 1958 c. 13		
Section 52 (2) (in the definition of "the Customs Acts").	"the Customs and Excise Act 1952".	"the Customs and Excise Management Act 1979".

SCHEDULE 4—*continued*

Section or Schedule	Words or provision replaced	Replacement
	MAGISTRATES' COURTS ACT (NORTHERN IRELAND) 1964 c. 21	
Section 62 (3).	"section 286 (2) of the Customs and Excise Act 1952".	"section 150 (2) of the Customs and Excise Management Act 1979".
Section 64 (3).	"section 285 (3) of the Customs and Excise Act 1952".	"section 149 (3) of the Customs and Excise Management Act 1979".
	WEIGHTS AND MEASURES ACT (NORTHERN IRELAND) 1967 c. 6	
Section 15 (5) (*b*).	"the Customs and Excise Act 1952".	"the Customs and Excise Management Act 1979".
	PLANT HEALTH ACT (NORTHERN IRELAND) 1967 c. 28	
Section 2 (2).	"the Customs and Excise Act 1952".	"the Customs and Excise Management Act 1979".
	MISCELLANEOUS TRANSFERRED EXCISE DUTIES ACT (NORTHERN IRELAND) 1972 c. 11	
Section 73.	"the Customs and Excise Act 1952".	"the Customs and Excise Management Act 1979".

Section 177 (2)

SCHEDULE 5

TRANSITORY CONSEQUENTIAL AMENDMENTS OF ENACTMENTS RELATING TO PURCHASE TAX

Purchase Tax Act 1963

1. In section 1 (3) (*a*) of the Purchase Tax Act 1963 (in this Schedule referred to as "the 1963 Act") for the words "section 11 of the Customs and Excise Act 1952" there shall be substituted the words "section 17 of the Customs and Excise Management Act 1979".

2.—(1) In section 25 of the 1963 Act the amendments specified in this paragraph shall be made.

(2) In subsection (1)—

(*a*) for the words "the Customs and Excise Act 1952" there shall be substituted the words "the Customs and Excise Management Act 1979"; and

(*b*) after the word "customs", in each place where it occurs, there shall be inserted the words "or excise".

(3) In subsection (2)—

(*a*) the words "of the Customs and Excise Act 1952" shall be omitted;

(*b*) in paragraph (*a*), for the words "sections 34 (4), 35 and 36" there shall be substituted the words "section 43 (5) of the Customs and Excise Management Act 1979, and sections 10 and 11 of the Customs and Excise Duties (General Reliefs) Act 1979";

(*c*) in paragraph (*b*), for the words "section 37" there shall be substituted the words "section 5 of the Customs and Excise Duties (General Reliefs) Act 1979";

(*d*) in paragraph (*c*), for the words "section 259" there shall be substituted the words "section 126 of the Customs and Excise Management Act 1979"; and (*e*) in paragraph (*d*), for the words "section 272" there shall be substituted the words "section 12 of the Customs and Excise Duties (General Reliefs) Act 1979".

(4) In subsection (3)—

(*a*) for the words "section 258 of the Customs and Excise Act 1952" there shall be substituted the words "section 125 of the Customs and Excise Management Act 1979"; and

(*b*) for the words "section 260" there shall be substituted the words "section 127".

(5) In subsection (4), for the words "Section 46 of the Customs and Excise Act 1952" there shall be substituted the words "Section 51 of the Customs and Excise Management Act 1979".

3.—(1) In section 34 of the 1963 Act the amendments specified in this paragraph shall be made.

(2) In subsection (1) for the words "the Customs and Excise Act 1952" and "the said Act of 1952" there shall be substituted the words "the Customs and Excise Management Act 1979".

(3) In subsection (2)—

(*a*) for the words "Sections 290 (2) and 301 (2) of the Customs and Excise Act 1952" there shall be substituted the words "Sections 154 (2) and 167 (4) of the Customs and Excise Management Act 1979"; and

(*b*) after the words "duty of excise" there shall be inserted the words "for the time being chargeable on goods produced or manufactured in the United Kingdom".

(4) For subsection (3) there shall be substituted the following subsection—

"(3) Section 156 of the Customs and Excise Management Act 1979 shall apply to this Act as it applies to the outlying provisions of the customs and excise Acts within the meaning of that section; and the reference in subsection (2) of that section to Part XI of that Act includes a reference to that Part as applied in relation to penalties under this Act by subsection (1) of this section."

4. In Schedule 2 to the 1963 Act, in paragraph 2 (*b*) for the words "duties of customs" there shall be substituted the words "duties (whether of customs or excise)".

Finance Act 1964

5. In section 10 (2) (*b*) of the Finance Act 1964—

(*a*) for the words "subsection (1) above" there shall be substituted the words "section 1 (4) of the Customs and Excise Management Act 1979"; and

(*b*) for the words "section 307 of the Act of 1952" there shall be substituted the words "section 1 (1) of that Act".

Finance Act 1967

6. In section 9 (1) of the Finance Act 1967 for the words "the Act of 1952" there shall be substituted the words "the Customs and Excise Management Act 1979".

Section 177 (3)

SCHEDULE 6

REPEALS

PART I

ENACTMENTS OF THE PARLIAMENT OF THE UNITED KINGDOM

Chapter	Short Title	Extent of Repeal
15 & 16 Geo. 6 & 1 Eliz. 2. c. 44.	The Customs and Excise Act 1952.	Parts I, II, III, IX, X, XI and XII except the following provisions, that is to say— sections 35 to 37, 41 to 43, 237, 241 to 243, 263 (3) to (5), in the proviso to section 271 (3), paragraph (i), section 272, so much of section 307 (1) as is repealed by the Alcoholic Liquor Duties Act 1979, sections 309 (1), (3) and (4) and 310 and section 315 (*c*) and (*d*). Schedule 7. Schedule 10, except paragraph 15.
1 & 2 Eliz. 2. c. 34.	The Finance Act 1953.	Sections 33 (1) and 35 (2).
5 & 6 Eliz. 2. c. 49.	The Finance Act 1957.	Sections 5 and 42 (2) (*a*). Schedule 2.
6 & 7 Eliz. 2. c. 11.	The Isle of Man Act 1958.	In section 2 (1), the words from " shall not be paid " to " but ".
6 & 7 Eliz. 2. c. 56.	The Finance Act 1958.	Section 40 (2) (*b*).
7 & 8 Eliz. 2. c. 58.	The Finance Act 1959.	Section 37 (2) (*a*).
8 & 9 Eliz. 2. c. 44.	The Finance Act 1960.	In section 79, subsections (2) and (3) (*a*) and, in subsection (6), the words from " or any tobacco dealer's licence " onwards.
9 & 10 Eliz. 2. c. 36.	The Finance Act 1961.	Sections 11 and 37 (2).
10 & 11 Eliz. 2. c. 44.	The Finance Act 1962.	In section 34, in subsection (2) the words from " Part I " to " 1952 and ".
10 & 11 Eliz. 2. c. 58.	The Pipe-lines Act 1962.	Section 56.
1963 c. 25.	The Finance Act 1963.	Section 7. In section 73, subsection (3) and, in subsection (4), the words from " Part I " to " 1952 and ".
1964 c. 49.	The Finance Act 1964.	Sections 10 (1) and 26 (2) and (3).

SCHEDULE 6—continued

Chapter	Short Title	Extent of Repeal
1966 c. 18.	The Finance Act 1966.	Sections 10 and 11. In Schedule 2, paragraph 1, except the words from "section 107 (1)" to "spirits)".
1967 c. 54.	The Finance Act 1967.	Section 3. In section 4 (5), paragraph (*a*) (i) and (v). In section 5, in subsection (1), paragraphs (*a*) and (*b*) and subsection (2). In Schedule 6, paragraphs 5, 6, and 12. In Schedule 9, paragraph 7.
1967 c. 80.	The Criminal Justice Act 1967.	Section 93 (4). In section 106 (2) (*b*) the words "and (4)".
1968 c. 44.	The Finance Act 1968.	Sections 6 and 61 (3).
1968 c. 59.	The Hovercraft Act 1968.	In the Schedule, paragraph 4 (*c*).
1969 c. 39.	The Age of Majority (Scotland) Act 1969.	In Schedule 1, the entry relating to the Customs and Excise Act 1952.
1969 c. 46.	The Family Law Reform Act 1969.	In Schedule 1, the entry relating to the Customs and Excise Act 1952.
1970 c. 24.	The Finance Act 1970.	Section 5. Section 7 (5) and (8). Section 36 (3). In Schedule 2, paragraph 5.
1971 c. 12.	The Hydrocarbon Oil (Customs & Excise) Act 1971.	Section 22. In Schedule 6, paragraph 1.
1971 c. 23.	The Courts Act 1971.	In Schedule 9, the entry relating to the Customs and Excise Act 1952.
1971 c. 38.	The Misuse of Drugs Act 1971.	Section 26.
1971 c. 68.	The Finance Act 1971.	Section 11. In section 69 (3), the words from "sections 3" to "1952". Schedule 1.
1972 c. 25.	The Betting and Gaming Duties Act 1972.	In Schedule 2, paragraph 7. In Schedule 4, paragraph 10.
1972 c. 41.	The Finance Act 1972.	Section 17 (5). Section 55 (4). Section 134 (3) (*a*).
1972 c. 68.	The European Communities Act 1972.	Section 5 (4) and (7) to (9). In Schedule 4, paragraph 2.
1973 c. 51.	The Finance Act 1973.	Section 2. Section 59 (3) (*a*).

SCHEDULE 6—*continued*

Chapter	Short Title	Extent of Repeal
1974 c. 30.	The Finance Act 1974.	Section 1 (7) and (8). In section 57 (3) (*a*), the words from "except so far" to "1952 and".
1975 c. 7.	The Finance Act 1975.	Section 4.
1975 c. 45.	The Finance (No. 2) Act 1975.	Section 1 (7) and (8). Sections 8 and 16. In section 75, in subsection (2), the words from "and in Part I" onwards and subsection (3) (*a*). In Schedule 3, paragraphs 1, 14, 23, 39 to 41, 43 and, in paragraph 44, sub-paragraph (*c*). In Schedule 6, paragraphs 1 to 4.
1976 c. 40.	The Finance Act 1976.	Section 15. Section 132 (3) (*a*). In Schedule 3, paragraphs 2 to 4 and 6.
1977 c. 36.	The Finance Act 1977.	Sections 8 and 9. In Schedule 6, paragraph 21.
1977 c. 45.	The Criminal Law Act 1977.	In Schedule 5, in paragraph 1, sub-paragraphs (1) (*a*) and (2) (*c*).
1978 c. 42.	The Finance Act 1978.	Sections 3 to 5 and 79. In Schedule 12, paragraphs 7 (1), 11 to 14, 16 to 19 (except paragraph 19 (7) (*d*)) and 21 to 24.

PART II

ENACTMENTS OF THE PARLIAMENT OF NORTHERN IRELAND

Chapter	Short Title	Extent of Repeal
1954 c. 8 (N.I.).	The Excise (Amendment) Act (Northern Ireland) 1954.	Sections 1 and 3.
1969 c. 28 (N.I.).	The Age of Majority Act (Northern Ireland) 1969.	In Schedule 1, the entry relating to the Customs and Excise Act 1952.

Section 177 (4)

SCHEDULE 7

SAVING AND TRANSITIONAL PROVISIONS

1. Notwithstanding the repeal by this Act of section 258 of the Customs and Excise Act 1952, of paragraph 5 of Schedule 2 to the Finance Act 1970, and of paragraph 2 (8) of Schedule 4 to the European Communities Act 1972, that section (together with Schedule 6) as it had effect immediately before the entry date within the meaning of the said Act of 1972, shall continue to have effect for

cases in which the value of goods falls to be determined as at a time before that date.

2. Notwithstanding the repeal by this Act of subsections (2) and (5) of section 283 of the Customs and Excise Act 1952, those subsections shall continue to have effect in relation to offences under Part I of, and paragraph 22 of Schedule 7 to, the Finance Act 1972; and, accordingly, in section 38 (8) of, and paragraph 22 (5) of Schedule 7 to, that Act (as amended by Schedule 4 to this Act) the reference in that section and in that paragraph to sections 145 to 155 of this Act shall be construed as including a reference to the said section 283 (2) and (5).

3. Notwithstanding the repeal by this Act of section 308 (3) of the Customs and Excise Act 1952, section 277 of the Customs Consolidation Act 1876 does not apply in relation to any Act passed after 1st January 1953.

4. Nothing in the repeal by this Act of paragraph 1 of Schedule 3 to the Finance (No. 2) Act 1975 shall affect the operation of section 1 (3) of the Isle of Man Act 1958 in relation to provisions which fell to be construed immediately before the commencement of this Act as provided in that paragraph.

5. The repeal by this Act of section 5 (4) of the European Communities Act 1972 (which, so far as it relates to enactments contained in this Act, is re-enacted by section 1 (7) of this Act) shall not affect the application of any law not contained in this Act which relates to customs duties.

6. The repeal by this Act of any enactment already repealed by section 75 (5) of the Finance (No. 2) Act 1975 and specified in Part I of Schedule 14 to that Act shall not affect the operation of the saving in paragraph 2 in that Part in relation to that enactment.

7. The repeal by this Act of section 8 (4) of the Finance (No. 2) Act 1975 and the repeal by any of the Customs and Excise Acts 1979 of any provision of Part I of Schedule 3 to that Act shall not affect the right to any drawback or other relief under any enactment amended by that provision in respect of customs duty charged before the end of 1975.

8. Any such reference as is specified in paragraph 1 of Schedule 3 to the Finance (No. 2) Act 1975 ("customs duty", "excise duty" and associated references), being a reference in—

(*a*) any instrument of a legislative character made under the customs and excise Acts which was in force at the end of 1975; or

(*b*) any local and personal or private Act which was then in force,

shall continue to be construed as provided by that paragraph notwithstanding the repeal of that paragraph by this Act.

9. Any such reference as is specified in sub-paragraph (2), (6) or (8) of paragraph 19 of Schedule 12 to the Finance Act 1978 ("customs Acts", "excise Acts", "excise trade", "excise trader", "customs airport" and "customs station"), being a reference in—

(*a*) any instrument in force immediately before the commencement of this Act; or

(*b*) any local and personal or private Act then in force,

shall continue to be construed as provided by the said sub-paragraph (2), (6) or (8), as the case may be, notwithstanding the repeal of that sub-paragraph by this Act.

10.—(1) Any provision of this Act relating to anything done or required or authorised to be done under or in pursuance of the Customs and Excise Acts 1979 shall have effect as if any reference to those Acts included a reference to the Customs and Excise Act 1952.

(2) Any provision of this Act relating to anything done or required or authorised to be done under, in pursuance of or by reference to that provision or any other provision of this Act shall have effect as if any reference to that provision, or that other provision, as the case may be, included a reference to the corresponding provision of the enactments repealed by this Act.

11. Any functions which, immediately before the commencement of this Act, fall to be performed on behalf of any other person by the Commissioners or by officers or by any person appointed by the Commissioners shall continue to be so performed by them unless and until other arrangements are made, notwithstanding that those functions are not expressly mentioned in this Act.

12.—(1) The repeal by this Act of subsection (4) of section 316 of the Customs and Excise Act 1952 shall not affect any such right or privilege as is referred to in that subsection.

(2) Where by any enactment, grant or other instrument, any right or privilege not relating to customs or excise has at any time been granted by reference to the then existing limits of any port or approved wharf appointed or approved for the purposes of customs and excise, then, subject to any provision contained in that instrument, nothing in any order made or other thing done under section 19 or 20 of this Act shall affect that right or privilege.

Customs and Excise Duties (General Reliefs) Act 1979

(1979 c. 3)

ARRANGEMENT OF SECTIONS

An Act to consolidate certain enactments relating to reliefs and exemptions from customs and excise duties, section 7 of the Finance Act 1968 and certain other related enactments.

[22nd February 1979]

General Note

This Act consolidates certain enactments relating to reliefs and exemptions from customs and excise duties, s. 7 of the Finance Act 1968 and other related enactments.

S. 1 provides for reliefs from customs duty for conformity with EEC and other international obligations; s. 2 deals with reliefs from customs duty referable to EEC practices; s. 3 gives power to exempt particular importations of certain goods from customs duty; s. 4 concerns the administration of reliefs under s. 1 and similar EEC reliefs; s. 5 gives relief from customs duty of certain goods from Channel Islands; s. 6 gives relief from duty of certain goods from Isle of Man; s. 7 deals with duty on imported legacies; s. 8 gives relief from duty on trade samples, labels, etc.; s. 9 provides for relief from duty on antiques and prizes; s. 10 gives relief from duty on certain U.K. goods re-imported; s. 11 gives relief from excise duty on certain foreign goods re-imported; s. 12 deals with supply of duty-free goods to naval ships; s. 13 enables Commissioners to provide for reliefs from duty and VAT for persons entering the U.K.; s. 14 concerns produce of the sea or continental shelf; s. 15 relates to false statements in connection with reliefs from customs duties; s. 16 provides for annual reports to Parliament; s. 17 gives power to make orders and regulations; s. 18 is the interpretation provisions; s. 19 contains consequential amendments, repeals and transitional provisions; s. 20 deals with citation and commencement.

This Act received the Royal Assent on February 22, 1979, and came into force on April 1, 1979.

Parliamentary Debates

Hansard, H.L. Vol. 397, cols. 556, 1170; Vol. 398, col. 832.

Table of Derivations

CUSTOMS AND EXCISE ACT 1952

1952	1979	1952	1979	1952	1979
s. 35 (1) (3)		s. 42	s. 8	s. 306A	s. 5
(4) (6) (7)	s. 10	43	9	307 (1) ..	5
36	11	272	12	309 (1) (3)	
37	5	283 (2) (5)	Sch. 1	(4)	6
41	7	306	s. 17 (1) (2)	310	Sch. 1

IMPORT DUTIES ACT 1958

1958	1979	1958	1979	1958	1979
s. 4	s. 16, Sch. 2,	s. 6 (5) (6) .	s. 3 (6) (7)	s. 15 (1) ...	ss. 1 (4)–(6),
5 (1)	para. 5	10 (1) ...	15		14 (1), 18
	1 (1) (4)–(6)	12 (4) ...	14 (1)	Sch. 3,	
(1A) ...	ss. 1 (1), 3 (1)	13 (1) ...	Sch. 2,	paras. 4, 5 .	s. 1 (4)–(6)
(4)	s. 4 (1) (2)		para. 13	para. 8 ...	1 (2) (3)
(8)	4 (3)	(2) ...	s. 17 (1)	Sch. 4,	
6 (1)	3 (1) (2)	(3) ...	17 (3)	para. 2 ...	3 (2)
(2) (3) .	3 (3) (4)	(4) ...	17 (4) (5)		
(4)	3 (5)				

FINANCE ACT 1960

1960	1979
s. 10 (1)	s. 3 (5)

DEFENCE (TRANSFER OF FUNCTIONS) ACT 1964

1964	1979
s. 1	s. 12

FINANCE ACT 1966

1966	1979
s. 10 (1) (9).	s. 18

Finance Act 1967

1967	1979
s. 2 (1) (2)	s. 14 (2)–(4)
(3)	17 (3)

National Loans Act 1968

1968	1979
s. 1 (8)	ss. 4 (3), 10, 11

Finance Act 1968

1968	1979
s. 7	s. 13
(4)	17 (1)
(5)	17 (3) (4) (6)

Finance Act 1969

1969	1979
s. 54	s. 3 (1) (3)–(5)
(2) (*a*)	3 (6) (7)

Finance Act 1972

1972	1979
s. 55 (2) (3)	s. 13

European Communities Act 1972

1972	1979
s. 2	s. 17 (1)
(4)	17 (2)
4	ss. 1 (1), 3 (1) (3)–(6), 4 (1) (2), 16, 17 (1) (5), Sch. 2, para. 5
s. 5 (3)	ss. 1 (1), 2, 3 (1), 14 (2), 16, 17 (3) (4), Sch. 2, para. 5
(6)	s. 2
(6A)	2
Sch. 2, para. 2 (1).	17 (1)
para. 2 (2).	17 (2)
Sch. 4, para. 1 (1).	ss. 1 (1), 3 (1) (3)–(7), 4 (1) (2), 16, 17 (1)
para. 1 (3).	s. 3 (1)
para. 1 (5).	17 (5), Sch. 2, para. 5

Criminal Procedure (Scotland) Act 1975

1975	1979
s. 193A	s. 15
289B (1) (6)	15

Finance (No. 2) Act 1975

1975	1979
Sch. 3, para. 1	s. 6
para. 1 (1)	ss. 7, 13, Sch. 1
para. 10	s. 6
para. 11	Sch. 1

Criminal Law Act 1977

1977	1979
s. 28 (2) (7)	s. 15
32 (1)	15

Finance Act 1978

1978	1979
s. 6 (8)	ss. 2, 19 (3)
Sch. 12, para. 9	s. 5
para. 10	9
para. 15	12
para. 18	5
Sch. 12, para. 19 (7) (*a*)	Sch. 1
(7) (*d*)	s. 3 (5)
para. 19 (8)	Sch. 1
para. 24	s. 15
Sch. 12, para. 25	ss. 1 (1), 3 (1)
para. 26	s. 17 (4), Sch. 2, para. 5

SECRETARY OF STATE FOR TRADE AND INDUSTRY ORDER 1970 (S.I. 1970 No. 1537)

1970	**1979**
Art. 2 (1) ..	s. 14 (3) (4)

CUSTOMS DUTIES (ECSC) RELIEF REGULATIONS 1976 (S.I. 1976 No. 2130)

1976	**1979**
Regs. 1, 2 ..	s. 1 (2) (3)

INWARD PROCESSING RELIEF REGULATIONS 1977 (S.I. 1977 No. 910)

1977	**1979**
Reg. 7 (1) ..	s. 15

CUSTOMS AND EXCISE (RELIEF FOR RETURNED GOODS) REGULATIONS 1977 (S.I. 1977 No. 1785)

1977	**1979**
Regs. 1, 2 ..	ss. 10, 11

Principal reliefs from customs duties

Reliefs from customs duty for conformity with Community obligations and other international obligations, etc.

1.—(1) The Secretary of State may, in accordance with subsections (2) to (6) below, by order provide for relieving goods from the whole or part of any customs duty chargeable on goods imported into the United Kingdom.

(2) Goods of any description may be relieved from customs duty if and in so far as the relief appears to the Secretary of State to be necessary or expedient with a view to—

(*a*) conforming with any Community obligations; or

(*b*) otherwise affording relief provided for by or under the Community Treaties or any decisions of the representatives of the governments of the member States of the Coal and Steel Community meeting in Council.

(3) Goods of any description may be relieved from customs duty if and in so far as the relief appears to the Secretary of State to be necessary or expedient with a view to conforming with an international agreement relating to matters other than commercial relations.

(4) Exposed cinematograph film may be relieved from customs duty if certified as provided by the order to be of an educational character.

(5) Relief given by virtue of subsection (4) above may be restricted with a view to securing reciprocity in countries or territories outside the United Kingdom.

(6) Articles recorded with sound, other than exposed cinematograph film, may be relieved from customs duty (other than duty chargeable on similar articles not so recorded) if the articles are not produced in quantity for general sale as so recorded.

Reliefs from customs duty referable to Community practices

2.—(1) The Secretary of State may by regulations make such provision as regards reliefs from customs duty chargeable on goods imported into the United Kingdom as appears to him to be expedient having regard to the practices adopted or to be adopted in other member States, whether by law or administrative action and whether or not for conformity with Community obligations.

(2) Regulations under this section may amend or repeal accordingly any of sections 1, 3, 4 and 15 of this Act.

Power to exempt particular importations of certain goods from customs duty

3.—(1) Subject to the provisions of this section, the Secretary of State may direct that payment shall not be required of the whole or part of any customs duty which is chargeable on any goods imported or proposed to be imported into the United Kingdom if he is satisfied—

(*a*) that the goods qualify for relief under this section; and

(*b*) that in all the circumstances it is expedient for the relief to be given.

(2) The following goods qualify for relief under this section, that is to say, articles intended and reasonably required—

(*a*) for the purpose of subjecting the articles, or any material or component in the articles, to examination or tests with a view to promoting or improving the manufacture in the United Kingdom of goods similar to those articles or to that material or component, as the case may be; or

(*b*) for the purpose of subjecting goods capable of use with those or similar articles (including goods which might be used as materials or components in such articles or in which such articles might be used as materials or components) to examination or tests with a view to promoting or improving the manufacture in the United Kingdom of those or similar goods.

(3) Any direction of the Secretary of State under this section may be given subject to such conditions as he thinks fit.

(4) Where a direction given by the Secretary of State under this section is subject to any conditions, and it is proposed to use or dispose of the goods in any manner for which the consent of the Secretary of State is required by the conditions, the Secretary of State may consent to the goods being so used or disposed of subject to payment of the duty which would have been payable but for the direction or such part of the duty as the Secretary of State thinks appropriate in the circumstances.

(5) The Secretary of State shall not give a direction under this section except on a written application made by the importer, and a direction under this section shall have effect to such extent (if any) as the Commissioners may allow if the goods have been released from customs and excise control without the importer having given to the Commissioners notice of the direction or of his application or intention to apply for it.

(6) Any notice to the Commissioners under subsection (5) above shall be in such form as they may require, and the Commissioners on receiving any such notice or at any time afterwards may impose any such conditions as they see fit for the protection of the revenue (including conditions requiring security for the observance of any conditions subject to which relief is granted).

(7) A direction of the Secretary of State under this section shall have effect only if and so long as any conditions of the relief, including any conditions imposed by the Commissioners under subsection (6) above, are complied with; but where any customs duty is paid on the importation of any goods, and the Commissioners are satisfied that by virtue of a direction subsequently given and having effect under this section payment of the duty is not required, then the duty shall be repaid.

Administration of reliefs under section 1 and administration or implementation of similar Community reliefs

4.—(1) The Secretary of State may by order make provision for the administration of any relief under section 1 above or for the implementation or administration of any like relief provided for by any Community instrument.

(2) An order under this section may in particular—

(*a*) impose or authorise the imposition of conditions for securing that goods relieved from duty as being imported for a particular purpose are used for that purpose or such other conditions as appear expedient to secure the object or prevent abuse of the relief;

(*b*) where the relief is limited to a quota of imported goods, provide for determining the allocation of the quota or for enabling it to be determined by the issue of certificates or licences or otherwise;

(*c*) confer on a government department or any other authority or person functions in connection with the administration of the relief or the enforcement of any condition of relief;

(*d*) authorise any government department having any such functions to make payments (whether for remuneration or for expenses) to persons advising the department or otherwise acting in the administration of the relief;

(*e*) require the payment of fees by persons applying for the relief or applying for the registration of any person or premises in connection with the relief;

(*f*) authorise articles for which relief is claimed to be sold or otherwise disposed of if the relief is not allowed and duty is not paid.

(3) Any expenses incurred by a government department by virtue of any order under this section shall be defrayed out of money provided by Parliament, and any fees received by a government department by virtue of any such order shall be paid into the Consolidated Fund.

Reliefs from duties for Channel Islands or Isle of Man goods

Relief from customs duty of certain goods from Channel Islands

5.—(1) Subject to subsection (2) below, any goods which are the produce or growth of any of the Channel Islands or which have been manufactured in any of those islands from—

(*a*) materials which are such produce or growth; or

(*b*) materials not chargeable with any duty in the United Kingdom; or

(*c*) materials so chargeable upon which that duty has been paid and not drawn back,

may be imported without payment of any customs duty chargeable thereon.

(2) Subsection (1) above shall not apply in relation to any goods unless the master of the ship or commander of the aircraft in which the goods are imported produces to the proper officer at the place of importation a certificate from the Lieutenant-Governor or other proper authority of the island from which the goods are imported that a declaration in such form and containing such particulars as the Commissioners may direct has been made before a magistrate of that island by the person exporting the goods therefrom that the goods are goods to which this section applies.

(3) Directions under subsection (2) above may make different provision for different circumstances and may be varied or revoked by subsequent directions thereunder.

Relief from duty of certain goods from Isle of Man and supplementary provisions

6.—(1) Without prejudice to section 174 (1) of the Customs and Excise Management Act 1979 but subject to the provisions of this section, goods removed into the United Kingdom from the Isle of Man shall be deemed, for the purposes of any charge of duty on goods imported into the United Kingdom, not to be imported.

(2) Where in the case of any goods which are the produce or growth of the Isle of Man, or which have been manufactured in that island from materials which are such produce or growth, a duty of excise is chargeable on like goods or materials manufactured or produced in the United Kingdom, a like duty of excise shall be payable on the removal of those goods into the United Kingdom from the Isle of Man.

(3) Any goods manufactured in the Isle of Man wholly or partly from imported materials, being materials—

(*a*) which, if they had been imported into the United Kingdom, would have been chargeable with customs or excise duty; and

(*b*) which on their importation into the Isle of Man either were not charged with customs or excise duty or were charged with a lower amount by way of customs or excise duty than would have been payable on their importation into the United Kingdom,

shall on their removal into the United Kingdom from the Isle of Man be chargeable with customs or excise duty as if they were being imported.

(4) Schedule 1 to this Act shall have effect for the purpose of restricting the removal into the United Kingdom of certain dutiable goods imported or removed to the Isle of Man.

Miscellaneous reliefs from customs and excise duties

Relief from customs or excise duty on imported legacies

7. Where it is shown to the satisfaction of the Commissioners that—

(*a*) any imported goods were chattels or corporeal moveables belonging to or in the possession of a deceased person which had been used before his death and were not at the time of his death used or held by him for business purposes; and

(*b*) the importation thereof is by or for a person resident in the United Kingdom who upon that death becomes entitled thereto by virtue of any testamentary disposition or intestacy,

the Commissioners may remit or repay any customs or excise duty which would otherwise be payable or which has been paid on the importation thereof.

Relief from customs or excise duty on trade samples, labels, etc.

8. The Commissioners may allow the delivery without payment of customs or excise duty on importation, subject to such conditions and restrictions as they see fit—

(*a*) of trade samples of such goods as they see fit, whether imported as samples or drawn from the goods on their importation;

(*b*) of labels or other articles supplied without charge for the purpose of being re-exported with goods manufactured or produced in, and to be exported from, the United Kingdom.

Relief from customs or excise duty on antiques, prizes, etc.

9. The Commissioners may allow the delivery without payment of customs or excise duty on importation—

(*a*) of any goods (other than spirits or wine) which are proved to the satisfaction of the Commissioners to have been manufactured or produced more than 100 years before the date of importation;

(*b*) of articles which are shown to the satisfaction of the Commissioners to have been awarded abroad to any person for distinction in art, literature, science or sport, or for public service, or otherwise as a record of meritorious achievement or conduct, and to be imported by or on behalf of that person.

Reliefs from excise duties

Relief from excise duty on certain United Kingdom goods re-imported

10.—(1) Without prejudice to any other enactment relating to excise, the following provisions of this section shall have effect in relation to goods manufactured or produced in the United Kingdom which are re-imported into the United Kingdom after exportation therefrom.

(2) If the goods are at the date of their re-importation excise goods, they may on re-importation be delivered for home use without payment of excise duty if it is shown to the satisfaction of the Commissioners—

(*a*) that at the date of their exportation the goods were not excise goods or, if they were then excise goods, that the excise duty had been paid before their exportation; and

(*b*) that no drawback in respect of the excise duty and no allowance has been paid on their exportation or that any such drawback or allowance so paid has been repaid to the Consolidated Fund; and

(*c*) that the goods have not undergone any process outside the United Kingdom since their exportation.

(3) If the goods both are at the date of their re-importation and were at the date of their exportation excise goods, but they were exported without the excise duty having been paid from a warehouse or from the place where they were manufactured or produced, then, where the following conditions are satisfied, that is to say—

(*a*) it is shown to the satisfaction of the Commissioners that they have not undergone any process outside the United Kingdom since their exportation; and

(*b*) any allowance paid on their exportation is repaid to the Consolidated Fund,

the goods may on their re-importation, subject to such conditions and restrictions as the Commissioners may impose, be entered and removed without payment of excise duty for re-warehousing or for return to the place where they were manufactured or produced, as the case may be.

(4) Nothing in this section shall authorise the delivery for home use of any goods not otherwise eligible therefor.

(5) In this section—

"excise goods" means goods—

(*a*) of a class or description chargeable at the time in question with a duty of excise; or

(*b*) in the manufacture or preparation of which any goods of such a class or description have been used;

"the excise duty" means the duty by virtue of which the goods are or were at the time in question excise goods.

Relief from excise duty on certain foreign goods re-imported

11.—(1) Without prejudice to any other enactment relating to excise but subject to subsection (2) below, goods manufactured or produced outside the United Kingdom which are re-imported into the United Kingdom after exportation therefrom may on their re-importation be delivered without payment of excise duty for home use, where so eligible, if it is shown to the satisfaction of the Commissioners—

(*a*) that no excise duty was chargeable thereon at their previous importation or that any excise duty so chargeable was then paid; and

(*b*) that no drawback has been paid or excise duty refunded on their exportation or that any drawback so paid or excise duty so refunded has been repaid to the Consolidated Fund; and

(*c*) that the goods have not undergone any process outside the United Kingdom since their exportation.

(2) For the purposes of this section goods which on their previous importation were entered for transit or transhipment or were permitted to be delivered without payment of excise duty as being imported only temporarily with a view to subsequent re-exportation and which were re-exported accordingly shall on their re-importation be deemed not to have been previously imported.

Relief for goods for Her Majesty's ships

Supply of duty-free goods to Her Majesty's ships

12.—(1) The Treasury may by regulations provide that, subject to any prescribed conditions, goods of any description specified in the regulations which are supplied either—

(*a*) to any ship of the Royal Navy in commission of a description so specified, for the use of persons serving in that ship, being persons borne on the books of that or some other ship of the Royal Navy or a naval establishment; or

(*b*) to the Secretary of State, for the use of persons serving in ships of the Royal Navy or naval establishments,

shall for all or any purposes of any excise duty or drawback in respect of those goods be treated as exported, and a person supplying or intending to supply goods as mentioned in paragraph (*a*) or (*b*) above shall be treated accordingly as exporting or intending to export them.

(2) Regulations made under this section with respect to goods of any description may regulate or provide for regulating the quantity allowed to any ship or establishment, the manner in which they are to be obtained and their use or distribution.

(3) The regulations may—

(*a*) contain such other incidental or supplementary provisions as appear to the Treasury to be necessary for the purposes of this section, including any adaptations of the customs and excise Acts; and

(*b*) make different provision in relation to different cases, and in particular in relation to different classes or descriptions of goods or of ships or establishments.

(4) In subsection (1) above "prescribed" means prescribed by regulations under this section or, in pursuance of any such regulations, by the Commissioners after consultation with the Secretary of State.

(5) Before making any regulations under this section, the Treasury shall consult with the Secretary of State and with the Commissioners.

(6) The powers conferred by this section shall apply for the purposes of customs duty as they apply for the purposes of excise duty but shall not so apply after such day as the Commissioners may by order appoint.

Personal reliefs

Power to provide, in relation to persons entering the United Kingdom, for reliefs from duty and value added tax and for simplified computation of duty and tax

13.—(1) The Commissioners may by order make provision for conferring on persons entering the United Kingdom reliefs from duty and value added tax; and any such relief may take the form either of an exemption from payment of duty and tax or of a provision whereby the sum payable by way of duty or tax is less than it would otherwise be.

(2) Without prejudice to subsection (1) above, the Commissioners may by order make provision whereby, in such cases and to such extent as may be specified in the order, a sum calculated at a rate specified in the order is treated as the aggregate amount payable by way of duty and tax in respect of goods imported by a person entering the United Kingdom; but any order making such provision shall enable the person concerned to elect that duty and tax shall be charged on the goods in question at the rate which would be applicable apart from that provision.

(3) An order under this section—

(*a*) may make any relief for which it provides subject to conditions, including conditions which are to be complied with after the importation of the goods to which the relief applies;

(*b*) may contain such incidental and supplementary provisions as the Commissioners think necessary or expedient, including provisions for the forfeiture of goods in the event of non-compliance with any condition subject to which they have been relieved from duty or tax; and

(*c*) may make different provision for different cases.

(4) In this section—

" duty " means customs or excise duty chargeable on goods imported into the United Kingdom and, in the case of excise duty, includes any addition thereto by virtue of section 1 of the Excise Duties (Surcharges or Rebates) Act 1979; and

" value added tax " or " tax " means value added tax chargeable on the importation of goods.

(5) Nothing in any order under this section shall be construed as authorising any person to import any thing in contravention of any prohibition or restriction for the time being in force with respect thereto under or by virtue of any enactment.

Produce of the sea or continental shelf

Produce of the sea or continental shelf

14.—(1) Fish, whales or other natural produce of the sea, or goods produced or manufactured therefrom at sea, if brought direct to the United Kingdom, shall—

(*a*) in the case of goods which, under any enactment or instrument having the force of law, are to be treated as originating in the United Kingdom, be deemed for the purposes of any charge to customs duty not to be imported; and

(*b*) in the case of goods which, under any enactment or instrument having the force of law, are to be treated as originating in any other country or territory, be deemed to be consigned to the United Kingdom from that country.

(2) Any goods brought into the United Kingdom which are shown to the satisfaction of the Commissioners to have been grown, produced or

manufactured in any area for the time being designated under section 1 (7) of the Continental Shelf Act 1964 and to have been so brought direct from that area shall be deemed for the purposes of any charge to customs duty not to be imported.

(3) The Secretary of State may by regulations prescribe cases in which, with a view to exempting any goods from any duty, or charging any goods with duty at a reduced or preferential rate, under any of the enactments relating to duties of customs the continental shelf of any country prescribed by the regulations, or of any country of a class of countries so prescribed, shall be treated for the purposes of such of those enactments or of any instruments made thereunder as may be so prescribed as if that shelf formed part of that country and any goods brought from that shelf were consigned from that country.

(4) In subsection (3) above " continental shelf ", in relation to any country means—

(*a*) if that country is the United Kingdom, any area for the time being designated under section 1 (7) of the Continental Shelf Act 1964;

(*b*) in any other case, the seabed and subsoil of the submarine areas adjacent to the coast, but outside the seaward limits of the territorial waters, of that country over which the exercise by that country of sovereign rights in accordance with international law is recognised or authorised by Her Majesty's Government in the United Kingdom.

False statements etc. in connection with reliefs from customs duties

False statements etc. in connection with reliefs from customs duties

15.—(1) If a person—

(*a*) for the purpose of an application for relief from customs duty under section 1 or 3 above or under a Community instrument; or

(*b*) for the purpose of an application for an authorisation under regulations made under section 2 above,

makes any statement or furnishes any document which is false in a material particular to any government department or to any authority or person on whom functions are conferred by or under section 1, 3 or 4 above or a Community instrument, then—

(i) any decision allowing the relief or granting the authorisation applied for shall be of no effect; and

(ii) if the statement was made or the document was furnished knowingly or recklessly, that person shall be guilty of an offence under this section.

(2) A person guilty of an offence under this section shall be liable—

(*a*) on summary conviction, to a fine not exceeding the prescribed sum, or to imprisonment for a term not exceeding 3 months, or to both; or

(*b*) on conviction on indictment, to a fine of any amount or to imprisonment for a term not exceeding 2 years, or to both.

(3) In subsection (2) (*a*) above " the prescribed sum " means—

(*a*) if the offence was committed in England, Wales or Northern Ireland, the prescribed sum within the meaning of section 28 of the Criminal Law Act 1977 (£1,000 or other sum substituted by order under section 61 (1) of that Act);

(*b*) if the offence was committed in Scotland, the prescribed sum within the meaning of section 289B of the Criminal Procedure (Scotland) Act 1975 (£1,000 or other sum substituted by order under section 289D (1) of that Act).

(4) References in Parts XI and XII of the Customs and Excise Management Act 1979 to an offence under the customs and excise Acts shall not apply to an offence under this section.

Supplementary provisions

Annual reports to Parliament

16. As soon as may be after the end of each financial year the Secretary of State shall lay before each House of Parliament a report on the exercise during that year of the powers conferred by sections 1, 3 and 4 above with respect to the allowance of exemptions and reliefs from customs duties (including the power to amend or revoke orders providing for any exemption or relief from customs duties).

Orders and regulations

17.—(1) Any power to make orders or regulations under this Act shall be exercisable by statutory instrument.

(2) Any statutory instrument containing regulations under section 2 or 12 above shall be subject to annulment in pursuance of a resolution of either House of Parliament except where, in the case of regulations under section 2, a draft of the regulations has been approved by resolution of each House of Parliament.

(3) Any statutory instrument containing an order under section 1, 4 or 13 above or regulations under section 14 (3) above shall be subject to annulment in pursuance of a resolution of the House of Commons except in a case falling within subsection (4) below.

(4) Subject to subsection (5) below, where an order under section 1, 4 or 13 above restricts any relief from duty or tax the statutory instrument containing the order shall be laid before the House of Commons after being made and, unless the order is approved by that House before the end of the period of 28 days beginning with the day on which it was made, it shall cease to have effect at the end of that period but without prejudice to anything previously done under the order or to the making of a new order.

In reckoning the said period of 28 days no account shall be taken of any time during which Parliament is dissolved or prorogued or during which the House of Commons is adjourned for more than 4 days.

(5) Subsection (4) above does not apply in the case of an instrument containing an order under section 1 or 4 above which states that it does not restrict any relief otherwise than in pursuance of a Community obligation.

(6) For the purposes of this section restricting any relief includes removing or reducing any relief previously conferred.

Interpretation

18.—(1) This Act and the other Acts included in the Customs and Excise Acts 1979 shall be construed as one Act but where a provision of this Act refers to this Act that reference is not to be construed as including a reference to any of the others.

(2) Any expression used in this Act or in any instrument made under this Act to which a meaning is given by any other Act included in the

Customs and Excise Acts 1979 has, except where the context otherwise requires, the same meaning in this Act or in any such instrument as in that Act; and for ease of reference the Table below indicates the expressions used in this Act to which a meaning is given by any other such Act—

Customs and Excise Management Act 1979

" the Commissioners "
" the Customs and Excise Acts 1979 "
" the customs and excise Acts "
" customs and excise airport "
" goods "
" hovercraft "
" importer "
" master "
" officer " and " proper " in relation to an officer
" port "
" ship "
" transit and transhipment "
" warehouse "

Alcoholic Liquor Duties Act 1979

" spirits "
" wine "

(3) This Act applies as if references to ships included references to hovercraft.

Consequential amendments, repeals and transitional provision

19.—(1) The enactments specified in Schedule 2 to this Act shall be amended in accordance with the provisions of that Schedule.

(2) The enactments specified in Part I of Schedule 3 to this Act are hereby repealed to the extent specified in the third column of that Schedule and the regulations specified in Part II of that Schedule are hereby revoked to the extent so specified.

(3) References to import duties in instruments in force at the commencement of this Act shall, on and after that commencement, be construed—

(*a*) in the case of references in orders under section 5 or directions under section 6 of the Import Duties Act 1958, as references to customs duties charged under section 5 (1) or (2) of the European Communities Act 1972;

(*b*) in the case of references in such orders or directions made by virtue of section 5 (1A) of the said Act of 1958 or in regulations under section 5 (6) of the European Communities Act 1972, as references to customs duties (whether so charged or charged under the Customs Duties (Dumping and Subsidies) Act 1969 or section 6 (1) of the Finance Act 1978).

Citation and commencement

20.—(1) This Act may be cited as the Customs and Excise Duties (General Reliefs) Act 1979 and is included in the Acts which may be cited as the Customs and Excise Acts 1979.

(2) This Act shall come into operation on 1st April 1979.

SCHEDULES

Section 6 (4)

SCHEDULE 1

Restrictions on Removal of Goods into United Kingdom from Isle of Man

1. Where any goods which, if they were imported into the United Kingdom, would be chargeable with customs or excise duty are imported into the Isle of Man and on that importation either are not charged with any customs or excise duty than would have been payable on their importation into the United Kingdom, then—

(*a*) if the goods are cleared out of charge in the Isle of Man for home use or to be dealt with in any other manner in the Isle of Man, they shall not thereafter be removed into the United Kingdom;

(*b*) in any other case, the goods shall not be removed from the Isle of Man into the United Kingdom until they have been cleared for that purpose by the proper officer and, except in the case of goods reported on arrival for removal into the United Kingdom in the same ship or aircraft and in continuance of the same voyage or flight, until security has been given to the satisfaction of the Commissioners for the due delivery thereof at some port or customs and excise airport in the United Kingdom.

2. Where any goods—

(*a*) manufactured or produced in the United Kingdom and chargeable with a duty of excise on being so manufactured or produced or on being sent out from the premises of the manufacturer; or

(*b*) imported into the United Kingdom and chargeable on that importation with a duty of customs or excise,

have been removed from the United Kingdom into the Isle of Man without payment of that duty or on drawback of the excise duty, then, save with the permission of the Commissioners and subject to such conditions as they see fit to impose, neither those goods nor any other goods in the manufacture or preparation of which those goods have been used shall thereafter be removed from the Isle of Man into the United Kingdom.

3. Any goods removed into the United Kingdom contrary to paragraph 1 or 2 above shall be liable to forfeiture, and any person concerned in the removal of the goods shall be liable on summary conviction to a penalty of three times the value of the goods or £100, whichever is the greater.

Section 19 (1)

SCHEDULE 2

Consequential Amendments

Agriculture and Horticulture Act 1964

1. At the end of paragraph 1 (2) of the Schedule to the Agriculture and Horticulture Act 1964 there shall be added the words " nor the operation of sections 1 to 4 and 14 to 16 of the Customs and Excise Duties (General Reliefs) Act 1979 ".

Finance Act 1972

2. In section 17 of the Finance Act 1972, after the subsection (2) inserted by paragraph 10 of Schedule 4 to the Customs and Excise Management Act 1979 there shall be inserted the following subsection—

" (2A) The provisions of the Customs and Excise Duties (General Reliefs) Act 1979 other than sections 7, 8 and 9 (*b*) (various reliefs for imported goods other than legacies, trade samples and prizes) shall also be excepted from the enactments which are to have effect as mentioned in subsection (1) of this section."

European Communities Act 1972

3. For section 5 (3) of the European Communities Act 1972 (in this Schedule

referred to as "the Act of 1972") there shall be substituted the following subsection—

"(3) Schedule 2 to this Act shall also have effect in connection with the powers to make orders conferred by subsections (1) and (2) above.".

4. In section 6 (5) of the Act of 1972, for paragraph (*b*), there shall be substituted the following paragraph—

"(*b*) sections 1, 3, 4, 5, 6 (including Schedule 1), 7, 8, 9, 12, 13, 15, 17 and 18 of the Customs and Excise Duties (General Reliefs) Act 1979 but so that—

(i) any references in sections 1, 3 and 4 to the Secretary of State shall include the Ministers; and

(ii) the reference in section 15 to an application for an authorisation under regulations made under section 2 of that Act shall be read as a reference to an application for an authorisation under regulations made under section 2 (2) of this Act;".

5. In Schedule 2 to the Act of 1972 there shall be added at the end the following paragraphs—

"4.—(1) The power to make orders under section 5 (1) or (2) of this Act shall be exercisable in accordance with the following provisions of this paragraph.

(2) The power to make such orders shall be exercisable by statutory instrument and includes power to amend or revoke any such order made in the exercise of that power.

(3) Any statutory instrument containing any such order shall be subject to annulment in pursuance of a resolution of the House of Commons except in a case falling within sub-paragraph (4) below.

(4) Subject to sub-paragraph (6) below, where an order imposes or increases any customs duty, or restrict any relief from customs duty under the said section 5, the statutory instrument containing the order shall be laid before the House of Commons after being made and, unless the order is approved by that House before the end of the period of 28 days beginning with the day on which it was made, it shall cease to have effect at the end of that period, but without prejudice to anything previously done under the order or to the making of a new order.

In reckoning the said period of 28 days no account shall be taken of any time during which Parliament is dissolved or prorogued or during which the House of Commons is adjourned for more than 4 days.

(5) Where an order has the effect of altering the rate of duty on any goods in such a way that the new rate is not directly comparable with the old, it shall not be treated for the purposes of sub-paragraph (4) above as increasing the duty on those goods if it declares the opinion of the Treasury to be that, in the circumstances existing at the date of the order, the alteration is not calculated to raise the general level of duty on the goods.

(6) Sub-paragraph (4) above does not apply in the case of an instrument containing an order which states that it does not impose or increase any customs duty or restrict any relief from customs duty otherwise than in pursuance of a Community obligation.

5. As soon as may be after the end of each financial year the Secretary of State shall lay before each House of Parliament a report on the exercise during that year of the powers conferred by section 5 (1) and (2) of this Act with respect to the imposition of customs duties and the allowance of exemptions and reliefs from duties so imposed (including the power to amend or revoke orders imposing customs duties or providing for any exemption or relief from duties so imposed).".

Finance Act 1977

6. In section 10 (4) of the Finance Act 1977, for the words "those sections" there shall be substituted the words "the said section 6".

Section 19 (2)

SCHEDULE 3

Repeals and Revocations

Part I

Enactments Repealed

Chapter	Short Title	Extent of Repeal
15 & 16 Geo. 6 & 1 Eliz. 2. c. 44.	The Customs and Excise Act 1952.	Sections 35 to 37 and 41 to 43. Section 272. Sections 309 (1), (3) and (4) and 310.
6 & 7 Eliz. 2. c. 6.	The Import Duties Act 1958.	Sections 4, 5 and 6. Section 10 (1). Sections 12 (4) and 13. Sections 15 and 16. In Schedule 3, paragraphs 4, 5 and 8. In Schedule 4, paragraph 2.
8 & 9 Eliz. 2. c. 44.	The Finance Act 1960.	Section 10 (1).
1967 c. 54.	The Finance Act 1967.	Section 2.
1968 c. 44.	The Finance Act 1968.	Section 7.
1969 c. 32.	The Finance Act 1969.	Section 54.
1972 c. 41.	The Finance Act 1972.	Section 55 (2) and (3).
1972 c. 68.	The European Communities Act 1972.	In section 5, subsections (5), (6) and (6A). In Schedule 4, paragraph 1.
1975 c. 45.	The Finance (No. 2) Act 1975.	In Schedule 3, paragraphs 10, 11 and 13.
1977 c. 36.	The Finance Act 1977.	Section 12.
1978 c. 42.	The Finance Act 1978.	Section 6 (8). In Schedule 12, paragraphs 9, 10, 15, 19 (7) (*d*), 20, 25 and 26.

Part II

Regulations Revoked

Year and Number	Title	Extent of Revocation
1976/2130.	The Customs Duties (ECSC) Relief Regulations 1976.	All the regulations.
1977/910.	The Inward Processing Relief Regulations 1977.	Regulation 7 (1).
1977/1785.	The Customs and Excise (Relief for Returned Goods) Regulations 1977.	All the regulations.
1978/1148.	The Customs Duties (Inward and Outward Processing Relief) Regulations 1978.	Regulation 2.

Alcoholic Liquor Duties Act 1979

(1979 c. 4)

ARRANGEMENT OF SECTIONS

PART I

PRELIMINARY

Part VI

General Control Provisions

An Act to consolidate the enactments relating to the excise duties on spirits, beer, wine, made-wine and cider together with certain other enactments relating to excise.

[22nd February 1979]

General Note

This Act consolidates enactments relating to the excise duties on spirits, beer, wine, made-wine and cider together with certain other enactments relating to excise.

Pt. I (ss. 1–4) contains preliminary provisions: s. 1 defines the alcoholic liquors dutiable under the Act; s. 2 is a provision for ascertaining the strength, weight and volume of spirits and other liquors; s. 3 gives the meaning of and method of ascertaining gravity of liquids; s. 4 is the interpretation section.

Pt. II (ss. 5–35) concerns duty on spirits: s. 5 provides for the charge of excise duty on spirits; s. 6 gives power to exempt angostura bitters from duty; s. 7 gives exemption to spirits in articles used for medical purposes; s. 8 deals with repayment of duty in respect of spirits used for medical or scientific purposes; s. 9 provides for remission of duty on spirits used for methylation; s. 10 concerns remission of duty on spirits for use in art or manufacture; s. 11 gives relief from duty on imported goods not for human consumption containing spirits; s. 12 deals with licences to manufacture spirits; s. 13 empowers Commissioners to make regulations as to the manufacture of spirits; s. 14 provides for an attenuation charge; s. 15 relates to a distiller's warehouse; s. 16 controls the racking of duty-paid spirits at distillery; s. 17 specifies offences in connection with removal of spirits from distillery; s. 18 concerns rectifiers' and compounders' licences; s. 19 enables Commissioners to make regulations as to rectifying and compounding; s. 20 gives a penalty for excess or deficiency in rectifier's stock; s. 21 makes restrictions relating to rectifiers; s. 22 provides for drawback on British compounds; s. 23 makes an allowance for British compounds; s. 24 restricts the carrying on of other trades by distiller or rectifier; s. 25 gives the penalty for unlawful manufacture of spirits, etc.; s. 26 provides for the importation and exportation of spirits; s. 27 deals with spirits consignment and spirits advice notes; s. 28 regulates the keeping and production of spirits advice and consignment notes; s. 29 specifies offences in connection with spirits advice and consignment notes; s. 30 makes special provisions as to spirits advice and consignment notes; s. 31 restricts delivery of immature spirits for home use; s. 32 restricts transfer of British spirits in warehouse; s. 33 places restrictions on use of certain goods relieved from spirits duty; s. 34 prohibits grogging; s. 35 deals with returns as to importation, manufacture, sale or use of alcohols.

Pt. III (ss. 36–53) concerns duty on beer: s. 36 provides for a charge of excise duty on beer; s. 37 sets out the charge of duty on beer brewed in the U.K.; s. 38 deals with the duty on beer brewed in the U.K. for sale; s. 39 concerns duty on beer brewed by private brewers; s. 40 makes a charge of duty on imported beer; s. 41 exempts from duty beer brewed for private consumption; s. 42 provides for drawback on exportation, removal to warehouses and shipment as stores; s. 43 provides for warehousing of beer for exportation, etc.; s. 44 deals with remission of duty on beer used for research; s. 45 concerns repayment of duty on beer used in the production or manufacture of other beverages; s. 46 provides for remission of duty on spoilt beer; s. 47 deals with licences to brew beer; s. 48 provides for licences to use premises for adding solutions to beer; s. 49 empowers Commissioners to regulate manufacture of beer by brewers for sale; s. 50 concerns regulations as respects sugar kept by brewers for sale; s. 51 gives power to require production of books by brewers; s. 52 specifies offences by brewers for sale; s. 53 makes special provisions as to holders of limited licences to brew beer.

Pt. IV (ss. 54–61) concerns the duty on wine and made-wine: s. 54 provides for the charge of excise duty on wine; s. 55 deals with the charge of excise duty on made-wine; s. 56 regulates the making of wine and made-wine and provides for charging duty thereon; s. 57 relates to the mixing of made-wine and spirits in warehouse; s. 58 deals with the mixing of wine and spirits in warehouse; s. 59 prohibits the rendering of imported wine or made-wine sparkling in warehouse; s. 60 concerns repayment of duty on imported wine used in the production of other beverages; s. 61 provides for remission of duty on spoilt wine or made-wine.

Pt. V (ss. 62–64) deals with excise duty on cider; s. 62 imposes the duty on cider; s. 63 provides for the repayment of duty on imported cider used in the production of other beverages; s. 64 deals with remission of duty on spoilt cider.

Pt. VI (ss. 65–88) contains general control provisions: s. 65 concerns excise licences for dealing wholesale in certain alcoholic liquors; s. 66 exempts the sale of certain alcoholic liquors from licensing; s. 67 regulates the keeping of dutiable alcoholic liquors by wholesalers and retailers; s. 68 imposes a penalty for excess in stock of wholesaler or retailer of spirits; s. 69 contains miscellaneous provisions as to wholesalers and retailers of spirits; s. 70 specifies general offences in connection with sale of spirits; s. 71 imposes a penalty for mis-describing liquor as spirits; s. 72 lists offences by wholesaler or retailer of beer; s. 73 gives a penalty for mis-describing substances as beer; s. 74 deems liquor to be wine or spirits; s. 75 gives licence or authority to manufacture and deal wholesale in methylated spirits; s. 76 licenses the retailing of methylated spirits; s. 77 empowers Commissioners to make regulations relating to methylated spirits; s. 78 makes additional provisions as to methylated spirits; s. 79 provides for inspection of premises; s. 80 prohibits use of methylated spirits as a beverage or medicine; s. 81 licenses the keeping of stills otherwise than as a distiller; s. 82 gives power to make regulations with respect to stills; s. 83 gives power to enter premises of person keeping or using still; s. 84 provides for reduced duty on excise licence for sale of spirits for medical purposes; s. 85 reduces duty on part-year licences; s. 86 also deals with duty on part-year licences; s. 87 gives relief from duty on discontinuance of trade; s. 88 provides for payment of licence duty in two instalments.

Pt. VII (ss. 89–93) contains miscellaneous provisions: s. 89 is a saving provision for Cambridge University and Vintners company; s. 90 gives general power to make regulations; s. 91 concerns directions under the Act; s. 92 contains consequential amendments, repeals and saving and transitional provisions; s. 93 deals with citation and commencement.

The Act received the Royal Assent on February 22, 1979, and came into force on April 1, 1979.

Parliamentary Debates

Hansard, H.L. Vol. 397, cols. 417, 1169; Vol. 398, col. 832.

Table of Derivations

Customs and Excise Act 1952

1952	1979
s. 93	s. 12
94	13
95	14
96	15
97	16
98	17
99	18
100	19
101	20
102	21
103	22
104	23
105	24
106	25
107	26
109	31
110	32
111	10
112	8
113	33
114	34
115 (2) (3)	35
116	75
117	76
118	77
119	78
120	79
121	80
122	9
125 (1) ..	47 (1) (2)
(2) ..	47 (3) (4)
(3)–(5)	47 (5)–(7)
126	48
127	49
128	50

1952	1979
s. 129	s. 51
130	52
131	53
132	37
133 (1)–(8)	38 (1)–(9)
133 (8) proviso .	38 (10) (11)
134	39
135	40
137	42
138	43
140	56
142 (1) ..	57
144 (1) ..	58
145 (3)–(5)	59
146 (1) ..	65 (1) (2)
146 (3) ..	65 (4)
146 (4)–(6)	65 (6)–(8)
147 (1) ..	65 (5)
148 (4) ..	4 (4)
157 (1) ..	66
158	67
159	68
160	69
161	70
162	71
163	72
164	73
165	74
166	89
167	84
168	85
169 (2) ..	87 (1) (2)
169 (3) ..	87 (3)
169 (4) ..	87 (5)

1952	1979
s. 169 (5) ..	s. 87 (6) (7)
170	88
171	3
172	2
226	81
227	82
228	83
237	86
241 (1A) .	28
241 (2) ..	28
242	29
243	30
263 (3) ..	46 (1)
263 (4) ..	ss. 46 (3), 61, 64
263 (5) ..	s. 46 (3), 61, 64
283 (2) (5)	ss. 8, 10, 13, 15–22, 24, 25, 28, 29, 31, 33–35, 40, 44, 46 (2) (3), 47 (7), 48–56, 59, 61, 62, 64, 65 (7), 67–73, 75, 77, 78, 80–82, 84
306	s. 90
306A	91
307 (1) ..	ss. 1 (1)–(3), 4 (1), 47 (2), 87 (1)
315 (*e*) ..	s. 88

Finance Act 1953

1953	1979
s. 2	s. 38 (10) (11)

Medical Act 1956

1956	1979
s. 52 (1)	s. 84

Finance Act 1958

1958	1979
s. 6 (1)	s. 1 (8)
6 (2)	35

Finance Act 1959

1959	1979
s. 2 (1)	s. 65 (3)
3 (2)	84
3 (3)	ss. 85, 86
3 (4)	s. 87 (4) (8)

Finance Act (Northern Ireland) Act 1959

1959	1979
s. 12 (1)	s. 65 (3)
13 (2)	84
13 (3)	ss. 85, 86
13 (4)	s. 87 (4) (8)

Finance Act 1960

1960	1979
s. 3 (1)	s. 27 (1) (2) (5)
3 (2)	ss. 4 (1), 27 (1) (2) (5)
Sch. 1, para. 1 .	s. 28
Sch. 1, para. 2 .	29
Sch. 1, para. 3 .	30

Weights and Measures Act 1963

1963	1979
s. 59 (*a*)	ss. 4 (4), 65 (8)
59 (6)	s. 4 (1)

Finance Act 1963

1963	1979
s. 6 (1)	s. 41
6 (2)	47 (2) (4)
6 (3)	4 (1)
Sch. 2,	
para. 1 (2).	s. 47 (1) (2)
para. 1 (3).	47 (4)
para. 1 (4).	47 (5)
para. 1 (5).	47 (7)
Sch. 2,	
para. 2 ...	s. 53
para. 3 ...	39
para. 4 ...	ss. 4 (1), 47 (2)

Finance Act (Northern Ireland) 1963

1963	1979
s. 19 (1) ...	s. 47 (5)
19 (2) ...	47 (2) (4)
19 (3) ...	ss. 4 (1), 53
Sch. 2,	
para. 1 (2).	s. 47 (1) (2)
para. 1 (3).	47 (4)
para. 1 (4).	47 (5)
Sch. 2,	
para. 1 (5).	s. 47 (7)
para. 2 ...	53
para. 3 ...	4 (1)

Finance Act 1964

1964	1979
s. 1 (5)	s. 11
2 (5)	ss. 1 (3), 4 (1)
2 (5) (*b*) .	s. 73

Finance Act 1966

1966	1979
s 10 (2)	s. 26
10 (9)	ss. 4 (1), 26
Sch. 2, paras. 1, 2 .	s. 26

Finance Act 1967

1967	1979
s. 4 (1)	ss. 12, 48
4 (2)	s. 85
4 (4)	12
4 (5) (*b*) .	25
5 (1)	ss. 71, 87 (4)
6 (2) (3) .	s. 27 (3) (4)
6 (5)	ss. 4 (1), 27 (5)
Sch. 5,	
para. 2 ...	s. 42
para. 3 ...	46 (1)

1967	1979
Sch. 5,	
para. 4 (1)	s. 44
(2)	
para. 4 (3).	47 (5)
Sch. 6,	
para. 1 ...	76
para. 3 ...	70
para. 4 ...	71
paras. 7–9.	4 (1)
para. 10 ..	87 (4) (6)–(8)

1967	1979
Sch. 6,	
para. 11 ..	s. 27 (1) (2) (5)
Sch. 9,	
para. 1 ...	21
para. 2 ...	65 (4)
para. 3 ...	28
paras. 4, 5.	29
para. 6 ...	30

Finance Act (Northern Ireland) 1967

1967	1979
s. 15 (6)	s. 76
17 (1)	25

Finance Act 1968

1968	1979
s. 1 (3)	s. 31

Theatres Act 1968

1968	1979
s. 19 (1)	s. 71
Sch. 2	71

Hovercraft Act 1968

1968	1979
Sch., para. 4 .	s. 4 (1)

Decimal Currency Act 1969

1969	1979
s. 10 (1)	ss. 12, 18, 47 (4), 48, 75, 76, 81

Finance Act 1969

1969	1979
Sch. 7, para. 2 .	s. 57

Finance Act 1970

1970	1979
s. 6 (1)	ss. 1 (7), 6
6 (2) (*a*) .	1 (7)

Finance Act 1972

1972	1979
s. 57 (3)	s. 7
(*a*) .	8
(*b*) .	22
(*c*) .	33

Finance Act 1974

1974	1979
s. 4	s. 31

CRIMINAL PROCEDURE (SCOTLAND) ACT 1975

1975	1979
s. 193A	s. 17
289B (1)	17
(6)	4 (1)
289C (5)	ss. 35, 53, 72

FINANCE (NO. 2) ACT 1975

1975	1979
s. 9	s. 5
10 (1)	36
10 (2)	ss. 42, 43
14 (1)–(4)	s. 54
14 (5)	s. 1 (4)
15 (1)–(5)	55
15 (6)	ss. 1 (1), (5), 4 (4), 22, 24, 57, 65 (1) (2) (6) (8), 66, 67, 76
Sch. 3,	
para. 1 (2)	13, 32, 41, 44, 49, 51
para. 3	s. 22

1975	1979
Sch. 3,	
para. 4	s. 31
para. 5	ss. 9, 10
para. 6	8
para. 7	33
para. 9	46 (1)
para. 15	6
para. 24	7
para. 25	24
para. 26	42
para. 27	56
para. 29 (*a*)	57
para. 31 (*a*)	58
para. 32	59
para. 33	65 (4)
para. 34	s. 85

1975	1979
Sch. 3,	
para. 35	s. 87 (1)
para. 36	88
para. 37	2
para. 42	ss. 46 (2) (3), 61, 64
para. 44 (*b*)	s. 1 (4)
para. 44 (*d*)	1 (5)
para. 44 (*d*) (ii)	4 (1)
Sch. 6,	
para. 5	20
para. 6	21
para. 7	23
para. 8	31

FINANCE ACT 1976

1976	1979
s. 2 (1)–(6)	s. 62
2 (8)	1 (6)
3 (1)	24

1976	1979
s. 3 (2) (3)	s. 69
Sch. 3,	
para. 1	2
para. 5	64
para. 7 (*a*)	1 (6)

1976	1979
Sch. 3,	
para. 7 (*b*)	s. 1 (5)
para. 9 (*a*)	55
para. 9 (*b*)	1 (5)

FINANCE ACT 1977

1977	1979
s. 1 (1)	s. 5
1 (2)	36

1977	1979
s. 1 (3)	Sch. 1
1 (4)	Sch. 2
1 (5)	s. 62

1977	1979
Sch. 1	Sch. 1
Sch. 2	Sch. 2

CRIMINAL LAW ACT 1977

1977	1979
s. 27 (1)	s. 17
28 (2)	17
(7)	4 (1)
31 (6)	ss. 35, 53, 72
32 (1)	s. 17

FINANCE ACT 1978

1978	1979
s. 2	ss. 45, 60, 63
Sch. 12,	
para. 1 (2)	s. 4 (1)
para. 1 (3) (*a*)	35
para. 1 (3) (*b*)	42
para. 1 (3) (*c*)	58

1978	1979
Sch. 12,	
para. 1 (3) (*d*)	s. 70
para. 1 (3) (*e*)	ss. 71, 73
para. 1 (3) (*f*)	s. 74
para. 1 (4)	ss. 4 (1), 22, 42, 43

1978	1979
Sch. 12,	
para. 1 (5)	s. 56
para. 1 (6)	ss. 2, 3
para. 2	s. 11
para. 3	1 (4)
para. 4	1 (5)
para. 5	62

DECIMAL CURRENCY (REVENUE DUTIES) ORDER 1970 (S.I. 1970 No. 1718)

1970	1979
Art. 7	s. 23

CUSTOMS AND EXCISE (WAREHOUSE) REGULATIONS 1978 (S.I. 1978 No. 1603)

1978	1979
Arts. 1–4	....ss. 15, 22, 42, 43, 48, 57, 58

PART I

PRELIMINARY

The alcoholic liquors dutiable under this Act

1.—(1) Subsections (2) to (8) below define for the purposes of this Act the alcoholic liquors which are subject to excise duty under this Act, that is to say—

(*a*) spirits,
(*b*) beer,
(*c*) wine,
(*d*) made-wine, and
(*e*) cider;

and in this Act " dutiable alcoholic liquor " means any of those liquors and " duty " means excise duty.

(2) " Spirits " means, subject to subsections (7) and (8) below, spirits of any description and includes all liquors mixed with spirits and all mixtures, compounds or preparations made with spirits but does not include methylated spirits.

(3) " Beer " includes ale, porter, stout and any other description of beer, and any liquor which is made or sold as a description of beer or as a substitute for beer and which on analysis of a sample thereof at any time is found to be of a strength exceeding 2° of proof, but does not include—

(*a*) black beer the worts whereof before fermentation were of a specific gravity of 1200° or more; and
(*b*) liquor made elsewhere than upon the licensed premises of a brewer for sale which on analysis of a sample at any time is found to be of an original gravity not exceeding 1016° and to be of a strength not exceeding 2° of proof.

(4) " Wine " means any liquor obtained from the alcoholic fermentation of fresh grapes or of the must of fresh grapes, whether or not the liquor is fortified with spirits or flavoured with aromatic extracts.

(5) " Made-wine " means any liquor obtained from the alcoholic fermentation of any substance or by mixing a liquor so obtained or derived from a liquor so obtained with any other liquor or substance but does not include wine, beer, black beer, spirits or cider.

(6) " Cider " means cider (or perry) of a strength less than 8·7 per cent. of alcohol by volume (at a temperature of 20°C) obtained from the fermentation of apple or pear juice without the addition at any time of any alcoholic liquor or of any liquor or substance which communicates colour or flavour other than such as the Commissioners may allow as appearing to them to be necessary to make cider (or perry).

(7) Angostura bitters, that is to say, the aromatic flavouring essence commonly known as angostura bitters, shall be deemed not to be spirits, but this subsection does not apply for the purposes of sections 2, 5, 6 and 27 to 30 below.

(8) Methyl alcohol, notwithstanding that it is so purified or prepared as to be drinkable, shall not be deemed to be spirits nor shall naphtha or any mixture or preparation containing naphtha or methyl alcohol and not containing spirits as defined in subsection (2) above.

Ascertainment of strength, weight and volume of spirits and other liquors

2.—(1) For the purposes of the Customs and Excise Acts 1979, the strength, weight or volume of any spirits shall be ascertained in accordance with the following provisions of this section.

(2) Spirits shall be deemed to be at proof if the volume of the ethyl alcohol contained therein made up to the volume of the spirits with distilled water has a weight equal to that of twelve-thirteenths of a volume of distilled water equal to the volume of the spirits, the volume of each liquid being computed as at 51°F.

(3) " Degree of proof ", " degree over proof " and " degree under proof " shall be construed by reference to a scale on which 100° denotes the strength of spirits at proof and—

(*a*) 101°, or 1 degree over proof, denotes the strength of spirits which would be at proof if there were added thereto such quantity of distilled water as would increase by 1 per cent. the volume of the spirits computed as at 50°F;

(*b*) 99°, or 1 degree under proof, denotes the strength of spirits which would be at proof if there were removed therefrom such quantity of distilled water as would reduce by 1 per cent. the volume of the spirits computed as at 50°F;

and so in proportion for any other number of degrees.

(4) The equivalent at proof of any spirits not at proof shall for the purposes of the Customs and Excise Acts 1979 be deemed to be their volume—

(*a*) multiplied by the number of degrees of proof representing their strength; and

(*b*) divided by 100.

(5) The Commissioners may make regulations prescribing the means to be used for ascertaining for any purpose the strength, weight or volume of spirits, and any such regulations may provide that in ascertaining for any purpose the strength of any spirits any substance contained therein which is not ethyl alcohol or distilled water may be treated as if it were.

(6) Different regulations may be made under subsection (5) above for different purposes.

(7) This section shall apply to methylated spirits and to any fermented liquor as it applies to spirits but, in relation to wine, made-wine or cider shall not apply so as to prevent the strength, weight or volume of wine, made-wine or cider from being ascertained for the purpose of charging duty thereon by methods other than that provided in this section.

Meaning of and method of ascertaining gravity of liquids

3.—(1) For the purposes of the Customs and Excise Acts 1979—

(*a*) " gravity ", in relation to any liquid, means the ratio of the weight of a volume of the liquid to the weight of an equal volume of distilled water, the volume of each liquid being computed as at 60°F;

(*b*) where the gravity of any liquid is expressed as a number of degrees that number shall be the said ratio multiplied by 1,000; and

(*c*) " original gravity ", in relation to any liquid in which fermentation has taken place, means its gravity before fermentation.

(2) The gravity of any liquid at any time shall be ascertained by such means as the Commissioners may approve, and the gravity so ascertained shall be deemed to be the true gravity of the liquid.

(3) Subject to subsection (5) below, where for any purposes of the

Customs and Excise Acts 1979 it is necessary to ascertain the original gravity of worts in which fermentation has commenced or of any liquid produced from such worts, that gravity shall be determined in such manner as the Commissioners may by regulations prescribe.

(4) Different regulations may be made under subsection (3) above in relation to different liquids.

(5) Where the original gravity of any worts has been determined in accordance with regulations made under subsection (3) above for the purpose of charging duty under section 38 below by reference to the quantity and original gravity of worts produced, a deduction of $\frac{3}{4}°$ shall be allowed from the original gravity so determined, so however as not to reduce the original gravity by reference to which the duty is charged below the gravity of the worts as ascertained by the proper officer in accordance with subsection (2) above.

Interpretation

4.—(1) In this Act, unless the context otherwise requires,—

" authorised methylator " means a person authorised to methylate spirits under section 75 (1) below;

" beer " has the meaning given by section 1 above;

" black beer " means beer of the description called or similar to black beer, mum, spruce beer or Berlin white beer, and any other preparation (whether fermented or not) of a similar character;

" brewer " and " brewer for sale " have the meanings given by section 47 below;

" British compounded spirits " means spirits which have, in the United Kingdom, had any flavour communicated thereto or ingredient or material mixed therewith, not being methylated spirits;

" case ", in relation to dutiable alcoholic liquor, means 1 dozen units each consisting of a container holding not less than 23 nor more than 28 fluid ounces, or the equivalent of that number of such units made up wholly or partly of containers of a larger or smaller size;

" cider " has the meaning given by section 1 above;

" compounder " means a person holding a licence as a compounder under section 18 below;

" distiller " means a person holding a distiller's licence under section 12 below;

" distiller's licence " has the meaning given by section 12 (1) below;

" distiller's warehouse " means a place of security provided by a distiller and approved by the Commissioners under section 15 (1) below;

" distillery " means premises where spirits are manufactured, whether by distillation of a fermented liquor or by any other process;

" dutiable alcoholic liquor " has the meaning given by section 1 (1) above;

" duty " has the meaning given by section 1 (1) above and " duty-paid ", " duty-free " and references to drawback shall be construed accordingly;

" gravity " and " original gravity " have the meanings given by section 3 above;

" justices' licence " and " justices' on-licence "—

(*a*) in the application of this Act to England and Wales have the meanings respectively given to them by sections 1 (1) and 1 (2) (*a*) of the Licensing Act 1964 and in both cases include a canteen licence granted under Part X and an occasional licence granted under section 180 of that Act;

(*b*) in the application of this Act to Northern Ireland mean a licence corresponding to the relevant licence such as is mentioned in paragraph (*a*) of this definition;

" licensed ", in relation to a producer of wine or of made-wine, means a producer who holds a licence to produce wine or made-wine respectively under subsection (2) of section 54 or 55 below;

" licensed methylator " means a person holding a licence under section 75 (2) below;

" limited licence to brew beer " has the meaning given by section 47 (2) below;

" made-wine " has the meaning given by section 1 above;

" the Management Act " means the Customs and Excise Management Act 1979;

" methylated spirits " means spirits mixed in the United Kingdom with some other substance in accordance with regulations made under section 77 below;

" the prescribed sum ", in relation to the penalty provided for an offence, means—

(*a*) if the offence was committed in England or Wales or in Northern Ireland, the prescribed sum within the meaning of section 28 of the Criminal Law Act 1977 (£1,000 or other sum substituted by order under section 61 (1) of that Act);

(*b*) if the offence was committed in Scotland, the prescribed sum within the meaning of section 289B of the Criminal Procedure (Scotland) Act 1975 (£1,000 or other sum substituted by order under section 289D (1) of that Act);

" producer of made-wine " includes a person who renders made-wine sparkling, and " produce ", in relation to made-wine, shall be construed accordingly;

" producer of wine " includes a person who renders wine sparkling, and " produce ", in relation to wine, shall be construed accordingly;

" proof ", in relation to the strength of spirits, has the meaning given by section 2 above;

" rectifier " means a person holding a licence as a rectifier under section 18 below;

" registered club " means a club which is for the time being registered within the meaning of the Licensing Act 1964 or which is for the time being a registered club within the meaning of the Licensing (Scotland) Act 1976 or which is for the time being a registered club within the meaning of the Registration of Clubs Act (Northern Ireland) 1967;

" retailer " means—

(*a*) in relation to dutiable alcoholic liquor, a person who sells such liquor by retail;

(*b*) in relation to methylated spirits, a person holding a licence under section 76 below;

" Scottish licence " includes a licence of a type described in

Schedule 1 to the Licensing (Scotland) Act 1976 (other than an off-sale licence), an occasional licence granted in terms of section 33 of the said Act, an occasional permission granted in terms of section 34 of the said Act, and a licence granted in terms of section 40 of the said Act;
section 34 of the said Act, and a licence granted in terms of section 40 of the said Act;

" spirits " has the meaning given by section 1 above;

" spirits advice note " and " spirits consignment note " have the meanings given by section 27 (5) below;

" spirits of wine " means plain spirits of a strength of not less than 43° over proof manufactured in the United Kingdom;

" wholesale ", in relation to dealing in dutiable alcoholic liquor, has the meaning given by section 65 (8) below;

" wholesaler " means a person holding a licence under section 65 below;

" wine " has the meaning given by section 1 above.

(2) This Act and the other Acts included in the Customs and Excise Acts 1979 shall be construed as one Act but where a provision of this Act refers to this Act that reference is not to be construed as including a reference to any of the others.

(3) Any expression used in this Act or in any instrument made under this Act to which a meaning is given by any other Act included in the Customs and Excise Acts 1979 has, except where the context otherwise requires, the same meaning in this Act or in any such instrument as in that Act; and for ease of reference the Table below indicates the expressions used in this Act to which a meaning is given by any other such Act—

Management Act

" the Commissioners "
" container "
" the Customs and Excise Acts 1979 "
" excise warehouse "
" goods "
" hovercraft "
" importer "
" licence year "
" nautical mile "
" night "
" occupier "
" officer " and " proper " in relation to an officer
" ship " and " British ship "
" shipped "
" shipment "
" stores "
" tons register "
" warehouse "
" warehousing regulations ".

(4) For the purposes of this Act, selling by retail, in relation to dutiable alcoholic liquor, means the sale at any one time to any one person of quantities not exceeding the following, that is to say—

(*a*) in the case of spirits, wine or made-wine, 2 gallons or 1 case;

(*b*) in the case of beer or cider, $4\frac{1}{2}$ gallons or 2 cases.

PART II

SPIRITS

Charge of excise duty

Spirits: charge of excise duty

5. There shall be charged on spirits—

(*a*) imported into the United Kingdom; or

(*b*) distilled, or manufactured by any other process whatsoever, in the United Kingdom,

a duty of excise at the rates shown in the following Table—

TABLE

Description of spirits	*Rates of duty (per proof gallon)* £
1. Spirits warehoused for 3 years or more	27·0900
2. Spirits not warehoused or warehoused for less than 3 years	27·1650

Reliefs from excise duty

Power to exempt angostura bitters from duty

6. On the importation of the aromatic flavouring essence commonly known as angostura bitters, the Commissioners may, subject to such conditions as they see fit to impose, direct the bitters to be treated for the purposes of the charge of duty on spirits as not being spirits.

Exemption from duty of spirits in articles used for medical purposes

7. Duty shall not be payable on any spirits contained in an article imported or delivered from warehouse which is recognised by the Commissioners as being used for medical purposes.

Repayment of duty in respect of spirits used for medical or scientific purposes

8.—(1) If any person proves to the satisfaction of the Commissioners that any spirits on which duty has been paid have been delivered to him and have been used—

(*a*) solely in the manufacture or preparation of any article recognised by the Commissioners as being used for medical purposes; or

(*b*) for scientific purposes,

he shall, subject to such conditions as the Commissioners may by regulations impose, be entitled to obtain from the Commissioners the repayment of the duty paid thereon.

(2) If any person contravenes or fails to comply with any regulation made under this section he shall be liable on summary conviction to a penalty of £100.

Remission of duty on spirits for methylation

9. The Commissioners may, subject to such conditions as they see fit to impose, permit spirits to be delivered from warehouse for methylation without payment of the duty chargeable thereon.

Remission of duty on spirits for use in art or manufacture

10.—(1) Where, in the case of any art or manufacture carried on by any person in which the use of spirits is required, it is proved to the satisfaction of the Commissioners that the use of methylated spirits is unsuitable or detrimental, the Commissioners may, if they think fit and subject to such conditions as they see fit to impose, authorise that person to receive, and permit the delivery from warehouse to that person of, spirits for use in that art or manufacture without payment of the duty chargeable thereon.

(2) If any person contravenes or fails to comply with any condition imposed under this section then, in addition to any other penalty he may have incurred, he shall be liable on summary conviction to a penalty of £50.

Relief from duty on imported goods not for human consumption containing spirits

11. On the importation of goods not for human consumption containing spirits as a part or ingredient thereof, the Commissioners may, subject to such conditions as they may think fit to impose, direct the goods to be treated for the purposes of the charge of duty on spirits (and in particular the charge under section 126 of the Management Act) as not containing spirits.

Manufacture of spirits

Licence to manufacture spirits

12.—(1) No person shall manufacture spirits, whether by distillation of a fermented liquor or by any other process, unless he holds an excise licence for that purpose under this section (referred to in this Act as a " distiller's licence ").

(2) A licence granted under this section shall expire on the 30th September next after it is granted.

(3) On any licence granted under this section there shall be charged an excise licence duty of £15·75.

(4) The Commissioners may refuse to grant a distiller's licence in respect of any premises on which, from their situation with respect to premises used by a rectifier, brewer for sale or vinegar-maker, they think it inexpedient to allow the manufacture of spirits.

(5) Where the largest still to be used on any premises in respect of which a distiller's licence is sought for the manufacture of spirits by distillation of a fermented liquor is of less than 400 gallons capacity, the Commissioners may refuse to grant the licence or may grant it only subject to such conditions as they see fit to impose.

(6) The Commissioners may refuse to grant a distiller's licence in respect of any premises situated in an area where the Commissioners are not satisfied that convenient living accommodation for the officers to be placed in charge of the distillery can be found unless the distiller undertakes to provide to the satisfaction of the Commissioners lodgings for those officers which satisfy the conditions specified in subsections (7) and (8) below.

(7) The lodgings must be conveniently situated with respect to the distillery but must not form part of the distillery or of the distiller's dwelling house.

(8) The rent unfurnished of the lodgings must either be agreed

between the distiller and the Commissioners or, in default of agreement, must be equal—

(*a*) if the lodgings are in England or Wales, to their gross value for the purposes of section 19 of the General Rate Act 1967;

(*b*) if the lodgings are in Scotland, to their gross annual value ascertained in accordance with the provisions of section 6 (2) to (4) of the Valuation and Rating (Scotland) Act 1956 for the purpose of making up the valuation roll;

(*c*) if the lodgings are in Northern Ireland, to their annual value ascertained in accordance with section 531 of the Income and Corporation Taxes Act 1970.

(9) If a distiller to whom a licence has been granted upon his giving the undertaking mentioned in subsection (6) above fails to provide lodgings in accordance with that undertaking or to keep those lodgings in repair, or if he in any way interferes with the use and enjoyment of those lodgings by the officer residing therein, the Commissioners may suspend or revoke the licence.

Power to make regulations relating to manufacture of spirits

13.—(1) The Commissioners may, with a view to the protection of the revenue, make regulations—

(*a*) regulating the manufacture of spirits, whether by distillation of a fermented liquor or by any other process;

(*b*) for securing and collecting the duty on spirits manufactured in the United Kingdom; and

(*c*) regulating the removal of spirits from a distillery;

and different regulations may be made in respect of manufacture for different purposes or by different processes.

(2) Where—

(*a*) the Commissioners are satisfied that any process of manufacture carried on by any person involving the manufacture of spirits is primarily directed to the production of some article other than spirits; or

(*b*) the Commissioners see fit in the case of any person manufacturing spirits by any process other than distillation of a fermented liquor,

they may direct that, subject to compliance with such conditions as they think proper to impose, such of the provisions of this Act relating to the manufacture of, or manufacturers of, spirits or such of any regulations made under this section as may be specified in the direction shall not apply in the case of that person.

(3) If, save as provided in subsection (2) above, any person contravenes or fails to comply with any regulation made under subsection (1) above he shall, subject to subsection (4) below, be liable on summary conviction to a penalty of £1,000, and any spirits, and any vessels, utensils and materials used for distilling or otherwise manufacturing or for preparing spirits, in respect of which the offence was committed shall be liable to forfeiture.

(4) The Commissioners may by any regulation under subsection (1) above provide a penalty of an amount less than that specified in subsection (3) above for any contravention of or failure to comply with that regulation.

(5) If any person in whose case a direction is given by the Commissioners under subsection (2) above acts in contravention of or fails to comply with any condition imposed under that subsection which is applicable in his case, he shall be liable on summary conviction to a

penalty of £100, and any spirits in respect of which the offence was committed shall be liable to forfeiture.

Duty on spirits—attenuation charge

14.—(1) In the case of a distillery where spirits are manufactured by distillation of a fermented liquor, the duty on spirits shall, in addition to being charged on the spirits distilled, be chargeable in respect of each distillation period in accordance with the following provisions of this section.

(2) There shall be calculated the quantity of spirits at proof capable of being produced from any wort and wash made at the distillery on the assumption that from every 100 gallons of wort and wash 1 gallon of spirits at proof will be produced for every 5 degrees of attenuation, that is to say, for every 5 degrees of difference between the highest gravity of the wort and the lowest gravity of the wash before distillation, and so in proportion for any less number of gallons of wort and wash or any less number of degrees of attenuation.

(3) The gravity of wort or wash for the purposes of subsection (2) above shall be taken as that declared by the distiller except that, if either gravity is found by the proper officer before distillation and the gravity so found is, in the case of wort, higher or, in the case of wash, lower than that declared by the distiller, the gravity to be taken shall be that so found by the proper officer.

(4) There shall be ascertained the quantity computed at proof of the spirits and feints produced at the distillery after deducting the feints remaining at the end of the last preceding distillation period.

(5) If the quantity calculated under subsection (2) above exceeds the quantity ascertained under subsection (4) above the duty on spirits shall, subject to subsection (6) below, be charged and become payable immediately on that excess.

(6) The Commissioners may make such allowance as in their opinion is reasonable from any charge under this section on proof to their satisfaction that the charge arises wholly or in part on account of the removal of wash for the separation of yeast or on account of the loss or destruction of wort or wash by unavoidable accident.

(7) In this section, " distillation period " means the period prescribed by regulations under section 13 (1) above for the purpose of taking account of feints and spirits produced.

Distiller's warehouse

15.—(1) A distiller may provide in association with his distillery a place of security for the deposit of spirits manufactured at that distillery and, if that place is approved by the Commissioners and entry is made thereof by the distiller, may deposit therein without payment of duty any spirits so manufactured.

(2) If the place of security so provided is outside the distillery, the Commissioners may attach to their approval such conditions as they see fit, and if those conditions are not for the time being observed, that place shall be deemed not to have been approved by the Commissioners.

(3) A place of security for the time being approved by the Commissioners under subsection (1) above is referred to in this Act as a " distiller's warehouse ".

(4) A distiller who provides a distiller's warehouse shall, to the satisfaction of the Commissioners, provide accommodation at the warehouse for the officer in charge thereof, and if he fails so to do he shall be liable on summary conviction to a penalty of £50; but nothing in

this subsection shall prejudice any power of the Commissioners to require the provision of accommodation as a condition of their approval of any other premises or place under the Customs and Excise Acts 1979.

(5) A distiller who, after the approval of a distiller's warehouse provided by him, makes without the previous consent of the Commissioners any alteration therein or addition thereto shall be liable on summary conviction to a penalty of £200.

(6) The Commissioners may make regulations—

(*a*) regulating the warehousing of spirits in a distiller's warehouse;

(*b*) permitting, in so far as it appears to them necessary in order to meet the circumstances of any special case and subject to such conditions as they see fit to impose, the deposit by a distiller in his distiller's warehouse without payment of duty of spirits other than spirits manufactured at the distillery associated with that warehouse;

(*c*) for securing the duties on spirits so warehoused;

and subject to any such regulations, the provisions of Parts VIII and X of the Management Act, except sections 92 and 96, shall apply in relation to a distiller's warehouse and spirits warehoused therein as they apply in relation to an excise warehouse approved under subsection (1) of section 92 of that Act and goods warehoused therein.

(7) If any person contravenes or fails to comply with any regulation made under subsection (6) above he shall, subject to subsection (8) below, be liable on summary conviction to a penalty of £1,000, and any spirits in respect of which the offence was committed shall be liable to forfeiture.

(8) The Commissioners may by any regulation under subsection (6) above provide a penalty of an amount less than that specified in subsection (7) above for any contravention of or failure to comply with that regulation.

(9) The Commissioners may at any time for reasonable cause revoke or vary the terms of their approval of a distiller's warehouse.

Racking of duty-paid spirits at distillery

16.—(1) The Commissioners may, with a view to the protection of the revenue, make regulations regulating the racking at a distillery of duty-paid spirits.

(2) If any person contravenes or fails to comply with any regulation made under this section, he shall be liable on summary conviction to a penalty of £50 and any spirits in respect of which the offence was committed shall be liable to forfeiture.

(3) If on an officer's taking stock of duty-paid spirits racked at a distillery, a greater quantity of spirits computed at proof is found at the place of racking than ought to be there according to any accounts required by regulations made under this section to be kept thereof, then—

(*a*) duty shall be charged on the excess; and

(*b*) except as provided in subsection (4) below, if the excess amounts to more than 1 per cent. of the quantity of spirits computed at proof lawfully brought into the place of racking since stock was last taken, that excess shall be liable to forfeiture, and the distiller shall be liable on summary conviction to a penalty of double the duty so charged.

(4) Paragraph (*b*) of subsection (3) above shall not apply where the excess is less than 1 gallon at proof.

Offences in connection with removal of spirits from distillery, etc.

17.—(1) If any person—

(*a*) conceals in or without the consent of the proper officer removes from a distillery any wort, wash, low wines, feints or spirits; or

(*b*) knowingly buys or receives any wort, wash, low wines, feints or spirits so concealed or removed; or

(*c*) knowingly buys or receives or has in his possession any spirits which have been removed from the place where they ought to have been charged with duty before the duty payable thereon has been charged and either paid or secured, not being spirits which have been condemned or are deemed to have been condemned as forfeited,

he shall be guilty of an offence under this section and may be detained, and the goods shall be liable to forfeiture.

(2) A person guilty of an offence under this section shall be liable—

(*a*) on summary conviction, to a penalty of the prescribed sum or three times the value of the goods, whichever is the greater, or to imprisonment for a term not exceeding 6 months, or to both; or

(*b*) on conviction on indictment, to a penalty of any amount, or to imprisonment for a term not exceeding 2 years, or to both.

Rectifying and compounding of spirits

Rectifier's and compounder's licences

18.—(1) No person shall rectify or compound spirits and keep a still for that purpose unless he holds an excise licence under this section as a rectifier.

(2) Except as permitted by the Commissioners and subject to such conditions as they see fit to impose, no other person shall compound spirits unless he holds an excise licence under this section as a compounder.

(3) Any licence granted under this section shall expire on the 30th September next after it is granted.

(4) On any licence granted under this section there shall be charged an excise licence duty of £15·75.

(5) The Commissioners may refuse to grant any person a licence as a rectifier in respect of any premises on which, from their situation with respect to a distillery, they think it inexpedient to allow the keeping of a still for rectifying or compounding spirits.

(6) Without prejudice to section 25 below and except as provided by this section, if any person rectifies or compounds spirits otherwise than under and in accordance with an excise licence under this Act so authorising him, he shall be liable on summary conviction to a penalty of £500.

Regulation of rectifying and compounding

19.—(1) The Commissioners may, with a view to the protection of the revenue, make regulations—

(*a*) regulating the rectifying and compounding of spirits;

(*b*) regulating the receipt, storage, removal and delivery of spirits by rectifiers and compounders;

and different regulations may be made under this section for rectifiers and compounders.

(2) If any person contravenes or fails to comply with any regulation made under this section, he shall, subject to subsection (3) below, be liable on summary conviction to a penalty of £500, and any spirits and any other article in respect of which the offence was committed shall be liable to forfeiture.

(3) The Commissioners may by any regulation under this section provide a penalty of an amount less than that specified in subsection (2) above for any contravention of or failure to comply with that regulation.

Penalty for excess or deficiency in rectifier's stock

20.—(1) If at any time when an account is taken by an officer and a balance struck of the spirits in the stock of a rectifier any excess is found, that excess shall be liable to forfeiture, and the rectifier shall be liable on summary conviction to a penalty of double the duty on a like quantity of plain spirits at proof charged at the highest rate.

(2) If at any time when an account is taken and a balance struck as mentioned in subsection (1) above any deficiency is found which cannot be accounted for to the satisfaction of the Commissioners and which when computed at proof exceeds 5 per cent. of the aggregate of—

(*a*) the balance so computed struck when an account was last taken; and

(*b*) any quantity of spirits so computed since lawfully received by the rectifier,

the rectifier shall be liable on summary conviction to a penalty of double the duty on a quantity of plain spirits at proof charged at the highest rate equal to the quantity by which the deficiency exceeds the said 5 per cent.

(3) For the purposes of any such account and of this section—

(*a*) spirits used by a rectifier in warehouse in pursuance of warehousing regulations shall be deemed not to be spirits in his stock as a rectifier; and

(*b*) where a rectifier also carries on the trade of a wholesaler of spirits on the same premises, all spirits in his possession (other than spirits so used) shall be deemed to be spirits in his stock as a rectifier.

Restrictions relating to rectifiers

21.—(1) A rectifier shall not distil or extract feints or spirits from any other material then spirits on which duty has been duly paid.

(2) A rectifier shall not have in his possession—

(*a*) except for duty-paid spirits, any materials capable of being distilled into feints or spirits;

(*b*) any spirits for which he has not received a proper spirits advice note or spirits consignment note.

(3) If a rectifier contravenes subsection (1) or (2) above, or if his still is found to contain any materials capable of being distilled as aforesaid other than duty-paid spirits, whether or not mixed with spirits on which duty has been duly paid, he shall be liable on summary conviction to a penalty of £500 or double the duty on a quantity of plain spirits at proof charged at the highest rate equal to the quantity of the materials or spirits in respect of which the offence was committed, whichever is the greater.

(4) If a rectifier is convicted more than once under this section, his licence shall become void and he shall be disqualified from holding a licence as a rectifier for a period of 3 years from the date of his latest conviction.

(5) Spirits used in warehouse in pursuance of warehousing regulations shall be treated for the purposes of this section as duty-paid spirits.

Drawback on British compounds and spirits of wine

22.—(1) Subject to the provisions of this section and to such conditions and restrictions as the Commissioners may by regulations impose, a rectifier or compounder may warehouse in an excise warehouse on drawback any British compounded spirits or spirits of wine rectified or compounded by him from duty-paid spirits and not containing any methyl alcohol or any wine, made-wine or other fermented liquor.

(2) British compounded spirits may be warehoused under this section for exportation, for use in any permitted operation in warehouse, for use as stores or, except in the case of tinctures other than perfumed spirits, for home use.

(3) Spirits of wine may be warehoused under this section—

(*a*) for exportation, for use in any permitted operation in warehouse, or for use as stores; or

(*b*) if of a strength of not less than 50° over proof, for delivery for use in art or manufacture under section 10 above; or

(*c*) if of a strength of not less than 74° over proof, for home use.

(4) The Commissioners may, subject to such conditions and restrictions as they may by regulations impose, allow drawback on tinctures or spirits of wine exported or, except in the case of spirits of wine, shipped as stores by a rectifier or compounder direct from his premises.

(5) Subject to subsection (6) below, the amount of any drawback payable under this section shall be calculated by reference to the quantity of the British compounded spirits or spirits of wine computed at proof and shall be an amount equal to the duty at the appropriate rate chargeable on a like quantity of spirits at the date when duty was paid on the spirits from which the British compounded spirits or spirits of wine were rectified or compounded.

(6) The Commissioners may, in the case of tinctures exported or shipped as stores by a rectifier or compounder direct from his premises, make such addition to the quantity of spirits as they see fit in respect of waste.

(7) No drawback shall be payable under this section in the case of medicinal spirits in respect of which a repayment of duty has been obtained under section 8 above.

(8) British compounded spirits warehoused under this section for home use shall upon delivery from warehouse for that purpose be chargeable with the same rate of duty as spirits warehoused by a distiller.

(9) If any person contravenes or fails to comply with any regulation made under this section then, in addition to any other penalty he may have incurred under the Customs and Excise Acts 1979, he shall be liable on summary conviction to a penalty of £100, and any article in respect of which the offence was committed shall be liable to forfeiture.

(10) In this section " tinctures " means medicinal spirits, flavouring essences, perfumed spirits and such other articles containing spirits as the Commissioners may by regulations specify as tinctures.

Allowance on British compounds

23.—(1) Where any British compounded spirits—

(*a*) having been warehoused, are on removal from warehouse exported or shipped as stores; or

(*b*) are permitted under section 22 above to be exported or shipped as stores on drawback direct from the premises of a rectifier or compounder; or

(*c*) are used in warehouse for fortifying wine or for any other purpose for which spirits are permitted by or under this or any other Act to be used in warehouse,

there shall, subject to the provisions of this section and to such conditions as the Commissioners see fit to impose, be paid in respect of each gallon of those spirits computed at proof an allowance of £0·02.

(2) In the case of British compounded spirits of a strength exceeding 11° over proof which are deposited in a warehouse, the allowance mentioned in subsection (1) above may, subject as aforesaid, instead of being paid as provided in that subsection be paid on the warehousing of the spirits.

(3) No allowance shall be payable on any British compounded spirits under this section if those spirits were compounded in warehouse in pursuance of warehousing regulations or, in any other case, unless it is proved to the satisfaction of the Commissioners that the spirits have been distinctly altered in character by redistillation with or by the addition of flavouring or other matter.

(4) Any allowance on British compounded spirits under this section—

(*a*) when paid on their exportation or shipment as stores, shall be paid to the person by whom security is given for that exportation or shipment;

(*b*) when paid on their use in warehouse, shall be paid to the person upon whose written request they are so used;

(*c*) when paid on their warehousing, shall be paid to the person in whose name they are warehoused.

General provisions relating to manufacture of spirits and British compounds

Restriction on carrying on of other trades by distiller or rectifier

24.—(1) A distiller or rectifier shall not—

(*a*) carry on upon his premises the trade of a brewer for sale, producer of wine or of made-wine, maker of cider, vinegar-maker, refiner of sugar, wholesaler or retailer of wine, made-wine or beer, or retailer of methylated spirits or cider; or

(*b*) carry on the trade of a distiller or, as the case may be, rectifier on any premises communicating otherwise than by a public roadway with other premises on which any such trade as is mentioned in paragraph (*a*) above or that of a wholesaler of spirits is carried on.

(2) Save with the permission of the Commissioners and subject to compliance with such conditions as they see fit to impose, a distiller or rectifier shall not—

(*a*) carry on upon his premises the trade of a retailer of spirits; or

(*b*) carry on the trade of a distiller or, as the case may be, rectifier on any premises communicating otherwise than by a public roadway with other premises on which the trade of retailer of spirits is carried on.

(3) Save with the permission of the Commissioners and subject to compliance with such conditions as they see fit to impose, a distiller or rectifier shall not be concerned or interested in the trade of a retailer of spirits carried on within 2 miles of his distillery or, as the case may be, rectifying house.

(4) If a person contravenes any provision of this section or contravenes or fails to comply with any condition imposed thereunder, he shall be liable on summary conviction to a penalty of £200.

Penalty for unlawful manufacture of spirits, etc.

25.—(1) Save as provided by or under this Act, any person who, otherwise than under and in accordance with an excise licence under this Act so authorising him—

(*a*) manufactures spirits, whether by distillation of a fermented liquor or by any other process; or

(*b*) has in his possession or uses a still for distilling, rectifying or compounding spirits; or

(*c*) distils or has in his possession any low wines or feints; or

(*d*) not being a vinegar-maker, brews or makes or has in his possession any wort or wash fit for distillation,

shall be liable on summary conviction to a penalty of £1,000.

(2) Where there is insufficient evidence to convict a person of an offence under subsection (1) above, but it is proved that such an offence has been committed on some part of premises belonging to or occupied by that person in such circumstances that it could not have been committed without his knowledge, that person shall be liable on summary conviction to a penalty of £100.

(3) Any person found on premises on which spirits are being unlawfully manufactured or on which a still is being unlawfully used for rectifying or compounding spirits may be detained.

(4) All spirits and stills, vessels, utensils, wort, wash and other materials for manufacturing, distilling or preparing spirits—

(*a*) found in the possession of any person who commits an offence under subsection (1) above; or

(b) found on any premises on which such an offence has been committed,

shall be liable to forfeiture.

(5) Notwithstanding any other provision of the Customs and Excise Acts 1979 relating to goods seized as liable to forfeiture, any officer by whom any thing is seized as liable to forfeiture under subsection (4) above may at his discretion forthwith spill, break up or destroy that thing.

(6) Without prejudice to any other power conferred by the Customs and Excise Acts 1979, if any officer has reasonable grounds for suspecting that any thing liable to forfeiture under this section is in or upon any land or other premises in Northern Ireland, he may enter upon those premises, if need be by force, and search them and seize and remove any thing which he has reasonable grounds to believe to be so liable.

General provisions relating to spirits

Importation and exportation of spirits

26.—(1) Save as permitted by the Commissioners, spirits shall not be imported—

(*a*) in any ship of less than 40 tons register; or

(*b*) in containers of a capacity of less than 9 gallons each unless in bottles properly packed in cases.

(2) Save as permitted by the Commissioners, spirits other than bottled spirits shall not be exported, or be removed to the Isle of Man, or be

brought to any place or be waterborne for exportation or for removal to the Isle of Man, in containers holding less than 9 gallons each.

(3) Any spirits imported, exported, removed, brought or waterborne contrary to this section shall be liable to forfeiture.

(4) Where any ship is or has been, in the case of a British ship, within 12 or, in any other case, within 3 nautical miles of the coast of the United Kingdom while having on board or attached in any manner thereto any spirits in containers other than such as are permitted by or under subsection (1) of this section, the ship and any such spirits found therein shall be liable to forfeiture.

(5) For the purposes of subsection (1) above, all hovercraft (of whatever size) shall be treated as ships of less than 40 tons register and subsection (4) above shall apply as if any reference to a ship included a reference to a hovercraft.

Spirits consignment and spirits advice notes

27.—(1) Where any spirits are sent out from the stock of a rectifier or compounder or, otherwise than in the circumstances specified in subsection (2) below, are sent out from the stock of a wholesaler or retailer, the person sending them out shall, subject to any dispensation granted by the Commissioners, send to the person to whom they are sent a spirits consignment note, and shall send it either with the spirits or so that it is either delivered or posted on the day on which the spirits are sent out.

(2) The circumstances referred to in subsection (1) above in relation to a wholesaler or retailer are that—

(*a*) in the case of spirits sent out from the stock of a wholesaler, the spirits are sent out in a quantity not exceeding 1 gallon at a time and are sold by him by retail to a person who is not a wholesaler or retailer of spirits; and

(*b*) in the case of spirits sent out from the stock of a retailer, the spirits are sent out in a quantity not exceeding 1 gallon of the same denomination at a time for one person.

(3) The person by whom any spirits—

(*a*) are sent out from a distillery; or

(*b*) are removed from a warehouse; or

(*c*) not being spirits to which the requirement imposed by subsection (1) above to send a spirits consignment note applies, are otherwise removed from any place in the United Kingdom to any other such place in a quantity exceeding 1 gallon of the same denomination at a time for any one person,

shall, subject to any dispensation granted by the Commissioners, send to the person to whom the spirits are to be delivered a spirits advice note, and shall send that note either with the spirits or so that it is either delivered or posted on the day on which the spirits are sent out or removed.

(4) A distiller shall not send out from his distillery, or, save as permitted by the Commissioners in the case of samples, remove from a distiller's warehouse associated with his distillery, any spirits in a quantity of less than 9 gallons.

(5) In this Act—

" spirits advice note " means a document containing such particulars as the Commissioners may direct;

" spirits consignment note " means a consignment note or similar document containing such particulars as the Commissioners may direct.

Regulations about the keeping and production of spirits advice and spirits consignment notes, etc.

28.—(1) As respects spirits in the case of which a requirement is imposed by this Act that a spirits advice note or a spirits consignment note shall be sent in connection with their removal, the Commissioners may make regulations requiring the keeping and production of such notes and copies thereof, and of stock books.

(2) If any person contravenes or fails to comply with any regulation made under this section he shall, except in the circumstances specified in subsection (3) below, be liable on summary conviction to a penalty of £200.

(3) No liability shall be incurred under subsection (2) above for failure to keep or produce a spirits advice note, spirits consignment note or copy of such a note in accordance with any such regulation if it is proved that the note or, as the case may be, the note and any copy thereof was or were lost or destroyed by accident.

Offences in connection with spirits advice and spirits consignment notes

29.—(1) Where a spirits advice note or a spirits consignment note is required by this Act in connection with the removal of any spirits, then if any person—

(*a*) sends out or causes to be sent out, any spirits without the proper spirits advice note or spirits consignment note being duly sent; or

(*b*) requests, obtains or uses, or causes or permits to be requested, obtained or used, a spirits advice note or a spirits consignment note for any purpose otherwise than in accordance with the terms thereof; or

(*c*) in any manner uses or causes or permits the use of any spirits advice note or spirits consignment note so that the taking or checking of any account or the making of any examination by an officer is or may be frustrated or evaded; or

(*d*) produces or causes or permits the production of any spirits advice note or spirits consignment note to an officer as having been received with or in connection with any spirits other than those to which it relates,

he shall, in addition to any other punishment to which he may have become liable, be liable on summary conviction to a penalty of three times the value of any spirits in respect of which the offence was committed or £100, whichever is the greater.

(2) Any spirits—

(*a*) in connection with the removal of which a spirits advice note is required by this Act which are found in the course of being, or to have been, sent out, removed or received—

(i) without a proper spirits advice note having been duly sent, or

(ii) in contravention of section 27 (4) above; or

(*b*) in the case of which an altered or untrue spirits advice note has been sent,

shall be liable to forfeiture, and any person in whose possession any such spirits are found shall be liable on summary conviction to a penalty of three times the value of the goods or £100, whichever is the greater.

Special provisions as to spirits advice and spirits consignment notes

30.—(1) If in any proceedings under section 29 above, any question arises as to the accuracy of the description of any spirits in a spirits advice note or spirits consignment note—

(*a*) the burden of proof that the spirits correspond with the description shall lie on the person claiming that the spirits so correspond, who shall furnish that proof by the evidence of two persons competent to decide by examination of the spirits;

(*b*) the description of spirits shall not be deemed to be inaccurate by reason only of the fact that they are of a strength differing from that specified in the spirits advice note or spirits consignment note where the actual strength is not more than 1° of proof above or 2° of proof below that so specified.

(2) If a distiller, rectifier or compounder or a wholesaler or retailer of spirits is convicted of an offence in relation to spirits under section 29 above, the Commissioners may revoke his licence and refuse to re-grant him a licence during the remainder of the period for which the revoked licence would have been in force.

Restriction on delivery of immature spirits for home use

31.—(1) No spirits shall be delivered for home use unless they have been warehoused for a period of at least 3 years or, in the case of rum, at least 2 years. But this subsection shall not apply—

(*a*) to spirits delivered for any purpose for which they may for the time being be delivered without payment of duty; or

(*b*) to spirits delivered for methylation under section 9 above or for use in art or manufacture under section 10 above; or

(*c*) to spirits which have been warehoused on drawback; or

(*d*) to mixtures, compounds or preparations charged with duty on importation in respect of the spirits contained in them or used in their preparation or manufacture; or

(*e*) subject to such conditions as the Commissioners may by regulations impose, to spirits delivered to a rectifier or compounder, a manufacturing chemist or a manufacturer of perfumes for use in his manufacture, or to such other persons for such purposes as the Commissioners see fit to authorise for the purposes of this paragraph; or

(*f*) subject to such conditions as aforesaid, to spirits delivered for scientific purposes under section 8 above; or

(*g*) subject to such conditions as aforesaid, to imported Geneva, perfumed spirits or liqueurs; or

(*h*) to imported compounded spirits of any kind specified for the purposes of this paragraph in regulations made by the Commissioners; or

(*i*) to the supply of spirits of wine for the purpose of making medicines to registered medical practitioners, hospitals and persons entitled to carry on the business of a chemist and druggist; or

(*j*) to spirits compounded in warehouse in pursuance of warehousing regulations.

(2) For the purposes of this section, in the case of imported spirits, any period which is shown to the satisfaction of the Commissioners to have elapsed between the dates of manufacture and importation shall be treated as a period during which the spirits have been warehoused.

(3) If any person procures or attempts to procure the delivery of spirits in contravention of this section or contravenes or fails to comply with any regulation made thereunder, he shall be liable on summary conviction to a penalty of £100, and any spirits in respect of which the offence was committed shall be liable to forfeiture.

Restriction on transfer of British spirits in warehouse

32.—(1) No spirits in a distiller's warehouse may be transferred to a purchaser until the distiller has given such security for the payment of duty as the Commissioners may require, and any spirits so transferred shall not again be transferred while those spirits remain in that warehouse.

(2) Spirits manufactured in the United Kingdom chargeable with duty which has not been paid which are in any warehouse other than a distiller's warehouse shall not be transferred into the name of a purchaser until the purchaser produces to the officer in charge of the warehouse a written order for the delivery of the spirits signed by the person in whose name they are warehoused and countersigned by the occupier of the warehouse or a servant of his acting for him at the warehouse.

(3) Any spirits duly transferred in accordance with the provisions of this section shall be discharged from any liability under the Customs and Excise Acts 1979 in respect of the non-payment of any duty or penalty by the transferor.

Restrictions on use of certain goods relieved from spirits duty

33.—(1) If any person uses otherwise than for a medical or scientific purpose—

(*a*) any mixture which has on importation been relieved to any extent of the duty chargeable in respect of the spirits contained in it or used in its preparation or manufacture by reason of being a mixture which is recognised by the Commissioners as being used for medical purposes; or

(*b*) any article containing spirits which were exempted from duty under section 7 above; or

(*c*) any article manufactured or prepared from spirits in respect of which repayment of duty has been obtained under section 8 above; or

(*d*) any article in respect of which he has paid or agreed to pay a price fixed on the assumption that a repayment of duty will be obtained as mentioned in paragraph (*c*) above,

he shall, unless he has complied with the requirements specified in subsection (2) below, be liable on summary conviction to a penalty of three times the value of the mixture or article so used or £100, whichever is the greater, and any article in his possession in the preparation or manufacture of which the mixture or article has been used shall be liable to forfeiture.

(2) The requirements with which a person must comply to avoid incurring liability under subsection (1) above are that—

(*a*) he must obtain the consent of the Commissioners in writing to the use of the mixture or article otherwise than for a medical or scientific purpose; and

(*b*) he must pay to the Commissioners an amount equal to the difference between the duty charged on the mixture and the duty which would have been chargeable if it had not been a mixture recognised as mentioned in subsection (1) (*a*) above, or to the amount of the duty repaid or assumed to be repayable, as the case may be.

(3) The Commissioners may make regulations for the purpose of enforcing the provisions of this section.

(4) Regulations under subsection (3) above may in particular require any person carrying on any trade in which spirits, or mixtures or articles containing or prepared or manufactured with spirits, are in the opinion of the Commissioners likely to be or to have been used—

(*a*) to give and verify particulars of the materials which he is using or has used and of any such mixtures or articles which he has sold; and

(*b*) to produce any books of account or other documents of whatever nature relating to any such materials, mixtures or articles.

(5) If any person contravenes or fails to comply with any regulation made under subsection (3) above he shall be liable on summary conviction to a penalty of £100.

(6) In this section " mixture " includes a preparation and a compound, and any reference to a mixture or article includes a reference to any part thereof.

Prohibition of grogging

34.—(1) No person shall—

(*a*) subject any cask to any process for the purpose of extracting any spirits absorbed in the wood thereof; or

(*b*) have on his premises any cask which is being subjected to any such process or any spirits extracted from the wood of any cask.

(2) Any person contravening any provision of this section shall be liable on summary conviction to a penalty of £50.

(3) All spirits extracted contrary to this section and every cask which is being subjected to any such process or which, being upon premises upon which spirits so extracted are found, has been subjected to any such process shall be liable to forfeiture.

Returns as to importation, manufacture, sale or use of alcohols

35.—(1) The Commissioners may, in so far as it seems to them expedient so to do for the purposes of protecting the revenue arising from the duties on spirits, make regulations requiring importers, manufacturers, sellers or users of—

(*a*) the following alcohols, that is to say, methyl, propyl, butyl or amyl alcohol, or

(*b*) any of the isomeric forms of such alcohols,

to furnish returns containing such particulars as may be prescribed by the regulations in respect of the importation, manufacture, sale or use by any such persons of any of the articles specified in paragraphs (*a*) and (*b*) above.

(2) Provision may be made by any regulations under this section for requiring persons by whom and premises on which any such articles are manufactured to be registered.

(3) If any person contravenes or fails to comply with any regulation made under this section he shall be liable on summary conviction to a penalty of £25.

Part III

Beer

Charge of excise duty

Beer: charge of excise duty

36. There shall be charged on beer—

(*a*) imported into the United Kingdom; or

(*b*) brewed in the United Kingdom,

a duty of excise at the rate of £17·4240 for every 36 gallons, that rate being, however, increased in the case of beer of an original gravity exceeding 1030° by £0·5808 for each additional degree.

Computation of excise duty

Charge of duty on beer brewed in the United Kingdom: general

37.—(1) The quantity of worts and the gravity thereof by reference to which the duty on beer brewed in the United Kingdom is charged shall, according as is provided in sections 38 and 39 below, be either—

(*a*) the quantity and the original gravity of the worts produced; or

(*b*) the quantity of worts of an original gravity of 1055° deemed to have been brewed from the materials used.

(2) For the purpose of ascertaining the quantity of worts of an original gravity of 1055° deemed to have been brewed from the materials used, a brewer shall be deemed, subject to subsection (4) below, to have brewed 36 gallons of worts of that gravity for every unit of materials recorded by him in pursuance of regulations under section 49 or 53 below or used by him in any brewing.

(3) For the purposes of subsection (2) above "unit of materials" means—

(*a*) 84 pounds weight of malt or corn of any description; or

(*b*) 56 pounds weight of sugar; or

(*c*) a quantity of malt, corn and sugar, or of any two of those materials, which by relation to paragraph (*a*) and (*b*) above is the equivalent of either of the quantities mentioned in those paragraphs.

(4) In the case of a brewer for sale, where any materials used for brewing by the brewer are proved to the satisfaction of the Commissioners to be of such a description or nature that some deduction from the quantity deemed to have been brewed should be made, the Commissioners shall make such a deduction from that quantity as will in their opinion afford just relief to the brewer.

(5) In subsection (3) above "sugar" includes—

(*a*) any saccharine substance, extract or syrup;

(*b*) rice;

(*c*) flaked maize and any other description of corn which in the opinion of the Commissioners is prepared in a manner similar to flaked maize;

(*d*) any other material capable of being used in brewing except malt or corn;

and "corn" in that subsection means corn other than corn included in the foregoing definition of sugar.

(6) In the case of a brewer for sale, this section and section 38 below shall have effect as if priming and colouring solutions were worts.

Charge of duty on beer brewed in the United Kingdom: brewer for sale

38.—(1) The duty on beer brewed by a brewer for sale shall be charged and paid in accordance with the following provisions of this section.

(2) In respect of each brewing, duty shall first be charged by reference to the quantity and original gravity of the worts produced, as recorded by the brewer in pursuance of regulations made under section 49 below or as ascertained by the proper officer, whichever quantity and whichever gravity is the greater, less 6 per cent. of that quantity.

(3) There shall be ascertained in respect of each brewing—

(*a*) the quantity of worts of an original gravity of 1055° which is the equivalent of the worts produced; and

(*b*) the quantity of worts of that gravity deemed to have been brewed from the materials used in accordance with section 37 (2) above;

and if the quantity mentioned in paragraph (*b*) above, less 4 per cent., exceeds the quantity mentioned in paragraph (*a*) above duty shall in addition be charged on the excess, less 6 per cent. thereof.

(4) For the purposes of subsection (3) (*a*) above, the equivalent therein mentioned shall be taken to be the quantity of the worts produced—

(*a*) multiplied by the number, less 1000, of the degrees representing their original gravity; and

(*b*) divided by 55.

(5) If at any time while any worts are in the collecting or fermenting vessels at a brewery the original gravity of the worts is found to exceed by 5° or more the gravity recorded by the brewer in pursuance of regulations made under section 49 below or that ascertained by the proper officer, those worts may be deemed to be the produce of a fresh brewing and be charged with duty accordingly.

(6) Where beer has been prepared by a process of mixing by a brewer for sale and the aggregate amount charged in respect of duty on the several constituents of the beer exceeds the amount which would have been so charged on the mixture, the Commissioners may, subject to such conditions as they see fit to impose, remit or repay the excess.

(7) The conditions which may be imposed under subsection (6) above include conditions as to the method of computing the amount which would have been charged in respect of duty on the mixture and of ascertaining any matter by reference to which that amount is to be computed.

(8) Subject to subsection (9) below, the amount payable in respect of duty shall become due immediately duty is charged by the proper officer.

(9) The Commissioners may cause the charge to be made up at the close of each month in respect of all the brewings during that month, and, in that case, the aggregate of the quantities of worts produced and the aggregate of the quantities of worts deemed to have been brewed from the materials used shall be treated as worts produced or deemed to have been brewed in one brewing and, subject to subsection (10) below, the Commissioners may, if they think fit, allow payment of the duty to be deferred upon such terms as they see fit.

(10) Where the Commissioners allow payment of duty to be deferred under subsection (9) above the date of payment shall be—

(*a*) in the case of worts of beer to which this paragraph applies, such date as may be so allowed, not being later than the twenty-fifth day of the twelfth month after the month in which the duty was charged;

(*b*) in any other case, such date as may be so allowed, not being later than the twenty-fifth day of the month next following that in which the duty was charged.

(11) Paragraph (*a*) of subsection (10) above applies to worts of beer of an original gravity of or exceeding 1070° and worts of lager beer, being in each case beer kept for a period of at least three months on the entered premises in which it is brewed, but does not apply to priming or colouring solutions.

Charge of duty on beer brewed in the United Kingdom: private brewer

39.—(1) The duty on beer brewed by the holder of a limited licence to brew beer or of a corresponding licence in Northern Ireland shall be charged and paid in accordance with subsections (2) and (3) below.

(2) Duty shall be charged by reference to the quantity of worts of an original gravity of 1055° deemed to have been brewed from the materials used in accordance with section 37 (2) above, less 6 per cent. of that quantity.

(3) The charge of duty shall be made up and the amount payable in respect thereof shall be paid at such times as the Commissioners may appoint.

Charge of duty on imported beer

40.—(1) When any beer is imported or is removed into the United Kingdom from the Isle of Man, the importer of or person so removing the beer shall deliver to the proper office in such form and manner as the Commissioners may direct a declaration of the original gravity thereof; and, for the purpose of charging duty on the beer, the original gravity thereof shall be taken to be the original gravity stated in the declaration or the original gravity as ascertained by the proper officer, whichever is the higher.

(2) If the original gravity as ascertained by the proper officer exceeds by 2° or more that stated in the declaration, the beer shall be liable to forfeiture; and if the original gravity as so ascertained exceeds by 5° or more that stated in the declaration, the importer of or person removing the beer, and any agent of his by whom the declaration was made, shall each be liable on summary conviction to a penalty of £100.

Reliefs from excise duty

Exemption from duty of beer brewed for private consumption

41. The duty on beer brewed in the United Kingdom shall not be chargeable on beer brewed by a person who—

(*a*) brews only for his own domestic use or for consumption by farm labourers employed by him in the actual course of their labour or employment; and

(*b*) is not also a wholesaler or retailer of beer.

Drawback on exportation, removal to warehouse, shipment as stores, etc.

42.—(1) This section applies to—

(*a*) beer which has been brewed by a brewer for sale;

(*b*) beer which has been imported, or which has been removed into the United Kingdom from the Isle of Man.

(2) Subject to the provisions of this section and to such conditions as the Commissioners see fit to impose, drawback shall be allowable—

(*a*) on the removal by any person of any beer to which this section applies to an excise warehouse on the premises of a licensed producer of made-wine; or

(*b*) on the exportation or removal to the Isle of Man by any person of any such beer; or

(*c*) on the shipment as stores by any person of any such beer;

and shall also be allowable, subject as aforesaid, in the case of any beer to which this section applies which it is shown to the satisfaction of the Commissioners is being exported, removed or shipped as mentioned in paragraph (*b*) or (*c*) above as an ingredient of other goods.

(3) In the case of beer brewed in the United Kingdom, the person intending to remove, export or ship the beer shall produce to the proper officer a declaration made by the brewer in such form and manner as the Commissioners may direct stating the date upon which the beer was brewed and the original gravity thereof and that the proper duty has been charged thereon.

(4) In the case of beer brewed outside the United Kingdom, the person intending to remove, export or ship the beer shall produce to the proper officer in such form and manner as the Commissioners may direct a declaration that the proper duty has been charged and paid thereon.

(5) The amount of the drawback payable under this section in respect of any duty paid shall be calculated according to the rate of drawback applicable during the period of currency of the rate at which the duty was paid to like beer charged with that rate of duty during that period.

(6) Drawback under this section shall, where it is shown to the satisfaction of the Commissioners that duty has been paid, be allowed at the same rate as the rate at which the duty is charged; but as respects beer of an original gravity of less than 1030° the amount of drawback allowable shall not exceed the amount of the duty shown to the satisfaction of the Commissioners to have been paid.

Warehousing of beer for exportation, etc.

43.—(1) Subject to any regulations made by the Commissioners, a brewer for sale or a wholesaler of beer shall be entitled to warehouse in an excise warehouse for exportation or for use as stores any beer on which duty has been charged, and to add to the beer in warehouse finings for clarification or any other substance sanctioned by the Commissioners for the purpose of preparing the beer for exportation or for use as stores.

(2) Subject to subsection (3) below, where the duty charged in respect of any beer warehoused under this section has been paid, drawback shall be allowed and paid as if the beer had been exported at the time of the warehousing.

(3) Subsections (3) to (5) of section 42 above shall apply in relation to beer warehoused on drawback under this section as if the beer were being exported at the date of its warehousing.

(4) Drawback under this section shall, where it is shown to the satisfaction of the Commissioners that duty has been paid, be allowed at the same rate as the rate at which the duty is charged; but as respects beer of an original gravity of less than 1030° the amount of drawback allowable shall not exceed the amount of the duty shown to the satisfaction of the Commissioners to have been paid.

Remission or repayment of duty on beer used for purposes of research or experiment

44.—(1) Where it is proved to the satisfaction of the Commissioners that any beer brewed in the United Kingdom which is chargeable with duty is to be used only for the purposes of research or of experiments in brewing, the Commissioners may, if they think fit and subject to such conditions as they see fit to impose, remit or repay the duty chargeable on that beer.

(2) If any person contravenes or fails to comply with any condition imposed under subsection (1) above, then, in addition to any other penalty he may have incurred, he shall be liable on summary conviction to a penalty of £50.

Repayment of duty on beer used in the production or manufacture of other beverages, etc.

45. The Commissioners may by regulations provide for duty charged on beer which is used as an ingredient in the production or manufacture of—

(*a*) any beverage of an alcoholic strength not exceeding 2° of proof; or

(*b*) any such article (other than a beverage) as the Commissioners may determine having regard to the alcoholic content thereof,

to be repaid subject to such conditions as may be imposed by or under the regulations.

Remission or repayment of duty on spoilt beer

46.—(1) Where it is proved to the satisfaction of the Commissioners in the case of any brewer for sale that—

(*a*) any materials upon which a charge of duty has been made, or

(*b*) any worts or beer (whether manufactured by him or not),

have been destroyed or become spoilt or otherwise unfit for use by unavoidable accident while on the entered premises of the brewer and, in the case of any such substances which have become spoilt or unfit for use, have been destroyed with the permission and in the presence of the proper officer, the Commissioners shall remit or repay any duty charged or paid in respect thereof.

(2) Where it is shown to the satisfaction of the Commissioners that any beer which has been removed from the entered premises of a brewer for sale has accidentally become spoilt or otherwise unfit for use and, in the case of beer delivered to another person, has been returned to the brewer as so spoilt or unfit, the Commissioners shall, subject to compliance with such conditions as they may by regulations impose, remit or repay any duty charged or paid in respect of the beer.

(3) If any person contravenes or fails to comply with any regulation made under subsection (2) above, he shall be liable on summary conviction to a penalty of £50.

Brewing of beer

Licences to brew beer

47.—(1) No person shall brew beer unless he holds an excise licence under this section to brew beer or is exempted from holding one by subsection (5) below.

(2) An excise licence under this section may—

(*a*) authorise the person to whom it is granted to brew beer for sale; or

(*b*) authorise the person to whom it is granted to brew beer not for sale and only for his own domestic use or for consumption by any persons employed by him in the actual course of their employment;

and in this Act—

"brewer" means a person holding a licence under this section;

"brewer for sale" means a person holding a licence to brew beer for sale; and

"limited licence to brew beer" means a licence to brew beer as mentioned in paragraph (*b*) above.

(3) Any licence granted under this section shall expire on the 30th September next after it is granted.

(4) On every licence to brew beer there shall be charged an excise licence duty of the following amount, that is to say—

(*a*) in the case of a licence to brew beer for sale, £15·75;
(*b*) in the case of a limited licence to brew beer, £0·20.

(5) A licence to brew beer shall not be required—

(*a*) for the brewing of beer only for the brewer's own domestic use or for consumption by farm labourers employed by the brewer in the actual course of their labour or employment; or

(*b*) for the brewing of beer (with the authority of the Commissioners and subject to compliance with such conditions as they see fit to impose) solely for the purposes of research or of experiments in brewing;

but this subsection shall not exempt any person who is also a wholesaler or retailer of beer.

(6) The Commissioners may refuse to grant a licence under this section in respect of any premises on which, from the situation of those premises with respect to a distillery, they think it inexpedient to allow the brewing of beer.

(7) If any person, except as permitted by subsection (5) above, brews beer otherwise than under and in accordance with a licence under this section, he shall be liable on summary conviction to a penalty of £500 and all worts, beer and vessels, utensils and materials for brewing in his possession shall be liable to forfeiture.

Licence to use premises for adding solutions to beer

48.—(1) A brewer for sale shall not use for the purpose of adding priming or colouring solutions to beer any premises other than premises entered by him for the brewing of beer or an excise warehouse unless he holds an excise licence for that purpose under this section.

(2) A licence granted under this section shall expire on the 30th September next after it is granted.

(3) On any licence granted under this section there shall be charged an excise licence duty of £15·75.

(4) If any brewer for sale uses any premises for the purpose mentioned in subsection (1) above contrary to this section or otherwise than in accordance with any licence granted to him in respect thereof under this section, he shall be liable on summary conviction to a penalty of £100.

Power to regulate manufacture of beer by brewers for sale

49.—(1) The Commissioners may, with a view to the protection of the revenue, make regulations—

(*a*) regulating the manufacture of beer by brewers for sale;
(*b*) for securing the duties on beer brewed by brewers for sale;
(*c*) regulating with respect to brewers for sale the preparation, use, storage and removal of priming and colouring solutions;
(*d*) for enabling such solutions to be warehoused without payment of the duty chargeable on beer;
(*e*) regulating the addition of such solutions to beer at premises in respect of which a licence has been granted under section 48 above;
(*f*) for applying to such solutions, subject to such modifications and exceptions as may be specified in the regulations, any provision of, or of any instrument made under, any enactment relating to or containing provisions incidental to the duty on beer brewed in the United Kingdom.

(2) Any person contravening or failing to comply with any regulation made under this section shall be liable on summary conviction to a penalty

of £100, and any article in respect of which the offence was committed shall be liable to forfeiture.

Regulations as respects sugar kept by brewers for sale

50.—(1) The Commissioners may make regulations as respects—

(*a*) the receipt, storage, removal and disposal of sugar by brewers for sale;

(*b*) the books and other documents relating to sugar to be kept by brewers for sale;

(*c*) the powers of officers to inspect and take copies of any such book or other document and to take stock of the sugar in the possession of any brewer for sale.

(2) If any brewer for sale contravenes or fails to comply with any regulation made under this section he shall be liable on summary conviction to a penalty of £50.

(3) If, on taking stock at any time, the proper officer finds that the quantity of any description of sugar in the possession of any brewer for sale differs from the quantity of that description which ought to be in his possession according to any book or other document kept by him in pursuance of any regulations made under this section, then—

(*b*) if the quantity in his possession is less by more than 2 per cent. to be in his possession, the excess shall be liable to forfeiture;

(*b*) if the quantity in his possession is less by more than 2 per cent. than the quantity which ought to be in his possession, the deficiency above 2 per cent. shall, unless accounted for to the satisfaction of the Commissioners, be deemed to have been used in the brewing of beer without particulars thereof having been recorded in pursuance of regulations made under section 49 above, and duty shall be charged in respect thereof as if that deficiency had been so used.

(4) In this section " sugar " means sugar of any description and any saccharine substance, extract or syrup.

Power to require production of books by brewers for sale

51.—(1) Where the Commissioners are satisfied that it is necessary for the purpose of securing the collection of the duty on beer brewed in the United Kingdom, any person specially authorised in writing in that behalf by the Commissioners may require any brewer for sale to produce to that person any book or document whatsoever relating to his business as a brewer.

(2) If any brewer for sale fails to comply with any requirement imposed under subsection (1) above within a period of one hour he shall, on summary conviction, be liable to a penalty of £100 and to a further penalty of £10 for every day or part of a day thereafter during which the failure continues.

Offences by brewers for sale

52.—(1) If any brewer for sale conceals any worts or beer so as to prevent an officer from taking an account thereof, or after particulars of any worts or beer have been recorded by the brewer in pursuance of regulations made under section 49 above, mixes any sugar with those worts or with that beer so as to increase the quantity or the gravity or original gravity thereof, he shall be liable on summary conviction to a penalty of £100, and the worts or beer in respect of which the offence was committed shall be liable to forfeiture.

(2) If any brewer for sale adds to beer before it is delivered from his entered premises anything other than—

(*a*) water;

(*b*) finings for the purpose of clarification; or

(*c*) such other substances as may be sanctioned by the Commissioners,

he shall be liable on summary conviction to a penalty of £50.

(3) If any beer to which anything other than any substance falling within paragraph (*a*), (*b*) or (*c*) of subsection (2) above has been added is found in the possession of a brewer for sale, he shall be liable on summary conviction to a penalty of £50 and the beer shall be liable to forfeiture.

(4) In this section " sugar " means sugar of any description and any saccharine substance, extract or syrup, and includes any material capable of being used in brewing except malt or corn.

Special provisions as to holders of limited licences to brew beer

53.—(1) A limited licence to brew beer shall be granted in respect of one set of premises only, being premises occupied by the brewer.

For the purposes of this subsection the land and buildings within one curtilage, or any lands and buildings in Scotland with their parts and pertinents, shall be treated as one set of premises.

(2) A limited licence to brew beer granted to any person shall not be transferred to any other person except the widow, personal representatives, liquidator or trustee in bankruptcy of the person to whom the licence was granted.

(3) The Commissioners may make regulations prescribing the documents to be kept by holders of limited licences to brew beer and otherwise for securing any duty payable on, and safeguarding the revenue in connection with the brewing of, beer brewed by the holders of limited licences to brew beer.

(4) If any holder of a limited licence to brew beer—

(*a*) contravenes or fails to comply with any provision of this section or any regulation made thereunder; or

(*b*) sells or offers for sale any beer brewed by him,

he shall be liable on summary conviction to a penalty of £25.

(5) An officer may at all reasonable times enter and inspect any premises used for the purposes of brewing by the holder of a limited licence to brew beer and examine the vessels and utensils used by him for the purposes of brewing, and take samples of any worts, beer or materials for brewing in the possession of the brewer.

Part IV

Wine and Made-Wine

Wine: charge of excise duty

54.—(1) There shall be charged on wine—

(*a*) imported into the United Kingdom; or

(*b*) produced in the United Kingdom by a person who is required by subsection (2) below to be licensed to produce wine for sale,

a duty of excise at the rates shown in Schedule 1 to this Act and the duty shall, in so far as it is chargeable on wine produced in the United Kingdom, be charged and paid in accordance with regulations under section 56 below.

(2) Subject to subsection (4) below, a person who, on any premises in the United Kingdom, produces wine for sale must hold an excise licence under this subsection in respect of those premises for that purpose.

(3) On any licence under subsection (2) above there shall be charged an excise licence duty at the rate of £5·25 per annum.

(4) A person who, in warehouse, produces wine for sale by rendering it sparkling in accordance with warehousing regulations need not hold an excise licence under subsection (2) above in respect of those premises.

(5) If any person who is required by subsection (2) above to hold a licence under that subsection in respect of any premises produces wine on those premises without being the holder of a licence under that subsection in respect of those premises he shall be liable on summary conviction to a penalty of £500 and the wine and all vessels, utensils and materials for producing wine found in his possession shall be liable to forfeiture.

Made-wine: charge of excise duty

55.—(1) There shall be charged on made-wine—

(*a*) imported into the United Kingdom; or

(*b*) produced in the United Kingdom by a person who is required by subsection (2) below to be licensed to produce made-wine for sale,

a duty of excise at the rates shown in Schedule 2 to this Act and the duty shall, in so far as it is chargeable on made-wine produced in the United Kingdom, be charged and paid in accordance with regulations under section 56 below.

(2) Subject to subsections (4) and (5) below, a person who, on any premises in the United Kingdom, produces made-wine for sale must hold an excise licence under this subsection in respect of those premises for that purpose.

(3) On any licence under subsection (2) above there shall be charged an excise licence duty at the rate of £5·25 per annum.

(4) A person who, in warehouse, produces made-wine for sale by rendering it sparkling in accordance with warehousing regulations need not hold an excise licence under subsection (2) above in respect of those premises.

(5) A person need not hold an excise licence under subsection (2) above in respect of premises on which he produces made-wine for sale so long as all the following conditions are satisfied in relation to the production of made-wine by him on those premises, that is to say—

(*a*) the duty chargeable on each alcoholic ingredient used by him has become payable before he uses it;

(*b*) the ingredients he uses do not include cider or black beer;

(*c*) he does not increase by fermentation the alcoholic strength of any liquor or substance used by him; and

(*d*) he does not render any made-wine sparkling.

(6) If any person who is required by subsection (2) above to hold a licence under that subsection in respect of any premises produces made-wine on those premises without being the holder of a licence under that subsection in respect of those premises he shall be liable on summary conviction to a penalty of £500 and the made-wine and all vessels, utensils and materials for producing made-wine found in his possession shall be liable to forfeiture.

Power to regulate making of wine and made-wine and provide for charging duty thereon

56.—(1) The Commissioners may with a view to managing the duties on wine and made-wine produced in the United Kingdom for sale make regulations—

(*a*) regulating the production of wine and made-wine for sale, and the issue, renewal and cancellation of excise licences therefor;

(*b*) for determining the duty and the rates thereof and in that connection prescribing the method of charging the duty;

(*c*) prohibiting or restricting the use of wine in the production of made-wine;

(*d*) for securing and collecting the duty;

(*e*) for relieving wine or made-wine from the duty in such circumstances and to such extent as may be prescribed in the regulations.

(2) If any person contravenes or fails to comply with any regulation made under this section, he shall be liable on summary conviction to a penalty of £50 and any article in respect of which the offence was committed shall be liable to forfeiture.

Mixing of made-wine and spirits in warehouse

57. The Commissioners may, subject to such conditions as they see fit to impose, permit the mixing in an excise warehouse with made-wine (whether imported into or produced in the United Kingdom) of duty-free spirits in a proportion not exceeding 20 gallons of proof spirits to 100 gallons of made-wine, so, however, that the mixture shall not by virtue of this section be raised to a greater strength than 32° of proof.

Mixing of wine and spirits in warehouse

58.—(1) The Commissioners may, subject to such conditions as they see fit to impose, permit the mixing in an excise warehouse with wine (whether imported into or produced in the United Kingdom) of duty-free spirits in a proportion not exceeding 10 gallons of proof spirits to 100 gallons of wine, so, however, that the mixture shall not, except as provided by subsection (2) below, be raised to a greater strength than 40° of proof.

(2) If the Commissioners are satisfied that it is necessary for the preservation of the wine, they may permit the fortification of wine by virtue of this section for exportation only to a greater strength than 40° of proof.

Rendering imported wine or made-wine sparkling in warehouse

59.—(1) Neither imported wine nor imported made-wine shall be rendered sparkling, whether by aeration, fermentation or any other process, except in warehouse in accordance with warehousing regulations.

(2) Any person who contravenes subsection (1) above and any person who is concerned in such a contravention shall be liable on summary conviction to a penalty of £100.

(3) All imported wine and imported made-wine rendered or being rendered sparkling in contravention of subsection (1) above, and all machinery, utensils, bottles and materials (including wine or made-wine) used or intended to be used in any process for rendering any wine or made-wine sparkling in contravention of that subsection shall be liable to forfeiture.

Repayment of duty on imported wine or made-wine used in the production or manufacture of other beverages, etc.

60.—(1) The Commissioners may by regulations provide for duty charged on imported wine or imported made-wine which is used as an ingredient in the production or manufacture of—

(*a*) any beverage of an alcoholic strength not exceeding 2° of proof; or

(*b*) any such article (other than a beverage) as the Commissioners may determine having regard to the alcoholic content thereof,

to be repaid subject to such conditions as may be imposed by or under the regulations.

(2) The Commissioners may by regulations provide for duty charged on imported wine which is converted into vinegar to be repaid subject to such conditions as may be imposed by or under the regulations.

Remission or repayment of duty on spoilt wine or made-wine

61.—(1) Where it is shown to the satisfaction of the Commissioners that any wine or made-wine which has been removed from the entered premises of a licensed producer of wine or of made-wine has accidentally become spoilt or otherwise unfit for use and, in the case of wine or made-wine delivered to another person, has been returned to the producer as so spoilt or unfit, the Commissioners shall, subject to compliance with such conditions as they may by regulations impose, remit or repay any duty charged or paid in respect of the wine or made-wine.

(2) If any person contravenes or fails to comply with any regulation made under subsection (1) above, he shall be liable on summary conviction to a penalty of £50.

PART V

CIDER

Excise duty on cider

62.—(1) There shall be charged on cider—

(*a*) imported into the United Kingdom; or

(*b*) made in the United Kingdom by a person who is required by subsection (2) below to be registered as a maker of cider,

a duty of excise at the rate of £0·2420 a gallon.

(2) Subject to subsection (3) below, a person who, on any premises in the United Kingdom, makes cider for sale must be registered with the Commissioners in respect of those premises.

(3) The Treasury may by order made by statutory instrument provide for exempting from subsection (2) above makers of cider whose production does not exceed such limit as is specified in the order and who comply with such other conditions as may be so specified.

(4) If any person who is required by subsection (2) above to be registered in respect of any premises makes cider on those premises without being registered in respect of them, he shall be liable on summary conviction to a penalty of £500 and the cider and all vessels, utensils and materials for making cider found in his possession shall be liable to forfeiture.

(5) The Commissioners may with a view to managing the duty on cider made in the United Kingdom make regulations—

(*a*) regulating the making of cider for sale and the registration and cancellation of registration of makers of cider;

(*b*) for determining the duty and the rate thereof and in that connection prescribing the method of charging the duty;

(*c*) for securing and collecting the duty;

(*d*) for relieving cider from the duty in such circumstances and to such extent as may be prescribed in the regulations.

(6) If any person contravenes or fails to comply with any regulation made under subsection (5) above, he shall be liable on summary conviction to a penalty of £50 and any article in respect of which the offence was committed shall be liable to forfeiture.

Repayment of duty on imported cider used in the production or manufacture of other beverages, etc.

63. The Commissioners may by regulations provide for duty charged on imported cider which is used as an ingredient in the production or manufacture of—

(*a*) any beverage of an alcoholic strength not exceeding 2° of proof; or

(*b*) any such article (other than a beverage) as the Commissioners may determine having regard to the alcoholic content thereof,

to be repaid subject to such conditions as may be imposed by or under the regulations.

Remission or repayment of duty on spoilt cider

64.—(1) Where it is shown to the satisfaction of the Commissioners that any cider which has been removed from the entered premises of a registered maker of cider has accidentally become spoilt or otherwise unfit for use and, in the case of cider delivered to another person, has been returned to the maker as so spoilt or unfit, the Commissioners shall, subject to compliance with such conditions as they may by regulations impose, remit or repay any duty charged or paid in respect of the cider.

(2) If any person contravenes or fails to comply with any regulation made under subsection (1) above, he shall be liable on summary conviction to a penalty of £50.

Part VI

General Control Provisions

Sale of dutiable alcoholic liquors

Excise licence for dealing wholesale in certain alcoholic liquors

65.—(1) Subject to the provisions of this section, no person shall deal wholesale in any of the alcoholic liquors to which this section applies, that is to say, spirits, beer, wine and made-wine, unless he holds an excise licence for that purpose under this section in respect of that liquor.

(2) A licence granted under this section shall expire on the 30th June next after it is granted.

(3) On any licence granted under this section there shall be charged an excise licence duty of £5.

(4) Subject in the case of a distiller to section 27 (4) above, any alcoholic liquor to which this section applies which is the produce of a licenced manufacturer may be dealt in wholesale without an excise licence under this section—

(*a*) at the premises where it is manufactured; or

(*b*) if the liquor is supplied to the purchaser direct from the premises where it is manufactured, at any other place by the manufacturer or a servant or agent of his.

In this subsection "licensed manufacturer" means a distiller, rectifier, compounder, brewer for sale or licensed producer of wine or of made-wine.

(5) Without prejudice to subsection (4) above, an excise licence under this section as a wholesale dealer in spirits shall not, except with the permission of the Commissioners and subject to such conditions as they see fit to impose, be granted to a distiller in respect of any premises within 2 miles of his distillery.

(6) A person holding a licence under this section in respect of wine may deal wholesale at his licensed premises in made-wine as well as wine without taking out a further licence under this section.

(7) If, save as permitted by this section, any person deals wholesale in any alcoholic liquor to which this section applies otherwise than under and in accordance with a licence under this Act so authorising him he shall be liable on summary conviction to a penalty of £100.

(8) For the purposes of this section, dealing wholesale means the sale at any one time to any one person of quantities not less than the following, namely—

(*a*) in the case of spirits, wine or made-wine, 2 gallons or 1 case; or

(*b*) in the case of beer, $4\frac{1}{2}$ gallons or 2 cases.

Excise licence not required for sale of certain alcoholic liquors

66.—(1) Subject to subsection (2) below, an excise licence shall not be required for the sale wholesale of—

(*a*) any liquor which, whether made on the premises of a brewer for sale or elsewhere, is found on analysis of a sample thereof at any time to be of an original gravity not exceeding 1016° and of a strength not exceeding 2° of proof;

(*b*) perfumes;

(*c*) flavouring essences recognised by the Commissioners as not being intended for consumption as or with dutiable alcoholic liquor;

(*d*) spirits, wine or made-wine so medicated as to be, in the opinion of the Commissioners, intended for use as a medicine and not as a beverage.

(2) Subsection (1) (*a*) above shall not apply to Northern Ireland.

Power to regulate keeping of dutiable alcoholic liquors by wholesalers and retailers

67.—(1) The Commissioners may, with a view to the protection of the revenue, make regulations regulating the keeping of spirits, beer, wine, made-wine or cider respectively by wholesalers and retailers.

(2) If any person contravenes or fails to comply with any regulation made under this section, he shall be liable on summary conviction to a penalty of £100, and any liquor, container or utensil in respect of which the offence was committed shall be liable to forfeiture.

Penalty for excess in stock of wholesaler or retailer of spirits

68. If at any time on the taking of an account by an officer of the spirits in the stock or possession of a wholesaler or retailer of spirits the quantity of those spirits computed at proof is found to exceed the quantity which ought to be in his possession according to any stock book required under this Act to be kept by the wholesaler or retailer, the excess shall be liable to forfeiture and the wholesaler or retailer shall be liable on summary conviction to a penalty of double the duty on a like quantity of plain spirits at proof charged at the highest rate.

Miscellaneous provisions as to wholesalers and retailers of spirits

69.—(1) A wholesaler of spirits shall not carry on his business on any premises communicating otherwise than by a public roadway with any premises entered or used by a distiller or rectifier.

(2) Save with the permission of the Commissioners and subject to compliance with such conditions as they see fit to impose, a retailer of spirits shall not—

(*a*) carry on his business on any premises which are entered or used by a distiller or rectifier or which communicate otherwise than by a public roadway with any premises; or

(*b*) be concerned or interested in the business of a distiller or rectifier carried on upon any premises within 2 miles of any premises at which he sells spirits by retail.

(3) If any person contravenes or fails to comply with subsection (1) or (2) above or any condition imposed under subsection (2) above, he shall be liable on summary conviction to a penalty of £200.

(4) A retailer of spirits shall not, unless he is also a wholesaler of spirits, sell or send out spirits to a rectifier or to a wholesaler or retailer of spirits, nor shall he buy or receive spirits from another such retailer who is not also such a wholesaler; and if he contravenes or fails to comply with this subsection he shall be liable on summary conviction to a penalty of £50.

General offences in connection with sale of spirits

70.—(1) If any person hawks spirits, or, save as permitted by the Customs and Excise Acts 1979 or some other Act, sells or exposes for sale any spirits otherwise than on premises in respect of which he holds an excise licence as a wholesaler of spirits or a justice's licence (or in Scotland, a Scottish licence) authorising him to sell spirits, the spirits shall be liable to forfeiture and he shall be liable on summary conviction to a penalty of £100 and may be detained.

(2) If any person knowingly sells or delivers or causes to be sold or delivered any spirits in order that they may be unlawfully consumed or brought into home use, then, in addition to any other punishment he may have incurred, he shall be liable on summary conviction to a penalty of £100.

(3) If any person receives, buys or procures any spirits from a person not authorised to sell or deliver them, he shall be liable on summary conviction to a penalty of £100.

(4) If any spirits delivered in bottle from a warehouse for home use are sold by a wholesaler or retailer of spirits at a strength lower than that by reference to which the duty chargeable thereon was computed, he shall be liable on summary conviction to a penalty of £50.

(5) For the purposes of this section " Scottish licence " includes an off-licence in terms of Schedule 1 to the Licensing (Scotland) Act 1976.

Penalty for mis-describing liquor as spirits

71.—(1) If any person—

(*a*) for the purpose of selling any liquor, describes the liquor (whether in any notice or advertisement or on any label or wrapper, or in any other manner whatsoever) by any name or words such as to indicate that the liquor is, or is a substitute for, or bears any resemblance to, any description of spirits, or that the liquor is wine fortified or mixed with spirits or any description of spirits; or (*b*) sells, offers for sale, or has in his possession for the purpose of sale, any liquor so described,

that person shall be guilty of an offence under this section unless he proves that the duty chargeable on spirits has been paid in respect of not less than 97½ per cent. of the liquor.

(2) Notwithstanding anything in this section—

(*a*) the name " port " or " sherry " or the name of any other description of genuine wine; or

(*b*) a name which, before 4th May 1932, was used to describe a liquor containing vermouth and spirits, the quantity of vermouth being not less than the quantity of spirits computed at proof,

shall not, for the purposes of this section, be treated as being in itself such a description as to give such an indication as is mentioned in subsection (1) (*a*) above.

(3) Notwithstanding anything in this section, a person who has sold, offered for sale, or had in his possession for the purpose of sale, any liquor described only by any such name as is mentioned in subsection (2) (*a*) above shall not be guilty of an offence under this section by reason that the liquor has been described by some other person (not being the agent or servant of the first mentioned person) by that name in association with some other description such as to give such an indication as is mentioned in subsection (1) (*a*) above.

(4) Any person guilty of an offence under this section shall be liable on summary conviction to a penalty of £100; and on the conviction of a person under this section the court may direct that any liquor and other article by means of or in relation to which the offence has been committed shall be forfeited, and any liquor or other article so directed to be forfeited shall be destroyed or otherwise disposed of as the court may direct.

(5) Nothing in this section as it applies to England and Wales or Northern Ireland shall apply to any liquor which is prepared—

(*a*) on any premises in respect of which a justices' on-licence is in force; or

(*b*) in a registered club; or

(*c*) on any premises, or on board any aircraft, vessel or vehicle in the case of which, by virtue of section 199 (*c*) or (*d*) of the Licensing Act 1964, a justices' licence is not required,

for immediate consumption on those premises, in that club or on board that aircraft, vessel or vehicle, as the case may be.

(6) Nothing in this section as it applies to Scotland shall apply to any liquor which is prepared—

(*a*) on any premises in respect of which a Scottish licence is in force; or

(*b*) in any registered club; or

(*c*) in any theatre, or on board any aircraft, vessel or vehicle in the case of which, by virtue of section 138 (1) (*b*) or (*c*) of the Licensing (Scotland) Act 1976, a Scottish licence is not required,

for immediate consumption on those premises, in that club, at that theatre or on board that aircraft, vessel or vehicle, as the case may be.

Offences by wholesaler or retailer of beer

72.—(1) If any wholesaler or retailer of beer dilutes any beer or adds anything to beer other than finings for the purpose of clarification he shall be liable on summary conviction to a penalty of £50.

(2) If any beer which has been diluted or to which anything other

than finings for the purpose of clarification has been added is found in the possession of a wholesaler or retailer of beer he shall be liable on summary conviction to a penalty of £50 and the beer shall be liable to forfeiture.

(3) Subject to subsection (4) below, if a wholesaler or retailer of beer receives or has in his custody or possession any sugar of any description or any saccharine substance, extract or syrup, except such as he proves to be for domestic use, or any preparation for increasing the gravity of beer, he shall be liable on summary conviction to a penalty of £50 and the article in question shall be liable to forfeiture.

(4) Where a wholesaler or retailer of beer carries on upon the same premises the trade of a brewer for sale or of a grocer, subsection (3) above shall not apply to sugar and other preparations duly held by him in accordance with regulations made under section 50 above as a brewer for sale, or to sugar or syrup kept by him for sale in the ordinary course of his trade as a grocer.

Penalty for mis-describing substances as beer

73.—(1) If any person—

(*a*) for the purpose of selling any substance, describes the substance (whether in any notice or advertisement, or on any label, or in any other manner whatsoever) by any name or words such as to indicate that the substance is, or is a substitute for, or bears any resemblance to, beer or any description of beer; or

(*b*) sells, offers for sale or has in his possession for the purpose of sale any substance so decribed,

that person shall be guilty of an offence under this section unless he proves that the duty chargeable on beer has been paid in respect of the whole of the substance.

(2) Black beer the worts whereof before fementation were of a specific gravity of 1200° or more is not a substance to which this section applies; and for the purposes of this section the name " black beer " shall not in itself be taken to be such a description as to give such an indication as is mentioned in subsection (1) (*a*) above.

(3) For the purposes of this section the name " ginger beer " or " ginger ale " shall not in itself be taken to be such a description as to give such an indication as is mentioned in subsection (1) (*a*) above.

(4) Any person guilty of an offence under this section shall be liable on summary conviction to a penalty of £100; and on the conviction of a person under this section the court may order that any article by means of or in relation to which the offence has been committed shall be forfeited, and any article so directed to be forfeited shall be destroyed or otherwise disposed of as the court may direct.

Liquor to be deemed wine or spirits

74. For the purposes of this Act, as against any person selling or offering for sale the liquor in question—

(*a*) any liquor sold or offered for sale as wine or under the name by which any wine is usually designated or known shall be deemed to be wine; and

(*b*) any fermented liquor which is of a strength exceeding 40° of proof, not being imported wine delivered for home use in that state on which the appropriate duty has been duly paid, shall be deemed to be spirits.

Paragraph (*a*) above is without prejudice to any liability under section 71 above.

Methylated spirits

Licence or authority to manufacture and deal wholesale in methylated spirits

75.—(1) The Commissioners may authorise any distiller, rectifier or compounder to methylate spirits, and any person so authorised is referred to in this Act as an " authorised methylator ".

(2) No person other than an authorised methylator shall methylate spirits or deal wholesale in methylated spirits unless he holds an excise licence as a methylator under this section.

(3) A licence granted under this section shall expire on the 30th September next after it is granted.

(4) On any licence granted under this section there shall be charged an excise licence duty of £10·50.

(5) Any person who, not being an authorised methylator, methylates spirits otherwise than under and in accordance with a licence under this section shall be liable on summary conviction to a penalty of £50.

(6) The Commissioners may at any time revoke or suspend any authorisation or licence granted under this section.

(7) For the purposes of this section, dealing wholesale means the sale at any one time to any one person of a quantity of methylated spirits of not less than 5 gallons or such smaller quantity as the Commissioners may by regulations specify.

Licence to retail methylated spirits

76.—(1) No person shall sell methylated spirits by retail unless he holds an excise licence for that purpose under this section.

(2) A licence granted under this section shall expire on the 30th September next after it is granted.

(3) On any licence granted under this section there shall be charged an excise licence duty of £0·50.

(4) A licence under this section shall not be granted—

(*a*) to a distiller, rectifier or compounder; or

(*b*) in England, Wales or Northern Ireland, to a person holding a justice's on-licence in respect of spirits, beer, wine or made-wine; or

(*c*) in Scotland—

(i) to a person holding a Scottish licence in respect of spirits, beer, wine or made-wine, or

(ii) to any other person except in accordance with the Methylated Spirits (Sale by Retail) (Scotland) Act 1937.

(5) For the purposes of this section, sale by retail means the sale at any one time to any one person of a quantity of methylated spirits not exceeding 4 gallons.

Power to make regulations relating to methylated spirits

77.—(1) The Commissioners may with a view to the protection of the revenue make regulations—

(*a*) regulating the methylation of spirits and the supply, storage, removal, sale, delivery, receipt, use and exportation or shipment as stores of methylated spirits;

(*b*) prescribing the spirits which may be used, and the substances which may be mixed therewith, for methylation;

(*c*) permitting spirits to be methylated in warehouse;

(*d*) permitting the sale without a licence of such methylated spirits as may be specified in the regulations;

(*e*) regulating the importation, receipt, removal, storage and use of spirits for methylation;

(*f*) regulating the storage and removal of substances to be used in methylating spirits;

(*g*) prescribing the manner in which account is to be kept of stocks of methylated spirits in the possession of authorised or licensed methylators and of retailers of methylated spirits;

(*h*) for securing any duty chargeable in respect of methylated spirits of any class.

(2) Different regulations may be made under this section with respect to different classes of methylated spirits or different kinds of methylated spirits of any class.

(3) If any person contravenes or fails to comply with any regulation under this section, he shall be liable on summary conviction to a penalty of £100.

(4) If, save as permitted by any regulation under this section, any person sells methylated spirits otherwise than under and in accordance with a licence under section 75 or 76 above, he shall be liable on summary conviction to a penalty of £50.

(5) Any spirits or methylated spirits in respect of which an offence under subsection (3) or (4) above is committed shall be liable to forfeiture.

(6) Nothing in any regulations made under this section shall prejudice the operation of the Methylated Spirits (Sale by Retail) (Scotland) Act 1937.

Additional provisions relating to methylated spirits

78.—(1) If, at any time when an account is taken and a balance struck of the quantity of any kind of methylated spirits in the possession of an authorised or licensed methylator, that quantity computed at proof differs from the quantity so computed which ought to be in his possession according to any accounts required by regulations made under section 77 above to be kept thereof, then, subject to subsection (2) below—

(*a*) if the former quantity exceeds the latter, the excess, or such part thereof as the Commissioners may determine, shall be liable to forfeiture;

(*b*) if the former quantity is less than the latter, the methylator shall on demand by the Commissioners pay on the deficiency or such part thereof as the Commissioners may specify the duty payable on spirits.

(2) Subsection (1) above shall not apply if the excess is not more than 1 per cent. or the deficiency is not more than 2 per cent. of the aggregate computed at proof of—

(*a*) the balance struck when an account was last taken; and

(*b*) any quantity which has since been lawfully added to the methylator's stock.

(3) If any person authorised by regulations made under section 77 above to supply any kind of methylated spirits knowingly supplies such spirits to any person not authorised by those regulations to receive them, he shall, without prejudice to any penalty he may have incurred, pay thereon the duty payable on spirits.

(4) If any person other than an authorised or licensed methylator has in his possession any methylated spirits obtained otherwise than from a person authorised by regulations under the said section 77 to supply

those spirits, he shall be liable on summary conviction to a penalty of £100 and the methylated spirits shall be liable to forfeiture.

Inspection of premises, etc.

79. Without prejudice to any other power conferred by the Customs and Excise Acts 1979, an officer may in the daytime enter and inspect the premises of any person authorised by regulations made under section 77 above to receive methylated spirits, and may inspect and examine any methylated spirits thereon and take samples of any methylated spirits or of any goods containing methylated spirits, paying a reasonable price for each sample.

Prohibition of use of methylated spirits, etc. as a beverage or medicine

80.—(1) If any person—

(*a*) prepares or attempts to prepare any liquor to which this section applies for use as a beverage or as a mixture with a beverage; or

(*b*) sells any such liquor, whether so prepared or not, as a beverage or mixed with a beverage; or

(*c*) uses any such liquor or any derivative thereof in the preparation of any article capable of being used wholly or partially as a beverage or internally as a medicine; or

(*d*) sells or has in his possession any such article in the preparation of which any such liquor or any derivative thereof has been used; or

(*e*) except as permitted by the Commissioners and in accordance with any conditions imposed by them, purifies or attempts to purify any such liquor or, after any such liquor has once been used, recovers or attempts to recover the spirit or alcohol contained therein by distillation or condensation or in any other manner,

he shall be liable on summary conviction to a penalty of £100 and the liquor in respect of which the offence was committed shall be liable to forfeiture.

(2) Nothing in this section shall prohibit the use of any liquor to which this section applies or any derivative thereof—

(*a*) in the preparation for use as a medicine of sulphuric ether, chloroform, or any other article which the Commissioners may by order specify; or

(*b*) in the making for external use only of any article sold or supplied in accordance with regulations made by the Commissioners under section 77 above; or

(*c*) in any art or manufacture,

or the sale or possession of any article permitted to be prepared or made by virtue of paragraph (*a*) or (*b*) above where the article is sold or possessed for use as mentioned in that paragraph.

(3) The liquors to which this section applies are methylated spirits, methyl alcohol, and any mixture containing methylated spirits or methyl alcohol.

Still licences

Licence for keeping still otherwise than as a distiller, etc.

81.—(1) Subject to the provisions of this section, no person shall keep or use a still otherwise than as a distiller, rectifier, or compounder unless he holds an excise licence for that purpose under this section.

(2) A licence granted under this section shall expire on the 5th July next after it is granted.

(3) On any licence granted under this section there shall be charged an excise licence duty of £0·50.

(4) The Commissioners may permit, subject to such conditions as they see fit to impose, the keeping and use without a licence under this section of a still—

(*a*) kept by a person who makes or keeps stills solely for the purpose of sale; or

(*b*) kept or used for experimental, analytical or scientific purposes; or

(*c*) kept or used for the manufacture of any article other than spirits.

(5) If any person required to hold a licence under this section keeps or uses a still otherwise than under and in accordance with such a licence, he shall be liable on summary conviction to a penalty of £100 and the still shall be liable to forfeiture.

(6) If any person hoding a licence under this section is convicted of any offence whatever in relation to methylated spirits, the Commissioner may suspend or revoke his licence.

Power to make regulations with respect to stills

82.—(1) The Commissioners may, with a view to the protection of the revenue, make regulations—

(*a*) regulating the keeping and use of stills by persons other than distillers or rectifiers;

(*b*) regulating the manufacture of stills;

(*c*) prohibiting, except in such cases and upon such conditions as may be prescribed by the regulations, the keeping or use by persons other than distillers or rectifiers of stills of greater capacity than 50 gallons;

(*d*) regulating the removal of stills or parts thereof.

(2) If any person contravenes or fails to comply with any regulation made under this section he shall be liable on summary conviction to a penalty of £100 and any still or part thereof in respect of which the offence was committed shall be liable to forfeiture.

Power of entry on premises of person keeping or using still

83.—(1) Without prejudice to any other power conferred by the Customs and Excise Acts 1979, an officer may, subject to subsection (2) below, at any time enter upon the premises of any person licensed or permitted to keep a still under section 81 above and examine any still or retort kept or used by that person.

(2) No officer shall exercise the powers conferred on him by subsection (1) above by night unless he is accompanied by a constable.

Relief from, and payment by instalments of, liquor licence duties

Reduced duty on excise licence for sale of spirits for medical purposes, etc.

84.—(1) Any manufacturing or wholesale chemist and druggist who—

(*a*) requires an excise licence for the purposes only of selling spirits of wine wholesale for medicinal purposes to registered medical practitioners, duly registered pharmaceutical chemists, chemists and druggists or persons requiring the spirits for use for scientific purposes in any laboratory; and

(*b*) undertakes not to sell spirits otherwise than for those purposes and to those persons, may obtain that licence on payment of a reduced excise licence duty of £2.

(2) The Commissioners may attach such conditions to any licence granted on payment of a reduced duty under this section as they think expedient for the protection of the revenue.

(3) If any person holding a licence granted on payment of a reduced duty under this section sells spirits in any manner contrary to his undertaking or to the conditions attached to his licence he shall be liable on summary conviction to a penalty of £50.

Reduced duty on part-year licences generally

85.—(1) This section applies to any excise licence under this Act other than—

(*a*) a licence to which section 86 below applies; and

(*b*) a limited licence to brew beer.

(2) Where an excise licence to which this section applies is granted after the commencement of the licence year—

(*a*) to a person who has not within the 2 years immediately preceding held a similar licence; or

(*b*) in respect of premises in respect of which the person to whom the licence is granted has not within that period held a similar licence,

the proper officer may grant the licence on payment of such sum as bears to the duty payable thereon apart from this section the same proportion as the period for which the licence will be in force bears to a year.

Reduced duty on certain part-year licences

86.—(1) This section applies to an excise licence granted under the following provisions of this Act for the following purposes respectively, that is to say—

(*a*) under section 65, to deal wholesale in any alcoholic liquor to which that section applies;

(*b*) under section 75, to manufacture and deal wholesale in methylated spirits;

(*c*) under section 76, to sell methylated spirits by retail;

(*d*) under section 81, to keep or use a still.

(2) Subject to subsection (3) below, where any licence to which this section applies is granted more than 3 months after the commencement of the licence year—

(*a*) to a person who has not within the 2 years immediately preceding held a similar licence; or

(*b*) in respect of premises in respect of which the person to whom the licence is granted has not within that period held a similar licence,

the proper officer may grant the licence upon payment of such proportion of the full duty chargeable thereon as is specified in the following table in relation to the month during which the licence is taken out, that is to say—

Month from the commencement of the licence year	*Proportion of full duty*
4th to 6th	$\frac{3}{4}$
7th to 9th	$\frac{1}{2}$
10th to 12th	$\frac{1}{4}$

(3) In its application to a wholesaler who has been granted relief under section 87 (3) below on his trade being temporarily discontinued, subsection (2) above shall apply as respects the grant, on his first

resuming his trade thereafter, of his new licence as a wholesaler as if paragraphs (*a*) and (*b*) thereof were omitted.

Relief from duty on discontinuance of trade

87.—(1) Where a distiller, rectifier, compounder, brewer for sale, beer-primer, producer of wine or of made-wine or a wholesaler satisfies the Commissioners that his trade has been permanently discontinued he shall, subject to subsections (2) and (4) below, be entitled to surrender his licence and obtain relief from excise duty in respect of the period of the licence unexpired at the date when the trade was discontinued.

In this subsection " beer-primer " means a person who holds a licence under section 48 above.

(2) No relief shall be granted under subsection (1) above where the trade has been discontinued owing to the disqualification either of the premises or of the trader by reason of the conviction of the trader of some offence.

(3) Where a wholesaler satisfies the Commissioners that his trade has been temporarily discontinued—

(*a*) by reason of the premises in respect of which his licence was granted having been destroyed or seriously damaged or closed with a view to their demolition or alteration; or

(*b*) by reason of any circumstances directly or indirectly attributable to any war in which Her Majesty may be or have been engaged; or

(*c*) in Great Britain, by reason of the compulsory acquisition or the proposed compulsory acquisition of the said premises;

he shall, subject to subsection (4) below, on making application as provided in subsection (5) below and surrendering his licence, be entitled to relief from excise licence duty in respect of the period of the licence unexpired at the date when the trade was discontinued.

In this subsection, " compulsory acquisition " includes acquisition by agreement by any authority or persons for a purpose for which the authority or persons could be authorised to acquire the premises compulsorily.

(4) A wholesaler shall not be entitled to relief from duty under subsection (1) or (3) above unless his trade is discontinued within 9 months after the commencement of the licence year.

(5) An application for relief from duty under subsection (3) above shall be made to the Commissioners within one month after the discontinuance of the trade or within such longer period as the Commissioners may in any special case allow, and before making the application the licence holder shall give notice to the registered owner of the licensed premises of his intention to make it.

(6) Relief from excise licence duty under this section shall be granted by the Commissioners by repayment or, in so far as the duty has not been paid, by remission of the appropriate amount of duty.

(7) The appropriate amount of duty is, except where the relief is due to a wholesaler, such part of the full amount of duty for a year as bears to that amount the same proportion as the period in respect of which the licence holder is entitled to relief bears to a year.

(8) Where the relief is due to a wholesaler, the appropriate amount of duty is such proportion of the full amount of duty for the year as is specified in the following table in relation to the month during which the trade is discontinued, that is to say—

Month from the commencement of the licence year	*Proportion of full duty*
1st to 3rd	$\frac{3}{4}$
4th to 6th	$\frac{1}{2}$
7th to 9th	$\frac{1}{4}$

Payment of licence duty in two instalments

88.—(1) Where the excise licence duty payable by any person on the grant to him of a licence as a distiller, rectifier, compounder, brewer, producer of wine or of made-wine or as a wholesaler, or the aggregate amount of the duties payable on two or more such licences granted to him in respect of the same premises, amounts to not less than £20, the licence or licences may, at the option of that person, be granted upon payment of half only of the duty or aggregate amount so payable.

(2) Where a licence is granted in pursuance of subsection (1) above upon payment of half only of the duty or aggregate amount of the duty, the second half of that duty or amount shall be paid immediately after the expiration of 6 months from the commencement of the appropriate licence year, or on 1st February next following the grant of the licence or licences, whichever is the earlier.

(3) If default is made in payment of the second half of the duty or amount payable under subsection (2) above the licence or licences shall be of no effect so long as the default continues.

(4) Any sum remaining unpaid in any case in respect of the said second half may be recovered either as a debt due to the Crown or by distress on the licensed premises, and the proper officer may, subject to subsection (5) below, for the purpose of such distress by warrant signed by him authorise any person to distrain upon the premises and to sell any thing so distrained by public auction after giving 6 days' notice of the sale.

(5) A distress shall not be levied under subsection (4) above unless notice in writing requiring the payment of the sum unpaid has been served on the holder of the licence or licences by leaving the notice at the premises or by sending it by post addressed to him at those premises.

(6) The proceeds of any such sale shall be applied in or towards payment of the costs and expenses of the distress and sale and the payment of the sum due, and the surplus, if any, shall be paid to the holder of the licence or licences.

(7) In the application of this section to Scotland, any reference to distress, or to levying distress, shall be construed as a reference to poinding.

Part VII

Miscellaneous

Saving for certain privileges relating to sale of wine

Saving for Cambridge University and Vintners company

89. Nothing in this Act shall affect—

(*a*) any privilege in relation to the sale of wine enjoyed at 1st January 1953 by the University of Cambridge, or the chancellor, masters or scholars thereof, or by any person to whom that privilege has been transferred in pursuance of any Act;

(*b*) the exemption from the obligation to take out an excise licence for the sale of wine enjoyed at that date by the Company of the master, wardens and commonalty of Vintners of the City of London.

But—

(i) the exemption in paragraph (*b*) above shall not extend to freemen of the said company who have obtained the freedom by redemption only;

(ii) no freeman of the said company shall be entitled to that exemption in respect of more than one set of premises at any one time; and

(iii) no person shall be entitled to that exemption unless he previously makes entry of the premises on which he intends to sell wine.

General

Regulations

90.—(1) Any power to make regulations conferred by this Act shall be exercisable by statutory instrument.

(2) A statutory instrument containing regulations under this Act shall be subject to annulment in pursuance of a resolution of either House of Parliament.

Directions

91. Directions given under any provision of this Act may make different provision for different circumstances and may be varied or revoked by subsequent directions thereunder.

Consequential amendments, repeals and saving and transitional provisions

92.—(1) The enactments specified in Schedule 3 to this Act shall be amended in accordance with the provisions of that Schedule.

(2) The enactments specified in Parts I and II of Schedule 4 to this Act are hereby repealed to the extent specified in the third column of that Schedule and the instrument specified in Part III of that Schedule is hereby revoked to the extent so specified.

(3) Any provision of this Act relating to anything done or required or authorised to be done under or by reference to that provision or any other provision of this Act shall have effect as if any reference to that provision, or that other provision, as the case may be, included a reference to the corresponding provision of the enactments repealed by this Act.

(4) Where an offence has been committed under section 129 of the Customs and Excise Act 1952 proceedings may be taken under section 51 of this Act in respect of the continuance of the offence under section 129 after the commencement of this Act in the same manner as if the offence had been committed under section 51 of this Act.

(5) Where an offence has been committed under section 102 of the Customs and Excise Act 1952 before the commencement of this Act subsection (4) of section 21 of this Act shall apply on a conviction of an offence under that section as it would apply had the earlier offence been committed under section 21.

(6) The repeal by this Act of sections 103 and 112 of the Customs and Excise Act 1952 shall not affect the right to drawback under section 103 in respect of medicinal spirits in respect of which a repayment of duty had been made before 8th August 1972 or the right to a repayment of duty under section 112 in respect of spirits used for medical purposes

before that date (being the date on which the amendments made in those provisions by section 57 of the Finance Act 1972 came into operation).

(7) The repeal by this Act of section 243 of the Customs and Excise Act 1952 and section 3 (4) of the Finance Act 1960 shall not affect the operation of the saving in relation to spirits distilled before 1st August 1969 contained in paragraph 1 of Schedule 7 to the Finance Act 1969 (which repealed subsection (1 (*b*) of that section except in relation to spirits distilled before that date).

(8) Nothing in this section shall be taken as prejudicing the operation of sections 15 to 17 of the Interpretation Act 1978 (which relate to the effect of repeals).

Citation and commencement

93.—(1) This Act may be cited as the Alcoholic Liquor Duties Act 1979 and is included in the Acts which may be cited as the Customs and Excise Acts 1979.

(2) This Act shall come into operation on 1st April 1979.

SCHEDULES

Section 54

SCHEDULE 1

WINE: RATES OF DUTY

Description of wine (in strengths measured by reference to the following percentages of alcohol by volume at a temperature of 20° C.)	Rates of duty (per gallon)
	£
Wine of an alcoholic strength—	
not exceeding 15 per cent.	3·2500
exceeding 15 but not exceeding 18 per cent.	3·7500
exceeding 18 but not exceeding 22 per cent.	4·4150
exceeding 22 per cent.	4·4150 plus £0·4700 for every 1 per cent. or part of 1 per cent. in excess of 22 per cent.;
	each of the above rates of duty being, in the case of sparkling wine, increased by £0·7150 per gallon.

Section 55

SCHEDULE 2

MADE-WINE: RATES OF DUTY

Description of made-wine (in strengths measured by reference to the following percentages of alcohol by volume at a temperature of 20° C.)	Rates of duty (per gallon)
	£
Made-wine of an alcoholic strength—	
not exceeding 10 per cent.	2·1100
exceeding 10 but not exceeding 15 per cent.	3·1600
exceeding 15 but not exceeding 18 per cent.	3·4750
exceeding 18 per cent.	3·4750 plus £0·4700 for every 1 per cent. or part of 1 per cent. in excess of 18 per cent.;
	each of the above rates of duty being, in the case of sparkling made-wine, increased by £0·3300 per gallon.

Section 92 (1)

SCHEDULE 3

CONSEQUENTIAL AMENDMENTS

Food and Drugs Act 1955

1. In section 3 (4) of the Food and Drugs Act 1955, for the words " section one hundred and sixty-one of the Customs and Excise Act 1952 " there shall be substituted the words " section 70 of the Alcoholic Liquor Duties Act 1979."

Food and Drugs (Scotland) Act 1956

2. In section 3 (4) of the Food and Drugs (Scotland) Act 1956, for the words " section one hundred and sixty-one of the Customs and Excise Act 1952 " there shall be substituted the words " section 70 of the Alcoholic Liquor Duties Act 1979 ".

Weights and Measures Act 1963

3. In section 58 of the Weights and Measures Act 1963, in the definition of " intoxicating liquor," for the words " has the same meaning as for the purposes of the Customs and Excise Act 1952 " there shall be substituted the words " means spirits, beer, wine, made-wine or cider as defined in section 1 of the Alcoholic Liquor Duties Act 1979; ".

4. In Part VI of Schedule 4 to the Weights and Measures Act 1963, for paragraph 1 there shall be substituted the following paragraph—

" 1. In this Part of this Schedule—

(*a*) the expressions " beer " and " cider " have the same meanings respectively as in the Alcoholic Liquor Duties Act 1979;

(*b*) the expression " wine " means imported wine; and

(*c*) the expression " British wine " means any liquor which is made from fruit and sugar or from fruit or sugar mixed with any other material and which has undergone a process of fermentation in the manufacture thereof, and includes British wines, made wines, mead and metheglin."

Licensing Act 1964

5.—(1) The Licensing Act 1964 shall be amended as provided in this paragraph.

(2) In section 181, for the words " dealer's licence under section 146 of the Customs and Excise Act 1952 " there shall be substituted the words " wholesaler's licence under section 65 of the Alcoholic Liquor Duties Act 1979 " and for the words " dealer's licence " in the other two places where they occur there shall be substituted the words " wholesaler's licence ".

(3) In section 201 (1)—

(a) in the definition of " sale by retail," for the words following " section " there shall be substituted the words " 4 (4) of the Alcoholic Liquor Duties Act 1979 "; and

(b) in the appropriate place in alphabetical order there shall be inserted the following definition (in place of the definition repealed by this Act)—

" wine " means wine or made-wine as defined in section 1 of the Alcoholic Liquor Duties Act 1979.

(4) In Part II of Schedule 9, in paragraph 4, for the words " section 307 of the Customs and Excise Act 1952) " there shall be substituted the words " section 1 of the Alcoholic Liquor Duties Act 1979)".

Weights and Measures Act (Northern Ireland) 1967

6. In section 41 of the Weights and Measures Act (Northern Ireland) 1967, in the definition of " intoxicating liquor ", for the words " has the same meaning as for the purposes of the Customs and Excise Act 1952 " there shall be substituted the words " means spirits, beer, wine, made-wine or cider as defined in section 1 of the Alcoholic Liquor Duties Act 1979; ".

7. In Part VI of Schedule 2 to the Weights and Measures Act (Northern Ireland) 1967, for paragraph 1 there shall be substituted the following paragraph—

" 1. In this Part of this Schedule—

(a) the expressions " beer " and " cider " have the same meanings respectively as in the Alcoholic Liquor Duties Act 1979;

(b) the expression " wine " means imported wine; and

(c) the expression " British wine " means any liquor which is made from fruit and sugar or from fruit or sugar mixed with any other material and which has undergone a process of fermentation in the manufacture thereof, and includes British wines, made wines, mead and metheglin."

Licensing Act (Northern Ireland) 1971

8.—(1) The Licensing Act (Northern Ireland) 1971 shall be amended as provided in this paragraph.

(2) In section 76 (1), for the words " section 146 of the Customs and Excise Act 1952 " there shall be substituted the words " section 65 of the Alcoholic Liquor Duties Act 1979 ".

(3) In section 76 (2) (b), for the words " section 146 or 167 " there shall be substituted the words " section 65 or 84 " and for the words " Act of 1952 " there shall be substituted the words " Act of 1979 ".

(4) In section 84 (5), for the words " section 148 (4) of the Customs and Excise Act 1952 " there shall be substituted the words " section 4 (4) of the Alcoholic Liquor Duties Act 1979 ".

(5) In section 85 (c), for the words " section 167 of the Customs and Excise Act 1952 " there shall be substituted the words " section 84 of the Alcoholic Liquor Duties Act 1979 ".

Licensing (Scotland) Act 1976

9. In section 139 (1) of the Licensing (Scotland) Act 1976 the following amendments shall be made, that is to say—

(a) in the definitions of " made-wine " and " wine ", for the words " Customs and Excise Act 1952 " there shall be substituted the words " section 1 of the Alcoholic Liquor Duties Act 1979 ";

(b) in the definition of " wholesaler's excise licence ", for the words from " section 146 " to the end, there shall be substituted the words " section 65 of the Alcoholic Liquor Duties Act 1979 ".

Section 92 (2)

SCHEDULE 4

REPEALS

PART I

ENACTMENTS OF THE PARLIAMENT OF THE UNITED KINGDOM

Chapter	Short title	Extent of repeal
53 & 54 Vict. c. 8.	The Customs and Inland Revenue Act 1890.	Section 31 (2).
15 & 16 Geo. 6 & 1 Eliz. 2, c. 44.	The Customs and Excise Act 1952.	Part IV. Sections 226 to 228. Section 237. Sections 241 to 243. Section 263 (3) to (5). In section 307 (1), the definitions of "authorised methylator", "beer", "beer-primer", "brewer" and "brewer for sale", "British compounded spirits", "British spirits", "case", "cider", "compounder", "dealer", "distiller" and "distillery", "distiller's warehouse", "gravity" and "original gravity", "intoxicating liquor", "justices' licence" and "justices' on-licence", "licensed methylator", "limited licence to brew beer", "made-wine", "methylated spirits", "producer of wine", "producer of made-wine", "proof", "rectifier", "registered club", "retail", "retailer", "spirits", "spirits of wine" "wholesale" and "wine". In section 315, paragraphs (*c*) and (*d*). In Schedule 10, paragraph 15.
1 & 2 Eliz. 2. c. 34.	The Finance Act 1953.	Section 2.
6 & 7 Eliz. 2. c. 56.	The Finance Act 1958.	Section 6.
7 & 8 Eliz. 2. c. 58.	The Finance Act 1959.	Section 2 (1) and (5). Section 3 (2), (3), (4) and (5).
8 & 9 Eliz. 2. c. 44.	The Finance Act 1960.	Section 3. Schedule 1.
1963 c. 25.	The Finance Act 1963.	Section 6. Schedule 2.
1963 c. 31.	The Weights and Measures Act 1963.	Section 59. In Schedule 10, paragraph 1 (*d*).
1964 c. 49.	The Finance Act 1964.	Section 1 (5). Section 2 (5) and (6).
1966 c. 18.	The Finance Act 1966.	In Schedule 2, in paragraph 1, the words from "section 107 (1)" to "spirits)" and paragraph 2.
1967 c. 54.	The Finance Act 1967.	Section 1 (5). Section 4 except, in subsection (5), paragraphs (*a*) (i) and (v). Section 6. In Schedule 5, paragraphs 2, 3 and 4. In Schedule 6, paragraphs 1, 3, 4, 7, 8, 9, 10 and 11. In Schedule 9, paragraphs 1 to 6.
1968 c. 44.	The Finance Act 1968.	Section 1 (3).
1968 c. 54.	The Theatres Act 1968.	In Schedule 2 the amendment in section 162 of the Customs and Excise Act 1952.
1969 c. 32.	The Finance Act 1969.	Section 1 (5) (*b*). In Schedule 7, paragraph 2.

SCHEDULE 4—*continued*

Chapter	Short title	Extent of repeal
1970 c. 24.	The Finance Act 1970.	Section 6 (1) and (2) (*a*). Section 7, except subsections (5) and (8).
1972 c. 41.	The Finance Act 1972.	Section 57 (3) and (4).
1974 c. 30.	The Finance Act 1974.	Section 4.
1975 c. 45.	The Finance (No. 2) Act 1975.	Sections 9 and 10. Sections 14 and 15. In Schedule 3, paragraphs 3 to 7, 9, 15, 24 to 37, 42, in paragraph 44, subparagraphs (*a*), (*b*) and (*d*) and paragraphs 45 to 47. Schedules 4 and 5. In Schedule 6, paragraphs 5, 6, 7 and 8.
1976 c. 40.	The Finance Act 1976.	Sections 2 and 3. In Schedule 3, paragraphs 1, 5, 7 and 9.
1976 c. 66.	The Licensing (Scotland) Act 1976.	In Schedule 7, paragraphs 3 and 4.
1977 c. 36.	The Finance Act 1977.	Section 1 (1) to (5), (8) and (9). Schedules 1 and 2.
1978 c. 42.	The Finance Act 1978.	Section 2. In Schedule 12, paragraphs 1 to 5.

PART II

ENACTMENTS OF THE PARLIAMENT OF NORTHERN IRELAND

Chapter	Short title	Extent of repeal
1959 c. 9 (N.I.)	The Finance Act (Northern Ireland) 1959.	Section 12 (1) and (5). Section 13 (2) to (5). Section 18 (5).
1963 c. 22 (N.I.)	The Finance Act (Northern Ireland) 1963.	Section 19. Section 22 (6). Schedule 2.
1967 c. 20 (N.I.)	The Finance Act (Northern Ireland) 1967.	Section 15 (1) (*b*) and (6). Section 17. Section 21 (6). In Schedule 2, the amendment in the Finance Act (Northern Ireland) 1959.

PART III

NORTHERN IRELAND INSTRUMENT

Year and Number	Title	Extent of revocation
1976/1214 (N.I. 23).	The Poisons (Northern Ireland) Order 1976.	In Schedule 2, paragraph 1.

Hydrocarbon Oil Duties Act 1979

(1979 c. 5)

ARRANGEMENT OF SECTIONS

An Act to consolidate the enactments relating to the excise duties on hydrocarbon oil, petrol substitutes, power methylated spirits and road fuel gas. [22nd February 1979]

General Note

This Act consolidates the enactments relating to the excise duties on hydrocarbon oil, petrol substitutes, power methylated spirits and road fuel gas.

S. 1 defines hydrocarbon oil; s. 2 contains provisions supplementing s. 1; s. 3 provides for hydrocarbon oil as an ingredient of imported goods; s. 4 deals with petrol substitutes and power methylated spirits; s. 5 defines "road fuel gas"; s. 6 imposes excise duty on hydrocarbon oil; s. 7 imposes excise duty on petrol substitutes and power methylated spirits; s. 8 concerns excise duty on road fuel gas; s. 9 deals with oil delivered for home use for certain industrial purposes; s. 10 places restrictions on the use of duty-free oil; s. 11 provides for rebate of duty on heavy oil; s. 12 exempts fuel for road vehicles from rebate; s. 13 imposes penalties for misuse of rebated heavy oil; s. 14 gives a rebate on light oil for use as furnace fuel; s. 15 provides for drawback of duty on exportation of certain goods; s. 16 gives drawback of duty on exportation of power methylated spirits; s. 17 concerns heavy oil used by horticultural producers; s. 18 relates to fuel for ships in home waters; s. 19 deals with fuel used in fishing boats; s. 20 provides for oil being contaminated or accidentally mixed in warehouse; s. 21 empowers Commissioners to make regulations with respect to commodities dutiable under the Act; s. 22 prohibits use of petrol substitutes on which duty has not been paid; s. 23 prohibits use of road fuel gas on which duty has not been paid; s. 24 controls use of duty-free and rebated oil; s. 25 confers general power to make regulations; s. 26 concerns the giving of directions under the Act; s. 27 is the interpretation section; s. 28 contains consequential amendments, repeals, savings and transitional provisions; s. 29 deals with citation and commencement.

The Act received the Royal Assent on February 22, 1979, and came into force on April 1, 1979.

Parliamentary Debates

Hansard, H.L. Vol. 397, cols. 417, 1169; Vol. 398, col. 832.

Table of Derivations

Customs and Excise Act 1952

1952	1979
s. 283 (2) (5)	ss. 10, 13, 14 (2)–(10), 18, 21, 22, 23, 24
306	s. 25

Hydrocarbon Oil (Customs and Excise) Act 1971

1971	1979	1971	1979	1971	1979
s. 1	s. 1	s. 10 (2)	s. 27 (1)	s. 20 (3)	s. 22
2	2	11	13	21	24
3	4	12 (1)–(8)	14 (1)–(10)	(1)	ss. 9 (5), 14 (1)
4 (2)	6 (2)	13	15	23	s. 27 (1) (2)
5	3	14	16	Sch. 1	Sch. 1
6	7	15	17	Sch. 2	Sch. 2
7 (1)–(3)	9 (1)–(4)	16	18	Sch. 3	Sch. 3
(4)	(5)	17	19	Sch. 4	Sch. 4
(5)	(1)–(4)	18	20	para. 1	ss. 9 (5), 14 (1)
8	10	19	21	Sch. 5	Sch. 5
9	11	20 (1)	21	Sch. 6,	
10	12	20 (2) (*a*)	21	para. 3	Sch. 6
		(*b*)	22		

Finance Act 1971

1971	1979	1971	1979	1971	1979
s. 3 (1)–(4)	s. 8	s. 3 (7) (*b*)	s. 23	s. 3 (9) (*a*)	s. 28
(6)	21, Sch. 3	(8)	ss. 5, 8, 23, 27 (1), Sch. 3	(*b*)	23
(7) (*a*)	s. 21			(10) (11)	8

Criminal Procedure (Scotland) Act 1975

1975	1979
s. 193A	ss. 10, 13, 14 (2)–(10)
289B (1)	10, 13, 14 (2)–(10)

FINANCE ACT 1976

1976	1979
s. 9	s. 6 (1)
10	Sch. 1

FINANCE (No. 2) ACT 1975

1975	1979	1975	1979	1975	1979
s. 11	s. 6 (1)	Sch. 3		Sch. 3,	
Sch. 3,		para. 18	s. 10	para. 21	s. 19
para. 16	6 (2)	para. 19	17	para. 22	Sch. 3
para. 17	7	para. 20	18		

FINANCE ACT 1977

1977	1979
s. 4 (1) (*a*)	s. 6 (1)
(*b*)	ss. 7, 8, Sch. 6
(*c*)	Sch. 6
4 (2) (3)	s. 11
4 (4)	14 (1)

CRIMINAL LAW ACT 1977

1977	1979
s. 27	ss. 10, 13, 14 (2)–(10)
28 (2)	10, 13, 14 (2)–(10)
32 (1)	10, 13, 14 (2)–(10)

FINANCE ACT 1978

1978	1979
Sch. 12, para. 8	s. 1, 2, 4, 24, Sch. 5
para. 18	26

EXCISE DUTIES (GAS AS ROAD FUEL) ORDER 1972 (S.I. 1972 No. 567)

1972	1979
Arts. 1–3	s. 8

AMENDMENT OF UNITS OF MEASUREMENT (HYDROCARBON OIL, ETC.) ORDER 1977
(S.I. 1977 No. 1866)

1977	1979	1977	1979	1977	1979
Art. 2 (*a*)	s. 1	Art. 2 (*d*)	s. 11	Art. 2 (*f*)	s. 22
(*b*)	2	(*e*)	14 (1)	3	5
(*c*)	4			4	6 (1)

CUSTOMS AND EXCISE (WAREHOUSE) REGULATIONS 1978 (S.I. 1978 No. 1603)

1978	1979
Regs. 1–4	ss. 15, 16

The dutiable commodities

Hydrocarbon oil

1.—(1) Subsections (2) to (4) below define the various descriptions of oil referred to in this Act.

(2) " Hydrocarbon oil " means petroleum oil, coal tar, and oil produced from coal, shale, peat or any other bituminous substance, and all liquid hydrocarbons, but does not include such hydrocarbons or bituminous or asphaltic substances as are—

(*a*) solid or semi-solid at a temperature of 15°C, or

(*b*) gaseous at a temperature of 15°C and under a pressure of 1013·25 millibars.

(3) " Light oil " means hydrocarbon oil—

(*a*) of which not less than 90 per cent. by volume distils at a temperature not exceeding 210°C, or (*b*) which gives off an inflammable vapour at a temperature of less than 23°C when tested in the manner prescribed by the Acts relating to petroleum.

(4) " Heavy oil " means hydrocarbon oil other than light oil.

Provisions supplementing s. 1

2.—(1) The method of testing oil for the purpose of ascertaining its classification in accordance with section 1 above shall, subject to subsection (3) (*b*) of that section, be such as the Commissioners may direct.

(2) Subject to subsection (3) below, the Treasury may from time to time direct that, for the purposes of any duty of excise for the time being chargeable on hydrocarbon oil, any specified description of light oil shall be treated as being heavy oil.

(3) The Treasury shall not give a direction under subsection (2) above in relation to any description of oil unless they are satisfied that the description is one which should, according to its use, be classed with heavy oil.

(4) For the purposes of the Customs and Excise Acts 1979, the production of hydrocarbon oil includes—

(*a*) the obtaining of one description of hydrocarbon oil from another description of hydrocarbon oil; and

(*b*) the subjecting of hydrocarbon oil to any process of purification or blending,

as well as the obtaining of hydrocarbon oil from other substances or from any natural source.

(5) Where heavy oil having a temperature exceeding 15°C is measured for the purpose of ascertaining the amount of any duty of excise chargeable, or of any rebate or drawback allowable, on the oil and the Commissioners are satisfied that the oil is artificially heated, the duty shall be charged or the rebate or drawback shall be allowed on the number of litres which, in the opinion of the Commissioners, the oil would have measured if its temperature had been 15°C.

Hydrocarbon oil as ingredient of imported goods

3. Where imported goods contain hydrocarbon oil as a part or ingredient thereof, the oil shall be disregarded in the application to the goods of section 126 of the Management Act (charge of duty on manufactured or composite imported articles) unless in the opinion of the Commissioners the goods should, according to their use, be classed with hydrocarbon oil.

Petrol substitutes and power methylated spirits

4.—(1) In this Act " petrol substitute " means any liquid intended to take the place of petrol as fuel for internal combustion piston engines, being neither hydrocarbon oil nor power methylated spirits.

(2) In subsection (1) above, " liquid " does not include a substance which is gaseous at a temperature of 15°C and under a pressure of 1013·25 millibars.

(3) In this Act " power methylated spirits " means spirits methylated in such manner as may be prescribed by regulations made under section 77 of the Alcoholic Liquor Duties Act 1979 for methylated spirits of that class.

Road fuel gas

5. In this Act " road fuel gas " means any substance which is gaseous at a temperature of 15°C and under a pressure of 1013·25 millibars, and which is for use as fuel in road vehicles.

Charging provisions

Excise duty on hydrocarbon oil

6.—(1) Subject to subsection (2) below, there shall be charged on hydrocarbon oil—

(*a*) imported into the United Kingdom; or

(*b*) produced in the United Kingdom and delivered for home use from a refinery or from other premises used for the production of hydrocarbon oil or from any bonded storage for hydrocarbon oil, not being hydrocarbon oil chargeable with duty under paragraph (*a*) above,

a duty of excise at the rate of £0·0660 a litre in the case of light oil and £0·0770 a litre in the case of heavy oil.

(2) Where imported hydrocarbon oil is removed to a refinery, the duty chargeable under subsection (1) above shall, instead of being charged at the time of the importation of that oil, be charged on the delivery of any goods from the refinery for home use and shall be the same as that which would be payable on the importation of like goods.

Excise duty on petrol substitutes and power methylated spirits

7. A duty of excise at the same rate as the duty of excise on light oil shall be charged—

(*a*) on any petrol substitute which is sent out from the premises of a person producing or dealing in petrol substitutes and which was not acquired by him duty paid under this paragraph; and

(*b*) on spirits used for making power methylated spirits (payable by the methylator immediately after the spirits have been so used).

Excise duty on road fuel gas

8.—(1) A duty of excise shall be charged on road fuel gas which is sent out from the premises of a person producing or dealing in road fuel gas and on which the duty charged by this section has not been paid.

(2) The like duty of excise shall be charged on the setting aside for use, or on the use, by any person, as fuel in a road vehicle, of road fuel gas on which the duty charged by this section has not been paid.

(3) The rate of the duty under this section shall be prescribed by order made by the Treasury, and in exercising their power under this subsection the Treasury shall select the rate (whether for all road fuel gas or for a particular kind of road fuel gas) which in their opinion is for the time being the nearest convenient and suitable rate corresponding with the rate of excise duty on light oil.

In comparing the excise duty chargeable under this section with that on light oil account shall be taken of relative average calorific values and of other relevant factors.

(4) An order made under subsection (3) above—

(*a*) may express the rate of duty by reference to any method of measuring the road fuel gas;

(*b*) may prescribe different rates for different kinds of road fuel gas; and

(c) may prescribe a rate which depends in whole or in part on the rate for the time being of excise duty charged on light oil.

(5) The power to make orders under subsection (3) above shall be exercisable by statutory instrument, and any statutory instrument by which the power is exercised shall be subject to annulment in pursuance of a resolution of the House of Commons.

(6) For the purposes of this Act, so far as it relates to the excise duty chargeable under this section, road fuel gas shall be deemed to be used as fuel in a road vehicle if, but only if, it is used as fuel for the engine provided for propelling the vehicle, or for an engine which draws its fuel from the same supply as that engine.

(7) Subsection (2) above shall not apply to road fuel gas delivered to, or in the stock of, the person otherwise chargeable if it was delivered to, or stocked by, him before 3rd July 1972.

Delivery of oil without payment of duty

Oil delivered for home use for certain industrial purposes

9.—(1) The Commissioners may permit hydrocarbon oil to be delivered for home use to an approved person, without payment of excise duty on the oil, where—

(a) it is to be put by him to a use qualifying for relief under this section; or

(b) it is to be supplied by him in the course of a trade of supplying oil for any such use.

(2) The uses of hydrocarbon oil qualifying for relief under this section are—

(a) use in the manufacture or preparation of any article, not being hydrocarbon oil or an article which in the opinion of the Commissioners should, according to its use, be classed with hydrocarbon oil; and

(b) use for cleaning plant, in connection with the use of the plant in the manufacture or preparation of such an article,

but do not include the use of oil as fuel or, except as provided by subsection (3) below, as a lubricant.

(3) Where, in the manufacture or preparation of an article described in subsection (2) (a) above, hydrocarbon oil is used for preventing or reducing friction, adhesion or contact—

(a) between parts or components of the article; or

(b) between the article or a part or component of the article and any plant used in the manufacture or preparation, or any part or component of plant so used,

that use of the oil is to be included among the uses qualifying for relief under this section.

(4) Where the Commissioners are authorised to give permission under subsection (1) above in the case of any oil, but the permission is for any reason not given, they shall, if satisfied that the oil has been put by an approved person to a use qualifying for relief under this section, repay to him the amount of the excise duty paid on the oil, less any rebate allowed in respect of the duty.

(5) In this section—

(a) " an approved person " means a person for the time being approved in accordance with regulations made for any of the purposes of subsection (1) or (4) above under section 24 (1) below; and (*b*) " plant " means any machinery, apparatus, equipment or vessel.

Restrictions on the use of duty-free oil

10.—(1) Except with the consent of the Commissioners, no oil in whose case delivery without payment of duty has been permitted under section 9 above shall—

(*a*) be put to a use not qualifying for relief under that section; or

(*b*) be acquired or taken into any vehicle, appliance or storage tank in order to be put to such a use.

(2) In giving their consent for the purposes of subsection (1) above, the Commissioners may impose such conditions as they think fit.

(3) A person who—

(*a*) uses or acquires oil in contravention of subsection (1) above; or

(*b*) is liable for oil being taken into a vehicle, appliance or storage tank in contravention of that subsection,

shall be liable on summary conviction to a penalty of three times the value of the oil or £100, whichever is the greater; and the Commissioners may recover from him an amount equal to the excise duty on like oil at the rate in force at the time of the contravention.

(4) A person who supplies oil having reason to believe that it will be put to a use not qualifying for relief under section 9 above shall be liable on summary conviction to a penalty of three times the value of the oil or £100, whichever is the greater, if that use without the consent of the Commissioners would contravene subsection (1) above.

(5) A person who, with the intent that the restrictions imposed by subsection (1) above should be contravened,—

(*a*) uses or acquires oil in contravention of that subsection; or

(*b*) supplies oil having reason to believe that it will be put to a use not qualifying for relief under section 9 above, being a use which, without the consent of the Commissioners, would contravene that subsection,

shall be guilty of an offence under this subsection.

(6) A person who is liable for oil being taken into a vehicle, appliance or storage tank in contravention of subsection (1) above shall be guilty of an offence under this subsection where the oil was taken in with the intent by him that the restrictions imposed by that subsection should be contravened.

(7) A person guilty of an offence under subsection (5) or (6) above shall be liable—

(*a*) on summary conviction, to a penalty of the prescribed sum or of three times the value of the oil in question, whichever is the greater, or to imprisonment for a term not exceeding 6 months, or to both; or

(*b*) on conviction on indictment, to a penalty of any amount or to imprisonment for a term not exceeding 2 years, or to both.

(8) For the purposes of this section, a person is liable for oil being taken into a vehicle, appliance or storage tank in contravention of subsection (1) above if he is at the time the person having the charge of the vehicle, appliance or tank, or is its owner, except that if a person other than the owner is, or is for the time being, entitled to possession of it, that person and not the owner is liable.

(9) Any oil acquired, or taken into a vehicle, appliance or storage

tank as mentioned in subsection (1) above, or supplied as mentioned in subsection (4) or (5) above, shall be liable to forfeiture.

Rebate of duty

Rebate on heavy oil

11.—(1) Subject to sections 12 and 13 below, where heavy oil charged with the excise duty on hydrocarbon oil is delivered for home use, there shall be allowed on the oil at the time of delivery a rebate of duty at a rate—

(*a*) in the case of kerosene other than aviation turbine fuel, of £0·0022 a litre less than the rate at which the duty is for the time being chargeable;

(*b*) in the case of aviation turbine fuel, and heavy oil other than kerosene, of £0·0055 a litre less than the rate at which the duty is for the time being chargeable.

(2) In this section—

(*a*) " aviation turbine fuel " means kerosene which is intended to be used as fuel for aircraft engines and is allowed to be delivered for that purpose without being marked in accordance with the regulations made for the purposes of this section;

(*b*) " kerosene " means heavy oil of which more than 50 per cent. by volume distils at a temperature not exceeding 240°C.

Rebate not allowed on fuel for road vehicles

12.—(1) If, on the delivery of heavy oil for home use, it is intended to use the oil as fuel for a road vehicle, a declaration shall be made to that effect in the entry for home use and thereupon no rebate shall be allowed in respect of that oil.

(2) No heavy oil on whose delivery for home use rebate has been allowed shall—

(*a*) be used as fuel for a road vehicle; or

(*b*) be taken into a road vehicle as fuel,

unless an amount equal to the amount for the time being allowable in respect of rebate on like oil has been paid to the Commissioners in accordance with regulations made under section 24 (1) below for the purposes of this section.

(3) For the purposes of this section and section 13 below—

(*a*) heavy oil shall be deemed to be used as fuel for a road vehicle if, but only if, it is used as fuel for the engine provided for propelling the vehicle or for an engine which draws its fuel from the same supply as that engine; and

(*b*) heavy oil shall be deemed to be taken into a road vehicle as fuel if, but only if, it is taken into it as part of that supply.

Penalties for misuse of rebated heavy oil

13.—(1) A person who—

(*a*) uses heavy oil in contravention of section 12 (2) above; or

(*b*) is liable for heavy oil being taken into a road vehicle in contravention of that subsection,

shall be liable on summary conviction to a penalty of three times the value of the oil or £100, whichever is the greater; and the Commissioners may recover from him an amount equal to the rebate on like oil at the rate in force at the time of the contravention.

(2) A person who supplies heavy oil having reason to believe that it will be put to a particular use shall be liable on summary conviction to a penalty of three times the value of the oil or £100, whichever is the greater, where that use would, if a payment under subsection (2) of section 12 above were not made in respect of the oil, contravene that subsection.

(3) A person who, with the intent that the restrictions imposed by section 12 above should be contravened,—

(*a*) uses heavy oil in contravention of subsection (2) of that section; or

(*b*) supplies heavy oil having reason to believe that it will be put to a particular use, being a use which would, if a payment under that subsection were not made in respect of the oil, contravene that subsection,

shall be guilty of an offence under this subsection.

(4) A person who is liable for heavy oil being taken into a road vehicle in contravention of subsection (2) of section 12 above shall be guilty of an offence under this subsection where the oil was taken in with the intent by him that the restrictions imposed by that section should be contravened.

(5) A person guilty of an offence under subsection (3) or (4) above shall be liable—

(*a*) on summary conviction, to a penalty of the prescribed sum or of three times the value of the oil in question, whichever is the greater, or to imprisonment for a term not exceeding 6 months, or to both; or

(*b*) on conviction on indictment, to a penalty of any amount, or to imprisonment for a term not exceeding 2 years, or to both.

(6) Any heavy oil—

(*a*) taken into a road vehicle as mentioned in section 12 (2) above or supplied as mentioned in subsection (2) or (3) above; or

(*b*) taken as fuel into a vehicle at a time when it is not a road vehicle and remaining in the vehicle as part of its fuel supply at a later time when it becomes a road vehicle,

shall be liable to forfeiture.

(7) For the purposes of this section, a person is liable for heavy oil being taken into a road vehicle in contravention of section 12 (2) above if he is at the time the person having the charge of the vehicle or is its owner, except that if a person other than the owner is, or is for the time being, entitled to possession of it, that person and not the owner is liable.

Rebate on light oil for use as furnace fuel

14.—(1) On light oil charged with the excise duty on hydrocarbon oil, and delivered for home use as furnace fuel for burning in vaporised or atomised form by a person for the time being approved in accordance with regulations made for the purposes of this subsection under section 24 (1) below, there shall be allowed at the time of delivery a rebate of duty at a rate of £0·0055 a litre less than the rate at which the duty is charged.

(2) Except with the consent of the Commissioners, no oil in whose case rebate has been allowed under this section shall—

(*a*) be put to a use otherwise than as mentioned in subsection (1) above; or

(*b*) be acquired or taken into any vehicle, appliance or storage tank in order to be put to such a use.

(3) In giving their consent for the purposes of subsection (2) above, the Commissioners may impose such conditions as they think fit.

(4) A person who—

(*a*) uses or acquires oil in contravention of subsection (2) above; or

(*b*) is liable for oil being taken into a vehicle, appliance or storage tank in contravention of that subsection,

shall be liable on summary conviction to a penalty of three times the value of the oil or £100, whichever is the greater; and the Commissioners may recover from him the amount of the rebate allowed on the oil.

(5) A person who supplies oil having reason to believe that it will be used otherwise than as mentioned in subsection (1) above shall be liable on summary conviction to a penalty of three times the value of the oil or £100, whichever is the greater, if that use without the consent of the Commissioners would contravene subsection (2) above.

(6) A person who, with the intent that the restrictions imposed by subsection (2) above should be contravened,—

(*a*) uses or acquires oil in contravention of that subsection; or

(*b*) supplies oil having reason to believe that it will be put to a use otherwise than as mentioned in subsection (1) above, being a use which, without the consent of the Commissioners, would contravene subsection (2) above,

shall be guilty of an offence under this subsection.

(7) A person who is liable for oil being taken into a vehicle, appliance or storage tank in contravention of subsection (2) above shall be guilty of an offence under this subsection where the oil was taken in with the intent by him that the restrictions imposed by that subsection should be contravened.

(8) A person guilty of an offence under subsection (6) or (7) above shall be liable—

(*a*) on summary conviction, to a penalty of the prescribed sum or of three times the value of the oil in question, whichever is the greater, or to imprisonment for a term not exceeding 6 months, or to both; or

(*b*) on conviction on indictment, to a penalty of any amount, or to imprisonment for a term not exceeding 2 years, or to both.

(9) For the purposes of this section, a person is liable for oil being taken into a vehicle, appliance or storage tank in contravention of subsection (2) above if he is at the time the person having the charge of the vehicle, appliance or tank, or is its owner, except that if a person other than the owner is, or is for the time being, entitled to possession of it, that person and not the owner is liable.

(10) Any oil acquired, or taken into a vehicle, appliance or storage tank, as mentioned in subsection (2) above, or supplied as mentioned in subsection (5) or (6) above, shall be liable to forfeiture.

Drawback

Drawback of duty on exportation etc. of certain goods

15.—(1) A drawback equal to any amount shown to the satisfaction of the Commissioners to have been paid in respect of the goods in question by way of the excise duty on hydrocarbon oil shall be allowed on the exportation, shipment as stores or warehousing in an excise warehouse for use as stores of—

(*a*) any hydrocarbon oil; or

(*b*) any article in which there is contained any hydrocarbon oil which was used, or which formed a component of any article used, as an ingredient in the manufacture or preparation of the article.

(2) The Treasury may by order direct as respects articles of any class or description specified in the order that, subject to the provisions of the order, drawback shall be allowed under subsection (1) above in respect of hydrocarbon oil (or goods containing it) used as a material, solvent, extractant, preservative or finish in the manufacture or preparation of the articles.

(3) On the making of an order under subsection (2) above this Act shall have effect, subject to the provisions of the order and of this section, as if the reference in subsection (1) (*b*) above to an article in which there is contained any hydrocarbon oil used as an ingredient in the manufacture or preparation of the article included a reference to an article of the class or description specified in the order.

(4) An order made under subsection (2) above as respects articles of any class or description—

(*a*) may provide for drawback to be allowed in respect of hydrocarbon oil (or goods containing it) used as a material, solvent, extractant, preservative or finish in the manufacture or preparation not directly of articles of that class or description but of articles incorporated in them; and

(*b*) may provide that the quantity of hydrocarbon oil as respects duty on which drawback is to be allowed shall be determined by reference to average quantities or otherwise.

(5) The power to make orders under subsection (2) above shall be exercisable by statutory instrument, and any statutory instrument by which the power is exercised shall be subject to annulment in pursuance of a resolution of the House of Commons.

Drawback of duty on exportation etc. of power methylated spirits

16. On power methylated spirits which are exported, shipped as stores or warehoused in an excise warehouse for use as stores there shall be allowed a drawback equal to the amount of excise duty shown to the satisfaction of the Commissioners to have been paid in respect of those spirits.

Miscellaneous reliefs

Heavy oil used by horticultural producers

17.—(1) If, on an application made for the purposes of this section by a horticultural producer, it is shown to the satisfaction of the Commissioners that within the period for which the application is made any quantity of heavy oil has been used by the applicant as mentioned in subsection (2) below, then, subject as provided below, the applicant shall be entitled to obtain from the Commissioners repayment of the amount of any excise duty which has been paid in respect of the quantity so used, unless that amount is less than £2·50.

(2) A horticultural producer shall be entitled to repayment under this section in respect of oil used by him—

(*a*) in the heating, for the growth of horticultural produce primarily with a view to the production of horticultural produce for sale, of any building or structure, or of the earth or other growing medium in it; or

(*b*) in the sterilisation of the earth or other growing medium to be used for the growth of horticultural produce as mentioned in paragraph (*a*) above in any building or structure.

(3) Where any quantity of oil is used partly for any such purpose as is mentioned in subsection (2) above and partly for another purpose, such part of that quantity shall be treated as used for each purpose as may be determined by the Commissioners.

(4) An application under this section shall be made for a period of 6 months ending with June or December and within 3 months following that period, unless the Commissioners otherwise allow, and shall be made in such manner as the Commissioners may direct.

(5) The Commissioners may require an applicant for repayment under this section—

(*a*) to state such facts concerning the hydrocarbon oil delivered to or used by him, or concerning the production of horticultural produce by him, as they may think necessary to deal with the application;

(*b*) to furnish them in such form as they may require with proof of any statement so made; and

(*c*) to permit an officer to inspect any premises or plant used by him for the production of horticultural produce or in or for which any such oil was used.

(6) If—

(*a*) the facts required by the Commissioners under subsection (5) (*a*) above are not stated; or

(*b*) proof of the matters referred to in subsection (5) (*b*) above is not furnished to the satisfaction of the Commissioners; or

(*c*) an applicant fails to permit inspection of premises or plant as required under the subsection (5) (*c*) above,

the facts shall be deemed for the purposes of this section to be such as the Commissioners may determine.

(7) In this section—

(*a*) " horticultural produce " has the meaning assigned to it by Schedule 2 to this Act; and

(*b*) " horticultural producer " means a person growing horticultural produce primarily for sale.

Fuel for ships in home waters

18.—(1) If, on an application made for the purposes of this subsection in such manner as the Commissioners may direct by the owner of a ship specified in the application, not being a pleasure yacht, it is shown to the satisfaction of the Commissioners—

(*a*) that at any time within the period of 6 months preceding the date of the application (or within such longer period preceding that date as the Commissioners may in any special case allow) any quantity of heavy oil has been used as fuel for the machinery of the ship while engaged on a voyage in home waters; and

(*b*) that no drawback was allowable on the shipment of the oil,

the applicant shall be entitled to obtain from the Commissioners repayment of the amount of any excise duty which has been paid in respect of the quantity so used, unless that amount is less than £5.

(2) Subject to subsections (3) and (4) below, heavy oil in a warehouse or refinery may, on an application made for the purposes of this subsection in such manner as the Commissioners may direct by the owner of a ship specified in the application, not being a pleasure yacht, and on the prescribed security being given, be delivered without payment of

excise duty to the applicant for use as fuel for the machinery of the ship while engaged on a voyage in home waters.

(3) At any time not later than 12 months after any oil has been delivered as mentioned in subsection (2) above the Commissioners may require the applicant to prove in the prescribed manner that the whole of the oil, or such of it as is not on board the ship or has not been relanded with the sanction of the proper officer, has been used as so mentioned.

(4) If proof of any matter relating to the use of any oil, required by the Commissioners under subsection (3) above is not furnished to their satisfaction, any duty which but for the provisions of subsection (2) above would have been payable on the delivery of the oil shall become payable by the applicant on demand made by the Commissioners in the prescribed manner.

(5) If, where oil has been delivered from a warehouse or refinery without payment of duty on an application under subsection (2) above, a person—

(*a*) uses the oil or any part of it otherwise than as fuel for the machinery of the ship specified in the application while engaged on a voyage in home waters; or

(*b*) relands the whole or any part of the oil at any place in the United Kingdom without the sanction of the proper officer,

he shall be liable on summary conviction to a penalty of three times the value of the whole of the oil so delivered or £100, whichever is the greater; and in the case of an offence under paragraph (*b*) of this subsection the oil relanded shall be liable to forfeiture.

(6) In this section—

(*a*) " owner ", in relation to an application, includes a charterer to whom the specified ship is demised, or, in a case where the application relates to oil used, or for use, on a ship while undergoing trials for the purpose of testing her hull or machinery, the builder or other person conducting the trials;

(*b*) " prescribed " means prescribed by regulations made by the Commissioners; and

(*c*) " voyage in home waters ", in relation to a ship, means a voyage in which the ship is at all times either at sea or within the limits of a port.

(7) This section shall apply as if references to ships included references to hovercraft (and " pleasure yacht ", " voyage ", " reland " and other expressions shall be construed accordingly).

Fuel used in fishing boats, etc.

19.—(1) Subsection (3) below shall have effect in the case of—

(*a*) any fishing boat entered in the fishing boat register under the Merchant Shipping Act 1894 and used for the purposes of fishing by a person gaining a substantial part of his livelihood by fishing, whether he is the owner of the boat or not; or

(*b*) any lifeboat owned by the Royal National Lifeboat Institution (in this subsection called " the Institution "); or

(*c*) any tractor or gear owned by the Institution and used for the purpose of launching or hauling in any lifeboat owned by it,

in respect of which an application is made to the Commissioners for the purposes of this section by the owner or master of the fishing boat or, as the case may be, by the Institution.

(2) Paragraphs (*b*) and (*c*) of subsection (1) above shall apply to hovercraft as if hovercraft were boats or vessels.

(3) Subject to the provisions of this section, if it appears to the satisfaction of the Commissioners that the applicant has at any time within the period of 6 months preceding the date of the application or within such longer period preceding that date as the Commissioners may in any special case allow, used any quantity of hydrocarbon oil on board that boat or for the purposes of that tractor or gear, the applicant shall be entitled to obtain from the Commissioners repayment of any excise duty which has been paid in respect of the oil so used.

(4) An application for the purposes of this section shall be made in such manner as the Commissioners may direct.

(5) No person who has previously made application under this section for repayment of duty shall be entitled to make a further application until the expiration of at least 3 months from the date on which the last preceding application was made.

(6) This section shall have effect in relation to excise duty paid in respect of power methylated spirits as it has effect in relation to excise duty paid in respect of hydrocarbon oil.

Oil contaminated or accidently mixed in warehouse

20.—(1) Where in the case of hydrocarbon oil which has been delivered for home use it is shown to the satisfaction of the Commissioners—

(*a*) that since it was so delivered the oil has been deposited unused in an oil warehouse; and

(*b*) that it has been so deposited by reason of having become contaminated or by reason of its consisting of different descriptions of hydrocarbon oil which have accidentally become mixed; and

(*c*) that at the time when it was so deposited it was oil or, as the case may be, was a mixture of oils, on which the appropriate duty of excise had been paid and not repaid and on which drawback had not been allowed,

then, subject to any conditions which the Commissioners see fit to impose for the protection of the revenue, the Commissioners may make to the occupier of that warehouse a payment in accordance with subsection (2) below.

(2) The payment referred to in subsection (1) above shall be a payment of an amount appearing to the Commissioners to be equal to the excise duty which would have been payable if—

(*a*) the oil had not become contaminated or mixed; and

(*b*) it had first been delivered for home use at the time when it was deposited in the warehouse and the duty had first become chargeable on that delivery.

(3) In this section " oil warehouse " means a place of security approved by the Commissioners under section 92 of the Management Act for the depositing, keeping and securing of hydrocarbon oil, and includes a refinery.

Administration and enforcement

Regulations with respect to hydrocarbon oil, petrol substitutes and road fuel gas

21.—(1) The Commissioners may, with a view to the protection of the revenue, make regulations—

(*a*) for any of the purposes specified in Part I of Schedule 3 to this Act (which relates to hydrocarbon oil);

(*b*) for any of the purposes specified in Part II of that Schedule (which relates to petrol substitutes);

(*c*) for any of the purposes specified in Part III of that Schedule (which relates to road fuel gas).

(2) In the case of regulations made for the purposes mentioned in subsection (1) (*a*) above, different regulations may be made for different classes of hydrocarbon oil; and the power to make such regulations shall include power to make regulations—

(*a*) regulating the allowance and payment of drawback under or by virtue of section 15 above; and

(*b*) for making the allowance and payment of drawback by virtue of an order under subsection (2) of that section subject to such conditions as the Commissioners see fit to impose for the protection of the revenue.

(3) A person who contravenes or fails to comply with any regulation made under this section shall be liable on summary conviction to a penalty of three times the value of any goods in respect of which the offence was committed or £100, whichever is the greater; and the goods shall be liable to forfeiture.

Prohibition on use of petrol substitutes on which duty has not been paid

22.—(1) A person who uses as fuel for an internal combustion piston engine any liquid which is neither hydrocarbon oil nor power methylated spirits and on which he knows or has reasonable cause to believe that the excise duty on petrol substitutes has not been paid shall be liable on summary conviction to a penalty of three times the value of the goods in respect of which the offence was committed or £100, whichever is the greater; and the goods shall be liable to forfeiture.

(2) In subsection (1) above, " liquid " does not include any substance which is gaseous at a temperature of 15°C and under a pressure of 1013·25 millibars.

Prohibition on use etc. of road fuel gas on which duty has not been paid

23.—(1) A person who—

(*a*) uses as fuel in; or

(*b*) takes as fuel into,

a road vehicle any road fuel gas on which he knows or has reasonable cause to believe that the excise duty chargeable under section 8 above has not been paid shall be liable on summary conviction to a penalty of three times the value of the goods in respect of which the offence was committed or £100, whichever is the greater; and the goods shall be liable to forfeiture.

(2) For the purposes of subsection (1) (*b*) above, road fuel gas shall be deemed to be taken into a road vehicle as fuel if, but only if, it is taken into it as part of the supply of fuel for the engine provided for propelling the vehicle or for an engine which draws its fuel from the same supply as that engine.

Control of use of duty-free and rebated oil

24.—(1) The Commissioners may make regulations for any of the purposes of section 9 (1) or (4), section 12 or section 14 (1) above, and in particular for the purposes specified in Schedule 4 to this Act.

(2) Regulations made for the purposes of section 12 above may provide for restricting (whether by reference to locality, the obtaining of a licence from the Commissioners or other matters) the cases in which

payments to the Commissioners under subsection (2) of that section are to be effective for the purposes of that subsection.

(3) For the purposes of the Customs and Excise Acts 1979, the presence in any hydrocarbon oil of a marker which, in regulations made under this section, is prescribed in relation to—

(a) oil delivered without payment of duty under section 9 above; or

(b) rebated heavy oil or rebated light oil,

shall be conclusive evidence that that oil has been so delivered or, as the case may be, that the rebate in question has been allowed.

(4) A person who contravenes or fails to comply with any regulation made under this section shall be liable on summary conviction to a penalty of three times the value of any goods in respect of which the offence was committed or £100, whichever is the greater; and the goods shall be liable to forfeiture.

(5) Schedule 5 to this Act shall have effect with respect to any sample of hydrocarbon oil taken in pursuance of regulations made under this section.

Supplementary

Regulations

25. Any power to make regulations under this Act shall be exercisable by statutory instrument, and any statutory instrument by which the power is exercisd shall be subject to annulment in pursuance of a resolution of either House of Parliament.

Directions

26. Directions given under any provision of this Act may make different provision for different circumstances and may be varied or revoked by subsequent directions thereunder.

Interpretation

27.—(1) In this Act—

"heavy oil" has the meaning given by section 1 (4) above;

"hydrocarbon oil" has the meaning given by section 1 (2) above;

"light oil" has the meaning given by section 1 (3) above;

"the Management Act" means the Customs and Excise Management Act 1979;

"petrol substitute" shall be construed in accordance with section 4 (1) and (2) above;

"power methylated spirits" has the meaning given by section 4 (3) above;

"the prescribed sum", in relation to the penalty provided for an offence, means—

(a) if the offence was committed in England, Wales or Northern Ireland, the prescribed sum within the meaning of section 28 of the Criminal Law Act 1977 (£1,000 or other sum substituted by order under section 61 (1) of that Act);

(b) if the offence was committed in Scotland, the prescribed sum within the meaning of section 289B of the Criminal Procedure (Scotland) Act 1975 (£1,000 or other sum substituted by order under section 289D (1) of that Act);

" rebate " means rebate of duty under section 11 or 14 above, and " rebated " has a corresponding meaning;

" refinery " means any premises approved by the Commissioners for the treatment of hydrocarbon oil;

" road fuel gas " has the meaning given by section 5 above; and

" road vehicle " means a vehicle constructed or adapted for use on roads, but does not include any vehicle of a kind specified in Schedule 1 to this Act.

(2) This Act and the other Acts included in the Customs and Excise Acts 1979 shall be construed as one Act but where a provision of this Act refers to this Act that reference is not to be construed as including a reference to any of the others.

(3) Any expression used in this Act or in any instrument made under this Act to which a meaning is given by any other Act included in the Customs and Excise Acts 1979 has, except where the context otherwise requires, the same meaning in this Act or in any such instrument as in that Act; and for ease of reference the Table below indicates the expressions used in this Act to which a meaning is given by any other such Act—

Management Act

" the Commissioners "
" container "
" the Customs and Excise Acts 1979 "
" excise warehouse "
" goods "
" hovercraft "
" occupier "
" officer " and " proper " in relation to an officer
" port "
" ship "
" shipment "
" stores "
" warehouse "

Alcoholic Liquor Duties Act 1979

" methylated spirits "
" spirits ".

Consequential amendments, repeals, savings and transitional provisions

28.—(1) The enactments and order specified in Schedule 6 to this Act shall be amended in accordance with the provisions of that Schedule.

(2) The enactments specified in Schedule 7 to this Act are hereby repealed to the extent specified in the third column of that Schedule.

(3) Any provision of this Act relating to anything done or required or authorised to be done under or by reference to that provision or any other provision of this Act shall have effect as if any reference to that provision, or that other provision, as the case may be, included a reference to the corresponding provision of the enactments repealed by this Act.

(4) The repeal by subsection (2) above of the Hydrocarbon Oil (Customs & Excise) Act 1971 shall not affect the operation of the saving

in paragraph 2 in Part I of Schedule 14 to the Finance (No. 2) Act 1975 in relation to the provisions of the said Act of 1971 repealed by section 75 (5) of the said Act of 1975 and specified in that Part.

(5) The Amendment of Units of Measurement (Hydrocarbon Oil, etc.) Order 1977 is hereby revoked.

(6) Nothing in this section shall be taken as prejudicing the operation of sections 15 to 17 of the Interpretation Act 1978 (which relate to the effect of repeals).

Citation and commencement

29.—(1) This Act may be cited as the Hydrocarbon Oil Duties Act 1979 and is included in the Acts which may be cited as the Customs and Excise Acts 1979.

(2) This Act shall come into operation on 1st April 1979.

SCHEDULES

Section 27 (1)

SCHEDULE 1

VEHICLES WHICH ARE NOT ROAD VEHICLES WITHIN THE MEANING OF THIS ACT

Vehicles excluded from definition of "road vehicle"

1. Any vehicle while it is not used on a public road and no vehicle excise licence is in force in respect of it.

2. The following—

(*a*) any vehicle exempted from vehicle excise duty by section 4 (1) (*h*) of the Vehicles (Excise) Act 1971 (road construction vehicles) or section 7 (1) of that Act (vehicles used only for passing to and from land in the same occupation);

(*b*) a vehicle of any of the following descriptions which is not chargeable with duty as a goods vehicle, namely an agricultural machine, digging machine, mobile crane, works truck, mowing machine or fisherman's tractor mentioned in Schedule 3 to that Act;

(*c*) a road roller.

Interpretation

3. In paragraph 1 above "public road" means a road which is repairable at the public expense.

4. In this Schedule "vehicle excise licence", "vehicle excise duty" and "duty" means a licence and duty under the Vehicles (Excise) Act 1971; but a vehicle in respect of which there is current a certificate or document in the form of a licence issued in pursuance of regulations under section 23 of that Act shall be treated as a vehicle for which a road licence is in force.

5. In the application of this Schedule to Northern Ireland, for any reference to the Vehicles (Excise) Act 1971 there shall be substituted a reference to the Vehicles (Excise) Act (Northern Ireland) 1972.

Section 17 (7)

SCHEDULE 2

MEANING OF "HORTICULTURAL PRODUCE" FOR PURPOSES OF RELIEF UNDER SECTION 17

In section 17 of this Act "horticultural produce" means—

(*a*) fruit;

(*b*) vegetables of a kind grown for human consumption, including fungi, but not including maincrop potatoes or peas grown for seed, for harvesting dry or for vining;

(*c*) flowers, pot plants and decorative foliage;

(*d*) herbs;

(*e*) seeds other than pea seeds, and bulbs and other material, being seeds, bulbs or material for sowing or planting for the production of—

(i) fruit,

(ii) vegetables falling within paragraph (*b*) above,

(iii) flowers, plants or foliage falling within paragraph (*c*) above, or

(iv) herbs,

or for reproduction of the seeds, bulbs or other material planted; or

(*f*) trees and shrubs, other than trees grown for the purpose of afforestation;

but does not include hops.

Section 21 (1)

SCHEDULE 3

Subjects for Regulations under Section 21

Part I

Hydrocarbon Oil

1. Prohibiting the porduction of hydrocarbon oil or any description of hydrocarbon oil except by a person holding a licence.

2. Fixing the date of expiration of any such licence.

3. Regulating the production, storage and warehousing of hydrocarbon oil or any description of hydrocarbon oil and the removal of any such oil to or from premises used for the production of any such oil.

4. Prohibiting the refining of hydrocarbon oil elsewhere than in a refinery.

5. Prohibiting the incorporation of gas in hydrocarbon oil elsewhere than in a refinery.

6. Regulating the use and storage of hydrocarbon oil in a refinery.

7. Regulating or prohibiting the removal to a refinery of hydrocarbon oil in respect of which any rebate has been allowed.

8. Regulating the removal of imported hydrocarbon oil to a refinery without payment of the excise duty on such oil.

9. Making provision for securing payment of the excise duty on any imported hydrocarbon oil recevied into a refinery.

10. Relieving from the excise duty chargeable on hydrocarbon oil produced in the United Kingdom any such oil intended for exportation or shipment as stores.

11. Generally for securing and collecting the excise duty chargeable on hydrocarbon oil produced in the United Kingdom.

Part II

Petrol Substitutes

12. Prohibiting the production of petrol substitutes, and dealing in petrol substitutes on which the excise duty has not been paid, except by persons holding a licence.

13. Fixing the date of expiration of any such licence.

14. Regulating the production, dealing in, storage and warehousing of petrol substitutes and their removal to and from premises used therefor.

15. Relieving from the excise duty petrol substitutes intended for exportation or shipment as stores.

16. Generally for securing and collecting the excise duty.

In this Part of this Schedule "the excise duty" means the excise duty on petrol substitutes.

PART III

ROAD FUEL GAS

17. Prohibiting the production of gas, and dealing in gas on which the excise duty has not been paid, except by persons holding a licence.

18. Fixing the date of expiration of any such licence.

19. Regulating the production, dealing in, storage and warehousing of gas and the removal of gas to and from premises used therefor.

20. Requiring containers for gas to be marked in the manner prescribed by the regulations.

21. Conferring power to require information relating to the supply or use of gas and containers for gas to be given by producers of and dealers in gas, and by the person owning or possessing or for the time being in charge of any road vehicle which is constructed or adapted to use gas as fuel.

22. Requiring a person owning or possessing a road vehicle which is constructed or adapted to use gas as fuel to keep such accounts and records in such manner as may be prescribed by the regulations, and to preserve such books and documents relating to the supply of gas to or by him, or the use of gas by him, for such period as may be so prescribed.

23. Requiring the production of books or documents relating to the supply or use of gas or the use of any road vehicle.

24. Authorising the entry and inspection of premises (other than private dwelling-houses) and the examination of road vehicles, and authorising, or requiring the giving of facilities for, the inspection of gas found on any premises entered or on or in any road vehicle.

25. Generally for securing and collecting the excise duty.

In this Part of this Schedule "the excise duty" means the excise duty chargeable under section 8 of this Act on gas, and "gas" means road fuel gas.

Section 24 (1)

SCHEDULE 4

SUBJECTS FOR REGULATIONS UNDER SECTION 24

As to grant of relief under sections 9 and 14

1. Regulating the approval of persons for purposes of section 9 (1) or (4) or 14 (1) of this Act, whether individually or by reference to a class, and whether in relation to particular descriptions of oil or generally; enabling approval to be granted subject to conditions and providing for the conditions to be varied, or the approval revoked, for reasonable cause.

2. Enabling permission under section 9 (1) of this Act to be granted subject to conditions as to the giving of security and otherwise.

3. Requiring claims for repayment under section 9 (4) of this Act to be made at such times and in respect of such periods as are prescribed; providing that no such claim shall lie where the amount to be paid is less than the prescribed minimum; and preventing, where such a claim lies, the payment of drawback.

As to mixing of oil

4. Imposing restrictions on the mixing with other oil of any rebated oil or oil delivered without payment of duty.

As to marking of oil

5. Requiring as a condition of allowing rebate on, or delivery without payment of duty of, any oil (subject to any exceptions provided by or under the regulations) that there shall have been added to that oil, at such times, in such manner and in such proportions as may be prescribed, one or more prescribed markers, with or without a prescribed colouring substance (not being a prescribed marker), and that a declaration to that effect is furnished.

6. Prescribing the substances which are to be used as markers.

7. Providing that the presence of a marker shall be disregarded if the proportion in which it is present is less than that prescribed for the purposes of this paragraph.

8. Prohibiting the addition to any oil of any prescribed marker or prescribed colouring substance except in such circumstances as may be prescribed.

9. Prohibiting the removal from any oil of any prescribed marker or prescribed colouring substance.

10. Prohibiting the addition to oil of any substance, not being a prescribed marker, which is calculated to impede the identification of a prescribed marker.

11. Regulating the storage or movement of prescribed markers.

12. Requiring any person who adds a prescribed marker to any oil to keep in such manner and to preserve for such period as may be prescribed such accounts and records in connection with his use of that marker as may be prescribed, and requiring the production of the accounts and records.

13. Requiring, in such circumstances or subject to such exceptions as may be prescribed, that any drum, storage tank, delivery pump or other container or outlet which contains any oil in which a prescribed marker is present shall be marked in the prescribed manner to indicate that the oil is not to be used as road fuel or for any other prohibited purpose.

14. Requiring any person who supplies oil in which a prescribed marker is present to deliver to the recipient a document containing a statement in the prescribed form to the effect that the oil is not to be used as road fuel or for any other prohibited purpose.

15. Prohibiting the sale of any oil the colour of which would prevent any prescribed colouring substance from being readily visible if present in the oil.

16. Prohibiting the importation of oil in which any prescribed marker, or any other substance which is calculated to impede the identification of a prescribed marker, is present.

As to control of storage, supply etc. of oil, entry of premises etc.

17. Regulating the storage or movement of oil.

18. Restricting the supplying of oil in respect of which rebate has been allowed and not repaid or on which excise duty has not been paid.

19. Requiring a person owning or possessing a road vehicle which is constructed or adapted to use heavy oil as fuel to keep such accounts and records in such manner as may be prescribed, and to preserve such books and documents relating to the supply of heavy oil to or by him, or the use of heavy oil by him, for such period as may be prescribed.

20. Requiring the production of books or documents relating to the supply or use of oil or the use of any vehicle.

21. Authorising the entry and inspection of premises (other than private dwelling-houses) and the examination of vehicles, and authorising, or requiring the giving of facilities for, the inspection of oil found on any premises entered or on or in any vehicle and the taking of samples of any oil inspected.

Interpretation

22. In this Schedule—

"oil" means hydrocarbon oil;

"prescribed" means prescribed by regulations made under section 24 of this Act;

and section 12 (3) (*a*) of this Act shall apply for the purposes of paragraph 19 above as it applies for the purposes of that section.

Section 24 (5)

SCHEDULE 5

Sampling

1. The person taking a sample—

(a) if he takes it from a motor vehicle, shall if practicable do so in the presence of a person appearing to him to be the owner or person for the time being in charge of the vehicle;

(b) if he takes the sample on any premises but not from a motor vehicle, shall if practicable take it in the presence of a person appearing to him to be the occupier of the premises or for the time being in charge of the part of the premises from which it is taken.

2.—(1) The result of an analysis of a sample shall not be admissible—

(a) in criminal proceedings under the Customs and Excise Acts 1979; or

(b) on behalf of the Commissioners in any civil proceedings under those Acts,

unless the analysis was made by an authorised analyst and the requirements of paragraph 1 above (where applicable) and of the following provisions of this paragraph have been complied with.

(2) The person taking a sample must at the time have divided it into three parts (including the part to be analysed), marked and sealed or fastened up each part, and—

(a) delivered one part to the person in whose presence the sample was taken in accordance with paragraph 1 above, if he requires it; and

(b) retained one part for future comparison.

(3) Where it was not practicable to comply with the relevant requirements of paragraph 1 above, the person taking the sample must have served notice on the owner or person in charge of the vehicle or, as the case may be, the occupier of the premises informing him that the sample has been taken and that one part of it is available for delivery to him, if he requires it, at such time and place as may be specified in the notice.

3.—(1) Subject to sub-paragraph (2) below, in any such proceedings as are mentioned in paragraph 2 (1) above a certificate purporting to be signed by an authorised analyst and certifying the presence of any substance in any such sample of oil as may be specified in the certificate shall be evidence, and in Scotland sufficient evidence, of the facts stated in it.

(2) Without prejudice to the admissibility of the evidence of the analyst (which shall be sufficient in Scotland as well as in England), such a certificate shall not be admissible as evidence—

(a) unless a copy of it has, not less than 7 days before the hearing, been served by the prosecutor or, in the case of civil proceedings, the Commissioners on all other parties to the proceedings; or

(b) if any of those other parties, not less than 3 days before the hearing or within such further time as the court may in special circumstances allow, serves notice on the prosecutor or, as the case may be, the Commissioners requiring the attendance at the hearing of the person by whom the analysis was made.

4.—(1) Any notice required or authorised to be given under this Schedule shall be in writing.

(2) Any such notice shall be deemed, unless the contrary is shown, to have been received by a person if it is shown to have been left for him at his last-known residence or place of business in the United Kingdom.

(3) Any such notice may be given by post, and the letter containing the notice may be sent to the last-known residence or place of business in the United Kingdom of the person to whom it is directed.

(4) Any such notice given to the secretary or clerk of a company or body of persons (incorporated or unincorporated) on behalf of the company or body shall be deemed to have been given to the company or body; and for the purpose of the foregoing provisions of this paragraph any such company or body of persons having an office in the United Kingdom shall be treated as resident at that office or, if it has more than one, at the registered or principal office.

(5) Where any such notice is to be given to any person as the occupier of any land, and it is not practicable after reasonable inquiry to ascertain—

(a) what is the name of any person being the occupier of the land; or

(*b*) whether or not there is a person being the occupier of the land,
the notice may be addressed to the person concerned by any sufficient description of the capacity in which it is given to him.

(6) In any case to which sub-paragraph (5) above applies, and in any other case where it is not practicable after reasonable inquiry to ascertain an address in the United Kingdom for the service of a notice to be given to a person as being the occupier of any land, the notice shall be deemed to have been received by the person concerned on being left for him on the land, either in the hands of a responsible person or conspicuously affixed to some building or object on the land.

(7) Sub-paragraphs (2) to (6) above shall not affect the validity of any notice given otherwise than in accordance with those sub-paragraphs.

5. In this Schedule " authorised analyst " means—

(*a*) the Government Chemist or a person acting under his direction;

(*b*) the Government Chemist for Northern Ireland or a person acting under his direction;

(*c*) any chemist authorised by the Treasury to make analyses for the purposes of this Schedule; or

(*d*) any other person appointed as a public analyst or deputy public analyst under—

section 89 of the Food and Drugs Act 1955,
section 27 of the Food and Drugs (Scotland) Act 1956, or
section 31 of the Food and Drugs Act (Northern Ireland) 1958.

6. References in this Schedule to the taking of a sample or to a sample shall be construed respectively as references to the taking of a sample in pursuance of regulations under section 24 of this Act and to a sample so taken.

7. This Schedule shall have effect in its application to a vehicle of which a person other than the owner is, or is for the time being, entitled to possession as if for references to the owner there were substituted references to the person entitled to possession.

Section 28 (1)

SCHEDULE 6

CONSEQUENTIAL AMENDMENTS

Finance Act 1965 *and Finance Act* (*Northern Ireland*) 1965

1. In section 92 (2) of the Finance Act 1965 and section 14 (2) of the Finance Act (Northern Ireland) 1966 (grants towards duty on bus fuel) for the words " hydrocarbon oil " there shall be substituted the words " heavy oil ".

Transport Act 1968

2. In section 69 of the Transport Act 1968 (revocation etc. of operators' licences), in subsection (4) (*e*), after the words " section 200 of the Customs and Excise Act 1952 " there shall be inserted the words " section 11 of the Hydrocarbon Oil (Customs & Excise) Act 1971 or section 13 of the Hydrocarbon Oil Duties Act 1979 ".

Finance Act 1972

3. In Item 4 of Group 7 in Schedule 4 to the Finance Act 1972 for the words " the Hydrocarbon Oil (Customs and Excise Act 1971 " there shall be substituted the words " the Hydrocarbon Oil Duties Act 1979 ".

4. In Note (3) to Group 7 in Schedule 4 to the Finance Act 1972 for the words from " gas " to " road vehicles and " there shall be substituted the words " road fuel gas (within the meaning of the Hydrocarbon Oil Duties Act 1979) ".

5. In Note (4) to Group 7 in Schedule 4 to the Finance Act 1972 the words " or is to be " shall be omitted and at the end of that Note there shall be added the words " or on which a duty of excise has been or is to be charged without relief from, or rebate of, such duty by virtue of the provisions of the Hydrocarbon Oil Duties Act 1979 ".

Excise Duties (Gas as Road Fuel) Order 1972

6. In Article 3 of the Excise Duties (Gas as Road Fuel) Order 1972 for the words "hydrocarbon oil" there shall be substituted the words "light oil".

Finance (No. 2) Act 1975

7. In Note (1) to Group 8 in Schedule 7 to the Finance (No. 2) Act 1975 for the words "the Hydrocarbon Oil (Customs & Excise) Act 1971" there shall be substituted the words "the Hydrocarbon Oil Duties Act 1979".

Section 28 (2)

SCHEDULE 7

REPEALS

Chapter	Short title	Extent of repeal
1971 c. 12.	The Hydrocarbon Oil (Customs & Excise) Act 1971.	The whole Act, except section 22 and paragraphs 1 and 2 of Schedule 6.
1971 c. 68.	The Finance Act 1971.	Section 3, except subsection (5). Section 6 (2).
1972 c. 41.	The Finance Act 1972.	In Schedule 4, in Note (4) to Group 7, the words "or is to be".
1975 c. 45.	The Finance (No. 2) Act 1975.	Section 11. In Schedule 3, paragraphs 2 and 16 to 22.
1976 c. 40.	The Finance Act 1976.	Sections 9 and 10.
1977 c. 36.	The Finance Act 1977.	Section 4.
1978 c. 42.	The Finance Act 1978.	In Schedule 12, paragraph 8.

Matches and Mechanical Lighters Duties Act 1979

(1979 c. 6)

SECT.

An Act to consolidate the enactments relating to the excise duties on matches and mechanical lighters. [22nd February 1979]

General Note

This Act consolidates the enactments relating to the excise duties on matches and mechanical lighters.

S. 1 imposes excise duty on matches; s. 2 provides for licences to manufacture matches; s. 3 empowers Commissioners to make regulations about matches; s. 4 defines mechanical lighters; s. 5 deals with the prescribed component; s. 6 imposes excise duty on mechanical lighters; s. 7 concerns regulations about mechanical lighters; s. 8 is the interpretation section; s. 9 contains repeals and consequential amendments; s. 10 deals with citation and commencement.

The Act received the Royal Assent on February 22, 1979, and came into force on April 1, 1979.

Parliamentary debates

Hansard, H.L. Vol. 397, cols. 418, 1170; Vol. 398, col. 832.

Table of Derivations

CUSTOMS AND EXCISE ACT 1952

1952	1979	1952	1979	1952	1979
s. 219	s. 2	s. 221 (2) ..	s. 6 (4)	s. 222 (2) ..	s. 5 (2)–(5)
220 (1) ..	3 (1) (2)	(3) (*b*)	6 (5)	(5)–(7)	5 (2)–(5)
(2) ..	3 (3)	(*c*)	7 (4)	283 (2) (5)	ss. 2, 3 (3), 6 (5), 7 (4)
(3) ..	1 (2)	(4) ..	4 (1)	306	3 (4), 7 (5)
221 (1) ..	7 (1)	222 (1) ..	4 (2)		

FINANCE ACT 1953

1953	1979
s. 3 (3)	s. 5 (1)

FINANCE ACT 1960

1960	1979
s. 7 (1)	s. 4 (1)
(3)	7 (2) (3)
(4)	7 (1)

FINANCE ACT 1963

1963	1979
s. 4 (2)	s. 3 (1) (2)

FINANCE (NO. 2) ACT 1975

1975	1979
s. 12	s. 1 (1)
13	6 (1)–(3)
Sch. 3,	
para. 1 (2) .	3 (1) (2)
para. 8	4 (2)
para. 12 ...	5 (1)
para. 38 ...	7 (1)

FINANCE ACT 1978

1978	1979
Sch. 12,	
para. 6 (1)...	ss. 1 (2), 3 (1) (2)
para. 6 (2) (*a*)	4 (1), 6 (4), 7 (1)

Matches

Excise duty on matches

1.—(1) There shall be charged on matches—

(*a*) imported into the United Kingdom; or

(*b*) manufactured in the United Kingdom and sent out from the premises of a manufacturer of matches,

a duty of excise at the rate of £0·49 for every 7,200 matches (and so in proportion for any less number of matches).

(2) For the purposes of the duty chargeable under subsection (1) above, a match which has more than one point of ignition shall be reckoned as so many matches as there are points of ignition.

Licences to manufacture matches

2.—(1) No person shall manufacture matches unless he holds an excise licence for that purpose granted under this section.

(2) A licence granted under this section shall expire on the 31st March next after it is granted.

(3) On any licence granted under this section there shall be charged an excise licence duty of £1.

(4) If any person manufactures matches otherwise than under and in accordance with a licence granted under this section, he shall be liable on summary conviction to a penalty of £50 and the matches shall be liable to forfeiture.

Regulations about matches

3.—(1) The Commissioners may, with a view to the protection of the revenue, make regulations—

(*a*) regulating the manufacture of matches and the removal of matches from the premises of a licensed manufacturer;

(*b*) for securing and collecting the excise duty chargeable on matches manufactured in the United Kingdom;

(*c*) providing for the remission or repayment of excise duty on defective matches;

(*d*) for authorising the removal from the premises of a licensed manufacturer without payment of excise duty of matches removed for exportation or shipment as stores or for warehousing, or removed to other premises of that manufacturer or to premises of another licensed manufacturer;

(*e*) for securing that there is on every container of matches a notification of the contents, or the minimum or maximum contents, of the container.

(2) In subsection (1) above " licensed manufacturer " means a person who holds a licence granted under section 2 above.

(3) If any person contravenes or fails to comply with any regulation made under subsection (1) above, he shall be liable on summary conviction to a penalty of £50, and any article in respect of which the offence was committed shall be liable to forfeiture.

(4) The power to make regulations under subsection (1) above shall be exercisable by statutory instrument and any statutory instrument by which the power is exercised shall be subject to annulment in pursuance of a resolution of either House of Parliament.

Mechanical lighters

Mechanical lighters

4.—(1) For the purposes of this Act " mechanical lighter " means any portable contrivance intended to provide a means of ignition, whether by spark, flame or otherwise, being a mechanical, chemical, electrical, or similar contrivance.

(2) For the purposes of this Act—

(*a*) any component which is, in accordance with section 5 below, the prescribed component of a mechanical lighter; or

(*b*) any assembly which includes such a component,

shall be deemed to be a mechanical lighter; and any reference in this Act to a manufacturer of mechanical lighters includes a reference to a person by whom any prescribed component of a mechanical lighter, or assembly which includes such a component, has been manufactured in the course of a business carried on by him, notwithstanding that he has not carried on the manufacture at a time when such a component or assembly is deemed to be a mechanical lighter.

The prescribed component

5.—(1) Until otherwise provided by an order under subsection (2) below, for the purposes of section 4 (2) above the prescribed component of an imported mechanical lighter shall be the body.

(2) Subject to subsection (1) above, in section 4 (2) above the " prescribed component ", in relation to a mechanical lighter falling within any class or description of mechanical lighters, means such one of the component parts of a lighter of that class or description as the Treasury may by order designate for this purpose as being the component part or one of the component parts in such a lighter least likely to require replacement.

(3) The power to make orders under subsection (2) above shall be exercisable by statutory instrument and any statutory instrument by which the power is exercised shall be laid before the House of Commons after being made.

(4) A statutory instrument made under subsection (2) above which extends the incidence of duty shall cease to have effect on the expiration of a period of 28 days from the date on which it is made unless at some time before the expiration of that period it has been approved by a resolution of the House of Commons, but without prejudice to anything previously done under it or to the making of a new order.

In reckoning any such period no account shall be taken of any time during which Parliament is dissolved or prorogued or during which the House of Commons is adjourned for more than 4 days.

(5) A statutory instrument made under subsection (2) above which

does not extend the incidence of duty shall be subject to annulment in pursuance of a resolution of the House of Commons.

Excise duty on mechanical lighters

6.—(1) There shall be charged on mechanical lighters—

(*a*) imported into the United Kingdom; or

(*b*) manufactured in the United Kingdom and sent out from the premises of a manufacturer of mechanical lighters,

a duty of excise at the rate of £0·20 for each lighter.

(2) The duty chargeable under subsection (1) above shall be chargeable on mechanical lighters which when imported or sent out as mentioned in that subsection are incomplete as well as on lighters which at that time are complete.

(3) No duty shall be chargeable under this section on a mechanical lighter which is shown to the satisfaction of the Commissioners to be constructed solely for the purposes of igniting gas for domestic use.

(4) The Commissioners may, subject to such conditions as they see fit to impose, exempt from the duty chargeable under this section any mechanical lighters which are shown to their satisfaction to be intended to be used as parts of miners' lamps.

(5) If, save as permitted under subsection (4) above or regulations under section 7 (1) below, a manufacturer of mechanical lighters sends out from his premises any mechanical lighter without payment of the duty chargeable on it under this section, he shall be liable on summary conviction to a penalty of £50, and any article in respect of which the offence was committed shall be liable to forfeiture.

Regulations about mechanical lighters

7.—(1) The Commissioners may make regulations—

(*a*) prohibiting the manufacture of mechanical lighters (including the assembling of parts of mechanical lighters, whether to form complete mechanical lighters or not) except by a person who holds a licence granted for that purpose under the regulations;

(*b*) for fixing the date of the expiration of licences granted under the regulations;

(*c*) for regulating the manufacture of mechanical lighters and the removal of them from the place of manufacture with a view to securing and collecting the excise duty chargeable on them;

(*d*) for requiring every manufacturer of mechanical lighters to give security by bond or otherwise—

(i) for the keeping of such records as, in pursuance of regulations under this subsection, he may be required to produce to an officer; and

(ii) for the payment of all excise duty payable by him;

(*e*) providing for the delivery to and receipt by manufacturers licensed under the regulations of mechanical lighters imported into or manufactured in the United Kingdom without payment of the excise duty chargeable on them;

(*f*) for authorising the removal from the premises of a manufacturer licensed under the regulations without payment of excise duty of mechanical lighters for exportation or shipment as stores or for warehousing for exportation or for use as stores;

(g) for the remission or repayment, subject to such conditions as may be prescribed in the regulations, of any excise duty chargeable or paid on mechanical lighters—

(i) which have been destroyed or have become unfit for use by unavoidable accident before removal from a manufacturer's premises; or

(ii) which have been sent back to the place of manufacture as being defective.

(2) Where an officer finds that the number of mechanical lighters in the stock or possession of a manufacturer of mechanical lighters is less than the manufacturer's recorded number, then, except in so far as the deficiency is explained by the manufacturer to the satisfaction of the Commissioners, mechanical lighters to the number of the deficiency shall be deemed to have been sent out from the premises of the manufacturer on the day on which the deficiency first came to the notice of the officer.

(3) In subsection (2) above the " recorded number ", in relation to a manufacturer of mechanical lighters, means the number of mechanical lighters which, according to records or other documents produced by him in pursuance of regulations under subsection (1) above to the officer concerned, ought to be in his stock or possession.

(4) If any person contravenes or fails to comply with any regulation made under subsection (1) above, he shall be liable on summary conviction to a penalty of £50, and any article in respect of which the offence was committed shall be liable to forfeiture.

(5) The power to make regulations under subsection (1) above shall be exercisable by statutory instrument and any statutory instrument by which the power is exercised shall be subject to annulment in pursuance of a resolution of either House of Parliament.

Supplementary

Interpretation

8.—(1) In this Act " mechanical lighter " has the meaning given by section 4 (1) above.

(2) This Act and the other Acts included in the Customs and Excise Acts 1979 shall be construed as one Act but where a provision of this Act refers to this Act that reference is not to be construed as including a reference to any of the others.

(3) Any expression used in this Act or in any instrument made under this Act to which a meaning is given by any other Act included in the Customs and Excise Acts 1979 has, except where the context otherwise requires, the same meaning in this Act or in any such instrument as in that Act; and for ease of reference the Table below indicates the expressions used in this Act to which a meaning is given by any other such Act—

Customs and Excise Management Act 1979

" the Commissioners "
" the Customs and Excise Acts 1979 "
" container "
" officer "
" shipment "
" stores "
" warehousing ".

Repeals and consequential amendments

9.—(1) The enactments specified in the Schedule to this Act are hereby repealed to the extent specified in the third column of that Schedule.

(2) In section 17 of the Finance Act 1972, after the subsection (2A) inserted by paragraph 2 of Schedule 2 to the Customs and Excise Duties (General Reliefs) Act 1979, there shall be inserted the following subsection—

> " (2B) Section 6 (4) of the Matches and Mechanical Lighters Duties Act 1979 (exemption of certain mechanical lighters) shall also be excepted from the enactments which are to have effect as mentioned in subsection (1) of this section.".

(3) In Note (2) to Group 1 in Schedule 7 to the Finance (No. 2) Act 1975, and in Note (2) to Group 8 in that Schedule, for the words " section 221 (4) of the Customs and Excise Act 1952 " there shall be substituted the words " section 4 (1) of the Matches and Mechanical Lighters Duties Act 1979 ".

(4) Nothing in subsection (2) or (3) above shall prejudice the operation of sections 15 to 17 of the Interpretation Act 1978 (which relate to the effect of repeals).

Citation and commencement

10.—(1) This Act may be cited as the Matches and Mechanical Lighters Duties Act 1979 and is included in the Acts which may be cited as the Customs and Excise Acts 1979.

(2) This Act shall come into operation on 1st April 1979.

SCHEDULE

Section 9 (1)

REPEALS

Chapter	Short title	Extent of repeal
15 & 16 Geo. 6 & 1 Eliz. 2 c. 44.	The Customs and Excise Act 1952.	Sections 219 to 222.
1 & 2 Eliz. 2 c. 34.	The Finance Act 1953.	Section 3 (3) and (5).
8 & 9 Eliz. 2 c. 44.	The Finance Act 1960.	In section 7, in subsection (1), from the beginning to the words "or similar contrivance", and subsections (3) and (4).
1963 c. 25.	The Finance Act 1963.	Section 4 (2).
1975 c. 45.	The Finance (No. 2) Act 1975.	Sections 12 and 13. In Schedule 3, paragraphs 8, 12 and 38.
1978 c. 42.	The Finance Act 1978.	In Schedule 12, paragraph 6.

Tobacco Products Duty Act 1979

(1979 c. 7)

ARRANGEMENT OF SECTIONS

An Act to consolidate the enactments relating to the excise duty on tobacco products. [22nd February 1979]

General Note

This Act consolidates the enactments relating to the excise duty on tobacco products.

S. 1 defines tobacco products; s. 2 provides for the charge and remission of tobacco products duty; s. 3 imposes an additional duty on higher tar cigarettes; s. 4 deals with the calculation of duty in case of cigarettes more than 9 cm. long; s. 5 concerns the retail price of cigarettes; s. 6 provides for alteration of rates of duty; s. 7 empowers Commissioners to make regulations for management of duty; s. 8 concerns a charge in cases of default; s. 9 confers general power to make regulations; s. 10 is the interpretation section; s. 11 contains repeals, savings and transitional and consequential provisions; s. 12 deals with citation and commencement.

The Act received the Royal Assent on February 22, 1979, and came into force on April 1, 1979.

Parliamentary Debates

Hansard, H.L. Vol. 397, cols. 418, 1170; Vol. 398, col. 832.

Table of Derivations

CUSTOMS AND EXCISE ACT 1952

1952	1979
s. 283 (2) (5)	s. 7 (2)
306	9

FINANCE ACT 1976

1976	1979
s. 4 (1)	s. 2 (1)
(2)	2 (2)
(3)	7 (1)
s. 4 (4)	s. 7 (2)
(5)	1 (2)
(6)	1 (1) (6)
s. 5	s. 5
6 (1)–(5)	6 (1)–(4)
7	8

FINANCE ACT 1977

1977	1979
s. 2 (2)	ss. 4, 6 (5)
(4)	1 (3)–(6)
s. 2 (5)–(7)	s. 1 (3)–(5)
3 (1)	Sch. 1
s. 3 (5)	s. 7 (1)

FINANCE ACT 1978

1978	1979
s. 1 (1) (2)	s. 3
(3)	ss. 4, 6 (5)
Sch. 12, para. 7 (2) .	s. 6 (1)-(4)

Tobacco products

1.—(1) In this Act " tobacco products " means any of the following products, namely,—

(*a*) cigarettes;

(*b*) cigars;

(*c*) hand-rolling tobacco;

(*d*) other smoking tobacco; and

(*e*) chewing tobacco,

which are manufactured wholly or partly from tobacco or any substance used as a substitute for tobacco, but does not include herbal smoking products.

(2) Subject to subsection (3) below, in this Act " hand-rolling tobacco " means tobacco—

(*a*) which is sold or advertised by the importer or manufacturer as suitable for making into cigarettes; or

(*b*) of which more than 25 per cent. by weight of the tobacco particles have a width of less than 0·6 mm.

(3) The Treasury may by order made by statutory instrument provide that in this Act references to cigarettes, cigars, hand-rolling tobacco, other smoking tobacco and chewing tobacco shall or shall not include references to any product of a description specified in the order, being a product manufactured as mentioned in subsection (1) above but not including herbal smoking products; and any such order may amend or repeal subsection (2) above.

(4) Subject to subsection (5) below, a statutory instrument by which there is made an order under subsection (3) above shall be laid before the House of Commons after being made; and unless the order is approved by that House before the expiration of 28 days beginning with the date on which it was made, it shall cease to have effect on the expiration of that period, but without prejudice to anything previously done under it or to the making of a new order.

In reckoning any such period no account shall be taken of any time during which Parliament is dissolved or prorogued or during which the House of Commons is adjourned for more than 4 days.

(5) Subsection (4) above shall not apply to any order containing a statement by the Treasury that the order does not extend the incidence of the duty or involve a greater charge to duty or a reduction of any relief; and a statutory instrument by which any such order is made shall be subject to annulment in pursuance of a resolution of the House of Commons.

(6) In this section " herbal smoking products " means products commonly known as herbal cigarettes or herbal smoking mixtures.

Charge and remission or repayment of tobacco products duty

2.—(1) There shall be charged on tobacco products imported into or manufactured in the United Kingdom a duty of excise at the rates shown, subject to section 3 below, in the Table in Schedule 1 to this Act.

(2) Subject to such conditions as they see fit to impose, the Commissioners shall remit or repay the duty charged by this section where

it is shown to their satisfaction that the products in question have been—

(*a*) exported or shipped as stores; or

(*b*) used solely for the purposes of research or experiment;

and the Commissioners may by regulations provide for the remission or repayment of the duty in such other cases as may be specified in the regulations and subject to such conditions as they see fit to impose.

Additional duty on higher tar cigarettes

3.—(1) In the case of any cigarette having a tar yield of not less than 20 mg. the Table in Schedule 1 to this Act shall have effect as if the rate of duty in paragraph 1 were increased by £2·25 per thousand cigarettes.

(2) The Commissioners may make regulations—

(*a*) prescribing how the tar yield of cigarettes is to be determined for the purposes of this section;

(*b*) without prejudice to section 2 (2) above, enabling the whole or any part of the additional duty imposed by this section to be remitted or repaid in such cases as may be specified in the regulations or determined by the Commissioners and subject to such conditions as they see fit to impose.

Calculation of duty in case of cigarettes more than 9 cm. long

4. For the purposes of the references to a thousand cigarettes in paragraph 1 in the Table in Schedule 1 to this Act and in section 3 (1) above any cigarette more than 9 cm. long (excluding any filter or mouthpiece) shall be treated as if each 9 cm. or part thereof were a separate cigarette.

Retail price of cigarettes

5.—(1) For the purposes of the duty chargeable at any time under section 2 above in respect of cigarettes of any description, the retail price of the cigarettes shall be taken to be—

(*a*) in a case in which paragraph (*b*) below does not apply, the highest price at which cigarettes of that description are normally sold by retail at that time in the United Kingdom;

(*b*) in any case where—

(i) there is a price recommended by the importer or manufacturer for the sale by retail at that time in the United Kingdom of cigarettes of that description; and

(ii) duty is tendered and accepted by reference to that price,

the price so recommended.

(2) The duty in respect of any number of cigarettes shall be charged by reference to the price which, in accordance with subsection (1) above, is applicable to cigarettes sold in packets of 20 or of such other number as the Commissioners may determine in relation to cigarettes of the description in question; and the whole of the price of a packet shall be regarded as referable to the cigarettes it contains notwithstanding that it also contains a coupon, token, card or other additional item.

(3) In any case in which duty is chargeable in accordance with paragraph (*a*) of subsection (1) above—

(*a*) the question as to what price is applicable under that paragraph shall, subject to subsection (4) below, be determined by the Commissioners; and (*b*) the Commissioners may require security (by deposit of money or otherwise to their satisfaction) for the payment of duty to be given pending their determination.

(4) Any person who has paid duty in accordance with a determination of the Commissioners under subsection (3) (*a*) above and is dissatisfied with their determination may require the question of what price was applicable under subsection (1) (*a*) above to be referred to the arbitration of a referee appointed by the Lord Chancellor, not being an official of any government department.

(5) If, on a reference to him under subsection (4) above, the referee determines that the price was lower than that determined by the Commissioners, they shall repay the duty overpaid together with interest on the overpaid duty from the date of the overpayment at such rate as the referee may determine.

(6) The procedure on any reference to a referee under subsection (4) above shall be such as may be determined by the referee; and the referee's decision on any such reference shall be final and conclusive.

Alteration of rates of duty

6.—(1) The Treasury may by order made by statutory instrument increase or decrease any of the rates of duty for the time being in force under the Table in Schedule 1 to this Act by such percentage of the rate, not exceeding 10 per cent., as may be specified in the order, but any such order shall cease to be in force at the expiration of a period of one year from the date on which it takes effect unless continued in force by a further order made under this subsection.

(2) In relation to any order made under subsection (1) above to continue, vary or replace a previous order so made, the reference in that subsection to the rate for the time being in force is a reference to the rate that would be in force if no order under that subsection had been made.

(3) A statutory instrument under subsection (1) above by which there is made an order increasing the rate in force at the time of making the order shall be laid before the House of Commons after being made; and unless the order is approved by that House before the expiration of 28 days beginning with the date on which it was made, it shall cease to have effect on the expiration of that period, but without prejudice to anything previously done under it or to the making of a new order.

In reckoning any such period no account shall be taken of any time during which Parliament is dissolved or prorogued or during which the House of Commons is adjourned for more than 4 days.

(4) A statutory instrument made under subsection (1) above to which subsection (3) above does not apply shall be subject to annulment in pursuance of a resolution of the House of Commons.

(5) For the purposes of this section—

(*a*) the percentage and the amount per thousand cigarettes in paragraph 1 in the Table in Schedule 1 to this Act shall be treated as separate rates of duty; and

(*b*) the increase specified in section 3 (1) above shall be treated as a rate of duty separate from that applying apart from the increase.

Regulations for management of duty

7.—(1) The Commissioners may with a view to managing the duty charged by section 2 above make regulations—

(*a*) prescribing the method of charging the duty and for securing and collecting the duty;

(*b*) for the registration of premises for the safe storage of tobacco products and for requiring the deposit of tobacco products in, and regulating their treatment in and removal from, premises so registered;

(*c*) for the registration of premises where—

(i) tobacco products are manufactured;

(ii) materials for the manufacture of tobacco products are grown, produced, stored or treated; or

(iii) refuse from the manufacture of tobacco products is stored or treated,

and for regulating the storage and treatment in, and removal from, premises so registered of such materials and refuse;

(*d*) for requiring the keeping and preservation of such records, and the making of such returns, as may be specified in the regulations; and

(*e*) for the inspection of goods, documents and premises.

(2) If any person fails to comply with any regulation made under subsection (1) above he shall be liable on summary conviction to a penalty of £200, and any article in respect of which, or found on premises in respect of which, the offence was committed shall be liable to forfeiture.

Charge in cases of default

8.—(1) Where the records or returns kept or made by any person in pursuance of regulations under section 2 or 7 above show that any tobacco products or materials for their manufacture are or have been in his possession or under his control, the Commissioners may from time to time require him to account for those products or materials.

(2) Unless a person required under subsection (1) above to account for any products or materials proves—

(*a*) that duty has been paid or secured under section 7 above in respect of the products or, as the case may be, products manufactured from the materials; or

(*b*) that the products or materials are being or have been otherwise dealt with in accordance with regulations under section 2 or 7 above,

the Commissioners may require him to pay duty under section 2 above in respect of those products or, as the case may be, in respect of such products as in their opinion might reasonably be expected to be manufactured from those materials.

(3) Where a person has failed to keep or make any records or returns required by regulations under section 2 or 7 above, or it appears to the Commissioners that any such records or returns are inaccurate or incomplete, they may require him to pay any duty under section 2 above which they consider would have been shown to be due if proper records or returns had been kept or made.

Regulations

9. Any power to make regulations under this Act shall be exercisable by statutory instrument and any statutory instrument by which the power is exercised shall be subject to annulment in pursuance of a resolution of either House of Parliament.

Interpretation

10.—(1) In this Act—

" hand-rolling tobacco " has the meaning given by section 1 (2) above; and

" tobacco products " has the meaning given by section 1 (1) above.

(2) This Act and the other Acts included in the Customs and Excise Acts 1979 shall be construed as one Act but where a provision of this Act refers to this Act that reference is not to be construed as including a reference to any of the others.

(3) Any expression used in this Act or in any instrument made under this Act to which a meaning is given by any other Act included in the Customs and Excise Acts 1979 has, except where the context otherwise requires, the same meaning in this Act or in any such instrument as in that Act; and for ease of reference the Table below indicates the expressions used in this Act to which a meaning is given by any other such Act—

Customs and Excise Management Act 1979

" the Commissioners "
" the Customs and Excise Acts 1979 "
" goods "
" importer "
" shipped "
" stores ".

Repeals, savings and transitional and consequential provisions

11.—(1) The enactments specified in Schedule 2 to this Act are hereby repealed to the extent specified in the third column of that Schedule, but subject to the provision at the end of that Schedule.

(2) Any provision of this Act relating to anything done or required or authorised to be done under or by reference to that provision or any other provision of this Act shall have effect as if any reference to that provision, or that other provision, as the case may be, included a reference to the corresponding provision of the enactments repealed by this Act.

(3) In section 3 (2) of the Finance Act 1977 (which makes provision in consequence of the replacement from 1st January 1978 of duty under section 4 of the Finance Act 1964 with duty under section 4 of the Finance Act 1976) for the words " the said Act of 1964 " there shall be substituted the words " the Finance Act 1964 ", for the words " the said Act of 1976 " there shall be substituted the words " the Finance Act 1976 " and after the words " the said 1st January " there shall be inserted the words " or under section 2 of the Tobacco Products Duty Act 1979 on or after 1st April 1979 ".

(4) Nothing in this section shall be taken as prejudicing the operation of sections 15 to 17 of the Interpretation Act 1978 (which relate to the effect of repeals).

Citation and commencement

12.—(1) This Act may be cited as the Tobacco Products Duty Act 1979 and is included in the Acts which may be cited as the Customs and Excise Acts 1979.

(2) This Act shall come into operation on 1st April 1979.

SCHEDULES

Section 2 (1)

SCHEDULE 1

TABLE OF RATES OF TOBACCO PRODUCTS DUTY

TABLE

1. Cigarettes	An amount equal to 30 per cent. of the retail price plus £9·00 per thousand cigarettes.
2. Cigars	£9·50 per pound.
3. Hand-rolling tobacco	£9·20 per pound.
4. Other smoking tobacco and chewing tobacco	£3·30 per pound.

Section 11 (1)

SCHEDULE 2

REPEALS

Chapter	Short Title	Extent of Repeal
15 & 16 Geo. 6 & 1 Eliz. 2. c. 44.	The Customs and Excise Act 1952.	In the proviso to section 27 (3), paragraph (i).
1976 c. 40.	The Finance Act 1976.	Sections 4, 5, 6 (1) to (5) and 7.
1977 c. 36.	The Finance Act 1977.	Sections 2 (2) and (4) to (8) and 3 (1) and (5).
1978 c. 42.	The Finance Act 1978.	Section 1. In Schedule 12, paragraph 7 (2).

The repeal in section 271 (3) of the Customs and Excise Act 1952 does not affect drawback by virtue of events occurring on or before 30th June 1978.

Excise Duties (Surcharges or Rebates) Act 1979

(1979 c. 8)

An Act to consolidate the provisions of section 9 of and Schedules 3 and 4 to the Finance Act 1961 with the provisions amending them. [22nd February 1979]

General Note

This Act consolidates s. 9 of and Scheds. 3 and 4 to the Finance Act 1961 with the provisions amending them.

S. 1 provides for surcharges or rebates of amounts due for excise duties; s. 2 deals with orders under s. 1; s. 3 concerns the application of certain enactments; s. 4 contains interpretation, consequential amendments, repeals and saving provisions; s. 5 deals with citations and commencement.

The Act received the Royal Assent on February 22, 1979, and came into force on April 1, 1979.

Parliamentary debates

Hansard, H.L. Vol. 397, cols. 556, 1171; Vol. 398, col. 832.

Table of Derivations

FINANCE ACT 1961

1961	1979	1961	1979	1961	1979
s. 9 (1)	s. 1 (2)	s. 9 (9)	s. 1 (1)	Sch. 4,	
(2)	1 (2)–(4)	(10) ...	3 (3)	para. 2 ...	s. 1 (3)
(3)	1 (1)	37 (3) ...	4 (1)	para. 4 ...	1 (6)
(4) (*c*) .	1 (2) (5)	Sch. 3,		para. 7 ...	1 (7)
(5)	1 (5)	(1) (2)			
(7)	3 (1)	para. 2	2 (6) (7)		
(8)	3 (2)	para. 3 ...	2 (5)		

FINANCE ACT 1964

1964	1979	1964	1979	1964	1979
s. 8 (2)	s. 1 (1)	s. 8 (4)	s. 1 (2)	s. 8 (6)	s. 2 (8) (9)
(3)	ss. 1 (2), 2 (3)	(5)	2 (3)–(5)	26 (3) ...	4 (1)

FINANCE ACT 1968

1968	1979
s. 10 (2)	s. 1 (1)

HYDROCARBON OIL (CUSTOMS & EXCISE) ACT 1971

1971	1979
Sch. 6, para. 2 ..	s. 1 (7)

FINANCE ACT 1971

1971	1979
s. 3 (5)	s. 1 (1)

EUROPEAN COMMUNITIES ACT 1972

1972	1979
s. 5 (3)	s. 1 (1)

NORTHERN IRELAND CONSTITUTION ACT 1973

1973	1979
s. 40 (2)	s. 1 (1)

FINANCE (NO. 2) ACT 1975

1975	1979
s. 8 (4)	s. 1 (1)
14 (5)	1 (1)
15 (6)	1 (1)
Sch. 3, para. 1 .	1 (1)

FINANCE ACT 1976

1976	1979
s. 2 (7)	s. 1 (1)
6 (6)	1 (1)
Sch. 3, paras. 8, 9	1 (1)

FINANCE ACT 1977

1977	1979
s. 10 (4)	s. 1 (1)

FINANCE ACT 1978

1978	1979
s. 6 (4)	s. 1 (1)
10	2 (2)

Surcharges or rebates of amounts due for excise duties

1.—(1) This section applies to the following groups of excise duties, namely—

(*a*) those chargeable in respect of spirits (other than power methylated spirits), beer, wine, made-wine and cider;

(*b*) those chargeable in respect of hydrocarbon oil, petrol substitutes, power methylated spirits and road fuel gas;

(*c*) all other duties of excise except—

(i) that chargeable on tobacco products;

(ii) those payable on a licence; and

(iii) those with respect to which the Parliament of Northern Ireland would, if the Northern Ireland Constitution Act 1973 had not been passed, have had power to make laws.

(2) If it appears to the Treasury that it is expedient, with a view to regulating the balance between demand and resources in the United Kingdom, that an order under this section should be made with respect to one or more of the groups of duties to which this section applies, the Treasury may by order provide for an adjustment—

(*a*) of every liability to a duty within that group or any of those groups; and

(*b*) of every right to a drawback, rebate or allowance in connection with such a duty,

by the addition to or deduction from the amount payable or allowable of such percentage, not exceeding 10 per cent., as may be specified in the order.

(3) The adjustment under this section of a liability to duty shall be made where the duty becomes due while the order is in force with respect to it, except that if the duty pool betting duty it shall instead be made where the bets (whenever made) are made by reference to an event taking place while the order is in force with respect to the duty.

(4) The adjustment under this section of a right to any drawback, rebate or allowance in respect of a duty or goods charged with a duty shall be made where the right arises while the order is in force with respect to the duty (whenever the duty became due); but in calculating the amount to be adjusted any adjustment under this section of the liability to the duty shall be disregarded.

(5) A repayment of any duty within a group to which this section applies or of drawback or allowance in respect of such a duty or goods chargeable with such a duty shall be calculated by reference to the amount actually paid or allowed (after effect was given to any adjustment falling to be made under this section) but save as aforesaid this section does not require the adjustment of any such repayment.

(6) Subsection (5) above shall apply to any payment under section 94 or 95 of the Customs and Excise Management Act 1979 (deficiency in goods in or from warehouse) in the case of goods warehoused on drawback which could not lawfully be entered for home use (being a payment of an amount equal to the drawback and any allowance paid in respect of the goods) as if it were a repayment of drawback or allowance.

(7) The preceding provisions of this section shall apply to repayments of duty under the following provisions of the Hydrocarbon Oil Duties Act 1979—

(*a*) section 9 (4) (repayment of duty on oil put to an industrial use which would have qualified it for duty-free delivery);

(*b*) section 17 (relief for heavy oil used by horticultural producers);

(*c*) section 18 (relief for heavy oil used as fuel in ships in home waters);

(*d*) section 19 (relief for oil etc. used in fishing boats, lifeboats and lifeboat launching gear),

as if the repayments were drawbacks and not repayments.

Orders under s. 1

2.—(1) The following provisions of this section shall have effect with respect to orders under section 1 above.

(2) No order shall be made or continue in force after the end of August 1979 or such later date as Parliament may hereafter determine.

(3) An order may specify different percentages for different groups of duties but must apply uniformly to all the duties within the same group.

(4) An order may not provide for additions in the case of one or more groups and deductions in the case of another or others.

(5) An order may be made so as to come into operation at different times of day for different duties, whether or not within the same group.

(6) The power to make an order shall be exercisable by statutory instrument.

(7) Any statutory instrument by which an order is made shall be laid before the House of Commons after being made, and the order shall cease to have effect at the end of 21 days after that on which it is made unless at some time before the end of those 21 days the order is approved by a resolution of that House.

(8) Except in the case of such an order as is mentioned in subsection (9) below, in reckoning the period of 21 days specified in subsection (7) above no account shall be taken of any time during which Parliament is dissolved or prorogued or during which the House of Commons is adjourned for more than 4 days.

(9) Subsection (8) above does not apply to an order which, with respect to all or any of the groups of duties,—

(*a*) specifies a percentage by way of addition to duty, or increases a percentage so specified; or

(*b*) withdraws, or reduces, a percentage specified by way of deduction from duty.

Application of certain enactments

3.—(1) The enactments relating to the collection or recovery or otherwise to the management of any duty within a group to which section 1 above applies shall apply to the amount of any adjustment under that section as if it were duty, drawback, rebate or allowance, as the case may be.

(2) For the purposes of subsections (1) and (2) of section 10 of the Finance Act 1901 (adjustment of contract prices and variation of duties) the beginning or ending of a period during which an order under section 1 above is in force with respect to any duty, or the variation of a percentage specified in such an order, shall be treated as an increase or decrease (as the case may require) of that duty; and references in those subsections to an amount paid on account of an increase of duty, to having had the benefit of a decrease of duty, and to the amount of the decrease of duty shall be construed accordingly.

(3) For the purposes of section 2 of the Isle of Man Act 1958 (Isle of Man share of equal duties) the amount of equal duties collected in the Isle of Man and the United Kingdom, or in the Isle of Man, shall be calculated by reference to the amount so collected in respect of such duties after giving effect to any addition or deduction provided for under section 1 above or any corresponding provisions of the law of the Isle of Man.

Interpretation, consequential amendments, repeals and saving

4.—(1) Any expression used in this Act and in any Act included in the Customs and Excise Acts 1979 has the same meaning in this Act as in that Act.

(2) The enactments specified in Schedule 1 to this Act shall be amended in accordance with the provisions of that Schedule.

(3) The enactments specified in Schedule 2 to this Act are hereby repealed to the extent specified in the third column of that Schedule.

(4) If at the commencement of this Act an order under section 9 of the Finance Act 1961 is in force, the order shall have effect as if made under this Act.

Citation and commencement

5.—(1) This Act may be cited as the Excise Duties (Surcharges or Rebates) Act 1979.

(2) This Act shall come into operation on 1st April 1979.

SCHEDULES

Section 4 (2)

SCHEDULE 1

CONSEQUENTIAL AMENDMENTS

Finance (No. 2) Act 1964

1. In section 9 (8) of the Finance (No. 2) Act 1964, for the words " section 9 of the Finance Act 1961 " there shall be substituted the words " section 1 of the Excise Duties (Surcharges or Rebates) Act 1979 ".

Finance Act 1965

2. In section 92 (2) of the Finance Act 1965, for the words " section 9 of the Finance Act 1961 " there shall be substituted the words " section 1 of the Excise Duties (Surcharges or Rebates) Act 1979 ".

Finance Act 1966

3. In section 2 (12) of the Finance Act 1966, for the words "section 9 of the Finance Act 1961" there shall be substituted the words "section 1 of the Excise Duties (Surcharges or Rebates) Act 1979".

Section 4 (3)

SCHEDULE 2

REPEALS

Chapter	Short title	Extent of Repeal
9 & 10 Eliz. 2 c. 36.	The Finance Act 1961.	Section 9. Schedules 3 and 4.
1964 c. 49.	The Finance Act 1964.	Section 8.
1968 c. 44.	The Finance Act 1968.	Section 10 (2).
1971 c. 12.	The Hydrocarbon Oil (Customs & Excise) Act 1971.	In Schedule 6, paragraph 2.
1971 c. 68.	The Finance Act 1971.	Section 3 (5).
1976 c. 40.	The Finance Act 1976.	Section 6 (6). In Schedule 3, paragraph 8.
1978 c. 42.	The Finance Act 1978.	In section 6 (4) the words preceding "any duty" and the words "and any such duty". Section 10.

Films Act 1979

(1979 c. 9)

An Act to amend section 6 of the Films Act 1960.

[22nd February 1979]

General Note

This Act amends the Films Act 1960.

S. 1 substitutes a new s. 6 (1) of the Films Act 1960; s. 2 gives the short title.

The Act received the Royal Assent on February 22, 1979, and came into force on that date.

Parliamentary debates

Hansard, H.C. Vol. 959, col. 1438; Vol. 961, col. 990; H.L. Vol. 398, cols. 12, 1201 and 1922.

Amendment of section 6 of Films Act 1960

1. For subsection (1) of section 6 of the Films Act 1960 there shall be substituted the following subsection:—

" (1) Where—

(*a*) a film registered as a foreign film (other than a Community film) is to be or is being exhibited at a cinema; and

(*b*) before or while it is exhibited there an application for a direction under this section is made to the Secretary of State by the exhibitor who exhibits films at that cinema,

the Secretary of State may, if he thinks fit, direct that, if the period during which the film is exhibited at that cinema is or includes such a continuous period exceeding eight weeks as is specified in the direction, the requirements imposed by section 1 of this Act shall be deemed to be complied with in relation to that cinema in the relevant year, if they are so complied with in that year and the succeeding year taken together.".

Citation

2. This Act may be cited as the Films Act 1979; and the Films Acts 1960 to 1970, section 8 of the European Communities Act 1972 and this Act may be cited together as the Films Acts 1960 to 1979.

Public Lending Right Act 1979

(1979 c. 10)

ARRANGEMENT OF SECTIONS

SECT.

An Act to provide public lending right for authors, and for connected purposes. [22nd March 1979]

General Note

This Act provides for public lending right for authors.

S. 1 deals with the establishment of public lending right; s. 2 relates to the Central Fund; s. 3 provides for the administration of the scheme; s. 4 establishes a register of books and their authors; s. 5 deals with citation and interpretation. The Act extends to Northern Ireland.

The Act received the Royal Assent on March 22, 1979, and comes into force on a day to be appointed.

Parliamentary debates

Hansard, H.C. Vol. 957, cols. 355, 1360; Vol. 958, col. 30; Vol. 959, col. 1439; Vol. 961, cols. 1393; H.L. Vol. 398, cols. 142, 988; Vol. 399, col. 13.

Establishment of public lending right

1.—(1) In accordance with a scheme to be prepared and brought into force by the Secretary of State, there shall be conferred on authors a right, known as " public lending right ", to receive from time to time out of a Central Fund payments in respect of such of their books as are lent out to the public by local library authorities in the United Kingdom.

(2) The classes, descriptions and categories of books in respect of which public lending right subsists, and the scales of payments to be made from the Central Fund in respect of it, shall be determined by or in accordance with the scheme; and in preparing the scheme the Secretary of State shall consult with representatives of authors and library authorities and of others who appear to be likely to be affected by it.

(3) The Secretary of State shall appoint an officer to be known as the Registrar of Public Lending Right; and the Schedule to this Act has effect with respect to the Registrar.

(4) The Registrar shall be charged with the duty of establishing and maintaining in accordance with the scheme a register showing the books in respect of which public lending right subsists and the persons entitled to the right in respect of any registered book.

(5) The Registrar shall, in the case of any registered book, determine in accordance with the scheme the sums (if any) due by way of public lending right; and any sum so determined to be due shall be recoverable from the Registrar as a debt due to the person for the time being entitled to that right in respect of the book.

(6) Subject to any provision made by the scheme, the duration of public lending right in respect of a book shall be from the date of the book's first publication (or, if later, the beginning of the year in which

application is made for it to be registered) until 50 years have elapsed since the end of the year in which the author died.

(7) Provision shall be made by the scheme for the right—

(*a*) to be established by registration;

(*b*) to be transmissible by assignment or assignation, by testamentary disposition or by operation of law, as personal or moveable property;

(*c*) to be claimed by or on behalf of the person for the time being entitled;

(*d*) to be renounced (either in whole or in part, and either temporarily or for all time) on notice being given to the Registrar to that effect.

The Central Fund

2.—(1) The Central Fund shall be constituted by the Secretary of State and placed under the control and management of the Registrar.

(2) There shall be paid into the Fund from time to time such sums, out of money provided by Parliament, as the Secretary of State with Treasury approval determines to be required for the purpose of satisfying the liabilities of the Fund; but in respect of the liabilities of any one financial year of the Fund the total of those sums shall not exceed £2 million less the total of any sums paid in that year, out of money so provided, under paragraph 2 of the Schedule to this Act (pay, pension, etc. of Registrar).

(3) With the consent of the Treasury, the Secretary of State may from time to time by order in a statutory instrument increase the limit on the sums to be paid under subsection (2) above in respect of financial years beginning after that in which the order is made; but no such order shall be made unless a draft of it has been laid before the House of Commons and approved by a resolution of that House.

(4) There shall be paid out of the Central Fund—

(*a*) such sums as may in accordance with the scheme be due from time to time in respect of public lending right; and

(*b*) the administration expenses of the Registrar and any other expenses and outgoings mentioned in this Act which are expressed to be payable from the Fund.

(5) Money received by the Registrar in respect of property disposed of, or otherwise in the course of his functions, or under this Act, shall be paid into the Central Fund, except in such cases as the Secretary of State otherwise directs with the approval of the Treasury; and in any such case the money shall be paid into the Consolidated Fund.

(6) The Registrar shall keep proper accounts and other records and shall prepare in respect of each financial year of the Fund statements of account in such form as the Secretary of State may direct with Treasury approval; and those statements shall, on or before 31st August next following the end of that year, be transmitted to the Comptroller and Auditor General, who shall examine and certify the statements and lay copies thereof, together with his report thereon, before each House of Parliament.

The scheme and its administration

3.—(1) As soon as may be after this Act comes into force, the Secretary of State shall prepare the draft of a scheme for its purposes and lay a copy of the draft before each House of Parliament.

(2) If the draft scheme is approved by a resolution of each House,

the Secretary of State shall bring the scheme into force (in the form of the draft) by means of an order in a statutory instrument, to be laid before Parliament after it is made; and the order may provide for different provisions of the scheme to come into force on different dates.

(3) The scheme shall be so framed as to make entitlement to public lending right dependent on, and its extent ascertainable by reference to, the number of occasions on which books are lent out from particular libraries, to be specified by the scheme or identified in accordance with provision made by it.

(4) For this purpose, " library "—

(*a*) means any one of a local library authority's collections of books held by them for the purpose of being borrowed by the public; and

(*b*) includes any such collection which is taken about from place to place.

(5) The scheme may provide for requiring local library authorities—

(*a*) to give information as and when, and in the form in which, the Registrar may call for it or the Secretary of State may direct, as to loans made by them to the public of books in respect of which public lending right subsists, or of other books; and

(*b*) to arrange for books to be numbered, or otherwise marked or coded, with a view to facilitating the maintenance of the register and the ascertainment and administration of public lending right.

(6) The Registrar shall, by means of payments out of the Central Fund, reimburse to local library authorities any expenditure incurred by them in giving effect to the scheme, the amount of that expenditure being ascertained in accordance with such calculations as the scheme may prescribe.

(7) Subject to the provisions of this Act (and in particular to the foregoing provisions of this section), the scheme may be varied from time to time by the Secretary of State, after such consultation as is mentioned in section 1 (2) above, and the variation brought into force by an order in a statutory instrument, subject to annulment in pursuance of a resolution of either House of Parliament; and the variation may comprise such incidental and transitional provisions as the Secretary of State thinks appropriate for the purposes of continuing the scheme as varied.

(8) The Secretary of State shall in each year prepare and lay before each House of Parliament a report on the working of the scheme.

The register

4.—(1) The register shall be kept in such form, and contain such particulars of books and their authors, as may be prescribed.

(2) No application for an entry in the register is to be entertained in the case of any book unless it falls within a class, description or category of books prescribed as one in respect of which public lending right subsists.

(3) The scheme shall provide for the register to be conclusive both as to whether public lending right subsists in respect of a particular book and also as to the persons (if any) who are for the time being entitled to the right.

(4) Provision shall be included in the scheme for entries in the register to be made and amended, on application made in the prescribed manner and supported by prescribed particulars (verified as prescribed) so as to

indicate, in the case of any book, who (if any one) is for the time being entitled to public lending right in respect of it.

(5) The Registrar may direct the removal from the register of every entry relating to a book in whose case no sum has become due by way of public lending right for a period of at least 10 years, but without prejudice to a subsequent application for the entries to be restored to the register.

(6) The Registrar may require the payment of fees, according to prescribed scales and rates, for supplying copies of entries in the register; and a copy of an entry, certified under the hand of the Registrar or an officer of his with authority in that behalf (which authority it shall be unnecessary to prove) shall in all legal proceedings be admissible in evidence as of equal validity with the original.

(7) It shall be an offence for any person, in connection with the entry of any matter whatsoever in the register, to make any statement which he knows to be false in a material particular or recklessly to make any statement which is false in a material particular; and a person who commits an offence under this section shall be liable on summary conviction to a fine of not more than £1,000.

(8) Where an offence under subsection (7) above which has been committed by a body corporate is proved to have been committed with the consent or connivance of, or to be attributable to any neglect on the part of, a director, manager, secretary or other similar officer of the body corporate, or any person who was purporting to act in any such capacity, he (as well as the body corporate) shall be guilty of that offence and be liable to be proceeded against accordingly.

Where the affairs of a body corporate are managed by its members, this subsection applies in relation to the acts and defaults of a member in connection with his functions of management as if he were a director of the body corporate.

Citation, etc.

5.—(1) This Act may be cited as the Public Lending Right Act 1979.

(2) In this Act any reference to " the scheme " is to the scheme prepared and brought into force by the Secretary of State in accordance with sections 1 and 3 of this Act (including the scheme as varied from time to time under section 3 (7); and—

" local library authority " means—

(*a*) a library authority under the Public Libraries and Museums Act 1964,

(*b*) a statutory library authority within the Public Libraries (Scotland) Act 1955, and

(*c*) an Education and Library Board within the Education and Libraries (Northern Ireland) Order 1972;

" prescribed " means prescribed by the scheme;

" the register " means the register required by section 1 (4) to be established and maintained by the Registrar; and

" the Registrar " means the Registrar of Public Lending Right.

(3) This Act comes into force on a day to be appointed by an order made by the Secretary of State in a statutory instrument to be laid before Parliament after it has been made.

(4) This Act extends to Northern Ireland.

Section 1 (3)

SCHEDULE

The Registrar of Public Lending Right

1. The Registrar shall hold and vacate office as such in accordance with the terms of his appointment; but he may at any time resign his office by notice in writing addressed to the Secretary of State; and the Secretary of State may at any time remove a person from the office of Registrar on the ground of incapacity or misbehaviour.

2.—(1) There shall be paid to the Registrar out of money provided by Parliament such remuneration and allowances as the Secretary of State may determine with the approval of the Minister for the Civil Service.

(2) In the case of any such holder of the office of Registrar as may be determined by the Secretary of State with that approval, there shall be paid out of money so provided such pension, allowance or gratuity to or in respect of him, or such contributions or payments towards provision of such a pension, allowance or gratuity, as may be so determined.

3. If, when a person ceases to hold office as Registrar, it appears to the Secretary of State that there are special circumstances which make it right that he should receive compensation, there may (with the approval of the Minister for the Civil Service) be paid to him out of the Central Fund a sum by way of compensation of such amount as may be so determined.

4. In the House of Commons Disqualification Act 1975, in Part III of Schedule 1 (other disqualifying offices), the following shall be inserted at the appropriate place in alphabetical order—

"Registrar of Public Lending Right";

and the like insertion shall be made in Part III of Schedule 1 to the Northern Ireland Assembly Disqualification Act 1975.

5.—(1) The Registrar of Public Lending Right shall be by that name a corporation sole, with a corporate seal.

(2) He is not to be regarded as the servant or agent of the Crown.

6. The Documentary Evidence Act 1968 shall have effect as if the Registrar were included in the first column of the Schedule to that Act, as if the Registrar and any person authorised to act on his behalf were mentioned in the second column of that Schedule, and as if the regulations referred to in that Act included any documents issued by the Registrar or by any such person.

7.—(1) The Registrar may appoint such assistant registrars and staff as he thinks fit, subject to the approval of the Secretary of State as to their numbers; and their terms and conditions of service, and the remuneration and allowances payable to them, shall be such as the Registrar may determine.

(2) The Registrar may direct, in the case of persons appointed by him under this paragraph—

(*a*) that there be paid to and in respect of them such pensions, allowances and gratuities as he may determine;

(*b*) that payments be made towards the provision for them of such pensions, allowances and gratuities as he may determine; and

(*c*) that schemes be provided and maintained (whether contributory or not) for the payment to and in respect of them of such pensions, allowances and gratuities as he may determine.

(3) Any money required for the payment of remuneration and allowances under this paragraph, and of pensions, allowances and gratuities, and otherwise for the purposes of sub-paragraph (2) above, shall be paid from the Central Fund.

(4) The approval of the Secretary of State and the Minister for the Civil Service shall be required for any directions or determination by the Registrar under this paragraph.

8. Anything authorised or required under this Act (except paragraph 7 of this Schedule), or by or under the scheme, to be done by the Registrar may be done by any assistant registrar or member of the Registrar's staff who is authorised generally or specially in that behalf in writing by the Registrar.

Electricity (Scotland) Act 1979

(1979 c. 11)

ARRANGEMENT OF SECTIONS

PART I

THE BOARDS

Constitution

PART III

An Act to consolidate certain enactments relating to the North of Scotland Hydro-Electric Board and the South of Scotland Electricity Board and to functions of the Secretary of State in relation to the generation and distribution of electricity in Scotland with amendments to give effect to recommendations of the Scottish Law Commission. [22nd March 1979]

General Note

This Act consolidates certain enactments relating to electricity Boards in Scotland and to functions of the Secretary of State in relation to the generation and distribution of electricity in Scotland.

Pt. I (ss. 1–31) deals with the constitution, functions and duties of Boards: s. 1 provides for the constitution of Boards; s. 2 defines the districts of the Boards; s. 3 sets out the functions of the Boards; s. 4 specifies the general duties of the Boards in exercising their functions; s. 5 lists the duties of the Boards in relation to the amenity of the environment; s. 6 sets out the duty of the North Board in relation to economic development; s. 7 gives the Boards ancillary powers; s. 8 empowers the Boards to enter into agreements with each other, and with other persons; s. 9 governs the purchase and supply of electricity; s. 10 deals with contractual schemes; s. 11 authorises the acquisition of land for constructional schemes; s. 12 relates to the compulsory purchase of land; s. 13 gives ancillary powers in relation to land; s. 14 empowers the Boards to conduct experiments; s. 15 provides for research into heating from electricity; s. 16 enables the Boards to enter into agreements for technical assistance overseas; s. 17 deals with the establishment of Consultative Councils; s. 18 relates to the general fund; s. 19 concerns the general reserve fund of the South Board; s. 20 sets out sums which are to be chargeable by the South Board to revenue account; s. 21 provides for application of surplus revenues of the South Board; s. 22 deals with the fixing and variation of tariffs; s. 25 empowers the Treasury to guarantee loans to the Boards; s. 26 authorises the Boards to issue stock; s. 27 gives the Boards power to borrow; s. 28 deals with the application of money borrowed; s. 29 places a limit on the aggregate of amounts outstanding; s. 30 deals with accounts and audit; s. 31 relates to exemption from taxes.

Pt. II (ss. 32–38) defines the powers of the Secretary of State; s. 32 relates to the Secretary's powers; s. 33 empowers Secretary to give directions; s. 34

authorises transfer orders; s. 35 concerns control of new private hydro-electric generating stations; s. 36 deals with compensation for members and officers of the Boards; s. 37 empowers the Secretary to make regulations concerning pension rights; s. 38 deals with inquiries.

Pt. III (ss. 39–47) contains general and miscellaneous provisions; s. 39 relates to disputes between the Boards; s. 40 provides for the making of orders and regulations; s. 41 sets out offences and penalties; s. 42 deals with annual reports, statistics and returns; s. 43 empowers Boards to promote and oppose private legislation; s. 44 concerns service of notices; s. 45 is the interpretation section; s. 46 contains transitional and saving provisions and consequential amendments and repeals; s. 47 contains the short title, extent and commencement. The Act extends to Scotland only, except for para. 1 (*b*) of Sched. 3 which extends also to England and Wales.

The Act received the Royal Assent on March 22, 1979, and came into force on April 22, 1979.

Parliamentary debates

Hansard, H.L. Vol. 396, cols. 27, 662; Vol. 397, cols. 418, 848; H.C. Vol. 964, col. 412.

Table of Derivations

INTERPRETATION ACT 1889

1889	1979
s. 32 (1)	s. 2 (4)

HYDRO-ELECTRIC DEVELOPMENT (SCOTLAND) ACT 1943

1943	1979
s. 1	s. 1
2 (1)	ss. 2 (1), 3 (1)
2 (1) (*a*) (*c*)	s. 3 (2)
2 (2)	3 (3)
(3)	6
(4)	8 (1) (*b*)
3 (*b*)	7 (4)
(*c*)	ss. 7 (3), 11 (1)
5 (1)	s. 10 (1)
proviso	10 (3)
(2)	10 (2), Sch. 5, para. 1
(3)	s. 10 (2), Sch. 5, paras. 2, 3
(4)	s. 10 (2), Sch. 5, para. 4
proviso	s. 10 (2), Sch. 5, para. 5
(5)	s. 10 (2), Sch. 5, para. 6
(6)	s. 10 (2), Sch. 5, paras. 7, 8
(7)	s. 10 (2), Sch. 5, para. 9

1943	1979
s. 7	Sch. 5, para. 10
8 (1)–(5)	s. 11 (2)–(6)
9 (1)	5
(2)	s. 5, Sch. 4, paras. 1, 2
(3)–(6)	s. 5, Sch. 4, paras. 3–6
(7)	s. 5, Sch. 11
10	s. 18
10A	22
11 (1) (2)	28 (1) (2)
(3)	28 (3) (4)
(4)	28 (5)
11A (1) (2)	19 (1) (2)
(2) (*a*)	19 (3)
(*b*)	19 (4)
(3)	19 (6)
(4)	19 (5)
12 (1)	27 (1)–(3)
(2)	27 (4) (5)
(3)	27 (6)
proviso	27 (7)
(4)	27 (8) (9)
(5)	27 (9)
13 (1) (2)	26 (1) (2)
(3)	26 (3) (4)
14	25
15 (1) (2)	30 (1) (2)
(3)	30 (3) (4)

1943	1979
s. 16 (2) (3)	s. 9 (1)
(3A)	9 (2)
(4) (5)	9 (3) (4)
22	35 (1)
proviso	35 (2)
23	42
24	38 (2)
25	14
26	35 (3)
27	45 (1)
28	45 (1)
Sch. 1, para. 1	Sch. 1, paras. 1,2
paras. 5–14	Sch. 1, paras. 3–12
Sch. 2	Sch. 2, para. 1
Sch. 3, paras. 1, 2	Sch. 6, paras. 1, 2
paras. 4–9	Sch. 6, paras. 3–8
Sch. 6, paras. 1–11	Sch. 8, paras. 1–11

STATUTORY INSTRUMENTS ACT 1946

1946	1979
s. 1 (2)	s. 40 (1)
5 (2)	Sch. 5, para. 6

ELECTRICITY ACT 1947

1947	1979
s. 1 (2)	ss. 2 (1), 45 (1)
(3)	s. 8 (3), 45 (1)
(4)	8 (2)
(4) (*a*) (*c*)	8 (1) (*a*)
(5)	8 (1) (*a*) (2)
(6)	4
(7)	2 (1), 3 (1)
2 (1) (2)	4
(3)	7 (1)
proviso	7 (2)
(5)	7 (3)
(7)	8 (3) (4)
(8)	ss. 4, 7 (1) (3), 8 (4)
4 (2)	s. 2 (2) (4), Sch. 2, para. 7
(3)	s. 2 (3), Sch. 2, para. 3
(4)	ss. 2 (3), 40 (4)
(5)	s. 2 (3), Sch. 2, paras. 4, 5
(6)	2 (3)
(7)	ss. 2 (2) (3), 40 (4), Sch. 2, paras. 3–7
(8)	Sch. 2, paras. 3–7
5 (1)–(4)	s. 33 (1)–(4)
(7)	33 (1)–(4)
7A (1)	17 (1)
(2) (3)	17 (2), Sch. 7, paras. 1, 2
(4)–(7)	17 (2), Sch. 7, paras. 5–8
s. 7A (8)	s. 17 (2), Sch. 7, paras. 9, 10
(9)–(11)	s. 17 (2)
(12) (13)	17 (2), Sch. 7, paras. 3, 4
8 (4)	s. 17 (2) Sch. 7, para. 11
9 (1)	s. 12 (1) (2)
(2)	12 (3)–(5)
(3)	12 (6)
(4)	12 (1)(2)
10	43
11	31
19 (1) (2)	34
44 (1)	21 (1)
44 (1) (*a*) (*b*)	21 (2) (3)
45 (1) (2)	20
47 (7)	29
50 (1)	15 (1)
(2) (3)	15 (2)
(4)	40 (3)
51 (1) (2)	13 (8) (9)
54 (1)	37 (1)
(2)	37 (3)
(3)	37 (4) (5)
(4)	37 (2)
(7)	37 (1)
(8)	37 (6)
55 (1)	36 (2)
(2)	36 (4)
(4)	36 (3)
(5)	36 (4)
(7)	40 (4) (6)
s. 57 (5)	s. 34
61 (1)	41 (1)
(2)	40 (6)
62 (2)	41 (2)
63	44, Sch. 9
64 (1) (2)	s. 40 (6)
(3)	(2)
(7)	(7)
66 (1) (2)	s. 38 (1) (2)
67 (1)	ss. 8 (3) 45 (1)
67 (3)	s. 45 (2)
68 (2)	12 (2) (4)
(3)	ss. 12 (5),
68 (4)	43, 45 (1)
69 (1)	s. 45 (1)
Sch. 1	45 (1)
Sch. 4, Part II	ss. 3 (1)–(3), 5 (2), 9 (1) (3) (4), 10 (1) (3), 25 (1), 27 (1) (4) (6), 28 (1) (2) (5), 30 (1) (3) (4), 35, 42, 45 (1), Sch. 1, paras. 1, 3, 12, Sch. 2, para. 1, Sch. 4, para. 3, Sch. 5, paras. 2–5, 9

HYDRO-ELECTRIC DEVELOPMENT (SCOTLAND) ACT 1952

1952	1979
s. 1 (1)	s. 29 (1)

ELECTRICITY REORGANISATION (SCOTLAND) ACT 1954

1954	1979
s. 1 (1)	s. 32
(2)	ss. 32, 37 (1) (2) (5)
2 (1)	1, 2 (1), Sch. 2, para. 2
(2)	2 (1), 3 (1), 4, 5 (1), 7, 8 (1) (*a*), 10, 11 (1), 12 (1), 13 (8), 14, 15 (1), 31
10 (3)	s. 29 (1)
11 (1)–(4)	39 (1)–(4)
14 (2)	45 (2)
17	45 (1)
Sch. 1, Pt. I	ss. 3 (1)–(3), 5 (2), 6, 9
Sch. 1, Pt. I	10 (1)(3), 11 (1)–(3) (5) (6), 14, 18, 19, 22, 25 (1) (5) (6), 26 (1)–(3), 27 (1) (2) (4)–(6), 28, 30 (1)–(3), 35, 42, 45 (1), Sch. 1, paras. 1–8, 10–12, Sch. 2, paras. 3–7, Sch. 4, paras. 1–6, Sch. 5,
Sch. 1, Pt. I	paras. 2–4, 8–10, Sch. 6, paras. 1, 3–5, 7, 8, Sch. 8, paras. 2, 3
Pt. II	ss. 2 (3), 8 (1) (*a*) (2) (4), 10 (1), 12 (1)–(5), 13 (8), 15 (2), 20, 21, 29 (1), 33, 34, 37 (1) (2) (5), 38 (1), 43, 45 (1), Sch. 7, para. 11
Sch. 2, Pt. II	ss. 2 (2), 8 (1) (*a*)

Electricity Act 1957

1957	1979
s. 1	s. 45 (1)
3	45 (1)
5 (2)	17 (1) (2)
28 (1)	3 (2), Sch. 3, para. 1
(2)	3 (4), Sch. 3, para. 1
(5)	s. 3 (4), Sch. 3, para. 2
(6)	s. 3 (4)
(7)	3 (4), Sch. 3, para. 4
(8)	s. (4), Sch. 3, para. 5
s. 28 (9)	ss. 3 (4), 45 (1), Sch. 3, paras. 2, 3
29	s. 23
35 (1)	13 (1)
(2)	13 (2) (5)
(3) (4)	13 (6) (7)
(5)	13 (2)–(7)
40 (1)	45 (1), Sch. 3, paras. 2–4
(3)	45 (2)
43 (1)	45 (1)
Sch. 1, Pt. II	s. 17 (1) (2), Sch. 7, paras. 1–10
Sch. 4, Pt. I	ss. 4, 7 (3), 8 (2) (3), 15 (1), 20, 34, 37 (6), 38 (1), 44
Pt. II	8 (1) (*b*), 9 (2), 22 (1)

House of Commons Disqualification Act 1957

1957	1979
Sch. 4, Pt. I	s. 17 (2)

Tribunals and Inquiries Act 1958

1958	1979
s. 15	s. 37 (5)
Sch. 2, Pt. II	37 (5)

Electricity (Borrowing Powers) Act 1959

1959	1979
s. 1 (1) (*b*) (ii)	s. 29 (1)

Electricity (Borrowing Powers) (Scotland) Act 1962

1962	1979
s. 1	s. 29 (1)

Electricity and Gas Act 1963

1963	1979
s. 2 (1)	s. 24 (1)
(3) (4)	24 (2) (3)
s. 2 (6) (7)	s. 24 (4) (5)
3	36 (1)
Sch. 1	29 (1) (2)
Sch. 2	s. 29 (1)
Sch. 3	29 (1)

Redundancy Payments Act 1965

1965	1979
s. 44	ss. 36 (4), 37 (5)
Sch. 7, para. 7	36 (4), 37 (5)

Gas and Electricity Act 1968

1968	1979
s. 5	s. 16

Electricity (Scotland) Act 1969

1969	1979
s. 2	Sch. 1, para. 9

Post Office Act 1969

1969	1979
Sch. 4, para. 8 (*f*)	s. 12 (6)
(*h*)	Sch. 3, para. 5
para. 93 (1)	s. 13 (4)

Chronically Sick and Disabled Persons Act 1970

1970	1979
s. 14 (1)	s. 17 (1)

ELECTRICITY ACT 1972

1972	1979
s. 1 (2)	s. 29 (1)
(3)	40 (3)
Sch.	34

TOWN AND COUNTRY PLANNING (SCOTLAND) ACT 1972

1972	1979
s. 168	s. 13 (7)
265 (8)	13 (2)
s. 266 (1)	s. 13 (3)
(2)	13 (5)
(5)	13 (7)
s. 266 (6)	s. 13 (4)
275 (1)	13 (4) (7)

LOCAL GOVERNMENT (SCOTLAND) ACT 1973

1973	1979
s. 1	Sch. 2, para. 1
Sch. 1	Sch. 2, para. 1

STATUTORY CORPORATIONS (FINANCIAL PROVISIONS) ACT 1974

1974	1979
Sch. 2	s. 29

STATUTORY CORPORATIONS (FINANCIAL PROVISIONS) ACT 1975

1975	1979
s. 5 (1)	s. 27 (1)
Sch. 2	27 (1)
Sch. 3, para. 1	17 (2)
Sch. 3, paras. 2–4	s. 17 (2), Sch. 7, paras. 11–14
para. 5	s. 17 (2)
paras. 6–9	17 (2), Sch. 7, paras. 15–18
Sch. 4, para. 1 (*a*)	s. 27 (1) (2)
(*b*)	27 (2) (8) (9)

ELECTRICITY (FINANCIAL PROVISIONS) (SCOTLAND) ACT 1976

1976	1979
s. 1 (1)	s. 29 (1)
3 (1)	40 (5)
(2)	40 (7)

SCOTTISH LAW COMMISSION'S REPORT

Recommendation No.	1979
1	s. 2 (3), Sch. 2, para. 5
2	s. 8 (2)
3	13 (3) (6) (7)
4	33 (4)
5	41 (1)

PART I

Constitution of Boards

1.—(1) The North of Scotland Hydro-Electric Board established by section 1 of the Act of 1943 (in this Act referred to as " the North Board ") and the South of Scotland Electricity Board established by section 2 of the Act of 1954 (in this Act referred to as " the South Board ") shall continue in existence, and are referred to in this Act as " the Boards ".

(2) Schedule 1 shall have effect in relation to the constitution and proceedings of the Boards.

Definition and variation of districts

2.—(1) Subject to the provisions of this section, the districts of the North and South Boards shall continue to be as defined in Parts I and II of Schedule 2 respectively.

(2) Subject to subsection (3), the Secretary of State may, after giving to each Board an opportunity to make representations, by order vary the districts defined in Schedule 2 and any such variation may include the formation of a new district from any part of an existing district or parts of existing districts, or the amalgamation with an existing district of the whole or part of any other existing district.

(3) Part III of Schedule 2 shall have effect in relation to any order made under subsection (2).

(4) In subsection (2), " existing " means existing immediately before the order in question is made.

Principal functions

Functions of the Boards

3.—(1) Subject to the provisions of this Act, the Boards shall be responsible for initiating and undertaking the development of all means of generation of electricity within their respective districts.

(2) Subject to any directions of the Secretary of State and the provisions of this Act, it shall, so far as practicable, be the duty—

(*a*) of the South Board—

(i) to plan and carry out an efficient and economic distribution of supplies of electricity to persons in their district;

(ii) to provide supplies of electricity to meet the requirements for haulage or traction of railway undertakers in their district;

(*b*) of the North Board—

(i) to provide supplies of electricity required to meet the demands of ordinary consumers in their district;

(ii) to provide supplies of electricity suitable for the needs of large power users in their district, including the requirements for haulage or traction of railway undertakers.

(3) Subject to any duty of the North Board to supply electricity to the South Board, the duties imposed on the North Board under head (i) of paragraph (*b*) of subsection (2) shall have priority over all other demands for the electricity generated by them.

(4) Schedule 3 shall have effect in relation to the supply of electricity by the Boards to railway undertakers under subsection (2).

General duties in exercising functions

4. In exercising and performing their functions the Boards shall, subject to and in accordance with any directions given by the Secretary of State under section 33—

(*a*) promote the use of all economical methods of generating, transmitting and distributing electricity;

(*b*) secure so far as practicable, the development, extension to rural areas and cheapening of supplies of electricity;

(*c*) avoid undue preference in the provision of such supplies;

(*d*) promote the simplification and standardisation of methods of charge for such supplies;

(*e*) promote the standardisation of systems of supply and types of electrical fittings;

(*f*) promote the welfare, health and safety of persons in their employment and in consultation with any organisation appearing to them to be appropriate make provision for advancing the skill of persons employed by them and for improving the efficiency of their equipment and of the manner in which that equipment is to be used, including provision by them, and the assistance of the provision by others, of facilities for training and education;

(*g*) conduct research into matters affecting the supply of electricity and assist other persons conducting such research.

Duty in relation to amenity

5.—(1) In the exercise of their functions the Boards shall have regard in relation to their respective districts to the desirability of preserving the beauty of the scenery and any object of architectural or historical interest and of avoiding as far as possible injury to fisheries and to the stock of fish in any waters.

(2) For the purpose of giving advice and assistance to the Secretary of State and to each of the Boards, the Secretary of State shall appoint two Committees (in this Act referred to as the Amenity Committee and the Fisheries Committee respectively); and Schedule 4 shall have effect in relation to the constitution, proceedings and functions of those Committees.

Duty of North Board in relation to economic development

6. The North Board shall, so far as their powers and duties permit, collaborate in the carrying out of any measures for the economic development and social improvement of the whole or any part of their district.

Powers and duties

Ancillary powers

7.—(1) Subject to subsection (2), each of the Boards shall have power—

(*a*) to manufacture electrical plant and electrical fittings;

(*b*) to sell, hire or otherwise supply electrical plant and electrical fittings and to instal, repair, maintain or remove any electrical plant and electrical fittings;

(*c*) to carry on all such other activities as may appear to the Board concerned to be requisite, advantageous or convenient for them to carry on for or in connection with the performance of their duties under this Act, or with a view to making the best use of any assets vested in them.

(2) Subsection (1) shall not apply to the manufacture of electrical plant or electrical fittings for export.

(3) The Boards may do anything and enter into any transaction (whether or not involving the expenditure, the borrowing in accordance with the provisions of this Act or the lending of money, the acquisition of any property or rights or the disposal of any property or rights not in their opinion required for the proper exercise and performance of their functions) which in their opinion is calculated to facilitate the proper exercise or performance of any of their functions under this Act or is incidental or conducive thereto.

(4) The Boards may collect for the purposes of their powers and duties under this Act information as to the requirements of the whole or any part of their respective districts in respect of electricity.

Powers of Boards to enter into agreements with each other, and with other persons

8.—(1) Subject to this section and section 9 either of the Boards may by agreement—

(*a*) with each other—

(i) give to or acquire from the other Board bulk supplies of electricity;

(ii) supply electricity to consumers in the district of the other Board;

(*b*) with the Generating Board or with any person or body of persons carrying on an electricity undertaking outside Great Britain, provide bulk supplies of electricity for the Generating Board or for that undertaking

(2) If either of the Boards are unable to obtain the agreement of the other Board under head (ii) of paragraph (*a*) of subsection (1), they may apply to the Secretary of State for an authorisation to supply electricity to consumers in such part of the district of the other Board as may be specified in the application, and if the Secretary of State gives such authorisation the Board which has applied for it shall have power to supply electricity in accordance with it.

(3) Either of the Boards may by agreement with the other Board use for the purposes of any of their functions any works, plant or other property of the other Board.

(4) If it appears to the Secretary of State that such use cannot be obtained by agreement between the Boards and is required by one of them for the purpose of securing efficient and economical services he may by order authorise such use by that Board on such terms and conditions (including the payment of money) as he may determine.

Purchase and supply of electricity

9.—(1) Either of the Boards may purchase electricity from the other Board on such terms and conditions as they may agree.

(2) Either of the Boards may purchase electricity from any other person (other than an Area Board) on such terms and conditions as may be agreed with that person but—

(*a*) where any purchase of electricity is made by either of the Boards from a person in the district of the other Board any such purchase shall require the approval of that other Board; or

(*b*) where any purchase of electricity is made by either of the Boards from a person in the area of an Area Board, any such purchase shall require the approval of the Generating Board.

(3) The South Board and the North Board may enter into and carry into effect agreements for the construction by either Board of such main transmission lines as are necessary for the delivery of electricity purchased under this section, and for that purpose the powers of either Board shall be exercisable in the district of the other.

(4) Any question between the Boards under this section shall be determined by an arbiter appointed by the Secretary of State.

Constructional schemes

10.—(1) Each of the Boards shall in respect of their respective districts prepare schemes (in this Act referred to as " contructional schemes ") with a view to the execution of works necessary for the generation of electricity by water power, other than works required for the replacement or renewal of works already authorised.

(2) Schedule 5 shall have effect in relation to constructional schemes.

(3) If the Secretary of State is satisfied that a proposed extension of existing works involves only works of a minor character he may, subject to such conditions as he may think fit to impose, authorise the Board concerned to execute those works without the preparation of a constructional scheme.

Acquisition of land etc. for purposes of constructional schemes

11.—(1) For the purpose of carrying out any scheme confirmed under section 10, the Board authorised to carry out the scheme so confirmed may, subject to the provisions of this Act,

(*a*) acquire such land,

(*b*) abstract, divert and use such water,

(*c*) divert such roads, and

(*d*) construct, operate and maintain such works and plant,

as may be necessary for that purpose, and do any other thing necessary for the effective exercise and discharge of their powers and duties.

(2) Subject to the provisions of the Land Compensation (Scotland) Acts 1963 and 1973, and of this section, the Lands Clauses Acts and section 6 and sections 70 to 78 of the Railways Clauses Consolidation (Scotland) Act 1845 shall apply in accordance with the provisions of Schedule 6 for the purposes of the acquisition of land which either of the Boards are authorised by a constructional scheme to acquire.

(3) If it appears to the Board concerned necessary or expedient for the purpose of carrying out a constructional scheme to enter upon and take possession of any land which they are authorised by the scheme to acquire, they may, after giving not less than 28 days' notice by registered post to the persons appearing from the valuation roll to be the owners and occupiers of that land, enter upon and take possession of that land, and may give such directions as appear to them to be necessary or expedient in connection with the taking of possession of that land.

(4) A certified copy of any direction to give up possession of and remove from any land given under subsection (3) shall be sufficient warrant for ejection against any occupier or any party in his right in the event of non-compliance with any such direction.

(5) Land of which either of the Boards are in possession in pursuance of subsection (3) may, notwithstanding any restriction imposed on the use of that land under any enactment or otherwise, be used, subject to the provisions of the scheme, by the Board in such manner as they think expedient for the purpose of carrying out the scheme.

(6) Where in the exercise of the powers conferred on them by subsection (3) either of the Boards have taken possession of any land, they shall as soon as may be proceed with the acquisition of the land and shall, if they are unable to acquire the land by agreement, serve notice to treat.

Compulsory purchase of land

12.—(1) This section applies to land required by either of the Boards for any purpose connected with the discharge of their functions, not being land required by them for the purposes of a constructional scheme under section 10.

(2) The Secretary of State may authorise either of the Boards to purchase compulsorily any land to which this section applies and the Acquisition of Land (Authorisation Procedure) (Scotland) Act 1947 shall apply in relation to any such compulsory purchase as if the Board making the purchase were a local authority within the meaning of that Act and

as if this Act had been in force immediately before the commencement of that Act.

(3) Either of the Boards may be authorised under this section to purchase compulsorily a right to place an electric line across land, whether above or below ground, and a right to repair and maintain the line, without purchasing any other interest in the land.

(4) The said Act of 1947 shall have effect in relation to compulsory purchase under subsection (3) as if references to the land comprised in the compulsory purchase order were construed as references to the land across which the line is to be placed and as if references to the obtaining or taking possession of the land comprised in the order were construed as references to the exercise of the right to place the line across land.

(5) In this section " land " includes servitudes and other rights over land.

(6) Section 14 of the Schedule to the Electric Lighting (Clauses) Act 1899 shall, so far as it relates to the Post Office, apply to the placing of an electric line in pursuance of any right purchased under subsection (3) as it applies to the execution of works involving the placing of lines in, under, along or across any street or public bridge.

Ancillary powers in relation to land

13.—(1) Without prejudice to any other rights of entry exercisable by the Boards, any person duly authorised in writing by either of the Boards may, subject to the provisions of this section, at any reasonable time enter upon and survey any land, not being land covered by buildings or used as a garden or pleasure ground, for the purpose of ascertaining whether the land would be suitable for use for the purposes of any functions of the Board.

(2) In subsection (1) the power conferred to survey land includes power, subject to subsection (4), to search and bore for the purpose of ascertaining the nature of the subsoil.

(3) Any person duly authorised by either of the Boards under subsection (1) to enter on any land shall, if so required, produce evidence of his authority before so entering and shall not demand admission as of right to any land which is occupied unless 28 days' notice of the intended entry has been given to the occupier.

(4) Where a person proposes to carry out works authorised by virtue of subsection (2)—

(*a*) he shall not carry out those works unless notice of his intention to do so was included in the notice given under subsection (3); and

(*b*) if the land in question is held by statutory undertakers, and those undertakers object to the proposed works on the grounds that the carrying out of the works would be seriously detrimental to the carrying on of their undertaking, the works shall not be carried out except with the authority of the Secretary of State.

In this subsection " statutory undertakers " has the meaning given by the Town and Country Planning (Scotland) Act 1972 and includes the Post Office.

(5) Any person who wilfully obstructs a person acting in the exercise of his powers under subsection (1) shall be guilty of an offence and liable on summary conviction to a fine not exceeding £20.

(6) Where in the exercise of any power conferred by subsection (1) any damage is caused to land or to corporeal moveables, any person interested in the land or moveables may recover compensation in respect of that damage from the Board by whom or on whose behalf the power

is exercised; and where in consequence of the exercise of any such power any person is disturbed in his enjoyment of any land or moveables he may recover from that Board compensation in respect of the disturbance.

(7) Any question of disputed compensation under subsection (6) shall be referred to and determined by the Lands Tribunal for Scotland, and in relation to the determination of any such question sections 9 and 11 of the Land Compensation (Scotland) Act 1963 shall apply.

(8) Where either of the Boards—

(*a*) acquire a bulk supply of electricity which is received by them outside their district, or

(*b*) provide a supply of electricity outside their district,

that Board may, in accordance with proposals submitted by them to the Secretary of State and approved by him, exercise outside their district for the purpose of such acquisition or the provision of such supply any powers exercisable within their district by that Board under this Act or the Electricity (Supply) Acts or any local enactment, being powers relating to the breaking up of streets, railways and tramways which would not be so exercisable apart from this subsection.

(9) The powers conferred by subsection (8) shall be exercisable in like manner and subject to the like provisions and restrictions as they are exercisable by the Board concerned for the purpose of the supply of electricity in the district of that Board.

Power to conduct experiments

14. Either of the Boards may conduct experiments or trials for the improvement of methods of generation, distribution or use of electricity in the special conditions and circumstances in their respective districts and may for that purpose incur such expenditure as they may think fit.

Research into heating from electricity

15.—(1) It shall be the duty of the Boards to investigate methods by which heat obtained from or in connection with the generation of electricity may be used for the heating of buildings in neighbouring localities or for any other useful purpose, and the Boards may accordingly conduct or assist others in conducting research into any matters relating to such methods of using heat.

(2) Either of the Boards may provide or assist other persons to provide for the heating of buildings by any such methods or otherwise for the use of heat so obtained, and may, in accordance with a scheme submitted by the Board concerned to the Secretary of State and approved by order made with or without modification by him, exercise for those purposes the powers conferred by section 13 (8) for the purposes of that section, and section 13 (9) shall apply in relation to the manner in which those powers are exercisable.

Agreements for technical assistance overseas

16.—(1) The Boards may, with the consent of the Secretary of State, enter into and carry out agreements with the relevant Minister in pursuance of which the Boards, or one or other of them, may act at the expense of the Minister as the instrument by means of which technical assistance is furnished by him in exercise of the power conferred on him by section 1 (1) of the Overseas Aid Act 1966.

(2) In this section " the relevant Minister " means the Minister of the Crown by whom is exercisable the powers conferred on the Minister of Overseas Development by that section 1 (1) as originally enacted.

Consultation

Consultative Councils

17.—(1) The Consultative Councils established for the districts of each of the Boards under section 7A of the Act of 1947 shall continue in existence.

(2) Schedule 7 shall have effect in relation to the constitution, proceedings and functions of those Councils.

Finance

General Fund

18.—(1) It shall be the duty of each of the Boards so to exercise and perform their functions under this Act as to secure that their respective revenues are not less than sufficient to meet their outgoings properly chargeable to revenue account, taking one year with another.

(2) All sums received by the Boards on revenue account from whatever source, including any interest on money invested, shall in the case of each Board be credited to and form part of a fund to be called the " general fund ".

General reserve fund of the South Board

19.—(1) The South Board shall continue to maintain the general reserve fund established in pursuance of section 11A of the Act of 1943.

(2) The South Board shall contribute to the general reserve fund such sums at such times as the Board may determine, and the management of the fund and the application of the monies contained in the fund shall, subject to the provisions of this section, be as the Board may determine.

(3) No part of the general reserve fund shall be applied otherwise than for the purposes of the South Board.

(4) The Secretary of State may, with the approval of the Treasury, give directions of a general or specific character to the South Board as to any matter relating to the management of the general reserve fund, the carrying of sums to the credit thereof, or the application thereof.

(5) One of the purposes of the general reserve fund is the prevention of frequent fluctuations in the charges made by the South Board, and the powers of the Board in relation to the said fund shall be exercised accordingly.

(6) The provisions of this section shall be without prejudice to the power of the South Board to establish appropriate reserves for replacements or other purposes.

Sums which are to be chargeable by the South Board to revenue account

20. The South Board shall charge to the general fund in every year all charges which are proper to be made to revenue account including in particular—

(*a*) proper allocations to the general reserve fund;
(*b*) proper provision for the redemption of capital;
(*c*) proper provision for depreciation of assets or for renewal of assets; and
(*d*) all payments (including the payments which are by the relevant provision of this Act or by any other relevant enactment to be deemed to be capital payments) which fall to be made in that year to any local authority under this Act or the Act of 1947 in respect of any loan by that local authority;

and references in this Act to outgoings properly chargeable to revenue account shall be construed accordingly.

Application of surplus revenues of the South Board

21.—(1) Subject to the provisions of this section any excess of the revenues of the South Board for any financial year over their outgoings for that year properly chargeable to revenue account shall be applied for such purposes as that Board may determine.

(2) No part of any such excess shall be applied otherwise than for the purposes of the South Board.

(3) The Secretary of State may, with the approval of the Treasury, give directions of a general or specific character to the South Board as to the application of any such excess.

Fixing and variation of tariffs

22.—(1) The prices to be charged by each Board for the supply of electricity shall be in accordance with such tariffs as may be fixed by that Board from time to time.

(2) The tariffs fixed under subsection (1) shall be so framed as to show the methods by which, and the principles on which, the charges are to be made as well as the prices which are to be charged, and shall be published in such manner as in the opinion of each Board will secure adequate publicity for them.

(3) A tariff fixed by either of the Boards in respect of a supply of electricity by virtue of the provisions of this Act may include a rent or other charge in respect of electrical fittings provided by the Board on the premises of the consumer.

(4) Notwithstanding anything in the foregoing provisions of this section, in cases where the tariffs in force are not appropriate owing to special circumstances a Board may enter into an agreement with any consumer for the supply of electricity to him on such terms as may be specified in the agreement.

(5) The Boards in fixing tariffs and making agreements under this section shall not show undue preference to any person or class of persons and shall not exercise any undue discrimination against any person or class of persons.

Maximum charges for reselling electricity supplied by the Boards

23.—(1) Either of the Boards may publish a notice fixing maximum charges in consideration of which electricity supplied by the Board may be resold by persons to whom it is so supplied or by any class of such persons specified in the notice.

(2) Any notice under this section shall be published in such manner as in the opinion of the Board concerned will secure adequate publicity for it, and the maximum charges fixed by any such notice may be varied by a subsequent notice published by that Board in accordance with this subsection.

(3) Different maximum charges may be fixed by either Board under this section for different classes of cases, whether by reference to different parts of the district of the Board concerned or by reference to different tariffs under which electricity is supplied by that Board or by reference to any other relevant circumstances.

(4) If, in consideration of the resale of any electricity supplied by either of the Boards in circumstances to which a notice published by that Board under this section applies, any person requires the payment of

charges exceeding the maximum charges applicable thereto in accordance with the notice, the amount of the excess shall be recoverable by the person to whom the electricity is resold.

Exchequer advances to the Boards

24.—(1) The Secretary of State may, with the approval of the Treasury, advance to the Boards or either of them any sums which the Boards have power to borrow.

(2) Any advances made by the Secretary of State under subsection (1) shall be repaid to him at such times and by such methods, and interest thereon shall be paid to him at such rates and at such times, as he may with the approval of the Treasury from time to time direct.

(3) The Treasury may issue out of the National Loans Fund to the Secretary of State such sums as are necessary to enable him to make advances under this section.

(4) Any sums received by the Secretary of State under subsection (2) shall be paid into the National Loans Fund.

(5) In respect of each financial year the Secretary of State shall prepare, in such form and manner as the Treasury may direct, an account of sums issued to him under this section and of the sums to be paid into the National Loans Fund under subsection (4) and of the disposal by him of those sums respectively, and shall send it to the Comptroller and Auditor General not later than the end of November following that financial year; and the Comptroller and Auditor General shall examine, certify and report on the account and lay copies of it, together with his report, before each House of Parliament.

Power to Treasury to guarantee loans to the Boards

25.—(1) Subject to the provisions of this section, the Treasury may guarantee, in such manner and on such conditions as they think fit, the payment of the interest and principal of any loan proposed to be raised by either Board, or of either the interest or the principal.

(2) Such sums as may from time to time be required by the Treasury for fulfilling any guarantees given under this section shall be charged on and issued out of the Consolidated Fund.

(3) The repayment to the Treasury of any sums so issued out of the Consolidated Fund, together with interest thereon at such rate as the Treasury may fix, shall be a charge on the undertaking and all the revenues of the Board next after the principal and interest of the guaranteed loan and any sinking fund payments for the repayment of the principal thereof, and in priority to any other charges not existing at the date on which the loan is raised.

(4) All sums paid from time to time in or towards the repayment of any sum issued out of the Consolidated Fund under this section shall be paid into the Exchequer.

(5) Immediately after a guarantee is given under this section, the Treasury shall lay a statement of the guarantee before each House of Parliament.

(6) Where any sum is issued out of the Consolidated Fund under this section the Treasury shall forthwith lay before each House of Parliament a statement that that sum has been issued.

Power to issue stock

26.—(1) The Boards may for the purpose of raising money which they are authorised to borrow under this Act, create and issue stock.

(2) Any stock issued by either of the Boards and the interest thereon shall be charged on the undertaking and all the revenues of that Board.

(3) Subject to the provisions of this Act, any stock created by the Boards under this section shall be issued, transferred, dealt with, and redeemed according to regulations to be made by the Secretary of State with the approval of the Treasury.

(4) Regulations made under subsection (3) may apply for the purposes of this section, with or without modifications, any provisions of any Act relating to stock issued by a local authority.

Power of the Boards to borrow

27.—(1) Subject to the provisions of this section, either of the Boards may for the purposes to which this section applies, with the consent of the Secretary of State (which shall require the approval of the Treasury) and subject to regulations to be made by the Secretary of State with the approval of the Treasury, borrow money in sterling or foreign currency from any source, whether within or outwith the United Kingdom, in such manner and subject to such provisions as to repayments as may be prescribed

(2) Each Board shall have such powers as may be prescribed with respect to reborrowing for the purpose of paying off a loan previously raised under this section.

(3) Regulations under subsection (1) may provide—

(*a*) for either of the Boards to borrow temporarily; and

(*b*) for the application, with or without modifications, of any enactments relating to borrowing by local authorities.

(4) The purposes to which this section applies are—

(*a*) the acquisition of such land and the acquisition or construction of such works as the Boards are authorised to acquire or construct;

(*b*) the provision of working capital;

(*c*) providing temporarily for any current expenses properly chargeable to revenue;

(*d*) the making of any other payment which the Boards are authorised to make and which ought in the opinion of the Secretary of State to be spread over a term of years, including the payment of interest on money borrowed for capital expenditure for such period as may be determined by the Secretary of State with the approval of the Treasury, not exceeding the period during which the expenditure remains unremunerative.

(5) Any money borrowed for any of the purposes to which this section applies, and the interest on any such money, shall be charged on the undertaking and all the revenues of the Board concerned.

(6) It shall be lawful for any annual provision required to be made by the North Board for the repayment of money borrowed under this section to be suspended subject to such conditions and for such period, not exceeding the period during which the relative expenditure remains unremunerative, as the Secretary of State, with the approval of the Treasury, may determine.

(7) Where any annual provision is suspended under subsection (6) that suspension shall not be for a period exceeding 5 years from the commencement of the financial year following that in which such expenditure is incurred.

(8) The amount outstanding in respect of the principal of any sums of foreign currency borrowed under this section or section 3 of the Gas and Electricity Act 1968, and of any sums of sterling borrowed from

outwith the United Kingdom under this section, shall be included in the aggregate of the amounts outstanding in respect of loans raised by the Boards which is subject to the limit imposed by section 29.

(9) Nothing in subsection (8) shall—

(*a*) prevent the Boards from borrowing in excess of the limit mentioned in that subsection for the purpose of repaying the principal of any such sums borrowed by them under this section or the said section 3, or for the purpose of redeeming any securities issued under either of those sections which they are required or entitled to redeem;

(*b*) be taken as exempting the Boards from the provisions of any order under section 1 of the Borrowing (Control and Guarantees) Act 1946 or from the provisions of the Exchange Control Act 1947.

Application of money

28.—(1) All money borrowed by either of the Boards shall be applied to the purpose for which it is authorised to be borrowed up to the amount required for that purpose, and any excess over that amount and all other capital money received by the Board in respect of their undertaking, including money arising from the disposal of lands acquired by the Board for the purposes of any scheme, shall be applied towards the discharge of any loan, or, with the approval of the Secretary of State, to any other purpose to which capital may properly be applied.

(2) In the case of the North Board there shall be paid out of the general fund all the expenses of the Board which are properly chargeable to revenue including, without prejudice to the generality of this provision—

(*a*) interest on money borrowed and the sums required to be set aside for the repayment thereof;

(*b*) payments to the reserve fund;

(*c*) the salaries, fees and allowances to members of the Board;

(*d*) the salaries, remuneration, allowances of, and payments made for the purpose of providing superannuation allowances and gratuities for, the members and the secretary, officers and servants of the Board or their representatives; and

(*e*) expenditure on the operation, maintenance and repair of the works, machinery and plant forming part of the undertaking of the Board.

(3) The North Board may provide out of revenue a reserve fund by setting aside such sums as they think reasonable and investing such sums, and the resulting income thereof, in securities of Her Majesty's Government in the United Kingdom or securities guaranteed as to principal and interest by the Government, not being securities of that Board.

(4) The reserve fund shall be applicable to meet any deficiency at any time existing in the income of the North Board from their undertaking or to meet any extraordinary claim or demand at any time arising against the Board in respect of their undertaking.

(5) The North Board may make provision for the carrying forward of such working balance as they may consider reasonably necessary and may, with the approval of the Secretary of State, apply any surplus revenues in payment of expenses chargeable to capital.

Limit on aggregate of amount outstanding

29.—(1) The aggregate of the amounts outstanding in respect of—

(a) the principal of any stock issued (other than stock issued to the Central Authority under section 47 of the Act of 1947 and transferred to the South Board by virtue of section 5 (1) of the Act of 1954); and

(b) any loans raised by the Boards; and

(c) any advances, whether temporary or otherwise, made to either of those Boards under section 42 of the Finance Act 1956 or under section 2 of the Electricity and Gas Act 1963, or under section 24,

shall not at any time exceed the sum of £1,500 million, or such greater sum not exceeding £1,950 million as the Secretary of State may by order specify.

(2) Nothing in this section shall prevent the Boards from borrowing in excess of the said sum for the purposes of redeeming any stock which they are required or entitled to redeem or of repaying any such loans or any such advances.

Accounts and audit

30.—(1) The Boards shall each cause proper books of account and other books in relation thereto to be kept and shall prepare an annual statement of accounts in such form as the Secretary of State with the approval of the Treasury may direct, being a form which shall conform with the best commercial standards and which shall be such as to secure the provision of separate information as respects the generation of electricity, the distribution of electricity and each of the main other activities of the Board concerned and to show as far as may be the financial and operating results of each such activity.

(2) The accounts of each Board and their officers shall be audited by an auditor appointed by the Secretary of State and the audit shall be conducted in such manner as may be prescribed.

(3) As soon as the accounts of either of the Boards have been audited that Board shall send copies to the Secretary of State, together with copies of any report of the auditor, and shall publish the accounts in such manner as the Secretary of State may direct, and shall place copies of the accounts on sale at a reasonable price.

(4) The Secretary of State shall lay before each House of Parliament a copy of the accounts of each of the Boards and of any reports thereon sent to him under subsection (3).

Exemption from taxes

31.—(1) Subject to the provisions of this section, nothing in this Act shall exempt either of the Boards from any liability for tax, duty, rate, levy or other charge whatsoever, whether general or local.

(2) For the purposes of section 52 of the Finance Act 1946 (which exempts from stamp duty certain documents connected with nationalisation schemes) any transfer of property from one of the Boards to the other effected by an order made under this Act shall be deemed to be part of the initial putting into force of such a scheme.

PART II

POWERS OF SECRETARY OF STATE

Powers of the Secretary of State

32. The Secretary of State shall continue to exercise the functions transferred to him by subsections (1) and (2) of section 1 of the Act of 1954 (functions relating to the generation and supply of electricity in Scotland and matters connected therewith).

Power to give directions

33.—(1) The Secretary of State may after consultation with either of the Boards give to that Board such directions of a general character as to the exercise and performance by the Board of their functions under this Act as appear to the Secretary of State to be requisite in the national interest, and the Board shall give effect to any such directions.

(2) In carrying out such measures of reorganisation, or such works of development, as involve substantial outlay on capital account, the Boards shall act in accordance with a general programme settled from time to time in consultation with the Secretary of State.

(3) In the exercise and performance of their functions as to training, education and research the Boards shall act in accordance with a general programme settled from time to time in consultation with the Secretary of State.

(4) The Secretary of State may, after consultation with either of the Boards, give to that Board directions as to the use or disposal of any assets vested in them, being assets which are not connected with the generation, transmission or distribution of electricity; and the Board shall give effect to any such directions.

Transfer orders

34. The Secretary of State may, after consulting the Boards, provide by order—

(*a*) for the transfer to either of the Boards of any property, rights, liabilities and obligations vested in the other Board;

(*b*) for the modification of agreements so far as necessary for giving effect to the transfer of rights, liabilities and obligations thereunder from one of the Boards to the other, and, in a case where part only of the rights, liabilities and obligations under any agreement are transferred, for substituting for the agreement separate agreements in the requisite terms, and for any apportionments and indemnities consequent thereon;

(*c*) in connection with the transfer to one of the Boards of part of the land comprised in any lease vested in the other Boards for the severance of that lease and for apportionments and indemnities consequent thereon;

(*d*) for such other financial adjustments between the Boards as may be required in consequence of any such order, and for any other matters supplementary to or consequential on the matters aforesaid for which provision appears to the Secretary of State to be necessary or expedient, including the application to the Board to whom the transfer is made of the provisions of any local enactment applicable to the Board from whom the transfer is made.

Control of new private hydro-electric generating stations

35.—(1) It shall not be lawful, except with the consent of the Secretary of State given after consultation with the North Board or the South Board, as the case may be, for any body or person to establish in the district of either Board a new private generating station operated by water power and having plant with a rating exceeding 50 kilowatts, or to extend any existing private generating station so operated in that district by the installation of plant with a rating exceeding 50 kilowatts.

(2) The Secretary of State shall not refuse his consent to the establishment or extension of any such station if he is satisfied that such establishment or extension would not prejudice the exercise or performance by the Board concerned of their powers or duties regarding the development of further means of generation of electricity by water power.

(3) Where consent is given by the Secretary of State under subsection (1) to any body or person, nothing in this Act shall prevent that body or person from exercising any powers otherwise competent to them in relation to the construction or extension of the station and the carrying out of any other works necessary for the operation of the station.

Compensation for members and officers of the Boards

36.—(1) Where a person ceases otherwise than on the expiry of his term of office to be a member of either of the Boards and it appears to the Secretary of State that there are special circumstances which make it right that that person should receive compensation, the Secretary of State may, with the approval of the Minister for the Civil Service, require the Board concerned to make to that person a payment of such amount as may be determined by the Secretary of State with the approval of the Minister for the Civil Service.

(2) The Secretary of State shall by regulations require the Boards and any Board established by order made under section 2 to pay, in such cases and to such extent as may be specified in the regulations, compensation to officers of those Boards who suffer loss of employment or loss or diminution of emoluments or pension rights or whose position is worsened in consequence of—

(*a*) the transfer of any property, rights, liabilities and obligations vested in one of those Boards to another of those Boards under section 34 (*a*) or paragraph 6 (*a*) of Schedule 2, or

(*b*) the disposal in any other manner of any such property, rights, liabilities or obligations.

(3) Different regulations may be made under subsection (2) in relation to different classes of persons, and any such regulations may be made so as to have effect from a date prior to the date of making, provided that any such regulation so made shall not place any person other than any of those Boards in a worse position than he would have been if the regulations had not been so made.

(4) Regulations made under subsection (2)—

(*a*) shall prescribe the procedure to be followed in making claims for compensation, and the manner in which, and the person by whom, the question whether any or all the compensation is payable is to be determined; and

(*b*) may in particular contain provisions enabling appeals from any determination under paragraph (*a*) to be brought, in such cases and subject to such conditions as may be prescribed before a tribunal established under section 12 of the Industrial Training Act 1964; and

(*c*) shall, in such cases and to such extent as may be specified in the regulations, extend to persons to whom the said subsection would have applied, but for any service in Her Majesty's Forces and in such other employment as may be specified in the regulations.

Pension rights

37.—(1) The Secretary of State may make regulations—

(*a*) for providing pensions to or in respect of persons who are or have been in the employment of either of the Boards or of a Consultative Council established for the district of either of the Boards;

(*b*) for the establishment and administration of pension schemes and pension funds for the purpose of providing the pensions mentioned in paragraph (*a*);

(*c*) for the continuance, amendment, repeal or revocation of existing pension schemes, whenever constituted, relating in whole or in part to that purpose and of enactments relating thereto, and of trust deeds, rules or other instruments made for that purpose;

(*d*) for the transfer in whole or in part, or for the extinguishing, of liabilities under any such existing pension schemes, and for the transfer in whole or in part, or winding up, of pension funds held for the purposes of any such existing pension scheme, not being, in the case of a transfer, a diversion of any such funds to purposes other than those mentioned in paragraph (*a*); and

(*e*) for making any consequential provision, including—

(i) provision for the dissolution or winding up of any body whose continued existence has by reason of regulations made under this section become unnecessary;

(ii) provision as to the manner in which questions arising under the regulations are to be determined; and

(iii) provision for adapting, modifying or repealing enactments, whether of general or special application.

(2) Regulations made under subsection (1) may contain provisions authorising any person who, being a participant in any pension scheme to which the regulations relate, becomes a member of one of the Boards being treated as if his service as a member of the Board were service in the employment of the Board; and the pension rights of any such person resulting from the operation of any such provision shall not be affected by any provision of this Act which requires that the pensions if any, which are to be paid in the case of members of the Board are to be determined by the Secretary of State with the approval of the Minister for the Civil Service.

(3) Subject to subsection (4), regulations made under subsection (1) shall be so framed as to ensure that persons having existing pension rights are not by reason of any provisions of the regulations made under this section placed in any worse position than their position under the existing scheme.

(4) Regulations shall not be invalid by reason only that they do not comply with subsection (3), but if the Secretary of State is satisfied, or it is determined under subsection (5), that they do not so comply, the Secretary of State shall as soon as possible after being so satisfied, or, as the case may be, after it is so determined, make amending regulations to comply with subsection (3).

(5) Any dispute as to whether regulations made under subsection (1) comply with subsection (3) shall be referred to a tribunal established under section 12 of the Industrial Training Act 1964.

(6) Regulations made under subsection (1) may be made so as to have effect from a date prior to the date of making, provided that any such regulation so made shall not place any person other than either of

the Boards in a worse position than he would have been if the regulations had not been so made.

Inquiries

38.—(1) The Secretary of State may in any case where he deems it advisable to do so cause an inquiry to be held in connection with any matter arising under this Act, the Act of 1957 or the Electricity (Supply) Acts.

(2) Schedule 8 shall have effect in relation to any inquiry caused to be held by the Secretary of State under this section.

Part III

General and Miscellaneous

Disputes between the Boards

39.—(1) Subject to the provisions of this Act, any question or dispute arising between the Boards shall, failing agreement between them, be determined by the Secretary of State or by an arbiter appointed by the Secretary of State.

(2) Any arbiter so appointed shall have the like powers for securing the attendance of witnesses and the production of documents and with regard to the examination of witnesses on oath and the awarding of expenses as if the arbitration were under a submission.

(3) The arbiter may, and if so directed by the Court of Session shall, state a case for the opinion of that Court on any question of law arising in the proceedings.

(4) Any award of the Secretary of State or as the case may be of an arbiter under this section may be recorded in the Books of Council and Session for execution and may be enforced accordingly.

Orders and regulations

40.—(1) Any power of the Secretary of State to make regulations or orders under this Act shall be exercisable by statutory instrument.

(2) A statutory instrument made under the powers conferred by sections 8 (4), 34, 37 (1), paragraph 3 of Schedule 7, or, subject to subsection (4), by section 2 (2), shall be subject to annulment in pursuance of a resolution of either House of Parliament.

(3) A statutory instrument made under the powers conferred by section 15 (2) shall be subject to special parliamentary procedure.

(4) No order shall be made in the exercise of the power conferred by section 2 (2) the effect of which is to increase or reduce the total number of districts or to constitute a new district for which a new Board is required to be established and no regulations shall be made under section 36 (2) relating to compensation to officers unless a draft of the order or regulations has been laid before Parliament and has been approved by a resolution of each House of Parliament.

(5) No order shall be made in the exercise of the power conferred by section 29 unless a draft of the order has been laid before the Commons House of Parliament and has been approved by resolution of that House.

(6) Where a power to make regulations or orders is exercisable by the Secretary of State by virtue of sections 2 (2), 8 (4), 15 (2), 34, 36 (2), 37 (1) or paragraph 3 of Schedule 7, any regulations or order, as the case may be, made in the exercise of that power may—

(*a*) provide for the determination of questions of fact or of law which may arise in giving effect to the regulations or order;

(*b*) regulate (otherwise than in relation to any court proceedings) any matters relating to the practice and procedure to be followed in connection with the determination of such questions, including—

(i) provision as to the mode of proof of any matters;

(ii) provision as to parties and their representation;

(iii) provision for the right of the Secretary of State or other authorities to appear and be heard in court proceedings or otherwise; and

(iv) provision as to awarding expenses of proceedings for the determination of such questions, determining the amount of such expenses, and the enforcement of awards of expenses;

(*c*) provide for extending any period prescribed by any such regulations or order as a period within which anything is required to be done;

(*d*) in the case of regulations, provide that any person offending against them shall be liable on summary conviction to a fine not exceeding £100 and that, if the offence in respect of which he is so convicted is continued after the conviction, he shall be guilty of a further offence and shall be liable on summary conviction to a fine not exceeding £5 for each day on which the offence is so continued.

(7) Any power conferred on the Secretary of State by this Act to make orders includes power to vary or revoke any orders so made.

Offences and penalties

41.—(1) If any person, in giving any information, making any claim or giving any notice for the purposes of sections 4 (*g*), 12, 15, 36 (2) to (4) and 37 or of any regulation made thereunder, knowingly or recklessly makes any statement which is false in a material particular, he shall be liable—

(*a*) on summary conviction, to imprisonment for a term not exceeding 3 months, or to a fine not exceeding £100, or to both;

(*b*) on conviction on indictment, to imprisonment for a term not exceeding 2 years, or to a fine not exceeding £500, or to both.

(2) Where an offence under subsection (1) has been committed by a body corporate, every person who at the time of the commission of the offence was a director, general manager, or secretary or other similar officer of the body corporate, or was purporting to act in any such capacity, shall be deemed to be guilty of that offence unless he proves that the offence was committed without his consent or connivance and that he exercised all such diligence to prevent the commission of the offence as he ought to have exercised having regard to the nature of his functions in that capacity and to all the circumstances.

Annual reports, statistics and returns

42.—(1) The Boards shall each annually, at such date and in such form as the Secretary of State may require, make to him a report dealing generally with the operations of the Board during the preceding year, and such report shall set out any direction given by the Secretary of State to the Board during that year unless the Secretary of State has notified the Board that in his opinion it is against the interests of national security to do so; and any such report shall be laid before Parliament and shall be on sale at a reasonable charge to the public at the offices of the Board.

(2) Each of the Boards shall furnish to the Secretary of State such returns, accounts and information regarding the property and activities of the Board as he may require, and shall, in such manner and at such times as he may require, afford to him facilities for the verification of the information furnished.

Power of Boards to promote and oppose private legislation

43. The Boards may with the consent of the Secretary of State promote an order under the Private Legislation Procedure (Scotland) Act 1936 and may oppose any such order.

Service of notices etc.

44. Schedule 9 shall have effect in relation to the service of notices or other documents under this Act.

Interpretation

45.—(1) In this Act, unless the context otherwise requires—

" Act of 1943 " means the Hydro-Electric Development (Scotland) Act 1943;

" Act of 1947 " means the Electricity Act 1947;

" Act of 1954 " means the Electricity Reorganisation (Scotland) Act 1954;

" Act of 1957 " means the Electricity Act 1957;

" Area Board " means an Area Board within the meaning of section 1 of the Act of 1947, being an Area Board whose area is within England and Wales;

" the Boards " has the meaning given by section 1, and any reference to a Board shall be construed as a reference to one or other of the Boards;

" bulk supply " means a supply of electricity to be used for the purposes of distribution;

" Central Authority " means the Central Electricity Authority established by section 1 of the Act of 1947 and dissolved by section 1 of the Act of 1957;

" constructional scheme " has the meaning given by section 10;

" Consultative Councils " shall be construed in accordance with section 17;

" electric line " means a wire or wires, conductor, or other means used for the purpose of conveying, transmitting, or distributing electricity with any casing, coating, covering, tube, pipe, or insulator enclosing, surrounding, or supporting the same, or any part thereof, or any apparatus connected therewith for the purpose of conveying, transmitting, or distributing electricity or electric currents;

" electrical fittings " means electric lines, fittings, apparatus and appliances designed for use by consumers of electricity for lighting, heating, motive power and other purposes for which electricity can be used;

" electrical plant " means any plant, equipment, apparatus and appliances used for the purposes of generating, transmitting and distributing electricity, but not including any electrical fittings;

" Electricity Council " means the Electricity Council established by section 3 of the Act of 1957;

" Electricity (Supply) Acts " means the Electricity (Supply) Acts 1882 to 1936;

" financial year " in relation to either of the Boards means the financial year prescribed for that Board by the Secretary of State under section 30;

" general fund " has the meaning given by section 18;

" general reserve fund " shall be construed in accordance with section 19;

" the Generating Board " means the Central Electricity Generating Board established by section 2 of the Act of 1957;

" generating station " has the meaning given by section 36 of the Electricity (Supply) Act 1919;

" land " includes an interest in land and references to entering upon or taking possession of land shall be construed accordingly; and any reference to land shall include a reference to salmon fishings;

" large power user " means a consumer (other than either of the Boards) with a demand for a supply of not less than 5,000 kilowatts;

" lease " includes an agreement for a lease and any tenancy agreement;

" local authority " means a regional, islands or district council;

" local enactment " means any enactment other than a public general act;

" main transmission lines " has the meaning given by the Electricity (Supply) Act 1919;

" North Board " has the meaning given by section 1;

" ordinary consumer " means any consumer other than a large power user or the South Board;

" pension ", in relation to any person, means a pension, whether or not, of any kind whatsoever payable to or in respect of him, and includes a gratuity so payable and a return of contributions to a pension fund, with or without interest thereon or any other addition thereto;

" pension fund " means a fund established for the purposes of paying pensions;

" pension rights " includes, in relation to any person, all forms of right to or eligibility for the present or future payment of a pension to or in respect of that person, and any expectation of the accruer of a pension to or in respect of that person under any customary practice and includes a right of allocation in respect of the present or future payment of a pension;

" pension scheme " includes any form of arrangements for the payment of pensions, whether subsisting by virtue of an Act, trust, contract or otherwise;

" prescribed " means prescribed by regulations made by the Secretary of State;

" railway undertakers " means any body authorised by any enactment to carry goods and passengers by railway;

" South Board " has the meaning given by section 1;

" telegraphic line " has the meaning given by the Telegraph Act 1878.

(2) Except insofar as the context otherwise requires, any reference in this Act to an enactment shall be construed as a reference to that

enactment as amended by or under any other enactment including this Act.

(3) In this Act, except where otherwise indicated—

(a) the reference to a numbered Part, section or schedule is a reference to the Part or section of, or the schedule to, this Act so numbered, and

(b) the reference in a section to a numbered subsection is a reference to the subsection of that section so numbered, and

(c) a reference in a section, subsection or schedule to a numbered or lettered paragraph is a reference to the paragraph of that section, subsection or schedule so numbered or lettered.

Transitional and saving provisions and consequential amendment and repeals

46.—(1) Schedule 10 (transitional and saving provisions) and Schedule 11 (consequential amendment) shall have effect, but the provisions of those Schedules shall not be taken as prejudicing the operation of section 38 of the Interpretation Act 1889 (which relates to the effect of repeals).

(2) The enactments specified in Schedule 12 are hereby repealed to the extent shown in column 3 of that Schedule.

Short title, extent and commencement

47.—(1) This Act may be cited as the Electricity (Scotland) Act 1979.

(2) Subject to subsection (3), this Act extends to Scotland only.

(3) Paragraph 1 (b) of Schedule 3 shall extend also to England and Wales.

(4) This Act shall come into force on the expiry of the period of one month beginning on the date of its passing.

SCHEDULES

Section 1 (2)

SCHEDULE 1

CONSTITUTION AND PROCEEDINGS OF THE BOARDS

1. The Boards shall each be appointed by the Secretary of State and shall consist of a Chairman, and not less than 4 nor more than 8 other members of whom one or more may be appointed Deputy Chairman or Chairmen.

2. A person shall be disqualified from being appointed or being a member of either of the Boards if he is an undischarged bankrupt or if he has granted a trust deed for behoof of creditors, or entered into a composition contract.

3. A member of either of the Boards shall hold office for such term and on such conditions as the Secretary of State may determine at the time of his appointment, but may at any time resign his office by notice in writing given to the Secretary of State.

4. Any member of either of the Boards shall, if he is interested in any company with which the Board has made or proposes to make any contract, disclose to the Board the fact and nature of his interest, and shall take no part in any deliberation or decision of the Board relating to that contract; and the disclosure shall be forthwith recorded in the minutes of the Board.

5. Where any member of either of the Boards is absent from the meetings of the Board for more than 6 months consecutively, except for some reason approved by the Secretary of State, the Secretary of State shall forthwith declare the office of that member to be vacant and thereupon the office shall become vacant.

6. Each of the Boards shall be a body corporate and subject to the quorum of the Board not being less than 3, shall have power to regulate their own procedure.

7. Either of the Boards may act notwithstanding a vacancy in their number.

8. The Boards shall have their offices in Scotland.

9. Each Board shall have a common seal and the seal of each Board shall be authenticated by the signature of the secretary to the Board or some person authorised by the Board to act in that behalf.

10. Every document purporting to be an instrument issued by either of the Boards and

(*a*) to be sealed with the seal of the Board authenticated in the manner provided by paragraph 9, or

(*b*) to be signed by the secretary to the Board or by a person authorised by the Board to act in that behalf.

shall be received in evidence and be deemed to be such an instrument or document without further proof unless the contrary is shown.

11. Each Board shall appoint a secretary and such other officers and servants as the Board may determine.

12. There shall be paid to the members of each Board such salaries or fees and allowances for expenses as the Secretary of State with the approval of the Minister for the Civil Service may determine, and there shall be paid to the secretary, officers and servants of each Board such salaries, remuneration and allowances as the Board may determine; and on the retirement or death of any member in whose case it may be so determined to make such provision there shall be paid such a pension to or in respect of that member as may be so determined.

Section 2

SCHEDULE 2

DISTRICTS

PART I

NORTH DISTRICT

1. The district of the North Board (in this Act referred to as the North District) shall consist of—

(*a*) the following regions:—Highland, Grampian and Tayside, and

(i) in the Central Region—In Stirling District, the former parishes of Balfron, Buchanan, Drymen, Fintry, Gargunnock, Killearn and Kippen;

(ii) in Strathclyde Region—Argyll and Bute District, that part of Cunninghame District, formerly in the County of Bute, and that part of Dunbarton District formerly comprising the parishes of Arrochar, Kilmaronock and Luss;

(*b*) the Islands Areas.

PART II

SOUTH DISTRICT

2. The district of the Board (in this Act referred to as the South District) shall consist of all of Scotland other than the North District.

PART III

ORDERS VARYING DISTRICTS

3. If any question arises as to the exact boundary between the North District and the South District as defined by any order made under section 2 it shall be determined by the Secretary of State after giving to the Boards an opportunity to make representations in relation to that question.

4. An order so made shall state whether the districts affected by the order are to be regarded as the districts of the Boards or whether any such district is to be regarded as a new district.

5. An order so made which includes the formation of a new district shall establish for that district a new Board which shall be known by such name as may be specified in the order and Schedule 1 shall have effect in relation to any such new Board as it has effect in relation to the Boards, and any such new Board shall have the like functions as the South Board.

6. An order made under section 2 shall, so far as it appears to the Secretary of State to be necessary or expedient in consequence of the variation of districts or the establishment of a new Board provide—

(*a*) for the transfer of property, rights, liabilities and obligations from one Board to another;

(*b*) for the modification of agreements for the purposes of giving effect to the transfer of rights, liabilities and obligations under any such agreement from one Board to another and, in a case where part of the rights, liabilities and obligations under any agreement are transferred, for substituting for that agreement separate agreements in the requisite terms and for any consequent apportionments and indemnities;

(*c*) for the purpose of transferring part of the land comprised in any lease vested in any such Board to another such Board, for the severance of that lease and for consequent apportionments and indemnities;

(*d*) for dissolving any Board the whole of whose functions are to be exercised by another Board or Boards and for winding up the affairs of the Board to be dissolved; and

(*e*) for such other financial adjustments between the Boards concerned as may be required in consequence of any such transfer,

and for any other matter supplementary to or consequential on the matters aforesaid, including the continuation of legal proceedings.

7. An order made under section 2 shall define by reference to a map the new districts or new boundaries constituted by the order, and copies of the map shall be made available for inspection at such places and such times as may be published by the Secretary of State in the Edinburgh Gazette and in such other newspapers circulating in the districts concerned as the Secretary of State thinks fit, and shall also be made available for inspection to Members of each House of Parliament when the order is laid before Parliament.

Section 3 (4)

SCHEDULE 3

Supply of Electricity to Railways

1. A supply of electricity to railway undertakers under section 3 may be provided—

(*a*) by either of the Boards in their own district;

(*b*) in England or Wales by the South Board with the approval of the Generating Board;

(*c*) in the South District by the Generating Board with the approval of the South Board;

(*d*) in the district of either of the Boards by the other of them with the approval of the Board in whose district the supply is provided.

2. The terms and conditions on which electricity is supplied by either of the Boards to railway undertakers under section 3 shall be such as may be agreed between the Board concerned and the undertakers or in default of such agreement, as may be determined by the Secretary of State, being such terms and conditions as in the opinion of that Board or, as the case may be, of the Secretary of State, will not cause a financial loss to result to that Board from the provision of the supply.

3. Where the terms and conditions mentioned in paragraph 2 are determined by the Secretary of State that determination—

(*a*) shall not extend to the terms and conditions on which any electricity so supplied may be used by the undertakers for other purposes, and

(*b*) shall not be taken to preclude the Board concerned and the undertakers from subsequently varying the terms and conditions so determined by agreement between them.

4. Either of the Boards may enter into an agreement with any railway undertakers to whom the Board are to supply electricity under section 3 for purposes of haulage and traction whereby any of that electricity may be used by the undertakers for other purposes on such terms and conditions as may be specified in the agreement.

5. Without prejudice to any other enactment providing for protection of telegraphic lines belonging to or used by the Post Office, any electricity supplied to railway undertakers under section 3 shall be used in such manner as not to cause or to be likely to cause any interference (whether by induction or otherwise) with any such telegraphic line or with telegraphic communication by means of any such line.

Section 5 (2)

SCHEDULE 4

CONSTITUTION AND FUNCTIONS OF AMENITY COMMITTEE AND FISHERIES COMMITTEE

1. The Amenity Committee and the Fisheries Committee shall consist of such number of persons as the Secretary of State may think proper for them respectively, and shall have the function of giving advice and assistance to the Secretary of State and to each of the Boards on questions of amenity and fisheries respectively.

2. The Boards shall furnish to each of those Committees any maps, plans, drawings or information which the Committee may reasonably require, and shall give to each Committee reasonable facilities for inspection.

3. The Boards shall before and during the preparation of a constructional scheme under section 10, and may at any other time, consult the Amenity Committee and the Fisheries Committee; and upon being so consulted or at any other time each of those Committees may make recommendations to the Board concerned; and that Board shall transmit a copy of every such recommendation to the Secretary of State, together with an intimation as to whether or not they are prepared to accept it.

4. If either of the Boards is not prepared to accept any recommendation made to them under paragraph 3, the Secretary of State after considering any representations made to him may—

(*a*) if the recommendation relates to a scheme which has been submitted to him for confirmation but has not yet been confirmed, refuse to confirm the scheme, and

(*b*) in the case of any other recommendation (not being a recommendation involving the execution by either of the Boards of any works authorised by a confirmed scheme otherwise than in the manner set out in that scheme), require that Board to give effect to it;

and where a requirement is imposed on a Board under sub-paragraph (*b*) that Board shall thereupon be bound to carry out the requirement.

5. The Boards shall not, without giving prior notice to the Amenity Committee of their intention to do so, use or permit to be used for the exhibition of advertisements any part of any land or building owned or leased by them in connection with a constructional scheme under section 10.

6. Each of the Boards shall defray any expenses reasonably incurred by the Amenity Committee and the Fisheries Committee up to such amounts and in such proportions as the Secretary of State may from time to time approve.

Section 10

SCHEDULE 5

CONSTRUCTIONAL SCHEMES

1. A constructional scheme shall contain particulars with regard to such matters, and shall be accompanied by such maps, drawings and plans, as the Secretary of State may require.

2. When either of the Boards have prepared a constructional scheme they shall submit it to the Secretary of State for confirmation and shall publish, in such form and in such newspapers as the Secretary of State may require, a notice stating

that the scheme has been prepared and submitted for confirmation and specifying the situation of any works proposed to be undertaken and of any land proposed to be acquired.

3. The Board concerned shall send copies of that notice to the persons appearing from the valuation roll to be the owners and the occupiers of any land proposed to be acquired, and shall also deposit a copy of the scheme and keep copies available for inspection and sale at the offices of the Board and at one or more other convenient places; and the notice so published shall state where the copies of the scheme are deposited and shall also specify a period of 40 days within which, and the manner in which objection thereto may be made to the Secretary of State.

4. Subject to paragraph 5, if on the expiry of the time within which objection may be made to a constructional scheme the Secretary of State on considering the scheme together with any objections made thereto, and after holding such inquiry (if any) as he thinks fit, is of the opinion that it is in the public interest that the Board should be authorised to carry out the scheme, he may make an order confirming the scheme without amendment or with such amendments as the Board may submit.

5. Where any person who has lodged an objection to the scheme requests that an inquiry shall be held, the Secretary of State shall, unless he is of the opinion that the objection is frivolous, cause an inquiry to be held before confirming the scheme.

6. Every order made by the Secretary of State confirming a constructional scheme shall be laid before Parliament as soon as may be after it is made, together with a copy of the scheme as confirmed, and shall be subject to annulment by a resolution of either House of Parliament.

7. A constructional scheme shall become operative on the expiry of the period within which the order confirming the scheme might be annulled without its being so annulled.

8. The Board shall thereon deposit copies of the scheme as confirmed and give notice of the places where such copies are available for inspection and sale in like manner as under paragraph 3.

9. As soon as may be after notice has been given in accordance with paragraph 8 the Board shall proceed with the construction of the works specified in the scheme and may do all things necessary for giving effect to the scheme.

10. A scheme confirmed under this Schedule may be amended or revoked by a subsequent scheme prepared and confirmed in the like manner and subject to the like conditions as the original scheme.

Section 11 (2)

SCHEDULE 6

Adaptations and Modifications of the Lands Clauses Acts and of the Railways Clauses Consolidation (Scotland) Act, 1845

1. The scheme shall be deemed to be the special Act, and—

(*a*) in the Lands Clauses Acts references to the promoters of the undertaking shall be construed as references to the Board concerned, and

(*b*) in the Railways Clauses Consolidation (Scotland) Act, 1845—

(i) references to the railway company shall be construed as references to that Board, and

(ii) references to the railway shall be construed as references to the land acquired or to any works which have been or may be constructed thereon, or to any use to which the land is or may be put, according to the context.

2. Sections 83 to 88 and section 90 of the Lands Clauses Consolidation (Scotland) Act, 1845, and the provisions of that Act relating to access to the special Act, shall not apply.

3. No person shall be required to sell a part only of any house, building or manufactory or of any land which forms part of a park or garden belonging to a house, if he is willing and able to sell the whole of the house, building, manufactory,

park or garden, unless the arbiter by whom compensation is to be assessed determines—

(*a*) in the case of a house, building or manufactory that the part proposed to be taken can be taken without material detriment to the house, building or manufactory; or

(*b*) in the case of a park or garden, that such part can be taken without seriously affecting the amenity or convenience of the house;

and if the arbiter so determines, compensation shall be awarded in respect of the severance of the part so proposed to be taken, in addition to the value of that part, and thereupon the person interested shall be required to sell to the Board that part of the house, building, manufactory, park or garden.

4.—(1) In assessing the sums to be included in the compensation payable to any person by way of compensation in respect of the injurious affection of, or the severance of the land acquired from, any land in which that person has an interest, account shall be taken of any increase, ascribable to any use to which the land acquired is intended to be put, in the value of his interest in any land which at the relevant time was held with the land acquired.

(2) In this paragraph the expression " the relevant time " means, in connection with the acquisition of any land, immediately before the date of the service of the notice to treat relating to the land, or, if possession of the land had then already been taken by the Board in exercise of the power conferred on them by section 11 (3), immediately before the taking of possession.

5. In assessing the compensation payable in respect of the acquisition of any land, no account shall be taken of any change in the value of the land attributable to anything done by the Board in the exercise of their powers under section 11 (5), but the value of the land shall be computed by reference to the circumstances existing at the date of the notice given in pursuance of section 11 (3).

6. The compensation payable in respect of the acquisition of a servitude over any land shall be the difference between the value of the land free from that servitude and the value of that land subject to that servitude.

7. Any person empowered to sell or convey any land to the Board shall have power to grant to them a servitude over that land.

8.—(1) The Board concerned may sell, feu, or lease for such periods and for such consideration as they may think fit any land and property for the time being belonging to them which they do not require for the purposes of any scheme.

(2) On so disposing of any land, the Board concerned may reserve to themselves all or any part of the water rights or any servitude belonging thereto, and may so dispose of any land subject to such other reservations, conditions, and restrictions as they may think fit.

Section 17

SCHEDULE 7

Consultative Councils

Constitution, Proceedings and Functions

1. Each of the Consultative Councils established for the respective districts of the Board shall consist of a chairman appointed by the Secretary of State and of not less than 20 or more than 30 other persons so appointed of whom—

(*a*) not less than two-fifths or more than three-fifths shall be appointed from a panel of persons nominated by such associations as appear to the Secretary of State to represent local authorities in the district;

(*b*) the remainder shall be appointed after consultation with such bodies as the Secretary of State thinks fit to represent agriculture, commerce, industry, labour and the general interests of consumers of electricity and other persons or organisations interested in the development of electricity in the district.

2. In the appointment of any person under sub-paragraph (*a*) of paragraph 1, the Secretary of State shall have particular regard to that person's ability to exercise a wide and impartial judgment on the matters to be dealt with by the Council generally; and in making appointments under sub-paragraph (*b*) of that

paragraph the Secretary of State shall have particular regard to any nominations made to him by the bodies mentioned in that sub-paragraph of persons who are recommended by them as having both adequate knowledge of the requirements of the interests to be represented and also the ability to exercise a wide and impartial judgment on the matters to be dealt with by the Council generally.

3. The Secretary of State may make regulations with respect to—

(*a*) the appointment of, and the tenure and the vacation of office by, the members of a Consultative Council and the appointment of a person to act in the place of the Chairman of such a Council;

(*b*) the quorum, proceedings, meetings and determinations of a Consultative Council;

(*c*) any other matters supplementary or incidental to the matters aforesaid for which provision appears to the Secretary of State to be necessary or expedient.

4. Subject to the provisions of any regulations made under paragraph 3, a Consultative Council may regulate their own procedure.

5. Each of the Councils—

(*a*) shall consider any matter affecting the distribution of electricity in their district, including the variation of tariffs and the provision of new or improved services and facilities within the district, being a matter which is the subject of a representation made to them by consumers or other persons requiring supplies of electricity in that district, or which appears to them to be a matter to which consideration ought to be given apart from any such representation, and where action appears to them to be requisite as to any such matter, shall notify their conclusions to the Board; and

(*b*) shall consider and report to the Board on any such matter which may be referred to them by that Board.

6. Each of the Councils shall be informed by the Board of that Board's general plans and arrangements for exercising and performing their functions under this Act and may make representations thereon to that Board.

7. The Board shall consider any conclusions, reports and representations notified or made to them by the Council for their district under paragraphs 5 and 6, and the Council may after consultation with the Board make representations to the Secretary of State on matters arising therefrom.

8. Where representations have been so made to the Secretary of State and it appears to him after consultation with the Board and with the Council that a defect is disclosed in that Board's general plans and arrangements for the exercise and performance of their functions under this Act, the Secretary of State may give to the Board such directions as he thinks fit for remedying the defect.

9. Each of the Councils shall prepare and submit to the Secretary of State a scheme for the appointment by them of committees or individuals to be local representatives of the Council in such localities as may be specified in the scheme; and it shall be the duty of such committees and individuals to consider the particular circumstances and requirements of those localities with respect to the distribution of electricity and to make representations to the Council thereon, and to be available for receiving on behalf of the Council representations from consumers in those localities; and if the scheme is approved by the Secretary of State the Consultative Council shall put it into effect.

10. Under a scheme prepared and submitted under paragraph 8 a member of a Council shall be eligible for appointment either as a member of a Committee or as an individual, but membership of the Council shall not be a necessary qualification for such an appointment.

11. A Council may make to the Board concerned a report on the exercise and performance by the Council of their functions during any financial year of the Board and any such report shall be made to the Board as soon as possible after the end of that financial year and the Board shall include that report in the report made by them under section 42.

Council Chairmen

12. There shall be paid to the chairman of a Council such remuneration as the

Secretary of State may determine; and in the case of a person remunerated under this paragraph there shall be no obligation to remunerate him also under paragraph 12 of Schedule 1.

13. If the Secretary of State so determines in the case of a person who has been remunerated under paragraph 12, he shall pay such pension to or in respect of that person, or make such payments towards the provision of such a person, as the Secretary of State may determine.

14. If a person in receipt of remuneration under paragraph 12 ceases to hold the office by virtue of which he receives it, and it appears to the Secretary of State that there are special circumstances which make it right that that person should receive compensation, that person shall be paid a sum of such amount as the Secretary of State may determine.

Council's Administration, Personnel etc.

15. A Council may, subject to the approval of the Secretary of State as to numbers, appoint such officers as appear to the Council to be requisite for the performance of their functions, including those of any committee or individual appointed under paragraph 9.

16. The Secretary of State shall provide the Council with funds wherewith to pay—

(*a*) to their members, and to members of any such committee, or to any such individual, as is mentioned above such travelling and other allowances; and

(*b*) to the officers of a Council, such remuneration, and such travelling and other allowances,

as the Secretary of State may determine, and wherewith also to defray such other expenses in connection with their functions as he may determine to be appropriate; and he may make arrangements for Councils to be provided with office accommodation.

17.—(1) There shall be paid, to or in respect of persons who are or have been officers of Consultative Councils such pensions as the Secretary of State may determine or arrangements shall be made for the payment of such pensions.

(2) A Consultative Council may, if the Secretary of State determines that they should do so, assume in respect of such persons as are referred to in sub-paragraph (1) any liabilities incurred by either of the Boards under or in pursuance of section 37.

(3) The Secretary of State shall provide Consultative Councils with funds wherewith to pay pensions under sub-paragraph (1) or to finance any arrangements under that sub-paragraph, and to discharge any liabilities assumed by Councils under sub-paragraph (2).

Supplementary

18.—(1) The consent of the Minister for the Civil Service shall be required for any determination or approval by the Secretary of State under paragraphs 12 to 17.

(2) In this Schedule "pension" includes allowance and gratuity payable on retirement or otherwise.

Section 38

SCHEDULE 8

Provisions as to Inquiries

1. The Secretary of State shall appoint a person to hold the inquiry and to report thereon to him.

2. The person appointed to hold the inquiry shall notify the Board concerned and any person who has lodged objections to the matter which is the subject of the inquiry, and shall publish in such newspaper or newspapers as the Secretary of State may direct a notice of the time when and the place where the inquiry is to be held.

3. Except with the sanction of the person appointed to hold the inquiry, no person other than the Board or a person who has lodged objections to the matter which is the subject of the inquiry shall be entitled to appear or to be represented at the inquiry.

4. The person appointed to hold the inquiry may, on the motion of any party thereto, or of his own motion, require any person by notice in writing—

(*a*) to attend at the time and place set forth in the notice to give evidence or to produce any books or documents in his custody or under his control which relate to any matter in question at the inquiry; or

(*b*) to furnish within such reasonable period as is specified in the notice such information relating to any matter in question at the inquiry as the person appointed to hold the inquiry may think fit and as the person so required is able to furnish:

Provided that no person shall be required in obedience to such a notice to attend at any place which is more than 10 miles from the place where he resides unless the necessary expenses are paid or tendered to him.

5. The person appointed to hold the inquiry may administer oaths and examine witnesses on oath and may accept, in lieu of evidence on oath by any person, a statement in writing by that person.

6. The inquiry shall be held in public.

7. Any person who refuses or wilfully neglects to attend in obedience to a notice issued under paragraph 4, or who wilfully alters, suppresses, conceals, destroys, or refuses to produce, any book or document which he may be required by any such notice to produce, or who refuses or wilfully neglects to comply with any requirement under paragraph 4 of the person appointed to hold the inquiry, shall be liable on summary conviction to a fine not exceeding £20 or to imprisonment for a period not exceeding 3 months.

8. The Secretary of State shall communicate to each party to the inquiry the recommendations made by the person appointed to hold it.

9. The expenses incurred by the Secretary of State in relation to the inquiry (including such reasonable sum as the Secretary of State may determine for the services of the person appointed to hold the inquiry) shall be paid by such of the parties to the inquiry as the Secretary of State may direct.

10. The Secretary of State may make directions as to the expenses incurred by the parties to the inquiry and as to the parties by whom such expenses shall be paid.

11. Any direction by the Secretary of State under paragraph 9 or paragraph 10 requiring any party to pay expenses may be recorded in the Books of Council and Session for execution and may be enforced accordingly.

Section 44

SCHEDULE 9

Service of Notices

Any notice or other document required or authorised to be given, delivered or served by or under this Act, or under any enactment applied by this Act, may be given, delivered or served either—

(*a*) by delivering it to the person to whom it is to be given or delivered or on whom it is to be served; or

(*b*) by leaving it at the usual or last known place of abode of that person; or

(*c*) by sending it by registered post or recorded delivery service addressed to that person at his usual or last known place of abode; or

(*d*) in the case of an incorporated company or body, by delivering it to the secretary or clerk of the company or body at their registered or principal office or sending it by registered post or recorded delivery service addressed to the secretary or clerk of the company or body at that office; or

(*e*) if it is not practicable after reasonable enquiry to ascertain the name or address of a person to whom it should be given or delivered, or on whom it should be served, as being a person having any interest in land, by addressing it to him by the description of the person having that interest in the premises (naming them) to which it relates, and delivering it to some person on the premises or, if there is no person on the premises to whom it can be delivered, affixing it, or a copy of it, to some conspicuous part of the premises.

Section 46 (1)

SCHEDULE 10

Transitional and Saving Provisions

1. In so far as any regulation, order, licence, permit, notice, entry, directive, warrant or other instrument made, issued or given, under any enactment repealed by this Act, or any such other thing done or having effect as if done under any such enactment, could have been made, issued, given or done under a corresponding provision of this Act, it shall not be invalidated by the repeal but shall have effect as if made, issued, given or done under that corresponding provision.

2. Without prejudice to paragraph 1, any provision of this Act relating to anything done or required or authorised to be done under or by reference to that provision or any other provision of this Act shall have effect as if any reference to that provision, or that other provision, as the case may be, included a reference to the corresponding provision of the enactments repealed by this Act.

3. Without prejudice to the generality of paragraphs 1 and 2, any scheme or agreement made, or any charge or tariff imposed, under any enactment repealed by this Act, shall continue to have effect as if made or imposed under the corresponding provision of this Act.

4.—(1) Nothing in this Act shall affect the enactments repealed by this Act in their operation in relation to offences committed before the commencement of this Act.

(2) Where an offence, for the continuance of which a penalty may be provided, has been committed under an enactment repealed by this Act, proceedings may be taken under this Act in respect of the continuance of the offence after the commencement of this Act in the same manner as if the offence had been committed under the corresponding provision of this Act.

5. Where any enactment or document refers, either expressly or by implication, to an enactment repealed by this Act, the reference shall, except where the context otherwise requires, be construed as, or as including, a reference to the corresponding provision of this Act.

6. Nothing in this Act shall affect the operation of the provisions of section 57 (1) of or of Schedule 4 Part I to the Act of 1947 (adaptation and modification of Electricity (Supply) Acts) and references in any of the provisions of the Electricity (Supply) Acts, to those Acts, and any reference therein to one or more of those Acts, being a reference which, by virtue of the construction of those Acts as one, is to be construed as a reference to all the said Acts shall in their application to Scotland be construed as containing a reference to this Act.

7. Nothing in this Act shall affect the operation of the provisions of section 57 (2) of or of Schedule 4 Part III to the Act of 1947 (incorporation of the Schedule to the Electric Lighting (Clauses) Act 1899) and those provisions shall have effect in relation to the provisions of this Act as they had effect immediately before the coming into operation of this Act in relation to the provisions of the Act of 1947, with the adaptations and modifications subject to which they so had effect.

8. Notwithstanding the repeal by this Act of section 2 (9) of the Act of 1947 (capacity of Boards as statutory corporations), the provisions of that subsection shall continue to have effect in relation to the provisions of this Act as they had effect in relation to the provisions of the Act of 1947 immediately before the coming into operation of this Act.

9. The repeal by the Statutory Corporations (Financial Provisions) Act 1975 of section 3 of the Gas and Electricity Act 1968 shall not affect anything done or any right established under that section before the passing of the said Act of 1975.

10. Nothing in section 32 shall affect the functions of the Secretary of State under the Schedule to the Electric Lighting (Clauses) Act 1899 as incorporated with the Act of 1947, so far as that Schedule relates to the certification of meters and the measurement of electricity, or under the Electricity Supply (Meters) Act 1936, being the functions formerly exercised by the Minister of Fuel and Power and referred to in section 1 (4) of the Act of 1954, as originally enacted.

11. Notwithstanding the repeal by this Act of Section 51 of the Act of 1947 (power to break up streets), any powers exercisable by an Area Board in Scotland

by virtue of that section immediately before the coming into force of this Act, shall continue to be so exercisable thereafter.

12.—(1) Section 24 shall have effect without prejudice to the operation of any provisions of section 42 of the Finance Act 1956 in relation to advances made to the Boards before 18th December 1963, and the provisions of the said section 42 shall, notwithstanding its repeal by section 4 (2) of the Electricity and Gas Act 1963, continue to operate in relation to any such advances.

(2) Notwithstanding the repeal by this Act of section 2 (8) of the said Act of 1963, any account prepared under section 24 (5) shall include any sums received by the Secretary of State under section 42 (4) of the Finance Act 1956 in respect of the financial year to which the account relates; and the Secretary of State shall not be required to prepare an account under the said section 42.

13. Notwithstanding the repeal by this Act—

(*a*) of section 38 (4) of the Act of 1947 (amendments to Schedule 4 of the Act of 1943);

(*b*) of Schedule 4 Part II to the Act of 1947 (amendments to the Act of 1943);

(*c*) of Schedule 1 Part I to the Act of 1954 (amendments to the Act of 1943);

(*d*) of Schedule 1 Part II to the Act of 1954 (amendments to Act of 1947),

the amendments made by the said section 38 (4) to Schedule 4 of the Act of 1943 and by the said Schedule 4 Part II to the Act of 1947 to sections 2 (1) (*d*), 16 (1), 17, 27 and Schedule 4 of the Act of 1943 and by the said Schedule 1 Part I to the Act of 1954 to sections 2 (1) (*d*), 16 (1), 17 and Schedule 4 and by the said Schedule 1 Part II to the Act of 1954 to sections 1 (4) and (5), 2 (8A), 4, 19, 60 and 67 of the Act of 1947 shall continue to have the same effect in relation to that Schedule and to those sections and Schedules as they had immediately before the coming into force of this Act.

14. Notwithstanding the repeal by this Act of section 55 (6) of the Act of 1947 (saving of rights in respect of compensation), regulations made under section 36 (2) shall not prejudice the rights of any person arising in consequence of events which occurred before 1st April 1948 under—

(*a*) section 16 of the Electricity (Supply) Act 1919;

(*b*) section 15 of and the Fourth Schedule to the Electricity (Supply) Act 1926;

(*c*) the Compensation of Displaced Officers (War Service) (Electricity Undertakings) Order 1946,

including those sections and that Schedule as applied by any other enactment, with or without modifications and adaptations.

Section 46 (1)

SCHEDULE 11

Consequential Amendment

The Salmon Fisheries (Scotland) Act 1868

In Schedule G to the Salmon Fisheries (Scotland) Act 1868, at the end, add the following paragraph:—

"8. Nothing in this Schedule shall apply to any dam, aqueduct, pipe or other work constructed under the Electricity (Scotland) Act 1979 or under any enactment repealed by that Act."

Section 46 (2)

SCHEDULE 12

Repeals

Chapter	Short Title	Extent of Repeal
6 & 7 Geo. 6. c. 32.	The Hydro-Electric Development (Scotland) Act 1943.	The whole Act, except sections 2 (1) (*d*), 16 (1), 17, 27 in so far as it defines "maximum number of kilowatts" and other expressions, 28 and Schedule 4.
10 & 11 Geo. 6. c. 54.	The Electricity Act 1947.	The whole Act except sections 1 (3), 2 (8A), 4 (8), 13, 22, 54 (5), 57 (1) and 2, 60, 67, 68 (1) to (3) and 69, Schedule 2 and Schedule 4 Parts I and III, and in so far as they relate to any matter affecting one of the Boards and the Generating Board or an Area Board, sections 1 (4) and (5), 2 (7), 4 (2) to (7), 11 (2) and 19.
2 & 3 Eliz. 2. c. 60.	The Electricity Reorganisation (Scotland) Act 1954.	The whole Act, except sections 1 (3), 10 (2), 15 (1), 16, 17 and, in Schedule 1, Part III.
5 & 6 Eliz. 2. c. 48.	The Electricity Act 1957.	Sections 28 and 35. In section 29— in subsection (1), the words "or either of the Scottish Electricity Boards"; in subsection (3), the words "or District"; in subsection (4), the words "or Scottish Electricity Board". In Schedule 4 Part II, the entries relating to section 2 and section 10A of the Act of 1943.
1963, c. 59.	The Electricity and Gas Act 1963.	In section 2— in subsection (1), the words from "and the Secretary of State" to the words "South of Scotland Electricity Board"; and the words "or Board in question"; in subsections (3) and (6), the words "or the Secretary of State"; in subsections (4) and (7), the words "and the Secretary of State"; subsection (8); in subsection (9), the words "and Boards". In section 3— in subsection (2), paragraphs (*d*) and (*e*); subsection (3). In section 4, subsection (3). In Schedule 1, the entry relating to the Act of 1947.
1968 c. 39.	The Gas and Electricity Act 1968.	The whole Act.
1969 c. 1.	The Electricity (Scotland) Act 1969.	The whole Act.
1972 c. 17.	The Electricity Act 1972.	The whole Act except sections 2 and 4.
1975 c. 55.	The Statutory Corporations (Financial Provisions) Act 1975.	In Schedule 2, the references to the North Board and the South Board. In Schedule 3, Part I, except paragraph 5. In Schedule 4, paragraphs 1 and 4.
1976 c. 61.	The Electricity (Financial Provisions) (Scotland) Act 1976.	Section 1.

Wages Councils Act 1979 *

(1979 c. 12)

ARRANGEMENT OF SECTIONS

PART I

WAGES COUNCILS

* Annotations by Gwyneth Pitt, Lecturer in Law, University of Leeds.

An Act to consolidate the enactments relating to wages councils and statutory joint industrial councils. [22nd March 1979]

General Note

This Act makes no alteration to the previous law, but merely consolidates the Wages Councils Act 1959 (which was itself a consolidating measure) and the relevant provisions of the Employment Protection Act 1975. The main changes introduced by the Employment Protection Act were first, the extension of the power to make orders to other terms and conditions of employment besides wages and holidays; secondly, to give a limited power to make retrospective orders; thirdly, to enable wages councils to make orders by their own authority, thus cutting out the stage of submitting proposals to the Secretary of State for Employment for his approval; and fourthly, the institution of statutory joint industrial councils (S.J.I.C.s) to provide an intermediate stage in the transition from wages council to free collective bargaining.

At present there are 43 wages councils, covering about three million workers in over 418,000 establishments in occupations as diverse as Coffin Furniture and Cerement Making and the Ostrich and Fancy Feather and Artificial Flower industry. However, the majority are in the retail, catering and hairdressing trades. These are typical of wages council industries in being low-paid, substantially staffed by women, and difficult for trade unions to organise. About 150 wages inspectors police the Act, and their essential role is demonstrated by the fact that in 1977 over £1,500,000 was found to be owing to a total of almost 27,000 workers.

Parliamentary debates

There are no reported parliamentary debates.

Commencement

The Act came into force on April 22, 1979, one month after it received the Royal Assent: see s. 32.

Northern Ireland

The Act may be extended to Northern Ireland by Order in Council: see s. 27.

Abbreviations

1959 Act—Wages Councils Act 1959.

1975 Act—Employment Protection Act 1975.

Table of Derivations

WAGES COUNCIL ACT 1959

1959	1979	1959	1979	1959	1979
s. 1	s. 1	s. 11 (4)–(8)	s. 14 (7)–(12)	s. 24	s. 28
2	2	12	15	27 (3)	32 (2)
3	3	13	16	Sch. 1,	
4	4	14	17	paras. 1, 2	Sch. 1, paras. 1, 2
5	5	15	18	para. 2A	Sch. 1, para. 3
6	6	16	19	paras. 3–8	Sch. 1, paras. 4–9
7	25	17	20	Sch. 2	Sch. 2
8	8	18	21	Sch. 3	Sch. 3
9 (2)–(5)	7	19	22		
10	9	20	23		
11 (1)–(3A)	14 (1)–(5)	22	29		
		23	30		

CIVIL EVIDENCE ACT 1968

1968	1979
Sch.	s. 22

TRANSPORT ACT 1968

1968	1979
Sch. 11	s. 22

EQUAL PAY ACT 1970

1970	1979
s. 4 (1A)	s. 14 (6)

INDUSTRIAL RELATIONS ACT 1971

1971	1979
Sch. 8	s. 5

EUROPEAN COMMUNITIES ACT 1972

1972	1979
Sch. 4, para. 9 (4)	s. 22

SOCIAL SECURITY ACT 1973

1973	1979
Sch. 27, para. 21	s. 17

TRADE UNION AND LABOUR RELATIONS ACT 1974

1974	1979
Sch. 3, para. 9 (3)	s. 5
(8)	Sch. 1, para. 3

EMPLOYMENT PROTECTION ACT 1975

1975	1979	1975	1979	1975	1979
s. 89 (1)	ss. 1–3, 6, 7, 25, 29, 30, Sch. 1, paras. 1, 5–9	s. 96	s. 26	Sch. 7, Pt. IV,	
(2)	Sch. 2	117	24	para. 3	s. 25
90	s. 10	127 (1) (*a*) (*f*) (*g*)	27 (1)	para. 4	16
91	ss. 10, 15	127 (2)–(4)	27 (2)–(4)	para. 5	17
92	s. 11	129 (6)	32 (3)	para. 6	ss. 19, 20, 22, 23
93	12	Sch. 7,		para. 7	s. 20
94	13	Pt. I	14 (1)–(5) (7)–(12)	para. 8	22
(2)	Sch. 1, para. 1	Pt. II	15	para. 9	28
95	s. 24	Pt. III	Sch. 2	para. 10	Sch. 1, para. 5
		Pt. IV,		Sch. 8	Sch. 4
		para. 1	ss. 16, 19	Sch. 16, Pt. IV, para. 13 (8)	s. 14 (6)
		para. 2	s. 4		

ROAD TRAFFIC (DRIVERS' AGES AND HOURS OF WORK) ACT 1976

1976	1979
s. 2 (3)	s. 22

EMPLOYMENT (CONTINENTAL SHELF) ACT 1978

1978	1979
s. 1 (1)	s. 27 (7)
2	27 (5)

PART I

WAGES COUNCILS

Establishment of wages councils

1.—(1) Subject to the provisions of this Part of this Act, the Secretary of State may by order establish a wages council to perform, in relation to the workers described in the order and their employers, the functions specified in relation to wages councils in the subsequent provisions of this Part of this Act.

(2) An order establishing a wages council may be made by the Secretary of State either—

(*a*) if he is of opinion that no adequate machinery exists for the effective regulation of the remuneration of the workers described in the order and that, having regard to the remuneration existing among those workers, or any of them, it is expedient that such a council should be established; or

(*b*) if he thinks fit, to give effect to a recommendation of the Advisory, Conciliation and Arbitration Service (" the Service ") made on the reference to it, in accordance with section 2 below, of an application made in accordance therewith for the establishment of a wages council; or

(*c*) if he thinks fit, to give effect to the recommendation of the Service made in a case where the Secretary of State, being of opinion that no adequate machinery exists for the effective regulation of the remuneration of any workers or the existing machinery is likely to cease to exist or be adequate for that purpose and a reasonable standard of remuneration among those workers will not be maintained, refers to the Service the question whether a wages council should be established with respect to any of those workers and their employers.

(3) Schedule 1 to this Act shall have effect with respect to the making of orders establishing wages councils.

(4) Schedule 2 to this Act shall have effect with respect to the constitution, officers and proceedings of wages councils.

DERIVATION
1959 Act, s. 1.

GENERAL NOTE
This section gives the Secretary of State for Employment power to set up a wages council either on his own initiative or on the recommendation of ACAS where he considers that no adequate machinery exists for the effective regulation of wages. In practice, this always means where there is no adequate trade union organisation able to carry on free collective bargaining with the employer. In fact, no new wages council has been established since the Rubber Proofed Garment Making Industry wages council in 1956.

Applications for wages council orders

2.—(1) An application for the establishment of a wages council with respect to any workers and their employers may be made to the Secretary of State either—

(a) by a joint industrial council, conciliation board or other similar body constituted by organisations representative respectively of those workers and their employers; or

(b) jointly by any organisation of workers and any organisation of employers which claim to be organisations that habitually take part in the settlement of remuneration and conditions of employment for those workers;

on the ground, in either case, that the existing machinery for the settlement of remuneration and conditions of employment for those workers is likely to cease to exist or be adequate for that purpose.

(2) Where such an application as aforesaid is made to him, the Secretary of State—

(a) subject to subsection (3) below, if he is satisfied that there are sufficient grounds to justify the reference of the application to the Service, and in the case of an application under paragraph (b) of subsection (1) above, that the claim of the organisations habitually to take part in the settlement of remuneration and conditions of employment for those workers is well-founded, shall refer the application to the Service to inquire into and report on the application;

(b) if he is not so satisfied shall notify the applicants to that effect, in which case no further steps shall be taken on the application unless and until he is so satisfied by fresh facts brought to his notice:

Provided that before taking either of the said courses, the Secretary of State may require the applicants to furnish such information, if any, in relation to the application as he considers necessary.

(3) If, on considering an application under subsection (1) above, it appears to the Secretary of State either—

(a) that there is a joint industrial council, conciliation board or other similar body constituted by organisations of workers and organisations of employers, being a council, board or body which would or might be affected by the establishment of a wages council in pursuance of the application; or

(b) that there are organisations of workers and organisations of employers representative respectively of workers other than workers to whom the application relates and their employers, who would or might be affected by the establishment of a wages council as aforesaid;

being a council, board or body, or, as the case may be, organisations, which are parties to joint voluntary machinery for the settlement of remuneration and conditions of employment but are not parties to the application for a wages council, the Secretary of State shall, before deciding to refer the application to the Service give notice of the application to that council, board or body or, as the case may be, to those organisations, shall consider any observations in writing which may be submitted to him by them within such period as he may direct, not being less than one month from the date of the notice, and, if he decides to refer the application to the Service, shall transmit a copy of the observations to the Service.

(4) If, before an application is referred to the Service, it is withdrawn by the applicants, no further proceedings shall be had thereon.

DERIVATION
1959 Act, s. 2.

General Note

Under the wording of this section, it is necessary for there to be a joint application by both sides of the industry (s. 2 (1) (*a*) (*b*)). Contrast with s. 5 (1) (*c*) which permits applications for the abolition of a wages council to be made solely by an organisation of workers. This may be of little practical importance, however, in view of the unlikelihood of any new wages councils being set up.

On receiving an application the Secretary of State should refer it to ACAS if he thinks there are sufficient grounds. Before doing so, however, he should inform any other employers' or workers' bodies who might be affected by the establishment of a Council and allow time for their comments on the application.

Proceedings on references as to establishment of wages councils

3.—(1) Where the Secretary of State makes any such reference as is mentioned in paragraph (*b*) or (*c*) of subsection (2) of section 1 above, it shall be the duty of the Service to consider not only the subject matter of the reference but also any other question or matter which, in the opinion of the Service, is relevant thereto, and in particular to consider whether there are any other workers (being workers who, in the opinion of the Service, are engaged in work which is complementary, subsidiary or closely allied to the work performed by the workers specified in the reference or any of them) whose position should be dealt with together with that of the workers, or some of the workers, specified as aforesaid; and in relation to any such reference, any reference in this Part of this Act to the workers with whom the Service is concerned shall be construed as a reference to the workers specified as aforesaid and any such other workers as aforesaid.

(2) If the Service is of opinion with respect to the workers with whom it is concerned or any of those workers whose position should, in the opinion of the Service, be separately dealt with—

(*a*) that there exists machinery set up by agreement between organisations representing workers and employers respectively which is, or can be made by improvements which it is practicable to secure, adequate for regulating the remuneration and conditions of employment of those workers; and

(*b*) that there is no reason to believe that that machinery is likely to cease to exist or be adequate for that purpose,

the Service shall report to the Secretary of State accordingly and may include in its report any suggestions which it may think fit to make as to the improvement of that machinery.

(3) Where any such suggestions are so included, the Secretary of State shall take such steps as appear to him to be expedient and practicable to secure the improvements in question.

(4) If the Service is of opinion with respect to the workers with whom it is concerned or any of those workers whose position should, in the opinion of the Service, be separately dealt with—

(*a*) that machinery for regulating the remuneration and conditions of employment of those workers is not, and cannot be made by any improvements which it is practicable to secure, adequate for that purpose, or does not exist; or

(*b*) that the existing machinery is likely to cease to exist or be adequate for that purpose,

and that as a result a reasonable standard of remuneration among those workers is not being or will not be maintained, the Service may make a report to the Secretary of State embodying a recommendation for the establishment of a wages council in respect of those workers and their employers.

(5) In considering for the purposes of section 1 above whether any machinery is, or is likely to remain, adequate for regulating the remuneration and conditions of employment of any workers, the Service shall consider not only what matters are capable of being dealt with by that machinery, but also to what extent those matters are covered by the agreements or awards arrived at or given thereunder, and to what extent the practice is, or is likely to be, in accordance with those agreements or awards.

DERIVATION

1959 Act, s. 3.

GENERAL NOTE

This section governs the conduct of proceedings by ACAS when a reference is made to it. It has a wide power to consider not only the workers specified in the reference, but any others engaged in connected work. If there is machinery for collective bargaining which could be made adequate, ACAS should so report to the Secretary of State, and may suggest improvements to the machinery, which the Secretary of State should try to implement. If there is no adequate machinery and ACAS is of the opinion that without it the level of remuneration will not be maintained at a reasonable standard, then ACAS should recommend the establishment of a wages council.

Abolition of, or variation of field of operation of, wages councils

4.—(1) The Secretary of State may at any time abolish a wages council by order made—

(*a*) to give effect to an application in that behalf made to him in accordance with section 5 below, or

(*b*) without any such application, subject however to the provisions of section 6 below.

(2) The Secretary of State may at any time by order vary the field of operation of a wages council.

(3) The power of the Secretary of State to make an order under this section varying the field of operation of a wages council shall include power to vary that field by excluding from it any employers to whom there for the time being applies, as members of an organisation named in the order, an agreement, to which the organisation or any other organisation of which it is a member or on which it is represented, is a party, regulating remuneration or other terms or conditions of employment of their employees.

(4) Any organisation so named shall if it has not already done so furnish the Secretary of State with a list of its members and shall from time to time, and also if so required by the Secretary of State, furnish him with particulars of any changes in their membership which have occurred since the list was furnished or, as the case may be, when particulars were last furnished to him.

(5) An order under this section abolishing or varying the field of operation of one or more wages councils may include provision for the establishment of one or more wages councils operating in relation to all or any of the workers in relation to whom the first mentioned council or councils would have operated but for the order, and such other workers, if any, as may be specified in the order.

(6) Where an order of the Secretary of State under this section directs that any workers shall be excluded from the field of operation of one wages council and brought within the field of operation of another, the order may provide that anything done by, or to give effect to proposals made by, the first-mentioned council shall have effect in relation to those

workers as if it had been done by, or to give effect to proposals made by, the second-mentioned council and may make such further provision as appears to the Secretary of State to be expedient in connection with the transition.

(7) Where an order of the Secretary of State under this section directs that a wages council shall be abolished or shall cease to operate in relation to any workers, then, save as is otherwise provided by the order, anything done by, or to give effect to proposals made by the wages council shall, except as respects things previously done or omitted to be done, cease to have effect or, as the case may be, cease to have effect or, as the case may be, cease to have effect in relation to the workers in relation to whom the council ceases to operate.

(8) Schedule 1 to this Act shall have effect with respect to the making of orders under this section.

DERIVATION

1959 Act, s. 4, as amended by 1975 Act, Sched. 7, Pt. IV.

GENERAL NOTE

This section gives the Secretary of State power to abolish a wages council in accordance with ss. 5 and 6 of this Act, or to vary it in accordance with this section.

Subss. (3) *and* (4)

These were added for the first time by the 1975 Act, and implement an overdue rationalisation of the Secretary's powers recommended by the Donovan Commission in 1968 (Cmnd. 3623, paras. 263, 1030). It should be possible to exclude individual employers in order to encourage improved company and plant bargaining, as the existence of a wages council covering a particular type of employment might make an employer reluctant to engage in collective bargaining as well. Where there are satisfactory collective bargaining arrangements it is unnecessary that the employer should be obliged to observe also the detailed statutory requirements. However, the power to exempt should be used with caution, as it is clear from *N.U.G.S.A.T.* v. *Albury Bros.* [1978] I.R.L.R. 505 that membership of an employers' association which has collective bargaining arrangements with a trade union does not imply that the individual employer has recognised the trade unions for the purposes of collective bargaining.

As to making, revocation and variation of wages council orders, see Sched. 1.

Applications for abolition of wages councils

5.—(1) An application such as is mentioned in paragraph (*a*) of subsection (1) of section 4 above may be made to the Secretary of State either—

(*a*) by a joint industrial council, conciliation board or other similar body constituted by organisations of workers and organisations of employers which represent respectively substantial proportions of the workers and employers with respect to whom that wages council operates; or

(*b*) jointly by organisations of workers and organisations of employers which represent respectively substantial proportions of the workers and employers aforesaid; or

(*c*) by any organisation of workers which represents a substantial proportion of the workers with respect to whom that wages council operates.

(2) The grounds on which any such application may be made are that the existence of a wages council is no longer necessary for the purpose of maintaining a reasonable standard of remuneration for the workers with respect to whom that wages council operates.

Derivation

1959 Act, s. 5, as amended by the Industrial Relations Act 1971, Sched. 8.

General Note

Subs. (1) (*c*) was added by the Industrial Relations Act 1971 and implements the recommendation of the Donovan Commission (Cmnd. 3623, paras. 233, 262, 1030). The Ministry of Labour's evidence to the Donovan Commission indicated that employers were frequently opposed to the abolition of wages councils, preferring to rely on statutory machinery rather than to engage in more direct bargaining. Thus the statutory condition of a joint application could not be met. Now, therefore, it is possible for a trade union alone to apply. It is curious that the old Industrial Relations Act terminology (" organisation of workers ") has been retained. Contrast s. 2 above: there must be a joint application to establish a wages council.

Subs. (2)

Until the 1971 reform, the grounds for abolition were that the organisations making the application provided machinery adequate for the effective regulation of remuneration and conditions of employment. The present ground was introduced in accordance with the general policy recommended by the Donovan Commission of easing the path to abolition. (See Cmnd. 3623, paras. 230–234, 262, 1030.)

References to the Service as to variation or revocation of wages council orders

6.—(1) The Secretary of State—

(*a*) shall in any case where an application for the abolition of a wages council has been made to him under section 5 above and he does not thereupon proceed to the making of an order giving effect to the application,

(*b*) may in any other case where he is considering whether to exercise his power under section 4 above to abolish or vary the field of operation of a wages council;

refer to the Service the question whether the council should be abolished or, as the case may be, its field of operation varied.

(2) On a reference under this section of a question as to the abolition of a wages council the Service, if of the opinion that it is expedient to do so, may make a report to the Secretary of State recommending—

(i) the abolition of the wages council to which the reference relates, or

(ii) the narrowing of the field of operation of the council,

and (in either case), if the Service is of the opinion that it is expedient as aforesaid, also recommending the transfer of workers to the field of operation of another wages council, whether already existing or to be established.

(3) On a reference under this section as to the variation of the field of operation of a wages council the Service may make a report to the Secretary of State recommending any such variation (including the transfer of workers to the field of operation of any other wages council, whether already existing or to be established) which appears to the Service desirable in all the circumstances.

Derivation

1959 Act, s. 6, as amended by the Industrial Relations Act 1971, Sched. 8.

General Note

It is implicit in this section that the Secretary of State may abolish a wages council under s. 5 without referring the question to ACAS first. However, if he decides not to make an order after an application under s. 5, he must refer the question to ACAS, and he may do so where he is considering whether to exercise his power under s. 4. It is likely that in practice all questions of abolition will be referred first to ACAS.

Subs. (2)

Until the 1971 reform, it was necessary on such a reference to have regard to the extent to which there was adequate machinery to regulate remuneration and conditions of employment, and to whether the workers involved should be transferred to another wages council. This is no longer necessary, for the policy reasons already referred to (see note to s. 5 above).

Supplemental provisions

7.—(1) On any reference under this Part of this Act to the Service, the Service shall make all such investigations as appear to it to be necessary and shall publish in the prescribed manner a notice stating the questions which it is its duty to consider by virtue of the reference and further stating that it will consider representations with respect thereto made to it in writing within such period as may be specified in the notice, not being less than forty days from the date of the publication thereof; and it shall consider any representations made to it within that period and then make such further inquiries as it considers necessary including, so far as it considers necessary, the hearing of oral evidence.

(2) Any power conferred by this Part of this Act on the Secretary of State to make an order giving effect to a recommendation of the Service shall be construed as including power to make an order giving effect to that recommendation with such modifications as he thinks fit, being modifications which, in his opinion, do not effect important alterations in the character of the recommendation.

(3) Where the Secretary of State receives any report from the Service he may, if he thinks fit, refer the report back to the Service and the Service shall thereupon reconsider it having regard to any observations made by him and shall make a further report, and the like proceedings shall be had on any such further report as in the case of an original report.

(4) The Secretary of State shall publish every report made to him by the Service under this Part of this Act:

Provided that where he refers a report back to the Service, he shall not be bound to publish it until he publishes the further report of the Service.

DERIVATION

1959 Act, s. 9 (2)–(5).

Advisory committees

8.—(1) A wages council may request the Secretary of State to appoint a committee for any of the workers within the field of operation of the council and the Secretary of State shall appoint a committee accordingly, and the council may refer to it for a report and recommendations any matter relating to those workers which the council thinks it expedient so to refer.

(2) Schedule 3 to this Act shall have effect with respect to committees appointed under this section.

DERIVATION

1959 Act, s. 8.

General duty of wages councils to consider references by government departments

9.—(1) A wages council shall consider, as occasion requires, any matter referred to it by the Secretary of State or any government department with reference to the industrial conditions prevailing as respects the workers and employers in relation to whom it operates, and shall make a report upon the matter to the Secretary of State or, as the case may be, to that department.

(2) A wages council may, if it thinks it expedient so to do, make of its own motion a recommendation to the Secretary of State or any government department with reference to the said conditions and, where such a recommendation is so made, the Secretary of State or, as the case may be, that department, shall forthwith take it into consideration.

DERIVATION
1959 Act, s. 10.

PART II

STATUTORY JOINT INDUSTRIAL COUNCILS

Conversion of wages councils to statutory joint industrial councils

10.—(1) The Secretary of State may by order made in accordance with the following provisions of this section provide that a wages council shall become a statutory joint industrial council having the functions conferred on statutory joint industrial councils by the provisions of Part III of this Act.

(2) The Secretary of State may make an order under this section with respect to a wages council—

(*a*) on an application made to him by the employers' association or trade union nominated in relation to the council or by that association and union jointly; or

(*b*) without an application under paragraph (*a*) above, but after consultation with the employers' association and trade union so nominated.

(3) An order under this section shall not be made on an application by an employers' association or trade union alone unless the Secretary of State has consulted every employers' association and trade union nominated in relation to the wages council in question and (whether so nominated or not) all organisations of employers and workers which in his opinion represent a substantial proportion of employers and workers respectively in relation to whom that council operates.

(4) The Secretary of State shall before making an order under this section refer the question whether he should do so to the Service, and the Service shall inquire into it and report on that question.

(5) Part I of Schedule 4 to this Act shall have effect with respect to the constitution, officers and proceedings of statutory joint industrial councils and Part II of that Schedule shall have effect with respect to the transition of a wages council to a statutory joint industrial council.

DERIVATION
1975 Act, s. 90.

GENERAL NOTE

Wages councils are curious beasts in that the ultimate sign of their success is their own demise. Perhaps because of a natural aversion to suicide, they have not been particularly successful by this criterion. Thus the Employment Protection Act 1975 introduced the new concept of the statutory joint industrial council (S.J.I.C.) as a halfway house to ease the transition from wages council to voluntary collective bargaining. The crucial difference from a wages council is that the S.J.I.C. will have no independent members (see Sched. 4, para. 1). It is felt that often there is too much reliance on the independent members to solve an issue, with the result that neither the employers' side nor the workers' side makes a real effort to come to an agreement (see, *e.g.* ACAS Report No. 13 on the Toy Manufacturing Wages Council, Chap. 9). It is hoped that without independent members both sides will have to try harder to reach a consensus, which will enhance the growth of good industrial relations and make voluntary collective bargaining a more feasible proposition. However, there are safeguards if the parties are unable to agree (see s. 11 below).

So far, no S.J.I.C. has been set up, although one has been recommended for the toy manufacturing industry (see ACAS Report No. 13). Perhaps predictably, all the trade unions involved were in favour of such a conversion and all but one employer opposed it.

Subs. (2)

The application for a conversion need not be made jointly, although if it is not so made then every employers' association and trade union which might be affected must be consulted (subs. (3)).

Subs. (4)

All questions of conversion from wages council to S.J.I.C. must be investigated by ACAS.

Disputes between employers' and workers' representatives

11.—(1) If in the opinion of either the persons appointed to represent employers or the persons appointed to represent workers on a statutory joint industrial council, a dispute has arisen on any question and cannot be settled by the members of the council, those persons may request the Service to attempt to bring about a settlement of the dispute and the Service shall attempt to do so accordingly.

(2) If the Service is unable to bring about a settlement of any such dispute, the Service shall refer the dispute for settlement to the arbitration of—

(*a*) one or more persons appointed by the Service for that purpose (not being an officer or servant of the Service); or

(*b*) the Central Arbitration Committee.

(3) Where more than one arbitrator is appointed under subsection (2) (*a*) above, the Service shall appoint one of the arbitrators to act as chairman.

(4) Any determination of the arbitrator, arbitrators or Committee on a dispute referred to him, them or it under this section shall be final and binding on the statutory joint industrial council and its members, and the council shall make an order under section 14 below or take any steps which may be necessary to give effect to the determination.

(5) Part I of the Arbitration Act 1950 shall not apply to an arbitration under this section.

(6) In the application of this section to Scotland, references to an arbitrator shall be construed as references to an arbiter.

DERIVATION

1975 Act, s. 92.

GENERAL NOTE

If there is a dispute between members of a statutory joint industrial council which the council itself cannot settle, then either side may refer the matter to ACAS who will bring about a settlement by conciliation. If ACAS is unable to do this, then ultimately the question can be referred either to arbitrators appointed by ACAS or to the C.A.C., who will make a binding decision on the matter.

It is to be hoped that this procedure will be used very much as a last resort: otherwise the S.J.I.C. will simply become a more cumbersome form of wages council. This can probably be ensured by informal pressure by ACAS.

Abolition of statutory joint industrial councils

12.—(1) If the Secretary of State is of the opinion that, in the event of the abolition of a statutory joint industrial council, adequate machinery would be established for the effective regulation of the remuneration and other terms and conditions of employment of the workers within the council's field of operation and is likely thereafter to be maintained, he may by order abolish the council.

(2) An order under this section may be made on the application of the statutory joint industrial council concerned or without such an application, but shall not be made without such an application unless the Secretary of State has consulted the council.

(3) The Secretary of State shall before making an order under this section refer the question whether he should do so to the Service, and the Service shall inquire into it and report on that question.

(4) Where an order under this section abolishes a statutory joint industrial council, then, save as is otherwise provided by the order, anything done by the council shall, except as respects things previously done or omitted to be done, cease to have effect.

Derivation
1975 Act, s. 93.

General Note
The requirement for abolishing a wages council is now simply that it is no longer necessary for the maintenance of a reasonable level of remuneration (see s. 5 above). It seems curious that the old ground, that adequate machinery would be established, has been reproduced here.

Supplemental provisions

13.—(1) In sections 10 to 12 above " nominated ", in relation to an employers' association or trade union, means, an association or union for the time being nominated under paragraph 1 (2) of Schedule 2 to this Act to appoint persons to represent employers or workers on the wages council in question.

(2) Schedule 1 to this Act shall apply in relation to an order under section 10 above providing that a wages council shall become a statutory joint industrial council and in relation to an order under section 12 above abolishing a statutory joint industrial council.

Derivation
1975 Act, s. 94.

Part III

Orders Regulating Terms and Conditions of Employment

Power to fix terms and conditions of employment

14.—(1) A wages council or a statutory joint industrial council may make an order, subject to and in accordance with the provisions of this section,—

(*a*) fixing the remuneration,
(*b*) requiring holidays to be allowed,
(*c*) fixing any other terms and conditions,

for all or any of the workers in relation to whom the council operates.

(2) An order under this section requiring a holiday to be allowed for a worker—

(*a*) shall not be made unless both holiday remuneration in respect of the period of the holiday and remuneration other than holiday remuneration have been or are being fixed under this Part of this Act for that worker;

(*b*) shall provide for the duration of the holiday being related to the duration of the period for which the worker has been employed or engaged to be employed by the employer who is to allow the holiday; and

(*c*) subject as aforesaid, may make provision as to the times at which or the periods within which, and the circumstances in which, the holiday shall be allowed.

(3) Any order under this section fixing holiday remuneration may contain provisions—

(*a*) as to the times at which, and the conditions subject to which, that remuneration shall accrue and shall become payable, and

(*b*) for securing that any such remuneration which has accrued due to a worker during his employment by any employer shall, in the event of his ceasing to be employed by that employer before he becomes entitled to be allowed a holiday by him, nevertheless become payable by the employer to the worker.

(4) Before making an order under this section the council shall make such investigations as it thinks fit and shall—

(*a*) publish in the prescribed manner notice of the council's proposals with respect to any new terms and conditions of employment (that is to say, any terms and conditions of employment differing from any then in force by virtue of an order made under this section); and

(*b*) give the prescribed notice for the purpose of informing, so far as practicable, all persons affected by the proposals, stating the place where copies of the proposals may be obtained and the period (which shall not be less than fourteen days from the date of publication of the notice) within which written representations with respect to the proposals may be sent to the council.

(5) After considering any written representations made with respect to any such proposals within the said period and making such further inquiries as the council considers necessary, or if no such representations are made within that period, after the expiration of that period, the council may make an order—

(*a*) giving effect to the proposals; or

(*b*) giving effect to them with such modifications as the council thinks fit having regard to any such representations;

but if it appears to the council that, having regard to the nature of any proposed modifications, an opportunity should be given to persons concerned to consider the modifications, the council shall again publish the proposals and give notice under subsection (4) above, and that subsection and this subsection shall apply accordingly.

(6) Subsections (4) and (5) above have effect subject to the provisions of subsection (1A) of section 4 of the Equal Pay Act 1970.

(7) An order under this section shall have effect as regards any terms as to remuneration as from a date specified in the order, which may be a date earlier than the date of the order but not earlier than the date on which the council agreed on those terms prior to publishing the original proposals to which effect is given, with or without modifications, by the order; but where any such order fixing workers' remuneration applies to any worker who is paid wages at intervals not exceeding seven days and the date so specified does not correspond with the beginning of the period

for which the wages are paid (hereafter in this section referred to as a wages period), the order shall, as respects that worker, have effect as from the beginning of the next wages period following the date specified in the order.

(8) Any increase in remuneration payable by virtue of an order under this section in respect of any time before the date of the order shall be paid by the employer within a period specified in the order, being—

(*a*) in the case of a worker who is in the employment of the employer on the date of the order, a period beginning with that date;

(*b*) in the case of a worker who is no longer in the employment of the employer on that date, a period beginning with the date on which the employer receives from the worker or a person acting on his behalf a request in writing for the remuneration;

but if, in the case of a worker falling within paragraph (*a*) of this subsection who is paid wages at intervals not exceeding seven days, pay day (the day on which wages are normally paid to him) for any wages period falling wholly or partly within the period so specified occurs within seven days from the end of that specified period, any such remuneration shall be paid not later than pay day.

(9) As soon as a council has made an order under this section it shall give the prescribed notice of the making and contents of the order and shall then and subsequently give such notice of other prescribed matters affecting its operation for the purpose of informing, so far as practicable, all persons who will be affected by it.

(10) An order under this section may make different provision for different cases and may amend or revoke previous orders under this section.

(11) A document purporting to be a copy of an order made by a council under this section and to be signed by the secretary of the council shall be taken to be a true copy of the order unless the contrary is proved.

(12) An order under this section shall not prejudice any rights conferred on any worker by or under any other enactment.

DERIVATION

1959 Act, s. 11, as substituted by 1975 Act, s. 89 (2) and Sched. 7, Pt. I.

GENERAL NOTE

This section, introduced by the 1975 Act, changes the 1959 Act in three important respects. First, it is no longer necessary for the Secretary of State to approve the council's proposals (s. 14 (1)); secondly, orders can now be made about all terms and conditions (s. 14 (1) (*c*)), and thirdly, there is a limited power to make retrospective orders (s. 14 (7)). These alterations should help to make wages councils more effective.

Subs. (1)

Previously only remuneration and holiday entitlement could be the subject of orders.

Subs. (3)

For computation of remuneration, see s. 17.

Subs. (4)

"Prescribed" means prescribed by regulations made by the Secretary of State (see s. 28). At present, these are the Wages Councils and Statutory Joint Industrial Councils (Notices) Regulations 1975 (S.I. 1975 No. 2138).

Subs. (6)

Thus where a wages council or S.J.I.C. order needs amendment in order to comply with the Equal Pay Act, it is not necessary to comply with subss. (4) and (5).

Subs. (7)

This gives a limited power to make an order for remuneration retrospectively, but it must not be effective from a day earlier than the date on which the council agreed the terms.

Subs. (8)

It is unfortunate that an ex-employee will have to put in a request in writing in order to get back-dated pay. Since it is well known that those employed in wages councils industries are frequently ignorant of the existence of the council, let alone the contents of council orders, it seems likely that in most cases back pay will never be claimed.

Effect and enforcement of orders under section 14

15.—(1) If a contract between a worker to whom an order under section 14 above applies and his employer provides for the payment of less remuneration than the statutory minimum remuneration, it shall have effect as if the statutory minimum remuneration were substituted for the remuneration provided for in the contract, and if any such contract provides for the payment of any holiday remuneration at times or subject to conditions other than those specified in the order, it shall have effect as if the times or conditions specified in the order were substituted for those provided for in the contract.

(2) If any such contract fixes terms and conditions other than those relating to remuneration or wages which are less favourable than the corresponding terms and conditions specified in an order under section 14 above it shall have effect as if the corresponding terms and conditions were substituted for those fixed by the contract.

(3) If an employer fails—

(*a*) to pay a worker to whom an order under section 14 above applies remuneration not less than the statutory minimum remuneration; or

(*b*) to pay him arrears of remuneration before the expiration of the period specified in the order; or

(*c*) to pay him holiday remuneration at the times and subject to the conditions specified in the order; or

(*d*) to allow to any such worker the holidays fixed by the order;

he shall for each offence be liable on summary conviction to a fine not exceeding £100.

(4) Where proceedings are brought under subsection (3) above in respect of an offence consisting of a failure to pay remuneration not less than the statutory minimum remuneration, or to pay arrears of remuneration, and the employer or any other person charged as a person to whose act or default the offence was due is found guilty of the offence, then, subject to subsection (5) below,—

(*a*) evidence may be given of any failure on the part of the employer to pay any such remuneration or arrears during the two years ending with the date of the offence to any worker employed by him; and

(*b*) on proof of the failure, the court may order the employer to pay such sum as is found by the court to represent the difference between the amount of any such remuneration or arrears which ought to have been paid during that period to any such worker, if the provisions of this Part of this Act had been complied with, and the amount actually so paid.

(5) Evidence of any failure to pay any such remuneration or arrears may be given under subsection (4) above only if—

(*a*) the employer or any other person charged as aforesaid has been convicted of the offence consisting of the failure; and

(*b*) notice of intention to adduce such evidence has been served with the summons or warrant.

(6) The powers given by this section for the recovery of sums due from an employer to a worker shall not be in derogation of any right to recover such sums by civil proceedings.

(7) In the application of this section to Scotland—

(*a*) in subsection (4), the words " or any other person charged as a person to whose act or default the offence was due " shall be omitted; and

(*b*) in subsection (5), in paragraph (*a*) the words " or any other person charged as aforesaid " shall be omitted, and in paragraph (*b*) for the words " summons or warrant " there shall be substituted the word " complaint ".

DERIVATION

1959 Act, s. 12, as substituted by the 1975 Act, s. 89 (2) and Sched. 7, Pt. II.

GENERAL NOTE

Subs. (1) *and* (2)

The orders work by being implied into the individual worker's contract of employment, and can thus be enforced by him at civil law in the usual way subject to the usual limitations periods.

Subs. (3)

In fact prosecutions are rarely brought in practice. In 1977 when almost 27,000 workers had arrears paid to them, only seven employers were prosecuted for their failure to observe minimum conditions.

Subs. (4)

This permits an action to be brought for up to two years' back pay where criminal proceedings are taken against an employer for failure to comply with an order. This is subject, however, to subs. (5).

Permits to infirm and incapacitated persons

16.—(1) If, as respects any worker employed or desiring to be employed in such circumstances that an order under section 14 above applies or will apply to him, the council which made the order is satisfied, on application being made to it for a permit under this section either by the worker or the employer or a prospective employer, that the worker is affected by infirmity or physical incapacity which renders him incapable of earning the statutory minimum remuneration or makes it inappropriate for other terms and conditions fixed by the order to apply to him, it may, if it thinks fit, grant, subject to any conditions it may determine, a permit authorising his employment at less than the statutory minimum remuneration or dispensing with a term or condition specified in the permit; and while the permit is in force the remuneration authorised by the permit shall, if the conditions specified in the permit are complied with, be deemed to be the statutory minimum remuneration or, as the case may be, the terms and conditions fixed by the order shall be deemed to be observed.

(2) Where an employer employs any worker in reliance on any document purporting to be a permit granted under subsection (1) above authorising the employment of that worker at less than the statutory minimum remuneration, or dispensing with a term or condition specified

in the permit, then, if the employer has notified the council in question that, relying on that document, he is employing or proposing to employ that worker at a specified remuneration or without compliance with any such term or condition, the document shall, notwithstanding that it is not or is no longer a valid permit relating to that worker, be deemed, subject to the terms thereof and as respects only any period after the notification, to be such a permit until notice to the contrary is received by the employer from the council.

DERIVATION

1959 Act, s. 13, as amended by the 1975 Act, Sched. 7, Pt. IV.

GENERAL NOTE

This section allows exemption from compliance with the statutory minimum conditions in respect of individual workers who are too infirm or incapacitated to earn the minimum. The permit is granted by the wages council or S.J.I.C.

This power is used sparingly: for example, in 1977 only 21 new permits were issued, 32 renewed and 41 cancelled.

Computation of remuneration

17.—(1) Subject to the provisions of this Part of this Act, any reference therein to remuneration shall be construed as a reference to the amount obtained or to be obtained in cash by the worker from his employer after allowing for the worker's necessary expenditure, if any, in connection with his employment, and clear of all deductions in respect of any matter whatsoever, except any reduction lawfully made—

(*a*) under the Income Tax Acts, the enactments relating to social security or any enactment requiring or authorising deductions to be made for the purposes of a superannuation scheme;

(*b*) at the request in writing of the worker, either for the purposes of a superannuation scheme or a thrift scheme or for any purpose in the carrying out of which the employer has no beneficial financial interest, whether directly or indirectly; or

(*c*) in pursuance of, or in accordance with, such a contract in that behalf as is mentioned in section 1, 2 or 3 of the Truck Act 1896 and in accordance with the provisions of that section.

(2) Notwithstanding subsection (1) above, orders under section 14 above may contain provisions authorising specified benefits or advantages, being benefits or advantages provided, in pursuance of the terms and conditions of the employment of workers, by the employer or by some other person under arrangements with the employer and not being benefits or advantages the provision of which is illegal by virtue of the Truck Acts 1831 to 1940, or of any other enactment, to be reckoned as payment of wages by the employer in lieu of payment in cash, and defining the value at which any such benefits or advantages are to be reckoned.

(3) If any payment is made by a worker in respect of any benefit or advantage provided as mentioned in the foregoing subsection, then,—

(*a*) if the benefit or advantage is authorised by virtue of that subsection to be reckoned as therein mentioned, the amount of the payment shall be deducted from the defined value for the purposes of the reckoning;

(*b*) if the benefit or advantage is authorised by virtue of that subsection to be reckoned as therein mentioned, any excess of the amount of the payment over the defined value shall be treated for the purposes of subsection (1) above as if it had been a deduction not being one of the excepted deductions therein mentioned;

(c) if the benefit or advantage is specified in an order under section 14 above as one which has been taken into account in fixing the statutory minimum remuneration, the whole of the payment shall be treated for the purposes of subsection (1) above as if it had been a deduction not being one of the excepted deductions therein mentioned.

(4) Nothing in this section shall be construed as authorising the making of any deduction, or the giving of remuneration in any manner, which is illegal by virtue of the Truck Acts 1831 to 1940, or of any other enactment.

DERIVATION
1959 Act, s. 14.

GENERAL NOTE
In effect, remuneration means net pay. By subs. (2), the monetary value of "perks" may be included, minus any payment which the worker had to make for the benefit or advantage (subs. (3)).

Apportionment of remuneration

18. Where for any period a worker receives remuneration for work for part of which he is entitled to statutory minimum remuneration at one or more time rates and for the remainder of which no statutory minimum remuneration is fixed, the amount of the remuneration which is to be attributed to the work for which he is entitled to statutory minimum remuneration shall, if not apparent from the terms of the contract between the employer and the worker, be deemed for the purposes of this Part of this Act to be the amount which bears to the total amount of the remuneration the same proportion as the time spent on the part of the work for which he is entitled to statutory minimum remuneration bears to the time spent on the whole of the work.

DERIVATION
1959 Act, s. 15.

GENERAL NOTE
This section deals with situations where a worker is engaged on work, some of which is covered by a wages council or S.J.I.C. order, and the rest of which is not. The formula is logical, but one can imagine difficulties in applying it in practice.

Employers not to receive premiums

19.—(1) Where a worker to whom an order under section 14 above applies is an apprentice or learner, it shall not be lawful for his employer to receive directly or indirectly from him, or on his behalf or on his account, any payment by way of premium:

Provided that nothing in this section shall apply to any such payment duly made in pursuance of any instrument of apprenticeship not later than four weeks after the commencement of the apprenticeship or to any such payment made at any time if duly made in pursuance of any instrument of apprenticeship approved for the purposes of this proviso by a wages council or by a statutory joint industrial council.

(2) If any employer acts in contravention of this section, he shall be liable on summary conviction in respect of each offence to a fine not exceeding £100, and the court may, in addition to imposing a fine, order him to repay to the worker or other person by whom the payment was made the sum improperly received by way of premium.

DERIVATION
1959 Act, s. 16.

Records and notices

20.—(1) The employer of any workers to whom an order under section 14 above applies shall keep such records as are necessary to show whether or not the provisions of this Part and Part IV of this Act are being complied with as respects them, and the records shall be retained by the employer for three years.

(2) The employer of any workers shall post in the prescribed manner such notices as may be prescribed for the purpose of informing them of any proposal or order under section 14 above affecting them, and, if it is so prescribed, shall give notice in any other prescribed manner to the said workers of the said matters and of such other matters, if any, as may be prescribed.

(3) If an employer fails to comply with any of the requirements of this section he shall be liable on summary conviction to a fine not exceeding £100.

DERIVATION
1959 Act, s. 17.

GENERAL NOTE

Subs. (1)
While appreciating the pressures of space which an employer may have, it is nevertheless doubtful whether a three-year period is long enough.

Subs. (2)
As to the meaning of "prescribed," see the note to s. 14 above.

PART IV

MISCELLANEOUS

Offences and enforcement

Criminal liability of agent and superior employer, and special defence open to employer

21.—(1) Where the immediate employer of any worker is himself in the employment of some other person and that worker is employed on the premises of that other person, that other person shall for the purposes of Part III and this Part of this Act be deemed to be the employer of that worker jointly with the immediate employer.

(2) Where an employer is charged with an offence under Part III or this Part of this Act, he shall be entitled, upon information duly laid by him and on giving to the prosecution not less than three days' notice in writing of his intention, to have any other person to whose act or default he alleges that the offence in question was due brought before the court at the time appointed for the hearing of the charge; and if, after the commission of the offence has been proved, the employer proves that the offence was due to the act or the default of that other person, that other person may be convicted of the offence, and, if the employer further proves that he has used all due diligence to secure that the provisions of Part III and this Part of this Act and any relevant regulation or order made thereunder are complied with, he shall be acquitted of the offence.

(3) Where a defendant seeks to avail himself of the provisions of subsection (2) above—

(a) the prosecution, as well as the person whom the defendant charges with the offence, shall have the right to cross-examine him if he gives evidence and any witnesses called by him in support of his pleas and to call rebutting evidence;

(b) the court may make such order as it thinks fit for the payment of costs by any party to the proceedings to any other party thereto.

(4) Where it appears to an officer acting for the purposes of Part III and this Part of this Act that an offence has been committed in respect of which proceedings might be taken under this Act against an employer, and the officer is reasonably satisfied that the offence of which complaint is made was due to an act or default of some other person and that the employer could establish a defence under subsection (2) above, the officer may cause proceedings to be taken against that other person without first causing proceedings to be taken against the employer.

In any such proceedings the defendant may be charged with and, on proof that the offence was due to his act or default, be convicted of, the offence with which the employer might have been charged.

(5) Subsections (2) to (4) above shall not apply to Scotland, but—

(a) where an offence for which an employer is, under this Act, liable to a fine was due to an act or default of an agent of the employer or other person, then, whether proceedings are or are not taken against the employer, that agent or other person may be charged with and convicted of the offence, and shall be liable on conviction to the same punishment as might have been inflicted on the employer if he had been convicted of the offence;

(b) where an employer who is charged with an offence under this Act proves to the satisfaction of the court that he has used due diligence to secure compliance with the provisions of Part III and this Part of this Act and any relevant regulation or order made thereunder and that the offence was due to the act or default of some other person, he shall be acquitted of the offence.

DERIVATION
1959 Act, s. 18.

Officers

22.—(1) The Secretary of State, with the approval of the Minister for the Civil Service as to numbers and salaries, may appoint officers to act for the purposes of Part III and this Part of this Act, and may, in lieu of or in addition to appointing any officers under this section, arrange with any government department that officers of that department shall act for the said purposes.

(2) Every officer acting for the purposes of Part III and this Part of this Act shall be furnished by the Secretary of State with a certificate of his appointment or authority so to act, and, when so acting, shall, if so required by any person affected, produce the certificate to him.

(3) An officer acting for the purposes of Part III and this Part of this Act shall have power for the performance of his duties—

(a) to require the production of wages sheets or other records of wages kept by an employer, and records of payments made to homeworkers by persons giving out work, and any other such records as are required by this Act to be kept by employers, and to inspect and examine those sheets or records and copy any material part thereof;

(*b*) to require the production of any licence or certificate granted under the Transport Act 1968, and of any records kept in pursuance of Part VI of the Transport Act 1968 or of the applicable Community rules within the meaning of the said Part VI, and to examine any such licence, certificate or records and copy it or them or any material part therof;

(*c*) to require any person giving out work and any homeworker to give any information which it is in his power to give with respect to the names and addresses of the persons to whom the work is given out or from whom the work is received, as the case may be, and with respect to the payments to be made for the work;

(*d*) at all reasonable times to enter any premises at which any employer to whom an order under section 14 above applies carries on his business (including any place used, in connection with that business, for giving out work to homeworkers and any premises which the officer has reasonable cause to believe to be used by or by arrangement with the employer to provide living accommodation for workers);

(*e*) to inspect and copy any material part of any list of homeworkers kept by an employer or person giving out work to homeworkers;

(*f*) to examine, either alone or in the presence of any other person, as he thinks fit, with respect to any matters under Part III or this Part of this Act, any person whom he has reasonable cause to believe to be or to have been a worker to whom an order under section 14 above applies or applied or the employer of any such person or a servant or agent of the employer employed in the employer's business, and to require every such person to be so examined, and to sign a declaration of the truth of the matters in respect of which he is so examined:

Provided that no person shall be required under paragraph (*f*) above to give information tending to criminate himself or, in the case of a person who is married, his or her wife or husband.

(4) In England or Wales, an officer acting for the purposes of Part III and this Part of this Act may institute proceedings for any offence under this Act and may, although not of counsel or a solicitor, conduct any such proceedings:

Provided that an officer may not conduct proceedings for an offence under section 24 below unless he instituted those proceedings.

(5) An officer acting for the purposes of Part III and this Part of this Act who is authorised in that behalf by general or special directions of the Secretary of State may, if it appears to him that a sum is due from an employer to a worker on account of the payment to him of remuneration less than the statutory minimum remuneration, institute on behalf of and in the name of that worker civil proceedings for the recovery of that sum and in any such proceedings the court may make an order for the payment of costs by the officer as if he were a party to the proceedings.

The power given by this subsection for the recovery of sums due from an employer to a worker shall not be in derogation of any right of the worker to recover such sums by civil proceedings.

(6) Any person who obstructs an officer acting for the purposes of Part III and this Part of this Act in the exercise of any power conferred by this section, or fails to comply with any requirement of such an officer

made in the exercise of any such power, shall be liable on summary conviction to a fine not exceeding £100:

Provided that it shall be a defence for a person charged under this subsection with failing to comply with a requirement to prove that it was not reasonably practicable to comply therewith.

DERIVATION

1959 Act, s. 19.

GENERAL NOTE

There are at present about 150 wages inspectors although the figure is expected to increase by up to 10 per cent. Their role in enforcing the Act is crucial, yet because there are so few, at present employers are only visited once every six years. It is hoped to bring this down to a four-year cycle, but it is submitted that a far more regular cycle of inspection is required.

Penalties for false entries in records, producing false records or giving false information

23. If any person makes or causes to be made or knowingly allows to be made any entry in a record required by this Act to be kept by employers, which he knows to be false in a material particular, or for purposes connected with Part III or the preceding provisions of this Part of this Act produces or furnishes, or causes or knowingly allows to be produced or furnished, any wages sheet, record, list or information which he knows to be false in a material particular, he shall be liable on summary conviction to a fine not exceeding £400 or to imprisonment for a term not exceeding three months, or to both such fine and such imprisonment.

DERIVATION

1959 Act, s. 20.

GENERAL NOTE

Again, this section is rarely used. In 1977 there were only seven prosecutions for this offence (*cf.* note to s. 15 above).

Power to obtain information

24.—(1) The Secretary of State may, for the purpose of, or in connection with the enforcement of, an order under section 14 above, by notice in writing require an employer within the field of operation of a council making such an order to furnish such information as may be specified or described in the notice.

(2) A notice under this section may specify the way in which, and the time within which, it is to be complied with, and may be varied or revoked by a subsequent notice so given.

(3) If a person refuses or wilfully neglects to furnish any information which he has been required to furnish by a notice under subsection (i) above, he shall be liable on summary conviction to a fine not exceeding £100.

(4) If a person, in purporting to comply with a requirement of a notice under subsection (1) above, knowingly or recklessly makes any false statement he shall be liable on summary conviction to a fine not exceeding £400.

(5) Section 21 above shall not apply in relation to an offence under this section.

(6) Where an offence under this section committed by a body corporate is proved to have been committed with the consent or connivance

of, or to be attributable to any neglect on the part of, any director, manager, secretary or other similar officer of the body corporate, or any person who was purporting to act in any such capacity, he as well as the body corporate shall be guilty of that offence and shall be liable to be proceeded against and punished accordingly.

(7) Where the affairs of the body corporate are managed by its members, subsection (6) above shall apply in relation to the acts and defaults of a member in connection with his functions of management as if he were a director of the body corporate.

DERIVATION

1975 Act, ss. 95, 117.

GENERAL NOTE

Since the power to issue questionnaires was given in 1975 it has been found useful for improving the effectiveness of the Inspectorate. It is possible in this way to get enough information from employers to decide where visits are most necessary.

Central co-ordinating committees

Central co-ordinating committees

25.—(1) The Secretary of State may, if he thinks fit to do so, by order establish a central co-ordinating committee in relation to any two or more wages councils or statutory joint industrial councils, or wages councils and statutory joint industrial councils, or abolish, or vary the field of operation of, any central co-ordinating committee so established:

Provided that, except where subsection (2) or (3) below applies, the Secretary of State shall, before making any such order, consult the wages councils or statutory joint industrial councils, or, as the case may be, the wages councils and the statutory joint industrial councils, concerned.

(2) Where the Service makes a recommendation for the establishment of a wages council or statutory joint industrial council it may include in its report a recommendation for the establishment, in relation to any council established in accordance with the recommendation and any other council (including a council proposed to be established by another recommendation embodied in the same report), of a central co-ordinating committee, or for the variation of the field of operation of an existing central co-ordinating committee so that it operates also in connection with any council established in accordance with the recommendation.

(3) Where the Service makes a recommendation for the abolition of a wages council or statutory joint industrial council, it may include in its report a recommendation for the variation of the field of operation of an existing central co-ordinating committee so that it no longer operates in relation to the council to be abolished, or a recommendation for the abolition of any central co-ordinating committee theretofore operating in relation to the council to be abolished.

(4) The Secretary of State may by order give effect to a recommendation made under subsection (2) or (3) above.

(5) It shall be the duty of any central co-ordinating committee from time to time—

(*a*) to consider whether the field of operation of the councils in relation to which it is established is properly divided as between the councils and to report thereon to the Secretary of State;

(*b*) to make recommendations to the councils with respect to the principles to be followed by them in the exercise of their powers under this Act;

(c) to consider any question referred to it by the Secretary of State or by the councils or any two or more of them, and to report thereon to the Secretary of State, or to the councils which referred the question, as the case may be.

(6) Schedule 2 to this Act shall have effect with respect to the constitution, officers and proceedings of central co-ordinating committees.

DERIVATION
1959 Act, s. 7.

Reports on regulation of terms and conditions of employment

Reports by Service on regulation of terms and conditions of employment

26. The Service shall, if requested to do so by the Secretary of State—

(a) inquire into and report on the development by agreement of machinery for the regulation of the remuneration and terms and conditions of employment of workers within the field of operation of a wages council or statutory joint industrial council and the question whether, in order to maintain a reasonable standard of remuneration and terms and conditions of employment of those workers, it is necessary to regulate their remuneration and other terms and conditions of employment by means of orders under section 14 above;

(b) inquire into and report on the operation generally of this Act;

(c) publish a report made under paragraph (a) or (b) above.

DERIVATION
1975 Act, s. 96.

Power to extend wages councils legislation

Extension of this Act and N.I. legislation

27.—(1) Her Majesty may by Order in Council provide that—

(a) the provisions of this Act, and

(b) the provisions of any legislation (that is to say any enactment of the Parliament of Northern Ireland and any provision made by or under a Measure of the Northern Ireland Assembly) for the time being in force in Northern Ireland which makes provision for purposes corresponding to any of the purposes of the provisions of this Act,

shall, to such extent and for such purposes as may be specified in the Order, apply (with or without modification) to or in relation to any person in employment to which this section applies.

(2) This section applies to employment for the purposes of any activities—

(a) in the territorial waters of the United Kingdom; or

(b) connected with the exploration of the sea bed or subsoil or the exploitation of their natural resources in any designated area; or

(c) connected with the exploration or exploitation, in a foreign sector of the continental shelf, of a cross-boundary petroleum field.

(3) An Order in Council under subsection (1) above—

(*a*) may make different provision for different cases;

(*b*) may provide that all or any of the provisions of any Act mentioned in that subsection, as applied by such an Order, shall apply to individuals whether or not they are British subjects and to bodies corporate whether or not they are incorporated under the law of any part of the United Kingdom (notwithstanding that the application may affect their activities outside the United Kingdom);

(*c*) may make provision for conferring jurisdiction on any court or class of court specified in the Order, or on industrial tribunals, in respect of offences, causes of action or other matters arising in connection with employment to which this section applies;

(*d*) without prejudice to the generality of subsection (1) above or of paragraph (*a*) above, may provide that the enactments referred to in that subsection shall apply in relation to any person in employment for the purposes of such activities as are referred to in subsection (2) above in any part of the areas specified in paragraphs (*a*) and (*b*) of that subsection;

(*e*) may exclude from the operation of section 3 of the Territorial Waters Jurisdiction Act 1878 (consents required for prosecutions) proceedings for offences under the enactments referred to in subsection (1) above in connection with employment to which this section applies;

(*f*) may provide that such proceedings shall not be brought without such consent as may be required by the Order.

(4) Any jurisdiction conferred on any court or tribunal under this section shall be without prejudice to jurisdiction exercisable apart from this section by that or any other court or tribunal.

(5) In this section—

" cross-boundary petroleum field " means a petroleum field that extends across the boundary between a designated area and a foreign sector of the continental shelf;

" designated area " means an area designated under section 1 (7) of the Continental Shelf Act 1964;

" foreign sector of the continental shelf " means an area which is outside the territorial waters of any State and within which rights are exercisable by a State other than the United Kingdom with respect to the sea bed and subsoil and their natural resources;

" petroleum field " means a geological structure identified as an oil or gas field by the Order in Council concerned.

DERIVATION
1975 Act, s. 127.

Supplemental

Interpretation

28. In this Act—

" employers' association " means any organisation representing employers and any association of such organisations or of employers and such organisations;

" homeworkers " means a person who contracts with a person, for the purposes of that person's business, for the execution of work to be done in a place not under the control or management of the person with whom he contracts, and who does not normally make use of the services of more than two persons in the carrying out of contracts for the execution of work with statutory minimum remuneration;

" organisation ", in relation to workers, means a trade union and, in relation to employers, means an employers' association;

" prescribed " means prescribed by regulations made by the Secretary of State;

" the Service " means the Advisory, Conciliation and Arbitration Service;

" statutory joint industrial council " means a council established by an order made under section 10 above;

" statutory minimum remuneration " means remuneration (including holiday remuneration) fixed by an order made under section 14 above;

" statutory provision " means a provision contained in or having effect under any enactment;

" superannuation scheme " means any enactment, rules, deed or other instrument, providing for the payment of annuities or lump sums to the persons with respect to whom the instrument has effect on their retirement at a specified age or on becoming incapacitated at some earlier age, or to the personal representatives or the widows, relatives or dependants of such persons on their death or otherwise, whether with or without any further or other benefits;

" thrift scheme " means any arrangement for savings, for providing money for holidays or for other purposes, under which a worker is entitled to receive in cash sums equal to or greater than the aggregate of any sums deducted from his remuneration or paid by him for the purposes of the scheme;

" time rate " means a rate where the amount of the remuneration is to be calculated by reference to the actual number of hours worked;

" trade union " has the meaning given by section 28 of the Trade Union and Labour Relations Act 1974;

" wages council " means a wages council established by an order under section 1 above;

" worker " means any person—

(*a*) who has entered into or works under a contract with an employer (whether express or implied, and, if express, whether oral or in writing) whether it be a contract of service or of apprenticeship or any other contract whereby he undertakes to do or perform personally any work or services for another party to the contract who is not a professional client of his; or

(*b*) whether or not he falls within the foregoing provision, who is a homeworker;

but does not include any person who is employed casually and otherwise than for the purposes of the business of the employer or other party to the contract;

" work with statutory minimum remuneration " means work of a description for which, when executed by a worker, statutory minimum remuneration is provided under Part III of this Act.

DERIVATION

1959 Act, s. 24, as amended by 1975 Act, Sched. 7, Pt. IV.

Orders and regulations

29.—(1) The Secretary of State may make regulations for prescribing anything which by this Act is authorised or required to be prescribed.

(2) Any power to make orders or regulations conferred on the Secretary of State by this Act shall be exercisable by statutory instrument.

(3) Any statutory instrument containing any order of the Secretary of State made under Part I or II of this Act or regulations made under any of the provisions of this Act shall (together, in the case of an order, with any report of the Service relating thereto) be laid before Parliament after being made, and shall be subject to annulment in pursuance of a resolution of either House of Parliament.

(4) Any power conferred by this Act to prescribe the manner in which anything is to be published shall include power to prescribe the date which is to be taken for the purposes of this Act as the date of publication.

DERIVATION
1959 Act, s. 22.

Expenses

30. The expenses of the Secretary of State in carrying this Act into effect, and any expenses authorised by the Secretary of State with the consent of the Treasury to be incurred by a wages council, the Service, or a central co-ordinating committee established under this Act by order of the Secretary of State, shall be defrayed out of moneys provided by Parliament.

DERIVATION
1959 Act, s. 23.

Transitional provisions, amendments and repeals

31.—(1) The transitional provisions and savings in Schedule 5 to this Act shall have effect, but nothing in that Schedule shall be construed as prejudicing section 16 of the Interpretation Act 1978 (effect of repeals).

(2) The enactments specified in Schedule 6 to this Act shall have effect subject to the amendments specified in that Schedule.

(3) The enactments specified in the first column of Schedule 7 to this Act are hereby repealed to the extent specified in the third column of that Schedule.

Short title, commencement and extent

32.—(1) This Act may be cited as the Wages Councils Act 1979.

(2) This Act shall come into force on the expiry of the period of one month beginning with the date on which it is passed.

(3) This Act, except section 27, paragraphs 4 and 5 of Schedule 6 and the repeal of section 127 (1) (*a*) of the Employment Protection Act 1975 provided for in Schedule 7, shall not extend to Northern Ireland.

SCHEDULES

Sections 1, 4 and 13 SCHEDULE 1

ORDERS RELATING TO WAGES COUNCILS AND STATUTORY JOINT INDUSTRIAL COUNCILS

1. In this Schedule, except in so far as the context otherwise requires, "order"

means an order, whether made in pursuance of the recommendation of the Service or not, under section 1, 4, 10 or 12 of this Act.

2. Before making an order, the Secretary of State shall publish, in the prescribed manner, notice of his intention to make the order, specifying a place where copies of a draft thereof may be obtained and the time (which shall not be less than forty days from the date of the publication) within which any objection made with respect to the draft order must be sent to him.

3. In relation to the making of an order under section 4 of this Act in pursuance of an application made in accordance with section 5 (1) (*c*) of this Act, paragraph 2 above shall have effect as if, before the words "shall publish", there were inserted the words "after consultation with the wages council concerned and with all such organisations of employers as in his opinion represent a substantial proportion of employers with respect to whom the wages council operates".

4. Every objection made with respect to the draft order must be in writing, and must state—

(*a*) the specific grounds of objection, and

(*b*) the omissions, additions or modifications asked for,

and the Secretary of State shall consider any such objection made by or on behalf of any person appearing to him to be affected, being an objection sent to him within the time specified in the notice, but shall not be bound to consider any other objection.

5.—(1) If there is no objection which the Secretary of State is required by paragraph 4 above to consider or if, after considering any such objection, he is of the opinion that it satisfies one of the following conditions, that is to say—

(*a*) in the case of an order to be made in pursuance of a recommendation of the Service, the objection was made to the Service and was expressly dealt with in the report embodying the recommendations; or

(*b*) in the case of such an order as is referred to in paragraph (*a*) above, the objection is one the subject-matter of which was considered by the Service and was expressly dealt with in that report or is such that a further inquiry into that subject-matter would serve no useful purpose; or

(*c*) in any case, the objection will be met by a modification which he proposes to make under this paragraph, or is frivolous,

he may make the order either in the terms of the draft or subject to such modifications, if any, as he thinks fit, being modifications which, in his opinion, do not effect important alterations in the character of the draft order as published.

(2) The Secretary of State shall not form an opinion as to any matter mentioned in paragraph (*b*) of sub-paragraph (1) above without consulting the Service.

6. Where the Secretary of State does not proceed under paragraph 5 above, he may, if he thinks fit, either—

(*a*) amend the draft order, in which case all the provisions of this Schedule shall have effect in relation to the amended draft order as they have effect in relation to an original draft order; or

(*b*) refer the draft order to the Service for inquiry and report, in which case he shall consider the report of the Service and may then, if he thinks fit, make an order either in the terms of the draft or with such modifications as he thinks fit.

7.—(1) Where any objection is made to the Secretary of State and, under sub-paragraph (*b*) of paragraph 6 above, he refers the draft order to the Service, the Secretary of State shall notify to the Service the objections which he wishes the Service to take into account, and the questions which it is the duty of the Service to consider and report on by virtue of the reference shall be all questions affecting the draft order which arise on or in connection with the objections so notified.

(2) The Secretary of State shall include in the objections which he notifies to the Service all the objections which, under paragraph 4 above, he is himself required to consider, other than any objections which he thinks fit to exclude, in the case of an order in pursuance of a recommendation of the Service, on the ground that, in his opinion, they were made to the Service and were expressly dealt with in the report embodying the recommendation or, in any case, on the ground that they are in the Secretary of State's opinion frivolous.

8.—(1) Where any of the councils affected by an order under section 4 or 12 of this Act is one of the councils in relation to which a central co-ordinating committee has been established under section 25 of this Act, the Secretary of State, before making the order, shall consult that committee and take into consideration any observations which it may make to him within fourteen days from the date on which he consults it.

(2) Where an order under section 4 of this Act directs that a wages council shall cease to operate in relation to any workers, and that another existing wages council shall operate in relation to them, but save as aforesaid, does not affect the field of operation of any wages council, paragraphs 2 to 7 above shall not apply but before making the order the Secretary of State shall consult the councils concerned.

(3) On the reference under sub-paragraph (*b*) of paragraph 6 above of a draft order for the abolition, or variation of the field of operation, of a wages council, subsection (2), or, as the case may be, (3) of section 6 of this Act shall apply as it would apply to the like reference under that section; and the power of the Secretary of State under the sub-paragraph (*b*) to modify the draft in making an order shall include power to make any alterations necessary to give effect to a recommendation of the Service, with or without modifications.

9. An order shall come into operation on the date on which it is first issued by Her Majesty's Stationery Office or on such later date as is specified in the order.

DERIVATION

1959 Act, Sched. I, as amended by 1975 Act, Sched. 7, Pt. IV.

Sections 1 and 25

SCHEDULE 2

CONSTITUTION, OFFICERS AND PROCEEDINGS OF WAGES COUNCILS AND CO-ORDINATING COMMITTEES

1.—(1) A wages council or, subject to paragraph 2 below, a central co-ordinating committee shall consist of—

(*a*) not more than three persons appointed by the Secretary of State as being independent persons;

(*b*) such number of persons appointed to represent employers and workers on the council or committee as falls within the limits for the time being specified for the purposes of this paragraph by the Secretary of State.

(2) Subject to sub-paragraphs (4) and (5) below, the persons appointed under sub-paragraph (1) above to represent employers shall be appointed by one or more employers' associations for the time being nominated for that purpose by the Secretary of State and those so appointed to represent workers shall be appointed by one or more trade unions so nominated.

(3) A nominated employers' association or trade union shall on making such an appointment inform the secretary of the wages council or central co-ordinating committee, in writing, of that appointment.

(4) If the nominated employers' association or the nominated trade union are unable to agree on such an appointment, they shall consult the Secretary of State who may make the appointment on their behalf.

(5) If it appears to the Secretary of State that an insufficient number of persons has been appointed to represent either employers or workers on a wages council or central co-ordinating committee he may, after consultation with such persons or organisations as he thinks fit, himself appoint such number of persons for the purpose as will secure a sufficiency of representatives of employers or workers, as the case may be, on the council or committee.

(6) Of the independent persons appointed under sub-paragraph (1) (*a*) above, one shall be appointed by the Secretary of State to act as chairman, and another may be appointed by the Secretary of State to act as chairman in the absence of the chairman.

2.—(1) A central co-ordinating committee operating in relation only to two or more statutory joint industrial councils shall consist of equal numbers of persons appointed by one or more employers' associations to represent employers on the committee and of persons appointed by one or more trade unions to represent workers on the committee.

(2) Any such committee shall elect a chairman and deputy chairman from among its members.

3. The Secretary of State may on the application of a wages council or central co-ordinating committee make such changes in the number of members or the machinery for appointing them as is necessary or expedient in the circumstances.

4. The Secretary of State may appoint a secretary and such other officers as he thinks fit of a wages council or central co-ordinating committee.

5. The proceedings of a wages council or central co-ordinating committee shall not be invalidated by reason of any vacancy therein or by any defect in the appointment of a member.

6.—(1) A wages council or central co-ordinating committee may delegate any of its functions, other than the power to make orders under section 14 of this Act, to a committee or sub-committee consisting of such number of members of the council as the council or committee thinks fit.

(2) The number of members representing employers and the number of members representing workers on a committee of a council or any such sub-committee shall be equal.

7. The Secretary of State may make regulations as to the meetings and procedure of a wages council or central co-ordinating committee and of any committee or, as the case may be, sub-committee thereof, including regulations as to the quorum and the method of voting, but, subject to the provisions of this Act and to any regulations so made, a wages council or central co-ordinating committee and any committee or, as the case may be, sub-committee thereof may regulate its procedure in such manner as it thinks fit.

8.—(1) A member of a wages council or central co-ordinating committee shall hold and vacate office in accordance with the terms of his appointment, but the period for which he is to hold office, shall, without prejudice to his re-appointment, not exceed five years.

(2) Where the term for which the members of a wages council or central co-ordinating committee were appointed comes to an end before their successors are appointed, those members shall, except so far as the Secretary of State or, as the case may be, the appointing body otherwise directs, continue in office until the new appointments take effect.

9. There may be paid to the members of a wages council or central co-ordinating committee appointed under paragraph 1 (*a*) above such remuneration, and to any member of any such council or committee such travelling and other allowances, as the Secretary of State may, with the consent of the Minister for the Civil Service, determine, and all such remuneration and allowances shall be defrayed as part of the expenses of the Secretary of State in carrying this Act into effect.

DERIVATION
1975 Act, Sched. 7, Pt. III.

Section 8

SCHEDULE 3

PROVISIONS AS TO ADVISORY COMMITTEES

1.—(1) Any committee appointed by the Secretary of State at the request of a wages council shall consist of—

(*a*) a chairman chosen as being an independent person;

(*b*) persons who appear to the Secretary of State to represent the employers in relation to whom the committee will operate; and

(*c*) persons who appear to the Secretary of State to represent the workers in relation to whom the committee will operate.

(2) On any such committee the persons appointed under head (*b*), and the persons appointed under head (*c*), of sub-paragraph (1) above shall be equal in number.

2.—(1) The appointment of a member of any such committee as aforesaid shall be for such term as may be determined by the Secretary of State before his appointment and shall be subject to such conditions as may be so determined.

(2) Where the term for which the members of an advisory committee were appointed comes to an end before the Secretary of State has appointed the persons who are to serve as members of the committee after the expiration of that term, they shall, except so far as the Secretary of State otherwise directs, continue in office until the new appointments take effect.

3. There may be paid to the chairman of any such committee as aforesaid such fees, and to any member of any such committee such travelling and other allowances, as the Secretary of State may, with the consent of the Minister for the Civil Service, determine, and all such fees and allowances shall be defrayed out of moneys provided by Parliament.

DERIVATION
1959 Act, Sched. 3.

Section 10

SCHEDULE 4

STATUTORY JOINT INDUSTRIAL COUNCILS

PART I

CONSTITUTION, ETC.

1.—(1) A statutory joint industrial council (hereafter in this Part of this Schedule referred to as a council) shall consist of equal numbers (being numbers within the limits specified by the Secretary of State) of persons appointed by a nominated employers' association to represent employers on the council and of persons appointed by a nominated trade union to represent workers on the council.

(2) A nominated employers' association or trade union shall on making such an appointment inform the secretary of the council, in writing, of that appointment.

2.—(1) On the conversion of a wages council to a statutory joint industrial council—

(*a*) the limits as to the number of persons to be appointed to represent employers and workers on that wages council which are immediately before the date on which that council becomes a statutory joint industrial council for the time being specified by the Secretary of State, shall continue, subject to sub-paragraph (2) below, to be the limits in relation to that statutory joint industrial council; and

(*b*) an employers' association or trade union which immediately before the date on which that wages council becomes a statutory joint industrial council is for the time being nominated by the Secretary of State for the purpose of appointing persons to represent employers or workers on that wages council, shall continue, subject to sub-paragraph (2) below, to be so nominated in relation to that statutory joint industrial council.

(2) The Secretary of State may, on the application of a statutory joint industrial council, make such changes in the number of members of the council or in the machinery for appointing them as are necessary or expedient in the circumstances.

3. A council shall elect a chairman and deputy chairman from among its members.

4. The proceedings of a council shall not be invalidated by reason of any vacancy among its members or by any defect in the appointment of a member.

5.—(1) A council may delegate any of its functions, other than the power to make orders under section 14 of this Act, to a committee consisting of such number of members of the council as the council thinks fit.

(2) The number of members representing employers and the number of members representing workers on a committee of a council shall be equal.

6. A council may regulate its own procedure.

7.—(1) A member of a council shall hold and vacate office in accordance with the terms of his appointment, but the period for which he is to hold office shall, without prejudice to his re-appointment, not exceed five years.

(2) Where the term for which the members of a council were appointed comes

to an end before their successors are appointed, those members shall, except so far as the appointing body otherwise directs, continue in office until the new appointments take effect.

8. The Secretary of State may pay to the members of a council such travelling and other allowances, including allowances for loss of remunerative time, as the Secretary of State may, with the consent of the Minister for the Civil Service, determine.

9. The expenses of a statutory joint industrial council, to such an extent as may be approved by the Secretary of State with the consent of the Treasury, shall be paid by the Secretary of State.

10. The Secretary of State may appoint a secretary and such other officers of a council as he thinks fit.

Part II

Transitional Provisions

11. Any of the following things done by, to or in relation to a wages council, that is to say—

any order made under section 14 of this Act;

any proposals published in relation to making of such an order, any notice published and representations made with respect thereto;

any permit issued under section 16 of this Act;

any approval given under the proviso to section 19 (1) of this Act;

shall as from the date when that council becomes a statutory joint industrial council be treated as having been done by, to or in relation to the latter council.

12. The persons who immediately before the date on which a wages council becomes a statutory joint industrial council are the members of the wages council appointed by an employers' association or trade union shall, subject to paragraph 2 (2) above, become and continue to be members of the statutory joint industrial council as if they had been appointed under paragraph 1 above.

13. The persons who immediately before the date on which a wages council becomes a statutory joint industrial council are the secretary and officers of the wages council shall on that date become the secretary and officers of the statutory joint industrial council.

Derivation

1975 Act, Sched. 8.

Section 31

SCHEDULE 5

Transitional Provisions

1. The repeals effected by this Act shall not affect any right of a worker to recover sums from his employer on account of the payment to the worker of remuneration less than the statutory minimum remuneration, or the power of an officer of the Secretary of State to institute on behalf of and in the name of the worker civil procedings for the enforcement of that right or the power of the court in such proceedings to make an order for the payment of costs by the officer.

2. A member of a wages council or central co-ordinating committee who, immediately before the commencement of this Act, is by virtue of paragraph 11 (3) of Schedule 17 to the Employment Protection Act 1975 treated as having been appointed by a nominated employers' association or trade union shall continue to be so treated.

3. Any reference in any enactment or document made before the passing of the Wages Councils Act 1945 (28th March 1945), other than an enactment repealed by that Act, to a trade board shall be construed as including a reference to a wages council.

Section 31

SCHEDULE 6

CONSEQUENTIAL AMENDMENTS

Post Office Act 1969 (c. 48)

1. In section 81 (1) of the Post Office Act 1969, for the words "the Wages Councils Act 1959" there are substituted the words "Wages Councils Act 1979".

Equal Pay Act 1970 (c. 41)

2. In section 4 of the Equal Pay Act 1970—

(*a*) in subsections (1), (1A), and (2), for the words "section 11 of the Wages Councils Act 1959", in each place where they occur, there are substituted the words "section 14 of the Wages Councils Act 1979"; and

(*b*) in subsection (1A), for the words "subsections (3) and (3A) of the said section 11" there are substituted the words "subsections (4) and (5) of the said section 14"; and

(*c*) in subsection (3), for the words "section 12 (1) or (1A) of the Wages Councils Act 1959", "in section 12 (1) or (1A)" and "section 11 (8)" there are substituted the words "section 15 (1) or (2) of the Wages Councils Act 1979", "in section 15 (1) or (2)" and "section 14 (12)" respectively.

Attachment of Earnings Act 1971 (c. 32)

3. In Schedule 3 to the Attachment of Earnings Act 1971, in paragraph 3 (*c*), for the words "Wages Councils Act 1959" there are substituted the words "Wages Councils Act 1979".

House of Commons Disqualification Act 1975 (c. 24)

4. In Part III of Schedule 1 to the House of Commons Disqualification Act 1975, in the first entry relating to wages councils, for the words "paragraph 1 (*a*) of Schedule 2 to the Wages Councils Act 1959 or Chairman of a Committee appointed under paragraph 1 (1) (*a*) of Schedule 3 to that Act" there are substituted the words "paragraph 1 (1) (*a*) of Schedule 2 to the Wages Councils Act 1979 or chairman of a committee appointed under paragraph 1 (1) (*a*) of Schedule 3 to that Act".

Northern Ireland Assembly Disqualification Act 1975 (c. 25)

5. In Part III of Schedule 1 to the Northern Ireland Assembly Disqualification Act 1975, in the first entry relating to wages councils, for the words "paragraph 1 (*a*) of Schedule 2 to the Wages Councils Act 1959 or Chairman of a Committee appointed under paragraph 1 (1) (*a*) of Schedule 3 to that Act" there are substituted the words "paragraph 1 (1) (*a*) of Schedule 2 to the Wages Councils Act 1979 or chairman of a committee appointed under paragraph 1 (1) (*a*) of Schedule 3 to that Act".

Employment Protection (Consolidation) Act 1978 (c. 44)

6. In section 18 (2) of the Employment Protection (Consolidation) Act 1978 for paragraph (*a*) there is substituted the following paragraph—

"(*a*) section 14 of the Wages Councils Act 1979;".

Section 31

SCHEDULE 7

Repeals

Chapter	Short title	Extent of repeal
7 & 8 Eliz. 2 c. 69.	Wages Councils Act 1959.	The whole Act.
1968 c. 64.	Civil Evidence Act 1968.	In the Schedule, the paragraph relating to the Wages Councils Act 1959.
1968 c. 73.	Transport Act 1968.	In Schedule 11, the paragraph relating to the Wages Councils Act 1959.
1972 c. 68.	European Communities Act 1972.	In Schedule 4, in paragraph 9 (4), the words " and in section 19 (3) (*b*) of the Wages Councils Act 1959 ".
1973 c. 38.	Social Security Act 1973.	In Schedule 27, paragraph 21.
1974 c. 52.	Trade Union and Labour Relations Act 1974.	In Schedule 3, paragraph 9.
1975 c. 71.	Employment Protection Act 1975.	Sections 89 to 96. In section 127 (1), paragraph (*a*). Schedules 7 and 8. In Schedule 17, paragraph 11 and, in paragraph 12, the words " section 11 of the Wages Councils Act 1959 ".
1976 c. 3.	Road Traffic (Drivers' Ages and Hours of Work) Act 1976.	In section 2 (3), the words " section 19 (3) (*b*) of the Wages Councils Act 1959 ".

Agricultural Statistics Act 1979

(1979 c. 13)

Arrangement of Sections

An Act to consolidate certain enactments relating to agricultural statistics. [22nd March 1979]

General Note

This Act consolidates certain enactments relating to agricultural statistics.

S. 1 gives power to obtain agricultural statistics; s. 2 provides for the furnishing of information as to dealings in land used for agriculture; s. 3 restricts the disclosure of information; s. 4 gives penalties for failing to furnish information; s. 5 deals with service of notices; s. 6 is the interpretation section; s. 7 contains amendments and repeals; s. 8 deals with citation, commencement and extent. This Act does not extend to Scotland or Northern Ireland.

The Act received the Royal Assent on March 22, 1979, and came into force on April 22, 1979.

Parliamentary debates

Hansard, H.L. Vol. 396, col. 1410; Vol. 397, col. 418; Vol. 398, col. 1106; H.C. Vol. 964, col. 410.

Table of Derivations

Agriculture Act 1947

1947	1979	1947	1979	1947	1979
s. 78 (1) ...	s. 1 (1)	s. 78 (6) ...	s. 6 (1)	s. 106	s. 1 (5)
(1A) ..	6 (1) (2)	79	2 (1)	107	5 (1)–(5)
(2)–(4)	1 (2)–(4)	80	3	108 (1) ..	2 (2)
(5) ...	5 (6)	81 (2) ...	6 (1)	109	6 (2)
		(1) (2) .	4 (1) (2)		

Industrial Training Act 1964

1964	1979
s. 2B	s. 3

Agriculture (Miscellaneous Provisions) Act 1972

1972	1979
s. 18	s. 1 (1)

European Communities Act 1972

1972	1979
s. 12	s. 3

Criminal Law Act 1977

1977	1979
s. 28 (2) ...	s. 4 (2)
(7) ...	6 (1)
32 (1) ...	4 (2)

Agriculture (Miscellaneous Provisions) Act 1976

1976	1979
s. 6 (1) (*a*) ...	s. 1 (1)
(*b*) ...	6 (1) (2)

Interpretation Act 1978

1978	1979
s. 22 (1) ...	s. 6 (1)
Sch. 2, para. 5 (6) .	6 (1)

Transfer of Functions (Wales) (No. 1) Order 1978

1978	1979
Art. 2 (1)	ss. 1 (1) (2), 2 (1), 3, 6 (1)
Sch. 1	1 (1), 2 (1), 3, 6 (1)

Power to obtain agricultural statistics

1.—(1) Where it appears to the appropriate Minister expedient so to do for the purpose of obtaining statistical information relating to agriculture, he may serve on any owners or occupiers of land used for agriculture, or of land which he has reason to believe may be so used, notices requiring them to furnish in writing, in such form and manner and to such person as may be specified in the notice, and within such time and with respect to such date or dates or such period or periods as may be so specified, the information referred to in the notice (including, as respects paragraphs (*d*) to (*f*) of this subsection, the information referred to in the notice as to quantities, values, expenditure and receipts) relating to—

(*a*) the situation, area and description of relevant land owned or occupied by them, the date of acquisition of the land, and the date at which so much of it as is comprised in any agricultural unit became comprised in that unit, and the rates payable in respect of the land,

(*b*) the names and addresses of the owners and occupiers of the land,

(*c*) whether the land or any, and if so what, part of it is let and at what rent,

(*d*) the character and use of different parts of the land, the time at which any use of such parts was begun or will become fully effective, and their produce at any time during the period beginning one year before, and ending one year after, the time at which the information is required to be furnished,

(*e*) fixed and other equipment, livestock, and the stocks of agricultural produce and requisites held in respect of the land, and the provision and maintenance of such equipment, livestock and requisites and the provision of agricultural services for the benefit of the land,

(*f*) the methods and operations used on the land, the marketing or other disposal of its produce, any payments received under any enactment in respect of such produce, and the provision of agricultural services otherwise than for the benefit of the land,

(*g*) the number and description of persons employed on the land, or employed by the occupier in disposing of its produce, and the remuneration paid to, and hours worked by, persons so employed or such persons of different descriptions.

(2) For the purpose of obtaining statistical information relating to agriculture, any person authorised by the appropriate Minister in that behalf may, after giving not less than 24 hours notice and on producing if so required evidence of his authority to act for the purposes of this

subsection, orally require the owner or occupier of land to furnish to him within a reasonable time, and either orally or in writing as the said owner or occupier may elect, such information, whether or not specified in the notice, as the said person authorised by the appropriate Minister may require, being information which the owner or occupier, as the case may be, could have been required to furnish under subsection (1) above.

(3) References in subsections (1) and (2) above to the owner of land include references to a person exercising, as servant or agent of the owner, functions of estate management in relation to the land, and references in those subsections to the occupier of land include references to a person responsible for the control of the farming of the land as servant or agent of the occupier of the land.

(4) No person shall be required under this section to furnish any balance sheet or profit and loss account, but this subsection shall not prevent the requiring of information by reason only that it is or might be contained as an item in such a balance sheet or account.

(5) Section 106 of the Agriculture Act 1947 (provisions as to entry and inspection) shall have effect for the purposes of this section as it has effect for the purposes of that Act.

Information as to dealings in land used for agriculture

2.—(1) The appropriate Minister may by regulation require that parties to any sale of land which immediately before the completion of the transaction was being used for agriculture, or to any grant, assignment or surrender of a tenancy of such land for an interest not less than that of a tenant for a year, shall within the period from the completion of the transaction prescribed by the regulations furnish to him, in such manner as may be so prescribed, information as to the names and addresses of the parties to the transaction and the situation and extent of the land affected by it.

(2) Regulations under subsection (1) above shall be made by statutory instrument and shall be laid before Parliament forthwith after being made, and if either House of Parliament, within the period of 40 days beginning with the day on which the regulations are laid before it, resolves that an Address be presented to Her Majesty praying that the regulations be annulled, no further proceedings shall be taken under the regulations after the date of the resolution, and Her Majesty may by Order in Council revoke the regulations, so, however, that any such resolution and revocation shall be without prejudice to the validity of anything previously done under the regulations or to the making of new regulations.

Restriction on disclosure of information

3.—(1) Subject to subsection (2) below, no information relating to any particular land or business which has been obtained under section 1 or 2 above shall be published or otherwise disclosed without the previous consent in writing of the person by whom the information was furnished and every other person who is an owner or the occupier of the land and whose interests may in the opinion of the appropriate Minister be affected by the disclosure.

(2) Nothing in subsection (1) above shall restrict the disclosure of information—

(*a*) to the Minister in charge of any Government department, to any authority acting under an enactment for regulating the marketing of any agriculture produce, or to any person exercising functions on behalf of any such Minister or authority for the purpose of the exercise of those functions;

(*b*) to an authority having power under any enactment to give permission for the development of land, for the purpose of assisting that authority in the preparation of proposals relating to such development or in considering whether or not to give such permission;

(*c*) if the disclosure is confined to situation, extent, number and kind of livestock, character of land, and name and address of owner and occupier, to any person to whom the appropriate Minister considers that the disclosure is required in the public interest;

(*d*) to any person for the purposes of any criminal proceedings under section 4 below or for the purposes of any report of such proceedings;

(*e*) to the Agricultural Training Board under section 2B of the Industrial Training Act 1964; or

(*f*) to an institution of the European Communities under section 12 of the European Communities Act 1972,

or the use of information in any manner which the appropriate Minister thinks necessary or expedient in connection with the maintenance of the supply of food in the United Kingdom.

Penalties

4.—(1) Any person who without reasonable excuse fails to furnish information in compliance with a requirement under section 1 or 2 above shall be liable on summary conviction to a fine not exceeding £50.

(2) If any person—

(*a*) in purported compliance with a requirement imposed under section 1 or 2 above knowingly or recklessly furnishes any information which is false in any material particular, or

(*b*) publishes or otherwise discloses any information in contravention of section 3 above,

he shall be liable on summary conviction to imprisonment for a term not exceeding 3 months or to a fine not exceeding the prescribed sum or to both, or on conviction on indictment to imprisonment for a term not exceeding 2 years or to a fine or to both.

Service of notices

5.—(1) Any notice authorised by this Act to be served on any person shall be duly served if it is delivered to him, or left at his proper address or sent to him by post in a registered letter.

(2) Any such notice authorised to be served on an incorporated company or body shall be duly served if served on the secretary or clerk of the company or body.

(3) For the purposes of this section and of section 7 of the Interpretation Act 1978, the proper address of any person on whom any such notice is to be served shall, in the case of the secretary or clerk of any incorporated company or body be that of the registered or principal office of the company or body, and in any other case be the last known address of the person in question.

(4) Where any such notice is to be served on a person as being the

person having any interest in land, and it is not practicable after reasonable inquiry to ascertain his name or address, the notice may be served by addressing it to him by the description of the person having that interest in the land (naming it), and delivering the notice to some responsible person on the land or by affixing it, or a copy of it, to some conspicuous object on the land.

(5) Where any such notice is to be served on any person as being the owner of the land and the land belongs to an ecclesiastical benefice a copy shall be served on the Church Commissioners.

(6) Without prejudice to subsections (1) to (5) above, any notice under this Act to be served on an occupier shall be deemed to be duly served if it is addressed to him by the description of " the occupier " of the land in question and sent by post to, or delivered to some person on, the land.

Interpretation

6.—(1) In this Act—

" the appropriate Minister " means, in relation to England, the Minister of Agriculture, Fisheries and Food and, in relation to Wales, the Secretary of State;

" land " includes messuages, tenements and hereditaments, houses and buildings of any tenure;

" livestock " includes creatures kept for any purpose;

" owner " means, in relation to land, a person, other than a mortgagee not in possession, who is for the time being entitled to dispose of the fee simple of the land, and includes also a person holding, or entitled to the rents and profits of, the land under a lease or agreement;

" the prescribed sum " means the prescribed sum within the meaning of section 28 of the Criminal Law Act (£1,000 or other sum substituted by order under section 61 (1) of that Act); and

" relevant land " in the case of any owner or occupier of land used for agriculture, means the aggregate of—

(*a*) the land owned or occupied by him which is comprised in any agricultural unit; and

(*b*) any other land owned or occupied by him which is either—

(i) used for forestry; or

(ii) not used for any purpose, but capable of use for agriculture or forestry,

but which, if used as agricultural land by the occupier of that agricultural unit, would be comprised in that unit.

(2) Section 109 of the Agriculture Act 1947 (interpretation) shall have effect for the purposes of this Act as it has effect for the purposes of that Act except that the definition of " livestock " shall be omitted from subsection (3).

Amendments and repeals

7.—(1) The enactments specified in Schedule 1 to this Act shall have effect subject to the amendments set out in that Schedule, being amendments consequential on the foregoing provisions of this Act.

(2) The enactments specified in Schedule 2 to this Act are hereby repealed to the extent specified in column 3 of that Schedule.

Citation, etc.

8.—(1) This Act may be cited as the Agricultural Statistics Act 1979.

(2) This Act shall come into force at the expiry of the period of one month beginning on the date on which it is passed.

(3) This Act does not extend to Scotland or Northern Ireland.

SCHEDULES

SCHEDULE 1

CONSEQUENTIAL AMENDMENTS

Agricultural Marketing Act 1958

1. In section 5 (4) of the Agricultural Marketing Act 1958 (list of producers) for the words "eighty of the Agriculture Act 1947" there shall be substituted the words "three of the Agricultural Statistics Act 1979".

Public Records Act 1958

2. At the end of Schedule 2 to the Public Records Act 1958 (enactments prohibiting disclosure of information obtained from the public) there shall be added—

"The Agricultural Statistics Act 1979 Section 3."

Industrial Training Act 1964

3. At the end of section 2B of the Industrial Training Act 1964 (disclosure of information to Agricultural Training Board) there shall be added the words "or section 1 of the Agricultural Statistics Act 1979".

European Communities Act 1972

4. In section 12 of the European Communities Act 1972 (furnishing of information to Communities) for the words "80 of the Agriculture Act 1947" there shall be substituted the words "3 of the Agricultural Statistics Act 1979".

Section 7

SCHEDULE 2

ENACTMENTS REPEALED

Chapter	Short Title	Extent of Repeals
10 & 11 Geo. 6. c. 48.	Agriculture Act 1947.	Sections 78 to 81.
6 & 7 Eliz. 2. c. 51.	Public Records Act 1958.	In Schedule 2, the entry relating to section 80 of the Agriculture Act 1947.
1972 c. 62.	Agriculture (Miscellaneous Provisions) Act 1972.	Section 18.
1976 c. 55.	Agriculture (Miscellaneous Provisions) Act 1976.	Section 6. Schedule 2.

Capital Gains Tax Act 1979 *

(1979 c. 14)

Arrangement of Sections

Part I

General

Capital gains tax and corporation tax

* Annotations by John Walters, M.A., Barrister.

An Act to consolidate Part III of the Finance Act 1965 with related provisions in that Act and subsequent Acts.

[22nd March 1979]

General Note

This Act consolidates the enactments relating to capital gains tax which were originally contained in the Finance Act 1965 and succeeding Finance Acts. Capital gains tax applies to individuals, including partnerships and trustees. Chargeable gains accruing to companies are chargeable to corporation tax and the principal provisions enacting that charge are contained in I.C.T.A. 1970, ss. 265 to 281 and are not printed here. However, the provisions of this Act, except where otherwise stated, are relevant in ascertaining and computing the chargeable gains of companies which are charged to corporation tax.

Commencement

The Act came into force on April 6, 1979 (see s. 156).

Parliamentary debates

Hansard, H.L. Vol. 397, col. 1554; Vol. 398, col. 694; Vol. 399, col. 8, H.C. Vol. 964, col. 410.

Abbreviations

I.C.T.A.	=	Income and Corporations Taxes Act 1970.
F.A.	=	Finance Act (followed by relevant date).
F. (No. 2) A. 1975	=	Finance (No. 2) Act 1975.

Table of Derivations

FINANCE ACT 1965

1965	1979
s. 19	s. 1
20 (1)	2 (1)
(2)	12 (1) (2)
(3)	3
(4) (5)	4 (1) (2)
(6)	7
(7)	ss. 14 (1), 29 (4)
22 (1) (2)	s. 19 (1) (2)
(3)	20 (1)
(4)	19 (3)
(5)	46 (1)
(6)–(8)	23 (1)–(3)
(9)	ss. 20 (3), 28 (1), 106
(10)	s. 28 (2) (3)
23 (1) (2)	29 (1) (2)
(3)–(5)	22 (1)–(3)
(6)	29 (3)
(7)	29 (5)
24 (1)	49 (1)
(5)–(7)	49 (2)–(4)
(9)	49 (10)
(11)	49 (6)
25 (1)	52 (1) (2)
(2)	53
(3)	54 (1)
(4)	55 (1)
(8)	54 (2)
(9)	52 (4)
(10)	55 (4)
(11)	52 (3)
(12)	55 (6)
25A	Sch. 6, para. 15
26	s. 153
27 (1)	130
(2)	6
(4)	71
(5)	133
(6)	131
(7)	19 (4)
(8)	19 (5)
(9)	71
(10)	ss. 19 (4), 71, 130
28 (1) (2)	s. 143 (1) (2)
(3)	143 (3) (4)
29 (1)	101 (1)–(4)
(2)–(4)	102 (1)–(3)
(5)–(6)	103 (1) (2)
(7)	101 (5)

1965	1979
s. 29 (8) (a)	s. 101 (6)
(b)	
(bb)	101 (7)
(c)	101 (6)
(9)	104
(10)	105
(12)	101 (9)
(13) (a)	101 (7)
(b)	102 (4)
30 (1)–(6)	128 (1)–(6)
31 (1)–(9)	147 (1)–(9)
33 (1)	115 (1)
(2)	116 (1)
(3)	115 (3)
(5)	115 (4)
(6)	ss. 118, 119 (1) (2)
(7)–(9)	s. 115 (5)–(7)
(10)	121 (1) (2)
(11) (12)	115 (8) (9)
34 (1)	124 (1)
(2)–(6)	124 (4)–(8)
35	145
38 (1)	ss. 92 (a), 96
(2)	92 (a), 97 (1) (2)
39	s. 10
40 (1)	13 (1) (3)
(2)	13 (2)
(a)	13 (1)
(3) (4)	13 (5) (6)
41 (1)–(9)	15 (1)–(9)
42	17
43 (1)	18 (1)
(2) (3)	18 (3) (4)
44 (1)–(5)	s. 150 (1)–(5), Sch. 6, para. 2 (1)–(5)
45 (1)	ss. 12 (3), 47 (2) (3), 51, 64, 155 (1), Sch. 3, para. 10 (1)
(3)	s. 155 (2)
(4)	24
(5)	20 (2)
(6)	14 (2)
(7)	60

1965	1979
s. 45 (8)	ss. 92 (a) (b), 93
(9)	s. 32 (4)
(10)	155 (5)
94 (1)	99 (1)
(3)	ss. 92 (d), 99 (2)
(9)	s. 99 (3)
Sch. 6,	
para. 1	30
para. 2 (1)–(3)	31 (1)–(3)
para. 3 (5)	Sch. 6, para. 12 (2)
para. 3 (7)	Sch. 6, para. 12 (4)
para. 3 (8)	Sch. 6, para. 12 (1)
para. 4 (1) (2)	32 (1) (2)
para. 5	33
para. 6 (1)–(6)	34 (1)–(6)
para. 7 (1)–(4)	35 (1)–(4)
para. 8	36
para. 9	37
para. 10	38
para. 11	39
para. 12	141
para. 13 (1)	21 (1)
para. (13) (2)–(4)	21 (3)–(5)
para. 13 (5)	21 (7)
para. 14 (1)	40 (1)
para. 14 (5)	40 (2)
para. 15	41
para. 16 (2)	47 (1)
para. 17	42
para. 18	74
para. 19 (1)	113 (1)
para. 19 (1) (b)	113 (2)
(2)–(4)	113 (3)–(4)
para. 20	11
para. 21	43
para. 21 (4)	Sch. 6, para. 12 (4)
para. 22 (1) (2)	Sch. 5, para. 1 (1) (2)

Finance Act 1965—*cont.*

1965	1979
Sch. 6,	
para. 22 (3)	Sch. 6, para. 3
para. 22 (4)	Sch. 5, para. 2 (1)
para. 22 (5)	Sch. 5, para. 1 (3)
para. 22 (6)	Sch. 5, para. 2 (2)
para. 23	Sch. 5, para. 9
para. 24	para. 11
para. 25	
(1) (2)	para. 12 (1) (2)
(3) (4)	para. 12 (4) (5)
para. 26	
(1)–(3)	para. 13 (1)–(3)
(4)	para. 13 (5)
(6)	para. 13 (6)
para. 27	para. 14
para. 28	para. 15
para. 29	para. 16
para. 30	para. 17
Sch. 7,	
para. 1	
(1)–(3)	s. 122 (1)–(3)
para. 2 (1)	65 (2) (7)
(2)–(3)	65 (3)–(4)
(5)–(7)	65 (5)–(7)
(8)	65 (4) (7)
para. 3 (1)	72 (1)
(2)	72 (2) (5)
(3)	72 (3)
Sch. 7,	
para. 3 (4)	s. 72 (5)
para. 4 (1)	77 (1)
(*a*)	77 (2)
(2)	78
(3)–(4)	79 (1)–(2)
(5)	79 (3), 80 (1)
(7)	77 (3)
para. 5 (1)	82 (1)
(3)	82 (3)
para. 6	85 (1)
para. 7 (1)	ss. 85 (2) (3), 86 (1)
(2)	s. 85 (2)
(3)	ss. 85 (2), 86 (2)
para. 9	
(1)–(3)	s. 142 (1)–(3)
para. 10	
(1)–(3)	140 (1)–(3)
para. 11	
(1)–(4)	13 (1)–(4)
para. 12	144
para. 13	58
para. 14	
(1)–(3)	137 (1)–(3)
(4)	ss. 13 (2)–(4), 137 (4)
(5)	s. 137 (5)
(6)	ss. 137 (6), 138 (2)
(7) (8)	s. 137 (7) (8)
para. 15	
(1) (2)	25 (1) (2)
Sch. 7,	
para. 15	
(3) (4)	s. 25 (4) (5)
para. 16	151
para. 17	
(1)–(4)	62 (1)–(4)
(5)	62 (5) (6)
para. 18	
(1)–(2)	75 (1)–(3)
para. 19	59
para. 20	
(1) (2)	44 (1) (2)
para. 21	
(1)–(8)	63 (1)–(8)
Sch. 8,	
paras. 1–4	Sch. 3, paras. 1–4
para. 5	
(1) (2)	Sch. 3, para. 5 (1) (2)
(4)–(6)	Sch. 3, para. 5 (3)–(5)
paras. 6, 7	Sch. 3, paras. 6, 7
para. 9	Sch. 3, para. 9
para. 10	
(1) (2)	Sch. 3, para. 10 (2) (3)
Sch. 10,	
para. 3	
(1)–(5)	s. 45 (1)–(5)
para. 4 (1)	8 (1) (2)
(2)	8 (3)
(3)	8 (4)
para. 12	48
para. 13	154

Finance Act 1966

1966	1979
Sch. 10,	
para. 1	
(1)–(4)	s. 55 (2)–(5)
para. 2	
(1) (2)	125 (1) (2)
para. 4	108
para. 6 (1)	Sch. 5, para. 14 (1)
Sch. 10,	
para. 7 (1)	s. 81 (1)
(2)	ss. 80 (2), 81 (2)
(3)	77 (1), 82 (1), 85 (2)
(4)	s. 81 (3)
Sch. 10,	
para. 8	s. 73
para. 9	ss. 21 (2), 73, 83 (4), 109 (1)
para. 10	
(1)–(3)	s. 61 (1)–(3)
(5) (6)	61 (4) (5)

Finance Act 1967

1967	1979
s. 35 (2)	s. 143 (3)
37	112
Sch. 13,	
para. 2 (1)	ss. 115 (2), 116 (1)
para. 2 (2)	s. 121 (3)
para. 3	21 (6) Sch. 5, para. 18
Sch. 13,	
para. 4 (1)	s. 83 (1)
para. 4 (2)	ss. 82 (2), 83 (2)
para. 4 (3) (4)	s. 83 (3) (4)
para. 4 (5)	82 (3)
para. 5	75 (4)
Sch. 13,	
para. 6	s. 35 (5)
para. 8	Sch. 3, para. 5 (1)
para. 10 (1)	s. 15 (10)

Finance Act 1968

1968	1979
s. 32 (1) (2)	Sch. 5, para. 3 (1)
(4)	Sch. 5, para. 3 (2)
(5)	Sch. 5. para. 3 (3)
s. 32 (6)	Sch. 5, paras. 3 (1) (2), 8 (1)
(7)	Sch.5, para. 3 (3)
Sch. 11,	
para. 1 (1)	Sch. 5, para. 3 (3)
para. 1	
(3)–(7)	Sch. 5, para. 4 (2)–(6)

Finance Act 1968—*cont.*

1968	1979
Sch. 11,	
para. 1 (9)	Sch. 5, para. 4 (7)
para. 2	Sch. 5, para. 5
para. 3	Sch. 5, para. 6
para. 4	Sch. 5, para. 7
Sch. 12,	
para. 1 (1)–(4)	s. 127 (1)–(4)
para. 1 (5)	Sch. 5, para. 15
Sch. 12,	
para. 1 (6)	s. 127 (5)
para. 2 (1)	103 (3)
para. 3 (1)	119 (1)
para. 3 (2) (3)	119 (3) (4)
para. 4 (1) (2)	s. 50 (1) (2)
para. 5 (1)	Sch. 5, para. 12 (3)
para. 7 (1)–(6)	Sch. 3, para. 8
Sch. 12,	
para. 7 (7)	Sch. 3, para. 9
para. 8 (1)	s. 134 (1) (4)
para. 8 (2)	134 (5)
para. 15 (1) (2)	86 (3)
para. 22 (1)–(3)	16 (1)–(3)
para. 23 (1)	16 (4)

Finance Act 1969

1969	1979
s. 41 (1)	ss. 64, 67 (1)
41 (2)	s. 64, Sch. 2
Sch. 8, Pt. 1	Sch. 2
Sch. 14,	
para. 1 (1)–(4)	Sch. 6, para. 17
para. 2 (1) (2)	Sch. 6, para. 18
para. 3 (1)	s. 135
para. 4	15 (5)
para. 6	47 (3)
Sch. 14,	
para. 7	s. 101 (7)
para. 8 (3)	52 (2)
para. 9	46 (2)
para. 10 (1)–(4)	107 (1)–(4)
para. 10 (5)	109 (1)
para. 10 (6)	107 (5)
para. 10 (8) (9)	107 (6) (7)
para. 11	110
para. 12	62 (3)
para. 14 (1)	122 (1) (3)
Sch. 14,	
para. 14 (2)	s. 122 (2)
para. 15 (1)–(4)	123 (1)–(4)
para. 15 (7)	123 (2)
para. 15 (8)	123 (5)
para. 16 (1)–(5), (7)	117
para. 16 (9)	121 (3)
para. 17	118
para. 22 (3) (4)	98 (1) (2)
para. 22 (5)	86 (3)

Income and Corporation Taxes Act 1970

1970	1979
Sch. 15,	
para. 6 (1)	s. 10
(2)	155 (1)
(3)	32 (3)
(4)	35 (5)
(5)	16 (4)
(6)	98 (1)
para. 7	18 (2)
Sch. 15,	
para. 11	ss. 12 (2) (3), 14 (2), 15 (5), 16 (2), (3), 17, 34 (4), 45 (3) (4), 60, 63 (3), 93, 97 (1), 107 (1), 119 (4), 155 (2), Sch. 3,
Sch. 15, para. 11—*cont.*	paras. 5–7, 9, Sch. 5, paras. 4 (3), 5, Sch. 6, para. 12 (3)
para. 12 (1) (*a*)	s. 31 (2)
(*b*)	34 (3)
(*c*)	34 (4)
(*d*)	34 (6)

Finance Act 1971

1971	1979
s. 58 (1)	ss. 137 (4) (9), 139
(2)	s. 137 (4)
(3)	138 (1) (2)
(4)	ss. 137 (9), 138 (4), 139
59 (1)	Sch. 6, para. 9
Sch. 3,	
para. 10	s. 97 (1)
Sch. 6,	
para. 91	74
Sch. 8,	
para. 16 (1)	34 (4) (7)
Sch. 9,	
para. 3	Sch. 6, para. 22 (3)
para. 5	Sch. 6, para. 21
Sch. 10,	
para. 1 (1)	s. 66 (4), Sch. 6, para. 13
Sch. 10,	
para. 1 (2)	s. 66 (3)
para. 2	Sch. 6, para. 13
para. 4 (1)–(3)	s. 67 (1)–(3)
para. 5	65 (1), Sch. 5, paras. 2 (3), 13 (4)
para. 6 (1)	s. 66 (1)
(2)	66 (2) (4)
para. 7	68
para. 8	69
para. 9 (1)	70 (1) (7)
para. 9 (2)	70 (2) (7)
para. 9 (3)	70 (4)
para. 10	27
para. 11	111
Sch. 12,	
para. 1	49 (1)
Sch. 12,	
para. 2	s. 49 (10)
para. 3	49 (5)
para. 4	47 (2)
para. 5	44 (2)
para. 6	56 (1)
para. 7	55 (1)
para. 8	55 (1)
para. 9	56 (2)
para. 10	57
para. 11	Sch. 6, para. 16
para. 13	s. 147 (3)
para. 15	Sch. 6, para. 9
para. 16	s. 61 (2)
para. 17 (*a*)	50 (1)
para. 18	Sch. 6, para. 9
Sch. 14, Pt. V	Sch. 6, para. 2 (2)

Finance Act 1972

1972	1979
s. 112 (1)	ss. 92 (*d*), 94 (1)
(2)–(10)	92 (*d*), 94 (1)–(10)
(12)	s. 94 (11)
(13)	92 (*b*) (*c*)
113	ss. 92 (*d*), 97 (3), 100
s. 114 (1)	s. 95
(2)	150 (4), Sch. 5, para. 1 (1), Sch. 6, para. 1 (4)
115	s. 76
116 (1)	40 (1)
117	8
s. 118	s. 121 (1)
119 (1)–(3)	146 (1)–(3)
Sch. 24, para. 1	124 (8)
para. 2	74
Sch. 28, Pt. VI, Note 3	Sch. 5, para. 8 (2)

Finance Act 1973

1973	1979
s. 37	s. 115 (2)
51 (1)–(3)	152
(4)	Sch. 6, para. 5
54	Sch. 6, para. 4
Sch. 16, para. 15 (1)	s. 142 (2)
Sch. 20 para. 4	Sch. 6, para. 6
para. 5	Sch. 6, para. 7
para. 6	Sch. 6, para. 8
Sch. 21, para. 4	s. 150 (3), Sch. 6, para. 4

Finance Act 1974

1974	1979
s. 31	s. 121 (1)
48 (2)	Sch. 5, para. 9 (1) (2)
(3)	Sch. 5, para. 9 (1)
(4)	Sch. 5, para. 9 (5)
Sch. 8, para. 6	Sch. 6, para. 23

Finance Act 1975

1975	1979
s. 39	s. 149 (8)
53	146 (1) (3)
Sch. 12, para. 2	153
para. 12	Sch. 6, para. 15
para. 13	s. 153
para. 17	Sch. 6, para. 16

Finance (No. 2) Act 1975

1975	1979
s. 34 (7)	s. 89 (1)
44 (4)	7
57 (1)	8 (3)
(2)	ss. 8 (2), 9 (1)
s. 57 (3)–(5)	s. 9 (2)–(4)
59 (1) (2)	70 (3)
(3)–(6)	70 (4)–(7)
60	25 (3)
s. 61 (1)	s. 140 (1)
62	90
Sch. 8, para. 1	89(1)
para. 5	89 (1) (2)

Finance Act 1976

1976	1979
s. 52 (3)	s. 45 (1)
53	84
53 (8)	Sch. 6, para. 20 (4)
s. 55	s. 148
56 (1)	149 (1) (8)
(2)–(7)	149 (2)–(7)
90	149 (8)
Sch. 11, para. 1	s. 147 (1)
para. 1 (2)	Sch. 6, para. 24

Finance Act 1977

1977	1979
s. 40 (1)	s. 85(1)
(2)	87 (1)
(3) (*a*)	87 (2)
(3) (*b*)	88(1)
s. 40 (4)–(7)	s. 88 (2)–(5)
(8)	87 (4)
(9)	ss. 87 (3)–(5), 139
s. 40 (10)	Sch. 7, para. 2 (4)
43 (1)–(8)	s. 26
(9)	Sch. 6, para. 11

FINANCE ACT 1978

1978	1979
ss. 44 (1)–(6)	s. 5
(8) (*a*)	94 (3)
(*b*)	ss. 97 (3), 100
45 (1) ...	s. 128 (1) (3) (5)
(2) ...	128 (2)
(3) ...	128 (4)
(4) ...	128 (5)
46 ...	126
47 (1) ...	115 (7)
(2) ...	ss. 120, 121 (3)
s. 48 (1) ...	s. 124 (1)–(3)
(2) (3)	124 (5) (6)
(4) ...	124 (8)
49	136
50	101 (8)
51 (1) ...	107 (3)
52 (1) ...	49 (6)–(9)
Sch. 7	Sch. 1
Sch. 8, para. 1 ...	Sch. 4, paras. 1, 3
Sch. 8, para. 2 (1)–(3)	Sch. 4, para. 2
(4)	Sch. 4, para. 3
paras. 3–7	Sch. 4, paras. 4–8
Sch. 11, para. 2 (1)	s. 149 (1)
para. 2 (2)	149 (6)

PART I

GENERAL

Capital gains tax and corporation tax

Taxation of capital gains

1.—(1) Tax shall be charged in accordance with this Act in respect of capital gains, that is to say chargeable gains computed in accordance with this Act and accruing to a person on the disposal of assets.

(2) In the circumstances prescribed by the provisions of Part XI of the Taxes Act (taxation of companies and certain other bodies and associations) the tax shall be chargeable in accordance with those provisions, and all the provisions of this Act have effect subject to those provisions.

(3) Subject to the said provisions, capital gains tax shall be charged for all years of assessment in accordance with the following provisions of this Act.

GENERAL NOTE

This is the main charging section and subs. (1) imposes the tax in respect of gains (computed in accordance with the rules contained in ss. 28 to 43 and Sched. 5) accruing on the disposal (defined in s. 19 (2)) of assets (defined in s. 19 (1)). In particular the circumstance that the assets were acquired before April 7, 1965, does not provide immunity from the tax. The tax only applies on a disposal (actual or deemed).

Subs. (2) exempts from the tax gains accruing to entities liable to corporation tax with the result that the charge will normally only apply to individuals including trustees.

Capital gains tax

Persons chargeable

2.—(1) Subject to any exceptions provided by this Act, a person shall be chargeable to capital gains tax in respect of chargeable gains accruing to him in a year of assessment during any part of which he is resident in the United Kingdom, or during which he is ordinarily resident in the United Kingdom.

(2) This section is without prejudice to the provisions of section 12 below (non-resident with UK branch or agency), and of section 38 of the Finance Act 1973 (territorial sea of the United Kingdom).

GENERAL NOTE

Subs. (1) makes a person liable to the tax on any gain accruing to him in any year of assessment during which he is either resident or ordinarily resident in the

U.K. Subs. (2) provides that the scope of persons brought within the charge by s. 12 of this Act (*q.v.*) and s. 38 of the Finance Act 1973, shall not be limited by subs. (1).

Rate of tax

3. The rate of capital gains tax shall be 30 per cent.

GENERAL NOTE

The rate of tax has remained unaltered at 30 per cent. since its introduction in 1965–66. This is subject to the relief conferred by s. 5.

Gains chargeable to tax

4.—(1) Capital gains tax shall be charged on the total amount of chargeable gains accruing to the person chargeable in the year of assessment, after deducting—

(*a*) any allowable losses accruing to that person in that year of assessment, and

(*b*) so far as they have not been allowed as a deduction from chargeable gains accruing in any previous year of assessment, any allowable losses accruing to that person in any previous year of assessment (not earlier than the year 1965-66).

(2) In the case of a woman who in a year of assessment is a married woman living with her husband any allowable loss which, under subsection (1) above, would be deductible from the chargeable gains accruing in that year of assessment to the one but for an insufficiency of chargeable gains shall, for the purposes of that subsection, be deductible from chargeable gains accruing in that year of assessment to the other:

Provided that this subsection shall not apply in relation to losses accruing in a year of assessment to either if, before 6th July in the year next following that year of assessment, an application is made by the man or the wife to the inspector in such form and manner as the Board may prescribe.

GENERAL NOTE

Subs. (1) provides that the tax shall be charged on the balance of the gains left after deducting any losses realised in the year of assessment and any unrelieved losses from earlier years (not being years earlier than 1965–66). Only in the circumstances specified in s. 49 (2) can losses be set against the gains of earlier years.

Subs. (2) provides that, in the case of a husband and wife living together, any losses of the one which are unrelieved under subs. (1) can be applied against the chargeable gains of the other accruing in the same year of assessment as the losses, unless before July 6 in the next following year an application is made that the subsection is not to apply. It is considered that the election must specifically refer to the capital gains tax.

Relief for gains less than £9,500

5.—(1) An individual shall not be chargeable to capital gains tax for a year of assessment if his taxable amount for that year does not exceed £1,000.

(2) If an individual's taxable amount for a year of assessment exceeds £1,000 but does not exceed £5,000, the amount of capital gains tax to which he is chargeable for that year shall be 15 per cent. of the excess over £1,000.

(3) If an individual's taxable amount for a year of assessment exceeds £5,000, the amount of capital gains tax to which he is chargeable for that year shall not exceed £600 plus one-half of the excess over £5,000.

(4) For the purposes of this section an individual's taxable amount for a year of assessment is the amount on which he is chargeable under section 4 (1) above for that year but—

(*a*) where the amount of chargeable gains less allowable losses accruing to an individual in any year of assessment does not exceed £1,000, no deduction from that amount shall be made for that year in respect of allowable losses carried forward from a previous year or carried back from a subsequent year in which the individual dies, and

(*b*) where the amount of chargeable gains less allowable losses accruing to an individual in any year of assessment exceeds £1,000, the deduction from that amount for that year in respect of allowable losses carried forward from a previous year or carried back from a subsequent year in which the individual dies shall not be greater than the excess.

(5) Where in a year of assessment—

(*a*) the amount of chargeable gains accruing to an individual does not exceed £1,000, and

(*b*) the aggregate amount or value of the consideration for all the disposals of assets made by him (other than disposals gains accruing on which are not chargeable gains) does not exceed £5,000,

a statement to the effect of paragraphs (*a*) and (*b*) above shall, unless the inspector otherwise requires, be sufficient compliance with any notice under section 8 of the Taxes Management Act 1970 requiring the individual to make a return of the chargeable gains accruing to him in that year.

(6) Schedule 1 to this Act shall have effect as respects the application of this section to husbands and wives, personal representatives and trustees.

General Note

This section provides a new exemption to take the place of the small disposals exemption (abolished with effect from the tax year 1977–78) and the alternative charge for chargeable gains accruing to individuals, allowing assessments under Sched. D, Case VI (abolished with effect from the tax year 1978–79). The new exemption for individuals provides as follows:

(i) a taxable amount (defined as the net amount on which an individual is chargeable under s. 4 (1)) of less than £1,000 in a year shall be free of tax;

(ii) a taxable amount in a year between £1,000 and £5,000 shall be subject to tax at 15 per cent.;

(iii) on a taxable amount of over £5,000, tax cannot exceed one-half of the excess amount over £5,000, plus £600.

The relief will only be beneficial if the taxable amount concerned is less than £9,500. No deductions in respect of losses carried forward from previous years are made (*i.e.* there is no utilisation of such losses) if the chargeable gains reduced by the losses for the current year of assessment result in the taxable amount being less than £1,000. Where the taxable amounts exceed £1,000 the extent of the losses carried forward to be utilised will equal that excess, bringing the taxable amount down to £1,000. This, therefore, saves the allowable losses for future years.

A full return of an individual's chargeable gains need not be made if the taxable amount does not exceed £1,000 and the aggregate consideration for his disposals in that year is not greater than £5,000.

Sched. 1 to the Act contains special rules relating to husbands and wives, personal representatives and trustees. No carrying forward of any unutilised part of this relief from one year to another is allowed.

Small gifts

6. A gain accruing to an individual on a disposal by way of gift of an asset the market value of which does not exceed £100 shall not be a chargeable gain, but this section shall not apply to gifts made by the same individual in the same year of assessment the total value of which exceeds £100.

General Note

This section affords exemption from tax where the total value of the gifts (*not* the capital gains) made by an individual in any year of assessment does not exceed £100. The disposal of any item which is not a chargeable asset is disregarded when considering whether the relief conferred by this section applies; thus an individual could give away savings certificates worth, say, £200, and still be entitled to claim this relief if other chargeable assets which he gave away did not possess a value in excess of £100.

Time for payment of tax

7. Capital gains tax assessed on any person in respect of gains accruing in any year shall be payable by that person at or before the expiration of the three months following that year, or at the expiration of a period of thirty days beginning with the date of the issue of the notice of assessment, whichever is the later.

General Note

The tax is payable on or before July 6 following the year of assessment in which the gains accrue, or within 30 days of the issue of the notice of assessment being made, whichever is the later. See ss. 29–41, and s. 57 of the Taxes Management Act 1970 and the Capital Gains Tax Regulations 1967 for provisions regarding assessments and appeals.

Postponement of payment of tax

8.—(1) Where the whole or part of any assets falling within subsection (3) below—

(*a*) is disposed of by way of gift, or

(*b*) is under section 54 (1) or 55 (1) below (settled property) deemed to be disposed of,

the capital gains tax chargeable on a gain accruing on the disposal may, at the option of the person liable to pay it, be paid by eight equal yearly instalments or sixteen half-yearly instalments.

(2) Payment of capital gains tax in accordance with subsection (1) above shall be subject to the payment of interest under Part IX (except sections 87 and 88) of the Taxes Management Act 1970 except as provided by section 9 below.

(3) The assets referred to in subsection (1) above are—

(*a*) land or an estate or interest in land,

(*b*) any shares or securities of a company which, immediately before the disposal, gave control of the company to the person by whom the disposal was made or deemed to be made,

(*c*) any shares or securities of a company not falling under paragraph (*b*) above and not quoted on a recognised stock exchange in the United Kingdom or elsewhere, and

(*d*) any assets used exclusively for the purposes of a trade, profession or vocation which, immediately before the disposal, was carried on (whether alone or in partnership) by the person by whom the disposal was made or deemed to be made.

(4) Where tax is payable by instalments by virtue of this section the first instalment shall be due at the expiration of twelve months from the

time of the disposal, and subject to section 9 below, the interest on the unpaid portion of the tax shall be added to each instalment and paid accordingly; but the tax for the time being unpaid, with interest to the date of payment, may be paid at any time, and shall become due and payable forthwith if—

(*a*) the disposal was by way of gift to a person connected with the donor, or was deemed to be made under section 54 (1) or 55 (1) below, and

(*b*) the assets are disposed of for valuable consideration under a subsequent disposal (whether or not the subsequent disposal is made by the person who acquired them under the first disposal).

General Note

The right to pay capital gains tax by eight yearly or 16 half-yearly instalments is applied to disposals of certain types of assets by way of gift as well as to deemed disposals of such assets where they are settled property. The assets which qualify for this treatment are land, shares or securities of companies which gave the person making the disposal control of the company immediately prior to the disposal, unquoted shares or securities (without any condition as to control of the company) and business assets.

The instalments payable include interest on the tax still outstanding unless the conditions provided by s. 9 are satisfied.

A subsequent disposal for valuable consideration by any person, when the first disposal was a gift to a connected person or a deemed disposal, causes the outstanding tax on the first disposal to be payable immediately.

Postponement of payment of tax: further provisions

9.—(1) Subject to the following provisions of this section, where capital gains tax is payable—

(*a*) by instalments under section 8 above, and

(*b*) in respect of the disposal of assets falling within paragraph (*b*), (*c*) or (*d*) of subsection (3) of that section,

the tax shall, for the purpose of any interest to be added to each instalment, be treated as carrying interest from the date at which the instalment is payable.

(2) Subsection (1) above does not apply to tax payable in respect of the disposal of shares or securities of a company falling within paragraph (*a*) of subsection (3) below unless it also falls within paragraph (*b*) or (*c*) of that subsection.

(3) The companies referred to in subsection (2) above are—

(*a*) any company whose business consists wholly or mainly of one or more of the following, that is to say, dealing in shares or securities, land or buildings, or making or holding investments,

(*b*) any company whose business consists wholly or mainly in being a holding company (within the meaning of section 154 of the Companies Act 1948) of one or more companies not falling within paragraph (*a*) above and

(*c*) any company whose business is that of a jobber (as defined in section 477 of the Taxes Act) or discount house and is carried on in the United Kingdom.

(4) Subsection (1) above applies only to the extent to which—

(*a*) the market value of the assets in respect of the disposal of which the tax concerned is payable, plus

(*b*) the market value of any assets which the same person has or is deemed to have previously disposed of and in respect of the disposal of which the tax also fell within that subsection,

does not exceed £250,000.

General Note

This section extends to capital gains tax the capital transfer tax facility to pay tax on the disposal of certain assets by instalments free of interest. The right extends to cases where tax is payable by instalments under s. 8 and the assets disposed of come within s. 8 (3) (*b*), (*c*) or (*d*).

Subs. (2) specifically excludes disposals of shares in companies whose business consists of dealing in shares or securities, or in land or buildings or in making or holding investments from the benefit of subs. (1) save in the circumstances specified in subs. (3) (*b*) or (*c*). Subs. (4) provides that the right to pay tax by instalments free of interest is not available to the extent that the market value of the assets together with any other assets previously disposed of by the same person in respect of which the right has applied exceeds £250,000.

The foreign element

Double taxation relief

10.—(1) For the purpose of giving relief from double taxation in relation to capital gains tax and tax on chargeable gains charged under the law of any country outside the United Kingdom, in Chapters I and II of Part XVIII of the Taxes Act, as they apply for the purposes of income tax, for references to income there shall be substituted references to capital gains and for references to income tax there shall be substituted references to capital gains tax meaning, as the context may require, tax charged under the law of the United Kingdom or tax charged under the law of a country outside the United Kingdom.

(2) Any arrangements set out in an order made under section 347 of the Income Tax Act 1952 before 5th August 1965 (the date of the passing of the Finance Act 1965) shall so far as they provide (in whatever terms) for relief from tax chargeable in the United Kingdom on capital gains have effect in relation to capital gains tax.

(3) So far as by virtue of this section capital gains tax charged under the law of a country outside the United Kingdom may be brought into account under the said Chapters I and II as applied by this section, that tax, whether relief is given by virtue of this section in respect of it or not, shall not be taken into account for the purposes of those Chapters as they apply apart from this section.

(4) Section 518 of the Taxes Act (disclosure of information for purposes of double taxation) shall apply in relation to capital gains tax as it applies in relation to income tax.

General Note

This section provides that double taxation relief is to be given for capital gains tax in the same manner as it is given for income tax.

Allowance for foreign tax

11. Subject to section 10 above, the tax chargeable under the law of any country outside the United Kingdom on the disposal of an asset which is borne by the person making the disposal shall be allowable as a deduction in the computation under Chapter II of Part II of this Act.

General Note

This section allows for foreign tax paid on the disposal of a chargeable asset (unless allowed under s. 10 by way of double tax relief) to be deducted when computing liability to capital gains tax.

Non-resident with United Kingdom branch or agency

12.—(1) Subject to any exceptions provided by this Act, a person shall be chargeable to capital gains tax in respect of chargeable gains accruing to him in a year of assessment in which he is not resident and not ordinarily resident in the United Kingdom but is carrying on a trade in the United Kingdom through a branch or agency, and shall be so chargeable on chargeable gains accruing on the disposal—

(*a*) of assets situated in the United Kingdom and used in or for the purposes of the trade at or before the time when the capital gain accrued, or

(*b*) of assets situated in the United Kingdom and used or held for the purposes of the branch or agency at or before that time, or assets acquired for use by or for the purposes of the branch or agency.

(2) This section shall not apply to a person who, by virtue of Part XVIII of the Taxes Act (double taxation agreements), is exempt from income tax chargeable for the year of assessment in respect of the profits or gains of the branch or agency.

(3) In this Act, unless the context otherwise requires, " branch or agency " means any factorship, agency, receivership, branch or management, but does not include any person within the exemptions in section 82 of the Taxes Management Act 1970 (general agents and brokers).

GENERAL NOTE

This section makes a non-resident who conducts a trade here through a branch or agency (which are defined) liable to the tax on any gain accruing from the sale of the assets situated here and used in or acquired for the purposes of the trade or the agency. Subs. (2) creates an exception where the profits of the branch are immune from income tax by reason of a double taxation treaty.

Foreign assets: delayed remittances

13.—(1) Subsection (2) below applies where—

(*a*) chargeable gains accrue from the disposal of assets situated outside the United Kingdom, and

(*b*) the person charged or chargeable makes a claim and shows that the conditions set out in subsection (3) below are, so far as applicable, satisfied as respects those gains (" the qualifying gains ").

(2) For the purposes of capital gains tax—

(*a*) the amount of the qualifying gains shall be deducted from the amounts on which the claimant is assessed to capital gains tax for the year in which the qualifying gains accrued to the claimant, but

(*b*) the amount so deducted shall be assessed to capital gains tax on the claimant (or his personal representatives) as if it were an amount of chargeable gains accruing in the year of assessment in which the conditions set out in subsection (3) below cease to be satisfied.

(3) The said conditions are—

(*a*) that the claimant was unable to transfer the qualifying gains to the United Kingdom, and

(*b*) that that inability was due to the laws of the territory where the income arose, or to the executive action of its government, or to the impossibility of obtaining foreign currency in that territory, and

(*c*) that the inability was not due to any want of reasonable endeavours on the part of the claimant.

(4) Where under an agreement entered into under arrangements made by the Secretary of State in pursuance of section 1 of the Overseas

Investment and Export Guarantees Act 1972 or section 11 of the Export Guarantees and Overseas Investment Act 1978 any payment is made by the Exports Credits Guarantee Department in respect of any gains which cannot be transferred to the United Kingdom, then, to the extent of the payment, the gains shall be treated as gains with respect to which the conditions mentioned in subsection (3) above are not satisfied (and accordingly cannot cease to be satisfied).

(5) No claim under this section shall be made in respect of any chargeable gain more than six years after the end of the year of assessment in which that gain accrues.

(6) The personal representatives of a deceased person may make any claim which he might have made under this section if he had not died.

General Note

This section affords relief to a taxpayer who can establish that the non-remittance of his gains realised abroad was due to the circumstances set out in subs. (3) : the relief is similar to that applied to ordinary income by s. 418 (1)–(6) I.C.T.A. 1970. The relief ceases and the gains are chargeable to tax when it becomes possible to remit the gain (subs. (2) (*b*)). Subs. 5 stipulates that the relief can only be claimed up to six years after the year in which the gain accrued. The relief is extended to the personal representatives of an individual who would himself have been able to claim (subs. (6)).

Foreign assets of person with foreign domicile

14.—(1) In the case of individuals resident or ordinarily resident but not domiciled in the United Kingdom, capital gains tax shall not be charged in respect of gains accruing to them from the disposal of assets situated outside the United Kingdom (that is chargeable gains accruing in the year 1965–66 or a later year of assessment) except that the tax shall be charged on the amounts (if any) received in the United Kingdom in respect of those chargeable gains, any such amounts being treated as gains accruing when they are received in the United Kingdom.

(2) For the purposes of this section there shall be treated as received in the United Kingdom in respect of any gain all amounts paid, used or enjoyed in or in any manner or form transmitted or brought to the United Kingdom, and subsections (4) to (7) of section 122 of the Taxes Act (under which income applied outside the United Kingdom in payment of debts is, in certain cases, treated as received in the United Kingdom) shall apply as they would apply for the purposes of subsection (3) of the said section 122 if the gain were income arising from possessions out of the United Kingdom.

General Note

Subs. (1) provides that individuals who, though resident or ordinarily resident, are not domiciled here are only liable for gains derived from assets outside the U.K. to the extent that such gains are remitted here.

Subs. (2) applies to capital gains tax the provisions of s. 122 (4)–(7) I.C.T.A. 1970, which extend the remittance rule for income tax to sums applied outside the U.K. in repaying certain debts.

Non-resident company

15.—(1) This section applies as respects chargeable gains accruing to a company—

(*a*) which is not resident in the United Kingdom, and

(*b*) which would be a close company if it were resident in the United Kingdom.

(2) Subject to this section, every person who at the time when the chargeable gain accrues to the company is resident or ordinarily resident

in the United Kingdom, who, if an individual, is domiciled in the United Kingdom, and who holds shares in the company, shall be treated for the purposes of this Act as if a part of the chargeable gain had accrued to him.

(3) That part shall be equal to the proportion of the assets of the company to which that person would be entitled on a liquidation of the company at the time when the chargeable gain accrues to the company.

(4) If the part of a chargeable gain attributable to a person under subsection (2) above is less than one-twentieth, the said subsection (2) shall not apply to that person.

(5) This section shall not apply in relation to—

(*a*) any amount in respect of the chargeable gain which is distributed, whether by way of dividend or distribution of capital or on the dissolution of the company, to persons holding shares in the company, or creditors of the company, within two years from the time when the chargeable gain accrued to the company, or

(*b*) a chargeable gain accruing on the disposal of assets, being tangible property, whether movable or immovable, or a lease of such property, where the property was used, and used only, for the purposes of a trade carried on by the company wholly outside the United Kingdom, or

(*c*) a chargeable gain accruing on the disposal of currency or of a debt within section 135 (1) below (foreign currency bank accounts), where the currency or debt is or represents money in use for the purposes of a trade carried on by the company wholly outside the United Kingdom, or

(*d*) to a chargeable gain in respect of which the company is chargeable to tax by virtue of section 246 (2) (*b*) of the Taxes Act (gains corresponding to those charged under section 12 above).

(6) Subsection (5) (*a*) above shall not prevent the making of an assessment in pursuance of this section but if, by virtue of that paragraph, this section is excluded all such adjustments, whether by way of repayment or discharge of tax or otherwise, shall be made as will give effect to the provisions of that paragraph.

(7) The amount of capital gains tax paid by a person in pursuance of subsection (2) above (so far as not reimbursed by the company) shall be allowable as a deduction in the computation under this Act of a gain accruing on the disposal by him of the shares by reference to which the tax was paid.

(8) So far as it would go to reduce or extinguish chargeable gains accruing by virtue of this section to a person in a year of assessment this section shall apply in relation to a loss accruing to the company on the disposal of an asset in that year of assessment as it would apply if a gain instead of a loss had accrued to the company on the disposal, but shall only so apply in relation to that person; and subject to the preceding provisions of this subsection this section shall not apply in relation to a loss accruing to the company.

(9) If the person owning any of the shares in the company at the time when the chargeable gain accrues to the company is itself a company which is not resident in the United Kingdom but which would be a close company if it were resident in the United Kingdom, an amount equal to the amount apportioned under subsection (3) above out of the chargeable gain to the shares so owned shall be apportioned among the issued shares of the second-mentioned company, and the holders of those shares shall

be treated in accordance with subsection (2) above, and so on through any number of companies.

(10) If any tax payable by any person by virtue of subsection (2) above is paid by the company to which the chargeable gain accrues, or in a case under subsection (9) above is paid by any such other company, the amount so paid shall not for the purposes of income tax, capital gains tax or corporation tax be regarded as a payment to the person by whom the tax was originally payable.

GENERAL NOTE

This section applies to a non-resident "close company" (as defined in ss. 282 and 283 I.C.T.A. 1970) and provides that when any capital gain accrues to such a company, a proportional part of the gain shall be attributed to any shareholder resident or ordinarily resident in the U.K. and, being an individual, domiciled in the U.K., and shall be treated as part of his chargeable gains. The company's gain is apportioned among the shareholders in the same proportions as the assets of the company would be on a liquidation and each shareholder who comes within subs. (2) will be liable to pay tax on his part of the gain.

The section is excluded in respect of a shareholder whose share of a gain is less than one-twentieth (see subs. (4)) and in four cases set out in subs. (5): the first is where the gain is distributed to the shareholders within two years (see subs. (6) when this happens after a shareholder has been assessed); the second is where the gain accrues on the disposal of tangible movable property used for the company's trade outside the U.K.; the third is where the gain accrues on the disposal of currency or a debt within s. 135, which represents money in use for the company's trade outside the U.K.; the fourth is where the company, although non-resident, is itself taxable on the gain (see s. 246 (2) (*b*) I.C.T.A. 1970).

A person so charged is allowed to deduct any tax on capital gains attributed to him (in so far as not reimbursed by the company) in computing any gain which he derives on a disposal of shares in the company (subs. (7)).

Subs. (8) provides that the section shall apply in relation to a disposal resulting in a loss instead of a gain, only to the extent that it will offset a gain apportioned to the shareholders under this section in the same year.

Subs. (9) provides for capital gains tax to be sub-apportioned through "non-resident close companies" which are shareholders in the "non-resident close company" making the gain so that their shareholders become liable if they themselves come within subs. (2).

Under subs. (10), if any tax payable by a person under subs. (2) is paid by the company to which the chargeable gain accrues, such tax is not to be regarded for tax purposes as a payment by the company to the person by whom the tax was originally payable.

Non-resident group of companies

16.—(1) This section has effect for the purposes of section 15 above.

(2) Sections 273 to 275 and 276 (1) of the Taxes Act shall apply in relation to non-resident companies which are members of a non-resident group of companies, as they apply in relation to companies resident in the United Kingdom which are members of a group of companies.

(3) Section 278 and 279 of the Taxes Act shall apply for the said purposes as if for any reference therein to a group of companies there were substituted a reference to a non-resident group of companies, and as if references to companies were references to companies not resident in the United Kingdom.

(4) For the purposes of this section—

(*a*) a " non-resident group " of companies—

(i) in the case of a group, none of the members of which are resident in the United Kingdom, means that group, and

(ii) in the case of a group, two or more members of which are not resident in the United Kingdom means the members which are not resident in the United Kingdom;

(*b*) " group " shall be construed in accordance with subsections (1) (without paragraph (*a*)), (3) and (4) of section 272 of the Taxes Act.

General Note

This section qualifies the effect of s. 15 above. If the company is a member of a " non-resident group " (as defined in subs. (4)) and the disposal is within the group, then the question of whether a gain accrues which can be apportioned to the shareholders is to be determined as if the provisions of ss. 273–275, 276 (1), 278, and 279 I.C.T.A. 1970 applied. It will be recalled that for disposals within a group, the general rule under s. 273 I.C.T.A. 1970 is that there is a " no gain, no loss " consideration.

Non-resident trust

17.—(1) This section applies as respects chargeable gains accruing to the trustees of a settlement if the trustees are not resident and not ordinarily resident in the United Kingdom, and if the settlor, or one of the settlors, is domiciled and either resident or ordinarily resident in the United Kingdom, or was domiciled and either resident or ordinarily resident in the United Kingdom when he made his settlement.

(2) Any beneficiary under the settlement who is domiciled and either resident or ordinarily resident in the United Kingdom during any year of assessment shall be treated for the purposes of this Act as if an apportioned part of the amount, if any, on which the trustees would have been chargeable to capital gains tax under section 4 (1) above, if domiciled and either resident or ordinarily resident in the United Kingdom in that year of assessment, had been chargeable gains accruing to the beneficiary in that year of assessment; and for the purposes of this section any such amount shall be apportioned in such manner as is just and reasonable between persons having interests in the settled property, whether the interest be a life interest or an interest in reversion, and so that the chargeable gain is apportioned, as near as may be, according to the respective values of those interests, disregarding in the case of a defeasible interest the possibility of defeasance.

(3) For the purposes of this section—

(*a*) if in any of the three years ending with that in which the chargeable gain accrues a person has received a payment or payments out of the income of the settled property made in exercise of a discretion he shall be regarded, in relation to that chargeable gain, as having an interest in the settled property of a value equal to that of an annuity of a yearly amount equal to one-third of the total of the payments so received by him in the said three years, and

(*b*) if a person receives at any time after the chargeable gain accrues a capital payment made out of the settled property in exercise of a discretion, being a payment which represents the chargeable gain in whole or part then, except so far as any part of the gain has been attributed under this section to some other person who is domiciled and resident or ordinarily resident in the United Kingdom, that person shall, if domiciled and resident or ordinarily resident in the United Kingdom, be treated as if the chargeable gain, or as the case may be the part of the chargeable gain represented by the capital payment, had accrued to him at the time when he received the capital payment.

(4) In the case of a settlement made before 6th April 1965—

(*a*) subsection (2) above shall not apply to a beneficiary whose interest is solely in the income of the settled property, and who cannot, by means of the exercise of any power of appointment or power of revocation or otherwise, obtain for himself, whether with or without the consent of any other person, any part of the capital represented by the settled property, and

(*b*) payment of capital gains tax chargeable on a gain apportioned to a beneficiary in respect of an interest in reversion in any part of the capital represented by the settled property may be postponed until that person becomes absolutely entitled to that part of the settled property, or disposes of the whole or any part of his interest, unless he can, by any means described in paragraph (*a*) above, obtain for himself any of it at any earlier time,

and for the purposes of this subsection, property added to a settlement after the settlement is made shall be regarded as property under a separate settlement made at the time when the property is so added.

(5) In any case in which the amount of any capital gains tax payable by a beneficiary under a settlement in accordance with the provisions of this section is paid by the trustees of the settlement that amount shall not for the purposes of taxation be regarded as a payment to the beneficiary.

(6) This section shall not apply in relation to a loss accruing to the trustees of the settlement.

(7) In this section " settlement " and " settlor " have the meanings given by section 454 (3) of the Taxes Act and " settled property " shall be construed accordingly.

GENERAL NOTE

This section applies a somewhat similar procedure to that described in s. 15 to cover the case where a non-resident trust makes a gain and the settlor was domiciled and either resident or ordinarily resident in the U.K. either when the gain was made or when the settlement was made. A proportion of the capital gains arising to such a trust is attributed to any beneficiary domiciled and resident or ordinarily resident in the U.K. the proportion being determined by reference to the interest of the beneficiary under the settlement. The task of apportioning "as is just and reasonable" may be extremely difficult in the case of discretionary trusts and subs. (3) attempts to deal with this situation.

Subs. (4) limits the operation of the section in respect of settlements made before April 6, 1965, in certain respects. If the trust makes a loss this is not apportioned (subs. (6)). If the trustees pay the tax assessed on a beneficiary under this section that is not a payment to the beneficiary for the purposes of income tax at basic or higher rates or corporation tax (subs. (5)).

The meaning of "settlement" within this section has been considered in *Chinn* v. *Hochstrasser* [1977] 1 W.L.R. 1337, reversed in the Court of Appeal [1979] 1 W.L.R. 411. An arrangement is capable of being a "settlement" only if there is an act of bounty effected thereby by the settlor in favour of others. Leave to appeal to the House of Lords has been granted.

Residence etc. and location of assets

18.—(1) In this Act " resident " and " ordinarily resident " have the same meanings as in the Income Tax Acts.

(2) Section 207 of the Taxes Act (disputes as to domicile or ordinary residence) shall apply in relation to capital gains tax as it applies for the purposes mentioned in that section.

(3) Subject to section 12 (1) above, an individual who is in the United Kingdom for some temporary purpose only and not with any view or intent to establish his residence in the United Kingdom shall be

charged to capital gains tax on chargeable gains accruing in any year of assessment if and only if the period (or the sum of the periods) for which he is resident in the United Kingdom in that year of assessment exceeds six months.

(4) For the purposes of this Act—

(*a*) the situation of rights or interests (otherwise than by way of security) in or over immovable property is that of the immovable property,

(*b*) subject to the following provisions of this subsection, the situation of rights or interests (otherwise than by way of security) in or over tangible movable property is that of the tangible movable property,

(*c*) subject to the following provisions of this subsection, a debt, secured or unsecured, is situated in the United Kingdom if and only if the creditor is resident in the United Kingdom,

(*d*) shares or securities issued by any municipal or governmental authority, or by any body created by such an authority, are situated in the country of that authority,

(*e*) subject to paragraph (*d*) above, registered shares or securities are situated where they are registered and, if registered in more than one register, where the principal register is situated,

(*f*) a ship or aircraft is situated in the United Kingdom if and only if the owner is then resident in the United Kingdom, and an interest or right in or over a ship or aircraft is situated in the United Kingdom if and only if the person entitled to the interest or right is resident in the United Kingdom,

(*g*) the situation of good-will as a trade, business or professional asset is at the place where the trade, business or profession is carried on,

(*h*) patents, trade-marks and designs are situated where they are registered, and if registered in more than one register, where each register is situated, and copyright, franchises, rights and licences to use any copyright material, patent, trade-mark or design are situated in the United Kingdom if they, or any rights derived from them, are exercisable in the United Kingdom,

(*i*) a judgment debt is situated where the judgment is recorded.

General Note

This section provides that "residence" and "ordinary residence" shall have the same meanings as in the law of income tax and allows for disputes as to domicile or ordinary residence to be determined in accordance with s. 207 I.C.T.A. 1970 (subs. (2)). It also sets out rules for deciding the situation of the assets specified in subs. (4).

Part II

Gains and Losses

Chapter I

Disposals

Disposal of assets

19.—(1) All forms of property shall be assets for the purposes of this Act, whether situated in the United Kingdom or not, including—

(*a*) options, debts and incorporeal property generally, and

(*b*) any currency other than sterling, and

(*c*) any form of property created by the person disposing of it, or otherwise coming to be owned without being acquired.

(2) For the purposes of this Act—

(*a*) references to a disposal of an asset include, except where the context otherwise requires, references to a part disposal of an asset, and

(*b*) there is a part disposal of an asset where an interest or right in or over the asset is created by the disposal, as well as where it subsists before the disposal, and generally, there is a part disposal of an asset where, on a person making a disposal, any description of property derived from the asset remains undisposed of.

(3) Subject to the provisions of this Act, a person's acquisition of an asset and the disposal of it to him shall for the purposes of this Act be deemed to be for a consideration equal to the market value of the asset—

(*a*) where he acquires the asset otherwise than by way of a bargain made at arm's length and in particular where he acquires it by way of gift or by way of distribution from a company in respect of shares in the company, or

(*b*) where he acquires the asset wholly or partly for a consideration that cannot be valued, or in connection with his own or another's loss of office or employment or diminution of emoluments, or otherwise in consideration for or recognition of his or another's services or past services in any office or employment or of any other service rendered or to be rendered by him or another.

(4) It is hereby declared that winnings from betting, including pool betting, or lotteries or games with prizes are not chargeable gains, and no chargeable gain or allowable loss shall accrue on the disposal of rights to winnings obtained by participating in any pool betting or lottery or game with prizes.

(5) It is hereby declared that sums obtained by way of compensation or damages for any wrong or injury suffered by an individual in his person or in his profession or vocation are not chargeable gains.

GENERAL NOTE

Subs. (1)

This subsection provides an extremely wide definition of chargeable assets, especially as para. (*c*) expands the definition to include cases where there has been no acquisition. Illustrations of property which is created by the taxpayer are goodwill, copyright and paintings; para. (*c*) causes the consideration obtained on the disposal of such assets to be subject to capital gains tax unless exempt under one of the relieving provisions.

In *O'Brien* v. *Benson's Hosiery* (*Holdings*) *Ltd.* [1978] 3 W.L.R. 609, it was held that an employer's contract of personal service with his employee, being an asset to which the concept of market value was entirely inappropriate, was not "property" within s. 19 (1), notwithstanding the width of the terms in which the subsection is drafted.

Subs. (2)

By defining part disposals as including the granting of an interest in an asset, each of the following transactions (and many others) ranks as a disposal for the purposes of capital gains tax, unless it gives to a charge to income tax: granting a licence to use a patent or a copyright, a licence to remove minerals or dig sand or earth, a licence to tip rubbish, the grant of sporting or fishing rights, or a licence to fell trees (unless the trees qualify for the relief contained in s. 113). Two common cases which will be treated as part disposals are the granting of a lease and the sale of part of a larger holding of shares of the same class.

The Revenue has expressed the following views on the subject of part disposals: unless it appears from the facts at the time of acquisition that more than one asset (given its natural meaning) was acquired, a single acquisition of land (with or without buildings), whether obtained by purchase under one contract at an inclusive price or by gift or inheritance as a whole, should normally be regarded as a single asset (even though it comprises distinguishable elements such as house and garden, farm-houses, buildings, woodlands, cottages, etc.).

On the other hand, in the case of acquisitions by purchase, there may be contemporary evidence showing that the acquisition comprised more than one asset. For example, correspondence, etc., during negotiations leading up to a purchase may show that the contract price was based upon the sum rounded up or down of a number of valuation units; the land may have been offered for sale by auction in lots; or the rent roll of an estate may show separate tenants paying substantial rents for individual properties such as farms. In such cases it may be possible to make a satisfactory apportionment of the purchase price.

Where estates of small let properties (*e.g.* terraced urban dwelling-houses) are acquired, blocks of a size convenient to hold as investments are normally regarded as single assets, but in practice no objection is taken to treating individual dwelling-houses as separate assets and apportioning the cost of the larger unit on the basis of such evidence as is available. As a general rule, single buildings in multiple occupation such as blocks of flats or office suites are regarded as single assets, but again no objection is normally taken to treating individual flats, etc., as separate assets if it appears that similar flats, etc., in the same ownership or in the locality have commonly been sold singly as independent dwellings (see *Taxation*, November 8, 1969, at p. 105).

Subs. (3)

This subsection provides that where an asset is acquired in the circumstances listed, its value for the purposes of the capital gains tax is to be its market value at the date when the acquisition takes place. Para. (*a*) covers disposals by way of gift (subject to the exemption contained in s. 6 of this Act).

Donationes mortis causa are beyond the scope of this subsection: s. 49 (5). This subsection does not apply for the purpose of calculating the consideration given for the acquisition of shares in pursuance of a share option scheme as defined in Sched. 12, F.A. 1972: see s. 76. For gifts to charities, see s. 146 and the commentary thereto.

In *Harrison* v. *Nairn Williamson Ltd.* [1978] 1 W.L.R. 145, it was held that subs. (3) is not prevented from applying merely because an acquisition of an asset in a particular case is not consequent upon disposal of the asset by another person. In that case, the asset, loan stock issued otherwise than by way of a bargain made at arm's length, was held to have an acquisition cost for tax purposes equal to its market value at the date of acquisition which was different to the sum paid by the taxpayer for the asset.

On the other hand an acquisition otherwise than by way of a bargain made at arm's length is essential to bring the subsection into play: *cf. Berry* v. *Warnett* [1978] 1 W.L.R. 957, when the subsection was held not to apply in the context of a tax avoidance scheme because the parties to the transaction concerned were at arm's length.

Subs. (4)

This subsection provides that the sale of a betting or lottery ticket is not a chargeable disposal, and shall therefore be ignored when computing either gains or losses for the purposes of the charge to tax.

Subs. (5)

This subsection exempts damages for tort in respect of personal or professional injury from the charge to capital gains tax.

Capital sums derived from assets

20.—(1) Subject to sections 21 and 23 (1) below, and to any other exceptions in this Act, there is for the purposes of this Act a disposal of assets by their owner where any capital sum is derived from assets notwithstanding that no asset is acquired by the person paying the capital sum, and this subsection applies in particular to—

(*a*) capital sums received by way of compensation for any kind of damage or injury to assets or for the loss, destruction or dissipation of assets or for any depreciation or risk of depreciation of an asset,

(*b*) capital sums received under a policy of insurance of the risk of any kind of damage or injury to, or the loss or depreciation of, assets,

(*c*) capital sums received in return for forfeiture or surrender of rights, or for refraining from exercising rights, and

(*d*) capital sums received as consideration for use or exploitation of assets.

(2) In the case of a disposal within paragraph (*a*), (*b*), (*c*) or (*d*) of subsection (1) above the time of the disposal shall be the time when the capital sum is received as described in that subsection.

(3) In this section " capital sum " means any money or money's worth which is not excluded from the consideration taken into account in the computation under Chapter II below.

GENERAL NOTE

This section provides that a chargeable disposal takes place when a capital sum is derived from assets even though no asset is received by the person paying the capital sum. Illustrations of such circumstances are the redemption of a bond or debenture on maturity, and of the particular instances cited, illustrations are: (*a*) compensation for damage; (*b*) insurance moneys; (*c*) compensation for waiver of restrictive covenants; and (*d*) a premium for user (subs. (1)). The chargeable disposal occurs at the time of receipt of the capital sum in the case of the instances specified in subs. (1).

Subs. (3) defines what is meant by "capital sum" in these circumstances. The cases of *I.R.C.* v. *Montgomery* [1975] 2 W.L.R. 326; *Davis* v. *Powell* [1977] 1 W.L.R. 258 and *Marren* v. *Ingles* [1979] S.T.C. 58 illustrate the proper construction which is to be given to the expression "capital sum derived from assets."

Capital sums: compensation and insurance money

21.—(1) If the recipient so claims, receipt of a capital sum within paragraph (*a*), (*b*), (*c*) or (*d*) of section 20 (1) above derived from an asset which is not lost or destroyed shall not be treated for the purposes of this Act as a disposal of the asset if—

(*a*) the capital sum is wholly applied in restoring the asset, or

(*b*) (subject to subsection (2) below), the capital sum is applied in restoring the asset except for a part of the capital sum which is not reasonably required for the purpose and which is small as compared with the whole capital sum, or

(*c*) (subject to subsection (2) below), the amount of the capital sum is small, as compared with the value of the asset,

but, if the receipt is not treated as a disposal, all sums which would, if the receipt had been so treated, have been brought into account as consideration for that disposal in the computation under Chapter II below of a gain accruing on the disposal shall be deducted from any expenditure allowable under Chapter II below as a deduction in computing a gain on the subsequent disposal of the asset.

(2) If the allowable expenditure is less than the consideration for the disposal constituted by the receipt of the capital sum (or is nil)—

(*a*) paragraphs (*b*) and (*c*) of subsection (1) above shall not apply, and

(*b*) if the recipient so elects (and there is any allowable expenditure)—

(i) the amount of the consideration for the disposal shall be reduced by the amount of the allowable expenditure, and

(ii) none of that expenditure shall be allowable as a deduction in computing a gain accruing on the occasion of the disposal or any subsequent occasion.

In this subsection " allowable expenditure " means expenditure which, immediately before the disposal, was attributable to the asset under paragraphs (*a*) and (*b*) of section 32 (1) below.

(3) If, in a case not falling within subsection (1) (*b*) above, a part of a capital sum within paragraph (*a*) or paragraph (*b*) of section 20 (1) above derived from an asset which is not lost or destroyed is applied in restoring the asset, then if the recipient so claims, that part of the capital sum shall not be treated as consideration for the disposal deemed to be effected on receipt of the capital sum but shall be deducted from any expenditure allowable under Chapter II below as a deduction in computing a gain on the subsequent disposal of the asset.

(4) If an asset is lost or destroyed and a capital sum received by way of compensation for the loss or destruction, or under a policy of insurance of the risk of the loss or destruction, is within one year of receipt, or such longer period as the inspector may allow, applied in acquiring an asset in replacement of the asset lost or destroyed the owner shall if he so claims be treated for the purposes of this Act—

(*a*) as if the consideration for the disposal of the old asset were (if otherwise of a greater amount) of such amount as would secure that on the disposal neither a gain nor a loss accrues to him, and

(*b*) as if the amount of the consideration for the acquisition of the new asset were reduced by the excess of the amount of the capital sum received by way of compensation or under the policy of insurance, together with any residual or scrap value, over the amount of the consideration which he is treated as receiving under paragraph (*a*) above.

(5) A claim shall not be made under subsection (4) above if part only of the capital sum is applied in acquiring the new asset but if all of that capital sum except for a part which is less than the amount of the gain (whether all chargeable gain or not) accruing on the disposal of the old asset is so applied, then the owner shall if he so claims be treated for the purposes of this Act—

(*a*) as if the amount of the gain so accruing were reduced to the amount of the said part (and, if not all chargeable gain, with a proportionate reduction in the amount of the chargeable gain), and

(*b*) as if the amount of the consideration for the acquisition of the new asset were reduced by the amount by which the gain is reduced under paragraph (*a*) of this subsection.

(6) Subsections (4) and (5) above have effect subject to paragraph 18 of Schedule 5 to this Act (application to gain which in consequence of that Schedule is not all chargeable gain).

(7) This section shall not apply in relation to a wasting asset.

General Note

This section provides (subs. (1)) that where a capital sum is received within para. (*a*), (*b*), (*c*) or (*d*) of s. 20 (1), and the asset concerned is not a wasting asset, there is no disposal on the receipt of the capital sum if the following conditions are fulfilled. First, the asset is not lost or destroyed. Secondly, the capital sum received is applied as in para. (*a*) or (*b*) of s. 21 (1) or is small as compared with the value of the asset (para. (*c*)). If subs. (1) applies, then all sums which would have been brought into account as consideration if the receipt of the capital sum had constituted a disposal of the asset, are deducted from any expenditure allowable as a deduction in computing a gain on the subsequent disposal of the asset. Subs. (1) applies only if the recipient of the capital sum so claims.

Subs. (2) qualifies subs. (1) in that if the capital sum received is greater than the allowable expenditure on the asset immediately before the receipt, paras. (*b*) and (*c*) of subs. (1) shall not apply. If the recipient so elects he may (para. (*b*)) deduct the allowable expenditure from the capital sum received in computing the gain chargeable on the disposal deemed by s. 20. In that case the allowable expenditure may not be taken into account on the occasion of a subsequent disposal of the asset.

Subs. (3) provides that when an asset is not lost or destroyed and part of the capital sum received within s. 20 (1) (*a*) or (*b*) is applied in restoring the asset, but the case is not within s. 21 (1) (*b*), the recipient may claim that the part of the capital sum received which is applied in the restoration shall be excluded from the consideration for the deemed disposal. However, that part is to be deducted from any expenditure allowable as a deduction in computing a gain on the subsequent disposal of the asset.

Subss. (4) and (5) apply in the case when the asset is lost or destroyed and the capital sum received by way of compensation is within one year (or such longer period as the inspector may allow) applied in acquiring an asset in replacement. In such a case, if the owner so claims, the old asset is treated as disposed of for a consideration which gives no gain and no loss on the disposal and the allowable cost of the replacement asset is reduced by the excess of the compensation received and any residual or scrap value of the old asset over the amount of consideration deemed to be received which gives no gain and no loss on the disposal of the old asset (subs. (4)).

If part only of the compensation payment is applied in replacing the old asset, a claim can only be made under subs. (4) if that part exceeds the cost of acquisition and improvement of the old asset. In such a case the balance is treated as a gain accruing on the disposal deemed by s. 20 (1) and the amount applied in the replacement is deducted from the allowable cost of the replacement asset (subs. (5)).

Para. 18 of Sched. 5 has effect where the old asset was held before April 6, 1965, to limit the exclusion of allowable expenditure under subs. (4) or (5) to the amount of chargeable gain (or a proportion thereof) avoided by a claim under the subsection.

Assets lost or destroyed, or whose value becomes negligible

22.—(1) Subject to the provisions of this Act and, in particular to section 137 below (options), the occasion of the entire loss, destruction, dissipation or extinction of an asset shall, for the purposes of this Act, constitute a disposal of the asset whether or not any capital sum by way of compensation or otherwise is received in respect of the destruction, dissipation or extinction of the asset.

(2) If, on a claim by the owner of an asset, the inspector is satisfied that the value of an asset has become negligible, he may allow the claim and thereupon this Act shall have effect as if the claimant had sold, and immediately re-acquired, the asset for a consideration of an amount equal to the value specified in the claim.

(3) For the purposes of subsections (1) and (2) above, a building and any permanent or semi-permanent structure in the nature of a building, may be regarded as an asset separate from the land on which it is situated, but where either of those subsections applies in accordance with this subsection, the person deemed to make the disposal of the building or structure shall be treated as if he had also sold, and immediately re-acquired, the site of the building or structure (including in the site any land occupied for purposes ancillary to the use of the building or structure) for a consideration equal to its market value at that time.

General Note

This section provides that the total destruction of an asset is to be treated as a disposal irrespective of whether a sum within s. 20 (1) is thereupon received, but without prejudice to any other express provision and in particular to the provisions relating to options, contained in s. 137.

Subs. (2) enables a taxpayer whose asset has deteriorated to a negligible value to "crystallise" his loss by agreeing a new value with the Inspector. Thus, for example, where a company has failed and its shares have become of negligible value it is not necessary to sell the shares in order to establish the loss.

Subs. (3) provides that for the purposes of subss. (1) and (2) a building may be regarded as a separate asset from its site, but if a claim is made under this subsection the taxpayer must take account of the value which the cleared site would possess.

Mortgages and charges

23.—(1) The conveyance or transfer by way of security of an asset or of an interest or right in or over it, or transfer of a subsisting interest or right by way of security in or over an asset (including a retransfer on redemption of the security), shall not be treated for the purposes of this Act as involving any acquisition or disposal of the asset.

(2) Where a person entitled to an asset by way of security or to the benefit of a charge or incumbrance on an asset deals with the asset for the purpose of enforcing or giving effect to the security, charge or incumbrance his dealings with it shall be treated for the purposes of this Act as if they were done through him as nominee by the person entitled to it subject to the security, charge or incumbrance; and this subsection shall apply to the dealings of any person appointed to enforce or give effect to the security, charge or incumbrance as receiver and manager or judicial factor as it applies to the dealings of the person entitled as aforesaid.

(3) An asset shall be treated as having been acquired free of any interest or right by way of security subsisting at the time of any acquisition of it, and as being disposed of free of any such interest or right subsisting at the time of the disposal; and where an asset is acquired subject to any such interest or right the full amount of the liability thereby assumed by the person acquiring the asset shall form part of the consideration for the acquisition and disposal in addition to any other consideration.

General Note

This section provides that any dealings with an asset by way of security for a mortgage or charge shall not be treated as acquisitions or disposals for the purposes of a charge to tax. Subs. (3) is in similar terms to those applied for the purposes of stamp duty on a conveyance by s. 57 of the Stamp Act 1891.

Hire-purchase

24. A hire-purchase or other transaction under which the use and enjoyment of an asset is obtained by a person for a period at the end of which the property in the asset will or may pass to that person shall be treated for the purposes of this Act, both in relation to that person and in relation to the person from whom he obtains the use and enjoyment of the asset, as if it amounted to an entire disposal of the asset to that person at the beginning of the period for which he obtains the use and enjoyment of the asset, but subject to such adjustments of tax, whether by way of repayment or discharge of tax or otherwise, as may be required where the period for which that person has the use and enjoyment of the asset terminates without the property in the asset passing to him.

GENERAL NOTE

This section treats a hire-purchase or similar transaction as an entire disposal from the outset subject to any necessary adjustments if the whole of the transaction does not proceed to completion.

Value shifting

25.—(1) Without prejudice to the generality of the provisions of this Act as to the transactions which are disposals of assets, any transaction which under the following subsections is to be treated as a disposal of an asset shall be so treated (with a corresponding acquisition of an interest in the asset) notwithstanding that there is no consideration and so far as, on the assumption that the parties to the transaction were at arm's length, the party making the disposal could have obtained consideration, or additional consideration, for the disposal the transaction shall be treated as not being at arm's length and the consideration so obtainable, or the additional consideration so obtainable added to the consideration actually passing, shall be treated as the market value of what is acquired.

(2) If a person having control of a company exercises his control so that value passes out of shares in the company owned by him or a person with whom he is connected, or out of rights over the company exercisable by him or by a person with whom he is connected, and passes into other shares in or rights over the company, that shall be a disposal of the shares or rights out of which the value passes by the person by whom they were owned or exercisable.

(3) A loss on the disposal of an asset shall not be an allowable loss to the extent to which it is attributable to value having passed out of other assets, being shares in or rights over a company which by virtue of the passing of value are treated as disposed of under subsection (2) above.

(4) If, after a transaction which results in the owner of land or of any other description of property becoming the lessee of the property there is any adjustment of the rights and liabilities under the lease, whether or not involving the grant of a new lease, which is as a whole favourable to the lessor, that shall be a disposal by the lessee of an interest in the property.

(5) If an asset is subject to any description of right or restriction the extinction or abrogation, in whole or in part, of the right or restriction by the person entitled to enforce it shall be a disposal by him of the right or restriction.

GENERAL NOTE

This section provides that where a transaction within subs. (2), (4) or (5) is not made for full consideration it shall be deemed to be made for a consideration equal to market value. Subs. (2) in particular provides that if a person, either by himself or with his associates (defined in s. 303, I.C.T.A. 1970), exercises control (defined in s. 302, I.C.T.A. 1970) of a company so that value passes out of his shares or those of a person with whom he is connected (see s. 63 of this Act) and passes into other shares, that constitutes a disposal of the shares for such consideration or additional consideration as the disponer could have obtained if the parties to the transaction had been at arm's length.

Subs. (3) prevents a capital gains tax avoidance device for the creation of artificial losses. An example of this device is as follows:

> X purchases all the issue share capital in A Co. for £900. A Co. purchases all the shares of one class in B Co. for £900 and obtains control of B Co. The remaining shares in B Co. are shares of a different class and are purchased by X for £100. A Co. exercises its control over B Co. so that value passes out of the shares owned by it and into the shares owned by X. After this A Co.'s shares in B Co. are worth £100 and X's shares are worth £900. No chargeable gain will arise to A Co. on this transaction under subs. (2).

If X now sells his shares in A Co. he will obtain at the most £100, assuming that A Co. owns no assets but the shares in B Co. The difference between £900 and £100 would, but for this section, be an allowable loss, but subs. (3) prevents relief for such a loss being given.

The phrase "exercises his control" in subs. (2) has been given a broad construction (so that control can be exercised both by positive acts and by omissions) in *Floor* v. *Davis* [1978] 3 W.L.R. 360.

Value shifting: further provisions

26.—(1) This section has effect as respects the disposal of an asset if a scheme has been effected or arrangements have been made (whether before or after the disposal) whereby—

(*a*) the value of the asset has been materially reduced, and

(*b*) a tax-free benefit has been or will be conferred—

(i) on the person making the disposal or a person with whom he is connected, or

(ii) subject to subsection (3) below, on any other person.

(2) For the purposes of subsection (1) (*b*) above a benefit is conferred on a person if he becomes entitled to any money or money's worth or the value of any asset in which he has an interest is increased or he is wholly or partly relieved from any liability to which he is subject; and a benefit is tax-free unless it is required, on the occasion on which it is conferred on the person in question, to be brought into account in computing his income, profits or gains for the purposes of income tax, capital gains tax or corporation tax.

(3) This section shall not apply by virtue of subsection (1) (*b*) (ii) above if it is shown that avoidance of tax was not the main purpose or one of the main purposes of the scheme or arrangements in question.

(4) Where this section has effect in relation to any disposal, any allowable loss or chargeable gain accruing on the disposal shall be calculated as if the consideration for the disposal were increased by such amount as appears to the inspector, or on appeal the Commissioners concerned, to be just and reasonable having regard to the scheme or arrangements and the tax-free benefit in question.

(5) Where—

(*a*) by virtue of subsection (4) above the consideration for the disposal of an asset has been treated as increased, and

(*b*) the benefit taken into account under subsection (1) (*b*) above was an increase in the value of another asset,

any allowable loss or chargeable gain accruing on the first disposal of the other asset after the increase in its value shall be calculated as if the consideration for that disposal were reduced by such amount as appears to the inspector, or on appeal the Commissioners concerned, to be just and reasonable having regard to the scheme or arrangements in question and the increase made in relation to the disposal mentioned in paragraph (*a*) above.

(6) References in this section to a disposal do not include references to any disposal falling within—

(*a*) section 44 (1) below (disposals between husband and wife), or

(*b*) section 49 (4) below (disposals by personal representatives to legatees), or

(*c*) section 273 (1) of the Taxes Act (disposals within a group of companies).

(7) In relation to the disposal by a company of an asset consisting of shares in another company the reference in subsection (1) (*a*) above to a reduction in the value of the asset does not include a reference to any reduction attributable to—

(*a*) the payment of a dividend by the second company at a time when it and the first company are members of the same group of companies within the meaning of section 272 of the Taxes Act, or

(*b*) the disposal of any asset by the second company at such a time, being a disposal falling within section 273 (1) of that Act.

(8) In relation to a case in which the disposal of an asset precedes its acquisition the reference in subsection (1) (*a*) above to a reduction shall be read as including a reference to an increase.

GENERAL NOTE

This section is an anti-avoidance measure to combat certain schemes designed to create artificial losses. These schemes have generally involved either a shift in value from an equitable interest which was a chargeable asset to one which was not, or the reduction in the value of a chargeable debt.

For the section to apply, a scheme must have been entered into or arrangements must have been made under which the value of an asset disposed of has been materially reduced and a tax-free benefit (defined in subs. (2)) has been conferred upon a person. It is irrelevant on whom the tax-free benefit is conferred save that if it is on some person other than the person making the disposal or a person connected with him, the defence provided for in subs. (3) is available.

The section counteracts the tax advantage obtained by the scheme not by taxing the person who obtains the tax-free benefit, but by modifying the allowable loss or chargeable gain made by the person disposing of the asset. The consideration received for the disposal of the asset is to be increased by such amount as is "just and reasonable" in the mind of either the Inspector or, on appeal, the Commissioners. Likewise on the disposal of an asset the value of which has been increased in consequence of the arrangements, the consideration received on its disposal is for capital gains tax purposes to be reduced, so far as is "just and reasonable." In most cases it can be anticipated that the increase and decrease in consideration will balance each other out.

Subs. (7) prevents the section from applying where, prior to the sale of shares in a liquidation of a subsidiary company there is a payment of a dividend out of that subsidiary company or a transfer of an asset out of it to another member of the group.

Time of disposal and acquisition where asset disposed of under contract

27.—(1) Where an asset is disposed of and acquired under a contract the time at which the disposal and acquisition is made is the time the contract is made (and not, if different, the time at which the asset is conveyed or transferred).

This subsection has effect subject to section 20 (2) above, and subsection (2) below.

(2) If the contract is conditional (and in particular if it is conditional on the exercise of an option) the time at which the disposal and acquisition is made is the time when the condition is satisfied.

GENERAL NOTE

This section is important as it lays down a general rule that for capital gains tax purposes a disposal occurs at the time of contract, unless the contract is conditional in which case the relevant time is the date upon which the condition is satisfied.

CHAPTER II

COMPUTATION

Chargeable gains

28.—(1) The amount of the gains accruing on the disposal of assets shall be computed in accordance with this Chapter, and subject to the other provisions of this Act.

(2) Every gain shall, except as otherwise expressly provided, be a chargeable gain.

(3) Schedule 5 to this Act (which restricts the amount of chargeable gains accruing on the disposal of assets owned on 6th April 1965) shall have effect.

General Note

This section provides that the amount of chargeable gains on a disposal shall be computed in accordance with the rules contained in Chap. II (ss. 28–43).

Subs. (2) provides that all gains are chargeable unless exempted, but the provisions of Sched. 5 apply to restrict chargeable gains accruing on the disposal of assets held by the disponer on April 6, 1965, to the amount of gain treated as accruing after that date.

Losses

29.—(1) Except as otherwise expressly provided, the amount of a loss accruing on a disposal of an asset shall be computed in the same way as the amount of a gain accruing on a disposal is computed.

(2) Except as otherwise expressly provided, all the provisions of this Act which distinguish gains which are chargeable gains from those which are not, or which make part of a gain a chargeable gain, and part not, shall apply also to distinguish losses which are allowable losses from those which are not, and to make part of a loss an allowable loss, and part not; and references in this Act to an allowable loss shall be construed accordingly.

(3) A loss accruing to a person in a year of assessment during no part of which he is resident or ordinarily resident in the United Kingdom shall not be an allowable loss for the purposes of this Act unless, under section 12 above (non-resident with U.K. branch or agency), he would be chargeable to capital gains tax in respect of a chargeable gain if there had been a gain instead of a loss on that occasion.

(4) In accordance with section 14 (1) above (foreign assets of person with foreign domicile), losses accruing on the disposal of assets situated outside the United Kingdom to an individual resident or ordinarily resident but not domiciled in the United Kingdom shall not be allowable losses.

(5) Except as provided by section 49 below (death), an allowable loss accruing in a year of assessment shall not be allowable as a deduction from chargeable gains accruing in any earlier year of assessment, and relief shall not be given under this Act more than once in respect of any loss or part of a loss, and shall not be given under this Act if and so far as relief has been or may be given in respect of it under the Income Tax Acts.

General Note

Subss. (1) and (2) provide that, except as otherwise provided, losses are to be computed on the same basis as gains.

Subs. (3) restricts the losses deductible by a non-resident to those incurred in respect of assets on the disposal of which a chargeable gain is, under s. 12 of this Act, capable of accruing.

Subs. (4) specifies that individuals to whom s. 14 (1) applies (liability only on remitted gains) cannot obtain any capital loss relief on the disposal of assets situate abroad.

Subs. (5) provides that losses cannot be used to offset gains obtained in earlier years except when they accrue in the year of the disponer's death. It also provides that no loss can be allowed more than once.

Computation of gains

Introductory

30. The following provisions of this Chapter, and Schedule 5 to this Act, shall have effect for computing for the purposes of this Act the amount of a gain accruing on the disposal of an asset.

General Note

The rules for computing gains are contained in ss. 31 to 43 of and Sched. 5 to this Act.

Consideration chargeable to tax on income

31.—(1) There shall be excluded from the consideration for a disposal of assets taken into account in the computation under this Chapter of the gain accruing on that disposal any money or money's worth charged to income tax as income of, or taken into account as a receipt in computing income or profits or gains or losses of, the person making the disposal for the purposes of the Income Tax Acts.

(2) Subsection (1) above shall not be taken as excluding from the consideration so taken into account any money or money's worth which is taken into account in the making of a balancing charge under the Capital Allowances Act 1968 (including the provisions of the Taxes Act which under that Act are to be treated as contained in the said Act of 1968).

(3) This section shall not preclude the taking into account in a computation under this Chapter, as consideration for the disposal of an asset, of the capitalised value of a rentcharge (as in a case where a rentcharge is exchanged for some other asset) or of the capitalised value of a ground annual or feu duty, or of a right of any other description to income or to payments in the nature of income over a period, or to a series of payments in the nature of income.

General Note

S. 31 excludes from the tax any consideration received on a disposal which falls to be included in a computation for income tax, subject to the two exceptions of amounts taken into account in computing balancing charges and capitalised income payments.

Expenditure: general

32.—(1) Except as otherwise expressly provided, the sums allowable as a deduction from the consideration in the computation under this Chapter of the gain accruing to a person on the disposal of an asset shall be restricted to—

(*a*) the amount or value of the consideration, in money or money's worth, given by him or on his behalf wholly and exclusively for the acquisition of the asset, together with the incidental costs to him of the acquisition or, if the asset was not acquired by him, any expenditure wholly and exclusively incurred by him in providing the asset,

(*b*) the amount of any expenditure wholly and exclusively incurred on the asset by him or on his behalf for the purpose of enhancing the value of the asset, being expenditure reflected in the state or nature of the asset at the time of the disposal, and any expenditure wholly and exclusively incurred by him in establishing, preserving or defending his title to, or to a right over, the asset,

(*c*) the incidental costs to him of making the disposal.

(2) For the purposes of this section and for the purposes of all other provisions of this Act the incidental costs to the person making the disposal of the acquisition of the asset or of its disposal shall consist of expenditure wholly and exclusively incurred by him for the purposes of the acquisition or, as the case may be, the disposal, being fees, commission or remuneration paid for the professional services of any surveyor or valuer, or auctioneer, or accountant, or agent or legal adviser and costs of transfer or conveyance (including stamp duty) together—

(*a*) in the case of the acquisition of an asset, with costs of advertising to find a seller, and

(*b*) in the case of a disposal, with costs of advertising to find a buyer and costs reasonably incurred in making any valuation or apportionment required for the purposes of the computation under this Chapter, including in particular expenses reasonably incurred in ascertaining market value where required by this Act.

(3) Except as provided by section 269 of the Taxes Act (companies: interest charged to capital), no payment of interest shall be allowable under this section.

(4) Any provision in this Act introducing the assumption that assets are sold and immediately re-acquired shall not imply that any expenditure is incurred as incidental to the sale or re-acquisition.

GENERAL NOTE

S. 32 describes the expenditure which can be allowed in computing chargeable gains. In *I.R.C.* v. *Richards' Executors* [1971] 1 W.L.R. 571 fees were paid to a solicitor for obtaining confirmation (the Scots equivalent of probate) of some shares being included in the estate and commission was paid to the solicitors upon the subsequent sale of the shares. It was held that the fees were "expenditure wholly and exclusively incurred by (the executors) as establishing (their) title" to the shares (subs. (1) (*b*)) and that the commission was within subs. (1) (*c*).

The phrase "consideration given wholly and exclusively for the acquisition of an asset" was considered in *Cleveleys Investment Trust Co.* v. *I.R.C.* [1975] S.T.C. 457, where it was held that in order to qualify under s. 32 (1) (*a*) the main object of incurring the expenditure (as opposed to an incidental or ancillary object) must be the acquisition of the asset.

A case on s. 32 (1) (*b*) was *Emmerson* v. *Computer Time International Ltd.* [1977] 1 W.L.R. 734, where it was argued by the taxpayer company that arrears of rent paid by it so that it should have a lease which it could assign with the landlord's consent was enhancement expenditure. This argument failed, the court holding that the expenditure was incurred by the tenant in discharging its obligations under the lease and could not qualify under s. 32 (1) (*b*).

Exclusion of expenditure by reference to tax on income

33.—(1) There shall be excluded from the sums allowable under section 32 above as a deduction in the computation under this Chapter any expenditure allowable as a deduction in computing the profits or gains or losses of a trade, profession or vocation for the purposes of income tax or allowable as a deduction in computing any other income or profits or gains or losses for the purposes of the Income Tax Acts and any expenditure which, although not so allowable as a deduction in computing any losses, would be so allowable but for an insufficiency of income or profits or gains; and this subsection applies irrespective of whether effect is or would be given to the deduction in computing the amount of tax chargeable or by discharge or repayment of tax or in any other way.

(2) Without prejudice to the provisions of subsection (1) above there shall be excluded from the sums allowable under section 32 above as a

deduction in the computation under this Chapter any expenditure which, if the assets, or all the assets to which the computation relates, were, and had at all times been, held or used as part of the fixed capital of a trade the profits or gains of which were (irrespective of whether the person making the disposal is a company or not) chargeable to income tax would be allowable as a deduction in computing the profits or gains or losses of the trade for the purposes of income tax.

GENERAL NOTE

S. 33 describes the expenditure which cannot be allowed when computing gains or losses for the purpose of the charge. Expenditure which qualifies as a trading expense for income tax purposes is excluded, as is (subs. (2)) any expenditure which would so qualify if the assets disposed of had been part of the fixed capital of a trade whose profits were chargeable to income tax. Thus, for example, any expenditure incurred in the repair of an asset as opposed to its improvement would not be allowed.

Restriction of losses by reference to capital allowances and renewals allowances

34.—(1) Section 33 above shall not require the exclusion from the sums allowable as a deduction in the computation under this Chapter of any expenditure as being expenditure in respect of which a capital allowance or renewals allowance is made, but the amount of any losses accruing on the disposal of an asset shall be restricted by reference to capital allowances and renewals allowances as follows.

(2) In the computation under this Chapter of the amount of a loss accruing to the person making the disposal, there shall be excluded from the sums allowable as a deduction any expenditure to the extent to which any capital allowance or renewals allowance has been or may be made in respect of it.

(3) If the person making the disposal acquired the asset—

(*a*) by a transfer by way of sale in relation to which an election under paragraph 4 of Schedule 7 to the Capital Allowances Act 1968 was made, or

(*b*) by a transfer to which section 35 (2) to (4) or section 48 (2) of that Act applies,

(being enactments under which a transfer is treated for the purposes of capital allowances as being made at written down value), the preceding provisions of this section shall apply as if any capital allowance made to the transferor in respect of the asset had (except so far as any loss to the transferor was restricted under those provisions) been made to the person making the disposal (that is the transferee); and where the transferor acquired the asset by such a transfer, capital allowances which by virtue of this subsection can be taken into account in relation to the transferor shall also be taken into account in relation to the transferee (that is the person making the disposal), and so on for any series of transfers before the disposal.

(4) In this section " capital allowance " means—

(*a*) any allowance under the Capital Allowances Act 1968 (including the provisions of the Taxes Act which under that Act are to be treated as contained in the said Act of 1968) or under Chapter I of Part III of the Finance Act 1971, other than an allowance under section 79 (1) of the Taxes Act (relief for cost of maintenance of agricultural land),

(*b*) any relief given under section 76 of the Taxes Act (expenditure on sea walls), and

(*c*) any deduction in computing profits or gains allowable under section 141 of the Taxes Act (cemeteries).

(5) In this section " renewals allowance " means a deduction allowable in computing the profits or gains of a trade, profession or vocation for the purpose of income tax by reference to the cost of acquiring an asset for the purposes of the trade, profession or vocation in replacement of another asset, and for the purposes of this Chapter a renewals allowance shall be regarded as a deduction allowable in respect of the expenditure incurred on the asset which is being replaced.

(6) The amount of capital allowances to be taken into account under this section in relation to a disposal include any allowances falling to be made by reference to the event which is the disposal, and there shall be deducted from the amount of the allowances the amount of any balancing charge to which effect has been or is to be given by reference to the event which is the disposal, or any earlier event, and of any balancing charge to which effect might have been so given but for the making of an election under section 40 of the Capital Allowances Act 1968 (option in case of replacement of machinery or plant).

(7) Where the disposal is of machinery or plant in relation to expenditure on which allowances or charges have been made under Chapter I of Part III of the Finance Act 1971, and neither paragraph 5 (assets used partly for trade purposes and partly for other purposes) nor paragraph 6 (wear and tear subsidies) of Schedule 8 to that Act applies, the capital allowances to be taken into account under this section are to be regarded as equal to the difference between the capital expenditure incurred, or treated as incurred, under that Chapter on the provision of the machinery or plant by the person making the disposal and the disposal value required to be brought into account in respect of the machinery or plant.

General Note

This section contains special provisions where capital allowances have been granted on the asset disposed of.

First, expenditure on which capital allowances or renewals allowances (defined in subss. (4) and (5)) have been made is not disallowed under s. 33.

Secondly, capital losses arising on the disposal of assets in respect of which such allowances have been made are restricted. No capital loss is allowed to the extent of the net amount of such allowances made in respect of the asset disposed of. That net amount is ascertained after taking into account any allowances or charges which fall to be made by reference to the event which is the disposal (subs. (6)).

Where an allowance or charge has been made in respect of the asset under Chap. I, Pt. III, F.A. 1971, subs. (7) sets out the quantum of allowances which are to be taken into account under this section.

Part disposals

35.—(1) Where a person disposes of an interest or right in or over an asset, and generally wherever on the disposal of an asset any description of property derived from that asset remains undisposed of, the sums which under paragraphs (*a*) and (*b*) of section 32 (1) above are attributable to the asset shall, both for the purposes of the computation under this chapter of the gain accruing on the disposal and for the purpose of applying this Chapter in relation to the property which remains undisposed of, be apportioned.

(2) The apportionment shall be made by reference—

(*a*) to the amount or value of the consideration for the disposal on the one hand (call that amount or value A), and

(*b*) to the market value of the property which remains undisposed of on the other hand (call that market value B), and accordingly the fraction of the said sums allowable as a deduction in computing under this Chapter the amount of the gain accruing on the disposal shall be $\frac{A}{A+B}$, and the remainder shall be attributed to the property which remains undisposed of.

(3) Any apportionment to be made in pursuance of this section shall be made before operating the provisions of section 34 above and if, after a part disposal, there is a subsequent disposal of an asset the capital allowances or renewals allowances to be taken into account in pursuance of that section in relation to the subsequent disposal shall, subject to subsection (4) below, be those referable to the sums which under paragraphs (*a*) and (*b*) of section 32 (1) above are attributable to the asset whether before or after the part disposal, but those allowances shall be reduced by the amount (if any) by which the loss on the earlier disposal was restricted under the provisions of section 34 above.

(4) This section shall not be taken as requiring the apportionment of any expenditure which, on the facts, is wholly attributable to what is disposed of, or wholly attributable to what remains undisposed of.

(5) It is hereby declared that this section, and all other provisions for apportioning on a part disposal expenditure which is deductible in computing a gain, are to be operated before the operation of, and without regard to—

(*a*) section 44 (1) below (disposals between husband and wife),

(*b*) sections 115 and 121 below (replacement of business assets), but without prejudice to the provisions of subsection (8) of the said section 115,

(*c*) section 273 (1) of the Taxes Act (transfers within a group of companies), or

(*d*) any other enactment making an adjustment to secure that neither a gain nor a loss occurs on a disposal.

GENERAL NOTE

This section deals with part disposals. A part disposal occurs whenever on the disposal of an asset any description of property derived from the asset remains undisposed of.

On a part disposal, the allowable cost of the asset under s. 32 (1) (*a*) and (*b*) is apportioned between the part disposed of and the part retained by reference to the value of those parts immediately after the part disposal. This is the $\frac{A}{A+B}$ formula provided by subs. (2).

Subs. (3) deals with the interaction of ss. 34 and 35.

Subs. (4) provides that where, on the facts, expenditure is wholly attributable to the part disposed of or the part retained, such attribution is allowed in precedence to the apportionment under this section.

Subs. (5) provides that this measure is to be applied (so as to reduce the expenditure admissible on the eventual disposal of the asset retained) before applying the exemption relating to transfer between husband and wife and within groups of companies, before applying the "roll-over" procedure, and generally before any other provision which has the effect of securing that there is neither a chargeable gain nor an allowable loss.

Assets derived from other assets

36. If and so far as, in a case where assets have been merged or divided or have changed their nature or rights or interests in or over assets have been created or extinguished, the value of an asset is derived from any other asset in the same ownership, an appropriate proportion of the sums allowable as a deduction in a computation under this Chapter in respect of the other asset under paragraphs (*a*) and (*b*) of section 32 (1) above shall, both for the purpose of the computation of a gain accruing on the disposal of the first-mentioned asset and, if the other asset remains in existence, on a disposal of that other asset, be attributed to the first-mentioned asset.

GENERAL NOTE

S. 36 makes provision for assets which are derived from other assets. The allowable cost of the original asset is to be apportioned " appropriately " between the original asset (if it remains in existence) and the asset which is derived from it.

Wasting assets

37.—(1) In this Chapter " wasting asset " means an asset with a predictable life not exceeding fifty years but so that—

(*a*) freehold land shall not be a wasting asset whatever its nature, and whatever the nature of the buildings or works on it,

(*b*) " life ", in relation to any tangible movable property, means useful life, having regard to the purpose for which the tangible assets were acquired or provided by the person making the disposal,

(*c*) plant and machinery shall in every case be regarded as having a predictable life of less than fifty years, and in estimating that life it shall be assumed that its life will end when it is finally put out of use as being unfit for further use, and that it is going to be used in the normal manner and to the normal extent and is going to be so used throughout its life as so estimated,

(*d*) a life interest in settled property shall not be a wasting asset until the predictable expectation of life of the life tenant is fifty years or less, and the predictable life of life interests in settled property and of annuities shall be ascertained from actuarial tables approved by the Board.

(2) In this Chapter " the residual or scrap value ", in relation to a wasting asset, means the predictable value, if any, which the wasting asset will have at the end of its predictable life as estimated in accordance with this section.

(3) The question what is the predictable life of an asset, and the question what is its predictable residual or scrap value at the end of that life, if any, shall, so far as those questions are not immediately answered by the nature of the asset, be taken, in relation to any disposal of the asset, as they were known or ascertainable at the time when the asset was acquired or provided by the person making the disposal.

GENERAL NOTE

S. 37 provides a definition of the term " wasting asset."

Wasting assets: straightline restriction of allowable expenditure

38.—(1) In the computation under this Chapter of the gain accruing on the disposal of a fasting asset it shall be assumed—

(*a*) that any expenditure attributable to the asset under section 32 (1) (*a*) above after deducting the residual or scrap value, if any, of the asset, is written off at a uniform rate from its full amount at the time when the asset is acquired or provided to nothing at the end of its life, and

(*b*) that any expenditure attributable to the asset under section 32 (1) (*b*) above is written off from the full amount of that expenditure at the time when that expenditure is first reflected in the state or nature of the asset to nothing at the end of its life, so that an equal daily amount is written off day by day.

(2) Thus, calling the predictable life of a wasting asset at the time when it was acquired or provided by a person making the disposal L, the period from that time to the time of disposal T (1), and, in relation to any expenditure attributable to the asset under section 2 (1) (*b*) above, the period from the time when that expenditure is first reflected in the state or nature of the asset to the said time of disposal T (2), there shall be excluded from the computation under this Chapter—

(*a*) out of the expenditure attributable to the asset under section 32 (1) (*a*) above a fraction $\frac{T (1)}{L}$ of an amount equal to the amount of that expenditure minus the residual or scrap value, if any, of the asset, and

(*b*) out of the expenditure attributable to the asset under section 32 (1) (*b*) above a fraction $\frac{T (2)}{L - (T (1) - T (2))}$ of the amount of the expenditure.

(3) If any expenditure attributable to the asset under section 32 (1) (*b*) above creates or increases a residual or scrap value of the asset, the provisions of subsection (1) (*a*) above shall be applied so as to take that into account.

General Note

S. 38 prescribes the rules whereby the initial cost and allowable enhancement expenditure is written off at a uniform rate for the purposes of the charge. This has the effect of reducing the amount of an allowable loss or enhancing a chargeable gain. Short leases are specially dealt with in Sched. 3.

Wasting assets qualifying for capital allowances

39.—(1) Section 38 above shall not apply in relation to a disposal of an asset—

(*a*) which, from the beginning of the period of ownership of the person making the disposal to the time when the disposal is made, is used and used solely for the purposes of a trade, profession or vocation and in respect of which that person has claimed or could have claimed any capital allowance in respect of any expenditure attributable to the asset under paragraph (*a*) or paragraph (*b*) of section 32 (1) above, or

(*b*) on which the person making the disposal has incurred any expenditure which has otherwise qualified in full for any capital allowance.

(2) In the case of the disposal of an asset which, in the period of ownership of the person making the disposal, has been used partly for the purposes of a trade, profession or vocation and partly for other purposes, or has been used for the purposes of a trade, profession or vocation for part of that period, or which has otherwise qualified in part only for capital allowances—

(*a*) the consideration for the disposal, and any expenditure attributable to the asset by paragraph (*a*) or paragraph (*b*) of section 32 (1) above shall be apportioned by reference to the extent to which that expenditure qualified for capital allowances, and

(*b*) the computation under this Chapter shall be made separately in relation to the apportioned parts of the expenditure and consideration, and

(*c*) section 38 above shall not apply for the purposes of the computation in relation to the part of the consideration apportioned to use for the purposes of the trade, profession or vocation, or to the expenditure qualifying for capital allowances, and

(*d*) if an apportionment of the consideration for the disposal has been made for the purposes of making any capital allowance to the person making the disposal or for the purpose of making any balancing charge on him, that apportionment shall be employed for the purposes of this section, and

(*e*) subject to paragraph (*d*) above, the consideration for the disposal shall be apportioned for the purposes of this section in the same proportions as the expenditure attributable to the asset is apportioned under paragraph (*a*) above.

GENERAL NOTE

S. 39 provides that the disposal of assets qualifying for capital allowances and used solely for the purposes of a trade, profession or vocation, shall be exempted from the application of the provisions of s. 38. Subs. (2) provides for apportionments in cases where the user of the asset has in part qualified under subs. (1) and in part not so qualified.

Consideration due after time of disposal

40.—(1) If the consideration, or part of the consideration, taken into account in the computation under this Chapter is payable by instalments over a period beginning not earlier than the time when the disposal is made, being a period exceeding eighteen months, then, if the person making the disposal satisfies the Board that he would otherwise suffer undue hardship, the tax on a chargeable gain accruing on the disposal may, at his option, be paid by such instalments as the Board may allow over a period not exceeding eight years and ending not later than the time at which the last of the first-mentioned instalments is payable.

(2) In the computation under this Chapter consideration for the disposal shall be brought into account without any discount for postponement of the right to receive any part of it and, in the first instance, without regard to a risk of any part of the consideration being irrecoverable or to the right to receive any part of the consideration being contingent; and if any part of the consideration so brought into account is subsequently shown to the satisfaction of the inspector to be irrecoverable, such adjustment, whether by way of discharge or repayment of tax or otherwise, shall be made as is required in consequence.

GENERAL NOTE

This section deals with consideration due after the time of a disposal.

Subs. (2) provides the basic rule, which is that the disposal is complete at the time it is effected and, in the first instance, the whole of the consideration is to be taken into account at that time without any discount for the postponement of the right to receive any part of it. Also, no discount is allowed for the risk of any part of the consideration being irrevocable or for the right to receive any part of it being contingent. A subsequent adjustment may be allowed if the inspector is satisfied that in fact any part of the consideration is irrecoverable.

Subs. (1) gives a discretion to the Board to allow payment of tax by instalments over a period not exceeding eight years in cases where (a) the consideration is due by instalments over a period of more than 18 months, and (b) the taxpayer satisfies the Board that he would suffer undue hardship by having to pay the tax immediately in the normal way.

For a consideration of subs. (2), see *Randall* v. *Plumb* [1975] 1 W.L.R. 633 and *Marren* v. *Ingles* [1979] S.T.C. 58.

Contingent liabilities

41.—(1) In the first instance no allowance shall be made in the computation under this Chapter—

(*a*) in the case of a disposal by way of assigning a lease of land or other property, for any liability remaining with, or assumed by, the person making the disposal by way of assigning the lease which is contingent on a default in respect of liabilities thereby or subsequently assumed by the assignee under the terms and conditions of the lease,

(*b*) for any contingent liability of the person making the disposal in respect of any covenant for quiet enjoyment or other obligation assumed as vendor of land, or of any estate or interest in land, or as a lessor,

(*c*) for any contingent liability in respect of a warranty or representation made on a disposal by way of sale or lease of any property other than land.

(2) If it is subsequently shown to the satisfaction of the inspector that any such contingent liability has become enforceable, and is being or has been enforced, such adjustment, whether by way of discharge or repayment of tax or otherwise, shall be made as is required in consequence.

General Note

This section provides that no allowance is to be made in the first instance in computing a chargeable gain for contingent liabilities of the kinds mentioned in subs. (1) assumed by a vendor or lessor. If any such contingent liability subsequently becomes enforceable, provision is made in subs. (2) for a retrospective adjustment of the tax liability.

In *Randall* v. *Plumb* [1975] 1 W.L.R. 633, it was held that contingent liabilities assumed by a vendor or lessor which are not of the types specified in subs. (1) are to be taken account of, as a matter of valuation, in arriving at the consideration for the disposal concerned.

Expenditure reimbursed out of public money

42. There shall be excluded from the computation under this Chapter any expenditure which has been or is to be met directly or indirectly by the Crown or by any Government, public or local authority whether in the United Kingdom or elsewhere.

General Note

S. 42 excludes from the computation any expenditure met by the Crown or any Government or any public or local authority in the U.K. or elsewhere.

Supplemental

43.—(1) No deduction shall be allowable in a computation under this Chapter more than once from any sum or from more than one sum.

(2) References in this Chapter to sums into account as receipts or as expenditure in computing profits or gains or losses for the purposes of income tax shall include references to sums which would be so taken into account but for the fact that any profits or gains of a trade, profession, employment or vocation are not chargeable to income tax or that losses are not allowable for those purposes.

(3) In this Chapter references to income or profits charged or chargeable to tax include references to income or profits taxed or as the case may be taxable by deduction at source.

(4) For the purposes of any computation under this Chapter any necessary apportionments shall be made of any consideration or of any

expenditure and the method of apportionment adopted shall, subject to the express provisions of this Chapter, be such method as appears to the inspector or on appeal the Commissioners concerned to be just and reasonable.

(5) In this Chapter " capital allowance " and " renewals allowance " have the meanings given by subsections (4) and (5) of section 34 above.

General Note

S. 43 contains supplementary provisions.

Part III

Persons and Trusts

Married persons

Husband and wife

44.—(1) If, in any year of assessment, and in the case of a woman who in that year of assessment is a married woman living with her husband, the man disposes of an asset to the wife, or the wife disposes of an asset to the man, both shall be treated as if the asset was acquired from the one making the disposal for a consideration of such amount as would secure that on the disposal neither a gain nor a loss would accrue to the one making the disposal.

(2) This section shall not apply—

(*a*) if until the disposal the asset formed part of trading stock of a trade carried on by the one making the disposal, or if the asset is acquired as trading stock for the purposes of a trade carried on by the one acquiring the asset, or

(*b*) if the disposal is by way of donatio mortis causa,

but this section shall have effect notwithstanding the provisions of section 62 (transactions between connected persons) or section 122 (appropriations to and from stock in trade) below, or of any other provisions of this Act fixing the amount of the consideration deemed to be given on a disposal or acquisition.

General Note

This section provides that disposals between a husband and wife who are living together (within the construction provided by s. 42, I.C.T.A. 1970—see s. 155 (2) of this Act) are deemed to be for a consideration which will give the disponer no gain and no loss, except in the case of assets which have been the trading stock of the disponer or will become part of the stock-in-trade of the acquiring spouse or if the assets are disposed of by way of *donatio mortis causa.*

Tax on married woman's gains

45.—(1) Subject to this section, the amount of capital gains tax on chargeable gains accruing to a married woman in—

(*a*) a year of assessment, or

(*b*) any part of a year of assessment, being a part beginning with 6th April,

during which she is a married woman living with her husband shall be assessed and charged on the husband and not otherwise but this subsection shall not affect the amount of capital gains tax chargeable on a man apart from this subsection nor result in the additional amount of capital gains tax charged on a man by virtue of this subsection being different from the amount which would otherwise have remained chargeable on the married woman.

(2) Subsection (1) above shall not apply in relation to a husband and wife in any year of assessment if, before 6th July in the year next following that year of assessment, an application is made by either the husband or wife, and such an application duly made shall have effect not only as respects the year of assessment for which it is made but also for any subsequent year of assessment:

Provided that the applicant may give, for any subsequent year of assessment, a notice to withdraw that application and where such a notice is given the application shall not have effect with respect to the year for which the notice is given or any subsequent year.

A notice of withdrawal under this proviso shall not be valid unless it is given within the period for making, for the year for which the notice is given, an application similar to that to which the notice relates.

(3) Returns under section 8 or 42 (5) of the Taxes Management Act 1970 as respects chargeable gains accruing to a married woman may be required either from her or, if her husband is liable under subsection (1) above, from him.

(4) Section 40 (collection from wife of tax assessed on husband attributable to her income) and section 41 (right of husband to disclaim liability for tax on deceased wife's income) of the Taxes Act shall apply with any necessary modifications in relation to capital gains tax as they apply in relation to income tax.

(5) An application or notice of withdrawal under this section shall be in such form and made in such manner as may be prescribed by the Board.

General Note

This section provides (subs. (1)) that, except in the year of assessment in which she marries and any year in which she is not living with her husband, a married woman's chargeable gains are to be assessed on her husband. No adjustment in the amount of tax chargeable (as compared with the liability which would have arisen had the woman been unmarried) is caused by this procedure.

Subs. (1) does not apply if either the husband or the wife make an application under subs. (2) within the time limit provided therein and in the form and manner prescribed by the Board (subs. (5)).

Subss. (3) and (4) are administrative provisions dealing with returns and collection of tax.

Trustees, nominees and personal representatives

Nominees and bare trustees

46.—(1) In relation to assets held by a person as nominee for another person, or as trustee for another person absolutely entitled as against the trustee, or for any person who would be so entitled but for being an infant or other person under disability (or for two or more persons who are or would be jointly so entitled), this Act shall apply as if the property were vested in, and the acts of the nominee or trustee in relation to the assets were the acts of, the person or persons for whom he is the nominee or trustee (acquisitions from or disposals to him by that person or persons being disregarded accordingly).

(2) It is hereby declared that references in this Act to any asset held by a person as trustee for another person absolutely entitled as against the trustee are references to a case where that other person has the exclusive right, subject only to satisfying any outstanding charge, lien or other right of the trustees to resort to the asset for payment of duty, taxes, costs or other outgoings, to direct how that asset shall be dealt with.

General Note

This section provides that where a person holds assets as nominee for another person or as trustee for another person absolutely entitled as against the trustee, then for capital gains tax purposes the assets are treated as vested in the person in whom the beneficial ownership resides.

The provision also applies in relation to assets held by a trustee for a person who would be absolutely entitled as against the trustee but for being an infant or other person under disability. This provision has been construed as not applying to assets held by a trustee for infants contingently on their attaining 21 or marrying under that age: *Tomlinson* v. *Glyns Executor and Trustee Co.* [1969] 3 W.L.R. 310. In such a case, therefore, the assets are treated as in the ownership of the trustee. Where two or more persons are jointly absolutely entitled as against the trustee to assets held by the trustee, the assets are treated as belonging to the beneficiaries in the share in which they are jointly so entitled. In *Kidson* v. *Macdonald* [1974] 2 W.L.R. 566, it was held that the expression " jointly so entitled " does not import the technical considerations of joint tenancies but includes all situations (*e.g.* tenancies in common) where to or more persons are between them absolutely entitled as against the trustee.

In *Booth* v. *Ellard* [1978] 1 W.L.R. 927, it was held that the interests of persons jointly absolutely entitled as against the trustee in the property held by the trustee must be concurrent, not successive, and qualitatively the same (*i.e.* they should have the same rights as each other in the property *pro-rata* to the shares in the property to which they are entitled). See also: *Cochrane* v. *I.R.C.* [1974] S.T.C. 335, and *Crowe* v. *Appleby* [1975] 1 W.L.R. 1539.

Subs. (2) elaborates the meaning of the expression " absolutely entitled as against the trustee." In *Stephenson* v. *Barclays Bank Trust Co. Ltd.* [1975] 1 W.L.R. 882, it was held that the phrase " charge, lien or other right of the trustees " referred to the trustees' personal right of indemnity as against the trust funds and was not apt to cover another beneficial interest arising under the same instrument.

Expenses in administration of estates and trusts

47.—(1) In the case of a gain accruing to a person on the disposal of, or of a right or interest in or over, an asset to which he became absolutely entitled as legatee or as against the trustees of settled property—

(*a*) any expenditure within section 32 (2) above incurred by him in relation to the transfer of the asset to him by the personal representatives or trustees, and

(*b*) any such expenditure incurred in relation to the transfer of the asset by the personal representatives or trustees,

shall be allowable as a deduction in the computation under Chapter II of Part II above of the gain accruing to that person on the disposal.

(2) In this Act, unless the context otherwise requires, " legatee " includes any person taking under a testamentary disposition or on an intestacy or partial intestacy, whether he takes beneficially or as trustee, and a person taking under a donatio mortis causa shall be treated (except for the purposes of section 49 below (death)) as a legatee and his acquisition as made at the time of the donor's death.

(3) For the purposes of the definition of " legatee " above, and of any reference in this Act to a person acquiring an asset " as legatee ", property taken under a testamentary disposition or on an intestacy or partial intestacy includes any asset appropriated by the personal representatives in or towards satisfaction of a pecuniary legacy or any other interest or share in the property devolving under the disposition or intestacy.

General Note

This section deals with the case where an asset which a person acquired either as legatee or by becoming absolutely entitled as against trustees is disposed of by him.

In the computation arising by reason of that disposal, incidental expenditure (within s. 32 (2)) incurred in relation to the transfer of the asset to the disponer from the personal representatives or trustees is deductible whether that expenditure was incurred by the disponer or by the personal representatives or trustees.

Subss. (2) and (3) explains what is meant by "legatee." The term includes a person taking on an intestacy. It is also provided that a person taking under a *donatio mortis causa* takes as a legatee and his acquisition is treated as taking place at the time of the donor's death.

Liability for tax

48.—(1) Capital gains tax chargeable in respect of chargeable gains accruing to the trustees of a settlement or capital gains tax due from the personal representatives of a deceased person may be assessed and charged on and in the name of any one or more of those trustees or personal representatives, but where an assessment is made in pursuance of this subsection otherwise than on all the trustee or all the personal representatives the persons assessed shall not include a person who is not resident or ordinarily resident in the United Kingdom.

(2) Subject to section 46 above, chargeable gains accruing to the trustees of a settlement or to the personal representatives of a deceased person, and capital gains tax chargeable on or in the name of such trustees or personal representatives, shall not be regarded for the purposes of this Act as accruing to, or chargeable on, any other person, nor shall any trustee or personal representative be regarded for the purposes of this Act as an individual.

General Note

This section imposes liability to pay the capital gains tax chargeable on disposals of assets comprised in settlements and the estates of deceased persons upon any one or more of the trustees and personal representatives, respectively, in their capacities as trustees and personal representatives and not as individuals.

Death

Death: general provisions

49.—(1) For the purposes of this Act the assets of which a deceased person was competent to dispose—

(*a*) shall be deemed to be acquired on his death by the personal representatives or other person on whom they devolve for a consideration equal to their market value at the date of the death, but

(*b*) shall not be deemed to be disposed of by him on his death (whether or not they were the subject of a testamentary disposition).

(2) Allowable losses sustained by an individual in the year of assessment in which he dies may, so far as they cannot be deducted from chargeable gains accruing in that year, be deducted from chargeable gains accruing to the deceased in the three years of assessment preceding the year of assessment in which the death occurs, taking chargeable gains accruing in a later year before those accruing in an earlier year.

(3) In relation to property forming part of the estate of a deceased person the personal representatives shall for the purposes of this Act be treated as being a single and continuing body of persons (distinct from the persons who may from time to time be the personal representatives), and that body shall be treated as having the deceased's residence, ordinary residence, and domicile at the date of death.

(4) On a person acquiring any asset as legatee (as defined in section 47 above)—

(*a*) no chargeable gain shall accrue to the personal representatives, and

(*b*) the legatee shall be treated as if the personal representatives' acquisition of the asset had been his acquisition of it.

(5) Notwithstanding section 19 (3) above (gifts) no chargeable gain shall accrue to any person on his making a disposal by way of donatio mortis causa.

(6) Subject to subsections (7) and (8) below, where within the period of two years after a person's death any of the dispositions (whether effected by will, under the law relating to intestacy or otherwise) of the property of which he was competent to dispose are varied, or the benefit conferred by any of those dispositions is disclaimed, by an instrument in writing made by the persons or any of the persons who benefit or would benefit under the dispositions—

(*a*) the variation or disclaimer shall not constitute a disposal for the purposes of this Act, and

(*b*) this section shall apply as if the variation had been effected by the deceased or, as the case may be, the disclaimed benefit had never been conferred.

(7) Subsection (6) above does not apply to a variation unless the person or persons making the instrument so elect by written notice given to the Board within six months after the date of the instrument or such longer time as the Board may allow.

(8) Subsection (6) above does not apply to a variation or disclaimer made for any consideration in money or money's worth other than consideration consisting of the making of a variation or disclaimer in respect of another of the dispositions.

(9) Subsection (6) above applies whether or not the administration of the estate is complete or the property has been distributed in accordance with the original dispositions.

(10) In this section references to assets of which a deceased person was competent to dispose are references to assets of the deceased which (otherwise than in right of a power of appointment or of the testamentary power conferred by statute to dispose of entailed interests) he could, if of full age and capacity, have disposed of by his will, assuming that all the assets were situated in England and, if he was not domiciled in the United Kingdom, that he was domiciled in England, and include references to his severable share in any assets to which, immediately before his death, he was beneficially entitled as a joint tenant.

General Note

Subs. (1) provides that the devolution of assets on death is deemed not to be a disposal (subs. (1) (*b*)). Further, the deceased's assets are deemed to be acquired on his death by the personal representatives or other person on whom they devolve for their then market value (subs. (1) (a)). Thus any increase in the value of an asset held until death is exempt from capital gains tax.

Subs. (2) provides for a form of terminal loss relief. Any surplus losses for the year of assessment in which the deceased dies may be carried back and set off against the chargeable gains of the three preceding years of assessment, taking the gains of later years before those of earlier years.

Subs. (3) treats personal representatives as a continuing body of persons having the same residence, ordinary residence and domicile as the deceased had at the date of his death.

Subs. (4) has the effect of exempting personal representatives from capital gains tax in respect of any assets which they distribute to a legatee, but the legatee (for the purpose of any subsequent disposal by him) is treated as having acquired the asset at the time and for the consideration for which the personal representatives acquired it. "Legatee" is defined by s. 47 (2) to include a person who takes either beneficially or as a trustee. No chargeable gain is to accrue to any person on his making a disposal by way of *donatio mortis causa* (subs. (5)).

Subs. (6) is couched in general terms and applies to any re-arrangement of beneficial interests arising on the death of a deceased which are effected within two years of the death by a deed or other instrument, commonly known as a family arrangement. It brings the exemption into line with that given for capital transfer tax purposes by s. 68 of the Finance Act 1978. The exemption operates if:

(i) within two years after a death;

(ii) there is a variation of the dispositions of the property of which the deceased was competent to dispose or a disclaimer of a benefit conferred by such a disposition;

(iii) by an instrument in writing (not necessarily a "deed of family arrangement" or similar instrument);

(iv) made by any or all of the beneficiaries or potential beneficiaries of the dispositions varied.

The effect is that the variation or disclaimer is not a disposal but instead it is treated as if the deceased had made the variation or not conferred the benefit disclaimed.

Subs. (7) provides that to obtain the benefit of this exemption all the parties to the instrument must so elect within six months of its date or such longer time as allowed by the Board. This election must be unanimous otherwise the variation or disclaimer will be a disposal. It is made clear that an arrangement involving consideration other than the redistribution of the property disposed of by the deceased will not qualify for the exemption (subs. (8)). However, it does not matter that any of the parties to the variation have prior to the variation received a benefit from the property (subs. (9)). The same cannot be true of disclaimers in that under the general law the taking of a benefit prevents a disclaimer.

The definition in subs. (10) of "competent to dispose" resembles that contained in s. 22 (2) (*a*) of the Finance Act 1894, which defined the term for the purposes of estate duty, but is different in that it excludes property over which the deceased had a general power of appointment and includes property of which the deceased had been a joint tenant. Subs. (1), the effect of which is explained above, deals with assets of which the deceased was "competent to dispose."

Death: application of law in Scotland

50.—(1) The provisions of this Act, so far as relating to the consequences of the death of an heir of entail in possession of any property in Scotland subject to an entail, whether sui juris or not, or of a proper liferenter of any property, shall have effect subject to the provisions of this section.

(2) For the purposes of this Act, on the death of any such heir or liferenter the heir of entail next entitled to the entailed property under the entail or, as the case may be, the person (if any) who, on the death of the liferenter, becomes entitled to possession of the property as fiar shall be deemed to have acquired all the assets forming part of the property at the date of the deceased's death for a consideration equal to their market value at that date.

General Note

S. 50 contains provisions similar to those of s. 49, relating to the application to the law of Scotland of liability to tax on death.

Settlements

Meaning of "settled property"

51. In this Act, unless the context otherwise requires, "settled property" means any property held in trust other than property to which section 46 above (nominees and bare trustees) applies.

This definition has effect subject to section 61 (4) (insolvents' assets) and 93 (unit trusts) below.

GENERAL NOTE

S. 51 defines "settled property" as, in effect, property which is held in trust other than that to which s. 46 applies. Property held by a trustee or assignee in bankruptcy or under a deed of arrangement is not settled property for the purposes of the tax: see s. 61 (4).

Trustees of settlements

52.—(1) In relation to settled property, the trustees of the settlement shall for the purposes of this Act be treated as being a single and continuing body of persons (distinct from the persons who may from time to time be the trustees), and that body shall be treated as being resident and ordinarily resident in the United Kingdom unless the general administration of the trusts is ordinarily carried on outside the United Kingdom and the trustees or a majority of them for the time being are not resident or not ordinarily resident in the United Kingdom.

(2) Notwithstanding subsection (1) above, a person carrying on a business which consists of or includes the management of trusts, and acting as trustee of a trust in the course of that business, shall be treated in relation to that trust as not resident in the United Kingdom if the whole of the settled property consists of or derives from property provided by a person not at the time (or, in the case of a trust arising under a testamentary disposition or on an intestacy or partial intestacy, at his death) domiciled, resident or ordinarily resident in the United Kingdom, and if in such a case the trustees or a majority of them are or are treated in relation to that trust as not resident in the United Kingdom, the general administration of the trust shall be treated as ordinarily carried on outside the United Kingdom.

(3) For the purposes of this section, and of sections 54 (1) and 55 (1) below, where part of the property comprised in a settlement is vested in one trustee or set of trustees and part in another (and in particular where settled land within the meaning of the Settled Land Act 1925 is vested in the tenant for life and investments representing capital money are vested in the trustees of the settlement), they shall be treated as together constituting and, in so far as they act separately, as acting on behalf of a single body of trustees.

(4) If tax assessed on the trustees, or any one trustee, of a settlement in respect of a chargeable gain accruing to the trustees is not paid within six months from the date when it becomes payable by the trustees or trustee, and before or after the expiration of that period of six months the asset in respect of which the chargeable gain accrued, or any part of the proceeds of sale of that asset, is transferred by the trustees to a person who as against the trustees is absolutely entitled to it, that person may at any time within two years from the time when the tax became payable be assessed and charged (in the name of the trustees) to an amount of capital gains tax not exceeding tax chargeable on an amount equal to the amount of the chargeable gain and, where part only of the asset or of the proceeds was transferred, not exceeding a proportionate part of that amount.

GENERAL NOTE

Subs. (1) provides that trustees shall be treated as a continuing body of persons, distinct from the persons who are from time to time trustees. It further provides that they shall be treated as resident in the U.K. unless both the general administration of the trust is transacted abroad and a majority of the trustees are not resident or not ordinarily resident in the U.K. (subs. (2)). If the settlor was, at the time he made the settlement, or on his death (where the trust takes effect on death), not domiciled, resident or ordinarily resident in the U.K. then (a) any professional trustees are deemed to be non-resident; and (b) if a majority of the trustees are non-resident or deemed to be non-resident the general administration of the trust is deemed to be carried on abroad, irrespective of the amount of general administration actually carried out by the professional or non-resident trustee.

Subs. (3) prevents the reduction of liability by splitting up the settled property of one trust into various smaller parcels by reason only that parts of the settled property are vested in different trustees.

Subs. (4) enables the capital gains tax to be recovered from a beneficiary. Where the trustees fail to discharge their liability to the tax within six months of its becoming payable and either during, or subsequent to, that six-month period transfer the asset to a beneficiary, the tax can be recovered from him at any time within two years of the tax becoming payable.

Gifts in settlement

53. A gift in settlement, whether revocable or irrevocable, is a disposal of the entire property thereby becoming settled property notwithstanding that the donor has some interest as a beneficiary under the settlement and notwithstanding that he is a trustee, or the sole trustee, of the settlement.

General Note

This section provides that a gift in settlement, whether revocable or irrevocable, is a disposal of the assets settled, notwithstanding that the settlor retains a beneficial interest in the property or that the settlement is created by a declaration of trust so that the assets remain legally vested in the settlor.

In *Berry* v. *Warnett* [1978] 1 W.L.R. 957, it was held that a transaction between parties at arm's length is incapable of being a gift in settlement.

Person becoming absolutely entitled to settled property

54.—(1) On the occasion when a person becomes absolutely entitled to any settled property as against the trustee all the assets forming part of the settled property to which he becomes so entitled shall be deemed to have been disposed of by the trustee, and immediately reacquired by him in his capacity as a trustee within section 46 (1) above, for a consideration equal to their market value.

(2) On the occasion when a person becomes absolutely entitled to any settled property as against the trustee, any allowable loss which has accrued to the trustee in respect of property which is, or is represented by, the property to which that person so becomes entitled (including any allowable loss carried forward to the year of assessment in which that occasion falls), being a loss which cannot be deducted from chargeable gains accruing to the trustee in that year, but before that occasion, shall be treated as if it were allowable loss accruing at that time to the person becoming so entitled, instead of to the trustee.

General Note

The effect of subs. (1) is to treat any asset which is settled property as having been disposed of by the trustees for a consideration equal to its current market value whenever a beneficiary becomes absolutely entitled to it. For the meaning of "absolutely entitled" as against the trustee, see s. 46.

On the question of what constitutes an appropriation of trust funds between various persons interested in a joint trust fund, the Revenue has stated that where separate funds are held upon separate trusts there are separate settlements (even though they are created by one instrument) and that the only evidence of appropriation that is required is an appropriation account signed by all the trustees showing how the fund has been divided. The allocation of unused losses at the date of appropriation should be made between the separate funds on the lines of subs. (2) (see (1970) 67 L.S.Gaz. 13).

Subs. (2) enables a beneficiary to claim the benefit of any unrelieved loss of the trustee in respect of the assets to which he becomes entitled.

See on the interpretation of subs. (1): *Stephenson* v. *Barclays Bank Trust Co. Ltd.* [1975] 1 W.L.R. 882; *Hoare Trustees* v. *Gardner* [1978] 2 W.L.R. 832.

Termination of life interest etc.

55.—(1) On the termination at any time after 6th April 1965 of a life interest in possession in all or any part of settled property, the whole or a corresponding part of each of the assets forming part of the settled property and not ceasing at that time to be settled property shall be deemed for the purposes of this Act at that time to be disposed of and immediately reacquired by the trustee for a consideration equal to the whole or a corresponding part of the market value of the asset.

For the purposes of this subsection a life interest which is a right to part of the income of settled property shall be treated as a life interest in a corresponding part of the settled property.

(2) Subsection (1) above shall not apply on the occasion of the termination of the trusts of the settlement as respects any part of the settled property by the exercise of a power for that purpose contained in the settlement or of a statutory power of advancement or by the surrender of a life interest in such a part for the purpose of advancement, if all the property as respects which the life interest terminates thereby ceases to be settled under the settlement.

(3) Subsection (1) above shall apply where the person entitled to a life interest in possession in all or any part of settled property dies (although the interest does not then terminate) as it applies on the termination of such a life interest.

(4) In this section " life interest " in relation to a settlement—

(*a*) includes a right under the settlement to the income of, or the use or occupation of, settled property for the life of a person other than the person entitled to the right, or for lives,

(*b*) does not include any right which is contingent on the exercise of the discretion of the trustee or the discretion of some other person, and

(*c*) subject to subsection (5) below, does not include an annuity, notwithstanding that the annuity is payable out of or charged on settled property or the income of settled property.

(5) In this section the expression " life interest " shall include entitlement to an annuity created by the settlement if—

(*a*) some or all of the settled property is appropriated by the trustees as a fund out of which the annuity is payable, and

(*b*) there is no right of recourse to settled property not so appropriated, or to the income of settled property not so appropriated,

and, without prejudice to subsection (6) below, the settled property so appropriated shall, while the annuity is payable, and on the occasion of the death of the annuitant, be treated for the purposes of this section as being settled property under a separate settlement.

(6) If there is a life interest in a part of the settled property and, where that is a life interest in income, there is no right of recourse to, or to the income of, the remainder of the settled property, the part of the settled property in which the life interest subsists shall while it subsists be treated for the purposes of this section as being settled property under a separate settlement.

General Note

If the termination of a life interest (defined by subs. (4)) does not bring the settlement to an end, the termination is treated as causing a disposal and re-acquisition at their current market value of all the assets in the settlement in which the life interest subsists (subs. (1)) (but see s. 56). By subs. (2), the notional disposal of the settled property under subs. (1) is excluded in cases where by reason of the exercise of a power of appointment or advancement the life interest terminates in part of the settled property. Normally in these circumstances there will be a charge under s. 54 (1).

Subs. (3) provides for a charge to capital gains tax on the death of a person entitled to a life interest in possession in settled property, although the life interest does not then terminate. The definition contained in subs. (4) includes the user and enjoyment of land or chattels, but excludes contingent interests and has been expanded to include certain annuities (subs. (5)).

Subs. (6), which in certain circumstances deems settled property to be held under separate settlements, only applies where there is no right of recourse to the other settled property or its income; it would not apply when two or more persons are entitled between them to the income of a trust fund as they could each then look to the whole of the income for their share. It would, however, apply where property had been apportioned to a particular share of income and was not available for any other share (see *Pexton* v. *Bell; Crowe* v. *Appleby* [1976] 1 W.L.R. 885).

Death of life tenant: exclusion of chargeable gain

56.—(1) Where, by virtue of section 54 (1) above, the assets forming part of any settled property are deemed to be disposed of and re-acquired by the trustee on the occasion when a person becomes absolutely entitled thereto as against the trustee, then, if that occasion is the termination of a life interest (within the meaning of section 55 above) by the death of the person entitled to that interest—

(*a*) no chargeable gain shall accrue on the disposal, and

(*b*) if on the death the property reverts to the disponer the disposal and re-acquisition under that subsection shall be deemed to be for such consideration as to secure that neither a gain nor a loss accrues to the trustee, and shall, if the trustee had first acquired the property at a date earlier than 6th April 1965, be deemed to be at that earlier date.

(2) Where section 55 (1) above applies on the death of the person entitled to the life interest referred to therein, no chargeable gain shall accrue on the disposal deemed to be made under that section.

General Note

Subs. (1) provides that if the occasion of a person becoming absolutely entitled to trust property is the death of a life tenant within s. 54 (1), any increase in the value of the settled property up to the date when the property ceases to be settled property is free from capital gains tax. An exception to this is the case of settled property reverting to the disponer, which is adjudged to be on a no gains—no loss basis (subs. (1) (*b*)).

By subs. (2), where the life interest referred to in s. 55 (1) ends by reason of the death of the life tenant no chargeable gain arises on the notional disposal. Therefore, any increase in the value of the settled property up to the date of the life tenant's death is free from capital gains tax. In the case of concurrent life interests the death of one of the life tenants brings about a notional disposal and re-acquisition at market value (without any charge to capital gains tax) of the fraction A/100 of each asset in the fund, where A is the percentage of the income of the fund the deceased enjoyed. In such a case, part of any increase in the value of the assets of the fund up to the death of the co-life tenant is free from capital gains tax.

Death of annuitant

57. Sections 54 (1) and 55 (1) above shall apply, where an annuity which is not a life interest is terminated by the death of the annuitant, as they apply on the termination of a life interest by the death of the person entitled thereto.

In this section " life interest " has the same meaning as in section 55 above.

General Note

For the purposes of both ss. 55 (1) and 56 (1) an annuitant is treated as a life tenant.

Disposal of interests in settled property

58.—(1) No chargeable gain shall accrue on the disposal of an interest created by or arising under a settlement (including, in particular, an annuity or life interest, and the reversion to an annuity or life interest) by the person for whose benefit the interest was created by the terms of the settlement or by any other person except one who acquired, or derives his title from one who acquired, the interest for a consideration in money or money's worth, other than consideration consisting of another interest under the settlement.

(2) Subject to subsection (1) above, where a person who has acquired an interest in settled property (including in particular the reversion to an annuity or life interest) becomes, as the holder of that interest, absolutely entitled as against the trustee to any settled property, he shall be treated as disposing of the interest in consideration of obtaining that settled property (but without prejudice to any gain accruing to the trustee on the disposal of that property deemed to be effected by him under section 54 (1) above).

General Note

S. 58 exempts disposals of annuities and interests under settlements from the charge in all circumstances except that of an interest which has at any time been acquired for money or money's worth.

Other cases

Gifts: recovery from donee

59.—(1) If in any year of assessment a chargeable gain accrues to any person on the disposal of an asset by way of gift and any amount of capital gains tax assessed on that person for that year of assessment is not paid within twelve months from the date when the tax becomes payable the donee may, by an assessment made not later than two years from the date when the tax became payable, be assessed and charged (in the name of the donor) to capital gains tax on an amount not exceeding the amount of the chargeable gain so accruing, and not exceeding the grossed up amount of that capital gains tax unpaid at the time when he is so assessed, grossing up at the marginal rate of tax, that is to say taking capital gains tax on a chargeable gain at the amount which would not have been chargeable but for that chargeable gain.

(2) A person paying any amount of tax in pursuance of this section shall be entitled to recover a sum of that amount from the donor.

(3) References in this section to a donor include, in the case of an individual who has died, references to his personal representatives.

(4) In this section references to a gift include references to any transaction otherwise than by way of a bargain made at arm's length so far as money or money's worth passes under the transaction without full consideration in money or money's worth, and " donor " and " donee " shall be construed accordingly; and this section shall apply in relation to a gift made by two or more donors with the necessary modifications and subject to any necessary apportionments.

General Note

S. 59 provides for recovery from the donee one year after it falls due of capital gains tax unpaid by the donor.

Partnerships

60. Where two or more persons carry on a trade or business in partnership—

(*a*) tax in respect of chargeable gains accruing to them on the disposal of any partnership assets shall, in Scotland as well as elsewhere in the United Kingdom, be assessed and charged on them separately, and

(*b*) any partnership dealings shall be treated as dealings by the partners and not by the firm as such, and

(*c*) section 153 (1) (2) of the Taxes Act (residence of partnerships) shall apply in relation to tax chargeable in pursuance of this Act as it applies in relation to income tax.

General Note

S. 60 deals with partnerships; it provides that gains on partnership assets shall be assessed on the partners individually and that partnership dealings shall be treated as dealings by the partners rather than by the firm.

Insolvents' assets

61.—(1) In relation to assets held by a person as trustee or assignee in bankruptcy or under a deed of arrangement this Act shall apply as if the assets were vested in, and the acts of the trustee or assignee in relation to the assets were the acts of, the bankrupt or debtor (acquisitions from or disposals to him by the bankrupt or debtor being disregarded accordingly), and tax in respect of any chargeable gains which accrue to any such trustee or assignee shall be assessable on and recoverable from him.

(2) Assets held by a trustee or assignee in bankruptcy or under a deed of arrangement at the death of the bankrupt or debtor shall for the purposes of this Act be regarded as held by a personal representative of the deceased and—

(*a*) subsection (1) above shall not apply after the death, and

(*b*) section 49 (1) above (under which assets passing on a death are deemed to be acquired by the persons on whom they devolve) shall apply as if any assets held by a trustee or assignee in bankruptcy or under a deed of arrangement at the death of the bankrupt or debtor were assets of which the deceased was competent to dispose and which then devolved on the trustee or assignee as if he were a personal representative.

(3) Assets vesting in a trustee in bankruptcy after the death of the bankrupt or debtor shall for the purposes of this Act be regarded as held by a personal representative of the deceased, and subsection (1) above shall not apply.

(4) The definition of " settled property " in section 51 above shall not include any property as being property held by a trustee or assignee in bankruptcy or under a deed of arrangement.

(5) In this section " deed of arrangement " means a deed of arrangement to which the Deeds of Arrangement Act 1914 or any corresponding enactment forming part of the law of Scotland or Northern Ireland applies.

General Note

S. 61 deals with the case where chargeable assets are owned by a person who becomes bankrupt or makes a deed of arrangement with his creditors. The transfer of the assets to the trustee is not to be treated as a disposal and a subsequent disposal by the trustee is treated as a disposal by the bankrupt or debtor. However, any tax due as a result of such a disposal will be payable by the trustee (see *Re McMeekin (a bankrupt)* [1974] S.T.C. 429).

Transactions between connected persons

62.—(1) This section shall apply where a person acquires an asset and the person making the disposal is connected with him.

(2) Without prejudice to the generality of section 19 (3) above the person acquiring the asset and the person making the disposal shall be treated as parties to a transaction otherwise than by way of a bargain made at arm's length.

(3) If on the disposal a loss accrues to the person making the disposal, it shall not be deductible except from a chargeable gain accruing to him on some other disposal of an asset to the person acquiring the asset mentioned in subsection (1) above, being a disposal made at a time when they are connected persons:

Provided that this subsection shall not apply to a disposal by way of gift in settlement if the gift and the income from it is wholly or primarily applicable for educational, cultural or recreational purposes, and the persons benefiting from the application for those purposes are confined to members of an association of persons for whose benefit the gift was made, not being persons all or most of whom are connected persons.

(4) Where the asset mentioned in subsection (1) above is an option to enter into a sale or other transaction given by the person making the disposal a loss accruing to the person acquiring the asset shall not be an allowable loss unless it accrues on a disposal of the option at arm's length to a person who is not connected with him.

(5) In a case where the asset mentioned in subsection (1) above is subject to any right or restriction enforceable by the person making the disposal, or by a person connected with him, then (the amount of the consideration for the acquisition being, in accordance with subsection (2) above, deemed to be equal to the market value of the asset) that market value shall be—

(*a*) what its market value would be if not subject to the right or restriction, minus—

(*b*) the market value of the right or restriction or the amount by which its extinction would enhance the value of the asset to its owner, whichever is the less:

Provided that if the right or restriction is of such a nature that its enforcement would or might effectively destroy or substantially impair the value of the asset without bringing any countervailing advantage either to the person making the disposal or a person connected with him or is an option or other right to acquire the asset or, in the case of incorporeal property, is a right to extinguish the asset in the hands of the person giving the consideration by forfeiture or merger or otherwise, that market value of the asset shall be determined, and the amount of the gain accruing on the disposal shall be computed, as if the right or restriction did not exist.

(6) Subsection (5) above shall not apply to a right of forfeiture or other right exercisable on breach of a covenant contained in a lease of land or other property, and shall not apply to any right or restriction under a mortgage or other charge.

General Note

This section deals with transactions between connected persons (defined in s. 63). Subs. (2) provides that such transactions are treated as being otherwise than by way of a bargain made at arm's length. Accordingly they are deemed to be made for a consideration equal to market value: see s. 19 (3) (*a*).

Subs. (3) provides restrictions on the allowability of losses arising on transactions between connected persons. The general rule is that such losses are allowable only against chargeable gains accruing to the disponer on some other disposal of an asset to the same connected person at a time when they are connected persons. The proviso excludes from this general rule certain gifts in settlement.

Subs. (4) provides further restrictions on the deductibility of losses where a person disposes of an option to a connected person.

Subs. (5) provides a formula for ascertaining market value for the purposes of the section where the asset disposed of is subject to any right or restriction enforceable by the disponer or a person connected with him. See subs. (6) for limitations on the application of subs. (5).

Connected persons: interpretation

63.—(1) Any question whether a person is connected with another shall for the purposes of this Act be determined in accordance with the following subsections of this section (any provision that one person is connected with another being taken to mean that they are connected with one another).

(2) A person is connected with an individual if that person is the individual's husband or wife, or is a relative, or the husband or wife of a relative, of the individual or of the individual's husband or wife.

(3) A person, in his capacity as trustee of a settlement, is connected with any individual who in relation to the settlement is a settlor, with any person who is connected with such an individual and with a body corporate which, under section 454 of the Taxes Act, is deemed to be connected with that settlement (" settlement " and " settlor " having for the purposes of this subsection the meanings assigned to them by subsection (3) of the said section 454).

(4) Except in relation to acquisitions or disposals of partnership assets pursuant to bona fide commercial arrangements, a person is connected with any person with whom he is in partnership, and with the husband or wife or a relative of any individual with whom he is in partnership.

(5) A company is connected with another company—

(*a*) if the same person has control of both, or a person has control of one and persons connected with him, or he and persons connected with him, have control of the other, or

(*b*) if a group of two or more persons has control of each company, and the groups either consist of the same persons or could be regarded as consisting of the same persons by treating (in one or more cases) a member of either group as replaced by a person with whom he is connected.

(6) A company is connected with another person, if that person has control of it or if that person and persons connected with him together have control of it.

(7) Any two or more persons acting together to secure or exercise control of a company shall be treated in relation to that company as connected with one another and with any person acting on the directions of any of them to secure or exercise control of the company.

(8) In this section " relative " means brother, sister, ancestor or lineal descendant.

General Note

S. 63 defines connected persons for the purposes of the previous section.

Part IV

Shares and Securities

Chapter I

General

Interpretation

64.—(1) In this Act, unless the context otherwise requires—

"gilt-edged securities" has the meaning given by Schedule 2 to this Act,

"shares" includes stock,

"class", in relation to shares or securities, means a class of shares or securities of any one company.

(2) For the purposes of this Act shares or debentures comprised in any letter of allotment or similar instrument shall be treated as issued unless the right to the shares or debentures thereby conferred remains provisional until accepted, and there has been no acceptance.

General Note

This section and Sched. 2 define shares and gilt-edged securities for the purposes of capital gains tax and stipulate the point at which they are to be treated as issued.

Rules of identification

Pooling

65.—(1) This section has effect subject to—

(*a*) section 66 below, and

(*b*) paragraphs 3 and 13 (2) of Schedule 5 to this Act,

and this section shall not apply to gilt-edged securities.

(2) Any number of securities of the same class held by one person in one capacity shall for the purposes of this Act be regarded as indistinguishable parts of a single asset (in this section referred to as a holding) growing or diminishing on the occasions on which additional securities of the class in question are acquired, or some of the securities of the class in question are disposed of.

(3) Without prejudice to the generality of subsection (2) above, a disposal of securities in a holding, other than the disposal outright of the entire holding, is a disposal of part of an asset and the provisions of this Act relating to the computation of a gain accruing on a disposal of part of an asset shall apply accordingly.

(4) Shares, or securities of a company, shall not be treated for the purposes of this section as being of the same class unless they are so treated by the practice of a recognised stock exchange in the United Kingdom or elsewhere or would be so treated if dealt with on such a stock exchange, but shall be treated in accordance with this section notwithstanding that they are identified in some other way by the disposal or by the transfer or delivery giving effect to it.

(5) This section shall apply separately in relation to any securities held by a person to whom they were issued as an employee of the company or of any other person on terms which restrict his rights to dispose of them, so long as those terms are in force, and, while applying separately to any such securities, shall have effect as if the owner held them in a capacity other than that in which he holds any other securities of the same class.

(6) Nothing in this section shall be taken as affecting the manner in which the market value of any asset is to be ascertained.

(7) In this section " securities " means—

(*a*) shares, or securities of a company, and

(*b*) subject to the exclusion of gilt-edged securities in subsection (1) above, any other assets where they are of a nature to be dealt in without identifying the particular assets disposed of or acquired.

General Note

This section provides the general rule that all shares or securities of the same class and all holdings of the same quality of a commodity held by one person in one capacity are treated as a single asset growing or diminishing as shares, etc. are acquired or disposed of. This scheme is commonly known as "pooling" on account of the concept of a pool of shares.

Accordingly a disposal of securities in a holding other than the disposal outright of the entire holding is a part disposal (subs. (2)).

Exceptions to the general rule are:

(1) Securities of the same kind which are acquired and disposed of by the same person on the same day and in the same capacity (s. 66);

(2) gilt-edged securities as defined in Sched. 2;

(3) quoted securities held on April 6, 1965, where an election for pooling has not been made (paras. 3 to 7, Sched. 5);

(4) unquoted shares, commodities, etc., held on April 6, 1965 (para. 13, Sched. 5);

(5) securities held by a person to whom they were issued as an employee on terms which restrict his rights to dispose of them, so long as those terms are in force: such securities constitute a separate "pool" (s. 65 (5)).

Disposal on or before day of acquisition

66.—(1) The following provisions shall apply where securities of the same kind are acquired or disposed of by the same person on the same day and in the same capacity—

(*a*) all the securities so acquired shall be treated as acquired by a single transaction and all the securities so disposed of shall be treated as disposed of by a single transaction, and

(*b*) all the securities so acquired shall, so far as their quantity does not exceed that of the securities so disposed of, be identified with those securities.

(2) Where the quantity of the securities so disposed of exceeds the quantity of the securities so acquired, then so far as the excess—

(*a*) is not required by paragraph 2 (2), 3 (3) or 13 (3) of Schedule 5 to this Act to be identified with securities held on or acquired before 6th April 1965, and

(*b*) cannot be treated under section 65 above as diminishing a holding,

it shall be treated as diminishing a quantity subsequently acquired, and a quantity so acquired at an earlier date, rather than one so acquired at a later date.

(3) Shares shall not be treated for the purposes of this section as being of the same kind unless they are treated as being of the same class by the practice of a recognised stock exchange in the United Kingdom or elsewhere or would be so treated if dealt with on such a stock exchange.

(4) In this section " securities " includes shares and any assets dealt with without identifying the particular assets disposed of or acquired, and in the case of gilt-edged securities subsection (2) above has effect subject to section 68 below.

GENERAL NOTE

This section provides rules of identification where securities of the same kind are acquired and disposed of by the same person in the same capacity. The rules of identification are important, *inter alia,* in arriving at the amount of expenditure allowable in the computation of a gain arising on a disposal within the section.

Gilt-edged securities

Exemption for long-term gains

67.—(1) A gain which accrues on the disposal by any person of gilt-edged securities shall not be a chargeable gain except where the disposal occurs within 12 months after the acquisition of the securities.

(2) So much of subsection (1) above as excepts a disposal occurring within 12 months after the acquisition of the securities shall not apply where the person disposing of the securities had acquired them—

(*a*) by devolution on death or as legatee, or

(*b*) if they were settled property, on becoming absolutely entitled thereto as against the trustee.

(3) Where, in the case of a man and his wife, section 44 above applies in relation to the acquisition of any securities by the one from the other, and the one making the acquisition subsequently disposes of the securities by a disposal to which that section does not apply, he shall be treated for the purposes of the exception in subsection (1) above as if he had acquired the securities when the other did.

GENERAL NOTE

Where gilt-edged securities are disposed of after 12 months from being acquired (for the applicable rules of identification of securities disposed of with those acquired, see ss. 68 and 69) any gain arising is not chargeable (subs. (1)).

Where the disponer acquired the securities by devolution on death, or as legatee, or on becoming absolutely entitled to them as against a trustee of settled property, any gain on their disposal is exempt even if it accrues within 12 months of their acquisition (subs. (2)).

Subs. (3) applies in the case of securities which were acquired by the disponer from his spouse within s. 44. The disponer's acquisition is for the purpose of this section deemed to have taken place at the time of the spouse's acquisition.

Identification (general)

68.—(1) The following provisions shall apply, for the purpose of identifying gilt-edged securities disposed of by any person with securities of the same kind acquired by him in the same capacity.

(2) Securities disposed of at an earlier date shall be identified before securities disposed of at a later date, and their identification shall have effect also for determining what securities might be comprised in the later disposal.

(3) Securities disposed of shall be identified with securities acquired within the twelve months preceding the disposal rather than with securities not so acquired, and with securities so acquired at an earlier date rather than with securities so acquired at a later date.

(4) This section has effect subject to section 66 (1) above, and 69 below.

GENERAL NOTE

This section provides the general rule for identification of gilt-edged securities disposed of with those acquired. Securities disposed of are identified as far as possible with those acquired within 12 months preceding the disposal and within that 12-month period with securities acquired earlier rather than later (subs. (3)). Securities disposed of at an earlier date are identified before those disposed of at a later date (subs (2)).

Identification: disposal to husband or wife and third person

69.—(1) Where, in the case of a man and his wife living with him, one of them—

(*a*) disposes of gilt-edged securities of any kind to the other, and

(*b*) disposes of gilt-edged securities of the same kind to a third person,

then, if under the preceding provisions of this Chapter any of the securities disposed of to the husband or wife would be identified with securities acquired within the twelve months preceding the disposal and any of the securities disposed of to the third person with securities not so acquired, the securities disposed of to the third person shall be identified with securities so acquired before any securities disposed of to the husband or wife are so identified.

(2) If there is more than one disposal to the wife or husband, or to a third party, the provisions of this section shall be applied to securities disposed of at an earlier date before they are applied to securities disposed of at a later date, and the identification of the securities disposed of at the earlier date shall have effect also for determining what securities might be comprised in the later disposal.

General Note

S. 69 prevents a taxpayer from using these identification rules to avoid a charge to tax by making disposals to his spouse. Thus, if a taxpayer acquired £500 of gilt-edged stock in 1976 and a further £500 of the same stock in July 1978, a disposal of £500 of that stock to his wife in, say, January 1979 (which is not chargeable to tax under s. 44 (1)) would apart from this section be matched with the acquisition in 1978; he could then sell the remaining stock to an outsider which would be matched with the purchase in 1976, so avoiding a charge to tax. This section reverses the order of identification so as to preserve the charge to tax.

Re-acquisition after sale at a loss

70.—(1) Where a loss accrues to a person on the disposal of gilt-edged securities and he re-acquires the same securities within the prescribed period after the disposal that loss shall not be deductible except from a chargeable gain accruing to him on the disposal of the securities re-acquired.

(2) Where a person disposes of gilt-edged securities and acquires gilt-edged securities of the same kind within the prescribed period after the disposal he shall be treated for the purposes of subsection (1) above as re-acquiring the securities disposed of (or such quantity of them as does not exceed the quantity acquired) but so that—

(*a*) there cannot be in relation to the same disposal more than one re-acquisition of the same security, nor can there be by the same acquisition of a security a re-acquisition in relation to more than one disposal, and

(*b*) if an acquisition could be treated as a re-acquisition of securities disposed of either at an earlier or at a later date it shall be treated as a re-acquisition of the securities disposed of at the earlier date, and

(*c*) if securities disposed of by the same disposal could be treated as re-acquired at an earlier or at a later date they shall be treated as re-acquired at the earlier date.

(3) Where a person who holds gilt-edged securities (the " original holding ") acquires securities of the same kind (an " additional

holding ") and within the prescribed period after the acquisition disposes of securities of that kind, he shall be treated for the purposes of subsection (1) above as if he had within the prescribed period after the disposal re-acquired the securities disposed of or such quantity of them as does not exceed the original holding or the additional holding, whichever is the less.

Paragraphs (*a*), (*b*) and (*c*) of subsection (2) above shall have effect in relation to the acquisition of the additional holding as if it were a re-acquisition of the securities disposed of.

(4) In the case of a man and his wife living with him—

(*a*) the preceding provisions of this section shall, with the necessary modifications, apply also where a loss on the disposal accrues to one of them and the acquisition after the disposal is made by the other,

(*b*) paragraph (*a*) above shall have effect in relation to subsection (3) above as if the acquisition of the additional holding were an acquisition after the disposal.

(5) In the case of companies in the same group subsections (1), (2) and (3) above shall, with the necessary modifications, apply also where a loss on the disposal accrues to one of them and the acquisition is made by the other.

(6) In this section references to the acquisition of securities shall not include references—

(*a*) to acquisition as trading stock, or

(*b*) in the case of a company which is a member of a group, to acquisition from another company which is a member of that group throughout the prescribed period before and after the disposal.

(7) In this section—

" group " has the meaning given in section 272 of the Taxes Act;

" the prescribed period " means—

(*a*) in the case of an acquisition through a stock exchange, one month;

(*b*) in the case of an acquisition otherwise than as aforesaid, six months;

" trading stock ", in relation to a company carrying on life assurance business as defined in section 323 of the Taxes Act, does not include investments held in connection with that business except in so far as they are referable to general annuity business or pension business as defined in that section;

and references to a person's holding, acquiring and disposing of securities are references to his doing so in the same capacity.

General Note

This section restricts relief for losses accruing on the disposal of gilt-edged securities where there is a re-acquisition of the same securities within one month of the sale at a loss (where the acquisition is through a stock exchange) or within six months of the sale at a loss (where the acquisition is not through a stock exchange). In such circumstances the loss is only allowable against a chargeable gain accruing on the disposal of the securities re-acquired (subs. (1)).

Subss. (2)–(5) provide identification rules for the purposes of subs. (1) so that it can be ascertained whether the securities re-acquired are for those purposes the same as those disposed of.

Subs. (6) provides that for the purposes of this section no account is to be taken of securities held as trading stock.

Savings certificates, etc.

Exemption for government non-marketable securities

71.—(1) Savings certificates and non-marketable securities issued under the National Loans Act 1968 or the National Loans Act 1939, or any corresponding enactment forming part of the law of Northern Ireland, shall not be chargeable assets, and accordingly no chargeable gain shall accrue on their disposal.

(2) In this section—

(*a*) " savings certificates " means savings certificates issued under section 12 of the National Loans Act 1968, or section 7 of the National Debt Act 1958, or section 59 of the Finance Act 1920, and any war savings certificates as defined in section 9 (3) of the National Debt Act 1972, together with any savings certificates issued under any enactment forming part of the law of Northern Ireland and corresponding to the said enactments, and

(*b*) " non-marketable securities " means securities which are not transferable, or which are transferable only with the consent of some Minister of the Crown, or the consent of a department of the Government of Northern Ireland, or only with the consent of the National Debt Commissioners.

General Note

This section provides that neither saving certificates, as defined by subs. (2) (*a*), nor non-marketable securities, as defined by subs. (2) (*b*), are chargeable assets. It is considered that subs. (2) (*b*) exempts tax reserve certificates from the charge.

Capital distribution in respect of shares, etc.

Distribution which is not a new holding within Chapter II

72.—(1) Where a person receives or becomes entitled to receive in respect of shares in a company any capital distribution from the company (other than a new holding as defined in section 77 below) he shall be treated as if he had in consideration of that capital distribution disposed of an interest in the shares.

(2) If the inspector is satisfied that the amount distributed is small, as compared with the value of the shares in respect of which it is distributed, and so directs—

(*a*) the occasion of the capital distribution shall not be treated for the purposes of this Act as a disposal of the asset, and

(*b*) the amount distributed shall be deducted from any expenditure allowable under this Act as a deduction in computing a gain or loss on the disposal of the shares by the person receiving or becoming entitled to receive the distribution of capital.

(3) A person who is dissatisfied with the refusal of the inspector to give a direction under this section may appeal to the Commissioners having jurisdiction on an appeal against an assessment to tax in respect of a gain accruing on the disposal.

(4) Where the allowable expenditure is less than the amount distributed (or is nil)—

(*a*) subsections (2) and (3) above shall not apply, and

(*b*) if the recipient so elects (and there is any allowable expenditure)—

(i) the amount distributed shall be reduced by the amount of the allowable expenditure, and

(ii) none of that expenditure shall be allowable as a deduction in computing a gain accruing on the occasion of the capital distribution, or on any subsequent occasion.

In this subsection " allowable expenditure " means the expenditure which immediately before the occasion of the capital distribution was attributable to the shares under paragraphs (*a*) and (*b*) of section 32 (1) above.

(5) In this section—

(*a*) the " amount distributed " means the amount or value of the capital distribution,

(*b*) " capital distribution " means any distribution from a company, including a distribution in the course of dissolving or winding up the company, in money or money's worth except a distribution which in the hands of the recipient constitutes income for the purposes of income tax.

General Note

A capital distribution is as a general rule to be treated as consideration received on a disposal or part disposal by the recipient of the shares in respect of which the capital distribution is made (subs. (1)).

Capital distribution is defined in subs. (5) (*b*) to include a distribution on a liquidation but any amount which is income for the purposes of income tax is excluded from the definition.

If the inspector is satisfied that the amount of the capital distribution is small as compared with the value of the shares concerned, there is no disposal but the amount of the capital distribution is deducted from the allowable expenditure of the shares concerned (subs. (2)).

Subs. (4) deals with the position where the allowable expenditure of the shares immediately before the capital distribution is less than the amount distributed or is nil. In these circumstances subs. (2) is excluded.

Disposal of right to acquire shares

73.—(1) Where a person receives or becomes entitled to receive in respect of any shares in a company a provisional allotment of shares in or debentures of the company and he disposes of his rights section 72 above shall apply as if the amount of the consideration for the disposal were a capital distribution received by him from the company in respect of the first-mentioned shares, and as if that person had, instead of disposing of the rights, disposed of an interest in those shares.

(2) If under Schedule 5 to this Act it is to be assumed that, at a time after the creation of the rights and before their disposal, the said person sold and immediately re-acquired the shares in respect of which the rights were created, the same assumption shall be made as respects the rights.

(3) This section shall apply in relation to rights obtained in respect of debentures of a company as it applies in relation to rights obtained in respect of shares in a company.

General Note

This section deals with bonus and rights issues which are offered to share or debenture holders in a company and disposed of by them as rights and not taken up. The sums received for the rights will be treated as a capital distribution from the company of the same amount and s. 72 applies accordingly.

Close companies

Disposal of shares: relief in respect of income tax consequent on shortfall in distributions

74.—(1) If in pursuance of paragraph 5 of Schedule 16 to the Finance

Act 1972 (consequences for income tax of apportionment of income etc. of close company) a person is assessed to income tax, then, in the computation under Chapter II of Part II of this Act of the gain accruing on a disposal by him of any shares forming part of his interest in the company to which the relevant apportionment relates, the amount of the income tax paid by him, so far as attributable to those shares, shall be allowable as a deduction.

(2) Subsection (1) above shall not apply in relation to tax charged in respect of undistributed income which has, before the disposal, been subsequently distributed and is then exempt from tax by virtue of sub-paragraph (6) of the said paragraph 5 or in relation to tax treated as having been paid by virtue of sub-paragraph (2) (*b*) of that paragraph.

(3) For the purposes of this section the income assessed to tax shall be the highest part of the individual's income for the year of assessment in question, but so that if the highest part of the said income is taken into account under this section in relation to an assessment to tax the next highest part shall be taken into account in relation to any other relevant assessment, and so on.

(4) For the purpose of identifying shares forming part of an interest in a company with shares subsequently disposed of which are of the same class, shares bought at an earlier time shall be deemed to have been disposed of before shares bought at a later time.

(5) The provisions of this section shall be construed as if this section formed part of the said paragraph 5.

General Note

S. 74 provides that on a disposal or part disposal of shares which have been the subject of an apportionment of the income of a close company, to the extent that the income has not been subsequently distributed the income tax suffered shall be allowed as a deduction from the consideration received. This has the effect of reducing the gain or enhancing the loss arising on a disposal of such shares.

Shares in close company transferring assets at an undervalue

75.—(1) If after 6th April 1965 a company which is a close company transfers an asset to any person otherwise than by way of a bargain made at arm's length and for a consideration of an amount or value less than the market value of the asset an amount equal to the difference shall be apportioned among the issued shares of the company, and the holders of those shares shall be treated in accordance with the following provisions of this section.

(2) For the purposes of the computation under Chapter II of Part II of this Act of a gain accruing on the disposal of any of those shares by the person owning them on the date of transfer an amount equal to the amount so apportioned to that share shall be excluded from the expenditure allowable as a deduction under section 32 (1) (*a*) above from the consideration for the disposal.

(3) If the person owning any of the said shares at the date of transfer is itself a close company an amount equal to the amount apportioned to the shares so owned under subsection (1) above to that close company shall be apportioned among the issued shares of that close company, and the holders of those shares shall be treated in accordance with subsection (2) above, and so on through any number of close companies.

(4) This section shall not apply where the transfer of the asset is a disposal to which section 273 (1) of the Taxes Act (transfers within a group of companies) applies.

General Note

S. 75 is designed to prevent the creation of artificial losses on shares and deals with the case where a close company transfers assets at an undervalue. Subs. (1) is not confined to transfers to shareholders but includes any transfer at an undervalue no matter to whom made, *e.g.* for charitable or public purposes. An exception is the case where the transfer of assets is a disposal to which s. 273 (1), I.C.T.A. 1970, applies (*i.e.* a transfer within a group of companies). Where s. 75 applies the amount of the undervalue is apportioned among the shares of the close company and the amounts so apportioned go to reduce the allowable expenditure of the shares in the holders' hands.

Share option schemes

Consideration for acquisition of shares under share option schemes

76. Section 19 (3) above (assets deemed acquired and disposed of at market value) shall not apply in calculating the consideration for the acquisition of shares in pursuance of a share option scheme as defined in Schedule 12 to the Finance Act 1972.

General Note

The provisions deeming acquisition and cost to be at market value are not to apply to the acquisition cost of shares under recognised share option schemes.

Chapter II

Reorganisation of Share Capital, Conversion of Securities, Etc.

Reorganisation or reduction of share capital

Application of sections 78 to 81

77.—(1) For the purposes of this section and sections 78 to 81 below " reorganisation " means a reorganisation or reduction of a company's share capital, and in relation to the reorganisation—

(*a*) " original shares " means shares held before and concerned in the reorganisation,

(*b*) " new holding " means, in relation to any original shares, the shares in and debentures of the company which as a result of the reorganisation represent the original shares (including such, if any, of the original shares as remain).

(2) The reference in subsection (1) above to the reorganisation of a company's share capital includes—

(*a*) any case where persons are, whether for payment or not, allotted shares in or debentures of the company in respect of and in proportion to (or as nearly as may be in proportion to) their holdings of shares in the company or of any class of shares in the company, and

(*b*) any case where there are more than one class of share and the rights attached to shares of any class are altered.

(3) The reference in subsection (1) above to a reduction of share capital does not include the paying off of redeemable share capital, and where shares in a company are redeemed by the company otherwise than by the issue of shares or debentures (with or without other consideration) and otherwise than in a liquidation, the shareholder shall be treated as disposing of the shares at the time of the redemption.

General Note

S. 77 contains various definitions relating to the reorganisation or reduction of the share capital of a company or unit trust scheme, provided for in ss. 78 to 81. A redemption of share capital otherwise than either on a liquidation or by the issue of shares or debentures is treated as a disposal (subs. (3)) (see *Floor* v. *Davis* [1978] 3 W.L.R. 360).

Equation of original shares and new holding

78. Subject to sections 79 to 81 below, a reorganisation shall not be treated as involving any disposal of the original shares or any acquisition of the new holding or any part of it, but the original shares (taken as a single asset) and the new holding (taken as a single asset) shall be treated as the same asset acquired as the original shares were acquired.

General Note

This section provides that a reorganisation of share capital does not constitute a disposal for the purposes of the charge but the new shares and the original shares are treated as the same asset acquired when the original shares were acquired.

Consideration given or received by holder

79.—(1) Where, on a reorganisation, a person gives or becomes liable to give any consideration for his new holding or any part of it, that consideration shall in relation to any disposal of the new holding or any part of it be treated as having been given for the original shares, and if the new holding or part of it is disposed of with a liability attaching to it in respect of that consideration, the consideration given for the disposal shall be adjusted accordingly:

Provided that there shall not be treated as consideration given for the new holding or any part of it any surrender, cancellation or other alteration of the original shares or of the rights attached thereto, or any consideration consisting of any application, in paying up the new holding or any part of it, of assets of the company or of any dividend or other distribution declared out of those assets but not made.

(2) Where on a reorganisation a person receives (or is deemed to receive), or becomes entitled to receive, any consideration, other than the new holding, for the disposal of an interest in the original shares, and in particular—

(*a*) where under section 72 above he is to be treated as if he had in consideration of a capital distribution disposed of an interest in the original shares, or

(*b*) where he receives (or is deemed to receive) consideration from other shareholders in respect of a surrender of rights derived from the original shares,

he shall be treated as if the new holding resulted from his having for that consideration disposed of an interest in the original shares (but without prejudice to the original shares and the new holding being treated in accordance with section 78 above as the same asset).

(3) Where for the purpose of subsection (2) above it is necessary in computing the gain or loss accruing on the disposal of the interest in the original shares mentioned in subsection (2) above to apportion the cost of acquisition of the original shares between what is disposed of and what is retained, the apportionment shall be made in the like manner as under section 80 (1) below.

General Note

Subs. (1) provides that any consideration given for the new holding on a reorganisation, other than an alteration of rights, is to be treated as given for the original holding. By subs. (2), a shareholder who receives cash or any other consideration other than the new holding on a reorganisation or reduction of capital is treated as having disposed of an interest in his shares for the consideration, though this does not prevent any shares he also receives from being treated as part of his original holding.

Part disposal of new holding

80.—(1) Where for the purpose of computing the gain or loss accruing to a person from the acquisition and disposal of any part of the new holding it is necessary to apportion the cost of acquisition of any of the original shares between what is disposed of and what is retained, the apportionment shall be made by reference to market value at the date of the disposal (with such adjustment of the market value of any part of the new holding as may be required to offset any liability attaching thereto but forming part of the cost to be apportioned).

(2) This section has effect subject to section 8 (12) below.

General Note

This section provides that where it is necessary to apportion the cost of acquisition between what is disposed of and what is retained in order to obtain the cost of acquisition of the new holding, this shall be done by reference to market value on the day of disposal.

Composite new holdings

81.—(1) This section shall apply to a new holding—

(*a*) if it consists of more than one class of shares in or debentures of the company and one or more of those classes is of shares or debentures which, at any time not later than the end of the period of three months beginning with the date on which the reorganisation took effect, or of such longer period as the Board may by notice in writing allow, had quoted market values on a recognised stock exchange in the United Kingdom or elsewhere, or

(*b*) if it consists of more than one class of rights of unit holders and one or more of those classes is of rights the prices of which were published daily by the managers of the scheme at any time not later than the end of that period of three months (or longer if so allowed).

(2) Where for the purpose of computing the gain or loss accruing to any person from the acquisition and disposal of the whole or any part of any class of shares or debentures or rights of unit holders forming part of a new holding to which this section applies it is necessary to apportion costs of acquisition between what is disposed of and what is retained, the cost of acquisition of the new holding shall first be apportioned between the entire classes of shares or debentures or rights of which it consists by reference to market value on the first day (whether that day fell before the reorganisation took effect or later) on which market values or prices were quoted or published for the shares, debentures or rights as mentioned in subsection (1) (*a*) or (1) (*b*) above (with such adjustment of the market value of any class as may be required to offset any liability attaching thereto but forming part of the cost to be apportioned).

(3) For the purposes of this section the day on which a reorganisation involving the allotment of shares or debentures or unit holders' rights takes effect is the day following the day on which the right to renounce any allotment expires.

GENERAL NOTE

This section deals with the apportionment of the costs of acquisition of certain new holdings as between what is disposed of and what is retained on a disposal of part of the new holding. The new holdings concerned are ones which consist of more than one class of units or shares or debentures, one or more of which classes were at any time during three months from the date of the reorganisation quoted or had their prices published (subs. (1)). The apportionment is to be made by reference to market value on the first day on which market values or prices were quoted or published for the shares, debentures or units concerned (subs. (2)). Adjustment is to be made as required for any liability attaching to the shares, debentures or units.

Conversion of securities

Equation of converted securities and new holding

82.—(1) Sections 78 to 81 above shall apply with any necessary adaptations in relation to the conversion of securities as they apply in relation to a reorganisation (that is to say a reorganisation or reduction of a company's share capital).

(2) This section has effect subject to sections 83 and 84 below.

(3) For the purposes of this section and section 83 below—

(*a*) " conversion of securities " includes—

(i) a conversion of securities of a company into shares in the company, and

(ii) a conversion at the option of the holder of the securities converted as an alternative to the redemption of those securities for cash, and

(iii) any exchange of securities effected in pursuance of any enactment (including an enactment passed after this Act) which provides for the compulsory acquisition of any shares or securities and the issue of securities or other securities instead,

(*b*) " security " includes any loan stock or similar security whether of the Government of the United Kingdom or of any other government, or of any public or local authority in the United Kingdom or elsewhere, or of any company, and whether secured or unsecured.

GENERAL NOTE

Subject to ss. 83 and 84 below, this section provides that the rules relating to reorganisation provided by ss. 78 to 81 above are to apply to conversions of securities (as defined in subs. (3)). Thus ordinary shares obtained on exercising the rights of conversion conferred by a convertible debenture are treated as having been acquired at the same time and for the same consideration as the debenture itself. To the extent that there is no consideration receivable on the conversion other than the new shares, the conversion is not a disposal for capital gains tax purposes.

Premiums on conversion of securities

83.—(1) This section applies where, on a conversion of securities, a person receives, or becomes entitled to receive, any sum of money (in this section called " the premium ") which is by way of consideration (in addition to his new holding) for the disposal of the converted securities.

(2) If the inspector is satisfied that the premium is small, as compared with the value of the converted securities, and so directs—

(*a*) receipt of the premium shall not be treated for the purposes of this Act as a disposal of part of the converted securities, and (*b*) the premium shall be deducted from any expenditure allowable under this Act as a deduction in computing a gain or loss on the disposal of the new holding by the person receiving or becoming entitled to receive the premium.

(3) A person who is dissatisfied with the refusal of the inspector to give a direction under subsection (2) above may appeal to the Commissioners having jurisdiction on an appeal against an assessment to tax in respect of a gain accruing to him on a disposal of the securities.

(4) Where the allowable expenditure is less than the premium (or is nil)—

(*a*) subsections (2) and (3) above shall not apply, and

(*b*) if the recipient so elects (and there is any allowable expenditure)—

(i) the amount of the premium shall be reduced by the amount of the allowable expenditure, and

(ii) none of that expenditure shall be allowable as a deduction in computing a gain accruing on the occasion of the conversion, or on any subsequent occasion.

(5) In subsection (4) above " allowable expenditure " means expenditure which immediately before the conversion was attributable to the converted securities under paragraphs (*a*) and (*b*) of section 32 (1) above.

GENERAL NOTE

S. 83 provides that where a cash sum is received or receivable on the conversion of securities and the inspector is satisfied that it is small compared with the value of the securities, he may direct that the receipt is not to be treated as a disposal of part of the securities but is to be deducted from the expenditure allowable on the eventual disposal of the new holding. There is to be an appeal against the inspector's decision.

Where the allowable expenditure for the original securities is less than the premium or is nil, the provisions of subss. (2) and (3) are not to apply. There will therefore be a part disposal. Where the recipient of the premium elects under subs. (4) (*b*), all the allowable expenditure for the original securities is deducted from the amount of the premium and the balance is chargeable gain; and the allowable expenditure so deducted cannot be deducted on any subsequent occasion.

Compensation stock

84.—(1) This section has effect where gilt-edged securities are exchanged for shares in pursuance of any enactment (including an enactment passed after this Act) which provides for the compulsory acquisition of any shares and the issue of gilt-edged securities instead.

(2) The exchange shall not constitute a conversion of securities within section 82 above and accordingly the gilt-edged securities shall not be treated as having been acquired on any date earlier than that on which they were issued or for any consideration other than the value of the shares as determined for the purposes of the exchange.

(3) The exchange shall be treated as not involving any disposal of the shares by the person from whom they were compulsorily acquired but—

(*a*) there shall be calculated the gain or loss that would have accrued to him if he had then disposed of the shares for a consideration equal to the value mentioned in subsection (2) above, and

(*b*) on a subsequent disposal of the whole or part of the gilt-edged securities by the person to whom they were issued—

(i) there shall be deemed to accrue to him (in addition to any gain or loss that actually accrues)) the whole or a corresponding part of the gain or loss mentioned in paragraph (*a*) above, and

(ii) if the disposal is within section 67 (1) above (exemption for gilt-edged securities) that section shall have effect only in relation to any gain or loss that actually accrues and not in relation to any gain or loss that is deemed to accrue as aforesaid.

(4) Where a person to whom gilt-edged securities of any kind were issued as mentioned in subsection (1) above disposes of securities of that kind, the securities of which he disposes—

(*a*) shall, so far as possible, be identified with any securities of that kind which he has acquired otherwise than as mentioned in subsection (1) above within the twelve months preceding the disposal, and

(*b*) so far as they cannot be identified as aforesaid, shall be identified (without regard to sections 66, 68 (3) and 69 above) with securities which were issued to him as mentioned in subsection (1) above, taking those issued earlier before those issued later.

(5) Subsection (3) (*b*) above shall not apply to any disposal falling within the provisions of—

(*a*) section 44 (1) above (disposals between husband and wife),

(*b*) section 49 (4) above (disposals by personal representatives to legatees), or

(*c*) section 273 (1) of the Taxes Act (disposals within a group of companies);

but a person who has acquired the securities on a disposal falling within those provisions (and without there having been a previous disposal not falling within those provisions or a devolution on death) shall be treated for the purposes of subsections (3) (*b*) and (4) above as if the securities had been issued to him.

(6) Where the gilt-edged securities to be exchanged for any shares are not issued until after the date on which the shares are compulsorily acquired but on that date a right to the securities is granted, this section shall have effect as if the exchange had taken place on that date, as if references to the issue of the securities and the person to whom they were issued were references to the grant of the right and the person to whom it was granted and references to the disposal of the securities included references to disposals of the rights.

(7) In this section " shares " includes securities within the meaning of section 82 above.

(8) This section has effect subject to section 54 of the Finance Act 1976 (compulsory acquisition from certain companies of aircraft and shipbuilding shares).

General Note

This section applies to compulsory acquisitions of shares or securities (*e.g.* on nationalisation) where gilt-edged securities are issued in exchange for shares or securities. Without this section capital gains tax would generally be avoided altogether in the case of compulsory acquisitions where gilt-edged securities are issued in exchange for shares since this type of exchange is an express conversion of securities under s. 82 (3) (*a*) (iii) and thus involves no disposal of the shares. And the gilts will normally be exempt from capital gains tax under s. 67 (1). This section provides that any gain (or loss) on the shares is to be calculated at the time of the exchange but defers the charge (or allowance) until the gilts are subsequently disposed of.

Subs. (1)

The section is to apply where shares are exchanged for gilts under any Act that empowers the compulsory acquisition of shares and the issue of gilts in their place.

Subs. (2)

This explicitly provides that the exchange is not a conversion of securities for the purposes of s. 82. The gilts are to be treated as acquired at the time of the exchange and for a consideration equal to the value of the exchanged shares. This will be important if the gilts are disposed of within 12 months of the exchange.

Subs. (3)

This provides that the exchange of shares for gilts is not itself a disposal for capital gains tax purposes but that there is to be calculated the gain or loss that would have accrued on the exchange had it been. This gain or loss (or a corresponding part of it) will be charged or allowed in addition to any actual gain or loss on the subsequent disposal of all or part of the gilts. The exemption conferred by s. 67 (1) (exemption for the disposal of gilts 12 months after their acquisition), will only apply to the actual gains or losses on the gilts and not to the deferred gains or losses on the shares.

Subs. (4)

If a person who has received compensation gilts disposes of any gilts of that kind, the gilts disposed of are to be identified first with any gilts of that kind (other than the compensation gilts) which he has acquired in the 12 months before the disposal, and then, when those non-compensation gilts are exhausted, with the compensation gilts, beginning first with those issued at the earliest date before going on to those issued later.

Subs. (5)

The deferred gain or loss on the shares is not brought into account on certain categories of disposal of the compensation gilts. These categories are disposals by personal representatives to legatees, disposals between husband and wife and disposals within a group of companies. The person who has received the gilts as a result of such a disposal is treated as if the compensation gilts had originally been issued to him.

Subs. (6)

If the gilts are issued after the date when the shares are compulsorily acquired (as is likely when there are negotiations over the value of the acquired shares) but on the date of acquisition a right to the gilts is granted, then the section takes effect as if references to the issue of securities were references to the granting of the right to them, etc. Without this subsection, the section would have been easily avoidable: for the person whose shares are acquired could, by granting a right to the gilts before he received them, dispose of the gilts before the exchange had taken place.

Company reconstructions and amalgamations

Exchange of securities for those in another company

85.—(1) Subsection (3) below has effect where a company (company A) issues shares or debentures to a person in exchange for shares in or debenture of another company (company B) and—

(*a*) company A holds, or in consequence of the exchange will hold, more than one quarter of the ordinary share capital (as defined in section 526 (5) of the Taxes Act) of company B, or

(*b*) company A issues the shares or debentures in exchange for shares as the result of a general offer—

(i) which is made to members of company B or any class of them (with or without exceptions for persons connected with company A), and

(ii) which is made in the first instance on a condition such that if it were satisfied company A would have control of company B.

(2) Subsection (3) below also has effect where under section 86 below persons are to be treated as exchanging shares or debentures for shares or debentures held by them in consequence of the arrangement there mentioned.

(3) Subject to the provisions of sections 87 and 88 below, sections 78 to 81 above shall apply with any necessary adaptations as if the two companies mentioned in subsection (1) above, or as the case may be in section 86 below, were the same company and the exchange were a reorganisation of its share capital.

General Note

This section deals with company reconstructions and amalgamations, where shares in one company are exchanged for shares in another company. The general rule is that where the conditions in subs. (1) (*a*) or (*b*) are satisfied, the reconstruction or amalgamation is treated as if the two companies were one company and there was a reorganisation of that one company; so that ss. 78 to 81 apply *mutatis mutandis* (subs. (3)).

The conditions in subs. (1) are:

(*a*) that the acquiring company holds or in consequence of the exchange will hold more than one quarter of the ordinary share capital of the acquired company, or

(*b*) that the acquiring company issues the shares or debentures in exchange for shares in the acquired company as a result of a general offer which is made to the members of the acquired company (or any class of them) with or without exceptions for persons connected with the acquiring company; and which is made in the first instance on condition that on acceptance of the general offer the acquiring company will have control of the acquired company.

On the construction of this section see *Floor* v. *Davis* [1978] 3 W.L.R. 360.

Reconstruction or amalgamation involving issue of securities

86.—(1) Where—

(*a*) an arrangement between a company and the persons holding shares in or debentures of the company, or any class of such shares or debentures, is entered into for the purposes of or in connection with a scheme of reconstruction or amalgamation, and

(*b*) under the arrangement another company issues shares or debentures to those persons in respect of and in proportion to (or as nearly as may be in proportion to) their holdings of shares in or debentures of the first-mentioned company, but the shares in or debentures of the first-mentioned company are either retained by those persons or cancelled,

then those persons shall be treated as exchanging the first-mentioned shares or debentures for those held by them in consequence of the arrangement (any shares or debentures retained being for this purpose regarded as if they had been cancelled and replaced by a new issue), and subsections (2) and (3) of section 85 above shall apply accordingly.

(2) In this section " scheme of reconstruction or amalgamation " means a scheme for the reconstruction of any company or companies or the amalgamation of any two or more companies, and references to shares or debentures being retained include their being retained with altered rights or in an altered form whether as the result of reduction, consolidation, division or otherwise.

(3) This section, and section 85 (2) above, shall apply in relation

to a company which has no share capital as if references to shares in or debentures of a company included references to any interests in the company possessed by members of the company.

GENERAL NOTE

This section applies where, on a reconstruction or amalgamation, the acquiring company issues shares or debentures to the holders of shares or debentures in the acquired company in respect of and in proportion to the shares or debentures in the acquired company; but so that the shares or debentures in the acquired company are either cancelled or retained by the holders.

In such circumstances, the shares or debentures in the acquiring company (and any shares or debentures in the acquired company which are retained) are treated as though they had been exchanged for the shares or debentures in the acquired company and s. 85 (2) and (3) are to apply accordingly.

Restriction on application of sections 85 and 86

87.—(1) Subject to subsection (2) below, and section 88 below, neither section 85 nor section 86 above shall apply to any issue by a company of shares in or debentures of that company in exchange for or in respect of shares in or debentures of another company unless the exchange, reconstruction or amalgamation in question is effected for bona fide commercial reasons and does not form part of a scheme or arrangements of which the main purpose, or one of the main purposes, is avoidance of liability to capital gains tax or corporation tax.

(2) Subsection (1) above shall not affect the operation of section 85 or 86 in any case where the person to whom the shares or debentures are issued does not hold more than 5 per cent. of, or of any class of, the shares in or debentures of the second company mentioned in subsection (1) above.

(3) For the purposes of subsection (2) above shares or debentures held by persons connected with the person there mentioned shall be treated as held by him.

(4) If any tax assessed on a person (the chargeable person) by virtue of subsection (1) above is not paid within six months from the date when it is payable, any other person who—

(*a*) holds all or any part of the shares or debentures that were issued to the chargeable person, and

(*b*) has acquired them without there having been, since their acquisition by the chargeable person, any disposal of them not falling within section 44 (1) above or section 273 of the Taxes Act (disposals between spouses or members of a group of companies),

may, at any time within two years from the time when the tax became payable, be assessed and charged (in the name of the chargeable person) to all or, as the case may be, a corresponding part of the unpaid tax; and a person paying any amount of tax under this subsection shall be entitled to recover a sum of that amount from the chargeable person.

(5) In this section references to shares or debentures include references to any interests or options to which this Chapter applies by virtue of section 86 (3) above (interests in a company with no share capital) or section 139 below (quoted options).

GENERAL NOTE

As a general rule the reliefs provided by ss. 85 and 86 are not to apply to any issue of shares or debentures by the acquiring company in exchange for or in respect of shares or debentures in the acquired company unless the transaction is effected for *bona fide* commercial reasons and does not form part of a scheme of tax avoidance. This restriction is not to apply in the two following cases: (1)

where the person concerned (*i.e.* the potential taxpayer) to whom shares or debentures in the acquiring company are issued does not together with any persons connected with him hold more than 5 per cent. of, or of any class of, the shares or debentures of the acquired company; and (2) where clearance has been given under s. 88.

It is thought that "avoidance of liability" to tax in this section includes deferral of such liability, at any rate where such deferral is so significant as to amount to complete avoidance for all practical purposes.

Subs. (4) provides a means of recovery of tax unpaid after six months where the tax liability arose because of the application of subs. (1). Assessments may be made within two years from the time when the tax first became payable on any person who acquired the shares issued to the chargeable person either by a transfer between spouses or between group members. The person paying the tax has a right to recover that amount from the chargeable person. This section was originally introduced to counter avoidance schemes such as that used by the taxpayers in *Floor* v. *Davis* [1978] 3 W.L.R. 360.

Procedure for clearance in advance

88.—(1) Section 87 above shall not affect the operation of section 85 or 86 above in any case where, before the issue is made, the Board have, on the application of either company mentioned in section 87 (1) above, notified the company that the Board are satisfied that the exchange, reconstruction or amalgamation will be effected for bona fide commercial reasons and will not form part of any such scheme or arrangements as are mentioned in section 87 (1) above.

(2) Any application under subsection (1) above shall be in writing and shall contain particulars of the operations that are to be effected and the Board may, within thirty days of the receipt of the application or of any further particulars previously required under this subsection, by notice require the applicant to furnish further particulars for the purpose of enabling the Board to make their decision; and if any such notice is not complied with within thirty days or such longer period as the Board may allow, the Board need not proceed further on the application.

(3) The Board shall notify their decision to the applicant within thirty days of receiving the application or, if they give a notice under subsection (2) above, within thirty days of the notice being complied with.

(4) If the Board notify the applicant that they are not satisfied as mentioned in subsection (1) above or do not notify their decision to the applicant within the time required by subsection (3) above, the applicant may within thirty days of the notification or of that time require the Board to transmit the application, together with any notice given and further particulars furnished under subsection (2) above, to the Special Commissioners; and in that event any notification by the Special Commissioners shall have effect for the purposes of subsection (1) above as if it were a notification by the Board.

(5) If any particulars furnished under this section do not fully and accurately disclose all facts and considerations material for the decision of the Board or the Special Commissioners, any resulting notification that the Board or Commissioners are satisfied as mentioned in subsection (1) above shall be void.

General Note

This section provides a procedure for obtaining clearance from the Revenue before an issue has taken place, that s. 87 is not to apply in a particular case.

Stock dividends

Stock dividends: consideration for new holding

89.—(1) In applying section 79 (1) above in relation to the issue of any share capital to which section 34 of the Finance (No. 2) Act 1975 (stock dividends) applies as involving a reorganisation of the company's share capital, there shall be allowed, as consideration given for so much of the new holding as was issued as mentioned in—

(*a*) subsection (4), (5) or (6) of the said section 34, or

(*b*) paragraph 3 (1) of Schedule 8 to that Act,

(read in each case with subsection (3) of the said section 34) an amount equal to what is, for that much of the new holding, the appropriate amount in cash within the meaning of paragraph 1 of the said Schedule 8.

(2) This section shall have effect notwithstanding the proviso to section 79 (1) above.

General Note

Where a stock dividend (within s. 34, F. (No. 2) A. 1975) is received, for capital gains tax purposes there is a reorganisation of the share capital of the company concerned, and "the appropriate amount in cash" within para. 1, Sched. 8, F. (No. 2) A. 1975 is allowed as consideration given for the stock dividend when applying s. 79 (1) above to the reorganisation.

Capital gains on certain stock dividends

90.—(1) This section applies where a company issues any share capital to which section 34 of the Finance (No. 2) Act 1975 applies in respect of shares in the company held by a person as trustee, and another person is at the time of the issue absolutely entitled thereto as against the trustee or would be so entitled but for being an infant or other person under disability (or two or more other persons are or would be jointly so entitled thereto).

(2) Notwithstanding paragraph (*a*) of section 77 (2) above the case shall not constitute a reorganisation of the company's share capital for the purposes of sections 77 to 79 above.

(3) Notwithstanding section 19 (3) (*a*) above (disposal at market value) the person who is or would be so entitled to the share capital (or each of the persons who are or would be jointly so entitled thereto) shall be treated for the purposes of section 32 (1) (*a*) above as having acquired that share capital, or his interest in it, for a consideration equal to the appropriate amount in cash within the meaning of paragraph 1 of Schedule 8 to the Finance (No. 2) Act 1975.

General Note

This section deals with the situation where stock dividends to which s. 34, F. (No. 2) A. 1975 applies are allotted to trustees in a case where a beneficiary is absolutely entitled to them (or would be but for some legal disability). As the capital gains tax rules would not otherwise provide a satisfactory measure of cost to the beneficiary this section provides, first that the new shares do not form part of the trustees' holding and, secondly, that the cost to the beneficiary of the new shares is the amount on which income tax is charged under s. 34 ("the appropriate amount in cash" within para. 1, Sched. 8, F. (No. 2) A. 1975).

Quoted options

Application of Chapter II to quoted options

91. The preceding provisions of this Chapter have effect subject to section 139 below (quoted option to be regarded for the purposes of this Chapter as the shares which could be acquired by exercising the option).

GENERAL NOTE

S. 77 to 90 have effect subject to s. 139 which deals with quoted options.

CHAPTER III

UNIT TRUSTS ETC.

Preliminary

Interpretation

92. In this Act—

(*a*) " unit trust scheme " has the meaning given by section 26 (1) of the Prevention of Fraud (Investments) Act 1958 or section 22 of the Prevention of Fraud (Investments) Act (Northern Ireland) 1940,

(*b*) " authorised unit trust " has the meaning given by section 358 of the Taxes Act,

(*c*) " investment trust " has the meaning given by section 359 of the Taxes Act,

(*d*) " court investment fund " means a common investment fund established under section 1 of the Administration of Justice Act 1965.

GENERAL NOTE

This section defines the unit trusts and investment trusts with which Chap. III is concerned.

Application of Act to unit trusts

93. This Act shall apply in relation to any unit trust scheme as if—

(*a*) the scheme were a company,

(*b*) the rights of the unit holders were shares in the company, and

(*c*) in the case of an authorised unit trust, the company were resident and ordinarily resident in the United Kingdom.

GENERAL NOTE

For capital gains tax purposes a unit trust scheme is treated as if it were a company, the units being shares in the company. In the case of an authorised unit trust, the company is treated as resident and ordinarily resident in the U.K.

General

Reduction of tax liability on disposal of units or shares

94.—(1) Subject to subsections (2) and (6) below, this section applies to disposals of shares in—

(*a*) authorised unit trusts,

(*b*) unit trust schemes to which section 97 below applies,

(*c*) investment trusts, and

(*d*) any court investment fund.

(2) Paragraphs (*a*), (*b*) and (*c*) of subsection (1) above do not apply to any share of a class to which there would not be attributable in a liquidation of the trust the whole or a substantial part—

(*a*) of the assets of the trust representing gains on capital, or

(*b*) if those assets would be so attributable to two or more classes of shares, of a proportion of those assets corresponding to the proportion of all the issued shares of those classes represented by the issued shares of the class in question.

Where there are shares on which different amounts have been paid up the proportion mentioned in paragraph (*b*) above shall be calculated by reference to the amount paid up on the issued share capital of each class of shares.

(3) Where gains accrue to a person in any year of assessment on any disposals to which this section applies, the capital gains tax to which he is chargeable for that year shall be reduced by a credit equal to whichever of the following amounts is the smallest—

(*a*) the amount of that tax,

(*b*) an amount equal to 10 per cent. of the total chargeable gains accruing to him in that year on disposals to which this section applies,

(*c*) an amount equal to 10 per cent. of the total amount of chargeable gains accruing to him in that year on which capital gains tax is chargeable.

(4) Subsection (3) above shall have effect in relation to the corporation tax chargeable on a company for an accounting period in which gains accrue to it on any disposals to which this section applies as it has effect in relation to the capital gains tax chargeable on a person other than a company, and shall so have effect as if—

(*a*) references to a year of assessment were references to an accounting period, and

(*b*) for the total amount of chargeable gains mentioned in paragraph (*c*) of that subsection there were substituted the amount of gains charged to corporation tax for the accounting period in question increased, where subsection (5) below applies, in accordance with that subsection.

In this subsection " gains charged to corporation tax " means the profits on which corporation tax falls finally to be borne after deducting the income charged to corporation tax as defined in section 85 (6) of the Finance Act 1972 (read with section 110 (4) of that Act) except that, in relation to an accounting period for which the company claims a credit for foreign tax, those gains shall be determined in accordance with section 100 (5) of that Act.

(5) In relation to an accounting period for which any reduction falls to be made under section 93 of the Finance Act 1972 in the amount to be included in respect of chargeable gains in the company's total profits, the gains mentioned in subsection (4) (*b*) above shall be increased by multiplying by the inverse of the fraction of that amount remaining after the reduction; and if under subsection (3) or (4) of the said section 93 the reduction falls to be made by reference to different portions of that amount, the increase under this subsection shall be made similarly, using the inverse of the fractions of those portions remaining after any reduction.

(6) Where a person disposes of a share—

(*a*) which at the time of disposal is a qualifying share (that is to say, a share falling within subsection (1) (*a*), (*b*) or (*c*) above) but has not at all times while in the ownership of that person been a qualifying share, or

(*b*) which at the time of disposal is not a qualifying share but has previously while in his ownership been such a share,

this section shall apply to the disposal, but for the purposes of subsection (3) (*b*) above the gain accruing on the disposal shall be treated as reduced in proportion to the time for which the share was in the ownership of that person without being a qualifying share.

(7) Where under Chapter II above the share of which a person disposes falls to be identified with another asset or other assets previously held by him, subsection (6) above shall have effect as if—

(*a*) his period of ownership of the share disposed of included his period of ownership of the other asset or assets, and

(*b*) the share disposed of had or had not been a qualifying share at any time during that additional period according to whether or not the other asset or any of those other assets was a qualifying share at that time.

(8) Where a person disposes of a share which at the time of disposal is a qualifying share and which he has received on a conversion of—

(*a*) a share other than a qualifying share, or

(*b*) loan stock,

previously held by him, being a conversion pursuant to rights in that behalf attached to the share or stock previously held, subsections (6) and (7) above shall have effect as if that share or stock had been a qualifying share throughout any time for which the company by which it was issued was a body of the kind mentioned in paragraph (*a*), (*b*) or (*c*) of subsection (1) above.

(9) Where the gain accruing on a disposal to which this section applies falls to be computed in accordance with paragraph 14 (2) (*b*) of Schedule 5 to this Act (unquoted securities held before 6th April 1965 which are subsequently converted or exchanged)—

(*a*) the period of ownership of the share disposed of shall not be treated under subsection (7) (*a*) above as having begun before the time mentioned in the said paragraph 14 (2) (*b*); and

(*b*) for the purposes of subsection (3) (*b*) above the gain shall be taken to be that mentioned in sub-paragraph (ii) of the said paragraph 14 (2) (*b*) reduced, where applicable, in accordance with subsections (6) and (7) above.

(10) For the purposes of subsections (6) to (8) above no account shall be taken of any period of ownership before 6th April 1965; and nothing in Chapter II above shall be construed as enabling any asset to be treated as having been a qualifying share at any time when it was not such in fact.

(11) For the purposes of this section loan stock issued by an investment trust before 11th April 1972, being loan stock to which there would be attributable in a liquidation of the trust the whole of the assets of the trust representing gains on capital, shall be treated as shares in the trust falling within subsection (1) above.

GENERAL NOTE

This section provides for a credit against capital gains tax or corporation tax on chargeable gains from disposals of shares in authorised unit trusts, unit trusts for pension schemes, investment trusts and court investment funds provided the shares participate in the capital gains of the trust or fund (subs. (2)). The credit is equivalent, subject to subs. (3), to 10 per cent. of the chargeable gains. The credit is independent of the chargeable gains, if any, realised by the trust or fund in which the shares are held.

The alternative ceilings to the credit prevent it being used for relief of other chargeable gains or for loss relief (subs. (3)).

Subss. (4) and (5) adapt the credit to the corporation tax system where the shareholder is a company.

Unit trusts

Valuation of assets and rights

95. Nothing in any trust deed executed before 1st September 1972 and regulating any authorised unit trust, or any unit trust scheme to which section 97 below applies, shall preclude the managers of the trust or the trustee, in valuing the assets of the trust at any time during an accounting period, from making a deduction for any tax for which the trust may become liable in respect of its net gains in that period up to that time.

In this section " net gains " means the excess, if any, of chargeable gains over the allowable losses deductible from those gains as those gains and losses are computed for the charge to tax on the trust.

General Note

This section empowers the managers and trustees of authorised unit trusts and unit trusts for pension schemes to value their assets after providing for tax on the net capital gains up to the time of the valuation.

Unit trusts for exempt unit holders

96. If throughout a year of assessment all the issued units in a unit trust scheme are assets such that any gain accruing if they were disposed of by the unit holder would be wholly exempt from capital gains tax or corporation tax (otherwise than by reason of residence) gains accruing to the unit trust scheme in that year of assessment shall not be chargeable gains.

General Note

S. 96 provides an exemption from tax on the capital gains of a unit trust where all the units are held in such a way (*e.g.* by charities or approved superannuation schemes, but not by reason only of the residence of the holder) that the unit holders are exempt from tax on their gains.

Unit trusts for pension schemes

97.—(1) This section applies to a unit trust scheme for any year of assessment if throughout that year all the issued units in the unit trust scheme constitute investments to which section 208 (2) of the Taxes Act or section 21 (7) of the Finance Act 1970 (pension schemes) applies, each being an investment such that any gain accruing if it were disposed of by the unit holder would either be wholly exempt from capital gains tax or corporation tax, or be so exempt as to not less than 85 per cent.

(2) Of all the gains accruing to the unit trust scheme in the year of assessment one-tenth (that is one-tenth of what would apart from this subsection be chargeable gains) shall be chargeable gains.

(3) The rate of capital gains tax payable on chargeable gains accruing to a unit trust scheme to which this section applies in the year of assessment shall be 10 per cent.

General Note

This section applies to a unit trust scheme for any year of assessment throughout which all the issued units are held by pension funds so that any gain on the disposal of any of the units would be exempt from capital gains tax or corporation tax as to not less than 85 per cent. Only one-tenth of what would otherwise be chargeable gains on disposals of assets by the unit trust scheme shall be chargeable gains (subs. (2)) and capital gains tax shall be charged on such chargeable gains at the rate of 10 per cent. (subs. (3)). Where this section applies, the effective rate of capital gains tax is 1 per cent.

Transfer of company's assets to unit trust which later comes within section 96 or 97

98.—(1) Where section 267 of the Taxes Act (roll-over for assets transferred on company reconstruction or amalgamation) has applied on the transfer of a company's business (in whole or in part) to a unit trust scheme to which at the time of the transfer neither section 96 nor section 97 applied, then if—

(*a*) at any time after the transfer the unit trust scheme becomes in a year of assessment one to which either of those sections does apply, and

(*b*) at the beginning of that year of assessment the unit trust scheme still owns any of the assets of the business transferred,

the unit trust scheme shall be treated for all the purposes of this Act as if immediately after the transfer it had sold, and immediately re-acquired, the assets referred to in paragraph (*b*) above at their market value at that time.

(2) Notwithstanding any limitation on the time for making assessments, an assessment to corporation tax chargeable in consequence of subsection (1) above may be made at any time within six years after the end of the year of assessment referred to in subsection (1) above, and where under this section a unit trust scheme is to be treated as having disposed of, and re-acquired, an asset of a business, all such recomputations of liability in respect of other disposals and all such adjustments of tax, whether by way of assessment or by way of discharge or repayment of tax, as may be required in consequence of the provisions of this section shall be carried out.

General Note

This section applies where the roll-over relief for business assets transferred on a company reconstruction or amalgamation provided by s. 267, I.C.T.A. 1970 has applied on the transfer of a business to a unit trust scheme which at the time of the transfer was not within s. 96 or 97 above.

When such a unit trust scheme subsequently comes within s. 96 or 97 and at the beginning of the year of assessment in which this happens still owns any of the assets in respect of which s. 267 relief has been given, s. 267 relief in relation to those retained assets is effectively withdrawn and the unit trust scheme is treated as if immediately after the retained assets were transferred to it, it sold and reacquired them at their market value at that time.

Court investment funds, etc.

Funds in court

99.—(1) For the purposes of section 46 above (nominees and bare trustees) funds in court held by the Accountant General shall be regarded as held by him as nominee for the persons entitled to or interested in the funds, or as the case may be for their trustees.

(2) Where funds in court standing to an account are invested or, after investment, are realised the method by which the Accountant General effects the investment or the realisation of investments shall not affect the question whether there is for the purposes of this Act an acquisition, or as the case may be a disposal, of an asset representing funds in court standing to the account, and in particular there shall for those purposes be an acquisition or disposal of shares in a court investment fund notwithstanding that the investment in such shares of funds in court standing to an account, or the realisation of funds which have been so invested, is effected by setting off, in the Accountant General's

accounts, investment in one account against realisation of investments in another.

(3) In this section " funds in court " means—

(*a*) money in the Supreme Court, money in county courts and statutory deposits described in section 14 of the Administration of Justice Act 1965, and

(*b*) any such moneys as are mentioned in section 30 of the said Act of 1965 (which relates to Northern Ireland) and money in a county court in Northern Ireland,

and investments representing such money; and references in this section to the Accountant General are references to the Accountant General of the Supreme Court of Judicature in England and, in relation to money within paragraph (*b*) above and investments representing such money, include references to the Accountant General of the Supreme Court of Judicature of Northern Ireland or any other person by whom such funds are held.

GENERAL NOTE

This section deals with funds held in court. Such funds are defined and stated to fall within s. 46, as being held by the court merely as nominee. The mode of investment of funds in court is not to affect the substantial capital gains tax treatment of any gains or losses accruing to the persons beneficially entitled on the investment of such funds and the realisation of such investments.

Reduced rate of tax

100. The rate of capital gains tax payable on chargeable gains accruing to a court investment fund shall be 10 per cent.

GENERAL NOTE

Capital gains tax at a rate of 10 per cent. is chargeable on the gains of court investment funds.

PART V

LAND

Private residences

Relief on disposal of private residence

101.—(1) This section applies to a gain accruing to an individual so far as attributable to the disposal of, or of an interest in—

(*a*) a dwelling-house or part of a dwelling-house which is, or has at any time in his period of ownership been, his only or main residence, or

(*b*) land which he has for his own occupation and enjoyment with that residence as its garden or grounds up to the permitted area.

(2) In this section " the permitted area " means, subject to subsections (3) and (4) below, an area (inclusive of the site of the dwelling-house) of one acre.

(3) In any particular case the permitted area shall be such area, larger than one acre, as the Commissioners concerned may determine if satisfied that, regard being had to the size and character of the dwelling-house, that larger area is required for the reasonable enjoyment of it (or of the part in question) as a residence.

(4) Where part of the land occupied with a residence is and part is not within subsection (1) above, then (up to the permitted area) that

part shall be taken to be within subsection (1) above which, if the remainder were separately occupied, would be the most suitable for occupation and enjoyment with the residence.

(5) So far as it is necessary for the purposes of this section to determine which of two or more residences is an individual's main residence for any period—

(*a*) the individual may conclude that question by notice in writing to the inspector given within two years from the beginning of that period, or given by the end of the year 1966–67, if that is later, but subject to a right to vary that notice by a further notice in writing to the inspector as respects any period beginning not earlier than two years before the giving of the further notice,

(*b*) subject to paragraph (*a*) above, the question shall be concluded by the determination of the inspector, which may be as respects either the whole or specified parts of the period of ownership in question,

and notice of any determination of the inspector under paragraph (*b*) above shall be given to the individual who may appeal to the General Commissioners or the Special Commissioners against that determination within thirty days of service of the notice.

(6) In the case of a man and his wife living with him—

(*a*) there can only be one residence or main residence for both, so long as living together, and, where a notice under subsection (5) (*a*) above affects both the husband and the wife, it must be given by both, and

(*b*) any notice under subsection (5) (*b*) above which affects a residence owned by the husband and a residence owned by the wife shall be given to each and either may appeal under that subsection.

(7) In this section, and sections 102 to 105 below, " the period of ownership " where the individual has had different interests at different times shall be taken to begin from the first acquisition taken into account in arriving at the expenditure which under Chapter II of Part II of this Act is allowable as a deduction in computing under that Chapter the amount of the gain to which this section applies, and in the case of a man and his wife living with him—

(*a*) if the one disposes of, or of his or her interest in, the dwelling-house or part of a dwelling-house which is their only or main residence to the other, and in particular if it passes on death to the other as legatee, the other's period of ownership shall begin with the beginning of the period of ownership of the one making the disposal, and

(*b*) if paragraph (*a*) applies, but the dwelling-house or part of a dwelling-house was not the only or main residence of both throughout the period of ownership of the one making the disposal, account shall be taken of any part of that period during which it was his only or main residence as if it was also that of the other.

(8) If at any time (being a time after 30th July 1978) during an individual's period of ownership of a dwelling-house or part of a dwelling-house he—

(*a*) resides in living accommodation which is for him job-related within the meaning of paragraph 4A of Schedule 1 to the Finance Act 1974, and

(*b*) intends in due course to occupy the dwelling-house or part of a dwelling-house as his only or main residence,

this section, and sections 102 to 105 below, shall apply as if the dwelling-house or part of a dwelling-house were at that time occupied by him as a residence.

(9) Apportionments of consideration shall be made wherever required by this section or sections 102 to 105 below and, in particular, where a person disposes of a dwelling-house only part of which is his only or main residence.

GENERAL NOTE

This section defines the categories of gains accruing to individuals on disposals of private residences which are exempt from capital gains tax.

Subs. (1) limits the relief to gains accruing on the disposal of a dwelling-house which is or has been the taxpayer's only or main residence and land up to one acre (subject to subss. (3) and (4)) occupied with the house as garden or grounds.

It was held in *Varty* v. *Lynes* [1976] 1 W.L.R. 1091 that subs. (1) (*b*) did not apply to relieve a gain on a disposal of land which took place after the dwelling-house concerned had been disposed of. In *Makins* v. *Elson* [1977] 1 W.L.R. 221, a caravan jacked up and resting on bricks on its site in which a telephone, electricity and water supply had been installed qualified as a dwelling-house within the section.

Subs. (5) deals with the case where an individual has two or more residences. Para. (*a*) enables him by notice within two years of acquisition or by April 5, 1967, whichever is the later, to elect which residence shall be his main residence for the purposes of this section. Para. (*b*) provides that in default of such an election the inspector is to determine which is the individual's principal residence, but that the individual may within 30 days of such determination appeal to the General or Special Commissioners at his option.

Subs. (6) applies in the case of a man living with his wife. It provides by para. (*a*) that there can only be one main residence and that a nomination under subs. (5) (*a*) shall be made by both husband and wife. It provides by para. (*b*) that any notice under subs. (5) (*b*) shall be given to both husband and wife, either of whom may appeal.

Subs. (7) deals with the case of a residence owned at different times by a man and his wife, living with him. It provides by para. (*a*) that where the interest of one spouse is transferred to the other, whether *inter vivos* or on death, the recipient's period of ownership shall be treated as having begun at the beginning of the ownership of the other. It provides by para. (*b*) that on the disposal of a private residence from one spouse to the other where the residence was not the only or main residence of both throughout the period of ownership of the transferor spouse, the benefit of any period in which it was the transferor spouse's only or main residence shall be given to the transferee spouse.

Subs. (8) ensures that the relief shall not be affected if the individual ceases (or does not start) to occupy his dwelling-house (or part of it) for the following reasons, provided that he intends to occupy it in due course. The occupation must be prevented because he is occupying living accommodation provided by reason of his or his spouse's employment because

(i) it is necessary to enable performance of the duties of employment; or
(ii) enables the better performance of these duties and is customary; or
(iii) is part of special security arrangements, there being a special threat to the employee's security.

(There are special rules contained in Sched. 1, para. 4A (4)–(6) F.A. 1974, if the employer is a company and the employee is a director.)

This subsection only applies to periods occurring after the passing of the F.A. 1978.

Subs. (9) enables apportionments to be made where necessary.

Amount of relief

102.—(1) No part of a gain to which section 101 above applies shall be a chargeable gain if the dwelling-house or part of a dwelling-house has been the individual's only or main residence throughout the period

of ownership, or throughout the period of ownership except for all or any part of the last twelve months of that period.

(2) Where subsection (1) above does not apply, a fraction of the gain shall not be a chargeable gain, and that fraction shall be—

(*a*) the length of the part or parts of the period of ownership during which the dwelling-house or the part of the dwelling-house was the individual's only or main residence, but inclusive of the last twelve months of the period of ownership in any event, divided by

(*b*) the length of the period of ownership.

(3) For the purposes of subsections (1) and (2) above—

(*a*) a period of absence not exceeding three years (or periods of absence which together did not exceed three years), and in addition

(*b*) any period of absence throughout which the individual worked in an employment or office all the duties of which were performed outside the United Kingdom, and in addition

(*c*) any period of absence not exceeding four years (or periods of absence which together did not exceed four years) throughout which the individual was prevented from residing in the dwelling-house or part of the dwelling-house in consequence of the situation of his place of work or in consequence of any condition imposed by his employer requiring him to reside elsewhere, being a condition reasonably imposed to secure the effective performance by the employee of his duties,

shall be treated as if in that period of absence the dwelling-house or the part of the dwelling-house was the individual's only or main residence if both before and after the period there was a time when the dwelling-house was the individual's only or main residence.

In this subsection " period of absence " means a period during which the dwelling-house or the part of the dwelling-house was not the individual's only or main residence and throughout which he had no residence or main residence eligible for relief under this section.

(4) In this section " period of ownership " does not include any period before 6th April 1965.

General Note

Subs. (1) provides that the disposal of a dwelling-house is exempt from capital gains tax only if the house has been an individual's only or main residence throughout his period of ownership, the last 12 months being ignored.

Subs. (2) provides relief on a proportional basis where the terms of subs. (1) are not satisfied; the inclusion of the last 12 months as part of the period of ownership makes the relief more valuable to the taxpayer.

Subs. (3) treats as a period of residence:

(*a*) periods of absence not exceeding three years;

(*b*) periods of absence (unlimited in time) in which the individual worked in an employment or office all the duties of which were performed outside the U.K.; and

(*c*) periods of absence not exceeding four years throughout which the individual was prevented from residing in the dwelling-house in consequence of the situation or conditions of his work,

provided in every case that the residence was his sole or main residence both before and after such periods.

Subs. (4) defines " period of ownership " for the purposes of this section as excluding all time prior to April 6, 1965.

Amount of relief: further provisions

103.—(1) If the gain accrues from the disposal of a dwelling-house or part of a dwelling-house part of which is used exclusively for the purposes of a trade or business, or of a profession or vocation, the gain shall be apportioned and section 102 above shall apply in relation to the part of the gain apportioned to the part which is not exclusively used for those purposes.

(2) If at any time in the period of ownership there is a change in what is occupied as the individual's residence, whether on account of a reconstruction or conversion of a building or for any other reason, or there have been changes as regards the use of part of the dwelling-house for the purpose of a trade or business, or of a profession or vocation, or for any other purpose, the relief given by section 102 above may be adjusted in such manner as the Commissioners concerned may consider to be just and reasonable.

(3) Section 102 above shall not apply in relation to a gain if the acquisition of, or of the interest in, the dwelling-house or the part of a dwelling-house was made wholly or partly for the purpose of realising a gain from the disposal of it, and shall not apply in relation to a gain so far as attributable to any expenditure which was incurred after the beginning of the period of ownership and was incurred wholly or partly for the purpose of realising a gain from the disposal.

General Note

Subs. (1) excludes from the relief any part of the gain derived from any part of the dwelling-house used exclusively for the purposes of a business or trade, profession or vocation.

Subs. (2) provides for adjustment of relief in the case of a change in what is occupied as the individual's residence. It would apply where the individual divided his house into flats retaining one for his own occupation.

Subs. (3) describes the circumstances in which the relief does not apply. The exemption will not apply if the acquisition of the house was made wholly or partly for the purpose of realising a gain from the disposal. The wording makes it clear that an individual who buys a house intending to sell it at a profit does not get the benefit of the exemption merely by living in the house for a time before selling it.

Private residence occupied under terms of settlement

104. Sections 101 to 103 above shall also apply in relation to a gain accruing to a trustee on a disposal of settled property being an asset within section 101 (1) above where during the period of ownership of the trustee the dwelling-house or part of the dwelling-house mentioned in that subsection has been the only or main residence of a person entitled to occupy it under the terms of the settlement, and in those sections as so applied—

(*a*) references to the individual shall be taken as references to the trustee except in relation to the occupation of the dwelling-house or part of the dwelling-house, and

(*b*) the notice which may be given to the inspector under section 101 (5) (*a*) above shall be a joint notice by the trustee and the person entitled to occupy the dwelling-house or part of the dwelling-house.

General Note

This section applies the private residence relief of ss. 101 to 103 to property held on trust, where under the terms of the settlement an individual is entitled to occupy the residence, by treating the individual's occupation as that of the trustees.

In *Sansom* v. *Peay* [1976] 1 W.L.R. 1073, the occupation of a person who was an object of a discretionary settlement pursuant to the exercise by the trustees of an express power contained in the settlement was held to be occupation under the terms of the settlement within this section.

Private residence occupied by dependent relative

105.—(1) This section applies to a gain accruing to an individual so far as attributable to the disposal of, or of an interest in, a dwelling-house or part of a dwelling-house which is, or has at any time in his period of ownership been, the sole residence of a dependent relative of the individual, provided rent-free and without any other consideration.

(2) If the individual so claims, such relief shall be given in respect of it and its garden or grounds as would be given under sections 101 to 103 above if the dwelling-house (or part of the dwelling-house) had been the individual's only or main residence in the period of residence by the dependent relative, and shall be so given in addition to any relief available under those sections apart from this section.

(3) Not more than one dwelling-house (or part of a dwelling-house) may qualify for relief as being the residence of a dependent relative of the claimant at any one time nor, in the case of a man and his wife living with him, as being the residence of a dependent relative of the claimant or of the claimant's husband or wife at any one time.

(4) The inspector, before allowing a claim, may require the claimant to show that the giving of the relief claimed will not under subsection (3) above preclude the giving of relief to the claimant's wife or husband or that a claim to any such relief has been relinquished.

(5) In this section " dependent relative " means, in relation to an individual—

(*a*) any relative of his or of his wife who is incapacitated by old age or infirmity from maintaining himself, or

(*b*) his or his wife's mother who, whether or not incapacitated, is either widowed, or living apart from her husband, or a single woman in consequence of dissolution or annulment of marriage.

(6) If the individual mentioned in subsection (5) above is a woman the references in that subsection to the individual's wife shall be construed as references to the individual's husband.

General Note

This section extends the private residence relief to encompass cases where a residence has been provided free of rent or any other consideration, by an individual as the sole residence of a dependent relative, as defined in subs. (5). This extended relief is only available in respect of one dependent relative for each individual; and a husband and wife are treated as one person when considering whether they have utilised this relief.

Leases

Leases of land and other assets

106. Schedule 3 to this Act shall have effect as respects leases of land and of other assets.

General Note

This section brings into operation the detailed provisions of Sched. 3 which deals with computation of gains from disposals of leases.

Small part disposals

107.—(1) This section applies to a transfer of land forming part only of a holding of land, where—

(a) the amount or value of the consideration for the transfer is small, as compared with the market value of the holding as it subsisted immediately before the transfer, and

(b) the transfer is not one which, by virtue of section 44 above (transfers between husband and wife) or section 273 (1) of the Taxes Act (transfers within groups of companies), is treated as giving rise to neither a gain nor a loss.

(2) Subject to subsection (3) below, if the transferor so claims, the transfer shall not be treated for the purposes of this Act as a disposal, but all sums which, if it had been so treated, would have been brought into account as consideration for that disposal in the computation under Chapter II of Part II of this Act of a gain accruing on the disposal shall be deducted from any expenditure allowable under that Chapter as a deduction in computing a gain on any subsequent disposal of the holding.

(3) This section shall not apply—

(a) if the amount or value of the consideration for the transfer exceeds £10,000, or

(b) where in the year of assessment in which the transfer is made, the transferor made any other disposal of land, if the total amount or value of the consideration for all disposals of land made by the transferor in that year exceeds £10,000.

(4) No account shall be taken under subsection (3) above of any transfer of land to which section 108 below applies.

(5) In relation to a transfer which is not for full consideration in money or money's worth "the amount or value of the consideration" in this section shall mean the market value of the land transferred.

(6) For the purposes of this section the holding of land shall comprise only the land in respect of which the expenditure allowable under paragraphs (a) and (b) of section 32 (1) above would be apportioned under section 35 above if the transfer had been treated as a disposal (that is, as a part disposal of the holding).

(7) In this section references to a holding of land include references to any estate or interest in a holding of land, not being an estate or interest which is a wasting asset, and references to part of a holding shall be construed accordingly.

General Note

The purpose of this section seems to be that of saving the expense of valuing land remaining after a part disposal out of it, where the consideration for the part disposal is both modest (under £10,000—subs. (3)) and "small" in comparison to the value of the whole parcel (subs. (1)). Apart from this provision, a part disposal would render necessary a valuation of the land remaining undisposed of in order to apportion allowable expenditure in accordance with the $\frac{A}{A+B}$ formula. Under this section, however, if the taxpayer so elects, no capital gains tax computation is made on the part disposal, so that the need to apportion allowable expenditure does not arise (subs. (2)). Any gain or loss which would have been revealed by such a computation is reflected in the gain or loss arising on the disposal of the remaining land, for, where the section applies, the consideration received for the small part disposal is deducted from the amount of expenditure otherwise allowable in computing a gain on a subsequent disposal of the holding of land concerned.

Part disposal to authority with compulsory powers

108.—(1) This section applies to a transfer of land forming part only of a holding of land to an authority exercising or having compulsory powers where—

(*a*) the amount or value of the consideration for the transfer, or if the transfer is not for full consideration in money or money's worth, the market value of the land transferred, is small, as compared with the market value of the holding as it subsisted immediately before the transfer, and

(*b*) the transferor had not taken any steps by advertising or otherwise to dispose of any part of the holding or to make his willingness to dispose of it known to the authority or others.

(2) If the transferor so claims, the transfer shall not be treated for the purposes of this Act as a disposal, but all sums which, if it had been so treated, would have been brought into account as consideration for that disposal in the computation under Chapter II of Part II of this Act of a gain accruing on the disposal shall be deducted from any expenditure allowable under that Chapter as a deduction in computing a gain on any subsequent disposal of the holding.

(3) For the purposes of this section the holding of land shall comprise only the land in respect of which the expenditure allowable under paragraphs (*a*) and (*b*) of section 32 (1) above would be apportioned under section 35 above if the transfer had been treated as a disposal (that is, as a part disposal of the holding).

(4) In this section references to a holding of land include references to an estate or interest in a holding of land, not being an estate or interest which is a wasting asset, and references to part of a holding shall be construed accordingly.

(5) In this section "authority exercising or having compulsory powers" means, in relation to the land transferred, a person or body of persons acquiring it compulsorily or who has or have been, or could be, authorised to acquire it compulsorily for the purposes for which it is acquired, or for whom another person or body of persons has or have been, or could be, authorised so to acquire it.

General Note

This section deals in a similar manner to the provisions of s. 107, with the case of a part disposal of land to an authority having compulsory powers: if the consideration or market value of the part disposed of is small in relation to the market value of the total holding before the disposal then the transfer to the authority need not be treated as a part disposal, if the transferor so elects. Instead, any consideration will be treated as a deduction from the transferor's expenditure in the computation of chargeable gain when there is a subsequent disposal of the land retained.

It is a condition for the application of s. 107 that the transferor should not have taken any steps by advertising or otherwise to dispose of any part of the holding (subs. (1) (*b*)). Note that the £10,000 restriction contained in s. 106 (3), does not apply in cases within s. 107.

Part disposal: consideration exceeding allowable expenditure

109.—(1) The provisions of sections 107 (2) and 108 (2) above shall have effect subject to this section.

(2) Where the allowable expenditure is less than the consideration for the part disposal (or is nil)—

(*a*) the said provisions shall not apply, and

(*b*) if the recipient so elects (and there is any allowable expenditure)—

(i) the consideration for the part disposal shall be reduced by the amount of the allowable expenditure, and

(ii) none of that expenditure shall be allowable as a deduction in computing a gain accruing on the occasion of the part disposal or on any subsequent occasion.

In this subsection " allowable expenditure " means expenditure which, immediately before the part disposal, was attributable to the holding of land under paragraphs (*a*) and (*b*) of section 32 (1) above.

General Note

Where in a case of a part disposal of land which would otherwise come within s. 107 or s. 108 the allowable expenditure of the whole holding is less than the consideration for the part disposal (or is nil), those sections shall not apply. Instead it is open to the taxpayer to elect that s. 109 (2) (*b*) shall apply. If he so elects, in computing the chargeable gain on the part disposal the allowable expenditure relating to the whole holding is deductible from the consideration received (*i.e.* the balance is chargeable gain) and on any subsequent occasion none of that expenditure is allowable for capital gains tax purposes.

Compulsory acquisition

Compensation paid on compulsory acquisition

110.—(1) Where land or an interest in or right over land is acquired and the acquisition is, or could have been, made under compulsory powers, then in considering whether, under section 43 (4) above, the purchase price or compensation or other consideration for the acquisition should be apportioned and treated in part as a capital sum within section 20 (1) (*a*) above (disposal arising on receipt of capital sum), whether as compensation for loss of goodwill or for disturbance or otherwise, or should be apportioned in any other way, the fact that the acquisition is or could have been made compulsorily, and any statutory provision treating the purchase price or compensation or other consideration as exclusively paid in respect of the land itself, shall be disregarded.

(2) In any case where land or an interest in land is acquired as mentioned in subsection (1) above from any person and the compensation or purchase price includes an amount in respect of severance of the land comprised in the acquisition or sale from other land in which that person is entitled in the same capacity to an interest, or in respect of that other land as being injuriously affected, there shall be deemed for the purposes of this Act to be a part disposal of that other land.

General Note

Subs. (1)

In a case of a disposal of land to an authority which either was or could have been compelled by the authority using its compulsory purchase powers, this section directs that the statutory provisions dealing with land compensation are to be disregarded where any apportionment of the consideration received is made under s. 43 (4), for instance as between capital and income receipts.

Subs. (2)

In a case of a disposal within subs. (1) above, where the consideration received includes sums in respect of compensation for severance or injurious affection in respect of other land in the ownership of the disponee which is not disposed of by the disposal, for capital gains tax purposes there is deemed to be a part disposal of such other land.

Time of disposal and acquisition

111. Where an interest in land is acquired, otherwise than under a contract, by an authority possessing compulsory purchase powers the time at which the disposal and acquisition is made is the time at which the compensation for the acquisition is agreed or otherwise determined (variations on appeal being disregarded for this purpose) or, if earlier

(but after 20th April 1971), the time when the authority enter on the land in pursuance of their powers.

GENERAL NOTE

This section provides that land compulsorily acquired by a local authority is disposed of when the compensation is agreed or otherwise determined (appeals being disregarded for this purpose) or, if earlier (but after April 20, 1971), when the authority enters the land.

Agricultural land and woodlands

Grants for giving up agricultural land

112. For the purposes of capital gains tax, a sum payable to an individual by virtue of a scheme under section 27 of the Agriculture Act 1967 (grants for relinquishing occupation of uncommercial agricultural units) shall not be treated as part of the consideration obtain by him for, or otherwise as accruing to him on, the disposal of any asset.

GENERAL NOTE

Under the Agriculture Act 1967, grants may be made by the appropriate Minister to tenants who relinquish occupation of uncommercial agricultural units. Such grants, whether paid by lump sum or as an annuity, are to be exempt from capital gains tax (*cf. Davis* v. *Powell* [1977] 1 W.L.R. 258).

Woodlands

113.—(1) (*a*) Consideration for the disposal of trees standing or felled or cut on land assessed to income tax or corporation tax under Schedule B, and

(*b*) capital sums received under a policy of insurance in respect of the destruction of or damage or injury to trees by fire or other hazard on such land,

shall be excluded from the computation under Chapter II of Part II of this Act of the gain accruing on the disposal if the person making the disposal is the person assessed to the tax under Schedule B.

(2) Subsection (1) (*b*) above has effect notwithstanding section 20 (1) above (disposal arising on receipt of capital sum).

(3) In the computation under Chapter II of Part II above so much of the cost of woodland in the United Kingdom shall be disregarded as is attributable to trees growing on the land.

(4) In the computation under Chapter II of Part II above of the gain accruing on a disposal of woodland in the United Kingdom so much of the consideration for the disposal as is attributable to trees growing on the land shall be excluded.

(5) References in this section to trees include references to saleable underwood.

GENERAL NOTE

This section deals with the interaction of capital gains tax and income tax or corporation tax assessed under Sched. B (woodlands managed on a commercial basis).

Where land is assessed to tax under Sched. B, consideration for the disposal of trees standing or felled or cut on such land, and capital sums received under insurance policies in respect of trees on such land, are excluded from any capital gains tax computation of the gain accruing on the disposal of such land if the disponer is the person assessed under Sched. B (subs. (1)).

In a computation of a chargeable gain arising on a disposal of woodland in the U.K., so much of the consideration and so much of the cost as is attributable to trees growing on the land is to be excluded (subss. (3) and (4)).

Development land tax etc.

Interaction with development land tax and other taxation

114. The provisions of this Act have effect subject to—

(*a*) the Development Land Tax Act 1976, and in particular Schedule 6 to that Act,

(*b*) the taxation of development gains under Part III of the Finance Act 1974, which is to be terminated in accordance with the provisions of the Development Land Tax Act 1976.

(*c*) the extension of the taxation of chargeable gains by Chapter II of the said Part III (the first letting charge), subject to termination in accordance with the said Act of 1976.

GENERAL NOTE

S. 114 states that the capital gains tax provisions take effect subject to the legislation contained in the Development Land Tax Act 1976 which relates to the interaction of capital gains tax and other taxes.

PART VI

PROPERTY: FURTHER PROVISIONS

Replacement of business assets

Roll-over relief

115.—(1) If the consideration which a person carrying on a trade obtains for the disposal of, or of his interest in, assets (in this section referred to as " the old assets ") used, and used only, for the purposes of the trade throughout the period of ownership is applied by him in acquiring other assets, or an interest in other assets (in this section referred to as " the new assets ") which on the acquisition are taken into use, and used only, for the purposes of the trade, and the old assets and new assets are within the classes of assets listed in section 118 below, then the person carrying on the trade shall, on making a claim as respects the consideration which has been so applied, be treated for the purposes of this Act—

(*a*) as if the consideration for the disposal of, or of the interest in, the old assets were (if otherwise of a greater amount or value) of such amount as would secure that on the disposal neither a gain nor a loss accrues to him, and

(*b*) as if the amount or value of the consideration for the acquisition of, or of the interest in, the new assets were reduced by the excess of the amount or value of the actual consideration for the disposal of, or of the interest in, the old assets over the amount of the consideration which he is treated as receiving under paragraph (*a*) above,

but neither paragraph (*a*) nor paragraph (*b*) above shall affect the treatment for the purposes of this Act of the other party to the transaction involving the old assets, or of the other party to the transaction involving the new assets.

(2) Where subsection (1) (*a*) above applies to exclude a gain which, in consequence of Schedule 5 to this Act, is not all chargeable gain, the amount of the reduction to be made under subsection (1) (*b*) above shall be the amount of the chargeable gain, and not the whole amount of the gain.

(3) This section shall only apply if the acquisition of, or of the interest in, the new assets takes place, or an unconditional contract for the acquisition is entered into, in the period beginning twelve months before and ending three years after the disposal of, or of the interest in, the old assets, or at such earlier or later time as the Board may by notice in writing allow:

Provided that, where an unconditional contract for the acquisition is so entered into, this section may be applied on a provisional basis without waiting to ascertain whether the new assets, or the interest in the new assets, is acquired in pursuance of the contract, and, when that fact is ascertained, all necessary adjustments shall be made by making assessments or by repayment or discharge of tax, and shall be so made notwithstanding any limitation on the time within which assessments may be made.

(4) This section shall not apply unless the acquisition of, or of the interest in, the new assets was made for the purpose of their use in the trade, and not wholly or partly for the purpose of realising a gain from the disposal of, or of the interest in, the new assets.

(5) If, over the period of ownership or any substantial part of the period of ownership, part of a building or structure is, and part is not, used for the purposes of a trade, this section shall apply as if the part so used, with any land occupied for purposes ancillary to the occupation and use of that part of the building or structure, were a separate asset, and subject to any necessary apportionments of consideration for an acquisition or disposal of, or of an interest in, the building or structure and other land.

(6) If the old assets were not used for the purposes of the trade throughout the period of ownership this section shall apply as if a part of the asset representing its use for the purposes of the trade having regard to the time and extent to which it was, and was not, used for those purposes, were a separate asset which had been wholly used for the purposes of the trade, and this subsection shall apply in relation to that part subject to any necessary apportionment of consideration for an acquisition or disposal of, or of the interest in, the asset.

(7) This section shall apply in relation to a person who, either successively or at the same time, carries on two or more trades as if both or all of them were a single trade.

(8) The provisions of this Act fixing the amount of the consideration deemed to be given for the acquisition or disposal of assets shall be applied before this section is applied.

(9) Without prejudice to section 43 (4) above (general provision for apportionments), where consideration is given for the acquisition or disposal of assets some or part of which are assets in relation to which a claim under this section applies, and some or part of which are not, the consideration shall be apportioned in such manner as is just and reasonable.

General Note

Ss. 115 to 121 inclusive deal with "roll-over" relief on the replacement of business assets. The principle of the relief is that when a gain accrues on the disposal of a business asset, the liability to tax can be deferred if the proceeds of disposal are reinvested in other business assets. This is done by deducting the gain accruing on the disposal from the allowable capital gains tax cost of the new business assets. Where companies within a group are concerned, see s. 276, I.C.T.A. 1970.

Subs. (1) provides that the old and new business assets must, while they are in the taxpayer's ownership, be used only for the purposes of the same trade. They must also be within the classes of assets in s. 118. Any claim for relief under this section does not affect the tax liability of other parties to transactions of sale and purchase.

Subs. (2) provides an adjustment to the relief in cases where the old assets were held on April 6, 1965, and therefore under Sched. 5 only part of the gain (attributable to the period of ownership since April 6, 1965) is chargeable. In such a case the deduction from the allowable cost of the new asset is limited to the amount of the chargeable gain. In order to qualify for the relief (unless the Board extend the period) the new assets must be acquired within one year before or three years after the disposal of the old assets; for this purpose the provisions of the section are applied on a provisional basis where within that period an unconditional contract is entered into for the acquisition of new assets (subs. (3)).

Subs. (4) confines the relief to new assets which are acquired for the purpose of their use in the trade not for the purpose of making a gain on their disposal. See subs. (7) where the person carries on two trades.

Subs. (5) requires apportionments to be made where part of a building is not used for trade purposes for all or part of the period of ownership, and subs. (6) provides for apportionment of relief on a time basis where a building has not been used for the purposes of the trade throughout the period of ownership.

A person carrying on two or more trades, whether at the same time or one after the other, is now to be treated as if carrying on a single trade (subs. (7)). It is unnecessary for the trades to be concerned with the same goods or services.

Subs. (8) provides that the true consideration on a disposal or acquisition shall be found, in accordance with the provisions of this Act, before this section is applied.

Subs. (9) provides that where necessary, apportionments of consideration shall be made in a just and reasonable manner.

Assets only partly replaced

116.—(1) Section 115 (1) above shall not apply if part only of the amount or value of the consideration for the disposal of, or of the interest in, the old assets is applied as described in that subsection, but if all of the amount or value of the consideration except for a part which is less than the amount of the gain (whether all chargeable gain or not) accruing on the disposal of, or of the interest in, the old assets is so applied, then the person carrying on the trade, on making a claim as respects the consideration which has been so applied, shall be treated for the purposes of this Act—

(*a*) as if the amount of the gain so accruing were reduced to the amount of the said part (and, if not all chargeable gain, with a porportionate reduction in the amount of the chargeable gain), and

(*b*) as if the amount or value of the consideration for the acquisition of, or of the interest in, the new assets were reduced by the amount by which the gain is reduced (or as the case may be the amount by which the chargeable gain is proportionately reduced) under paragraph (*a*) of this subsection,

but neither paragraph (*a*) nor paragraph (*b*) above shall affect the treatment for the purposes of this Act of the other party to the transaction involving the old assets, or of the other party to the transaction involving the new assets.

(2) Subsections (3) to (9) of section 115 above shall apply as if this section formed part of that section.

General Note

This section deals with the case where part only of the consideration received for the old assets is applied in the purchase of the new assets.

A claim can be made if the part of the consideration which is not reinvested is less than the gain accruing on the disposal of the old assets. In such a case the part of the gain not reinvested is immediately chargeable (with an adjustment if the asset was held on April 6, 1965) and the balance of the chargeable gain goes to reduce the allowable cost of the new assets.

New assets which are depreciating assets

117.—(1) Sections 115 and 116 above shall have effect subject to the provisions of this section in which—

(*a*) the " held over gain " means the amount by which, under those sections, and apart from the provisions of this section, any chargeable gain on one asset (called " asset No. 1 ") is reduced, with a corresponding reduction of the expenditure allowable in respect of another asset (called " asset No. 2 "),

(*b*) any reference to a gain of any amount being carried forward to any asset is a reference to a reduction of that amount in a chargeable gain coupled with a reduction of the same amount in expenditure allowable in respect of that asset.

(2) If asset No. 2 is a depreciating asset, the held over gain shall not be carried forward, but the claimant shall be treated as if so much of the chargeable gain on asset No. 1 as is equal to the held over gain did not accrue until—

(*a*) the claimant disposes of asset No. 2, or

(*b*) he ceases to use asset No. 2 for the purposes of a trade carried on by him, or

(*c*) the expiration of a period of ten years beginning with the acquisition of asset No. 2,

whichever event comes first.

(3) If, in the circumstances specified in subsection (4) below, the claimant acquires an asset (called " asset No. 3 ") which is not a depreciating asset, and so claims under section 115 or 116 above—

(*a*) the gain held over from asset No. 1 shall be carried forward to asset No. 3, and

(*b*) the claim which applies to asset No. 2 shall be treated as withdrawn (so that subsection (2) above does not apply).

(4) The circumstances are that asset No. 3 is acquired not later than the time when the chargeable gain postponed under subsection (2) above would accrue and, assuming—

(*a*) that the consideration for asset No. 1 was applied in acquiring asset No. 3, and

(*b*) that the time between the disposal of asset No. 1 and the acquisition of asset No. 3 was within the time limited by section 115 (3) above,

the whole amount of the postponed gain could be carried forward from asset No. 1 to asset No. 3; and the claim under subsection (3) above shall be accepted as if those assumptions were true.

(5) If part only of the postponed gain could be carried forward from asset No. 1 to asset No. 3, and the claimant so requires, that and the other part of the postponed gain shall be treated as derived from two separate assets, so that, on that claim—

(*a*) subsection (3) above applies to the first-mentioned part, and

(*b*) the other part remains subject to subsection (2) above.

(6) For the purposes of this section, an asset is a depreciating asset at any time if—

(*a*) at that time it is a wasting asset, as defined in section 37 above, or

(*b*) within the period of ten years beginning at that time it will become a wasting asset (so defined).

GENERAL NOTE

This section places some restriction on the use of ss. 115 and 116, its purpose being to prevent the disappearance of gains by their "roll-over" into allowable expenditure on depreciating assets. Where s. 115 or 116 applies and the new asset being acquired with the proceeds of the old is a depreciating asset (defined in subs. (6)), then, instead of the gain on the old asset being deducted from the expenditure allowable in respect of the new asset, the payment of tax on the gain is held over for the shortest of (*a*) 10 years after the acquisition of the new asset; or (*b*) until the new asset is disposed of; or (*c*) until it is no longer used for the purposes of the taxpayer's trade.

Subss. (3) and (4) contain provisions enabling the normal "roll-over" rules to apply to the gains on the original asset where a further non-depreciating asset is acquired before the happening of the first of those events. For the purposes of this provision, members of a group of companies are treated as one person.

Relevant classes of assets

118. The classes of assets for the purposes of section 115 (1) above are as follows.

Class 1. Assets within heads A and B below.

Head A

1. Any building or part of a building and any permanent or semi-permanent structure in the nature of a building, occupied (as well as used) only for the purposes of the trade.

2. Any land occupied (as well as used) only for the purposes of the trade.

Head A has effect subject to section 119 below.

Head B

Fixed plant or machinery which does not form part of a building or of a permanent or semi-permanent structure in the nature of a building.

Class 2

Ships, aircraft and hovercraft ("hovercraft" having the same meaning as in the Hovercraft Act 1968).

Class 3

Goodwill.

GENERAL NOTE

This section defines the classes of assets for the purposes of s. 115 (1). It should be noted that buildings and fixed plant or machinery are in the same class.

Temperley v. *Visibell Ltd.* [1974] S.T.C. 64 is a case on the meaning of "land occupied (as well as used) only for the purposes of the trade" (Class 1, Head A (2)).

Assets of Class 1

119.—(1) This section has effect as respects head A of Class 1 in section 118 above.

(2) Head A shall not apply where the trade is a trade—

(*a*) of dealing in or developing land, or

(*b*) of providing services for the occupier of land in which the person carrying on the trade has an estate or interest.

(3) Where the trade is a trade of dealing in or developing land, but a profit on the sale of any land held for the purposes of the trade would not form part of the trading profits, then, as regards that land, the trade shall be treated for the purposes of subsection (2) (*a*) of this section as if it were not a trade of dealing in or developing land.

(4) A person who is a lessor of tied premises shall be treated as if he

occupied (as well as used) those tied premises only for the purposes of the relevant trade.

This subsection shall be construed in accordance with section 140 (2) of the Taxes Act (income tax and corporation tax on tied premises).

General Note

This section enables the "roll-over" relief of ss. 115 and 116 on disposals of business assets to be claimed by a land dealer in respect of land which is not part of his trading stock (subs. (3)).

Subs. (4) provides that a lessor of tied premises shall be treated as if he used those premises for the purposes of the relevant trade carried on there and not as his residence.

No roll-over relief is available under Head A of Class 1 (land and buildings) where the taxpayer's trade is the provision of services for the occupier of land in which the taxpayer has an estate or interest.

Trade carried on by family company: business assets dealt with by individual

120. In relation to a case where—

(*a*) the person disposing of, or of his interest in, the old assets and acquiring the new assets, or an interest in them, is an individual, and

(*b*) the trade or trades in question are carried on not by that individual but by a company which, both at the time of the disposal and at the time of the acquisition referred to in paragraph (*a*) above, is his family company, within the meaning of section 124 below,

any reference in sections 115 to 119 above to the person carrying on the trade (or the two or more trades) includes a reference to that individual.

General Note

The "roll-over" relief in ss. 115 to 119 is also available in cases where the assets are sold and acquired by an individual but the trade is carried on by a family trading company of the individual, *e.g.* a farm is owned by an individual but actually farmed by his family company. Relief is available on the sale of the farm and acquisition of a new farm. This provision will not apply if the land or other asset is owned by a company or trustees but the trade is actually carried on by the individual.

For the definition of "family company" in relation to an individual, see s. 124.

Activities other than trades, and interpretation

121.—(1) Sections 115 to 120 above shall apply with the necessary modifications—

(*a*) in relation to the discharge of the functions of a public authority, and

(*b*) in relation to the occupation of woodlands where the woodlands are managed by the occupier on a commercial basis and with a view to the realisation of profits, and

(*c*) in relation to a profession, vocation, office or employment, and

(*d*) in relation to such of the activities of a body of persons whose activities are carried on otherwise than for profit and are wholly or mainly directed to the protection or promotion of the interests of its members in the carrying on of their trade or profession as are so directed, and

(*e*) in relation to the activities of an unincorporated association or other body chargeable to corporation tax, being a body not established for profit whose activities are wholly or mainly carried on otherwise than for profit, but in the case of assets within head A of class 1 only if they are both occupied and used by the body, and in the case of other assets only if they are used by the body,

as they apply in relation to a trade.

(2) In sections 115 to 120 above and this section the expressions "trade", "profession", "vocation", "office" and "employment" have the same meanings as in the Income Tax Acts, but not so as to apply the provisions of the Income Tax Acts as to the circumstances in which, on a change in the persons carrying on a trade, a trade is to be regarded as discontinued, or as set up and commenced.

(3) Sections 115 to 120 above, and this section, shall be construed as one.

GENERAL NOTE

Subs. (1) extends the application of ss. 115 to 120 above to the following activities which might arguably not be trades:

(a) the discharge of its functions by a public authority;
(b) the occupation of woodlands managed on a commercial basis;
(c) a profession, vocation, office or employment;
(d) non-profit making activities of trade and professional associations; and
(e) non-profit making activities of unincorporated associations not established for profit (*e.g.* charities).

Subs. (2) applies certain income tax meanings to expressions used in the roll-over provisions but not so as to import the income tax provisions relating to deemed cessations and commencements of trades. Therefore, no disposals and acquisitions of assets are deemed for capital gains tax purposes by reason only of a cessation of a trade being deemed to occur for income tax purposes.

Stock in trade

Appropriations to and from stock

122.—(1) Subject to subsection (3) below, where an asset acquired by a person otherwise than as trading stock of a trade carried on by him is appropriated by him for the purposes of the trading stock (whether on the commencement of the trade or otherwise) and, if he had then sold the asset for its market value, a chargeable gain or allowable loss would have accrued to him, he shall be treated as having thereby disposed of the asset by selling it for its then market value.

(2) If at any time an asset forming part of the trading stock of a person's trade is appropriated by him for any other purpose, or is retained by him on his ceasing to carry on the trade, he shall be treated as having acquired it at that time for a consideration equal to the amount brought into the accounts of the trade in respect of it for tax purposes on the appropriation or on his ceasing to carry on the trade, as the case may be.

(3) Subsection (1) above shall not apply in relation to a person's appropriation of an asset for the purposes of a trade if he is chargeable to income tax in respect of the profits of the trade under Case I of Schedule D, and elects that instead the market value of the asset at the time of the appropriation shall, in computing the profits of the trade for purposes of tax, be treated as reduced by the amount of the chargeable gain or increased by the amount of the allowable loss referred to in that subsection, and where that subsection does not apply by reason of such an election, the profits of the trade shall be computed accordingly:

Provided that if a person making an election under this subsection is at the time of the appropriation carrying on the trade in partnership with others, the election shall not have effect unless concurred in by the others.

General Note

This section deals with appropriations of assets to or from stock in trade while remaining in the ownership of the same person.

Subs. (1), which has effect subject to any election made under subs. (3), provides that the appropriation of an asset not forming part of a person's stock-in-trade to stock-in-trade is, for capital gains tax purposes, a deemed disposal and reacquisition of that asset at its market value.

Subs. (2) provides that where an asset is appropriated from stock-in-trade for any other purpose its acquisition cost for capital gains tax purposes is the value brought into the accounts of the trade in respect of it for tax purposes. This will be its market value if the rule in *Sharkey* v. *Wernher* [1956] A.C. 58 applies.

Subs. (3) provides that where an asset is appropriated for trading purposes, so long as the profits of the trade concerned are within the charge to tax under Case I of Sched. D, the taxpayer can elect that subs. (1) shall not apply. Instead the trading profits are to be computed as though the asset was brought into account at its capital gains tax cost to the taxpayer (adjustments being made if the asset was held by him on April 6, 1965).

An election under subs. (3) may therefore have the effect either that a capital loss is relieved as though it were a trading loss or that a capital gain is taxed as though it were a trading profit.

Transfer of business to a company

Roll-over relief on transfer of business

123.—(1) This section shall apply for the purposes of this Act where a person who is not a company transfers to a company a business as a going concern, together with the whole assets of the business, or together with the whole of those assets other than cash, and the business is so transferred wholly or partly in exchange for shares issued by the company to the person transferring the business.

Any shares so received by the transferor in exchange for the business are referred to below as " the new assets ".

(2) The amount determined under subsection (4) below shall be deducted from the aggregate (referred to below as " the amount of the gain on the old assets ") of the chargeable gains less allowable losses.

(3) For the purpose of computing any chargeable gain accruing on the disposal of any new asset—

(*a*) the amount determined under subsection (4) below shall be apportioned between the new assets as a whole, and

(*b*) the sums allowable as a deduction under section 32 (1) (*a*) above shall be reduced by the amount apportioned to the new asset under paragraph (*a*) above;

and if the shares which comprise the new assets are not all of the same class, the apportionment between the shares under paragraph (*a*) above shall be in accordance with their market values at the time they were acquired by the transferor.

(4) The amount referred to in subsections (2) and (3) (*a*) above shall not exceed the cost of the new assets but, subject to that, the said amount shall be a fraction $\frac{A}{B}$ of the amount of the gain on the old assets where—

" A " is the cost of the new assets, and

" B " is the value of the whole of the consideration received by the transferor in exchange for the business;

and for the purposes of this subsection " the cost of the new assets " means any sums which would be allowable as a deduction under section

32 (1) (*a*) above if the new assets were disposed of as a whole in circumstances giving rise to a chargeable gain.

(5) References in this section to the business, in relation to shares or consideration received in exchange for the business, include references to such assets of the business as are referred to in subsection (1) above.

GENERAL NOTE

This section provides a form of roll-over relief where a business is transferred by an individual to a company in exchange for shares in that company.

Where: (i) an individual transfers to a company a business as a going concern, together with the whole assets of the business or together with the whole of those assets other than cash; and

(ii) the business is so transferred wholly or partly in exchange for shares issued by the company to the person transferring the business,

the total of chargeable gains arising on the transfer is reduced in the proportion that the value of the shares given by the company bears to the value of the whole consideration given for the business assets. Thus, if the sole consideration given for the business assets is shares in the transferee company, any chargeable gains arising on the transfer are reduced to nil, but if, say, shares worth £10,000 are given together with £5,000 cash, the relief extends only to two-thirds of any gains.

The amount by which the total chargeable gains arising on the transfer is reduced is deducted from the allowable cost of the shares on any subsequent disposal of them, that amount being apportioned between shares of different classes according to their values at the time of the transfer of the business to the company.

Whilst, strictly, an agreement by the company to take over business liabilities forms part of the consideration given for the business, the Revenue has announced that in practice such liabilities will be disregarded for the purposes of this paragraph (see (1971) 94 Tax. 220).

Transfer of business on retirement

Relief on transfer

124.—(1) If an individual who has attained the age of 60 years—

(*a*) disposes by way of sale or gift of the whole or part of a business, or

(*b*) disposes by way of sale or gift of shares or securities of a company,

and throughout a period of at least one year ending with the disposal the revelant conditions have been fulfilled, relief shall be given under this section in respect of gains accruing to him on the disposal.

(2) For the purposes of subsection (1) above the relevant conditions are fulfilled at any time if at that time,—

(*a*) in the case of a disposal falling within paragraph (*a*) of that subsection, the business in question is owned either by the individual or by a company with respect to which the following conditions are at that time fulfilled, namely,—

(i) it is a trading company,

(ii) it is the individual's family company, and

(iii) he is a full-time working director of it;

and

(*b*) in the case of a disposal falling within paragraph (*b*) of that subsection, either the conditions in sub-paragraphs (i) to (iii) of paragraph (*a*) above are fulfilled with respect to the company in question or the individual owns the business which, at the time of the disposal, is owned by the company;

and in relation to a particular disposal the period, up to a maximum of 10 years, which ends with the disposal and throughout which the relevant conditions are fulfilled is in this section referred to as " the qualifying period ".

(3) The amount available for relief under this section shall be—

(*a*) in the case of an individual who has attained the age of 65 years, the relevant percentage of £50,000, and

(*b*) in the case of an individual who has not attained that age, the relevant percentage of the aggregate of £10,000 for every year by which his age exceeds 60 and a corresponding part of £10,000 for any odd part of a year;

and for the purpose of this subsection " the relevant percentage " means a percentage determined according to the length of the qualifying period on a scale rising arithmetically from 10 per cent. where that period is precisely one year to 100 per cent. where it is ten years.

(4) Where subsection 1 (*a*) above applies the gains accruing to the individual on the disposal of chargeable business assets comprised in the disposal by way of sale or gift shall be aggregated, and only so much of that aggregate as exceeds the amount available for relief under this section shall be chargeable gains (but not so as to affect liability in respect of gains accruing on the disposal of assets other than chargeable business assets).

(5) Where subsection (1) (*b*) above applies—

(*a*) the gains which accrue to the individual on the disposal of the shares or securities shall be aggregated, and

(*b*) of a proportion of that aggregate sum which is equal to the proportion which the part of the value of the company's chargeable assets at the time of the disposal which is attributable to the value of the company's chargeable business assets bears to the whole of that value, only so much as exceeds the amount available for relief under this section shall constitute chargeable gains (but not so as to affect liability in respect of gains representing the balance of the said aggregate sum),

and for the purposes of paragraph (*b*) above every asset is a chargeable asset except one, on the disposal of which by the company at the time of the disposal of the shares or securities, no chargeable gain would accrue.

(6) So far as the amount available for relief under this section is applied in giving relief to an individual as respects a disposal it shall not be applied in giving relief to that individual as respects any other disposal (and the relief shall be applied in the order in which any disposals take place).

(7) In arriving at the aggregate under subsection (4) or subsection (5) above—

(*a*) the respective amounts of the gains shall be computed in accordance with the provisions of this Act (other than this section) fixing the amount of chargeable gains, and

(*b*) any allowable loss which accrues on the disposal shall be deducted,

and the provisions of this section shall not affect the computation of the amount of any allowable loss.

(8) In this section—

" chargeable business asset " means an asset (including goodwill but not including shares or securities or other assets held as investments) which is, or is an interest in, an asset used for the purposes of a trade, profession, vocation, office or employment carried on by the individual, or as the case may be by the individual's family company, other than an asset on the disposal of which no chargeable gain accrues or (where the disposal is of shares or securities in the family company) on the disposal of which no chargeable gain would accrue if the family company disposed of the asset at the time of the disposal of the shares or securities,

"family company" means, in relation to an individual, a company the voting rights in which are—

(*a*) as to not less than 25 per cent., exercisable by the individual, or

(*b*) as to not less than 51 per cent., exercisable by the individual or a member of his family, and, as to not less than 5 per cent., exercisable by the individual himself,

"family" means, in relation to an individual, the husband or wife of the individual, and a relative of the individual or the individual's husband or wife, and "relative" means brother, sister, ancestor or lineal descendant,

"full time working director" means a director who is required to devote substantially the whole of his time to the service of the company in a managerial or technical capacity,

"trade", "profession", "vocation", "office" and "employment" have the same meanings as in the Income Tax Acts,

"trading company" has the meaning given by paragraph 11 of Schedule 16 to the Finance Act 1972;

and in this section references to the disposal of the whole or part of a business include references to the disposal of the whole or part of the assets provided or held for the purposes of an office or employment.

GENERAL NOTE

This section gives relief from capital gains tax on the transfer of a business on retirement or otherwise.

To qualify, the following conditions must be satisfied (subs. (1));

(*a*) the individual making the disposal must be 60 years of age or over;

(*b*) there must be a disposal by way of sale or gift;

(*c*) the disposal must be either (i) the whole or part of a business (which includes an interest in a partnership according to the Revenue) which is owned by the individual or a family trading company of which the individual is a full-time director; or (ii) shares or securities of a family trading company of which the individual is a full-time director; and

(*d*) the above conditions have been satisfied for a period of one year ending with the date of the disposal.

The amount of relief available is dependent upon the age of the individual and the length of time that the above conditions have been satisfied in the years immediately preceding the disposal up to a maximum of 10 years (known as the "qualifying period") (subs. (2)). This must be a continuous period when all the conditions were satisfied.

Subs. (3) provides that an individual over 65 is entitled to the "relevant percentage" of £50,000. A person aged between 60 and 65 is entitled to the "relevant percentage" of £10,000 for each year by which his age exceeds 60 and a corresponding part of £10,000 for any additional part of a year.

The relevant percentage is $\frac{\text{qualifying period}}{10} \times 100$ per cent. For example, a farmer aged 66 sells his farm having satisfied all the conditions for five years. The relevant percentage will be $\frac{5}{10} \times 100 = 50$ per cent. The relief will be £50,000 × 50 per cent. = £25,000.

Where the disposal is of the whole or part of a business (subs. (1) (*a*)), the relief is set against the amount of gains accruing to the individual on the disposal of chargeable business assets (defined in subs. (8)) only (subs. (4)).

The manner in which the part of the chargeable gains accruing on the disposal of shares in a family company which qualifies for this relief is calculated is set out in subs. (5).

The proportion is:

$$\frac{\text{value of chargeable business assets of company}}{\text{value of chargeable assets of company}}$$

This excludes assets of the company from the calculation which are not chargeable to capital gains tax, such as cash.

The terms "chargeable business asset," "family company," "family" and "full-time working director" are defined in subs. (8). Also certain other definitions are imported by subs. (8).

For the distinction between a business and mere assets, see *McGregor* v. *Adcock* [1977] 1 W.L.R. 864.

Transfer by way of capital distribution from family company

125.—(1) Subject to subsection (2) below, section 124 (1) (*b*) above shall apply where under section 72 above (distribution which is not a new holding) the individual is treated as disposing of interests in shares or securities of a company in consideration of a capital distribution from the company in the course of dissolving or winding up the company as it applies where he disposes of shares or securities of a company by way of sale or gift.

(2) Subsection (1) above shall not apply if the capital distribution consists wholly of chargeable business assets of the company, and if it consists partly of chargeable business assets (and partly of money or money's worth), relief shall only be given under section 124 above in respect of that proportion of the gains accruing on the disposal which the part of the capital distribution not consisting of chargeable business assets bears to the entire capital distribution.

GENERAL NOTE

This section extends relief under s. 124 to the case where instead of disposing of shares or securities in a company by way of sale or gift (s. 124 (1) (*b*)), the individual receives a capital distribution from the company in the course of dissolving or winding up the company (*i.e.* on liquidation) (subs. (1)).

Where, however, all or part of the capital distribution consists of chargeable business assets of the company, relief under s. 124 is either denied or restricted to the percentage of the gains accruing on the disposal which is represented by that part of the total capital distribution which does not consist of chargeable business assets.

Gifts of business assets

Relief for gifts of business assets

126.—(1) If an individual (in this section referred to as " the transferor ") makes a disposal, otherwise than under a bargain at arm's length, to a person resident or ordinarily resident in the United Kingdom (in this section referred to as " the transferee ") of—

(*a*) an asset which is, or is an interest in, an asset used for the purposes of a trade, profession or vocation carried on by the transferor or by a company which is his family company, or

(*b*) shares or securities of a trading company which is the transferor's family company,

then, subject to subsection (2) below, the provisions of subsection (3) below shall apply in relation to the disposal if a claim for relief under this section is made by the transferor and the transferee.

(2) Subsection (3) below does not apply in relation to a disposal if—

(*a*) in the case of a disposal of an asset, any gain accruing to the transferor on the disposal is (apart from this section) wholly relieved under section 124 above, or

(*b*) in the case of a disposal of shares or securities, the proportion determined under subsection (5) (*b*) of section 124 above of any gain accruing to the transferor on the disposal is (apart from this section) wholly relieved under that section.

(3) Where a claim for relief is made under this section in respect of a disposal—

(*a*) the amount of any chargeable gain which, apart from this section, would accrue to the transferor on the disposal, and

(*b*) the amount of the consideration for which, apart from this section, the transferee would be regarded for the purposes of capital gains tax as having acquired the asset or, as the case may be, the shares or securities,

shall each be reduced by an amount equal to the held-over gain on the disposal.

(4) Part I of Schedule 4 to this Act shall have effect for extending the relief provided for by virtue of subsections (1) to (3) above in the case of agricultural property and for applying it in relation to settled property.

(5) Subject to Part II of Schedule 4 to this Act (which provides for reductions in the held-over gain in certain cases) and subsection (6) below, the reference in subsection (3) above to the held-over gain on a disposal is a reference to the chargeable gain which would have accrued on that disposal apart from subsection (3) above and (in appropriate cases) section 124 above, and in subsection (6) below that chargeable gain is referred to as the unrelieved gain on the disposal.

(6) In any case where—

(*a*) there is actual consideration (as opposed to the consideration equal to the market value which is deemed to be given by virtue of section 19 (3) above) for a disposal in respect of which a claim for relief is made under this section, and

(*b*) that actual consideration exceeds the sums allowable as a deduction under section 32 above,

the held-over gain on the disposal shall be the amount by which the unrelieved gain on the disposal exceeds the excess referred to in paragraph (*b*) above.

(7) Subject to subsection (8) below, in this section and Schedule 4 to this Act—

(*a*) " family company " has the meaning given by section 124 (8) above,

(*b*) " trading company " has the meaning given by paragraph 11 of Schedule 16 to the Finance Act 1972, and

(*c*) " trade ", " profession " and " vocation " have the same meaning as in the Income Tax Acts.

(8) In this section and Schedule 4 to this Act and in determining whether a company is a trading company for the purposes of this section and that Schedule, the expression " trade " shall be taken to include the occupation of woodlands where the woodlands are managed by the occupier on a commercial basis and with a view to the realisation of profits.

GENERAL NOTE

This section provides for a roll-over relief where the assets of a business or shares in a family trading company are disposed of other than for full consideration.

This is intended to ease the tax burden on the transfer of a business from, say, one generation of a family to the next.

To qualify for this relief the disposal must:

(i) not be made as part of a bargain at arm's length;

(ii) be made to a " transferee " who is both resident and ordinarily resident in the United Kingdom;

(iii) concern either (*a*) assets (or interests in them) of a business carried on by the transferor or his family, or (*b*) shares and securities in the transferor's family trading company;

(iv) create a chargeable gain which is not wholly relieved by reason of any retirement relief available to the transferor.

For these purposes, " family company " has the same meaning as in s. 124 (8), which means that the transferor must have the right to exercise at least 25 per cent. of the company's voting rights, or 51 per cent. are exercisable by the transferor and his family and at least 5 per cent. by the transferor.

In the case of a disposal satisfying these requirements, the amount of the chargeable gain accruing to the transferor and the amount of the consideration deemed to have been given by the transferee shall be reduced by the " held-over gain."

This sum (subject to Part II of Sched. 4) equals the chargeable gain reduced by the excess (if any) of the actual consideration given over the deductions allowable in accordance with s. 32.

Payment of capital gains tax is therefore postponed at least until the next disposal of the particular asset or shares. On that occasion (unless this or some other relief then applies) the burden of the tax postponed by the claim will be borne by the transferee, rather than the transferor.

The relief as it applies to agricultural property and settled property is dealt with in Sched. 4.

For the purposes of this relief, the occupation of woodlands if the occupier manages them on a commercial basis and with a view to the realisation of profits is to be treated as a trade (subs. (8)).

Movable property

Wasting assets

127.—(1) Subject to the provisions of this section, no chargeable gain shall accrue on the disposal of, or of an interest in, an asset which is tangible movable property and which is a wasting asset.

(2) Subsection (1) above shall not apply to a disposal of, or of an interest in, an asset—

(*a*) if, from the beginning of the period of ownership of the person making the disposal to the time when the disposal is made, the asset has been used and used solely for the purposes of a trade, profession or vocation and if that person has claimed or could have claimed any capital allowance in respect of any expenditure attributable to the asset or interest under paragraph (*a*) or paragraph (*b*) of section 32 (1) above (allowable expenditure), or

(*b*) if the person making the disposal has incurred any expenditure on the asset or interest which has otherwise qualified in full for any capital allowance.

(3) In the case of the disposal of, or of an interest in, an asset which, in the period of ownership of the person making the disposal, has been used partly for the purposes of a trade, profession or vocation and partly for other purposes, or has been used for the purposes of a trade, profession or vocation for part of that period, or which has otherwise qualified in part only for capital allowances—

(*a*) the consideration for the disposal, and any expenditure attributable to the asset or interest by virtue of section 32 (1) (*a*)

and (*b*) above, shall be apportioned by reference to the extent to which that expenditure qualified for capital allowances, and

(*b*) the computation under Chapter II of Part II above shall be made separately in relation to the apportioned parts of the expenditure and consideration, and

(*c*) subsection (1) above shall not apply to any gain accruing by reference to the computation in relation to the part of the consideration apportioned to use for the purposes of the trade, profession or vocation, or to the expenditure qualifying for capital allowances.

(4) Subsection (1) above shall not apply to a disposal of commodities of any description by a person dealing on a terminal market or dealing with or through a person ordinarily engaged in dealing on a terminal market.

(5) This section shall be construed as one with Chapter II of Part II above.

General Note

S. 127 removes entirely from the ambit of capital gains tax and corporation tax in respect of capital gains, assets which are tangible movable property and are wasting assets (subs. (1)). There is an exception, however, for assets which qualify for capital allowances (subs. (2)). Where assets so qualify only in part, appropriate apportionments are made (subs. (3)). Although tangible movable property qualifying for capital allowances remains within the scope of the taxes, it should be recalled that losses accruing on such property will not be allowable to the extent that capital allowances have been made. Subs. (4) is intended to take out of the exemption speculative dealings in commodities such as wheat or cocoa beans.

Chattel exemption

128.—(1) Subject to this section a gain accruing on a disposal of an asset which is tangible movable property shall not be a chargeable gain if the amount or value of the consideration for the disposal does not exceed £2,000.

(2) Where the amount or value of the consideration for the disposal of an asset which is tangible movable property exceeds £2,000, there shall be excluded from any chargeable gain accruing on the disposal so much of it as exceeds five-thirds of the difference between—

(*a*) the amount or value of the consideration, and

(*b*) £2,000.

(3) Subsections (1) and (2) above shall not affect the amount of an allowable loss accruing on the disposal of an asset, but for the purposes of computing under this Act the amount of a loss accruing on the disposal of tangible movable property the consideration for the disposal shall, if less than £2,000, be deemed to be £2,000 and the losses which are allowable losses, shall be restricted accordingly.

(4) If two or more assets which have formed part of a set of articles of any description all owned at one time by one person are disposed of by that person, and—

(*a*) to the same person, or

(*b*) to persons who are acting in concert or who are connected persons,

whether on the same or different occasions, the two or more transactions shall be treated as a single transaction disposing of a single asset, but with any necessary apportionments of the reductions in chargeable gains, and in allowable losses, under subsections (2) and (3) above.

(5) If the disposal is of a right or interest in or over tangible movable property—

(*a*) in the first instance subsections (1), (2) and (3) above shall be applied in relation to the asset as a whole, taking the consideration as including the market value of what remains undisposed of, in addition to the actual consideration,

(*b*) where the sum of the actual consideration and that market value exceeds £2,000, the part of any chargeable gain that is excluded from it under subsection (2) above shall be so much of the gain as exceeds five-thirds of the difference between that sum and £2,000 multiplied by the fraction equal to the actual consideration divided by the said sum, and

(*c*) where that sum is less than £2,000 any loss shall be restricted under subsection (3) above by deeming the consideration to be the actual consideration plus the said fraction of the difference between the said sum and £2,000.

(6) This section shall not apply—

(*a*) in relation to a disposal of commodities of any description by a person dealing on a terminal market or dealing with or through a person ordinarily engaged in dealing on a terminal market, or

(*b*) in relation to a disposal of currency of any description.

General Note

Subs. (1) exempts from the charge any gain derived from tangible movable property where the consideration for the disposal is less than £2,000, and subs. (2) provides that where a tangible movable is sold for more than £2,000 the gain shall not exceed five-thirds of the excess of the consideration over £2,000.

The effect of subs. (3) is to restrict the amount of losses on the disposal of tangible movable property by treating the disposal consideration of such property as £2,000 even though it was less in fact.

A chargeable gain on the disposal of a set of items cannot be avoided by making separate disposals of individual items to one person or to persons acting in concert or connected. The transaction would be treated as a single disposal (subs. (4)).

The provisions of this section do not apply to disposals of commodities through a terminal market or currency.

Subs. (5) provides rules on the application of the exemption to part disposals.

Leases of property other than land

129. Schedule 3 to this Act has effect, to the extent specified in paragraph 9 of that Schedule, as respects leases of property other than land.

General Note

This section gives effect to Sched. 3 as respects leases of property other than land: see Sched. 3, para. 9.

Passenger vehicles

130. A mechanically propelled road vehicle constructed or adapted for the carriage of passengers, except for a vehicle of a type not commonly used as a private vehicle and unsuitable to be so used, shall not be a chargeable asset; and accordingly no chargeable gain or allowable loss shall accrue on its disposal.

General Note

This section provides that a private motor vehicle, suitable for carrying passengers, shall not be a chargeable asset for the purposes of capital gains tax.

Decorations for valour or gallant conduct

131. A gain shall not be a chargeable gain if accruing on the disposal by any person of a decoration awarded for valour or gallant conduct which he acquired otherwise than for consideration in money or money's worth.

General Note

This section exempts a gain on the disposal of a decoration for valour or gallant conduct by the original recipient or by someone who acquired it otherwise than for consideration in money or money's worth.

Other property

Commodities and other assets without earmark

132. Sections 65 and 66 above (rules of identification), and paragraph 13 of Schedule 5 to this Act (assets held on 6th April 1965) have effect, to the extent there specified, as respects assets dealt with without identifying the particular assets disposed of or acquired.

General Note

This section provides that assets not capable of being identified with particularity within a holding shall be dealt with for the purposes of identification in accordance with ss. 65 and 66 and Sched. 5, para. 13.

Foreign currency for personal expenditure

133. A gain shall not be a chargeable gain if accruing on the disposal by an individual of currency of any description acquired by him for the personal expenditure outside the United Kingdom of himself or his family or dependants (including expenditure on the provision or maintenance of any residence outside the United Kingdom).

General Note

This section provides that no individual shall be liable to capital gains tax on any gain accruing to him on the disposal of foreign currency acquired by him for the personal expenditure of himself or his family or his dependants outside the United Kingdom.

Debts

134.—(1) Where a person incurs a debt to another, whether in sterling or in some other currency, no chargeable gain shall accrue to that (that is the original) creditor or his personal representative or legatee on a disposal of the debt, except in the case of the debt on a security (as defined in section 82 above).

(2) Subject to the provisions of sections 82 and 85 above (conversion of securities and company amalgamations), and subject to subsection (1) above, the satisfaction of a debt or part of it (including a debt on a security as defined in section 82 above) shall be treated as a disposal of the debt or of that part by the creditor made at the time when the debt or that part is satisfied.

(3) Where property is acquired by a creditor in satisfaction of his debt or part of it, then subject to the provisions of sections 82 and 85 above the property shall not be treated as disposed of by the debtor or acquired by the creditor for a consideration greater than its market value at the time of the creditor's acquisition of it; but if under subsection (1) above (and in a case not falling within either of the said sections 82 and 85) no chargeable gain is to accrue on a disposal of the debt by the creditor

(that is the original creditor), and a chargeable gain accrues to him on a disposal by him of the property, the amount of the chargeable gain shall (where necessary) be reduced so as not to exceed the chargeable gain which would have accrued if he had acquired the property for a consideration equal to the amount of the debt or that part of it.

(4) A loss accruing on the disposal of a debt acquired by the person making the disposal from the original creditor or his personal representative or legatee at a time when the creditor or his personal representative or legatee is a person connected with the person making the disposal, and so acquired either directly or by one or more purchases through persons all of whom are connected with the person making the disposal, shall not be an allowable loss.

(5) Where the original creditor is a trustee and the debt, when created, is settled property, subsections (1) and (4) above shall apply as if for the references to the original creditor's personal representative or legatee there were substituted references to any person becoming absolutely entitled, as against the trustee, to the debt on its ceasing to be settled property, and to that person's personal representative or legatee.

GENERAL NOTE

No chargeable gain (or allowable loss) can accrue on the disposal of a debt by the original creditor or his personal representative or legatee, except in the case of a debt on a security (subs. (1)).

Where, subject to subs. (1), a chargeable gain is capable of accruing on the disposal of a debt, the satisfaction of it or a part of it is treated as a disposal of it or that part (subs. (2)).

Where property is acquired by a creditor in satisfaction of a debt, as a general rule the consideration for which the property passes is to be treated for capital gains tax purposes, both as concerns the debtor and the creditor, as no more than the market value of the property at the time the creditor acquires it. However, if the property is acquired by the creditor in circumstances where no chargeable gain can accrue on the debt and the property is later disposed of by the creditor, he can on that later occasion bring into account the amount of the debt in satisfaction of which the property was acquired as the allowable cost of the property, if to do so would reduce the chargeable gain then accruing (subs. (3)).

No allowable loss can accrue on the disposal of a debt by a person who has acquired it directly or indirectly from a connected person who was, when he disposed of the debt, the original creditor (subs. (4)).

Where the debt is settled property and trustees are the original creditor, subss. (1) and (4) apply to disposals by the trustees, any person becoming absolutely entitled as against them and the personal representatives and legatees of such a person (subs. (5)).

In *Cleveleys Investment Trust Co.* v. *I.R.C.* (1971) 47 T.C. 300, the taxpayer lent £25,000 to a company on receipt of an undertaking that in due course the company would reconstruct its capital and issue shares to the taxpayer as fully paid without further consideration passing. *Held,* the asset so acquired by the taxpayer was not a debt or a debt on a security within s. 134, but incorporeal property on the disposal of which an allowable loss accrued.

In *Aberdeen Construction Group Ltd.* v. *I.R.C.* [1978] 2 W.L.R. 648, consideration was given to the meaning of "debt on a security" within the section. *Per* Lord Wilberforce (at p. 653), such a debt is one which may be unsecured and which has, if not a marketable character, at least such characteristics as enable it to be dealt in and if necessary converted into shares and other securities. This dictum was applied in *W. T. Ramsay Ltd.* v. *I.R.C.* [1978] 1 W.L.R. 1313.

Debts: foreign currency bank accounts

135.—(1) Subject to subsection (2) below, section 134 (1) above shall not apply to a debt owed by a bank which is not in sterling and which is represented by a sum standing to the credit of a person in an account in the bank.

(2) Subsection (1) above shall not apply to a sum in an individual's bank account representing currency acquired by the holder for the personal expenditure outside the United Kingdom of himself or his family or dependants (including expenditure on the provision or maintenance of any residence outside the United Kingdom).

General Note

This section provides that s. 134 (1) does not apply to a debt owed by a bank, not in sterling, which is represented by a sum standing to the credit of a person in the bank, unless such sum represents moneys required for personal expenditure outside the United Kingdom by the creditor or his family or dependants.

Relief in respect of loans to traders

136.—(1) In this section " a qualifying loan " means a loan in the case of which—

(*a*) the money lent is used by the borrower wholly for the purposes of a trade carried on by him, not being a trade which consists of or includes the lending of money, and

(*b*) the borrower is resident in the United Kingdom, and

(*c*) the borrower's debt is not a debt on a security as defined in section 82 above;

and for the purposes of paragraph (*a*) above money used by the borrower for setting up a trade which is subsequently carried on by him shall be treated as used for the purposes of that trade.

(2) In subsection (1) above references to a trade include references to a profession or vocation; and where money lent to a company is lent by it to another company in the same group, being a trading company, that subsection shall apply to the money lent to the first-mentioned company as if it had used it for any purpose for which it is used by the other company while a member of the group.

(3) If, on a claim by a person who has made a qualifying loan, the inspector is satisfied that—

(*a*) any outstanding amount of the principal of the loan has become irrecoverable, and

(*b*) the claimant has not assigned his right to recover that amount, and

(*c*) the claimant and the borrower were not each other's spouses, or companies in the same group, when the loan was made or at any subsequent time,

this Act shall have effect as if an allowable loss equal to that amount had accrued to the claimant when the claim was made.

(4) If, on a claim by a person who has guaranteed the repayment of a loan which is, or but for subsection (1) (*c*) above would be, a qualifying loan, the inspector is satisfied that—

(*a*) any outstanding amount of, or of interest in respect of, the principal of the loan has become irrecoverable from the borrower, and

(*b*) the claimant has made a payment under the guarantee (whether to the lender or a co-guarantor) in respect of that amount, and

(*c*) the claimant has not assigned any right to recover that amount which has accrued to him (whether by operation of law or otherwise) in consequence of his having made the payment, and

(*d*) the lender and the borrower were not each other's spouses, or companies in the same group, when the loan was made or at any subsequent time and the claimant and the borrower were not each other's spouses, and the claimant and the lender were not companies in the same group, when the guarantee was given or at any subsequent time,

this Act shall have effect as if an allowable loss had accrued to the claimant when the payment was made; and the loss shall be equal to the payment made by him in respect of the amount mentioned in paragraph (*a*) above less any contribution payable to him by any co-guarantor in respect of the payment so made.

(5) Where an allowable loss has been treated under subsection (3) or (4) above as accruing to any person and the whole or any part of the outstanding amount mentioned in subsection (3) (*a*) or, as the case may be, subsection (4) (*a*) is at any time recovered by him, this Act shall have effect as if there had accrued to him at that time a chargeable gain equal to so much of the allowable loss as corresponds to the amount recovered.

(6) For the purposes of subsection (5) above, a person shall be treated as recovering an amount if he (or any other person by his direction) receives any money or money's worth in satisfaction of his right to recover that amount or in consideration of his assignment of the right to recover it; and where a person assigns such a right otherwise than by way of a bargain made at arm's length he shall be treated as receiving money or money's worth equal to the market value of the right at the time of the assignment.

(7) No amount shall be treated under this section as giving rise to an allowable loss or chargeable gain in the case of any person if it falls to be taken into account in computing his income for the purposes of income tax or corporation tax.

(8) Where an allowable loss has been treated as accruing to a person under subsection (4) above by virtue of a payment made by him at any time under a guarantee—

(*a*) no chargeable gain shall accrue to him otherwise than under subsection (5) above, and

(*b*) no allowable loss shall accrue to him under this Act,

on his disposal of any rights that have accrued to him (whether by operation of law or otherwise) in consequence of his having made any payment under the guarantee at or after that time.

(9) References in this section to an amount having become irrecoverable do not include references to cases where the amount has become irrecoverable in consequence of the terms of the loan, of any arrangements of which the loan forms part, or of any act or omission by the lender or, in a case within subsection (4) above, the guarantor.

(10) In this section—

(*a*) " spouses " means spouses who are living together (construed in accordance with section 155 (2) below),

(*b*) " trading company " has the meaning given by paragraph 11 of Schedule 16 to the Finance Act 1972, and

(*c*) " group " shall be construed in accordance with section 272 of the Taxes Act.

(11) Subsection (3) above applies where the loan is made after 11th April 1978 and subsection (4) above applies where the guarantee is given after that date.

General Note

This section permits a claim to be made for an allowable loss by a lender or guarantor (but not to persons interested under a contract of indemnity) if a loan becomes irrecoverable. The following conditions must be satisfied:

(*a*) the money lent must be used for, or in setting up, a trade (which includes a profession or vocation) other than the lending of money. By virtue of subs. (2) the relief is extended to the case where the borrower is a company which lends the money to another company of the group;
(*b*) the borrower is resident in the United Kingdom;
(*c*) the borrower's debt is not a debt on a security within s. 82;
(*d*) the amount has become irrecoverable;
(*e*) the right to recover it has not been assigned;
(*f*) the loan was not made between spouses or companies in the same group;
(*g*) the loss is not included in the claimant's accounts for the purposes of income or corporation tax;
(*h*) in the case of a claim by a guarantor the guarantor must have made a payment under the guarantee and the guarantor and the borrower must not be spouses or companies in the same group;
(*i*) in the case of a claim by the lender the loan must have been made after April 11, 1978, and in the case of a guarantor the guarantee must have been made after April 11, 1978, though the loan may have been made before then.

It would seem that no claim can be made by a person to whom the right has been assigned, as opposed to the original lender.

Any amount subsequently recovered after a claim pursuant to this provision is to be treated as a chargeable gain. Under subs. (6) there is an extended meaning given to recovery.

Options and forfeited deposits

137.—(1) Without prejudice to section 19 above (general provisions about the disposal of assets), the grant of an option, and in particular—

(*a*) the grant of an option in a case where the grantor binds himself to sell what he does not own, and because the option is abandoned, never has occasion to own, and
(*b*) the grant of an option in a case where the grantor binds himself to buy what, because the option is abandoned, he does not acquire,

is the disposal of an asset (namely of the option), but subject to the following provisions of this section as to treating the grant of an option as part of a larger transaction.

(2) If an option is exercised the grant of the option and the transaction entered into by the grantor in fulfilment of his obligations under the option shall be treated as a single transaction and accordingly—

(*a*) if the option binds the grantor to sell, the consideration for the option is part of the consideration for the sale, and
(*b*) if the option binds the grantor to buy, the consideration for the option shall be deducted from the cost of acquisition incurred by the grantor in buying in pursuance of his obligations under the option.

(3) The exercise of an option by the person for the time being entitled to exercise it shall not constitute the disposal of an asset by that person, but, if an option is exercised then the acquisition of the option (whether directly from the grantor or not) and the transaction entered into by the person exercising the option in exercise of his rights under the option shall be treated as a single transaction and accordingly—

(*a*) if the option binds the grantor to sell, the cost of acquiring the option shall be part of the cost of acquiring what is sold, and
(*b*) if the option binds the grantor to buy, the cost of the option shall be treated as a cost incidental to the disposal of what is bought by the grantor of the option.

(4) The abandonment of—

(*a*) a quoted option to subscribe for shares in a company, or

(*b*) an option to acquire assets exercisable by a person intending to use them, if acquired, for the purpose of a trade carried on by him,

shall constitute the disposal of an asset (namely of the option); but the abandonment of any other option by the person for the time being entitled to exercise it shall not constitute the disposal of an asset by that person.

(5) In the case of an option relating to shares or securities this section shall apply subject to the provisions of section 65 above (rules for identification: pooling) and, accordingly, the option may be regarded, in relation to the grantor or in relation to the person entitled to exercise the option, as relating to part of a holding (as defined in section 65 above) of shares or securities.

(6) This section shall apply in relation to an option binding the grantor both to sell and to buy as if it were two separate options with half the consideration to each.

(7) In this section references to an option include references to an option binding the grantor to grant a lease for a premium or enter into any other transaction which is not a sale, and references to buying and selling in pursuance of an option shall be construed accordingly.

(8) This section shall apply in relation to a forfeited deposit of purchase money or other consideration money for a prospective purchase or other transaction which is abandoned as it applies in relation to the consideration for an option which binds the grantor to sell and which is not exercised.

(9) In subsection (4) (*a*) above, and in sections 138 and 139 below, " quoted option " means an option of a kind which, at the time of the abandonment or other disposal, is quoted on a recognised stock exchange within the meaning of section 535 of the Taxes Act, and there dealt in in the same manner as shares.

General Note

As a general rule, the grant of an option is the disposal of an asset, namely the option (subs. (1)).

Where an option is exercised, the grant of it and the transaction entered into by the grantor pursuant to his obligations under the option are treated as a single transaction, and the consideration for the grant is amalgamated with any consideration passing as a result of the exercise of the option (subs. (2)).

The exercise of an option does not constitute the disposal of an asset but the acquisition of the option by the person exercising it, and the transaction entered into by him consequent upon the the exercise of it, are treated as a single transaction and the consideration given for acquiring the option is amalgamated with any consideration passing as a result of the exercise of the option (subs. (3)).

The abandonment of an option does not constitute the disposal of an asset by a person unless it is either:

(*a*) a quoted option (as defined in subs. (9)) to subscribe for shares in a company; or

(*b*) an option to acquire trading assets intended for use in a trade carried on by that person (subs. (4)).

This section applies to forfeited deposits of purchase-money as it applies in relation to the consideration for an option which binds the grantor to sell but is not exercised by the prospective purchaser (subs. (8)).

Options: application of rules as to wasting assets

138.—(1) Section 38 above (wasting assets: restriction of allowable expenditure) shall not apply—

(*a*) to a quoted option to subscribe for shares in a company, or (*b*) to an option to acquire assets exercisable by a person intending to use them, if acquired, for the purpose of a trade carried on by him.

(2) In relation to the disposal by way of transfer of an option (other than a quoted option to subscribe for shares in a company) binding the grantor to sell or buy quoted shares or securities, the option shall be regarded as a wasting asset the life of which ends when the right to exercise the option ends, or when the option becomes valueless, whichever is the earlier.

Subsections (6) and (7) of section 137 above shall apply in relation to this subsection as they apply in relation to that section.

(3) The preceding provisions of this section are without prejudice to the application of sections 37 to 39 above (wasting assets) to options not within those provisions.

(4) In this section—

(*a*) " quoted option " has the meaning given by section 137 (9) above,

(*b*) " quoted shares or securities " means shares or securities which have a quoted market value on a recognised stock exchange in the United Kingdom or elsewhere.

General Note

This section provides that the two classes of options specified in s. 137 (4) are not to be treated as wasting assets for the purposes of s. 38. Otherwise, in relation to a disposal by way of transfer (not by the abandonment or exercise of an option), options to buy (not subscribe for) or sell quoted shares are wasting assets with lives ending when the right to exercise them expires or, if earlier, when they become valueless.

Quoted options treated as part of new holdings

139.—(1) If a quoted option to subscribe for shares in a company is dealt in (on the stock exchange where it is quoted) within three months after the taking effect, with respect to the company granting the option, of any reorganisation, reduction, conversion or amalgamation to which Chapter II of Part IV above applies, or within such longer period as the Board may by notice in writing allow—

(*a*) the option shall, for the purposes of the said Chapter II (under which a holding prior to the reorganisation or reduction of capital, conversion or amalgamation is to be treated as the same as the resulting new holding) be regarded as the shares which could be acquired by exercising the option, and

(*b*) section 150 (3) below shall apply for determining its market value.

(2) In this section " quoted option " has the meaning given by section 137 (9) above.

General Note

If a quoted option to subscribe for shares in a company is dealt in on the stock exchange where it is quoted within three months after a reorganisation, reduction, conversion or amalgamation affecting the company's share capital takes effect, the option is to be regarded for the purposes of Chap. II, Pt. IV, above as the shares which could be acquired by exercising it.

Part VII

Other Provisions

Insurance

Policies of insurance

140.—(1) The rights of the insurer under any policy of insurance shall not constitute an asset on the disposal of which a gain may accrue, whether the risks insured relate to property or not; and the rights of the insured under any policy of insurance of the risk of any kind of damage to, or the loss or depreciation of, assets shall constitute an asset on the disposal of which a gain may accrue only to the extent that those rights relate to assets on the disposal of which a gain may accrue or might have accrued.

(2) Notwithstanding subsection (1) above, sums received under a policy of insurance of the risk of any kind of damage to, or the loss or depreciation of, assets are for the purposes of this Act, and in particular for the purposes of section 20 above (disposal of assets by owner where any capital sum is derived from assets), sums derived from the assets.

(3) In this section " policy of insurance " does not include a policy of assurance on human life.

General Note

Rights of the insurer under an insurance policy (not being a life policy) are not assets on the disposal of which a chargeable gain (or allowable loss) can accrue.

Rights of an insured under an insurance policy (not being a life policy) are assets on the disposal of which a chargeable gain can accrue only to the extent that they relate to an asset on the disposal of which a chargeable gain might have accrued (subs. (1)).

Nothing in subs. (1) is to prevent sums received under a policy of insurance of the risk of damage to or loss of assets being sums derived from the assets insured (for the purposes of s. 20) (subs. (2)). The section as now drafted reverses the actual decision in *I.R.C.* v. *Montgomery* [1975] Ch. 266, although the case remains of general persuasive authority.

Disallowance of insurance premiums as expenses

141. Without prejudice to the provisions of section 33 above (exclusion of expenditure by reference to tax on income), there shall be excluded from the sums allowable as a deduction in the computation under Part II of Chapter II above of the gain accruing to a person on the disposal of an asset any premiums or other payments made under a policy of insurance of the risk of any kind of damage or injury to, or loss or depreciation of, the asset.

General Note

S. 141 prevents insurance premiums from being deducted as expenses when computing the amount of any gain.

Underwriters

142.—(1) An underwriting member of Lloyd's or of an approved association of underwriters shall, subject to the following provisions of this section, be treated for the purposes of this Act as absolutely entitled as against the trustees to the investments of his premiums trust fund, his special reserve fund (if any) and any other trust fund required or authorised by the rules of Lloyd's or the association in question, or required by the underwriting agent through whom his business or any part of it is carried on, to be kept in connection with the business.

(2) The trustees of any premiums trust fund shall, subject to subsection (3) below, be assessed and charged to capital gains tax as if subsection (1) above had not been passed.

(3) The assessment to be made on the trustees of a fund by virtue of subsection (2) above for any year of assessment shall not take account of losses accruing in any previous year of assessment, and if for that or any other reason the tax paid on behalf of an underwriting member for any year of assessment by virtue of assessments so made exceeds the capital gains tax for which he is liable, the excess shall, on a claim by him, be repaid.

(4) For the purposes of subsections (2) and (3) above the underwriting agent may be treated as a trustee of the premiums trust fund.

GENERAL NOTE

S. 142 deals with Lloyd's underwriters and clarifies their position in relation to the operation of their various trust funds. It also makes provision for how the assessments on such funds are to be made (subs. (3)).

Life assurance and deferred annuities

143.—(1) This section has effect as respects any policy of assurance or contract for a deferred annuity on the life of any person.

(2) No chargeable gain shall accrue on the disposal of, or of an interest in, the rights under any such policy of assurance or contract except where the person making the disposal is not the original beneficial owner and acquired the rights or interest for a consideration in money or money's worth.

(3) Subject to subsection (2) above, the occasion of—

(*a*) the payment of the sum or sums assured by a policy of assurance, or

(*b*) the transfer of investments or other assets to the owner of a policy of assurance in accordance with the policy,

and the occasion of the surrender of a policy of assurance, shall be the occasion of a disposal of the rights under the policy of assurance.

(4) Subject to subsection (2) above, the occasion of the payment of the first instalment of a deferred annuity, and the occasion of the surrender of the rights under a contract for a deferred annuity, shall be the occasion of a disposal of the rights under the contract for a deferred annuity and the amount of the consideration for the disposal of a contract for a deferred annuity shall be the market value at that time of the right to that and further instalments of the annuity.

GENERAL NOTE

This section excludes any chargeable gain on disposal of a life policy or contract for a deferred annuity except where the person making the disposal is not the original beneficial owner and acquired his interest for a consideration in money or money's worth. In the latter case, subs. (3) treats such a person as making a disposal when payment is first made under the life policy or deferred annuity contract or when under a policy providing for a transfer of investments or other assets to the owner of the policy, such transfer is effected.

Subs. (4) provides that on the disposal of a deferred annuity contract, whether on the payment of the first instalment or on the surrender of rights to the contract, such disposal is to be treated as having been made at market value.

Superannuation funds, annuities and annual payments

Superannuation funds, annuities and annual payments

144. No chargeable gain shall accrue to any person on the disposal of a right to, or to any part of—

(*a*) any allowance, annuity or capital sum payable out of any superannuation fund, or under any superannuation scheme, established solely or mainly for persons employed in a profession, trade, undertaking or employment, and their dependants,

(*b*) an annuity granted otherwise than under a contract for a deferred annuity by a company as part of its business of granting annuities on human life, whether or not including instalments of capital, or an annuity granted or deemed to be granted under the Government Annuities Act 1929, or

(*c*) annual payments which are due under a covenant made by any person and which are not secured on any property.

General Note

S. 144 exempts from charge to tax any gain accruing to a person on the disposal of any sum payable from a superannuation fund or similar body, or under an annuity other than those covered by the provisions of s. 143 and those payable by covenanted but unsecured annual payments.

Other exemptions and reliefs

Charities

145.—(1) Subject to subsection (2) below a gain shall not be a chargeable gain if it accrues to a charity and is applicable and applied for charitable purposes.

(2) If property held on charitable trusts ceases to be subject to charitable trusts—

(*a*) the trustees shall be treated as if they had disposed of, and immediately re-acquired, the property for a consideration equal to its market value, any gain on the disposal being treated as not accruing to a charity, and

(*b*) if and so far as any of that property represents, directly or indirectly, the consideration for the disposal of assets by the trustees, any gain accruing on that disposal shall be treated as not having accrued to a charity,

and an assessment to capital gains tax chargeable by virtue of paragraph (*b*) above may be made at any time not more than three years after the end of the year of assessment in which the property ceases to be subject to charitable trusts.

General Note

Subs. (1) exempts charities from the charge to tax. This exemption only applies to a gain accruing to a charity on a disposal of its own assets, which gain is applicable and applied for charitable purposes.

Subs. (2) deals with the case where property held on charitable trusts ceases to be subject to such trusts: there is then a notional disposal at market value by the trustees of the property so that any accrued gain becomes chargeable. Further, any gain on a prior disposal by the trustees (which would have been exempt while the property was subject to the charitable trusts) is treated as a chargeable gain to the extent that consideration for the disposal that gave rise to the former gain is represented by assets in the hands of the trustees at the time when the property ceases to be held on charitable trusts.

Gifts to charities etc.

146.—(1) Subsection (2) below shall apply where a disposal of an asset is made otherwise than under a bargain at arm's length—

(*a*) to a charity, or

(*b*) to any of the bodies mentioned in paragraph 12 of Schedule 6 to the Finance Act 1975 (gifts for national purposes, etc.).

(2) Section 19 (3) above (consideration deemed to be equal to market value) and section 17 (3) below shall not apply; but if the disposal is by way of gift (including a gift in settlement) or for a consideration not exceeding the sums allowable as a deduction under section 32 above, then—

(*a*) the disposal and acquisition shall be treated for the purposes of this Act as being made for such consideration as to secure that neither a gain nor a loss accrues on the disposal, and

(*b*) where, after the disposal, the asset is disposed of by the person who acquired it under the disposal, its acquisition by the person making the earlier disposal shall be treated for the purposes of this Act as the acquisition of the person making the later disposal.

(3) Where, otherwise than on the termination of a life interest (within the meaning of section 55 above) by the death of the person entitled thereto, any assets or parts of any assets forming part of settled property are, under section 54 or 55 above, deemed to be disposed of and re-acquired by the trustee, and—

(*a*) the person becoming entitled as mentioned in section 54 (1) above is a charity, or a body mentioned in paragraph 12 of Schedule 6 to the Finance Act 1975 (gifts for national purposes, etc.) or

(*b*) any of the assets which, or parts of which, are deemed to be disposed of and re-acquired under section 55 (1) above are held for the purposes of a charity, or a body mentioned in the said paragraph 12,

then, if no consideration is received by any person for or in connection with any transaction by virtue of which the charity or other body becomes so entitled or the assets are so held, the disposal and re-acquisition of the assets to which the charity or other body becomes so entitled or of the assets or parts of the assets which are held as mentioned in paragraph (*b*) above shall, notwithstanding sections 54 and 55 above, be treated for the purposes of this Act as made for such consideration as to secure that neither a gain nor a loss accrues on the disposal.

GENERAL NOTE

Capital gains tax relief is given for disposals, otherwise than by way of a bargain made at arm's length, to a charity or one of the bodies concerned with the national heritage listed in Sched. 6, para. 12, F.A. 1975. Subs. (2) provides that if the disposal is by way of gift, or for a consideration not exceeding the transferor's allowable cost, the disposal is treated as made for a consideration which gives the transferor no gain and no loss. The transferee takes over the allowable cost and acquisition date of the transferor, although in the case of a charity, this is important only if the property subsequently ceases to be subject to charitable trusts (see s. 145 (1)). If the disposal, although not at arm's length, is for a consideration exceeding the transferor's allowable cost, the transferor's liability to tax is computed by reference to the actual consideration, since s. 19 (3) is excluded.

The relief extends to deemed disposals of settled property, provided no consideration passes (subs. (3)).

Works of art etc.

147.—(1) A gain accruing on the disposal of an asset by way of gift shall not be a chargeable gain if the asset is property falling within sub-paragraph (2) of paragraph 13 of Schedule 6 to the Finance Act 1975 (gifts for public benefit) and the Treasury give a direction in relation to it under sub-paragraph (1) of that paragraph.

(2) A gain shall not be a chargeable gain if it accrues on the disposal of an asset with respect to which a capital transfer tax undertaking or an undertaking under the following provisions of this section has been given and—

(*a*) the disposal is by way of sale by private treaty to a body mentioned in paragraph 12 of the said Schedule 6 (museums, etc.), or is to such a body otherwise than by sale, or

(*b*) the disposal is to the Board in insurance of paragraph 17 of Schedule 4 to the said Act of 1975 or in accordance with directions given by the Treasury under section 50 or 51 of the Finance Act 1946 (acceptance of property in satisfaction of tax).

(3) Subsection (4) below shall have effect in respect of the disposal of any asset which is property which has been or could be designated under section 77 of the Finance Act 1976, being—

(*a*) a disposal by way of gift, including a gift in settlement, or

(*b*) a disposal of settled property by the trustee on an occasion when, under section 54 (1) or 55 (1) above, the trustee is deemed to dispose of and immediately re-acquire settled property (other than any disposal on which by virtue of section 56 above no chargeable gain or allowable loss accrues to the trustee),

if the requisite undertaking described in the said section 77 (maintenance, preservation and access) is given by such person as the Treasury think appropriate in the circumstances of the case.

(4) The person making a disposal to which subsection (3) above applies and the person acquiring the asset on the disposal shall be treated for all the purposes of this Act as if the asset was acquired from the one making the disposal for a consideration of such an amount as would secure that on the disposal neither a gain nor a loss would accrue to the one making the disposal.

(5) If—

(*a*) there is a sale of the asset and capital transfer tax is chargeable under section 78 of the Finance Act 1976 (or would be chargeable if a capital transfer tax undertaking as well as an undertaking under this section had been given), or

(*b*) the Treasury are satisfied that at any time during the period for which any such undertaking was given it has not been observed in a material respect,

the person selling that asset or, as the case may be, the owner of the asset shall be treated for the purposes of this Act as having sold the asset for a consideration equal to its market value, and, in the case of a failure to comply with the undertaking, having immediately re-acquired it for a consideration equal to its market value.

(6) The period for which an undertaking under this section is given shall be until the person beneficially entitled to the asset dies or it is disposed of, whether by sale or gift or otherwise; and if the asset subject to the undertaking is disposed of—

(*a*) otherwise than on sale, and

(*b*) without a further undertaking being given under this section,

subsection (5) above shall apply as if the asset had been sold to an individual.

References in this subsection to a disposal shall be construed without regard to any provision of this Act under which an asset is deemed to be disposed of.

(7) Where under subsection (5) above a person is treated as having sold for a consideration equal to its market value any asset within section 77 (1) (*c*), (*d*) or (*e*) of the Finance Act 1976, he shall also be treated as having sold and immediately re-acquired for a consideration equal to its market value any asset associated with it; but the Treasury may direct that the preceding provisions of this subsection shall not have effect in any case in which it appears to them that the entity consisting of the asset and any assets associated with it has not been materially affected.

For the purposes of this subsection two or more assets are associated with each other if one of them is a building falling within the said section 77 (1) (*c*) and the other or others such land or objects as, in relation to that building, fall within the said section 77 (1) (*d*) or (*e*).

(8) If in pursuance of subsection (5) above a person is treated as having on any occasion sold an asset and capital transfer tax becomes chargeable on the same occasion, then, in determining the value of the asset for the purposes of that tax, an allowance shall be made for the capital gains tax chargeable on any chargeable gain accruing on that occasion.

(9) In this section " capital transfer tax undertaking " means an undertaking under sections 76 to 81 of the Finance Act 1976 or section 31 or 34 of the Finance Act 1975.

General Note

This section confers various exemptions for gains accruing on the disposal by way of gift (subs. (1)), or sale by private treaty (subs. (2) (*a*)), or to the Board in satisfaction of tax (subs. (2) (*b*)), or by way of gift in settlement or on the deemed disposal of settled property (subss. (3) and (4)), where the property is of importance to the national heritage and the terms on which the disposal is made ensure the maintenance and preservation of it and reasonable public access to it. There are also provisions to recoup tax if the approved terms on which the disposal is made are not adhered to (subss. (5) to (7)).

Maintenance funds for historic buildings

148.—(1) This section applies where a person disposes of an asset to trustees in circumstances such that the disposal is a transfer of value which by virtue of section 84 of the Finance Act 1976 (capital transfer tax: maintenance funds for historic buildings) is an exempt transfer.

(2) The person making the disposal and the person acquiring the asset on the disposal shall be treated for all the purposes of this Act as if the asset was acquired from the one making the disposal for a consideration of such an amount as would secure that on the disposal neither a gain nor a loss would accrue to the one making the disposal.

General Note

This section provides that no gain or loss is to arise on a disposal which is an exempt transfer under s. 84, F.A. 1976 (maintenance funds for historic buildings). The trustees shall be treated as acquiring the asset for its existing base cost.

Employee trusts

149.—(1) Where—

(*a*) a close company disposes of an asset to trustees in circumstances such that the disposal is a disposition which by virtue of section 90 of the Finance Act 1976 (employee trusts) is not a transfer of value for the purposes of capital transfer tax, or

(*b*) an individual disposes of an asset to trustees in circumstances such that the disposal is an exempt transfer by virtue of section 67 of the Finance Act 1978 (employee trusts: capital transfer tax),

this Act shall have effect in relation to the disposal in accordance with subsections (2) and (3) below.

(2) Section 19 (3) above (consideration deemed to be equal to market value) shall not apply to the disposal; and if the disposal is by way of gift or is for a consideration not exceeding the sums allowable as a deduction under section 32 above—

(*a*) the disposal, and the acquisition by the trustees, shall be treated for the purposes of this Act as being made for such consideration as to secure that neither a gain nor a loss accrues on the disposal, and

(*b*) where the trustees dispose of the asset, its acquisition by the company or individual shall be treated as its acquisition by the trustees.

(3) Where the disposal is by a close company, section 75 (1) above (assets disposed of for less than market value) shall apply to the disposal as if for the reference to market value there were substituted a reference to market value or the sums allowable as a deduction under section 32 above, whichever is the less.

(4) Subject to subsection (5) below, this Act shall also have effect in accordance with subsection (2) above in relation to any disposal made by a company other than a close company if—

(*a*) the disposal is made to trustees otherwise than under a bargain made at arm's length, and

(*b*) the property disposed of is to be held by them on trusts of the description specified in paragraph 17 (1) of Schedule 5 to the Finance Act 1975 (that is to say, those in relation to which the said section 90 of the Finance Act 1976 has effect) and the persons for whose benefit the trusts permit the property to be applied include all or most of either—

(i) the persons employed by or holding office with the company, or

(ii) the persons employed by or holding office with the company or any one or more subsidiaries of the company.

(5) Subsection (4) above does not apply if the trusts permit any of the property to be applied at any time (whether during any such period as is referred to in the said paragraph 17 (1) or later) for the benefit of—

(*a*) a person who is a participator in the company (" the donor company "), or

(*b*) any other person who is a participator in any other company that has made a disposal of property to be held on the same trusts as the property disposed of by the donor company, being a disposal in relation to which this Act has had effect in accordance with subsection (2) above, or

(*c*) any other person who has been a participator in the donor company or any such company as is mentioned in paragraph (*b*) above at any time after, or during the ten years before, the disposal made by that company, or

(*d*) any person who is connected with a person within paragraph (*a*), (*b*) or (*c*) above.

(6) The participators in a company who are referred to in subsection (5) above do not include any participator who—

(*a*) is not beneficially entitled to, or to rights entitling him to acquire, 5 per cent. or more of, or of any class of the shares comprised in, its issued share capital, and

(*b*) on a winding-up of the company would not be entitled to 5 per cent. or more of its assets;

and in determining whether the trusts permit property to be applied as mentioned in that subsection, no account shall be taken—

(i) of any power to make a payment which is the income of any person for any of the purposes of income tax, or would be the income for any of those purposes of a person not resident in the United Kingdom if he were so resident, or

(ii) if the trusts are those of a profit sharing scheme approved under the Finance Act 1978, of any power to appropriate shares in pursuance of the scheme.

(7) In subsection (4) above " subsidiary " has the same meaning as in the Companies Act 1948 and in subsections (5) and (6) above " participator " has the meaning given in section 303 (1) of the Taxes Act, except that it does not include a loan creditor.

(8) In this section " close company " includes a company which, if resident in the United Kingdom, would be a close company as defined in section 155 (1) below.

General Note

Disposals of assets by close companies (defined in subs. (8) to include certain non-resident companies) and individuals to trustees of employee trusts, which are exempt transfers for capital transfer tax purposes (see s. 90, F.A. 1976, and s. 67, F.A. 1978), are also favourably treated for capital gains tax purposes.

S. 19 (3) (consideration deemed to be equal to market value) does not apply on such disposals and, except where the consideration passing exceeds the transferor's allowable cost for the assets (when the actual consideration is taken account of), the disposal is deemed to take place for a consideration which gives the transferor no gain and no loss. The trustees are deemed to have acquired the asset transferred at the time the transferor acquired it (thus giving them the benefit of any relief for gains accruing before April 6, 1965). The charge under s. 75 above (where assets are transferred by a close company at an undervalue) is also modified to an extent in the case of such disposals (subs. (3)). Disposals by companies other than close companies to trustees of employee trusts are similarly treated if the conditions of subs. (5) are met.

Part VIII

Supplemental

Valuation

Valuation: general

150.—(1) In this Act " market value " in relation to any assets means the price which those assets might reasonably be expected to fetch on a sale in the open market.

(2) In estimating the market value of any assets no reduction shall be made in the estimate on account of the estimate being made on the assumption that the whole of the assets is to be placed on the market at one and the same time.

(3) The market value of shares or securities listed in The Stock Exchange Daily Official List shall, except where in consequence of special

circumstances prices quoted in that List are by themselves not a proper measure of market value, be as follows—

(*a*) the lower of the two prices shown in the quotations for the shares or securities in The Stock Exchange Daily Official List on the relevant date plus one-quarter of the difference between those two figures, or

(*b*) halfway between the highest and lowest prices at which bargains, other than bargains done at special prices, were recorded in the shares or securities for the relevant date,

choosing the amount under paragraph (*a*) if less than that under paragraph (*b*), or if no such bargains were recorded for the relevant date, and choosing the amount under paragraph (*b*) if less than that under paragraph (*a*):

Provided that—

(i) this subsection shall not apply to shares or securities for which The Stock Exchange provides a more active market elsewhere than on the London trading floor, and

(ii) if the London trading floor is closed on the relevant date the market value shall be ascertained by reference to the latest previous date or earliest subsequent date on which it is open, whichever affords the lower market value.

(4) In this Act " market value " in relation to any rights of unit holders in any unit trust scheme the buying and selling prices of which are published regularly by the managers of the scheme shall mean an amount equal to the buying price (that is the lower price) so published on the relevant date, or if none were published on that date, on the latest date before.

(5) In relation to an asset of a kind the sale of which is subject to restrictions imposed under the Exchange Control Act 1947 such that part of what is paid by the purchaser is not retainable by the seller the market value, as arrived at under subsection (1), subsection (3) or subsection (4) above, shall be subject to such adjustment as is appropriate having regard to the difference between the amount payable by a purchaser and the amount receivable by a seller.

(6) The provisions of this section, with sections 151 to 153 below, have effect subject to Part I of Schedule 6 to this Act (market value at a time before the commencement of this Act).

General Note

This section defines market value for the purposes of computing a gain. Subss. (1) and (2) follow the language of s. 7 (5), F.A. 1894, and s. 60 (2), F. (1909–10) A. 1910, and decisions on their construction will be authorities for the construction of these subsections.

Subss. (3) and (4) set out the provisions for ascertaining the market value of quoted securities and of units whose value is published. The slightly different method adopted for valuing shares held on April 6, 1965, under Sched. 6, para. 3, should be noted.

Subs. (3) provides that the market value of quoted shares and securities is to be ascertained by reference to Stock Exchange prices except " where in consequence of special circumstances prices (so quoted) are by themselves not a proper measure of market value." A taxpayer contended that the market value at April 6, 1965, of quoted shares that he had held ought not to be based upon the Stock Exchange prices at that date because at that date, unknown to the Stock Exchange, a takeover of the company in which the stock was held was imminent. This contention was rejected on the ground that such a circumstance could not be regarded as " special " in the sense of " unusual ": *Crabtree* v. *Hinchcliffe* [1972] A.C. 707.

Where a figure for " market value " must be ascertained for an asset for which, if it were actually sold, the sale consideration would not all be retainable by the seller because of exchange control regulations, subs. (5) provides for an adjustment to be made to recognise this fact.

This section takes effect subject to the provisions relating to valuation contained in Pt. I of Sched. 6 (subs. (6)).

Assets disposed of in a series of transactions

151. **If a person is given, or acquires from one or more persons with whom he is connected, by way of two or more gifts or other transactions, assets of which the aggregate market value, when considered separately in relation to the separate gifts or other transactions, is less than their aggregate market value when considered together, then for the purposes of this Act their market value, where relevant, shall be taken to be the larger market value, to be apportioned rateably to the respective disposals.**

General Note

S. 151 is capable of producing some odd results. Suppose that X & Co. has an issued capital of 100 shares, and that A owns them all in June 1974. At that date the shares are worth £2 each as part of a majority holding and £1 each as part of a minority holding. In June 1974, A gives 25 shares to his son B and in June 1978, by which time the shares are worth £20 as part of a majority holding, he gives 26 more shares.

Plainly the notional consideration for the 1978 gift is 26 × £20, but perhaps less obviously, the capital gains tax computation for the 1974 gift will have to be done again, and strictly, it produces a notional consideration of 25 × £20 for that gift—even though the value of all the issued shares was then only 100 × £2!

If B had disposed of some of the shares comprised in the first gift before their value had risen, the capital gains tax computation for that disposal would have to be done again so as to reveal a loss of £18 per share.

The section produces rather less complex results if the two parcels are valued together as follows: (a) as at the time of the first gift for the purpose of ascertaining the market value of the first parcel; and (b) as at the time of the second gift for the purpose of ascertaining the market value of the second parcel, and this is how the Revenue interprets the provision. The Revenue also regards the making of additional assessments under these provisions as sufficient reason for allowing an election to be made outside the normal time limits (under Sched. 5, para. 12). But an election once made cannot be withdrawn (Sched. 5, para. 12 (4)).

In a statement in (1969) 93 Tax. the Revenue indicated that it interprets the expression "is given or acquired" as covering gifts *inter vivos*, gifts under a will and acquisition by the exercise of an option granted by a deceased person (either during life or by will) to purchase property from his personal representatives. It would seem therefore that the Revenue does not regard sales at an undervalue as being within the provision (on the question of whether this is the true construction of the provision, see [1970] B.T.R. 349).

It is not clear how the Revenue have concluded that personal representatives are "connected persons" (see s. 63).

Unquoted shares and securities

152.—**(1) The provisions of subsection (3) below shall have effect in any case where, in relation to an asset to which this section applies, there falls to be determined by virtue of section 150 (1) above the price which the asset might reasonably be expected to fetch on a sale in the open market.**

(2) The assets to which this section applies are shares and securities which are not quoted on a recognised stock exchange, within the meaning of section 535 of the Taxes Act, at the time as at which their market value for the purposes of tax on chargeable gains falls to be determined.

(3) For the purposes of a determination falling within subsection (1) above, it shall be assumed that, in the open market which is postulated

for the purposes of that determination, there is available to any prospective purchaser of the asset in question all the information which a prudent prospective purchaser of the asset might reasonably require if he were proposing to purchase it from a willing vendor by private treaty and at arm's length.

General Note

This section deals with the valuation of unquoted shares and securities. Subs. (3) provides that in determining the price that might be fetched on the open market a prospective purchaser shall be assumed to have all the information of a prudent person, purchasing by private agreement in a transaction at arm's length.

This provision reverses for the purpose of capital gains tax the effect of the decision in *Re Lynall* [1972] A.C. 680 where it was held that, in ascertaining the open market value of shares in an unquoted company, it should not be assumed that information that would have been made available to a prospective purchaser would be available in the " open market."

Value determined for capital transfer tax

153. Where on the death of any person capital transfer tax is chargeable on the value of his estate immediately before his death and the value of an asset forming part of that estate has been ascertained (whether in any proceedings or otherwise) for the purposes of that tax, the value so ascertained shall be taken for the purposes of this Act to be the market value of that asset at the date of the death.

General Note

This section provides that a valuation of assets for capital transfer tax purposes carried out on the event of a death, shall also be adopted as providing the market value figure when computing any liability to capital gains tax on any of the assets.

Other provisions

Income tax decisions

154. Any assessment to income tax or decision on a claim under the Income Tax Acts, and any decision on an appeal under the Income Tax Acts against such an assessment or decision, shall be conclusive so far as under Chapter II of Part II of this Act, or any other provision of this Act, liability to tax depends on the provisions of the Income Tax Acts.

General Note

This section makes income tax assessments conclusive for capital gains tax purposes in determining such questions as whether the gain in question is part of the profits of a trade.

Interpretation

155.—(1) In this Act, unless the context otherwise requires—

" allowable loss " has the meaning given by section 29 above,

" the Board " means the Commissioners of Inland Revenue,

" chargeable gain " has the meaning given by section 28 (2) above,

" chargeable period " means a year of assessment or an accounting period of a company for purposes of corporation tax,

" close company " has the meaning given by sections 282 and 283 of the Taxes Act,

" company " includes any body corporate or unincorporated

association but does not include a partnership, and shall be construed in accordance with section 93 above (application of Act to unit trusts),

"control" shall be construed in accordance with section 302 of the Taxes Act,

"inspector" means any inspector of taxes,

"land" includes messuages, tenements, and hereditaments, houses and buildings of any tenure,

"married woman living with her husband": see subsection (2) below,

"part disposal" has the meaning given by section 19 (2) above,

"personal representatives" has the meaning given by section 432 (4) of the Taxes Act,

"quoted" on a stock exchange, or recognised stock exchange, in the United Kingdom: see subsection (3) below,

"the Taxes Act" means the Income and Corporation Taxes Act 1970,

"trade" has the same meaning as in the Income Tax Acts,

"trading stock" has the meaning given by section 137 (4) of the Taxes Act,

"wasting asset" has the meaning given by section 37 above and paragraph 1 of Schedule 3 to this Act,

"year of assessment" means, in relation to capital gains tax, a year beginning on 6th April and ending on 5th April in the following calendar year, and "1979–80" and so on indicate years of assessment as in the Income Tax Acts.

(2) References in this Act to a married woman living with her husband shall be construed in accordance with section 42 (1) (2) of the Taxes Act.

(3) References in this Act to quotation on a stock exchange in the United Kingdom or a recognised stock exchange in the United Kingdom shall be construed as references to listing in the Official List of The Stock Exchange.

(4) The Table below indexes other general definitions in this Act.

Expression defined	*Reference*
"Absolutely entitled as against the trustee"	S. 46 (2).
"Authorised unit trust"	S. 92.
"Branch or agency"	S. 12 (3).
"Class", in relation to shares or securities	S. 64 (1).
"Connected", in references to persons being connected with one another	S. 63.
"Court investment fund"	S. 92.
"Gilt-edged securities"	Schedule 2.
"Investment trust"	S. 92.
"Issued", in relation to shares or debentures	S. 64 (2).
"Lease" and cognate expressions	Paragraph 10 (1) of Schedule 3.
"Legatee"	S. 47 (2) (3).
"Market value"	Ss. 150 to 153; Part I of Schedule 6.
"Resident" and "ordinarily resident"	S. 18 (1).
"Settled property"	S. 51.
"Shares"	S. 64 (1).
"Unit trust scheme"	S. 92.

(5) References in the Income Tax Acts to profits or gains shall not include references to chargeable gains.

GENERAL NOTE

Subs. (1) contains further definitions applicable to this Act and the other subsections contain a number of ancillary provisions including (subs. (4)) a useful index of general definitions in this Act.

PART IX

GENERAL

Commencement

156.—(1) Except as otherwise provided by this Part of this Act, this Act shall come into force in relation to tax for the year 1979–80 and subsequent years of assessment, and tax for other chargeable periods beginning after 5th April 1979.

(2) The following provisions of this Act, that is—

(*a*) so much of any provision of this Act as authorises the making of any order or other instrument,

(*b*) except where the tax concerned is all tax for chargeable periods to which this Act does not apply, so much of any provision of this Act as confers any power or imposes any duty the exercise or performance of which operates or may operate in relation to tax for more than one chargeable period,

shall come into force for all purposes on 6th April 1979 to the exclusion of the corresponding enactments repealed by this Act.

GENERAL NOTE

This section provides that this Act shall come into effect on April 6, 1979, and the provisions of the Act shall apply to tax assessable in the year 1979–80 and all subsequent years.

Savings, transitory provisions and consequential amendments

157.—(1) Schedule 6 to this Act, which contains transitory provisions and savings, shall have effect, and the repeals made by section 158 (1) below have effect subject to that Schedule.

(2) For the avoidance of doubt it is hereby declared that this Act has effect subject to those provisions of the Taxes Act and other enactments relating to chargeable gains which are not repealed by this Act; and with a view to preserving the existing effect of such enactments as are mentioned in Schedule 7 to this Act, they shall be amended in accordance with that Schedule.

(3) The provisions of the said Schedule 7, and the other provisions of this Part of this Act, are without prejudice to the provisions of the Interpretation Act 1978 as respects the effect of repeals.

(4) This section and the said Schedules 6 and 7 shall come into force on the passing of this Act.

GENERAL NOTE

S. 157 clarifies the position concerning the previous provisions concerned with capital gains tax which are herewith repealed, and confirms that the Act takes effect subject to those provisions which are not repealed and relate to chargeable gains.

Repeals

158.—(1) The enactments and instruments mentioned in Schedule 8 to this Act are hereby repealed to the extent specified in the third column of that Schedule.

(2) The said repeals shall come into force in accordance with section 156 above.

GENERAL NOTE

This section provides that the provisions listed in Sched. 8 shall be repealed.

Continuity and construction of references to old and new law

159.—(1) The continuity of the operation of the law relating to chargeable gains shall not be affected by the substitution of this Act for the repealed enactments.

(2) Any reference, whether express or implied, in any enactment, instrument or document (including this Act and any enactment amended by Schedule 7 to this Act) to, or to things done or falling to be done under or for the purposes of, any provision of this Act shall, if and so far as the nature of the reference permits, be construed as including, in relation to the times, years or periods, circumstances or purposes in relation to which the corresponding provision in the repealed enactments has or had effect, a reference to, or as the case may be to things done or falling to be done under or for the purposes of, that corresponding provision.

(3) Any reference, whether express or implied, in any enactment, instrument or document (including the repealed enactments and enactments, instruments and documents passed or made after the passing of this Act) to, or to things done or falling to be done under or for the purposes of, any of the repealed enactments shall, if and so far as the nature of the reference permits, be construed as including, in relation to the times, years or periods, circumstances or purposes in relation to which the corresponding provision of this Act has effect, a reference to, or as the case may be to things done or falling to be done under or for the purposes of, that corresponding provision.

(4) In this section " the repealed enactments " means the enactments repealed by this Act.

General Note

S. 159 provides that the continuity of the law relating to capital gains tax is not affected by the substitution of this Act for the former legislation which this Act consolidates and repeals.

Short title

160. This Act may be cited as the Capital Gains Tax Act 1979.

SCHEDULES

Section 5

SCHEDULE 1

Relief for Gains Less than £9,500

Preliminary

1. In this Schedule references to any subsections not otherwise identified are references to subsections of section 5 of this Act.

Husband and wife

2.—(1) For any year of assessment during which a married woman is living with her husband subsections (1) to (4) shall apply to them as if the amounts of £1,000, £5,000 and £600 were divided between them—

(*a*) in proportion to their respective taxable amounts for that year (disregarding for this purpose paragraphs (*a*) and (*b*) of subsection (4)), or

(*b*) where the aggregate of those amounts does not exceed £1,000 and allowable losses accruing to either of them in a previous year are carried forward from that year, in such other proportion as they may agree.

(2) Sub-paragraph (1) above shall also apply for any year of assessment during a part of which (being a part beginning with 6th April) a married woman is living with her husband but—

(*a*) her taxable amount for that year shall not include chargeable gains or allowable losses accruing to her in the remainder of the year, and

(*b*) subsections (1) to (4) shall apply to her (without the modification in sub-paragraph (1) above) for the remainder of the year as if it were a separate year of assessment.

3.—(1) For any year of assessment during which or during a part of which (being a part beginning with 6th April) the individual is a married man whose wife is living with him and in relation to whom section 45 (1) of this Act applies subsection (5) shall apply as if—

(*a*) the chargeable gains accruing to him in the year included those accruing to her in the year or the part of the year, and

(*b*) all the disposals of assets made by her in the year or the part of the year were made by him.

(2) Subsection (5) shall not apply for any year of assessment during which or during a part of which (being a part beginning with 6th April)—

(*a*) the individual is a married man whose wife is living with him but in relation to whom the said section 45 (1) does not apply, or

(*b*) the individual is a married woman living with her husband.

Personal representatives

4. For the year of assessment in which an individual dies and for the two next following years of assessment, subsections (1) to (5) shall apply to his personal representatives as they apply to an individual.

Trustees

5.—(1) For any year of assessment during the whole or part of which settled property is held on trusts which secure that, during the lifetime of a mentally disabled person or a person in receipt of attendance allowance, any of the property which is applied, and any income arising from the property, is applied only or mainly for the benefit of that person, subsections (1) to (5) shall apply to the trustees of the settlement as they apply to an individual.

(2) In this paragraph "mentally disabled person" means a person who by reason of mental disorder within the meaning of the Mental Health Act 1959 is incapable of administering his property or managing his affairs and "attendance allowance" means an allowance under section 35 of the Social Security Act 1975 or the Social Security (Northern Ireland) Act 1975.

6.—(1) For any year of assessment during the whole or part of which any property is settled property, not being a year of assessment for which paragraph 5 (1) above applies, subsections (1) to (5) shall apply to the trustees of a settlement as they apply to an individual but with the following modifications.

(2) In subsections (1), (4) and (5) for "£1,000" there shall be substituted "£500".

(3) For subsections (2) and (3) there shall be substituted—

"(2) If an individual's taxable amount for a year of assessment exceeds £500 the amount of capital gains tax to which he is chargeable for that year shall not exceed one-half of the excess."

(4) In subsection (5) for "£5,000" there shall be substituted "£2,500".

(5) This paragraph applies where the settlement was made before 7th June 1978.

General Note

This Schedule applies the capital gains tax relief for gains less than £9,500 (s. 5) to husbands and wives, personal representatives and trustees.

Husbands and wives. The relief given by s. 5 cannot be claimed by both the husband and wife if during the relevant year of assessment they are living together. Instead it is divided between them. The division will be in proportion to their respective taxable amounts taking into account for these purposes only, any losses carried forward from previous years. This is subject to one qualification in the case where their taxable amounts together do not exceed £1,000 and one or both of them has carried forward losses from previous years. In such a case they can agree to divide the relief between them in such proportions as they decide. In any year of assessment in which the spouses cease to live together for the purposes of this relief, the part of the year for which they are not living together is treated as a separate year of assessment as regards the wife.

Personal representatives. The relief may be claimed by a personal representative but only in respect of the year of assessment in which the deceased died and the two years of assessment following that one.

Trusts. The relief will apply in the same manner as for individuals to trusts providing that the capital and income is applied "only or mainly" for the benefit of a person who is mentally disabled or in receipt of an attendance allowance during that person's lifetime. As regards other trusts, the first £500 of taxable amount will not be charged to capital gains tax, and thereafter the tax will be limited to one-half the excess of the taxable amount over £500. The relief will not apply to settlements created after June 6, 1978, whether or not for the benefit of a mentally disabled person or one in receipt of an attendance allowance.

Section 64 (1)

SCHEDULE 2

Gilt-Edged Securities

Part I

1. For the purposes of this Act "gilt-edged securities" means the securities specified in Part II of this Schedule, and such of the following securities, denominated in sterling and issued after 15th April 1969, as may be specified by order made by the Treasury by statutory instrument, namely—

(*a*) stocks and bonds issued under section 12 of the National Loans Act 1968, and

(*b*) stocks and bonds guaranteed by the Treasury and issued under the Electricity (Scotland) Acts 1943 to 1954, the Electricity Acts 1947 and 1957 and the Gas Act 1972.

2. The Treasury shall cause particulars of any order made under paragraph 1 above to be published in the London and Edinburgh Gazettes as soon as may be after the order is made.

3. Section 14 (*b*) of the Interpretation Act 1978 (implied power to amend orders made by statutory instrument) shall not apply to the power of making orders under paragraph 1 above.

Part II

Existing Gilt-Edged Securities

Stocks and bonds charged on the National Loans Fund

11½%	Treasury Stock 1979
3 %	Treasury Stock 1979
10½%	Treasury Stock 1979
9 %	Treasury Convertible Stock 1980
4 %	British Overseas Airways Stock 1974–80
9½%	Treasury Stock 1980
3½%	Treasury Stock 1977–80
5¼%	Funding Loan 1978–80
13 %	Exchequer Stock 1980
11½%	Treasury Stock 1981
3½%	Treasury Stock 1979–81
9¾%	Treasury Stock 1981
8¼%	Exchequer Stock 1981
9½%	Exchequer Stock 1981
3 %	Exchequer Stock 1981
	Variable Rate Treasury Stock 1981
12¾%	Exchequer Stock 1981
8½%	Treasury Loan 1980–82
3 %	Treasury Stock 1982

14 % Treasury Stock 1982
2½% British Overseas Airways Stock 1977–82
Variable Rate Treasury Stock 1982
8¼% Treasury Stock 1982
9¼% Exchequer Stock 1982
8¾% Exchequer Stock 1983
3 % British Overseas Airways Stock 1980–83
3 % Exchequer Stock 1983
12 % Treasury Loan 1983
9¼% Treasury Stock 1983
10 % Exchequer Stock 1983
5½% Funding Stock 1982–84
12¼% Exchequer Stock 1985
8½% Treasury Loan 1984–86
6½% Funding Loan 1985–87
7¾% Treasury Loan 1985–88
3 % British Transport Stock 1978–88
5 % Treasury Stock 1986–89
13 % Treasury Stock 1990
8¼% Treasury Loan 1987–90
11¾% Treasury Stock 1991
5¾% Funding Loan 1987–91
12¾% Treasury Loan 1992
10 % Treasury Stock 1992
12¼% Exchequer Stock 1992
12½% Treasury Loan 1993
6 % Funding Loan 1993
13¾% Treasury Loan 1993
14½% Treasury Loan 1994
12½% Exchequer Stock 1994
9 % Treasury Loan 1994
12 % Treasury Stock 1995
10¼% Exchequer Stock 1995
12¾% Treasury Loan 1995
9 % Treasury Loan 1992–96
15¼% Treasury Loan 1996
13¼% Exchequer Loan 1996
13¼% Treasury Loan 1997
10½% Exchequer Stock 1997
8¾% Treasury Loan 1997
6¾% Treasury Loan 1995–98
15½% Treasury Loan 1998
12 % Exchequer Stock 1998
9½% Treasury Loan 1999
10½% Treasury Stock 1999
12 % Exchequer Stock 1999–2002
3½% Funding Stock 1999–2004
12½% Treasury Stock 2003–2005
8 % Treasury Loan 2002–2006
5½% Treasury Stock 2008–2012
7¾% Treasury Loan 2012–2015
2½% Treasury Stock 1986–2016
12 % Exchequer Stock 2013–2017
2½% Annuities 1905 or after
2¾% Annuities 1905 or after
2½% Consolidated Stock 1923 or after
4 % Consolidated Loan 1957 or after
3½% Conversion Loan 1961 or after
2½% Treasury Stock 1975 or after
3 % Treasury Stock 1966 or after
3½% War Loan 1952 or after

Securities issued by the Treasury under Part II of the Tithe Act 1936

3 % Redemption Stock 1986–96

Securities issued by certain public corporations and guaranteed by the Treasury

4¼% North of Scotland Electricity Stock 1974–79
4¼% British Electricity Stock 1974–79
3½% British Electricity Stock 1976–79
3½% North of Scotland Electricity Stock 1977–80
3 % British European Airways Stock 1980–83
3 % North of Scotland Electricity Stock 1989–92
3 % British Gas Stock 1990–95.

GENERAL NOTE

This schedule defines (Pt. I) and provides a list (Pt. II) of "gilt-edged securities" in accordance with s. 64 (1) and for use in the interpretation of ss. 67 to 70.

Section 106

SCHEDULE 3

LEASES

Leases of land as wasting assets: curved line restriction of allowable expenditure

1.—(1) A lease of land shall not be a wasting asset until the time when its duration does not exceed fifty years.

(2) If at the beginning of the period of ownership of a lease of land it is subject to a sub-lease not at a rackrent and the value of the lease at the end of the duration of the sub-lease, estimated as at the beginning of the period of ownership, exceeds the expenditure allowable under section 32 (1) (*a*) of this Act in computing the gain accruing on a disposal of the lease, the lease shall not be a wasting asset until the end of the duration of the sub-lease.

(3) In the case of a wasting asset which is a lease of land the rate at which expenditure is assumed to be written off shall, instead of being a uniform rate as provided by section 38 of this Act, be a rate fixed in accordance with the Table below.

(4) Accordingly, for the purposes of the computation under Chapter II of Part II of this Act of the gain accruing on a disposal of a lease, and given that—

(*a*) the percentage derived from the Table for the duration of the lease at the beginning of the period of ownership is P (1),

(*b*) the percentage so derived for the duration of the lease at the time when any item of expenditure attributable to the lease under section 32 (1) (*b*) of this Act is first reflected in the nature of the lease is P (2), and

(*c*) the percentage so derived for the duration of the lease at the time of the disposal is P (3),

then—

(i) there shall be excluded from the expenditure attributable to the lease under section 32 (1) (*a*) of this Act a fraction equal to $\frac{P(1) - P(3)}{P(1)}$, and

(ii) there shall be excluded from any item of expenditure attributable to the lease under section 32 (1) (*b*) of this Act a fraction equal to $\frac{P(2) - P(3)}{P(2)}$.

(5) This paragraph applies notwithstanding that the period of ownership of the lease is a period exceeding fifty years and, accordingly, no expenditure shall be written off under this paragraph in respect of any period earlier than the time when the lease becomes a wasting asset.

(6) Section 39 of this Act (wasting assets qualifying for capital allowances) shall apply in relation to this paragraph as it applies in relation to section 38.

TABLE

Years	Percentage	Years	Percentage
50 (or more)	100	25	81·100
49	99·657	24	79·622
48	99·289	23	78·055
47	98·902	22	76·399
46	98·490	21	74·635
45	98·059	20	72·770
44	97·595	19	70·791
43	97·107	18	68·697
42	96·593	17	66·470
41	96·041	16	64·116
40	95·457	15	61·617
39	94·842	14	58·971
38	94·189	13	56·167
37	93·497	12	53·191
36	92·761	11	50·038
35	91·981	10	46·695
34	91·156	9	43·154
33	90·280	8	39·399
32	89·354	7	35·414
31	88·371	6	31·195
30	87·330	5	26·722
29	86·226	4	21·983
28	85·053	3	16·959
27	83·816	2	11·629
26	82·496	1	5·983
		0	0

If the duration of the lease is not an exact number of years the percentage to be derived from the Table above shall be the percentage for the whole number of years plus one twelfth of the difference between that and the percentage for the next higher number of years for each odd month counting an odd 14 days or more as one month.

Premiums for leases

2.—(1) Subject to this Schedule where the payment of a premium is required under a lease of land, or otherwise under the terms subject to which a lease of land is granted, there is a part disposal of the freehold or other asset out of which the lease is granted.

(2) In applying section 35 of this Act to such a part disposal, the property which remains undisposed of includes a right to any rent or other payments, other than a premium, payable under the lease, and that right shall be valued as at the time of the part disposal.

3.—(1) This paragraph applies in relation to a lease of land.

(2) Where, under the terms subject to which a lease is granted, a sum becomes payable by the tenant in lieu of the whole or part of the rent for any period, or as consideration for the surrender of the lease, the lease shall be deemed for the purposes of this Schedule to have required the payment of a premium to the landlord (in addition to any other premium) of the amount of that sum for the period in relation to which the sum is payable.

(3) Where, as consideration for the variation or waiver of any of the terms of a lease, a sum becomes payable by the tenant otherwise than by way of rent, the lease shall be deemed for the purposes of this Schedule to have required the payment of a premium to the landlord (in addition to any other premium) of the amount of that sum for the period from the time when the variation or waiver takes effect to the time when it ceases to have effect.

(4) If under sub-paragraph (2) or (3) above a premium is deemed to have been received by the landlord, otherwise than as consideration for the surrender of the lease, then subject to sub-paragraph (5) below, both the landlord and the tenant shall be treated as if that premium were, or were part of, the consideration for the grant of the lease due at the time when the lease was granted, and the

gain accruing to the landlord on the disposal by way of grant of the lease shall be recomputed and any necessary adjustments of tax, whether by way of assessment for the year in which the premium is deemed to have been received, or by way of discharge or repayment of tax, made accordingly.

(5) If under sub-paragraph (2) or (3) above a premium is deemed to have been received by the landlord, otherwise than as consideration for the surrender of the lease, and the landlord is a tenant under a lease the duration of which does not exceed fifty years this Schedule shall apply as if an amount equal to the amount of that premium deemed to have been received had been given by way of consideration for the grant of the part of the sub-lease covered by the period in respect of which the premium is deemed to have been paid as if that consideration were expenditure incurred by the sub-lessee and attributable to that part of the sub-lease under section 32 (1) (*b*) of this Act.

(6) Where under sub-paragraph (2) above a premium is deemed to have been received as consideration for the surrender of a lease the surrender of the lease shall not be the occasion of any recomputation of the gain accruing on the receipt of any other premium, and the premium which is consideration for the surrender of the lease shall be regarded as consideration for a separate transaction consisting of the disposal by the landlord of his interest in the lease.

(7) Sub-paragraph (3) above shall apply in relation to a transaction not at arm's length, and in particular in relation to a transaction entered into gratuitously, as if such sum had become payable by the tenant otherwise than by way of rent as might have been required of him if the transaction had been at arm's length.

Sub-leases out of short leases

4.—(1) In the computation under Chapter II of Part II of this Act of the gain accruing on the part disposal of a lease which is a wasting asset by way of the grant of a sub-lease for a premium the expenditure attributable to the lease under paragraphs (*a*) and (*b*) of section 32 (1) of this Act shall be apportioned in accordance with this paragraph, and section 35 of this Act shall not apply.

(2) Out of each item of the expenditure attributable to the lease under paragraphs (*a*) and (*b*) of section 32 (1) of this Act there shall be apportioned to what is disposed of—

(*a*) if the amount of the premium is not less than what would be obtainable by way of premium for the said sub-lease if the rent payable under that sub-lease were the same as the rent payable under the lease, the fraction which, under paragraph 1 (3) of this Schedule, is to be written off over the period which is the duration of the sub-lease, and

(*b*) if the amount of the premium is less than the said amount so obtainable, the said fraction multiplied by a fraction equal to the amount of the said premium divided by the said amount so obtainable.

(3) If the sub-lease is a sub-lease of part only of the land comprised in the lease this paragraph shall apply only in relation to a proportion of the expenditure attributable to the lease under paragraphs (*a*) and (*b*) of section 32 (1) of this Act which is the same as the proportion which the value of the land comprised in the sub-lease bears to the value of that and the other land comprised in the lease; and the remainder of that expenditure shall be apportioned to what remains undisposed of.

Exclusion of premiums taxed under Schedule A etc.

5.—(1) Where by reference to any premium income tax has become chargeable under section 80 of the Taxes Act on any amount, that amount out of the premium shall be excluded from the consideration brought into account in the computation under Chapter II of Part II of this Act of a gain accruing on the disposal for which the premium is consideration except where the consideration is taken into account in the denominator of the fraction by reference to which an apportionment is made under section 35 of this Act (part disposals).

(2) Where by reference to any premium in respect of a sub-lease granted out of a lease the duration of which (that is of the lease) does not, at the time of granting the lease, exceed fifty years, income tax has become chargeable under section 80 of the Taxes Act on any amount that amount shall be deducted from any gain accruing on the disposal for which the premium is consideration as

computed in accordance with the provisions of this Act apart from this sub-paragraph, but not so as to convert the gain into a loss, or to increase any loss.

(3) Where income tax has become chargeable under section 82 of the Taxes Act (sale of land with right of re-conveyance) on any amount a sum of that amount shall be excluded from the consideration brought into account in the computation under Chapter II of Part II of this Act of a gain accruing on the disposal of the estate or interest in respect of which income tax becomes so chargeable, except where the consideration is taken into account in the denominator of the fraction by reference to which an apportionment is made under section 35 of this Act:

Provided that if what is disposed of is the remainder of a lease or a sub-lease out of a lease the duration of which does not exceed fifty years the preceding provisions of this sub-paragraph shall not apply but the said amount shall be deducted from any gain accruing on the disposal as computed in accordance with the provisions of this Act apart from this sub-paragraph, but not so as to convert the gain into a loss, or to increase any loss.

(4) References in sub-paragraphs (1) and (2) above to a premium include references to a premium deemed to have been received under subsection (3) or subsection (4) of section 80 of the Taxes Act (which correspond to paragraph 3 (2) and (3) of this Schedule).

(5) Section 31 of this Act (exclusion of consideration chargeable to tax on income) shall not be taken as authorising the exclusion of any amount from the consideration for a disposal of assets taken into account in the computation under Chapter II of Part II of this Act by reference to any amount chargeable to tax under Part III of the Taxes Act.

6.—(1) If under section 83 (2) of the Taxes Act (allowance where, by the grant of a sub-lease, a lessee has converted a capital amount into a right to income) a person is to be treated as paying additional rent in consequence of having granted a sub-lease, the amount of any loss accruing to him on the disposal by way of the grant of the sub-lease shall be reduced by the total amount of rent which he is thereby treated as paying over the term of the sub-lease (and without regard to whether relief is thereby effectively given over the term of the sub-lease), but not so as to convert the loss into a gain, or to increase any gain.

(2) Nothing in section 31 of this Act shall be taken as applying in relation to any amount on which tax is paid under section 81 of the Taxes Act (charge on assignment of lease granted at undervalue).

(3) If any adjustment is made under section 82 (2) (*b*) of the Taxes Act on a claim under that paragraph, any necessary adjustment shall be made to give effect to the consequences of the claim on the operation of this paragraph or paragraph 5 above.

7. If under section 80 (2) of the Taxes Act income tax is chargeable on any amount, as being a premium the payment of which is deemed to be required by the lease, the person so chargeable shall be treated for the purposes of the computation of any gain accruing to him as having incurred at the time the lease was granted expenditure of that amount (in addition to any other expenditure) attributable to the asset under section 32 (1) (*b*) of this Act.

Duration of leases

8.—(1) In ascertaining for the purposes of this Act the duration of a lease of land the following provisions shall have effect.

(2) Where the terms of the lease include provision for the determination of the lease by notice given by the landlord, the lease shall not be treated as granted for a term longer than one ending at the earliest date on which it could be determined by notice given by the landlord.

(3) Where any of the terms of the lease (whether relating to forfeiture or to any other matter) or any other circumstances render it unlikely that the lease will continue beyond a date falling before the expiration of the term of the lease, the lease shall not be treated as having been granted for a term longer than one ending on that date.

(4) Sub-paragraph (3) applies in particular where the lease provides for the rent to go up after a given date, or for the tenant's obligations to become in any other respect more onerous after a given date, but includes provision for the

determination of the lease on that date by notice given by the tenant, and those provisions render it unlikely that the lease will continue beyond that date.

(5) Where the terms of the lease include provision for the extension of the lease beyond a given date by notice given by the tenant this paragraph shall apply as if the term of the lease extended for as long as it could be extended by the tenant, but subject to any right of the landlord by notice to determine the lease.

(6) It is hereby declared that the question what is the duration of a lease is to be decided, in relation to the grant or any disposal of the lease, by reference to the facts which were known or ascertainable at the time when the lease was acquired or created.

Leases of property other than land

9.—(1) Paragraphs 2, 3, 4 and 8 of this Schedule shall apply in relation to leases of property other than land as they apply to leases of land, but subject to any necessary modifications.

(2) Where by reference to any capital sum within the meaning of section 492 of the Taxes Act (leases of assets other than land) any person has been charged to income tax on any amount, that amount out of the capital sum shall be deducted from any gain accruing on the disposal for which that capital sum is consideration, as computed in accordance with the provisions of this Act apart from this sub-paragraph, but not so as to convert the gain into a loss, or increase any loss.

(3) In the case of a lease of a wasting asset which is movable property the lease shall be assumed to terminate not later than the end of the life of the wasting asset.

Interpretation

10.—(1) In this Act, unless the context otherwise requires "lease"—

(*a*) in relation to land, includes an underlease, sublease or any tenancy or licence, and any agreement for a lease, underlease, sublease or tenancy or licence and, in the case of land outside the United Kingdom, any interest corresponding to a lease as so defined,

(*b*) in relation to any description of property other than land, means any kind of agreement or arrangement under which payments are made for the use of, or otherwise in respect of, property,

and "lessor", "lessee" and "rent" shall be construed accordingly.

(2) In this Schedule "premium" includes any like sum, whether payable to the intermediate or a superior landlord, and for the purposes of this Schedule any sum (other than rent) paid on or in connection with the granting of a tenancy shall be presumed to have been paid by way of premium except in so far as other sufficient consideration for the payment is shown to have been given.

(3) In the application of this Schedule to Scotland "premium" includes in particular a grassum payable to any landlord or intermediate landlord on the creation of a sublease.

General Note

This schedule provides special rules for leases in relation to the provisions dealing with wasting assets in s. 37.

Para. 1 (1). This provides that subject to para. 1 (2) (land subject to a sub-lease not at a rackrent), a lease shall not be treated as a wasting asset at any time when its unexpired term does not exceed 50 years. This paragraph also makes special rules for writing down the allowable expenditure for leases.

Paras. 2 and 3. These treat the receipt of a premium on the grant of a head lease as a part disposal of the freehold and provide detailed rules for computing gains on such part disposals (the provisions apply *mutatis mutandis* to the grant of a sublease out of a head lease, and so on).

Also, a sum paid on a surrender of a lease, or a waiver of its terms, is treated as the receipt of a premium and accordingly as a part disposal of the immediately superior interest in the land. See also para. 10 (2) which extends the meaning of "premium".

Para. 4. This provides the method of calculating the gain derived on the grant of a sub-lease at a premium out of a lease which is a wasting asset, but para. 4

is to be construed in accordance with para. 5 (1) (exclusion of premiums taxed under Sched. A, etc.).

Paras. 5, 6 and 7. These provide machinery whereby premiums which are taxed under income tax rules (and rules relating to corporation tax on income) are not also charged to capital gains tax.

Para. 8. This provides that a lease is not to be treated as continuing for a period longer than one ending at the earliest date at which it could be determined by notice given by the landlord. Where the terms of the lease provide for the rent to go up on a particular date (or otherwise for the lease to become more onerous to the tenant) and the tenant has an option to determine on that date the lease's duration will be treated as continuing only until then (sub-para. (4)). That is, in fact, one instance of the general principle that where the lease's terms or any other circumstances render the lease unlikely to continue beyond a particular date, it is to be treated as continuing only until then (sub-para. (3)). If the tenant has an option to extend the lease, its duration is taken to continue for as long as it may be extended by the tenant (sub-para. (5)). Para. 9 applies certain of the provisions of this schedule to leases of property other than land (*e.g.* machinery).

Section 126

SCHEDULE 4

Relief for Gifts of Business Assets

Part I

Agricultural Property and Settled Property

Agricultural property

1.—(1) This paragraph applies where—

(*a*) there is a disposal of an asset which is, or is an interest in, agricultural property within the meaning of Schedule 8 to the Finance Act 1975 (capital transfer tax relief for agricultural property), and

(*b*) apart from this paragraph, the disposal would not fall within section 126 (1) (*a*) of this Act by reason only that the agricultural property is not used for the purposes of a trade carried on as mentioned in that paragraph.

(2) Where this paragraph applies, section 126 (1) of this Act shall apply in relation to the disposal if the circumstances are such that a reduction in respect of the asset—

(*a*) is made under Schedule 8 to the Finance Act 1975 in relation to a chargeable transfer taking place on the occasion of the disposal, or

(*b*) would be so made if there were a chargeable transfer on that occasion and a claim were duly made under that Schedule.

Settled property

2.—(1) If a trustee is deemed, by virtue of section 54 (1) or 55 (1) of this Act (settled property), to have disposed of, and immediately re-acquired—

(*a*) an asset which is, or is an interest in, an asset used for the purposes of a trade, profession or vocation carried on by the trustee or by a relevant beneficiary, or

(*b*) shares or securities of a trading company as to which not not less than 25 per cent. of the voting rights are exercisable by the trustee at the time of the disposal and re-acquisition,

subsection (3) of section 126 of this Act shall apply in relation to the disposal if a claim for relief under that section is made by the trustee.

(2) Where subsection (3) of the said section 126 applies by virtue of sub-paragraph (1) above—

(*a*) a reference to the trustee shall be substituted for the reference in paragraph (*a*) of that subsection to the transferor and for the reference in paragraph (*b*) thereof to the transferee, and

(*b*) subsection (6) of that section shall not apply.

(3) In paragraph (*a*) of sub-paragraph (1) above, "relevant beneficiary" means—

(*a*) where the disposal is deemed to occur by virtue of section 54 (1) of this Act, a beneficiary who had an interest in possession in the settled property immediately before the disposal; and

(*b*) where the disposal is deemed to occur by virtue of section 55 (1) of this Act on the termination of a life interest in possession, the beneficiary whose interest it was.

3.—(1) This paragraph applies where—

(*a*) there is, by virtue of section 54 (1) or 55 (1) of this Act (settled property), a disposal of an asset which is, or is an interest in, agricultural property within the meaning of Schedule 8 to the Finance Act 1975, and

(*b*) apart from this paragraph, the disposal would not fall within paragraph (*a*) of paragraph 2 (1) above by reason only that the agricultural property is not used for the purposes of a trade as mentioned in the said paragraph (*a*).

(2) Where this paragraph applies, paragraph 2 (1) above shall apply in relation to the disposal if the circumstances are such that a reduction in respect of the asset—

(*a*) is made under Schedule 8 to the Finance Act 1975 in relation to a chargeable transfer taking place on the occasion of the disposal, or

(*b*) would be so made if there were a chargeable transfer on that occasion and a claim were duly made under that Schedule.

Part II

Reductions in Held-Over Gain

Application and interpretation

4.—(1) The provisions of this Part of this Schedule apply in cases where a claim for relief is made under section 126 of this Act.

(2) In this Part of this Schedule—

(*a*) "the principal provision" means section 126 (1) of this Act, or, as the case may require, sub-paragraph (1) of paragraph 2 above,

(*b*) "shares" includes securities,

(*c*) "the transferor" and "the transferee" have the same meaning as in section 126 of this Act, except that, in a case where paragraph 2 above applies, each of those expressions refers to the trustee mentioned in that paragraph, and

(*d*) "unrelieved gain", in relation to a disposal, has the same meaning as in section 126 (6) of this Act.

(3) Any reference in this Part of this Schedule to a disposal of an asset is a reference to a disposal which falls within paragraph (*a*) of the principal provision and any reference to a disposal of shares is a reference to a disposal which falls within paragraph (*b*) of that provision.

(4) In relation to a disposal of an asset or of shares, any reference in the following provisions of this Part of this Schedule to the held-over gain is a reference to the held-over gain on that disposal as determined under subsection (5) or, as the case may be, subsection (6) of section 126 of this Act (taking account, where paragraph 2 above applies, of sub-paragraph (2) (*b*) of that paragraph).

Reductions peculiar to disposals of assets

5. If, in the case of a disposal of an asset, the asset was not used for the purpose of the trade, profession or vocation referred to in paragraph (*a*) of the principal provision throughout the period of its ownership by the transferor, the amount of the held-over gain shall be reduced by multiplying it by the fraction of which the denominator is the number of days in that period of ownership and the numerator is the number of days in that period during which the asset was so used.

6. If, in the case of a disposal of an asset, the asset is a building or structure

and, over the period of its ownership by the transferor or any substantial part of that period, part of the building or structure was, and part was not, used for the purposes of the trade, profession or vocation referred to in paragraph (*a*) of the principal provision, there shall be determined the fraction of the unrelieved gain on the disposal which it is just and reasonable to apportion to the part of the asset which was so used, and the amount of the held-over gain (as reduced, if appropriate, under paragraph 5 above) shall be reduced by multiplying it by that fraction.

Reduction peculiar to disposal of shares

7.—(1) If, in the case of a disposal of shares, the chargeable assets of the company whose shares are disposed of include assets which are not business assets, the amount of the held-over gain shall be reduced by multiplying it by the fraction of which the denominator is the market value of the whole of the company's chargeable assets on the date of the disposal and the numerator is the market value of the company's chargeable business assets on that date.

(2) For the purpose of this paragraph—

(*a*) an asset is a business asset in relation to a company if it is or is an interest in an asset used for the purposes of a trade, profession or vocation carried on by the company, and

(*b*) an asset is a chargeable asset in relation to a company at any time if, on a disposal of it at that time, a chargeable gain would accrue to the company.

Reduction where gain partly relieved by retirement relief

8.—(1) If, in the case of a disposal of an asset—

(*a*) the disposal is of a chargeable business asset and is comprised in a disposal of the whole or part of a business in respect of gains accruing on which the transferor is entitled to relief under section 124 of this Act (transfer of business on retirement), and

(*b*) apart from this paragraph, the held-over gain on the disposal (as reduced, where appropriate, under the preceding provisions of this Part of this Schedule) would exceed the amount of the chargeable gain which, apart from section 126 of this Act, would accrue on the disposal,

the amount of that held-over gain shall be reduced by the amount of the excess.

(2) In sub-paragraph (1) above "chargeable business asset" has the same meaning as in section 124 of this Act.

(3) If, in the case of a disposal of shares,—

(*a*) the disposal is or forms part of a disposal of shares in respect of the gains accruing on which the transferor is entitled to relief under section 124 of this Act, and

(*b*) apart from this paragraph, the held-over gain on the disposal (as reduced, where appropriate, under paragraph 7 above) would exceed an amount equal to the relevant proportion of the chargeable gain which, apart from section 126 of this Act, would accrue on the disposal,

the amount of that held-over gain shall be reduced by the amount of the excess.

(4) In sub-paragraph (3) above "the relevant proportion," in relation to a disposal falling within paragraph (*a*) of that sub-paragraph, means the proportion determined under subsection (5) (*b*) of section 124 of this Act in relation to the aggregate sum of the gains which accrue on that disposal.

General Note

This Schedule is concerned with the relief conferred by s. 126 relating to disposals of business assets (including shares or securities in family trading companies) for less than full consideration.

Para. 1. This extends the relief to cover disposals for less than full consideration of agricultural property which is not used for the purposes of a trade so long as it does (or would if the transfer had been a chargeable transfer) qualify for capital transfer tax relief under Sched. 8, F.A. 1975.

Para. 2. This extends the roll-over relief to settled property in certain circumstances. It will apply whenever there is a deemed disposal under s. 54 (1) (on a person becoming absolutely entitled), or s. 55 (1) (termination of a life interest in possession) occasioning a deemed disposal and re-acquisition by the trustees.

To qualify in the case of a deemed disposal of an asset (or an interest in an asset) it must have been used in a trade carried on by the trustee or beneficiary interested in possession immediately prior to the date of the deemed disposal. In the case of shares in a trading company, the trustee at the date of the deemed disposal must have had the right to exercise not less than 25 per cent. of the voting rights. Agricultural property not being used to carry on a trade which is subject to a settlement will be within the roll-over relief in the same circumstances as non-settled agricultural property (see para. 1).

Paras. 4 to 8. These paragraphs apply to reduce the held-over gains in certain circumstances. As regards disposals of assets (or interests in assets) there will be a reduction in the following cases:

(*a*) if the asset (or interest) has not been used for the purposes of the trade during the whole of the transferor's period of ownership. Then the held-over gain is reduced by:

$$\frac{\text{number of days used in trade whilst owned by transferor}}{\text{number of days owned by transferor}};$$

(*b*) if a building or structure is used partly for the purposes of the trade and partly for other purposes then there will be an apportionment of the chargeable gain on a just and reasonable basis;

(*c*) if part of the chargeable gain is relieved by the application of the retirement relief when the disposal of the asset (or interest) is comprised in the disposal of the whole or part of a business.

As regards shares and securities there will be a reduction in the following cases:

(*a*) if certain of the chargeable assets of the company are not assets used for the purposes of the trade carried on by the company. Then the held-over gain will be reduced by:

$$\frac{\text{market value of chargeable business assets}}{\text{market value of all chargeable assets}};$$

(*b*) if part of the chargeable gain is relieved by application of the retirement relief.

Section 28 (3)

SCHEDULE 5

ASSETS HELD ON 6TH APRIL 1965

PART I

QUOTED SECURITIES

Deemed acquisition at 6th April 1965 value

1.—(1) This paragraph applies—

(*a*) to shares and securities which on 6th April 1965 have quoted market values on a recognised stock exchange in the United Kingdom or elsewhere, or which have had such quoted market values at any time in the period of six years ending on 6th April 1965, and

(*b*) to rights of unit holders in any unit trust scheme the prices of which are published regularly by the managers of the scheme.

(2) For the purposes of this Act it shall be assumed, wherever relevant, that any assets to which this paragraph applies were sold by the owner, and immediately re-acquired by him, at their market value on 6th April 1965.

(3) This paragraph shall not apply in relation to a disposal of shares or securities of a company by a person to whom those shares or securities were issued as an employee either of the company or of some other person on terms which restrict his rights to dispose of them.

Restriction of gain or loss by reference to actual cost

2.—(1) Subject to the rights of election conferred by paragraphs 4 to 7 below, paragraph 1 (2) above shall not apply in relation to a disposal of assets—

(*a*) if on the assumption in paragraph 1 (2) a gain would accrue on that disposal to the person making the disposal and either a smaller gain or a loss would so accrue (computed in accordance with Chapter II of Part II) if paragraph 1 (2) did not apply, or

(*b*) if on the assumption in paragraph 1 (2) a loss would so accrue and either a smaller loss or a gain would accrue if paragraph 1 (2) did not apply,

and accordingly the amount of the gain or loss accruing on the disposal shall be computed without regard to the preceding provisions of this Schedule except that in a case where this sub-paragraph would otherwise substitute a loss for a gain or a gain for a loss it shall be assumed, in relation to the disposal, that the relevant assets were sold by the owner, and immediately re-acquired by him, for a consideration such that, on the disposal, neither a gain nor a loss accrued to the person making the disposal.

(2) For the purpose of—

(*a*) identifying shares or securities held on 6th April 1965 with shares or securities previously acquired, and

(*b*) identifying the shares or securities held on that date with shares or securities subsequently disposed of, and distinguishing them from shares or securities acquired subsequently,

so far as that identification is needed for the purposes of sub-paragraph (1) above, and so far as the shares or securities are of the same class, shares or securities acquired at an earlier time shall be deemed to be disposed of before shares or securities acquired at a later time.

(3) Sub-paragraph (2) above has effect subject to section 66 of this Act (disposal on or before day of acquisition).

Exclusion of pooling

3.—(1) Subject to the rights of election conferred by paragraphs 4 to 7 below, section 65 of this Act (pooling of shares and other assets) shall not apply to quoted securities held on 6th April 1965.

(2) Where—

(*a*) a disposal was made out of quoted securities before 20th March 1968 (that is to say before the date on which the provisions re-enacted in sub-paragraph (1) above took effect), and

(*b*) by virtue of paragraph 2 of Schedule 7 to the Finance Act 1965 (re-enacted as section 65 of this Act) some of the quoted securities out of which the disposal was made were acquired before 6th April 1965, and some later

then in computing the gain accruing on any disposal of quoted securities the question of what remained undisposed of on the earlier disposal shall be decided on the footing that sub-paragraph (1) above had effect as respects that earlier disposal.

(3) The rules of identification in paragraph 2 (2) above shall apply for the purposes of this paragraph as they apply for the purposes of the said paragraph 2.

Election for pooling

4.—(1) If a person so elects, quoted securities covered by the election shall be excluded from paragraphs 2 and 3 above (so that neither paragraph 1 (2) above nor section 65 of this Act is excluded by those paragraphs as respects those securities).

(2) An election made by any person under this paragraph shall be as respects all disposals made by him at any time, including disposals made before the election but after 19th March 1968—

(*a*) of quoted securities of kinds other than fixed-interest securities and preference shares, or

(*b*) of fixed-interest securities and preference shares,

and references to the quoted securities covered by an election shall be construed accordingly.

Any person may make both of the elections.

(3) An election under this paragraph shall not cover quoted securities which the holder acquired on a disposal after 19th March 1968 in relation to which either of the following enactments (which secure that neither a gain nor a loss accrues on the disposal) applies, that is—

(*a*) section 44 of this Act (disposals between husband and wife),

(*b*) section 273 (1) of the Taxes Act (disposals within a group of companies), but this paragraph shall apply to the quoted securities so held if the person making the original disposal (that is to say the wife or husband of the holder, or the other member of the group of companies) makes an election covering quoted securities of the kind in question.

For the purpose of identifying quoted securities disposed of by the holder with quoted securities acquired by him on a disposal in relation to which either of the said enactments applies, so far as they are of the same class, quoted securities acquired at an earlier time shall be deemed to be disposed of before quoted securities acquired at a later time.

(4) For the avoidance of doubt it is hereby declared—

(*a*) that where a person makes an election under this paragraph as respects quoted securities which he holds in one capacity, that election does not cover quoted securities which he holds in another capacity, and

(*b*) that an election under this paragraph is irrevocable.

(5) An election under this paragraph shall be made by notice in writing to the inspector nor later than the expiration of two years from the end of the year of assessment or accounting period of a company in which the first relevant disposal is made, or such further time as the Board may allow.

(6) Subject to paragraph 5 below, in this paragraph the "first relevant disposal", in relation to each of the elections referred to in sub-paragraph (2) of this paragraph, means the first disposal after 19th March 1968 by the person making the election of quoted securities of the kind covered by that election.

(7) All such adjustments shall be made, whether by way of discharge or repayment of tax, or the making of assessments or otherwise, as are required to give effect to an election under this paragraph.

Election by principal company of group

5.—(1) In the case of companies which at the relevant time are members of a group of companies—

(*a*) an election under paragraph 4 above by the company which at that time is the principal company of the group shall have effect also as an election by any other company which at that time is a member of the group, and

(*b*) no election under that paragraph may be made by any other company which at that time is a member of the group.

(2) In this paragraph "the relevant time", in relation to a group of companies, and in relation to each of the elections referred to in paragraph 4 (2) above, is the first occasion after 19th March 1968 when any company which is then a member of a group disposes of quoted securities of a kind covered by that election, and for the purposes of paragraph 4 (5) above that occasion is, in relation to the group, "the first relevant disposal".

(3) This paragraph shall not apply in relation to quoted securities of either kind referred to in paragraph 4 (2) above which are owned by a company which, in some period after 19th March 1968 and before the relevant time, was not a member of the group if in that period it had made an election under paragraph 4 above in relation to securities of that kind (or was treated by virtue of this paragraph, in relation to another group, as having done so), or had made a disposal of quoted securities of that kind and did not make an election within the time limited by paragraph 4 (5) above.

(4) This paragraph shall apply notwithstanding that a company ceases to be a member of the group at any time after the relevant time.

(5) In this paragraph "company" and "group" shall be construed in accordance with subsections (1) and (2) of section 272 of the Taxes Act.

Pooling at value on 6th April 1965:
exchange of securities etc.

6.—(1) Where a person who has made only one of the elections under paragraph 4 above disposes of quoted securities which, in accordance with Chapter II of Part IV of this Act, are to be regarded as being or forming part of a new holding, the election shall apply according to the nature of the quoted securities disposed of, notwithstanding that under the said Chapter the new holding is to be regarded as the same asset as the original holding and that the election would apply differently to the original holding.

(2) Where the election does not cover the disposal out of the new holding, but

does cover quoted securities of the kind comprised in the original holding, then in computing the gain accruing on the disposal out of the new holding (in accordance with paragraph 3 above) the question of what remained undisposed of on any disposal out of the original holding shall be decided on the footing that paragraph 3 above applied to that earlier disposal.

(3) In the case converse to that in sub-paragraph (2) above (that is to say where the election covers the disposal out of the new holding, but does not cover quoted securities of the kind comprised in the original holding) the question of how much of the new holding derives from quoted securities held on 6th April 1965, and how much derives from other quoted securities, shall be decided as it is decided for the purposes of paragraph 3 above.

Underwriters

7. No election under paragraph 4 above shall cover quoted securities comprised in any underwriter's premiums trust fund, or premiums trust fund deposits, or personal reserves, being securities comprised in funds to which section 142 of this Act applies.

Interpretation of paragraphs 3 to 7

8.—(1) In paragraphs 3 to 7 above—

"quoted securities" means assets to which paragraph 1 above applies,

"fixed interest security" means any security as defined by section 82 of this Act,

"preference share" means any share the holder whereof has a right to a dividend at a fixed rate, but has no other right to share in the profits of the company.

(2) If and so far as the question whether at any particular time a share was a preference share depends on the rate of dividends payable on or before 5th April 1973, the reference in the definition of "preference share" in sub-paragraph (1) above to a dividend at a fixed rate includes a dividend at a rate fluctuating in accordance with the standard rate of income tax.

PART II

LAND REFLECTING DEVELOPMENT VALUE

Valuation at 6th April 1965

9.—(1) This paragraph shall apply in relation to a disposal of an asset which is an interest in land situated in the United Kingdom—

(*a*) if, but for this paragraph, the expenditure allowable as a deduction in computing under Chapter II of Part II of this Act the gain accruing on the disposal would include any expenditure incurred before 6th April 1965, and

(*b*) if the consideration for the asset acquired on the disposal exceeds the current use value of the asset at the time of the disposal, or if any material development of the land has been carried out after 17th December 1973 since the person making the disposal acquired the asset.

(2) For the purposes of this Act, including Chapter II of Part II, it shall be assumed in relation to the disposal and, if it is a part disposal, in relation to any subsequent disposal of the asset which is an interest in land situated in the United Kingdom that that asset was sold by the person making the disposal, and immediately reacquired by him, at its market value on 6th April 1965.

(3) Sub-paragraph (2) above shall apply in relation to any prior part disposal of the asset and, if tax has been charged, or relief allowed, by reference to that part disposal on a different footing, all such adjustments shall be made, whether by way of assessment or discharge or repayment of tax, as are required to give effect to the provisions of this sub-paragraph.

(4) Sub-paragraph (2) above shall not apply in relation to a disposal of assets—

(*a*) if on the assumption in that sub-paragraph a gain would accrue on that disposal to the person making the disposal and either a smaller gain or a loss would so accrue (computed in accordance with the provisions of Chapter II of Part II of this Act) if the said sub-paragraph (2) did not apply, or

(*b*) if on the assumption in the said sub-paragraph (2) a loss would so accrue and either a smaller loss or a gain would accrue if the said sub-paragraph (2) did not apply,

and accordingly the amount of the gain or loss accruing on the disposal shall be computed without regard to the provisions of this Schedule except that in a case where this sub-paragraph would otherwise substitute a loss for a gain or a gain for a loss it shall be assumed, in relation to the disposal, that the relevant assets were sold by the owner, and immediately re-acquired by him, for a consideration such that, on the disposal, neither a gain nor a loss accrued to the person making the disposal.

(5) For the purposes of this paragraph—

(*a*) "interest in land" has the meaning given by section 44 (1) of the Finance Act 1974,

(*b*) "material development" has the meaning given by paragraph 6 of Schedule 3 to the Finance Act 1974,

(*c*) the current use value of an interest in land shall be computed in accordance with Part I of the said Schedule 3, but so that, in relation to any material development which was begun before 18th December 1973, sub-paragraph (2) of paragraph 1 of that Schedule (definition of current use value) shall have effect as if the words from "other than" to the end of the sub-paragraph (which allow for the completion of duly authorised material development already begun) were omitted,

(*d*) paragraph 9 of the said Schedule 3 (date when material development is begun) shall apply as it applies for the purposes of that Schedule, and

(*e*) paragraph 14 of the said Schedule 3 (meaning of material development "carried out after" a particular date) shall apply as it applies for the purposes of paragraphs 11 to 13 of that Schedule.

Allowance for betterment levy

10. Paragraph 9 (1) above has effect subject to paragraph 21 (2) of Schedule 6 to this Act (valuation at 6th April 1965 on a claim under that paragraph).

Part III

Other Assets

Apportionment by reference to straightline growth of gain or loss over period of ownership

11.—(1) This paragraph applies subject to Parts I and II of this Schedule.

(2) On the disposal of assets by a person whose period of ownership began before 6th April 1965 only so much of any gain accruing on the disposal as is under this paragraph to be apportioned to the period beginning with 6th April 1965 shall be a chargeable gain.

(3) Subject to the following provisions of this Schedule, the gain shall be assumed to have grown at a uniform rate from nothing at the beginning of the period of ownership to its full amount at the time of the disposal so that, calling the part of that period before 6th April 1965, P, and the time beginning with 6th April 1965 and ending with the time of the disposal T, the fraction of the gain which is a chargeable gain is $\frac{T}{P + T}$.

(4) If any of the expenditure which is allowable as a deduction in the computation under Chapter II of Part II of this Act of the gain is within section 32 (1) (*b*) of this Act—

(*a*) the gain shall be attributed to the expenditure, if any, allowable under paragraph (*a*) of the said section 32 (1) as one item of expenditure, and to the respective items of expenditure under the said section 32 (1) (*b*) in proportion to the respective amounts of those items of expenditure,

(*b*) sub-paragraph (3) of this paragraph shall apply to the part of the gain attributed to the expenditure under the said section 32 (1) (*a*), (*c*) each part of the gain attributed to the items of expenditure under the said section 32 (1) (*b*) shall be assumed to have grown at a uniform rate from nothing at the time when the relevant item of expenditure was first reflected in the value of the asset to the full amount of that part of the gain at the time of the disposal,

so that, calling the respective proportions of the gain E(0), E(1), E(2) and so on (so that they add up to unity) and calling the respective periods from the times when the items under the said section 32 (1) (*b*) were reflected in the value of the asset to 5th April 1965 P(1), P(2) and so on, and employing also the abbreviations in sub-paragraph (3) above, the faction of the gain which is a chargeable gain is $E(0)\frac{T}{P+T}+E(1)\frac{T}{P(1)+T}+E(2)\frac{T}{P(2)+T}$ and so on.

(5) In a case within sub-paragraph (4) above where there is no initial expenditure (that is no expenditure under section 32 (1) (*a*) of this Act) or that initial expenditure is, compared with any item of expenditure under section 32 (1) (*b*), disproportionately small having regard to the value of the asset immediately before the subsequent item of expenditure was incurred, the part of the gain which is not attributable to the enhancement of the value of the asset due to any item of expenditure under the said section 32 (1) (*b*) shall be deemed to be attributed to expenditure incurred at the beginning of the period of ownership and allowable under section 32 (1) (*a*), and the part or parts of the gain attributable to expenditure under section 32 (1) (*b*) shall be reduced accordingly.

(6) The beginning of the period over which a gain, or a part of a gain, is under sub-paragraphs (3) and (4) above, to be treated as growing shall not be earlier than 6th April 1945, and this sub-paragraph shall have effect notwithstanding any provision in this Schedule or elsewhere in this Act.

(7) If in pursuance of section 35 of this Act (part disposals) an asset's market value at a date before 6th April 1965 is to be ascertained sub-paragraphs (3) to (5) above shall have effect as if that asset had been on that date sold by the owner, and immediately re-acquired by him, at that market value.

(8) If in pursuance of section 35 of this Act an asset's market value at a date on or after 6th April 1965 is to be ascertained sub-paragraphs (3) to (5) above shall have effect as if—

(*a*) the asset on that date had been sold by the owner, and immediately re-acquired by him, at that market value, and

(*b*) accordingly, the computation of any gain on a subsequent disposal of that asset shall be computed—

(i) by apportioning in accordance with this paragraph the gain or loss over a period ending on the said date (the date of the part disposal), and

(ii) by bringing into account the entire gain or loss over the period from the date of the part disposal to the date of subsequent disposal.

(9) For the purposes of this paragraph the period of ownership of an asset shall, where under section 36 of this Act (assets derived from other assets) account is to be taken of expenditure in respect of an asset from which the asset disposed of was derived, or where it would so apply if there were any relevant expenditure in respect of that other asset, include the period of ownership of that other asset.

(10) If under this paragraph part only of a gain is a chargeable gain, the fraction in 102 (2) of this Act (private residences: amount of relief) shall be applied to that part, instead of to the whole of the gain.

Election for valuation at 6*th April* 1965

12.—(1) If the person making a disposal so elects paragraph 11 of this Schedule shall not apply in relation to that disposal and it shall be assumed, both for the purposes of computing under Chapter II of Part II of this Act the gain accruing to that person on the disposal, and for all other purposes both in relation to that person and other persons, that the assets disposed of, and any assets of which account is to be taken in relation to the disposal under section 36 of this Act, being assets which were in the ownership of the said person on 6th April 1965, were on that date sold, and immediately re-acquired, by him at their market value on the said 6th April 1965.

(2) Sub-paragraph (1) above shall not apply in relation to a disposal of assets if on the assumption in that sub-paragraph a loss would accrue on that disposal

to the person making the disposal and either a smaller loss or gain would accrue if the said sub-paragraph (1) did not apply, but in a case where this sub-paragraph would otherwise substitute a gain for a loss it shall be assumed, in relation to the disposal, that the relevant assets were sold by the owner, and immediately re-acquired by him, for a consideration such that, on the disposal, neither a gain nor a loss accrued to the person making the disposal.

The displacement of sub-paragraph (1) above by this sub-paragraph shall not be taken as bringing paragraph 11 above into operation.

(3) An election under this paragraph shall be made by notice in writing to the inspector given within two years from the end of the year of assessment or accounting period of a company in which the disposal is made or such further time as the Board may by notice in writing allow.

(4) For the avoidance of doubt it is hereby declared that an election under this paragraph is irrevocable.

(5) An election may not be made under this paragraph as respects, or in relation to, an asset the market value of which at a date on or after 6th April 1965, and before the date of the disposal to which the election relates, is to be ascertained in pursuance of section 35 of this Act (part disposals).

Unquoted shares, commodities, etc.

13.—(1) This paragraph has effect as respects shares held by any person on 6th April 1965 other than shares which are to be treated under this Act as if disposed of and immediately re-acquired by him on that date.

(2) Section 65 of this Act (pooling of shares and other assets) shall not apply in relation to the shares while that person continues to hold them and, in particular, shall not apply in relation to a disposal of the shares by him.

(3) For the purpose of—

(*a*) identifying the shares so held on 6th April 1965 with shares previously acquired, and

(*b*) identifying the shares so held on that date with shares subsequently disposed of, and distinguishing them from shares acquired subsequently,

so far as the shares are of the same class shares bought at an earlier time shall be deemed to have been disposed of before shares bought at a later time.

(4) Sub-paragraph (3) above has effect subject to section 66 of this Act (disposal on or before day of acquisition).

(5) Shares shall not be treated for the purposes of this paragraph as being of the same class unless if dealt with on a recognised stock exchange in the United Kingdom or elsewhere they would be so treated, but shall be treated in accordance with this paragraph notwithstanding that they are identified in a different way by a disposal or by the transfer or delivery giving effect to it.

(6) This paragraph, without sub-paragraph (5), shall apply in relation to any assets, other than shares, which are of a nature to be dealt with without identifying the particular assets disposed of or acquired.

Reorganisation of share capital, conversion of securities, etc.

14.—(1) For the purposes of this Act, including Chapter II of Part II, it shall be assumed that any shares or securities held by a person on 6th April 1965 (identified in accordance with paragraph 13 above) which, in accordance with Chapter II of Part IV of this Act, are to be regarded as being or forming part of a new holding were sold and immediately re-acquired by him on 6th April 1965 at their market value on that date.

(2) If, at any time after 5th April 1965, a person comes to have, in accordance with the said Chapter II of Part IV, a new holding sub-paragraphs (3) to (5) of paragraph 11 above shall have effect as if—

(*a*) the new holding had at that time been sold by the owner, and immediately re-acquired by him, at its market value at that time, and

(*b*) accordingly, the amount of any gain on a disposal of the new holding or any part of it shall be computed—

(i) by apportioning in accordance with paragraph 11 above the gain or loss over a period ending at the said time, and

(ii) by bringing into account the entire gain or loss over the period from that time to the date of the disposal.

(3) This paragraph shall not apply in relation to a reorganisation of a company's share capital if the new holding differs only from the original shares in being a different number, whether greater or less, of shares of the same class as the original shares.

PART IV

MISCELLANEOUS

Capital allowances

15. If under any provision in this Schedule it is to be assumed that any asset was on 6th April 1965 sold by the owner, and immediately re-acquired by him, sections 34 and 39 of this Act (restriction of losses by reference to capital allowances, and wasting assets qualifying for capital allowances) shall apply in relation to any capital allowance or renewals allowance made in respect of the expenditure actually incurred by the owner in providing the asset, and so made for the year 1965–66 or for any subsequent year of assessment, as if it were made in respect of the expenditure which, on the said assumption, was incurred by him in re-acquiring the asset on 7th April 1965.

Assets transferred to close companies

16.—(1) This paragraph has effect where—

(*a*) at any time, including a time before 7th April 1965, any of the persons having control of a close company, or any person who is connected with a person having control of a close company, has transferred assets to the company, and

(*b*) paragraph 11 above applies in relation to a disposal by one of the persons having control of the company of shares or securities in the company, or in relation to a disposal by a person having, up to the time of disposal, a substantial holding of shares or securities in the company, being in either case a disposal after the transfer of the assets.

(2) So far as the gain accruing to the said person on the disposal of the shares is attributable to a profit on the assets so transferred, the period over which the gain is to be treated under paragraph 11 above as growing at a uniform rate shall begin with the time when the assets were transferred to the company, and accordingly a part of a gain attributable to a profit on assets transferred on or after 6th April 1965 shall all be a chargeable gain.

(3) This paragraph shall not apply where a loss, and not a gain, accrues on the disposal.

Husbands and wives

17. Where section 44 of this Act is applied in relation to a disposal of an asset by a man to his wife, or by a man's wife to him, then in relation to a subsequent disposal of the asset (not within section 44) the one making the disposal shall be treated for the purposes of this Schedule as if the other's acquisition or provision of the asset had been his or her acquisition or provision of it.

Compensation and insurance money

18. Where section 21 (4) (*a*) of this Act applies to exclude a gain which, in consequence of this Schedule, is not all chargeable gain, the amount of the reduction to be made under section 21 (4) (*b*) (corresponding reduction in allowable expenditure in respect of new asset) shall be the amount of the chargeable gain and not the whole amount of the gain; and in section 21 (5) (*b*) of this Act (corresponding reduction in allowable expenditure in respect of the new asset where part only of the consideration in respect of the old asset has been applied as such expenditure) for the reference to the amount by which the gain is reduced under section 21 (5) (*a*) there shall be substituted a reference to the amount by which the chargeable gain is proportionately reduced under the said section 21 (5) (*a*).

GENERAL NOTE

This schedule provides special rules for computing gains on assets held on

April 6, 1965 (the date when the tax was introduced) so as to exclude from the charge gains which accrued before that date.

Part I: quoted securities

Para. 1. This provides that all quoted shares or securities or units shall be treated as if they had been sold and immediately reacquired by their owners on April 6, 1965. That is, for capital gains tax purposes their cost is taken to be their value on that date. Shares issued to a person as an employee are excluded from this rule.

Para. 2. This provides the circumstances when market value on April 6, 1965, is not to be taken as the cost of quoted securities. These are where, by comparison with April 6, 1965, the historical cost of the securities shows a smaller gain or a loss instead of a gain, or a smaller loss, or a gain instead of a loss. Where the April 6, 1965, cost shows a gain, and historical cost a loss and *vice versa*, a disposal is taken to show no gain and no loss. Otherwise, where para. 2 applies, historical cost is taken as the allowable cost.

Unless the taxpayer so elects, the pooling provisions of s. 65 do not apply to quoted shares and securities held on April 6, 1965 (para. 3). Para. 4 provides for the election for pooling of quoted securities held on April 6, 1965. Where the election applies, April 6, 1965, value must be adopted for those securities entering the pool. Elections may (and may only) be made in respect of either or both of:

(*a*) all quoted securities of kinds other than fixed-interest securities and preference shares; and

(*b*) all fixed-interest securities and preference shares.

Elections under this paragraph are irrevocable (para. 4 (4) (*b*)).

Securities acquired between spouses and from other members of a group cannot be included in an election under this paragraph (para. 4 (3)).

Part II: land reflecting development value

If land, or an interest in land, situate within the United Kingdom is disposed of, and the disponer held it on April 6, 1965, para. 9 applies to the disposal if the consideration exceeds the current use value of the land at the time of the disposal or if any material development has been carried out on the land after December 17, 1973. The allowable cost of land within the paragraph shall not take account of the disponer's historical acquisition cost before April 6, 1965, but he is deemed to have disposed of and reacquired the land or interest on April 6, 1965, at its market value on that date. *Watkins* v. *Kidson* (*No.* 2) [1978] 2 All E.R. 785 is an interesting case on the construction of this provision before it was amended by F.A. 1974. The decision in that case is not authority for the interpretation of the present legislation.

Part III: other assets held on April 6, 1965

The rule under this part is that the appreciation in value of assets held on April 6, 1965, is treated by paras. 11 and 12 as accruing evenly over the period of ownership, except that any period before April 6, 1945, is to be disregarded. But a person can calculate his gain or loss by reference to the value of his asset on April 6, 1965, if he so elects (para. 12). See para. 12 (2) for the cases in which an election cannot be made. Elections under para. 12 are irrevocable and must be made before the end of two years after the year of assessment or accounting period in which the disposal is made.

Para. 14. This provides that any shares or securities held by a person on April 6, 1965, which are, under the rules relating to reorganisations of share capital, etc., to be regarded as being or forming part of a new holding are to be deemed to have been sold and reacquired by that person on April 6, 1965, at their market value on that date.

Para. 15. This relates the rules relating to the restriction of losses by reference to capital allowances to any deemed disposal and reacquisition on April 6, 1965.

Para. 16. This deals with a possible avoidance device where persons who have control of a close company transfer assets to that company (after April 6, 1965, for instance), and subsequently sell their shares for a consideration which reflects the growth in the value of the assets. Such persons are not permitted to rely on time apportionment under para. 11 above to exempt a part of the gain. So far as the gain on the disposal of the shares is attributable to a profit on the assets, the period over which the gain is treated as accruing at a uniform rate is to begin with the time the assets were transferred to the company rather than the beginning of the period of ownership of the shares.

Para. 17 deals with the disposal between spouses of assets held by the disponer-spouse on April 6, 1965. The disponee-spouse is treated for the purposes of Sched. 5 as if the other spouse's acquisition of the assets had been his or her own.

Section 157 (1)

SCHEDULE 6

TRANSITORY

PART I

VALUATION

Preliminary

1. This Part of this Schedule has effect in cases where the market value of an asset or any part of it at a time before the commencement of this Act is material to the computation of a gain under this Act, and in those cases—

(*a*) section 150 of this Act (which is the same as paragraph 2 below with the amendments in paragraph 4) shall not apply,

(*b*) section 152 of this Act shall only apply to the extent specified in paragraphs 5 to 8 below,

(but sections 151 and 153 of this Act shall apply in those cases as in later cases).

Original rules

2.—(1) "Market value" in relation to any assets means the price which those assets might reasonably be expected to fetch on a sale in the open market.

(2) In estimating the market value of any assets no reduction shall be made in the estimate on account of the estimate being made on the assumption that the whole of the assets is to be placed on the market at one and the same time:

Provided that where capital gains tax is chargeable, or an allowable loss accrues, in consequence of a death before 31st March 1971 and the market value of any property on the date of death taken into account for the purposes of that tax or loss has been depreciated by reason of the death the estimate of the market value shall take that depreciation into account.

(3) The market value of shares or securities quoted on the London Stock Exchange shall, except where in consequence of special circumstances prices so quoted are by themselves not a proper measure of market value, be as follows—

(*a*) the lower of the two prices shown in the quotations for the shares or securities in the Stock Exchange Official Daily List on the relevant date plus one-quarter of the difference between those two figures, or

(*b*) halfway between the highest and lowest prices at which bargains, other than bargains done at special prices, were recorded in the shares or securities for the relevant date,

choosing the amount under paragraph (*a*) if less than that under paragraph (*b*), or if no such bargains were recorded for the relevant date, and choosing the amount under paragraph (*b*) if less than that under paragraph (*a*):

Provided that—

(i) this sub-paragraph shall not apply to shares or securities for which some other stock exchange in the United Kingdom affords a more active market, and

(ii) if the London Stock Exchange is closed on the relevant date the market value shall be ascertained by reference to the latest previous date or earliest subsequent date on which it is open, whichever affords the lower market value.

(4) "Market value" in relation to any rights of unit holders in any unit trust scheme the buying and selling prices of which are published regularly by the managers of the scheme shall mean an amount equal to the buying price (that is the lower price) so published on the relevant date, or if none were published on that date, on the latest date before.

(5) In relation to an asset of a kind the sale of which is subject to restrictions imposed under the Exchange Control Act 1947 such that part of what is paid by the purchaser is not retainable by the seller the market value, as arrived at under sub-paragraph (1), (3) or (4) above, shall be subject to such adjustment as is appropriate having regard to the difference between the amount payable by a purchaser and the amount receivable by a seller.

(6) This paragraph has effect subject to the following provisions of this Part of this Schedule.

Value of quoted securities on 6th April 1965

3.—(1) For the purpose of ascertaining the market value of any shares or securities in accordance with paragraph 1 (2) of Schedule 5 to this Act, paragraph 2 above shall have effect subject to the provisions of this paragraph.

(2) Sub-paragraph (3) (*a*) of that paragraph shall have effect as if for the words, " one-quarter " there were substituted the words " one-half ", and as between the amount under paragraph (*a*) and the amount under paragraph (*b*) of that sub-paragraph the higher, and not the lower, amount shall be chosen.

(3) Sub-paragraph (4) of that paragraph shall have effect as if for the reference to an amount equal to the buying price there were substituted a reference to an amount halfway between the buying and selling prices.

(4) Where the market value of any shares or securities not within the said sub-paragraph (3) falls to be ascertained by reference to a pair of prices quoted on a stock exchange, an adjustment shall be made so as to increase the market value by an amount corresponding to that by which any market value is increased under sub-paragraph (2) above.

References to Stock-Exchange on or after 25th March 1973

4. Except in relation to anything done before 25th March 1973, paragraph 2 (3) above shall have effect subject to the following amendments—

(*a*) for the words " quoted on the London Stock Exchange " there shall be substituted the words " listed in The Stock Exchange Daily Official List " and for the words " so quoted " the words " quoted in that List ";

(*b*) for the words " the Stock Exchange Official Daily List " there shall be substituted the words " The Stock Exchange Daily Official List ";

(*c*) for the words " some other stock exchange in the United Kingdom affords a more active market " there shall be substituted the words " The Stock Exchange provides a more active market elsewhere than on the London trading floor "; and

(*d*) for the words " if the London Stock Exchange is closed " there shall be substituted the words " if the London trading floor is closed ".

Unquoted shares and securities: application of section 152 *to acquisitions before commencement of this Act*

5. Paragraphs 6 to 8 below shall have effect with respect to the application of section 152 of this Act, and in those paragraphs " asset " means an asset to which that section applies.

6. Subject to paragraphs 7 and 8 below, if the market value of an asset or any part of it at the time of its acquisition is material to the computation of any chargeable gain under this Act then, notwithstanding that the acquisition may have occurred before 6th July 1973 (the date on which the provision re-enacted in section 152 of this Act first came into operation as respects disposals) or that the market value of the asset at the time of its acquisition may have been fixed for the purposes of a contemporaneous disposal, section 152 of this Act shall apply for the purposes of the determination of the market value of the asset or, as the case may be, that part of it at the time of its acquisition.

Unquoted shares or securities: acquisition on death

7.—(1) This paragraph applies if, in a case where the market value of an asset at the time of its acquisition is material as mentioned in paragraph 6 above,—

(*a*) the acquisition took place on the occasion of a death occurring after 30th March 1971 and before 6th July 1973, and

(*b*) by virtue of paragraph 9 below, the principal value of the asset for the purposes of estate duty on that death would, apart from this paragraph, be taken to be the market value of the asset at the date of the death for the purposes of this Act.

(2) If the principal value referred to in sub-paragraph (1) (*b*) above falls to be determined as mentioned in section 55 of the Finance Act 1940 or section 15 of the Finance (No. 2) Act (Northern Ireland) 1946 (certain controlling shareholdings to be valued on an assets basis), nothing in section 152 of this Act shall affect the operation of paragraph 9 below for the purpose of determining the market value of the date of the death.

(3) If sub-paragraph (2) above does not apply, paragraph 9 below shall not apply as mentioned in sub-paragraph (1) (*b*) above and the market value of the asset on its acquisition at the date of the death shall be determined in accordance with paragraphs 2 and 6 above.

Unquoted shares or securities: prior part disposal

8.—(1) In any case where—

(*a*) before 6th July 1973 there has been a part disposal of an asset to which section 152 of this Act applies (in this paragraph referred to as "the earlier disposal"), and

(*b*) by virtue of any enactment, the acquisition of the asset or any part of it was deemed to be for a consideration equal to its market value, and

(*c*) on or after 6th July 1973 there is a disposal (including a part disposal) of the property which remained undisposed of immediately before that date (in this paragraph referred to as "the later disposal"),

sub-paragraph (2) below shall apply in computing any chargeable gain accruing on the later disposal.

(2) Where this sub-paragraph applies, the apportionment made by virtue of paragraph 7 of Schedule 6 to the Finance Act 1965 (corresponding to section 35 of this Act) on the occasion of the earlier disposal shall be recalculated on the basis that section 152 (3) of this Act was in force at the time, and applied for the purposes, of the determination of—

(*a*) the market value referred to in sub-paragraph (1) (*b*) above, and

(*b*) the market value of the property which remained undisposed of after the earlier disposal, and

(*c*) if the consideration for the earlier disposal was, by virtue of any enactment, deemed to be equal to the market value of the property disposed of, that market value.

Value determined for estate duty

9.—(1) Where estate duty (including estate duty leviable under the law of Northern Ireland) is chargeable in respect of any property passing on a death after 30th March 1971 and the principal value of an asset forming part of that property has been ascertained (whether in any proceedings or otherwise) for the purposes of that duty, the principal value so ascertained shall, subject to paragraph 7 (3) above, be taken for the purposes of this Act to be the market value of that asset at the date of the death.

(2) Where the principal value has been reduced under section 35 of the Finance Act 1968 or section 1 of the Finance Act (Northern Ireland) 1968 (tapering relief for gifts inter vivos etc.), the reference in sub-paragraph (1) above to the principal value as ascertained for the purposes of estate duty is a reference to that value as so ascertained before the reduction.

Part II

Assets Acquired Before Commencement

Events before commencement

10.—(1) The substitution of this Act for the corresponding enactments repealed by this Act shall not alter the effect of any provision enacted before this Act (whether or not there is a corresponding provision in this Act) so far as it determines whether and to what extent events in, or expenditure incurred in, or other amounts referable to, a period earlier than the chargeable periods to which this

Act applies may be taken into account for any tax purposes in a chargeable period to which this Act applies.

(2) Without prejudice to sub-paragraph (1) above, the repeals made by this Act shall not affect—

(a) the enactments specified in Part V of Schedule 14 to the Finance Act 1971 (charge on death) so far as their operation before repeal falls to be taken into account in chargeable periods to which this Act applies,

(b) the application of the enactments repealed by this Act to events before 6th April 1965 in accordance with paragraph 31 of Schedule 6 to the Finance Act 1965.

(3) This paragraph has no application to the law relating to the determination of the market value of assets (which is stated for all relevant times and occasions in Part I of this Schedule, with Part VIII of this Act).

PART III

OTHER TRANSITORY PROVISIONS

Value-shifting

11. Section 26 of this Act applies only where the reduction in value mentioned in subsection (1) of that section (or, in a case within subsection (8) of that section, the reduction or increase in value) is after 29th March 1977.

Assets acquired on disposal chargeable under Case VII of Schedule D

12.—(1) In this paragraph references to a disposal chargeable under Case VII are references to cases where the acquisition and disposal was in circumstances that the gain accruing on it was chargeable under Case VII of Schedule D, or where it would have been so chargeable if there were a gain so accruing.

(2) The amount or value of the consideration for the acquisition of an asset by the person acquiring it on a disposal chargeable under Case VII shall not under any provision of this Act be deemed to be an amount greater than the amount taken into account as consideration on that disposal for the purposes of Case VII.

(3) Any apportionment of consideration or expenditure falling to be made in relation to a disposal chargeable under Case VII in accordance with section 164 (4) of the Taxes Act, and in particular in a case where section 164 (6) of that Act (enhancement of value of land by acquisition of adjoining land) applied, shall be followed for the purposes of this Act both in relation to a disposal of the assets acquired on the disposal chargeable under Case VII and, where the disposal chargeable under Case VII was a part disposal, in relation to a disposal of what remains undisposed of.

(4) Sub-paragraph (3) above has effect notwithstanding section 43 (4) of this Act (general provisions for apportionment).

Unrelieved Case VII losses

13. Where no relief from income tax (for a year earlier than 1971–72) has been given in respect of a loss or part of a loss allowable under Case VII of Schedule D the loss or part shall, notwithstanding that the loss accrued before that year, be an allowable loss for the purposes of capital gains tax, but subject to any restrictions imposed by section 62 of this Act (transactions between connected persons).

Dispositions before 27th March 1974 which attract capital transfer tax

14. Paragraph 15 and 16 below have effect in respect of dispositions before 27th March 1974 where the disponer dies before 27th March 1981.

Gifts subject to capital transfer tax on death

15.—(1) Where the value of any asset comprised in a gift inter vivos is by virtue of section 22 (5) of the Finance Act 1975 included in the value of the estate of any person for the purposes of capital transfer tax, and at the time of that person's death the asset—

(*a*) is owned by the donee, or

(*b*) is property settled by the gift or property which for the purposes of section 38 of the Finance Act 1957 would by virtue of subsection (9) thereof be treated as property settled by the gift,

then, subject to sub-paragraph (2) below, the asset shall for the purposes of this Act be deemed to be disposed of and immediately re-acquired at that time by the donee or trustee for a consideration equal to the value so included; but no chargeable gain shall accrue on the disposal.

(2) Where the value so included is reduced by virtue of section 35 of the Finance Act 1968, the appropriate portion only of the asset shall be deemed to be so disposed of and re-acquired; and for this purpose the appropriate portion is the reduced value so included divided by the value before the reduction.

Life interest terminated on death on which capital transfer tax is chargeable

16. Where a life interest within the meaning of section 55 of this Act in settled property is terminated by the death of a person on whose death capital transfer tax is chargeable under section 22 of the Finance Act 1975 and, under subsection (5) of that section, a value falls to be included in respect of the settled property, then—

(*a*) if that value is the principal value of the property, section 56 of this Act shall apply as if that person had been entitled to the life interest at his death, and

(*b*) if that value is a value reduced by any percentage under paragraph 3 of Part II of Schedule 17 to the Finance Act 1969, any chargeable gain or allowable loss accruing on the disposal deemed to be made under section 54 (1) or 55 (1) of this Act shall be reduced by the complementary percentage, that is to say the percentage found by subtracting the first-mentioned percentage from one hundred per cent.

Devaluation of sterling: securities acquired with borrowed foreign currency

17.—(1) This paragraph applies where, in pursuance of permission granted under the Exchange Control Act 1947, currency other than sterling was borrowed before 19th November 1967 for the purpose of investing in foreign securities (and had not been repaid before that date), and it was a condition of the permission—

(*a*) that repayment of the borrowed currency should be made from the proceeds of the sale in foreign currency of the foreign securities so acquired or out of investment currency, and

(*b*) that the foreign securities so acquired should be kept in separate accounts to distinguish them from others in the same ownership,

and securities held in such a separate account on 19th November 1967 are in this paragraph referred to as "designated securities".

(2) In computing the gain accruing to the borrower on the disposal of any designated securities or on the disposal of any currency or amount standing in a bank account on 19th November 1967 and representing the loan the sums allowable as a deduction under section 32 (1) (*a*) of this Act shall be increased by multiplying by seven sixths:

Provided that the total amount of the increase so made in computing all gains (and losses) which are referable to any one loan (made before 19th November 1967) shall not exceed one sixth of the sterling parity value of that loan at the time it was made.

(3) Section 65 of this Act (rules for identification: pooling) shall apply separately in relation to any designated securities held in a particular account until such time as a disposal takes place on the occurrence of which the proviso to sub-paragraph (2) above operates to limit the increases which would otherwise be made under that sub-paragraph in allowable deductions.

(4) In this paragraph and paragraph 18 below "foreign securities" means securities expressed in a currency other than sterling, or shares having a nominal value expressed in a currency other than sterling, or the dividends on which are payable in a currency other than sterling.

Devaluation of sterling: foreign insurance funds

18.—(1) The sums allowable as a deduction under section 32 (1) (*a*) of this Act in computing any gains to which this paragraph applies shall be increased by multiplying by seven-sixths.

(2) This paragraph applies to gains accruing—

(*a*) to any underwriting member of Lloyd's or to any other approved association of underwriters, or

(*b*) to any company engaged in the business of marine protection and indemnity insurance on a mutual basis,

on the disposal by that person after 18th November 1967 of any foreign securities which on that date formed part of a trust fund—

(i) established by that person in any country or territory outside the United Kingdom, and

(ii) representing premiums received in the course of that person's business, and

(iii) wholly or mainly used for the purpose of meeting liabilities arising in that country or territory in respect of that business.

Gilt-edged securities past redemption date

19. So far as material for the purposes of this or any other Act, the definition of "gilt-edged securities" in Schedule 2 to this Act shall include any securities which were specified securities for the purposes of section 41 of the Finance Act 1969, and the redemption date of which fell before 1st January 1979.

Reorganisation of share capital, conversion of securities, etc.

20.—(1) Chapter II of Part IV of this Act has effect subject to the provisions of this paragraph.

(2) The substitution of the said Chapter II for the enactments repealed by this Act shall not alter the law applicable to any reorganisation or reduction of share capital, conversion of securities or company amalgamation taking place before the commencement of this Act.

(3) Sub-paragraph (2) above applies in particular to the law determining whether or not any assets arising on an event mentioned in that sub-paragraph are to be treated as the same asset as the original holding of shares, securities or other assets.

(4) Notwithstanding the preceding provisions of this paragraph, section 84 of this Act (compensation stock) shall apply where the compulsory acquisition took place after 6th April 1976, but before the commencement of this Act, as well as where it took place after the commencement of this Act.

Land: allowance for betterment levy

21.—(1) Where betterment levy charged in the case of any land in respect of an act or event falling within Case B or Case C or, if it was the renewal, extension or variation of a tenancy, Case F—

(*a*) has been paid, and

(*b*) has not been allowed as a deduction in computing the profits or gains or losses of a trade for the purposes of Case I of Schedule D;

then, if the person by whom the levy was paid disposes of the land or any part of it and so claims, the following provisions of this paragraph shall have effect for the purpose of applying Chapter II of Part II of, and Schedule 5 to, this Act to the disposal.

(2) Paragraph 9 of Schedule 5 to this Act (sales of land reflecting development value) shall apply where the condition stated in sub-paragraph (1) (*a*) thereof is satisfied, notwithstanding that the condition stated in sub-paragraph (1) (*b*) thereof is not satisfied.

(3) Subject to the following provisions of this paragraph, there shall be ascertained the excess, if any, of—

(*a*) the net development value ascertained for the purposes of the levy, over

(*b*) the increment specified in sub-paragraph (6) below;

and the amount of the excess shall be treated as an amount allowable under section 32 (1) (*b*) of this Act.

(4) Where the act or event in respect of which the levy was charged was a part disposal of the land, the said section 32 shall apply as if the part disposal had not taken place and sub-paragraph (5) below shall apply in lieu of sub-paragraph (3) above.

(5) the amount or value of the consideration for the disposal shall be treated as increased by the amount of any premium or like sum paid in respect of the part disposal, and there shall be ascertained the excess, if any, of—

(*a*) the aggregate specified in sub-paragraph (7) below, over

(*b*) the increment specified in sub-paragraph (6) below:

and the amount of the excess shall be treated as an amount allowable under section 32 (1) (*b*) of this Act.

(6) The increment referred to in sub-paragraphs (3) (*b*) and (5) (*b*) above is the excess, if any, of—

(*a*) the amount or value of the consideration brought into account under section 32 (1) (*a*) of this Act, over

(*b*) the base value ascertained for the purposes of the levy.

(7) The aggregate referred to in sub-paragraph (5) (*a*) above is the aggregate of—

(*a*) the net development value ascertained for the purposes of the levy, and

(*b*) the amount of any premium or like sum paid in respect of the part disposal, in so far as charged to tax under Schedule A (or, as the case may be, Case VIII of Schedule D), and

(*c*) the chargeable gain accruing on the part disposal.

(8) Where betterment levy in respect of more than one act or event has been charged and paid as mentioned in sub-paragraph (1) above sub-paragraphs (2) to (7) above shall apply without modifications in relation to the betterment levy in respect of the first of them; but in relation to the other or others sub-paragraph (3) or, as the case may be, (5) above shall have effect as if the amounts to be treated thereunder as allowable under section 32 (1) (*b*) of this Act were the net development value specified in sub-paragraph (3) (*a*) or, as the case may be, the aggregate referred to in sub-paragraph (5) (*a*) of this paragraph.

(9) Where the disposal is of part only of the land sub-paragraphs (2) to (8) above shall have effect subject to the appropriate apportionments.

(10) References in this paragraph to a premium include any sum payable as mentioned in subsection (3) or (4) of section 80 of the Taxes Act (sums payable in lieu of rent or as consideration for the surrender of lease or for variation or waiver of term) and, in relation to Scotland, a grassum.

Replacement of business assets

22.—(1) Sections 115 to 121 of this Act (which are substituted for section 33 of the Finance Act 1965 as amended by subsequent enactments) have effect subject to the provisions of this paragraph.

(2) The substitution of those sections for the enactments repealed by this Act shall not alter the effect of those repealed enactments so far as they apply where the acquisition of, or of the interest in, the new assets (but not the disposal of, or of the interests in, the old assets) was before the commencement of this Act.

(3) Where the said section 33 of the Finance Act 1965 applied on the acquisition, before 23rd July 1970, of, or of an interest in, any new assets and the adjustment required to be made under subsection (1) (*a*) or subsection (2) (*a*) of that section was, by virtue of paragraph 9 (5) of Schedule 14 to the Finance Act 1967 (allowance for development value), required to be computed as mentioned therein, any adjustment required to be made under section 115 (1) (*b*), or 116 (1) (*b*), of this Act shall also be so computed, notwithstanding the repeals made by the Finance Act 1971 (restoring development value).

Transfer of business to a company

23. Section 123 of this Act shall have effect as if after subsection (4) there were inserted as subsection (4A)—

" (4A) If any development gains within the meaning of Part III of the Finance Act 1974 accrue to the transferor in respect of his disposal of the assets included in the business, then for the purposes of subsection (4) above B (that is, the value of the whole of the consideration received by the transferor in exchange for the business) shall be taken to be what it would be if the value of the consideration other than shares so received by him were less by an amount equal to those gains".

Works of art etc.

24. The repeals made by this Act do not affect the continued operation of sections 31 and 32 of the Finance Act 1965, in the form in which they were before 13th March 1975, in relation to estate duty in respect of deaths occurring before that date.

Disposal before acquisition

25. The substitution of this Act for the corresponding enactments repealed by this Act shall not alter the effect of any provision enacted before this Act (whether or not there is a corresponding provision in this Act) so far as it relates to an asset which—

(*a*) was disposed of before being acquired, and
(*b*) was disposed of before the commencement of this Act.

Estate duty

26. Nothing in the repeals made by this Act shall affect any enactment as it applies to the determination of any principal value for the purposes of estate duty.

Income and corporation tax: premiums on leases

27. The repeal by this Act of section 116 (3) of the Finance Act 1972 shall not affect its application by paragraph 3 of Schedule 13 to that Act.

Validity of subordinate legislation

28. So far as this Act re-enacts any provision contained in a statutory instrument made in exercise of powers conferred by any Act, it shall be without prejudice to the validity of that provision, and any question as to its validity shall be determined as if the re-enacted provision were contained in a statutory instrument made under those powers.

Saving for Part II of this Schedule

29. The provisions of this Part of this Schedule are without prejudice to the generality of Part II of this Schedule.

GENERAL NOTE

This schedule contains transitory provisions which re-enact the original legislation as it was before various amendments were made (which took effect before the consolidation). This legislation is re-enacted here to govern the position in relation to events which happened before it was amended. For detailed commentary on this legislation the reader is referred to past editions of this publication.

Section 157 (2)

SCHEDULE 7

CONSEQUENTIAL AMENDMENTS

Taxes Management Act 1970 (*c.* 9)

1.—(1) The Taxes Management Act 1970 shall be amended as follows.

(2) In section 12 (2) for paragraph (*a*) substitute—

"(*a*) any assets exempted by the following provisions of the Capital Gains Tax Act 1979, namely—

(i) section 19 (4) (rights to winnings from pool betting, lotteries or games with prizes),

(ii) section 71 (government non-marketable securities),

(iii) section 130, 131 or 133 (passenger vehicles, decorations for valour or gallant conduct and foreign currency for personal expenditure)".

(3) In section 28 (1) for "section 41" (in both places) substitute "section

15 ", for " section 42 " (in both places) substitute " section 17 ", and for " Finance Act 1965 " substitute " Capital Gains Tax Act 1979 ".

Income and Corporation Taxes Act 1970 (*c.* 10)

2.—(1) The Taxes Act shall be amended as follows.

(2) In section 270 (3) for the words from " disposal " to the end of the subsection substitute—

" disposal, and the asset consists of specified securities, the company acquiring the asset shall be treated for the purposes of sections 67 to 70 of the Capital Gains Tax Act 1979 as acquiring it at the time when the other acquired it."

(3) At the end of section 270 (in place of the subsection (6) inserted by paragraph 12 of Schedule 10 to the Finance Act 1971) insert—

" (6) In this section " specified securities " means securities which are gilt-edged securities as defined by Schedule 2 to the Capital Gains Tax Act 1979."

(4) In section 279 (1) (a) after " 1965 " insert " but before 20th April 1977 ".

Finance Act 1974 (*c.* 30)

3. For paragraph 18 (6) of Schedule 3 to the Finance Act 1974 substitute—

" (6) The following provisions of the Capital Gains Tax Act 1979 shall, with any necessary modifications, apply for the purposes of this paragraph as they apply for the purposes of section 115 of that Act, namely—

(*a*) subsections (3) to (8) of the said section 115,

(*b*) section 119,

(*c*) section 121."

4. For paragraph 19 of Schedule 3 to the Finance Act 1974 substitute—

" 19.—(1) Paragraph 18 above shall have effect subject to the provisions of this paragraph, in which—

(*a*) the " tax reduction " means the reduction in the income tax or corporation tax to which the person carrying on the trade is chargeable which is made under sub-paragraph (3) of the said paragraph 18 in connection with a disposal of an asset (called " asset No. 1 ");

(*b*) the " expenditure reduction " means the related amount by which under sub-paragraph (4) of that paragraph, and apart from the provisions of this paragraph, the expenditure allowable in respect of another asset (called " asset No. 2 ") is reduced;

(*c*) any reference to an expenditure reduction of any amount being carried forward to any asset is a reference to a reduction of that amount in expenditure allowable in respect of that asset.

(2) If asset No. 2 is a depreciating asset, the expenditure reduction shall not be carried forward, but—

(*a*) when the claimant disposes of asset No. 2, or

(*b*) when he ceases to use asset No. 2 for the purposes of a trade carried on by him, or

(*c*) on the expiration of a period of ten years beginning with the acquisition of asset No. 2,

whichever event comes first, an amount equal to the tax reduction may be assessed to tax and recovered accordingly.

Any assessment to income tax or corporation tax under this paragraph shall be made under Case VI of Schedule D.

(3) If, in the circumstances specified in sub-paragraph (4) below, the claimant acquires an asset (called " asset No. 3 ") which is not a depreciating asset, and so claims under paragraph 18 above—

(*a*) the expenditure reduction shall be carried forward to asset No. 3, and

(*b*) the claim which applies to asset No. 2 shall be treated as withdrawn (so that sub-paragraph (2) above does not apply).

(4) The circumstances are that asset No. 3 is acquired not later than the occurrence of whichever of the events mentioned in sub-paragraph (2) above comes first and, assuming—

(*a*) that the consideration for asset No. 1 was applied in acquiring asset No. 3, and

(*b*) that the time between the disposal of asset No. 1 and the acquisition of asset No. 3 was within the time limited by section 115 (3) of the Capital Gains Tax Act 1979 as applied by paragraph 18 (6) above, the whole amount of the expenditure reduction could be carried forward from asset No. 1 to asset No. 3; and the claim under sub-paragraph (3) above shall be accepted as if those assumptions were true.

(5) For the purposes of this paragraph an asset is a depreciating asset at any time if—

(*a*) at that time it is a wasting asset as defined in section 37 (1) of the Capital Gains Tax Act 1979, or

(*b*) within the period of ten years beginning at that time it will become a wasting asset (so defined).

(6) This paragraph shall be construed as one with paragraph 18 above."

Finance (No. 2) Act 1975 (*c.* 45)

5. For paragraph 2 (2) of Schedule 8 to the Finance (No. 2) Act 1975 substitute—

" (2) Section 150 (3) of the Capital Gains Tax Act 1979 (market value of shares or securities listed in The Stock Exchange Daily Official List) shall apply for the purposes of this paragraph as it applies for the purposes of that Act."

Development Land Tax Act 1976 (*c.* 24)

6.—(1) Paragraph 5 of Schedule 6 to the Development Land Tax Act 1976 shall be amended as follows.

(2) In sub-paragraph (1) (a)—

(*a*) for " section 33 of the Finance Act 1965 " substitute " sections 115 to 121 of the Capital Gains Tax Act 1979 ", and

(*b*) for " applies " substitute " apply ".

(3) In sub-paragraph (2) for " section 33 of the Finance Act 1965 " substitute " sections 115 to 121 of the Capital Gains Tax Act 1979 ".

(4) In sub-paragraph (4)—

(*a*) for " section 33 of the Finance Act 1965 has effect subject to the provisions of paragraph 16 of Schedule 19 to the Finance Act 1969 " substitute " sections 115 and 116 of the Capital Gains Tax Act 1979 have effect subject to the provisions of section 117 of that Act ", and

(*b*) for " sub-paragraph (2) of that paragraph accrues in accordance with that sub-paragraph " substitute " subsection (2) of the said section 117 accrues in accordance with that subsection."

(5) In sub-paragraph (4) (*a*) for " that sub-paragraph " substitute " subsection (2) of the said section 117 ".

(6) In sub-paragraph (4) (*b*) for " sub-paragraph (3) of that paragraph " substitute " subsection (3) of the said section 117 ".

(7) In sub-paragraph (6)—

(*a*) for " section 33 of the Finance Act 1965 " substitute " sections 115 to 121 of the Capital Gains Tax Act 1979 ", and

(*b*) for " paragraph 16 of Schedule 19 to the Finance Act 1969 " substitute " section 117 of that Act ".

Finance Act 1976 (*c.* 40)

7. For section 54 (5) of the Finance Act 1976 substitute—

" (5) Subsection (6) of section 84 of the Capital Gains Tax Act 1979 (gilt-edged securities not issued until after the date when shares are compulsorily acquired) shall apply in relation to this section as it applies in relation to that section, and in this section—

" gilt-edged securities " has the meaning given by Schedule 2 to that Act;

" shares " includes securities within the meaning of section 82 of that Act."

Translation of references to Part III of Finance Act 1965

8. In the enactments specified in the Table below substitute " the Capital Gains Tax Act 1979 " (or " The Capital Gains Tax Act 1979 " if at the beginning of a sentence)—

(*a*) in the contexts in Part I of the Table, for " Part III of the Finance Act 1965 ",

(*b*) in the contexts in Part II of the Table, for " Part III of the Finance Act

1965", together with the words "(chargeable gains)" or "(capital gains)" or "(capital gains tax)" or "(tax on chargeable gains)" as the case may be.

TABLE

PART I

1. In the Taxes Management Act 1970 (c. 9)
   section 11 (1) (*b*)
   section 47 (1)
   section 57 (1) (a)
   section 111 (1)
   section 118 (1), in the definitions of "chargeable gain" and of "the Taxes Acts"
   section 119 (4).
2. In the Income and Corporation Taxes Act 1970 (c. 10)
   section 265 (4).
   section 268 (2)
   section 268A (2)
   section 273 (1)
   section 278 (3)
   section 279 (2)
   section 352 (7)
   section 526 (5), in the definition of "chargeable gain"
   section 540 (2).
3. In the Finance Act 1970 (c. 24)
   section 29 (1) (*b*)
   Schedule 6 paragraph 9.
4. In the Finance Act 1972 (c. 41)
   Schedule 12, Part VII, in the definition of "market value" in paragraph 6.
5. In the Finance Act 1973 (c. 51)
   section 38 (3)
   section 59 (3) (*c*).
6. In the Finance Act 1974 (c. 30)
   section 40 (3) (*a*)
   section 45 (1)
   section 57 (3) (*c*).
   Schedule 3 paragraph 18 (4)
   Schedule 9 paragraph 2 (3)
   Schedule 9 paragraph 17.
7. In the Finance Act 1975 (c. 7)
   section 51 (4)
   Schedule 10 paragraph 4 (1).
8. In the Development Land Tax Act 1976 (c. 24)
   section 47 (1), in the definition of "chargeable gain".
9. In the Finance Act 1976 (c. 40)
   section 67 (11) (*d*)
   section 132 (3) (*c*).
10. In the Finance Act 1977 (c. 36)
   section 42 (1) (see also entry above for section 268A (2) of the Taxes Act)
   section 45 (3).

PART II

REFERENCES TO PART III OF FINANCE ACT 1965 FOLLOWED BY DESCRIPTIVE WORDS

1. Section 74 (2) of the Post Office Act 1969 (c. 48).
2. Section 27 (1) of the Taxes Management Act 1970 (c. 9).
3. In the Income and Corporation Taxes Act 1970 (c. 10)
   section 321 (1) (*a*)
   section 525 (2).

4. In the Finance Act 1970 (c. 24)
   Schedule 3 paragraph 8 (1)
   Schedule 6 paragraph 3 (2) (*b*.)
5. Paragraph 15 of Schedule 9 to the Finance Act 1974 (c. 30).
6. In the Development Land Tax Act 1976 (c. 24)
   section 5 (6) (*b*)
   section 12 (5) (*c*)
   Schedule 8 paragraph 57 (1) (*b*).

Translation of references to enactments repealed and re-enacted

9. In the enactments specified in column 1 of the following Table for the words in column 2 substitute the words in column 3, adding, except as otherwise indicated, " of the Capital Gains Tax Act 1979 " (but in all cases saying " to " instead of " of " if the substituted words refer to a Schedule rather than a section).

TABLE

Enactment amended	*Words to be replaced*	*Corresponding provision of this Act*
	Taxes Management Act 1970 (*c.* 9)	
In the Taxes Management Act 1970 section		
12 (2) (*b*)	section 30 (6).	section 128 (6) (without adding more words).
25 (9)	subsections (1) and (8) of section 45 of the Finance Act 1965.	sections 64, 93 and 155 (1).
28 (2)	section 45 (1) of the Finance Act 1965.	section 51.
	subsections (1) and (8) of that section.	sections 64, 93 and 155 (1) of that Act (without adding more words).
	Income and Corporation Taxes Act 1970 (*c.* 10)	
In the Income and Corporation Taxes Act 1970 section		
186 (12) (*a*)	paragraph 4 (1) (*a*) of Schedule 6 to the Finance Act 1965.	section 32 (1) (*a*).
246 (2) (*b*)	Part III of the Finance Act 1965.	section 12.
265 (3) (*a*)	paragraph 5 (2) of Schedule 6 to the Finance Act 1965.	section 33 (2).
266 (5)	paragraph 3 of Schedule 7 to the Finance Act 1965.	section 72 (5) (*b*).
267 (1)	Part II of Schedule 6 to the Finance Act 1965.	Schedule 5.
267 (3)	subsection (1) or subsection (2) of section 38 of the Finance Act 1965.	section 96 or 97.
267 (3A)	subsections (4) to (7) of section 40 of the Finance Act 1977.	Subsections (2) to (5) of section 88.
	subsection (3) (*b*).	subsection (1) (without adding more words).
269 (1)	paragraph 4.	section 32 (without adding more words).
269 (1) (*a*)	paragraph 4 of Schedule 6 to the Finance Act 1965.	section 32.
270 (4) (*a*)	section 41 of the Finance Act 1969.	section 67.
270 (5) (*b*)	section 41 of the Finance Act 1969.	section 67.
273 (2)	Schedule 7 to the Finance Act 1965.	section 72.
	paragraph 3 of that Schedule.	that section (without adding more words).
274 (1) and (2)	paragraph 1 of Schedule 7 to the Finance Act 1965.	section 122.

Enactment amended	*Words to be replaced*	*Corresponding provision of this Act*
275 (1)	paragraph 6 of Schedule 6 to the Finance Act 1965.	section 34.
275 (2)	Part II of Schedule 6 to the Finance Act 1965.	Schedule 5.
276 (1)	section 33 of the Finance Act 1965.	sections 115 to 121.
276 (2)	paragraph 16 (2) of Schedule 19 to the Finance Act 1969.	section 117 (2).
	paragraph 16 (2).	section 117 (2) (without adding more words).
278 (4) (b)	section 33 of the Finance Act 1965.	sections 115 to 121.
279 (6)	paragraph 6 or paragraph 7 of Schedule 7 to the Finance Act 1965.	section 85 or section 86.
279 (7)	paragraph 7 of the said Schedule 7.	section 86.
280 (8)	section 23 (4) of the Finance Act 1965.	section 22 (2).
305 (2)	paragraph 2 (1) of Schedule 6 to the Finance Act 1965.	section 31 (1).
352 (7)	Part II of Schedule 6.	Schedule 5 (without adding more words).
359 (4)	subsections (1) and (8) of section 45 of the Finance Act 1965.	sections 64, 93 and 155 (1).
360 (2)	section 35 of the Finance Act 1965.	section 145.
474 (2)	Part III of the Finance Act 1965.	section 72 (5) (b).
488 (9)	section 29 of the Finance Act 1965.	sections 101 to 105.
	paragraph 2 of Schedule 12 to the Finance Act 1968.	section 103 (3) of that Act (without adding more words).
489 (11)	paragraph 1 of Schedule 7 to the Finance Act 1965.	section 122.
489 (12)	paragraphs 2 and 5 of Schedule 6 to the Finance Act 1965.	sections 31 and 33.
	Finance Act 1970 (c. 24)	
In the Finance Act 1970		
Schedule 3 paragraph 8 (1) ...	Part II of Schedule 6.	Schedule 5 (without adding more words).
	Finance Act 1972 (c. 41)	
In the Finance Act 1972		
section 79 (9)	paragraph 4 (1) (a) of Schedule 6 to the Finance Act 1965.	section 32 (1) (a).
Schedule 12 Part VIII paragraph 6 in the definition of "market value."	section 44.	section 150 (without adding more words).

Enactment amended	*Words to be replaced*	*Corresponding provision of this Act*
In the Finance Act 1973	*Finance Act* 1973 (*c.* 51)	
Schedule 16		
paragraph 5	paragraph 2 or 5 of Schedule 6 to the Finance Act 1965.	section 31 or 33.
paragraph 7	specified securities within the meaning of section 41 of the Finance Act 1969.	gilt-edged securities as defined in Schedule 2.
	Finance Act 1974 (*c.* 30)	
In the Finance Act 1974 section		
26 (2) (*a*)	section 20 (3) of the Finance Act 1965.	section 3.
30 (1)	paragraph 5 of Schedule 7 to the Finance Act 1965.	section 82.
38 (3) (*a*)	paragraph 4 (1) (*a*) and (*b*) of Schedule 6 to the Finance Act 1965.	section 32 (1) (*a*) and (*b*).
39 (4) (*a*)	section 45 (7) (*b*) of the Finance Act 1965.	section 60 (*b*).
41 (6)	section 45 (8) of the Finance Act 1965.	section 93.
41 (13)	paragraph 3 of Schedule 7 to the Finance Act 1965.	section 72.
42 (4) (*a*)	paragraph 13 (1) of Schedule 7 to the Finance Act 1965.	section 58 (1).
42 (4) (after paragraphs (*a*) and (*b*)).	paragraph 13 (1) (twice).	section 58 (1) (without adding more words).
42 (5)	paragraph 13 (2) of Schedule 7 to the Finance Act 1965.	section 58 (2).
42 (5) (*a*)	section 25 (3) of the Finance Act 1965.	section 54 (1).
42 (5) (*b*)	section 42 of the Finance Act 1965.	section 17.
42 (6)	section 42 (three times).	section 17 (without adding more words).
42 (7)	Schedule 6 to the Finance Act 1965.	Chapter II of Part II.
	paragraph 4 (1) (*a*) of that Schedule.	section 32 (1) (*a*).
43 (2)	section 38 (2) of the Finance Act 1965.	section 97.
44 (1) (definition of "securities")	paragraph 5 of Schedule 7 to the Finance Act 1965.	section 82.
44 (1) (definition of "shares")	section 45 (1) of the Finance Act 1965.	section 64 (1).

Enactment amended	*Words to be replaced*	*Corresponding provision of this Act*
Schedule 3		
paragraph 2 (3)	paragraph 7 (2) of Schedule 6 to the Finance Act 1965.	subsection (2) of section 35.
	paragraph 7 (4) of that Schedule.	subsection (4) of that section (without adding more words).
	that Schedule.	Chapter II of Part II of that Act (without adding more words).
paragraph 2 (4)	paragraph 4 (1) (*a*) and (*b*) of the said Schedule 6.	section 32 (1) (*a*) and (*b*).
	that Schedule.	Chapter II of Part II of that Act (without adding more words).
paragraph 2 (7)	paragraph 4 (1) (*a*) and (*b*) of Schedule 6 to the Finance Act 1965.	section 32 (1) (*a*) and (*b*).
	Schedule 8.	Schedule 3 (without adding more words).
paragraph 3	subsection (3) of section 22 of the Finance Act 1965.	subsection (1) of section 20.
paragraph 5 (2)	paragraph 4 (1) (*a*) and (*b*) of Schedule 6 to the Finance Act 1965.	section 32 (1) (*a*) and (*b*).
	Schedule 8.	Schedule 3 (without adding more words).
	the said Schedule 6.	Chapter II of Part II of that Act (without adding more words).
paragraph 11 (5) (*b*)	paragraph 4 (1) (*b*) of Schedule 6 to the Finance Act 1965.	section 32 (1) (*b*).
paragraph 12 (1)	Schedule 8 to the Finance Act 1965.	Schedule 3.
	paragraph 4 (1) (*b*) of Schedule 6 to the Finance Act 1965.	section 32 (1) (*b*) of that Act (without adding more words).
Cross-heading before paragraph 15.	paragraph 23 (4) of Schedule 6 to the Finance Act 1965.	paragraph 9 (4) of Schedule 5.
paragraph 15	paragraph 23 of Schedule 6 to the Finance Act 1965.	paragraph 9 of Schedule 5.
	Part II of that Schedule.	the said Schedule 5 (without adding more words).
paragraph 16 (1)	section 33 of the Finance Act 1965.	sections 115 to 121 (changing "applies" to "apply").
	the said section 33.	those sections (without adding more words).

Enactment amended	*Words to be replaced*	*Corresponding provision of this Act*
paragraph 17	subsection (1) (*b*) or (2) (*b*) of section 33 of the Finance Act 1965.	section 115 (1) (*b*) or 116 (1) (*b*).
	Part III of that Act.	that Act (without adding more words).
	subsection (1) (*b*) or (2) (*b*).	section 115 (1) (*b*) or 116 (1) (*b*) (without adding more words).
paragraph 18 (1) (*a*)	subsection (6) of section 33 of the Finance Act 1965.	section 118 (with section 119).
paragraph 18 (7)	Part III of the Finance Act 1965 providing generally for apportionments.	section 43 (4).
paragraph 18 (8)	section 33 (6) of the Finance Act 1965.	section 118.
	paragraph (*a*).	paragraph 1 (without adding more words).
	paragraph (*b*).	paragraph 2 (without adding more words).
paragraph 20 (1)	paragraph 6 of Schedule 7 to the Finance Act 1965.	section 85.
	paragraph 6.	section 85 (without adding more words).
paragraph 20 (2)	paragraph 6.	section 85 (without adding more words).
paragraph 21	subsection (3) of section 29 of the Finance Act 1965.	subsection (2) of section 102.
paragraph 22 (1)	section 34 of the Finance Act 1965.	section 124.
paragraph 22 (2)	section 34.	section 124 (without adding more words).
paragraph 22 (3)	subsection (1) of the said section 34.	the said section 124 (without adding more words).
	subsection (2) or (3).	subsection (4) or (5) (without adding more words).
paragraph 22 (5)	subsection (5) of the said section 34.	Subsection (7) of the said section 124 (without adding more words).
	subsection (2) or (3).	subsection (4) or (5) (without adding more words).
paragraph 22 (6)	section 34.	section 124 (without adding more words).
	subsection (4).	subsection (6) (without adding more words).
	the said subsection (1).	that section (without adding more words).
paragraph 22 (7)	section 34.	section 124 (without adding more words).
paragraph 23	paragraph 2 (1) of Schedule 6 to the Finance Act 1965.	section 31 (1).

Enactment amended	*Words to be replaced*	*Corresponding provision of this Act*
Schedule 6		
paragraph 2	section 20 (2) of the Finance Act 1965.	section 12.
Cross-heading before paragraph 6	paragraph 23 (4) of Schedule 6 to the Finance Act 1965.	paragraph 9 (4) of Schedule 5.
paragraph 6	paragraph 23 of Schedule 6 to the Finance Act 1965.	paragraph 9 of Schedule 5.
	Part II of that Schedule	the said Schedule 5 (without adding more words).
paragraph 7	subsection (3) of section 29 of the Finance Act 1965.	section 102 (2).
paragraph 9 (1)	paragraph 2 (1) of Schedule 6 to the Finance Act 1965.	section 31 (1).
Schedule 8		
paragraph 1	Subsections (1) and (2) of section 20 of the Finance Act 1965.	Sections 2 and 12.
paragraph 2	Section 41 of the Finance Act 1965.	Section 15.
paragraph 3	Section 42 of the Finance Act 1965.	Section 17.
	section 20 (4) of this Act.	section 4 (1) above (without adding more words).
paragraph 4	section 33 of the Finance Act 1965.	sections 115 to 121 (substituting "apply" for "applies").
	that section	those sections (without adding more words).
	the said section 33 in its application.	those sections in their application (without adding more words).
paragraph 5	Schedule 6 to the Finance Act 1965.	Chapter II of Part II.
	paragraph 4 (1) (*b*) of the said Schedule 6.	section 32 (1) (*b*) of that Act (without adding more words).
paragraph 7 (1)	paragraph 15 of Schedule 19 to the Finance Act 1969.	section 123.
	said paragraph 15.	said section 123 (without adding more words).
paragraph 7 (2) (*b*) (ii) ...	sub-paragraph (4) of the said paragraph 15.	subsection (4) of the said section 123 (without adding more words).
	that sub-paragraph.	that subsection (without adding more words).
paragraph 7 (5)	Schedule 6 to the Finance Act 1965.	Chapter II of Part II.
		section 32 (1) (*a*) and (*b*).
paragraph 7 (6)	paragraph 4 (1) (*a*) and (*b*) of the said Schedule 6.	Chapter II of Part II of that Act (without adding more words).
	that Schedule.	

Enactment amended	*Words to be replaced*	*Corresponding provision of this Act*
Schedule 9		
paragraph 14 (4)	Schedule 6 to the Finance Act 1965.	Chapter II of Part II.
paragraph 14 (5)	paragraph 4 (1) (*a*) and (*b*) of the said Schedule 6.	section 32 (1) (*a*) and (*b*).
	that Schedule.	Chapter II of Part II of that Act (without adding more words).
paragraph 14 (6)	paragraph 14 of Schedule 6 to the Finance Act 1965.	Section 40.
paragraph 15	paragraph 2 of Schedule 6 to that Act.	section 31 of that Act (without adding more words).
	that Schedule	Chapter II of Part II of that Act (without adding more words).
paragraph 16 (1)	Schedule 8 to the Finance Act 1965.	Schedule 3.
paragraph 16 (2)	Schedule 6 to the Finance Act 1965.	Chapter II of Part II.
	paragraph 4 (1) of that Schedule.	section 32 (1) of that Act (without adding more words).
	paragraph 7 of that Schedule.	section 35 of that Act (without adding more words).
	that Schedule.	the said Chapter II (without adding more words).
paragraph 16 (4)	Schedule 8 to the Finance Act 1965.	Schedule 3.
paragraph 18	Schedule 8 to the Finance Act 1965.	Schedule 3.
	paragraph 4 (1) (*b*) of Schedule 6 to the Finance Act 1965.	section 32 (1) (*b*) of that Act (without adding more words).
Schedule 10		
paragraph 1 (*a*)	section 25 (9) of, and paragraph 19 of Schedule 7 to, the Finance Act 1965.	sections 52 (4) and 59.
paragraph 2	paragraph 14 of Schedule 6 to the Finance Act 1965 and paragraph 4 of Schedule 10 to that Act and section 57 of the Finance (No. 2) Act 1975.	sections 8 and 40.
paragraph 5 (2) (*a*)	sections 41 and 42 of the Finance Act 1965.	sections 15 and 17.

Finance Act 1975 (*c.* 7)

In the Finance Act 1975		
section 51 (4)	paragraph 21 of Schedule 7 to.	section 63 of (without adding more words).
	that paragraph.	that section (without adding more words).

Enactment amended	*Words to be replaced*	*Corresponding provision of this Act*
Schedule 10		
paragraph 4 (1) (*b*)	paragraph 19 of Schedule 7 to.	section 59 of (without adding more words).
paragraph 27 (1)	paragraph 4 of Schedule 7 to the Finance Act 1965.	section 78.
paragraph 27 (1) (*a*)	that paragraph, or reduction of the share capital of a company.	section 77 (1) of that Act (without adding more words).
paragraph 27 (1) (*b*)	paragraph 5 of that Schedule.	section 82 of that Act (without adding more words).
paragraph 27 (1) (*c*)	paragraph 6 of that Schedule.	section 85 of that Act (without adding more words).
paragraph 27 (1) (*d*)	paragraph 7 of that Schedule.	section 86 of that Act (without adding more words).
paragraph 27 (1) (at end) ...	paragraph 4 of that Schedule applies by virtue of section 45 (8) of the Finance Act 1965.	the said section 78 applies by virtue of section 93.
paragraph 27 (2)	paragraph 4 of the said Schedule 7.	section 77 (1).
paragraph 29 (1)	section 26 of the Finance Act 1965.	section 153.
paragraph 34 (2)	Schedule 8 to the Finance Act 1965.	Schedule 3.
	Finance (No. 2) Act 1975 (*c.* 45)	
In the Finance (No. 2) Act 1975 section		
42 (10)	section 22 (2) (*b*) of the Finance Act 1965.	section 19 (2) (*b*).
58 (8)	paragraph 4 of Schedule 6 to the Finance Act 1965.	section 32.
	sub-paragraph (1) (*c*) of that paragraph.	subsection (1) (*c*) of that section (without adding more words).
	sub-paragraph (1) (*a*) and (*b*) of that paragraph.	subsection (1) (*a*) and (*b*) of that section (without adding more words).
58 (9)	sub-paragraph (1) of paragraph 6 of Schedule 10 to the Finance Act 1971.	section 66 (1).
	sub-paragraph (2) of that paragraph.	subsection (2) of the said section 66 (without adding more words).
	under sub-paragraph (1).	under subsection (1) (without adding more words).
58 (12)	paragraph 5 of Schedule 7 to the Finance Act 1965.	section 82.
	specified securities within the meaning of section 41 of the Finance Act 1969.	gilt-edged securities as defined in Schedule 2 to that Act (without adding more words).
Schedule 8		
paragraph 2 (3)	section 51 of the Finance Act 1973.	section 152.

Enactment amended	*Words to be replaced*	*Corresponding provision of this Act*
	Development Land Tax Act 1976 (*c.* 24)	
In the Development Land Tax Act 1976		
Schedule 6		
paragraph 1 (5) (*a*)	section 34 of the Finance Act 1965.	section 124 or 125.
paragraph 1 (5) (*b*)	section 38 (2).	section 97 (without adding more words).
paragraph 2 (2)	section 24 (1) of the Finance Act 1965.	section 49 (1).
paragraph 3 (2)	Schedule 8 to the Finance Act 1965.	Schedule 3.
paragraph 3 (10)	sub-paragraph (1) or sub-paragraph (4) of paragraph 5 of Schedule 8 to the Finance Act 1965.	paragraph 5 (1) or (3) of Schedule 3.
paragraph 4 (1) (*a*)	Schedule 8 to the Finance Act 1965.	Schedule 3.
	Schedule 6 to.	Chapter II of Part II of (without adding more words).
paragraph 4 (4) (*a*)	Schedule 8 to the Finance Act 1965.	Schedule 3.
Schedule 8		
paragraph 52 (1) (*c*)	the words from "Part III" to "1969".	the Capital Gains Tax Act 1979, section 123 of that Act (without adding more words).
	Finance Act 1976 (*c.* 40)	
In the Finance Act 1976		
section		
54 (3) (*a*)	section 53 (3) above.	section 84 (3).
54 (3) (*b*)	section 33 of the Finance Act 1965.	sections 115 to 121.
	that section.	section 118 of that Act (without adding more words).
67 (11) (*d*)	section 44.	section 150 (without adding more words).
67 (13)	paragraph 4 (1) (*a*) of Schedule 6 to the Finance Act 1965.	section 32 (1) (*a*).
82 (2)	section 31 of the Finance Act 1965.	section 147.
Schedule 10		
paragraph 4 (5)	paragraphs 4 to 7 of Schedule 7 to the Finance Act 1965.	sections 77 to 86.
Schedule 12		
paragraph 4 (1)	paragraph 4 of Schedule 7 to the Finance Act 1965.	section 78.
	section 53 of this Act.	section 84 of that Act (without adding more words).

Enactment amended	*Words to be replaced*	*Corresponding provision of this Act*
paragraph 4 (1) (*a*)	that paragraph, or reduction of the share capital of a company.	section 77 (1) of that Act (without adding more words).
paragraph 4 (1) (*b*)	paragraph 5 of that Schedule.	section 82 of that Act (without adding more words).
paragraph 4 (1) (*c*)	paragraph 6 of that Schedule.	section 85 of that Act (without adding more words).
paragraph 4 (1) (*d*)	paragraph 7 of that Schedule.	section 86 of that Act (without adding more words).
paragraph 4 (1) (at end) ...	paragraph 4 of that Schedule applies by virtue of section 45 (8) of the Finance Act 1965.	the said section 78 applies by virtue of section 93.
paragraph 4 (2)	the said paragraph 4.	section 77 (1).
paragraph 7 (2)	Schedule 8 to the Finance Act 1965.	Schedule 3.
Schedule 13	(see amendment in this Table of Finance Act 1975 Schedule 10 paragraph 34 (2)).	
	Finance Act 1977 (*c.* 36)	
In the Finance Act 1977 section		
41 (1)	(see amendment in this Table of section 267 (3A) of the Income and Corporation Taxes Act 1970).	———
46 (2) (*a*)	paragraph 4, 5, 6 or 7 of Schedule 7 to the Finance Act 1965.	sections 77 to 86.
46 (2) (*b*)	section 53 of the Finance Act 1976.	section 84 of that Act (without adding more words).
46 (6)	paragraph 5 of Schedule 7 to the said Act of 1965.	section 82.
	the words from " section 45 (8) " to " Finance Act 1971 ".	section 86 (7), 93 or 139 of that Act (without adding more words).
46 (7)	paragraph 6 or 7 of Schedule 7 to the said Act of 1965.	section 85 or 86.
	section 40 (2) above.	section 87 (1) of that Act (without adding more words).

Enactment amended	*Words to be replaced*	*Corresponding provision of this Act*
	Finance Act 1978 (*c.* 42)	
In the Finance Act 1978 section		
54 (2) (*a*)	paragraph 4 of Schedule 7 to the Finance Act 1965.	section 77 (1) (*b*).
57 (1)	paragraph 4 of Schedule 7 of the Finance Act 1965.	section 77 (1) (*b*).
57 (7)	Part III of the Finance Act 1965.	Chapter II of Part IV.
61 (1), in the definition of "market value".	Part III of the Finance Act 1965 (capital gains tax).	Part VIII.
61 (3) (*b*)	paragraph 3 of Schedule 7 to the Finance Act 1965.	section 72 (5) (*b*).
64 (5)	(see amendment in this Table of Finance Act 1976 Schedule 10 paragraph 4 (5)).	

General Note

This Schedule provides for amendments of other enactments consequent on the enactment of this consolidation Act.

Section 158

SCHEDULE 8

Repeals

Chapter	Short title	Extent of repeal
1965 c. 25.	Finance Act 1965.	Part III, except section 45 (12). Section 94. Schedules 6 to 9. Schedule 10, except paragraph 15.
1966 c. 18.	Finance Act 1966.	Section 43. Schedule 10.
1967 c. 54.	Finance Act 1967.	Section 32. Section 35. Section 37. Section 45 (3) (*h*). Schedule 13.
1968 c. 44.	Finance Act 1968.	Section 32. Section 34. Section 61 (5). Schedules 11 and 12.
1969 c. 32.	Finance Act 1969.	Sections 41 and 42. Section 61 (3) (*e*). Schedules 18 and 19.
1970 c. 9.	Taxes Management Act 1970.	Section 47 (4). In section 57 (3) (*c*) the words " or under any provision in the Finance Act 1965 ".
1970 c. 10.	Income and Corporation Taxes Act 1970.	In Schedule 15— paragraphs 6 and 7; in Part I of the Table in paragraph 11 the entries amending the Finance Act 1965; in Part II of that Table the entries amending— the Finance Act 1965 (except section 93), the Finance Act 1967, the Finance Act 1968, Schedules 18 and 19 to the Finance Act 1969; paragraph 12 (1).
1970 c. 24.	Finance Act 1970.	In section 28 (1) the words from " section 41 " to " 1969 and of ".
1971 c. 68.	Finance Act 1971.	Section 55, except subsection (5). Section 56. Sections 58 to 60. In section 69 (3) the words from " Part IV " to the end of the subsection. In Schedule 3 paragraph 10. In Schedule 6 paragraph 91. In Schedule 8 paragraph 16 (1). Schedule 9, except paragraph 4. Schedule 10. Schedule 12.
1972 c. 41.	Finance Act 1972.	Sections 112 to 119. In section 124 (2) the words " or gains " before paragraph (*a*), and in paragraph (*a*) the words " or gains " (in three places) and the words " or section 40 (1) of the Finance Act 1965.". Section 134 (3) (*c*). In Schedule 24 paragraphs 1 and 2.

Schedule 8—*continued*

Chapter	Short title	Extent of repeal
1973 c. 51.	Finance Act 1973.	Section 37. Section 51. In section 54 (1) the words " capital gains tax ". In Schedule 16 paragraph 15. Schedule 20. In Schedule 21 paragraph 4.
1974 c. 30.	Finance Act 1974.	Section 8 (8). Sections 31 to 33. Section 48. In section 57 (3) (*b*) the words from " and so far " to the end of the paragraph. In Schedule 8 paragraph 6.
1975 c. 7.	Finance Act 1975.	Section 53. In Schedule 12 paragraphs 12, 13 and 17.
1975 c. 45.	Finance (No. 2) Act 1975.	Section 44 (4). Section 57. Sections 59 to 64. In section 75 (3) (*c*) the words from " and so far " to the end of the paragraph. In Schedule 8 paragraph 5.
1976 c. 40.	Finance Act 1976.	Sections 52 and 53. Sections 55 and 56. In Schedule 11 paragraphs 1 and 6.
1977 c. 36.	Finance Act 1977.	Section 40. Section 43. In section 59 (3) (*c*) the words from " and, so far " to the end of the paragraph.
1978 c. 42.	Finance Act 1978.	Section 44. In section 45 subsections (1) to (4), and in subsection (6) the words from " and subsections (2) " to the end of the sub-section. Sections 46 to 52. In section 80 (3) (*c*) the words from " and so far " to the end of the paragraph. Schedules 7 and 8. In Schedule 11 paragraph 2.

Statutory instruments

Serial No.	Title	Extent of repeal
S.I. 1970/173.	Capital Gains Tax (Exempt Gilt-edged Securities) Order 1970.	The whole order.
S.I. 1970/1741.	Capital Gains Tax (Exempt Gilt-edged Securities) (No. 2) Order 1970.	The whole order.
S.I. 1971/793.	Capital Gains Tax (Exempt Gilt-edged Securities) Order 1971.	The whole order.
S.I. 1971/1366.	Capital Gains Tax (Exempt Gilt-edged Securities) (No. 2) Order 1971.	The whole order.
S.I. 1971/1786.	Capital Gains Tax (Exempt Gilt-edged Securities) (No. 3) Order 1971.	The whole order.
S.I. 1972/244.	Capital Gains Tax (Exempt Gilt-edged Securities) Order 1972.	The whole order.
S.I. 1972/1015.	Capital Gains Tax (Exempt Gilt-edged Securities) (No. 2) Order 1972.	The whole order.
S.I. 1973/241.	Capital Gains Tax (Exempt Gilt-edged Securities) Order 1973.	The whole order.
S.I. 1973/716.	Capital Gains Tax (Exempt Gilt-edged Securities) (No. 2) Order 1973.	The whole order.
S.I. 1973/1769.	Capital Gains Tax (Exempt Gilt-edged Securities) (No. 3) Order 1973.	The whole order.
S.I. 1974/693.	Capital Gains Tax (Exempt Gilt-edged Securities) Order 1974.	The whole order.
S.I. 1974/1071.	Capital Gains Tax (Exempt Gilt-edged Securities) (No. 2) Order 1974.	The whole order.
S.I. 1974/1907.	Capital Gains Tax (Exempt Gilt-edged Securities (No. 3) Order 1974.	The whole order.
S.I. 1975/354.	Capital Gains Tax (Exempt Gilt-edged Securities) Order 1975.	The whole order.
S.I. 1975/1129.	Capital Gains Tax (Exempt Gilt-edged Securities) (No. 2) Order 1975.	The whole order.
S.I. 1975/1757.	Capital Gains Tax (Exempt Gilt-edged Securities) (No. 3) Order 1975.	The whole order.
S.I. 1976/698.	Capital Gains Tax (Exempt Gilt-edged Securities) (No. 1) Order 1976.	The whole order.
S.I. 1976/1859.	Capital Gains Tax (Exempt Gilt-edged Securities) (No. 2) Order 1976.	The whole order.
S.I. 1977/347.	Capital Gains Tax (Exempt Gilt-edged Securities) (No. 1) Order 1977.	The whole order.
S.I. 1977/919.	Capital Gains Tax (Exempt Gilt-edged Securities) (No. 2) Order 1977.	The whole order.
S.I. 1977/1136.	Capital Gains Tax (Exempt Gilt-edged Securities) (No. 3) Order 1977.	The whole order.
S.I. 1977/1614.	Capital Gains Tax (Exempt Gilt-edged Securities) (No. 4) Order 1977.	The whole order.
S.I. 1978/141.	Capital Gains Tax (Exempt Gilt-edged Securities) (No. 1) Order 1978.	The whole order.
S.I. 1978/1312.	Capital Gains Tax (Exempt Gilt-edged Securities) (No. 2) Order 1978.	The whole order.
S.I. 1978/1838.	Capital Gains Tax (Exempt Gilt-edged Securities) (No. 3) Order 1978.	The whole order.

General Note

This Schedule provides for the repeal of other enactments consequent on the enactment of this consolidation Act.

House of Commons (Redistribution of Seats) Act 1979

(1979 c. 15)

An Act to increase the number of constituencies in Northern Ireland required by rule 1 in Schedule 2 to the House of Commons (Redistribution of Seats) Act 1949. [22nd March 1979]

General Note

This Act increases the number of constituencies in Northern Ireland.

S. 1 provides for the increase in number of Northern Ireland constituencies; s. 2 deals with citation.

The Act received the Royal Assent on March 22, 1979, and came into force on that date.

Parliamentary debates

Hansard, H.C. Vol. 957, col. 960; Vol. 959, col. 236; Vol. 960, col. 1839; H.L. Vol. 397, col. 1168; Vol. 398, col. 1408; Vol. 399, col. 758.

Increase of number of constituencies in Northern Ireland

1.—(1) In rule 1 of the rules for the redistribution of seats set out in Schedule 2 to the House of Commons (Redistribution of Seats) Act 1949 (referred to below in this section as " the principal Act ") for the figure " 12 " (the required number of constituencies for Northern Ireland) there shall be substituted the words " Not greater than 18 or less than 16 ".

(2) Notwithstanding subsection (1) above, in discharging their functions under section 2 of the principal Act, the Boundary Commission for Northern Ireland shall read rule 1 as if it required the number of constituencies in Northern Ireland to be 17, unless it appears to the Commission that Northern Ireland should for the time being be divided into 16 or (as the case may be) into 18 constituencies.

(3) In framing their first report after the passing of this Act under section 2 (1) of the principal Act, the Boundary Commission for Northern Ireland shall read rule 5 of those rules (under which the electorate of a constituency is to be brought as near the electoral quota as is practicable having regard to the other rules) in accordance with the definitions given in subsection (4) below instead of in accordance with rule 7 of those rules.

(4) In rule 5 as it applies by virtue of subsection (3) above—

(*a*) " electoral quota " shall mean a number obtained by dividing the aggregate electorate (as defined in paragraph (*b*) below) of all the constituencies in Northern Ireland by 17; and

(*b*) " electorate " shall mean, in relation to any constituency, the number of persons whose names appear on the register of parliamentary electors in force for the constituency at the passing of this Act under the Representation of the People Acts.

(5) For subsections (5) and (6) of section 28 of the Northern Ireland Constitution Act 1973 (effect of Orders in Council under the principal Act on elections to the Northern Ireland Assembly) there shall be substituted the following subsections—

" (5) An Order in Council under the said Act of 1949 for giving effect, with or without modifications, to the recommendations contained in a report or supplementary report of the Boundary Commission for Northern Ireland may make amendments consequential on giving effect to those recommendations in section 1 (1) of and in the Schedule to the said Act of 1973.

(6) The coming into force of any such Order in Council shall not affect any election to the Assembly before the next general election to the Assembly or affect the constitution of the Assembly then in being."

(6) In framing their first supplementary report after the passing of this Act under section 28 (supplementary reports with respect to the number of members to be returned to the Northern Ireland Assembly by each constituency in Northern Ireland), the Boundary Commission for Northern Ireland shall read subsection (3) of that section (which requires the ratio of the electorate of each constituency to the number of members to be returned by that constituency to be as far as practicable the same in every constituency) as if the electorate were defined by reference to the enumeration date.

Citation

2. This Act may be cited as the House of Commons (Redistribution of Seats) Act 1979, and shall be included among the Acts which may be cited as the Representation of the People Acts, and this Act and the House of Commons (Redistribution of Seats) Acts 1949 and 1958 may be cited together as the House of Commons (Redistribution of Seats) Acts 1949 to 1979.

Criminal Evidence Act 1979 *

(1979 c. 16)

An Act to amend paragraph (*f*) (iii) of the proviso to section 1 of the Criminal Evidence Act 1898 and corresponding enactments extending to Scotland and Northern Ireland.

[22nd March 1979]

General Note

Where A and B are tried together, and A gives evidence against B, this Act permits B to cross-examine A to show that A is a person of bad character. It implements a proposal of the Criminal Law Revision Committee contained in its Eleventh Report (Evidence—General), Cmnd. 4991, pp. 84, 178 and 219.

One principle of criminal evidence is that the accused's general bad character must be kept from the jury. Another is that the accused may attack the character of anyone who gives evidence against him in order to undermine the witness's credibility. These principles conflict where two or more persons are accused in the same proceedings, and one gives evidence against another. The Criminal Evidence Act 1898, s. 1 (*f*) (iii) resolved this conflict with a compromise:

> " A person charged and called as a witness in pursuance of this Act shall not be asked, and if asked shall not be required to answer, any question tending to show that he has committed or been convicted of or been charged with any offence other than that wherewith he is then charged, or is of bad character, unless— . . . he has given evidence against any other person *charged with the same offence*."

—a solution adopted for Scotland and for Northern Ireland as well. The words in italics meant that where A and B were charged in the same proceedings with the same offence, A could cross-examine B on his bad character if B gave evidence against him, but where the two accused were charged in the same proceedings with different offences, he could not. This was unsatisfactory. Whether joint defendants are charged with the same or different offences is often a technicality within the control of the prosecutor, and the reasons for promoting A's right to cross-examine B as to character above B's right to have his bad character kept from the jury in this general situation obtain at least as strongly where A and B are tried together for different offences as where they are tried together for the same offence (see Peter Mirfield, " The meaning of ' the same offence ' in s. 1 (*f*) (iii) " [1978] Crim.L.R. 725, 729). These problems were pointed out by the Criminal Law Revision Committee in its Eleventh Report, and again by the House of Lords in *R.* v. *Hills* [1978] 3 W.L.R. 423—a decision which accentuated the problems by putting the narrowest possible interpretation upon the words " charged with the same offence," so narrowing the application of s. 1 (*f*) (iii). Soon after *R.* v. *Hills*, Viscount Dilhorne, who had given the main speech in that case, introduced in the House of Lords a Bill which after an easy passage through both Houses became this Act.

Parliamentary Debates

Hansard, H.L. Vol. 398, cols. 243–250, 1906; H.C. Vol. 963, cols. 1722–1723; Vol. 964, col. 1058.

Extent

This Act extends to Scotland and to Northern Ireland.

Commencement

This Act came into force on April 22, 1979.

* Annotations by J. R. Spencer, M.A., LL.B., Lecturer in Law, Fellow of Selwyn College, Cambridge.

Amendment of section 1 of Criminal Evidence Act 1898, etc., and transitional provision

1.—(1) In paragraph (*f*) (iii) of the proviso to each of the following enactments, that is to say, section 1 of the Criminal Evidence Act 1898, sections 141 and 346 of the Criminal Procedure (Scotland) Act 1975 and section 1 of the Criminal Evidence Act (Northern Ireland) 1923 (under which an accused person who has given evidence against another person charged with the same offence may be cross-examined about his previous convictions and his bad character), for the words " with the same offence " there shall be substituted the words " in the same proceedings ".

(2) Notwithstanding subsection (1) above, a person charged with any offence who, before the coming into force of this Act, has given evidence against any other person charged in the same proceedings shall not by reason of that fact be asked or required to answer any question which he could not have been asked and required to answer but for that subsection.

General Note

Subs. 1 amends the Criminal Evidence Act 1898, s. 1 (*f*) (iii) and the corresponding Scottish and Northern Irish provisions by changing "charged with the same offence" into "charged in the same proceedings." It thereby permits A to cross-examine his co-accused B if B gives evidence against A, no matter what offences each is charged with. The wording adopted is even wider than what the Criminal Law Revision Committee proposed, which was "*jointly* charged with him in the same proceedings"—a formula which might have kept alive some of the difficulties which it was designed to remedy.

Subs. 2 prevents the change affecting the position of an accused who has already given evidence against his co-accused when the Act comes into effect.

Short title and commencement

2.—(1) This Act may be cited as the Criminal Evidence Act 1979.

(2) This Act shall come into force at the end of the period of one month beginning with the date on which it is passed.

General Note

This Act came into force on April 22, 1979.

Vaccine Damage Payments Act 1979 *

(1979 c. 17)

ARRANGEMENT OF SECTIONS

SECT.

An Act to provide for payments to be made out of public funds in cases where severe disablement occurs as a result of vaccination against certain diseases or of contact with a person who has been vaccinated against any of those diseases; to make provision in connection with similar payments made before the passing of this Act; and for purposes connected therewith. [22nd March 1979]

General Note

Background

Although adults may be advised to have specified vaccinations in certain circumstances the prime objective of the vaccination programme is to reduce the risk of children catching serious diseases. Vaccination is not compulsory in the United Kingdom although the D.H.S.S. and the Health Departments of Scotland, Wales and Northern Ireland strongly recommend that children be vaccinated against diphtheria, tetanus, whooping cough, poliomyelitis, measles, and tuberculosis, and rubella for girls only. In making these recommendations the D.H.S.S. offers detailed advice to general practitioners and health authorities on contra-indications to vaccination. The latest advice is contained in D.H.S.S. circular CMO (77) 7, dated March 31, 1977. In 1974 Area Health Authorities in England and Wales and Area Health Boards in Scotland took over from the former local health authorities statutory responsibility for providing local vaccination services.

The vaccination programmes have made a very significant contribution to improving the nation's health. Since vaccination against the diseases referred to above was introduced the number of people suffering from these diseases, and in particular the number of deaths, has decreased sharply. For example, when routine vaccination for poliomyelitis was introduced in 1955 there were 6,000 notifications of the disease and 270 deaths. In 1973 there were five notifications and no deaths.

In the early 1970s doubts about the safety and effectiveness of whooping cough vaccine were expressed by a section of the medical profession and by a group of parents of handicapped children. In 1973 two of these parents formed the Association of Vaccine Damaged Children with a view to launching a campaign to press the Government to set up a scheme of compensation for children injured as a result of vaccination. The publicity surrounding this campaign resulted in the Association receiving 1,200 letters from parents claiming that whooping cough vaccine was responsible for severe damage to their children. After initial resistance the D.H.S.S. referred these letters to the Committee on Safety of Medicines for investigation.

* Annotations by Richard Jones, M.A., Solicitor, Lecturer in the Department of Social Administration and School of Social Work, University College, Cardiff.

This investigation will take a "considerable time to complete" (H.C. Written Answer, June 30, 1977). During this period there was a dramatic reduction in the number of children who were being vaccinated against whooping cough. In England, by the end of 1972, 79 per cent. of children born in 1970 had been vaccinated against whooping cough. By 1976, in respect of children born in 1974, this figure had fallen to 38 per cent. There was also a smaller reduction in the number of children being vaccinated against other diseases. (For a review of the evidence on whooping cough vaccination see the report of the Joint Committee on Vaccination and Immunization, *Whooping Cough Vaccination*, HMSO, 1977.)

The Association's campaign for compensation was led in Parliament by Mr. Jack Ashley. Apart from arranging a number of (sometimes acrimonious) debates on the issue he also asked the Parliamentary Commissioner for Administration to investigate the cases of four children who were said to have suffered brain damage after whooping cough vaccinations. The Commissioner's report (Whooping Cough Vaccination, H.C. 571) criticised the D.H.S.S. for not having earlier recognised the desirability of alerting parents to the risks and contra-indications of vaccination. The Association also brought a complaint before the European Commission on Human Rights asserting that the Government were in breach of art. 2 of the European Convention on Human Rights (right to life) and art. 8 (right to respect for private and family life). The Commission decided that the complaint was not admissible.

The Government's initial response to the campaign was lukewarm and two reasons were given for not setting up a compensation scheme. First, it was felt that it would be wrong for the Government to pre-empt the report of the Royal Commission on Civil Liability and Compensation for Personal Injury, knowing that the question of vaccine damage to children was within its terms of reference. Secondly, there was resistance to the idea of discriminating between one set of handicapped children and another. However, intense parliamentary and public pressure and the decline in children being vaccinated persuaded the Government to approach the Chairman of the Royal Commission to inquire whether the Commission had reached any conclusions about vaccine damaged children. Immediately after the Government received Lord Pearson's reply that the Commission had agreed that "some kind of financial assistance should be made available for very serious injury resulting from vaccination recommended by a public health authority," the Secretary of State for Social Services, David Ennals, announced to the House of Commons on March 14, 1977, that the Government had "decided to accept in principle that there should be a scheme of payments for vaccine damaged children and that the scheme would apply to existing, as well as to new, cases." But the Government delayed reaching any conclusions about qualifying criteria for, or about other detailed aspects of, a compensation scheme until they had considered the report of the Royal Commission.

The Royal Commission's Report

The Commission's report (Cmnd. 7054), which was published in March 1978, devoted a separate chapter to the question of compensation for vaccine damaged children (paras 1377–1413). The Commission recognised that, although in certain cases it might be possible for servicemen who are vaccine damaged to receive compensation through the armed forces pension scheme, and civilians who are damaged by vaccination arising out of their work may be eligible for benefits under the industrial injuries scheme, the only possible source of compensation for the majority of vaccine damaged people is to claim damages in an action for negligence. However, as the Commission point out, an action in tort against a doctor who performs a vaccination in recognised circumstances and using recognised methods would be unlikely to succeed since the doctor could not be said to be acting outside the bounds of proper practice. (See H. Teff, "Compensating Vaccine-Damaged Children" (1977) 127 New L.J. 904, for a discussion on tortious liability.)

The Commission proposed that the vaccine damaged child should be considered with other severely disabled children, irrespective of cause of disablement, and be eligible for a new non-taxable disability income of £4 per week (at 1977 figures). Where vaccine damage can be proved to have followed from medical procedures recommended by the Government, the Commission recommend that those who suffer serious damage should be entitled to bring an action in tort against the Government on the basis of strict liability. The problem of proving causation was recognised and the Commission repeated the finding of the Joint Committee on Vaccination and Immunisation that there are no clinical tests which can distinguish convulsions that are caused by the whooping cough vaccine and convulsions that occur naturally. Nevertheless, they saw no need to suggest that the courts should adopt a different approach to the proof of causation than that of assessing the balance of probabilities as in the case of other tort actions.

Outline of the Act

As it became clear to the Government that they would need to give detailed and prolonged consideration to all of the recommendations made by the Royal Commission it was decided to take immediate action to introduce a scheme to compensate vaccine damaged children. Details of the scheme were announced in the House of Commons on May 9 and August 2, 1978, and the Bill was given its first reading in the House of Commons on January 24, 1979.

The first two sections constitute the essence of the scheme. They provide for a lump sum payment of £10,000 to be made to any person whom the Secretary of State is satisfied has suffered severe disablement as a result of vaccination. For the purposes of the scheme, such a person must satisfy certain criteria before payment can be made: he or she must have suffered 80 per cent. or greater disablement as a result of vaccination against specified diseases, must have been vaccinated in the United Kingdom or the Isle of Man after July 5, 1948, when the N.H.S. came into existence, and must, except for vaccination against rubella or poliomyelitis, have been vaccinated before reaching the age of 18. These sections also provide for people who have suffered disablement either because their mothers were vaccinated during pregnancy or because of contact with someone else who had been vaccinated against the disease, to receive payment.

S. 3 sets out the procedures by which claims will be submitted to the D.H.S.S. and determined, in the first instance, by the Secretary of State. The question of whether severe disablement has been caused by vaccination is to be decided on the balance of probability. S. 4 provides for independent medical tribunals to review cases disallowed by the Secretary of State because he is not satisfied that severe disablement has resulted from vaccination.

S. 5 enables the Secretary of State to reconsider a determination made on his behalf because of a change of circumstances since the original decision was made, or because of ignorance or a mistake regarding some material fact at the time of the original decision.

The procedure for payment is set out in s. 6. Payment will be made either direct to the disabled person, if he is over 18 and capable of managing his own affairs, or, if not, to trustees appointed by the Secretary of State. This section also makes it clear that payment does not prejudice the right of the disabled person to seek compensation through the courts.

S. 7 ensures that those who have claimed before the Bill received the Royal Assent, and whose claims have not succeeded, will be able to ask for their cases to be reviewed by the independent medical tribunals. Ss. 8 to 12 are of a technical nature.

Comment on the Act

Although the Bill was the subject of some detailed criticisms during its passage through Parliament it received all-party support and was not amended. The payment of £10,000 was criticised as being too small, the 80 per cent. condition was felt by some to be rigid and arbitrary, the lack of provision for those families whose children had died as a result of the vaccine damage before the scheme was announced was criticised, and there was a call for people who had been vaccinated before the July 5, 1948, qualifying date to be included in the scheme.

The rationale for providing compensation for this particular group of handicapped people is, that as vaccination is recommended by the State and is intended not only for the benefit of the individual but also for the benefit of the community at large the State ought to compensate where vaccination causes injury. There is a precedent for this approach in the pension scheme provided for the war disabled and during the debates on the Bill M.P.s attempted to identify other groups of handicapped people, such as women who had been injured through taking the contraceptive pill, who might qualify for compensation under this principle. One unintended consequence of this cause-based, as opposed to needs-based, approach to compensation for the handicapped could be to delay the introduction of a comprehensive compensation scheme for all handicapped people.

Commencement

The Act came into force on March 22, 1979, the day it received the Royal Assent.

Extent

This Act extends to Scotland, Northern Ireland and the Isle of Man.

Regulations

The Vaccine Damage Payments Regulations 1979 (S.I. 1979 No. 432) were made by the Secretary of State on April 5, 1979.

Parliamentary Debates

Hansard, H.C. Vol. 962, cols. 32–86 (Second Reading), cols. 1376–1424 (Committee); H.L. Vol. 399, cols. 303–321 (Second Reading).

Payments to persons severely disabled by vaccination

1.—(1) If, on consideration of a claim, the Secretary of State is satisfied—

(*a*) that a person is, or was immediately before his death, severely disabled as a result of vaccination against any of the diseases to which this Act applies; and

(*b*) that the conditions of entitlement which are applicable in accordance with section 2 below are fulfilled,

he shall in accordance with this Act make a payment of £10,000 to or for the benefit of that person or to his personal representatives.

(2) The diseases to which this Act applies are—

(*a*) diphtheria,
(*b*) tetanus,
(*c*) whooping cough,
(*d*) poliomyelitis,
(*e*) measles,
(*f*) rubella,
(*g*) tuberculosis,
(*h*) smallpox, and
(*i*) any other disease which is specified by the Secretary of State for the purposes of this Act by order made by statutory instrument.

(3) Subject to section 2 (3) below, this Act has effect with respect to a person who is severely disabled as a result of a vaccination given to his mother before he was born as if the vaccination had been given directly to him and, in such circumstances as may be prescribed by regulations under this Act, this Act has effect with respect to a person who is severely disabled as a result of contracting a disease through contact with a third person who was vaccinated against it as if the vaccination had been given to him and the disablement resulted from it.

(4) For the purposes of this Act, a person is severely disabled if he suffers disablement to the extent of 80 per cent. or more, assessed as for the purposes of section 57 of the Social Security Act 1975 or the Social Security (Northern Ireland) Act 1975 (disablement gratuity and pension).

(5) A statutory instrument under subsection (2) (*i*) above shall be subject to annulment in pursuance of a resolution of either House of Parliament.

DEFINITION

"Claim": s. 3 (1).

GENERAL NOTE

Subs. (1)

This specifies the amount of payment and provides for the Secretary of State to make payment.

"*claim.*" Claims should be made to the Vaccine Damage Payments Unit, Department of Health and Social Security, North Fylde Central Offices, Norcross, Blackpool FY5 3TA.

According to D.H.S.S. Circular HN (79) 7 issued in January 1979 it "is expected that, in the first instance, the Department will need to seek information from the claimant's general medical practitioner extracted from his record, and from any records in possession of the Area Health Authority."

"*Secretary of State.*" One of Her Majesty's Principal Secretaries of State (Interpretation Act 1978, s. 5 and Sched. 1).

"*satisfied.*" The question of whether a claimant's severe disablement results from vaccination against any of the diseases to which the Act applies is to be determined on the balance of probability (s. 3 (5)).

"*severely disabled.*" See subs. (4).

"*£10,000.*" This is a lump sum. During the debate on the Second Reading the Secretary of State announced that "the Supplementary Benefits Commission has agreed that if the damaged person is a child it will ignore the £10,000 payment. If the damaged person is an adult, the payment will be taken into account and the Commission will give sympathetic consideration to special circumstances" (H.C. Vol. 962, col. 47).

Subs. (2)

This lists the diseases for which vaccination has been offered as part of public vaccination policies since 1948.

"*by order.*" An order under s. 1 (2) (*i*) specifying a disease may provide that, in relation to vaccination against that disease, the conditions of entitlement specified in s. 2 (1) shall have effect subject to such conditions as may be specified in that order (s. 2 (2)).

Subs. (3)

This ensures that a payment may be made to a person who is severely disabled as a result of vaccination given to his mother before he was born and to a person severely disabled as a result of contracting a disease through contact with a third party.

"*result.*" This is to be determined on the balance of probability (s. 3 (5)).

"*regulations.*" "We do not know whether any payment will fall to be made under this provision but, if there is a case, the circumstances will have to be very minutely defined" (Mr. Alfred Morris, H.C. Vol. 962, col. 1388).

"*it.*" One of the diseases to which the Act applies.

Subs. (4)

The provisions as to the method of assessment of disablement can be found in Sched. 8 to the Social Security Act 1975 or the Social Security (Northern Ireland) Act 1975. The general principle of assessment is to take into account the disabilities incurred by the claimant as a result of the relevant loss of faculty ". . . to which the claimant may be expected, having regard to his physical and mental condition at the date of the assessment, to be subject during the period taken into account by the assessment as compared with a person of the same age and sex whose physical and mental condition is normal" (Sched. 8, para. 1 (*a*)). Apart from the element of comparison mentioned in para. 1 (*a*) the assessment is objective and "shall be made without reference to the particular circumstances of the claimant other than age, sex, and physical and mental condition" (Sched. 8, para. 1 (*c*)). This formulation pays little regard to the social consequences of disablement. Para. 1 (*d*) states: "the disabilities resulting from such loss of faculty as may be prescribed shall be taken as amounting to 100 per cent. disablement and other disabilities shall be assessed accordingly." No regulations have been made under this paragraph.

Conditions of entitlement

2.—(1) Subject to the provisions of this section, the conditions of entitlement referred to in section 1 (1) (*b*) above are—

(*a*) that the vaccination in question was carried out—
(i) in the United Kingdom or the Isle of Man, and
(ii) on or after 5th July 1948, and
(iii) in the case of vaccination against smallpox, before 1st August 1971;

(*b*) except in the case of vaccination against poliomyelitis or rubella, that the vaccination was carried out either at a time when the person to whom it was given was under the age of eighteen or at the time of an outbreak within the United Kingdom or the Isle of Man of the disease against which the vaccination was given; and

(*c*) that the disabled person was over the age of two on the date when the claim was made or, if he died before that date, that he died after 9th May 1978 and was over the age of two when he died.

(2) An order under section 1 (2) (*i*) above specifying a disease for the purposes of this Act may provide that, in relation to vaccination against that disease, the conditions of entitlement specified in subsection (1) above shall have effect subject to such modifications as may be specified in the order.

(3) In a case where this Act has effect by virtue of section 1 (3) above, the reference in subsection (1) (*b*) above to the person to whom a vaccination was given is a reference to the person to whom it was actually given and not to the disabled person.

(4) With respect to claims made after such date as may be specified in the order and relating to vaccination against such disease as may be so specified, the Secretary of State may by order made by statutory instrument—

(*a*) provide that, in such circumstances as may be specified in the order, one or more of the conditions of entitlement appropriate to vaccination against that disease need not be fulfilled; or

(*b*) add to the conditions of entitlement which are appropriate to vaccination against that disease, either generally or in such circumstances as may be specified in the order.

(5) Regulations under this Act shall specify the cases in which vaccinations given outside the United Kingdom and the Isle of Man to persons defined in the regulations as serving members of Her Majesty's forces or members of their families are to be treated for the purposes of this Act as carried out in England.

(6) The Secretary of State shall not make an order containing any provision made by virtue of paragraph (*b*) of subsection (4) above unless a draft of the order has been laid before Parliament and approved by a resolution of each House; and a statutory instrument by which any other order is made under that subsection shall be subject to annulment in pursuance of a resolution of either House of Parliament.

Definitions

"claims": s. 3 (1).
"disabled person": s. 3 (1).

General Note

This section contains the main conditions for entitlement, including the requirement that the vaccination took place in the United Kingdom or the Isle of Man after July 5, 1948, and in the case of smallpox, that the vaccination took place prior to August 1, 1971, when smallpox vaccination ceased to be part of the routine programme. In general these routine programmes relate only to vaccination of children and accordingly, except in the case of vaccination against rubella or poliomyelitis, there is a general condition that the vaccination took place when the person in question was under the age of 18, subject to an exception where vaccination takes place during an outbreak of the disease. Orders under subs. (4) may, however, modify these conditions.

Subs. (1)

"*5th July* 1948." The date of the establishment of the National Health Service.

"*poliomyelitis or rubella.*" Exceptions to the rule that the present routine public policy vaccination scheme is for the vaccination of children.

"*to whom it was given.*" See note to subs. (3).

"*outbreak.*" This is not defined. It is submitted that one identified case of a disease to which the Act applies could constitute an outbreak.

"*9th May* 1978." The date when the outline of the scheme was announced to the House of Commons.

Subs. (3)

Where a claim is made under s. 1 (3) the person to whom the vaccination was actually given must have been under the age of 18 at the time when the vaccination was carried out. The age limit of 18 years will not apply if the vaccination was against poliomyelitis or rubella or if the vaccination was given at the time of an outbreak within the United Kingdom or the Isle of Man of the disease against which the vaccination was given.

Subs. (5)

"*serving members of Her Majesty's forces.*" The scheme does not cover civilians employed in overseas service establishments or members of the diplomatic service serving abroad.

By reg. 5 of the Vaccine Damage Payments Regulations 1979 (S.I. 1979 No. 432), vaccinations given outside the United Kingdom and the Isle of Man to serving members of Her Majesty's forces or members of their families should be treated for the purposes of this Act as carried out in England where the vaccination in question has been given as part of medical facilities provided under arrangements made by or on behalf of the service authorities.

For the purposes of this subsection, "serving members of Her Majesty's forces" means a member of the naval, military or air forces of the Crown or any women's service administered by the Defence Council. The family of a serving member of Her Majesty's forces shall consist of the spouse of such member and the child or children whose requirements are provided by him (reg. 5 (2)).

Determination of claims

3.—(1) Any reference in this Act, other than section 7, to a claim is a reference to a claim for a payment under section 1 (1) above which is made—

(*a*) by or on behalf of the disabled person concerned or, as the case may be, by his personal representatives; and

(*b*) in the manner prescribed by regulations under this Act; and

(*c*) within the period of six years beginning on the latest of the following dates, namely, the date of the vaccination to which the claim relates, the date on which the disabled person attained the age of two and 9th May 1978;

and, in relation to a claim, any reference to the claimant is a reference to the person by whom the claim was made and any reference to the disabled person is a reference to the person in respect of whose disablement a payment under subsection (1) above is claimed to be payable.

(2) As soon as practicable after he has received a claim, the Secretary of State shall give notice in writing to the claimant of his determination whether he is satisfied that a payment is due under section 1 (1) above to or for the benefit of the disabled person or to his personal representatives.

(3) If the Secretary of State is not satisfied that a payment is due as

mentioned in subsection (2) above, the notice in writing under that subsection shall state the grounds on which he is not so satisfied.

(4) If, in the case of any claim, the Secretary of State—

(*a*) is satisfied that the conditions of entitlement which are applicable in accordance with section 2 above are fulfilled, but

(*b*) is not satisfied that the disabled person is or, where he has died, was immediately before his death severely disabled as a result of vaccination against any of the diseases to which this Act applies,

the notice in writing under subsection (2) above shall inform the claimant that, if an application for review is made to the Secretary of State, the matters referred to in paragraph (*b*) above will be reviewed by an independent medical tribunal in accordance with section 4 below.

(5) If in any case a person is severely disabled, the question whether his severe disablement results from vaccination against any of the diseases to which this Act applies shall be determined for the purposes of this Act on the balance of probability.

DEFINITION

" severely disabled ": s. 1 (4).

GENERAL NOTE

This section deals with the determination of claims. Claims will initially be considered by the Secretary of State and, if he is not satisfied that a payment is due, a notice stating the grounds for disallowance must be given. Where the notice states that the Secretary of State is not satisfied that the claimant is severely disabled as a result of vaccination, the notice must specify the arrangements for referring the question to a tribunal. Subs. (5) provides that the question whether the severe disablement results from vaccination is to be determined on the balance of probability.

Subs. (1)

" *section* 7." This section deals with cases where claims have been made prior to the Act receiving the Royal Assent.

Subs. (4)

" *died.*" The death must have occurred after May 9, 1978, with the person being over the age of two when he died (s. 2 (1) (*c*)).

Subs. (5)

" *balance of probability.*" This is the standard of proof generally required in civil cases. " If the evidence is such that the tribunal can say ' we think it more probable than not ', the burden is discharged, but if the probabilities are equal it is not ": *per* Denning J. in *Miller* v. *Minister of Pensions* [1947] 2 All E.R. 372, 373–374. " In some cases the decision will be relatively easy; the medical evidence will show that severe convulsions and brain damage occurred soon after vaccination, and unless the evidence of some other cause is very persuasive indeed, the claim will be accepted. At the other end of the spectrum there will be cases in which there is strong evidence pointing to a congenital condition, or some other cause, or in which the symptoms have first shown themselves a long time after vaccination. Many cases will fall somewhere between these two extremes ": *per* Lord Wells-Pestell, H.L. Vol. 44, cols. 306–307. As conclusive medical evidence will not be available in many cases the proximity of the vaccination to the occurrence of the handicap is likely to be a crucial factor in determining causation. The absence of medical records will prove problematic in some cases because most medical records are destroyed after a 20 to 25 years period.

Review of extent of disablement and causation by independent tribunals

4.—(1) Regulations under this Act shall make provision for inde-

pendent medical tribunals to determine matters referred to them under this section, and such regulations may make provision with respect to—

(*a*) the terms of appointment of the persons who are to serve on the tribunals;

(*b*) the procedure to be followed for the determination of matters referred to the tribunals;

(*c*) the summoning of persons to attend to give evidence or produce documents before the tribunals and the administration of oaths to such persons.

(2) Where an application for review is made to the Secretary of State as mentioned in section 3 (4) above, then, subject to subsection (3) below, the Secretary of State shall refer to a tribunal under this section—

(*a*) the question of the extent of the disablement suffered by the disabled person;

(*b*) the question whether he is or, as the case may be, was immediately before his death disabled as a result of the vaccination to which the claim relates; and

(*c*) the question whether, if he is or was so disabled, the extent of his disability is or was such as to amount to severe disablement.

(3) The Secretary of State may refer to differently constituted tribunals the questions in paragraphs (*a*) to (*c*) of subsection (2) above, and the Secretary of State need not refer to a tribunal any of those questions if—

(*a*) he and the claimant are not in dispute with respect to it; or

(*b*) the decision of a tribunal on another of those questions is such that the disabled person cannot be or, as the case may be, could not immediately before his death have been severely disabled as a result of the vaccination to which the claim relates.

(4) For the purposes of this Act, the decision of a tribunal on a question referred to them under this section shall be conclusive except in so far as it falls to be reconsidered by virtue of section 5 below.

DEFINITIONS

" claim ": s. 3 (1).
" claimant ": s. 3 (1)
" disabled person ": s. 3 (1).
" severe disablement: s. 1 (4).

GENERAL NOTE

This section provides for regulations to make provision for independent medical tribunals to determine whether disabled persons are severely disabled as a result of vaccination. Different issues may be referred to differently constituted tribunals. The section provides that the decisions of a tribunal on the questions referred to it are to be conclusive for the purposes of the Act. By s. 12 (3) (*b*) the expenses of those required to attend before tribunals shall be paid by the Secretary of State.

Regs. 7–10 of the Vaccine Damage Payments Regulations 1979 (S.I. 1979 No. 432) deal with review by tribunals. The tribunals, which shall be known as vaccine damage tribunals, shall consist of a chairman and two medical practitioners. The Secretary of State and the claimant shall have the right to be heard and may be represented at the hearing of a tribunal, which shall be in public except in so far as the chairman may for special reasons otherwise direct. The tribunal shall include in its written decision a statement of the reasons for its decision. Reg. 10 enables the tribunal to take into account medical evidence which in the opinion of the chairman it would be undesirable in the interests of the claimant or the disabled person to disclose.

Subs. (4)

" *conclusive.*" *I.e.* binding on the Secretary of State. However, a decision of a tribunal may be reconsidered by the Secretary of State under the provisions of s. 5.

Reconsideration of determinations and recovery of payments in certain cases

5.—(1) Subject to subsection (2) below, the Secretary of State may reconsider a determination that a payment should not be made under section 1 (1) above on the ground—

(*a*) that there has been a material change of circumstances since the determination was made, or

(*b*) that the determination was made in ignorance of, or was based on a mistake as to, some material fact,

and the Secretary of State may, on the ground set out in paragraph (*b*) above, reconsider a determination that such a payment should be made.

(2) Regulations under this Act shall prescribe the manner and the period in which—

(*a*) an application may be made to the Secretary of State for his reconsideration of a determination; and

(*b*) the Secretary of State may of his own motion institute such a reconsideration.

(3) The Secretary of State shall give notice in writing of his decision on a reconsideration under this section to the person who was the claimant in relation to the claim which gave rise to the determination which has been reconsidered and also, where the disabled person is alive and was not the claimant, to him; and the provisions of subsections (3) to (5) of section 3 and section 4 above shall apply as if—

(*a*) the notice under this subsection were a notice under section 3 (2) above; and

(*b*) any reference in those provisions to the claimant were a reference to the person who was the claimant in relation to the claim which gave rise to the determination which has been reconsidered.

(4) If, whether fraudulently or otherwise, any person misrepresents or fails to disclose any material fact and in consequence of the misrepresentation or failure a payment is made under section 1 (1) above, the person to whom the payment was made shall be liable to repay the amount of that payment to the Secretary of State unless he can show that the misrepresentation or failure occurred without his connivance or consent.

(5) Except as provided by subsection (4) above, no payment under section 1 (1) above shall be recoverable by virtue of a reconsideration of a determination under this section.

DEFINITIONS

"claim": s. 3 (1).
"claimant": s. 3 (1).
"disabled person": s. 3 (1).

GENERAL NOTE

This section enables the Secretary of State to reconsider a determination that a payment should or should not be made in certain circumstances. In the case where a determination has been made that a payment should be made, and the payment has been duly made, the sum paid can be recovered only in cases of misrepresentation or failure to disclose a material fact.

By reg. 11 of the Vaccine Damage Payments Regulations 1979 (S.I. 1979 No. 432), an application for reconsideration of a determination may be made to the Secretary of State within six years of the date of the notice of that determination. The Secretary of State may of his own motion institute a reconsideration of a determination within six years of the date of the notice of that determination but where it appears to him that a payment was made in consequence of a misrepresentation or failure to disclose any material facts he may institute a reconsideration of a determination at any time.

Subs. (1)

Note that the Secretary of State can only reconsider a determination that a payment should be made on the ground set out in para. (*b*). For liability to repay, see subs. (5)

"*material change of circumstances.*" In *Re Cement Makers' Federation Agreement* (*No.* 2) [1974] I.C.R. 445, the Restrictive Practices Court held that the phrase "material change in the relevant circumstances," in s. 22 (4) of the Restrictive Trade Practices Act 1956, meant a change in an essential part of the reasoning by which the court had reached its previous decision.

"*material fact.*" A fact which would influence the judgment of the Secretary of State.

Subs. (3)

This allows for the decision on a reconsideration to be reviewed by an independent medical tribunal.

Subs. (4)

"*fraudulently.*" This involves the use of deceit. "'Fraud' in my opinion, is a term that should be reserved for something dishonest and morally wrong . . ." (*per* Wills J., *Ex p. Watson* (1888) 21 Q.B.D. 301).

"*misrepresents.*" "In my opinion any behaviour, by words or conduct, is sufficient to be a misrepresentation if it is such as to mislead the other party. . . If it conveys a false impression that is enough": *per* Denning L.J., *Curtis* v. *Chemical Cleaning and Dyeing Co. Ltd.* [1951] 1 K.B. 805. See s. 9 for the offence of making a false statement for the purpose of obtaining any payment under the Act.

"*the person to whom the payment was made.*" The disabled person, or, where the disabled person has died, his personal representatives, or the trustees (s. 6 (1)–(3)).

"*connivance.*" Where a person assists in a wrongful act or, having a duty to interfere, fails to interfere to prevent the wrongful act taking place.

Payments to or for the benefit of disabled persons

6.—(1) Where a payment under section 1 (1) above falls to be made in respect of a disabled person who is over eighteen and capable of managing his own affairs, the payment shall be made to him.

(2) Where such a payment falls to be made in respect of a disabled person who has died, the payment shall be made to his personal representatives.

(3) Where such a payment falls to be made in respect of any other disabled person, the payment shall be made for his benefit by paying it to such trustees as the Secretary of State may appoint to be held by them upon such trusts or, in Scotland, for such purposes and upon such conditions as may be declared by the Secretary of State.

(4) The making of a claim for, or the receipt of, a payment under section 1 (1) above does not prejudice the right of any person to institute or carry on proceedings in respect of disablement suffered as a result of vaccination against any disease to which this Act applies; but in any civil proceedings brought in respect of disablement resulting from vaccination against such a disease, the court shall treat a payment made to or in respect of the disabled person concerned under section 1 (1) above as paid on account of any damages which the court awards in respect of such disablement.

DEFINITIONS

"claim": s. 3 (1).

"disabled person": s. 3 (1).

GENERAL NOTE

This section provides that, where the disabled person is over 18 and capable of managing his own affairs, the payment is to be made direct to him. In all other cases the payment is to be made to trustees, in accordance with trusts declared by the Secretary of State. Subs. (4) ensures that payments do not prejudice the right to institute proceedings in respect of disablement due to vaccination. Any payment made will, however, fall to be taken into account as paid in respect of any damages awarded.

Subs. (1)

"*Capable of managing his own affairs.*" A judgment to be made by the Secretary of State.

Subs. (2)

"*died.*" The death must have occurred after May 9, 1978, with the person being over the age of two when he died (s. 2 (1) (*c*)).

Subs. (3)

"*trustees.*" It is envisaged that the trustees will normally be the parents or relatives who are looking after the disabled person. In other cases the Public Trustee will probably be appointed to administer the trust (H.C. Vol. 962, col. 82).

"*trusts.*" The original proposal, given to the House of Commons in a written reply on August 2, 1978, was that one-half of the money would be held in trust for the benefit of the disabled person and the remainder would be used for the benefit of the family and their needs as a whole. It is now proposed to make an undivided payment subject to a single trust which enables the entirety of the payment to be spent for the benefit of the family as a whole. The trust deed will give a wide discretion to the trustees and the Government gave the following examples of the kind of expenditure that could be authorised under the trust: buying or extending the family home, buying a car or covering the cost of holidays for the whole family or for members of the family other than the disabled person (H.C. Vol. 962 col. 81).

Payments, claims etc. made prior to the Act

7.—(1) Any reference in this section to an extra-statutory payment is a reference to a payment of £10,000 made by the Secretary of State to or in respect of a disabled person after 9th May 1978 and before the passing of this Act pursuant to a non-statutory scheme of payments for severe vaccine damage.

(2) No such claim as is referred to in section 3 (1) above shall be entertained if an extra-statutory payment has been made to or for the benefit of the disabled person or his personal representatives.

(3) For the purposes of section 5 above, a determination that an extra-statutory payment should be made shall be treated as a determination that a payment should be made under section 1 (1) above; and in relation to the reconsideration of such a determination references in subsection (3) of section 5 above to the person who was the claimant in relation to the determination which has been reconsidered shall be construed as references to the person who made the claim for the extra-statutory payment.

(4) Subsections (4) and (5) of section 5 above and section 6 (4) above shall apply in relation to an extra-statutory payment as they apply in relation to a payment made under section 1 (1) above.

(5) For the purposes of this Act (other than this section) regulations under this Act may—

(*a*) treat claims which were made in connection with the scheme referred to in subsection (1) above and which have not been disposed of at the commencement of this Act as claims falling within section 3 (1) above; and

(*b*) treat information and other evidence furnished and other things done before the commencement of this Act in connection with any such claim as is referred to in paragraph (*a*) above as furnished or done in connection with a claim falling within section 3 (1) above.

General Note

This section deals with cases where claims have been made prior to the Act receiving the Royal Assent. Where payment has been made on such claims, on the authority of the Appropriation Act, no further payment can be made under the provisions in the Act but a determination prior to Royal Assent to make a payment may be reconsidered under the arrangements set out in s. 5. By regulations under subs. (5) a claim which has not been disposed of at the time of Royal Assent, will then be dealt with as a claim under the provisions in the Act.

Subs. (1)

"*passing of this Act.*" March 22, 1979.

Subs. (2)

"*claim.*" A claim for payment under s. 1 (1).

Subs. (3)

This enables the Secretary of State to reconsider a determination that an extra-statutory payment should be made on the ground that it was made in ignorance of, or was based on a mistake as to, some material fact. Provision is made for a reconsideration of a determination made under this subsection to be reviewed by an independent medical tribunal.

Subs. (5)

Reg. 6 of the Vaccine Damage Payments Regulations 1979 (S.I. 1979 No. 432) incorporates the provisions of paras. (*a*) and (*b*) of this subsection.

Regulations

8.—(1) Any reference in the preceding provisions of this Act to regulations under this Act is a reference to regulations made by the Secretary of State.

(2) Any power of the Secretary of State under this Act to make regulations—

(*a*) shall be exercisable by statutory instrument which shall be subject to annulment in pursuance of a resolution of either House of Parliament; and

(*b*) includes power to make such incidental or supplementary provision as appears to the Secretary of State to be appropriate.

(3) Regulations made by the Secretary of State may contain provision—

(*a*) with respect to the information and other evidence to be furnished in connection with a claim;

(*b*) requiring disabled persons to undergo medical examination before their claims are determined or for the purposes of a reconsideration under section 5 above;

(*c*) restricting the disclosure of medical evidence and advice tendered in connection with a claim or a reconsideration under section 5 above; and

(*d*) conferring functions on the tribunals constituted under section 4 above with respect to the matters referred to in paragraphs (*a*) to (*c*) above.

Definitions

"claim": s. 3 (1).

"disabled persons": s. 3 (1).

General Note

This section provides for regulations under the Act to be subject to the negative procedure and authorises the making of regulations as to the mode of making claims, medical examinations, the disclosure of medical evidence and the functions of tribunals. The Vaccine Damage Payments Regulations 1979 (S.I. 1979 No. 432) were made on April 5, 1979.

Fraudulent statements etc.

9.—(1) Any person who, for the purpose of obtaining any payment under this Act, whether for himself or some other person,—

(*a*) knowingly makes any false statement or representation, or

(*b*) produces or furnishes or causes or knowingly allows to be produced or furnished any document or information which he knows to be false in a material particular,

shall be liable on summary conviction to a fine not exceeding £1,000.

(2) In the application of subsection (1) above to the Isle of Man, for the words following " liable " there shall be substituted the words " on summary conviction, within the meaning of the Interpretation Act 1976 (an Act of Tynwald), to a fine of £400 and on conviction on information to a fine ".

General Note

This section provides for penalties for the making of a fraudulent claim.

Subs. (1)

" *person.*" This includes a body of persons corporate or unincorporate (Interpretation Act 1978, s. 5 and Sched. 1).

" *purpose.*" " ' Purpose ' connotes an intention by some person to achieve a result desired by him ": *per* Lord Diplock, *Sweet* v. *Parsley* [1969] 1 All E.R. 347, 363–364.

" *knowingly.*" *Mens rea* is required.

" *false in a material particular.*" Relevant material which creates a false impression (see *R.* v. *Kylsant* (*Lord*) [1932] 1 K.B. 442.)

Scotland

10.—(1) In the Scotland Act 1978, at the end of Part III of Schedule 10 (matters dealt with by certain enactments to be included, to the extent specified, in the groups of devolved matters) there shall be added the following entry:—

" The Vaccine Damage Payments Act 1979	Included, except for the matters dealt with in section 2 (5)."

(2) For the purpose of the following provisions of the Scotland Act 1978, this Act shall be deemed to have been passed before the passing of that Act, namely,—

(*a*) section 21 (2) (executive powers);

(*b*) subsections (1) and (2) of section 22 (subordinate instruments);

(*c*) section 60 (modification of enactments providing for payments out of moneys provided by Parliament etc.); and

(*d*) section 82 (construction and amendment of existing enactments).

General Note

This section amends the Scotland Act 1978 so as to provide for the subject matter of the Act, other than s. 2 (5), to be included in devolved matters for the purposes of that Act.

Wales

11.—(1) In Schedule 2 to the Wales Act 1978 (enactments under which, except as provided in the second column thereof, functions of Ministers of the Crown are exercisable as regards Wales by the Welsh Assembly) at the end of Part VI (health and social services) there shall be added the following entry:—

"The Vaccine Damage Payments Act 1979	The power to make regulations under section 2 (5) and, so far as it relates to any regulations made under that section, the power conferred by section 8 (2) (*b*)."

(2) For the purpose of the following provisions of the Wales Act 1978, this Act shall be deemed to have been passed before the passing of that Act, namely,—

(*a*) section 55 (modification of enactments providing for payments out of moneys provided by Parliament etc.);

(*b*) section 74 (construction of references to Ministers); and

(*c*) subsections (2) and (3) of section 77 (amendment of existing enactments).

General Note

This section amends the Wales Act 1978 so as to provide that, as regards Wales, the functions of the Secretary of State under the Act, other than the power to make regulations under s. 2 (5), will fall to be exercised by the Welsh Assembly.

Financial provisions

12.—(1) The Secretary of State shall pay to persons appointed to serve on tribunals under section 4 of this Act such remuneration and such travelling and other allowances as he may, with the consent of the Minister for the Civil Service, determine.

(2) The Secretary of State shall pay such fees as he considers appropriate to medical practitioners, as defined in Schedule 20 to the Social Security Act 1975, who provide information or other evidence in connection with claims.

(3) The Secretary of State shall pay such travelling and other allowances as he may determine—

(*a*) to persons required under this Act to undergo medical examinations;

(*b*) to persons required to attend before tribunals under section 4 above; and

(*c*) in circumstances where he considers it appropriate, to any person who accompanies a disabled person to such a medical examination or tribunal.

(4) There shall be paid out of moneys provided by Parliament—

(*a*) any expenditure incurred by the Secretary of State in making payments under section 1 (1) above;

(*b*) any expenditure incurred by the Secretary of State by virtue of subsections (1) to (3) above; and

(*c*) any increase in the administrative expenses of the Secretary of State attributable to this Act.

(5) Any sums repaid to the Secretary of State by virtue of section 5 (4) above shall be paid into the Consolidated Fund.

Definition

"disabled person": s. 3 (1).

General Note

Subs. (2).

"*medical practitioners.*" "A registered medical practitioner . . . includes a person outside the United Kingdom who is not a registered medical practitioner, but has qualifications corresponding (in the Secretary of State's opinion) to those of a registered medical practitioner." (Social Security Act 1975, Sched. 20).

Short title and extent

13.—(1) This Act may be cited as the Vaccine Damage Payments Act 1979.

(2) This Act extends to Northern Ireland and the Isle of Man.

General Note

Subs. (2)

"*Isle of Man.*" By administrative arrangement the cost of Isle of Man cases will fall on Isle of Man funds (H.C. Vol. 962, col. 1397).

Social Security Act 1979 *

(1979 c. 18)

ARRANGEMENT OF SECTIONS

An Act to amend the law relating to social security.
[22nd March 1979]

General Note

This Act is almost exclusively concerned with effecting amendment, on a variety of distinct matters, of the Social Security Act 1975, the Child Benefit Act 1975, the Social Security Pensions Act 1975, the Supplementary Benefits Act 1976 and the Social Security (Miscellaneous Provisions) Act 1977. It, together with the first, third and fifth of these Acts, may be cited as the Social Security Acts 1975 to 1979 (*post*, s. 21 (1)).

The Royal Assent was granted on March 22, 1979. The Act itself contains no interpretation provision but see Social Security Act 1975, Sched. 20, Social Security Pensions Act 1975, s. 66, and Supplementary Benefits Act 1976, s. 34.

* Annotations by Professor Harry Calvert, Dean of the Faculty of Law, University College, Cardiff.

Commencement

Ss. 11 and 12, Sched. 1, paras. 2–22, and Sched. 3, paras. 5–7, 11, 14–20, 22, 23, and 29 (*a*) (*b*) came into force on April 6, 1979 (s. 21 (3)). The rest of the Act came into force on March 22, 1979, except for s. 3 (3) so far as it relates to women who have attained the age of 60 but not the age of 65, which comes into force on a day or days to be appointed (s. 21 (2)).

By the Social Security Act 1979 (Commencement No. 1) Order 1979 (S.I. 1979 No. 369 (C. 10)), s. 3 (3) came into force in relation to women born on or after June 7, 1918, but before March 23, 1919, on March 29, 1979, for the purpose of making claims for mobility allowance, and on June 6, 1979, for all other purposes.

Abbreviations

In these notes, "the 1975 Act" means the Social Security Act 1975, "the Pensions Act," means the Social Security Pensions Act 1975," "the 1976 Act" means the Supplementary Benefits Act 1976 and "the 1977 Act" means the Social Security (Miscellaneous Provisions) Act 1977.

Extent

Except as otherwise stated in these notes, the Act does not extend to Northern Ireland (s. 21 (5), *post*).

Parliamentary Debates

See *Hansard,* H.C. Vol. 958, cols. 1111–1204 (Second Reading); Vol. 961, cols. 308–382 (Report and Third Reading); Standing Committee D, December 5, 7 and 12, 1978, and H.C. Paper No. 131 (14 Dec. 1978) (Committee); H.L. Official Report, Vol. 397, col. 1427 (1st R.); Vol. 398, cols. 924–939 (2nd R.); 1922–1977 (Committee); Vol. 399, cols. 15–46 (Report), cols. 299–303 (3rd R.); H.C. Vol. 964, cols. 1243–1266 (Lords amendments considered); H.L. Official Report Vol. 399, cols. 1301–1305 (consideration of Commons amendment to Lords amendment).

Interpretation

Interpretation

1. In this Act—

" the principal Act " means the Social Security Act 1975;

" the Pensions Act " means the Social Security Pensions Act 1975;

" the Act of 1976 " means the Supplementary Benefits Act 1976;

" the Act of 1977 " means the Social Security (Miscellaneous Provisions) Act 1977.

Allowances and pensions

Attendance allowance

2.—(1) Section 35 of the principal Act is amended as follows.

(2) In subsection (2) (*b*) for the words " immediately preceded " there are substituted the words " preceded immediately, or within such period as may be prescribed,".

(3) After subsection (2) there is inserted the following subsection—

" (2A) For the purposes of subsection (2) above a person who suffers from renal failure and is undergoing such form of treatment as may be prescribed shall, in such circumstances as may be prescribed, be deemed to satisfy or to be likely to satisfy one or both of those conditions.".

(4) In subsection (3), for the words " preceding 6 months " there are substituted the words " period of 6 months mentioned in subsection (2) (*b*) above ".

(5) In subsection (4) (*a*), for the words " mentioned in subsection

(2) (*b*) above " and " there mentioned " there are substituted, respectively, the words " immediately preceding the period for which the allowance is payable " and " mentioned in subsection (2) (*b*) above " and after the words " that period " there are inserted the words " of 6 months ".

(6) After subsection (5) there is inserted the following subsection—

" (5A) Regulations may provide that, in such circumstances and for such purposes as may be prescribed, a person who is, or is treated under the regulations as, undergoing treatment for renal failure in a hospital or other similar institution otherwise than as an in-patient shall be deemed not to satisfy or to be unlikely to satisfy one or both of the conditions mentioned in subsection (1) (*a*) and (*b*) above.".

DEFINITIONS

" Principal Act " means the 1975 Act (see s. 1 above).

" Prescribed " means prescribed by regulations made by the Secretary of State under the 1975 Act (1975 Act, Sched. 20, *sub nom.* " Prescribe," " Regulations ").

GENERAL NOTE

This section amends s. 35 of the 1975 Act dealing with attendance allowance and is concerned with the entitlement of kidney failure patients. Such patients undergoing dialysis. treatment at home were at first treated as entitled to lower rate allowance and then, as a result of a revised interpretation by the Attendance Allowance Board in 1977, refused it. (See decision R(A)4/78.) The section aims to re-establish entitlement in the generality of cases. Subs. (2) provides for the relaxation by regulations of the requirement that the six-month qualifying period for the allowance must immediately precede the period for which the allowance is claimed. Subs. (4) has a similar effect in relation to s. 37 (3) of the 1975 Act, and subs. (5) has a similar effect in relation to s. 35 (4) (*a*) of the 1975 Act. Subs. (3) allows the Secretary of State by regulations to provide that kidney failure sufferers undergoing prescribed treatment need not actually satisfy the attendance allowance conditions laid down by s. 35 (1) of the 1975 Act in order to be entitled to lower a higher rate allowance. Subs. (6) empowers the Secretary of State to exclude hospital outpatients receiving dialysis treatment in hospital from the allowance, the assumption being that their attendance needs are largely met by hospital staff.

Mobility allowance

3.—(1) Section 37A of the principal Act is amended as follows.

(2) In subsection (4) (increase in rate of mobility allowance) for the words " and such other matters as he thinks relevant " there are substituted the words " any changes in taxation which directly affect the cost of motoring for persons in receipt of mobility allowance and such other matters as he thinks relevant; and he shall lay before Parliament a statement setting out his conclusion and the reasons therefor as soon as is reasonably practicable.".

(3) In subsection (5) (periods for which mobility allowance is not payable)—

(*a*) in paragraph (*a*) (allowance not payable to a person for any period in which he is under the age of 5 or over pensionable age) for the words " pensionable age " there are substituted the words " the age of 75 "; and

(*b*) the following paragraph is inserted after paragraph (*a*)—

" (*aa*) in respect of a period in which he is over the age of 65 but under the age of 75 unless either—

(i) he had been entitled to a mobility allowance in respect of a period ending immediately before the date on which he attained the age of 65; or

(ii) he would have been so entitled but for paragraph (*b*) below and a claim for the allowance by or in respect of him is made before the date on which he attained the age of 66; ".

(4) The following subsections are inserted after subsection (6)—

" (6A) Regulations may provide that this section shall have effect in relation to prescribed categories of persons in respect of whom certificates issued in pursuance of regulations made under section 13 of the Social Security (Miscellaneous Provisions) Act 1977 (mobility allowance for person eligible for invalid carriage) are in force as if, in subsection (5), the words " or over the age of 75 " and paragraph (*aa*) were omitted.

(6B) Where, before the coming into force of this subsection, a person has been awarded a mobility allowance for a specified period ending with the date on which he will attain pensionable age, that award shall have effect as if it referred instead to a period ending with the date on which he will attain the age of 75 years.".

(5) Where an application for a certificate under the Mobility Allowance (Vehicle Scheme Beneficiaries) Regulations 1977 was refused before the commencement of the Mobility Allowance (Vehicle Scheme Beneficiaries) Amendment Regulations 1978 any question whether the application was properly refused shall be determined as if that commencement had preceded the refusal.

DEFINITIONS

" Principal Act " means the 1975 Act (see s. 1 above).

" Pensionable age " means, in the case of a man, 65; in the case of a woman, 60 (1975 Act, Sched. 20, *sub nom.* " pensionable age ").

" Regulations " means regulations made by the Secretary of State under the 1975 Act (1975 Act, Sched. 20, *sub nom.* " Regulations ").

GENERAL NOTE

This section amends s. 37A of the 1975 Act dealing with mobility allowance.

Subs. (2) specifies in greater detail the matters which the Secretary of State is required to consider relating to the uprating of mobility allowance.

Subs. (3) raises the age up to which entitlement may be retained to 75; subs. (4) is consequential; subs. (5) applies the stated regulations retrospectively to applications previously refused.

Amendment of provisions relating to earnings after retirement age

4.—(1) In section 30 of the principal Act (supplementary provisions about retirement pensions) the following subsection is inserted at the end—

" (6) The Secretary of State may by order—

(*a*) substitute for the period of 5 years mentioned in section 27 (5) of this Act and subsection (1) above a shorter period; and

(*b*) substitute for the ages of 65 and 70 mentioned in sections 26 (1) and (3), 36 (5), 37 (6) and 79 (2) (*a*) of this Act and subsection (3) above such lower ages as are appropriate in consequence of any provision made by virtue of paragraph (*a*) above.".

(2) In section 167 of the principal Act (Parliamentary control of orders and regulations)—

(*a*) in subsection (1) the following paragraph is inserted after paragraph (*b*)—

" (*c*) no order shall be made under section 30 (6),";

and

(*b*) in subsection (3) after the words " section 17 (3) " there is inserted " 30 (6),".

(3) In Part II of Schedule 15 to the principal Act (regulations not requiring prior submission to National Insurance Advisory Committee) the following paragraph is inserted after paragraph 17—

"17A. Regulations contained in a statutory instrument which states that it contains only provisions in consequence of an order under section 30 (6) of this Act.".

DEFINITION

"the principal Act" means the 1975 Act.

GENERAL NOTE

Subs. (1) empowers the Secretary of State by order to effect the following variations in pensionable age (presently 65 for men, 60 for women) and/or retiring age (presently 70 for men, 65 for women):

(a) reduction of the difference (presently five years—1975 Act, s. 27 (5)) between them; and, consequently,
(b) reduction of the period (presently five years—1975 Act, s. 30 (1)) during which the earnings rule, which may cause pension to be reduced, applies;
(c) reduction of the age under which a woman must become widowed or cease to be entitled to a widowed mother's allowance in order to qualify for widow's pension (presently 65—1975 Act, s. 26);
(d) reduction of retirement age for purposes of provision by regulations of continuation of entitlement to non-contributory invalidity pension (see 1975 Act, s. 36 (1) and (5)); or invalid care allowance (see 1975 Act, s. 37 (1) and (6));
(e) reduction of the age over which a category A or B retirement pension may be paid to a woman without claim on her ceasing to be entitled to a widow's benefit (1975 Act, s. 79 (2)).
(f) reduction of the age below which regulations may, on his election, treat a person who has retired as if he had not retired (1975 Act, s. 30 (3)).

Subs. (2) subjects orders under subs. (1) above to affirmative resolution procedure under s. 167 of the 1975 Act; subs. (3) provides for the exemption of such regulations from the requirement of prior submission to the National Insurance Advisory Committee under s. 139 of the 1975 Act.

Amendment of principal Act, Pensions Act and Act of 1977

5.—(1) The provisions of the principal Act, the Pensions Act and the Act of 1977 specified in Part I of Schedule 1 to this Act shall have effect subject to the amendments there specified (miscellaneous amendments of provisions relating to retirement and invalidity pensions).

(2) The provisions of the principal Act and the Pensions Act specified in Part II of Schedule 1 to this Act shall have effect subject to the amendments there specified (modification of certain provisions in relation to events occurring before 6th April 1979).

DEFINITION

"the principal Act" means the 1975 Act (see s. 1).

GENERAL NOTE

This section warrants the amendments detailed in Sched. 1, *post*.

Appeals and reviews, etc.

Appeals from and to Supplementary Benefit Appeal Tribunals

6.—(1) After section 15 of the Act of 1976 (appeals from Supplementary Benefits Commission) there is inserted the following section—

"**Appeals from Appeal Tribunal**

15A.—(1) The Secretary of State may by rules make provision for any party to proceedings before an Appeal Tribunal (whether under this or any other Act) to appeal to a National Insurance Commissioner against a decision of the tribunal.

(2) Rules under this section may, in particular, make provision—

(*a*) as to the cases and circumstances in which, and the conditions subject to which, appeals may be made, including provision either generally or in relation to specified classes of case for appeals—

(i) to be confined to points of law;

(ii) to be made only with leave;

(*b*) as to the manner in which, and the time within which, appeals are to be brought and (where appropriate) applications are to be made for leave to appeal;

(*c*) as to the procedure to be followed on appeals;

(*d*) as to the payment by the Secretary of State to persons attending proceedings before a Commissioner of travelling and other allowances (including compensation for loss of remunerative time).

(3) The power to make provision as to procedure under subsection (2) (*c*) above includes power to make provision as to the representation of one person in any proceedings by another person.

(4) Rules under this section may provide for a Commissioner hearing an appeal—

(*a*) to give any decision which might have been given by the tribunal;

(*b*) to refer the case to another tribunal, with directions;

(*c*) to dispose of the appeal in such other manner as may be specified;

and in any case where directions are given to a tribunal in accordance with rules under this section the tribunal shall proceed accordingly.

(5) In this section " National Insurance Commissioner " has the same meaning as in the Social Security Act 1975 and includes a Tribunal of Commissioners under section 116 of that Act."

(2) For Schedule 4 to the Act of 1976 (constitution, jurisdiction and proceedings of appeal tribunals) there is substituted the Schedule set out in Schedule 2 to this Act.

(3) In section 14 (2) of the Act of 1976 (power to make regulations) after paragraph (*e*) there is inserted the following paragraph—

" (*ee*) for suspending the payment of supplementary benefit pending the determination of questions; and ".

Definitions

" Appeal Tribunal " means the tribunal which has jurisdiction in accordance with s. 28 of the 1976 Act (1976 Act, s. 34 (1)).

" Supplementary Benefit " means any benefit under the 1976 Act and includes, except where the context otherwise requires, any payments under s. 10 (4) (*b*) of the 1976 Act (payments where a person is maintained in a re-establishment centre); (1976 Act, s. 34, *sub nom.* " supplementary benefits ").

General Note

By the Tribunals and Inquiries (Supplementary Benefit Appeal Tribunals) Order 1977 (S.I. 1977 No. 1735) provision was made, as a temporary measure, for appeal against the decision of an appeal tribunal to the High Court. This section provides for the institution of a new appeals procedure.

Subs. (1) creates power for the Secretary of State to provide by rules for appeals against the decision of an appeal tribunal to a National Insurance Commissioner (see 1975 Act, ss. 97, 101; Sched. 10).

Subs. (2) substitutes a new schedule in place of Sched. 4 to the 1976 Act, the new schedule (*post*) providing for, *inter alia,* the appointment of Senior Chairmen of Appeal Tribunals.

Subs. (3) confers upon the Secretary of State power to make regulations providing for the suspension of payment of supplementary benefit pending determination of questions. There is no entitlement until the question of entitlement has been determined by the Supplementary Benefit Commission (1976 Act, s. 2 (1)) and the new power would seem to be designed in order to suspend pending determination of questions on appeal.

Incompatible benefits

7. In section 86 of the principal Act (set-off of overpayments) the following subsection is substituted for subsection (2)—

"(2) Where on review or appeal a decision awarding or refusing a person benefit is revised, or is reversed or varied, but he retains any sums paid either in pursuance of the original decision or of any other decision awarding him benefit and those sums would not have been payable if the decision on the review or appeal had been given in the first instance, then, except in so far as regulations otherwise provide,—

(*a*) where the decision on the review or appeal reverses a decision refusing the person benefit, the decision on the review or appeal shall direct that those sums shall be treated as having been paid on account of that benefit (except to the extent that they exceed the amount of that benefit);

(*b*) in any other case, any subsequent decision awarding the person other benefit, being a benefit to which a right to any of those sums would by virtue of any such provision as is mentioned in subsection (1) above have disentitled him, shall direct that those sums shall be treated as having been paid on account of the other benefit (except to the extent that they exceed the amount of that other benefit).".

DEFINITIONS

"Benefit" means benefit under the 1975 Act or (as respects any period before April 6, 1975) under—

(a) the National Insurance Act 1946 or 1965, or

(b) the National Insurance (Industrial Injuries) Act 1946 or 1965 (1975 Act, Sched. 20, *sub nom.* "benefit").

"The principal Act" means the 1975 Act (see s. 1 above).

GENERAL NOTE

S. 86 (2) of the 1975 Act provided for setting-off against benefit to which he subsequently becomes entitled, any sums paid to a beneficiary in pursuance of a decision originally awarding him benefit but then revised, reversed or varied on review or appeal. The substitute subsection extends this so as to provide for set-off, where a benefit originally refused is awarded on review or appeal, of any sums paid on account of a different benefit which would not have been awarded had the above appeal or review decision been made originally.

Repayment of benefit

8. After subsection (2) of section 119 of the principal Act there is inserted the following subsection—

"(2A) Where, in pursuance of a decision, an amount of benefit was paid which would not have been paid if the facts established for the purpose of any subsequent decision by an insurance officer, local tribunal or Commissioner had been known and—

(*a*) the subsequent decision is given in relation to the same benefit but is not given on an appeal against or a review of the earlier decision; and

(*b*) the circumstances are not such as to enable the earlier decision to be reviewed;

the subsequent decision shall require repayment of that amount (except so much of it as is directed by the decision to be treated as having been properly paid) unless it is shown to the satisfaction of the insurance officer, tribunal or Commissioner that in the obtaining and receipt of the benefit the beneficiary, and any person acting for him, has throughout used due care and diligence to avoid overpayment.".

DEFINITIONS

"Benefit" means benefit under the 1975 Act or (as respects any period before April 6, 1975) under—

(*a*) the National Insurance Act 1946 or 1965, or

(*b*) the National Insurance (Industrial Injuries) Act 1946 or 1965 (1975 Act, Sched. 20, *sub nom.* "benefit").

"Commissioner" means the Chief National Insurance Commissioner or any National Insurance Commissioner. The expression includes a tribunal of three commissioners constituted under s. 116 of the 1975 Act (1975 Act, Sched. 20, *sub nom.* "commissioner").

"The principal Act" means the 1975 Act.

GENERAL NOTE

S. 119 of the 1975 Act required repayment of benefit overpaid only where the decision to pay it was reversed or varied on appeal or review, provided due care and diligence to avoid overpayment was exercised throughout. This section extends the scope of the requirement to repay. Repayment is now required where facts established in any subsequent decision about the same benefit are such that, had they been known, the original decision to award the benefit would not have been made, notwithstanding that the subsequent decision is not made on appeal and that there are insufficient grounds for review (see Decision R(S) 6/78).

Qualification of National Insurance Commissioners in Great Britain and Northern Ireland

9.—(1) In section 97 (3) of the principal Act, after the word " barristers " there is inserted the word " solicitors ".

(2) In section 97 (3) of the Social Security (Northern Ireland) Act 1975 after the word " barristers " there are inserted the words " or solicitors ".

DEFINITION

"The principal Act" means the 1975 Act.

GENERAL NOTE

This section provides that solicitors, as well as barristers, of 10 years' standing may be appointed as National Insurance Commissioners, both in Great Britain and Northern Ireland.

Subs. (2) applies to Northern Ireland.

Increases in rates, etc.

Revaluation of earnings factors

10.—(1) Section 21 of the Pensions Act (revaluation of earnings factors) is amended as follows.

(2) In subsection (2) (review of general level of earnings and of changes in that level) for the words " since the last review " there are substituted the words " since the end of the period taken into account for the last review ".

(3) For subsection (3) (increase of earnings factors) there is substituted the following subsection—

" (3) If on any such review the Secretary of State concludes, having regard to earlier orders under this section, that earnings factors for any previous tax year (not being earlier than 1978–79) have not, during the period taken into account for that review, maintained their value in relation to the general level of earnings, he shall prepare and lay before each House of Parliament the draft of an order directing that those earnings factors shall, for the purpose of any such calculation as in mentioned in subsection (1) above, be increased by such percentage of their amount, apart from earlier orders under this section, as he thinks necessary to make up that fall in their value together with other falls in their value which had been made up by such earlier orders.".

(4) For subsection (7) (provisions as to first review) there is substituted the following subsection—

" (7) The first review under this section shall be in the tax year 1979–80; and in relation to that review subsection (2) above shall have effect as if for the reference to the end of the period taken into account for the last review there were substituted a reference to the beginning of the latest twelve-month period for which figures are available at the time the review is carried out.".

Definition

" Earnings factor," in relation to a person's contributions of any class or classes, means the aggregate of his earnings factors derived from all these contributions (Pensions Act, s. 66 (2) ; 1975 Act, s. 13 (6)).

General Note

This section amends s. 21 of the Pensions Act as follows:

Subs. (2) enables the Secretary of State in the annual review to take account of the entire period since the end of the period covered by the last review (*cf.* the period since the last review under the pre-amended s. 21 (2)).

Subs. (3) enables the Secretary of State, in the annual review, to have regard to loss of value of earnings factors in tax years prior to the period of review.

Subs. (4) specifies the tax year of the first review.

Increase of official pensions

11.—(1) In section 59 of the Pensions Act (increase of official pensions), in subsection (5) for the words from " a person " to " by reference " (in the second place where they occur) there is substituted—

" (*a*) a person is entitled to a guaranteed minimum pension when an order under this section comes into force; and

(*b*) entitlement to that guaranteed minimum pension arises from an employment from which (either directly or by virtue of the payment of a transfer credit under section 38 of this Act) entitlement to the official pension also arises;

the amount by reference ".

(2) In subsection (7) of section 59, in the definition of " base period ", for the words from " the first " to the end there are substituted the words " 13th November 1978 (date of the relevant order under section 124 of the principal Act, increasing rates of benefit);".

(3) At the end of section 59 there is inserted the following subsection—

" (8) Where, for the purposes of this section, it is necessary to calculate the number of complete months in any period an incomplete month shall be treated as a complete month if it consists of at least 16 days.".

(4) After section 59 there is inserted the following section—

" Modification of effect of section 59 (5)

59A.—(1) This section applies where the amount by reference to which an increase in an official pension is to be calculated would, but for the provisions of this section, be reduced under section 59 (5) of this Act by an amount equal to the rate of a guaranteed minimum pension.

(2) The Minister for the Civil Service may direct that in such cases or classes of case as may be specified in the direction—

(*a*) no such reduction shall be made; or

(*b*) the reduction shall be of an amount less than the rate of the guaranteed minimum pension;

and in any case to which such a direction applies the increase shall, in respect of such period or periods as may be specified in the direction, be calculated in accordance with the direction, notwithstanding section 59 (5).

(3) A direction under this section may provide that where it has applied in any case and ceases to apply in that case, the rate of the official pension for any period following the date on which the direction ceases to apply shall, in such circumstances as may be specified in the direction, be calculated as if the direction had never applied.

(4) A direction under this section may provide that the rate of an official pension shall, in such circumstances as may be specified in the direction, be calculated as if the direction had been in force at all times during such period as may be so specified.

(5) A direction made under subsection (2) above may be varied or revoked by a subsequent direction.".

DEFINITIONS

"Base period" (as amended by subs. (2) hereof) means, in relation to a direction under section 59 (1) of the Pensions Act, "the period ending with the coming into force of that direction and beginning with the coming into force of the last previous direction or, if there was none, with 13th November 1978 . . ." (Pensions Act, s. 59 (7)).

"Guaranteed minimum pension" means any pension provided by an occupational pension scheme in accordance with the requirements of ss. 33 and 36 of the Pensions Act to the extent to which its weekly rate is equal to the earner's or widow's guaranteed minimum as determined for the purpose of those sections respectively (Pensions Act s. 26).

"Transfer credits" means rights allowed to an earner under the rules of an occupational pension scheme by reference to a transfer to that scheme of his accrued rights from another scheme (Pensions Act, s. 38).

GENERAL NOTE

This section amends s. 59 of the Pensions Act dealing with increases of official pensions. Subs. (1) provides that before the official pension is uprated only the guaranteed minimum pension, deriving from the period during which official pension rights accrue, is deducted. Subs. (2) amends the definition of "base period" as above. Subs. (3) provides a definition of "complete months." Subs. (4) provides for the Minister of the Civil Service by direction to modify the effect of s. 59 (5) of the Pensions Act.

Up-rating of increments in guaranteed minimum pensions

12. The following section is inserted in the principal Act after section 126—

" Up-rating of increments in guaranteed minimum pensions

126A.—(1) The Secretary of State shall in each tax year review the sums which are payable—

(*a*) by virtue of section 35 (6) of the Pensions Act (increments in guaranteed minimum pension where retirement is postponed), including such sums which are payable by virtue of section 36 (3) of that Act, to a person who is also entitled to a Category A or Category B retirement pension (in this section referred to as a " beneficiary "); and

(*b*) by virtue of this section to a beneficiary as part of his Category A or Category B retirement pension;

for the purpose of determining whether those sums have retained their value in relation to the general level of prices (estimated in such manner as the Secretary of State thinks fit) obtaining in Great Britain.

(2) If the Secretary of State concludes that those sums have not retained their value he shall prepare and lay before Parliament the draft of an order increasing the beneficiary's Category A or Category B retirement pension at least by an amount equal to the percentage of the aggregate of the sums under review by which in the opinion of the Secretary of State that aggregate amount would have to be increased in order to restore its value.

(3) If the draft order is approved by resolution of each House of Parliament the Secretary of State shall make the order in the form of the draft.

(4) Section 126 above (supplementary provisions as to up-rating orders) shall have effect as if—

(*a*) the reference therein to section 125 above included a reference to this section;

(*b*) the references to subsection (3) of that section included references to subsection (2) of this section; and

(*c*) the reference to an up-rating order included a reference to an order under this section.

(5) Where sums are payable to a person by virtue of section 35 (6) of the Pensions Act (including such sums payable by virtue of section 36 (3) of that Act) during a period ending with the date on which he became entitled to a Category A or Category B retirement pension, then, for the purpose of determining the amount of his Category A of Category B retirement pension, orders made under this section during that period shall be deemed to have come into force (consecutively in the order in which they were made) on the date on which he became entitled to that pension.".

DEFINITIONS

" Guaranteed minimum pensions " means any pension provided by an occupational pension scheme in accordance with the requirements of ss. 33 and 36 of the Pensions Act to the extent to which its weekly rate is equal to the earner's or widow's guaranteed minimum as determined for the purpose of those sections respectively (Pensions Act s. 26).

" Up-rating order " means an order made by the Secretary of State under s. 124 of the 1975 Act (1975 Act, Sched. 20, *sub nom.* " up-rating order ").

GENERAL NOTE

This section provides for the inflation-proofing of increments to guaranteed minimum pensions earned by contracted-out employees by reason of deferment of retirement. It replaces s. 3 (3) and (5) of the 1977 Act, repealed by s. 21 (4) and Sched. 3 hereof (*post*).

Miscellaneous

Maternity grant and death grant

13. The Secretary of State shall in the tax year 1978–79 and each subsequent tax year review the sums specified in Part II of Schedule 4 to the principal Act for the purpose of determining whether those sums have retained their value in relation to the general level of earnings or prices obtaining in Great Britain.

DEFINITION

" The principal Act " means the 1975 Act.

GENERAL NOTE

S. 124 of the 1975 Act authorises the Secretary of State to increase any benefit. S. 125 requires him to review and, on certain conditions, to uprate some, not including maternity grant and death grant the value of which have been eroded by inflation since instituted. This section requires him to review but not to uprate maternity and death grant annually. On review and uprating, see *Metzger* v. *Department of Health and Social Security* [1978] 3 All E.R. 753 (C.A.).

Adjustment of secondary Class I contributions for exceptions to redundancy provisions

14.—(1) The following subsection is inserted at the end of section 4 of the principal Act—

" (7) Regulations may provide for reducing secondary Class 1 contributions which are payable in respect of persons to whom section 81 (redundancy payments) of the Employment Protection (Consolidation) Act 1978 does not apply by virtue of section 144 (2), 145 or 149 of that Act."

(2) In section 134 of the principal Act (destination of contributions) the following words are inserted at the end of subsection (6) (power to modify section) " and in relation to any contributions which are reduced under section 4 (7) of this Act ".

DEFINITION

" The principal Act " means the 1975 Act.

GENERAL NOTE

Certain employees, *e.g.* registered dock workers, are excluded from the redundancy payment provisions of the Employment Protection (Consolidation) Act 1978. Under existing administrative practice, employers of such employees pay secondary Class 1 contributions minus the redundancy fund element. This section enables the making of regulations authorising that practice. Such regulations are exempted for six months from the requirement of reference to the National Insurance Advisory Committee (see s. 17, *post*).

Overlap with benefits under legislation of other Member States

15.—(1) The following subsections are inserted at the end of section 85 of the principal Act (overlapping benefits)—

" (4) Regulations may provide for adjusting benefit payable to or in respect of any person where there is payable in his case any such benefit as is described in subsection (5) below.

(5) Subsection (4) above applies to any benefit payable under the legislation of any member State other than the United Kingdom which is payable to or in respect of—

(*a*) the person referred to in that subsection;

(*b*) that person's wife or husband;

(*c*) any child or adult dependant of that person; or

(*d*) the wife or husband of any adult dependant of that person.".

(2) In Part II of Schedule 15 to the principal Act (regulations not requiring prior submission to National Insurance Advisory Committee) the following paragraph is inserted after paragraph 12—

" 12A. Regulations under section 85 (4) of this Act (overlap with benefits under legislation of other member States).".

(3) The following section is inserted in the Child Benefit Act 1975 after section 4—

"Overlap with benefits under legislation of other Member States

4A. Regulations may provide for adjusting child benefit payable in respect of any child in respect of whom any benefit is payable under the legislation of any member State other than the United Kingdom.".

DEFINITIONS

"regulations" means regulations made by the Secretary of State under the 1975 Act (1975 Act, Sched. 20, *sub nom.* "regulations").

"The principal Act" means the 1975 Act.

For the meaning of "child," see Child Benefit Act 1975, s. 2 (1).

GENERAL NOTE

This section enables the Secretary of State to make regulations adjusting benefit where there is an overlap of entitlement as between a benefit payable under the law of the United Kingdom (including child benefit) and a benefit payable under the legislation of another Member State of the E.E.C. Existing overlapping benefits regulations do not provide for adjustment in such a case (see Decision R(U)2/78).

Such regulations are exempted from the requirement of prior submission to the National Insurance Advisory Committee (subs. (2)).

Criminal proceedings

16. For the purposes of the Criminal Evidence Act 1965 as it applies in relation to proceedings for any offence which is connected with—

(*a*) the obtaining or receipt of any benefit under the Family Income Supplements Act 1970, the Industrial Injuries and Diseases (Old Cases) Act 1975, the Child Benefit Act 1975, the principal Act or the Act of 1976; or

(*b*) the failure to pay any Class 1 or Class 2 contribution (within the meaning of Part I of the principal Act),

" business " shall include the activities of the Secretary of State.

GENERAL NOTE

The Criminal Evidence Act 1965 was passed in order to enable business records to be allowed in evidence in stated circumstances, not only where the person having personal knowledge of the master record is not available (overturning the decision in *Myers* v. *D.P.P.* [1964] 3 W.L.R. 145). This section extends the meaning of "business" in that Act (see s. 1 (4) thereof) so as to embrace activities of the Secretary of State, so far as the stated proceedings are concerned.

Reference of regulations to National Insurance Advisory Committee

17. Section 139 (1) of the principal Act (reference of proposed regulations to the National Insurance Advisory Committee) shall not apply in relation to regulations—

(*a*) made under section 119 of the principal Act (effect of adjudication on payment and recovery) by virtue of paragraph 9 of Schedule 3 to this Act;

(*b*) made by virtue of section 14 of this Act; or

(*c*) made under paragraph 4 (*a*) of Schedule 1 to the principal Act (calculation and adjustment of amounts) in relation to contributions reduced under section 4 (7) of that Act;

and made within 6 months of the passing of this Act.

DEFINITIONS

"Regulations" means regulations made by the Secretary of State under the 1975 Act (1975 Act, Sched. 20 *sub nom.* "regulations").

"The principal Act" means the 1975 Act.

General Note

For the composition and functions of the National Insurance Advisory Committee, see 1975 Act, ss. 138, 139 and Sched. 15.

This section suspends for six months from the passing of the Act the requirement of reference of regulations to the Committee in the case of regulations:

(a) providing (i) as respects matters arising pending the determination of any claim or of any question affecting right to benefit or liability for contributions or out of the revision on appeal or review of any decision on any such matter (1975 Act, s. 119 (3)), or more particularly, (ii) as provided for in s. 119 (4) (see Sched. 3, para. 9, *post*);

(b) authorising deduction from secondary Class 1 contributions under s. 14 (*ante*);

(c) providing for calculating the amounts payable according to a scale prepared from time to time by the Secretary of State or otherwise adjusting them so as to avoid fractional amounts or otherwise facilitate computation so far as reduced contributions under s. 14 (*ante*) are concerned (1975 Act, Sched. 1, para. 4 (*a*)).

Treatment of insignificant amounts

18. The following section is inserted in the Pensions Act after section 60:—

"**Treatment of insignificant amounts**

60A. Where an amount is required to be calculated in accordance with the provisions of sections 6 (3), 35 (4) and (6) and 36 (3) of, and paragraphs 2 (3) and 4A of Schedule 1 to, this Act and, apart from this section, the amount so calculated is less than ½p, then, notwithstanding any other provision of this Act, that amount shall be taken to be zero, and other amounts so calculated shall be rounded to the nearest whole penny, taking ½p as nearest to the next whole penny above".

General Note

This section provides for fixing certain pension rates in whole pence where the method of calculation of such rates would otherwise result in fractions of a penny.

Enactments of same provisions for Northern Ireland

19. An Order in Council under paragraph 1 (1) (*b*) of Schedule 1 to the Northern Ireland Act 1974 (legislation for Northern Ireland in the interim period) which contains a statement that it operates only so far as to make for Northern Ireland provision corresponding to provisions contained in this Act—

(*a*) shall not be subject to paragraph 1 (4) and (5) of that Schedule (affirmative resolution of both Houses of Parliament), but

(*b*) shall be subject to annulment by resolution of either House.

General Note

The Northern Ireland Act 1974, Sched. 1, subjects Northern Ireland orders to affirmative resolution procedure. This section substitutes negative resolution procedure where the order states that its only function is to make provision for Northern Ireland corresponding to the provisions of the Act. The section applies to Northern Ireland.

Financial provisions

20.—(1) There shall be paid out of money provided by Parliament any increase attributable to any of the provisions of this Act in sums so payable under any other Act.

(2) Section 60 (1) of the Scotland Act 1978 (modification of enactments authorising payments out of money provided by Parliament etc.)

shall have effect as if subsection (1) above were contained in an Act passed before that Act.

(3) As respects any increase attributable to this Act in the expenses which under subsection (3) (*a*) of section 135 of the principal Act are to be paid out of money provided by Parliament, subsection (1) above is without prejudice to the provision made by subsection (5) of that section for reimbursement out of the National Insurance Fund.

General Note

This section authorises out of moneys provided by Parliament any increases of sums otherwise authorised rendered necessary by this Act.

Short title, etc.

21.—(1) This Act may be cited as the Social Security Act 1979, and this Act, the principal Act, the Pensions Act and the Act of 1977 may be cited together as the Social Security Acts 1975 to 1979.

(2) Section 3 (3) of this Act shall not come into force in relation to women who on the passing of this Act have attained the age of 60 but not the age of 65 until such day as the Secretary of State may by order made by statutory instrument appoint; and different days may be so appointed in relation to women of different ages.

An order under this subsection shall be laid before Parliament after being made.

(3) Sections 11 and 12 of, and paragraphs 2 to 22 of Schedule 1 and paragraphs 5, 6, 7, 11, 14 to 20, 22, 23, and 29 (*a*) and (*b*) of Schedule 3 to, this Act shall not come into force until 6th April 1979.

(4) The Acts and instruments mentioned in Schedule 3 to this Act shall have effect subject to the minor and consequential amendments specified in that Schedule.

(5) Sections 9 (2) and 19 of, and paragraphs 3 and 12 of Schedule 3 to, this Act, and this section so far as it applies for the purposes of those provisions, extend to Northern Ireland but the other provisions of this Act do not.

General Note

For commencement orders under subs. (2), see the Social Security Act 1979 (Commencement No. 1) Order 1979 (S.I. 1979 No. 369 (C. 10)).

SCHEDULES

Section 5 SCHEDULE 1

Amendment of Principal Act, Pensions Act and Act of 1977

Part I

Miscellaneous Amendments of Provisions Relating to Retirement and Invalidity Pensions

Principal Act

1. In section 15 (4) of the principal Act (disregard of certain amounts in calculating amount of pension by reference to which certain invalidity pensions are calculated) there are inserted after paragraph (*b*) the words " and

(*c*) if he is also entitled to an invalidity allowance, any increase under section 28 (7) or 29 (8) of this Act (increase in Category A and B retirement pensions by amount equal to invalidity allowance).".

2. In section 39 (1) (*c*) (ii) of the principal Act (certain increases to be disregarded in determining entitlement to Category D retirement pension) after the word "disregarding" there are inserted the words "any additional component, any increase so far as attributable to any additional component or to any increase in a guaranteed minimum pension, any graduated retirement benefit and".

3. In paragraph 5 of Schedule 3 to the principal Act (contribution conditions for retirement pensions etc.), for sub-paragraphs (6) and (7) (which provide for the second condition to be deemed to be satisfied in certain circumstances) there is substituted the following sub-paragraph—

"(6) The second condition shall be deemed to be satisfied notwithstanding that paragraphs (*a*) and (*b*) of sub-paragraph (3) above are not complied with as respects each of the requisite number of years if—

(*a*) those paragraphs are complied with as respects at least half that number of years (or at least 20 of them, if that is less than half); and

(*b*) in each of the other years the contributor concerned was, within the meaning of regulations, precluded from regular employment by responsibilities at home.".

Pensions Act

4. In section 8 (1) of the Pensions Act (provision for Category B retirement pension for a widower in certain circumstances) the following paragraph is substituted for paragraph (*c*)—

"(*c*) before her death she satisfied the contribution conditions specified in paragraph 5 of Part I of Schedule 3 to the principal Act."

5. In section 20 (1) of the Pensions Act (use of former spouse's contributions), after the words "those conditions" there are inserted the words "(but only in respect of any claim for a Category A retirement pension)".

6. In paragraph 4 of Schedule 1 to the Pensions Act (deferred retirement) there is inserted, after sub-paragraph (2), the following sub-paragraph—

"(3) Where—

(*a*) there is a period between the death of the former spouse and the date on which the surviving spouse becomes entitled to a Category A or Category B retirement pension, and

(*b*) one or more orders have come into force under section 124 of the principal Act (increases in rates of benefit) during that period,

the amount of the increase to which the surviving spouse is entitled under this paragraph shall be determined as if the order or orders had come into force before the beginning of that period.".

7. In the said Schedule 1, the following paragraph is inserted after paragraph 4—

"4A.—(1) Where a woman is entitled to a Category A or Category B retirement pension and—

(*a*) she has had a husband and he has died, and she was married to him when he died; and

(*b*) the husband either—

(i) was entitled to a guaranteed minimum pension with an increase under section 35 (6) of this Act; or

(ii) would have been so entitled if he had retired on the date of his death,

the rate of her pension shall be increased by an amount equal to the sum of the following amounts, that is to say, an amount equal to one-half of that increase; the appropriate amount; and an amount equal to any increase to which he had been entitled under this paragraph.

(2) Where a man is entitled to a Category A or Category B retirement pension and—

(*a*) he has had a wife and she has died, and he was married to her when she died; and

(*b*) he was over pensionable age when she died; and

(*c*) the wife either—

(i) was entitled to a guaranteed minimum pension with an increase under section 35 (6) of this Act; or

(ii) would have been so entitled if she had retired on the date of her death, the rate of his pension shall be increased by an amount equal to the sum of the following amounts, that is to say, an amount equal to that increase; the appropriate amount; and an amount equal to any increase to which she had been entitled under this paragraph.

(3) The "appropriate amount" means either—

(*a*) the amount by which the deceased person's Category A or Category B retirement pension had been increased under section 126A of the principal Act (up-rating of increments in guaranteed minimum pensions), or

(*b*) the amount by which his Category A or Category B retirement pension would have been so increased had he died immediately before his surviving spouse became entitled to a Category A or Category B retirement pension.

whichever is the greater.".

Act of 1977

8. In section 4 (1) of the Act of 1977 (provision for payment of Category D retirement pension and Category A or Category B retirement pension at the same time) for the words "a Category D retirement pension" there are substituted the words "a Category C or Category D retirement pension".

Part II

Modification of Certain Provisions in Relation to Events Occurring Before 6th April 1979

9. Expressions used in this Part of this Schedule and in the principal Act shall have the same meaning in this Part as they have in that Act.

Principal Act

10. In section 16 (rates at which invalidity allowance is payable)—

(*a*) the following paragraphs are substituted for paragraphs (*a*) and (*b*) of subsection (2)—

" (*a*) at the higher rate specified in relation thereto in Schedule 4, Part I, if—

(i) the qualifying date fell before 5th July 1948; or

(ii) on the qualifying date the beneficiary was under the age of 35; or

(iii) on the qualifying date the beneficiary was under the age of 40 and had not attained pensionable age before 6th April 1979;

(*b*) at the middle rate so specified if paragraph (*a*) above does not apply and either—

(i) on the qualifying date the beneficiary was under the age of 45; or

(ii) on the qualifying date the beneficiary was under the age of 50 and had not attained pensionable age before 6th April 1979; "; and

(*b*) the following subsection is inserted after subsection (2)—

" (2A) No payment shall be made by virtue of subsection (2) (*a*) (iii) or (*b*) (ii) above in respect of any period before 6th April 1979.".

11. Section 28 (2) (entitlement of married woman to Category A retirement pension) shall, notwithstanding its repeal by section 19 (4) of and Schedule 5 to the Pensions Act, continue to apply in relation to any woman who attained pensionable age before 6th April 1979.

12. In section 59 (increase of unemployability supplement) the following words are inserted at the end of subsection (1)—

"Provided that no payment shall be made by virtue of heads (*aa*) or (*bb*) of that paragraph in respect of any period before 6th April 1979.".

13. In paragraph 5 of Part V of Schedule 4 (weekly rates of the increase in unemployability supplement)—

(a) after paragraph (a) there is inserted the following paragraph—

"(aa) if head (a) above does not apply and on the qualifying date the beneficiary was under the age of 40 and he had not attained pensionable age before 6th April 1979 ... ... £4·15."

(b) in paragraph (b) for the words "head (a) above does" there are substituted the words "heads (a) and (aa) above do";

(c) for paragraph (c) there are substituted the following paragraphs—

"(bb) if heads (a), (aa) and (b) above do not apply and on the qualifying date the beneficiary was under the age of 50 and had not attained pensionable age before 6th April 1979 ... ... £2·60;

(c) in any other case ... ... £1·30".

Pensions Act

14. Section 8 (1) (Category B retirement pension for widower) shall not apply in any case where the death of the wife occurred before 6th April 1979.

15. Section 9 (special provision for surviving spouses) shall not apply in any case where the death of the wife or husband (as the case may be) occurred before 6th April 1979 and the surviving spouse had attained pensionable age before that date.

16. Section 10 (special provision for married women) shall not apply in any case where both the husband and the wife attained pensionable age before 6th April 1979.

17. Section 15 (invalidity pension for widows) shall not apply in relation to a widow unless she ceased to be entitled to a widow's allowance or a widowed mother's allowance after 5th April 1979.

18. Section 16 (invalidity pension for widowers) shall not apply in any case where the wife died before 6th April 1979.

19. Section 17 (which is superseded by paragraphs 10 and 13 above) is hereby repealed.

20. Section 20 (use of former spouse's contributions) shall not apply in relation to any person who attained pensionable age before 6th April 1979 if the termination of his marriage (or, if he had been married more than once, his last marriage) also occurred before that date.

21. In paragraph 2 (2) (b) of Schedule 1 (which defines "period of deferment" for the purpose of enabling an increase of pension to be paid where retirement is deferred) for the words from "in relation to" to the end there are substituted the words—

"(i) in relation to any person who attains pensionable age after 5th April 1979, means the period beginning with the date on which he attains that age and ending with the day before that of his retirement;

(ii) in relation to any person who reaches pensionable age before 6th April 1979, means the period beginning with that date and ending with the day before the date of retirement.".

22. In paragraph 4 of Schedule 1 (increase of pension where pensioner's deceased spouse had deferred his retirement) the following sub-paragraph is inserted at the end—

"(4) The preceding provisions of this paragraph shall not apply in any case where the deceased spouse died before 6th April 1979 and the widow or widower attained pensionable age before that date.".

General Note

Pt. I amends the 1975 Act (paras. 1–3), the Pensions Act (paras. 4–7), and the 1977 Act (para. 8) so as to prevent the duplicate payment of invalidity allowance to certain persons over pensionable age who have not retired. It provides that only a person's basic contributory pension is to be taken into account in deciding upon entitlement to a Category D pension. It enables a Category C pension to be paid together with earnings related additional component and effects other amendments affecting the retirement pensions of contracted out widows and widowers under the Pensions Act scheme.

Pt. II amends the above legislation so as to enable provision to be made, in the case of qualifying on or after April 6, 1979, for:

(a) Payment of a retirement pension to a widower on his deceased wife's contributions;
(b) supplementation of the survivor's retirement pension by reason of the deceased spouse's pension;
(c) supplementation of a married woman's retirement pension on her own contributions by reference to her husband's contributions;
(d) abolition of the married woman's " half-test " for retirement pension.

Section 6 (2)

SCHEDULE 2

SCHEDULE INSERTED IN ACT OF 1976 IN SUBSTITUTION FOR SCHEDULE 4

SCHEDULE 4

CONSTITUTION, JURISDICTION AND PROCEEDINGS OF APPEAL TRIBUNALS

1. Every tribunal shall consist of—

(*a*) one member drawn from a panel of persons appearing to the Secretary of State to have knowledge or experience of conditions in the area to which the panel relates and of the problems of people living on low incomes;
(*b*) one member drawn from a panel of persons appearing to the Secretary of State to represent work-people; and
(*c*) a person drawn from those selected by the Secretary of State to act as chairman of the tribunals.

2. Panels of the kinds mentioned in paragraph 1 above shall be constituted by the Secretary of State for the whole of Great Britain and each panel shall relate to such area as he thinks fit, and be composed of such persons as he sees fit to appoint.

3. Before appointing members to either of the panels, the Secretary of State may take into consideration recommendations from such organisations or persons as he considers appropriate.

4. A tribunal shall have jurisdiction in respect of the area to which the panels from whose members it is constituted relates.

5. So far as is practicable—

(*a*) each member of a panel shall be summoned in turn to serve on a tribunal;
(*b*) where several persons are selected to act as chairmen for a particular area they shall be invited in turn to preside over a tribunal;
(*c*) at least one of the members of the tribunal shall be of the same sex as the claimant.

6. The Secretary of State shall pay to the chairman of a tribunal such remuneration, and to any member thereof such travelling and other allowances (including compensation for the loss of remunerative time), as he may, with the consent of the Minister for the Civil Service, determine.

7.—(1) The Secretary of State shall assign to serve the tribunals having jurisdiction in respect of each area a clerk and such other officers and servants and shall pay them such salaries or fees and such allowances as he may, with the consent of the Minister for the Civil Service, determine.

(2) Before assigning a clerk under this paragraph the Secretary of State shall, if one or more Senior Chairmen have been appointed under paragraph 11 below, consult him or such one of them as he considers appropriate.

(3) The Secretary of State shall consider any representations made to him by a Senior Chairman as to the desirability of terminating the assignment of a clerk and shall take such action, if any, as he considers appropriate.

8. A person appointed to act as a member of a panel shall hold and vacate office in accordance with the terms of his appointment.

9.—(1) The Secretary of State may make rules—

(*a*) as to the procedure of tribunals and the procedure in connection with the bringing of matters before a tribunal, and as to the time within which matters may be brought before tribunals;

(*b*) as to the payment by the Secretary of State to persons attending proceedings before tribunals of travelling and other allowances (including compensation for loss of remunerative time);

(*c*) for authorising proceedings notwithstanding that the members of the tribunal are not all present.

(2) The power to make rules as to procedure under this paragraph includes power to make provision as to the representation of one person in any proceedings by another person.

(3) In any case where proceedings take place in accordance with rules made under sub-paragraph (1) (*c*) above the tribunal shall, notwithstanding anything in this Act, be deemed to be properly constituted, and the chairman shall have a second or casting vote.

10. Notwithstanding the preceding provisions of this Schedule—

(*a*) a tribunal shall have jurisdiction in respect of such area as the Secretary of State may direct; and

(*b*) the chairman and other members may, if the Secretary of State so directs, be drawn from among those selected or appointed in relation to different areas.

Senior Chairman

11.—(1) The Lord Chancellor may, after consultation with the Lord Advocate, appoint persons who are barristers, advocates or solicitors of not less than 7 years' standing to act in relation to the tribunals as Senior Chairmen.

(2) A person appointed under this paragraph to act as a Senior Chairman shall have such functions in relation to the tribunals, including the function of acting as chairman of a tribunal, as the Secretary of State may from time to time assign to him.

(3) Section 7 of the Tribunal and Inquiries Act 1971 (chairmen of certain tribunals) and paragraph 5 (*b*) above shall not apply in relation to a Senior Chairman acting as chairman of a tribunal by virtue of sub-paragraph (2) above.

(4) A Senior Chairman shall hold and vacate office in accordance with the terms of his appointment.

(5) The Secretary of State may pay, or make such payments towards the provision of, such remuneration, pensions, allowances or gratuities to or in respect of Senior Chairmen or any of them as, with the consent of the Minister for the Civil Service, he may determine.

(6) Senior Chairmen shall have such officers and staff as the Secretary of State may, with the consent of the Minister for the Civil Service as to numbers and as to remuneration and other terms and conditions of service, see fit to appoint.

General Note

The chief innovation effected by this Schedule is the provision, effected by para. 11, for the appointment by the Lord Chancellor, in consultation with the Lord Advocate, of barristers, advocates and solicitors of seven years' standing as Senior Chairmen of Supplementary Benefit Appeal Tribunals.

Section 21 (4)

SCHEDULE 3

Minor and Consequential Amendments

The Family Income Supplements Act 1970 (c. 55)

1. In section 7 (2) of the Family Income Supplements Act 1970 (appeals to Appeal Tribunals), for the words "be final" there are substituted the words "subject to section 15A of the Supplementary Benefits Act 1976 (appeal from Appeal Tribunals) be final.

Nothing in this subsection shall make a finding of fact or other determination embodied in or necessary to a decision, or on which it is based, conclusive for the purpose of a further decision.".

2. In section 10 (2) (*h*) of that Act (review of determinations by the Supplementary Benefits Commission and Appeal Tribunals), at the end there are inserted the words " or by a National Insurance Commissioner or Tribunal of Commissioners by virtue of rules under section 15A of the Supplementary Benefits Act 1976 ".

THE SOCIAL SECURITY ACT 1973 (C. 38)

3. In section 68 (1) of the Social Security Act 1973 (reference of proposed regulations to the Occupational Pensions Board) for the words from " (other than " to " passing of this Act) " there are substituted the words " (other than regulations made for the purpose only of consolidating other regulations revoked thereby) ".

THE SOCIAL SECURITY ACT 1975 (C. 14)

4. In section 4 (6) of the principal Act (Class 1 contributions), after the words " regulations under " there are inserted the words " subsection (7) or ".

5. In section 13 (5) of the principal Act (calculation of earnings factors) after the words " any tax year " there are inserted the words " (including earnings factors as increased by any order under section 21 of the Pensions Act).".

6. In section 14 (6) of the principal Act (disregard of certain increases in computing unemployment and sickness benefit) after paragraph (*a*) there is inserted the following paragraph—

" (*aa*) any increase under section 126A of this Act; ".

7. In section 15 (4) of the principal Act (disregard of certain increases in computing invalidity pension) after paragraph (*a*) there is inserted the following paragraph—

" (*aa*) any increase under section 126A of this Act; and ".

8. In section 110 (1) of the principal Act (review of decision of medical board or medical appeal tribunal) for the words from " in consequence of " to the end there are substituted the words " in ignorance of a material fact or was based on a mistake as to a material fact ".

9. In section 119 of the principal Act—

(*a*) in subsection (3) (*b*) there are inserted at the end the words " or out of a requirement to repay any amount by virtue of subsection (2A) above ";

(*b*) in subsection (4)—

(i) in paragraph (*c*) for the words " subsections (1) and (2) " there are substituted the words " subsections (1) to (2A) ";

(ii) in paragraph (*cc*) (inserted by Schedule 4 to the Pensions Act) the words " by way of a mobility allowance " are hereby repealed; and

(iii) in paragraph (*d*) after the words " subsection (1) " there are inserted the words " or (2A) ".

10. In paragraph 8 of Schedule 3 to the principal Act (satisfaction of contribution conditions) the following sub-paragraph is substituted for sub-paragraph (3)—

" (3) For the purposes of satisfaction by the contributor concerned of paragraph (*b*) of the first contribution condition for unemployment benefit, sickness benefit, a maternity grant or a maternity allowance, or of paragraph (*b*) of the contribution condition for a widow's allowance, all earnings factors derived from his contributions of a relevant class actually paid by him before the relevant time may be aggregated and that aggregate sum shall be treated as his earnings factor for the last complete year before the beginning of the benefit year in which the relevant time falls."

11. In paragraph 9 of Part I of Schedule 4 to the principal Act (as amended by paragraph 62 of Schedule 4 to the Pensions Act) for the words " £6·90 " there are substituted the words " £11·70 ".

THE HOUSE OF COMMONS DISQUALIFICATION ACT (C. 24)

12. In Part III of Schedule 1 to the House of Commons Disqualification Act 1975 (offices the holders of which are disqualified) at the end of the entry beginning " Chairman of an Appeal Tribunal " there are inserted the words " or Senior Chairman in relation to such a tribunal ".

THE SOCIAL SECURITY PENSIONS ACT 1975 (c. 60)

13. In sections 6 (3) and 35 (4) of the Pensions Act the words from "and rounding" to the end are hereby repealed.

14. In section 6 (4) of the Pensions Act (increase of earnings factors), for the words "any order or orders that have come into force under section 21 below" there are substituted the words "the last order under section 21 below to come into force".

15. In section 11 of the Pensions Act (application of earnings rule) after the words "the additional component" there are inserted the words ", of any increase so far as attributable to any additional component or to any increase in a guaranteed minimum pension".

16. In section 23 (1) (*c*) of the Pensions Act (up-rating of certain increases under Schedule 1) after the words "such pensions" there are inserted the words "or to increases in guaranteed minimum pensions".

17. In section 34 (6) of the Pensions Act (increase of earnings) for the words "any order or orders coming into force under section 21 above" there are substituted the words "the last order under section 21 above to come into force".

18. In section 35 of the Pensions Act (earner's guaranteed minimum)—

(*a*) in subsection (5) (increase of earnings factors) for the words "any order or orders that have come into force under section 21 above" there are substituted the words "the last order under section 21 above to come into force";

(*b*) in subsection (7) (early retirement) for the words "any order or orders that come into force under the said section 21" there are substituted the words "the last order under the said section 21 to come into force".

19. In section 37 (3) of the Pensions Act (earner's salary as factor of widow's pension) for the words "any order or orders coming into force under section 21 above" there are substituted the words "the last order under section 21 above to come into force".

20. In section 59 (7) of the Pensions Act, after the words "this section" (in the two places where they occur after the definition of "lump sum") there are inserted in each case the words "and section 59A of this Act".

21. In section 61 (2) of the Pensions Act (reference of proposed regulations to the Occupational Pensions Board) for the words from "to be made" to "passing of this Act" there are substituted the words "made for the purpose only of consolidating other regulations revoked thereby".

22. In sections 66 (2) and 68 (3) (*a*) of the Pensions Act, for the words "section 59" there are, in each case, substituted the words "sections 59 and 59A".

23. In paragraph 4 of Schedule 1 to the Pensions Act (deferred retirement) at the end of both sub-paragraph (1) and sub-paragraph (2) there are inserted the words "under this Schedule apart from paragraph 4A.".

THE SUPPLEMENTARY BENEFITS ACT 1976 (c. 71)

24. In section 2 (1) of the Act of 1976 (determination of benefit, subject to provisions of section 15 as to appeals) for the words "section 15" there are substituted the words "sections 15 and 15A".

25. In section 14 (2) (*d*) of the Act of 1976 (review of determinations), at the end there are inserted the words "or by a National Insurance Commissioner or Tribunal of Commissioners by virtue of rules under section 15A of this Act".

26. In section 15 of the Act of 1976 (appeals to Appeal Tribunals), in subsection (3) the words from "and any" to the end are omitted and at the end there is inserted the following subsection:—

"(4) Subject to section 15A of this Act, any determination of an Appeal Tribunal shall be final; but nothing in this section shall make any finding of fact or other determination embodied in or necessary to a decision, or on which it is based, conclusive for the purpose of any further decision.".

27. In section 33 of the Act of 1976 (rules and regulations) the following subsection is inserted after subsection (1)—

"(1A) Rules and regulations under this Act may make different provision for different classes of case and otherwise for different circumstances.".

28. In paragraph 8 of Schedule 2 to the Act of 1976 (increase of amount of award on appeal), in sub-paragraph (*a*) after the words " section 15 " there are inserted the words " or 15A ".

THE SOCIAL SECURITY (MISCELLANEOUS PROVISIONS) ACT 1977 (C. 5)

29. In the Act of 1977—

(*a*) section 3 (3) to (5),

(*b*) section 5 (2), and

(*c*) section 13 (2),

are hereby repealed.

THE EMPLOYMENT PROTECTION (CONSOLIDATION) ACT 1978 (C. 44)

30. In section 132 of the Employment Protection (Consolidation) Act 1978—

(*a*) in subsection (3) (*e*) for the words " and (3) " there are substituted the words " to (4) "; and

(*b*) in subsection (4) (*a*) for the words " and (2) " there are substituted the words " (2) and (2A) ".

THE SUPPLEMENTARY BENEFIT (APPEAL TRIBUNAL) RULES 1971 (S.I. No. 680)

31. Rule 2 of the Supplementary Benefit (Appeal Tribunal) Rules 1971 (tenure of office of members of Appeal Tribunals) is hereby revoked.

THE MOBILITY ALLOWANCE (VEHICLE SCHEME BENEFICIARIES) REGULATIONS 1977 (S.I. No. 1229)

32. In Regulation 6 of the Mobility Allowance (Vehicle Scheme Beneficiaries) Regulations 1977 the following paragraph is substituted for paragraph (*a*)—

" (*a*) section 37A (5) of the principal Act shall have effect as though the words " or over the age of 75 " and paragraph (*aa*) were omitted ;".

Administration of Justice (Emergency Provisions) (Scotland) Act 1979

(1979 c. 19)

An Act to provide for emergency arrangements for the administration of justice in Scotland; to suspend in part the operation of section 17 of the Stamp Act 1891; and for connected purposes. [22nd March 1979]

General Note

This Act provides for emergency arrangements for the administration of justice in Scotland.

S. 1 deals with the duration and effect of the Act; s. 2 provides for an extension of time limits; s. 3 defines the period of detention of unconvicted prisoners; s. 4 concerns the prosecution of offences and criminal diets; s. 5 makes arrangements for court proceedings during emergency period; s. 6 partially suspends operation of s. 17 of Stamp Act 1891; s. 7 gives short title and extent.

The Act received the Royal Assent on March 22, 1979, and came into force on that date.

Parliamentary debates

Hansard, H.C. Vol. 964, cols. 706, 1395, 1457; H.L. Vol. 399, cols. 1201, 1327.

Duration and effect of Act

1.—(1) This Act shall cease to be in force one month after the date prescribed by the Secretary of State by order made by statutory instrument; and the period from 23rd February 1979 until the prescribed date is in this Act referred to as " the emergency period ".

(2) This Act shall have effect, and shall be deemed always to have had effect, in relation to the whole of the emergency period.

Extension of time limits, etc.

2. Subject to sections 3 and 4 of this Act, where, by reference to any time-limit or period of time, the time, or the latest time, when for any purpose anything requires to be done in relation to legal proceedings, civil or criminal (including the institution of such proceedings), occurs during the emergency period, that thing may be done at any time which is not later than one month after the expiry of the emergency period.

Period of detention of unconvicted prisoners

3. Nothing in section 2 of this Act shall affect section 101 of the Criminal Procedure (Scotland) Act 1975 (prevention of delay in trials) but, in computing the period of 110 days for the purposes of that section, no account shall be taken of any period of detention of an accused person since committal until liberated in due course of law, being a period of detention which occurred during the emergency period.

Prosecution of offences and criminal diets

4.—(1) For the avoidance of doubt, any power to cite accused persons and witnesses to a criminal diet shall be exercisable during the emergency period notwithstanding that any ordinary sitting of the court has been suspended.

(2) Any criminal diet, which is due to be held on a date during the emergency period and which is not called or duly adjourned or continued,

shall be deemed to be adjourned, as if the accused person had failed to appear, to such date as the court may determine on an application by the prosecutor (which application need not be intimated to the accused person) made at any time which is not later than one month after the expiry of the emergency period, and such date shall be intimated to the accused person not less than seven days before it occurs.

Arrangements for court proceedings during emergency period

5.—(1) Without prejudice to any existing powers, a judge of any court may do anything during the emergency period in relation to legal proceedings, civil or criminal (including the institution of such proceedings), which could be done by the clerk of court, sheriff clerk or other officer of court, and in any particular case may with the consent of the Secretary of State authorise any person to do any such thing in relation to such proceedings.

(2) During the emergency period, a copy of any document lodged in court in connection with legal proceedings (civil or criminal) may be accepted by the court in lieu of the original; and any such copy shall be taken to be a true copy unless the contrary is proved.

(3) Any failure or omission of a judge or other person doing anything by virtue of subsection (1) above, in relation to the keeping of any record of proceedings, shall not invalidate the proceedings.

Partial suspension of operation of s. 17 of Stamp Act 1891, etc.

6. Section 17 of the Stamp Act 1891 (penalty for enrolling, etc., instrument not duly stamped) shall not have effect in relation to the Keeper of the Registers of Scotland while this Act is in force; and a deed recorded or registered in conformity with this section shall, notwithstanding section 14 of that Act, be available for any purpose provided that the deed is duly stamped within three months of its recording or registering, as the case may be, or such later time as the Commissioners of Inland Revenue may allow.

Short title and extent

7.—(1) This Act may be cited as the Administration of Justice (Emergency Provisions) (Scotland) Act 1979.

(2) This Act shall extend to Scotland only.

Consolidated Fund Act 1979

(1979 c. 20)

An Act to apply certain sums out of the Consolidated Fund to the service of the years ending on 31st March 1978 and 1979.
[22nd March 1979]

General Note

This Act authorises the issue of certain moneys out of the Consolidated Fund.

The Act received the Royal Assent on March 22, 1979, and came into force on that date.

Issue out of the Consolidated Fund for the year ending 31st March 1978

1. The Treasury may issue out of the Consolidated Fund of the United Kingdom and apply towards making good the supply granted to Her Majesty for the service of the year ending on 31st March 1978 the sum of £29,504,147·67.

Issue out of the Consolidated Fund for the year ending 31st March 1979

2. The Treasury may issue out of the Consolidated Fund of the United Kingdom and apply towards making good the supply granted to Her Majesty for the service of the year ending on 31st March 1979 the sum of £577,727,000.

Short title

3. This Act may be cited as the Consolidated Fund Act 1979.

Forestry Act 1979

(1979 c. 21)

An Act to re-state the power of the Forestry Commissioners to make grants and loans; and to provide for the metrication of enactments relating to forestry and forest lands. [29th March 1979]

General Note

This Act restates the power of the Forestry Commissioners to make grants and loans and provides for the metrication of enactments relating to forestry and forest lands.

S. 1 empowers the Forestry Commissioners to provide finance for forestry; s. 2 introduces the metrication of measurements; s. 3 contains the short title, commencement, etc. The Act does not extend to Northern Ireland.

The Act received the Royal Assent on March 29, 1979, and came into force on May 29, 1979.

Parliamentary debates

Hansard, H.L. Vol. 396, cols. 28, 818 and 1410; Vol. 397, col. 314; H.C. Vol. 961, col. 991; Vol. 965, col. 201.

Finance for forestry

1.—(1) The Forestry Commissioners may, with Treasury approval, make grants and loans to owners and lessees of land for and in connection with the use and management of the land for forestry purposes.

(2) Any such grant or loan shall be made out of the Forestry Fund and be on such terms and conditions as the Commissioners think fit.

Metrication of measurements

2.—(1) The Forestry Act 1967 is amended as shown in Schedule 1 to this Act (the amendments being to substitute metric units of measurement throughout the Act).

(2) The Forestry Commissioners may by regulations amend enactments to which this subsection applies so as to substitute—

(*a*) for any reference to a number of acres, a reference to a number of hectares;

(*b*) for any reference to a number of feet, a reference to a number of metres; and

(*c*) for any requirement that plans be made on the scale of 3 chains to an inch, a requirement that they be made on the scale of 1:2,500;

and for this purpose " number " includes a number less than unity.

(3) Subsection (2) applies to any local enactment contained in an Act (whether public general, local or private) relating to particular forest lands in England and Wales.

(4) Before making any such regulations, the Commissioners shall consult such persons and organisations as appear to them to be representative of interests likely to be affected.

(5) The regulations—

(*a*) may contain such incidental, supplementary and consequential provisions (if any) as the Commissioners consider expedient; and

(*b*) shall be made by statutory instrument subject to annulment by resolution of either House of Parliament.

Citation, etc.

3.—(1) This Act may be cited as the Forestry Act 1979; and the Forestry Act 1967 and this Act may be cited together as the Forestry Acts 1967 and 1979.

(2) The Forestry Act 1967 is repealed to the extent specified in Schedule 2 to this Act.

(3) This Act comes into force at the expiration of two months from the date on which it is passed.

(4) This Act does not extend to Northern Ireland.

SCHEDULES

Section 2 (1)

SCHEDULE 1

Metrication of 1967 Act

In section 9 (requirement of felling licence; exemptions from that requirement)—

in subsection (2) (*a*), for " 3 inches " and " 6 inches " substitute respectively " 8 centimetres " and " 15 centimetres ";

in subsection (3) (*a*), for " 4 inches " substitute " 10 centimetres ";

in subsection (3) (*b*), for " 825 cubic feet " and " 150 cubic feet ", substitute respectively " 30 cubic metres " and " 5.5 cubic metres ";

in subsection (5) (*a*), for " 3 inches " and " 4 inches ", substitute respectively " 8 centimetres " and " 10 centimetres ", and for " 825 cubic feet " and " 150 cubic feet " substitute respectively " 30 cubic metres " and " 5.5 cubic metres ";

in subsection (5) (*b*) for " 6 inches " substitute " 15 centimetres ";

in subsection (5) (*c*) for " 825 cubic feet " and " 150 cubic feet " substitute respectively " 30 cubic metres " and " 5.5 cubic metres "; and

in subsection (6) for " five feet " substitute " 1.3 metres ".

In section 43 (1) (satisfaction of contingent liability to Crown Estate), for five acres " substitute " 2 hectares ".

Section 3 (2)

SCHEDULE 2

Repeals in 1967 Act

Section 4.

In section 9 (6), the words from " and references to the cubic content " onwards.

Confirmation to Small Estates (Scotland) Act 1979

(1979 c. 22)

An Act to amend the law relating to confirmation to small estates in Scotland; and for connected purposes. [29th March 1979]

General Note

This Act amends the law relating to confirmation to small estates in Scotland.

S. 1 amends the Intestates Widows and Children (Scotland) Act 1875 and the Small Testate Estates (Scotland) Act 1876 in relation to the confirmation of small estates; s. 2 repeals various enactments; s. 3 contains the short title, extent, construction and commencement. The Act extends to Scotland only.

The Act received the Royal Assent on March 29, 1979, and comes into force on a day to be appointed.

Parliamentary debates

Hansard, H.C. Vol. 962, col. 798; Vol. 963, col. 858; H.L. Vol. 399, cols. 46, 870, and 1662.

Confirmation to small estates

1.—(1) In the Intestates Widows and Children (Scotland) Act 1875—

(*a*) in section 3 (confirmation to small intestate estate)—

(i) for the words " the net estate of an intestate is of a value less than one thousand pounds, and his gross estate is of a value less than three thousand pounds, his widow or any one or more of his children, or in the case of an intestate widow any one or more of her children," there shall be substituted the words " the whole estate of an intestate is of a value not exceeding £10,000 an applicant for confirmation thereto "; and

(ii) for the words " without the payment of any fee therefor save as is provided in Schedule C annexed to this Act " there shall be substituted the words " on payment of the requisite fee ";

(*b*) in section 5 (commissary clerk to be satisfied as to value of estate), for the words " either of the values " there shall be substituted the words " the value ";

(*c*) in section 7 (acts of sederunt), the words " ; but the total amount to be charged to applicants shall not in any case exceed the sums mentioned in Schedule C annexed to this Act " shall cease to have effect;

(*d*) in Schedule A (form of inventory and relative oath) for the words " 150*l*." there shall be substituted the words " £10,000 ";

(*e*) in Schedule B (form of confirmation) for the words " 150*l* " there shall be substituted the words " £10,000 "; and

(*f*) Schedule C (fees) shall cease to have effect.

(2) In the Small Testate Estates (Scotland) Act 1876—

(*a*) in section 3 (confirmation to small testate estate)—

(i) for the words " the net estate of a testate is of a value less than one thousand pounds, and his gross estate is of a value less than three thousand pounds the executor of such testate " there shall be substituted the words " the whole estate of a testate is of a value not exceeding £10,000 an applicant for confirmation thereto "; and

(ii) for the words " without the payment of any fee therefor save as is provided in Schedule C annexed to this Act " there shall be substituted the words " on payment of the requisite fee ";

(*b*) in section 5 (commissary clerk to be satisfied as to value of estate) for the words " either of the values " there shall be substituted the words " the value ";

(*c*) in section 7 (procedure and fees) the words " ; but the total amount to be charged to executors shall not in any case exceed the sums mentioned in Schedule C annexed to this Act " shall cease to have effect;

(*d*) in Schedule A (form of inventory and relative oath) for the words " 150*l*." there shall be substituted the words " £10,000 "; and

(*e*) Schedule C (fees) shall cease to have effect.

(3) The Secretary of State may by order made by statutory instrument amend the provisions mentioned in subsections (1) (*a*), (*d*) and (*e*) or (2) (*a*) and (*d*) above to alter the limit of value at or below which confirmation may be expeded under the said Act of 1875 or 1876 (as the case may be).

(4) An order under subsection (3) above shall be subject to annulment in pursuance of a resolution of either House of Parliament.

Repeals

2. The enactments mentioned in the Schedule to this Act are hereby repealed to the extent specified in the third column of that Schedule.

Short title, extent, construction and commencement

3.—(1) This Act may be cited as the Confirmation to Small Estates (Scotland) Act 1979 and extends to Scotland only.

(2) This Act, except this section, shall come into force on such date as the Secretary of State may by order made by statutory instrument appoint.

(3) For the purposes of sections 21, 22 and 82 (1) of the Scotland Act 1978 (which provide, respectively, for the exercise of executive powers, the making of subordinate legislation and construction) this Act shall be deemed to be an enactment passed before the passing of that Act.

Section 2

SCHEDULE

REPEALS

Chapter	Short Title	Extent of Repeal
38 & 39 Vict. c. 41.	The Intestates Widows and Children (Scotland) Act 1875.	In section 7 the words " ; but the total amount to be charged to applicants shall not in any case exceed the sums mentioned in Schedule C annexed to this Act ". Schedule C.
39 & 40 Vict. c. 24.	The Small Testate Estates (Scotland) Act 1876.	In section 7, the words " ; but the total amount to be charged to executors shall not in any case exceed the sums mentioned in Schedule C annexed to this Act ". Schedule C.
44 & 45 Vict. c. 12.	The Customs and Inland Revenue Act 1881.	Section 34.
9 & 10 Eliz. 2. c. 37.	The Small Estates (Representation) Act 1961.	The whole Act.

Public Health Laboratory Service Act 1979

(1979 c. 23)

An Act to extend the powers conferred by section 5 (2) (*c*) of the National Health Service Act 1977 and to amend certain provisions of that Act relating to the Public Health Laboratory Service Board. [29th March 1979]

General Note

This Act extends the powers conferred by s. 5 (2) (*c*) of the National Health Service Act 1977 and amends provisions relating to the Public Health Laboratory Service Board.

S. 1 amends s. 5 of the 1977 Act to provide for the extension of the public health laboratory service; s. 2 provides for payments to members of the Public Health Laboratory Service Board and its committees; s. 3 contains the short title and extent. The Act does not extend to Scotland or Northern Ireland.

The Act received the Royal Assent on March 29, 1979, and came into force on that date.

Parliamentary debates

Hansard, H.L. Vol. 396, cols. 421, 1442; Vol. 397, cols. 837, 1171; H.C. Vol. 962, col. 1326; Vol. 965, col. 417.

Extension of public health laboratory service

1.—(1) In section 5 of the National Health Service Act 1977 (miscellaneous services) in paragraph (*c*) of subsection (2) (provision of a microbiological service for the control of the spread of infectious diseases) for the words following " diseases " there shall be substituted " and carry on such other activities as in his opinion can conveniently be carried on in conjunction with that service ".

(2) After that subsection there shall be inserted—

" (2A) Charges may be made for services or materials supplied by virtue of paragraph (*c*) of subsection (2) above; and the powers conferred by that paragraph may be exercised both for the purposes of the health service and for other purposes.".

(3) In subsection (4) of that section (functions of Public Health Laboratory Service Board) for the words from " administration " to the end there shall be substituted " powers conferred by paragraph (*c*) of subsection (2) above as the Secretary of State may determine ".

(4) In Schedule 3 to that Act (constitution etc. of Public Health Laboratory Service Board) in paragraph 2 for the words from " the public " to the end there shall be substituted " its functions ".

Payments in respect of membership of Public Health Laboratory Service Board and its committees

2. In paragraph 12 of Schedule 3 to that Act (payment of travelling and other allowances) for the words from " travelling " to the end there shall be substituted " remuneration and allowances, and may make such provision for the payment of pensions, gratuities or allowances to or in respect of persons who have ceased to be members of the Board, as the Secretary of State may with the approval of the Minister for the Civil Service determine ".

Short title and extent

3.—(1) This Act may be cited as the Public Health Laboratory Service Act 1979.

(2) This Act does not extend to Scotland or Northern Ireland.

Appropriation Act 1979

(1979 c. 24)

An Act to appropriate the supplies granted in this Session of Parliament. [4th April 1979]

General Note

This Act received the Royal Assent on April 4, 1979.

The Schedules to the Act have not been reproduced here as they are of little or no legal interest.

Appropriation of sums voted for supply services

1. All sums granted by the Acts mentioned in Schedule (A) annexed to this Act out of the Consolidated Fund towards making good the supply granted to Her Majesty amounting, as appears by the said schedule, in the aggregate, to the sum of £23,344,270,047·67 are appropriated, and shall be deemed to have been appropriated as from the date of the passing of the Acts mentioned in the said Schedule (A), for the services and purposes expressed in Schedule (B) annexed hereto.

The abstract of schedules and schedules annexed hereto, with the notes (if any) to such schedules, shall be deemed to be part of this Act in the same manner as if they had been contained in the body thereof.

In addition to the said sums granted out of the Consolidated Fund, there may be applied out of any money directed, under section 2 of the Public Accounts and Charges Act 1891, to be applied as appropriations in aid of the grants for the services and purposes specified in Schedule (B) annexed hereto the sums respectively set forth in the last column of such parts of the said schedule as relate to the year ended 31st March 1979.

Short title

2. This Act may be cited as the Appropriation Act 1979.

Finance Act 1979

(1979 c. 25)

An Act to continue income tax and corporation tax at the existing rates; to increase the main personal reliefs from income tax; to withdraw child tax allowances; and to continue the limit on relief for interest imposed by paragraph 5 of Schedule 1 to the Finance Act 1974. [4th April 1979]

General Note

This Act continues income tax and corporation tax at the existing rates, increases the main personal reliefs, and withdraws child allowances.

S. 1 states the rate of income tax for 1979–80, and increases certain personal allowances; s. 2 charges corporation tax for 1979–80; s. 3 gives the short title.

The Act received the Royal Assent on April 4, 1979, and came into force on that date.

Parliamentary debates

Hansard, H.C. Vol. 965, cols. 1186 and 1259; H.L. vol. 399, cols. 1905 and 1914.

Income tax

1.—(1) Income tax for the year 1979–80 shall be charged at the same rates as for the year 1978–79.

(2) In section 8 of the Income and Corporation Taxes Act 1970 (personal reliefs)—

(*a*) in subsection (1) (*a*) (married) for " £1,535 " there shall be substituted " £1,675 ";

(*b*) in subsection (1) (*b*) (single) and (2) (wife's earned income relief) for " £985 " there shall be substituted " £1,075 ";

(*c*) in subsection (1A) (age allowance) for " £2,075 " and " £1,300 " there shall be substituted " £2,265 " and " £1,420 " respectively;

(*d*) in subsection (1B) (income limit for age allowance) for " £4,000 " there shall be substituted " £4,400 ";

and in section 14 (2) and (3) of that Act (additional relief for widows and others in respect of children) for " £550 " there shall be substituted " £600 ".

(3) Neither subsection (2) above nor section 22 (2) or (3) of the Finance Act 1977 shall require any change to be made in the amounts deductible or repayable under section 204 of the said Act of 1970 (pay as you earn) before 1st August 1979.

(4) No relief shall be given under section 10 of the said Act of 1970 (child tax allowances) for the year 1979–80 or any subsequent year of assessment except in the case of a child to whom section 25 or 26 of the said Act of 1977 applies.

(5) In paragraph 5 (1) of Schedule 1 to the Finance Act 1974 (limit on relief for interest on certain loans for the purchase or improvement of land) the references to £25,000 shall have effect for the year 1979–80 as well as for previous years of assessment.

Corporation tax

2.—(1) Corporation tax shall be charged for the financial year 1978 at the same rate as for the financial year 1977; and the small companies rate and the fraction mentioned in section 95 (2) of the Finance Act 1972 (marginal relief for small companies) shall also be the same for the financial year 1978 as for the financial year 1977.

(2) The rate of advance corporation tax for the financial year 1979 shall be the same as for the financial year 1978.

Short title

3. This Act may be cited as the Finance Act 1979.

Legal Aid Act 1979 *

(1979 c. 26)

ARRANGEMENT OF SECTIONS

An Act to amend certain enactments relating to legal aid and legal advice and assistance. [4th April 1979]

General Note

Throughout these annotations the Legal Aid Act 1974 is referred to as "the 1974 Act," the Legal Aid (Scotland) Act 1967 as "the 1967 Act," and the Legal Advice and Assistance Act 1972 as "the 1972 Act."

Introduction

This Act is the second part of a package of major improvements both in the terms of financial eligibility for legal aid and in the scope of the scheme. The Lord Chancellor introduced the whole package when speaking to new financial conditions regulations on November 14, 1978 (see H.L. Vol. 396, cols. 663–682). The improvements are to be financed primarily out of the savings made on the withdrawal of legal aid for undefended divorce work. Those savings were estimated to be around £6 million per year and the cost of the improvements in the Lord Chancellor's package are estimated to rise to £6 million per year by 1982–83.

The first part of the Lord Chancellor's package was the major up-rating of the figures for disposable income and capital and of the allowances for dependants which became effective on April 6, 1979, and which are to be found in the following statutory instruments:

For England and Wales:

* Annotations by Robin C. A. White, Lecturer in Law, University of Leicester.

Legal Advice and Assistance (Financial Conditions) Regulations 1979 (S.I. 1979 No. 166).

Legal Aid (General) (Amendment) Regulations 1979 (S.I. 1979 No. 263).

Legal Aid (Assessment of Resources) (Amendment) Regulations 1979 (S.I. 1979 No. 280).

Legal Advice and Assistance (Amendment) Regulations 1979 (S.I. 1979 No. 281).

Legal Advice and Assistance (Financial Conditions) (No. 2) Regulations 1979 (S.I. 1979 No. 350).

Legal Aid (Financial Conditions) Regulations 1979 (S.I. 1979 No. 351).

For Scotland:

Legal Advice and Assistance (Scotland) (Financial Conditions) Regulations 1979 (S.I. 1979 No. 156).

Legal Aid (Scotland) (Assessment of Resources) (Amendment) Regulations 1979 (S.I. 1979 No. 324).

Legal Advice and Assistance (Scotland) (Amendment) Regulations 1979 (S.I. 1979 No. 325).

Legal Aid (Scotland) (Financial Conditions) Regulations 1979 (S.I. 1979 No. 409).

Legal Advice and Assistance (Scotland) (Financial Conditions) (No. 2) Regulations 1979 (S.I. 1979 No. 410).

The effect of the changes made by the regulations for England and Wales is summarised in the *Law Society's Gazette,* April 4, 1979, at p. 342, and at [1979] L.A.G. Bul. 83. The Scottish regulations similarly amend the Scottish scheme. Those who find the plethora of regulations and amending regulations baffling will be pleased to learn that the Lord Chancellor indicated that work was in hand to consolidate the legal aid regulations and that once the regulations required under the new Act had been promulgated consolidated regulations would be made. He also indicated that a new edition of the *Legal Aid Handbook* would be prepared. It is to be hoped that Lord Hailsham as the new Lord Chancellor will implement these proposals.

The second part of the Lord Chancellor's package of improvements required amendment of the English and Scottish legislation and this is achieved in this Act. There are two important aspects of the Act. First, it creates a new species of help under the advice and assistance scheme, namely *assistance by way of representation.* Secondly, it confers on the Lord Chancellor (or Secretary of State for Scotland as the case may be) powers to make regulations concerning all aspects of financial eligibility; notable among these is the power to make regulations varying the proportion of disposable income in excess of the prescribed figure (currently £1,500 per annum) to be taken by way of contribution.

Assistance by way of representation

The regulations that will implement this part of the Act must be awaited to see exactly what this extension of the green form scheme is to encompass. In essence, it is a means of ensuring that for " small " cases (such as, for example, where large sums are not involved, or domestic proceedings in the magistrates' courts), the expensive administrative machinery of full assessment of merits and means by local committees and the Supplementary Benefits Commission is avoided by subsuming representation in such cases into the more simply administered green form scheme. The potential of assistance by way of representation is enormous, provided that an adequate figure is prescribed for the value of work a solicitor may undertake by way of such assistance. The new s. 2A of the 1974 Act and of the 1972 Act are drafted sufficiently widely to allow assistance by way of representation to extend to any court, tribunal or statutory inquiry, though it seems that initially it will cover domestic proceedings in magistrates' courts, thus transferring such proceedings from legal aid to the advice and assistance scheme. It will, presumably, also cover the criminal jurisdiction of magistrates since s. 2 (4) of the 1974 Act and s. 2 (4) of the 1972 Act are repealed. These subsections authorise remuneration of duty solicitors under the green form scheme. For assistance by way of representation it is envisaged that approval of an area committee will be required in the same way as is required when seeking an extension to exceed the basic limit under the green form scheme.

Power to make regulations

In addition to the matters already covered by the Lord Chancellor's (or Secretary of State for Scotland's) powers to make regulations, the Lord Chancellor (or Secretary of State for Scotland) now has:

(a) wide powers concerning the operation of assistance by way of representation; see general note to s. 1;

(b) powers to make regulations for the purpose of varying the value of work that may be done under the advice and assistance scheme, including power to prescribe different figures for different categories of work;

(c) powers to make regulations to provide different scales of contributions under the advice and assistance scheme according to the type of case;

(d) powers to make regulations to vary the proportion taken as contribution in excess of the prescribed figure of disposable income and to prescribe different maximum contributions for different cases.

What the Act does not do

(a) It is unfortunate that the Act does not amend the unsatisfactory mandatory operation of the statutory charge where legal aid is granted in civil proceedings. The introduction of some element of discretion would surely not have proved so controversial as to have threatened the passage of the Act. The point was raised by Mr. John Prescott, M.P. for Kingston upon Hull, East, but at that stage, as the Solicitor-General commented, it was too late in the life of Parliament to add provisions to the Bill by way of amendment.

(b) The Act does not increase the basic £25 limit on the value of work which can be done under the advice and assistance scheme. The figure has remained at £25 since 1973. It is, of course, a figure alterable by regulation, and once assistance by way of representation becomes operative, there will be a separate limit for such assistance which will need to be considerably higher than £25. When these regulations are promulgated, it is to be hoped that the basic figure of £25 will be raised as well.

(c) S. 16 of the 1974 Act remains unimplemented, but this is to be expected. To have done anything here would have been premature since the subject-matter of s. 16 is fairly and squarely within the remit of the Royal Commission on Legal Services which is due to report later in the year.

Commencement

The Act is to come into force on a day to be appointed, for England and Wales by the Lord Chancellor, and for Scotland by the Secretary of State for Scotland. Different dates may be prescribed for different provisions.

Extent

Pt. I applies to England and Wales, Pt. II to Scotland, and Pt. III to England and Wales, and Scotland. Only the protection from execution of certain property in the new s. 2A (6) of the 1974 Act and of the 1972 Act applies to Northern Ireland.

Parliamentary debates

Hansard, H.L. Vol. 398, cols. 893–924, and 2031; Vol. 399, cols. 1914–1916; H.C. Vol. 965, cols. 835–848.

PART I

PROVISIONS FOR ENGLAND AND WALES

Extension of assistance to representation in proceedings

1.—(1) In section 2 (scope of advice and assistance) of the Legal Aid Act 1974 (in this Act referred to as "the Act of 1974")—

(*a*) in subsection (1) for the words "the following provisions of this section" there shall be substituted the words "subsection (2) and section 2A below"; and (*b*) subsections (3) and (4) and, in subsection (6), the words from " and " onwards shall be omitted.

(2) After that section there shall be inserted the following section—

" **Representation in proceedings**

2A.—(1) In this Part of this Act ' assistance by way of representation ' means any assistance given to a person by taking on his behalf any step in the institution or conduct of any proceedings before a court or tribunal, or of any proceedings in connection with a statutory inquiry, whether by representing him in those proceedings or by otherwise taking any step on his behalf (as distinct from assisting him in taking such a step on his own behalf).

(2) Without prejudice to section 2 (2) above and subject to any prescribed exceptions, section 1 above does not apply to any assistance by way of representation unless it is approved by an appropriate authority in accordance with regulations made for the purposes of this section; and regulations so made may make different provision for different cases or classes of cases.

(3) Regulations may—

(*a*) describe the proceedings in relation to which assistance by way of representation may be approved by reference to the court, tribunal or statutory inquiry, to the issues involved, to the capacity in which the person requiring the assistance is concerned, or in any other way;

(*b*) specify, in relation to any proceedings so described, the assistance by way of representation which may be approved; and

(*c*) preclude the giving of approval in the case of persons who would not be eligible for assistance if paragraph (*a*) of section 1 (1) above were omitted or for the weekly sum specified in that paragraph there were substituted such lower weekly sum as may be prescribed.

(4) Regulations may also make provision—

(*a*) as to which committees, courts, tribunals or other persons or bodies of persons are to be appropriate authorities ;

(*b*) as to the procedure to be followed in applying for approval, the criteria for determining whether approval should be given and the conditions which should or may be imposed; and

(*c*) as to the circumstances in which approval may be withdrawn and the effect of its withdrawal.

(5) Where a person receives any assistance by way of representation in any civil proceedings before a court or any proceedings before a tribunal, then, except in so far as regulations otherwise provide, his liability by virtue of an order for costs made against him with respect to the proceedings shall not exceed the amount (if any) which is a reasonable one for him to pay having regard to all the circumstances, including the means of all the parties and their conduct in connection with the dispute ; and regulations shall make provision as to the court, tribunal or person by whom that amount is to be determined and the extent to which any determination of that amount is to be final.

(6) For the purposes of any inquiry under subsection (5) above as to the means of a person against whom an order for costs has been made, his dwelling house and household furniture and the tools and implements of his trade shall be left out of account except in such cases and to such extent as may be prescribed, and except as so

prescribed they shall, in all parts of the United Kingdom, be protected from seizure in execution to enforce the order.

(7) In this section ' statutory inquiry ' has the meaning assigned to it by section 19 (1) of the Tribunals and Inquiries Act 1971."

(3) In section 7 of the Act of 1974 (scope of legal aid)—

(*a*) in subsection (5) the words from " and may also " onwards shall be omitted; and

(*b*) after that subsection there shall be inserted the following subsection—

" (5A) A person may be refused legal aid if, in the particular circumstances of the case, it appears—

(*a*) unreasonable that he should receive it; or

(*b*) more appropriate that he should receive assistance by way of representation;

and regulations may prescribe the criteria for determining any question arising under paragraph (*b*) above."

(4) In section 13 of the Act of 1974 (power to award costs out of legal aid fund) after subsection (6) there shall be inserted the following subsection—

" (7) References in this section and section 14 below to legal aid include references to assistance by way of representation."

(5) In section 25 of the Act of 1974 (interpretation of Part I) after the definitions of " advice " and " assistance " there shall be inserted the following definition—

" ' assistance by way of representation ' has the meaning assigned to it by section 2A (1) above; ".

DEFINITION

" assistance by way of representation ": subs. (2).

GENERAL NOTE

The main thrust of this section is to add to the advice and assistance scheme a new component to be known as *assistance by way of representation.* This will be an extension of the green form scheme to cover representation in the inferior courts and tribunals. The definition of assistance by way of representation is wide enough to cover representation of any kind whether before a court, tribunal or statutory inquiry. It has, of course, been a serious difficulty to date that the green form scheme has permitted a solicitor to advise and assist a client with a case before a tribunal but at the very point when the client perhaps most needs the services of a solicitor, namely to appear on his behalf before the tribunal, the assistance provided by the scheme has ended. The best the solicitor has been able to do is to provide the client with a written statement and even for this the solicitor will usually need to have requested an extension. The Lord Chancellor did not, however, indicate the immediate inclusion of a number of tribunals in the list of cases for which assistance by way of representation would become available. The immediate plan is to use it for domestic proceedings in magistrates' courts, thus transferring these proceedings from civil legal aid to advice and assistance, which will save administrative costs, but not materially extend the scope of legal aid. It will presumably also be made clear that duty solicitors will be able to claim under assistance by way of representation. S. 2 (4) of the 1974 Act under which duty solicitors were remunerated has now gone.

The detailed operation of assistance by way of representation is to be laid down in regulations. It will be the coverage of these regulations that will determine the value of the new component. The regulations can limit the application of the new assistance in a number of ways:

(a) by limiting its application to particular courts, tribunals, or statutory inquiries;

(b) by limiting its application to cases involving particular types of issues;

(c) by limiting its application by reference to " the capacity in which the person requiring the assistance is concerned ";

(d) by limiting its application " in any other way ";

(e) by limiting the amount of work to be approved in relation to any proceedings; and

(f) apparently, by virtue of new s. 2A (3) (*c*), by imposing more stringent financial conditions for eligibility for assistance by way of representation.

With regard to (f) above, it will be most unsatisfactory if a party is financially eligible for advice and assistance, but is to be regarded as ineligible for assistance by way of representation in respect of the same problem. Surely, in most cases it will still be true that the initial advice will be by way of advice and assistance which might then need to be extended to provide representation.

There is also provision for establishing a "merits" test for assistance by way of representation. The provisions as to costs are brought into line with the costs rules where a person has a legal aid certificate. New s. 2A (5) contains exactly the same conditions as are to be found in s. 8 (3) and (4) of the 1974 Act. Ss. 13 and 14 are amended to make it clear that costs may be awarded out of the legal aid fund where a person is receiving assistance by way of representation.

The grounds for refusing a legal aid certificate are amended. The phrase "in the particular circumstances of the case" are deleted from the second limb of the merits test in s. 7 (5) of the 1974 Act, presumably leaving (at least in theory) a wider discretion on the part of the local and area committees to refuse legal aid if they consider it unreasonable for a party to receive it. A further ground of refusal is added, namely that it is more appropriate for the party to receive assistance by way of representation. It would seem from the fact that regulations may prescribe criteria for determining whether a legal aid certificate or assistance by way of representation will be more appropriate, that a kind of subsidiary merits test will arise here. As long as the limit on the value of the work that may be done under assistance by way of representation is not restrictive, then the effect for the assisted party will be minimal. It was perhaps considerations such as those mentioned above, coupled with the fact that *so much* is left to regulations, which led Lord Gifford to express a reservation about assistance by way of representation, when he commented, "I hope very much that this will not become a new kind of legal aid on the cheap" (H.L. Vol. 398, col. 919).

The other provisions of s. 1 repeal bits of the 1974 Act which are inconsistent with assistance by way of representation. Of particular interest is the repeal of the troublesome s. 2 (4) of the 1974 Act: see [1975] L.A.G. Bul. 41 and Legal Action Group, *Legal Aid—How to make the best use of it*, p. 19.

Financial limits on prospective cost of advice and assistance

2. In section 3 (2) of the Act of 1974 (financial limit on prospective cost of advice and assistance) for the words from " such larger sum " onwards there shall be substituted the words " such other sum as may be prescribed; and regulations made for the purposes of this subsection may prescribe different sums for different cases or classes of cases ".

General Note

It is sad to see that the opportunity was not taken in this Act to raise the now paltry limits in the basic value of work that can be done under the advice and assistance scheme. The figure of £25 has remained static since 1973. The figure of £45 for undefended divorce work is authorised by a blanket extension for this kind of work. S. 3 of the 1974 Act is amended to permit alteration (up or down) of the base value by regulation and for different figures to be prescribed for different kinds of case. Clearly the prescribed figure for assistance by way of representation is going to have to be much higher than the current figure for assistance in undefended divorce cases.

Contributions from persons receiving advice or assistance

3. In section 4 of the Act of 1974 (contributions from persons receiving advice or assistance)—

(*a*) in subsection (2) for the words from " such amount " onwards there shall be substituted the words " such amount as may be prescribed; and regulations made for the purposes of this subsection may prescribe different maximum payments for different amounts of disposable income and for different cases or classes of cases ";

(*b*) subsection (3) shall be omitted; and

(*c*) in subsection (4) for the words " any sum specified in subsection (2) or (3) " there shall be substituted the words " the sum specified in subsection (2) ".

General Note

This section amends s. 4 of the 1974 Act by removing the table of contributions from the Act and consequentially tidying up the section. Again, it will be possible for regulations to provide different contribution scales for different types of case.

Contributions from persons receiving legal aid

4.—(1) For section 9 (1) of the Act of 1974 (contributions from persons receiving legal aid) there shall be substituted the following subsection—

" (1) Where a person receives legal aid in connection with any proceedings, his contribution to the legal aid fund in respect of those proceedings may include—

(*a*) if his disposable income exceeds £1,500 a year, a contribution in respect of income not greater than one quarter of the excess or such other proportion of the excess or such amount as may be prescribed by regulations; and

(*b*) if his disposable capital exceeds £1,200, a contribution in respect of capital not greater than the excess or such lesser amount as may be so prescribed;

and regulations made for the purposes of this subsection may make different provision for different amounts of disposable income or disposable capital and for different cases or classes of cases."

(2) In section 20 (8) of that Act (regulations not to come into force unless or until approved by a resolution of each House of Parliament) for " 9 (2) " there shall be substituted " 9 (1) or (2) ".

General Note

The main change to s. 9 (1) of the 1974 Act is the substitution of one-quarter for one-third as the proportion of disposable income in excess of £1,500 per annum taken by way of contribution, and to permit the proportion to be altered by regulation. Again, different rates may be applied to different types of cases. Note that whereas the regulations increasing the figures for disposable income to £1,500 and for disposal capital to £1,200 became effective on April 6, 1979, the reduction of the proportion of the excess over £1,500 taken as contribution will only come into force on the coming into operation of this section.

Charge on property recovered for persons receiving legal aid

5.—(1) For section 9 (9) of the Act of 1974 (charge on property recovered for persons receiving legal aid) there shall be substituted the following subsections—

" (9) In this section references to the net liability of the legal aid fund on any person's account in relation to any proceedings are references to the aggregate amount of—

(*a*) the sums paid or payable out of that fund on his account in respect of those proceedings to any solicitor or counsel ; and

(*b*) if he has received any advice or assistance in connection with those proceedings or any matter to which those proceedings relate, any sums paid or payable out of that fund in respect of that advice or assistance to any solicitor,

being sums not recouped to that fund by sums which are recovered by virtue of an order or agreement for costs made in his favour with respect to those proceedings, or by virtue of any right of his to be indemnified against expenses incurred by him in connection with those proceedings.

(10) Where the solicitor acting for a person is a solicitor employed by the Law Society in employment to which section 16 below applies, references in subsection (9) above to sums payable out of the legal aid fund include references to sums which would have been so payable if the solicitor had not been so employed."

(2) Section 24 (6) of that Act (which is superseded by this section) shall cease to have effect.

GENERAL NOTE

This section makes a minor amendment to s. 9 of the 1974 Act to ensure that the statutory charge in favour of the legal aid fund extends to the amount outstanding on an assisted person's account for advice and assistance where, as will be usual, a person has received both advice and assistance and legal aid in connection with the same proceedings.

PART II

PROVISIONS FOR SCOTLAND

General Note to Part II

Part II contains the amendments to the 1972 Act and the 1967 Act giving effect in Scotland to the changes outlined for England and Wales in Pt. I of the Act. For this reason cross-reference is made to the corresponding sections of Pt. I for substantive comment, although, in reading those annotations, references to the 1972 Act and to the 1967 Act should be substituted for the references to the 1974 Act.

Extension of assistance to representation in proceedings

6.—(1) In section 2 (scope of advice and assistance) of the Legal Advice and Assistance Act 1972 (in this Act referred to as " the Act of 1972 ")—

(*a*) in subsection (1) for the words " the following provisions of this section " there shall be substituted the words " subsection (2) of this section and section 2A of this Act ";

(*b*) subsections (3) and (4) shall be omitted;

(*c*) for subsection (5) there shall be substituted the following subsection—

" (5) In the application of this section to Scotland, in subsection (2), for paragraphs (*a*) and (*b*) there shall be substituted the words ' at a time when he is receiving legal aid for the purposes of those proceedings '."; and

(*d*) subsection (6) shall be omitted.

(2) After that section there shall be inserted the following section—

" **Representation in proceedings**

2A.—(1) In this Part of this Act ' assistance by way of representation ' means any assistance given to a person by taking on his behalf any step in the institution or conduct of any proceedings before a court or tribunal, or of any proceedings in connection with a statutory inquiry, whether by representing him in those proceedings or by otherwise taking any step on his behalf (as distinct from assisting him in taking such a step on his own behalf).

(2) Without prejudice to section 2 (2) of this Act and subject to any prescribed exceptions, section 1 of this Act does not apply to any assistance by way of representation unless it is approved by an

appropriate authority in accordance with regulations made for the purposes of this section; and regulations so made may make different provision for different cases or classes of cases.

(3) Regulations may—

(a) describe the proceedings in relation to which assistance by way of representation may be approved by reference to the court, tribunal or statutory inquiry, to the issues involved, to the capacity in which the person requiring the assistance is concerned, or in any other way;

(b) specify, in relation to any proceedings so described, the assistance by way of representation which may be approved; and

(c) preclude the giving of approval in the case of persons who would not be eligible for assistance if paragraph (a) of section 1 of this Act were omitted or for the weekly sum specified in that paragraph there were substituted such lower weekly sum as may be prescribed.

(4) Regulations may also make provision—

(a) as to which committees, courts, tribunals or other persons or bodies of persons are to be appropriate authorities;

(b) as to the procedure to be followed in applying for approval, the criteria for determining whether approval should be given and the conditions which should or may be imposed; and

(c) as to the circumstances in which approval may be withdrawn and the effect of its withdrawal.

(5) Where a person receives any assistance by way of representation in any civil proceedings before a court or any proceedings before a tribunal, then, except in so far as regulations otherwise provide, his liability by virtue of an order for expenses made against him with respect to the proceedings shall not exceed the amount (if any) which is a reasonable one for him to pay having regard to all the circumstances, including the means of all the parties and their conduct in connection with the dispute; and regulations shall make provision as to the court, tribunal or person by whom that amount is to be determined and the extent to which any determination of that amount is to be final.

(6) For the purposes of any inquiry under subsection (5) of this section as to the means of a person against whom an order for expenses has been made, his dwelling house, wearing apparel and household furniture and the tools and implements of his trade shall be left out of account except in such cases and to such extent as may be prescribed, and except as so prescribed they shall, in all parts of the United Kingdom, be protected from diligence or any corresponding process in the execution of the award.

(7) In this section ' statutory inquiry ' has the meaning assigned to it by section 19 (1) of the Tribunals and Inquiries Act 1971."

(3) In section 1 (scope of legal aid) of the Legal Aid (Scotland) Act 1967 (in this Act referred to as " the Act of 1967 ")—

(a) in subsection (6) the words from " and may also " onwards shall be omitted; and

(b) after subsection (6A) there shall be inserted the following subsection—

" (6B) A person may be refused legal aid if, in the particular circumstances of the case, it appears—

(a) unreasonable that he should receive it; or

(*b*) more appropriate that he should receive assistance by way of representation;

and regulations may prescribe the criteria for determining any question arising under paragraph (*b*) of this subsection."

(4) In section 13 of the Act of 1967 (power to award expenses out of legal aid fund) after subsection (6) there shall be inserted the following subsection—

"(7) References in this section and section 14 of this Act to legal aid include references to assistance by way of representation."

(5) In section 20 of the Act of 1967 (interpretation and construction) before the definition of the expression "Law Society" there shall be inserted the following definition—

"the expression 'assistance by way of representation' has the meaning assigned to it by section 2A (1) of the Legal Advice and Assistance Act 1972;".

DEFINITION

"assistance by way of representation": subs. (2).

GENERAL NOTE

See note to s. 1.

Financial limits on prospective cost of advice and assistance

7.—In section 3 (2) of the Act of 1972 (financial limit on prospective cost of advice and assistance) for the words from "such larger sum" onwards there shall be substituted the words "such other sum as may be prescribed; and regulations made for the purposes of this subsection may prescribe different sums for different cases or classes of cases".

GENERAL NOTE

See note to s. 2.

Contributions from persons receiving advice or assistance

8.—(1) In section 4 of the Act of 1972 (contributions from persons receiving advice or assistance)—

(*a*) in subsection (2) for the words from "such amount" onwards there shall be substituted the words "such amount as may be prescribed; and regulations made for the purposes of this subsection may prescribe different maximum payments for different amounts of disposable income and for different cases or classes of cases";

(*b*) subsection (3) shall be omitted; and

(*c*) in subsection (4) for the words "any sum specified in subsection (2) of this section or in Schedule 1 to this Act" there shall be substituted the words "the sum specified in subsection (2) of this section".

(2) Schedule 1 to the Act of 1972 (clients' contributions) shall be omitted.

GENERAL NOTE

See note to s. 3.

Contributions from persons receiving legal aid

9. For section 3 (1) of the Act of 1967 (contributions from persons receiving legal aid) there shall be substituted the following subsection—

"(1) A person's contribution to the legal aid fund in respect of any proceedings may include—

(*a*) if his disposable income exceeds £1,500 a year, a contribution in respect of income not greater than one quarter of the excess or such other proportion of the excess or such amount as may be prescribed by regulations; and

(*b*) if his disposable capital exceeds £1,200, a contribution in respect of capital not greater than the excess or such lesser amount as may be so prescribed;

and regulations made for the purposes of this subsection may make different provision for different amounts of disposable income or disposable capital and for different cases or classes of cases."

General Note

See note to s. 4. Note the commencement provisions in relation to the reduction of the proportion of disposable income over £1,500 to be taken by way of contribution.

Payments out of property recovered for persons receiving legal aid

10.—(1) For section 3 (7) of the Act of 1967 (payments out of property recovered for persons receiving legal aid) there shall be substituted the following subsections—

" (7) In this section references to the net liability of the legal aid fund on any person's account in relation to any proceedings are references to the aggregate amount of—

(*a*) the sums paid or payable out of that on his account in respect of those proceedings to any solicitor; and

(*b*) if he has received any advice or assistance in connection with those proceedings or any matter to which those proceedings relate, any sums paid or payable out of that fund in respect of that advice or assistance to any solicitor,

being sums not recouped to that fund by sums which are recovered by virtue of an order or agreement for expenses made in his favour with respect to those proceedings, or by virtue of any right of his to be indemnified against expenses incurred by him in connection with those proceedings.

(8) Where the solicitor acting for a person is a solicitor employed by the Law Society in accordance with Part II of the Legal Advice and Assistance Act 1972, references in subsection (7) of this section to sums payable out of the legal aid fund include references to sums which would have been so payable if the solicitor had not been so employed."

(2) Section 17 (5) of the Act of 1967 (which is superseded by this section) shall cease to have effect.

General Note

See note to s. 5.

Part III

General

Financial provisions

11. There shall be defrayed out of moneys provided by Parliament any increase attributable to this Act in the sums payable out of moneys so provided under the Act of 1974 or the Act of 1967.

General Note

The note of the financial effects of the Act stated that the cost of the whole package of improvements will be within "the increases in expenditure rising to about £6 million a year by 1982–83 announced in Cmnd. 7439."

Interpretation, etc.

12.—(1) In this Act—

"the Act of 1967" means the Legal Aid (Scotland) Act 1967;

"the Act of 1972" means the Legal Advice and Assistance Act 1972;

"the Act of 1974" means the Legal Aid Act 1974.

(2) This Act shall be treated for the purposes of the Scotland Act 1978 as if it had been passed before that Act.

GENERAL NOTE

Subs. (2) is destined to be of historical interest only. It takes account of the Scotland Act 1978, under which advice and assistance and legal aid are devolved matters.

Minor amendments and repeals

13.—(1) The enactments mentioned in Schedule 1 to this Act shall have effect subject to the amendments specified in that Schedule.

(2) The enactments mentioned in Schedule 2 to this Act are hereby repealed to the extent specified in the third column of that Schedule.

GENERAL NOTE

There are listed in Sched. 1 a number of minor and consequential amendments to the English and Scottish legal aid legislation. The penalties for breaking the rule of secrecy contained in the legislation, or for wilfully refusing to comply with the regulations requiring the giving of information, or for making false representations in connection with applications for legal aid, are all raised from fines of £100 maximum to fines of £500 maximum. Also worthy of note is the resulting subtle change of emphasis in s. 11 (6) of the 1974 Act and in s. 4 (5) of the 1967 Act which allow a discretion to depart from the existing link with the rules for the calculation of entitlement to supplementary benefit in fixing certain figures by which financial eligibility for legal aid is assessed.

Citation, commencement and extent

14.—(1) This Act may be cited as the Legal Aid Act 1979.

(2) This Act may be cited together with the Act of 1974 as the Legal Aid Acts 1974 and 1979 and may be cited together with the Act of 1967 and the Act of 1972 as the Legal Aid and Advice (Scotland) Acts 1967 to 1979.

(3) This Act shall come into force—

(*a*) in relation to England and Wales, on such date as the Lord Chancellor may by order made by statutory instrument appoint; and

(*b*) in relation to Scotland, on such date as the Secretary of State may by order made by statutory instrument appoint;

and different dates may be so appointed for different provisions or different purposes.

(4) An order under subsection (3) above may make such transitional provision as appears to the Lord Chancellor or, as the case may be, the Secretary of State to be necessary or expedient in connection with the provisions thereby brought into force.

(5) This Act, except—

(*a*) section 1 (2) so far as it relates to section 2A (6) of the Act of 1974;

(*b*) section 6 (2) so far as it relates to section 2A (6) of the Act of 1972; and

(*c*) paragraphs 8 and 19 of Schedule 1,

does not extend to Northern Ireland.

GENERAL NOTE

The new provisions in s. 2A (6) of the 1974 Act and of the 1972 Act are extended to Northern Ireland, but otherwise the Act does not extend to Northern Ireland.

SCHEDULES

Section 13 (1)

SCHEDULE 1

MINOR AMENDMENTS

The Legal Aid (Scotland) Act 1967

1. In section 2 (1) of the Legal Aid (Scotland) Act 1967 (financial conditions of legal aid) and in the proviso thereto for the word " larger ", wherever it occurs, there shall be substituted the word " other ".

2. In section 4 (5) of that Act (provision for applying the rules in Schedule 1 to the Supplementary Benefits Act 1976)—

(*a*) for the word " shall ", in the first place where it occurs, there shall be substituted the word " may ";

(*b*) the words " there shall be observed " shall be omitted; and

(*c*) for the words from " except that " onwards there shall be substituted the words " shall be observed to such extent as may be prescribed ".

3. In section 18 of that Act (offences)—

(*a*) in subsections (1) and (2) for the words " one hundred pounds " there shall be substituted " £500 "; and

(*b*) in proviso (i) to subsection (2) after the word " any " there shall be inserted the words " committee, court, tribunal or other ".

4. In section 20 of that Act (interpretation) in the definition of " person " after the word " unincorporate " there shall be inserted the words " which is not concerned in a representative, fiduciary or official capacity ".

The Legal Advice and Assistance Act 1972

5. In section 1 of the Legal Advice and Assistance Act 1972 (variation of limits of disposable income and disposable capital) for the word " larger ", wherever it occurs, there shall be substituted the word " other ".

6. In section 3 (5) of that Act (meaning of " regulations ") for the words " as so extended " there shall be inserted the words " as extended from time to time ".

7. In section 11 (1) of that Act (meaning of " prescribed ") for the words " as so extended " there shall be substituted the words " as extended from time to time ".

8. In section 14 (5) of that Act (Act not to form part of the Law of Northern Ireland) after the word " Except " there shall be inserted the words " for section 2A (6) and except ".

The Legal Aid Act 1974

9. In section 1 (2) of the Legal Aid Act 1974 (variation of limits on disposable income and disposable capital) the words " not less than £20 " and " not less than £125 " shall be omitted.

10. In section 2 (2) (*b*) of that Act (section 1 not to apply if there is a legal aid order) after the words " criminal proceedings " there shall be inserted the words " or any proceedings mentioned in subsection (3), (6) or (6A) of section 28 below ".

11. In section 5 (3) (*a*) of that Act (first charge for benefit of solicitor on any costs or property recovered) the words " or expenses " shall be omitted.

12. In section 6 (2) of that Act (variation of limits on disposable income and disposable capital) the words " not less than £700 " and " not less than £500 " shall be omitted.

13. In section 9 (2) of that Act (variation of amounts of free disposable income and free disposable capital) the words " not less than £250 " and " not less than £125 " shall be omitted.

14. In section 11 (6) of that Act (provision for applying the rules in Schedule 1 to the Supplementary Benefits Act 1976)—

(*a*) for the word " shall ", in the first place where it occurs, there shall be substituted the word " may ";

(*b*) the words "there shall be observed" shall be omitted; and
(*c*) for the words from "except that" onwards there shall be substituted the words "shall be observed to such extent as may be prescribed".

15. In section 21 (1) of that Act (advisory committee) after the word "and", in the first place where it occurs, there shall be inserted the words "to make to him recommendations on such matters so relating as they consider appropriate; and the Lord Chancellor".

16. In section 22 of that Act (secrecy)—
(*a*) in subsection (1) in paragraph (*a*) after the word "any" there shall be inserted the words "committee, court, tribunal or other"; and
(*b*) in subsection (3) for "£100" there shall be substituted "£500".

17. In section 23 (1) of that Act (proceedings for misrepresentation etc.) for "£100" there shall be substituted "£500".

18. In section 25 of that Act (interpretation of Part I) in the definition of "person" after the word "unincorporate" there shall be inserted the words "which is not concerned in a representative, fiduciary or official capacity".

19. In section 43 (5) of that Act (Act not to extend to Scotland or Northern Ireland) after the word "Act" there shall be inserted the words "(except sections 2A (6) and 8 (4))".

20. In Schedule 1 to that Act (proceedings for which legal aid may be given under Part I) paragraph 1 (*b*) shall be omitted.

GENERAL NOTE
See note to s. 13.

Section 13 (2) SCHEDULE 2

REPEALS

Chapter	Short title	Extent of repeal
1967 c. 43.	The Legal Aid (Scotland) Act 1967.	In section 1 (6) the words from "and may also" onwards. In section 4 (5) the words "there shall be observed". Section 17 (5).
1972 c. 50.	The Legal Advice and Assistance Act 1972.	In section 2, subsections (3), (4) and (6). Section 4 (3). Schedule 1. In Schedule 2, the entry relating to section 3 (7) of the Legal Aid (Scotland) Act 1967.
1974 c. 4.	The Legal Aid Act 1974.	In section 1 (2) the words "not less than £20" and "not less than £125". In section 2, subsections (3) and (4) and, in subsection (6), the words from "and" onwards. Section 4 (3). In section 5 (3) (*a*) the words "or expenses". In section 6 (2) the words "not less than £700" and "not less than £500". In section 7 (5) the words from "and may also" onwards. In section 9 (2) the words "not less than £250" and "not less than £125". In section 11 (6) the words "there shall be observed". Section 24 (6). In Schedule 1, paragraph 1 (*b*).

Kiribati Act 1979

(1979 c. 27)

An Act to make provision for and in connection with the attainment by the Gilbert Islands of fully responsible status as a Republic within the Commonwealth under the name of Kiribati. [19th June 1979]

General Note

This Act provides for the attainment by the Gilbert Islands of fully responsible status as the Republic of Kiribati.

S. 1 proclaims independence for Kiribati; s. 2 provides for the constitution of Kiribati as a republic; s. 3 deals with the operation of existing law; s. 4 makes consequential modifications to British Nationality Acts; s. 5 provides for retention of U.K. citizenship in certain cases; s. 6 relates to appeals to the Privy Council from the courts of Kiribati; s. 7 is the interpretation section; s. 8 gives the short title.

The Act received the Royal Assent on June 19, 1979, and came into force on that date.

Parliamentary debates

Hansard, H.C. Vol. 967, cols. 392, 1341; Vol. 968, col. 196; H.L. Vol. 400, cols. 595, 800, 836.

Independence of Kiribati

1.—(1) On and after 12th July 1979 (in this Act referred to as " Independence Day ") Her Majesty's Government in the United Kingdom shall have no responsibility for the government of Kiribati.

(2) No Act of the Parliament of the United Kingdom passed on or after Independence Day shall extend, or be deemed to extend, to Kiribati as part of its law.

Power to provide for constitution of Kiribati as Republic

2. Her Majesty may by Order in Council (which shall be laid before Parliament after being made) make provision for the constitution of Kiribati as a Republic on Independence Day.

Operation of existing law

3.—(1) Subject to the following provisions of this Act, all law to which this section applies, whether being a rule of law or a provision of an Act of Parliament or of any other enactment or instrument whatsoever, which is in force on Independence Day, or, having been passed or made before that day, comes into force thereafter, shall, unless and until provision to the contrary is made by Parliament or some other authority having power in that behalf, have the same operation in relation to Kiribati and persons and things belonging to or connected with Kiribati, as it would have had apart from this subsection if there had been no change in the status of Kiribati.

(2) This section applies to law of, or any part of, the United Kingdom, the Channel Islands and the Isle of Man and, in relation only to any enactment of the Parliament of the United Kingdom or any Order in Council made by virtue of any such enactment whereby any such enactment applies in relation to Kiribati, to law of any other country or territory to which that enactment or Order extends.

(3) Subsection (1) above shall not apply in relation to section 9 of the British Nationality Act 1948 as set out in Appendix C to Schedule 1 to the Immigration Act 1971.

(4) On and after Independence Day the provisions specified in the Schedule to this Act shall have effect subject to the amendments there specified.

(5) Subsection (4) above, and the Schedule to this Act, shall not extend to Kiribati as part of its law.

Consequential modifications of British Nationality Acts

4.—(1) On and after Independence Day the British Nationality Acts 1948 to 1965 shall have effect as if in section 1 (3) of the 1948 Act (Commonwealth countries having separate citizenship) there were added at the end the words " and Kiribati ".

(2) Except as provided by section 5 below, any person who immediately before Independence Day is a citizen of the United Kingdom and Colonies shall on that day cease to be such a citizen if he becomes on that day a citizen of Kiribati.

(3) Except as provided by section 5 below, a person who immediately before Independence Day is a citizen of the United Kingdom and Colonies and—

(*a*) who was born, or whose father was born, in Kiribati, or, in the case of a woman, who became a citizen of the United Kingdom and Colonies by reason of her marriage to a man who was born, or whose father was born, in Kiribati; and

(*b*) who on Independence Day does not become a citizen of Kiribati;

shall on Independence Day cease to be a citizen of the United Kingdom and Colonies if he is then a citizen of some other country.

(4) Section 6 (2) of the 1948 Act (registration as citizens of the United Kingdom and Colonies of women who have been married to such citizens) shall not apply to a woman by virtue of her marriage to a person who on Independence Day ceases to be such a citizen under subsection (2) or (3) above or who would have done so if living on that day.

(5) In accordance with section 3 (3) of the West Indies Act 1967, it is hereby declared that this and the following section extend to all associated states.

Retention of citizenship of the United Kingdom and Colonies in certain cases

5.—(1) A person shall not cease to be a citizen of the United Kingdom and Colonies under section 4 (2) or (3) above if he, his father or his father's father—

(*a*) was born in the United Kingdom or a relevant territory; or

(*b*) is or was a person naturalised in the United Kingdom and Colonies by virtue of a certificate of naturalisation granted in the United Kingdom or a relevant territory; or

(*c*) was, in the United Kingdom or a relevant territory, registered as a citizen of the United Kingdom and Colonies, or was so registered by a High Commissioner exercising functions under section 8 (2) or 12 (7) of the 1948 Act; or

(*d*) became a British subject by reason of the annexation of any territory included in a relevant territory;

or if his father or his father's father would, if living immediately before the commencement of the 1948 Act, have become a person naturalised in the United Kingdom and Colonies under section 32 (6) of that Act (previous local naturalisation in a colony or protectorate) by virtue of having enjoyed the privileges of naturalisation in a relevant territory.

(2) In subsection (1) above "relevant territory" means any territory which on Independence Day is a colony or an associated state, other than any territory which on that day is not a colony for the purposes of the 1948 Act as then in force (and accordingly does not include Kiribati).

(3) Subsection (1) (*c*) above shall not apply to a woman by virtue of her registration as a citizen of the United Kingdom and Colonies if that registration was effected under section 6 (2) of the 1948 Act (registration as citizens of the United Kingdom and Colonies of women who have been married to such citizens).

(4) A woman who is a citizen of the United Kingdom and Colonies, and is the wife of such a citizen, shall not herself cease to be such a citizen under section 4 (2) or (3) above unless her husband does so.

(5) Part III of the 1948 Act (supplementary provisions) as in force from time to time, except section 23 (legitimated children), shall have effect for the purposes of this section as if this section were included in that Act.

(6) A person born out of wedlock and legitimated (within the meaning of section 23 (2) of the 1948 Act) by the subsequent marriage of his parents shall be treated, for the purpose of determining whether he has by virtue of this Act ceased to be a citizen of the United Kingdom and Colonies, as if he had been born legitimate.

Appeals to the Privy Council

6.—(1) Her Majesty may by Order in Council confer on the Judicial Committee of the Privy Council such jurisdiction and powers as may be appropriate in cases in which provision is made by the law of Kiribati for appeals to the Committee from courts of Kiribati.

(2) An Order in Council under this section may contain such incidental and supplemental provisions as appear to Her Majesty to be expedient.

(3) Any such Order in Council may contain such transitional provisions as appear to Her Majesty to be expedient—

(*a*) in relation to appeals in which the records have been registered in the Office of the Judicial Committee on or before Independence Day; and

(*b*) in relation to petitions for leave to appeal filed in that Office on or before that date.

(4) Except so far as otherwise provided by or in accordance with an Order in Council under this section, and subject to such modifications as may be so provided, the Judicial Committee Act 1833 shall have effect in relation to appeals in respect of which jurisdiction is conferred under this section as it has effect in relation to appeals to Her Majesty in Council.

(5) An Order in Council under this section shall be laid before Parliament after being made.

Interpretation

7.—(1) In this Act, and in any amendment made by this Act in any other enactment, "Kiribati" means the territories which immediately before Independence Day constitute the colony of the Gilbert Islands.

(2) In this Act, "the 1948 Act" means the British Nationality Act 1948.

Short title

8. This Act may be cited as the Kiribati Act 1979.

Section 3

SCHEDULE

Consequential Amendments

Diplomatic immunities

1. In section 1 (5) of the Diplomatic Immunities (Conferences with Commonwealth Countries and Republic of Ireland) Act 1961, before the word "and" in the last place where it occurs there shall be inserted the word "Kiribati".

The Services

2. The expression "colony" in the Army Act 1955, the Air Force Act 1955 and the Naval Discipline Act 1957 shall not include Kiribati; and in the definitions of "Commonwealth force" in section 225 (1) and 223 (1) respectively of those Acts of 1955, and in the definition of "Commonwealth country" in section 135 (1) of that Act of 1957, at the end there shall be added the words "or Kiribati".

Visiting forces

3. In the Visiting Forces (British Commonwealth) Act 1933, section 4 (attachment and mutual powers of command) shall apply in relation to forces raised in Kiribati as it applies to forces raised in Dominions within the meaning of the Statute of Westminster 1931.

4. In the Visiting Forces Act 1952—

(*a*) in section 1 (1) (*a*) (countries to which the Act applies) at the end there shall be added the words "Kiribati or";

(*b*) in section 10 (1) (*a*), the expression "colony" shall not include Kiribati;

and, until express provision with respect to Kiribati is made by an Order in Council under section 8 of that Act (application to visiting forces of law relating to home forces), any such Order for the time being in force shall be deemed to apply to visiting forces to Kiribati.

Ships and aircraft

5. In section 427 (2) of the Merchant Shipping Act 1894, as set out in section 2 of the Merchant Shipping (Safety Convention) Act 1949, before the words "or in any" there shall be inserted the words "or Kiribati".

6. In the Whaling Industry (Regulation) Act 1934, the expression "British ship to which this Act applies" shall not include a British ship registered in Kiribati.

7. Kiribati shall not be a relevant overseas territory for the purposes of sections 21 (2) and 22 (3) of the Civil Aviation Act 1971.

8. Section 20 of the Colonial Stock Act 1877 (which relates to the jurisdiction of courts in the United Kingdom as to colonial stock) shall, in its application to stock of Kiribati, have effect as if for the second paragraph there were substituted—

"(2) Any person claiming to be interested in colonial stock to which this Act applies, or in any dividend thereon, may institute civil proceedings in the United Kingdom against the registrar in relation to that stock or dividend.

(3) Notwithstanding anything in the foregoing provisions of this section, the registrar shall not by virtue of an order made by any court in the United Kingdom in any such proceedings as are referred to in this section be liable to make any payment otherwise than out of moneys in his possession in the United Kingdom as registrar."

Commonwealth Institute

9. In section 8 (2) of the Imperial Institute Act 1925, as amended by the Commonwealth Institute Act 1958, (power to vary the provisions of the said Act of 1925 if an agreement for the purpose is made with the governments of certain territories which for the time being are contributing towards the expenses of the Commonwealth Institute) at the end there shall be added the words "and Kiribati".

Carriage by Air and Road Act 1979

(1979 c. 28)

Arrangement of Sections

An Act to enable effect to be given to provisions of certain protocols signed at Montreal on 25th September 1975 which further amend the convention relating to carriage by air known as the Warsaw Convention as amended at The Hague 1955; to modify article 26 (2) of the said convention both as in force apart from those protocols and as in force by virtue of them; to provide for the amendment of certain Acts relating to carriage by air or road in consequence of the revision of relevant conventions; and to replace references to gold francs in the Carriage of Goods by Road Act 1965 and the Carriage of Passengers by Road Act 1974 by references to special drawing rights. [4th April 1979]

General Note

This Act enables effect to be given to provisions of protocols signed at Montreal on September 25, 1975, and modifies art. 26 (2) of the Warsaw Convention; it also amends certain Acts relating to carriage by air or road.

S. 1 substitutes a new Sched. 1 to the Carriage by Air Act 1961 so as to give effect to Protocols Nos. 3 and 4; s. 2 modifies art. 26 (2) of the Warsaw Convention; s. 3 amends certain Acts in consequence of the revision of conventions relating to carriage by air or road; s. 4 replaces gold francs by special drawing rights for the purposes of certain relevant enactments; s. 5 relates to the conversion of special drawing rights into sterling; s. 6 contains supplemental provisions; s. 7 gives the short title.

The Act received the Royal Assent on April 4, 1979, and will come into force, except for s. 2, on a day to be appointed by Her Majesty in Council. S. 2 came into force on April 4, 1979 (s. 2 (2)).

Parliamentary debates

Hansard, H.L. Vol. 397, col. 1168; Vol. 398, col. 1234; Vol 399, col. 760; H.C. Vol. 965, cols. 1275, 1276.

Alterations of texts of carriage by air convention

1.—(1) For Schedule 1 to the Carriage by Air Act 1961 (which contains the English and French texts of the Warsaw Convention mentioned in the title to this Act as it has the force of law in the United Kingdom by virtue of section 1 of that Act) there shall be substituted Schedule 1 to this Act (which contains the English and French texts of that Convention as amended by provisions of protocols No. 3 and No. 4 which were signed at Montreal on 25th September 1975).

(2) The said Act of 1961 and the Carriage by Air (Supplementary Provisions) Act 1962 shall have effect with the amendments set out in Schedule 2 to this Act (which are consequential upon the changes of texts made by the preceding subsection or are connected with the coming into force of those texts).

(3) Neither of the preceding subsections shall affect rights and liabilities arising out of an occurrence which took place before the coming into force of that subsection or, if the subsection comes into force in pursuance of section 7 (2) of this Act for some purposes only, arising out of an occurrence which took place before it comes into force for those purposes.

Modification of article 26 (2) of carriage by air convention

2.—(1) In the Carriage by Air Act 1961, after section 4 there shall be inserted the following section—

Notice of partial loss

4A.—(1) In Article 26 (2) the references to damage shall be construed as including loss of part of the baggage or cargo in question and the reference to the receipt of baggage or cargo shall, in relation to loss of part of it, be construed as receipt of the remainder of it.

(2) It is hereby declared, without prejudice to the operation of any other section of this Act, that the reference to Article 26 (2) in the preceding subsection is to Article 26 (2) as set out in Part I and Part II of the First Schedule in this Act.

(2) This section shall come into force at the passing of this Act but shall not apply to loss which occurred before the passing of this Act.

Amendment of Acts relating to carriage by air or road in consequence of revision of relevant conventions

3.—(1) In the Carriage by Air Act 1961, after section 8 there shall be inserted the following section—

Amendments consequential on revision of Convention

8A.—(1) If at any time it appears to Her Majesty in Council that Her Majesty's Government in the United Kingdom have agreed to a revision of the Convention, Her Majesty may by Order in Council provide that this Act, the Carriage by Air (Supplementary Provisions) Act 1962 and section 5 (1) of the Carriage by Air and Road Act 1979 shall have effect subject to such exceptions, adaptations and modifications as Her Majesty considers appropriate in consequence of the revision.

(2) In the preceding subsection " revision " means an omission from, addition to or alteration of the Convention and includes replacement of the Convention or part of it by another convention.

(3) An Order in Council under this section shall not be made unless a draft of the Order has been laid before Parliament and approved by a resolution of each House of Parliament.

(2) In the Carriage by Air (Supplementary Provisions) Act 1962, after section 4 there shall be inserted the following section—

Amendments consequential on revision of Supplementary Convention

4A.—(1) Section 8A of the said Act of 1961 (which among other things enables Her Majesty in Council to alter that Act and this Act in consequence of any revision of the convention to which that Act relates) shall have effect in relation to a revision of the Convention in the Schedule to this Act as it has effect in relation to a revision of the Convention mentioned in that section but as if the reference in that section to the said Act of 1961 were omitted.

(2) An order under the said section 8A may relate both to that Act and this Act; and in the preceding subsection " revision ", in relation to the Convention in the Schedule to this Act, means an omission from, addition to or alteration of that Convention and includes replacement of that Convention or part of it by another convention.

(3) In the Carriage of Goods by Road Act 1965, after section 8 there shall be inserted the following section—

Amendments consequential on revision of Convention

8A.—(1) If at any time it appears to Her Majesty in Council that Her Majesty's Government in the United Kingdom have agreed to any revision of the Convention, Her Majesty may by Order in Council make such amendment of—

(*a*) the provisions set out in the Schedule to this Act; and

(*b*) the definition of, and references in this Act to, or to particular provisions of, the Convention; and

(*c*) section 5 (1) of the Carriage by Air and Road Act 1979,

as appear to Her to be appropriate in consequence of the revision.

(2) In the preceding subsection " revision " means an omission from, addition to or alteration of the Convention and includes replacement of the Convention or part of it by another convention.

(3) An Order in Council under this section shall not be made unless a draft of the Order has been laid before Parliament and approved by a resolution of each House of Parliament.

(4) In section 8 of the Carriage of Passengers by Road Act 1974 (of which subsection (1) enables amendments of the provisions of that Act mentioned in paragraphs (*a*) and (*b*) of that subsection to be made by Order in Council in consequence of any revision of the Convention mentioned in that subsection, whether the revision operates by way of amendment of the text of the Convention as then in force or takes the form of a new convention or part of a new convention having substantially the same effect as the provisions set out in the Schedule to that Act)—

(*a*) in subsection (1) the words from " whether " to " Act " where it first occurs shall be omitted;

(*b*) at the end of paragraph (*b*) of subsection (1) there shall be inserted the words " and

(*c*) of section 5 (1) of the Carriage by Air and Road Act 1979 "; and

(*c*) after subsection (1) there shall be inserted the following subsection—

(1A) In the preceding subsection " revision " means an omission from, addition to or alteration of the Convention and includes replacement of the Convention or part of it by another convention.

Replacement of gold francs by special drawing rights for the purposes of certain enactments relating to carriage by air or road

4.—(1) Schedule 1 to the Carriage by Air Act 1961 as originally enacted shall have effect with the following amendments, namely—

(*a*) in Article 22 of Part I of that Schedule (which among other things provided that the liability of a carrier is limited to two hundred and fifty thousand francs for each passenger and two hundred and fifty francs per kilogramme of cargo and registered baggage unless a higher limit is agreed and to five thousand francs for objects of which a passenger takes charge himself)—

(i) for the words " two hundred and fifty thousand francs " where they first occur and the words " two hundred and fifty francs " and " five thousand francs " there shall be substituted respectively the words " 16,600 special drawing rights ", " 17 special drawing rights " and " 332 special drawing rights ";

(ii) for the words " two hundred and fifty thousand francs " in the second place where they occur there shall be substituted the words " this limit ", and

(iii) for paragraph (5) there shall be substituted the following paragraph—

(5) The sums mentioned in terms of the special drawing right in this Article shall be deemed to refer to the special drawing right as defined by the International Monetary Fund. Conversion of the sums into national currencies shall, in case of judicial proceedings, be made according to the value of such currencies in terms of the special drawing right at the date of the judgment.;

(*b*) in Article 22 of Part II of that Schedule (which contains the corresponding provisions of the French text)—

(i) for the words " deux cent cinquante mille francs ", " deux cent cinquante francs " and " cinq mille francs " there shall be substituted respectively the words " 16.600 Droits de Tirage spéciaux ", " 17 Droits de Tirage spéciaux " and " 332 Droits de Tirage spéciaux ", and

(ii) for paragraph (5) there shall be substituted the following paragraph—

(5) Les sommes indiquées en Droits de Tirage spéciaux dans le présent article sont considérées comme se rapportant au Droit de Tirage spécial tel que défini par le Fonds monétaire international. La conversion de ces sommes en monnaies nationales s'effectuera en cas d'instance judiciaire suivant la valeur de ces monnaies en Droit de Tirage spécial à la date du jugement.;

but nothing in this subsection affects the provisions of Schedule 1 to this Act.

(2) The Schedule to the Carriage of Goods by Road Act 1965 (which contains the text of the Convention on the Contract for the International Carriage of Goods by Road as it has the force of law in the United Kingdom by virtue of section 1 of that Act) shall have effect with the following amendments, namely—

(*a*) for paragraph 3 of Article 23 (which provides that compensation for loss of goods shall not exceed 25 francs per kilogram of gross weight short) there shall be substituted the following paragraph—

3. Compensation shall not, however, exceed 8.33 units of account per kilogram of gross weight short.;

(b) at the end of Article 23 there shall be inserted the following paragraph—

7. The unit of account mentioned in this Convention is the Special Drawing Right as defined by the International Monetary Fund. The amount mentioned in paragraph 3 of this article shall be converted into the national currency of the State of the Court seised of the case on the basis of the value of that currency on the date of the judgment or the date agreed upon by the Parties. .

(3) The Schedule to the Carriage of Passengers by Road Act 1974 (which contains the text of the Convention on the Contract for the International Carriage of Passengers and Luggage by Road as it has the force of law in the United Kingdom by virtue of section 1 of that Act) shall have effect with the following amendments, namely—

(a) in paragraph 1 of Article 13 (which among other things provides that the total damages payable by a carrier in respect of the same occurrence shall not exceed 250,000 francs for each victim) for the words " 250,000 francs " there shall be substituted the words " 83,333 units of account ";

(b) in paragraph 1 of Article 16 (which among other things provides that compensation in respect of luggage shall not exceed 500 francs for each piece of luggage nor 2,000 francs for each passenger and that compensation in respect of personal effects shall not exceed 1,000 francs for each passenger) for the words " 500 francs "; " 2,000 francs " and " 1,000 francs " respectively there shall be submitted the words " 166.67 units of account ", " 666.67 units of account " and " 333.33 units of account ";

(c) for Article 19 (which provides that the franc referred to in the Convention shall be the gold franc specified in that Article) there shall be substituted the following Article—

Article 19

The Unit of Account mentioned in this Convention is the Special Drawing Right as defined by the International Monetary Fund. The amounts mentioned in articles 13 and 16 of this Convention shall be converted into the national currency of the State of the Court seised of the case on the basis of the value of that currency on the date of the judgment or the date agreed upon by the Parties. .

(4) If judgment in respect of a liability limited by the said Article 22, 23, 13 or 16 is given—

(a) in the case of a liability limited by the said Article 22, at a time when the amendments made by this section to that Article are in force for the purposes of the liability; or

(b) in any other case, at a time when the amendments made by this section to the other Article in question are in force,

then, notwithstanding that the liability arose before the amendments in question came into force, the judgment shall be in accordance with that Article as amended by this section and, in a case falling within the said Article 13 or 16, in accordance with the said Article 19 as so amended.

Conversion of special drawing rights into sterling

5.—(1) For the purposes of Articles 22 and 22A of Schedule 1 to this Act and the Articles 22, 23 and 19 mentioned in the preceding section as amended by that section, the value on a particular day of one special drawing right shall be treated as equal to such a sum in sterling as the International Monetary Fund have fixed as being the equivalent of one special drawing right—

(*a*) for that day; or

(*b*) if no sum has been fixed for that day, for the last day before that day for which a sum has been so fixed.

(2) A certificate given by or on behalf of the Treasury stating—

(*a*) that a particular sum in sterling has been fixed as aforesaid for a particular day; or

(*b*) that no sum has been so fixed for a particular day and that a particular sum in sterling has been so fixed for a day which is the last day for which a sum has been so fixed before the particular day,

shall be conclusive evidence of those matters for the purposes of the preceding subsection; and a document purporting to be such a certificate shall in any proceedings be received in evidence and, unless the contrary is proved, be deemed to be such a certificate.

(3) The Treasury may charge a reasonable fee for any certificate given by or on behalf of the Treasury in pursuance of the preceding subsection, and any fee received by the Treasury by virtue of this subsection shall be paid into the Consolidated Fund.

Supplemental

6.—(1) It is hereby declared that the powers to make Orders in Council conferred by—

(*a*) sections 8A, 9 and 10 of the Carriage by Air Act 1961 (which provide for the amendment of that Act and other Acts in consequence of a revision of the relevant convention and for the application of that Act to the countries mentioned in section 9 and to such carriage by air as is mentioned in section 10); and

(*b*) sections 8, 8A and 9 of the Carriage of Goods by Road Act 1965 (which provide for the resolution of conflicts between provisions of that Act and certain other provisions relating to carriage by road, for the amendment of that Act in consequence of a revision of the relevant convention and for the application of that Act to the countries mentioned in section 9); and

(*c*) sections 7, 8 and 9 of the Carriage of Passengers by Road Act 1974 (which provide as mentioned in the preceding paragraph),

include power to make Orders in Council in respect of the Act in question as amended by this Act.

(2) It is hereby declared that Schedule 1 to the said Act of 1961 as originally enacted or, if subsection (1) of section 4 of this Act has come into force, as amended by that subsection, remains in force in relation to any matter in relation to which Schedule 1 to this Act is not for the time being in force and that the reference to Schedule 1 to that Act in section 2 (1) (*b*) of the Carriage by Air (Supplementary Provisions) Act 1962 is to be construed as a reference to both the Schedules 1 aforesaid so far as each is for the time being in force.

(3) This Act binds the Crown.

(4) The following provisions (which are superseded by this Act) are hereby repealed, namely—

(*a*) section 4 (4) of the said Act of 1961;

(*b*) in section 8 (1) of the said Act of 1974 the words from " whether " to " Act " where it first occurs.

Short title and commencement

7.—(1) This Act may be cited as the Carriage by Air and Road Act 1979.

(2) This Act, except section 2, shall come into force on such day as Her Majesty may by Order in Council appoint, and—

(*a*) different days may be appointed in pursuance of this subsection for different provisions of this Act or for different purposes of the same provision;

(*b*) it is hereby declared that a day or days may be appointed in pursuance of this subsection in respect of subsection (1) of section 1 of this Act and Schedule 1 to this Act notwithstanding that the protocols mentioned in that subsection are not in force in accordance with the provisions in that behalf of those protocols.

SCHEDULES

Sections 1 (1), 4 (1), 5 (1), 6 (2), 7 (2)

SCHEDULE 1

THE WARSAW CONVENTION AS AMENDED AT THE HAGUE IN 1955 AND BY PROTOCOLS NO. 3 AND NO. 4 SIGNED AT MONTREAL IN 1975

PART I

THE ENGLISH TEXT

CHAPTER I

SCOPE—DEFINITIONS

Article 1

(1) This Convention applies to all international carriage of persons, baggage or cargo performed by aircraft for reward. It applies equally to gratuitous carriage by aircraft performed by an air transport undertaking.

(2) For the purposes of this Convention, the expression *international carriage* means any carriage in which, according to the agreement between the parties, the place of departure and the place of destination, whether or not there be a break in the carriage or a transhipment, are situated either within the territories of two High Contracting Parties or within the territory of a single High Contracting Party if there is an agreed stopping place within the territory of another State, even if that State is not a High Contracting Party. Carriage between two points within the territory of a single High Contracting Party without an agreed stopping place within the territory of another State is not international carriage for the purposes of this Convention.

(3) Carriage to be performed by several successive air carriers is deemed, for the purposes of this Convention, to be one undivided carriage if it has been regarded by the parties as a single operation, whether it has been agreed upon under the form of a single contract or of a series of contracts, and it does not lose its international character merely because one contract or a series of contracts is to be performed entirely within the territory of the same State.

Article 2

(1) This Convention applies to carriage performed by the State or by legally constituted public bodies provided it falls within the conditions laid down in Article 1.

(2) In the carriage of postal items the carrier shall be liable only to the relevant postal administration in accordance with the rules applicable to the relationship between the carriers and the postal administrations.

(3) Except as provided in paragraph (2) of this Article, the provisions of this Convention shall not apply to the carriage of postal items.

CHAPTER II

DOCUMENTS OF CARRIAGE

SECTION 1—PASSENGER TICKET

Article 3

(1) In respect of the carriage of passengers an individual or collective document of carriage shall be delivered containing:

(*a*) an indication of the places of departure and destination;

(*b*) if the places of departure and destination are within the territory of a single High Contracting Party, one or more agreed stopping places being within the territory of another State, an indication of at least one such stopping place.

(2) Any other means which would preserve a record of the information indicated in (*a*) and (*b*) of the foregoing paragraph may be substituted for the delivery of the document referred to in that paragraph.

(3) Non-compliance with the provisions of the foregoing paragraphs shall not affect the existence or the validity of the contract of carriage, which shall, none the less, be subject to the rules of this Convention including those relating to limitation of liability.

SECTION 2—BAGGAGE CHECK

Article 4

(1) In respect of the carriage of checked baggage, a baggage check shall be delivered, which, unless combined with or incorporated in a document of carriage which complies with the provisions of Article 3, paragraph (1), shall contain:

(*a*) an indication of the places of departure and destination;

(*b*) if the places of departure and destination are within the territory of a single High Contracting Party, one or more agreed stopping places being within the territory of another State, an indication of at least one such stopping place.

(2) Any other means which would preserve a record of the information indicated in (*a*) and (*b*) of the foregoing paragraph may be substituted for the delivery of the baggage check referred to in that paragraph.

(3) Non-compliance with the provisions of the foregoing paragraphs shall not affect the existence or the validity of the contract of carriage, which shall, none the less, be subject to the rules of this Convention including those relating to limitation of liability.

SECTION 3—DOCUMENTATION RELATING TO CARGO

Article 5

(1) In respect of the carriage of cargo an air waybill shall be delivered.

(2) Any other means which would preserve a record of the carriage to be performed may, with the consent of the consignor, be substituted for the delivery of an air waybill. If such other means are used, the carrier shall, if so requested by the consignor, deliver to the consignor a receipt for the cargo permitting identification of the consignment and access to the information contained in the record preserved by such other means.

(3) The impossibility of using, at points of transit and destination, the other means which would preserve the record of the carriage referred to in paragraph (2) of this Article does not entitle the carrier to refuse to accept the cargo for carriage.

Article 6

(1) The air waybill shall be made out by the consignor in three original parts.

(2) The first part shall be marked "for the carrier"; it shall be signed by the consignor. The second part shall be marked "for the consignee"; it shall be signed by the consignor and by the carrier. The third part shall be signed by the carrier and handed by him to the consignor after the cargo has been accepted.

(3) The signature of the carrier and that of the consignor may be printed or stamped.

(4) If, at the request of the consignor, the carrier makes out the air waybill, he shall be deemed, subject to proof to the contrary, to have done so on behalf of the consignor.

Article 7

When there is more than one package:

(*a*) the carrier of cargo has the right to require the consignor to make out separate air waybills;

(*b*) the consignor has the right to require the carrier to deliver separate receipts when the other means referred to in paragraph (2) of Article 5 are used.

Article 8

The air waybill and the receipt for the cargo shall contain:

(*a*) an indication of the places of departure and destination;

(*b*) if the places of departure and destination are within the territory of a single High Contracting Party, one or more agreed stopping places being within the territory of another State, an indication of at least one such stopping place; and

(*c*) an indication of the weight of the consignment.

Article 9

Non-compliance with the provisions of Articles 5 to 8 shall not affect the existence or the validity of the contract of carriage, which shall, none the less, be subject to the rules of this Convention including those relating to limitation of liability.

Article 10

(1) The consignor is responsible for the correctness of the particulars and statements relating to the cargo inserted by him or on his behalf in the air waybill or furnished by him or on his behalf to the carrier for insertion in the receipt for the cargo or for insertion in the record preserved by the other means referred to in paragraph (2) of Article 5.

(2) The consignor shall indemnify the carrier against all damage suffered by him, or by any other person to whom the carrier is liable, by reason of the irregularity, incorrectness or incompleteness of the particulars and statements furnished by the consignor or on his behalf.

(3) Subject to the provisions of paragraphs (1) and (2) of this Article, the carrier shall indemnify the consignor against all damage suffered by him, or by any other person to whom the consignor is liable, by reason of the irregularity, incorrectness or incompleteness of the particulars and statements inserted by the carrier or on his behalf in the receipt for the cargo or in the record preserved by the other means referred to in paragraph (2) of Article 5.

Article 11

(1) The air waybill or the receipt for the cargo is *prima facie* evidence of the conclusion of the contract, of the acceptance of the cargo and of the conditions of carriage mentioned therein.

(2) Any statements in the air waybill or the receipt for the cargo relating to the weight, dimensions and packing of the cargo, as well as those relating to the number of packages, are *prima facie* evidence of the facts stated; those relating to the quantity, volume and condition of the cargo do not constitute evidence against the carrier except so far as they both have been, and are stated in the air waybill to have been, checked by him in the presence of the consignor, or relate to the apparent condition of the cargo.

Article 12

(1) Subject to his liability to carry out all his obligations under the contract of carriage, the consignor has the right to dispose of the cargo by withdrawing it at the airport of departure or destination, or by stopping it in the course of the

journey on any landing, or by calling for it to be delivered at the place of destination or in the course of the journey to a person other than the consignee originally designated, or by requiring it to be returned to the airport of departure. He must not exercise this right of disposition in such a way as to prejudice the carrier or other consignors and he must repay any expenses occasioned by the exercise of this right.

(2) If it is impossible to carry out the orders of the consignor the carrier must so inform him forthwith.

(3) If the carrier obeys the orders of the consignor for the disposition of the cargo without requiring the production of the part of the air waybill or the receipt for the cargo delivered to the latter, he will be liable, without prejudice to his right of recovery from the consignor, for any damage which may be caused thereby to any person who is lawfully in possession of that part of the air waybill or the receipt for the cargo.

(4) The right conferred on the consignor ceases at the moment when that of the consignee begins in accordance with Article 13. Nevertheless, if the consignee declines to accept the cargo, or if he cannot be communicated with, the consignor resumes his right of disposition.

Article 13

(1) Except when the consignor has exercised his right under Article 12, the consignee is entitled, on arrival of the cargo at the place of destination, to require the carrier to deliver the cargo to him, on payment of the charges due and on complying with the conditions of carriage.

(2) Unless it is otherwise agreed, it is the duty of the carrier to give notice to the consignee as soon as the cargo arrives.

(3) If the carrier admits the loss of the cargo, or if the cargo has not arrived at the expiration of seven days after the date on which it ought to have arrived, the consignee is entitled to enforce against the carrier the rights which flow from the contract of carriage.

Article 14

The consignor and the consignee can respectively enforce all the rights given them by Articles 12 and 13, each in his own name, whether he is acting in his own interest or in the interest of another, provided that he carries out the obligations imposed by the contract of carriage.

Article 15

(1) Articles 12, 13 and 14 do not affect either the relations of the consignor and the consignee with each other or the mutual relations of third parties whose rights are derived either from the consignor or from the consignee.

(2) The provisions of Articles 12, 13 and 14 can only be varied by express provision in the air waybill or the receipt for the cargo.

Article 16

(1) The consignor must furnish such information and such documents as are necessary to meet the formalities of customs, octroi or police before the cargo can be delivered to the consignee. The consignor is liable to the carrier for any damage occasioned by the absence, insufficiency or irregularity of any such information or documents, unless the damage is due to the fault of the carrier, his servants or agents.

(2) The carrier is under no obligation to enquire into the correctness or sufficiency of such information or documents.

Chapter III

Liability of the carrier

Article 17

(1) The carrier is liable for damage sustained in case of death or personal injury of a passenger upon condition only that the event which caused the death or

injury took place on board the aircraft or in the course of any of the operations embarking or disembarking. However, the carrier is not liable if the death or injury resulted solely from the state of health of the passenger.

(2) The carrier is liable for damage sustained in case of destruction or loss of, or of damage to, baggage upon condition only that the event which caused the destruction, loss or damage took place on board the aircraft or in the course of any of the operations of embarking or disembarking or during any period within which the baggage was in charge of the carrier. However, the carrier is not liable if the damage resulted solely from the inherent defect, quality or vice of the baggage.

(3) Unless otherwise specified, in this Convention the term "baggage" means both checked baggage and objects carried by the passenger.

Article 18

(1) The carrier is liable for damage sustained in the event of the destruction or loss of, or damage to, cargo upon condition only that the occurrence which caused the damage so sustained took place during the carriage by air.

(2) However, the carrier is not liable if he proves that the destruction, loss of, or damage to, the cargo resulted solely from one or more of the following:

(*a*) inherent defect, quality or vice of that cargo;

(*b*) defective packing of that cargo performed by a person other than the carrier or his servants or agents;

(*c*) an act of war or an armed conflict;

(*d*) an act of public authority carried out in connection with the entry, exit or transit of the cargo.

(3) The carriage by air within the meaning of paragraph (1) of this Article comprises the period during which the cargo is in the charge of the carrier, whether in an airport or on board an aircraft, or, in the case of a landing outside an airport, in any place whatsoever.

(4) The period of the carriage by air does not extend to any carriage by land, by sea or by river performed outside an airport. If, however, such carriage takes place in the performance of a contract for carriage by air, for the purpose of loading, delivery or transhipment, any damage is presumed, subject to proof to the contrary, to have been the result of an event which took place during the carriage by air.

Article 19

The carrier is liable for damage occasioned by delay in the carriage by air of passengers, baggage or cargo.

Article 20

In the carriage of passengers, baggage and cargo, the carrier shall not be liable for damage occasioned by delay if he proves that he and his servants and agents have taken all necessary measures to avoid the damage or that it was impossible for them to take such measures.

Article 21

(1) In the carriage of passengers and baggage, if the carrier proves that the damage was caused or contributed to by the negligence or other wrongful act or omission of the person claiming compensation, the carrier shall be wholly or partly exonerated from his liability to such person to the extent that such negligence or wrongful act or omission caused or contributed to the damage. When by reason of the death or injury of a passenger compensation is claimed by a person other than the passenger, the carrier shall likewise be wholly or partly exonerated from his liability to the extent that he proves that the damage was caused or contributed to by the negligence or other wrongful act or omission of that passenger.

(2) In the carriage of cargo, if the carrier proves that the damage was caused by or contributed to by the negligence or other wrongful act or omission of the person claiming compensation, or the person from whom he derives his rights, the carrier shall be wholly or partly exonerated from his liability to the claimant to the extent that such negligence or wrongful act or omission caused or contributed to the damage.

Article 22

(1) (*a*) In the carriage of persons the liability of the carrier is limited to the sum of 100,000 special drawing rights for the aggregate of the claims, however founded, in respect of damage suffered as a result of the death or personal injury of each passenger. Where, in accordance with the law of the court seised of the case, damages may be awarded in the form of periodic payments, the equivalent capital value of the said payments shall not exceed 100,000 special drawing rights.

(*b*) In the case of delay in the carriage of persons the liability of the carrier for each passenger is limited to 4,150 special drawing rights.

(*c*) In the carriage of baggage the liability of the carrier in the case of destruction, loss, damage or delay is limited to 1,000 special drawing rights for each passenger.

(2) (*a*) The courts of the High Contracting Parties which are not authorised under their law to award the costs of the action, including lawyers' fees, shall, in actions relating to the carriage of passengers and baggage to which this Convention applies, have the power to award, in their discretion, to the claimant the whole or part of the costs of the action, including lawyers' fees which the court considers reasonable.

(*b*) The costs of the action including lawyers' fees shall be awarded in accordance with subparagraph (*a*) only if the claimant gives a written notice to the carrier of the amount claimed including the particulars of the calculation of that amount and the carrier does not make, within a period of six months after his receipt of such notice, a written offer of settlement in an amount at least equal to the compensation awarded within the applicable limit. This period will be extended until the time of commencement of the action if that is later.

(*c*) The costs of the action including lawyers' fees shall not be taken into account in applying the limits under this Article.

(3) The sums mentioned in terms of special drawing right in this Article shall be deemed to refer to the special drawing right as defined by the International Monetary Fund. Conversion of the sums into national currencies shall, in case of judicial proceedings, be made according to the value of such currencies in terms of the special drawing right at the date of the judgment.

Article 22A

(1) (*a*) In the carriage of cargo, the liability of the carrier is limited to a sum of 17 special drawing rights per kilogramme, unless the consignor has made, at the time when the package was handed over to the carrier, a special declaration of interest in delivery at destination and has paid a supplementary sum if the case so requires. In that case the carrier will be liable to pay a sum not exceeding the declared sum, unless he proves that that sum is greater than the consignor's actual interest in delivery at destination.

(*b*) In the case of loss, damage or delay of part of the cargo, or of any object contained therein, the weight to be taken into consideration in determining the amount to which the carrier's liability is limited shall be only the total weight of the package or packages concerned. Nevertheless, when the loss, damage or delay of a part of the cargo, or of an object contained therein, affects the value of other packages covered by the same air waybill, the total weight of such package or packages shall also be taken into consideration in determining the limit of liability.

(2) The limits prescribed in this Article shall not prevent the court in an action relating to the carriage of cargo from awarding in accordance with its own law, in addition, the whole or part of the court costs and of the other expenses of the litigation incurred by the plaintiff. The foregoing provision shall not apply if the amount of the damages awarded, excluding court costs and other expenses of the litigation, does not exceed the sum which the carrier has offered in writing to the plaintiff within a period of six months from the date of the occurrence causing the damage, or before the commencement of the action, if that is later.

(3) The sums mentioned in terms of special drawing right in this Article shall be deemed to refer to the special drawing right as defined by the International Monetary Fund. Conversion of the sums into national currencies shall, in case of judicial proceedings, be made according to the value of such currencies in terms of the special drawing right at the date of the judgment.

Article 23

(1) Any provision tending to relieve the carrier of liability or to fix a lower limit than that which is laid down in this Convention shall be null and void, but the nullity of any such provision does not involve the nullity of the whole contract, which shall remain subject to the provisions of this Convention.

(2) Paragraph (1) of this Article shall not apply to provisions governing loss or damage resulting from the inherent defect, quality or vice of the cargo carried.

Article 24

In the carriage of passengers, baggage and cargo, any action for damages, however founded, whether under this Convention or in contract or in tort or otherwise, can only be brought subject to the conditions and limits of liability set out in this Convention without prejudice to the question as to who are the persons who have the right to bring suit and what are their respective rights. Such limits of liability constitute maximum limits and may not be exceeded whatever the circumstances which gave rise to the liability.

Article 25A

(1) If an action is brought against a servant or agent of the carrier arising out of damage to which the Convention relates, such servant or agent, if he proves that he acted within the scope of his employment, shall be entitled to avail himself of the limits of liability which that carrier himself is entitled to invoke under this Convention.

(2) The aggregate of the amounts recoverable from the carrier, his servants and agents, in that case, shall not exceed the said limits.

Article 26

(1) Receipt by the person entitled to delivery of baggage or cargo without complaint is *prima facie* evidence that the same has been delivered in good condition and in accordance with the document of carriage.

(2) In the case of damage, the person entitled to delivery must complain to the carrier forthwith after the discovery of the damage, and, at the latest, within seven days from the date of receipt in the case of baggage and fourteen days from the date of receipt in the case of cargo. In the case of delay the complaint must be made at the latest within twenty-one days from the date on which the baggage or cargo have been placed at his disposal.

(3) Every complaint must be made in writing upon the document of carriage or by separate notice in writing despatched within the times aforesaid.

(4) Failing complaint within the times aforesaid, no action shall lie against the carrier, save in the case of fraud on his part.

Article 27

In the case of the death of the person liable, an action for damages lies in accordance with the terms of this Convention against those legally representing his estate.

Article 28

(1) An action for damages must be brought, at the option of the plaintiff, in the territory of one of the High Contracting Parties, either before the court having jurisdiction where the carrier is ordinarily resident, or has his principal place of business, or has an establishment by which the contract has been made or before the court having jurisdiction at the place of destination.

(2) In respect of damage resulting from the death, injury or delay of a passenger or the destruction, loss, damage or delay of baggage, the action may be brought before one of the courts mentioned in paragraph (1) of this Article, or in the territory of one of the High Contracting Parties, before the court within the jurisdiction of which the carrier has an establishment if the passenger has his ordinary or permanent residence in the territory of the same High Contracting Party.

(3) Questions of procedure shall be governed by the law of the court seised of the case.

Article 29

(1) The right to damages shall be extinguished if an action is not brought within two years, reckoned from the date of arrival at the destination, or from the date on which the aircraft ought to have arrived, or from the date on which the carriage stopped.

(2) The method of calculating the period of limitation shall be determined by the law of the court seised of the case.

Article 30

(1) In the case of carriage to be performed by various successive carriers and falling within the definition set out in the third paragraph of Article 1, each carrier who accepts passengers, baggage or cargo is subjected to the rules set out in this Convention, and is deemed to be one of the contracting parties to the contract of carriage in so far as the contract deals with that part of the carriage which is performed under his supervision.

(2) In the case of carriage of this nature, the passenger or his representative can take action only against the carrier who performed the carriage during which the accident or the delay occurred, save in the case where, by express agreement, the first carrier has assumed liability for the whole journey.

(3) As regards baggage or cargo, the passenger or consignor will have a right of action against the first carrier, and the passenger or consignee who is entitled to delivery will have a right of action against the last carrier, and further, each may take action against the carrier who performed the carriage during which the destruction, loss, damage or delay took place. These carriers will be jointly and severally liable to the passenger or to the consignor or consignee.

Article 30A

Nothing in this Convention shall prejudice the question whether a person liable for damage in accordance with its provisions has a right of recourse against any other person.

Provisions Relating to Combined Carriage

Article 31

(1) In the case of combined carriage performed partly by air and partly by any other mode of carriage, the provisions of this Convention apply only to the carriage by air, provided that the carriage by air falls within the terms of Article 1.

(2) Nothing in this Convention shall prevent the parties in the case of combined carriage from inserting in the document of air carriage conditions relating to other modes of carriage, provided that the provisions of this Convention are observed as regards the carriage by air.

Chapter V

General and Final Provisions

Article 32

Any clause contained in the contract and all special agreements entered into before the damage occurred by which the parties purport to infringe the rules laid down by this Convention, whether by deciding the law to be applied, or by altering the rules as to jurisdiction, shall be null and void. Nevertheless for the carriage of cargo arbitration clauses are allowed, subject to this Convention, if the arbitration is to take place within one of the jurisdictions referred to in the first paragraph of Article 28.

Article 33

Except as provided in paragraph (3) of Article 5, nothing in this Convention shall prevent the carrier either from refusing to enter into any contract of carriage or from making regulations which do not conflict with the provisions of this Convention.

Article 34

The provisions of Articles 3 to 8 inclusive relating to documents of carriage shall not apply in the case of carriage performed in extraordinary circumstances outside the normal scope of an air carrier's business.

Article 35

The expression "days" when used in this Convention means current days not working days.

Article 35A

No provision contained in this Convention shall prevent a State from establishing and operating within its territory a system to supplement the compensation payable to claimants under the Convention in respect of death, or personal injury, of passengers. Such a system shall fulfil the following conditions:

(*a*) it shall not in any circumstances impose upon the carrier, his servants or agents, any liability in addition to that provided under this Convention;

(*b*) it shall not impose upon the carrier any financial or administrative burden other than collecting in that State contributions from passengers if required so to do;

(*c*) it shall not give rise to any discrimination between carriers with regard to the passengers concerned and the benefits available to the said passengers under the system shall be extended to them regardless of the carrier whose services they have used;

(*d*) if a passenger has contributed to the system, any person suffering damage as a consequence of death or personal injury of such passenger shall be entitled to the benefits of the system.

Article 40A

(1) [*This paragraph is not reproduced. It defines "High Contracting Party".*]

(2) For the purposes of the Convention the word *territory* means not only the metropolitan territory of a State but also all other territories for the foreign relations of which that State is responsible.

[*Articles* 36, 37, 38, 39, 40, 41 *and* 42 *and the concluding words of the Convention are not reproduced. They deal, among other things, with the coming into force of the Convention. The former Article* 25 *is superseded by Article* 24.]

ADDITIONAL PROTOCOL

(*With reference to Article* 2)

The High Contracting Parties reserve to themselves the right to declare at the time of ratification or of accession that the first paragraph of Article 2 of this Convention shall not apply to international carriage by air performed directly by the State, its colonies, protectorates or mandated territories or by any other territory under its sovereignty, suzerainty or authority.

PART II

THE FRENCH TEXT

CHAPITRE IER

OBJET—DÉFINITIONS

Article 1er

(1) La présente Convention s'applique à tout transport international de personnes, bagages ou marchandises, effectué par aéronef contre rémunération. Elle s'applique également aux transports gratuits effectués par aéronef par une entreprise de transports aériens.

(2) Est qualifié *transport international*, au sens de la présente Convention, tout transport dans lequel, d'après les stipulations des parties, le point de départ et le point de destination, qu'il y ait ou non interruption de transport ou transbordement,

sont situés soit sur le territoire de deux Hautes Parties Contractantes, soit sur le territoire d'une seule Haute Partie Contractante si une escale est prévue sur le territoire d'une autre Etat, même si cet Etat n'est pas une Haute Partie Contractante. Le transport sans une telle escale entre deux points du territoire d'une seule Haute Partie Contractante n'est pas considéré comme international au sens de la présente Convention.

(3) Le transport à exécuter par plusieurs transporteurs par air successifs est censé constituer pour l'application de la présente Convention un transport unique lorsqu'il a été envisagé par les parties comme une seule opération, qu'il ait été conclu sous la forme d'un seul contrat ou d'une série de contrats, et il ne perd pas son caractre international par le fait qu'un seul contrat ou une série de contrats doivent être exécutés intégralement dans le territoire d'un même Etat.

Article 2

(1) La Convention s'applique aux transports effectués par l'Etat ou les autres personnes juridiques de droit public, dans les conditions prévues à l'article 1er.

(2) Dans le transport des envois postaux, le transporteur n'est responsable qu'envers l'administration postale compétente conformément aux règles applicables dans les rapports entre les transporteurs et les administrations postales.

(3) Les dispositions de la présente Convention autres que cells de l'alinéa (2) ci-dessus ne s'appliquent pas au transport des envois postaux.

Chapitre II

Titres de transport

Section 1—Billet de passage

Article 3

(1) Dans le transport de passagers, un titre de transport individuel ou collectif doit être délivré, contenant:

(*a*) l'indication des points de départ et de destination;

(*b*) si les points de départ et de destination sont situés sur le territoire d'une même Haute Partie Contractante et si une ou plusieurs escales sont prévues sur le territoire d'un autre Etat, l'indication d'une de ces escales.

(2) L'emploi de tout autre moyen constatant les indications qui figurent à l'alinéa (1) (*a*) et (*b*), peut se substituer à la déliverance du titre de transport mentionné audit alinéa.

(3) L'inobservation des dispositions de l'alinéa précédent n'affecte ni l'existence ni la validité du contrat de tranport, qui n'en sera pas moins soumis aux règles de la présente Convention, y compris celles qui portent sur la limitation de responsabilité.

Section 2—Bulletin de Bagages

Article 4

(1) Dans le transport de bagages enregistrés, un bulletin de bagages doit être délivré qui, s'il n'est pas combiné avec un titre de transport conforme aux dispositions de l'article 3, alinéa ler, ou n'est pas inclus dans un tel titre de transport, doit contenir:

(*a*) l'indication des points de départ et de destination;

(*b*) si les points de départ et de destination sont situés sur le territoire d'une même Haute Partie Contractante et si une ou plusieurs escales sont prévues sur le territoire d'un autre Etat, l'indication d'une de ces escales.

(2) L'emploi de tout autre mayen constatant les indications qui figurent à l'alinéa (1) (*a*) et (*b*), peut se substituter à la délivrance du bulletin de bagages mentionné audit alinéa.

(3) L'inobservation des dispositions de l'alinée précédent n'affecte ni l'existence ni la validité du contrat de transport, qui n'en sera pas moins soumis aux règles de la présente Convention, y compris celles qui portent sur la limitation de responsabilité.

SECTION 3—DOCUMENTATION RELATIVE AUX MARCHANDISES

Article 5

(1) Pour le transport de marchandises une lettre de transport aérien est émise.

(2) L'emploi de tout autre moyen constant les indications relatives au transport à exécuter peut, avec le consentement de l'expéditeur, se substituer à l'émission de la lettre de transport aérien. Si de tels autres moyens sont utilisés, le transporteur délivre à l'expéditeur, à la demande de ce dernier, un récépissé de la marchandise permettant l'identification de l'expédition et l'accès aux indications enregistrées par ces autres moyens.

(3) L'impossibilité d'utiliser, aux points de transit et de destination, les autres moyens permettant de constater les indications relatives au transport, visés à l'alinéa (2) ci-dessus, n'autorise pas le transporteur à refuser l'acceptation des marchandises en vue du transport.

Article 6

(1) La lettre de transport aérien est établie par l'expéditeur en trois exemplaires originaux.

(2) Le premier exemplaire porte la mention " pour le transporteur "; il est signé par l'expéditeur. Le deuxième exemplaire porte la mention " pour le destinataire "; il est signé par l'expéditeur et le transporteur. Le troisième exemplaire est signé par le transporteur et remis par lui à l'expéditeur après acceptation de la marchandise.

(3) La signature du transporteur et celle de l'expéditeur peuvent être imprimées ou remplacées par un timbre.

(4) Si, à la demande de l'expéditeur, le transporteur établit la lettre de transport aérien, il est considéré, jusqu'à preuve contraire, comme agissant au nom de l'expéditeur.

Article 7

Lorsqu'il y a plusieurs colis:

(*a*) le transporteur de marchandises a le droit de demander à l'expéditeur l'établissement de lettres de transport aérien distinctes;

(*b*) l'expéditeur a le droit de demander au transporteur la remise de récépissés distincts, lorsque les autres moyens visés à l'alinéa (2) de l'article 5 sont utilisés.

Article 8

La lettre de transport aérien et le récépissé de la marchandise contiennent:

(*a*) l'indication des points de départ et destination;

(*b*) si les points de départ et de destination sont situés sur le territoire d'une même Haute Partie Contractante et qu'une ou plusieurs escales soient prévues sur le terrtoire d'un autre Etat, l'indication d'une de ces escales;

(*c*) la mention du poids de l'expédition.

Article 9

L'inobservation des dispositions des articles 5 à 8 n'affecte ni l'existence ni la validité du contrat de transport, qui n'en sera pas moins soumis aux règles de la présente Convention, y compris celles qui portent sur la limitation de responsabilité.

Article 10

(1) L'expéditeur est responsable de l'exactitude des indications et déclarations concernant la marchandise inscrites par lui ou en son nom dans la lettre de transport aérien, ainsi que de celles fournies et faites par luiou en son nom au transporteur en vue d'être insérées dans le récépissé de la marchandise ou pour insertion dans les données enregistrées dans par les autres moyens prévus à l'alinéa (2) de l'article 5.

(2) L'expéditeur assume la responsabilité de tout dommage subi par le transporteur ou par toute autre personne à l'égard de laquelle la responsabilité du transporteur est engagée, à raison des indications et déclarations irrégulières, inexactes ou incomplètes fournies et faites par lui ou en son nom.

(3) Sous réserve des dispositions des alinéas (1) et (2) du présent article, le transporteur assume la responsabilité de tout dommage subi par l'expéditeur ou par toute autre personne à l'égard de laquelle la responsabilité de l'expéditeur est engagée,

à raison des indications et déclarations irrégulières, inexactes ou incomplètes insérées par lui ou en son nom dans le récépissé de la marchandise ou dans les données enregistrées par les autres moyens prévus à l'alinéa (2) de l'article 5.

Article 11

(1) La lettre de transport aérien et le récépissé de la marchandise font foi, jusqu'à preuve contraire, de la conclusion du contrat, de la réception de la marchandise et des conditions du transport qui y figurent.

(2) Les énonciations de la lettre de transport aérien et du récépissé de la marchandise, relatives au poids, aux dimensions et à l'emballage de la marchandise ainsi qu'au nombre des colis font foi jusqu'à preuve contraire; celles relatives à la quantité, au volume et à l'état de la marchandise ne font preuve contre le transporteur qu'autant que la vérification en a été faite par lui en présence de l'expéditeur, et constatée sur la lettre de transport aérien, ou qu'il s'agit d'énonciations relatives à l'état apparent de la marchandise.

Article 12

(1) L'expéditeur a le droit, sous la condition d'exécuter toutes les obligations résultant du contrat de transport, de disposer de la marchandise, soit en la retirant à l'aérodrome de départ ou de destination, soit en l'arrêtant en cours de route lors d'un atterrissage, soit en la faisant délivrer au lieu de destination ou en cours de route à une personne autre que le destinataire initialement désigné, soit en demandant son retour à l'aérodrome de départ, pour autant que l'exercise de ce droit ne porte préjudice ni au transporteur, ni aux autres expéditeurs et avec l'obligation de rembourser les frais qui en résultent.

(2) Dans les cas où l'exécution des ordres de l'expéditeur est impossible, le transporteur doit l'en aviser immédiatement.

(3) Si le transporteur se conforme aux ordres de disposition de l'expéditeur, sans exiger la production de l'exemplaire de la lettre de transport aérien ou du récépissé de la marchandise délivré à celui-ci, il sera reponsable, sauf son recours contre l'expéditeur, du préjudice qui pourra être causé par ce fait à celui qui est régulièrement en possession de la lettre de transport aérien ou du récépissé de la marchandise.

(4) Le droit de l'expéditeur cesse au moment où celui du destinataire commence, conformément à l'article 13. Toutefois, si le destinataire refuse la marchandise, ou s'il ne peut être atteint, l'expéditeur reprend son droit de disposition.

Article 13

(1) Sauf lorsque l'expéditeur a exercé le droit qu'il tient de l'article 12, le destinataire a le droit, dès l'arrivée de la marchandise au point de destination, de demander au transporteur de lui livrer la marchandise contre le paiement du montant des créances et contre l'exécution des conditions de transport.

(2) Sauf stipulation contraire, le transporteur doit aviser le destinataire dès l'arrivée de la marchandise.

(3) Si la perte de la marchandise est reconnue par le transporteur ou si, à l'expiration d'un délai de sept jours après qu'elle aurait dû arriver, la marchandise n'est pas arrivée, le destinataire est autorisé à faire valoir vis-à-vis du transporteur les droits résultant du contrat de transport.

Article 14

L'expéditeur et le destinataire peuvent faire valoir tous les droits qui leur sont respectivement conférés par les articles 12 et 13, chacum en son propre nom, qu'il agisse dans son propre intérêt ou dans l'intérêt d'autrui, à condition d'exécuter les obligations que le contrat de transport impose.

Article 15

(1) Les articles 12, 13 et 14 ne portent aucun préjudice ni aux rapports de l'expéditeur et du destinataire entre eux, ni aux rapports des tiers dont les droits proviennent, soit d l'expéditeur, soit du destinataire.

(2) Toute clause dérogeant aux stipulations des articles 12, 13 et 14 doit être inscrite dans la lettre de transport aérien ou dans le récépissé de la marchandise.

Article 16

(1) L'expéditeur est tenu de fournir les renseignements et les documents qui, avant la remise de la marchandise au destinataire, sont nécessaires à l'accomplissement des formalités de douane, d'octroi ou de police. L'expéditeur est responsable envers le transporteur de tous dommages qui pourraient résulter de l'absence, de l'insuffisance ou de l'irrégularité de ces renseignements et pièces, sauf les cas de faute de la part du transporteur ou de ses préposés.

(2) Le transporteur n'est pas tenu d'examiner si ces renseignements et documents sont exacts ou suffisants.

Chapitre III

Responsabilité du transporteur

Article 17

(1) Le transporteur est responsable du préjudice survenu en case de mort ou de toute lésion corporelle subie par un passager, par cela seul que le fait a causé la mort ou la lésion corporelle s'est produit à bord de l'aéronef ou au cours de toutes opérations d'embarquement ou de débarquement. Toutefois, le transporteur n'est pas responsable si la mort ou la lésion corporelle résulte uniquement de l'état de santé du passager.

(2) Le transporteur est responsable du dommage survenu en cas de destruction, perte on avarie de bagages, par cela seul que le fait qui a causé la destruction, la perte ou l'avarie s'est produit à bord de l'aéronef, au cours de toutes opérations d'embarquement ou de débarquement ou au cours de toute période durant laquelle le transporteur avait la garde des bagages. Toutefois, le transporteur n'est pas responsable si le dommage résulte uniquement de la nature ou du vice propre des bagages.

(3) Sous réserve de dispositions contraires, dans cette Convention le terme " bagages " désigne les bagages enregistrés aussi bien que les objets qu'emporte le passager.

Article 18

(1) Le transporteur est responsable du dommage survenu en cas de destruction, perte ou avarie de la marchandise par cela seul que le fait qui a causé le dommage s'est produit pendant le transport aérien.

(2) Toutefois, le transporteur n'est pas responsable s'il établit que la destruction, la perte ou l'avarie de la marchandise résulte uniquement de l'un ou de plusieurs des faits suivants:

(*a*) la nature ou le vice propre de la marchandise;

(*b*) l'emballage défectueux de la marchandise par une personne autre que le transporteur ou ses préposés;

(*c*) un fait de guerre ou un conflit armé;

(*d*) un acte de l'autorité publique accompli en relation avec l'entrée, la sortie ou le transit de la marchandise.

(3) Le transport aérien, au sens de l'alinéa (1) du présent article, comprend la période pendant laquelle les bagages ou marchandises se trouvent sous la garde du transporteur, que ce soit dans un aérodrome ou à bord d'un aéronef ou dans un lieu quelconque en cas d'atterrissage en dehors d'un aérodrome.

(4) La période du transport aérien ne couvre aucun transport terrestre, maritime ou fluvial effectué en dehors d'un aérodrome. Toutefois, lorsqu'un tel transport est effectué dans l'exécution du contrat de transport aérien en vue du chargement, de la livraison on du transbordement, tout dommage est présumé, sauf preuve contraire, résulter d'un événement survenu pendant le transport aérien.

Article 19

Le transporteur est responsable du dommage résultant d'un retard dans le transport aérien de voyagers, bagages ou marchandises.

Article 20

Dans le transport de passagers, de bagages et de marchandises, le transporteur n'est pas responsable du dommage résultant d'un retard s'il prouve que lui et ses préposés ont pris toutes les mesures nécessaires pour éviter le dommage ou qu'il leur était impossible de les prendre.

Article 21

(1) Dans le cas où il fait la preuve que la faute de la personne qui demande réparation a causé le dommage ou y a contribué, le transporteur est exonéré en tout ou en partie de sa responsabilité à l'égard de cette personne, dans la mesure où cette faute a causé le dommage ou y a contribué. Lorsqu'une demande en réparation est introduite par une personne autre que le passager, en raison de la mort ou d'une lésion corporelle subie par ce dernier, le transporteur est également exonéré en tout ou en partie de sa responsabilité dans la mesure où il prouve que la faute de ce passager a causé le dommage ou y a contribué.

(2) Dans le transport de marchandises, le transporteur est exonéré, en tout ou en partie, de sa responsabilité dans la mesure où il prouve que la faute de la personne qui demande réparation ou de la personne dont elle tient ses droits a causé le dommage ou y a contribué.

Article 22

(1) (*a*) Dans le transport de personnes, la responsabilité du transporteur est limitée à la somme de 100.000 Droits de Tirage spéciaux pour l'ensemble des demandes présentées, à quelque titre que ce soit, en réparation du dommage subi en conséquence de la mort on de lésions corporelles d'un passager. Dans le case où, d'après la loi du tribunal saisi, l'indemnité peut être fixée sous forme de rente, le capital de la rente ne dépasser 100.000 Droits de Tirage spéciaux.

(*b*) En cas de retard dans le transport de personnes, la responsabilité du transporteur est limitée à la somme de 4.150 Droits de Tirage spéciaux par passager.

(*c*) Dans le transport de bagages, la responsabilité du transporteur en cas de destruction, perte, avarie ou retard est limitée à la somme de 1.000 Droits de Tirage spéciaux par passager.

(2) (*a*) Les tribunaux des Hautes Parties Contractantes qui n'ont pas la faculté, en vertu de leur propre loi, d'allouer des frais de procès y compris des honoraires d'avocat auront, dans les instances auxquelles la présente Convention s'applique, le pouvoir d'allouer au demandeur, suivant leur appréciation, tout ou partie des frais de procès, y compris les honoraires d'avocat qu'ils jugent raisonnables.

(*b*) Les frais de procès y compris des honoraires d'avocat ne sont accordés, en vertu de l'alinéa (*a*), que si le demandeur a notifié par écrit au transporteur le montant de la somme réclamée, y compris les détails de calcul de cette somme, et si le transporteur n'a pas, dans un délai de six mois à compter de la réception de cette demande, fait par écrit une offre de règlement d'un montant au moins égal à celui des dommages-intérêts alloués par le tribunal à concurrence de la limite applicable. Ce délai est prorogé jusqu'au jour de l'introduction de l'instance si celle-ci est postérieure à l'expiration de ce délai.

(*c*) Les frais de procès y compris des honoraires d'avocat ne sont pas pris en considération pour l'application des limites prévues au présent article.

(3) Les sommnes indiquées en Droits de Tirage spéciaux dans le présent article sont considérées comme se rapportant au Droit de Tirage spécial tel que défini par le Fonds monétaire international. La conversion de ces sommes en monnaies nationales s'effectuera en cas d'instance judiciare suivant la valeur de ces monnaies en Droit de Tirage spécial à la date du jugement.

Article 22A

(1) (*a*) Dans le transport de marchandises, la responsabilité du transporteur est limitée à la somme de 17 Droits de Tirage spéciaux par kilogramme, sauf déclaration spéciale d'intérêt à la livraison faite par l'expéditeur au moment de la remise du colis au transporteur et moyennant le paiement d'une taxe supplémentaire éventuelle. Dans ce cas, le transporteur sera tenu de payer jusqu'à concurrence de la somme déclarée, à moins qu'il ne prouve qu'elle est supérieure à l'intérêt réel de l'expéditeur à la livraison.

(*b*) En cas de perte, d'avarie ou de retard d'une partie des marchandises, ou de tout object qui y est contenu, seul le poids total du ou des colis dont il s'agit est pris en considération pour déterminer la limite de responsabilité du transporteur. Toutefois, lorsque la perte, l'avarie ou le retard d'une partie des marchandises, ou d'un objet qui y est contenu, affecte la valeur d'autres colis couverts par la même lettre de transport aérien, le poids total de ces colis doit être pris en considération pour déterminer la limite de responsabilité.

(2) Les limites fixées par le présent article n'ont pas pour effet d'enlever au tribunal la faculté d'allouer en outre, conformément à sa loi, une somme correspondante à tout ou partie des dépens et autres frais du procès exposés par le demandeur. La disposition précédente ne s'applique pas lorsque le montant de l'indemnité allouée, non compris les dépens et autres frais de procès, ne dépasse pas la somme que le transporteur a offerte par écrit au demandeur dans un délai de six mois à dater du fait qui a causé le dommage ou avant l'introduction de l'instance si celle-ci est postérieure à ce délai.

(3) Les sommes indiquées en Droits de Tirage spéciaux dans le présent article sont considérées comme se rapportant au Droit de Tirage spécial tel que défini par le Fonds monétaire international. La conversion de ces sommes en monnaies nationales s'effectuera en cas d'instance judiciaire suivant la valeur de ces monnaies en Droit de Tirage spécial à la date du jugement.

Article 23

(1) Toute clause tendant à exonérer le transporteur de sa responsabilité ou à établir une limite inférieure à celle qui est fixée dans la présente Convention est nulle et de nul effet, mais la nullité de cette clause n'entraîne pas la nullité du contrat qui reste soumis aux dispositions de la présente Convention.

(2) L'alinéa ler du présent article ne s'applique pas aux clauses concernant la perte ou le dommage résultant de la nature ou du vice propre des marchandises transportées.

Articles 24

Dans le transport de passagers, de bagages et de marchandises, toute action en responsabilité introduite, à quelque titre que ce soit, que ce soit en vertu de la présente Convention, en raison d'un contrat ou d'un acte illicite ou pour toute autre cause, ne peut être exercée que dans les conditions et limites de responsabilité prévues par la présente Convention, sans préjudice de la détermination des personnes qui ont le droit d'agir et de leurs droits respectifs. Ces limits de responsabilité constituent un maximum et sont infranchissables, quelles que soient les circonstances qui sont à l'origine de la responsabilité.

Article 25A

(1) Si une action est intentée contre un préposé du transporteur à la suite d'un dommage visé par la Convention, ce préposé, s'il prouve qu'il a agi dans l'exercice de ses fonctions, pourra se prévaloir des limites de responsabilité que peut invoquer ce transporteur en vertu de la présente Convention.

(2) Le montant total de la réparation qui, dans ce cas, peut être obtenu du transporteur et de ses préposés ne doit pas dépasser lesdites limites.

Article 26

(1) La réception des bagages et marchandises sans protestation par le destinataire constituera présomption, sauf preuve contraire, que les marchandises ont été livrées en bon état et conformément au titre de transport.

(2) En cas d'avarie, le destinataire doit adresser au transporteur une protestation immédiatement après la découverte de l'avarie et, au plus tard, dans un délai de sept jours pour les bagages et de quatorze jours pour les marchandises à dater de leur réception. En cas de retard, la protestation devra être faite au plus tard dans les vingt et un jours à dater du jour où le bagage ou la marchandise auront été mis à sa disposition.

(3) Toute protestation doit être faite par réserve inscrite sur le titre de transport ou par un autre écrit expédié dans le délai prévu pour cette protestation.

(4) A défaut de protestation dans les délais prévus, toutes actions contre le transporteur sont irrecevables, sauf le cas de fraude de celui-ci.

Article 27

En cas de décès du débiteur, l'action en responsabilité, dans les limites prévues par la présente Convention, s'exerce contre ses ayants droit.

Article 28

(1) L'action en responsabilité devra être portée, au choix du demandeur, dans le territoire d'une des Hautes Parties Contractantes, soit devant le tribunal du domicile du transporteur, du siège principal de son exploitation ou du lieu où il possède un établissement par le soin duquel le contrat a été conclu, soit devant le tribunal du lieu de destination.

(2) En ce qui concerne le dommage résultant de la mort, d'une lésion corporelle ou du retard subi par un passager ainsi que de la destruction, perte, avarie ou retard des bagages, l'action en responsabilité peut être intentée devant l'un des tribunaux mentionnés à l'alinéa ler du prêsent article ou, sur le territoire d'une Haute Partie Contractante, devant le tribunal dans le ressort duquel le transporteur possède un établissement, si le passager a son domicile ou sa résidence permanente sur le territoire de la méme Haute Partie Contractante.

(3) La procédure réglée par la loi du tribunal saisi.

Article 29

(1) L'action en responsabilité doit être intentée, sous peine de déchéance, dans le délai de deux ans à compter de l'arrivée à destination ou du jour où l'aéronef aurait dú arriver, ou de l'arrêt transport.

(2) Le mode de calcul du délai est dêterminé par la loi du tribunal saisi.

Article 30

(1) Dans les cas de transport régis par la définition du troisième alinéa de l'article ler, à exécuter par divers transporteurs successifs, chaque transporteur acceptant des voyageurs, des bagages ou des marchandises est soumis aux régles établies par cette Convention, et est censé être une des parties contractantes du contrat de transport, pour autant que ce contrat ait trait à la partie du transport effectuée sous son contrôle.

(2) Au cas d'un tel transport, le voyageur ou ses ayants droit ne pourront recourir que contre le transporteur ayant effectué le transport au cours duquel l'accident ou le retard s'est produit, sauf dans le cas où, par stipulation expresse, le premier transporteur aura assuré la responsabilité pour tout le voyage.

(3) S'il s'agit de bagages ou de marchandises, l'expéditeur aura recours contre le premier transporteur et le destinataire qui a le droit à la délivrance contre le dernier, et l'un et l'autre pourront, en outre, agir contre le transporteur ayant effectué le transport au cours duquel la destruction, la perte, l'avarie ou le retard se sont produits. Ces transporteurs seront solidairement responsables envers l'expéditeur et le destinataire.

Article 30A

La présente Convention ne préjuge en aucune manière la question de savoir si la personne tenue pour responsable en vertu de ses dispositions a ou non un recours contre toute autre personne.

Chapitre IV

Dispositions relatives aux transports combinés

Article 31

(1) Dans le cas de transports combinés effectués en partie par air et en partie par tout autre moyen de transport, les stipulations de la présente Convention ne s'appliquent qu'au transport aérien et si celui-ci répond aux conditions de l'article ler.

(2) Rien dans la présente Convention n'empêche les parties, dans le cas de transports combinés, d'insérer dans le titre de transport aérien des conditions relatives à d'autres modes de transport, à condition que les stipulations de la présente Convention soient respectées en ce qui concerne le transport par air.

Chapitre V

Dispositions générales et finales

Article 32

Sont nulles toutes clauses du contrat de transport et toutes conventions particulières antérieures au dommage par lesquelles les parties dérogeraient aux règles de la présente Convention soit par une détermination de la loi applicable, soit par une modification des règles de compétence. Toutefois, dans le transport des marchandises, les clauses d'arbitrage sont admises, dans les limites de la présente Convention, lorsque l'arbitrage doit s'effectuer dans le lieux de compétence des tribunaux prévus à l'article 28, alinéa (1).

Article 33

Sous réserve des dispositions de l'alinéa (3) de l'article 5, rien dans la présente Convention ne peut empêcher un transporteur de refuser la conclusion d'un contrat de transport ou de formuler des règlements qui ne sont pas en contradiction avec les dispositions de la présente Convention.

Article 34

Les dispositions des articles 3 à 8 inclus relatives aux titres de transport ne sont pas applicables au transport effectué dans des circonstances extraordinaires en dehors de toute opération normale de l'exploitation aérienne.

Article 35

Lorsque dans la présente Convention il est question de jours, il s'agit de jours courants et non de jours ouvrables.

Article 35A

Rien dans la présente Convention ne prohibe l'institution par un Etat et l'application sur son territoire d'un système d'indemnisation complémentaire à celui prevu par la présente Convention en faveur des demandeurs dans le cas de mort ou de lésions corporelles d'un passager. Un tel systeme doit satisfaire aux conditions suivantes:

(*a*) en aucun cas il ne doit imposer au transporteur et à ses préposés une responsabilité quelconque s'ajoutant à celle stipulée par la Convention;

(*b*) il ne doit imposer au transporteur aucune charge financière ou administrative autre que la perception dans ledit Etat des contributions des passagers, s'il en est requis;

(*c*) il ne doit donner lieu à aucune discrimination entre les transporteurs en ce qui concerne les passagers intéressés et les avantages que ces derniers peuvent retirer du système doivent leur être accordés quel que soit le transporteur dont ils ont utilisé les services;

(*d*) lorsqu'un passager a contribué au système, toute personne ayant subi des dommages à la suite de la mort ou de lésions corporelles de ce passager pourra prétendre à bénéficier des avantages du système.

Article 40A

(1) ......

(2) Aux fins de la Convention, le mot *territoire* signifie non seulement le territoire métropolitan d'un Etat, mais aussi tous les territoires qu'il représente dans les relations extérieures.

Protocole additionnel

Ad Article 2

Les Hautes Parties Contractantes se réservent le droit de déclarer au moment de la ratification ou de l'adhésion que l'article 2, alinéa ler, de la présente Convention ne s'appliquera pas aux transports internationaux aériens effectués directement par l'Etat, ses colonies, protectorats, territoires sous mandat ou tout autre territoire sous sa souveraineté, sa suzeraineté ou son autorité.

Section 1 (2)

SCHEDULE 2

Consequential etc. Amendments of Carriage by Air Act 1961 and Carriage by Air (Supplementary Provisions) Act 1962

1. In section 1 (1) of the Carriage by Air Act 1961 (which provides for the Warsaw Convention as amended at The Hague 1955 to have the force of law in the United Kingdom) after the words " 1955, as " there shall be inserted the words " further amended by provisions of protocols No. 3 and No. 4 signed at Montreal on 25th September 1975 and ".

2. In section 2 (1) of that Act (which provides for Orders in Council to certify who are the High Contracting Parties to the Convention) after the words " who are " there shall be inserted the words " , either generally or in respect of specified matters,".

3. In section 3 of that Act and in that section as set out in section 11 (*b*) of that Act (which refer to liability under Article 17 of the Convention) for the words " Article 17 " there shall be substituted the words " Article 17 (1) ".

4. In section 4 of that Act (which relates to the limitations on liability in Article 22 of the Convention)—

(*a*) after the words " Article 22 " in subsections (1) and (5), except subsection (1) (*b*), there shall be inserted the words " and Article 22A " and after the words " Article 22 " in subsections (2) and (3) there shall be inserted the words " or Article 22A ";

(*b*) in subsection (1) (*b*) (which refers to paragraph (1) of Article 22) for the words " paragraph (1)" there shall be substituted the words " paragraph (1) (*a*)"; and

(*c*) subsection (4) (which relates to amounts which are to be taken as equivalent to sums expressed in francs) shall be omitted.

5. In section 4 of the Carriage by Air (Supplementary Provisions) Act 1962 (which refers to the date of the coming into force of Article 25A of Schedule 1 to the said Act of 1961) after the words " 1961 " there shall be inserted the words " as originally enacted ".

6. In paragraph 2 of Article III in Part I of the Schedule to the said Act of 1962 (which refers to the limits and the destination mentioned in Article 22 of the Convention), after the words " Article 22 " in both places there shall be inserted the words " or Article 22A "; and in paragraph 2 of Article III in Part II of that Schedule (which contains the corresponding French text) after the words " l'article 22 " in both places there shall be inserted the words " ou à l'article 22A ".

International Monetary Fund Act 1979

(1979 c. 29)

SECT. ARRANGEMENT OF SECTIONS

An Act to consolidate the enactments relating to the International Monetary Fund and to repeal, as obsolete, the European Monetary Agreement Act 1959 and the entries relating to it in Schedule 2 to the National Loans Act 1968. [4th April 1979]

General Note

This Act consolidates the enactments relating to the International Monetary Fund, and repeals the European Monetary Agreement Act 1959.

S. 1 provides that payments by the U.K. Government to the International Monetary Fund shall be paid out of the National Loans Fund; s. 2 relates to loans to the International Monetary Fund; s. 3 states that receipts from the International Monetary Fund shall be paid into the National Loans Fund; s. 4 empowers the Treasury to create and issue notes and other obligations to the Fund; s. 5 authorises provision to be made by Her Majesty in Council relating to the status, immunities and privileges of the Fund; s. 6 contains repeals; s. 7 gives the short title.

The Act received the Royal Assent on April 4, 1979, and came into force on May 4, 1979.

Parliamentary debates

Hansard, H.L. Vol 398, cols. 830 and 1105; Vol. 399, col. 1660; H.C. Vol. 965, col. 1377.

Table of Derivations

BRETTON WOODS AGREEMENT ACT 1945

1945	1979
s. 2 (1) (*b*)–(*d*) .	s. 1 (1) (*b*)–(*d*)
(2)	(3)
(4)	4
3 (1)	5 (1)
(2)	(2) (3)

INTERNATIONAL MONETARY FUND ACT 1962

1962	1979
Preamble ...	s. 2 (1) (5)
s. 1 (1)	(1) (4) (5)

NATIONAL LOANS ACT 1968

1968	1979
Sch. 2	ss. 1 (1), 3, 4 (2)

INTERNATIONAL MONETARY FUND ACT 1970

1970	1979
s. 2	s. 2 (4)

INTERNATIONAL FINANCE, TRADE AND AID ACT 1977

1977	1979	1977	1979	1977	1979
s. 1 (1)	s. 1 (1)	s. 1 (2)	s. 2 (2)	s. 2 (4)	s. 1 (1) (*d*)
(1) (*b*) .	1 (1) (*a*)	(3)	ss. 1 (2), 2 (3)	(5)	4 (1)
		2 (3)	s. 1 (1) (*b*)		

Payments to International Monetary Fund

1.—(1) All sums which the Government of the United Kingdom requires for the purpose of paying to the International Monetary Fund in accordance with the Fund's Articles of Agreement—

(*a*) subscriptions of such amounts as may from time to time be authorised by order of the Treasury in the event of proposals being made for increases in the United Kingdom's quota under section 3 (*a*) of Article III;

(*b*) any sums payable under section 11 of Article V (maintenance of value of assets);

(*c*) any sums required for implementing the guarantee required by section 3 of Article XIII (guarantee against loss resulting from failure or default of designated depository); and

(*d*) any compensation required to be paid to the Fund or any member of it under Schedule J or K (withdrawal of members and liquidation),

shall be paid out of the National Loans Fund.

(2) The power of the Treasury to make orders under subsection (1) (*a*) above shall be exercisable by statutory instrument; and no such order shall be made until a draft of it has been laid before and approved by a resolution of the House of Commons.

(3) All sums which the Government of the United Kingdom requires for the purpose of paying any charges payable to the International Monetary Fund under section 8 of Article V of the Fund's Articles of Agreement shall be paid out of the Exchange Equalisation Account.

Loans to Fund

2.—(1) The Treasury may lend the International Monetary Fund, in accordance with the Fund's borrowing arrangements, such sums not, in the aggregate, after allowing in accordance with the borrowing arrangements for repayments made under them, exceeding £357,142,857.

(2) The Treasury may by order raise or further raise the limit on lending imposed by subsection (1) above.

(3) The power of the Treasury to make orders under subsection (2) above shall be exercisable by statutory instrument; and no such order shall be made until a draft of it has been laid before and approved by a resolution of the House of Commons.

(4) Sums to be lent under this section shall be issued out of the National Loans Fund.

(5) In this section " the Fund's borrowing arrangements " means arrangements made by the International Monetary Fund for enabling it to borrow the currency of any member of the Fund taking part in the arrangements.

Receipts from Fund

3. Sums received by the Government of the United Kingdom from the International Monetary Fund (other than sums received by reason of the operation of the Exchange Equalisation Account) shall be paid into the National Loans Fund.

Power of Treasury to create and issue notes and other obligations to Fund

4.—(1) The Treasury may, if they think fit so to do, create and issue to the International Monetary Fund, in such form as they think fit, any such non-interest-bearing and non-negotiable notes or other obligations as are provided for by section 4 of Article III of the Fund's Articles of Agreement.

(2) The sums payable under any such notes or other obligations shall be charged on the National Loans Fund with recourse to the Consolidated Fund.

Immunities and privileges etc.

5.—(1) Without prejudice to the powers conferred by the International Organisations Act 1968 or any other Act, Her Majesty may by Order in Council make such provision as She may consider reasonably necessary for carrying into effect any of the provisions of the Articles of Agreement of the International Monetary Fund relating to the status, immunities and privileges of the Fund and its governors, executive directors, alternates, officers and employees, or as to the unenforceability of exchange contracts.

(2) Subject to subsection (3) below, Orders in Council made under this section may be so made as to extend to any of the Channel Islands, the Isle of Man, any colony and, to the extent that Her Majesty has jurisdiction there, to any country outside Her Majesty's dominions in which Her Majesty has jurisdiction in right of the Government of the United Kingdom.

(3) If, whether before or after the coming into force of this Act, effect is given by or under the law of any part of Her Majesty's dominions or other territory to the provisions of the Articles of Agreement of the International Monetary Fund specified in subsection (1) above, no Order in Council made under this section shall extend to that part of Her Majesty's dominions or other territory as respects any period as respects which effect is so given to those provisions.

Repeals and savings

6.—(1) The enactments specified in Part I of the Schedule to this Act (consequential repeals) and Part II of that Schedule (obsolete enactments) are hereby repealed to the extent specified in the third column of that Schedule.

(2) Without prejudice to sections 14 and 17 (2) of the Interpretation Act 1978 (implied powers to revoke, amend and re-enact subordinate legislation and savings for such legislation where enactments are repealed and re-enacted), any Order in Council made under section 3 of the Bretton Woods Agreements Act 1945 and in force immediately before this Act comes into force shall have effect, so far as it applies to the International Monetary Fund, as if made under section 5 above and may accordingly, so far as it so applies, be amended or revoked by an Order in Council under that section.

Short title and commencement

7.—(1) This Act may be cited as the International Monetary Fund Act 1979.

(2) This Act shall come into force on the expiration of the period of one month from the date on which it is passed.

SCHEDULE

Section 6

Enactments Repealed

Part I

Consequential Repeals

Chapter	Short Title	Extent of Repeal
9 & 10 Geo. 6. c. 19.	Bretton Woods Agreements Act 1945.	In the preamble, paragraph (*a*) In section 2, subsection (1) (*b*), (*c*) and (*d*), in subsection (2), the words from "and" to the end of the subsection, and in subsection (4), the words "the Fund or" and the words from "section", in the first place where it occurs, to "and", in the third place where it occurs. In section 3, in subsection (1), the words "the Fund Agreement and", "the Fund and" and "respective" and the words from "or any" to the end of the subsection, and in subsection (4), the words "the Fund or", in both places where they occur, and the words "of the said agreements".
7 & 8 Eliz. 2. c. 17.	International Bank and Monetary Fund Act 1959	In the preamble, the words from the beginning to "whereas", in the second place where it occurs.
10 & 11 Eliz. 2. c. 20.	International Monetary Fund Act 1962.	The whole Act.
1968 c. 13.	National Loans Act 1968.	In Schedule 2, the entry relating to section 2 (1) of the Bretton Woods Agreements Act 1945 and the entry relating to sums received from the International Monetary Fund.
1970 c. 49.	International Monetary Fund Act 1970.	The whole Act.
1977 c. 6.	International Finance, Trade and Aid Act 1977.	Sections 1 and 2.

Part II

Obsolete Enactments

Chapter	Short Title	Extent of Repeal
7 & 8 Eliz. 2. c. 11.	European Monetary Agreement Act 1959.	The whole Act.
1968 c. 13.	National Loans Act 1968.	In Schedule 2, the entries relating to the European Monetary Agreement Act 1959.

Exchange Equalisation Account Act 1979

(1979 c. 30)

ARRANGEMENT OF SECTIONS

SECT.

An Act to consolidate the enactments relating to the Exchange Equalisation Account. [4th April 1979]

General Note

This Act consolidates enactments relating to the Exchange Equalisation Account.

S. 1 continues the Exchange Equalisation Account and states for what purposes it is to be used; s. 2 relates to the funding of the Account; s. 3 provides for investment of the Account's funds; s. 4 provides for the annual examination and certification of the Account; s. 5 contains the short title and repeals.

The Act received the Royal Assent on April 4, 1979, and came into force on May 4, 1979.

Parliamentary debates

Hansard, H.L. Vol. 398, cols. 830 and 1106; Vol. 399, col. 1660; H.C. Vol. 395, col. 1377.

Table of Derivations

FINANCE ACT 1932

1932	1979
s. 24 (1)	s. 1 (1) (2)
(3)	ss. 1 (3) (*a*), 3 (1) (*a*)
(7)	s. 4
25 (7)	3 (3)

BRETTON WOODS AGREEMENT ACT 1945

1945	1979
s. 2 (2)	s. 1 (3) (*c*)

NATIONAL LOANS ACT 1968

1968	1979
s. 7 (1)–(3) ..	s. 2

FINANCE ACT 1946

1946	1979
s. 63	s. 1 (3) (*b*)

INTERNATIONAL FINANCE, TRADE AND AID ACT 1977

1977	1979
s. 3 (1)	s. 1 (3) (*d*)
(2)	3 (1) (*b*) (2)
(3)	4

The Exchange Equalisation Account

1.—(1) There shall continue to be an account called the Exchange Equalisation Account (in this Act referred to as " the Account ").

(2) The Account shall continue to be under the control of the Treasury.

(3) The Account is to be used—

(*a*) for checking undue fluctuations in the exchange value of sterling;

(*b*) for securing the conservation or disposition in the national interest of the means of making payments abroad;

(*c*) for the purpose specified in section 1 (3) of the International Monetary Fund Act 1979 (payment of charges under section 8 of Article V of the Articles of Agreement of the International Monetary Fund); and

(*d*) for carrying out any of the functions of the Government of the United Kingdom under those of the said Articles of Agreement which relate to special drawing rights.

The Account's funds

2.—(1) There shall be issued to the Account out of the National Loans Fund, at such times and in such manner as the Treasury may direct, such sums as the Treasury may determine.

(2) Sums issued to the Account under subsection (1) above or under section 7 (1) of the National Loans Act 1968 (which corresponded to subsection (1) above) and which are for the time being outstanding shall constitute a liability of the Account to the National Loans Fund.

(3) If at any time the Treasury are of opinion that the assets in sterling of the Account are for the time being in excess of what is required for the purposes of the Account, the Treasury may direct that the excess shall be paid into the National Loans Fund.

Investment of the Account's funds

3.—(1) The Treasury may cause any funds in the Account to be invested—

(*a*) in securities or in the purchase of gold, or

(*b*) in the acquisition of special drawing rights under the Articles of Agreement of the International Monetary Fund.

(2) Any special drawing rights received or disposed of by the Government of the United Kingdom shall, in the case of receipts, be treated as assets of the Account, and in the case of disposals, be transferred from the Account.

(3) In subsection (1) (*a*) above " securities " include securities and assets in currency of any country and in whatever form held.

Examination and certification of the Account

4. The Account shall in every year be examined by the Comptroller and Auditor General in such manner as he, in his discretion, thinks proper with a view to ascertaining whether the operations on and the transactions in connection with the Account have been in accordance with the provisions of this Act, and he shall certify to the House of Commons whether in his opinion, having regard to the result of the examination, the operations on and the transactions in connection with the Account have or have not been in accordance with the provisions of this Act.

Short title, repeals and commencement

5.—(1) This Act may be cited as the Exchange Equalisation Account Act 1979.

(2) The enactments specified in the Schedule to this Act are hereby repealed to the extent specified in the third column of that Schedule.

(3) This Act shall come into force on the expiration of the period of one month from the date on which it is passed.

Section 5

SCHEDULE

ENACTMENTS REPEALED

Chapter	Short title	Extent of repeal
22 & 23 Geo. 5. c. 25.	Finance Act 1932.	Section 24. In section 25 (7), the words " in sub-section (3) of the last preceding section of this Act and ".
9 & 10 Geo. 6. c. 64.	Finance Act 1946.	Section 63.
1968 c. 13.	National Loans Act 1968.	Section 7.
1977 c. 6.	International Finance Trade and Aid Act 1977.	Section 3.

Prosecution of Offences Act 1979 *

(1979 c. 31)

Arrangement of Sections

An Act to consolidate certain enactments relating to the prosecution of offences in England and Wales and to repeal certain obsolete enactments relating thereto. **[4th April 1979]**

General Note

The Act consolidates certain enactments relating to the prosecution of offences. The first part of the Act (ss. 1–6) prescribes the means of appointment and remuneration of the Director of Public Prosecutions and Assistant Directors and defines the Director's powers and duties in relation to criminal proceedings. The second part (ss. 6–7) makes saving provisions for arrest in cases where the consent of the D.P.P. or a Law Officer is required for prosecution and provides for the admissibility in evidence of such consents. The third part (ss. 8–12) deals with crime returns to the D.P.P. from the police, provides for the making of regulations, sets out relevant definitions and provides for consequential amendments and repeals.

Background

When on June 24, 1977, the Prime Minister announced the setting up of a Royal Commission on Criminal Procedure, he added that, pending the Commission's Report, studies would be made within Government of various matters relating to prosecuting authorities and procedures. In consequence a Working Party was set up chaired by the Deputy Director of Public Prosecutions and including representatives from the Home Office, Law Officers' Department, Association of Chief Police Officers, the Metropolitan Police Commissioner and the Prosecuting Solicitors' Society. The fruits of the Working Party's deliberations were (a) this Act; (b) the Prosecution of Offences Regulations 1978 (S.I. 1978 No. 1357); and (c) the Consents to Prosecutions Bill.

The Regulations which came into force on January 1, 1979, and continue in force under the 1979 Act (see note to s. 9) replace, with some modifications to take account of current practice, the Prosecution of Offences Regulations 1946 (S.I. 1946 No. 1467).

The Consents to Prosecutions Bill provided for the transfer of certain consent functions presently exercisable by the Law Officers to the D.P.P. (cl. 1); that such further transfers as between the Law Officers and the D.P.P. might be effected by

* Annotations by J. R. Leng, Lecturer in Law, University of Birmingham.

statutory instrument made by the Attorney-General and subject to the affirmative resolution procedure (cl. 2); and that the Solicitor-General might exercise any of the consent functions of the Attorney-General where so directed by him (cl. 3). The Bill, and particularly cl. 2, received some criticism in the Commons' Second Reading Committee (H.C. Vol. 964, col. 657) and at the Committee Stage (Report of Standing Committee B, March 27, 1979) on the ground that it would derogate from the Attorney-General's responsibility to Parliament, and was subsequently dropped by the Government.

Extent

The Act does not extend to Scotland or Northern Ireland.

Parliamentary debates

The Act was not debated at any stage in Parliament.

Commencement

The Act came into force on May 4, 1979 (s. 12).

Abbreviations

D.P.P.	=	Director of Public Prosecutions
1879	=	Prosecution of Offences Act 1879 (c. 22)
1884	=	Prosecution of Offences Act 1884 (c. 58)
1908	=	Prosecution of Offences Act 1908 (c. 3)
1925	=	Criminal Justice Act 1925 (c. 86)
1968	=	Criminal Appeal Act 1968 (c. 19)
1971	=	Courts Act 1971 (c. 23)
1975	=	Criminal Jurisdiction Act 1975 (c. 59)
"1946 Regulations"	=	Prosecution of Offences Regulations 1946 (S.I. 1946 No. 1467) (L. 17)
"1978 Regulations"	=	Prosecution of Offences Regulations 1978 (S.I. 1978 No. 1357) (L. 33), as amended by Prosecution of Offences (Amendment) Regulations 1978 (S.I. 1978 No. 1846) (L. 38)

Unless otherwise indicated, "reg." refers to the 1978 Regulations.

Table of Derivations

PROSECUTION OF OFFENCES ACT 1879

1879	1979
s. 2	s. 2 (1)
2A	3
5	5
8	9

PROSECUTION OF OFFENCES ACT 1884

1884	1979
s. 3	s. 8

PROSECUTION OF OFFENCES ACT 1908

1908	1979
s. 1 (1)	s. 1 (1) (2)
(2)	(3)
(4)	(1) (2)
(5)	(4)
2 (1)	2 (2)
(3)	4

CRIMINAL JUSTICE ACT 1925

1925	1979
s. 34	ss. 7, 10

POST OFFICE (AMENDMENT) ACT 1935

1935	1979
Sch. 2	s. 7

STATUTORY INSTRUMENTS ACT 1946

1946	1979
s. 1 (2)	s. 9

MENTAL HEALTH ACT 1959

1959	1979
Sch. 8	s. 7

ADMINISTRATION OF JUSTICE ACT 1965

1965	1979
s. 27	s. 9
Sch. 3	9

CRIMINAL JUSTICE ACT 1967

1967	1979
Sch. 6, para. 2	s. 2 (1)

CRIMINAL APPEAL ACT 1968

1968	1979
Sch. 5, Pt. 1 .	ss. 2 (1), 3

COURTS ACT 1971

1971	1979
Sch. 8,	
para. 2 ...	s. 3
para. 13 ..	2 (1)

CRIMINAL JURISDICTION ACT 1975

1975	1979
s. 12	s. 6
(3)	10

CRIMINAL LAW ACT 1977

1977	1979
Sch. 13	s. 5

The Director of Public Prosecutions

The Director of Public Prosecutions and Assistant Directors

1.—(1) The Secretary of State may appoint the Director of Public Prosecutions (in this Act referred to as " the Director "); but a person shall not be so appointed unless he is a barrister or solicitor of not less than ten years standing.

(2) The Secretary of State may also appoint such number of Assistant Directors of Public Prosecutions (in this Act referred to as " Assistant Directors ") as the Minister for the Civil Service sanctions; but a person shall not be so appointed unless he is a barrister or solicitor of not less than seven years standing.

(3) There shall be paid to the Director, and to any Assistant Director so appointed, such remuneration as the Minister for the Civil Service may determine.

(4) An Assistant Director may do any act or thing which the Director is required or authorised to do by or in pursuance of any Act, or otherwise.

DERIVATION

1908, s. 1 (1) (4) (5); The Minister for the Civil Service Order 1968 (S.I. 1968 No. 1656), art. 3 (2).

DEFINITIONS
"Assistant Director of Public Prosecutions": subs. (2).
"Director of Public Prosecutions": subs. (1).

Duties of Director

2.—(1) It shall be the duty of the Director, under the superintendence of the Attorney General—

(*a*) to institute, undertake or carry on such criminal proceedings (whether in the criminal division of the Court of Appeal, or in the House of Lords on appeal under Part II of the Criminal Appeal Act 1968 from the criminal division or from a divisional court of the Queen's Bench Division of the High Court, or in such a divisional court, or before the Crown Court, or before a magistrates' court, or otherwise); and

(*b*) to give such advice and assistance to chief officers of police, justices' clerks and other persons (whether officers or not) concerned in any criminal proceedings respecting the conduct of those proceedings,

as may be prescribed, or as may be directed, in a special case, by the Attorney General.

(2) The regulations shall provide for the Director's taking action in cases which appear to him to be of importance or difficulty, or which for any other reason require his intervention.

DERIVATION
1879, s. 2; 1908, s. 2 (1); Criminal Justice Act 1967 (c. 80), Sched. 6, para. 2; 1968, Sched. 5, Pt. I; 1971, Sched. 8, para. 13.

DEFINITIONS
"Director": ss. 1 (1) and 10.
"prescribed": s. 10.

GENERAL NOTE

S. 2 and regs. 3 and 4 give the D.P.P. wide discretion to give advice on, institute or take over at any stage criminal proceedings. The duty which was cast on the D.P.P. under reg. 1 of the 1946 Regulations to institute proceedings (a) in the case of an offence punishable by death, and (b) in any case referred to him by a government department in which he considered that proceedings should be instituted, has now been dispensed with. Under 1978, regs. 3 and 4 the sole criterion for his intervention whether by advice or by taking over the proceedings is that the case "appears to him to be of importance or difficulty or for some other reason appears to him to require his intervention." The effective exercise of this wide discretion is supported by the requirements that certain types of offence should be reported to the D.P.P. under ss. 5 (3) and 8 and regs. 6, 7 and 9. A stimulating critique of the manner in which succeeding Directors have interpreted this discretion and an examination of the control which may be exercised over it via the Attorney-General's responsibility to Parliament is found in Edwards, *Law Officers of the Crown* (1964).

The power to intervene may be exercised for various purposes, for instance to prevent the abandonment of a well-founded prosecution for lack of funds, to ensure adequate argument of complex issues or that the public interest is properly represented in cases of public importance, to prevent oppressive prosecutions, or where it is considered to be in the public interest to discontinue a prosecution. Where the D.P.P. intervenes to discontinue a prosecution by offering no evidence it appears that his discretion to do so is unfettered (*R.* v. *Turner* [1978] Crim.L.R. 754, *per* Mars-Jones J.), except perhaps where bad faith is alleged.

The power of the D.P.P. to authorise payment of certain prosecution costs under reg. 3 of the 1946 Regulations has been dispensed with. Prosecution costs may be payable out of central funds at the discretion of the court under the Costs in Criminal Cases Act 1952, s. 5, or the Courts Act 1971, s. 47 (1). However, if it appears that a prosecution will be discontinued through lack of funds, the correct course will now be for the D.P.P. to take over the prosecution. (See note to s. 5 (3).)

By reg. 5, the D.P.P. may employ a solicitor to act as his agent in the conduct of a prosecution and shall authorise the payment to an agent so employed of such costs and charges as he shall consider proper and reasonable.

Directions to Director to appear on appeals

3.—(1) Without prejudice to section 2 above, it shall be the duty of the Director to appear for the Crown or the prosecutor, when directed by the court to do so, on any appeal under—

(*a*) section 1 of the Administration of Justice Act 1960 (appeal from the High Court in criminal cases); or

(*b*) Part I or Part II of the Criminal Appeal Act 1968 (appeals from the Crown Court to the criminal division of the Court of Appeal and thence to the House of Lords).

(2) In subsection (1) above " the court " means—

(*a*) in the case of an appeal to or from the criminal division of the Court of Appeal, that division; and

(*b*) in the case of an appeal from a divisional court of the Queen's Bench Division, the divisional court.

DERIVATION

1879, s. 2A, as inserted by 1968, Sched. 5, Pt. I, and amended by 1971, Sched. 8, para. 2.

DEFINITIONS

" the court ": subs. (2).
" Director ": ss. 1 (1) and 10.

GENERAL NOTE

The D.P.P. may be directed to appear for the Crown on any criminal appeal by (a) the Court of Appeal, where the appeal is from the Crown Court to the Court of Appeal or from the Court of Appeal to the House of Lords; (b) the Divisional Court, where the appeal is from the Divisional Court to the House of Lords.

Saving for private prosecutions

4. Nothing in this Act shall preclude any person from instituting or carrying on any criminal proceedings; but the Director may undertake, at any stage, the conduct of those proceedings, if he thinks fit.

DERIVATION

1908, s. 2 (3).

DEFINITION

" Director ": ss. 1 (1) and 10.

GENERAL NOTE

See Note to s. 2.

Delivery of recognizances, etc. to Director

5.—(1) Where the Director gives notice to any justice that he has instituted or undertaken or is carrying on any criminal proceedings, the justice shall, at the prescribed time and in the prescribed manner or at the time and in the manner directed, in a special case, by the Attorney General, send the Director every recognizance, information, certificate, deposition, document and thing connected with those proceedings which the justice is required by law to deliver to the appropriate officer of the Crown Court.

(2) The Director shall—

(*a*) subject to the regulations, cause anything which is sent to him under subsection (1) above to be delivered to the appropriate officer of the Crown Court; and

(*b*) be under the same obligation (on the same payment) to deliver to an applicant copies of anything so sent as the said officer.

(3) It shall be the duty of every justices' clerk to send the Director, in accordance with the regulations, a copy of the information and of any depositions and other documents relating to any case in which a prosecution for an offence before the magistrates' court to which he is clerk is withdrawn or is not proceeded with within a reasonable time.

DERIVATION

1879, s. 5; 1971, Sched. 8, para. 2; Criminal Law Act 1977 (c. 45), Sched. 13.

DEFINITIONS

"Director": ss. 1 (1) and 10.
"prescribed": s. 10.
"regulations": s. 10.

GENERAL NOTE

By reg. 8 the documents, etc., which are required to be sent to the D.P.P. under s. 5 shall be sent within three days of the receipt of the notice from the D.P.P. requiring them to be sent. The transmission may be by post or other means.

The documents, etc., which the justices are required to send to the Crown Court are prescribed by the Magistrates' Courts Rules 1969 (S.I. 1969 No. 1920), r. 10 (2), as amended by the Magistrates' Courts (Amendment) Rules 1973 (S.I. 1973 No. 790). The D.P.P. is under the same duty to provide an accused person with copies of such documents as is the officer of the Crown Court.

Subs. (3)

By reg. 9 of the 1978 Regulations it was intended to modify the existing practice as to the reporting of withdrawals of, or delays in, prosecution so that a justices' clerk would only be under a duty to report such delay or withdrawal where "there is some ground for suspecting that there is no satisfactory reason for the withdrawal or failure to proceed." However, since subs. (3) re-enacts the mandatory terms of 1879, s. 5, it would seem that the justices' clerk remains under a duty to report in *all* cases of withdrawal or unreasonable failure to proceed.

Consents to prosecutions

Consents to prosecutions, etc.

6.—(1) This section applies to any enactment which prohibits the institution or carrying on of proceedings for any offence except—

(*a*) with the consent (however expressed) of a Law Officer of the Crown or of the Director; or

(*b*) where the proceedings are instituted or carried on by or on behalf of a Law Officer of the Crown or the Director,

and so applies whether or not there are other exceptions to the prohibition (and in particular whether or not the consent is an alternative to the consent of any other authority or person).

(2) An enactment to which this section applies—

(*a*) shall not prevent the arrest without warrant, or the issue or execution of a warrant for the arrest, of a person for any offence, or the remand in custody or on bail of a person charged with any offence; and

(*b*) shall be subject to any enactment concerning the apprehension or detention of children or young persons.

(3) In this section "enactment" includes any provision having effect under or by virtue of any act; and this section applies to enactments passed or made before the passing of this Act, or later.

DERIVATION
1975, s. 12.

DEFINITIONS
"consent": s. 10.
"Director": ss. 1 (1) and 10.
"enactment": subs. 3.
"Law Officer of the Crown": s. 10.

GENERAL NOTE
S. 6 provides that, notwithstanding a requirement in an enactment, whenever passed, that proceedings shall not be instituted for an offence except by or with the consent of a Law Officer or the D.P.P., a person charged with such an offence may be arrested or remanded in custody or on bail.

Consequential amendments to existing legislation are made by s. 11 (1) and Sched. 1.

Exceptionally by the Public Order Act 1936, s. 1 (2), as amended by Sched. 1 of the 1979 Act, a person remanded in custody by virtue of s. 6 is entitled to be released on bail without sureties after a period of eight days unless within that period the Attorney-General's consent to prosecution has been obtained.

1975, s. 12, which is re-enacted in s. 6 of the 1979 Act, extended to all parts of the United Kingdom. Since by s. 12 (3) the 1979 Act does not apply to Scotland or Northern Ireland 1975, s. 12, will remain in force in respect of Scotland and Northern Ireland.

Consents to be admissible in evidence

7. Any document purporting to be the consent of a Law Officer of the Crown or the Director for, or to, the institution of any criminal proceedings or the institution of criminal proceedings in any particular form and to be signed by a Law Officer of the Crown, the Director or an Assistant Director, as the case may be, shall be admissible as prima facie evidence without further proof.

DERIVATION
1925, s. 34; Post Office (Amendment) Act 1935 (c. 15), Sched. 2; Mental Health Act 1959 (c. 72), Sched. 8.

DEFINITIONS
"Assistant Director": s. 10.
"consent": s. 10.
"Director": ss. 1 (1) and 10.
"Law Officer of the Crown": s. 10.

GENERAL NOTE
The consent need not be in any particular form. In *R.* v. *Cain* [1975] 3 W.L.R. 131, it was argued that the consent given by the Attorney-General to a prosecution under the Explosive Substances Act 1883 did not sufficiently identify the consent with the particular charge where the consent was given in the form "I hereby consent to the prosecution of X (accused) of Y (address) for an offence contrary to the provisions of the said Act". The Court of Appeal held that the consent was sufficient. "Where consent is given in any terms it should be presumed that the Attorney-General has made the necessary and proper inquiries before giving his consent": *per* Lord Widgery, *ibid.* p. 136.

Where an enactment provides for the consent of the D.P.P. the consent may be given by an Assistant Director (s. 1 (4)). Where the Attorney-General's consent is required the consent may be given by the Solicitor-General if (a) the office of Attorney-General is vacant; or (b) the Attorney-General is unable to act owing to absence or illness; or (c) the Attorney-General authorises the Solicitor-General to act in any particular case (Law Officers Act 1944, s. 1).

Proceedings instituted without the required consent will be a nullity: *R.* v. *Angel* [1968] 52 Cr.App.R. 280, C.A.; *R.* v. *Withers* [1975] Crim.L.R. 647. However, the existence of a required consent is not one of the matters which the prosecution must prove at the trial. It is the duty of the clerk to the justices to satisfy himself that any consent requirement has been fulfilled before the issue of summons, thus unless the issue of lack of consent is raised by the accused before the close of the prosecution case the court may act on the presumption that the consent has been given: *Price* v. *Humphries* [1958] 2 All E.R. 725.

Miscellaneous and general

Crime returns of chief officers of police

8.—(1) The chief officer of every police area in England and Wales shall give the Director information with respect to indictable offences alleged to have been committed within his area and the manner of dealing with those offences.

(2) The information given under subsection (1) above shall contain such particulars, and be in such form, as may be required by the regulations.

DERIVATION

1884, s. 3.

DEFINITIONS

"Director": ss. 1 (1) and 10.
"the regulations": s. 10.

GENERAL NOTE

S. 8 and regs. 6 and 7 require chief officers of police to report to the D.P.P. alleged offences in cases where proceedings may only be instituted by or with the consent of the D.P.P., Attorney-General or Solicitor-General, and in certain other cases where due to possible complexity or sensitivity the D.P.P. may wish to advise on the desirability of prosecution or undertake the prosecution himself.

Reg. 6 (1) requires the chief officer of police to provide such information where it appears to him that there is a prima facie case for proceeding in the following cases—

(a) offences in which the prosecution has by statute to be undertaken by or requires the consent of the Attorney-General, the Solicitor-General or the D.P.P.;
(b) offences where it appears to the Chief Officer of Police that the advice or the assistance of the D.P.P. is desirable;
(c) offences punishable with death;
(d) offences of homicide except offences of causing death by reckless driving;
(e) offences of abortion;
(f) offences of treason felony, misprision of treason, sedition, seditious libel or libel on holders of public offices;
(g) (repealed, see below);
(h) offences under the following enactments:
  (i) Offences against the Person Act 1861, ss. 21, 23, 28, 29, 32 and 33;
  (ii) Forgery Act 1913, ss. 2 (1), 3 and 5, of uttering any such documents, seals or dies mentioned in those sections;
(i) conspiracies, attempts or incitements to commit any of the above offences;
(j) offences which may be the subject of an application under the Extradition Acts 1870 to 1935 or the Fugitive Offenders Act 1967.

The information which must be provided in the cases listed in reg. 6 (1) is specified in reg. 7 as follows—

(a) a full report of the circumstances;
(b) copies of the statements of any witnesses;
(c) copies of any material documents; and
(d) such information and material as the Director of Public Prosecutions may require of him.

Reg. 6 (2) imparts a degree of flexibility into the system of crime returns allowing the D.P.P. to take account of changes in the law or shifts in public concern without recourse to amending regulations. Reg. 6 (2) states: "The Chief Officer of every such police area shall give to the Director of Public Prosecutions such information as he may require with respect to such other cases as the Director of Public

Prosecutions may from time to time specify as appearing to him to be of importance or difficulty or for any other reason requiring his intervention."

The offences which for the time being are required to be reported to the D.P.P. pursuant to reg. 6 (2), where a prima facie case is disclosed, are as follows (this list does not have the force of law):

(a) Offences against the Perjury Act 1911, s. 1 and the Criminal Justice Act 1967, s. 89; subornation of these offences and conspiracy and incitement to commit them;
(b) conspiracy and attempt to pervert or defeat the course of justice;
(c) conspiracy to manufacture controlled drugs; large scale conspiracy to supply controlled drugs in large amounts;
(d) large scale conspiracy to contravene immigration laws;
(e) causing death by reckless driving where the deceased is a close relative of the accused;
(f) rape where one woman is raped by more than one man on the same occasion and where one man rapes several women;
(g) Offences against the Sexual Offences Act 1956, s. 7, as amended by the Mental Health Act 1959, s. 127;
(h) kidnapping;
(i) robbery involving the use of firearms where injury is caused;
(j) large scale robbery involving property or money exceeding £250,000 in value;
(k) arson involving grave damage to public property;
(l) coinage offences except those that are trivial;
(m) criminal libel;
(n) conspiracy and attempt and incitement to commit offences 6 to 13;
(o) offences in relation to the Backing of Warrants (Republic of Ireland) Act 1965, where the order is resisted under s. 2 (2) of the Act.
(p) cases in which questions of EEC law have been or seem likely to be raised, and all cases which have been referred by Crown Courts or magistrates' courts in England and Wales to the European Court of Justice (Home Office Circular 71/1979).

It should be noted that in contrast to the position under reg. 6 (1) where all relevant documents are required to be sent to the D.P.P., the information required to be supplied under reg. 6 (2) is "such information as [the D.P.P.] may require". This allows for concise reports of alleged offences to be sent. Since it would be particularly inconvenient in cases of alleged offences concerning obscene publications if all relevant documents were required to be sent, a practice has developed whereby at first instance the police simply send the D.P.P. a list of the publications on which they require his advice. Alleged offences concerning obscene publications and exhibitions were originally included in the list of offences required to be formally reported under reg. 6 (1) (*g*). This regulation has now been deleted under the Prosecution of Offences (Amendment) Regulations 1978 (S.I. 1978 No. 1846), and such offences will now be reported under reg. 6 (2), thereby accommodating the existing practice.

A further instance in which the Chief Officer of Police is under a duty to report an alleged offence to the D.P.P. is found in the Police Act 1964, s. 49. Where the Chief Officer has ordered a complaint against a police officer to be investigated under s. 49 (1), he is under a duty to send a report of the investigation to the D.P.P. unless satisfied that no criminal offence has been committed (s. 49 (3)). The Police Complaints Board may request a Chief Officer to report to the D.P.P. where it appears that information furnished to them is relevant to the question of criminal proceedings against a police officer and that that information has not been furnished to the D.P.P. The Chief Officer is under a duty to make such report unless such report has already been made or he is satisfied that the information is not relevant to the question of criminal proceedings (Police Act 1976, s. 5 (2)).

In the context of offences which must be reported to the D.P.P. attention is also drawn to s. 5 (3) and reg. 9 which require justices' clerks to report cases where an information has been laid before the magistrates but the case is withdrawn or not proceeded with within a reasonable time.

Regulations

9.—(1) **The Attorney General may, with the concurrence of the Secretary of State, make regulations for carrying this Act into effect.**

(2) The power to make the regulations shall be exercisable by statutory instrument, which shall be subject to annulment in pursuance of a resolution of either House of Parliament.

DERIVATION

1879, s. 8; Statutory Instruments Act 1946 (c. 36), s. 1 (2); Administration of Justice Act 1965 (c. 2), s. 27 and Sched. 3.

GENERAL NOTE

The 1978 Regulations made under the legislation repealed by this Act continue in force by virtue of Interpretation Act 1978, s. 17 (2) (*b*) which provides that "where an Act repeals and re-enacts, with or without modification, a previous enactment, then unless the contrary intention appears, — . . . in so far as any subordinate legislation made or things done under the enactment so repealed, or having effect as if so made or done, could have been made or done under the provision re-enacted, it shall have effect as if made or done under that provision." (See also Background Note above).

Interpretation

10. In this Act—

"Assistant Director" has the meaning given by section 1 above;

"consent" includes, sanction, fiat, direction or order;

"the Director" has the meaning given by section 1 above;

"a Law Officer of the Crown" means the Attorney General or the Solicitor General;

"prescribed" means prescribed by the regulations;

"the regulations" means the regulations made under section 9 above.

DERIVATION

1975, s. 12 (3), and 1925, s. 34.

Consequential amendments and repeals

11.—(1) The enactments specified in Schedule 1 to this Act shall have effect subject to the amendments there specified, being amendments consequential upon the provisions of this Act.

(2) The enactments specified in Part I of Schedule 2 to this Act (repeal of obsolete enactments) and those specified in Part II of that Schedule (consequential repeals) are hereby repealed to the extent specified in the third column of that Schedule.

Short title, commencement and extent

12.—(1) This Act may be cited as the Prosecution of Offences Act 1979.

(2) This Act shall come into force at the end of the period of one month beginning with the date on which it is passed.

(3) This Act shall not extend to Scotland or Northern Ireland.

SCHEDULES

Section 11

SCHEDULE 1

CONSEQUENTIAL AMENDMENTS

Public Order Act 1936 (1 *Edw.* 8 *&* 1 *Geo.* 6, *c.* 6)

In section 1 (2) of the Public Order Act 1936 (as amended by Schedule 5 to the Criminal Jurisdiction Act 1975), for the words "section 12 of the Criminal

Jurisdiction Act 1975" there shall be substituted the words "section 6 of the Prosecution of Offences Act 1979".

Representation of the People Act 1949 (c. 68)

In section 159 of the Representation of the People Act 1949, for the words "the Prosecution of Offences Act 1879" where they appear in subsections (4) and (9) there shall be substituted the words "the Prosecution of Offences Act 1979".

Theft Act 1968 (c. 60)

In subsection (5) of section 30 of the Theft Act 1968 (which was added by Schedule 5 to the Criminal Jurisdiction Act 1975), for the words "section 12 of the Criminal Jurisdiction Act 1975" there shall be substituted the words "section 6 of the Prosecution of Offences Act 1979".

Section 11

SCHEDULE 2

Repeals

Part I

Repeal of Obsolete Enactments

Chapter	Short Title	Extent of Repeal
42 & 43 Vict. c. 22.	Prosecution of Offences Act 1879.	In section 5, the words "justice or", in the first place where they occur, and the words from "A failure" onwards. Section 7.
8 Edw. 7. c. 3.	Prosecution of Offences Act 1908.	Section 2 (4).

Part II

Consequential Repeals

Chapter	Short Title	Extent of Repeal
42 & 43 Vict. c. 22.	Prosecution of Offences Act 1879.	The whole Act, so far as unrepealed.
47 & 48 Vict. c. 58.	Prosecution of Offences Act 1884.	The whole Act.
8 Edw. 7. c. 3.	Prosecution of Offences Act 1908.	The whole Act, so far as unrepealed.
15 & 16 Geo. 5. c. 86.	Criminal Justice Act 1925.	Section 34.
1965 c. 2.	Administration of Justice Act 1965.	Section 27.
1967 c. 80.	Criminal Justice Act 1967.	In Schedule 6, paragraph 2.
1968 c. 19.	Criminal Appeal Act 1968.	In Schedule 5, the entry relating to the Prosecution of Offences Act 1879.
1971 c. 23.	Courts Act 1971.	In Schedule 8, paragraph 13.
1975 c. 59.	Criminal Jurisdiction Act 1975.	Section 12. In section 14 (2) (*a*), the words "12 and".

Industry Act 1979

(1979 c. 32)

An Act to provide with respect to the limits on sums borrowed by, or paid by Ministers of the Crown to, the National Enterprise Board, the Scottish Development Agency and the Welsh Development Agency and subsidiaries of theirs, on sums paid by the Treasury in pursuance of guarantees of loans to the Board or either of those Agencies and on loans guaranteed by the Board or either of those Agencies or subsidiaries of the Scottish Development Agency. [4th April 1979]

General Note

This Act provides for the limits on sums borrowed by, or paid by, Ministers of the Crown to the National Enterprise Board, the Scottish Development Agency and the Welsh Development Agency.

S. 1 increases the limit on loans made and capital made available to the National Enterprise Board and other agencies; s. 2 gives the short title.

The Act received the Royal Assent on April 4, 1979, and came into force on that date.

Parliamentary debates

Hansard, H.C. Vol. 959, col. 1636; Vol. 961, col. 230; Vol. 964, col. 582; H.L. Vol. 399, cols. 758, 1445, and 1717.

Increase in limits on loans, etc., to National Enterprise Board, Scottish Development Agency and Welsh Development Agency

1.—(1) The following enactments, that is to say, section 8 of the Industry Act 1975, section 13 of the Scottish Development Agency Act 1975 and section 18 of the Welsh Development Agency Act 1975 (limits on loans made and capital made available to the National Enterprise Board, the Scottish Development Agency and the Welsh Development Agency and their wholly owned subsidiaries, and guarantees by, and in respect of loans to, that Board and those Agencies and any such subsidiary of the Scottish Development Agency) shall be amended in accordance with the following provisions of this section.

(2) In section 8 (2) (limit for National Enterprise Board of £700 million which can be raised by order under that subsection to £1,000 million), for the words " £700 million " and " £1,000 million " there shall be substituted the words " £3,000 million " and " £4,500 million " respectively.

(3) In section 13 (3) (limit for Scottish Development Agency of £200 million which can be raised by order under that subsection to £300 million), for the words " £200 million " and " £300 million " there shall be substituted the words " £500 million " and " £800 million " respectively.

(4) In section 18 (3) (limit for Welsh Development Agency of £100 million which can be raised by order under that subsection to £150 million), for the words " £100 million " and " £150 million " there shall be substituted the words " £250 million " and " £400 million " respectively.

(5) In sections 8, 13 and 18, for the words "wholly owned subsidiaries " and " wholly owned subsidiary ", wherever occurring, there

shall be substituted the words " subsidiaries " and " subsidiary " respectively.

(6) In sections 8 (4) (*b*), 13 (5) (*b*) and 18 (5) (*b*) (which bring within the relevant limit sums borrowed by a subsidiary of the Board or either of the Agencies only when it was such a subsidiary) for the words " when it was such a subsidiary " there shall be substituted the words " (whether or not it was such a subsidiary at the time any such sum was borrowed) ".

(7) In accordance with the foregoing provisions of this section sections 8, 13 and 18 shall have effect as set out in the Schedule to this Act.

Short title, etc.

2.—(1) This Act may be cited as the Industry Act 1979.

(2) The National Enterprise Board (Financial Limit) Order 1978 is hereby revoked.

Section 1 (7)

SCHEDULE

1975 Enactments as Amended

Industry Act 1975 (c. 68)

Financial limits

8.—(1) The aggregate amount outstanding, otherwise than by way of interest in respect of—

(*a*) the general external borrowing of the Board and their subsidiaries;
(*b*) sums issued by the Treasury in fulfilment of guarantees under paragraph 4 of Schedule 2 below and not repaid to the Treasury;
(*c*) sums paid to the Board under paragraph 5 (1) of that Schedule;
(*d*) loans guaranteed by the Board otherwise than under section 3 above;

shall not exceed the limit specified in subsection (2) below.

(2) The said limit shall be £3,000 million, but the Secretary of State may by order made with the consent of the Treasury raise the limit to not more than £4,500 million.

(3) Such an order shall not be made unless a draft of it has been approved by resolution of the House of Commons.

(4) In subsection (1) above " general external borrowing " means—

(*a*) in relation to the Board, sums borrowed by them other than—
(i) sums borrowed from a body corporate which is one of the Board's subsidiaries at the time of the loan;
(ii) any sums mentioned in subsection (1) (*b*) above; or
(iii) sums borrowed by the Board for the purpose of giving assistance under section 3 above; and
(*b*) in relation to a subsidiary of the Board, sums borrowed by it (whether or not it was such a subsidiary at the time any such sum was borrowed) other than sums borrowed from the Board or from another subsidiary;

but does not include any debt assumed by the Board under paragraph 6 (1) of Schedule 2 below.

Scottish Development Agency Act 1975 (c. 69)

Finances of the Agency

13.—(1) Schedule 2 to this Act (Financial and Administrative Provisions relating to the Agency) shall have effect with respect to the finances of, and certain administrative matters relating to, the Agency.

(2) The aggregate amount outstanding, otherwise than by way of interest, in respect of

(*a*) the general external borrowing of the Agency and their subsidiaries;

(b) sums issued by the Treasury in fulfilment of guarantees under paragraph 6 of Schedule 2 below and not repaid to the Treasury;

(c) sums paid to the Agency by the Secretary of State out of monies provided by Parliament less repayments to the Secretary of State by the Agency (other than payments made by virtue of paragraph 1 (3) of Schedule 2 to this Act) and less such sums paid in respect of the administrative expenses of the Agency;

(d) loans guaranteed by the Agency otherwise than under section 5 of this Act and loans guaranteed by a subsidiary of the Agency;

shall not exceed the limit specified in subsection (3) below.

(3) The said limit shall be £500 million, but the Secretary of State may, by order made with the consent of the Treasury, raise the limit to £800 million.

(4) Such an order shall not be made unless a draft of it has been approved by resolution of the House of Commons.

(5) In subsection (2) above, " general external borrowing " means—

(a) in relation to the Agency, sums borrowed by them other than—

(i) sums borrowed from a body corporate which is one of the Agency's subsidiaries at the time of the loan;

(ii) any sums mentioned in subsection (2) (b) above; or

(iii) sums borrowed by the Agency for the purpose of giving assistance under section 5 of this Act; and

(b) in relation to a subsidiary of the Agency, sums borrowed by it (whether or not it was such a subsidiary at the time any such sum was borrowed) other than sums borrowed from the Agency or from another subsidiary;

but does not include any debt assumed by the Agency under paragraph 7 (1) of Schedule 2 to this Act.

Welsh Development Agency Act 1975 (c. 70)

Finances of the Agency

18.—(1) Schedule 3 to this Act shall have effect.

(2) The aggregate amount outstanding, otherwise than by way of interest, in respect of—

(a) the general external borrowing of the Agency and their subsidiaries;

(b) sums issued by the Treasury in fulfilment of guarantees under paragraph 6 of Schedule 3 below and not repaid to the Treasury;

(c) sums paid to the Agency by the Secretary of State out of money provided by Parliament less repayments to the Secretary of State by the Agency and less such sums paid in respect of the administrative expenses of the Agency;

(d) loans guaranteed by the Agency otherwise than under section 12 above;

shall not exceed the limit specified in subsection (3) below.

(3) The said limit shall be £250 million but the Secretary of State may by order made with the consent of the Treasury raise the limit to £400 million.

(4) Such an order shall not be made unless a draft of it has been approved by resolution of the House of Commons.

(5) In subsection (2) above " general external borrowing " means—

(a) in relation to the Agency, sums borrowed by them other than—

(i) sums borrowed from a body corporate which is one of the Agency's subsidiaries at the time of the loan;

(ii) any sums mentioned in subsection (2) (b) above; or

(iii) sums borrowed by the Agency for the purpose of giving assistance under section 12 above; and

(b) in relation to a subsidiary of the Agency, sums borrowed by it (whether or not it was such a subsidiary at the time any such sum was borrowed) other than sums borrowed from the Agency or from another subsidiary;

but does not include any debt assumed by the Agency under paragraph 7 (1) of Schedule 3 to this Act.

Land Registration (Scotland) Act 1979 *

(1979 c. 33)

ARRANGEMENT OF SECTIONS

PART I

REGISTRATION OF INTERESTS IN LAND

PART II

INDEMNITY IN RESPECT OF REGISTERED INTERESTS IN LAND

PART III

SIMPLIFICATION AND EFFECT OF DEEDS

PART IV

MISCELLANEOUS AND GENERAL

* Annotations by J. M. Halliday, C.B.E., M.A., LL.D., Professor of Conveyancing, University of Glasgow.

An Act to provide a system of registration of interests in land in Scotland in place of the recording of deeds in the Register of Sasines; and for indemnification in respect of registered interests in land; to simplify certain deeds relating to land and to provide as to the effect of certain other such deeds; to enable tenants-at-will to acquire their landlords' interests in the tenancies; to provide for the fixing of fees payable to the Keeper of the Registers of Scotland; and for connected purposes.

[4th April 1979]

General Note

A Committee appointed by the Secretary of State for Scotland on September 25, 1959, under the chairmanship of the Rt. Hon. Lord Reid (the Reid Committee) recommended in their Report (Cmnd. 2032, July 1963) that an expert committee should be appointed immediately to consider proposals for the amendment of the conveyancing statutes and also that another expert committee should be appointed to work out the details of a scheme of registration of title to land.

The first of these committees under the chairmanship of Professor J. M. Halliday (the Halliday Committee) reported in 1966 (Report of Committee on Conveyancing Legislation and Practice, Cmnd. 3118, December 1966). Legislation followed on that Report, the Conveyancing and Feudal Reform (Scotland) Act 1970 and the Land Tenure Reform (Scotland) Act 1974, and some other minor recommendations are now given effect in Part III of this Act.

The second of these committees under the chairmanship of Professor G. L. F. Henry (the Henry Committee) reported in 1969 (Report on the Scheme for the Introduction and Operation of Registration of Title to Land in Scotland, Cmnd. 4137, October 1969). At the instigation of the Committee a registration of title pilot scheme was set up and operated in the Department of the Registers of Scotland, and the Report set out in detail the principles of a scheme of registration of title for Scotland after putting their ideas to a practical test. The scheme now incorporated in the Act follows in essential matters the proposals in the Report of the Henry Committee.

Part I

Part I of the Act establishes the Land Register of Scotland under the management and control of the Keeper of the Registers of Scotland. It is intended that registration of title should replace the recording of deeds in the Register of Sasines as the principal means of creating real rights in land. The system of registration of title will be introduced by a phased process, one area after another, with the ultimate objective of transferring the registration of titles to land wholly to the new system, when the Register of Sasines will be closed. As each area becomes operational the only method of creating certain interests in land will be by registration in the Land Register. In certain kinds of transactions the interest in land concerned will be registrable: these include grants of feus, long leases or securities by way of ground annual and transfers for valuable consideration. The expense of first registration will not be imposed on transfers by way of gift, where no valuable consideration is given. The creation of heritable securities over registered interests in land will likewise be registrable.

Applications for registration will be made to the Keeper, accompanied by such documents and other evidence as he may require. If the Keeper is satisfied with the sufficiency of the applicant's title he will prepare a title sheet for the particular interest containing a description of the land to which it refers, the nature of the interest, the rights and burdens affecting it and such other information relating to it as the Keeper thinks desirable. Thereafter the title sheet will be kept up to date as documents effecting further transactions relative to the interest are registered. Upon first registration the Keeper will issue to the applicant a land certificate in the form of an officially sealed copy of the title sheet. Where the subject of the application is a heritable security, no title sheet will be prepared but the security will be entered as a burden on the title sheet of the security subjects and the heritable creditor will receive a charge certificate.

Registered titles will rank in accordance with the respective dates of registration, subject to any express provision as to ranking contained in the relevant deeds.

Even after an area becomes operational the Register of Sasines will continue for certain purposes during a transitional period which will probably be of considerable duration. Deeds which give effect to transactions relating to land which do not involve an interest becoming registrable in the Land Register, such as gratuitous dispositions or the assignation of existing standard securities over unregistered interests, will continue to be recorded in the Register of Sasines. As more interests in land become registrable in the Land Register, however, the need for recording in the Register of Sasines in each operational area will steadily diminish and eventually, when comparatively few properties remain unregistered, the Secretary of State may by statutory order require those remaining interests in unregistered land to be registered and the Register of Sasines for that area will be closed.

Since the system of registration of title envisages that the Land Register will at all times show the current position as to titles registered upon it, the Keeper has power to rectify inaccuracies in the Register and he may be required to make such rectification by the Lands Tribunal for Scotland or a court. Where rectification of the Register would prejudice a proprietor in possession, however, there are limitations upon the exercise of the Keeper's powers and upon the competency of orders by the Lands Tribunal or the courts.

Part II

It is fundamental to the system of registration of title that a title which has been registered is guaranteed by an indemnity from the Keeper, whose liability under an indemnity will be met by the State. There will be some titles submitted for registration which do not sufficiently demonstrate the entitlement of the applicant to the interest for which registration is sought. Since the interest must be registered in order to bring the land concerned within the system, the Keeper may accept the application for registration but may exclude, wholly or partially, any right to indemnity. This Part of the Act sets out the right to indemnity with certain necessary qualifications.

The qualifications are contained in s. 12 of the Act which specifies various circumstances in which the right to indemnity is excluded. These include cases where the land has been registered with exclusion of indemnity becoming fortified by prescription with the result that it prevails over another registered title, or where the registered title is reduced under some provision of statute as in the case of a gratuitous alienation in bankruptcy, or where the claimant to indemnity has by his fraudulent or careless act or omission caused the loss. Indemnity is also excluded in respect of certain kinds of interest, such as ownership of minerals by the proprietor of the surface, and in respect of the enforceability of real burdens or errors or omissions in noting an overriding interest.

Special provisions are made with regard to the foreshore with the object of ensuring that the Crown Estate Commissioners are notified of applications for registration of interests in land which includes foreshore where the title of the applicant has not been fortified by prescriptive possession.

Part III

This Part of the Act relates to simplifications of deeds and the legal effect of these.

Those contained in s. 15 result from registration of title and come into operation only as the system is introduced in each operational area. The reference to the number of its title sheet will then sufficiently describe an interest in land, so that the existing statutory provisions as to description of land by reference will be superseded. Since the real burdens and conditions affecting an interest will appear on the title sheet, the provisions of the conveyancing statutes as to reference to burdens in conveyances will no longer be required. Nor will it be necessary to deduce title, since the Keeper can satisfy himself as to the sufficiency of the links in the title of an applicant for registration. A narration in any deed of the series of writs by which the grantor of a deed became entitled to obligations or rights of relief will also be unnecessary if these have been entered in the title sheet.

The simplifications contained in ss. 16 to 19 of the Act are general conveyancing reforms, not specifically related to registration of title, and come into effect immediately on the Act receiving the Royal Assent (April 4, 1979). They include the omission from deeds relating to interests in land of clauses of assignation of writs, assignation of rents and obligations of relief from feuduties, ground annuals and public burdens. Deeds of declaration of conditions executed under s. 32 of the Conveyancing (Scotland) Act 1874 will now be effective as regards all the land to which they relate immediately upon recording or registration unless the deeds expressly provide otherwise. Variations or discharges of land obligations will be binding on the singular successors of the parties. A new provision (in s. 19) will enable agreements to be entered into as to a common boundary, with a plan of the boundary, and recording or registration effected so as to render the agreement binding on singular successors.

Part IV

This Part of the Act contains (ss. 20–22) special provisions relating to tenancies-at-will, generally with the object of conferring upon a tenant-at-will the right to purchase the tenancy land. Provision is made for fixing the compensation payable to the landlord and the determination of questions with the landlord or heritable creditors.

S. 25 provides for appeals on matters of fact and law relating to anything done or omitted to be done by the Keeper under the Act to be made to the Lands Tribunal for Scotland, but without prejudice to any right of recourse at law to the courts.

The interpretation section (s. 28) includes an exhaustive definition of the new term " overriding interests " which broadly describes interests which may be real interests in land without requiring to be recorded in the Register of Sasines or registered in the Land Register.

Other general provisions relate to fees, financial provisions, rules, amendments or repeals and commencement of the Act.

Parliamentary debates

Hansard, H.L. Vol. 396, col. 1087; Vol. 397, cols. 72, 848, 883; Vol. 398, col. 1449; H.C. Vol. 965, col. 859.

Commencement

Ss. 1, 16–23 and 30 came into force on April 4, 1979 (see s. 30 (2)). The remaining sections come into force on a day or days to be appointed.

PART I

REGISTRATION OF INTERESTS IN LAND

The Land Register of Scotland

1.—(1) There shall be a public register of interests in land in Scotland to be known as the " Land Register of Scotland " (in this Act referred to as " the register ").

(2) The register shall be under the management and control of the Keeper of the Registers of Scotland (in this Act referred to as " the Keeper ") and shall have a seal.

(3) In this Act " registered " means registered in the register in accordance with this Act and " registrable ", " registration " and other cognate expressions shall be construed accordingly.

DEFINITIONS

" interests in land " and " land ": see s. 28 (1).

GENERAL NOTE

This section creates a public register of title to land in Scotland known as the Land Register of Scotland under the management and control of the Keeper of the Registers of Scotland. This register will in due course supersede the existing Register of Sasines but the legal effect of registration will be significantly different from that of registration in the Register of Sasines. Registration in the Register of Sasines creates a real right of property in land but the validity of the title so registered depends upon the sufficiency of the progress of title deeds evidencing the right and title of the granter of the recorded deed, and so in practice registration is preceded by an examination of that progress by the solicitor of the person on whose behalf the deed is registered. After the Land Register is in operation, registration will be the only method of creating a real right and before registration the Keeper will normally be satisfied as to the validity of the title to be registered and will guarantee its validity. The title of the grantee of a deed registered in the Register of Sasines is not guaranteed in this way.

Registration

2.—(1) Subject to subsection (2) below, an unregistered interest in land other than an overriding interest shall be registrable—

(*a*) in any of the following circumstances occurring after the commencement of this Act—

(i) on a grant of the interest in land in feu, long lease or security by way of contract of ground annual, but only to the extent that the interest has become that of the feuar, lessee or debtor in the ground annual;

(ii) on a transfer of the interest for valuable consideration;

(iii) on a transfer of the interest in consideration of marriage;

(iv) on a transfer of the interest whereby it is absorbed into a registered interest in land;

(v) on any transfer of the interest where it is held under a long lease, udal tenure or a kindly tenancy;

(*b*) in any other circumstances in which an application is made for registration of the interest by the person or persons having that interest and the Keeper considers it expedient that the interest should be registered.

(2) Subsection (1) above does not apply to an unregistered interest which is a heritable security, liferent or incorporeal heritable right; and subsection (1) (*a*) (ii) above does not apply where the interest on transference is absorbed into another unregistered interest.

(3) The creation over a registered interest in land of any of the following interests in land—

(i) a heritable security;

(ii) a liferent;

(iii) an incorporeal heritable right,

shall be registrable; and on registration of its creation such an interest shall become a registered interest in land.

(4) There shall also be registrable—

(*a*) any transfer of a registered interest in land including any transfer whereby it is absorbed into another registered interest in land;

(*b*) any absorption by a registered interest in land of another registered interest in land;

(*c*) any other transaction or event which (whether by itself or in conjunction with registration) is capable under any enactment or rule of law of affecting the title to a registered interest in land but which is not a transaction or event creating or affecting an overriding interest.

(5) The Secretary of State may, by order made by statutory instrument, provide that interests in land of a kind or kinds specified in the order, being interests in land which are unregistered at the date of the making of the order other than overriding interests, shall be registered; and the provisions of this Act shall apply for the purposes of such

registration with such modifications, which may include provision as to the expenses of such registration, as may be specified in the order.

(6) In this section, "enactment" includes sections 17, 18 and 19 of this Act.

DEFINITIONS

"commencement of this Act": see s. 30 (2) and (3).
"feu": see s. 28 (1).
"heritable security": see s. 28 (1).
"incorporeal heritable right": see s. 28 (1).
"interest in land": see s. 28 (1).
"the Keeper": see ss. 1 (2) and 28 (1).
"long lease": see s. 28 (1).
"overriding interest": see s. 28 (1).
"registered": see s. 1 (3).
"registrable" and "registration": see s. 1 (3).
"unregistered": for definition of "registered," see s. 1 (3).

GENERAL NOTE

This section prescribes the circumstances in which an interest in land becomes registrable in the Land Register. The Report of the Committee appointed to prepare a detailed scheme for the Introduction and Operation of Registration of Title to Land in Scotland (the Henry Committee) (Cmnd. 4137, October 1969) recommended that registration should be compulsory on the first transfer for valuable consideration of a separate tenement of lands (para. 11). It was apparently thought to be inequitable to impose the expense of the first registration on the occasion of a gratuitous transfer. The Henry Committee, in agreement with the recommendation of the Report of the Committee on Conveyancing Legislation and Practice (the Halliday Committee) (Cmnd. 3118, December 1966) (para. 101), recommended that, for the purpose of the creation of a real right under a registrable lease, such leases should be registered in the Land Register (para. 33). The Henry Committee also recommended that lands held under kindly tenancy and udal tenure should be registered in the Land Register. This section implements these recommendations. It provides in subs. (1) (*a*) (i) to (iv) for the compulsory registration in an area where the provisions of the Act have come into force (an operational area) on the occasion of (i) the grant of a feu, long lease or security by way of contract of ground annual *quoad* the interest of the feuar, lessee or debtor in the ground annual; (ii) the transfer of an interest in land for valuable consideration; (iii) the transfer of such an interest in consideration of marriage; and (iv) the transfer of such an interest whereby it is absorbed into an interest in land which is registered. It also provides in subs. (1) (*a*) (v) for registration of any transfer of an interest where it is held under a long lease, udal tenure or kindly tenancy. The provisions of s. 3 (3) ensure that a real right to the interest of a lessee under a long lease, a proprietor under udal tenure or a kindly tenant will only be obtained by registration.

Subs. (1)

This subsection authorises registration of an interest in land, hitherto unregistered, in any of the several circumstances specified in the subsection. If the land is situated wholly or partially (see s. 11 (2)) in an operational area, registration of the interest in the Land Register will be compulsory, not in the sense that the law requires its registration, but as the only means whereby the owner of the interest can obtain a real right, since registration in the Register of Sasines will only be competent in respect of an interest in land in an operational area to the limited extent and for the restricted purposes authorised by s. 8. A registrable interest does not include the relatively less important interests which are designated overriding interests as defined in s. 28 (1), and the subsection does not apply to the interests excluded from its application by subs. (2), *infra*.

Where land is feued, let on long lease, or made the subject of a contract of ground annual, the interest of the feuar, lessee or debtor in the ground annual is registrable. Although the Land Tenure Reform (Scotland) Act 1974 prohibits the creation of feuduties or ground annuals, grants of feus and contracts of ground annual are normally made for valuable consideration by way of a capital payment and by the imposition of onerous obligations upon the feuar or debtor in the ground annual. Moreover, feu grants, long leases and contracts of ground annual create conditions and define responsibilities in relation to land which are of importance to the parties and may affect interests in other land. As transactions usually made for valuable consideration which involve the creation of important conditions and obligations affecting land it is necessary that they come within the scope of the scheme of registration. In relation to leases it is only where the lease granted is a long lease as defined in s. 28 (1), *i.e.* a lease having a duration exceeding 20 years or which can be extended at the request of the lessee beyond 20 years, that the lessee's interest is registrable: leases of lesser duration are overriding interests.

The transfer of an interest for valuable consideration covers the commonest case, a disposition of land on sale for a full price. When land situated within an operational area is sold a first registration will be made.

The transfer of an interest in consideration of marriage is included among the circumstances which render the interest registrable since marriage is regarded as valuable consideration. A transfer of an interest on the occasion of a marriage does not make the interest registrable: the transfer must be in consideration of the marriage, in the sense that it must be conditioned to take effect only on the marriage taking place, *e.g.* a marriage contract. For judicial interpretation of similar phraseology in revenue statutes, see *Re Park* (*decd.*) (*No.* 2) [1972] Ch. 385.

When an unregistered interest is absorbed into an interest which has already been registered, it will be necessary to show on the title sheet of the registered interest the enlargement of it which results from the absorption. Examples are: (1) when a superiority interest has already been registered and a feuar either voluntarily surrenders the *dominium utile* by conveying it to the superior *ad perpetuam remanentiam* or the feu is irritated; or (2) when a long lease terminates and the lessor's registered interest as owner of the land is thereby enlarged. In such circumstances registration may be made whether or not valuable consideration has been given.

In terms of s. 3 (3), a lessee under a long lease, a proprietor under udal tenure, or a kindly tenant can only obtain a real right by registration. Accordingly it is necessary to provide in subs. (1) (*a*) (v) that the interest of any such person is registrable on the occasion of transfer of the interest.

Subs. (1) (*b*) is designed to permit voluntary registration of an interest in circumstances other than those specified in subs. (1) (*a*). It is anticipated that the Keeper will welcome voluntary applications for registration of interests in land situated within an operational area, but it may be that the volume of required first registrations will tax the resources of the system to such an extent that it would be impracticable or seriously inconvenient for the Keeper to accept a significant number of voluntary applications for registration also. The subsection therefore gives the Keeper discretion to decline such applications. There may be circumstances in which voluntary registration may facilitate subsequent compulsory registrations, *e.g.* where the owner of land which is being developed with a view to feuing or selling individual plots holds on a title which has not been registered, it may simplify both the conveyancing procedures and first registrations of the individual plots if the owner's interest in the whole area is registered voluntarily in the first place. Again, where an estate has been acquired in parcels and the titles to the later acquisitions have been registered but not those of the earlier acquisitions; in such circumstances voluntary registration of the unregistered titles will enable future transactions affecting any part of the estate to be carried out by the conveyancing methods appropriate to registered interests.

Subs. (2)

This subsection makes it clear that first registration is not required when the interest transferred in the circumstances of s. 2 (1) is an unregistered interest in a heritable security, liferent or incorporeal heritable right. These interests are all something less than full ownership of land and it would not be appropriate to require first registration when such lesser rights are transferred. It should be noted that an incorporeal heritable right does not include salmon fishings (s. 28 (1)): these have always been regarded as praedial interests which can be separately owned rather than as rights of a subordinate character.

The subsection also exempts from first registration the transfer of an interest in land where the interest transferred is absorbed into another unregistered interest.

For example, where the superior acquires the *dominium utile,* or the feuar acquires the superiority of his feu, and both interests are unregistered, the merging of one estate with the other does not require a first registration.

Subs. (3)

This subsection applies in circumstances where there already exists a registered interest and there is then created on that interest a heritable security, liferent or incorporeal heritable right: the creation of such heritable security, liferent or incorporeal heritable right is then registrable. The provisions of this subsection relate only to the *creation* of such lesser interests: their *transfer* is dealt with under subs. (4). The subsection covers only the creation of, for example, a heritable security *after* the interest of the owner of the land has already been registered: if the security was created *before* the interest of the owner was first registered, the Keeper will already have transferred the security interest to the Land Register by entering its provisions in the title sheet in pursuance of s. 6 (1) and (2).

Subs. (4)

This subsection relates to the situation where an interest in land has already been registered and makes registrable certain subsequent transactions affecting the registered interest. These are: (1) any transfer of the registered interest, *e.g.* a disposition of it on sale; (2) any absorption by one registered interest of another registered interest, *e.g.* consolidation of the superiority and the property where the interests of both the superior and the feuar have previously been registered; and (3) any transaction or event which can have a legal effect upon the title to the registered interest (not being a transaction or event which merely creates or affects an overriding interest). The transaction or event may be of a character which would formerly have involved the recording of a deed in the Register of Sasines, such as the assignation of a registered heritable security, or it may be an event of such a kind that it would not have required such recording, *e.g.* the death of one of the parties to a title taken in the names of A and B and the survivor. In cases of the latter sort it is thought that the Keeper will bring the title sheet up to date by deleting the interest of the predeceaser which will then be absorbed into the interest of the survivor. There may be problems in the operation of this provision, particularly as to the nature of the evidence of transmission or cessation of an interest which the Keeper will require. For example, the Keeper may not be in safety in accepting a death certificate as evidence of the passing of the interest of the predeceaser to the survivor, even when it appears from the registered title that there is a contractual destination to the survivor, in the light of the decision in *Hay's Tr.* v. *Hay's Trs.,* 1951 S.C. 329. Also, when a heritable security is extinguished by negative prescription will there not now be some necessity for the debtor to provide a declarator of the court in order to secure the deletion of the creditor's registered interest from the title sheet?

Subs. (5)

The programme for the change to registration of title involves a phrased introduction of registration in the Land Register by the provisions of the Act being brought into operation by order in successive operational areas (ss. 11 and 30 (2)). Thereupon, in each area as it becomes operational, first registrations will be induced by s. 2 (1) (*a*) and voluntary first registrations will normally be accepted under s. 2 (1) (*b*). Ultimately, in each area a stage will be reached when a substantial majority of interests in land within the area will have been registered in the Land Register and it will be desirable to enable the division of the Register of Sasines for that area to be closed. This subsection empowers the Secretary of State to require that interests in land in that area which have not yet been registered in the Land Register be so registered in order that all registrable interests in the area may be included in the Land Register, when the Register of Sasines so far as relating to that area will cease to operate.

Subs. (6)

Subs. (4) (*c*) makes registrable any transaction or event which is capable under any enactment of affecting the title to a registered interest in land. Ss. 17, 18 and 19 make provisions as to when a deed of declaration of conditions, a variation or discharge of a land obligation or an agreement as to a common boundary become real obligations or binding on singular successors. This subsection ensures that the effect of the events contemplated in ss. 17, 18 and 19 will be registrable.

Effect of registration

3.—(1) Registration shall have the effect of—

(*a*) vesting in the person registered as entitled to the registered interest in land a real right in and to the interest and in and to any right, pertinent or servitude, express or implied, forming part of the interest, subject only to the effect of any matter entered in the title sheet of that interest under section 6 of this Act so far as adverse to the interest or that person's entitlement to it and to any overriding interest whether noted under that section or not;

(*b*) making any registered right or obligation relating to the registered interest in land a real right or obligation;

(*c*) affecting any registered real right or obligation relating to the registered interest in land,

insofar as the right or obligation is capable, under any enactment or rule of law, of being vested as a real right, or being made real or, as the case may be, of being affected as a real right.

In this subsection, " enactment " includes sections 17, 18 and 19 of this Act.

(2) Registration shall supersede the recording of a deed in the Register of Sasines but, subject to subsection (3) below, shall be without prejudice to any other means of creating or affecting real rights or obligations under any enactment or rule of law.

(3) A—

(*a*) lessee under a long lease;

(*b*) proprietor under udal tenure;

(*c*) kindly tenant,

shall obtain a real right in and to his interest as such only by registration; and registration shall be the only means of making rights or obligations relating to the registered interest in land of such a person real rights or obligations or of affecting such real rights or obligations.

(4) The date—

(*a*) at which a real right or obligation is created or as from which it is affected under this section;

(*b*) of entry of a feuar of a registrable interest in land with his superior,

shall be the date of registration.

(5) Where an interest in land has been registered, any obligation to assign title deeds and searches relating to that interest in land or to deliver them or make them forthcoming or any related obligation shall be of no effect in relation to that interest or to any other registered interest in land.

This subsection does not apply—

(*a*) to a land or charge certificate issued under section 5 of this Act;

(*b*) where the Keeper has, under section 12 (2) of this Act, excluded indemnity under Part II of this Act.

(6) It shall not be necessary for an uninfeft proprietor of an interest in land which has been registered to expede a notice of title in order to complete his title to that interest if evidence of sufficient midcouples or links between the uninfeft proprietor and the person last infeft are produced to the Keeper on any registration in respect of that interest and, accordingly, section 4 of the Conveyancing (Scotland) Act 1924 (completion of title by person uninfeft) shall be of no effect in relation to such an interest in land.

This subsection does not apply to the completion of title under

section 74 or 76 of the Lands Clauses Consolidation (Scotland) Act 1845 (procedure on compulsory purchase of lands).

(7) Nothing in this section affects any question as to the validity or effect of an overriding interest.

DEFINITIONS

"charge certificate": see s. 5 (3).
"deed": see s. 28 (1).
"interest in land": see s. 28 (1).
"the Keeper": see ss. 1 (2) and 28 (1).
"land certificate": see s. 5 (2).
"long lease": see s. 28 (1).
"overriding interest": see s. 28 (1).
"registered": see s. 1 (3).
"registration": see s. 1 (3).
"title sheet": see s. 6 (1).

GENERAL NOTE

This section defines the legal effect of registration in the Land Register. Broadly expressed, registration has the effect of making a registered interest in land, such as ownership, a real right subject to any adverse registered interest and to any overriding interest whether noted in the title sheet or not. It also makes any registered right an obligation real *quoad* both the creditor's interest and as a burden on the land. It further provides that a real right to the interests of a lessee under a long lease, a proprietor under udal tenure and a kindly tenant can only be obtained by registration, so that the alternative of making such rights real by possession will no longer be effective. The date of creation of the real right is the date of registration. An obligation to assign writs will now be ineffective save as regards a land or charge certificate or in cases where the Keeper has excluded indemnity. Notices of title will no longer require to be expede to complete the title of an uninfeft proprietor of a registered interest.

Subs. (1)

The effect of registration is to vest in the registered proprietor of the interest a real right therein and also, following the recommendation in para. 23 of the Henry Report, in any rights, pertinents or servitudes pertaining to it. The vested real right is subject to any adverse interest entered in the title sheet and also to any overriding interest whether noted in the title sheet or not. Registration also makes real any registered right or obligation relating to the registered interest and affects any existing registered real right or obligation which relates to the interest that is registered. These provisions are qualified by the general requirement that the right or obligation is such that it is capable in law of being vested as a real right. This is a proper qualification which preserves the established distinction between a praedial interest in land, which is capable of separate ownership, and rights which are merely incidents of other property such as trout fishing and shooting, which cannot be the subjects of separate ownership (*Patrick* v. *Napier* (1867) 5 M. 683; *Earl of Galloway* v. *Duke of Bedford* (1902) 4 F. 851; 9 S.L.T. 472; *Beckett* v. *Bisset,* 1921, 2 S.L.T. 33).

The final paragraph of the subsection ensures that the obligations created real and binding on singular successors in ss. 17, 18 and 19 are accorded that effect on registration—see note to s. 2 (6), *supra.*

Subs. (2)

The effect of s. 8 (4) is that, once an area becomes operational, the Keeper will reject deeds submitted for recording in the Register of Sasines if they relate to transactions in registrable interests which should enter the Land Register, so that registration therein will supersede recording in the Register of Sasines. There are certain kinds of real rights and obligations, however, which could be created without recording of any deed in the Register of Sasines, *e.g.* the creation of a servitude by prescription, and the creation of such real rights and obligations under the rules of the existing law remains competent. That general reservation, however, is subject to the new provision in s. 3 (3) which restricts the method of obtaining a real right to the interests therein specified to registration.

Subs. (3)

This subsection implements the recommendations of the Halliday Report (para. 101) and the Henry Report (paras. 33 and 34).

The Registration of Leases (Scotland) Act 1857 authorised registration of long leases in the Register of Sasines but the alternative method of constituting the lessee's right real by possession remained competent (*Rodger* v. *Crawfords* (1867) 6 M. 24). Problems arose from this duality of method and it would have been illogical to preserve it in a system of registration of title.

"Udal tenure" is a form of allodial tenure, Norse in origin, peculiar to Orkney and Shetland. In contrast to feudal principles, the owner of udal lands has no superior. Many properties in Orkney and Shetland have been converted to feudal holding and titles to them are recorded in the Register of Sasines. They will now be brought within the system of registration of title.

"Kindly tenancy" is a special form of tenure in Lochmaben, originating from grants by King Robert the Bruce to vassals on the lands of his castle there. Its characteristics are those of ownership rather than tenancy. This tenure also will now be brought within the new system.

The effect of the subsection is to ensure that titles under all these forms of tenure become registered in the Land Register since that will be the only method for the holders of land under such tenures to obtain a real right.

Subs. (4)

Under existing law, recording of a deed conferring a right to land is equivalent to the former sasine which made the right real and also implies entry with the superior (Conveyancing (Scotland) Act 1874, s. 4), and the date of recording is the criterion of preference in competition (Titles to Land Consolidation (Scotland) Act 1868, s. 142). This subsection preserves these rules in relation to registration in the Land Register.

Subs. (5)

This subsection makes unenforceable any obligation to assign, deliver or produce title deeds and searches relating to a registered interest. The principle will now be that a registered title will have been examined by the Keeper on first registration and in effect guaranteed by the Keeper (s. 12) backed by a state guarantee (s. 24). The land certificate or the charge certificate will vouch the interest of the person whose title is registered and the title sheet will disclose all relevant information regarding the registered interest and burdens affecting it, apart from overriding interests. In these circumstances it will be unnecessary to examine prior deeds: only the land or charge certificate need be furnished.

An exception from the general provision is plainly required where for any reason the Keeper has excluded indemnity under s. 12 (2): in such cases it will still be necessary for a person transacting with the holder of the registered title to examine prior writs and make his own decision as to the sufficiency of the title.

Subs. (6)

Under the present system, the proprietor of an interest in land who does not have a recorded title, such as the executor of a deceased proprietor, can obtain infeftment by expeding a notice of title and recording it in the Register of Sasines using the appropriate form of notice of title prescribed by the Conveyancing (Scotland) Act 1924, s. 4 and Sched. B. Under the system of registration of title the Keeper can examine the links or midcouples which connect the right of the uninfeft proprietor to the last infeft proprietor and, if satisfied as to their sufficiency, may register the uninfeft proprietor's interest without the need of requiring him to expede a notice of title. Accordingly the provisions of s. 4 of the 1924 Act no longer have effect in relation to a registered interest.

The final sentence of the subsection relates to a specialty in the code for compulsory acquisition of land. Ss. 74 and 76 of the Lands Clauses Consolidation (Scotland) Act 1845 provide for the situation where the owner of land compulsorily acquired fails to grant a conveyance of it or is unable to produce a good title; in these circumstances the acquiring body may deposit the price and procure a title by expeding and recording a notarial instrument. The present Act does not interfere with the existing statutory code and the method of completing the title of an acquiring body which it prescribes remains unchanged.

Subs. (7)

This subsection removes a possible doubt in relation to overriding interests. Subs. (1), in effect, and subs. (3) expressly make registration the only means of creating or affecting real rights or obligations. The essence of an overriding interest, however, is that although it is not registered it can affect an interest which is. The object of the subsection is to preserve that position.

Applications for registration

4.—(1) Subject to subsection (2) below, an application for registration shall be accepted by the Keeper if it is accompanied by such documents and other evidence as he may require.

(2) An application for registration shall not be accepted by the Keeper if—

(*a*) it relates to land which is not sufficiently described to enable him to identify it by reference to the Ordnance Map;

(*b*) it relates to land which is a souvenir plot, that is a piece of land which, being of inconsiderable size or no practical utility, is unlikely to be wanted in isolation except for the sake of mere ownership or for sentimental reasons or commemorative purposes; or

(*c*) it is frivolous or vexatious;

(*d*) a deed which—

(i) accompanies the application;

(ii) relates to a registered interest in land; and

(iii) is executed after that interest has been registered,

does not bear a reference to the number of the title sheet of that interest.

(3) On receipt of an application for registration, the Keeper shall forthwith note the date of such receipt, and that date shall be deemed for the purposes of this Act to be the date of registration either—

(*a*) where the application, after examination by the Keeper, is accepted by him, or

(*b*) where the application is not accepted by him on the grounds that it does not comply with subsection (1) or (2) (*a*) or (*d*) above but, without being rejected by the Keeper or withdrawn by the applicant, is subsequently accepted by the Keeper on his being satisfied that it does so comply, or has been made so to comply.

DEFINITIONS

"interest in land": see s. 28 (1).
"the Keeper": see ss. 1 (2) and 28 (1).
"land": see s. 28 (1).
"registered": see s. 1 (3).
"registration": see s. 1 (3).

GENERAL NOTE

S. 4 describes the procedure on applications for registration, the circumstances in which the Keeper may decline to accept an application, and the determination of the date of registration in relation to the receipt of an application.

Subs. (1)

The Keeper must accept an application for registration if it is accompanied by such documents and information as he may require. It is anticipated that rules will be made under s. 27 which will, *inter alia,* prescribe the form of application for registration.

Subs. (2)

This subsection sets out various circumstances in which the Keeper may decline to accept an application for registration.

He may refuse to accept an application if it relates to land which is not sufficiently described to enable him to identify it on the Ordnance Map. The system of registration of title depends upon mapping and the description of the land to be entered in the title sheet will be based on the Ordnance Map. The scale of the map to be used in an application is not specified but presumably the scale most appropriate to show the land will be used in each case. It would appear from the wording of the subsection that the responsibility of ensuring that the land is accurately described in relation to the map rests ultimately upon the Keeper.

The Keeper may also decline to accept an application for registration if it relates to a souvenir plot, i.e. one which is very small or useless for practical purposes, or if the application is frivolous or vexatious. Attempts to register small plots, or frivolous or vexatious registrations, have occurred occasionally in relation to the Register of Sasines and under registration of title in England, and it is proper that the Keeper should have discretion to refuse applications for registration in such cases.

Where an interest in land has already been registered, it is essential that a reference to the number of the title sheet be made in the relevant deed which accompanies an application. When an interest is first registered a title number will be assigned to it which will appear on the land certificate and on any charge certificate which relates to it. In terms of s. 15 (1) it will be sufficient in subsequent transactions to describe the land by reference to its number on the title sheet, and specification of the number in an application relating to a subsequent transaction affecting the interest will facilitate the work of the Keeper in identifying the interest in the Land Register.

A refusal by the Keeper to accept an application for registration will be subject to appeal under s. 25.

Subs. (3)

The date of receipt of an application is deemed to be the date of registration, which is of importance since the date of registration is made the criterion of preference as between titles to registered interests *inter se* and as between titles to registered interests and titles under deeds recorded in the Register of Sasines (s. 7).

The date of receipt of the application will be the date of registration where the application is in order and acceptable. Even if it is insufficient as originally presented by reason of non-compliance with the requirements of identification of the land on the Ordnance Map or of failure to quote the number of the title sheet, the application will retain its date of registration if the matter is rectified and, without the application having been rejected by the Keeper or withdrawn by the applicant, subsequently accepted by the Keeper.

Completion of registration

5.—(1) The Keeper shall complete registration—

(*a*) in respect of an interest in land which is not a heritable security, liferent or incorporeal heritable right—

(i) if the interest has not previously been registered, by making up a title sheet for it in the register in accordance with section 6 of this Act, or

(ii) if the interest has previously been registered, by making such amendment as is necessary to the title sheet of the interest;

(*b*) in respect of an interest in land which is a heritable security, liferent or incorporeal heritable right or in respect of the matters registrable under section 2 (4) of this Act by making such amendment as is necessary to the title sheet of the interest in land to which the heritable security, liferent, incorporeal heritable right or matter, as the case may be, relates,

and in each case by making such consequential amendments in the register as are necessary.

(2) Where the Keeper has completed registration under subsection (1) (*a*) above, he shall issue to the applicant a copy of the title sheet,

authenticated by the seal of the register; and such copy shall be known as a land certificate.

(3) Where the Keeper has completed registration in respect of a heritable security, he shall issue to the applicant a certificate authenticated by the seal of the register; and such certificate shall be known as a charge certificate.

(4) A land certificate shall be accepted for all purposes as sufficient evidence of the contents of the title sheet of which the land certificate is a copy; and a charge certificate shall be accepted for all purposes as sufficient evidence of the facts stated in it.

(5) Every land certificate and charge certificate shall contain a statement as to indemnity by the Keeper under Part II of this Act.

DEFINITIONS

"heritable security": see s. 28 (1).
"incorporeal heritable right": see s. 28 (1).
"interest in land": see s. 1 (3).
"register": see s. 1 (1).
"registered": see s. 1 (3).
"registrable": see s. 1 (3).
"registration": see s. 1 (3).

GENERAL NOTE

This section describes the process of registration, the making up of a title sheet on first registration or the amendment of the title sheet upon subsequent transactions or upon registration of a heritable security, liferent or incorporeal right affecting a registered interest, and the issue of copies of the title sheet, land certificates and charge certificates.

Subs. (1)

Upon first registration of an interest in land (other than one which is a heritable security, liferent or incorporeal heritable right) the Keeper will make up a title sheet for it: if the interest has already been registered he will amend the existing title sheet appropriately to give effect to the subsequent transaction.

Where the registration is of a heritable security, liferent or incorporeal heritable right, or is required in respect of the transfer or absorption of a registered interest or of any other of the events specified in s. 2 (4), registration will be effected by making the necessary amendment to the existing title sheet of the interest affected.

Subs. (2)

Upon completion of registration the Keeper will issue to the applicant an authenticated copy of the title sheet, the land certificate. In practice the land certificate will dispense with the need to examine the earlier progress of titles. On the sale of a heritable property the seller will produce the certificate which will provide all relevant information regarding the property and will be supported by the Keeper's indemnity. Thereupon the appropriate document of transfer will be executed by the seller and the purchaser will submit it for registration. Inquiry will still be necessary in respect of overriding interests, which may not always be noted on the copy title sheet.

Subs. (3)

Where the interest to be registered relates to a heritable security, a charge certificate will be issued. The applicant will normally be the creditor and the certificate will evidence the fact that the security has been registered and shown on the title sheet of the burdened land. It should be kept in view that a charge certificate does not guarantee that the amount of the secured loan is or will remain the sum stated in the standard security registered against the land. The Keeper has no knowledge of the state of accounting between the creditor and the debtor: he simply gives effect to an application to enter a standard security as a charge against the debtor's interest in the land. Moreover, after issue of the charge certificate payments may be made to account of the indebtedness which may not have been communicated to the Keeper. The charge certificate is guaranteed by the Keeper, but only in the sense that the title of the creditor to the charge as and when it entered the title sheet was valid. There is no right to indemnity where there is an issue as to the amount due under a heritable security at any particular date (s. 12 (3) (*o*)).

Subs. (4)

This subsection states the evidential force of a land certificate and a charge certificate.

Subs. (5)

The purpose of this subsection is to ensure that each land certificate and charge certificate discloses the extent of the indemnity given by the Keeper.

The title sheet

6.—(1) Subject to subsection (3) below, the Keeper shall make up and maintain a title sheet of an interest in land in the register by entering therein—

(*a*) a description of the land which shall consist of or include a description of it based on the Ordnance Map, and, where the interest is that of the proprietor of the *dominium utile* or the lessee under a long lease and the land appears to the Keeper to extend to 2 hectares or more, its area as calculated by the Keeper;

(*b*) the name and designation of the person entitled to the interest in the land and the nature of that interest;

(*c*) any subsisting entry in the Register of Inhibitions and Adjudications adverse to the interest;

(*d*) any heritable security over the interest;

(*e*) any enforceable real right pertaining to the interest or subsisting real burden or condition affecting the interest;

(*f*) any exclusion of indemnity under section 12 (2) of this Act in respect of the interest;

(*g*) such other information as the Keeper thinks fit to enter in the register.

(2) The Keeper shall enter a real right or real burden or condition in the title sheet by entering its terms or a summary of its terms therein; and such a summary shall, unless it contains a reference to a further entry in the title sheet wherein the terms of the real right, burden or condition are set out in full be presumed to be a correct statement of the terms of the right, burden or condition.

(3) The Keeper's duty under subsection (1) above shall not extend to entering in the title sheet any over-feuduty or over-rent exigible in respect of the interest in land, but he may so enter any such over-feuduty or over-rent.

(4) Any overriding interest which appears to the Keeper to affect an interest in land—

(*a*) shall be noted by him in the title sheet of that interest if it has been disclosed in any document accompanying an application for registration in respect of that interest;

(*b*) may be so noted if—

(i) application is made to him to do so;

(ii) the overriding interest is disclosed in any application for registration; or

(iii) the overriding interest otherwise comes to his notice.

In this subsection " overriding interest " does not include the interest of a lessee under a lease which is not a long lease.

(5) The Keeper shall issue, to any person applying, a copy, authenticated as the Keeper thinks fit, of any title sheet, part thereof, or of any document referred to in a title sheet; and such copy, which shall be known as an office copy, shall be accepted for all purposes as sufficient evidence of the contents of the original.

DEFINITIONS

"heritable security": see s. 28 (1).
"interest in land": see s. 28 (1).
"the Keeper": see s. 1 (2).
"land": see s. 28 (1).
"long lease": see s. 28 (1).
"overriding interest": see s. 28 (1), as modified in subs. (4).
"the register": see s. 1 (1).
"registration": see s. 1 (3).

GENERAL NOTE

This section sets out in detail the particulars which will be entered in a title sheet and those which may be so entered or noted.

Subs. (1)

This subsection requires the Keeper to enter in the title sheet:

(*a*) A description of the land concerned, consisting of or including a description of it based on the Ordnance Map. Most modern titles contain a statement of the area of the land involved although in some modern developments, for reasons of economy, the area of new building plots is not specified. Many older titles do not contain a statement of total area. Where the area is stated in the deeds or other information furnished to the Keeper on application for first registration it is anticipated that it will be recorded in the title sheet. A description based on a reference to the Ordnance Map of appropriate scale should, however, even in the absence of a statement of area, identify the land with reasonable accuracy.

Where the interest registered is that of the proprietor of the *dominium utile* or the lessee under a long lease and the area appears to be two hectares or more, the area as calculated by the Keeper is to be entered on the title sheet. The area of two hectares or more will exclude the vast majority of urban or suburban dwelling-houses and small business properties; in the case of the latter the Keeper may enter the area of the land if that information is furnished to him but otherwise he need not calculate it, since that would be a formidable task. Interests in land of two hectares or more will form a relatively small proportion of registrable interests, possibly about 5 per cent. of the whole, and there is some value in having disclosed on the Land Register the larger holdings of land in Scotland and the size of each. The Keeper's indemnity does not extend to a guarantee of the accuracy of the areas so calculated by him (s. 12 (3) (*e*)).

(*b*) The name and designation of the person entitled to the interest and the nature of the interest, *e.g.* owner of *dominium utile*, lessee under long lease, superior or creditor in a ground annual. This will show whether the subject of the title sheet is a superiority, or property, or a long leasehold.

(*c*) Any subsisting entry in the Register of Inhibitions and Adjudications adverse to the registered interest. This will include inhibitions, adjudications, notices of litigiosity, abbreviations in sequestration, etc., all of which may affect the right of the owner of the registered interest to deal with it. It does not appear how an inhibition obtained by a creditor after registration of the title will be incorporated in the register, *e.g.* whether the Keeper will have the responsibility of relating the person inhibited to the registered title or titles of his property or properties, but no doubt this will be clarified in the rules to be made under s. 27.

(*d*) Any heritable security over the interest. If there is an existing heritable security when the proprietor of the burdened interest first registers, the security will be transferred from the Register of Sasines and noted in the title sheet of the burdened interest. When a new heritable security is created and the creditor registers his interest, the security will be entered in the title sheet of the burdened interest.

(*e*) Any enforceable real right pertaining to the interest or a subsisting real burden or condition affecting that interest. This provision may cause problems in practice. A real burden or condition may not be enforceable because of defect in expression, as by lack of precision, or may have become unenforceable through absence of a praedial interest to do so or by acquiescence. Hence the provision in s. 12 (3) (*g*) that the Keeper's indemnity does not cover loss arising from inability to enforce a real burden or condition entered in the register unless the Keeper expressly assumes responsibility for its enforceability. The problem will remain, as under the present system, of real burdens and conditions *ex facie* affecting a title which in practice are obsolete or unenforceable.

(*f*) Since the land certificate is a copy of the title sheet, anything appearing on the title sheet which the Keeper wishes to exclude from his indemnity must be specified in it.

(*g*) The Keeper may have knowledge from other registers or other title sheets of information which may be of value in relation to the interest concerned, and it may be appropriate to enter it on the title sheet of that interest.

Subs. (2)

The Keeper has the option of entering the real right or burden in full or summarising it. If a summary is made, it will be presumed to be accurate but it would appear that the presumption is rebuttable.

Subs. (3)

In older titles it is often difficult to ascertain the amount of over-feuduties or over-rents which affect a relatively small part of lands feued or leased. Where information as to over-feuduty or over-rent is available, the Keeper may enter it, but he is not obliged to make time-consuming investigation in order to ascertain it.

Subs. (4)

Overriding interests are defined in s. 28 (1). If such an interest is disclosed in the application for registration, the Keeper *must* note it on the title sheet. If it is not so disclosed, the Keeper *may* in his discretion note it if it comes to his notice in any of the ways described in subs. (4) (*b*). The interest of a lessee under a lease of 20 years or less is not to be so noted: it might well be misleading to do so since the lease may have expired or been continued by tacit relocation without the Keeper's knowledge.

Subs. (5)

In conformity with the established practice that in Scotland land registers are public, the new Land Register and information contained in it are available to any person.

Ranking

7.—(1) Without prejudice to any express provision as to ranking in any deed or any other provision as to ranking in, or having effect by virtue of, any enactment or rule of law, the following provisions of this section shall have effect to determine the ranking of titles to interests in land.

(2) Titles to registered interests in land shall rank according to the date of registration of those interests.

(3) A title to a registered interest and a title governed by a deed recorded in the Register of Sasines shall rank according to the respective dates of registration and recording.

(4) Where the date of registration or recording of the titles to two or more interests in land is the same, the titles to those interests shall rank equally.

DEFINITIONS

"interest in land": see s. 28 (1).
"Register of Sasines": see s. 28 (1).
"registered": see s. 1 (3).
"registration": see s. 1 (3).

GENERAL NOTE

This section regulates the priority of (i) deeds registered in the Land Register, and (ii) deeds registered in the Land Register and deeds recorded in the Register of Sasines. The date of registration, or the respective dates of registration and recording, will be the criteria of preference.

The statutory provisions are without prejudice to express provisions in any deed. For example, two registered standard securities may contain ranking clauses: the provisions of these clauses will regulate priority notwithstanding the order in which the standard securities are respectively registered. It is possible that ranking agreements may be contained in unregistered or unrecorded deeds. In general, the effect of such an agreement will be contractual as between the parties; the statutory provisions will regulate the priority of their interests in the land but the agreement may nevertheless alter contractually that situation as between the parties *inter se*. For example, advances may be made by A and B upon standard securities which contain no ranking clauses, but by unregistered or unrecorded agreement A's security will have preference over that of B. If B's security is registered first then as a matter of heritable right it will rank before that of B, but by reason of the agreement B will require to account to A for any sums received by enforcement of his security before the balance is applied towards B's advance.

Likewise the statutory provisions are without prejudice to any rule of law. If A owns land in an operational area and his title is still recorded in the Register of Sasines and he grants a feu of part of it to B, but B delays in registering his title, and before he does so A grants a standard security to C over the whole of his land which is recorded in the Register of Sasines, then, when B later registers his title to the feu in the Land Register, C will have preference over B by virtue of s. 7 (3). If, however, C was aware of the existence of the feu grant to B when he made his advance, he will be unable to enforce that priority in a question with B because of the common law rules as to good faith (*Stodart* v. *Dalzell* (1876) 4 R. 236; *Petrie* v. *Forsyth* (1874) 2 R. 214).

It may be noted that the section effects a minor change as regards the determination of priorities in relation to recording in the Register of Sasines. At present priority is regulated by the time of receipt of a deed as recorded in the presentment book, and is preferred in ranking to a deed received later on the same day (Register of Sasines Act 1693; Land Registers (Scotland) Act 1868, s. 6; Titles to Land Consolidation (Scotland) Act 1868, s. 142). Once an area becomes operational, however, priority of ranking in the Register of Sasines, and also in the Land Register, will be determined only by the day of recording or registration.

Continuing effectiveness of recording in Register of Sasines

8.—(1) Subject to subsection (3) below, the only means of creating or affecting a real right or a real obligation relating to anything to which subsection (2) below applies shall be by recording a deed in the Register of Sasines.

(2) This subsection applies to—

(*a*) an interest in land which is to be transferred or otherwise affected by—

(i) an instrument which, having been recorded before the commencement of this Act in the Register of Sasines with an error or defect; or

(ii) a deed which, having been recorded before the commencement of this Act in the Register of Sasines with an error or defect in the recording,

has not, before such commencement, been re-presented, corrected as necessary, for the purposes of recording of new under section 143 of the Titles to Land Consolidation (Scotland) Act 1868;

In this paragraph, " instrument " has the same meaning as in section 3 of the said Act of 1868.

(*b*) a registered interest in land which has been absorbed, otherwise than by operation of prescription, into another interest in land the title to which is governed by a deed recorded in the Register of Sasines;

(*c*) anything which is not registrable under subsections (1) to (4) of section 2 of this Act and in respect of which, immediately before the commencement of this Act, a real right or obligation could be created or affected by recording a deed in the Register of Sasines.

(3) Nothing in subsection (1) above shall prejudice any other means, other than by registration, of creating or affecting real rights or obligations under any enactment or rule of law.

(4) Except as provided in this section, the Keeper shall reject any deed submitted for recording in the Register of Sasines.

DEFINITIONS

"instrument": see Titles to Land Consolidation (Scotland) Act 1868, s. 3.
"interest in land": see s. 28 (1).
"the Keeper": see s. 1 (2).
"Register of Sasines": see s. 28 (1).
"registered": see s. 1 (3).
"registrable": see s. 1 (3).

GENERAL NOTE

The provisions of this section are transitional. The drafting scheme of the section is to provide that, once an area has become operational, recording of deeds in the Register of Sasines will be refused (subs. (4)), but permits such recording of deeds in certain circumstances, *e.g.* where the transaction to which the deed relates does not attract registration in the Land Register under s. 2.

Subs. (1)

The general effect of ss. 2 and 3 of the Act is to ensure that, when an area has become operational, a right in a registrable interest in land will be made real by registration in the Land Register, although that is without prejudice to any other means of creating a right real, *e.g.* the constitution of a servitude by positive prescription. Subs. (1) of this section provides that recording in the Register of Sasines will be the only method of creating or affecting a real right or obligation where subs. (2) applies, again subject to the qualification that it is without prejudice to any means, other than registration, of creating or affecting real rights or obligations (subs. (3)).

Subs. (2)

(*a*) Where an instrument as defined in s. 3 of the Titles to Land Consolidation (Scotland) Act 1868, *e.g.* a notice of title, contains an error or defect, or where there has been an error or defect in the recording of any deed, it is competent under s. 143 of that Act to correct the instrument and record the corrected version, or to record the deed of new. If the area should become operational when the process of correction or re-recording has not been completed, it will still be competent to complete the process in the Register of Sasines.

(*b*) In certain circumstances a registered interest may become absorbed in an interest which is as yet unregistered, *e.g.* where the registered interest of the feuar in the *dominium utile* is acquired by the superior whose title is still recorded only in the Register of Sasines. In such cases the deed which effects the absorption will be recorded in the Register of Sasines and the title sheet of the feuar's interest in the Land Register will be closed under s. 2 (4) (*c*). Absorption by the operation of prescription is excepted. If the title to a superiority is recorded in the Register of Sasines and the title to the *dominium utile* is registered in the Land Register, and the same person is the proprietor of both so that consolidation would be effected after 10 years by prescription, it would seem necessary to remove the interest in the *dominium utile* from the Land Register by the closing of the title sheet, using s. 2 (4) (*c*), before consolidation would operate.

(*c*) Anything in respect of which a real right or interest could be created by recording a deed in the Register of Sasines, but which is not registrable under s. 2 (1)–(4), may still be done by recording in the Register of Sasines, *e.g.* a disposition of land by way of gift.

Subs. (3)

This subsection preserves the competency of creating real rights or obligations other than by way of registration, *e.g.* the creation by positive prescription of a servitude of access.

Subs. (4)

This provision will ensure that the Register of Sasines is gradually phased out in operational areas.

Rectification of the register

9.—(1) Subject to subsection (3) below, the Keeper may, whether on being so requested or not, and shall, on being so ordered by the court or the Lands Tribunal for Scotland, rectify any inaccuracy in the register by inserting, amending or cancelling anything therein.

(2) Subject to subsection (3) (*b*) below, the powers of the court and of the Lands Tribunal for Scotland to deal with questions of heritable right or title shall include power to make orders for the purposes of subsection (1) above.

(3) If rectification under subsection (1) above would prejudice a proprietor in possession—

(*a*) the Keeper may exercise his power to rectify only where—

(i) the purpose of the rectification is to note an overriding interest or to correct any information in the register relating to an overriding interest;

(ii) all persons whose interests in land are likely to be affected by the rectification have been informed by the Keeper of his intention to rectify and have consented in writing;

(iii) the inaccuracy has been caused wholly or substantially by the fraud or carelessness of the proprietor in possession; or

(iv) the rectification relates to a matter in respect of which indemnity has been excluded under section 12 (2) of this Act;

(*b*) the court or the Lands Tribunal for Scotland may order the Keeper to rectify only where sub-paragraph (i), (iii) or (iv) of paragraph (*a*) above applies.

(4) In this section—

(*a*) " the court " means any court having jurisdiction in questions of heritable right or title;

(*b*) " overriding interest " does not include the interest of a lessee under a lease which is not a long lease.

DEFINITIONS

" the court ": see subs. (4).
" interest in land ": see s. 28 (1).
" the Keeper ": see s. 1 (2).
" overriding interest ": see s. 28 (1), as qualified by subs. (4).
" register ": see s. 1 (1).

GENERAL NOTE

This section provides for rectification of the Land Register, either by the Keeper or by order of the Lands Tribunal for Scotland or the court.

The Keeper may rectify the Register either on his own initiative or when requested to do so. If, however, rectification would prejudice the interest of a proprietor in possession the Keeper may rectify only where (i) the purpose is to note or to correct an overriding interest (not being the interest of a lessee under a short lease); (ii) all persons concerned have been notified and have consented in writing to the rectification; (iii) the inaccuracy is the fault of the proprietor in possession; or (iv) the rectification relates to a matter in respect of which indemnity has been excluded.

Any person aggrieved by a refusal to rectify may appeal to the Lands Tribunal

(s. 25 (1)) and there will be a right of further appeal to the Court of Session, and the Keeper may be ordered by the Lands Tribunal or the court to effect rectification.

Positive prescription in respect of registered interests in land

10. Section 1 of the Prescription and Limitation (Scotland) Act 1973 shall have effect as if—

(*a*) after " followed " in paragraph (*b*) of subsection (1) there were inserted " (i) " and for the words from " then " to the end of that subsection there were inserted " , or

(ii) registration of that interest in favour of that person in the Land Register of Scotland, subject to an exclusion of indemnity under section 12 (2) of the Land Registration (Scotland) Act 1979,

then, as from the expiration of the said period, the validity of the title so far as relating to the said interest in the particular land shall be exempt from challenge.

(1A) Subsection (1) above shall not apply where—

(*a*) possession was founded on the recording of a deed which is invalid *ex facie* or was forged; or

(*b*) possession was founded on registration in respect of an interest in land in the Land Register of Scotland proceeding on a forged deed and the person appearing from the Register to be entitled to the interest was aware of the forgery at the time of registration in his favour ";

(*b*) at the end of subsection (2) there were added " or which is registrable in the Land Register of Scotland.".

Definitions

" interest in land ": see s. 28 (1).
" registrable ": see s. 1 (3).
" registration ": see s. 1 (3).

General Note

The amendments to s. 1 of the Prescription and Limitation (Scotland) Act 1973 are designed to continue the benefit of positive prescription in rendering a title unchallengeable in the only case under a registration of title system where that may still be useful, *i.e.* where the registration of a title has been made subject to an exclusion of indemnity. That benefit will not be available, however, if the registration proceeded on a forged deed and the person entitled to the interest was aware of the forgery when his title was registered.

Transitional provisions for Part I

11.—(1) If an application for registration relates to land no part of which is in an operational area, the Keeper may nevertheless accept that application as if it related to land wholly within an operational area, and if the Keeper has so accepted such an application, the provisions of this Act relating to registration then in force shall apply in relation to that application.

(2) An application for registration which relates to land which is partly in an operational area shall be treated as if it related to land wholly in that area, and the provisions of this Act relating to registration in force shall apply in relation to that application.

(3) In this section an " operational area " means an area in respect of which the provisions of this Act relating to registration have come into operation.

Definitions

" the Keeper ": see s. 1 (2).

"operational areas": see subs. (3).
"registration": see s. 1 (3).

GENERAL NOTE

This section deals with the situations where application is made to register an interest in (i) land wholly outwith an operational area, and (ii) land partly within an operational area. In the former case, the Keeper has a discretion to register the interest or not to do so. In the latter case, the application will be treated as if it related to land wholly within the operational area and will be registrable accordingly.

PART II

INDEMNITY IN RESPECT OF REGISTERED INTERESTS IN LAND

Indemnity in respect of loss

12.—(1) Subject to the provisions of this section, a person who suffers loss as a result of—

(*a*) a rectification of the register made under section 9 of this Act;

(*b*) the refusal or omission of the Keeper to make such a rectification;

(*c*) the loss or destruction of any document while lodged with the Keeper;

(*d*) an error or omission in any land or charge certificate or in any information given by the Keeper in writing or in such other manner as may be prescribed by rules made under section 27 of this Act,

shall be entitled to be indemnified by the Keeper in respect of that loss.

(2) Subject to section 14 of this Act, the Keeper may on registration in respect of an interest in land exclude, in whole or in part, any right to indemnity under this section in respect of anything appearing in, or omitted from, the title sheet of that interest.

(3) There shall be no entitlement to indemnity under this section in respect of loss where—

(*a*) the loss arises as a result of a title prevailing over that of the claimant in a case where—

(i) the prevailing title is one in respect of which the right to indemnity has been partially excluded under subsection (2) above, and

(ii) such exclusion has been cancelled but only on the prevailing title having been fortified by prescription;

(*b*) the loss arises in respect of a title which has been reduced as a gratuitous alienation or fraudulent preference, or has been reduced or varied by an order under section 6 (2) of the Divorce (Scotland) Act 1976 (orders relating to settlements and other dealings);

(*c*) the loss arises in consequence of the making of a further order under section 5 (2) of the Presumption of Death (Scotland) Act 1977 (effect on property rights of recall or variation of decree of declarator of presumed death);

(*d*) the loss arises as a result of any inaccuracy in the delineation of any boundaries shown in a title sheet, being an inaccuracy which could not have been rectified by reference to the Ordnance Map, unless the Keeper has expressly assumed responsibility for the accuracy of that delineation;

(*e*) the loss arises, in the case of land extending to 2 hectares or more the area of which falls to be entered in the title sheet of an interest in that land under section 6 (1) (*a*) of this Act, as a result of the Keeper's failure to enter such area in the title sheet or, where he has so entered such area, as a result of any inaccuracy in the specification of that area in the title sheet;

(*f*) the loss arises in respect of an interest in mines and minerals and the title sheet of any interest in land which is or includes the surface land does not expressly disclose that the interest in mines and minerals is included in that interest in land;

(*g*) the loss arises from inability to enforce a real burden or condition entered in the register, unless the Keeper expressly assumes responsibility for the enforceability of that burden or condition;

(*h*) the loss arises in respect of an error or omission in the noting of an overriding interest;

(*j*) the loss is suffered by—

(i) a beneficiary under a trust in respect of any transaction entered into by its trustees or in respect of any title granted by them the validity of which is unchallengeable by virtue of section 2 of the Trusts (Scotland) Act 1961 (validity of certain transactions by trustees), or as the case may be, section 17 of the Succession (Scotland) Act 1964 (protection of persons acquiring title), or

(ii) a person in respect of any interest transferred to him by trustees in purported implement of trust purposes;

(*k*) the loss arises as a result of an error or omission in an office copy as to the effect of any subsisting adverse entry in the Register of Inhibitions and Adjudications affecting any person in respect of any registered interest in land, and that person's entitlement to that interest is neither disclosed in the register nor otherwise known to the Keeper;

(*l*) the claimant is the proprietor of the dominant tenement in a servitude, except insofar as the claim may relate to the validity of the constitution of that servitude;

(*m*) the claimant is a superior, a creditor in a ground annual or a landlord under a long lease and the claim relates to any information—

(i) contained in the feu writ, the contract of ground annual or the lease, as the case may be, and

(ii) omitted from the title sheet of the interest of the superior, creditor or landlord,

(except insofar as the claim may relate to the constitution or amount of the feuduty, ground annual or rent and adequate information has been made available to the Keeper to enable him to make an entry in the register in respect of such constitution or amount or to the description of the land in respect of which the feuduty, ground annual or rent is payable);

(*n*) the claimant has by his fraudulent or careless act or omission caused the loss;

(*o*) the claim relates to the amount due under a heritable security.

(4) A refusal or omission by the Keeper to enter in a title sheet—

(*a*) any over-feuduty or over-rent exigible in respect of a registrable interest;

(*b*) any right alleged to be a real right on the ground that by virtue of section 6 of this Act he has no duty to do so since it is unenforceable,

shall not by itself prevent a claim to indemnity under this section.

DEFINITIONS

"charge certificate": see s. 5 (3).

" feu ": see s. 28 (1).
" heritable security ": see s. 28 (1).
" interest in land ": see s. 28 (1).
" the Keeper ": see s. 1 (2).
" land certificate ": see s. 5 (2).
" long lease ": see s. 28 (1).
" office copy ": see s. 6 (5).
" overriding interest ": see s. 28 (1).
" register ": see s. 1 (1).
" registered ": see s. 1 (3).
" registration ": see s. 1 (3).
" title sheet ": see s. 6.

GENERAL NOTE

This section provides the necessary corollary to s. 9. If a person suffers loss as a result of rectification of the Land Register, or a refusal to rectify it, he will be entitled to be indemnified by the Keeper. The Keeper will also be liable to indemnify loss which results from loss or destruction of any document lodged with him, or from errors or omissions in land certificates or charge certificates. The right to indemnity may, in particular cases, be excluded, in whole or in part, in respect of anything appearing in or omitted from the title sheet of the interest. There are, however, certain circumstances, listed in subs. (3), where there is no entitlement to indemnity.

Subs. (1)

This subsection specifies the matters which may result in financial loss and in respect of which the Keeper will be liable to indemnify.

Subs. (2)

In certain circumstances, *e.g.* when a title which is defective or doubtful is submitted for registration, or where there is doubt whether a real burden has been properly constituted, the Keeper may restrict the indemnity. Clearly he cannot be expected to guarantee at public expense an unsatisfactory title or right. As regards the foreshore there are special provisions as to indemnity in s. 14.

Subs. (3)

This subsection specifies circumstances in which there will be no entitlement to indemnity, *viz.*:

(*a*) The kind of situation envisaged is that A registers a title to land which includes a small area X, A having demonstrated to the Keeper that he has possessed the area X. Subsequently B registers a title to adjoining land which is sufficient in respect of its terms to include area X but, since A has already registered a title which includes that area, the Keeper excludes his indemnity in respect of B's registered title as regards that area. Later A ceases to exercise possession of area X and permits B to possess it for the period of positive prescription, so that B may then obtain from the Keeper an unqualified land certificate which includes area X. Since the loss to A has been caused by his own failure to exercise possession, he will be unable to claim indemnity.

(*b*) Gratuitous alienations or fraudulent preferences, and settlements or dealings reducible under s. 6 of the Divorce (Scotland) Act 1976, are transactions designed wrongfully to defeat the rights of other persons. When a title has been obtained by a transaction of that character, there is no right to indemnity when it is reduced by the court.

(*c*) Under s. 2 (2) of the Presumption of Death (Scotland) Act 1977, the court may determine any question relating to an interest in property which may arise in consequence of the death of a missing person, and under s. 5 (2) of that Act the court may subsequently, when a decree under s. 2 has been varied or recalled, make a further order in relation to rights of property. When that occurs, any loss suffered as a result of the further order will not entitle the person whose registered title is affected by the further order to indemnity.

(*d*) There will be cases where the description of a boundary in the title deeds submitted on first registration are not reconcilable with the Ordnance Map. Where the discrepancy cannot be clarified to the satisfaction of the Keeper he may state on the title sheet that the boundary is not guaranteed. There will be no entitlement to indemnity in such circumstances if it transpires later that it is not accurately delineated.

(*e*) The Keeper is required under s. 6 (1) (*a*) to calculate the area of the land when the title sheet is that of the interest of the proprietor of the *dominium utile* or a lessee under a long lease. That does not affect the validity of the title, and so there is no entitlement to indemnity if the Keeper fails to enter the area on the title sheet or enters it incorrectly.

(*f*) Since the law presumes that ownership of land extends *ad centrum,* a title to surface includes minerals unless they have been excepted or reserved. In many cases, especially where the minerals are or were of little commercial value, it is unclear from the title deeds of the land whether minerals have been thus excluded. The Report of the Henry Committee (para. 31) recommended that if there was no specific inclusion of mines and minerals in the title deeds submitted to the Keeper there should be no guarantee thereof.

(*g*) It would be impracticable for the Keeper to guarantee that real burdens or conditions appearing in a title progress were enforceable. Deeds which incorporate such burdens or conditions by reference normally qualify the reference by words such as " so far as valid and subsisting ", and the Keeper cannot be expected to verify that the burdens or conditions have not become unenforceable, *e.g.* by acquiescence or loss of interest to enforce.

(*h*) The character of overriding interests makes it impracticable for the Keeper to ensure that they are disclosed in every case. The Keeper will note them on the title sheet if they are disclosed in the documents furnished on an application for registration and may do so if they are otherwise brought or come to his notice (s. 6 (4)), but he cannot be expected to accept responsibility for the accuracy or comprehensiveness of the notes of them appearing on a title sheet.

(*j*) S. 2 of the Trusts (Scotland) Act 1961 protects the title of persons who enter into certain kinds of transaction with trustees against challenge on the ground that the action of the trustees was at variance with the terms or purposes of the trust. S. 17 of the Succession (Scotland) Act 1964 protects the title of any person who has acquired from an executor or from any person deriving title directly from an executor any interest in or security over heritable property in good faith and for value against challenge on the ground that the executor's confirmation was reducible or had been reduced or that the title should not have been transferred by the executor to the person from whom the acquisition was made. Neither of these sections, however, protect the trustees or the executor, as the case may be, from claims by the beneficiaries who may have suffered loss through the transactions. The object of para. (i) of this subsection is to protect the Keeper against any beneficiary in respect of a title registered by him as a result of any such transaction.

Para. (ii) of the subsection protects the Keeper against any claim by a person who has suffered loss where trustees have transferred any interest in land in purported implement of trust purposes and the Keeper has registered his title to that interest and the transaction is subsequently reduced.

(*k*) In terms of s. 6 (1) (*c*) the Keeper is required to enter in the title sheet any subsisting entry in the Register of Inhibitions and Adjudications adverse to the title registered. It would appear that the Keeper's liability to enter any such entry in the title sheet (and so in the land certificate) is absolute. Where, however, the Keeper furnishes an office copy of a title sheet, as he is required to do under s. 6 (5), he will only be liable in indemnity if he makes an error or omission as to the effect of a subsisting entry in the personal register in a question with a person whose title to the registered interest affected by the entry is disclosed in the Land Register or is otherwise known to the Keeper.

(*l*) A servitude may be lost by non-use or may be extinguished by change of circumstances (*Winans* v. *Lord Tweedmouth* (1888) 15 R. 540; *Rutherglen Mags.* v. *Bainbridge* (1886) 13 R. 745). The Keeper may be unaware of such events. Accordingly it is only where the Keeper has erred in deciding whether a servitude has or has not been validly created that he will be liable to indemnify the proprietor of the dominant tenement.

(*m*) The Keeper will not be liable in indemnity where he has omitted to enter in the title sheet of the interest of a superior, creditor in a ground-annual, or landlord in a long lease, information contained in the feu writ, contract of ground annual or lease themselves. The proprietors of these interests have or ought to have information as to the terms of the constituting deeds and persons acquiring from them should have that information communicated to them. Moreover, detailed conditions contained in, say, a long lease may have been varied or become unenforceable through the actings of parties. If, however, the Keeper has had adequate information which enabled him to verify the constitution and amount of the feuduty, ground annual or rent and make an appropriate entry in the title sheet of the creditor's interest, then that information is guaranteed and the Keeper will be liable in indemnity if the title sheet is wrong as regards these matters.

(*n*) The Keeper is not liable to indemnify a claimant whose fraudulent or careless action or omission has caused the loss. S. 13 (4) provides that the indemnity will be reduced to the extent by which the action or omission of the claimant has contributed to the loss.

(*o*) The amount due under a heritable security may vary from time to time, for example by periodic repayments of an advance from a building society, by special payments to account of the secured loan or by compensation or set off. The Keeper may have no knowledge of such events and so is not liable to indemnify any person in respect of loss arising through reliance upon the statement of the amount due under a heritable security in a land certificate or charge certificate.

Subs. (4)

The Keeper need not enter in the title sheet any over-feuduty or over-rent exigible in respect of a registered interest (s. 6 (3)) nor need he enter a real right or burden which he considers to be unenforceable (s. 6 (1) (*e*)). If he refuses or omits to do so, however, that will not preclude a claim for indemnity if, for example, there is some significant over-rent payable or a real burden which he has refused to enter is in fact enforceable.

Provisions supplementary to section 12

13.—(1) Subject to any order by the Lands Tribunal for Scotland or the court for the payment of expenses in connection with any claim disposed of by the Lands Tribunal under section 25 of this Act or the court, the Keeper shall reimburse any expenditure reasonably and properly incurred by a person in pursuing a *prima facie* well-founded claim under section 12 of this Act, whether successful or not.

(2) On settlement of any claim to indemnity under the said section 12, the Keeper shall be subrogated to all rights which would have been available to the claimant to recover the loss indemnified.

(3) The Keeper may require a claimant, as a condition of payment of his claim, to grant, at the Keeper's expense, a formal assignation to the Keeper of the rights mentioned in subsection (2) above.

(4) If a claimant to indemnity has by his fraudulent or careless act or omission contributed to the loss in respect of which he claims indemnity, the amount of the indemnity to which he would have been entitled had he not so contributed to his loss shall be reduced proportionately to the extent to which he has so contributed.

DEFINITIONS

"the court": see s. 9 (4).

"the Keeper": see s. 1 (2).

GENERAL NOTE

Since the indemnity is guaranteed by the state, it is reasonable that a person who has *prima facie* a valid claim to indemnity should recover the expense of pursuing it, even if it should ultimately prove to be unsuccessful. Where the claim is disposed of by the Lands Tribunal or the court, however, the Tribunal or the court will determine the matter of expenses.

Where the Keeper settles a claim to indemnity, he will be subrogated to all rights which would have been available to the claimant to recover the loss, and may be required to assign such rights to the Keeper.

As to contributions to loss by a claimant who has been fraudulent or careless, see note to s. 12 (3) (*n*) *supra*.

The foreshore

14.—(1) If—

(*a*) it appears to the Keeper that—

(i) an interest in land which is registered or in respect of which an application for registration has been made consists, in whole or in part, of foreshore or a right in foreshore, or might so consist, and

(ii) discounting any other deficiencies in his title in respect of that foreshore or right in foreshore, the person registered or, as the case may be, applying to be registered as entitled to the interest will not have an unchallengeable title in respect of the foreshore or the right in foreshore until prescription against the Crown has fortified his title in that respect, and

(*b*) the Keeper wholly excludes or proposes wholly to exclude rights to indemnity in respect of that person's entitlement to that foreshore or that right in foreshore, and is requested by that person not to do so,

the Keeper shall notify the Crown Estate Commissioners that he has been so requested.

(2) If the Crown Estate Commissioners have—

(*a*) within one month of receipt of the notification referred to in subsection (1) above, given to the Keeper written notice of their interest, and

(*b*) within three months of that receipt informed the Keeper in writing that they are taking steps to challenge that title,

the Keeper shall—

(i) during the prescriptive period, or

(ii) until such time as it appears to the Keeper that the Commissioners are no longer taking steps to challenge that title or that their challenge has been unsuccessful,

whichever is the shorter, continue wholly to exclude or, as the case may be, wholly exclude right to indemnity in respect of that person's entitlement to that foreshore or that right in foreshore.

(3) This section, or anything done under it, shall be without prejudice to any other right or remedy available to any person in respect of foreshore or any right in foreshore.

DEFINITIONS

"interest in land": see s. 28 (1).
"the Keeper": see s. 1 (2).
"registered": see s. 1 (3).
"registration": see s. 1 (3).

GENERAL NOTE

The foreshore is part of the *regalia minora* and can be alienated by the Crown. It is possible for a riparian proprietor who has a title sufficient in respect of its terms to include the foreshore to acquire ownership of it by uninterrupted possession for the prescriptive period which, by reason of the special problems of supervision, remains at 20 years when positive prescription of foreshore is pled against the Crown (Prescription and Limitation (Scotland) Act 1973, s. 1 (4)). The Henry Committee recognised that in relation to registration of title special treatment should be accorded to the foreshore by the inclusion of provisions for the protection of the Crown's interest (para. 30). This section contains these special provisions.

Subs. (1)

Where an application is made for registration of a title which includes, or may include, foreshore, and the Keeper is satisfied that prescription has run against the Crown in respect of the foreshore involved, he may register the title including the foreshore. If, however, the Keeper is not satisfied that prescription has so run and proposes to exclude rights to indemnity in relation to the title or right of the applicant to the foreshore, he must notify the Crown Estate Commissioners of the application.

Subs. (2)

If the Crown Estate Commissioners within one month of receipt of the notification give written notice to the Keeper of their interest, and within three months of that receipt inform the Keeper that they are taking steps to challenge the applicant's title, then the Keeper must continue to exclude indemnity *quoad* the foreshore for the prescriptive period or until it appears to the Keeper that the Commissioners are no longer persisting in their challenge or that their challenge has been unsuccessful.

Subs. (3)

This subsection makes clear that the section relates only to rights of indemnity; it in no way affects or prejudices rights to foreshore, which are determined by the existing law.

PART III

SIMPLIFICATION AND EFFECT OF DEEDS

Simplification of deeds relating to registered interests

15.—(1) Land in respect of which an interest has been registered shall be sufficiently described in any deed relating to that interest if it is described by reference to the number of the title sheet of that interest, and accordingly, section 13 of and Schedule G to the Titles to Land Consolidation (Scotland) Act 1868, section 61 of the Conveyancing (Scotland) Act 1874, sections 8 and 24 (2) of and Schedules D and J to the Conveyancing (Scotland) Act 1924 and Note 1 of Schedule 2 to the Conveyancing and Feudal Reform (Scotland) Act 1970 (sufficiency of description by reference) shall not apply to such a deed.

(2) It shall not be necessary in any deed relating to a registered interest in land to insert or refer to any real burden, condition, provision or other matter affecting that interest if that real burden, condition, provision or other matter has been entered in the title sheet of that interest under section 6 (1) (*e*) of this Act, and, accordingly, in such a case—

(*a*) sections 10 and 146 of and Schedule D to the Titles to Land Consolidation (Scotland) Act 1868, in section 32 of the Conveyancing (Scotland) Act 1874, the words from the beginning to " shall be sufficient " and in section 9 of the Conveyancing (Scotland) Act 1924, the proviso to subsection (1), subsections (3) and (4) and Schedule E to the said Act of 1924 (importation of burdens etc. by reference) shall not apply to such a deed; and

(*b*) such a deed shall import for all purposes a full insertion of the real burden, condition, provision or other matter.

(3) It shall not be necessary in any deed relating to a registered interest in land, being a deed referred to in section 3 of the Conveyancing (Scotland) Act 1924 or section 12 of the Conveyancing and Feudal Reform (Scotland) Act 1970 (dispositions etc. by persons uninfeft), to deduce title, if evidence of sufficient midcouples or links between the uninfeft proprietor and the person last infeft are produced to the Keeper on registration in respect of that interest in land and, accordingly, in such a case, section 5 of and Form 1 of Schedule A and Note 2 of Schedule K to the said Act of 1924 and Notes 2 and 3 (*b*) of Schedule 2 to the Conveyancing and Feudal Reform (Scotland) Act

1970 (further provisions to deduction of title) as well as the said section 3 and the said section 12, shall not apply to such a deed, which shall be as valid as if it had contained a clause of deduction of title.

(4) It shall not be necessary, in connection with any deed relating to a registered interest in land, to include an assignation of any obligation or right of relief or to narrate the series of writs by which the grantor of the deed became entitled to enforce that obligation or exercise that right if the obligation or right has been entered in the title sheet of that interest and, accordingly, in such a case—

(*a*) section 50 of and Schedule M to the Conveyancing (Scotland) Act 1874 (form and effect of assigning right of relief or other right affecting land) shall not apply to such a deed; and

(*b*) such a deed shall for all purposes import a valid and complete assignation of that obligation or right.

DEFINITIONS

"interest in land": see s. 28 (1).
"land": see s. 28 (1).
"registered": see s. 1 (3).
"title sheet": see s. 6.

GENERAL NOTE

The introduction of registration of title affords an opportunity to carry further the process of simplification of deeds by statutory provisions which assign specific meanings to relatively brief standard clauses. Indeed, it will now be possible to dispense with certain clauses and deeds altogether. S. 15, which comes into operation only with the introduction of registration of title, effects a major simplification in the description of an interest in land by reference to the number of its title sheet, and dispenses altogether with clauses in deeds referring to earlier deeds for burdens and conditions, clauses of deduction of title and assignations of obligations or rights of relief.

Subs. (1)

Where an interest in land has been registered, all that is necessary for its description is a reference to the number of the title sheet. The provisions as to description of land in the various older statutes mentioned are now disapplied in the case of deeds relating to a registered interest.

Subs. (2)

Once a real burden, condition or provision affecting a registered interest has been entered on its title sheet it will be unnecessary to insert or refer to it in any deed relating to that interest. The requirement of feudal law that real burdens and conditions must be inserted or referred to in the dispositive clause of a recorded conveyance is now superseded as regards a deed relating to a registered interest by the statutory provision in para. (*b*) that such a deed shall import full insertion, and the provisions of the older conveyancing statutes specified in para. (*a*), which permitted importation of burdens by reference, are disapplied.

Subs. (3)

Where a registered interest in land is transferred by an uninfeft proprietor, the Keeper can satisfy himself as to the sufficiency and validity of the links or midcouples connecting the uninfeft proprietor to the title of the person last infeft. In such a case there is no need to incorporate in the deed transferring the interest a clause of deduction of title, and the various statutory provisions relating to such clauses are accordingly disapplied.

Subs. (4)

There are certain obligations or rights of relief which do not automatically run with the land on a conveyance of it and require to be specially assigned to the grantee if he is to have the benefit of them. A statutory form for assignation of these was provided in the Conveyancing (Scotland) Act 1874 (s. 50 and Sched. M). Where the obligation or right has been entered in the title sheet of a registered interest in land it is not necessary to continue expressly to assign the obligation or right in a deed relating to the registered interest. Accordingly the subsection provides that such a deed shall import a valid and complete assignation of the obligation or right and the provisions of the 1874 Act are disapplied.

Omission of certain clauses in deeds

16.—(1) It shall not be necessary to insert in any deed executed after the commencement of this Act which conveys an interest in land a clause of assignation of writs and any such deed shall, unless specially qualified, import an assignation to the grantee of the title deeds and searches and all deeds not duly recorded, and shall—

(*a*) impose on the grantor or any successor an obligation—

(i) to deliver to the grantee all title deeds and searches relating exclusively to the interest conveyed;

(ii) to make forthcoming to the grantee and his successors at his or their expense on all necessary occasions any title deeds and searches which remain in the possession of the grantor or any successor and which relate partly to the interest conveyed; and

(*b*) import an assignation to the grantee by the grantor of his right to require any person having custody thereof to exhibit or deliver any title deeds and searches remaining undelivered; and

(*c*) impose on the grantee or any successor an obligation to make forthcoming on all necessary occasions to any party having an interest therein any deeds and searches which have been delivered to the grantee but which relate partly to interests other than the interest conveyed to the grantee.

(2) It shall not be necessary to insert in any deed executed after the commencement of this Act which grants land in feu a clause of assignation of writs, and any such deed shall, unless specially qualified, import an assignation to the grantee of the title deeds and searches to the effect of maintaining and defending the right of the grantee in the feu; and the superior shall be held to be obliged for that purpose to make the title deeds and searches forthcoming to the grantee on all necessary occasions at the latter's expense.

(3) It shall not be necessary to insert in any deed conveying an interest in land executed after the commencement of this Act a clause of assignation of rents or a clause of obligation of relief, and any such deed so executed shall, unless specially qualified, import—

(*a*) an assignation of the rents payable

(i) in the case of backhand rents, at the legal terms following the date of entry, and

(ii) in the case of forehand rents, at the conventional terms following that date;

(*b*) an obligation on the grantor to relieve the grantee of all feuduties, ground annuals, annuities and public, parochial and local burdens exigible in respect of the interest prior to the date of entry and, in the case of a grant of land in feu, of all feuduties payable by the grantor to his superiors from and after the date of entry.

DEFINITIONS

"commencement of this Act": April 4, 1979—see s. 30 (2).
"deed": see s. 28 (1).
"feu": see s. 28 (1).
"interest in land": see s. 28 (1).

GENERAL NOTE

This section introduces a general conveyancing reform, applicable to any deed executed after April 4, 1979, whether relating to an interest registered in the Land Register or relating to an interest recorded in the Register of Sasines. The report of the Halliday Committee recommended that forms of feu grants and dispositions should be prescribed and the import of the clauses defined by statute (para. 95) and the model forms suggested in Pt. II of Appendix E to the Report omitted certain clauses altogether and defined the import of the deeds without their inclusion. This section largely implements that policy. It makes it unnecessary to include clauses of assignation of writs, assignation of rents, and obligations of relief, and prescribes the effect of the deeds without such clauses. The provisions of the section are permissive, not obligatory, and the clauses may still be incorporated although it will only be advisable to do so where the import of the clauses differs from that which the section would imply.

Subs. (1)

This subsection applies to deeds which convey an interest in land, *e.g.* a disposition. It is unnecessary to include in such a deed a clause of assignation of writs, and the effect of the deed, omitting the clause, is defined as being that which a normal clause of assignation of writs would contain in the former conveyancing practice. If it is desired that the provisions as to assignation of writs in any particular case should differ from the effect described in the subsection, a specific clause should be inserted in appropriate terms.

Subs. (2)

This subsection applies to assignation of writs in feu grants. It is now unnecessary to include therein a clause of assignation of writs. The effect of the deed, omitting the clause, will be that defined in the subsection, which is in accordance with the normal provision hitherto included in such a deed.

Subs. (3)

This subsection renders it unnecessary to include in any deed conveying an interest in land a clause of assignation of rents or a clause of obligation of relief and then proceeds to define the import of the deed, unless specially qualified, in these matters.

(*a*) As regards rent, the deed, unless specially qualified, imports (i) *quoad* backhand rents, an assignation of the rents payable at the legal terms following the date of entry; and (ii) *quoad* forehand rents, an assignation of the rents payable at the conventional terms following the date of entry. No express provision is made as regards rents which are neither backhand nor forehand, but in law the grantee of the conveyance will be entitled to the rents payable for the possession following the term of entry. Those provisions may be compared with the import of a clause of assignation of rents as defined in s. 8 of the Titles to Land Consolidation (Scotland) Act 1868. There may be differences in effect between the two sets of statutory provisions, particularly in relation to arable rents payable backhand and pastoral rents payable at the legal terms. In certain circumstances the insertion or the omission of a clause of assignation of rents may produce different results, since s. 8 of the 1868 Act is not repealed.

(*b*) As regards obligations of relief, the deed, unles specially qualified, imports an obligation on the grantor to relieve the grantee of all feuduties, ground annuals and public, parochial and local burdens exigible in respect of the interest before the date of entry and, in the case of feu grants, of all overfeuduties from and after the date of entry. That involves no change from the normal provisions implied by an obligation of relief in dispositions by s. 8 of the 1868 Act as usually varied in practice in the case of feu grants.

Deeds of declaration of conditions

17.—(1) A land obligation specified in a deed executed after the commencement of this Act under section 32 of the Conveyancing (Scotland) Act 1874 (deeds of conditions etc.) shall—

(*a*) on the recording of such deed in the Register of Sasines;

(*b*) on the obligation being registered,

become a real obligation affecting the land to which it relates, unless it is expressly stated in such deed that the provisions of this section are not to apply to that obligation.

(2) In this section " land obligation " has the meaning assigned to it by section 1 (2) of the Conveyancing and Feudal Reform (Scotland) Act 1970.

DEFINITIONS

" commencement of this Act ": April 4, 1979—see s. 30 (2).
" deed ": see s. 28 (1).
" land obligation ": see subs. (2).
" Register of Sasines ": see s. 28 (1).
" registered ": see s. 1 (3).

GENERAL NOTE

This section implements a recommendation of the Halliday Committee (para. 83). There was some doubt whether conditions specified in a deed of conditions executed in pursuance of the powers contained in s. 32 of the Conveyancing (Scotland) Act 1874 became real on recording of the deed or whether they only became real when they were incorporated by reference in a subsequent conveyance of part of the land to which they applied. The general view was that the conditions became real only in the latter event because of the requirement of feudal law that real burdens must be contained in the dispositive clause of a recorded conveyance. In some circumstances, *e.g.* a deed of conditions relating to an existing tenement of flatted houses, it is desirable that the conditions be made real immediately as regards all the flats; in other cases, *e.g.* a deed of conditions relating to an estate which it is proposed to feu in lots, it may be preferred to create the conditions real only in respect of each lot as it is feued off. The section provides that land obligations will become real immediately upon recording of the deed of conditions in the Register of Sasines or upon the obligation being registered in the Land Register, unless the deed contains an express statement that the provisions of the section do not apply.

Variations and discharges of land obligations

18.—(1) The terms of any—

(*a*) deed recorded in the Register of Sasines, whether before or after the commencement of this Act, whereby a land obligation is varied or discharged;

(*b*) registered variation or discharge of a land obligation,

shall be binding on the singular successors of the person entitled to enforce the land obligation, and of the person on whom the land obligation was binding.

(2) In this section " land obligation " has the meaning assigned to it by section 1 (2) of the Conveyancing and Feudal Reform (Scotland) Act 1970.

DEFINITIONS

" commencement of this Act ": April 4, 1979—see s. 30 (2).
" deed ": see s. 28 (1).
" land obligation ": see subs. (2).
" Register of Sasines ": see s. 28 (1).
" registered ": see s. 1 (3).

GENERAL NOTE

The object of this section is to remove doubts whether a deed varying or waiving feudal conditions, such as a minute of waiver granted by a superior, is valid against successors of the superior who has granted it, or is personal to the grantor. The section is expressed to comprehend all land obligations as defined in the Conveyancing and Feudal Reform (Scotland) Act 1970, s. 1 (2), and applies to all deeds recorded in the Register of Sasines whereby a land obligation is varied or discharged and to all variations or discharges of land obligations registered in the Land Register. In all such cases the variations or discharges will be binding on the singular successors of both parties.

Agreement as to common boundary

19.—(1) This section shall apply where the titles to adjoining lands disclose a discrepancy as to the common boundary and the proprietors of those lands have agreed to, and have executed a plan of, that boundary.

(2) Where one or both of the proprietors holds his interest or their interest in the land or lands by virtue of a deed or, as the case may be, deeds recorded in the Register of Sasines, the agreement and plan may be recorded in the Register of Sasines and on being so recorded shall be binding on the singular successors of that proprietor or, as the case may be, those proprietors and on all other persons having an interest in the land or, as the case may be, the lands.

(3) Where one or both of the interests in the lands is or are registered interests, the plan with a docquet thereon executed by both proprietors referring to the agreement shall be registrable as affecting that interest or those interests, and on its being so registered its effect shall be binding on the singular successors of the proprietor of that interest or, as the case may be, the proprietors of those interests and on all other persons having an interest in the land or, as the case may be, the lands.

DEFINITIONS

" deed ": see s. 28 (1).
" interest in land ": see s. 28 (1).
" land ": see s. 28 (1).
" Register of Sasines ": see s. 28 (1).
" registered ": see s. 1 (3).
" registrable ": see s. 1 (3).

GENERAL NOTE

The object of this section is to enable proprietors of lands having a common boundary to agree in writing as to the boundary and have it delineated on a plan, and, once that agreement and plan have been recorded in the Register of Sasines, or the plan with a docquet thereon executed by both proprietors referring to the agreement is registered in the Land Register, as the case may be, the effect will be that the agreement and plan will be binding upon singular successors of the parties and upon all other parties who may have an interest.

This section came into force on April 4, 1979.

PART IV

MISCELLANEOUS AND GENERAL

Tenants-at-will

20.—(1) A tenant-at-will shall be entitled, in accordance with this section, to acquire his landlord's interest as such in the land which is subject to the tenancy-at-will (hereinafter referred to as the " tenancy land ").

(2) Subject to section 21 (2) of this Act, a tenant-at-will who wishes to acquire his landlord's interest under this section shall serve notice on him in, or as nearly as may be in, the form set out in Schedule 1 to this Act.

(3) There shall be payable by the tenant-at-will to his landlord by way of compensation in respect of an acquisition of tenancy land such amount as may be agreed between them or, failing agreement, an amount equal to—

(*a*) the value of the tenancy land, not including any buildings thereon, but assuming that planning permission for residential purposes has been granted in respect of it; or (*b*) one twenty-fifth of the value of the tenancy land, including any buildings thereon,

whichever is the lesser, together with—

(i) subject to subsection (4) below, such further amount as may be required to discharge any heritable security over the tenancy land or, where the heritable security is granted over land including the tenancy land, such further amount (being such proportion of the sum secured over the land which includes the tenancy land as may reasonably be regarded as attributable to the tenancy land) as is required to restrict the heritable security so as to disburden the tenancy land; and

(ii) such further amount as may be required to redeem any feuduty, ground annual or other periodic payment falling to be redeemed under section 5 of the Land Tenure Reform (Scotland) Act 1974.

(4) In respect of any acquisition under this section, the amount mentioned in paragraph (i) of subsection (3) above shall not exceed ninety per cent. of the amount fixed by virtue of paragraph (*a*) or (*b*) of that subsection.

(5) The tenant-at-will shall reimburse the expenses reasonably and properly incurred by the landlord in conveying his interest in the tenancy land to the tenant-at-will, including the expenses of any discharge, restriction or redemption under subsection (3) above.

(6) The landlord shall, on there being tendered to him the compensation and expenses specified in this section, convey his interest in the tenancy land to his tenant-at-will on such terms and conditions (additional to those relating to compensation and expenses under subsections (3), (4) and (5) above) as may be agreed between them or, failing agreement, as may be appropriate to the circumstances of the case and free of all heritable securities, and all such feuduties, ground annuals or other periodical payments as are mentioned in subsection (3) (ii) above.

(7) A heritable creditor whose security is over the tenancy land or land which includes the tenancy land, on there being tendered to him the amount mentioned in paragraph (i) of subsection (3) above (as read with subsection (4) above) and his reasonable expenses, shall discharge or, as the case may be, restrict the security so as to disburden the tenancy land.

(8) In this section and in sections 21 and 22 of this Act, " tenant-at-will " means a person—

(*a*) who, not being—

(i) a tenant under a lease;

(ii) a kindly tenant; or

(iii) a tenant or occupier by virtue of any enactment,

is by custom and usage the occupier (actual or constructive) of land on which there is a building or buildings erected or acquired for value by him or any predecessor of his;

(*b*) who is under an obligation to pay a ground rent to the owner of the land in respect of the said land but not in respect of the building or buildings on it, or would have been under such an obligation if the ground rent had not been redeemed; and

(*c*) whose right of occupancy of the land is without ish.

(9) In subsections (5) and (6) above, references to the conveying of the landlord's interest in tenancy land shall be construed in accordance with section 21 (10) of this Act.

DEFINITIONS

" heritable security ": see s. 28 (1).

" land ": see s. 28 (1).

" tenant-at-will ": see subs. (8).

GENERAL NOTE

A tenancy-at-will is an anomalous type of holding which is found occasionally in certain rural and mining areas. Generally it involves the renting of land for building a house without formal title but subject to payment of a rent, transferable by receipt for the price and intimation of the change to the landlord of his factor. The holding is perpetual, without any specified ish. Tenants-at-will were recognised in the Housing (Financial Provisions) (Scotland) Act 1978, Sched. 2, para. 29, which enabled them to obtain grants. There are disadvantages in this type of holding in respect that the tenant-at-will, having no recorded title, cannot normally borrow on the security of his house, and he cannot require the landlord to grant him a formal title. The purpose of this section is to entitle him to acquire his landlord's interest and obtain a conveyance of it on the terms prescribed in the section.

Subs. (1)

This is the leading provision which confers upon a tenant-at-will the right to acquire his landlord's interest in the land. The words "as such" indicate that the interest which can be acquired is only that which enabled the landlord to grant the tenancy-at-will. If the landlord is a feuar, then the *dominium utile* will be conveyed; if the landlord is also the owner of the superiority, and there has been no consolidation of the superiority and the property, the landlord may retain the superiority interest.

Subs. (2)

The tenant-at-will may serve a notice on the landlord in the form of Sched. 1 to the Act, which requires the landlord to make over his interest to the tenant-at-will. Procedure where the landlord is unknown or untraceable is provided in s. 21 (2).

Subs. (3)

This subsection provides a formula for the compensation payable to the landlord if the parties cannot reach agreement upon the amount. The amount is the lesser of (a) the value of the site excluding the buildings but on the basis that planning permission for residential purposes has been granted; or (b) one twenty-fifth of the value of the land and buildings, with the addition of (i) any amount required to discharge any heritable security over the tenancy land or have it restricted so as to disburden the tenancy land; and (ii) any amount required to redeem any feuduty, ground annual or other periodic payment falling to be redeemed under s. 5 of the Land Tenure Reform (Scotland) Act 1974.

Subs. (4)

It is improbable that any security will have been granted by the landlord or his predecessor over the tenancy land alone; normally any security will extend over the larger area which includes it. This subsection restricts the repayment which can be asked by the heritable creditor to disburden the tenancy land to 90 per cent. of the amount payable under para. (*a*) or (*b*) of subs. (3).

Subs. (5)

The tenant-at-will is made responsible for the expenses of the conveyance to him of the landlord's interest and of the discharge or restriction of any heritable security and the redemption of the feuduty, ground annual or periodic charge.

Subs. (6)

Upon tender by the tenant-at-will of the compensation and expense above mentioned the landlord is required to convey his interest in the tenancy land on such terms and conditions as may be agreed between the parties. If the parties cannot agree on such terms and conditions they will be determined by the Lands Tribunal for Scotland under s. 21 (1) (*e*).

Subs. (7)

The creditor in a heritable security over land which includes the tenancy land is required to grant the necessary discharge or restriction of his security on tender of the amount due to him under subs. (3) (i) as qualified by subs. (4), plus reasonable expenses.

Subs. (8)

This subsection defines a tenant-at-will for the purposes of this section and ss. 21 and 22. The definition is largely by exclusion and by reference to custom and usage.

Subs. (9)

In effect, by reference to s. 21 (10), this subsection ensures that the conveyance to be granted by the landlord to a tenant-at-will will be a feu grant or, where the landlord is a tenant, an assignation of the lease *quoad* the tenancy land.

Provisions supplementary to section 20

21.—(1) Any question arising under section 20 of this Act as to—

(*a*) whether a person is a tenant-at-will;

(*b*) the extent or boundaries of any tenancy land;

(*c*) the value of any tenancy land or as to what proportion of any sum secured over any land may reasonably be regarded as attributable to any tenancy land included in that land;

(*d*) whether any expenses are reasonably and properly incurred;

(*e*) what are appropriate terms and conditions,

shall be determined, on the application of the tenant-at-will, a person claiming to be the tenant-at-will or the landlord, by the Lands Tribunal for Scotland.

(2) The Lands Tribunal for Scotland may, on the application of a tenant-at-will who wishes to acquire his landlord's interest in the tenancy land under section 20 of this Act, if they are satisfied that such landlord is unknown or cannot be found, make an order—

(*a*) dispensing with notice under section 20 (2) above;

(*b*) fixing an amount by way of compensation in accordance with section 20 (3) of this Act;

(*c*) determining appropriate terms and conditions on which the landlord's interest in the tenancy land should be conveyed,

for the purposes of the acquisition by the tenant-at-will of his landlord's said interest.

(3) If the landlord—

(*a*) fails to convey his interest in accordance with section 20 (6) of this Act, or

(*b*) is unknown or cannot be found,

the tenant-at-will may apply to the sheriff for an order dispensing with the execution by the landlord of the conveyance in favour of the tenant-at-will and directing the sheriff clerk to execute the conveyance instead of the landlord, and on making such an order the sheriff may require the tenant-at-will to consign in court any sums payable by the tenant-at-will under section 20 (3) and (5) of this Act or, as the case may be, any sums specified in an order under subsection (2) above.

(4) Where, in pursuance of an order made by the sheriff under this section, a conveyance is executed by the sheriff clerk on behalf of the landlord, such conveyance shall have the like force and effect as if it had been executed by such landlord.

(5) The sheriff may, on the application of any party, order the investment, payment or distribution of any sums consigned in court under subsection (3) above, and in so doing the sheriff shall have regard to the respective interests of any parties appearing to have a claim on such sums.

(6) Nothing in section 5 of the Sheriff Courts (Scotland) Act 1907 shall entitle any party to an application to the sheriff under this section to require it to be remitted to the Court of Session on the grounds that it relates to a question of heritable right or title.

(7) A landlord shall have power to execute a valid conveyance in pursuance of this section notwithstanding that he may be under any such disability as is mentioned in section 7 of the Lands Clauses Consolidation (Scotland) Act 1845.

(8) Where a person other than the landlord is infeft in the subjects to be conveyed, references in section 20 of this Act and in this section to the landlord shall be construed as references to the landlord and such other person for their respective rights.

(9) Any condition or provision to the effect that—

(*a*) the superior of any feu shall be entered to a right of pre-emption in the event of a sale thereof or any part thereof by the proprietor of the feu, or

(*b*) any other person with an interest in land shall be entitled to a right of pre-emption in the event of a sale thereof or of any part thereof by the proprietor for the time being,

shall not be capable of being enforced where the sale is by a landlord to his tenant-at-will under section 20 of this Act.

(10) In this section and in section 20 (5) and (6) of this Act, references to the conveying of the landlord's interest in the tenancy land shall be construed as references to a grant by him of a feu of that land or, where the landlord is a lessee under a lease, an assignation of the lease but only as regards the tenancy land and, in this section, " conveyance " shall be construed accordingly.

DEFINITIONS

" conveyance ": see subs. (10).
" feu ": see s. 28 (1).
" tenant-at-will ": see s. 20 (8).

GENERAL NOTE

This section contains provisions supplementary to s. 20, and deals with disputes and various special circumstances.

Subs. (1)

This subsection confers jurisdiction on the Lands Tribunal in respect of questions as to (*a*) whether a person is a tenant-at-will who is entitled to exercise the rights of such persons under the Act; (*b*) the extent or boundaries of the tenancy land (which may be ill-defined by reason of the undocumented character of the arrangement); (*c*) the value of the tenancy land or the proportion of any sum secured over land which may reasonably be regarded as attributable to the tenancy land; (*d*) whether the expenses, such as those claimed by the landlord or a heritable creditor under s. 20 (5), (6) or (7), are reasonable and properly incurred; and (*e*) what are appropriate terms and conditions to be inserted in a conveyance by the landlord under s. 20 (6).

Subs. (2)

This subsection authorises the Lands Tribunal, in circumstances where the landlord is unknown or cannot be found, to dispense with notice to him, to fix the compensation and to determine appropriate terms and conditions to be included in the conveyance to the tenant-at-will.

Subs. (3)

This subsection provides for the situation where the tenant-at-will cannot obtain a title to the tenancy land because the landlord fails to convey his interest or is unknown or untraceable. The tenant-at-will may apply to the sheriff for an order dispensing with the execution by the landlord of the conveyance and directing the sheriff clerk to execute a conveyance instead. This follows the precedent of s. 5 (1) of the Crofting Reform (Scotland) Act 1976. The sheriff may order consignation in court of any sums payable by the tenant-at-will under the Act as a condition of making the order.

Subs. (4)

The conveyance executed by the sheriff clerk will have the same force and effect as if it had been executed by the landlord himself.

Subs. (5)

This subsection enables the sheriff to invest or distribute the sums consigned under subs. (3), having regard to the interests of any parties appearing to have a claim thereto.

Subs. (6)

The jurisdiction of the sheriff under s. 21 is privative; removal to the Court of Session is incompetent.

Subs. (7)

S. 7 of the Lands Clauses Consolidation (Scotland) Act 1845 specifies a number of persons under legal disabilities, *e.g.* liferenters, trustees, tutors and curators. The subsection enables a landlord who may be under any such disability nevertheless to execute a valid conveyance to the tenant-at-will.

Subs. (8)

Where the landlord is not infeft, he and the person infeft are included in the term "landlord" under s. 20: they must execute a conveyance for their respective rights and interests. Where the landlord has the sole beneficial right he will be able to deduce title.

Subs. (9)

Any right of pre-emption competent to a superior or any other person will not be enforceable where the sale is to a tenant-at-will under s. 20. In effect the Act overrules the contractual right of pre-emption in such circumstances.

Subs. (10)

This subsection makes it plain that, where the landlord owns the land, the form of conveyance to be granted to the tenant-at-will is a feu; where the landlord is a lessee, the conveyance will be a partial assignation of the lease *quoad* the tenancy land.

Provisions supplementary to section 20: heritable creditors

22.—(1) The provisions of this section shall have effect where a heritable security over tenancy land or over land which includes tenancy land falls to be discharged or restricted under section 20 (7) of this Act.

(2) The heritable creditor shall be entitled for his interest to apply, and to be a party to an application, under section 21 (1) of this Act.

(3) The Lands Tribunal for Scotland, if they are satisfied that the heritable creditor is unknown or cannot be found, may, on the application of the tenant-at-will or his landlord or both, make an order fixing the amount required to discharge or restrict the heritable security so as to disburden the tenancy land.

(4) If the heritable creditor—

(*a*) fails to disburden the tenancy land in accordance with section 20 (7) of this Act, or

(*b*) is unknown or cannot be found,

the tenant-at-will or the landlord or both may apply to the sheriff for an order dispensing with the execution by the heritable creditor of the deed of discharge or restriction in favour of the landlord and directing the sheriff clerk to execute the deed instead of the heritable creditor and on making such an order the sheriff may require the landlord to consign in court any amount or expenses which the landlord requires to pay for the purposes of section 20 (3) (i), (4) and (5) of this Act to the heritable creditor or, as the case may be, any amount specified in an order under subsection (3) above.

(5) Where, in pursuance of an order made by the sheriff under this section, a deed of discharge or restriction is executed by the sheriff clerk on behalf of the heritable creditor, such deed shall have the like force and effect as if it had been executed by such heritable creditor.

(6) The sheriff may, on the application of any party, order the investment, payment or distribution of any amount consigned in court under subsection (4) above, and in so doing the sheriff shall have regard to the respective interests of any parties appearing to have a claim on such amount.

(7) Nothing in section 5 of the Sheriff Courts (Scotland) Act 1907 shall entitle any party to an application to the sheriff under this section to require it to be remitted to the Court of Session on the grounds that it relates to a question of heritable right or title.

(8) A heritable creditor shall have power to execute a valid deed of discharge or restriction in pursuance of this section notwithstanding that he may be under any such disability as is mentioned in section 7 of the Lands Clauses Consolidation (Scotland) Act 1845.

DEFINITIONS

"heritable security": see s. 28 (1).
"tenant-at-will": see s. 20 (8).

GENERAL NOTE

This section adapts for heritable creditors the general provisions of s. 21, such as the right of the creditor to apply to the Lands Tribunal for determination of questions (*cf.* s. 21 (1)), the fixing by the Lands Tribunal of the amount required to discharge or restrict the security where the creditor is unknown or cannot be found (*cf.* s. 21 (2)), the execution in such circumstances of a discharge or restriction by the sheriff clerk by order of the sheriff upon consignation and the effectiveness of the deed so executed (*cf.* s. 21 (3) and (4)), dealing with and disposal of the consigned amount by the sheriff (*cf.* s. 21 (5)), the sheriff's jurisdiction being privative (*cf.* s. 21 (6)) and the power of a heritable creditor under disability to execute a valid deed of discharge or restriction (*cf.* s. 21 (7)).

Fees

23. For section 25 of the Land Registers (Scotland) Act 1868 (power of Treasury to prepare amended tables of fees for registration), there shall be substituted the following section—

"**Fees**

25. The Secretary of State, with the consent of the Treasury, may from time to time by order made by statutory instrument fix fees payable in respect of registration or recording in any register under the management and control of the Keeper of the Registers of Scotland and in respect of the provision by the Keeper of searches, reports, certificates or other documents or copies of any document or of information from any such register; and the amount of the fees so fixed shall not be greater than is reasonably sufficient for defraying the expenses of the department of the Keeper, including the expenses of the improvement of the systems of such registration and recording.".

DEFINITION

"registration": see s. 1 (3).

GENERAL NOTE

This section replaces s. 25 of the Land Registers (Scotland) Act 1868 and is applicable to fees payable in respect of registration or recording in all registers under the control of the Keeper of the Registers of Scotland, including, *inter alia*, the Register of Sasines and the new Land Register, and in respect of the provision of searches, certificates, etc. It differs from the provision of the 1868 Act in that such fees will now be fixed by the Secretary of State, with the consent of the Treasury, but amended tables of fees are no longer required, as formerly, to be laid before the Lord President, the Lord Advocate and the Lord Justice Clerk.

Financial provisions

24. There shall be defrayed out of money provided by Parliament all expenses incurred by the Keeper in consequence of the provisions of this Act.

DEFINITION

"the Keeper": see s. 1 (2).

Appeals

25.—(1) Subject to subsections (3) and (4) below, an appeal shall lie, on any question of fact or law arising from anything done or omitted to be done by the Keeper under this Act, to the Lands Tribunal for Scotland.

(2) Subject to subsections (3) and (4) below subsection (1) above is without prejudice to any right of recourse under any enactment other than this Act or under any rule of law.

(3) Nothing in subsection (1) above shall enable the taking of an appeal if it is, under the law relating to *res judicata*, excluded as a result of the exercise of any right of recourse by virtue of subsection (2) above; and nothing in subsection (2) above shall enable the exercise of any right of recourse if it is so excluded as a result of the taking of an appeal under subsection (1) above.

(4) No appeal shall lie under this section, nor shall there be any right of recourse by virtue of this section in respect of a decision of the Keeper under section 2 (1) (*b*) or 11 (1) of this Act.

DEFINITION

"the Keeper": see s. 1 (2).

GENERAL NOTE

The Henry Committee suggested that a Land Registration Committee should be constituted to determine questions and disputes arising under registration of title (para. 49 (1)). Since the Committee reported, the Lands Tribunal for Scotland was brought into operation by the Conveyancing and Feudal Reform (Scotland) Act 1970 and it was considered to be the appropriate body to determine such matters. This section constitutes the Lands Tribunal as the appellate body on questions of fact and law arising from anything done or not done by the Keeper under the Act.

Subs. (1)

This subsection constitutes the Lands Tribunal as the body to whom an appeal will lie on any question of fact or law arising from anything done or omitted to be done by the Keeper under the Act, *e.g.* rectifying or refusing to rectify a title sheet under s. 9.

Subs. (2)

This subsection preserves, subject to subs. (3) and (4), all rights of recourse to the courts. The Lands Tribunal does not have exclusive jurisdiction on appeals.

Subs. (3)

If an appeal is decided by the Lands Tribunal the matter is *res judicata;* an appellant who has been unsuccessful before the Lands Tribunal cannot raise the same question anew before another court of first instance, but can only appeal against the decision of the Lands Tribunal. Similarly an appellant who has had an appeal decided by a court cannot raise it afresh before the Lands Tribunal but must appeal to a higher court.

Subs. (4)

No appeal will be competent against a decision of the Keeper under s. 2 (1) (*b*) (refusal by the Keeper to accept an application for registration where he considers it inexpedient to register the interest, *e.g.* where the application is voluntary and the acceptance of too many voluntary applications at the particular time would place an undue burden on the resources of the Keeper's department). Nor will an appeal be competent against a decision of the Keeper under s. 11 (1) (refusal of an application to register an interest in land which is outwith an operational area). These are matters within the Keeper's discretion.

Application to Crown

26. This Act shall apply to land held of the Crown and of the Prince and Steward of Scotland, and to land in which there is any other interest belonging to Her Majesty in right of the Crown or to a Government department, or held on behalf of Her Majesty for the purposes of a Government department, in like manner as it applies to other land.

Rules

27.—(1) The Secretary of State may, after consultation with the Lord President of the Court of Session, make rules—

(*a*) regulating the making up and keeping of the register;

(*b*) prescribing the form of any search, report or other document to be issued or used under or in connection with this Act and regulating the issue of any such document;

(*c*) regulating the procedure on application for any registration;

(*d*) prescribing the form of deeds relating to registered interests in land;

(*e*) concerning such other matters as seem to the Secretary of State to be necessary or proper in order to give full effect to the purposes of this Act.

(2) The power to make rules under this section shall be exerciseable by statutory instrument subject to annulment in pursuance of a resolution of either House of Parliament.

DEFINITIONS

"the register": see s. 1 (1).

"registered": see s. 1 (3).

"registration": see s. 1 (3).

GENERAL NOTE

This section authorises the Secretary of State, after consultation with the Lord President, to make rules for the operation of the Land Register, the procedure on applications for registration, the forms of deeds and documents, etc.

Interpretation, etc.

28.—(1) In this Act, except where the context otherwise requires—

"deed" has the meaning assigned to it by section 3 of the Titles to Land Consolidation (Scotland) Act 1868, section 3 of the Conveyancing (Scotland) Act 1874 and section 2 of the Conveyancing (Scotland) Act 1924;

"feu" includes blench holding and cognate expressions shall be construed accordingly;

"heritable security" has the same meaning as in section 9 (8) of the Conveyancing and Feudal Reform (Scotland) Act 1970;

"incorporeal heritable right" does not include a right to salmon fishings;

"interest in land" means any estate, interest, servitude or other heritable right in or over land, including a heritable security but excluding a lease which is not a long lease;

" the Keeper " has the meaning assigned by section 1 (2) of this Act;

" land " includes buildings and other structures and land covered with water;

" long lease " means a probative lease—

(*a*) exceeding 20 years; or

(*b*) which is subject to any provision whereby any person holding the interest of the grantor is under a future obligation if so requested by the grantee, to renew the lease so that the total duration could (in terms of the lease, as renewed, and without any subsequent agreement, express or implied, between the persons holding the interests of the grantor and the grantee) extend for more than 20 years;

" overriding interest " means, subject to sections 6 (4) and 9 (4) of this Act, in relation to any interest in land, the right or interest over it of—

(*a*) the lessee under a lease which is not a long lease;

(*b*) the lessee under a long lease who, prior to the commencement of this Act, has acquired a real right to the subjects of the lease by virtue of possession of them;

(*c*) a crofter or cottar within the meaning of section 3 or 28 (4) respectively of the Crofters (Scotland) Act 1955, or a landholder or statutory small tenant within the meaning of section 2 (2) or 32 (1) respectively of the Small Landholders (Scotland) Act 1911;

(*d*) the proprietor of the dominant tenement in a servitude;

(*e*) the Crown or any Government or other public department, or any public or local authority, under any enactment or rule of law, other than an enactment or rule of law authorising or requiring the recording of a deed in the Register of Sasines or registration in order to complete the right or interest;

(*f*) the holder of a floating charge whether or not the charge has attached to the interest;

(*g*) a member of the public in respect of any public right of way or in respect of any right held inalienably by the Crown in trust for the public;

(*h*) any person, being a right which has been made real, otherwise than by the recording of a deed in the Register of Sasines or by registration; or

(*i*) any other person under any rule of law relating to common interest or joint or common property, not being a right or interest constituting a real right, burden or condition entered in the title sheet of the interest in land under section 6 (1) (*e*) of this Act or having effect by virtue of a deed recorded in the Register of Sasines,

but does not include any subsisting burden or condition enforceable against the interest in land and entered in its title sheet under section 6 (1) of this Act;

" the register " and " registered " have the meanings assigned to them respectively by subsections (1) and (3) of section 1 of this Act;

" Register of Sasines " has the same meaning as in section 2 of the Conveyancing (Scotland) Act 1924;

" transfer " includes transfer by operation of law.

(2) This Act shall be deemed, for the purposes of the Scotland Act 1978, to have been passed before that Act.

General Note

Subs. (1)

"*deed*", as defined in the 1868, 1874 and 1924 Acts, embraces an extensive list of formal documents including decrees relating to land. The effect is to accord to "deed" a wide interpretation.

"*heritable security*", as defined in the 1970 Act, means "any security capable of being constituted over any interest in land by disposition or assignation of that interest in security of any debt and of being recorded in the Register of Sasines". The reference to recording of a deed in the Register of Sasines is, by virtue of s. 29 (2), now construed as a reference to registration in the Land Register.

"*incorporeal heritable right*" excludes salmon fishings which form a separate estate in land capable of ownership apart from the riparian lands and will have a separate title sheet in the Land Register.

"*interest in land*" means any estate or interest in land, any servitude or other heritable right in or over land, including a heritable security but excluding a lease which is not a long lease. Compare the definitions of "estate in land" in the Conveyancing (Scotland) Act 1874, s. 3, and of "interest in land" in the Conveyancing and Feudal Reform (Scotland) Act 1970, s. 9 (8) (*b*).

"*long lease*" is defined in different terminology but to the same general effect as the definition contained in the Land Tenure Reform (Scotland) Act 1974, s. 8 (4).

"*overriding interests*" may broadly be regarded as interests in land which can exist as real rights without being recorded in the Register of Sasines. They override interests in land or conditions of title that are so registered and their existence must be ascertained by enquiry if they are not evident on inspection, since they will not appear in a search. These overriding interests are accommodated in the system of registration of title as matters which may, but will not necessarily, be noted on the title sheet, and so enquiry will require as formerly to be made with regard to them. As regards the particular items specified in the definition:

(*a*) Leases other than long leases are not registrable in the Land Register. The burden of registering large numbers of short leases, often of brief duration and sometimes with frequent changes of tenant, would substantially increase the work of the Keeper. In any event the function of the Land Register relates to permanent or relatively long term interests in land.

(*b*) In terms of s. 3 (3) of the Act, the lessee's right in a long lease granted after the commencement of the Act will only be capable of being made real by registration, but existing rights under long leases which have been made real by the alternative of possession remain unaffected. As rights which were capable of being made real without recording in the Register of Sasines they are included amongst overriding interests.

(*c*) A crofter is the tenant of a croft as defined in s. 2 (1) of the Crofters (Scotland) Act 1955. A cottar, as defined in s. 28 (4) of that Act, is the occupier of a dwelling-house situated in the crofting counties who pays no rent, or the tenant of such a dwelling-house who resides therein and who pays an annual rent not exceeding £6, whether with or without garden ground but without arable or pastoral land. A landholder is defined in s. 2 (2) of the Small Landholders (Scotland) Act 1911 as including a crofter, every existing yearly tenant, every qualified leaseholder, every new holder and the successor of every such person in a holding as defined by s. 2 (1) of the Act who are his heirs and successors. A statutory small tenant is defined in s. 32 (1) of the 1911 Act as including a tenant from year to year or leaseholder, who is not an existing yearly tenant or a qualified leaseholder, and his successors as therein defined. All these persons have important rights, protected by statute, in relation to their tenancies which are not recorded in the Register of Sasines and will not be registrable in the Land Register.

(*d*) A servitude, either positive or negative, may be effectively created by writing which does not require to be recorded in the Register of Sasines, and a positive servitude may be acquired without any writing by possession for the prescriptive period or even by implication, *e.g.* as a servitude of necessity. The existence of a positive servitude should be evident to a singular successor from possession of it; a negative servitude is not susceptible of possession but must be of a recognised category. Servitudes may therefore exist without notice of their existence appearing either on the Register of Sasines or on the Land Register.

(*e*) Certain public bodies, *e.g.* the Post Office (for telephone wires or cables), and Electricity Boards (for power lines or cables), necessarily acquire rights over land for the construction and maintenance of such equipment. In view of the very large number of wayleave rights required to carry out their functions, the practice of such bodies is to enter into numerous wayleave agreements with individual landowners which are not recorded in the Register of Sasines.

(*f*) Although a floating charge may include land in the property over which the charge extends, the nature of a floating security is that the company which has granted it remains free to deal with the property subject to the charge, apart from any special restraints imposed contractually in the conditions of the floating charge itself. The scheme of the floating charge legislation is to provide for registration of such charges in the Register of Charges which forms part of the system of registration under the Companies Acts, and not to require registration of floating charges which cover land in the Register of Sasines. Even when the floating charge crystallises upon the appointment of a receiver or upon liquidation, notice of the occurrence of that event is given in the Companies Register under s. 13 (1) of the Companies (Floating Charges and Receivers) (Scotland) Act 1972 or s. 305 of the Companies Act 1948. It follows that for the purposes of the scheme of registration under the Land Registration (Scotland) Act 1979 floating charges, whether or not they have attached to the property to which they relate, are overriding interests.

(*g*) Public rights of way are normally created by use for the prescriptive period and there is no writing constituting them which can appear in the Land Register. Likewise rights vested inalienably in the Crown in trust for the public, *e.g.* right of public access to the foreshore, are fundamental rights, *regalia majora*, which need no document to establish their existence.

(*h*) This category is of the nature of a "sweeping up" provision, embracing any right which has been made real otherwise than by recording in the Register of Sasines or by registration in the Land Register. Examples are an agricultural charge under the Agricultural Credits (Scotland) Act 1929, ss. 5–9, or an ancient title created before registers of sasines were established, followed by uninterrupted possession for centuries (*Wallace* v. *St. Andrews University Court* (1904) 6 F. 1093).

(*i*) A right to common interest in flatted property stems from the common law of the tenement and may not be shown or mentioned in the title of each flat recorded in the Register of Sasines.

Subs. (2)

The Scotland Act 1978 has now been repealed.

Amendment and repeal of enactments

29.—(1) The enactments specified in Schedule 2 to this Act shall have effect subject to the amendments set out in that Schedule.

(2) Subject to subsection (3) below, any reference, however expressed, in any enactment passed before, or during the same Session as, this Act or in any instrument made before the passing of this Act under any enactment to the Register of Sasines or to the recording of a deed therein shall be construed as a reference to the register or, as the case may be, to registration.

(3) Subsection (2) above does not apply—

(*a*) to the enactments specified in Schedule 3 to this Act;

(*b*) for the purposes of the recording of a deed in the Register of Sasines under section 8 of this Act.

(4) The enactments specified in Schedule 4 to this Act are hereby repealed to the extent specified in the third column of that Schedule.

DEFINITIONS
"register": see s. 1 (1).
"Register of Sasines": see s. 28 (1).
"registration": see s. 1 (3).

Short title, extent and commencement

30.—(1) This Act may be cited as the Land Registration (Scotland) Act 1979 and extends to Scotland only.

(2) Sections 1, 16 to 23 of this Act, this section and so much of the remainder of this Part of this Act as relates to the aforesaid provisions of this Act shall come into operation on the passing of this Act, and the other provisions of this Act shall come into operation on the appointed day, being such day as the Secretary of State may by order made by statutory instrument appoint; and different days may be appointed under this subsection for different areas, or for different provisions of this Act.

(3) Any reference in any provision of this Act to the commencement of this Act shall be construed as a reference to the date on which that provision comes into operation.

GENERAL NOTE

Only ss. 1, 16 to 23, and 30 came into operation on April 4, 1979. The remaining sections relating to registration of title will be brought into operation by areas by orders made by statutory instruments.

SCHEDULES

Section 20

SCHEDULE 1

FORM OF NOTICE TO BE GIVEN BY A TENANT-AT-WILL WHO WISHES TO ACQUIRE HIS LANDLORD'S INTEREST AS SUCH IN THE TENANCY

To .... (1)

Take Notice that ....(2), as tenant-at-will of ....(3), requires you to make over to him your interest as landlord of the tenancy land in accordance with the provisions of the Land Registration (Scotland) Act 1979.

Dated this .... of .... 19......

Signed ....

Notes

(1) To be addressed to the landlord.
(2) Insert name and designation of tenant-at-will.
(3) Give the address or a short identifying description of the property to be acquired.

Section 29 (1)

SCHEDULE 2

AMENDMENT OF ENACTMENTS

The Land Registers (Scotland) Act 1868

1. In section 6 of the Land Registers (Scotland) Act 1868 (recording in Register of Sasines of writs transmitted by post) for "day, and hour" substitute "and day".

The Titles to Land Consolidation (Scotland) Act 1868

2. In section 142 of the Titles to Land Consolidation (Scotland) Act 1868, for

the words "day, and hour" substitute "and day", and for "at the same time" substitute "on the same day".

The Conveyancing Amendment (Scotland) Act 1938

3. In section 6 of the Conveyancing Amendment (Scotland) Act 1938 (provisions as to actions of declarator of irritancy)—
  (*a*) in subsection (1), after "action", where thirdly occurring, insert "or from an examination of the relevant title sheet in the Land Register of Scotland".
  (*b*) in subsection (2) after "search" insert "or examination".

The Conveyancing and Feudal Reform (Scotland) Act 1970

4. In section 28 of the Conveyancing and Feudal Reform (Scotland) Act 1970 (foreclosure)—
  (*a*) in subsection (3) at the end insert "or by an examination of the title sheet of the security subjects in the Land Register of Scotland.";
  (*b*) in subsection (5) after the words "unsold part thereof" where secondly occurring insert "or in accordance with section 15 of the Land Registration (Scotland) Act 1979".

The Housing (Scotland) Act 1974

5. In section 9 of the Housing (Scotland) Act 1974 (conditions of improvement grants), in subsection (9)—
  (*a*) in paragraph (i) after "tenant-at-will" insert "or was a tenant-at-will who, since applying, has acquired his landlord's interest in the tenancy";
  (*b*) in paragraph (ii), after "was" insert ", and continues to be,".

6. In paragraph 7 of Schedule 2 of the said Act of 1974 (consequences of breach of conditions under section 9)—
  (*a*) in sub-paragraph (*a*), after "tenant-at-will" insert "or was a tenant-at-will who, since applying, has acquired his landlord's interest in the tenancy,";
  (*b*) in sub-paragraph (*b*), after "was" insert ", and continues to be,".

Section 29 (3)

SCHEDULE 3

Enactments Referring to the Register of Sasines or to the Recording of a Deed in the Register of Sasines not Affected by Section 29 (2)

1. *The Real Rights Act* 1693
   The whole Act.

2. *The Register of Sasines Act* 1693
   The whole Act.

3. *The Register of Sasines Act* 1829
   Section 1.

4. *The Infeftment Act* 1845
   Sections 1 to 4 and Schedule B insofar as relating to section 1.

5. *The Registration of Leases (Scotland) Act* 1857
   (*a*) In section 6, from the beginning of the section to "to the extent assigned" and Schedule D.
   (*b*) Section 12.
   (*c*) Section 15.
   (*d*) Section 16.

6. *The Land Registers (Scotland) Act* 1868
   (*a*) Sections 2 and 3.
   (*b*) Sections 5 to 7.
   (*c*) Section 9.
   (*d*) Sections 12 to 14.
   (*e*) In section 19, the proviso.
   (*f*) Section 23.

7. *The Titles to Land Consolidation (Scotland) Act* 1868
   (*a*) Sections 9 and 10 and Schedules C and D.
   (*b*) Sections 12 and 13 and Schedules F and G insofar as relating to sections 12 and 13 respectively.
   (*c*) Section 17.
   (*d*) Section 19 and Schedule L.
   (*e*) Section 120.
   (*f*) Section 141.
   (*g*) Section 142.
   (*h*) Section 143.
   (*i*) Section 146.
   (*j*) Schedule D.
   (*k*) Schedule G.

8. *The Conveyancing (Scotland) Act* 1874
   (*a*) Section 8.
   (*b*) In section 32, from the beginning to " shall be sufficient " and Schedule H.
   (*c*) Section 61.
   (*d*) Schedule M.

9. *The Writs Execution (Scotland) Act* 1877
   Sections 5 and 6.

10. *The Registration of Certain Writs (Scotland) Act* 1891
   Section 1 (2).

11. *The Conveyancing (Scotland) Act* 1924
   (*a*) Section 3, form 1 of Schedule A and Note 2 to Schedule K.
   (*b*) Section 4 and, in Schedule B, forms 1 to 6 and Note 7, but not insofar as relating to the completion of title under section 74 or 76 of the Lands Clauses Consolidation (Scotland) Act 1845.
   (*c*) Section 8 and Schedule D.
   (*d*) Section 9 (3) and (4).
   (*e*) Section 10 (1) to (5) and Schedule F.
   (*f*) In section 24 (3) from " and such lease, before " to " Schedule B to this Act ".
   (*g*) Section 24 (2) and (5) and Schedule J.
   (*h*) Section 47.
   (*i*) Sections 48 and 49 (2).

12. *The Burgh Registers (Scotland) Act* 1926
   (*a*) Section 1 (1) (except the words from " and any writ " to " appropriate burgh register of sasines ") and Schedule 1 insofar as relating to section 1 (1) with that exception.
   (*b*) Section 1 (2).
   (*c*) Section 2 and Schedule 1 insofar as relating to section 2.
   (*d*) Section 5 and Schedule 1 insofar as relating to section 5.

13. *The Conveyancing Amendment (Scotland) Act* 1938
   Section 6 (1) and (2).

14. *The Public Registers and Records (Scotland) Act* 1948
   (*a*) Section 2.
   (*b*) Section 4.

15. *The Public Registers and Records (Scotland) Act* 1950
   Section 1 (1).

16. *The Conveyancing and Feudal Reform (Scotland) Act* 1970
   (*a*) Section 12 (1) and (2) and Notes 1, 2 and 3 to Schedule 2 insofar as relating to section 12 (2).
   (*b*) Section 28 (3).

17. *The Prescription and Limitation (Scotland) Act* 1973
   Section 1.

Section 29 (4)

SCHEDULE 4

REPEALS

Chapter	Short Title	Extent of Repeal
1693 c. 22.	The Real Rights Act 1693.	The words " and priority ".
1693 c. 23.	The Register of Sasines Act 1693.	The words " and houre ".
1868 c. 64.	The Land Registers (Scotland) Act 1868.	In section 6, the words " stamp the words ' by post ' ", and the words " and thereafter " and the words " transmitted by post " where secondly occurring.
1868 c. 101.	The Titles to Land Consolidation (Scotland) Act 1868.	In section 142, the words " transmitted by post in terms of the Land Writs Registration (Scotland) Act 1868.".

Credit Unions Act 1979 *

(1979 c. 34)

ARRANGEMENT OF SECTIONS

An Act to enable certain societies in Great Britain to be registered under the Industrial and Provident Societies Act 1965 as credit unions; to make further provision with respect to societies so registered; to make provision with respect to the taxation of

* Annotations by Eva Lomnicka, M.A., LL.B., Barrister, Lecturer in Laws, Kings College, London.

societies so registered and of Northern Ireland credit unions; to enable reciprocal arrangements to be made in relation to Northern Ireland credit unions; to facilitate the amendment of the Industrial and Provident Societies Act (Northern Ireland) 1969; and for connected purposes. [4th April 1979]

General Note

Background

A credit union was described by Mr. Denzil Davies M.P., Minister of State at the Treasury, when introducing the second reading of the Credit Unions Bill as "a self-help association, run on mutual lines, in which members agree to pool part of their savings in order to provide themselves with a source of low-cost credit". In short, a credit union is a financial co-operative. It is therefore surprising that despite the popularity of the co-operative principle in Britain, there were only some 50 credit unions in Britain at the time of the passing of this Act. In contrast, the credit union movement is widespread throughout the rest of the world, both in developed and developing countries. Thus in the U.S.A. about one-sixth of consumer credit is provided through credit unions and in Canada almost one-third of the adult population belongs to the movement.

Credit unions are said to have been devised over a century ago by Wilhelm Raiffeisen, Mayor of the small country town of Flammerfeld in Bavaria, to enable the people to help themselves through a financially difficult period. His efforts led to the rapid spread of the concept throughout Germany and then to both the rural and urban communities in Italy. On seeing credit unions flourishing in Europe, Alphonse Desjardins imported the idea to Canada at the turn of this century and caused it to spread across the border to the U.S.A. There, Ed Filene, a Boston merchant, did much to found and organise credit unions in the States. Meanwhile the credit union movement had taken root in the developing world, especially in India and the West Indies.

The reason normally given for the lack of a significant credit union movement in Great Britain was the lack of an appropriate statutory framework for such associations. Some 10 credit unions were registered under the Companies Acts (as companies limited by guarantee) and another four under the Industrial and Provident legislation, but neither framework was entirely satisfactory, as was shown by the fact that most credit unions preferred to remain as unregistered societies. Further, in Northern Ireland, Pt. III of the Industrial and Provident Societies Act (Northern Ireland) 1969 provided for the first time legislation specially catering for credit unions and the following decade saw credit unions flourish in that part of the United Kingdom.

In 1971, the Crowther Committee on Consumer Credit (Cmnd. 4596 at para. 9.2.13) stated that:

> "We think, however, there is a prima facie case for encouraging the credit union movement and for taking steps to make its existence, its aims and its methods widely known in the hope that it may take root here and more credit unions be formed in Britain"

and pressure grew for legislation here. An abortive attempt was made by Mr. John Roper M.P. in 1972 when he introduced (as a Private Member's Bill) a Credit Unions Bill modelled on the Northern Irish legislation. But finally, both the desire to encourage credit unions and to ensure that they were adequately regulated and supervised led the Labour Government to publish a draft Credit Unions Bill on July 25, 1978, in the White Paper "Banking and Credit Unions Bills" (Cmnd. 7303). Following consultations and with the support of the National Consumer Council, the National Federation of Credit Unions and the Credit Union League of Great Britain, this Credit Unions Bill was introduced on January 26, 1979, and received the Royal Assent on April 4, 1979. It too follows the precedent of the Northern Irish legislation to a large extent.

The Act

The Credit Unions Act 1979 provides for the registration of credit unions under the Industrial and Provident Societies Act 1965 and therefore for their supervision by the Chief Registrar of Friendly Societies. It contains special provisions applicable to such credit unions, in particular, the conditions they must fulfil for registration, how they must operate and how they are to be supervised. But except in so far as the Credit Unions Act 1979 provides otherwise, the Industrial and Provident legislation applies to credit unions as it does to other industrial and provident societies (see further, "*Credit Unions and the Industrial and Provident Acts* 1965–1978," *post*). Therefore the Credit Unions Act 1979 together with the Industrial and Provident legislation provides for the first time a distinctive legislative framework for credit unions in Great Britain.

For registration as a credit union, a society must fulfil certain conditions (s. 1). It must have at least 21 (s. 6 (1)) and generally not more than 5,000 (s. 6 (2)) members. Its objects must be those and only those set out in the Act (s. 1 (3)) and it must generally restrict its membership to persons with a "common bond" (s. 1 (2) (*b*), (4)–(6)). Its rules must contain, *inter alia,* those matters set out in Sched. 1 (s. 4 (1)) and its registered office must be in Great Britain. Provision is made for those credit unions already registered as ordinary industrial and provident societies under the Industrial and Provident Societies Act 1965 to be re-registered as credit unions (s. 2). Every credit union so registered must have the words "credit union" and "limited" in its name and restrictions are put on the use of the term "credit union" by any other person (s. 3).

To become a member (and only natural persons can be members of a credit union) an individual must hold at least one fully paid-up share (s. 5). The shares of a credit union must be of £1 denomination and, subject to the rules, may be paid for in full or in instalments (s. 7). The maximum interest in shares per member is £2,000 and each member, irrespective of shareholding, has only one vote. The shares must be non-transferable and withdrawable at not less than 60 days notice—although restrictions are placed on the withdrawal of shares in certain circumstances (s. 7). Subject to the rules, members who cease to have a common bond with the others may remain as members (called "non-qualifying members") but their rights as members are to some extent modified.

Apart from raising money by issuing shares, credit unions are also permitted to borrow money within the restrictions laid down (s. 10). Further, they are able to take deposits of up to £250 in total from persons who are too young to become members, which deposits are to be kept separate, held in trust and invested in narrower-range investments (s. 9). Otherwise they are expressly prohibited from taking deposits (s. 8) and thus prevented from developing into deposit-taking institutions.

A credit union is empowered to loan up to £2,000 in excess of a member's paid-up shareholding, to a member for a provident or productive purpose (s. 11). Maximum repayment periods and maximum interest chargeable are laid down and the Chief Registrar is empowered to limit, by order, the aggregate lending of credit unions. Otherwise, the terms of the loan are left to the discretion of the credit union.

To prevent credit unions developing into significant land-owning institutions, a credit union is only empowered to hold such land as is required for its own premises and for taking security for loans (s. 12). Further, the Chief Registrar is empowered to specify the manner in which a credit union's surplus funds (as defined) may be invested (s. 13). If they are not so invested and if they are not kept in cash, the surplus funds must be kept in an account with an authorised bank.

The mode of calculation of a credit union's profit (or loss) and the manner in which the profits are to be applied are laid down (s. 14). In particular, a credit union is obliged first to establish and maintain a general reserve of between 10 and 20 per cent. of the total assets and then to distribute 90 per cent. of the remaining profits by paying a dividend of not more than 8 per cent. on shares or by giving a rebate of interest on loans to members or by (subject to restrictions) donating money for certain purposes.

A credit union is obliged to insure against the fraud or other dishonesty of its officers or employees up to certain prescribed limits (s. 15), and a credit union may enter into insurance arrangements approved by the appropriate registrar to protect its members against other losses (s. 16).

The powers of the registrars are enlarged and modified in relation to credit unions. Thus the appropriate registrar may require the production of books, accounts and documents and the furnishing of financial and other information (s. 17). He may cancel or suspend a credit union's registration or petition for its winding up in specified circumstances (s. 20). The Chief Registrar may appoint inspectors of the affairs of a credit union and/or call a special meeting of the credit union (s. 18). He further has the power to suspend certain activities of the credit union (s. 19 and Sched. 2).

The relevant provisions of the 1965 Act as to the amalgamation of registered societies and transfer of engagements between them are modified in relation to credit unions (s. 21). Further, the relevant provision in the 1965 Act enabling a registered society to convert into or amalgamate with or transfer engagements to a company registered under the Companies Acts is stated to be inapplicable to credit unions (s. 22). On the other hand, a company registered under the Companies Acts is able to convert, if specified conditions are fulfilled, into a credit union (s. 23).

Subject to various conditions, a credit union is able to display at its registered office (only) interim unaudited accounts (s. 24).

Special treatment for the purposes of taxation is accorded to credit unions (s. 25).

Credit unions are prohibited from having subsidiaries (s. 26) and undischarged bankrupts and persons convicted on indictment for fraud or dishonesty are prohibited from being officers or performing certain other functions in relation to a credit union (s. 27). The provisions in the 1965 Act as to criminal offences are extended and modified in relation to offences under this Act (s. 28).

An interpretation section is included in the Act and the interpretation provisions of the 1965 Act are made applicable to this Act (s. 31). Finally, arrangements may be made to enable credit unions registered in Britain to operate in Northern Ireland and *vice versa* (s. 32).

Credit Unions and the Industrial and Provident Societies Acts 1965–1978

It has been seen that the Industrial and Provident Societies Acts 1965–1978 (*i.e.* the Industrial and Provident Societies Act 1965, the Industrial and Provident Societies Act 1967 (see s. 8 (1) thereof), the Friendly and Industrial and Provident Societies Act 1968 (see s. 23 (2) thereof), the Industrial and Provident Societies Act 1975 (see s. 3 (2) thereof) and the Industrial and Provident Societies Act 1978 (see s. 3 (2) thereof)) apply, except in so far as the Credit Unions Act 1979 provides otherwise, to credit unions.

The 1965 Act is modified in relation to credit unions as follows:

(i) The following provisions of the 1965 Act do *not* apply to credit unions:

s. 1 (see 1979 Act, ss. 2 (1) and 1)
s. 6 (see 1979 Act, ss. 31 (3) and 6 (2))
s. 11 (see 1979 Act, s. 4 (5))
s. 12 (see 1979 Act, s. 31 (3))
s. 19 (see 1979 Act, ss. 31 (3) and 5 (1))
s. 21 (see 1979 Act, ss. 31 (3) and 11)
s. 30 (see 1979 Act, ss. 31 (3) and 12)
s. 31 (see 1979 Act, ss. 31 (3) and 13)
s. 52 (see 1979 Act, s. 22)
s. 76 (see 1979 Act, s. 32 (1))
Sched. 1 (see 1979 Act, s. 2 (1) and Sched. 1)

(ii) By virtue of the nature of credit unions the following provisions of the 1965 Act cannot apply: ss. 2 (2), 4, 7 (2), (4) and (5), 14 (3), 16 (1) (*c*) (iii), 56 and Sched. 2.

(iii) The following provisions of the 1965 Act are modified in their application to credit unions:

s. 2 (1) (see 1979 Act, s. 6 (1) (*a*))
s. 2 (3) (see 1979 Act, s. 2 (2))
s. 10 (3) (see 1979 Act, s. 4 (3))
s. 16 (1) (*a*) (i) (see 1979 Act, s. 6 (1) (*b*))
s. 16 (1) (*c*) (i) & (ii) (see 1979 Act, s. 20 (1) (*a*) (*b*))
s. 48 (1) (see 1979 Act, s. 17 (1))
s. 53 (1) (see 1979 Act, s. 23 (2))
s. 53 (2) (see 1979 Act, s. 6 (1) (*c*))
ss. 61–66 (see 1979 Act, s. 28 (1)–(4))
s. 68 (see 1979 Act, s. 28 (1))

Commencement

Ss. 32 and 33 came into operation on the passing of the Act (April 4, 1979) and the other provisions will come into operation on days to be appointed by order by the Treasury: s. 33 (2). Ss. 1, 2, 3 (1) (4), 4–14, 16–31, and Scheds. 1–3 came into operation on August 20, 1979 (S.I. 1979 No. 936 (C. 25)).

Extent

The Act extends to Scotland.

With the exception of s. 25 (taxation) and s. 32 (4), the Act does not extend to Northern Ireland: s. 33 (4).

Parliamentary debates

Hansard, H.C. Vol. 962, cols. 799–848; Standing Committee A, cols. 3–164; Vol. 965, cols. 859–895; H.L. Vol. 399, cols. 1710, 1805.

Abbreviations

All references in the notes to the sections are to the Credit Unions Act 1979, unless otherwise stated. The abbreviation "the 1965 Act" refers (as it does in the Credit Unions Act 1979 itself, see s. 31 (1)) to the Industrial and Provident Societies Act 1965.

Registration as a credit union

Registration under the Industrial and Provident Societies Act 1965

1.—(1) Subject to sections 6 (4) and 15 (1) below and to sections 2 (1) and 7 (1) of the Industrial and Provident Societies Act 1965 (in this Act referred to as "the 1965 Act"), a society may be registered under that Act if—

(*a*) it is shown to the satisfaction of the appropriate registrar that the conditions specified in subsection (2) below are fulfilled;

(*b*) the rules of the society comply with section 4 (1) below; and

(*c*) the place which under those rules is to be the society's registered office is situated in Great Britain;

and a society which is so registered by virtue of this section shall be registered as, and is in this Act referred to as, a "credit union".

(2) The conditions referred to in subsection (1) (*a*) above are—

(*a*) that the objects of the society are those, and only those, of a credit union; and

(*b*) that admission to membership of the society is restricted to persons all of whom fulfil a specific qualification which is stated in the rules and is appropriate to a credit union (whether or not any other qualifications are also required by the rules) and that in consequence a common bond exists between members of the society.

(3) The objects of a credit union are—

(*a*) the promotion of thrift among the members of the society by the accumulation of their savings;

(*b*) the creation of sources of credit for the benefit of the members of the society at a fair and reasonable rate of interest;

(*c*) the use and control of the members' savings for their mutual benefit; and

(*d*) the training and education of the members in the wise use of money and in the management of their financial affairs.

(4) The qualifications for admission to membership which are appropriate to a credit union are—

(*a*) following a particular occupation;

(*b*) residing in a particular locality;

(*c*) being employed in a particular locality;

(*d*) being employed by a particular employer;

(*e*) being a member of a bona fide organisation or being otherwise associated with other members of the society for a purpose other than that of forming a society to be registered as a credit union;

and such other qualifications as are for the time being approved by the appropriate registrar.

(5) In ascertaining whether a common bond exists between the members of a society, the appropriate registrar—

(*a*) shall have regard to the nature of the qualification for admission to membership of the society, and

(*b*) may, if he considers it proper in the circumstances of the case, treat the fact that admission to membership is restricted as mentioned in subsection (2) (*b*) above as sufficient evidence of the existence of a common bond.

(6) For the purposes of this Act, if the rules of a credit union so provide, a person shall be treated as fulfilling a qualification for admission to membership stated in those rules if he is a member of the same household as, and is a relative of, another person who is a member of the credit union and fulfils that qualification directly.

Definitions

"appropriate registrar": 1965 Act, s. 73 (1) (*c*).
"credit union": s. 31 (1).
"registered office": 1965 Act, s. 74.
"relative": s. 31 (1).

General Note

This section provides for the registration of societies as credit unions under the 1965 Act. To qualify for registration as a credit union, a society must fulfil each of the following conditions.

(i) *Maximum membership*: Its membership (see note to s. 5) must not exceed the maximum laid down by virtue of s. 6 (2): s. 6 (4).

(ii) *Minimum membership*: Its membership must not be less than 21. Further, its application for registration must be signed by 21 members and the secretary of the society: 1965 Act s. 2 (1) (*a*) and (*b*), as modified in relation to credit unions by s. 6 (1) (*a*) of this Act. See also s. 27 (*a*)

(iii) *Insurance*: The appropriate registrar must be satisfied that on registration the credit union will be insured in accordance with s. 15: s. 15 (1).

(iv) *Objects*: It must be shown to the satisfaction of the appropriate registrar that the objects of the society are "those, and only those" listed in subs. (3): s. 1 (*a*) and subs. (2). Thus the society must have all those objects and no others. The objects specified in subs. (3) are rather vaguely phrased but they seek to ensure that the society benefits its members by enabling them to save together and thus have a source of low-cost credit. In practice, a credit union receiving subscriptions from members under s. 7 and lending money to members under s. 11 (note the maximum interest chargeable under subs. (5)) will of necessity be carrying out objects (*a*), (*b*) and (*c*). Further, it is submitted that object (*d*) would be fulfilled by giving members the opportunity of asking financial advice of the committee or officers and of gaining experience in financial matters by helping to run the credit union. It is important to note that credit unions cannot have any objects apart from those listed in subs. (3). This limits their sphere of activity considerably and will inhibit the future development and diversification of the operations of credit unions. See also, 1965 Act, s. 7 (1) (*a*) (a society which has withdrawable share capital—which a credit union has by virtue of s. 7 (4) of this Act—cannot be registered with the object of carrying on the business of banking).

A credit union must list its objects in its rules: ss. 1 (1) (*b*), 4 (1) and Sched. 1, para. 2.

(v) "*Common bond*": It must be shown to the satisfaction of the appropriate registrar that a "common bond" exists between the members. This means that the membership of the credit union must have something in common by fulfilling a specific qualification for admission. That specific qualification must be stated in the rules (subs. (2) (*b*), s. 4 (1) and Sched. 1, para. 4) and must be "appropriate to a credit union" within the meaning of subs. (4). Subs. (4) gives five examples of appropriate qualifications but leaves the appropriate registrar with a discretion to approve others. The first four examples are self-explanatory and enable local communities and persons at a common work-place, for instance, to form credit unions. Clubs and associations which exist for the purposes apart from forming a credit union (for example, motoring clubs, sports clubs, trade unions) will fall within example (*e*). But if there is any doubt whether a group of individuals fulfils an appropriate qualification within (*a*) to (*e*), then the approval of the appropriate registrar to their particular qualification can be sought. However, it is important to note that the mere specification of an appropriate qualification will not necessarily mean that the appropriate registrar will find a common bond between the members. As Mr. Denzil Davies M.P. explained (H.C. Vol. 962, col. 803):

> "It is also necessary to ensure that the common bond is a real one. A society whose only qualification for admission to membership was one which was so wide as to lack any real element of community, would not provide the necessary foundation of mutual trust and co-operation. For example, a requirement that all members must reside, or be employed, in Greater London would be unlikely to be acceptable as a qualification for registration even though, on the face of it, it might be said to meet the criterion of residence in a particular locality."

Note also, subs. (5).

There are two exceptions to the requirement that all members of a credit union must actually satisfy the appropriate requirement. The first is in subs. (6), the second is in s. 5 (5) and both are subject to the credit union's rules.

It was considered desirable that a credit union should be able (by a provision in its rules) to admit not only individuals who actually fulfilled the appropriate requirement but also relatives belonging to such a member's household. Thus by subs. (6), provided the rules so allow and provided an individual is already a member who actually ("directly") fulfils the appropriate qualification, all those who belong to his household and who fall within the definition of a "relative" are treated as fulfilling a qualification for admission. Thus they may also become members with the same rights (including the right to vote: s. 5 (9)) and liabilities as those who qualify "directly." Disquiet was expressed during the Committee stage of the Bill (H.C. Standing Committee A, col. 16) that subs. (6) was a means whereby one member, by causing those belonging to his household to join, could in practice increase his voting strength (see further, note to s. 5). Further, the use of the expression "member of the same household" creates difficulties of interpretation. It seems to connote more than just living under the same roof (*cf.* Industrial and Provident Societies Act (Northern Ireland) 1969, s. 78: "resides . . . in the same house"), but in interpreting "household" for the purposes of the Housing Act 1969, s. 58 (1) in *Simmons* v. *Pizzey* [1977] 3 W.L.R. 1, at p. 17, Lord Hailsham said: "I should have supposed in any case that both the expression 'household' and membership of it is a question of fact and degree, there being no certain indicia the presence or absence of which is by itself conclusive". And note the wide meaning given to the word "relative" in s. 31 (1).

The second category of persons who need not actually satisfy the qualification requirement are "non-qualifying members" (see s. 5 (5) and (7) as well as note to s. 5). As discussed in the note to s. 5, these are not in exactly the same position as members qualifying whether directly or by virtue of subs. (6).

There is apparently nothing to prevent a member holding his shares on trust or as nominee for another (see note to s. 7). It is submitted that it is the trustee, not the beneficial owner, who is the "member" for the purposes of this Act as it is the trustee who actually holds the allotted share—albeit on trust (see the discussion on the meaning of "member" in note to s. 5). As the common bond must exist between "members", it is the trustee and not the beneficial owner who must fulfil the appropriate qualification.

(vi) *Rules*: The rules of the society must comply with s. 4 (1) (see note thereto and Sched. 1): subs. (1) (*b*). By reason of the 1965 Act, s. 2 (1) (*b*), an application for registration of a credit union must be accompanied by two copies of the rules so that the appropriate registrar may satisfy himself that this condition is indeed fulfilled.

(vii) *Registered office*: The credit union's registered office (which must be stated in the rules: s. 4 (1) and Sched. 1, para. 3) must be in Great Britain. If a credit union subsequently wishes to change the situation of its registered office it must comply with the 1965 Act, s. 10 (2). For form of notice and acknowledgment of registration of change in the situation of the registered office, see Industrial and Provident Societies Regulations 1965 (S.I. 1965 No. 1995), reg. 2 (1), Sched. 1, Forms I and J, and for fees, see *ibid.* Sched. 2 (as substituted by S.I. 1977 No. 2022). See further, 1965 Act, s. 44 (register of members and officers to be kept at the registered office) and s. 8 (society whose registered office is in one registration area carrying on business in another). For the position of credit unions registered in Great Britain wishing to operate in Northern Ireland, see s. 32.

On being satisfied that a society has fulfilled these conditions, the appropriate registrar is obliged to register the society (1965 Act, s. 2 (3), as modified in relation to credit unions by s. 2 (2) of this Act) as a credit union: subs. (1). An appeal against the refusal of the appropriate registrar to register a credit union may be made to the High Court (in England and Wales) or to the Court of Session (in Scotland) by virtue of the 1965 Act, s. 18. For the English procedure, see R.S.C. Ord. 55, r. 4, and Ord. 93, rr. 10 (2), 12.

For form of application to register, see the Industrial and Provident Societies Regulations 1965 (S.I. 1965 No. 1995), reg. 2 (1), Sched. 1, Form A, and for form of acknowledgment of registration see *ibid.* reg. 2 (1), Sched. 1, Form B. For fees see *ibid.* Sched. 2 (as substituted by S.I. 1977 No. 2022).

Effect of Registration

On registration, the credit union comes under the general supervision of the Chief Registrar of Friendly Societies and the assistant registrars. In particular, the credit union becomes subject to the Industrial and Provident legislation as applied to credit unions by this Act (see "*Credit Unions and the Industrial and Provident Societies Acts* 1965–1978" in the General Note to this Act). By the 1965 Act, s. 3, it becomes a body corporate by its registered name, with perpetual succession and a common seal and with limited liability.

The Consumer Credit Act 1974

Prima facie, the Consumer Credit Act 1974 applies to credit unions and they may require to be licensed under that Act. Unlike friendly societies, industrial and provident societies are not listed in s. 16 (1) of that Act as bodies which can apply to have certain of their credit agreements exempted, but in view of the maximum interest chargeable by reason of s. 11 (5) of this Act, loan agreements credit unions make with members may nevertheless be exempt (see further, note to s. 11, heading (v)).

Supplementary and transitional provisions as to registration

2.—(1) Section 1 of, and Schedule 1 to, the 1965 Act (societies which may be registered and matters to be provided for in their rules) shall not apply in relation to registration as a credit union.

(2) In section 2 (3) of the 1965 Act (acknowledgment of registration) as it applies to registration as a credit union the reference to compliance with the provisions of the 1965 Act shall be construed, subject to subsection (1) above, as a reference to compliance with the provisions as to registration of both that Act and this Act.

(3) A society whose objects are wholly or substantially those of a credit union within the meaning of section 1 (3) above shall not be registered under the 1965 Act otherwise than as a credit union and, except in the case of a registration made before the commencement of this Act, any such registration shall be void.

(4) A society which at the commencement of this Act is registered under the 1965 Act but whose objects are wholly or substantially those of a credit union within the meaning of section 1 (3) above shall take all reasonable steps to have its existing registration cancelled and become registered as a credit union.

(5) Where in accordance with subsection (4) above a society's existing registration is cancelled on its registration as a credit union, the society shall, notwithstanding anything in section 16 (7) or section 3 of the 1965 Act, be taken for all purposes to be the same body corporate before and after the change of registration.

(6) If a society to which subsection (4) above applies does not become registered as a credit union within such reasonable period after the commencement of this Act as the appropriate registrar may allow, the registrar may proceed to cancel or suspend its existing registration under section 16 or section 17 of the 1965 Act in the same way as in the case of a society which no longer fulfils one of the conditions specified in section 1 (2) of that Act; and an appeal shall lie under section 18 of that Act where it would lie in such a case.

DEFINITIONS

" appropriate registrar ": 1965 Act, s. 73 (1) (*c*).
" credit union ": ss. 1 (1), 31 (1).
" the 1965 Act ": s. 31 (1).

GENERAL NOTE

Subss. (1) *and* (2)

See " *Credit Unions and the Industrial and Provident Societies Acts* 1965–1978 " in the General Note to this Act. S. 1 of and Sched. 1 to this Act replace s. 1 of and Sched. 1 to the 1965 Act in relation to credit unions.

Subss. (3)–(6)

As to the commencement of this Act, see s. 33 (2) and (3).

As to cancellation of registration, see 1965 Act, s. 16 and s. 18 (appeals).

As to suspension of registration, see 1965 Act, ss. 17 and 18 (appeals).

After the commencement of this Act, a society whose objects are wholly or substantially those within s. 1 (3) can only be registered under the Industrial and Provident Societies legislation as a credit union (subs. (3)). There is, of course, nothing to prevent such a society alternatively registering under the Companies Acts or existing as an unincorporated association, but both these possibilities are considerably less attractive to such a society. In particular, the society will not be able to call itself a credit union (s. 3 (2)) and may not enjoy the tax advantages provided by s. 25.

The objects of a society must be " *those, and only those* " within s. 1 (3) (see s. 1 (2) (*a*)) before it can be registered as a credit union. Therefore it would seem that a society whose objects are only substantially within s. 1 (3) is obliged to vary them before it can be registered under the 1965 Act. The society may either omit those objects which do not fall within s. 1 (3), thus becoming a society whose objects are wholly those within s. 1 (3) and therefore qualifying for registration as a credit union, or it may vary its objects so that they are less than substantially those within s. 1 (3) and register as an ordinary industrial and provident society.

As was mentioned in the General Note to the Act (see " *Background* "), there are a few existing credit unions already registered as industrial and provident societies under the 1965 Act. When the Credit Unions Act 1979 comes into force, such a society whose objects are wholly or substantially within s. 1 (3) of this Act is obliged to take all reasonable steps to cancel its existing registration (see 1965 Act, s. 16 (1) (*b*)) and re-register as a credit union. It has a " reasonable period " to do so, otherwise the appropriate registrar has a discretion to cancel or suspend its existing registration. " All reasonable steps " would include the variation of its objects (if its objects are only substantially within s. 1 (3), to ensure they become wholly within s. 1 (3)) and of its rules and membership to ensure that this Act is complied with (see further, note to s. 1). It is submitted that although in subs. (4) the obligation to take all reasonable steps appears to apply both to the cancellation and the re-registration as a credit union, in practice a registered society unwilling to comply with this Act need not register as a credit union. Of course it cannot remain registered as an ordinary industrial and provident society (the appropriate registrar in the exercise of his discretion in subs. (6) will no doubt eventually cancel or suspend the registration) but it seems it could register under the Companies Acts (see 1965 Act, s. 52—s. 22 of this Act does not apply as the society is not a "credit union" within the meaning of this Act) or become an unincorporated association.

For the conversion of a company into a credit union, see s. 23.

Use of name "credit union", etc.

3.—(1) The name of every society registered as a credit union shall contain the words "credit union".

(2) Subject to subsection (3) below, a person shall not, unless registered as a credit union,—

(*a*) use in reference to himself a name, title or descriptive expression containing the words "credit union" or any cognate term or any derivative of those words; or

(*b*) represent himself as being a credit union;

and any person who contravenes this subsection shall be guilty of an offence and liable on summary conviction to a fine not exceeding £500.

(3) Subsection (2) above does not apply to—

(*a*) the use by an officer or employee of a credit union of a title or descriptive expression indicating his office or post with the credit union; or

(*b*) the use with reference to an association or group of credit unions of a name which has been approved in writing by the chief registrar.

(4) For the purposes of section 5 (5) of the 1965 Act (societies which may be permitted to have a name which does not contain the word "limited") the objects of a credit union shall not be regarded as wholly charitable or benevolent.

DEFINITIONS

"chief registrar": 1965 Act, s. 73 (1) (*a*).

"credit union": ss. 1 (1), 31 (1).

"officer": 1965 Act, s. 74 (as amended by the Friendly and Industrial and Provident Societies Act 1968, s. 20 (1) (*a*) and Sched. 1, para. 11).

"person": Interpretation Act 1978, s. 5 and Sched. 1.

"the 1965 Act": s. 31 (1).

GENERAL NOTE

Subss. (1) *and* (4)*—registered name*

There are three important provisions which the registered name of a credit union must satisfy.

First, by subs. (1) every credit union is obliged to include the words "credit union" in its name.

Secondly, by the 1965 Act, s. 5 (2), the name must end with the word "limited" (and see 1965 Act, s. 3). The 1965 Act gives the appropriate registrar the discretion to register a society by a name not ending in "limited" if he is satisfied that its objects are "wholly charitable or benevolent," but by virtue of subs. (4) of this section a credit union's objects are not regarded as such.

Thirdly, by s. 5 (1) of the 1965 Act, registration under a name which the appropriate registrar considers "undesirable" is not permitted (see the similar provisions in the Registration of Business Names Act 1916, s. 14, the Companies Act 1948, s. 17, the Building Societies Act 1962, s. 2 (2), the Friendly Societies Act 1974, s. 8 (3) and the Consumer Credit Act 1974, s. 25 (1) (*b*)). In practice it is prudent to consult the appropriate registrar as to the suitability of a proposed name before a formal application for registration is made. However, there is no provision enabling a name to be reserved pending a formal application for registration.

For the display and use of the registered name and offences relating thereto, see 1965 Act, s. 5 (6) and (7).

For the mode of changing the registered name and consequences, see 1965 Act, ss. 5 (3), (4), 10 (2) (*b*) and 18 (1) (*b*) (appeals). For form of application for approval and acknowledgment of registration of change of name, see the Industrial and Provident Societies Regulations 1965 (S.I. 1965 No. 1995), reg. 2 (1) and Sched. 1, Forms C and K, and for fees see *ibid.* reg. 13 and Sched. 2 (as substituted by S.I. 1977 No. 2022).

Subss. (3) *and* (4)

The reputation and good name of duly registered credit unions are safeguarded by restricting the use of the term " credit union " in two respects.

First, the use of the words " credit union " or any similar or derivative terms is closely circumscribed. By subs. (2) (*a*) the use of such words and terms by a person other than a registered credit union is prohibited but subs. (3) creates two exceptions. The first enables an officer (as defined) or employee of a credit union to describe himself as such: subs. (3) (*a*). Thus, for example, the treasurer or secretary or committee member of a registered credit union may call himself such. But the exception does not extend to any auditor (see the definition of " officer ") or ordinary member of a credit union nor to an independent contractor who renders services to it.

Secondly, with the written approval of the chief registrar, the National Federation of Credit Unions, the Credit Union League of Great Britain and the World Council of Credit Unions will be able to continue to use these names: subs. (3) (*b*).

However, a company registered under the Companies Acts or an unincorporated association which functions as a credit union will not be able to refer to itself as such.

Criminal sanctions are provided for breaches of these provisions. See also, the 1965 Act, ss. 63 (continuing offences), and 66 as modified in relation to credit unions by s. 28 (3) of this Act (institution of proceedings), and this Act, s. 28 (1), (5) (offences by bodies corporate) and (6) (defences).

Rules and membership

Rules

4.—(1) The rules of a credit union shall be in such form as the appropriate registrar may determine and shall contain—

(*a*) provision with respect to the matters mentioned in Schedule 1 to this Act; and

(*b*) such additional provision as the appropriate registrar may determine.

(2) The rules of a credit union may not be amended except by a resolution passed by not less than two-thirds of the members present at a general meeting called for the purpose after the giving of such notice as is by the rules required for such a resolution.

(3) In section 10 (3) of the 1965 Act (acknowledgment of registration of amendment of rules where not contrary to the Act) as it applies to credit unions the reference to the 1965 Act shall be construed as including a reference to this Act.

(4) The Treasury may by regulations under section 71 of the 1965 Act vary the fee which under section 15 of that Act may be charged by a credit union for supplying a person with a copy of its registered rules.

(5) Section 11 of the 1965 Act (power to make rules as to fund for purchase of government securities) shall not apply to credit unions.

DEFINITIONS

" appropriate registrar ": 1965 Act, s. 73 (1) (*c*).
" credit union ": ss. 1 (1), 31 (1).
" meeting ": 1965 Act, s. 75.
" registered rules ": 1965 Act, s. 74.
" the 1965 Act ": s. 31 (1).
" Treasury ": Interpretation Act 1978, s. 5 and Sched. 1.

General Note

Subs. (1)

The rules of a credit union approximate to the memorandum and articles of a company registered under the Companies Acts.

A credit union is generally free to make such provision in its rules as it wishes as long as the rules comply with statute and "are not otherwise unlawful": 1965 Act, s. 13 (4). Thus subs. (1) must first be satisfied. The appropriate registrar has considerable powers (subject to the right of appeal given in the 1965 Act, s. 18 (1) (*a*) and (*b*)) over the specific content of the rules and may, for example, consider that a particular quorum for a general meeting is too low (see Sched. 1, para. 5).

In drawing up the rules, the following provisions of this Act should also be borne in mind: s. 1 (6) (rules may extend membership to relatives in the same household as a member), s. 5 (5) (rules may disallow a member who ceases to be qualified for membership from remaining a member, albeit a "non-qualifying member"), s. 5 (8) (rules may disallow a non-qualifying member from purchasing shares and receiving loans), s. 5 (9) (rule as to chairman's casting vote), and s. 7 (1) (rules may provide for mode of subscription for shares). And note s. 5 (2) (rules must not require a person to hold more than £5 in fully paid-up shares). See also the following provisions of the 1965 Act: ss. 13 (1) (2), 20, 33 (1) (*b*), 41, 46 (2) and 60 (1). Further, a credit union may wish to provide for a membership fee in its rules.

See also the 1965 Act, s. 14 (the effect of the rules on members), s. 13 (supplementary provisions as to rules) and s. 9 (acknowledgment of registration of rules).

Subss. (2) and (3)

For a discussion of the meaning of "member", see note to s. 5.

As to the amendment of the rules, see 1965 Act, ss. 10 and 18 (1) (*b*) (appeals). See also Sched. 1, para. 5 of this Act.

From subs. (3) it is clear that it is not two-thirds of the total membership but only two-thirds of the members present at a quorate (see Sched. 1, para. 5) general meeting who can validly amend the rules. The two-thirds majority may be compared with the three-quarters majority needed for the alteration of the articles of association or objects of a company under the Companies Act (Companies Act 1948, ss. 10 (1), 141 (2)).

Subs. (4)

S. 15 of the 1965 Act imposes an obligation on a registered society to deliver a copy of its rules to any person (not necessarily a member) who demands one and pays a fee. Subs. (4) empowers the Treasury to vary this fee in relation to credit unions.

Subs. (5)

For the powers of investment of a credit union, see s. 13. Further, by s. 31 (1), s. 12 of the 1965 Act is inapplicable to credit unions.

For forms of application in relation to the registration and amendment of rules, see the Industrial and Provident Societies Regulations 1965 (S.I. 1965 No. 1995), regs. 2 (1), 3 and 4, Sched. 1, Forms D, E, F, G and H. For fees see *ibid.* Sched. 2 (as substituted by S.I. 1977 No. 2022).

Membership and voting rights

5.—(1) Only individuals shall be members of a credit union.

(2) A person shall not be a member of a credit union unless he holds at least one fully paid-up share in that credit union, but the rules of the credit union shall not require a person to hold more than £5 in fully paid-up shares as a condition of membership.

(3) A member of a credit union shall not have or claim any interest in the shares of the credit union exceeding £2,000.

(4) The chief registrar may, by order made with the consent of the Treasury, from time to time amend subsection (3) above so as to substitute for the sum for the time being specified in that subsection

such other sum, not being less than £2,000, as may be specified in the order.

(5) A member of a credit union who ceases to fulfil the qualifications for admission to membership shall be entitled, subject to subsection (6) below, to retain his membership unless the rules of the credit union provide otherwise; and, subject to section 21 (4) below, in this Act the expression " non-qualifying member ", in relation to a credit union, means a person who remains a member of the credit union by virtue of this subsection.

(6) The number of non-qualifying members of a credit union shall not at any time exceed ten per cent. of the total membership of the credit union.

(7) Non-qualifying members of a credit union shall be left out of account in determining for any purpose whether a common bond exists between the members of the credit union.

(8) A non-qualifying member of a credit union shall be entitled, except so far as the rules of the credit union may provide otherwise, to purchase shares and, subject to section 11 (3) below, to receive loans.

(9) Subject to any provision in the rules of a credit union as to voting by a chairman who has a casting vote, on every matter which is determined by a vote of members of a credit union every member shall be entitled to vote and shall have one vote only.

DEFINITIONS

" chief registrar ": 1965 Act, s. 73 (1) (*a*).
" credit union ": ss. 1 (1), 31 (1).
" person ": Interpretation Act 1978, s. 5 and Sched. 1.
" Treasury ": Interpretation Act 1978, s. 5 and Sched. 1.

GENERAL NOTE

Subs. (1)—" *individual* "

The term " individual " is not defined in the Act. Other statutory definitions of " individual " either expressly (see, for example, Registration of Business Names Act 1916, s. 22) or impliedly (see, for example, Consumer Credit Act 1974, s. 189) exclude corporate bodies and it is submitted (despite *G.N.R.* v. *G.C.R. Co.* (1899) 10 Ry. & Can. Tr. Cases 266, which held the contrary in relation to the now repealed Railway Canal Traffic Act 1888, s. 9 (*c*)), that corporations cannot be members of a credit union. This view is supported by the fact that although the 1965 Act, s. 19, makes provision for a body corporate holding shares in a registered society, s. 31 (3) of this Act lists that s. 19 as inapplicable to credit unions.

Subss. (2)–(4) *and* (9)—" *member* "

To be a member of a credit union an individual must satisfy two conditions. First, he must fall within that category of individuals who qualify for admission to membership (see s. 1 (1) (*a*), (2) (*b*), (4)–(6)). Secondly, he must fulfil a shareholding qualification: subs. (2). By s. 7 (1), the shares must be of £1 denomination and although shares may (subject to the rules) be paid for by instalments, a share is only actually allotted when it has been paid for in cash. To become a member an individual must hold at least one fully paid-up £1 share. Thus if an individual subscribes for 10 shares and pays 10p towards each share (thus paying £1 in sum to the credit union) he will not be a member until he has fully paid for at least one share. The rules may increase the minimum shareholding qualification but not beyond £5 in fully paid-up shares. A rule which sought to impose a higher qualification would not be accepted by the appropriate registrar (ss. 1 (1) (*b*) and 4, and the 1965 Act, s. 13 (4)).

A distinction must therefore be drawn between a member's allotted shares, which are fully paid-up (and he must of course hold at least one of these) and a member's subscribed for but not yet allotted shares, which are not fully paid-up. Thus a member may have paid £1,000 into a credit union, having 750 allotted shares and another 500 subscribed for shares towards each of which he has paid 50p. It would seem that subs. (3) has this distinction in mind when it sets the maximum amount of money a member can pay into a credit union at £2,000 (an amount variable upwards by order: subs. (4)). "*Shall not have . . . shares*" seems to refer to allotted shares and "*shall not . . . claim any interest in . . . shares*" seems to refer to subscribed for but not fully paid-up shares. The latter phrase would also appear wide enough to cover a beneficial interest in shares. In the note to s. 1 it was submitted that in the case of a trust of shares, it is the trustee who is the "member" and not the beneficial owner. Therefore, as long as an individual is not a member by virtue of having any paid-up shares in his own name, he may have a beneficial interest in shares exceeding £2,000—for example by being a beneficiary under two trusts, each trustee holding 2,000 shares on trust for him. However, once an individual is a member, then any beneficial interest he also has in shares on trust for him must be included in the calculation of his shareholding for the purposes of subs. (3).

Sched. 1, para. 7 makes it clear that the rules may specify a lower maximum than that in subs. (3). It seems the phrase "*maximum amount of the interest in the shares*" in para. 7 is apt to cover allotted and subscribed for shares as well as beneficial interests in shares.

The limitation in subs. (3) was considered necessary to restrict the size of credit unions and to ensure that they remained small saving institutions. Further, in view of the tax advantages the dividends on credit union shares enjoy (see note to s. 25), a limitation on the amount which can be invested will inhibit credit unions developing into significant tax avoidance devices.

Irrespective of the size of a member's stake in a credit union, each member is only entitled to one vote: subs. (9).

Only members of a credit union may receive loans under s. 11.

It is submitted below that the term "member" when used in this Act normally includes a "non-qualifying member." Further, it is clear that a deposit under s. 9 (1) does not render the depositor a member but that an individual treated as qualifying for admission under s. 1 (6) who fulfils the shareholding requirement, becomes a member with the same rights and liabilities as one who qualifies "directly."

As to the position of persons under 18 as members, see 1965 Act, s. 20 (as amended by the Family Law Reform Act 1969, s. 1 (3) and Sched. 1, Pt. I) and note to s. 9. See also *Steinberg* v. *Scala* (*Leeds*) *Ltd.* [1923] 2 Ch. 452 (minor as a shareholder). Further, members under 18 cannot receive loans: s. 11 (1).

As to register of members (and officers) see 1965 Act, s. 44.

Subss. (6)–(8)—"*non-qualifying member*"

The term "non-qualifying member" is defined in subs. (5) (and given an extended meaning in relation to the amalgamation of credit unions or transfers, by s. 21 (4)). A member who ceases to qualify for admission is normally allowed to remain a member, albeit a "non-qualifying member." However, the rules may disallow such an individual from remaining a member, in which case the credit union will have no non-qualifying members.

By subs. (6), more than 10 per cent. of the "total membership" cannot comprise non-qualifying members. The limitation is expressed in terms of membership, not in terms of proportion of shareholding, no doubt because voting strength does not depend on the size of a member's shareholding (subs. (9)). The total membership would be ascertained by discovering the number of individuals fulfilling the minimum shareholding requirement (see discussion of "member" above). Then the proportion thereof who had ceased to qualify for admission would have to be calculated and kept below 10 per cent.

It is submitted that by virtue of subs. (5) ("shall be entitled . . . to retain his membership . . . remains a member"), a non-qualifying member is included in the term "member" whenever that term is used in this and the 1965 Act, except when non-qualifying members are specifically mentioned and different rules applied to them.

Thus it would seem that, for example, a non-qualifying member would be considered a member for the purposes of ss. 4 (2) (amendment of rules), 5 (2) (shareholding qualification), 5 (3) (maximum stake), 5 (9) (voting), 6 (maximum and minimum number of members), 7 (1) (allotting of shares), 14 (3) (application of profits), 16 (1) (guarantee funds), 19 (suspension of operation of credit union), 20 (2) (*a*) (winding-up of credit union)—but not s. 20 (1) (*b*) or s. 20 (2) (*c*), by virtue of s. 5 (7)—and 25 (taxation). But a non-qualifying member would not be a member who "fulfils" a qualification for admission for the purposes of s. 1 (6).

However, non-qualifying members are treated differently in the following provisions:

(i) Subs. (6)—Discussed above.

(ii) Subs. (7)—This is of importance when the appropriate registrar is considering whether to register a credit union (s. 1 (1) (*a*) and (2) (*b*)), or to apply to wind-up a credit union (s. 20 (2) (*c*)), or to cancel the registration (s. 20 (1) (*b*)), or to register an amalgamation or transfer (s. 21 (3) (*b*) —and note the extended meaning given to "non-qualifying member" in s. 21 (4)).

(iii) Subs. (8)—For the avoidance of doubt this subsection provides that a non-qualifying member is entitled to increase his shareholding, subject to two qualifications. First, the rules may of course prevent a credit union having any non-qualifying members altogether (see above and s. 5 (5)), but if they do not do so, the rules may still modify such members' rights to purchase more shares. Secondly, the limit in subs. (3) must not be breached. Of course an increase in shareholding would not increase a member's voting strength as each member only has one vote (subs. (9)).

(iv) Subs. (8)—Again for the avoidance of doubt this subsection provides that a non-qualifying member is entitled to receive loans, but once more subject to two qualifications. First, the rules may again modify this right. Secondly, the loan must not cause a non-qualifying member's liability to the credit union to exceed his paid-up shareholding: s. 11 (3) (see further, note thereto).

(v) S. 7 (5)—A non-qualifying member is not allowed to withdraw any shares if this would reduce his paid-up shareholding to less than his liability (see further, note to s. 7).

Considering (iv) and (v), if a member who still qualifies for admission takes a loan which causes his liability to exceed his paid-up shareholding (by up to £2,000—see s. 11 (2)) and then ceased to so qualify, he is not obliged immediately to repay so much of his loan as exceeds his shareholding. S. 11 (3) merely prevents a credit union from *making* a loan which causes liability to exceed shareholding. It does not prevent a non-qualifying member from having liabilities exceeding shareholding but in such a situation the member will not be able to withdraw any shares (s. 7 (5)).

Sex and Race Discrimination

As credit unions are not concerned with providing facilities or services "to the public or a section of the public" but only to those who at least qualify for membership, they would not prima facie be in breach of either s. 29 of the Sex Discrimination Act 1975 or s. 20 of the Race Relations Act 1976 if they discriminated on the grounds of sex or race (see *Charter* v. *Race Relations Board* [1973] A.C. 868; *Race Relations Board* v. *Dockers' Labour Club and Institute* [1974] 1 All E.R. 713). However, if a credit union has 25 or more members, s. 25 of the Race Relations Act 1976 will apply to render it unlawful to discriminate on the grounds of race either in admitting to membership or in providing facilities and services to members. Note, however, *ibid.*, s. 26 (1). There is no equivalent provision in the Sex Discrimination Act 1975 (and see s. 34 thereof).

Contravention of section

If this section is breached the Chief Registrar, with the consent of the Treasury, could suspend the operation of the credit union under s. 19 or the appropriate registrar could cancel (with the consent of the Treasury) or suspend its registration under the 1965 Act, s. 16 (1) (*c*) (i) (as modified in relation to credit unions by s. 20 (1) (*a*) of this Act) and s. 17 (1) respectively. Further, the appropriate registrar could petition for the winding-up of the credit union under s. 20 (2) (*b*) of this Act.

For criminal sanctions, see 1965 Act, ss. 61 (as amended by the Criminal Justice Act 1967, s. 92 (1) and Sched. 3, Pt. I), 62, 63, 66 (as modified in relation to credit unions by s. 28 (3) of this Act), 68, and see this Act, s. 28 (1) and (6).

For "by order" in subs. (4), see s. 29.

Minimum and maximum number of members

6.—(1) The minimum number of members of a credit union shall be twenty-one and, accordingly, in the following provisions, namely—

(*a*) section 2 (1) of the 1965 Act, as it applies to registration as a credit union and to an application therefor,

(*b*) section 16 (1) (*a*) (i) of that Act, as it applies to the cancellation of such a registration,

(*c*) section 53 (2) of that Act, as it applies to the conversion of a company into a credit union, and

(*d*) section 222 (*d*) of the Companies Act 1948 as it applies by virtue of section 55 (*a*) of the 1965 Act to the presentation of a petition for winding up a credit union,

for the word " seven " there shall be substituted the words " twenty-one ".

(2) Subject to the following provisions of this section, the maximum number of members of a credit union shall be five thousand.

(3) The Treasury may, after consultation with the chief registrar, by order made by statutory instrument, from time to time amend subsection (2) above so as to substitute for the maximum number of members for the time being provided for in that subsection such other maximum number as may be specified in the order, but no such order shall be made unless a draft of it has been laid before and approved by a resolution of each House of Parliament.

(4) Subject to subsection (5) below a society shall not be registered as a credit union if the number of its members exceeds the maximum for the time being provided for in subsection (2) above.

(5) The appropriate registrar may grant exemption from the maximum number for the time being provided for in subsection (2) above—

(*a*) to a credit union,

(*b*) to a society or company seeking registration as a credit union, and

(*c*) in respect of a credit union proposed to be created by amalgamation,

if he is satisfied that exemption would be in the public interest and in the interests of the members and would not jeopardise the existence of a common bond between them.

(6) An exemption under subsection (5) above may be granted on such conditions as the appropriate registrar thinks fit, and those conditions shall include, in particular, a condition that the number of members shall not exceed such other maximum as may be specified by him.

DEFINITIONS

" appropriate registrar ": 1965 Act, s. 73 (1) (*c*).
" chief registrar ": 1965 Act, s. 73 (1) (*a*).
" credit union ": ss. 1 (1), 31 (1).

GENERAL NOTE

This section lays down both the minimum and maximum number of members a credit union may have. For a discussion of the meaning of " member," see note to s. 5.

Subs. (1)

The minimum is set at 21 and it is unclear why the minimum of seven laid down in the 1965 Act for ordinary industrial and provident societies (s. 2 (1) (*a*) thereof) was not retained. In consequence of this modification, " 21 " is substituted for " 7 " in certain statutory provisions as they apply to credit unions.

Subss. (2), (3), (5) *and* (6)

The maximum is set at 5,000 (subss. (2) and (4)) and this maximum may be raised in two ways.

First, the maximum may be raised for credit unions generally by statutory instrument (subs. (3)). The overall maximum membership for credit unions is an important figure. It determines the scale of operation of credit unions and therefore their very nature and role in the credit market. Thus it was thought necessary to allow a general increase in this figure only by the affirmative resolution procedure in Parliament rather than by the more usual (and swifter) negative resolution procedure which gives less opportunity for debate, used for other orders made under this Act (see s. 29).

Secondly, the maximum may be raised for particular credit unions (or proposed credit unions), if the appropriate registrar grants an exemption (subs. (5)). Although a wide discretion is given to the registrar, he must nevertheless be satisfied on the three counts stated in subs. (5). (For the meaning of " common bond " see s. 1 (2) (*b*) and (5) and note to s. 1). Further, he is obliged to fix a new maximum figure for membership of the credit union. In exercising this discretion the appropriate registrar would appear to be acting in an administrative capacity. In particular, the appeals procedure from certain decisions by the appropriate registrar in the 1965 Act, s. 18, does not apply and it is difficult to see how a decision of the registrar on this matter could be challenged. But see the powers of the Ombudsman in relation to the Chief Registrar of Friendly Societies: Parliamentary Commissioner Act 1967, s. 4 (1) and Sched. 2.

Examples of when an exemption might be granted would be if an employer had more than 5,000 employees or a club had more than 5,000 members and those employees or members wished to form a credit union.

Subs. (4)

No society may be registered if its initial members are below the minimum (1965 Act, s. 2 (1) as modified in relation to credit unions by s. 6 (1) (*a*) of this Act) or above the maximum (subs. (4)).

Contravention of section

If a credit union breaches the maximum or minimum, the Chief Registrar, with the consent of the Treasury, could suspend its operations under s. 19 or the appropriate registrar could petition for its winding up under s. 20 (2) (*b*). Further, if the minimum is breached, the appropriate registrar could cancel the credit union's registration under the 1965 Act, s. 16 (1) (*a*) (*i*) (as modified in relation to credit unions by s. 6 (1) (*b*) of this Act) or suspend its registration under the 1965 Act, s. 17 (1). If the maximum is breached, the appropriate registrar could cancel (with the consent of the Treasury) the credit union's registration under the 1965 Act, s. 16 (1) (*c*) (i) (as modified in relation to credit unions by s. 20 (1) (*b*) of this Act) or suspend its registration under the 1965 Act, s. 17 (1).

For criminal sanctions, see note to s. 5 (under the heading " *Contravention of section* ").

Operation of credit union

Shares

7.—(1) All shares in a credit union shall be of £1 denomination and may, subject to the rules of the credit union, be subscribed for either in full or by periodical or other subscriptions but no share shall be allotted to a member until it has been fully paid in cash.

(2) Shares in a credit union shall not be transferable and a credit union shall not issue to a member a certificate denoting ownership of a share.

(3) Nothing in subsection (2) above shall affect the operation of section 24 (1) of the 1965 Act (transfer in pursuance of nomination on death of nominator).

(4) Subject to subsection (5) below, shares in a credit union shall be withdrawable but a credit union shall not issue shares except on terms enabling it to require not less than sixty days' notice of withdrawal.

(5) If a withdrawal of shares would reduce a member's paid-up shareholding in the credit union to less than his total liability (including contingent liability) to the credit union whether as borrower, guarantor or otherwise, then—

(*a*) in the case of a non-qualifying member the withdrawal shall not be permitted; and

(*b*) in any other case the withdrawal shall be permitted only at the discretion of the committee.

DEFINITIONS

" committee ": 1965 Act, s. 74.
" credit union ": ss. 1 (1), 31 (1).
" non-qualifying member ": ss. 5 (5), 21 (4), 31 (1).
" the 1965 Act ": s. 31 (1)

GENERAL NOTE

For a discussion of the meaning of " member " and " non-qualifying member," see note to s. 5.

The shares in a credit union must fulfil the following conditions:

(i) They must be of £1 denomination: subs. (1). Thus shares which are multiples and fractions of £1 are not permitted, but see below as to payment for shares.

(ii) They must not be transferable (subs. (2)), although a member may by a signed written statement nominate another (or others) to become entitled on his death to his shares in the credit union (see further, 1965 Act, ss. 23 and 24 as amended by the Administration of Estates (Small Payments) Act 1965, ss. 2, 4 (1), (3), 7 (6) and Scheds. 2 and 4): subs. (3). See also, 1965 Act, ss. 25 (as amended by the Administration of Estates (Small Payments) Act 1965), 27 (intestacy). But the 1965 Act, s. 24 (1) gives the committee of the credit union the option of either allotting the shares to the nominee of the deceased member or paying the nominee their full value. If the nominee is an " individual " (see note to s. 5) and fulfils the qualifications for admission to the credit union (see s. 1 (1) (*a*), (2) (*b*), (4) and (6)), the committee may transfer the shares to him provided, if the nominee is already a member, s. 5 (3) is not thereby breached. But the committee may always choose not to transfer but to pay the nominee the shares' value in lieu. The committee should adopt this course of action if the nominee does not qualify for admisssion or if s. 5 (3) would be breached. Otherwise the Chief Registrar could suspend the credit union's operations under s. 19 or the appropriate registrar could cancel (with the consent of the Treasury) the union's registration (1965 Act, s. 16 (1) (*c*) (i) and (ii) as modified in relation to credit unions by s. 20 (1) of this Act) or suspend its registration (1965 Act, s. 17 (1)), or petition for its winding up (s. 20 (2)). Further, criminal sanctions are applicable: 1965 Act, s. 61.

The general non-transferability of shares is necessary to ensure that the strict conditions as to membership of a credit union are not inadvertently breached.

It is submitted that subs. (2) does not prevent a member declaring a trust of his shares for another. See further, note to s. 1 where it was submitted that such a trustee and not the beneficial owner would remain the " member " for the purposes of this Act.

(iii) They must be withdrawable: subs. (4). Two limitations are however placed on the withdrawal of shares.

First, a credit union is obliged to issue shares on such terms that it may require at least 60 days' notice of withdrawal (see also, Sched. 1, para. 8). Although the terms of issue must contain such a provision, no doubt a credit union could waive the 60 days' notice in any given case. It could do so if it had the cash value of the shares readily available, but subs. (4) ensures that a credit union could insist on the 60-day period if it had problems raising the money due to a run on the credit union, for example.

Secondly, subs. (5) restricts the right to withdraw if a withdrawal would reduce a member's " *paid-up shareholding* " to less than his " *total liability (including contingent liability) to the credit union whether as borrower, guarantor or otherwise.*"

" *Paid-up shareholding* " is an ambiguous phrase. By subs. (1) only fully paid-up shares can be allotted, so arguably " paid-up shareholding " refers only to the amount paid for allotted shares, disregarding part-payments made for subscribed for (but not allotted) shares. But such an interpretation renders the word "paid-up" otiose. Thus it is submitted that "paid-up shareholding" refers to the total amount paid by a member both for fully paid-up allotted shares and for partly paid for subscribed shares. However, it seems clear that deposits made under s. 9 (1) would not be included in the phrase.

The reference to "*total liability*" is broadly phrased and seems to cover any form of actual or potential liability a member has to a credit union. It would include loans received under s. 11 (1) and liability for interest thereon, any contingent liability under a guarantee given by one member in respect of a loan to another, any potential liability of an officer-member under security given by virtue of the 1965 Act, s. 41 (and see Sched. 4 thereof) and any liability of an office-member under the 1965 Act, s. 42.

If the withdrawal of shares would cause the "paid-up shareholding" to be less than the "total liability," then the committee has a discretion as to whether to permit it. No doubt in exercising this discretion it would bear in mind that it is desirable for a member to retain a substantial link with the credit union by way of shareholding but that by s. 11 (2) a member may borrow up to £2,000 in excess of his paid-up shareholding. But in allowing a withdrawal, it must ensure that s. 11 (2), which states that the amount on loan to a member must not at any time be more than £2,000 in excess of his paid-up shareholding, is not contravened.

A non-qualifying member cannot withdraw any shares in such circumstances, even if the committee has no objection (see further, note to s. 5 under the heading "*non-qualifying member*").

For a further limitation on the withdrawal of shares (where money borrowed by a credit union is not repaid when due) see s. 10 (5).

These limitations on the withdrawal of shares do not apply to the withdrawal of deposits made under s. 9 (1).

A consequence of a credit union of necessity having withdrawable share capital is that by the 1965 Act, s. 7 (1) (*b*), a credit union is not permitted to carry on the business of banking (but see in any event the limitations on the objects a credit union may have, imposed by s. 1 (1) (*a*), (2) (*a*) and (3)).

(iv) The maximum dividend payable on shares is fixed by s. 14 (4) and dividends are only payable on paid-up shares (s. 14 (3) (*a*)). For the tax position of dividends, see s. 25.

Subject to (i)–(iv), a credit union may make such provision in its rules as to shares as it wishes (see 1965 Act, s. 13 (4)). Although subs. (1) allows shares to be subscribed for either in full or by instalments, the rules may modify this by, for example, not permitting payment by instalments or by stating the mode of payment by instalments. Further, the rules may provide for classes of shares.

See also s. 8 (1) (subscription for shares not within the prohibition against deposit taking).

Contravention of section

The powers of the chief and appropriate registrars on breach of this section are the same as those listed in note to s. 5.

For criminal sanctions, see note to s. 5.

General prohibition on deposit-taking

8.—(1) Subject to sections 9 and 10 below, a credit union shall not accept a deposit from any person except by way of subscription for its shares.

(2) In this section and section 9 below a "deposit" means a sum of money paid on terms—

(*a*) under which it will be repaid, with or without interest or at a premium, and either on demand or at a time or in circumstances agreed by or on behalf of the person making the payment and the credit union; and

(*b*) which are not referable to the provision of property or services or to the giving of security.

(3) For the purposes of subsection (2) (*b*) above, money is paid on terms which are referable to the provision of property or services or to the giving of security if, and only if,—

(*a*) it is paid by way of advance or part-payment for the sale, hire or other provision of property or services of any kind and is repayable only in the event that the property or services is or are not in the fact sold, hired or otherwise provided; or

(*b*) it is paid by way of security for payment for the provision of property or services of any kind provided or to be provided by the credit union; or

(*c*) it is paid by way of security for the delivery up or return of any property, whether in a particular state of repair or otherwise.

(4) If a credit union accepts a deposit in contravention of this section it shall be guilty of an offence and liable on conviction on indictment or on summary conviction to a fine which on summary conviction shall not exceed the statutory maximum.

(5) The fact that a deposit is taken in contravention of this section shall not affect any civil liability arising in respect of the deposit or the money deposited.

DEFINITIONS

"credit union": ss. 1 (1), 31 (1).
"person": Interpretation Act 1978, s. 5 and Sched. 1.
"statutory maximum": s. 31 (1).

GENERAL NOTE

Subss. (2) and (3) define "deposit" in terms almost identical to the Banking Act 1979, s. 1 (4) and (6) respectively.

Subs. (1) then ensures that credit unions do not develop into deposit-taking institutions (which are generally regulated by the Banking Act 1979) by prohibiting a credit union from accepting a deposit (as defined) from any person. However, this prohibition does not apply to:

(i) the taking of money as subscriptions for shares (see s. 7 (1));
(ii) the taking of deposits within s. 9 (1);
(iii) the borrowing of money in accordance with s. 10.

As regards these three activities, the Banking Act 1979, s. 2 (1) and Sched. 1, para. 11, exempt credit unions from the general prohibition in s. 1 of that Act against certain persons taking deposits (but note s. 2 (2) of that Act). It has already been seen that in any event a credit union cannot carry on the business of banking (1965 Act, s. 7 (1) (*b*), and note to s. 7, (iii)).

There is nothing to prevent a credit union accepting sums of money which do not fall within the definition of "deposit." Therefore, a credit union could charge a membership fee or accept donations to its funds.

Contravention of section—subss. (4) *and* (5)

Subss. (4) and (5) are again similar in terms to the Banking Act 1979, s. 1 (7) and (8).

For further provisions relevant to the criminal sanction in subs. (4), see 1965 Act, ss. 62 (as modified in relation to credit unions by s. 28 (4) of this Act), 63, 66 (as modified in relation to credit unions by s. 28 (3) of this Act) and 68, and this Act, s. 28 (1) and (6).

Although contravention of this section does not affect any civil liability in respect of the deposit, it could induce the Chief Registrar or appropriate registrar to exercise his powers (listed in the note to s. 5 under the heading "*Contravention of section*").

Deposits by persons too young to be members

9.—(1) A credit union may take deposits up to a total of £250 from a person who is under the age at which, by virtue of section 20 of the 1965 Act, he may become a member of the credit union; and nothing in section 7 (3) of the 1965 Act shall apply to any such deposits.

(2) Any deposit received by a credit union as mentioned in subsection (1) above shall be held by it on trust for the depositor and all such

deposits shall be kept in a fund apart from the general funds of the credit union and shall be invested only in the manner specified in Part I or Part II of Schedule 1 to the Trustee Investments Act 1961 (narrower-range investments).

(3) The moneys which from year to year are earned by the investment of deposits in accordance with subsection (2) above shall, after deduction of the expenses incurred in operating the separate fund referred to in that subsection, be distributed as interest to the depositors.

(4) The chief registrar may, by order made with the consent of the Treasury, from time to time amend subsection (1) above so as to substitute for the maximum amount for the time being provided for in that subsection such other amount, being not less than £250, as may be specified in the order.

(5) An order under subsection (4) above may contain such transitional, consequential, incidental or supplementary provisions as appear to the chief registrar to be necessary or appropriate, and in particular may make any such provision in connection with the alteration of the limit in subsection (1) above as is made by section 1 of the Industrial and Provident Societies Act 1978 in connection with the alterations made by that section in the limits in section 7 (3) of the 1965 Act.

DEFINITIONS

" chief registrar ": 1965 Act, s. 73 (1) (*c*).
" credit union ": ss. 1 (1), 31 (1).
" deposit ": s. 8 (2).
" person ": Interpretation Act 1978, s. 5 and Sched. 1.
" the 1965 Act ": s. 31 (1).
" Treasury ": Interpretation Act 1978, s. 5 and Sched. 1.

GENERAL NOTE

For a discussion of the meaning of " member," see note to s. 5.

Although by s. 8 (1) a credit union is generally prohibited from taking deposits, one important exception is contained in subs. (1).

By the 1965 Act, s. 20 (as amended by the Family Law Reform Act 1969, s. 1 (3) and Sched. 1, Pt. I), an individual under 18 but over 16 may, unless the rules provide otherwise, be a member of a credit union although he cannot hold specified posts. Thus by subs. (1), individuals under 16 or under 18 if the rules do not permit members below this age, may make deposits up to £250 (which is variable upwards by order: subss. (4) and (5)). The Banking Act 1979, s. 2 (1) and Sched. 1, para. 11, exempt such deposits from that Act (but see s. 2 (2) thereof).

The exception in subs. (1) was considered desirable to enable children of members (although the exception is not limited to such children) to establish a link with a credit union early in their lives. But once an individual attains the age when he may become a member, he is not permitted to make further deposits. There are no statutory provisions governing the withdrawal of such deposits: ss. 7 (4) (5) and 10 (5) only apply to the withdrawal of shares and the 1965 Act, s. 7 (3), is made inapplicable by s. 9 (1) of this Act. So it seems the depositor has the choice, subject to the rules, of either leaving his money on deposit indefinitely or (under the rule in *Saunders* v. *Vautier* (1841) Cr. & Ph. 240) claiming it after he comes of age.

It is submitted that although subs. (1) talks of deposits " from a person who is under the age . . . ," a deposit by a parent of such a child intended to be for the child would fall within the exception. Further, it is submitted that the child and not the parent would be the " depositor " for the purposes of subss. (2) and (3).

Subs. (2) renders the credit union statutory trustee of any deposits for the depositor. Further, the credit union is obliged to keep all the deposits in a separate fund and to invest it only in investments listed in Pts. I and II of Sched. 1 to the Trustee Investments Act 1961. Thus unlike most other trust funds, this fund cannot be divided and half invested in the wider-range investments list in Pt. III of that Schedule. The investment income, after deduction of expenses, must then be distributed (a term which would include adding it to the capital) amongst the depositors. Thus such deposits cannot be used for the general purposes of the credit union and, for the avoidance of doubt, s. 13 is stated not to apply to them (s. 13 (5) (*b*)).

It is submitted in notes to ss. 7 and 11 that such deposits are not included in the phrase "paid-up shareholding" for the purposes of ss. 7 (5) and 11 (3), in the note to s. 10 that such deposits are not included in the "total paid-up share capital" for the purposes of s. 10 (1) and in the note to s. 19 that the taking of deposits is not "borrowing" within s. 19 (1) (*a*).

Contravention of section

Breach of this section renders the powers of the Chief Registrar and appropriate registrar listed in the note to s. 5 applicable and has the same criminal consequences as contravention of s. 5 (see note to s. 5 under heading "*Contravention of section*").

As to "by order" in subs. (4), see s. 29.

Power to borrow money

10.—(1) A credit union may borrow money from an authorised bank or temporarily from another credit union or an association of credit unions but the amount so borrowed and not repaid shall not at any time exceed in the aggregate one half of the total paid-up share capital.

(2) A temporary loan obtained by a credit union from an authorised bank shall be disregarded for the purposes of the limit on borrowing imposed by subsection (1) above if the credit union has obtained the consent in writing of the chief registrar.

(3) A person dealing with a credit union shall not be obliged to satisfy himself or to inquire whether the limit on borrowing by that credit union imposed by subsection (1) above has been or is being observed, but if a person who lends money to a credit union or takes security in connection with such a loan has, at the time when the loan is made or the security is given, actual notice of the fact that the limit has been or is thereby exceeded, the debt or security shall be unenforceable.

(4) Subject to subsection (3) above, no transaction with a credit union shall be invalid or ineffectual solely by reason of the fact that the limit on borrowing by that credit union imposed by subsection (1) above has been or is thereby exceeded.

(5) Where money borrowed by a credit union is not repaid on written demand on the date on which repayment is due, the credit union shall not make any loans or permit the withdrawal of any shares until the repayment is made.

(6) If a credit union borrows in excess of the limit imposed by subsection (1) above or makes loans or permits withdrawals in contravention of subsection (5) above, it shall be guilty of an offence and liable on conviction on indictment or on summary conviction to a fine which on summary conviction shall not exceed the statutory maximum.

DEFINITIONS

"authorised bank": s. 31 (1).
"chief registrar": 1965 Act, s. 73 (1) (*c*).
"credit union": ss. 1 (1), 31 (1).
"person": Interpretation Act 1978, s. 5 and Sched. 1.
"statutory maximum": s. 31 (1).

GENERAL NOTE

Subss. (1) *and* (2)

The powers of a credit union to borrow are limited by this section in the following respects.

First, the only sources from which it may borrow are (a) an authorised bank (as defined in s. 31 (1)), or (b) another credit union, or (c) an association of credit unions.

Secondly, although it may theoretically borrow for an indefinite period from an authorised bank (but see subs. (2) and discussion thereof below), it may only borrow temporarily from another credit union or an association of credit unions. (It is clear that "temporarily" qualifies both the latter sources.) There is no guidance as to how short the period of the loan must be or what other factors would render it "temporary" within this section. For a discussion of loans between credit unions, see note to s. 13.

Thirdly, money so borrowed must not exceed half of the credit union's "*total paid-up share capital.*" It seems this phrase refers to the sum of the subscriptions received for shares, whether allotted or only partly paid (see s. 7 (1)), but it would not include deposits received under s. 9 (1). It is clear, however, that "a temporary loan" from the credit union's bankers is to be disregarded in calculating the money borrowed for this purpose, provided the Chief Registrar consents: subs. (2). It appears that "temporary loan" would include an overdraft incurred for a short period when there is greater than usual demand for money (for example, Christmas). But again it is unclear how long an overdraft or other bank loan must be outstanding before it ceases to be "temporary." In practice, because interest payable on bank loans will normally exceed the interest chargeable to members (see s. 11 (5)), financial considerations will preclude a credit union maintaining a bank loan for any length of time. Of course, a credit union is permitted to borrow indefinitely from an authorised bank (see subs. (1)) but then the sum so borrowed must be included for the purposes of ascertaining whether the statutory limitation on borrowing is exceeded.

The paid-up share capital will, of course, vary as shares are subscribed for and withdrawn. Apart from cases where there are limitations on the withdrawal of shares (discussed in note to s. 7 under heading (iii)), a credit union cannot prevent a member from withdrawing his shares. Thus if such a withdrawal would cause a breach of subs. (1), it seems that the credit union can only avoid such a breach by reducing the amount it has borrowed by, for example, realising some of its investments and using the proceeds to repay its creditors.

Subss. (3), (4) *and* (6)—*breach of statutory limit in subs.* (1)

The criminal penalty in subs. (6) is incurred if a credit union "borrows" in excess of the limit in subs. (1). (See further those sections of the 1965 Act and this Act listed in note to s. 8 under the heading "*Contravention of section.*") Although "borrows" seems to suggest that there must be a fresh loan which causes the statutory limit to be exceeded (or a further loan when the limit is already exceeded), it is submitted that anything which causes the limit to be exceeded would render the credit union (and others, see 1965 Act, s. 62, as modified in relation to credit unions by s. 28 (4) of this Act) liable to prosecution under subs. (6). Thus any withdrawal of share capital or any accumulation of interest payable as well as any loan taken which causes the amount borrowed to exceed the statutory limit, would mean the credit union "borrows in excess" of the limit within subs. (6). This view is supported by the wording of subs. (1) which talks of the limit not being exceeded "at any time."

In addition, breach of the statutory limit could induce the Chief Registrar or the appropriate registrar to exercise his powers (those listed in note to s. 5 under the heading "*Contravention of section*").

With one exception, breach of the statutory limit does not render any "transactions with a credit union" invalid: subs. (4). This exception is contained in subs. (3).

If a creditor actually knows (constructive notice is apparently not enough) at the time he makes a loan or takes security (knowledge at some later time is not enough) of the breach, his debt or security is "unenforceable" (subs. (3), which also specifically states that such a creditor is not bound to make inquiries as to the observance of the limit). Subs. (3) does not render the debt or security void, only "unenforceable". Therefore any payments made voluntarily by the debtor pursuant to the loan agreement are not recoverable (see *Orakpo* v. *Manson Investments Ltd.* [1978] A.C. 95 at p. 106, a decision on the Moneylenders Act 1927, s. 6). However, any enforcement of the loan or security, whether judicial or extra-judicial, whether direct or indirect, is not permitted. Thus the creditor will not be able by subrogation to claim any rights against the credit union's property if his money has been used to purchase that property or to discharge any previous security over it (*Orakpo* (*supra*), overruling *Congresbury Motors Ltd.* v. *Anglo–Belge Finance Co. Ltd.*

[1971] Ch. 81). Further, the court will order the cancellation and delivery up of any security without obliging the debtor to repay the loan (*Cohen* v. *J. Lester Ltd.* [1939] 1 K.B. 504; *Kasum* v. *Bada-Egbe* [1956] A.C. 539; *Barclay* v. *Prospect Mortgages Ltd.* [1974] 1 W.L.R. 837—all on the Moneylenders Acts).

Otherwise (unless the relevant registrar decides to use his powers) it seems a credit union is permitted to carry on functioning despite a breach of the limit. Thus it may allow the withdrawal of deposits made under s. 9 (1), it may make loans (*cf.* subs. (5)) to members under s. 11 or to other credit unions and it may invest under s. 13. Indeed such transactions, as well as loans taken in circumstances where subs. (3) does not render them unenforceable and as well as withdrawal of shares, are all as " transactions with a credit union " expressly saved from civil invalidity by subs. (4).

Subs. (5)

In contrast to the position if the statutory limit on borrowing is breached, if a credit union fails to repay a loan when due after a written demand, its assets are to some extent frozen. Thus it cannot make any loans (either to members under s. 11 or to other credit unions) nor can it permit the withdrawal of shares. But it seems it can allow the withdrawal of deposits made under s. 9 (1) and it can invest under s. 13 (unless the particular investment is regarded as a " loan ").

If subs. (5) is breached, the criminal penalty in subs. (6) may be incurred. See further those provisions of the 1965 Act and this Act listed in note to s. 8 under the heading "*Contravention of section.*" In addition, the relevant registrars have the same powers as those in relation to the breach of the statutory limit in subs. (1) (see above, *i.e.* those listed in note to s. 5).

However, the civil consequences of making loans or allowing the withdrawal of shares in breach of subs. (5) are not expressly provided for in the same way as for the breach of the statutory limit on borrowing.

See also the Industrial and Provident Societies Act 1967 and the Industrial and Provident Societies Regulations 1967 (S.I. 1967 No. 1310) (charges on property).

Loans

11.—(1) Subject to the provisions of this section, a credit union may make to a member who is of full age a loan for a provident or productive purpose, upon such security (or without security) and terms as the rules of the credit union may provide.

(2) The total amount on loan to a member of a credit union shall not at any time be more than £2,000 (or such other sum as may from time to time be specified) in excess of his total paid-up shareholding in the credit union at that time.

(3) Without prejudice to subsection (2) above, a credit union shall not at any time make a loan to a non-qualifying member if the making of the loan would cause that member's total liability (including contingent liability) to the credit union, whether as borrower, guarantor or otherwise, to exceed his total paid-up shareholding in the credit union at that time.

(4) The maximum period within which a loan by a credit union must be repaid shall be five years in the case of a secured loan and two years in the case of an unsecured loan, or such other period as may from time to time be specified.

(5) A credit union may charge interest on loans made by it but such interest shall be at a rate not exceeding one per cent. per month, or such other rate as may from time to time be specified, on the amount of the loan outstanding and such interest shall be inclusive of all administrative and other expenses incurred in connection with the making of the loan.

(6) A credit union shall not at any time make a loan to a member if the making of such a loan would bring the total amount outstanding on loans to members above such limit as may from time to time be specified.

(7) In this section " specified " means specified by order made by the chief registrar with the consent of the Treasury.

DEFINITIONS

" chief registrar ": 1965 Act, s. 73 (1) (*a*).
" credit union ": ss. 1 (1), 31 (1).
" month ": Interpretation Act 1978, s. 5 and Sched. 1.
" non-qualifying member ": ss. 5 (5), 21 (4) and 31 (1).
" Treasury ": Interpretation Act 1978, s. 5 and Sched. 1.

GENERAL NOTE

For a discussion of the meaning of " member " and " non-qualifying member," see note to s. 5.

This section empowers a credit union to make secured or unsecured loans to members (but members only—although see the investment powers in s. 13, in particular s. 13 (5) (*a*)) if the following conditions are fulfilled:

(i) The member must be of full age, *i.e.* over 18 (see the Family Law Reform Act 1969, s. 1 (1) and (2)). As to minors as members of a credit union, see 1965 Act, s. 20, and note to s. 9.

(ii) The loan must be for a " provident or productive purpose." These criteria, which have a somewhat Victorian tenor, are not defined but they seek to limit the type of expenditure credit unions are to finance. " Provident " construed narrowly connotes expenditure which will eventually save money (for example, a cycle or season ticket to save fares or a washing machine to save laundry bills). " Productive " could merely mean financially productive (a car used for work, a greenhouse to grow vegetables) or it could also mean productive of well-being (leisure and luxury expenditure). It is submitted that these words, which are disjunctive, should be interpreted broadly if credit unions are to be a significant source of credit for their members.

(iii) The maximum amount permitted to be loaned is generally governed by two factors.

(a) The member's " *total paid-up shareholding* " must be ascertained. It is submitted that " total " adds nothing to the meaning of " paid-up shareholding ", which has been discussed in the note to s. 7 (under heading (iii)). Then, if he is a non-qualifying member, his position is governed by subs. (3) which has been considered in the note to s. 5 (under heading " *Subss.* (6)–(8)—' *non-qualifying member* ' "). But if he still qualifies for admission to membership, the maximum amount he may borrow is ascertained by adding £2,000 (a figure which may be increased or decreased by order: subs. (6)) to his total paid-up shareholding and deducing the amount (if any) he already has " *on loan.*" In so far as the phrase " *total liability,*" etc., is not used (*c.f.* subs. (3) and s. 7 (5)), no account need be taken of any other liability a member may be under (for example, contingent liability under a guarantee).

(b) An order made under subs. (6) may limit the total amount any credit union may have on loan to its members. Then, a loan may not be made to a member if any such limit has been reached by that credit union.

(iv) Subs. (4) lays down the maximum possible periods for loans (which maximum periods may be varied by order: subs (7)). A distinction is made between " secured " and " unsecured " loans. These terms are not defined and it is unclear if a "secured " loan would only be one where the creditor had rights over the debtor's property (for example, a mortgage) or whether it would include one where the creditor merely had a personal guarantee from a third party (see, for example, the wide definition of " security " in s. 189 of the Consumer Credit Act 1974 and *Temperance Loan Fund Ltd.* v. *Rose* [1932] 2 K.B. 522 in relation to s. 6 of the Moneylenders Act 1927).

(v) The maximum amount of interest chargeable is 1 per cent. per month (a rate which is variable by order: subs. (7)) on the reducing monthly balance: subs. (5). This approximates to an annual rate of 12⅔ per cent. To calculate the interest for the purposes of subs (5), it seems that all other payments made by the member in order to obtain the loan (" all administrative and other expenses "), for example, surveyors' fees for valuing any real security, are to be included. A similar approach is adopted in the calculating of the " rate of total charge for credit " for the purposes of the Consumer Credit Act 1974, s. 20. However, the calculation provisions (in S.I. 1977 No. 327) are far more detailed and complex. Therefore, the annual equivalent rate of interest calculated for the purposes of subs. (5) above will not necessarily be the same as the rate of total charge for credit (which is expressed as an annual rate) for the purposes of the Consumer Credit Act 1974. It is submitted, however, that in calculating both the maximum rate of interest for the purposes of subs. (5) and the rate of total charge for credit for the purposes of the Consumer Credit Act 1974, any payments made by an individual to acquire shares in order to become a member of a credit union (and thus qualify for a loan) would not need to be included in the calculation. (For a further discussion, see Guest and Lloyd, *Encyclopedia of Consumer Credit Law,* para. 3–044.) A credit union will have to calculate the rate of total charge for credit for each transaction in order to determine the impact of the Consumer Credit Act 1974. Prima facie, the 1974 Act applies to credit unions. But many of its provisions are inapplicable to " exempt agreements " and certain agreements where the rate of total charge for credit is below 13 per cent. per annum are exempt (1974 Act, s. 16 (5) (*b*) and S.I. 1977 No. 326, Art. 3 (1) (*c*)). Thus it is likely that most loans to members made by credit unions will be exempt. But ss. 43–47 (advertising) and s. 52 (quotations) of the Consumer Credit Act 1974 may apply even if exempt agreements are made and therefore if a credit union wishes to advertise or quote its rate of interest, it must do so in terms of the rate of total charge for credit calculated in accordance with the regulations made under the 1974 Act and not in terms of the rate calculated for the purposes of subs. (5).

(vi) The rules may specify other conditions (subs. (1) and Sched. 1, para. 9), in particular, whether credit insurance must be taken out. If the member has to pay the premium, this must be included in calculating the rate of interest he is charged (see (v) above).

Subject to these conditions, whether to grant a loan and on what terms (as to security and mode of repayment, for instance) lies in the discretion of the committee of the credit union.

The limitations in this section do not apply to loans to other credit unions (see further, note to s. 13). See also, s. 10 (5) (a credit union may not make loans if it has failed after a written request to repay a loan due).

As to " by order " in subs. (7), see s. 29.

Contravention of section

As to the criminal consequences of breach of this section and as to the powers of the relevant registrars on such a breach, see the provisions listed in the note to s. 5 under the heading " *Contravention of section* ".

Power to hold land for limited purposes

12.—(1) A credit union may hold, purchase or take on lease in its own name any land for the purpose of conducting its business thereon but, subject to subsection (3) below, for no other purpose, and may sell, exchange, mortgage or lease any such land, and erect, alter or pull down buildings on it.

(2) In the application of subsection (1) above to Scotland—

(*a*) for the word " exchange " there shall be substituted the word " excamb ", and

(*b*) for the word " mortgage " there shall be substituted the words " grant a heritable security over ".

(3) A credit union shall have power to hold any interest in land so far as is necessary for the purpose of making loans to its members on the security of an interest in land and of enforcing any such security.

(4) In any case where—

(*a*) in England or Wales, a credit union becomes absolutely entitled to any interest in land by foreclosure or by release or other extinguishment of a right of redemption, or

(*b*) in Scotland, a credit union acquires an interest in land by the exercise of any right which it holds as creditor in a heritable security,

the credit union shall sell that interest as soon as may be conveniently practicable.

(5) If a credit union continues to hold any interest in land in contravention of subsection (4) above it shall be guilty of an offence and liable on conviction on indictment or on summary conviction to a fine which on summary conviction shall not exceed the statutory maximum.

(6) No person shall be bound to inquire as to the authority for any dealing with land by a credit union; and the receipt of a credit union shall be a discharge for all moneys arising from or in connection with any dealing with land by it.

DEFINITIONS

" credit union ": ss. 1 (1), 31 (1).
" heritable security ": 1965 Act, s. 74.
" land ": 1965 Act, s. 74; Interpretation Act 1978, s. 5 and Sched. 1.
" person ": Interpretation Act 1978, s. 5 and Sched. 1.
" statutory maximum ": s. 31 (1).

GENERAL NOTE

This section places restrictions on the power of a credit union to hold land. Note that s. 30 of the 1965 Act, which enables a registered society to hold land, is excluded in relation to credit unions by s. 31 (3) of this Act.

A credit union may only hold land in two circumstances.

First, it may hold land as premises for its own activities: subs. (1). Secondly, it may hold land as security for loans to its members (but apparently not for loans to other credit unions nor for loans made by virtue of the investment powers in s. 13): subs (3). But by subs. (4), if a credit union becomes entitled to an interest in land held as security through the debtor losing his right of redemption, it must sell that interest " as soon as may be conveniently practicable ". In this subsection " foreclosure " and " release " are self-explanatory. The extinguishment of a right of redemption by the expiry of the limitation period under the Limitation Act 1939, s. 12 would be an example of an " *other extinguishment or a right of redemption.*" There is no statutory obligation on the credit union to take reasonable care to obtain the true market price. If the credit union were selling as mortgagee it would be under such an obligation at common law (*Cuckmere Brick Co. Ltd.* v. *Mutual Finance Co. Ltd.* [1971] Ch. 949—but note the more onerous obligation on a building society selling as mortgagee imposed by the Building Societies Act 1962, s. 36). But as it would be selling as absolute owner, it would seem it is not under such an obligation (and see *Barclays Bank Ltd.* v. *Thienel* (1978) 247 E.G. 385, D.C.).

These restrictions preclude credit unions speculating in land and becoming property companies. But note subs. (6).

For a discussion of the meaning of " member " see note to s. 5.

See also 1965 Act, ss. 33 (discharge of mortgages in England and Wales), 34 (discharge of securities in Scotland), and 35 (receipts).

Contravention of section

Only breach of subs (4) incurs the specific criminal penalty in subs. (5), but breach of subs. (1) would incur a criminal penalty under the 1965 Act, s. 61 as amended by the Criminal Justice Act, s. 92 (1) and Sched. 3, Pt. 1. See further, those provisions of the 1965 Act and this Act listed in the note to s. 8 under the heading " *Contravention of section.*"

The powers of the relevant registrars on breach of subs. (1) or (4) are those listed in the note to s. 5 under the heading " *Contravention of section.*"

Investments

13.—(1) A credit union may not invest any part of its surplus funds except in a manner authorised by an order made by the chief registrar with the consent of the Treasury; and such an order may contain provisions authorising the application of the funds of a credit union in any form of investment subject to any limitations as to amount, whether by reference to a fixed sum or by reference to a proportion of the total investments of the credit union or otherwise.

(2) Any surplus funds of a credit union which are not either—

(*a*) invested in accordance with subsection (1) above, or

(*b*) kept in cash in the custody of officers of the credit union,

shall be kept by the credit union on current account with, or otherwise on loan to, an authorised bank.

(3) Where an institution ceases to be an authorised bank and any funds of a credit union are on loan to that institution, the credit union shall take all practicable steps to call in and realise the loan within the period of three months from the time when the institution ceased to be an authorised bank or, if that is not possible, as soon after the end of that period as possible.

(4) In this section " surplus funds ", in relation to a credit union, means funds not immediately required for its purposes.

(5) Nothing in this section shall—

(*a*) prevent a credit union from making a temporary loan to another credit union; or

(*b*) apply to funds held on trust as mentioned in section 9 (2) above.

(6) If a credit union contravenes the provisions of this section, it shall be guilty of an offence and liable on conviction on indictment or on summary conviction to a fine which on summary conviction shall not exceed the statutory maximum.

DEFINITIONS

" authorised bank ": s. 31 (1).

" chief registrar ": 1965 Act, s. 73 (1) (*a*).

" credit union ": ss. 1 (1), 31 (1).

" officer ": 1965 Act, s. 74 as amended by the Friendly and Industrial and Provident Societies Act 1968, s. 20 (1) (*a*) and Sched. 1, para. 11.

" statutory maximum ": s. 31 (1).

" Treasury ": Interpretation Act 1978, s. 5 and Sched. 1.

GENERAL NOTE

This section defines " surplus funds " (subs. (4)) and circumscribes their application. It is submitted that this definition precludes a credit union choosing to apply its funds in accordance with s. 13 in preference to making loans to its members. The making of such loans is one of a credit union's " purposes " (see its objects listed in s. 1 (3), especially s. 1 (3) (*b*)) and only if funds are not immediately required for this do they become " surplus funds " and so applicable in accordance with s. 13. For the avoidance of doubt, deposits taken under s. 9 (1) and kept separate by virtue of s. 9 (2) are excluded from the definition of "surplus funds": subs. (5) (*b*).

Surplus funds may be kept in cash in the custody of a credit union's officers: subs. (2) (*b*). But if such funds are to be invested (and there is no statutory obligation to do so) they must be invested in accordance with the order to be made under subs. (1). It is expected that this order will be similar to those made under the Building Societies Act 1962, s. 58 (see the Building Societies (Authorised Investments) (No. 2) Order 1977, (S.I. 1977 No. 2052)). Funds not kept or applied in either of these two ways must be paid into an " authorised bank " (as defined, and note the obligation in subs. (3) to realise this loan if the bank ceases to be authorised).

Subs. (5) (*a*)

A combination of this subsection and s. 10 (1) obliquely permits a credit union to lend some of its funds temporarily to another credit union. Two points arise. First, the difficulties in knowing when a loan ceases to be " temporary " have already been noted (see the note to s. 10 under heading " *Subss.* (1) *and* (2)"). Secondly, this permission is not confined to " surplus funds " but extends to all the funds of a credit union.

The provisions in s. 11 circumscribing the terms of loans to members, of course would not apply to loans to other credit unions. Further, it would seem that s. 12

does not permit a credit union making a loan to another credit union secured on land (see note thereto).

Contravention of section

Any contravention of s. 13 attracts the criminal penalty in subs. (6) (as to which see also the provisions of the 1965 Act and this Act listed in the note to s. 8 under the heading "*Contravention of section*").

Further, such contravention would empower the relevant registrars to use those powers listed in the note to s. 5 under the head "*Contravention of section.*"

Computation and application of profits

14.—(1) In ascertaining the profit or loss resulting from the operations of a credit union during any year of account all operating expenses in that year shall be taken into account (including payments of interest) and provision shall be made for depreciation of assets, for tax liabilities and for bad and doubtful debts, but no provision shall be made in respect of amounts to be paid by way of dividend.

(2) A credit union shall out of its profits from year to year establish and maintain a general reserve, as follows—

(*a*) if at the end of any year of account the amount standing to general reserve before any transfer under this subsection is less than 10 per cent. of total assets, the credit union shall transfer to general reserve not less than 20 per cent. of its profits for that year or such lesser sum as is required to bring the general reserve up to 10 per cent. of total assets;

(*b*) if at the end of any year of account the amount standing to general reserve before any transfer under this subsection is more than 20 per cent. of total assets, the credit union shall transfer to the revenue account and treat as revenue for that year a sum not less than that required to reduce the general reserve to 20 per cent. of total assets;

(*c*) subject to paragraphs (*a*) and (*b*) above, a credit union may at the end of any year of account—

(i) transfer to general reserve from the profits of that year, or

(ii) transfer from general reserve to the revenue account and treat as revenue for that year,

such sum as the credit union may in general meeting determine, provided that the general reserve is not thereby reduced to less than 10 per cent. or increased to more than 20 per cent. of total assets.

(3) Not less than 90 per cent. of the amount available for distribution in respect of any year of account, that is to say, the profit of that year reduced or increased by any transfer to or from general reserve in accordance with subsection (2) above, shall be applied in such one or more of the following ways as the credit union shall in general meeting determine—

(*a*) subject to subsection (4) below, in the payment to members of dividends on the amount of their paid-up shares;

(*b*) as a rebate of interest paid by or due from members who have received loans from the credit union, such rebate being proportional to the interest paid by or due from such members during that year of account; and

(*c*) subject to subsection (5) below, for social, cultural or charitable purposes.

(4) The dividend payable on any shares of a credit union shall not exceed a rate of 8 per cent. per annum or such other rate as may from time to time be specified by order made by the chief registrar with the consent of the Treasury.

(5) No part of the amount available for distribution in respect of any year of account shall be applied by a credit union for the purposes mentioned in subsection (3) (*c*) above unless a dividend of not less than 3 per cent. per annum is paid for that year on all paid-up shares of the credit union; and the total sum applied for those purposes out of the amount available for distribution in respect of any year of account shall not exceed 10 per cent. of that amount.

(6) Where in accordance with subsection (3) above a credit union in general meeting determines that an amount shall be applied in any of the ways mentioned in paragraphs (*a*) to (*c*) of that subsection, that amount may, unless the determination is that it be distributed or expended forthwith, be so applied by being appropriated to a fund to be distributed or expended from time to time or at some future date; and where in accordance with that subsection a credit union in general meeting determines that an amount shall be applied for a purpose falling within paragraph (*c*) of that subsection, that amount may, unless the determination is that it be expended in some specific manner, be expended for that purpose at the discretion of the committee.

(7) Nothing in this section applies to income arising from, or to expenses incurred by a credit union in operating, such a trust fund as is referred to in section 9 (2) above.

DEFINITIONS

" charitable ": s. 31 (1).
" chief registrar ": 1965 Act, s. 73 (1) (*a*).
" committee ": 1965 Act, s. 74.
" credit union ": ss. 1 (1), 31 (1).
" meeting ": 1965 Act, s. 74.
" Treasury ": Interpretation Act 1978, s. 5 and Sched. 1.
" year of account ": Friendly and Industrial and Provident Societies Act 1968, s. 21 (1).

GENERAL NOTE

In computing its annual profit, a credit union must comply with subs. (1). The annual profit must be ascertained before (and must therefore be inclusive of) any dividend to be paid and must take account of the items stated. Further, for the avoidance of doubt, deposits made under s. 9 (1) and kept separately in accordance with s. 9 (2), are stated to be outside the provisions of s. 14: subs. (7).

Subs. (2)

As a first call on the profit, a credit union must build up and then maintain a general reserve in accordance with subs. (2). But when the general reserve stands at between 10 and 20 per cent. of the total assets, a discretion is given to the credit union to make transfers between the general reserve and the revenue account: subs. (2) (*c*). For credit unions to be financially sound and stable, an adequate reserve is obviously desirable, but the tying up of the profits in accordance with subs. (2), leaving correspondingly less for dividends and rebates of interest (see subs. (3)) will weigh against a new credit union trying to attract members in its initial years.

Subss. (3)–(6)

Having complied with subs. (2) as to its general reserve, a credit union is then obliged to apply at least 90 per cent. of the profits remaining, " *the amount available for distribution* " (which may be less or greater than the annual profit, depending on whether amounts have been transferred to or from the general reserve) in one or more of the ways listed in subs. (3) (*a*), (*b*) and (*c*). It is for the general meeting (see also Sched. 1, para. 5) to decide how to allocate the remaining profit, within the limits set by subs. (3).

A dividend (or various dividends on different classes of shares) may be paid on *paid-up* shares, but such dividend (or dividends) must not exceed that rate provided for in subs. (4): subs. (3) (*a*). Further, members (but not other creditors, for example, other credit unions) may be given a rebate in accordance with subs. (3) (*b*).

Finally, up to 10 per cent. of *the amount available for distribution* (not 10 per cent of the total annual profit calculated in accordance with subs. (1) nor 10 per cent. of the amount actually being distributed under subs. (3)) may be applied for " social, cultural or charitable purposes " as long as a dividend of at least 3 per cent. is paid on all paid-up shares: subs. (3) (c). By subs. (6), the general meeting having allocated a sum for item (*c*) may leave the precise details of how it is to be spent to the committee.

Although " charitable " has a distinct legal meaning (and note the meaning in English law is applied in Scotland for the purposes of this Act by virtue of s. 31 (1)), " social, cultural " are imprecise words of much wider import. It seems, however, that the expenditure must still be *intra vires* the credit union's objects (listed in s. 1 (3)) and therefore for the members' benefit. This creates problems. A charitable purpose must generally be for the " public benefit " (see *Dingle* v. *Turner* [1972] A.C. 601) and it is doubtful if the members of a credit union would normally be considered a sufficient section of the public to fulfil the public benefit requirement. Therefore, in so far as the Act clearly contemplates that expenditure for a charitable purpose may be *intra vires* a credit union's objects, it is submitted that expenditure may still be *intra vires* if it benefits a class wider than the members themselves. However, admittedly this view is somewhat difficult to reconcile with the fact that most such expenditure would only come within object (*c*) in s. 1 (3) and that talks of members' " mutual benefit." It is further submitted that not all the members need benefit. It is sufficient if only some of them do—just as only some members will benefit from an application of funds under subs. (3) (*a*) or (*b*). Finally it is submitted that " benefit " should be given a wide interpretation so that taking satisfaction from the fact that contributions have been made to, for example, charitable objects of special interest but no direct benefit to some members is sufficient (see, in the context of the power of advancement, a similar wide interpretation of " benefit " in *Re Clore* [1966] 1 W.L.R. 955).

Therefore it seems that the committee has a very wide discretion as to the application of funds under subs. (3) (*c*), but the fact that a 3 per cent. dividend has priority and that only a small proportion of the amount available for distribution can be so spent, together with the powers of the general meeting to determine itself the destination of the funds, will in practice limit the importance of this discretion.

Although a credit union must allocate at least 90 per cent. of *the amount available* for distribution in accordance with subs. (3), it need not immediately pay over the allocation sums. It may (subject to a direction of the general meeting to the contrary) pay the allocated sums into a fund and carry them forward from year to year. This gives a credit union a measure of flexibility to accumulate profits.

For a discussion of the meaning of " member " see note to s. 5.

For " by order " in subs. (4), see s. 29.

Contravention of section

As to the criminal consequences for breach of this section and the powers of the relevant registrars on such a breach, see the provisions listed in the note to s. 5 under the heading " *Contravention of section.*"

Insurance and other arrangements

Insurance against fraud or other dishonesty

15.—(1) A society shall not be registered as a credit union unless the appropriate registrar is satisfied that on registration there will be in force in relation to that society a policy of insurance complying with the requirements of this section; and a credit union shall at all times maintain in force such a policy and if it fails to do so shall be guilty of an offence and liable on summary conviction to a fine not exceeding £200.

(2) In order to comply with this section, a policy of insurance—

(*a*) subject to such exceptions as may be prescribed, must insure the credit union in respect of every description of loss suffered or liability incurred by reason of the fraud or other dishonesty of any of its officers or employees;

(b) must so insure the credit union up to a limit of not less than £20,000 (or such other figure as may be prescribed) in respect of any one claim, except that the liability of the insurer may be restricted to an amount not less than £100,000 (or such other figure as may be prescribed) in respect of the total of the claims made in any one year;

(c) must not, except with the consent in writing of the chief registrar, provide in relation to any claim for any amount greater than one per cent. of the limit referred to in paragraph (b) above to be met by the credit union; and

(d) must be issued by a person who is permitted under the Insurance Companies Act 1974 or the corresponding provision for the time being in force in Northern Ireland to carry on in Great Britain or Northern Ireland insurance business of a relevant class or who has corresponding permission under the law of another member State.

(3) In paragraphs (a) and (b) of subsection (2) above "prescribed" means prescribed by regulations made by the chief registrar with the consent of the Treasury.

(4) Regulations made by virtue of paragraph (b) of that subsection may provide for different figures in relation to different descriptions of credit union, whether by reference to the amount of the assets of the credit union or to such other factors as appear to the chief registrar to be appropriate; and if such regulations do so provide the reference in paragraph (c) of that subsection to the limit referred to in the said paragraph (b) shall be construed as a reference to the limit applicable to the credit union in question.

DEFINITIONS

"appropriate registrar": 1965 Act, s. 73 (1) (c).
"chief registrar": 1965 Act, s. 73 (1) (a).
"credit union": ss. 1 (1), 31 (1).
"officer": 1965 Act, s. 74 as amended by Friendly and Industrial and Provident Societies Act 1968, s. 20 (1) (a) and Sched. 1, para. 11.
"Treasury": Interpretation Act 1978, s. 5 and Sched. 1.

GENERAL NOTE

This section is self-explanatory. First, it makes it a condition of registration of a credit union that on registration a policy of insurance complying with this section will be in force. Secondly, it obliges a credit union to maintain such a policy "at all times."

By s. 33 (2) and (3), this section may be brought into force later than the rest of the Act, to enable appropriate policies to be negotiated.

See also s. 16 (guarantee funds).

Contravention of section

Breach of this section incurs the criminal penalty in subs. (1). See further the provisions of the 1965 Act and this Act listed in the note to s. 8 under the heading "*Contravention of section.*"

The powers of the relevant registrars on breach are those listed in the note to s. 5 under the heading "*Contravention of section.*"

Guarantee funds

16.—(1) Subject to the provisions of this section, a credit union, or any two or more credit unions, may enter into arrangements with a person carrying on the business of insurance for the purpose of making funds available to meet losses incurred by members of a credit union which is a party to the arrangements; and any two or more credit unions may enter into any other kind of arrangements for that purpose.

(2) Subject to subsection (3) below, a credit union shall have power to make contributions under arrangements made in accordance with subsection (1) above, and such arrangements may in particular provide for the vesting of a fund in trustees appointed under the arrangements.

(3) Arrangements under subsection (1) above shall not come into force and no contribution shall be made thereunder by a credit union, until they have been approved by the appropriate registrar; and the appropriate registrar shall not approve any such arrangements unless they provide that any variation of their terms shall also require his approval.

DEFINITIONS

" appropriate registrar ": 1965 Act, s. 73 (1) (*c*).
" credit union ": ss. 1 (1) and 31 (1).
" person ": Interpretation Act 1978, s. 5 and Sched. 1.

GENERAL NOTE

This section enables (but does not, in contrast to s. 15, oblige) a credit union to make insurance arrangements to protect its members, provided those arrangements are approved by the appropriate registrar in accordance with subs. (3).

For a discussion of the meaning of " member " see note to s. 5.

Contravention of section

For the criminal penalties and powers of the relevant registrars on breach of this section see the note to s. 5 under the heading " *Contravention of section.*"

Powers of registrar

Power to require information

17.—(1) In relation to a credit union, the powers of the appropriate registrar under subsection (1) of section 48 of the 1965 Act to require the production of books, accounts and other documents and the furnishing of information in connection with the exercise of certain of his powers under that Act—

(*a*) shall apply also in connection with the exercise of his functions under this Act; and

(*b*) shall extend to the chief registrar in connection with the exercise of his functions under this Act;

and subsections (2) and (3) of section 48 of the 1965 Act (penalties and defraying expenses) shall apply accordingly.

(2) Without prejudice to section 39 of the 1965 Act (duty to furnish annual returns), the appropriate registrar may from time to time by notice in writing served on a credit union require it to furnish, within such period as may be specified in the notice, a financial statement or periodic financial statements in such form and containing such information as may be so specified.

(3) If a credit union fails without reasonable excuse to comply with a notice under subsection (2) above it shall be guilty of an offence and liable on summary conviction to a fine not exceeding £200.

DEFINITIONS

" appropriate registrar ": 1965 Act, s. 73 (1) (*c*).
" chief registrar ": 1965 Act, s. 73 (1) (*a*).
" credit union ": ss. 1 (1), 31 (1).
" the 1965 Act ": s. 31 (1).

GENERAL NOTE

The appropriate registrar already has powers to order, on the application of 10 members of the society, an inspection of the society's books under s. 47 of the 1965 Act. Further, he may by written notice require production of certain information under s. 48 of the 1965 Act. Subs. (1) applies and modifies this latter power in relation to credit unions. Failure to comply with such a request incurs the criminal penalty under s. 48 (2) of the 1965 Act.

By s. 39 of the 1965 Act as amended by the Friendly and Industrial and Provident Societies Act 1968, all registered societies are obliged to furnish annual returns to the appropriate registrar. Subs. (2) gives the appropriate registrar the additional power in relation to credit unions to require by written notice further financial statements. Failure to comply with such a request incurs the criminal penalty in subs. (3) (and see also the provisions of the 1965 Act and this Act listed in the note to s. 8 under the heading *"Contravention of section"*).

See also, 1965 Act, ss. 45 (1) (restrictions on inspection of books) and 46 (inspection of books by members).

The exercise of the powers under this section may reveal factors which would induce the relevant registrars to use their powers to suspend the operations of the credit union under s. 19 of this Act or to apply to wind up the credit union under s. 20 of this Act or to suspend or cancel the registration of the credit union under ss. 17 and 16 of the 1965 Act (as modified in relation to credit unions by this Act).

Power to appoint inspector and call meeting

18.—(1) Without prejudice to section 49 of the 1965 Act (appointment of inspector or calling of special meeting upon application of members of registered society), where the chief registrar is of the opinion that an investigation should be held into the affairs of a credit union or that the affairs of the credit union call for consideration by a meeting of the members, he may, with the consent of the Treasury, appoint an inspector to investigate and report on the affairs of the credit union or may call a special meeting of the credit union, or may (either on the same or on different occasions) both appoint such an inspector and call such a meeting.

(2) All expenses of and incidental to an investigation or meeting held pursuant to subsection (1) above shall be defrayed out of the funds of the credit union, or by the members or officers or former members or officers of the credit union in such proportions as the chief registrar shall direct.

(3) Subsections (5) and (6) of the said section 49 (power to prescribe time and place of meeting, procedure, power to require evidence to be given, etc.) shall apply in relation to an inspector appointed or meeting called in accordance with this section.

DEFINITIONS

"chief registrar": 1965 Act, s. 73 (1) (*a*).

"credit union": ss. 1 (1), 31 (1).

"meeting": 1965 Act, s. 74.

"officer": 1965 Act, s. 74 as amended by the Friendly and Industrial and Provident Societies Act 1968, s. 20 (1) (*a*) and Sched. 1, para. 11.

"the 1965 Act": s. 31 (1).

"Treasury": Interpretation Act 1978, s. 5 and Sched. 1.

GENERAL NOTE

By s. 49 of the 1965 Act, the Chief Registrar has the power, with the consent of the Treasury, upon the application of one-tenth of the membership (or 100 members if the membership is in excess of 1,000) to order an inspection or call a special meeting of a registered society. In relation to credit unions, s. 18 gives the Chief Registrar (again with the consent of the Treasury) the power to order an inspection and/or call a special meeting on his own initiative. This could be the preliminary step to the Chief Registrar invoking his powers under s. 19 (suspension of the operations of a credit union) or to the appropriate registrar invoking his powers under s. 20 (2) (winding up), or under s. 16 of the 1965 Act as modified in relation to credit unions by this Act (cancellation of registration), or under s. 17 of the 1965 Act (suspension of registration).

For a discussion of the meaning of "member," see note to s. 5.

Power to suspend operations of credit union

19.—(1) If, with respect to any credit union, the chief registrar considers it expedient to do so having regard to the interests of all the members of the credit union or in the interests of potential members of the credit union, he may, with the consent of the Treasury, give a direction prohibiting the credit union to such extent and subject to such conditions as may be specified in the direction from carrying on any one or more of the following activities, that is to say,—

(*a*) borrowing money;

(*b*) accepting a payment representing the whole or any part of an amount due by way of subscription for a share in the credit union other than a payment which fell due before the making of the order;

(*c*) lending money; and

(*d*) repaying share capital;

and Schedule 2 to this Act shall have effect in relation to the giving of a direction under this section.

(2) Nothing in any direction given under this section shall make it unlawful for a credit union to borrow from an authorised bank if the credit union has obtained the consent in writing of the chief registrar.

(3) For the purposes of this section and of any direction given under it, if any indebtedness of a member to a credit union is set off to any extent against the share capital credited to him, then, to that extent, the setting off shall be treated as a repayment of that share capital.

(4) A direction given under this section may be revoked by the chief registrar with the consent of the Treasury and notice of the revocation shall be published in the same manner as notice of the giving of the direction.

(5) Where a direction under this section is revoked, any obligation of any person to make a payment to the credit union which fell due at a time when the credit union was prohibited by the direction from accepting it shall be suspended for a period equal to the period for which the prohibition was in force.

(6) Subject to subsection (5) above, any obligation to make to a credit union a payment which the credit union is prohibited from accepting by a direction under this section shall be wholly rescinded.

(7) If a credit union contravenes a direction under this section it shall be guilty of an offence and liable on conviction on indictment or on summary conviction to a fine which on summary conviction shall not exceed the statutory maximum.

DEFINITIONS

"authorised bank": s. 31 (1).
"chief registrar": 1965 Act, s. 73 (1) (*a*).
"credit union": ss. 1 (1), 31 (1).
"statutory maximum": s. 31 (1).
"Treasury": Interpretation Act 1978, s. 5 and Sched. 1.

GENERAL NOTE

Under the 1965 Act, the Chief Registrar has no power to suspend the operations of a registered society. Thus the power conferred on him by this section is new and confined to credit unions. (But the Chief Registrar has a similar power in relation to friendly societies under the Friendly Societies Act 1974, s. 88 and the Registrar of Building Societies has a similar power in relation to building societies under the Building Societies Act 1962, s. 48.) The power is exercisable by the giving of a direction, with the consent of the Treasury, in accordance with Sched. 2. The right of appeal against certain decisions of the appropriate registrar given by the 1965 Act, s. 18, does not extend to the decision of the Chief Registrar to give such a direction. But the decision could be challenged by certiorari (see

R. v. *Registrar of Building Societies, ex p. a Building Society* [1960] 1 W.L.R. 669, C.A.).

The possible content of the direction is limited by subs. (1). Not all the activities of a credit union may be suspended but only those which fall within (*a*)–(*d*). It is doubtful if the receipt of deposits under s. 9 (1) would be "*borrowing*" within (*a*). "*Lending money*" ((*c*)) would clearly cover loans to members (under s. 11) and to other credit unions (see s. 13 (5) (*a*)) but it is doubtful if this phrase is intended to cover investment by way of loan under s. 13 or the paying of funds into a bank account under s. 13 (2). "*Repaying share capital*" ((*d*)) is given an extended meaning by subs. (3) (see the 1965 Act, s. 22 (2) which enables a society to so set-off any sum credited to a member against any indebtedness). Subs. (3) was rendered necessary by the view expressed by Greene M.R. in *Lloyd* v. *Francis* [1937] 4 All E.R. 489, C.A. that set-off within the predecessor of s. 22 (2) of the 1965 Act was a different process from the withdrawal of shares. But the application of profits under s. 14 (see especially, s. 14 (3)) seemingly cannot be prohibited.

Contravention of direction

As for the criminal sanction for breach of a direction, see subs. (7) and the provisions of the 1965 Act and this Act listed in the note to s. 8 under the heading "*Contravention of sections.*" Further, note the powers of the relevant registrars listed in the note to s. 5 under the heading "*Contravention of section,*" and see especially s. 20 (2) (*b*).

Cancellation or suspension of registration and petition for winding up

20.—(1) In subsection (1) of section 16 of the 1965 Act (grounds for cancellation of registration) as it applies to credit unions—

(*a*) in paragraph (*c*) (i) the reference to violation of any of the provisions of the 1965 Act shall be construed as including a reference to violation of any of the provisions of this Act; and

(*b*) in paragraph (*c*) (ii) the reference to the fact that neither of the conditions in section 1 (2) of that Act is fulfilled shall be construed as a reference to the fact that there is no longer a common bond between the members of a credit union;

and section 17 (1) of that Act (suspension of registration on grounds which would justify cancellation) and section 18 of that Act (appeals) shall apply accordingly.

(2) A petition for the winding up of a credit union may be presented to the court by the appropriate registrar if it appears to him that—

(*a*) the credit union is unable to pay sums due and payable to its members, or is able to pay such sums only by obtaining further subscriptions for shares or by defaulting in its obligations to creditors; or

(*b*) there has been, in relation to that credit union, a failure to comply with any provision of, or of any direction given under, this Act or the Industrial and Provident Societies Acts 1965 to 1978; or

(*c*) there is no longer a common bond between the members of the credit union;

or in any other case where it appears to him that the winding up of the credit union is in the public interest or is just and equitable having regard to the interests of all the members of the credit union.

DEFINITIONS

"appropriate registrar": 1965 Act, s. 73 (1) (*c*).
"credit union": ss. 1 (1), 31 (1).
"the 1965 Act": s. 31 (1).

GENERAL NOTE

The appropriate registrar has powers under ss. 16 and 17 of the 1965 Act to respectively cancel and suspend the registration of a society on a variety of grounds.

The society may appeal against such a decision (1965 Act, s. 18). Subs. (1) modifies these sections in their application to credit unions (and see s. 6 (1) (*b*)). As to restrictions on the cancellation of the registration of a society, see 1965 Act, s. 59.

Subs. (2) empowers the appropriate registrar to petition for the dissolution of a credit union on the variety of grounds therein set out. The last ground, that the winding up is "just and equitable having regard to the interests of all the members" makes it clear that the conflicting interests of all the different categories of members (for example, those who are net creditors and those who are net debtors of the credit union) must be taken into account.

A credit union may also be dissolved by virtue of the 1965 Act, s. 55, and see *ibid.* ss. 57 (liability of members in winding up under s. 55 (*a*)), 58 (instrument of dissolution in relation to s. 55 (*b*)), and 59 (restrictions on dissolution in accordance with s. 55).

For a discussion of the meaning of "member" see the note to s. 5 and of the meaning of "common bond" see the note to s. 1 under heading "(v)").

Amalgamations, transfers of engagements and conversions

Amalgamations and transfers of engagements

21.—(1) In their application to credit unions, sections 50 and 51 of the 1965 Act (amalgamations of registered societies and transfers of engagements between them) shall have effect subject to the provisions of subsections (2) and (3) of this section.

(2) A credit union shall not amalgamate with or transfer its engagements to or accept a transfer of engagements from any registered society which is not a credit union.

(3) The appropriate registrar shall not register a special resolution under section 50 or section 51 of the 1965 Act if in his opinion—

(*a*) the proposed amalgamation or transfer of engagements would result in a contravention of any provision of this Act or of the Industrial and Provident Societies Acts 1965 to 1978; or

(*b*) there would be no common bond between the members of the proposed amalgamated credit union or, as the case may be, the credit union which proposes to accept the transfer of engagements.

(4) In this Act the expression "non-qualifying member", in relation to an amalgamated credit union or a credit union which has accepted a transfer of engagements, includes a person who does not fulfil the qualifications for admission to membership of that credit union but became a member of it by virtue of the amalgamation or transfer of engagements, having been immediately before the amalgamation or transfer a non-qualifying member of one of the amalgamating credit unions or, as the case may be, the credit union from which the transfer of engagements was made.

DEFINITIONS

"appropriate registrar": 1965 Act, s. 73 (1) (*c*).
"credit union": ss. 1 (1), 31 (1).
"registered society": 1965 Act, s. 74.
"the 1965 Act": s. 31 (1).

GENERAL NOTE

As well as ss. 50 and 51 of the 1965 Act, see also ss. 54 (saving for rights of creditors on an amalgamation or transfer) and 59 (restriction on transfer of society's engagements under s. 51).

For a discussion of the meaning of "member," see the note to s. 5, and of the meaning of "common bond," see the note to s. 1 under heading "(v)."

For the form of application for registration of a special resolution pursuant to ss. 50 and 51 of the 1965 Act and for form of relevant declarations, see the

Industrial and Provident Societies Regulations 1965 (S.I. 1965 No. 1995), regs. 2 (1), 6, 7, 9 and Sched. 1, Forms, T, U, V, W and Y. For fees, see *ibid.* Sched. 2 (as substituted by S.I. 1977 No. 2022).

No conversion of credit union into company, etc.

22. Section 52 of the 1965 Act (conversion of registered society into company or amalgamation with, or transfer of engagements from registered society to, company) shall not apply to credit unions.

Definitions
"credit union": ss. 1 (1), 31 (1).
"registered society": 1965 Act, s. 74.
"the 1965 Act": s. 31 (1).

General Note
Although a credit union cannot by special resolution under s. 52 of the 1965 Act convert itself into or amalgamate with or transfer its engagements to a company registered under the Companies Acts, there is nothing to prevent it dissolving itself under s. 55 of the 1965 Act and then registering and functioning under the Companies Acts. However, in practice, the Industrial and Provident legislation (as extended to and modified in relation to credit unions by this Act) is more appropriate to those societies who wish to function as credit unions. Thus, for example, a company registered under the Companies Acts will not be able to use the name "credit union" (see s. 3 (2) and the note thereto) nor (unless the principle of mutuality applies) claim the tax advantages given by s. 25.

Conversion of company into credit union

23.—(1) In its application to the conversion of a company into a credit union, section 53 of the 1965 Act (conversion of company into registered society) shall have effect subject to the provisions of this section.

(2) In subsection (1) of that section the words from "and for this purpose" to the end (which refer to the limitation on shareholdings applicable to societies other than credit unions) shall be omitted.

(3) A company shall not be registered as a credit union in accordance with that section unless the appropriate registrar is satisfied—

(*a*) that either there are no outstanding deposits by members with the company or that, in the case of every such outstanding deposit, the member concerned has consented in writing to the deposit being converted into an equivalent amount of shares in the credit union immediately upon the company being registered as a credit union;

(*b*) that in no case does the nominal value of the company's shares held by any member, together with the amount of any deposit of his which is to be converted as mentioned in paragraph (*a*) above, exceed the maximum shareholding for the time being permitted by section 5 (3) above in the case of a member of a credit union; and

(*c*) that, except in a case where an exemption has been granted to the company under subsection (5) of section 6 above, the number of its members does not exceed the maximum for the time being provided for in subsection (2) of that section in relation to a credit union.

Definitions
"appropriate registrar": 1965 Act, s. 73 (1) (*c*).
"credit union": ss. 1 (1), 31 (1).
"registered society": 1965 Act, s. 74.
"the 1965 Act": s. 31 (1).

GENERAL NOTE

This section ensures, *inter alia,* that when a company registered under the Companies Acts is converted into a credit union under s. 53 of the 1965 Act, the credit union does not contravene the requirements of this Act as to the maximum shareholding or maximum membership.

General and miscellaneous

Modifications of requirements as to audit of accounts

24.—(1) A credit union may display at its registered office, but only at that office, an interim revenue account or balance sheet which has not been audited, provided that—

(*a*) the latest audited revenue account and balance sheet are displayed side by side with the interim revenue account or balance sheet; and

(*b*) the interim revenue account or balance sheet so displayed is marked in clearly legible characters and in a prominent position with the words " UNAUDITED REVENUE ACCOUNT " or, as the case may be, " UNAUDITED BALANCE SHEET ".

(2) Paragraphs (*a*) and (*b*) of subsection (5) of section 3 of the Friendly and Industrial and Provident Societies Act 1968 (requirements as to audit) shall not apply in relation to any such interim revenue account or balance sheet as is referred to in subsection (1) above and section 39 (1) of the 1965 Act (annual returns) shall not apply to any such interim balance sheet.

DEFINITIONS

" credit union ": ss. 1 (1), 31 (1).
" registered office ": 1965 Act, s. 74.
" the 1965 Act ": s. 31 (1).

GENERAL NOTE

For the accounts of societies registered under the 1965 Act, see generally the Friendly and Industrial and Provident Societies Act 1968, which repeals and replaces ss. 37 and 38 of the 1965 Act and amends s. 39 thereof. See also the 1965 Act, s. 40 (display of latest balance-sheet at registered office). But note subs. (2).

Contravention of section

If the unaudited account does not comply with subs. (1), the criminal penalty in s. 61 of the 1965 Act (as amended by the Criminal Justice Act 1967, s. 92 (1) and Sched. 3, Pt. I) may be incurred. See also the provisions of the 1965 Act and this Act listed in the note to s. 8 under the heading " *Contravention of section.*" Further, theoretically, the relevant registrars could exercise those powers listed in the note to s. 5 under the heading " *Contravention of section.*"

Taxation

25.—(1) After section 340 of the Income and Corporation Taxes Act 1970 there shall be inserted the following section—

" **Credit Unions**

340A.—(1) Subject to subsection (2) below, in computing for the purposes of corporation tax the income of a credit union for any accounting period—

(*a*) neither the activity of the credit union in making loans to its members nor in placing on deposit or otherwise investing from time to time its surplus funds shall be regarded as the carrying on of a trade or part of a trade; and (*b*) interest received by the credit union on loans made by it to its members shall not be chargeable to tax under Case III of Schedule D or otherwise.

(2) Paragraph (*b*) of subsection (1) above shall not apply to an accounting period of a credit union for which the credit union is obliged to make a return under section 340 (5) of this Act and has not done so within three months after the end of that accounting period or such longer period as the inspector shall allow.

(3) No share interest, loan interest or annuity or other annual payment paid or payable by a credit union in any accounting period shall be deductible in computing for the purposes of corporation tax the income of the credit union for that period from any trade carried on by it or be treated for those purposes as a charge on income.

(4) A credit union shall not be regarded as an investment company for the purposes of section 304 or section 306 of this Act (management expenses and capital allowances).

(5) In the case of a credit union registered under the Industrial and Provident Societies Act (Northern Ireland) 1969 before the passing of the Credit Unions Act 1979, the preceding provisions of this section shall apply to the accounting period beginning on or after 1st October 1979.

(6) For the year 1978–79 and the next six following years of assessment there shall be disregarded for all purposes of the Income Tax Acts any share interest paid to a member by a credit union and a credit union shall not be obliged under section 340 (5) of this Act to make a return in respect of any such payment.

(7) In this section—

" credit union " means a society registered as a credit union under the Industrial and Provident Societies Act 1965 or the Industrial and Provident Societies Act (Northern Ireland) 1969;

" share interest " and " loan interest " have the same meaning as in section 340 of this Act;

" surplus funds ", in relation to a credit union, means funds not immediately required for its purposes;

and references to the payment of share interest or loan interest include references to the crediting of such interest.".

(2) In section 340 of the Income and Corporation Taxes Act 1970 (industrial and provident societies, etc.)—

(*a*) in subsection (1) (share and loan interest to be deductible or constitute a charge on income) after the words " subject to subsection (6) below " there shall be inserted the words " and to section 340A (3) of this Act "; and

(*b*) at the beginning of subsection (3) (share and loan interest to be chargeable under Case III of Schedule D) and at the beginning of subsection (5) (duty to make return of payments made without deduction of tax) there shall be inserted the words " Subject to section 340A (6) of this Act.".

General Note

"*Share interest*" is defined in s. 340 of the Income and Corporation Taxes Act 1970 as meaning "any interest, dividend, bonus or other sum payable to a shareholder of the society by reference to the amount of his holding in the share capital of the society." In the case of credit unions, it includes any dividend paid by virtue of s. 14 (3) (*a*) but not any rebate of interest under s. 14 (3) (*b*) as such a rebate is calculated by reference to the interest paid or due from a member on his loan, not by reference to the amount of his shareholding.

"*Loan interest*" is defined in s. 340 of the Income and Corporation Taxes Act 1970 as meaning "any interest payable by the society in respect of any mortgage, loan, loan stock or deposit." In the case of credit unions, it includes interest paid on loans taken under s. 10.

In addition to the Income and Corporation Taxes Act 1970 s. 340, for the taxation of industrial and provident societies in general, see *ibid.* s. 345 and the Finance Act 1972, s. 96 (special rate of corporation tax).

The effect of the addition of this new subsection to s. 340 of the Income and Corporation Taxes Act 1970 is as follows.

First, any internal profits made by credit unions from dealings with their members are exempted from corporation tax: subs. (1) (*a*) of s. 340A. Arguably the principle of mutuality would in any event have rendered credit unions so exempt, but as the Inland Revenue takes the view that credit unions are not mutually trading (see H.C. Vol. 962, cols. 814, 845; Standing Committee A, col. 116) this provision was inserted to put the existence of the exemption beyond doubt. As a corollary, a credit union cannot claim investment company status for the purposes of management expenses and capital allowances: subs. (4) of s. 340A. In any event, subs. (1) (*a*) of s. 340A, in stating that credit unions are not trading, prevents expenses being deducted or set off against investment income.

Secondly, interest on loans to members is also not taxable (subs. (1) (*b*) of s. 340A), provided a return is made by the credit union as provided in subs. (2) of s. 340A.

Thirdly, there is no exemption as regards a credit union's outside investment income which is consequently liable to corporation tax at the special rate applicable to industrial and provident societies (see above—at present 40 per cent.). Further, subss. (1) (*a*) and (4) of s. 340A prevent a credit union claiming relief for management expenses incurred in making such investments against this investment income, although in practice such expenses would be very small. Subs. (5) of s. 340A in effect ensures that Northern Irish credit unions will cease to pay 20 per cent. corporation tax on outside investment income and will start to pay the same rate as credit unions in Great Britain. Northern Irish credit unions already enjoy the other exemptions discussed above.

Fourthly, until and including the year of account 1984–85 no tax will be charged on dividends paid to members: subs. (6) of s. 340A. (By a concession, members of Northern Irish credit unions already enjoy this privilege, but this subsection now puts this concession on a statutory basis as far as they are concerned.) Thus for six years credit unions will enjoy a privilege not enjoyed by shareholders in other industrial and provident societies, building societies or other savings institutions. However, it is probable that eventually the tax position of small savers in all institutions, including credit unions, will become the same.

Subs. (3) of s. 340A in effect renders s. 340 (1) inapplicable to credit unions.

Prohibition on subsidiaries

26. A credit union shall not have any subsidiary within the meaning of section 15 of the Friendly and Industrial and Provident Societies Act 1968.

DEFINITION

"credit union": ss. 1 (1), 31 (1).

GENERAL NOTE

For the criminal consequences and powers of the relevant registrars on breach of this section, see the provisions listed in the note to s. 5 under the heading "*Contravention of section.*"

Prohibition on undischarged bankrupts and other persons

27. A person who is an undischarged bankrupt or who has been convicted on indictment of any offence involving fraud or dishonesty shall not—

(*a*) sign an application form for registration of a credit union; or

(*b*) act as a member of the committee of a credit union; or

(c) directly or indirectly take part in or be concerned in the management of a credit union; or

(d) permit his name to be put forward for election or appointment to any office in a credit union;

and where a person holding any office in a credit union becomes ineligible by virtue of this section to hold that office, he shall forthwith cease to hold that office.

DEFINITIONS

"committee": 1965 Act, s. 74.

"credit union": ss. 1 (1), 31 (1).

"person": Interpretation Act 1978, s. 5 and Sched. 1.

GENERAL NOTE

As to "*application form for registration of a credit union*" in para. (a), see the 1965 Act, s. 2 (1) (b).

There is, of course, nothing to prevent an undischarged bankrupt or one who has been convicted on indictment of any offence involving fraud or dishonesty from merely being a member of a credit union as long as he does not do anything within paras. (a)—(d).

The rehabilitation provisions of the Rehabilitation of Offenders Act 1974 will not cause this disqualification to be removed once a person's conviction is "spent" under that Act (see s. 7 (1) (d) thereof).

Contravention of section

The criminal consequences and the powers of the relevant registrars on breach of this section are those listed in the note to s. 5 under the heading "*Contravention of section.*"

Provisions as to offences

28.—(1) Subject to subsections (2) and (3) below, in sections 61 to 66 and section 68 of the 1965 Act (general provisions as to offences by registered societies, their officers and others) as they apply to credit unions references to the 1965 Act shall include references to this Act.

(2) Section 63 of the 1965 Act (continuing act or default to constitute a new offence every week) shall not apply to an offence under section 12 (5) above.

(3) Without prejudice to the operation of subsection (1) above in relation to offences under the 1965 Act committed by or in relation to a credit union, section 66 (2) of that Act (extension of time limit for summary prosecutions in certain cases) shall not apply to proceedings for an offence under this Act.

(4) Where under section 62 of the 1965 Act (offences by registered societies to be also offences by officers, etc.) as it applies by virtue of subsection (1) above an individual is convicted on indictment of an offence under this Act, he shall be liable not only to a fine but, in the alternative or in addition, to imprisonment for a term not exceeding two years.

(5) Where an offence under this Act which has been committed by a body corporate other than a registered society is proved to have been committed with the consent or connivance of, or to be attributable to any neglect on the part of, any director, manager, secretary or similar officer of the body corporate, or any person who was purporting to act in any such capacity, he as well as the body corporate shall be guilty of that offence and shall be liable to be proceeded against and published accordingly.

(6) In any proceedings for an offence under this Act it shall be a defence for the person charged to prove that he took all reasonable precautions and exercised all due diligence to avoid the commission of such an offence by himself or any person under his control.

DEFINITIONS

"credit union": ss. 1 (1), 31 (1).

"officer": 1965 Act, s. 74, as amended by Friendly and Industrial and Provident Societies Act 1968, s. 20 (1) (*a*) and Sched. 1, para. 11.

"person": Interpretation Act 1978, s. 5 and Sched. 1.

"registered society": 1965 Act, s. 74.

"the 1965 Act": s. 31 (1).

GENERAL NOTE

Subs. (1)

This subsection extends the general provisions of the 1965 Act as to criminal sanctions for breach of the 1965 Act to breaches of this Act, subject to the limitation in subs. (3) and the additional penalty in subs. (4).

Subs. (5)

This subsection is in the standard form for imposing personal liability on individuals for corporate crimes (see, for example, the almost identical wording in the Customs and Excise Act 1952, s. 305 (3); the Trade Descriptions Act 1968, s. 20; the Fair Trading Act 1972, s. 132; the Consumer Credit Act 1974, s. 169; the Health and Safety at Work etc. Act 1974, s. 37 (1); the Consumer Safety Act 1978, s. 7 (4) and the Banking Act 1979, s. 41 (1)). For the meaning of "*manager*" and "*other officer,*" see *Registrar of Restrictive Trading Agreements* v. *W. H. Smith Ltd.* [1969] 1 W.L.R. 1460 (a decision of the Restrictive Trade Practices Act 1956, s. 15 (3)). For "*consent or connivance of, or . . . neglect,*" see *Huckerby* v. *Elliot* [1970] 1 All E.R. 189, D.C. (a decision under the Customs and Excise Act 1952, s. 305 (3)).

Subs. (6)

Again, this subsection is similarly worded to the Trade Descriptions Act 1968, s. 24 (1) (*b*), the Fair Trading Act 1972, s. 25 (1) (*b*), the Consumer Credit Act 1974, s. 168 (1) (*b*), the Consumer Safety Act 1978, s. 2 (6), and the Banking Act 1979, s. 41 (3). For "*all reasonable precautions and . . . all due diligence,*" see *Naish* v. *Gore* [1971] 3 All E.R. 737 and *Tesco Supermarkets Ltd.* v. *Nattrass* [1972] A.C. 153 (both decisions on the Trade Descriptions Act).

Orders made by the chief registrar

29.—(1) Any power to make an order conferred on the chief registrar by any provision of this Act, except Schedule 3 to this Act, shall be exercisable by statutory instrument which shall be subject to annulment in pursuance of a resolution of either House of Parliament.

(2) The Statutory Instruments Act 1946 shall apply to orders made by the chief registrar in the exercise of any power to which subsection (1) above applies notwithstanding that he is not a Minister of the Crown.

DEFINITION

"chief registrar": 1965 Act, s. 73 (1) (*a*).

GENERAL NOTE

For the powers of the Chief Registrar to make orders (with the consent of the Treasury), see ss. 5 (4), 9 (4), 11 (7) (and (2), (4), (5) and (6)) and 13 (1), as well as Sched. 3, para. 1.

The orders made by virtue of these powers are subject to the negative resolution procedure. In contrast, an order altering the maximum possible membership of a credit union is subject to the less common affirmative resolution procedure, which of course gives more opportunity for debate (see s. 6 (3) and note thereto). This distinction was made in the Act because it was considered that the general alteration of the maximum size of credit unions would change the very nature of those institutions whereas the other alterations would be less fundamental.

For the power of the Treasury to make regulations for the purposes of the 1965 Act, see s. 71 thereof (as extended by the Industrial and Provident Societies Act 1967, s. 1 (4), and the Insurance Companies Act 1974, ss. 20 (3), 40 (7), and note s. 4 (4) of this Act). By virtue of s. 28 (4) of this Act, s. 71 of the 1965 Act also applies for the purposes of this Act.

Expenses and fees

30.—(1) There shall be paid out of moneys provided by Parliament any increase attributable to this Act in the administrative expenses of the chief registrar and any assistant registrar.

(2) Any fees received by the chief registrar or any assistant registrar by virtue of this Act shall be paid into the Consolidated Fund.

DEFINITIONS

"assistant registrar": 1965 Act, s. 73 (1) (*a*).
"chief registrar": 1965 Act, s. 73 (1) (*a*).

Interpretation, etc.

31.—(1) In this Act—

"authorised bank" means—

(*a*) a recognised bank or municipal bank within the meaning of the Banking Act 1979;

(*b*) a trustee savings bank within the meaning of section 3 of the Trustee Savings Banks Act 1969;

(*c*) the National Savings Bank; and

(*d*) the Post Office in the exercise of its powers to provide banking services;

and, so long as the powers conferred on the chief registrar by Schedule 3 to this Act remain exercisable, includes an institution for the time being designated by him in accordance with that Schedule;

"charitable", in the application of this Act to Scotland, shall be construed in the same way as in the Income Tax Acts;

"credit union", except in the expression "Northern Ireland credit union", means a society registered under the 1965 Act by virtue of section 1 above;

"the 1965 Act" means the Industrial and Provident Societies Act 1965;

"non-qualifying member", in relation to a credit union, has the meaning assigned to it by sections 5 (5) and 21 (4) above;

"relative", in relations to any person, means any of the following—

(*a*) his spouse;

(*b*) any lineal ancestor, lineal descendant, brother, sister, aunt, uncle, nephew, niece or first cousin of his or his spouse; and

(*c*) the spouse of any relative within paragraph (*b*) above;

and for the purpose of deducing any such relationship an illegitimate child or step-child shall be treated as a child born in wedlock;

"spouse" includes former spouse and reputed spouse; and

"statutory maximum", in relation to a fine on summary conviction, means—

(*a*) in England and Wales, the prescribed sum within the meaning of section 28 of the Criminal Law Act 1977; and

(*b*) in Scotland, the prescribed sum within the meaning of section 289B of the Criminal Procedure (Scotland) Act 1975;

(which in each case was at the passing of this Act £1,000).

(2) Section 67 and sections 70 to 74 of the 1965 Act (supplementary provisions as to recovery of costs, fees, regulations, documents, meaning of "chief registrar", etc. and general interpretation provisions) shall apply for the purposes of this Act as they apply for the purposes of that Act.

(3) In its application to credit unions the 1965 Act shall have effect subject to the provisions of this Act and with the omission of the following

provisions (which are replaced by, or are inconsistent with, provisions of this Act), that is to say sections 6, 12, 19, 21, 30 and 31.

DEFINITION

"chief registrar": 1965 Act, s. 73 (1) (*a*).

GENERAL NOTE

Subs. (1)

"*charitable.*" Generally, the meaning of charitable in Scottish law differs from that in English law, but subs. (1) ensures that the English meaning prevails in Scotland for the purposes of this Act (see s. 14 (3) (*c*)) as well as for the purposes of income tax (see *I.R.C.* v. *City of Glasgow Police Athletic Association* [1953] A.C. 380 at p. 403).

"*statutory maximum.*" See ss. 8 (4), 10 (6), 12 (5), 13 (6) and 19 (7).

Subss. (2) *and* (3)

See further "*Credit Unions and the Industrial and Provident Societies Acts* 1965–1978" in the note to this Act.

Northern Ireland

32.—(1) The Treasury may make reciprocal arrangements with the Department of Commerce for Northern Ireland or such other authority as may be specified for the purposes of this subsection by any Measure of the Northern Ireland Assembly with a view to securing that, on or after the commencement of this Act,—

(*a*) the law applicable in England and Wales to credit unions registered at the central office and the law applicable in Scotland to credit unions registered by the assistant registrar for Scotland may be applied, in such cases and subject to such modifications as may be provided in the arrangements, to Northern Ireland credit unions; and

(*b*) the law applicable in Northern Ireland to Northern Ireland credit unions may be applied, in such cases and subject to such modifications as may be provided in the arrangements, to credit unions registered at the central office or by the assistant registrar for Scotland;

and section 76 of the 1965 Act (which enables societies registered in Northern Ireland to be treated for certain purposes as if they were registered under that Act) shall not apply to Northern Ireland credit unions.

(2) The Treasury may by regulations under section 71 of the 1965 Act make provision for giving effect to any arrangements made under subsection (1) above, and such regulations may in particular—

(*a*) confer rights and obligations (appropriate to credit unions) under this Act and the Industrial and Provident Societies Acts 1965 to 1978 on Northern Ireland credit unions in such circumstances as may be specified in the regulations;

(*b*) confer functions on the chief registrar, the central office and the assistant registrar for Scotland in relation to Northern Ireland credit unions; and

(*c*) make such modifications of this Act, the Industrial and Provident Societies Acts 1965 to 1978 and the Government of Ireland (Companies, Societies, etc.) Order 1922 as appear to the Treasury to be expedient to give effect to the arrangements.

(3) In this section " Northern Ireland credit union " means a society registered as a credit union under the law of Northern Ireland.

(4) An Order in Council made under paragraph 1 (1) (*b*) of Schedule 1 to the Northern Ireland Act 1974 which contains a statement that its purposes correspond to those of this Act shall be subject to annulment

in pursuance of a resolution of either House of Parliament instead of the Order, or a draft of the Order, being subject to the procedure set out in paragraph 1 (4) or (5) of that Schedule.

DEFINITIONS

"assistant registrar": 1965 Act, s. 73 (1) (*a*).
"central office": 1965 Act, s. 73 (1) (*a*).
"credit union": ss. 1 (1), 31 (1).
"the 1965 Act": s. 31 (1).

GENERAL NOTE

In Northern Ireland, credit unions are governed by Pt. III of the Industrial and Provident Societies Act (Northern Ireland) 1969, and although the Credit Unions Act 1979 to a large extent draws on the precedent of the Northern Irish legislation, there are significant differences between the two bodies of legislation. In particular, they are administered by different registration authorities. Bearing in mind that Northern Irish credit unions may have members in Great Britain and that credit unions registered in Great Britain may have members in Northern Ireland, this section enables regulations to be made (following the making of such reciprocal arrangements as are described in subs. (1)) applying the law applicable to credit unions registered in Great Britain to Northern Irish credit unions and vice versa.

Short title, commencement and extent

33.—(1) This Act may be cited as the Credit Unions Act 1979.

(2) This section and section 32 above shall come into operation on the passing of this Act and the other provisions of this Act shall come into operation on such day as the Treasury may appoint by order made by statutory instrument; and different days may be so appointed for different provisions.

(3) Any reference in this Act to the commencement of any provision of this Act shall be construed as a reference to the day appointed under this section for the coming into operation of that provision.

(4) With the exception of section 25 and section 32 (4) above, this Act does not extend to Northern Ireland.

SCHEDULES

Section 4 (1)

SCHEDULE 1

MATTERS TO BE PROVIDED FOR IN RULES OF CREDIT UNION

1. The name of the society, which shall comply with section 3 (1) above and with subsections (1) and (2) of section 5 of the 1965 Act (name not to be undesirable and to end with the word "limited").

2. The objects of the society.

3. The place which is to be the registered office of the society to which all communications and notices to the society may be addressed.

4. The qualifications for, and the terms of, admission to membership of the society, including any special provision for the insurance of members in relation to their shares.

5. The mode of holding meetings, including provision as to the quorum necessary for the transaction of any description of business, and the mode of making, altering or rescinding rules.

6. The appointment and removal of a committee, by whatever name, and of managers or other officers and their respective powers and remuneration.

7. Determination (subject to section 5 (3) of this Act) of the maximum amount of the interest in the shares of the society which may be held by any member.

8. Provision for the mode of withdrawal of shares and for payment of the balance due thereon on withdrawing from the society.

9. The mode and circumstances in which loans to members are to be made and repaid, including any special provision for the insurance of members in relation to loans made to them.

10. Provision for the custody and use of the society's seal.

11. Provision for the audit of accounts by one or more auditors appointed by the society in accordance with the requirements of the Friendly and Industrial and Provident Societies Act 1968.

12. Provision for the withdrawal of members from the society and for the claims of the representatives of deceased members or the trustees of the property of bankrupt members, or, in Scotland, members whose estate has been sequestrated, and for the payment of nominees.

13. Provision for terminating the membership of members in order to comply with—

(*a*) the limit on the number of members of a credit union for the time being provided for in subsection (2) of section 6 above or, if a conditional exemption has been granted under subsection (5) of that section, any other limit which may be specified as a condition of that exemption; and

(*b*) the limit provided for in subsection (6) of section 5 above on the number of non-qualifying members of a credit union;

and for the repayment of the shares held by, and of any loans made to, a member whose membership is terminated for such a purpose.

14. Provision for the dissolution of the society, including provision requiring any assets remaining after the payment of debts, repayment of share capital and discharge of other liabilities—

(*a*) to be transferred to another credit union; or

(*b*) if not so transferred, to be applied for charitable purposes.

Section 19

SCHEDULE 2

Procedure in Relation to Directions Under Section 19

1. Not less than fourteen days before giving a direction, the chief registrar shall serve on the credit union concerned, and on every member of its committee, a notice stating that he proposes to give such a direction and specifying the nature of the direction he proposes to give and the considerations which have led him to conclude that he should give such a direction.

2. The chief registrar shall consider any representations with respect to the notice which may be made to him by the credit union within such period as he may allow, not being less than fourteen days from the date on which the credit union is served with the notice, and, if the credit union so requests, shall afford it an opportunity of being heard by him within that period.

3.—(1) On giving such a direction the chief registrar shall serve the direction on the credit union and shall serve on every member of its committee a notice of the giving of the direction.

(2) The direction and notices served in accordance with sub-paragraph (1) above shall be accompanied by a notice specifying the considerations which have led the chief registrar to conclude that he should give the direction.

(3) The chief registrar shall not have power to give such a direction unless all the considerations so specified were those, or were among those, which were specified in the notice under paragraph 1 above.

4. A notice under this Schedule may be served on a member of the committee of a credit union by sending it by post to his address, or latest address, as notified to the chief registrar by him or by the credit union.

5. Failure to serve a notice under this Schedule on a committee member shall not affect the validity of a direction.

6. Notice of the giving of a direction shall be published by the chief registrar in the Gazette and in any other manner which appears to him to be necessary for informing the public.

Section 31 (1)

SCHEDULE 3

TEMPORARY POWERS TO DESIGNATE AUTHORISED BANKS

Powers of chief registrar

1.—(1) The chief registrar may, by order made with the consent of the Treasury, designate as an authorised bank for the purposes of this Act any body corporate or partnership carrying on the business of banking.

(2) An order under sub-paragraph (1) above may be varied or revoked by a subsequent order made by the chief registrar with the consent of the Treasury.

(3) Any order made under this paragraph shall be published in the Gazette.

Duration of powers

2.—(1) When it appears to the Treasury that, the relevant provisions of the Banking Act 1979 having come into operation, there are in existence such number of recognised banks (within the meaning of that Act) as to render no longer necessary the powers conferred by paragraph 1 above, the Treasury shall by order made by statutory instrument provide that those powers may no longer be exercised.

(2) An institution which, immediately before the date on which the Treasury order referred to in sub-paragraph (1) above comes into effect, was an authorised bank for the purposes of this Act solely by virtue of an order of the chief registrar under this Schedule shall cease to be an authorised bank for those purposes on that date.

Independent Broadcasting Authority Act 1979

(1979 c. 35)

An Act to confer power on the Independent Broadcasting Authority to equip themselves to transmit a television broadcasting service additional to those of the British Broadcasting Corporation and to that provided by the Authority under the Independent Broadcasting Authority Act 1973.

[4th April 1979]

General Note

This Act confers power on the Independent Broadcasting Authority to equip themselves to transmit an additional broadcasting service.

S. 1 relates to the provision of transmitting equipment for a new television broadcasting service; s. 2 contains financial provisions; s. 3 deals with the short title and extent. The Act extends to Northern Ireland.

The Act received the Royal Assent on April 4, 1979, and came into force on that date.

Parliamentary debates

Hansard, H.C. Vol. 962, col. 401; Vol. 963, col. 1167; Vol. 965, col. 679; H.L. Vol. 399, cols. 1711, 1769 and 1807.

Provision of transmitting equipment for new television broadcasting service

1.—(1) With a view to the provision (whether by the Independent Broadcasting Authority themselves or by any other body of persons) of a television broadcasting service additional to those of the British Broadcasting Corporation and to that already provided by the Authority under the Independent Broadcasting Authority Act 1973, the Authority shall have power (without regard to any time limit under section 2 (1) of that Act) to do all such things as are in their opinion necessary or expedient for the purpose of equipping themselves to transmit the programmes included in any such additional service.

(2) Without prejudice to the generality of the power conferred by subsection (1) above, the Authority shall have power for the purpose there mentioned—

(*a*) to establish and install stations for wireless telegraphy (within the meaning of the Wireless Telegraphy Act 1949); and

(*b*) to arrange for the provision and equipment of, or, if need be, themselves to provide and equip studios and other premises for television broadcasting purposes.

(3) Without prejudice to the generality of the preceding provisions of this section and subsection (3) of section 3 of the Act of 1973 (extent of Authority's powers), that subsection shall be construed as applying in relation to activities undertaken and in relation to property or rights acquired or held by the Authority for the purposes of this section.

(4) The reference in paragraph 3 (3) of Schedule 1 to that Act (capacity of the Authority as a statutory corporation) to the powers of the Authority under that Act shall be construed as including a reference to the powers of the Authority under this section.

(5) Nothing in this section shall be construed as authorising the Authority to do, otherwise than under and in accordance with a licence under section 1 of the Wireless Telegraphy Act 1949, anything for the doing of which such a licence is requisite under that Act.

Financial provisions

2.—(1) Notwithstanding anything in section 25 (5) of the Act of 1973 (reserve fund for either branch of the Authority's undertaking not to be applied otherwise than for the purposes of that branch) the Authority may apply any current surplus on any of their television services branch reserves to meet any expenditure incurred by them for the purposes of section 1 of this Act, but the sums so applied by virtue of this section shall not in the aggregate exceed £10 million.

(2) In subsection (1) above " surplus " means, in relation to any of the Authority's television services branch reserves, any amount credited to that reserve which appears to the Authority to exceed the amount for the time being required to provide an adequate fund for expenditure for the purposes of that reserve.

(3) For the purpose of enabling the Authority to discharge their function under section 1 of this Act the Secretary of State may with the consent of the Treasury make advances to the Authority out of moneys provided by Parliament.

(4) The aggregate amount outstanding by way of principal in respect of sums advanced to the Authority under this section shall not at any time exceed £18 million.

(5) Any sums advanced under this section shall be repaid to the Secretary of State at such times and by such methods, and interest on those sums shall be paid to him at such times and at such rates, as he may from time to time direct with the consent of the Treasury.

(6) All sums received by the Secretary of State in pursuance of subsection (5) above shall be paid into the Consolidated Fund.

(7) References in this section to the Authority's television services branch reserves are references to—

(*a*) the reserve fund established under section 25 (4) of the Act of 1973 for the branch of the Authority's undertaking consisting of the provision of television broadcasting services; and

(*b*) any other reserves established by the Authority by way of provision for depreciation or for any other matter for which the Authority are required to provide in discharging their duty under section 25 (2) of that Act in relation to that branch of their undertaking.

Short title, etc.

3.—(1) This Act may be cited as the Independent Broadcasting Authority Act 1979.

(2) In this Act " the Act of 1973 " means the Independent Broadcasting Authority Act 1973, and " the Authority " means the Independent Broadcasting Authority.

(3) It is hereby declared that this Act extends to Northern Ireland.

(4) Her Majesty may by Order in Council direct that all or any of the provisions of this Act shall extend to the Isle of Man or any of the Channel Islands with such adaptations and modifications, if any, as may be specified in the Order.

Nurses, Midwives and Health Visitors Act 1979 *

(1979 c. 36)

ARRANGEMENT OF SECTIONS

An Act to establish a Central Council for Nursing, Midwifery and Health Visiting, and National Boards for the four parts of the United Kingdom; to make new provision with respect to the education, training, regulation and discipline of nurses, midwives and health visitors and the maintenance of a single professional register; to amend an Act relating to the Central Council for Education and Training in Social Work; and for purposes connected with those matters. [4th April 1979]

* Annotations by John Finch, Lecturer in Law, University of Leicester.

General Note

This Act, which received Royal Assent on April 4, 1979, represents the first legislative product of the full and searching deliberations of the Briggs Committee in 1972 (Report of the Committee on Nursing) Cmnd. 5115, published in October 1972 and reprinted in 1977). For Lord Briggs himself it must have been a particularly happy event to deliver his maiden speech in the House of Lords in support of the Bill, thus representing the first fruits of his Committee's earlier labours.

This relatively short Act received a considerable amount of parliamentary attention—in all, some 718 columns of *Hansard* were devoted to it. Even so, the Act in its final form shows relatively few signs of amendment from the original Bill presented to the Commons. The reason for all the debate and accompanying extra-parliamentary discussion was the fact that this, the spearhead of a major reorganisation of the nursing and allied professions (midwives, health visitors) was based on certain attitudes and evaluations in respect of nursing and allied services which were clearly open to debate, and which in fact received very extensive attention especially in the House of Commons. Despite the Bill's having all-party support, there was more than an element of party politics in the debates and Committee discussions. Indeed, some adverse comparisons of this preliminary reorganisation with the major overall reorganisation of the National Health Service as a whole (1973, c. 32) produced at times a certain courteous acrimony.

This form of legislation, pioneered by Sir Geoffrey Howe, Q.C., in relation to legislation on the entry of the United Kingdom into the EEC, creates a legislative skeleton to be fleshed out at a later date (or, rather, at a number of later dates) by way of statutory instruments. However, where the respective roles and functions of three similar but different professions (nursing, midwifery, health visiting) are being stated and evaluated in terms of work areas and job demands, the creation of a skeleton for a new education and training body is not by any means a simple straightforward task. The variety of legitimate demands from these three professions, and also from diverse interest groups and representative bodies within each, needed to be canvassed in order that future perspectives could be, as it were, projected back in time to the initial legislative framework for the newly structured profession(s). It is clear from the debates and discussion that a set of formulae needed to be found such as to satisfy not only proper representation of professional interests and claims but also the occasionally politically-coloured evaluations of the varying parliamentary opinions involved in the passage of the Bill.

Secondary legislation introduced pursuant to the Act will take the form of statutory instruments subject to negative resolution. While such a procedure will no doubt be viewed in many quarters with some relief, Members nevertheless have an extremely full and well-argued debate on principles and policies in issue in the amalgamation of these three professions if it is their wish to raise questions as to the form, content or scope of the secondary legislation. The 404 columns of Committee B's deliberations are sufficient to instruct even the most untutored.

The purpose of the Act is to replace the existing separate bodies responsible for the education, training and regulation of the professions by a single central United Kingdom council supported by powerful national boards in each of the four countries. It will, for the first time, bring the professions under one umbrella and, for the first time, bring together the nurses, midwives and health visitors of England and Wales, Scotland and Northern Ireland. The Act does not of itself make any change in the substance of professional education and training, but it paves the way for the professions themselves to initiate a new system of integrated training on the lines recommended by the Briggs Report when the substantial resources which such a change would require are available.

When Richard Crossman, in March 1970, announced in Parliament that he had invited Lord Briggs—then Professor Asa Briggs—to chair a committee whose terms of reference were

> "To review the role of the nurse and the midwife in the hospital and the community and the education and training required for that role, so that the best use is made of available manpower to meet present needs and the needs of an integrated health service,"

it was against the background that though there had been many other committees and many reports, both official and unofficial, during the previous 30 years, never before had the subject been looked at in the context of an integrated health service.

The main purpose of the Act is to establish a United Kingdom Central Council for Nursing, Midwifery and Health Visiting, and four national boards. The Central Council is to prepare and maintain a central register of qualified nurses, midwives and health visitors and to determine, by means of rules, education and training requirements and other conditions for admission to the register.

The new bodies will replace all the existing statutory training bodies—the General Nursing Council for England and Wales, the General Nursing Council for Scotland and the Northern Ireland Council for Nursing and Midwifery, the Central Midwives Board for England and Wales, the Central Midwives Board for Scotland and the Council for the Education and Training of Health Visitors—and will also take over the functions of the three non-statutory bodies—the Joint Board for Clinical Nursing Studies, its Scottish equivalent, and the Panel of Assessors for District Nurse Training.

The Act is concerned with the government of the professions by the requirement that nurses, midwives and health visitors should be registered for practice in their professions and by the enforcement of standards of professional conduct through a disciplinary process. These provisions are vital to the protection of the public and will ensure that those who care for us are in all respects qualified to do so.

In the new structure, nurses, midwives and health visitors will form the majority on national boards and on the Central Council. Indeed the majority on the Council will be directly nominated from the national boards. More importantly, after an initial term during which all members will be appointed by Ministers, the majority on each national board will be directly elected by the professions themselves, as soon as the necessary electoral arrangements can be worked out. This is not something new for nurses, but it is a major change for midwives and for health visitors.

S. 1 establishes the new United Kingdom Central Council. Its detailed membership will be prescribed by Ministers but the crucial feature is the high degree of cross-membership with the four national boards, each of which will nominate in equal numbers, members of the Council. Those nominated by national boards will form the majority on the Council and, as is to be expected in a body that is concerned with nurses, midwives and health visitors, that majority will be members of the three professions.

S. 2 deals with six principal functions which are to be exercised by the Central Council. Four of these were in the Bill as it was originally presented in the Commons, and the last two were added each as the result of protracted debate.

S. 3 deals with specialist standing committees of the Council. They will be established by order. In particular, there is a requirement to constitute a midwifery committee. In the original Bill this was envisaged as a committee which the Council should consult on all matters relating to midwifery and which might discharge such of the Council's functions as were assigned to it. This requirement remains in the Act, but in the body of a new s. 4 which goes on to state that the Council shall assign to the Committee any matter involving a proposal to make, amend or revoke rules under s. 15 (*infra*) (rules regulating the practice of midwives); and such matters may be finally dealt with by the Committee if the Council so authorise.

There is also power under s. 3 to establish other specialist committees, including those for district and mental nursing and for clinical nursing studies—that is, the whole range of post-basic specialities such as intensive care, renal nursing, operating theatre nursing and the care of the elderly.

S. 5 establishes the national boards; s. 6 deals with the functions of national boards in relation to training and investigating cases of alleged misconduct; s. 7 deals with standing committees of national boards; s. 8 deals with joint standing committees which serve both the Council and the Boards; and s. 9 empowers the Secretary of State by order to provide for the constitution of training committees, such committees to be charged with assisting the boards in the exercise of their training functions.

S. 10 is, in a sense, the practical kernel of the Bill. It requires the Council to prepare and maintain a professional register of qualified nurses, midwives and health visitors, which will replace all the existing registers and rolls. Ss. 11 and 12 deal with admissions to and removal from the register; s. 13 deals with the right of a person aggrieved by a decision to remove from the register to appeal to an "appropriate court" (specified in s. 13 (2)); s. 14 provides for the offence of false claim of professional qualification, with intent to deceive.

Ss. 15 to 17 restate, in relation to the Council and the Boards, provisions for existing legislation on the practice of midwifery. In particular, they require the Council to make rules governing midwifery practice and restate the provision for establishing local supervision of midwifery practice. The presence of this group of clauses is a recognition of the separate characteristics of midwifery and the need, in order to protect the public, to have adequate control over the way in which midwives operate. Ss. 19 to 21 deal with the finance of the Council and Boards. The remaining clauses are of a technical nature.

The Act has eight schedules. Scheds. 1 and 2 deal with the constitution of the Council and Boards respectively and set out in detail their procedures and methods of working. Sched. 3 deals with disciplinary proceedings before the Council and Boards. Sched. 4, added during the passage of the Bill, deals with qualification of auditors. Sched. 5 contains transitional provisions relating to the transfer of staff, property, and so on, from the existing to the new bodies.

Sched. 6 contains the adaptations required for Northern Ireland and its National Board. The constitutional position in Northern Ireland is different from that elsewhere in the United Kingdom, and it is necessary to adapt United Kingdom legislation to take account of that. Sched. 7 contains amendments of other Acts. Sched. 8 deals with Acts that are to be repealed by the Bill.

In introducing the details of the Bill at the stage of the Second Reading in the Commons Mr. Ennals, the then Secretary of State for Health and Social Services, made a firm commitment to the quality of manning to be achieved in the newly established Boards and Committees in terms of the specialist knowledge and expertise required for a proper fulfilment of their role. It is for this reason that the Act now contains powers for Ministers to set up further specialist standing committees, within the overall framework, to look after specialist interests as and when such is thought desirable or necessary. Among the groups or " interests " so to be catered for are the growing number of nurses working in occupational health services, mental nurses, district nurses, sick children's nurses, and others. (The second and fourth of these groups already have a specialist register for their own respective spheres of professional activity.) Little was said in the introduction of the Bill as it originally stood about the highly important " specialist " group to be provided for directly by the principal legislation itself, namely health visitors. Any omission here was, however, more than amply compensated by debate and especially by discussion in Commons Standing Committee B.

Lest it ever be thought that the new legislation arose in part from a dissatisfaction with the operations of existing bodies, statutory and non-statutory, within the nursing, midwives' and health visitors' professions, Mr. Ennals had this to say:

> " I should like to pay tribute to the existing statutory and other bodies, which have done yeoman service over the years and may well feel sad, and perhaps a little hurt, at being supplanted by a new statutory framework. As the Briggs Report said: ' It is in no sense because we fail to recognise the achievement of these bodies that we recommend in the interests of the professions there should be one single central statutory organisation to supervise training and education to safeguard and, when possible, to raise professional standards.' I certainly endorse fully those remarks and others in the report about the achievement of the present bodies. They have all done a splendid job over the years, and we are all deeply grateful for their work. The restructuring to be achieved by the Bill is not required because the present organisations have failed. It is required to strengthen and develop the organisation and prepare it for the future. It is required to give nursing, midwifery and health visiting that ' authoritative voice ' that the Briggs Committee felt was essential."

Finally, a principal problem which the Bill experienced in its none-too-easy passage through Parliament was the achievement of a working compromise between the policy, which permeated the Briggs Report, of bringing three related professions within a common statutory framework, and the necessity, readily apparent from lengthy debates centred especially on s. 1 (Constitution of the Central Council) of preserving the identity and thus the special interests of each of the three groups. This was especially necessary in the case of midwives (who have a full and specific identity in the principal legislation) and health visitors (who are not, in the event, as fully provided for).

The Briggs Report made 75 recommendations, of which the first five are accommodated in this Act. The remainder, relating in the main to specific issues in education and training, remains to be implemented by statutory instrument.

Parliamentary debates

See *Hansard,* H.C. Vol. 958, cols. 35–126; Standing Committee B, cols. 1–404; Vol. 962, cols. 413–509; H.L. Vol. 398, cols. 1643–1681; Vol. 399, cols. 504–557, 1473–1496 and 1726–1729; H.C. Vol. 965, cols. 1351–1357.

Extent

The Act extends to Northern Ireland.

Commencement

Ss. 21 (2) and 24 came into force on April 4, 1979. The remainder of the Act comes into force on a day or days to be appointed.

The Central Council

Constitution of Central Council

1.—(1) There shall be a corporate body known as the United Kingdom Central Council for Nursing, Midwifery and Health Visiting.

(2) The Council shall consist of the number of members, being not more than 45, prescribed by the Secretary of State by order.

(3) Of the members of the Council—

(*a*) the majority shall be members of the National Boards established by section 5 below and be nominated by the Boards (in equal numbers) in accordance with Part I of Schedule 1 to this Act; and

(*b*) the other members shall be persons appointed by the Secretary of State.

(4) The Secretary of State's appointments shall be made from among persons who either are nurses, midwives, health visitors or registered medical practitioners, or have such qualifications and experience in education or other fields as, in the Secretary of State's opinion, will be of value to the Council in the performance of its functions.

(5) The Secretary of State shall have especially in mind the need to secure that qualifications and experience in the teaching of nurses, midwives and health visitors are adequately represented on the Council.

(6) The Council shall have—

(*a*) a chairman appointed from among its members (initially by the Secretary of State and, as from such later day as he may by order appoint, by the Council itself); and

(*b*) a deputy chairman appointed by the Council from among its members.

(7) Part II of Schedule 1 to this Act shall have effect with respect to the constitution and administration, etc. of the Central Council.

DEFINITIONS

" National Boards " and " Boards ": s. 23 (1), referring to s. 5 (1).

" registered medical practitioners ": Medical Act 1978, s. 30.

" The Central Council ": s. 23 (1), referring to s. 1 (1).

GENERAL NOTE

This section, essential to the whole structure which the Act proceeds to build upon it, was the subject of very full and sometimes hotly contested debate.

Subs. (2)

The maximum number of members of the General Council, set in the Act as in the original Bill at 45, was the subject of some comment in Committee. In the debates which took place on the Medical Bill in 1977 a figure of 98 was accepted as the appropriate maximum number for membership of the General Medical Council, representing about 60,000 doctors. The number of people in question in the present Act is in the region of 500,000. The maximum figure of 45 was eventually agreed to, it being noted that it was the quality of representation in respect of the three allied professions, as distinct from its mere quantity, which should be the paramount consideration. The nomination (subs. (3)) to the Central Council by the National Boards in equal numbers was found particularly pleasing by Mr. Enoch Powell, M.P. for Down, South, himself a one-time Minister of Health, and a member of Standing Committee B.

Subs. (4)

The expression "registered medical practitioners" gives cause for no surprise, but it was preferred in Committee to the original formulation "who . . . . have such qualification in . . . medicine." The original formulation could have been interpreted to include such persons as osteopaths and chiropractors, who are therefore now excluded (unless, of course, they are also registered medical practitioners).

Subs. (5)

This subsection simply serves to underline the very considerable difference in numbers within the three allied professions. The provision appears to look both to an adequate representation of nurses, who number over 400,000 (though areas of specialist interest, such as mental or sick child nursing should by inference be covered also) and also to an adequate showing in favour of the (numerically) minority interest of the 7,000 or so health visitors.

Functions of Council

2.—(1) The principal functions of the Central Council shall be to establish and improve standards of training and professional conduct for nurses, midwives and health visitors.

(2) The Council shall ensure that the standards of training they establish are such as to meet any Community obligation of the United Kingdom.

(3) The Council shall by means of rules determine the conditions of a person's being admitted to training, and the kind and standard of training to be undertaken, with a view to registration.

(4) The rules may also make provision with respect to the kind and standard of further training available to persons who are already registered.

(5) The powers of the Council shall include that of providing, in such manner as it thinks fit, advice for nurses, midwives and health visitors on standards of professional conduct.

(6) In the discharge of its functions the Council shall have proper regard for the interests of all groups within the professions, including those with minority representation.

DEFINITIONS

"Central Council": s. 23 (1), referring to s. 1 (1).

"Community obligation": see European Communities Act 1972, Sched. 1, Pt. II: "Community obligation" means any obligation created or arising by or under the Treaties, whether an enforceable Community obligation or not.

"registration": s. 23 (1), referring to s. 10 (1).

"rules": s. 23 (1).

"training": s. 23 (1).

GENERAL NOTE

S. 2 sets out the functions of the Council, the first four having been part of the original Bill and subss. (5) and (6) having been added at a later stage. Subs. (5) relates to advisory powers which are to be on a discretionary basis. It was at one stage proposed in Committee B that the Central Council should be invested with powers similar to those possessed by the General Medical Council under the Medical Act 1978 (c. 12). An opposition amendment proposing that the Central Council should have similar powers in this respect to the General Medical Council was, by leave, withdrawn on the assurance from the then Minister of Health that he would review the matter at a subsequent date. There appears to be nothing to prevent such provision for rule-making power being introduced in the form of secondary legislation at some later date if such transpires to be either necessary or desirable.

Subs. (1)

It is certainly not the intention of the Act to pass adverse comment on the quality of existing training schemes and methods. The object of this subsection is simply to look to yet higher quality which, following the philosophy of the Briggs Committee, is now envisaged.

Subs. (2)

The content of this provision is by no means an unexpected inclusion, but neither was the discussion among " pro- " and " anti-Marketeers " especially in Standing Committee B. It was suggested by one Member that any such " ensuring " of the meeting of Community obligations should be made subject to an affirmative resolution of each House. On the other hand, one Member pointed to the " obligations " which might naturally arise in relation to many other distinguished institutions in the world outside the Community. It became clear, however, that " Community obligation " was being interpreted by the majority of those present in Standing Committee B in a legalistic rather than any other way. And the majority of those voting (there were some abstentions) on the motion to make such steps subject to affirmative resolution of each House of Parliament were against the proposal.

Subs. (3)

A proposal to have " education " specifically included in the wording of subs. (3) failed despite clear statements in the Briggs Report in relation to projected improvements in the area of nurse education. Even though the educational objectives of the Report can be, as it were, fleshed out by secondary legislation in the fullness of time, the same could presumably be said of training also. Nevertheless " training " is in, and " education " is out, in respect of s. 2. However, in s. 23 (1), " training includes education."

Subs. (6)

This provision added by way of amendment to the Bill, serves simply but usefully to underline the concern which was (and probably still is) expressed in a variety of quarters about certain interest groups being, as it were, swamped by the big battalions. Such interest groups include not only midwives and health visitors (and especially the latter, for there is narrower specific provision for them in the principal legislation than there is for the midwives) but also sub-groups within the nursing profession, such as, for instance, mental or sick children's nurses, who may have certain particular interests or opinions to be represented on the Council and the Boards.

Standing committees of Council

3.—(1) The Secretary of State shall by order constitute as standing committees of the Council a Midwifery Committee and a Finance Committee.

(2) The Council shall consult the Finance Committee on all financial matters.

(3) The Secretary of State may by order constitute other standing committees of the Council and (to the extent prescribed by the order) require the Council to consult them on, or empower them to discharge functions of the Council with respect to, other matters including in particular—

(*a*) training;

(*b*) clinical nursing studies;

(*c*) mental nursing; and

(*d*) occupational health nursing.

(4) An order constituting a standing committee of the Council—

(*a*) may provide for persons who are not members of the Council to be appointed as members of that committee; and (*b*) shall provide for a majority on the committee to be persons who work or have worked in the professional field with which it is primarily concerned.

DEFINITIONS

"Council": see s. 23 (1), referring to s. 1 (1).

"training": includes education—see s. 23 (1).

GENERAL NOTE

Subs. (3) (*d*)

"*occupational health nursing*" was added to the original provisions following a division in Committee B which decided by nine votes to three in favour of its inclusion. It is a useful and unsurprising addition, especially in view of the specific references to occupational health nursing during the Commons debate on the Second Reading of the Bill.

The Midwifery Committee

4.—(1) Of the members of the Council's Midwifery Committee the majority shall be practising midwives.

(2) The Council shall consult the Committee on all matters relating to midwifery and the Committee shall, on behalf of the Council, discharge such of the Council's functions as are assigned to them either by the Council or by the Secretary of State by order.

(3) The Council shall assign to the Committee any matter involving a proposal to make, amend or revoke rules under section 15 below; and—

(*a*) the Committee shall consider the proposal and report on it to the Council;

(*b*) the Council shall take no action on the report until they have consulted the National Boards with respect to the matters dealt with in it.

(4) The Secretary of State shall not approve rules relating to midwifery practice unless satisfied that they are framed in accordance with recommendations of the Council's Midwifery Committee.

(5) Any matter which is assigned to the Midwifery Committee otherwise than under subsection (3) shall be finally dealt with by the Committee on behalf of the Council, so far as the Council expressly authorise the Committee to deal finally with it; and the Committee shall make a report to the Council as to the way in which they have dealt with the matter.

DEFINITIONS

"Council": s. 23 (1), referring to s. 1 (1).

"rules": s. 23 (1).

GENERAL NOTE

S. 4 (2) was originally s. 3 (2) in the Bill until the later stages of the deliberations of Standing Committee B. It reflects the influence on arrangements, practices, policies and rules which were until the passing of the Act in existence within the closely organised midwives' profession. (The new clause was, remarkably, introduced and discussed as a "New Clause 1" in which position it would have looked a trifle odd.)

The National Boards and their relationship to the Central Council

Constitution of National Boards

5.—(1) England, Wales, Scotland and Northern Ireland shall each have a National Board for Nursing, Midwifery and Health Visiting, and the Board shall be corporate bodies.

(2) Each of the National Boards shall have the number of members prescribed by the Secretary of State by order, the maximum being, in the case of the National Board for Northern Ireland, 35 members and, in the case of the other National Boards, 45 members.

(3) Until the appointed day, the members of each National Board shall be persons appointed by the Secretary of State for a term of office ending not later than that day.

(4) With effect from the appointed day, each of the Boards shall consist—

(*a*) of members directly appointed by the Secretary of State; and

(*b*) of elected members, that is to say members appointed by him on being elected under an electoral scheme to be prepared and approved as set out in Part I of Schedule 2 to this Act;

and, in the case of each Board, the numbers of members who are directly appointed and of elected members shall be as prescribed for that Board by the Secretary of State by order, but so that the elected members form a majority on the Board.

(5) In the case of each Board—

(*a*) the majority of those appointed under subsection (3) shall be persons who are nurses, midwives or health visitors; and

(*b*) the Secretary of State's direct appointments under subsection (4) (*a*) shall be made from among persons who either—

(i) are nurses, midwives, health visitors or registered medical practitioners, or

(ii) have such qualifications and experience in education or other fields as, in his opinion, will be of value to the Board in the performance of its functions.

(6) The Secretary of State shall have especially in mind the need to secure that qualifications and experience in the teaching of nurses, midwives and health visitors are adequately represented on each Board.

(7) Each of the Boards shall have a chairman and a deputy chairman appointed from among its members.

(8) The chairman shall—

(*a*) until the appointed day, be a person appointed by the Secretary of State;

(*b*) on and after that day, be a person appointed by the Board;

and the deputy chairman shall at all times be a person appointed by the Board.

(9) Part II of Schedule 2 to this Act shall have effect with respect to the constitution and administration, etc. of the National Boards.

(10) In this section and in Schedule 2, " the appointed day " means a day appointed by the Secretary of State by order, which must be not more than three years from the coming into force of this section.

DEFINITIONS

" elected members ": s. 23 (1) referring to s. 5 (4) (*b*).

" National Board " and " Boards ": s. 23 (1), referring back to this section.

" prescribed ": s. 23 (1).

" registered medical practitioners ": Medical Act 1978 (c. 12), s. 30.

GENERAL NOTE

Subs. (2)

Standing Committee B divided equally on a proposal to increase the membership of the National Board for Northern Ireland from 30 to 35 and the Chairman of the Committee, in accordance with precedent, cast his votes for the Noes. However, the number was later increased to 35 in view of the greater flexibility which this larger number would be able to inject into the representation of the variety of interests and groups who can legitimately expect such representation.

Subs. (10)

The phrase " which must be not more than three years from the coming into force of this section " was added to the Bill as it originally stood in response to fears voiced in some quarters that the powers given to the Secretary of State by subss. (3) and (4) could conceivably result in " jobs for the boys " in perpetuity. The additional phrase gives legislative confirmation to Ministerial assurances to the contrary.

Functions of Boards

6.—(1) The National Boards shall in England, Wales, Scotland and Northern Ireland respectively—

(*a*) provide, or arrange for others to provide, at institutions approved by the Board—

(i) courses of training with a view to enabling persons to qualify for registration as nurses, midwives or health visitors or for the recording of additional qualifications in the register; and

(ii) courses of further training for those already registered;

(*b*) ensure that such courses meet the requirements of the Central Council as to their content and standard;

(*c*) hold, or arrange for others to hold, such examinations as are necessary to enable persons to satisfy requirements for registration or to obtain additional qualifications;

(*d*) collaborate with the Council in the promotion of improved training methods; and

(*e*) carry out investigations of cases of alleged misconduct, with a view to proceedings before the Central Council or a committee of the Council for a person to be removed from the register.

(2) The National Boards shall discharge their functions subject to and in accordance with any applicable rules of the Council and shall have proper regard for the interests of all groups within the professions, including those with minority representation.

DEFINITIONS

" Central Council ": s. 23 (1), referring to s. 1 (1).
" National Boards ": s. 23 (1), referring to s. 5 (1).
" registration ": s. 23 (1), referring to s. 10 (1).
" training ": s. 23 (1).

GENERAL NOTE

Subs. (1) (*e*)

Para. (*e*) read " investigate cases of alleged misconduct " in the Bill as it originally stood. This formulation contained an ambiguity which was identified on Second Reading by Enoch Powell (Down, South). It was possible to construe that in investigating cases of alleged misconduct the National Boards would themselves be able to determine what constitutes misconduct, rather than the Central Council. The disciplinary function will, as is now made abundantly clear, be a function of the Central Council as it will be the guardian of the register (see ss. 10 (1) *et seq.*). It is therefore a decision for the Central Council whether someone should be placed on the register or removed from it because of the qualifications he has or for reasons of professional misconduct, as the case may be.

Standing committees of Boards

7.—(1) The Secretary of State shall for each of the National Boards by order constitute as standing committees of the Board a Midwifery Committee and a Finance Committee.

(2) Of the members of the Board's Midwifery Committee the majority shall be practising midwives.

(3) Each Board shall consult its Midwifery Committee on all matters relating to midwifery and the Committee shall, on behalf of the Board,

discharge such of the Board's functions as are assigned to them by the Board or by the Secretary of State by order.

(4) In particular, the Board, when consulted by the Central Council with respect to matters dealt with in a report of the latter's Midwifery Committee, shall seek the views of its own Midwifery Committee on those matters.

(5) Each Board shall consult its Finance Committee on all financial matters.

(6) In the case of any Board, the Secretary of State may by order constitute other standing committees of the Board and (to the extent prescribed by the order) require the Board to consult them on, or empower the committee to discharge functions of the Board with respect to, any other matters including any of those mentioned in section 3 (3).

(7) An order constituting a standing committee of a National Board—

(*a*) may provide for persons who are not members of the Board to be appointed as members of that committee; and

(*b*) shall provide for a majority on the committee to be persons who work or have worked in the professional field with which it is primarily concerned.

DEFINITIONS

"National Boards": s. 23 (1), referring to s. 5 (1).

"order": s. 23 (1).

"practising": for person to be treated as "practising" he [and she] must be working in some capacity by virtue of a qualification in nursing, midwifery or health visiting as the case may be : s. 23 (1).

Joint committees of Council and Boards

8.—(1) The Secretary of State shall by order constitute a joint committee of the Central Council and the National Boards, called the Health Visiting Joint Committee.

(2) Of the members of the Health Visiting Joint Committee, the majority shall be practising health visitors.

(3) The Council and each of the Boards shall consult the Joint Committee on all matters relating to health visiting and shall not act on any such matters before receiving a recommendation of the Joint Committee which shall be made within such period of time as the Council or Board shall specify; and the Committee shall, on behalf of the Council or of any Board, discharge such of the functions of the Council or the Board as are assigned to it by the body otherwise charged with those functions, or by the Secretary of State by order.

(4) The Secretary of State may by order constitute other joint committees of the Council and the National Boards and (to the extent prescribed by the order)—

(*a*) require the Council and the Boards to consult the appropriate joint committee on such matters as may be assigned to it; and

(*b*) authorise any such committee to discharge functions of the Council or a Board with respect to any matters including any of those mentioned in section 3 (3).

(5) There may in particular be constituted under subsection (4) a joint committee to be concerned with district nursing.

(6) Joint committees shall be constituted from members of the Council and of the Boards, in such numbers and proportions as the Secretary of State's order may specify; and his order—

(*a*) may provide for persons who are not members of the Council or of any Board to be appointed as members of the joint committee;

(*b*) shall provide for a majority on the joint committee to be persons who work or have worked in the professional field with which it is primarily concerned.

DEFINITIONS
"by order": s. 23 (1).
"Central Council": s. 23 (1), referring to s. 1 (1).
"National Boards": s. 23 (1), referring to s. 5 (1).
"practising": s. 23 (1).

Local training committees

9.—(1) The Secretary of State may by order provide for the constitution of training committees of the Boards for such areas of England, Wales, Scotland and Northern Ireland as the other may prescribe.

(2) The committees shall be charged with assisting the Boards in the exercise of their training functions, being the functions specified in section 6 (1) (*a*) to (*c*) above.

(3) The committees shall discharge the training functions of the Boards to such extent and in such cases as may be prescribed or (subject to orders under this section) the Boards may direct.

(4) The committees shall carry out their functions in accordance with directions given to them by the Boards.

(5) Orders under this section may make provision for persons who are not members of a Board to be appointed as members of any of its training committees.

(6) Before making an order under this section, and before varying or revoking such an order, the Secretary of State shall consult the Central Council and have regard to any proposals made by the Council after it has consulted the Boards for the parts of the United Kingdom affected.

DEFINITIONS
"Boards": s. 23 (1), referring to s. 5 (1).
"by order": s. 23 (1).
"training": "includes education"—s. 23 (1).

Registration

The professional register

10.—(1) The Central Council shall prepare and maintain a register of qualified nurses, midwives and health visitors.

(2) The register shall be divided into such parts as the Secretary of State may by order determine, the parts being indicative of different qualifications and different kinds and standards of training; and in this Act references to parts of the register are to the parts so determined.

(3) The Council may by rules make provision—

(*a*) as to the documentary and other evidence to be produced, and the fees to be paid, by those applying for registration or for additional qualifications to be recorded, or for any entry in the register to be altered or restored;

(*b*) as to the keeping of the register and the means of obtaining access to, and copies of extracts from it;

(*c*) for a person's registration to remain effective without limitation of time (subject to removal from the register for misconduct or otherwise) or to lapse after a specified period or in specified cases, or to be subject to renewal as and when provided by the rules.

(4) The Secretary of State may by order provide—

(*a*) for persons to be registered in one or more parts of the register by virtue of having been included in one or more of the registers, rolls or lists maintained under enactments repealed by this Act, or having been certified under any of those enactments;

(*b*) for a specified part of the register to be closed, as from a date specified by the order, so that on or after that date no further persons can become registered in that part;

(*c*) for a specified part of the register to be sub-divided into two or more parts, or for two or more parts to be combined into one.

(5) The Secretary of State shall consult the Central Council before making, varying or revoking any order under this section.

(6) A certificate issued and duly authenticated by the Council stating that a person is, or was at any date, or is not, or was not at any date, registered shall be evidence in all courts of law of the fact stated in the certificate.

(7) In any enactment or instrument (past or future, and including this Act) " registered ", in relation to nurses, midwives and health visitors, means registered in the register maintained under this section by virtue of qualifications in nursing, midwifery or health visiting, as the case may be.

(8) Orders under subsection (2) may, by reference to the part or parts in which a person is registered, prescribe the more advanced qualifications which he must have in order to be treated as a qualified nurse for the purposes of any particular enactment or instrument.

DEFINITIONS

" by order ": s. 23 (1).
" Central Council ": s. 23 (1), referring to s. 1 (1).
" register ": see also s. 23 (1).
" registration ": see also s. 23 (1).

GENERAL NOTE

S. 10 is, in a sense, the practical kernel of the Act. It requires the Council to prepare and maintain a professional register of qualified nurses, midwives and health visitors, which will replace all existing registers and rolls. The distinction as we now know it between State Registered Nurses and State Enrolled Nurses will as such disappear, though future nurse *education*—which was the practical kernel of the Briggs Report—will presumably cater for a variety of needs and aspirations within the nursing professions.

Admission to register

11.—(1) A person seeking admission to a part of the register must make application to the Central Council in accordance with the Council's rules.

(2) Subject to subsection (4) below, the applicant shall be registered in that part (on payment of such fee as may be required by the rules) if he satisfies the Council that he is of good character and has the appropriate professional qualifications.

(3) He is to be regarded as having those qualifications if—

(*a*) he has in the United Kingdom undergone the training, and passed the examinations, required by the Council's rules for admission to that part of the register; or

(*b*) being a national of any member State of the European Communities, he has professional qualifications, obtained in a member State other than the United Kingdom, which the

Secretary of State has by order designated as having Community equivalence for purposes of registration in that part; or

(c) he has, elsewhere than in the United Kingdom, undergone training in nursing, midwifery or health visiting (as the case may be) and either—

(i) that training is recognised by the Central Council as being to a standard sufficient for registration in that part; or

(ii) it is not so recognised, but the applicant has undergone in the United Kingdom or elsewhere such additional training as the Council may require.

(4) In the case of an applicant within subsection (3) (b) or (c), the rules may either—

(a) make it an additional condition of his being registered that he has the necessary knowledge of English; or

(b) require him to have that knowledge within a period specified by the rules (failing which his registration will lapse at the end of the period).

(5) " National " in relation to a member State of the European Communities, means the same as it does for the purposes of the Community Treaties.

DEFINITIONS

" Central Council ": s. 23 (1), referring to s. 1 (1).

" European Communities " and " National ": see European Communities Act 1972 (c. 68).

" register ": s. 23 (1).

" training ": " includes education "—s. 23 (1).

GENERAL NOTE

Subs. (3) (b)

Cf. Medical Act 1978 (c. 12), ss. 17, 18.

Subs. (4)

The Bill as it originally stood contained the following proviso in the case of knowledge of the English language: " but this (requirement) does not apply in the case of a national of any Member State of the European Communities, whose professional qualifications are designated as having Community equivalence." Standing Committee B inserted the requirement of a proficiency in English, and this requirement now appears, in a rather different form to that which the Committee proposed, in paras. (a) and (b). The latter paragraph is reminiscent of a similar arrangement for doctors under the provisions of the Medical Act 1978 (c. 12). There is additionally, in any case, an EEC directive (77/452) which states: " Member States shall see to it that, where appropriate, the persons concerned acquire, in their own interest and that of their patients, the linguistic knowledge necessary for the exercise of their profession in the host Member States." It is very proper that the Act now specifically provides for the linguistic facility for, despite the very excellent medical and associated qualifications which foreign nurses may have, it is a fact of life that the ill and the dying may have delicate feelings to impart, and if the nurse cannot understand them or reply suitably in the patient's language, the patient may suffer as a consequence.

Subs. (5)

For the meaning of " the Community Treaties " see European Communities Act 1972 (c. 68), s. 1 (2) and (3); Sched. 1, Pt. I.

Removal from, and restoration to, register

12.—(1) The Central Council shall by rules determine circumstances in which, and the means by which—

(*a*) a person may, for misconduct or otherwise, be removed from the register or a part of it, whether or not for a specified period;

(*b*) a person who has been removed from the register or a part of it may be restored to it; and

(*c*) an entry in the register may be removed, altered or restored.

(2) Committees of the Council shall be constituted by the rules to hear and determine proceedings for a person's removal from, or restoration to, the register or for the removal, alteration or restoration of any entry.

(3) The committees shall be constituted from members of the Council; and the rules shall so provide that the members of a committee constituted to adjudicate upon the conduct of any person are selected with due regard to the professional field in which that person works.

(4) The rules shall make provision as to the procedure to be followed, and the rules of evidence to be observed, in such proceedings, whether before the Council itself or before any committee so constituted, and for the proceedings to be in public except in such cases (if any) as the rules may specify.

(5) Schedule 3 to this Act has effect with respect to the conduct of proceedings to which this section applies.

DEFINITIONS

"Central Council": s. 23 (1) referring to s. 1 (1)

"register": s. 23 (1), referring to s. 10 (1).

"rules": s. 23 (1).

Appeals

13.—(1) A person aggrieved by a decision to remove him from the register, or to remove or alter any entry in respect of him, may, within 3 months after the date on which notice of the decision is given to him by the Council, appeal to the appropriate court; and on the appeal—

(*a*) the court may give such directions in the matter as it thinks proper, including directions as to the costs of the appeal; and

(*b*) the order of the court shall be final.

(2) The appropriate court for the purposes of this section is the High Court, the Court of Session or the High Court in Northern Ireland, according as the appellant's ordinary place of residence is in England and Wales, Scotland or Northern Ireland at the time when notice of the decision is given.

DEFINITIONS

"Council": s. 23 (1), referring to s. 1 (1).

"register": s. 23 (1), referring to s. 10 (1).

GENERAL NOTE

Subs. (2)

While some disquiet was voiced in Committee B about the appeal to the High Court (or other appropriate court), it was accepted that, ever since the Nurses Act 1919, this has been regarded by all concerned as a satisfactory way of going about matters in this area. The judiciary will operate as an appellate board, in addition to its already existing functions at common law as a review body.

False claim of professional qualification

14.—(1) A person commits an offence if, with intent to deceive (whether by words or in writing or by the assumption of any name or description, or by the wearing of any uniform or badge or by any other kind of conduct)—

(*a*) he falsely represents himself to possess qualifications in nursing, midwifery or health visiting; or (*b*) he falsely represents himself to be registered in the register, or in a particular part of it.

(2) A person commits an offence if—

(*a*) with intent that any person shall be deceived, he causes or permits another person to make any representation about himself which, if made by himself with intent to deceive would be an offence in him under subsection (1); or

(*b*) with intent to deceive, makes with regard to another person any representation which—

(i) is false to his own knowledge, and

(ii) if made by the other with that intent would be an offence in the other under that subsection.

(3) A person guilty of an offence under this section shall be liable on summary conviction to a fine of not more than £500.

Miscellaneous provisions about midwifery

Rules as to midwifery practice

15.—(1) The Council shall make rules regulating the practice of midwives and these rules may in particular—

(*a*) determine the circumstances in which, and the procedure by means of which, midwives may be suspended from practice;

(*b*) require midwives to give notice of their intention to practise to the local supervising authority for the area in which they intend to practise; and

(*c*) require registered midwives to attend courses of instruction in accordance with the rules.

(2) If rules are made requiring midwives to give the notice referred to in subsection (1) (*b*), it is then the duty of the local supervising authority to inform the National Board of any notices given to them in compliance with the rules.

DEFINITIONS

"Council": s. 23 (1), referring to s. 1 (1).

"National Board": s. 23 (1), referring to s. 5 (1).

"rules": s. 23 (1).

GENERAL NOTE

Subs. (2)

This amendment was introduced at the request of midwifery bodies which wish to see more involvement of the national boards in the control of practices. It will allow the national boards to keep a record of those midwives who are practising within their sphere of responsibility. It will thus help in assessing the need for refresher courses which the national boards have to provide in their areas. This will ease the administration of the system.

Local supervision of midwifery practice

16.—(1) The following bodies shall be local supervising authorities for midwives—

(*a*) in England, Regional Health Authorities;

(*b*) in Wales, Area Health Authorities;

(*c*) in Scotland, Health Boards; and

(*d*) in Northern Ireland, Health and Social Services Boards.

(2) Each local supervising authority shall—

(*a*) exercise general supervision, in accordance with rules under section 15, over all midwives practising within its area;

(*b*) report any prima facie case of misconduct on the part of a midwife which arises in its area to the National Board for the part of the United Kingdom in which the authority acts;

(*c*) have power in accordance with the Council's rules to suspend a midwife from practice.

(3) The Council may by rules prescribe the qualifications of persons who may be appointed by a local supervising authority to exercise supervision over midwives within its area, and no person shall be so appointed who is not qualified in accordance with the rules.

(4) The National Boards are responsible for providing the authorities with advice and guidance in respect of the exercise of their functions under this section.

DEFINITIONS

"Council": s. 23 (1), referring to s. 1 (1).

"Regional Health Authorities," "Area Health Authorities," "Health Boards," "Health and Social Services Boards": see National Health Service Act 1977 (c. 49), especially s. 8.

"rules": s. 23 (1).

Attendance by unqualified persons at childbirth

17.—(1) A person other than a registered midwife or a registered medical practitioner shall not attend a woman in childbirth.

(2) Until the day appointed by the Secretary of State by an order under paragraph 3 (1) of Schedule 4 to the Sex Discrimination Act 1975, a man who is a registered midwife shall not attend a woman in childbirth except in a place approved in writing by or on behalf of the Secretary of State.

(3) Subsections (1) and (2) do not apply—

(*a*) where the attention is given in a case of sudden or urgent necessity; or

(*b*) in the case of a person who, while undergoing training with a view to becoming a medical practitioner or to becoming a midwife, attends a woman in childbirth as part of a course of practical instruction in midwifery recognised by the General Medical Council or one of the National Boards.

(4) A person who contravenes subsection (1) or (2) shall be liable on summary conviction to a fine of not more than £500.

DEFINITIONS

"registered medical practitioner": see Medical Act 1978 (c. 12), s. 30.

GENERAL NOTE

Subs. (2)

Under the original rules of the Royal College of Midwives, men were unable to act in the capacity as midwives. This position was reversed by the Sex Discrimination Act 1975 (c. 65). Nevertheless, certain disabilities still exist, and these are provided for in subs. (2).

Jury service in Scotland

18. Practising midwives shall be exempt from serving on any jury in Scotland.

Financial provisions

Finances of Council and Boards

19.—(1) The Central Council and the National Boards may each charge such fees, in respect of such matters, as are determined by them respectively with the approval of the Secretary of State, including fees in connection with the training, qualification, examination and certification of nurses, midwives and health visitors.

(2) Subject to this section, fees received by the Council and Boards shall be applied to defray the expenses of the Council and Boards respectively.

(3) The Secretary of State may make grants to the Council and the Boards towards expenses incurred, or to be incurred, by them with the approval of the Secretary of State in connection with—

(*a*) the initial establishment of the Council and Boards;

(*b*) the promotion by the Council and Boards of improvements in the education and training of nurses, midwives and health visitors;

(*c*) the performance by the National Boards of their duties under paragraphs (*a*) and (*b*) of section 6 (1) above.

(4) The Council shall reimburse the Boards in respect of expenditure incurred by them with the former's approval in so far as that expenditure is not defrayed by fees received by the Boards, or funded by the Secretary of State with grants under subsection (3).

(5) Any sums required by the Secretary of State for making grants under subsection (3) shall be paid out of money provided by Parliament.

DEFINITIONS

" Central Council ": s. 23 (1), referring to s. 1 (1).

" National Boards ": s. 23 (1), referring to s. 5 (1).

Accounts of Council and Boards

20.—(1) The Central Council and each of the National Boards shall—

(*a*) keep proper accounts, and such records in relation to the accounts, as the Secretary of State may direct; and

(*b*) in respect of each financial year, prepare a statement of accounts in such form as the Secretary of State may with the approval of the Treasury direct.

(2) The accounts of the Council and of each of the Boards shall be audited in such manner and by such persons (qualified in accordance with Schedule 4) as the Secretary of State may direct; and copies of the statements of account, together with the auditors' reports, shall be sent to the Secretary of State who shall send them to the Comptroller and Auditor General not later than 30th November in the year following that for which the accounts are made up.

(3) The Comptroller and Auditor General shall examine the statements of account and auditors' reports, certify the statements and prepare a report on the results of his examination.

(4) For the purposes of his examination, the Comptroller and Auditor General may inspect the accounts of the Council and Boards and any records relating to them.

(5) The Council and each of the Boards shall annually, within such time as may be limited by the Secretary of State, submit a report to him on the performance of their respective functions during the period since their last such report.

(6) The Secretary of State shall lay before each House of Parliament—

(*a*) copies of the statements of account certified by the Comptroller and Auditor General, and the auditors' reports in respect of the Council and each of the Boards, together with copies of the report made by the Comptroller and Auditor General under subsection (3); and

(*b*) copies of the reports submitted by the Council and each of the Boards under subsection (5).

Miscellaneous and general

Dissolution of existing bodies, etc.

21.—(1) The following bodies are dissolved by virtue of this subsection—

the General Nursing Council for England and Wales;
the General Nursing Council for Scotland;
the Central Midwives Board;
the Central Midwives Board for Scotland;
the Northern Ireland Council for Nurses and Midwives; and
the Council for the Education and Training of Health Visitors;

and the Health Visiting and Social Work (Training) Act 1962 (which established the last-mentioned Council and also another body not dissolved by this Act) has effect accordingly.

(2) All those persons who at the passing of this Act hold office as members of—

the General Nursing Council for England and Wales;
the General Nursing Council for Scotland; or
the Northern Ireland Council for Nurses and Midwives,

shall continue in that office until the Council's dissolution.

(3) Part I of Schedule 5 to this Act has effected in connection with the transfer to the Central Council and the National Boards of the staff, property, rights and liabilities of the bodies mentioned in subsection (1); and Part II of that Schedule has effect with respect to the disposal of disciplinary proceedings begun before subsection (1) comes into force.

(4) In section 3 (1) (*a*) of the Health Visiting and Social Work (Training) Act 1962 (functions of Central Council for Education and Training in Social Work) for " in the health and welfare services " there is substituted " in connection with health and welfare services provided in the United Kingdom by local authorities, the Department of Health and Social Services for Northern Ireland and voluntary organisations "; and accordingly the Central Council for Education and Training in Social Work Order 1977 is revoked so far as it extends the functions of that Council to include social work required in services provided under the enactments specified in the Order.

Central Council rules

22.—(1) The Council may make rules for the purpose of giving effect to this Act, and in particular with respect to anything which by this Act is required or authorised to be determined by rules.

(2) Rules under this Act may make different provision in relation to England, Wales, Scotland and Northern Ireland respectively.

(3) Before making any rules under this Act, the Council shall consult—

(*a*) representatives of any group of persons who appear likely to be affected by the proposed rules; and

(*b*) the National Boards for the parts of the United Kingdom to which the proposed rules are to extend.

(4) Rules under section 12 shall not come into force until approved by order by the Lord Chancellor and, in the case of rules which apply to proceedings in Scotland, the Lord Advocate; otherwise, rules come into force only when approved by the Secretary of State by order.

Interpretation and supplementary

23.—(1) In this Act—

" by order " means by order in a statutory instrument;

" the Central Council " and " the Council " mean the body established by section 1 (1);

"elected members" has the meaning given by section 5 (4) (*b*);
"the National Boards" and "the Boards" mean the bodies established by section 5 (1);
"prescribed" means prescribed by the Secretary of State by order;
"the professional register" means the register maintained by the Council under section 10 (1), and "registration" and "register" shall be construed accordingly;
"rules" means rules made by the Council; and
"training" includes education;

and for a person to be treated as "practising" he must be working in some capacity by virtue of a qualification in nursing, midwifery or health visiting as the case may be.

(2) Orders under this Act shall be subject to annulment by resolution of either House of Parliament; but this does not apply to—

(*a*) orders under section 22 (4), Schedule 2, Part I, Schedule 3 or Schedule 5, Part I; or

(*b*) orders appointing a day for the purposes of any provision of this Act.

(3) Schedule 6 to this Act has effect for adapting the provisions of this Act there mentioned in their application to Northern Ireland and to the National Board for Nursing, Midwifery and Health Visiting for Northern Ireland.

(4) The enactments specified in Schedule 7 are amended as there specified.

(5) The enactments specified in Schedule 8 are repealed to the extent there specified.

Citation, etc.

24.—(1) This Act may be cited as the Nurses, Midwives and Health Visitors Act 1979.

(2) This Act, except section 21 (2) and this section (which shall come into force on the passing of this Act), shall come into force on such day as the Secretary of State may by order appoint; and different days may be appointed for different provisions of this Act.

(3) This Act extends to Northern Ireland.

SCHEDULES

Section 1

SCHEDULE 1

CONSTITUTION ETC. OF CENTRAL COUNCIL

PART I

NOMINATION OF MEMBERS OF CENTRAL COUNCIL BY NATIONAL BOARDS

1.—(1) Each of the National Boards shall nominate as members of the Central Council the number of members of the Board, being not less than 5, prescribed by the Secretary of State by order.

(2) The persons nominated by each of the Boards shall include at least—

(*a*) two practising nurses;
(*b*) one practising midwife;
(*c*) one practising health visitor; and
(*d*) one person engaged in the teaching of nursing, midwifery or health visiting.

Part II

Other provisions with respect to constitution etc. of Central Council

Tenure of office of members and chairman etc.

2.—(1) In the first instance, members of the Council shall hold office for a period ending on a day appointed by the Secretary of State by order, which day is not to be more than three years from the coming into force of section 1.

(2) After that day, members shall hold office for a period prescribed by the Secretary of State by order, being not less than 3 and not more than 5 years.

3.—(1) Where the place of a member becomes vacant before the expiration of his term of office (whether by death, resignation or otherwise) the vacancy shall be filled as follows—

(*a*) if the former member was a member nominated by a National Board, that Board shall nominate another of its members to be a member of the Council; or

(*b*) if the former member was appointed by the Secretary of State, the vacancy shall be filled by an appointment made by the Secretary of State.

(2) In nominating a person under sub-paragraph (1) (*a*), a Board shall have regard to the requirements of paragraph 1 (2); and, in making an appointment under sub-paragraph (1) (*b*), the Secretary of State shall have regard to the qualification by virtue of which the former member was appointed.

(3) Where a person is nominated or appointed as a member of the Council under sub-paragraph (1) above, he shall (subject to paragraph 4 (2) and (3)) hold office for the remainder of the term of office of the former member whose place he fills.

4.—(1) If the chairman or deputy chairman ceases to be a member of the Council, he shall also cease to be chairman or deputy chairman.

(2) Where a member of the Council or of any of its committees is absent from meetings for more than 6 months consecutively or is disqualified from practising as a nurse, midwife or health visitor, the Council may by resolution declare his office to be vacant.

(3) A nominated member who ceases to be a member of the National Board which nominated him shall cease to be a member of the Council.

5. In Part III of Schedule 1 to the House of Commons Disqualification Act 1975 (disqualifying offices), the following entry is inserted at the appropriate place in alphabetical order—

> " Chairman of the United Kingdom Central Council for Nursing, Midwifery and Health Visiting, if appointed by the Secretary of State under section 1 (6) (*a*) of the Nurses, Midwives and Health Visitors Act 1979."

Procedure

6.—(1) The Council may act notwithstanding—

(*a*) any vacancy among its members, or

(*b*) that in consequence of one or more vacancies, the nominated members cease to form the majority of the total membership of the Council.

(2) At any meeting of the Council the quorum shall be 15 members including at least one nominated member from each of the National Boards.

(3) The Council may constitute committees of itself, for the purpose of transacting particular business of the Council.

(4) Persons who are not members of the Council may be appointed by it as members of such committees; but not more than one-third of the members of such a committee shall be persons appointed by virtue of this sub-paragraph.

(5) The Council may, by means of standing orders, regulate its own procedure and that of its standing committees and of any joint committee constituted by or under section 8, and that of any committees constituted under sub-paragraph (3) above, and may, to such extent and in such cases as may be permitted or required by orders of the Secretary of State or by its rules and standing orders, act through those standing and other committees.

(6) Before making any standing orders regarding the procedure of any joint committee constituted by or under section 8, the Council shall consult each of the National Boards.

(7) No defect in the appointment of any member shall invalidate any proceedings of the Council or of its committees or of any joint committee.

Remuneration, allowances and pensions

7. The Council may pay—

(*a*) to its employees such remuneration, and make such provision for the payment of pensions, allowances or gratuities to or in respect of them, as the Secretary of State may, with the consent of the Minister for the Civil Service, approve;

(*b*) to its chairman and members and to other persons appointed to serve on its standing and other committees, or on any joint committee constituted by or under section 8, such travelling and other allowances as the Secretary of State may determine with the approval of the Minister for the Civil Service.

Documents

8. A document purporting to be duly executed under the seal of the Council or to be signed on its behalf shall be received in evidence and shall be deemed to be so executed or signed unless the contrary is proved.

Section 5

SCHEDULE 2

CONSTITUTION ETC. OF NATIONAL BOARDS

PART I

ELECTIONS TO NATIONAL BOARDS

1.—(1) The Central Council shall, within the period of two years following the coming into force of section 1 (1) of this Act, submit an electoral scheme to the Secretary of State for his approval, and the Secretary of State shall, if he approves it, give effect to the scheme by order.

(2) The Council shall by the scheme determine as respects each Board the professional, residential or other qualifications which a person must have to be eligible to vote or be elected in the election held under the scheme.

(3) The scheme may be varied from time to time by the Central Council, subject to the approval of the Secretary of State to be signified by order.

(4) No order shall be made under this paragraph unless a draft of the order has been approved by resolution of each House of Parliament.

PART II

OTHER PROVISIONS WITH RESPECT TO NATIONAL BOARDS

Tenure of office of members and chairmen

2.—(1) With effect from the appointed day, members of each of the Boards shall hold office for a period prescribed by the Secretary of State by order, being not less than 3 and not more than 5 years.

(2) Such an order may make different provision with regard to elected and appointed members respectively.

3.—(1) Where the place of a member becomes vacant before the expiration of his term of office (whether by death, resignation or otherwise) the vacancy shall be filled—

(*a*) if the former member was an elected member, by an appointment made by the Secretary of State of a person (proposed by the Board) who would be qualified for election to that place;

(*b*) if the former member was appointed by the Secretary of State, by an appointment made by the Secretary of State having regard to the qualification by virtue of which the former member was appointed.

(2) Persons so appointed shall (subject to paragraph 4 (2) and (3)) hold office for the remainder of the term of office of the former member.

4.—(1) If the chairman or deputy chairman of a Board ceases to be a member of that Board, he shall also cease to be chairman or deputy chairman.

(2) Where a member of a Board or of any of its committees is absent from meetings for more than 6 months consecutively or is disqualified from practising as a nurse, midwife or health visitor, the Board may by resolution declare his office to be vacant.

(3) An elected member, or a member appointed under paragraph 3 (1) (*a*) who ceases to hold the qualification by virtue of which he was elected or appointed shall cease to be a member and his place shall become vacant.

5.—(1) In Part III of Schedule 1 to the House of Commons Disqualification Act 1975 (disqualifying offices), the following entry is inserted at the appropriate place in alphabetical order—

> " Chairman of any of the National Boards constituted under the Nurses, Midwives and Health Visitors Act 1979, if appointed by the Secretary of State under section 5 (8) (*a*) of that Act ".

(2) In Schedule 1 to the Northern Ireland Assembly Disqualification Act 1975, in Part III the following entry is inserted at the appropriate place in alphabetical order—

> " Chairman of the National Board for Nursing, Midwifery and Health Visiting for Northern Ireland ".

Procedure

6.—(1) A Board may act notwithstanding—

(*a*) any vacancy among its members, or

(*b*) that in consequence of one or more vacancies, the elected members cease to form the majority of the total membership of the Board.

(2) At any meeting of a Board the quorum shall be 15 members (10 in the case of the Board for Northern Ireland).

(3) A Board may constitute committees of itself, for the purpose of transacting particular business of the Board.

(4) A Board may appoint as members of such committees persons who are not members of the Board; but not more than one-third of the members of such a committee shall be persons appointed by virtue of this sub-paragraph.

(5) A Board may, by means of standing orders, regulate its own procedure and that of its standing and other committees and may, to such extent and in such cases as may be permitted or required by orders of the Secretary of State and by its standing orders, act through those standing and other committees and through joint committees constituted by or under section 8:

Provided that standing orders shall not be made by a Board so as to conflict with any rules of the Central Council.

(6) No defect in the appointment of any member shall invalidate any proceedings of a Board, or of any of its standing or other committees.

Remuneration, allowances and pensions

7. A Board may pay—

(*a*) to its employees such remuneration, and make such provision for the payment of pensions, allowances or gratuities to or in respect of them, as the Secretary of State may, with the consent of the Minister for the Civil Service, approve;

(*b*) to its chairman and members and to other persons appointed to serve on its standing and other committees, such travelling and other allowances as the Secretary of State may determine with the approval of the Minister for the Civil Service.

Documents

8. A document purporting to be duly executed under the seal of a Board or to be signed on its behalf shall be received in evidence and shall be deemed to be so executed or signed unless the contrary is proved.

Section 12 (5)

SCHEDULE 3

Proceedings before Council and committees

1. For purposes of proceedings under section 12 before the Council or a committee in England and Wales—

(a) the Council or committee may administer oaths;

(b) a solicitor to the Council, and any person entitled to appear at the proceedings, may sue out writs of subpoena ad testificandum and duces tecum (but not so as to compel a person to produce a document which he could not be compelled to produce on the trial of an action); and

(c) section 49 of the Supreme Court of Judicature (Consolidation) Act 1925 (subpoena valid throughout United Kingdom) applies as in relation to causes or matters in the High Court.

2.—(1) For purposes of proceedings under section 12 before the Council or a committee in Scotland—

(a) the Council or committee may administer oaths; and

(b) the Court of Session shall, on the application of any party to the proceedings, have the same such powers as are mentioned in sub-paragraph (2) below as it has in an action in that court.

(2) The powers mentioned above are—

(a) to grant warrant for the citation of witnesses and havers to give evidence or to produce documents before the Council or committee, and for the issue of second diligence against any witness or haver failing to appear after due citation;

(b) to grant warrant for the recovery of documents; and

(c) to grant commissions to persons to take the evidence of witnesses or to examine havers and receive their exhibits and productions.

3.—(1) The Central Council shall appoint assessors (either generally or for any particular proceedings or class of proceedings) to advise the Council or committees on questions of law arising in the proceedings.

(2) Assessors shall be barristers, advocates or solicitors of not less than 10 years' standing.

(3) The Council shall pay to assessors such remuneration as it may determine.

4.—(1) The Lord Chancellor and, for proceedings in Scotland, the Lord Advocate may by order make provision with regard to the functions of assessors.

(2) In particular, provision may be made—

(a) requiring assessors, when advising the Council or any of its committees, to do so in the presence of the parties or, where advice is given in private, requiring the parties to be notified of the advice tendered by the assessors; and

(b) requiring the parties to be informed in cases where the assessors' advice is not accepted.

Section 20 (2)

SCHEDULE 4

Qualification of Auditors

1. A person is qualified for the purposes of section 20 (2) if he is a member of one of the recognised professional bodies.

2. Those bodies are—

the Institute of Chartered Accountants in England and Wales;
the Institute of Chartered Accountants of Scotland;
the Association of Certified Accountants; and
the Institute of Chartered Accountants in Ireland.

3. A person is also qualified if he is a member of a body of accountants established in the United Kingdom and recognised by the Secretary of State for the purposes of section 161 (1) (a) of the Companies Act 1948.

4. A Scottish firm is qualified if each of the partners in it is so.

Section 21

SCHEDULE 5

Transitional provisions, etc.

Part I

Transfer of property and staff etc. from existing bodies

1. In this Schedule—

"the new statutory bodies" means the Central Council and the four National Boards;

"the replaced statutory bodies" means the bodies mentioned in section 21 (1) of this Act.

2.—(1) The Secretary of State may by order provide for the transfer on the day specified by the order—

(*a*) to the employment of one or other of the new statutory bodies of any persons who immediately before that day were employed by one of the replaced statutory bodies;

(*b*) to any one or other of the new statutory bodies of such of the property, rights and liabilities, which immediately before that day were property, rights and liabilities of one or other of the replaced statutory bodies, as may be specified by the order.

(2) The reference in sub-paragraph (1) (*b*) above to rights and liabilities does not include rights and liabilities under any contract of employment.

(3) An order under sub-paragraph (1) (*a*) above shall, in the case of any persons transferred by the order, provide for the scales of remuneration applicable to them in the employment of the new statutory body and, taken as a whole, the other terms and conditions of that employment to be in general no less favourable than the scales of remuneration, terms and conditions enjoyed by them immediately before the transfer.

(4) Any such order shall so provide and have effect that, for the purposes of any enactment specified in it, the employments from which and to which persons are transferred by the order are to be treated as one continuous employment.

3. Orders under paragraph 2 shall provide for persons suffering loss of employment in consequence of the dissolution of any of the replaced statutory bodies (whether or not they are entitled to payments in respect of that loss of employment under legislation relating to redundancy) to be entitled, in such circumstances as the order may specify, to compensation payable by the Central Council on scales laid down by the Secretary of State with the approval of the Minister for the Civil Service.

4. Any dispute arising as to whether or not—

(*a*) the terms of employment with one of the new statutory bodies are, or would be, less favourable to a person than those on which he was employed at the time when the employment was offered to him; or

(*b*) whether or not a person's refusal of employment with one of those bodies was reasonable,

and any dispute concerning the compensation referred to in paragraph 3, shall be referred to and determined by an industrial tribunal.

5. Any property, rights and liabilities (other than rights and liabilities under a contract of employment) which are vested in or incumbent on any of the replaced statutory bodies immediately before the day on which the replaced statutory bodies are dissolved and are not transferred on that day by virtue of an order under paragraph 2 (1) (*b*) above shall by virtue of this sub-paragraph be transferred to, and vest in or become incumbent on, the Central Council on that day.

6.—(1) Where a person formerly employed by any of the replaced statutory bodies claims to have a right of action against that body arising from his employment by them but is unable to pursue his claim because of the dissolution of the body, he may bring his claim—

(*a*) if he is transferred to the employment of one or other of the new statutory bodies, against that body; or

(*b*) in any other case, against the Central Council.

(2) The body against whom a claim is brought by virtue of sub-paragraph (1) shall be liable in the same manner and to the same extent as the replaced statutory body would have been liable if it had not been dissolved.

PART II

CONTINUATION OF DISCIPLINARY PROCEEDINGS

7. Where on the appointed day any disciplinary proceedings—

(*a*) are pending before any of the replaced statutory bodies or before any committee of theirs; or

(*b*) have begun but the body or committee seized of them has not communicated its decision to the person who is the subject of the proceedings,

that body or committee shall refer the proceedings to the Central Council and the Council shall dispose of the matter in whatever way it thinks just.

8. An appeal by a person aggrieved by a decision of any of the replaced statutory bodies or any committee of theirs to remove or suspend him from one of the registers, rolls or lists maintained under any of the enactments repealed by this Act which is pending or proceeding before any court on the appointed day may be continued and disposed of as if the provision of the repealed enactments under which the appeal was brought had remained in force.

9. In this Part of this Schedule "the appointed day" means the day appointed by the Secretary of State by order for the purposes of this Part.

Section 23 (3)

SCHEDULE 6

ADAPTATIONS FOR NORTHERN IRELAND AND ITS NATIONAL BOARD

1. In sections, 5, 7, 9, 17, 19, 20, 22 and 23, and Schedules 2, 3 and 4, as they apply to Northern Ireland and to the National Board for Nursing, Midwifery and Health Visiting for Northern Ireland, there are made the adaptations provided for by this Schedule.

2. Subject to the following provisions of this Schedule, in the provisions of this Act specified in column 1 of the Table set out below, for any reference specified in column 2 substitute the reference specified in column 3.

TABLE

Provision	*Reference*	*Substituted reference*
Sections 5 (3), (4) (*a*), (5), (6) and (8) (*a*) and 20 (5) and (6) and Schedule 2, paragraph 3.	The Secretary of State.	The Head of the Department of Health and Social Services for Northern Ireland.
Sections 7, 9, 17 (2), 19 (1), (3) and (4) and 20 (1) and (2) and Schedule 2, paragraphs 6 (5) and 7.	The Secretary of State.	The Department of Health and Social Services for Northern Ireland.
Section 17 (2).	Schedule 4 to the Sex Discrimination Act 1975.	Schedule 5 to the Sex Discrimination (Northern Ireland) Order 1976.
Section 20 (1) (*b*).	The Treasury.	The Department of Finance for Northern Ireland.
Section 20.	The Comptroller and Auditor General.	The Comptroller and Auditor General for Northern Ireland.
Section 20 (5).	Each House of Parliament.	The Northern Ireland Assembly.
Section 22 (4) and Schedule 3, paragraph 4.	The Lord Chancellor,	The Lord Chief Justice of Northern Ireland.
Schedule 2, paragraph 7.	The Minister for the Civil Service.	The Department of the Civil Services for Northern Ireland.
Schedule 4, paragraph 3.	The Secretary of State.	The Department of Commerce for Northern Ireland.
Schedule 4, paragraph 3.	Section 161 (1) (*a*) of the Companies Act 1948.	Section 155 (1) (*a*) of the Companies Act (Northern Ireland) 1960.

3. In section 23 (1)—

(*a*) in the definition of " by order ", at the end add the words " or in the case of an order under section 7 or 9 made by the Department of Health and Social Services for Northern Ireland or an order under section 22 (4) or paragraph 4 of Schedule 3 made by the Lord Chief Justice of Northern Ireland means by order made by statutory rule for the purposes of the Statutory Rules Act (Northern Ireland) 1958 " ;

(*b*) in the definition of " prescribed " after the words " Secretary of State " insert the words " or, as the case may be, the Department of Health and Social Services for Northern Ireland ".

4. In section 23 (2) at the end add—

" (*c*) orders made by the Department of Health and Social Services for Northern Ireland under section 7 or 9;

and the orders mentioned in paragraph (*c*) shall be subject to negative resolution as defined by section 41 (6) of the Interpretation Act (Northern Ireland) 1954 as if they were statutory instruments within the meaning of that Act.".

5. In paragraph 1 of Schedule 3, for " in England and Wales " substitute " in Northern Ireland " and for paragraph 1 (*c*) substitute—

" (*c*) section 67 of the Judicature (Northern Ireland) Act 1978 (subpoena valid throughout United Kingdom) applies as in relation to causes or matters in the High Court in Northern Ireland."

Section 23 (4)

SCHEDULE 7

Amendments of enactments

Nursing Homes Registration (Scotland) Act 1938 (*c.* 73)

1. In section 1 (3) (*d*) of the Nursing Homes Registration (Scotland) Act 1938, for " certified " substitute " registered " and for " pupil midwife " substitute " student midwife " ; and after section 1 (3) insert—

" (3A) In relation to any nursing home, a person is to be treated as a qualified nurse if he possesses such qualifications as the Secretary of State considers to be requisite in the provision of nursing care for patients in that home."

2. In section 5 (1), for " qualified nurse " substitute " registered nurse ".

3. In section 10—

(*a*) omit the definitions of " qualified nurse " and " certified midwife " ;

(*b*) for the definition of " pupil midwife " substitute—

" " student midwife " means a person who is undergoing training with a view to becoming a registered midwife, and for that purpose attending women in childbirth, as part of a course of practical instruction in midwifery recognised by the National Board for Nursing, Midwifery and Health Visiting for Scotland " ; ".

Nurses (Scotland) Act 1951 (*c.* 55)

4. In section 27 of the Nurses (Scotland) Act 1951—

(*a*) in subsection (1), for paragraphs (*a*) to (*c*) substitute—

" (*a*) registered nurses and registered midwives; and " and make paragraph (*d*) into paragraph (*b*) ;

(*b*) in subsection (3), for " registered nurse " substitute " registered and qualified nurse ".

5. In section 29, for " registered nurse " substitute " registered and qualified nurse ".

6. In section 32, omit the definition of " certified midwife ".

Births and Deaths Registration Act 1953 (*c.* 20)

7. In section 11 (1) and (1A) of the Births and Deaths Registration Act 1953, for " certified midwife " substitute " registered midwife ".

Nurses Agencies Act 1957 (*c.* 16)

8. In section 1 of the Nurses Agencies Act 1957—

(*a*) in subsection (1), for paragraphs (*a*) to (*c*) substitute—

" (*a*) registered nurses and registered midwives; and " and make paragraph (*d*) into paragraph (*b*) ;

(b) in subsection (3), for "registered nurse" substitute "registered and qualified nurse".

9. In section 3 (2), for "registered nurse" substitute "registered and qualified nurse".

10. In section 8, omit the definitions of "certified midwife", "enrolled nurse" and "registered nurse", and the word "and" immediately preceding the latter.

Health Visiting and Social Work (Training) Act 1962 (*c.* 33)

11. In paragraph 4 of Schedule 1 to the Health Visiting and Social Work (Training) Act 1962, for "General Nursing Council for England and Wales" substitute "United Kingdom Central Council for Nursing, Midwifery and Health Visiting".

Registration of Births, Deaths and Marriages (Scotland) Act 1965 (*c.* 49)

12. In section 21 (2) and (3) of the Registration of Births, Deaths and Marriages (Scotland) Act 1965, for "certified midwife" substitute "registered midwife".

13. Omit section 21 (6).

Medicines Act 1968 (*c.* 67)

14. In section 11 of the Medicines Act 1968—

(a) in subsection (1) for "a registered nurse or as a certified midwife" substitute "a registered and qualified nurse or a registered midwife";

(b) omit subsection (2).

Commissioner for Complaints Act (Northern Ireland) 1969 (*c.* 25 *N.I.*)

15. In Schedule 1 to the Commissioner for Complaints Act (Northern Ireland) 1969, in Part II insert the following entry at the appropriate point in alphabetical order—

"The National Board for Nursing, Midwifery and Health Visiting for Northern Ireland."

Nursing Homes and Nursing Agencies Act (Northern Ireland) 1971 (*c.* 32 *N.I.*)

16. In section 2 (e) of the Nursing Homes and Nursing Agencies Act (Northern Ireland) 1971, before "midwife" insert "registered" and for "pupil midwife" substitute "student midwife"; and at the end of section 2 insert—

"(2) In relation to any nursing home, a person is to be treated as a qualified nurse if he possesses such qualifications as the Department of Health and Social Services for Northern Ireland considers to be requisite in the provision of nursing care for patients in that home."

17. In section 10 (1)—

(a) omit the definitions of "Joint Council", "qualified nurse", and "the register of nurses";

(b) for the definition of "pupil midwife" substitute–

"" student midwife" means a person who is undergoing training with a view to becoming a registered midwife, and for that purpose attending women in childbirth, as part of a course of practical instruction in midwifery recognised by the National Board for Nursing, Midwifery and Health Visiting for Northern Ireland".

18. Omit section 10 (2).

19. In section 11—

(a) in subsection (1), for paragraphs (a) to (c) substitute—

"(a) registered nurses and registered midwives; and" and make paragraph (d) into paragraph (b);

(b) in subsection (3) for "registered nurse" substitute "registered and qualified nurse".

20. In section 19 omit the definitions of "enrolled nurse" and "registered nurse".

21. In section 20 omit the definitions of "the Act of 1970" and "midwife".

22. In Schedule 1, omit the entry relating to the Nurses and Midwives Act (Northern Ireland) 1970.

Nursing Homes Act 1975 (*c.* 37)

23. In section 4 (*e*) of the Nursing Homes Act 1975, for " certified " substitute " registered " and for " pupil midwife " substitute " student midwife "; and at the end of section 4 insert—

" (2) In relation to any nursing home, a person is to be treated as a qualified nurse if he possesses such qualifications as the Secretary of State considers to be requisite in the provision of nursing care for patients in that home."

24. In section 20 (1)—

(*a*) for the definition of " pupil midwife " substitute—

" " student midwife " means a person who is undergoing training with a view to becoming a registered midwife, and for that purpose attending women in childbirth, as part of a course of practical instruction in midwifery recognised by the National Board for Nursing, Midwifery and Health Visiting for England or for Wales ";

(*b*) omit the definition of " qualified nurse ".

25. Omit section 20 (2).

Sex Discrimination Act 1975 (*c.* 65)

26. In paragraph 3 (1) of Schedule 4 to the Sex Discrimination Act 1975, for the words " the issue " to " section 20) " substitute " registration as midwives under the Nurses, Midwives and Health Visitors Act 1979 ".

Restrictive Trade Practices Act 1976 (*c.* 34)

27. In Schedule 1 to the Restrictive Trade Practice Act 1976, for paragraph 6 substitute—

" 6. The services of nurses ".

National Health Service Act 1977 (*c.* 49)

28. In section 128 (1) of the National Health Service Act 1977, omit the definition of " certified midwife " and " registered nurse "; and in Schedule 4, paragraph 1 (5) (*c*), for " certified " substitute " registered ".

National Health Service (Scotland) Act 1978 (*c.* 29)

29. In section 108 (1) of the National Health Service (Scotland) Act 1978, omit the definitions of " certified midwife " and " registered nurse ".

Interpretation Act 1978 (*c.* 30)

30. In Schedule 1 to the Interpretation Act 1978 (words and expressions defined) at the appropriate place in alphabetical order insert—

" Registered " in relation to nurses, midwives and health visitors, means registered in the register maintained by the United Kingdom Central Council for Nursing, Midwifery and Health Visiting by virtue of qualifications in nursing, midwifery or health visiting, as the case may be.

Employment Protection (Consolidation) Act 1978 (*c.* 44)

31. In section 33 (5) of the Employment Protection (Consolidation) Act 1978, for " certified midwife " substitute " registered midwife "; and in section 153 (1) omit the definition of " certified midwife ".

Scotland Act 1978 (*c.* 51)

32. In Schedule 13 to the Scotland Act 1978, at the end of Part II add—

United Kingdom Central Council for Nursing, Midwifery and Health Visiting.	Nurses, Midwives and Health Visitors Act 1979, section 1.
Standing committees of the Central Council constituted by Order.	The said Act, section 3.
National Board for Nursing, Midwifery and Health Visiting for Scotland.	The said Act, section 5.
Standing committees of the National Board for Scotland constituted by order.	The said Act, section. 7.

Joint committees of the Central Council and the National Boards for Nursing, Midwifery and Health Visiting constituted by order.	The said Act, section 8.
Local training committees of the National Board for Scotland constituted by order.	The said Act, section 9.

Wales Act 1978 (*c.* 52)

33. In Schedule 7 to the Wales Act 1978, at the end of Part II, add—

United Kingdom Central Council for Nursing, Midwifery and Health Visiting.	Nurses, Midwives and Health Visitors Act 1979, section 1.
Standing committees of the Central Council constituted by order.	The said Act, section 3.
National Board for Nursing, Midwifery and Health Visiting for Wales.	The said Act, section 5.
Standing committees of the National Board for Wales constituted by order.	The said Act, section 7.
Joint committees of the Central Council and the National Boards for Nursing, Midwifery and Health Visiting constituted by order.	The said Act, section 8.
Local training committees of the National Board for Wales constituted by order.	The said Act, section 9.

Health and Personal Social Services Order (*Northern Ireland*) 1972 (*S.I.* 1972/1265 (*N.I.* 14))

34. In Article 17 (1) of the Health and Personal Social Services Order (Northern Ireland) 1972, after sub-paragraph (*c*), insert—

"(*d*) provide such facilities and accommodation for persons training with a view to qualification for registration as nurses and midwives as the National Board for Nursing, Midwifery and Health Visiting for Northern Ireland may require in discharging functions under section 6 (1) (*a*) of the Nurses, Midwives and Health Visitors Act 1979;".

35. After Article 17 (1), insert—

"(1A) The Health and Social Services Board in whose area a school for the training of nurses and midwives is situated shall—

(*a*) employ, for the period of the person's training with a view to qualification for registration as a nurse or midwife, any person accepted for such training by it and the National Board for Nursing, Midwifery and Health Visiting for Northern Ireland;

(*b*) in assigning duties to any such person during that period, comply with the training requirements of the United Kingdom Central Council for Nursing, Midwifery and Health Visiting.".

Births and Deaths Registration (*Northern Ireland*) *Order* 1976 (*S.I.* 1976/1041 (*N.I.* 14))

36. In Article 2 (2) of the Births and Deaths Registration (Northern Ireland) Order 1976 omit the definition of "midwife"; and in Article 15 for "midwife" substitute "registered midwife".

Sex Discrimination (*Northern Ireland*) *Order* 1976 (*S.I.* 1976/1042 (*N.I.* 15))

37. In paragraph 3 (1) of Schedule 5 to the Sex Discrimination (Northern Ireland) Order 1976, for the words from "the issue" to "Article 22)" substitute "registration as midwives under the Nurses, Midwives and Health Visitors Act 1979".

Industrial Relations (No. 2) (Northern Ireland) Order 1976
(*S.I.* 1976/2147 (*N.I.* 28))

38. In Article 15 (4) of the Industrial Relations (No. 2) (Northern Ireland) Order 1976, for " certified midwife " substitute " registered midwife "; and in Article 32 omit the definition of " certified midwife ".

SCHEDULE 8

Repeals

Chapter	Short title	Extent of repeal
1 & 2 Geo. 6 c. 72.	The Nursing Homes Registration (Scotland) Act 1938.	In section 10, the definitions of " qualified nurse " and " certified midwife ".
14 & 15 Geo. 6. c. 53.	The Midwives Act 1951.	The whole Act.
14 & 15 Geo. 6. c. 54.	The Midwives (Scotland) Act 1951.	The whole Act.
14 & 15 Geo. 6. c. 55.	The Nurses (Scotland) Act 1951.	Parts I, II and (except section 36 (1) and (2)) IV, and in section 32 the definition of " certified midwife ". Schedules 1 and 4.
1 & 2 Eliz. 2. c. 47.	The Emergency Laws (Miscellaneous Provisions) Act 1953.	Section 6.
5 & 6 Eliz. 2. c. 15.	The Nurses Act 1957.	The whole Act.
5 & 6 Eliz. 2. c. 16.	The Nurses Agencies Act 1957.	In section 8, the definitions of " certified midwife ", " enrolled nurse " and " registered nurse ", and the word " and " immediately preceding the latter definition.
7 & 8 Eliz. 2. c. 72.	The Mental Health Act 1959.	In Schedule 7, the entry relating to the Nurses Act 1957.
8 & 9 Eliz. 2. c. 61.	The Mental Health (Scotland) Act 1960.	In Schedule 4, the entry relating to the Nurses (Scotland) Act 1951.
9 & 10 Eliz. 2. c. 14.	The Nurses (Amendment) Act 1961.	The whole Act.
10 & 11 Eliz. 2. c. 33.	The Health Visiting and Social Work (Training) Act 1962.	Section 3 (5).
1964 c. 44.	The Nurses Act 1964.	The whole Act.
1965 c. 49.	The Registration of Births and Marriages (Scotland) Act 1965.	Section 21 (6).
1967 c. 16.	The Teachers of Nursing Act 1967.	The whole Act.
1967 c. 80.	The Criminal Justice Act 1967.	In Schedule 3, Part I, the entries relating to the Midwives Act 1951 and the Midwives (Scotland) Act 1951.
1968 c. 46.	The Health Services and Public Health Act 1968.	In Part I of Schedule 3, in the first entry relating to the Health Visiting and Social Work (Training) Act 1962, the words " 3 and "; and the second entry relating to that Act.
1968 c. 49.	The Social Work (Scotland) Act 1968.	In Schedule 8, paragraph 60.
1968 c. 67.	The Medicines Act 1968.	In section 11 (1), the words " or, in relation to " onwards. Section 11 (2).
1969 c. 25 (N.I.).	The Commissioner for Complaints Act (Northern Ireland) 1969.	In Schedule 1, in Part II, the entry relating to the Northern Ireland Council for Nurses and Midwives.
1969 c. 47.	The Nurses Act 1969.	The whole Act.
1970 c. 11 (N.I.).	The Nurses and Midwives Act (Northern Ireland) 1970	The whole Act.

SCHEDULE 8—*continued*

Chapter	Short title	Extent of repeal
1971 c. 32 (N.I.).	The Nursing Homes and Nursing Agencies Act (Northern Ireland) 1971.	In section 10 (1), the definitions of " Joint Council ", " qualified nurse " and " the register of nurses ". Section 10 (2). In section 19, the definitions of " enrolled nurse " and " registered nurse ". In section 20, the definitions of " the Act of 1970 " and " midwife ". In Schedule 1, the entry relating to the Nurses and Midwives Act (Northern Ireland) 1970.
1975 c. 24.	The House of Commons Disqualification Act 1957.	In Schedule 1, Part III, the entry relating to the Chairman of the Northern Ireland Council for Nurses and Midwives.
1975 c. 25.	The Northern Ireland Assembly Disqualification Act 1975.	In Schedule 1, in Part III, the entry relating to the Chairman of the Northern Ireland Council for Nurses and Midwives.
1975 c. 37.	The Nursing Homes Act 1975.	In section 20 (1), the definition of " qualified nurse ". Section 20 (2). Section 20 (4) and (5).
1975 c. 65.	The Sex Discrimination Act 1975.	In Schedule 4, paragraph 3 (2) and (3). In Schedule 5, paragraph 2.
1977 c. 45.	The Criminal Law Act 1977.	In Schedule 6, the entries relating to the Midwives Act 1951, the Midwives (Scotland) Act 1951, the Nurses (Scotland) Act 1951 and the Nurses Act 1957.
1977 c. 49.	The National Health Service Act 1977.	In section 128 (1) the definition of " certified midwife ". In Schedule 15, paragraphs 15 to 17.
1978 c. 29.	The National Health Service (Scotland) Act 1978.	In section 108 (1) the definitions of " certified midwife " and " registered nurse ". In Schedule 16, paragraph 7.
1978 c. 44.	The Employment Protection (Consolidation) Act 1978.	In section 153 (1) the definition of " certified midwife ".

Orders in Council

Number	Short title	Extent of repeal
S.I. 1972/1073 (N.I. 10).	The Superannuation (Northern Ireland) Order 1972.	In Schedule 6, paragraph 7.
S.I. 1972/1245 (N.I. 14).	The Health and Personal Social Services (Northern Ireland) Order 1972.	In Schedule 16, Part II, paragraphs 84 to 95.
S.I. 1976/1041 (N.I. 14).	The Births and Deaths Registration (Northern Ireland) Order 1976.	In Article 2 (2) the definition of " midwife ".
S.I. 1976/1042 (N.I. 15).	The Sex Discrimination (Northern Ireland) Order 1976.	Article 22 (4). In Schedule 5, paragraph 3 (2) and (3).
S.I. 1976/2147. (N.I. 28).	The Industrial Relations (No. 2) (Northern Ireland) Order 1976.	In Article 32 the definition of " certified midwife ".
S.I. 1977/1240.	The Central Council for Education and Training in Social Work Order 1977.	Article 3. Schedule 1.

Banking Act 1979 *

(1979 c. 37)

ARRANGEMENT OF SECTIONS

PART I

CONTROL OF DEPOSIT-TAKING

* Annotations by F. R. Ryder, LL.B., F.I.B., Barrister, former Group International Legal Adviser to the Midland Bank.

An Act to regulate the acceptance of deposits in the course of a business; to confer functions on the Bank of England with respect to the control of institutions carrying on deposit-taking businesses; to give further protection to persons who are depositors with such institutions; to make provision with respect to advertisements inviting the making of deposits; to restrict the use of names and descriptions associated with banks and banking; to prohibit fraudulent inducement to make a deposit; to amend the Consumer Credit Act 1974 and the law with respect to instruments to which section 4 of the Cheques Act 1957 applies; to repeal certain enactments relating to banks and banking; and for purposes connected therewith.

[4th April 1979]

General Note

This statute, given its Royal Assent on April 4, 1979, after an accelerated passage through Parliament for political reasons, represents a departure from the principles of laissez-faire in an area where it was once most strongly ensconced. The functions of the Bank of England could be compared to those of a headmaster; its legal authority was never questioned but its actual authority was real; no-one sought the "Board of Governors." In the days of the Capital Issues Committee the wishes of the Chancellor as to bank overdrafts were conveyed to the City by Treasury Directives, the Bank of England being the arbiter of the application of the principle that one bank would not take business if the other had refused it on the ground that it was contrary to the Directive. The door was open legally in that borrowing in the ordinary course of business from a banker payable on demand was exempt (S.I. 1958 No. 1208).

The change stems from two reasons: the secondary banking crisis, and harmonisation of "banking law" (*sic*) being pursued by the EEC. In part, at least, the former may be traced to a legal decision (*United Dominions Trust* v. *Kirkwood* [1966] 2 Q.B. 431). Kirkwood had borrowed money from UDT and, *faute de mieux,* the defence was raised that UDT were unregistered moneylenders whereas they contended that they were exempt as carrying on the "business of banking" (Moneylenders Act 1927, s. 6 (*d*)). Although, when the case went to the Court of Appeal, a majority decision was given in favour of UDT, no doubt was left that in any future case proof that a substantial proportion of the business of a company claiming to be carrying on the business of banking was, in fact, so engaged would require precise satisfaction. This would involve evidence of the conduct of current accounts and the payment and collection of cheques. Diplock L.J. said that if the evidence were more closely probed in another case it did not follow that the result would be the same (*ibid.* p. 475). To save other finance houses from the fate that nearly overtook UDT, s. 123 of the Companies Act 1967 was passed enabling the Board of Trade (as it then was) to certify that "they were satisfied that a person could probably be treated as bona fide carrying on the business of banking." That was to be conclusive evidence and available as an alternative to the proof of a sufficient proportion of business involving the activity quoted above from the UDT case. From such certificates, at least in part, came the secondary banks, quite a number of whom lent long and borrowed short, which, with the fall in property values, caused failures that would have been far more numerous had the Bank of England not obtained co-operation from the traditional bankers in establishing the "lifeboat" fund. This latter, whilst in one way illustrating the flexibility of the virtually unwritten sanction, also reflected a weakness now being removed. The Bank of England will control by statute not only the banks but "licensed deposit takers," a new category likely to involve those institutions that have not been traditionally regarded as banks.

A second influence in the introduction of this legislation has been EEC Directive 1977/780 aimed at achieving harmonisation of "banking law" within the Community. It should perhaps be mentioned that banking law in Continental countries is regarded as the body of statutory law governing the constitution of banks and administration of banking, in contradistinction to the meaning usually applied hitherto in the United Kingdom and in most of the English speaking world generally, which involves the legal relationship between banker and customer, especially in relation to the payment and collection of cheques (which have most of the implications of other bills of exchange). An earlier draft of a Directive caused consternation. In fact the present Directive represents a measure of compromise and the Committee which it sets up is intended to achieve a further degree of harmonisation. An incidental consequence may be that the Directive, although not incorporated in the law *ipso facto* as part of the statute law as would be a "Regulation," may be subject to the interpretation of the Luxembourg Court, and thus necessitate a variation in the statute, although this is an unlikely possibility.

The Preamble to the Act has been slightly extended during the passage through Parliament to include amendments of the Consumer Credit Act 1974 and of the Cheques Act 1957. The main achievements are:

(1) The regulation of deposit taking.

(2) The control of all deposit takers—recognised banks *and* licensed institutions by the Bank of England.

(3) Further protection than previously for depositors with licensed institutions, including a fund.

(4) Strengthened prohibition of fraudulent inducement to make a deposit.

(5) Restriction of the use of banking names.

(6) Amendment of Consumer Credit Act 1974 (to give certain exclusions to bank overdrafts) and the amendment and repeal of other statutes affecting banking.

It is in the control given formally to the Bank of England that the greatest change takes place. Previously there was tacit *de facto* control of the banks but now this is formal; of more importance, however, is the control of the other deposit takers which at best was tenuous and at worst was non-existent. The measure of control stemming from the Act of 1964 was slight and debatable.

Extent

The Act extends to Northern Ireland.

Commencement

The Act comes into force when the Treasury appoints by Statutory Instrument, but different days may be appointed for different provisions *or* for *different purposes* of the *same* provision (s. 52 (3)).

Parliamentary debates

Hansard, H.C. Vol. 957, col. 1209; Vol. 958, col. 1500; Vol. 962, col. 1593; H.L. Vol. 398, col. 1267; Vol. 399, cols. 77, 1744.

Part I

Control of Deposit-Taking

Ambit of control

Control of deposit-taking and meaning of " deposit "

1.—(1) Except as provided by section 2 below, no person may accept a deposit in the course of carrying on a business which is a deposit-taking business for the purposes of this Act.

(2) Subject to subsection (3) below, a business is a deposit-taking business for the purposes of this Act if—

(*a*) in the course of the business money received by way of deposit is lent to others, or

(*b*) any other activity of the business is financed, wholly or to any material extent, out of the capital of or the interest on money received by way of deposit.

(3) Notwithstanding that paragraph (*a*) or paragraph (*b*) of subsection (2) above applies to a business, it is not a deposit-taking business for the purposes of this Act if, in the normal course of the business,—

(*a*) the person carrying it on does not hold himself out to accept deposits on a day to day basis; and

(*b*) any deposits which are accepted are accepted only on particular occasions, whether or not involving the issue of debentures or other securities.

(4) Subject to subsection (5) below, in this Act " deposit " means a sum of money paid on terms—

(*a*) under which it will be repaid, with or without interest or a premium, and either on demand or at a time or in circumstances agreed by or on behalf of the person making the payment and the person receiving it; and

(*b*) which are not referable to the provision of property or services or to the giving of security;

and references in this Act to money deposited and to the making of deposits shall be construed accordingly.

(5) Except in so far as any provision of this Act otherwise provides, in this Act " deposit " does not include—

(*a*) a loan made by the Bank, a recognised bank or a licensed institution; or

(*b*) a loan made by a person for the time being specified in Schedule 1 to this Act; or

(*c*) a loan made by a person, other than a person falling within paragraph (*a*) or paragraph (*b*) above, in the course of a business of lending money carried on by him; or

(*d*) a sum which is paid by one company to another at a time when one is a subsidiary of the other or both are subsidiaries of another company; or

(*e*) a sum which is paid to an institution by a person who at the time it is paid is a director, controller or manager of the institution or the wife, husband, son or daughter of such a person.

(6) For the purposes of subsection (4) (*b*) above, money is paid on terms which are referable to the provision of property or services or to the giving of security if, and only if,—

(*a*) it is paid by way of advance or part payment for the sale, hire or other provision of property or services of any kind and is repayable only in the event that the property or services is or are not in fact sold, hired or otherwise provided; or

(*b*) it is paid by way of security for payment for the provision of property or services of any kind provided or to be provided by the person by whom or on whose behalf the money is accepted; or

(*c*) it is paid by way of security for the delivery up or return of any property, whether in a particular state of repair or otherwise.

(7) Any person who accepts a deposit in contravention of subsection (1) above shall be liable—

(*a*) on summary conviction to a fine not exceeding the statutory maximum; and

(*b*) on conviction on indictment to imprisonment for a term not exceeding two years or to a fine or both.

(8) The fact that a deposit is taken in contravention of this section shall not affect any civil liability arising in respect of the deposit or the money deposited.

General Note

It is to be borne in mind that the primary purpose of the Act is control, involving offences. It does not *aim* to alter the civil law; these changes are largely incidental. The proposals were outlined in a White Paper in 1976 (Cmnd. 6584) and the draft Bill was published early as part of another White Paper in July 1978 (Cmnd. 7303) to allow for consultation with the many interests involved. The EEC Directive, mentioned in the General Note to this Act above, has to be implemented by the end of 1979. The task of this section is fundamental—to define deposit—and is difficult because prima facie almost every loan is a deposit. The Protection of Depositors Act 1963, now finally repealed by the Act, was far less ambitious being concerned with the provision of information and the control of advertisements; banks, within the definition of a " banking or discount company " in the Eighth Schedule to the Companies Act 1948, were excluded and other advertisers could not hold out that they were engaged in banking. The interpretation of that definition of " bank " was regarded by the Board of Trade as burdensome.

Subs. (1)

Here we have the basic prohibition against accepting a deposit other than as permitted in s. 2. It is limited to doing so in the course of a deposit-taking business. During the Committee stage of the Bill it was pointed out that, strictly speaking, one might carry on a deposit-taking business without taking a deposit (December 5, 1978)—obviously unsuccessfully. This accounts for the "comprehensive" character of the definition. "Deposit" is defined in subss. (2) to (6) below.

Subs. (2)

The *first* category of the subsection includes the traditional banking operation comprehending the current account as well as the deposit account. Unlike, for example, an estate agent who is under a duty *not* to use money, deposited with him temporarily, for his own purposes, a banker has only the obligation to repay the *debt* when called upon (in the case of a current account most usually upon presentation of a cheque). Pending the time when the banker has to fulfil his obligation he has no duty to keep the money deposited in any particular form (*cf. Joachimson* v. *Swiss Bank Corp.* [1918] 2 K.B. 833 at p. 848 and *Midland Bank* v. *Conway Borough Council* [1965] 1 W.L.R. 1165). A "banker" also collects cheques (see *United Dominions Trust* v. *Kirkwood* [1966] 2 Q.B. 431), but other deposit-takers also may lend money to third parties; for instance, the taking of deposits and finance of hire-purchase transactions thereout is an understood function.

The *second* category is probably more controversial. "Any material extent" is a question of discretion. Previously, a discretion in any matter exercised by the Bank of England went almost invariably unquestioned, at all events in the courts, even if a pretext for doing so could have been conjured up. Now these matters of "degree," so to speak, are open to appeal to a tribunal (see ss. 11 and 12, *infra*). The reference to "capital of or interest on" the money may refer to a possible contention that utilisation of *interest* on money received *differs* from utilisation of the money. This definition appears to go beyond that in the EEC Directive (77/780) where "credit institution" is defined as "an undertaking whose business is to receive deposits or other repayable funds from the public and to grant credits for its own account."

Subs. (3)

This subsection is a further contribution to the definition in that there is an indication of what is *not* a deposit-taking business, thus excluding deposits taken in the circumstances described. There have to be two characteristics in order that the business is *not* a deposit-taking business: that there is no holding out on a day-to-day basis *and* that in fact the deposit is accepted only on particular occasions. Thus the occasional raising of capital, perhaps loan capital, would be excluded if the business were not a deposit-taking business *and* the occasion of the receipt of the money was explicable as associated with an event or occasion peculiar to the recipient.

Subs. (4)

This makes it clear that the circumstances of repayment may be wide without taking the transaction out of the definition although there is the reservation in favour of transactions appearing in subs. (6). "Sum of money" would include cheques received for collection and credit, or "short bills," *i.e.* bills not due when received; but not bills discounted (or purchased).

Subs. (5)

Loans by persons whose normal business includes lending obviously have to be excluded since, taken in reverse, they are of the nature of a deposit. Inter-company lending within a group is subject to a similar analysis. It is seemingly intended to be family loans to small businesses; this may, however, be more controversial. On the one hand, the mechanism may be abused; on the other hand the loss of a regular source of loan finance not in the category outlined may cause hardship. (An "associate" in the Consumer Credit Act 1974 is more widely defined in relation to s. 184.)

Subs. (6)

This explains the provision in subs. (4), above, extending to all kinds of advance payments or cash security in respect of hire or purchase of goods, services or property, including house purchase.

Subs. (7)

The statutory maximum is £1,000. Compare provisions of Criminal Law Amendment Act 1977.

Subs. (8)

This is most significant, otherwise all the cases concerning illegality and the enhanced position of a defendant would arise in application of the maxim of *in pari delicto potior est conditio defendentis,* although the rigours appear to be diminishing (*cf. Nash* v. *Halifax Building Society* [1979] 2 All E.R. 19 where what appeared might be an illegal second mortgage was upheld).

Exceptions from prohibition in section 1 (1)

2.—(1) The prohibition in section 1 (1) above on the acceptance of a deposit does not apply to—

(*a*) the Bank; or

(*b*) a recognised bank; or

(*c*) a licensed institution; or

(*d*) a person for the time being specified in Schedule 1 to this Act;

and does not apply to a transaction prescribed for the purposes of this section regulations made by the Treasury.

(2) The Treasury may from time to time by order made by statutory instruments—

(*a*) add a person to the list set out in Schedule 1 to this Act, or

(*b*) remove a person from that list (whether that person was included in the list as originally enacted or was added to it by virtue of this subsection).

(3) A statutory instrument containing an order under paragraph (*a*) of subsection (2) above shall be subject to annulment in pursuance of a resolution of either House of Parliament and no order under paragraph (*b*) of that subsection shall be made unless a draft of it has been laid before Parliament and approved by a resolution of each House.

(4) In the case of a body which on the appointed day was carrying on a deposit-taking business in the United Kingdom, the prohibition in section 1 (1) above on the acceptance of a deposit does not apply—

(*a*) at any time during the period of six months beginning on that day; nor

(*b*) if within that period the body makes an application for recognition or a licence, at any time after the end of that period and before the date on which the body is granted recognition or, as the case may be, a licence or on which the Bank notifies the body of its decision to refuse to grant it recognition or a licence.

(5) Regulations under subsection (1) above may prescribe transactions by reference to any factors appearing to the Treasury to be appropriate and, in particular, by reference to all or any of the following, namely,—

(*a*) the amount of the deposit;

(*b*) the total liability of the body concerned to its depositors;

(*c*) the circumstances in which or the purpose for which the deposit is made; and

(*d*) the identity of the person by whom the deposit is made or accepted.

(6) The power to make regulations under subsection (1) above shall be exercisable by statutory instrument which shall be subject to annulment in pursuance of a resolution of either House of Parliament.

General Note

This section is the source of the most far-reaching effects of the Act. It divides recognised banks from deposit-takers. What is more, from this division comes the right to the description of banker, specifically a matter of greatest concern to those previously using it from whom it is to be taken away. The significant Schedule (Sched. 2) is the one containing the criteria on which the Bank of England is to take its decisions. It would seem that while the decisions are to be governed by the criteria, they contain deliberate scope for the traditional wisdom to be pursued with an element of discretion. There must be no conflict with the EEC Directive in the specific exemptions or the description of bank, but it is to be noted that the Directive deals only with credit institutions and would not extend to deposit-takers who use the deposits for investment in their own businesses. This Act is of wider import.

Subs. (1)

There are the two main categories, "recognised banks" and "licensed institutions," exempted with others, from the prohibition in s. 1 (1). More are specifically exempted in Sched. 1, *and* the Treasury have also specific powers to prescribe transactions to which the prohibition is not to apply. Close examination of the criteria is appended to Sched. 2.

Subs. (2)

This reflects the power of variation of the list of exemptions although it has to be effected by Statutory Instrument with the accompanying formality of approval by Parliament, indicated below. (This could be a way of resolving the problems associated with solicitors as deposit-takers.)

Subs. (3)

The *addition* necessitates a resolution of *either* House of Parliament whereas the *removal* (as indicated by the Minister in Standing Committee A, First Sitting, December 5, 1978) was sufficiently serious to justify approval by a resolution of both Houses.

Subs. (4)

It is thought that there will be three months or more before the Act comes into force so, in practice there is, say, nine months plus any time taken for the decision of the Bank.

Subs. (5)

The exemption of transactions obviously may be based on a wide variety of reasons. Reference was made in the First Sitting to Industrial and Provident Societies as an example, and elsewhere, there was criticism of the possible inclusion of Crown Agents who hold money for non-specified purposes on behalf of principals.

The system of recognition and licensing by the Bank

Recognition and licences

3.—(1) Recognition as a bank for the purposes of this Act may be granted by the Bank on an application in that behalf by the institution concerned.

(2) A full licence to carry on a deposit-taking business may be granted to an institution by the Bank on an application in that behalf or on an application for recognition or on the revocation of the institution's recognition.

(3) Subject to subsection (5) below,—

(*a*) the Bank shall not grant to an institution recognition as a bank unless it is satisfied that the criteria in Part I of Schedule 2 to this Act are fulfilled with respect to the institution; and

(*b*) the Bank shall not grant a full licence to an institution unless it is satisfied that the criteria in Part II of that Schedule are fulfilled with respect to the institution.

(4) The Bank shall grant neither recognition nor a licence to an institution which is not a body corporate if the whole of the assets available to the institution are owned by a single individual.

(5) In the case of an institution whose principal place of business is in a country or territory outside the United Kingdom, the Bank may regard itself as satisfied that the criteria in paragraphs 3 and 6 of Schedule

2 to this Act or, as the case may be, paragraphs 7 and 10 of that Schedule are fulfilled if—

(*a*) the relevant supervisory authorities inform the Bank that they are satisfied with respect to the management of the institution and its overall financial soundness; and

(*b*) the Bank is satisfied as to the nature and scope of the supervision exercised by those authorities.

(6) In subsection (5) above " the relevant supervisory authorities " in relation to an institution whose principal place of business is in a country or territory outside the United Kingdom means the authorities which exercise functions corresponding to those of the Bank under this Act in the country or territory where the institution's principal place of business is.

(7) A grant of recognition and a full licence shall remain in force until—

(*a*) it is surrendered by notice in writing given by the institution concerned to the Bank; or

(*b*) it is revoked in accordance with the following provisions of this Act.

(8) The provisions of Part I of Schedule 3 to this Act shall have effect with regard to transitional licences and the provisions of Part II of that Schedule shall have effect with respect to the grant of recognition to certain institutions which were in existence on 9th November 1978.

General Note

Subss. (1) (2) *and* (3)

It is to be observed that the authority to the Bank is permissive as to both recognition as a bank and licence to carry on a deposit-taking business. This does not mean that a decision does not have to be justified as a bona fide exercise of discretion on appeal. On the other hand, subs. (3) prohibits the Bank from granting recognition or a licence *unless* it is satisfied that criteria stipulated are fulfilled.

Subs. (4)

The exclusion of a one-man business conforms with the EEC Directive. A " credit institution " is an undertaking.

Subs. (5)

This is controversial. The provisions of the Schedule relate respectively to recognitions and licences but the double requirement means that the Bank of England are not dealing with matters entirely within their purview. The Bank of England has to be informed that the supervisory body abroad is satisfied with the management *and* itself to be satisfied with the supervision exercised abroad—the latter being an aspect that could perhaps be controversial. It has been suggested that even implied non-approval could cause political embarrassment.

Subs. (6)

It will not always be easy to find a precise counterpart abroad to the Bank of England.

Subs. (7)

For revocation, see s. 6.

Subs. (8)

For definition of transitional licence, which applies primarily to deposit-taking, not recognition, see s. 10 and Sched. 3. It must have been in light relief that in the Third Sitting of Standing Committee A (December 12, 1978), thought was expressed that a transitional licence might, like an " L " licence for a motor-cyclist, seemingly continue indefinitely, or at least for an eviternity.

Annual report and list of recognised and licensed institutions

4.—(1) The Bank shall, as soon as practicable after the end of each of its financial years, make a report to the Chancellor of the Exchequer on its activities in that year in the exercise of the functions conferred on it by this Act.

(2) Every report under this section shall contain a list of the institutions which are recognised or licensed under this Act at the end of the financial year of the Bank to which the report relates.

(3) Every report under this section shall set out the principles on which the Bank is acting, at the end of the financial year of the Bank to which the report relates, with respect to—

(*a*) the interpretation and application of the criteria to be fulfilled by institutions applying for recognition or a licence; and

(*b*) the interpretation and application of the grounds for revocation of recognition or a licence;

and shall specify any material change in those principles which was made in the course of the year in question or is proposed to be made in the following years.

(4) The Chancellor of the Exchequer shall lay a copy of every report made by the Bank under this section before each House of Parliament and the Bank shall arrange for the publication of every such report in such manner as it thinks appropriate.

(5) Any reference in this section to a financial year of the Bank is a reference to a period of twelve months ending on the last day of February.

(6) The Bank shall make available to any person, on request and on payment of such charge (if any) as the Bank may reasonably demand to cover the cost of preparation, a list of all the institutions which are recognised or licensed under this Act either at the date of the request or at such earlier date, being not more than one month earlier, as may be specified in the list.

General Note

This section requires a report on activity annually up to the last day of February, which is in fact the present end of the year for the Bank of England. Its contents will be vital: "the interpretation and appreciation of the criteria" for recognition or a licence and the grounds for revocation. This is so important that one must surely anticipate guidance at an early stage when the applications are being prepared. The Chancellor does not appear to be answerable strictly on individual cases, but the fact that the *Annual* Report will be laid before Parliament will enable the principles to be questioned. Some relation may be sought to enable the preliminary guidance to be similarly raised; on the other hand the whole object of the legislation is to perpetuate, at least through an opaque glass, the undoubted but confidential wisdom of the past. Whether wisdom is lost by revelation time will tell. Secrecy, in law and in practice, is the quintessence of banking domestically and, one hopes, internationally. Once the first principles are established there should be little annual change except in so far as may flow from interpretations of the EEC Directive and perhaps also of the Appeal Tribunals (see ss. 11 and 12) under this Act. However, if the tail wags the dog too much, the extent to which the City operates flexibly may be detrimentally reduced. The list of authorised banks for purposes of the Exchange Control legislation will no doubt still remain. Guidelines issued by the Bank may be expected in September 1979.

Recognition and licences: procedure on applications

5.—(1) An application for recognition or for a full licence—

(*a*) shall be made in such manner as the Bank may specify, either generally or in any particular case; and (*b*) shall be accompanied by such information as the Bank may reasonably require, either generally or in any particular case, in order to reach a decision on the application.

(2) If required to do so by notice in writing from the Bank given at any time after an application falling within subsection (1) above has been made and before a decision has been reached on the application, the applicant shall furnish to the Bank such additional information as the Bank may reasonably require in order to reach a decision.

(3) Any person who knowingly or recklessly furnishes any information which is false or misleading in a material particular in connection with an application falling within subsection (1) above shall be liable—

(*a*) on summary conviction to a fine not exceeding the statutory maximum; and

(*b*) on conviction on indictment to imprisonment for a term not exceeding two years or to a fine or both.

(4) If, on an application falling within subsection (1) above, the Bank proposes to refuse to grant recognition or, in the case of an application for a licence, to refuse to grant the licence applied for, the Bank—

(*a*) shall give notice in writing to the applicant of the action it proposes to take with respect to the application and of the reasons for that proposed action; and

(*b*) in the notice under paragraph (*a*) above shall also inform the applicant of the right to make representations in writing with respect to the proposed action of the Bank within such period of not less than twenty-eight days as may be specified in the notice; and

(*c*) before reaching a decision on the application shall take account of any representations made as mentioned in paragraph (*b*) above.

(5) If, on an application falling within subsection (1) above, the Bank refuses to grant recognition or, as the case may be, the licence applied for, then subject to subsection (6) below, the Bank shall give notice in writing to the applicant of its decision and the reasons for it before the expiry of the period of six months beginning with the date on which the application was received by the Bank.

(6) In any case where, under subsection (2) above, the Bank requires additional information with respect to an application, the latest time for the giving of a notice under subsection (5) above with respect to that application shall be the expiry of whichever of the following periods first expires, namely—

(*a*) the period of six months beginning on the date on which the additional information is furnished to the Bank; and

(*b*) the period of twelve months beginning on the date on which the application was received by the Bank.

General Note

This section provides the mechanism for applications. It contains all the provisions one would expect and forms the right to call, if need be, for further information and the penalty for false information. In addition there is the opportunity during the rather short period of 14 days for the applicant to make further representations, in that he will receive preliminary notice of refusal (subs. (4)). There is also the obligation of the Bank of England to answer the application within six months which can be extended to 12 when further information is sought by the Bank. These times coincide with the EEC Directive (art. 3 (6)).

Revocation of recognition or licence

Grounds for revocation of recognition or licence

6.—(1) The powers of the Bank under section 7 below to revoke recognition or a licence shall become exercisable with respect to an institution if it appears to the Bank that—

(*a*) any of the information required to be furnished by the institution in connection with its application was false or misleading in a material particular; or

(*b*) the institution has not carried on any deposit-taking business within the period of twelve months beginning on the date on which it was granted recognition or, as the case may be, on which the licence took effect, or has ceased to carry on any such business for a period of more than six months; or

(*c*) any of the criteria in Part I or Part II of Schedule 2 to this Act which is applicable to the institution is not being or has not been fulfilled with respect to it; or

(*d*) in the case of an institution whose principal place of business is in a country or territory outside the United Kingdom, the authorities which exercise in that country or territory functions corresponding to those of the Bank under this Act have withdrawn from the institution the authority which in that country or territory corresponds to the authority conferred in the United Kingdom by recognition or a licence; or

(*e*) the institution is a body corporate and any of the events referred to in subsection (2) below has occurred with respect to it; or

(*f*) the institution is a partnership and any of the events referred to in subsection (3) below has occurred with respect to it; or

(*g*) the institution is an unincorporated institution other than a partnership and is formed under the law of another member State and an event has occurred with respect to it which, in that member State, appears to the Bank to correspond, as near as may be, with any of the events specified in paragraphs (*a*) to (*d*) of subsection (2) or paragraphs (*a*) to (*f*) of subsection (3) below; or

(*h*) the institution has failed to comply with any obligation imposed by this Act; or

(*i*) the institution has in any other way so conducted its affairs as to threaten the interests of its depositors.

(2) The events referred to in subsection (1) (*e*) above are—

(*a*) the making of a winding-up order;

(*b*) the passing of a resolution for voluntary winding up;

(*c*) the appointment of a receiver or manager of the body's undertaking; and

(*d*) the taking of possession, by or on behalf of the holders of any debenture secured by a floating charge, of any property of the body comprised in or subject to the charge;

and also, in the case of a body corporate formed under the law of a country or territory outside the United Kingdom, any event which appears to the Bank to correspond under that law with any of the events specified above.

(3) The events referred to in subsection (1) (*f*) above are—

(*a*) the dissolution of the partnership;

(*b*) the making of a winding-up order against the firm under Part IX of the Companies Act 1948 or the Companies Act (Northern Ireland) 1960 (unregistered companies);

(*c*) if one of the partners is a body corporate, the occurrence with respect to that partner of one of the events specified in subsection (2) above;

(*d*) in England and Wales, the making of a receiving order against the firm or against one of the partners or one of the partners executing an instrument to which the Deeds of Arrangement Act 1914 applies;

(*e*) in Scotland, the making of an award of sequestration on the estate of the partnership or one of the partners, or the partnership or one of the partners executing a trust deed for creditors or entering into a composition contract; and

(*f*) in Northern Ireland, the making of an order of adjudication of bankruptcy against one of the partners or one of the partners making a composition or arrangement with his creditors;

and also, in the case of a partnership whose principal place of business is in a country or territory outside the United Kingdom, any event which appears to the Bank to correspond in that country or territory with any of the events specified above.

(4) It shall be a ground for revoking a full licence held by an institution that the Bank proposes to grant recognition to the institution with effect from the time of the revocation of the licence.

(5) It shall be a ground for revoking a conditional licence held by an institution that the Bank proposes to grant a full licence to the institution with effect from the time of the revocation of the conditional licence.

GENERAL NOTE

Subs. (1)

The first four grounds reflect the EEC Directive (art. 8). Para. (*a*) is obvious. Para. (*b*) presumably does not necessitate the taking of a deposit since there could be a holding out, and for that matter a seeking of business, without there being a taking of a deposit. Para. (*c*) may come into effect immediately as will be seen from the powers given to the Bank under s. 8. This latter is dictated by the need for expedition where deposit-taking is to cease, although it will not always have been appreciated by the bank or deposit-taker that it is in breach, as for example, when "net assets" are no longer at the figure required by Sched. 2, para. 5. It is then likely that the Bank may treat the breach with discretion although there is power to do otherwise, but it is to be remembered that, although a new statute has been passed, the intention is to continue, at least so far as bankers are concerned, an extra-legal authority that has grown up over the centuries. Para. (*d*) is bound to be in general terms, although it is not clear that the Bank can effect revocation if it is no longer satified as to the "nature and scope of the supervision exercised by the authorities," as required by s. 3 (5) (*b*). Para. (*e*) refers to any body corporate—not just to one incorporated in the home countries—and is expanded later in the section regarding foreign institutions, as is a partnership mentioned in para. (*f*). Para. (*g*) refers to foreign institutions which may be regarded, strictly speaking, as unincorporated. It is to be observed that it is one formed in a "Member State," not any territory outside the United Kingdom; an example of a borderline case would be a "société en nom collectif." Para. (*h*) appears to be designed to catch omissions and para. (*i*) likewise. At the Third Sitting of Standing Committee A, a proposal was moved to change the latter (para. (*i*)) to being "so adverse to the interests of its depositors as to be inequitable," but the Minister remarked that such phraseology was appropriate to contracts (having been culled from the Fair Trading Act 1973), not to conduct—and, in practice, he did "not think it would make very much difference."

Subs. (2)

These events make the powers under s. 7 exercisable by the Bank in the case of a limited company arise when the authority of the directors has been taken over, although in two instances, (*c*) and (*d*), it *may* possibly revert to them at a later date, the "receiver and manager" carrying on the business temporarily. The powers of the Bank have "become exercisable" (see subs. (1)). It would appear to be in their discretion not to exercise them although one wonders whether there is a duty for which a mandatory injunction could be obtained for unreasonably forbearing to exercise such powers. Here again this is presumably a sanction that is not intended to hang over the head of the Bank so long as there is the bona fide exercise of a discretion. The final part of the subsection (and of the next) is the expansion mentioned and is about the only solution to the difficult problem—however ambitious the draftsman.

Subs. (3)

Para. (*b*) relates to the wide description of unregistered companies. Examples are companies established by Royal Charter (*Re Bank of South Australia* [1895] 1 Ch. 578), a friendly society (*Re Victoria Society, Knottingly* [1892] 1 Ch. 154), a building society (*Re Queens Building Society* (1871) L.R. 6 Ch. 815), and a dissolved foreign company with assets in the United Kingdom (*Re Azoff-Don Commercial Bank* [1954] Ch. 315). Para. (*c*) is because the dissolution of the partnership would not follow automatically upon the dissolution of a corporate partner. As to para. (*d*), the receiving order does not necessitate ultimate bankruptcy but the event justifies the power arising from the clause (in Scotland sequestration is preceded by "notour" bankruptcy).

Subss. (4) *and* (5)

These subsections are basically consequential.

Revocation: powers and procedure

7.—(1) Where the powers of the Bank under this section have become exercisable with respect to an institution, the Bank may—

(*a*) revoke the recognition or licence of the institution and take such action as it considers appropriate under section 8 below; or

(*b*) revoke the recognition or licence of the institution and grant it a conditional licence or, if the institution is already the holder of such a licence, grant it another conditional licence subject to different conditions.

(2) Where the powers of the Bank under this section have become exercisable with respect to a recognised bank but it appears to the Bank that the circumstances are not such as to justify proceedings under subsection (1) above, the Bank may revoke the institution's recognition and grant it a full licence.

(3) Subject to subsection (4) below, where the Bank proposes to act under subsection (1) or subsection (2) above,—

(*a*) the Bank shall give the institution concerned notice in writing of its intention specifying the reasons why it proposes to act; and

(*b*) the provisions of Part I of Schedule 4 to this Act shall apply.

(4) In any case where—

(*a*) the powers of the Bank under this section have become exercisable with respect to an institution, and

(*b*) the Bank considers that urgent action is necessary,

the Bank may, without prior notice under subsection (3) above, by notice in writing given to the institution concerned exercise its powers under paragraph (*b*) of subsection (1) above; and where the Bank exercises those powers by virtue of this subsection, the provisions of Part II of Schedule 4 to this Act shall apply instead of the provisions of Part I of that Schedule.

(5) In Schedule 4 to this Act "the principal section" means this section and—

(*a*) in Part I of that Schedule a "notice of intention to act" means a notice given under subsection (3) (*a*) above; and

(*b*) in Part II of that Schedule an "immediate revocation notice" means a notice given under subsection (4) above.

(6) The power of the Bank to revoke a licence by virtue of subsection (4) or subsection (5) of section 6 above shall be exercisable by notice in writing given to the institution concerned.

GENERAL NOTE

Subs. (1)

The power is to give a conditional licence (see s. 10) or to give other instructions (s. 8).

Subs. (2)

Circumstances justifying reduction to a "full licence" from "recognition" are perhaps difficult to envisage where a bank seeks to retain its status, unless there is agreement or the circumstances are blatant.

Subss. (3)–(6)

The position following notice is examined when considering Sched. 4, from which it can be seen that a conditional licence—which can prohibit deposits (s. 10)—can supervene immediately. This is strong control but reflects the reaction against the past laxity. Immediate revocation is also detailed in Sched. 4 (*q.v.*). In fact all deposit-taking authority can be revoked by the Bank at any time.

Power to give directions in connection with termination of deposit-taking authority

8.—(1) Subject to sections 9 and 11 (5) below, the Bank may give directions under this section to an institution—

(*a*) at the same time as the Bank gives the institution notice under subsection (3) (*a*) of section 7 above of its intention to take action under subsection (1) (*a*) of that section; or

(*b*) at any time after such a notice has been given to the institution (whether before or after its recognition or licence is revoked); or

(*c*) at any time after the institution has surrendered its recognition or licence.

(2) Directions under this section shall be such as appear to the Bank to be desirable in the interests of depositors, whether for the purpose of safeguarding the assets of the institution or otherwise, and a direction under this section may do all or any of the following, namely—

(*a*) prohibit the institution from dealing with or disposing of its assets in any manner specified in the direction;

(*b*) prohibit it from entering into any transaction or class of transaction so specified;

(*c*) prohibit it from soliciting deposits either generally or from persons who are not already depositors; and

(*d*) require it to take certain steps or pursue a particular course of action.

(3) A direction under this section shall be in writing and shall specify the reasons why the Bank considers it should be given.

(4) The power of the Bank to give a direction under this section includes power to vary such a direction by a further direction; and a direction under this section may be revoked by a notice in writing (which may be contained in a later direction) given to the institution concerned by the Bank.

(5) Any person who fails to comply with a direction for the time being in force under this section shall be liable—

(*a*) on summary conviction to a fine not exceeding the statutory maximum; and

(*b*) on conviction on indictment to imprisonment for a term not exceeding two years or to a fine or both.

General Note

Subs. (1)

S. 9 elaborates the power given to the Bank by this section, and s. 11 (5) terminates its operation when an appeal is successful. The section outlines the mechanism of the Bank to direct institutions, whether recognised banks or licensed deposit-takers, at the time of giving first notice (under s. 7 (3) and before or after the licence or status has been revoked or surrendered). The directions do not continue indefinitely, expiring automatically unless confirmed (see s. 9 below).

Subs. (2)

The extent of the authority of the Bank may be seen. Each of the four categories is aimed at protecting the *interests* of *depositors*—theoretically, perhaps, even wider than the *deposits*—which are not protected against inflation. This of course is too fine a line to be realistic but nevertheless shows that only a prima facie reason is required to prohibit the deposit-taker from dealing with the deposits in any way the Bank thinks undesirable, or from any transaction specified, or from soliciting new deposits; yet again, by para. (*d*), the deposit-taker may be required to pursue certain actions. These obligations appear, perhaps, to overlap.

Subs. (3)

It is true that there has to be a written reason for a direction. The reason will have to be valid in the eyes of the Bank, but the provision will not have to outline the connection between the reason and the direction.

Subss. (4) *and* (5)

These ensure the right to vary the direction and to impose the penalty.

Duration of directions and direction-making power

9.—(1) A direction under section 8 above shall cease to have effect at the expiry of the period of twenty-eight days beginning on the day on which it was given unless, before the expiry of that period, the Bank gives notice in writing to the institution concerned confirming the direction.

(2) In deciding whether to give a notice under subsection (1) above confirming a direction, the Bank shall take into account any written representations made by or on behalf of the institution concerned within the period of fourteen days beginning with the date on which the direction was given.

(3) In any case where—

(*a*) the Bank has given an institution notice under subsection (3) (*a*) of section 7 above of its intention to take action under subsection (1) (*a*) of that section, and

(*b*) subsequently the Bank gives notice to the institution under paragraph 2 of Schedule 4 to this Act of a decision to take no further action or to take some other course of action,

any direction under section 8 above previously given to the institution shall cease to have effect on the giving of the notice referred to in paragraph (*b*) above and no further direction may be given to the institution under that section in reliance on the notice mentioned in paragraph (*a*) above having been given.

(4) No direction may be given to an institution under section 8 above after it has ceased to have any liability in respect of deposits for which it had a liability at a time when it was recognised or licensed; and any such direction which is in force with respect to an institution shall cease to have effect when the institution ceases to have any such liability.

General Note

The duration has to be limited, in that it must cease to affect deposit-takers and not operate indefinitely.

Subs. (1)

The authority ceases after 28 days but the Bank can save the termination by giving notice of confirmation.

Subs. (2)

That the Bank is to take into account representations by the institution affected merely reflects the spirit in which it is intended to operate the law.

Subs. (3)

Where there has been a notice of revocation and later the Bank gives notice of its intention to take no further action, as it may under Sched. 4, any directions given under s. 8 (above) are also to cease.

Subs. (4)

This makes it clear that once an institution ceases to have liability for deposits taken when it was licensed, the power to direct *ends*—as does any direction outstanding.

Conditional licences

10.—(1) A conditional licence is a licence which, subject to section 11 (3) below, is granted to an institution by the Bank in the exercise of its powers under section 7 (1) (*b*) above and gives the institution authority to carry on a deposit-taking business conditionally upon its complying with conditions imposed by the Bank and set out in the licence.

(2) The conditions of a conditional licence granted to an institution—

(*a*) shall be such as the Bank considers necessary in order to secure the protection of the depositors of that institution; and

(*b*) may require the institution to take certain steps or to refrain from adopting or pursuing a particular course of action or to restrict the scope of its business in a particular way; and

(*c*) may be varied from time to time by agreement between the Bank and the institution.

(3) Without prejudice to the generality of subsection (2) (*b*) above, the conditions of a conditional licence may—

(*a*) impose limitations on the acceptance of deposits, the granting of credit or the making of investments;

(*b*) prohibit the soliciting of deposits, either generally or from persons who are not already depositors; and

(*c*) require the removal of any director, controller or manager.

(4) In the case of an institution holding a conditional licence, a failure to comply with any of the conditions of the licence shall be treated for the purposes of this Act as a failure by the institution to comply with such an obligation as is referred to in section 6 (1) (*h*) above.

(5) A conditional licence may be surrendered by notice in writing given by the institution concerned to the Bank.

(6) Unless previously revoked or surrendered, a conditional licence shall expire at the end of the period of one year beginning on the date on which it was granted or on such earlier date as may be specified in the licence.

General Note

The principle of a conditional licence—that it is not to extend beyond 12 months—enables any mandatory or restrictive condition to be attached. It can amount to next to nothing or be cathartic. It may well be used pending investigation as to whether a full licence (that is a licence for a deposit-taker) is to be removed—or for that matter when a recognition is removed. It is wide except that there is the maximum period of a year—but one could not expect it otherwise. As well as being part of control it gives opportunity to condition the decision to circumstances. It may give a very wide discretion but it is a matter of policy that detailed stipulation which could hamper the exercise of maximum wisdom is avoided. It is in this type of Act that one expects to find latitude—where legal rights are replacing a discretion that in the past had no formal bounds.

Subs. (1)

As well as operating within the scope set out above, it is to be noted that it is subject to appeal.

Subss. (2) *and* (3)

These subsections show how wide are the powers. We see, as in s. 8 (3), on the one hand it being ensured that the object of the protection of the depositors is achieved; on the other there are available the powers to vary the conditions. It appears that anything that can be directed can be couched in the form of a conditional licence (presumably in the latter if you fail to use the licence you can ignore the condition—but that will probably have little practical attractions).

Subs. (4)

It is stated in this subsection that failure to comply with the condition in a licence is to amount to failure to comply with s. 6 (1) (*h*), which means that the Bank can revoke a licence or recognition as the case may be, that is to say the powers become exercisable. Of course until action is taken by the Bank, the conditional licence is still held but may not be used.

Appeals

Appeals from decisions of the Bank

11.—(1) Any institution which is aggrieved by a decision of the Bank—

(*a*) to refuse to grant recognition or a licence to it, or

(*b*) to grant a licence to it on an application for recognition, or

(*c*) to revoke its recognition or licence, or

(*d*) to give it a direction under section 8 above,

may appeal against the decision to the Chancellor of the Exchequer who, in accordance with regulations under section 12 below, shall refer the matter for a hearing before persons appointed for the purpose.

(2) If the Bank revokes recognition or a licence in the exercise of its powers under section 7 (1) (*b*) above, then, on an appeal against the decision to revoke, the appellant institution may challenge any of the conditions of the conditional licence granted to it, whether or not it also challenges the decision itself.

(3) On the determination of an appeal under this section, the Chancellor of the Exchequer may confirm, vary or reverse the decision appealed against, and may—

(*a*) take any action which the Bank could have taken at the time it took the decision appealed against; and

(*b*) give such directions as he thinks just for the payment of costs or expenses by any party to the appeal.

(4) Notice of the Chancellor of the Exchequer's decision on the appeal together with a statement of his reasons for the decision shall be given to the appellant and to the Bank and, unless the Chancellor otherwise directs, the decision shall come into operation on such notice being given to the appellant.

(5) Where an institution is successful in an appeal to the Chancellor of the Exchequer against a decision of the Bank to revoke all authority of the institution to carry on a deposit-taking business and, prior to that decision, the Bank gave such a notice as is referred to in subsection (1) (*a*) of section 8 above, then, on the Chancellor's coming into operation,—

(*a*) any directions previously given to the institution under that section shall cease to have effect; and

(*b*) no further direction may be given to the institution under that section in reliance on that notice having been given.

General Note

This form of appeal, like much of the rest of the statute, reflects the extent to which it is sought to protect the *Bank* from embarrassment. Admittedly such a policy is merited by the delicacy of the area with which the Act deals. It is to be noted that the appeal is made nominally to the Chancellor who is to be advised by a tribunal, yet to be constituted. However, while he is likely to follow its decisions there is no legal obligation to do so, however perverse his attitude may appear to be.

Subss. (1)–(4)

Appeals may be made against a refusal to grant a licence or a "bank" recognition, or against any revocation of such status or against any direction. If a conditional licence only is granted then (see s. 7 (1) (*b*)), an appeal lies against the inclusion of the condition. Then it is open to the Chancellor (presumably recommended by the tribunal) to vary the condition as well as remove it. In fact, any other decision the Bank could have taken originally may be substituted as a result of the appeal. An appeal result, with reasons, will be the subject of notice (strictly notification?) to the parties, when normally the decision will come into operation.

Subs. (5)

Where there is a successful appeal against a decision of the Bank to revoke deposit-taking (following the exercise of revocation powers pursuant to ss. 7 (1) (*a*), (3) (*a*) and 8 (1) (*a*), which embody the process of revocation) these notices and any directions under s. 9 cease to have effect; also no further directions pursuant to the notices can be given.

Regulations with respect to appeals

12.—(1) Provision may be made by regulations with respect to appeals under section 11 above—

(*a*) as to the period within which and the manner in which such appeals are to be brought;

(*b*) as to the persons (in this subsection referred to as "appointed persons") by whom such appeals are to be heard on behalf of the Chancellor of the Exchequer;

(*c*) as to the manner in which such appeals are to be conducted, including provision for any hearing before appointed persons to be held in private;

(*d*) for requiring any person, on tender of the necessary expenses of his attendance, to attend and give evidence or produce documents in his custody or under his control;

(*e*) for taxing or otherwise settling any costs or expenses directed to be paid under section 11 (3) (*b*) above and for the enforcement of any such direction; and

(*f*) as to any other matter connected with such appeals.

(2) Subject to subsection (3) below, regulations under this section shall be made by the Treasury after consultation with the Council on Tribunals and shall be made by statutory instrument which shall be subject to annulment in pursuance of a resolution of either House of Parliament.

(3) Regulations under this section with respect to Scottish appeals, that is to say, appeals where the institution concerned—

(*a*) is a company registered in Scotland, or

(*b*) has its principal or prospective principal place of business in the United Kingdom in Scotland,

shall be made by the Lord Advocate after consultation with the Council on Tribunals which shall consult with its Scottish Committee.

(4) A person who, having been required in accordance with regulations under this section to attend and give evidence, fails without reasonable

excuse to attend or give evidence shall be liable on summary conviction to a fine not exceeding £1,000.

(5) A person who intentionally alters, suppresses, conceals, destroys or refuses to produce any document which he has been required to produce in accordance with regulations under this section, or which he is liable to be so required to produce, shall he liable—

(*a*) on summary conviction to a fine not exceeding the statutory maximum; and

(*b*) on conviction on indictment to imprisonment for a term not exceeding two years or to a fine or both.

(6) The Treasury may, out of money provided by Parliament, pay to any persons appointed as mentioned in paragraph (*b*) of subsection (1) above such fees and make good to them such expenses as the Treasury may determine.

General Note

There are to be regulations as to the period during which appeals are to be brought, the constitution of the tribunal, as to the conduct of the appeals, the attendance of witnesses and the taxing of costs.

Subs. (2)

The regulations are to be made by statutory instrument (after the consultation with the Council on Tribunals). The Council on Tribunals, consisting of between 10 and 15 members appointed by the Lord Chancellor, has a duty to consider the working of tribunals and since 1959 it has been mandatory for Ministers to approve procedural rules only after reference to the Council. One of its functions is to keep under review the working of statutory tribunals. It is at present governed by the Tribunals and Inquiries Act 1971.

Subs. (3)

Scottish banks are registered in Scotland and English banks normally in England, although there have been for a century or more branches of Scottish banks in England (only very recently has the reverse applied also). There appears to be no instance, however, with a Scottish bank of a head office or registered office being situated in a particular country for tax purposes or the benefit of the legal provisions obtaining locally.

Subss. (4)–(6)

These provisions ensure the practical functioning of the Tribunal.

Further appeal on points of law

13.—(1) An appeal shall lie to the Court at the instance of the institution concerned or of the Bank on any question of law arising from any decision of the Chancellor of the Exchequer on an appeal under section 11 above; and if the Court is of opinion that the decision appealed against was erroneous in point of law, it shall remit the matter to the Chancellor with the opinion of the Court for re-hearing and determination by him.

(2) In subsection (1) above " the Court " means the High Court, the Court of Session or a judge of the High Court in Northern Ireland according to whether,—

(*a*) if the institution concerned is a company registered in the United Kingdom, it is registered in England and Wales, Scotland or Northern Ireland; and

(*b*) in the case of any other institution, its principal or prospective principal place of business in the United Kingdom is situated in England and Wales, Scotland or Northern Ireland.

(3) No appeal to the Court of Appeal or to the Court of Appeal in Northern Ireland shall be brought from a decision under subsection (1)

above except with the leave of that court or of the court or judge from whose decision the appeal is brought.

(4) An appeal shall lie, with the leave of the Court of Session or the House of Lords, from any decision of the Court of Session under this section, and such leave may be given on such terms as to costs, expenses or otherwise as the Court of Session or the House of Lords may determine.

GENERAL NOTE

Subs. (1)

"Question of law". This is a point arising on the presumption that all the facts are not in dispute. As well as the need to give a legal interpretation to statute or to the common law it can relate to the incorrect admission of evidence or to the exercise of a discretion.

The remission for re-hearing is a logical consequence. In Standing Committee A on January 16, 1979, the following comment on errors of law was read from the Minister's Notes:

> "Errors of law may include the misinterpretation of statutes or other legal documents; misinterpretation of rules of common law, considering the wrong questions, taking irrelevant considerations into account when purporting to apply the law to the facts; admitting inadmissible evidence or rejecting admissible and relevant evidence; exercising discretion on the basis of incorrect legal principles; giving decisions which disclose faulty legal reasoning or which are inadequate to fulfil the duty to give reasons; and making errors with regard to the burden of proof."

Presumably any of the aspects is available for consideration in the High Court (and, if need be, above), if they emerge from the activity of the tribunal or of any variation of their findings that, exceptionally, the Chancellor may exercise.

Subss. (3) *and* (4)

Although nothing is said of the right to appeal from the Court of Appeal to the House of Lords, this is normally available with the leave of the Court of Appeal or of the House of Lords, if the relevant statute does not prohibit it.

Duties of licensed institutions

Duty to notify changes of directors etc.

14.—(1) A licensed institution shall give written notice to the Bank of the fact that any person has become or ceased to be a director, controller or manager of the institution.

(2) A notice required to be given by subsection (1) above shall be given before the expiry of the period of twenty-one days beginning with the day next following that on which the relevant fact comes to the knowledge of the institution.

(3) Any institution which fails to give a notice required by this section shall be liable on summary conviction to a fine not exceeding £1,000.

GENERAL NOTE

"*Director, controller or manager*" is defined in s. 49 of this Act. There are only 21 days in which to give the notice. (One wonders whether "notification" would be open to misunderstanding.) There is ample time but a normal company routine may not in practice accomplish the matter in time. In practice, however, there is a considerable difference between being liable to a fine and being fined. That is no answer technically to the length of the period of notice, but in practice the controversy about time (in Committee) is unlikely to cause difficulty. If a bank were involved, recognition could be withdrawn and the institution would become a licensed institution within this section; the conduct of withholding information would justify the loss of status if it were deliberate.

Audited accounts of licensed institutions to be open to inspection

15.—(1) At each place within the United Kingdom at which it holds itself out to accept deposits, a licensed institution shall keep a copy of its most recent audited accounts; and during normal business hours that copy shall be made available for inspection by any person on request.

(2) If an institution fails to comply with subsection (1) above, then, for each occasion on which it fails, it shall be liable on summary conviction to a fine not exceeding £500.

General Note

It is to be noted that this section and s. 14 refer to "licensed institutions" only, the information presumably being received in the ordinary course from the recognised banks.

Audited accounts are required but in this statute there is no reference to auditors' qualifications. This would not be practicable with foreign corporations, presumably (for English companies, see Companies Act 1948, s. 161, and Companies Act 1967, s. 13). Harmonisation of company law with the EEC may further affect this matter. The Fourth Directive will relate to accounts.

Powers of the Bank

Powers to obtain information and require production of documents

16.—(1) The Bank may by notice in writing served on a licensed institution—

(*a*) require the institution to furnish to the Bank, at such time or times as may be specified in the notice, such information as the Bank may reasonably require about the nature and conduct of the institution's business and its plans for future development; and

(*b*) require the institution to furnish to the Bank, together with the information required under paragraph (*a*) above, a report by an accountant approved by the Bank on that information or on such aspects of it as may be specified in the notice.

(2) The Bank may by notice in writing served on a licensed institution require the institution to produce, within such time and at such place as may be specified in the notice, such books or papers as may be so specified, being books or papers which the Bank may reasonably require for the purpose of obtaining information falling within paragraph (*a*) of subsection (1) above.

(3) Where, by virtue of subsection (2) above, the Bank has power to require the production of any books or papers from a licensed institution, the Bank shall have the like power to require production of those books or papers from any person who appears to the Bank to be in possession of them; but where any person from whom such production is required claims a lien on books or papars produced by him, the production shall be without prejudice to the lien.

(4) Where, by virtue of subsection (2) or subsection (3) above, the Bank requires the production by a licensed institution or any other person of books or papers, the Bank may—

(*a*) if the books or papers are produced, take copies of them or extracts from them and require that person, or any other person who is a present or past director, controller or manager of, or is or was at any time employed by, the institution, to provide an explanation of any of them; and

(*b*) if the books or papers are not produced, require the person who was required to produce them to state, to the best of his knowledge and belief, where the books or papers are.

(5) If and so long as an institution which was formerly a recognised bank or licensed institution—

(*a*) is neither recognised nor licensed, but

(*b*) continues to have any liability in respect of any deposit for which it had a liability at a time when it was recognised or licensed,

the provisions of this section shall apply in relation to it as if it were a licensed institution.

(6) Any person who, when required to do so under this section, fails without reasonable excuse to furnish any information or accountant's report, to produce any books or papers, or to provide any explanation or make any statement, shall be liable on summary conviction to a fine not exceeding £1,000.

(7) Any person who, in purported compliance with a requirement under this section, furnishes any information, provides any explanation or makes any statement which he knows or has reasonable cause to believe to be false or misleading in a material particular, shall be liable—

(*a*) on summary conviction to a fine not exceeding the statutory maximum; and

(*b*) on conviction on indictment to imprisonment for a term not exceeding two years or to a fine or both.

(8) Nothing in this section or in section 17 below shall compel the production by a solicitor of a document containing a privileged communication made by him or to him in that capacity.

General Note

It is to be observed that this section dealing with the powers of the Bank to obtain information and require the production of documents still relates only to licensed institutions and not also to recognised banks.

Subs. (1) (*a*)

Reasonable information about the business is one thing; to ask similarly about institutions' ideas for the future is more ambitious. It will be no doubt to the advantage of the licensed institutions to give such prior information in that they will get the benefit and help of the Bank; on the other hand to prove that *at a particular time* the obligations were not satisfied would be a difficulty. A negative averment is always a heavy burden and the "devil himself knoweth not the mind of man."

Subs. (1) (*b*)

The report of an approved accountant on both of the above requirements is more tangible if, in the latter case, some plans have been intimated to the accountant by the institution. Admittedly, only in perverse instances is there likely to be difficulty in applying the provisions which, basically, extend to licensed institutions the powers exercised traditionally with the recognised banks.

Subs. (2)

If the specified books and papers exist *and* are nominated there is no problem. "Plans" in the previous subsection were not confined to documents—information was being sought.

Subs. (3)

This is clear enough. There is no protection for any third person, except so far as lien—of, say, an accountant or solicitor for fees—is concerned. It is to be noted that there is no exception for the banker-customer secrecy if information as to financial weakness, for example, is known to the institution's bankers only as part of the confidentiality of the banker-customer contract (*cf. Tournier* v. *National Provincial Bank of England* [1921] 1 K.B. 461). A similar power existed under the Protection of Depositors Acts, but this appears to have been subject to provisions in the Companies Act 1967, ss. 111 and 118, which gave a measure of relief to bankers.

Subss. (4)–(7)

These add little that is not consequential in that there has to be a sanction. The protection of a solicitor's privilege is to be noted in subs. (8).

Investigations on behalf of the Bank

17.—(1) If it appears to the Bank desirable to do so in the interests of the depositors of a recognised bank or licensed institution, the Bank may appoint one or more competent persons to investigate and report to the Bank on the state and conduct of the business of the bank or institution concerned, or any particular aspect of that business.

(2) If a person appointed under subsection (1) above thinks it necessary for the purposes of his investigation, he may also investigate the business of any body corporate which is or has at any relevant time been—

(*a*) a holding company or subsidiary of the body whose business is under investigation;

(*b*) a subsidiary of a holding company of that body; or

(*c*) a holding company of a subsidiary of that body.

(3) It shall be the duty of every director, controller, manager and agent of a body whose business is under investigation (whether by virtue of subsection (1) or subsection (2) above)—

(*a*) to produce to the persons appointed under subsection (1) above all books and papers relating to the body concerned which are in custody or power; and

(*b*) to attend before the persons so appointed when required to do so; and

(*c*) otherwise to give to those persons all assistance in connection with the investigation which he is reasonably able to give.

(4) Any director, controller, manager or agent of a body who—

(*a*) without reasonable excuse fails to produce any books or papers which it is his duty to produce under subsection (3) above, or

(*b*) without reasonable excuse fails to attend before the persons appointed under subsection (1) above when required to do so, or

(*c*) without reasonable excuse fails to answer any question which is put to him by persons so appointed with respect to a business of any body corporate which is being investigated by virtue of subsection (2) above,

shall be liable on summary conviction to a fine not exceeding £1,000.

(5) Any director, controller, manager or agent of a body who knowingly or recklessly furnishes to any person appointed under subsection (1) above any information which is false or misleading in a material particular, shall be liable—

(*a*) on summary conviction to a fine not exceeding the statutory maximum; and

(*b*) on conviction on indictment to imprisonment for a term not exceeding two years or to a fine or both.

(6) In this section—

(*a*) " holding company " shall be construed in accordance with section 154 of the Companies Act 1948 or section 148 of the Companies Act (Northern Ireland) 1960;

(*b*) any reference to a director, controller, manager or agent of a body includes a reference to a person who has been but no longer is a director, controller, manager or agent of that body; and

(*c*) " agent ", in relation to a body whose business is under investigation, includes its bankers and solicitors and any

persons, whether officers of the body or not, who are employed as its auditors.

GENERAL NOTE

Subs. (1)

The setting up of investigations is applicable to both recognised banks and licensed institutions. There have to be no specific circumstances—merely that the Bank of England thinks it desirable.

Subs. (2)

Similarly the investigation of holders and subsidiaries by way of addition is a matter of discretion.

Subs. (3)

We have again the somewhat anomalous additions to " director " of " controller " and " manager " defined in s. 49 below. It is they who have to " produce books," to attend and be asked to attend.

Subs. (4)

Thus the production of the books, the attendance and answering of questions must be in the absence of reasonable excuse.

Subs. (5)

There are penalties on the same parties for " knowingly or recklessly " giving false information.

Subs. (6)

The definitions are important. " Holding company " (s. 154 of the Companies Act 1948) is familiar (briefly being a member of and controlling the composition of the board, holding more than half the equity capital or being a parent company of a parent company means that the company is a subsidiary) but paras. (*b*) and (*c*) are of interest—" controller " and " manager " include former controllers or managers but otherwise are defined in s. 49. " Agent," restricted in its definition to this section, includes " its bankers and solicitors and any persons . . . who are employed as auditors." Bankers are losing their right to secrecy in a number of areas although the privilege of solicitors is preserved, but for an agent it could be a matter of difficulty. (Much more detailed provisions along similar lines are contained in the Companies Act 1948, s. 167, as expanded in the Companies Act 1967, ss. 3 (1), 39 and 50 (*a*). Bankers and solicitors are included specifically in s. 167 (5) of the Companies Act 1948). S. 116 (1) of the same Act preserves the solicitors' privilege but the protection of the bankers' secrecy is more limited. None appears in this section. In fact bankers are included specifically with no limitation.

Winding up on petition from the Bank

18.—(1) On a petition presented by the Bank by virtue of this section, the court having jurisdiction under the Companies Act 1948 may wind up a recognised bank or licensed institution under that Act if—

(*a*) the institution is unable to pay sums due and payable to its depositors or is able to pay such sums only by defaulting in its obligations to its other creditors; or

(*b*) the value of the institution's assets is less than the amount of its liabilities.

(2) If a petition is presented by the Bank by virtue of this section for the winding up of a recognised bank or licensed institution which, apart from this subsection, would be excluded from being an unregistered company for the purposes of Part IX of the Companies Act 1948 by virtue of—

(*a*) paragraph (*c*) of section 398 of that Act (exclusion of partnerships etc. having less than eight members), or

(b) paragraph (d) of that section (exclusion of limited partnerships registered in England and Wales or Northern Ireland),

the court shall have jurisdiction, and the Companies Act 1948 shall have effect, as if the institution concerned were an unregistered company within the meaning of Part IX of that Act.

(3) If and so long as an institution which was formerly a recognised bank or licensed institution—

(a) is neither recognised nor licensed, but

(b) continues to have any liability in respect of any deposit for which it had a liability at a time when it was recognised or licensed,

the provisions of this section shall apply in relation to it as if it were a licensed institution.

(4) In its application to Northern Ireland, this section shall have effect—

(a) with the substitution of a reference to the Companies Act (Northern Ireland) 1960 for any reference to the Companies Act 1948;

(b) with the substitution of a reference to paragraph (d) of section 348 of the Companies Act (Northern Ireland) 1960 for the reference in paragraph (a) of subsection (2) above to paragraph (c) of section 398 of the Companies Act 1948; and

(c) with the omission of paragraph (b) of subsection (2) above.

GENERAL NOTE

Subs. (1)

We see here two definitions of insolvency different from ss. 222 and 223 of the Companies Act 1948; first, inability to pay depositors what is due and payable without defaulting on other obligations is peculiar to deposit-takers although it savours a little of *Patrick* v. *Lyon* [1933] Ch. 786, " inability to pay debts as they become due " (for purpose of s. 322 in relation to validity of a floating charge). However, the value of assets being less than liabilities concerns an aspect left to the discretion of the court, and influenced by representatives of other creditors where a petition is presented for the liquidation of a company. There was some discussion at the Fourth Sitting of Standing Committee A on Tuesday, January 16, 1979, as to whether deposits were " due and payable " whether or not they were demanded, but the Minister recalled that the phraseology had caused no trouble in relation to the Protection of Depositors Act 1963. (A somewhat similar authority was given to the " Board of Trade " in the Protection of Depositors Act 1963.)

Subs. (2)

This section forms a convenient extension of authority to the businesses mentioned.

Subs. (3)

Here the Act applies to institutions, whether formerly recognised banks or holding full licences, that have lost their status; but have not yet repaid all their deposits.

Subs. (4)

This is solely for Northern Ireland application.

Confidentiality of information obtained by the Bank

19.—(1) Subject to the provisions of this section and section 20 below, no information obtained under or for the purposes of this Act and relating to the business or other affairs of any person may be disclosed (otherwise than to an officer or employee of the Bank) except—

(a) with the consent of the person to whom the information relates; or

(b) to the extent that it is information which is at the time of the disclosure, or has previously been, available to the public from other sources; or (*c*) in the form of a summary or collection of information so framed as not to enable information relating to any particular person to be ascertained from it.

(2) Nothing in subsection (1) above prohibits the disclosure of information—

(*a*) with a view to the institution of, or otherwise for the purposes of, any criminal proceedings, whether under this Act or otherwise;

(*b*) in connection with any other proceedings arising out of this Act; or

(*c*) in order to enable the Bank to comply with any obligation imposed on it by or under this Act.

(3) If, in order to enable the Bank properly to discharge any of its functions under this Act, the Bank considers it necessary to seek advice from any qualified person on any matter of law, accountancy, valuation or other matter requiring the exericse of professional skill, nothing in subsection (1) above prohibits the disclosure to that person of such information as may appear to the Bank to be necessary to ensure that he is properly informed with respect to the matters on which his advice is sought.

(4) Nothing in subsection (1) above prohibits the disclosure of information—

(*a*) to the Treasury in circumstances where, in the opinion of the Bank, it is desirable or expedient that the information should be so disclosed in the interest of depositors or in the public interest; or

(*b*) to the Deposit Protection Board established under Part II of this Act in order to enable that Board to perform any of their functions under that Part.

(5) Nothing in subsection (1) above prohibits the disclosure to the Secretary of State of information relating to a body corporate to which section 165 or section 172 of the Companies Act 1948 applies if it appears to the Bank that there may be circumstances relating to the body corporate in which the Secretary of State might wish to appoint inspectors under—

(*a*) sub-paragraph (i) or sub-paragraph (ii) of paragraph (*b*) of the said section 165 (investigation of cases of fraud, etc.); or

(*b*) the said section 172 (investigation of ownership of company, etc.).

(6) Nothing in subsection (1) above prohibits the disclosure to the authorities which exercise in a country or territory outside the United Kingdom functions corresponding to those of the Bank under this Act of information which was furnished by or relates to a recognised bank or licensed institution which—

(*a*) carries on or proposes to carry on a deposit-taking business in that country or territory, whether directly, through a subsidiary or otherwise, or

(*b*) has or proposes to acquire an interest in an institution which carries on or proposes to carry on a deposit-taking business in that country or territory, or

(*c*) is a subsidiary of, or appears to the Bank to be otherwise associated with, an institution which is established under the law of that country or territory or whose principal place of business is, or is proposed to be, in that country or territory,

if it appears to the Bank that the disclosure of the information would assist those authorities in the exercise of those functions.

(7) Any person who discloses information in contravention of subsection (1) above shall be liable—

(*a*) on summary conviction to a fine not exceeding the statutory maximum; and

(b) on conviction on indictment to imprisonment for a term not exceeding two years or to a fine or both.

(8) In the application of this section to Northern Ireland,—

(a) for any reference in subsection (5) above to section 165 or section 172 of the Companies Act 1948 there shall be substituted respectively a reference to section 159 or section 165A of the Companies Act (Northern Ireland) 1960; and

(b) for any reference in that subsection to the Secretary of State there shall be substituted a reference to the Department of Commerce for Northern Ireland.

GENERAL NOTE

Associated with the confidentiality is the concern as to the degree of disclosure permitted.

Subs. (1)

The three provisions are reasonable—consent, availability of information from other sources, and, as collected information, without revealing individual details.

Subs. (2)

These provisions are very wide, if not unexpected.

Subs. (3)

Solicitors, counsel and chartered accountants must all come in this category.

Subs. (4)

Disclosure here is also unobjectionable.

Subs. (5)

The investigation of fraud and company ownership presumably should also be unimpaired by absence of information that is known to the Bank.

Subs. (6)

This must be permitted to reciprocate and will be a practical necessity when an institution is going to set up abroad. (It stems from the EEC Directive, art. 12, but the policy of the Act is to treat all foreign countries alike.)

The remaining subss. (7) and (8) concern firms and Northern Ireland.

Information disclosed to the Bank from other sources

20.—(1) If and so far as it appears to the Secretary of State that the disclosure of any information will enable the Bank better to discharge its functions under this Act (but not otherwise),—

(a) information obtained by the Secretary of State under section 109 or section 110 of the Companies Act 1967 (inspection of companies' books and papers) may be disclosed to the Bank, notwithstanding the provision as to security of information contained in section 111 of that Act; and

(b) where the information is contained in a report made by inspectors appointed under section 164, section 165 or section 172 of the Companies Act 1948 (investigation of affairs or ownership of companies and certain other bodies corporate) the Secretary of State may furnish a copy of the report to the Bank.

(2) If and so far as it appears to the Department of Commerce for Northern Ireland that the disclosure of any information will enable the Bank better to discharge its functions under this Act (but not otherwise),—

(*a*) information obtained by the Department under Article 107 or Article 108 of the Companies (Northern Ireland) Order 1978 (inspection of companies' books and papers) may be disclosed to the Bank, notwithstanding the provision as to security of information contained in Article 109 of that Order; and

(*b*) where the information is contained in a report made by inspectors under section 158, section 159, section 165A of the Companies Act (Northern Ireland) 1960 (investigation of affairs or ownership of companies and certain other bodies corporate) the Department may furnish a copy of the report to the Bank.

(3) Subsection (1) of section 19 above does not apply to information which has been disclosed to the Bank by virtue of subsection (1) or subsection (2) above, but—

(*a*) except as provided by paragraph (*b*) below, nothing in this Act authorises any further disclosure of that information in contravention of section 111 of the Companies Act 1967 or, as the case may require, Article 109 of the Companies (Northern Ireland) Order 1978; and

(*b*) with respect to that information the references in subsections (3) to (6) of section 19 above to subsection (1) of that section shall be construed as including a reference to the said section 111 or, as the case may require, Article 109.

(4) If information is disclosed to the Bank by the authorities which exercise, in a country or territory outside the United Kingdom, functions corresponding to those of the Bank under this Act,—

(*a*) subsection (1) of section 19 above applies to that information as it applies to information obtained under or for the purposes of this Act; but

(*b*) the references in subsections (4) to (6) of that section to the disclosure of information do not extend to the disclosure of that information.

General Note

Subs. (1)

This section is complementary to s. 19. It deals with information that may be disclosed to the Bank if it will help it to discharge its functions better—quite a wide mandate. The information is particularised by ss. 109 and 110 of the Companies Act 1967, by which the Department of Trade are given authority to require production of books and papers (without prejudice to any lien); they may take copies and demand statements. By s. 110 there is provision for entry and search. The Department is authorised to make this information available to the Bank of England. The authority under s. 16 relates to licensed institutions but ss. 17 to 20 to both categories. Presumably if information were required relating to a collateral company the Department of Trade could obtain it and pass it to the Bank within the general wide mandate. S. 164 of the Companies Act 1948 relates to reports made on applications at the request of members; s. 165 gives similar powers following a court order or a special resolution of the company or if there are reasons to suspect fraud. These powers have been extended by ss. 35 to 42 of the Companies Act 1967. S. 172 relates to the investigation of the true beneficial ownership of a company.

Subs. (3)

This extends the Companies Act protection (s. 111 of the 1967 Act) as to further disclosure in place of s. 19 (1) of this Act, which is excluded.

Subs. (4)

S. 19 (1) *is* to apply to information received by the Bank from other central banks although the exemptions relating to further disclosure (s. 19 (4)–(6)) do not. This latter limitation accords with the EEC Directive (art. 12 (3)). Application in practice would call for somewhat arbitrary decisions as to differentiation.

Part II

The Deposit Protection Scheme

The Board and the Fund

The Deposit Protection Board

21.—(1) There shall be a body corporate to be known as the Deposit Protection Board (in this Part of this Act referred to as " the Board ") which—

(*a*) shall hold, manage and apply in accordance with the following provisions of this Part of this Act, a fund to be known as the Deposit Protection Fund (in this Part of this Act referred to as " the Fund "); and

(*b*) shall levy contributions for the Fund, in accordance with the following provisions of this Part of this Act, from recognised banks and licensed institutions; and

(*c*) shall have such other functions as are conferred on the Board by those provisions.

(2) The provisions of Schedule 5 to this Act shall have effect with respect to the Board.

General Note

In some ways this is the most controversial aspect of the statute because there is the implication that the existence of the Scheme will encourage depositors to exercise less caution than they should when deciding to deposit money. It is to relate to both recognised banks and licensed deposit-takers. The Fund is to be £5–£6 millions and is to cover 75 per cent. of the amount deposited—up to a maximum £10,000 sterling (there is no protection for currency deposits). Subject to a maximum, contributions are to be 0·6 per cent. of the deposit base of the Bank or licensed institution. If an institution becomes insolvent the Board have a right to be consulted, as would a creditor in the realisation of assets. There was much parliamentary debate regarding the exemption of Government-backed entities particularly National Girobank. The Board manages, administers and levies contributions. It is a legal entity—a body corporate—and its constitution, administration and organisation are contained in Sched. 5.

The Deposit Protection Fund

22.—(1) The Fund shall consist of—

(*a*) initial, further and special contributions levied by the Board under sections 24 to 26 below;

(*b*) moneys borrowed by the Board under section 26 (3) below;

(*c*) moneys credited to the Fund in accordance with subsection (1) or subsection (5) of section 32 below; and

(*d*) income credited to the Fund in accordance with subsection (3) below.

(2) The moneys constituting the Fund shall be placed by the Board in an account with the Bank.

(3) So far as possible, the Bank shall invest moneys placed with it under subsection (2) above in Treasury bills payable not more than ninety-one days from the date of issue; and any income from moneys so invested shall be credited to the Fund.

(4) The administrative expenses of the Board shall be defrayed out of the Fund.

(5) There shall be chargeable to the Fund—

(*a*) payments to meet administrative expenses of the Board in accordance with subsection (4) above;

(*b*) repayments of special contributions under section 26 (2) below;

(*c*) moneys required for the repayment of the Board's borrowings under section 26 (3) below; and

(*d*) payments under section 28 below.

General Note

The Fund is made up of three types of contributions (initial, further and special), borrowed moneys, payments from liquidators of insolvent institutions, and income from Treasury Bills on which the Fund is invested (after being placed in a separate account at the Bank).

The Fund is charged with administrative expenses, repayments of special contributions (see below), moneys to repay borrowings and payments to claimants under the Scheme.

Contributions to the Fund

Contributory institutions and general provisions as to contributions

23.—(1) All recognised banks and licensed institutions which are not excluded by an order under subsection (2) below shall be liable to contribute to the Fund and are in this Act referred to as " contributory institutions ".

(2) The Treasury may by order exclude from subsection (1) above—

(*a*) a body corporate formed under the law of a country or territory outside the United Kingdom, or

(*b*) any other description of institution of which the principal place of business is in a country or territory outside the United Kingdom,

if they are satisfied, after consultation with the Board, that, under the law of that country or territory or by virtue of arrangements which are in force there, sterling deposits with the United Kingdom offices of that institution are as well protected as they would be under this Part of this Act.

(3) The power to make an order under subsection (2) above shall be exercisable by statutory instrument which shall be subject to annulment in pursuance of a resolution of either House of Parliament.

(4) Contributions to the Fund shall be levied on a contributory institution by the Board by service on the institution of a notice specifying the amount due, which shall be paid by the institution not later than twenty-one days after the date on which the notice is served.

(5) Subject to section 27 below, on each occasion on which contributions are to be levied from contributory institutions (other than the occasion of the levy of an initial contribution from a particular institution under subsection (2) of section 24 below),—

(*a*) a contribution shall be levied from each of the contributory institutions; and

(*b*) the amount of the contribution of each institution shall be ascertained by applying to the institution's deposit base the percentage determined by the Board for the purpose of the contributions levied on that occasion.

(6) In relation to any contribution, the deposit base of an institution is the amount which the Board determine as representing the average, over such period preceding the levying of the contribution as appears to the Board to be appropriate, of sterling deposits with the United Kingdom offices of that institution, other than—

(*a*) secured deposits;

(*b*) deposits which had an original term to maturity of more than five years; and

(c) deposits in respect of which the institution has in the United Kingdom issued a sterling certificate of deposit.

(7) In its application to this section, subsection (5) of section 1 of this Act shall have effect with the omission of paragraphs (b) and (c).

GENERAL NOTE

Subs. (1)

Unless excluded, all banks and licensed institutions are contributories.

Subs. (2)

Where there is cover abroad satisfactory to the Bank extending to English branches, then it may order that no contribution arises in respect of those branches. (If the "branches"—despite their names—were separate legal entities, as in one or two instances, this would not be possible.) Often schemes abroad will apply, however, only to local territory.

Subs. (3)

Nevertheless, the above is only possible in any event as a result of a Treasury Order, which results from a statutory instrument (it can be annulled by a resolution of either House).

Subs. (4)

The 21 days was at one time intended to be 14 days.

Subs. (5)

This is simply that the contribution is based on the "deposit base" of the particular institution.

Subs. (6)

This raises the question of the calculation of the deposit base. It consists of sterling deposits (including current account credit balances) *other than* those for which certificates of deposit have been issued, those originally having five years or more to run, and "secured deposits." Probably the only frequent instance of secured deposits is in the discount market where bills are ear-marked as cover for deposits of money by, say, a clearing banker. Remotely, a company taking finance from a private source may give a security for its repayment.

Subs. (7)

This means that deposits for this section (that is for calculating the deposit base) *do* include loans by persons listed in Sched. 1 (such as the Post Office, a building society, a stockbroker or a local authority) as well as a loan to the institution made in the course of a business of lending money.

Initial contributions

24.—(1) On or as soon as possible after the appointed day the Board shall levy from all institutions which on that day are contributory institutions initial contributions which produce in the aggregate a total of not less than £5 million and not more than £6 million.

(2) Subject to subsection (5) below, where an institution becomes a contributory institution after the appointed day, the Board shall levy from it, on or as soon as possible after the day on which it becomes a contributory institution, an initial contribution of an amount determined in accordance with subsection (3) or subsection (4) below.

(3) Where the institution concerned has a deposit base, then, subject to subsection (1) of section 27 below, the amount of an initial contribution levied under subsection (2) above shall be such percentage of the deposit base as the Board consider appropriate to put the institution on a basis of equality with the other contributory institutions, having regard to—

(a) the initial contributions levied under subsection (1) above, and (*b*) so far as they are attributable to an increase in the size of the Fund resulting from an order under subsection (2) of section 25 below, further contributions levied under that section.

(4) Where the institution concerned has no deposit base, the amount of an initial contribution levied under subsection (2) above shall be the minimum amount for the time being provided for in section 27 (1) below.

(5) The Board may waive an initial contribution under subsection (2) above if it appears to them that the institution concerned is to carry on substantially the same business as that previously carried on by one or more institutions which are or were contributory institutions.

GENERAL NOTE

Subs. (1)

The rate will depend, of course, on the percentage of the base required to raise £5 to £6 million. The appointed day can be later than that on which the Act comes into force (see s. 52). The Bank will want to know of the contributors first, presumably.

Subs. (2)

After the appointed day the Board makes the levy as soon as possible.

Subs. (3)

This merely indicates the way on which the amount is calculated (allowing for any increase in the total fund that may be thought justified), in particular in relation to those not included in the first general levy.

Subs. (4)

This is £2,500.

Subs. (5)

As with so much, not unreasonably, there is the discretion—in this case to regard the new institution as a continuation of the old.

Further contributions

25.—(1) If at the end of any financial year of the Board the amount standing to the credit of the Fund is less than £3 million, the Board may, with the approval of the Treasury, levy further contributions from contributory institutions so as to restore the amount standing to the credit of the Fund to a minimum of £5 million and a maximum of £6 million.

(2) If at any time it appears to the Treasury to be desirable in the interest of depositors to increase the size of the Fund, the Treasury may, after consultation with the Board, by order made by statutory instrument amend subsection (1) above so as to substitute for the sums for the time being specified in that subsection such larger sums as may be specified in the order; but no such order shall be made unless a draft of it has been laid before and approved by a resolution of each House of Parliament.

(3) An order under subsection (2) above may authorise the Board forthwith to levy further contributions from contributory institutions so as to raise the amount standing to the credit of the Fund to a figure between the new minimum and maximum amounts provided for by the order.

GENERAL NOTE

The permanent increase of the Fund requires a resolution of both Houses. No parliamentary authority is necessary for a levy if the Fund is less than £3 million and the levy is on the specific occasion—one might think to meet an isolated instance requiring restoration of the Fund to £5–£6 million.

Special contributions and power to borrow

26.—(1) If it appears to the Board that payments in any financial year of the Board under section 28 below are likely to exhaust the Fund, the Board may, with the approval of the Treasury, levy special contributions from contributory institutions to meet the Fund's commitments in the year.

(2) Where, at the end of any financial year of the Board in the course of which special contributions were levied, moneys representing the whole or part of those contributions remain in the Fund, those moneys shall be repaid by the Board to the institutions from which they were levied *pro rata* according to the amount of the special contribution made by each of them.

(3) If in the course of operating the Fund it appears to the Board desirable to do so, the Board may borrow for temporary purposes up to a total outstanding at any time of £10 million or such larger sum as, after consultation with the Board, the Treasury may from time to time prescribe by order made by statutory instrument.

(4) A statutory instrument made under subsection (3) above shall be subject to annulment in pursuance of a resolution of either House of Parliament.

(5) Any amount borrowed by virtue of subsection (3) above shall be disregarded in ascertaining whether the amount standing to the credit of the Fund is such that the Board may exercise their power to levy further contributions under subsection (1) of section 25 above.

GENERAL NOTE

S. 26 deals with the contingency element and the money raised is separate from the cash fund. This eliminates a growing unused cash fund as distinct from a stand-by.

Subs. (1)

With Treasury approval there may be a levy if a shortfall is anticipated over the year as a result of payments out of the Fund.

Subs. (2)

The *above* levy is repaid on a pro-rata basis.

Subs. (3)

The maximum amount that the Fund may borrow is £10 million unless the Treasury provide for a greater maximum by statutory instrument.

Subs. (4)

The statutory instrument may be annulled by either House.

Subs. (5)

Temporary borrowings are not to affect the power of the Board to levy further contributions.

Maximum and minimum contributions

27.—(1) Subject to subsection (5) below, the amount of the initial contribution levied from a contributory institution shall be not less than £2,500.

(2) Subject to subsection (5) below, the amount of the initial contribution or any further contribution levied from a contributory institution shall not exceed £300,000.

(3) No contributory institution shall be required to pay a further or special contribution if, or to the extent that, the amount of that

contribution, together with previous initial, further and special contributions made by the institution, after allowing for any repayments made to it under section 26 (2) above or section 32 below, amounts to more than 0·3 per cent. of the institution's deposit base as ascertained for the purpose of the contribution in question.

(4) Nothing in subsection (3) above—

(*a*) shall entitle an institution to repayment of any contribution previously made; or

(*b*) shall prevent the Board from proceeding to levy contributions from other contributory institutions in whose case the limit in that subsection has not been reached.

(5) The Treasury may from time to time, after consultation with the Board, by order made by statutory instrument amend subsection (1) or subsection (2) above so as to substitute for the sum for the time being specified in that subsection such other sum as may be specified in the order.

(6) No order shall be made under subsection (5) above unless a draft of it has been laid before and approved by a resolution of each House of Parliament.

GENERAL NOTE

S. 27 is concerned with maximum and minimum contributions, respectively £300,000 and £2,500, but a statutory instrument reflecting the decision of the Treasury can change these figures although both Houses of Parliament must approve such resolution. After allowing for any reimbursement the overall net maximum contribution is to be 0·6 per cent. of the deposit base with a further 0·3 per cent. in respect of further and special contributions.

Payments out of the Fund

Payments to depositors when institution become insolvent

28.—(1) Subject to the provisions of this section, if at any time an institution becomes insolvent and at that time—

(*a*) it is a recognised bank or licensed institution which is not excluded from being a contributory institution by an order under section 23 (2) above; or

(*b*) it is neither recognised nor licensed but is an institution which was formerly a recognised bank or licensed institution and, at the time when it ceased to have either recognition or a licence, was not excluded as mentioned in paragraph (*a*) above;

the Board shall as soon as practicable pay out of the Fund to a depositor who has a protected deposit with that institution an amount equal to three-quarters of his protected deposit.

(2) The Board may decline to make any payment under subsection (1) above to a person who, in the opinion of the Board, had any responsibility for, or may have profited directly or indirectly from, the circumstances giving rise to the institution's financial difficulties.

(3) For the purposes of this Part of this Act, a body corporate becomes insolvent—

(*a*) on the making of a winding-up order against it; or

(*b*) on the passing of a resolution for a creditors' voluntary winding up;

or, in the case of a body corporate formed under the law of a country or territory outside the United Kingdom, on the occurrence of an event which appears to the Board to correspond under that law with either of the events specified above.

(4) For the purposes of this Part of this Act, a partnership becomes insolvent—

(*a*) on the making of a winding-up order against the firm under Part IX of the Companies Act 1948 or the Companies Act (Northern Ireland) 1960 (unregistered companies); or

(*b*) in England and Wales, on the making of a receiving order against the firm; or

(*c*) in Scotland, on the making of an award of sequestration on the estate of the partnership; or

(*d*) in Northern Ireland, on the making of an order of adjudication of bankruptcy against any of the partners;

or, in the case of a partnership whose principal place of business is in a country or territory outside the United Kingdom, on the occurrence of an event which appears to the Board to correspond under the law of that country or territory with any of the events specified above.

(5) For the purposes of this Part of this Act, an unincorporated institution which is formed under the law of another member State and is not a partnership becomes insolvent on the occurrence of an event which, under the law of that member State, appears to the Board to correspond, as near as may be, with any of the events specified in paragraphs (*a*) and (*b*) of subsection (3) or paragraphs (*a*) to (*d*) of subsection (4) above.

(6) Notwithstanding that the Board may not yet have made or become liable to make a payment under this section, in relation to an institution falling within subsection (1) above,—

(*a*) the Board shall at all times be entitled to receive any notice or other document required to be sent to a creditor of the institution whose debt has been proved; and

(*b*) a duly authorised representative of the Board shall be entitled—

(i) to attend any meeting of creditors of the institution;

(ii) to be a member of any committee of inspection appointed under section 20 of the Bankruptcy Act 1914;

(iii) to be a commissioner under section 72 of the Bankruptcy (Scotland) Act 1913; and

(iv) to be a member of any committee of inspection appointed by virtue of Part V or Part IX of the Companies Act 1948 or the Companies Act (Northern Ireland) 1960;

but where a representative of the Board exercises the right to be a member of a committee of inspection or to be a commissioner by virtue of paragraph (*b*) above, he may not be removed except with the consent of the Board and, for the purposes of any provision made by or under any enactment or Northern Ireland legislation which specifies a minimum or maximum number of members of such committee or such commission, his appointment hereunder shall be disregarded.

(7) In relation to an insolvent institution which is a partnership, any reference in this Part of this Act to the liquidator shall be construed, where the case so requires, as a reference—

(*a*) to the trustee in bankruptcy or, in Northern Ireland, the official assignee in bankruptcy; or

(*b*) in England and Wales, where no adjudication of bankruptcy occurs, to any trustee appointed in pursuance of a composition or scheme of arrangement to administer the firm's property or manage its business or distribute the composition and, where an adjudication of bankruptcy is annulled under subsection (2) of section 21 of the Bankruptcy Act 1914, to any person in whom the property of the firm is vested under that subsection; or

(*c*) in Scotland, where the sequestration is declared at an end by a competent court, to any trustee or other person appointed to administer the firm's property or manage its business or distribute a composition in pursuance of any deed of arrangement or other settlement or arrangement by way of composition between the firm and its creditors.

General Note

Subs. (1)

The required conditions are:

(a) insolvency, *and either*

(b) being a recognised bank or licensed institution, *or*

(c) having been one of those institutions at the time that it lost its licence.

Subs. (2)

This excludes those who, in the opinion of the Board, had any responsibility for the circumstances of the institution's financial embarrassment or have profited from those happenings.

Subs. (3)

A winding-up order or resolution is clear enough; the equivalent abroad has to be left with the Board to decide.

Subs. (4)

The circumstances with a partnership are also clear. A limited partnership can be wound up under Pt. IX of the Companies Act 1948. Again, the equivalent for the foreign partnership has to be left to the Board.

Subs. (5)

Such a contingency also has to be left to the discretion of the Board.

Subs. (6)

This enables the Board to participate as a creditor in the insolvency administration of an institution although no payment out has been made. It is not to count in relation to a maximum or minimum of membership of a committee in which it participates.

Subs. (7)

This covers instances where, in the case of a partnership being insolvent, other persons are in similar positions to a liquidator in the case of an insolvency of a limited company.

Note: If a company that is insolvent has appointed a receiver it would appear that he would be unaffected. There is no liquidation; but when this does happen the Receiver will still be in control.

Protected deposits

29.—(1) Subject to the provisions of this section, in relation to an institution falling within subsection (1) of section 28 above, any reference in this Act to a depositor's protected deposit is a reference to the total liability of the institution to him, limited to a maximum of £10,000, in respect of the principal amounts of sterling deposits made with United Kingdom offices of the institution.

(2) For the purposes of subsection (1) above, no account shall be taken of any liability unless proof of the debt which gives rise to it has been lodged with the liquidator of the insolvent institution or, in the case of an institution which is—

(*a*) a body corporate formed under the law of a country or territory outside the United Kingdom, (*b*) a partnership whose principal place of business is in such a country or territory, or

(*c*) any other unincorporated institution formed under the law of another member State,

unless an act has been done which appears to the Board to correspond under the law of that country or territory or, as the case may be, under the law of that member State with the lodging of such a proof with the liquidator of the institution.

(3) The Treasury, after consultation with the Board, may by order made by statutory instrument amend subsection (1) above so as to substitute for the sum for the time being specified in that subsection such larger sum as may be specified in the order; and no such order shall be made unless a draft of it has been laid before Parliament and approved by a resolution of each House.

(4) The reference in subsection (1) above to the principal amount of a sterling deposit includes any interest or premium which has been so credited to the deposit in question as to constitute an accretion to the principal.

(5) In determining the total liability of an institution to a depositor for the purposes of subsection (1) above, no account shall be taken of any liability in respect of a deposit if—

(*a*) it is a secured deposit; or

(*b*) it is a deposit which had an original term to maturity of more than five years; or

(*c*) the institution is no longer recognised or licensed and the deposit was made after it ceased to be either recognised or licensed, unless, at the time the deposit was made, the depositor did not know and could not reasonably be expected to have known that the institution was no longer recognised or licensed.

(6) Unless the Board otherwise direct in any particular case, in determining the total liability of an institution to a depositor for the purposes of subsection (1) above, there shall be deducted the amount of any liability of the depositor to the institution—

(*a*) in respect of which a right of set-off existed immediately before the institution became insolvent against any such sterling deposit as is referred to in subsection (1) above, or

(*b*) in respect of which such a right would then have existed if the deposit in question had been repayable on demand and the liability in question had fallen due.

(7) In its application to this section and sections 30 and 31 below, subsection (5) of section 1 of this Act shall have effect—

(*a*) with the omission of paragraphs (*b*) and (*c*), and

(*b*) as if the reference in paragraph (*a*) to a loan made by the Bank, a recognised bank or a licensed institution did not include a loan made by any of those bodies as trustees,

and any reference in this Part of this Act to a protected deposit or, in the context of such a deposit, to a depositor shall be construed accordingly.

GENERAL NOTE

Subs. (1)

The liabilities are limited to the first £10,000.

Subs. (2)

Proof is necessary for the acknowledgment of the claim. It has to be lodged with the Board—there are comparative steps for entities based abroad.

Subs. (3)

Both Houses have to approve any increase in the £10,000.

Subs. (4)

This relates only to the calculation of the maximum of £10,000—any accretions are included.

Subs. (5)

There are three types of deposit excluded when calculating a deposit-base (see s. 23 (5))—secured deposits and those having five years or more originally to run. The third category is where the recognised bank or institution eventuates to be no longer recognised or licensed and depositors did not know or could not reasonably have been expected to know of the absence of such status.

Subs. (6)

This covers the deduction of a set-off in two instances—where immediately before insolvent liquidation money was owing by the depositor on current account or on a term loan to the bank, then there is a right of set-off. (This would seem to exist even though the institution had agreed to forgo its rights against the depositor (*cf. National Westminster Bank* v. *Halesowen* [1972] A.C. 785).)

Subs. (7)

As to para. (*a*), see s. 23 (7) with similar provisions. As to para. (*b*) this will include deposits made by a bank as a trustee of a will, for example.

Trustee deposits and joint deposits

30.—(1) For the purposes of sections 28 and 29 above, where any persons are entitled to a deposit as trustees, then, unless the deposit is held on trust for a person absolutely entitled to it as against the trustees, the trustees shall be treated as a single and continuing body of persons, distinct from the persons who may from time to time be the trustees and if the same persons are entitled as trustees to different deposits under different trusts, they shall be treated as a separate and distinct body with respect to each of those trusts.

(2) For the purpose of this section, a deposit is held on trust for a person absolutely entitled to it as against the trustees where that person has the exclusive right, subject only to satisfying any outstanding charge, lien or other right of the trustees to resort to the deposit for payment of duty, taxes, costs or other outgoings, to direct how the deposit shall be dealt with.

(3) Any reference in subsection (1) or subsection (2) above to a person absolutely entitled to a deposit as against the trustees includes a reference to two or more persons who are so entitled jointly; and in the application of subsection (2) above to Scotland the words from " subject " to " outgoings " shall be omitted.

(4) For the purposes of sections 28 and 29 above and the following provisions of this section, where a deposit is held on trust for any person absolutely entitled to it or, as the case may be, for two or more persons so entitled jointly, that person or, as the case may be, those persons jointly shall be treated as entitled to the deposit without the intervention of any trust.

(5) For the purposes of sections 28 and 29 above, where two or more persons are jointly entitled to a deposit and subsection (1) above does not apply, each of them shall be treated as having a separate deposit of an amount produced by dividing the amount of the deposit to which they are jointly entitled by the number of persons who are so entitled.

(6) The Board may decline to make any payment under section 28 above in respect of a deposit until the person claiming to be entitled to

it informs the Board of the capacity in which he is entitled to the deposit; and if it appears to the Board—

(a) that the persons entitled to a deposit are so entitled as trustees, or

(b) that subsection (4) above applies to a deposit, or

(c) that two or more persons are jointly entitled to a deposit otherwise than as trustees,

the Board may decline to make any payment under that section in respect of the deposit until sufficient information has been disclosed to them to enable them to determine what payment (if any) should be made under that section and to whom.

(7) In this section " jointly entitled " means—

(a) in England and Wales and Northern Ireland, beneficially entitled as joint tenants, tenants in common or as coparceners; and

(b) in Scotland, beneficially entitled as joint owners or owners in common.

GENERAL NOTE

The background of this problem arises from the fact that the destiny of the payment from the Fund will be determined by the Act; at all events merely to reimburse the account with 75 per cent. of the loss on the first £10,000 would leave the position uncertain for the account holders, particularly if they were trustees. Where there are joint account holders, who hold on the basis that the survivor takes, there is not much difficulty; neither is there where they hold as trustees for a number who share equally. It is where there is a life interest and, say, three remainders that there is a problem as to where the loss (or the benefit) is to fall such as whether three remaindermen could amount to three claimants. A fairly simple—some might say almost obvious—solution has been adopted for most instances. The deposit is to be treated as a simple deposit of £10,000 and payment made to the trustees. There are, however, variations.

Subs. (1)

The first point to notice is that money held on trust is additional to the deposit held personally by the trustees. Also if the trustees hold additional deposits on behalf of separate trusts they are treated as a separate claim. The exception is when it is held for one person absolutely entitled. If it were held for two persons absolutely, the trustees may have duties to perform in which event they would not be bare trustees (but see subs. (3) *infra*). The point of the subsection is that where the moneys are not held absolutely for beneficiaries (as elaborated below) payment is made to the trustee or trustees.

Subs. (2)

This defines holding absolutely. If money is held for two persons, the trustee may have duties. If the duty is payment of a tax or discharge of costs or expenses then for this section of the Act, it is held "absolutely." (The law was reviewed on the subject in *Re Blandy-Jenkins' Estate* [1917] 1 Ch. 46.)

Subs. (3)

It will be seen that subs. (2) includes *two* or *more* parties jointly notwithstanding the outstanding obligation of a charge, such as for tax. In other words, if money was held on trust for two or more it is not to be treated without investigation as *other* than for these persons beneficially.

Subs. (4)

This eliminates the trust where the deposit comes within the definition of subs. (2) or subs. (3).

Subs. (5)

This is the *pro rata* sharing where the beneficiaries are absolutely entitled (within the meaning of this section).

Subs. (6)

This is precautionary so that the Board may withhold payment whilst it receives sufficient evidence to apply the foregoing sections.

Subs. (7)

With joint tenants the benefit devolves upon the survivors, and with tenants in common the beneficial interests are shared equally and devolve on the event of death, with the rest of the estate of the deceased. Coparcenary was a form of inheritance by daughters in which they had, under the law before 1926, joint estate (or seisin) but took equally, there being no right of survivorship. It could still arise as a beneficial interest on the death of someone who was of unsound mind on January 1, 1926, or in relation to an entailed interest devolving on daughters although, otherwise, it is within the abolition effected by the Administration of Estates Act 1925, s. 45.

Joint owners in Scotland have no separate estates or rights of property—only one right, passing on death to other joint owners. Owners in common have " shares " of which disposition can be forced—normally an equal distribution.

Liability of insolvent institutions in respect of payments made by the Board

31.—(1) This section applies where—

(*a*) an institution is insolvent; and

(*b*) the Board have made, or are under a liability to make, a payment under section 28 above by virtue of the institution becoming insolvent;

and in the following provisions of this section a payment falling within paragraph (*b*) above is referred to as an " insolvency payment " and the person to whom such a payment has been or is to be made is referred to as " the depositor ".

(2) Where this section applies—

(*a*) the institution concerned shall become liable to the Board, as in respect of a contractual debt incurred immediately before the institution became insolvent, for an amount equal to the amount of the insolvency payment;

(*b*) the liability of the institution to the depositor in respect of any deposit or deposits of his (in this section referred to as " the liability to the depositor ") shall be reduced by an amount equal to the insolvency payment made or to be made to him by the Board; and

(*c*) the duty of the liquidator of the insolvent institution to make payments to the Board on account of the liability referred to in paragraph (*a*) above (in this section referred to as " the liability to the Board ") and to the depositor on account of the liability to him (after taking account of paragraph (*b*) above) shall be varied in accordance with subsection (3) below.

(3) The variation referred to in subsection (2) (*c*) above is as follows:—

(*a*) in the first instance the liquidator shall pay to the Board instead of to the depositor any amount which, apart from this section, would be payable on account of the liability to the depositor, except in so far as that liability relates to a secured deposit or a deposit which had an original term to maturity of more than five years or a deposit which is not a sterling deposit; and

(*b*) if at any time the total amount paid to the Board by virtue of paragraph (*a*) above and in respect of the liability to the Board equals the amount of the insolvency payment made to the depositor, the liquidator shall thereafter pay to the depositor instead of to the Board any amount which, apart from this section, would be payable to the Board in respect of the liability to the Board.

(4) In the case of a deposit which, for the purposes of section 30 above, is held on trust for a person absolutely entitled to it as against the trustees or, as the case may be, for two or more persons so entitled jointly, any reference in the preceding provisions of this section to the liability to the depositor shall be construed as a reference to the liability of the institution concerned to the trustees.

(5) The Board may by notice in writing served on the liquidator of an insolvent institution require him, at such time or times and at such place as may be specified in the notice,—

(*a*) to furnish to the Board such information, and

(*b*) to produce to the Board such books or papers specified in the notice,

as the Board may reasonably require to enable them to carry out their functions under this Part of this Act.

(6) Where, as a result of an institution having become insolvent, any books or papers have come into the possession of the Official Receiver or, in Northern Ireland, the official assignee for company liquidations or in bankruptcy, he shall permit any person duly authorised by the Board to inspect the books or papers for the purpose of establishing—

(*a*) the identity of those of the institution's depositors to whom the Board are liable to make a payment under section 28 above; and

(*b*) the amount of the protected deposit held by each of those depositors.

(7) Rules may be made—

(*a*) for England and Wales, under section 365 of the Companies Act 1948 and section 132 of the Bankruptcy Act 1914;

(*b*) for Scotland, under section 365 of the Companies Act 1948 and section 32 of the Sheriff Courts (Scotland) Act 1971; and

(*c*) for Northern Ireland, under section 317 of the Companies Act (Northern Ireland) 1960 and section 55 of the Judicature (Northern Ireland) Act 1978;

for the purpose of integrating the procedure provided for in this section into the general procedure on winding-up or bankruptcy.

General Note

Subs. (1)

When a payment is being made by the Board (under s. 28 above) and the institution with which the deposit was made becomes insolvent, the expression "insolvency payment" is used.

Subs. (2)

The institution becomes liable to the Board for the amount of the insolvency payment; the liability to the depositor is reduced by the amount paid to him by the Board and the liquidator pays dividends to the Board on account. (The practical effect is that dividends are used first to reimburse the Board and later to repay the balance owed to the depositor.)

Subs. (3)

This confirms the position described above, it being remembered that types of deposit excluded from the scheme are of course outside the reimbursement.

Subs. (4)

The mechanism also applies to such payments in respect of joint deposits and trustees' deposits. Where payment has been made to beneficiaries absolutely entitled the dividend due to the Board will of course be that receivable by the trustees.

Subs. (5)

This is more easy than having to apply through the depositor.

Subs. (6)

It also binds any official who may have the books.

Subs. (7)

Further rules are likely for procedural purposes associated with the rules for bankruptcies and company winding up.

Repayments in respect of contributions

Repayments in respect of contributions

32.—(1) Any moneys received by the Board under section 31 above shall not form part of the Fund but, for the remainder of the financial year of the Board in which they are received, shall be retained and, so far as appears to the Board appropriate, shall be invested in Treasury bills payable not more than ninety-one days from the date of issue; and any income arising from moneys so invested during the remainder of the year shall be credited to the Fund.

(2) The Board shall prepare a scheme for the making of repayments to institutions out of moneys falling within subsection (1) above in respect of—

(*a*) special contributions, and

(*b*) so far as they are not attributable to an increase in the size of the Fund resulting from an order under subsection (2) of section 25 above, further contributions levied under that section,

which have been made in the financial year of the Board in which the moneys were received or in any previous such financial year.

(3) A scheme under subsection (2) above—

(*a*) shall provide for the making of repayments first in respect of special contributions and then, if those contributions can be repaid in full (taking into account any previous repayments under this section and under section 26 (2) above), in respect of further contributions;

(*b*) may make provision for repayments in respect of contributions made by an institution which has ceased to be a contributory institution to be made to a contributory institution which, in the opinion of the Board, is its successor; and

(*c*) subject to paragraph (*b*) above, may exclude from the scheme further contributions levied from institutions which have ceased to be contributory institutions.

(4) As soon as practicable after the end of the financial year of the Board in which any moneys are received by them as mentioned in subsection (1) above, the Board shall make out of those moneys the payments required by the scheme under subsection (2) above.

(5) If in any financial year of the Board the payments made under subsection (4) above (in that and any previous years) in pursuance of a scheme or schemes under subsection (2) above are sufficient to provide for repayment in full of all the contributions to which the scheme or, as the case may be, the schemes related, any balance remaining of the moneys received by the Board as mentioned in subsection (1) above shall be credited to the Fund.

General Note

This section is intended to deal with accretions to the Fund through dividends on liquidations which take it beyond £5 to £6 millions. These will have been received in the manner described under s. 31 (above).

Subs. (1)

The receipts are first invested in 90-day Treasury Bills (*i.e.* a reasonably short-dated form of Government security).

Subs. (2)

It is to be noted that the parties being repaid are those who made the further contributions (s. 25) and special contributions (s. 26).

Subs. (3)

Repayment first of special contributions and then of further contributions is the reverse order of call—that is, the last levied are the first repaid, as between the two types of contributions. It is to be noted that further (but not special) contributions may be excluded where institutions have ceased to contribute, either because they have lost their status or perhaps, in the case of a foreign bank, the Bank of England is satisfied with the contingency arrangements in their home country (see s. 23 (2)).

Subs. (4)

The effect of this may be that the " scheme " by its terms must conform to this requirement; that is to say, the scheme must provide for repayment as soon after the end of the financial year as possible.

Subs. (5)

If all the contributions are repaid remaining dividends from liquidators are credited to the Fund.

Tax treatment of contributions and repayments

33. In computing for the purposes of the Tax Acts the profits or gains arising from the trade carried on by a contributory institution,—

(*a*) to the extent that it would not be deductible apart from this subsection, any sum expended by the institution in paying a contribution to the Fund may be deducted as an expense; and

(*b*) any payment which is made to the institution by the Board under section 26 (2) above or pursuant to a scheme under section 32 (2) above shall be treated as a trading receipt.

General Note

This section was inserted after parliamentary discussion. All contributions are now deductible for tax.

Part III

Advertisements and Banking Names

Advertisements for deposits

Control of advertisements for deposits

34.—(1) After consultation with the Bank, the Treasury may by regulations made by statutory instrument regulate the issue, form and content of advertisements inviting the making of deposits.

(2) Regulations under this section may make different provision with respect to different descriptions of advertisement and different descriptions of advertisers and, in particular,—

(*a*) may prohibit the issue of advertisements of, or by persons of, particular descriptions; and (*b*) may make provision for the exclusion from all or any of the provisions of the regulations of advertisements of particular descriptions or advertisements issued by persons of particular descriptions; and

(*c*) may make provision with respect to matters which must be, as well as to matters which may not be, included in advertisements.

(3) Any person who issues an advertisement in contravention of regulations under this section shall be liable—

(*a*) on summary conviction to a fine not exceeding the statutory maximum; and

(*b*) on conviction on indictment to imprisonment for a term not exceeding two years or to a fine or to both.

(4) In this section " advertisement " includes every form of advertising, whether in a publication, by the display of notices, signs, labels, showcards or goods, by distribution of samples, by means of circulars, catalogues, price lists or other documents, by an exhibition of photographic or cinematographic films, or of pictures or models, by way of sound broadcasting or television, or in any other manner; and references to the issue of an advertisement shall be construed accordingly.

(5) For the purposes of this section—

(*a*) an advertisement issued by any person by way of display or exhibition in a public place shall be treated as issued by him on every day on which he causes or permits it to be displayed or exhibited;

(*b*) an advertisement which contains information which is intended or might reasonably be presumed to be intended to lead directly or indirectly to the making of deposits shall be treated as an advertisement inviting deposits;

(*c*) an advertisement issued by any person on behalf of or to the order of another person shall be treated as an advertisement issued by that other person; and

(*d*) an advertisement inviting deposits with a person specified in the advertisement shall be presumed, unless the contrary is proved, to have been issued by that person.

(6) A statutory instrument containing regulations under this section shall be subject to annulment in pursuance of a resolution of either House of Parliament.

General Note

This section is to be read in the light of the repeal, by this Act, of the remainder of the Protection of Depositors Act 1963.

Subs. (1)

The regulations that will be issued are likely to be very similar to those under the Protection of Depositors Act 1963. They require, *inter alia,* country of incorporation, names of officials, bankers. Reference to interest had to include the minimum amount, period and notice. If assets were stated liabilities were also to be indicated. Deposits, if claimed to be guaranteed, had to give some particulars of the extent of the cover. Reference to bank, and its derivatives, was primarily limited to those satisfying the Department of Trade that they were a bank within the Eighth Schedule to the Companies Act 1948. A conditional licence could further particularise as to the manner of seeking deposits. The regulations will apply to recognised banks, licensed deposit-takers, exempted bodies and those excluded from the statute in that they take isolated items on deposit. There will no doubt be new provisions, in that references in an advertisement to a " licence issued under the Banking Act," by a deposit-taker, or to the " security of the Deposit Insurance Scheme " will have to be monitored if they are not to be misleading.

Subs. (2)

The regulations could be comprehensive in that they may direct inclusion of certain matters, or forbid such inclusion, or may prohibit advertisements by particular persons.

Subs. (4)

The width of the description should be noticed. Circulars, catalogues, broadcasting, television, films, any form of publication are included.

Subs. (5)

Continuous issue is a continuous offence. The possibility of an invitation is enough. The principal, not the agent, is responsible. Of most importance, the institution that is specified in the advertisement will be presumed to have issued it until proved otherwise.

Specific prohibitions etc. directed at licensed institutions

35.—(1) Subject to subsections (3) and (4) below, if the Bank considers that an advertisement for deposits issued or proposed to be issued by a licensed institution is misleading, the Bank may give the institution concerned a direction under this section.

(2) A direction under this section shall be in writing and may contain all or any of the following, namely,—

(*a*) a prohibition on the issue of advertisements of a specified kind;

(*b*) a requirement that advertisements of a particular description shall be modified in a specified manner;

(*c*) a prohibition on the issue of any advertisements which are, wholly or substantially, repetitions of an advertisement which has been issued and which is identified in the direction; and

(*d*) a requirement to take all practical steps to withdraw from display in any place any advertisements or any advertisements of a particular description specified in the direction.

(3) Not less than seven days before giving a direction under this section, the Bank shall give the institution concerned notice in writing of its intention, specifying the reasons why it proposes to act.

(4) In any case where—

(*a*) the Bank has given notice under subsection (3) above, and

(*b*) within the period of seven days beginning on the date on which the notice was given, written representations are made to the Bank by or on behalf of the institution concerned,

the Bank shall take those representations into account in deciding whether or not to proceed to give the direction.

(5) A direction under this section—

(*a*) may be revoked or varied by a further direction under this section; and

(*b*) may be revoked by the Bank by notice in writing given to the institution concerned.

(6) Subsections (4) and (5) of section 34 above shall apply in relation to this section as they apply in relation to that.

(7) Any person who fails to comply with a direction under this section shall be liable—

(*a*) on summary conviction to a fine not exceeding the statutory maximum; and

(*b*) on conviction on indictment to imprisonment for a term not exceeding two years or to a fine or to both.

GENERAL NOTE

Subs. (1)

There is the power for the Bank to give specific instructions about an advertisement that it considers misleading.

Subs. (2)

The kind or manner may be directed to be changed in a specific way; repetitions of any advertisement can be forbidden. Advertisements of a type or from a particular place may be the subject of direction for withdrawal.

Subs. (3)

Seven days' notice must be given of an intention to give a direction, including the reasons. It appears that there is no appeal (other, presumably, than on points of law) on a direction regarding an advertisement.

Subs. (4)

The consideration of contrary representations is an obvious obligation.

Subs. (5)

Revocation and variation are part of the panoply of control.

Subs. (6)

This relates to the definition of advertisement.

Banking names and descriptions

Restriction on use of certain names and descriptions

36.—(1) Subject to the provisions of this section and section 37 below, no person carrying on a business of any description in the United Kingdom, other than—

(*a*) the Bank,

(*b*) the central bank of a member State other than the United Kingdom,

(*c*) a recognised bank,

(*d*) a trustee savings bank,

(*e*) the Central Trustee Savings Bank Limited, and

(*f*) the Post Office, in the exercise of its powers to provide banking services,

may use any name or in any other way so describe himself or hold himself out as to indicate, or reasonably be understood to indicate, that he is a bank or banker or is carrying on a banking business.

(2) Nothing in this Part of this Act or in the preceding Parts of this Act affects the determination of any question whether a licensed institution or other person is a bank or banker for purposes other than those of this Act, and accordingly nothing in subsection (1) above shall prohibit a person who is not a recognised bank from using the expression " bank " or " banker " or a similar expression with reference to himself in any case where—

(*a*) he wishes to comply with or take advantage of any relevant provision of law or custom; and

(*b*) it is necessary for him to use that expression in order to be able to assert that he is complying with or entitled to take advantage of that provision.

(3) In subsection (2) above " relevant provision of law or custom " means any enactment, any instrument made under an enactment, any international agreement, any rule of law or any commercial usage or practice which confers any benefit on, or otherwise has effect only in relation to, a person by virtue of his being a bank or banker.

(4) Without prejudice to any provision made by virtue of section 34 above, nothing in subsection (1) above shall prohibit a licensed institution which provides at least two of the services specified in paragraph 2 (2) of Schedule 2 to this Act from using the expression "banking services" in relation to any of the services provided by it except—

(*a*) where the use is in such immediate conjunction with the name of the institution that the expression might reasonably be thought to form part of its name; or

(*b*) where the expression appears on any notice or sign or in other writing which is for the time being so displayed as to be visible to persons frequenting any place or building to which the public has access.

(5) Subsection (1) above does not prohibit the use by—

(*a*) a savings bank specified in subsection (6) below, or

(*b*) a municipal bank, or

(*c*) a body of persons certified as a school bank by either a trustee savings bank or the National Savings Bank, or a recognised bank,

of a name or description if the name contains an indication, or when the description is used it is accompanied by a statement, that the bank or body concerned is a savings bank, a municipal bank or, as the case may be, a school bank.

(6) The savings banks referred to in subsection 5 (*a*) above are—

(*a*) the National Savings Bank;

(*b*) any penny savings bank;

(*c*) any savings bank established before 28th July 1863 under an Act passed in the fifty-ninth year of King George the Third intituled an Act for the Protection of Banks for Savings in Scotland, which has not since become a trustee savings bank; and

(*d*) the British Railways Savings Bank established under section 32 of the British Railways Act 1966.

(7) Subsection (1) above does not prohibit the use by—

(*a*) a licensed institution which is a wholly owned subsidiary (within the meaning of section 150 (4) of the Companies Act 1948) of a recognised bank, or

(*b*) a company which has a wholly owned subsidiary (within the meaning of that section) which is a recognised bank,

of a name which includes the name of that recognised bank for the purpose of indicating the connection between the two companies.

(8) Subsection (1) above does not prohibit the use by a licensed institution which has its principal place of business in a country or territory outside the United Kingdom of the name under which the institution carries on business in that country or territory if the name is used in immediate conjunction with the description "licensed deposit-taker" and, where the name appears in writing, if that description is at least as prominent as the name.

(9) Subsection (1) above does not prohibit the use by a person who carries on business at a representative office of an overseas institution of a name under which the overseas institution carries on a deposit-taking business in a country or territory outside the United Kingdom if the name is used in immediate conjunction with the description "representative office" and, where the name appears in writing, if that description is at least as prominent as the name; and in this subsection "overseas institution" and "representative office" have the same meaning as in section 40 below.

(10) Where on an application for—

(*a*) registration of a name under the Registration of Business Names Act 1916, or

(*b*) the first registration of a company, or the registration of a company by a new name, under the Companies Act 1948 or the Companies Act (Northern Ireland) 1960,

it appears to the registrar concerned that the use of the name by the person seeking to register it would contravene subsection (1) above, the registration shall not be made.

(11) A person who contravenes subsection (1) above shall be liable on summary conviction to a fine not exceeding £1,000; and where the contravention involves a public display or exhibition of the offending name, description or other matter, there shall be a fresh contravention of the subsection on each day on which that person causes or permits the display or exhibition to continue.

General Note

Associated with the dichotomy of recognition of banks and the licensing of deposit-takers, this restriction of the use of the name bank or banking is the most controversial provision of the Act. There are many contexts in which it is used: first, the one relating to the taking of deposits which is one of the essential functions of a bank; secondly, in statutes that are amended by this Act (Sched. 6, Pt. I); thirdly, in statutes that are specifically saved by this Act (Sched. 6, Pt. II); fourthly, those not mentioned at all in the Act, which will come within the comprehensive and oblique provision of s. 36 (2) above.

Subs. (1)

A " Member State " is one of the Nine EEC Members. This subsection contains the primary prohibition on the use of a banking name " describing himself as or holding out as to indicate, or reasonably to be understood as to indicate " that he is a bank. This is wide in that it embraces the understanding of a reasonable man. Whatever the strict meaning, the production by a prosecution of reasonable men as witnesses is alone enough, despite any doubt as to the interpretation that could or should be placed on what has been written. Possibly it is an answer to get a number of reasonable men who think otherwise. Holding out depends on what is evidenced, not intention. The reference to the reasonable men gives an indication of the type of evidence that is to be accepted. It may not extend the definition but it does not narrow it. For " trustee savings bank," see s. 50. The Central Trustee Savings Bank Limited is the central body established.

It is to be noticed that the restriction refers to " persons carrying on business in the United Kingdom " so international institutions like the European Investment Bank would not be affected. For that matter any bank without an office here is unaffected. Some of the old banks that are kept alive only for their names and their convenience in relation to conveyancing will be exempt under this subsection. The Post Office exemption covers the National Girobank activity.

Subs. (2)

This section, expanded from its original form, is one of the most difficult in the statute because of its width. It is certainly more explicit than as at first drafted. It repays careful analysis. *Nothing* in Pt. I, II or III of the Act *is to affect the determination of any question* whether a licensed institution or other person (that is anyone other than a recognised bank) *is a bank* for purposes *other* than this Act. Therefore, anyone who could call himself a banker under the old law can still do so for particular purposes, but he must *not* use the name to suggest that he is carrying on business as such. He can take deposits if he has a deposit-taking licence; he can therefore do all that was and is necessary to satisfy the definition as contained in *United Dominions Trust Ltd.* v. *Kirkwood* [1966] 2 Q.B. 431—run current and deposit accounts, pay cheques and collect cheques. For most of the other definitions, the requirement of taking deposits is essential. At all events the payment of cheques will usually have necessitated the accumulation of a credit balance. The section then goes on " accordingly nothing shall prohibit." Presumably " accordingly " cannot delimit wider wording in the first part of the section. That is the first point to be clarified. In other words could the whole of the relief contained in the following two requirements, (2) (*a*) and (2) (*b*) extend but not restrict the significance? It may be intended to cut down the umbrella that has been opened. Yet, so long as the word " banker " is not used, the whole of the previous law is to be unaffected. Then one would be left a number of examples (excluding of course matters specifically amended by the statute). The law relating to crossed cheques would enable, for example, a licensed deposit-taker who carried on banking in the old, traditional meaning (that is the *United Dominions Trust* v. *Kirkwood* meaning) to present crossed cheques over a bank counter and demand payment. The Bills of Exchange Act 1882 has many illustrations. It seems, on the other hand, that, as mentioned, examples of " banker " in the old sense necessitate the taking of deposits. Thus in addition, of course, to recognised banks, only licensed institutions will come within the section even on its widest interpretation, apart perhaps from some foreign entities.

Subs. (3)

The amplification is extremely wide and generous but on the narrower interpretation of subs. (2) it has to be necessary to use the expression " banker." Yet all the previous law is unsullied, so long as the determination as to whether a party is a banker is for purposes other than those of this Act. For example, one has to plead that one is a banker for the purpose of the Cheques Act 1957. This is the kind of instance included on any interpretation. For the Bills of Exchange Act 1882 the meaning of banker is still " someone who carries on the business of banking."

Subs. (4)

This enables a licensed institution that provides two out of five of the " wide range of services " contained in para. 2 (2) of Sched. 2 to use the expression " banking services " so long as it is used in a way that cannot suggest that the phrase is part of the name and that where it is written and displayed it is not visible in a public place. This definition probably includes the banking hall; at least for purposes of the criminal law the definition covers places where people enter by implied invitation. The banking hall would be a public place but the manager's room may well not be. The concession is not to prejudice the restriction contained in s. 34 relating to advertisement control. An obvious part of the concession is inclusion in a letter heading.

Subs. (5)

There are minor exceptions from the prohibition relating to savings and minor banks.

Subs. (6)

This expands the details of the savings banks within the preceding exception.

Subs. (7)

This exception is where a licensed institution is a *wholly-owned* subsidiary of a recognised bank and includes the name of that recognised bank in its title for the purpose of showing the connection. (X Bank Finance Company is presumably an example; X Bank for Finance of Industry would not, perhaps, be one.)

Subs. (8)

A licensed institution (licensed in the United Kingdom in accordance with *this* Act) which has its main place of business abroad may use the name under which it carries on business abroad, so long as the description " licensed deposit-taker " is equally prominent.

Subs. (9)

Where a foreign institution has a representative office (see s. 40) in the United Kingdom the name that is used abroad can be used so long as it is done in immediate conjunction with the description " representative office " and with equal prominence.

Transitory exceptions from section 36 (1)

37.—(1) If on the appointed day an institution is carrying on a deposit-taking business in the United Kingdom, nothing in section 36 (1) above shall apply to the institution at any time when, by virtue of section 2 (4) above, it is not prohibited by section 1 (1) above from accepting a deposit.

(2) For a period of twelve months beginning on the appointed day, nothing in section 36 (1) above shall apply to a person who on that day is carrying on in the United Kingdom a business other than a deposit-taking business.

(3) Notwithstanding anything in section 36 above, if an institution ceases (otherwise than on becoming a recognised bank) to be entitled to the benefit of subsection (1) above, the institution shall be entitled—

(*a*) to continue to use any existing registered business or company name for a period of twelve months, and

(*b*) to continue to use any other description for a period of six months,

each period beginning on the date on which the institution ceased to benefit from subsection (1) above.

(4) If, at any time when an institution or other person is entitled to use a registered business or company name by virtue only of the preceding provisions of this section, that name is changed so as to avoid any contravention of section 36 (1) above, then—

(*a*) throughout the period or, as the case may be, the remainder of the period of twelve months specified in subsection (2) or, as the case may be, subsection (3) above, and

(*b*) for a further period of twelve months,

the institution or other person shall be entitled, in any context where it uses the new name, to include a reference to the name by which it was formerly known, together with some indication that that name is no longer in use.

(5) Notwithstanding anything in section 36 above, if an institution ceases to be a recognised bank, the institution shall be entitled to continue to use any existing registered business or company name or any other description for a period of six months beginning on the date when it ceases to be a recognised bank.

GENERAL NOTE

S. 2 (4) provides for the *transitional* implication in relation to the restriction on the use of a banking name and of holding-out to be a banker. The basic prohibition contained in s. 36 (1) does not apply while the temporary period of grace obtains in relation to an application. This is contained in s. 2 (4), giving six months and any part of the ensuing six months taken by the Bank to make its decision whether to grant a licence.

Subs. (2)

Any company not carrying on deposit-taking has 12 months by the end of which it must give up using the name. For historic reasons, a company may have called itself " bankers "—perhaps because of its relationship to the rest of a commercial group. This inclusion may eventually have to go but there is to be a " twilight " 12 months. (It could be needed in relation to its status abroad.)

Subs. (3)

There is the concession of the company name being used for 12 months (or the description for six months). These periods commence when the authority under s. 2 (4) to carry on with a licensed activity ceases.

Subs. (4)

Any change of name to avoid the use of a banking name prohibited by the statute can be deferred for a further 12 months.

Subs. (5)

This provides six months' grace during which the formal name may be used after an institution ceases to be a bank.

Part IV

Miscellaneous and General

Amendments of Consumer Credit Act 1974

38.—(1) In section 74 of the Consumer Credit Act 1974 (certain agreements excluded from Part V of that Act) after subsection (3) (certain overdraft agreements excluded only where the Director General of Fair Trading makes a determination) there shall be inserted the following subsection:—

" (3A) Notwithstanding anything in subsection (3) (*b*) above, in relation to a debtor-creditor agreement under which the creditor is the Bank of England or a bank within the meaning of the Bankers' Books Evidence Act 1879, the Director shall make a determination that subsection (1) (*b*) above applies unless he considers that it would be against the public interest to do so ";

and in subsection (4) of that section (certain agreements in writing falling within subsection (1) (*b*) or (*c*) subject to regulations as to form and content) for " (1) (*b*) or (*c*) ", in each place where it occurs, there shall be substituted " (1) (*c*) ".

(2) Nothing in sections 114 to 122 of the Consumer Credit Act 1974 (pledges) shall be taken to apply to bearer bonds and, accordingly, in paragraph (*a*) of subsection (3) of section 114 of that Act (exclusion of pledges of documents of title) after the word " title " there shall be inserted the words " or of bearer bonds ".

(3) In section 185 (2) of the Consumer Credit Act 1974 (which relates to dispensing notices given by one of two or more debtors to whom running-account credit is provided) at the end of the proviso there shall be added the following paragraph:—

" (*c*) a dispensing notice which is operative in relation to an agreement shall be operative also in relation to any subsequent agreement which, in relation to the earlier agreement, is a modifying agreement ".

General Note

The first of these amendments is of considerable importance; the others are non-controversial. The Consumer Credit Act became law in 1974 but much of it was a shell to be filled in by subordinate legislation following negotiation. The principle adopted was that the Act was aimed against transactions, not parties. The concept of differentiating " bankers " was anathema to the progenitors of the legislation.

Subs. (1)

The Act, very rightly in relation to many transactions, embodied much formality to protect the unsuspecting borrower. However, the implication was that bank overdrafts to private individuals and partnerships, otherwise within the limits of the Act would be similarly embroiled. This could have stultified much of the flexibility of the overdraft system. The difficulty was in some measure anticipated and the Consumer Credit Act 1974 provided for a determination—a form of subsidiary legislation—to be made pursuant to s. 74 of the Act, but agreement with the Banks could not be achieved. Now the onus has been placed more clearly on the Director of Fair Trading, it being indicated that bankers within the meaning of the Bankers' Books Evidence Act 1879 are to be exempted from the formality so long as it is not considered that the position of depositors will be prejudiced. Quite what reservation may be made is not known but it is thought that the general run of overdrafts will be free from the irritation that would otherwise have persisted. By the amendment to the Bankers' Books Evidence Act 1879 effected by Sched. 6, Pt. I, to this Act, deposit-takers will enjoy the benefit of the determination.

Subs. (2)

This eliminates a doubt, not well founded, that a receipt of bearer bonds may have been a " pledge " if deposited as security.

Subs. (3)

This is a drafting amendment.

Fraudulent inducement to make a deposit

39.—(1) Any person who, on or after the appointed day, by any statement, promise or forecast which he knows to be misleading, false or deceptive, or by any dishonest concealment of material facts, or by the reckless making (dishonestly or otherwise) of any statement, promise or forecast which is misleading, false or deceptive, induces or attempts to induce another person—

(*a*) to make a deposit with him or with any other person, or

(*b*) to enter into or offer to enter into any agreement for that purpose,

shall be liable on conviction on indictment to imprisonment for a term not exceeding seven years or to a fine or both.

(2) In subsection (1) above " deposit " does not include a loan made to an institution upon terms involving the issue of debentures or other securities but, subject to that, in its application to subsection (1) above, subsection (5) of section 1 of this Act shall have effect with the omission of paragraphs (*b*) to (*e*).

(3) Nothing in this section shall be construed as empowering a court in Scotland, other than the High Court of Justiciary, to pass for any offence under this section a sentence of imprisonment for a term exceeding two years.

(4) Subsections (1) to (3) above have effect in substitution for subsections (1) and (2) of section 1 of the Protection of Depositors Act 1963 or, in Northern Ireland, section 1 of the Protection of Depositors Act (Northern Ireland) 1964; and nothing in this Act shall affect any liability of any person under either of those sections in respect of anything done or omitted to be done before the appointed day.

General Note

This re-enacts s. 1 of the Protection of Depositors Act 1963 which is repealed. It created the offence of fraudulent inducement to make a deposit, and subs. (3) re-enacts s. 2 of that Act regarding Scotland. Subs. (2) excludes secured loans which come within the ambit of the Prevention of Fraud Investment Act 1958, s. 13. The Protection of Depositors Act 1963 achieved the differentiation by the definition of deposit. That definition incidentally *includes* the exceptions in subs. (5) (*b*) to (*e*) in s. 1 of this Act, within the definition of deposit for this purpose.

Representative offices of overseas deposit-taking institutions

40.—(1) If, on or after the appointed day, a representative office is established in the United Kingdom by an overseas institution which does not carry on a deposit-taking business there, then, within the period of one month beginning with the date on which that office is established, the institution shall give notice in writing to the Bank of the establishment of the office.

(2) If, before the appointed day, a representative office has been established in the United Kingdom by an overseas institution which does not carry on a deposit-taking business there, then, within the

period of six months beginning with the appointed day, the institution shall give notice in writing to the Bank of the existence of the office.

(3) Any reference in this section to an overseas institution is a reference to an institution which carries on a deposit-taking business in a country or territory outside the United Kingdom and which is either—

(*a*) a body corporate formed under the law of such a country or territory, or

(*b*) any other description of institution of which the principal place of business is in such a country or territory,

and in relation to such an institution any reference in this section to a representative office is a reference to premises from which the deposit-taking business of the institution or any other activity of the institution which falls within paragraph 2 (2) of Schedule 2 to this Act is promoted or assisted in any way.

(4) Where the Bank has received notice from an institution under subsection (1) or subsection (2) above, the Bank may by notice in writing given to the institution require it to furnish to the Bank, within the period of one month beginning with the date on which the notice is given,—

(*a*) in the case of an institution which is required in connection with the establishment of a representative office in Great Britain after the appointed day to deliver certain documents to the Registrar of Companies under section 407 (1) of the Companies Act 1948, copies of those documents; and

(*b*) in the case of an institution which is not so obliged, or which has a representative office established before the appointed day, the like information as would be contained in the documents which the institution would be required to deliver as mentioned in paragraph (*a*) above if it were a company to which the said section 407 (1) applied and had established a place of business within Great Britain immediately before the notice was given to it under this subsection.

(5) If at any time an overseas institution which has been required to furnish information or documents under subsection (4) above—

(*a*) is required to deliver a return to the Registrar of Companies under section 409 of the Companies Act 1948 containing particulars of an alteration in the matters referred to in that section (alterations of memorandum, directors, persons authorised to accept service etc.), or

(*b*) is required, in connection with ceasing to have a representative office in Great Britain, to give notice to the Registrar under subsection (2) of section 413 of that Act of the fact that it has ceased to have a place of business in either part of Great Britain,

the institution shall deliver a copy of the return, or, as the case may be, shall also give notice, to the Bank; and if at any time such an institution would be required to deliver such a return or give such a notice as is mentioned in paragraph (*a*) or paragraph (*b*) above if it were a company to which the said section or subsection applied and its representative office were a place of business, it shall make such a return or give such a notice to the Bank.

(6) Subsections (4) and (5) above shall apply in the case of a representative office established in Northern Ireland—

(*a*) with the substitution for the references in those subsections to Great Britain of references to Northern Ireland, and (*b*) with the substitution for the references in those subsections to subsection (1) of section 407, section 409 and subsection (2) of section 413 of the Companies Act 1948 of references to, respectively, sections 356, 358 and 362 of the Companies Act (Northern Ireland) 1960.

(7) An institution which fails to comply with any provision of this section shall be liable on summary conviction to a fine not exceeding £1,000.

General Note

Representative officers of English banks have often been permitted where branches were illegal. A branch is not a representative office merely because it does not take deposits (for some years English banks had establishments in New York that did not take deposits from the public—there was also the intermediate category of agency). It appears that, for the purposes of this Act, a representative office of an overseas institution—bank or other deposit-taking institution—is one that does not take deposits here.

Subs. (1)

This creates a duty for such a representative to notify the Bank of England.

Subs. (2)

An existing representative has to notify within six months of the Act coming into force.

Subs. (3)

The definition means that the institution is either formed under foreign law or has its principal place of business abroad, but has premises here from which deposit-taking or any other activity included in the wide range of banking facilities is promoted.

Subs. (4)

S. 407 (1) of the Companies Act 1948 requires a copy of the constitution, names of directors and secretary and particulars of persons authorised to accept service. Some representatives will demur that they do not carry on a business and are not liable to service in the United Kingdom. (Quite what effect this section will have is open to doubt.) It seems that representation will entail an obligation to accept service here solely because the institution in the country of control is, primarily, engaged in a banking activity.

Subs. (5)

This covers the obligation to advise changes as would be the case if the company have registered as an " overseas " company.

Offences

41.—(1) Where an offence under this Act committed by a body corporate is proved to have been committed with the consent or connivance of, or to be attributable to any neglect on the part of, any director, manager, secretary or other similar officer of the body corporate, or any person who was purporting to act in any such capacity, he, as well as the body corporate, shall be guilty of that offence and be liable to be proceeded against and punished accordingly.

(2) Where the affairs of a body corporate are managed by its members, subsection (1) above shall apply in relation to the acts and defaults of a member in connection with his functions of management as if he were a director of the body corporate.

(3) In any proceedings for an offence under this Act it shall be a defence for the person charged to prove that he took all reasonable precautions and exercised all due diligence to avoid the commission of such an offence by himself or any person under his control.

(4) Without prejudice to subsection (3) above, in any proceedings for an offence under section 34 or section 36 above committed by the publication of an advertisement it shall be a defence for the person charged to prove that he is a person whose business is to publish or arrange for the publication of advertisements and that he received the advertisement for publication in the ordinary course of business and did not know and had no reason to suspect that its publication would amount to such an offence.

(5) No proceedings for an offence under this Act shall be instituted—

(*a*) in England and Wales, except by or with the consent of the Director of Public Prosecutions or the Bank; or

(*b*) in Northern Ireland, except by or with the consent of the Director of Public Prosecutions for Northern Ireland or the Bank.

(6) Summary proceedings for any offence under this Act may, without prejudice to any jurisdiction exercisable apart from this subsection, be taken against an institution, including an unincorporated institution, at any place at which it has a place of business, and against an individual at any place at which he is for the time being.

General Note

This is a reminder that the primary object of the Act is control, the sanctions for which are the punishment of the offences created. It gives protection relating to what would be offences by innocent publishers and deals with the prosecution of institutions on the one hand and individuals on the other.

Subs. (1)

A director, manager, secretary or similar officer (or anyone purporting to hold that office) is to be guilty of an offence as well as the institution, if he has connived at, agreed or caused by his neglect the particular offence. Here the meanings in s. 49 of "director," "controller" and "manager" do not apply. "Director" will presumably have the meaning of s. 455 of the Companies Act 1948 being "one occupying the position by whatever name called." The secretary of a company is a question of fact but one would think that a "manager" depends on what he does and not what he is called literally. It is one who takes part in management.

Subs. (2)

This would appear intended where members take part in management as where they may attend a board meeting, and participate.

Subs. (3)

This provision puts the onus on the defendant to give evidence that he exercised due diligence and took reasonable care.

Subs. (4)

This absolves publishers from offences under ss. 34 and 36.

Subs. (6)

Summary proceedings may be taken against an institution at its place of business or against an official where he is for the time being.

Offences committed by unincorporated institutions

42.—(1) Proceedings for an offence alleged to have been committed under this Act by an unincorporated institution shall be brought in the name of that institution (and not in that of any of its members) and, for the purposes of any such proceedings, any rules of court relating to the service of documents shall have effect as if the institution were a corporation.

(2) A fine imposed on an unincorporated institution on its conviction of an offence under this Act shall be paid out of the funds of the institution.

(3) Section 33 of the Criminal Justice Act 1925 and Schedule 2 to the Magistrates' Courts Act 1952 (procedure on charge of offence against a corporation) shall have effect in a case in which an unincorporated institution is charged in England or Wales with an offence under this Act in like manner as they have effect in the case of a corporation so charged.

(4) In relation to any proceedings on indictment in Scotland for an offence alleged to have been committed under this Act by an unincorporated institution, section 74 of the Criminal Procedure (Scotland) Act 1975 (proceedings on indictment against bodies corporate) shall have effect as if the institution were a body corporate.

(5) Section 18 of the Criminal Justice Act (Northern Ireland) 1945 and Schedule 5 to the Magistrates' Courts Act (Northern Ireland) 1964 (procedure on charge of offence against a corporation) shall have effect in a case in which an unincorporated institution is charged in Northern Ireland with an offence under this Act in like manner as they have effect in the case of a corporation so charged.

(6) Where a partnership is guilty of an offence under this Act, every partner, other than a partner who is proved to have been ignorant of or to have attempted to prevent the commission of the offence, shall also be guilty of that offence and be liable to be proceeded against and punished accordingly.

(7) Where any other unincorporated institution is guilty of an offence under this Act, every officer of the institution who is bound to fulfil any duty whereof the offence is a breach, or if there is no such officer then every member of the committee or other similar governing body, other than a member who is proved to have been ignorant of or to have attempted to prevent the commission of the offence, shall also be guilty of that offence and be liable to be proceeded against and punished accordingly.

GENERAL NOTE

Subs. (1)

Although it is unincorporated, proceedings may be brought against an institution—as is provided in respect of similar bodies under s. 80 of the Insurance Companies Act 1974.

Subs. (3)

This deals with such matters as where decisions may be taken to deal with cases summarily and the form of authority required from representatives.

Subs. (6)

The onus lies on the partner to prove absence of knowledge.

Subs. (7)

A breach of duty as an officer means liability for an offence under this Act. There is a similar provision in s. 98 (5) of the Friendly Societies Act 1974.

Exclusion of certain provisions relating to rehabilitation of offenders

43.—(1) Section 4 (2) of the Rehabilitation of Offenders Act 1974 (questions relating to previous convictions which have become spent) shall not apply in relation to any question put to any person with respect to the previous convictions, offences, conduct or circumstances of an individual if—

(a) the question is put by or on behalf of the Bank and the individual is a director, controller or manager of an institution which is recognised or licensed or which has made an application for recognition or a licence which has not been disposed of; or

(b) the question is put by or on behalf of a recognised or licensed institution or an institution which has made an application for recognition or a licence which has not yet been disposed of and the individual is, or is seeking to become, a director, controller or manager of the institution.

(2) Section 4 (3) (b) of the Rehabilitation of Offenders Act 1974 (spent convictions not to be ground for dismissal etc. from offices, professions, occupations or employment) shall not—

(a) prevent the Bank from refusing to grant a licence to an institution or from revoking a licence held by an institution on the ground that, by reason of a previous conviction, an individual is not a fit and proper person to be a director, controller or manager of the institution; or

(b) apply in relation to the dismissal or exclusion of an individual from being a director, controller or manager of an institution which is recognised or licensed or which has made an application for recognition or a licence which has not yet been disposed of.

(3) For the purposes of subsections (1) and (2) above, an application by an institution is not disposed of until the decision of the Bank on the application is communicated to the institution.

(4) In section 7 (2) of the Rehabilitation of Offenders Act 1974 (exclusion of certain proceedings from the effect of rehabilitation set out in section 4 (1) of that Act) at the end of paragraph (f) there shall be added the words " or,

(g) in any proceedings arising out of any such decision of the Bank of England as is referred to in section 11 (1) of the Banking Act 1979, including proceedings on appeal to any court ".

(5) In the application of subsections (1) and (2) above to Northern Ireland, for the references to sections 4 (2) and 4 (3) (b) of the Rehabilitation of Offenders Act 1974 there shall be substituted references to Articles 5 (2) and 5 (3) (b) of the Rehabilitation of Offenders (Northern Ireland) Order 1978, respectively.

(6) In Article 8 (2) of the Rehabilitation of Offenders (Northern Ireland) Order 1978 (exclusion of certain proceedings from the effect of rehabilitation set out in Article 5 (1) of that Order) at the end of sub-paragraph (e) there shall be added the words " or,

(f) in any proceedings arising out of any such decision of the Bank of England as is referred to in section 11 (1) of the Banking Act 1979, including proceedings on appeal to any court.".

General Note

Subs. (1)

The 1974 Act provides that after a lapse of time convictions become " spent," then they need not be disclosed. This section excludes the impact of that Act in relation to questions regarding " director, controller or manager " of a recognised bank or licensed institution whether put by the Bank of England or by the recognised bank to the individuals concerned. " Director," " controller " and " manager " are defined in s. 49.

Subs. (2)

Similarly, a licence may be refused or a dismissal effected that would otherwise have conflicted with s. 4 (3) (b) of the Rehabilitation of Offenders Act 1974; also a licence may be revoked in disregard of that Act. (The requirement of being a fit and proper person does not apply to directors, controllers and managers of recognised banks in that its absence is not a ground for revocation of recognition.)

Subs. (4)

This excludes proceedings before the Chancellor's Tribunal from the impact of s. 4 (1) of the Rehabilitation of Offenders Act 1974 and adds the inset clause to the list of such items contained in that Act.

Evidence

44. In any proceedings, a certificate purporting to be signed by the Chief Cashier or a Deputy Chief Cashier of the Bank and certifying—

(*a*) that a particular institution is or is not recognised or licensed or was or was not recognised or licensed at a particular time, or

(*b*) the date on which recognition or a licence was granted to a particular institution, or

(*c*) the date on which an institution ceased to be recognised or to hold a licence, or a licence of a particular description, or

(*d*) the nature of the licence held by a particular institution at any time and, in the case of a conditional or transitional licence, the date of its expiry,

shall be admissible in evidence and, in Scotland, shall be sufficient evidence of the facts stated in the certificate.

General Note

This is, of course, not conclusive evidence.

Service of notices

45.—(1) This section has effect in relation to any notice, directions or other document required or authorised by or under this Act to be given to or served on any person other than the Bank.

(2) Any such document may be given to or served on the person in question—

(*a*) by delivering it to him;

(*b*) by leaving it at his proper address; or

(*c*) by sending it by post to him at that address.

(3) Any such document may,—

(*a*) in the case of a body corporate, be given to or served on the secretary or clerk of that body; and

(*b*) in the case of any other description of institution, be given to or served on a controller of the institution.

(4) For the purposes of this section and section 7 of the Interpretation Act 1978 (service of documents by post) in its application to this section, the proper address of any person to or on whom a document is to be given or served shall be his last known address, except that—

(*a*) in the case of a body corporate or its secretary or clerk, it shall be the address of the registered or principal office of that body in the United Kingdom; and

(*b*) in the case of any other description of institution or a person having the control or management of its business, it shall be that of the principal office of the institution in the United Kingdom.

(5) If the person to or on whom any document mentioned in subsection (1) above is to be given or served has specified an address within the United Kingdom, other than his proper address within the meaning of subsection (4) above, as the one at which he or someone on his behalf

will accept documents of the same description as that document, that address shall also be treated for the purposes of this section and section 7 of the Interpretation Act 1978 as his proper address.

General Note

This section applies to all *notices* under the Act whether " given " or " served." " Given " could refer to oral notice received in relation to the suspension of payment in bankruptcy proceedings (*cf.* Bankruptcy Act 1914, s. 1 (*h*)). The " proper address " is the last known address, except that for a corporate body it shall be the registered address or principal address; with any other institution it is again its principal office in the United Kingdom. S. 7 of the Interpretation Act 1978 provides for the service of documents by post.

Repeal of certain enactments relating to banks and banking

46. The following enactments are hereby repealed:—

(*a*) section 21 of the Bank Charter Act 1844 and section 13 of the Bank Notes (Scotland) Act 1845 (which require banks to make a return to the Commissioners of Inland Revenue of the names of their principals and places of business);

(*b*) in section 4 (2) of the Limited Partnerships Act 1907 (which provides that a partnership registered under that Act may not have more than a certain number of partners), the words " in the case of a partnership carrying on the business of banking, of more than ten persons, and, in the case of any other partnership ";

(*c*) in section 155 of the Companies Act 1948 and section 149 of the Companies Act (Northern Ireland) 1960 (which lay down requirements as to the signature of the balance sheet of a registered company), subsection (2) (which lays down special requirements for banking companies);

(*d*) section 429 of the said Act of 1948 and section 377 of the said Act of 1960 (which, subject to certain exceptions, prohibit the formation otherwise than as a registered company of a company, association or partnership of more than ten persons for the purpose of carrying on the business of banking);

(*e*) section 430 of the said Act of 1948 and section 378 of the said Act of 1960 (which require banking companies proposing to become registered with limited liability to give notice to all persons having an account with them);

(*f*) section 431 of the said Act of 1948 and section 379 of the said Act of 1960 (which exclude liabilities in respect of notes issued by a bank in the United Kingdom from the principle of limited liability); and

(*g*) in subsection (1) of section 433 of the said Act of 1948 and section 381 of the said Act of 1960 (which require certain companies to post up in their business premises a bi-annual statement of their financial position), the words " a limited banking company or ".

General Note

The effect of the repealed enactments is shown in parentheses in each case. The reasons for the repeals are:

(*a*) The information required is now provided by this Act to the Bank of England.

(*b*) The distinction is presumably no longer necessary.

(*c*) The signature of the extra director is no longer thought to be a necessary assurance for the public.

(*d*) The maximum is now 20 with no special differentiation for banking as provided by s. 434 (1) of the Companies Act 1948.
(*e*) The general provisions obtaining where an unlimited company is going to register as a limited company presumably provide sufficient protection (see Companies Act 1948, s. 44).
(*f*) Only Scottish and Irish Banks still issue their own notes; the last English Bank to have that privilege was Fox Fowler & Co. in 1921, when they amalgamated with a joint stock bank.
(*g*) It is no longer, presumably, considered necessary for such publication in view of the precautions now taken following the passing of this Act.

Defence of contributory negligence

47. In any circumstances in which proof of absence of negligence on the part of a banker would be a defence in proceedings by reason of section 4 of the Cheques Act 1957, a defence of contributory negligence shall also be available to the banker notwithstanding the provisions of section 11 (1) of the Torts (Interference with Goods) Act 1977.

General Note

This section represents an opportunity that was taken to eliminate doubts that were cast upon one aspect of the law relating to the collecting bankers. Strictly if a banker collects a cheque for someone who has no right, the cheque has been converted (*cf. Lloyds Bank* v. *Chartered Bank of India, Australia and China* [1929] 1 K.B. 40), the value of the piece of paper being regarded as the value of the cheque. Banks are protected by (in part) s. 4 of the Cheques Act 1957 if they collect such a cheque, *inter alia,* without negligence, upon which there are many cases. Another aspect was raised in the case of *Lumsden* v. *London Trustee Savings Bank* [1977] 2 Lloyd's Rep. 114. There, a fraudulent clerk had opened a banking account in circumstances in which the bank had been negligent and thus the protection of s. 4 was lost. There had, however, been an element of negligence in the conduct of the plaintiffs in that they had drawn their cheques carelessly. The Bank alleged that they should not bear *all* the loss on the ground that the Contributory Negligence Act 1945 applies to tort as well as contract. The Bank was held liable for a percentage of the loss only. Then the Torts (Interference with Goods) Act 1977 was passed, which by s. 11 (1) states: "contributory negligence is no defence in proceedings founded in conversion. . . ." This immediately threw doubt upon the *Lumsden* decision mentioned above. This section says that where the absence of negligence would be a defence by reason of s. 4 of the Cheques Act 1957, "a defence of contributory negligence" is also to be available. In the *Lumsden* case, the bank could not rely on s. 4 of the Cheques Act because to do so it had to have collected without negligence which is one of the stipulated conditions for the protection to be available. It was thus open to liability for conversion. The new law is that in such proceedings contributory negligence is to be available. This will be part of the conversion. (The proof of the absence of negligence does not, of course, relate to the tort of negligence but to the availability of the statutory immunity for which it is a pre-condition). The section, however, achieves the object; it was introduced quite late in the passage of the Bill.

Municipal banks

48.—(1) References in this Act to a municipal bank are to a company within the meaning of the Companies Act 1948 which—
(*a*) carries on a deposit-taking business,
(*b*) is connected with a local authority as mentioned in subsection (2) below, and
(*c*) has its deposits guaranteed by that local authority in accordance with subsection (5) below.

(2) The connection referred to in paragraph (*b*) of subsection (1) above between a company and a local authority is that—
(*a*) the company's articles of association provide that the shares in the company are to be held only by members of the local authority; and

(b) substantially all the funds lent by the company are lent to the local authority.

(3) Where on 9th November 1978 a company, or its predecessor,—

(a) was carrying on a deposit-taking business, and

(b) was connected with a local authority as mentioned in subsection (2) above,

that local authority or its successor may for the purposes of this Act resolve to guarantee deposits with the company.

(4) A resolution passed by a local authority under subsection (3) above may not be rescinded.

(5) Where a local authority has passed a resolution under subsection (3) above, that local authority and any local authority which is its successor shall be liable, if the company concerned defaults in payment, to make good to a depositor the principal and interest owing in respect of any deposit with the company, whether made before or after the passing of the resolution.

(6) For the purposes of this section—

(a) one company is the predecessor of another if that other succeeds to its obligations in respect of its deposit-taking business; and

(b) one local authority is the successor of another if, as a result of, or in connection with, an order under Part IV of the Local Government Act 1972 or Part II of the Local Government (Scotland) Act 1973 (change of local government area), it becomes connected as mentioned in subsection (2) above with a company formerly so connected with that other local authority.

(7) In the Scotland Act 1978, at the end of Part III of Schedule 10 (matters dealt with by certain enactments to be included, to the extent specified, in the groups of devolved matters) there shall be added the following entry—

" The Banking Act 1979 section 48 (3) to (6). Included."

General Note

Municipal banks, which are few and principally in Scotland, would have difficulty in meeting the statutory stipulations; therefore the deposits are being guaranteed irrevocably by the relevant local authority. The moneys are lent to the local authority and the shares are held by the local authority. The section also covers successorship of the local authority or of the company.

Meaning of " director ", " controller " and " manager "

49.—(1) Except in section 41 above, in this Act the expressions " director ", " controller " and " manager ", in relation to an institution, shall be construed in accordance with the provisions of this section.

(2) " Director ", in relation to an institution, includes—

(a) any person who occupies the position of a director, by whatever name called; and

(b) in the case of an institution established in a country or territory outside the United Kingdom, any person, including a member of a managing board, who occupies a position appearing to the Bank to be analogous to that of a director of a company registered under the Companies Act 1948;

and in the case of a partnership the expression " director ", where it is used in subsections (4) and (5) below, includes a partner.

(3) " Controller ", in relation to an institution, means—

(*a*) a managing director of the institution or of another institution of which it is a subsidiary or, in the case of an institution which is a partnership, a partner;

(*b*) a chief executive of the institution or of another institution of which it is a subsidiary;

(*c*) a person in accordance with whose directions or instructions the directors of the institution or of another institution of which it is a subsidiary (or any of them) are accustomed to act; and

(*d*) a person who, either alone or with any associate or associates, is entitled to exercise, or control the exercise of, fifteen per cent. or more of the voting power at any general meeting of the institution or of another institution of which it is a subsidiary.

(4) " Manager ", in relation to an institution, means a person (other than the chief executive) employed by the institution who, under the immediate authority of a director or chief executive of the institution—

(*a*) exercises managerial functions; or

(*b*) is responsible for maintaining accounts or other records of the institution.

(5) In this section " chief executive ", in relation to an institution, means a person who is employed by the institution and who either alone or jointly with one or more other persons, is or will be responsible under the immediate authority of the directors for the conduct of the business of the institution.

(6) Without prejudice to subsection (5) above, in relation to an institution whose principal place of business is in a country or territory outside the United Kingdom, the expression " chief executive " also includes a person who is employed by the institution and who, either alone or jointly with one or more other persons, is or will be responsible for the conduct of its deposit-taking business in the United Kingdom.

(7) In this section " associate ", in relation to any person, means—

(*a*) the wife or husband or son or daughter of that person;

(*b*) any company of which that person is a director;

(*c*) any person who is an employee or partner of that person; and

(*d*) if that person is a company—

(i) any director of that company;

(ii) any subsidiary of that company; and

(iii) any director or employee of any such subsidiary;

and for the purposes of this section " son " includes step-son and " daughter " includes step-daughter.

General Note

Except in relation to offences (s. 41), " director," " controller " and " manager " have special meanings in this statute (ss. 10, 14, 16, 17, 43, 45, Scheds. 2, para. 7, and 5).

Subs. (2)

(*a*) *Director* accords with the definition in the Companies Act 1948, s. 455. As to (*b*), the intention may be clear but the section is inevitably imprecise (for example, the Vorstand and the Aufsichtsrat of the German Company may have inspired the clause, the Vorstand being the " managing board ").

Subs. (3)

Controller means:

(*a*) managing director of a company or of a subsidiary; or a partner;

(*b*) a chief executive of the institution or of a parent institution; or

(c) someone under whose authority the directors are accustomed to act, which contains the weakness that the formal power of the controller may disappear in fact;

(d) the 15 per cent. of the voting control is one that no doubt has been found to have practical effect.

Subs. (4)

As to (*a*) that a manager is one who manages immediately under a Managing Director or Chief Executive is reasonably clear but as to (*b*), the responsibility for maintaining accounts or other records is wide, although there is the necessity of being *immediately* below the chief executive or managing director.

Subs. (5)

A chief executive (or joint chief executives) being immediately responsible to the Board accords with modern habits.

Subs. (6)

A chief executive from abroad can extend to the responsibility of the deposit-taking in a branch. This would be the person responsible for, say, the main London branch of a foreign institution.

Subs. (7)

The definition of "associate" is for the purpose of this section *only*. It relates to subs. (3) (*d*) defining "controller" when the definition of controlling is dependent on voting power. It is very broad in relation to a company of which a person is a director and includes his employees.

Interpretation

50.—(1) In this Act—

"the appointed day", and similar expressions, shall be construed in accordance with section 52 (4) below;

"the Bank" means the Bank of England;

"conditional licence" shall be construed in accordance with section 10 of this Act;

"contributory institution" has the meaning assigned to it by section 23 of this Act;

"debenture" has the same meaning as in the Companies Act 1948;

"deposit" and "deposit-taking business" shall be construed in accordance with section 1 of this Act;

"enactment" includes an enactment of the Parliament of Northern Ireland and a Measure of the Northern Ireland Assembly;

"full licence" means a licence granted under section 3 (2) of this Act;

"institution", except in the expression "unincorporated institution", means a body corporate or a partnership or any other association of two or more persons formed under the law of another member State and, accordingly, except in the expression "licensed institution", includes a recognised bank;

"licence" means a full licence, a conditional licence or a transitional licence and "licensed institution" shall be construed accordingly;

"local authority" means—

(*a*) in England and Wales, a local authority within the meaning of the Local Government Act 1972, the Common Council of the City of London or the Council of the Isles of Scilly;

(*b*) in Scotland, a local authority within the meaning of the Local Government (Scotland) Act 1973; and

(*c*) in Northern Ireland, a district council within the meaning of the Local Government Act (Northern Ireland) 1972;

" municipal bank " shall be construed in accordance with section 48 above;

" penny savings bank " has the same meaning as in section 16 of the National Savings Bank Act 1971;

" recognition " means recognition as a bank for the purposes of this Act and any reference to a recognised bank or institution shall be construed accordingly;

" statutory maximum ", in relation to a fine on summary conviction, means—

(*a*) in England and Wales and Northern Ireland, the prescribed sum, within the meaning of section 28 of the Criminal Law Act 1977 (at the passing of this Act £1,000); and

(*b*) in Scotland, the prescribed sum, within the meaning of section 289B of the Criminal Procedure (Scotland) Act 1975 (at the passing of this Act £1,000);

and for the purposes of the application of this definition in Northern Ireland the provisions of the Criminal Law Act 1977 which relate to the sum mentioned in paragraph (*a*) above shall extend to Northern Ireland;

" subsidiary " shall be construed in accordance with section 154 of the Companies Act 1948 or section 148 of the Companies Act (Northern Ireland) 1960;

" transitional licence " means a licence granted under paragraph 1 of Schedule 3 to this Act;

" trustee savings bank " has the meaning assigned to it by section 3 of the Trustee Savings Banks Act 1969; and

" unincorporated institution " means a partnership or any other association of two or more persons which is not a body corporate.

(2) Any reference in this Act to any provision of Northern Ireland legislation, within the meaning of section 24 of the Interpretation Act 1978, includes a reference to any subsequent provision of that legislation which, with or without modification, re-enacts the provision referred to in this Act.

GENERAL NOTE

Of the words included, " institution " merits separate comment. The most striking feature of the Act is that it will divide deposit-takers into two groups—recognised banks and licensed institutions, a distinction encountered first in s. 2. From the definition, it is clear that " institution " includes a recognised bank, which is of a higher category than licensed institution. This latter, however, has a special meaning in that a deposit-taker authorised by the Bank of England will be a licensed institution, but in the case of a recognised bank it will not *also* be a licensed institution, although it will be an institution.

Consequential amendments and repeals

51.—(1) The amendments in Part I of Schedule 6 to this Act being amendments consequential on the provisions of this Act, shall have effect, subject to the savings in Part II of that Schedule.

(2) The enactments mentioned in Schedule 7 to this Act are hereby repealed to the extent specified in the third column of that Schedule.

General Note

The consequential amendments are considered under Sched. 6.

Short title, commencement and extent

52.—(1) This Act may be cited as the Banking Act 1979.

(2) This Act extends to Northern Ireland.

(3) This Act shall come into operation on such day as the Treasury may appoint by order made by statutory instrument; and different days may be so appointed for different provisions of this Act and for such different purposes of the same provision as may be specified in the order.

(4) Any reference in any provision of this Act to " the appointed day " shall be construed as a reference to the day appointed for the purposes of any provision of this Act—

(*a*) shall be construed as a reference to the day appointed under this section for the coming into operation of that provision; and

(*b*) where different days are appointed for different purposes of that provision, shall be construed, unless an order under this section otherwise provides, as a reference to the first day so appointed.

General Note

This section has already been considered separately in relation to s. 2 above. It is worth repeating, however, that whilst the appointed day for the Act will not be likely to be for, say, six months, different days may be named for different provisions and different purposes within those provisions. The appointment by the Treasury will have to be scrutinised carefully to see that the differentiations are clear beyond doubt.

SCHEDULES

Section 2

SCHEDULE 1

Exceptions from Prohibition in Section 1

1. The central bank of each member State other than the United Kingdom.

2. The National Savings Bank.

3. The Post Office.

4. A trustee savings bank or penny savings bank.

5. A municipal bank.

6. A building society within the meaning of the Building Societies Act 1962 or the Building Societies Act (Northern Ireland) 1967.

7. A society which is registered within the meaning of the Friendly Societies Act 1974 or is registered or deemed to be registered under the Friendly Societies Act (Northern Ireland) 1970.

8. Any institution or unincorporated institution which is for the time being authorised, by virtue of section 3 of the Insurance Companies Act 1974 or Article 7 of the Insurance Companies (Northern Ireland) Order 1976, to carry on insurance business of a class relevant for the purposes of Part I of that Act or, as the case may be, Part II of that Order.

9. A member of The Stock Exchange in the course of business as a stockbroker or stockjobber.

10. A loan society whose rules are certified, deposited and enrolled in accordance with the Loan Societies Act 1840.

11. A credit union within the meaning of the Industrial and Provident Societies Act (Northern Ireland) 1969 or the Credit Unions Act 1979.

12. A body of persons certified as a school bank by a trustee savings bank, the National Savings Bank or a recognised bank.

13. A local authority.

14. Any other body which by virtue of any enactment has power to issue a precept to a local authority in England or Wales, or a requisition to a local authority in Scotland.

General Note

These entities are exempt from the prohibition against taking deposits; this is additional to the Bank of England itself, recognised banks and licensed institutions. Brief comment is appended on each category.

Para. 1. *EEC Central Banks* are excluded from the Directive, but a central bank from a third country needs recognition.

Para. 2. *National Savings Bank.* The Department of National Savings, of which the National Savings Bank is a part, is answerable to Parliament through the Treasury.

Para. 3. *The Post Office* is exempt because it is already subject to supervision by the Treasury.

Para. 4. *The Trustee Savings Banks* are in the course of transition and when they become involved more actively in private, if not also, in commercial, banking, may come within the general control created by the Act. A "Penny Savings Bank" is a minor form of savings bank where the maximum deposit is £5; they are linked to National Savings Banks.

Para. 5. *Municipal Banks.* See s. 48.

Para. 6. *Building Societies* are supervised by the Chief Registrar of Friendly Societies and may become subject to a similar scheme or to more substantial control.

Para. 7. *Friendly Societies* take deposits and make loans; thus they needed exclusion (none has been registered in recent years and their functions may be superseded by credit unions (established under the Credit Unions Act 1979) which are exempt (see para. 11 below)).

Para. 8. This enables the wide range of insurance companies covered by that Act to take deposits.

Para. 9. *A Member of The Stock Exchange.* This would have caused embarrassment if absent, because of cash received. It was added in the course of the passage of the Bill through Parliament.

Para. 10. There are very few loan societies registered under the Act and the total deposits are thought to be under £20,000.

Para. 11. See the Credit Unions Act 1979—a new form.

Para. 12. This depends on the certificates.

Para. 13. This is an authority that is subject to the Local Government Acts.

Para. 14. Bodies with power to issue precepts to local authorities include such institutions as River Boards.

Section 3 (3)

SCHEDULE 2

Minimum Criteria for Deposit-Taking Institutions

Part I

Recognised Banks

1.—(1) Subject to sub-paragraph (2) below, the institution enjoys, and has for a reasonable period of time enjoyed, a high reputation and standing in the financial community.

(2) In the case of—

(*a*) an institution which is not yet carrying on a deposit-taking business, or

(*b*) an institution which has not carried on such a business long enough to have earned the reputation and standing referred to in sub-paragraph (1) above,

the criteria in sub-paragraph (1) above may be taken to be fulfilled if control of the institution lies with one or more bodies of appropriate standing.

(3) In sub-paragraph (2) above the expression "body of appropriate standing" means a recognised bank or an institution which enjoys, and has for a reasonable period of time enjoyed, a high reputation and standing in the financial community.

(4) Section 534 of the Income and Corporation Taxes Act 1970 (meaning of "control" in certain contexts) shall apply for the purposes of sub-paragraph (2)

above as it applies for purposes of provisions of the Taxes Acts which apply to that section.

2.—(1) The institution provides in the United Kingdom or, in the case of an institution which is not yet carrying on a deposit-taking business in the United Kingdom, will provide there either a wide range of banking services or a highly specialised banking service.

(2) For the purposes of this Part of this Schedule, an institution shall not be regarded as providing a wide range of banking services at any time unless, subject to sub-paragraph (3) below, it provides at that time all of the following services, namely,—

(*a*) current or deposit account facilities in sterling or foreign currency for members of the public or for bodies corporate or the acceptance of funds in sterling or foreign currency in the wholesale money markets;

(*b*) finance in the form of overdraft or loan facilities in sterling or foreign currency for members of the public or for bodies corporate or the lending of funds in sterling or foreign currency in the wholesale money markets;

(*c*) foreign exchange services for domestic and foreign customers;

(*d*) finance through the medium of bills of exchange and promissory notes together with finance for foreign trade and documentation in connection with foreign trade; and

(*e*) financial advice for members of the public and for bodies corporate or investment management services and facilities for arranging the purchase and sale of securities in sterling or foreign currency.

(3) Any question whether an institution is to be regarded for the purposes of this Schedule as providing at any time either a wide range of banking services or a highly specialised banking service shall be determined by the Bank and, for the purpose of that determination the Bank may—

(*a*) with regard to the provision of a wide range of banking services, disregard the fact that the institution does not or will not provide one or two of the services specified in paragraphs (*c*) to (*e*) of sub-paragraph (2) above; and

(*b*) have regard to the nature and scope of a particular service provided or to be provided by an institution in determining whether the institution is to be regarded as providing or as going to provide that service for the purposes of this paragraph.

3. The business of the institution is or, in the case of an institution which is not yet carrying on a deposit-taking business, will be carried on with integrity and prudence and with those professional skills which are consistent with the range and scale of the institution's activities.

4. At least two individuals effectively direct the business of the institution.

5.—(1) Without prejudice to paragraph 6 below but subject to sub-paragraph (2) below, the institution will at the time recognition is granted to it have net assets which amount to not less than—

(*a*) £5 million, if it is an institution which provides or will provide a wide range of banking services; and

(*b*) £250,000, if it provides or will provide a highly specialised banking service.

(2) Sub-paragraph (1) above does not apply to an institution which, on the day appointed for the purposes of subsection (4) of section 2 of this Act, was carrying on a deposit-taking business in the United Kingdom if—

(*a*) the grant of recognition referred to in that sub-paragraph is made pursuant to an application made at any time during the period referred to in paragraph (*a*) of that subsection; and

(*b*) the institution has carried on such a business continuously throughout the period beginning on 9th November 1978 and ending on the date of its application for recognition.

(3) In sub-paragraph (1) above " net assets ", in relation to a body corporate, means paid-up capital and reserves.

(4) After consultation with the Bank, the Treasury may by order vary either or both of the sums specified in sub-paragraph (1) above.

(5) The power to make an order under sub-paragraph (4) above shall be exercisable by statutory instrument which shall be subject to annulment in pursuance of a resolution of either House of Parliament.

6.—(1) The institution maintains or, in the case of an institution which is not yet carrying on a deposit-taking business, will maintain net assets which together with other financial resources available to the institution of such a nature and amount as are considered appropriate by the Bank, are of an amount which is commensurate with the scale of the institution's operations.

(2) In sub-paragraph (1) above "net assets", in relation to a body corporate, means paid-up capital and reserves.

Part II

Licensed Institutions

7. Every person who is a director, controller or manager of the institution is a fit and proper person to hold that position.

8. At least two individuals effectively direct the business of the institution.

9.—(1) Without prejudice to paragraph 10 (1) (*a*) below but subject to sub-paragraph (2) below, the institution will at the time the licence is granted to it have net assets which amount to not less than £250,000 or such larger sum as the Treasury, after consultation with the Bank, may by order specify.

(2) This paragraph does not apply to an institution which on 9th November 1978 was carrying on a deposit-taking business in the United Kingdom.

(3) In sub-paragraph (1) above "net assets", in relation to a body corporate, means paid-up capital and reserves.

(4) The power to make an order under sub-paragraph (1) above shall be exercisable by statutory instrument which shall be subject to annulment in pursuance of a resolution of either House of Parliament.

10.—(1) The institution conducts or, in the case of an institution which is not yet carrying on a deposit-taking business, will conduct its business in a prudent manner and, in particular,—

(*a*) maintains or, as the case may require, will maintain net assets of such amount as, together with other financial resources available to it of such a nature and amount as are considered appropriate by the Bank, is sufficient to safeguard the interests of its depositors, having regard to the factors specified in sub-paragraph (2) below; and

(*b*) maintains or, as the case may require, will maintain adequate liquidity having regard to the relationship between its liquid assets and its liabilities and also to the times at which its liabilities fall due and its assets mature; and

(*c*) makes or, as the case may require, will make adequate provision for bad and doubtful debts and obligations of a contingent nature.

(2) The factors referred to in sub-paragraph (1) (*a*) above are—

(*a*) the scale and nature of the liabilities of the institution and the sources and amounts of deposits accepted by it; and

(*b*) the nature of its assets and the degree of risk attached to them.

(3) In sub-paragraph (1) (*a*) above "net assets" in relation to a body corporate, means paid-up capital and reserves.

General Note

This Schedule is probably the most important part of the Act. This is because it sets out the factors that will determine whether an institution is classified as a "bank," or whether it is a licensed institution and not allowed to describe itself as a bank or as doing banking, or whether it comes within neither of these descriptions. Obviously, the ability to hold out that you are banking is a privilege that will be given up with great reluctance and sought eagerly. The categorisation is important because the granting by the Department of Trade of licences to describe an institution as carrying on banking led in part to the secondary banking crisis, as can be seen from the history of events resulting in the life-boat rescue by which the clearing banks, in conjunction with the Bank of England, rescued the majority of troubled secondary banks from insolvent liquidation. Only those institutions that satisfy the Schedule will now be able to claim the classification. It is perhaps well to note the way in which the Schedule is applied. By s. 3 (3), the Bank of England is not to grant recognition as a bank or a full licence as a deposit-taking institution *unless* it is content that all criteria are satisfied.

Part I

Recognised Banks

Para. 1 (1). There are two imponderables: "a reasonable time" and "a high reputation and standing in the financial community." Material factors will be applicable, ability of management and even financial reputation of customers may contribute to one fundamentally in a subjective judgment. Other banks will themselves by their opinions contribute. (In fact, in *United Dominions Trust* v. *Kirkwood* [1966] 2 Q.B. 431, Lord Denning said that UDT had only succeeded in that case because of its reputation and standing in the City of London as a banker.) Of course, the selection of authorised dealers for the Exchange Control Act 1947 are based, without statutory direction, on similar factors. This fundamental aspect of reputation lies in the views of the Bank of England and any argument against them in a tribunal must be persuasive rather than evidence that claims to convince as of right, so frequently the case in legal hearings.

Para. 1 (2). Here there is the problem of "appropriate standing" which may come near to begging the question. It is a reason for granting banking status to an institution not yet carrying on a deposit-taking business or which has not carried on long enough to earn the reputation mentioned in the previous paragraph. The control must belong to an institution of "appropriate" standing (meaning satisfying para. 1 (1)).

Para. 1 (3) says that the "body of appropriate standing" is any of the high reputation and standing mentioned in para. 1; so to satisfy para. 1 (2) above, one presumes it to mean a bank highly regarded having a subsidiary—such as a consortium bank—or that it exercises control as in para. 1 (4).

Para. 1 (4) refers to the definition of control (in relation to the power vested in the appropriate body) in s. 534 of the Income and Corporation Taxes Act 1970 which is, in the case of a company, "by means of holding shares or the possession of voting power or by any power conferred by the articles of association by which the affairs of the company are conducted in accordance with the wishes of the other person." In the case of a partnership, control stems from a share in over half the assets or in the partnership income.

Para. 2 (1). The first paragraph has dealt with reputation. The second deals with functions. There has to be either a wide range of banking services or a highly specialised banking service.

Para. 2 (2). The wide range of banking services are clear and understandable. The first are current or deposit accounts in sterling or currency or acceptance of such moneys in the wholesale market. It is to be noted that either of the alternatives in group (*a*) is sufficient. Again there are the various forms of loan as alternatives with group (*b*). Foreign exchange services do not appear to be itemised and may not have to be complete services. In (*d*), bill finance presumably includes documentary credits. Finally, in (*e*), financial advice may savour of the merchant bank fighting takeovers but the alternative of investment services will be equally familiar in the City of London.

Para. 2 (3). The limitation to provision of three services to attain a wide range is clear and provides no obvious difficulty. It is (*a*) and (*b*) plus (*c*), (*d*) or (*e*). However, the reference in relation to a "highly specialised banking service" is troublesome; one can only think that there is a reference to a highly specialised service *that must be seen to be a regular feature* and not just an occasional item of that activity or facility. On the face of the words the sentence almost begs the question. Another possible suggestion is that para. (*b*) relates to the wide range of services. If so the drafting is oblique, if not obscure.

Para. 3. This is *one* of the things with which the Bank of England has to be satisfied. It must be remembered that the *aggregate* in the schedule determines the banking classification; the Bank must be satisfied, and from this the contrary would be to establish that the Bank was unreasonably dissatisfied. (This provision particularly is a reminder that, unlike most statutes, the object is to perpetuate within a legal framework the *de facto* control that has grown up during the past 200 years. Yet this has to be subject to the tribunal decisions and the further appeal on points of law.)

Para. 4. This comes from the EEC Directive, para. 3 (2). In the event of death, and there being no legal entity, that is to say a form of partnership, there is a continuity.

Para. 5 (1). This sub-paragraph does not apply during an application for recognition by deposit-takers doing business on November 9, 1978, if their application is successful. It is not to detract from the right given to the Bank in para. 6 to require commensurate "net assets . . . together with financial resources" (*vide infra*). There is, so to speak, a "double-stop." "Net assets" is a matter for accountants and therefore open to argument in that the definition in sub-para.

(3) (*infra*) of "capital and reserves" does not take the matter a lot further. For this reason para. 5 is largely a guide, being subject to the over-riding discretion in para. 6. It is further to be noted that the £250,000 minimum is a requisite amount only if the institution seeking recognition is one with the "highly specialised banking service" mentioned in para. 2 (3) (*b*) above and therefore is associated with discretion or, one might also say, selection, more than much of the remainder of the Act.

Para. 5 (2). This means that an institution is exempt if on November 9, 1978, it was carrying on a deposit-taking business in the United Kingdom, from the capital requirement, although the second requirement of net assets mentioned above and contained in subs. (3) still applies. However, the exemption is as indicated in the above Note, only during the transitional period pending the decision. The maxima are not expected to cause embarrassment in most instances.

Para. 5 (3). See comment to para. 5 (1). This definition is in relation only to a "body corporate."

Para. 5 (4). This power to make changes is included in many statutes in these days of constant inflation.

Para. 5 (5). The above variation by statutory instrument calls only for a resolution of *either* House for annulment.

Para. 6 (1). This applies to all institutions seeking recognition, new or old.

Part II

Licensed institutions

This Part of Sched. 2 represents the requirements for deposit-takers who do not seek recognition as "banks." It will apply to those institutions that fail in their applications for banking status and accept the status of a licensed institution, to existing institutions taking deposits to provide sources of lending, and to those institutions taking deposits to finance their own businesses.

Para. 7. This is less demanding than para. 3 above.

Para. 8. This is the same as para. 4 above.

Para. 9 (1). This figure is subject to increase as with para. 5 above.

Para. 9 (2). It is not applicable to deposit-takers carrying on business on November 9, 1978, that is to say, such institution does not have to evidence the *specific* figures by way of "net assets" (but see para. 10 (1) (*a*) to which it is subject).

Para. 9 (3) and (4). Compare with para. 5 (3) and (5) above.

Para. 10 (1). Requires maintenance of assets, liquidity and adequate provision for bad and doubtful debts (including contingent liabilities). This phraseology appears broad; the control is new in practice to deposit-takers, unlike most banks.

Para. 10 (2). This is, in a way, a demand for adequate capital (incidentally, so often the commercial bankers' cry); it has to be measured in the light of the proportion of easily realisable assets.

Para. 10 (3). This is as before.

Section 3 (8)

SCHEDULE 3

Transitional Provisions

Part I

Transitional Licences

1.—(1) A transitional licence to carry on a deposit-taking business may be granted to an institution by the Bank—

(*a*) on an application in that behalf by the institution concerned; or

(*b*) on an application by that institution for recognition or a full licence.

(2) The Bank shall not grant a transitional licence to an institution unless—

(*a*) the institution was on the appointed day carrying on a deposit-taking business in the United Kingdom; and

(*b*) the Bank is satisfied that the criteria in paragraphs 7 and 8 of Schedule 2 above are fulfilled; and

(c) it appears to the Bank that, although at the time of the application the remainder of the criteria for the grant of a full licence are not fulfilled, all those criteria will be fulfilled within a reasonable time.

2. Section 5 of this Act shall apply in relation to an application for a transitional licence as it applies in relation to an application for a full licence.

3.—(1) The authority conferred by a transitional licence may be made conditional upon the institution to which it is granted complying with conditions imposed by the Bank and set out in the licence.

(2) Where a transitional licence is granted subject to conditions by virtue of sub-paragraph (1) above, subsections (2) and (3) of section 10 of this Act shall apply in relation to the conditions of the licence as they apply in relation to the conditions of a conditional licence.

4.—(1) Subject to sub-paragraph (2) and (3) below, a transitional licence held by an institution shall expire at the end of the period of two years beginning on the date on which the licence was granted or, if the institution is granted more than one transitional licence, beginning on the date on which the first of those licences was granted.

(2) A transitional licence may be so granted as to expire at a time earlier than it would expire in accordance with sub-paragraph (1) above.

(3) A transitional licence—

(a) may be surrendered by notice in writing given by the institution concerned to the Bank; or

(b) may be revoked in accordance with the provisions of Part I of this Act.

5.—(1) In the case of an institution holding a transitional licence which is granted subject to conditions, a failure to comply with any of those conditions shall be treated for the purposes of this Act as a failure by the institution to comply with such an obligation as is referred to in section 6 (1) (h) of this Act.

(2) It shall be a ground for revoking a transitional licence held by an institution that the Bank proposes to grant a full licence to the institution with effect from the time of the revocation of the transitional licence.

(3) The power of the Bank to revoke a licence by virtue of sub-paragraph (2) above shall be exercisable by notice in writing given to the institution concerned.

6.—(1) In their application to an institution which is the holder of a transitional licence, section 7 of this Act and Schedule 4 below shall have effect as if for paragraph (b) of subsection (1) of that section there were substituted the following paragraph:—

" (b) revoke the transitional licence held by the institution and grant it a transitional licence subject to conditions or, as the case may require, subject to conditions different from those in the licence which is revoked ".

(2) In a case where a notice under subsection (3) (a) or subsection (4) of section 7 of this Act is given to an institution which is the holder of a transitional licence, Part I or, as the case may require, Part II of Schedule 4 below shall have effect as if any reference therein to a conditional licence were a reference to a transitional licence.

7.—(1) In its application to an institution to which a transitional licence has been granted, section 11 of this Act shall have effect as if at the end of paragraph (b) of subsection (1) there were added the words " to grant it a transitional licence on an application for a full licence or, on an application for a transitional licence, to grant such a licence subject to conditions, or ".

(2) If an institution is granted a transitional licence subject to conditions, then, on an appeal under section 11 of this Act against the decision to grant the transitional licence, the appellant institution may challenge any of the conditions of that licence, whether or not it also challenges the decision itself.

Part II

Transitional Grant of Recognition

8. The provisions of this Part of this Schedule apply to an institution which—

(a) on 9th November 1978 was, and at the time of its application for recognition continues to be, either a company within the meaning of the Companies Act 1948 or any other body corporate having its place of central management and control in the United Kingdom; and (*b*) does not, apart from this Part of this Schedule, qualify for the grant of recognition.

9. Notwithstanding anything in section 3 (3) of this Act, the Bank may grant recognition to an institution to which this Part of this Schedule applies (whether or not it would otherwise qualify for the grant of a licence) if the Bank is satisfied—

(*a*) that the institution carries on, and has since 9th November 1978 continuously carried on, a deposit-taking business but that the whole, or substantially the whole of that business is and has been carried on outside the United Kingdom; and

(*b*) that, with the exception of the criteria in paragraph 2 of Schedule 2 to this Act, the criteria in Part I of that Schedule are fulfilled with respect to the institution; and

(*c*) that the criteria in paragraph 2 of Schedule 2 to this Act would be fulfilled with respect to the institution if the reference in sub-paragraph (1) of that paragraph to the provision of a wide range of banking services were not limited to the provision of that range of services within the United Kingdom.

General Note

This schedule is incorporated into the legislation by s. 3 (8). Pt. I relates to transitional licences and Pt. II to institutions that were in business on November 9, 1978, and who sought recognition.

Part I

Para. 1 (1). It may be granted to an institution on an application for a transitional licence or an application for a full licence or for recognition.

Para. 1 (2). The essential requirement is that if a licence cannot be granted because some of the criteria cannot be satisfied at the time, there is a reasonable chance of their being satisfied later. The criteria of subs. (7) or (8) (*q.v.*) also have to be satisfied.

Para. 2. The formalities of application contained in s. 5 (which pertain to applications generally) are to apply to applications for a transitional licence.

Para. 3 (1). There appear to be no restrictions on the conditions that may be included in a transitional licence.

Para. 3 (2). The same terms apply to conditions as contained in s. 10 (2) (*a*) and (*b*), which deal with the width of conditions that may be imposed.

Para. 4 (1). The maximum period is two years; or if more than one licence is granted, the aggregate must be limited to that period.

Para. 4 (2). It can be granted to expire in a shorter period.

Para. 4 (3). It can be surrendered or revoked like any other licence.

Para. 5 (1). Failure to comply with a condition contained in a transitional licence has the same effect as the breach of any other condition (see s. 6 (1) (*h*)).

Para. 5 (2) and (3). A transitional licence will, of course, be revoked if a full licence is going to be granted—written notice being as stipulated.

Para. 6 (1) and (2). This applies the powers and provisions relating to revocation of licences to transitional licences.

Para. 7 (1). Enables an appeal to be made in respect of transitional licences and also an appeal to be made against the conditions contained in a transitional conditional licence.

Part II

Para. 8. This applies to a special category of applicant for permission.

Para. 9. This type for which recognition is specially applicable has three requirements, all of which must obtain for the paragraph to apply. They are: (1) the carrying on of a deposit-taking business substantially outside the U.K. since November 9, 1978; (2) the satisfaction of all the criteria contained in Pt. I of Sched. 2 necessary to obtain a banking recognition *other* than the wide range of banking services and the highly specialised service; and (3) that the requirement of the " wide range " would have been satisfied if activity in territory outside the U.K. were included.

Section 7

SCHEDULE 4

Revocation of Recognition or Licence

Part I

Procedure Where Notice of Intention to Act is Given

1.—(1) Where the Bank has given to an institution notice of intention to act, then, before taking any action under the principal section, the Bank shall take into account any representations made by or on behalf of the institution concerned within the period of fourteen days beginning with the date on which the notice was given.

(2) After taking account of representations in accordance with sub-paragraph (1) above, the Bank shall decide whether—

(*a*) to proceed with the proposal in the notice of intention to act; or

(*b*) to take no further action; or

(*c*) to take some other course of action open to it under sub-paragraph (3) or sub-paragraph (4) below.

(3) If the proposal in the notice of intention to act was for action under paragraph (*a*) of subsection (1) of the principal section, the Bank may decide to take action under paragraph (*b*) of that subsection or, in the case of a recognised bank, to take action under subsection (2) of that section.

(4) If the proposal in the notice of intention to act was for action under paragraph (*b*) of subsection (1) of the principal section and the institution concerned is a recognised bank, the Bank may decide to take action under subsection (2) of the principal section.

(5) Where the Bank gives notice of intention to act under paragraph (*b*) of subsection (1) of the principal section and, after taking account of representations in accordance with sub-paragraph (1) above, decides to take action under that paragraph but to grant a conditional licence subject to conditions which are different from those stated in the notice of intention to act, the Bank shall be treated for the purposes of this Act as having decided to proceed with the proposal in the notice.

2.—(1) The Bank shall give the institution concerned notice in writing of its decision under paragraph 1 above within the period of twenty-eight days beginning with the date on which the notice of intention to act was given and, except where the decision is to take no further action, the Bank shall set out in the notice under this paragraph the reasons for its decision.

(2) Where the Bank gives notice under this paragraph of its decision to take action under paragraph (*a*) of subsection (1) of the principal section the notice shall have the effect of revoking the recognition or licence of the institution concerned but shall not come into force until—

(*a*) the expiry of the period within which an appeal against that decision may be brought under section 11 of this Act; or

(*b*) if such an appeal is brought within that period, it is determined on that appeal that the decision should be confirmed and that determination comes into operation.

(3) Where the Bank gives notice under this paragraph of its decision to take action under paragraph (*b*) of subsection (1) of the principal section, the notice shall have the effect of revoking the recognition or licence of the institution concerned and granting it a conditional licence subject to such conditions as may be specified in the notice.

(4) Where the Bank gives notice under this paragraph of its intention to take action under subsection (2) of the principal section the notice shall have the effect of revoking the recognition of the institution concerned and granting it a full licence.

(5) Where the Bank has given to an institution notice of intention to act but has not given a notice under this paragraph within the period of twenty-eight days referred to in sub-paragraph (1) above, the Bank shall be treated for the purposes of this Act as having given to that institution, immediately before the expiry of that period, notice of a decision under paragraph 1 above to take no further action.

Part II

Procedure Where Immediate Revocation Notice is Given

3. An immediate revocation notice given to an institution shall specify the reasons why the Bank has acted.

4.—(1) If representations are made by or on behalf of the institution concerned within the period of fourteen days beginning with the date on which the immediate revocation notice was given, the Bank shall review its decision in the light of those representations and may decide—

(*a*) to confirm its original decision; or

(*b*) to rescind its original decision; or

(*c*) in the case of a recognised bank, to revoke the institution's recognition and grant it a full licence.

(2) If, after taking account of representations in accordance with sub-paragraph (1) above, the Bank decides to confirm the revocation of the recognition or licence of an institution but to grant to it a conditional licence subject to conditions which are different from those stated in the immediate revocation notice, the Bank shall be treated for the purposes of this Act as having decided to confirm its original decision.

5.—(1) The Bank shall give the institution concerned notice in writing of its decision under paragraph 4 above within the period of twenty-eight days beginning with the date on which the immediate revocation notice was given and, except where the decision is to rescind the original decision, the Bank shall set out in the notice under this paragraph the reasons for its decision.

(2) Where the Bank gives notice under this paragraph of its decision to confirm its original decision and sub-paragraph (2) of paragraph 4 above applies, the notice under this paragraph shall have the effect of varying the terms of the conditional licence previously granted with effect from the date, and in accordance with the terms, of the notice.

(3) Where the Bank gives notice under this paragraph of its decision to rescind its original decision, the recognition in question shall be deemed never to have been revoked.

(4) Where the Bank gives notice of a decision under paragraph 4 (1) (*c*) above,—

(*a*) the institution's recognition shall be deemed not to have been revoked by the immediate revocation notice; and

(*b*) the notice under this paragraph shall have the effect of revoking that recognition and granting a full licence to the institution with effect from the date of the notice under this paragraph.

General Note

This amplifies s. 7 dealing with the mechanics of revocation. It will be remembered that there are two circumstances of revocation; where notice is first given (s. 7 (3)) and where revocation is immediate (s. 7 (4)).

Where notice is first given

Para. 1 (1). Representations submitted within 14 days have to be taken into account.

Para. 1 (2). The Bank decides to go ahead, take no action or take a third type or action, mentioned in para. 1 (3) or 1 (4) below.

Para. 1 (3). If the notice of intention had been for a revocation of a full licence or for a " recognition " the Bank grants a conditional licence, or in the case of a bank, grants a full licence replacing the recognition.

Para. 1 (4). If the notice of intention had been for the grant of a conditional licence as a result of a revocation of recognition, the Bank may instead grant a full licence (that is, for deposit-taking instead of full banking status).

Para. 1 (5). This is making a conditional notice equivalent to an earlier conditional notice subject to different conditions. The reason for the provision is that the Bank cannot be shown to be inactive (as not taking action within the meaning of para. 1 (2)), merely varying existing conditions and not taking a positive step—at least this could be a purpose behind the somewhat obscure provision.

Para. 2 (1). This is the requirement for reasons to be given to be included in the 28 days' notice.

Para. 2 (2). This delays the termination until an appeal is heard or time for notice of appeal has expired.

Para. 2 (3). Where notice to revoke a licence or recognition has been given as well as for a conditional licence in replacement, the condition in the notice is immediately applicable.

Para. 2 (4). This means that the full licence of the deposit-taker is granted automatically on the revocation of the bank. This would be where the Bank decided that the position was not serious enough to revoke entirely.

Para. 2 (5). Where notice of intention has been given but nothing further has been done within the 28 days, it is to be regarded as implying no further action.

Where immediate action is to be taken

Para. 3. There must be reasons given.

Para. 4 (1). Within 14 days the Bank *must* confirm or rescind its decision or, if the subject be a bank, grant a deposit-taking licence instead.

Para. 4 (2). The confirmation may be accompanied by a conditional licence (even if the condition is different from that indicated in relation to the original decision to grant a conditional licence).

Para. 5 (1). 28 days' notice with reasons are required in respect of the above decision.

Para. 5 (2). Where the decision is to revoke recognition and grant a conditional licence, the conditions varying the terms of the conditional licence take effect forthwith.

Para. 5 (3). A provision that a revocation shall be deemed never to have happened can have complex effects in law—although it is unlikely to cause trouble in this context.

Para. 5 (4). Similar comment is applicable here.

It is not inappropriate to sound a note of warning about the complexity of the provisions of Scheds. 3 and 4 and the sections of the Act to which they are appended. The system is evidently designed to show precision in situations that are delicate. However, from the very efforts at exactitude may stem controversy and dispute, in circumstances where tense practical situations may exist. The Bank of England has exercised a discretion in the past and, particularly when there is pressure of time, the formalities now enacted may provide an over-legalistic and procedural influence on the practical consequences.

Section 21

SCHEDULE 5

THE DEPOSIT PROTECTION BOARD

Constitution

1.—(1) The Board shall consist of three *ex officio* members, namely—

(*a*) the Governor of the Bank for the time being, who shall be the chairman of the Board,

(*b*) the Deputy Governor of the Bank for the time being, and

(*c*) the Chief Cashier of the Bank for the time being,

and such ordinary members as shall from time to time be appointed under sub-paragraph (2) below.

(2) The Governor of the Bank shall appoint as ordinary members of the Board—

(*a*) three persons who are directors, controllers or managers of contributory institutions; and

(*b*) persons who are officers or employees of the Bank.

(3) Each *ex officio* member of the Board may appoint an alternate member, being an officer or employee of the Bank, to perform his duties as a member in his absence.

(4) Each ordinary member of the Board may appoint an appropriately qualified person as an alternate member to perform his duties as a member in his absence; and for this purpose a person is appropriately qualified for appointment as an alternate—

(*a*) by a member appointed under paragraph (*a*) of sub-paragraph (2) above, if he is a director, controller or manager of a contributory institution; and

(*b*) by a member appointed under paragraph (*b*) of that sub-paragraph, if he is either an officer or employee of the Bank.

(5) Ordinary and alternate members of the Board shall hold and vacate office in accordance with the terms of their appointment.

Proceedings

2.—(1) The Board shall determine their own procedure, including the quorum necessary for their meetings.

(2) The validity of any proceedings of the Board shall not be affected by any vacancy among the *ex officio* members of the Board or by any defect in the appointment of any ordinary or alternate member.

3.—(1) The fixing of the common seal of the Board shall be authenticated by the signature of the chairman of the Board or some other person authorised by the Board to act for that purpose.

(2) A document purporting to be duly executed under the seal of the Board shall be received in evidence and deemed to be so executed unless the contrary is proved.

Accounts, audit and annual report

4.—(1) The Board may determine their own financial year.

(2) It shall be the duty of the Board—

(*a*) to keep proper accounts and proper records in relation to the accounts; and

(*b*) to prepare in respect of any period beginning with the appointed day and ending with the beginning of the Board's first financial year and in respect of each of their financial years, a statement of accounts showing the state of affairs and income and expenditure of the Board.

(3) A statement of accounts prepared in accordance with sub-paragraph (2) (*b*) above shall be audited by auditors appointed by the Board and the auditors shall report to the Board stating whether in their opinion the provisions of paragraph 4 (2) above have been complied with.

(4) A person shall not be qualified to be appointed as auditor by the Board under sub-paragraph (3) above unless—

(*a*) he is a member of, or a Scottish firm in which all the partners are members of, one or more bodies of accountants established in the United Kingdom and for the time being recognised for the purposes of section 161 (1) (*a*) of the Companies Act 1948 by the Secretary of State; or

(*b*) he is for the time being authorised to be appointed as auditor of a company under section 161 (1) (*b*) of that Act as having similar qualifications obtained outside the United Kingdom.

(5) It shall be the duty of the Board, as soon as possible after the end of any such period as is mentioned in sub-paragraph (2) (*b*) above and of each of their financial years, to prepare a report on the performance of their functions during that period or, as the case may be, during that financial year.

(6) It shall be the duty of the Board to publish, in such manner as they think appropriate, every statement of account prepared in accordance with sub-paragraph (2) (*b*) above and every report prepared in accordance with sub-paragraph (5) above.

General Note

It will be remembered that the Board holds and manages the Fund, levies contributions and makes payments to depositors. It consists of the Governor, Deputy Governor and Chief Cashier of the Bank of England, three officials from contributory institutions. In addition there are members of the staff of the Bank. This appears, therefore, to give the Bank of England a majority.

The Board determines its own quorum and procedure and has a seal to be authenticated by the Chairman or someone else nominated for that purpose by the Board. It has to keep records and accounts for producing and publishing an annual or other statements, audited by persons qualified in accordance with the Companies Act 1948, s. 161 (*a*). In practice this means English, Scottish or Irish chartered accountants, members of the Certified and Incorporated Accountants and anyone having specific approval of the Department of Trade.

Section 51 (1)

SCHEDULE 6

Consequential Amendments

Part I

Enactments Amended

The Bankers' Books Evidence Act 1879 (*c.* 11)

1. For section 9 of the Bankers' Books Evidence Act 1879 (meaning of "bank", "banker", and "bankers' books" for the purposes of that Act) there shall be substituted the following section:—

" Interpretation of " bank ", " banker " and " bankers' books "

9.—(1) In this Act the expressions " bank " and " banker " mean—

(*a*) a recognised bank, licensed institution or municipal bank, within the meaning of the Banking Act 1979;

(*b*) a trustee savings bank within the meaning of section 3 of the Trustee Savings Bank Act 1969;

(*c*) the National Savings Bank; and

(*d*) the Post Office, in the exercise of its powers to provide banking services.

(2) Expressions in this Act relating to " bankers' books " include ledgers, day books, cash books, account books and other records used in the ordinary business of the bank, whether those records are in written form or are kept on microfilm, magnetic tape or any other form of mechanical or electronic data retrieval mechanism."

The Agricultural Credits Act 1928 (*c.* 43)

2. In subsection (7) of section 5 of the Agricultural Credits Act 1928 (agricultural charges on farming stock and assets) for the definition of " Bank " there shall be substituted the following definition:—

" " Bank " means the Bank of England, a recognised bank or licensed institution within the meaning of the Banking Act 1979, a trustee savings bank within the meaning of section 3 of the Trustee Savings Banks Act 1969 or the Post Office, in the exercise of its powers to provide banking services ".

The Agricultural Credits (*Scotland*) *Act* 1929 (*c.* 13)

3. In subsection (2) of section 9 of the Agricultural Credits (Scotland) Act 1929 (interpretation), for the definition of " Bank " there shall be substituted the following definition:—

" " Bank " means the Bank of England, a recognised bank or licensed institution within the meaning of the Banking Act 1979, a trustee savings bank within the meaning of section 3 of the Trustee Savings Banks Act 1969 or the Post Office, in the exercise of its powers to provide banking services ".

The Prevention of Fraud (*Investments*) *Act* (*Northern Ireland*) 1940 (*c.* 9) (*N.I.*)

4.—(1) Subsection (1) of section 12 of the Prevention of Fraud (Investments) Act (Northern Ireland) 1940 (penalty for fraudulently inducing persons to invest money) shall be amended as follows:—

(*a*) after the words " the reckless making " there shall be inserted the words " (dishonestly or otherwise) "; and

(*b*) for paragraph (*b*) there shall be substituted the following paragraph:—

" (*b*) to take part or offer to take part in any arrangements with respect to property other than securities, being arrangements the purpose or effect, or pretended purpose or effect of which is to enable persons taking part in the arrangements (whether by becoming owners of the property or any part of the property or otherwise) to participate in or receive profits or income alleged to arise or to be likely to arise from the acquisition, holding, management or disposal of such property, or sums to be paid or alleged to be likely to be paid out of such profits or income."

(2) In the proviso to subsection (3) of section 13 of the said Act of 1940, for the words from " any arrangements " to the end there shall be substituted the words " any such arrangements as are mentioned in paragraph (*b*) of subsection (1) of the last preceding section ".

The Prevention of Fraud (*Investments*) *Act* 1958 (*c.* 45)

5.—(1) Subsection (1) of section 13 of the Prevention of Fraud (Investments) Act 1958 (penalty for fraudulently inducing persons to invest money) shall be amended as follows:—

(*a*) after the words " the reckless making " there shall be inserted the words " (dishonestly or otherwise) ";

(*b*) for paragraph (*b*) there shall be substituted the following paragraph:—

" (*b*) to take part or offer to take part in any arrangements with respect to property other than securities, being arrangements the purpose or effect, or pretended purpose or effect, of which is to enable persons taking part in the arrangements (whether by becoming owners of the property or any part of the property or otherwise) to participate in or receive profits or income alleged to arise or to be likely to arise from the acquisition, holding, management or disposal of such property, or sums to be paid or alleged to be likely to be paid out of such profits or income."

(2) In the proviso to subsection (3) of section 14 of the said Act of 1958, for the words from "any arrangements" to the end there shall be substituted the words "any such arrangements as are mentioned in paragraph (*b*) of subsection (1) of the last preceding section".

The Building Societies Act 1962 (*c.* 37)

6. In subsection (5) of section 59 of the Building Societies Act 1962 (institutions which may be authorised to hold surplus funds of building societies) for the words "a body corporate or partnership carrying on the business of banking" there shall be substituted the words "a recognised bank within the meaning of the Banking Act 1979".

The Building Societies Act (*Northern Ireland*) 1967 (*c.* 31) (*N.I.*)

7. In subsection (5) of section 59 of the Building Societies Act (Northern Ireland) 1967 (institutions which may be authorised to hold surplus funds of building societies) for the words "a body corporate or partnership carrying on the business of banking" there shall be substituted the words "a recognised bank within the meaning of the Banking Act 1979".

The Industrial and Provident Societies Act (*Northern Ireland*) 1969 (*c.* 24) (*N.I.*)

8. At the end of section 87 of the Industrial and Provident Societies Act (Northern Ireland) 1969 (investment of surplus funds of credit unions) there shall be added the following subsection:—

"(7) In this section "bank" means—

(*a*) a recognised bank or municipal bank within the meaning of the Banking Act 1979;

(*b*) a trustee savings bank within the meaning of section 3 of the Trustee Savings Banks Act 1969; and

(*c*) the National Savings Bank."

The Solicitors Act 1974 (*c.* 47)

9. In subsection (1) of section 87 of the Solicitors Act 1974 (interpretation of expressions used in that Act), in the definition of "bank"—

(*a*) in paragraph (*a*) after the word "England" there shall be inserted the words "the Post Office, in the exercise of its powers to provide banking services, or a recognised bank within the meaning of the Banking Act 1979"; and

(*b*) in paragraph (*b*) for the words "a company as to which the Secretary of State is satisfied" there shall be substituted the words "any other company as to which, immediately before the repeal of the Protection of Depositors Act 1963, the Secretary of State was satisfied";

and the expression "bank" in any instrument made under the said Act of 1974 which is in force immediately before the appointed day shall be construed accordingly.

The Solicitors (*Scotland*) *Act* 1976 (*c.* 6)

10. In subsection (1) of section 5 of the Solicitors (Scotland) Act 1976 (extension of power of Council to make rules regarding certain accounts)—

(*a*) after the words "National Savings Bank" there shall be inserted the words "the Post Office, in the exercise of its powers to provide banking services, a recognised bank within the meaning of the Banking Act 1979"; and

(*b*) for the words "company as to which the Secretary of State is satisfied" there shall be substituted the words "other company as to which, immediately before the repeal of the Protection of Depositors Act 1963, the Secretary of State was satisfied";

and the expression "bank" in any instrument made under the said Act of 1976 or under the Solicitors (Scotland) Act 1949 which is in force immediately before the appointed day shall be construed accordingly.

The Home Purchase Assistance and Housing Corporation Guarantee Act 1978 (*c.* 27)

11. In Part I of the Schedule to the Home Purchase Assistance and Housing Corporation Guarantee Act 1978 (lending institutions) in paragraph 7 for the words "Companies which have satisfied the Secretary of State" there shall be substituted the words "Recognised banks, within the meaning of the Banking Act 1979, and any other companies as to which, immediately before the repeal of the Protection of Depositors Act 1963, the Secretary of State was satisfied".

The Home Purchase Assistance (*Northern Ireland*) *Order* 1978 (1978/1043) (*N.I.* 13)

12. In Part I of the Schedule to the Home Purchase Assistance (Northern Ireland) Order 1978 (lending institutions) in paragraph 4 for the words "Companies which have satisfied the Department of Commerce" there shall be substituted the words "Recognised banks, within the meaning of the Banking Act 1979, and any other companies as to which, immediately before the repeal of the Protection of Depositors Act (Northern Ireland) 1964, the Department of Commerce was satisfied".

PART II

SAVINGS

The Bankers' Books Evidence Act 1879 (*c.* 11)

13. Nothing in paragraph 1 above shall affect the operation of the Bankers' Books Evidence Act 1879 in relation to any entry in any banker's book made, or relating to a transaction carried out,—

(*a*) before the day appointed for the purposes of that paragraph; or

(*b*) at a time when the bank or banker in question was permitted to accept deposits by virtue of subsection (4) of section 2 of this Act.

The Agricultural Credits Act 1928 (*c.* 43)

14. Nothing in paragraph 2 above shall affect the validity of, or the rights and obligations of the parties to, an agricultural charge within the meaning of the Agricultural Credits Act 1928 made before the day appointed for the purposes of that paragraph.

The Agricultural Credits (*Scotland*) *Act* 1929 (*c.* 13)

15. Nothing in paragraph 3 above shall affect the validity of, or the rights and obligations of the parties to, an agricultural charge within the meaning of the Agricultural Credits (Scotland) Act 1929 made before the day appointed for the purposes of that paragraph.

The Building Societies Act 1962 (*c.* 37)

16. Nothing in paragraph 6 above shall affect the authority of any body corporate or partnership which immediately before the day appointed for the purposes of that paragraph was designated by order of the Chief Registrar under section 59 of the Building Societies Act 1962 or the power of the Chief Registrar to remove the authority of such a body or partnership by a subsequent order made on or after that day.

The Building Societies Act (*Northern Ireland*) 1967 (*c.* 31) (*N.I.*)

17. Nothing in paragraph 7 above shall affect the authority of any body corporate or partnership which immediately before the day appointed for the purposes of that paragraph was designated by order of the registrar under section 59 of the Building Societies Act (Northern Ireland) 1967 or the power of the registrar to

remove the authority of such a body or partnership by a subsequent order made on or after that day.

The Industrial and Provident Societies Act
(Northern Ireland) 1969 (*c.* 24) (*N.I.*)

18. Nothing in paragraph 8 above shall affect the authority of any body which immediately before the day appointed for the purposes of that paragraph was authorised by order of the registrar under section 87 of the Industrial and Provident Societies Act (Northern Ireland) 1969 or the power of the registrar to remove the authority of such a body by a subsequent order made on or after that day.

19. The savings contained in this Part of this Schedule are without prejudice to section 16 of the Interpretation Act 1978 (general savings).

General Note

Most of these changes are consequential. However, in the case of the Bankers' Books Evidence Act 1879 there is more to be said. The Act was intended to save the practical inconvenience of bringing bankers' books to court. First, the ledgers were needed by the bank concerned to record the daily entries, and secondly, one would trust that the larger hand-written ledgers contained in the one bound volume (A to C perhaps) were required for posting—there would also have been quite a number of entries relating to other customers which had to be kept covered—that is undisclosed. The Act also contains provisions enabling books to be inspected on a magistrate's authority—a discretion usually easily granted but about which a Divisional Court recently warned as to the degree of care to be exercised (*Williams* v. *Summerfield* [1972] 3 W.L.R. 131).

A banker for this purpose was previously obliquely defined by reason of being an institution required by the Bank Charter Act 1844 to make a return to the Revenue. S. 432 of the Companies Act 1948 eliminated the need for these returns where a return under s. 124 (the standard obligation of all companies) had been made *together* with an indication of the places where the business of banking was carried on; *secondly,* such a bank was to be a banker for the purpose of the 1879 Act.

Now there are two major changes. "Banker" for the purpose of the 1879 Act is to be "a recognised bank, *licensed institution* or municipal bank within the meaning of the Banking Act." That is to say that licensed institutions including deposit-takers with no semblance of aspiration to be bankers can claim the benefits of the 1879 Act. These benefits, which also apply to Trustee Savings Banks, the National Savings Bank, and the Post Office (as a provider of banking services), enable certified copies to be produced, although they are secondary evidence, and for inspection and the taking of copies by a magistrate's order as an alternative.

A second change eliminates the controversy as to what could be produced by way of records that were *not* books. There appears to be no limitation so long as the records are used in the ordinary business of the bank. The modern appendages of computer film-tape or "retrieval mechanisms" are covered by procedure contained in the Civil Evidence Act 1968, s. 9, as to the way such evidence to be produced in lieu of books is to be permitted, when accounts are operated by computer statements verified as described in the Act.

Para. 2. The Agricultural Credits Act 1928 enables finance secured by agricultural charges (a form of security peculiar to the Act) to be made available by banks. The meaning is now changed to recognised banks *and* licensed institutions as well as Trustee Savings Banks and Post Office banking institutions.

Para. 3. A similar change is extended to the counterpart Scottish Act, although it should be mentioned that its operation has considerable differences from the English statute.

Paras. 4 *and* 5. These amendments are consequential because the Prevention of Fraud Acts were amended by the Protection of Depositors Acts, which themselves have been amended by this Act.

Paras. 6 *and* 7. These stem from the provisions that building society surplus moneys must be deposited with a bank.

Para. 8. This appears to tie in with a provision for depositing surplus funds with a bank. The 1979 Act definition applies.

Paras. 9 *and* 10. These relate to the operation of client accounts and other trust accounts.

Paras. 11 *and* 12. Formerly these Acts contained the "Protection of Depositors Act" definition of banker; now the Banking Act 1979 definition is substituted.

Section 51 (2)

SCHEDULE 7

Enactments Repealed

Chapter	Short Title	Extent of Repeal
1844 c. 32.	The Bank Charter Act 1844.	Section 21.
1845 c. 38.	The Bank Notes (Scotland) Act 1845.	Section 13.
1880 c. 20.	The Inland Revenue Act 1880.	Section 57. Schedule 3.
1907 c. 24.	The Limited Partnerships Act 1907.	In section 4, in subsection (2), the words from " in the case of a partnership " to " any other partnership ".
1948 c. 38.	The Companies Act 1948.	In section 155, subsection (2). Sections 429 to 432. In section 433, in subsection (1), the words " a limited banking company or ". In section 434, in subsection (1), the words " (other than the business of banking)".
1960 c. 22 (N.I.).	The Companies Act (Northern Ireland) 1960.	In section 149, subsection (2). Sections 377 to 380. In section 381, in subsection (1), the words " a limited banking company or ". In section 382, in subsection (1), the words " (other than the business of banking)".
1963 c. 16.	The Protection of Depositors Act 1963.	The whole Act, so far as unrepealed.
1964 c. 22 (N.I.).	The Protection of Depositors Act (Northern Ireland) 1964.	The whole Act, so far as unrepealed.
1967 c. 81.	The Companies Act 1967.	Section 119. In section 120, in subsection (1), the words "(other than the business of banking)". In section 121, in subsection (1), the words " (other than a partnership carrying on the business of banking)"; and in subsection (2), the words " (other than a partnership carrying on the business of banking)". Section 127.
1968 c. 25. (N.I.).	The Financial Provisions Act (Northern Ireland) 1968.	In Schedule 1, in paragraph 1, the entry relating to the Protection of Depositors Act (Northern Ireland) 1964.
1969 c. 48.	The Post Office Act 1969.	In section 40, the words from " but shall not " to the end. In Part III of Schedule 6, the provision amending the Bankers' Books Evidence Act 1879.
1976 c. 4.	The Trustee Savings Banks Act 1976.	In Schedule 5, paragraphs 4 to 7.
1976 c. 10.	The Post Office (Banking Services) Act 1976.	Section 1 (2).
1976 c. 69.	The Companies Act 1976.	In Schedule 1, the paragraph amending section 432 (1) of the Companies Act 1948. In Schedule 2, the paragraphs amending the Protection of Depositors Act 1963.
S.I. 1978/1042 (N.I. 12).	The Companies (Northern Ireland) Order 1978.	Article 133. In Article 134 (1), the words " (other than the business of banking)".

SCHEDULE 7—*continued*

Chapter	Short Title	Extent of Repeal
S.I. 1978/1042 (N.I. 12)—*cont.*	The Companies (Northern Ireland) Order 1978—*cont.*	In Article 135, in paragraph (1) the words " (other than a partnership carrying on the business of banking)", in paragraph (2), the words " (other than a partnership carrying on the business of banking)". In Schedule 6, in Part II the amendments of the Protection of Depositors Act (Northern Ireland) 1964.

Estate Agents Act 1979 *

(1979 c. 38)

ARRANGEMENT OF SECTIONS

An Act to make provision with respect to the carrying on of and to persons who carry on, certain activities in connection with

* Annotations by C. M. Douglas, LL.B., Solicitor, Senior Lecturer in Law, Preston Polytechnic, and R. G. Lee, LL.B., Lecturer in Law, University of Lancaster.

the disposal and acquisition of interests in land; and for purposes connected therewith. [4th April 1979]

General Note

At present a person can adopt the title of "estate agent" without any particular qualification or other indication of competence or, indeed, honesty. The Act does not change this but introduces a mechanism, operated by the Director-General of Fair Trading, whereby an estate agent can be judged unfit to practise. The fitness of an individual for "estate agency work" (which is the central definition in the Act) is established by reference to certain requirements contained in the Act. These include indemnity insurance; a separate client deposit account; full disclosure of an agent's personal interest in property; and complete information on the likely charges and other liabilities at the outset of the agent's appointment.

The Act is the culmination of many attempts to regulate the activities of estate agents by legislation, and otherwise. The full history is given below, but an understanding of the immediate history will lead to an appreciation of some of the idiosyncracies of the Act. Traditionally, regulation had been designed as control by licensing, usually overseen by a national body commanding the support of professional institutions. It had always been difficult to satisfy the various professional institutions and conflict had arisen between those in the profession who warmly welcomed the idea and those who bitterly opposed it. Additionally, registration was seen as exceedingly bureaucratic.

The Act is substantially the same as a Private Member's Bill introduced by Labour M.P., Bryan Davies, in the previous session. That Bill, in departing from the idea of registration, found the key to success. It had been anticipated that the Government Bill would follow the Davies format but it seemed reasonable to expect that the various criticisms which had been made would be met. This did not happen.

Nonetheless, the Act goes much further than was originally intended. This is because the Lords' amendments which were considered on the day of dissolution after the defeat of the Labour Government, were accepted in full. The major effect of this was to extend the Act to cover dealings with commercial as well as residential property. This has had two effects: first, there has been only scant consideration of resource implications and, secondly, although the measure began life as a piece of consumer protection it now protects many persons other than the consumer. Yet, strangely, there are many consumer problems which the Act makes no attempt to handle. Before examining these it is worth outlining the provisions of the Act.

Ss. 1 and 2 define the activity ("estate agency work") controlled by the Act. These sections also exclude certain other activities from control.

Ss. 3–8 and Scheds. 1 and 2 deal with orders made by the Director-General of Fair Trading which either exclude unfit persons from engaging in estate agency work, or warn of a likely exclusion. A system for the revocation or variation of orders is instituted, as is an appeals procedure. Orders made are to be registered by the Director.

Ss. 9–11 secure the provision of information for the Director and give powers of entry and inspection in order to assist in this. However, there are restrictions on the disclosure of any information obtained.

Ss. 12–17 are concerned with the safeguarding of "clients' money." This is done by ensuring that all clients' money is held by the estate agent as trustee (except in Scotland). In addition the estate agent is obliged to take out indemnity insurance cover.

Ss. 18–21 regulate other aspects of estate agency work. Full information of a client's prospective liabilities must be provided by an estate agent. Pre-contract deposits are to be kept within prescribed limits, except in Scotland where they are banned. If an estate agent has a personal interest in any transaction, this must be disclosed to the client.

Ss. 22 and 23 ensure that estate agents satisfy certain minimum requirements. Generally, minimum standards will be laid down by the Secretary of State, but the Act specifically excludes bankrupts from engaging in estate agency work except as employees.

Ss. 24–27 lay down the responsibilities for supervision and enforcement of the Act.

Ss. 28–36 contain various supplementary information including provisions as to offences; the service of notices; interpretation; finance and commencement.

It was claimed throughout the debates on the Act that these provisions would impose control only on a small minority of estate agents who engage in the malpractices covered. However, if this is the case it seems strange (especially since initially this was claimed to be a consumer protection measure) that various unfair and dishonest practices involving only a few rogue agents, and a few wider abuses, are left untouched by the Act. The Department of Prices and Consumer Protection published a consultative document entitled "The Regulation of Estate Agency" in November 1975. That listed the following six unfair practices:

(i) agents buying and selling property in circumstances where their interests conflict with those of their clients;

(ii) involvement of estate agents in disreputable mortgage-broking activities;

(iii) misdescription of property, and failure to give essential information about it;

(iv) persuading clients to use their services on the basis of terms or conditions which are unfair or oppressive;

(v) actively soliciting custom from bereaved relatives; and

(vi) financial inducement to local deliverymen to report possible removals.

Of these only (i) is fully covered. In addition there are certain matters which are the subject of much complaint but on which the Act is silent. A good example of this is the problem of the contract race—a topical one at the time of writing. It is curious that although the Bill passed through Parliament at the time of a very active house market, the problems associated with such a market, especially contract-racing and gazumping, were ignored. Other difficulties remain. Estate agency contracts escape largely unscathed, in spite of grave problems faced by the consumer in relation to both sole agency agreements and estate agency commissions. A review of other major omissions is contained below.

Background

The Estate Agents Act 1979 has a most remarkable history, stretching over some 90 years. The first parliamentary attempt at regulation began in 1888 with a Private Member's Bill. In all there were 12 such Bills before the 13th Bill, and the first Government Bill, was successful. In fairness, it was the 12th Bill that was the significant one since for the first time, there was a move away from registration by a system of licensing by a licensing body guaranteeing certain minimum standards. Whilst even this Bill, which avoided the previous stumbling-block, failed, it was adopted by the Government due to wide-ranging support for the measure at a time when non-controversial legislation was all a minority Government could afford. On the day of dissolution of Parliament, the Act was passed in a finale quite suited to its dramatic history. That history is now outlined.

1888 A Private Member's Bill seeks the registration of architects, engineers, and surveyors but meets with massive opposition in the House of Commons and is withdrawn at the time of the second reading.

1914 A lengthy Bill entitled "the Auctioneers and Estate Agents Registration Bill" is introduced by a Private Member. It defined an Estate Agent as:

> "Any person who on behalf of any other person and for or in consideration of any payment or other remuneration whether monetary or otherwise (a) values, sells, buys, lets, takes on lease or otherwise deals with or disposes of land of any tenure or buildings, or any estate or interest in land of any tenure or buildings, or (b) negotiates for the sale, purchase, letting or taking on lease or for any other dealing with or disposition of land of any tenure or buildings or any estate or interest in land of any tenure or buildings."

The Bill lapses at the end of the session, and any renewal of interest is forestalled by the outbreak of war.

1921 The Auctioneers' and Estate Agents' Institute and the Surveyors' Institution arrange talks on registration.

1923 Another Private Member's Bill, "the Landed Property Practitioners (Registration) Bill" is introduced, at the instigation of the above two bodies and the Land Agents' Society. Solicitors, accountants and engineers are exempt. Two societies, the National Society of Landed Property Practitioners and the Auctioneers and Estate Agents' Association, form in opposition to the Bill but, failing to reach a high position in the Private Members' ballot, the Bill fails.

1924 The National Society of Landed Property Practitioners (above) becomes the Incorporated Society of Auctioneers and Landed Property Agents, and begins to work towards registration.

1928 A further Bill is prepared, proposing to set up a registration board of recognised bodies. Leave to introduce the Bill was not granted.

1929 There is canvassing of M.P.s by both the Incorporated Society of Auctioneers and Landed Property Agents, and the National Association of Auctioneers. The latter conclude that a registration measure would not pass through the Commons, but that registration providing real protection for the public might achieve some support, and a Registration Bill establishing a guarantee fund is prepared but gains no support from other professional bodies.

1931 Architects succeed in their pressure for a Registration Act.

1934 The Chartered Surveyors' Institution (R.I.C.S.), the Land Agents' Society and the Auctioneers' and Estate Agents' Institute, in a joint statement reject the idea of registration. Although the other professional bodies issue counter statements the effect of these is the establishment of a select committee of the Lords under Lord Mersey.

1936 Following the report of the Mersey Committee, three bills are prepared; one by the National Association of Auctioneers; one by the other major professional bodies; and one, quite independently of the profession, by a Private Member, Sir Reginald Clarry. The final one of these—the Auctioneers and House Agents Bill—actually wins the support of the National Association of Auctioneers, but although it is introduced into the Commons, it fails in the face of widespread opposition by parties not consulted.

1939 The issue is dropped on the outbreak of war but both the R.I.C.S. and the Auctioneers' and Estate Agents' Institute have standing committees during wartime considering registration.

1943 There is a tentative enquiry by the latter body concerning the prospects of introducing a Bill.

1944 The same body makes another inquiry of the Commons.

1945 Following these inquiries this body publish the report of their committee supporting the idea of statutory control for the future, but rejecting any immediate measure as impractical. The R.I.C.S. publish their committee report which recommends non-pursuance of registration.

1947 The Irish Auctioneers and House Agents Act is passed. This is a licensing measure and introduces bonding, and renews British interest.

1949 National Association of Auctioneers, Rating Surveyors and Valuers amalgamate with the Valuers' Institution (I.S.V.A.).

1952 A joint conference of the major professional bodies, terminating three years of discussion ends in division.

1953 The Accommodation Agencies Act 1953, controlling the activities of letting agents, is passed.

1959 The four major bodies announce their agreement on the provision of a Bill.

1960 An R.I.C.S. questionnaire seeking support for the Bill and the idea of registration shows opinion to be clearly favourable.

1961 There follows Parliamentary pressure, and some Government prevarication on the subject of estate agents' registration.

1962 As the possibilities of a Bill become stronger, unattached estate agents form themselves into a body, the National Association of Estate Agents (N.A.E.A.), to pressure against registration. A revised Bill drafted by Parliamentary counsel is published. The revision would seem to indicate, if not Government support for the measure, at least acceptance that it might become law. Entitled "The Estate Agents Bill," it is fairly wide ranging, covering both the sale and letting of residential and commercial property. It provides for minimum standards of competence, overseen by an Estate Agents Council, which body also makes rules for the keeping of client accounts and good accountancy procedures. There is also a compensation fund for persons suffering loss due to the default of a registered agent. It is introduced into the Commons.

1963 There is sustained opposition to this Bill by the National Association of Estate Agents, who suggest a licensing measure as an alternative. The Bill fails to obtain a second reading. This is because under the threat of the Bill being talked out, Sir Harry Legge-Bourke moved early that the question be put. Although carried by 54 votes to six, this is contrary to the requirement of at least 100 members in support of the standing order.

1964 Under the 10-minute rule an Estate Agents Bill is introduced. It aims at the placing of much estate agency work in the hands of local authorities. This is in line with the policy of the 1964 Labour administration to develop municipal house agencies, but again, although leave is given to introduce the Bill, it makes no progress. In spite of the failure of these measures they have the value of instigating urgent action on the part of the professional bodies. All the professional bodies except the National Association of Estate Agents join together for talks, but on an indication by the Government that only a proposal from all bodies would be acceptable, an invitation is given to the National Association and is taken up.

1966 These moves lead to a draft Bill introduced by the first balloted private member, and given its second reading in January 1966. It provides for an Estate Agents Council to regulate activities of estate agents, including maximum fees to be charged, and arrangements for accounting, auditing, and payment of interest. Accountants, solicitors, and architects are to be given exemption. The second reading is carried, and the committee work begins only to be interrupted by the dissolution of Parliament.

1967 Faced with considerable losses incurred in the promotion of the Bill, and the fact that the new Labour administration is committed to a heavy legislative programme not including estate agency measures, the societies decide to introduce voluntary regulation. In October 1967 the Estate Agents Council is formed.

1968 Another Private Member's Bill, "The Fraser Bill," seeks provision for the Estate Agents Council to have certain powers regarding bonding, safeguarding of deposits, and clients' money. The Bill fails after the first reading.

1969 The Report of the Monopolies Commission is published. Monopoly conditions are found to be prevailing, contrary to public interest—they also recommend that scales of fees should cease to be published, and rules discouraging competition should be withdrawn.
The Estate Agents Council is wound up. A statement from the President of the Board of Trade regrets that it had "not proved practicable for the Council to continue its work."

1970 An order implementing the main recommendations of the Monopolies Commission passes through Parliament.

1971 One year after the order no reports of its contravention have been received.

1972 A proposal by the N.A.E.A. for a licensing provision is sent to the Secretary of State for Trade and Industry. It is followed by proposals from the R.I.C.S. and I.S.V.A., and a debate in the Commons but there is no immediate promise or legislation.

1974 A Private Member's Bill entitled the Estate Agents (Regulation) Bill which seeks to regulate certain estate agency practices, especially sole selling right agreements, is given a first reading in the Commons. It fails to achieve a second reading.

1975 The preparation of a consultative document is announced, and published later in the year.

1976 Yet another Private Member's Bill, which once again fails after the first reading.

1978 A Private Member's Bill is introduced by Labour M.P. Bryan Davies.

It has a second reading and its Commons committee stages, but lapses at the end of the session. However, the Government adopt a very similar Bill in the next session.

1979 The Estate Agents Act received Royal Assent.

For a full account of the history of attempts to regulate estate agency work, see the series of articles by Bennion, *Estates Gazette,* May/June 1967.

The Act

The Act has three main goals. These are: (1) to allow the Director-General of Fair Trading to prohibit certain estate agents from engaging in estate agency work by means of a register of unfit persons; (2) to require estate agents to maintain a separate client account; and (3) to ensure that an estate agent receiving clients' money is covered by insurance against failing to account for such money.

In order to achieve this, the Act contains 36 sections and two lengthy schedules. In spite of this there is a surprising absence of detail. Indeed, it could be argued that the Act is an enabling Act in that it contains provisions for a large amount of detail to be filled in at a later date by means of ministerial regulations and orders. For example, s. 16 (2) allows the Secretary of State to specify certain arrangements (*e.g.* indemnity insurance) whereby loss of client's money by an estate agent's default or dishonesty is made good. The Secretary of State can also lay down the terms and conditions governing such arrangements and even specify persons to be exempted the necessity of compliance with them.

Another, and from an estate agent's point of view more disturbing, power is contained in s. 22 whereby the Secretary of State may at any time in the future lay down standards of competence prescribed in terms of practical experience, or professional or academic qualifications, which a person must attain before he may engage in estate agency work. Furthermore, the Secretary may delegate such power to an "established body" should he choose to specify one.

The stated purpose of the Bill was "to impose a measure of control on certain activities of estate agents with a view to affording protection to users of their services" (explanatory and financial memorandum), *i.e.* it was seen as being first and foremost a consumer protection measure. Therefore, it was perhaps acceptable that the Secretary of State had a discretion to extend some of the provisions, should the need arise, for increased consumer protection in this field. It must be borne in mind, however, that with the acceptance of the Lords' amendments, this is arguably no longer a consumer protection measure.

The omissions

If this is still the aim of the Act then many other points often raised by the consumer remain unanswered. For example, in spite of the recommendations of the 1976 White Paper, descriptions of properties by estate agents generally remain outside the scope of the Trade Descriptions Acts 1968 and 1972, leaving the consumer to rely on common law remedies. However, an estate agent is less likely to be sued for malpractice or incompetence than many other professional people. One of the grounds on which the Director-General can decide a person is unfit to carry on estate agency work is that the estate agent is guilty of a breach of a legal duty (s. 3). Whilst one of the most common consumer complaints against estate agents relates to their descriptions of property, it would seem that no matter how idiosyncratic or inaccurate the wording used by the agent and no matter how much time and money is spent by an individual viewing totally unsuitable property there is no legal sanction against the agent. Consequently, it is unlikely that the Director-General will be able to issue such an order unless the Secretary of State declares that the practice is undesirable (s. 3 (1) (*d*)).

Another example appears in the field of estate agents' contracts. The problem of "the contract race," a topical one at the time of writing, could become more so when the demand for houses increases and gazumping once more comes to the fore. The Act is silent on both these points. Often the gazumping is on the part of the vendor, but the estate agent is blamed. Mr. Andrew McKay M.P. suggested during the second reading that gazumping be made illegal so as to protect estate agents from such criticism and the consequent damage to their reputation (H.C. Vol. 958, col. 646). In some parts of the country a more serious defect can occur in relation to the particular terminology used, by virtue of which the unwary vendor may find himself bound by a sole agency agreement. Furthermore, under some contracts, commission may be payable even though the estate agent has not introduced a " ready, willing and able " purchaser. In addition the Act does not attempt to regulate the amount of commission chargeable, in spite of the fact that there is provision to limit the amount taken as a pre-contract deposit (s. 19).

A common misapprehension is that the Act is a registration measure. It is not. Even after it becomes law the present system of anyone being able to set up in practice will continue. Registration in any shape or form is only operative once a person has been declared unfit to practise (ss. 3–8). It provides for a blacklist rather than a register or directory of practitioners. Critics of the Act regard this as closing the stable door after the horse has bolted, and claim it is an omission of a vital, further protection which could have been afforded to the consumer. In fairness, the type of system chosen does have the effect of cutting out the rot, whilst leaving the majority of honest estate agents untroubled.

Enforcement

The weights and measures authorities are faced with the imposition of a further duty to enforce yet another statute, and one wonders just what priority the authorities will give to this particular statute. No doubt, as with other matters dealt with by the weights and measures authorities, the standard of vigilance will vary from region to region. The choice of this enforcement authority rather than, say, a separate enforcement body under the Director-General is another matter of compromise imposed by finance. As long as the Act was designed to cover estate agency work on residential property, the compromise, although undesirable, was understandable. Given the scope of the Act, it is to be hoped that the burden will not be so great as to render the measure unenforceable.

Conclusion

As Bryan Davies pointed out in debate at the time of the second reading, the Act is not revolutionary (H.C. Vol. 958, col. 653). In the same debate other members mentioned the need for wider proposals; Ken Weetch spoke of a structured attack on the cost of moving house (H.C. Vol. 958, col. 645), but it is doubtful whether this measure will provide even one weapon in such an attack. A close survey of the Act leaves one wondering whether, after a 90-year wait, this measure is worth-while. The point is continually made in debate that the Act seeks only to guard against the " rogue " estate agent. However, as will be shown, many activities of such agents may fall outside the scope of the Act. There are three reasons for this: the first is that the definition of estate agency work is sufficiently loose to allow the " rogue " to work as an estate agent but outside the Act (see notes to s. 1, especially subs. (4)); the second is that many of the fringe activities, engaged in by the less reputable of the profession, fall outside the Act. (This is especially true of their activities with regard to lettings and rents (see notes to ss. 1, 2, 12 and 13)); finally one must bear in mind the known abuses (mentioned above) not covered by the Act.

This is quite apart from criticisms that can be levelled against various other provisions in the Act, including the problems of enforcement. It is true, and again this was stressed throughout the Parliamentary proceedings on the Bill, that the honest estate agent has nothing to fear from this Act. The problem may well be that neither does the dishonest one.

Extent

The Act applies to Scotland (s. 35), and to Northern Ireland (s. 36).

Commencement

The Act is not yet in operation. Parts may become operative during 1980, but individual provisions will be brought into force by regulation thereafter (see further s. 36).

Parliamentary debates

For parliamentary debates and Committee Stages, see *Hansard*, H.L. Vol. 398, cols. 142, 1216–1234; Vol. 399, cols. 77–154, 1745–1761; H.C. Vol. 958, cols. 618–700; Vol. 961, cols. 1373–1393; Vol. 965, cols. 1358–1359; H.C. Standing Committee E, cols. 1–144. For Debates and Committee Stages on the earlier Private Member's Bill (*supra*), see H.C. Vol. 943, cols. 885–953; Vol. 949, cols. 631–727, 1702–1709, H.C. Standing Committee C, cols. 1–116.

Application of Act

Estate agency work

1.—(1) This Act applies, subject to subsections (2) to (4) below to things done by any person in the course of a business (including a business in which he is employed) pursuant to instructions received from another person (in this section referred to as " the client ") who wishes to dispose of or acquire an interest in land—

(*a*) for the purpose of, or with a view to, effecting the introduction to the client of a third person who wishes to acquire or, as the case may be, dispose of such an interest; and

(*b*) after such an introduction has been effected in the course of that business, for the purpose of securing the disposal or, as the case may be, the acquisition of that interest;

and in this Act the expression " estate agency work " refers to things done as mentioned above to which this Act applies.

(2) This Act does not apply to things done—

(*a*) in the course of his profession by a practising solicitor or a person employed by him; or

(*b*) in the course of credit brokerage, within the meaning of the Consumer Credit Act 1974; or

(*c*) in the course of insurance brokerage by a person who is for the time being registered under section 2, or enrolled under section 4, of the Insurance Brokers (Registration) Act 1977; or

(*d*) in the course of carrying out any survey or valuation pursuant to a contract which is distinct from that under which other things falling within subsection (1) above are done; or

(*e*) in connection with applications and other matters arising under the Town and Country Planning Act 1971 or the Town and Country Planning (Scotland) Act 1972 or the Planning (Northern Ireland) Order 1972.

(3) This Act does not apply to things done by any person—

(*a*) pursuant to instructions received by him in the course of his employment in relation to an interest in land if his employer is the person who, on his own behalf, wishes to dispose of or acquire that interest; or

(*b*) in relation to any interest in any property if the property is subject to a mortgage and he is the receiver of the income of it; or

(*c*) in relation to a present, prospective or former employee of his or of any person by whom he also is employed if the things are done by reason of the employment (whether past, present or future).

(4) This Act does not apply to the publication of advertisements or the dissemination of information by a person who does no other acts which fall within subsection (1) above.

(5) In this section—

(*a*) " practising solicitor " means, except in Scotland, a solicitor who is qualified to act as such under section 1 of the Solicitors Act 1974 or article 4 of the Solicitors (Northern Ireland) Order 1976, and in Scotland includes a firm of practising solicitors;

(*b*) " mortgage " includes a debenture and any other charge on property for securing money or money's worth; and

(*c*) any reference to employment is a reference to employment under a contract of employment.

DEFINITION

" interest in land " : s. 2.

GENERAL NOTE

This section introduces the central definition of " estate agency work," and specifies those activities to which the Act does not apply.

It is important to note that there is no provision similar to that of s. 189 (2) of the Consumer Credit Act 1974, which has the effect of exempting from the requirements of that Act any person who only occasionally enters into transactions of the type controlled. Consequently, difficulties arise in respect of the activities of a duly appointed holder of a fiduciary office; for example executors, administrators, trustees for incapable persons, trustees of a settlement, and in bankruptcy.

Subs. (1)

" *estate agency work.*" There is no attempt to define " estate agent." This is because it was felt that it was not possible to define the range of persons or bodies engaged in the work of estate agency. This is similar to the position under the Consumer Credit Act 1974, and there is evidence that under that Act many people failed to realise that they came within the scope of the licensing provisions (see Annual Reports of the Director General of Fair Trading, 1976, p. 20).

" *things done.*" The vague nature of this phrase gives rise to certain difficulties; as to which, see s. 1 (4).

" *in the course of a business.*" See note to s. 16 (4). This includes a business in which a person is employed. Problems have arisen in the past concerning the interpretation of these words (see, for example, the Trade Descriptions Act 1968 and *Havering London Borough* v. *Stevenson* [1970] 1 W.L.R. 1375; *Fletcher* v. *Sledmore* [1973] R.T.R. 371; *Fletcher* v. *Budgen* [1974] 1 W.L.R. 1056; see also the Unfair Contract Terms Act 1977).

The phrase is meant to protect private sales of houses but it refers to " a business " and not to an " estate agency business." Any person engaging in " estate agency work," even on a single occasion, is brought within the Act. The inclusion of employees could lead to secretaries/receptionists, who in a small office might take instructions from a client, incurring liability under the Act. However, provided an employee does not receive deposits he has no obligations under the client account provisions (s. 14) and provided he does not receive clients' money he has no obligations in respect of indemnity (s. 16). On the other hand a secretary/receptionist might receive and misappropriate " clients' money " (see s. 13) or ostensibly, in the course of his employment, sell his own house without disclosing an interest (see s. 21). In both of these circumstances the Act would apply so as to bar such a person from employment in estate agency work in the future (see s. 3). Thus the consumer need not take steps to identify the person in the estate agent's office with whom he is dealing. Arguably, whether by design or otherwise, this operates as a disincentive to vigilance on the part of the consumer.

As to whether voluntary activities are to be included as " in the course of a business," see the discussion of the Law Commission's Second Report on Exemption Clauses (Law Com. No. 69) Pt. III, 1975, p. 50, para. 127.

" *instructions.*" These are not defined. There is no requirement for instructions to be in writing which raises questions as to the degree of formality, if any, required. Whilst it might be the case that instructions to estate agents are often informal in order to quicken the transaction, there are two main effects:

(a) The comments (*supra*) concerning the liability of the secretary/receptionist are reinforced. Very often it is this person who will take informal instructions.

(b) In the course of many businesses, *e.g.* banking, accountancy, etc., informal discussions may seem tantamount to instructions and may be included within the Act. Whether liability would arise in such situations would depend whether, on the facts, any part of the Act has been breached.

"*dispose of or acquire.*" See s. 2.

"*interest in land.*" See s. 2. As this Act began life in an earlier session as a Private Member's Bill (*supra*) with the consequential restraints on financial and departmental support, commercial property was felt to be outside its ambit. It was designed as a simple consumer protection measure in the belief that commercial consumers were well able to look after themselves. This philosophy was adopted by the Government, included in their Bill, and survived criticism in the Commons. The deletion of "residential," the first-tabled Lords' amendment, was carried in the Committee of that House, and in a flurry of activity on the day of dissolution, finally agreed to by the Commons. This phrase was thus adopted.

The intention of this amendment was that, for example, the small businessman who buys or sells a shop, with or without residential accommodation, is as well protected as any private purchaser/vendor. However, there was a total lack of debate in the Commons on the far-reaching effect of this amendment. This becomes apparent on an examination of later sections.

Subs. (2)

"*in the course of his profession by a practising solicitor.*" See s. 1 (5). In Scotland the title "solicitor and estate agent" is frequently adopted and is in fact permitted by the Scottish Law Society. Thus it was felt that s. 1 (2) (*a*) was a necessary exemption, in view of the fact that (a) internal standards of competence for solicitors were fixed at a level involving academic and practical qualification, and also (b) the major reforms in the Act (*e.g.* client account, indemnity insurance, supervision of the profession, etc.) were more than adequately covered by Law Society Regulations.

In England under the Solicitor's Practice Rules 1936–72, r. 3:7 provides that:

"A solicitor who wishes to engage in another profession or business must satisfy two tests:

(a) The other profession or business must be an honourable one that does not detract from his status as a solicitor.

(b) It must not involve him in a breach of a rule of the Solicitor's Practice Rules 1971."

R. 3:18:2 gives the specific example of a person practising as a solicitor and also as an auctioneer and estate agent and concludes that this would almost inevitably lead to a breach of r. 1 of the Solicitor's Practice Rules (Professional Purposes Committee 1:4 1946, p. 58 (Cmnd. 3638)). However, a solicitor who incidentally, in the course of his practice, comes within the definition of estate agency work (for example, a solicitor inviting offers for a house whilst acting for a mortgagee in possession) is exempt from the provisions. Members of other professions who might be called upon to effect introductions (*e.g.* accountants winding up estates) will be jealous of such exemption. The argument used in favour of exempting solicitors was that otherwise they would be subject to double jeopardy.

Subs. (2) (*b*)

See s. 145 of the Consumer Credit Act 1974. The exemption is included so that credit brokers would also escape double jeopardy.

Subs. (2) (*c*)

S. 2 of the 1977 Act imposes a system of registration in respect of individual insurance brokers, and s. 4 requires the Insurance Brokers Registration Council (established by the Act) to maintain a list of bodies corporate carrying on business as insurance brokers. Because there is provision in that Act for a code of conduct (s. 10) and indemnity insurance (s. 12), insurance brokers would have been liable to double jeopardy.

Subs. (2) (*d*)

The purpose of this exemption is to ensure that a surveyor or valuer acting in good faith is not caught by the definition of estate agency work. No doubt the legislature were concerned particularly with building society surveyors. The difficulty is that many estate agents are also valuers and/or surveyors, and it may be a problem for the judiciary to decide whether or not a particular valuation or survey falls within "estate agency work" (s. 1 (1)). For example, in contemplation of a future sale of his property a person obtains a valuation from a local estate agent. If this is substantially below the market value because the agent has an undisclosed person interested in the purchase of the property certain questions arise. Is the valuation within s. 1 (1) or will it remain outside this subsection until the estate agent receives instructions to sell? What if there is a considerable delay between valuation and sale? Will the courts decide that if the delay is unreasonably long there is no scope for the operation of s. 1 (1)? These questions are not easily answered.

The concept of a "survey or valuation pursuant to a contract" yet remaining distinct from estate agency work can be difficult to grasp. The Act could have demanded that its provisions, in particular those relating to standards of competence (s. 22), apply to all persons engaged in valuation or survey work.

Subs. (2) (*e*)

These acts give the Secretary of State for the Environment the power either to acquire or to authorise a local authority to compulsorily acquire any land within their area subject to the conditions contained therein. A similar power to acquire land is granted to the Secretary of State for the Environment himself. The authorities also have the power to dispose of land which has been held for planning purposes. The power is also subject to restraints: ss. 112–123 of the Town and Country Planning Act 1971; ss. 102–122 of the Town and Country (Scotland) Planning Act 1972; Planning (Northern Ireland) Order 1972.

Subs. (3)

"*in the course of his employment.*" See P. S. Atiyah, *Vicarious Liability in the Law of Torts* (1967), Part V, and see *Smith* v. *Martin* [1911] 2 K.B. 775; *London County Council* v. *Cattermoles* (*Garages*) *Ltd.* [1953] 1 W.L.R. 997; *Canadian Pacific Railways* v. *Lockhart* [1942] A.C. 591. This apparently simple provision is open to ambiguity. Presumably the intention is to cover the straightforward disposal or acquisition of the interest in land by the employee, on behalf of the employer, in the course of employment unconnected with estate agency work. However, the following are some of the problems which could arise:

(a) An estate agent's secretary could assist in the disposal or acquisition of his employer's property, and still be covered by this exemption. This may be significant if the secretary failed to disclose the employer's personal interest in the transaction, since this would normally breach s. 21.

(b) There would seem to be an obvious discrepancy between the words "in the course of his employment" and on "his own behalf." Apart from a personal secretary, which type of employee could act purely to further the personal interest of the employer and yet remain within the course of his employment?

Subs. (4)

If a person is engaged merely in the dissemination of information, then he falls outside the Act unless, according to this section, he does other acts falling within the definition of estate agency work. The purpose of this is to allow for the display of a newspaper advertisement without the publishers falling within the scope of the Act. However, the following should be noted.

(a) Certain fringe activities, *e.g.* computer agencies, may not be caught by the Act. The consumer may, nonetheless, need protection against agencies if they act without disclosing their own interests relating to the purchase or acquisition of the properties on their print-outs.

(b) It is vital to know, for the purposes of this section, which other Acts fall within subs. (1). Much depends on the interpretation of the ugly phrase "things done" (*supra*). For example, it is not inconceivable, particularly in the North of England where estate agents do not always handle deposits, that the only thing done is a valuation. If, therefore, the estate agent accepted the seller's own valuation or did not advise the purchaser as to valuation on an acquisition, he may be deemed to be engaged solely in disseminating information and thereby gain exemption from the Act.

Perhaps the only way to evade this unhappy conclusion is to include as "things done" the preparation of any materials to disseminate. In this way only publishers would remain exempt.

Subs. (5)

There is a full definition section (s. 33). However, the definitions of mortgage and employment are clearly intended for this section only. Both of these terms appear in other sections throughout the Act, so this was clearly necessary. The point is easily understood with reference to "employment," which is defined here as work done under a contract of employment, *i.e.* a contract of service. Thus in s. 1 (3) (*a*) work done in the course of his employment covers work done whilst under a contract for services. Consequently it would be highly unsatisfactory if this definition of employment applied throughout, because estate agents would fall outside the scope of the word "employment" whenever it is used; see, *e.g.* s. 3 (3) (*a*).

There is a great deal of material on the crucial distinction between the contract of service and the contract for services. See P. S. Atiyah, *Vicarious Liability in the Law of Torts* (1967) chaps. 1–4; P. O'Higgins, "When is an Employee not an Employee?" [1967] C.L.J. 27; for the relevant case law, see *Yewens* v. *Noakes* (1880) 6 Q.B.D. 530; *Cassidy* v. *Minister of Health* [1951] 2 K.B. 343; *Morren* v. *Swinton and Pendlebury Borough Council* [1965] 1 W.L.R. 576; *Stevenson, Jordan and Harrison* v. *Macdonald and Evans* [1952] 1 T.L.R. 101; *Beloff* v. *Pressdram* [1973] 1 All E.R. 241; *Ready-Mixed Concrete (South East) Ltd.* v. *Minister of Pensions* [1968] 2 Q.B. 494; *Argent* v. *Minister of Social Security* [1968] 1 W.L.R. 1749; *Ferguson* v. *John Dawson and Partners* [1976] 1 W.L.R. 1213; *Massey* v. *Crown Life Assurance Co.* [1978] 1 W.L.R. 676.

Interests in land

2.—(1) Subject to subsection (3) below, any reference in this Act to disposing of an interest in land is a reference to—

(*a*) transferring a legal estate in fee simple absolute in possession; or

(*b*) transferring or creating, elsewhere than in Scotland, a lease which, by reason of the level of the rent, the length of the term or both, has a capital value which may be lawfully realised on the open market; or

(*c*) transferring or creating in Scotland any estate or interest in land which is capable of being owned or held as a separate interest and to which a title may be recorded in the Register of Sasines;

and any reference to acquiring an interest in land shall be construed accordingly.

(2) In subsection (1) (*b*) above the expression "lease" includes the rights and obligations arising under an agreement to grant a lease.

(3) Notwithstanding anything in subsections (1) and (2) above, references in this Act to disposing of an interest in land do not extend to disposing of—

(*a*) the interest of a creditor whose debt is secured by way of a mortgage or charge of any kind over land or an agreement for any such mortgage or charge; or

(*b*) in Scotland, the interest of a creditor in a heritable security as defined in section 9 (8) of the Conveyancing and Feudal Reform (Scotland) Act 1970.

General Note

S. 2 originally defined interests in residential property but as a consequence of including business properties this section was amended by deleting the word "residential" whenever it occurred. It now defines interest in land which is crucial to the definition of estate agency work (s. 1 (1)). It is now made clear that the words "disposal" and "acquisition" in s. 1 (1) relate only to purchase and sale transactions. This is in spite of a claim in the Explanatory and Financial Memorandum of the original Bill that:

> "The purpose of the Bill is to impose a measure of control on certain activities of estate agents with a view to affording protection to *users* of their services." (our italics)

The limited approach adopted may raise problems for both landlord and tenant. In situations in which estate agents manage property on behalf of landlords, a service charge may be payable by the tenant to the agent. Failure to maintain the services at the required standard and/or misappropriation of the payments is naturally to the disadvantage of both landlord and tenant. Additionally, a landlord may be involved in dispute with, or vulnerable to an action by, a tenant, in respect of sums paid over to an agent who has absconded. The sums involved may take various forms; if not advanced rent, they may be a deposit, returnable at the end of the letting, quarter, month, etc. Such sums might be substantial if, for example, they are in respect of furnished premises or commercial properties in Central London.

There may be deposits intended to cover dilapidations. Difficulties can arise where there are differences of opinion regarding the state of the property, and the consequent refund on surrender, or where the estate agent retains the deposit for an unreasonable length of time.

Whilst vendors and purchasers of property will normally receive protection by way of solicitor's advice, a good number of tenants and small landlords do not have this advantage. An extension of the Act to these areas was opposed by the Government in both Houses on a variety of grounds. These were: that it would involve increased expenditure; that there was a lack of consultation on these problems; that the loss of deposits of rent was a different type of problem to that intended to be resolved by this legislation; and finally because the Accommodation Agencies Act 1953 overcomes the worse abuses in this area. All of these excuses must be treated with caution. The lack of expenditure did not prevent an even greater and arguably less deserving extension of the Act to commercial properties. The lack of consultation was the result of the narrow terms of reference of the consultative document. Deposits of rent could easily have been included in the definition of clients' money (s. 12). Finally, the 1953 Act applies only premiums.

Subs. (1) (*b*)

This subsection was introduced at the time of the third reading in the Commons to close the potential loophole where the capital sum paid for the transfer of the property is in fact consideration not for the transfer of the lease but is a premium for goodwill, fixtures and fittings.

Subs. (1) (*c*)

See s. 8 of the Conveyancing & Feudal Reform (Scotland) Act 1970.

Subs. (2)

Whilst subs. (1) is concerned with legal interests in property, subs. (2) extends the definition to equitable interests by including an agreement to grant a lease.

Orders by Director General of Fair Trading

Orders prohibiting unfit persons from doing estate agency work

3.—(1) The power of the Director General of Fair Trading (in this Act referred to as "the Director") to make an order under this section with respect to any person shall not be exercisable unless the Director is satisfied that that person—

(*a*) has been convicted of—

(i) an offence involving fraud or other dishonesty or violence, or

(ii) an offence under any provision of this Act, other than section 10 (6), section 22 (3) or section 23 (4), or

(iii) any other offence which, at the time it was committed, was specified for the purposes of this section by an order made by the Secretary of State; or

(*b*) has committed discrimination in the course of estate agency work; or

(*c*) has failed to comply with any obligation imposed on him under any of sections 15 and 18 to 21 below; or

(*d*) has engaged in a practice which, in relation to estate agency work, has been declared undesirable by an order made by the Secretary of State;

and the provisions of Schedule 1 to the Act shall have effect for supplementing paragraphs (*a*) and (*b*) above.

(2) Subject to subsection (1) above, if the Director is satisfied that any person is unfit to carry on estate agency work generally or of a particular description he may make an order prohibiting that person—

(*a*) from doing any estate agency work at all; or

(*b*) from doing estate agency work of a description specified in the order;

and in determining whether a person is so unfit the Director may, in addition to taking account of any matters falling within subsection (1) above, also take account of whether, in the course of estate agency work or any other business activity, that person has engaged in any practice which involves breaches of a duty owed by virtue of any enactment, contract or rule of law and which is material to his fitness to carry on estate agency work.

(3) For the purposes of paragraphs (*c*) and (*d*) of subsection (1) above,—

(*a*) anything done by a person in the course of his employment shall be treated as done by his employer as well as by him, whether or not it was done with the employer's knowledge or approval, unless the employer shows that he took such steps as were reasonably practicable to prevent the employee from doing that act, or from doing in the course of his employment acts of that description; and

(*b*) anything done by a person as agent for another person with the authority (whether express or implied, and whether precedent or subsequent) of that person shall be treated as done by that other person as well as by him; and

(*c*) anything done by a business associate of a person shall be treated as done by that person as well, unless he can show that the act was done without his connivance or consent.

(4) In an order under this section the Director shall specify as the grounds for the order those matters falling within paragraphs (*a*) to (*d*) of subsection (1) above as to which he is satisfied and on which, accordingly, he relies to give him power to make the order.

(5) If the Director considers it appropriate, he may in an order under this section limit the scope of the prohibition imposed by the order to a particular part of or area within the United Kingdom.

(6) An order under paragraph (*a*) (iii) or paragraph (*d*) of subsection (1) above—

(*a*) shall be made by statutory instrument;

(*b*) shall be laid before Parliament after being made; and

(*c*) shall cease to have effect (without prejudice to anything previously done in reliance on the order) after the expiry of the period of twenty-eight days beginning with the date on which it was made unless within that period it has been approved by a resolution of each House of Parliament.

(7) In reckoning for the purposes of subsection (6) (*c*) above any period of twenty-eight days, no account shall be taken of any period during which Parliament is dissolved or prorogued or during which both Houses are adjourned for more than four days.

(8) A person who fails without reasonable excuse to comply with an order of the Director under this section shall be liable on conviction on indictment or on summary conviction to a fine which on summary conviction shall not exceed the statutory maximum.

DEFINITIONS

"business associate": ss. 31 (1), 33 (1).
"discrimination": Sched. 1, para. 2.
"estate agency work": ss. 1 (1), 33 (1).
"statutory maximum": s. 33 (1).

GENERAL NOTE

The Director-General is given the power to issue orders prohibiting any person from engaging in estate agency work if he considers that person to be unfit to practise on one or more of the grounds specified in the section. The prohibition may be of a general or limited nature.

The grounds are widely drafted and include conviction for crimes of violence, contravention of certain provisions of the Act, a finding of discrimination committed in the course of estate agency work, and the engaging in of any practice in relation to estate agency work which is declared by the Secretary of State to be undesirable.

The aim has been to ensure that the Director has effective control, but at the same time, a sufficient degree of flexibility when considering an agent's fitness to practice. It should be noted that the existence of one of the specified grounds may not in itself lead to prohibition. They are merely events which could trigger action by the Director.

The powers of the Director under ss. 3 and 4 may be compared with the R.I.C.S. rules of conduct, which allow that body to take any one of five courses of action:

"(a) to admonish the Member;
(b) to require the Member to give an undertaking to refrain from continuing or repeating the conduct which is found to have constituted the contravention;
(c) to reprimand the Member;
(d) to suspend the Member from membership of the Institution for such period as the Institution may determine;
(e) to expel the Member from the Institution."

Subs. (1)

"*exercisable.*" This indicates that the wrong-doings under subs. (1) (*a*) (*b*) (*c*) and (*d*) will not lead automatically to prohibition from estate agency work. It will allow the Director to set up an inquiry once he has established, to his own satisfaction, that the wrong-doing is of such a nature as to render that person unfit to practise as an estate agent.

Subs. (1) (*a*) (i)

This is also s. 25 (2) (*a*) of the Consumer Credit Act 1974. A common complaint throughout the passage of the Bill was that violence is not referrable to estate agency work. Unlike subs. (1) (*b*), these offences need not occur "in the course of estate agency work." An obvious difficulty would lie in proving that a rape (for example) took place "in the course of estate agency work." However, as it stands, this subsection grants, to the Director, the power to make a prohibition order on the basis of an estate agent's conviction for assault/battery on his wife or child.

"*an offence of violence.*" This is not defined.

Subs. (1) (*a*) (ii)

S. 10 (6) provides for a penalty for disclosure of information contrary to s. 10; s. 22 (3), a penalty for practising as an estate agent but without having reached the requisite standard of competence; s. 23 (4), a penalty for engaging in estate agency work having been adjudged bankrupt.

Subs. (1) (*a*) (iii)

See subss. (6) and (7).

Sub. (1) (*b*)

Sched. 1, para. 2 outlines the circumstances in which discrimination is deemed to have been committed for the purposes of the Act. The schedule is limited to sex discrimination under the Sex Discrimination Act 1975 and discrimination on grounds of race under the Race Relations Act 1976. The agent must have been the subject of action under these Acts before he shall be deemed to have committed discrimination for the purposes of this subsection. Therefore, the power of the Director to issue a prohibition order is dependent upon the enforcement of the anti-discrimination legislation, which has been the subject of some criticism: see Coussins J., *The Equality Report* (1976), pp. 108–115; W. B. Creighton, "Enforcing the Sex Discrimination Act" (1976) 51 I.L.J. 42; Byrne & Lovenduski, "Sex Equality and the Law," *British Journal of Law and Society,* Vol. 5, p. 148 (1978).

It follows that the agent is liable to double jeopardy in respect of any act of discrimination under the 1975 and 1976 Acts, which takes place "in the course of estate agency work." The counter argument is that the inclusion of discrimination as grounds for a prohibition order will assist the agent in resisting pressure from a vendor to discriminate, particularly in respect of race.

Subs. (1) (*c*)

S. 15 deals with interest on clients' money; s. 18 with information to clients of prospective liabilities; ss. 19 and 20 with the regulation (England) and prohibition (Scotland) of pre-contract deposits; s. 21 with transactions in which the estate agent has a personal interest.

Subs. (1) (*d*)

Various activities of estate agents which have been criticised by the general public are not controlled by the Act (see General Note to the Act). However, the regulations of the Secretary of State may be wide enough to cover these omissions. For the power to make regulations, see subss. (6) and (7).

Subs. (2)

As is noted above, the grounds in subs. (1) are merely trigger events. They may lead to an investigation by the Director, in the course of which he has the discretion to consider those matters contained in this subsection.

"*he may make an order.*" "May" indicates that even if grounds exist under both subss. (1) and (2), the Director still retains complete discretion as to whether or not an order shall be issued.

"*estate agency work at all.*" This would allow for a complete prohibition order. The fear is that such a sanction is so severe that the Director may feel reluctant to use it. However, the Director can resort to other less stringent forms of orders (subs. (2) (*b*) and s. 4).

"*of a description specified.*" This is ambiguous. It is unclear whether the description could include a geographical limitation (subs. (5)) or a prohibition relating simply to one type of activity within estate agency work (*e.g.* the handling of pre-contract deposits). The words "at all" in subs. (2) (*a*) render the latter explanation the more likely.

"*taking account of any matters.*" There is provision for the Director to be notified of various findings and convictions which may be relevant to his functions under this Act (s. 9 (5) (6)). However, the converse does not apply. The Director has no duty to report his decision to, for example, the Equal Opportunities Commission. The more significant question is whether or not there is any onus on the Director to consult with the Commission. As to the Director's duty to consult with the Secretary of State, see s. 25 (2).

"*or any other business activity.*" This is intended to allow the Director some measure of control over those persons with, *e.g.* a long history of fraud. There exists the safeguard that there must be a trigger event under subs. (1) before this could become relevant.

Subs. (3)

"*in the course of his employment.*" See note to s. 1 (3) and (5).

Subs. (4)

It is important to know the grounds upon which the Director has relied in making an order, since these may determine the date when the order will lapse (s. 5 (4) (5)).

Subs. (5)

This is presumably to allow for the different provisions applying to Scotland. For example, a limitation as to the amount of any pre-contract deposit which an agent may receive would have to specifically exclude Scotland (s. 20).

Subs. (6)

This provides for the affirmative resolution of each House of Parliament.

As to affirmative and negative resolutions, see Wade, *Administrative Law* (4th ed., 1977), p. 732.

Warning orders

4.—(1) If the Director is satisfied that—

(*a*) in the course of estate agency work any person has failed to comply with any such obligation as is referred to in section 3 (1) (*c*) above (in this section referred to as a "relevant statutory obligation") or has engaged in such a practice as is referred to in section 3 (1) (*d*) above, and

(*b*) if that person were again to fail to comply with a relevant statutory obligation or, as the case may be, were to continue to engage in that practice, the Director would consider him unfit as mentioned in subsection (2) of section 3 above and would proceed to make an order under that section,

the Director may by order notify that person that he is so satisfied.

(2) An order under this section shall state whether, in the opinion of the Director, a further failure to comply with a relevant statutory obligation or, as the case may be, continuation of the practice specified in the order would render the person to whom the order is addressed unfit to carry on estate agency work generally or estate agency work of a description specified in the order.

(3) If, after an order has been made under this section, the person to whom it is addressed fails to comply with a relevant statutory obligation or, as the case may be, engages in the practice specified in the order then, for the purposes of this Act, that fact shall be treated as conclusive evidence that he is unfit to carry on estate agency work as stated in the order in accordance with subsection (2) above; and the Director may proceed to make an order under section 3 above accordingly.

DEFINITIONS

"director": s. 33 (1).

"estate agency work": ss. 1 (1), 33 (1).

GENERAL NOTE

The Director has no power to issue warning orders in respect of a conviction under s. 3 (1) (*a*) or a finding of discrimination under s. 3 (1) (*b*). With respect to obligations under s. 3 (1) (*c*) and practices under s. 3 (1) (*d*), the Director has a discretion to warn that a future contravention of these subsections could lead to a prohibition order. The Director must be satisfied that the agent would be declared unfit to practise following any such contravention.

The idea of warning orders was introduced at the time of the Private Member's Bill, where it was described as "a shot across the bows or a warning signal" (Standing Committee C, April 26, 1978, cols. 59–60). The section was considerably redrafted before its incorporation in the Government Bill. It was intended only to issue warnings in respect of a practice contrary to s. 3 (1) (*d*). In committee it was extended to cover s. 3 (1) (*c*), but not s. 3 (1) (*a*) or (*b*). A point of distinction is that the former contains no criminal penalties whereas the latter do.

Under s. 8, both prohibition and warnings orders are recorded on a register, open to inspection by members of the public. The agent has been given no time limit within which to remedy conduct specified in the warning order prior to its registration. Therefore, the "warning signal" effectively serves as a sanction.

This is unfortunate because it is easy to envisage minor breaches which could be remedied as soon as a warning is received.

Subs. (1) (*a*)

An obligation under s. 3 (1) (*c*) is an obligation under s. 15, 18, 19, 20 or 21, and a practice under s. 3 (1) (*d*) is one declared undesirable by the Secretary of State.

Subs. (1) (*b*)

See subss. (2) and (3).

Subs. (2)

By virtue of subs. (1) (*b*) the Director has to be satisfied that a further failure to comply would render an agent wholly or partially unfit. It may be necessary to draw this to the agent's attention but the word " whether " introduces an ambiguity. One possible interpretation is that it is open to the Director to state that a further failure would not render an agent unfit. This would have two effects.

(i) to negate the purpose of a warning order.

(ii) to render subs. (3) redundant.

Subs. (3)

Once a warning order is issued, a further failure to comply with a relevant statutory obligation, or engaging again in a practice specified by virtue of s. 3 (1) (*d*), will render the agent liable to immediate prohibition. The wording is open to the following criticisms:

(i) If a warning order has been issued following the breach of a relevant statutory obligation, does the subsequent non-compliance, under subs. (3), have to be with the relevant statutory obligation? For example, a warning order is issued following an agent's non-payment of interest on clients' money (s. 15). This is remedied but shortly afterwards he fails to fully inform a client of prospective liabilities.

(ii) Ambiguity is caused by the use of the word " order " to relate to both orders made by the Secretary of State under delegated powers and orders made under ss. 3 and 4 by the Director.

(iii) If the warning order specifies a practice (s. 3 (1) (*d*)) which the agent must cease, and the agent fails to comply with a relevant statutory obligation then on a literal interpretation of the subsection, this will be treated as " conclusive evidence." However, the reverse does not apply.

The resolution of these difficulties may depend upon the format of the warning orders adopted by the Director. It seems that the Director need not be specific as to the grounds upon which he relies under s. 4 (*cf.* s. 3 (4)).

Supplementary provisions as to orders under sections 3 and 4

5.—(1) The provisions of Part I of Schedule 2 to this Act shall have effect—

(*a*) with respect to the procedure to be followed before an order is made by the Director under section 3 or section 4 above; and

(*b*) in connection with the making and coming into operation of any such order.

(2) Where an order is made by the Director under section 3 or section 4 above against a partnership, it may, if the Director thinks it appropriate, have effect also as an order against some or all of the partners individually, and in such a case the order shall so provide and shall specify the names of the partners affected by the order.

(3) Nothing in section 62 of the Sex Discrimination Act 1975, section 53 of the Race Relations Act 1976 or Article 62 of the Sex Discrimination (Northern Ireland) Order 1976 (restriction of sanctions for breaches of those Acts and that Order) shall be construed as applying to the making of an order by the Director under section 3 above.

(4) In any case where—

(*a*) an order of the Director under section 3 above specifies a conviction as a ground for the order, and

(*b*) the conviction becomes spent for the purposes of the Rehabilitation of Offenders Act 1974 or any corresponding enactment for the time being in force in Northern Ireland,

then, unless the order also specifies other grounds which remain valid, the order shall cease to have effect on the day on which the conviction becomes so spent.

(5) In any case where—

(*a*) an order of the Director under section 3 above specifies as grounds for the order the fact that the person concerned committed discrimination by reason of the existence of any such finding or notice as is referred to in paragraph 2 of Schedule 1 to this Act, and

(*b*) the period expires at the end of which, by virtue of paragraph 3 of that Schedule, the person concerned would no longer be treated for the purposes of section 3 (1) (*b*) above as having committed discrimination by reason only of that finding or notice,

then, unless the order also specifies other grounds which remain valid, the order shall cease to have effect at the end of that period.

DEFINITIONS

"Director": s. 33 (1).
"discrimination": Sched. 1, para. 2.

GENERAL NOTE

These supplementary provisions achieve four objectives:

(i) they give effect to Sched. 2;
(ii) they deal with the effect of s. 3 and orders on a partnership;
(iii) they clarify the effect of ss. 3 & 4 in relation to discrimination on the grounds of sex, race and previous convictions;
(iv) they provide for the lapsing of orders.

Subs. (1)

Pt. I of Sched. 2 deals with orders and decisions of the Director made under ss. 3, 4 and 6. By virtue of Pt. I, the Director must give notice of any proposal to any person affected. A proposal (defined in para. 1 (*b*) of the Schedule) is a proposal to make a s. 3 or 4 order or a decision under s. 6 (4) and (5). The notice given by the Director is to allow for representations which must be heard in accordance with paras. 3–5 of the Schedule. Pt. I of Sched. 2 also concerns the means by which the Director will arrive at a decision and notify a person affected.

Subs. (3)

S. 62 of the Sex Discrimination Act 1975, s. 53 of the Race Relations Act 1976 and art. 62 of the Sex Discrimination (Northern Ireland) Order 1976 provide that the contravention of any of these enactments shall incur only such sanctions as are available under the enactment breached. These provisions obviously had to be by-passed in order to give effect to the Director's powers relating to discrimination.

Subs. (4)

"*a conviction as a ground.*" A conviction can directly be a ground for an order; for example, an offence involving fraud or dishonesty or violence under s. 3 (1) (*a*) (i). However, a criminal conviction may be taken into account as part of a host of factors under s. 3 (2). In the former, the order will lapse on the day the conviction becomes spent. In the latter case, the Director must specify the other, perhaps more significant, grounds upon which he is relying when he makes the order if he does not wish the order to lapse with the conviction.

It was thought that the protection was necessary for two reasons:

(a) Some of the offences used as a ground for the prohibition order had already attracted criticism as being only questionably relevant.

(b) Other offences might simply be taken into account if material (s. 3 (2)). This could give the Director vast power unless offences lapsed.

Subs. (5)

Sched. 1, para. 3 allows for the expiry of any act of discrimination after a period of five years, and if this order is to remain valid thereafter it must be for some other stated reason.

Revocation and variation of orders under sections 3 and 4

6.—(1) On an application made to him by the person in respect of whom the Director has made an order under section 3 or section 4 above, the Director may revoke or vary the order.

(2) An application under subsection (1) above—

(*a*) shall state the reasons why the applicant considers that the order should be revoked or varied;

(*b*) in the case of an application for a variation, shall indicate the variation which the applicant seeks; and

(*c*) shall be accompanied by the prescribed fee.

(3) If the Director decides to accede to an application under subsection (1) above, he shall give notice in writing of his decision to the applicant and, upon the giving of that notice, the revocation or, as the case may be, the variation specified in the application shall take effect.

(4) The Director may decide to refuse an application under subsection (1) above—

(*a*) where it relates to an order under section 3 above, if he considers that the applicant remains unfit to carry on any estate agency work at all or, as the case may be, estate agency work of the description which is prohibited by the order; and

(*b*) where it relates to an order under section 4 above, if he considers that the applicant may again fail to comply with a relevant statutory obligation or, as the case may be, again engage in the practice specified in the order.

(5) If, on an application under subsection (1) above, the Director decides that—

(*a*) he cannot accede to the application because he considers that the applicant remains unfit to carry on any estate agency work at all in a particular part of or area within the United Kingdom or remains unfit to carry on estate agency work of a particular description (either throughout the United Kingdom or in a particular part of or area within it) or, as the case may be, remains likely to fail to comply with a relevant statutory obligation or to engage in a particular practice, but

(*b*) the order to which the application relates could, without detriment to the public, be varied in favour of the applicant,

the Director may make such a variation accordingly.

(6) The provisions of Part II of Schedule 2 to this Act shall have effect in relation to any application to the Director under subsection (1) above and the provisions of Part I of that Schedule shall have effect—

(*a*) with respect to the procedure to be followed before the Director comes to a decision under subsection (4) or subsection (5) above; and

(*b*) in connection with the making and coming into operation of such a decision.

(7) In this section " relevant statutory obligation " has the meaning assigned to it by section 4 (1) (*a*) above.

DEFINITIONS
"Director": s. 33 (1).
"estate agency work": ss. 1 (1), 33 (1).
"prescribed fee": s. 33 (1).

GENERAL NOTE

S. 6 and Sched. 2 enable the Director to vary or revoke an order made by him under ss. 3 and 4. They also make provisions for the procedures to be followed in connection with applications for revocation and variation. The section is necessary for those orders of the Director which will not automatically lapse (*i.e.* all warning orders and prohibition orders made under s. 3 (1) (*c*) and (*d*)). It also allows for the early revocation of a prohibition order under s. 3 (1) (*a*) and (*b*).

Every application for revocation gives the Director the opportunity to review the conduct of those persons who have in the past indulged in malpractice and therefore merit further surveillance. On the other hand, the procedure can be seen as unnecessarily cumbersome, and could simply be replaced by the lapsing of all orders. Unless an estate agent takes the trouble to see an order revoked, he may be tainted with it long after it has ceased to be relevant.

There is no time limit within which the Director must answer any application, but the usual administrative law remedies, in particular mandamus, are available.

Subs. (2)

The application must be in writing (s. 29 (3)).

Subs. (2) (*b*)

This is consistent with s. 3 (2) (*b*).

Subs. 2 (*c*)

The fee is prescribed by the Secretary of State and subject to the negative resolution of the House (ss. 33 and 34) (see note to s. 3 (6)).

It is envisaged that the fee will simply cover the cost of registration as with the inspection of the Register of Companies, of Business Names and the Land Registry.

Subs. (3)

See note to subs. (4).

Subs. (4)

Unlike subs. (3) there is no requirement for the refusal to be in writing. S. 29 (1) states that any notice must be in writing. The problem is whether or not a decision to refuse an application amounts to a notice under s. 29 (1). Arguably the answer must be in the affirmative otherwise there would be no onus in this Act on the Director to communicate his decision.

Subs. (5)

This is open to the criticism that it allows the Director to engage in speculation as to an estate agent's future conduct.

Subs. (6).

This is again consistent with ss. 3 (2) (*b*) and 6 (2) (*b*).

Sched. 2, Pt. II, deals with the form of applications. Sched. 2, Pt. I, outlines the procedure for the Director's handling of applications.

Appeals

7.—(1) A person who receives notice under paragraph 9 of Schedule 2 to this Act of—

(*a*) a decision of the Director to make an order in respect of him under section 3 or section 4 above, or

(*b*) a decision of the Director under subsection (4) or subsection (5) of section 6 above on an application made by him,

may appeal against the decision to the Secretary of State.

(2) On an appeal under subsection (1) above the Secretary of State may give such directions for disposing of the appeal as he thinks just, including a direction for the payment of costs or expenses by any party to the appeal.

(3) The Secretary of State shall make provision by regulations with respect to appeals under subsection (1) above—

(*a*) as to the period within which and the manner in which such appeals are to be brought;

(*b*) as to the persons by whom such appeals are to be heard on behalf of the Secretary of State;

(*c*) as to the manner in which such appeals are to be conducted;

(*d*) for taxing or otherwise settling any costs or expenses directed to be paid under subsection (2) above and for the enforcement of any such direction; and

(*e*) as to any other matter connected with such appeals;

and such regulations shall be made by statutory instrument which shall be subject to annulment in pursuance of a resolution of either House of Parliament.

(4) If the appellant is dissatisfied in point of law with a decision of the Secretary of State under this section he may appeal against that decision to the High Court, the Court of Session or a judge of the High Court in Northern Ireland.

(5) No appeal to the Court of Appeal or to the Court of Appeal in Northern Ireland shall be brought from a decision under subsection (4) above except with the leave of that Court or of the court or judge from whose decision the appeal is brought.

(6) An appeal shall lie, with the leave of the Court of Session or the House of Lords, from any decision of the Court of Session under this section, and such leave may be given on such terms as to costs or otherwise as the Court of Session or the House of Lords may determine.

DEFINITION

"Director": s. 33 (1).

GENERAL NOTE

The Secretary of State is given wide powers to provide for a system of appeal from the decision of the Director. There are similar powers contained in the Consumer Credit Act 1974, and it seems safe to assume the appeals procedure will operate in a broadly similar way (see ss. 41 and 182 of the 1974 Act and Consumer Credit Licensing (Appeals) Regulations 1976 (S.I. 1976 No. 837)). In that case appeal would lie to a body consisting of a legally qualified chairman and two assessors. Such a body would advise the Secretary of State with whom the final decision would lie. This is significant since the Secretary of State is not a tribunal within Sched. 1 to the Tribunal and Inquiries Act 1971. This has two effects:

(a) The Council on Tribunals will not be required to approve any regulations made under this section.

(b) S. 12 (1) of the 1971 Act does not apply; therefore, the Secretary of State need only give reasons following appeal to meet the requirements of the rules of natural justice (on the need to give reasons, see (Wade, *Administrative Law* (4th ed., 1977), pp. 463 *et seq.*)).

The function of the Secretary of State and of any tribunal acting under this section is clearly judicial. (See further s. 24 for the nature of the functions of the Director in reaching the initial decision.)

Subs. (1)

Sched. 2, para. 9, provides for the notification of decisions by the Director including the reasons for, and the facts which justify the decision. If the Director fails to make, or delays unduly in the making of, a decision, the position is unclear. Could this constitute an implied refusal and thus form the ground for an appeal to the Secretary of State? Alternatively, an application for judicial review would lie (see generally Wade, *Administrative Law* (4th ed., 1977), chap. 19 (Remedies for enforcing public duties). Also *R.* v. *Tower Hamlets London Borough Council, ex p. Kayne-Levenson* [1975] Q.B. 431; *R.* v. *Secretary of State for the Home Department, ex p. Phansopkar* [1976] Q.B. 606; *Sheffield Corporation* v. *Luxford* [1929] 2 K.B. 180).

Subs. (1) (*a*)

S. 3 relates to prohibition orders, s. 4 relates to warning orders.

Subs. (1) (*b*)

S. 6 (4) deals with refusal of an application for revocation or variation; s. 6 (5) deals with variation of an order made under s. 3 or 4.

Subs. (2)

Presumably the Secretary of State will give directions of a similar nature to those given by, for example, a county court registrar at a pre-trial review (see County Court Rules, Ord. 21). The Secretary of State seems to have a discretion as to the necessity of direction on any appeal. There is no provision similar to s. 1 (4) of the Consumer Credit Act 1974 which allows a direction for payment of costs to the Secretary of State to be made a rule of the High Court. The omission may give rise to problems of enforcement.

Subs. (3)

There is a tendency to use an enabling provision in one Act, and adopt it automatically in a later Act in which it is much less appropriate. The Consumer Credit Act 1974 has 193 sections and five schedules and covers a variety of interests. This made it difficult to include detailed provisions for appeal in the text of the Act. The Estate Agents Act is of limited application and contains only 36 sections and two schedules, yet the same enabling section is present. It is not even certain, for instance, whether estate agents will be represented on any tribunal formed. (See note to subs. (3) (*b*)).

"*shall make provision by regulation.*" The word "shall" was introduced to replace "may" by a Lords amendment (H.L. Vol. 399, col. 141). Other enabling provisions remain unchanged (*e.g.* s. 14 (3)). Any regulations made under this subsection will be subject to the negative resolution of either House (see note to s. 3 (6)).

Subs. (3) (*b*)

See the General Note to this section. There was a promise of consultation "with estate agents' organisations" as to the composition of the panel from which tribunal members will be drawn (H.L. Vol. 399, col. 134; see also note to s. 36).

Subs. (4)

"*appellant.*" This excludes the Director.

"*point of law.*" The courts are usually willing to interpret this provision liberally (see *Instrumatic Ltd.* v. *Supabrase Ltd.* [1969] 1 W.L.R. 519 at 521 *per* Lord Denning M.R.; *Edwards* v. *Blairstow* [1956] A.C. 14; *Ward* v. *James* [1966] 1 Q.B. 273).

Register of orders etc.

8.—(1) The Director shall establish and maintain a register on which there shall be entered particulars of every order made by him under section 3 or section 4 above and of his decision on any application for revocation or variation of such an order.

(2) The particulars referred to in subsection (1) above shall include—

(*a*) the terms of the order and of any variation of it; and

(*b*) the date on which the order or variation came into operation or is expected to come into operation or if an appeal against the decision is pending and the order or variation has in consequence not come into operation, a statement to that effect.

(3) The Director may, of his own motion or on the application of any person aggrieved, rectify the register by the addition, variation or removal of any particulars; and the provisions of Part II of Schedule 2 to this Act shall have effect in relation to an application under this subsection.

(4) If it comes to the attention of the Director that any order of which particulars appear in the register is no longer in operation, he shall remove those particulars from the register.

(5) Any person shall be entitled on payment of the prescribed fee—

(*a*) to inspect the register during such office hours as may be specified by a general notice made by the Director and to take copies of any entry, or

(*b*) to obtain from the Director a copy, certified by him to be correct, of any entry in the register.

(6) A certificate given by the Director under subsection (5) (*b*) above shall be conclusive evidence of the fact that, on the date on which the certificate was given, the particulars contained in the copy to which the certificate relates were entered on the register; and particulars of any matters required to be entered on the register which are so entered shall be evidence and, in Scotland, sufficient evidence of those matters and shall be presumed, unless the contrary is proved, to be correct.

DEFINITIONS

"Director": s. 33 (1).
"general notice": s. 33 (1).
"prescribed fee": s. 33 (1).

GENERAL NOTE

The provisions may be compared with s. 35 of the Consumer Credit Act 1974. The Director is charged with the task of establishing and maintaining a register of those orders which are made under ss. 3 and 4 as amended by ss. 5, 6 and 7. There are effectively three ways of securing the removal of an entry from the register. These are as follows:

1. By an application by an estate agent for revocation or variation under s. 6.
2. By an application by a person aggrieved under s. 8 (3).
3. By bringing the non-removal of an entry to the attention of the Director under s. 8 (4). In the final case the rectification is mandatory. In addition the Director may, of his own motion, rectify the register.

The Act is silent about whether or not a person who has suffered loss by reason of an inaccurate registration can obtain damages. A comparison with the system of land registration under the Land Registration Act 1925 is useful. Basically, the State insures all titles to land but no indemnity is payable if the applicant was guilty of lack of proper care (see s. 83 (5) (*a*) of the Land Registration Act 1925). To a large extent rectification and indemnity are complementary (see ss. 82 and 83 of the Land Registration Act 1925; but see also *Epps* v. *Esso Petroleum* [1973] 1 W.L.R. 1071; *Freer* v. *Unwins Ltd.* [1976] 2 W.L.R. 609; *Re Chowoods Registered Land* [1933] Ch. 574).

Subs. (1)

S. 3 relates to prohibition orders, s. 4 relates to warning orders.

"*revocation or variation.*" See s. 6.

The Director must register his decision on any application under s. 6 even if this is a refusal. This could be to the disadvantage of an estate agent as is shown by the following example:

Two agents each receive a warning order in 1980. Between 1980 and 1985, one agent applies annually for revocation but is refused, the other does not bother. In 1985 a member of the public applies for a certified copy of the entries against each agent (subs. (5) (*b*)). The obvious disparity in the entries will be to the disadvantage of the agent who appears to have been under the constant surveillance of the Director.

As most inspections will presumably be by obtaining a certified copy, the format of these will be of importance.

Subs. (2) (*a*)
This is consistent with s. 3 (2) (*b*) and s. 6 (2) (*b*).

Subs. (2) (*b*)
"*An appeal.*" See s. 7. This could operate largely against the agent. For example, if a prohibition order is issued against an agent in error and the agent appeals, until such time as the appeal is successful there is an entry on the register noting the prohibition order. However, the register will state that the order is not yet operative.

Subs. (3)
"*any person aggrieved.*" This is intended to cover complaints not only by agents but also by clients who claim that the details registered were inadequate. An application by an aggrieved person must be in writing and must meet any formalities specified by the Director. Failure to comply with these requirements would allow the Director to refuse to proceed with an application (Sched. 2, Pt. II).

Subs. (4)
This applies to particulars entered on the register but no longer in operation. These would include:

1. An order made under s. 3 (1) (*a*) or (*b*) which has now lapsed.
2. An order which the Director has agreed to revoke under s. 6 (1) but which still appears on the register.
3. An order which has ceased to be operative due to the quashing of a conviction on appeal (s. 9 (5)).

Subs. (5)
See notes to s. 6 (2) (*c*).

Subs. (6)
See note to subs. (4).

Information, entry and inspection

Information for the Director

9.—(1) The Director may, for the purpose of assisting him—

(*a*) to determine whether to make an order under section 3 or section 4 above, and

(*b*) in the exercise of any of his functions under sections 5, 6 and 8 above and 13 and 17 below,

by notice require any person to furnish to him such information as may be specified or described in the notice or to produce to him any documents so specified or described.

(2) A notice under this section—

(*a*) may specify the way in which and the time within which it is to be complied with and, in the case of a notice requiring the production of documents, the facilities to be afforded for making extracts, or taking copies of, the documents; and

(*b*) may be varied or revoked by a subsequent notice.

(3) Nothing in this section shall be taken to require a person who has acted as counsel or solicitor for any person to disclose any privileged communication made by or to him in that capacity.

(4) A person who—

(*a*) refuses or wilfully neglects to comply with a notice under this section, or

(*b*) in furnishing any information in compliance with such a notice, makes any statement which he knows to be false in a material particular or recklessly makes any statement which is false in a material particular, or

(*c*) with intent to deceive, produces in compliance with such a notice a document which is false in a material particular,

shall be liable on conviction on indictment or on summary conviction to a fine which, on summary conviction, shall not exceed the statutory maximum.

(5) In section 131 of the Fair Trading Act 1973 (which provides for the Director to be notified by courts of convictions and judgments which may be relevant to his functions under Part III of that Act) after the words " this Act " there shall be inserted the words " or under the Estate Agents Act 1979 ".

(6) It shall be the duty of—

(*a*) the Equal Opportunities Commission,

(*b*) the Equal Opportunities Commission for Northern Ireland, and

(*c*) the Commission for Racial Equality,

to furnish to the Director such information relating to any finding, notice, injunction or order falling within paragraph 2 of Schedule 1 to this Act as in their possession and appears to them to be relevant to the functions of the Director under this Act.

DEFINITIONS

" Director ": s. 33 (1).
" statutory maximum ": s. 33 (1).

GENERAL NOTE

The effect of this section is to enable the Director to call for information to assist him in discharging his functions under the Act. It has broad equivalents in other legislation (see ss. 7 and 166 of the Consumer Credit Act 1974, and ss. 44–66 of the Fair Trading Act 1973).

Subss. (1) *and* (2)

S. 3 deals with prohibition orders, s. 4 with warning orders.

The Director's functions under ss. 5, 6, 8, 13 and 17 are as follows:

(i) giving notices, hearing representations and notification of decisions regarding orders under ss. 3 and 4 (s. 5);

(ii) revoking or varying entries on the register (s. 6);

(iii) maintaining the register (s. 8);

(iv) prohibition of a person from holding clients' money and appointing trustees to hold and deal with that money (s. 13);

(v) granting of exemptions from insurance provisions (s. 17).

" *any person.*" This will include a body of persons corporate or unincorporate (Interpretation Act 1889, s. 19).

Subs. (3)

" *privileged communication.*" See *Jones* v. *Great Central Railway* [1910] A.C. 5; statements made by a prospective client to a solicitor attract privilege even though the solicitor does not take on the case: see *Minter* v. *Priest* [1930] A.C. 558.

Subs. (4)

" *wilfully neglects.*" In *R.* v. *Downes* (1875) 1 Q.B.D. 25, *per* Mellor J., it was said that to wilfully neglect to do something is to intentionally or purposely omit to do it. See also *Cooper* v. *Cooper* (1941) 65 C.L.R. 162 (*per* Rich C.J.): " The phrase connotes a deliberate and intentional act of a culpable nature."

Subs. (5)

Cf. s. 166 of the Consumer Credit Act 1974, and Pt. III of the Fair Trading Act 1973, *i.e.* ss. 34–43 of that Act.

" *judgments.*" This includes any orders or decrees: s. 131 (2) of the Fair Trading Act 1973.

Subs. (6)

This would appear to conflict with s. 61 of the Sex Discrimination Act 1975 and s. 52 of the Race Relations Act 1976 which have not been formally amended.

Sched. 1, para. 2, outlines the circumstances in which a person is deemed to have committed discrimination.

Restriction on disclosure of information

10.—(1) Subject to subsections (3) to (5) below, no information obtained under or by virtue of this Act about any individual shall be disclosed without his consent.

(2) Subject to subsections (3) to (5) below, no information obtained under or by virtue of this Act about any business shall be disclosed except, so long as the business continues to be carried on, with the consent of the person for the time being carrying it on.

(3) Subsections (1) and (2) above do not apply to any disclosure of information made—

(*a*) for the purpose of facilitating the performance of any functions under this Act, the Trade Descriptions Act 1968, the Fair Trading Act 1973, the Consumer Credit Act 1974 or the Restrictive Trade Practices Act 1976 of any Minister of the Crown, any Northern Ireland department, the Director or a local weights and measures authority in Great Britain, or

(*b*) in connection with the investigation of any criminal offence or for the purposes of any criminal proceedings, or

(*c*) for the purposes of any civil proceedings brought under or by virtue of this Act or any of the other enactments specified in paragraph (*a*) above.

(4) For the purpose of enabling the Director to use, in connection with his functions under this Act, information obtained by him in the exercise of functions under certain other enactments, the following amendments shall be made in provisions restricting disclosure of information, namely,—

(*a*) at the end of paragraph (*a*) of subsection (2) of section 133 of the Fair Trading Act 1973 there shall be added the words " the Estate Agents Act 1979, or ";

(*b*) in paragraph (*a*) of subsection (3) of section 174 of the Consumer Credit Act 1974 after the words " Fair Trading Act 1973 " there shall be added the words " or the Estate Agents Act 1979 "; and

(*c*) at the end of paragraph (*a*) of subsection (1) of section 41 of the Restrictive Trade Practices Act 1976 there shall be added the words " or the Estate Agents Act 1979 ".

(5) Nothing in subsections (1) and (2) above shall be construed—

(*a*) as limiting the particulars which may be entered in the register; or

(*b*) as applying to any information which has been made public as part of the register.

(6) Any person who discloses information in contravention of this section shall be liable on summary conviction to a fine not exceeding the statutory maximum and, on conviction on indictment, to imprisonment for a term not exceeding two years or to a fine or both.

DEFINITIONS

" Director ": s. 33 (1).

" statutory maximum ": s. 33 (1).

GENERAL NOTE

These provisions prohibit the disclosure of information obtained by virtue of this Act except with the consent of the person to whom the information relates, or who carries on a business to which the information relates. Exceptions are contained within the section. Disclosure of information contrary to the section is an offence (*cf.* Consumer Credit Act 1974, s. 174).

Powers of entry and inspection

11.—(1) A duly authorised officer of an enforcement authority, at all reasonable hours and on production, if required, of his credentials may—

(*a*) if he has reasonable cause to suspect that an offence has been committed under this Act, in order to ascertain whether it has been committed, enter any premises (other than premises used only as a dwelling);

(*b*) if he has reasonable cause to suspect that an offence has been committed under this Act, in order to ascertain whether it has been committed, require any person—

(i) carrying on, or employed in connection with, a business to produce any books or documents relating to it, or

(ii) having control of any information relating to a business recorded otherwise than in a legible form, to provide a document containing a legible reproduction of the whole or any part of the information;

and take copies of, or of any entry in, the books or documents;

(*c*) seize and detain any books or documents which he has reason to believe may be required as evidence in proceedings for an offence under this Act;

(*d*) for the purpose of exercising his powers under this subsection to seize books and documents, but only if and to the extent that it is reasonably necessary for securing that the provisions of this Act are duly observed, require any person having authority to do so to break open any container and, if that person does not comply, break it open himself.

(2) An officer seizing books or documents in exercise of his powers under this section shall not do so without informing the person from whom he seizes them.

(3) If and so long as any books or documents which have been seized under this section are not required as evidence in connection with proceedings which have been begun for an offence under this Act, the enforcement authority by whose officer they were seized shall afford to the person to whom the books or documents belong and to any person authorised by him in writing reasonable facilities to inspect them and to take copies of or make extracts from them.

(4) If a justice of the peace, on sworn information in writing, or, in Scotland, a sheriff or a justice of the peace, on evidence on oath,—

(*a*) is satisfied that there is reasonable ground to believe either—

(i) that any books or documents which a duly authorised officer has power to inspect under this section are on any premises and their inspection is likely to disclose evidence of the commission of an offence under this Act, or

(ii) that an offence under this Act has been, or is being or is about to be, committed on any premises; and

(*b*) is also satisfied either—

(i) that admission to the premises has been or is likely to be refused and that notice of intention to apply for a warrant under this subsection has been given to the occupier, or

(ii) that an application for admission, or the giving of such a notice, would defeat the object of the entry or that the premises are unoccupied or that the occupier is temporarily

absent and it might defeat the object of the entry to wait for his return,

the justice or, as the case may be, the sheriff may by warrant under his hand, which shall continue in force for a period of one month, authorise an officer of an enforcement authority to enter the premises, by force if need be.

(5) An officer entering premises by virtue of this section may take such other persons and equipment with him as he thinks necessary, and on leaving premises entered by virtue of a warrant under subsection (4) above shall, if the premises are unoccupied or the occupier is temporarily absent, leave them as effectively secured against trespassers as he found them.

(6) The Secretary of State may by regulations provide that, in cases specified in the regulations, an officer of a local weights and measures authority is not to be taken to be duly authorised for the purposes of this section unless he is authorised by the Director.

(7) The power to make regulations under subsection (6) above shall be exercisable by statutory instrument which shall be subject to annulment in pursuance of a resolution of either House of Parliament.

(8) Nothing in this section shall be taken to require a person who has acted as counsel or solicitor for any person to produce a document containing a privileged communication made by or to him in that capacity or authorises the seizing of any such document in his possession.

DEFINITION

"enforcement authority": ss. 26 (1), 33 (1).

GENERAL NOTE

Examples of enforcement powers similar to those contained within this section are to be found in the Merchandise Marks Act 1887; the Weights and Measures Act 1963; the Trade Descriptions Act 1968; the Consumer Credit Act 1974; and the Consumer Safety Act 1978. See also the Finance Act 1976, Sched. 6.

The section would appear to work as follows:

If a duly authorised officer has a reasonable cause to suspect that an offence has been committed, then he may exercise his powers under subs. (1) (*a*) and (*b*). He has the power, therefore, to enter the premises and require documents to be produced from which he may make copies.

A duly authorised officer has the power to seize and detain books and documents (subs. (1) (*c*)) if he has reason to believe that these may be required as evidence in proceedings under the Act. Proceedings need not have commenced (*cf.* subs. (3): "proceedings which have been begun"); in order to assist with this seizure and detention, he can require containers to be broken open or, on a refusal, open the containers himself (subs. (1) (*a*)).

The agent may refuse entry or resist the exercise of the powers under subs. (1) (*b*). In such a case, the officer may obtain a warrant (subs. (4)). More seriously, provided the officer has a reasonable cause to suspect an offence has been committed, an agent, refusing entry, could be charged with obstruction under s. 27 (1).

Subs. (1)

"*duly authorised officer.*" See note to s. 27.

Subs. (1) (*a*)

"*reasonable cause to suspect.*" This subsection differs from the equivalent sections in the Trade Descriptions Act 1968 (s. 28 (1) (*a*)) and the Consumer Credit Act 1974 (s. 162 (1) (*a*)). Both of these sections allow entry as a matter of routine, and without suspicion. The change in this Act is due to a Lords' amendment pressed on the basis that an "innuendo of suspicion . . . is caused by a visit from a Trading Standards Officer" (H.L. Vol. 399, cols. 881, 893). It was also said that this would allow "fishing expeditions" on the part of the enforcement authorities (H.L. Vol. 399, col. 872).

The answer to the first of these arguments is that the role of the Trading Standards Officer is largely advisory. For example, in 1978 in South Yorkshire, 40,000 complaints resulted in 9,000 investigations but only 101 prosecutions. In fact, from the layman's point of view, a greater innuendo will now be induced by a visit to the agents of a duly authorised officer, since he must have a reasonable suspicion of an offence.

The answer to the second argument, that as it stood the Bill allowed "fishing expeditions," is as follows:

As the clause stood in the original Bill there was a power to enter but nothing more. It barred any possibility that an officer entering the estate agents' office, in his official capacity, could be accused of trespass, because the implied licence given to the public to enter the premises did not extend to him. It also allowed for the easy enforcement of certain parts of the Act (see for example s. 16 (4) (*a*) which demands that certain information be displayed at the place of business).

"*any offence under this Act.*" This will presumably exclude ss. 15 and 18 to 21, breaches of which may lead to service of prohibition orders (s. 3) but carry no criminal penalty. This reasoning is reinforced by s. 3 (1) (*c*) which refers to these sections as "obligations" (*cf.* s. 162 (1) (*a*) of the Consumer Credit Act 1974 which refers to "breaches" of the Act, thus including purely civil breaches).

"*any premises.*" These are not restricted to estate agency premises (see note to subs. (1) (*b*)). The definition adopted here would give powers of entry and inspection in respect of the residential part of mixed residential/business accommodation. The point does not seem to have arisen under s. 162 (1) (*a*) of the Consumer Credit Act 1974.

Subs. 1 (*b*)

"*reasonable cause to suspect.*" See note to subs. (1) (*a*).

"*an offence . . . under this Act.*" See note to subs. (1) (*a*).

"*carrying on or employed in connection with a business.*" Because "employed" does not refer to employed under a contract of service (*cf.* s. 1 (5) (*c*)), and because "business" is not restricted to an estate agency business, the following are persons who may be required to produce books or documents:

(i) The estate agent's cleaner.
(ii) The accountant auditing the estate agent's books.
(iii) The cleaner of the above accountant.

This is reinforced by the wording "any premises" (subs. (1) (*a*); see also note to subs. (2)).

Subs. (1) (*c*)

There is no compensation section (*cf.* Consumer Credit Act 1974, s. 163).

Subs. (1) (*d*)

There is a conflict in the wording of this subsection. It is difficult to see how the powers can be exercised for the purpose of subs. (1) (*c*), and at the same time, to the extent necessary for securing the observance of the provisions of the Act. This is because subs. (1) (*c*) is restricted to seizure in order to obtain evidence of an offence, but many of the provisions of the Act are not offences as such (*e.g.* relevant statutory obligations).

Given that this section envisages powers of entry and seizure in the absence of the occupier (subss. (4) and (5)), it seems strange that the only power to break open containers is on the non-compliance of "any person having authority." Since this last phrase is not defined, could it include persons other than the occupier (also undefined) (subs. (4)) ? Even if this is so, problems will arise when the premises are empty, and the authorised officer enters with his "equipment" (subs. (5)) following a warrant. Unless the warrant grants the power to search, and subs. (4) does not allow for this, the powers of the officer are restricted to those under subs. (1) (*c*) and (*d*). Therefore, strictly, the officer would not be able to break open containers in empty premises because he has not received the non-compliance of "any person having authority." Can non-compliance be implied or presumed from conduct (*cf.* subs. (4) (*b*) (i)) ?

Subs. (2)

"*any premises.*" See note to subs. (1) (*b*).

Subss. (4) and (5) clearly recognise the possibility of a person, whose books or documents are seized, not being present at the time (see note to subs. (1) (*d*)). Therefore, although this subsection is not specific on the point, the officer ought to inform a person following seizure. However, if the books are seized from, *e.g.* an accountant, there is no requirement to inform the estate agent.

Subs. (3)

This is in order that the estate agent's business may continue during the investigation (*cf.* Finance Act 1976, Sched. 6, para. 200 (5), which allows reasonable access to seized documents " for the continued conduct of the business ").

See also General Note to this section.

Subs. (4)

This subsection provides for warrants to be issued to authorised officers authorising entry into any premises (see note to subs. (1) (*b*)), by force if necessary. However, the officer must be able to meet one of the conditions in both subs. (1) (*a*) and (*b*).

Subs. (4) (*a*)

This introduces the new wording " reasonable ground to believe " (and not *suspect* as within subs. (1) (*a*) and (*b*))

" *Writing.*" See the Interpretation Act 1889, s. 20.

Subs. (4) (*a*) (i)

The belief must be that books are on the premises and " likely to disclose evidence." This is not practically different to subs. (1) (*b*) (*supra*) but it must also be coupled with a condition under subs. (4) (*b*).

Subs. (4) (*a*) (ii)

This would include an offence under s. 27 (obstruction). Therefore, once obstruction is committed, a condition under subs. (4) (*a*) is immediately satisfied.

Subs. (4) (*b*)

See note to subs. (1) (*d*) as to unoccupied premises.

Subs. (5)

The Act provides no remedy for a breach of the requirement to leave premises secured. An agent suffering loss as a result of a breach could claim damages for breach of statutory duty.

Subs. (6)

Perhaps in acknowledgment of the wide powers given in this section, it is envisaged that only certain officers in the Weights and Measures Authorities may be " authorised " for the purposes of this Act (*cf.* s. 162 (5) of the Consumer Credit Act 1974).

Subs. (7)

Regulations under subs. (6) will be subject to the negative resolution of either House. See note to s. 3 (6).

Subs. (8)

See note to s. 9 (3).

Clients' money and accounts

Meaning of " clients' money " etc.

12.—(1) In this Act " clients' money ", in relation to a person engaged in estate agency work, means any money received by him in the course of that work which is a contract or pre-contract deposit—

(*a*) in respect of the acquisition of an interest in land in the United Kingdom, or (*b*) in respect of a connected contract,

whether that money is held or received by him as agent, bailee, stakeholder or in any other capacity.

(2) In this Act "contract deposit" means any sum paid by a purchaser—

(*a*) which in whole or in part is, or is intended to form part of, the consideration for acquiring such an interest as is referred to in subsection (1) (*a*) above or for a connected contract; and

(*b*) which is paid by him at or after the time at which he acquires the interest or enters into an enforceable contract to acquire it.

(3) In this Act "pre-contract deposit" means any sum paid by any person—

(*a*) in whole or in part as an earnest of his intention to acquire such an interest as is referred to in subsection (1) (*a*) above, or

(*b*) in whole or in part towards meeting any liability of his in respect of the consideration for the acquisition of such an interest which will arise if he acquires or enters into an enforceable contract to acquire the interest, or

(*c*) in respect of a connected contract,

and which is paid by him at a time before he either acquires the interest or enters into an enforceable contract to acquire it.

(4) In this Act "connected contract", in relation to the acquisition of an interest in land, means a contract which is conditional upon such an acquisition or upon entering into an enforceable contract for such an acquisition (whether or not it is also conditional on other matters).

DEFINITIONS

"estate agency work": ss. 1 (1), 33 (1).
"interest in land": s. 2.

GENERAL NOTE

The purpose of the section is to define "clients' money." This it does in terms of "contract" and "pre-contract" deposits (as defined in the section) received by a person engaged in estate agency work. A "contract deposit" (see s. 12 (2)) will include any sum which is paid to the agent at or after exchange of contracts. The sum must form, or be intended to form, part of the purchase price, or be paid in respect of a "connected contract" (s. 12 (4)). A "pre-contract deposit" is intended to refer to deposits given by a prospective purchaser as a sign of good faith until exchange of contracts (s. 12 (3) (*a*)). In practice this leaves the agent with several options open to him; he can take the property off the market; tell subsequent enquirers that negotiations are in progress with another prospective purchaser; or finally, remain silent on the point and engage either in a contract race, or gazumping or both. The Act is silent on the desirability of these practices but the Secretary of State has the power under s. 3 to declare them undesirable. As with "contract deposits," a "pre-contract deposit" can include money paid in respect of a "connected contract" (s. 12 (3) (*c*)).

The main criticism of the section has been forcibly expressed in the following terms: "Once one establishes the principle that money held temporarily by an estate agent on behalf of his client should be protected, it is difficult to see what justification there can be for limiting that protection to money defined as a deposit" (Standing Committee E, col. 111). Most estate agents also act as rent collectors and managers of property. Some are agents for building societies and insurance companies. As such, moneys are paid to them which are not within s. 12. However, the general law of agency will apply in all of these instances. Therefore, in most cases of the agent's default or insolvency, the burden will fall upon the landlord, building society or insurance company (*Scott* v. *Surman* (1742) Willes 400; *Re Strachan. ex p. Cooke* (1876) 4 Ch.D. 123; *Taylor* v. *Plumer* (1815) 3 M. & S. 562. See also the Factors Act 1889, s. 12 (2). This distinction was excusable when the Bill was purely a consumer protection measure, but given the extension of the Act to cover commercial property this is no longer justifiable. In addition, it is doubtful whether the laymen will understand the distinction.

Subs. (1)

"*agent.*" An estate agent may take clients' money as "agent for the vendor." The vendor is entitled to call for the money to be paid over to him pending the outcome of the negotiations.

"*bailee.*" The phrase "as agent, bailee, stakeholder or in any other capacity" can be found in the Solicitors' Accounts Rules 1967, r. 2. It is doubtful if "bailee" is an appropriate inclusion in this section because bailment is the delivery or transfer of possession of a chattel, usually a personal chattel.

"*stakeholder.*" If a person engaged in estate agency work receives clients' money as stakeholder he must hold the money pending the outcome of negotiations. Until exchange of contracts the prospective purchaser may withdraw and the pre-contract deposit must be returned to him at his request. After exchange of contracts, clients' money will be held in accordance with the terms of that contract. Thus, the money does not "belong" to the vendor when held by a "stakeholder" (see *Barrington* v. *Lee* [1972] 1 Q.B. 326, C.A., and s. 13 (1) (*b*)).

Subs. (1) (*b*)

See subs. (4) and s. 33 (1).

Subs. (2)

See s. 21 (4).

Subs. (2) (*a*)

"*in whole or in part.*" There are five possible interpretations of this phrase:

(1) that the whole of the contract deposit is to form part of the consideration for acquiring an interest in land;

(2) that the whole of the contract deposit is to form part of the consideration in respect of a connected contract;

(3) that part of the contract deposit is to form part of the consideration for acquiring an interest in land and the remainder is to be treated as part of the consideration in respect of a connected contract;

(4) as in (3) (above) but that the remainder is to be treated as surplus to requirements (as to which, see below);

(5) that part of the contract deposit is to form part of the consideration for a connected contract and the remainder is again surplus.

Presumably, in (4) and (5) above the agent will hold the surplus money on trust for the purchaser (s. 13 (1) (*a*)). However, this presumption presupposes that the surplus money is treated as contract deposit.

"*connected contract.*" See subs. (4) and s. 33 (1).

Subs. (2) (*b*)

"*at or after the time at which he acquires the interest.*" It is difficult to imagine a situation in which the purchaser of property will pay a contract deposit to an estate agent at the time of completion of the purchase. Furthermore, it is impossible to envisage circumstances in which the purchaser would pay a contract deposit to an estate agent *after* completion of the purchase.

Subs. (3)

See s. 21 (4).

The subsection is designed to cover money paid to the agent which is:

(i) a sign of good faith (see general note to s. 12);

(ii) intended to become a contract deposit under subs. (2) (*a*); and

(iii) concerned with a connected contract.

"*any person.*" Whilst subs. (2) is clearly limited to the purchaser/vendor/estate agent triangle, this subsection is obviously much wider in application. The intention is to cover situations in which, *e.g.* the father of the prospective purchaser pays over a pre-contract deposit on behalf of his son. However, subs. (3) (*b*) is inconsistent for "he" (*i.e.* the father in our example) is never likely to acquire an interest.

"*in whole or in part.*" See notes to subs. (2) (*a*).

"*at a time before he . . . acquires the interest.*" If a purchaser has exchanged contracts (*i.e.* entered into "an enforceable contract to acquire" an interest in land) then any such money paid will be governed by subs. (2). Therefore, these words would seem superfluous.

Subs. (4)

The subsection is intended to cover the purchase or intended purchase of personal chattels from the vendor. However, because mortgage or insurance premiums are not specifically included within the definition of "clients' money" (see general note to s. 12) it is possible that such sums could be protected by virtue of this subsection. The argument is that if such sums are paid over to the agent by a prospective purchaser, then that payment is in respect of a connected contract.

Clients' money held on trust or as agent

13.—(1) It is hereby declared that clients' money received by any person in the course of estate agency work in England, Wales or Northern Ireland—

(*a*) is held by him on trust for the person who is entitled to call for it to be paid over to him or to be paid on his direction or to have it otherwise credited to him, or

(*b*) if it is received by him as stakeholder, is held by him on trust for the person who may become so entitled on the occurrence of the event against which the money is held.

(2) It is hereby declared that clients' money received by any person in the course of estate agency work in Scotland is held by him as agent for the person who is entitled to call for it to be paid over to him or to be paid on his direction or to have it otherwise credited to him.

(3) The provisions of sections 14 and 15 below as to the investment of clients' money, the keeping of accounts and records and accounting for interest shall have effect in place of the corresponding duties which would be owed by a person holding clients' money as trustee, or in Scotland as agent, under the general law.

(4) Where an order of the Director under section 3 above has the effect of prohibiting a person from holding clients' money the order may contain provision—

(*a*) appointing another person as trustee, or in Scotland as agent, in place of the person to whom the order relates to hold and deal with clients' money held by that person when the order comes into effect; and

(*b*) requiring the expenses and such reasonable remuneration of the new trustee or agent as may be specified in the order to be paid by the person to whom the order relates or, if the order so provides, out of the clients' money;

but nothing in this subsection shall affect the power conferred by section 41 of the Trustee Act 1925 or section 40 of the Trustee Act (Northern Ireland) 1958 to appoint a new trustee to hold clients' money.

(5) For the avoidance of doubt it is hereby declared that the fact that any person has or may have a lien on clients' money held by him does not affect the operation of this section and also that nothing in this section shall prevent such a lien from being given effect.

DEFINITIONS

"clients' money": ss. 13 (1), 33 (1).

"Director": s. 33 (1).

"estate agency work": ss. 33 (1), 1 (1).

GENERAL NOTE

The effect of the section is to ensure that clients' money is deemed to be trust money, as soon as it is received by the agent. As a result the money will not form part of the agent's assets on his insolvency. This is a similar provision to that governing money in a solicitor's client account. (See *Re a Solicitor* [1952] Ch. 328; *cf. Brown* v. *I.R.C.* [1965] A.C. 244). At common law, if an agent became bankrupt whilst in possession of clients' money, either the purchaser or vendor had to bear the loss (see *Goding* v. *Frazer* [1967] 1 W.L.R. 286 (Sachs J.); *Barrington* v. *Lee* [1972] 1 Q.B. 326, C.A.; *Potters* v. *Loppert* [1973] Ch. 399; *Sorrell* v. *Finch* [1976] 2 W.L.R. 833, H.L.). The section also ensures that if the agent should default in paying over clients' money, the beneficiary will have available the remedy of tracing subject to the usual restraints (see Hanbury and Maudsley, *Modern Equity* (10th ed.), pp. 563–576).

The general law of trusts is thus imported into the Act with the exception that ss. 14 and 15 of the Act are to be read in place of the general trust law relating to the investment of clients' money, the keeping of accounts and records and accounting for interest (subs. (3)). Subs. (4) is subject to s. 41 of the Trustee Act 1925 and s. 40 of the Trustee Act (Northern Ireland) 1958. These latter two sections contain the powers of the court to appoint new trustees.

The above applies to England, Wales and Northern Ireland. The section contains separate provisions for Scotland. In Scotland, clients' money received by an estate agent is to be held by him as agent and not as trustee.

Subs. (1)

Subs. (1) (*a*) is intended to cover money received by an agent in the capacities outlined in s. 12 (1), except that subs. (1) (*b*) applies specifically to the estate agent holding money as stakeholder. However, in the last resort clients' money will only be protected in so far as the remedy of tracing is available to the beneficiary (see General Note to the section).

Additionally, it will still be necessary for the courts to settle disputes between vendor and purchaser as to who is entitled to the "trust money" (see note to s. 12 (1)).

Subs. (2).

"*in Scotland.*" See note to s. 9.

Subs. (3)

S. 14 relates to the opening and keeping of clients' accounts, the keeping of account and records relating to clients' money and the auditing of clients' accounts.

S. 15 deals with interest on clients' money.

Subs. (4)

S. 3 relates to prohibition orders.

The subsection gives the Director the power to appoint a new trustee or agent in place of the prohibited estate agent/trustee. In addition, the Director may, in the prohibition order, authorise payment of a salary and/or expenses to be made either by the prohibited estate agent or out of clients' money. Under s. 3 (*b*), a failure to comply with a prohibition order can result in a criminal penalty. From the point of view of the beneficiary (*i.e.* vendor or purchaser), the Director's power to order payment of the new trustee's salary and/or expenses out of clients' money may seem unfair. However, the vendor is presumably in no worse a position than having to pay the original estate agent's commission. The same is not true for the purchaser.

Keeping of client accounts

14.—(1) Subject to such provision as may be made by accounts regulations, every person who receives clients' money in the course of estate agency work shall, without delay, pay the money into a client account maintained by him or by a person in whose employment he is.

(2) In this Act a "client account" means a current or deposit account which—

(*a*) is with an institution authorised for the purposes of this section, and

(*b*) is in the name of a person who is or has been engaged in estate agency work; and

(*c*) contains in its title the word "client".

(3) The Secretary of State may make provision by regulations (in this section referred to as "accounts regulations") as to the opening and keeping of client accounts, the keeping of accounts and records relating to clients' money and the auditing of those accounts; and such regulations shall be made by statutory instrument which shall be subject to annulment in pursuance of a resolution of either House of Parliament.

(4) As to the opening and keeping of client accounts, accounts regulations may in particular specify—

(*a*) the institutions which are authorised for the purposes of this section;

(*b*) any persons or classes of persons to whom, or any circumstances in which, the obligation imposed by subsection (1) above does not apply;

(*c*) any circumstances in which money other than clients' money may be paid into a client account; and

(*d*) the occasions on which, and the persons to whom, money held in a client account may be paid out.

(5) As to the auditing of accounts relating to clients' money, accounts regulations may in particular make provision—

(*a*) requiring such accounts to be drawn up in respect of specified accounting periods and to be audited by a qualified auditor within a specified time after the end of each such period;

(*b*) requiring the auditor to report whether in his opinion the requirements of this Act and of the accounts regulations have been complied with or have been substantially complied with;

(*c*) as to the matters to which such a report is to relate and the circumstances in which a report of substantial compliance may be given; and

(*d*) requiring a person who maintains a client account to produce on demand to a duly authorised officer of an enforcement authority the latest auditor's report.

(6) Subject to subsection (7) below, "qualified auditor" in subsection (5) (*a*) above means—

(*a*) a person who is a member of one or more bodies of accountants established in the United Kingdom and for the time being recognised by the Secretary of State for the purposes of section 161 (1) (*a*) of the Companies Act 1948 or, in Northern Ireland, recognised by the Department of Commerce for Northern Ireland for the purposes of section 155 (1) (*a*) of the Companies Act (Northern Ireland) 1960; or

(*b*) a person who is for the time being authorised by the Secretary of State under section 161 (1) (*b*) of the Companies Act 1948 or, in Northern Ireland, by the Department of Commerce for Ireland under section 155 (1) (*b*) of the Companies Act (Northern Ireland) 1960; or

(*c*) in the case of a client account maintained by a company, a person who is qualified to audit the accounts of the company by virtue of section 13 (1) of the Companies Act 1967 (unqualified auditors of former exempt private companies); or

(*d*) a Scottish firm of which all the members are qualified auditors within paragraph (*a*) to (*c*) above.

(7) A person is not a qualified auditor for the purposes of subsection (5) (*a*) above if, in the case of a client account maintained by a company, he is disqualified from auditing the accounts of the company by subsection (2), subsection (3) or subsection (4) of either section 161 of the Companies Act 1948 or section 155 of the Companies Act (Northern Ireland) 1960.

(8) A person who—

(*a*) contravenes any provision of this Act or of accounts regulations as to the manner in which clients' money is to be dealt with or accounts and records relating to such money are to be kept, or

(*b*) fails to produce an auditor's report when required to do so by accounts regulations,

shall be liable on summary conviction to a fine not exceeding £500.

DEFINITIONS

"clients' money": ss. 33 (1), 12 (1).
"enforcement authority": s. 26 (1).
"estate agency work": ss. 33 (1), 1 (1).

GENERAL NOTE

The general requirement of this section is that clients' money (s. 12) received by a person engaged in estate agency work is to be held in a clients' account (s. 13 (1)). There is a similar duty imposed on solicitors who are required to pay money received by them on account of their clients into a clients' account (see the Solicitors' Accounts Rules 1969). The section enables the Secretary of State to make provision, by regulation, as to the manner in which such accounts are to be opened, maintained and audited. The section is open to criticism on the grounds that a suitable working model is to be found in the system governing solicitors (see the Solicitors' Accounts Rules 1969 and the Accountants' Report Rules 1967) which could have been incorporated. In addition the Department of Prices and Consumer Protection had ample time to do this between the original Private Member's Bill and the Government Bill.

S. 15 (4) provides for the contracting out of accounts regulations.

Subs. (1)

"*accounts regulations.*" S. 14 (3).

"*without delay.*" Presumably this means on the day the money is received or on the next banking business day.

Subs. (2)

This can be compared with the definition of "client account" to be found in r. 2 of the Solicitors' Accounts Rules 1967. It will be appreciated that under r. 2 the account must be held with a bank and, for the purpose of r. 2, a bank does not include a building society or any other association which is not registered under the appropriate Act (see subss. (2) (*a*) and (4) (*a*) and also note to s. 15 (4)).

Subs. (2) (*a*)

"*institution authorised.*" See subs. (4) (*a*).

Subs. (2) (*c*)

"*client.*" No definition is contained in the Act. For the purposes of this section, the definition used in r. 2 of the Solicitors' Accounts Rules 1967 could be adapted and utilised: "'Client' shall mean any person on whose account a solicitor holds or receives client's money."

Subs. (3)

The power of the Secretary of State to prescribe regulations is subject to the negative resolution of either House (see note to s. 3 (6)).

"*opening and keeping of clients' accounts.*" See subs. (4).

"*client accounts.*" See subs. (2).

"*the keeping of accounts and records relating to clients' money.*" Although subss. (4) and (5) detail the type of matter which the accounts regulations may specify, they are limited to the opening and keeping of clients' accounts (subs. (4)) and the auditing of accounts (subs. (5)). No guidelines are given as to the particulars which may be specified, by regulation, in respect of the manner in which the accounts and records, relating to clients' money, are to be kept. The regulations ought to require: books of account to be kept written up to date; the maintenance of either a clients' cash book or, as a minimum, a clients' column of a cash book; finally, again as a minimum requirement, the keeping of a clients' ledger or a clients' column of a ledger. Every person engaged in estate agency work ought to be required to preserve, for a specific period of time, all accounts, books, ledgers, and records kept by him.

"*auditing of those accounts.*" See subs. (5).

Subs. (4)

"*accounts regulations.*" See subs. (3).

"*may.*" There is no onus on the Secretary of State to specify in the regulations any of the particulars referred to in this subsection.

Subs. (4) (*a*)

"*institutions which are authorised.*" See note to subs. (2), and s. 15 (4).

Estate agents often assist a prospective purchaser in finding a mortgage. Consequently, an estate agents' connection with a building society attracts business. It would be advantageous, therefore, if building societies were designated authorised institutions. No doubt when designating an institution "authorised," the Secretary of State will take into account the reliability of the organisation, its financial standing, the way it conducts business, the immediate availability of current or deposit account money.

Subs. (4) (*b*)

This is intended to cover groups who are already required (either by statute or by their own internal, professional regulations) to maintain client accounts. The obvious example is accountants.

Subs. (4) (*c*)

For example, estate agent's money which may have to be paid into a client account in order to open or maintain the account; money to replace any sum which has been withdrawn from the client account in contravention of the Act.

Subs. (4) (*d*)

For example, money inadvertently paid into client account; the declaration of commission (*cf.* r. 7 (*a*) (ii) and (iv) of the Solicitors' Accounts Rules 1967); payment to a third party at the client's request.

Subs. (5)

"*accounts regulations.*" See subs. (3).

"*money.*" See note to subs. (4).

The Accountants' Report Rules 1967 which govern the auditing of solicitors' accounts may be used as a guideline.

"*specific accounting periods.*" For example, between November 1 and the following October 31 (see the Accountants' Report Rules 1967).

Subs. (5) (*a*)

"*qualified auditor.*" See subs. (6).

Subs. (5) (*b*)

"*auditor.*" This is no doubt intended to mean "qualified auditor" (see subs. (6)).

"*to report.*" The wording used in the Private Member's Bill of 1977 was "to certify." The amendment was made because the latter phrase was inappropriate in the context of an expression of opinion.

Interest on clients' money

15.—(1) Accounts regulations may make provision for requiring a person who has received any clients' money to account, in such cases as may be prescribed by the regulations, to the person who is or becomes entitled to the money for the interest which was, or could have been, earned by putting the money in a separate deposit account at an institution authorised for the purposes of section 14 above.

(2) The cases in which a person may be required by accounts regulations to account for interest as mentioned in subsection (1) above may be defined, amongst other things, by reference to the amount of the sum held or received by him or the period for which it is likely to be retained, or both.

(3) Except as provided by accounts regulations and subject to subsection (4) below, a person who maintains a client account in which he keeps clients' money generally shall not be liable to account to any person for interest received by him on money in that account.

(4) Nothing in this section or in accounts regulations shall affect any arrangement in writing, whenever made, between a person engaged in estate agency work and any other person as to the application of, or of any interest on, money in which that other person has or may have an interest.

(5) Failure of any person to comply with any provision of accounts regulations made by virtue of this section may be taken into account by the Director in accordance with section 3 (1) (*c*) above and may form the basis of a civil claim for interest which was or should have been earned on clients' money but shall not render that person liable to any criminal penalty.

(6) In this section " accounts regulations " has the same meaning as in section 14 above.

DEFINITIONS

" client account ": ss. 14 (2), 33 (1).
" clients' money ": ss. 12 (1), 33 (1).
" Director ": s. 33 (1).

GENERAL NOTE

The section, which is not mandatory, states that accounts regulations may require an estate agent to account for the interest on any clients' money held by him (subs. (1)).

It is a corollary to the declaration in s. 13 that clients' money received by any person in the course of estate agency work is trust money. At common law, it was held that the liability of an estate agent who, as stakeholder, received money in respect of a pre-contract deposit, was founded on contract or quasi-contract and not on trust principles (see *Potters* v. *Loppert* [1973] Ch. 399, *per* Pennycuick V.-C.).

The Secretary of State is given the power by accounts regulations to make provision for the payment of interest. Any such regulations will be subject to a written arrangement between the parties (subs. (4)). A failure to comply with the regulations will not give rise to criminal liability (unlike a failure under s. 14). The plaintiff will have recourse to the civil law courts.

The Solicitors' Accounts (Deposit Interest) Rules 1965 provide a useful model.

***Subs.* (1)**

" *accounts regulations.*" Subs. (6).

" *may.*" The making of regulations under the section is not mandatory.

" *to the person who is or becomes entitled to the money.*" This wording ensures that whether the estate agent receives money as stakeholder, agent, bailee or in any other capacity he will still be covered by the accounts regulations (see note to s. 12 (1)); compare r. 2 of the Solicitors' Accounts (Deposit Interest) Rules 1965 which provides for the payment of interest to "the client." When a person holds money as a stakeholder under general law, the stake money does not belong to anybody until the happening of the deciding event. Thus, the solicitor holding money as stakeholder could keep the interest earned upon it as neither s. 8 of the Solicitors Act 1965, nor the Solicitors' Account (Deposit Interest) Rules 1965 applied to it.

" *which was or could have been.*" The agent will not be able to avoid the operation of the section by claiming that he had failed to put the money in the requisite deposit account.

"*separate deposit account.*" See notes to s. 14. The phrase is not defined in the section; presumably the requirements of s. 14 (2) will be implicitly incorporated. The word "separate" indicates that the account should be further designated by reference to the identity of the client or matter concerned.

"*institution authorised.*" See notes to subs. (2).

Subs. (2)

"*accounts regulations.*" See subs. (6). The subsection is not mandatory but the overall requirement ought to be the maintenance of an equitable balance as between the amount and the known time-factor so as to ensure fairness to the person entitled. For example, a sum in excess of £1,000 might call for payment of interest to the person entitled to it, even though it is held for a short period, *e.g.* one month. On the other hand £200 held for two years might also call for payment of interest.

Subs. (3)

"*accounts regulations.*" See subs. (6). This ensures that, except as provided by the accounts regulations, an estate agent is entitled to retain personally interest on clients' money placed generally in a client's account.

Subs. (4)

"*accounts regulations.*" See subs. (6). This provides for the contracting out of accounts regulations (see general note to s. 14).

Subs. (5)

This provides an exception to s. 14 (8).

Insurance cover for clients' money

16.—(1) Subject to the provisions of this section, a person may not accept clients' money in the course of estate agency work unless there are in force authorised arrangements under which, in the event of his failing to account for such money to the person entitled to it, his liability will be made good by another.

(2) The Secretary of State may by regulations made by statutory instrument, which shall be subject to annulment in pursuance of a resolution of either House of Parliament,—

(*a*) specify any persons or classes of persons to whom subsection (1) above does not apply;

(*b*) specify arrangements which are authorised for the purposes of this section including arrangements to which an enforcement authority nominated for the purpose by the Secretary of State or any other person so nominated is a party;

(*c*) specify the terms and conditions upon which any payment is to be made under such arrangements and any circumstances in which the right to any such payment may be excluded or modified;

(*d*) provide that any limit on the amount of any such payment is to be not less than a specified amount;

(*e*) require a person providing authorised arrangements covering any person carrying on estate agency work to issue a certificate in a form specified in the regulations certifying that arrangements complying with the regulations have been made with respect to that person; and

(*f*) prescribe any matter required to be prescribed for the purposes of subsection (4) below.

(3) Every guarantee entered into by a person (in this subsection referred to as "the insurer") who provides authorised arrangements covering another person (in this subsection referred to as "the agent") carrying on estate agency work shall enure for the benefit of every person from whom the agent has received clients' money as if—

(a) the guarantee were contained in a contract made by the insurer with every such person; and

(b) except in Scotland, that contract were under seal; and

(c) where the guarantee is given by two or more insurers, they had bound themselves jointly and severally.

(4) No person who carries on estate agency work may describe himself as an " estate agent " or so use any name or in any way hold himself out as to indicate or reasonably be understood to indicate that he is carrying on a business in the course of which he is prepared to act as a broker in the acquisition or disposal of interests in land unless, in such manner as may be prescribed,—

(a) there is displayed at his place of business, and

(b) there is included in any relevant document issued or displayed in connection with his business,

any prescribed information relating to arrangements authorised for the purposes of this section.

(5) For the purposes of subsection (4) above,—

(a) any business premises at which a person carries on estate agency work and to which the public has access is a place of business of his; and

(b) " relevant document " means any advertisement, notice or other written material which might reasonably induce any person to use the services of another in connection with the acquisition or disposal of an interest in land.

(6) A person who fails to comply with any provision of subsection (1) or subsection (4) above or of regulations under subsection (2) above which is binding on him shall be liable on conviction on indictment or on summary conviction to a fine which, on summary conviction, shall not exceed the statutory maximum.

DEFINITIONS

" clients' money ": ss. 12 (1), 33 (1).
" enforcement authority ": ss. 26 (1), 33 (1).
" estate agency work ": ss. 1 (1), 33 (1).
" interest in land ": s. 2.
" statutory maximum ": s. 33 (1).

GENERAL NOTE

The section implements one of the two alternative proposals originally envisaged as methods of providing an indemnity against an estate agent's failure to account for clients' money (see *The Regulation of Estate Agency: A Consultative Document*). Under the section, an estate agent is prohibited from accepting clients' money unless he has the protection of an authorised indemnity bond. The insurance will cover fraud and dishonesty. There is no need to ensure cover against bankruptcy because clients' money is deemed trust money and not available as part of the bankrupt's assets (see note to s. 13). The alternative to guarantee bonds was the establishment of a compensation fund, to which all estate agents would be required to contribute as a condition to carrying on business. The objections to the latter scheme are that, in the absence of a single body governing estate agents, the operation of such a fund would be an additional burden on the government. In addition, the amount of the fund would have to be frequently reviewed and the estate agent's contribution to it would probably lead, directly, to an increase in his charges.

The section is another example of power to legislate being delegated to the Secretary of State. Although he is not obliged to, the Secretary of State has the power, by regulations, to recognise and authorise various forms of insurance arrangements, including the laying down of a minimum premium (s. 16 (1) (b) (c) and (d)). He may, also, specifically exempt certain estate agents from the insurance requirements.

Subs. (1)

"*authorised arrangements.*" See subs. (2) (*b*).

"*the person entitled to it.*" See notes to s. 15 (1). Any estate agent breaching this subsection will be criminally liable (subs. (6)).

Subs. (2)

This subsection contains the list of matters about which the Secretary of State may regulate. The word "may" ensures that the list is not exhaustive and indicates that the Secretary of State has a complete discretion. The power of the Secretary of State to prescribe regulations is subject to the negative resolution of either House (see note to s. 3 (6)).

Subs. (2) (*a*)

See notes to s. 17. The purpose of this subsection is to enable the Secretary of State to grant an exemption to those estate agents who, by reason of their religious beliefs, are unable to be involved in any form of compulsory insurance. There is a similar provision in s. 12 (4) (*h*) of the Insurance Brokers (Registration) Act 1977. There is no provision for reimbursing a person who has lost money as a result of an uninsured estate agent's default.

Subs. (2) (*d*)

The Department of Prices and Consumer Protection had originally tentatively suggested the sum of £25,000, with the power to vary the amount as property values, and consequently deposits, increase (*The Regulation of Estate Agency*: *A Consultative Document*, para. 25). However, this figure would represent only (for example) 25 deposits of £1,000 or 10 deposits of £2,500.

Subs. (2) (*e*)

"*authorised arrangements.*" See subs. (2) (*b*).

A certificate of insurance may be issued and, possibly, displayed at the estate agent's office (see subs. (4) and s. 11 as to powers of entry for purposes of inspection).

Subs. (3)

"*authorised arrangements.*" See subs. (2) (*b*).

"*has received clients' money.*" The subsection is intended to ensure that the privity of contract rule shall not be a bar to a person who has given clients' money to a defaulting estate agent, being able to recover under the contract of insurance between the estate agent and the insurer (see also subs. (3) (*a*)). The wording indicates that the benefit of the insurance policy is limited to a person who has paid clients' money to the agent. Such a person may not, however, be entitled to receive the money. An example would be: a purchaser pays a contract deposit of £2,000 to the estate agent as stakeholder (see note to s. 12 (1)). The determining event is to be completion. After completion the estate agent fraudulently absconds with the money. At common law and under s. 13 (1) (6), the person entitled to receive the money is the vendor. However, under s. 16 (3) the purchaser alone has the benefit of any insurance policy. In these circumstances the vendor is not aided by the Act at all, but will have to rely either on suing the purchaser at common law or the estate agent in equity.

Subs. (3) (*b*)

The exclusion of Scotland is because the English law concept of "contract under seal" is not known to the law of Scotland.

Subs. (3) (*c*)

"*person.*" See note to s. 9 (1) (*b*).

Subs. (4)

"*carries on.*" "The phrase 'carrying on' implies a repetition or series of acts" (*per* Brett L.J., *Smith* v. *Anderson* (1880) 15 Ch.D. 247; see *Re Government's Stock Investment Co.* (1891) 60 L.J.Ch. 47; *Re Siddall* (1885) 29 Ch.D. 1; *Crowther* v. *Thorley* (1884) 50 L.T. 43; *Re Thomas* (1885) 14 Q.B.D. 379; *England* v. *Webb* (1898) A.C. 758).

"*reasonably understood to indicate.*" "The Lord Chief Justice told the jury that . . . if reasonably meant anything else than in good faith, it meant, 'according to his reason,' as contradistinguished from 'caprice' . . . The direction of the Lord Chief Justice was right" (*Booth* v. *Clive* (1851) 10 C.B. 827, at pp. 834, 837).

"*carrying on a business in the course of which.*" The business need not be an estate agency business as such. Thus an accountant, stockbroker or any other businessman not specifically excluded by s. 1 would be subject to the requirements of the subsection (but see note to "carries on" above). Presumably the, for example, accountant would have to either engage in estate agency work or indicate that he proposed to so engage on more than one occasion before he is caught by the subsection (for a definition of "business," see 38 *Halsbury's Laws* (3rd ed.), pp. 10, 11; *Rolls* v. *Miller* (1884) 27 Ch.D. 71, C.A., *per* Lindley L.J. at p. 88; *Re Griffin, ex p. Board of Trade* (1890) 60 L.J.Q.B. 235, C.A., *per* Lord Esher M.R. at p. 237; *Re Williams' Will Trusts* [1953] Ch. 138, *per* Danckwerts J. at pp. 141, 142; *Abernethie* v. *Kleiman Ltd.* [1970] 1 Q.B. 10, C.A., *per* Widgery L.J. at p. 19) (see also s. 192 (3) (*c*), Sched. 4, para. 36, to the Consumer Credit Act 1974 and notes to s. 1 (3)).

"*prepared to act.*" See note to "carrying on a business" above.

"*broker.*" See 1 *Halsbury's Laws* (4th ed.), p. 173; *Milford* v. *Hughes* (1846) 16 M. & W. 174, *per* Alderson B. at p. 177. (See also "Broker for Sale," 34 *Halsbury's Laws* (3rd ed.), p. 27).

"*prescribed information.*" See subs. (2) (*f*).

"*arrangement authorised.*" See subs. (2) (*b*).

Subs. (4) (*a*)

"*place of business.*" See subs. (5) (*a*).

Subs. (4) (*b*)

"*relevant document.*" See subs. (5) (*b*)

Subs. (5) (*a*)

"*business premises.*" See definition adopted in s. 202, Pt. VIII, Chap. II of the Income and Corporation Taxes Act 1970.

Subs. (6)

See notes to subs. (1).

Exemptions from section 16

17.—(1) If, on an application made to him in that behalf, the Director considers that a person engaged in estate agency work may, without loss of adequate protection to consumers, be exempted from all or any of the provisions of subsections (1) of section 16 above or of regulations under subsection (2) of that section, he may issue to that person a certificate of exemption under this section.

(2) An application under subsection (1) above—

(*a*) shall state the reasons why the applicant considers that he should be granted a certificate of exemption; and

(*b*) shall be accompanied by the prescribed fee.

(3) A certificate of exemption under this section—

(*a*) may impose conditions of exemption on the person to whom it is issued;

(*b*) may be issued to have effect for a period specified in the certificate or without limit of time.

(4) If and so long as—

(*a*) a certificate of exemption has effect, and

(*b*) the person to whom it is issued complies with any conditions of exemption specified in the certificate,

that person shall be exempt, to the extent so specified, from the provisions of subsection (1) of section 16 above and of any regulations made under subsection (2) of that section.

(5) If the Director decides to refuse an application under subsection (1) above he shall give the applicant notice of his decision and of the reasons for it, including any facts which in his opinion justify the decision.

(6) If a person who made an application under subsection (1) above is aggrieved by a decision of the Director—

(*a*) to refuse his application, or

(*b*) to grant him a certificate of exemption subject to conditions,

he may appeal against the decision to the Secretary of State; and subsections (2) to (6) of section 7 above shall apply to such an appeal as they apply to an appeal under that section.

(7) A person who fails to comply with any condition of exemption specified in a current certificate of exemption issued to him shall be liable on conviction on indictment or on summary conviction to a fine which, on summary conviction, shall not exceed the statutory maximum.

DEFINITIONS

"Director": s. 33 (1).
"estate agency work": ss. 1 (1), 33 (1).
"prescribed fee": s. 33 (1).
"statutory maximum": s. 33 (1).

GENERAL NOTE

Under s. 16 (2) (*a*) the Secretary of State may specify any persons or classes of persons who are exempted from the insurance requirement laid down in s. 16 (1). S. 17 provides a course of action for those people who do not have the benefit of the s. 16 (2) (*a*) exemption. Such persons may apply to the Director-General for a certificate of exemption. If the Director is satisfied (and the matter is in his absolute discretion) that exemption can be given without loss to the consumer, then he will grant the certificate. The exemption may be absolute or limited (subs. 3).

Subs. (1)

S. 16 (1) relates to insurance cover for clients' money; s. 16 (2) sets out the matters which may be specified in the Secretary of State's regulations.

"*an application made to him in that behalf.*" Presumably, the application will be in writing, although this is not specified. It would seem from the wording that anybody can make an application on behalf of an estate agent, but see subs. (2) (*a*).

"*a person.*" See notes to s. 9 (1).

"*without loss of adequate protection to consumers.*" It is difficult to envisage the circumstances in which an estate agent can satisfy the Director-General that he has protected consumers against his own fraud or against his absconding with their money. "Consumers" is not defined in the Act. Is it reasonable to suppose, after the extension to cover both residential and commercial properties (see note to s. 2 and General Note), that everybody, including a large business organisation, is a consumer for the purposes of the Act?

Subs. (2) (*c*)

See note to subs. (1).

Subs. (3) (*a*)

"*the person.*" See note to s. 9 (1).

Subs. (4)

"*the person.*" See note to s. 9 (1).

Subs. (5)

The onus on the Director is mandatory but the Director need not specify all the factors which he took into account or which came to his attention.

Subs. (6)

S. 7 (2) deals with the Secretary of State's power to give directions; s. 7 (3) relates to the Secretary of State's power to make provision by regulation with respect to appeals; s. 7 (4) to (6) relate to appeals from the decision of the Secretary of State.

"*a person.*" See note to s. 9 (1).

Subs. (7)

"*a person.*" See note to s. 9 (1).

Regulation of other aspects of estate agency work

Information to clients of prospective liabilities

18.—(1) Subject to subsection (2) below, before any person (in this section referred to as " the client ") enters into a contract with another (in this section referred to as " the agent ") under which the agent will engage in estate agency work on behalf of the client, the agent shall give the client—

(*a*) the information specified in subsection (2) below; and

(*b*) any additional information which may be prescribed under subsection (4) below.

(2) The following is the information to be given under subsection (1) (*a*) above—

(*a*) particulars of the circumstances in which the client will become liable to pay remuneration to the agent for carrying out estate agency work;

(*b*) particulars of the amount of the agent's remuneration for carrying out estate agency work or, if that amount is not ascertainable at the time the information is given, particulars of the manner in which the remuneration will be calculated;

(*c*) particulars of any payments which do not form part of the agent's remuneration for carrying out estate agency work or a contract or pre-contract deposit but which, under the contract referred to in subsection (1) above, will or may in certain circumstances be payable by the client to the agent or any other person and particulars of the circumstances in which any such payments will become payable; and

(*d*) particulars of the amount of any payment falling within paragraph (*c*) above or, if that amount is not ascertainable at the time the information is given, an estimate of that amount together with particulars of the manner in which it will be calculated.

(3) If, at any time after the client and the agent have entered into such a contract as is referred to in subsection (1) above, the parties are agreed that the terms of the contract should be varied so far as they relate to the carrying out of estate agency work or any payment falling within subsection (2) (*c*) above, the agent shall give the client details of any changes which, at the time the statement is given, fall to be made in the information which was given to the client under subsection (1) above before the contract was entered into.

(4) The Secretary of State may by regulations—

(*a*) prescribe for the purposes of subsection (1) (*b*) above additional information relating to any estate agency work to be performed under the contract; and

(*b*) make provision with respect to the time and the manner in which the obligation of the agent under subsection (1) or subsection (3) above is to be performed;

and the power to make regulations under this subsection shall be exercisable by statutory instrument which shall be subject to annulment in pursuance of a a resolution of either House of Parliament.

(5) If any person—

(*a*) fails to comply with the obligation under subsection (1) above with respect to a contract or with any provision of regulations under subsection (4) above relating to that obligation, or

(*b*) fails to comply with the obligation under subsection (3) above with respect to any variation of a contract or with any provision of regulations under subsection (4) above relating to that obligation,

the contract or, as the case may be, the variation of it shall not be enforceable by him except pursuant to an order of the court under subsection (6) below.

(6) If, in a case where subsection (5) above applies in relation to a contract or a variation of a contract, the agent concerned makes an application to the court for the enforcement of the contract or, as the case may be, of a contract as varied by the variation,—

(*a*) the court shall dismiss the application if, but only if, it considers it just to do so having regard to prejudice caused to the client by the agent's failure to comply with his obligation and the degree of culpability for the failure; and

(*b*) where the court does not dismiss the application, it may nevertheless order that any sum payable by the client under the contract or, as the case may be, under the contract as varied shall be reduced or discharged so as to compensate the client for prejudice suffered as a result of the agent's failure to comply with his obligation.

(7) In this section—

(*a*) references to the enforcement of a contract or variation include the withholding of money in pursuance of a lien for money alleged to be due under the contract or as a result of the variation; and

(*b*) "the court" means any court having jurisdiction to hear and determine matters arising out of the contract.

DEFINITIONS

"contract deposit": ss. 12 (2), 33 (1).
"estate agency work": ss. 1 (1), 33 (1).
"pre-contract deposit": ss. 12 (3), 33 (1).

GENERAL NOTE

The intention of these requirements is to ensure that an estate agent discloses to a client full details of the circumstances, particulars and amount of any payments to be made. This should be done before the contract is entered into, and all payments for which the prospective purchaser will become liable must be disclosed. The section was described at the time of the second reading in the Commons as "the price display part of the Bill" (H.C. Vol. 958, col. 626). Failure to comply with these requirements could result in the contract being unenforceable by the estate agent. Thus the sanction for non-compliance lies with the civil and not the criminal courts.

Subs. (1)

Having avoided, with great determination, any definition of either "client" or "agent" throughout the Act, the parliamentary draftsmen eventually succumbed. The results are that under subs. (1), a prospective purchaser may become a "client," for example, by consulting an estate agent and asking him to find suitable property.

The estate agent will have to disclose any prospective liability to the purchaser.

"*person.*" See note to s. 9 (1).

Subs. (2)

"*person.*" See note to s. 9 (1).

Broadly these requirements are in line with the suggestions of the Law Reform Committee's paper "*The Regulation of Estate Agency*" commenting on the Consultative Document of the Department of Prices and Consumer Protection. That suggested that the Act might "govern the terms of the estate agent's contract with his client, the vendor, by requiring clear statements in the contract on such matters as the time when the commission is due, whether commission is payable if the vendor himself finds a purchaser, and whether there are extra charges for such things as advertising. We think, however, that the level of the agent's remuneration should not be fixed."

It should be noted that under subs. (2) (*b*), it is necessary to give particulars of the manner in which the remuneration will be calculated, but in subs. (2) (*d*), as well as this, an account must be given of any other payments not forming part of the agent's remuneration. This would seem to be anomalous.

Subs. (4)

As subs. (2) seems to be specific and comprehensive this subsection appears to be unnecessary, and also because the powers could be widely interpreted and, for example, could be used to limit estate agents' fees (Standing Committee E, cols. 126–128). The regulations are subject to negative resolution of either House (see note to s. 3 (6)).

Subs. (5)

"*person.*" See note to s. 9 (1).

"*fails to comply with the obligation.*" See note to s. 27 (1) below.

Subs. (6)

"*just.*" "The expression 'just' . . . must mean that which is right and fitting with regard to public interests." See *Re an application under Solicitors Act 1843* (1899) 80 L.T. 720, 722, *per* Wills J. concerning appeal against non-issue of practising certificate (see the Solicitors Act 1957, s. 13).

"*prejudice suffered.*" See generally the Sale of Food and Drugs Act 1875 in which prejudice to the purchaser has been held to include not merely pecuniary loss or injury but simply prejudice suffered by a customer in receiving without his knowledge, an article other than that demanded (see *Hoyle* v. *Hitchman* (1879) 4 Q.B. 233).

Subs. (7)

"*lien.*" See note to s. 13 (5).

Regulation of pre-contract deposits outside Scotland

19.—(1) No person may, in the course of estate agency work in England, Wales or Northern Ireland, seek from any other person (in this section referred to as a "prospective purchaser") who wishes to acquire an interest in land in the United Kingdom, a payment which, if made, would constitute a pre-contract deposit in excess of the prescribed limit.

(2) If, in the course of estate agency work, any person receives from a prospective purchaser a pre-contract deposit which exceeds the prescribed limit, so much of that deposit as exceeds the prescribed limit shall forthwith be either repaid to the prospective purchaser or paid to such other person as the prospective purchaser may direct.

(3) In relation to a prospective purchaser, references in subsections (1) and (2) above to a pre-contract deposit shall be treated as references to the aggregate of all the payments which constitute pre-contract deposits in relation to his proposed acquisition of a particular interest in land in the United Kingdom.

(4) In this section " the prescribed limit " means such limit as the Secretary of State may by regulations prescribe; and such a limit may be so prescribed either as as a specific amount or as a percentage or fraction of a price or other amount determined in any particular case in accordance with the regulations.

(5) The power to make regulations under this section shall be exercisable by statutory instrument which shall be subject to annulment in pursuance of a resolution of either House of Parliament.

(6) Failure by any person to comply with subsection (1) or subsection (2) above may be taken into account by the Director in accordance with section 3 (1) (*c*) above but shall not render that person liable to any criminal penalty nor constitute a ground for any civil claim, other than a claim for the recovery of such an excess as is referred to in subsection (2) above.

(7) This section does not form part of the law of Scotland.

DEFINITIONS

" Director ": s. 33 (1).
" estate agency work ": ss. 1 (1), 33 (1).
" interest in land ": s. 2.
" pre-contract deposit ": ss. 12 (3), 33 (1).

GENERAL NOTE

According to the Consultative Document on " the Regulation of Estate Agency," the Department of Prices and Consumer Protection considered prohibiting estate agents from holding deposits but rejected the idea. A pre-contract deposit is a useful tool for the estate agent in so much as a prospective purchaser who withdraws from a transaction usually will inform the estate agent immediately if he wishes to regain a deposit. In fact the prohibition suggested above could have created more difficulties than it solved. Unless the acceptance of pre-contract deposits was banned altogether, it could have led to the vendor himself demanding sums of money. Also, a prohibition would have been difficult to enforce particularly in situations of excessive demand on the house market. In such circumstances other abuses, such as contract-racing, could have appeared.

The Consultative Document therefore suggested the alternative of an indemnity insurance scheme and, initially, it was not intended to regulate pre-contract deposits. The section was only introduced when it was realised that it might be impossible to find adequate insurance cover unless there was some guaranteed limit on pre-contract deposits. There was an assurance in the Committees of both Houses that the Secretary of State had no plans to make regulations under this section unless it became vital in order to secure adequate insurance (Standing Committee E, col. 129, H.L. Vol. 399, cols. 923–924).

The estate agent in England, Wales and Northern Ireland is prohibited from seeking or receiving a pre-contract deposit in the limited circumstances outlined in s. 21 (4).

Subs. (1)

" person." See note to s. 9 (1).

" in England, Wales, or Northern Ireland." The problem arises both here and in s. 20 as to what amounts to, *e.g.* " estate agency work in Scotland." It is submitted that since " estate agency work " is " things done . . . pursuant to instructions," if the instructions are given in Scotland then what follows is " estate agency work " in Scotland. It matters not whether the land is in England or Scotland.

Subs. (2)

" such other person." *Cf.* the wording of s. 13 (1) (2).

Subs. (3)

Because the definition in s. 12 (3) of pre-contract deposit covers " any sum paid . . . in whole or in part," this section aims to fill the loophole that various sums could be taken in respect of the same property all of which are pre-contract deposits but none of which is above the prescribed limit.

Subs. (5)

See general note to this section. Regulations are subject to negative resolution of either House (see also note to s. 3 (6)).

Subs. (6)

Subs. (3) (1) (*c*) introduces the concept of a relevant statutory obligation upon which the Director may base a s. 3 or 4 order.

Subs. (7)

See note to s. 20.

Prohibition of pre-contract deposits in Scotland

20.—(1) No person may, in the course of estate agency work in Scotland, seek or accept from any person (in this section referred to as a " prospective purchaser ") who wishes to acquire an interest in land in the United Kingdom a payment which, if made, would constitute a pre-contract deposit or, as the case may be, which constitutes such a deposit.

(2) If, in the course of estate agency work in Scotland, any person receives from a prospective purchaser a payment which constitutes a pre-contract deposit, it shall forthwith be either repaid to the prospective purchaser or paid to such person as the prospective purchaser shall direct.

(3) Failure by any person to comply with subsection (1) or subsection (2) above may be taken into account by the Director in accordance with section 3 (1) (*c*) above but shall not render that person liable to any criminal penalty nor constitute a ground for any civil claim, other than a claim under subsection (2) above for the recovery of the pre-contract deposit.

(4) This section forms part of the law of Scotland only.

General Note

The position in Scotland is referred to in s. 1 (2) (*a*). Solicitors in Scotland not only undertake the work of estate agents, but in many cases hold themselves out as " estate agents." Independent firms of estate agents handle a relatively small proportion of sales of heritage (immovable property) in Scotland.

Under Scottish law, a contract for the sale of heritage must be in writing and probative of both parties. However, this normally takes the form of missives (letters of offer and acceptance), so that there is a concluded contract at a stage roughly equivalent to that at which property in England would be described as " sold subject to contract." Consequently the sale of heritage is a much more straightforward matter in Scotland. Estate agency work may consist simply of placing advertisements, receiving offers to purchase, and, where necessary, dispatching the offer to a solicitor for acceptance.

Solicitors do not normally enter into formal contracts with clients when undertaking estate agency work. They have come to regard it as a preliminary to conveyancing. However, the Law Society of Scotland sanctions a fee between 1 and 1½ per cent. of the sale price where a conveyancing scale fee is also to be charged, and up to 2½ per cent. in other cases.

The exclusion of practising solicitors or persons employed by them (s. 1 (2) (*a*)) means in effect that a very high proportion of estate agents in Scotland are not affected by this Act. The significance of this cannot be fully ascertained until the regulations to be made under this Act are compared with those which regulate the professional activities of Scottish solicitors. It may be noted that they do not at present labour under legal obligations such as those contained in ss. 18 and 21 of this Act.

In the light of this, a concluded bargain for the sale of heritage is reached at an early stage. Money paid before conclusion of missives is rare, although it is the practice of some local authorities in placing local authority housing on the market to accept a small good faith deposit which then gives the purchaser a short time to arrange finance.

Subs. (1)

See note to s. 19 (1) on words " in England, Wales, or Northern Ireland."

Transactions in which an estate agent has a personal interest

21.—(1) A person who is engaged in estate agency work (in this section referred to as an " estate agent ") and has a personal interest in any land shall not enter into negotiations with any person with respect to the acquisition or disposal by that person of any interest in that land until the estate agent has disclosed to that person the nature and extent of his personal interest in it.

(2) In any case where the result of a proposed disposal of an interest in land or of such a proposed disposal and other transactions would be that an estate agent would have a personal interest in that land, the estate agent shall not enter into negotiations with any person with respect to the proposed disposal until he has disclosed to that person the nature and extent of that personal interest.

(3) Subsections (1) and (2) above apply where an estate agent is negotiating on his own behalf as well as he is negotiating in the course of estate agency work.

(4) An estate agent may not seek or receive a contract or pre-contract deposit in respect of the acquisition or proposed acquisition of—

(*a*) a personal interest of his in land in the United Kingdom; or

(*b*) any other interest in any such land in which he has a personal interest.

(5) For the purposes of this section, an estate agent has a personal interest in land if—

(*a*) he has a beneficial interest in the land or in the proceeds of sale of any interest in it; or

(*b*) he knows or might reasonably be expected to know that any of the following persons has such a beneficial interest, namely,—

(i) his employer or principal, or

(ii) any employee or agent of his, or

(iii) any associate of his or of any person mentioned in sub-paragraphs (i) or (ii) above.

(6) Failure by an estate agent to comply with any of the preceding provisions of this section may be taken into account by the Director in accordance with section 3 (1) (*c*) above but shall not render the estate agent liable to any criminal penalty nor constitute a ground for any civil claim.

DEFINITIONS

" associate ": s. 32.
" contract deposit ": ss. 12 (2), 33 (1).
" Director ": s. 33 (1).
" estate agency work ": ss. 1 (1), 33 (1).
" interest in land ": s. 2.
" pre-contract deposit ": ss. 12 (3), 33 (1).

GENERAL NOTE

This requires an estate agent to declare a personal interest in respect of any property for which he is attempting to secure the disposal or acquisition. " Personal interest " is defined to include the interest of an associate, and of an employer or employee. In particular, this is an attempt to curb the abuse of a person ostensibly acting as an agent on behalf of an undisclosed principal and buying property cheaply, to sell at a substantial profit at a later date. This reflects the original consumer protection philosophy of the Act (see General Note) and is a simple enough provision, allowing the purchaser to obtain an independent valuation, or take his business elsewhere.

Subs. (1)

As noted above, the common abuse in failing to disclose a personal interest is when the estate agent is secretly purchasing a property on his own behalf. However, the section applies to interests in land in which the agent already has a personal interest. This must be disclosed to a person acquiring the property. It is not easy to envisage the likely abuse on the part of the estate agent in such a situation. In addition, an estate agent with a personal interest must disclose this to another person before he enters into negotiations for the " disposal by that person " of the land. It seems unlikely that a person could sell land in which, unknown to him, the agent had an interest. However, due to the wide definition of " personal interest " this is by no means impossible. What is less clear is the type of abuse anticipated in such a situation.

" *person.*" See note to s. 9 (1). This section would extend to the sale of office premises belonging to a firm of estate agents.

Subs. (2)

This covers the situation referred to in the General Note to this section. It is submitted that the word " proposed " is supernumerary.

Subs. (4)

See General Note to this section.

Subs. (6)

This renders a failure to comply with this section a breach of a " relevant statutory obligation " (see ss. 3 and 4).

Standards of competence

22.—(1) The Secretary of State may by regulations made by statutory instrument make provision for ensuring that persons engaged in estate agency work satisfy minimum standards of competence.

(2) If the Secretary of State exercises his power to make regulations under subsection (1) above, he shall in the regulations prescribe a degree of practical experience which is to be taken as evidence of competence and, without prejudice to the generality of subsection (1) above, the regulations may, in addition,—

(*a*) prescribe professional or academic qualifications which shall also be taken to be evidence of competence;

(*b*) designate any body of persons as a body which may itself specify professional qualifications the holding of which is to be taken as evidence of competence;

(*c*) make provision for and in connection with the establishment of a body having power to examine and inquire into the competence of persons engaged or professing to engage in estate agency work; and

(*d*) delegate to a body established as mentioned in paragraph (*c*) above powers of the Secretary of State with respect to the matters referred to in paragraph (*a*) above;

and any reference in the following provisions of this section to a person who has attained the required standard of competence is a reference to a person who has that degree of practical experience which, in accordance with the regulations, is to be taken as evidence of competence or, where the regulations so provide, holds such qualifications or otherwise fulfils such conditions as, in accordance with the regulations, are to be taken to be evidence of competence.

(3) After the day appointed for the coming into force of this subsection,—

(*a*) no individual may engage in estate agency work on his own account unless he has attained the required standard of competence;

(*b*) no member of a partnership may engage in estate agency work on the partnership's behalf unless such number of the partners as may be prescribed have attained the required standard of competence; and (*c*) no body corporate or unincorporated association may engage in estate agency work unless such numbers and descriptions of the officers, members or employees as may be prescribed have attained the required standard of competence;

and any person who contravenes this subsection shall be liable on conviction on indictment or on summary conviction to a fine which, on summary conviction, shall not exceed the statutory maximum.

(4) In subsection (3) above "prescribed" means prescribed by the Secretary of State by order made by statutory instrument, which shall be subject to annulment in pursuance of a resolution of either House of Parliament.

(5) No regulations shall be made under this section unless a draft of them has been laid before Parliament and approved by a resolution of each House.

DEFINITIONS

"estate agency work": ss. 1 (1), 33 (1).
"statutory maximum": s. 33 (1).
"unincorporated association": s. 33 (1).

GENERAL NOTE

This was one of the more controversial clauses in the Bill. The section enables the Secretary of State to make provision by regulation to ensure that there is a minimum standard of competence which all estate agents must meet. However, because in the past professional or academic qualifications have been unnecessary, there is provision for the Secretary of State to prescribe a degree of practical experience which can be taken as evidence of competence. Therefore, although not a licensing measure, the full use of the powers under this section could lead to a restriction upon entry into estate agency work which hitherto has not existed. It is not difficult to see the advantages to be gained from adopting a minimum standard. These include:

(i) the economy as compared with a licensing system;
(ii) the fact that if a professional body screens entrants and possibly exercises its own sanctions (including expulsion), the workload of the Director-General is lightened;
(iii) the existence of a minimum standard ought to facilitate the provision of indemnity insurance now necessary (s. 16);
(iv) certain provisions of the Act will, themselves, demand a minimum standard of competence on the part of estate agents (*e.g.* client accounts and related duties).

Against this, fears were expressed in committee (Standing Committee E, col. 131) that this section might lead to a monopoly, and it was pointed out in debate (H.C. Vol. 958, cols. 620–621) that estate agents' charges were well below those in most other countries of the western world. These fears are probably not well-grounded; it seems that whatever the system adopted, it will be flexible, and probably prescribe various differing criteria to establish competence. It was recognised in committee that there may be estate agents who do not wish to join a professional body, and the then Secretary of State seemed quite prepared to allow for this (Standing Committee E, col. 132).

It may be some time before the powers under this section are used. The Minister in the Commons said of the regulations, "they are not even a twinkle in the draftsman's or parliamentary counsel's eye. The power is included partly because the Bill is intended to endure for, I hope, several decades" (Standing Committee E, col. 135). Moreover, a Government spokesman in the Lords said, "the Government are not wedded to the idea of imposing standards of competence at all," and later, "the Government see no reason to impose any standards unless and until the need for them is apparent" (H.L. Vol. 399, cols. 925–926).

Subs. (1)

See note to subs. (3). Note that the competence is for "estate agency work" which may or may not include matters involving expertise (*e.g.* surveying or valuing; see note to s. 1 (1)).

Subs. (2)

This would seem to make it mandatory for the Secretary of State to prescribe a degree of experience which is to be "taken as evidence of competence." However, there would seem to be complete discretion as to the degree of experience prescribed, although any regulations made are subject to affirmative resolution of each House (subs. 5).

The words "in addition" cause some confusion. There are three possible meanings to the subsection. They are:

(i) that the use of "in addition" means that practical experience will always be required and therafter, at the discretion of the regulations, the provisions of paras. (*a*)–(*d*) may have to be met;

(ii) that, as above, practical experience will be required but professional or academic requirements may "also" be demanded "in addition," under para. (*d*). However, this would not apply to the requirements of paras. (*b*)–(*d*). The word "itself" in para (*b*), for example, indicates that the requirement of para. (*b*) will be sufficient without practical experience;

(iii) that the words "in addition" merely mean "as well as" or even "instead of," and the requirements of paras. (*a*)–(*d*) may all be seen as an alternative to practical experience.

It is submitted that the last explanation is correct. It is reinforced by the use of the word "or" in the latter part of the section. Moreover, in time the regulations may lay down academic qualifications. If these had to be held "in addition" to practical experience, it would defeat the aim of the section which is to ensure that long-standing estate agents with good practical experience do not suffer. It would also mean that a qualification could never be sufficient in itself.

Subs. (3)

"*day appointed.*" See s. 36.

Subss. (4) *and* (5)

See note to s. 3 (6). See also General Note to this section.

Bankrupts not to engage in estate agency work

23.—(1) An individual who is adjudged bankrupt after the day appointed for the coming into force of this section or, in Scotland, whose estate is sequestrated after that day shall not engage in estate agency work of any description except as an employee of another person.

(2) The prohibition imposed on an individual by subsection (1) above shall cease to have effect if and when—

(*a*) the adjudication of bankruptcy against him is annulled, or, in Scotland, the sequestration of his estate is recalled; or

(*b*) he obtains his discharge.

(3) The reference in subsection (1) above to employment of an individual by another person does not include employment of him by a body corporate of which he is a director or controller.

(4) If a person engages in estate agency work in contravention of subsection (1) above he shall be liable on conviction on indictment or on summary conviction to a fine which on summary conviction shall not exceed the statutory maximum.

Definitions

"controller": ss. 31 (5), 33 (1)

"estate agency work": ss. 1 (1), 33 (1).

"statutory maximum": s. 33 (1)

"the day appointed for the coming into force of this section": s. 36.

General Note

This section prohibits bankrupts engaging in estate agency work except as employees.

Subs. (1)

"*An individual.*" The subsection does not apply to companies registered under the Companies Act 1948. Under existing law the consequences of a compulsory or creditors' voluntary liquidation are that the company must cease to carry on business except for the purposes of beneficial winding up.

"*adjudged bankrupt.*" See Bankruptcy Act 1914, s. 26.

"*person.*" See note to s. 9 (1).

Subs. (2) (*a*)

See ss. 21 (2) and 29 of the Bankruptcy Act 1914 for annulling the adjudication.

Subs. (2) (*b*)

An individual who is adjudged bankrupt can be discharged on his own application (s. 26 of the Bankruptcy Act 1914); by court order (s. 7 of the Insolvency Act 1976); or on the application of the official receiver (s. 8 (2) of the Insolvency Act 1976).

Supervision, enforcement, publicity etc.

Supervision by Council on Tribunals

24.—(1) The Tribunals and Inquiries Act 1971 shall be amended as follows (the amendments bringing the adjudicating functions of the Director under this Act under the supervision of the Council on Tribunals)—

(*a*) in section 8 (2) and section 19 (4), for "5A" there shall be substituted "6A"; and

(*b*) in Schedule 1, paragraph 5A is hereby repealed and after paragraph 6 there shall be inserted—

"**Fair Trading**

6A. The Director General of Fair Trading in respect of his functions under the Consumer Credit Act 1974 (c. 39) and the Estate Agents Act 1979 (c. 38), and any member of the Director's staff authorised to exercise those functions under paragraph 7 of Schedule 1 to the Fair Trading Act 1973 (c. 41)."

(2) Any member of the Council on Tribunals or of the Scottish Committee of the Council, in his capacity as such, may attend any hearing of representations conducted in accordance with Part I of Schedule 2 to this Act.

DEFINITION

"Director": s. 33 (1).

GENERAL NOTE

The Director (and his authorised staff) become a tribunal within Sched. 1 to Tribunals and Inquiries Act 1971 when exercising adjudicating functions under this Act. The Secretary of State in exercising his functions will remain outside the scope of that schedule.

"*adjudicating functions.*" These are not defined in this Act. In s. 1 (1) (*b*) of the Consumer Credit Act 1974, these are described as "the issue, variation, suspension and revocation of licences . . ." Under this Act, this would apply to certain functions of the Director under ss. 3, 4, 5, 6, and 8.

"*5A.*" This amendment was introduced by s. 3 of the Consumer Credit Act 1974. S. 6A effectively incorporates the earlier s. 5A.

"*s.* 8 (2)." The effect of this is to ensure that by amending the 1971 Act, whenever the Secretary of State wishes to terminate a person's membership of a tribunal, he does not require judicial consents.

"*s.* 19 (4)." This eliminates the need, by amendment to the 1971 Act, for the Director to comply with certain procedural requirements normally operative upon tribunals.

General duties of Director

25.—(1) Subject to section 26 (3) below, it is the duty of the Director—

(*a*) generally to superintend the working and enforcement of this Act, and

(*b*) where necessary or expedient, himself to take steps to enforce this Act.

(2) It is the duty of the Director, so far as appears to him to be practicable and having regard both to the national interest and the interests of persons engaged in estate agency work and of consumers, to keep under review and from time to time advise the Secretary of State about—

(*a*) social and commercial developments in the United Kingdom and elsewhere relating to the carrying on of estate agency work and related activities; and

(*b*) the working and enforcement of this Act.

(3) The Director shall arrange for the dissemination, in such form and manner as he considers appropriate, of such information and advice as it may appear to him expedient to give the public in the United Kingdom about the operation of this Act.

DEFINITIONS

"Director": s. 33 (1).

"estate agency work": ss. 1 (1), 33 (1).

GENERAL NOTE

This section is similar to s. 1 of the Consumer Credit Act 1974. It may also be compared with the general functions of the Director under s. 2 of the Fair Trading Act 1973. To the Director's functions under these and other Acts are now added the various powers and duties in relation to estate agency work, and the general duties laid down in this section.

"*s.* 26 (3)." This bars the Director from instituting proceedings in Scotland.

"*enforcement.*" See s. 26.

"*national interest.*" These words appear in s. 1 (2) of the Consumer Credit Act 1974. Arguably this could cover the effect of credit on the national economy. It would seem the words are less relevant in this instance.

"*time to time.*" This will cover both requests from the Secretary of State for information, and information which the Director brings to the attention of the Secretary of State because he considers it expedient to do so. In addition, under s. 125 (1), Fair Trading Act 1973, the Director is required to "make to the Secretary of State a report on his activities" at the end of each calendar year, or as soon as is practicable thereafter.

Enforcement authorities

26.—(1) Without prejudice to section 25 (1) above, the following authorities (in this Act referred to as "enforcement authorities") have a duty to enforce this Act—

(*a*) the Director,

(*b*) in Great Britain, a local weights and measures authority, and

(*c*) in Northern Ireland, the Department of Commerce for Northern Ireland.

(2) Where a local weights and measures authority in England and Wales propose to institute proceedings for an offence under this Act it shall, as between the authority and the Director, be the duty of the authority to give the Director notice of the intended proceedings, together with a summary of the facts on which the charges are to be founded, and postpone the institution of the proceedings until either—

(*a*) twenty-eight days have expired since that notice was given, or

(*b*) the Director has notified them of receipt of the notice and summary.

(3) Nothing in this section or in section 25 above authorises an enforcement authority to institute proceedings in Scotland for an offence.

(4) Every local weights and measures authority shall, whenever the Director requires, report to him in such form and with such particulars as he requires on the exercise of their functions under this Act.

(5) Where a complaint is made to the Secretary of State that all or any of the functions of a local weights and measures authority under this Act are not being properly discharged in any area, or he is of the opinion that an investigation should be made relating to the proper discharge of those functions in any area, he may cause a local inquiry to be held.

(6) Subsections (2), (3) and (5) of section 250 of the Local Government Act 1972 (evidence and costs at local inquiries), and, in a case where the Secretary of State so directs, subsection (4) of that section (costs of department), shall apply to an inquiry held under subsection (5) above as if it were an inquiry held in pursuance of that section.

(7) The person holding an inquiry under subsection (5) above shall make a written report of the results to the Secretary of State, who shall publish it together with such observations on it (if any) as he thinks fit.

(8) In the application of this section to Scotland, for the references in subsection (6) above to subsections (2), (3) and (5) of section 250 of the Local Government Act 1972 and subsection (4) of that section, there shall be substituted respectively references to subsections (4), (5) and (8) of section 210 of the Local Government (Scotland) Act 1973 and subsection (7) of that section.

DEFINITION

"Director": s. 33 (1).

GENERAL NOTE

There is in practice a two-tier system of enforcement. Following the Local Government Act 1972, there are 36 weights and measures authorities, and these will be responsible for local enforcement. The functions of this Act can be discharged jointly by two or more such authorities by virtue of s. 10 of the Local Government Act 1972. However, in practice each authority will deal with contraventions in its own area, and it is usual to find standards of vigilance in enforcement varying from region to region.

The Director is, therefore, to be informed of prosecutions by the authorities (subs. (2)). This will assist in avoiding duplication in enforcement, and help maintain uniform standards. If the weights and measures authorities remain responsible for local enforcement the Director is left free to deal with more widespread abuses, and fulfil his general duties under s. 25.

See further notes to ss. 27 (3) and 34.

Subs. (1)

"*local weights and measures authority.*" See Local Government Act 1972, s. 201.

Subs. (2)

"*an offence under this Act.*" *I.e.* a contravention of ss. 3, 10, 14, 16, 17, 22, 23, 27.

"*the duty of the authority.*" The duty owed only to the Director. A failure to meet this duty would not serve as a defence to an agent prosecuted under the Act.

"*give the Director notice.*" A notice of intended prosecution must include a summary of the facts. This notice must be given 28 days prior to the institution of proceedings, or, failing that, the proceedings must be postponed until the Director has acknowledged the notice. The Director has no power under this section to prevent a prosecution, since his consent is not required. The notice is for information only. It is possible but unlikely that the power to prevent prosecution could be inferred from s. 25 (1) (*a*) (but see below, subss. (4)–(8)).

Subs. (3)

As a general rule, prosecutions in Scotland are public, the responsibility of the Lord Advocate and only a few statutes give power to other authorities to initiate prosecutions. This subject ensures only the Lord Advocate has the power under this Act.

Subss. (4)–(8)

In the light of the provisions of subs. (2) that the Director must receive notice of proceedings instituted by weights and measures authorities but cannot prevent such proceedings, these powers should be noted. The Director can demand a report from an authority (subs. (4)) and then, if dissatisfied, complain to the Secretary of State. The Secretary of State has the power, upon complaint by any person, to institute a local inquiry, the results of which the Secretary of State must publish along with his own comments.

Obstruction and personation of authorised officers

27.—(1) Any person who—

(*a*) wilfully obstructs an authorised officer, or

(*b*) wilfully fails to comply with any requirement properly made to him under section 11 above by an authorised officer, or

(*c*) without reasonable cause fails to give an authorised officer other assistance or information he may reasonably require in performing his functions under this Act, or

(*d*) in giving information to an authorised officer, makes any statement which he knows to be false,

shall be liable on summary conviction to a fine not exceeding £500.

(2) A person who is not an authorised officer but purports to act as such shall be liable on summary conviction to a fine not exceeding £1,000.

(3) In this section " authorised officer " means a duly authorised officer of an enforcement authority who is acting in pursuance of this Act.

(4) Nothing in subsection (1) above requires a person to answer any question or give any information if to do so might incriminate that person or that person's husband or wife.

General Note

Cf. Trade Descriptions Act 1968, s. 29; Consumer Credit Act 1974, s. 165; Consumer Safety Act 1978, Sched. 2, para. 10.

See also notes to s. 11.

Subs. (1)

" wilfully obstructs." *I.e.* " intentionally and without lawful excuse " (see *Arrowsmith* v. *Jenkins* [1963] 2 Q.B. 561, which concerns the interpretation of these words in s. 121 (1) of the Highways Act 1959. It is for the prosecution to show that the behaviour was intentional (*Rice* v. *Connelly* [1966] 2 Q.B. 414). There is no necessity for physical force (*Borrow* v. *Howland* (1876) 74 L.T. 787 in which a householder was found to have wilfully obstructed another by refusal of entry to the house (s. 116 of the Public Health (London) Act 1891)). However, there must be something more than the failure to take positive steps unless there is a legal duty to act (see *Swallow* v. *London County Council* [1916] 1 K.B. 224). But see *" other assistance "* (below).

" wilfully fails to comply." *Cf.* the Road Traffic Act 1960, s. 134, and see note to *" wilfully obstructs "* and s. 9 (4) (*b*).

" without reasonable cause fails." *Cf.* the wording of the Public Health (London) Act 1891, s. 30 (2), and *Wandsworth Corporation* v. *Baines* [1906] 1 K.B. 470, 477, 479, in which similar words were read throughout as " reasonable excuse " (*per* Alverstone C.J.).

" other assistance." Thus under s. 11 (1) (*d*) a refusal to open a container would give the authorised officer the right not only to open the container but also to institute proceedings for a contravention of this section. In addition, these words would seem to be sufficiently widely drafted to extend to assistance or information not specifically required within the Act (but see note on *" wilfully obstructs "* and *Swallow* v. *London County Council* (*supra*)).

" false." See s. 9 (4) (*b*).

Subs. (3)

In common with both the Trade Descriptions Act 1968 and the Consumer Credit Act 1974, there is no duty on the local weights and measures authority to appoint inspectors for local enforcement (*cf.* Weights and Measures Act 1963). Therefore, whilst in practice this may be done, under the Act any officer of the authority is an authorised officer.

Subs. (4)

The definition under s. 32 (3) by which " spouse " can include both " a former spouse and a reputed spouse " would not apply here. This would apply only to a marriage which is valid at the time of the questioning.

Supplementary

General provisions as to offences

28.—(1) In any proceedings for an offence under this Act it shall be a defence for the person charged to prove that he took all reasonable precautions and exercised all due diligence to avoid the commission of an offence by himself or any person under his control.

(2) Where an offence under this Act committed by a body corporate is proved to have been committed with the consent or connivance of, or to be attributable to any neglect on the part of, any director, manager, secretary or other similar officer of the body corporate, or any person who was purporting to act in any such capacity, he as well as the body corporate shall be guilty of that offence and shall be liable to be proceeded against and punished accordingly.

General Note

Cf. s. 24 (1) (*b*) of the Trade Descriptions Act 1968; ss. 25 (1) (*b*) and 132 of the Fair Trading Act 1973; ss. 168 (1) (*b*) and 169 of the Consumer Credit Act 1974.

Subs. (1)

The defence given here is limited to any offence under the Act (see note to s. 11) which prevents its use in the case of a prohibition order based on the breach of a relevant statutory obligation (s. 3 (1) (*c*)).

" *reasonable precautions* " and " *due diligence*." There will always need to be an adequate system to prevent contravention of the Act. However, one departure from the safe system (*e.g.* by a junior member of staff) will not bar the person from proving the exercise of all due diligence (*Tesco Supermarkets* v. *Nattrass* [1972] A.C. 153) (*cf. J. H. Dewhurst* v. *Coventry Corporation* [1970] 1 Q.B. 20).

Subs. (2)

" *consent or connivance*." Connivance has been said to be " culpable acquiescence " (*Boulting* v. *Boulting* (1864) 3 Sw. & T. 329), but it may be rather more than that. Some element of encouragement may be needed (*Godfrey* v. *Godfrey* [1965] A.C. 444). Knowledge would seem to be essential for both connivance and consent (*Re Caughey* (1876) 1 Ch.D. 521).

" *neglect*." " The omission to do some duty which the party is able to do " (*per* Patteson J., *King* v. *Burrell* (1840) 12 A. & E. 460, at p. 468).

" *officer*." See note to s. 31 (4).

Service of notices etc.

29.—(1) Any notice which under this Act is to be given to any person by the Director shall be so given—

(*a*) by delivering it to him, or

(*b*) by leaving it at his proper address, or

(*c*) by sending it by post to him at that address.

(2) Any such notice may,—

(*a*) in the case of a body corporate or unincorporated association, be given to the secretary or clerk of that body or association; and

(*b*) in the case of a partnership, be given to a partner or a person having the control or management of the partnership business.

(3) Any application or other document which under this Act may be made or given to the Director may be so made or given by sending it by post to the Director at such address as may be specified for the purposes of this Act by a general notice.

(4) For the purposes of subsections (1) and (2) above and section 7 of the Interpretation Act 1978 (service of documents by post) in its application to those subsections, the proper address of any person to whom a notice is to be given shall be his last-known address, except that—

(*a*) in the case of a body corporate or their secretary or clerk, it shall be the address of the registered or principal office of that body;

(*b*) in the case of an unincorporated association or their secretary or clerk, it shall be that of the principal office of that association;

(*c*) in the case of a partnership or a person having the control or management of the partnership business, it shall be that of the principal office of the partnership;

and for the purposes of this subsection the principal office of a company registered outside the United Kingdom or of an unincorporated association or partnership carrying on business outside the United Kingdom shall be their principal office within the United Kingdom.

(5) If the person to be given any notice mentioned in subsection (1) above has specified an address within the United Kingdom other than his proper address, within the meaning of subsection (4) above, as the one at which he or someone on his behalf will accept notices under this Act, that address shall also be treated for the purposes mentioned in subsection (4) above as his proper address.

DEFINITIONS

"Director": s. 33 (1).
"general notice": s. 33 (1).
"unincorporated association": s. 33 (1).

GENERAL NOTE

The marginal note states that this section is concerned with the "service of notices, etc." In fact the section deals with the way in which notices should be given by the Director. This is some improvement on the Consumer Credit Act 1974 which uses "give" and "serve" interchangeably, and it follows the solution adopted by Bennion in his restatement of that Act (*Consumer Credit Control*, 1977). For the instances in which the giving of notices will be required, see ss. 3, 4, 6 and 7, and Sched. 2. See also s. 8 (2) and (3) on refusal of revocation orders, and as to whether or not a refusal will require a notice under this section. The Act is silent as to the result of a failure to comply with this section. Presumably documents not given in line with this section are to be treated as not being given at all.

The word "give" has been said to have allowed for both oral and written notices, as opposed to the word "serve" which raises the implication of a written notice (*Wilson* v. *Nightingale* (1846) 8 Q.B. 1034). However, it is clear from Sched. 2, para. 9, to the Act that all notices must be in writing. It has been said that if the notice is in writing, the word "give" has the same meaning as the word "serve," and therefore, the posting of the notice would be sufficient (*Re* 88 *Berkeley Road, N.W.* 9; *Rickwood* v. *Turnsek* [1971] Ch. 648). Subs. (1) (*c*) seems to confirm this.

Subs. (1)

"*delivering.*" A document delivered to a business address and received by another person who promises to deliver it to the person to whom it is addressed has been held to be effective service (*Morecambe and Heysham Corporation* v. *Warwick* (1958) 56 L.G.R. 283).

"*leaving.*" *Cf.* Law of Property Act 1925, s. 196 (3)—notice "left for him." See *Cannon Brewery Ltd.* v. *Signal Press Ltd.* (1928) 44 T.L.R. 486.

"*proper address.*" Subs. (4).

Subs. (2) (*a*)

A secretary is "no longer a mere clerk" (*Panorama Developments* (*Guildford*) *Ltd.* v. *Fidelis Furnishing Fabrics Ltd.* [1971] 2 Q.B. 711, *per* Lord Denning M.R.). A statement of the status of the secretary is contained therein.

Subs. (2) (*b*)

See note to s. 31 (4) below.

Subs. (4)

S. 7 of the Interpretation Act 1978 allows that service can be effected by properly addressing, pre-paying, and posting a letter which would be delivered in the ordinary course of the post. Subs. (4) states what is to be the proper address for the purpose of that section (*cf.* Town and Country Planning Act 1971, s. 283).

Subs. (5)

The word "also" in this subsection would seem to indicate that, even if a person specifies to the Director (for example) an address to which he wishes a notice to be sent under subs. (1), service at a proper address, within subs. (4), is sufficient.

Orders and regulations

30.—(1) Before making any order or regulations under any provision of this Act to which this subsection applies, the Secretary of State shall consult the Director, such bodies representative of persons carrying on estate agency work, such bodies representative of consumers and such other persons as he thinks fit.

(2) Subsection (1) above applies to paragraphs (*a*) (iii) and (*d*) of section 3 (1) above and to sections 14, 15, 16, 18, 19 and 22 above.

(3) Any power of the Secretary of State to make orders or regulations under this Act—

(*a*) may be so exercised as to make different provision in relation to different cases or classes of cases and to exclude certain cases or classes of case; and

(*b*) includes power to make such supplemental, incidental and transitional provisions as he think fit.

DEFINITIONS

"Director": s. 33 (1).

"estate agency work": ss. 1 (1), 33 (1).

GENERAL NOTE

This section presumably aims to reassure interest groups worried by the vast enabling powers contained in the Act, particularly those contained in s. 22. As Wade points out (*Administrative Law* (4th ed., 1977), p. 729), such consultations are "one of the firmest and most carefully observed conventions." (See also J. F. Garner, "Consultation in Subordinate Legislation" [1964] P.L. 105.) There would seem to be a conflict between subss. (1) and (2). Subs. (1) imposes a duty to consult in respect of *any* order, and subs. (2) goes on to mention specific sections to which subs. (1) will apply. The problem is whether there is a duty to consult in the case of regulations under a section not referred to in subs. (2), *e.g.* under s. 7.

The Act does not go as far as those statutes, *e.g.* the Factories Act 1961, or the Offices, Shops and Railway Premises Act 1963, which allow for disclosure of draft regulations and, in some instances, public inquiry. Nor does the Act require consultation with specific bodies (*cf.* Protection of Birds Act 1954, s. 13). As to the detail on duties to consult, see *Port-Louis Corporation* v. *Att.-Gen. of Mauritius* [1965] A.C. 1111; *Legg* v. *Inner London Education Authority* [1972] 1 W.L.R. 1245; *Lee* v. *Department of Education and Science* (1967) 66 L.G.R. 211; *Sinfield* v. *London Transport Executive* [1976] Ch. 550.

Subs. (1)

"*shall consult.*" For the mandatory nature of this requirement and the effect of failure to comply, see *Agricultural, Horticultural and Forestry Training Board* v. *Aylesbury Mushrooms Ltd.* [1972] 1 W.L.R. 190.

Subs. (3) (*a*)

Cf. s. 182 (2) of the Consumer Credit Act 1974, and see, for example, the Consumer Credit (Total Charge for Credit) Regulations 1977 (S.I. 1977 No. 327).

Meaning of "business associate" and "controller"

31.—(1) The provisions of this section shall have effect for determining the meaning of "business associate" and "controller" for the purposes of this Act.

(2) As respects acts done in the course of a business carried on by a body corporate, every director and controller of that body is a business associate of it.

(3) As respects acts done in the course of a business carried on by a partnership, each partner is a business associate of every other member of the partnership and also of the partnership itself and, in the case of a partner which is a body corporate, every person who, by virtue of subsection (2) above, is a business associate of that body is also a business associate of every other member of the partnership.

(4) As respects acts done in the course of a business carried on by an unincorporated association, every officer of the association and any other person who has the management or control of its activities is a business associate of that association.

(5) In relation to a body corporate "controller" means a person—

(*a*) in accordance with whose directions or instructions the directors of the body corporate or of any other body corporate which is its controller (or any of them) are accustomed to act; or

(*b*) who, either alone or with any associate or associates, is entitled to exercise, or control the exercise of, one third or more of the voting power at any general meeeting of the body corporate or of another body corporate which is its controller.

DEFINITION

"unincorporated association": s. 33 (1).

GENERAL NOTE

Ss. 31 and 32 effectively define "associate." This is necessary for the purposes of s. 21. In fact, s. 31 defines "business associate" and s. 32 defines "associate," but by virtue of s. 32 (1), "associate" includes "business associate." S. 31 overcomes certain difficulties to be found in the Consumer Credit Act 1974. In s. 184 of that Act, "associate" was defined without reference to business associates, except that s. 25 (3) provided that "associate" should include a "business associate." However, "business associate" was not defined, which attracted adverse comment (see, *e.g.* Goode, *The Consumer Credit Act* (1976), p. 52, para. 533). Moreover, the problems were heightened by the fact that the definition of "controller" was to be found hidden in the lengthy interpretation section (s. 189). Therefore, in the present Act, the simple expedient of defining "business associate" and "controller" within one section has been adopted.

Subs. (2)

"*in the course of a business.*" See note to s. 1 (1).

"*Director.*" See the Companies Act 1948, ss. 176 *et seq.*

Subs. (3)

A partner may be a business associate of:

(i) other partners;

(ii) the partnership itself;

(iii) the directors and controllers of a body corporate which is itself a partner.

"*in the course of a business.*" See note to s. 1 (1).

"*partnership.*" See the Partnership Act 1890, ss. 1 and 2.

Subs. (4)

"*officer.*" This term is not defined in the Act. It may be safe to assume the definition contained in the Companies Act 1948, s. 455. This would include a director; any person occupying the position of director but referred to by another title; and a manager or secretary.

"*control.*" This would seem to be deliberately someone other than a "controller" (subs. (5)) (*cf.* application form for a standard licence under the Consumer Credit Act 1974 which speaks of "a person who exercises control over general policy").

Subs. (5)

The tests posed under paras. (*a*) and (*b*) are distinct from each other. They apply to a body corporate only. The first is a test which envisages a chain of companies with actual control vested in only one of the chain. The second test is made by reference to voting power. Again, this is applicable to situations in which there exists a chain of companies. Although the tests are alternatives, the controller under (*b*) will normally be the controller under (*a*) in any given situation.

As regards control by voting power, because a controller must have one third of the votes it seems that there can be more than one controller. This is reinforced by the words in subs. (2): "every . . . controller."

Meaning of "associate"

32.—(1) In this Act "associate" includes a business associate and otherwise has the meaning given by the following provisions of this section.

(2) A person is an associate of another if he is the spouse or a relative of that other or of a business associate of that other.

(3) In subsection (2) above "relative" means brother, sister, uncle, aunt, nephew, niece, lineal ancestor or linear descendant, and references to a spouse include a former spouse and a reputed spouse; and for the purposes of this subsection a relationship shall be established as if an illegitimate child or step-child of a person had been a child born to him in wedlock.

(4) A body corporate is an associate of another body corporate—

(*a*) if the same person is a controller of both, or a person is a controller of one and persons who are his associates, or he and persons who are his associates, are controllers of the other; or

(*b*) if a group of two or more persons is a controller of each company, and the groups either consist of the same persons or could be regarded as consisting of the same persons by treating (in one or more cases) a member of either group as replaced by a person of whom he is an associate.

(5) An unincorporated association is an associate of another unincorporated association if any person—

(*a*) is an officer of both associations;

(*b*) has the management or control of the activities of both associations; or

(*c*) is an officer of one association and has the management or control of the activities of the other association.

(6) A partnership is an associate of another partnership if—

(*a*) any person is a member of both partnerships; or

(*b*) a person who is a member of one partnership is an associate of a member of the other partnership; or

(*c*) a member of one partnership has an associate who is also an associate of a member of the other partnership.

DEFINITIONS

"business associate": s. 32 (1).
"controller": s. 32 (1).
"unincorporated association": s. 33 (1).

GENERAL NOTE

The definition of "associate" is vital in relation to the disclosure of a personal interest in land to clients (s. 21). This section is similar in many details to s. 184 of the Consumer Credit Act 1974. The definition is a wide one, and the interpretation is not made easier by the structure of some of the subsections. The word "associate" has been used to describe both individual (subss. (2) and (3)) and corporate (subss. (4) (5) and (6)) relationships.

Subs. (1)

See generally s. 31.

Subs. (2)

"*spouse.*" See subs. (3).
"*relative.*" See subs. (3); *e.g.* the nephew of an estate agent's partner is an associate.

Subs. (3)

"*lineal ancestor or linear descendant.*" See *Knowles* v. *Att.-Gen.* [1951] P. 54, at 69.
"*former spouse.*" *Cf.* Matrimonial Causes Act 1965, s. 26.
"*reputed spouses.*" Questions of reputed spouses generally arise on questions of legitimacy following the cohabitation of the man and woman (see *Re Haynes* (1906) 94 L.T. 431).
"*illegitimate child or step-child.*" With regard to the definition of relative, any illegitimate child shall be treated as a child born in wedlock. Thus "niece" will include the step-daughter of the brother of any person.

Subs. (4) (*a*)

E.g. A controls company X. A is also in partnership with B. B's former wife controls company Z. Companies X and Z are associates.

Subs. (4) (*b*)

E.g. estate agents A, B and C control company X (Estates) Ltd. Their wives D, E and F control company Z (Knitwear) Ltd. Companies X and Z are associates.

Subs. (5)

"*officer.*" See note to s. 31 (4).
"*control.*" See note to s. 31 (4).

Subs. (6) (*c*)

E.g. the member of one partnership has a spouse who is the reputed spouse of a member of another partnership!

General interpretation provisions

33.—(1) In this Act, unless the context otherwise requires,—

"associate" has the meaning assigned to it by section 32 above and "business associate" has the meaning assigned to it by section 31 above;

"client account" has the meaning assigned to it by section 14 (2) above;

"clients' money" has the meaning assigned to it by section 12 (1) above;

"connected contract", in relation to the acquisition of an interest in land, has the meaning assigned to it by section 12 (4) above;

"contract deposit" has the meaning assigned to it by section 12 (2) above;

"controller", in relation to a body corporate, has the meaning assigned to it by section 31 (5) above;

"Director" means the Director General of Fair Trading;

"enforcement authority" has the meaning assigned to it by section 26 (1) above;

"estate agency work" has the meaning assigned to it by section 1 (1) above;

"general notice" means a notice published by the Director at a time and in a manner appearing to him suitable for securing that the notice is seen within a reasonable time by persons likely to be affected by it;

"pre-contract deposit" has the meaning assigned to it by section 12 (3) above;

"prescribed fee" means such fee as may be prescribed by regulations made by the Secretary of State;

"the statutory maximum", in relation to a fine on summary conviction, means—

(*a*) in England and Wales and Northern Ireland, the prescribed sum within the meaning of section 28 of the Criminal Law Act 1977 (at the passing of this Act £1,000); and

(*b*) in Scotland, the prescribed sum within the meaning of section 289B of the Criminal Procedure (Scotland) Act 1975 (at the passing of this Act £1,000);

and for the purposes of the application of this definition in Northern Ireland the provisions of the Criminal Law Act 1977 which relate to the sum mentioned in paragraph (*a*) above shall extend to Northern Ireland; and

"unincorporated association" does not include a partnership.

(2) The power to make regulations under subsection (1) above prescribing fees shall be exercisable by statutory instrument which shall be subject to annulment in pursuance of a resolution of either House of Parliament.

General Note

"*general notice.*" This is the definition used in the Consumer Credit Act 1974, s. 189 (1).

"*prescribed fee.*" Any fee prescribed is subject to the negative resolution of either House: see note to s. 3 (6).

"*unincorporated association.*" This would otherwise be a partnership within the meaning of the Partnership Act 1890, s. 1.

Financial provisions

34.—(1) There shall be defrayed out of moneys provided by Parliament—

(*a*) any expenses incurred by the Secretary of State in consequence of the provisions of this Act; and

(*b*) any increase attributable to this Act in the sums payable out of moneys so provided under any other Act.

(2) Any fees paid to the Director under this Act shall be paid into the Consolidated Fund.

Definition

"Director": s. 33 (1).

General Note

At the time of the publication of the Bill, the total increase in public expenditure, with all subordinate legislation in force, was said to be "not greater than £6,000,000 per annum." Of this, the administrative expenditure at central government level was described as "insignificant." Most of this money would be provided to the local authorities by Parliament through the annual rate support grant. In Northern Ireland the equivalent money for enforcement was to go to the Department of Commerce, with their increase in expenditure said to be "negligible" (Explanatory and Financial Memorandum to the Bill). Presumably the vast extension of the Bill to cover all interests in land (as defined by s. 2) will demand a radical reappraisal of these figures if enforcement is to be reasonably stringent.

Scotland

35.—(1) In the Scotland Act 1978, at the end of Part III of Schedule 10 (matters dealt with by certain enactments to be included, to the extent specified, in the groups of devolved matters) there shall be added the following entry—

"The Estate Agents Act 1979 (c. 38).	Included, except so far as relates to fees paid or to be paid to the Director General of Fair Trading."

(2) For the purpose of the following provisions of the Scotland Act 1978, this Act shall be deemed to have been passed before the passing of that Act, namely—

(*a*) section 21 (2) (executive powers);
(*b*) subsections (1) and (2) of section 22 (subordinate instruments);
(*c*) section 60 (modification of enactments providing for payments out of moneys provided by Parliament etc.); and
(*d*) section 82 (construction and amendment of existing enactments).

General Note

This section rendered the Act a devolved measure under the terms of the devolution settlement contained in the Scotland Act 1978. This was because the measure was labelled a housing not a consumer protection enactment. It would have allowed the Scottish Assembly to make alternative provision if it so desired, but until such time as the assembly was constituted, the Estate Agents Act 1979 would be applicable to and operative in Scotland. With the result of the referendum and subsequent repeal of the Scotland Act 1978, the provisions of the Estate Agents Act 1979 apply to Scotland, but s. 35 is rendered redundant.

Short title, commencement and extent

36.—(1) This Act may be cited as the Estate Agents Act 1979.

(2) This Act shall come into force on such day as the Secretary of State may by order made by statutory instrument appoint and different days may be so appointed for different provisions and for different purposes.

(3) This Act extends to Northern Ireland.

General Note

This allows the Secretary of State to appoint a day, by statutory instrument, on which the Act will become operative. It also allows him to appoint different days for different provisions within the Act. These will include those provisions referred to in s. 30 (2). In committee of the House of Lords, it was said of this section, whilst debating s. 7:

"This approach was adopted so as to enable my right honourable friend to make proper administrative arrangements at central and local authority level; to carry out consultations (including, for instance, with the estate agents' organisations about the make-up of the panel from which will be drawn tribunal members to advise my right honourable friend on appeals); to ensure sufficient prior publicity to allow estate agents to prepare for the necessary changes in their working arrangements and so on."

SCHEDULES

Section 3 (1)

SCHEDULE 1

Provisions Supplementary to Section 3 (1)

Spent convictions

1. A conviction which is to be treated as spent for the purposes of the Rehabilitation of Offenders Act 1974 or any corresponding enactment for the time being in force in Northern Ireland shall be disregarded for the purposes of section 3 (1) (*a*) of this Act.

Discrimination

2. A person shall be deemed to have committed discrimination for the purposes of section 3 (1) (*b*) of this Act in the following cases only, namely,—

(*a*) where a finding of discrimination has been made against him in proceedings under section 66 of the Sex Discrimination Act 1975 (in this Schedule referred to as "the 1975 Act") and the finding has become final;

(*b*) where a non-discrimination notice has been served on him under the 1975 Act and the notice has become final;

(*c*) if he is for the time being subject to the restraints of an injunction or order granted against him in proceedings under section 71 (persistent discrimination) or section 72 (4) (enforcement of sections 38 to 40) of the 1975 Act;

(*d*) if, on an application under section 72 (2) (*a*) of the 1975 Act, there has been a finding against him that a contravention of section 38, section 39 or section 40 of that Act has occurred and that finding has become final;

(*e*) where a finding of discrimination has been made against him in proceedings under section 57 of the Race Relations Act 1976 (in this Schedule referred to as "the 1976 Act") and the finding has become final;

(*f*) where a non-discrimination notice has been served on him under the 1976 Act and the notice has become final;

(*g*) if he is for the time being subject to the restraints of an injunction or order granted against him in proceedings under section 62 (persistent discrimination) or section 63 (4) (enforcement of sections 29 to 31) of the 1976 Act; or

(*h*) if, on an application under section 63 (2) (*a*) of the 1976 Act, there has been a finding against him that a contravention of section 29, section 30 or section 31 of that Act has occurred and that finding has become final;

and the finding, notice, injunction or order related or relates to discrimination falling within Part III of the 1975 Act or the 1976 Act (discrimination in fields other than employment).

3. After the expiry of the period of five years beginning on the day on which any such finding or notice as is referred to in paragraph 2 above became final, no person shall be treated for the purposes of section 3 (1) (*b*) of this Act as having committed discrimination by reason only of that finding or notice.

4.—(1) So far as paragraphs 2 and 3 above relate to findings and notices under the 1975 Act, subsections (1) and (4) of section 82 of that Act (general interpretation provisions) shall have effect as if those paragraphs were contained in that Act.

(2) So far as paragraphs 2 and 3 above relate to findings and notices under the 1976 Act, subsections (1) and (4) of section 78 of that Act (general interpretation provisions) shall have effect as if those paragraphs were contained in that Act.

5. In the application of paragraphs 2 to 4 above to Northern Ireland references to the 1975 Act shall be construed as references to the Sex Discrimination (Northern Ireland) Order 1976, and in particular—

(*a*) the references to sections 38, 39 and 40 of the 1975 Act shall be construed as references to Articles 39, 40 and 41 of that Order;

(*b*) the reference to subsections (1) and (4) of section 82 of the 1975 Act shall be construed as a reference to paragraphs (1), (2) and (5) of Article 2 of that Order; and

(*c*) other references to numbered sections of the 1975 Act shall be construed as references to the Articles of that Order bearing the same number;

and there shall be omitted sub-paragraphs (*e*) to (*h*) of paragraph 2, sub-paragraph (2) of paragraph 4 and so much of paragraph 3 as relates to findings or notices under the 1976 Act.

General Note

"*Spent convictions.*" See ss. 3 (1) (2); 5 (4); 8 (4) (6); 9 (5).

"*Discrimination.*" See ss. 3 (1) (2); 5 (3) (5); 8 (4) (6); 9 (6).

Sections 5, 6 and 8 (3)

SCHEDULE 2

PROCEDURE ETC.

PART I

ORDERS AND DECISIONS UNDER SECTIONS 3, 4 AND 6

Introductory

1.—(1) In this Schedule—

(*a*) subject to sub-paragraph (2) below, references to " the person affected " are to the person in respect of whom the Director proposes to make, or has made, an order under section 3 or section 4 of this Act, or who has made an application under section 6 of this Act for the variation or revocation of such an order; and

(*b*) references to the Director's " proposal " are to any proposal of his to make such an order or to make a decision under subsection (4) or subsection (5) of section 6 of this Act on such an application.

(2) In the case of a proposal of the Director to make an order under section 3 or section 4 of this Act against a partnership where, by virtue of section 5 (2) of this Act, he intends that the order shall have effect as an order against some or all of the partners individually, references in the following provisions of this Schedule to the person affected shall be construed, except where the contrary is provided, as references to each of the partners affected by the order, as well as to the partnership itself.

Notice of proposal

2.—(1) The Director shall give to the person affected a notice informing him of the proposal and of the Director's reason for it; but paragraph 1 (2) above shall not apply for the purposes of this sub-paragraph.

(2) In the case of a proposal to make an order, the notice under sub-paragraph (1) above shall inform the person affected of the substance of the proposed order and, in the case of a proposal to make an order under section 3 of this Act, shall—

(*a*) set out those matters falling within subsection (1) of that section which the Director intends should be specified as the grounds for the order, and

(*b*) specify any other matters of which the Director has taken account under subsection (2) of that section, and

(*c*) if the Director proposes to rely on section 4 (3) of this Act to establish the unfitness of the person affected, state that fact.

(3) The notice given under sub-paragraph (1) above shall invite the person affected, within such period of not less than twenty-one days as may be specified in the notice,—

(*a*) to submit to the Director his representations in writing as to why the order should not be made or, as the case may be, should be varied or revoked in accordance with the application, and

(*b*) to give notice to the Director, if he thinks fit, that he wishes to make such representations orally,

and where notice is given under paragraph (*b*) above the Director shall arrange for the oral representations to be heard.

Hearing of representations

3. Where the Director receives notice under paragraph 2 (3) (*b*) above he shall give the person affected not less than twenty-one days notice, or such shorter notice as the person affected may consent to accept, of the date, time and place at which his representations are to be heard.

4.—(1) In the course of the hearing of oral representations the Director shall, at the request of the person affected, permit any other person (in addition to the person affected) to make representations on his behalf or to give evidence or to introduce documents for him.

(2) The Director shall not refuse to admit evidence solely on the grounds that it would not be admissible in a court of law.

5. If the Director adjourns the hearing he shall give the person affected reasonable notice of the date, time and place at which the hearing is to be resumed.

Decision

6.—(1) The Director shall take into account in deciding whether to proceed with his proposal any written or oral representations made in accordance with the preceding provisions of this Schedule.

(2) If the Director considers that he should proceed with his proposal but for a reason which differs, or on grounds which differ, from those set out in the notice of the proposal under paragraph 2 above, he shall give a further notice under that paragraph.

(3) In any case where—

(*a*) a notice under paragraph 2 above gives more than one reason for the proposal or (in the case of a proposal to make an order under section 3 of this Act) sets out more than one matter which the Director intends should be specified as the grounds for the order, and

(*b*) it appears to the Director that one or more of those reasons should be abandoned or, as the case may be, that one or more of those matters should not be so specified,

the Director may nevertheless decide to proceed with his proposal on the basis of any other reason given in the notice or, as the case may be, on any other grounds set out in the notice.

7. If the Director decides not to proceed with his proposal he shall give notice of that decision to the person affected and, in the case of a notice of a decision on an application under section 6 of this Act, such a notice shall be combined with a notice under subsection (3) of that section.

8. If the Director decides to proceed with his proposal he may, if he thinks fit having regard to any representations made to him,—

(*a*) where the proposal is for the making of an order, make the order in a form which varies from that of the proposed order mentioned in the notice under paragraph 2 above, or

(*b*) where the proposal is to vary an order, make a variation other than that mentioned in the notice under paragraph 2 above, or

(*c*) where the proposal is to refuse to revoke an order, vary the order.

Notification of decision

9.—(1) Notice of the decision to make the order, and of the terms of the order or, as the case may be, notice of the decision on the application for variation or revocation of the order, shall be given to the person affected, together with the Director's reasons for his decision, including the facts which in his opinion justify the decision.

(2) The notice referred to in sub-paragraph (1) above shall also inform the person affected of his right to appeal against the decision and of the period within which an appeal may be brought and of how notice of appeal may be given.

10.—(1) Subject to sub-paragraph (2) below, the order to which the decision relates or, as the case may be, any variation of an order for which the decision provides shall not come into operation until any appeal under section 7 (1) of this Act and any further appeal has been finally determined or the period within which such an appeal may be brought has expired.

(2) Where the Director states in the notice referred to in paragraph 9 (1) above that he is satisfied that there are special circumstances which require it, an order shall come into operation immediately upon the giving of notice of the decision to make it.

Part II

Applications Under Sections 6 (1) and 8 (3)

11. Any reference in this Part of this Schedule to an application is a reference to an application to the Director under section 6 (1) of section 8 (3) of this Act, and any reference to the applicant shall be construed accordingly.

12. An application shall be in writing and be in such form and accompanied by such particulars as the Director may specify by general notice.

13. The Director may by notice require the applicant to publish details of his application at a time or times and in a manner specified in the notice.

14. If an application does not comply with paragraph 12 above or if an applicant fails to comply with a notice under section 9 of this Act requiring the furnishing of information or the production of documents in connection with the application, the Director may decline to proceed with the application.

GENERAL NOTE

See ss. 3 (1) (2) (4); 5 (2); 6 (1) (4) (5); 7 (1); 8 (1) (3).

Merchant Shipping Act 1979 *

(1979 c. 39)

ARRANGEMENT OF SECTIONS

* Annotations by D. R. Thomas, LL.B., M.A., Lecturer in Law, University College, Cardiff.

An Act to make amendments of the law relating to pilotage, carriage by sea, liability of shipowners and salvors and pollution from ships and other amendments of the law relating to shipping, pollution and seamen. [4th April 1979]

General Note

The Merchant Shipping Act 1979 is an important statute of great significance in the realm of merchant shipping and related areas. It is a lengthy and complex statute which deals with a variety of not always related matters. In many regards the Act is several statutes in the garb of one and many of the matters incorporated in the Act might readily, and possibly with better effect, have been the subject of separate Acts of Parliament. The Act was nearly lost on the fall of the last Labour government on a motion of confidence and was only saved in the little time that remained before dissolution by the general all-party support that existed for the Bill and the willingness of the House of Lords to waive its constitutional obligation as a reviewing chamber. In the result the Bill sped with breathtaking speed through its final parliamentary stages which was in marked contrast to the almost four years it took for the Bill to be introduced into Parliament. In many instances the Act is merely an enabling statute empowering the making of regulations.

The theme underlying much of the Act is the safety of ships and seafarers. It makes provision for the reorganisation of pilotage with the aim of securing a pilotage service which is uniformly efficient and adaptable to the benefits of technological advance. The Act gives wide powers to make regulations to promote safety and health in United Kingdom ships and to strengthen the powers of the

Department of Trade inspectors in this regard. The Act represents a substantial step towards the elimination of the differences in the employment safety legislation between terrestrial and maritime employees and adopts a formula similar to that in the Health and Safety at Work, etc. Act 1974. The Act modernises the system of discipline aboard ships and attempts to deal with the problem of intoxication on board fishing vessels. These and other administrative adjustments effected by the Act are principally the domestic developments. On a wider perspective, the Act confirms the response of Parliament to the urgent problem of oil pollution and enables several recent international agreements in this field to be ratified. The Act also gives the force of law to recent international conventions in the sphere of the international carriage of passengers and their luggage, and in the important area of limitation of liability.

In the realm of international agreements the Act attempts to counter the all too frequent delay with which such agreements are brought into force as a part of international law by permitting effect to be given to such agreements following ratification by the United Kingdom Government and notwithstanding that such agreements are not in force internationally. Finally, the Act undertakes a comprehensive review of the system of penalties in force under the merchant shipping legislation and related statutes with the effect that practically all the former maximum limits are raised and with the more serious offences made subject to a maximum fine of £50,000. Under the Act penalties are also inflation-proofed with future adjustments capable of being made by regulation.

The Act was preceded by a substantial amount of consultation with interested bodies and by a White Paper, "*Action on Safety and Pollution at Sea*," Cmnd. 7217, 1978. The Act implements, or has been influenced by, or anticipates a number of working party and advisory reports. These may be enumerated as follows:

(i) "*Marine pilotage in the United Kingdom*," report by the Steering Committee on Pilotage, June 1974, HMSO.

(ii) Report of the Advisory Committee on Pilotage, July 1977, HMSO.

(iii) Report of the Steering Committee on the Safety of Merchant Seamen at work, 1978, HMSO.

(iv) Report of the Working Group on the Occupational Safety of Fishermen, 1979, HMSO.

(v) Report of the Working Group on Discipline in the Merchant Navy, 1975, HMSO.

(vi) Report of the Working Group on Discipline in the Fishing Industry, 1975, HMSO.

The Act also enables the United Kingdom to ratify the following conventions and protocols:

(1) The Athens Convention relating to the Carriage of Passengers and their luggage by sea, 1974 (Cmnd. 6326) and a Protocol of 1976 (Cmnd. 6765).

(2) The London Convention on Limitation of Liability for Maritime Claims 1976 (Cmnd. 7035).

(3) International Convention on the Standards of Training Certification and Watchkeeping of Seafarers 1978 (I.L.O. Convention No. 147).

(4) International Convention for the Prevention of Pollution from Ships 1973 (Cmnd. 5748) and the 1978 Protocol to that Convention.

(5) A Protocol of November 2, 1973, to the International Convention relating to Intervention on the High Seas in cases of Oil Pollution Casualties 1969 (Cmnd. 6038).

(6) The Protocols of 1976 to the International Convention on Civil Liability for Oil Pollution Damage 1969 (Cmnd. 7028) and the International Convention on Civil liability for Oil Pollution Damage 1969 (Cmnd. 7028) and the International Convention on the Establishment of an International Fund for Compensation for Oil Pollution Damage 1971 (Cmnd. 7029).

The Act

S. 1 provides for the establishment of a corporate body to be styled the "Pilotage Commission" and together with Sched. 1 makes provision for its membership and administrative operation.

Ss. 2 and 3 relate to the financing and borrowing powers of the Pilotage Commission. S. 2 enables the Commission to make a scheme or schemes requiring pilotage authorities to make payments towards the Commission's expenses. Each such scheme is subject to the approval of the Secretary of State before it may come into force. S. 2 entitles the Commission to borrow money up to specified amounts for the purpose of carrying out its functions. The Secretary of State is also empowered to lend money to the Commission.

S. 4 sets out the advisory functions of the Pilotage Commission and specifies the classes of person to whom the advice is to be directed. The Secretary of State may also confer additional functions upon the Commission.

S. 5 requires the Pilotage Commission to publish an annual report as soon as possible after March 31 in each year. A copy of the accounts and auditor's report are to be included in the annual report.

S. 6 imposes a particular duty on the Pilotage Commission to keep under review the organisation of pilotage in the United Kingdom, the numbers of pilots required for efficient pilotage in the various pilotage districts and the extent to which compulsory pilotage ought to be extended. To implement its proposals in these regards the Commission may in certain circumstances apply for a pilotage order or make by-laws.

S. 7 provides for the making of regulations in connection with the procedure of making and coming into force of pilotage orders.

S. 8 makes amendments to s. 11 of the Pilotage Act 1913 which is concerned with compulsory pilotage. It also sets out a new s. 11 which will in due course supersede the amended s. 11. The effect of this section is to restrict the exceptions to compulsory pilotage.

S. 9 empowers a pilotage authority by means of a list of charges, to make pilotage charges operative in its district in respect of the services of a pilot and in respect of the pilotage services of the district. The section contains provision for objections to the list to be made to the Pilotage Commission which has the power to cancel or alter such list.

S. 10 empowers a pilotage authority to refuse to grant or renew a pilotage certificate when the numbers of persons holding a pilot's licence or pilotage certificate are in the view of the Commission appropriate for the district. In such circumstances the Secretary of State is also empowered to revoke a pilotage certificate which has been granted by a pilotage authority. Provision is made for the repeal of the section by order but not before 10 years has elapsed after the clause has come into force.

S. 11 makes it clear that a pilotage authority has a power to employ licensed pilots and their assistants and to enter into pilotage agreements with shipowners. Provision is made that self-employed licensed pilots may not be employed by a pilotage authority unless a majority of their number so resolve.

S. 12 authorises the Pilotage Commission to establish and maintain a pilots' pension and compensation scheme. Provision is also made for the transfer of the assets or liabilities existing under any established scheme to the new scheme.

S. 13 makes amendments to the Pilotage Act 1913 and also increases the amount of some of the maximum fines specified in the 1913 Act.

Ss. 14–16, and Sched. 3 enable effect to be given to the Athens Convention relating to the Carriage of Passengers and their Luggage by Sea 1974 (Cmnd. 6326) and a Protocol thereto dated November 19, 1976. S. 14 provides for the Athens Convention as set out in Sched. 3, Pt. I, together with the adaptations and clarifications set out in Pt. II, to have the force of law. It also provides to the same effect with regard to the Protocol which is provided for in Pt. III to the Schedule. When Pt. III is brought into effect the whole of Sched. 3 will subsist subject to its provisions. Any future adjustments which may become necessary as a result of any revision of the Convention may be made by Order in Council. S. 15 is supplementary and enables the Athens Convention to be extended to the Isle of Man, the Channel Islands, the colonies and dependent territories. S. 16 enables interim effect, subject to modification, to be given to the Athens Convention before s. 14 is brought into force. It also empowers Orders in Council to be made applying the Athens Convention, subject to modification, to domestic carriage.

Ss. 17–19 and Scheds. 4 and 5 enable effect to be given to the London Convention on Limitation of Liability for Maritime Claims 1976 (Cmnd. 7035) and necessary consequential amendments to existing legislation resulting therefrom. S. 17 gives the force of law to the Convention which is set out in Sched. 4, Pt. I, as adapted and clarified by Pt. II of the Schedule. S. 18, reproducing preceding legislation but in amended form, provides for the exclusion of liability of a shipowner, master, member of the crew or servant in respect of damage or loss of property by reason of fire on board a ship, and in respect of the damage or loss of valuables. The exclusion of liability is confined to negligent conduct and does not apply when the damage or loss is intentionally or recklessly caused. S. 19 enables ss. 17 and 18 to be extended with modification to the Isle of Man, the Channel Islands, the colonies and dependent territories. It also gives effect to the consequential amendments specified in Sched. 5.

S. 20 enables effect to be given by Order in Council to the International Convention for the Prevention of Pollution from Ships, which constitutes Attachment 1 to the final act of the International Conference on Marine Pollution signed in London on November 2, 1973, and a Protocol thereto which constitutes Attachment 2 to the final act of the International Conference on Tanker Safety and Pollution Prevention signed in London on February 17, 1978; a Protocol relating to Intervention on the High Seas in Cases of Marine Pollution by substances other than Oil which constitutes Attachment 2 to the final act of the International Conference on Marine Pollution signed in London on November 2, 1973; any other convention relating to the prevention or control of pollution of the sea. Power is conferred to enable a convention to be brought into effect notwithstanding that it has not entered into force internationally.

Ss. 21 and 22 are concerned with safety and health on ships. S. 21 enables the Secretary of State to make safety regulations to secure the general safety of ships and the safety and health of those employed on board ships. The power is confined to United Kingdom ships but may be extended to other ships when the regulation attempts to give effect to an international agreement which the United Kingdom Government has ratified. S. 22 contains supplementary provisions to s. 21, including a power to repeal and modify enactments and instruments which are replaced or affected by the safety regulations.

S. 23 enables fundamental changes to the disciplinary régime on board ships to be effected by regulation. The section empowers the Secretary of State to approve disciplinary regulations embodied in codes of conduct in relation to the mercantile marine and local industrial agreements in the case of the fishing industry. The section also empowers the Secretary of State to establish or approve a disciplinary body to hear and determine complaints made against seamen by a master or shipowner. Provision is also made for the powers of such bodies.

S. 24 extends the power to make regulations under s. 9 of the Merchant Shipping Act 1970, which relates to deductions from the wages of a seaman, so as to enable deductions to be made from the wages of persons employed in fishing vessels by a body established or approved under s. 23.

S. 25 makes it a criminal offence to take or possess unauthorised liquor on board a fishing vessel. The section provides prescribed defences and power is given to authorised persons to conduct searches aboard the fishing vessel and to take possession of unauthorised liquor.

Ss. 26–28 are concerned with the appointment and powers of Department of Trade Inspectors in respect of the merchant shipping legislation and regulations made thereunder. S. 26 extends the power to appoint inspectors so as to secure the adequate supervision of the safety regulations made under this Act and the terms of any approval, licence, consent, direction or exemption given by virtue of such regulations. S. 27 re-enacts, but in greater detail, the powers of the inspectorate. S. 28 makes it an offence wilfully to obstruct inspectors and makes other provisions supplementary to s. 27.

S. 29 amends s. 61 of the Merchant Shipping Act 1970, and extends the circumstances when the Secretary of State may cause an inquiry to be instituted into the cause of death of a person in a United Kingdom registered ship. It also enables the Secretary of State to institute an inquiry where, in consequence of injury or disease while master or a seaman of a United Kingdom ship, such person is discharged from the ship and subsequently dies outside the United Kingdom and the death occurs within one year from the date of the discharge. The section also provides for an inquiry when the Secretary of State considers that a person may have died in or been lost from a ship, with a view to ascertaining whether such person has in fact died or been lost, and, if so, to ascertain also the cause of death.

S. 30 amends s. 72 of the Merchant Shipping Act 1970 in relation to the returns required to be made by masters of deaths in United Kingdom registered ships and of deaths outside the United Kingdom of persons employed in such ships. It enables the Secretary of State to make regulations requiring the Registrar General of Shipping and Seamen to record the death in circumstances when the master cannot and the death has been established by an inquest or post-mortem. It also imposes a duty on coroners to send particulars to the Registrar General of Shipping and Seamen.

S. 31 amends s. 85 of the Merchant Shipping Act 1894 and empowers the making of regulations for the purpose of ascertaining the tonnage of the space occupied by deck cargo for the purpose of ascertaining the dues payable for the space so occupied.

S. 32 amends s. 464 of the Merchant Shipping Act 1894 and s. 55 of the Merchant Shipping Act 1970 in relation to preliminary inquiries and formal investigations into shipping casualties. The amendments allow such inquiries and investigations to be held where there occurs serious personal injury not resulting in loss of life or where there has occurred a "near miss" incident which in the opinion of the Secretary of State might have resulted in a shipping casualty.

S. 33 repeals ss. 637, 640 and 641 of the Merchant Shipping Act 1894 and amends s. 668 (4) of the same Act so as to make an alteration in the composition of the Commissioners of Northern Lighthouses.

S. 34 repeals ss. 670–672 and 675 of the Merchant Shipping Act 1894, relating to colonial light dues, as spent. Also repealed is s. 677 (M) of the same Act relating to the publication of information about foreign lighthouses. The section also enables orders to be made extending the meaning of "buoys and beacons" in Pt. XI of the 1894 Act.

S. 35 amends s. 503 of the Merchant Shipping Act 1894 and s. 17 of this Act so as to remove a shipowner's and salvor's right to limit liability in respect of loss of life or personal injury caused to a person on board or employed in connection with the ship under a contract of service governed by United Kingdom law.

S. 36 repeals as spent provisions of the Merchant Shipping (Mercantile Marine Fund) Act 1898 relating to colonial light dues and provides a simplified procedure for the alteration of light dues. The section also authorises the United Kingdom's share of expenditure on certain lighthouses in the Red Sea to be deducted from the General Lighthouse Fund. The section also makes amendment to the 1898 Act following upon the transfer of certain lighthouses off the coast of Sri Lanka to the Government of that country.

S. 37 makes miscellaneous amendments to the Merchant Shipping Act 1970 and the Prevention of Oil Pollution Act 1971.

S. 38 enables effect to be given to a Protocol of November 19, 1976, to the International Convention on Civil Liability for Oil Pollution Damage 1969 (Cmnd. 4403) and a Protocol dated November 19, 1976, to the International Convention on the Establishment of an International Fund for Compensation for Oil Pollution Damage 1971 (Cmnd. 506). The effect of both Protocols is to substitute the special drawing right of the International Monetary Fund for the gold franc as the unit of account.

S. 39 amends s. 11 of the Merchant Shipping Act 1970 and s. 24 of the Attachment of Earnings Act 1971 so as to make a seaman's wages subject to attachment in relation to maintenance orders. The section also amends Scottish law so as to make the wages of a seaman of a fishing vessel subject to arrestment and the wages of other seamen subject to arrestment in relation to maintenance orders.

S. 40 clarifies and extends the Government's defensive powers under s. 14 of the Merchant Shipping Act 1974.

S. 41 empowers the Secretary of State to provide by order that anything designed or adapted for use at sea shall, or shall not be, a ship for the purpose of the Merchant Shipping Acts and the Prevention of Oil Pollution Act 1971, and instruments made thereunder.

S. 42 amends the Merchant Shipping Act 1894 so as to alter the time limits within which certain summary prosecutions may be instituted.

S. 43 and Sched. 6 make provision for altering the penalties for offences under the Merchant Shipping Acts and the Prevention of Oil Pollution Act 1971. Provision is also made for inflation-proofing penalties.

S. 44 repeals s. 457 of the Merchant Shipping Act 1894 and create a new offence relating to a dangerously unsafe ship.

S. 45 makes amendments to the offences set out in ss. 27, 28 and 30 of the Merchant Shipping Act 1970.

S. 46 relates to offences by officers of corporate bodies.

Ss. 47–52 contain various supplementary provisions to the Act. Sched. 7 effects a number of repeals.

Commencement

The Act received the Royal Assent on April 4, 1979. By the Merchant Shipping Act 1979 (Commencement No. 1) Order 1979 (S.I. 1979 No. 807 (C. 19)), ss. 1–6, 12, 13 (1) (part), 16, 20–22, 26, 32 (1), 33, 34, 35 (1), 36 (1) (3), 37 (1)–(3) (5) (7) (8), 39–41, 47 (1) (2) (part) (3), 48, 49, 50 (1) (2) (4) (part), 51 (1) (3) and 52, and Scheds. 1, 2 (part) and 7 (part) came into force on August 1, 1979; ss. 27, 28, 46 (part), 47 (2) (part) and 50 (4) (part), and Sched. 7 (part) came into force on October 1, 1979; ss. 13 (1) (part) (2)–(4), 29, 30, 42–45, 47 (2) (part) and 50 (4) (part), and Scheds. 2 (part), 6 and 7 (part) come into force on January 1, 1980.

Parliamentary debates

Hansard, H.C. Vol. 959, cols. 778, 847; Vol. 965, col. 770; H.L. Vol. 399, cols. 1867, 1919.

The Pilotage Commission

Constitution of Commission

1.—(1) There shall be a body corporate, to be called the Pilotage Commission (and hereafter in this Act referred to as " the Commission "), which shall be constituted in accordance with the following provisions of this section.

(2) The Commission shall consist of not less than ten and not more than fifteen persons appointed by the Secretary of State from among the following, namely—

(*a*) licensed pilots;

(*b*) persons appearing to the Secretary of State to have wide practical experience of the management of ships;

(*c*) persons appearing to the Secretary of State to have wide practical experience of the administration of pilotage services;

(*d*) persons appearing to the Secretary of State to have wide practical experience of the management of docks or harbours;

(*e*) other persons appearing to the Secretary of State to have special knowledge or experience likely to be of value to the Commission in connection with the performance of its functions;

and it shall be the duty of the Secretary of State to appoint as members of the Commission at least one person from each of the categories of persons mentioned in paragraphs (*a*) to (*d*) of this subsection and to appoint one member to be the chairman of the Commission.

(3) It shall be the duty of the Secretary of State—

(*a*) before appointing as a member a person in any category of persons which is mentioned in paragraphs (*a*) to (*d*) of subsection (2) of this section, to consult on the appointment such persons as the Secretary of State considers are representative of the persons in the United Kingdom in the category in question;

(*b*) before appointing as a member a person in the category of persons which is mentioned in paragraph (*e*) of that subsection, to consult on the appointment—

(i) such persons as the Secretary of State considers are representative of the persons in the United Kingdom in all the categories of persons mentioned in the said paragraphs (*a*) to (*d*), and

(ii) such other persons, if any, as he considers appropriate;

(*c*) before appointing a member to be the chairman of the Commission, to consult on the appointment such persons as the

Secretary of State considers are representative of the persons in the United Kingdom in all the categories of persons mentioned in the said paragraphs (*a*) to (*d*).

(4) The provisions of Schedule 1 to this Act shall have effect with respect to the Commission.

(5) It is hereby declared that the Commission is not to be regarded as the servant or agent of the Crown or as enjoying any status, privilege or immunity of the Crown or as exempt from any tax, duty, rate, levy or other charge whatsoever, whether general or local, and that its property is not to be regarded as property of or held on behalf of the Crown.

(6) In Part II of Schedule 1 to the House of Commons Disqualification Act 1975, after the entry relating to the Performing Right Tribunal there shall be inserted the words " The Pilotage Commission "; and in Part II of Schedule 1 to the Northern Ireland Assembly Disqualification Act 1975, after the entry relating to the said Tribunal there shall be inserted the words aforesaid.

DEFINITIONS

" the Commission ": s. 50 (2). " functions ": s. 50 (2).

GENERAL NOTE

This section is probably the most significant part of the Act in so far as it relates to pilotage (ss. 1–13). It provides for the creation and membership of a new body entitled the Pilotage Commission which is to be a corporate entity but not a Crown body. The section is to be read in conjunction with Sched. 1, which makes further provisions relating to the tenure and remuneration of members, the proceedings of the Commission and the employment of administrative staff. The " Commission " when set up will be an expert body with an essentially advisory role and with an obligation to keep pilotage under review and secure its uniform and efficient development. The Pilotage Commission, although it assumes many of the responsibilities which under the Pilotage Act 1913 were those of the Secretary of State, does not displace the Secretary of State, nor the local pilotage authorities nor the former contribution of Trinity House. The Secretary of State continues to possess the sole power to grant pilotage orders and to receive representations and appeals under the Pilotage Act 1913 except in relation to pilotage charges whereby, under s. 9, objections are to be made to the Commission. But even in this latter case the Commission may be compelled to act in accordance with the directions of the Secretary of State (s. 9 (5)).

Payments by pilotage authorities to Commission

2.—(1) The Commission may make a scheme or schemes requiring pilotage authorities to pay to the Commission from time to time, in respect of the expenses of the Commission in performing its functions, such sums as are determined under the scheme or schemes; and such a scheme—

(*a*) may provide for the payment of different sums by different authorities;

(*b*) must contain provision requiring the Commission to indicate how the sums to be payable under the scheme for periods determined under it are related to the Commission's estimates of its expenditure during those periods;

(*c*) may be revoked or varied by a subsequent scheme made by virtue of this subsection;

but a scheme made by virtue of this subsection shall not come into force unless it has been confirmed by the Secretary of State.

(2) It shall be the duty of the Commission, immediately after it has submitted such a scheme to the Secretary of State for confirmation—

(*a*) to send a copy of the scheme to each pilotage authority by which sums are to be payable under the scheme; and

(*b*) to publish in a manner approved by the Secretary of State a notice which—

(i) states that the scheme has been so submitted, and

(ii) specifies a place where a copy of the scheme may be obtained free of charge by any licensed pilot, any harbour authority and any shipowner, and

(iii) states that any person mentioned in paragraph (*a*) or sub-paragraph (ii) above and any person appearing to the Secretary of State to represent any persons so mentioned may, within a period specified in the notice of not less than 42 days beginning with the date of first publication of the notice, object to the scheme by giving to the Secretary of State a statement in writing setting out his objections to the scheme and the reasons for the objections.

(3) The Secretary of State may, after considering any statement of objections and of reasons for objections to a scheme which is given to him by a person and within the period mentioned in paragraph (*b*) (iii) of the preceding subsection, by order confirm the scheme either without modification or, after consulting the Commission about any modifications he proposes to make to the scheme, with such modifications as he thinks fit; but the Secretary of State shall not have power to make a modification of a scheme which would increase the amount of any sum payable in pursuance of the scheme.

(4) Any sum payable to the Commission by a pilotage authority in pursuance of a scheme made by virtue of this section may be recovered by the Commission in any court of competent jurisdiction.

DEFINITIONS

"the Commission": s. 50 (2).
"functions": s. 50 (2).
"modifications": s. 50 (2).

GENERAL NOTE

This section makes it plain that the Commission is to be financed from within the pilotage industry. It enables the Commission to set up a scheme or schemes requiring pilotage authorities to make contributions to the expenses of the Commission. The schemes of levy may vary as between different pilotage authorities. By s. 9 (1) (*c*) the charge levied may be introduced as a cost factor in the charges made by the pilotage authorities. There is given to interested persons the right to object to any scheme presented and no proposed scheme may be implemented without the approval of the Secretary of State.

Other financial provisions relating to Commission

3.—(1) The Commission may borrow in sterling any sum which it requires for the purpose of carrying out its functions, but the aggregate amount of the principal of sums borrowed by the Commission which is outstanding at any time shall not exceed £200,000 or such larger amount, not exceeding £500,000, as the Secretary of State may specify by order.

(2) The Secretary of State may out of money provided by Parliament lend to the Commission, with the consent of the Treasury and on such terms as he may determine with the consent of the Treasury, any sum which the Commission has power to borrow in pursuance of the preceding subsection; and any sum received by the Secretary of State by way of interest on or the payment of a loan made by virtue of this subsection shall be paid into the Consolidated Fund.

(3) It shall be the duty of the Commission—

(*a*) to keep proper accounts and proper records in relation to the accounts; and (*b*) to prepare in respect of the period of 12 months ending with the 31st March in each year a statement of those accounts in such form as the Secretary of State may direct with the approval of the Treasury; and

(*c*) to cause the accounts kept and the statement prepared for each such period to be audited by auditors appointed by the Commission with the approval of the Secretary of State.

(4) A person shall not be qualified to be appointed as an auditor in pursuance of the preceding subsection unless he is a member of one or more of the following bodies—

the Institute of Chartered Accountants in England and Wales;
the Institute of Chartered Accountants of Scotland;
the Association of Certified Accountants;
the Institute of Chartered Accountants in Ireland;
any other body of accountants established in the United Kingdom and for the time being recognised for the purposes of section 161 (1) (*a*) of the Companies Act 1948 by the Secretary of State;

but a Scottish firm may be so appointed if each of the partners in the firm is qualified to be so appointed.

DEFINITIONS

"the Commission": s. 50 (2).
"functions": s. 50 (2).

GENERAL NOTE

The section enables the Commission to borrow money up to a prescribed amount for the purpose of performing its functions. The Secretary of State is empowered to lend such sums as may be required and it is anticipated that when the Commission is initially constituted it will require a floating loan of £50,000.

Functions of Commission

4.—(1) It shall be the duty of the Commission to give to the Secretary of State, and to pilotage authorities, dock and harbour authorities, pilots and shipowners, such advice as the Commission considers appropriate for any of the following purposes, namely—

(*a*) securing by means of pilotage the safety of navigation in ports of and waters off the coasts of the United Kingdom;

(*b*) ensuring that efficient pilotage services are provided for those ports and waters and, in particular, that suitable equipment is provided in connection with those services;

(*c*) ensuring that the terms of service of pilots providing those services are fair; and

(*d*) promoting standards, in the qualifications which entitle persons to apply for pilots' licences and in the training of pilots, which are uniform for areas which the Commission considers are of the same kind.

(2) The Secretary of State may by order confer on the Commission such functions, in addition to the functions conferred on the Commission by this Act, as he considers appropriate for any of the purposes mentioned in the preceding subsection.

(3) Without prejudice to the generality of the preceding subsection, an order in pursuance of that subsection may in particular provide for the making of schemes under which payments may be made by the Commission for the purpose of compensating pilots and their assistants for loss of employment or reductions in earnings suffered by them in consequence of changes in the organisation of pilotage services or of the

granting of pilotage certificates to nationals of member States of the Economic Community other than the United Kingdom.

(4) The Commission shall have power to do anything which is calculated to facilitate, or is conducive or incidental to, the performance of any of its functions.

DEFINITIONS

"the Commission": s. 50 (2).

"functions": s. 50 (2).

GENERAL NOTE

This section enumerates in broad terms the advisory functions of the Pilotage Commission. The obligation to give advice is not confined to pilots, pilotage authorities and the Secretary of State but extends to shipowners and harbour authorities. Additional functions may by order made by the Secretary of State be conferred upon the Commission. The section stands alongside s. 6 which imposes particular duties upon the Commission.

Annual report

5. It shall be the duty of the Commission—

(*a*) to prepare and publish, as soon as possible after the 31st March in each year, a report on the performance of its functions during the period of 12 months ending with that date;

(*b*) to include in the report a copy of the statement of accounts prepared in respect of that period in pursuance of section 3 (3) (*b*) of this Act and a copy of the auditors' report on the statement and on the accounts to which the statement relates; and

(*c*) to deliver a copy of the report to the Secretary of State before it is published;

and it shall be the duty of the Secretary of State to lay before Parliament copies of each report of which he receives a copy in pursuance of this section.

DEFINITIONS

"the Commission": s. 50 (2).

"functions": s. 50 (2).

GENERAL NOTE

To the annual report must be appended a copy of the annual statement of account and auditor's report (see s. 3 (3)). Persons qualified to act as auditors are specified in s. 3 (4).

Other provisions relating to pilotage

Review of pilotage services and non-compulsory pilotage areas

6.—(1) It shall be the duty of the Commission—

(*a*) to keep under consideration the organisation of pilotage services at ports in and waters off the coasts of the United Kingdom, to consider suggestions for changes in the organisation of those services which are made to the Commission by persons appearing to the Commission to be interested in the organisation of them and to make proposals for such changes in the organisation of those services as the Commission considers appropriate;

(*b*) without prejudice to the generality of the preceding paragraph, to consider what numbers of pilots are needed in order to provide efficient pilotage services in pilotage districts and to make to the pilotage authorities concerned such recommendations about the numbers as the Commission considers appropriate; and

(*c*) to carry out such investigations as the Commission considers appropriate in order to ascertain whether pilotage should be made compulsory at places in or off the coasts of the United Kingdom where it is not compulsory and to make proposals for pilotage to be made compulsory at such places as the Commission considers appropriate in consequence of the investigations.

(2) Accordingly sections 1 and 2 of the Pilotage Act 1913 (which among other things provide for the Secretary of State to initiate changes in the organisation of pilotage services and changes in byelaws to achieve uniformity of administration) shall cease to have effect and section 22 of that Act (which provides for information to be furnished to the Secretary of State by pilotage authorities) shall have effect as if—

(*a*) the duties imposed by that section to deliver returns and furnish statements of accounts to the Secretary of State and to allow inspection of books and documents by him or a person appointed by him were duties to deliver the returns and furnish the statements to the Commission and to allow inspection by the Commission or a person appointed by the Commission; and

(*b*) in subsection (1) the words " and any returns so delivered shall, as soon as may be, be laid before both Houses of Parliament " were omitted; and

(*c*) in subsection (4) for the first reference to the Secretary of State there were substituted a reference to the Commission.

(3) If the Commission considers that a pilotage order or byelaws should be made for the purpose of giving effect to such a proposal as is mentioned in paragraph (*a*) or (*c*) of subsection (1) of this section and that an application for such an order or for confirmation of byelaws which are appropriate for that purpose has not been made to the Secretary of State by a pilotage authority affected by the proposal within a period which the Commission considers reasonable in the circumstances, the Commission may apply to the Secretary of State for a pilotage order for that purpose or, as the case may be, may exercise for that purpose the power to make byelaws which is conferred on the pilotage authority by section 17 (1) of the Pilotage Act 1913.

(4) It shall be the duty of the Commission—

(*a*) before it performs a function conferred on it by subsection (1) of this section, to consult the persons in the United Kingdom who the Commission considers are likely to be affected by the performance of the function or to consult persons appearing to the Commission to represent those persons; and

(*b*) to send to the Secretary of State, and to publish in such manner as the Commission thinks fit, copies of the returns and statements received by the Commission by virtue of subsection (2) (*a*) of this section;

and it shall be the duty of the Secretary of State to lay before Parliament copies of any document he receives in pursuance of paragraph (*b*) of this subsection.

DEFINITIONS

" the Commission ": s. 50 (2).
" functions ": s. 50 (2).

General Note

The section specifies particular duties to be performed by the Pilotage Commission. The section gives to the Commission the reviewing role which under the Pilotage Act 1913 was vested in the Secretary of State. Again the role of the Commission is advisory and the instigation of change, whether it be for a pilotage order or change in the by-laws, must come from the local pilotage authorities. It is only if they delay unreasonably in acting on the advice given that the Commission may assume an active role in effecting the desired change and apply for a pilotage order under s. 7 (4) (*b*) of the Pilotage Act 1913 or assume the pilotage authority's power to make by-laws under s. 17 (1) of the same Act. Under the section the Commission's most important obligation and also probably its most contentious, will be a consideration of the extent, if any, compulsory pilotage ought to be extended.

Procedure connected with making and coming into force of pilotage orders

7.—(1) The Secretary of State may by regulations make provision as to the notices to be given, the other steps to be taken and the payments to be made in connection with an application for a pilotage order, and the regulations must include provision for notice of the application to be advertised and for any person who objects to the application and who appears to the Secretary of State to have a substantial interest in the pilotage services in the area to which the application relates to be given an opportunity of making representations in writing to the Secretary of State about the application.

(2) Where the Secretary of State makes a pilotage order in consequence of such an application, then—

(*a*) if before the order is made either—

(i) no objection to the application has been made in accordance with regulations made by virtue of the preceding subsection, or

(ii) every objection so made to the application has been withdrawn,

the statutory instrument containing the order shall be subject to annulment in pursuance of a resolution of either House of Parliament; and

(*b*) if an objection so made to the application has not been withdrawn before the order is made the order shall be subject to special parliamentary procedure, and the Statutory Orders (Special Procedure) Act 1945 shall have effect accordingly but as if—

(i) sections 2 and 10 (2) of that Act (which relate to preliminary proceedings) were omitted, and

(ii) that Act extended to Northern Ireland and, in the application of section 7 (3) of that Act to Northern Ireland, for any reference to a local authority and the Secretary of State there were substituted respectively a reference to a district council and the Department of the Environment for Northern Ireland.

(3) Subsections (5) and (6) of section 7 of the Pilotage Act 1913 and paragraphs 1 to 6, 8 and 9 of Schedule 1 to that Act (which relate to applications for pilotage orders and contain provisions as to the pilotage orders which do and do not require confirmation by Parliament) shall cease to have effect.

General Note

For pilotage orders, see the Pilotage Act 1913, s. 7. This section alters the former procedure which was set out in s. 7 of the 1913 Act and the First Schedule thereto.

Compulsory pilotage

8.—(1) In section 11 of the Pilotage Act 1913 (which relates to compulsory pilotage)—

(*a*) in subsection (2) (which provides that if a ship is not under pilotage as required by that section the master of it shall be liable to a fine not exceeding double the amount of the pilotage dues that could be demanded for the conduct of the ship) after the word " liable " there shall be inserted the words " on summary conviction " and for the words " could be demanded for the conduct of the ship " there shall be substituted the words " (disregarding any increase in the dues attributable to failure to comply with the requirements of byelaws in force in the district about requests for pilots) would have been payable in respect of the ship if it had been under pilotage as so required ";

(*b*) subsection (3) (*b*) (which provides that pleasure yachts are excepted ships) and subsections (4) and (5) (which enable byelaws to provide that ships mentioned in those subsections shall be excepted ships) shall cease to have effect; and

(*c*) at the end of paragraph (*c*) of subsection (3) (which provides that fishing vessels are excepted ships) there shall be inserted the words " of which the registered length is less than 47·5 metres ";

but nothing in the preceding provisions of this subsection or in any repeal by this Act of a provision of the said section 11 affects that section as set out in subsection (3) of this section.

(2) Any byelaws which, immediately before the preceding subsection comes into force, were in force by virtue of subsection (4) of the said section 11 shall continue in force thereafter and may be revoked as if the said subsection (4) were still in force.

(3) For the said section 11 as amended by subsection (1) of this section there shall be substituted the following section—

11.—(1) Subject to subsection (3) of this section, a ship which is being navigated in a pilotage district in circumstances which the Pilotage Order for the district specifies as circumstances in which pilotage in the district is compulsory shall be—

(*a*) under the pilotage of a licensed pilot of the district who, in any such case as is specified in byelaws made under this Act by the pilotage authority for the district, is accompanied by an assistant who is also a licensed pilot of the district or, if the byelaws so provide, has a qualification specified in the byelaws; or

(*b*) under the pilotage of a master or first mate who possesses a pilotage certificate for the district and is bona fide acting as master or first mate of the ship.

(2) Without prejudice to the generality of the preceding subsection but subject to the following subsection, a ship which is being navigated in a port in a pilotage district at a time when—

(*a*) there is a defect in its hull, machinery or equipment which might affect materially the navigation of the ship; and

(*b*) the pilotage authority for the district have, at the request of the body managing or regulating the port, given notice to the master of the ship stating that the ship is to be under pilotage,

shall be under such pilotage as is mentioned in paragraph (*a*) or (*b*) of the preceding subsection.

(3) The preceding provisions of this section shall not apply to a ship belonging to Her Majesty, and a pilotage authority may by byelaws under this Act provide that a ship which is of a kind described in the byelaws by reference to its type, size or cargo shall not be required by virtue of the Pilotage Order for the authority's district to be under such pilotage as is mentioned in subsection (1) of this section; and in this Act " excepted ship " means, in relation to a pilotage district, a ship belonging to Her Majesty and any other ship of a kind described in byelaws made by virtue of this subsection by the pilotage authority for the district.

(4) If any ship is not under pilotage as required by subsection (1) or (2) of this section, and either—

(*a*) the master of the ship has not complied with the requirements of byelaws made under this Act, by the pilotage authority for the district in question, about requests for pilots; or

(*b*) a licensed pilot of the district has offered to take charge of the ship,

then, subject to the following subsection, the master of the ship shall be guilty of an offence and liable on summary conviction to a fine not exceeding whichever of the following is the greater, namely, one thousand pounds or double the amount of the pilotage dues which would have been payable in respect of the ship if it had been under pilotage as so required and, where the master has not complied as aforesaid, if he had so complied.

(5) It shall be a defence in proceedings for an offence under the preceding subsection to prove that on the occasion to which the charge relates the ship was being navigated in the pilotage district in question only so far as was necessary to avoid serious danger to the ship.

(4) Without prejudice to the generality of subsection (2) of section 52 of this Act, an order in pursuance of that subsection which brings the preceding subsection into force may provide that it shall come into force in relation only to such pilotage districts as are specified in the order.

(5) The Secretary of State may by order provide that the provisions of the Pilotage Act 1913 relating to compulsory pilotage shall, notwithstanding anything in section 12 of that Act (which provides that those provisions are not to apply to certain craft while they are employed and navigating as mentioned in that section), apply to such of the craft so mentioned as are specified in the order.

(6) Section 13 of the Pilotage Act 1913 (which provides for a ship to be exempt from compulsory pilotage in a district if it is there for the purpose of taking or landing a pilot from another district) and section 14 of that Act (which relates to the defence of compulsory pilotage and is spent) shall cease to have effect.

General Note

This section amends the Pilotage Act 1913, s. 11, in a manner which reduces the exceptions to the requirement of compulsory pilotage. Eventually the amended s. 11 will be replaced by an entirely new s. 11 which is set out in subs. (3). The effect of the new section will be to restrict further the categories of " excepted ships " which will include only Crown vessels and those specified in the by-laws of the pilotage district. It will be for each pilotage authority, having regard to local conditions and circumstances, to determine which vessels are to be exempt. The new s. 11 eradicates the former blanket statutory exceptions.

Pilotage charges

9.—(1) A pilotage authority may make in the prescribed form a list of the charges to be paid, by persons who make use in the district of the authority of the services of a pilot licensed by the authority, for the services of the pilot and in respect of the pilotage services of the district; and without prejudice to the generality of the preceding provisions of this subsection—

(*a*) the charges for the services of a pilot may be or include charges in respect of an assistant for the pilot and in respect of the fees and expenses of the pilot and any assistant of his during periods spent outside the district of the authority in anticipation or in consequence of his activities as a pilot or assistant;

(*b*) the charges for the services of a pilot, in a case where the master of the relevant ship has not complied with the requirements of byelaws made under this Act by the authority about requests for pilots, may be greater than, but not more than one and a half times, the charges for those services in a case where the master has so complied;

(*c*) the charges in respect of the pilotage services of the district may be or include charges in respect of the cost of providing, maintaining and operating pilot boats for the district, charges in respect of other costs of providing and maintaining the pilotage organisation provided by the authority and charges in respect of sums payable or paid by the authority to the Commission by virtue of section 2 of this Act; and

(*d*) the list may provide for the payment of different charges in connection with different circumstances, may provide for a charge which is not paid within a prescribed period after it becomes due to be increased periodically in accordance with a prescribed scale and may alter or cancel any previous list made by the authority by virtue of this section.

(2) The charges specified in a list made in pursuance of this section shall not be payable in respect of any use of the services of a pilot before the expiration of the period of 28 days beginning with the day when the list was first published in the prescribed manner; and if at any time after that day an objection to the list is made in writing to the Commission in accordance with the following subsection the Commission may, after giving the authority which made the list an opportunity of commenting in writing to the Commission on the objection and considering any comments then made by the authority, serve in a prescribed manner on the authority a notice in writing cancelling the list or altering the list in a manner specified in the notice and providing that the cancellation or alteration shall have effect on and after a day so specified which is not earlier than the date of service of the notice.

(3) An objection to a list must—

(*a*) be made by—

(i) a majority of the pilots licensed for the district to which the list relates by the authority which made the list or, if the objection is to a particular charge in the list, by a majority of those pilots who are customarily employed in providing the services to which the charge relates, or

(ii) three or more persons who are owners of ships which are customarily navigated in the district of the authority, or

(iii) a dock or harbour authority whose area lies within the district of the authority, or

(iv) any other person appearing to the Commission to have a substantial interest in the list; and (*b*) be so made on one or more of the following grounds, namely—

(i) that one or more of the charges in the list should not be payable or should not be payable in a case specified in the objection;

(ii) that the amount of one or more of the charges in the list should be reduced or increased or should be reduced or increased in a case so specified.

(4) The alteration or cancellation of list made in pursuance of this section shall not affect charges payable in pursuance of the list in respect of the use of the services of a pilot before the alteration or cancellation took effect.

(5) If the Secretary of State directs the Commission to give to an authority by which a list has been made in pursuance of this section a notice in writing cancelling the list, or altering it in a manner specified in the direction, with effect from a day so specified, it shall be the duty of the Commission to comply with the direction.

(6) It shall be the duty of an authority which has made a list in pursuance of this section to send copies of the list to the Secretary of State and the Commission and, unless it has been cancelled, to keep copies of the list, or if it has been altered of the altered list, available during office hours at the principal office of the authority for inspection free of charge and purchase at a reasonable price by members of the public.

(7) Any reference to pilotage dues in the Pilotage Act 1913 shall be construed as a reference to charges payable by virtue of this section, and in this section " prescribed " means prescribed by regulations made by the Secretary of State.

(8) In paragraph (*f*) of section 17 (1) of the Pilotage Act 1913 (which among other things enables byelaws to fix the rates of pilotage dues and to provide for the collection and distribution of them) the words from the beginning to " scales and " shall be omitted and for the words " collection and " there shall be substituted the words " collection (either before or after the performance of services to which they relate) and for the "; but any byelaws made by an authority by virtue of the omitted words and in force immediately before the date when this subsection comes into force shall remain in force on and after that date but—

(*a*) may be revoked by byelaws made by the authority and confirmed by the Secretary of State; and

(*b*) shall not apply to services provided or to be provided after the date when charges first became payable by reference to a list made by the authority in pursuance of this section.

DEFINITION

" pilotage authority ": s. 8 (1) of the Pilotage Authorities (Limitation of Liability) Act 1936.

GENERAL NOTE

This section replaces and extends upon a pilotage authority's power to fix pilotage dues by by-laws under the Pilotage Act 1913, s. 17 (1) (*f*). This latter provision, however, continues in force in respect of the collection and distribution of charges payable. All references to pilotage dues in the preceding pilotage legislation will following the enactment of this section relate to the charges stipulated therein.

Refusal and cancellation of pilotage certificates

10.—(1) A pilotage authority shall not be obliged to grant a pilotage certificate if the Commission considers—

(*a*) that without the certificate the number of persons holding pilots' licences for the authority's district and the number of persons holding pilotage certificates for the district are appropriate for the district; or

(*b*) that if the certificate were granted functions by virtue of it would probably be performed wholly or mainly in a particular area in the authority's district and that without the certificate the number of persons holding pilots' licences by virtue of which functions are performed wholly or mainly in that area and the number of persons holding pilots' certificates by virtue of which functions are so performed are adequate for the area;

and accordingly, for the purposes of paragraph (*a*) of section 27 (1) of the Pilotage Act 1913 (which among other things enables a complaint to be made to the Secretary of State if an authority have refused or failed to grant a pilotage certificate without reasonable cause) a pilotage authority shall have reasonable cause for refusing or failing to grant a pilotage certificate if by virtue of this subsection the authority are not obliged to grant it.

(2) If—

(*a*) a majority of the persons holding pilots' licences for the district of a pilotage authority; or

(*b*) a majority of the persons who hold pilots' licences for the district of a pilotage authority and appear to the Commission to perform functions by virtue of the licences wholly or mainly within a particular area in the district,

make representations in writing to the Secretary of State, within the period of two months beginning with the day when a pilotage certificate is granted by the authority, requesting him to revoke the certificate—

(i) on the ground, in the case of a request by a majority mentioned in paragraph (*a*) above, that apart from the holder of the certificate the number of persons holding pilots' licences for the district and the number of persons holding pilotage certificates for the district are in the opinion of the Commission appropriate for the district; or

(ii) on the ground, in the case of a request by a majority mentioned in paragraph (*b*) above, that in the opinion of the Commission the holder of the certificate is likely to perform functions by virtue of the certificate wholly or mainly within the area in question and that, apart from him, the number of persons who hold pilots' licences by virtue of which functions are in the opinion of the Commission performed wholly or mainly in that area and the number of persons who hold pilotage certificates by virtue of which functions are in the opinion of the Commission so performed are in the opinion of the Commission appropriate for that area,

the Secretary of State may, after giving to the holder of the certificate and the authority an opportunity of making representations in writing to him about the request, give to the holder a notice in writing revoking the certificate; and the certificate shall cease to have effect when the holder receives the notice.

(3) The Secretary of State may, by an order made after the expiration of the period of ten years beginning with the date when this section comes

into force, repeal subsections (1) and (2) of this section; and such an order may contain such transitional provisions as the Secretary of State considers are appropriate in connection with the repeal.

DEFINITIONS

"the Commission": s. 50 (2).

"functions": s. 50 (2).

"pilotage authority": s. 8 (1) of the Pilotage Authorities (Limitation of Liability) Act 1936.

GENERAL NOTE

The subject of pilotage certificates is governed by the Pilotage Act 1913, s. 23, as amended by Sched. 2 to this Act. A pilotage authority may grant a pilotage certificate to any person who is a bona fide master or first mate of any ship if the pilotage authority is satisfied that such a person possesses sufficient skill, experience and local knowledge to be capable of piloting his ship or ships to which the certificate relates. The effect of the pilotage certificate is to permit the master or first mate to act also as a pilot for the ship. The current section is protective of the interest of licensed pilots in that it gives a pilotage authority a power to refuse a certificate in circumstances when the Pilotage Commission considers there already exist a sufficient number of licensed pilots and holders of pilotage certificates. Also, when a pilotage authority so acts, it will have acted with "reasonable cause" for the purpose of any appeal under the Pilotage Act 1913, s. 27. The section also contains a power to revoke a pilotage certificate granted by a pilotage authority. Following the amendment of s. 23 of the Pilotage Act 1913 by s. 13 (1) of, and Sched. 2, para. 8, to this Act, pilotage certificates may be applied for by a national of a Member State of the European Economic Community, if the ship in respect of which the application relates is also registered in a Member State. The section provides a safeguard against any sudden influx of new certificate holders which this amendment may result in.

Employment of pilots by pilotage authorities

11.—(1) A pilotage authority shall have and be deemed always to have had—

(*a*) power to employ pilots licensed by the authority and, as assistants for such pilots, persons who are or are not pilots so licensed; and

(*b*) power to make arrangements with shipowners and other persons under which payments are made to the authority in respect of services of persons employed by the authority by virtue of the preceding paragraph.

(2) If a majority of the persons who for the time being hold pilots' licences for the district of a pilotage authority and are not employed by the authority resolve that the authority shall not be entitled to exercise the power mentioned in the preceding subsection to employ, as pilots or assistants, any pilots licensed by the authority, the authority shall not be entitled to exercise that power until the resolution is revoked by a majority of such persons as aforesaid; and—

(*a*) the Secretary of State may by regulations make provision with respect to the passing and revocation of resolutions for the purposes of this subsection and with respect to records of resolutions and of the revocation of them; but

(*b*) nothing in the preceding provisions of this subsection shall affect any contract of employment in force when a resolution is passed in pursuance of those provisions.

DEFINITION

"pilotage authority": s. 8 (1) of the Pilotage Authorities (Limitation of Liability) Act 1936.

General Note

This section makes it clear that in addition to licensing pilots a pilotage authority may also directly employ pilots. Subs. (2) provides a protection to licensed pilots who are self-employed by providing that in a district where the pilots are so self-employed the pilotage authority may not exercise its power to employ them directly unless a majority of their number approve. In respect of any vicarious liability which may arise from the employment relationship, a pilotage authority will be able to avail itself of the limitation of liability provisions contained in the Pilotage Authorities (Limitation of Liability) Act 1936 as amended by s. 19 (1) of and Sched. 5 to this Act.

Pilots' pension and compensation schemes

12.—(1) The Commission may establish and maintain a scheme for the payment of pensions and other benefits to and in respect of pilots and former pilots.

(2) Such a scheme may include provision for the assets and liabilities of any pilots' benefit fund established by virtue of section 17 (1) (*j*) of the Pilotage Act 1913 to become, with the consent of the managers of the fund, assets and liabilities of the scheme instead of assets and liabilities of the fund; and the managers of any such fund shall have power to give their consent for the purposes of this subsection and to wind up the fund to which their consent relates.

(3) The Commission may establish and maintain a scheme under which payments may be made for the purpose of compensating pilots and their assistants for loss of employment or reductions in earnings suffered by them in consequence of incidents over which they have no control.

Definition

"the Commission": s. 50 (2).

Miscellaneous amendments etc. of Pilotage Act 1913

13.—(1) The Pilotage Act 1913 shall have effect with the amendments specified in Schedule 2 to this Act, and in that Schedule references to sections are to sections of that Act.

(2) In each provision of the Pilotage Act 1913 which is specified in the first column of the following table, for the words specified in relation to that provision in the second and third columns of the table (which state respectively the amount of the maximum fine authorised by that provision for Great Britain and the Isle of Man and for other places) there shall be substituted the words specified in relation to that provision in the fourth column of the table.

Table

Provision of Act	*Old amount for Great Britain and Isle of Man*	*Old amount for other places*	*New amount*
Sections 20 (4), 36 (2) and 50.	Twenty-five pounds	Ten pounds	Two hundred pounds
Sections 34 (1) and 37.	Fifty pounds	Twenty pounds	One thousand pounds
Sections 30 (3) and (4), 41 and 42.	Fifty pounds	Fifty pounds	Five hundred pounds
Section 48 (1) and (2).	One hundred pounds	One hundred pounds	Five hundred pounds
Section 47.	One hundred pounds	One hundred pounds	One thousand pounds

(3) In the following provisions of the Pilotage Act 1913 as in force elsewhere than in Great Britain and the Isle of Man, namely sections 17 (1) (*e*), 39 (2), 43 (3) and 45 (3) (which authorise fines not exceeding twenty pounds), for the words " twenty pounds " there shall be substituted the words " fifty pounds ".

(4) Nothing in any of the preceding provisions of this section applies to an offence committed before the provision comes into force.

(5) It is hereby declared that any reference to a ship in section 30 of the Pilotage Act 1913 (which authorises a licensed pilot to supersede an unlicensed pilot) and section 43 (2) of that Act (which relates to the display of a pilot signal) does not include a ship which a person is piloting or ordered to pilot, in a dockyard port within the meaning of the Dockyard Ports Regulation Act 1865, in the course of his duties as a servant of the Crown; but nothing in this subsection shall be construed as derogating from any immunity which affects a ship apart from this subsection.

Carriage of passengers and luggage by sea

Scheduled convention to have force of law

14.—(1) The provisions of the Convention relating to the Carriage of Passengers and their Luggage by Sea as set out in Part I of Schedule 3 to this Act (hereafter in this section and in Parts II and III of that Schedule referred to as " the Convention ") shall have the force of law in the United Kingdom.

(2) The provisions of Part II of that Schedule shall have effect in connection with the Convention and the preceding subsection shall have effect subject to the provisions of that Part.

(3) On and after the date when this subsection and Part III of Schedule 3 to this Act come into force Parts I and II of that Schedule shall have effect with the modifications specified in the said Part III.

(4) If it appears to Her Majesty in Council that there is a conflict between the provisions of this section or of Part I or II of Schedule 3 to this Act and any provisions relating to the carriage of passengers or luggage for reward by land, sea or air in—

(*a*) any convention which has been signed or ratified by or on behalf of the government of the United Kingdom before the passing of this Act (excluding the Convention); or

(*b*) any enactment of the Parliament of the United Kingdom giving effect to such a convention,

She may by Order in Council make such modifications of this section or that Schedule or any such enactment as She considers appropriate for resolving the conflict.

(5) If it appears to Her Majesty in Council that the government of the United Kingdom has agreed to any revision of the Convention She may by Order in Council make such modifications of Parts I and II of Schedule 3 to this Act as She considers appropriate in consequence of the revision.

(6) Nothing in subsection (1), (2) or (3) of this section or in any modification made by virtue of subsection (4) or (5) of this section shall affect any rights or liabilities arising out of an occurrence which took place before the day on which the said subsection (1), (2) or (3), or as the case may be the modification, comes into force.

(7) This section shall bind the Crown, and any Order in Council made by virtue of this section may provide that the Order or specified provisions of it shall bind the Crown.

DEFINITION

"modifications": s. 50 (2).

GENERAL NOTE

This section has the effect of incorporating into the domestic law of the United Kingdom the Convention relating to the Carriage of Passengers and Their Luggage by Sea 1974 (Cmnd. 6326), commonly referred to as the Athens Convention, and a Protocol to the Convention of November 19, 1976. The text of the Convention is set out in Sched. 3, Pt. I as supplemented and clarified by Pt. II of the Schedule. The Protocol is set out in Pt. III of the same Schedule and when this latter part of the Schedule is eventually brought into effect the whole Schedule will take effect subject to the modifications specified in it.

The Athens Convention applies to the international carriage of passengers and their luggage in the circumstances specified in art. 2 (1) of the Convention. Art. 1 provides the definitions of the basic concepts of the Convention. The broad theme of the Convention is to impose certain basic responsibilities on both carrier and performing carrier subject to an entitlement to limit that liability to certain prescribed sums. The carrier and performing carrier are liable for the death or personal injury to a passenger and for the loss or damage to luggage caused by their fault or neglect or that of their servants or agents. The carrier is made vicariously liable for negligence on the part of the performing carrier but where both carrier and performing carrier are in breach of duty their liability is joint and several. There is, however, no liability for valuables unless they have been deposited with the carrier for safe-keeping. Under the Convention, the burden of proof lies with the claimant although in important circumstances liability is presumed unless the contrary is proved.

The limits of liability specified in the Convention are 700,000 gold francs in the case of death or personal injury (although a higher per capita limit may be fixed by a State Party to the Convention in relation to carriers who are nationals of such a State); 12,500 gold francs in respect of loss or damage to cabin luggage; 50,000 gold francs in respect of vehicles and luggage carried in or on the vehicle; 18,000 gold francs in respect of other luggage and valuables deposited for safe-keeping. By agreement in writing, the parties to the contract may agree to higher limits. The amounts specified relate to the aggregate of claims. Where it can be shown that the damage complained of has been intentionally or recklessly caused, the right to limit liability is lost. The effect of the Protocol when brought into force will be to replace the gold franc by a unit of account as the measure of liability, each unit of account being a special drawing right as defined by the International Monetary Fund.

Any contractual provision which, prior to the cause of action, attempts to dilute the obligations of the carrier or extends his rights is null and void.

The Athens Convention does not apply to gratuitous carriage nor does it apply when the carriage by sea is part of a mixed mode of transport in respect of which another international convention applies, *e.g.* the International Convention concerning the Carriage of Passengers and Luggage by Rail 1970 (Cmnd. 5211), and the Additional Convention to the International Convention concerning the Carriage of Passengers and Luggage by Rail given statutory force by the Carriage by Railway Act 1972; the International Convention concerning the Carriage of Goods by Rail 1970 and Protocol of 25.2.71, given contractual effect under British Rail Consignment Note BR 20105/114 (see also Sched. 63, Pt. II, para. 2, to this Act); the Convention on the Contract for the International Carriage of Passengers and Luggage by Road (Cmnd. 5622) given effect by the Carriage of Passengers by Road Act 1974.

A claim under the Athens Convention may only be brought in a court of a State Party to the Convention in the circumstances specified in art. 17 of the Convention. The effect of this article is restrictive for it slightly diminishes the availability of the Admiralty action *in rem* under the Administration of Justice Act 1956, s. 1 (1) (*f*), in respect of claims under the Convention which are also within the jurisdiction of the Admiralty Court.

For the relationship between the Athens Convention and the Convention on Limitation for Maritime Claims 1976 (see s. 17) and other statutory rights of limitation, see Sched. 3, Pt. II, paras. 12 and 13.

The Athens Convention applies only to negligent liability in respect of passengers and their luggage. Other aspects of the legal relationship appertaining to the performance of the contract, such as delay, deviation, failure to execute the voyage with reasonable dispatch, or the provision of reasonable accommodation are not incorporated and therefore continue to be governed by the common law and the Unfair Contract Terms Act 1977. The Athens Convention was in fact anticipated by s. 28 of the latter Act, the effect of which was to permit international carriers to adopt the provisions of the Convention without falling foul of the "reasonableness test" which under the 1977 Act is in most cases the determinant of the validity of an excluding or limiting contractual term. When the Convention comes into force, s. 28 will cease to have any relevance and art. 18 of the Convention will become the governing provision.

Provisions supplementary to s. 14

15.—(1) Her Majesty may by Order in Council provide that the preceding section and Schedule 3 to this Act shall extend, with such modifications, if any, as are specified in the Order, to any of the following countries, namely—

(*a*) the Isle of Man;
(*b*) any of the Channel Islands;
(*c*) any colony;
(*d*) any country outside Her Majesty's dominions in which Her Majesty has jurisdiction in right of the government of the United Kingdom.

(2) A draft of an Order in Council proposed to be made by virtue of subsection (4) or (5) of the preceding section shall not be submitted to Her Majesty in Council unless the draft has been approved by a resolution of each House of Parliament; and any statutory instrument made by virtue of subsection (1) of this section shall be subject to annulment in pursuance of a resolution of either House of Parliament.

(3) An order made by virtue of section 52 (2) of this Act which appoints a day for the coming into force of Part III of Schedule 3 to this Act may contain such transitional provisions as the Secretary of State considers appropriate in connection with the coming into force of that Part.

DEFINITION
"modifications": s. 50 (2).

GENERAL NOTE
This section appears to follow the standard constitutional practice when the United Kingdom Government is giving statutory force to an international convention which ought, in the general interest, to be accepted globally. The power which the section provides is not exercised except after full consultation and with the agreement of the territories concerned. Moreover, the power exists alongside the right of the various local legislations to implement the Convention by domestic statutes. In most instances the issue is not whether the provisions of a Convention ought to be extended to an overseas territory but the precise constitutional device by which it is to be achieved.

Application of Schedule 3 to international carriage before coming into force of s. 14 (1) and (2) and to domestic carriage

16.—(1) Her Majesty may by Order in Council provide that, during any period before the coming into force of subsections (1) and (2) of section 14 of this Act, Part I of Schedule 3 to this Act—

(*a*) shall have the force of law in the United Kingdom, with such modifications as are specified in the Order, in relation to, and to matters connected with, any contract of carriage for international carriage which is made in the United Kingdom and any contract of carriage for international carriage under which a place in the United Kingdom is the place of departure or destination; and (*b*) shall, as modified in pursuance of the preceding paragraph, have effect in relation to, and to matters connected with, any such contract subject to the provisions of Part II of that Schedule or to those provisions with such modifications as are specified in the Order.

(2) Her Majesty may by Order in Council provide that Part I of Schedule 3 to this Act—

(*a*) shall have the force of law in the United Kingdom, with such modifications as are specified in the Order, in relation to, and to matters connected with, a contract of carriage where the places of departure and destination under the contract are in the area consisting of the United Kingdom, the Channel Islands and the Isle of Man and under the contract there is no intermediate port of call outside that area; and

(*b*) shall, as modified in pursuance of the preceding paragraph, have effect in relation to, and to matters connected with, any such contract subject to the provisions of Part II of that Schedule or to those provisions with such modifications as are specified in the Order.

(3) An Order in Council made by virtue of subsection (1) or (2) of this section may contain such provisions, including provisions modifying section 28 of the Unfair Contract Terms Act 1977 (which relates to certain contracts as respects which the Convention mentioned in section 14 (1) of this Act does not have the force of law in the United Kingdom), as the Secretary of State considers appropriate for the purpose of dealing with matters arising in connection with any contract to which the said section 28 applies before the Order is made.

(4) If an order appointing a day for the coming into force of subsections (1) and (2) of section 14 of this Act is made in pursuance of section 52 (2) of this Act at a time when an Order in Council made by virtue of subsection (1) of this section is in force, the order appointing the day may contain such provisions as the Secretary of State considers appropriate (including provisions modifying provisions of Schedule 3 to this Act as they have effect by virtue of those subsections) for the purpose of dealing with matters arising, in connection with such a contract as is mentioned in subsection (1) of this section, in consequence of the coming into force of subsections (1) and (2) of the said section 14.

(5) An Order in Council made by virtue of subsection (1) or (2) of this section may provide that the Order or specified provisions of it shall bind the Crown; but a draft of an Order in Council proposed to be made by virtue of either of those subsections shall not be submitted to Her Majesty in Council, and no order shall be made containing provisions authorised by the preceeding subsection, unless the draft of the Order in Council or, as the case may be, a draft of the other order has been approved by a resolution of each House of Parliament.

(6) In subsections (1) and (2) of this section expressions to which meanings are assigned by article 1 of the Convention set out as mentioned in section 14 (1) of this Act have those meanings but any reference to a contract of carriage excludes such a contract which is not for reward.

DEFINITION

"modifications": s. 50 (2).

GENERAL NOTE

This section allows for an interim régime whereby the Athens Convention may be brought into effect prior to the coming into force of s. 14. It also provides a power by which the Convention may be extended so as to apply also to domestic contracts of passage.

Liability of shipowners and salvors

Limitation of liability

17.—(1) The provisions of the Convention on Limitation of Liability for Maritime Claims 1976 as set out in Part I of Schedule 4 to this Act (hereafter in this section and in Part II of that Schedule referred to as " the Convention ") shall have the force of law in the United Kingdom.

(2) The provisions of Part II of that Schedule shall have effect in connection with the Convention, and the preceding subsection shall have effect subject to the provisions of that Part.

General Note

This section when brought into effect will replace s. 503 of the Merchant Shipping Act 1894, as amended by the Merchant Shipping (Liability of Shipowners and Others) Act 1958. The effect of the section will be to give the force of law to the Convention on Limitation of Liability for Maritime Claims 1976 (Cmnd. 7035) which is set out in Sched. 4, Pt. I, to the Act and supplemented by Pt. II of the same Schedule. The 1976 Convention, familiarly known as the London Convention, replaces the International Convention relating to the Limitation of Liability of Sea-going Ships, signed in Brussels on October 10, 1957. Although the London Convention was ultimately drafted and introduced by I.M.C.O. its genesis can be traced to the Hamburg Conference of the C.M.I. in 1974.

The London Convention continues in the general pattern of the former law in that specified claims are made subject to monetary limitations assessed by reference to the tonnage of the ship concerned. There are, however, significant amendments.

First, for the purposes of the Convention a ship's tonnage relates to gross tonnage calculated in accordance with Annex I of the International Convention on Tonnage Measurement of Ships, 1969.

Secondly, the range of claims subject to limitation is increased. Of particular significance, the Convention gives the privilege of limitation to salvors in respect of specified claims. This is undoubtedly a response to the increasing judicial inclination, culminating in the House of Lords' decision in *The Tojo Maru* [1972] A.C. 242, to refuse to ascribe any legal privilege to salvors arising from their status and the tenets of public policy which envelops the services they render. Apart from claims against salvors, the privilege of limitation is also extended to claims resulting from delay in the carriage by sea of cargo, passengers or their luggage, claims in respect of removal, destruction or the rendering harmless of the cargo of the ship, and claims arising in respect of measures taken in order to avert or minimise loss in circumstances when the person liable may limit his liability under the Convention, and also for loss caused by such measures. The Convention also provides that the benefit of limitation extends to the insurer of any claim which is subject to limitation.

Thirdly, the Convention materially alters the circumstances when the right to limitation is lost. Under s. 503, the right to limitation is dependant upon the claim arising without the " actual fault or privity " of the shipowner. The privilege of limitation is lost under the Convention if it can be shown that the loss resulted from the shipowner's or salvor's " personal act or omission, committed with the intent to cause such loss, or recklessly and with knowledge that such loss would probably result " (art. 4). The formula under s. 503 was particularly imprecise and uncertain, particularly the word " privity," and triggered a substantial amount of litigation. The new formula under the Convention probably avoids much of this uncertainty but at the same time substantially reduces the occasions when the right to limit may be circumvented and a full and complete liability implemented on the wrongdoer. This is the inevitable consequence of the need under the Convention to show that the loss was intentionally or recklessly caused before the right to limitation is lost. As the Minister responsible for the Bill, Mr. Clinton Davies, observed during the House of Commons Committee stage, " the new words would, in fact, be more severe and designed to ensure that the limitation was unbreakable in normal cases."

Fourthly, the Convention broadly raises the limits of liability, although they continue to be generous in favour of the wrongdoer, and also the method of calculating the limitation fund. The Poincaré franc applied under the former law is replaced by units of account, each such unit being a special drawing right as defined by the International Monetary Fund. For the method of ascertaining the sterling equivalent of a special drawing right, see Sched. 4, Pt. II, para. 7. Also the mechanics of the limitation process by which units of account are related to the tonnage of the ship is applied with greater specificity of gradations under the London Convention than was formerly the case. Separate provision is made in relation to the liability of salvors not operating from any ship or operating solely on the ship which is benefiting from his services. Particular provision is also made for small ships of less than 300 gross tons.

Fifthly, the Convention awards a priority to claims in respect of death anl personal injury. Where personal injury and property claims subsist alongside each other and that part of the limitation fund constituted in respect of the personal injury claims is insufficient to meet the claim in full, the residue may be pursued into that part of the fund constituted by reference to the property claims and in relation to which the personal injury and property claims rank rateably (art. 6 (2)).

Sixthly, the Convention specifies that the claims set out therein may be subject to limitation of liability even if brought by way of recourse or indemnity under a contract or otherwise.

Alongside art. 3 of the Convention, which enumerates claims excepted from limitation, should be considered s. 35 of this Act which further excludes from limitation any claim advanced by a person employed on board a ship under a contract of service.

Exclusion of liability

18.—(1) Subject to subsection (3) of this section, the owner of a British ship shall not be liable for any loss or damage in the following cases, namely—

(*a*) where any property on board the ship is lost or damaged by reason of fire on board the ship; or

(*b*) where any gold, silver, watches, jewels or precious stones on board the ship are lost or damaged by reason of theft, robbery or other dishonest conduct and their nature and value were not at the time of shipment declared by their owner or shipper to the owner or master of the ship in the bill of lading or otherwise in writing.

(2) Subject to subsection (3) of this section, where the loss or damage arises from anything done or omitted by any person in his capacity as master or member of the crew or (otherwise than in that capacity) in the course of his employment as a servant of the owner of the ship, the preceding subsection shall also exclude the liability of—

(*a*) the master, member of the crew or servant; and

(*b*) in a case where the master or member of the crew is the servant of a person whose liability would not be excluded by that subsection apart from this paragraph, the person whose servant he is.

(3) This section does not exclude the liability of any person for any loss or damage resulting from any such personal act or omission of his as is mentioned in article 4 of the Convention in Part I of Schedule 4 to this Act.

(4) In this section " owner ", in relation to a ship, includes any part owner and any charterer, manager or operator of the ship.

DEFINITIONS

"master": s. 742 of the Merchant Shipping Act 1894.

"ship": s. 742 of the Merchant Shipping Act 1894.

"British ship": *Chartered Mercantile Bank of India* v. *Netherlands India S.N. Co.* (1883) 10 Q.B.D. 521, *per* Brett L.J. at pp. 534–536; *Union Bank of London* v. *Lenanton* (1878) 3 C.P.D. 243, *per* Cockburn C.J.

General Note

This section re-enacts s. 502 of the Merchant Shipping Act 1894, as amended by s. 3 of the Merchant Shipping (Liability of Shipowners and Others) Act 1958. The language of the former statutes has been modernised, and words and phrases of ambiguous, if not meaningless, import have been omitted. For example, the phrase "making away with" and the word "secreting" in relation to the different means by which valuables might be lost or damaged for the purpose of s. 502 (11), are no longer reproduced. S. 18 also clears up any ambiguity that might have existed under s. 3 of the 1958 statute as to the extent of the immunity enjoyed by master and members of the crew. All persons within the ambit of the section are only entitled to immunity from suit if the damage or loss contemplated by the section did not arise from a personal act or omission committed with intent to cause such damage or loss, or recklessly and with knowledge that such damage or loss would probably occur. This is the effect of subs. (3) which incorporates art. 4 of the London Convention set out in Sched. 4, Pt. I. The section continues to be applicable only to British ships.

Provisions supplementary to ss. 17 and 18

19.—(1) The enactments mentioned in Schedule 5 to this Act shall have effect with the amendments there specified (which are consequential on sections 17 and 18 of this Act).

(2) Her Majesty may by Order in Council provide that the said sections 17 and 18, the preceding subsection and Schedules 4 and 5 to this Act shall extend, with such modifications, if any, as are specified in the Order, to any of the following countries, namely—

(*a*) the Isle of Man;

(*b*) any of the Channel Islands;

(*c*) any colony;

(*d*) any country outside Her Majesty's dominions in which Her Majesty has jurisdiction in right of the government of the United Kingdom.

(3) Any statutory instrument made by virtue of the preceding subsection shall be subject to annulment in pursuance of a resolution of either House of Parliament.

(4) Nothing in the said sections 17 and 18 or the said Schedule 4 shall apply in relation to any liability arising out of an occurrence which took place before the coming into force of those sections, and subsection (1) of this section and Schedule 5 to this Act shall not affect the operation of any enactment in relation to such an occurrence.

Definitions

"modifications": s. 50 (2).

General Note

Subs. (1) brings into force necessary amendments in associated legislation principally with the aim of making the new formula incorporated in art. 4 of the Convention of widespread application and also the method adopted in the Convention for calculating the limited liability of a ship. Subs. (2) enable the Convention to be extended in its application to overseas territories in the same manner as s. 15 operates in relation to the Athens Convention. The observations made in relation to s. 15 are equally applicable to this section. When brought into effect, ss. 17 and 18 and the Schedule thereto will apply only to occurrences which take place after they have been brought into force.

Prevention of pollution from ships etc.

Prevention of pollution from ships etc.

20.—(1) Her Majesty may by Order in Council make such provision as She considers appropriate for the purpose of giving effect to any provision of any of the following which have been ratified by the United Kingdom, namely—

(*a*) the International Convention for the Prevention of Pollution from Ships (including its protocols, annexes and appendices) which constitutes attachment 1 to the final act of the International Conference on Marine Pollution signed in London on 2nd November 1973;

(*b*) the Protocol relating to Intervention on the High Seas in Cases of Marine Pollution by Substances other than Oil which constitutes attachment 2 to the final act aforesaid;

(*c*) the Protocol relating to the said Convention which constitutes attachment 2 to the final act of the International Conference on Tanker Safety and Pollution Prevention signed in London on 17th February 1978;

(*d*) any international agreement not mentioned in the preceding paragraphs which relates to the prevention, reduction or control of pollution of the sea or other waters by matter from ships;

and in paragraph (*d*) of this subsection the reference to an agreement includes an agreement which provides for the modification of another agreement, including the modification of an agreement mentioned in paragraphs (*a*) to (*c*) of this subsection.

(2) The powers conferred by the preceding subsection to make provision for the purpose of giving effect to an agreement include power to provide for the provision to come into force although the agreement has not come into force.

(3) Without prejudice to the generality of subsection (1) of this section, an Order under that subsection may in particular include provision—

(*a*) for applying for the purpose mentioned in that subsection any enactment or instrument relating to the pollution of the sea or other waters and any of the following enactments, namely—

sections 446 to 450 of the Merchant Shipping Act 1894 (which relate to dangerous goods),

sections 55 to 58 of the Merchant Shipping Act 1970 (which relate to investigations of shipping casualties),

sections 10 to 13 of and Schedules 2 and 3 to the Merchant Shipping Act 1974 (which relate to oil tankers);

(*b*) with respect to the carrying out of surveys and inspections for the purpose aforesaid, the issue, duration and recognition of certificates for that purpose and the payment in connection with such a survey, inspection or certificate of fees of amounts determined with the approval of the Treasury;

(*c*) for repealing the provisions of any enactment or instrument so far as it appears to Her Majesty that those provisions are not required having regard to any provision made or proposed to be made by virtue of this section;

(*d*) with respect to the application of the Order to the Crown and the extra-territorial operation of any provision made by or under the Order;

(*e*) for the extension of any provisions of the Order, with or without modifications, to any of the Channel Islands, the Isle of Man, any colony and any country or place outside Her Majesty's dominions in which Her Majesty has jurisdiction in right of the government of the United Kingdom;

(*f*) for imposing penalties in respect of any contravention of a provision made by or under the Order, not exceeding, in respect of any one contravention, a fine of £1,000 on summary conviction and imprisonment for two years and a fine on conviction on indictment; and

(*g*) for detaining any ship in respect of which such a contravention is suspected to have occurred and, in relation to such a ship, for applying section 692 of the Merchant Shipping Act 1894 (which relates to the detention of a ship) with such modifications, if any, as are prescribed by the Order;

and nothing in any of the preceding provisions of this subsection shall be construed as prejudicing the generality of any other of those provisions and in particular paragraph (*f*) shall not prejudice paragraph (*a*).

(4) An Order under subsection (1) of this section may—

(*a*) make different provision for different circumstances;

(*b*) provide for exemptions from any provisions of the Order;

(*c*) provide for the delegation of functions exercisable by virtue of the Order;

(*d*) include such incidental, supplemental and transitional provisions as appear to Her Majesty to be expedient for the purposes of the Order;

(*e*) authorise the making of regulations and other instruments for any of the purposes of this section (except the purposes of paragraphs (*a*) and (*c*) of the preceding subsection) and apply the Statutory Instruments Act 1946 to instruments made under the Order; and

(*f*) provide that any enactment or instrument applied by the Order shall have effect as so applied subject to such modifications as may be specified in the Order.

(5) An Order in Council in pursuance of paragraph (*b*) or (*d*) of subsection (1) of this section may apply to areas of land or sea or other waters within the seaward limits of the territorial waters of the United Kingdom notwithstanding that the agreement in question does not relate to those areas.

(6) A draft of an Order in Council proposed to be made by virtue of subsection (1) of this section shall not be submitted to Her Majesty in Council unless the draft has been approved by a resolution of each House of Parliament or the Order is to contain a statement that it is made only for any of the following purposes, namely, the purpose of giving effect to an agreement mentioned in paragraphs (*a*) to (*c*) of that subsection, the purpose of providing as authorised by subsection (2) of this section in relation to such an agreement and the purposes of the preceding subsection, or the Order extends only to a territory mentioned in subsection (3) (*e*) of this section; and a statutory instrument containing an Order which contains such a statement shall be subject to annulment in pursuance of a resolution of either House of Parliament.

DEFINITIONS

"convention": s. 50 (2).
"modification": s. 50 (2).

GENERAL NOTE

This section gives wide powers by which the International Conventions specified, together with any future conventions, may be implemented by Orders in Council. The section also represents a response to the growing disquiet of recent years at the length of time it takes for international agreement in the realm of pollution from ships to come into force. The delay is principally caused by the laggardliness of certain Member States of I.M.C.O., which is the organisation principally concerned with the international control of marine pollution and which instigates most of the international conventions. This dilatoriness was also adversely commented upon in the EEC Commission Document COM (78) 184 published on April 28, 1978. The section attempts to overcome the effects of such delay by empowering the adoption of the whole or part of a convention before it has come into force and thereby securing its application to British registered ships and foreign registered ships when in U.K. ports. The government has, however, made it known that it will not unilaterally legislate a convention in this manner unless it has first ratified the convention and is also satisfied that there has been an unreasonable delay on the part of foreign maritime states in taking similar action. Where a convention is timetabled there can be no question of unreasonable delay until the expiration of the schedule period of time. Orders in Council made under the section are subject to the affirmative resolution procedure.

Many of the penalties under the previous marine pollution by oil legislation are increased by s. 43 of and Sched. 6 to the Act.

Safety and health on ships

Safety and health on ships

21.—(1) The Secretary of State may by regulations make such provision as he considers appropriate for all or any of the following purposes, namely—

(*a*) for securing the safety of United Kingdom ships and persons on them and for protecting the health of persons on United Kingdom ships;

(*b*) for giving effect to any provisions of an international agreement ratified by the United Kingdom so far as the agreement relates to the safety of other ships or persons on them or to the protection of the health of persons on other ships.

(2) In the preceding subsection " United Kingdom ship " means a ship which—

(*a*) is registered in the United Kingdom; or

(*b*) is not registered under the law of any country but is wholly owned by persons each of whom is either a citizen of the United Kingdom and Colonies or a body corporate which is established under the law of a part of the United Kingdom and has its principal place of business in a part of the United Kingdom;

and the power conferred by the preceding subsection to make provision for giving effect to an agreement includes power to provide for the provision to come into force although the agreement has not come into force.

(3) Regulations in pursuance of subsection (1) of this section (hereafter in this section and in the following section referred to as " safety regulations ") may in particular make provision with respect to any of the following matters, namely—

(*a*) the design, construction, maintenance, repair, alteration, inspection, surveying and marking of ships and their machinery and equipment;

(*b*) the packaging, marking, loading, placing, moving, inspection, testing and measuring of cargo and anything on a ship which is not cargo, machinery or equipment;

(*c*) the carrying out of any operation involving a ship;

(*d*) the use of the machinery and equipment of a ship and of anything on a ship which is not cargo, machinery or equipment;

(*e*) the manning of ships, including the employment on ships of persons qualified to attend to the health and safety of persons on the ships;

(*f*) the arrangements for ensuring communication between persons in different parts of a ship and between persons in the ship and other persons;
(*g*) the access to, presence in and egress from a ship, and different parts of it, of persons of any description;
(*h*) the ventilation, temperature and lighting of different parts of a ship;
(*i*) the steps to be taken to prevent or control noise, vibration and radiation in and from a ship and the emission in or from a ship of smoke, gas and dust;
(*j*) the steps to be taken to prevent, detect and deal with outbreaks of fire on a ship;
(*k*) the steps to be taken to prevent any collision involving a ship and in consequence of any collision involving a ship;
(*l*) the steps to be taken, in a case where a ship is in distress or stranded or wrecked, for the purpose of saving the ship and its machinery, equipment and cargo and the lives of persons on or from the ship, including the steps to be taken by other persons for giving assistance in such a case;
(*m*) the removal, by jettisoning or otherwise, of its equipment and of other things from a ship for the purpose of avoiding, removing or reducing danger to persons or property;
(*n*) the steps to be taken, in a case where danger of any kind occurs or is suspected on a ship, for removing or reducing the danger and for warning persons who are not on the ship of the danger or suspected danger;
(*o*) the making of records and the keeping of documents relating to ships and the keeping and use on a ship of information to facilitate the navigation of the ship;
(*p*) the keeping of registers and the issue of certificates in cases for which registration or a certificate is required by virtue of the regulations;
(*q*) the furnishing of information; and
(*r*) the payment of fees of amounts determined with the approval of the Treasury.

(4) Safety regulations—
(*a*) may make provision in terms of approvals given by the Secretary of State or another person and in terms of any document which the Secretary of State or another person considers relevant from time to time;
(*b*) may provide for the cancellation of an approval given in pursuance of the regulations and for the alteration of the terms of such an approval; and
(*c*) must provide for any approval in pursuance of the regulations to be given in writing and to specify the date on which it takes effect and the conditions (if any) on which it is given.

(5) Without prejudice to subsection (1) (*b*) of the following section, safety regulations may provide—
(*a*) for the granting by the Secretary of State or another person, on such terms (if any) as the Secretary of State or other person may specify, of exemptions from specified provisions of the regulations for classes of cases or individual cases; and
(*b*) for the alteration or cancellation of exemptions granted in pursuance of the regulations.

(6) Safety regulations may provide—
(*a*) that in such cases as are prescribed by the regulations a ship

shall be liable to be detained and that section 692 of the Merchant Shipping Act 1894 (which relates to the detention of a ship) shall have effect, with such modifications (if any) as are prescribed by the regulations, in relation to the ship;

(*b*) that, in such cases of contraventions of the regulations as are prescribed by the regulations, such persons as are so prescribed shall each be guilty of an offence and liable on summary conviction to a fine not exceeding £1,000 or, on conviction on indictment, to imprisonment for a term not exceeding two years and a fine;

(*c*) that, notwithstanding anything in the preceding paragraph, a person convicted summarily of an offence under the regulations of a kind which is stated by the regulations to correspond to an offence under an enactment specified in the regulations which authorises or authorised a fine on summary conviction of a maximum amount exceeding £1,000 shall be liable to a fine not exceeding that maximum amount.

DEFINITION

"contravention": s. 50 (2).

GENERAL NOTE

This section gives the Secretary of State a wide power to make safety regulations with a view to securing the safety of ships and seafarers, and for protecting the health of those employed on board ships. The section only applies to United Kingdom ships, which concept is defined in subs. (2). Under the section, however, the regulations may be extended to "other ships" where the regulation derives from an international agreement which the U.K. has ratified and notwithstanding that the international agreement is not yet in force. In this regard the section follows the same pattern as that adopted under s. 20. Regulations made under the section are variously subject to both affirmative and negative resolution processes (see s. 49). Regulations which are derived from international agreements not yet in force and which are to apply to non-United Kingdom ships are subject to the affirmative approval of Parliament (s. 49 (3)).

The section is analogous to the scheme under the Health and Safety at Work, etc. Act 1974 and represents a determined policy to bring the regulation of safety and health on ships into line with those relating to persons on land. The particular matters encountered in subs. (3) are not exhaustive but merely illustrative of the kind of regulations which may be made under subs. (1). The whole section has been drafted broadly so as to provide flexibility and permit the government to respond expeditiously to changed circumstances, scientific development and to enable it to ratify speedily appropriate international conventions, *e.g.* the International Convention on the Training, Certification and Watch-Keeping of Seafarers, 1978 (ILO Convention No. 147). A particular aim of the section is to replace the voluntary system of accident reporting which has previously prevailed by a statutory scheme of universal application. See also the Merchant Shipping Act 1970, s. 19. It is contemplated that when regulations are ultimately made they will provide for a separate injury annex to the log book.

Provisions supplementary to s. 21

22.—(1) Safety regulations may—

(*a*) make different provision for different circumstances and, in particular, make provision for an individual case;

(*b*) be made so as to apply only in such circumstances as are prescribed by the regulations;

(*c*) be made so as to extend outside the United Kingdom;

(*d*) contain such incidental, supplemental and transitional provisions as the Secretary of State considers appropriate.

(2) Where the Secretary of State proposes to make safety regulations or he or another person proposes to give an approval in pursuance of safety regulations it shall be the duty of the Secretary of State or other person, before he gives effect to the proposal, to consult such persons in the United Kingdom (if any) as he considers will be affected by the proposal.

(3) The Secretary of State may by regulations—

(*a*) make such repeals or other modifications of provisions of the Merchant Shipping Acts, of any instruments made under those Acts and of the Anchors and Chain Cables Act 1967 as he considers appropriate in consequence or in anticipation of the making of safety regulations;

(*b*) make such repeals or other modifications of provisions of any enactment passed and any instrument made before the passing of this Act as he considers appropriate in connection with any modification made or to be made in pursuance of the preceding paragraph;

(*c*) provide for anything done under a provision repealed or otherwise modified by virtue of either of the preceding paragraphs to have effect as if done under safety regulations and make such other transitional provision and such incidental and supplemental provision as he considers appropriate in connection with any modification made by virtue of either of those paragraphs.

(4) Nothing in subsections (3) to (6) of the preceding section or subsection (1) of this section shall be construed as prejudicing the generality of subsection (1) of the preceding section.

Discipline

Breaches by seamen of codes of conduct and local industrial agreements

23.—(1) For the purpose of maintaining discipline on board ships registered in the United Kingdom the Secretary of State may by regulations make provision—

(*a*) for the hearing on shore in the United Kingdom, by a body established or approved by the Secretary of State in pursuance of the regulations, of a complaint by the master or owner of a ship registered in the United Kingdom, other than a fishing vessel, alleging that during a period when a person (hereafter in this subsection referred to as " the seaman ") was employed on board the ship he contravened, either on or off the ship and in the United Kingdom or elsewhere, a provision of a code of conduct approved by the Secretary of State for the purposes of this section;

(*b*) for enabling the body to dismiss the complaint if it finds the allegation not proved and, if it finds the allegation proved, to warn or reprimand the seaman or to recommend to the Secretary of State that the seaman shall, either for a period specified in the recommendation or permanently, cease to be entitled to a discharge book in pursuance of section 71 of the Merchant Shipping Act 1970 and shall be required to surrender any such book which has been issued to him;

(*c*) for enabling the seaman to appeal against such a recommendation to another body established or approved as aforesaid and for enabling the body to confirm or cancel the recommendation or, in the case of a recommendation that the seaman shall cease to be entitled to a discharge book permanently or for a particular period, to substitute for it a recommendation that he shall cease to be so entitled, instead of permanently, for a period specified in the substituted recommendation or, instead of for the particular period, for a shorter period so specified;

(*d*) for securing that a recommendation in pursuance of regulations made by virtue of paragraph (*b*) above that the seaman shall permanently cease to be entitled to a discharge book is not submitted to the Secretary of State unless it has been confirmed, either on appeal or otherwise, by a body which is or was authorised by regulations made by virtue of the preceding paragraph to entertain an appeal against the recommendation;

(*e*) for the establishment or approval for the purposes of this section of such number of bodies as the Secretary of State thinks fit and with respect to the composition, jurisdiction and procedure of any body established or approved for those purposes;

(*f*) for the payment out of money provided by Parliament of such remuneration and allowances as the Secretary of State may with the consent of the Minister for the Civil Service determine to any member of a body established by the Secretary of State in pursuance of the regulations;

and regulations made by virtue of this subsection may make different provision for different circumstances and may contain such incidental and supplemental provisions as the Secretary of State considers appropriate.

(2) In relation to fishing vessels registered in the United Kingdom the preceding subsection shall have effect with the substitution for paragraph (*a*) of the following paragraph—

(*a*) for the hearing on shore in the United Kingdom, by a body established or approved by the Secretary of State in pursuance of the regulations, of a complaint by the master or owner of a fishing vessel registered in the United Kingdom alleging that during a period when a person (hereafter in this subsection referred to as " the seaman ") was employed on board the vessel, he contravened, either on or off the vessel and in the United Kingdom or elsewhere, a local industrial agreement relating to his employment in the vessel and for requiring the body to have regard to the agreement in determining whether the allegation is proved;

and regulations made by virtue of the preceding subsection may include provision authorising persons to determine, for the purposes of that paragraph, what agreements are or were local industrial agreements and which local industrial agreement relates or related to a person's employment in a particular vessel.

(3) Without prejudice to the generality of subsection (1) of this section, regulations made by virtue of that subsection may include provision for any proceedings in pursuance of the regulations to take place notwithstanding the absence of the seaman to whom the proceedings relate; and nothing in regulations made by virtue of that subsection or done in pursuance of regulations so made shall be construed as affecting any power to institute, prosecute, entertain or determine proceedings (including criminal proceedings) under any other enactment or at common law.

(4) When the Secretary of State proposes to make any regulations in pursuance of subsection (1) of this section it shall be his duty, before

he makes the regulations, to consult about the proposal such organisations in the United Kingdom as he considers are representative of persons likely to be affected by the regulations.

(5) The power conferred by section 71 of the Merchant Shipping Act 1970 to make regulations relating to discharge books—

(*a*) shall include power to provide for a person to cease to be entitled to a discharge book in consequence of a recommendation made by virtue of this section;

(*b*) includes power to provide for the re-issue of discharge books which have been surrendered in consequence of such a recommendation.

(6) A person who, in the United Kingdom or elsewhere—

(*a*) obtains employment as a seaman on board a ship registered in the United Kingdom and does so when he is disentitled to a discharge book by virtue of regulations made by virtue of paragraph (*a*) of the preceding subsection; or

(*b*) employs as such a seaman a person who he knows or has reason to suspect is disentitled as aforesaid,

shall be guilty of an offence and liable on summary conviction to a fine not exceeding £1,000 or, on conviction on indictment, to imprisonment for a term not exceeding two years or a fine or both.

(7) Sections 34 to 38 of the Merchant Shipping Act 1970 and paragraph 2 of Schedule 2 to that Act (which relate to discipline on board ships registered in the United Kingdom) shall cease to have effect.

DEFINITION

"contravention": s. 50 (2).

GENERAL NOTE

This section enables regulations to be made with a view to modernising and making more acceptable to the contemporary seaman the disciplinary régime on board ship. It is the culmination of a process commenced in the Merchant Shipping Act 1970, continued in the Merchant Shipping Act 1974, and implements the recommendations of the Working Group on Disciplinary Needs for Seagoing Employment in the Merchant Navy, published in November 1975. The section replaces the long-established authority of the master to impose on board fines and introduces a régime whereunder disciplinary matters are deferred for consideration by shore-based disciplinary committees subject to a right of appeal. The section repeals the former power to make disciplinary regulations under the Merchant Shipping Act 1970, which in future will emerge by agreement from the industry in the form of "codes of conduct" in the case of the Merchant Navy and "local industrial agreements" in the case of the fishing industry, which the Secretary of State has a power to approve by regulation. In the case of the Merchant Navy, a new disciplinary code was agreed between the General Council of British Shipping, the various seafarers' unions and the Department of Trade and brought into effect on January 1, 1979. The section enables statutory backing to be given to this code and future modifications to it. The section does not affect the various statutory crimes relating to conduct on board ship and enacted in the Merchant Shipping Act 1970, although by s. 43 of and Sched. 6 to this Act the penalties in respect of such offences are raised. The section applies to ships registered in the United Kingdom.

Determination of amount of deductions from seamen's wages

24. The power to make regulations conferred by section 9 of the Merchant Shipping Act 1970 (which among other things relates to deductions from the wages of a seaman) shall include power to provide that the amount of a deduction of a description specified in the regulations from wages in respect of employment in a fishing vessel is to be determined by a body established or approved by the Secretary of State in pursuance of regulations made by virtue of the preceding section.

Unauthorised liquor on fishing vessels

25.—(1) A person who, in the United Kingdom or elsewhere—

(*a*) takes any unauthorised liquor on board a fishing vessel registered in the United Kingdom; or

(*b*) has any unauthorised liquor in his possession on board such a vessel; or

(*c*) permits another person to take on board such a vessel, or to have in his possession on board such a vessel, any unauthorised liquor; or

(*d*) wilfully obstructs another person in the exercise of powers conferred on the other person by subsection (3) of this section,

shall, subject to the following subsection, be guilty of an offence and liable on summary conviction to a fine not exceeding £1,000 or, on conviction on indictment, to imprisonment for a term not exceeding two years or a fine or both.

(2) It shall be a defence in proceedings for an offence under paragraph (*a*) or (*b*) of the preceding subsection to prove—

(*a*) that the accused believed that the liquor in question was not unauthorised liquor in relation to the vessel in question and that he had reasonable grounds for the belief; or

(*b*) that the accused did not know that the liquor in question was in his possession;

and it shall be a defence in proceedings for an offence under paragraph (*c*) of the preceding subsection to prove as mentioned in paragraph (*a*) of this subsection.

(3) If an authorised person has reason to believe that an offence under (*a*) or (*b*) of subsection (1) of this section has been committed by another person in connection with a fishing vessel, the authorised person—

(*a*) may go on board the vessel and search it and any property on it and may, if the other person is on board the vessel, search him there in an authorised manner; and

(*b*) may take possession of any liquor which he finds on the vessel and has reason to believe is unauthorised liquor and may detain the liquor for the period needed to ensure that the liquor is available as evidence in proceedings for the offence.

(4) In this section—

" an authorised manner " means a manner authorised by regulations made by the Secretary of State;

" authorised person ", in relation to a vessel, means a mercantile marine superintendent, a proper officer as defined by section 97 (1) of the Merchant Shipping Act 1970, a person appointed in pursuance of section 76 (1) (*c*) of that Act (which relates to inspectors), the master of the vessel in question, the owner of the vessel and any person instructed by the said master or owner to prevent the commission of offences under subsection (1) of this section in relation to the vessel;

" liquor " means spirits, wine, beer, cider, perry and any other fermented, distilled or spirituous liquor; and

" unauthorised liquor " means, in relation to a vessel, liquor as to which permission to take it on board the vessel has been given neither by the master nor the owner of the vessel nor by a person authorised by the said owner to give such permission.

(5) Any reference in the preceding subsection to the owner of a vessel shall be construed—

(*a*) as excluding any member of the crew of the vessel; and (*b*) subject to the preceding paragraph, as a reference to the person or all the persons who, in the certificate of registry of the vessel, is or are stated to be the registered owner or owners of the vessel.

GENERAL NOTE

This section applies only to fishing vessels registered in the United Kingdom and represents an attempt to deal with the problem of drinking and intoxication on board fishing vessels, which has been highlighted in several recent formal inquiries and by the Working Group on the Disciplinary Needs for Seagoing Employment in the Fishing Industry, 1975. Under s. 28 of the Merchant Shipping Act 1970, as amended by s. 45 (2) of this Act, it is also an offence for a seaman to be drunk on board a fishing vessel whilst in the performance of his duties of employment.

Inspectors

Extension of power to appoint Department of Trade inspectors

26. In section 728 of the Merchant Shipping Act 1894 (under which the Secretary of State may appoint a person as an inspector to report to him whether, among other things, the provisions of regulations made by virtue of that Act have been complied with) after the words " by virtue of this Act " there shall be inserted the words " or the terms of any approval, licence, consent, direction or exemption given by virtue of such regulations ".

GENERAL NOTE

This section extends the power to appoint Department of Trade inspectors by extending upon the terms of s. 728 of the Merchant Shipping Act 1894.

Powers of Department of Trade inspectors

27.—(1) An inspector appointed in pursuance of section 728 of the Merchant Shipping Act 1894—

(*a*) may at any reasonable time (or, in a situation which in his opinion is or may be dangerous, at any time)—

(i) enter any premises in the United Kingdom, or

(ii) board any ship which is registered in the United Kingdom wherever it may be and any other ship which is present in the United Kingdom or the territorial waters of the United Kingdom,

if he has reason to believe that it is necessary for him to enter the premises or board the ship for the purpose of performing his functions as such an inspector;

(*b*) may, on entering any premises by virtue of paragraph (*a*) above or on boarding a ship by virtue of that paragraph, take with him any other person authorised in that behalf by the Secretary of State and any equipment or materials required to assist him in performing the said functions;

(*c*) may make such examination and investigation as he considers necessary for the purpose of performing the said functions;

(*d*) may, as regards any premises or ship which he has power to enter or board, give a direction requiring that the premises or ship or any part of the premises or ship or any thing in the premises or ship or such a part shall be left undisturbed (whether generally or in particular respects) for so long as it reasonably necessary for the purposes of any examination or investigation under paragraph (*c*) above;

(*e*) may take such measurements and photographs and make such recordings as he considers necessary for the purpose of any examination or investigation under paragraph (*c*) above;

(*f*) may take samples of any articles or substances found in any premises or ship which he has power to enter or board and of the atmosphere in or in the vicinity of any such premises or ship;

(*g*) may, in the case of any article or substance which he finds in any such premises or ship and which appears to him to have caused or to be likely to cause danger to health or safety, cause it to be dismantled or subjected to any process or test (but not so as to damage or destroy it unless that is in the circumstances necessary for the purpose of performing the said functions);

(*h*) may, in the case of any such article or substance as is mentioned in paragraph (*g*) above, take possession of it and detain it for so long as is necessary for all or any of the following purposes, namely—

(i) to examine it and do to it anything which he has power to do under that paragraph,

(ii) to ensure that it is not tampered with before his examination of it is completed,

(iii) to ensure that it is available for use as evidence in any proceedings for an offence under the Merchant Shipping Acts or under regulations made by virtue of any provision of those Acts;

(*i*) may require any person who he has reasonable cause to believe is able to give any information relevant to any examination or investigation under paragraph (*c*) above—

(i) to attend at a place and time specified by the inspector, and

(ii) to answer (in the absence of persons other than any persons whom the inspector may allow to be present and a person nominated to be present by the person on whom the requirement is imposed) such questions as the inspector thinks fit to ask, and

(iii) to sign a declaration of the truth of his answers;

(*j*) may require the production of, and inspect and take copies of or of any entry in,—

(i) any books or documents which by virtue of any provision of the Merchant Shipping Acts are required to be kept; and

(ii) any other books or documents which he considers it necessary for him to see for the purposes of any examination or investigation under paragraph (*c*) above;

(*k*) may require any person to afford him such facilities and assistance with respect to any matters or things within that person's control or in relation to which that person has responsibilities as the inspector considers are necessary to enable him to exercise any of the powers conferred on him by this subsection.

(2) It is hereby declared that nothing in the preceding provisions of this section authorises a person unnecessarily to prevent a ship from proceeding on a voyage.

(3) The Secretary of State may by regulations make provision as to the procedure to be followed in connection with the taking of samples under subsection (1) (*f*) above and subsection (6) below and provision as to the way in which samples that have been so taken are to be dealt with.

(4) Where an inspector proposes to exercise the power conferred by subsection (1) (*g*) above in the case of an article or substance found in any premises or ship, he shall, if so requested by a person who at the time is present in and has responsibilities in relation to the premises or ship, cause anything which is to be done by virtue of that power to be done in the presence of that person unless the inspector considers that its being done in that person's presence would be prejudicial to the safety of that person.

(5) Before exercising the power conferred by subsection (1) (*g*) above, an inspector shall consult such persons as appear to him appropriate for the purpose of ascertaining what dangers, if any, there may be in doing anything which he proposes to do under that power.

(6) Where under the power conferred by subsection (1) (*h*) above an inspector takes possession of any article or substance found in any premises or ship, he shall leave there, either with a responsible person or, if that is impracticable, fixed in a conspicuous position, a notice giving particulars of that article or substance sufficient to identify it and stating that he has taken possession of it under that power; and before taking possession of any such substance under that power an inspector shall, if it is practicable for him to do so, take a sample of the substance and give to a responsible person at the premises or on board the ship a portion of the sample marked in a manner sufficient to identify it.

(7) No answer given by a person in pursuance of a requirement imposed under subsection (1) (*i*) above shall be admissible in evidence against that person or the husband or wife of that person in any proceedings except proceedings in pursuance of subsection (1) (*c*) of the following section in respect of a statement in or a declaration relating to the answer; and a person nominated as mentioned in the said subsection (1) (*i*) shall be entitled, on the occasion on which the questions there mentioned are asked, to make representations to the inspector on behalf of the person who nominated him.

General Note

This section replaces s. 729 of the Merchant Shipping Act 1894, and sets out the powers of inspectors in greater detail than under the previous legislation.

Provisions supplementary to s. 27

28.—(1) A person who—

(*a*) wilfully obstructs a Department of Trade inspector in the exercise of any power conferred on him by the preceding section; or

(*b*) without reasonable excuse, does not comply with a requirement imposed in pursuance of the preceding section or prevents another person from complying with such a requirement; or

(*c*) without prejudice to the generality of the preceding paragraph, makes a statement or signs a declaration which he knows is false, or recklessly makes a statement or signs a declaration which is false, in purported compliance with a requirement made in pursuance of subsection (1) (*i*) of the preceding section,

shall be guilty of an offence and liable on summary conviction to a fine not exceeding £1,000 or, on conviction on indictment, to imprisonment for a term not exceeding two years or a fine or both.

(2) In relation to a person, other than a Department of Trade inspector, who has the powers conferred on such an inspector by the preceding section—

(*a*) that section and the preceding subsection shall have effect as if for references to such an inspector there were substituted references to the person; and

(*b*) that section shall have effect as if for references to the functions of such an inspector there were substituted references to the functions in connection with which those powers are conferred on the person.

(3) Nothing in the preceding section shall be taken to compel the production by any person of a document of which he would on grounds of legal professional privilege be entitled to withhold production on an order for discovery in an action in the High Court or, as the case may be, on an order for the production of documents in an action in the Court of Session.

(4) A person who complies with a requirement imposed on him in pursuance of paragraph (*i*) (i) or (*k*) of subsection (1) of the preceding section shall be entitled to recover from the person who imposed the requirement such sums in respect of the expenses incurred in complying with the requirement as are prescribed by regulations made by the Secretary of State, and the regulations may make different provision for different circumstances; and any payments in pursuance of this subsection shall be made out of money provided by Parliament.

(5) References in the Merchant Shipping Acts to a Department of Trade inspector are to an inspector appointed in pursuance of section 728 of the Merchant Shipping Act 1894.

(6) Sections 729 and 730 of the Merchant Shipping Act 1894 (which relate to the powers and to obstruction of inspectors shall cease to have effect and the following enactments (which provide for certain persons to have the powers of a Department of Trade inspector in connection with the functions there mentioned) shall cease to have effect, namely—

section 420 (3) of the Merchant Shipping Act 1894 and in sections 369 (3) and 431 (1) of that Act the words from " and " onwards;

in section 7 (2) of the Merchant Shipping Act 1964 the words from " and for that purpose " to " Acts ";

section 11 (2) of the Merchant Shipping (Load Lines) Act 1967 and in sections 17 (1) and 24 (6) of that Act the words from " and " onwards;

in section (1) (3) of the Fishing Vessels (Safety Provisions) Act 1970 the words from " and " onwards;

and in section 14 (3) of the Merchant Shipping (Safety Convention) Act 1949 (which also provides as aforesaid) for the words from " shall have all the powers " onwards there shall be substituted the words " may go on board the ship and inspect it and anything on it ".

(7) Without prejudice to the operation of section 17 (2) of the Interpretation Act 1978 (which relates to the repeal and re-enactment of enactments)—

(*a*) in sections 386 (2), 459 (6), 463 (5), 465 (2), 471 (3) (*b*), 488 (2) and 517 (3) of the Merchant Shipping Act 1894 (which refer to the powers of a Department of Trade inspector under that Act) for the words " under this Act " there shall be substituted the words " under section 27 of the Merchant Shipping Act 1979 ";

(*b*) in sections 55 (2) and 61 (2) of the Merchant Shipping Act 1970 and in paragraph 5 (2) of Schedule 2 to that Act (which refer to the powers conferred on an inspector by section 729 of the Merchant Shipping Act 1894) for the words " section 729 of the Merchant Shipping Act 1894 " there shall be substituted the words " section 27 of the Merchant Shipping Act 1979 "; and

(c) in section 18 of the Prevention of Oil Pollution Act 1971 (which among other things applies the said section 729 to inspectors appointed under the said section 18)—

(i) in subsection (3) for the words " Section 729 of the Merchant Shipping Act 1894 " there shall be substituted the words " Sections 27 and 28 (1), (3) and (4) of the Merchant Shipping Act 1979 " and for paragraph (a) there shall be substituted the following paragraph—

(a) any reference to a ship included any vessel, any reference to the Merchant Shipping Acts (except the second reference in sub-paragraph (iii) of section 27 (1) (h)) were a reference to this Act and the reference in that sub-paragraph to regulations were omitted;

(ii) in subsections (4) and (5) for the words " under section 729 " there shall be substituted the words " under section 27 " and in subsection (5) the words from " and in subsection (3) " onwards shall be omitted;

(iii) in subsection (8) after the words " by virtue of this section " there shall be inserted the words " and the obstruction is not punishable by virtue of the said section 28 (1) ".

General Note

This section replaces s. 730 of the Merchant Shipping Act 1894.

Deaths on ships

Inquiries as to whether person has died on United Kingdom ship etc.

29.—(1) In section 61 of the Merchant Shipping Act 1970 (which among other things provides for an inquiry into the death of a person in a ship registered in the United Kingdom),—

(a) at the end of subsection (1) (a) there shall be inserted the words " in a boat or life-raft from such ship; or "; and

(b) after subsection (1) there shall be inserted the following subsections—

(1A) Subject to subsection (4) of this section, where it appears to the Secretary of State that—

(a) in consequence of an injury sustained or a disease contracted by a person, when he was the master of or a seaman employed in a ship registered in the United Kingdom, he ceased to be employed in the ship and subsequently died; and

(b) the death occurred in a country outside the United Kingdom during the period of one year beginning with the day when he so ceased,

the Secretary of State may arrange for an inquiry into the cause of the death to be held by a superintendent or proper officer.

(1B) Subject to subsection (4) of this section, where it appears to the Secretary of State that a person may—

(a) have died in a ship registered in the United Kingdom or in a boat or life-raft from such a ship; or

(b) have been lost from such a ship, boat or life-raft and have died in consequence of having been so lost,

the Secretary of State may arrange for an inquiry to be held by a superintendent or proper officer into whether the person died as aforesaid and, if the superintendent or officer finds that he did, into the cause of the death.

(2) In subsection (3) (*a*) of that section (which provides for a report of the findings of an inquiry under that section to be made available to the next of kin of the deceased if the deceased was employed in the ship) for the words " if the person to whom the report relates " and for the words " deceased person's name " there shall be substituted the words " name of the person to whom the report relates ".

(3) In section 97 (5) of the said Act of 1970 (which provides that references in that Act to dying in a ship include dying in a ship's boat and being lost from a ship's boat) after the word " Act " there shall be inserted the words " (except section 61) ".

General Note

This section extends the circumstances in which the Secretary of State may cause an inquiry to be conducted into the death of a person in a U.K. registered ship or, in certain circumstances, of a person formerly employed on a U.K. registered ship.

Record of certain deaths on ships etc.

30.—(1) At the end of subsection (1) of section 72 of the Merchant Shipping Act 1970 (of which paragraph (*a*) enables regulations to be made requiring the master of a ship registered in the United Kingdom to make a return of any death occurring in the ship and of the death outside the United Kingdom of any person employed in the ship) there shall be inserted the words

" : and

(*c*) requiring the Registrar General of Shipping and Seamen to record such information as may be specified in the regulations about such a death as is mentioned in paragraph (*a*) above in a case where it appears to him that the master of the ship cannot perform the duty imposed on him by virtue of that paragraph in respect of the death because he has himself died or is incapacitated or missing and either—

(i) the death in question has been the subject of an inquest held by the coroner or an inquiry held in pursuance of section 61 of this Act or in pursuance of the Fatal Accidents and Sudden Deaths Inquiry (Scotland) Act 1976 and the findings of the inquest or inquiry include a finding that the death occurred, or

(ii) a post-mortem examination, or a preliminary investigation in Northern Ireland, has been made of the deceased's body and in consequence the coroner is satisfied that an inquest is unnecessary, or

(iii) in Scotland, it does not appear to the Lord Advocate, under section 1 (1) (*b*) of the said Act of 1976, to be expedient in the public interest that an inquiry under that Act should be held.";

and in subsection (2) of that section (which enables regulations to require a certified copy of a return under that section to be sent to the appropriate Registrar General concerned with the registration of deaths) after the word " return " there shall be inserted the words " or record ".

(2) Where—

(*a*) an inquest is held on a dead body or touching a death or a post-mortem examination, or a preliminary investigation in Northern Ireland, is made of a dead body as a result of which the coroner is satisfied that an inquest is unnecessary; and

(b) it appears to the coroner that the death in question is such as is mentioned in paragraph (a) of section 72 (1) of the Merchant Shipping Act 1970 or in that paragraph as extended (with or without amendments) by virtue of section 92 of that Act,

it shall be the duty of the coroner to send to the Registrar General of Shipping and Seamen particulars in respect of the deceased of a kind prescribed by regulations made by the Secretary of State.

GENERAL NOTE

This section amends and extends s. 72 of the Merchant Shipping Act 1970.

Miscellaneous

Dues for space occupied by deck cargo

31.—(1) In section 85 of the Merchant Shipping Act 1894 (which relates to dues for space occupied by deck cargo) for subsection (3) (which among other things makes provision about the way in which the space is to be ascertained and recorded) there shall be substituted the following subsection—

(3) The Secretary of State may, by regulations made by statutory instrument, make provision—

(a) as to the manner in which (including the persons by whom) the tonnage of the space is to be ascertained, recorded and verified;

(b) as to the occasions on which and the persons by whom and to whom records of the said tonnage are to be produced;

(c) for a contravention of the regulations to be an offence punishable on summary conviction by a fine not exceeding £500 or such less sum as is prescribed by the regulations;

(d) for such incidental and supplemental matters as the Secretary of State considers appropriate in connection with the regulations,

and may make different provision by the regulations for different circumstances; and any statutory instrument made by virtue of this subsection shall be subject to annulment in pursuance of a resolution of either House of Parliament.

(2) Accordingly in section 1 (2) (c) of the Merchant Shipping Act 1965 (under which tonnage regulations may provide for the ascertainment of the space to be taken into account for the purposes of the said section 85 and may exempt any space from being taken into account for those purposes) for the words from " provide " to " be " there shall be substituted the words " exempt any space from being ", and the words from " and may " to " those purposes " shall cease to have effect.

DEFINITION

" contravention ": s. 50 (2).

Shipping casualties

32.—(1) In section 464 of the Merchant Shipping Act 1894 (which specifies the shipping casualties which may be the subject of inquiries and investigations under Part VI of that Act)—

(a) in paragraph (4) (which refers to loss of life by reason of a casualty happening to or on board a ship) after the word " life " there shall be inserted the words " or serious personal injury " and after the word " ship " there shall be inserted the words " , or any boat or life-raft from a ship,";

(*b*) after that paragraph there shall be inserted the following paragraph—

(4A) when any person is lost from a ship, or any boat or life-raft from a ship, on or near the coasts of the United Kingdom;

(*c*) after paragraph (7) there shall be inserted the following paragraph—

(8) when events occur which the Secretary of State determines are of a kind likely to cause events which, if they occurred, would constitute a shipping casualty by virtue of any of the preceding paragraphs.

(2) In section 55 of the Merchant Shipping Act 1970 (which relates to inquiries and investigations into shipping casualties)—

(*a*) after the words " loss of life " in subsection (1) (*b*) there shall be inserted the words " or serious personal injury "; and

(*b*) after subsection (1) there shall be inserted the following subsection—

(1A) Where an incident has occurred which the Secretary of State considers was or is capable of causing a casualty into which he could require an inquiry in pursuance of the preceding subsection, the powers to hold an inquiry or an investigation or both which are conferred on him by paragraphs (i) and (ii) of that subsection shall be exercisable in relation to the incident as if it were such a casualty.

(3) Accordingly in section 56 (1) of the Merchant Shipping Act 1970 (which relates to an investigation under section 55 of that Act into a casualty) after the word " casualty " there shall be inserted the words " or incident ".

General Note

This section extends the preceding statutory law relating to the shipping inquiries and investigations by extending their scope so as to include occasions when serious injury results, and to " near miss " incidents at sea which are of a kind likely to cause shipping casualties.

Commissioners of Northern Lighthouses and Irish Lights

33.—(1) Sections 640 and 641 of the Merchant Shipping Act 1894 (which provide for the control by the Trinity House of certain activities of the Commissioners of Northern Lighthouses and the Commissioners of Irish Lights) and section 637 of that Act (which authorises the Trinity House and their servants to enter lighthouses in a lighthouse area which are vested in the said Commissioners or the Trinity House) shall cease to have effect.

(2) In section 668 (4) of the Merchant Shipping Act 1894 (which authorises the Commissioners of Northern Lighthouses to elect not more than four other persons as members of their body) for the words " four other persons " there shall be substituted the words " five other persons; but a person shall not be elected in pursuance of this subsection after section 33 (2) of the Merchant Shipping Act 1979 comes into force unless either he appears to the Commissioners to have special knowledge and experience of nautical matters or three persons who so appear are members of the said body ".

Repeal of spent provisions, and amendment of Part XI, of Merchant Shipping Act 1894

34.—(1) Sections 670 to 672 of the Merchant Shipping Act 1894 (which relate to colonial light dues and became spent after the abolition of the dues in 1960) shall cease to have effect.

(2) In section 677 of that Act, paragraph (*m*) (which provides for the payment out of money provided by Parliament of the cost of publishing information about foreign lighthouses, buoys and beacons) shall be omitted.

(3) The Secretary of State may by order provide that references or a particular reference to a buoy or beacon in Part XI of that Act shall be construed as including, in such circumstances as are specified in the order, equipment of a kind so specified which is intended as an aid to the navigation of ships.

Amendment of s. 503 of Merchant Shipping Act 1894 etc.

35.—(1) Nothing in section 503 of the Merchant Shipping Act 1894 (which relates to the limitation of liability in certain cases of loss of life, injury or damage) shall apply to any liability in respect of loss of life or personal injury caused to, or loss of or damage to any property of, a person who is on board or employed in connection with the ship in question if—

(*a*) he is so on board or employed under a contract of service governed by the law of any part of the United Kingdom; and

(*b*) the liability arises from an occurrence which took place after the coming into force of this subsection and before the coming into force of the following subsection;

and in this subsection " ship " has the same meaning as in the said section 503.

(2) The provisions having the force of law under section 17 of this Act shall not apply to any liability in respect of loss of life or personal injury caused to, or loss of or damage to any property of, a person who is on board the ship in question or employed in connection with that ship or with the salvage operations in question if—

(*a*) he is so on board or employed under a contract of service governed by the law of any part of the United Kingdom; and

(*b*) the liability arises from an occurrence which took place after the coming into force of this subsection;

and in this subsection " ship " and " salvage operations " have the same meaning as in those provisions.

GENERAL NOTE

This section has already been commented upon when considering s. 17. The section makes it clear that neither under s. 503 of the Merchant Shipping Act 1894 nor under the London Convention on Limitation of Liability for Maritime Claims 1976, when brought into effect by s. 17, may a shipowner or salvor limit his liability for loss of life, personal injury, loss or damage to property, in respect of claims advanced by persons employed on board ship, for example, seaman, master, pilot, or any other person on board in the circumstances specified, *e.g.* caterers. The section also secures that claims by servants of shipowners and salvors are excepted claims under art. 3 (*e*) of the 1976 Convention.

Amendments of Merchant Shipping (Mercantile Marine Fund) Act 1898

36.—(1) Section 2 (1) and (2) of the Merchant Shipping (Mercantile Marine Fund) Act 1898 (which relate to colonial light dues and of which subsection (1) became spent after the abolition of the dues in 1960) shall cease to have effect; and in section 2 (3) of that Act (which among other things provides for the payment out of the General Lighthouse Fund of contributions in respect of the lighthouse on Cape Spartel, Morocco) for the words " lighthouse on Cape Spartel, Morocco " there shall be substituted the words " lights on the islands of Abu Ail and Jabal at Tair in the Red Sea ".

(2) For subsection (2) of section 5 of that Act (which enables the scales, rules and exemptions set out in Schedule 2 to that Act for the levying of light duties to be altered by Order in Council) there shall be substituted the following subsection—

(2) The Secretary of State may by statutory instrument make regulations with respect to the amounts and the levying of such dues (including the cases in which the dues are not to be levied) and the regulations may make different provision for different circumstances; and any statutory instrument made by virtue of this subsection shall be subject to annulment in pursuance of a resolution of either House of Parliament.

(3) In Schedule 3 to the said Act of 1898, paragraph II (which relates to certain lighthouses off the coast of Sri Lanka as to which an arrangement was made on 27th February 1976 between the government of that country and the government of the United Kingdom providing for their transfer to the government of that country) shall be omitted; but any expenditure incurred by the government of the United Kingdom in pursuance of that arrangement either before or after the passing of this Act shall be defrayed out of the General Lighthouse Fund.

Amendments of ss. 15, 43, 52, 54, 76 (1), 92 and 101 (4) of Merchant Shipping Act 1970 and s. 23 of the Prevention of Oil Pollution Act 1971

37.—(1) Section 15 of the Merchant Shipping Act 1970 (which among other things provides that where a seaman's employment in a ship ends because the ship is wrecked or lost or is sold abroad or ceases to be registered in the United Kingdom he shall in certain cases be entitled to wages for two months after the ending of the employment) shall apply to a master as it applies to a seaman; and in subsection (1) of that section (which makes the wages payable in the case of wreck or loss unless it is proved that the seaman did not make reasonable efforts to save the ship and the persons and property carried on it) the words from " unless " onwards shall be omitted.

(2) The power to make regulations conferred by section 43 of the Merchant Shipping Act 1970 (which authorises the Secretary of State to make regulations requiring certain ships to carry the number specified in the regulations of officers and other seamen who are qualified in accordance with the regulations) shall include power to make regulations providing that existing certificates shall, except in such cases as are specified in the regulations, be deemed for the purposes of such of the provisions of that Act as are so specified to be issued in pursuance of that section and to confer on the persons to whom they were issued such qualifications for the purposes of that section as are so specified.

(3) In the preceding subsection " existing certificate " means a certificate granted in pursuance of section 93, 99 or 414 of the Merchant Shipping Act 1894 (which relate to certificates of competency or service as masters, mates and engineers and as skippers and second hands of fishing boats), a certificate referred to in an Order in Council made by virtue of section 102 of that Act (which relates to Commonwealth certificates of competency), a certificate granted in pursuance of subsection (2) of section 27 of the Merchant Shipping Act 1906 or by an institution approved in pursuance of that subsection (which relates to cooks) and a certificate granted in pursuance of section 5 of the Merchant Shipping Act 1948 (which relates to seamen who may be rated as A.B.).

(4) At the end of sections 52 (3) and 54 (2) of the Merchant Shipping Act 1970 (which respectively make provision for the rules which are to govern inquiries into the fitness or conduct of officers and of seamen other than officers) there shall be inserted the words " ; and the persons holding the inquiry shall for the purpose of the inquiry have the powers conferred on an inspector by section 27 of the Merchant Shipping Act 1979.".

(5) In section 76 (1) of the Merchant Shipping Act 1970 (which enables inspections to be carried out for the purpose of seeing that the provisions of the Merchant Shipping Acts and regulations and rules made under those Acts are complied with)—

(*a*) references to the Merchant Shipping Acts shall include references to this Act and,

(*b*) after the words " regulations and rules made thereunder " there shall be inserted the words " or that the terms of any approval, licence, consent, direction or exemption given by virtue of such regulations ".

(6) Without prejudice to the operation of section 50 (1) of this Act, in section 92 of the Merchant Shipping Act 1970 (which among other things enables provisions of that Act to be extended to unregistered British ships) the references to that Act shall be construed as including references to sections 23 and 25 of this Act.

(7) At the end of section 101 (4) of the Merchant Shipping Act 1970 (which authorises the appointment of different days for the coming into force of different provisions of that Act) there shall be inserted the words " or for different purposes of the same provision ".

(8) In section 23 of the Prevention of Oil Pollution Act 1971 (which among other things authorises the Secretary of State to exempt from provisions of that Act certain discharges of crude oil produced as a result of operations for exploring the seabed or for exploiting its resources) for the words from " crude oil " onwards there shall be substituted the word " oil ".

Replacement of gold francs by special drawing rights for certain purposes of Merchant Shipping (Oil Pollution) Act 1971 and Merchant Shipping Act 1974

38.—(1) In section 4 of the Merchant Shipping (Oil Pollution) Act 1971 (which among other things enables a ship's owner to limit in certain circumstances his liability under section 1 of that Act so that it does not exceed 2,000 gold francs for each ton of the ship's tonnage or 210 million gold francs, whichever is less)—

(*a*) for the words " 2,000 gold francs " and " 210 million gold francs " in subsection (1) (*b*) there shall be substituted respectively the words " 133 special drawing rights " and " 14 million special drawing rights "; and

(*b*) subsections (3) to (5) (which relate to the value of gold francs) shall cease to have effect.

(2) In section 5 of that Act (which among other things relates to payment into court of the amount of a limit determined in pursuance of that section), after subsection (2) there shall be inserted the following subsection—

(2A) A payment into court of the amount of a limit determined in pursuance of this section shall be made in sterling; and—

(*a*) for the purpose of converting such an amount from special drawing rights into sterling one special drawing right shall be treated as equal to such a sum in sterling as the International Monetary Fund have fixed as being the equivalent of one special drawing right for—

(i) the day on which the determination is made, or

(ii) if no sum has been so fixed for that day, the last day before that day for which a sum has been so fixed;

(*b*) a certificate given by or on behalf of the Treasury stating—

(i) that a particular sum in sterling has been so fixed for the day on which the determination was made, or

(ii) that no sum has been so fixed for that day and that a particular sum in sterling has been so fixed for a day which is the last day for which a sum has been so fixed before the day on which the determination was made,

shall be conclusive evidence of those matters for the purposes of this Act;

(*c*) a document purporting to be such a certificate shall, in any proceedings, be received in evidence and, unless the contrary is proved, be deemed to be such a certificate.

(3) For the purposes of sections 10 (2) and 11 (1) of that Act (which refer to Article VII of the International Convention on Civil Liability for Oil Pollution Damage signed in Brussels in 1969) references in that Article to Article V of the Convention shall be construed as references to Article V as amended by Article II of the protocol dated 19th November 1976 to the Convention; and in section 14 (2) of that Act (which refers to the limit prescribed by the said Article V) for the words " Article V thereof " there shall be substituted the words " Article V of the Convention as amended by Article II of the protocol dated 19th November 1976 to the Convention ".

(4) The Merchant Shipping Act 1974 shall have effect with the following amendments, namely—

(*a*) section 1 (6) and (7) (which relate to the value of gold francs) shall cease to have effect;

(*b*) in section 2 (7) (*a*) (which provides for a person's contributions to the International Fund there mentioned to be of an amount determined under articles 11 and 12 of the convention which established the Fund) and in section 4 (10) (which provides for the liability of the said Fund to be subject to the limits imposed by article 4 of the said convention) after the words " the Fund Convention " there shall be inserted the words " (as amended by Article III of the protocol dated 19th November 1976 to that Convention) ";

(*c*) at the end of section 4 (which relates to compensation from the said Fund for persons suffering pollution damage) there shall be inserted the following subsection—

(13) Any steps taken to obtain payment of an amount or a reduced amount in pursuance of such a judgment as is mentioned in subsection (12) above shall be steps to obtain payment in sterling; and—

(*a*) for the purpose of converting such an amount from special drawing rights into sterling one special drawing right shall be treated as equal to such a sum in sterling as the Internatoinal Monetary Fund have fixed as being the equivalent of one special drawing right for—

(i) the day on which the judgment is given, or

(ii) if no sum has been so fixed for that day, the last day before that day for which a sum has been so fixed;

(*b*) a certificate given by or on behalf of the Treasury stating—

(i) that a particular sum in sterling has been so fixed for the day on which the judgment was given, or

(ii) that no sum has been so fixed for that day and that a particular sum in sterling has been so fixed for a day which is the last day for which a sum has been so fixed before the day on which the judgment was given,

shall be conclusive evidence of those matters for the purposes of this Act;

(*c*) a document purporting to be such a certificate shall, in any proceedings, be received in evidence and, unless the contrary is proved, be deemed to be such a certificate.;

(*d*) in section (5) (1) (*a*) and (*b*) (which specify the portion of the aggregate amount of a liability for which the said Fund is to give indemnity) for the words " 1,500 francs " and " 2,000 francs " there shall be substituted respectively the words " 100 special drawing rights " and " 133 special drawing rights " and for the words " 125 million francs " and " 210 million francs " there shall be substituted respectively the words " 8,333,000 special drawing rights " and " 14 million special drawing rights ";

(*e*) at the end of section 5 there shall be inserted the following subsection—

(8) For the purpose of converting into sterling the amount in special drawing rights adjudged to be payable by the Fund by way of indemnity in such proceedings as are mentioned in subsection (4) of this section, paragraphs (*a*) to (*c*) of subsection (13) of section 4 of this Act shall have effect—

(*a*) if the liability in question has been limited in pursuance of section 5 of the Merchant Shipping (Oil Pollution) Act 1971, as if—

(i) for the reference in the said paragraph (*a*) to the amount there mentioned there were substituted a reference to the amount adjudged as aforesaid, and

(ii) for any reference to the day on which the judgment is or was given there were substituted a reference to the day on which the determination of the limit was made in pursuance of the said section 5; and

(*b*) if the liability in question has not been so limited, with the modification made by paragraph (*a*) (i) of this subsection and as if for any reference to the day on which the judgment is or was given there were substituted a reference to the day on which the said amount was so adjudged.;

(*f*) in section 6 (5) (*a*) (which refers to provisions of the said article 4 as set out in Schedule 1 to that Act) after the words " as set out " there shall be inserted the words " as amended ";

(*g*) in Schedule 1 for the words " 450 million francs " wherever they occur there shall be substituted the words " 30 million special drawing rights " and for the words " 900 million francs " there shall be substituted the words " 60 million special drawing rights ".

(5) It is hereby declared that the powers to make Orders in Council conferred by section 18 of the said Act of 1971 and section 20 of the said Act of 1974 (which provide for the extension of those Acts to any of the countries mentioned in those sections and for those Acts to have effect as if references in them to the United Kingdom included references to any of those countries) include power to make Orders in Council in respect of those Acts as amended by this section.

(6) An order made by virtue of section 52 (2) of this Act which appoints a day for the coming into force of any of the preceding provisions of this section may contain such transitional provisions as the Secretary of State considers appropriate in connection with the coming into force of the provision in question.

General Note

This section enables effect to be given to Protocols, both dated November 19, 1976, to two Conventions, the first being the International Convention on Civil Liability for Oil Pollution Damage 1969 (Cmnd. 4403), and the second the International Convention on the Establishment of an International Fund for Compensation for Oil Pollution Damage 1971 (Cmnd. 5061). The effect in each case is to substitute the special drawing right of the International Monetary Fund for the gold franc as the unit of account.

Attachment of earnings

39.—(1) At the beginning of paragraph (*e*) of section 24 (2) of the Attachment of Earnings Act 1971 (under which wages of a seaman are not to be treated as earnings for the purposes of that Act unless he is a seaman of a fishing boat) there shall be inserted the words " except in relation to a maintenance order ".

(2) As respects Scotland, the wages of a seaman of a fishing boat shall cease to be exempt from arrestment and the wages of any other seaman shall cease to be exempt from arrestment under a maintenance order; and in this subsection " maintenance order " means an order of any court or authority enforceable in Scotland for the payment of any periodical or capital sum due or awarded in respect of a marriage or other family relationship.

(3) Accordingly section 11 (1) (*a*) of the Merchant Shipping Act 1970 (which provides that the wages of a seaman employed in a ship registered in the United Kingdom shall not be subject to attachment or arrestment) shall have effect, as respects England and Wales, subject to the said Act of 1971 as amended by subsection (1) of this section and, as respects Scotland, subject to the preceding subsection.

General Note

This section eradicates an anomaly which existed in the law whereby the wages of a merchant seaman were immune from attachment for the purpose of securing payments under a maintenance order. Scots law is also amended so as to achieve the same result.

Foreign action affecting shipping

40.—(1) In section 14 of the Merchant Shipping Act 1974 (which relates to foreign action affecting shipping)—

(*a*) in subsection (3) (which among other things enables provision to be made for regulating matters mentioned in that subsection) after paragraph (*d*) there shall be inserted the words " and in this subsection ' regulating ', except in relation to the rates which may or must be charged for carrying goods, includes imposing a prohibition ";

(*b*) in subsection (8) (which prohibits the disclosure of information otherwise than with the informant's consent or for the purposes of the section) after paragraph (*c*) there shall be inserted the words " or

(*d*) in pursuance of a Community obligation to a Community institution ";

(*c*) in subsection (11) (which defines expressions used in that section) after the words " United Kingdom " there shall be inserted the words " and ' agency or authority of a foreign government ' includes any undertaking appearing to the Secretary of State to be, or to be acting on behalf of, an undertaking which is in effect owned or controlled (directly or indirectly) by a State other than the United Kingdom "; and

(*d*) after that subsection there shall be inserted the following subsection—

(11A) A recital in an order under this section that the persons who have adopted, or propose to adopt, the measures or practices in question are a foreign govenment, or an agency or authority of a foreign government, shall be conclusive.

(2) In paragraph 2 of Schedule 4 to the said Act of 1974 (which relates to the making of orders under subsection (3) (*d*) of section 14) after sub-paragraph (3) there shall be inserted the following sub-paragraph—

(4) Nothing in this paragraph prejudices subsection (6) of the principal section. .

General Note

This section clarifies and extends the government's defensive powers set out in Pt. III of the Merchant Shipping Act 1974 against certain types of foreign shipping activity.

Application of Merchant Shipping Acts to certain structures etc.

41.—(1) The Secretary of State may by order provide that a thing designed or adapted for use at sea and described in the order is or is not to be treated as a ship for the purposes of any provision specified in the order of the Merchant Shipping Acts or the Prevention of Oil Pollution Act 1971 or an instrument made by virtue of any of those Acts; and such an order may—

(*a*) make different provision in relation to different occasions;

(*b*) if it provides that a thing is to be treated as a ship for the purposes of a provision specified in the order, provide that the provision shall have effect in relation to the thing with such modifications as are so specified.

(2) Where the Secretary of State proposes to make an order in pursuance of the preceding subsection it shall be his duty, before he makes the order, to consult such persons about the proposal as appear to him to represent the persons in the United Kingdom who he considers are likely to be affected by the order.

General Note

The object of this section is to enable speedy action to be taken to bring within the ambit of the specified legislation any conceivable structure or thing at sea which is not a ship (itself a concept variously defined in different statutes) nor an oil-rig attached to the sea bed, for example, mobile rigs and the range of other peculiar craft which are being produced by the advanced technology of our times.

Offences

Alteration of time for certain summary prosecutions

42.—(1) Subsection (1) of section 683 of the Merchant Shipping Act 1894 (which prevents convictions in summary proceedings in the United Kingdom for certain offences unless the proceedings are begun within the times limited by that subsection) shall not apply to summary proceedings for an indictable offence; and at the end of that subsection there shall be inserted the words " and, in the case of a summary conviction, before the expiration of three years beginning with the date on which the offence was committed ".

(2) The said subsection (1) shall not prevent a conviction for an offence in summary proceedings begun before the expiration of three years beginning with the date on which the offence was committed and before—

(*a*) the expiration of the period of six months beginning with the day when evidence which the Secretary of State considers is sufficient to justify a prosecution for the offence came to his knowledge; or

(*b*) the expiration of two months beginning with the day when the accused was first present in the United Kingdom after the expiration of the period mentioned in the preceding paragraph if throughout that period the accused was absent from the United Kingdom.

(3) For the purposes of the preceding subsection—

(*a*) a certificate of the Secretary of State stating that evidence came to his knowledge on a particular day shall be conclusive evidence of that fact; and

(*b*) a document purporting to be a certificate of the Secretary of State and to be signed on his behalf shall be presumed to be such a certificate unless the contrary is proved.

(4) Section 18 of the Criminal Law Act 1977 (which among other things contains a provision for England and Wales which corresponds to the first provision in subsection (1) of this section) shall not apply to an offence under the Merchant Shipping Acts; but nothing in the preceding provisions of this section, except subsection (1), applies to an offence committed before this section comes into force.

(5) In the application of this section to Scotland—

(*a*) in subsection (2) (*a*) for the words from " Secretary " to " knowledge " there shall be substituted the words " Lord Advocate considers is sufficient to justify a prosecution for the offence came to his knowledge, or, where such evidence is reported to him by the Secretary of State, the expiration of the period of six months beginning with the day when it came to the knowledge of the Secretary of State ";

(*b*) in subsection (3) (*a*) and (*b*) for the words " Secretary of State " there shall be substituted the words " Lord Advocate or the Secretary of State, as the case may be,".

Alteration of penalties

43.—(1) A person guilty of an offence under any of the enactments mentioned in the first column of Part I, II, III or IV of Schedule 6 to this Act (which among other things relate to the matters mentioned in the second column of those Parts and provide for maximum fines on summary conviction of from £2 to £50 in the case of enactments mentioned in Part I of that Schedule, from £5 to £100 in the case of enactments mentioned in Part II of that Schedule and from £5 to £400 in the case of enactments mentioned in Parts III and IV of that Schedule) shall be liable on summary conviction to a fine not exceeding—

(*a*) £50 if the enactment is mentioned in the said Part I;

(*b*) £200 if the enactment is mentioned in the said Part II;

(*c*) £500 if the enactment is mentioned in the said Part III; and

(*d*) £1,000 if the enactment is mentioned in the said Part IV,

instead of the fine to which he would be liable for the offence apart from this subsection.

(2) A person guilty of an offence under any of the enactments mentioned in the first column of Part V of that Schedule (which among other things relate to the matters mentioned in the second column of that Part and provide for maximum fines of from £20 to £1,000 on summary conviction and in some cases for a fine on conviction on indictment) shall be liable—

(*a*) on conviction on indictment to a fine; and

(*b*) on summary conviction to a fine not exceeding £1,000,

instead of the fine to which he would be liable for the offence apart from this subsection.

(3) The enactments mentioned in Parts VI and VII of that Schedule (which provide for various penalties for the offences under the Merchant Shipping Acts and the Prevention of Oil Pollution Act 1971 which are mentioned in those Parts) shall have effect with the amendments specified in those Parts.

(4) If it appears to the Secretary of State that the maximum amount of a fine on summary conviction for the time being specified in a provision of the Merchant Shipping Acts or the Prevention of Oil Pollution Act 1971 should be altered in consequence of a change in the value of money since 17th July 1978 or, if the amount has been altered in pursuance of this subsection, since it was last so altered, he may by order provide that the provision shall have effect with the substitution for the amount aforesaid of an amount specified in the order which he considers is justified by the change; and such an order may provide that paragraph (*b*) of section 680 (1) of the Merchant Shipping Act 1894 (which as amended by the said Part VII provides that certain offences made punishable by a fine not exceeding £1,000 can only be prosecuted summarily) and section 703 of that Act (which as so amended provides for penalties and jurisdiction in Scotland) shall have effect with the substitution for the amounts for the time being specified in that paragraph and the said section 703 of the different amounts specified in the order.

(5) An order under subsection (1) of section 61 of the Criminal Law Act 1977 (which enables the sums specified in certain enactments to be altered in consequence of changes in the value of money) in respect of the prescribed sum mentioned in section 28 of that Act and an order under section 289D (1) of the Criminal Procedure (Scotland) Act 1975 (which makes corresponding provision for Scotland) shall not apply to a sum specified in a provision of the Acts mentioned in the preceding subsection.

(6) Nothing in any of the preceding provisions of this section or an order under subsection (4) of this section applies to an offence committed before the provision or, as the case may be, the order comes into force.

Offence in respect of dangerously unsafe ship

44.—(1) If—

(*a*) a ship in a port in the United Kingdom; or

(*b*) a ship registered in the United Kingdom which is in any other port,

is, having regard to the nature of the service for which the ship is intended, unfit by reason of the condition of the ship's hull, equipment or machinery or by reason of undermanning or by reason of overloading or improper loading to go to sea without serious danger to human life, then, subject to the following subsection, the master and the owner of the ship shall each be guilty of an offence and liable on conviction on indictment to a fine and on summary conviction to a fine not exceeding £50,000.

(2) It shall be a defence in proceedings for an offence under the preceding subsection to prove that at the time of the alleged offence—

(*a*) arrangements had been made which were appropriate to ensure that before the ship went to sea it was made fit to do so without serious danger to human life by reason of the matters aforesaid which are specified in the charge; or

(*b*) it was reasonable not to have made such arrangements.

(3) No proceedings for an offence under subsection (1) of this section shall be begun—

(*a*) in England and Wales, except by or with the consent of the Secretary of State or the Director of Public Prosecutions;

(*b*) in Northern Ireland, except by or with the consent of the Secretary of State or the Director of Public Prosecutions for Northern Ireland.

(4) Section 457 of the Merchant Shipping Act 1894 (under which it is an offence to send an unseaworthy ship to sea) shall cease to have effect.

General Note

This section supersedes s. 457 of the Merchant Shipping Act 1894, and replaces the offence there created in relation to an unseaworthy ship by a new offence appertaining to a dangerously unsafe ship. In many regards the two concepts are synonymous but differ materially in their ambit of application. The new offence is not confined to British ships but applies to all ships when in port in the United Kingdom and only to United Kingdom registered ships when in a foreign port. The section does not affect s. 2 of the Merchant Shipping Act 1921 which relates to unsafe lighters, barges and other like vessels.

Amendment of certain offences provisions of Merchant Shipping Act 1970

45.—(1) In section 27 (1) of the Merchant Shipping Act 1970 (which among other things penalises certain acts and omissions by the master or a member of the crew of a ship which are likely to cause the loss or destruction of or serious damage to the ship)—

(*a*) for the words " or any member of the crew of " there shall be substituted the words " of or any seaman employed in "; and

(*b*) after the words " to the ship " in paragraph (*a*) and the words " preserve the ship " in paragraph (*b*) there shall be inserted the words " or its machinery, navigational equipment or safety equipment ".

(2) In section 28 of that Act (under which a seaman employed in a ship commits an offence if while on duty he is under the influence of drink or a drug to such an extent that his capacity to carry out his duties is impaired) for the word " ship " there shall be substituted the words

" fishing vessel ", for the words " on duty " there shall be substituted the words " on board the vessel " and for the words " his duties " there shall be substituted the words " the duties of his employment ".

(3) In section 95 (1) (*a*) of that Act, (which among other things provides that section 30 of that Act, of which paragraph (*c*) (iii) penalises combinations by seaman to impede the ship, does not apply to fishing vessels) for the words " 30 and " there shall be substituted the words " and 30 (*a*) and (*b*), sub-paragraphs (i) and (ii) of section 30 (*c*) and sections ".

General Note

This section both extends and confines certain offences enacted in the Merchant Shipping Act 1970. The offence of misconduct endangering the ship (s. 27) is extended so as to cover damage to a ship's machinery, navigational or safety equipment. The offence of concerted action impeding the progress or navigation of a ship (s. 30 (*c*) (iii)) is extended to fishing vessels. The offence of drunkenness, etc. on duty (s. 28) is restricted to seamen employed on a fishing vessel but is made applicable whether they are on duty or not.

Offences by officers of bodies corporate

46.—(1) Where such an offence as is mentioned in section 23 (6), 28 (1) or 44 (1) of this Act which has been committeed by a body corporate is proved to have been committed with the consent or connivance of, or to be attributable to any neglect on the part of, a director, manager, secretary or other similar officer of the body corporate or any person who was purporting to act in any such capacity, he as well as the body corporate shall be guilty of that offence and shall be liable to be proceeded against and punished accordingly.

(2) Where the affairs of a body corporate are managed by its members the preceding subsection shall apply in relation to the acts and defaults of a member in connection with his functions of management as if he were a director of the body corporate.

Supplemental

Power to extend Act to certain countries etc.

47.—(1) Her Majesty may by Order in Council provide that any provision of this Act which is mentioned in the following subsection and specified in the Order and any instrument so specified which is in force under that provision shall, with such modifications (if any) as are so specified—

(*a*) extend to a relevant country so specified as part of the law of the country; or

(*b*) apply to ships registered in a relevant country so specified and to masters and seamen employed in the ships as they apply to ships registered in the United Kingdom and to masters and seamen employed in them; or

(*c*) extend and apply as aforesaid.

(2) The provisions of this Act referred to in the preceding subsection are sections 21 to 52 (except sections 33, 34, 36, 38, 42 and 44 and this section) and Schedule 7 (except so far as it relates to the Pilotage Act 1913); and in that subsection " a relevant country " means a country mentioned in section 15 (1) of this Act.

(3) Any statutory instrument made by virtue of subsection (1) of this section shall be subject to annulment in pursuance of a resolution of either House of Parliament.

Application to hovercraft

48. The enactments and instruments with respect to which provision may be made by Order in Council in pursuance of section 1 (1) (*h*) of the Hovercraft Act 1968 shall include this Act and any instrument made under it.

Orders and regulations

49.—(1) Any power to make an order or regulations conferred on the Secretary of State by this Act shall be exercisable by statutory instrument.

(2) Section 738 of the Merchant Shipping Act 1894 (which among other things provides for the publication in the London Gazette, the laying before Parliament and the alteration and revocation of Orders in Council made under that Act or any Act amending that Act) shall not apply to an Order in Council made under this Act.

(3) No order shall be made in pursuance of section 3 (1), 4 (2), 8 (5), 10 (3) or 34 (3) of this Act and no regulations relating to an international agreement which has not been laid before Parliament before the passing of this Act shall be made in pursuance of section 21 (1) (*b*) of this Act unless a draft of the order or regulations has been approved by resolution of each House of Parliament.

(4) Any statutory instrument containing an order made by virtue of section 2 (3), 41 (1) or 43 (4) of this Act or paragraph 11 of Part II of Schedule 3 or paragraph 3 or 5 of Part II of Schedule 4 to this Act or containing regulations made by virtue of section 11 (2) (*a*), 21 (1), 22 (3), 23 (1), 25 (4) or 30 (2) of this Act (except regulations made by virtue of section 21 (1) of which a draft has been approved as mentioned in the preceding subsection) shall be subject to annulment in pursuance of a resolution by either House of Parliament.

(5) Any statutory instrument containing an order made by virtue of paragraph 8 (1) of Part II of Schedule 4 to this Act shall be laid before Parliament after being made.

Interpretation and repeals

50.—(1) This Act shall be construed as one with the Merchant Shipping Acts.

(2) In this Act—

" the Commission " means the Pilotage Commission;

" contravention " includes failure to comply;

" functions " includes powers and duties;

" the Merchant Shipping Acts " means the Merchant Shipping Acts 1894 to 1977 and, except in sections 22 (3) (*a*) and 37 (5) of this Act and the preceding subsection, this Act; and

" modifications " includes additions, omissions and alterations, and related expressions shall be construed accordingly.

(3) Section 4 of the Aliens Restriction (Amendment) Act 1919 (which prohibits an alien from holding a pilotage certificate for a pilotage district in the United Kingdom except in certain cases) shall cease to have effect.

(4) The enactments mentioned in the first and second columns of Schedule 7 to this Act are hereby repealed to the extent specified in the third column of that Schedule; but nothing in Part I of that Schedule shall affect the operation of any enactment in relation to such an occurrence as mentioned in section 19 (4) of this Act.

Expenses etc.

51.—(1) There shall be paid out of money provided by Parliament—

(*a*) any administrative expenses incurred by a Minister of the Crown or a government department under this Act; and

(*b*) any increase attributable to this Act in the sums which, under any other Act, are payable out of money so provided.

(2) The Treasury shall be entitled to charge a reasonable fee for any certificate given by or on behalf of the Treasury in pursuance of any provision contained in subsection (2) or (4) (*c*) of section 38 of this Act or paragraph 4 of Part III of Schedule 3 or paragraph 7 of Part II of Schedule 4 to this Act.

(3) Any fees received by a Minister of the Crown by virtue of this Act shall be paid into the Consolidated Fund.

Citation and commencement

52.—(1) This Act may be cited as the Merchant Shipping Act 1979 and this Act and the Merchant Shipping Acts 1894 to 1977 may be cited together as the Merchant Shipping Acts 1894 to 1979.

(2) This Act shall come into force on such day as the Secretary of State may appoint by order, and different days may be appointed in pursuance of this subsection for different provisions of this Act or for different purposes of the same provision.

GENERAL NOTE

For commencement, see the Merchant Shipping Act 1979 (Commencement No. 1) Order 1979 (S.I. 1979 No. 807 (C. 19)), and the General Note at the beginning of this Act.

SCHEDULES

Section 1 (4)

SCHEDULE 1

FURTHER PROVISIONS RELATING TO CONSTITUTION ETC. OF PILOTAGE COMMISSION

Tenure of members

1. Subject to paragraphs 2 to 4 of this Schedule, a person shall hold and vacate office as a Commissioner or the Chairman in accordance with the terms of the instrument appointing him to that office.

2. A person shall not be appointed as a Commissioner and a Commissioner shall not be appointed as the Chairman for a term of more than three years; but a person may be reappointed as a Commissioner and a Commissioner may be reappointed as the Chairman on or after the date on which he ceases to be a Commissioner or, as the case may be, ceases to be the Chairman.

3.—(1) A person may at any time resign his office as a Commissioner or the Chairman by giving to the Secretary of State a notice in writing signed by that person and stating that he resigns that office.

(2) If the Chairman ceases to be a Commissioner he shall cease to be the Chairman.

4. If the Secretary of State is satisfied that a Commissioner—

(*a*) has been absent from the meetings of the Commission for a period longer than six consecutive months without the permission of the Commission; or

(*b*) is incapacitated by physical or mental illness; or

(*c*) is otherwise unable or unfit to discharge the functions of a Commissioner,

the Secretary of State may declare his office as a Commissioner to be vacant and shall notify the declaration in such manner as the Secretary of State thinks fit; and thereupon the office shall become vacant.

Remuneration of members

5. The Commission shall pay to each Commissioner such remuneration and allowances as the Secretary of State may determine with the consent of the Minister for the Civil Service.

6. Where a person ceases to be a Commissioner otherwise than on the expiry of his term of office and it appears to the Secretary of State that there are special circumstances which make it right for that person to receive compensation, the Secretary of State may with the consent of the Minister for the Civil Service direct the Commission to make to that person a payment of such amount as the Secretary of State may determine with the consent of the said Minister; and it shall be the duty of the Commission to comply with the direction.

Proceedings

7. The quorum of the Commission and the arrangements relating to meetings of the Commission shall be such as the Commission may determine.

8.—(1) A Commissioner who is in any way directly or indirectly interested in a contract made or proposed to be made by the Commission, or in any other matter whatsoever which falls to be considered by the Commission, shall disclose the nature of his interest at a meeting of the Commission and the disclosure shall be recorded in the minutes of the meeting; and the Commissioner shall not—

(*a*) in the case of a contract, take part in any deliberation or decision of the Commission with respect to the contract; and

(*b*) in the case of any other matter, take part in any decision of the Commission with respect to the matter if the Commission decides that the interest in question might affect prejudicially the Commissioner's consideration of the matter.

(2) A notice given by a Commissioner at a meeting of the Commission to the effect that he is a member or employee of a specified company or firm and is to be regarded as interested in any contract which is made after the date of the notice with the company or firm shall, for the purposes of the preceding sub-paragraph, be a sufficient disclosure of his interest in relation to any contract so made.

(3) A Commissioner need not attend in person at a meeting of the Commission in order to make a disclosure which he is required to make under this paragraph if he takes reasonable steps to secure that the disclosure is made by a notice which is taken into consideration and read at such a meeting.

9. The validity of any proceedings of the Commission shall not be affected by any vacancy among the Commissioners or by any defect in the appointment of a Commissioner.

Staff

10. The Commission may employ such persons as it considers are needed to assist the Commission in the performance of its functions and may pay to them such remuneration and allowances as the Commission considers appropriate.

11. The Commission may—

(*a*) pay, to or in respect of persons formerly employed by the Commission, pensions, allowances or gratuities of such amounts as the Commission may determine;

(*b*) make such payments towards the provision of any of the said benefits as the Commission may determine;

(*c*) maintain such schemes as the Commission may determine, whether contributory or not, for the payment of any of the said benefits.

12. If a person employed by the Commission becomes a Commissioner and was by reference to his employment by the Commission a participant in a pension scheme maintained by the Commission in pursuance of the preceding paragraph, the Commission may determine that his service as a Commissioner shall be treated for the purposes of the scheme as service as an employee of the Commission.

Instruments

13. The fixing of the common seal of the Commission shall be authenticated by the signature of the Chairman or of another Commissioner authorised by the Commission to authenticate it.

14. A document purporting to be duly executed under the seal of the Commission shall be received in evidence and shall, unless the contrary is proved, be deemed to be so executed.

Interpretation

15. In the preceding provisions of this Schedule "the Chairman" and "a Commissioner" mean respectively the chairman of the Commission and a member of the Commission.

Section 13 (1)

SCHEDULE 2

MISCELLANEOUS AMENDMENTS OF PILOTAGE ACT 1913

1. In paragraph (*h*) of section 7 (1) (which enables a pilotage order to provide that pilotage shall become or cease to be compulsory in specified areas subject to provision being also made for the payment of compensation to the pilots concerned in certain cases where pilotage ceases to be compulsory) for the words from the beginning to "also made" there shall be substituted the words "make provision as to the circumstances in which pilotage in a pilotage district is to be compulsory, subject to provision being also made, in a case where pilotage ceases to be compulsory in connection with the rearrangement of the district,".

2. Section 8 (2) (which relates to pilotage districts and authorities as they were constituted at the passing of the Pilotage Act 1913 and is spent) shall cease to have effect.

3. Section 9 (which provides for the appointment of a committee to give advice to the Secretary of State about the performance of his functions under the Pilotage Act 1913) shall cease to have effect.

4. Section 10 (1) (which relates to areas in which pilotage was and was not compulsory at the passing of the Pilotage Act 1913 and is spent) shall cease to have effect.

5.—(1) In paragraphs (*k*), (*l*), (*m*) and (*p*) of section 17 (1) (which among other things provide for byelaws relating to pilotage certificates for masters and mates) before the words "mates" and "mate" wherever they occur there shall be inserted the word "first".

(2) In section 17 (which authorises a pilotage authority to make byelaws for the purposes mentioned in subsection (1) of that section) after subsection (3) there shall be inserted the following subsection—

(4) A byelaw may make different provision for different circumstances.

6. In section 18 (of which paragraphs (*a*) to (*c*) specify the persons who may make objections to or proposals for a byelaw relating to a port) at the end of paragraph (*c*) there shall be inserted the words "or

(*d*) the Pilotage Commission;".

7. In section 20 (4) (which penalises a person who fails to return a pilot's licence as required by that section) after the words "fails" there shall be inserted the words "without reasonable excuse".

8.—(1) In section 23 (1) (which provides for the grant of pilotage certificates to masters and mates of ships except in the cases mentioned in the proviso)—

(*a*) before the word "mate" wherever it occurs there shall be inserted the word "first";

(*b*) in paragraph (*a*) of the proviso (which prohibits the grant of a pilotage certificate to a person who is not a British subject except in special cases) for the words "except in the cases for which special provision is made by this Act" there shall be substituted the words "or a national of a member State of the Economic Community other than the United Kingdom and the ship is registered under the law of a member State of the Economic Community"; and

(*c*) after paragraph (*b*) of the proviso there shall be inserted the words "; and

(*c*) In any district where a byelaw is in force prohibiting the grant of a pilotage certificate in respect of a vessel of a description specified in the byelaws, the pilotage authority shall not grant a certificate in respect of such a vessel";

but nothing in paragraph (*b*) of this sub-paragraph affects the validity or prevents the renewal of any pilotage certificate which, immediately before the day when that paragraph comes into force, is in force in respect of a ship which is not registered under the law of a member State of the Economic Community.

(2) In section 23 (3) (which provides that a pilotage certificate shall not be in

force for more than one year but may be renewed annually) after the word " may " there shall be inserted the words " if held by the master or first mate of a ship ".

(3) In section 23 (4) and (5) (which refer to pilotage certificates for masters and mates and for more than one ship of substantially the same class) before the word " mate " wherever it occurs there shall be inserted the word " first " and after the word " class " there shall be inserted the words " and registered as mentioned in paragraph (*a*) in subsection (1) of this section.".

9. Section 24 (which specifies the special cases mentioned in sub-paragraph (1) of the preceding paragraph) shall cease to have effect.

10.—(1) In section 27 (1) (*a*) (which refers to a pilotage certificate for a master or mate) before the word " mate " there shall be inserted the word " first ".

(2) In section 27 (which provides for complaints to the Secretary of State about pilotage authority's conduct in connection with pilots' licences and pilotage certificates and examinations for them) after subsection (1) there shall be inserted the following subsection—

(1A) The Secretary of State may—

(*a*) before he considers a complaint as required by the preceding subsection, ask the Pilotage Commission for its advice on the complaint; and

(*b*) when considering the complaint as so required, have regard to the Commission's advice on the complaint.

11.—(1) In section 30 (2) (which relate to dues payable in a case where an unlicensed pilot is superseded by a licensed pilot) for the words from " a proportionate " to " of the licensed pilot " there shall be substituted the words " an appropriate proportion of the pilotage dues payable in respect of the ship " and the words " to the licensed pilot and " shall be omitted.

(2) In section 30 (3) (which penalises a pilot not licensed for a district if he pilots or attempts to pilot a ship in the district after a licensed pilot for the district has offered to pilot the ship) for the word " after " there shall be substituted the words " when he knows that ".

12. In section 31 (which relates to the furnishing of information by the master to the pilot of a ship about her draught, length and beam and provides that a master who refuses to comply with a request for the information or makes or is party to the making of a false statement in answer to such a request shall be liable to a fine not exceeding £50)—

(*a*) after the word " beam " in subsection (1) there shall be inserted the words " and to provide him with such other information relating to the ship or its cargo as the pilot specifies and is necessary to enable him to carry out his duties as the pilot of the ship ";

(*b*) for subsection (2) there shall be substituted the following subsections—

(2) It shall be the duty of the master of a ship to bring to the notice of each licensed pilot who pilots the ship any defects in, and any matter peculiar to, the ship and its machinery and equipment of which the master knows and which might affect materially the navigation of the ship.

(3) The master of a ship who—

(*a*) refuses to comply with a request made to him in pursuance of subsection (1) of this section; or

(*b*) makes a statement which he knows is false; or recklessly makes a statement which is false, in answer to such a request or is privy to the making by another person in answer to such a request of a statement which the master knows is false; or

(*c*) fails without reasonable excuse to perform the duty imposed on him by the preceding subsection,

shall be guilty of an offence and liable to a fine not exceeding one thousand pounds in the case of an offence under paragraph (*b*) of this subsection and five hundred pounds in any other case.

13.—(1) In section 32 (1) (which provides that a ship while being moved within a harbour in a pilotage district shall, except in certain cases, be deemed to be a ship navigating in a pilotage district) for the words " a ship navigating " there shall be substituted the words " being navigated ".

(2) Section 32 (2) (which provides that a ship which is navigating in a closed dock or other work in a pilotage district is deemed to be in a district where pilotage is not compulsory) shall cease to have effect.

(3) Without prejudice to the generality of subsection (2) of section 52 of this Act, an order in pursuance of that subsection which brings into force the preceding sub-paragraph or Schedule 7 to this Act so far as that Schedule relates to section 32 (2) may provide that it shall come into force in relation only to such pilotage districts as are specified in the order.

14. Section 33 (2) (under which a licensed pilot is required to produce, to a person employing him who requests him to do so, his copies of the Pilotage Act 1913 and of the pilotage order and any byelaws in force in the pilotage district) shall cease to have effect.

15. In section 35 (under which a pilot who in pursuance of byelaws under the Pilotage Act 1913 has given a bond, of which the penalty mut not exceed £100, shall not be liable for neglect or lack of skill beyond the penalty of the bond and the amount of his pilotage dues)—

(*a*) for subsection (1) there shall be substituted the following subsection—

(1) A licensed pilot, a person authorised to act as the assistant of a licensed pilot by the authority who licensed the pilot and the pilotage authority who employ a licensed pilot or such an assistant shall not be liable—

(*a*) in the case of a pilot or assistant, for neglect or want of skill; and

(*b*) in the case of a pilotage authority, for neglect or want of skill by the pilot or assistant of by the authority in employing the pilot or assistant,

beyond the amount of one hundred pounds and the amount of the pilotage dues in respect of the voyage during which the liability arose.;

(*b*) subsection (2) and in subsection (3) the words " his " and " pilot's " shall be omitted; and

(*c*) in subsection (3) after the word " pilot " where it first occurs and the words " by the pilot " and the words " from the pilot " there shall be inserted the words " , assistant or pilotage authority ".

16. In section 36 (2) (which penalises a licensed pilot who refuses to produce his licence in accordance with that section) after the word " refuses " there shall be inserted the words " without reasonable excuse ".

17. In section 39—

(*a*) in subsection (1) (which requires a pilot boat to carry the marks mentioned in paragraph (*a*), to be painted in the colours mentioned in paragraph (*b*) and to display the flag described in paragraph (*c*)) paragraphs (*a*) and (*b*) shall be omitted; and

(*b*) in subsection (2) (which provides for a fine for failure to comply with subsection (1)) the words " that the pilot boat possesses all the above characteristics and " and the words from " and also " to " concealed " shall be omitted.

18. In section 42 (which among other things penalises the master of a ship on which a pilot flag is displayed when no authorised pilot is on board) after the words " shall, unless " there shall be inserted the words " in the case of a pilot flag he proves that he took all reasonable precautions and exercised all due diligence to avoid displaying the flag and ".

19. In section 43 (3) (which penalises a master who fails to display a pilot signal as required by that section) after the word " fails " there shall be inserted the words " without reasonable excuse ".

20.—(1) In section 44 (2) (which requires a master of a ship who accepts the services of a pilot to facilitate his getting on board the ship) for the words " getting on board " there shall be substituted the words " and any assistant of his getting on board and subsequently leaving ".

(2) In section 44 (3) (which provides that a master who fails to comply with the provisions of that section shall be liable to a fine not exceeding double the amount of the dues that could be demanded for the conduct of the ship) after the words " fails " there shall be inserted the words " without reasonable excuse ", after the word " liable " there shall be inserted the words " on summary conviction " and for the words " could be demanded for the conduct of the ship " there shall be substituted the words " (disregarding any increase in the dues attributable to failure to comply with the requirements of byelaws in force in the district about requests for pilots) are payable in respect of the ship or would have been so payable if he had complied with those provisions or five hundred pounds, whichever is the greater ".

21. In section 45 (3) (which penalises the master of a ship if he misuses or permits another person to misuse a pilot signal) after the word " If " there shall be inserted the words " without reasonable excuse ".

22. In section 46 (which provides that a pilot of a ship who through breach or neglect of duty or through drunkenness endangers the ship or persons on the ship shall be guilty of a misdemeanour) for the words from " in respect of each offence " onwards there shall be substituted the words " be guilty of an offence and liable—

(i) on summary conviction, to imprisonment for a term not exceeding three months or a fine of an amount not exceeding one thousand pounds or both;

(ii) on conviction on indictment, to imprisonment for a term not exceeding two years or a fine or both.".

23. In section 48 (1) (under paragraph (*a*) of which it is an offence, punishable with a fine not exceeding one hundred pounds, for a licensed pilot to keep licensed premises or to sell liquor, tobacco or tea and under paragraph (*d*) of which it is an offence so punishable for a licensed pilot to act as a pilot whilst suspended and under paragraph (*g*) of which it is an offence so punishable for a licensed pilot to refuse or delay, when not prevented by illness or other reasonable cause, to pilot a ship which he is properly requested to pilot),—

(*a*) paragraph (*a*) shall be omitted;

(*b*) for the word " whilst " in paragraph (*d*) there shall be substituted the words " when he knows he is "; and

(*c*) in paragraph (*g*) for the words " when not prevented by illness or other " there shall be substituted the word " without ".

24. In section 50 (which penalises a pilot who demands or receives, and a master who offers or pays, dues at any other rate, whether greater or less than the authorised rates) for the words from " dues " to " demanded " there shall be substituted the words " pilotage dues of amounts which he knows are greater or less than the amounts authorised ".

25. In section 51 (which provides that if a ship with a licensed pilot on board leads another ship which has no such pilot, the pilot shall be entitled to the same pilotage rate for the other ship as if he had piloted it) for the words from " pilot so leading " to " as if he " there shall be substituted the words " same pilotage dues shall be payable in respect of the last-mentioned ship as if the pilot ".

26. Section 56 (which provides that expenditure under the Pilotage Act 1913 out of money provided by Parliament must not exceed £6,000 a year), section 58 (which provides for the apportionment of the income of pilotage authorities in cases which no longer arise) and section 59 (which contains savings which are no longer required) shall cease to have effect.

27. In section 61 (which relates to the extent and application of the Pilotage Act 1913) the reference to that Act shall be construed as including the provisions of this Act relating to pilotage except paragraph 2 of Schedule 5.

Sections 14, 15, 16, 49 (4), 51 (2) SCHEDULE 3

Convention relating to the Carriage of Passengers and their Luggage by Sea

Part I

Text of Convention

Article 1

Definitions

In this Convention the following expressions have the meaning hereby assigned to them:

1. (*a*) " carrier " means a person by or on behalf of whom a contract of carriage has been concluded, whether the carriage is actually performed by him or by a performing carrier;

(*b*) " performing carrier " means a person other than the carrier, being the owner, charterer or operator of a ship, who actually performs the whole or a part of the carriage;

2. " contract of carriage " means a contract made by or on behalf of a carrier for the carriage by sea of a passenger or of a passenger and his luggage, as the case may be;

3. " ship " means only a seagoing vessel, excluding an air-cushion vehicle;

4. " passenger " means any person carried in a ship,

(a) under a contract of carriage, or

(b) who, with the consent of the carrier, is accompanying a vehicle or live animals which are covered by a contract for the carriage of goods not governed by this Convention;

5. " luggage " means any article or vehicle carried by the carrier under a contract of carriage, excluding:

(a) articles and vehicles carried under a charter party, bill of lading or other contract primarily concerned with the carriage of goods, and

(b) live animals;

6. " cabin luggage " means luggage which the passenger has in his cabin or is otherwise in his possession, custody or control. Except for the application of paragraph 8 of this Article and Article 8, cabin luggage includes luggage which the passenger has in or on his vehicle;

7. " loss of or damage to luggage " includes pecuniary loss resulting from the luggage not having been re-delivered to the passenger within a reasonable time after the arrival of the ship on which the luggage has been or should have been carried, but does not include delays resulting from labour disputes;

8. " carriage " covers the following periods:

(a) with regard to the passenger and his cabin luggage, the period during which the passenger and/or his cabin luggage are on board the ship or in the course of embarkation or disembarkation, and the period during which the passenger and his cabin luggage are transported by water from land to the ship or vice-versa, if the cost of such transport is included in the fare or if the vessel used for the purpose of auxiliary transport has been put at the disposal of the passenger by the carrier. However, with regard to the passenger, carriage does not include the period during which he is in a marine terminal or station or on a quay or in or on any other port installation;

(b) with regard to cabin luggage, also the period during which the passenger is in a marine terminal or station or on a quay or in or on any other port installation if that luggage has been taken over by the carrier or his servant or agent and has not been re-delivered to the passenger;

(c) with regard to other luggage which is not cabin luggage, the period from the time of its taking over by the carrier or his servant or agent on shore or on board until the time of its re-delivery by the carrier or his servant or agent;

9. " international carriage " means any carriage in which, according to the contract of carriage, the place of departure and the place of destination are situated in two different States, or in a single State if, according to the contract of carriage or the scheduled itinerary, there is an intermediate port of call in another State.

Article 2

Application

1. This Convention shall apply to any international carriage if:

(a) the ship is flying the flag of or is registered in a State Party to this Convention, or

(b) the contract of carriage has been made in a State Party to this Convention, or

(c) the place of departure or destination, according to the contract of carriage, is in a State Party to this Convention.

2. Notwithstanding paragraph 1 of this Article, this Convention shall not apply when the carriage is subject, under any other international convention concerning the carriage of passengers or luggage by another mode of transport, to a civil liability regime under the provisions of such convention, in so far as those provisions have mandatory application to carriage by sea.

ARTICLE 3

Liability of the carrier

1. The carrier shall be liable for the damage suffered as a result of the death of or personal injury to a passenger and the loss of or damage to luggage if the incident which caused the damage so suffered occurred in the course of the carriage and was due to the fault or neglect of the carrier or of his servants or agents acting within the scope of their employment.

2. The burden of proving that the incident which caused the loss or damage occurred in the course of the carriage, and the extent of the loss or damage, shall lie with the claimant.

3. Fault or neglect of the carrier or of his servants or agents acting within the scope of their employment shall be presumed, unless the contrary is proved, if the death of or personal injury to the passenger or the loss of or damage to cabin luggage arose from or in connection with the shipwreck, collision, stranding, explosion or fire, or defect in the ship. In respect of loss of or damage to other luggage, such fault or neglect shall be presumed, unless the contrary is proved, irrespective of the nature of the incident which caused the loss or damage. In all other cases the burden of proving fault or neglect shall lie with the claimant.

ARTICLE 4

Performing carrier

1. If the performance of the carriage or part thereof has been entrusted to a performing carrier, the carrier shall nevertheless remain liable for the entire carriage according to the provisions of this Convention. In addition, the performing carrier shall be subject and entitled to the provisions of this Convention for the part of the carriage performed by him.

2. The carrier shall, in relation to the carriage performed by the performing carrier, be liable for the acts and omissions of the performing carrier and of his servants and agents acting within the scope of their employment.

3. Any special agreement under which the carrier assumes obligations not imposed by this Convention or any waiver of rights conferred by this Convention shall affect the performing carrier only if agreed by him expressly and in writing.

4. Where and to the extent that both the carrier and the performing carrier are liable, their liability shall be joint and several.

5. Nothing in this Article shall prejudice any right of recourse as between the carrier and the performing carrier.

ARTICLE 5

Valuables

The carrier shall not be liable for the loss of or damage to monies, negotiable securities, gold, silverware, jewellery, ornaments, works of art, or other valuables, except where such valuables have been deposited with the carrier for the agreed purpose of safe-keeping in which case the carrier shall be liable up to the limit provided for in paragraph 3 of Article 8 unless a higher limit is agreed upon in accordance with paragraph 1 of Article 10.

ARTICLE 6

Contributory fault

If the carrier proves that the death of or personal injury to a passenger or the loss of or damage to his luggage was caused or contributed to by the fault or neglect of the passenger, the court seized of the case may exonerate the carrier wholly or partly from his liability in accordance with the provisions of the law of that court.

ARTICLE 7

Limit of liability for personal injury

1. The liability of the carrier for the death of or personal injury to a passenger shall in no case exceed 700,000 francs per carriage. Where in accordance with the law of the court seized of the case damages are awarded in the form of periodical income payments, the equivalent capital value of those payments shall not exceed the said limit.

2. Notwithstanding paragraph 1 of this Article, the national law of any State Party to this Convention may fix, as far as carriers who are nationals of such State are concerned, a higher *per capita* limit of liability.

Article 8
Limit of liability for loss of or damage to luggage

1. The liability of the carrier for the loss of or damage to cabin luggage shall in no case exceed 12,500 francs per passenger, per carriage.

2. The liability of the carrier for the loss of or damage to vehicles including all luggage carried in or on the vehicle shall in no case exceed 50,000 francs per vehicle, per carriage.

3. The liability of the carrier for the loss of or damage to luggage other than that mentioned in paragraphs 1 and 2 of this Article shall in no case exceed 18,000 francs per passenger, per carriage.

4. The carrier and the passenger may agree that the liability of the carrier shall be subject to a deductible not exceeding 1,750 francs in the case of damage to a vehicle and not exceeding 200 francs per passenger in the case of loss of or damage to other luggage, such sum to be deducted from the loss or damage.

Article 9
Monetary unit and conversion

1. The franc mentioned in this Convention shall be deemed to refer to a unit consisting of 65·5 milligrams of gold of millesimal fineness 900.

2. The amounts referred to in Articles 7 and 8 shall be converted into the national currency of the State of the court seized of the case on the basis of the official value of that currency, by reference to the unit defined in paragraph 1 of this Article, on the date of the judgment or the date agreed upon by the parties.

Article 10
Supplementary provisions on limits of liability

1. The carrier and the passenger may agree, expressly and in writing, to higher limits of liability than those prescribed in Articles 7 and 8.

2. Interest on damages and legal costs shall not be included in the limits of liability prescribed in Articles 7 and 8.

Article 11
Defences and limits for carriers' servants

If an action is brought against a servant or agent of the carrier or of the performing carrier arising out of damage covered by this Convention, such servant or agent, if he proves that he acted within the scope of his employment, shall be entitled to avail himself of the defences and limits of liability which the carrier or the performing carrier is entitled to invoke under this Convention.

Article 12
Aggregation of claims

1. Where the limits of liability prescribed in Articles 7 and 8 take effect, they shall apply to the aggregate of the amounts recoverable in all claims arising out of the death of or personal injury to any one passenger or the loss of or damage to his luggage.

2. In relation to the carriage performed by a performing carrier, the aggregate of the amounts recoverable from the carrier and the performing carrier and from their servants and agents acting within the scope of their employment shall not exceed the highest amount which could be awarded against either the carrier or the performing carrier under this Convention, but none of the persons mentioned shall be liable for a sum in excess of the limit applicable to him.

3. In any case where a servant or agent of the carrier or of the performing carrier is entitled under Article 11 of this convention to avail himself of the limits of liability prescribed in Articles 7 and 8, the aggregate of the amounts recoverable from the carrier, or the performing carrier as the case may be, and from that servant or agent, shall not exceed those limits.

ARTICLE 13

Loss of right to limit liability

1. The carrier shall not be entitled to the benefit of the limits of liability prescribed in Articles 7 and 8 and paragraph 1 of Article 10, if it is proved that the damage resulted from an act or omission of the carrier done with the intent to cause such damage, or recklessly and with knowledge that such damage would probably result.

2. The servant or agent of the carrier or of the performing carrier shall not be entitled to the benefit of those limits if it is proved that the damage resulted from an act or omission of that servant or agent done with the intent to cause such damage, or recklessly and with knowledge that such damage would probably result.

ARTICLE 14

Basis for claims

No action for damages for the death of or personal injury to a passenger, or for the loss of or damage to luggage, shall be brought against a carrier or performing carrier otherwise than in accordance with this Convention.

ARTICLE 15

Notice of loss or damage to luggage

1. The passenger shall give written notice to the carrier or his agent:

(*a*) in the case of apparent damage to luggage:

(i) for cabin luggage, before or at the time of disembarkation of the passenger;

(ii) for all other luggage, before or at the time of its re-delivery;

(*b*) in the case of damage to luggage which is not apparent, or loss of luggage, within fifteen days from the date of disembarkation or re-delivery or from the time when such re-delivery should have taken place.

2. If the passenger fails to comply with this Article, he shall be presumed, unless the contrary is proved, to have received the luggage undamaged.

3. The notice in writing need not be given if the condition of the luggage has at the time of its receipt been the subject of joint survey or inspection.

ARTICLE 16

Time-bar for actions

1. Any action for damages arising out of the death of or personal injury to a passenger or for the loss of or damage to luggage shall be time-barred after a period of two years.

2. The limitation period shall be calculated as follows:

(*a*) in the case of personal injury, from the date of disembarkation of the passenger;

(*b*) in the case of death occurring during carriage, from the date when the passenger should have disembarked, and in the case of personal injury occurring during carriage and resulting in the death of the passenger after disembarkation, from the date of death, provided that this period shall not exceed three years from the date of disembarkation;

(*c*) in the case of loss of or damage to luggage, from the date of disembarkation or from the date when disembarkation should have taken place, whichever is later.

3. The law of the court seized of the case shall govern the grounds of suspension and interruption of limitation periods, but in no case shall an action under this Convention be brought after the expiration of a period of three years from the date of disembarkation of the passenger or from the date when disembarkation should have taken place, whichever is later.

4. Notwithstanding paragraphs 1, 2 and 3 of this Article, the period of limitation may be extended by a declaration of the carrier or by agreement of the parties

after the cause of action has arisen. The declaration or agreement shall be in writing.

ARTICLE 17

Competent jurisdiction

1. An action arising under this Convention shall, at the option of the claimant, be brought before one of the courts listed below, provided that the court is located in a State Party to this Convention:

(*a*) the court of the place of permanent residence or principal place of business of the defendant, or

(*b*) the court of the place of departure or that of the destination according to the contract of carriage, or

(*c*) a court of the State of the domicile or permanent residence of the claimant, if the defendant has a place of business and is subject to jurisdiction in that State, or

(*d*) a court of the State where the contract of carriage was made, if the defendant has a place of business and is subject to jurisdiction in that State.

2. After the occurrence of the incident which has caused the damage, the parties may agree that the claim for damages shall be submitted to any jurisdiction or to arbitration.

ARTICLE 18

Invalidity of contractual provisions

Any contractual provision concluded before the occurrence of the incident which has caused the death of or personal injury to a passenger or the loss of or damage to his luggage, purporting to relieve the carrier of his liability towards the passenger or to prescribe a lower limit of liability than that fixed in this Convention except as provided in paragraph 4 of Article 8, and any such provision purporting to shift the burden of proof which rests on the carrier, or having the effect of restricting the option specified in paragraph 1 of Article 17, shall be null and void, but the nullity of that provision shall not render void the contract of carriage which shall remain subject to the provisions of this Convention.

ARTICLE 19

Other conventions on limitation of liability

This Convention shall not modify the rights or duties of the carrier, the performing carrier, and their servants or agents provided for in international conventions relating to the limitation of liability of owners of seagoing ships.

ARTICLE 20

Nuclear damage

No liability shall arise under this Convention for damage caused by a nuclear incident:

(*a*) if the operation of a nuclear installation is liable for such damage under either the Paris Convention of 29 July 1960 on Third Party Liability in the Field of Nuclear Energy as amended by its Additional Protocol of 28 January 1964, or the Vienna Convention of 21 May 1963 on Civil Liability for Nuclear Damage, or

(*b*) if the operator of a nuclear installation is liable for such damage by virtue of a national law governing the liability for such damage, provided that such law is in all respects as favourable to persons who may suffer damage as either the Paris or the Vienna Conventions.

ARTICLE 21

Commercial carriage by public authorities

This Convention shall apply to commercial carriage undertaken by States or Public Authorities under contracts of carriage within the meaning of Article 1.

PART II

PROVISIONS HAVING EFFECT IN CONNECTION WITH CONVENTION

Interpretation

1. In this Part of this Schedule any reference to a numbered article is a reference to the article of the Convention which is so numbered and any expression to which a meaning is assigned by article 1 of the Convention has that meaning.

Provisions adapting or supplementing specified articles of the Convention

2. For the purposes of paragraph 2 of article 2, provisions of such an international convention as is mentioned in that paragraph which apart from this paragraph do not have mandatory application to carriage by sea shall be treated as having mandatory application to carriage by sea if it is stated in the contract of carriage for the carriage in question that those provisions are to apply in connection with the carriage.

3. The reference to the law of the court in article 6 shall be construed as a reference to the Law Reform (Contributory Negligence) Act 1945 except that in relation to Northern Ireland it shall be construed as a reference to section 2 of the Law Reform (Miscellaneous Provisions) Act (Northern Ireland) 1948.

4. The Secretary of State may by order provide that, in relation to a carrier whose principal place of business is in the United Kingdom, paragraph 1 of article 7 shall have effect with the substitution for the limit for the time being specified in that paragraph of a different limit specified in the order (which shall not be lower than the limit specified in that paragraph at the passing of this Act or, if paragraph 1 of Part III of this Schedule has come into force, specified in paragraph 1 of article 7 as amended by paragraph 1 of that Part).

5. The values which in pursuance of article 9 shall be considered as the official values in the United Kingdom of the amounts in francs for the time being specified in articles 7 and 8 shall be such amounts in sterling as the Secretary of State may from time to time by order specify.

6. It is hereby declared that by virtue of article 12 the limitations on liability there mentioned in respect of a passenger or his luggage apply to the aggregate liabilities of the persons in question in all proceedings for enforcing the liabilities or any of them which may be brought whether in the United Kingdom or elsewhere.

7. Article 16 shall apply to an arbitration as it applies to an action; and section 27 (3) and (4) of the Limitation Act 1939 and section 72 (2) and (3) of the Statute of Limitation (Northern Ireland) 1958 (which determine when an arbitration is deemed to commence) shall apply for the purposes of article 16 as they apply for the purposes of those Acts.

8. The court before which proceedings are brought in pursuance of article 17 to enforce a liability which is limited by virtue of article 12 may at any stage of the proceedings make such orders as appear to the court to be just and equitable in view of the provisions of article 12 and of any other proceedings which have been or are likely to be begun in the United Kingdom or elsewhere to enforce the liability in whole or in part; and without prejudice to the generality of the preceding provisions of this paragraph such a court shall, where the liability is or may be partly enforceable in other proceedings in the United Kingdom or elsewhere, have jurisdiction to award an amount less than the court would have awarded if the limitation applied solely to the proceedings before the court or to make any part of its award conditional on the results of any other proceedings.

Other provisions adapting or supplementing the Convention

9. Any reference in the Convention to a contract of carriage excludes a contract of carriage which is not for reward.

10. If Her Majesty by Order in Council declares that any State specified in the Order is a party to the Convention in respect of a particular country the Order shall, subject to the provisions of any subsequent Order made by virtue of this paragraph, be conclusive evidence that the State is a party to the Convention in respect of that country.

11. The Secretary of State may by order make provision—

(*a*) for requiring a person who is the carrier in relation to a passenger to give to the passenger, in a manner specified in the order, notice of such of the provisions of Part I of this Schedule as are so specified;

(b) for a person who fails to comply with a requirement imposed on him by the order to be guilty of an offence and liable on summary conviction to a fine of an amount not exceeding £500.

Application of ss. 502 *and* 503 *of Merchant Shipping Act* 1894 *and sections* 17 *and* 18 *of this Act*

12. Nothing in section 502 of the Merchant Shipping Act 1894 or section 18 of this Act (which among other things limit a shipowner's liability for the loss or damage of goods in certain cases) shall relieve a person of any liability imposed on him by the Convention.

13. It is hereby declared that nothing in the Convention affects the operation of section 503 of the Merchant Shipping Act 1894 or section 17 of this Act (which limit a shipowner's liability in certain cases of loss of life, injury or damage).

Part III

Modifications of parts I and II in consequence of protocol of 19th November 1976

1. In Part I of this Schedule, in article 7 of the Convention, for the words "700,000 francs" or any other words which, by virtue of paragraph 4 of Part II of this Schedule, are specified in that article in the place of those words there shall be substituted the words "46,666 units of account".

2. In the said Part I, in article 8 of the Convention, for the word "francs" wherever it occurs there shall be substituted the words "units of account" and for the figures "12,500", "50,000", "18,000", "1,750" and "200" here shall be substituted respectively the figures "833", "3,333", "1,200", "117" and "13".

3. In the said Part I for article 9 there shall be substituted the following—

Article 9

Unit of account and conversion

The Unit of Account mentioned in this Convention is the Special Drawing Right as defined by the International Monetary Fund. The amounts mentioned in Articles 7 and 8 shall be converted into the national currency of the State of the Court seized of the case on the basis of the value of that currency on the date of the judgment or the date agreed upon by the Parties.

4. In Part II of this Schedule for paragraph 5 there shall be substituted the following—

5.—(1) For the purpose of converting from special drawing rights into sterling the amounts mentioned in articles 7 and 8 of the Convention in respect of which a judgment is given, one special drawing right shall be treated as equal to such a sum in sterling as the International Monetary Fund have fixed as being the equivalent of one special drawing right for—

(a) the day on which the judgment is given; or

(b) if no sum has been so fixed for that day, the last day before that day for which a sum has been so fixed.

(2) A certificate given by or on behalf of the Treasury stating—

(a) that a particular sum in stering has been fixed as mentioned in the preceding sub-paragraph for a particular day; or

(b) that no sum has been so fixed for that day and a particular sum in sterling has been so fixed for a day which is the last day for which a sum has been so fixed before the particular day,

shall be conclusive evidence of those matters for the purposes of articles 7 to 9 of the Convention; and a document purporting to be such a certificate shall, in any proceedings, be received in evidence and, unless the contrary is proved, be deemed to be such a certificate.

Sections 17, 18, 19, 49, 51 (2) SCHEDULE 4

CONVENTION ON LIMITATION OF LIABILITY FOR MARITIME CLAIMS 1976

PART I

TEXT OF CONVENTION

CHAPTER I. THE RIGHT OF LIMITATION

ARTICLE 1

Persons entitled to limit liability

1. Shipowners and salvors, as hereinafter defined, may limit their liability in accordance with the rules of this Convention for claims set out in Article 2.

2. The term " shipowner " shall mean the owner, charterer, manager or operator of a seagoing ship.

3. Salvor shall mean any person rendering services in direct connexion with salvage operations. Salvage operations shall also include operations referred to in Article 2, paragraph 1 (*d*), (*e*) and (*f*).

4. If any claims set out in Article 2 are made against any person for whose act, neglect or default the shipowner or salvor is responsible, such person shall be entitled to avail himself of the limitation of liability provided for in this Convention.

5. In this Convention the liability of a shipowner shall include liability in an action brought against the vessel herself.

6. An insurer of liability for claims subject to limitation in accordance with the rules of this Convention shall be entitled to the benefits of this Convention to the same extent as the assured himself.

7. The act of invoking limitation of liability shall not constitute an admission of liability.

ARTICLE 2

Claims subject to limitation

1. Subject to Articles 3 and 4 the following claims, whatever the basis of liability may be, shall be subject to limitation of liability:

(*a*) claims in respect of loss of life or personal injury or loss of or damage to property (including damage to harbour works, basins and waterways and aids to navigation), occurring on board or in direct connexion with the operation of the ship or with salvage operations, and consequential loss resulting therefrom;

(*b*) claims in respect of loss resulting from delay in the carriage by sea of cargo, passengers or their luggage;

(*c*) claims in respect of other loss resulting from infringement of rights other than contractual rights, occurring in direct connexion with the operation of the ship or salvage operations;

(*d*) claims in respect of the raising, removal, destruction or the rendering harmless of a ship which is sunk, wrecked, stranded or abandoned, including anything that is or has been on board such ship;

(*e*) claims in respect of the removal, destruction or the rendering harmless of the cargo of the ship;

(*f*) claims of a person other than the person liable in respect of measures taken in order to avert or minimize loss for which the person liable may limit his liability in accordance with this Convention, and further loss caused by such measures.

2. Claims set out in paragraph 1 shall be subject to limitation of liability even if brought by way of recourse or for indemnity under a contract or otherwise. However, claims set out under paragraph 1 (*d*), (*e*) and (*f*) shall not be subject to limitation of liability to the extent that they relate to remuneration under a contract with the person liable.

ARTICLE 3

Claims excepted from limitation

The rules of this Convention shall not apply to:

(*a*) claims for salvage or contribution in general average;

(*b*) claims for oil pollution damage within the meaning of the International Convention on Civil Liability for Oil Pollution Damage dated 29th November 1969 or of any amendment or Protocol thereto which is in force;

(*c*) claims subject to any international convention or national legislation governing or prohibiting limitation of liability for nuclear damage;

(*d*) claims against the shipowner of a nuclear ship for nuclear damage;

(*e*) claims by servants of the shipowner or salvor whose duties are connected with the ship or the salvage operations, including claims of their heirs, dependants or other persons entitled to make such claims, if under the law governing the contract of service between the shipowner or salvor and such servants the shipowner or salvor is not entitled to limit his liability in respect of such claims, or if he is by such law only permitted to limit his liability to an amount greater than that provided for in Article 6.

ARTICLE 4

Conduct barring limitation

A person liable shall not be entitled to limit his liability if it is proved that the loss resulted from his personal act or omission, committed with the intent to cause such loss, or recklessly and with knowledge that such loss would probably result.

ARTICLE 5

Counterclaims

Where a person entitled to limitation of liability under the rules of this Convention has a claim against the claimant arising out of the same occurrence, their respective claims shall be set off against each other and the provisions of this Convention shall only apply to the balance, if any.

CHAPTER II. LIMITS OF LIABILITY

ARTICLE 6

The general limits

1. The limits of liability for claims other than those mentioned in Article 7, arising on any distinct occasion, shall be calculated as follows:

(*a*) in respect of claims for loss of life or personal injury,

(i) 333,000 Units of Account for a ship with a tonnage not exceeding 500 tons,

(ii) for a ship with a tonnage in excess thereof, the following amount in addition to that mentioned in (i):

for each ton from 501 to 3,000 tons, 500 Units of Account;
for each ton from 3,001 to 30,000 tons, 333 Units of Account;
for each ton from 30,001 to 70,000 tons, 250 Units of Account, and
for each ton in excess of 70,000 tons, 167 Units of Account,

(*b*) in respect of any other claims,

(i) 167,000 Units of Account for a ship with a tonnage not exceeding 500 tons,

(ii) for a ship with a tonnage in excess thereof the following amount in addition to that mentioned in (i):

for each ton from 501 to 30,000, 167 Units of Account;
for each ton from 30,001 to 70,000 tons, 125 Units of Account; and
for each ton in excess of 70,000 tons, 83 Units of Account.

2. Where the amount calculated in accordance with paragraph 1 (*a*) is insufficient to pay the claims mentioned therein in full, the amount calculated in accordance with paragraph 1 (*b*) shall be available for payment of the unpaid balance of claims under paragraph 1 (*a*) and such unpaid balance shall rank rateably with claims mentioned under paragraph 1 (*b*).

3. The limits of liability for any salvor not operating from any ship or for any salvor operating solely on the ship to, or in respect of which he is rendering salvage services, shall be calculated according to a tonnage of 1,500 tons.

ARTICLE 7

The limit for passenger claims

1. In respect of claims arising on any distinct occasion for loss of life or personal injury to passengers of a ship, the limit of liability of the shipowner thereof shall be an amount of 46,666 Units of Account multiplied by the number of passengers which the ship is authorised to carry according to the ship's certificate, but not exceeding 25 million Units of Account.

2. For the purpose of this Article " claims for loss of life or personal injury to passengers of a ship " shall mean any such claims brought by or on behalf of any person carried in that ship:

(*a*) under a contract of passenger carriage, or

(*b*) who, with the consent of the carrier, is accompanying a vehicle or live animals which are covered by a contract for the carriage of goods.

ARTICLE 8

Unit of Account

1. The Unit of Account referred to in Articles 6 and 7 is the Special Drawing Right as defined by the International Monetary Fund. The amounts mentioned in Articles 6 and 7 shall be converted into the national currency of the State in which limitation is sought, according to the value of that currency at the date the limitation fund shall have been constituted, payment is made, or security is given which under the law of that State is equivalent to such payment.

ARTICLE 9

Aggregation of claims

1. The limits of liability determined in accordance with Article 6 shall apply to the aggregate of all claims which arise on any distinct occasion:

(*a*) against the person or persons mentioned in paragraph 2 of Article 1 and any person for whose act, neglect or default he or they are responsible; or

(*b*) against the shipowner of a ship rendering salvage services from that ship and the salvor or salvors operating from such ship and any person for whose act, neglect or default he or they are responsible; or

(*c*) against the salvor or salvors who are not operating from a ship or who are operating solely on the ship to, or in respect of which, the salvage services are rendered and any person for whose act, neglect or default he or they are responsible.

2. The limits of liability determined in accordance with Article 7 shall apply to the aggregate of all claims subject thereto which may arise on any distinct occasion against the person or persons mentioned in paragraph 2 of Article 1 in respect of the ship referred to in Article 7 and any person for whose act, neglect or default he or they are responsible.

ARTICLE 10

Limitation of liability without constitution of a limitation fund

1. Limitation of liability may be invoked notwithstanding that a limitation fund as mentioned in Article 11 has not been constituted.

2. If limitation of liability is invoked without the constitution of a limitation fund, the provisions of Article 12 shall apply correspondingly.

3. Questions of procedure arising under the rules of this Article shall be decided in accordance with the national law of the State Party in which action is brought.

CHAPTER III. THE LIMITATION FUND

ARTICLE 11

Constitution of the fund

1. Any person alleged to be liable may constitute a fund with the Court or other competent authority in any State Party in which legal proceedings are instituted in respect of claims subject to limitation. The fund shall be constituted in the sum of such of the amounts set out in Articles 6 and 7 as are applicable to claims

for which that person may be liable, together with interest thereon from the date of the occurrence giving rise to the liability until the date of the constitution of the fund. Any fund thus constituted shall be available only for the payment of claims in respect of which limitation of liability can be invoked.

2. A fund may be constituted, either by depositing the sum, or by producing a guarantee acceptable under the legislation of the State Party where the fund is constituted and considered to be adequate by the Court or other competent authority.

3. A fund constituted by one of the persons mentioned in paragraph 1 (*a*), (*b*) or (*c*) or paragraph 2 of Article 9 or his insurer shall be deemed constituted by all persons mentioned in paragraph 1 (*a*), (*b*) or (*c*) or paragraph 2, respectively.

ARTICLE 12

Distribution of the fund

1. Subject to the provisions of paragraphs 1 and 2 of Article 6 and of Article 7, the fund shall be distributed among the claimants in proportion to their established claims against the fund.

2. If, before the fund is distributed, the person liable, or his insurer, has settled a claim against the fund such person shall, up to the amount he has paid, acquire by subrogation the rights which the person so compensated would have enjoyed under this Convention.

3. The right of subrogation provided for in paragraph 2 may also be exercised by persons other than those therein mentioned in respect of any amount of compensation which they may have paid, but only to the extent that such subrogation is permitted under the applicable national law.

4. Where the person liable or any other person establishes that he may be compelled to pay, at a later date, in whole or in part any such amount of compensation with regard to which such person would have enjoyed a right of subrogation pursuant to paragraphs 2 and 3 had the compensation been paid before the fund was distributed, the Court or other competent authority of the State where the fund has been constituted may order that a sufficient sum shall be provisionally set aside to enable such person at such later date to enforce his claim against the fund.

ARTICLE 13

Bar to other actions

1. Where a limitation fund has been constituted in accordance with Article 11, any person having made a claim against the fund shall be barred from exercising any right in respect of such a claim against any other assets of a person by or on behalf of whom the fund has been constituted.

2. After a limitation fund has been constituted in accordance with Article 11, any ship or other property, belonging to a person on behalf of whom the fund has been constituted, which has been arrested or attached within the jurisdiction of a State Party for a claim which may be raised against the fund, or any security given, may be released by order of the Court or other competent authority of such State. However, such release shall always be ordered if the limitation fund has been constituted:

(*a*) at the port where the occurrence took place, or, if it took place out of port, at the first port of call thereafter; or

(*b*) at the port of disembarkation in respect of claims for loss of life or personal injury; or

(*c*) at the port of discharge in respect of damage to cargo; or

(*d*) in the State where the arrest is made.

3. The rules of paragraphs 1 and 2 shall apply only if the claimant may bring a claim against the limitation fund before the Court administering that fund and the fund is actually available and freely transferable in respect of that claim.

ARTICLE 14

Governing law

Subject to the provisions of this Chapter the rules relating to the constitution and distribution of a limitation fund, and all rules of procedure in connection therewith, shall be governed by the law of the State Party in which the fund is constituted.

CHAPTER IV. SCOPE OF APPLICATION

ARTICLE 15

This Convention shall apply whenever any person referred to in Article 1 seeks to limit his liability before the Court of a State Party or seeks to procure the release of a ship or other property or the discharge of any security given within the jurisdiction of any such State.

PART II

PROVISIONS HAVING EFFECT IN CONNECTION WITH CONVENTION

Interpretation

1. In this Part of this Schedule any reference to a numbered article is a reference to the article of the Convention which is so numbered.

Right to limit liability

2. The right to limit liability under the Convention shall apply in relation to any ship whether seagoing or not, and the definition of " shipowner " in paragraph 2 of article 1 shall be construed accordingly.

Claims subject to limitation

3.—(1) Paragraph 1 (*d*) of article 2 shall not apply unless provision has been made by an order of the Secretary of State for the setting up and management of a fund to be used for the making to harbour or conservancy authorities of payments needed to compensate them for the reduction, in consequence of the said paragraph 1 (*d*), of amounts recoverable by them in claims of the kind there mentioned, and to be maintained by contributions from such authorities raised and collected by them in respect of vessels in like manner as other sums so raised by them.

(2) Any order under sub-paragraph (1) above may contain such incidental and supplemental provisions as appear to the Secretary of State to be necessary or expedient.

(3) If immediately before the coming into force of section 17 of this Act an order is in force under section 2 (6) of the Merchant Shipping (Liability of Shipowners and Others) Act 1958 (which contains provisions corresponding to those of this paragraph) that order shall have effect as if made under this paragraph.

Claims excluded from limitation

4.—(1) The claims excluded from the Convention by paragraph (*b*) of article 3 are claims in respect of any liability incurred under section 1 of the Merchant Shipping (Oil Pollution) Act 1971.

(2) The claims excluded from the Convention by paragraph (*c*) of article 3 are claims made by virtue of any of sections 7 to 11 of the Nuclear Installations Act 1965.

The general limits

5.—(1) In the application of article 6 to a ship with a tonnage less than 300 tons that article shall have effect as if—

(*a*) paragraph (*a*) (i) referred to 166,667 Units of Account; and

(*b*) paragraph (*b*) (i) referred to 83,333 Units of Account.

(2) For the purposes of article 6 and this paragraph a ship's tonnage shall be its gross tonnage calculated in such manner as may be prescribed by an order made by the Secretary of State.

(3) Any order under this paragraph shall, so far as appears to the Secretary of State to be practicable, give effect to the regulations in Annex I of the International Convention on Tonnage Measurement of Ships 1969.

Limit for passenger claims

6.—(1) In the case of a passenger steamer within the meaning of Part III of the Merchant Shipping Act 1894 the ship's certificate mentioned in paragraph 1 of article 7 shall be the passenger steamer's certificate issued under section 274 of that Act.

(2) In paragraph 2 of article 7 the reference to claims brought on behalf of a person includes a reference to any claim in respect of the death of a person under the Fatal Accidents Act 1976, the Fatal Accidents (Northern Ireland) Order 1977 or the Damages (Scotland) Act 1976.

Units of Account

7.—(1) For the purpose of converting the amounts mentioned in articles 6 and 7 from special drawing rights into sterling one special drawing right shall be treated as equal to such a sum in sterling as the International Monetary Fund have fixed as being the equivalent of one special drawing right for—

(*a*) the relevant date under paragraph 1 of article 8; or

(*b*) if no sum has been so fixed for that date, the last preceding date for which a sum has been so fixed.

(2) A certificate given by or on behalf of the Treasury stating—

(*a*) that a particular sum in sterling has been fixed as mentioned in the preceding sub-paragraph for a particular date; or

(*b*) that no sum has been so fixed for that date and that a particular sum in sterling has been so fixed for a date which is the last preceding date for which a sum has been so fixed,

shall be conclusive evidence of those matters for the purposes of those articles; and a document purporting to be such a certificate shall, in any proceedings, be received in evidence and, unless the contrary is proved, be deemed to be such a certificate.

Constitution of fund

8.—(1) The Secretary of State may from time to time, with the concurrence of the Treasury, by order prescribe the rate of interest to be applied for the purposes of paragraph 1 of article 11.

(2) Where a fund is constituted with the court in accordance with article 11 for the payment of claims arising out of any occurrence, the court may stay any proceedings relating to any claim arising out of that occurrence which are pending against the person by whom the fund has been constituted.

Distribution of fund

9. No lien or other right in respect of any ship or property shall affect the proportions in which under article 12 the fund is distributed among several claimants.

Bar to other actions

10. Where the release of a ship or other property is ordered under paragraph 2 of article 13 the person on whose application it is ordered to be released shall be deemed to have submitted to (or, in Scotland, prorogated) the jurisdiction of the court to adjudicate on the claim for which the ship or property was arrested or attached.

Meaning of "court"

11. References in the Convention and the preceding provisions of this Part of this Schedule to the court are—

(*a*) in relation to England and Wales, references to the High Court;

(*b*) in relation to Scotland, references to the Court of Session;

(*c*) in relation to Northern Ireland, references to the High Court of Justice in Northern Ireland.

Meaning of "ship"

12. References in the Convention and in the preceding provisions of this Part of this Schedule to a ship include references to any structure (whether completed or in course of completion) launched and intended for use in navigation as a ship or part of a ship.

Meaning of " State Party "

13. An Order in Council made for the purposes of this paragraph and declaring that any State specified in the Order is a party to the Convention shall, subject to the provisions of any subsequent Order made for those purposes, be conclusive evidence that the State is a party to the Convention.

Section 19

SCHEDULE 5

LIABILITY OF SHIPOWNERS AND SALVORS: CONSEQUENTIAL AMENDMENTS

The Merchant Shipping (Liability of Shipowners and Others) Act 1900

1.—(1) In section 2 (1) of the Merchant Shipping (Liability of Shipowners and Others) Act 1900 for the reference to the actual fault or privity of the owners or authority there shall be substituted a reference to any such personal act or omission of the owners or authority as is mentioned in article 4 of the Convention in Part I of Schedule 4 to this Act.

(2) The limit of liability under that section shall be ascertained by applying to the ship mentioned in subsection (1) the method of calculation specified in paragraph 1 (*b*) of article 6 of the Convention read with paragraph 5 (1) and (2) of Part II of that Schedule.

(3) Articles 11 and 12 of the Convention in Part I of that Schedule and paragraphs 8 and 9 of Part II of that Schedule shall apply for the purposes of that section.

The Pilotage Authorities (Limitation of Liability) Act 1936

2.—(1) In section 1 (1) of the Pilotage Authorities (Limitation of Liability) Act 1936 for the reference to the actual fault or privity of the pilotage authority there shall be substituted a reference to any such personal act or omission of the authority as is mentioned in article 4 of the Convention in Part I of Schedule 4 to this Act.

(2) In section 4 of that Act for the words from " by or under " to " subsequent Acts " there shall be substituted the words " under section 17 or 18 of the Merchant Shipping Act 1979 ".

The Crown Proceedings Act 1947

3. For section 5 of the Crown Proceedings Act 1947, including that Act as it applies in Northern Ireland, there shall be substituted—

" 5.—(1) The provisions of sections 17 and 18 of the Merchant Shipping Act 1979 and of Schedule 4 to that Act (liability of shipowners and salvors) shall apply in relation to His Majesty's ships as they apply in relation to other ships.

(2) In this section " ships " has the same meaning as in those provisions."

The Hovercraft Act 1968

4. In section 1 (1) (*i*) of the Hovercraft Act 1968 for the words " Part VIII of the Merchant Shipping Act 1894 ", " that Part " and " the said Part VIII " there shall be substitutel respectively the words " sections 17 and 18 of the Merchant Shipping Act 1979 ", " those sections " and " the said sections of the Merchant Shipping Act 1979 ".

The Carriage of Goods by Sea Act 1971

5. In section 6 (4) of the Carriage of Goods by Sea Act 1971 for the words from " section 502 " to " 1958 " there shall be substituted the words " section 18 of the Merchant Shipping Act 1979 (which ".

The Merchant Shipping (Oil Pollution) Act 1971

6.—(1) In sections 5 (4) (*b*) and 7 (*b*) of the Merchant Shipping (Oil Pollution) Act 1971 for the words " the Merchant Shipping (Liability of Shipowners and Others) Act 1958 " there shall be substituted the words " the Merchant Shipping Act 1979 ".

(2) For section 15 (2) of that Act there shall be substituted—

"(2) For the purposes of section 17 of the Merchant Shipping Act 1979 (limitation of liability) any liability incurred under this section shall be deemed to be a liability in respect of such damage to property as is mentioned in paragraph 1 (a) of article 2 of the Convention in Part I of Schedule 4 to that Act."

Section 43

SCHEDULE 6

ALTERATION OF PENALTIES

PART I

MAXIMUM FINE OF £50 ON SUMMARY CONVICTION

Enactment	*Subject matter*
Merchant Shipping Act 1894 (c. 60)—	
section 111 (4)	Engaging of seamen by unauthorised person.
section 112 (2)	Receiving remuneration from seamen for engagement.
section 280 (2)	Surrender of passenger steamer's certificate.
section 281 (2)	Display of passenger steamer's certificate.
section 287	Miscellaneous offences in connection with passenger steamers.
section 373 (4)	Use of unregistered fishing boat.
section 385 (5)	Failure to record or report occurrences on fishing boats.
section 417 (4)	Transfer of fish from fishing boats to collecting vessels.
section 543 (2)	Failure by manufacturer to mark information on anchor.
section 722 (2)	Use or supply of unauthorised forms.
Merchant Shipping (International Labour Conventions) Act 1925 (c. 42)—	
section 4	Employment in ships of persons under 18.
Merchant Shipping (Safety and Load Line Conventions) Act 1932 (c. 9)—	
section 12 (2)	Failure to return memorandum about life-saving appliances.
section 31 (2)	Failure to give notice of Atlantic routes used by passenger line.
Merchant Shipping Act 1970 (c. 36)—	
section 8 (5), including section 8 (5) as set out in Schedule 2	Delivery to seaman of account of wages.
section 78	Unauthorised persons on ship in port.
section 89 (4)	Impeding arrest of deserter from foreign ship.

PART II

MAXIMUM FINE OF £200 ON SUMMARY CONVICTION

Enactment	*Subject matter*
Merchant Shipping Act 1894 (c. 60)—	
section 7 (5)	Marking of ships.
section 15 (2)	Delivery up of ship's certificate of registry for purpose of navigation.
section 18 (3)	Delivery up of ship's provisional certificate of registry to registrar.
section 20 (4)	Delivery up of certificate on change of ownership of ship.
section 21 (3)	Notice and delivery up of certificate on loss of ship or transfer to person not qualified to own British ship.
section 44 (11)	Production of certificates on sale of ship to person not qualified to own British ship.
section 47 (8)	Breach of rules as to name of ship.
section 59 (3)	Registration of particulars of ship's managing owner or manager.
section 74 (2)	Failure to hoist national colours.
section 536 (1)	Unauthorised boarding of vessel which is wrecked or in distress.
section 726 (3)	Failure to give information and assistance to surveyor of ship.
Merchant Shipping (Safety and Load Line Conventions) Act 1932 (c. 9)—	
section 27	Going to sea without approved signalling lamp.
section 29 (2)	Form of steering orders.
Merchant Shipping Act 1970 (c. 36)—	
section 22 (4) excluding paragraphs (*a*) and (*b*)	Master's failure to arrange for seamen to complain to proper officer about food.
section 23 (3)	Master's failure to arrange for seamen to complain to proper officer about conditions on board.
section 47	Production of certificates of qualification.
section 51 (4)	Employment in ships of persons under 18.
section 59	Failure to deliver certificate as required by section 52, 53, 54 or 56.
section 74	Handing over of documents on change of master.
paragraph 3 of Part I of Schedule 2	Production of certificates of qualification.
Prevention of Oil Pollution Act 1971 (c. 60)—	
section 10 (5)	Restrictions on transfer of oil at night.
section 18 (8) except so far as it relates to obstruction	Failure to comply with requirement to produce book or records or to certify true copy.

Part III

Maximum Fine of £500 on Summary Conviction

Enactment	*Subject matter*
Merchant Shipping Act 1894 (c. 60)—	
section 10 (3)	False statement in certificate given by builder of ship.
section 518	Failure to deliver wreck or particulars of wreck to receiver.
section 519 (2)	Retaining cargo washed up from wreck.
section 536 (2)	Impeding assistance for a ship in distress or removing its cargo.
section 666 (2)	Injuring lighthouses, lightships and similar equipment.
Merchant Shipping (Safety and Load Line Conventions) Act 1932 (c. 9)—	
section 24 (3)	Failure to report danger to navigation.
Merchant Shipping Act 1970 (c. 36)—	
section 1 (8)	Breach of provisions about crew agreements.
section 21 (4)	Breach of regulations about food.
section 22 (4) (*a*) and (*b*) ...	Retention of use of food which is unfit or of wrong quality.
section 24 (2)	Inadequate medical stores.
section 68 (6)	Destruction and mutilation of official log book.
section 70 (4)	False statement to obtain British seaman's card.
section 86 (2)	Going to sea without appropriate charts etc.
paragraph 4 (2) of Part I of Schedule 2	Maximum period of duty for seamen employed in fishing vessels.
Merchant Shipping (Oil Pollution) Act 1971 (c. 59)—	
section 10 (7)	Carrying and production of certificate in respect of insurance cover for oil pollution damage.
Prevention of Oil Pollution Act 1971 (c. 60)—	
section 18 (8) so far as it relates to obstruction	Failure to comply with requirements to produce book or records or to certify true copy.

Part IV

Maximum Fine of £1,000 on Summary Conviction

Enactment	*Subject matter*
Merchant Shipping Act 1894 (c. 60)—	
section 436 (4)	Recording of ship's draught.
section 488 (4)	Obstruction of survey of ship.
section 689 (4)	Conveyance from abroad of offenders and witnesses.
Merchant Shipping (Load Lines) Act 1967 (c. 27)—	
section 5	Observance of marking requirements of ship.

SCHEDULE 6—*continued*

Enactment	*Subject matter*
Merchant Shipping Act 1970 (c. 36)—	
section 20 (6)	Contravention of crew accommodation regulations.
section 43 (5)	False statement to obtain certificate of competence.
section 48 (2)	Going to sea with inadequate arrangements for translating orders to foreign crew.
section 50 (2)	False statement to obtain special certificate of competence.
section 73 (2)	Failure to report shipping casualty.
section 76 (4)	Obstruction of inspections and surveys.
Prevention of Oil Pollution Act 1971 (c. 60)—	
section 11 (3)	Failure to report discharge of oil into waters of harbour.
Merchant Shipping Act 1974 (c. 43)—	
section 3 (5)	Unauthorised disclosure of information.
section 14 (8)	Unauthorised disclosure of information.
paragraph 4 (3) of Schedule 2 ...	Obstruction of inspection or survey of foreign oil tanker.

PART V

FINE ON CONVICTION ON INDICTMENT AND MAXIMUM FINE OF £1,000 ON SUMMARY CONVICTION

Enactment	*Subject matter*
Merchant Shipping Act 1894 (c. 60)—	
section 285 (5)	Safety equipment for passenger steamers.
section 286	Unauthorised weight on safety valve of passenger steamer.
section 413 (2)	Fishing boat sailing without certificated skipper and second hand.
section 413 (3)	Service or employment of uncertificated person as skipper or second hand of fishing boat.
section 430 (1)	Provision of life-saving appliances for ships.
section 432 (2)	Adjustment of compasses and provision of hose in ship.
section 433	Unauthorised weight on safety valve of steamship.
The Merchant Shipping Act 1906 (c. 48)—	
section 16 (2)	Passengers not to be carried on more than one deck below water line.
Merchant Shipping (Safety and Load Line Conventions) Act 1932 (c. 9)—	
section 30 (2)	Avoidance of danger from ice.
Merchant Shipping (Safety Convention) Act 1949 (c. 43)—	
section 5 (5)	Breach of rules for direction-finders.
section 6 (3)	Breach of rules about radio navigational aids.

SCHEDULE 6—*continued*

Enactment	*Subject matter*
section 6 (4)	Using unauthorised apparatus for signals to or from radio navigational aids.
section 12 (3) (*b*)	Steamer other than passenger steamer going to sea without certificates.
section 12 (6)	Compliance with conditions of exemption certificate.
section 19 (2)	Compliance with rules about closing of openings in ships' hull.
section 21 (3)	Misuse of distress signals.
section 23 (3)	Breach of rules about carriage of dangerous goods.
section 24 (1)	Failure to take precautions in loading grain to prevent it from shifting.
section 24 (2)	Entering port with grain which was loaded without precautions to prevent it from shifting.
Merchant Shipping Act 1964 (c. 47)—	
section 5 (2)	Going to sea without safety construction certificate.
section 7 (1)	Breach of cargo ship construction and survey rules.
Merchant Shipping (Load Lines) Act 1967 (c. 27)—	
section 3 (2)	Breach of load line rules in respect of British ship.
section 4 (4)	Taking or sending ship to sea with load line submerged.
section 9 (3)	Going to sea without load line certificate.
section 13 (3)	Breach of load line rules in respect of foreign ship.
section 24 (4)	Breach of deck cargo regulations.
Fishing Vessels (Safety Provisions) Act 1970 (c. 27)—	
section 1 (4)	Contravention of construction rules.
section 4 (2)	Going to sea without certificates of compliance with construction and other rules.
Merchant Shipping Act 1970 (c. 36)—	
section 45	Going to sea undermanned.
section 46 (1)	Unqualified person going to sea as qualified.

PART VI

MISCELLANEOUS PENALTIES ON SUMMARY CONVICTION

Maximum fines of £50

1. In section 373 (5) (*d*) of the Merchant Shipping Act 1894 (which enables regulations relating to the registration of fishing boats to provide for fines for breaches of the regulations of up to £50 in some cases and £20 in others) for the words from " fines " to " pounds " there shall be substituted the words " fines not exceeding fifty pounds ".

2. In subsection (2) of section 77 of the Merchant Shipping Act 1906 (which provides that the master of a ship carrying cattlemen to the United Kingdom who fails to make a return of particulars of the cattlemen as required by that section shall be liable on summary conviction to a fine not exceeding £100 and that a cattleman who refuses to give information required for the purposes of a return under

that section shall be liable on summary conviction to imprisonment for up to 3 months) for the words " one hundred pounds " there shall be substituted the words " fifty pounds " and for the words from " imprisonment " onwards there shall be substituted the words " such a fine ".

3. In subsection (4) of section 6 of the Merchant Shipping Act 1970 (which provides that a person shall be liable to a fine of up to £50 if he acts in contravention of subsection (1) of that section and £20 if he acts in contravention of subsection (2) of that section) after the words " subsection (1) " there shall be inserted the words " or subsection (2) " and the words from " and if " onwards shall be omitted.

4. In sections 68 (5), 69 (5), 70 (2), 71 (2) and 72 (4) of the Merchant Shipping Act 1970 (which relate respectively to official log books, lists of crews, British seamen's cards, discharge books and returns of births and deaths on ships and authorise regulations under the section in question to provide for maximum fines of £10 in the case of sections 70 (2) and 71 (2) and £20 in the case of sections 68 (5), 69 (5) and 72 (4) for contraventions of the regulations) for the word " £10 " or, as the case may be, " £20 " there shall be substituted the word " £50 ".

Maximum fines of £200 *and* £20 *a day*

5. In subsection (2) of section 48 of the Merchant Shipping Act 1894 (which among other things provides that if default is made in registering an alteration of a ship or in registering a ship anew as required by that section the owner shall be liable to a fine of up to £100 and a further fine of up to £5 for each day during which the offence continues after conviction) for the words " one hundred pounds " there shall be substituted the words " two hundred pounds " and for the words " five pounds " there shall be substituted the words " twenty pounds ".

6. In subsections (2) (*d*) and (6A) of section 1 of the Merchant Shipping Act 1965 (which authorise tonnage regulations to provide for fines not exceeding £100 for the contraventions and failures there mentioned) for the words " one hundred pounds " in subsection (2) (*d*) and the word " £100 " in subsection (6A) there shall be substituted the word " £200 ".

7. In Schedule 1 to the Merchant Shipping (Load Lines) Act 1967 (which among other things provides for a fine of up to £50 on summary conviction of an offence under section 281 (3) of the Merchant Shipping Act 1894 of not posting up a passenger steamer's certificate) in column 3 of the entry relating to the said section 281 (3) for the word " £50 " there shall be substituted the word " £200 ".

8. In sections 2 (2), 3 (4), 62 (6) and 65 (3) of the Merchant Shipping Act 1970 (which relate respectively to crew agreements, the discharge of seamen, the return of seamen left overseas and the property of deceased seamen and authorise regulations under the section in question to provide for maximum fines of £50 in the case of section 2 (2) and £100 in other cases for contraventions of the regulations) for the word " £50 " or, as the case may be, " £100 " there shall be substituted the word " £200 ".

9. In section 77 (1) of the Merchant Shipping Act 1970 (under which the punishment for stowing away is a fine not exceeding £100 or imprisonment not exceeding three months) for the words from " £100 " onwards there shall be substituted the word " £200 ".

Miscellaneous

10. In section 667 (3) of the Merchant Shipping Act 1894 (under which a person who fails to comply with a notice to extinguish or screen a light which may be mistaken for a lighthouse is guilty of a common nuisance and is also liable to a fine not exceeding £100) for the words from " a common nuisance " onwards there shall be substituted the words " an offence and liable to a fine not exceeding one thousand pounds ".

11. In subsection (2) of section 723 of the Merchant Shipping Act 1894 (which provides that a person who fails to produce a log book or document which he is required to produce under that section or who refuses to allow the same to be inspected or copied or commits any other offence mentioned in that subsection shall be liable to a fine not exceeding £50 in some cases and £20 in others)—

(*a*) for the words " or refuses to allow the same " there shall be substituted the words " that person shall be liable to a fine not exceeding two hundred pounds and if any person on being so required refuses to allow such a book or document "; and

(b) for the words from "for each offence" onwards there shall be substituted the words "be liable to a fine not exceeding one thousand pounds".

12. Subsection (4) of section 724 of the Merchant Shipping Act 1894 (which provides that a surveyor of ships who receives unauthorised remuneration in respect of the duties he performs under that Act shall be liable to a fine not exceeding £50) shall be omitted.

13. In section 76 (3) of the Merchant Shipping Act 1906 (under which the master of a ship carrying passengers who fails to make a return of particulars of the passengers as required by that section or makes a false return and a passenger who refuses to give information required for such a return or gives false information is liable on summary conviction to a fine not exceeding £50 in some cases and £20 in others) for the words from "not exceeding" onwards there shall be substituted the words "not exceeding fifty pounds in the case of a failure or refusal and two hundred pounds in the case of a false return or false information."

14. In subsection (5) of section 24 of the Merchant Shipping (Safety Convention) Act 1949 (under which a master of a ship carrying grain who fails to deliver to customs the notice required by that section or delivers such a notice which is false in a material particular is liable to a fine not exceeding £100) for the words "one hundred pounds" there shall be substituted the words "two hundred pounds in the case of a failure and five hundred pounds in the case of a false statement".

15. In Schedule 1 to the Merchant Shipping (Load Lines) Act 1967 (under which any of the following offences, namely, an offence under section 283 of the Merchant Shipping Act 1894 of carrying passengers in excess, an offence under section 21 of the Merchant Shipping Act 1906 of not complying with provisions requiring a passenger steamer to be surveyed and to have a passenger steamer's certificate and an offence under section 12 (3) (a) of the Merchant Shipping (Safety Convention) Act 1949 of going to sea without appropriate certificates, is punishable on summary conviction with a fine of up to £1,000 in some cases and £400 in others)—

(a) in column 3 of the entry relating to the said section 283, for the word "£400" there shall be substituted the word "£50,000"; and

(b) in column 3 of the entries relating to the said sections 21 and 12 (3) (a), for the word "£400" there shall be substituted the word "£1,000".

16. In subsection (8) of section 9 of the Prevention of Oil Pollution Act 1971 (under which a harbour authority is liable to a fine not exceeding £10 for each day on which it fails to comply with a direction to provide oil reception facilities) for the word "£10" there shall be substituted the words "£500 and to a further fine not exceeding £50".

17. In section 17 (5) of the said Act of 1971 (which among other things provides for a fine of up to £500 on summary conviction of an offence of making a false entry in a record relating to oil) for the word "£500" in the third place where it occurs there shall be substituted the word "£1,000".

18. In subsection (6) of section 3 of the Merchant Shipping Act 1974 (under paragraph (a) of which a person who fails to provide information as required by that section is liable on summary conviction to a fine not exceeding £1,000 in some cases and £400 in others and under paragraph (b) of which a person who provides false information is so liable) for paragraph (i) there shall be substituted the words "(i) on summary conviction to a fine not exceeding £500 in the case of an offence under paragraph (a) of this subsection and not exceeding £1,000 in the case of an offence under paragraph (b) of this subsection, and".

19. In subsection (9) of section 14 of the Merchant Shipping Act 1974 (under paragraph (a) of which a person who fails to provide information as required by that section is liable on summary conviction to a fine not exceeding £400 and under paragraph (b) of which a person who provides false information is so liable), for the word "£400" there shall be substituted the words "500 in the case of an offence under paragraph (a) of this subsection and not exceeding £1,000 in the case of an offence under paragraph (b) of this subsection".

20. In paragraph 3 (2) of Schedule 5 to the Merchant Shipping Act 1974 (under which a person who commits an offence created by regulations relating to submersible or supporting apparatus is liable on summary conviction to a fine not exceeding £1,000 in some cases and £400 in others unless the regulations prescribe a lower limit) for paragraph (a) there shall be substituted the words "(a) on summary conviction a fine not exceeding £1,000".

Part VII

Other Penalties

The Merchant Shipping Act 1894

1. At the end of section 66 of the Merchant Shipping Act 1894 as it has effect in Scotland (which among other things provides that a person who forges a document mentioned in that section shall be guilty of felony) there shall be inserted the words "and liable on conviction on indictment to imprisonment for not more than seven years".

2. In section 73 of the Merchant Shipping Act 1894 (which among other things provides that if unauthorised colours are hoisted on board a vessel belonging to a British subject the master or owner of the vessel and the person who hoists the colours shall be guilty of an offence for which he is liable on conviction on indictment to a fine in some cases and to a fine of up to £500 in others or on summary conviction to a fine of up to £1,000 in some cases and £100 in others)—

(*a*) in subsection (2) for the words from "incur a fine" onwards there shall be substituted the words "be liable on conviction on indictment to a fine or on summary conviction to a fine not exceeding one thousand pounds"; and

(*b*) subsections (4) and (5) shall be omitted.

3. In section 271 of the Merchant Shipping Act 1894 (which among other things provides that, except in certain cases, no ship shall proceed to sea or on any voyage or excursion with more than twelve passengers on board unless a certificate as to survey under Part III of that Act is in force in respect of the ship) after subsection (2) there shall be inserted the following subsection—

(3) If a ship proceeds to sea or on any voyage or excursion when it is prohibited from doing so by subsection (1) of this section, the owner and the master of the ship shall each be guilty of an offence and liable on conviction on indictment to a fine or on summary conviction to a fine not exceeding one thousand pounds.

4. Subsection (3) of section 360 of the Merchant Shipping Act 1894 (which provides that a person employed under Part III of that Act who demands or takes unauthorised remuneration for performing his duty under that Part shall for each offence be liable to a fine not exceeding £50) shall be omitted.

5. In section 419 (2) of the Merchant Shipping Act 1894 (which provides that if an infringement of the collision regulations is caused by the wilful default of the master or owner of a ship he shall be guilty of a misdemeanour) for the words "guilty of a misdemeanour" there shall be substituted the words "liable, on conviction on indictment, to a fine and imprisonment for a term not exceeding two years or, on summary conviction,—

(*a*) to a fine not exceeding fifty thousand pounds and imprisonment for a term not exceeding six months in the case of an infringement of Rule 10 (*b*) (i) of the regulations set out in Schedule 1 to the Collision Regulations and Distress Signals Order 1977; and

(*b*) to a fine not exceeding £1,000 in any other case".

6. In subsection (3) of section 422 of the Merchant Shipping Act 1894 (which among other things provides that if a person in charge of a vessel involved in a collision with another vessel fails without reasonable cause to render assistance to the other vessel or persons on her as required by subsection (1) (*a*) of that section or to give the name of his vessel and certain other information to the person in charge of the other vessel as required by subsection (1) (*b*) of that section he shall be guilty of a misdemeanour) for the words "a misdemeanour, and" there shall be substituted the words "an offence and—

(*a*) in the case of a failure to comply with subsection (1) (*a*) of this section, liable on conviction on indictment to a fine and imprisonment for a term not exceeding two years and on summary conviction to a fine not exceeding fifty thousand pounds and imprisonment for a term not exceeding six months; and

(*b*) in the case of a failure to comply with subsection (1) (*b*) of this section, liable on conviction on indictment to a fine and on summary conviction to a fine not exceeding one thousand pounds,

and in either case".

7. In subsection (2) of section 446 of the Merchant Shipping Act 1894 (which among other things provides that a person who sends dangerous goods by ship without marking the goods and giving notice about them as required by that section shall be liable to a fine not exceeding £100 or, if he shows that he was merely an agent in the shipment and was not aware that the goods were dangerous, then to a smaller fine)—

(*a*) for the words from " liable " to " shows that he " there shall be substituted the words " liable on conviction on indictment to a fine or on summary conviction to a fine not exceeding one thousand pounds; but it shall be a defence to show that the accused "; and

(*b*) the words from " then " onwards shall be omitted.

8. In section 447 of the Merchant Shipping Act 1894 (under which, among other things, a person who sends dangerous goods by ship under a false description or with a false description of the sender is liable on conviction on indictment to a fine in some cases and to a fine of up to £500 in others) for the words from " liable " onwards, there shall be substituted the words " liable on conviction on indictment to a fine or on summary conviction to a fine not exceeding one thousand pounds ".

9. In paragraph (*a*) of subsection (1) of section 680 of the Merchant Shipping Act 1894 (under which, except in certain cases, an offence under that Act, which is declared to be a misdemeanour is punishable on conviction on indictment by a fine or by imprisonment not exceeding two years or on summary conviction with imprisonment for a term not exceeding six months or with a fine not exceeding £1,000 in some cases and £100 in others)—

(*a*) for the words " or by imprisonment " there shall be substituted the words " and by imprisonment ";

(*b*) for the words from " or with a fine " onwards there shall be substituted the words " and with a fine not exceeding one thousand pounds ";

and in paragraph (*b*) of that subsection (under which an offence under that Act which is punishable by a fine not exceeding £100 can only be prosecuted summarily except in certain cases) for the words " one hundred pounds " there shall be substituted the words " one thousand pounds ".

10. In section 692 (1) of the Merchant Shipping Act 1894 (which among other things provides that if a ship which is detained in pursuance of that section proceeds to sea before it is released the master and the owner of the ship and any other person who sends it to sea shall be liable to a fine not exceeding £200) for the words from " liable " onwards there shall be substituted the words " liable on conviction on indictment to a fine and on summary conviction to a fine not exceeding fifty thousand pounds.".

11. In section 692 (2) of the Merchant Shipping Act 1894 (which among other things provides that the master and the owner of a ship which takes to sea an officer authorised to detain the ship or certain other officials shall be liable to a fine of which the maximum amount varies with the circumstances) for the words from " to a fine " onwards there shall be substituted the words " on conviction on indictment to a fine or on summary conviction to a fine not exceeding one thousand pounds ".

12. In section 696 (2) of the Merchant Shipping Act 1894 (under which, among other things, a person who obstructs the service on the master of a ship of any document under that Act about the detention of ships as unseaworthy is liable to a fine not exceeding £25 in some cases and £10 in others) for the words from " to a fine " to " and " there shall be substituted the words " on conviction on indictment to a fine or on summary conviction to a fine not exceeding one thousand pounds, and ".

13. In section 702 of the Merchant Shipping Act 1894 (which provides for prosecution on indictment in Scotland)—

(*a*) after the words " High Court of Justiciary ", there shall be inserted the words " or the sheriff court "; and

(*b*) after the word " punishable " there shall be inserted the words ", subject to any maximum penalty prescribed in respect of any particular offence in this Act,".

14. For section 703 of the Merchant Shipping Act 1894 (which provides for summary proceedings in Scotland) there shall be substituted the following section—

703. In Scotland—

(*a*) any offence under this Act may be tried in a summary manner before the sheriff court and if so tried shall, subject to any other penalty prescribed in respect of any particular offence in this Act, on summary conviction be punishable with imprisonment for a term not exceeding six months and with a fine not exceeding one thousand pounds;

(*b*) all prosecutions in respect of offences under this Act in respect of which the maximum penalty which may be imposed does not exceed imprisonment for a period of three months or a fine of two hundred pounds or both may be tried in a summary manner before the district court.

The Merchant Shipping Act 1921

15. In section 2 (1) of the Merchant Shipping Act 1921 (under which a person who, among other things, uses in navigation a lighter or similar vessel which is so unsafe as to endanger human life is liable on summary conviction to a fine of up to £100 or to imprisonment for up to 6 months) for the words from "liable" onwards there shall be substituted the words "liable on conviction on indictment to a fine or on summary conviction to a fine not exceeding one thousand pounds".

The Merchant Shipping (*Safety Convention*) *Act* 1949

16. In subsection (5) of section 3 of the Merchant Shipping (Safety Convention) Act 1949 (under which a radio officer who contravenes certain radio rules is liable to a fine not exceeding £10 and, if other radio rules are contravened in relation to a ship, the owner or master is liable on conviction on indictment to a fine in some cases and a fine not exceeding £500 in others or on summary conviction to a fine not exceeding £1,000 in some cases and £100 in others)—

(*a*) for the word "£10" there shall be substituted the word "£500"; and

(*b*) for the words from "on indictment" onwards there shall be substituted the words "on indictment to a fine or on summary conviction to a fine not exceeding £1,000".

The Merchant Shipping (*Load Lines*) *Act* 1967

17. In section 4 of the Merchant Shipping (Load Lines) Act 1967 (of which subsection (2) provides that if any ship is loaded in contravention of subsection (1) of that section the owner or master shall be liable on summary conviction to a fine not exceeding £400 and to an additional fine not exceeding an amount calculated in accordance with subsection (3) of that section in terms of £400 for each inch or part of an inch by which the load line is or would have been submerged)—

(*a*) in subsection (2) for the words "on summary conviction—

(*a*) to a fine not exceeding £400, and"

there shall be substituted the words "—

(*a*) on conviction on indictment to a fine;"

and at the beginning of paragraph (*b*) there shall be inserted the words "on summary conviction to a fine not exceeding £1,000 and"; and

(*b*) in subsection (3) for the words from "£400" to "complete inches" there shall be substituted the words "£1,000 for each complete centimetre" and the words following paragraph (*b*) shall be omitted.

The Merchant Shipping Act 1970

18. In section 19 (5) of the Merchant Shipping Act 1970 (which authorises safety regulations to make a contravention of the regulations punishable on summary conviction with a fine not exceeding £200 if the offence is committed by the master or owner of the ship and £20 if it is committed by another person) for the words from "summary conviction" onwards there shall be substituted the words "conviction on indictment with a fine and on summary conviction with a fine not exceeding £1,000".

19. In section 27 (1) of the Merchant Shipping Act 1970 (under which the master or a member of the crew of a ship registered in the United Kingdom who improperly endangers the ship or persons on board the ship is liable on conviction on indictment to imprisonment for up to 2 years or to a fine and on summary conviction to a fine not exceeding £1,000 in some cases and £400 in others)—

(a) for the words "or to a fine" there shall be inserted the words "and a fine"; and

(b) for the words from "summary conviction" onwards there shall be substituted the words "summary conviction to a fine not exceeding £1,000".

20. In section 28 of the Merchant Shipping Act 1970 (which provides that a seaman who is under the influence of drink or drugs while on duty to such an extent that his capacity to carry out his duties is impaired shall be liable on summary conviction to a fine not exceeding £50) for the words from "summary conviction" onwards there shall be substituted the words "conviction on indictment to imprisonment for a term not exceeding two years and a fine and, on summary conviction, to a fine not exceeding £1,000".

21. In section 30 of the Merchant Shipping Act 1970 (which provides among other things that a seaman employed in a ship registered in the United Kingdom who persistently neglects his duty or disobeys orders or combines with other seamen to do so or to impede the ship's progress shall be liable on summary conviction to a fine not exceeding £100) for the words from "summary conviction" to "£100" there shall be substituted the words "conviction on indictment, to imprisonment for a term not exceeding two years and a fine and, on summary conviction, to a fine not exceeding £1,000".

The Merchant Shipping Act 1974

22. In paragraph 5 of Schedule 2 to the Merchant Shipping Act 1974 (which among other things authorises oil tanker construction rules to provide for a person who breaks the rules to be liable on summary conviction to a fine of up to £100) for the word "£100" there shall be substituted the word "£1,000" and at the end of sub-paragraph (1) there shall be inserted the words "and on conviction on indictment to a fine".

Sections 47 (2), 50 (4)

SCHEDULE 7

Enactments Repealed

Part I

Enactments relating to liability of shipowners and salvors

Chapter	Short title	Extent of repeal
57 & 58 Vict. c. 60.	The Merchant Shipping Act 1894.	Part VIII.
63 & 64 Vict. c. 32.	The Merchant Shipping (Liability of Shipowners and Others) Act 1900.	Section 2 (2) and (3).
6 Edw. 7. c. 48.	The Merchant Shipping Act 1906.	Section 69.
1 & 2 Geo. 5. c. 42.	The Merchant Shipping Act 1911.	Section 1 (2).
11 & 12 Geo. 5. c. 29.	The Merchant Shipping Act 1921.	In section 1 the words "and VIII".
6 & 7 Eliz. 2. c. 62.	The Merchant Shipping (Liability of Shipowners and Others) Act 1958.	The whole Act except section 11 so far as applying to the Merchant Shipping (Liability of Shipowners and Others) Act 1900.
1965 c. 47.	The Merchant Shipping Act 1965.	Section 5 (2). In Schedule 1, the entry relating to the Crown Proceedings Act 1947.
1965 c. 57.	The Nuclear Installations Act 1965.	In section 14 (1) the words from "and section 503" to "shipowners)".
1971 c. 59.	The Merchant Shipping (Oil Pollution) Act 1971.	Section 4 (1) (a). Section 8A.
1974 c. 43.	The Merchant Shipping Act 1974.	Section 4 (1) (c) (ii) together with the word "or" preceding it. Section 9.

PART II

OTHER ENACTMENTS

Chapter	Short title	Extent of repeal
57 & 58 Vict. c. 60.	The Merchant Shipping Act 1894.	Section 73 (4) and (5). Section 360 (3). In section 369 (3) the words from "and" onwards. Section 420 (3). In section 431 (1) the words from "and" onwards. In section 446 (2) the words from "then" onwards. Section 457. Section 468. Section 637. In section 638 the words from "but" to "of this Act". Sections 640 and 641. Sections 670 to 672 and 675. Section 677 (*m*). Section 724 (4). Sections 729 and 730.
61 & 62 Vict. c. 44.	The Merchant Shipping (Mercantile Marine Fund) Act 1898.	Section 2 (1) and (2). Section 5 (3). In section 7 the words "or out of colonial light dues" and the definition of "Basses Lights Fund". Schedule 2. In Schedule 3, paragraph II.
6 Edw. 7. c. 48.	The Merchant Shipping Act 1906.	Section 82 (2).
2 & 3 Geo. 5. c. 31.	The Pilotage Act 1913.	Sections 1, 2 and 6. In section 7, in paragraph (*c*) of subsection (1) the words from "distinguishing" to "in which pilotage is compulsory", paragraph (*a*) of subsection (4), and subsections (5) and (6). Sections 8 (2), 9 and 10. In section 11, paragraph (*b*) of subsection (3), and subsections (4) and (5). Sections 13 and 14. In section 17 (1), in paragraph (*f*) the words from the beginning to "scales and", in paragraph (*h*) the words from "sums required" to "or any", and paragraph (*i*). In section 22 (1) the words from "and any returns" onwards. Section 24. In section 30 (2) the words "to the licensed pilot and". In section 32 (2), 33 (2) and 34 (2) and (3). In section 35, subsection (2) and in subsection (3) the words "his" and "pilot's". In section 39, paragraphs (*a*) and (*b*) of subsection (1) and in subsection (2) the words "that the pilot boat possesses all the above characteristics and" and the words from "and also" to "concealed". Sections 48 (1) (*a*), 56, 58 and 59. In Schedule 1, paragraphs 1 to 6, 8 and 9.
9 & 10 Geo. 5. c. 92.	The Aliens Restriction (Amendment) Act 1919.	Section 4.

SCHEDULE 7—*continued*

Chapter	Short title	Extent of repeal
12 & 13 Geo. 6. c. 43.	The Merchant Shipping (Safety Convention) Act 1949.	Section 24 (4).
1964 c. 47.	The Merchant Shipping Act 1964.	In section 7 (2) the words from " and for that purpose " to " Acts ".
1965 c. 47.	The Merchant Shipping Act 1965.	In section 1 (2) (*c*) the words from " and may " to " those purposes ". In Schedule 1 the entry relating to section 85 (3) of the Merchant Shipping Act 1894.
1967 c. 27.	The Merchant Shipping (Load Lines) Act 1967.	In section 4 (3) the words from " and, if " onwards. Section 11 (2). In sections 17 (1) and 24 (6) the words from " and " onwards. Section 27 (4). In Schedule 1, the entry relating to section 281 (2) of the Merchant Shipping Act 1894.
1970 c. 27.	The Fishing Vessels (Safety Provisions) Act 1970.	In section 1 (3) the words from " and " onwards.
1970 c. 36.	The Merchant Shipping Act 1970.	In section 6 (4) the words from " and if " onwards. In section 15 (1) the words from " unless " onwards. Sections 34 to 38. In section 95 (1) (*a*) the words " 34 to 38 ". In section 99 (1) the words from " except " to " to this Act ". In Schedule 2, paragraph 2. In Schedule 5, in the entries relating to the Merchant Shipping Act 1894, the words " Section 271 (3) ".
1971 c. 59.	The Merchant Shipping (Oil Pollution) Act 1971.	Section 4 (3) to (5).
1971 c. 60.	The Prevention of Oil Pollution Act 1971.	In section 18 (5) the words from " and in subsection (3) " onwards.
1974 c. 43.	The Merchant Shipping Act 1974.	Section 1 (6) and (7). Section 19 (2), (5) and (6).
1975 c. 21.	The Criminal Procedure (Scotland) Act 1975.	In Schedule 7C the entry relating to the Merchant Shipping Act 1894.
1977 c. 45.	The Criminal Law Act 1977.	In Schedule 6 the entry relating to the Merchant Shipping Act 1894.

Representation of the People Act 1979

(1979 c. 40)

An Act to facilitate polling on the same day at a general election and district council elections, and to postpone certain parish or community council elections. [4th April 1979]

General Note

This Act facilitates polling on the same day at a general election and district council elections and postpones certain parish or community council elections.

S. 1 provides for modification of election rules; s. 2 postpones polling at parish or community council elections; s. 3 deals with citation.

The Act received the Royal Assent on April 4, 1979, and came into force on that date.

Parliamentary debates

Hansard, H.C. Vol. 965, cols. 769, 1027 and 1063; H.L. Vol. 399, cols. 1796, 1866, and 1867.

Modification of election rules

1. If the present Parliament is dissolved and a new Parliament summoned by a proclamation made on such date that the date of the poll at the election of Members for the new Parliament is the same as that of the poll at the next ordinary elections of district councillors to be held in England and Wales after the passing of this Act, the provisions (whether made by or under any Act) relating to—

(*a*) the conduct, in England and Wales, of the parliamentary election; and

(*b*) the conduct of the elections of district councillors;

shall have effect subject to the provisions of the Schedule to this Act.

Postponement of poll at parish or community council elections

2.—(1) Any poll at an election of parish or community councillors to be held on the same date as the polls mentioned in section 1 above shall be postponed for three weeks and the expenses of the returning officers attributable to the postponement shall be charged on and paid out of the Consolidated Fund.

(2) The date to which the poll is so postponed shall be taken to be the day of election for the purposes of the timetable in paragraph 1 of the Local Elections (Parishes and Communities) Rules 1973.

(3) Any nomination submitted for an election which is postponed as a result of this Act shall, if otherwise valid and if not withdrawn, be valid for the postponed election.

Citation

3. This Act may be cited as the Representation of the People Act 1979 and shall be included among the Acts that may be cited as the Representation of the People Acts.

SCHEDULE

Modification of Election Rules

Polling stations, presiding officers and clerks

1. Only polling stations used for the parliamentary election may be used for an election of district councillors and the duty to appoint and pay the presiding officer and clerks at each polling station shall be performed by the returning officer for the parliamentary election.

Hours of poll

2. Polling at all elections shall be between the hours of seven in the morning and ten at night.

Notices to Voters

3. Where a polling station is used both for the parliamentary and for a district council election the notices inside and outside the polling station may be combined so as to relate to both elections and may be modified for that purpose.

Appointment of polling agents

4. All notices of the appointment of polling agents to attend at a polling station shall be sent to the returning officer for the parliamentary election.

Absent voters, proxies and postal proxies

5. Regulations 35 of the Representation of the People Regulations 1974 (disregard of applications) shall apply to a district council election as if it were a parliamentary election.

6. Regulation 5 (1) (*b*) of the Representation of the People Regulations 1974 (certain functions of registration officers to be performed by acting returning officers) shall not apply.

Ballot papers

7. Ballot papers used in a district council election shall be easily distinguishable, in such manner as the Secretary of State directs, from those used in the parliamentary election.

8.—(1) On the front of every ballot paper there shall be printed at the top, in small capitals, an indication of the election to which it relates, thus—

PARLIAMENTARY ELECTION
or
DISTRICT COUNCIL ELECTION

and a statement of the number of candidates for whom the elector may vote, thus—
YOU MAY VOTE FOR NOT MORE THAN CANDIDATE(S).

(2) If the constituency or district concerned is in Wales the indication and statement shall also be printed in Welsh, thus—

ETHOLIAD SENEDDOL
or
ETHOLIAD CYNGOR DOSBARTH
and
NI CHEWCH BLEIDLEISIO DROS FWY NA YMGEISYDD

each line being printed immediately below the corresponding English line.

Ballot boxes

9. At each polling station used for the parliamentary and a district council election the same boxes shall be used at both elections.

Procedure on close of poll

10.—(1) All ballot boxes shall be delivered to the returning officer for the parliamentary election.

(2) All other items which at any polling station are, after the close of the poll in either election, to be made up into a separate packet shall be combined into a single packet with the corresponding items in the other election for which the polling station is used and shall be delivered to the returning officer for the parliamentary election together with the separate ballot paper accounts in respect of each of the elections.

The count

11.—(1) The returning officer for the parliamentary election shall open all ballot boxes and shall record separately the number of ballot papers used in each election.

(2) The returning officer for the parliamentary election shall verify all ballot paper accounts which are delivered to him.

(3) After verifying each ballot paper account, the returning officer shall separate the ballot papers relating to the election of district councillors for each area, and put them into separate containers together with a statement of the number of ballot papers in each container.

(4) The containers shall then be delivered to the returning officer for the election of district councillors, each labelled with a description of the area to which the ballot papers in it relate.

Pneumoconiosis etc. (Workers' Compensation) Act 1979 *

(1979 c. 41)

SECT. ARRANGEMENT OF SECTIONS

An Act to make provision for lump sum payments to or in respect of certain persons who are, or were immediately before they died, disabled by pneumoconiosis, byssinosis or diffuse mesothelioma; and for connected purposes. [4th April 1979]

General Note

This Act provides for lump sum payments to be made by the Department of Employment to persons disabled by industrial lung diseases caused by various kinds of noxious dust at work. If the disease causes death, certain dependants (specified in s. 3) are also entitled to such payments. The relevant diseases are pneumoconiosis (including silicosis, asbestosis, and kaolinosis), byssinosis (caused by cotton or flax dust) and diffuse mesothelioma (for definitions, see the Note to s. 1 (3) below).

It is not enough, however, that the person is or was disabled by disease. He (or she) must in addition:—

(i) be or have been entitled to disablement benefit (whether or not actually being paid it) under the system of special " national insurance " compensation (now under the Social Security Act 1975) for the victims of prescribed industrial diseases (s. 2). This means that the person must be or have been disabled by not less than 1 per cent. (1975 Act, s. 57) by one of the relevant diseases, contracted in an occupation for which it is prescribed (see the detailed note below to s. 1 of this Act). Thus the lump sum benefits are linked to, but are not part of, the system of social security benefits administered by the Department of Health and Social Security; *and*

(ii) be unable to recover damages, by court action, from any employer(s) who might be liable to him (*e.g.* because of negligent lack of precautions against dust) because such employer has ceased to carry on business (s. 2).

The amounts of lump sums (expected to vary between £300 and £10,000) are to be specified by regulations (s. 1) and statements by the Minister of State in the House of Commons indicated that the regulations are expected to follow in amount etc., a voluntary scheme in existence since 1974 by which the National Coal Board compensates the victims of pneumoconiosis contracted in its mines.

The Royal Commission on Civil Liability and Compensation for Personal Injury (the " Pearson " Commission) in its report (1978, Cmnd. 7054) reported adversely to the singling out of a special category of those to receive from the State lump sum compensation where there was a failure of the existing system of compensation by way of actions in tort for damages (see the Report, paras. 888–892) but this Act means that the recommendations of the Pearson Commission on this point have not been followed. The Act represents the first " bridge " between the two systems of compensation for accidents and diseases at work, *i.e.* claiming damages in tort (based on " fault liability ") on the one hand and, on the other, claiming special social security benefits (not dependent on " fault ") from the State.

* Annotations by Michael J. Goodman, M.A., Ph.D., Solicitor.

Commencement

The Act received the Royal Assent on April 4, 1979, and came into force on July 4, 1979 (s. 10).

Regulations

See the Pneumoconiosis etc. (Workers' Compensation) Determination of Claims Regulations 1979 (S.I. 1979 No. 727).

Parliamentary debates

See *Hansard,* H.C. Vol. 965, cols. 1079–1128; H.L. Vol. 399, cols. 1797, 1919.

Extent

The Act does not extend to Northern Ireland.

Lump sum payments

1.—(1) If, on a claim by a person who is disabled by a disease to which this Act applies, the Secretary of State is satisfied that the conditions of entitlement mentioned in section 2 (1) below are fulfilled, he shall in accordance with this Act make to that person a payment of such amount as may be prescribed by regulations.

(2) If, on a claim by the dependant of a person who, immediately before he died, was disabled by a disease to which this Act applies, the Secretary of State is satisfied that the conditions of entitlement mentioned in section 2 (2) below are fulfilled, he shall in accordance with this Act make to that dependant a payment of such amount as may be so prescribed.

(3) The diseases to which this Act applies are pneumoconiosis, byssinosis and diffuse mesothelioma.

(4) Regulations under this section may prescribe different amounts for different cases or classes of cases or for different circumstances.

DEFINITIONS

"dependant": s. 3.

GENERAL NOTE

This section provides for lump sum payments to be made by the Department of Employment to persons disabled by industrial lung diseases caused by various kinds of noxious dust at work. The amounts of lump sums (expected to vary between £300 and £10,000) are to be specified by regulations. Statements by the Minister of State in the House of Commons indicated that the regulations are expected to follow in amount, etc., a voluntary scheme in existence since 1974 by which the National Coal Board compensates the victims of pneumoconiosis contracted in its mines.

Subs. (1)

"*a person who is disabled by a disease to which this Act applies.*" This means a person (male or female—Interpretation Act 1978, s. 6) who is disabled by at least 1 per cent. (Social Security Act 1975, s. 57) by pneumoconiosis, byssinosis, or diffuse mesothelioma (see note to subs. (3), below) and is consequently entitled to social security disablement benefit (see notes to s. 2, below). Such person must be in effect unable to recover damages from his employer(s) because such employer has ceased to carry on business (s. 2 (1), below). The "Secretary of State" is in effect the Department of Employment but there will clearly have to be close liaison with the Department of Health and Social Security, who operate the existing scheme of payment of disablement benefit. The mode of claim is to be prescribed by regulations (see s. 4, below) and with the 12 months' period set out in s. 4.

Subs. (2)

A "dependant", as defined in s. 3 below, will be entitled to claim the lump sums under this Act if the deceased had not received any such lump sum but would at his death have had a potential claim (as to which see the note to subs. (1) above),—s. 2 (2).

Subs. (3)

"*Pneumoconiosis.*" This is defined by the Social Security (Industrial Injuries) (Prescribed Diseases) Regulations 1975 (S.I. 1975 No. 1537) as follows: "fibrosis of the lungs due to silica dust, asbestos dust or other dust, and includes the condition of the lungs known as dust reticulation but does not include byssinosis." This definition will be directly applicable (see s. 10 (2) of this Act) as entitlement to disablement benefit under the 1975 Regulations is a pre-condition to a claim for a lump sum under this Act. Moreover, Sched. I, Pt. II of the 1975 Regulations contains a detailed list of 12 occupations for which pneumoconiosis is prescribed and it follows that only workers in those occupations (*e.g.* in mining, quarrying, handling asbestos, and boiler scaling), or (if dead) their dependants, will be able to claim lump sums under this Act.

"*Byssinosis.*" This is not defined in this Act or in the 1975 Regulations but is in fact a lung disease caused by cotton or flax dust and is prescribed (by reg. 2 (*c*) of the 1975 Regulations) for "any occupation in any room where any process up to and including the winding or beaming process is performed in factories in which the spinning or manipulation of raw or waste cotton or of flax is carried on." The former requirement that the worker should have been in such an occupation for at least five years was revoked by the Social Security (Industrial Injuries) (Prescribed Diseases) Amendment (No. 2) Regulations 1979 (S.I. 1979 No. 265).

"*Diffuse mesothelioma.*" This is defined by Reg. 1 and Sched. 1, Pt. I (No. 44) of the 1975 Regulations as "primary malignant neoplasm of the mesothelium (diffuse mesothelioma) of the pleura or of the peritoneum." A "neoplasm" is an autonomous new growth in part of the body, in this case either of part of the lung (the "pleura") or of the abdomen (the "peritoneum"). Diffuse mesothelioma is prescribed by the 1975 Regulations (Sched. 1, Pt. I, No. 44), for four occupations (detailed therein) involving work with asbestos.

Conditions of entitlement

2.—(1) In the case of a person who is disabled by a disease to which this Act applies, the conditions of entitlement are—

(*a*) that disablement benefit is payable to him in respect of the disease;

(*b*) that every relevant employer of his has ceased to carry on business; and

(*c*) that he has not brought any action, or compromised any claim, for damages in respect of the disablement.

(2) In the case of the dependant of a person who, immediately before he died, was disabled by a disease to which this Act applies, the conditions of entitlement are—

(*a*) that no payment under this Act has been made to the deceased in respect of the disease;

(*b*) that death benefit is payable to or in respect of the dependant by reason of the deceased's death as a result of the disease, or that disablement benefit was payable to the deceased in respect of the disease immediately before he died;

(*c*) that every relevant employer of the deceased has ceased to carry on business; and

(*d*) that neither the deceased nor his personal representatives nor any relative of his has brought any action, or compromised any claim, for damages in respect of the disablement or death.

(3) In this section—

"death benefit" means industrial death benefit under section 76 of the Social Security Act 1975, or death benefit under a a scheme made, or having effect as if made, under section 5 of the Industrial Injuries and Diseases (Old Cases) Act 1975;

"disablement benefit" means disablement benefit under section 76 of the Social Security Act 1975 or under any corresponding provision of the former Industrial Injuries Acts, or an allowance under a scheme made, or having effect as if made, under section 5 of the Industrial Injuries and Diseases (Old Cases) Act 1975 or under any corresponding provision of the former Old Cases Acts;

"the former Industrial Injuries Acts" means the National Insurance (Industrial Injuries) Act 1946 and the National Insurance (Industrial Injuries) Act 1965;

"the former Old Cases Acts" means the Pneumoconiosis and Byssinosis Benefit Act 1951 and the Industrial Injuries and Diseases (Old Cases) Act 1967;

"relevant employer", in relation to a person disabled by a disease to which this Act applies, means any person by whom he was employed at any time during the period during which he was developing the disease and against whom he might have or might have had a claim for damages in respect of the disablement.

(4) For the purposes of this section any action which has been dismissed otherwise than on the merits (as for example for want of prosecution or under any enactment relating to the limitation of actions) shall be disregarded.

DEFINITIONS

"death benefit": s. 2 (3).
"dependant": s. 3.
"disablement benefit": s. 2 (3).
"relevant employer": s. 2 (3).
"the former Industrial Injuries Acts": s. 2 (3).
"the former Old Cases Acts": s. 2 (3).

GENERAL NOTE

For a general statement as to the conditions of entitlement to lump sums under this Act, see the General Notes to the Act and to s. 1 thereof. This section elaborates and adds to the specification of those persons entitled to claim, as set out in section 1, above. It requires that the claimant (or, if dead, his dependant(s)) should be entitled to disablement benefit under the Social Security legislation (as to which, see the Note to s. 1 (3) above) *and* be in effect unable to recover damages from his employers(s) because such employer has ceased to carry on business (s. 2 (1) and (4)).

Subs. (1)

"a person who is disabled by a disease to which this Act applies." I.e. a person who is disabled by at least 1 per cent. by pneumoconiosis, byssinosis, or diffuse mesothelioma (see s. 1 (3) and the Note thereto).

"disablement benefit is payable to him in respect of the disease." This means disablement benefit under the social security legislation (see detailed definition in s. 2 (3)). Questions of entitlement to such benefit are decided by the adjudicating authorities under that legislation, *e.g.* the medical boards and medical appeal tribunals (see, now, the Social Security (Industrial Injuries) (Prescribed Diseases) Amendment Regulations 1979 (S.I. 1979 No. 264)). Presumably this condition is satisfied if no claim to disablement benefit has in fact been made, provided there is entitlement to it.

"every relevant employer of his has ceased to carry on business." "Relevant employer" is defined in subs. (3)—see the Note thereto, below. "Ceased to carry on business" is not defined in this Act or elsewhere. The expression presumably extends to cases where the employer's business activities are defunct (at least in relation to the occupation where the disease was contracted), even though the

employer, if a company, has not gone into liquidation or been struck off the register of companies.

"has not brought any action, or compromised any claim, for damages in respect of the disablement." This does not include a case where an action has been brought but dismissed otherwise than on the merits (s. 2 (4)). If, however, an action has at any time been brought and has not been dismissed, no claim can be made under this Act. A claimant will therefore have to apply to the Court to dismiss his action, *e.g.* on a withdrawal by him, before he can make a claim under this Act.

Subs. (2)

"dependant." This is defined in s. 3 below. For "disease to which this Act applies" see the Notes to s. 1 and s. 2 (1), above. If a person was at his death disabled by one of the specified diseases, a dependant may claim a lump sum under this Act if *either* disablement benefit was at the date of the death "payable to the deceased" *or* death benefit is payable to the dependant because the deceased died of the disease. For "payable" see note to subs. (1) above. Here again no action in court must have been brought by either the deceased or his personal representative (executor or administrator)—*cf.* note to subs. (1), above.

Subs. (3)

"death benefit," "disablement benefit." See the Note to subs. (1) above. The Industrial Injuries and Diseases (Old Cases) Acts 1967 and 1975 deal with social security benefits payable to those who had claims under earlier legislation for pneumoconiosis or byssinosis prior to the coming into force of the National Insurance Acts on July 5, 1948.

"Relevant employer." The expression "against whom he might have or might have had a claim for damages in respect of the disablement" presumably means no more than that the employer employed the claimant in a prescribed occupation (see Note to s. 1 (3) above) and that questions of liability in tort and whether or not an action would be time-barred (under the Limitation Acts 1939–1975) are not relevant. If this interpretation is correct, then, the fact, for example, that the claimant worked 20 years ago (when he had started to develop the disease) for an employer who is still in business will prevent the claimant succeeding under this Act even though (i) the claimant has worked for many employers since, all of whom have ceased business and (ii) an action against the employer of 20 years ago might be time barred, or liable to fail for want of proof of fault.

Subs. (4)

For a discussion of the points raised by this subsection see the Notes to Subs. (1) and (3) above. For dismissals of an action for want of prosecution, see the Encyclopedia of Health and Safety at Work, Vol. I, para. 1056a. The enactments "relating to the limitation of actions" are the Limitation Acts 1939–1975, which contain detailed provisions as to the time-limits for bringing actions. For an account of them in this context, see the Encyclopedia of Health and Safety at Work, Vol. I, para. 1–056.

Dependants

3.—(1) In this Act "dependant", in relation to a person who, immediately before he died, was disabled by a disease to which this Act applies, means—

(*a*) if he left a spouse who was residing with him or was receiving or entitled to receive from him periodical payments for her maintenance, that spouse;

(*b*) if paragraph (*a*) above does not apply but he left a child or children who fall within subsection (2) below, that child or those children;

(*c*) if neither of the preceding paragraphs applies but he left a reputed spouse who was residing with him, that reputed spouse;

(*d*) if none of the preceding paragraphs applies, any relative or relatives of his who fall within subsection (2) below and who were, in the opinion of the Secretary of State, wholly or mainly dependent on him at the date of his death.

(2) A person falls within this subsection if, at the relevant date, he was—

(*a*) under the age of 16;

(*b*) under the age of 21 and not gainfully employed full-time; or

(*c*) permanently incapable of self-support;

and in this subsection " relevant date " means the date of the deceased's death or the date of the coming into force of this Act, whichever is the later.

(3) Where any payment under this Act falls to be made to two or more persons, the payment shall be made to one of them or divided between some or all of them as the Secretary of State thinks fit.

(4) In this section—

" child " includes posthumous child;

" relative " means brother, sister, lineal ancestor or lineal descendant;

and for the purposes of this section a relationship shall be established as if any illegitimate child or step child of a person had been a child born to him in wedlock.

(5) In the application of subsection (1) above to Scotland, for paragraph (*c*) there shall be substituted the following paragraph—

" (*c*) if neither of the preceding paragraphs applies but he left a person residing with him who, but for some impediment to marriage, would be entitled to obtain a declarator of marriage with him by cohabitation with habit and repute, that person; ".

DEFINITIONS

" child ": s. 3 (4).
" dependant ": s. 3.
" disabled by a disease to which this Act applies ": ss. 1 (3) and 2 (1).
" relative ": s. 3 (4).

GENERAL NOTE

This section defines which dependants of a deceased person, who was at his or her death disabled by a specified disease, may make claims for lump sums under this Act, provided they satisfy the requirements of s. 2 (2), above (see the Note to that subsection). If more than one dependant is entitled to the lump sum payment, the Department of Employment may make the whole payment to one of them, or divide it between them, as it thinks fit (subs. (3)). Possibly, the Regulations to be made under s. 1, above, will make further provision on this point.

Subs. (1)

" disabled by a disease to which this Act applies." See ss. 1 (3) and 2 (1) and the Notes thereto.

" reputed spouse." This does not apply to Scotland, where the definition in subs. (5) is substituted.

Subs. (2)

A person attains a given age on his birthday—Family Law Reform Act 1969, s. 9.

" gainfully employed." See *Vandyk* v. *Minister of Pensions* [1955] 1 Q.B. 29.

Subs. (3)

See the General Note to this section.

Subs. (4)

The limitation of ancestors and descendants to lineals means that, *e.g.* cousins of the deceased cannot claim, though they may be entitled to a share of the deceased's estate on intestacy. However, illegitimate and step-children can claim.

Subs. (5)

See the Note to subs. (1) above.

Determination of claims

4.—(1) Any reference in this Act to a claim under section 1 above is a reference to a claim under that section which is made—

(*a*) in the manner prescribed by regulations; and

(*b*) within the period of 12 months beginning with the relevant date or within such further period as the Secretary of State may allow.

(2) The Secretary of State may, if he thinks fit, before determining any claim under section 1 above, appoint a person to hold an inquiry into any question arising on the claim, or any matters arising in connection therewith, and to report on the question, or on those matters, to the Secretary of State.

(3) Section 94 of the Social Security Act 1975 (appeal on question of law) shall apply in relation to any question of law arising in connection with the determination by the Secretary of State of any claim under section 1 above as it applies in relation to any question of law arising in connection with the determination by the Secretary of State of any question within section 93 (1) of that Act.

(4) In this section " relevant date "—

(*a*) in the case of a person disabled by a disease to which this Act applies, means the date on which disablement benefit first became payable to him in respect of the disease or the date of the coming into force of this Act, whichever is the later;

(*b*) in the case of the dependant of a person who, immediately before he died, was disabled by a disease to which this Act applies, means the date of the deceased's death or the date of the coming into force of this Act, whichever is the later.

DEFINITION

" relevant date ": s. 4 (4).

GENERAL NOTE

This section provides for the making and determination of claims for the lump sum benefits specified in ss. 1 and 2 of this Act.

Subs. (1)

As the 12 months' period for making a claim runs only from the date that the Act came into force (July 4, 1979—s. 10), for cases where disablement by the prescribed diseases had occurred before that date, there may be a considerable number of claims in the first year, estimated by the Department of Employment as totalling £5 million, but thereafter being only £70,000 per annum.

For regulations made under this subsection, see the Pneumoconiosis etc. (Workers' Compensation) Determination of Claims Regulations 1979 (S.I. 1979 No. 727), which provide that claims shall be in writing, in such form as the Secretary of State may determine. Application forms are obtainable from the Department of Employment, HSL 6, Rex House, 4–12 Regent Street, London SW1, and for Wales from Companies House, Crown Way, Maindy, Cardiff, where forms in Welsh are also available.

The " relevant date " from which the 12 months' period runs is defined in subs. (4).

Subss. (2) *and* (3)

These subsections provide for determination of questions arising on claims under this Act. Subs. (2) provides for the holding of an inquiry by an appointed person and extends to matters of fact and law. Presumably, however, medical questions as to the prescribed diseases will continue to be answered by the medical boards and medical appeal tribunals under the aegis of the Department of Health and Social Security and factual decisions as to whether or not a claimant worked in a prescribed occupation will continue to be decided by insurance officers, with appeal to the local National Insurance Tribunal, and thence to the National Insurance Commissioners.

S. 94 of the Social Security Act 1975 (which subs. (3) makes applicable to determination of questions of law under this Act) provides that the High Court may hear such questions, either on a reference to it by the Secretary of State or on an appeal by a claimant from the Secretary of State's decision. The decision of the High Court is final and no appeal lies from it (1975 Act, s. 94 (7)).

Subs. (4)

The effect of this subsection is that the 12 months' time limit for claims prescribed by subs. (1) runs from the date of coming into force of this Act (July 4, 1979—s. 10) for cases where the date of disablement by, or death from, a prescribed disease was before July 4, 1979, but for all subsequent cases, the 12 months will run in effect from the earliest date a claim could have been made. In cases where this was not realised and a claim is made outside the 12 months' period, reliance will have to be made on the Secretary of State allowing a further period for the claim (subs. (1)). His refusal to do so would not appear to be subject to appeal, as no point of law is involved (see Note to subss. (3) and (4)).

Reconsideration of determinations

5.—(1) Subject to subsection (2) below, the Secretary of State may reconsider a determination that a payment should not be made under this Act on the ground—

(*a*) that there has been a material change of circumstances since the determination was made; or

(*b*) that the determination was made in ignorance of, or was based on a mistake as to, some material fact;

and the Secretary of State may, on the ground set out in paragraph (*b*) above, reconsider a determination that such a payment should be made.

(2) Regulations shall prescribe the manner in which and the period within which—

(*a*) an application may be made to the Secretary of State for his reconsideration of a determination; and

(*b*) the Secretary of State may of his own motion institute such a reconsideration.

(3) Subsections (2) and (3) of section 4 above shall apply in relation to any reconsideration of a determination under this section as they apply in relation to the determination of a claim.

(4) If, whether fraudulently or otherwise, any person misrepresents or fails to disclose any material fact and in consequence of the misrepresentation or failure a payment is made under this Act, the person to whom the payment was made shall be liable to repay the amount of that payment to the Secretary of State unless he can show that the misrepresentation or failure occurred without his connivance or consent.

(5) Except as provided by subsection (4) above, no payment under this Act shall be recoverable by virtue of a reconsideration of a determination under this section.

General Note

This section contains provisions similar to those in the Social Security legislation as to reconsideration by the Department of Employment of its decisions as to whether or not a payment should be made under this Act. Such reconsideration can change an earlier decision *not* to make a payment and thus involve the making of a payment if that decision was made in ignorance of, or was based on a mistake as to, some material fact or there has been a material change of circumstances since the decision (subs. (1)). A reconsideration of a decision to make a payment can be made on the ground that the decision was made in ignorance of, or was based on a mistake as to, some material fact (subs. (1). However, such a reconsideration cannot require repayment to the Department of Employment of any sum paid unless it was due to misrepresentation or non-disclosure by any person of a material fact and the payee cannot show that that occurred without his own connivance or consent (subss. (4) and (5)).

Subs. (2)

For regulations made under this subsection, see the Pneumoconiosis etc. (Workers' Compensation) Determination of Claims Regulations 1979 (S.I. 1979 No. 727).

Payments for the benefit of minors etc.

6. Where a payment under this Act falls to be made to a person who is under the age of 18 or incapable of managing his own affairs, then, subject to section 3 (3) above, the payment shall be made for his benefit by paying it to such trustees as the Secretary of State may appoint to be held by them upon such trusts or, in Scotland, for such purposes and upon such conditions as may be declared by the Secretary of State.

General Note

A person attains the age of 18 on his 18th birthday (Family Law Reform Act 1969, s. 9). S. 3 (3) of this Act refers to the possibility that where more than one dependant claims the lump sum payment, *e.g.* an adult and a minor, the Department of Employment may make the whole payment to one of them, *e.g.* the adult.

Regulations

7.—(1) Any reference in the preceding provisions of this Act to regulations is a reference to regulations made by the Secretary of State.

(2) Any power of the Secretary of State to make regulations under this Act shall be exercisable by statutory instrument and includes power to make such incidental, supplementary or transitional provision as the Secretary of State thinks fit.

(3) No regulations shall be made under section 1 above unless a draft of the regulations has been laid before, and approved by a resolution of, each House of Parliament.

(4) Any statutory instrument containing regulations made under any other provision of this Act shall be subject to annulment in pursuance of a resolution of either House of Parliament.

General Note

For regulations made under this Act, see the Pneumoconiosis etc. (Workers' Compensation) Determination of Claims Regulations 1979 (S.I. 1979 No. 727).

Subs. (2)

For provisions as to the making of regulations by statutory instrument, see the Statutory Instruments Act 1946 (as amended).

Fraudulent statements etc.

8. Any person who, for the purpose of obtaining a payment under this Act, whether for himself or some other person—

(*a*) knowingly makes any false statement or representation; or

(*b*) produces or furnishes or causes or knowingly allows to be produced or furnished any document or information which he knows to be false in a material particular,

shall be liable on summary conviction to a fine not exceeding £1,000.

Financial provisions

9.—(1) There shall be paid out of moneys provided by Parliament—

(*a*) any expenditure incurred by the Secretary of State in making payments under this Act; and

(*b*) any increase in the administrative expenses of the Secretary of State which is attributable to this Act.

(2) Any sums repaid to the Secretary of State by virtue of section 5 (4) above shall be paid into the Consolidated Fund.

GENERAL NOTE

Estimates by the Department of Employment of expenditure under this Act are that, in the first 12 months after the coming into force of this Act, claims may total up to £5 million but thereafter will approximate to £70,000 per year. Additional staff costs and administrative expenses will total £130,000 in the first year, but should thereafter not exceed £20,000 per annum.

Short title, construction, commencement and extent

10.—(1) This Act may be cited as the Pneumoconiosis etc. (Workers' Compensation) Act 1979.

(2) Except where the context otherwise requires, any expression to which a meaning is assigned by the Social Security Act 1975, or by any regulations made under that Act, has that meaning also for the purposes of this Act.

(3) This Act shall come into force on the expiration of a period of three months beginning with the day on which it is passed.

(4) This Act does not extend to Northern Ireland.

GENERAL NOTE

Subs. (2)

S. 168 of and Sched. 20 to the Social Security Act 1975 contain definitions for the purposes of that legislation. Definitions are also contained in the Social Security (Industrial Injuries) (Prescribed Diseases) Regulations 1975 (S.I. 1975 No. 1537) (as amended)—see the Note to s. 1 (3) above.

Subs. (3)

As this Act was passed on April 4, 1979, it came into force on July 4, 1979.

Arbitration Act 1979 *

(1979 c. 42)

Arrangement of Sections

An Act to amend the law relating to arbitrations and for purposes connected therewith. [4th April 1979]

General Note

Judicial review of arbitration awards

The main purpose of this Act is to provide a new procedure for judicial review of arbitration awards.

As is pointed out in the Preface to *Russell on Arbitration* (19th ed.) there is a never-ending war between two irreconcilable principles, the high principle which demands justice though the heavens fall, and the low principle which demands that there shall be an end to litigation. The high principle favours judicial review; the low does not.

The words "judicial review" are used advisedly. There are many techniques for reviewing decisions of inferior tribunals, and opinions vary as to the suitability of any particular technique for any particular situation. Techniques range from prerogative orders through cases stated towards appeals *stricto sensu,* though even appeals *stricto sensu* can in fact vary as to the matters which can be reviewed and the extent to which the appeal is a genuine rehearing in which the lower decision is irrelevant, or a process of having to find fault to a greater or lesser degree with the inferior decision if it is to be reversed. There is also the technique, relevant in the present context, of having a court decide a preliminary point for an inferior tribunal; preliminary points in court are normally a mere procedural convenience; but when the preliminary point is decided by a court, and the main hearing is before an inferior tribunal, that necessarily results in a kind of judicial review.

Up to the date of the passing of the Arbitration Act 1979, arbitrations in the United Kingdom managed to get the worst of all possible worlds *quoad* judicial review.

In the first place, the fact that there was a judicial review at all found little favour with countless foreign parties to contracts who had agreed to arbitration in the belief that it was as final in the United Kingdom as it was in their own countries. The official discussions of the situation have one and all recognised that this disappointment of expectations had been losing the United Kingdom a great deal of arbitration work, United Kingdom arbitration and arbitrators being universally admired and sought after but for the element of judicial review which was by many accounted a defect.

In the second place, when the judicial review came, it came not by way of appeal—however limited—but in two rather unsatisfactory ways of proceeding: the first was the procedure by way of case stated, and this was provided for by statute, the latest Act (that of 1950) making the relevant provision in s. 21; the second was the common law procedure of setting aside or remitting an award on the ground of error on the face of the award.

Both these methods of judicial review had been ingeniously expanded so that by 1976 Ormrod L.J. could say in *The Ciechocinek* [1976] 1 Lloyd's Rep. 489 at 497, cited in Russell (19th ed.), p. 24 "It is sometimes said that the onlooker sees more

* Annotations by Anthony Walton, Q.C.

of the game than the players. It seems to me, very much an onlooker in this field, that we are witnessing the evolution of a general form of appeal on law from arbitrators to the court."

In effect the new Act has determined to fulfil this prophecy and has given the law one last push in the direction in which it was seen to be going. But of course in so doing, statute could do what the common law and ingenious development could not do, and has provided for a genuine appeal *stricto sensu,* thereby (it is to be hoped) removing the infelicities and circumscriptions of the old procedure.

Two new procedures for judicial review have accordingly been provided, namely (1) a new procedure for appeal *stricto sensu* on points of law, and (2) a new procedure for the determination by the court of a preliminary point of law. Pursuant to this new policy, the old statutory provisions for the stating of a case (Arbitration Act 1950, s. 21) have been abolished, as have the common law jurisdictions to set aside or remit an award on the ground of errors on the face of the award (see s. 1).

Further, as ancillary to the new jurisdiction to provide appeals from arbitral tribunals on points of law, there are ancillary provisions to compel arbitral tribunals to state the reasons for their awards (see s. 1 (5) and (6)). This may throw some light on the nature of the proposed appeal. According to the new scheme, evidently, the nature of the inferior decision is not irrelevant.

At the same time, the new Act has allowed for the exclusion of both these methods of judicial review (and the ancillary jurisdiction) thereby enabling a foreign party to a United Kingdom arbitration agreement to approach more nearly his supposed ideal of a dispute which is determined solely by arbitration (see ss. 3, 4).

New provisions for appeal from arbitrator

It is now provided that an appeal *stricto sensu* may lie from an arbitrator to the High Court, but this right of appeal is limited as follows:

1. It only lies on a point of law (s. 1 (2)).
2. It must " arise out of " an award made on an arbitration agreement (s. 1 (2)).

As to " arising out of," reference may be made to the construction of similar words relating to the scope of a submission (for which see Russell (19th ed.), pp. 92 *et seq.*). The arbitration agreement must be in writing (s. 7 (1) (*e*), and Arbitration Act 1950, s. 32).

3. Either: (A) all the parties must consent (s. 1 (3) (*a*)), or (B) the High Court has granted leave. But the High Court cannot grant leave unless:
   (a) there is no valid exclusion agreement (see generally under heading " Exclusion of right to judicial review ");
   (b) the High Court considers that, having regard to all the circumstances, the determination of the question of law concerned could substantially affect the rights of one or more of the parties to the arbitration agreement (s. 1 (3) (*b*) and (4)).

In order that an appeal (if it takes place) may be effective the court has power to order an arbitrator to give reasons for his decision (as to which, see heading " Requirement that arbitrator shall give reasons ").

The court may impose conditions on the granting of leave (as to which, see notes to s. 1).

In certain circumstances an appeal lies to the Court of Appeal from a decision of the High Court on an appeal under s. 1 (as to which, see heading " Appeals to the Court of Appeal ").

On the determination of the appeal the High Court may by order (a) confirm, vary or set aside the award; or (b) remit the award to the reconsideration of the arbitrator or umpire together with the court's opinion on the question of law which was the subject of the appeal. When there is a remission the arbitrator or umpire must, unless otherwise directed, make his award within three months from the date of the order (s. 1 (2)).

Where the award of an arbitrator or umpire is varied on appeal, the award as varied has effect as if it were the award of the arbitrator or umpire (s. 1 (8)).

Requirement that arbitrator shall give reasons

In order that an appeal (where an appeal is permitted) may be effective there is provision that the arbitrator can be made to state the reasons for his award in sufficient detail to enable the court to consider any question of law arising out of the award (s. 1 (5) and (6)).

In course of time there will undoubtedly be learning on the matter of how precisely the court will frame its order, and in what manner the arbitrator should comply with it. An analogy may perhaps be drawn with the old law of the way in which arbitrators should find facts (not evidence) and state them so that the court could see how the question of law arose, under the now repealed procedure for stating a case (for which reference may be made to Russell (19th ed.), pp. 293–324). It is too soon to tell to what extent the old law will be found helpful to the new.

However, the arbitrator will not be compelled to give reasons unless:

1 (a). In a case where no (as opposed to no sufficient) reason is given, then before the award was made one of the parties to the reference gave notice to the arbitral tribunal that a reasoned award would be required;

1 (b) *or* (in such a case) that there is some special reason why such a notice was not given;
and

2 (a) in every case (whether a case of no reason or of no sufficient reasons) an application is made to the High Court to compel the arbitral tribunal to give reasons by one party with the consent of all the other parties;

2 (b) *or* in a case where there is no exclusion agreement (see under heading "Exclusion of right to judicial review") the court gives leave.

Appeals to the Court of Appeal

It is elementary that there is no appeal from the decision of any court unless it is provided by statute. The new Act provides for certain appeals, but—*sub silentio*—prohibits others.

There is no appeal to the Court of Appeal from a decision of the High Court granting or refusing leave to appeal from the arbitrator under s. 1 (3) (*b*) or granting or refusing an application to compel the arbitrator to state his reasons under s. 1 (5) (*b*).

Under s. 1 there is only an appeal from a decision of the High Court given on an appeal from the arbitral tribunal (see s. 1 (7)).

However, in the case of the jurisdiction under s. 2 to determine a preliminary point of law, there is an appeal to the Court of Appeal from a decision of the High Court "*under this section*" (see s. 2 (3)) so that not only is there an appeal from a decision on the point of law concerned, but there must also be an appeal (in theory) from the refusal or grant of an application asking the court to determine a point of law.

But the words "in theory" are used advisedly for this reason: no appeal to the Court of Appeal lies under either s. 1 or s. 2 in any case under each respective section where appeal is possible unless:

(a) the High Court or the Court of Appeal gives leave (ss. 1 (7) (*a*), 2 (3) (*a*)), *and*

(b) it is certified *by the High Court* that the question of law to which its decision relates either is one of general public importance or is one which for some other special reason should be considered by the Court of Appeal (ss. 1 (7) (*b*), 2 (3) (*b*)).

This will leave the High Court in precisely the dilemma in which the Patents Appeal Tribunal used to be under the Patents Act 1949, s. 14 (1) (*e*) "clearly obvious," and s. 87 (1) (*c*) "appeal on refusal under s. 14 (1) (*e*) with the leave of the Tribunal": in this case one patents judge took the firm view that if he refused an application on the grounds of obviousness that necessarily meant that it was a clear case so that he ought not to grant leave to appeal.

Under this new Act, it is not so much that a judge who does not consider that he ought to allow an appeal from an arbitrator on a point of law will be likely to take the view that he ought not to certify in accordance with the Act (thereby effectively blocking an appeal), but a judge who refuses an application to have a preliminary point of law determined by the court will already (under s. 2 (2)) have decided that the determination of the application probably will not produce substantial savings in costs to the parties and that if the arbitrator decides the point it is unlikely that leave to appeal would be given under s. 1 and accordingly would very probably decide that it was his duty to refuse to certify.

As to "special reason" for giving leave to appeal to the Court of Appeal other than the point being one of general public importance, this is another instance of the unfortunate habit of the legislature of leaving it to the courts to ascertain the precise ambit of the law.

Preliminary point of law

The new provisions are designed to give parties arbitrating the same facilities that litigants have to get preliminary points of law determined by the court. Heretofore in arbitrations this could only be done by invoking the provisions (of the Arbitration Act 1950, s. 21) which could not be ousted by agreement (see Russell (19th ed.), p. 89).

Now s. 2 provides for the determination of preliminary points of law, but this provision can be excluded (see ss. 3 and 4 and heading below "Exclusion of Right to Judicial Control").

The new facility is only available if one of the parties to the arbitration makes an application to the High Court for the purpose, and the application will not be successful unless *either* (1) all the other parties consent (s. 2 (1) (*b*)), *or* (2) the arbitral tribunal consents (s. 2 (1) (*a*)) and the High Court is satisfied of two matters, namely (a) that determination of the point might produce substantial savings in costs and (b) it considers that, having regard to all the circumstances, the determination of the question of law could substantially affect the rights of one or more of the parties (ss. 1 (4) and 2 (2)). Also of course, it is essential that the right to this judicial control has not been excluded.

Provision will be needed for the manner in which the application must be made, and the manner in which the point must be put before the court if the application is successful. It is not likely that the detailed learning on the manner in which a case had to be stated under the old law (for which see Russell (19th ed.), pp. 302 *et seq.*) will be of any assistance in this matter.

For the normal procedure with regard to preliminary points of law, see R.S.C., Ord. 18, r. 11.

One can expect the usual determined attempts to dress up questions of fact as questions of law in order to try and take advantage of this jurisdiction.

Exclusion of right to judicial review

Exclusion agreement. The right to judicial review by way of appeal (s. 1) or by determination of a preliminary point of law by the court (s. 2) can be ousted by agreement (ss. 3 and 4).

Since the jurisdiction to compel an arbitral tribunal to state the reasons for its award is ancillary to the jurisdiction to review the award judicially, it follows that any exclusion of the right to review the award judicially will automatically exclude the ancillary jurisdiction (s. 3 (1) (*b*)).

The basic rule for establishing such an exclusion is that the parties shall have entered into an agreement in writing which excludes the right of appeal under s. 1 *or* (emphasis added) the right to have a preliminary point determined under s. 2. The wording of the relevant provision (s. 3 (1)) is not altogether happy, and until some loose draftsmanship raises the question squarely, it will be prudent for an exclusion clause to exclude *both* methods of judicial review *nominatim.* Of course when there is an effective exclusion of both methods of review, the ouster of the jurisdiction to require the arbitral tribunal to state its reasons for the award is automatic.

It is also probably necessary to be very strict in the way the agreement is expressed (and this may prove to be a trap for the unwary foreigner). To be effective, an agreement must be by "the parties to the reference" and must exclude the right to review (in both sorts) "in relation to that (*i.e.* the relevant) award" or "in relation to an award to which the determination of the question of law is material" (s. 3 (1)). That does not end the matter because "an exclusion agreement may be expressed so as to relate to a particular award, to awards under a particular reference or to any other description of awards, whether arising out of the same reference or not; and an agreement may be an exclusion agreement for the purposes of the section whether it is entered into before or after the passing of the Act *and whether or not it forms part of an arbitration agreement*" (s. 3 (2)).

As a consequence it seems prima facie that it would be possible that parties who were likely to arbitrate between themselves from time to time could enter into blanket agreements, not being part of any arbitration agreement, to exclude judicial review. But s. 3 (4) provides that the following matter in any agreement shall *not* be sufficient to exclude judicial review, namely matter purporting:

(a) to prohibit or restrict access to the High Court, or

(b) to restrict the jurisdiction of that court, or

(c) to prohibit or restrict the making of a reasoned award.

Provision (c) is easy enough to understand—the mere ousting of the obligation to make a reasoned award will not oust the substantive right to judicial review. But provisions (a) and (b) seem to imply that the ouster of judicial review will have to be very specific. Until accepted exclusionary clauses have been judicially approved, it would be prudent to exclude specifically both rights of review *nominatim*, as already indicated above in connection with the wording of s. 3 (1).

Domestic arbitrations. If the arbitration agreement is a domestic arbitration agreement (as to which see s. 3 (7), a definition in complete consonance with the definition in the Arbitration Act 1975, s. 1 (4)) there is a further requirement for a successful exclusion agreement to be operative, namely that it must be entered into *after* the commencement of the relevant arbitration (s. 3 (6)). (For commencement, see the Arbitration Act 1950, s. 29 (2) and (3), and the Arbitration Act 1979, s. 7 (2).)

Other special cases. As well as domestic arbitrations, certain other arbitrations, namely:

(a) those involving Admiralty jurisdiction (s. 4 (1) (*a*));

(b) disputes arising out of contracts of insurance (s. 4 (1) (*b*)); and

(c) disputes arising out of a commodity contract (s. 4 (1) (*c*));

require (as one of the conditions for an exclusion agreement being operative) that the exclusion agreement is entered into *after* the commencement of the relevant arbitration (s. 4 (1) (i)).

The other condition for the exclusion being operative is the alternative that the award or question relates to a contract which is expressed to be governed by a law other than the law of England and Wales (s. 4 (1) (ii)). Note that the mere specification of a foreign law does not prevent the agreement being a domestic arbitration agreement.

"Commodity contract" is specially defined (s. 4 (2)) and there is provision for the Secretary of State to modify the application of the law to these special cases (s. 4 (3) and (4)).

Fraud. The Arbitration Act 1950, s. 24 (2), has not been repealed, and enables the court to quash an arbitration in a case where the agreement was to submit future disputes and a question arises whether a party has been guilty of fraud. But if the arbitration agreement is other than a domestic arbitration agreement and the parties have entered into an exclusion agreement in the manner outlined above, then except as the agreement otherwise provides, this jurisdiction is also ousted (s. 3 (3)).

Statutory arbitrations. Review by the court cannot be ousted by an exclusion agreement (s. 3 (5)).

Abolished jurisdiction relating to statement of case

The Arbitration Act 1950, s. 21, now ceases to have effect (s. 1) and is also repealed (s. 8 (3) (*b*)).

The jurisdiction under this section was dealt with in Russell (19th ed.), pp. 293–324. Broadly the section enabled (and on the direction of the court compelled) an arbitrator to state as a case for the opinion of the court:

(a) any question of law arising in the course of the reference, and

(b) an award or any part of an award,

and it was misconduct for an arbitrator, if asked to state a case, to make his award immediately so as to prevent himself being compelled to state such a case (Russell (19th ed.), p. 473).

This method of enabling the courts in effect to control the arbitrator and make sure that he did not go wrong in law suffered from many procedural defects and had been heavily criticised. It had been often noticed that the sister jurisdiction in Scotland knew no such procedure. However, now that the jurisdiction has been abolished in England, it is interesting to note that it will not be wholly lost to jurisprudence, for it has recently been extended to Scotland (Administration of Justice Act 1972, s. 3) to which the Arbitration Act of 1979 does not extend (see s. 8 (4)).

It is to be noted that of the present changes to the law, the new provision for the determination by the court of a preliminary point is the new substitute for the old procedure of stating a case on any question of law arising in the course of the reference, and the aim is in each case the same, the real difference being one of procedure only.

Abolished jurisdiction to impeach award for error on face

The jurisdiction to impeach for error on the face of the award (dealt with in Russell (19th ed.), pp. 437–447) was anomalous. As Russell puts it (on p. 437):

> "An award which, on its face, fails to comply with the requirements for a valid award (as to which see Russell (19th ed.), pp. 328–349), will be remitted or set aside. By a somewhat anomalous extension of this rule, notwithstanding that an arbitrator's decision is in general final, if an error of law is allowed to appear on the face of the award, this is a ground for setting it aside."

This statement of the position was different from the corresponding statement in the 18th edition (p. 357) in that, in the earlier edition, the position was stated as being "if an error *either of fact or law* is allowed to appear on the face of the award, this is a ground for setting it aside." This statement was altered to omit the words "either of fact or" because no convenient examples could be found of cases where awards were set aside for errors of fact on the face thereof. Cases where awards were remitted because (for example) the arbitrator had mis-named one of the parties in the award were hardly true support for the proposition that awards could be impeached for the kind of error usually characterised as one of fact (rather than a slip) appearing on the face of the award. Slips could, of course always be corrected either under the Arbitration Act 1950, s. 17, or by virtue of an inherent jurisdiction, and this position still holds good.

However, the new Act (s. 1 (1)) has abolished the jurisdiction to set aside or remit an award on the ground of errors of fact or law on the face of the award so that presumably the jurisdiction to set aside for errors of fact must have existed, unless the abolition has been widened *ex abundanti cautela*. It is possible that the real reason for the original existence of the jurisdiction to impeach for errors of fact appearing on the face was the necessity to cope with errors of law which, being errors as to *foreign* law, had in our law to be treated as errors of fact; or awards containing decisions on the existence and reasonableness of customs might perhaps have been assailed on the basis of error of fact rather than law. Further, had there been no abolition of the power to impeach on the ground of error of fact on the face of the award, the well-known pastime of dressing up errors of fact as errors of law might have been played in reverse by dressing up errors of law as errors of fact.

In any event it is not believed that real slips—such as the misnaming of a party in an award—cannot continue to be corrected by remission (under the Arbitration Act 1950, ss. 17 and 22) and of course the jurisdiction to set aside for misconduct (under the Arbitration Act 1950, s. 23) remains. However, at least one type of behaviour, formerly misconduct, is no longer so: it was formerly misconduct for an arbitrator, if asked to state a case, to make his award immediately so as to prevent himself being compelled to state such a case (Russell (19th ed.), p. 473). Plainly enough as this duty has been abolished it can no longer be misconduct to neglect it.

It should also be noted that the retention of the jurisdiction to set aside for misconduct does not indirectly retain the jurisdiction to set aside for mistake of law (or fact) on the face of the award for it was never misconduct to make a mistake either of fact or law (see Russell (19th ed.), pp. 475–477).

But the jurisdiction to set aside for admitted mistake (see Russell (19th ed.), pp. 452–457) is almost certainly affected by the repeal of the Arbitration Act 1950, s. 21. This jurisdiction always was particularly anomalous, and in so far as it went beyond the mere correction of slips (which could be effected anyway by the Arbitration Act 1950, s. 17, if not under an inherent jurisdiction) could have done so on no other basis than that "on the face of the award" was only one requirement for making certain that the error was an open one, and that a plain admission by the arbitrator would be an equally acceptable method of showing that the error was an open one. If that be so, the basis must now be taken to have been utterly removed.

Lastly, it may be noted that the relief formerly obtainable for error on the face of the award was extremely chancy, and depended on the arbitrator making a speaking award. But there was never any reason why the award should be a speaking award if the arbitrator had not been asked to state a case. This aspect of matters is now dealt with by the new requirements that an arbitrator should make a speaking award—obviously an assistance to any appeal tribunal reviewing his decision.

Minor amendments to the law of arbitration

The new Act has, besides its main purpose, two subsidiary purposes, namely to give arbitrators greater powers to enforce obedience to their interlocutory orders (s. 5) and to amend the law relating to the appointment and constitution of arbitral tribunals (s. 6).

Interlocutory orders

The old law (Arbitration Act 1950, s. 12) gave the High Court certain powers to control the interlocutory stages of an arbitration. But these powers were limited, and in particular the power to order pleadings was confined to the arbitrator. The question then arose as to what his powers were if a party defaulted in obedience to an order made in such a case or in any case in which the interlocutory order came from the arbitrator alone. The question is discussed in Russell (19th ed.), pp. 233 *et seq.*, but the arbitrator's powers to enforce obedience to his interlocutory orders were plainly unsatisfactorily limited. It is now expressly provided that if there is default in obeying an arbitrator's order, the High Court may make an order, in effect telling the arbitrator that he may go ahead with the reference in spite of the default (subject to any conditions imposed by the court).

In the case of a judge-arbitrator or judge-umpire, this power of the High Court in respect of interlocutory orders can be exercised by the judge-arbitrator or judge-umpire himself.

Appointment and constitution of arbitral tribunals

Under the old law (Arbitration Act 1950, s. 8) relating to umpires there were two infelicities. In the first place, s. 8 (1) provided that if there were to be two arbitrators they should appoint an umpire immediately after they were themselves appointed. However, if they eventually agreed the appointment of the umpire was fruitless. The new law (s. 6 (1)) provides that they can appoint the umpire at any time, and they are only compelled to do so " forthwith " when it is plain that they cannot agree on their award. In the second place, the Arbitration Act 1950, s. 9, provided that where the parties had referred their dispute to three arbitrators, an incautious method of appointing the third arbitrator (namely by letting the two parties' arbitrators choose him) would convert him into an umpire, which is most unlikely to have been the parties' intentions. It is now provided (s. 6 (2)) that any method of appointing three arbitrators will (unless a contrary intention is expressed) succeed in getting three arbitrators, and not two arbitrators only plus one umpire. The inescapable consequence is of course that the award of any two of the arbitrators shall be binding.

There are also very minor amendments to the Arbitration Act 1950, s. 10 (1) (*c*) (as it now is), set out below under " Alterations made to existing Acts " (s. 6 (3)), and a provision for filling a lacuna in the old law relating to default in the appointment of an arbitrator (s. 6 (4)). Under the old law, the court had certain powers to appoint an arbitrator which included cases where the parties themselves did not appoint, or an appointed arbitrator refused to act or did not act; but there was no power for the court to appoint if the choice was left to a third party (as was often provided for, the choice being left to, *e.g.*, the President of some institution) and the third party would not appoint. No doubt the occasions on which such third parties refused to appoint must have been rare, but in any event there now is power for the court to appoint in default, on the new procedure being followed.

Alterations made to existing Acts

Arbitration Act 1950

S. 8 (1) (Russell (19th ed.), p. 519) has (by the Arbitration Act 1979, s. 6 (1)) been amended so as to read as follows:

"8 (1). Unless a contrary intention is expressed therein, every arbitration agreement shall, where the reference is to two arbitrators, be deemed to include a provision that the two arbitrators may appoint an umpire at any time after they are themselves appointed and shall do so forthwith if they cannot agree" (*scilicet on their award, and not on the appointment of an umpire*).

S. 9 (Russell (19th ed.), p. 519). In effect s. 9 (1) is repealed and subs. (2) now governs. The machinery (Arbitration Act 1979, s. 6 (2)) is that a new section is substituted for the old one as follows:

"9. Unless the contrary intention is expressed in the arbitration agreement, in any case where there is a reference to three arbitrators, the award of any two of the arbitrators shall be binding."

S. 10 (Russell (19th ed.), p. 520). What is now s. 10 (1) (*c*) has been amended (Arbitration Act 1979, ss. 6 (3) and 8 (3) (*a*)) and a new subs. (2) has been added (Arbitration Act 1979, s. 6 (4)), the relevant portions of the 1950 Act now reading as follows:

"10 (1) (*c*) where the parties or two arbitrators are required or are at liberty to appoint an umpire or third arbitrator and do not appoint him."

"10 (2) In any case where—

(*a*) an arbitration agreement provides for the appointment of an arbitrator or umpire by a person who is neither one of the parties nor an existing arbitrator (whether the provision applies directly or in default of agreement by the parties or otherwise), and

(*b*) that person refuses to make the appointment or does not make it within the time specified in the agreement or, if no time is so specified, within a reasonable time,

any party to the agreement may serve the person in question with a written notice to appoint an arbitrator or umpire and, if the appointment is not made within seven clear days after the service of the notice, the High Court or a judge thereof may, on the application of the party who gave the notice, appoint an arbitrator or umpire who shall have the like powers to act in the reference and make an award as if he had been appointed in accordance with the terms of the agreement."

S. 14 (Russell (19th ed.), p. 523) is extended so that any reference in the Arbitration Act 1979 to an award includes a reference to an interim award (Arbitration Act 1979, s. 7 (1) (*a*)).

S. 21 (Russell (19th ed.), p. 525). This is repealed and ceases to have effect (Arbitration Act 1979, ss. 1, 8 (3) (*b*)).

S. 24 (2) (Russell (19th ed.), p. 527). This is restricted. In any case where (a) an arbitration agreement other than a domestic arbitration agreement, provides for disputes between the parties to be referred to arbitration, (b) a dispute to which the agreement relates involves the question whether a party has been guilty of fraud and (c) the parties have entered into an exclusion agreement which is applicable to any award made on the reference to that dispute, then (except in so far as the exclusion agreement otherwise provides) the High Court shall not exercise its powers under this subsection.

S. 28 (Russell (19th ed.), p. 530) is extended so that any reference in the Arbitration Act 1979 to an order has in effect provided that it may be made on such terms as to costs, etc., as may be just (Arbitration Act 1979, s. 7 (1) (*b*)).

S. 29 (2) and (3) (Russell (19th ed.), p. 530) are extended so as to determine when an arbitration is commenced for the purposes of the Arbitration Act 1979, ss. 3 (6) and 4 (1) (i) (Arbitration Act 1979, s. 7 (2)).

S. 30 (Russell (19th ed.), p. 531) is extended so as to make the Arbitration Act 1979 bind the Crown (Arbitration Act 1979, s. 7 (1) (*c*)).

S. 31 (Russell (19th ed.), p. 531) is extended so as to apply the Arbitration Act 1979 to statutory arbitrations (Arbitration Act 1979, s. 7 (1) (*d*)) and the Act cannot be excluded by agreement (Arbitration Act 1979, s. 3 (5)). But the reference in s. 31 (1) to arbitration under any other Act, does not extend to arbitration under the County Courts Act 1959, s. 92, and nothing in the Arbitration Act 1950, Pt. I, or the Arbitration Act 1979 applies to arbitration under the said s. 92 (Arbitration Act 1979, s. 7 (3)).

S. 32 (Russell (19th ed.), p. 531) is extended to the Arbitration Act 1979 to make that Act applicable only to written agreements (Arbitration Act 1979, s. 7 (1) (*e*)).

Administration of Justice Act 1970

S. 4 (5) (Russell (19th ed.), p. 545) (jurisdiction of the High Court to be exercisable by the Court of Appeal in relation to judge-arbitrators and judge-umpires) is restricted in its application. It does not apply in relation to the new power of the High Court to make an interlocutory order under the Arbitration Act 1979, s. 5, but in the case of a reference to a judge-arbitrator or judge-umpire that power is exercisable, as in the case of any other reference to arbitration, by the High Court, and also by the judge-arbitrator or judge-umpire himself (Arbitration Act 1979, s. 5 (3)) in his capacity as judge of the High Court (*ibid.* s. 5 (4)), without derogation from any powers conferred upon him *qua* arbitrator, whether by an arbitration agreement or otherwise (*ibid.* s. 5 (5)).

Sched. 3, para. 9 (Russell (19th ed.), p. 547). In sub-para. (1) the words " 21 (1) and (2) " are repealed and sub-para. (2) is repealed (Arbitration Act 1979, s. 8 (3) (*c*)).

Commencement

The Act received the Royal Assent on April 4, 1979, and came into operation on August 1, 1979: see the Arbitration Act 1979 (Commencement) Order 1979 (S.I. 1979 No. 750 (C. 16)).

Extent

The Act forms part of the law of England and Wales only: s. 8 (4).

Parliamentary debates

The genesis of the Act lies in the suggestions made by the Hon. Mr. Justice Donaldson for the reform of arbitration law set out in *The Times*, March 3, 1978, and mentioned in the Preface to Russell. These suggestions were followed by the publication of the Report on Arbitration of the Commercial Court Committee in July 1978 (Cmnd. 7284) of which the Hon. Mr. Justice Donaldson was Chairman. The Act was introduced in the House of Lords so that the main parliamentary debates are to be found as follows: H.L. Vol. 397, cols. 434–464 (Second Reading); H.L. Vol. 398, cols. 1465–1481 (Third Reading); H.C. Vol. 964, cols. 635–656 (Second Reading); and H.C. Vol. 965, cols. 1064–1078 (Committee).

Judicial review of arbitration awards

1.—(1) In the Arbitration Act 1950 (in this Act referred to as " the principal Act ") section 21 (statement of case for a decision of the High Court) shall cease to have effect and, without prejudice to the right of appeal conferred by subsection (2) below, the High Court shall not have jurisdiction to set aside or remit an award on an arbitration agreement on the ground of errors of fact or law on the face of the award.

(2) Subject to subsection (3) below, an appeal shall lie to the High Court on any question of law arising out of an award made on an arbitration agreement; and on the determination of such an appeal the High Court may by order—

(*a*) confirm, vary or set aside the award; or

(*b*) remit the award to the reconsideration of the arbitrator or umpire together with the court's opinion on the question of law which was the subject of the appeal;

and where the award is remitted under paragraph (*b*) above the arbitrator or umpire shall, unless the order otherwise directs, make his award within three months after the date of the order.

(3) An appeal under this section may be brought by any of the parties to the reference—

(*a*) with the consent of all the other parties to the reference; or

(*b*) subject to section 3 below, with the leave of the court.

(4) The High Court shall not grant leave under subsection (3) (*b*) above unless it considers that, having regard to all the circumstances, the determination of the question of law concerned could substantially affect the rights of one or more of the parties to the arbitration agreement; and the court may make any leave which it gives conditional upon the applicant complying with such conditions as it considers appropriate.

(5) Subject to subsection (6) below, if an award is made and, on an application made by any of the parties to the reference,—

(*a*) with the consent of all the other parties to the reference, or

(*b*) subject to section 3 below, with the leave of the court,

it appears to the High Court that the award does not or does not sufficiently set out the reasons for the award, the court may order the arbitrator or umpire concerned to state the reasons for his award in sufficient detail to enable the court, should an appeal be brought under this section, to consider any question of law arising out of the award.

(6) In any case where an award is made without any reason being given, the High Court shall not make an order under subsection (5) above unless it is satisfied—

(*a*) that before the award was made one of the parties to the reference gave notice to the arbitrator or umpire concerned that a reasoned award would be required; or

(*b*) that there is some special reason why such a notice was not given.

(7) No appeal shall lie to the Court of Appeal from a decision of the High Court on an appeal under this section unless—

(*a*) the High Court or the Court of Appeal gives leave; and

(*b*) it is certified by the High Court that the question of law to which its decision relates either is one of general public importance or is one which for some other special reason should be considered by the Court of Appeal.

(8) Where the award of an arbiter or umpire is varied on appeal, the award as varied shall have effect (except for the purposes of this section) as if it were the award of the arbitrator or umpire.

DEFINITIONS

"Arbitration agreement": see s. 7 (1) (*e*) and the Arbitration Act 1950, s. 32; the agreement must be in writing.

GENERAL NOTE

For the effect of this section, see the introductory General Note under headings "New provisions for appeal from arbitrator," "Requirement that arbitrator shall give reasons," "Appeals to Court of Appeal," "Abolished jurisdiction relating to statement of case," "Abolished jurisdiction to impeach award for error on face," and "Alterations made to existing Acts." As to the rights given by this section being excluded by agreement, see ss. 3 and 4 and notes thereto, and the introductory General Note under heading "Exclusion of right to judicial review."

Subs. (4)

Note that the court may impose conditions on the giving of leave to appeal.

Conditions envisaged include conditions designed to ensure that the motive for an appeal is not mere delay, and may comprise conditions that a minimum sum due to a successful party should be paid over to him and/or that the sum in dispute should be secured, if seen fit by bringing that sum into court, and/or that other security should be given either as to moneys in dispute or costs. In the case of continuing wrongs, conditions might include conditions as to cesser.

Subs. (6)

Note that this subsection only applies where the arbitrator gives no reasons. If he gives inadequate reasons this subsection does not apply so that it will not be necessary to show that a notice was given or that there is some special reason why it was not given. As to what constitutes a "special reason," this is unfortunately wide drafting and it will be possible to try and bring almost any unusual circumstance within its ambit before the law is clarified by judicial decisions: the reason probably most in mind was the case where no notice was given because the arbitrator led the parties to suppose that he was going to give a reasoned notice.

The new Act also suggests another possible reason, namely where the agreement itself obliges the arbitral tribunal not to give reasons: this, however, will not oust the jurisdiction for judicial review (s. 3 (4) (*c*)).

Semble no notice given by the parties need be in writing, and a request from counsel during the course of the proceedings would be sufficient.

Determination of preliminary point of law by court

2.—(1) Subject to subsection (2) and section 3 below, on an application to the High Court made by any of the parties to a reference—

(*a*) with the consent of an arbitrator who has entered on the reference or, if an umpire has entered on the reference, with his consent, or

(*b*) with the consent of all the other parties,

the High Court shall have jurisdiction to determine any question of law arising in the course of the reference.

(2) The High Court shall not entertain an application under subsection (1) (*a*) above with respect to any question of law unless it is satisfied that—

(*a*) the determination of the application might produce substantial savings in costs to the parties; and

(*b*) the question of law is one in respect of which leave to appeal would be likely to be given under section 1 (3) (*b*) above.

(3) A decision of the High Court under this section shall be deemed to be a judgment of the court within the meaning of section 27 of the Supreme Court of Judicature (Consolidation) Act 1925 (appeals to the Court of Appeal), but no appeal shall lie from such a decision unless—

(*a*) the High Court or the Court of Appeal gives leave; and

(*b*) it is certified by the High Court that the question of law to which its decision relates either is one of general public importance or is one which for some other special reason should be considered by the Court of Appeal.

DEFINITIONS

"entered on the reference": arbitrators enter upon a reference as soon as they have accepted their appointment and have communicated with each other about the reference: *Iossifoglu* v. *Coumantaros* [1941] 1 K.B. 396; an umpire enters upon a reference when he enters the reference in lieu of the arbitrators.

GENERAL NOTE

For the effect of these provisions see the introductory General Note under headings "Preliminary point of law" and "Appeals to the Court of Appeal." For the jurisdiction for which this is a substitute see *ibid.* "Abolished jurisdiction relating to statement of case." As to the rights given by this section being excluded by agreement see ss. 3 and 4 and notes thereto, and the General Note under heading "Exclusion of right to judicial review."

Exclusion agreements affecting rights under sections 1 and 2

3.—(1) Subject to the following provisions of this section and section 4 below—

(*a*) the High Court shall not, under section 1 (3) (*b*) above, grant leave to appeal with respect to a question of law arising out of an award, and (*b*) the High Court shall not, under section 1 (5) (*b*) above, grant leave to make an application with respect to an award, and

(*c*) no application may be made under section 2 (1) (*a*) above with respect to a question of law,

if the parties to the reference in question have entered into an agreement in writing (in this section referred to as an " exclusion agreement ") which excludes the right of appeal under section 1 above in relation to that award or, in a case falling within paragraph (*c*) above, in relation to an award to which the determination of the question of law is material.

(2) An exclusion agreement may be expressed so as to relate to a particular award, to awards under a particular reference or to any other description of awards, whether arising out of the same reference or not; and an agreement may be an exclusion agreement for the purposes of this section whether it is entered into before or after the passing of this Act and whether or not it forms part of an arbitration agreement.

(3) In any case where—

(*a*) an arbitration agreement, other than a domestic arbitration agreement, provides for disputes between the parties to be referred to arbitration, and

(*b*) a dispute to which the agreement relates involves the question whether a party has been guilty of fraud, and

(*c*) the parties have entered into an exclusion agreement which is applicable to any award made on the reference of that dispute,

then, except in so far as the exclusion agreement otherwise provides, the High Court shall not exercise its powers under section 24 (2) of the principal Act (to take steps necessary to enable the question to be determined by the High Court) in relation to that dispute.

(4) Except as provided by subsection (1) above, sections 1 and 2 above shall have effect notwithstanding anything in any agreement purporting—

(*a*) to prohibit or restrict access to the High Court; or

(*b*) to restrict the jurisdiction of that court; or

(*c*) to prohibit or restrict the making of a reasoned award.

(5) An exclusion agreement shall be of no effect in relation to an award made on, or a question of law arising in the course of a reference under, a statutory arbitration, that is to say, such an arbitration as is referred to in subsection (1) of section 31 of the principal Act.

(6) An exclusion agreement shall be of no effect in relation to an award made on, or a question of law arising in the course of a reference under, an arbitration agreement which is a domestic arbitration agreement unless the exclusion agreement is entered into after the commencement of the arbitration in which the award is made or, as the case may be, in which the question of law arises.

(7) In this section " domestic arbitration agreement " means an arbitration agreement which does not provide, expressly or by implication, for arbitration in a State other than the United Kingdom and to which neither—

(*a*) an individual who is a national of, or habitually resident in, any State other than the United Kingdom, nor

(*b*) a body corporate which is incorporated in, or whose central management and control is exercised in, any State other than the United Kingdom,

is a party at the time the arbitration agreement is entered into.

DEFINITIONS

" exclusion agreement ": see s. 3 (1), (2) and (4) and the discussion in General Note under heading " Exclusion agreement."

"domestic arbitration agreement": see s. 3 (7). This definition is practically identical with that in the Arbitration Act 1975, s. 1 (4), but in that Act the concluding words are "at the time the proceedings are commenced" and in this Act the concluding words are "at the time the arbitration agreement is entered into."

"powers under s. 24 (2) of the principal Act": s. 24 (2) states "Where an agreement between any parties provides that disputes which may arise in the future between them shall be referred to arbitration, and a dispute which so arises involves the question whether any such party has been guilty of fraud, the High Court shall, so far as may be necessary to enable that question to be determined by the High Court, have power to order that the agreement shall cease to have effect and power to give leave to revoke the authority of any arbitrator or umpire appointed by or by virtue of the agreement."

"commencement of the arbitration": see Definitions under s. 4.

General Note

For the effect of these provisions see the introductory General Note under the heading "Exclusion of right to judicial review." The position as regards exclusion of these rights is also affected by s. 4. See also under the heading "Alterations made to existing Acts" for the effect on ss. 24 (2) and 31 (1) of the Arbitration Act 1950.

Exclusion agreements not to apply in certain cases

4.—(1) Subject to subsection (3) below, if an arbitration award or a question of law arising in the course of a reference relates, in whole or in part, to—

(*a*) a question or claim falling within the Admiralty jurisdiction of the High Court, or

(*b*) a dispute arising out of a contract of insurance, or

(*c*) a dispute arising out of a commodity contract,

an exclusion agreement shall have no effect in relation to the award or question unless either—

(i) the exclusion agreement is entered into after the commencement of the arbitration in which the award is made or, as the case may be, in which the question of law arises, or

(ii) the award or question relates to a contract which is expressed to be governed by a law other than the law of England and Wales.

(2) In subsection (1) (*c*) above "commodity contract" means a contract—

(*a*) for the sale of goods regularly dealt with on a commodity market or exchange in England or Wales which is specified for the purposes of this section by an order made by the Secretary of State; and

(*b*) of a description so specified.

(3) The Secretary of State may by order provide that subsection (1) above—

(*a*) shall cease to have effect; or

(*b*) subject to such conditions as may be specified in the order, shall not apply to any exclusion agreement made in relation to an arbitration award of a description so specified;

and an order under this subsection may contain such supplementary, incidental and transitional provisions as appear to the Secretary of State to be necessary or expedient.

(4) The power to make an order under subsection (2) or subsection (3) above shall be exercisable by statutory instrument which shall be subject to annulment in pursuance of a resolution of either House of Parliament.

(5) In this section "exclusion agreement" has the same meaning as in section 3 above.

DEFINITIONS

"exclusion agreement": see ss. 3 (1), (2) and (4) and 4 (5), and the discussion in the General Note, under the heading "Exclusion agreement."

"Admiralty jurisdiction": See R.S.C., Ord. 75; Administration of Justice Act 1956, ss. 1–8; Hovercraft Act 1968; Oil in Navigable Waters Act 1971; Prevention of Oil Pollution Act 1971; Merchant Shipping (Oil Pollution) Act 1971; Merchant Shipping Act 1974.

"commodity contract": a contract (a) for the sale of goods regularly dealt with on a commodity market or exchange in England or Wales which is specified for the purposes of Arbitration Act 1979, s. 4 by an order made by the Secretary of State; and (b) of a description so specified (Arbitration Act 1979, s. 4 (2)).

"commencement of the arbitration": an arbitration shall be deemed to be commenced when one party to the arbitration agreement serves on the other party or parties a notice requiring him or them to appoint or concur in appointing an arbitrator, or, where the arbitration agreement provides that the reference shall be to a person named or designated in the agreement, requiring him or them to submit the dispute to the person so named or designated.

Any such notice may be served either—

(*a*) by delivering it to the person on whom it is to be served; or

(*b*) by leaving it at the usual or last known place of abode in England of that person; or

(*c*) by sending it by post in a registered letter addressed to that person at his usual or last known place of abode in England;

as well as in any other manner provided in the arbitration agreement; and where a notice is sent by post in manner prescribed by paragraph (*c*), service thereof shall, unless the contrary is proved, be deemed to have been effected at the time at which the letter would have been delivered in the ordinary course of post. (Arbitration Act 1979, s. 7 (2); Arbitration Act 1950, s. 29 (2) and (3)).

GENERAL NOTE

For the general effect of these provisions see the introductory General Note under the heading "Exclusion of right to judicial review." The position as regards exclusion of these rights is also affected by s. 3.

Interlocutory orders

5.—(1) If any party to a reference under an arbitration agreement fails within the time specified in the order or, if no time is so specified, within a reasonable time to comply with an order made by the arbitrator or umpire in the course of the reference, then, on the application of the arbitrator or umpire or of any party to the reference, the High Court may make an order extending the powers of the arbitrator or umpire as mentioned in subsection (2) below.

(2) If an order is made by the High Court under this section, the arbitrator or umpire shall have power, to the extent and subject to any conditions specified in that order, to continue with the reference in default of appearance or of any other act by one of the parties in like manner as a judge of the High Court might continue with proceedings in that court where a party fails to comply with an order of that court or a requirement of rules of court.

(3) Section 4 (5) of the Administration of Justice Act 1970 (jurisdiction of the High Court to be exercisable by the Court of Appeal in relation to judge-arbitrators and judge-umpires) shall not apply in relation to the power of the High Court to make an order under this section, but in the case of a reference to a judge-arbitrator or judge-umpire that power shall be exercisable as in the case of any other reference to arbitration and also by the judge-arbitrator or judge-umpire himself.

(4) Anything done by a judge-arbitrator or judge-umpire in the exercise of the power conferred by subsection (3) above shall be done by him in his capacity as judge of the High Court and have effect as if done by that court.

(5) The preceding provisions of this section have effect notwithstanding anything in any agreement but do not derogate from any powers conferred on an arbitrator or umpire, whether by an arbitration agreement or otherwise.

(6) In this section " judge-arbitrator " and " judge-umpire " have the same meaning as in Schedule 3 to the Administration of Justice Act 1970.

DEFINITIONS

" judge-arbitrator " and " judge-umpire ": a judge of the Commercial Court appointed as arbitrator or, as the case may be, as umpire by or by virtue of an arbitration agreement.

GENERAL NOTE

The effect of this section has been fully set out in the introductory General Note (under heading " Interlocutory orders ") together with its effect on the existing legislation in the table there provided (under heading " Alterations made to existing Acts ").

Minor amendments relating to awards and appointment of arbitrators and umpires

6.—(1) In subsection (1) of section 8 of the principal Act (agreements where reference is to two arbitrators deemed to include provision that the arbitrators shall appoint an umpire immediately after their own appointment)—

(*a*) for the words " shall appoint an umpire immediately " there shall be substituted the words " may appoint an umpire at any time "; and

(*b*) at the end there shall be added the words " and shall do so forthwith if they cannot agree ".

(2) For section 9 of the principal Act (agreements for reference to three arbitrators) there shall be substituted the following section:—

" **Majority award of three arbitrators**

9. Unless the contrary intention is expressed in the arbitration agreement, in any case where there is a reference to three arbitrators, the award of any two of the arbitrators shall be binding."

(3) In section 10 of the principal Act (power of court in certain cases to appoint an arbitrator or umpire) in paragraph (*c*) after the word " are ", in the first place where it occurs, there shall be inserted the words " required or are " and the words from " or where " to the end of the paragraph shall be omitted.

(4) At the end of section 10 of the principal Act there shall be added the following subsection:—

" (2) In any case where—

(*a*) an arbitration agreement provides for the appointment of an arbitrator or umpire by a person who is neither one of the parties nor an existing arbitrator (whether the provision applies directly or in default of agreement by the parties or otherwise), and

(*b*) that person refuses to make the appointment or does not make it within the time specified in the agreement or, if no time is so specified, within a reasonable time,

any party to the agreement may serve the person in question with a written notice to appoint an arbitrator or umpire and, if the appointment is not made within seven clear days after the service of the notice, the High Court or a judge thereof may, on the application of the party who gave the notice, appoint an arbitrator or umpire who shall have the like powers to act in the reference and make an award as if he had been appointed in accordance with the terms of the agreement."

General Note

The effect of this section has been fully set out in the introductory General Note (under the heading "Appointment and constitution of arbitral tribunals") together with its effect on the existing legislation in the table there provided (under the heading "Alterations made to existing Acts").

Application and interpretation of certain provisions of Part I of principal Act

7.—(1) References in the following provisions of Part I of the principal Act to that Part of that Act shall have effect as if the preceding provisions of this Act were included in that Part, namely,—

(*a*) section 14 (interim awards);

(*b*) section 28 (terms as to costs of orders);

(*c*) section 30 (Crown to be bound);

(*d*) section 31 (application to statutory arbitrations); and

(*e*) section 32 (meaning of " arbitration agreement ").

(2) Subsections (2) and (3) of section 29 of the principal Act shall apply to determine when an arbitration is deemed to be commenced for the purposes of this Act.

(3) For the avoidance of doubt, it is hereby declared that the reference in subsection (1) of section 31 of the principal Act (statutory arbitrations) to arbitration under any other Act does not extend to arbitration under section 92 of the County Courts Act 1959 (cases in which proceedings are to be or may be referred to arbitration) and accordingly nothing in this Act or in Part I of the principal Act applies to arbitration under the said section 92.

General Note

This section applies certain provisions of the Arbitration Act 1950 ("the principal Act") to the Arbitration Act 1979, the effect being to extend the application of those provisions. Their effect is included in the account of alterations to existing legislation, for which see the introductory General Note "Alterations made to existing Acts."

Short title, commencement, repeals and extent

8.—(1) This Act may be cited as the Arbitration Act 1979.

(2) This Act shall come into operation on such day as the Secretary of State may appoint by order made by statutory instrument; and such an order—

(*a*) may appoint different days for different provisions of this Act and for the purposes of the operation of the same provision in relation to different descriptions of arbitration agreement; and

(*b*) may contain such supplementary, incidental and transitional provisions as appear to the Secretary of State to be necessary or expedient.

(3) In consequence of the preceding provisions of this Act, the following provisions are hereby repealed, namely—

(*a*) in paragraph (*c*) of section 10 of the principal Act the words from " or where " to the end of the paragraph;

(*b*) section 21 of the principal Act;

(*c*) in paragraph 9 of Schedule 3 to the Administration of Justice Act 1970, in sub-paragraph (1) the words " 21 (1) and (2) " and sub-paragraph (2).

(4) This Act forms part of the law of England and Wales only.

General Note

Subs. (3)

This subsection does not give a complete picture of the alterations made to existing legislation, for which see the introductory General Note: "Alterations made to existing Acts."

Subs. (4)

The Act applies only to England and Wales. As to Scotland, see Administration of Justice (Scotland) Act 1972, s. 3.

Crown Agents Act 1979

(1979 c. 43)

ARRANGEMENT OF SECTIONS

An Act to reconstitute as a body corporate, and make other provision with respect to, the Crown Agents for Oversea Governments and Administrations, including the establishment of a Board to realise certain of their assets.

[4th April 1979]

General Note

This Act reconstitutes as a body corporate, and makes other provision with respect to, the Crown Agents for Overseas Governments and Administrations.

S. 1 reconstitutes the Crown Agents as a body corporate; s. 2 vests property, rights and liabilities in the Crown Agents; s. 3 outlines the general functions of the Crown Agents; s. 4 concerns authorised agency activities; s. 5 deals with non-agency activities; s. 6 specifies ancillary powers of the Crown Agents; s. 7 imposes a duty to act as agents of certain governments on request; s. 8 relates to prefunding of agency activities; s. 9 outlines the duties of the Crown Agents with respect to management of activities; s. 10 empowers the Minister to obtain information from the Crown Agents; s. 11 provides for annual reports; s. 12 regulates control by the Crown Agents of subsidiaries; s. 13 sets out the general financial duties of the Crown Agents; s. 14 relates to directions by the Minister as to reserves of the Crown Agents and their wholly-owned subsidiaries; s. 15 deals with management of liquid assets of the Crown Agents and their wholly-owned subsidiaries; s. 16 provides for payments to the Minister; s. 17 relates to the Crown Agents' commencing capital debt; s. 18 outlines the borrowing powers of the Crown Agents and their wholly-owned subsidiaries; s. 19 places a limit on certain liabilities of the Crown Agents and their subsidiaries; s. 20 allows the Minister to make grants and loans to the Agents; s. 21 provides for Treasury guarantees; s. 22 relates to accounts and audit; s. 23 empowers the Minister to give directions with respect to financial matters; s. 24 imposes a duty on the Crown Agents to insure against insurable financial risks; s. 25 establishes the Crown Agents Holding and Realisation Board; s. 26 concerns the position with respect to recoverable grants paid to unincorporated agents; s. 27 exempts the Crown Agents from certain revenue provisions; s. 28 makes provision as to revenues of, and alienations by former Agents; s. 29 deals with administrative expenses incurred by the Minister; s. 30 provides for orders, regulations and consents under the Act; s. 31 is the interpretation section; s. 32 contains consequential amendments, transitional provisions and repeals; s. 33 deals with citation and extent. The Act extends to Northern Ireland.

The Act received the Royal Assent on April 4, 1979, and came into force on that date.

Parliamentary debates

Hansard, H.C. Vol. 961, col. 730; Vol. 962, col. 585; H.L. Vol. 399, cols. 1796, 1834, and 1919.

The Crown Agents for Oversea Governments and Administrations

Reconstitution of Crown Agents as body corporate

1.—(1) On such day as the Minister may by order appoint (in this Act referred to as " the appointed day ")—

(*a*) there shall come into being a body corporate named the Crown Agents for Oversea Governments and Administrations, which shall function under and in accordance with the provisions of this Act; and

(*b*) the term of office of each of the unincorporated Agents shall expire, but without prejudice to his eligibility for appointment under this section to membership of the Crown Agents for a term of office beginning on that day.

(2) In this Act—

(*a*) " the Crown Agents " means the body corporate established by this section;

(*b*) " the unincorporated Agents " means the persons for the time being holding office under the Crown as Crown Agents for Oversea Governments and Administrations; and

(*c*) " the Minister " means the Minister of Overseas Development.

(3) The Crown Agents shall consist of not less than six nor more than ten members appointed by the Minister; and the Minister shall appoint one member to be the chairman, and another member to be the deputy chairman, of the Crown Agents.

(4) Any appointment under subsection (3) may be on either a full-time or a part-time basis.

(5) The Crown Agents, despite their name—

(*a*) are to be regarded as agents of the Crown only in so far as they act as agents of the Crown by virtue of any provision of this Act expressly authorising them to do so; and

(*b*) are not to be regarded as servants of the Crown or as enjoying any status, privilege or immunity of the Crown,

and their property is not to be regarded as property of, or held on behalf of, the Crown; but nothing in this Act shall be taken to derogate from any privilege, immunity or exemption of the Crown in relation to any matter as respects which the Crown Agents act as agents of the Crown by virtue of any such provision as is mentioned in paragraph (*a*).

(6) Schedule 1 shall have effect with respect to the Crown Agents.

(7) The Minister may, after consultation with the Crown Agents, by order specify a different name by which the Crown Agents are to be known; and an order under this subsection may make such provision as appears to the Minister to be necessary or expedient in consequence of the change of name effected thereby, including provision for amending enactments (whether contained in this or any other Act).

Vesting in Crown Agents of property, rights and liabilities

2.—(1) Subject to the provisions of this section, on the appointed day there shall vest in the Crown Agents by virtue of this Act—

(*a*) all property (in whoever vested) which, immediately before the appointed day, is held by or on behalf of the Crown in connection with the functions of the unincorporated Agents in their capacity as such; and

(*b*) all rights, liabilities and obligations (in whoever vested) which, immediately before that day, are enjoyed by, or incumbent on, the Crown in that connection.

(2) Subsection (1) does not apply to any property, rights, liabilities or obligations as to which it is provided by paragraph 7 of Schedule 5 that on the appointed day they are to vest in the Crown Agents Holding and Realisation Board established by section 25.

(3) Subsection (1) (*a*) does not apply to any property which, immediately before the appointed day, is vested in any person as nominee of the unincorporated Agents or any of them in their capacity as such; and accordingly, subject to paragraph 7 (2) of Schedule 5, any such property shall as from that day continue vested in that person as nominee, but (by virtue of subsection (1) (*b*)) as nominee of the Crown Agents and not of any other person.

(4) Schedule 2 shall have effect for the purpose of supplementing the preceding provisions of this section.

(5) In this section and Schedule 2 " the Crown " means the Crown in right of Her Majesty's Government in the United Kingdom.

General functions of Crown Agents

3.—(1) Subject to the following provisions of this Act, the Crown Agents shall have power—

(*a*) to do, as agents of any scheduled authority or body, but not as agents of any other person, anything which they are by or under this Act given power to do as agents; and

(*b*) to do, otherwise than as agents, anything which they are by or under this Act given power to do in their own right.

(2) It shall be the duty of the Minister, in deciding whether or how far to make use of any power conferred on him by this Act, and in particular his powers under section 10 to require the Crown Agents to furnish him with information, to have regard to the special nature of the relationship between the Crown Agents and the scheduled authorities and bodies for whom they act as agents.

(3) In this Act " scheduled authority or body " means an authority or body of any description specified in Part I of Schedule 3, and references to the scheduled authorities and bodies shall be construed accordingly.

(4) Part II of Schedule 3 shall have effect for the purpose of supplementing subsection (3).

Authorised agency activities

4.—(1) As agents of any scheduled authority or body the Crown Agents shall have power to carry on anywhere in the world any of the activities mentioned in Schedule 4 on behalf of their principal; and references in that Schedule to the principal shall be construed accordingly.

(2) The Minister may from time to time, with the approval of the Treasury and after consultation with the Crown Agents, by order impose on the Crown Agents, for any period specified in the order, an overall limit on the amount of funds which may be accepted by them under paragraph 10 of Schedule 4 during that period.

(3) The Minister may by order confer on the Crown Agents power, as agents of any scheduled authority or body, to carry on anywhere in the world any activity not mentioned in Schedule 4 which in his opinion it would be appropriate for the Crown Agents to have power to carry on as agents.

(4) An order under subsection (3) conferring power to carry on any activity—

(*a*) may be framed so as to confer power to carry on that activity only in accordance with conditions specified in the order; and

(*b*) may be made so as to have effect from any date not earlier than the appointed day.

Authorised non-agency activities

5.—(1) The Crown Agents shall have power to carry on in their own right anywhere in the world any of the following activities—

(*a*) providing any of the services mentioned in subsection (2) to scheduled authorities and bodies, but not to any other person;

(*b*) procuring, subject to subsection (3), movable property of any kind, being property for which the Crown Agents anticipate a demand on the part of one or more of the scheduled authorities and bodies, and selling any such property to any such authority or body or (subject to subsection (3)) to any other person.

(2) The services referred to in subsection (1) (*a*) are—

(*a*) technical inspection services (including testing);

(*b*) giving professional or technical advice;

(*c*) carrying out feasibility studies;

(*d*) supervision and management of projects;

(*e*) appraisal of proposals;

(*f*) certification in connection with contracts;

(*g*) consultancy services;

(*h*) training services;

(*i*) provision and management of staff;

(*j*) services as a trustee or nominee;

(*k*) acting as registrar, and performing related functions, for the purposes of any loan raised by a scheduled authority or body;

(*l*) subject to subsection (3), procuring movable property of any kind, being property required by one or more of the scheduled authorities and bodies, and selling it to such of those authorities and bodies as require it;

(*m*) subject to subsection (3), assembling, installing, commissioning or maintaining any equipment procured and sold in pursuance of paragraph (*l*);

(*n*) providing on commercial terms—

(i) short-term credit in cases where a payment falls to be made by the Crown Agents, as agents of any scheduled authority or body, before the principal has done any of the things mentioned in section 8 (2) (*a*) and (*b*); or

(ii) subject to subsection (3), credit in connection with the sale of any movable property in pursuance of subsection (1) (*b*) or paragraph (*l*).

(3) The following powers of the Crown Agents under subsection (1), namely—

(*a*) the power under subsection (1) (*a*) to procure movable property in pursuance of subsection (2) (*l*);

(*b*) the power under subsection (1) (*a*) to provide any of the services mentioned in subsection (2) (*m*);

(*c*) the power under subsection (1) (*a*) to provide credit as mentioned in subsection (2) (*n*) (ii);

(*d*) the power under subsection (1) (*b*) to procure movable property; and

(*e*) the power under subsection (1) (*b*) to sell property procured under subsection (1) (*b*) to a person other than a scheduled authority or body,

shall be exercisable only with the consent of the Minister.

(4) Where as agents of any scheduled authority or body the Crown Agents receive any sum for disbursement or investment on behalf of the principal, they shall have power in their own right, pending the disbursement or investment of that sum on behalf of the principal, to make use of it for their own benefit by investing it in their own name in accordance with regulations.

(5) The Minister may by order confer on the Crown Agents power in their own right to carry on anywhere in the world any activity not authorised by subsection (1).

(6) Any order under subsection (5) conferring power to carry on any activity may be framed so as to confer power to carry on that activity only in accordance with conditions specified in the order.

(7) No order shall be made under subsection (5) unless a draft of the order has been laid before Parliament and approved by a resolution of each House of Parliament.

Ancillary powers

6.—(1) Subject to the provisions of this section, the Crown Agents shall have power to do anywhere in the world anything which is calculated to facilitate the carrying on of the activities authorised by or under sections 4 and 5 or is incidental or conducive to the carrying on of any of those activities, including, without prejudice to the generality of the preceding provision, power to acquire, hold and dispose of interests in other bodies corporate and to form or take part in forming bodies corporate.

(2) Except with the consent of the Minister the Crown Agents shall not have power in their own right—

(*a*) to acquire any interest in a body corporate; or

(*b*) to transfer any interest of theirs in a wholly owned subsidiary of the Crown Agents to a person other than—

(i) another wholly owned subsidiary of the Crown Agents; or

(ii) a person who is to hold it as nominee of the Crown Agents or of a wholly owned subsidiary of the Crown Agents;

(*c*) to form or take part in forming a body corporate; or

(*d*) to enter into a partnership or any other form of joint venture with any person other than a subsidiary of the Crown Agents.

(3) The Crown Agents—

(*a*) shall not have power in their own right—

(i) to acquire any land otherwise than for occupation or (as regards rights in or over land) enjoyment by the Crown Agents or a subsidiary of the Crown Agents; or

(ii) to guarantee any obligation (however arising) incurred by any other person not being such a subsidiary; and

(*b*) except with the consent of the Minister, shall not have power in their own right to guarantee any obligation (however arising) incurred by such a subsidiary.

(4) Nothing in this section shall—

(*a*) give the Crown Agents power to engage in their own right in any field of activity not expressly authorised by or under section 5; or

(*b*) preclude the Crown Agents from holding any property or right, meeting any liability or fulfilling any obligation which under section 2 vests in them on the appointed day.

Duty to act as agents of certain governments etc. on request

7. Except in so far as the Minister may otherwise direct, it shall be the duty of the Crown Agents, if so requested by a scheduled authority or body being either—

(*a*) a government within paragraph 1 of Part 1 of Schedule 3; or

(*b*) a public authority or public body established under the law of any colony or associated state or of any country or territory outside Her Majesty's dominions in which Her Majesty has jurisdiction in right of Her Government in the United Kingdom,

to carry on as agents of that authority or body such of the activities authorised by or under section 4 as are specified in the request, and to do so on terms similar to those on which they carry on the activities in question for other scheduled authorities and bodies.

Pre-funding of agency activities

8.—(1) Where as agents of any scheduled authority or body the Crown Agents undertake any activity involving the making of payments by them on behalf of the principal, the following provisions of this section shall apply.

(2) It shall be the duty of the Crown Agents to ensure, so far as they are able to do so, that before any particular payment falls to be made by them on behalf of the principal, the principal will have either—

(*a*) paid or caused to be paid to them a sum sufficient to enable them to make the payment; or

(*b*) caused to be issued to them an irrevocable letter of credit that will enable them to recover the sum required to make the payment.

(3) Subject to subsection (5), any sum which the Crown Agents receive for disbursement or investment on behalf of the principal may, pending its disbursement or investment on his behalf, be invested by the Crown Agents in their own name and for their own benefit in accordance with regulations made under section 5 (4).

(4) As consideration for their use of any sum invested by them for their own benefit under subsection (3) the Crown Agents shall be liable to pay interest thereon to the principal; and the Crown Agents shall not be liable to account to the principal for any profit accruing to them from that use.

(5) Where—

(*a*) the Crown Agents receive for disbursement or investment on behalf of the principal a sum which, or a part of which, will not be needed by them for that purpose until a future date; and

(*b*) the period from the receipt of that sum to the date when it, or that part of it, will be, or is likely to be, so needed is long enough for it to be appropriate, as a matter of good investment management, for the Crown Agents to invest the sum, or that part of it, on behalf of the principal,

the Crown Agents shall invest the sum, or that part of it, on behalf of the principal at his risk in accordance with his general or specific instructions or, in default of such instructions, by placing it on deposit at his risk at a bank.

In this subsection " bank " means the Bank of England or—

(i) in relation to any time before such date as the Minister may, after consultation with the Treasury, determine, a bank which is both an authorised dealer and an authorised depositary as respectively defined in section 42 (1) of the Exchange Control Act 1947; and

(ii) in relation to any time on or after that date, a recognised bank within the meaning of the Banking Act 1979, or the Post Office in the exercise of its powers to provide banking services.

(6) Where—

(*a*) a payment falls to be made on some future date by the Crown Agents on behalf of the principal; and

(*b*) to enable them to make that payment the Crown Agents need to realise investments for the time being held by them on behalf of the principal in consequence of subsection (5),

the Crown Agents may realise the necessary investments a reasonable time before the payment falls to be made.

(7) Where the Crown Agents realise any investments in pursuance of subsection (6), subsections (3) and (5) shall apply in the case of the proceeds as they apply in the case of any other sum received by them for disbursement or investment on behalf of the principal.

Duties with respect to management of activities

9.—(1) The Crown Agents shall at any time when the Minister so requires—

(*a*) undertake a review of the affairs of the Crown Agents and their subsidiaries for the purpose of determining how the management of the activities of the Crown Agents and their subsidiaries can most efficiently be organised; and

(*b*) make a report to the Minister on the Crown Agents' conclusions arising from the review.

(2) The Minister shall lay before each House of Parliament a copy of any report under subsection (1), and may, after doing so and consulting the Crown Agents, give the Crown Agents such directions as he considers appropriate for securing that the management of the activities of the Crown Agents and their subsidiaries is organised in the most efficient manner.

Power of Minister to obtain information from Crown Agents

10.—(1) The Crown Agents shall furnish the Minister with such information as he may from time to time require with respect to such of the matters mentioned in subsection (2) as he may specify in writing.

(2) Those matters are the activities (past, present and future), the plans, the property and the financial position of the Crown Agents or of any subsidiary of the Crown Agents, and in particular (but without prejudice to the foregoing provision) the position with respect to any sums received by the Crown Agents from the Minister by way of loan or grant under this Act.

(3) Any information which the Crown Agents are required to furnish to the Minister under subsection (1) shall be furnished in such manner and at such time or times as he may specify in writing; but the Crown Agents shall only be required under that subsection to furnish information which they have or which they can reasonably be expected to obtain.

(4) The Crown Agents shall afford the Minister facilities for verifying any information furnished to him under this section in such manner and at such times as he may reasonably request.

Annual reports

11.—(1) After the end of each accounting year the Crown Agents shall, within such time as the Minister may direct, make to the Minister, in such form as he may direct, a report on the performance by them of their functions during that year and on their policies, programmes and plans.

(2) The report of the Crown Agents for any accounting year shall set out any direction given to them under this Act during that year, except any direction in the case of which the Minister has notified to the Crown Agents his opinion that it is against the national interest for it to be included in the report.

(3) The Minister shall lay a copy of every report made to him under this section before each House of Parliament.

Control by Crown Agents of subsidiaries

12.—(1) As regards any subsidiary of the Crown Agents, the Crown Agents—

(*a*) shall ensure that no person other than a member of the Crown Agents is appointed as a director of the subsidiary unless his appointment has been approved by the Minister or is made in accordance with any general arrangements for the appointment of directors of the subsidiary which are for the time being so approved;

(*b*) shall secure that (notwithstanding anything in the subsidiary's memorandum or articles of association) the subsidiary does not, either alone or in association with any other person, engage in any activity which the Crown Agents are not empowered to carry on; but

(*c*) shall not by virtue of paragraph (*b*) be obliged to prevent the subsidiary from carrying on with the consent of, or in accordance with the terms of any general authority given by, the Minister and in accordance with any conditions attached by him thereto, any activity which the Crown Agents would have power to carry on if the consent or authority had been given to them.

(2) As regards any wholly owned subsidiary of the Crown Agents, the Crown Agents shall secure that (notwithstanding anything in the subsidiary's memorandum or articles of association) the subsidiary does not, except with the consent of the Minister—

(*a*) issue any of its shares, stock or debentures to a person other than—

(i) the Crown Agents or another wholly owned subsidiary of the Crown Agents; or

(ii) a person who is to hold them as a nominee of the Crown Agents or of a wholly owned subsidiary of the Crown Agents; or

(*b*) transfer any interest of the subsidiary in another wholly owned subsidiary of the Crown Agents to a person not within paragraph (*a*) (i) or (ii).

Financial provisions

General financial duties of Crown Agents

13.—(1) Without prejudice to the following provisions of this section, it shall be the duty of the Crown Agents so to perform their functions, and so to exercise their control over their subsidiaries, as to secure that, taking one year with another, the combined revenues of the Crown Agents and their subsidiaries are not less than sufficient—

(*a*) to meet the total outgoings of the Crown Agents and their subsidiaries properly chargeable to revenue account; and

(*b*) to enable the Crown Agents and their subsidiaries to make such allocations to reserve as the Crown Agents consider adequate, and as may be necessary to comply with any directions given by the Minister under section 14.

(2) The Minister may determine, for any period specified in the determination, the overall rate of return which he considers it appropriate for the Crown Agents and their subsidiaries, taken as a whole, to achieve in that period; and the Minister shall give the Crown Agents notice of any determination under this subsection.

(3) In determining an overall rate of return for any period under subsection (2) the Minister shall among other things have regard to the overall rate of return which, in the absence of any determination under that subsection, he would expect the Crown Agents and their subsidiaries, taken as a whole, to achieve in that period with a view to satisfying the requirements of subsection (1).

(4) A determination under subsection (2)—

(*a*) shall be made only with the approval of the Treasury and after consultation with the Crown Agents;

(*b*) may relate to a period beginning before the date on which it is made; and

(*c*) may be varied by a further determination under that subsection relating to the same period.

(5) During any period as respects which a determination has been made under subsection (2) the Crown Agents shall perform their functions and exercise their control over their subsidiaries with a view to achieving in that period an overall rate of return not less than that specified by the determination as for the time being in force.

Directions by Minister as to reserves of Crown Agents and their wholly owned subsidiaries

14.—(1) The Miinster may from time to time, with the approval of the Treasury and after consultation with the Crown Agents, give the Crown Agents directions—

(*a*) requiring them to allocate to reserve generally or to reserve for a particular purpose, or to cause any wholly owned subsidiary of the Crown Agents so to allocate, either a specified amount or such amount as the Crown Agents consider adequate; or

(*b*) requiring them to re-allocate for a specified purpose, or to cause any such wholly owned subsidiary so to re-allocate, the whole or part of any amount previously allocated by the Crown Agents or the subsidiary to reserve for some other purpose; or

(*c*) with respect to the application by the Crown Agents or any such wholly owned subsidiary of amounts allocated to reserve;

but no such directions shall require any amount to be allocated, re-allocated or (subject to section 16 (3)) applied otherwise than for the purposes of the Crown Agents and their wholly owned subsidiaries.

(2) Directions under subsection (1) requiring the allocation of any amount to reserve may provide for it to be so allocated either at a specified time or during the course of a specified period.

Management of liquid assets of Crown Agents and their wholly owned subsidiaries

15. Any money for the time being standing to the credit of the Crown Agents, other than money held by them as agents, shall be held or invested by them in accordance with regulations; and the Crown Agents shall ensure that any money for the time being standing to the credit of any wholly owned subsidiary of the Crown Agents, other than money held by the subsidiary as agent, is held or invested by it in accordance with regulations.

Payments to Minister

16.—(1) If for any accounting year there is an excess of revenue of the Crown Agents over the total sum required by them—

(*a*) to meet the total outgoings of the Crown Agents properly chargeable to revenue account; and

(*b*) to enable the Crown Agents to make such allocations to reserve as they consider adequate, and as may be necessary to comply with any directions under section 14 requiring them to make allocations to reserve,

the Minister may, with the approval of the Treasury and after consultation with the Crown Agents, give the Crown Agents directions requiring them to pay the whole or part of the excess to the Minister.

(2) Subject to any directions given to them under subsection (1), the Crown Agents may deal with any such excess as is mentioned in that subsection either—

(*a*) by applying it for such of the purposes of the Crown Agents as they may determine; or

(*b*) by allocating it to reserve, whether generally or for a particular purpose,

or partly in one of those ways and partly in the other.

(3) The Minister may, with the approval of the Treasury and after consultation with the Crown Agents, direct the Crown Agents to pay to the Minister the whole or part of the sum for the time being standing to the credit of any reserve of the Crown Agents.

(4) Any sums received by the Minister in pursuance of this section shall be paid into the Consolidated Fund.

Crown Agents' commencing capital debt

17.—(1) The Crown Agents shall on the appointed day assume a debt due to the Minister (in this Act referred to as their " commencing capital debt ") in respect of the property and rights transferred to them by virtue of section 2.

(2) The amount of the Crown Agents' commencing capital debt shall be such as the Minister may, with the approval of the Treasury, specify by notice in writing given to the Crown Agents; and the Treasury shall be deemed to have issued to the Minister out of the National Loans Fund on the appointed day a sum equal to that amount.

(3) The arrangement is for repaying the Crown Agents' commencing capital debt, and, subject to the following provisions of this section, the other terms of that debt shall be such as the Minister may from time to time, after consultation with the Crown Agents, determine.

(4) For any part of the initial period interest shall be payable on the Crown Agents' commencing capital debt or any portion of that debt only if the Minister so determines; and for any part of that period for which interest on the debt or any portion thereof is payable, the rate of interest shall be such as the Minister may from time to time determine.

(5) As from the end of the initial period interest on the amount outstanding in respect of the principal of the Crown Agents' commencing capital debt shall be payable at such rate as the Minister may from time to time determine.

(6) Different rates may be determined under subsection (4) or (5) with respect to different portions of the debt.

(7) Any sums received by the Minister by way of interest on or repayment of the Crown Agents' commencing capital debt shall be paid into the National Loans Fund.

(8) The approval of the Treasury shall be required for any determination by the Minister under this section; but section 5 (2) of the National Loans Act 1968 (criteria for fixing or approving rates of interest) shall not apply to approval by the Treasury of a rate of interest on the Crown Agents' commencing capital debt or any portion thereof for any part of the initial period.

(9) For the purposes of this section " the initial period " means the period of five years or, if the Minister by order so provides, seven years beginning with the appointed day.

(10) No order shall be made under subsection (9) unless a draft thereof has been laid before and approved by a resolution of the House of Commons.

Borrowing powers of Crown Agents and their wholly owned subsidiaries

18.—(1) Subject to section 19, the Crown Agents may borrow money in accordance with the provisions of subsections (2) to (5), and not otherwise.

(2) The Crown Agents may borrow temporarily, by way of overdraft or otherwise—

(*a*) in sterling from the Minister; or

(*b*) with the consent of the Minister or in accordance with any general authority given by him, in sterling or a currency other than sterling from a person other than the Minister,

such sums as the Crown Agents may require for meeting their obligations and performing their functions or for enabling any of their wholly owned subsidiaries to meet the obligations and perform the functions of that subsidiary.

(3) The Crown Agents may borrow, otherwise than by way of temporary loan—

(*a*) in sterling from the Minister; or

(*b*) with the consent of the Minister, in sterling from the Commission of the European Communities or the European Investment Bank or in a currency other than sterling from a person other than the Minister,

such sums as the Crown Agents may require for any of the purposes mentioned in subsection (2).

(4) The Minister shall not give any consent or authority under subsection (2) or (3) except with the approval of the Treasury.

(5) The Crown Agents may borrow from any of their wholly owned subsidiaries without any consent, approval or other authority.

(6) It shall be the duty of the Crown Agents to secure that no wholly owned subsidiary of theirs borrows money otherwise than from the Crown Agents or another wholly owned subsidiary of the Crown Agents.

(7) References in this and the following section to borrowing by the Crown Agents or by a subsidiary of theirs do not include—

(*a*) receiving money in the capacity of an agent or in the capacity of the provider of any goods or services; or

(*b*) in the case of any sum received by the Crown Agents as agents, making use of it for the Crown Agents' own benefit as mentioned in section 5 (4).

Limit on certain liabilities of Crown Agents and their subsidiaries

19.—(1) The aggregate of the following amounts, namely—

(*a*) the amounts outstanding in respect of the principal of money borrowed by the Crown Agents under section 18 otherwise than from a wholly owned subsidiary of theirs;

(*b*) the amount outstanding in respect of the principal of the Crown Agents' commencing capital debt; and

(*c*) all liabilities which for the time being are to be taken into account for the purposes of this subsection by virtue of subsection (2),

shall not at any time exceed £50 million or such greater sum, not exceeding £80 million, as the Minister may from time to time, with the consent of the Treasury, by order specify.

(2) Where any asset is being leased or hired by the Crown Agents or any of their subsidiaries at any time in circumstances such that, in the relevant accounts, if made up to that time—

(*a*) that asset would be capitalised; and

(*b*) the present and future liabilities of the Crown Agents or the subsidiary, as the case may be, under the lease or hiring agreement would be shown,

the aggregate of those liabilities, as they would be shown in those accounts, shall be taken into account for the purposes of subsection (1) in its application to that time.

(3) For the purposes of subsection (2) "the relevant accounts" means:

(*a*) in the case of an asset leased or hired by the Crown Agents, a statement of accounts dealing with the Crown Agents and complying with any requirements duly notified to the Crown Agents under section 22 (4);

(*b*) in the case of an asset leased or hired by a subsidiary of the Crown Agents, a statement of consolidated accounts dealing with the Crown Agents and that subsidiary and complying with any such requirements.

(4) No order shall be made under subsection (1) unless a draft thereof has been laid before and approved by a resolution of the House of Commons.

(5) Section 18 (7) applies for the purposes of this section.

Grants and loans by Mnister

20.—(1) The Minister may, with the approval of the Treasury—

(*a*) make to the Crown Agents out of money provided by Parliamentary grants of such amounts as the Minister thinks fit;

(*b*) give the Crown Agents directions providing that the whole or part of a grant made under paragraph (*a*) is not to be used by them otherwise than—

(i) for the purposes of such of their functions as are specified in the directions or as the Minister may, with the approval of the Treasury, from time to time determine; and

(ii) in accordance with such conditions as are so specified or as the Minister may, with the like approval, from time to time determine.

(2) The Minister may, with the approval of the Treasury, lend to the Crown Agents any sums which they have power to borrow from him under section 18; and the Treasury may issue to the Minister out of the National Loans Fund any sums necessary to enable him to make loans under this subsection.

(3) Any loans made under subsection (2) shall be repaid to the Minister at such times and by such methods, and, subject to subsection (4), interest thereon shall be paid to him at such rates and at such times, as he may from time to time determine.

(4) In the case of any loan made to the Crown Agents under subsection (2) in the initial period, being a loan obtained by them for the purpose of repaying the whole or part of their commencing capital debt—

(*a*) interest on that loan or any portion thereof shall be payable for any part of the initial period only if the Minister so determines; and

(*b*) for any part of that period for which interest on that loan or any portion thereof is payable, the rate of interest shall be such as the Minister may from time to time determine.

(5) The approval of the Treasury shall be required for any determination by the Minister under subsection (3) or (4); but, in the case of a

loan to which subsection (4) applies, section 5 (2) of the National Loans Act 1968 (criteria for fixing or approving rates of interest) shall not apply to approval by the Treasury of a rate of interest on that loan or any portion thereof for any part of the initial period.

(6) All sums received by the Minister under subsection (3) or (4) shall be paid into the National Loans Fund.

(7) In respect of each financial year the Minister shall prepare, in such form as the Treasury may direct, an account of—

(*a*) any sums issued to him under subsection (2) or received by him under subsection (3) or (4); and

(*b*) any sums received by him by way of interest on, or repayment of, the Crown Agents' commencing capital debt,

and the disposal by him of any sums so received, and shall send the account to the Comptroller and Auditor General not later than the end of the month of November following the financial year to which it relates; and the Comptroller and Auditor General shall examine, certify and report on the account and lay copies of it and of his report before each House of Parliament.

(8) For the purposes of this section " the initial period " has the same meaning as it has for the purposes of section 17.

Treasury guarantees

21.—(1) The Treasury may guarantee, in such manner and on such conditions as they think fit, the repayment of the principal of, the payment of interest on, and the discharge of any other financial obligation in connection with, any sums borrowed by the Crown Agents from a person other than the Minister.

(2) Immediately after a guarantee is given under this section the Treasury shall lay a statement of the guarantee before each House of Parliament.

(3) Any sum required for fulfilling a guarantee given under this section shall be charged on and issued out of the Consolidated Fund.

(4) Where any sum is so issued for fulfilling any such guarantee—

(*a*) the Crown Agents shall make to the Treasury, at such time and in such manner as the Treasury may from time to time direct, payments of such amounts as the Treasury may so direct in or towards repayment of that sum and payments of interest on the amount outstanding for the time being in respect of that sum at such rate as the Treasury may so direct; and

(*b*) the Treasury shall, as soon as possible after the end of each financial year beginning with that in which the sum is issued and ending with that in which all liability in respect of the principal of the sum and in respect of interest thereon is finally discharged, lay before each House of Parliament a statement relating to the sum.

(5) Any sums received by the Treasury in pursuance of subsection (4) (*a*) shall be paid into the Consolidated Fund.

Accounts and audit

22.—(1) Subject to the following provisions of this section, it shall be the duty of the Crown Agents—

(*a*) to keep proper accounts and proper records in relation thereto; and (*b*) to prepare in respect of each accounting year a statement of accounts dealing with, and giving a true and fair view of the state of affairs, profit or loss, and source and application of funds of, the Crown Agents.

(2) If the Minister with the approval of the Treasury so directs, it shall be the duty of the Crown Agents to prepare, in respect of each accounting year during which the direction is in force, such of the following statements of accounts as are specified in the direction, namely a statement or statements of consolidated accounts dealing with, and giving a true and fair view of the state of affairs, profit or loss, and source and application of funds of—

(*a*) the Crown Agents and all of their subsidiaries; or

(*b*) the Crown Agents and one or more of their subsidiaries specified in the direction; or

(*c*) two or more subsidiaries of the Crown Agents so specified.

(3) A direction under subsection (2) requiring the preparation of a statement or statements of consolidated accounts dealing with the Crown Agents and all or one or more of their subsidiaries.

(*a*) may provide that where, in respect of any accounting year, the statement or statements prepared in accordance with the direction show the profit or loss of the Crown Agents for that year, the statement prepared in respect of that year under subsection (1) (*b*) need not contain a profit and loss account; and

(*b*) may provide that the statement prepared under subsection (1) (*b*) in respect of any accounting year during which the direction is in force need not contain a statement of the source and application of funds.

(4) Every statement of accounts prepared by the Crown Agents under this section shall conform to the best commercial standards and, subject to that, shall comply with any requirement which the Minister has, with the approval of the Treasury, notified in writing to the Crown Agents relating to—

(*a*) the information to be contained in the statement;

(*b*) the manner in which the information is to be presented; and

(*c*) the methods and principles according to which the statement is to be prepared.

(5) The accounts kept, and all statements prepared, by the Crown Agents in pursuance of the preceding provisions of this section shall be audited by auditors appointed for each accounting year by the Minister after consultation with the Crown Agents.

(6) A person shall not be qualified for appointment under subsection (5) unless he is a member of one or more bodies of accountants established in the United Kingdom and for the time being recognised for the purposes of section 161 (1) (*a*) of the Companies Act 1948 by the Secretary of State.

(7) As soon as the accounts kept, and the statement or statements prepared, by the Crown Agents in pursuance of the preceding provisions of this section have been audited, the Crown Agents shall send to the Minister a copy of the statement or statements, together with a copy of any report made by the auditors on the statement or statements or on the accounts of the Crown Agents; and the Minister shall lay a copy of every statement and report of which a copy is received by him in pursuance of this subsection before each House of Parliament.

(8) It shall be the duty of the Crown Agents to secure that the requirements of subsections (5) and (7) with respect to the accounts and statements relating to any particular accounting year are complied with

within seven months after the end of that year or within such longer period as the Minister may for any special reason allow in relation to that year.

Power of Minister to give directions with respect to financial matters

23.—(1) Without prejudice to any other power conferred on the Minister by this Act, the Minister may, with the approval of the Treasury and after consultation with the Crown Agents, give the Crown Agents directions with respect to any financial matter connected with any of the functions which they are performing or propose to perform in their own right (including the exercise of rights conferred by the holding of interests in bodies corporate).

(2) A direction under this section may be general or specific in character, but shall not confer on the Crown Agents power to do anything which they would not have power to do apart from the direction.

Duty to insure against insurable financial risks

24. It shall be the duty of the Crown Agents to secure, so far as is reasonably practicable, that they and their subsidiaries are appropriately insured against financial risks arising from the activities in which they engage, whether as agents or in their own right.

The Crown Agents Holding and Realisation Board

The Crown Agents Holding and Realisation Board

25.—(1) On the appointed day there shall come into being a body corporate named the Crown Agents Holding and Realisation Board (in this Act referred to as " the Board ") which shall function under and in accordance with the provisions of this section and Schedule 5 and such of the other provisions of this Act as (by virtue of that Schedule or otherwise) apply in relation to the Board.

(2) The Board shall consist of the persons for the time being holding office as members of the Crown Agents; and the persons for the time being holding office as the chairman and the deputy chairman of the Crown Agents shall be respectively the chairman and the deputy chairman of the Board.

(3) Subject to the provisions of Schedule 5, it shall be the duty of the Board, acting in accordance with such instructions as may from time to time be given by the Minister under paragraph 21 of that Schedule—

(*a*) to secure the realisation of the Board's assets and the assets of the Board's subsidiaries and the application of the proceeds in or towards discharging the liabilities of the Board and their subsidiaries;

(*b*) to secure that while any particular asset of the Board or any of the Board's subsidiaries remains unrealised, it is held and managed as advantageously as is consistent with its eventual realisation; and

(*c*) to discharge the liabilities of the Board and of each of their subsidiaries so far as not discharged in pursuance of paragraph (*a*).

(4) The Board are not to be regarded as servants or agents of the Crown or as enjoying any status, privilege or immunity of the Crown, and their property is not to be regarded as property of, or held on behalf of, the Crown.

(5) Schedule 5 shall have effect with respect to the Board, their powers and duties, and their eventual dissolution.

Position with respect to recoverable grants paid to unincorporated Agents

26.—(1) The liability of the unincorporated Agents to make, at the direction of the Minister, repayments in respect of the sums totalling £175 million paid to them by the Minister by way of recoverable grant (that is to say the sums of £85 million and £90 million so paid on 24th December 1974 and 28th March 1978 respectively) shall cease on the day before the appointed day, and shall accordingly not become a liability of the Crown Agents or the Board.

(2) If for any accounting year—

(*a*) there is an excess of revenue of the Board over the total sums properly chargeable by the Board to revenue account; and

(*b*) under paragraph 14 (2) of Schedule 5 the Minister has power to direct the Board to pay the whole or a part of that excess into the Consolidated Fund,

then, in deciding whether to give the Board such a direction, the Minister shall have regard to the fact that the sum of £175 million mentioned in subsection (1) would have been recoverable at his direction but for that subsection.

Miscellaneous and general

Exemptions

27.—(1) The Board and every wholly owned subsidiary of the Board shall be exempt from corporation tax

(2) Stamp duty shall not be chargeable on any declaration of trust in respect of any land situated outside the United Kingdom which is made by the Minister on the appointed day for the benefit of the Crown Agents.

(3) The provisions of the Moneylenders Acts 1900 to 1927 and the Moneylenders Acts (Northern Ireland) 1900 to 1969 shall not apply—

(*a*) to the Crown Agents or the Board; or

(*b*) to any body corporate the whole of whose issued share capital is held by or on behalf of the Board.

Provisions as to revenue of, and alienations by, former Agents

28.—(1) Revenue received (before or after the passing of this Act) by the former Agents or any of them on behalf of the Crown shall not be treated as being, or as having at any time been, required to be paid into the Consolidated Fund by virtue of section 1 of the Civil List Act 1952 (payment of hereditary revenues into that Fund) or any corresponding earlier enactment.

(2) The former Agents shall be deemed not to be, and never to have been, subject to any restraint on alienation imposed on the Crown by section 5 of the Crown Lands Act 1702.

(3) In this section " the former Agents " means the persons from time to time holding office under the Crown (whether as the Crown Agents for Oversea Governments and Administration or by any other name) as the persons appointed to act as agents or trustees for oversea governments and administrations, and in subsection (2) includes persons who have ceased to hold office as aforesaid.

Administrative expenses

29. Any administrative expenses incurred by the Minister in connection with the provisions of this Act shall be defrayed out of money provided by Parliament.

Orders, regulations and consents

30.—(1) An order or regulations made by the Minister under any provision of this Act—

(*a*) may make different provision in relation to different cases or circumstances;

(*b*) may make the consent or approval of the Minister material for the purposes of any provision of the order or regulations; and

(*c*) may contain such supplementary, incidental and transitional provisions as appear expedient to the Minister.

(2) Any power of the Minister to make an order under any provision of this Act shall be exercisable by statutory instrument.

(3) Any order made under any provision of this Act, except—

(*a*) an order under section 1 (1) or 31 (2) or paragraph 24 (2) of Schedule 5; and

(*b*) an order which is required to be laid before Parliament or the House of Commons in draft,

shall be subject to annulment in pursuance of a resolution of either House of Parliament.

(4) Any consent given by the Minister under this Act—

(*a*) may be given either generally or so as to apply only to the doing of specified things by or in relation to specified persons;

(*b*) may, if given generally, be revoked by the Minister; and

(*c*) may in any case be given either unconditionally or subject to such conditions as the Minister thinks fit.

(5) Where any body corporate is given power by or under this Act to do something only with the consent of the Minister, then, if that consent is given subject to conditions, the body corporate shall not have power to do anything by virtue of that consent except in accordance with the conditions.

Interpretation

31.—(1) In this Act—

" accounting year " means, subject to subsection (2) and to any order under subsection (3) altering the meaning of that expression in relation to the Crown Agents, a period of twelve months ending with the 31st December in any year;

" the appointed day " means the day appointed by the Minister under section 1 (1);

" the Board " means the Crown Agents Holding and Realisation Board;

" commencing capital debt ", in relation to the Crown Agents, has the meaning given by section 17 (1);

" the Crown Agents " means the body corporate established by section 1;

" financial year ", in relation to the unincorporated Agents, means a period of twelve months ending with the 31st December in any year;

" functions " includes powers and duties;

" the Minister " means the Minister of Overseas Development;

" pension ", in relation to any person, means a pension, whether contributory or not, of any kind whatever payable to or in respect of him, and includes an allowance or a gratuity so payable (whether on retirement or otherwise) and a return of contributions to a pension fund or of insurance premiums, with or without interest or any other addition;

" performance ", in relation to functions, includes the exercise of powers as well as the performance of duties, and " perform " shall be construed accordingly;

" regulations " means regulations made by the Minister with the approval of the Treasury;

" scheduled authority or body " has the meaning given by section 3 (3);

" subsidiary " shall be construed in accordance with section 154 of the Companies Act 1948 or section 148 of the Companies Act (Northern Ireland) 1960, and " wholly owned subsidiary " shall be construed in accordance with section 150 (4) of that Act of 1948 or section 144 (5) of that Act of 1960;

" the unincorporated Agents " has the meaning given by section 1 (2) (*b*).

(2) For the purposes of this Act the first accounting year shall be the period of whatever length beginning with such date (whether the same as, or earlier or later than, the appointed day) as the Minister may by order prescribe and ending with the 31st December next after the appointed day.

(3) The Minister may, after consultation with the Crown Agents, by order direct that, in relation to the Crown Agents, the definition of " accounting year " in subsection (1) shall have effect with the substitution for the 31st December (or any date for the time being substituted therefor under this subsection of such date as may be prescribed by the order; and where an order is made under this subsection then, in relation to the Crown Agents, the duration of the accounting year in which the first altered accounting year is to begin, or of the preceding accounting year, shall be shortened or extended, as the order may provide, by not more than six months so as to end with the date prescribed by the order.

(4) Any provision of this Act conferring a power to give directions or instructions shall be construed as imposing, on any person to whom directions or instructions are given thereunder, a duty to comply with those directions or instructions.

Consequential amendments, transitional provisions and repeals

32.—(1) The enactment mentioned in Part I of Schedule 6 shall have effect as from the appointed day subject to the amendments there specified (being amendments consequential on the provisions of this Act).

(2) This Act shall have effect subject to the transitional provisions contained in Part II of Schedule 6.

(3) The enactments mentioned in Schedule 7 are hereby repealed as from the appointed day to the extent specified in the third column of that Schedule.

Citation and extent

33.—(1) This Act may be cited as the Crown Agents Act 1979.

(2) This Act extends to Northern Ireland.

SCHEDULES

Section 1

SCHEDULE 1

Supplementary Provisions as to Constitution Etc. of Crown Agents

Appointment and tenure of members

1. It shall be the duty of the Minister—

(a) to satisfy himself, before he appoints a person to be a member of the Crown Agents, that he will have no such financial or other interest as is likely to affect prejudicially the performance of his functions as a member; and

(b) to satisfy himself from time to time with respect to each member that he has no such interest;

and a person who is a member or whom the Minister proposes to appoint as a member shall, whenever requested by the Minister to do so, furnish the Minister with such information as he may specify with a view to carrying out his duty under this paragraph.

2. Subject to the following provisions of this Schedule, a person shall hold and vacate office as a member or the chairman or deputy chairman of the Crown Agents in accordance with the terms of the instrument appointing him to that office.

3. A person may at any time resign his office as a member or the chairman or deputy chairman by giving to the Minister a signed notice in writing stating that he resigns that office.

4. Where a member becomes or ceases to be the chairman or deputy chairman, the Minister may vary the terms of the instrument appointing him a member so as to alter the date on which he is to vacate office as a member.

5. If the chairman or deputy chairman ceases to be a member, he shall cease to be the chairman or deputy chairman, as the case may be.

6.—(1) If the Minister is satisfied that a member—

(a) has been absent from meetings of the Crown Agents for a period longer than three consecutive months without the permission of the Crown Agents; or

(b) has become bankrupt or made an arrangement with his creditors; or

(c) is incapacitated by physical or mental illness; or

(d) is otherwise unable or unfit to discharge the functions of a member,

the Minister may declare his office as a member vacant, and shall notify the declaration in such manner as he thinks fit; and thereupon the office shall become vacant.

(2) In the application of sub-paragraph (1) to Scotland, for the references in paragraph (b) to a member's having become bankrupt and to a member's having made an arrangement with his creditors there shall be substituted respectively a reference to sequestration of a member's estate having been awarded and to a member's having made a trust deed for behoof of his creditors or a composition contract.

Remuneration etc. of members

7. The Crown Agents shall pay to each of their members such remuneration and such reasonable allowances in respect of expenses as the Minister may determine with the approval of the Minister for the Civil Service.

8.—(1) If the Minister so determines in the case of any person who is or has been a member of the Crown Agents, the Crown Agents shall pay or make arrangements for the payment of such pension to or in respect of that person as the Minister may determine.

(2) Where a person ceases to be a member of the Crown Agents otherwise than on the expiry of his term of office and it appears to the Minister that there are special circumstances which make it right for that person to receive compensation, the Minister may direct the Crown Agents to make to that person a payment of such amount as the Minister may determine.

(3) The approval of the Minister for the Civil Service shall be required for any determination or direction by the Minister under this paragraph.

Disqualification of members of Crown Agents for House of Commons and Northern Ireland Assembly

9. As from the appointed day the references to the Crown Agents for Overseas Governments and Administrations in Part II of Schedule 1 to the House of Commons Disqualification Act 1975 and Part II of Schedule 1 to the Northern Ireland Assembly Disqualification Act 1975 (bodies of which all members are disqualified) are to be read as referring to the Crown Agents and not the unincorporated Agents.

Proceedings

10. The quorum of the Crown Agents and the arrangements relating to their meetings shall be such as the Crown Agents may determine.

11.—(1) A member who is in any way directly or indirectly interested in a contract made or proposed to be made by the Crown Agents (whether as agents or in their own right), or in any other matter whatsoever which falls to be considered by them, shall disclose the nature of his interest at a meeting of the Crown Agents, and the disclosure shall be recorded in the minutes of the meeting.

(2) The member shall not—

(*a*) in the case of any such contract, take part in any deliberation or decision of the Crown Agents with respect to the contract; and

(*b*) in the case of any other matter, take part in any deliberation or decision of the Crown Agents with respect to the matter if the Crown Agents decide that the interest in question might prejudicially affect the member's consideration of the matter.

(3) For the purposes of this paragraph, a notice given by a member at a meeting of the Crown Agents to the effect that he is a member of a specified body corporate or firm and is to be regarded as interested in any contract which is made with the body corporate or firm after the date of the notice, and in any other matter whatsoever concerning the body corporate or firm which falls to be considered by the Crown Agents after that date, shall be a sufficient disclosure of his interest.

(4) A member need not attend in person at a meeting of the Crown Agents in order to make a disclosure which he is required to make under this paragraph, if he takes reasonable steps to secure that the disclosure is made by a notice which is taken into consideration and read at such a meeting.

12. The validity of any proceedings of the Crown Agents shall not be affected by any vacancy among the members or by any defect in the appointment of a member or by any failure to comply with the requirements of paragraph 11.

Staff

13.—(1) The Crown Agents may appoint, on such terms and conditions as they think fit, such officers and servants of the Crown Agents as they think fit.

(2) In the case of any person to be employed by them on and after the appointed day who immediately before that day was employed by the unincorporated Agents, the Crown Agents shall ensure that, so long as he is engaged in duties reasonably comparable to those in which he was engaged immediately before he joined the Crown Agents' staff, the terms and conditions of his employment, taken as a whole, are not less favourable than those which he then enjoyed.

(3) In relation to any person who—

(*a*) is in the employment of the unincorporated Agents immediately before the appointed day; and

(*b*) is as from that day employed by the Crown Agents,

Schedule 13 to the Employment Protection (Consolidation) Act 1978 (ascertainment, for the purposes of that Act and section 119 of the Employment Protection Act 1975, of the length of an employee's period of employment and whether that employment has been continuous) shall have effect as if his employment under the unincorporated Agents had been Crown employment within the meaning of paragraph 19 of that Schedule.

14.—(1) The Crown Agents may pay such pensions as they think fit to or in respect of any of their employees, make such payments as they think fit towards the provision of pensions to or in respect of any of their employees, or provide and maintain such schemes as they think fit (whether contributory or not) for the payment of pensions to or in respect of any of their employees, and may manage the investment of funds for the trustees of any such scheme.

(2) If an employee of the Crown Agents becomes a member and was by reference to his employment by the Crown Agents a participant in a pension scheme maintained by the Crown Agents for the benefit of any of their employees—

(a) the Crown Agents may determine that his service as a member shall be treated for the purposes of the scheme as service as an employee of the Crown Agents whether or not any benefits are to be payable to or in respect of him by virtue of paragraph 8 (1) ; but

(b) if the Crown Agents determine as aforesaid in his case, any discretion as to the benefits payable to or in respect of him which the scheme confers on the Crown Agents shall be exercised by them only with the consent of the Minister given with the approval of the Minister for the Civil Service.

15.—(1) Except so far as they are satisfied that adequate machinery exists for achieving the purposes mentioned in sub-paragraph (2), it shall be the duty of the Crown Agents to consult any organisation appearing to them to be appropriate with a view to the conclusion between the Crown Agents and that organisation of such agreements as appear to the parties to be desirable with respect to the establishment and maintenance of machinery for the purposes mentioned in that sub-paragraph.

(2) Those purpose are—

(a) the settlement by negotiation of terms and conditions of employment of persons employed by the Crown Agents and their wholly owned subsidiaries;

(b) the resolution of trade disputes, within the meaning of the Trade Union and Labour Relations Act 1974;

(c) the promotion and encouragement of measures affecting efficiency, in any respect, in the carrying on of their activities by the Crown Agents and their wholly owned subsidiaries; and

(d) the discussion of other matters of mutual interest to the parties to the agreements.

Performance of functions

16. The Crown Agents may authorise any member or employee of the Crown Agents to perform on behalf of the Crown Agents such of the Crown Agents' functions (including the power conferred on the Crown Agents by this paragraph) as are specified in the authorisation.

Instruments and contracts

17. The fixing of the common seal of the Crown Agents shall be authenticated by the signature of their secretary or some other person authorised by them to act for that purpose.

18.—(1) A document purporting to be duly executed under the seal of the Crown Agents shall be received in evidence and shall, unless the contrary is proved, be deemed to be so executed.

(2) A document purporting to be signed on behalf of the Crown Agents shall be received in evidence and shall, unless the contrary is proved, be deemed to be so signed.

Section 2

SCHEDULE 2

SUPPLEMENTARY PROVISIONS AS TO VESTING OF PROPERTY ETC.

1. In this Schedule " the former Agents " means the persons who at any material time before the appointed day held office under the Crown (whether as the Crown Agents for Oversea Governments and Administrations or by any other name) as the persons appointed to act as agents or trustees for oversea governments and administrations.

2. Every agreement to which the former Agents or any of them in their capacity as such were a party immediately before the appointed day, whether in writing or not and whether or not of such nature that rights, liabilities and obligations under it could be assigned by the former Agents or any of them, shall have effect as from that day as if—

(a) the Crown Agents had been a party to the agreement;

(*b*) for any reference (however worded, and whether express or implied) to the former Agents or any of them there were substituted, as respects anything falling to be done on or after the appointed day, a reference to the Crown Agents; and

(*c*) for any reference (however worded, and whether express or implied) to any member or officer of the former Agents, not being a party to the agreement and beneficially interested therein, there were substituted, as respects anything falling to be done on or after the appointed day, a reference to such person as the Crown Agents may appoint, or, in default of appointment, to the member or officer of the Crown Agents who corresponds as nearly as may be to the member or officer of the former Agents.

3.—(1) Every agreement, whether in writing or not, and every document (not being an agreement to which paragraph 2 applies or an enactment) which refers whether specifically or generally to the former Agents or any of them in their capacity as such shall be construed in accordance with the provisions of that paragraph so far as applicable.

(2) The agreements to which sub-paragraph (1) applies include any agreement to which paragraph 2 would apply but for the fact that rights, liabilities or obligations under it which were previously vested in one of the former Agents as a party to the agreement are, immediately before the appointed day, vested in a person who is not a party to the agreement.

4. Without prejudice to the generality of paragraphs 2 and 3, where any right, liability or obligation vests in the Crown Agents by virtue of this Act, the Crown Agents and all other persons shall, as from the appointed day, have the same rights, powers and remedies (and, in particular, the same rights as to the taking or resisting of legal proceedings or the making or resisting of applications to any authority) for ascertaining, perfecting or enforcing that right, liability or obligation as they would have had if it had at all times been a right, liability or obligation of the Crown Agents.

5. Without prejudice to the generality of paragraphs 2 and 3, any legal proceedings or applications to any authority pending on the appointed day—

(*a*) by the Crown in connection with the unincorporated Agents, or by the unincorporated Agents; or

(*b*) against—

(i) the Crown in connection with the unincorporated Agents or any of them; or

(ii) the former Agents of any of them; or

(iii) any other person as the successor of any of the former Agents,

shall, so far as they relate to any property, right, liability or obligation vesting in the Crown Agents by virtue of this Act or to any agreement or document which has effect in accordance with paragraph 2 or 3, be continued by or against the Crown Agents to the exclusion (where applicable) of the Crown or, as the case may be, the relevant person or persons mentioned in sub-paragraph (*a*) or (*b*).

6.—(1) If any question arises whether any particular item of property or any particular right, liability or obligation vested or will vest in the Crown Agents on the appointed day by virtue of this Act, that question shall be referred to and determined by the Minister.

(2) A certificate issued by or under the authority of the Minister and stating the result of any determination under sub-paragraph (1) shall be conclusive for all purposes.

Section 3

SCHEDULE 3

Scheduled Authorities and Bodies

Part I

Descriptions of Authorities and Bodies for whom Crown Agents can Act as Agents

1. The government of any colony or associated state or of any country or territory outside Her Majesty's dominions in which Her Majesty has jurisdiction in right of Her Government in the United Kingdom.

2. The government of any other country or territory outside the United Kingdom (including, in the case of any territory which is under both a local and a central government, the local as well as the central government).

3. Any department of the Government of the United Kingdom or of the Government of Northern Ireland, and any Minister of the Crown in charge of such a department.

4. Any organisation whose members consist of or include two or more of the following, namely sovereign Powers or the Governments of such Powers.

5. Any non-profit-making authority or body of an international character established by or under any treaty or other international agreement.

6. Any public authority or public body established under the law of—

(*a*) any part of the United Kingdom; or

(*b*) any country or territory outside the United Kingdom.

7. Any organisation or body established for charitable purposes.

8. Any body corporate the whole of whose issued share capital is held, directly or through a nominee, by an authority or body within any of paragraphs 1 to 7.

9. Any body corporate for the time being approved by the Minister for the purposes of this paragraph, being a body more than half (but less than the whole)' of whose issued share capital is held as mentioned in paragraph 8.

10. The trustees of any pension fund maintained by any authority or body within any of paragraphs 1 to 9.

11. Any body corporate for the time being approved by the Minister for the purposes of this paragraph, being a co-operative established under the law of any country or territory outside the United Kingdom.

Part II

Supplementary

1. If any question arises whether a particular authority or body is a scheduled authority or body, that question shall be referred to and determined by the Minister.

2. A determination by the Minister under the preceding paragraph—

(*a*) shall be conclusive for the purposes of this Act; but

(*b*) may (without prejudice to its previous operation) be revoked by the Minister at any time if satisfied that the authority or body to which it relates has, in consequence of a change in its status or for any other reason, ceased to be or, as the case may be, become a scheduled authority or body.

Section 4

SCHEDULE 4

Authorised Agency Activities

1. Procuring movable property of any kind.
2. Making arrangements for and in connection with the conveyance of movable property of any kind to any destination (including arrangements for its insurance and inspection).
3. Obtaining professional advice on projects, and negotiating and making contracts for the preparation of projects and the carrying out of feasibility studies.
4. Acquiring and disposing of land, doing anything in connection with any land, and arranging for anything to be done in connection with any land.
5. Negotiating and making contracts for the design, production or supply of coins, medallions, currency notes, postage stamps and other documents.
6. Selling coins, medallions, currency notes and postage stamps to dealers.
7. Recruiting staff.
8. Making travel and other arrangements for staff and other persons.
9. Paying remuneration, allowances, expenses and pensions.
10. Accepting funds for investment on behalf of the principal and managing the investment of funds so accepted, but only at the risk of, and (subject to section 8 (5)) in accordance with general or specific instructions given by, the principal.

11. Making or receiving payments in accordance with standing or other instructions given by the principal.
12. Managing operations relating to the raising and servicing of loans.
13. Administering and managing the provision or utilisation of financial, technical or other assistance of any kind.
14. Negotiating and making contracts for the assembly, installation, commissioning or maintenance of equipment.

Section 25

SCHEDULE 5

Provisions Relating to Crown Agents Holding and Realisation Board

Absence of members from Board meetings

1. The power of the Minister to declare vacant the office of a member of the Crown Agents by virtue of paragraph 6 (1) (*a*) of Schedule 1 shall include power to declare vacant the office of such a member who, in his capacity as member of the Board, has been absent from meetings of the Board for a period longer than three consecutive months without the permission of the Board.

Payment of allowances to members

2. The Board shall pay to each of their members such reasonable allowances in respect of expenses as the Minister may determine with the approval of the Minister for the Civil Service.

Proceedings

3. Paragraphs 10 to 12 of Schedule 1 shall apply to the Board as they apply to the Crown Agents.

Performance of functions

4. The Board may authorise any member of the Board or any employee of the Crown Agents to perform on behalf of the Board such of the Board's functions (including the power conferred on the Board by this paragraph) as are specified in the authorisation.

Instruments and contracts

5. The fixing of the common seal of the Board shall be authenticated by the signature of any person authorised by the Board to act for the purpose.

6. Paragraph 18 of Schedule 1 shall apply in relation to the Board as it applies in relation to the Crown Agents.

Vesting in Board of property, rights and liabilities

7.—(1) On the appointed day there shall by virtue of this Act vest in the Board the interest of Four Millbank Holdings Limited in shares issued by the following companies (in this paragraph referred to as "the Companies"), namely Four Millbank Investments Limited and Four Millbank Securities Limited.

(2) In so far as the rights, liabilities and obligations referred to in section 2 (1) (*b*) consist of rights, liabilities and obligations enjoyed by, or incumbent on, the Crown in connection with—

(*a*) either of the Companies or any subsidiary of either of them; or

(*b*) any shares in either of the Companies; or

(*c*) any property which immediately before the appointed day is vested in either of the Companies or in any subsidiary of either of them,

those rights, liabilties and obligations shall (subject to sub-paragraph (3)) on the appointed day vest in the Board by virtue of this Act, and not in the Crown Agents.

(3) The rights, liabilities and obligations which vest in the Board by virtue of sub-paragraph (2) shall not include any right, liability or obligation under or arising out of a contract of employment.

(4) In so far as any agreement or other document to which paragraph 2 or paragraph 3 (1) of Schedule 2 applies relates to any property, right, liability or obligation vesting in the Board by virtue of sub-paragraph (1) or (2) of this paragraph, paragraph 2 of that Schedule shall, in its application to that agreement or document, have effect—

(a) as if any reference to the Crown Agents were a reference to the Board; and
(b) as if in paragraph 2 (c) the resulting reference to the officer of the Board who corresponds as nearly as may be to the officer of the former Agents were a reference to the officer of the Crown Agents acting for the Board who so corresponds.

(5) Paragraphs 4, 5 and 6 of Schedule 2 shall have effect in relation to the Board as they have effect in relation to the Crown Agents, any reference to paragraph 2 or paragraph 3 of that Schedule being for this purpose read as a reference to that paragraph as modified by sub-paragraph (4) of this paragraph.

(6) If it appears to the Minister that any liability which has vested in the Crown Agents under section 2 is one which should be borne by the Board rather than by the Crown Agents, he may instruct the Board to indemnify the Crown Agents against that liability and any expenses which have been or may be incurred by the Crown Agents in connection therewith.

(7) In this paragraph " the Crown " means the Crown in right of Her Majesty's Government in the United Kingdom.

Ancillary powers

8.—(1) Subject to the provisions of this paragraph, the Board shall have power to do anywhere in the world anything which is calculated to facilitate the performance of their functions (other than those conferred on them by this sub-paragraph) or is incidental or conducive to the performance of any such function, including, without prejudice to the generality of the preceding provision, power to acquire, hold and dispose of interests in other bodies corporate and to form or take part in forming bodies corporate.

(2) The Board, if so instructed by the Minister under paragraph 21, shall (notwithstanding sub-paragraph (3) (g)) have power—
(a) to remit the whole or part of any liability towards the Board of any subsidiary of the Board; and
(b) to cause any such subsidiary to remit the whole or part of any liability towards itself of any other subsidiary of the Board.

(3) Except with the consent of the Minister the Board shall not have power—
(a) to acquire any interest in a body corporate;
(b) to form or take part in forming a body corporate;
(c) to enter into a partnership or any other form of joint venture with any person other than a subsidiary of the Board;
(d) to acquire land;
(e) to guarantee any obligation (however arising) incurred by any person other than a subsidiary of the Board;
(f) to lend money to any person other than a subsidiary of the Board;
(g) as regards any debt to or other financial liability towards the Board, to accept in satisfaction thereof less than the full amount thereof in money or money's worth.

(4) The Board shall not have power—
(a) to employ staff;
(b) to use any office accommodation, office equipment or other office facilities except under arrangements made under sub-paragraph (5); or
(c) except with the consent of the Minister, to engage the services of any person as consultant or adviser to the Board.

(5) The Board may make arrangements with the Crown Agents for the use by the Board—
(a) of the services of any person in the employment of, or who acts as consultant or adviser to, the Crown Agents; and
(b) of any office accommodation, office equipment or other office facilities for the time being occupied or used by the Crown Agents in the course of their business;

and any such arrangements may provide for payment to be made by the Board to the Crown Agents in respect of any such use at such rates as may be agreed from time to time between the parties with the approval of the Minister.

(6) Nothing in this paragraph shall preclude the Board from holding any property or right, meeting any liability or fulfilling any obligation which under paragraph 7 vests in them on the appointed day.

Duties with respect to management of activities

9. Section 9 shall apply to the Board as it applies to the Crown Agents.

Power of Minister to obtain information from Board

10. Section 10 shall apply to the Board as it applies to the Crown Agents.

Annual reports

11. Section 11 shall apply to the Board as it applies to the Crown Agents.

Control by Board of subsidiaries

12.—(1) Subject to sub-paragraph (2), section 12 shall apply in relation to the Board and their subsidiaries as it applies in relation to the Crown Agents and their subsidiaries, but with the omission, in subsection (2), of " wholly owned ", wherever occurring.

(2) In the case of any subsidiary of the Board, the duty of the Board under section 12 (1) (*b*), as applied by sub-paragraph (1), shall not apply as regards—

(*a*) the doing of anything by the subsidiary for the purpose of realising any of the subsidiary's assets; or

(*b*) the doing by the subsidiary of anything mentioned in paragraph 8 (4).

Management of liquid assets of Board and their subsidiaries

13. Any money for the time being standing to the credit of the Board shall be held or invested by them in accordance with regulations; and the Board shall ensure that any money for the time being standing to the credit of any subsidiary of the Board is held or invested by it in accordance with regulations.

Application of surplus revenue of Board

14.—(1) If for any accounting year there is an excess of revenue of the Board over the total sums properly chargeable by the Board to revenue account, the excess shall be applied by the Board in such manner as the Minister, with the approval of the Treasury and after consultation with the Board, may direct.

(2) If it appears to the Minister, after consultation with the Board, that the whole or a part of any such excess is surplus to the requirements of the Board, he may under this paragraph, with the approval of the Treasury, direct the Board to pay the whole or, as the case may be, that part of that excess into the Consolidated Fund.

(3) The account required to be prepared by the Minister in respect of any financial year under section 20 (7) in its application to the Board shall include particulars of any sums required to be paid into the Consolidated Fund under this paragraph during that year.

Borrowing by the Board and their subsidiaries

15.—(1) Subject to paragraph 16, the Board may borrow money in accordance with the provisions of section 18 (2) to (4), as applied by sub-paragraph (2), and not otherwise.

(2) Subsections (2) to (4) of section 18 shall apply in relation to the Board and their subsidiaries as they apply in relation to the Crown Agents and their subsidiaries, but with the omission of " wholly owned ", wherever occurring.

(3) It shall be the duty of the Board to secure that, except with the consent of the Minister given with the approval of the Treasury, no subsidiary of theirs borrows money otherwise than from the Board or another subsidiary of the Board.

Limit on indebtedness of Board and their subsidiaries

16.—(1) The aggregate of the following amounts, namely—

(*a*) the amounts outstanding in respect of the principal of money borrowed by the Board under the provisions applied by paragraph 15 (2) otherwise than from a subsidiary of theirs; and

(*b*) the amounts outstanding in respect of the principal of money borrowed by any subsidiary of the Board otherwise than from the Board or another subsidiary of the Board, shall not at any time exceed £275 million or such greater sum, not exceeding £325 million, as the Minister may from time to time, with the consent of the Treasury, by order specify.

(2) No order shall be made under sub-paragraph (1) unless a draft thereof has been laid before and approved by a resolution of the House of Commons.

Grants and loans by Minister

17. Section 20 shall apply to the Board as it applies to the Crown Agents, but—

(*a*) as if in subsection (2) the reference to section 18 were a reference to the provisions applied by paragraph 15 (2) of this Schedule; and

(*b*) with the omission of—

(i) subsections (4), (7) (*b*) and (8);

(ii) the references to subsection (4) in subsections (3), (6) and (7); and

(iii) in subsection (5), the words from " or (4) " onwards.

Treasury guarantees

18.—(1) The Treasury may on or after the appointed day guarantee, in such manner and on such conditions as they think fit, the discharge of any financial liability to which this sub-paragraph applies.

(2) Sub-paragraph (1) applies to—

(*a*) any financial liability which has on the appointed day vested in the Board under paragraph 7;

(*b*) any financial liability of the Board, not falling within paragraph (*a*), which immediately before that day was a financial liability of the unincorporated Agents or any of them in their capacity as such;

(*c*) any financial liability incurred by the Board towards a person other than the Minister in substitution for a liability falling within any (including this) paragraph of this sub-paragraph or to enable the Board to discharge a liability so falling.

(3) Where the Treasury have given a guarantee under this paragraph in respect of a financial liability to which sub-paragraph (1) applies, then, if the terms or condtions of that ilability are subsequently varied with the approval of the Treasury given before the variation takes effect, the Treasury may continue to guarantee the discharge of the liability notwithstanding the variation.

(4) In this paragraph " financial liability " includes any form of financial obligation.

19. Section 21 shall apply in relation to the Board as it applies in relation to the Crown Agents, but as if any reference to a guarantee given under that section included a reference to a guarantee given under paragraph 18.

Accounts and audit

20.—(1) Subsections (1) to (4) of section 22 shall apply in relation to the Board and their subsidiaries as they apply in relation to the Crown Agents and their subsidiaries.

(2) Every statement of accounts prepared by the Board in respect of any accounting year in pursuance of the provisions applied by sub-paragraph (1) shall be submitted to the Minister at such time as he may direct.

(3) The Minister shall send each statement of accounts submitted to him under sub-paragraph (2) to the Comptroller and Auditor General not later than the end of the month of May following the accounting year to which the statement relates; and the Comptroller and Auditor General shall examine, certify and report on the statement and shall lay copies of it and of his report before each House of Parliament not later than the end of the month of July following that accounting year.

(4) The Board shall, for the purpose of enabling the Comptroller and Auditor General to perform his functions under sub-paragraph (3), permit any person authorised in that behalf by the Comptroller and Auditor General to inspect and make copies of any of the Board's accounts, books, documents or papers and shall afford to any such person such explanation thereof as he may reasonably require.

Power of Minister to give instructions

21.—(1) Without prejudice to any other power conferred on the Minister by this Act, the Minister may give the Board instructions with respect to any matter connected with any of their functions.

(2) An instruction under this paragraph relating to any financial matter shall be given only with the approval of the Treasury and after consultation with the Board; and any other instruction under this paragraph shall be given only after consultation with the Board.

(3) An instruction under this paragraph may be general or specific in character, but shall not confer on the Board power to do anything which they would not have power to do apart from the instruction.

Duty to insure against insurable financial risks

22. It shall be the duty of the Board to secure, so far as is reasonably practicable, that they and their subsidiaries are appropriately insured against financial risks arising in the course of the performance by them of their functions under this Act.

Dissolution of Board

23.—(1) If at any time it appears to the Minister that the duties of the Board under section 25 (3) (*a*) and (*c*) have been substantially discharged, he may by order made with the approval of the Treasury prescribe a day (in this and the following paragraph referred to as "the prescribed day") and make such provision as appears to him necessary or expedient for for winding up the aiffrs of the Board.

(2) Such an order shall make provision—

(*a*) for the transfer, by virtue of the order, of any property, rights, liabilities or obligations which the Board may have immediately before the prescribed day to a Minister of the Crown or his nominees or agents or to the Crown Agents, and for the disposal thereof; and

(*b*) for the payment into the Consolidated Fund of sums transferred by or accruing under the order to any Minister of the Crown, and the payment out of money provided by Parliament of any sums to be provided for the purposes of the order.

(3) No order shall be made under this paragraph unless a draft of the order has been laid before Parliament and approved by a resolution of each House of Parliament.

(4) In this paragraph "Minister of the Crown" means the holder of an office in Her Majesty's Government in the United Kingdom, and includes the Treasury.

24.—(1) If the prescribed day is not the 1st January, the accounting year then current shall, in relation to the Board, be deemed to have ended with the day before the prescribed day.

(2) As soon as the Minister is satisfied that the requirements of the following provisions, namely—

(*a*) section 11 in its application to the Board; and

(*b*) paragraph 20, including the provisions of section 22 (1) to (4) as thereby applied,

have been complied with on the part of the Board in respect of accounting years down to and including the one ending immediately before the prescribed day, he shall by order dissolve the Board; and thereupon any further liabilities incurred by the Board on or after the prescribed day in complying with the said provisions or otherwise shall become liabilities of the Minister.

(3) In relation to any statement of accounts relating to the accounting year ending immediately before the prescribed day, paragraph 20 (3) shall have effect with the omission of the words from "not later" (where first occurring) to "relates" and of the words from "not later" (where last occurring) onwards.

Section 32

SCHEDULE 6

Consequential Amendments and Transitional Provisions

Part I

Consequential Amendments

Public Records Act 1958 (*c.* 51)

In Schedule 1 to the Public Records Act 1958 (definition of public records), in Part II of the Table at the end of paragraph 3 (establishments and organisations whose records are public records)—

(*a*) in the entry beginning "Crown Agents", for "Crown Agents for Overseas Governments and Administrations" substitute "Crown Agents for Oversea Governments and Administrations (before and after their reconstitution as a body corporate)"; and

(*b*) after that entry insert the entry—

"Crown Agents Holding and Realisation Board.".

Part II

Transitional Provisions

Final accounts of unincorporated Agents

1.—(1) If by the appointed day—

(*a*) the unincorporated Agents have not prepared a statement of accounts in respect of their last full financial year; or

(*b*) the statement of accounts prepared by them in respect of that year has not been audited,

the following sub-paragraph shall apply.

(2) It shall be the duty of the Crown Agents and the Board, acting jointly—

(*a*) to prepare in respect of the period between the beginning of the last full financial year of the unincorporated Agents and the beginning of the first accounting year a statement of accounts dealing with the unincorporated Agents; and

(*b*) to submit that statement to the Minister within such time after the appointed day as the Minister may direct.

2.—(1) If—

(*a*) on the appointed day the circumstances are such that sub-paragraph 1 (2) does not apply; and

(*b*) the beginning of the first accounting year does not coincide with the end of the last full financial year of the unincorporated Agents,

the following sub-paragraph shall apply.

(2) It shall be the duty of the Crown Agents and the Board, acting jointly—

(*a*) to prepare in respect of the period between the end of the last full financial year of the unincorporated Agents and the beginning of the first accounting year a statement of accounts dealing with the unincorporated Agents; and

(*b*) to submit that statement to the Minister within such time after the appointed day as the Minister may direct.

3. Without prejudice to section 30 (1) (*c*), an order under section 31 (2) may contain such supplementary, incidental and transitional provisions as the Minister thinks fit with respect to any statement of accounts to be submitted to him under paragraph 1 or 2.

Final report on affairs of unincorporated Agents

4.—(1) If by the appointed day the unincorporated Agents have not made to the Minister a report on the performance by them of their functions during their last full financial year, the following sub-paragraph shall apply.

(2) The Crown Agents and the Board, acting jointly, shall, within such time after that day as the Minister may direct, make to the Minister, in such form as he may direct, a report on the performance by the unincorporated Agents of their functions during the period mentioned in paragraph 1 (2) (*a*).

(3) If—

(*a*) by the appointed day the unincorporated Agents have made to the Minister such a report as is mentioned in sub-paragraph (1); and

(*b*) the condition specified in paragraph 2 (1) (*b*) is fulfilled,

the preceding sub-paragraph shall apply, but with the substitution of a reference to the period mentioned in paragraph 2 (2) (*a*) for the reference to the period mentioned in paragraph 1 (2) (*a*).

Section 32

SCHEDULE 7

Repeals

Chapter	Short title	Extent of repeal
1965 c. 74.	Superannuation Act 1965.	In section 39 (1), in paragraph 7, the entry relating to the Crown Agents for Oversea Governments and Administrations.
1975 c. 81.	Moneylenders (Crown Agents) Act 1975.	The whole Act.

Leasehold Reform Act 1979 *

(1979 c. 44)

An Act to provide further protection, for a tenant in possession claiming to acquire the freehold under the Leasehold Reform Act 1967, against artificial inflation of the price he has to pay. [4th April 1979]

General Note

This Act was passed specifically to negative the effect of the device considered by the House of Lords in *Jones* v. *Wrotham Park Settled Estates* [1979] 2 W.L.R. 132 (the title of the appeal being strictly *Wentworth Securities Ltd.* v. *Jones*). Under s. 9 (1) of the Leasehold Reform Act 1967, the calculation of the purchase price of the freehold upon proposed acquisition by a qualified lessee consists of the value of that freehold subject to certain assumptions including the assumption that the tenant had exercised the statutory right arising under s. 14 of the 1967 Act to claim an extended 50-year lease at a modern ground rent (whether or not such a claim had been made in fact).

The device in question consisted of the grant by the freeholder, Wentworth Securities, shortly after the date of the application to enfranchise, of an intermediate lease to an associated company, Wrotham Park Settled Estates. Under that intermediate lease the initial rent, for a 300-year term subject to the lease sought to be enfranchised, was a peppercorn but upon any grant of any sub-lease by the mesne lessor it had then to pay the freeholder a full rack rent. The effect was to increase the price for the freehold from £300, which it would have been without the intermediate lease, to £4,000 with that lease. Several speeches in the House of Lords indicated that such a result ran counter to Parliament's intentions in 1967, and this Acts seeks to provide a safeguard not included in the earlier legislation. It was acknowledged during the passage of the Bill that it is so framed as to catch *any* transaction which has the penalised result, whether an avoidance device or not. The Bill originally was drafted so as to apply to any transaction since February 18, 1966 (publication date of the White Paper leading to the 1967 Act) but this was lost in the passage of the Bill and February 15, 1979, the date of the First Reading of the Bill, substituted. The Government spokesman declared an intention to re-introduce such retrospective provisions in future legislation.

Parliamentary debates

Hansard H,C. Vol. 963, col. 1287; Vol. 965, col. 1269; H.L. Vol. 399, cols. 1905 and 1939.

Extent

This Act extends to England and Wales only.

Commencement

The Act came into force on April 4, 1979.

Price to tenant on enfranchisement

1.—(1) As against a tenant in possession claiming under section 8 of the Leasehold Reform Act 1967, the price payable on a conveyance for giving effect to that section cannot be made less favourable by reference to a transaction since 15th February 1979 involving the creation or transfer of an interest superior to (whether or not preceding) his own, or an alteration since that date of the terms on which such an interest is held.

* Annotations by J. E. Adams, LL.B., Solicitor, Professor of Law, Queen Mary College, University of London.

(2) References in this section to a tenant claiming are to his giving notice under section 8 of his desire to have the freehold.

(3) Subsection (1) applies to any claim made on or after the commencement date (which means the date of the passing of this Act), and also to a claim made before that date unless by then the price has been determined by agreement or otherwise.

GENERAL NOTE

As this Act is clearly *in pari materia* with the Act of 1967 words and phrases in it defined in the earlier Act or by decisions under it will be given the same meaning. "Tenancy", but not "tenant" as such, is defined in s. 37 (1) of the earlier Act and extensions of the meaning for various purposes of the Act will be found in ss. 6 and 7.

The word "transaction" has undoubtedly been used as a word of the widest import, having been so construed in the context of other legislation in a variety of fields.

Citation and extent

2.—(1) This Act may be cited as the Leasehold Reform Act 1979; and the 1967 Act and this Act may be cited together as the Leasehold Reform Acts 1967 and 1979.

(2) This Act extends to England and Wales only.

Weights and Measures Act 1979

(1979 c. 45)

Arrangement of Sections

Part I

Packaged Goods

An Act to make further provision with respect to weights and measures. [4th April 1979]

General Note

This Act makes further provision with respect to weights and measures.

Pt. I (ss. 1–15) relates to packaged goods: s. 1 sets out the duties of packers and importers of packages; s. 2 contains enforcement provisions; s. 3 specifies offences under the Act; s. 4 deals with local administration of Pt. I; s. 5 makes special provision for certain packages; s. 6 establishes the Metrological Co-ordinating Unit; s. 7 outlines the functions of the Unit; s. 8 provides for supervision by the Unit of certain functions of inspectors; s. 9 concerns annual reports by the Unit; s. 10 relates to accounts and audit; s. 11 gives the Secretary of State power to extend or transfer the Unit's functions and to abolish the Unit; s. 12 deals with disclosure of information; s. 13 allows for modification of Pt. I by regulations; s. 14 is the interpretation section for Pt. I; s. 15 contains supplemental provisions.

Pt. II (ss. 16–20) amends the Weights and Measures Act 1963; s. 16 amends ss. 11 and 14 of the 1963 Act relating to weighing or measuring equipment for use for trade; s. 17 amends s. 12 with respect to approved patterns of equipment for use in trade; s. 18 alters certain penalties set out in the 1963 Act; s. 19 relates to the measurement of beer and cider; s. 20 makes other amendments to the 1963 Act.

Pt. III (ss. 21–24) contains general provisions; s. 21 provides for application of the Act to Northern Ireland; s. 22 sets out provisions relating to expenses, etc.; s. 23 concerns repeals; s. 24 deals with citation, interpretation and commencement.

The Act received the Royal Assent on April 4, 1979, and came into force on that date except for ss. 1–5, 8–13, 15, 20 (part), 23 (part) and Scheds. 1, 2, 5, para. 16, and Sched. 7 which come into force on January 1, 1980; s. 20 (part) and Sched. 5, para. 1 which come into force on October 4, 1979; and ss. 6, 7 and 19 and Sched. 3 which come into force on a day to be appointed.

Parliamentary debates

Hansard, H.C. Vol. 958, col. 434; Vol. 961, col. 59; Vol. 965, col. 1268; H.L. Vol. 399, cols. 1905 and 1939.

Part I

Packaged Goods

Quantity control

Duties of packers and importers of packages

1.—(1) It shall be the duty of a person who is the packer or importer of relevant packages to ensure that when a group of the packages marked with the same nominal quantity is selected in the prescribed manner and the packages in the group or such a portion of the group as is so selected are tested in the prescribed manner by an inspector—

(*a*) the total quantity of the goods shown by the test to be included in the packages tested divided by the number of those packages is not less than the nominal quantity on those packages; and

(*b*) the number of non-standard packages among those tested is not greater than the number prescribed as acceptable in relation to the number tested.

(2) Regulations in pursuance of the preceding subsection with respect to the manner of selecting or testing packages may, without prejudice to the generality of the powers to make regulations conferred by that subsection or to the generality of section 15 (2) (*b*) of this Act, make provision by reference to a document other than the regulations (which may be or include a code of practical guidance issued by the Secretary of State).

(3) Where, as a result of a test in respect of a group of packages which is carried out when the packages are in the possession of the packer or importer of the packages or another person, it is shown that the packer or importer of the packages has failed to perform the duty imposed on

him by subsection (1) of this section in respect of the packages, then, without prejudice to the liability of the packer or importer under subsection (1) of the following section in respect of the failure, it shall be the duty of the person in possession of the packages to keep them in his possession—

(*a*) except so far as he is authorised by or under regulations to dispose of them; or

(*b*) if he is the packer or importer of them, until he has performed his duty under subsection (1) of this section in respect of the group.

(4) It shall be the duty of a person who is the packer or importer of a relevant package to ensure that the container included in the package is marked before the prescribed time and in the prescribed manner with—

(*a*) a statement of quantity in prescribed units either of weight or of volume, as regulations require; and

(*b*) his name and address or a mark which enables his name and address to be readily ascertained by an inspector or—

(i) if he is the packer of the package, the name and address of a person who arranged for him to make up the package or a mark which enables that name and address to be readily ascertained by an inspector,

(ii) if he is the importer of the package, the name and address of the packer of the package or of a person who arranged for the packer to make up the package or a mark which enables the name and address of the packer or the said person to be readily ascertained by an inspector; and

(*c*) if regulations so provide, a mark allocated to him by a scheme in pursuance of section 7 (4) of this Act for the purpose of enabling the place where the package was made up to be ascertained.

(5) If at the time when a relevant package is made up or imported the container included in the package is not marked with such a statement as is mentioned in paragraph (*a*) of the preceding subsection, it shall be the duty of the packer or, as the case may be, of the importer of the package to decide what statement he proposes to mark on the container in pursuance of that paragraph and to make at that time, and to maintain for the prescribed period, a record of the statement; and the container shall, until the time mentioned in that subsection or any earlier time at which it is actually marked in the prescribed manner in pursuance of that paragraph, be treated for the purposes of this Part of this Act as marked with the statement in the record.

(6) It shall be the duty of a person who makes up packages either—

(*a*) to use suitable equipment of the prescribed kind in an appropriate manner in making up the packages; or

(*b*) to carry out at the prescribed time a check which is adequate to show whether he has performed the duty imposed on him by subsection (1) of this section in respect of the packages and—

(i) to use suitable equipment of the prescribed kind in an appropriate manner in carrying out the check, and

(ii) to make, and to keep for the prescribed period, an adequate record of the check.

(7) It shall be the duty of a person who is the importer of relevant packages—

(*a*) to carry out at the prescribed time such a check as is mentioned in paragraph (*b*) of the preceding subsection and to comply with sub-paragraphs (i) and (ii) of that paragraph in connection with the check; or

(*b*) to obtain before the prescribed time, and to keep for the prescribed period, documents containing such information about the packages as is adequate to show that the person is likely to have complied with his duty under subsection (1) of this section in relation to the packages.

(8) Without prejudice to the generality of the powers to make regulations conferred by subsection (6) or (7) of this section or to the generality of section 15 (2) (*b*) of this Act, regulations may provide—

(*a*) for equipment not to be equipment for the purposes of the subsection in question unless it is made from materials and on principles specified in the regulations and is inspected, tested and certified as provided by the regulations and for the payment of fees in respect of the inspection, testing and certification of equipment as so provided;

(*b*) for questions as to the suitability of equipment, the appropriate manner of using equipment and the adequacy of checks, records and information to be determined for those purposes by reference to documents other than the regulations (which may be or include codes or parts of codes of practical guidance issued or approved by the Secretary of State);

(*c*) that the use and the possession for use, for the purposes of subsection (6) or (7) of this section, of a thing which is equipment for the purposes of the subsection in question shall not constitute a contravention of section 9A (1) (*b*) of the principal Act (which among other things prohibits the use for trade of any measure or weight not mentioned in Schedule 3 to that Act).

Enforcement

2.—(1) A person who fails to perform a duty imposed on him by the preceding section shall be guilty of an offence.

(2) If an inspector has reasonable cause to believe that a person has failed to perform the duty imposed on him by subsection (1) of the preceding section in relation to a group of packages, the inspector may give to the person in possession of the packages instructions in writing specifying the packages and requiring him to keep the packages at a place specified in the instructions and at the disposal of the inspector for the period of twenty-four hours beginning with the time when the inspector gives him the instructions or for such shorter period as the inspector may specify; and if the person to whom the instuctions are given fails without reasonable cause to comply with the instructions he shall be guilty of an offence.

(3) If an inspector has reasonable cause to believe that a person has failed to perform the duty imposed on him by subsection (6) or (7) of the preceding section, then—

(*a*) the inspector may give to the person such instructions in writing as the inspector considers appropriate with a view to ensuring that the person does not subsequently fail to perform that duty; and

(*b*) Schedule 1 to this Act shall have effect with respect to the instructions;

and if the instructions or the instructions with modifications come into force in pursuance of that Schedule and the person fails without reasonable cause to comply with them he shall be guilty of an offence.

(4) If a person—

(*a*) purports to comply with his duty under sub-paragraph (ii) of subsection (6) (*b*) of the preceding section or that sub-paragraph as applied by subsection (7) (*a*) of that section by making a record which he knows is false in a material particular; or

(*b*) purports to comply with his duty under subsection (7) (*b*) of that section by reference to a document containing information which he knows is false in a material particular; or

(*c*) with intent to deceive, alters any record kept for the purposes of subsection (5) of the preceding section or sub-paragraph (ii) of subsection (6) (*b*) of that section or that sub-paragraph as applied by subsection (7) (*a*) of that section or any document kept for the purposes of subsection (7) (*b*) of that section,

he shall be guilty of an offence.

(5) If a person has in his possession for sale, agrees to sell or sells a relevant package which is inadequate and either—

(*a*) he is the packer or importer of the package; or

(*b*) he knows that the package is inadequate,

he shall be guilty of an offence; and if the packer of a relevant package which is inadequate, and which was made up by him in the course of carrying out arrangements with another person for the packer to make up packages, delivers the package to or to the order of a person to whom it falls to be delivered in pursuance of the arrangements, the packer shall be guilty of an offence.

(6) For the purposes of sections 22 and 24 of the principal Act (which among other things make it an offence to sell certain goods otherwise than in a particular quantity and make it an offence to give short weight) the quantity of the goods in a relevant package shall be deemed to be the nominal quantity on the package.

(7) No action shall lie in respect of a failure to perform a duty imposed by the preceding section.

Offences

3.—(1) A person guilty of an offence under the preceding section (hereafter in this section referred to as " a relevant offence ") shall be liable on summary conviction—

(*a*) in the case of an offence under subsection (4) of that section, to imprisonment for a term not exceeding six months and a fine not exceeding £1,000;

(*b*) in any other case, to a fine not exceeding £1,000.

(2) Proceedings for a relevant offence shall not be instituted in England and Wales except by or on behalf of a local weights and measures authority or the chief officer of police for a police area; and subsections (2) and (4) of section 51 of the principal Act (which provide that proceedings for certain offences under that Act shall not be instituted unless among other things notice of the date and nature of the alleged offence has been served on the accused and shall not be instituted after the expiry of a period mentioned in the said subsection (2)) shall apply to a relevant offence as they apply to an offence under section 24 of that Act but as if in paragraph (*a*) of the said subsection (2) the words from " and where " to " those articles " were omitted.

(3) Section 50 of the principal Act (which relates to offences by corporations) shall apply to a relevant offence as it applies to an offence under that Act.

(4) Where a person is charged with an offence under subsection (1) of the preceding section of failing to perform the duty imposed on him by section 1 (1) of this Act in respect of any packages, it shall be a defence to prove that the test in question took place when the packages were not in his possession and by reference to a nominal quantity which was not on the packages when they were in his possession.

(5) Where the importer of packages is charged with an offence under subsection (1) of the preceding section of failing to perform the duty imposed on him by section 1 (1) of this Act in respect of the packages, it shall be a defence to prove—

(*a*) that in respect of the packages the accused performed the duty imposed on him by paragraph (*b*) of section 1 (7) of this Act; and

(*b*) that within the prescribed period after obtaining the documents mentioned in that paragraph relating to the packages he took all reasonable steps to verify the information contained in the documents and that when the relevant test in pursuance of the said section 1 (1) began he believed and had no reason to disbelieve that the information was true; and

(*c*) that before the beginning of the period of seven days ending with the date when the hearing of the charge began he served on the prosecutor a copy of the said documents and a notice which stated that the accused intended to rely on them in proving a defence under this subsection; and

(*d*) that he took all reasonable steps to ensure that the quantity of goods in each of the packages did not alter while the packages were in his possession.

(6) Where a person is charged with an offence under subsection (1) of the preceding section of failing to perform the duty imposed on him by paragraph (*b*) of subsection (4) of section 1 of this Act in respect of a package, it shall be a defence to prove—

(*a*) that the container included in the package was marked at the time and in the manner mentioned in that subsection with a mark as to which he had, before that time, given notice to an inspector stating that the mark indicated a name and address specified in the notice; and

(*b*) that at the time aforesaid the name and address were such as are mentioned in relation to him in that paragraph.

(7) Where a person is charged with an offence under subsection (1) of the preceding section or an offence alleged to have been committed by him, as the packer or importer of a package, under subsection (5) of that section, it shall be a defence to prove that he took all reasonable precautions and exercised all due diligence to avoid the commission of the offence.

Local administration

4.—(1) It shall be the duty of a local weights and measures authority to enforce the provisions of this Part of this Act within the area of the authority.

(2) Schedule 2 to this Act shall have effect with respect to the powers and duties of inspectors and the other matters there mentioned.

(3) The following provisions of the principal Act (which relate to annual reports by local weights and measures authorities, to the investigation of a complaint that the functions of such an authority are not being properly discharged and to breaches by inspectors of their duties under that Act) shall have effect with the following modifications,

namely, in section 38 (1) the reference to the purposes of that Act, in sections 38 (1) and 39 (3) the references to functions under that Act and in section 45 (1) (*c*) the reference to a duty imposed by or under that Act shall include respectively references to the purposes of, to functions under and to a duty imposed by or under this Part of this Act.

(4) Nothing in the preceding provisions of this section authorises a weights and measures authority to institute proceedings in Scotland for an offence.

Special provision for certain packages

5.—(1) Subsections (2) to (7) of this section apply only to packages containing goods of a prescribed quantity, and references to packages in those subsections shall be construed accordingly.

(2) If in the course of carrying on a business—

(*a*) a person marks a package with the EEC mark and is neither the packer nor the importer of the package nor a person acting on behalf of the packer or importer of the package; or

(*b*) a person marks a package with a mark so closely resembling the EEC mark as to be likely to deceive,

the person shall be guilty of an offence.

(3) For the purposes of this Part of this Act a person who brings a package marked with the EEC mark into the United Kingdom does not import the package if he shows that the package is from a member State of the Economic Community in which it was liable to be tested under a law corresponding to section 1 (1) of this Act and, except in such cases as are determined by or under regulations, has not since leaving that State been in a country which is not such a member State.

(4) Subject to the following subsection it shall be the duty of—

(*a*) the packer of packages which are marked with the EEC mark and which he intends to export from the United Kingdom; and

(*b*) a person who intends to import packages which are so marked and to export them from the United Kingdom to a place in another member State of the Economic Community; and

(*c*) a person who intends to import packages, to mark them with the EEC mark and to export them as mentioned in the preceding paragraph,

to give before the prescribed time and in the prescribed manner, to the local weights and measures authority for the area in which the packages were packed or, as the case may be, in which the place of intended import is situated, a notice containing such information about the packages as is prescribed and, in the case of a person who has given such a notice in pursuance of paragraph (*b*) or (*c*) of this subsection, such further information about the packages in question as an inspector may specify in a notice served on the person by the inspector; and a person who fails without reasonable cause to perform a duty imposed on him by this subsection shall be guilty of an offence.

(5) Regulations may enable an inspector to give notice to any person providing that, until an inspector informs the person in writing that the notice is cancelled, any paragraph of the preceding subsection which is specified in the notice shall not apply to the person or shall not apply to him as respects packages of a kind specified in the notice or a place so specified.

(6) In this section " the EEC mark " means such mark as may be prescribed; and, without prejudice to the generality of section 15 (2) (*b*)

of this Act, regulations prescribing a mark in pursuance of this subsection may contain such provisions as the Secretary of State considers appropriate with respect to the dimensions of the mark and the manner and position in which it is to be applied to the container included in a package and may provide for a mark which is not in accordance with those provisions to be disregarded for the purposes of prescribed provisions of this section.

(7) Subsections (1) to (3) of section 3 of this Act shall apply to an offence under this section as they apply to an offence under section 2 (1) of this Act.

Co-ordination of control

The Metrological Co-ordinating Unit

6.—(1) There shall be a body corporate, to be called the National Metrological Co-ordinating Unit (and hereafter in this Act referred to as " the Unit "), which shall consist of not less than five persons and not more than fifteen persons appointed by the Secretary of State.

(2) A person shall not be qualified for appointment in pursuance of the preceding subsection unless he is a member of a local authority; and it shall be the duty of the Secretary of State, before he makes such an appointment, to consult a body which in his opinion represents such local authorities as he considers appropriate in connection with the appointment.

In this subsection " local authority " means any of the following councils, namely, the council of a county or a district in England or Wales, the council of a region or an islands area in Scotland, the council of a London borough, the Common Council of the City of London and the Council of the Isles of Scilly.

(3) The provisions of Schedule 3 to this Act shall have effect with respect to the Unit.

(4) The Secretary of State may, out of money provided by Parliament, make payments to the Unit from time to time for the purpose of enabling the Unit to defray the whole or part of its expenses.

(5) It is hereby declared that the Unit is not to be regarded as the servant or agent of the Crown or as enjoying any status, privilege or immunity of the Crown or as exempt from any tax, duty, rate, levy or other charge whatsoever, whether general or local, and that its property is not to be regarded as property of or held on behalf of the Crown.

Functions of Unit

7.—(1) It shall be the duty of the Unit—

(*a*) to keep under review the operation of this Part of this Act and to carry out such research in connection with the review as the Unit considers appropriate;

(*b*) to make available, to local weights and measures authorities and to packers and importers of packages, such information as the Unit considers appropriate in connection with the operation of this Part of this Act;

(*c*) to give advice to local weights and measures authorities about arrangements to be made by the authorities for the purpose of discharging the duty imposed on them by section 4 (1) of this Act and about such other matters as the Unit considers appropriate in connection with the operation of this Part of this Act;

(*d*) to seek to collaborate, with any authority in a place outside Great Britain appearing to the Unit to have functions which correspond to those of the Unit or to those conferred on a local weights and measures authority by this Part of this Act, about matters which are connected with packages and are of interest to the Unit and the authority;

(*e*) to give advice to the Secretary of State about such documents as are mentioned in section 1 (8) (*b*) of this Act which are prepared by persons appearing to the Secretary of State to represent the interests of packers or importers of packages;

(*f*) to make and maintain a record of the names and addresses of packers and importers of packages and of—

(i) the kind of packages which they make up or import, and

(ii) the marks of which particulars have been furnished by them in pursuance of the following subsection;

(*g*) to make and maintain a record of the names and addresses of persons who make measuring container bottles in any member State of the Economic Community and of the marks put on the bottles for the purpose of enabling the makers of them to be identified:

(*h*) to perform any duty conferred on the Unit by the preceding paragraphs in accordance with any directions given to the Unit by the Secretary of State.

(2) The Unit may serve, on any person carrying on business as a packer or importer of packages, a notice requiring him—

(*a*) to furnish the Unit from time to time with particulars of the kind specified in the notice of any marks which, otherwise than in pursuance of section 1 (4) (*c*) of this Act, are applied from time to time, to packages made up or as the case may be imported by him, for the purpose of enabling the place where the packages were made up to be ascertained; and

(*b*) if he has furnished particulars of a mark in pursuance of the notice and the mark ceases to be applied for the purpose aforesaid to packages made up or imported by him, to give notice of the cesser to the Unit;

but a notice given by the Unit in pursuance of this subsection shall not require a person to furnish information which he does not possess.

(3) A person who fails without reasonable cause to comply with a notice served on him in pursuance of the preceding subsection shall be guilty of an offence and liable on summary conviction to a fine not exceeding £1,000; and—

(*a*) section 50 of the principal Act (which relates to offences by corporations) shall apply to an offence under this subsection as it applies to an offence under that Act; but

(*b*) proceedings for an offence under this subsection shall not be instituted in England or Wales except by or on behalf of the Director of Public Prosecutions or the Unit.

(4) It shall be the duty of the Unit—

(*a*) if the Secretary of State so directs, to prepare a scheme which—

(i) allocates, to persons carrying on business as packers or importers of packages, marks from which there can be ascertained the places where packages made up or imported by them were made up, and

(ii) specifies the kinds of packages to which each mark is to be applied;

(*b*) to make from time to time such alterations of the scheme as the Unit considers appropriate and the Secretary of State approves;

(*c*) to give, to each person to whom a mark is for the time being allocated by the scheme, a notice which specifies the mark, states that it has been allocated to him in pursuance of the scheme and specifies the kinds of packages to which it is to be applied.

(5) The functions conferred on the Secretary of State by regulation 6 of the 1977 Regulations (which relates to the approval by the Secretary of State of marks identifying the makers of measuring container bottles) are hereby transferred to the Unit, and accordingly references to the Secretary of State in that regulation shall be construed as references to the Unit; but any approval given by the Secretary of State in pursuance of that regulation before this subsection comes into force shall have effect thereafter as if given by the Unit.

(6) In this section and the following section—

" measuring container bottle " has the same meaning as in the 1977 Regulations or, if regulations so provide, such other meaning as is prescribed; and

" the 1977 Regulations " means the Measuring Container Bottles (EEC Requirements) Regulations 1977.

Supervision by Unit of certain functions of inspectors

8.—(1) The Unit may serve on any local weights and measures authority in Great Britain a notice requiring the authority—

(*a*) to furnish the Unit with information, of such a kind as is specified in the notice (and, if the notice so provides, relating only to persons so specified or packages or measuring container bottles of a kind so specified), with respect to relevant functions which inspectors appointed by the authority have performed or propose to perform during a period so specified; or

(*b*) to arrange for the performance by an inspector, in relation to persons, premises or equipment specified in the notice or packages or measuring container bottles of a kind so specified and during a period so specified, of such relevant functions as are so specified and to make to the Unit a report containing information of a kind so specified about the results of complying with the notice;

and, subject to paragraph (*b*) (ii) of subsection (3) of this section, it shall be the duty of the authority to comply with the requirements of the notice.

(2) In the preceding subsection " relevant functions " means the function of carrying out a test in pursuance of section 1 (1) of this Act, functions conferred on an inspector by paragraph 1 of Schedule 2 to this Act and regulation 8 (1) of the 1977 Regulations (which relates to inspection for the purposes of the 1977 Regulations) and such other functions conferred on an inspector by this Part of this Act as are prescribed; and in relation to a notice served in pursuance of paragraph (*b*) of the preceding subsection the inspector in question shall be treated as having such reasonable cause as is mentioned in sub-paragraph (1) (*a*) and (*b*) of the said paragraph 1 and paragraph (*b*) of the said regulation 8 (1).

(3) If the Unit is of opinion that a local weights and measures authority has not complied with a requirement contained in a notice served on the authority in pursuance of subsection (1) of this section,

the Unit may refer the matter to the Secretary of State who, if he is also of that opinion, may—

(*a*) serve a notice on the authority requiring it to comply with the requirement within a period specified in the notice; or

(*b*) in the case of a requirement in pursuance of paragraph (*b*) of subsection (1) of this section—

(i) make such arrangements as the Secretary of State considers appropriate for securing that the requirement is complied with by persons acting on his behalf,

(ii) serve on the authority a notice stating that he proposes to make the arrangements and prohibiting the authority from complying with the requirement,

(iii) by an instrument in writing appoint a person specified in the instrument to be an inspector for the purpose of carrying out the arrangements and to exercise accordingly for that purpose any power which by virtue of this Part of this Act or the 1977 Regulations is conferred on an inspector, and

(iv) recover from the authority the reasonable cost of making and carrying out the arrangements.

Annual reports by Unit

9.—(1) It shall be the duty of the Unit to make in each year a report to the Secretary of State on the performance during the preceding year of its functions, and it shall be the duty of the Secretary of State to publish, in such manner as he thinks fit, each report received by him in pursuance of this subsection.

(2) In preparing such a report the Unit shall have regard to the need for excluding, so far as it is practicable to do so, any matter which relates to the private affairs of an individual or which relates specifically to the affairs of a particular person where the publication of that matter would, in the opinion of the Unit, seriously and prejudicially affect the interests of that individual or person.

(3) For the purposes of the law of defamation every publication of such a report shall be absolutely privileged.

Accounts and audit

10.—(1) It shall be the duty of the Unit—

(*a*) to keep proper accounts and proper records in relation to the accounts; and

(*b*) to prepare in respect of each accounting year, in such form as the Secretary of State may with the approval of the Treasury direct, a statement of those accounts; and

(*c*) to send the statement to the auditors for the time being appointed in pursuance of this subsection and to do so within six months beginning with the last day of the accounting year to which the statement relates;

and the accounts kept and the statements prepared in pursuance of this subsection shall be audited by auditors appointed by the Treasury.

(2) As soon as the accounts and statement of accounts of the Unit for any accounting year have been audited, the Unit shall send to the Secretary of State a copy of the statement and a copy of any report made by the auditors on the statement or on the accounts of the Unit, and it shall be the duty of the Secretary of State to lay before each House of Parliament a copy of every statement and report of which a copy is received by him in pursuance of this subsection.

(3) On and after 1st April 1980 the preceding provisions of this section shall have effect with the following amendments—

(*a*) in subsection (1) the words from " in such " to " direct " in paragraph (*b*) shall be omitted and for the words " appointed by the Treasury " there shall be substituted the words " appointed by the Unit ";

(*b*) after that subsection there shall be inserted the following subsection—

(1A) A person shall not be qualified to be so appointed unless he is a member of one or more of the following bodies—

the Institute of Chartered Accountants in England and Wales;

the Institute of Chartered Accountants of Scotland;

the Association of Certified Accountants;

the Institute of Chartered Accountants in Ireland;

any other body of accountants established in the United Kingdom and for the time being recognised for the purposes of section 161 (1) (*a*) of the Companies Act 1948 by the Secretary of State;

but a Scottish firm may be so appointed if each of the partners in the firm is qualified to be so appointed.;

(*c*) for subsection (2) there shall be substituted the following subsection—

(2) It shall be the duty of the Unit to include, in the first report it makes in pursuance of section 9 of this Act after the accounts and statement of accounts of the Unit for any accounting year have been audited, a copy of the statement and of any report made by the auditors on the statement or the accounts.

(4) The Secretary of State may, before 1st April 1980 or any later date for the time being specified in the preceding subsection by virtue of this subsection, direct that the preceding subsection shall have effect with the substitution for the reference to the date there specified of a later date specified in the direction.

(5) In this section " accounting year " means the period of twelve months ending with 31st March in any year except that a particular accounting year shall, if the Secretary of State so directs, be such other period not longer than two years as is specified in the direction.

Power to extend or transfer Unit's functions and to abolish Unit

11.—(1) The Secretary of State may by order confer on the Unit such functions as he thinks fit in addition to the functions conferred on the Unit by this Act.

(2) The Secretary of State may by order—

(*a*) transfer any function of the Unit to himself;

(*b*) establish a body and transfer to it any function of the Unit and any function transferred by virtue of the preceding paragraph;

(*c*) where all the functions of the Unit are transferred by virtue of the preceding paragraphs, abolish the Unit.

(3) An order made by virtue of this section may—

(*a*) make such modifications of section 6 (1) to (3) and (5) of this Act and Schedule 3 to this Act, and of references to the Unit in any provision of this Act except section 6, as the Secretary of State considers appropriate in connection with the conferring or transfer of any function, the establishment of a body or the abolition of the Unit in pursuance of this section;

(b) contain such supplemental and transitional provisions as the Secretary of State considers appropriate as aforesaid.

(4) If the Secretary of State proposes to make an order in pursuance of this section it shall be his duty, before he makes the order, to consult a body which in his opinion represents such local authorities (within the meaning of section 6 (2) of this Act) as he considers appropriate in connection with the proposal.

(5) The Secretary of State may make payments out of money provided by Parliament, to any body established by virtue of this section, for the purpose of enabling the body to defray its expenses.

(6) The powers to make orders conferred by this section shall be exercisable by statutory instrument; but no order shall be made by virtue of this section unless a draft of the order has been laid before and approved by a resolution of each House of Parliament.

Miscellaneous

Disclosure of information

12.—(1) If a person discloses information which—

(a) relates to a trade secret or secret manufacturing process; and

(b) was obtained by him by virtue of this Part of this Act when he was a member of the Unit, a person employed by the Unit, an inspector, a person who accompanied an inspector by virtue of paragraph 3 (1) of Schedule 2 to this Act or a person appointed by the Secretary of State in pursuance of section 8 (3) (b) (iii) of this Act,

he shall be guilty of an offence unless the disclosure was made in the performance of his duty as a member, inspector or other person mentioned in paragraph (b) of this subsection, or, in the case of an inspector, was made to the Unit in consequence of a request by the Unit.

(2) For the purposes of the preceding subsection information disclosing the identity of the packer of a package or the identity of the person who arranged with the packer of a package for the package to be made up shall be treated as a trade secret unless the information has previously been disclosed in a manner which made it available to the public.

(3) A person guilty of an offence under this section shall be liable, on summary conviction, to a fine not exceeding the statutory maximum and, on conviction on indictment, to imprisonment for a term not exceeding two years and a fine; and in this subsection " the statutory maximum " means the prescribed sum within the meaning of section 28 of the Criminal Law Act 1977 as respects England and Wales and section 289B of the Criminal Procedure (Scotland) Act 1975 as respects Scotland (which is £1,000 or another sum fixed by order to take account of changes in the value of money).

Power to modify Part I

13. Regulations may provide—

(a) that in relation to packages of a prescribed kind the provisions of this Part of this Act, except this section, shall have effect with prescribed modifications;

(b) for the said provisions to apply, with prescribed modifications, to goods of a prescribed kind which are not comprised in packages.

Interpretation of Part I

14.—(1) In this Part of this Act—

" container " includes any wrapping;

" functions " includes powers and duties;

" goods ", in relation to a package, excludes the container included in the package;

" importer ", in relation to a package, means, subject to section 5 (3) of this Act, the person by whom or on whose behalf the package is entered for customs purposes on importation;

" modifications " includes additions, omissions and alterations;

" nominal quantity ", in relation to a package, means the units of weight or volume prescribed for the package and the number of them in the statement of quanity marked on the container included in the package (any other matter in the statement being disregarded);

" notice " means notice in writing;

" package " means, subject to section 5 (1) of this Act, a container containing prescribed goods together with the goods in the container in a case where—

(*a*) the goods are placed for sale in the container otherwise than in the presence of a person purchasing the goods; and

(*b*) none of the goods can be removed from the container without opening it;

" packer " means, in relation to a package, the person who placed in the container included in the package the goods included in it;

" prescribed ", except in section 12 (3), means prescribed by regulations;

" regulations " means regulations made by the Secretary of State by virtue of this Part of this Act;

" relevant package " means a package which is made up in the United Kingdom or imported on or after 1st January 1980 or, if the goods in the package became prescribed goods after that date, on or after the date on which they became prescribed goods;

" the Unit " has the meaning assigned to it by section 6 (1) of this Act;

and other expressions used in this Part of this Act and defined by subsection (1) of section 58 of the principal Act have in this Part of this Act the meanings assigned to them by that subsection.

(2) For the purposes of this Part of this Act a package is non-standard if the quantity of the goods it contains is less by more than a prescribed amount than the nominal quantity on the package and is inadequate if the quantity of the goods it contains is less by more than twice that amount than the nominal quantity on the package.

(3) Regulations may make provision, in relation to a package which comprises more than one container or goods of more than one kind, as to which of the containers or goods shall be disregarded for the purposes of prescribed provisions of this Part of this Act.

(4) If two or more different nominal quantities are marked on a package, each of those quantities except the one which indicates the larger or largest quantity shall be disregarded for the purposes of this Part of this Act.

(5) In this Part of this Act, except this subsection, references to this Part of this Act include Schedules 1 to 3 to this Act.

Supplemental

15.—(1) Section 57 of the principal Act (which among other things enables provisions of that Act to be applied with modifications to the Crown by Order in Council) shall have effect as if the references to that Act in subsection (1) of that section included the provisions of this Part of this Act except this subsection.

(2) Any power to make regulations conferred by this Part of this Act—

(*a*) includes power to make different provision for different circumstances and provision relating only to specified circumstances;

(*b*) includes power to make provision by reference to documents which do not form part of the regulations and to include in the regulations such supplemental and incidental provisions as the Secretary of State considers appropriate; and

(*c*) shall be exercisable by statutory instrument;

and any statutory instrument made by virtue of this subsection shall be subject to annulment in pursuance of a resolution of either House of Parliament.

(3) When the Secretary of State proposes to make regulations it shall be his duty, before he makes the regulations, to consult on the proposal such organisations as he considers are representative of interests which would be substantially affected by the regulations.

(4) Any document required or authorised by virtue of this Part of this Act to be served on a person may be so served—

(*a*) by delivering it to him or by leaving it at his proper address or by sending it by post to him at that address; or

(*b*) if the person is a body corporate, by serving it in accordance with the preceding paragraph on the secretary or clerk of that body; or

(*c*) if the person is a partnership, by serving it as aforesaid on a partner or on a person having the control or management of the partnership business.

(5) For the purposes of the preceding subsection and section 7 of the Interpretation Act 1978 (which relates to the service of documents by post) in its application to the preceding subsection, the proper address of any person on whom a document is to be served by virtue of this Part of this Act shall be his last known address except that—

(*a*) in the case of service on a body corporate or its secretary or clerk it shall be the address of the registered or principal office of the body;

(*b*) in the case of service on a partnership or a partner or a person having the control or management of a partnership business it shall be the principal office of the partnership;

and for the purposes of this subsection the principal office of a company registered outside the United Kingdom or a partnership carrying on business outside the United Kingdom is its principal office within the United Kingdom.

(6) A statement applied to a package in pursuance of section 1 (4) (*a*) of this Act shall be deemed not to be a trade description within the meaning of the Trade Descriptions Act 1968.

(7) It is hereby declared that a person discharges the duty imposed on him by section 1 (1) of this Act in respect of a group of packages if the quantity of goods in each package is or exceeds the nominal quantity on the package.

PART II

AMENDMENTS OF WEIGHTS AND MEASURES ACT 1963

Weighing or measuring equipment for use for trade

16.—(1) In section 11 of the principal Act (which relates to weighing or measuring equipment for use for trade)—

(*a*) in paragraph (*b*) of subsection (3) after the word " error " there shall be inserted the words " and by virtue of subsection (5) of this section is not required to be stamped as mentioned in paragraph (*c*) of this subsection ";

(*b*) in subsection (4) the words from " or of " to " that section " shall be omitted;

(*c*) after subsection (5) there shall be inserted the following subsections—

(5A) Where a person submits equipment to an inspector under this section, the inspector may require the person to provide the inspector with such assistance in connection with the testing of the equipment as the inspector reasonably considers it necessary for the person to provide and shall not be obliged to proceed with the test until the person provides it; but a failure to provide the assistance shall not constitute an offence under section 49 of this Act.

(5B) If an inspector refuses to pass as fit for use for trade any equipment submitted to him under this section and is requested by the person by whom the equipment was submitted to give reasons for the refusal, the inspector shall give to that person a statement of those reasons in writing.;

(*d*) in subsection (6) for the words " been retested by an inspector " there shall be substituted the words " again been passed under this section " and for the words " be retested " there shall be substituted the words " be again so passed ".

(2) In accordance with the preceding subsection the said section 11 is to have effect as set out in Schedule 4 to this Act.

(3) In section 14 of the principal Act, after subsection (1) (which among other things enables provision to be made by regulations with respect to the testing of weighing or measuring equipment for use for trade) there shall be inserted the following subsection—

(1A) Regulations under the foregoing subsection with respect to the testing of equipment may provide—

(*a*) that where a group of items of equipment of the same kind is submitted for testing and prescribed conditions are satisfied with respect to the group, the testing may be confined to a number of items determined by or under the regulations and selected in the prescribed manner; and

(*b*) that if items so selected satisfy the test other items in the group shall be treated as having satisfied it.

Approved patterns of equipment for use for trade

17.—(1) In section 12 of the principal Act (which relates to the approval of patterns of equipment for use for trade)—

(*a*) in subsection (1) the words from " on payment " to " determine " and the words from " and may " onwards shall be omitted;

(*b*) after subsection (1) there shall be inserted the following subsection—

(1A) The foregoing subsection applies to a pattern consisting of an approved pattern with modifications as it applies to other patterns, and in this subsection " approved pattern " means a pattern in respect of which a certificate of approval under the foregoing subsection is in force.;

(*c*) in subsection (2)—

(i) for the words from " the foregoing subsection " to " purpose " there shall be substituted the words " subsection (1) of this section may be granted or renewed subject to such conditions as the Secretary of State thinks fit ",

(ii) for the words " knowing that such a condition " there shall be substituted the words—

" (*a*) knowing that a condition other than a condition mentioned in section 12A (1) (*b*) of this Act ",

and

(iii) for the words " or disposes " there shall be substituted the words—

" or

(*b*) knowing that any condition has been imposed with respect to any equipment, disposes ";

(*d*) in subsection (3) the words " or authorisation " wherever they occur and the words " or incorporating the modification " shall be omitted; and

(*e*) after subsection (3) there shall be inserted the following subsection—

(3A) The provisions of the last foregoing subsection relating to offences and forfeiture shall not apply in consequence of the revocation of a certificate of approval if the notice of the revocation published under that subsection states that instead of those provisions of section 12A (4) of this Act are to apply in consequence of the revocation.

(2) In accordance with the preceding subsection the said section 12 is to have effect as set out in Schedule 4 to this Act.

(3) After the said section 12 there shall be inserted the following section—

Provisions supplementary to s. 12

12A.—(1) A certificate of approval under section 12 (1) of this Act—

(*a*) shall, unless previously revoked and subject to the next following paragraph, cease to have effect on the expiration of the period of ten years beginning with the date when it was granted or last renewed;

(*b*) may, without prejudice to the generality of section 12 (2) of this Act, be granted or renewed subject to a condition under which it ceases to be in force on the expiration of a specified period of less than ten years; and

(*c*) may be renewed by the Secretary of State on an application made in such manner and during such period as may be prescribed and on payment, except in such cases as the Secretary of State may determine, of a fee of an amount ascertained in such manner as the Secretary of State may determine with the approval of the Treasury.

(2) Where such an application as is mentioned in paragraph (*c*) of the last foregoing subsection is made for the renewal of a certificate mentioned in that subsection, the certificate shall continue in force

until the Secretary of State gives to the applicant, in such manner as may be prescribed, notice of the Secretary of State's decision with respect to the application.

(3) Where a person submits a pattern of equipment to the Secretary of State under section 12 (1) of this Act the Secretary of State may—

(*a*) require the person to provide such assistance as the Secretary of State thinks fit in connection with the examination in question (and shall not be obliged to proceed with the examination until the person provides it);

(*b*) require the person to pay in respect of the examination a fee of an amount ascertained as aforesaid;

(*c*) if he is satisfied that equipment of that pattern is suitable for use for trade, require the person to deposit with the Secretary of State parts of equipment of that pattern or a model or drawings of such equipment or parts of it and withhold a certificate of approval of the pattern or, as the case may be, a declaration in pursuance of section 13 (2) of this Act in respect of the pattern until the person complies with the requirement.

(4) Where a certificate of approval under section 12 (1) of this Act ceases to have effect by the effluxion of time or by virtue of a notice under subsection (2) of this section or is revoked in a case falling within section 12 (3A) of this Act, then—

(*a*) the certificate shall continue in force in relation to any equipment of the pattern in question which we used for trade at a time when the certificate was in force otherwise than by virtue of this paragraph; but

(*b*) if a person—

(i) knows that the certificate has ceased to have effect or been revoked as aforesaid, and

(ii) supplies to another person equipment of that pattern which is marked with a stamp and which was not used for trade at such time,

he shall be guilty of an offence and the equipment supplied shall be liable to be forfeited.

(5) Each of the following instruments, namely—

(*a*) a certificate of approval granted under section 12 of this Act and in force immediately before the day when this subsection comes into force; and

(*b*) an authorisation of modifications so granted and in force; and

(*c*) a certificate which is deemed by virtue of section 12 (5) of this Act to be a certificate of approval so granted and is in force as aforesaid,

shall have effect on and after that day as if it were a certificate of approval so granted on that day and, in the case of a certificate of approval actually granted subject to a condition relating to a specified period, as if that condition were imposed by virtue of subsection (1) (*b*) of this section and provided for the certificate to cease to be in force on the expiration of a period equal to that period and beginning with the day when the certificate was actually granted.

(6) The power conferred by section 12 (3) of this Act to revoke a certificate of approval of a pattern shall, in the case of a certificate in respect of which an authorisation of modifications has effect by

virtue of subsection (5) of this section as if it were a further certificate of approval, include power to revoke the first-mentioned certificate as it has effect apart from the modifications without revoking it as it has effect with the modifications.

(7) It is hereby declared that subsection (3) of section 12 of this Act and the provisions of subsection (2) of that section relating to offences and forfeiture apply to a certificate continued in force by virtue of subsection (2) or subsection (4) (*a*) of this section.

(4) In subsection (1) of section 52 of the principal Act (which as amended by the following section provides for offences under the provisions of that Act mentioned in that subsection to be punishable on summary conviction by a fine of up to £200) after the figures " 12 (3)," there shall be inserted the figures " 12A (4),".

Alteration of penalties

18.—(1) In subsection (1) of section 52 of the principal Act (which provides for offences under the provisions of that Act mentioned in that subsection to be punishable on summary conviction by a fine of up to £50)—

(*a*) the words " 31 and 49 (1) " shall be omitted; and

(*b*) for the word " £50 " there shall be substituted the word " £200 ".

(2) In subsection (2) of that section (which provides that a person guilty of an offence under provisions of that Act other than those mentioned in subsection (1) of that section shall be liable on summary conviction to a fine of up to £100, or up to £250 in the case of a second or subsequent offence under the same provision, or to imprisonment for up to three months or to both) for the words from " shall be liable " onwards there shall be substituted the words " and the following subsection shall be liable on summary conviction to a fine not exceeding £1,000.".

(3) After subsection (2) of that section there shall be inserted the following subsection—

(3) A person guilty of an offence under section 16 (3) or 20 (3) (*b*) of this Act or paragraph 6 of Part I of Schedule 6 to this Act shall be liable on summary conviction to a fine not exceeding £1,000 or to imprisonment for a term not exceeding six months or to both, and a person guilty of an offence under section 48 (5) of this Act shall be liable, on summary conviction, to a fine not exceeding £1,000 and, on conviction on indictment, to imprisonment for a term not exceeding two years or to a fine or to both. .

Beer and cider

19. In ascertaining the quantity of any beer or cider for any of the purposes of Part VI of Schedule 4 to the principal Act or section 22 or 24 of that Act (which respectively regulate particular transactions and penalise short weight etc.), the gas comprised in any foam on the beer or cider shall be disregarded; and in this section " beer " and " cider " have the same meanings as in the said Part VI.

Other amendments of principal Act

20. The provisions of the principal Act mentioned in Schedule 5 to this Act shall have effect with the amendments specified in that Schedule, and in that Schedule references to sections and Schedules are to sections and Schedules of that Act.

PART III

GENERAL

Application to Northern Ireland

21. Schedule 6 to this Act shall have effect for modifying this Act in its application to Northern Ireland.

Expenses etc.

22.—(1) Any administrative expenses of the Secretary of State under this Act shall be defrayed out of money provided by Parliament; and any sums received by the Secretary of State by virtue of this Act shall be paid into the Consolidated Fund.

(2) There shall be defrayed out of money provided by Parliament or paid into the Consolidated Fund any increase attributable to this Act in the sums which, by virtue of any other Act, are payable out of money so provided or, as the case may be, into that Fund.

Repeals

23.—(1) Section 6 of the Weights and Measures Act 1859 as set out in Schedule 6 to the Weights and Measures Act 1878 (which relates to the provision of sales etc. by owners of markets) shall cease to have effect.

(2) The enactments mentioned in the first and second columns of Schedule 7 to this Act are hereby repealed to the extent specified in the third column of that Schedule.

Citation, interpretation and commencement

24.—(1) This Act may be cited as the Weights and Measures Act 1979, and the principal Act and the Weights and Measures &c. Act 1976 and this Act may be cited together as the Weights and Measures Acts 1963 to 1979.

(2) In this Act " the principal Act " means the Weights and Measures Act 1963.

(3) The provisions of this Act mentioned in paragraphs (*a*) to (*c*) of this subsection shall come into force as provided by those paragraphs, that is to say—

(*a*) Part I (except sections 6, 7 and 14), Schedules 1 and 2, paragraph 16 of Schedule 5 and section 20 so far as it relates to that paragraph, and section 23 and Schedule 7, except so far as they relate to provisions of the principal Act and the Weights and Measures &c. Act 1976 other than section 60 of the principal Act and the figures " 60 (3) " in section 54 (4) (*c*) of that Act, shall come into force on 1st January 1980;

(*b*) sections 6, 7 and 19 and Schedule 3 shall come into force on such date as the Secretary of State may appoint by order made by statutory instrument, and different dates may be appointed in pursuance of this paragraph for different provisions and for different purposes of the same provision; and

(*c*) paragraph 1 of Schedule 5 and section 20 so far as it relates to that paragraph shall come into force on the expiration of the period of six months beginning with the date of the passing of this Act;

and accordingly, except as provided by those paragraphs this Act comes into force on the date of the passing of this Act.

SCHEDULES

Section 2 (3)

SCHEDULE 1

Instructions under section 2 (3)

1. Instructions given to a person by an inspector in pursuance of section 2 (3) of this Act shall not come into force until the expiration of the prescribed period beginning with the day when the instructions are given to him and, if during that period the person gives notice to the inspector that he objects to the instructions, shall not come into force except as agreed in writing by the person or as directed by the Secretary of State.

2. Where in pursuance of the preceding paragraph a person gives to an inspector notice of objection to instructions, it shall be the duty of the inspector to refer the instructions to the Unit and it shall be the duty of the Unit to seek to obtain the person's agreement in writing to the instructions either without modifications or with such modifications as the Unit considers acceptable; and if at the expiration of the prescribed period beginning with the day when the instructions are received by the Unit the Unit considers that it has not obtained the person's agreement as aforesaid, it shall be the duty of the Unit to refer the instructions to the Secretary of State.

3. Where instructions are referred to the Secretary of State in pursuance of the preceding paragraph, it shall be his duty—

(*a*) to invite representations in writing about the instructions from the Unit, from the inspector who gave them and from the person to whom they were given and to consider any representations made in response to the invitations within the periods specified in the invitations; and

(*b*) to direct that the instructions shall come into force, without modifications or with modifications specified in the direction, on a day so specified or shall not come into force and to give notice of the direction to the Unit and to the inspector and the person in question.

Section 4 (2)

SCHEDULE 2

Powers and Duties of inspectors etc.

1.—(1) An inspector may, within the area for which he is appointed an inspector and on production if so requested of his credentials, at all reasonable times—

(*a*) enter any premises (except premises used only as a private dwelling) as to which he has reasonable cause to believe that packages are made up on the premises or that imported packages belonging to the importer of them are on the premises or that relevant packages intended for sale are on the premises;

(*b*) inspect and test any equipment which he has reasonable cause to believe is used in making up packages in the United Kingdom or in carrying out a check mentioned in subsections (6) and (7) of section 1 of this Act;

(*c*) inspect, and measure in such manner as he thinks fit, any thing which he has reasonable cause to believe is or contains or is contained in a package, and, if he considers it necessary to do so for the purpose of inspecting the thing or anything in it, break it open;

(*d*) inspect and take copies of, or of any thing purporting to be, a record, document or certificate mentioned in subsections (5) to (8) of section 1 of this Act;

(*e*) require any person on premises which the inspector is authorised to enter by virtue of paragraph (*a*) of this sub-paragraph to provide such assistance as the inspector reasonably considers necessary to enable the inspector to exercise effectively any power conferred on him by paragraphs (*a*) to (*d*) of this sub-paragraph;

(*f*) require any person to give to the inspector such information as the person possesses about the name and address of the packer and of any importer of a package which the inspector finds on premises he has entered by virtue of this sub-paragraph or the following paragraph.

(2) An inspector may serve, on any person carrying on business as the packer or importer of packages in the area for which the inspector is appointed an inspector, a notice requiring the person—

(*a*) to furnish the inspector from time to time with particulars of the kind specified in the notice of any marks which, otherwise than in pursuance of section 1 (4) (*c*) of this Act, are applied from time to time, to packages made up in that area by the person or as the case may be to packages imported by him, for the purpose of enabling the place where the packages were made up to be ascertained; and

(*b*) if the person has furnished particulars of a mark in pursuance of the notice and the mark ceases to be applied for the purpose aforesaid to such packages as aforesaid, to give notice of the cesser to the inspector;

but a notice given by an inspector in pursuance of this sub-paragraph shall not require a person to furnish information which the person does not possess.

2. If a justice of the peace, on sworn information in writing—

(*a*) is satisfied that there is reasonable ground to believe that a package or a thing containing a package or that any such equipment, record, document or certificate as is mentioned in sub-paragraph (1) of the preceding paragraph is on any premises or that an offence under section 2 of this Act is being or is about to be committed on any premises; and

(*b*) is also satisfied either—

(i) that admission to the premises has been refused or that a refusal is apprehended and that notice of the intention to apply for a warrant has been given to the occupier, or

(ii) that an application for admission or the giving of such a notice would defeat the object of the entry or that the premises are unoccupied or that the occupier is temporarily absent and it might defeat the object of the entry to await his return,

the justice may by warrant under his hand, which shall continue in force for a period of one month, authorise an inspector to enter the premises if need be by force.

In the application of this paragraph to Scotland "justice of the peace" includes a sheriff.

3.—(1) An inspector entering any premises by virtue of paragraph 1 or 2 of this Schedule may take with him such other persons and such equipment as he considers necessary.

(2) It shall be the duty of an inspector who leaves premises which he has entered by virtue of paragraph 2 of this Schedule and which are unoccupied or of which the occupier is temporarily absent to leave the premises as effectively secured against trespassers as he found them.

4. Where an inspector has reasonable cause to believe that an offence under section 2 or 5 of this Act or this Schedule has been committed and that any equipment, record, document, package or thing containing or contained in a package may be required as evidence in proceedings for the offence he may seize it and detain it for as long as it is so required.

5.—(1) A local weights and measures authority shall have power to purchase goods, and to authorise any of its officers to purchase goods on behalf of the authority, for the purpose of ascertaining whether an offence under section 2 or 5 (2) of this Act has been committed.

(2) If an inspector breaks open a package in pursuance of paragraph 1 (1) (*c*) of this Schedule otherwise than on premises occupied by the packer or importer of the package and the package is not inadequate, it shall be the duty of the inspector, if the owner of the package requests him to do so, to buy the package on behalf of the local weights and measures authority for the area in which he broke it open.

6. A person who wilfully obstructs an inspector acting in pursuance of this Schedule or Part I of this Act or who without reasonable cause fails to comply with a requirement made of him in pursuance of paragraph 1 (1) (*e*) or (*f*) or 1 (2) of this Schedule shall be guilty of an offence; and subsections (1) to (3) of section 3 of this Act shall apply to such offences as they apply to an offence under section 2 (1) of this Act.

Sections 6 (3), 11 (3) (a)

SCHEDULE 3

Further provisions relating to constitution of Metrological Co-ordinating Unit

Tenure of members

1.—(1) Subject to the following paragraph, a member shall hold office as a member until the Secretary of State gives him notice that his appointment as a member is terminated.

(2) Without prejudice to the generality of the Secretary of State's power to give notices in pursuance of the preceding sub-paragraph, it shall be his duty to give a member such a notice if the Secretary of State is satisfied that the member is no longer a membeer of any local authority.

2. A person may at any time resign his office as a member by giving to the Secretary of State a notice signed by that person and stating that he resigns that office.

Proceedings

3. The quorum of the Unit and the arrangements relating to meetings of the Unit shall be such as the Unit may determine.

4. The validity of any proceedings of the Unit shall not be affected by any vacancy among the members or by any defect in the appointment of a member.

Chairman

5. The Unit may appoint a member to be the chairman of the Unit and may terminate an appointment made in pursuance of this paragraph.

6. A person shall cease to hold office as the chairman of the Unit if he ceases to be a member.

Staff

7. The Unit may employ, on such terms as are applicable to comparable employment in the service of a local authority, such persons as are needed to assist the Unit in the performance of its functions.

Instruments

8. The fixing of the common seal of the Unit shall be authenticated by the signature of the chairman or of any other member authorised by the Unit to authenticate it.

9. A document purporting to be duly executed under the seal of the Unit shall be received in evidence and shall, unless the contrary is proved, be deemed to be so executed.

Interpretation

10. In the preceding provisions of this Schedule "member", except in relation to a local authority, means member of the Unit, and "local authority" has the same meaning as in section 6 (2) of this Act.

Sections 16 (2), 17 (2)

SCHEDULE 4

Sections 11 and 12 of principal act

Weighing or measuring equipment for use for trade

11.—(1) The provisions of this section shall apply to the use for trade of weighing or measuring equipment of such classes or descriptions as may be prescribed.

(2) No person shall use any article for trade as equipment to which this section applies, or have any article in his possession for such use, unless that article, or equipment to which this section applies in which that article is incorporated or to the operation of which the use of that article is incidental, has been passed by an inspector as fit for such use and, except as otherwise expressly provided by or under this Act, bears a stamp indicating that it has been so

passed which remains undefaced otherwise than by reason of fair wear and tear; and if any person contravenes this subsection, he shall be guilty of an offence and any article in respect of which the offence was committed shall be liable to be forfeited.

(3) Any person requiring any equipment to which this section applies to be passed as fit for use for trade shall submit the equipment to an inspector in such manner as the local weights and measures authority may direct and, subject to the provisions of this Act and of any regulations made under section 14 thereof and to the payment by that person of the prescribed fee, the inspector shall—

(*a*) test the equipment by means of such local or working standards and testing equipment as he considers appropriate or, subject to any conditions which may be prescribed, by means of other equipment which has already been tested and which the inspector considers suitable for the purpose; and

(*b*) if the equipment submitted falls within the prescribed limits of error and by virtue of subsection (5) of this section is not required to be stamped as mentioned in paragraph (*c*) of this subsection, give to the person submitting it a statement in writing to the effect that it is passed as aforesaid; and

(*c*) except as otherwise expressly provided by or under this Act, cause it to be stamped with the prescribed stamp;

and each inspector shall keep a record of every such test carried out by him:

Provided that, except as otherwise expressly provided by or under this Act, no weight or measure shall be stamped as mentioned in paragraph (*c*) of this subsection unless it has been marked in the prescribed manner with its purported value.

(4) Where any equipment submitted to an inspector under subsection (3) of this section is of a pattern in respect of which a certificate of approval granted under section 12 of this Act is for the time being in force, the inspector shall not refuse to pass or stamp the equipment on the ground that it is not suitable for use for trade:

Provided that if the inspector is of opinion that the equipment is intended for use for trade for a particular purpose for which it is not suitable, he may refuse to pass or stamp it until the matter has been referred to the Board, and the Board's decision thereon shall be final.

(5) The requirements of subsections (2) and (3) of this section with respect to stamping and marking shall not apply to any weight or measure which is too small to be stamped or marked in accordance with those requirements.

(5A) Where a person submits equipment to an inspector under this section, the inspector may require the person to provide the inspector with such assistance in connection with the testing of the equipment as the inspector reasonably considers it necessary for the person to provide and shall not be obliged to proceed with the test until the person provides it; but a failure to provide the assistance shall not constitute an offence under section 49 of this Act.

(5B) If an inspector refuses to pass fit for use for trade any equipment submitted to him under this section and is requested by the person by whom the equipment was submitted to give reasons for the refusal, the inspector shall give to that person a statement of those reasons in writing.

(6) In the case of any equipment which is required by regulations made under section 14 of this Act to be passed and stamped under this section only after it has been installed at the place where it is to be used for trade, if after the equipment has been so passed and stamped it is dismantled and reinstalled, whether in the same or some other place, it shall not be used for trade after being so reinstalled until it has again been passed under this section; and if any person knowingly uses that equipment in contravention of this subsection, or knowingly causes or permits any other person so to use it, or knowing that the equipment is required by virtue of this subsection to be again so passed disposes of it to some other person without informing him of that requirement, he shall be guilty of an offence and the equipment shall be liable to be forfeited.

(7) Subject to the last foregoing subsection, a stamp applied to any equipment under this section shall have the like validity throughout Great Britain as it has in the place in which it was originally applied, and accordingly that equipment shall not be required to be re-stamped because it is used in any other place;

and any equipment to which this section applies which has been duly stamped before the commencement of this section under any enactment specified in Part I of Schedule 9 to this Act shall be treated for the purposes of this Act as if it had been duly stamped under this section.

(8) Nothing in any local Act passed before this Act shall make unlawful the use for trade as equipment to which this section applies of any article such use of which is not unlawful under this section or require any such article to be stamped otherwise than as required by this section.

(9) If at any time the Board are satisfied that, having regard to the law for the time being in force in Northern Ireland, any of the Channel Islands or the Isle of Man, it is proper so to do, they may by order provide for any equipment to which this section applies duly stamped in accordance with that law, or treated for the purposes of that law as if duly stamped in accordance therewith, to be treated for the purposes of this Act as if it had been duly stamped in Great Britain under this section.

Approved patterns of equipment for use for trade

12.—(1) Where any pattern of weighing or measuring equipment is submitted to the Board for the purpose by any person in such manner as may be prescribed, the Board shall examine in such manner as they think fit the suitability for use for trade of equipment of that pattern, having regard in particular to the principle, materials and methods used or proposed to be used in its construction, and if the Board are satisfied that such equipment is suitable for use for trade then, subject to section 13 (2) of this Act, they shall issue a certificate of approval of that pattern and cause particulars thereof to be published.

(1A) The foregoing subsection applies to a pattern consisting of an approved pattern with modifications as it applies to other patterns, and in this subsection "approved pattern" means a pattern in respect of which a certificate of approval under the foregoing subsection is in force.

(2) A certificate of approval under subsection (1) of this section may be granted or renewed subject to such conditions as the Secretary of State thinks fit; and if any person—

(*a*) knowing that a condition other than a condition mentioned in section 12A (1) (*b*) of this Act has been imposed with respect to any equipment, uses, or causes or permits any other person to use, that equipment in contravention of that condition; or

(*b*) knowing that any condition has been imposed with respect to any equipment, disposes of that equipment to any other person in a state in which it could be used for trade without informing that other person of that condition,

he shall be guilty of an offence and the equipment shall be liable to be forfeited.

(3) The Board, after consultation with such persons appearing to them to be interested as they think fit, may at any time revoke any certificate granted under this section, and shall cause notice of any such revocation to be published; and where the Board so revoke any certificate, then if any person, knowing that the certificate has been revoked, and save as may be permitted by any fresh certificate granted in respect thereof, uses for trade, or has in his possession for such use, or causes or permits any other person so to use, any equipment of the pattern in question, or disposes of any such equipment to any other person in a state in which it could be so used without informing that other person of the revocation, he shall be guilty of an offence and the equipment shall be liable to be forfeited.

(3A) The provisions of the last foregoing subsection relating to offences and forfeiture shall not apply in consequence of the revocation of a certificate of approval if the notice of the revocation published under that subsection states that instead of those provisions the provisions of section 12A (4) of this Act are to apply in consequence of the revocation.

(4) Any equipment of a pattern in respect of which a certificate of approval has been granted under this section may, and in such cases as may be prescribed shall, be marked in the prescribed manner so as to identify it with the pattern in question.

(5) A certificate granted under section 6 of the Weights and Measures Act 1904 in respect of any pattern of weighing or measuring equipment shall be deemed for the purposes of this Act to be a certificate of approval of that pattern granted under this section.

Section 20

SCHEDULE 5

OTHER AMENDMENTS OF PRINCIPAL ACT

1. In section 4 (5) (which provides for certificates of fitness for local standards to be in force for periods of two, five and ten years) for the words from "following period" to "ten years" there shall be substituted the words "prescribed period"; but the amendment made by this paragraph shall not affect a certificate of fitness which is in force immediately before the date when this paragraph comes into force.

2. In section 5 (which requires local weights and measures authorities to provide working standards and testing and stamping equipment) after subsection (1) there shall be inserted the following subsection—

(1A) An authority may, with the approval of the Secretary of State—

(*a*) provide a particular working standard or item of equipment as required by subsection (1) of this section by making arrangements with another person for the standard or item to be made available by him;

(*b*) make arrangements with another person for standards or equipment provided by the authority under subsection (1) of this section, except stamping equipment, to be made available to the other person;

and the provisions of subsection (3) of this section relating to the premises at which things are to be kept shall not apply to things which are the subject of arrangements under paragraph (*a*) of this subsection.

Nothing in the preceding provisions of this subsection prejudices the operation of the Local Authorities (Goods and Services) Act 1970, section 101 of the Local Government Act 1972 or section 56 of the Local Government (Scotland) Act 1973 (which among other things enable a local authority to arrange for the provision of goods or services and the discharge of its functions by another local authority).

3.—(1) In subsection (1) of section 6 (which among other things enables certain articles and equipment to be accepted, on payment of a fee, for testing for accuracy by the Secretary of State)—

(*a*) the words from "and on payment" to "determine" shall be omitted; and

(*b*) after the word "accuracy" there shall be inserted the words "or compliance with any specification"; and

(*c*) at the end of paragraph (*b*) there shall be inserted the words "and

(*c*) any other metrological equipment, and

(*d*) any article for use in connection with equipment mentioned in paragraph (*b*) or (*c*) above,";

and at the end of the subsection there shall be inserted the words "The Secretary of State may charge, in respect of any article or equipment accepted by him in pursuance of this subsection, a fee of an amount ascertained in such manner as he may determine with the approval of the Treasury.".

(2) In subsection (3) of section 6 (of which the proviso limits the fee for a certain test of apparatus to £15 or a higher sum specified by order) the proviso shall be omitted.

4. Section 7 (which provides for the establishment and constitution of the Commission on Units and Standards of Measurement) and section 8 (which relates to the functions of the Commission) shall be omitted.

5. In subsection (1) of section 15 (which among other things makes it an offence to alter or deface a stamp on weighing or measuring equipment used for trade)—

(*a*) after paragraph (*d*) there shall be inserted the words "; or

(*e*) severs or otherwise tampers with any wire, cord or other thing by means of which a stamp is attached to the equipment"; and

(*b*) in the proviso (under which certain provisions of that subsection do not apply to things done by specified persons in the course of adjusting or repairing the equipment in question) before the words "in the course of" there shall be inserted the words ", and paragraph (*e*) of this subsection shall not apply to anything done,".

6. In subsection (9) of section 24 (which excludes certain transactions from the provisions of that section) paragraph (*b*) (which relates to the sale of goods with a view to their industrial or constructional use) shall be omitted.

7. In section 26, for subsection (1) (under which it is a defence for a person charged with an offence under Part IV of the principal Act in respect of any goods to prove that the commission of the offence was due to a mistake or to an accident or some other cause beyond his control and that he took all reasonable precautions and exercised all due diligence to avoid the commission of such an offence in respect of the goods by himself or any person under his control) there shall be substituted the following subsection—

> (1) In any proceedings for an offence under this Part of this Act or an instrument made thereunder, it shall be a defence for the person charged to prove that he took all reasonable precautions and exercised all due diligence to avoid the commission of the offence.

but the amendment made by this paragraph and the repeal by this Act of section 26 (4) (which is consequential upon that amendment) shall not apply in relation to an offence committed before the date when this paragraph comes into force.

8. For section 27 (which relates to offences due to the default of a third person) there shall be substituted the following section—

> 27.—(1) If in any case the defence provided by section 26 (1) of this Act involves an allegation that the commission of the offence in question was due to the act or default of another person or due to reliance on information supplied by another person, the person charged shall not, without the leave of the court, be entitled to rely on the defence unless, before the beginning of the period of seven days ending with the date when the hearing of the charge began, he served on the prosecutor a notice giving such information identifying or assisting in the identification of the other person as was then in his possession.
>
> (2) Where the commission by any person of an offence under this Part of this Act or an instrument made thereunder is due to the act or default of some other person, the other person shall be guilty of the offence and may be charged with and convicted of the offence whether or not proceedings are taken against the first-mentioned person.
>
> (3) Where by virtue of subsection (2) of this section a person is charged with an offence with which some other person might have been charged, the reference in section 26 (7) of this Act to articles or goods sold by or in the possession of the person charged shall be construed as a reference to articles or goods sold by or in the possession of that other person.

but the amendment made by this paragraph shall not apply in relation to an offence committed before the date when this paragraph comes into force.

9. Section 28 (which relates to offences originating in certain countries outside Great Britain) shall be omitted; but the repeal by this Act of that section shall not affect the application of that section to an offence committed before the date when this paragraph comes into force.

10. In section 38 (1) (which as amended by section 4 (3) of this Act requires each local weights and measures authority to make a report to the Secretary of State about the operation during each financial year of the arrangements made to give effect in the area of the authority to the purposes of the principal Act and Part I of this Act)—

(*a*) the reference to those arrangements shall include arrangements for giving effect to functions relating to weights and measures which are conferred on the authority otherwise than by or under the principal Act and Part I of this Act and which are specified, in a notice in writing given to the authority by the Seecretary of State and not withdrawn, as functions to which this paragraph applies; and

(*b*) the reference to functions under the principal Act shall include functions so specified.

11. In section 42 (which among other things provides for examinations to be held for the purpose of ascertaining whether persons are qualified for appointment as inspectors) after subsection (1) there shall be inserted the following subsection—

> (1A) The Secretary of State may if he thinks fit arrange with some other person for that person to hold examinations for the purpose aforesaid.

and in subsection (3) of that section (which relates to the fees for any such examination as aforesaid) after the word "aforesaid" there shall be inserted the words "which is held by the Secretary of State".

12. For subsection (1) of section 44 (which provides that no reduction in an inspector's fees shall be made for assistance given in the inspection, testing or

stamping of equipment except where the assistance is given by a manufacturer of the equipment) there shall be substituted the following subsection—

(1) Where a person gives assistance in connection with the inspection, testing or stamping of weighing or measuring equipment by an inspector, the local weights and measures authority may reduce, by a sum which the authority considers is reasonable by reference to the assistance, the amount of any payment falling to be made by that person to the inspector in respect of the inspection, testing or stamping.

13.—(1) In subsection (2) of section 48, for paragraph (*b*) (which authorises an inspector to seize and detain any document which is displayed with certain goods and relates to the price or quantity of them and which may be required as evidence in proceedings under the principal Act) there shall be substituted the following paragraph—

(*b*) any document or goods which the inspector has reason to believe may be required as evidence in proceedings for an offence under this Act.

(2) In subsection (5) of section 48 (which penalises a person who improperly discloses information about any manufacturing process or trade secret which he has obtained in a work-place he entered by virtue of that section) before the word "manufacturing" there shall be inserted the word "secret".

14. In section 51 (of which subsection (2) provides among other things that proceedings for an offence mentioned in that subsection shall not be instituted unless in certain cases a notice giving particulars of the alleged offence has been served on the accused within fifteen days from the date of the alleged offence and shall not be instituted after three months from that date)—

(*a*) in subsection (2) (*b*) for the words "fifteen days beginning with the date aforesaid" there shall be substituted the words "thirty days beginning with the date when evidence which the person proposing to institute the proceedings considers is sufficient to justify a prosecution for the offence came to his knowledge";

(*b*) in subsection (2) (*c*) for the words from "three months" onwards there shall be substituted the words "twelve months beginning with the date mentioned in paragraph (*a*) of this subsection or three months beginning with the date mentioned in paragraph (*b*) of this subsection, whichever first occurs"; and

(*c*) after subsection (3) there shall be inserted the following subsection—

(4) For the purposes of subsection (2) of this section—

(*a*) a certificate of a person who institutes proceedings for an offence mentioned in that subsection which states that evidence came to his knowledge on a particular date shall be conclusive evidence of that fact; and

(*b*) a document purporting to be a certificate of such a person and to be signed by him or on his behalf shall be presumed to be such a certificate unless the contrary is proved.

but the amendments made by this paragraph shall not apply in relation to an offence committed before the date when this paragraph comes into force.

15. In subsection (1) of section 58 (which assigns meanings to certain expressions used in the principal Act), in the definition of "credentials" for the words "authority in writing from a person who is for the time being a justice of the peace (or, in Scotland, either the sheriff or a justice of the peace)" there shall be substituted the words "authority in writing from the local weights and measures authority who appointed him".

16. Section 60 (which relates to cran and quarter cran measures) shall be omitted.

17. In Part II of Schedule 1 and Schedule 1A, for the word "Dekare" there shall be substituted the word "Decare".

18. In paragraph 3 of Part VI of Schedule 4 (which provides for certain liquors to be sold by retail for consumption on the premises of the seller only in one of the quantities there mentioned and for the quantity to be the same for all those liquors)—

(*a*) after the word "retail" there shall be inserted the words ", by or on behalf of the licensee of licensed premises or a licensed canteen within the meaning of the Licensing Act 1964, or the Licensing (Scotland) Act 1976,"; and (*b*) after the word " same " there shall be inserted the words " for those parts of the premises of which he is the licensee and ".

19. In paragraph 1 of Part IX of Schedule 4 (of which sub-paragraph (*d*), as amended by the Weights and Measures Act 1963 (Cereal Breakfast Foods and Oat Products) Order 1975, provides that the foods to which that Part applies include rolled oats) sub-paragraph (*d*) shall be omitted.

20. For Part XII of Schedule 4 there shall be substituted the following—

Part XII

Tables of permitted weights for containers

Table A

Gross weight	Permitted weight of container
Not exceeding 500g	5g
Exceeding 500g	a weight at the rate of 10g per kg of the gross weight.

Table B

Gross weight	Permitted weight of container
Not exceeding 500g	9g
Exceeding 500g but not exceeding 1kg ..	a weight at the rate of 16g per kg of the gross weight.
Exceeding 1kg but not exceeding 2kg ..	a weight at the rate of 12g per kg of the gross weight.
Exceeding 2kg	a weight at the rate of 10g per kg of the gross weight.

Table C

Gross weight	Permitted weight of container
Not exceeding 250g	a weight at the rate of 120g per kg of the gross weight.
Exceeding 250g but not exceeding 1kg ..	a weight at the rate of 100g per kg of the gross weight.
Exceeding 1kg but not exceeding 3kg ..	a weight at the rate of 90g per kg of the gross weight.
Exceeding 3kg	a weight at the rate of 60g per kg of the gross weight.

21. At the end of paragraph 1 of Part VIII of Schedule 7 (which lists miscellaneous goods which are to be sold by or marked with net weight) there shall be inserted the words " (*f*) rolled oats ".

Section 21

SCHEDULE 6

Application to Northern Ireland

1. Sections 6, 8 to 11 and 22 and Schedules 3 and 4 shall be omitted.

2. Subject to the following provisions of this Schedule, for any such reference as is specified in column 1 of the table set out below there shall be substituted the reference specified in column 2.

TABLE

Reference	*Substituted references*
The Secretary of State (except the references in sections 1 (2) and (8) (*b*), 5 (6), 7 (5) and 24 (3) (*b*)).	The Department of Commerce for Northern Ireland.
Section 9A.	Section 3A.
Schedule 3.	Schedule 1.
Section 22.	Section 16.
Section 24.	Section 18.
A local weights and measures authority.	The Department of Commerce for Northern Ireland.
Section 51.	Section 33.
The Unit.	The Department of Commerce for Northern Ireland.
Section 58.	Section 41.
Section 57.	Section 37.
Section 11.	Section 5.
Section 14 (except the reference to section 24 (3) (*a*)).	Section 8.
Section 12 (except the reference in section 14 (1)).	Section 6.
Section 12A.	Section 6A.
The Treasury.	The Department of Finance for Northern Ireland.
Section 13.	Section 7.
Section 52.	Section 34.
Section 31.	Section 25 (1).
Section 49.	Section 29.
Section 16.	Section 10.
Section 20.	Section 14.
Section 48.	Section 28.
Schedule 4.	Schedule 2.
Schedule 6.	Schedule 4.
Section 60.	Section 4 (4).

3. In section 1 (2) and (8) (*b*) after the words " Secretary of State " there shall be inserted the words " or, as the case may be, the Department of Commerce for Northern Ireland ".

4. In section 3—

(*a*) in subsection (2)—

(i) for the words " England and Wales " there shall be substituted the words " Northern Ireland ";

(ii) for the words " chief officer of police for a police area " there shall be substituted the words " Director of Public Prosecutions for Northern Ireland ";

(iii) for the word " (4) " there shall be substituted the word " (3) ";

(*b*) subsection (3) shall be omitted.

5. In section 4—

(*a*) in subsection (1) the words " within the area of the authority " shall be omitted;

(*b*) for subsection (3) there shall be substituted the following subsection—

(3) In section 32 (1) (*c*) of the principal Act (which relates to breaches by inspectors of their duties under that Act) the reference to a duty imposed by or under that Act shall include a reference to a duty imposed by or under this Part of this Act;

(*c*) subsection (4) shall be omitted.

6. In section 5—

(*a*) in subsection (4) the words from " for the area " to " is situated " shall be omitted;

(*b*) in subsection (6) after the words " Secretary of State " there shall be inserted the words " or, as the case may be, the Department of Commerce for Northern Ireland ";

(*c*) in subsection (7) for the words " to (3) " there shall be substituted the words " and (2) ".

7. In section 7—

(*a*) in subsection (1)—

(i) in paragraph (*b*) the words " to local weights and measures authorities and " shall be omitted;

(ii) paragraph (*c*) shall be omitted;

(iii) in paragraph (*d*) for the words " Great Britain " there shall be substituted the words " Northern Ireland " and the words from " or to those " to " of this Act " shall be omitted;

(iv) paragraphs (*e*), (*g*) and (*h*) shall be omitted;

(*b*) in subsection (3)—

(i) paragraph (*a*) shall be omitted;

(ii) in paragraph (*b*) for the words " England or Wales " there shall be substituted the words " Northern Ireland " and after the word " Prosecutions " there shall be inserted the words " for Northern Ireland ";

(*c*) in subsection (4)—

(i) in paragraph (*a*) the words " if the Secretary of State so directs " shall be omitted;

(ii) in paragraph (*b*) the words " and the Secretary of State approves " shall be omitted.

8. In section 12—

(*a*) in subsection (1) for the words in paragraph (*b*) from " a member " onwards there shall be substituted the words " an inspector or a person who accompanied an inspector by virtue of paragraph 3 (1) of Schedule 2 to this Act ", for the words " a member, inspector " there shall be substituted the word " an inspector " and the words from " or, in the case " onwards shall be omitted;

(*b*) in subsection (3) in the definition of " statutory maximum " for the reference to England and Wales there shall be substituted a reference to Northern Ireland,

and for the purposes of the definition of " statutory maximum " as so amended the provisions of the Criminal Law Act 1977 which relate to the sum mentioned in that definition shall extend to Northern Ireland.

9. In section 14—

(*a*) in subsection (1) the definition of " the Unit " shall be omitted;

(*b*) in subsection (5) for the words " to 3 " there shall be substituted the words " and 2 ".

10. In section 15—

(*a*) in subsection (2) for the words from " by statutory instrument " to the end of the subsection there shall be substituted the words " by statutory rule for the purposes of the Statutory Rules Act (Northern Ireland) 1958, and shall be subject to negative resolution as defined by section 41 (6) of the Interpretation Act (Northern Ireland) 1954 as if it were a statutory instrument within the meaning of that Act ";

(*b*) subsections (4) and (5) shall be omitted.

11. In section 16—

(*a*) in subsection (1) (*a*)—

(i) for the word " error " there shall be substituted the word " prescribed ";

(ii) for the words " paragraph (*c*) of this subsection " there shall be substituted the words " sub-paragraph (ii) ";

(*b*) subsection (2) shall be omitted.

12. In section 17—

(*a*) in subsection (1) (*c*) (i) for the words " the foregoing subsection " there shall be substituted the words " subsection (1) ";

(*b*) subsection (2) shall be omitted.

13. In section 24—

(*a*) in subsection (2) for the word " 1963 " there shall be substituted the words " (Northern Ireland) 1967 ";

(*b*) in subsection (3)—

(i) in paragraph (*a*) the words from " paragraph 16 " to " that paragraph " and the words " and the figures ' 60 (3) ' in section 54 (4) (*c*) of that Act," shall be omitted;

(ii) in paragraph (*b*) the words " and Schedule 3 " shall be omitted;
(iii) paragraph (*c*) shall be omitted.

14. In Schedule 1—
(*a*) in paragraph 2 the words from " and it shall " to the end of the paragraph shall be omitted;
(*b*) in paragraph 3 the words " from the Unit " and the words " the Unit and to " shall be omitted.

15. In Schedule 2—
(*a*) in paragraph 1 (1) the words " within the area for which he is appointed an inspector and " shall be omitted;
(*b*) in paragraph 1 (2) the words " in the area for which the inspector is appointed an inspector " shall be omitted;
(*c*) in paragraph 2 for the word " information " there shall be substituted the word " complaint " and the words from " In the application " to the end of the paragraph shall be omitted;
(*d*) in paragraph 5 (2) the words " for the area in which he broke it open " shall be omitted;
(*e*) in paragraph 6 for the words " to (3) " there shall be substituted the words " and (2) ".

16. For Schedule 5 there shall be substituted the following Schedule—

Schedule 5

Other amendments of principal act

1. In section 2 (which requires the Department to provide working standards and testing and stamping equipment) after subsection (1) there shall be inserted the following subsection—

(1A) The Department may—
(*a*) provide a particular working standard or item of equipment as required by subsection (1) of this section by making arrangements with another person for the standard or item to be made available by him;
(*b*) make arrangements with another person for standards or equipment provided by the Department under subsection (1) of this section, except stamping equipment, to be made available to the other person.

2. In subsection (1) of section 9 (which among other things makes it an offence to alter or deface a stamp on weighing or measuring equipment used for trade), after paragraph (d) there shall be inserted the words " ; or
(*e*) severs or otherwise tampers with any wire, cord or other thing by means of which a stamp is attached to the equipment ";
and in subsection (2) of that section (under which certain provisions of the said subsection (1) do not apply to things done by specified persons in the course of adjusting or repairing the equipment in question) before the words " in the course of " there shall be inserted the words " , and paragraph (e) of that subsection shall not apply to anything done,".

3. In subsection (9) of section 18 (which excludes certain transactions from the provisions of that section) paragraph (*b*) (which relates to the sale of goods with a view to their industrial or constructional use) shall be omitted.

4. In section 20, for subsection (1) (under which it is a defence for a person charged with an offence under Part IV of the principal Act in respect of any goods to prove that the commission of the offence was due to a mistake or to an accident or some other cause beyond his control and that he took all reasonable precautions and exercised all due diligence to avoid the commission of such an offence in respect of the goods by himself or any person under his control) there shall be substituted the following subsection—

(1) In any proceedings for an offence under this Part of this Act or an instrument made thereunder, it shall be a defence for the person charged to prove that he took all reasonable precautions and exercised all due diligence to avoid the commission of the offence.

but the amendment made by this paragraph and the repeal by this Act of section 20 (4) (which is consequential upon that amendment) shall not apply in relation to an offence committed before that date when this paragraph comes into force.

5. For section 21 (which relates to offences due to the default of a third person) there shall be substituted the following section—

21.—(1) If in any case the defence provided by section 20 (1) of this Act involves an allegation that the commission of the offence in question was due to the act or default of another person or due to reliance on information supplied by another person, the person charged shall not, without the leave of the court, be entitled to rely on the defence unless, before the beginning of the period of seven days ending with the date when the hearing of the charge began, he served on the prosecutor a notice giving such information identifying or assisting in the identification of the other person as was then in his possession.

(2) Where the commission by any person of an offence under this Part of this Act or an instrument made thereunder is due to the act or default of some other person, the other person shall be guilty of the offence and may be charged with and convicted of the offence whether or not proceedings are taken against the first-mentioned person.

(3) Where by virtue of subsection (2) of this section a person is charged with an offence with which some other person might have been charged, the reference in section 20 (7) of this Act to articles or goods sold by or in the possession of the person charged shall be construed as a reference to articles or goods sold by or in the possession of that other person.

but the amendment made by this paragraph shall not apply in relation to an offence committed before the date when this paragraph comes into force.

6. Section 22 (which relates to offences originating in certain countries outside Northern Ireland) shall be omitted; but the repeal by this Act by that section shall not affect the application of that section to an offence committed before the date when this paragraph comes into force.

7.—(1) In subsection (2) of section 28, for paragraph (*b*) (which authorises an inspector to seize and detain any document which is displayed with certain goods and relates to the price or quantity of them and which may be required as evidence in proceedings under the principal Act) there shall be substituted the following paragraph—

(*b*) any document or goods which the inspector has reason to believe may be required as evidence in proceedings for an offence under this Act.

(2) In subsection (5) of section 28 (which penalises a person who improperly discloses information about any manufacturing process or trade secret which he has obtained in a work-place he has entered by virtue of that section) before the word "manufacturing" there shall be inserted the word "secret".

8. In section 33 (of which subsection (2) provides among other things that proceedings for an offence mentioned in that subsection shall not be instituted unless in certain cases a notice giving particulars of the alleged offence has been served on the accused within fifteen days from the date of the alleged offence and shall not be instituted after three months from that date)—

(*a*) in subsection (2) (*b*) for the words "fifteen days beginning with the date aforesaid" there shall be substituted the words "thirty days beginning with the date when evidence which the person proposing to institute the proceedings considers is sufficient to justify a prosection for the offence came to his knowledge";

(*b*) in subsection (2) (*c*) for the words from "three months" onwards there shall be substituted the words "twelve months beginning with the date mentioned in paragraph (*a*) of this subsection or three months beginning with the date mentioned in paragraph (b) of this subsection, whichever first occurs"; and

(*c*) after subsection (2) there shall be inserted the following subsection—

(3) For the purposes of subsection (2) of this section—

(*a*) a certificate of a person who institutes proceedings for an offence mentioned in that subsection which states that evidence came to his knowledge on a particular date shall be conclusive evidence of that fact; and

(*b*) a document purporting to be a certificate of such a person and to be signed by him or on his behalf shall be presumed to be such a certificate unless the contrary is proved,

but the amendments made by this paragraph shall not apply in relation to an offence committed before the date when this paragraph comes into force.

9. Section 38 (2) (which limits the fee for certain tests of apparatus to £15 or to a higher sum specified by order) shall be omitted.

10. For subsection (1) of section 40 (which provides that no reduction in an inspector's fees shall be made for assistance given in the inspection, testing or stamping of equipment except where the assistance is given by a manufacturer of the equipment) there shall be substituted the following subsection—

(1) Where a person gives assistance in connection with the inspection, testing or stamping of weighing or measuring equipment by an inspector, the Department may reduce, by a sum which the Department considers reasonable by reference to the assistance, the amount of any payment falling to be made by that person to the inspector in respect of the inspection, testing or stamping.

11. In paragraph 1 of Part IX of Schedule 2 (of which sub-paragraph (*d*), as amended by the Cereal Breakfast Foods and Oat Products Order (Northern Ireland) 1975, provides that the foods to which that Part applies include rolled oats) sub-paragraph (*d*) shall be omitted.

12. For Part XII of Schedule 2 there shall be substituted the following—

Part XII

Tables of permitted weights for containers

Table A

Gross weight	Permitted weight of container
Not exceeding 500g	5g
Exceeding 500g	a weight at the rate of 10g per kg of the gross weight.

Table B

Gross weight	Permitted weight of container
Not exceeding 500g	9g
Exceeding 500g but not exceeding 1kg ..	a weight at the rate of 16g per kg of the gross weight.
Exceeding 1kg but not exceeding 2kg ..	a weight at the rate of 12g per kg of the gross weight.
Exceeding 2kg	a weight at the rate of 10g per kg of the gross weight.

Table C

Gross weight	Permitted weight of container
Not exceeding 250g	a weight at the rate of 120g per kg of the gross weight.
Exceeding 250g but not exceeding 1kg ..	a weight at the rate of 100g per kg of the gross weight.
Exceeding 1kg but not exceeding 3kg ..	a weight at the rate of 90g per kg of the gross weight.
Exceeding 3kg	a weight at the rate of 60g per kg of the gross weight.

13. At the end of paragraph 1 of Part VIII of Schedule 5 (which lists miscellaneous goods which are to be sold by or marked with net weight) there shall be inserted the words " (*f*) rolled oats ".

Section 23 (2)

SCHEDULE 7

ENACTMENTS REPEALED

Chapter	Short title	Extent of repeal
55 Geo. 3. c. 94.	The Herring Fishery (Scotland) Act 1815.	Section 13.
41 & 42 Vict. c. 49.	The Weights and Measures Act 1878.	Section 86. Schedule 6.
52 & 53 Vict. c. 23.	The Herring Fishery (Scotland) Act 1889.	Section 4.
8 Edw. 7. c. 17.	The Cran Measures Act 1908.	The whole Act.
1963 c. 31.	The Weights and Measures Act 1963.	In section 2 (3), the words from the beginning to " section 8 of this Act ". In section 6, the words from " and on " to " determine " in subsection (1) and the proviso in subsection (3). Sections 7 and 8. In section 9A (7) the figure " 60 ". In section 11 (4), the words from " or of " to " that section ". In section 12, in subsection (1) the words from " on payment " to " determine " and the words from " and may " onwards, and in subsection (3) the words " or authorisation " wherever they occur and the words " or incorporating the modification ". In section 13 (1), the words from " or of " onwards. Section 24 (9) (*b*). Section 26 (4). Section 28. In section 29 (3), the words from " and nothing " onwards. In section 52 (1), the words " 31 and 49 (1) ". In section 54, in subsection (3) paragraphs (*b*) and (*c*), and in subsection (4) paragraph (*b*) and the figures " 8 (2) " and " 60 (3) " in paragraph (*c*). Section 60. In paragraph 1 of Part IX of Schedule 4, sub-paragraph (*d*).
1967 c. 6 (N.I.)	The Weights and Measures Act (Northern Ireland) 1967.	In section 3A (7) the figures " 4 (4) ". Section 4 (4). In section 5 (4), the words from " or of " to " that section ". In section 6, in subsection (1) the words from " on payment " to " determine " and the words from " and may " onwards, and in subsection (3) the words " or authorisation " wherever they occur and the words " or incorporating the modification ". In section 7 (1), the words from " or of " onwards. Section 18 (9) (*b*). Section 20 (4). Section 22. In section 23 (3), the words from " and nothing " onwards. In section 34 (1), the words " 25 (1) and 29 (1) ". Section 38 (2).

SCHEDULE 7—*continued*

Chapter	Short title	Extent of repeal
1967 c. 6 (N.I. —*cont.*	The Weights and Measures Act (Northern Ireland) 1967—*cont.*	In paragraph 1 of Part IX of Schedule 2, sub-paragraph (*d*).
1971 c. 23.	The Courts Act 1971.	In Part I of Schedule 9, the words " Cran Measures Act 1908 . . . Section 9 (6) ".
1976 c. 77.	The Weights and Measures &c. Act 1976.	Sections 2 (3) (*c*), 7 (5) and 10 (5) (*b*).
1976 c. 86.	The Fishery Limits Act 1976.	In Schedule 2, paragraph 9.

Ancient Monuments and Archaeological Areas Act 1979

(1979 c. 46)

ARRANGEMENT OF SECTIONS

PART I

ANCIENT MONUMENTS

Protection of scheduled monuments

PART II

ARCHAEOLOGICAL AREAS

An Act to consolidate and amend the law relating to ancient monuments; to make provision for the investigation, preservation and recording of matters of archaeological or historical interest and (in connection therewith) for the regulation of operations or activities affecting such matters; to provide for the recovery

of grants under section 10 of the Town and Country Planning (Amendment) Act 1972 or under section 4 of the Historic Buildings and Ancient Monuments Act 1953 in certain circumstances; and to provide for grants by the Secretary of State to the Architectural Heritage Fund. [4th April 1979]

General Note

This Act consolidates and amends the law relating to ancient monuments and makes provision for the investigation, preservation and recording of matters of archaeological or historical interest.

Pt. I (ss. 1–32) relates to ancient monuments: s. 1 makes provision for a schedule of monuments; s. 2 deals with the control of works affecting scheduled monuments; s. 3 provides for the grant of scheduled monument consent by order of the Secretary of State; s. 4 sets out the duration, modification and revocation provisions of scheduled monument consent; s. 5 allows for the execution of works for preservation of a scheduled monument by the Secretary of State in cases of urgency; s. 6 grants powers of entry for inspection of scheduled monuments; s. 7 provides for compensation for refusal of scheduled monument consent; s. 8 allows for recovery of compensation under s. 7 where consent is subsequently given; s. 9 grants compensation where works affecting a scheduled monument cease to be authorised; s. 10 provides for compulsory acquisition of ancient monuments by the Secretary of State; s. 11 deals with acquisition by agreement or gift of ancient monuments; s. 12 grants power to place ancient monuments under guardianship; s. 13 sets out the effect of guardianship; s. 14 states the methods for terminating guardianship; s. 15 provides for the acquisition and guardianship of land in the vicinity of an ancient monument; s. 16 relates to the acquisition of easements and other similar rights over land in the vicinity of an ancient monument; s. 17 deals with agreements concerning ancient monuments and land in their vicinity; s. 18 outlines the powers of limited owners for the purposes of ss. 12, 16 and 17; s. 19 allows the public access to monuments under public control; s. 20 makes provision for public facilities in connection with ancient monuments; s. 21 provides for the transfer of ancient monuments between local authorities and the Secretary of State; s. 22 allows for the continued existence of Ancient Monuments Boards; s. 23 relates to the annual reports of the Ancient Monuments Boards; s. 24 concerns expenditure by the Secretary of State or local authorities on acquisition and preservation of ancient monuments; s. 25 allows for advice and superintendence by the Secretary of State; s. 26 empowers the Secretary of State to authorise entry on land believed to contain an ancient monument; s. 27 contains general provisions as to compensation for depreciation under Pt. I; s. 28 states the offence of damaging certain ancient monuments; s. 29 provides for compensation orders for damages to monuments under guardianship in England and Wales; s. 30 concerns disposal of land acquired under Pt. I; s. 31 deals with voluntary contributions towards expenditure under Pt. I; s. 32 contains interpretation provisions relating to Pt. I.

Pt. II (ss. 33–41) relates to archaeological areas: s. 33 deals with destination of areas of archaeological importance; s. 34 concerns the appointment of investigating authorities for areas of archaeological importance; s. 35 states the notice required of operations in areas of archaeological importance; s. 36 provides for the certificate to accompany operations notices under s. 35; s. 37 exempts certain operations from s. 35; s. 38 outlines the powers of investigating authorities to enter and excavate site of operations covered by an operations notice; s. 39 grants power to the investigating authority to investigate in advance of operations notice any site which may be acquired compulsorily; s. 40 sets out other powers of entry on site of operations covered by an operations notice; s. 41 concerns the interpretation of Pt. II.

Pt. III (ss. 42–65) contains miscellaneous and supplemental provisions: s. 42 places restrictions on the use of metal detectors; s. 43 grants power of entry for survey and valuation; s. 44 contains supplementary provisions with respect to powers of entry; s. 45 provides for expenditure on archaeological investigation; s. 46 allows for compensation for damage caused by the exercise of certain powers under this Act; s. 47 contains general provisions with respect to claims for compensation under the Act; s. 48 provides for recovery of grants for expenditure in conservation areas and on historic buildings; s. 49 enables the Secretary to make grants to the

Architectural Heritage Fund; s. 50 applies the Act, with certain exceptions, to Crown land; s. 51 relates to ecclesiastical property; s. 52 relates to the application of the Act to the Isles of Scilly; s. 53 concerns monuments in territorial waters; s. 54 relates to the treatment and preservation of finds; s. 55 provides for proceedings for questioning validity of certain orders, etc.; s. 56 deals with the service of documents; s. 57 grants power to require information as to interests in land; s. 58 outlines offences by corporations; s. 59 concerns prosecution of offences in Scotland; s. 60 deals with regulations and orders under the Act; s. 61 is the general interpretation section; s. 62 makes special provision for Scotland; s. 63 makes special provision for Wales; s. 64 contains transitional provisions, consequential amendments and repeals; s. 65 contains the short title, commencement and extent. The Act does not extend to Northern Ireland.

The Act received the Royal Assent on April 4, 1979, and comes into force on a day to be appointed.

Parliamentary debates

Hansard, H.L. Vol. 397, col. 1167; Vol. 398, col. 453; Vol. 399, col. 1468; H.C. Vol. 965, cols. 1375, 1376.

PART I

ANCIENT MONUMENTS

Protection of scheduled monuments

Schedule of monuments

1.—(1) The Secretary of State shall compile and maintain for the purposes of this Act (in such form as he thinks fit) a schedule of monuments (referred to below in this Act as " the Schedule ").

(2) The Secretary of State shall on first compiling the Schedule include therein—

(*a*) any monument included in the list last published before the commencement of this Act under section 12 of the Ancient Monuments Consolidation and Amendment Act 1913; and

(*b*) any monument in respect of which the Secretary of State has before the commencement of this Act served notice on any person in accordance with section 6 (1) of the Ancient Monuments Act 1931 of his intention to include it in a list to be published under section 12.

(3) Subject to subsection (4) below, the Secretary of State may on first compiling the Schedule or at any time thereafter include therein any monument which appears to him to be of national importance.

(4) The power of the Secretary of State under subsection (3) above to include any monument in the Schedule does not apply to any structure which is occupied as a dwelling house by any person other than a person employed as the caretaker thereof or his family.

(5) The Secretary of State may—

(*a*) exclude any monument from the Schedule; or

(*b*) amend the entry in the Schedule relating to any monument (whether by excluding anything previously included as part of the monument or adding anything not previously so included, or otherwise).

(6) As soon as may be after—

(*a*) including any monument in the Schedule under subsection (3) above;

(*b*) amending the entry in the Schedule relating to any monument; or

(*c*) excluding any monument from the Schedule;

the Secretary of State shall inform the owner and (if the owner is not the occupier) the occupier of the monument, and any local authority in whose area the monument is situated, of the action taken and, in a case falling within paragraph (*a*) or (*b*) above, shall also send to him or them a copy of the entry or (as the case may be) of the amended entry in the Schedule relating to that monument.

(7) The Secretary of State shall from time to time publish a list of all the monuments which are for the time being included in the Schedule, whether as a single list or in sections containing the monuments situated in particular areas; but in the case of a list published in sections, all sections of the list need not be published simultaneously.

(8) The Secretary of State may from time to time publish amendments of any list published under subsection (7) above, and any such list (as amended) shall be evidence of the inclusion in the Schedule for the time being—

(*a*) of the monuments listed; and

(*b*) of any matters purporting to be reproduced in the list from the entries in the Schedule relating to the monuments listed.

(9) An entry in the Schedule recording the inclusion therein of a monument situated in England and Wales shall be a local land charge.

(10) It shall be competent to record in the Register of Sasines—

(*a*) a certified copy of the entry or (as the case may be) the amended entry in the Schedule relating to any monument in Scotland which is heritable; and

(*b*) where any such monument is excluded from the Schedule and a certified copy of the entry in the Schedule relating to it has previously been so recorded under paragraph (*a*) above, a certificate issued by or on behalf of the Secretary of State stating that it has been so excluded.

(11) In this Act "scheduled monument" means any monument which is for the time being included in the Schedule.

Control of works affecting scheduled monuments

2.—(1) If any person executes or causes or permits to be executed any works to which this section applies he shall be guilty of an offence unless the works are authorised under this Part of this Act.

(2) This section applies to any of the following works, that is to say—

(*a*) any works resulting in the demolition or destruction of or any damage to a scheduled monument;

(*b*) any works for the purpose of removing or repairing a scheduled monument or any part of it or of making any alterations or additions thereto; and

(*c*) any flooding or tipping operations on land in, on or under which there is a scheduled monument.

(3) Without prejudice to any other authority to execute works conferred under this Part of this Act, works to which this section applies are authorised under this Part of this Act if—

(*a*) the Secretary of State has granted written consent (referred to below in this Act as "scheduled monument consent") for the execution of the works; and

(*b*) the works are executed in accordance with the terms of the consent and of any conditions attached to the consent.

(4) Scheduled monument consent may be granted either unconditionally or subject to conditions (whether with respect to the manner in which or the persons by whom the works or any of the works are to be executed or otherwise).

(5) Without prejudice to the generality of subsection (4) above, a condition attached to a scheduled monument consent may require that the Secretary of State or a person authorised by the Secretary of State be afforded an opportunity, before any works to which the consent relates are begun, to examine the monument and its site and carry out such excavations therein as appear to the Secretary of State to be desirable for the purpose of archaeological investigation.

(6) Without prejudice to subsection (1) above, if a person executing or causing or permitting to be executed any works to which a scheduled monument consent relates fails to comply with any condition attached to the consent he shall be guilty of an offence, unless he proves that he took all reasonable precautions and exercised all due diligence to avoid contravening the condition.

(7) In any proceedings for an offence under this section in relation to works within subsection (2) (*a*) above it shall be a defence for the accused to prove that he took all reasonable precautions and exercised all due diligence to avoid or prevent damage to the monument.

(8) In any proceedings for an offence under this section in relation to works within subsection (2) (*a*) or (*c*) above it shall be a defence for the accused to prove that he did not know and had no reason to believe that the monument was within the area affected by the works or (as the case may be) that it was a scheduled monument.

(9) In any proceedings for an offence under this section it shall be a defence to prove that the works were urgently necessary in the interests of safety or health and that notice in writing of the need for the works was given to the Secretary of State as soon as reasonably practicable.

(10) A person guilty of an offence under this section shall be liable—

(*a*) on summary conviction or, in Scotland, on conviction before a court of summary jurisdiction, to a fine not exceeding the statutory maximum; or

(*b*) on conviction on indictment to a fine.

(11) Part I of Schedule 1 to this Act shall have effect with respect to applications for, and the effect of, scheduled monument consent.

Grant of scheduled monument consent by order of the Secretary of State

3.—(1) The Secretary of State may by order grant scheduled monument consent for the execution of works of any class or description specified in the order, and any such consent may apply to scheduled monuments of any class or description so specified.

(2) Any conditions attached by virtue of section 2 of this Act to a scheduled monument consent granted by an order under this section shall apply in such class or description of cases as may be specified in the order.

(3) The Secretary of State may direct that scheduled monument consent granted by an order under this section shall not apply to any scheduled monument specified in the direction, and may withdraw any direction given under this subsection.

(4) A direction under subsection (3) above shall not take effect until notice of it has been served on the occupier or (if there is no occupier) on the owner of the monument in question.

(5) References below in this Act to a scheduled monument consent do not include references to a scheduled monument consent granted by an order under this section, unless the contrary intention is expressed.

Duration, modification and, revocation of scheduled monument consent

4.—(1) Subject to subsection (2) below, if no works to which a scheduled monument consent relates are executed or started within the period of five years beginning with the date on which the consent was granted, or such longer or shorter period as may be specified for the purposes of this subsection in the consent, the consent shall cease to have effect at the end of that period (unless previously revoked in accordance with the following provisions of this section).

(2) Subsection (1) above does not apply to a scheduled monument consent which provides that it shall cease to have effect at the end of a period specified therein.

(3) If it appears to the Secretary of State to be expedient to do so, he may by a direction given under this section modify or revoke a scheduled monument consent to any extent he considers expedient.

(4) Without prejudice to the generality of the power conferred by subsection (3) above to modify a scheduled monument consent, it extends to specifying a period, or altering any period specified, for the purposes of subsection (1) above, and to including a provision to the effect mentioned in subsection (2) above, or altering any period specified for the purposes of any such provision.

(5) Part II of Schedule 1 to this Act shall have effect with respect to directions under this section modifying or revoking a scheduled monument consent.

Execution of works for preservation of a scheduled monument by Secretary of State in cases of urgency

5.—(1) If it appears to the Secretary of State that any works are urgently necessary for the preservation of a scheduled monument he may enter the site of the monument and execute those works, after giving the owner and (if the owner is not the occupier) the occupier of the monument not less than seven days' notice in writing of his intention to do so.

(2) Where the Secretary of State executes works under this section for repairing any damage to a scheduled monument—

(*a*) any compensation order previously made in respect of that damage under section 35 of the Powers of Criminal Courts Act 1973 (compensation orders against convicted persons) in favour of any other person shall be enforceable (so far as not already complied with) as if it had been made in favour of the Secretary of State; and

(*b*) any such order subsequently made in respect of that damage shall be made in favour of the Secretary of State.

Powers of entry for inspection of scheduled monuments, etc.

6.—(1) Any person duly authorised in writing by the Secretary of State may at any reasonable time enter any land for the purpose of inspecting any scheduled monument in, on or under the land with a view to ascertaining its condition and—

(*a*) whether any works affecting the monument are being carried out in contravention of section 2 (1) of this Act; or

(*b*) whether it has been or is likely to be damaged (by any such works or otherwise).

(2) Any person duly authorised in writing by the Secretary of State may at any reasonable time enter any land for the purpose of inspecting any scheduled monument in, on or under the land in connection with—

(*a*) any application for scheduled monument consent for works affecting that monument; or

(*b*) any proposal by the Secretary of State to modify or revoke a scheduled monument consent for any such works.

(3) Any person duly authorised in writing by the Secretary of State may at any reasonable time enter any land for the purpose of—

(*a*) observing the execution of the land of any works to which a scheduled monument consent relates; and

(*b*) inspecting the condition of the land and scheduled monument in question after the completion of any such works;

so as to ensure that the works in question are or have been executed in accordance with the terms of the consent and of any conditions attached to the consent.

(4) Any person duly authorised in writing by the Secretary of State may at any reasonable time enter any land on which any works to which a scheduled monument consent relates are being carried out for the purpose of—

(*a*) inspecting the land (including any buildings or other structures on the land) with a view to recording any matters of archaeological or historical interest; and

(*b*) observing the execution of those works with a view to examining and recording any objects or other material of archaeological or historical interest, and recording any matters of archaeological or historical interest, discovered during the course of those works.

(5) Any person duly authorised in writing by the Secretary of State may enter any land in, on or under which a scheduled monument is situated, with the consent of the owner and (if the owner is not the occupier) of the occupier of the land, for the purpose of erecting and maintaining on or near the site of the monument such notice boards and marker posts as appear to the Secretary of State to be desirable with a view to preserving the monument from accidental or deliberate damage.

(6) References in this section to scheduled monument consent include references to consent granted by order under section 3 of this Act.

Compensation for refusal of scheduled monument consent.

7.—(1) Subject to the following provisions of this section, where a person who has an interest in the whole or any part of a monument incurs expenditure or otherwise sustains any loss or damage in consequence of the refusal, or the granting subject to conditions, of a scheduled monument consent in relation to any works of a description mentioned in subsection (2) below, the Secretary of State shall pay to that person compensation in respect of that expenditure, loss or damage.

References in this section and in section 8 of this Act to compensation being paid in respect of any works are references to compensation being paid in respect of any expenditure incurred or other loss or damage sustained in consequence of the refusal, or the granting subject to conditions, of a scheduled monument consent in relation to those works.

(2) The following are works in respect of which compensation is payable under this section—

(*a*) works which are reasonably necessary for carrying out any development for which planning permission had been granted (otherwise than by a general development order) before the time when the monument in question became a scheduled monument and was still effective at the date of the application for scheduled monument consent;

(*b*) works which do not constitute development, or constitute development such that planning permission is granted therefor by a general development order; and

(*c*) works which are reasonably necessary for the continuation of any use of the monument for any purpose for which it was in use immediately before the date of the application for scheduled monument consent.

For the purposes of paragraph (*c*) above, any use in contravention of any legal restrictions for the time being applying to the use of the monument shall be disregarded.

(3) The compensation payable under this section in respect of any works within subsection (2) (*a*) above shall be limited to compensation in respect of any expenditure incurred or other loss or damage sustained by virtue of the fact that, in consequence of the Secretary of State's decision, any development for which the planning permission in question was granted could not be carried out without contravening section 2 (1) of this Act.

(4) A person shall not be entitled to compensation under this section by virtue of subsection (2) (*b*) above if the works in question or any of them would or might result in the total or partial demolition or destruction of the monument, unless those works consist solely of operations involved in or incidental to the use of the site of the monument for the purposes of agriculture or forestry (including afforestation).

(5) In a case where scheduled monument consent is granted subject to conditions, a person shall not be entitled to compensation under this section by virtue of subsection (2) (*c*) above unless compliance with those conditions would in effect make it impossible to use the monument for the purpose there mentioned.

(6) In calculating, for the purposes of this section, the amount of any loss or damage consisting of depreciation of the value of an interest in land—

(*a*) it shall be assumed that any subsequent application for scheduled monument consent in relation to works of a like description would be determined in the same way; but

(*b*) if, in the case of a refusal of scheduled monument consent, the Secretary of State, on refusing that consent, undertook to grant such consent for some other works affecting the monument in the event of an application being made in that behalf, regard shall be had to that undertaking.

(7) References in this section to a general development order are references to a development order made as a general order applicable (subject to such exceptions as may be specified therein) to all land.

Recovery of compensation under section 7 on subsequent grant of consent

8.—(1) Subject to the following provisions of this section, this section applies—

(*a*) in a case where compensation under section 7 of this Act was paid in consequence of the refusal of a scheduled monument consent, if the Secretary of State subsequently grants scheduled monument consent for the execution of all or any of the works in respect of which the compensation was paid; and

(*b*) in a case where compensation under that section was paid in consequence of the granting of a scheduled monument consent subject to conditions, if the Secretary of State subsequently so modifies that consent that those conditions, or any of them, cease to apply to the execution of all or any of the works in respect of which the compensation was paid or grants a new consent in respect of all or any of those works free from those conditions, or any of them.

(2) This section does not apply in any case unless—

(*a*) the compensation paid exceeded £20; and

(*b*) the Secretary of State has caused notice of the payment of compensation to be deposited with the local authority of each area (in Scotland) or with the council of each district or

London borough (in England and Wales) in which the monument in question is situated or (where it is situated in the City of London, the Inner Temple or the Middle Temple) with the Common Council of the City of London.

(3) In granting or modifying a scheduled monument consent in a case to which this section applies the Secretary of State may do so on terms that no works in respect of which the compensation was paid are to be executed in pursuance of the consent until the recoverable amount has been repaid to the Secretary of State or secured to his satisfaction.

Subject to subsection (4) below, in this subsection " the recoverable amount " means such amount (being an amount representing the whole of the compensation previously paid or such part thereof as the Secretary of State thinks fit) as the Secretary of State may specify in giving notice of his decision on the application for scheduled monument consent or (as the case may be) in the direction modifying the consent.

(4) Where a person who has an interest in the whole or any part of a monument is aggrieved by the amount specified by the Secretary of State as the recoverable amount for the purposes of subsection (3) above, he may require the determination of that amount to be referred to the Lands Tribunal or (in the case of a monument situated in Scotland) to the Lands Tribunal for Scotland; and in any such case the recoverable amount for the purposes of that subsection shall be such amount (being an amount representing the whole or any part of the compensation previously paid) as that Tribunal may determine to be just in the circumstances of the case.

(5) A notice deposited under subsection (2) (*b*) above shall specify the decision which gave rise to the right to compensation, the monument affected by the decision, and the amount of the compensation.

(6) A notice so deposited in the case of a monument situated in England and Wales shall be a local land charge; and for the purposes of the Local Land Charges Act 1975 the council with whom any such notice is deposited shall be treated as the originating authority as respects the charge thereby constituted.

(7) A notice so deposited in the case of any monument situated in Scotland which is heritable may be recorded in the Register of Sasines.

Compensation where works affecting a scheduled monument cease to be authorised

9.—(1) Subject to the following provisions of this section, where any works affecting a scheduled monument which were previously authorised under this Part of this Act cease to be so, then, if any person who has an interest in the whole or any part of the monument—

(*a*) has incurred expenditure in carrying out works which are rendered abortive by the fact that any further works have ceased to be so authorised; or

(*b*) has otherwise sustained loss or damage which is directly attributable to that fact;

the Secretary of State shall pay to that person compensation in respect of that expenditure, loss or damage.

(2) Subsection (1) above only applies where the works cease to be authorised under this Part of this Act—

(*a*) by virtue of the fact that a scheduled monument consent granted by order under section 3 of this Act ceases to apply to any scheduled monument (whether by virtue of variation or revocation of the order or by virtue of a direction under subsection (3) of that section); or

(b) by virtue of the modification or revocation of a scheduled monument consent by a direction given under section 4 of this Act; or

(c) in accordance with paragraph 8 of Schedule 1 to this Act, by virtue of the service of a notice of proposed modification or revocation of a scheduled monument consent under paragraph 5 of that Schedule.

(3) A person shall not be entitled to compensation under this section in a case falling within subsection (2) (a) above unless, on an application for scheduled monument consent for the works in question, consent is refused, or is granted subject to conditions other than those which previously applied under the order.

(4) For the purposes of this section, any expenditure incurred in the preparation of plans for the purposes of any works, or upon other similar matters preparatory thereto, shall be taken to be included in the expenditure incurred in carrying out those works.

(5) Subject to subsection (4) above, no compensation shall be paid under this section in respect of any works carried out before the grant of the scheduled monument consent in question, or in respect of any other loss or damage (not being loss or damage consisting of depreciation of the value of an interest in land) arising out of anything done or omitted to be done before the grant of that consent.

Acquisition of ancient monuments

Compulsory acquisition of ancient monuments

10.—(1) The Secretary of State may acquire compulsorily any ancient monument for the purpose of securing its preservation.

(2) The Acquisition of Land (Authorisation Procedure) Act 1946 shall apply to any compulsory acquisition by the Secretary of State under this section of an ancient monument situated in England and Wales as it applies to a compulsory acquisition by another Minister in a case falling within section 1 (1) of that Act.

(3) The Acquisition of Land (Authorisation Procedure) (Scotland) Act 1947 shall apply to any compulsory acquisition by the Secretary of State under this section of an ancient monument situated in Scotland as it applies to a compulsory acquisition by another Minister or by the Secretary of State under section 58 of the National Health Service (Scotland) Act 1972 in a case falling within section 1 (1) of the said Act of 1947.

(4) For the purpose of assessing compensation in respect of any compulsory acquisition under this section of a monument which, immediately before the date of the compulsory purchase order, was scheduled, it shall be assumed that scheduled monument consent would not be granted for any works which would or might result in the demolition, destruction or removal of the monument or any part of it.

Acquisition by agreement or gift of ancient monuments

11.—(1) The Secretary of State may acquire by agreement any ancient monument.

(2) Any local authority may acquire by agreement any ancient monument situated in or in the vicinity of their area.

(3) The Secretary of State or any local authority may accept a gift (whether by deed or will) of any ancient monument.

(4) The provisions of Part I of the Compulsory Purchase Act 1965 (so far as applicable) other than sections 4 to 8, section 10 and section 31, shall apply in relation to any acquisition under subsection (1) or (2) above of an ancient monument situated in England and Wales.

(5) For the purpose of any acquisition under subsection (1) or (2) above of any ancient monument situated in Scotland which is heritable—

(*a*) the Lands Clauses Acts (with the exception of the provisions excluded by subsection (6) below) and sections 6 and 70 to 78 of the Railways Clauses Consolidation (Scotland) Act 1845 (as originally enacted and not as amended by section 15 of the Mines (Working Facilities and Support) Act 1923) shall be incorporated with this section; and

(*b*) in construing those Acts for the purposes of this section, this section shall be deemed to be the special Act and the Secretary of State or the local authority acquiring the monument shall be deemed to be the promoter of the undertaking or company (as the case may require).

(6) The provisions of the Lands Clauses Acts excluded from being incorporated with this section are—

(*a*) those which relate to the acquisition of land otherwise than by agreement;

(*b*) those which relate to access to the special Act; and

(*c*) sections 120 to 125 of the Lands Clauses Consolidation (Scotland) Act 1845.

Guardianship of ancient monuments

Power to place ancient monument under guardianship

12.—(1) Subject to subsection (4) below, a person who has—

(*a*) an interest of any description mentioned in subsection (3) below in an ancient monument situated in England and Wales; or

(*b*) any heritable interest in an ancient monument situated in Scotland;

may, with the consent of the Secretary of State, constitute him by deed guardian of the monument.

(2) Subject to subsection (4) below, a person who has any such interest in an ancient monument may with the consent of any local authority in or in the vicinity of whose area the monument is situated constitute that authority by deed guardians of the monument.

(3) The interests in an ancient monument situated in England and Wales which qualify a person to establish guardianship of the monument under subsection (1) or (2) above are the following—

(*a*) an estate in fee simple absolute in possession;

(*b*) a leasehold estate or interest in possession, being an estate or interest for a term of years of which not less than forty-five are unexpired or (as the case may be) renewable for a term of not less than forty-five years; and

(*c*) an interest in possession for his own life or the life of another, or for lives (whether or not including his own), under any existing or future trust for sale under which the estate or interest for the time being subject to the trust falls within paragraph (*a*) or (*b*) above.

(4) A person who is not the occupier of an ancient monument may not establish guardianship of the monument under this section unless the occupier is also a party to the deed executed for the purposes of subsection (1) or (2) above.

(5) Any person who has an interest in an ancient monument may be a party to any such deed in addition to the person establishing the guardianship of the monument and (where the latter is not the occupier) the occupier.

(6) In relation to any monument of which the Secretary of State or any local authority have been constituted the guardians under this Act, references below in this Act to the guardianship deed are references to the deed executed for the purposes of subsection (1) or (as the case may be) subsection (2) above.

(7) A guardianship deed relating to any ancient monument situated in England and Wales shall be a local land charge.

(8) A guardianship deed relating to any ancient monument situated in Scotland may be recorded in the Register of Sasines.

(9) Every person deriving title to any ancient monument from, through or under any person who has executed a guardianship deed shall be bound by the guardianship deed unless—

(*a*) in the case of a monument in England and Wales, he derives title by virtue of any disposition made by the person who executed the deed before the date of the deed; or

(*b*) in the case of a monument in Scotland, he is a person who in good faith and for value acquired right (whether completed by infeftment or not) to his interest in the monument before the date of the deed.

(10) The Secretary of State or a local authority shall not consent to become guardians of any structure which is occupied as a dwelling house by any person other than a person employed as the caretaker thereof or his family.

(11) Except as provided by this Act, any person who has any estate or interest in a monument under guardianship shall have the same right and title to, and estate or interest in, the monument in all respects as if the Secretary of State or (as the case may be) the local authority in question had not become guardians of the monument.

Effect of guardianship

13.—(1) The Secretary of State and any local authority shall be under a duty to maintain any monument which is under their guardianship by virtue of this Act.

(2) The Secretary of State and any local authority shall have full control and management of any monument which is under their guardianship by virtue of this Act.

(3) With a view to fulfilling their duty under subsection (1) above to maintain a monument of which they are the guardians, the Secretary of State or any local authority shall have power to do all such things as may be necessary for the maintenance of the monument and for the exercise by them of proper control and management with respect to the monument.

(4) Without prejudice to the generality of the preceding provisions of this section, the Secretary of State or any local authority shall have power—

(*a*) to make any examination of a monument which is under their guardianship by virtue of this Act;

(*b*) to open up any such monument or make excavations therein for the purpose of examination or otherwise; and

(*c*) to remove the whole or any part of any such monument to another place for the purpose of preserving it.

(5) The Secretary of State or any local authority may at any reasonable time enter the site of a monument which is under their guardianship by virtue of this Act for the purpose of exercising any of their powers under this section in relation to the monument (and may authorise any other person to exercise any of those powers on their behalf).

(6) Subsections (2) to (4) above are subject to any provision to the contrary in the guardianship deed.

(7) In this Part of this Act " maintenance " includes fencing, repairing, and covering in, of a monument and the doing of any other act or thing which may be required for the purpose of repairing the monument or protecting it from decay or injury, and " maintain " shall be construed accordingly.

Termination of guardianship

14.—(1) Subject to the following provisions of this section, where the Secretary of State or a local authority have become guardians of any monument under this Act, they may by agreement made with the persons who are for the time being immediately affected by the operation of the guardianship deed—

(*a*) exclude any part of the monument from guardianship; or

(*b*) renounce guardianship of the monument;

but except as provided above the monument shall remain under guardianship (unless it is acquired by its guardians) until an occupier of the monument who is entitled to terminate the guardianship gives notice in writing to that effect to the guardians of the monument.

An occupier of a monument is entitled to terminate the guardianship of the monument if—

(*a*) he has any interest in the monument which would qualify him to establish guardianship of the monument under section 12 of this Act; and

(*b*) he is not bound by the guardianship deed.

(2) A local authority shall consult with the Secretary of State before entering into any agreement under this section.

(3) Neither the Secretary of State nor a local authority may enter into any such agreement unless he or they are satisfied with respect to the part of the monument or (as the case may be) with respect to the whole of the monument in question—

(*a*) that satisfactory arrangements have been made for ensuring its preservation after termination of the guardianship; or

(*b*) that it is no longer practicable to preserve it (whether because of the cost of preserving it or otherwise).

(4) An agreement under this section must be made under seal in the case of a monument situated in England and Wales.

(5) Where in the case of a monument situated in Scotland the guardianship deed has been recorded in the Register of Sasines in accordance with section 12 of this Act an agreement under this section relating to that monument may also be so recorded.

Acquisition and guardianship of land in the vicinity of an ancient monument, etc.

Acquisition and guardianship of land in the vicinity of an ancient monument

15.—(1) References in sections 10 to 12 of this Act to an ancient monument shall include references to any land adjoining or in the vicinity of an ancient monument which appears to the Secretary of State or a local authority to be reasonably required for any of the following purposes, that is to say—

(*a*) the maintenance of the monument or its amenities;

(*b*) providing or facilitating access to the monument;

(*c*) the exercise of proper control or management with respect to the monument;

(*d*) the storage of equipment or materials for the purpose mentioned in paragraph (*a*) above; and

(*e*) the provision of facilities and services for the public for or in connection with affording public access to the monument;

(and one of those purposes shall accordingly be sufficient to support the compulsory acquisition of any such land under section 10 (1) of this Act, instead of the purpose there mentioned).

(2) Land may be acquired or taken into guardianship by virtue of this section for any of the purposes relating to an ancient monument mentioned in subsection (1) above either at the same time as the monument or subsequently.

(3) The Secretary of State and any local authority shall have full control and management of any land which is under their guardianship by virtue of this Act after being taken into guardianship by virtue of this section for a purpose relating to any ancient monument, and shall have power to do all such things as may be necessary—

(*a*) for the exercise by them of proper control and management with respect to the land; and

(*b*) for the use of the land for any of the purposes relating to the monument mentioned in subsection (1) above.

(4) The Secretary of State and any local authority may at any reasonable time enter any land which is under their guardianship by virtue of this Act for the purpose of exercising their power under subsection (3) above (and may authorise any other person to do so, and to exercise that power, on their behalf).

(5) Section 14 (1) and (2) of this Act shall apply in relation to any land taken into guardianship by virtue of this section for any purpose relating to an ancient monument as they apply in relation to a monument, but, apart from any termination of guardianship by virtue of that section, any such land shall also cease to be under guardianship if the monument in question ceases to be under guardianship otherwise than by virtue of being acquired by its guardians or ceases to exist.

(6) References below in this Act, in relation to any monument of which the Secretary of State or a local authority are the owners or guardians by virtue of this Act, to land associated with that monument (or to associated land) are references to any land acquired or taken into guardianship by virtue of this section for a purpose relating to that monument, or appropriated for any such purpose under a power conferred by any other enactment.

Acquisition of easements and other similar rights over land in the vicinity of an ancient monument

16.—(1) The Secretary of State may acquire, by agreement or compulsorily, over land adjoining or in the vicinity of any monument which is under his ownership by virtue of this Act, any easement which appears to him to be necessary—

(*a*) for any of the purposes relating to that monument mentioned in section 15 (1) of this Act; or

(*b*) for the use of any land associated with that monument for any of those purposes.

(2) A local authority may by agreement acquire over land adjoining or in the vicinity of any monument which is under their ownership by virtue of this Act any such easement as the Secretary of State may acquire by virtue of subsection (1) above.

(3) The power of acquiring an easement under subsection (1) or (2) above shall include power to acquire any such easement by the grant of a new right.

(4) The Secretary of State or any local authority may acquire, for the benefit of any monument or land under his or their guardianship by virtue of this Act, a right of any description which he or they would be authorised to acquire under any of the preceding provisions of this section if the monument or land was under his or their ownership by virtue of this Act, and those provisions shall apply accordingly in any such case.

(5) Any right to which subsection (4) above applies—

(*a*) shall be treated for the purposes of its acquisition under this section and in all other respects as if it were a legal easement; and

(*b*) may be enforced by the guardians for the time being of the monument or land for whose benefit it was acquired as if they were the absolute owner in possession of that monument or land.

(6) Any right to which subsection (4) above applies which is acquired by agreement under this section for a purpose relating to any monument under guardianship, or for the use of any land associated with any such monument for any purpose relating to that monument—

(*a*) subject to any provision to the contrary in the agreement under which it was acquired, may be revoked by the grantor; and

(*b*) may be revoked by any successor in title of the grantor as respects any of the land over which it is exercisable in which he has an interest;

if the monument ceases to be under guardianship otherwise than by virtue of being acquired by its guardians or ceases to exist.

(7) References above in this section to an easement or (as the case may be) to a legal easement shall be construed in relation to land in Scotland as references to a servitude.

(8) Any right to which subsection (4) above applies—

(*a*) shall be a local land charge, if it relates to land in England and Wales; and

(*b*) may be recorded in the Register of Sasines, if it relates to land in Scotland.

(9) The Acquisition of Land (Authorisation Procedure) Act 1946 shall apply to any compulsory acquisition by the Secretary of State under this section of any easement over land in England and Wales as it applies to a compulsory acquisition by another Minister in a case falling within section 1 (1) of that Act.

(10) The Acquisition of Land (Authorisation Procedure) (Scotland) Act 1947 shall apply to any compulsory acquisition by the Secretary of State under this section of any servitude over land in Scotland as it applies to a compulsory acquisition by another Minister or by the Secretary of State under section 58 of the National Health Service (Scotland) Act 1972 in a case falling within section 1 (1) of the said Act of 1947.

(11) The provisions of Part I of the Compulsory Purchase Act 1965 (so far as applicable) other than sections 4 to 8, section 10 and section 31, shall apply in relation to any acquistion by agreement under this section of any easement over land in England and Wales.

(12) For the purposes of any acquisition by agreement under this section of any servitude over land in Scotland—

(*a*) the Lands Clauses Acts (with the exception of the provisions excluded by subsection (13) below) and sections 6 and 70 to 78 of the Railways Clauses Consolidation (Scotland) Act 1845 (as originally enacted and not as amended by section 15 of the Mines (Working Facilities and Support) Act 1923) shall be incorporated with this section; and

(b) in construing those Acts for the purposes of this section, this section shall be deemed to be the special Act and the Secretary of State or the local authority acquiring the servitude shall be deemed to be the promoter of the undertaking or company (as the case may require).

(13) The provisions of the Lands Clauses Act excluded from being incorporated with this section are—

(a) those which relate to the acquisition of land otherwise than by agreement;

(b) those which relate to access to the special Act; and

(c) sections 120 to 125 of the Lands Clauses Consolidation (Scotland) Act 1845.

Agreements concerning ancient monuments, etc.

Agreements concerning ancient monuments and land in their vicinity

17.—(1) The Secretary of State may enter into an agreement under this section with the occupier of an ancient monument or of any land adjoining or in the vicinity of an ancient monument.

(2) A local authority may enter into an agreement under this section with the occupier of any ancient monument situated in or in the vicinity of their area or with the occupier of any land adjoining or in the vicinity of any such ancient monument.

(3) Any person who has an interest in an ancient monument or in any land adjoining or in the vicinity of an ancient monument may be a party to an agreement under this section in addition to the occupier.

(4) An agreement under this section may make provision for all or any of the following matters with respect to the monument or land in question, that is to say—

(a) the maintenance and preservation of the monument and its amenities;

(b) the carrying out of any such work, or the doing of any such other thing, in relation to the monument or land as may be specified in the agreement;

(c) public access to the monument or land and the provision of facilities and information or other services for the use of the public in that connection;

(d) restricting the use of the monument or land;

(e) prohibiting in relation to the monument or land the doing of any such thing as may be specified in the agreement; and

(f) the making by the Secretary of State or (as the case may be) by the local authority of payments in such manner, of such amounts and on such terms as may be so specified (and whether for or towards the cost of any work provided for under the agreement or in consideration of any restriction, prohibition or obligation accepted by any other party thereto);

and may contain such incidental and consequential provisions as appear to the Secretary of State or (as the case may be) to the local authority to be necessary or expedient.

(5) Where an agreement under this section expressly provides that the agreement as a whole or any restriction, prohibition or obligation arising thereunder is to be binding on the successors of any party to the agreement (but not otherwise), then, as respects any monument or land in England and Wales, every person deriving title to the monument or land in question from, through or under that party shall be bound by the agreement, or (as the case may be) by that restriction, prohibition or obliga-

tion, unless he derives title by virtue of any disposition made by that party before the date of the agreement.

(6) An agreement under this section relating to any monument or land in Scotland and containing any such provision as is mentioned in subsection (5) above may be recorded in the Register of Sasines, and that subsection shall apply to any such agreement which is so recorded or (as the case may be) to any restriction, prohibition or obligation to which that provision relates.

(7) Neither—

(*a*) section 84 of the Law of Property Act 1925 (power of Lands Tribunal to discharge or modify restrictive covenants); nor

(*b*) sections 1 and 2 of the Conveyancing and Feudal Reform (Scotland) Act 1970 (power of Lands Tribunal for Scotland to vary or discharge land obligations);

shall apply to an agreement under this section.

(8) Nothing in any agreement under this section to which the Secretary of State is a party shall be construed as operating as a scheduled monument consent.

Powers of limited owners

Powers of limited owners for purposes of sections 12, 16 and 17

18.—(1) Subject to section 12 of this Act, a person may establish guardianship of any land under subsection (1) or (2) of that section or join in executing a guardianship deed for the purposes of that section notwithstanding that he is a limited owner of the land.

(2) A person may—

(*a*) grant any easement, servitude or other right over land which the Secretary of State or any local authority are authorised to acquire under section 16 of this Act; or

(*b*) enter into an agreement under section 17 of this Act with respect to any land;

notwithstanding that he is a limited owner of the land.

(3) For the purposes of this section—

(*a*) a body corporate or corporation sole is a limited owner of any land in which it has an interest; and

(*b*) any other persons are limited owners of land in which they have an interest only if they hold that interest in one or other of the capacities mentioned in subsection (4) below.

(4) The capacities referred to in subsection (3) (*b*) above are the following—

(*a*) as tenant for life or statutory owner within the meaning of the Settled Land Act 1925;

(*b*) as trustees for sale within the meaning of the Law of Property Act 1925;

(*c*) as liferenter or heir of entail in possession (in Scotland); and

(*d*) as trustees for charities or as commissioners or trustees for ecclesiastical, collegiate or other public purposes.

(5) The Trusts (Scotland) Act 1921 shall have effect as if among the powers conferred on trustees by section 4 of that Act (general powers of trustees) there were included a power to do any of the following acts in relation to the trust estate or any part of it, that is to say—

(*a*) to execute a guardianship deed;

(*b*) to grant any servitude or other right which the Secretary of State or any local authority are authorised to acquire under section 16 of this Act; and

(*c*) to enter into an agreement under section 17 of this Act.

(6) Subject to subsection (7) below, where a person who is a limited owner of any land by virtue of holding an interest in the land in any of the capacities mentioned in subsection (4) above executes a guardianship deed in relation to the land the guardianship deed shall bind every successive owner of any estate or interest in the land.

(7) Where the land to which a guardianship deed relates is at the date of the deed subject to any incumbrance not capable of being overreached by the limited owner in exercise of any powers of sale or management conferred on him by law or under any settlement or other instrument, the deed shall not bind the incumbrancer.

(8) Subject to subsection (9) below, where an agreement under section 17 of this Act to which a limited owner is a party expressly provides that the agreement as a whole or any restriction, prohibition or obligation arising thereunder is to be binding on his successors (but not otherwise), subsections (6) and (7) above shall apply to the agreement or (as the case may be) to the restriction, prohibition or obligation in question as they apply to a guardianship deed.

(9) Subsection (8) above does not apply to an agreement relating to any land in Scotland unless it is recorded in the Register of Sasines.

Public access to monuments under public control

Public access to monuments under public control

19.—(1) Subject to the following provisions of this section, the public shall have access to any monument under the ownership or guardianship of the Secretary of State or any local authority by virtue of this Act.

(2) The Secretary of State and any local authority may nevertheless control the times of normal public access to any monument under their ownership or guardianship by virtue of this Act and may also, if they consider it necessary or expedient to do so in the interests of safety or for the maintenance or preservation of the monument, entirely exclude the public from access to any such monument or to any part of it, for such period as they think fit:

Provided that—

(*a*) the power of a local authority under this subsection to control the times of normal public access to any monument shall only be exercisable by regulations under this section; and

(*b*) the power of a local authority under this subsection entirely to exclude the public from access to any monument with a view to its preservation shall only be exercisable with the consent of the Secretary of State.

(3) The Secretary of State and any local authority may by regulations under this section regulate public access to any monument, or to all or any of the monuments, under their ownership or guardianship by virtue of this Act and any such regulations made by the Secretary of State may also apply to any monument, or to all or any of the monuments, under his control or management for any other reason.

(4) Without prejudice to the generality of subsection (3) above, regulations made by the Secretary of State or a local authority under this section may prescribe the times when the public are to have access to monuments to which the regulations apply and may make such provision as appears to the Secretary of State or to the local authority in question to be necessary for—

(*a*) the preservation of any such monument and its amenities or of any property of the Secretary of State or local authority; and (*b*) prohibiting or regulating any act or thing which would tend to injure or disfigure any such monument or its amenities or to disturb the public in their enjoyment of it;

and may prescribe charges for the admission of the public to any such monument or to any class or description of monuments to which the regulations apply.

(5) Without prejudice to subsections (3) and (4) above, the Secretary of State and any local authority shall have power to make such charges as they may from time to time determine for the admission of the public to any monument under their ownership or guardianship by virtue of this Act or (in the case of the Secretary of State) to any monument otherwise under his control or management.

(6) Notwithstanding subsection (1) above, any person authorised in that behalf by the Secretary of State or by a local authority may refuse admission—

(*a*) to any monument under the ownership or guardianship of the Secretary of State or (as the case may be) of that local authority by virtue of this Act; or

(*b*) (in the case of the Secretary of State) to any monument otherwise under his control or management;

to any person he has reasonable cause to believe is likely to do anything which would tend to injure or disfigure the monument or its amenities or to disturb the public in their enjoyment of it.

(7) If any person contravenes or fails to comply with any provision of any regulations under this section, he shall be liable on summary conviction or, in Scotland, on conviction before a court of summary jurisdiction, to a fine not exceeding £50.

(8) Regulations made by a local authority under this section shall not take effect unless they are submitted to and confirmed by the Secretary of State, and the Secretary of State may confirm any such regulations either with or without modifications.

(9) In relation to any monument under guardianship, subsection (1) above is subject to any provision to the contrary in the guardianship deed.

Provision of facilities for the public in connection with ancient monuments

20.—(1) The Secretary of State and any local authority may provide such facilities and information or other services for the public for or in connection with affording public access—

(*a*) to any monument under their ownership or guardianship by virtue of this Act; or

(*b*) (in the case of the Secretary of State) to any monument otherwise under his control or management;

as appear to them to be necessary or desirable.

(2) Facilities and information or other services for the public may be provided under this section in or on the monument itself or on any land associated with the monument.

(3) The Secretary of State and any local authority shall have power to make such charges as they may from time to time determine for the use of any facility or service provided by them for the public under this section.

Transfer of ownership and guardianship of ancient monuments

Transfer of ancient monuments between local authorities and Secretary of State

21.—(1) Subject to subsection (2) below, the Secretary of State and any local authority may, in respect of any monument of which they are the owners or guardians by virtue of this Act or any land associated with any such monument, enter into and carry into effect any agreements for the transfer—

(*a*) from the Secretary of State to the local authority;

(*b*) from the local authority to the Secretary of State; or

(*c*) from the local authority to another local authority;

of that monument or land or (as the case may be) of the guardianship of that monument or land.

(2) Where the Secretary of State or the local authority in question are guardians of a monument or associated land, they may not enter into an agreement under this section with respect to that monument or land without the consent of the persons who are for the time being immediately affected by the operation of the guardianship deed.

Ancient Monuments Boards

Ancient Monuments Boards

22.—(1) The advisory boards constituted under section 15 of the Ancient Monuments Consolidation and Amendment Act 1913 shall continue to exist under the names by which they were respectively known immediately before the commencement of this Act, that is to say—

(*a*) the Ancient Monuments Board for England;

(*b*) the Ancient Monuments Board for Scotland; and

(*c*) the Ancient Monuments Board for Wales.

(2) The Ancient Monuments Board for England shall consist of members representing the following bodies, that is to say—

The Royal Commission on Historical Monuments (England)
The Society of Antiquaries of London
The Royal Academy of Arts
The Royal Institute of British Architects
The Trustees of the British Museum
The British Academy

and of such other members as the Secretary of State may appoint.

(3) The Ancient Monuments Board for Scotland shall consist of members representing the following bodies, that is to say—

The Royal Commission on the Ancient and Historical Monuments of Scotland
The Royal Incorporation of Architects in Scotland
The Society of Antiquaries of Scotland

and of such other members as the Secretary of State may appoint.

(4) The Ancient Monuments Board for Wales shall consist of members representing the following bodies, that is to say—

The Royal Commission on Ancient and Historical Monuments (Wales)
The National Museum of Wales
The Cambrian Archaeological Association
The Royal Institute of British Architects

and of such other members as the Secretary of State may appoint.

(5) References in this Act and in any other enactment to the Ancient Monuments Board shall be construed—

(*a*) in relation to England, as references to the Ancient Monuments Board for England;

(*b*) in relation to Scotland, as references to the Ancient Monuments Board for Scotland; and

(*c*) in relation to Wales, as references to the Ancient Monuments Board for Wales.

(6) It shall be the function of the Ancient Monuments Board to advise the Secretary of State with respect to the exercise of his functions under this Act, whether generally or in relation to any particular case or classes of case.

(7) Without prejudice to the generality of subsection (6) above the Ancient Monuments Board may advise the Secretary of State with respect to any of the following, that is to say—

(*a*) the inclusion of any monument in the Schedule under section 1 (3) of this Act;

(*b*) the exclusion of any monument from the Schedule;

(*c*) the amendment of the entry in the Schedule relating to any monument;

(*d*) the termination of guardianship by an agreement under section 14 of this Act; and

(*e*) the disposal (in accordance with section 30 of this Act) of any land acquired under section 10, 11 or 21 of this Act.

(8) The Secretary of State may by regulations under this section amend subsection (2), (3) or (4) above.

Annual reports of Ancient Monuments Boards

23. The Ancient Monuments Board for England, the Ancient Monuments Board for Scotland and the Ancient Monuments Board for Wales shall each, before such date in every year as the Secretary of State may fix, send to the Secretary of State a report on the discharge by them of their functions during the previous year, and the Secretary of State shall lay a copy of each such report before each House of Parliament.

Miscellaneous and supplemental

Expenditure by Secretary of State or local authority on acquisition and preservation of ancient monuments, etc.

24.—(1) The Secretary of State may defray or contribute towards the cost of the acquisition by any person of any ancient monument.

(2) The Secretary of State may undertake, or assist in, or defray or contribute towards the cost of the removal of any ancient monument or of any part of any such monument to another place for the purpose of preserving it, and may at the request of the owner undertake, or assist in, or defray or contribute towards the cost of the preservation, maintenance and management of any ancient monument.

(3) The Secretary of State may contribute towards the cost of the provision of facilities or services for the public by a local authority under section 20 of this Act.

(4) Any local authority may at the request of the owner undertake, or assist in, or defray or contribute towards the cost of the preservation, maintenance and management of any ancient monument situated in or in the vicinity of their area.

(5) No expenses shall be incurred by the Secretary of State or any local authority under this section in connection with any monument which is occupied as a dwelling house by any person other than a person employed as the caretaker thereof or his family.

Advice and superintendence by Secretary of State

25.—(1) The Secretary of State may give advice with reference to the treatment of any ancient monument.

(2) The Secretary of State may also, if in his opinion it is advisable, superintend any work in connection with any ancient monument if invited

to do so by the owner, and shall superintend any such work, whether required to do so by the owner or not, in connection with any scheduled monument, if in his opinion it is advisable.

(3) The Secretary of State may make a charge for giving advice and superintendence under this section or may give it free of charge, as he thinks fit.

Power of entry on land believed to contain an ancient monument

26.—(1) A person duly authorised in writing by the Secretary of State may at any reasonable time enter any land in, on or under which the Secretary of State knows or has reason to believe there is an ancient monument for the purpose of inspecting the land (including any building or other structure on the land) with a view to recording any matters of archaeological or historical interest.

(2) Subject to subsection (3) below, a person entering any land in exercise of the power conferred by subsection (1) above may carry out excavations in the land for the purpose of archaeological investigation.

(3) No excavation shall be made in exercise of the power conferred by subsection (2) above except with the consent of every person whose consent to the making of the excavation would be required apart from this section.

General provisions as to compensation for depreciation under Part I

27.—(1) For the purpose of assessing any compensation to which this section applies, the rules set out in section 5 of the Land Compensation Act 1961 or, in relation to land in Scotland, the rules set out in section 12 of the Land Compensation (Scotland) Act 1963 shall, so far as applicable and subject to any necessary modifications, have effect as they have effect for the purpose of assessing compensation for the compulsory acquistion of an interest in land.

(2) This section applies to any compensation payable under section 7 or 9 of this Act in respect of any loss or damage consisting of depreciation of the value of an interest in land.

(3) Where an interest in land is subject to a mortgage—

(*a*) any compensation to which this section applies, which is payable in respect of depreciation of the value of that interest, shall be assessed as if the interest were not subject to the mortgage;

(*b*) a claim for any such compensation may be made by any mortgagee of the interest, but without prejudice to the making of a claim by the person entitled to the interest;

(*c*) no compensation to which this section applies shall be payable in respect of the interest of the mortgagee (as distinct from the interest which is subject to the mortgage); and

(*d*) any compensation to which this section applies which is payable in respect of the interest which is subject to the mortgage shall be paid to the mortgagee, or, if there is more than one mortgagee, to the first mortgagee, and shall in either case be applied by him as if it were proceeds of sale.

Offence of damaging certain ancient monuments

28.—(1) A person who without lawful excuse destroys or damages any protected monument—

(*a*) knowing that it is a protected monument; and

(*b*) intending to destroy or damage the monument or being reckless as to whether the monument would be destroyed or damaged; shall be guilty of an offence.

(2) This applies to anything done by or under the authority of the owner of the monument, other than an act for the execution of expected works, as it applies to anything done by any other person.

In this subsection subsection " excepted works " means works for which scheduled monument consent has been given under this Act (including any consent granted by order under section 3).

(3) In this section " protected monument " means any scheduled monument and any monument under the ownership or guardianship of the Secretary of State or a local authority by virtue of this Act.

(4) A person guilty of an offence under this section shall be liable—

(*a*) on summary conviction, to a fine not exceeding the statutory maximum or to imprisonment for a term not exceeding six months or both; or

(*b*) on conviction on indictment, to a fine or to imprisonment for a term not exceeding two years or both.

Compensation orders for damage to monuments under guardianship in England and Wales

29. Where the owner or any other person is convicted of an offence involving damage to a monument situated in England and Wales which was at the time of the offence under the guardianship of the Secretary of State or any local authority by virtue of this Act, any compensation order made under section 35 of the Powers of Criminal Courts Act 1973 (compensation orders against convicted persons) in respect of that damage shall be made in favour of the Secretary of State or (as the case may require) in favour of the local authority in question.

Disposal of land acquired under Part I

30.—(1) Subject to the following provisions of this section, the Secretary of State or any local authority may dispose of any land acquired by them under section 10, 11 or 21 of this Act.

(2) A local authority shall consult with the Secretary of State before disposing of any land under this section.

(3) Subject to subsection (4) below, where the land in question is or includes a monument, the Secretary of State or (as the case may be) the local authority may only dispose of it on such terms as will in their opinion ensure the preservation of the monument.

(4) Subsection (3) above does not apply in any case where the Secretary of State or (as the case may be) the local authority are satisfied that it is no longer practicable to preserve the monument (whether because of the cost of preserving it or otherwise).

Voluntary contributions towards expenditure under Part I

31. The Secretary of State or any local authority may receive voluntary contributions for or towards the cost of any expenditure incurred by them under this Part of this Act (whether in relation to any particular monument or land or otherwise).

Interpretation of Part I

32.—(1) In this Part of this Act " maintenance " and " maintain " have the meanings given by section 13 (7) of this Act, and expressions to which a meaning is given for the purposes of the Town and Country Planning Act 1971 or (as regards Scotland) for the purposes of the Town and Country Planning (Scotland) Act 1972 have the same meaning as in the said Act of 1971 or (as the case may require) as in the said Act of 1972.

(2) References in this Part of this Act to a monument, in relation to the acquistion or transfer of any monument (whether under a power conferred by this Part of this Act or otherwise), include references to any interest in or right over the monument.

(3) For the purposes of this Part of this Act the Secretary of State or a local authority are the owners of a monument by virtue of this Act if the Secretary of State or (as the case may be) the local authority have acquired it under section 10, 11 or 21 of this Act.

Part II

Archaeological Areas

Designation of areas of archaeological importance

33.—(1) The Secretary of State may from time to time by order designate as an area of archaeological importance any area which appears to him to merit treatment as such for the purposes of this Act.

(2) A local authority may from time to time by order designate as an area of archaeological importance any area within the area of that local authority which appears to them to merit treatment as such for the purposes of this Act.

(3) An order under this section designating an area as an area of archaeological importance (whether made by the Secretary of State or by a local authority) is referred to below in this Act as a designation order.

(4) The Secretary of State may at any time by order vary or revoke a designation order, but his power to vary such an order is confined to reducing the area designated by the order.

(5) A designation order relating to an area in England and Wales shall be a local land charge.

(6) Schedule 2 to this Act shall have effect with respect to the making, and with respect to the variation and revocation, of designation orders.

Investigating authorities for areas of archeological importance

34.—(1) The Secretary of State may at any time appoint any person whom he considers to be competent to undertake archaelogical investigations to exercise in relation to any area of archaeological importance the functions conferred by the following provisions of this Part of this Act on the investigating authority for an area of archaeological importance, and any such appointment shall be on such terms and for such period as the Secretary of State thinks fit.

(2) A person's appointment as investigating authority may be cancelled at any time by the Secretary of State.

(3) On appointing or cancelling the appointment of any person as investigating authority for an area of archaeological importance, the Secretary of State shall notify each local authority in whose area the area of archaeological importance in question is wholly or partly situated.

(4) Where there is for the time being no person holding appointment under this section as the investigating authority for an area of archaeological importance, the functions of the investigating authority for that area under this Part of this Act shall be exercisable by the Secretary of State.

(5) A person duly authorised in writing by any person by whom the functions of an investigating authority under this Part of this Act are for the time being exercisable may act on his behalf in the exercise of those functions.

Notice required of operations in areas of archaeological importance

35.—(1) Subject to section 37 of this Act, if any person carries out, or causes or permits to be carried out, on land in an area of archaeological importance any operations to which this section applies—

(*a*) without having first served a notice relating to those operations which complies with subsections (4) and (5) below; or

(*b*) within six weeks of serving such a notice;

he shall be guilty of an offence.

(2) Subject to section 37 of this Act, this section applies to any of the following operations, that is to say—

(*a*) operations which disturb the ground;

(*b*) flooding operations; and

(*c*) tipping operations.

(3) In this Part of this Act the person carrying out or proposing to carry out any operations is referred to, in relation to those operations, as " the developer ", and a notice complying with subsections (4) and (5) below is referred to as an " operations notice ".

(4) A notice required for the purposes of this section—

(*a*) shall specify the operations to which it relates, the site on which they are to be carried out, the date on which it is proposed to begin them and, where the operations are to be carried out after clearance of the site, the developer's estimated date for completion of the clearance operations;

(*b*) shall be accompanied by a certificate in the prescribed form which satisfies the requirements of section 36 of this Act; and

(*c*) shall be in the prescribed form.

(5) A notice required for the purposes of this section shall be served by the developer—

(*a*) in the case of land in England and Wales, on the district council or London borough council or (as the case may be) on each district council or London borough council in whose area the site of the operations is wholly or partly situated; or

(*b*) in the case of land in Scotland, on the local authority or (as the case may be) on each local authority in whose area the site of the operations is wholly or partly situated; or

(*c*) in a case where the developer is any such council or local authority, on the Secretary of State.

(6) Regulations made by the Secretary of State may prescribe the steps to be taken by any council or local authority on whom an operations notice is served in accordance with subsection (5) above.

(7) Where an operations notice is served with respect to operations which are to be carried out after clearance of any site, the developer shall notify the investigating authority for the area of archaeological importance in question of the clearance of the site immediately on completion of the clearance operations.

(8) If in a case falling within subsection (7) above the developer carries out, or causes or permits to be carried out, any of the operations to which the operations notice relates without having first notified the investigating authority of the clearance of the site in accordance with that subsection, this section shall have effect in relation to those operations as if the operations notice had not been served.

(9) A person guilty of an offence under this section shall be liable—

(*a*) on summary conviction or, in Scotland, on conviction before a court of summary jurisdiction, to a fine not exceeding the statutory maximum; or

(*b*) on conviction on indictment to a fine.

(10) Without prejudice to section 222 of the Local Government Act 1972, any such council as is mentioned in subsection (5) (*a*) above may

institute proceedings for an offence under this section in respect of operations on any site situated partly in their area notwithstanding that the operations are confined to a part of the site outside their area; and if it appears to any such council or, in Scotland, to any local authority—

(*a*) that any operations are being, or are about to be, carried out in contravention of this section on any site situated wholly or partly in their area; and

(*b*) that the site contains or is likely to contain anything of archaeological or historical interest which will be disturbed, damaged, destroyed or removed without proper archaeological investigation if operations are carried out on the site without regard for the provisions of this Part of this Act;

that council or local authority may take proceedings in the High Court or, in Scotland, in any court of competent jurisdiction for the purpose of securing an injunction or interdict prohibiting those operations from being carried out in contravention of this section.

Certificate to accompany operations notice under section 35

36.—(1) A person is qualified to issue a certificate for the purposes of section 35 (4) (*b*) of this Act if he either—

(*a*) has an interest in the site of the operations which (apart from any restrictions imposed by law) entitles him to carry out the operations in question; or

(*b*) has a right to enter on and take possession of that site under section 11 (1) or (2) of the Compulsory Purchase Act 1965 (powers of entry on land subject to compulsory purchase) or, in the case of a site in Scotland, under paragraph 3 (1) of Schedule 2 to the Acquisition of Land (Authorisation Procedure) (Scotland) Act 1947.

(2) Statutory undertakers are qualified to issue a certificate for the purposes of section 35 (4) (*b*) of this Act if they are entitled by or under any enactment to carry out the operations in question.

(3) Any such certificate—

(*a*) shall be signed by or on behalf of a person or persons qualified in accordance with subsection (1) or (2) above to issue it;

(*b*) shall state that the person issuing the certificate has an interest within paragraph (*a*) or (as the case may be) a right within paragraph (*b*) of subsection (1) above or, in the case of a certificate issued by statutory undertakers, shall state that it is so issued and specify the enactment by or under which they are entitled to carry out the operations in question; and

(*c*) if the person issuing the certificate is not the developer, shall state that he has authorised the developer to carry out the operations.

(4) If any person issues a certificate which purports to comply with the requirements of this section and which contains a statement which he knows to be false or misleading in a material particular, or recklessly issues a certificate which purports to comply with those requirements and which contains a statement which is false or misleading in a material particular, he shall be guilty of an offence and liable on summary conviction or, in Scotland, on conviction before a court of summary jurisdiction, to a fine not exceeding £200.

Exemptions from offence under section 35

37.—(1) Section 35 of this Act does not apply to any operations carried out with the consent of the investigating authority for the area of archaeological importance in question.

(2) The Secretary of State may by order direct that section 35 shall not apply to the carrying out, or to the carrying out by any class or description of persons specified in the order, of operations of any class or description so specified; and an exemption conferred by an order under this subsection may be either unconditional or subject to any conditions specified in the order.

(3) The Secretary of State may direct that any exemption conferred by an order under subsection (2) above shall not apply to the carrying out on any land specified in the direction, or to the carrying out on any land so specified by any class or description of persons so specified, of operations of any class or description so specified, and may withdraw any direction given under this subsection.

(4) A direction under subsection (3) above shall not take effect until notice of it has been served on the occupier or (if there is no occupier) on the owner of the land in question.

(5) In any proceedings for an offence under section 35 consisting in carrying out, or causing or permitting to be carried out, any operations which disturb the ground, it shall be a defence for the accused to prove that he took all reasonable precautions and exercised all due diligence to avoid or prevent disturbance of the ground.

(6) In any proceedings for an offence under section 35 it shall be a defence for the accused to prove either—

(*a*) that he did not know and had no reason to believe that the site of the operation was within an area of archaeological importance;

(*b*) that the operations were urgently necessary in the interests of safety or health and that notice in writing of the need for the operations was given to the Secretary of State as soon as reasonably practicable.

Powers of investigating authority to enter and excavate site of operations covered by an operations notice

38.—(1) Where an operations notice is served with respect to any operations, the investigating authority for the area of archaeological importance in which the site of the operations is situated shall thereupon have a right to enter, at any reasonable time, the site and any land giving access to the site, for either or both the following purposes, that is to say—

(*a*) for the purpose of inspecting the site (including any buildings or other structures on the site) with a view to recording any matters of archaeological or historical interest and determining whether it would be desirable to carry out any excavations in the site; and

(*b*) for the purpose of observing any operations carried out on the site with a view to examining and recording any objects or other material of archaeological or historical interest, and recording any matters of archaeological or historical interest, discovered during the course of those operations.

(2) Where—

(*a*) an operations notice is served with respect to any operations; and

(*b*) the investigating authority for the area of archaeological importance in which the site of the operations is situated serves notice in accordance with subsection (3) below of its intention to excavate the site;

the investigating authority shall have a right to carry out excavations in the site for the purpose of archaeological investigation at any time during the period allowed for excavation in accordance with subsection (4) below.

(3) The investigating authority shall only have a right to excavate the site of any operations in accordance with subsection (2) above if before the end of the period of four weeks beginning with the date of service of the operations notice the authority—

(*a*) serves notice in the prescribed form of its intention to excavate on the developer; and

(*b*) serves a copy of that notice on any council (in England and Wales) or local authority (in Scotland) served with the operations notice and also (unless the functions of the investigating authority are for the time being exercisable by the Secretary of State) on the Secretary of State.

(4) The period allowed for excavation under subsection (2) above is the period of four months and two weeks beginning—

(*a*) with the date immediately following the end of the period of six weeks beginning with the date of service of the operations notice; or

(*b*) where the operations specified in the operations notice are to be carried out after clearance of the site, with the date of receipt of the notification of clearance of the site required under section 35 (7) of this Act or with the date first mentioned in paragraph (*a*) above (whichever last occurs); or

(*c*) with any earlier date agreed between the investigating authority and the developer.

(5) Where—

(*a*) the investigating authority has served notice of its intention to excavate the site in accordance with subsection (3) above; and

(*b*) the period of six weeks beginning with the date of service of the operations notice has expired;

the investigating authority shall have a right to carry out excavations in the site for the purpose of archaeological investigation notwithstanding that the period allowed for excavation in accordance with subsection (4) above has not yet begun, but only if the authority does not thereby obstruct the execution on the site by the developer of clearance operations or any other operations to which section 35 of this Act does not apply.

(6) The investigating authority may at any reasonable time enter the site and any land giving access to the site for the purpose of exercising a right to excavate the site in accordance with subsection (2) or (5) above.

(7) If operations to which the operations notice relates are carried out on the site at a time when the investigating authority has a right to excavate the site in accordance with subsection (2) or (5) above section 35 of this Act shall have effect in relation to those operations as if the operations notice had not been served (subject, however, to any exemption or defence conferred by or under section 37 of this Act).

(8) The Secretary of State may at any time direct—

(*a*) that an investigating authority shall comply with any conditions specified in the direction in exercising any of its powers under the preceding provisions of this section in relation to any site; or

(*b*) that any such power shall cease to be exercisable by an investigating authority in relation to the whole or any part of any site;

and may vary or revoke any direction given under paragraph (*a*) above.

(9) On giving a direction under subsection (8) above the Secretary of State shall serve a copy of the direction on each of the following persons, that is to say—

(*a*) the investigating authority;

(*b*) any council (in England and Wales) or local authority (in Scotland) served with the operations notice in question;

(*c*) the developer; and

(*d*) any person other than the developer by whom the certificate accompanying the operations notice in accordance with section 35 (4) (*b*) of this Act was issued;

and on varying or revoking any such direction the Secretary of State shall notify the same persons (giving particulars of the effect of any variation).

Power of investigating authority to investigate in advance of operations notice any site which may be acquired compulsorily

39.—(1) If an authority possessing compulsory purchase powers notifies the investigating authority for any area of archaeological importance that it proposes to carry out, or to authorise someone else to carry out, on any site in the area, any operations of a description mentioned in section 35 (2) of this Act (other than exempt operations), the investigating authority shall thereupon have a right to enter, at any reasonable time, the site and any land giving access to the site, for the purpose mentioned in section 38 (1) (*a*) of this Act.

In this subsection " exempt operations " means operations excluded from the application of section 35 by an order under section 37 of this Act.

(2) The right of an investigating authority to enter any site by virtue of subsection (1) above shall cease at the end of the period of one month beginning with the day on which it is first exercised.

(3) Section 38 (8) of this Act shall apply in relation to the power of entry under this section as it applies in relation to the powers of an investigating authority under that section.

(4) Section 38 (9) of this Act shall not apply in relation to a direction under section 38 (8) with respect to the exercise of the power of entry under this section, but on giving any such direction the Secretary of State shall serve a copy of the direction on each of the following persons, that is to say—

(*a*) the investigating authority;

(*b*) the authority possessing compulsory purchase powers; and

(*c*) the owner and (if the owner is not the occupier) the occupier of the site in question;

and on varying or revoking any such direction the Secretary of State shall notify the same persons (giving particulars of the effect of any variation).

(5) In this section " authority possessing compulsory purchase powers " means any person or body of persons who could be or have been authorised to acquire an interest in land compulsorily.

Other powers of entry on site of operations covered by an operations notice

40. Where an operations notice is served with respect to any operations—

(*a*) any person duly authorised in writing by the Secretary of State may at any reasonable time enter the site of the operations for the purpose of inspecting the site (including any building or other structure on the site) and recording any matters of archaeological or historical interest observed in the course of that inspection; and

(*b*) any person duly authorised in writing by the Royal Commission on Historical Monuments may at any reasonable time enter the site for the purpose of inspecting any building or other structure on the site and recording any matters of archaeological or historical interest observed in the course of that inspection.

Interpretation of Part II

41.—(1) In this Part of this Act—

(*a*) " the developer " and " operations notice " have the meanings respectively given by section 35 (3) of this Act;

(*b*) references to a London borough council include references to the Common Council of the City of London;

(*c*) references to operations on any land include references to operations in, under or over the land in question;

(*d*) references to the clearance of any site are references to the demolition and removal of any existing building or other structure on the site and the removal of any other materials thereon so as to clear the surface of the land (but do not include the levelling of the surface or the removal of materials from below the surface); and

(*e*) references to clearance operations are references to operations undertaken for the purpose of or in connection with the clearance of any site.

(2) For the purposes of this Part of this Act, the investigating authority for an area of archaeological importance is the person for the time being holding appointment as such under section 34 of this Act or (if there is no such person) the Secretary of State.

Part III

Miscellaneous and Supplemental

Restrictions on use of metal detectors

Restrictions on use of metal detectors

42.—(1) If a person uses a metal detector in a protected place without the written consent of the Secretary of State he shall be guilty of an offence and liable on summary conviction or, in Scotland, on conviction before a court of summary jurisdiction, to a fine not exceeding £200.

(2) In this section—

" metal detector " means any device designed or adapted for detecting or locating any metal or mineral in the ground; and

" protected place " means any place which is either—

(*a*) the site of a scheduled monument or of any monument under the ownership or guardianship of the Secretary of State or a local authority by virtue of this Act; or

(*b*) situated in an area of archaeological importance.

(3) If a person without the written consent of the Secretary of State removes any object of archaeological or historical interest which he has discovered by the use of a metal detector in a protected place he shall be guilty of an offence and liable on summary conviction to a fine not exceeding the statutory maximum or on conviction on indictment to a fine.

(4) A consent granted by the Secretary of State for the purposes of this section may be granted either unconditionally or subject to conditions.

(5) If any person—

(*a*) in using a metal detector in a protected place in accordance with any consent granted by the Secretary of State for the purposes of this section; or

(*b*) in removing or otherwise dealing with any object which he has discovered by the use of a metal detector in a protected place in accordance with any such consent;

fails to comply with any condition attached to the consent, he shall be guilty of an offence and liable, in a case falling within paragraph (*a*) above, to the penalty provided by subsection (1) above, and in a case falling within paragraph (*b*) above, to the penalty provided by subsection (3) above.

(6) In any proceedings for an offence under subsection (1) above, it shall be a defence for the accused to prove that he used the metal detector for a purpose other than detecting or locating objects of archaeological or historical interest.

(7) In any proceedings for an offence under subsection (1) or (3) above, it shall be a defence for the accused to prove that he had taken all reasonable precautions to find out whether the place where he used the metal detector was a protected place and did not believe that it was.

Powers of entry

Power of entry for survey and valuation

43.—(1) Any person authorised under this section may at any reasonable time enter any land for the purpose of surveying it, or estimating its value, in connection with any proposal to acquire that or any other land under this Act or in connection with any claim for compensation under this Act in respect of any such acquisition or for any damage to that or any other land.

(2) A person is authorised under this section if he is an officer of the Valuation Office of the Inland Revenue Department or a person duly authorised in writing by the Secretary of State or other authority proposing to make the acquisition which is the occasion of the survey or valuation or (as the case may be) from whom in accordance with this Act compensation in respect of the damage is recoverable.

(3) Subject to section 44 (9) of this Act, the power to survey land conferred by this section shall be construed as including power to search and bore for the purposes of ascertaining the nature of the subsoil or the presence of minerals therein.

Supplementary provisions with respect to powers of entry

44.—(1) A person may not in the exercise of any power of entry under this Act, other than that conferred by section 43, enter any building or part of a building occupied as a dwelling house without the consent of the occupier.

(2) Subject to the following provisions of this subsection, a person may not in the exercise of any power of entry under this Act demand admission as of right to any land which is occupied unless prior notice of the intended entry has been given to the occupier—

(*a*) where the purpose of the entry is to carry out any works on the land (other than excavations in exercise of the power under section 26 or 38 of this Act), not less than fourteen days before the day on which admission is demanded; or

(*b*) in any other case, not less than twenty-four hours before admission is demanded.

This subsection does not apply in relation to the power of entry under section 5 of this Act.

(3) A person seeking to enter any land in exercise of any power of entry under this Act shall, if so required by or on behalf of the owner or occupier thereof, produce evidence of his authority before entering.

(4) Any power of entry under this Act shall be construed as including power for any person entering any land in exercise of the power of entry

to take with him any assistance or equipment reasonably required for the purpose to which his entry relates and to do there anything reasonably necessary for carrying out that purpose.

(5) Without prejudice to subsection (4) above, where a person enters any land in exercise of any power of entry under this Act for the purpose of carrying out any archaeological investigation or examination of the land, he may take and remove such samples of any description as appear to him to be reasonably required for the purpose of archaeological analysis.

(6) Subject to subsection (7) below, where any works are being carried out on any land in relation to which any power of entry under this Act is exercisable, a person acting in the exercise of that power shall comply with any reasonable requirements or conditions imposed by the person by whom the works are being carried out for the purpose of preventing interference with or delay to the works.

(7) Any requirements or conditions imposed by a person by whom any works are being carried out shall not be regarded as reasonable for the purposes of subsection (6) above if compliance therewith would in effect frustrate the exercise of the power of entry or the purpose of the entry; and that subsection does not apply where the works in question are being carried out in contravention of section 2 (1) or (6) or 35 of this Act.

(8) Any person who intentionally obstructs a person acting in the exercise of any power of entry under this Act shall be guilty of an offence and liable on summary conviction or, in Scotland, on conviction before a court of summary jurisdiction, to a fine not exceeding £200.

(9) Where under section 43 of this Act a person proposes to carry out any works authorised by virtue of subsection (3) of that section—

(*a*) he shall not carry out those works unless notice of his intention to do so was included in the notice required by subsection (2) (*a*) above; and

(*b*) if the land in question is held by statutory undertakers, and those undertakers object to the proposed works on the grounds that the carrying out thereof would be seriously detrimental to the carrying on of their undertaking, the works shall not be carried out except with the authority of the Secretary of State.

Financial provisions

Expenditure on archaeological investigation

45.—(1) The Secretary of State may undertake, or assist in, or defray or contribute towards the cost of, an archaeological investigation of any land which he considers may contain an ancient monument or anything else of archaeological or historical interest.

(2) Any local authority may undertake, or assist in, or defray or contribute towards the cost of, an archaeological investigation of any land in or in the vicinity of their area, being land which they consider may contain an ancient monument or anything else of archaeological or historical interest.

(3) The Secretary of State or any local authority may publish the results of any archaeological investigation undertaken, assisted, or wholly or partly financed by them under this section in such manner and form as they think fit.

(4) Without prejudice to the application, by virtue of section 53 of this Act, of any other provision of this Act to land which is not within Great Britain, the powers conferred by this section shall be exercisable

in relation to any such land which forms part of the sea bed within the seaward limits of United Kingdom territorial waters adjacent to the coast of Great Britain.

Compensation for damage caused by exercise of certain powers under this Act

46.—(1) Subject to subsection (2) below, where, in the exercise in relation to any land of any power to which this section applies, any damage has been caused to that land or to any chattels on that land, any person interested in that land or those chattels may recover compensation in respect of that damage from the Secretary of State or other authority by or on whose behalf the power was exercised.

(2) Where any such damage is caused in the exercise of any such power by or on behalf of any person for the time being holding appointment as the investigating authority for an area of archaeological importance under section 34 of this Act, compensation shall be recoverable in accordance with this section from the Secretary of State instead of from that person.

(3) This section applies to any power to enter, or to do anything, on any land under any of the following sections of this Act, that is to say, sections 6, 26, 38, 39, 40 and 43.

(4) References in subsection (1) above to chattels shall be construed in relation to Scotland as references to moveables.

General provisions with respect to claims for compensation under this Act

47.—(1) Any claim for compensation under this Act shall be made within the time and in the manner prescribed.

(2) Any question of disputed compensation under this Act shall be referred to and determined by the Lands Tribunals or (in the case of any land situated in Scotland) by the Lands Tribunal for Scotland.

(3) In relation to the determination of any such question, the provisions of sections 2 and 4 of the Land Compensation Act 1961 or (as the case may be) of sections 9 and 11 of the Land Compensation (Scotland) Act 1963 shall apply, but the references in section 4 of the Act of 1961 and section 11 of the Act of 1963 to the acquiring authority shall be construed as references to the authority by whom the compensation claimed is payable under this Act.

Recovery of grants for expenditure in conservation areas and on historic buildings

48.—(1) After section 10 of the Town and Country Planning (Amendment) Act 1972 (grants and loans for preservation or enhancement of character or appearance of conservation areas) there shall be inserted the following section—

" **Recovery of grants under section 10**

10A.—(1) This section applies to any grant under section 10 above made on terms that it shall be recoverable under this section; but any such grant shall only be regarded for the purposes of this section as so made if before or on making the grant the Secretary of State gives to the grantee notice in writing—

(*a*) summarising the effect of this section; and

(*b*) specifying the period during which the grant is to be recoverable in accordance with subsection (5) below in the case of a grant made for the purpose mentioned in subsection (4) below.

(2) The period specified under subsection (1) (*b*) above in the case of any grant shall be a period beginning with the day on

which the grant is made and ending not more than ten years after that day.

(3) If any condition subject to which a grant to which this section applies was made is contravened or not complied with, the Secretary of State may recover the amount of the grant or such part of it as he thinks fit from the grantee.

(4) The following provisions of this section have effect where a grant to which this section applies is made to any person for the purpose of defraying in whole or in part any expenditure in relation to any particular property; and references in those provisions to the relevant interest are references to the interest held by the grantee in that property on the day on which the grant is made.

(5) If, during the period specified for the purposes of this subsection under subsection (1) (*b*) above, the grantee disposes of the relevant interest or any part of it by way of sale or exchange or lease for a term of not less than twenty-one years, the Secretary of State may recover the amount of the grant or such part of it as he thinks fit from the grantee.

(6) If a person becomes entitled by way of gift from the grantee, whether directly or indirectly (but otherwise than by will) to a part of the relevant interest, a disposal by the donee in any manner mentioned in subsection (5) above of the interest so acquired by him in the property, or any part of that interest, shall be treated for the purposes of that subsection as a disposal by the grantee of a part of the relevant interest.

(7) If a person becomes entitled by way of any such gift to the whole of the relevant interest subsection (5) above shall have effect as if the donee were the grantee.

(8) Nothing in subsection (3) or (5) above shall be taken as conferring on the Secretary of State a right to recover (by virtue of a breach of more than one condition or disposals of several parts of an interest in property) amounts in the aggregate exceeding the amount of the grant."

(2) After section 4 of the Historic Buildings and Ancient Monuments Act 1953 (grants for preservation of historic buildings, their contents and adjoining land) there shall be inserted the following section—

" **Recovery of grants under section 4**

4A.—(1) This section applies to any grant under section 4 of this Act made on terms that it shall be recoverable under this section; but any such grant shall only be regarded for the purposes of this section as so made if before or on making the grant the Secretary of State gives to the grantee notice in writing—

(*a*) summarising the effect of this section; and

(*b*) specifying the period during which the grant is to be recoverable in accordance with subsection (4) below in the case of a grant made for the purpose there mentioned.

(2) The period specified under subsection (1) (*b*) above in the case of any grant shall be a period beginning with the day on which the grant is made and ending not more than ten years after that day.

(3) If any condition subject to which a grant to which this section applies was made is contravened or not complied with, the Secretary of State may recover the amount of the grant or such part of it as he thinks fit from the grantee.

(4) If, during the period specified under subsection (1) (*b*) above in the case of a grant to which this section applies made to any person for the purpose of defraying in whole or in part any expendi-

ture on the repair, maintenance or upkeep of any property, the grantee disposes in any manner mentioned in subsection (5) below of the interest, or any part thereof, held by him in the property on the day on which the grant is made (referred to below in this section as " the relevant interest "), the Secretary of State may recover the amount of the grant or such part of it as he thinks fit from the grantee.

(5) Subsection (4) above only applies where the grantee disposes of the relevant interest or any part of it by way of sale or exchange or lease for a term of not less than twenty-one years.

(6) If a person becomes entitled by way of gift from the grantee, whether directly or indirectly (but oherwise than by will) to a part of the relevant interest, a disposal by the donee in any manner mentioned in subsection (5) above of the interest so acquired by him in the property, or any part of that interest, shall be treated for the purposes of subsection (4) above as a disposal by the grantee of a part of the relevant interest.

(7) If a person becomes entitled by way of any such gift to the whole of the relevant interest subsection (4) above shall have effect (except for the purpose of determining the relevant interest) as if the donee were the grantee.

(8) Nothing in subsection (3) or (4) above shall be taken as conferring on the Secretary of State a right to recover (by virtue of a breach of more than one condition or disposals of several parts of an interest in property) amounts in the aggregate exceeding the amount of the grant."

Grants to the Architectural Heritage Fund

49.—(1) The Secretary of State may make grants to the institution registered under the Charities Act 1960 under the name of the Architectural Heritage Fund.

(2) A grant under this section may be made subject to such conditions as the Secretary of State may think fit to impose.

Application to special cases

Application to Crown land

50.—(1) Notwithstanding any interest of the Crown in Crown land, but subject to the following provisions of this section—

(*a*) a monument which for the time being is Crown land may be included in the Schedule; and

(*b*) any restrictions or powers imposed or conferred by any of the provisions of this Act shall apply and be exercisable in relation to Crown land and in relation to anything done on Crown land otherwise than by or on behalf of the Crown, but not so as to affect any interest of the Crown therein.

(2) Except with the consent of the appropriate authority—

(*a*) no power under this Act to enter, or to do anything, on any land shall be exercisable in relation to land which for the time being is Crown land; and

(*b*) no interest in land which for the time being is Crown land shall be acquired compulsorily under Part I of this Act.

(3) In relation to any operations proposed to be carried out on Crown land otherwise than by or on behalf of the Crown, an operations notice served under section 35 of this Act shall not be effective for the purposes of that section unless it is accompanied by a certificate from the appro-

priate authority in the prescribed form consenting to the exercise in relation to that land in connection with those operations of the powers conferred by sections 38 and 40 of this Act.

(4) In this section " Crown land " means land in which there is a Crown interest or a Duchy interest; " Crown interest " means an interest belonging to Her Majesty in right of the Crown, or belonging to a Government department, or held in trust for Her Majesty for the purposes of a Government department, and includes any estate or interest held in right of the Prince and Steward of Scotland; " Duchy interest " means an interest belonging to Her Majesty in right of the Duchy of Lancaster, or belonging to the Duchy of Cornwall; and for the purposes of this section " the appropriate authority ", in relation to any land—

(*a*) in the case of land belonging to Her Majesty in right of the Crown and forming part of the Crown Estate, means the Crown Estate Commissioners, and, in relation to any other land belonging to Her Majesty in right of the Crown, means the Government department having the management of that land;

(*b*) in relation to land belonging to Her Majesty in right of the Duchy of Lancaster, means the Chancellor of the Duchy;

(*c*) in relation to land belonging to the Duchy of Cornwall, means such person as the Duke of Cornwall, or the possessor for the time being of the Duchy of Cornwall, appoints;

(*d*) in the case of land belonging to a Government department or held in trust for Her Majesty for the purposes of a Government department, means that department;

and, if any question arises as to what authority is the appropriate authority in relation to any land, that question shall be referred to the Treasury, whose decision shall be final.

In this subsection " Government department " includes any Minister of the Crown.

Ecclesiastical property

51.—(1) Without prejudice to the provisions of the Acquisition of Land (Authorisation Procedure) Act 1946 with respect to notices served under that Act, where under any of the provisions of this Act a notice is required to be served on an owner of land, and the land is ecclesiastical property, a like notice shall be served on the Church Commissioners.

(2) Where the fee simple of any ecclesiastical property is in abeyance, the fee simple shall for the purposes of this Act be treated as being vested in the Church Commissioners.

(3) Any sum which under section 7, 9 or 46 of this Act is payable in relation to land which is ecclesiastical property, and apart from this subsection would be payable to an incumbent, shall be paid to the Church Commissioners, to be applied for the purposes for which the proceeds of a sale by agreement of the land would be applicable under any enactment or Measure authorising, or disposing of the proceeds of, such a sale.

(4) Where any sum is recoverable under section 8 of this Act in respect of land which is ecclesiastical property the Church Commissioners may apply any money or securities held by them in the payment of that sum.

(5) In this section " ecclesiastical property " means land belonging to an ecclesiastical benefice of the Church of England, or being or forming part of a church subject to the jurisdiction of a bishop of any diocese of the Church of England or the site of such a church, or being or forming part of a burial ground subject to such jurisdiction.

Application to the Isles of Scilly

52. The Secretary of State may, after consultation with the Council of the Isles of Scilly, by order provide for the application to those Isles of the provisions of this Act—

(*a*) as if those Isles were a district and the Council of the Isles were the council of that district; and

(*b*) in other respects subject to such modifications as may be specified in the order.

Monuments in territorial waters

53.—(1) A monument situated in, on or under the sea bed within the seaward limits of United Kingdom territorial waters adjacent to the coast of Great Britain (referred to below in this section as a monument in territorial waters) may be included in the Schedule under section 1 (3) of this Act, and the remaining provisions of this Act shall extend accordingly to any such monument which is a scheduled monument (but not otherwise).

(2) The entry in the Schedule relating to any monument in territorial waters shall describe the monument as lying off the coast of England, or of Scotland, or of Wales; and any such monument shall be treated for the purposes of this Act as situated in the country specified for the purposes of this subsection in the entry relating to the monument in the Schedule.

(3) In relation to any monument in territorial waters which is under the ownership or guardianship of the Secretary of State or any local authority by virtue of this Act, references in this Act to land associated with the monument (or to associated land) include references to any part of the sea bed occupied by the Secretary of State or by a local authority for any such purpose relating to the monument as is mentioned in section 15 (1) of this Act.

(4) Without prejudice to any jurisdiction exercisable apart from this subsection, proceedings for any offence under this Act committed in United Kingdom territorial waters adjacent to the coast of Great Britain may be taken, and the offence may for all incidental purposes be treated as having been committed, in any place in Great Britain.

(5) It is hereby declared that, notwithstanding that by virtue of this section this Act may affect individuals or bodies corporate outside the United Kingdom, it applies to any individual whether or not he is a British subject, and to any body corporate whether or not incorporated under the law of any part of the United Kingdom.

(6) A constable shall on any monument in territorial waters have all the powers, protection and privileges which he has in the area for which he acts as constable.

(7) References in this section to the sea bed do not include the seashore or any other land which, though covered (intermittently or permanently) by the sea, is within Great Britain.

Supplemental

Treatment and preservation of finds

54.—(1) Where a person enters any land in exercise of any power of entry under this Act for any of the following purposes, that is to say—

(*a*) to carry out any excavations in the land or any operations affecting any ancient monument situated in, on or under the land;

(*b*) to observe any operations on the land in exercise of the power under section 6 (3) (*a*) or (4) (*b*) or 38 (1) (*b*) of this Act; or (*c*) to carry out any archaeological examination of the land;

he may take temporary custody of any object of archaeological or historical interest discovered during the course of those excavations or operations or (as the case may be) during the course of that examination, and remove it from its site for the purpose of examining, testing, treating, recording or preserving it.

(2) The Secretary of State or other authority by or on whose behalf the power of entry was exercised may not retain the object without the consent of the owner beyond such period as may be reasonably required for the purpose of examining and recording it and carrying out any test or treatment which appears to the Secretary of State or to that other authority to be desirable for the purpose of archaeological investigation or analysis or with a view to restoring or preserving the object.

(3) Nothing in this section shall affect any right of the Crown in relation to treasure trove.

Proceedings for questioning validity of certain orders, etc.

55.—(1) If any person—

(*a*) is aggrieved by any order to which this section applies and desires to question the validity of that order, on the grounds that it is not within the powers of this Act, or that any of the relevant requirements have not been complied with in relation to it; or

(*b*) is aggrieved by any action on the part of the Secretary of State to which this section applies and desires to question the validity of that action, on the grounds that it is not within the powers of this Act, or that any of the relevant requirements have not been complied with in relation to it;

he may, within six weeks from the relevant date, make an application under this section to the High Court or (in Scotland) to the Court of Session.

(2) This section applies to any designation order and to any order under section 33 (4) of this Act varying or revoking a designation order.

(3) This section applies to action on the part of the Secretary of State of either of the following descriptions, that is to say—

(*a*) any decision of the Secretary of State on an application for scheduled monument consent; and

(*b*) the giving by the Secretary of State of any direction under section 4 of this Act modifying or revoking a scheduled monument consent.

(4) In subsection (1) above "the relevant date" means—

(*a*) in relation to an order, the date on which notice of the making of the order is published (or, as the case may be, first published) in accordance with Schedule 2 to this Act; and

(*b*) in relation to any action on the part of the Secretary of State, the date on which that action is taken.

(5) On any application under this section the High Court or (in Scotland) the Court of Session—

(*a*) may by interim order suspend the operation of the order or action, the validity whereof is questioned by the application, until the final determination of the proceedings;

(*b*) if satisfied that the order or action in question is not within the powers of this Act, or that the interests of the applicant have been substantially prejudiced by a failure to comply with any of the relevant requirements in relation thereto, may quash that order or action in whole or in part.

(6) In this section "the relevant requirements" means—

(*a*) in relation to any order to which this section applies, any requirements of this Act or of any regulations made under this Act which are applicable to that order; and

(*b*) in relation to any action to which this section applies, any requirements of this Act or of the Tribunals and Inquiries Act 1971 or of any regulations or rules made under this Act or under that Act which are applicable to that action.

(7) Except as provided by this section, the validity of any order or action to which this section applies shall not be questioned in any legal proceedings whatsoever; but nothing in this section shall affect the exercise of any jurisdiction of any court in respect of any refusal or failure on the part of the Secretary of State to take a decision on an application for scheduled monument consent.

Service of documents

56.—(1) Any notice or other document required or authorised to be served under this Act may be served either—

(*a*) by delivering it to the person on whom it is to be served; or

(*b*) by leaving it at the usual or last known place of abode of that person or, in a case where an address for service has been given by that person, at that address; or

(*c*) by sending it in a pre-paid registered letter, or by the recorded delivery service, addressed to that person at his usual or last known place of abode or, in a case where an address for service has been given by that person, at that address; or

(*d*) in the case of an incorporated company or body, by delivering it to the secretary or clerk of the company or body at their registered or principal office, or sending it in a pre-paid registered letter, or by the recorded delivery service, addressed to the secretary or clerk of the company or body at that office.

(2) Where any such notice or document is required or authorised to be served on any person as being the owner or occupier of any monument or other land—

(*a*) it may be addressed to the "owner" or (as the case may require) to the "occupier" of that monument or land (describing it) without further name or description; and

(*b*) if the usual or last known place of abode of the person in question cannot be found, it may be served by being affixed conspicuously to the monument or to some object on the site of the monument or (as the case may be) on the land.

Power to require information as to interests in land

57.—(1) For the purpose of enabling the Secretary of State or a local authority to exercise any function under this Act, the Secretary of State or the local authority may require the occupier of any land and any person who, either directly or indirectly, receives rent in respect of any land to state in writing the nature of his interest therein, and the name and address of any other person known to him as having an interest therein, whether as a freeholder, owner of the dominium utile, mortgagee, lessee, or otherwise.

(2) Any person who, having been required under this section to give any information, fails without reasonable excuse to give that information, shall be guilty of an offence and liable on summary conviction or, in Scotland, on conviction before a court of summary jurisdiction, to a fine not exceeding £200.

(3) Any person who, having been so required to give any information, knowingly makes any mis-statement in respect of it, shall be guilty of an offence and liable—

(*a*) on summary conviction or, in Scotland, on conviction before a court of summary jurisdiction, to a fine not exceeding the statutory maximum; or

(*b*) on conviction on indictment to a fine.

Offences by corporations

58.—(1) Where an offence under this Act which has been committed by a body corporate is proved to have been committed with the consent or connivance of, or to be attributable to any neglect on the part of, a director, manager, secretary or other similar officer of the body corporate, or any person who was purporting to act in any such capacity, he, as well as the body corporate, shall be guilty of that offence and be liable to be proceeded against accordingly.

(2) In subsection (1) above the expression " director ", in relation to any body corporate established by or under an enactment for the purpose of carrying on under national ownership an industry or part of an industry or undertaking, being a body corporate whose affairs are managed by the members thereof, means a member of that body corporate.

Prosecution of offences: Scotland

59. Notwithstanding anything in section 331 of the Criminal Procedure (Scotland) Act 1975, summary proceedings in Scotland for an offence under this Act may be commenced at any time within one year from the date on which evidence sufficient in the opinion of the prosecutor to warrant proceedings came to his knowledge; and a certificate purporting to be signed by the prosecutor stating that date shall be conclusive.

Regulations and orders

60.—(1) Any order or regulations made under this Act may make different provision for different cases to which the order or (as the case may be) the regulations apply.

(2) Any power of the Secretary of State to make regulations under this Act, and the power to make orders under sections 3, 37, 52, 61 and 65 of this Act shall be exercisable by statutory instrument; and any statutory instrument containing any such regulations or order, other than one containing regulations under section 19 of this Act, shall be subject to annulment in pursuance of a resolution of either House of Parliament.

Interpretation

61.—(1) In this Act—

" ancient monument " has the meaning given by subsection (12) below;

" area of archaeological importance " means an area designated as such under section 33 of this Act;

" designation order " means an order under that section;

" enactment " includes an enactment in any local or private Act of Parliament, and an order, rule, regulation, bye-law or scheme made under an Act of Parliament;

" flooding operations " means covering land with water or any other liquid or partially liquid substance;

" functions " includes powers and duties;

"guardianship deed" has the meaning given by section 12 (6) of this Act;

"land" means—

(*a*) in England and Wales, any corporeal hereditament;

(*b*) in Scotland, any heritable property;

including a building or a monument and, in relation to any acquisition of land, includes any interest in or right over land;

"local authority" means—

(*a*) in England and Wales, the council of a county or district, the Greater London Council, the council of a London borough, and the Common Council of the City of London; and

(*b*) in Scotland, the planning authority within the meaning of Part IX of the Local Government (Scotland) Act 1973;

"monument" has the meaning given by subsection (7) below;

"owner", in relation to any land in England and Wales means (except for the purposes of paragraph 2 (1) of Schedule 1 to this Act and any regulations made for the purposes of that paragraph) a person, other than a mortgagee not in possession, who, whether in his own right or as trustee for any other person, is entitled to receive the rack rent of the land, or where the land is not let at a rack rent, would be so entitled if it were so let;

"possession" includes receipt of rents and profits or the right to receive rents and profits (if any);

"prescribed" means prescribed by regulations made by the Secretary of State;

"the Schedule" has the meaning given by section 1 (1) of this Act;

"scheduled monument" has the meaning given by section 1 (11) of this Act and references to "scheduled monument consent" shall be construed in accordance with section 2 (3) and 3 (5) of this Act;

"the statutory maximum" means—

(*a*) in England and Wales the prescribed sum within the meaning of section 28 of the Criminal Law Act 1977 (that is to say, £1,000 or another sum fixed by order under section 61 of that Act to take account of changes in the value of money); and

(*b*) in Scotland—

(i) on conviction in the sheriff court, the prescribed sum within the meaning of section 289B of the Criminal Procedure (Scotland) Act 1975 (that is to say, £1,000 or another sum fixed by order under section 289D of that Act for that purpose);

(ii) on conviction in the district court, the sum of £200;

"tipping operations" means tipping soil or spoil or depositing building or other materials or matter (including waste materials or refuse) on any land; and

"works" includes operations of any description and, in particular (but without prejudice to the generality of the preceding provision) flooding or tipping operations and any operations undertaken for purposes of agriculture (within the meaning of the Town and Country Planning Act 1971 or, as regards

Scotland, the Town and Country Planning (Scotland) Act 1972) or forestry (including afforestation).

(2) In this Act "statutory undertakers" means—

(*a*) persons authorised by any enactment to carry on any railway, light railway, tramway, road transport, water transport, canal, inland navigation, dock, harbour, pier or lighthouse undertaking, or any undertaking for the supply of electricity, gas, hydraulic power or water;

(*b*) the British Airports Authority, the Civil Aviation Authority, the National Coal Board, the Post Office and any other authority, body or undertakers which by virtue of any enactment are to be treated as statutory undertakers for any of the purposes of the Town and Country Planning Act 1971 or of the Town and Country Planning (Scotland) Act 1972; and

(*c*) any other authority, body or undertakers specified in an order made by the Secretary of State under this paragraph.

(3) For the purposes of sections 14 (1) and 21 (2) of this Act and paragraph 6 (1) (*b*) and (2) (*b*) of Schedule 3 to this Act a person shall be taken to be immediately affected by the operation of a guardianship deed relating to any land if he is bound by that deed and is in possession or occupation of the land.

(4) For the purposes of this Act "archaeological investigation" means any investigation of any land, objects or other material for the purpose of obtaining and recording any information of archaeological or historical interest and (without prejudice to the generality of the preceding provision) includes in the case of an archaeological investigation of any land—

(*a*) any investigation for the purpose of discovering and revealing and (where appropriate) recovering and removing any objects or other material of archaeological or historical interest situated in, on or under the land; and

(*b*) examining, testing, treating, recording and preserving any such objects or material discovered during the course of any excavations or inspections carried out for the purposes of any such investigation.

(5) For the purposes of this Act, an archaeological examination of any land means any examination or inspection of the land (including any buildings or other structures thereon) for the purpose of obtaining and recording any information of archaeological or historical interest.

(6) In this Act references to land associated with any monument (or to associated land) shall be construed in accordance with section 15 (6) of this Act.

(7) "Monument" means (subject to subsection (8) below)—

(*a*) any building, structure or work, whether above or below the surface of the land, and any cave or excavation;

(*b*) any site comprising the remains of any such building, structure or work or of any cave or excavation; and

(*c*) any site comprising, or comprising the remains of, any vehicle, vessel, aircraft or other movable structure or part thereof which neither constitutes nor forms part of any work which is a monument within paragraph (*a*) above;

and any machinery attached to a monument shall be regarded as part of the monument if it could not be detached without being dismantled.

(8) Subsection (7) (*a*) above does not apply to any ecclesiastical building for the time being used for ecclesiastical purposes, and subsection (7) (*c*) above does not apply—

(*a*) to a site comprising any object or its remains unless the situation of that object or its remains in that particular site is a matter of public interest;

(*b*) to a site comprising, or comprising the remains of, any vessel which is protected by an order under section 1 of the Protection of Wrecks Act 1973 designating an area round the site as a restricted area.

(9) For the purposes of this Act, the site of a monument includes not only the land in or on which it is situated but also any land comprising or adjoining it which appears to the Secretary of State or a local authority, in the exercise in relation to that monument of any of their functions under this Act, to be essential for the monument's support and preservation.

(10) References in this Act to a monument include references—

(*a*) to the site of the monument in question; and

(*b*) to a group of monuments or any part of a monument or group of monuments.

(11) References in this Act to the site of a monument—

(*a*) are references to the monument itself where it consists of a site; and

(*b*) in any other case include references to the monument itself.

(12) " Ancient monument " means—

(*a*) any scheduled monument; and

(*b*) any other monument which in the opinion of the Secretary of State is of public interest by reason of the historic, architectural, traditional, artistic or archaeological interest attaching to it.

(13) In this section " remains " includes any trace or sign of the previous existence of the thing in question.

Special provision for Scotland

62.—(1) This Act shall be treated as if it had been passed before the Scotland Act 1978 for the purposes of the following provisions of that Act (which adapt certain provisions of earlier legislation in their application to devolved matters)—

section 21 (2) (exercise by a Scottish Secretary of executive powers and duties of Ministers of the Crown);

section 22 (1) and (2) (powers of Scottish Secretary and Assembly with respect to subordinate instruments);

section 60 (1) (money formerly payable out of or into United Kingdom funds to be payable out of or into the Scottish Consolidated Fund);

section 74 (2) (construction of references to property vested in a Government department);

section 78 (reports formerly required to be laid before Parliament to be laid instead before the Scottish Assembly); and

section 82 (1) and (3) (construction of references to Ministers of the Crown and power to make consequential amendments in earlier legislation).

(2) The reference in Schedule 5 to that Act to sections 4 to 6 of the Historic Buildings and Ancient Monuments Act 1953 shall be construed as including a reference to the section 4A inserted in the said Act of 1953 by section 48 (2) of this Act.

(3) Part III of Schedule 10 to the Scotland Act 1978 (which lists devolved and non-devolved matters dealt with in enactments) shall be amended by the addition at the end thereof of the following entry—

" The Ancient Monuments and Archaeological Areas Act 1979.	The function under section 44 (9) in respect of land held by excepted statutory undertakers and the power of the Treasury to determine questions under section 50 (4) are not included."

(4) In this Act, in relation to any land in Scotland, " occupier " means an occupier with an interest in that land which is heritable and, if there is no such occupier, the owner thereof shall be deemed to be the occupier.

(5) In relation to land in Scotland, any reference in this Act—

(*a*) to a mortgage shall be construed as a reference to a heritable security;

(*b*) to a mortgagee shall be construed as a reference to a creditor in a heritable security; and

(*c*) to a first mortgagee shall be construed as a reference to a creditor in a heritable security which ranks prior to any other heritable security over the same land.

Special provision for Wales

63.—(1) This Act shall be treated as if it had been passed before the Wales Act 1978 for the purposes of the following provisions of that Act (which adapt certain provisions of earlier legislation in relation to the exercise by the Welsh Assembly of its functions)—

section 55 (money formerly payable out of or into United Kingdom funds to be payable out of or into the Welsh Consolidated Fund);

section 74 (construction of references to Ministers of the Crown and to property vested in a Government department);

section 76 (reports formerly required to be laid before Parliament to be sent instead to the Welsh Assembly); and

section 77 (2) (power to make consequential amendments in earlier legislation).

(2) In Part VIII of Schedule 2 to that Act (Land Use and Development), in the entry relating to the Town and Country Planning (Amendment) Act 1972, for the words " section 10 " there shall be substituted the words " sections 10 and 10A ".

(3) In Part XII of Schedule 2 to the Wales Act 1978 (Ancient Monuments and Historic Buildings), for the entry relating to the Ancient Monuments Acts 1913 to 1974 there shall be substituted the following entry—

" *Enactment*	*Excluded functions*
The Ancient Monuments and Archaeological Areas Act 1979.	The function under section 44 (9) in respect of land held by excepted statutory undertakers. The functions under section 50 except so far as exercisable in relation to land vested in or held for the purposes of the Assembly. The function under section 61 (2) (*c*)."

(4) The references in Part XII of Schedule 2 and in Schedule 3 to that Act to Part I and sections 4 to 6 of the Historic Buildings and

Ancient Monuments Act 1953 respectively shall each be construed as including a reference to the section 4A inserted in the said Act of 1953 by section 48 (2) of this Act.

(5) In Schedule 11 to that Act, paragraph 2 (which relates to the Ancient Monuments Consolidation and Amendment Act 1913) shall be omitted.

Transitional provisions, consequential amendments and repeals

64.—(1) Schedule 3 to this Act shall have effect for the purposes of the transition to the provisions of this Act from the law previously in force.

(2) The enactments specified in Schedule 4 to this Act shall have effect subject to the amendments specified in that Schedule, being amendments consequential on the provisions of this Act.

(3) The enactments specified in Schedule 5 to this Act are hereby repealed to the extent specified in the third column of that Schedule.

Short title, commencement and extent

65.—(1) This Act may be cited as the Ancient Monuments and Archaeological Areas Act 1979.

(2) This Act shall come into force on such day as may be appointed by order of the Secretary of State, and different days may be appointed for different purposes; and a reference in any provision of this Act to the commencement of this Act is a reference to the day appointed for the coming into force of that provision.

(3) This Act does not extend to Northern Ireland.

SCHEDULES

Sections 2 and 4

SCHEDULE 1

Control of Works Affecting Scheduled Monuments

PART I

Applications for Scheduled Monument Consent

1.—(1) Provision may be made by regulations under this Act with respect to the form and manner in which applications for scheduled monument consent are to be made, the particulars to be included therein and the information to be provided by applicants or (as the case may be) by Secretary of State in connection therewith.

(2) Any scheduled monument consent (including scheduled monument consent granted by order under section 3 of this Act) shall (except so far as it otherwise provides) enure for the benefit of the monument and of all persons for the time being interested therein.

2.—(1) The Secretary of State may refuse to entertain an application for scheduled monument consent unless it is accompanied by one or other of the following certificates signed by or on behalf of the applicant, that is to say—

(*a*) a certificate stating that, at the beginning of the period of twenty-one days ending with the application, no person other than the applicant was the owner of the monument;

(*b*) a certificate stating that the applicant has given the requisite notice of the application to all the persons other than the applicant who, at the beginning of that period, were owners of the monument;

(*c*) a certificate stating that the applicant is unable to issue a certificate in accordance with either of the preceding paragraphs, that he has given the requisite notice of the application to such one or more of the persons mentioned in paragraph (*b*) above as are specified in the certificate, that he has taken such steps as are reasonably open to him to ascertain the names and addresses of the remainder of those persons and that he has been unable to do so;

(d) a certificate stating that the applicant is unable to issue a certificate in accordance with paragraph (a) above, that he has taken such steps as are reasonably open to him to ascertain the names and addresses of the persons mentioned in paragraph (b) above and that he has been unable to do so.

(2) Any certificate issued for the purposes of sub-paragraph (1) above—

(a) shall contain such further particulars of the matters to which the certificate relates as may be prescribed by regulations made for the purposes of this paragraph; and

(b) shall be in such form as may be so prescribed;

and any reference in that sub-paragraph to the requisite notice is a reference to a notice in the form so prescribed.

(3) Regulations made for the purposes of this paragraph may make provision as to who, in the case of any monument, is to be treated as the owner for those purposes.

(4) If any person issues a certificate which purports to comply with the requirements of this paragraph and which contains a statement which he knows to be false or misleading in a material particular, or recklessly issues a certificate which purports to comply with those requirements and which contains a statement which is false or misleading in a material particular, he shall be guilty of an offence and liable on summary conviction or, in Scotland, on conviction before a court of summary jurisdiction, to a fine not exceeding £200.

3.—(1) The Secretary of State may grant scheduled monument consent in respect of all or any part of the works to which an application for scheduled monument consent relates.

(2) Before determining whether or not to grant scheduled monument consent on any application therefor, the Secretary of State shall either—

(a) cause a public local inquiry to be held; or

(b) afford to the applicant, and to any other person to whom it appears to the Secretary of State expedient to afford it, an opportunity of appearing before and being heard by a person appointed by the Secretary of State for the purpose.

(3) Before determining whether or not to grant scheduled monument consent on any application therefor the Secretary of State—

(a) shall in every case consider any representations made by any person with respect to that application before the time when he considers his decision thereon (whether in consequence of any notice given to that person in accordance with any requirements of regulations made by virtue of paragraph 2 above or of any publicity given to the application by the Secretary of State, or otherwise); and

(b) shall also, if any inquiry or hearing has been held in accordance with sub-paragraph (2) above, consider the report of the person who held it.

(4) The Secretary of State shall serve notice of his decision with respect to the application on the applicant and on every person who has made representations to him with respect to the application.

4.—(1) Subsections (2) to (5) of section 250 of the Local Government Act 1972 (evidence and costs at local inquiries) shall apply to a public local inquiry held in pursuance of paragraph 3 (2) above in relation to a monument situated in England and Wales as they apply where a Minister or the Secretary of State causes an inquiry to be held under subsection (1) of that section.

(2) Subsections (2) to (8) of section 210 of the Local Government (Scotland) Act 1973 (evidence and expenses at local inquiries) shall apply to a public local inquiry held in pursuance of paragraph 3 (2) above in relation to a monument situated in Scotland as they apply where a Minister or the Secretary of State causes an inquiry to be held under sub-section (1) of that section.

Part II

Modification and Revocation of Scheduled Monument Consent

5.—(1) Before giving a direction under section 4 of this Act modifying or revoking a scheduled monument consent the Secretary of State shall serve a notice of proposed modification or revocation on—

(*a*) the owner of the monument and (if the owner is not the occupier) the occupier of the monument; and

(*b*) any other person who in the opinion of the Secretary of State would be affected by the proposed modification or revocation.

(2) A notice under this paragraph shall—

(*a*) contain a draft of the proposed modification or revocation and a brief statement of the reasons therefor; and

(*b*) specify the time allowed by sub-paragraph (5) below for making objections to the proposed modification or revocation and the manner in which any such objections can be made.

(3) Where the effect of a proposed modification (or any part of it) would be to exclude any works from the scope of the scheduled monument consent in question or in any manner to affect the execution of any of the works to which the consent relates, the notice under this paragraph relating to that proposed modification shall indicate that the works affected must not be executed after the receipt of the notice or (as the case may require) must not be so executed in a manner specified in the notice.

(4) A notice of proposed revocation under this paragraph shall indicate that the works to which the scheduled monument consent in question relates must not be executed after receipt of the notice.

(5) A person served with a notice under this paragraph may make an objection to the proposed modification or revocation at any time before the end of the period of twenty-eight days beginning with the date on which the notice was served.

6.—(1) If no objection to a proposed modification or revocation is duly made by a person served with notice thereof in accordance with paragraph 5 above, or if all objections so made are withdrawn, the Secretary of State may give a direction under section 4 of this Act modifying or revoking the scheduled monument consent in question in accordance with the notice.

(2) If any objection duly made as mentioned in sub-paragraph (1) above is not withdrawn, then, before giving a direction under section 4 of this Act with respect to the proposed modification or revocation, the Secretary of State shall either—

(*a*) cause a public local inquiry to be held; or

(*b*) afford to any such person an opportunity of appearing before and being heard by a person appointed by the Secretary of State for the purpose.

(3) If any person by whom an objection has been made avails himself of the opportunity of being heard, the Secretary of State shall afford to each other person served with notice of the proposed modification or revocation in accordance with paragraph 5 above, and to any other person to whom it appears to the Secretary of State expedient to afford it, an opportunity of being heard on the same occasion.

(4) Before determining in a case within sub-paragraph (2) above whether to give a direction under section 4 of this Act modifying or revoking the scheduled monument consent in accordance with the notice, the Secretary of State—

(*a*) shall in every case consider any objections duly made as mentioned in sub-paragraph (1) above and not withdrawn; and

(*b*) shall also, if inquiry or hearing has been held in accordance with sub-paragraph (2) above, consider the report of the person who held it.

(5) After considering any objections and report he is required to consider in accordance with sub-paragraph (4) above the Secretary of State may give a direction under section 4 of this Act modifying or revoking the scheduled monument consent either in accordance with the notice or with any variation appearing to him to be appropriate.

7. As soon as may be after giving a direction under section 4 of this Act the Secretary of State shall send a copy of the direction to each person served with notice of its proposed effect in accordance with paragraph 5 above and to any other person afforded an opportunity of being heard in accordance with paragraph 6 (3) above.

8.—(1) Where in accordance with sub-paragraph (3) of paragraph 5 above a notice under that paragraph indicates that any works specified in the notice must not be executed after receipt of the notice, the works so specified shall not be regarded as authorised under Part I of this Act at any time after the relevant service date.

(2) Where in accordance with that sub-paragraph a notice under that paragraph indicates that any works specified in the notice must not be executed after receipt of the notice in a manner so specified, the works so specified shall not be regarded as authorised under Part I of this Act if executed in that manner at any time after the relevant service date.

(3) Where in accordance with sub-paragraph (4) of paragraph 5 above a notice under that paragraph indicates that the works to which the scheduled monument consent relates must not be executed after receipt of the notice, those works shall not be regarded as authorised under Part I of this Act at any time after the relevant service date.

(4) The preceding provisions of this paragraph shall cease to apply in relation to any works affected by a notice under paragraph 5 above—

(*a*) if within the period of twenty-one months beginning with the relevant service date the Secretary of State gives a direction with respect to the modification or revocation proposed by that notice in accordance with paragraph 6 above, on the date when he gives that direction;

(*b*) if within that period the Secretary of State serves notice on the occupier or (if there is no occupier) on the owner of the monument that he has determined not to give such a direction, on the date when he serves that notice; and

(*c*) in any other case, at the end of that period.

(5) In this paragraph " the relevant service date " means, in relation to a notice under paragraph 5 above with respect to works affecting any monument, the date on which that notice was served on the occupier or (if there is no occupier) on the owner of the monument.

9.—(1) Subject to sub-paragraph (2) below, subsections (2) to (5) of section 250 of the Local Government Act 1972 (evidence and costs at local inquiries) shall apply to a public local inquiry held in pursuance of paragraph 6 (2) above as they apply where a Minister or the Secretary of State causes an inquiry to be held under subsection (1) of that section.

(2) Subsection (4) of that section (costs of the Minister causing the inquiry to be held to be defrayed by such local authority or party to the inquiry as the Minister may direct) shall not apply except in so far as the Secretary of State is of opinion, having regard to the object and result of the inquiry, that his costs should be defrayed by any party thereto.

(3) In the application of this paragraph to Scotland, in sub-paragraph (1) for the words " subsections (2) to (5) of section 250 of the Local Government Act 1972 (evidence and costs at local inquiries) " there shall be substituted the words " subsections (2) to (8) of section 210 of the Local Government (Scotland) Act 1973 (evidence and expenses at local inquiries) ", and in sub-paragraph (2) for the words " subsection (4) of that section (costs " there shall be substituted the words " subsection (7) of that section (expenses ".

Section 33

SCHEDULE 2

DESIGNATION ORDERS

Designation orders by the Secretary of State

1.—(1) A designation order made by the Secretary of State shall describe by reference to a map the area affected.

(2) The map shall be to such a scale, and the order in such form, as the Secretary of State considers appropriate.

2. Before making a designation order the Secretary of State shall—

(*a*) consult each of the local authorities concerned; and

(*b*) publish notice of his proposal to make the order;

in accordance with paragraph 3 below.

3.—(1) The consultation required by sub-paragraph (*a*) of paragraph 2 above shall precede the publication of the notice required by sub-paragraph (*b*) of that paragraph.

(2) The notice required by paragraph 2 (*b*) above—

(*a*) shall be published in two successive weeks in the London Gazette and in one or more local newspapers circulating in the locality in which the area affected is situated;

(*b*) shall state that the Secretary of State proposes to make the order, describing the area affected and the effect of the order; and

(*c*) shall indicate where (in accordance with paragraphs 4 and 5 below) a copy of the draft order and of the map to which it refers may be inspected.

4. Copies of the draft order and of the map to which it refers—

(*a*) shall be deposited with each of the local authorities concerned on or before the date on which notice of the Secretary of State's proposal to make the order is first published in accordance with paragraph 3 (2) (*a*) above; and

(*b*) shall be kept available for public inspection by each of those authorities, free of charge, at reasonable hours and at a convenient place, until the Secretary of State makes the order or notifies the local authority in question that he has determined not to make it.

5. Copies of the draft order and of the map to which it refers shall similarly be kept available by the Secretary of State, until he makes the order or determines not to make it.

6. The Secretary of State may make the order, either without modifications or with such modification only as consists in reducing the area affected, at any time after the end of the period of six weeks beginning with the date on which notice of his proposal to make the order is first published in accordance with paragraph 3 (2) (*a*) above.

7. On making the order, the Secretary of State shall—

(*a*) publish notice in two successive weeks in the London Gazette and in one or more local newspapers circulating in the locality in which the area affected is situated, stating that the order has been made and describing the area affected and the effect of the order; and

(*b*) deposits a copy of the order and of the map to which it refers with each local authority concerned.

Designation orders by a local authority

8.—(1) A designation order made by a local authority shall describe by reference to a map the area affected.

(2) The map shall be to such a scale, and the order in such form as may be prescribed.

9. Before making a designation order a local authority shall—

(*a*) consult any other local authority concerned; and

(*b*) publish notice of their proposal to make the order;

in accordance with paragraph 10 below.

10.—(1) The consultation required by sub-paragraph (*a*) of paragraph 9 above shall precede the publication of the notice required by sub-paragraph (*b*) of that paragraph.

(2) The notice required by paragraph 9 (*b*) above shall be in the prescribed form and shall otherwise comply with paragraph 3 (2) above (with the necessary modifications).

11. Copies of the draft order and of the map to which it refers—

(*a*) shall be deposited with each of the local authorities concerned (other than the local authority proposing to make the order) on or before the date on which notice of the proposal to make the order is first published in accordance with paragraph 3 (2) (*a*) above as applied by paragraph 10 above; and

(*b*) shall be kept available for public inspection by each of the local authorities concerned, free of charge at reasonable hours and at a convenient place, until the local authority proposing to make the order either make it or determine not to make it and, in the case of any other local authority concerned, notify that local authority of their determination.

12. The local authority may make the order, either without modifications or with such modification only as consists in reducing the area affected, and submit it to the Secretary of State for confirmation, at any time after the end of the period of six weeks beginning with the date on which notice of their proposal to make the order is first published in accordance with paragraph 3 (2) (*a*) above as applied by paragraph 10 above.

13. A designation order made by a local authority shall not take effect unless it is confirmed by the Secretary of State, and the Secretary of State may confirm any such order either without modifications or with such modification only as consists in reducing the area affected.

14. If the Secretary of State confirms the order the local authority shall on being notified that the order has been confirmed—

(*a*) publish notice of the making of the order in the manner and form prescribed; and

(*b*) deposit a copy of the order and of the map to which it refers with any other local authority concerned.

15. The Secretary of State may by regulations prescribe the procedure to be followed by a local authority in submitting a designation order for confirmation by the Secretary of State.

Operation of designation orders

16.—(1) A designation order made by the Secretary of State shall not come into operation until the end of the period of six months beginning with the date on which it is made.

(2) A designation order made by a local authority and confirmed by the Secretary of State shall not come into operation until the end of the period of six months beginning with the date on which it is confirmed.

Variation and revocation of designation orders

17.—(1) An order varying or revoking a designation order shall describe by reference to a map the area affected by the designation order and (in the case of an order varying a designation order) the reduction of that area made by the order.

(2) The map shall be to such a scale, and the order in such form, as the Secretary of State considers appropriate.

18. Before and on making an order varying or revoking a designation order the Secretary of State shall follow the procedure laid down for the making by him of a designation order, and paragraphs 2 to 7 above shall accordingly apply in any such case (taking references to the area affected as references to the area affected by the designation order).

Scotland

19. In relation to a designation order relating to an area in Scotland, references in this Schedule to the London Gazette shall be construed as references to the Edinburgh Gazette.

Interpretation

20.—(1) In this Schedule "the area affected" means, in relation to a designation order, the area to which the order for the time being relates.

(2) For the purposes of this Schedule a local authority is a local authority concerned in relation to a designation order (or in relation to an order varying or revoking a designation order) if the area affected by the designation order, or any part of that area, is within the area of that local authority.

Section 64 (1)

SCHEDULE 3

Transitional Provisions

1.—(1) Where an interim preservation notice is in force with respect to any monument immediately before the commencement of this Act, sections 10 (3) (*a*) and (*c*) and 12 (1), (2) (*b*), (3) (*b*) and (4) of the Historic Buildings and Ancient Monuments Act 1953 shall continue to apply to the notice and monument respectively as if this Act had not been passed, unless and until the monument is included in the Schedule under section 1 (3) of this Act.

(2) So long as by virtue of sub-paragraph (1) above section 12 (1) of the Historic Buildings and Ancient Monuments Act 1953 continues to apply after the commencement of this Act to any monument which is under guardianship by virtue of this Act, section 28 of this Act shall have effect in relation to that monument as

if for the reference in subsection (2) of that section to a scheduled monument consent there were substituted a reference to the consent of the Secretary of State under section 12 (1).

2.—(1) Subject to sub-paragraph (2) below, where a guardianship order made under section 12 (5) of the Historic Buildings and Ancient Monuments Act 1953 is in force immediately before the commencement of this Act that order shall continue in force notwithstanding the repeal by this Act of section 12 (5), and the provisions of this Act shall apply while the order is in force as if the Secretary of State had been constituted guardian of the monument by a deed not containing any restriction not contained in the order and executed by all the persons who, at the time when the order was made, were able by deed to constitute the Secretary of State guardian of the monument.

(2) A guardianship order continued in force by this paragraph may be revoked at any time by the Secretary of State.

3.—(1) Where within the period of three months immediately preceding the commencement of this Act a person has given notice in accordance with section 6 (2) of the Ancient Monuments Act 1931 of his intention to execute or permit to be executed any such work in relation to a monument as is there mentioned the notice shall have effect for the purposes of this Act as an application for scheduled monument consent for the execution of that work.

(2) Where—

(*a*) a monument becomes a scheduled monument under this Act; and

(*b*) before it is included in the Schedule any person has applied for the consent of the Secretary of State for the execution of any works affecting the monument which would otherwise be prohibited by section 12 (1) of the Historic Buildings and Ancient Monuments Act 1953 (consent required for certain works in relation to a monument subject to an interim preservation notice or preservation order);

then, in a case where the Secretary of State's decision on the application has not been notified to the person in question before the monument is included in the Schedule, the application shall have effect for the purposes of this Act as an application for scheduled monument consent for the execution of those works.

(3) The Secretary of State shall consider and determine any application for scheduled monument consent which has effect as such by virtue of this paragraph notwithstanding that any requirements of regulations made by virtue of paragraph 1 or any requirements of paragraph 2 of Schedule 1 to this Act are not satisfied in relation to that application.

4.—(1) Subject to the following provisions of this paragraph, where a person has given notice as mentioned in paragraph 3 (1) above with respect to any work more than three months before the commencement of this Act, the notice shall have effect for the purposes of this Act as if it were a scheduled monument consent for the execution of that work granted by the Secretary of State under section 2 of this Act on the date of the commencement of this Act (and it may be modified or revoked by the Secretary of State under section 4 of this Act accordingly).

(2) This paragraph does not apply in any case where an interim preservation notice or a preservation order is in force with respect to the monument in question immediately before the commencement of this Act.

(3) A scheduled monument consent which has effect as such by virtue of this paragraph shall not cease to have effect by virtue of section 4 (1) of this Act if any of the work to which it relates has been executed or started before the commencement of this Act.

5.—(1) Subject to sub-paragraph (2) below, where—

(*a*) a monument becomes a scheduled monument under this Act; and

(*b*) before it is included in the Schedule the Secretary of State has granted consent for the execution of any works affecting the monument under section 12 (1) of the Historic Buildings and Ancient Monuments Act 1953;

that consent shall have effect for the purposes of this Act as if it were a scheduled monument consent for the execution of those works granted by the Secretary of State under section 2 of this Act on the date when the monument became a scheduled monument (and it may be modified or revoked by the Secretary of State under section 4 of this Act accordingly).

(2) A scheduled monument consent which has effect as such by virtue of this paragraph shall not cease to have effect by virtue of section 4 (1) of this Act if any of the works to which it relates have been executed or started before the monument becomes a scheduled monument.

6.—(1) Section 13 (2) of this Act shall not apply to any monument of which the Secretary of State or a local authority have been constituted guardians before the commencement of this Act, except where either—

(*a*) the guardianship deed provided for control and management of the monument by the guardians; or

(*b*) the persons for the time being immediately affected by the operation of the guardianship deed have consented to the exercise of control and management of the monument by the guardians.

(2) Section 19 (1) of this Act shall not apply to any monument of which the Secretary of State or a local authority had been constituted guardians before 15th August 1913 (being the date of commencement of the Ancient Monuments Consolidation and Amendment Act 1913), except where either—

(*a*) the guardianship deed provided for public access to the monument; or

(*b*) the persons for the time being immediately affected by the operation of the guardianship deed have consented to the public having access to the monument.

(3) Where any land adjoining or adjacent to a monument (in addition to its site) was acquired or taken into guardianship before the commencement of this Act under any enactment repealed by this Act, it shall be regarded for the purposes of this Act as having been acquired or taken into guardianship for a purpose relating to that monument by virtue of section 15 of this Act.

7. Notwithstanding the repeal by this Act of the Field Monuments Act 1972, the provisions of that Act shall continue to apply in relation to any acknowledgement payment agreement within the meaning of that Act which is in force immediately before the commencement of this Act.

8. Any reference in any document (including an enactment) to an enactment repealed by this Act shall be construed as or (as the case may be) as including a reference to the corresponding enactment in this Act.

9. Nothing in the preceding provisions of this Schedule shall be construed as prejudicing the effect of section 16 or 17 of the Interpretation Act 1978 (effect of repeals).

10. In this Schedule—

"interim preservation notice" means a notice served under section 10 (1) of the Historic Buildings and Ancient Monuments Act 1953; and

"preservation order" means an order made under section 11 (1) of that Act.

Section 64 (2)

SCHEDULE 4

Consequential Amendments

1. In section 44 (3) of the Electricity (Supply) Act 1926 (protection of ancient monuments from prejudicial effect of placing electric lines above ground), for the words "the Ancient Monuments Consolidation and Amendment Act 1913" there shall be substituted the words "the Ancient Monuments and Archaeological Areas Act 1979".

2. In section 47 (*d*) of the Coast Protection Act 1949 (saving for law relating to ancient monuments), for the words "the Ancient Monuments Acts 1913 to 1931" there shall be substituted the words "the Ancient Monuments and Archaeological Areas Act 1979".

3.—(1) In sections 5 (2) (*b*) and 8 (1) (*c*) of the Historic Buildings and Ancient Monuments Act 1953, for the words "the ancient Monuments Consolidation and Amendment Act 1913" there shall be substituted the words "the Ancient Monuments and Archaeological Areas Act 1979".

(2) In section 8 (4) of that Act, for the words "the said Act of 1913" there shall be substituted the words "the said Act of 1979".

4. In section 9 (1) of the Coal Mining (Subsidence) Act 1957 (special provision for subsidence damage in case of ancient monuments, etc.), for paragraphs (*a*) and (*b*) there shall be substituted the following paragraphs—

" (*a*) for the time being included in the Schedule of monuments compiled and maintained under section 1 of the Ancient Monuments and Archaeological Areas Act 1979; or

(*b*) notified to the Board by the Secretary of State as an ancient monument within the meaning of that Act for the time being under the care of the Secretary of State ".

5. In section 6 (4) (*b*) of the Land Powers (Defence) Act 1958 (restriction on use of land for training purposes)—

(*a*) for the words from " a list " to " 1913 " there shall be substituted the words " the Schedule compiled and maintained under section 1 of the Ancient Monuments and Archaeological Areas Act 1979 "; and

(*b*) the words from " or which " to " 1953 " shall cease to have effect, except in relation to a monument to which paragraph 1 (1) of Schedule 3 to this Act applies.

6. In section 17 (2) of the Building (Scotland) Act 1959 (requirements with respect to operations under that Act to be subject to special controls for ancient monuments and historic buildings)—

(*a*) for paragraph (*a*) there shall be substituted the following paragraph—

" (*a*) a building which is for the time being included in the Schedule of monuments compiled and maintained under section 1 of the Ancient Monuments and Archaeological Areas Act 1979 ";

(*b*) paragraph (*d*) and the words " or, as the case may be, the said Act of 1953 " shall cease to have effect, except in relation to a monument to which paragraph 1 (1) of Schedule 3 to this Act applies; and

(*c*) for the words " the said Act of 1931 " there shall be substituted the words " the said Act of 1979 or ".

7. In section 3 (3) (*a*) of the Flood Prevention (Scotland) Act 1961 (Act not to authorise contraventions of certain enactments), for the words " the Ancient Monuments Acts 1913 to 1953 " there shall be substituted the words " the Ancient Monuments and Archaeological Areas Act 1979 ".

8. In section 2 (5) of the Faculty Jurisdiction Measure 1964 (limit on authority conferred by faculty for demolition of church), for the words " the Ancient Monuments Acts 1913 to 1953 " there shall be substituted the words " the Ancient Monuments and Archaeological Areas Act 1979 ".

9. In section 7 (8) of the Mines (Working Facilities and Support) Act 1966 (right to apply for restrictions on working minerals to secure support)—

(*a*) for the words " the Ancient Monuments Consolidation and Amendment Act 1913 " there shall be substituted the words " the Ancient Monuments and Archaeological Areas Act 1979 "; and

(*b*) the words " or Part II of the Historic Buildings and Ancient Monuments Act 1953 " shall be omitted.

10. In paragraph 2 (*d*) of Schedule 1 to the General Rate Act 1967 (exemption from rates for certain unoccupied property)—

(*a*) the words from " is the " to " or " shall cease to have effect, except in relation to a monument to which paragraph 1 (1) of Schedule 3 to this Act applies; and

(*b*) for the words from " a list " to " those Acts " there shall be substituted the words " the Schedule compiled and maintained under section 1 of the Ancient Monuments and Archaeological Areas Act 1979 ".

11. In sections 56 (1) and 58 (2) of the Town and Country Planning Act 1971 (exclusion of certain buildings from control of works under sections 55 and 58 respectively), for paragraphs (*b*) and (*c*) there shall be substituted the following paragraph—

" (*b*) a building for the time being included in the Schedule of monuments compiled and maintained under section 1 of the Ancient Monuments and Archaeological Areas Act 1979 ".

12. In sections 54 (1) and 56 (2) of the Town and Country Planning (Scotland) Act 1972 (exclusion of certain buildings from control of works under sections 53 and 56 respectively) for paragraphs (*b*) and (*c*) there shall be substituted the following paragraph—

" (*b*) a building for the time being included in the Schedule of monuments compiled and maintained under section 1 of the Ancient Monuments and Archaeological Areas Act 1979 ".

13. In section 131 (2) of the Local Government Act 1972 (general powers of local authority with respect to dealings in land not to affect certain enactments), for paragraph (*f*) there shall be substituted the following paragraph—

"(*f*) the Ancient Monuments and Archaeological Areas Act 1979".

14. In section 182 (1) of the Local Government (Scotland) Act 1973 (functions of local authorities under the Ancient Monuments Acts to be district planning functions), for the words "the Ancient Monuments Acts 1913 and 1931" there shall be substituted the words "the Ancient Monuments and Archaeological Areas Act 1979".

15. In paragraph 17 (3) (*c*) of Schedule 4 to the Finance Act 1975 (acceptance of certain objects in satisfaction of tax), for the words "the Ancient Monuments Consolidation and Amendment Act 1913" there shall be substituted the words "the Ancient Monuments and Archaeological Areas Act 1979".

16. In section 111 of the Land Drainage Act 1976 (protection of ancient monuments), for the words "the Ancient Monuments Acts 1913 to 1972" there shall be substituted the words "the Ancient Monuments and Archaeological Areas Act 1979".

Section 64 (3)

SCHEDULE 5

Enactments Repealed

Chapter	Short Title	Extent of Repeal
45 & 46 Vict. c. 73.	The Ancient Monuments Protection Act 1882.	The Schedule.
3 & 4 Geo. 5. c. 32.	The Ancient Monuments Consolidation and Amendment Act 1913.	The whole Act.
21 & 22 Geo. 5. c. 16.	The Ancient Monuments Act 1931.	The whole Act.
9 & 10 Geo. 6. c. 49.	The Acquisition of Land (Authorisation Procedure) Act 1946.	In section 1 (2), paragraph (*c*) and the word "or" immediately preceding it. In section 8 (1), the definition of "ancient monument". In Schedule 1, paragraph 12.
10 & 11 Geo. 6. c. 42.	The Acquisition of Land (Authorisation Procedure) (Scotland) Act 1947.	In section 1 (2), paragraph (*c*) and the word "or" immediately preceding it. In section 7 (1), the definition of "ancient monument". In Schedule 1, paragraph 12.
1 & 2 Eliz. 2. c. 49.	The Historic Buildings and Ancient Monuments Act 1953.	Parts II and III. Section 20. Section 22 (2). The Schedule.
6 & 7 Eliz. 2. c. 30.	The Land Powers (Defence) Act 1958.	In section 6 (4) (*b*), the words from "or which" to "1953".
7 & 8 Eliz. 2. c. 24.	The Building (Scotland) Act 1959.	In section 17 (2), paragraph (*d*) and the words "or, as the case may be, the said Act of 1953".
1966 c. 4.	The Mines (Working Facilities and Support) Act 1966.	In section 7 (8), the words from "or Part II" to "1953".
1967 c. 9.	The General Rate Act 1967.	In paragraph 2 (*d*) of Schedule 1, the words from "is the" to "or".
1967 c. 80.	The Criminal Justice Act 1967.	In Schedule 3, the entries relating to the Ancient Monuments Consolidation and Amendment Act 1913 and the Ancient Monuments Act 1931.
1968 c. 72.	The Town and Country Planning Act 1968.	Section 59.
1969 c. 30.	The Town and Country Planning (Scotland) Act 1969.	Section 59.
1971 c. 78.	The Town and Country Planning Act 1971.	In Schedule 23, the entry relating to the Town and Country Planning Act 1968.
1972 c. 43.	The Field Monuments Act 1972.	The whole Act.

SCHEDULE 5—*continued*

Chapter	Short Title	Extent of Repeal
1972 c. 52.	The Town and Country Planning (Scotland) Act 1972.	In Schedule 21, the entry relating to the Town and Country Planning (Scotland) Act 1969.
1973 c. 65.	The Local Government (Scotland) Act 1973.	In Schedule 23, paragraph 1.
1974 c. 32.	The Town and Country Amenities Act 1974.	In section 13 (1), paragraph (*c*) and the word "and" immediately preceding that paragraph.
1976 c. 57.	The Local Government (Miscellaneous Provisions) Act 1976.	In Schedule 1, paragraph 5.
1976 c. 75.	The Development of Rural Wales Act 1976.	In Schedule 4, paragraph 5.
1978 c. 52.	The Wales Act 1978.	In Schedule 11, paragraph 2.

Nothing in this Schedule shall affect the operation of any enactment in relation to a monument to which paragraph 1 (1) of Schedule 3 to this Act applies.

Finance (No. 2) Act 1979

(1979 c. 47)

ARRANGEMENT OF SECTIONS

PART I

VALUE ADDED TAX AND EXCISE DUTIES

An Act to grant certain duties, to alter other duties, and to amend the law relating to the National Debt and the Public Revenue, and to make further provision in connection with Finance.

[26th July 1979]

General Note

This Act received the Royal Assent on July 26, 1979, and came into force on that date, except for s. 2 which came into force on June 12, 1979, and s. 3 which came into force on August 13, 1979.

Parliamentary debates

Hansard, H.C. Vol. 970, cols. 1813, 1940; H.L. Vol. 401, cols. 1532, 1822.

Abbreviations

I.C.T.A. 1970	=	Income and Corporation Taxes Act 1970, c. 10.
F.A. 1972	=	Finance Act 1972, c. 41.
F.A. 1975	=	Finance Act 1975, c. 7.
F. (No. 2) A. 1975	=	Finance (No. 2) Act 1975, c. 45.
F.A. 1976	=	Finance Act 1976, c. 40.
F.A. 1977	=	Finance Act 1977, c. 36.
F.A. 1979	=	Finance Act 1979, c. 25.

PART I

VALUE ADDED TAX AND EXCISE DUTIES

Increase of value added tax.

1.—(1) As from 18th June 1979—

(*a*) section 17 of the Finance (No. 2) Act 1975 and Schedule 7 to that Act (higher rate of value added tax) shall cease to have effect; and

(*b*) in section 9 (1) of the Finance Act 1972 (standard rate of value added tax) for the words " eight per cent." there shall be substituted the words " fifteen per cent.".

(2) Subsection (1) (*a*) above does not affect Note (7) of Group 9 or item 1 of Group 17 of Schedule 4 to the said Act of 1972 (which contain exceptions from zero-rating expressed by reference to items in Schedule 7 to the said Act of 1975).

(3) Subsection (1) (*b*) above does not affect the rate of tax on any supply of telephone services provided by the Post Office or the District Council of Kingston upon Hull by means of their public switched telephone exchange systems, being services in respect of which—

(*a*) the Post Office issue a tax invoice which includes a rental charge for a rental quarter beginning before 1st November 1979; or

(*b*) the Council issue a tax invoice which includes a rental charge for a rental period beginning before that date or charges for calls made in a period ending before 1st September 1979.

In this subsection " tax invoice " has the same meaning as in section 7 of the said Act of 1972.

(4) Where a supply in fact made wholly or partly before the said 18th June, or a supply which, apart from the other provisions of the said section 7, would be treated as so made by subsection (2) or (3) of that section, is treated under those other provisions as made on or after that date, the person making the supply may account for and pay tax on the supply or, as the case may be, on the relevant part of it as if the rate of tax had not been increased by subsection (1) (*b*) above.

(5) Where a person avails himself of subsection (4) above in relation to a supply in respect of which he is required by regulations to issue a tax invoice, any provision of the regulations requiring the amount of tax chargeable or the rate of tax to be stated in the invoice shall be construed as referring to the amount and rate that apply by virtue of that subsection.

GENERAL NOTE

Subs. (1)

The higher rate of 12½ per cent. is abolished and both former rates are unified at 15 per cent. from June 18, 1979.

Subs. (2)

The repeal of the higher rate Schedule does not affect the references to it in the zero-rating Schedule.

Subs. (3)

This prevents telephone bills for a period spanning June 18, 1979, having to be apportioned.

Subs. (4)

The normal rule in F.A. 1972, s. 7 (5), that where an invoice is issued within 14 days (or longer period allowed by H.M. Customs and Excise) after the actual time of supply, the supply is deemed to be made at the time the invoice is issued, does not apply to supplies made before the increase in rates. Thus on a sale of goods on, say, June 14, 1979, a tax invoice at the old 8 per cent. can still be issued after the change. In the case of a supply of services, the amount can be apportioned and the new rate applied only to the part after the change.

Subs. (5)

Where invoices are issued as permitted by subs. (4) showing tax at the old rate, this must be so stated.

Hydrocarbon oil etc.

2.—(1) In section 6 (1) of the Hydrocarbon Oil Duties Act 1979 (duty of £0·0660 a litre in case of light oil and £0·0770 a litre in case of heavy oil) for " £0·0660 " and " £0·0770 " there shall be substituted respectively " £0·0810 " and " £0·0920 ".

(2) In section 11 (1) (*b*) of that Act (rebate on aviation turbine fuel and heavy oil other than kerosene at rate of £0·0055 a litre less than the rate at which duty is for the time being chargeable) for " £0·0055 " there shall be substituted " £0·0066 ".

(3) In section 14 (1) of that Act (rebate on light oil delivered to approved person for use as furnace fuel at rate of £0·0055 a litre less than the rate at which duty is charged) for " £0·0055 " there shall be substituted " £0·0066 ".

(4) This section shall be deemed to have come into force at 6 o'clock in the evening of 12th June 1979.

GENERAL NOTE

This section introduces a higher rate of duty on hydrocarbon oil and has the effect, *inter alia*, of increasing the price of petrol over and above the increase consequential upon the rise in VAT.

Tobacco products

3.—(1) In paragraph 1 of the Table in Schedule 1 to the Tobacco Products Duty Act 1979 (duty on cigarettes) for " 30 per cent. " and " £9·00 " there shall be substituted respectively " 21 per cent." and " £11·77 ".

(2) This section shall come into force on 13th August 1979.

GENERAL NOTE

This section alters the rates of duty payable on cigarettes—it does not affect the rate of duty applicable to cigars, hand-rolling tobacco and other smoking and chewing tobacco. There is an additional charge for high tar cigarettes and cigarettes over 9 cm. The Tobacco Products Duty Act 1979 consolidates the enactments relating to excise duty on tobacco products.

Continuation of regulator powers

4. In section 2 (2) of the Excise Duties (Surcharges or Rebates) Act 1979 (which provides that no order under section 1 of that Act shall be made or continue in force after the end of August 1979) for the words " August 1979 " there shall be substituted the words " August 1980 ".

General Note

This section continues the regulator powers under the Excise Duties (Surcharges or Rebates) Act 1979 by another year, *i.e.* to August 1980. S. 2 of that Act deals with orders made under s. 1 which provides for surcharges or rebates of amounts due for excise duty which may become payable where the Treasury decides that it should be expedient to regulate the balance between demand and resources in the United Kingdom by the making of such an order.

Part II

Income Tax, Corporation Tax and Capital Gains Tax

Charge of income tax for 1979–80

5.—(1) Income tax for the year 1979–80 shall be charged at the basic rate of 30 per cent.; and—

(*a*) in respect of so much of an individual's total income as does not exceed £750 at the rate of 25 per cent.;

(*b*) in respect of so much of an individual's total income as exceeds £10,000 at such higher rates as are specified in the Table below; and

(*c*) in respect of so much of the investment income included in an individual's total income as exceeds £5,000 at the additional rate of 15 per cent.

Table

Part of excess over £10,000	*Higher rate*
The first £2,000	40 per cent.
The next £3,000	45 per cent.
The next £5,000	50 per cent.
The next £5,000	55 per cent.
The remainder	60 per cent.

(2) This section has effect in substitution for section 1 (1) of the Finance Act 1979 but does not require any change to be made in the amounts deductible or repayable under section 204 of the Taxes Act (pay as you earn) before 6th October 1979.

General Note

The reductions in the rates of income tax proposed by the present Government are given effect to by this section. The reductions in the higher rates of tax are particularly noticeable, the highest rate on earned income now being 60 per cent., reached when taxable income exceeds £25,000.

The additional rate of tax on investment income has been simplified. There is now a single rate of 15 per cent. alone, rather than two rates of 10 per cent. and 15 per cent. There is no special relief given in respect of investment income for persons over 65. Presumably it was thought that the raising to £5,000 of the level under which no additional rate is payable did away with the necessity for such relief to be given.

The reductions in the rate of tax given effect to by this section will only be implemented in the P.A.Y.E. system after October 6, 1979.

Rate of advance corporation tax for financial year 1979

6. The rate of advance corporation tax for the financial year 1979 shall be three-sevenths.

General Note

For the financial year 1978 the rate of advance corporation tax was thirty-three sixty-sevenths.

The financial year for companies commences on April 1, 1979.

Corporation tax: small companies

7.—(1) The fraction mentioned in subsection (2) of section 95 of the Finance Act 1972 (marginal relief for small companies) shall for the financial year 1978 be three-twentieths.

(2) For the financial year 1978 and subsequent financial years subsection (3) of the said section 95 shall have effect with the substitution for any reference to £50,000 of a reference to £60,000 and with the substitution for any reference to £85,000 of a reference to £100,000.

(3) Where by virtue of subsection (2) above the said section 95 has effect with different relevant amounts in relation to different parts of the same accounting period, those parts shall be treated for the purposes of that section as if they were separate accounting periods and the profits and income of the company for that period (as defined in that section) shall be apportioned between those parts.

General Note

F.A. 1979, s. 2 maintained the small companies rate at 42 per cent. for the financial year 1978. This section makes no change to that rate but increases the applicability of the relief. For the financial year 1978 the rate is now to apply to companies with profits not exceeding £60,000 as opposed to £50,000 in 1977. Marginal relief is given to companies with profits of up to £100,000 as opposed to £85,000. In consequence of these changes the fraction by reference to which marginal relief is given is to be altered from one-seventh to three-twentieths.

Alteration of personal reliefs

8.—(1) Sections 8 and 14 of the Taxes Act shall have effect with the following amendments instead of those specified in section 1 (2) of the Finance Act 1979.

(2) In section 8 (personal reliefs)—

(*a*) in subsection (1) (*a*) (married) for " £1,535 " there shall be substituted " £1,815 ";

(*b*) in subsection (1) (*b*) (single) and (2) (wife's earned income relief) for " £985 " there shall be substituted " £1,165 ";

(*c*) in subsection (1A) (age allowance) for " £2,075 " and " £1,300 " there shall be substituted " £2,455 " and " £1,540 " respectively;

(*d*) in subsection (1B) (income limit for age allowance) for " £4,000 " there shall be substituted " £5,000 ".

(3) In section 14 (2) (additional relief for widows and others in respect of children) for " £550 " there shall be substituted " £650 ".

General Note

Subs. (2) increases the married man's allowance by £280 to £1,815 and the single person's allowance and the wife's earned income allowance by £180 to £1,165. The age allowances are increased by £380 for a married person and by £240 for a single person. The income limit as regards age allowance is increased by £1,000 to £5,000. In the event that the total income of the person exceeds that limit the relief is reduced by £2 for every £3 over the limit.

Subs. (3) increases the additional relief in respect of one-parent families by £100 to £650.

Exemption of pensions in respect of death due to war service etc.

9.—(1) Payments of pensions or allowances to which this section applies shall not be treated as income for any purposes of the Income Tax Acts.

(2) This section applies to—

(*a*) any pension or allowance payable by or on behalf of the Department of Health and Social Security under so much of any Order in Council, Royal Warrant, order or scheme as relates to death due to—

(i) service in the armed forces of the Crown or war-time service in the merchant navy, or

(ii) war injuries;

(*b*) any pension or allowance at similar rates and subject to similar conditions which is payable by the Ministry of Defence in respect of death due to peace-time service in the armed forces of the Crown before 3rd September 1939; and

(*c*) any pension or allowance which is payable under the law of a country other than the United Kingdom and is of a character substantially similar to a pension or allowance falling within paragraph (*a*) or (*b*) above.

(3) Where a pension or allowance falling within subsection (2) above is withheld or abated by reason of the receipt of another pension or allowance not falling within that subsection, there shall be treated as falling within that subsection so much of the other pension or allowance as is equal to the pension or allowance that is withheld or, as the case may be, to the amount of the abatement.

(4) This section applies for the year 1979–80 and subsequent years of assessment.

General Note

Under F.A. 1976, s. 31, 50 per cent. of war widows' pensions are exempt from income tax. This section provides for them to be totally exempt.

The main benefits covered by this provision are the war widows' pension, the war widows' age allowance and the special temporary allowance awarded to widows of the most severely disabled war servicemen. The exemption will also apply to pensions or allowances of a comparable nature paid by other countries. It is to be noted that in so far as the benefits covered by this provision are abated in consequence of the receipt of other allowances those other allowances are to be exempt to the extent of that abatement.

Relief for interest: extension of transitional provisions

10. In section 19 (4) (*b*) and (*c*) of the Finance Act 1974 (transitional relief for interest payable before 6th April 1980) for " 1980 " there shall be substituted " 1982 "; and the same amendment shall be made in section 122 (1) (*c*) of the Taxes Act and paragraph 2 (1) (*c*) and (2) of Schedule 12 to that Act (transitional relief for interest payable before that date to non-residents out of foreign income).

General Note

The Finance Act 1974 imposed restrictions on the tax relief available for interest payments. Prior to that, annual or short interest was generally deductible when computing a person's total income. As a result of the restrictions, interest on overdrafts ceased to be deductible and interest on other loans is now only deductible if the loan was made for certain specific purposes. However, in respect of debts incurred on or before March 26, 1974, transitional relief was granted for interest payable before April 6, 1980. This transitional relief has now been extended by two years to cover interest payments made before April 6, 1982. This extension has been made also in respect of the transitional relief applicable to interest payable to a non-resident out of foreign investment income.

Withdrawal of child tax allowances: consequential provisions

11.—(1) The Taxes Act shall have effect with the amendments specified in Schedule 1 to this Act, being amendments consequential on section 1 (4) of the Finance Act 1979 (withdrawal of child tax allowances).

(2) This section has effect for the year 1979–80 and subsequent years of assessment.

Social Security Pensions Act: consequential provisions

12.—(1) The Income Tax Acts shall have effect with the amendments specified in Schedule 2 to this Act, being amendments consequential on the Social Security Pensions Act 1975 and the Social Security Pensions (Northern Ireland) Order 1975.

(2) This section has effect for the year 1979–80 and subsequent years of assessment.

General Note

Sched. 2 effects a number of amendments consequent upon the Social Security Pensions Act 1975 (which Act took effect on April 6, 1979) and in particular s. 10 of that Act which increases in certain circumstances a Category A retirement pension due to a married woman.

Relief for increase in stock values

13. Schedule 5 to the Finance Act 1976 (relief for increase in stock values) shall have effect with the amendments specified in Schedule 3 to this Act, being amendments which—

(*a*) reduce the profit restriction for persons other than companies;

(*b*) permit claims for partial relief; and

(*c*) provide for the writing-off of past relief.

Capital allowances: motor vehicles

14.—(1) Section 43 of the Finance Act 1971 (which excludes from first-year allowances road vehicles not falling within paragraph (*a*), (*b*) or (*c*) of that section) shall be amended in accordance with subsections (2) and (3) below.

(2) The existing provisions of that section shall become subsection (1) and in paragraph (*c*) (vehicles provided for hire to, or the carriage of, members of the public in the ordinary course of a trade) after " (*c*) " there shall be inserted the words " subject to subsection (2) below,".

(3) After the said paragraph (*c*) there shall be inserted—

" (2) Subsection (1) (*c*) above applies to a vehicle only if—

(*a*) the following conditions are satisfied—

(i) the number of consecutive days for which it is on hire to, or used for the carriage of, the same person will normally be less than thirty; and

(ii) the total number of days for which it is on hire to, or used for the carriage of, the same person in any period of twelve months will normally be less than ninety; or

(*b*) it is provided for hire to a person who will himself use it wholly or mainly for hire to, or the carriage of, members of the public in the ordinary course of a trade and in a manner complying with the conditions specified in paragraph (*a*) above.

(3) For the purposes of subsection (2) above persons who are connected with each other within the meaning of section 533 of the Taxes Act shall be treated as the same person; and that subsection does not affect vehicles provided wholly or mainly for the use of persons in receipt of a mobility allowance under the Social Security Act 1975 or the Social Security (Northern Ireland) Act 1975.".

(4) In paragraph 9 of Schedule 8 to the said Act of 1971 (which defines the vehicles to which the special rules in paragraphs 10 to 12 apply as those not falling within paragraph (*a*), (*b*) or (*c*) of section 43) for the words " section 43 of this Act " there shall be substituted the words " section 43 (1) of this Act ".

(5) In paragraphs 10 to 12 of that Schedule (special capital allowance

rules for motor vehicles) for " £5,000 " and " £1,250 " wherever they occur there shall be substituted respectively " £8,000 " and " £2,000 ".

(6) After paragraph 12 of that Schedule there shall be inserted—

" 12A. The Treasury may by order increase or further increase the sums of money specified in paragraphs 10, 11 and 12 above; and any such order shall be made by statutory instrument subject to annulment in pursuance of a resolution of the House of Commons.".

(7) Subject to subsection (8) below, this section applies in relation to expenditure incurred after 12th June 1979, and for the purposes of this subsection expenditure is incurred on the date when the sums in question become payable.

(8) This section does not affect the operation of the said section 43 in relation to any expenditure on the provision of a vehicle if the expenditure consists of the payment of sums payable under a contract entered into on or before the said 12th June and the vehicle is brought into use not later than 12th June 1980.

GENERAL NOTE

This provision imposes a restriction on the availability of 100 per cent. first year capital allowances for vehicles provided for hire to, or the carriage of, members of the public in the ordinary course of a trade. It also relaxes the rules relating to cars costing more than £5,000.

It was intended by the Revenue that the 100 per cent. first year capital allowance in respect of hired cars would apply only to cars hired on a short term basis. However, following a decision before the Special Commissioners in 1975 the allowance has also been available for cars leased over a long period. Hence the boom in the car-leasing industry.

Certain restrictions are now to be imposed. In order to qualify for the 100 per cent. first year allowance (rather than the usual 25 per cent.) the car must not be let or hired to the same person: (*a*) for a period of consecutive days exceeding 30; or (*b*) for 90 or more days in any period of 12 months unless that person will hire it out " in the ordinary cause of a trade " in such a manner that conditions (*a*) and (*b*) are fulfilled.

The restrictions do not apply in the case of cars leased wholly or mainly for use by disabled persons receiving mobility allowances.

There is the qualification regarding these restrictions that they should be the normal situation. In calculating the periods any connected persons will be treated as one.

The restrictions will apply as regards any expenditure incurred after June 12, 1979, unless the expenditure consists of payments pursuant to a contract made on or before June 12, 1979, *and* the vehicle is used not later than June 12, 1980 (this would seem to exclude from the saving clause, expenditure relating to a replacement vehicle brought into use after June 12, 1980, even if the contract was made before June 12, 1979).

The restriction of the capital allowance for vehicles costing more than £5,000 and not qualifying for 100 per cent. first year allowance to £1,250 is to be relaxed. It is not now to operate for cars costing less than £8,000. The restriction is to be increased from £1,250 to £2,000.

Deduction rate for sub-contractors in the construction industry

15. Section 69 (4) of the Finance (No. 2) Act 1975 (which requires deductions to be made from payments to certain sub-contractors in the construction industry) shall have effect in relation to payments made on or after 6th November 1979 with the substitution for the words " 33 per cent." of the words " 30 per cent.".

GENERAL NOTE

The reduction in the deduction rate applicable to certain sub-contractors in the construction industry is in line with the reduction of the basic rate of income tax from 33 per cent. to 30 per cent. This reduction is only to operate after November 6, 1979.

United States Double Taxation Convention

16.—(1) The arrangements to which effect may be given by virtue of an Order in Council under Section 497 of the Taxes Act (double taxation relief) shall include the arrangements contained in the Convention mentioned in subsection (2) below notwithstanding that those arrangements withdraw relief from tax for periods before the making of the Order.

(2) The Convention referred to above is the Convention between the Government of the United Kingdom of Great Britain and Northern Ireland and the Government of the United States of America for the avoidance of double taxation and the prevention of fiscal evasion with respect to taxes on income and capital gains which was signed on 31st December 1975.

GENERAL NOTE

The Income and Corporation Taxes Act (s. 497), provides for Double Taxation Conventions to take effect by means of an Order in Council. The present convention with the United States confers certain reliefs for residents of the United States. It is intended to replace this by a new Convention signed on December 31, 1975, taking effect from April 1975 (with a transitional period running to April 6, 1976). This would have the effect of retrospectively withdrawing the relief. There is some doubt as to whether s. 497 in its present form permits this. Consequently this section expressly provides for such retrospective withdrawal.

Compensation for delay in national savings payments

17.—(1) There shall be disregarded for all purposes of income tax, corporation tax and capital gains tax any sums paid by the Department for National Savings as compensation for delay in making any such payments or repayments as are mentioned in subsection (2) below, being delay attributable to industrial action by staff of the Department between 22nd February 1979 and 4th May 1979.

(2) The payments and repayments referred to above are—

(*a*) payments or dividends or interest on stocks and securities registered on the National Savings Stock Register;

(*b*) repayments of national savings certificates;

(*c*) repayments of contributions, and payments of bonuses or interest, under certified contractual saving schemes as defined by section 415 (2) of the Taxes Act;

(*d*) payments of premium savings bond prizes and repayments of premium savings bonds;

(*e*) repayments of money deposited in the National Savings Bank.

(3) This section does not affect the tax treatment of interest to which a person is entitled under any express provision in that behalf contained in the terms of issue of any such stock, securities or certificates as are mentioned in paragraph (*a*) or (*b*) of subsection (2) above, in the conditions applying to a contract made under any such scheme as is mentioned in paragraph (*c*) of that subsection or in the National Savings Bank Act 1971.

GENERAL NOTE

This section introduces relief for any compensation payments made as a consequence of delay due to a strike at the Department of National Savings between February 22, 1979, and May 4, 1979. The payments referred to are set out in subs. (2) and the relief is granted in respect of income tax, capital gains tax and corporation tax. The section has no application to the tax treatment of interest to which a person may be entitled.

Part III

Petroleum Revenue Tax

Increase of rate

18.—(1) In section 1 (2) of the Oil Taxation Act 1975 (rate of petroleum revenue tax) for the words " 45 per cent " there shall be substituted the words " 60 per cent ".

(2) This section shall have effect in relation to chargeable periods ending after 31st December 1978.

General Note

The rate of PRT is increased in relation to chargeable periods ending after December 31, 1978, by this section. As PRT is deducted in computing profits for corporation tax purposes, an increase in PRT is offset by a decrease in corporation tax liability.

Reduction of uplift for allowable expenditure

19.—(1) In section 2 (9) (*b*) (ii) and (*c*) (ii) of the Oil Taxation Act 1975 (uplift of 75 per cent. of allowable expenditure) for " 75 per cent." there shall be substituted " 35 per cent.".

(2) Subject to subsection (3) below, subsection (1) above has effect in relation to expenditure incurred in pursuance of a contract entered into on or after 1st January 1979.

(3) Where expenditure is incurred in pursuance of a contract entered into before the said 1st January but is attributable to a request for an alteration or addition made, or other instruction given, on or after that date by or on behalf of the person incurring the expenditure to another party to the contract, subsection (1) above shall have effect in relation to that expenditure as if the percentage to be substituted for 75 per cent. were $66\frac{2}{3}$ per cent.

(4) Where under paragraph 2 (4) (*a*) of Schedule 5 to the said Act of 1975 or that paragraph as applied by Schedule 6 to that Act (claims for allowable expenditure) a claim states that any expenditure is claimed as qualifying for supplement under section 2 (9) (*b*) (ii) or (*c*) (ii) of that Act, then, if by virtue of this section those provisions have effect in relation to different parts of that expenditure with different percentages—

(*a*) the claim shall distinguish between those parts;

(*b*) in paragraph 3 (1) (*b*), 6 (1) (*b*), 6 (2), 7 (1) and 8 (2) of that Schedule, and in those paragraphs as applied by the said Schedule 6, references to expenditure allowed or which ought to be allowed as qualifying for supplement or to expenditure which does so qualify shall be construed as referring separately to each of those parts; and

(*c*) in paragraph 5 (1) (*a*) of that Schedule, and in that paragraph as so applied, the reference to the amount or total of the amounts stated under the said paragraph 3 (1) (*b*) shall be construed as a reference to any amount so stated by virtue of paragraph (*b*) above.

(5) Where by virtue of subsection (4) above different amounts are stated under paragraph 3 (1) (*b*) of the said Schedule 5 the reference in paragraph 3 (1) (*c*) of that Schedule to an amount equal to the relevant percentage of the amount stated under paragraph 3 (1) (*b*) shall be construed as a reference to an amount arrived at by applying the appropriate percentage to each of those amounts and aggregating the result.

General Note

An "uplift" for PRT purposes is available in relation to expenditure undertaken to bring about the commencement of production from an oilfield or well, or a substantial increase in the rate of production (or to prevent substantial decline) as well as for other purposes. (It also ranks for immediate write-off in full as an expense.) This section reduces the rate of uplift from 75 per cent. to 35 per cent. for expenditure incurred under contracts entered into on or after January 1, 1979. In the case of specific sums committed for specific works under contracts entered into before January 1, 1979, there would still be a 75 per cent. uplift. Other qualifying expenditure made under such contracts would attract uplift at 66⅔ per cent.

Extension of allowable expenditure

20.—(1) In section 3 (1) (*f*) of the Oil Taxation Act 1975 (which allows expenditure of transporting oil from the field to the place where it is first landed in the United Kingdom) and in paragraph (*b*) of the definition of "production purposes" in section 12 (1) of that Act, after the words "in the United Kingdom" there shall be inserted the words "or to the place in the United Kingdom at which the seller in a sale at arm's length could reasonably be expected to deliver it or, if there is more than one place at which he could reasonably be expected to deliver it, the one nearest to the place of extraction;".

(2) In paragraph 2 of Schedule 4 to that Act (restriction on allowable expenditure where incurred in transactions between specified persons), for paragraphs (*a*) to (*c*) of sub-paragraph (2) there shall be substituted the words "they are connected within the meaning of section 533 of the Taxes Act".

(3) This section shall have effect in relation to any expenditure in respect of which a claim is made after 31st December 1978.

General Note

This section introduces two relaxations in the rules for expenditure relief (which is dealt with by s. 3 of the Oil Taxation Act 1975). The original rules allowed expenditure relief only on a limited basis—it only allows the cost of transporting oil to a landing point in the United Kingdom which was an important point from the point of view of calculating overall liability to PRT and to the amount of uplift which was applicable. This section now extends the deduction to costs incurred up to the point where the oil could reasonably be expected to be delivered to a prospective purchaser.

Subs. (2)

This permits a person to deduct payments made to a fellow licensee in calculating liability for PRT. The fellow licensee may be a subsidiary or another company involved contractually in the exploitation of the same block. Formerly the asset or service supplied was restricted (so far as allowable expenses were concerned) to the supplier's cost.

Reduction of oil allowance and metrication of measurements

21.—(1) Section 8 of the Oil Taxation Act 1975 (oil allowance) shall be amended as follows:—

(*a*) in subsection (2) (oil allowance for each chargeable period), for the words "500,000 long tons" there shall be substituted the words "250,000 metric tonnes";

(*b*) in subsections (3) and (5) (participator's share of oil allowance and amount of allowance utilised in a chargeable period), for the words "long tons", wherever they occur, there shall be substituted the words "metric tonnes";

(*c*) in subsection (6) (total oil allowance for an oil field), for the words "10 million long tons", wherever they occur, there shall be substituted the words "5 million metric tonnes"; and (*d*) in subsection (7) (equivalent of long ton)—

(i) for the words " 40,000 cubic feet " there shall be substituted the words " 1,100 cubic metres "; and

(ii) for the words " long ton " there shall be substituted the words " metric tonne ".

(2) In section 1 (4) of that Act, in the definition of " the critical half year "—

(*a*) for the words " long tons " there shall be substituted the words " metric tonnes ";

(*b*) for the words " 40,000 cubic feet " there shall be substituted the words " 1,100 cubic metres "; and

(*c*) for the words " long ton " there shall be substituted the words " metric tonne ".

(3) In section 10 (5) of that Act (equivalent of long ton)—

(*a*) for the words "40,000 cubic feet " there shall be substituted the words " 1,100 cubic metres "; and

(*b*) for the words " long ton " there shall be substituted the words " metric tonne ".

(4) Subsections (1) and (2) above shall have effect respectively in relation to chargeable periods ending after 31st December 1978 and half years ending after that date and subsection (3) above shall be deemed to have come ito force on 1st January 1979.

GENERAL NOTE

Under this provision the " oil allowance " (that is the amount of oil extracted from each field each year which is free of PRT) is reduced to half a million metric tonnes per year, subject to a cumulative limit of five million metric tonnes per field.

The section also metricates amounts mentioned in the Oil Taxation Act 1975.

Taxation of British National Oil Corporation

22.—(1) Section 9 (1) of the Petroleum and Submarine Pipe-lines Act 1975 (exemption of British National Oil Corporation and its wholly owned subsidiaries from petroleum revenue tax) shall not have effect in relation to chargeable periods ending after 30th June 1979; and the provisions of subsections (2) and (3) below, being transitional provisions, shall have effect—

(*a*) in the case of subsection (2), for the purpose of computing the assessable profit or allowable loss accruing from any oil field to that Corporation or any company which is or has been one of those subsidiaries; and

(*b*) in the case of subsection (3), for the purpose of computing the assessable profit or allowable loss accruing from any oil field to any of the following persons (in this section referred to as " relevant persons ") that is to say, that Corporation, any such company and any person having an interest in an oil field, being an interest the whole or part of which in any chargeable period ending before 1st July 1979 constituted the interest in that oil field of that Corporation or one of those subsidiaries.

(2) In relation to any oil field, section 2 of the Oil Taxation Act 1975 shall have effect with respect to the chargeable period ending next after 30th June 1979 as if in subsections (6) (*b*) (ii) and (7) (*b*) (royalty repaid and paid in period to be taken into account) for the words " in the period " there were substituted the words " in or before the period ".

(3) If for any chargeable period—

(*a*) there is an amount to be taken into account by virtue of paragraph (*b*) or (*c*) of subsection (9) the said section 2 (allowable expenditure) or both those paragraphs; and

(*b*) the whole or any part of that amount is attributable to expenditure incurred before 1st July 1979.

that amount or as the case may be, that part (including so much of it as is so taken into account by virtue of sub-paragraph (ii) of the said paragraph (*b*) or (*c*)) shall be deemed for the purposes of that Act, except section 9, to be reduced by the relevant amount or, as the case may be, by so much of the relevant amount as has not been taken into account under this subsection in computing the assessable profit or allowable loss accruing to the relevant person in question or any other person in an earlier chargeable period.

(4) In this section "the relevant amount", in relation to an oil field, means the aggregate gross profit, as defined in section 2 (4) of the Oil Taxation Act 1975, accruing in chargeable periods ending before 1st July 1979 in respect of so much of the interest of the relevant person in question in that oil field as in any of those chargeable periods constituted the interest in that oil field of the British National Oil Corporation or one of its wholly owned subsidiaries; and in this subsection "wholly owned subsidiary" has the same meaning as in the Petroleum and Submarine Pipe-lines Act 1975.

General Note

This section ends the exemption given by the Petroleum and Submarine Pipelines Act 1975 to the B.N.O.C. in respect of PRT. The exemption is removed for chargeable periods ending after June 30, 1979.

Subs. (2)

This sets out consequential amendments to the Oil Taxation Act 1975, s. 2. That section makes provision for the rules and method to be followed in computing a participator's assessable profits and allowable losses from each field. Subss. (6) and (7) of the 1975 Act are designed to ensure that over the life of a field the total net deduction for royalty will equal the net amount of royalty paid, without any need to upset the tight schedule for making returns under Sched. 2, para. 2, or to re-open or amend past returns and assessments. This is a transitional provision.

Subs. (3)

This is another transitional provision in respect of allowable expenditure under the Oil Taxation Act 1975, s. 2 (9), concerning expenditure incurred before July 1, 1979. It provides that where there is an amount of allowable expenditure in respect of expenditure incurred before July 1, 1979, then the allowable amount (or where appropriate a part of that amount) shall be reduced by the relevant amount (or where appropriate a part of the relevant amount) which is defined as the aggregable gross profit of an oil field (as defined in the Oil Taxation Act 1975, s. 2 (4)), accruing in chargeable periods ending before July 1, 1979, in respect of the interest in that oil field of B.N.O.C. or any of its subsidiaries.

Part IV

Miscellaneous and Supplementary

Capital transfer tax: extension of transitional relief

23.—(1) For the references to 1st April 1980 in—

(*a*) paragraph 12 (6) of Schedule 5 to the Finance Act 1975 (earliest date for 10-year periodic charge on settlements without interests in possession); and

(*b*) paragraph 14 (2) of that Schedule (earliest date at which capital distribution bears tax at full rate).

there shall be substituted references to 1st April 1982.

(2) This section does not affect tax chargeable by virtue of sub-paragraph (2) of paragraph 12 of the said Schedule 5 (annual charge where trustees are non-resident) in respect of any year ending before 1st January 1979; but where in the case of any settlement tax has been charged by virtue of that sub-paragraph in respect of one or more years in a period that would have ended with a relevant anniversary but for this section, tax shall not be chargeable by virtue of that sub-paragraph in respect of the first year or years (up to a corresponding number) in respect of which tax would be so chargeable in the period ending with the date that becomes the first relevant anniversary by virtue of this section.

GENERAL NOTE

The transitional relief from CTT for distribution from settlements in which no interest in possession subsists is hereby extended, at the current rate of 20 per cent. of the full rates, for a further two years to March 31, 1982, therefore the starting date for the periodic charge to CTT will be deferred to April 1, 1982.

Subs. (2)

This subsection deals with a similar settlement but where the trustees are non-resident. The tax treatment of non-resident discretionary trusts is provided for under F.A. 1975, Sched. 5, para. 12 (2), and the charge is calculated upon the basis of a deemed yearly capital distribution chargeable at 3 per cent. of the rate which would apply to an ordinary capital distribution. The effect of subs. (2) is to provide that no tax shall become chargeable in respect of the first year or years in relation to a period, the first relevant anniversary (as defined in para. 12 (6)) of which falls to be calculated by virtue of the new transitional provisions under this section (*i.e.* after April 1, 1982). This amendment is made necessary by the fact that hitherto under para. 12 (6) tax was not chargeable on a tenth anniversary falling before April 1, 1980, although this does not prevent an annual charge being imposed before that date (except for any year ending before January 1, 1976).

Development land tax

24.—(1) With respect to chargeable realised development value accruing to any person on the disposal of an interest in land on or after 12th June 1979, section 1 (3) of the Development Land Tax Act 1976 (the rate of tax) shall be amended—

(*a*) by substituting " 60 per cent." for " 80 per cent."; and

(*b*) by the omission of the words " Subject to section 13, below ".

(2) With respect to financial years ending after 12th June 1979, section 12 of that Act (exemption for first £10,000 of realised development value) shall be amended by substituting " £50,000 " for " £10,000 ", in each place where it occurs but, of the £50,000 relief available to any person under that section for the financial year ending on 31st March 1980, not more than £10,000 may be attributed to realised development value which accrued to him before 12th June 1979.

(3) For the purposes of section 13 of that Act (reduced rate of 66⅔ per cent. on first £150,000 of chargeable realised development value accruing in any financial year ending on or before 31st March 1980) the period beginning on 1st April 1979 and ending immediately before 12th June 1979 shall be treated as an interim financial year; and nothing in that section shall apply with respect to chargeable realised development value accruing to any person on the disposal of an interest in land on or after 12th June 1979.

(4) In section 40 of that Act (deduction on account of development land tax from consideration for disposals by non-residents) subsection (2)

(exemption where consideration does not exceed £10,000) shall be amended with respect to disposals on or after 12th June 1979 by substituting " £50,000 " for " £10,000 ".

(5) In Schedule 6 to that Act (interaction of development land tax with other taxes)—

(a) nothing in sub-paragraphs (5) to (9) of paragraph 4 or sub-paragraphs (3) to (9) of paragraph 6 (which in the case of certain DLT disposals in interim financial years give rise to a charge to tax under Case VI of Schedule D) shall cause any person to be treated as having received, in a year of assessment after the year 1978–79, a payment chargeable under Case VI of Schedule D; and

(b) paragraph 9 (effect on apportionment of income of close companies in cases where development land tax charged at 66⅔ per cent.) shall not have effect with respect to any accounting period which ends after 5th April 1979.

(6) With respect to disposals on or after 12th June 1979, Schedules 7 and 8 of that Act shall be amended, in consequence of the preceding provisions of this section, in accordance with Schedule 4 to this Act.

General Note

This provision reduces the rate of development land tax and increases the exemption available to individuals.

From June 12, 1978, any development value realised on the disposal of an interest in land is chargeable at the rate of 60 per cent. and the reduced rate of 66⅔ per cent. and the principal rate of 80 per cent.

The exemption available to individuals for financial years ending after June 12, 1979, is increased from £10,000 to £50,000 save that in respect of development value realised on disposals before June 12, 1979, the exemption remains at £10,000.

Subs. (5) prevents the clawback rules from applying after April 5, 1979. These rules applied when there was a sale of land held as trading stock which resulted in a higher income tax liability than for development land tax.

Short title, interpretation, construction and repeals

25.—(1) This Act may be cited as the Finance (No. 2) Act 1979.

(2) In this Act " the Taxes Act " means the Income and Corporation Taxes Act 1970.

(3) Part II of this Act so far as it relates to income tax shall be construed as one with the Income Tax Acts and so far as it relates to corporation tax shall be construed as one with the Corporation Tax Acts.

(4) Part III of this Act shall be construed as one with Part I of the Oil Taxation Act 1975.

(5) The enactments mentioned in Schedule 5 to this Act are hereby repealed to the extent specified in the third column of that Schedule, but subject to any provision at the end of any Part of that Schedule.

SCHEDULES

Section 11

SCHEDULE 1

Withdrawal of Child Tax Allowances: Consequential Provisions

Relative taking charge of unmarried person's young brother or sister

1. Section 13 of the Taxes Act shall cease to have effect.

Additional personal allowance

2.—(1) Section 14 of the Taxes Act shall be amended as follows.

(2) In subsection (2) after the words " Subject to subsections (3) and (4) below " there shall be inserted the words " and to section 14A below " and for

paragraphs (*a*) and (*b*) there shall be substituted the words "that a qualifying child is resident with him for the whole or part of the year,".

(3) For subsection (3) there shall be substituted—

"(3) A claimant is entitled to only one deduction under subsection (2) above for any year of assessment irrespective of the number of qualifying children resident with him in that year."

(4) After subsection (4) there shall be added—

"(5) For the purposes of this section a qualifying child means, in relation to any claimant and year of assessment, a child who—

(*a*) is born in, or is under the age of sixteen years at the commencement of, the year or, being over that age at the commencement of that year, is receiving full-time instruction at any university, college, school or other educational establishment; and

(*b*) is a child of the claimant or, not being such a child, is born in, or is under the age of eighteen years at the commencement of, the year and maintained for the whole or part of that year by the claimant at his own expense.

(6) In subsection (5) (*a*) above the reference to a child receiving full-time instruction at an educational establishment includes a reference to a child undergoing training by any person ("the employer") for any trade, profession or vocation in such circumstances that the child is required to devote the whole of his time to the training for a period of not less than two years.

For the purpose of a claim in connection with a child undergoing training, the inspector may require the employer to furnish particulars with respect to the training of the child in such form as may be prescribed by the Board.

(7) If any question arises under this section whether a child is receiving full-time instruction at an educational establishment, the Board may consult the Secretary of State for Education and Science.

In the application of this subsection to Scotland and Northern Ireland, the Secretary of State and the Department of Education for Northern Ireland shall respectively be substituted for the Secretary of State for Education and Science.

(8) In subsection (5) (*b*) above the reference to a child of the claimant includes a reference to a stepchild of his, an illegitimate child of his if he has married the other parent after the child's birth and an adopted child of his if the child was under the age of eighteen years when he was adopted.

(9) Notwithstanding anything in section 9 of the Family Law Reform Act 1969 or any corresponding enactment in force in Northern Ireland or any rule of law in Scotland, for the purposes of subsection (5) above a child whose birthday falls on 6th April shall be taken to be over the age of sixteen at the commencement of the year which begins with his sixteenth birthday and over the age of eighteen at the commencement of the year which begins with his eighteenth birthday.".

3. After section 14 of the Taxes Act there shall be inserted the following section—

"**Apportionment of relief under s. 14**

14A.—(1) Where for any year of assessment two or more individuals are entitled to relief under section 14 above in connection with the same child—

(*a*) the amount specified in subsection (2) of that section shall be apportioned between them; and

(*b*) the deduction to which each of them is entitled under that section shall, subject to subsection (2) below, be equal to so much of that amount as is apportioned to him.

(2) Where for any year of assessment amounts are apportioned to an individual under this section in respect of two or more children the deduction to which he is entitled for that year under section 14 above shall be equal to the sum of those amounts or the amount specified in subsection (2) of that section, whichever is the less.

(3) Any amount required to be apportioned under this section shall be apportioned between the individuals concerned in such proportions as may be agreed between them or, in default of agreement, in proportion to the length of the periods for which the child in question is resident with them respectively in the year of assessment; and where the proportions are not so agreed, the apportionment shall be made by such body of General Commissioners, being the General

Commissioners for a division in which one of the individuals resides, as the Board may direct, or, if none of the individuals resides in Great Britain, by the Special Commissioners.

(4) Where a claim is made under section 14 above and it appears that, if the claim is allowed, an apportionment will be necessary under this section, the Board may if they think fit direct that the claim itself shall be dealt with by any specified body of Commissioners which could under this section be directed to make the apportionment and that the same Commissioners shall also make any apportionment which proves to be necessary; and where a direction is given under this subsection no other body of Commissioners shall have jurisdiction to determine the claim.

(5) The Commissioners making any apportionment under this section shall hear and determine the case in like manner as an appeal, but any individual who is, or but for the provisions of this section would be, entitled to relief in connection with the child shall be entitled to appear and be heard by the Commissioners or to make representations to them in writing.

(6) For the purposes of this section an individual shall not be regarded as entitled to relief under section 14 above for any year of assessment in connection with the same child as another individual if there is another child in connection with which he, and he alone, is entitled to relief under that section for that year."

Exemption of social security benefits in respect of children etc.

4.—(1) In section 219 (1) (*a*) of the Taxes Act the word "and" shall be omitted and at the end there shall be inserted the words ", child's special allowance and guardian's allowance and except so much of any benefit as is attributable to an increase in respect of a child."

(2) In section 219 (2) of the Taxes Act for the words "and payments of child benefit" there shall be substituted the words ", payments of child benefit, payments by way of an allowance under section 70 of the Social Security Act 1975 or section 70 of the Social Security (Northern Ireland) Act 1975 and payments excepted by subsection (1) above from the charge to tax imposed by that subsection".

General Note

This Schedule contains various provisions consequential upon the withdrawal of child tax allowances (save in the circumstances specified in F.A. 1977, ss. 25 and 26) by F.A. 1979, s. 1 (4).

Para. 1. The relief in s. 13 given in respect of a relative taking charge of an unmarried person's young brother or sister is now to be abolished.

Para. 2. S. 14 gives an additional personal allowance to one parent families so as to equate their position with two parent families where the higher married man's allowance is available. The relief in s. 14 was drawn by reference to the child tax allowance in that the s. 14 relief was only available where child tax allowance could be claimed. With the abolition of child tax allowance s. 14 is now amended by this paragraph. Essentially the amendments are consequential, in that relief will only be available when conditions can be met that would have had to be met in order for child tax allowances to be obtained.

Para. 3. S. 14 relief is available where a "qualifying child" is resident with a person for the "whole or part of the year." Clearly there is a possibility of more than one person being in a position to claim the allowance and the addition of a new s. 14A is to deal with this eventuality. Broadly s. 14A is drafted in similar terms to I.C.T.A. 1970, s. 11, the provision dealing with the apportionment of child tax allowances. It is noteworthy, however, that while s. 11 apportionment is in the absence of agreement to be made by reference to the amount or value of provision made for a child the s. 14A apportionment is in the absence of agreement to be made by reference to the length of residence of a child with each person in question.

Para. 4. This paragraph excludes certain benefits from tax. When child tax allowances were originally reduced, F.A. 1977, s. 23 (3) applied in order to prevent certain families from being worse off in consequence. Now that child tax allowances are totally abolished this paragraph provides total exemption for the payments concerned.

Section 12

SCHEDULE 2

SOCIAL SECURITY PENSIONS ACT: CONSEQUENTIAL PROVISIONS

1. For section 8 (2) (*b*) of the Taxes Act (under which wife's earned income relief is available in respect of a Category A retirement pension and a mobility allowance) there shall be substituted—

" (*b*) no payment of benefit under the Social Security Acts except—

(i) a Category A retirement pension (exclusive of any increase under section 10 of the Social Security Pensions Act 1975 or the Northern Ireland equivalent); and

(ii) a mobility allowance,

shall be treated as earned income ".

2. In section 16 of the Taxes Act (dependent relative relief where dependant's income does not exceed the basic retirement pension by more than a specified amount) for subsections (2A) and (2B) there shall be substituted—

" (2A) For the purposes of this section " the basic retirement pension " for any year means the aggregate of the payments to which a person would be entitled in that year on account of a Category A retirement pension under the Social Security Acts if the weekly rate of his pension consisted (and consisted only) of the full amount of the basic component."

3. In section 219 (1) (*a*) of the Taxes Act (benefits charged to or exempt from tax under Schedule E)—

(*a*) for the word " or " there shall be substituted the words ", Part II of the Social Security Pensions Act 1975,";

(*b*) after the words " the Social Security (Northern Ireland) Act 1975 " there shall be inserted the words " or Part III of the Social Security Pensions (Northern Ireland) Order 1975 ".

4. In section 526 (5) of the Taxes Act (interpretation) after the definition of " qualifying distribution " there shall be inserted—

" 'the Social Security Acts' means the Social Security Acts 1975 or the Social Security (Northern Ireland) Acts 1975;".

5. In paragraph 1 of Schedule 4 to the Finance Act 1971 (benefits excluded from wife's earnings in cases of separate taxation) for paragraph (*b*) there shall be substituted—

" (*b*) any payment of benefit under the Social Security Acts except a Category A retirement pension (exclusive of any increase under section 10 of the Social Security Pensions Act 1975 or the Northern Ireland equivalent)."

GENERAL NOTE

This deals with a number of amendments consequent upon the Social Security Pensions Act 1975.

Para. 1. This deals with the benefits which qualify as earned income of a wife for the purposes of personal relief. Prior to this a Category A retirement pension is treated as earned income. By virtue of para. 1 it is to continue to be treated in this manner save as to so much of it as relates to an increase in the pension due to the Social Security Pensions Act 1975, s. 10. A person will be entitled to an increase if that person would have been entitled to both a Category A retirement pension and a Category B retirement pension but for s. 27 (*b*) of the Social Security Act 1975 (which prevents a person from being entitled to more than one retirement pension) and the basic component of the Category A pension falls short of the weekly rates specified in Sched. 4, para. 9, to that Act by reason of a deficiency of contribution. In such a case the component is increased by the amount of the shortfall or the amount of the weekly rate of the Category B pension whichever is the smaller.

Para. 2. Dependent relative relief is available provided that the total income of the relative does not exceed by more than £100 the basic retirement pension for that year of the person. If it exceeds that amount then some marginal relief is available. The amendment in para. 2 simplifies the definition of "basic retirement pension" and limits the amount to the flat rate pension disregarding any additional amount due to the earnings related element.

Para. 3. This charges to income tax under Sched. E the benefits within Pt. II of the Social Security Pensions Act 1975 (which includes invalidity benefits).

Para. 5. In determining a wife's earnings in a case of separate taxation from her husband the treatment of a Category A retirement pension is as set out in para. 1 above. This means that a wife's earnings will not include any increase in her retirement pension attributable to her husband's contributions.

Section 13

SCHEDULE 3

Stock Relief

Amount of stock relief

1.—(1) In paragraph 1 (2) of Schedule 5 to the Finance Act 1976 (stock relief for purposes of income tax to be amount of increase in stock value less 15 per cent. of relevant income) for "15 per cent." there shall be substituted "10 per cent.".

(2) This paragraph has effect in relation to periods of account ending after 5th April 1979.

Claims for partial relief

2.—(1) In paragraph 1 (2) of the said Schedule 5 after "(2)" there shall be inserted the words "Subject to sub-paragraph (4) below" and after paragraph 1 (3) of that Schedule there shall be inserted—

"(4) A person may, in making a claim for relief under this paragraph in respect of any period of account, specify an amount of relief less than that stated in sub-paragraph (2) above and, if he does so, the relief to which he is entitled under this paragraph in respect of that period shall be the amount specified in the claim."

(2) In paragraph 9 (2) of the said Schedule 5 after "(2)" there shall be inserted the words "Subject to sub-paragraph (4) below" and after paragraph 9 (3) of that Schedule there shall be inserted—

"(4) A company may, in making a claim for relief under this paragraph in respect of any period of account, specify an amount of relief less than that stated in sub-paragraph (2) above and, if it does so, the relief to which it is entitled under this paragraph in respect of that period shall be the amount specified in the claim."

(3) Sub-paragraph (1) above has effect in relation to periods of account ending after 5th April 1979 and sub-paragraph (2) above in relation to periods of account ending after 31st March 1979.

Write-off of past relief

3.—(1) In sub-paragraph (2) of paragraph 26 of the said Schedule 5 (definition of unrecovered past stock relief) after "(2)" there shall be inserted the words "Subject to sub-paragraphs (3) to (5) below," and after that sub-paragraph there shall be inserted—

"(3) There shall be excluded from the amount of unrecovered past relief in any period of account so much of that amount (if any) as is attributable to relief allowed under Part I or Part II of this Schedule in respect of any period of account which ended six years or more before the beginning of the first-mentioned period.

(4) There shall be excluded from the amount of unrecovered past relief in any period of account beginning after—

(*a*) the end of the period or last period of account ending in the financial year 1978 (in the case of a company) or the year 1978–79 (in other cases); or (*b*) if there is no such period of account, the end of the period of account current at the end of that financial year or year of assessment, as the case may be,

so much of that amount (if any) as is attributable to Schedule 10 relief.

(5) For the purpose of attributing the amount of unrecovered past relief in any period to Schedule 10 relief or to relief allowed under Part I or Part II of this Schedule in respect of any previous period it shall be assumed that relief is recovered from later periods before earlier periods."

(2) In sub-paragraph (5) of paragraph 25 of the said Schedule 5 (special provisions for the recovery of relief in cases of election for herd basis) for the words from the beginning to "made" there shall be substituted the words "(5) Subject to sub-paragraph (5A) below, the amount on which the charge is to be made" and after that sub-paragraph there shall be inserted—

"(5A) The amount on which the charge is to be made in respect of any period of account ("the period of charge") shall not exceed the amount of unrecovered past relief attributed to the herd at the point of election less—

(*a*) so much (if any) of the amount of that unrecovered past relief at that point as is attributable to relief allowed under Part I or Part II of this Schedule in respect of any period of account which ended six years or more before the beginning of the period of charge; and

(*b*) if the period of charge begins after the end of the period of account mentioned in paragraph 26 (4) (*a*) or (*b*) below, so much (if any) of the amount of that unrecovered past relief at that point as is attributable to Schedule 10 relief; and

(*c*) the aggregate of the amounts on which charges have been made under this paragraph in respect of earlier periods of account for which the election has effect."

General Note

This Schedule contains the detailed provisions amending the stock relief given by F.A. 1976, Sched. 5.

Para. 1. This paragraph reduces the profit restriction on stock relief as regards unincorporated businesses. The profit restriction of 15 per cent. will remain for companies.

Para. 2. A criticism of stock relief in its past form has been that it has not allowed partial claims for relief. This could create unfairness in that it could prevent companies from benefiting from double taxation relief in a year in which a substantial amount of stock relief could be claimed and could prevent sole traders from obtaining the benefit of their personal allowances if they claimed the relief. This criticism has now been met by this paragraph.

Para. 3. This paragraph provides a write-off for past stock relief obtained. The write-off provided for is as follows:

(*a*) Any unrecovered relief given under F.A. 1975, s. 18, and F. (No. 2) A. 1975, Sched. 10. This will broadly be a write-off of any unrecovered relief obtained in 1973–74 and 1974–75. For this purpose the unrecovered relief is to be determined immediately after the end of the period of account ending in 1978–79 or in the absence of such a period of account, the end of the period of account current at the end of 1978 financial year or 1978–79 tax year.

(*b*) Any unrecovered relief after it has been outstanding for six years. Such write-off will occur immediately after the sixth anniversary of the end of the period of account for which the relief is given. As the first relief qualifying for write-off will be that given in 1975–76, write-off will first occur at the beginning of the period of account in 1981–82 (assuming constant annual periods of account are kept).

It is important to note that in determining what relief has been unrecovered under the claw-back system and recoveries made are to be set against relief obtained in later rather than earlier years. Thus if for instance in year seven a sale of stock might occur leading to claw-back such a sale would not affect the amount of write-off available in respect of relief obtained in year one so long as in the intervening period sufficient relief has been obtained to cover the claw-back.

Sub.-para. (2) of para. 3 contains consequential provisions relating to the write-off of past relief so as to make the write-off apply to relief obtained in respect of farm animals for which an election for a herd basis has been made.

Section 24

SCHEDULE 4

Development Land Tax

1. In paragraph 1 of Schedule 7 to the Development Land Tax Act 1976 (cases where notice of acquisition is to be given) after "exceeds", in sub-paragraphs (1) and (5) (*b*), there shall be inserted "the aggregate of £50,000 and".

2.—(1) In paragraph 5 of that Schedule (the formula deduction) in sub-paragraph (3) (disposals where formula deduction is nil and determination of "the exempt amount") for the words from the beginning to "does not exceed" there shall be substituted "In relation to a material disposal, any reference in the following provisions of this paragraph to 'the exempt amount' is a reference to" and for the words from "£10,000" to the end of the sub-paragraph there shall be substituted "£50,000".

(2) Sub-paragraphs (4) and (5) of that paragraph (the formula deduction for other disposals in interim financial years) shall be omitted.

(3) In sub-paragraph (6) of that paragraph (the formula deduction for other disposals) the words from the beginning to "then" shall be omitted and, in paragraph (*b*), for "80 per cent." there shall be substituted "60 per cent.".

(4) In sub-paragraph (7) of that paragraph ("the appropriate percentage" to be determined by regulations) for "such" there shall be substituted "30 per cent. or such other".

(5) In sub-paragraph (8) of that paragraph the words "sub-paragraph (4) (*b*) or, as the case may be" shall be omitted.

3. In paragraph 7 (3) of that Schedule (application of formula deduction where there is an advance payment of compensation) for "sub-paragraphs (4) (*a*) and" there shall be substituted "sub-paragraph".

4. In paragraphs 35 (1) and 38 (3) of Schedule 8 to that Act (notices of disposals and of events giving rise to liability for tax) for "£10,000", in each place where it occurs, there shall be substituted "£50,000".

General Note

This Schedule makes a number of amendments resulting from the reduction in the rate of D.L.T. and the increase in the exemption available to individuals.

Section 25

SCHEDULE 5

Repeals

Part I

Value Added Tax

Chapter	Short title	Extent of repeal
1975 c. 7.	The Finance Act 1975.	Section 1.
1975 c. 45.	The Finance (No. 2) Act 1975.	Section 17. Section 18 (3) (*b*) and (*c*). Schedule 7.
1976 c. 40.	The Finance Act 1976.	Section 17.

These repeals take effect on 18th June 1979 and the repeal of Schedule 7 to the Finance (No. 2) Act 1975 has effect subject to section 1 (2) of this Act.

SCHEDULE 5—*continued*

PART II

INCOME TAX AND CORPORATION TAX

Chapter	Short title	Extent of repeal
1970 c. 10.	The Income and Corporation Taxes Act 1970.	Section 13. In section 15 the figure "13". In section 219 (1) (*a*) the word "and". Section 365 (3).
1971 c. 68.	The Finance Act 1971.	Section 18 (1) (*a*). In Schedule 4, in paragraph 3 (3) the figure "13".
1973 c. 51.	The Finance Act 1973.	Section 12 (2) (*c*).
1975 c. 18.	The Social Security (Consequential Provisions) Act 1975.	In Schedule 2 paragraph 36.
1975 c. 60.	The Social Security Pensions Act 1975.	In Schedule 4 paragraphs 12 and 20.
1976 c. 40.	The Finance Act 1976.	Section 29 (5). Section 31. In section 36 (8) (*b*) (i) the figure "13". Section 43.
1977 c. 36.	The Finance Act 1977.	Section 22 (1) (*e*). Section 23 (3) and (4).
1978 c. 42.	The Finance Act 1978.	Section 18. Section 19 (1), (3) and (4). Section 20 (4).
1979 c. 25.	The Finance Act 1979.	Section 1 (1), (2) and (3). In section 2, in subsection (1), the words "and the fraction mentioned in section 95 (2) of the Finance Act 1972 (marginal relief for small companies)", and subsection (2).

1. The repeal of section 43 of the Finance Act 1976 has effect in relation to expenditure to which section 14 (5) of this Act applies.

2. The repeal of section 1 (1) of the Finance Act 1979 has effect subject to section 5 (2) of this Act.

3. Subject as aforesaid, the repeals relating to income tax have effect for the year 1979–80 and subsequent years of assessment.

PART III

PETROLEUM REVENUE TAX

Chapter	Short title	Extent of repeal
1975 c. 74.	Petroleum and Submarine Pipe-lines Act 1975.	Section 9 (1). Section 15 (2) (*d*).

The repeal of section 9 (1) has effect for chargeable periods ending after 30th June 1979.

SCHEDULE 5—*continued*

PART IV

DEVELOPMENT LAND TAX

Chapter	Short title	Extent of repeal
1976 c. 24.	The Development Land Tax Act 1976.	In section 1 (3) the words " Subject to section 13 below ". Section 13. In Schedule 6, sub-paragraphs (5) to (9) of paragraph 4, sub-paragraphs (3) to (9) of paragraph 6 and paragraph 9. In Schedule 7, in paragraph 5, sub-paragraphs (4) and (5), in sub-paragraph (6) the words from the beginning to " then " and in sub-paragraph (8) the words " sub-paragraph (4) (*b*) or, as the case may be ".
1978 c. 42.	The Finance Act 1978.	Section 76.

1. The repeals in Schedule 6 to the Development Land Tax Act 1976 take effect in accordance with section 24 (5) of this Act.

2. The other repeals have effect with respect to disposals on or after 12th June 1979.

Pensioners' Payments and Social Security Act 1979

(1979 c. 48)

ARRANGEMENT OF SECTIONS

An Act to make provision for lump sum payments to pensioners and to modify section 125 of the Social Security Act 1975.

[26th July 1979]

General Note

This Act provides for lump sum payments to pensioners and modifies the Social Security Act 1975.

S. 1 provides for a lump sum payment of £10 to pensioners to be made in December 1979; s. 2 contains definitions; s. 3 relates to the administration of payments; s. 4 deals with payments for 1980 and subsequent years; s. 5 modifies the Social Security Act 1975, s. 125; s. 6 contains financial provisions; s. 7 relates to Northern Ireland; s. 8 contains the short title.

The Act received the Royal Assent on July 26, 1979, and came into force on that date.

Parliamentary debates

Hansard, H.L. Vol. 401, cols. 473, 1034.

Lump sum payments to pensioners

Payments for 1979

1.—(1) Any person who—

(*a*) is present or ordinarily resident in the United Kingdom or any other member state of the Communities at any time during the relevant week; and

(*b*) is entitled to a payment of a qualifying benefit in respect of a period which includes a day in that week or is to be treated as entitled to a payment of a qualifying benefit in respect of such a period,

shall, subject to subsection (3) of this section and sections 2 and 3 of this Act, be entitled to payment by the Secretary of State of a sum of £10.

(2) Subject as aforesaid, any person entitled to a payment under the preceding subsection shall, if he and his spouse have attained pensionable age not later than the end of the relevant week and his spouse satisfies the condition mentioned in paragraph (*a*) of that subsection and if—

(*a*) he is entitled in respect of his spouse to an increase in the payment of qualifying benefit mentioned in paragraph (*b*) of that subsection; or (*b*) he is to be treated as so entitled and the relevant qualifying benefit is not a supplementary pension; or

(*c*) his and his spouse's requirements and resources fall to be aggregated under paragraph 3 (1) of Schedule 1 to the Supplementary Benefits Act 1976 or to the Supplementary Benefits (Northern Ireland) Order 1977,

be entitled to payment by the Secretary of State of a further sum of £10.

(3) Only one sum shall be payable under this section in respect of any person.

(4) A sum payable under this section shall not be treated as benefit for the purposes of any enactment or instrument under which entitlement to the relevant qualifying benefit arises or is to be treated as arising.

(5) A payment and the right to receive a payment—

(*a*) under this section; or

(*b*) under regulations relating to widows which are, within the period of two months beginning with the date of the passing of this Act, made by the Secretary of State under any enactment relating to police and contain a statement that the regulations provide for payments corresponding to payments under this section,

shall be disregarded for all purposes of income tax and for the purposes of any enactment or instrument under which regard is had to a person's means.

Interpretation of provisions as to payments

2.—(1) In this Act " qualifying benefit " means—

(*a*) any of the following benefits under the Social Security Act 1975 or the Social Security (Northern Ireland) Act 1975 (each of which is hereafter in this section referred to as " the Social Security Act "), namely—

(i) a retirement pension;

(ii) an invalidity pension;

(iii) a widow's allowance, widowed mother's allowance or widow's pension;

(iv) a non-contributory invalidity pension;

(v) an invalid care allowance;

(vi) an industrial death benefit by way of widow's or widower's pension;

(*b*) an attendance allowance;

(*c*) an unemployability supplement or allowance;

(*d*) a war disablement pension;

(*e*) a war widow's pension;

(*f*) a supplementary pension.

(2) In this Act—

" attendance allowance " has the meaning assigned to it by any regulations in force on the passing of this Act under the Family Income Supplements Act 1970 or the Family Income Supplements Act (Northern Ireland) 1971;

" pensionable age " means—

(*a*) in the case of a man, the age of 65;

(*b*) in the case of a woman, the age of 60;

" the relevant week " means the week beginning with 3rd December 1979;

" retirement pension " includes graduated retirement benefit, if paid periodically;

" supplementary pension " means a supplementary pension under section 1 (1) (*a*) of the Supplementary Benefits Act 1976 or article 3 (1) (*a*) of the Supplementary Benefits (Northern Ireland) Order 1977;

" unemployability supplement or allowance " has the meaning assigned to it by Schedule 5 to the Social Security Act;

" war disablement pension " means—

(*a*) any retired pay, pension or allowance granted in respect of disablement under powers conferred by or under the Air Force (Constitution) Act 1917, the Personal Injuries (Emergency Provisions) Act 1939, the Pensions (Navy, Army, Air Force and Mercantile Marine) Act 1939, the Polish Resettlement Act 1947, the Home Guard Act 1951 or the Ulster Defence Regiment Act 1969;

(*b*) without prejudice to paragraph (*a*) of this definition, any retired pay or pension to which subsection (1) of section 365 of the Income and Corporation Taxes Act 1970 applies;

" war widow's pension " means any widow's pension or allowance granted in respect of a death due to service or war injury and payable by virtue of any enactment mentioned in paragraph (*a*) of the preceding definition or a pension or allowance for a widow granted under any scheme mentioned in subsection (2) (*e*) of the said section 365;

and each of the following expressions, namely, " attendance allowance ", " unemployability supplement or allowance ", " war disablement pension " and " war widow's pension ", includes any payment which the Secretary of State accepts as being analogous to it.

(3) For the purposes of the preceding section the Channel Islands, the Isle of Man and Gibraltar shall be treated as though they were part of the United Kingdom.

(4) A person shall be treated for the purposes of subsection (1) (*b*) of the preceding section as entitled to a payment of qualifying benefit if he would be so entitled—

(*a*) in the case of a qualifying benefit other than a supplementary pension;

(i) but for the fact that he or his spouse is entitled to receive some other payment out of public funds;

(ii) but for the operation of section 30 (1) of the Social Security Act;

(iii) but for the terms of any arrangement to which section 92 of that Act applies and by which he is bound;

(iv) but for the fact that he has not made a claim for the payment;

(*b*) in the case of a supplementary pension, but for the fact that his or his spouse's earnings were exceptionally of an amount which resulted in his having ceased to be entitled to the pension.

(5) A person shall be treated for the purposes of subsection (2) (*b*) of the preceding section as entitled in respect of his spouse to an increase in a payment of qualifying benefit if he would be so entitled—

(*a*) but for the fact that he or his spouse is entitled to receive some other payment out of public funds;

(*b*) but for the operation of any provision of section 30 (1), 45 (2) or (3) or 66(4) of the Social Security Act or any regulations made under section 66 (3) of that Act whereby entitlement to benefit is affected by the amount of a person's earnings in a given period; or

(*c*) but for such terms as are mentioned in paragraph (*a*) (iii) of the preceding subsection; or

(*d*) but for the fact that he has not made a claim for the increase.

(6) For the purposes of the preceding section a person shall be deemed not to be entitled to a payment of a war disablement pension unless not later than the end of the relevant week—

(*a*) he has attained the age of 70 in the case of a man or 65 in the case of a woman; or

(*b*) he is treated under section 27 (3) of the Social Security Act as having retired from regular employment.

(7) Two persons who are not married to each other and are living together as husband and wife shall be treated as spouses for the purposes of the preceding section if—

(*a*) the qualifying benefit to which the man is entitled is a supplementary pension; and

(*b*) their requirements and resources fall to be aggregated as mentioned in subsection (2) (*c*) of that section.

Administration of payments

3.—(1) A determination by the competent authority that a person is entitled or not entitled to payment of a qualifying benefit in respect of a period which includes a day in the relevant week shall be conclusive for the purposes of section 1 of this Act; and in this subsection " competent authority " means, in relation to a payment of any description of qualifying benefit, an authority who ordinarily determines whether a person is entitled to such a payment.

(2) Any question arising under section 1 or 2 of this Act, other than one determined or falling to be determined under the preceding subsection, shall be determined by the Secretary of State whose decision shall, except as provided by the following subsection, be final.

(3) The Secretary of State may reverse a decision under the preceding subsection on new facts being brought to his notice or if he is satisfied that the decision was given in ignorance of, or was based on a mistake as to, some material fact.

(4) The Secretary of State may—

(*a*) require any person to make a claim in writing for a payment under section 1 of this Act;

(*b*) require such information and evidence to be furnished by a person who has applied for a payment under that section as may in the opinion of the Secretary of State be necessary for the purpose of determining whether that person is or was entitled to such a payment.

(5) The Secretary of State may make any payment under section 1 of this Act at any time and in any manner that he thinks appropriate and, in particular, may make such a payment to someone other than the person entitled to it, but on that person's behalf, if in the circumstances of the case he considers it appropriate so to do.

(6) The right of any person to payment of any sum under section 1 of this Act shall be extinguished if payment is not obtained within twelve months, or such longer period as the Secretary of State may in any particular case allow, from the date which the Secretary of State determines to be the date on which that person became entitled to that payment.

(7) Notwithstanding anything in subsections (5) and (6) of this section, a payment under section 1 of this Act to which, apart from this subsection, a person is entitled by virtue of subsection (4) or (5) of the preceding section shall not be made after the expiration of the period of one year beginning with the last day of the relevant week unless a claim for the payment was made in the prescribed manner before the expiration of that period.

In this subsection " prescribed " means prescribed by regulations made by the Secretary of State by statutory instrument, and any statutory instrument made by virtue of this subsection shall be subject to annulment in pursuance of a resolution of either House of Parliament.

Payments for 1980 and subsequent years

4.—(1) It shall be the duty of the Secretary of State, in the year 1980 and each subsequent year,—

(*a*) to lay before each House of Parliament a draft of an order under this section; and

(*b*) if the draft is approved by a resolution of each House, to make by statutory instrument an order in the form of the draft.

(2) An order under this section must provide that sections 1 to 3 of this Act are to have effect as if—

(*a*) for references to the relevant week there were substituted references to a week in the current year which begins with a day not earlier than the second Monday in November of that year and is specified in the order; and

(*b*) for references to the passing of this Act there were substituted references to the making of the order.

(3) If it appears to the Secretary of State that, having regard to the economic situation in the United Kingdom, the standard of living in the United Kingdom and such other matters as he considers relevant, the sums to be payable by virtue of an order under this section should be larger than £10, the order may provide that sections 1 to 3 of this Act are to have effect, in relation to the week specified in the order, as if for references to £10 in section 1 (1) and (2) there were substituted references to a larger sum so specified.

Modification of s. 125 of Social Security Act 1975

Modification of 1975 c. 14 s. 125

5. The Secretary of State shall not be required by virtue of section 125 of the Social Security Act 1975 (which provides among other things for reviews of the amount of the earnings of a beneficiary's wife which must be exceeded before a pension is reduced by reference to the excess in pursuance of section 45 (3) or 66 (4) of that Act) to review a sum specified in section 45 (3) or 66 (4) of that Act or to prepare and lay before Parliament the draft of an order relating to such a sum.

Supplemental

Financial provisions

6.—(1) A sum paid to a person under section 1 of this Act shall be so paid—

(*a*) out of the National Insurance Fund if the relevant qualifying benefit to which he is entitled or treated as entitled is a benefit payable out of that Fund;

(*b*) out of money provided by Parliament if the said benefit is a benefit payable out of such money;

(*c*) out of the Northern Ireland National Insurance Fund if the said benefit is a benefit payable out of that Fund; and

(*d*) out of money appropriated from the Consolidated Fund of Northern Ireland if the said benefit is a benefit payable out of such money.

(2) Any administrative costs incurred in Great Britain under this Act by a government department shall be defrayed out of money provided by

Parliament, but so much of those costs as relates to sums payable out of the National Insurance Fund shall be repaid to the Consolidated Fund out of the other Fund.

(3) Any administrative costs incurred in Northern Ireland under this Act by a government department (including a Northern Ireland department) shall be paid out of money appropriated from the Consolidated Fund of Northern Ireland, but so much of those costs as relates to sums payable out of the Northern Ireland National Insurance Fund shall be repaid into the Consolidated Fund of Northern Ireland out of the other Fund.

(4) Where any payments fall to be made into a Fund in pursuance of subsection (2) or (3) of this section, the payments shall be taken to be of such amounts, and payments on account of them shall be made at such times and in such manner, as the Secretary of State may determine in accordance with any directions of the Treasury.

Additional provisions relating to Northern Ireland

7.—(1) The preceding provisions of this Act, except sections 4 and 5, shall have effect, in relation to a person who is or is treated as entitled to a benefit payable as is mentioned in subsection (1) (*c*) or (*d*) of the preceding section, as if for any reference to the Secretary of State (except in sections 1 (5) (*b*) and 3 (7)) or to the Treasury there were substituted respectively a reference to the Department of Health and Social Services for Northern Ireland and the Department of Finance for Northern Ireland.

(2) In relation to a payment under section 1 of this Act which falls to be paid out of a Fund mentioned in subsection (1) (*c*) or (*d*) of the preceding section, section 3 (7) of this Act shall have effect as if for the second paragraph there were substituted the following—

> In this section " prescribed " means prescribed by regulations made, by statutory rule for the purposes of the Statutory Rules Act (Northern Ireland) 1958, by the Department of Health and Social Services for Northern Ireland; and a statutory rule made by virtue of this subsection shall be subject to negative resolution as defined by section 41 (6) of the Interpretation Act (Northern Ireland) 1954 as if it were a statutory instrument within the meaning of that Act.

Citation and repeals

8.—(1) This Act may be cited as the Pensioners' Payments and Social Security Act 1979 and shall be included among the Acts which may be cited together as the Social Security Acts 1975 to 1979.

(2) In section 125 (1) (*c*) of the Social Security Act 1975 the words " 45 (3) and 66 (4) " and the words " of those provisions " are hereby repealed.

Education Act 1979 *

(1979 c. 49)

An Act to repeal sections 1, 2 and 3 of the Education Act 1976 and to make provision as to certain proposals submitted or transmitted to the Secretary of State under the said section 2.
[26th July 1979]

General Note

This two-section Act repeals the three sections of the Education Act 1976 which imposed on local education authorities and voluntary school governing and managing bodies the duty to give effect to the "comprehensive principle" in secondary education and enabled the Secretary of State for Education and Science to require local education authorities and, in certain circumstances, voluntary school governing and managing bodies, to submit schemes for comprehensive re-organisation. It also contains transitional provisions for dealing with plans submitted in accordance with requirements of the Secretary of State under the 1976 Act, enabling local education authorities or governors or managers to opt to retain them or to abandon them.

Commencement

The Act came into force on receiving the Royal Assent on July **26, 1979.**

Extent

The Act does not apply to Scotland or Northern Ireland.

Parliamentary Debates

Hansard, H.C. Vol. 967, col. 392; Report of Standing Committee A, cols. 1–158; H.L. Vol. 401, cols. 1287–1293, 1306–1368, 1509–1521, 1532, 1565, 1822–1839.

Abolition of duty to give effect to comprehensive principle

1.—(1) In the Education Act 1976—

section 1 (the comprehensive principle);

section 2 (submission of proposals for giving effect to comprehensive principle); and

section 3 (approval and implementation of proposals submitted under section 2),

are hereby repealed.

(2) The following provisions of this section apply to proposals submitted or transmitted to the Secretary of State under section 2 which have been treated, by virtue of a direction under subsection (1) of section 3, as if they had been submitted to him by a local education authority under subsection (1) or by the managers or governors of a voluntary school under subsection (2) of section 13 of the Education Act 1944 (establishing, maintaining, changing character of, enlarging or ceasing to maintain county school or voluntary school).

(3) Where any proposals to which this subsection applies have been approved under subsection (4) of section 13, the Secretary of State may, on the application of the local education authority, managers or governors concerned, revoke the approval.

(4) Where any proposals to which this subsection applies have not been so approved but public notice of them has been given under subsection (3) of section 13, the local education authority, managers or

* Annotations by Sir Ashley Bramall, M.A., Barrister.

governors concerned may elect that, notwithstanding the repeals effected by subsection (1) above, the proposals shall continue to be treated as if they had been submitted to the Secretary of State under subsection (1) or (2) of that section; but no such election shall have effect unless it is made in writing to the Secretary of State before 31st December 1979.

DEFINITIONS

"Secretary of State": in England this means the Secretary of State for Education and Science and in Wales the Secretary of State for Wales.

"local education authority": this is now defined by s. 30 (1) of the London Government Act 1963 and s. 192 (1) of the Local Government Act 1972.

"managers or governors": see s. 17 of the Act of 1944.

"voluntary school": this is defined by s. 9 (2) of the Act of 1944 as a maintained school established otherwise than by a local education authority.

GENERAL NOTE

This is the only operative section of the Act and contains the repeal of ss. 1, 2 and 3 of the Education Act 1976 and the transitional provisions for dealing with schemes submitted in accordance with the requirements of the Secretary of State under that Act.

Subs. (1)

S. 1 of the 1976 Act established the principle that secondary education was to be provided only in schools where the arrangements for admission were not based on selection by reference to aptitude and ability, subject to exceptions for schools for those suffering from disability and for schools mainly teaching music and dancing. S. 2 of that Act provided machinery for securing the implementation of the principle. It empowered the Secretary of State to require local education authorities, and in certain circumstances voluntary school governing or managing bodies, to submit to him proposals for its implementation in the whole or a specified part of the authority's area, and to require revised proposals if the original proposals were unsatisfactory in a specified manner. S. 3 enabled the Secretary of State to treat any proposals made under s. 2 as being submitted for his consent under s. 13 of the Education Act 1944.

Subs. (2)

This introduces provisions made in the two following subsections for dealing with action already taken by the Secretary of State or local education authorities to implement the 1976 Act.

It is to be observed that s. 4 of the 1976 Act has not been repealed. That section added two subsections to s. 13 of the Education Act 1944. The effect of those new subsections was to compel local education authorities and voluntary school managers and governors who have obtained the Secretary of State's permission to cease to maintain a school, or to change the character of a school, to carry out the plans for which they have obtained permission. Similar provisions apply under s. 13 to plans to establish or maintain new schools and to the enlargement of school premises.

The present Act leaves this general position unchanged, but subs. (3) enables local education authorities to secure the cancellation of approvals given by the Secretary of State as a result of submissions which arose (a) from a direction by the Secretary of State under s. 2 of the 1976 Act, (b) from a submission by a local education authority or voluntary managers or governors under that section, and (c) from a direction by the Secretary of State under s. 3 of the 1976 Act that such submission was to be treated as a proposal submitted under s. 13 (1) or (2) of the 1944 Act. Subs. (4) deals with proposals for which approval has not been given.

Subs. (3)

Where the three conditions referred to in (*a*), (*b*) and (*c*) above are fulfilled the local education authority, or voluntary managing or governing body, may apply to the Secretary of State to revoke the approval. There is no time limit for the application to revoke, but it appears that the Secretary of State has discretion whether or not to revoke and if he does not do so s. 13 of the Act of 1944 will compel the carrying out of the proposal.

Subs. (4)

This subsection deals with proposals to which the same conditions apply, which have reached the stage that the local education authority, or the voluntary managing or governing body, have given public notice of the proposal under s. 13 (3) of the 1944 Act, but which the Secretary of State has not approved.

The subsection treats the repeals under subs. (1) as though they took away from the Secretary of State the power to deal with the proposal as a submission under s. 13 (1) or (2) of the 1944 Act. There seems to be no warrant for this, since s. 3 (1) of the 1976 Act gave power to direct that proposals shall be treated as though submitted under s. 13 (1) or (2). Since all cases to which subs. (4) applies are *ex definitione* ones on which the Secretary of State has already made such a direction, it is difficult to see how the repeals have invalidated that direction. The approval to the proposal is not given under the 1976 Act, to which the repeals apply, but under the 1944 Act, which is unaffected by the repeals.

The effect of subs. (4), however, is to require the local education authority, or the managers or governors, who desire to have their proposal approved in spite of the manner in which it originally came to be made, to give notice of their wish before December 31, 1979. In that event it appears that the Secretary of State has no discretion and must treat the proposal as validly submitted under s. 13 of the 1944 Act. He has then, of course, discretion under that section whether or not to agree to the proposal.

Citation, construction and extent

2.—(1) This Act may be cited as the Education Act 1979.

(2) The Education Acts 1944 to 1976 and this Act may be cited together as the Education Acts 1944 to 1979.

(3) This Act shall be construed as one with the Education Act 1944.

(4) This Act does not extend to Scotland or Northern Ireland.

European Assembly (Pay and Pensions) Act 1979

(1979 c. 50)

ARRANGEMENT OF SECTIONS

An Act to make provision for the payment of salaries and pensions, and the provision of allowances and facilities, to or in respect of Representatives to the Assembly of the European Communities. [26th July 1979]

General Note

This Act provides for the payment of salaries and pensions to Representatives to the European Assembly; it also makes provision for allowances and facilities.

S. 1 provides for salaries of Representatives, and sets out the basis on which they are to be calculated; s. 2 provides for allowances; s. 3 relates to grants to Representatives losing their seats; s. 4 empowers the Secretary of State to provide for pensions; s. 5 sets out the salary for the purpose of calculating pension benefits; s. 6 provides for payment of block transfer value into another pension scheme; s. 7 relates to expenses and receipts; s. 8 contains definitions; s. 9 gives the short title; the Act extends to Northern Ireland.

The Act received the Royal Assent on July 26, 1979, and came into force on that date.

Parliamentary debates

Hansard, H.C. Vol. 967, col. 1241; H.L. Vol. 401, cols. 1368, 1672, 2052.

Salaries of Representatives

1.—(1) A salary shall be payable to every Representative in accordance with this section.

(2) The yearly rate of the salary payable to a Representative for any period shall be—

(*a*) in the case of a period not within paragraph (*b*), the same as that of a Member's ordinary salary for that period;

(*b*) in the case of a period for which a salary is payable to him pursuant to any resolution or combination of resolutions of the House of Commons relating to the remuneration of Members, a rate equal to one-third of that of a Member's ordinary salary for that period.

(3) The salary payable under this section to a Representative shall be payable—

(*a*) in the case of a Representative elected at a general election of representatives to the Assembly, for the period beginning with the opening of the first session of the Assembly following his election and ending with—

(i) the day before the opening of the first session of the Assembly following the next such general election; or

(ii) if he ceases to be a Representative before that day, his last day as a Representative;

(*b*) in the case of a Representative elected otherwise than at such a general election, for the period beginning with the day of his election and ending as mentioned in paragraph (*a*).

(4) The salary payable under this section to a Representative shall be payable in sterling monthly in arrears, the payments being made into such account at a bank in the United Kingdom as he may nominate for the purpose.

(5) If the rate of a Member's ordinary salary for any period is changed retrospectively, the yearly rates given for that period by subsection (2) shall change accordingly.

Allowances

2.—(1) The Secretary of State may with the concurrence of the Treasury by order make provision with respect to the allowances and facilities which, in such circumstances and subject to fulfilment of such conditions as may be prescribed by the order, are to be available to Representatives in connection with the performance within the United Kingdom of their duties as Representatives.

(2) An order under this section may make different provision with respect to different circumstances.

(3) No order shall be made under this section unless a draft thereof has been laid before, and approved by resolution of, each House of Parliament.

Grants to Representatives losing their seats

3.—(1) Where a person who is a Representative immediately before the end of any five-year period stood for election to the Assembly (whether for the same or a different constituency in the United Kingdom) at the general election of representatives to the Assembly held in that period and was not elected, he shall be entitled to a grant equal to three months' salary under section 1 as a Representative at the rate applicable to him immediately before the end of that period.

(2) In this section "five-year period" means a period of five years for which representatives have been elected to the Assembly; but if any such period is extended or curtailed, the references in subsection (1) to the end of that period shall be construed accordingly.

Pensions

4.—(1) The Secretary of State may by order make provision with respect to the pensions which, subject to the fulfilment of such requirements and conditions as may be prescribed by the order, are to be or may be paid by the Treasury to or in respect of persons who have ceased to be Representatives.

(2) Any such provision shall include provision for the appointment of persons as managers to perform such functions in connection with the administration of provisions contained in orders under this section as may be conferred on them by any such order, and may include provision for the removal of managers so appointed.

(3) Without prejudice to the generality of subsection (1), an order under this section may

(*a*) make provision as to the periods of service as a Representative which are to be taken into account for pension purposes;

(*b*) provide for deductions to be made by the Treasury from Representatives' salaries at a prescribed rate by way of contributions towards the cost of providing the pensions payable by virtue of this section;

(*c*) provide for transfer values to be paid or received by the Treasury;

(*d*) make the opinion, satisfaction or approval of the managers appointed in pursuance of subsection (2) material for the purposes of any provision of the order;

(*e*) make different provision with respect to different classes of persons and different circumstances;

(*f*) include transitional and other supplemental provisions;

(*g*) be made so as to have effect from a date before the making of the order.

(4) An order under this section may provide for any statutory provision relating to any matter connected with the pensions payable to or in respect of Members to have effect with respect to or in connection with Representatives, with such additions, omissions, amendments or other modifications as may be specified in the order.

In this subsection " statutory provision " means any provision contained in an Act or in any instrument made under an Act (including an instrument passed or made after the passing of this Act).

(5) The Secretary of State shall from time to time lay before each House of Parliament a report on the operation of any provisions in force under this section.

(6) As regards such reports—

(*a*) the first shall be so laid not more than five years after the coming into force of the first order made under this section;

(*b*) each subsequent report shall be so laid not more than five years after the date by which the previous report was so laid; and

(*c*) each report shall cover the period since the previous report or, in the case of the first report, since the coming into force of the first order under this section.

(7) In Schedule 2 to the Pensions (Increase) Act 1971 (which specifies the pensions referred to in that Act as " official pensions "), after paragraph 3A there shall be inserted—

" *European Assembly*

3B. A pension payable under an order made under section 4 of the European Assembly (Pay and Pensions) Act 1979.".

Salary for purpose of calculating pension benefits

5.—(1) For the purpose of calculating the rate or amount of any pension payable by virtue of section 4 the yearly rate of the salary payable to a Representative under this Act for any period shall be regarded as being—

(*a*) in the case of a period not within section 1 (2) (*b*), the same as that of a Member's pensionable salary for that period;

(*b*) in the case of a period within section 1 (2) (*b*), a rate equal to one-third of that of a Member's pensionable salary for that period.

(2) If the rate of a Member's pensionable salary for any period is changed retrospectively, the yearly rates given for that period by subsection (1) shall change accordingly.

Provision for payment of block transfer value into another pension scheme

6.—(1) At any time after he has made an order under section 4 the Secretary of State may by order direct that, on a specified date, there shall be paid into or for the purposes of a specified overseas fund or scheme a specified sum representing the aggregate value on that date of the accrued pension rights of all Representatives and other persons under the relevant pension provisions, excluding (if the order so provides) those of persons of any specified class.

(2) Before making an order under this section the Secretary of State shall consult with—

(*a*) the managers appointed under the relevant pension provisions; and

(*b*) such persons representing the interests of Representatives and other persons having pension rights under the relevant pension provisions as he considers appropriate,

and shall not make such an order unless he has been informed by or on behalf of the persons administering the overseas fund or scheme in question that they are willing to accept the sum proposed to be specified in the order.

(3) For the purposes of this section the aggregate value on any date of the accrued pension rights mentioned in subsection (1) shall be taken to be such sum as for those purposes may be certified by the Government Actuary.

(4) In this section—

"overseas fund or scheme" means a fund or scheme which is established outside the United Kingdom or wholly or primarily administered outside the United Kingdom and which is approved by the Commissioners of Inland Revenue and the Occupational Pensions Board for the purposes of this section;

"the relevant pension provisions", in relation to an order under this section, means all such provisions contained in orders made under section 4 as are in force when the order is made.

Expenses and receipts

7.—(1) There shall be charged on and paid out of the Consolidated Fund—

(*a*) all salaries payable under section 1;

(*b*) any grant payable under section 3;

(*c*) all pensions and other sums payable by the Treasury under the provisions of any order made under section 4 or of any enactment or instrument so far as it has effect with respect to or in connection with Representatives by virtue of such an order; and

(*d*) any sum directed to be paid as mentioned in subsection (1) of section 6 by an order under that section.

(2) Any sums required by a secondary Class 1 contributor for the purpose of paying any secondary Class 1 contributions which are payable by him in respect of an earner in consequence of the earner's employment in the office of Representative for the constituency of Northern Ireland shall be paid out of the Consolidated Fund of the United Kingdom.

Expressions used in this subsection and Part I of the Social Security (Northern Ireland) Act 1975 have the same meanings in this subsection as in that Part.

(3) There shall be paid out of money provided by Parliament—

(*a*) any expenses incurred by the Secretary of State in providing allowances or facilities in pursuance of any order made under section 2;

(*b*) any administrative expenses incurred by a government department in consequence of this Act; and

(*c*) any increase attributable to this Act in the sums payable out of money so provided under any other Act.

(4) Any sums received by a government department in consequence of this Act shall be paid into the Consolidated Fund.

Interpretation and orders

8.—(1) In this Act—

"the Assembly" means the Assembly of the European Communities;

"constituency" means an Assembly constituency;

"Member" means a Member of the House of Commons;

"a Member's ordinary salary" and "a Member's pensionable salary" have the meaning given by section 3 (6) of the Parliamentary and other Pensions Act 1972;

"pension" includes a gratuity, and "pension rights" shall be construed accordingly;

"Representative" means a representative to the Assembly elected for a constituency in the United Kingdom.

(2) Every order under this Act shall be made by statutory instrument, and, unless made under section 2, shall be subject to annulment in pursuance of a resolution of either House of Parliament.

Short title and extent

9.—(1) This Act may be cited as the European Assembly (Pay and Pensions) Act 1979.

(2) This Act extends to Northern Ireland.

Appropriation (No. 2) Act 1979

(1979 c. 51)

An Act to apply a sum out of the Consolidated Fund to the service of the year ending on 31st March 1980, to appropriate the supplies granted in this Session of Parliament, and to repeal certain Consolidated Fund and Appropriation Acts.

[27th July 1979]

General Note

This Act received the Royal Assent on July 27, 1979.

The Schedules to the Act have not been reproduced here as they are of little or no legal interest.

Grant Out of the Consolidated Fund

Issue out of the Consolidated Fund for the year ending 31st March 1980

1. The Treasury may issue out of the Consolidated Fund of the United Kingdom and apply towards making good the supply granted to Her Majesty for the service of the year ending on 31st March 1980 the sum of £31,112,689,100.

Appropriation of Grant

Appropriation of sums voted for supply services

2. All sums granted by this Act (being sums further to those granted by the Consolidated Fund (No. 2) Act 1978 and appropriated for various services and purposes by the Appropriation Act 1979) out of the said Consolidated Fund towards making good the supply granted to Her Majesty amounting, in the aggregate, to the sum of £31,112,689,100 are appropriated, and shall be deemed to have been appropriated as from the date of the passing of this Act for the services and purposes expressed in Schedule (A) annexed hereto.

The abstract of Schedule (A) and Schedule annexed hereto, with the notes (if any) to such schedules, shall be deemed to be part of this Act in the same manner as if they had been contained in the body thereof.

In addition to the said sums granted out of the Consolidated Fund, there may be applied out of any money directed, under section 2 of the Public Accounts and Charges Act 1891, to be applied as appropriations in aid of the grants for the services and purposes specified in Schedule (A) annexed hereto the sums respectively set forth in the last column of the said schedule.

Repeals

3. The enactments mentioned in Schedule (B) annexed to this Act are hereby repealed.

Short title

4. This Act may be cited as the Appropriation (No. 2) Act 1979.

Southern Rhodesia Act 1979

(1979 c. 52)

An Act to provide for the grant of a constitution for Zimbabwe to come into effect on the attainment by Southern Rhodesia, under any Act hereafter passed for that purpose, of fully responsible status as a Republic under the name of Zimbabwe, and to make other provision with respect to Southern Rhodesia.

[14th November 1979]

General Note

This Act provides for the grant of a constitution for Zimbabwe and related matters.

S. 1 empowers the Crown to provide a constitution for Zimbabwe; s. 2 gives power to bring particular provisions of the new constitution into force before the appointed day; s. 3 contains miscellaneous provisions with respect to Southern Rhodesia; s. 4 contains the short title and extent.

The Act received the Royal Assent on November 14, 1979, and came into force on that date.

Parliamentary debates

Hansard, H.C. Vol. 973, cols. 663, 907, 1033; H.L. Vol. 402, col. 1095.

Power to provide constitution for Zimbabwe

1.—(1) Her Majesty may by Order in Council provide a constitution for Zimbabwe to come into effect on the day (in this Act referred to as " the appointed day ") on which, in accordance with such provision in that behalf as may after the passing of this Act be made by Act of Parliament, Southern Rhodesia becomes independent as a Republic under the name of Zimbabwe.

(2) Her Majesty may by Order in Council revoke the Constitution of Southern Rhodesia 1961, and may make such transitional provision as appears to Her Majesty to be necessary or expedient in connection with the coming into effect of the new constitution or the revocation of the said Constitution of 1961.

(3) Any Order in Council under this section shall be laid before Parliament after being made.

(4) Subsection (1) is without prejudice to any power conferred on Her Majesty by section 2.

Power to bring particular provisions of new constitution into force before appointed day

2.—(1) For the purpose of enabling the new constitution to function as from the appointed day and, in particular, of enabling elections for the purposes thereof to be held before that day, Her Majesty may by Order in Council make such provision as appears to Her to be necessary or expedient, including provision for bringing particular provisions of that constitution into force, with or without modifications, before that day.

(2) Different provisions of the new constitution may be brought into force under this section at different times before the appointed day; but any modifications to which any provisions of that constitution are by virtue of this section subject immediately before the appointed day shall cease to have effect on that day.

(3) An Order in Council under this section shall be laid before Parliament after being made and shall expire at the end of the period of twenty-eight days beginning with the day on which it was made unless during that period it is approved by resolution of each House of Parliament.

The expiration of an Order in pursuance of this subsection shall not affect the operation of the Order as respects things previously done or omitted to be done or the power to make a new Order; and in calculating the period aforesaid no account shall be taken of any time during which Parliament is dissolved or prorogued or during which both Houses are adjourned for more than four days.

Other powers with respect to Southern Rhodesia

3.—(1) Her Majesty may by Order in Council—

(*a*) make provision for and in connection with the government of Southern Rhodesia in the period up to the appointed day;

(*b*) make such provision in relation to Southern Rhodesia, or persons or things in any way belonging to or connected with Southern Rhodesia, as appears to Her to be necessary or expedient—

(i) in consequence of any unconstitutional action taken therein; or

(ii) in connection with the repeal, revocation, expiration or lapse of any statutory provision relating to sanctions.

(2) In subsection (1) "statutory provision relating to sanctions" means—

(*a*) any Order in Council made under section 2 of the Southern Rhodesia Act 1965; and

(*b*) any statutory provision (wherever in force) implementing any resolution of the Security Council of the United Nations providing for the imposition of economic or other sanctions or other measures directed against Southern Rhodesia or against any persons at any time purporting to exercise authority therein.

(3) Without prejudice to the generality of subsection (1), an Order in Council thereunder may make provision—

(*a*) for conferring power to make laws for the peace, order and good government of Southern Rhodesia, including laws having extra-territorial operation;

(*b*) for suspending or modifying the provisions of the Constitution of Southern Rhodesia 1961;

(*c*) for suspending or modifying the operation of any enactment or instrument in relation to Southern Rhodesia or persons or things in any way belonging to or connected with Southern Rhodesia;

and any provision made by or under such an Order may apply to things done or omitted outside as well as within the United Kingdom or other country or territory to which the Order extends.

(4) Subject to subsection (5), the following Orders in Council, namely—

(*a*) the Southern Rhodesia Constitution Order 1965 and any Order in Council made thereunder;

(*b*) the Southern Rhodesia (British Nationality Act 1948) Order 1965;

(*c*) the Southern Rhodesia (Matrimonial Jurisdiction) Order 1970; and

(*d*) the Southern Rhodesia (Immunity for Persons attending Meetings and Consultations) (No. 2) Order 1979,

shall continue in force notwithstanding the expiration of section 2 of the Southern Rhodesia Act 1965, but shall have effect after the expiration of that section with such modifications, if any, as Her Majesty may from time to time by Order in Council prescribe.

(5) Her Majesty may by Order in Council revoke any Order saved by subsection (4).

(6) Section 2 (3) shall apply to any Order in Council made under this section.

Citation etc.

4.—(1) This Act may be cited as the Southern Rhodesia Act 1979.

(2) In this Act—

"the appointed day" has the meaning given by section 1 (1);

"modifications" includes additions, omissions and alterations, and related expressions shall be construed accordingly;

"the new constitution" means the constitution provided by Order in Council under section 1 (1);

"statutory provision" means a provision contained in an Act or in subordinate legislation within the meaning of the Interpretation Act 1978.

(3) An Order in Council under any provision of this Act may make or authorise the making of such incidental, supplementary and consequential provisions as appear to Her Majesty to be expedient for the purposes of the Order.

(4) Any administrative expenses incurred by the Secretary of State in consequence of the provisions of this Act shall be paid out of money provided by Parliament.

(5) This Act extends to Southern Rhodesia, the Channel Islands, the Isle of Man and any colony, and (to the extent of Her Majesty's jurisdiction therein) to any foreign country or territory in which for the time being Her Majesty has jurisdiction.

Charging Orders Act 1979 *

(1979 c. 53)

Arrangement of Sections

An Act to make provision for imposing charges to secure payment of money due, or to become due, under judgments or orders of court; to provide for restraining and prohibiting dealings with, and the making of payments in respect of, certan securities; and for connected purposes. [6th December 1979]

General Note

This Act is based on the recommendations contained in the Law Commission's Report on Charging Orders (1976 Law Com. No. 74). This was in response to a Joint Memorandum prepared by the Law Reform Committees of the Bar Council and Law Society.

The main purpose of the Act is to cure the defects in s. 35 of the Administration of Justice Act 1956. These were:

1. A charging order on land did not operate by itself to give the judgment creditor any preference over other creditors on the bankruptcy or winding up of the debtor. He had to take another purely formal step. S. 4 of this Act remedies this defect.

2. A beneficial interest in land held on trust for sale could not be the subject matter of a charging order as it was not an interest in land but an interest in the proceeds of sale. S. 2 of this Act has altered the law in this respect.

3. It was uncertain whether a judgment debtor, having satisfied the judgment could obtain a court order formally discharging his land. An affirmative answer has been given by s. 3 (5) of this Act.

Changes have also been made in the law relating to charging orders on securities.

Commencement

The Act was passed on December 6, 1979, and will come into force on such day as the Lord Chancellor may appoint by order made by statutory instrument.

Extent

This Act does not extend to Scotland or Northern Ireland.

Parliamentary debates

Hansard, H.L. Vol. 401, cols. 10–17, 1507–1508, 1631–1632, 2052; H.C. Vol. 972, cols. 770–779; Vol. 974, col. 345; H.L. Vol. 403, col. 336.

* Annotations by Angela Sydenham, M.A., LL.B., Solicitor.

Charging orders

Charging orders

1.—(1) Where, under a judgment or order of the High Court or a county court, a person (the "debtor") is required to pay a sum of money to another person (the "creditor") then, for the purpose of enforcing that judgment or order, the appropriate court may make an order in accordance with the provisions of this Act imposing on any such property of the debtor as may be specified in the order a charge for securing the payment of any money due or to become due under the judgment or order.

(2) The appropriate court is—

(*a*) in a case where the property to be charged is a fund in court, the court in which that fund is lodged;

(*b*) in a case where paragraph (*a*) above does not apply and the order to be enforced is a maintenance order of the High Court, the High Court or a county court;

(*c*) in a case where neither paragraph (*a*) nor paragraph (*b*) above applies and the judgment or order to be enforced is a judgment or order of the High Court for a sum exceeding £2,000, the High Court; and

(*d*) in any other case, a county court.

In this section "maintenance order" has the same meaning as in section 2 (*a*) of the Attachment of Earnings Act 1971.

(3) An order under subsection (1) above is referred to in this Act as a "charging order".

(4) Where a person applies to the High Court for a charging order to enforce more than one judgment or order, that court shall be the appropriate court in relation to the application if it would be the appropriate court, apart from this subsection, on an application relating to one or more of the judgments or orders concerned.

(5) In deciding whether to make a charging order the court shall consider all the circumstances of the case and, in particular, any evidence before it as to—

(*a*) the personal circumstances of the debtor, and

(*b*) whether any other creditor of the debtor would be likely to be unduly prejudiced by the making of the order.

Definition

"Judgment or order": s. 6 (2).

General Note

This section provides that subject to certain exceptions, a charging order may be granted by the High Court in respect of a High Court judgment debt of over £2,000 and by the county court in other cases.

Subs. (1) establishes the jurisdiction of the court to make charging orders for the purpose of enforcing money judgments or orders. It replaces s. 35 (1) of the Administration of Justice Act 1956; s. 141 (1) of the County Courts Act 1959; R.S.C., Ord. 52, r. 2; C.C.R., Ord. 25, r. 6A.

A judgment creditor thus becomes a secured creditor.

Subs. (2). *Fund* in court: This includes money and investments. Fund was substituted for the word money as originally drafted so as to avoid any ambiguities in construction. (See *Perrin* v. *Morgan* [1943] A.C. 399.)

The aim of the subsection is to transfer most of the jurisdiction from the High Court to the county court. This encourages a debtor to attend the hearing which means that the court is better able to exercise its discretion: see subs. (5). Moreover the county court is more accustomed to exercise a discretion of this kind than the High Court.

The county court now has power to grant a charging order in respect of a

High Court judgment debt not exceeding £2,000. This reverses the unreported decision in *London Borough of Merton* v. *Sammon* (Croydon County Ct., October 1972).

"£2,000." This figure will be kept in line with the limit imposed from time to time on the county court's jurisdiction in contract and tort cases: s. 7.

Which county court?

(a) An application for a charging order to enforce a county court judgment debt is made by interlocutory application in the proceedings in which the judgment is obtained and will be heard by the same court as gives the judgment.

(b) An application for a charging order to enforce in the county court a judgment of the High Court will be covered by a rule to be made by the County Court Rule Committee. This will probably be the court for the district in which the defendant or one of the defendants resides or carries on business.

(c) Proceedings for the *enforcement* of a charging order should be commenced in the court in which the order itself was made.

In the Attachment of Earnings Act 1971, s. 2 (*a*), "maintenance order" means order specified in Sched. 1 to that Act and includes such an order which has been discharged if any arrears are recoverable thereunder.

Sched. 1 specifies 10 such orders to which the Act applies.

Subs. (5). As a charging order by itself will now make a judgment creditor a secured creditor the Law Commission was anxious that charging orders should not be automatic. The court is therefore given a wide discretion in deciding whether or not to grant a charging order. This should stop charging orders being made which are really unfair to the debtor. The court should also take into account any other creditors who might be unfairly prejudiced. This gives legislative effect to the point made in *Rainbow* v. *Moorgate Properties Ltd.* [1975] 2 All E.R. 821.

"any evidence before it." This emphasises the importance of the debtor being present in person. (See note to subs. (2).) The court is not required to institute inquiries of its own.

Property which may be charged

2.—(1) Subject to subsection (3) below, a charge may be imposed by a charging order only on—

(*a*) any interest held by the debtor beneficially—

(i) in any asset of a kind mentioned in subsection (2) below, or

(ii) under any trust; or

(*b*) any interest held by a person as trustee of a trust ("the trust"), if the interest is in such an asset or is an interest under another trust and—

(i) the judgment or order in respect of which a charge is to be imposed was made against that person as trustee of the trust, or

(ii) the whole beneficial interest under the trust is held by the debtor unencumbered and for his own benefit, or

(iii) in a case where there are two or more debtors all of whom are liable to the creditor for the same debt, they together hold the whole beneficial interest under the trust unencumbered and for their own benefit.

(2) The assets referred to in subsection (1) above are—

(*a*) land,

(*b*) securities of any of the following kinds—

(i) government stock,

(ii) stock of any body (other than a building society) incorporated within England and Wales,

(iii) stock of any body incorporated outside England and Wales or of any state or territory outside the United Kingdom, being stock registered in a register kept at any place within England and Wales,

(iv) units of any unit trust in respect of which a register of the unit holders is kept at any place within England and Wales, or

(c) funds in court.

(3) In any case where a charge is imposed by a charging order on any interest in an asset of a kind mentioned in paragraph (b) or (c) of subsection (2) above, the court making the order may provide for the charge to extend to any interest or dividend payable in respect of the asset.

DEFINITIONS

" charging orders ": s. 6 (1).
" debtor ": s. 1 (1).
" creditor ": s. 1 (1).
" building society ": s. 6 (1).
" stock ": s. 6 (1).
" government stock ": s. 6 (1).
" unit trust ": s. 6 (1).

GENERAL NOTE

This section sets out the property capable of being charged by a charging order. The range of chargeable interests is the same whether the interest to be charged is held by the debtor beneficially or is held by the trustees in circumstances set out in s. 2 (1) (b) (i) (ii) (iii). In the first case the creditor can proceed against the debtor; in the second against the trustees. A charging order takes effect as an equitable charge.

Subs. (1) (a) (i). A charge may be imposed on the debtor's beneficial interest whether legal or absolute or not in any of the assets mentioned in s. 2 (2), or on his equitable interest in assets of any kind to which he is entitled under a trust.

The difficulty about equitable charges is that a purchaser without notice of such charges will take free of them. The assets mentioned in subs. (2) are only those in relation to which a creditor chargee can ensure by registration or otherwise that a purchaser from the debtor will have notice of the charge, *e.g.* in the case of legal estates in land, registration as a writ or order affecting land under s. 6 L.C.A. 1972, where the land is unregistered, or protection by notice on the register s. 49, L.R.A. 1925, as amended by s. 3 (3), Charging Orders Act 1979, where the land is registered.

A charge, necessarily equitable, on the debtor's beneficial interest under a trust, poses two main problems. First, such a charge cannot be registered under the Land Charges Act 1925. S. 35 (3) of the Administration of Justice Act 1956 stipulates that a charging order cannot be made unless the charge would be capable of registration in the register of land charges or at the Land Registry. Thus as it was incapable of such registration a beneficial interest under a trust could not be the subject matter of a charging order. See Cross L.J. in *Irani Finance Ltd.* v. *Singh* [1971] Ch. 59 (C.A.). Secondly, following the *Irani* case where the trust was a trust for sale the doctrine of conversion meant that the beneficiary had not an interest in land but in the proceeds of sale. S. 35 of the Administration of Justice Act 1956 provided that a charging order may only be made in respect of " any such *land* or interest in *land* of the debtor as may be specified in the order."

The effect of s. 2 (1) (a) (ii) is that beneficial interests under strict settlements, bare trusts and trusts for sale can now be charged. It does not matter what the trust assets are. The creditor charge should protect his interest by giving notice to the trustees. This will preserve his priority against a purchaser of the debtor's equitable interest. See s. 137, L.P.A. 1925. On the sale of the legal estate the creditor's interest will be overreached and attach to the purchase money. The danger here is where the trustees are the same as the judgment debtors.

The consequences of such an order are not only that a receiver can be appointed to collect the debtor's share of the income but that an application can be made to the court for an order for the sale of the beneficial interest charged. These remedies will only be of real practical use where the property is producing income or where a purchaser would obtain vacant possession of the property. However, even if these conditions do not apply debtors might be persuaded that a better price would be obtained if a sale of the legal estate were effected. Further, under s. 30, L.P.A. 1925, the chargee creditor could apply to the court as "a person interested" for an order directing the trustees to sell the trust property. The creditor would then be able to levy equitable execution on the debtor's share of the cash proceeds. It seems unlikely, however, that a sale would be ordered at the instigation of the chargee if it would defeat the purpose of the trust: *Jones* v. *Challenger* [1961] 1 Q.B. 176. A judgment creditor who has merely obtained an order appointing a receiver of a debtor's interest, as distinct from a charging order, has previously not been considered to be within the ambit of s. 30, L.P.A. 1925 (*Stevens* v. *Hutchinson* [1953] Ch. 299), but for a recent decision to the contrary, see *Levermore* v. *Levermore* [1979] 1 W.L.R. 1277.

Subs. (2) (*b*) (i). This is the straightforward case where the debt had been incurred by the trustees for the purposes of the trust, *i.e.* not by the trustees in their personal capacity.

Subs. (2) (*b*) (ii). In this case under the doctrine of *Saunders* v. *Vautier* (1841) 4 Beav. 115, affd. Cr. & Ph. 240, the debtor is entitled to call for the legal estate. He should not therefore be able to escape by technical means, having the charge placed on the legal estate. This is only appropriate where there are no third party rights which would be prejudiced by giving the creditor chargee priority.

Subs. (2) (*b*) (iii). The background to this paragraph can be found in *Irani Finance* v. *Singh* [1971] Ch. 59 and *National Westminster Bank Ltd.* v. *Allen* [1971] 2 Q.B. 718. The essential requirements for the operation of this section are (1) the beneficiaries under the trust must be liable to the creditor for the same debt, *i.e.* there must be unity of the debt; (2) together the beneficiaries are entitled to the whole beneficial interest free of any third party's equitable rights.

Provided these requirements are fulfilled a charge can be imposed on the trustees legal estate or lesser interest even where the trustees are not the same persons as the beneficiaries.

This provision applies where the debtor's interest is held under a sub-trust as well as where it is under a direct trust of assets within subs. (2).

Provisions supplementing sections 1 and 2

3.—(1) A charging order may be made either absolutely or subject to conditions as to notifying the debtor or as to the time when the charge is to become enforceable, or as to other matters.

(2) The Land Charges Act 1972 and the Land Registration Act 1925 shall apply in relation to charging orders as they apply in relation to other orders or writs issued or made for the purpose of enforcing judgments.

(3) In section 49 of the Land Registration Act 1925 (protection of certain interests by notice) there is inserted at the end of subsection (1) the following paragraph—

"(*g*) charging orders (within the meaning of the Charging Orders Act 1979) which in the case of unregistered land may be protected by registration under the Land Charges Act 1972 and which, notwithstanding section 59 of this Act, it may be deemed expedient to protect by notice instead of by caution.".

(4) Subject to the provisions of this Act, a charge imposed by a charging order shall have the like effect and shall be enforceable in the same courts and in the same manner as an equitable charge created by the debtor by writing under his hand.

(5) The court by which a charging order was made may at any time, on the application of the debtor or of any person interested in any property to which the order relates, make an order discharging or varying the charging order.

(6) Where a charging order has been protected by an entry registered under the Land Charges Act 1972 or the Land Registration Act 1925, an order under subsection (5) above discharging the charging order may direct that the entry be cancelled.

(7) The Lord Chancellor may by order made by statutory instrument amend section 2 (2) of this Act by adding to, or removing from, the kinds of asset for the time being referred to there, any asset of a kind which in his opinion ought to be so added or removed.

(8) Any order under subsection (7) above shall be subject to annulment in pursuance of a resolution of either House of Parliament.

DEFINITIONS

"charging order": s. 6 (1).
"debtor": s. 1 (1).

GENERAL NOTE

S. 3 contains supplementary provisions relating to the effect of a charging order, its discharge or variation and the manner in which it may be protected.

Subss. (1) (2) and (3) reproduce existing law in relation to charging orders on land.

The provisions of subss. (1) and (3) also cover orders affecting interests in securities, in money in court or under trusts.

Subs. (3). S. 59, L.R.A. 1925, provides that a charging order should be protected by a caution. A caution is, however, unsatisfactory as it is subject to the warning off procedure. S. 49, L.R.A. 1925, provides several cases where even if the registered proprietor does not agree to the entry of a notice the applicant can obtain an order of the court authorising the registration of such notice. This has now been extended to charging orders, the consent of the proprietor not being a relevant consideration.

Subs. (5) generalises the existing power to discharge or vary charging orders on securities contained in R.S.C., Ord. 50, r. 7, and C.C.R., Ord. 25, r. 6A (6).

Subs. (6). An order under subs. (4) should contain a direction that any entry on the register in respect of the original charging order should be removed.

Subss. (7) (8) enable the list of assets in s. 2 (2) to be reviewed and kept up to date. The power is exercisable by the Lord Chancellor and can be annulled by Parliament.

Completion of execution

4. In section 40 of the Bankruptcy Act 1914 and in section 325 of the Companies Act 1948 (which restrict the rights of creditors under execution or attachment) there is substituted, in each case for subsection (2), the following subsection:—

"(2) For the purposes of this Act—

(*a*) an execution against goods is completed by seizure and sale or by the making of a charging order under section 1 of the Charging Orders Act 1979;

(*b*) an attachment of a debt is completed by the receipt of the debt; and

(*c*) an execution against land is completed by seizure, by the appointment of a receiver, or by the making of a charging order under the said section 1."

GENERAL NOTE

This section reverses the effect of *Re Overseas Aviation Engineering* (*G.B.*) *Ltd.* [1963] 1 Ch. 24. A charging order not only amounts to execution but the making of such an order by itself amounts to the completion of an execution for the purposes of s. 40 of the Bankruptcy Act 1914 and s. 325 of the Companies Act 1948.

A judgment creditor therefore obtains priority as a secured creditor simply by obtaining a charging order and need take no further steps. Should the debtor subsequently go bankrupt (or be wound up) the creditor chargee will not lose the benefit of his charge.

Note: If on the application for a charging order it appears that the bankruptcy or winding up of the debtor is imminent the court may in its discretion decline to make the order if it would thereby unfairly prejudice other unsecured creditors. s. 1 (5) (*b*).

"Goods" include securities.

Stop orders and notices

Stop orders and notices

5.—(1) In this section—

"stop order" means an order of the court prohibiting the taking, in respect of any of the securities specified in the order, of any of the steps mentioned in subsection (5) below;

"stop notice" means a notice requiring any person or body on whom it is duly served to refrain from taking, in respect of any of the securities specified in the notice, any of those steps without first notifying the person by whom, or on whose behalf, the notice was served; and

"prescribed securities" means securities (including funds in court) of a kind prescribed by rules of court made under this section.

(2) The power to make rules of court under section 99 of the Supreme Court of Judicature (Consolidation) Act 1925 shall include power by any such rules to make provision—

(*a*) for the court to make a stop order on the application of any person claiming to be entitled to an interest in prescribed securities;

(*b*) for the service of a stop notice by any person claiming to be entitled to an interest in prescribed securities.

(3) The power to make rules of court under section 102 of the County Courts Act 1959 shall include power by any such rules to make provision for the service of a stop notice by any person entitled to an interest in any securities by virtue of a charging order made by a county court.

(4) Rules of court made by virtue of subsection (2) or (3) above shall prescribe the person or body on whom a copy of any stop order or a stop notice is to be served.

(5) The steps mentioned in subsection (1) above are—

(*a*) the registration of any transfer of the securities;

(*b*) in the case of funds in court, the transfer, sale, delivery out, payment or other dealing with the funds, or of the income thereon;

(*c*) the making of any payment by way of dividend, interest or otherwise in respect of the securities; and

(*d*) in the case of units of a unit trust, any acquisition of or other dealing with the units by any person or body exercising functions under the trust.

(6) Any rules of court made by virtue of this section may include such incidental, supplemental and consequential provisions as the authority making them consider necessary or expedient, and may make different provision in relation to different cases or classes of case.

DEFINITIONS

"dividend": s. 6 (1).

"unit trust": s. 6 (1).

GENERAL NOTE

This section enlarges the powers of the Rule Committees to make rules of court to prevent dealings, without notice to the creditor, in securities which are subject to a charging order.

Subs. (1) "*prescribed securities.*" Statutory authority is now given to the Supreme Court Rule Committee to amend and revise the types of securities to which stop orders and stop notices may apply.

Subs. (3). A creditor with a charging order made by a county court can now serve a stop notice. This procedure was formerly only available in the High Court. A stop notice ensures that a creditor has warning of any disposition of the securities in question. The charging order is sufficient in itself to establish the interest of the chargee.

High Court procedure in relation to stop notices founded on charging orders will probably be different from those applying in other cases (where the filing of affidavit evidence is necessary).

Subs. (6). Power is given by this subsection to make different provision for different assets.

Supplemental

Interpretation

6.—(1) In this Act—

" building society " has the same meaning as in the Building Societies Act 1962;

" charging order " means an order made under section 1 (1) of this Act;

" debtor " and " creditor " have the meanings given by section 1 (1) of this Act;

" dividend " includes any distribution in respect of any unit of a unit trust;

" government stock " means any stock issued by Her Majesty's government in the United Kingdom or any funds of, or annuity granted by, that government;

" stock " includes shares, debentures and any securities of the body concerned, whether or not constituting a charge on the assets of that body;

" unit trust " means any trust established for the purpose, or having the effect, of providing, for persons having funds available for investment, facilities for the participation by them, as beneficiaries under the trust, in any profits or income arising from the acquisition, holding, management or disposal of any property whatsoever.

(2) For the purposes of section 1 of this Act references to a judgment or order of the High Court or a county court shall be taken to include references to a judgment, order, decree or award (however called) of any court or arbitrator (including any foreign court or arbitrator) which is or has become enforceable (whether wholly or to a limited extent) as if it were a judgment or order of the High Court or a county court.

(3) References in section 2 of this Act to any securities include references to any such securities standing in the name of the Accountant General.

General Note

This is the interpretation section.

Subs. (2). By virtue of the Judgments Extension Act 1868 Orders in Council under the Administration of Justice Act 1920, the Foreign Judgments (Reciprocal Enforcement) Act 1933 and the Arbitration Act 1950 certain judgments and orders are enforceable as if they were High Court or county court judgments. This reproduces the existing law.

Subs. (3). This also reproduces existing law.

Consequential amendment, repeals and transitional provisions

7.—(1) In section 192 of the County Courts Act 1959 (power to raise limits of jurisdiction) subsection (2) (as substituted by section 10 of the Administration of Justice Act 1969) is amended by inserting, at the end, the following paragraph—

" (*e*) section 1 (2) (*c*) of the Charging Orders Act 1979 ".

(2) Section 35 of the Administration of Justice Act 1956 and section 141 of the County Courts Act 1959 (which relate to the powers of courts

to make charging orders) are hereby repealed; and in section 36 (2) and (3) of the Act of 1956 and section 142 (2) and (3) of the Act of 1959 for the words " the last preceding section " (in section 36) and " the last foregoing section " (in section 142) there are substituted, in each case, the words " section 1 of the Charging Orders Act 1979 ".

(3) Any order made or notice given under any enactment repealed by this Act or under any rules of court revoked by rules of court made under this Act (the " new rules ") shall, if still in force when the provisions of this Act or, as the case may be, the new rules come into force, continue to have effect as if made under this Act or, as the case may be, under the new rules.

(4) Any notice of such an order registered in the register maintained under the Land Registration Act 1925 which would have been registrable by virtue of the paragraph inserted in section 49 (1) of that Act by section 3 (3) of this Act, if section 3 (3) had been in force when the notice was registered, shall have effect as if registered by virtue of that paragraph.

General Note

This section contains transitional provisions, makes consequential amendments and repeals other enactments.

Subs. (1). This enables the limit of the county court's jurisdiction to be raised as in contract and tort cases.

Subs. (2) repeals the existing statutory provisions relating to charging orders on land. The law relating to orders affecting securities is contained in the rules of court.

Subs. (3) preserves the effect of existing charging orders, stop orders and stop notices.

Subs. (4) gives retrospective effect to notices of charging orders registered before the Act in the register at the Land Registry.

Short title, commencement and extent

8.—(1) This Act may be cited as the Charging Orders Act 1979.

(2) This Act comes into force on such day as the Lord Chancellor may appoint by order made by statutory instrument.

(3) This Act does not extend to Scotland or Northern Ireland.

General Note

This section gives the title, commencement and extent of the Act.

Subs. (2). This provides time for the Rules of the Supreme Court and the County Court Rules to be reviewed in the light of the Act, so that the Act and new rules may come into force simultaneously.

Sale of Goods Act 1979*

(1979 c. 54)

ARRANGEMENT OF SECTIONS

PART I

CONTRACTS TO WHICH ACT APPLIES

PART II

FORMATION OF THE CONTRACT

Contract of sale

Formalities of contract

Subject matter of contract

The price

Conditions and warranties

Sale by sample

PART III

EFFECTS OF THE CONTRACT

Transfer of property as between seller and buyer

Transfer of title

PART IV

PERFORMANCE OF THE CONTRACT

* Annotations by W. H. Thomas, Solicitor.

An Act to consolidate the law relating to the sale of goods.

[6th December 1979]

General Note

This Act consolidates all the amendments made to the Sale of Goods Act 1893 throughout its long existence but, apart from minor insertions to take account of the alterations made by the Unfair Contract Terms Act 1977, it makes no new law. The whole of the 1893 Act is repealed with the exception of s. 26 (which deals with the effect on goods of writs of execution). It is not clear why this section was not included in the Act for tidiness if for no other reason; it might have meant that section numbering would have caused difficulties as the Act retains the familiar sections with which generations of law students have wrestled. It is also not certain why this consolidation took place now since the Law Commissions are at work following a reference made in January 1979 by the Lord Chancellor. This reference, which followed a Private Member's Bill introduced to re-define "merchantable quality" is in three parts and requires the Law Commissions to consider:

(a) whether the undertakings as to the quality and fitness of goods implied under the law relating to the sale of goods, hire-purchase and other contracts for the supply of goods require amendment;

(b) the circumstances in which a person, to whom goods are supplied under a contract of sale, hire-purchase or other contract for the supply of goods, is entitled, where there has been a breach by the supplier of a term implied by statute to:

(i) reject the goods and treat the contract as repudiated;

(ii) claim against the supplier a diminution in or extinction of the price;

(iii) claim damages against the supplier;

(c) the circumstances in which, by reason of the 1893 Act, a buyer loses the right to reject the goods.

In view of the matters to be considered as a result of this reference, it might have been thought better to leave the Act as it was until a more substantial amendment took place following the Report of the Law Commissions.

Because of the changes in the law made by the Supply of Goods (Implied Terms) Act 1973 (and, indeed, by the Misrepresentation Act 1967) transitional provisions are made throughout the Act to cover contracts made before the date of commencement of the Act (January 1, 1980) but after the dates on which the two Acts came into force. These provisions are contained in Sched. 1; other consequential amendments are set forth in Sched. 2.

Commencement and Extent

The Act came into force on January 1, 1980; it provides for modifications to apply to contracts made after April 22, 1967, and May 18, 1973. The Act extends to Scotland and to Northern Ireland and where appropriate reference is made to the law in those countries.

Abbreviations

1893 — Sale of Goods Act 1893.
1973 — Supply of Goods (Implied Terms) Act 1973.
1974 — Consumer Credit Act 1974.
1977 — Unfair Contract Terms Act 1977.

Parliamentary Debates

For parliamentary debates and committee stages, see H.L. Vol. 400, col. 1112; Vol. 402, col. 991; H.C. Vol. 974, col. 1445.

Table of Derivations

Factors Act 1889

1889	1979
s. 1 (1)	s. 26

Factors (Scotland) Act 1890

1890	1979
s. 1	s. 26

Sale of Goods Act 1893

1893	1979
s. 1 (1)	s. 2 (1) (2)
(2)	2 (3)
(3)	2 (4) (5)
(4)	2 (6)
2	3
3	4
5	5
6	6
7	7
8 (1)	8 (1)
(2)	8 (2) (3)
9	9
10 (1)	10 (1) (2)
(2)	10 (3)
11 (1)	11 (1)
(*a*)	11 (2)
(*b*)	11 (3)
(*c*)	11 (4)
(2)	11 (1) (5)
(3)	11 (6)
12	Sch. 1, para. 3
(1) (*a*)	s. 12 (1)
(*b*)	12 (2)
(2)	12 (3)
(*a*)	12 (4)
(*b*)	12 (5)
13 (1)	13 (1) (2)
(2)	13 (3)
14	Sch. 1, paras. 5, 6
(1)	s. 14 (1)
(2)	14 (2)
(3)	14 (3)
(4)	14 (4)
(5)	14 (5)
15	Sch. 1, para. 7
(1)	s. 15 (1)
(2)	15 (2)
s. 16	s. 16
17	17
18	18
19	19
20	20 (1)
proviso 1	20 (2)
proviso 2	20 (3)
21	21
22 (1)	22 (1)
(3)	22 (2)
23	23
25 (1)	24
(2)	25 (1) (2)
(3)	26
27	27
28	28
29 (1)	29 (1) (2)
(2)	29 (3)
(3)	29 (4)
(4)	29 (5)
(5)	29 (6)
30 (1)	30 (1)
(2)	30 (2) (3)
(3)	30 (4)
(4)	30 (5)
31	31
32	32
33	33
34	34
35	35
36	36
37	37
38	38
39	39
40	40
41	41
42	42
43	43
44	44
s. 45	s. 54
46 (1)	46 (1)–(3)
(2)	46 (4)
47	47
48	48
49	49
50	50
51	51
52	52
53	53
54	54
55	Sch. 1, paras. 11, 12
(1)	s. 55 (1)
(2)	55 (2)
55A	Sch. 1, para. 13 (1) (3)
56	s. 59
57	60
58	57
59	58
61	62
(6)	Sch. 1, paras. 11, 13 (1) (3)
62 (1)	ss. 39 (2), 41 (2), 61 (1) (2), Sch. 1, paras. 11, 13 (1) (3)
(1A)	ss. 14 (6), 15 (3), Sch. 1, para. 5
(2)	s. 61 (3)
(3)	61 (4)
(4)	61 (5)
63	1 (1)

Statute Law Revision Act 1908

1908	1979
s. 1, proviso	s. 1 (1)

Misrepresentation Act 1967

1967	1979
s. 4 (2)	s. 35 (1)
5	1 (2), Sch. 1, paras. 2, 10
12 (1)	Sch. 1, para. 8

Criminal Law Act 1967

1967	1979
s. 12 (1)	s. 1 (2)

Misrepresentation Act (Northern Ireland) 1967

1967	1979
s. 5	Sch. 1, paras. 1, 10

Criminal Law Act (Northern Ireland) 1967

1967	1979
s. 14 (1)	Sch. 1, para. 8

Supply of Goods (Implied Terms) Act 1973

1973	1979	1973	1979	1973	1979
s. 1	s. 12	s. 5 (1)	Sch. 1, para. 13 (1) (3)	s. 7 (2)	ss. 14 (6), 15 (3), Sch. 1, para. 5
2	13 (1)–(3)	6	Sch. 1, paras. 11, 13 (1) (3)	18 (5) ...	s. 1 (2), Sch. 1, paras. 3, 4, 6, 7, 12, 15
3	14 (1) (2) (4) (5), Sch. 1, para. 5	7 (1)	s. 61 (1), Sch. 1, paras. 11, 13 (1) (3)		
4	s. 55 (1) (2), Sch. 1, para. 11				

Consumer Credit Act 1974

1974	1979
s. 192 (4)....	s. 1 (2), Sch. 1, para. 5
Sch. 4,	
para. 3 ...	61 (1)
para. 4 ...	25 (2)

Unfair Contract Terms Act 1977

1977	1979
s. 31 (2)	s. 1 (2), Sch. 1, paras. 11, 13 (1) (3), 14
Sch. 3	ss. 55 (1), 61 (1)
Sch. 4	Sch. 1, para. 13 (2)

Part I

Contracts to Which Act Applies

Contracts to which Act applies

1.—(1) This Act applies to contracts of sale of goods made on or after (but not to those made before) 1 January 1894.

(2) In relation to contracts made on certain dates, this Act applies subject to the modification of certain of its sections as mentioned in Schedule 1 below.

(3) Any such modification is indicated in the section concerned by a reference to Schedule 1 below.

(4) Accordingly, where a section does not contain such a reference, this Act applies in relation to the contract concerned without such modification of the section.

General Note

This section is new and is declaratory. It makes clear that the Act applies only to contracts made after January 1, 1894 (the date on which the 1893 Act came into force), and indicates the manner in which modifications to take account of changes in the law of 1967 and 1973 will be made—by reference to Sched. 1. Where no reference is made, the Act applies to any contract made after 1893 without modification.

Part II

Formation of the Contract

Contract of sale

Contract of sale

2.—(1) A contract of sale of goods is a contract by which the seller transfers or agrees to transfer the property in goods to the buyer for a money consideration, called the price.

(2) There may be a contract of sale between one part owner and another.

(3) A contract of sale may be absolute or conditional.

(4) Where under a contract of sale the property in the goods is transferred from the seller to the buyer the contract is called a sale.

(5) Where under a contract of sale the transfer of the property in the goods is to take place at a future time or subject to some condition later to be fulfilled the contract is called an agreement to sell.

(6) An agreement to sell becomes a sale when the time elapses or the conditions are fulfilled subject to which the property in the goods is to be transferred.

DERIVATION

1893, s. 1.

DEFINITIONS

" buyer ": s. 61 (1).
" contract of sale ": s. 61 (1).
" goods ": s. 61 (1).
" property ": s. 61 (1).
" sale ": s. 61 (1).
" seller ": s. 61 (1).

GENERAL NOTE

This section splits into six subsections the four in the 1893 Act. The price (see ss. 8 and 9) is a crucial factor in a contract for sale. Without a " money consideration " there may be a contract but it will not be one of sale—*Esso Petroleum* v. *Customs and Excise Commissioners* [1976] 1 W.L.R. 1. It may be a gift or a contract of exchange or barter. The money consideration need not be cash; a cheque or credit card or a voucher like a trading cheque which is redeemable for money will suffice—*Davies* v. *Customs and Excise Commissioners* [1975] 1 W.L.R. 204. The section differentiates between an " agreement to sell "—where the transfer of property in goods is conditional or is to take place in the future (see ss. 18 and 20)—and a " sale " where the property passes at the time of the making of the contract. A breach of a contract of sale—when the property has passed—gives the buyer remedies against the goods because they are *his*; a breach of an agreement, on the other hand, merely enables the buyer to sue for damages.

Capacity to buy and sell

3.—(1) Capacity to buy and sell is regulated by the general law concerning capacity to contract and to transfer and acquire property.

(2) Where necessaries are sold and delivered to a minor or to a person who by reason of mental incapacity or drunkenness is incompetent to contract, he must pay a reasonable price for them.

(3) In subsection (2) above " necessaries " means goods suitable to the condition in life of the minor or other person concerned and to his actual requirements at the time of the sale and delivery.

DERIVATION

1893, s. 2.

DEFINITIONS

" delivery ": s. 61 (1).
" property ": s. 61 (1).
" sale ": s. 61 (1).

GENERAL NOTE

There is a popular misunderstanding about the capacity of children to make contracts. People under 18 can and do contract on their own behalf for the sale and purchase of goods. They buy sweets and comics, books, clothes, food and motor vehicles. They may sell their own property or do so in the course of a business. A contract for the purchase of " necessaries " is valid and binding. In other cases the law is archaic and out of touch with the present day. S. 1 of the

Infants' Relief Act 1874 ("all contracts . . . for goods supplied or to be supplied (other than necessaries) . . . shall be absolutely void") and the cases with which practitioners are familiar are unreal, dealing as they do with racehorses, jewellery and expensive clothing invariably bought on credit. If a minor buys goods and pays for them—and most shopping transactions are on that basis—the money cannot be recovered unless there has been a complete failure of consideration, which is extremely rare. It is only when a seller tries to enforce a contract *against* a minor that the nature of the goods has to be considered. (The position of minors is admirably treated in Pt. V of Cheshire & Fifoot's *Law of Contract.*) See *Nash* v. *Inman* [1908] 2 K.B. 1 for a discussion of the liability to pay for necessaries.

The section provides that a "reasonable price" must be paid for necessaries, which suggests that a minor might bring an action to recover the excess over the "reasonable" figure which had been paid. It is assumed that the same criteria for judging reasonableness in the case of a minor would apply as in s. 8 (*post*).

If a mental patient's condition of mind is such that he does not know what he is doing—and this ought reasonably to have been known to the seller—any contract is voidable. A contract made in a lucid interval is binding. Necessaries sold and delivered have to be paid for at a reasonable price. A drunk has to pay for necessaries and is almost certainly liable to pay for other goods when he recovers.

Formalities of contract

How contract of sale is made

4.—(1) Subject to this and any other Act, a contract of sale may be made in writing (either with or without seal), or by word of mouth, or partly in writing and partly by word of mouth, or may be implied from the conduct of the parties.

(2) Nothing in this section affects the law relating to corporations.

Derivation

1893, s. 3.

Definition

"contract of sale": s. 2 (1) and s. 61 (1).

General Note

The only contracts of sale which have to be in writing are credit-sale agreements, conditional sale agreements (see s. 5 (1) of the Hire-Purchase Act 1965) and regulated consumer credit agreements which are for the sale of goods (see s. 61 of the Consumer Credit Act 1974). Otherwise there is complete freedom of contract; many traders seek to impose terms and conditions by reducing contracts to writing although the validity and effect of such attempts are open to question where there is any lapse of time between the making of the contract and its being written down. There may be argument whether the terms are contained in a document or notice which is a contractual document; see *Chapelton* v. *Barry U.D.C.* [1940] 1 K.B. 532; *McCutcheon* v. *David MacBrayne Ltd.* [1964] 1 W.L.R. 125. Where machines are used to sell goods—cigarettes, sweets, petrol, food, for example—it should be noted that the "offer" to sell is "made" by the machine; it is held out by its owner as being able to receive money in exchange for which goods will be made available. Acceptance of the offer takes place when the coin is inserted: *Thornton* v. *Shoe Lane Parking Ltd.* [1971] 2 W.L.R. 585. In supermarkets and self-service stores, the offer is made at the checkout: *Pharmaceutical Society of Great Britain* v. *Boots* [1953] 2 W.L.R. 427; and it is submitted that at a supermarket a separate contract is made for each item of goods bought.

Subject matter of contract

Existing or future goods

5.—(1) The goods which form the subject of a contract of sale may be either existing goods, owned or possessed by the seller, or goods to be manufactured or acquired by him after the making of the contract of sale, in this Act called future goods.

(2) There may be a contract for the sale of goods the acquisition of which by the seller depends on a contingency which may or may not happen.

(3) Where by a contract of sale the seller purports to effect a present sale of future goods, the contract operates as an agreement to sell the goods.

DERIVATION

1893, s. 5.

DEFINITIONS

"contract of sale": s. 2 (1) and s. 61 (1).
"goods": s. 61 (1).
"seller": s. 61 (1).

GENERAL NOTE

This section defines "future goods" and distinguishes them from existing goods which are either owned by or in the possession of the seller at the time the contract is made. A contract for future goods which became impossible to perform in full was held to be enforceable as to the part of the goods which was available: *H. R. & S. Sainsbury* v. *Street* [1972] 1 W.L.R. 834.

Goods which have perished

6. Where there is a contract for the sale of specific goods, and the goods without the knowledge of the seller have perished at the time when the contract is made, the contract is void.

DERIVATION

1893, s. 6.

DEFINITIONS

"contract of sale": s. 2 (1) and s. 61 (1).
"goods": s. 61 (1).
"seller": s. 61 (1).
"specific goods": s. 61 (1).

GENERAL NOTE

There are two criteria for this section to be effective; the subject-matter of the contract must be "specific goods" as defined and they must have perished at the time the contract was made. Destruction or perishing after the contract is not within this section. See *Barrow, Lane and Ballard* v. *Phillips* [1929] 1 K.B. 574; *Bell* v. *Lever Bros.* [1932] A.C. 161; *Solle* v. *Butcher* [1950] 1 K.B. 671.

Goods perishing before sale but after agreement to sell

7. Where there is an agreement to sell specific goods and subsequently the goods, without any fault on the part of the seller or buyer, perish before the risk passes to the buyer, the agreement is avoided.

DERIVATION

1893, s. 7.

DEFINITIONS

"contract of sale": s. 2 (1) and s. 61 (1).
"buyer": s. 61 (1).
"fault": s. 61 (1).
"goods": s. 61 (1).
"seller": s. 61 (1).
"specific goods": s. 61 (1).

GENERAL NOTE

There must have been an agreement to sell "specific goods" but they perished after the contract but before the risk has passed to the buyer: see *H. R. & S. Sainsbury* v. *Street* [1972] 1 W.L.R. 834.

The price

Ascertainment of price

8.—(1) The price in a contract of sale may be fixed by the contract, or may be left to be fixed in a manner agreed by the contract, or may be determined by the course of dealing between the parties.

(2) Where the price is not determined as mentioned in subsection (1) above the buyer must pay a reasonable price.

(3) What is a reasonable price is a question of fact dependent on the circumstances of each particular case.

DERIVATION

1893, s. 8.

DEFINITION

"contract of sale": s. 2 (1) and s. 61 (1).

GENERAL NOTE

The price is a fundamental ingredient of a contract for the sale of goods; it is the consideration without which the contract is of a different character. In many sales the price is that marked on goods, on a price ticket or is ascertainable by reference to a price list or catalogue. Subs. (2) deals with the situation where there is no agreed or ascertained price. Here the buyer has to pay a "reasonable" price. While subs. (3) states that what is a reasonable price is a question of fact, it is submitted that this is not the exclusive test. Recent legislation has imposed controls on the price mechanism in many sectors of trade and the imposition of resale price maintenance has been outlawed in most areas—in theory, at any rate. Reference should be made to the Prices Acts 1974 and 1975, the Resale Prices Act 1976, the Competition Act 1979 as well as to the extortionate credit bargain provisions of the Consumer Credit Act 1974 (ss. 137–140). The price charged may be affected by taxation, currently VAT. A reference has been made by the Office of Fair Trading under Pt. II of the Fair Trading Act 1973 on the question of the quotation of prices on which VAT is payable. See *Mack & Edwards (Sales) Ltd.* v. *McPhail Bros.* (1968) 112 S.J. 211; *Butler Machine Tool Co. Ltd.* v. *Ex-Cell-o Corp. (England) Ltd.* [1979] 1 W.L.R. 401—as authority for a subsequent price variation in a contract term.

Agreement to sell at valuation

9.—(1) Where there is an agreement to sell goods on the terms that the price is to be fixed by the valuation of a third party, and he cannot or does not make the valuation, the agreement is avoided; but if the goods or any part of them have been delivered to and appropriated by the buyer he must pay a reasonable price for them.

(2) Where the third party is prevented from making the valuation by the fault of the seller or buyer, the party not at fault may maintain an action for damages against the party at fault.

DERIVATION

1893, s. 9.

DEFINITIONS

"action": s. 61 (1).
"buyer": s. 61 (1).
"contract of sale": s. 2 (1) and s. 61 (1).
"delivery": s. 61 (1).

"fault": s. 61 (1).
"goods": s. 61 (1).
"seller": s. 61 (1).

Conditions and warranties

Stipulations about time

10.—(1) Unless a different intention appears from the terms of the contract, stipulations as to time of payment are not of the essence of a contract of sale.

(2) Whether any other stipulation as to time is or is not of the essence of the contract depends on the terms of the contract.

(3) In a contract of sale "month" prima facie means calendar month.

DERIVATION

1893, s. 10.

DEFINITION

"contract of sale": s. 2 (1) and s. 61 (1).

GENERAL NOTE

In the absence of agreement between the parties to a contract for the sale of goods time for payment is not of the essence. The effect of other stipulations as to time depends on the terms and nature of the contract. Where the contract is silent on time, it can be made essential on notice. Other references to time will be treated as essential unless a contrary intention appears in the contract. A time fixed for delivery of goods must be observed exactly. See *McDougall* v. *Aeromarine of Emsworth* [1958] 1 W.L.R. 1126; *Elmdove* v. *Keech* (1969) 113 S.J. 871; *Kolfor Plant Hire* v. *Tilbury Plant* (1977) 121 S.J. 390.

When condition to be treated as warranty

11.—(1) Subsections (2) to (4) and (7) below do not apply to Scotland and subsection (5) below applies only to Scotland.

(2) Where a contract of sale is subject to a condition to be fulfilled by the seller, the buyer may waive the condition, or may elect to treat the breach of the condition as a breach of warranty and not as a ground for treating the contract as repudiated.

(3) Whether a stipulation in a contract of sale is a condition, the breach of which may give rise to a right to treat the contract as repudiated, or a warranty, the breach of which may give rise to a claim for damages but not to a right to reject the goods and treat the contract as repudiated, depends in each case on the construction of the contract; and a stipulation may be a condition, though called a warranty in the contract.

(4) Where a contract of sale is not severable and the buyer has accepted the goods or part of them, the breach of a condition to be fulfilled by the seller can only be treated as a breach of warranty, and not as a ground for rejecting the goods and treating the contract as repudiated, unless there is an express or implied term of the contract to that effect.

(5) In Scotland, failure by the seller to perform any material part of a contract of sale is a breach of contract, which entitles the buyer either within a reasonable time after delivery to reject the goods and treat the contract as repudiated, or to retain the goods and treat the failure to perform such material part as a breach which may give rise to a claim for compensation or damages.

(6) Nothing in this section affects a condition or warranty whose fulfilment is excused by law by reason of impossibility or otherwise.

(7) Paragraph 2 of Schedule 1 below applies in relation to a contract made before 22 April 1967 or (in the application of this Act to Northern Ireland) 28 July 1967.

DERIVATION

1893, s. 11.

DEFINITIONS

"buyer": s. 61 (1).
"contract of sale": s. 2 (1) and s. 61 (1).
"delivery": s. 61 (1).
"goods": s. 61 (1).
"property": s. 61 (1).
"seller": s. 61 (1).
"specific goods": s. 61 (1).
"warranty": s. 61 (1).

GENERAL NOTE

Subs. (2)

When there has been a breach of condition the buyer has an option; he may waive the condition or may treat its breach as a breach of warranty, forego his right to rescind the contract and claim damages: *Sullivan* v. *Constable* (1932) 48 T.L.R. 369.

Subs. (3)

This contains one of the most difficult problems for the adviser to determine—what *is* a condition and how does it vary from a warranty. While the Act says that it depends on construction that is of little practical guidance to the buyer, particularly when the words used in the subsection remind one that what is called a warranty may in fact be a condition. Much of the protection given to buyers—whether traders or dealing as consumers—lies in the right of the buyer to rely always on the implied conditions in ss. 12 to 15. If new goods are defective does the defect amount to a breach of condition—thus permitting rejection and the return of the price; or is it merely a breach of warranty? If a new car develops a fault which can be rectified by the garage which sells it, is the fault a breach of condition or of warranty? In Scotland trivial defects have been held to be not sufficient to amount to a non-performance of a material part of the contract: *Millars of Falkirk* v. *Turpie,* 1976 S.L.T. 66 (see subs. (5) below). Where a car has developed a wide variety of defects over a period of months from its purchase new these were held to be breaches of condition of quality and fitness for use although in effect they were treated as breaches of warranty resulting in an award of damages to the consumer buyer: *Jackson* v. *Chrysler Acceptances* [1978] R.T.R. 474. For further discussion, see *Wallis* v. *Pratt* [1911] A.C. 394, *Oscar Chess* v. *Williams* [1957] 1 W.L.R. 370, and *Cehave N.V.* v. *Bremer Handelsgesellschaft m.b.H.* [1976] Q.B. 44.

Subs. (4)

This sets the limit on the buyer's right to reject by stating that once "acceptance" has taken place (see ss. 34 and 35, *post*) any breach of condition can *only* be treated as a breach of warranty. The buyer has to make up his mind very quickly whether or not to reject defective goods because as each day passes his position weakens: *Lee* v. *York Coach & Marine* [1977] R.T.R. 35. Part of the vice in this section is the use of the words warranty and condition each of which means different things to the individual who may be completely unaware of the legal distinction. When the word "stipulation" is also used the confusion grows. The Law Commission is considering whether, in time, to recommend replacing these technical words with one new word (see Law Com. No. 95 1979, para. 23).

Subs. (7)

This subsection provides that the Act does not apply the new law to contracts made before the passing of the Misrepresentation Act 1967.

Implied terms about title, etc.

12.—(1) In a contract of sale, other than one to which subsection (3) below applies, there is an implied condition on the part of the seller that in the case of a sale he has a right to sell the goods, and in the case of an agreement to sell he will have such a right at the time when the property is to pass.

(2) In a contract of sale, other than one to which subsection (3) below applies, there is also an implied warranty that—

(*a*) the goods are free, and will remain free until the time when the property is to pass, from any charge or encumbrance not disclosed or known to the buyer before the contract is made, and

(*b*) the buyer will enjoy quiet possession of the goods except so far as it may be disturbed by the owner or other person entitled to the benefit of any charge or encumbrance so disclosed or known.

(3) This subsection applies to a contract of sale in the case of which there appears from the contract or is to be inferred from its circumstances an intention that the seller should transfer only such title as he or a third person may have.

(4) In a contract to which subsection (3) above applies there is an implied warranty that all charges or encumbrances known to the seller and not known to the buyer have been disclosed to the buyer before the contract is made.

(5) In a contract to which subsection (3) above applies there is also an implied warranty that none of the following will disturb the buyer's quiet possession of the goods, namely—

(*a*) the seller;

(*b*) in a case where the parties to the contract intend that the seller should transfer only such title as a third person may have, that person;

(*c*) anyone claiming through or under the seller or that third person otherwise than under a charge or encumbrance disclosed or known to the buyer before the contract is made.

(6) Paragraph 3 of Schedule 1 below applies in relation to a contract made before 18 May 1973.

DERIVATION

1893, s. 12, as substituted by 1973, s. 1.

DEFINITIONS

"buyer": s. 61 (1).
"contract of sale": s. 2 (1) and s. 61 (1).
"goods": s. 61 (1).
"property": s. 61 (1).
"seller": s. 61 (1).
"warranty": s. 61 (1).

GENERAL NOTE

Although no new law is made by this section, it has been redrafted to make it clearer and easier to follow. Subss. (1) and (2) deal with all cases of contracts for the sale of goods except where there is a limitation on the title to be transferred. In the general case there is:

(a) an implied condition that the seller has the right to sell (or will have when the property is to pass);

(b) an implied warranty that the goods are free from undisclosed encumbrances; and

(c) an implied warranty for quiet possession (except for the rights of disclosed encumbrancers).

Where the seller cannot transfer title, so that there is a complete failure of consideration, the buyer is entitled to his money back in full, see *Rowland* v.

Divall [1923] 2 K.B. 500 and *Microbeads* v. *Vinhurst* [1975] 1 W.L.R. 218. The buyer always has a claim for damages for breach of condition if the seller *never* had the title to goods; but if the seller later receives title this is " fed " to the buyer, see *Butterworth* v. *Kingsway Motors* [1954] 1 W.L.R. 1286.

Subss. (3) *to* (5)

These subsections deal with the situation where it is known by the parties prior to the contract that the seller may have a limited or bare title and that the buyer is taking only such title. In this case there is no implied condition as to the right to sell but implied warranties:

(a) that all encumbrances which the seller knows of have been disclosed;
(b) that the seller will not disturb the buyer's quiet possession;
(c) that no third party (whose title is being transferred) will disturb the buyer's quiet possession; and
(d) that no unknown encumbrancer will do so.

It should be noted that liability for breach of any of the obligations arising from this section cannot be excluded or restricted by any contract term in any contract made on or after February 1, 1978 (s. 6, Unfair Contract Terms Act 1977).

Subs. (6)

This subsection provides that the Act does not apply the new law to contracts made before May 18, 1973, when the Supply of Goods (Implied Terms) Act 1973 came into force.

Sale by description

13.—(1) Where there is a contract for the sale of goods by description, there is an implied condition that the goods will correspond with the description.

(2) If the sale is by sample as well as by description it is not sufficient that the bulk of the goods corresponds with the sample if the goods do not also correspond with the description.

(3) A sale of goods is not prevented from being a sale by description by reason only that, being exposed for sale or hire, they are selected by the buyer.

(4) Paragraph 4 of Schedule 1 below applies in relation to a contract made before 18 May 1973.

DERIVATION

1893, s. 13 (subs. (3) added by 1973, s. 2).

DEFINITION

" contract of sale ": s. 2 (1) and s. 61 (1).

GENERAL NOTE

This section contains the first of the major implied conditions in contracts for the sale of goods. It also applies to all such contracts, private sales as well as those in the course of a business: *Beale* v. *Taylor* [1967] 1 W.L.R. 1193. Any type of indication applied to goods may amount to a description and, in contracts made on or after May 18, 1973, it does not now matter that the customer may have selected the goods himself in, for example, a supermarket or self-service shop. Where there is a sale by sample, the bulk of goods must correspond with any description as well as with the sample. See *Grant* v. *Australian Knitting Mills* [1936] A.C. 85, *Wallis* v. *Pratt* [1911] A.C. 394; *Robert A. Munro* v. *Meyer* [1930] 2 K.B. 312, *Godley* v. *Perry* [1960] 1 W.L.R. 9, *Leaf* v. *International Galleries* [1950] 2 K.B. 86, and *Ashington Piggeries* v. *Christopher Hill* [1972] A.C. 441.

It should be noted that as against a person dealing as a consumer, liability for breach of the obligations arising under this section cannot be excluded or restricted by reference to any contract term (s. 6 (2) of the Unfair Contract

Terms Act 1977) and as against a person dealing otherwise than as a consumer, liability for such breach can only be excluded or restricted in so far as the term satisfies the test of reasonableness (s. 6 (3) of the Unfair Contract Terms Act 1977).

Subs. (4)

This subsection provides that the Act does not apply the new law to contracts made before the coming into force of the Supply of Goods (Implied Terms) Act 1973.

Implied terms about quality or fitness

14.—(1) Except as provided by this section and section 15 below and subject to any other enactment, there is no implied condition or warranty about the quality or fitness for any particular purpose of goods supplied under a contract of sale.

(2) Where the seller sells goods in the course of a business, there is an implied condition that the goods supplied under the contract are of merchantable quality, except that there is no such condition—

(*a*) as regards defects specifically drawn to the buyer's attention before the contract is made; or

(*b*) if the buyer examines the goods before the contract is made, as regards defects which that examination ought to reveal.

(3) Where the seller sells goods in the course of a business and the buyer, expressly or by implication, makes known—

(*a*) to the seller, or

(*b*) where the purchase price or part of it is payable by instalments and the goods were previously sold by a credit-broker to the seller, to that credit-broker,

any particular purpose for which the goods are being bought, there is an implied condition that the goods supplied under the contract are reasonably fit for that purpose, whether or not that is a purpose for which such goods are commonly supplied, except where the circumstances show that the buyer does not rely, or that it is unreasonable for him to rely, on the skill or judgment of the seller or credit-broker.

(4) An implied condition or warranty about quality or fitness for a particular purpose may be annexed to a contract of sale by usage.

(5) The preceding provisions of this section apply to a sale by a person who in the course of a business is acting as agent for another as they apply to a sale by a principal in the course of a business, except where that other is not selling in the course of a business and either the buyer knows that fact or reasonable steps are taken to bring it to the notice of the buyer before the contract is made.

(6) Goods of any kind are of merchantable quality within the meaning of subsection (2) above if they are as fit for the purpose or purposes for which goods of that kind are commonly bought as it is reasonable to expect having regard to any description applied to them, the price (if relevant) and all the other relevant circumstances.

(7) Paragraph 5 of Schedule 1 below applies in relation to a contract made on or after 18 May 1973 and before the appointed day, and paragraph 6 in relation to one made before 18 May 1973.

(8) In subsection (7) above and paragraph 5 of Schedule 1 below references to the appointed day are to the day appointed for the purposes of those provisions by an order of the Secretary of State made by statutory instrument.

DERIVATION

1893, s. 14, as substituted by 1973, s. 3 (subs. (3) by 1974, Sched. 4, para. 3).

Definitions

"business": s. 61 (1).
"buyer": s. 61 (1).
"contract of sale": s. 2 (1) and s. 61 (1).
"goods": s. 61 (1).
"quality": s. 61 (1).
"seller": s. 61 (1).
"warranty": s. 61 (1).

General Note

First, it must be observed that there are three different ss. 14 which are in force depending on the date of the contract. For contracts made prior to May 18, 1973 (when the Supply of Goods (Implied Terms) Act came into force) the "original" section will apply and is contained in Sched. 1, para. 6, to this Act. For contracts made on or after May 18, 1973, but before the coming into force of that part of the Consumer Credit Act 1974 (which amends subs. (3) by adding references to "credit-brokers") on "the appointed day" (which has yet to arrive) the version of s. 14 contained in Sched. 1, para. 5, to the Act will continue to apply. *After* the "appointed day" the full text printed above will apply to all contracts made on or after "the appointed day." The notes which follow relate to the above section alone.

Subs. (1)

There are only implied into contracts for the sale of goods such conditions as appear in ss. 12, 13, this section and in s. 15, *post*. Although there is reference to "any other enactment" breach of statutory duty only gives a buyer a right of action if the Act specifically says so, see *Square* v. *Model Farm Dairies* [1939] 2 K.B. 365.

Subs. (2)

Breach of the implied condition of merchantable quality (defined below in subs. (6)) gives rise to a right to rescind and recover damages. As against a person dealing as consumer there can be no exclusion or restriction of liability for breach of the obligations arising from this and the following subsections (s. 6 (2) of the Unfair Contract Terms Act 1977) and as against a person dealing other than as a consumer liability for such breach can only be excluded or restricted in so far as any contract term purporting to do so is reasonable (s. 6 (3) of the Unfair Contract Terms Act 1977). In consumer cases a notice or contract term which seeks to limit liability may be an offence under the Consumer Transactions (Restrictions on Statements) Order 1976 (as amended). There are two notable exceptions to the general rule contained in the two provisos to this subsection both of which require action to be taken by the seller (for subs. (2) (*a*)) or the buyer (for subs. (2) (*b*)) *before* the contract is made. For reliance upon the first proviso, defects must be "specifically drawn" to the buyer's attention, which, it is submitted, means giving details rather than a general statement such as "seconds" or "shop-soiled."

Subs. (3)

Breach of the implied condition of fitness for purpose gives rise to a right to rescind and recover damages. The major difficulty is to determine what is "reasonable fitness" for any particular purpose. In the absence of standards the plaintiff is left with the difficulty of proving that what he has bought is unfit. In the case of a total failure of a machine to function this may be easy to establish. But intermittent faults, rapid wear and other defects may give rise to the defence of undue use, misuse or damage by the plaintiff; in this event, the plaintiff has a hard task. The buyer of goods which he intends to use for a less obvious purpose is also protected if he makes known the use to the seller. The burden is thus placed on sellers of goods either to be skilled and knowledgeable about their products or to make it quite plain that they have no specialised skill; but it is submitted that a seller of goods will be presumed to know, through experience and product-knowledge the main characteristics of the merchandise he sells.

Both these subsections apply to goods "sold in the course of a business"—which means *any* goods sold in *any* business. It would extend to a furniture shop selling a salesman's car; a solicitor selling a typewriter from his office; a grocer selling sweet jars, and is not confined (as it was prior to May 18, 1973) to goods which the seller normally sold in the course of his business.

Subs. (5)

This subsection brings within scope any agent who sells unless his principal is not selling in the course of a business and the buyer is informed or knows that fact.

Subs. (6)

This subsection contains the definition of merchantable quality introduced in 1973. Although there has been some debate among lawyers about this definition, and whether it is more restrictive than the previous meaning laid down by the House of Lords in 1936, judges appear to find no difficulty in deciding about particular cases. It is to be noted, however, that the cases show that judges may use " fitness for purpose " and " merchantable quality " interchangeably and may blur any real distinction between the two concepts. It is also difficult to see how one element in this section, which amounts to a condition implied into every contract, has to be defined by reference to description and fitness for purpose when these two matters are also conditions so implied. The Law Commission is studying the implied conditions following a reference in 1979 by the Lord Chancellor.

Subss. (7) *and* (8)

These subsections provide for transitional arrangements as outlined above.

For cases on s. 14 generally:

Harbutts " Plasticine " Ltd. v. *Wayne Tank & Pump Co. Ltd.* [1970] 1 Q.B. 447.
B. S. Brown Ltd. v. *Craiks Ltd.* [1970] 1 W.L.R. 752.
Jackson v. *Chrysler Acceptances Ltd.* [1978] R.T.R. 474.
Crowther v. *Shannon Motor Co.* [1975] 1 W.L.R. 30.
Bartlett v. *Sidney Marcus* [1965] 1 W.L.R. 1013.
Bristol Tramways v. *Fiat* [1910] 2 K.B. 831.
Grant v. *Australian Knitting Mills* [1936] A.C. 85.
Henry Kendall v. *William Lillico* [1969] 2 A.C. 31.
Lee v. *York Coach & Marine* [1977] R.T.R. 35.
Suisse Atlantique v. *N.V. Rotterdam* [1966] 2 W.L.R. 944.
Gascoigne v. *British Credit Trust Ltd.* [1978] C.L.Y. 711.
Frost v. *Aylesbury Dairy Co.* [1905] 1 K.B. 608.
Jackson v. *Watson* [1909] 2 K.B. 193.
Andrews v. *Hopkinson* [1957] 1 Q.B. 229.
McDonald v. *Empire Garages, The Times,* October 8, 1975.
Millars of Falkirk v. *Turpie,* 1976 S.L.T. 76.
Baldrey v. *Marshall* [1925] 1 K.B. 260.
Farnworth Finance v. *Attryde* [1970] 1 W.L.R. 1053.
Yeoman Credit v. *Apps* [1962] 2 Q.B. 508.

Sale by sample

Sale by sample

15.—(1) A contract of sale is a contract for sale by sample where there is an express or implied term to that effect in the contract.

(2) In the case of a contract for sale by sample there is an implied condition—

(*a*) that the bulk will correspond with the sample in quality;
(*b*) that the buyer will have a reasonable opportunity of comparing the bulk with the sample;
(*c*) that the goods will be free from any defect, rendering them unmerchantable, which would not be apparent on reasonable examination of the sample.

(3) In subsection (2) (*c*) above " unmerchantable " is to be construed in accordance with section 14 (6) above.

(4) Paragraph 7 of Schedule 1 below applies in relation to a contract made before 18 May 1973.

DERIVATION
1893, s. 15.

DEFINITIONS
" buyer ": s. 61 (1).
" contract of sale ": s. 2 (1) and s. 61 (1).
" goods ": s. 61 (1).
" merchantable quality ": s. 14 (6).
" quality ": s. 61 (1).

GENERAL NOTE
This section enacts a further series of implied conditions the breach of which gives rise to a right to rescind and recover damages. Liability for breach of these obligations cannot be excluded or restricted by reference to any contract term as against a person dealing as consumer (s. 6 (2) of the Unfair Contract Terms Act 1977) and as against any other person can only be effective in so far as the term meets the test of reasonableness (s. 6 (3) *idem*). See *Godley* v. *Perry* [1960] 1 W.L.R. 9 and *Ashington Piggeries* v. *Hill* [1972] A.C. 441.

Subs. (4)
This subsection provides that the Act does not apply the new law to contracts made before the coming into force of the Supply of Goods (Implied Terms) Act 1973.

PART III

EFFECTS OF THE CONTRACT

Transfer of property as between seller and buyer

Goods must be ascertained

16. Where there is a contract for the sale of unascertained goods no property in the goods is transferred to the buyer unless and until the goods are ascertained.

DERIVATION
1893, s. 16.

DEFINITIONS
" buyer ": s. 61 (1).
" contract of sale ": s. 2 (1) and s. 61 (1).
" goods ": s. 61 (1).
" property ": s. 61 (1).
" specific goods ": s. 61 (1).

GENERAL NOTE
See *Lacis* v. *Cashmarts* [1969] 2 Q.B. 400.

Property passes when intended to pass

17.—(1) Where there is a contract for the sale of specific or ascertained goods the property in them is transferred to the buyer at such time as the parties to the contract intend it to be transferred.

(2) For the purposes of ascertaining the intention of the parties regard shall be had to the terms of the contract, the conduct of the parties and the circumstances of the case.

DERIVATION
1893, s. 17.

DEFINITIONS
" buyer ": s. 61 (1).
" contract of sale ": s. 2 (1) and s. 61 (1).

"goods": s. 61 (1).
"property": s. 61 (1).

General Note

The Act defines future and specific goods but does not define unascertained goods. Until the subject-matter of the contract is known nothing can pass between seller and buyer.

Rules for ascertaining intention

18. Unless a different intention appears, the following are rules for ascertaining the intention of the parties as to the time at which the property in the goods is to pass to the buyer.

Rule 1.—Where there is an unconditional contract for the sale of specific goods in a deliverable state the property in the goods passes to the buyer when the contract is made, and it is immaterial whether the time of payment or the time of delivery, or both, be postponed.

Rule 2.—Where there is a contract for the sale of specific goods and the seller is bound to do something to the goods for the purpose of putting them into a deliverable state, the property does not pass until the thing is done and the buyer has notice that it has been done.

Rule 3.—Where there is a contract for the sale of specific goods in a deliverable state but the seller is bound to weigh, measure, test, or do some other act or thing with reference to the goods for the purpose of ascertaining the price, the property does not pass until the act or thing is done and the buyer has notice that it has been done.

Rule 4.—When goods are delivered to the buyer on approval or on sale or return or other similar terms the property in the goods passes to the buyer:—

(*a*) when he signifies his approval or acceptance to the seller or does any other act adopting the transaction;

(*b*) if he does not signify his approval or acceptance to the seller but retains the goods without giving notice of rejection, then, if a time has been fixed for the return of the goods, on the expiration of that time, and, if no time has been fixed, on the expiration of a reasonable time.

Rule 5.—(1) Where there is a contract for the sale of unascertained or future goods by description, and goods of that description and in a deliverable state are unconditionally appropriated to the contract, either by the seller with the assent of the buyer or by the buyer with the assent of the seller, the property in the goods then passes to the buyer; and the assent may be express or implied, and may be given either before or after the appropriation is made.

(2) Where, in pursuance of the contract, the seller delivers the goods to the buyer or to a carrier or other bailee or custodier (whether named by the buyer or not) for the purpose of transmission to the buyer, and does not reserve the right of disposal, he is to be taken to have unconditionally appropriated the goods to the contract.

Derivation

1893, s. 18.

DEFINITIONS

"bailee": s. 61 (1).
"buyer": s. 61 (1).
"contract of sale": s. 2 (1) and s. 61 (1).
"delivery": s. 61 (1).
"deliverable state": s. 61 (5).
"future goods": s. 61 (1).
"goods": s. 61 (1).
"property": s. 61 (1).
"seller": s. 61 (1).
"specific goods": s. 61 (1).

GENERAL NOTE

This section only comes into force if there is no term in the contract dealing with the time at which property in goods is to pass. Many commercial contracts do deal at length with this matter and it is tied to the transfer of risk (see s. 20 *infra*). Distinction is made in the Rules between specific goods and future goods. It should be noted in Rule 2 and Rule 3 that notice must be given to the buyer that what had to be done has been completed; but once that notice is given the property will pass. In Rule 4, the time in which the buyer has to act (where not specified in the contract) must be reasonable: see *Poole* v. *Smith's Car Sales (Balham) Ltd.* [1962] 1 W.L.R. 744 and *Tiffin* v. *Pitcher* [1969] C.L.Y. 3234. In Rule 5 "appropriation" may cause difficulties. Does it occur when the goods are ear-marked by the seller for delivery to the buyer? When goods are put in a delivery van or left in the street outside the buyer's premises? See *Philip Head* v. *Showfronts* [1970] Lloyd's Rep. 140; *Pignataro* v. *Gilroy* [1919] 1 K.B. 459; *Wardars (Import & Export)* v. *W. Norwood & Sons Ltd.* [1968] 2 W.L.R. 1440.

Reservation of right of disposal

19.—(1) Where there is a contract for the sale of specific goods or where goods are subsequently appropriated to the contract, the seller may, by the terms of the contract or appropriation, reserve the right of disposal of the goods until certain conditions are fulfilled; and in such a case, notwithstanding the delivery of the goods to the buyer, or to a carrier or other bailee or custodier for the purpose of transmission to the buyer, the property in the goods does not pass to the buyer until the conditions imposed by the seller are fulfilled.

(2) Where goods are shipped, and by the bill of lading the goods are deliverable to the order of the seller or his agent, the seller is prima facie to be taken to reserve the right of disposal.

(3) Where the seller of goods draws on the buyer for the price, and transmits the bill of exchange and bill of lading to the buyer together to secure acceptance or payment of the bill of exchange, the buyer is bound to return the bill of lading if he does not honour the bill of exchange, and if he wrongfully retains the bill of lading the property in the goods does not pass to him.

DERIVATION

1893, s. 19.

DEFINITIONS

"bailee": s. 61 (1).
"buyer": s. 61 (1).
"contract of sale": s. 2 (1) and s. 61 (1).
"delivery": s. 61 (1).
"goods": s. 61 (1).
"property": s. 61 (1).
"seller": s. 61 (1).
"specific goods": s. 61 (1).

Risk prima facie passes with property

20.—(1) Unless otherwise agreed, the goods remain at the seller's risk until the property in them is transferred to the buyer, but when the property in them is transferred to the buyer the goods are at the buyer's risk whether delivery has been made or not.

(2) But where delivery has been delayed through the fault of either buyer or seller the goods are at the risk of the party at fault as regards any loss which might not have occurred but for such fault.

(3) Nothing in this section affects the duties or liabilities of either seller or buyer as a bailee or custodier of the goods of the other party.

DERIVATION

1893, s. 20.

DEFINITIONS

" bailee ": s. 61 (1).
" buyer ": s. 61 (1).
" delivery ": s. 61 (1).
" fault ": s. 61 (1).
" goods ": s. 61 (1).
" property ": s. 61 (1).
" seller ": s. 61 (1).

GENERAL NOTE

In many commercial contracts the question of risk is dealt with by specific terms. There may be uncertainty or silence in which case the section will apply. Many traders (and consumers) are unaware of the significance of this aspect of transfer of property and the effect that receipt of goods may have upon insurance. A seller retaining title may wish to make certain that the goods are insured by the buyer; while he may stipulate this in the contract of sale, default in obtaining adequate cover may mean that the seller is unprotected by insurance. It is therefore better, in such a case, for the seller to insure and add the premium to the price. See *Borden (U.K.)* v. *Scottish Timber Products* [1979] 2 Lloyd's Rep. 168 (and on appeal [1979] 3 W.L.R. 672) and *Re Bond Worth* [1979] 3 W.L.R. 629.

Transfer of title

Sale by person not the owner

21.—(1) Subject to this Act, where goods are sold by a person who is not their owner, and who does not sell them under the authority or with the consent of the owner, the buyer acquires no better title to the goods than the seller had, unless the owner of the goods is by his conduct precluded from denying the seller's authority to sell.

(2) Nothing in this Act affects—

(*a*) the provisions of the Factors Acts or any enactment enabling the apparent owner of goods to dispose of them as if he were their true owner;

(*b*) the validity of any contract of sale under any special common law or statutory power of sale or under the order of a court of competent jurisdiction.

DERIVATION

1893, s. 21.

DEFINITIONS

" buyer ": s. 61 (1).
" contract of sale ": s. 2 (1) and s. 61 (1).
" goods ": s. 61 (1).
" seller ": s. 61 (1).

General Note

This section puts into statutory form the maximum *nemo dat quod non habet*. See *Central Newbury Car Auctions* v. *Unity Finance* [1957] 1 Q.B. 371 and *Cundy* v. *Lindsay* (1878) 3 App.Cas. 459. Note the proviso for sales under court orders or in the exercise of a statutory power of sale.

Market overt

22.—(1) Where goods are sold in market overt, according to the usage of the market, the buyer acquires a good title to the goods, provided he buys them in good faith and without notice of any defect or want of title on the part of the seller.

(2) This section does not apply to Scotland.

(3) Paragraph 8 of Schedule 1 below applies in relation to a contract under which goods were sold before 1 January 1968 or (in the application of this Act to Northern Ireland) 29 August 1967.

Derivation

1893, s. 22.

Definitions

"buyer": s. 61 (1).
"good faith": s. 61 (3).
"goods": s. 61 (1).
"seller": s. 61 (1).

General Note

There are markets overt in various parts of England—but not in Scotland and Wales. In the City of London, all shops are market overt if they sell goods in ordinary business hours between sunrise and sunset. See *Bishopsgate Motor Finance Co.* v. *Transport Brakes Ltd.* [1949] 1 K.B. 322; *Reid* v. *Metropolitan Police Commissioner* [1973] Q.B. 551. Subs. (3) preserves the law in force prior to the coming into force of the Misrepresentation Act 1967.

Sale under voidable title

23. When the seller of goods has a voidable title to them, but his title has not been avoided at the time of the sale, the buyer acquires a good title to the goods, provided he buys them in good faith and without notice of the seller's defect of title.

Derivation

1893, s. 23.

Definitions

"buyer": s. 61 (1).
"good faith": s. 61 (3).
"goods": s. 61 (1).
"sale": s. 61 (1).
"seller": s. 61 (1).

General Note

The essential feature of transactions to which this section applies is the creation of a voidable title: A sells to B under circumstances which give rise to the passing of a voidable title—fraud, mistake, undue influence. B then sells to C. If B's title has not been avoided, C will receive a good title so long as he acted in good faith without notice of the defective title.

See

Pierce v. *London Horse and Carriage Repository* [1922] W.N. 170.
Lewis v. *Averay* (*No.* 2) [1973] 1 W.L.R. 510.
Ingram v. *Little* [1960] 3 W.L.R. 504.
Car and Universal Finance v. *Caldwell* [1964] 2 W.L.R. 600.
Newtons of Wembley Ltd. v. *Williams* [1964] 3 W.L.R. 888.
Whitehorn Bros. v. *Davison* [1911] 1 K.B. 463.

Seller in possession after sale

24. Where a person having sold goods continues or is in possession of the goods, or of the documents of title to the goods, the delivery or transfer by that person, or by a mercantile agent acting for him, of the goods or documents of title under any sale, pledge, or other disposition thereof, to any person receiving the same in good faith and without notice of the previous sale, has the same effect as if the person making the delivery or transfer were expressly authorised by the owner of the goods to make the same.

DERIVATION

1893, s. 25 (1).

DEFINITIONS

"delivery": s. 1 (1).
"documents of title": s. 61 (1).
"good faith": s. 61 (3).
"goods": s. 61 (1).
"mercantile agent": s. 26.

GENERAL NOTE

The position of the parties to a contract after the sale is dealt with in this and the next section. Both are important commercially with the concept of "title retention" being prevalent. This section provides that where a seller of goods (a manufacturer, for example) retains either possession or title, the delivery of the goods by him or by an agent (a retailer, for example) to a third person in good faith, who has no notice of the previous sale, passes a good title to that third person as though the retailer had been authorised by the manufacturer. Thus in the normal course of trading, customers—either trade or consumer—who buy goods from a distributor who appears to be carrying on business in the usual way—and who have no notice of any retention of title by the manufacturer or supplier *to* the distributor will be fully protected in the title they receive. See *Worcester Works Finance* v. *Cooden Engineering Co.* [1971] 3 W.L.R. 661.

Buyer in possession after sale

25.—(1) Where a person having bought or agreed to buy goods obtains, with the consent of the seller, possession of the goods or the documents of title to the goods, the delivery or transfer by that person, or by a mercantile agent acting for him, of the goods or documents of title, under any sale, pledge, or other disposition thereof, to any person receiving the same in good faith and without notice of any lien or other right of the original seller in respect of the goods, has the same effect as if the person making the delivery or transfer were a mercantile agent in possession of the goods or documents of title with the consent of the owner.

(2) For the purposes of subsection (1) above—

(*a*) the buyer under a conditional sale agreement is to be taken not to be a person who has bought or agreed to buy goods, and

(*b*) "conditional sale agreement" means an agreement for the sale of goods which is a consumer credit agreement within the meaning of the Consumer Credit Act 1974 under which the purchase price or part of it is payable by instalments, and the property in the goods is to remain in the seller (notwithstanding that the buyer is to be in possession of the goods) until such conditions as to the payment of instalments or otherwise as may be specified in the agreement are fulfilled.

(3) Paragraph 9 of Schedule 1 below applies in relation to a contract under which a person buys or agrees to buy goods and which is made before the appointed day.

(4) In subsection (3) above and paragraph 9 of Schedule 1 below references to the appointed day are to the day appointed for the purposes of those provisions by an order of the Secretary of State made by statutory instrument.

Derivation
1893, s. 25 (2).

Definitions
"buyer": s. 61 (1).
"delivery': s. 61 (1).
"documents of title": s. 61 (1).
"good faith": s. 61 (2).
"goods": s. 61 (1).
"mercantile agent": s. 26.
"sale": s. 61 (1).
"seller": s. 61 (1).

General Note

Subs. (1) deals with the situation where a distributor of goods who is in possession of them with the suppliers' consent sells them to a third person. If the title to the goods is retained by the supplier the sale by the distributor to an innocent purchaser without notice of any title retention clause passes a good title. For cases on this and the preceding section, see:

Aluminium Industrie v. *Romalpa* [1976] 1 W.L.R. 676.
Borden (U.K.) Ltd. v. *Scottish Timber Products* [1979] 2 Lloyds Rep. 168 (and on appeal (1979) 123 S.J. 688).
Re Bond Worth (1979) 123 S.J. 216.
Re Hallett (1880) 13 Ch.D. 696.
Eastern Distributors v. *Goldring* [1957] 3 W.L.R. 237.
Belsize Motor Supply Co. v. *Cox* [1914] 1 K.B. 244.

Subs. (2) preserves the position of a person who buys goods under a conditional sale agreement and, by subs. (4), will come into force when the appropriate Commencement Order is made under Consumer Credit Act 1974.

Subs. (3) provides that the Act does not apply to contracts made before its coming into force.

Supplementary to sections 24 and 25

26. In sections 24 and 25 above "mercantile agent" means a mercantile agent having in the customary course of his business as such agent authority either—

(*a*) to sell goods, or
(*b*) to consign goods for the purpose of sale, or
(*c*) to buy goods, or
(*d*) to raise money on the security of goods.

Derivation
1893, s. 25 (3).

General Note
This section is a definition section.

Part IV

Performance of the Contract

Duties of seller and buyer

27. It is the duty of the seller to deliver the goods, and of the buyer to accept and pay for them, in accordance with the terms of the contract of sale.

DERIVATION

1893, s. 27.

DEFINITIONS

"buyer": s. 61 (1).
"contract of sale": s. 2 (1) and s. 61 (1).
"delivery": s. 61 (1).
"goods": s. 61 (1).
"seller": s. 61 (1).

GENERAL NOTE

This section contains the basis of the obligations between parties to a contract for the sale of goods.

Payment and delivery are concurrent conditions

28. Unless otherwise agreed, delivery of the goods and payment of the price are concurrent conditions, that is to say, the seller must be ready and willing to give possession of the goods to the buyer in exchange for the price and the buyer must be ready and willing to pay the price in exchange for possession of the goods.

DERIVATION

1893, s. 28.

DEFINITIONS

"buyer": s. 61 (1).
"delivery": s. 61 (1).
"goods": s. 61 (1).
"seller": s. 61 (1).

GENERAL NOTE

Anyone who buys goods will be expected to pay for them at the time of delivery—unless the contract contains different terms. The criminal law has been amended to try to cover shopping situations where goods are delivered by a trader but not paid for at the time by a person lacking the intent to pay. See Theft Act 1978.

Rules about delivery

29.—(1) Whether it is for the buyer to take possession of the goods or for the seller to send them to the buyer is a question depending in each case on the contract, express or implied, between the parties.

(2) Apart from any such contract, express or implied, the place of delivery is the seller's place of business if he has one, and if not, his residence; except that, if the contract is for the sale of specific goods, which to the knowledge of the parties when the contract is made are in some other place, then that place is the place of delivery.

(3) Where under the contract of sale the seller is bound to send the goods to the buyer, but no time for sending them is fixed, the seller is bound to send them within a reasonable time.

(4) Where the goods at the time of sale are in the possession of a third person, there is no delivery by seller to buyer unless and until the third person acknowledges to the buyer that he holds the goods on his behalf; but nothing in this section affects the operation of the issue or transfer of any document of title to goods.

(5) Demand or tender of delivery may be treated as ineffectual unless made at a reasonable hour; and what is a reasonable hour is a question of fact.

(6) Unless otherwise agreed, the expenses of and incidental to putting the goods into a deliverable state must be borne by the seller.

DERIVATION

1893, s. 29.

DEFINITIONS

" business ": s. 61 (1).
" buyer ": s. 61 (1).
" contract of sale ": s. 2 (1) and s. 61 (1).
" deliverable state ": s. 61 (5).
" delivery ": s. 61 (1).
" document of title ": s. 61 (1).
" goods ": s. 61 (1).
" seller ": s. 61 (1).
" specific goods ": s. 61 (1).

GENERAL NOTE

In commercial contracts there are usually terms dealing with delivery. In consumer contracts there may well not be any such terms.

Subs. (1) sets out the basic proposition that it is a matter for the construction of each contract to see what is intended.

Subs. (2) provides that in the absence of specific agreement the seller's place of business (or his residence—for the Act applies to private sales as well as trade ones)—is to be the place of delivery. If specific goods are at another place to the knowledge of *both* parties when the contract is made, that place is where delivery shall take place.

Subs. (3) makes provision for silence in the contract on time for delivery and imposes a duty of " reasonableness." See s. 10 (*ante*) for the general rules about time.

Subs. (4) makes it incumbent on a third party in whose possession goods may be to confirm that he is holding them on behalf of the buyer before delivery takes place.

Subs. (5) makes reasonableness for delivery a question of fact and raises interesting questions where goods are to be delivered to consumers, for example, who are at work during normal delivery times.

Subs. (6) is declaratory. There must be express agreement to relieve the seller of his duty to put goods into a deliverable state. What is the status of descriptive words such as " self-assembly " or " do-it-yourself " ? Would this enable a retailer selling such items to avoid assembling them himself?

Delivery of wrong quantity

30.—(1) Where the seller delivers to the buyer a quantity of goods less than he contracted to sell, the buyer may reject them, but if the buyer accepts the goods so delivered he must pay for them at the contract rate.

(2) Where the seller delivers to the buyer a quantity of goods larger than he contracted to sell, the buyer may accept the goods included in the contract and reject the rest, or he may reject the whole.

(3) Where the seller delivers to the buyer a quantity of goods larger than he contracted to sell and the buyer accepts the whole of the goods so delivered he must pay for them at the contract rate.

(4) Where the seller delivers to the buyer the goods he contracted to sell mixed with goods of a different description not included in the contract, the buyer may accept the goods which are in accordance with the contract and reject the rest, or he may reject the whole.

(5) This section is subject to any usage of trade, special agreement, or course of dealing between the parties.

DERIVATION

1893, s. 30.

DEFINITIONS
" buyer ": s. 61 (1).
" delivery ": s. 61 (1).
" goods ": s. 61 (1).
" seller ": s. 61 (1).

GENERAL NOTE
For the seller to be able to deliver more or less than the contract quantity there must be an express term in the contract. See *Re Bond Worth* [1979] 3 W.L.R. 629. In the absence of express agreement, the buyer is entitled to decide what he wants to do when confronted with a different quantity than he ordered. See *Jackson* v. *Rotax* [1910] 2 K.B. 937 and *Behrend & Co.* v. *Produce Brokers Co.* [1920] 3 K.B. 530.

Instalment deliveries

31.—(1) Unless otherwise agreed, the buyer of goods is not bound to accept delivery of them by instalments.

(2) Where there is a contract for the sale of goods to be delivered by stated instalments, which are to be separately paid for, and the seller makes defective deliveries in respect of one or more instalments, or the buyer neglects or refuses to take delivery of or pay for one or more instalments, it is a question in each case depending on the terms of the contract and the circumstances of the case whether the breach of contract is a repudiation of the whole contract or whether it is a severable breach giving rise to a claim for compensation but not to a right to treat the whole contract as repudiated.

DERIVATION
1893, s. 31.

DEFINITIONS
" buyer ": s. 61 (1).
" contract of sale ": s. 2 (1) and s. 61 (1).
" delivery ": s. 61 (1).
" goods ": s. 61 (1).
" seller ": s. 61 (1).

GENERAL NOTE
The contract must specifically provide for instalments. If it does not the buyer does not have to accept them. Subs. (2) deals with what is to happen where there are to be instalments but either side default. See *Maple Flock Co.* v. *Universal Furniture Products (Wembley) Ltd.* [1934] 1 K.B. 148.

Delivery to carrier

32.—(1) Where, in pursuance of a contract of sale, the seller is authorised or required to send the goods to the buyer, delivery of the goods to a carrier (whether named by the buyer or not) for the purpose of transmission to the buyer is prima facie deemed to be a delivery of the goods to the buyer.

(2) Unless otherwise authorised by the buyer, the seller must make such contract with the carrier on behalf of the buyer as may be reasonable having regard to the nature of the goods and the other circumstances of the case; and if the seller omits to do so, and the goods are lost or damaged in course of transit, the buyer may decline to treat the delivery to the carrier as a delivery to himself or may hold the seller responsible in damages.

(3) Unless otherwise agreed, where goods are sent by the seller to the buyer by a route involving sea transit, under circumstances in which it is usual to insure, the seller must give such notice to the buyer as may enable him to insure them during their sea transit; and if the seller fails to do so, the goods are at his risk during such sea transit.

DERIVATION
1893, s. 32.

DEFINITIONS
"buyer": s. 61 (1).
"contract of sale": s. 2 (1) and s. 61 (1).
"delivery": s. 61 (1).
"goods": s. 61 (1).
"seller": s. 61 (1).

GENERAL NOTE
Where a seller has to send goods to the buyer in order to fulfil the contract, delivery to a carrier is delivery to the buyer.

Subs. (2) provides that any contract of carriage unilaterally arranged by the seller must be reasonable having regard to the nature of the goods and the circumstances of the case. The buyer has a remedy where the contract of carriage is not reasonable. Sellers should therefore have regard to these factors when making a contract of carriage as well as to the terms and conditions of the carrier; the impact of the Unfair Contract Terms Act 1977 is in addition to the obligations imposed by this section.

See *Thomas Young & Sons Ltd.* v. *Hobson & Partners* (1949) 65 T.L.R. 365. It must be stressed that while delivery to a carrier is treated as delivery to the buyer, the delivery to the carrier does not deny the buyer's right to examine the goods for conformity to the contract.

Risk where goods are delivered at distant place

33. Where the seller of goods agrees to deliver them at his own risk at a place other than that where they are when sold, the buyer must nevertheless (unless otherwise agreed) take any risk of deterioration in the goods necessarily incident to the course of transit.

DERIVATION
1893, s. 33.

DEFINITIONS
"buyer": s. 61 (1).
"delivery": s. 61 (1).
"goods": s. 61 (1).
"seller": s. 61 (1).

GENERAL NOTE
To relieve the buyer from the consequences of deterioration in transit the contract must specifically so provide.

Buyer's right of examining the goods

34.—(1) Where goods are delivered to the buyer, and he has not previously examined them, he is not deemed to have accepted them until he has had a reasonable opportunity of examining them for the purpose of ascertaining whether they are in conformity with the contract.

(2) Unless otherwise agreed, when the seller tenders delivery of goods to the buyer, he is bound on request to afford the buyer a reasonable opportunity of examining the goods for the purpose of ascertaining whether they are in conformity with the contract.

DERIVATION
1893, s. 34.

DEFINITIONS
"buyer": s. 61 (1).
"contract of sale": s. 2 (1) and s. 61 (1).
"delivery": s. 61 (1).
"goods": s. 61 (1).
"seller": s. 61 (1).

GENERAL NOTE

This and the following section are key provisions in the working through of a contract for the sale of goods. As will be seen, acceptance in s. 35 is crucial; this section deals with the point immediately preceding that. Subs. (1) enacts that a buyer has a right to examine goods which are delivered to see if they conform unless he has done so before. This right cannot be avoided by contract terms. Subs. (2) says that when the seller tenders delivery, the buyer must have a reasonable opportunity to examine—unless the contract provides to the contrary. It is submitted that any electrical or mechanical goods cannot be tested for conformity until they have been used, and that the buyer must be given a reasonable chance to do this; being required to sign a delivery or acceptance note " goods received in good condition " would not, it is submitted, relieve the seller from liability until a test was made.

Acceptance

35.—(1) The buyer is deemed to have accepted the goods when he intimates to the seller that he has accepted them, or (except where section 34 above otherwise provides) when the goods have been delivered to him and he does any act in relation to them which is inconsistent with the ownership of the seller, or when after the lapse of a reasonable time he retains the goods without intimating to the seller that he has rejected them.

(2) Paragraph 10 of Schedule 1 below applies in relation to a contract made before 22 April 1967 or (in the application of this Act to Northern Ireland) 28 July 1967.

DERIVATION

1893, s. 35, and Misrepresentation Act 1967.

DEFINITIONS

" buyer ": s. 61 (1).
" delivery ": s. 61 (1).
" goods ": s. 61 (1).
" seller ": s. 61 (1).

GENERAL NOTE

The words in brackets were added by the 1967 Act.

This section covers the crucial stage in the contract. Once goods have been " accepted " by the buyer the right to reject is lost. The buyer is left with a claim for damages for breach of warranty—not rescission and breach of condition (see s. 11, *ante*). There are three categories of deemed acceptance:

(i) intimation to the seller;

(ii) delivery to the buyer followed by his doing something which is inconsistent with the seller's ownership; this would extend to the use of goods by a consumer—wiring them up, wearing them, washing them, etc., or to the sale of them by retail. See *E. & S. Ruben* v. *Faire Bros. Ltd.* [1949] 1 K.B. 254 and *Wallis* v. *Pratt* [1911] A.C. 394.

But this is subject to the words in brackets which preserve the right of the buyer to examine the goods for conformity within a reasonable time;

(iii) when the buyer retains the goods without rejecting within a reasonable time.

See:

Tiffin v. *Pitcher* [1969] C.L.Y. 3234.
Lee v. *York Coach & Marine* [1977] R.T.R. 35.
Leaf v. *International Galleries* [1950] 2 K.B. 86.
Mechan v. *Bow McLachlan & Co.*, 1910 S.C. 758.
Cf. Jackson v. *Chrysler Acceptances Ltd.* [1978] R.T.R. 474.
Sheridan v. *J. R. Calvert* (*Quarry Plant*) [1979] 2 C.L. (unreported).

Buyer not bound to return rejected goods

36. Unless otherwise agreed, where goods are delivered to the buyer, and he refuses to accept them, having the right to do so, he is not bound to return them to the seller, but it is sufficient if he intimates to the seller that he refuses to accept them.

DERIVATION
1893, s. 36.

DEFINITIONS
" buyer ": s. 61 (1).
" delivery ": s. 61 (1).
" goods ": s. 61 (1).
" seller ": s. 61 (1).

GENERAL NOTE
For the buyer to be required to return goods which he has rejected, the contract must so provide. It will be a question of fact whether any term or notice is incorporated into the contract. A buyer who finds that his seller will not collect rejected goods can claim damages for storage: *Kolfor Plant* v. *Tilbury Plant* (1977) 121 S.J. 390.

Buyer's liability for not taking delivery of goods

37.—(1) When the seller is ready and willing to deliver the goods, and requests the buyer to take delivery, and the buyer does not within a reasonable time after such request take delivery of the goods, he is liable to the seller for any loss occasioned by his neglect or refusal to take delivery, and also for a reasonable charge for the care and custody of the goods.

(2) Nothing in this section affects the rights of the seller where the neglect or refusal of the buyer to take delivery amounts to a repudiation of the contract.

DERIVATION
1893, s. 37.

DEFINITIONS
" buyer ": s. 61 (1).
" delivery ": s. 61 (1).
" goods ": s. 61 (1).
" seller ": s. 61 (1).

GENERAL NOTE
This section deals with the duty of the buyer to take delivery and sets out the consequences of his failure to do so. See s. 50 which sets out the measure of damages for non-acceptance.

PART V

RIGHTS OF UNPAID SELLER AGAINST THE GOODS

Preliminary

Unpaid seller defined

38.—(1) The seller of goods is an unpaid seller within the meaning of this Act—

(*a*) when the whole of the price has not been paid or tendered;
(*b*) when a bill of exchange or other negotiable instrument has been received as conditional payment, and the condition on which it

was received has not been fulfilled by reason of the dishonour of the instrument or otherwise.

(2) In this Part of this Act " seller " includes any person who is in the position of a seller, as, for instance, an agent of the seller to whom the bill of lading has been indorsed, or a consignor or agent who has himself paid (or is directly responsible for) the price.

DERIVATION
1893, s. 38.

DEFINITIONS
" goods ": s. 61 (1).
" seller ": s. 61 (1).

Unpaid seller's rights

39.—(1) Subject to this and any other Act, notwithstanding that the property in the goods may have passed to the buyer, the unpaid seller of goods, as such, has by implication of law—

(*a*) a lien on the goods or right to retain them for the price while he is in possession of them;

(*b*) in case of the insolvency of the buyer, a right of stopping the goods in transit after he has parted with the possession of them;

(*c*) a right of re-sale as limited by this Act.

(2) Where the property in goods has not passed to the buyer, the unpaid seller has (in addition to his other remedies) a right of withholding delivery similar to and co-extensive with his rights of lien or retention and stoppage in transit where the property has passed to the buyer.

DERIVATION
1893, s. 39.

DEFINITIONS
" buyer ": s. 61 (1).
" goods ": s. 61 (1).
" property ": s. 61 (1).
" unpaid seller ": s. 38.

Attachment by seller in Scotland

40. In Scotland a seller of goods may attach them while in his own hands or possession by arrestment or poinding; and such arrestment or poinding shall have the same operation and effect in a competition or otherwise as an arrestment or poinding by a third party.

DERIVATION
1893, s. 40.

DEFINITION
" seller ": s. 61 (1).

Unpaid seller's lien

Seller's lien

41.—(1) Subject to this Act, the unpaid seller of goods who is in possession of them is entitled to retain possession of them until payment or tender of the price in the following cases:—

(*a*) where the goods have been sold without any stipulation as to credit;

(b) where the goods have been sold on credit but the term of credit has expired;

(c) where the buyer becomes insolvent.

(2) The seller may exercise his lien or right of retention notwithstanding that he is in possession of the goods as agent or bailee or custodier for the buyer.

DERIVATION
1893, s. 41.

DEFINITIONS
"buyer": s. 61 (1).
"goods": s. 61 (1).
"insolvent": s. 61 (4).
"unpaid seller": s. 38.

GENERAL NOTE
Retention of possession is crucial to the exercise of a lien by an unpaid seller.

Part delivery

42. Where an unpaid seller has made part delivery of the goods, he may exercise his lien or right of retention on the remainder, unless such part delivery has been made under such circumstances as to show an agreement to waive the lien or right of retention.

DERIVATION
1893, s. 42.

DEFINITIONS
"delivery": s. 61 (1).
"goods": s. 61 (1).
"unpaid seller": s. 38.

Termination of lien

43.—(1) The unpaid seller of goods loses his lien or right of retention in respect of them—

(a) when he delivers the goods to a carrier or other bailee or custodier for the purpose of transmission to the buyer without reserving the right of disposal of the goods;

(b) when the buyer or his agent lawfully obtains possession of the goods;

(c) by waiver of the lien or right of retention.

(2) An unpaid seller of goods who has a lien or right of retention in respect of them does not lose his lien or right of retention by reason only that he has obtained judgment or decree for the price of the goods.

DERIVATION
1893, s. 43.

DEFINITIONS
"buyer": s. 61 (1).
"delivery": s. 61 (1).
"goods": s. 61 (1).
"unpaid seller": s. 38.

Stoppage in transit

Right of stoppage in transit

44. Subject to this Act, when the buyer of goods becomes insolvent the unpaid seller who has parted with the possession of the goods has the right of stopping them in transit, that is to say, he may resume possession of the goods as long as they are in course of transit, and may retain them until payment or tender of the price.

DERIVATION
1893, s. 44.

DEFINITIONS
"buyer": s. 61 (1).
"course of transit": s. 45 (1).
"goods": s. 61 (1).
"unpaid seller": s. 38.

Duration of transit

45.—(1) Goods are deemed to be in course of transit from the time when they are delivered to a carrier or other bailee or custodier for the purpose of transmission to the buyer, until the buyer or his agent in that behalf takes delivery of them from the carrier or other bailee or custodier.

(2) If the buyer or his agent in that behalf obtains delivery of the goods before their arrival at the appointed destination, the transit is at an end.

(3) If, after the arrival of the goods at the appointed destination, the carrier or other bailee or custodier acknowledges to the buyer or his agent that he holds the goods on his behalf and continues in possession of them as bailee or custodier for the buyer or his agent, the transit is at an end, and it is immaterial that a further destination for the goods may have been indicated by the buyer.

(4) If the goods are rejected by the buyer, and the carrier or other bailee or custodier continues in possession of them, the transit is not deemed to be at an end, even if the seller has refused to receive them back.

(5) When goods are delivered to a ship chartered by the buyer it is a question depending on the circumstances of the particular case whether they are in the possession of the master as a carrier or as agent to the buyer.

(6) Where the carrier or other bailee or custodier wrongfully refuses to deliver the goods to the buyer or his agent in that behalf, the transit is deemed to be at an end.

(7) Where part delivery of the goods has been made to the buyer or his agent in that behalf, the remainder of the goods may be stopped in transit, unless such part delivery has been made under such circumstances as to show an agreement to give up possession of the whole of the goods.

DERIVATION
1893, s. 45.

DEFINITIONS
"buyer": s. 61 (1).
"goods": s. 61 (1).
"seller": s. 38 (2) and s. 61 (1).

How stoppage in transit is effected

46.—(1) The unpaid seller may exercise his right of stoppage in transit either by taking actual possession of the goods or by giving notice of his claim to the carrier or other bailee or custodier in whose possession the goods are.

(2) The notice may be given either to the person in actual possession of the goods or to his principal.

(3) If given to the principal, the notice is ineffective unless given at such time and under such circumstances that the principal, by the exercise of reasonable diligence, may communicate it to his servant or agent in time to prevent a delivery to the buyer.

(4) When notice of stoppage in transit is given by the seller to the carrier or other bailee or custodier in possession of the goods, he must re-deliver the goods to, or according to the directions of, the seller; and the expenses of the re-delivery must be borne by the seller.

DERIVATION
1893, s. 46.

DEFINITIONS
" buyer ": s. 61 (1).
" delivery ": s. 61 (1).
" goods ": s. 61 (1).
" seller ": s. 38 (2) and s. 61 (1).
" unpaid seller ": s. 38.

Re-sale etc. by buyer

Effect of sub-sale etc. by buyer

47.—(1) Subject to this Act, the unpaid seller's right of lien or retention or stoppage in transit is not affected by any sale or other disposition of the goods which the buyer may have made, unless the seller has assented to it.

(2) Where a document of title to goods has been lawfully transferred to any person as buyer or owner of the goods, and that person transfers the document to a person who takes it in good faith and for valuable consideration, then—

(*a*) if the last-mentioned transfer was by way of sale the unpaid seller's right of lien or retention or stoppage in transit is defeated; and

(*b*) if the last-mentioned transfer was made by way of pledge or other disposition for value, the unpaid seller's right of lien or retention or stoppage in transit can only be exercised subject to the rights of the transferee.

DERIVATION
1893, s. 47.

DEFINITIONS
" buyer ": s. 61 (1).
" document of title ": s. 61 (1).
" good faith ": s. 61 (3).
" goods ": s. 61 (1).
" sale ": s. 61 (1).
" seller ": s. 38 (2) and s. 61 (1).
" unpaid seller ": s. 38.

Rescission: and re-sale by seller

Rescission: and re-sale by seller

48.—(1) Subject to this section, a contract of sale is not rescinded by the mere exercise by an unpaid seller of his right of lien or retention or stoppage in transit.

(2) Where an unpaid seller who has exercised his right of lien or retention or stoppage in transit re-sells the goods, the buyer acquires a good title to them as against the original buyer.

(3) Where the goods are of a perishable nature, or where the unpaid seller gives notice to the buyer of his intention to re-sell, and the buyer does not within a reasonable time pay or tender the price, the unpaid seller may re-sell the goods and recover from the original buyer damages for any loss occasioned by his breach of contract.

(4) Where the seller expressly reserves the right of re-sale in case the buyer should make default, and on the buyer making default re-sells the goods, the original contract of sale is rescinded but without prejudice to any claim the seller may have for damages.

DERIVATION

1893, s. 48.

DEFINITIONS

"buyer": s. 61 (1).
"contract of sale": s. 2 (1) and s. 61 (1).
"goods": s. 61 (1).
"unpaid seller": s. 38.

GENERAL NOTE

This section enables an unpaid seller to exercise various rights when the buyer is in default. It is important to note that the buyer from an unpaid seller gets a good title as against the defaulting buyer (subs. (2)). See *R. V. Ward* v. *Bignall* [1967] 1 Q.B. 534.

PART VI

ACTIONS FOR BREACH OF THE CONTRACT

Seller's remedies

Action for price

49.—(1) Where, under a contract of sale, the property in the goods has passed to the buyer and he wrongfully neglects or refuses to pay for the goods according to the terms of the contract, the seller may maintain an action against him for the price of the goods.

(2) Where, under a contract of sale, the price is payable on a day certain irrespective of delivery and the buyer wrongfully neglects or refuses to pay such price, the seller may maintain an action for the price, although the property in the goods has not passed and the goods have not been appropriated to the contract.

(3) Nothing in this section prejudices the right of the seller in Scotland to recover interest on the price from the date of tender of the goods, or from the date on which the price was payable, as the case may be.

DERIVATION

1893, s. 49.

DEFINITIONS

"action": s. 61 (1).
"buyer": s. 61 (1).
"contract of sale": s. 2 (1) and s. 61 (1).
"delivery": s. 61 (1).
"goods": s. 61 (1).
"property": s. 61 (1).
"seller": s. 61 (1).

GENERAL NOTE

This section contains the basic remedies for the seller of goods. By subs. (1) once the property has passed and the buyer defaults the seller may sue for the price. By subs. (2) the seller who has expressly provided for payment on a given day may sue for the price when the day has passed even though neither property has passed nor appropriation taken place.

Damages for non-acceptance

50.—(1) Where the buyer wrongfully neglects or refuses to accept and pay for the goods, the seller may maintain an action against him for damages for non-acceptance.

(2) The measure of damages is the estimated loss directly and naturally resulting, in the ordinary course of events, from the buyer's breach of contract.

(3) Where there is an available market for the goods in question the measure of damages is prima facie to be ascertained by the difference between the contract price and the market or current price at the time or times when the goods ought to have been accepted or (if no time was fixed for acceptance) at the time of the refusal to accept.

DERIVATION

1893, s. 50.

DEFINITIONS

"action": s. 61 (1).
"buyer": s. 61 (1).
"goods": s. 61 (1).
"seller": s. 61 (1).

GENERAL NOTE

Subs. (1) contains the remedy for the seller where the buyer refuses to accept and pay for the goods.

Subs. (2) states the rules of the calculation of the measure of damages. See:

Lazenby Garages v. *Wright* [1976] 1 W.L.R. 459.
Harlow and Jones v. *Panex* (*International*) [1967] 2 Lloyd's Rep. 509.
Thompson v. *Robinson* (*Gunmakers*) [1955] 2 W.L.R. 185.

Buyer's remedies

Damages for non-delivery

51.—(1) Where the seller wrongfully neglects or refuses to deliver the goods to the buyer, the buyer may maintain an action against the seller for damages for non-delivery.

(2) The measure of damages is the estimated loss directly and naturally resulting, in the ordinary course of events, from the seller's breach of contract.

(3) Where there is an available market for the goods in question the measure of damages is prima facie to be ascertained by the difference between the contract price and the market or current price of the goods at the time or times when they ought to have been delivered or (if no time was fixed) at the time of the refusal to deliver.

DERIVATION

1893, s. 51.

DEFINITIONS

"action": s. 61 (1).
"buyer": s. 61 (1).
"goods": s. 61 (1).
"seller": s. 61 (1).

Specific performance

52.—(1) In any action for breach of contract to deliver specific or ascertained goods the court may, if it thinks fit, on the plaintiff's application, by its judgment or decree direct that the contract shall be performed specifically, without giving the defendant the option of retaining the goods on payment of damages.

(2) The plaintiff's application may be made at any time before judgment or decree.

(3) The judgment or decree may be unconditional, or on such terms and conditions as to damages, payment of the price and otherwise as seem just to the court.

(4) The provisions of this section shall be deemed to be supplementary to, and not in derogation of, the right of specific implement in Scotland.

DERIVATION

1893, s. 52.

DEFINITIONS

"action": s. 61 (1).
"defendant": s. 61 (1).
"delivery": s. 61 (1).
"goods": s. 61 (1).
"plaintiff": s. 61 (1).
"specific goods": s. 61 (1).

Remedy for breach of warranty

53.—(1) Where there is a breach of warranty by the seller, or where the buyer elects (or is compelled) to treat any breach of a condition on the part of the seller as a breach of warranty, the buyer is not by reason only of such breach of warranty entitled to reject the goods; but he may—

(*a*) set up against the seller the breach of warranty in diminution or extinction of the price, or

(*b*) maintain an action against the seller for damages for the breach of warranty.

(2) The measure of damages for breach of warranty is the estimated loss directly and naturally resulting, in the ordinary course of events, from the breach of warranty.

(3) In the case of breach of warranty of quality such loss is prima facie the difference between the value of the goods at the time of delivery to the buyer and the value they would have had if they had fulfilled the warranty.

(4) The fact that the buyer has set up the breach of warranty in diminution or extinction of the price does not prevent him from maintaining an action for the same breach of warranty if he has suffered further damage.

(5) Nothing in this section prejudices or affects the buyer's right of rejection in Scotland as declared by this Act.

DERIVATION

1893, s. 53.

DEFINITIONS

"action": s. 61 (1).
"buyer": s. 61 (1).
"delivery": s. 61 (1).
"goods": s. 61 (1).
"quality": s. 61 (1).
"seller": s. 61 (1).
"warranty": s. 61 (1).

General Note

Parties to a contract must appreciate the distinction between warranty and condition and read this section with s. 11 (*ante*). Where there is a breach of warranty the remedy is an action for damages not for rescission.

See:

Collins v. *Martin-Bird, The Times,* December 6, 1963.
Jackson v. *Watson & Sons* [1909] 2 K.B. 193.
Tai Hing Cotton Mill v. *Kamsing Knitting Factory* [1978] 2 W.L.R. 62.
Jackson v. *Horizon Holidays* [1975] 1 W.L.R. 1468.
Jarvis v. *Swans Tours* [1973] 1 Q.B. 233.
Fothergill v. *Monarch Airlines* [1977] 3 W.L.R. 885.
Daily Office Cleaning Contractors v. *Shefford* [1977] R.T.R. 361.
Robbins of Putney v. *Meek* [1971] R.T.R. 345.

Interest, etc.

Interest, etc.

54. Nothing in this Act affects the right of the buyer or the seller to recover interest or special damages in any case where by law interest or special damages may be recoverable, or to recover money paid where the consideration for the payment of it has failed.

Derivation

1893, s. 54.

Definitions

" buyer ": s. 61 (1).
" seller ": s. 61 (1).

Part VII

Supplementary

Exclusion of implied terms

55.—(1) Where a right, duty or liability would arise under a contract of sale of goods by implication of law, it may (subject to the Unfair Contract Terms Act 1977) be negatived or varied by express agreement, or by the course of dealing between the parties, or by such usage as binds both parties to the contract.

(2) An express condition or warranty does not negative a condition or warranty implied by this Act unless inconsistent with it.

(3) Paragraph 11 of Schedule 1 below applies in relation to a contract made on or after 18 May 1973 and before 1 February 1978, and paragraph 12 in relation to one made before 18 May 1973.

Derivation

1893, s. 55, substituted by 1973, s. 4, amended by 1977.

Definitions

" contract of sale ": s. 2 (1) and s. 61 (1).
" warranty ": s. 61 (1).

General Note

This section has been the subject of considerable amendment in its time. The original section (printed in para. 12 of Sched. 1 (*post*)) was the provision which enabled those who so desired to avoid or limit their obligations as to fitness, quality and description in ss. 11 to 15. This remained the law until May 18, 1973, when the Supply of Goods (Implied Terms) Act came into force. That Act restricted the power to contract out as far as the new class of " consumer sales " were concerned; the replaced section is contained in para. 11 of Sched. 1 (*post*) for contracts made on or after May 18, 1973, and February 1, 1978 (when the Unfair Contract Terms Act 1977 came into force).

The effect of the Unfair Contract Terms Act is to alter the concept of a "consumer sale" and replace it with a contract made by a person "dealing as consumer." In such a case, terms in a contract limiting liability for the breach of the provisions of ss. 13, 14 and 15 are void. In other contracts of sale or hire purchase these terms are subject to the test of reasonableness: and in contracts under which goods pass but which are not sales or hire-purchase agreements—work and materials, bailment, exchange, for example—such terms are subject to both the test of reasonableness and the guidelines contained in Sched. 2 to the 1977 Act.

It should be noted that the Consumer Transactions (Restrictions on Statements) Order 1976 (as amended) makes it a criminal offence in certain circumstances to limit liability for the inalienable rights created by ss. 13 to 15.

Conflict of laws

56. Paragraph 13 of Schedule 1 below applies in relation to a contract made on or after 18 May 1973 and before 1 February 1978, so as to make provision about conflict of laws in relation to such a contract.

Derivation

This section is new.

General Note

This section retains, by reference to para. 13 of Sched. 1, the provisions of s. 5 (1) of the Supply of Goods (Implied Terms) Act 1973, for the purpose of contracts made between May 18, 1973, and February 1, 1978.

Auction sales

57.—(1) Where the goods are put up for sale by auction in lots, each lot is prima facie deemed to be the subject of a separate contract of sale.

(2) A sale by auction is complete when the auctioneer announces its completion by the fall of the hammer, or in other customary manner; and until the announcement is made any bidder may retract his bid.

(3) A sale by auction may be notified to be subject to a reserve or upset price, and a right to bid may also be reserved expressly by or on behalf of the seller.

(4) Where a sale by auction is not notified to be subject to a right to bid by or on behalf of the seller, it is not lawful for the seller to bid himself or to employ any person to bid at the sale, or for the auctioneer knowingly to take any bid from the seller or any such person.

(5) A sale contravening subsection (4) above may be treated as fraudulent by the buyer.

(6) Where, in respect of a sale by auction, a right to bid is expressly reserved (but not otherwise) the seller or any one person on his behalf may bid at the auction.

Derivation

1893, s. 58.

Definitions

"buyer": s. 61 (1).
"contract of sale": s. 2 (1) and s. 61 (1).
"goods": s. 61 (1).
"sale": s. 61 (1).
"seller": s. 61 (1).

General Note

This section sets out the rules for auctions, slightly rewritten for clarity in six subsections replacing four. It should be noted that by virtue of s. 12 (2) of the

Unfair Contract Terms Act 1977 the buyer at an auction—whoever he is—cannot be treated as dealing as consumer and thus none of the protections which are implied by this Act apply. As in any other offer, a bid may be withdrawn at any time until it is accepted and the contract is completed by the fall of the hammer.

Payment into court in Scotland

58. In Scotland where a buyer has elected to accept goods which he might have rejected, and to treat a breach of contract as only giving rise to a claim for damages, he may, in an action by the seller for the price, be required, in the discretion of the court before which the action depends, to consign or pay into court the price of the goods, or part of the price, or to give other reasonable security for its due payment.

DERIVATION
1893, s. 59.

DEFINITIONS
"action": s. 61 (1).
"buyer": s. 61 (1).
"goods": s. 61 (1).
"seller": s. 61 (1).

Reasonable time a question of fact

59. Where a reference is made in this Act to a reasonable time the question what is a reasonable time is a question of fact.

DERIVATION
1893, s. 56.

GENERAL NOTE
For references to time regard should be had to ss. 18 (4), 29 (3), 35, 37 and 48 (3). Comparison can also be made with s. 29 (5) where "reasonable hour" is used. The purpose of this section is to remove any uncertainty that formerly existed whether the reasonableness of time was a question of law or fact.

Rights etc. enforceable by action

60. Where a right, duty or liability is declared by this Act, it may (unless otherwise provided by this Act) be enforced by action.

DERIVATION
1893, s. 57.

DEFINITION
"action": s. 61 (1).

Interpretation

61.—(1) In this Act, unless the context or subject matter otherwise requires,—

"action" includes counterclaim and set-off, and in Scotland condescendence and claim and compensation;

"business" includes a profession and the activities of any government department (including a Northern Ireland department) or local or public authority;

"buyer" means a person who buys or agrees to buy goods;

"contract of sale" includes an agreement to sell as well as a sale;

"credit-broker" means a person acting in the course of a business of credit brokerage carried on by him, that is a business of effecting introductions of individuals desiring to obtain credit—

(*a*) to persons carrying on any business so far as it relates to the provision of credit, or

(*b*) to other persons engaged in credit brokerage;

" defendant " includes in Scotland defender, respondent, and claimant in a multiplepoinding;

" delivery " means voluntary transfer of possession from one person to another;

" document of title to goods " has the same meaning as it has in the Factors Acts;

" Factors Acts " means the Factors Act 1889, the Factors (Scotland) Act 1890, and any enactment amending or substituted for the same;

" fault " means wrongful act or default;

" future goods " means goods to be manufactured or acquired by the seller after the making of the contract of sale;

" goods " includes all personal chattels other than things in action and money, and in Scotland all corporeal moveables except money; and in particular " goods " includes emblements, industrial growing crops, and things attached to or forming part of the land which are agreed to be severed before sale or under the contract of sale;

" plaintiff " includes pursuer, complainer, claimant in a multiplepoinding and defendant or defender counterclaiming;

" property " means the general property in goods, and not merely a special property;

" quality ", in relation to goods, includes their state or condition;

" sale " includes a bargain and sale as well as a sale and delivery;

" seller " means a person who sells or agrees to sell goods;

" specific goods " means goods identified and agreed on at the time a contract of sale is made;

" warranty " (as regards England and Wales and Northern Ireland) means an agreement with reference to goods which are the subject of a contract of sale, but collateral to the main purpose of such contract, the breach of which gives rise to a claim for damages, but not to a right to reject the goods and treat the contract as repudiated.

(2) As regards Scotland a breach of warranty shall be deemed to be a failure to perform a material part of the contract.

(3) A thing is deemed to be done in good faith within the meaning of this Act when it is in fact done honestly, whether it is done negligently or not.

(4) A person is deemed to be insolvent within the meaning of this Act if he has either ceased to pay his debts in the ordinary course of business or he cannot pay his debts as they become due, whether he has committed an act of bankruptcy or not, and whether he has become a notour bankrupt or not.

(5) Goods are in a deliverable state within the meaning of this Act when they are in such a state that the buyer would under the contract be bound to take delivery of them.

(6) As regards the definition of " business " in subsection (1) above, paragraph 14 of Schedule 1 below applies in relation to a contract made on or after 18 May 1973 and before 1 February 1978, and paragraph 15 in relation to one made before 18 May 1973.

Savings: rules of law etc.

62.—(1) The rules in bankruptcy relating to contracts of sale apply to those contracts, notwithstanding anything in this Act.

(2) The rules of the common law, including the law merchant, except in so far as they are inconsistent with the provisions of this Act, and in particular the rules relating to the law of principal and agent and the effect of fraud, misrepresentation, duress or coercion, mistake, or other invalidating cause, apply to contracts for the sale of goods.

(3) Nothing in this Act or the Sale of Goods Act 1893 affects the enactments relating to bills of sale, or any enactment relating to the sale of goods which is not expressly repealed or amended by this Act or that.

(4) The provisions of this Act about contracts of sale do not apply to a transaction in the form of a contract of sale which is intended to operate by way of mortgage, pledge, charge, or other security.

(5) Nothing in this Act prejudices or affects the landlord's right of hypothec or sequestration for rent in Scotland.

Derivation
1893, s. 61.

Definition
" contract of sale ": s. 2 (1) and s. 61 (1).

Consequential amendments, repeals and savings

63.—(1) Without prejudice to section 17 of the Interpretation Act 1978 (repeal and re-enactment), the enactments mentioned in Schedule 2 below have effect subject to the amendments there specified (being amendments consequential on this Act).

(2) The enactments mentioned in Schedule 3 below are repealed to the extent specified in column 3, but subject to the savings in Schedule 4 below.

(3) The savings in Schedule 4 below have effect.

General Note
By subs. (2) there is created a fourth class of contract to which a different combination of legislation applies. There are those made before May 18, 1973; those made between that date and February 1, 1978; those made from February 1, 1978, until January 1, 1980; and those made after the coming into force of this Act. The Act applies to England, Wales, Scotland and Northern Ireland.

Short title and commencement

64.—(1) This Act may be cited as the Sale of Goods Act 1979.

(2) This Act comes into force on 1 January 1980.

SCHEDULES

Section 1 SCHEDULE 1

Modification of Act for Certain Contracts

Preliminary

1.—(1) This Schedule modifies this Act as it applies to contracts of sale of goods made on certain dates.

(2) In this Schedule references to sections are to those of this Act and references to contracts are to contracts of sale of goods.

(3) Nothing in this Schedule affects a contract made before 1 January 1894.

Section 11: condition treated as warranty

2. In relation to a contract made before 22 April 1967 or (in the application of this Act to Northern Ireland) 28 July 1967, in section 11 (4) after " or part of them," insert " or where the contract is for specific goods, the property in which has passed to the buyer,".

Section 12: *implied terms about title etc.*

3. In relation to a contract made before 18 May 1973 substitute the following for section 12:—

Implied terms about title, etc.

12. In a contract of sale, unless the circumstances of the contract are such as to show a different intention, there is—

(*a*) an implied condition on the part of the seller that in the case of a sale he has a right to sell the goods, and in the case of an agreement to sell he will have such a right at the time when the property is to pass;

(*b*) an implied warranty that the buyer will have and enjoy quiet possession of the goods;

(*c*) an implied warranty that the goods will be free from any charge or encumbrance in favour of any third party, not declared or known to the buyer before or at the time when the contract is made.

Section 13: *sale by description*

4. In relation to a contract made before 18 May 1973, omit section 13 (3).

Section 14: *quality or fitness* (*i*)

5. In relation to a contract made on or after 18 May 1973 and before the appointed day, substitute the following for section 14:—

Implied terms about quality or fitness

14.—(1) Except as provided by this section and section 15 below and subject to any other enactment, there is no implied condition or warranty about the quality or fitness for any particular purpose of goods supplied under a contract of sale.

(2) Where the seller sells goods in the course of a business, there is an implied condition that the goods supplied under the contract are of merchantable quality, except that there is no such condition—

(*a*) as regards defects specifically drawn to the buyer's attention before the contract is made; or

(*b*) if the buyer examines the goods before the contract is made, as regards defects which that examination ought to reveal.

(3) Where the seller sells goods in the course of a business and the buyer, expressly or by implication, makes known to the seller any particular purpose for which the goods are being bought, there is an implied condition that the goods supplied under the contract are reasonably fit for that purpose, whether or not that is a purpose for which such goods are commonly supplied, except where the circumstances show that the buyer does not rely, or that it is unreasonable for him to rely, on the seller's skill or judgment.

(4) An implied condition or warranty about quality or fitness for a particular purpose may be annexed to a contract of sale by usage.

(5) The preceding provisions of this section apply to a sale by a person who in the course of a business is acting as agent for another as they apply to a sale by a principal in the course of a business, except where that other is not selling in the course of a business and either the buyer knows that fact or reasonable steps are taken to bring it to the notice of the buyer before the contract is made.

(6) Goods of any kind are of merchantable quality within the meaning of subsection (2) above if they are as fit for the purpose or purposes for which goods of that kind are commonly bought as it is reasonable to expect having regard to any description applied to them, the price (if relevant) and all the other relevant circumstances.

(7) In the application of subsection (3) above to an agreement for the sale of goods under which the purchase price or part of it is payable by instalments any reference to the seller includes a reference to the person by whom any antecedent negotiations are conducted; and section 58 (3) and (5) of the Hire-Purchase Act 1965, section 54 (3) and (5) of the Hire-Purchase (Scotland) Act 1965 and section 65 (3) and (5) of the Hire-Purchase Act (Northern Ireland) 1966 (meaning of antecedent negotiations and related

expressions) apply in relation to this subsection as in relation to each of those Acts, but as if a reference to any such agreement were included in the references in subsection (3) of each of those sections to the agreements there mentioned.

Section 14: *quality or fitness* (*ii*)

6. In relation to a contract made before 18 May 1973 substitute the following for section 14:—

Implied terms about quality or fitness

14.—(1) Subject to this and any other Act, there is no implied condition or warranty about the quality or fitness for any particular purpose of goods supplied under a contract of sale.

(2) Where the buyer, expressly or by implication, makes known to the seller the particular purpose for which the goods are required, so as to show that the buyer relies on the seller's skill or judgment, and the goods are of a description which it is in the course of the seller's business to supply (whether he is the manufacturer or not), there is an implied condition that the goods will be reasonably fit for such purpose, except that in the case of a contract for the sale of a specified article under its patent or other trade name there is no implied condition as to its fitness for any particular purpose.

(3) Where goods are bought by description from a seller who deals in goods of that description (whether he is the manufacturer or not), there is an implied condition that the goods will be of merchantable quality; but if the buyer has examined the goods, there is no implied condition as regards defects which such examination ought to have revealed.

(4) An implied condition or warranty about quality or fitness for a particular purpose may be annexed by the usage of trade.

(5) An express condition or warranty does not negative a condition or warranty implied by this Act unless inconsistent with it.

Section 15: *sale by sample*

7. In relation to a contract made before 18 May 1973, omit section 15 (3).

Section 22: *market overt*

8. In relation to a contract under which goods were sold before 1 January 1968 or (in the application of this Act to Northern Ireland) 29 August 1967, add the following paragraph at the end of section 22 (1):—

" Nothing in this subsection affects the law relating to the sale of horses."

Section 25: *buyer in possession*

9. In relation to a contract under which a person buys or agrees to buy goods and which is made before the appointed day, omit section 25 (2).

Section 35: *acceptance*

10. In relation to a contract made before 22 April 1967 or (in the application of this Act to Northern Ireland) 28 July 1967, in section 35 (1) omit " (except where section 34 above otherwise provides) ".

Section 55: *exclusion of implied terms* (*i*)

11. In relation to a contract made on or after 18 May 1973 and before 1 February 1978 substitute the following for section 55:—

Exclusion of implied terms

55.—(1) Where a right, duty or liability would arise under a contract of sale of goods by implication of law, it may be negatived or varied by express agreement, or by the course of dealing between the parties, or by such usage as binds both parties to the contract, but the preceding provision has effect subject to the following provisions of this section.

(2) An express condition or warranty does not negative a condition or warranty implied by this Act unless inconsistent with it.

(3) In the case of a contract of sale of goods, any term of that or any other contract exempting from all or any of the provisions of section 12 above is void.

(4) In the case of a contract of sale of goods, any term of that or any other contract exempting from all or any of the provisions of section 13, 14 or 15 above is void in the case of a consumer sale and is, in any other case, not enforceable to the extent that it is shown that it would not be fair or reasonable to allow reliance on the term.

(5) In determining for the purposes of subsection (4) above whether or not reliance on any such term would be fair or reasonable regard shall be had to all the circumstances of the case and in particular to the following matters—

(*a*) the strength of the bargaining positions of the seller and buyer relative to each other, taking into account, among other things, the availability of suitable alternative products and sources of supply;

(*b*) whether the buyer received an inducement to agree to the term or in accepting it had an opportunity of buying the goods or suitable alternatives without it from any source of supply;

(*c*) whether the buyer knew or ought reasonably to have known of the existence and extent of the term (having regard, among other things, to any custom of the trade and any previous course of dealing between the parties);

(*d*) where the term exempts from all or any of the provisions of section 13, 14 or 15 above if some condition is not complied with, whether it was reasonable at the time of the contract to expect that compliance with that condition would be practicable;

(*e*) whether the goods were manufactured, processed, or adapted to the special order of the buyer.

(6) Subsection (5) above does not prevent the court from holding, in accordance with any rule of law, that a term which purports to exclude or restrict any of the provisions of section 13, 14 or 15 above is not a term of the contract.

(7) In this section " consumer sale " means a sale of goods (other than a sale by auction or by competitive tender) by a seller in the course of a business where the goods—

(*a*) are of a type ordinarily bought for private use or consumption; and

(*b*) are sold to a person who does not buy or hold himself out as buying them in the course of a business.

(8) The onus of proving that a sale falls to be treated for the purposes of this section as not being a consumer sale lies on the party so contending.

(9) Any reference in this section to a term exempting from all or any of the provisions of any section of this Act is a reference to a term which purports to exclude or restrict, or has the effect of excluding or restricting, the operation of all or any of the provisions of that section, or the exercise of a right conferred by any provision of that section, or any liability of the seller for breach of a condition or warranty implied by any provision of that section.

(10) It is hereby declared that any reference in this section to a term of a contract includes a reference to a term which although not contained in a contract is incorporated in the contract by another term of the contract.

(11) Nothing in this section prevents the parties to a contract for the international sale of goods from negativing or varying any right, duty or liability which would otherwise arise by implication of law under sections 12 to 15 above.

(12) In subsection (11) above " contract for the international sale of goods " means a contract of sale of goods made by parties whose places of business (or, if they have none, habitual residences) are in the territories of different States (the Channel Islands and the Isle of Man being treated for this purpose as different States from the United Kingdom) and in the case of which one of the following conditions is satisfied:—

(*a*) the contract involves the sale of goods which are at the time of the conclusion of the contract in the course of carriage or will be carried from the territory of one State to the territory of another; or (*b*) the acts constituting the offer and acceptance have been effected in the territories of different States; or

(*c*) delivery of the goods is to be made in the territory of a State other than that within whose territory the acts constituting the offer and the acceptance have been effected.

Section 55: *exclusion of implied terms* (*ii*)

12. In relation to a contract made before 18 May 1973 substitute the following for section 55:—

Exclusion of implied terms

55. Where a right, duty or liability would arise under a contract of sale by implication of law, it may be negatived or varied by express agreement, or by the course of dealing between the parties, or by such usage as binds both parties to the contract.

Section 56: *conflict of laws*

13.—(1) In relation to a contract made on or after 18 May 1973 and before 1 February 1978 substitute for section 56 the section set out in sub-paragraph (3) below.

(2) In relation to a contract made otherwise than as mentioned in sub-paragraph (1) above, ignore section 56 and this paragraph.

(3) The section mentioned in sub-paragraph (1) above is as follows:—

Conflict of laws

56.—(1) Where the proper law of a contract for the sale of goods would, apart from a term that it should be the law of some other country or a term to the like effect, be the law of any part of the United Kingdom, or where any such contract contains a term which purports to substitute, or has the effect of substituting, provisions of the law of some other country for all or any of the provisions of sections 12 to 15 and 55 above, those sections shall, notwithstanding that term but subject to subsection (2) below, apply to the contract.

(2) Nothing in subsection (1) above prevents the parties to a contract for the international sale of goods from negativing or varying any right, duty or liability which would otherwise arise by implication of law under sections 12 to 15 above.

(3) In subsection (2) above " contract for the international sale of goods " means a contract of sale of goods made by parties whose places of business (or, if they have none, habitual residences) are in the territories of different States (the Channel Islands and the Isle of Man being treated for this purpose as different States from the United Kingdom) and in the case of which one of the following conditions is satisfied:—

(*a*) the contract involves the sale of goods which are at the time of the conclusion of the contract in the course of carriage or will be carried from the territory of one State to the territory of another; or

(*b*) the acts constituting the offer and acceptance have been effected in the territories of different States; or

(*c*) delivery of the goods is to be made in the territory of a State other than that within whose territory the acts constituting the offer and the acceptance have been effected.

Section 61 (1): *definition of " business "* (*i*)

14. In relation to a contract made on or after 18 May 1973 and before 1 February 1978, in the definition of " business " in section 61 (1) for " or local or public authority " substitute ", local authority or statutory undertaker ".

Section 61 (1): *definition of " business "* (*ii*)

15. In relation to a contract made before 18 May 1973 omit the definition of " business " in section 61 (1).

Section 63

SCHEDULE 2

Consequential Amendments

War Risks Insurance Act 1939 (2 & 3 Geo. 6 c. 57)

1. In section 15 (1) (*e*) of the War Risks Insurance Act 1939 for " section sixty-two of the Sale of Goods Act 1893 " substitute " section 61 of the Sale of Goods Act 1979 ".

Law Reform (Frustrated Contracts) Act 1943 (6 & 7 Geo. 6 c. 40)

2. In section 2 (5) (*c*) of the Law Reform (Frustrated Contracts) Act 1943 for " section seven of the Sale of Goods Act 1893 " substitute " section 7 of the Sale of Goods Act 1979 ".

Frustrated Contracts Act (Northern Ireland) 1947 (c. 2)

3. In section 2 (5) (*c*) of the Frustrated Contracts Act (Northern Ireland) 1947 for " section seven of the Sale of Goods Act 1893 " substitute " section 7 of the Sale of Goods Act 1979 ".

Hire-Purchase Act 1964 (c. 53)

4. In section 27 (5) of the Hire-Purchase Act 1964 (as originally enacted and as substituted by Schedule 4 to the Consumer Credit Act 1974)—

(*a*) in paragraph (*a*) for " section 21 of the Sale of Goods Act 1893 " substitute " section 21 of the Sale of Goods Act 1979 ";

(*b*) in paragraph (*b*) for " section 62 (1) of the said Act of 1893 " substitute " section 61 (1) of the said Act of 1979 ".

Hire-Purchase Act 1965 (c. 66)

5. In section 20 of the Hire-Purchase Act 1965—

(*a*) in subsection (1) for " Section 11 (1) (*c*) of the Sale of Goods Act 1893 " substitute " Section 11 (4) of the Sale of Goods Act 1979 ";

(*b*) in subsection (3) for " sections 12 to 15 of the Sale of Goods Act 1893 " substitute " sections 12 to 15 of the Sale of Goods Act 1979 ".

6. In section 54 of the Hire-Purchase Act 1965 for " section 25 (2) of the Sale of Goods Act 1893 " substitute " section 25 (1) of the Sale of Goods Act 1979 ".

7. In section 58 (1) of the Hire-Purchase Act 1965 for " the Sale of Goods Act 1893 " substitute " the Sale of Goods Act 1979 ".

Hire-Purchase (Scotland) Act 1965 (c. 67)

8. In section 20 of the Hire-Purchase (Scotland) Act 1965 for " 1893 " substitute " 1979 ".

9. In section 50 of the Hire-Purchase (Scotland) Act 1965 for " section 25 (2) of the Sale of Goods Act 1893 " substitute " section 25 (1) of the Sale of Goods Act 1979 ".

10. In section 54 (1) of the Hire-Purchase (Scotland) Act 1965 for " the Sale of Goods Act 1893 " substitute " the Sale of Goods Act 1979 ".

Hire-Purchase Act (Northern Ireland) 1966 (c. 42)

11. In section 20 of the Hire-Purchase Act (Northern Ireland) 1966—

(*a*) in subsection (1) for " Section 11 (1) (*c*) of the Sale of Goods Act 1893 " substitute " Section 11 (4) of the Sale of Goods Act 1979 ";

(*b*) in subsection (3) for " 1893 " substitute " 1979 ".

12. In section 54 of the Hire-Purchase Act (Northern Ireland) 1966 for " section 25 (2) of the Sale of Goods Act 1893 " substitute " section 25 (1) of the Sale of Goods Act 1979 ".

13. In section 62 (5) of the Hire-Purchase Act (Northern Ireland) 1966 (as originally enacted and as substituted by Schedule 4 to the Consumer Credit Act 1974)—

(*a*) in paragraph (*a*) for " 1893 " substitute " 1979 ";

(*b*) in paragraph (*b*) for " section 62 (1) of the said Act of 1893 " substitute " section 61 (1) of the said Act of 1979 ".

14. In section 65 (1) of the Hire-Purchase Act (Northern Ireland) 1966 for "the Sale of Goods Act 1893" substitute "the Sale of Goods Act 1979".

Uniform Laws on International Sales Act 1967 (c. 45)

15. For section 1 (4) of the Uniform Laws on International Sales Act 1967 substitute the following:—

"(4) In determining the extent of the application of the Uniform Law on Sales by virtue of Article 4 thereof (choice of parties)—

(*a*) in relation to a contract made before 18 May 1973, no provision of the law of any part of the United Kingdom shall be regarded as a mandatory provision within the meaning of that Article;

(*b*) in relation to a contract made on or after 18 May 1973 and before 1 February 1978, no provision of that law shall be so regarded except sections 12 to 15, 55 and 56 of the Sale of Goods Act 1979;

(*c*) in relation to a contract made on or after 1 February 1978, no provision of that law shall be so regarded except sections 12 to 15 of the Sale of Goods Act 1979".

Supply of Goods (Implied Terms) Act 1973 (c. 13).

16. In section 14 (1) of the Supply of Goods (Implied Terms) Act 1973 (as originally enacted and as substituted by Schedule 4 to the Consumer Credit Act 1974) for "Section 11 (1) (*c*) of the principal Act" substitute "Section 11 (4) of the Sale of Goods Act 1979".

17. For the definition of "consumer sale" in section 15 (1) of the Supply of Goods (Implied Terms) Act 1973 substitute—

"consumer sale" has the same meaning as in section 55 of the Sale of Goods Act 1979 (as set out in paragraph 11 of Schedule 1 to that Act).

Consumer Credit Act 1974 (c. 39)

18. In section 189 (1) of the Consumer Credit Act 1974, in the definition of "goods", for "section 62 (1) of the Sale of Goods Act 1893" substitute "section 61 (1) of the Sale of Goods Act 1979".

Unfair Contract Terms Act 1977 (c. 50)

19. In section 6 of the Unfair Contract Terms Act 1977—

(*a*) in subsection (1) (*a*) for "section 12 of the Sale of Goods Act 1893" substitute "section 12 of the Sale of Goods Act 1979";

(*b*) in subsection (2) (*a*) for "section 13, 14 or 15 of the 1893 Act" substitute "section 13, 14 or 15 of the 1979 Act".

20. In section 14 of the Unfair Contract Terms Act 1977, in the definition of "goods", for "the Sale of Goods Act 1893" substitute "the Sale of Goods Act 1979".

21. In section 20 (1) (*a*) and (2) (*a*) of the Unfair Contract Terms Act 1977 for "1893" substitute (in each case) "1979".

22. In section 25 (1) of the Unfair Contract Terms Act 1977, in the definition of "goods", for "the Sale of Goods Act 1893" substitute "the Sale of Goods Act 1979".

Section 63

SCHEDULE 3

Repeals

Chapter	Short title	Extent of repeal
56 & 57 Vict. c. 71.	Sale of Goods Act 1893.	The whole Act except section 26.
1967 c. 7.	Misrepresentation Act 1967.	Section 4. In section 6 (3) the words ", except section 4 (2),".
1967 c. 14 (N.I.)	Misrepresentation Act (Northern Ireland) 1967.	Section 4.
1973 c. 13.	Supply of Goods (Implied Terms) Act 1973.	Sections 1 to 7. Section 18 (2).
1974 c. 39.	Consumer Credit Act 1974.	In Schedule 4, paragraphs 3 and 4.
1977 c. 50.	Unfair Contract Terms Act 1977.	In Schedule 3, the entries relating to the Sale of Goods Act 1893.

Section 63

SCHEDULE 4

SAVINGS

Preliminary

1. In this Schedule references to the 1893 Act are to the Sale of Goods Act 1893.

Orders

2. An order under section 14 (8) or 25 (4) above may make provision that it is to have effect only as provided by the order (being provision corresponding to that which could, apart from this Act, have been made by an order under section 192 (4) of the Consumer Credit Act 1974 bringing into operation an amendment or repeal making a change corresponding to that made by the order under section 14 (8) or 25 (4) above).

Offences

3. Where an offence was committed in relation to goods before 1 January 1969 or (in the application of this Act to Northern Ireland) 1 August 1969, the effect of a conviction in respect of the offence is not affected by the repeal by this Act of section 24 of the 1893 Act.

1893 Act, section 26

4. The repeal by this Act of provisions of the 1893 Act does not extend to the following provisions of that Act in so far as they are needed to give effect to or interpret section 26 of that Act, namely, the definitions of " goods " and " property " in section 62 (1), section 62 (2) and section 63 (which was repealed subject to savings by the Statute Law Revision Act 1908).

Things done before 1 *January* 1894

5. The repeal by this Act of section 60 of and the Schedule to the 1893 Act (which effected repeals and which were themselves repealed subject to savings by the Statute Law Revision Act 1908) does not affect those savings, and accordingly does not affect things done or acquired before 1 January 1894.

6. In so far as the 1893 Act applied (immediately before the operation of the repeals made by this Act) to contracts made before 1 January 1894 (when the 1893 Act came into operation), the 1893 Act shall continue so to apply notwithstanding this Act.

Justices of the Peace Act 1979*

(1979 c. 55)

ARRANGEMENT OF SECTIONS

PART I

GENERAL

* Annotations by Alec Samuels, J.P., Barrister, Reader in Law, University of Southampton.

General Note

The royal assent was given on December 6, 1979. The Act came into force on March 6, 1980, s. 72 (2). This Act is a consolidation Act, consolidating principally the Justices of the Peace Act 1949 and the Justices of the Peace Act 1968, but also other enactments going back to 1742. The Act relates to justices of the peace, justices' clerks and the administrative and financial arrangements for magistrates' courts and connected matters. The Act arises out of Justices of the

Peace Bill, the Law Commission Report No. 94 Cmnd. 7583, June 1979. See also the Report of the Joint Committee on Consolidation Bills H.L. 50–I and H.C. 184–I, Session 1979–1980, July 18, 1979. Notes on Clauses (supplied to the Joint Committee).

The Act of 1361 is not consolidated. The reason is that nobody knows for certain what is the correct wording! One version of it is that it is a power to bind over those of good fame and the other is that it is a power to bind over those not of good fame and nobody knows for certain which it is. Any reform or change in this matter would not be appropriate for a consolidation Act.

The expressions "magistrate" and "petty sessional court-house" are defined in the definition section, s. 70. LC in the annotations refers to the Law Commission Report.

Parliamentary Debates

See *Hansard,* H.L. Vol. 400, col. 1111; Vol. 402, cols. 604, 1391; H.C. Vol. 974, col. 1435; Vol. 975, col. 383.

Table of Derivations

JUSTICES JURISDICTION ACT 1742

1742	1979
s. 1	s. 65

JUSTICES PROTECTION ACT 1848

1848	1979
s. 1	s. 44
2	45
3	46
s. 4	ss. 47, 49 (1) (2)
5	s. 48 (1)
6	48 (2)
s. 7	s. 50
10	51
13	52

STIPENDIARY MAGISTRATES ACT 1858

1858	1979
s. 1	s. 16 (3)
2	16 (4)
3	16 (5)

LOCAL GOVERNMENT ACT 1888

1888	1979
s. 42 (12)	s. 66 (2)

METROPOLITAN POLICE COURTS ACT 1897

1897	1979
ss. 1, 8	s. 58 (3)

ADMINISTRATION OF JUSTICE (MISCELLANEOUS PROVISIONS) ACT 1938

1938	1979
Sch. 2	s. 48 (1)

JUSTICES OF THE PEACE ACT 1949

1949	1979
s. 1 (1)–(3)	s. 7 (1)–(3)
(5)	68 (1)
3 (1)	64 (1)
(2)–(4)	64 (2)–(4)
5	ss. 7 (4), 64 (5)
13 (1)	s. 18 (1)
(2)	17 (1)
(3)	17 (2)
(4)	17 (3)
(5)	18 (2) (4)
(5A)	18 (3)
(6)	18 (5)
16 (1)	19 (1)
(2)	19 (2) (3)
(5)	69
17	63 (1)
s. 18 (1)	s. 23 (1)
(2)	23 (2)
(3)	23 (3)
(4)	23 (5)
(5)	24 (1)
(6)	24 (2)
(7)	24 (3)
(8)	23 (4)
(9)	24 (6)
(10)	24 (5)
19 (1)	25 (1)
(2)	27 (1)
(3–(7)	27 (2)–(7)
(8)	25 (2)
(9)	25 (3)
(11)	25 (4)
20 (1)	26 (1)
s. 20 (2)	s. 26 (2)
(4) (5)	26 (3)–(5)
21 (1)	29 (1) (2)
(4)	Sch. 1, para. 14
23 (1)	Sch. 1, paras. 10, 11
(2)	Sch. 1, para. 10
(7)	Sch. 1, para. 11
25	s. 55
26 (1)	56 (1)
(2)	56 (2)
(3)	56 (2)–(4)
27 (1)	61 (1)–(3)
(2)	59 (1)–(3)

JUSTICES OF THE PEACE ACT 1949—*continued*

1949	1979
s. 27 (5) (6).	s. 59 (4) (5)
(7) ...	61 (2)
(9) ...	61 (4)
(10) ..	61 (7)
(*d*)	59 (6)
(12) ..	61 (5)
42	Sch. 1, para. 13
43 (1) ...	s. 59 (1)–(3)
44 (1) ...	ss. 4 (2), 18 (1) (6), 61 (7), 70
Sch. 2	Sch. 1, para. 15
Sch. 4,	
para. 1 (1).	s. 20 (1)
para. 1 (2).	20 (3)
para. 1 (2A)	20 (2)
para. 1 (4)–(6)	20 (4)–(6)
para. 1 (7).	21 (1) (3)
para. 1 (8).	21 (2)
para. 1 (9).	21 (4)
para. 2 ...	19 (3)
Sch. 4,	
para. 5 ...	s. 22 (3)
para. 6 ...	19 (4)
para. 7 ...	22 (7)
para. 8 ...	22 (6)
para. 9 (1).	22 (1)
para. 9 (2).	22 (2)
para. 10 ..	22 (4)
para. 11 ..	22 (5)

MAGISTRATES' COURTS ACT 1952

1952	1979
s. 116 (1)	s. 66 (1)
118 (3) (4) .	30 (1) (2)
121 (1)	16 (1)
Sch. 5	61 (1)

LICENSING ACT 1953

1953	1979
Pt. II	s. 27 (1)
s. 168 (1) (5) .	27 (1)
Sch. 10	27 (1)

METROPOLITAN MAGISTRATES' COURTS ACT 1959

1959	1979
s. 2 (1) (2) ..	s. 34 (1) (2)
(3)	67 (4)
(4)	34 (3)

LICENSING ACT 1964

1964	1979
Pt. VII	s. 27 (1)
Sch. 14, para. 1 ..	27 (1)

ADMINISTRATION OF JUSTICE ACT 1964

1964	1979
s. 2 (1)	s. 2 (1)
(3)	ss. 2 (2), 4 (2), 19 (1)–(3), 20 (1) (3), 21 (2), 23 (1) (2) (4), 24 (5), 57 (1) (2), 66 (1)
3	s. 3
9	33
10 (1) ...	31 (1)
(2)–(5)	31 (2)–(5)
(6)–(8)	32
13 (1) ...	ss. 19 (1)–(3), 20 (1), 23 (1) (4), 35 (1)
s. 13 (2)–(4)	s. 35 (2)–(4)
(5) ...	35 (5)
(6) ...	38 (3)
(7) ...	35 (6)
14	36
15 (1) (2).	37 (1) (2)
(3) ...	38 (4)
(4)–(6)	37 (3)–(5)
(7) ...	37 (6) (7)
(8) ...	ss. 25 (5), 27 (9)
16 (1) ...	s. 38 (1)
(2) ...	ss. 38 (2), 63 (2)
(3) ...	s. 38 (5)
17 (1) ...	58 (1)
(2) ...	58 (2)
(3) (4).	58 (4) (5)
(5) ...	57 (1) (2)
s. 27	s. 53
28	54
30 (1) (2).	67 (1) (2)
(5) ...	67 (5)
32	Sch. 1, para. 13
36	s. 36
(1) ...	ss. 37 (6) (7), 53 (4)
37 (4) ...	s. 60, Sch. 2, para. 26
38 (1) ...	s. 70
Sch. 3,	
para. 2 ...	26 (3)–(5)
para. 12 (1)	66 (2)
para. 20 (6)	57 (1) (2)
para. 20 (7)	59 (6)

JUSTICES OF THE PEACE ACT 1965

1965	1979
s. 1	s. 26 (3)–(5)

GENERAL RATE ACT 1967

1967	1979
ss. 2 (5), 116 (1) ..	s. 49 (1) (2)

Superannuation (Miscellaneous Provisions) Act 1967

1967	1979
s. 15 (8) (9) ..	s. 58 (2)

Justices of the Peace Act 1968

1968	1979
s. 1 (2)	s. 39 (1)
(3)	67 (3)
3	18 (3)
5 (1)	28 (1) (2)
(2)	27 (8)
(3)	28 (3) (4)
8 (2)	26 (3)–(5)
Sch. 2,	
para. 1 ...	39 (2)
para. 2 (1).	40 (1)
para. 2 (2).	40 (4)
para. 3 ...	40 (2)

1968	1979
Sch. 2,	
para. 4 ...	s. 40 (3)
Sch. 3,	
para. 1 (*b*)	ss. 41 (1), 57 (3), 59 (6)
para. 2 ...	s. 39 (3)
para. 3 ...	ss. 4 (2), 19 (2), 20 (1), 21 (2), 41 (1), 57 (3), 59 (6), 66 (1)

1968	1979
Sch. 3,	
para. 4 (4).	ss. 19 (3), 42
para. 8 ...	s. 30 (1) (2)
para. 15 ..	Sch. 1, para. 12
para. 16 ..	Sch. 1, para. 13
Sch. 5, Pt. II	s.26 (3)–(5)

Decimal Currency Act 1969

1969	1979
s. 10 (1), Sch. 1 ..	s. 52

Courts Act 1971

1971	1979
s. 3	s. 5 (2)
Sch. 7, para. 2 (1) ..	20 (2)
para. 3	22 (3)
Sch. 8, para. 2	ss. 54 (1), 61 (5), 64 (1)
para. 43 (1) .	s. 35 (5)

Superannuation Act 1972

1972	1979
Sch. 7, para. 5 ..	s. 59 (1)–(3)

Local Government Act 1972

1972	1979
s. 216	s. 69
217 (3) ..	4 (1)
(5) ..	55 (1)
Sch. 27,	
para. 1 ...	68 (1)
para. 5 (1).	19 (1)
para. 5 (2).	19 (2) (3)
para. 5 (4).	69
para. 6 (1).	23 (1)
para. 6 (2).	23 (2)
para. 6 (3).	24 (1) (2)
para. 6 (4).	23 (4)
para. 6 (5).	24 (6)

1972	1979
Sch. 27,	
para. 6 (6).	s. 24 (4)
para. 7 (1).	25 (2) (3)
para. 9 (1).	55 (1)
para. 9 (2).	55 (2)
para. 10 (4)	59 (6)
para. 13 ..	4 (2)
para. 14 (1)	20 (1)
para. 14 (2)	20 (2) (3)
para. 14 (3)–(5)	20 (4)–(6)
para. 14 (6)	21 (1) (3)
para. 14 (7)	21 (2)

1972	1979
Sch. 27,	
para. 14 (8)	s. 19 (3)
para. 14 (10)	22 (2)
para. 17 (2)	ss. 57 (1) (2), 59 (6)
para. 19 (1)	ss. 4 (2), 19 (2) (3), 41 (1), 57 (3)
Sch. 29,	
para. 1 (2).	s. 64 (1)

Criminal Justice Act 1972

1972	1979
s. 61 (1)	s. 61 (6)
(2)	59 (1)–(3)
62 (1)	63 (5)
(3)	62 (1) (2)
(4)	ss. 62 (1) (2), 63 (6)

Administration of Justice Act 1973

1973	1979
s. 1 (1)	ss. 1, 5 (1)
(2)	6 (1) (2), 11, Sch.1, para. 4
(3)	ss. 11, 43
(4)	8 (1), 11

1973	1979
s. 1 (6)	ss. 6 (2), 39 (1), 43
(7)	s. 68 (1) (2)
(8)	69
2 (1)	13 (1) (2)
(2)	13 (3)

1973	1979
s. 2 (3)	s. 16 (2)
(5)	14 (1)
(6)	ss. 13 (4) (5), 31 (1) (7)
(7)	s. 15
3 (1)	63 (3)

ADMINISTRATION OF JUSTICE ACT 1973—*continued*

1973	**1979**
s. 3 (2)	s. 63 (4)
20 (3) (*a*).	Sch. 1, para. 3
(*h*).	Sch. 1, para. 4
(5) ...	Sch. 1, paras. 7, 8
(6) ...	Sch. 1, para. 5
Sch. 1,	
para. 1 ...	s. 31 (6)
para. 1 (1).	14 (1)
para. 1 (2).	14 (2)
Sch. 1,	
para. 3 ...	s. 31 (6)
para. 4 (1)–(4)	8 (2)–(7)
para. 4 (5).	68 (2)
para. 4 (6).	8 (2)–(7)
para. 5 ...	9
para. 6 ...	10
para. 8 (1).	12 (1)
para. 8 (2) (3)	12 (2) (3)
para. 8 (3A)	12 (4)
para. 8 (4).	12 (5)
Sch. 1,	
para. 8 (5).	s. 12 (6)
para. 8 (6).	12 (7)
para. 9 (1).	71 (3), Sch. 1, para. 6
para. 9 (1) (*a*)	s. 7 (1)–(3)
para. 12 ..	59 (1)–(3)
Sch. 5,	
para. 14 ..	60

SOCIAL SECURITY ACT 1973

1973	**1979**
Sch. 27, para. 98 ..	s. 12 (1)

POWERS OF CRIMINAL COURTS ACT 1973

1973	**1979**
Sch. 5, para. 14 ..	Sch. 2, para. 26

SOCIAL SECURITY PENSIONS ACT 1975

1975	**1979**
Sch. 4, para. 5 ..	s. 58 (2)

ADMINISTRATION OF JUSTICE ACT 1977

1977	**1979**
s. 21 (1)	s. 17 (2)
(2)	18 (2)
Sch. 2, para. 5 ..	12 (4) (6)

DOMESTIC PROCEEDINGS AND MAGISTRATES' COURTS ACT 1978

1978	**1979**
s. 86	ss. 2 (2), 4 (2), 19 (1)–(3), 20 (1), 21 (2), 23 (1) (2) (4), 57 (1) (2)
Sch. 2, para. 10 ..	s. 17 (3)

An Act to consolidate certain enactments relating to justices of the peace (including stipendiary magistrates), justices' clerks and the administrative and financial arrangements for magistrates' courts, and to matters connected therewith, with amendments to give effect to recommendations of the Law Commission.

[6th December 1979]

PART I

GENERAL

Areas and commissions of the peace

Commission areas

1. There shall in England and Wales be a commission of the peace for the following areas (in this Act referred to as " commission areas ") and no others, that is to say—

(*a*) every county;
(*b*) every London commission area; and
(*c*) the City of London.

DERIVATION
1973, s. 1.

London commission areas

2.—(1) Subject to the provisions of section 3 of this Act, the following areas of Greater London, that is to say—

(*a*) an area to be known as the " inner London area ", consisting of the inner London boroughs;

(*b*) an area to be known as the " north-east London area ", consisting of the London Boroughs of Barking, Havering, Newham, Redbridge and Waltham Forest;

(*c*) an area to be known as the " south-east London area ", consisting of the London boroughs of Bexley, Bromley and Croydon;

(*d*) an area to be known as the " south-west London area ", consisting of the London boroughs of Kingston upon Thames, Merton, Richmond upon Thames and Sutton; and

(*e*) an area to be known as the " Middlesex area ", consisting of the London boroughs of Barnet, Brent, Ealing, Enfield, Haringey, Harrow, Hillingdon and Hounslow,

are in this Act referred to as " London commission areas ', and the areas specified in paragraphs (*b*) *to* (*e*) above are in this Act referred to as the " outer London areas ".

(2) Subject to the provisions of this Act, a London commission area shall be deemed to be a non-metropolitan county for all purposes of the law relating to commissions of the peace, justices of the peace, magistrates' courts, magistrates' courts committees, the keeper of the rolls, justices' clerks and matters connected with any of those matters; and references to a county in any enactment passed or instrument made before the 10th June 1964, and references to a non-metropolitan county in any enactment or instrument as amended or modified by or under the Local Government Act 1972, shall be construed accordingly.

(3) Subsection (2) above shall not apply to any enactment (including any enactment contained in this Act) to which apart from this subsection it would apply and which expressly refers in the same context both—

(*a*) to a county or counties or to a non-metropolitan county or non-metropolitan counties, and

(*b*) to a London commission area or London commission areas or any of those areas;

and the generality of subsection (2) above shall not be taken to be prejudiced by any enactment to which by virtue of this subsection that subsection does not apply.

DERIVATION
1964, s. 2.

GENERAL NOTE
For the sake of clarity the Act spells out in full the areas to which the provisions of the Act apply, instead of the former deeming provisions. LC para. 10.

Power to adjust London commission areas

3.—(1) Her Majesty may by Order in Council substitute for any one or more of the areas specified in section 2 (1) above any other area or areas comprising the whole or part of Greater London, or alter the boundaries of any area so specified; but the City of London shall not by virtue of any such Order be included in a London commission area.

(2) An Order in Council made under this section may contain such incidental, consequential, transitional or supplementary provisions as may be necessary or expedient for the purposes of the Order (including provisions amending this Act or any other enactment).

(3) Any statutory instrument made by virtue of this section shall be subject to annulment in pursuance of a resolution of either House of Parliament.

DERIVATION
1974, s. 3.

GENERAL NOTE
Since 1968 the City of London has been specifically a separate commission of the peace and this is accordingly specifically spelt out. LC para. 11.

Petty sessions areas

4.—(1) The following areas outside Greater London are petty sessions areas, that is to say—
(*a*) every non-metropolitan county which is not divided into petty sessional divisions;
(*b*) every petty sessional division of a non-metropolitan county;
(*c*) every metropolitan district which is not divided into petty sessional divisions; and
(*d*) every petty sessional division of a metropolitan district.

(2) In the following provisions of this Act "petty sessions area" means any of the following, that is to say—
(*a*) any of the areas outside Greater London specified in subsection (1) above;
(*b*) any London commission area which is not divided into petty sessional divisions;
(*c*) any petty sessional division of a London commission area; and
(*d*) the City of London.

DERIVATION
1949, s. 44 (1); 1964, s. 2 (3), 1972, s. 217 (3).

General form of commissions of the peace

5.—(1) The commission of the peace for any commission area shall be a commission under the Great Seal addressed generally, and not by name, to all such persons as may from time to time hold office as justices of the peace for the commission area.

(2) A commission of the peace issued after the commencement of this Act shall be framed so as to take account of the abolition of courts of quarter sessions by section 3 of the Courts Act 1971.

DERIVATION
1971, s. 3; 1973, s. 1 (1).

Justices other than stipendiary magistrates

Appointment and removal of justices of the peace

6.—(1) Subject to the following provisions of this Act, justices of the peace for any commission area shall be appointed on behalf and in the name of Her Majesty by instrument under the hand of the Lord Chancellor, and a justice so appointed may be removed from office in like manner.

(2) The preceding subsection does not apply to stipendiary magistrates and shall be without prejudice to the position of the Lord Mayor and aldermen as justices for the City of London by virtue of the charters of the City.

DERIVATION
1973, s. 1 (2) (6).

Residence qualification

7.—(1) Subject to the provisions of this section, a person shall not be appointed as a justice of the peace for a commission area in accordance with section 6 of this Act, nor act as a justice of the peace by virtue of any such appointment, unless he resides in or within fifteen miles of that area.

(2) If the Lord Chancellor is of opinion that it is in the public interest for a person to act as a justice of the peace for a particular area though not qualified to do so under subsection (1) above, he may direct that, so long as any conditions specified in the direction are satisfied, that subsection shall not apply in relation to that person's appointment as a justice of the peace for the area so specified.

(3) Where a person appointed as a justice of the peace for a commission area in accordance with section 6 of this Act is not qualified under the preceding provisions of this section to act by virtue of the appointment, he shall be removed from office as a justice of the peace in accordance with section 6 of this Act if the Lord Chancellor is of opinion that the appointment ought not to continue having regard to the probable duration and other circumstances of the want of qualification.

(4) No act or appointment shall be invalidated by reason only of the disqualification or want of qualification under this section of the person acting or appointed.

DERIVATION

1979, ss. 1, 5; 1973, Sched. 1, para. 9 (1).

Supplemental list for England and Wales

8.—(1) There shall be kept in the office of the Clerk of the Crown in Chancery a supplemental list for England and Wales as provided for by this Act (in this Act referred to as "the supplemental list").

(2) Subject to the following provisions of this section, there shall be entered in the supplemental list—

(*a*) the name of any justice of the peace who is of the age of 70 years or over and neither holds nor has held high judicial office within the meaning of the Appellate Jurisdiction Act 1876, and

(*b*) the name of any justice of the peace who holds or has held such office and is of the age of 75 years or over.

(3) A person who on the date when his name falls to be entered in the supplemental list in accordance with subsection (2) above holds office as chairman of the justices in a petty sessions area (whether by an election made, or having effect as if made, under section 17 of this Act, or, in the City of London, as Chief Magistrate or acting Chief Magistrate) shall have his name so entered on the expiry or sooner determination of the term for which he holds office on that date.

(4) The Lord Chancellor may direct that the name of a justice of the peace for any area shall be entered in the supplemental list if the Lord Chancellor is satisfied either—

(*a*) that by reason of the justice's age or infirmity or other like cause it is expedient that he should cease to exercise judicial functions as a justice for that area, or

(*b*) that the justice declines or neglects to take a proper part in the exercise of those functions.

(5) On a person's appointment as a justice of the peace for any area the Lord Chancellor may direct that his name shall be entered in the supplemental list, if that person is appointed a justice for that area on ceasing to be a justice for some other area.

(6) The name of a justice of the peace shall be entered in the supplemental list if he applies for it to be so entered and the application is approved by the Lord Chancellor.

(7) Nothing in this section shall apply to a person holding office as stipendiary magistrate.

DERIVATION
1973, ss. 1 (4), 5, Sched. 1, para. 4.

Removal of name from supplemental list

9.—(1) A person's name shall be removed from the supplemental list if he ceases to be a justice of the peace.

(2) The name of any person, if not required to be entered in the supplemental list by subsection (2) or subsection (3) of section 8 of this Act, shall be removed from the list if so directed by the Lord Chancellor.

DERIVATION
1973, Sched. 1, para. 5.

Effect of entry of name in supplemental list

10.—(1) Subject to the following subsections, a justice of the peace for any area, while his name is entered in the supplemental list, shall not by reason of being a justice for that area be qualified as a justice to do any act or to be a member of any committee or other body.

(2) Subsection (1) above shall not preclude a justice from doing all or any of the following acts as a justice, that is to say—

(*a*) signing any document for the purpose of authenticating another person's signature;

(*b*) taking and authenticating by his signature any written declaration not made on oath; and

(*c*) giving a certificate of facts within his knowledge or of his opinion as to any matter.

(3) The entry of a person's name in the supplemental list shall also not preclude him, if so authorised by the Lord Chancellor, from acting as a judge of the Crown Court so long as he has not attained the age of 72 years.

(4) No act or appointment shall be invalidated by reason of the disqualification under this section of the person acting or appointed.

DERIVATION
1973, Sched. 1, para. 6.

Records of justices of the peace

11.—(1) In each commission area, other than the City of London, such one of the justices as may be designated by the Lord Chancellor shall be keeper of the rolls.

(2) There shall be transmitted to the keeper of the rolls for each commission area, and be enrolled in the records of the justices for that area, a copy of any instrument appointing or removing a justice of the peace in that area in accordance with section 6 of this Act; and the keeper of the rolls shall be notified, in such manner as the Lord Chancellor may direct, of any resignation or death of a justice so appointed, and shall cause to be kept, and from time to time rectified, a record of those for the time being holding office by virtue of any such appointment.

(3) There shall be kept in the office of the Clerk of the Crown in Chancery a record of all persons for the time being holding office as justices of the peace by virtue of appointments made in accordance with section 6 of this Act, together with the instruments of appointment or removal.

DERIVATION
1973, s. 1 (2)–(4).

Travelling, subsistence and financial loss allowances

12.—(1) Subject to the provisions of this section, a justice of the peace shall be entitled—

(a) to receive payments by way of travelling allowance or subsistence allowance where expenditure on travelling or, as the case may be, on subsistence is necessarily incurred by him for the purpose of enabling him to perform any of his duties as a justice, and

(b) to receive payments by way of financial loss allowance where for that performance there is incurred by him any other expenditure to which he would not otherwise be subject or there is suffered by him any loss of earnings or of benefit under the enactments relating to social security which he would otherwise have made or received.

(2) For the purposes of this section, a justice following a course of instruction under a scheme made in accordance with arrangements approved by the Lord Chancellor, or a course of instruction provided by the Lord Chancellor, shall be deemed to be acting in the performance of his duties as a justice.

(3) A justice shall not be entitled to any payment under this section in respect of any duties, if in respect of those duties a payment of the like nature may be paid to him under arrangements made apart from this section or if regulations provide that this section shall not apply; and a stipendiary magistrate shall not be entitled to any payment under this section in respect of his duties as such.

(4) Allowances payable under this section shall be paid at rates determined by the Secretary of State with the consent of the Minister for the Civil Service.

(5) An allowance payable under this section in respect of duties as a justice in the Crown Court shall be paid by the Lord Chancellor; and an allowance otherwise payable under this section to a justice for any commission area in respect of his duties as such shall be paid by the appropriate authority in relation to that area, that is to say—

(a) in relation to the City of London, the Common Council;

(b) in relation to the inner London area, the Receiver;

(c) in relation to any of the outer London areas, the Greater London Council;

(d) in relation to a non-metropolitan county, the county council;

(e) in relation to a metropolitan county, the council of the metropolitan district which is or includes the petty sessions area for which the justice acts.

(6) Regulations may make provision as to the manner in which this section is to be administered, and in particular—

(a) for prescribing the forms to be used and the particulars to be provided for the purpose of claiming payment of allowances; and

(b) for avoiding duplication between payments under this section and under other arrangements where expenditure is incurred for more than one purpose, and otherwise for preventing abuses.

(7) Regulations for the purposes of this section shall be made by the Secretary of State by statutory instrument, which shall be subject to annulment in pursuance of a resolution of either House of Parliament.

DERIVATION
1973, Sched. 1, para. 8.

Stipendiary magistrates other than metropolitan stipendiary magistrates

Appointment and removal of stipendiary magistrates

13.—(1) It shall be lawful for Her Majesty to appoint a barrister or solicitor of not less than seven years' standing to be, during Her Majesty's pleasure, a whole-time stipendiary magistrate in any commission area or areas outside the inner London area and the City of

London, and to appoint more than one such magistrate in the same area or areas.

(2) A person so appointed to be a magistrate in any commission area shall by virtue of his office be a justice of the peace for that area.

(3) Any appointment of a stipendiary magistrate under this section shall be of a person recommended to Her Majesty by the Lord Chancellor, and a stipendiary magistrate appointed under this section shall not be removed from office except on the Lord Chancellor's recommendation.

(4) The number of stipendiary magistrates appointed under this section shall not at any time exceed forty or such larger number as Her Majesty may from time to time by Order in Council specify.

(5) Her Majesty shall not be recommended to make an Order in Council under subsection (4) above unless a draft of the Order has been laid before Parliament and approved by resolution of each House.

DERIVATION
1973, s. 2 (1) (2) (6).

Retirement of stipendiary magistrates

14.—(1) A stipendiary magistrate appointed on or after the 25th October 1968 shall vacate his office at the end of the completed year of service in the course of which he attains the age of 70:

Provided that where the Lord Chancellor considers it desirable in the public interest to retain him in office after that time, the Lord Chancellor may from time to time authorise him to continue in office up to such age not exceeding 72 as the Lord Chancellor thinks fit.

(2) A stipendiary magistrate appointed before the 25th October 1968 shall vacate his office at the end of the completed year of service in the course of which he attains the age of 72:

Provided that where the Lord Chancellor considers it desirable in the public interest to retain him in office after that time, the Lord Chancellor may from time to time authorise him to continue in office up to such age not exceeding 75 as the Lord Chancellor thinks fit.

DERIVATION
1973, s. 2 (5), Sched. 1, para. 1 (1) (2).

Acting stipendiary magistrate

15.—(1) Where it appears to the Lord Chancellor that it is expedient to do so in order to avoid delays in the administration of justice in any commission area in which a stipendiary magistrate can be appointed under section 13 of this Act, the Lord Chancellor—

(*a*) may authorise any person qualified to be so appointed to act as a stipendiary magistrate in the area during such period (not exceeding three months at one time) as the Lord Chancellor thinks fit, or

(*b*) may require so to act any stipendiary magistrate appointed under that section in another commission area.

(2) While acting as a stipendiary magistrate in any commission area under subsection (1) above, a person shall have the same jurisdiction, powers and duties as if he had been appointed stipendiary magistrate in that area and were a justice of the peace for that area.

(3) The Lord Chancellor may, out of moneys provided by Parliament, pay to any person authorised to act under this section, not being a stipendiary magistrate, such remuneration as he may, with the approval of the Minister for the Civil Service, determine.

DERIVATION
1973, s. 2 (7).

General Note

An acting stipendiary magistrate can be appointed by the Lord Chancellor to any commission area, including a commission area that normally has no stipendiary magistrate. LC para. 15.

Place of sitting and powers of stipendiary magistrates

16.—(1) Subject to subsection (5) below, nothing in the Magistrates' Courts Act 1952 requiring a magistrates' court to be composed of two or more justices, or to sit in a petty sessional court-house or an occasional court-house, or limiting the powers of a magistrates' court composed of a single justice, or when sitting elsewhere than in a petty sessional court-house, shall apply to any stipendiary magistrate sitting in a place appointed for the purpose.

(2) A stipendiary magistrate appointed under section 13 of this Act in any commission area shall sit at such court houses in the area, on such days and at such times as may be determined by, or in accordance with, directions given by the Lord Chancellor from time to time.

(3) Subject to subsection (5) below, a stipendiary magistrate so appointed, sitting at a place appointed for the purpose, shall have power to do any act, and to exercise alone any jurisdiction, which can be done or exercised by two justices under any law, other than any law made, after the 2nd August 1858 which contains an express provision to the contrary; and all the provisions of any Act which are auxiliary to the jurisdiction exercisable by two justices of the peace shall apply also to the jurisdiction of such a stipendiary magistrate.

(4) Subsection (3) above shall apply to cases where the act or jurisdiction in question is expressly required to be done or exercised by justices sitting or acting in petty sessions as it applies to other cases; and any enactment authorising or requiring persons to be summoned or to appear at petty sessions shall in the like cases authorise or require persons to be summoned or to appear before such a stipendiary magistrate at the place appointed for his sitting.

(5) Nothing in this section shall apply to the hearing or determination of domestic proceedings within the meaning of section 56 of the Magistrates' Courts Act 1952; and nothing in subsection (3) above shall apply to any act or jurisdiction relating to the grant or transfer of any licence.

Derivation

1858, ss. 1–3; 1952, s. 121 (1); 1973, s. 2 (3).

General Note

Domestic proceedings under the Domestic Proceedings and Magistrates' Courts Act 1978 must be kept separate from the criminal proceedings in magistrates' courts.

Part II

Organisation of Functions of Justices

General provisions

Chairman and deputy chairmen of justices

17.—(1) In any pettty sessions area there shall be a chairman and one or more deputy chairmen of the justices chosen from amongst themselves by the magistrates for the area by secret ballot.

(2) Subject to subsection (3) below, if the chairman or a deputy chairman of the justices for a petty sessions area is present at a meeting

of those justices, he shall preside unless he requests another justice to preside in accordance with rules made under the next following section.

(3) Subsection (2) above shall not confer on the chairman and deputy chairmen of the justices as such any right to preside in a juvenile or domestic court or at meetings of a committee or other body of justices having its own chairman, or at meetings when any stipendiary magistrate is engaged as such in administering justice.

DERIVATION

1949, s. 13 (2)–(4).

Rules as to chairmanship and size of bench

18.—(1) The number of justices (other than metropolitan stipendiary magistrates) sitting to deal with a case as a magistrates' court shall not be greater than the number prescribed by rules made under this section.

(2) Rules made under this section may make provision as to the manner in which section 17 of this Act and this section are to be administered, and in particular—

(*a*) as to the arrangements to be made for securing the presence on the bench of enough, but not more than enough, justices;

(*b*) as to the term of office and the procedure at an election of the chairman or a deputy chairman of the justices in a petty sessions area and the number of deputy chairmen to be elected in any such area; and

(*c*) as to the justices whom a chairman or deputy chairman of justices may request to preside at a meeting.

(3) The right of magistrates to vote at an election of the chairman or a deputy chairman of the justices in a petty sessions area may, by rules made under this section, be restricted with a view to securing that the election is made by magistrates experienced as such in the area.

(4) No rules shall be made under this section except on the advice of, or after consultation with, the rule committee established under section 15 of the Justices of the Peace Act 1949.

(5) Rules under this section shall be made by the Lord Chancellor by statutory instrument, which shall be subject to annulment in pursuance of a resolution of either House of Parliament.

DERIVATION

1949, ss. 13 (1) (5) (5A) (6), 15 (5), 44 (1); 1977, s. 21 (2).

DEFINITION

" magistrates' court ": Interpretation Act 1978, s. 5, Sched. 1 and Sched. 2, para. 4 (1) (*b*).

GENERAL NOTE

The obsolescent expression " court of summary jurisdiction " is superseded and replaced by the expression " magistrates' court." LC para. 5. See also ss. 29 (1), 61 (1) (*a*), (5) and (7) (*b*), and s. 64 (1) and (3).

Magistrates' courts committees

General provisions as to magistrates' courts committees

19.—(1) There shall continue to be committees (to be called " magistrates' courts committees ") set up in accordance with the following provisions of this Part of this Act, with such functions in relation to justices' clerks to the division into petty sessional divisions of non-metropolitan counties, metropolitan districts and the outer London areas, to the provision of courses of instruction for justices and to other matters of an administrative character as are or may be provided by or under this Act or as they may be authorised by the Secretary of State to undertake.

(2) Subject to subsection (3) below, there shall be a magistrates' courts committee for each area to which this subsection applies, that is to say—

(*a*) every non-metropolitan county;

(*b*) every metropolitan district;

(*c*) each of the outer London areas; and

(*d*) the City of London.

(3) There may be a single magistrates' courts committee for a composite area (in this Act referred to as a "joint committee area") consisting of two or more areas to which subsection (2) above applies, other than the City of London; but—

(*a*) there shall be a single magistrates' courts committee for such a composite area if, but only if, the area is for the time being directed by an order of the Secretary of State to be a joint committee area; and

(*b*) no order directing that a composite area shall be a joint committee area shall be made except on the application of the magistrates for each area to which subsection (2) above applies which is included in the composite area.

(4) Any order of the Secretary of State under subsection (3) above may, if it relates to an area for which a magistrates' courts committee is already acting, contain such consequential and transitional provisions for the preservation of rights and liabilities of that committee or otherwise as appear to the Secretary of State to be necessary or expedient.

DERIVATION

1949, s. 16 (1) (2), Sched. 4, para. 6; 1964, ss. 2 (3), 13 (1); 1968, Sched. 3, para. 3; 1972, Sched. 27, paras. 5, 14 and 19.

GENERAL NOTE

A joint committee area is expressly provided for the magistrates' court committee in order to avoid any possible doubt following local government reorganisation. LC para. 14.

Constitution of magistrates' courts committees

20.—(1) A magistrates' courts committee shall, subject to subsection (2) below,—

(*a*) in the case of a committee for a county, be composed of magistrates for the county;

(*b*) in the case of a committee for a metropolitan district, be composed of magistrates for the county comprising that district;

(*c*) in the case of a committee for any of the outer London areas or for the City of London, be composed of magistrates for that area or for the City, as the case may be; and

(*d*) in the case of a committee for a joint committee area, be composed of magistrates for such of the following as are applicable to it, that is to say, magistrates for each county, magistrates for the county comprising each metropolitan district, and magistrates for each London commission area, for which the committee acts.

(2) The magistrates' courts committee for any area may, with his consent, co-opt a judge of the High Court, Circuit judge or Recorder to serve as a member of the committee.

(3) The keeper of the rolls of a county shall by virtue of his office be a member of any magistrates' courts committee acting for the county or any district thereof; and the keeper of the rolls of a London com-

mission area shall by virtue of his office be a member of any magistrates' courts committee acting for that area.

(4) The magistrates' courts committee for an area to which section 19 (2) of this Act applies which is divided into petty sessional divisions shall (in addition to any person who is a member of the committee by virtue of subsection (2) or subsection (3) above) consist of such number of magistrates chosen from amongst themselves by the magistrates for each of the petty sessional divisions of that area as may be determined in accordance with regulations made by the Secretary of State under the next following section.

(5) The magistrates' courts committee for an area to which section 19 (2) of this Act applies which is not divided into petty sessional divisions shall (in addition to any person who is a member of the committee by virtue of subsection (2) or subsection (3) above) consist of such number of magistrates chosen from amongst themselves by the magistrates for that area as those magistrates may determine.

(6) The magistrates' courts committee for a joint committee area shall consist of the following persons, that is to say—

(*a*) any person who is a member of the committee by virtue of subsection (2) or subsection (3) above;

(*b*) in respect of any area to which section 19 (2) of this Act applies which is divided into petty sessional divisions and is included in the joint committee area, such number of magistrates, chosen from amongst themselves by the magistrates for each such petty sessional division, as may be determined in accordance with regulations made by the Secretary of State under the next following section; and

(*c*) in respect of any area to which section 19 (2) of this Act applies which is not divided into petty sessional divisions but is included in the joint committee area, such number of magistrates chosen from amongst themselves by the magistrates for the area so included as may for the time being be determined by, or in accordance with, the order directing that the composite area shall be a joint committee area.

DERIVATION

1949, s. 1 (1) (2A) (2) (4)–(6); 1964, s. 2 (3); 1968, Sched. 3, para. 3; 1972, Sched. 27, para. 14; 1978, s. 86.

Powers of Secretary of State in relation to magistrates' courts committees

21.—(1) The Secretary of State may by statutory instrument make general regulations about the constitution, procedure and quorum of magistrates' courts committees; but (except as provided by subsection (2) below) any such regulations shall have effect subject to the provisions of section 20 of this Act.

(2) Any such regulations may—

(*a*) lay down upper and lower limits for the number of members of which the magistrates' courts committee for an area to which section 19 (2) of this Act appplies which is not divided into petty sessional divisions may be composed, and

(*b*) direct that where, in an area to which section 19 (2) of this Act applies which is divided into petty sessional divisions, the total number of the divisions is less than that specified in the regulations, there shall from each division be such number of members on any magistrates' courts committee acting for the area as may be so specified.

(3) Any such regulations may also make provision with respect to the persons (other than the members, clerks and officers of the committee)

who may be entitled to attend the meetings of a magistrates' courts committee and the rights of such persons to make representations to the committee.

(4) The Secretary of State may give general or special directions with respect to summoning the first meeting of magistrates' courts committees.

DERIVATION

1949, Sched. 4, para. 1 (7)–(9); 1964, s. 2 (3); 1968, Sched. 3, para. 3; 1972, Sched. 27, para. 14 (6) (7).

Supplementary provisions as to magistrates' courts committees

22.—(1) A magistrates' courts committee shall appoint one of its members to be chairman of the committee and, subject to subsection (2) below, shall also appoint a clerk to the committee and may appoint such other officers (if any) as the Secretary of State may approve.

(2) Where there is a separate magistrates' courts committee for an area to which section 19 (2) of this Act applies which is not divided into petty sessional divisions, the clerk to the justices (that is to say—

(*a*) in the case of a non-metropolitan county, the county justices;

(*b*) in the case of a metropolitan district, the justices acting for that district;

(*c*) in the case of any of the outer London areas, the justices for that area; or

(*d*) in the case of the City of London, the justice for the City),

shall by virtue of his office be the clerk to the committee.

(3) Where the magistrates for a petty sessions area are required to meet for the purpose of carrying out any functions under section 20 of this Act, a meeting shall be convened by the magistrates' courts committee or, if there is no such committee in being or the Secretary of State considers it appropriate, by the Secretary of State.

(4) A magistrates' courts committee may act through sub-committees appointed by them.

(5) Subject to the provisions of this Act, a magistrates' courts committee shall have power to regulate its own procedure, including quorum.

(6) The proceedings of a magistrates' courts committee shall not be invalidated by reason of any vacancy therein or of any defect in the appointment of a member.

(7) A magistrates' courts committee shall be a body corporate.

DERIVATION

1949, Sched. 4, paras. 5, 9 (1) (2), 7, 8, 10, 11; 1972, Sched. 27, para. 14 (10).

GENERAL NOTE

It may be necessary to convene a meeting of magistrates for a petty sessional division, *e.g.* to elect representatives for the magistrates' courts committee, and the power so to convene is put beyond doubt. LC para. 8.

Powers and duties of committee as to petty sessional divisions

23.—(1) Subject to the provisions of this and the next following section, a magistrates' courts committee acting for a non-metropolitan county or metropolitan district or any of the outer London areas may at any time submit to the Secretary of State a draft order making such provision about the division of the county, district or area or any part thereof into petty sessional divisions as the committee think fit.

(2) It shall be the duty of such a committee, if directed to do so by the Secretary of State, to review the division of the county, district or area, as the case may be, or any part thereof into petty sessional divisions and, on completion of the review, to submit to the Secretary of

State either a draft order under subsection (1) above or a report giving reasons for making no change.

(3) Subject to the provisions of this and the next following section—

(*a*) where such a committee submit a draft order to the Secretary of State under this section, he may by statutory instrument make the order either in the terms of the draft or with such modifications as he thinks fit; and

(*b*) where such a committee fail to comply within six months with a direction of the Secretary of State under subsection (2) above, or the Secretary of State is dissatisfied with the draft order or report submitted in pursuance of such a direction, he may by statutory instrument make such order as he thinks fit about the division into petty sessional divisions of the area to which the direction related.

(4) An order under this section may provide for a non-metropolitan county or metropolitan district or any of the outer London areas ceasing to be divided into petty sessional divisions, and a direction under subsection (2) above may be given with respect to the division of a non-metropolitan county or metropolitan district or any of the outer London areas which is not for the time being so divided.

(5) Any order under this section may contain transitional and other consequential provisions.

DERIVATION

1949, s. 18 (1)–(4) (8); 1964, ss. 2 (3), 13 (1); 1972, Sched. 27, para. 6 (1) (2) (4); 1978, s. 86.

Procedure relating to s. 23

24.—(1) Before submitting to the Secretary of State a draft order or a report under section 23 of this Act about any area, a magistrates' courts committee—

(*a*) shall consult the council of the non-metropolitan county or metropolitan district concerned and the magistrates for any existing petty sessional division in the area; and

(*b*) in the case of a draft order, after complying with paragraph (*a*) above, shall send a copy of their proposals to every interested authority and take into consideration any objections made in the prescribed manner and within the prescribed time.

(2) A magistrates' courts committee submitting to the Secretary of State a draft order or a report under section 23 of this Act shall comply with such requirements (if any) as to notice as may be prescribed; and the Secretary of State, before making an order under that section about any area otherwise than in accordance with a draft submitted to him by the magistrates' courts committee, shall send a copy of his proposals to the committee, to the council of the non-metropolitan county or metropolitan district concerned, to the magistrates for any existing petty sessional division in the area and to every interested authority.

(3) Before making any order under section 23 of this Act the Secretary of State shall take into consideration any objections made in the prescribed manner and within the prescribed time, and may cause a local inquiry to be held.

(4) In its application to the outer London areas this section shall have effect as if any reference to the council of a non-metropolitan county were a reference to the Greater London Council.

(5) Subject to the provisions of Schedule 1 to this Act, the powers conferred by section 23 of this Act shall be in substitution for any other power to create or alter petty sessional divisions in a county or London

commission area, except powers conferred by any other provision of this Act.

(6) For the purposes of this section—

(*a*) " interested authority ", in relation to any order or draft order, means the council of any outer London borough, metropolitan county or metropolitan district which includes the whole or any part of the area to which the order relates; and

(*b*) an order shall be deemed to be made in accordance with a draft order if either it is made in terms of the draft order or the departures from the draft order do not, in the opinion of the Secretary of State, effect important alterations in the draft order.

DERIVATION

1949, s. 18 (5)–(7) (9) (10); 1964, s. 2 (3); 1972, Sched. 27, para. 6 (3) (5) (6).

Justices' clerks and their staffs

Appointment and removal of justices' clerks

25.—(1) Justices' clerks shall be appointed by the magistrates' courts committee and shall hold office during the pleasure of the committee; and a magistrates' courts committee may appoint more than one justices' clerk for any area.

(2) The approval of the Secretary of State shall be required—

(*a*) for any decision to increase the number of justices' clerks in a petty sessions area or to have more than one justices' clerk in a new petty sessions area;

(*b*) for any appointment of a justices' clerk;

(*c*) for the removal of the justices' clerk for a petty sessional division where the magistrates for the division do not consent to the removal.

(3) A magistrates' courts committee shall consult the magistrates for any petty sessional division on the appointment or removal of a justices' clerk for the division; and the Secretary of State, before approving the appointment or removal of a justices' clerk for such a division, shall consider any representations made to him by the magistrates for the division, and before approving the removal of any such clerk shall consider any representations made to him by the clerk.

(4) The magistrates' courts committee shall inform the Secretary of State of the age, qualification and experience of any person proposed to be appointed a justices' clerk and, if the Secretary of State so requires, of any other person offering himself for the appointment.

(5) Subsections (1) to (4) above shall not apply to the inner London area.

DERIVATION

1949, s. 19 (1) (8) (9) (11); 1964, s. 15 (8); 1972, Sched. 27, para. 7 (1).

Qualifications for appointment as justices' clerk

26.—(1) Except as provided by this section, no person shall be appointed as justices' clerk of any class or description unless either—

(*a*) at the time of appointment he is a barrister or solicitor of not less than five years' standing and is within any limit of age prescribed for appointments to a clerkship of that class or description, or

(*b*) he then is or has previously been a justices' clerk.

(2) A lower as well as an upper limit of age may be prescribed under subsection (1) above for appointments to any class or description of clerkship.

(3) A person not having the qualification as barrister or solicitor which is required by subsection (1) (*a*) above may be appointed a justices' clerk—

(*a*) if at the time of appointment he is a barrister or solicitor and has served for not less than five years in service to which this subsection applies, or

(*b*) if before the 1st January 1960 he had served for not less than ten years in service to which this subsection applies and, in the opinion of the magistrates' courts committee and of the Secretary of State, there are special circumstances making the appointment a proper one.

(4) Subsection (3) above applies to service in any one or more of the following capacities, that is to say, service as assistant to a justices' clerk and service before the 1st February 1969—

(*a*) as clerk to a stipendiary magistrate;

(*b*) as clerk to a magistrates' court for the inner London area or as clerk to a metropolitan stipendiary court;

(*c*) as clerk at one of the justice rooms of the City of London; or

(*d*) as assistant to any such clerk as is mentioned in paragraphs (*a*) to (*c*) above.

(5) A person may be appointed a justices' clerk notwithstanding that he is over the upper limit of age mentioned in subsection (1) of this section if he has served continuously in service to which subsection (3) above applies from a time when he was below that limit to the time of appointment.

DERIVATION

1949, s. 20 (1) (2) (4); 1964, Sched. 3, para. 2; 1965, s. 1; 1968, s. 8 (2), Sched. 5, Pt. II.

Conditions of service and staff of justices' clerks

27.—(1) A justices' clerk shall be paid a salary for his personal remuneration, and the salary shall be deemed to be remuneration for all business which he may by reason of his office as justices' clerk be called upon to perform, other than any duties as secretary to a licensing planning committee under Part VII of the Licensing Act 1964.

(2) A justices' clerk may be paid a single salary in respect of two or more clerkships.

(3) Subject to subsection (5) below, a justices' clerk shall be provided with the accommodation and staff, and the furniture, books and other things, proper to enable him to carry out his duties.

(4) A justices' clerk shall, in addition to his salary, be paid the amount of any expenses of a description specified when his salary is determined, being expenses incurred by him with the general or special authority of the magistrates' courts committee.

(5) Where a justices' clerk devotes part of his time to work other than the duties appertaining to his clerkship or clerkships, he may by arrangement with the magistrates' courts committee make use for the purpose of those duties of any accommodation, staff or equipment which he has for other purposes; and the sums payable to him under subsection (4) above may include payments for accommodation, staff or equipment so provided by him, whether or not he thereby incurs additional expense.

(6) Any staff provided for a justices' clerk shall be employed by the magistrates' courts committee but shall work under the direction of the

clerk, and subject to this Act the committee may make any arrangements they think fit for staff to be engaged and dismissed, and the terms of their employment fixed, on behalf of the committee.

(7) Before any such staff are engaged or dismissed (otherwise than by the clerk himself on behalf of the committee) the clerk shall be consulted.

(8) The power conferred by section 15 of the Justices of the Peace Act 1949 to make rules for regulating and prescribing the procedure and practice to be followed by justices' clerks shall, without prejudice to the generality of subsection (1) of that section, include power to provide that, subject to any exceptions prescribed by the rules, persons shall not be employed to assist a justices' clerk in any capacity so prescribed, or shall not be permitted to do on behalf of a justices' clerk any such acts as may be so prescribed, unless those persons are qualified (any age limits apart) to be appointed justices' clerk or have such other qualifications as may for any purpose be allowed by the rules.

(9) Subsections (1) to (7) above shall not apply to the inner London area.

DERIVATION

1949, s. 19 (2) (3)–(7); 1953, Pt. II, s. 168 (1) (5), Sched. 10; 1964, s. 15 (8), Pt. VII, Sched. 14, para. 1.

General powers and duties of justices' clerks

28.—(1) Rules made in accordance with section 15 of the Justices of the Peace Act 1949 may (except in so far as any enactment passed after the 25th October 1968 otherwise directs) make provision enabling things authorised to be done by, to or before a single justice of the peace to be done instead by, to or before a justices' clerk.

(2) Any enactment (including any enactment contained in this Act) or any rule of law regulating the exercise of any jurisdiction or powers of justices of the peace, or relating to things done in the exercise or purported exercise of any such jurisdiction or powers, shall apply in relation to the exercise or purported exercise thereof by virtue of subsection (1) above by the clerk to any justices as if he were one of those justices.

(3) It is hereby declared that the functions of a justices' clerk include the giving to the justices to whom he is clerk or any of them, at the request of the justices or justice, of advice about law, practice or procedure on questions arising in connection with the discharge of their or his functions, including questions arising when the clerk is not personally attending on the justices or justice, and that the clerk may, at any time when he thinks he should do so, bring to the attention of the justices or justice any point of law, practice or procedure that is or may be involved in any question so arising.

In this subsection the reference to the functions of justices or a justice is a reference to any of their or his functions as justices or a justice of the peace, other than functions as a judge of the Crown Court.

(4) The enactment of subsection (3) above shall not be taken as defining or in any respect limiting the powers and duties belonging to a justices' clerk or the matters on which justices may obtain assistance from their clerk.

DERIVATION

1968, s. 5 (1) (3).

GENERAL NOTE

The function of the clerk to advise the magistrates does not apply when the magistrates are sitting in the Crown Court. LC para. 12.

Functions of justices' clerk as collecting officer

29.—(1) A justices' clerk shall by virtue of his office be collecting officer of any magistrates' court of which he is the clerk.

(2) In his capacity as such a collecting officer, a justices' clerk—

(*a*) shall discharge all such functions as are conferred by any enactment on a collecting officer appointed by the justices for a petty sessional division under the Affiliation Orders Act 1914; and

(*b*) shall act under any order directing the payment of money to him which was made by any court under section 30 of the Criminal Justice Administration Act 1914 (which provided for periodical payments under court orders to be made through an officer of the court or other third party) and which continues to have effect in accordance with the provisions of paragraph 14 of Schedule I to this Act.

(3) Subsections (1) and (2) above shall have effect without prejudice to the provisions of section 52 of the Magistrates' Courts Act 1952 (periodical payments through justices' clerk) or section 53A of that Act (relating to payments required to be made to a child).

Derivation

1949, s. 21 (1).

General Note

The provisions in the Domestic Proceedings and Magistrates' Courts Act 1978 providing for payment direct to a child are not affected by the general provisions in this section.

Person acting as substitute clerk to justices

30.—(1) The provisions of this section shall have effect where, in any petty sessions area outside the inner London area, a person who is not the justices' clerk or one of the justices' clerks appointed in that petty sessions area by the magistrates' courts committee acts as clerk to the justices for that petty sessions area.

(2) Subject to any rules made under section 15 of the Justices of the Peace Act 1949 and to subsection (3) below, the person so acting shall be treated as having acted as deputy to the justices' clerk appointed by the magistrates' courts committee in that petty sessions area, and shall make a return to the justices' clerk so appointed of all matters done before the justices and of all matters that the clerk to the justices is required to register or record.

(3) In relation to a petty sessions area in which there are two or more justices' clerks appointed by the magistrates' courts committee, any reference in subsection (2) above to the justices' clerk so appointed shall be construed as a reference to such one of them as may be designated for the purpose by the committee.

Derivation

1952, s. 118 (3) (4); 1968, Sched. 3, para. 8.

General Note

Although there is only technically one "justices' clerk" for each petty sessional division he may have, and usually does have, various colleagues, deputies, assistants, court clerks, salaried staff, variously described, carrying out the duties of a justices' clerk, *e.g.* advising the magistrates. Apart from the clerk to the justices himself all such persons are to be treated as his deputy for the purpose of carrying out their duties. LC para. 9.

Part III

Inner London Area

Metropolitan stipendiary magistrates

Appointment, removal and retirement of metropolitan stipendiary magistrates

31.—(1) Metropolitan stipendiary magistrates shall be appointed by Her Majesty, and Her Majesty shall from time to time appoint such number of persons as is necessary; but the number of metropolitan stipendiary magistrates shall not at any time exceed sixty or such larger number as Her Majesty may from time to time by Order in Council specify.

(2) A person shall not be qualified to be appointed a metropolitan stipendiary magistrate unless he is a barrister or solicitor of not less than seven years' standing.

(3) The Lord Chancellor shall designate one of the metropolitan stipendiary magistrates to be the chief metropolitan stipendiary magistrate.

(4) The following provisions shall apply to each metropolitan stipendiary magistrate, that is to say—

(*a*) he shall by virtue of his office be a justice of the peace for each of the London commission areas and for the counties of Essex, Hertfordshire, Kent and Surrey;

(*b*) he shall not during his continuance in office practise as a barrister or solicitor;

(*c*) he may be removed from office by the Lord Chancellor for inability or misbehaviour.

(5) A metropolitan stipendiary magistrate who is by virtue of his office a justice of the peace for any area mentioned in subsection (4) above shall not, by reason only of his being a justice of the peace for that area by virtue of that office, be qualified to be chosen under section 17 (1) of this Act as chairman or deputy chairman of the justices for a petty sessional division of that area or to vote under that subsection at the election of any such chairman or deputy chairman.

(6) Section 14 of this Act shall apply to metropolitan stipendiary magistrates as well as to other stipendiary magistrates in England or Wales.

(7) Her Majesty shall not be recommended to make an Order in Council under subsection (1) above unless a draft of the Order has been laid before Parliament and approved by resolution of each House.

Derivation

1964, s. 10 (1)–(5); 1973, s. 2 (6).

Allocation and sittings of metropolitan stipendiary magistrates

32.—(1) The Lord Chancellor may assign metropolitan stipendiary magistrates to petty sessional divisions constituted under section 36 of this Act and may alter any assignment under this subsection; but the assignment of a magistrate to a particular division shall not preclude him from exercising jurisdiction for any other division of the inner London area.

(2) Metropolitan stipendiary magistrates shall sit at such courthouses provided for the inner London area under the following provisions of this Act, on such days and at such times as may be determined by, or in accordance with, directions given by the Lord Chancellor from time to time.

(3) The chief metropolitan stipendiary magistrate shall cause to be held, at least once in every quarter of a year, a meeting of all the metropolitan stipendiary magistrates, or such of them as are able to attend, and, if present, shall preside over the meeting.

DERIVATION
1964, s. 10 (6)–(8).

Jurisdiction of metropolitan stipendiary magistrates and lay justices

33.—(1) In the inner London area the jurisdiction conferred on justices of the peace by any enactment, by their commission or by the common law shall be exercisable both by metropolitan stipendiary magistrates and by justices of the peace for that area who are not metropolitan stipendiary magistrates (hereafter in this Part of this Act referred to as " lay justices ").

(2) Metropolitan stipendiary magistrates shall continue to exercise the jurisdiction conferred on them as such by any enactment; and the inner London area (having taken the place of the metropolitan stipendiary courts area) shall continue to be the area for which magistrates' courts are to be held by metropolitan stipendiary magistrates.

(3) Lay justices for the inner London area may, in addition to exercising the jurisdiction mentioned in subsection (1) above, exercise the jurisdiction conferred on metropolitan stipendiary magistrates as such by any enactment except the following, that is to say—

(*a*) the Extradition Acts 1870 to 1935;

(*b*) section 28 of the Pilotage Act 1913 (which relates to appeals by pilots against certain actions of pilotage authorities);

(*c*) section 25 of the Children and Young Persons Act 1933 (restrictions on persons under 18 going abroad for the purpose of performing for profit); and

(*d*) the Fugitive Offenders Act 1967;

but a magistrates' court consisting of lay justices for the inner London area shall not by virtue of this subsection try an information summarily or hear a complaint except when composed of at least two justices.

(4) Without prejudice to subsection (1) above, subsections (3) to (5) of section 16 of this Act shall have effect in relation to a metropolitan stipendiary magistrate as they have effect in relation to a stipendiary magistrate appointed under section 13 of this Act.

DERIVATION
1964, s. 9.

GENERAL NOTE
The Fugitive Offenders Act 1967 is taken to have re-enacted the Fugitive Offenders Act 1881 with modifications.

Acting metropolitan stipendiary magistrate

34.—(1) If it appears to the Lord Chancellor that it is expedient to do so in order to avoid delays in the administration of justice in the inner London area, he may authorise any person, who is a barrister or solicitor of not less than seven years' standing, to act as a metropolitan stipendiary magistrate during such period (not exceeding three months at any one time) as the Lord Chancellor thinks fit.

(2) All things required or authorised by law to be done by, to or before a metropolitan stipendiary magistrate may be done by, to or before any person acting as such in pursuance of this section.

(3) The Lord Chancellor may, out of moneys provided by Parliament, pay to any person authorised to act under this section such remuneration as he may, with the approval of the Minister for the Civil Service, determine.

DERIVATION

1959, s. 2 (1) (2) (4).

Provisions relating to committee of magistrates

Committee of magistrates for inner London area

35.—(1) No magistrates' courts committee shall be set up under Part II of this Act for the inner London area, but instead there shall continue to be a committee (to be known as the "committee of magistrates") set up for that area in accordance with the following provisions of this Part of this Act, with such functions in relation to—

(*a*) the division of that area into petty sessional divisions;

(*b*) the employment of clerks and other officers;

(*c*) the division of work between the metropolitan stipendiary magistrates and lay justices;

(*d*) the provision of courses of instruction for justices; and

(*e*) other matters of a financial or administrative character,

as are or may be provided by or under this Act or as the committee may be authorised by the Secretary of State to undertake.

(2) The chief metropolitan stipendiary magistrate shall by virtue of his office be a member of the committee of magistrates.

(3) In addition to the chief metropolitan stipendiary magistrate, the committee of magistrates shall consist of the following members, that is to say—

(*a*) one lay justice chosen from amongst themselves by the lay justices for each petty sessional division;

(*b*) three members of the juvenile court panel for the inner London area and the City of London, chosen jointly by the members of that panel and by any chairmen of the juvenile courts for that area and the City who are not members of that panel; and

(*c*) such number of metropolitan stipendiary magistrates nominated by the chief metropolitan stipendiary magistrate as is equal to the total number of members required to be chosen under paragraphs (*a*) and (*b*) above.

(4) The members of the committee of magistrates who are chosen or nominated under subsection (3) above shall hold office as such for the period of one year beginning on such date as the Secretary of State may direct, but may again be chosen or nominated as members of the committee.

(5) There shall be a chairman, a vice-chairman and deputy chairman of the committee of magistrates; and—

(*a*) the chief metropolitan stipendiary magistrate shall be the chairman;

(*b*) a metropolitan stipendiary magistrate chosen from amongst the members of the committee by the chief metropolitan stipendiary magistrate shall be vice-chairman; and

(*c*) a person chosen from amongst themselves by the lay justices who are members of the committee shall be the deputy chairman.

(6) Section 22 of this Act, with the exception of—

(*a*) so much of subsection (1) as relates to the chairman of a magistrates' courts committee; and

(*b*) subsection (3),

shall apply to the committee of magistrates as it applies to a magistrates' courts committee.

DERIVATION

1964, s. 13 (1)–(5) (7).

Petty sessional divisions in inner London area

36.—(1) The Secretary of State may, on the recommendation of or after consultation with the committee of magistrates, by order made by statutory instrument make provision for the division of the inner London area or any part of that area into petty sessional divisions.

(2) It shall be the duty of the committee of magistrates from time to time, and also when directed to do so by the Secretary of State, to take into consideration the division of the inner London area into petty sessional divisions and to recommend to the Secretary of State (giving reasons for their recommendation) whether or not to make any changes in those divisions and, if changes are recommended, what changes; and the Secretary of State shall not act otherwise than in accordance with any recommendation under this subsection except after consultation with the committee.

(3) An order under this section may contain transitional and other consequential provisions.

DERIVATION

1964, ss. 14, 36.

Justices' clerks and other officers

37.—(1) It shall be the duty of the committee of magistrates, subject to the following provisions of this section, to appoint—

(*a*) a principal chief clerk for the inner London area, one or more chief clerks for each petty sessional division of that area and one or more chief clerks for the juvenile courts for that area and the City of London, and

(*b*) such deputy chief clerks and other officers as may be necessary;

and the committee shall, where there is more than one chief clerk for such a division or for those courts, designate one of them to be the senior chief clerk for that division or for all those courts, as the case may be.

(2) The officers mentioned in subsection (1) (*a*) above shall rank as justices' clerks and be treated as such for the purposes of the enactments relating to justices' clerks, including (except where otherwise expressly provided) any such enactment contained in this Act.

(3) The justices' clerks and deputy chief clerks mentioned in subsection (1) above shall not be appointed or dismissed by the committee of magistrates without the approval of the Secretary of State, and —

(*a*) the committee shall inform the Secretary of State of the age, qualification and experience of any person proposed to be appointed such a clerk, and, if the Secretary of State so requires, of any other person offering himself for the appointment; and

(*b*) before approving the dismissal of any such clerk the Secretary of State shall consider any representations made to him by the clerk.

(4) The number of justices' clerks and of other officers employed by the committee of magistrates in each grade below that of principal chief clerk, the grades in which such officers below that of deputy clerk are to be employed and the terms and conditions of employment of all officers employed by the committee shall be such as may from time to time be determined by the committee.

(5) The following provisions of this subsection shall have effect with respect to determinations under subsection (4) above and related matters, that is to say—

(*a*) no such determination shall have effect unless confirmed, with or without modifications, by the Secretary of State;

(*b*) the committee of magistrates shall not make or refuse to make any such determination with respect to terms and conditions of employment except after consultation with persons appearing to the committee to represent the interests of the officers affected;

(*c*) any refusal of the committee to make any such determination with respect to any terms and conditions of employment may be reviewed by the Secretary of State, and on the review the Secretary of State may confirm the refusal or make such determination with respect to those terms and conditions as he thinks fit;

(*d*) in the case of any matter which falls to be determined under subsection (4) above and affects officers employed by the committee who immediately before the 1st April 1965—

(i) were clerks or other officers of metropolitan stipendiary courts, or

(ii) were justices' clerks or officers employed by the magistrates' courts committee for the county of London,

the functions of the Secretary of State under paragraphs (*a*) to (*c*) above shall be exercised in such manner as he thinks necessary for protecting the interests of those officers.

(6) The Secretary of State may by order made by statutory instrument amend subsection (1) (*a*) above by substituting for or adding to the offices therein mentioned such other offices as he thinks fit; and any such order may contain transitional and other consequential provisions (including provisions amending the preceding provisions of this section).

(7) Any statutory instrument containing an order under this section shall be subject to annulment in pursuance of a resolution of either House of Parliament.

DERIVATION
1964, ss. 15 (1) (2) (4)–(7), 36 (1).

Other functions for which committee is or may be responsible

38.—(1) It shall be the duty of the committee of magistrates to keep under consideration the division of work in the inner London area between the metropolitan stipendiary magistrates and the lay justices, and to give general directions as to the division of the work.

(2) The chief metropolitan stipendiary magistrate shall, subject to and in accordance with any directions given by the committee of magistrates, carry on the day to day administration of the magistrates' courts in the inner London area (including domestic courts and including juvenile courts for that area and the City of London).

(3) The principal chief clerk for the inner London area shall assist the chief metropolitan stipendiary magistrate to perform his duty under subsection (2) above of carrying on the day to day administration of the magistrates' courts in that area.

(4) In addition to exercising the functions conferred on them by, or by virtue of, the preceding provisions of this Part of this Act, the committee of magistrates shall consider any matters referred to them by the Lord Chancellor or the Secretary of State and, if required to do so, shall make recommendations on any matter so referred.

DERIVATION
1964, ss. 13 (6), 15 (3), 16 (1)–(3).

PART IV

CITY OF LONDON

Ex officio and appointed justices

39.—(1) The Lord Mayor and aldermen of the City shall by virtue of the charter granted by His late Majesty King George II dated the 25th August 1741 continue to be justices of the peace for the City:

Provided that any of them may be excluded by the Lord Chancellor from the exercise of his functions as a justice.

(2) The persons holding office as justices of the peace for the City shall constitute a single body of justices, without distinction between those holding office by virtue of the charter and those appointed; and the jurisdiction and powers of the Lord Mayor and aldermen as justices by virtue of the charter shall be the same in all respects as those of appointed justices.

(3) The establishment of the City as a separate commission area shall not be taken to have constituted new courts for the City; and the jurisdiction and powers of the justices of the peace for the City are in continuation of those formerly belonging exclusively to the justices holding office by virtue of the charter.

(4) In this Part of this Act "the City" means the City of London.

DERIVATION

1968, s. 1 (2), Sched. 2, para. 1, Sched. 3, para. 2; 1973, s. 1 (6).

Chairman and deputy chairmen of justices

40.—(1) The Lord Mayor for the time being, if not disqualified, shall be chairman of the justices, with the style of Chief Magistrate, instead of a chairman being elected under section 17 (1) of this Act; and, subject to subsection (3) below, the aldermen who have been Lord Mayor and are not disqualified (or, if there are more than eight such aldermen, the eight who were last Lord Mayor) shall be deputy chairmen in addition to any deputy chairmen elected under section 17 (1) above.

(2) For the purposes of this section a Lord Mayor or alderman is disqualified at any time while his name is entered in the supplemental list.

(3) In the event of a Lord Mayor being disqualified, then during his mayoralty the senior of the aldermen designated as deputy chairmen in subsection (1) above shall, instead of being a deputy chairman, be chairman of the justices as acting Chief Magistrate.

(4) Subsections (2) and (3) of section 17 of this Act shall apply to any Lord Mayor or alderman as chairman or deputy chairman of the justices as they apply to a chairman or deputy chairman elected under subsection (1) of that section.

DERIVATION

1968, Sched. 2, paras. 2–4.

Application of enactments to the City

41.—(1) Subject to the provisions of this Part of this Act, in any enactment relating to justices of the peace, magistrates' courts, justices' clerks or matters connected therewith (including, except in so far as it otherwise expressly provides, any such enactment passed after the passing of this Act)—

(*a*) any reference to a county or to county justices shall be taken to include the City or justices for the City, and (*b*) any reference to a county council shall be taken to include the Corporation of the City acting through the Common Council, and references to a county fund shall be taken to include the general rate fund of the City:

Provided that in any such enactment which refers in the same context both to a non-metropolitan county and to a metropolitan district, the reference to a non-metropolitan county shall be taken to include the City.

(2) Where any such enactment (including any enactment contained in this Act) expressly refers in the same context both—

(*a*) to a county or non-metropolitan county or to justices or magistrates for a county or non-metropolitan county, and

(*b*) to the City or to justices or magistrates for the City,

the operation of that enactment shall not be affected by, and shall be without prejudice to the generality of, subsection (1) above.

DERIVATION

1968, Sched. 3, paras. 1 (*b*), 3; 1972, Sched. 27, para. 19 (1).

GENERAL NOTE

For the avoidance of doubt express reference is made to any enactment passed in the future after the passing of this Act. LC para. 13.

No petty sessional divisions in the City

42. Nothing in section 41 above shall authorise the making of an order under section 23 of this Act for the division of the City into petty sessional divisions.

DERIVATION

1968, Sched. 3, para. 4 (4).

Records of appointed justices for the City

43. There shall be transmitted to the Lord Mayor, and be enrolled in the records of the justices for the City, a copy of any instrument appointing or removing a justice of the peace for the City in accordance with section 6 of this Act; and the Lord Mayor shall be notified, in such manner as the Lord Chancellor may direct, of any resignation or death of a justice for the City so appointed, and shall cause to be kept, and from time to time rectified, a record of those for the time being holding office as justices for the City by virtue of any such appointment.

DERIVATION

1973, s. 1 (3) (6).

PART V

PROTECTION OF JUSTICES AND INDEMNIFICATION OF JUSTICES AND JUSTICES' CLERKS

Acts done within jurisdiction

44. If apart from this section any action lies against a justice of the peace for an act done by him in the execution of his duty as such a justice, with respect to any matter within his jurisdiction as such a justice, the action shall be as for a tort, in the nature of an action on the case; and—

(*a*) in the statement or particulars of claim it shall be expressly alleged that the act in question was done maliciously and without reasonable and probable cause, and (*b*) if that allegation is not proved at the trial of the action, judgment shall be given for the defendant, if it is in the High Court, or, if it is in the county court, the plaintiff shall be non-suited or judgment shall be given for the defendant.

DERIVATION

1848, s. 1.

GENERAL NOTE

The continued use of the archaic expression "action on the case" is used in order to preserve the requirement that the plaintiff must prove damage, deriving from the 1848 Act, s. 1. This section relates to acts done within jurisdiction, s. 45 relates to acts done in excess of jurisdiction.

Acts outside or in excess of jurisdiction

45.—(1) This section applies—

(*a*) to any act done by a justice of the peace in a matter in respect of which by law he does not have jurisdiction or in which he has exceeded his jurisdiction, and

(*b*) to any act done under any conviction or order made or warrant issued by a justice of the peace in any such matter;

and in the following provisions of this section "the justice", in relation to any act falling within paragraph (*a*) above, means the justice of the peace by whom it is done, and, in relation to a conviction, order or warrant falling within paragraph (*b*) above, means the justice of the peace by whom the conviction or order is made or the warrant issued.

(2) Any person injured by an act to which this section applies may maintain an action against the justice without making any allegation in his statement or particulars of claim that the act complained of was done maliciously and without reasonable and probable cause.

(3) In respect of any act done under any such conviction or order as is mentioned in subsection (1) (*b*) above no action shall be brought against the justice until the conviction or order has been quashed, either on appeal or upon application to the High Court.

(4) In respect of any act done under any such warrant as is mentioned in subsection (1) (*b*) above which was issued by the justice to procure the appearance of a person (in this subsection referred to as "the complainant")—

(*a*) where the issue of the warrant has been followed by a conviction or order in the same matter, no action shall be brought by the complainant against the justice until the conviction or order has been quashed, either on appeal or upon application to the High Court, and

(*b*) where the issue of the warrant has not been followed by any such conviction or order, or the warrant was issued upon an information for an alleged indictable offence, no action shall be brought by the complainant against the justice if, before the issue of the warrant, a summons was issued and was served on the complainant (either personally or by leaving it for him with some person at his last or most usual place of abode) and he did not appear in accordance with the summons.

DERIVATION

1848, s. 2.

GENERAL NOTE

The phrase "conviction or order" is used in order to overcome the suggestion that "or order" was omitted by inadvertence in the Justices' Protection Act 1848, s. 2. See *O'Connor* v. *Isaacs* [1956] 2 Q.B. 288, C.A. LC para. 2.

Warrant granted on a conviction or order made by another justice

46. Where a conviction or order is made by a justice or justices of the peace, and another justice, in good faith and without collusion, grants a warrant of distress or warrant of commitment thereon, no action shall be brought against the justice who granted the warrant by reason of any defect in the conviction or order, or for any want of jurisdiction in the justice or justices who made it, but the action (if any) shall be brought against the justice or justices who made the conviction or order.

DERIVATION
1848, s. 3.

Exercise of discretionary powers

47. Where by an enactment a discretionary power is given to a justice of the peace, no action shall be brought against the justice by reason of the manner in which he exercises his discretion in the execution of the power.

DERIVATION
1848, s. 4.

Compliance with, or confirmation on appeal to, superior court

48.—(1) In all cases where a justice of the peace refuses to do any act relating to the duties of his office, the party requiring the act to be done may apply to the High Court for an order of mandamus; and, if the High Court makes the order, no action or proceeding whatsoever shall be commenced or prosecuted against the justice for having obeyed the order.

(2) Where a warrant of distress or warrant of commitment is granted by a justice of the peace upon any conviction or order which, whether before or after the granting of the warrant, is confirmed on appeal, no action for anything done under the warrant shall be brought against the justice by reason of any defect in the conviction or order.

DERIVATION
1848, ss. 5, 6.

Distress warrant for rates

49.—(1) Where a general rate has been made, approved and published, and a warrant of distress is issued against a person on whom the rate has been levied, no action shall be brought against the justice or justices who granted the warrant by reason of any irregularity or defect in the rate, or by reason that the person in question was not liable to the rate.

(2) Any reference in this section to a general rate shall—

(*a*) in relation to the City of London, be construed as including a reference to a poor rate, and

(*b*) in relation to the Inner Temple and the Middle Temple, be construed as a reference to any rate in the nature of a general rate.

(3) Subsection (2) above shall have effect without prejudice to the generality of section 26 of the Administration of Justice Act 1964 (whereby, for the purposes of the law relating to justices of the peace and other matters therein mentioned, the Temples are included in the City) in its application to this Act.

DERIVATION

1848, s. 4; 1967, ss. 2 (5), 116 (1).

GENERAL NOTE

The City of London and the Inner Temple and Middle Temple are separate rating areas, but are drawn in for the purpose of issuing a warrant of distress for rates.

Where action prohibited, proceedings may be set aside

50. If any action is brought in circumstances in which this Part of this Act provides that no action is to be brought, a judge of the court in which the action is brought may, on the application of the defendant and upon an affidavit as to the facts, set aside the proceedings in the action, with or without costs, as the judge thinks fit.

DERIVATION

1848, s. 7.

No action in county court if defendant justice objects

51. No action shall be brought in the county court against a justice of the peace for anything done by him in the execution of his office as such a justice if he objects to it; and if within six days after being served with a summons in any such action the justice, or his solicitor or agent, gives written notice to the plaintiff that the justice objects to being sued in the county court in respect of the cause of action in question, all subsequent proceedings in the county court in the action shall be null and void.

DERIVATION

1848, s. 10.

Limitation of damages

52.—(1) The provisions of this section shall have effect where, in any action brought against a justice of the peace for anything done by him in the execution of his office as such a justice, the plaintiff is (apart from this section) entitled to recover damages in respect of a conviction or order, and proves the levying or payment of a penalty or sum of money under the conviction or order as part of the damages which he seeks to recover, or proves that he was imprisoned under the conviction or order and seeks to recover damages for the imprisonment, but it is also proved—

(*a*) that the plaintiff was actually guilty of the offence of which he was so convicted, or that he was liable by law to pay the sum he was so ordered to pay, and

(*b*) where he was imprisoned, that he had undergone no greater punishment than that assigned by law for the offence of which he was so convicted or for non-payment of the sum he was so ordered to pay.

(2) In the circumstances specified in subsection (1) above, the plaintiff shall not be entitled to recover the amount of the penalty or sum levied or paid as mentioned in that subsection or (as the case may be) to recover any sum beyond the sum of one penny as damages for the imprisonment, and shall not be entitled to any costs.

DERIVATION

1848, s. 13; 1969, s. 10 (1), Sched. 1.

Indemnification of justices and justices' clerks

53.—(1) Subject to the provisions of this section and of section 54 below, a justice of the peace or justices' clerk may be indemnified out of local funds in respect of—

(*a*) any costs reasonably incurred by him in or in connection with proceedings against him in respect of anything done or omitted in the exercise or purported exercise of the duty of his office, or in taking steps to dispute any claim which might be made in such proceedings;

(*b*) any damages awarded against him or costs ordered to be paid by him in any such proceedings; or

(*c*) any sums payable by him in connection with a reasonable settlement of any such proceedings or claim;

and shall be entitled to be so indemnified if, in respect of the matters giving rise to the proceedings or claim, he acted reasonably and in good faith.

(2) Any question whether, or to what extent, a person is to be indemnified under this section shall be determined by the magistrates' courts committee for the area for which he acted at the material time; and a determination under this subsection with respect to any such costs or sums as are mentioned in paragraph (*a*) or paragraph (*c*) of subsection (1) above may, if the person claiming to be indemnified so requests, be made in advance before those costs are incurred or the settlement made, as the case may be:

Provided that any such determination in advance for indemnity in respect of costs to be incurred shall be subject to such limitations, if any, as the committee think proper and to the subsequent determination of the amount of the costs reasonably incurred and shall not affect any other determination which may fall to be made in connection with the proceedings or claim in question.

(3) An appeal shall lie to a person appointed for the purpose by the Lord Chancellor—

(*a*) on the part of the person claiming to be indemnified, from any decision of the magistrates' courts committee under subsection (2) above, other than a decision to postpone until after the conclusion of the proceedings any determination with respect to his own costs or to impose limitations on making a determination in advance for indemnity in respect of such costs;

(*b*) on the part of the local authority, from any determination of the magistrates' courts committee under that subsection, other than a determination in advance for indemnity in respect of costs to be incurred by the person claiming to be indemnified.

(4) The Lord Chancellor may by statutory instrument make rules prescribing the procedure to be followed in any appeal under this section; and any statutory instrument made by virtue of this subsection shall be subject to annulment in pursuance of a resolution of either House of Parliament.

(5) In this section " justices' clerk " includes a person appointed by a magistrates' court committee to assist a justices' clerk and any member of the staff of a part-time justices' clerk assisting the clerk in his duties as such; " local funds ", in relation to a justice or a justices' clerk, means funds out of which any salary or allowance to which he is entitled (or, if he is entitled to more than one, is entitled in the relevant capacity) is payable; and " local authority " means the authority responsible for the payment of any such salary or allowance.

(6) Subsection (5) above shall not apply to the inner London area, but in the application of the other provisions of this section to that area—

(*a*) for any reference to local funds there shall be substituted a reference to the metropolitan police fund;

(*b*) for any reference to a magistrates' courts committee there shall be substituted a reference to the committee of magistrates set up under section 35 of this Act; and

(*c*) for any reference to a local authority there shall be substituted a reference to the Receiver,

and "justices' clerk" includes any officer employed by the committee of magistrates.

DERIVATION
1964, s. 27, 36 (1).

Provisions as to prerogative proceedings and membership of Crown Court

54.—(1) Section 53 of this Act shall not apply to proceedings for an order of prohibition, mandamus or certiorari, or to proceedings arising out of anything done or omitted by any person in his capacity as a member of the Crown Court.

(2) The Lord Chancellor may, if he thinks fit, defray out of moneys provided by Parliament any costs awarded against a justice or justices' clerk in proceedings for an order of prohibition, mandamus or certiorari (other than proceedings relating to the jurisdiction of the Crown Court) or any part of such costs.

(3) In this section "justices' clerk" has the same meaning as in section 53 of this Act.

DERIVATION
1964, s. 28; 1971, Sched. 8, para. 2.

PART VI

ADMINISTRATIVE AND FINANCIAL ARRANGEMENTS

Duties of local authorities outside Greater London

55.—(1) Subject to the provisions of this Act, the council of each non-metropolitan county and of each metropolitan district shall provide the petty sessional court-houses and other accommodation, and the furniture, books, and other things, proper for the due transaction of the business, and convenient keeping of the records and documents, of the county justices or any committee of such justices, or for enabling the justices' clerk for the non-metropolitan county or metropolitan district or any part thereof to carry out his duties.

(2) The council of each non-metropolitan county or metropolitan district shall pay—

(*a*) any expenses of the magistrates' courts committee, or, in the case of a committee acting for the area of more than one such council, the proper proportion of those expenses; and

(*b*) the sums payable under Part II of this Act on account of a person's salary or expenses as justices' clerk for the non-metropolitan county or metropolitan district or any part thereof and the remuneration of any staff employed by the magistrates' courts committee to assist him, together with—

(i) secondary Class I contributions payable in respect of any such person or staff under Part I of the Social Security Act 1975, and

(ii) state scheme premiums so payable under Part III of the Social Security Pensions Act 1975; and

(c) so far as they are not otherwise provided for, all other costs incurred with the general or special authority of the magistrates' courts committee by the county justices.

(3) Subject to section 16 (2) of this Act, any accommodation provided under this section for any justices or justices' clerk may be outside the area for which the justices act and, in the case of a petty sessional court-house, shall be deemed to be in that area for the purposes of the jurisdiction of the justices when acting in the court-house.

(4) Two or more councils may arrange for accommodation, furniture, books or other things provided for the purposes of this section by one of them to be used also as if provided for those purposes by the other or each of the others.

DERIVATION

1949, s. 25; 1972, s. 217 (5), Sched. 27, para. 9.

GENERAL NOTE

This section regularises and authorises the payment by the magistrates' courts committee of social security contributions on behalf of its staff, correcting an oversight in the previous legislation. LC para. 7.

Provisions supplementary to s. 55

56.—(1) Subject to the provisions of this section—

(a) the petty sessional court houses and other accommodation, furniture, books and other things to be provided by a council under section 55 of this Act;

(b) the salary to be paid to a justices' clerk and the staff to be provided for him; and

(c) the nature and amount of the expenses which a magistrates' courts committee may incur in the discharge of any functions or may authorise to be incurred, including the sums payable to a justices' clerk in respect of accommodation, staff or equipment provided by him,

shall be such as may from time to time be determined by the magistrates' courts committee after consultation with the council or councils concerned.

(2) Where the expenses of the magistrates' courts committee, or the sums payable to or in respect of a justices' clerk holding more than one clerkship or to or in respect of staff provided for any such clerk, fall to be borne by more than one council, any question as to the manner in which they are to be borne by the councils concerned shall be determined by agreement between those councils or, in default of such agreement, shall be determined by the Secretary of State.

(3) Any council concerned which is aggrieved by a determination of a magistrates' courts committee under subsection (1) above may, within one month from the receipt by the council of written notice of the determination, appeal to the Secretary of State, whose decision shall be binding upon the magistrates' courts committee and any council concerned.

(4) The approval of the Secretary of State shall be required for any determination under subsection (1) above reducing the salary of a justices' clerk, unless the clerk consents to the reduction.

DERIVATION

1949, s. 26 (1)–(3).

Application of ss. 55 and 56 to outer London areas and City of London

57.—(1) The provisions of sections 55 and 56 of this Act shall have effect in relation to each of the outer London areas as if each such area were a non-metropolitan county and as if the Greater London Council were the council of that county.

(2) The sums payable by the Greater London Council under section 55 (2) as applied by subsection (1) above shall be chargeable only on the outer London boroughs.

(3) Sections 55 and 56 of this Act shall have effect in relation to the City of London as if in section 55 above—

(*a*) references to a non-metropolitan county and to county justices were references to the City and to justices for the City respectively, and

(*b*) any reference to the council of a non-metropolitan county were a reference to the Corporation of the City acting through the Common Council,

and references to a council in section 56 of this Act shall be construed accordingly.

DERIVATION

1964, ss. 2 (3), 17 (5), Sched. 3, para. 20 (6); 1968, Sched. 3, paras. 1 (*b*), 3; 1972, Sched. 27, paras. 17 (2), 19 (1); 1978, s. 86.

Corresponding arrangements in inner London area

58.—(1) The Receiver shall provide such court houses and other accommodation, and such furniture, books and other things, as the committee of magistrates may determine to be proper for the due transaction of the business, and convenient keeping of the records and documents, of magistrates' courts in the inner London area (including domestic courts and including juvenile courts for that area and the City of London) or for enabling the justices' clerks for that area (or for juvenile courts for that area and the City) to carry out their duties; but any determination under this subsection shall not have effect unless confirmed, with or without modifications, by the Secretary of State.

(2) The Receiver shall pay out of the metropolitan police fund—

(*a*) any expenses of the committee of magistrates, of such amount and of such a nature as may be approved by the Secretary of State;

(*b*) the sums payable by way of salary or expenses to justices' clerks and other officers employed by the committee of magistrates, together with—

(i) secondary Class I contributions payable in respect of those officers under Part I of the Social Security Act 1975, and

(ii) state scheme premiums so payable under Part III of the Social Security Pensions Act 1975; and

(*c*) any superannuation benefits payable in respect of such clerks and other officers under any enactment or instrument applied to them by regulations having effect in accordance with section 15 (9) of the Superannuation (Miscellaneous Provisions) Act 1967, other than benefits payable by the Greater London Council, and any superannuation contributions and other payments for which the committee of magistrates may be liable as their employer under any such enactment or instrument.

(3) Without prejudice to subsection (2) above, the expenses of and incidental to the magistrates' courts for the inner London area, except the salaries and superannuation allowances of metropolitan stipendiary magistrates, shall be paid out of the metropolitan police fund; and, if any question arises as to what expenses are expenses of or incidental to any such court, the question shall be determined by the Secretary of

State, with the concurrence of the Treasury so far as the question affects the amount of any charge on the Exchequer.

(4) Any accommodation provided under this section for any magistrates' court or justices' clerk may be outside the area for which the court or clerk acts, and, if outside that area, shall be deemed to be in that area for the purposes of the jurisdiction of the court.

(5) The Secretary of State, after consultation with the committee of magistrates, may assign court houses and other accommodation either to petty sessional divisions of the inner London area or to particular magistrates' courts for that area (including domestic courts and including juvenile courts for that area and the City of London) and may alter any assignment under this subsection.

DERIVATION

1897, ss. 1, 8; 1964, s. 17; 1967, s. 15 (8) (9); 1975, Sched. 4, para. 5.

Grants by Secretary of State to responsible authorities

59.—(1) The Secretary of State may out of moneys provided by Parliament pay to the responsible authorities grants towards the net cost to them in any year—

(*a*) of their functions under Part II or this Part of this Act, or under any such regulations as are mentioned in subsection (2) below, or, in the case of the Receiver, his corresponding functions; and

(*b*) of making payments under section 12 or section 53 of this Act.

(2) The regulations referred to in subsection (1) (*a*) above are any regulations made, or having effect as if made, under section 7 of the Superannuation Act 1972 with respect to persons appointed or deemed to have been appointed as justices' clerks, or employed by a magistrates' courts committee to assist a justices' clerk, under Part III of the Justices of the Peace Act 1949 or under Part II of this Act.

(3) The amount of any grant under this section shall not exceed 80 per cent. of the expenditure in respect of which it is made.

(4) The Secretary of State, with the concurrence of the Treasury, may by statutory instrument make regulations as to the manner in which income and expenditure of responsible authorities are to be taken into account in determining the net cost to them in any year of the matters mentioned in subsection (1) above; and for the purposes of this section any question as to that cost shall (subject to any such regulations) be determined by the Secretary of State.

(5) Grants under this section shall be paid at such times, in such manner and subject to such conditions as the Secretary of State may with the approval of the Treasury determine.

(6) In this section "responsible authority" means any of the following, namely, the council of a non-metropolitan county or metropolitan district, the Greater London Council, the Corporation of the City of London and the Receiver.

DERIVATION

1949, s. 27 (2) (5) (6) (10); 1964, Sched. 3, para. 20 (7); 1968, Sched. 3, paras. 1 (*b*), 3; 1972, Sched. 27, paras. 10 (4), 17 (2).

Special provision as to grants to Greater London Council

60.—(1) Any grant paid to the Greater London Council under section 59 of this Act shall be placed to the credit of the special London account out of which the relevant expenses of the Council are payable.

(2) In this section "the relevant expenses" means expenses under section 55 (2) as applied by section 57 (1) of this Act.

DERIVATION
1964, s. 37 (4); 1973, Sched. 5, para. 14.

Application of fines and fees

61.—(1) Subject to paragraphs (*a*) and (*b*) of section 114 (1) of the Magistrates Courts Act 1952 (which relates to the disposal of sums adjudged to be paid by a summary conviction) and to the following provisions of this section, there shall be paid to the Secretary of State—

(*a*) all fines imposed by a magistrates' court and all sums which become payable by virtue of an order of such a court and are by any enactment made applicable as fines so imposed or any class or description of such fines; and

(*b*) all other sums received by a justices' clerk by reason of his office except sums to which a person other than the Secretary of State is by law entitled and which are paid to that person.

(2) The sums payable to the Secretary of State by virtue of paragraph (*a*) of subsection (1) above shall not include—

(*a*) any sums which by or in pursuance of any provision in the enactments relating to those sums are directed to be paid to the Commissioners of Customs and Excise or to any other officer of theirs or person appointed by them; or

(*b*) any sums which by or in pursuance of any such provision are directed to be paid to or for the benefit of the party aggrieved, party injured or a person described in similar terms, or to or for the benefit of the family or relatives of a person described in any such terms or of a person dying in consequence of an act or event which constituted or was the occasion of an offence; or

(*c*) any sums which by or in pursuance of any such provision are directed to be applied in making good any default or repairing any damage or paying or reimbursing any expenses (other than those of the prosecution); or

(*d*) any sums which are directed to be paid to any person by or in pursuance of any such provision referring in terms to awarding or reimbursing a loss, or to damages, compensation or satisfaction for loss, damage, injury or wrong.

(3) Paragraph (*b*) of subsection (1) above shall not apply to sums received by a justices' clerk on account of his salary or expenses as such; and any sum paid to the Secretary of State by virtue of that paragraph shall be paid to him subject to its being repaid to any person establishing his title to it.

(4) The Secretary of State, with the concurrence of the Treasury, may by statutory instrument make regulations as to the times at which, and the manner in which, justices' clerks shall account for and pay the sums payable to him under this section, and as to the keeping, inspection and audit of accounts of justices' clerks, whether for the purposes of this section or otherwise.

(5) For the purposes of this section anything done by the Crown Court on appeal from a magistrates' court shall be treated as done by the magistrates' court.

(6) Any sums received by the Secretary of State under this section shall be paid by him into the Consolidated Fund.

(7) In this section " fine " includes—

(*a*) any pecuniary penalty, pecuniary forfeiture or pecuniary compensation payable under a conviction, and

(*b*) any non-pecuniary forfeiture on conviction by, or under an order of, a magistrates' court so far as the forfeiture is converted into or consists of money,

and " justices' clerk " includes a clerk of special sessions.

DERIVATION

1949, ss. 27 (1) (9) (10) (12), 44 (1); 1952, Sched. 5; 1972, s. 61 (1).

GENERAL NOTE

The expression " magistrates' court " is used instead of " court of summary jurisdiction." LC para. 5.

Defaults of justices' clerks and their staffs

62.—(1) The Secretary of State may, if he thinks fit, pay to any person any money due to that person which he has not received because of the default of a justices' clerk or of a person employed to assist a justices' clerk.

(2) In this section " justices' clerk " has the same meaning as in section 61 of this Act.

DERIVATION

1972, s. 62 (3) (4).

PART VII

MISCELLANEOUS AND SUPPLEMENTARY PROVISIONS

Courses of instruction

63.—(1) It shall be the duty of every magistrates' courts committee, in accordance with arrangements approved by the Lord Chancellor, to make and administer schemes providing for courses of instruction for justices of the peace of their area.

(2) It shall be the duty of the committee of magistrates, in accordance with arrangements approved by the Lord Chancellor, to make and administer schemes providing for courses of instruction for justices of the peace of the inner London area.

(3) There may be paid out of moneys provided by Parliament any expenses incurred by the Lord Chancellor in providing courses of instruction for justices of the peace.

(4) If courses of instruction are not provided for justices of the peace of any area as required by subsection (1) or subsection (2) above, then any expenses incurred by the Lord Chancellor in providing courses of instruction to make good the default shall be recoverable by him from the magistrates' courts committee or committee of magistrates in default; and any sums recovered by the Lord Chancellor under this subsection shall be paid into the Consolidated Fund.

(5) The Secretary of State may provide courses of instruction for justices' clerks and their staffs.

(6) In this section " justices' clerk " includes a clerk of special sessions.

DERIVATION

1949, s. 17; 1964, s. 16 (2); 1972, s. 62 (1) (4); 1973, s. 3 (1) (2).

Disqualification in certain cases of justices who are members of local authorities

64.—(1) A justice of the peace who is a member of a local authority within the meaning of the Local Government Act 1972 or the Local Government (Scotland) Act 1973 shall not act as a member of the

Crown Court or of a magistrates' court in any proceedings brought by or against, or by way of appeal from a decision of, the authority or any committee or officer of the authority.

(2) For the purposes of subsection (1) above—

(*a*) any reference to a committee of a local authority includes a joint committee, joint board, joint authority or other combined body of which that authority is a member or on which it is represented; and

(*b*) any reference to an officer of a local authority refers to a person employed or appointed by the authority, or by a committee of the authority, in the capacity in which he is employed or appointed to act.

(3) A justice of the peace who is a member of the Common Council of the City of London shall not act as a member of the Crown Court or of a magistrates' court in any proceedings brought by or against, or by way of appeal from a decision of, the Corporation of the City or the Common Council or any committee or officer of the Corporation or Common Council; and subsection (2) above shall apply for the purposes of this subsection, with the substitution, for references to a local authority, of references to the Corporation or the Common Council.

(4) Nothing in this section shall prevent a justice from acting in any proceedings by reason only of their being brought by a police officer.

(5) No act shall be invalidated by reason only of the disqualification under this section of the person acting.

DERIVATION

1949, ss. 3 (1)–(4), 5; 1971, Sched. 8, para. 2; 1972, Sched. 29, para. 1 (2).

GENERAL NOTE

A justice of the peace who is an elected councillor is disqualified from acting in any proceedings brought by or against, or by way of appeal from a decision of, the authority or any committee or officer of the authority, both in England and in Scotland. LC para. 4.

Justices not disqualified by reason of being ratepayers

65. A justice of the peace may perform any act in the execution of his office as such a justice in relation to the laws concerning rates leviable by a rating authority, notwithstanding that the justice is rated to or chargeable with such rates in the area affected by the act in question.

DERIVATION

1742, s. 1.

GENERAL NOTE

The mere fact that a justice of the peace is a ratepayer for the district or area does not in itself disqualify him from acting in matters concerning rates, *e.g.* the issue of a distress warrant for non-payment of rates. LC para. 1.

Acts done by justices outside their commission area

66.—(1) A justice of the peace for any commission area may act as a justice for that area in any commission area which adjoins the commission area for which he is a justice.

(2) Justices for the county of Surrey or the county of Kent may hold special or petty sessions for any division of their county at any place in Greater London; and for all purposes relating to sessions so held the place at which they are held shall be deemed to be within the county and the division for which the justices holding them are justices.

DERIVATION
1888, s. 42 (12); 1952, s. 116 (1); 1964, s. 2 (3), Sched. 3, para. 12 (1); 1968, Sched. 3, para. 3.

Promissory oaths of certain justices

67.—(1) Subject to the provisions of this section, any person who under this Act or under any other enactment is a justice of the peace for any area by virtue of any other office held by him shall, before acting as such a justice, take the oath of allegiance and judicial oath in accordance with the Promissory Oaths Acts.

(2) A person shall not be required by virtue of subsection (1) above to take those oaths as a justice of the peace by reason only of his being appointed under this Act or any other enactment to act temporarily as deputy for, or as if he were, the holder of another office to which that subsection applies; but those oaths may be taken by and administered to any such person notwithstanding anything in the Promissory Oaths Acts or any other enactment.

(3) A person shall not be required, on becoming a justice of the peace for any area, to take the oath of allegiance and judicial oath in accordance with the Promissory Oaths Acts if he has at any time done so as justice of the peace for whatever area.

(4) The oaths required by law to be taken by a metropolitan stipendiary magistrate may, in the case of a person authorised to act as such under section 34 of this Act, be taken before any of the metropolitan stipendiary magistrates.

(5) In this section "the Promissory Oaths Acts" means the Promissory Oaths Act 1868 and the Promissory Oaths Act 1871.

DERIVATION
1959, s. 2 (3); 1964, s. 30 (1) (2) (5); 1968, s. 1 (3).

Greater Manchester, Merseyside and Lancashire

68.—(1) Sections 6 (1), 7 and 11 of this Act shall have effect in relation to the counties of Greater Manchester, Merseyside and Lancashire with the substitution, for any reference to the Lord Chancellor, of a reference to the Chancellor of the Duchy of Lancaster.

(2) In relation to the entry in or removal from the supplemental list of the name of a person who is a justice of the peace only for any of the counties of Greater Manchester, Merseyside and Lancashire, subsections (4) to (6) of section 8 and section 9 of this Act shall have effect respectively with the substitution, for any reference to the Lord Chancellor, of a reference to the Chancellor of the Duchy of Lancaster.

DERIVATION
1949, s. 1 (5); 1972, Sched. 27, para. 1; 1973, s. 1 (7), Sched. 1, para. 4 (5).

Isles of Scilly

69. For the purposes of this Act the Isles of Scilly shall be deemed to form part of the county of Cornwall.

DERIVATION
1949, s. 16 (5); 1972, s. 216, Sched. 27, para. 5 (4); 1973, s. 1 (8).

Interpretation

70. In this Act, except in so far as the context otherwise requires,—

"commission area" has the meaning assigned to it by section 1 of this Act;

"joint committee area" has the meaning assigned to it by section 19 (3) of this Act;

"justices' clerk" means a clerk to the justices for a petty sessions area;

"London commission areas", "inner London area" and "outer London areas" have the meanings assigned to them by section 2 of this Act;

"magistrate", in relation to a county, a London commission area or the City of London, means a justice of the peace for the county, London commission area or the City, as the case may be, other than a justice whose name is for the time being entered in the supplemental list, and, in relation to a part of a county or of a London commission area, means a person who (in accordance with the preceding provisions of this definition) is a magistrate for that county or area and ordinarily acts in and for that part of it;

"officer" includes the holder of any place, situation or employment, and "office" shall be construed accordingly;

"petty sessional court-house" means any of the following, that is to say—

(*a*) a court-house or place at which justices are accustomed to assemble for holding special or petty sessions or for the time being appointed as a substitute for such a court-house or place (including, where justices are accustomed to assemble for either special or petty sessions at more than one court-house or place in a petty sessional division, any such court-house or place);

(*b*) a court-house or place at which a stipendiary magistrate is authorised by law to do alone any act authorised to be done by more than one justice of the peace;

"petty sessions area" has the meaning assigned to it by section 4 of this Act;

"prescribed" in Part II of this Act means prescribed by regulations made by the Secretary of State by statutory instrument;

"the Receiver" means the Receiver for the metropolitan police district;

"stipendiary magistrate" includes a metropolitan stipendiary magistrate;

"the supplemental list" has the meaning assigned to it by section 8 of this Act.

DERIVATION

1949, s. 44 (1); 1964, s. 38 (1).

GENERAL NOTE

The definition of petty sessional court-house contained in the Interpretation Act 1889 was repealed and not re-enacted in the Interpretation Act 1978. Therefore this Act contains an express definition but having the same effect as the Interpretation Act 1889, s. 13 (13). LC para. 6.

Transitional provisions and savings, amendments and repeals

71.—(1) The transitional provisions and savings in Schedule 1 to this Act shall have effect.

(2) Subject to subsection (1) above—

(*a*) the enactments specified in Schedule 2 to this Act shall have effect subject to the amendments specified in that Schedule; and

(b) the enactments specified in Schedule 3 to this Act are hereby repealed to the extent specified in the third column of that Schedule.

(3) Subject to any express amendment or repeal made by this Act, any enactment passed or instrument made before the 18th April 1973 and in force at the commencement of this Act shall have effect in relation to any time thereafter as if—

(a) any reference to a person appointed justice by a commission of the peace or to a person being removed from a commission of the peace were a reference to his being appointed or removed from office as a justice of the peace in accordance with section 6 of this Act; and

(b) any reference to a supplemental list kept by virtue of section 4 of the Justices of the Peace Act 1949 in connection with the commission of the peace for any area were a reference to the supplemental list for England and Wales kept under section 8 of this Act.

(4) The inclusion in this Act of any express transitional provision, saving or amendment shall not be taken as prejudicing the operation of sections 16 and 17 of the Interpretation Act 1978 (which relate to the effect of repeals).

DERIVATION
1973, Sched. 1, para. 9 (1).

Short title, commencement and extent

72.—(1) This Act may be cited as the Justices of the Peace Act 1979.

(2) This Act shall come into force at the end of the period of three months beginning with the day on which it is passed.

(3) This Act shall not extend to Scotland or to Northern Ireland.

SCHEDULES

SCHEDULE 1

TRANSITIONAL PROVISIONS AND SAVINGS

Interpretation

Section 71

1. In this Schedule—
"the Act of 1949" means the Justices of the Peace Act 1949;
"the Act of 1964" means the Administration of Justice Act 1964;
"the Act of 1968" means the Justices of the Peace Act 1968;
"the Act of 1972" means the Local Government Act 1972;
"the Act of 1973" means the Administration of Justice Act 1973.

General transitional provisions

2.—(1) In so far as anything done, or having effect as if done, under or in accordance with an enactment repealed by this Act could have been done under or in accordance with a corresponding provision in this Act, it shall not be invalidated by the repeal but shall have effect as if done under or in accordance with that provision.

(2) Sub-paragraph (1) above applies, in particular, to any regulation, order, rule, appointment or determination made, commission of the peace issued, meeting or sitting held, notice served or direction or consent given.

(3) Subject to the provisions of this Schedule, any document made, served or issued before the passing of this Act or at any time thereafter (whether before or after the commencement of this Act) and containing a reference, whether express or implied, to an enactment repealed by this Act, or having effect as if containing such a reference, shall, except in so far as the context otherwise requires, be construed as referring or (as the context requires) as including a reference to the corresponding provision of this Act.

(4) Where a period of time specified in an enactment repealed by this Act is current at the commencement of this Act, this Act shall have effect as if the corresponding provision thereof had been in force when that period began to run.

Commissions of the peace

3.—(1) Where a commission of the peace is in force immediately before the commencement of this Act as the commission of the peace for a commission area, the repeal of any enactment by this Act shall not affect its continuance in force as the commission of the peace for that commission area.

(2) Any order made under subsection (2) of section 217 of the Act of 1972 (which conferred power by order to specify which of two or more existing commissions of the peace should be treated as the sole commission of the peace for a county) which is in force immediately before the commencement of this Act shall continue to have effect notwithstanding the repeal of that subsection by this Act, and may be revoked or varied accordingly.

(3) Any commission of the peace in force immediately before the commencement of this Act which, by virtue of section 20 (3) (*a*) of the Act of 1973 (which related to commissions of the peace issued before the 1st April 1974), had effect as if addressed generally and not to named persons shall, until superseded by a new commission, continue to have effect as if addressed generally as required by section 5 of this Act.

Justices of the peace in office

4.—(1) Any person who immediately before the commencement of this Act was a justice of the peace and either—

(*a*) held that office by virtue of an appointment made in accordance with section 1 (2) of the Act of 1973, or

(*b*) under section 20 (3) (*b*) of that Act (which related to justices of the peace in office on the 1st April 1974 by virtue of a commission of the peace issued before that date) held that office as if appointed in accordance with section 1 (2) of that Act,

shall continue to hold that office as if appointed in accordance with section 6 of this Act; and the provisions of this Act relating to justices appointed in accordance with section 6 shall have effect in relation to him accordingly.

(2) In sub-paragraph (1) (*b*) above the reference to section 20 (3) (*b*) of the Act of 1973 shall be construed as including a reference to the provisions (where applicable) of section 217 (2) (*b*) of the Act of 1972 (which provided that, where one out of two or more commissions of the peace was chosen to be treated as the sole commission of the peace for a county, the names of the justices appointed by the other commission or other commissions were to be deemed to be included among the names of the justices specified in the commission so chosen).

5.—(1) The supplemental list for England and Wales kept under the Act of 1973, as in force immediately before the commencement of this Act, shall have effect as the supplemental list required to be kept under section 8 of this Act; and any name which immediately before the commencement of this Act was treated as included in the list by virtue of section 20 (4) of the Act of 1973 (which related to justices whose names were entered in a supplemental list immediately before the 1st April 1974) shall continue to be treated as so included until removed from the list in accordance with section 9 of this Act.

(2) Any person whose name immediately before the commencement of this Act was omitted from the supplemental list by virtue of the proviso to paragraph 4 (1) of Schedule 1 to the Act of 1973 (which made provision corresponding to section 8 (3) of this Act) shall have his name entered in the supplemental list on the expiry or sooner determination of the term of office by reason of which his name was omitted from the list.

6. The repeal by this Act of paragraph 9 (1) of Schedule 1 to the Act of 1973 (which made provision corresponding to section 71 (3) of this Act) shall not affect the operation of the said paragraph 9 (1) in relation to the period beginning on the 1st April 1974 and ending with the commencement of this Act.

Stipendiary magistrates (other than metropolitan stipendiary magistrates)

7. Any person who immediately before the commencement of this Act was a stipendiary magistrate in a commission area or commission areas and held that office either—

(*a*) by virtue of an appointment made under section 2 of the Act of 1973, or

(*b*) as if appointed under that section, being treated as if so appointed by virtue of section 20 (5) of that Act (which related to any person who immediately before 1st April 1974 held office as a stipendiary magistrate for any area under section 29 of the Act of 1949),

shall continue to hold office as stipendiary magistrate in that commission area or those commission areas (as the case may be) and (subject to paragraphs 8 and 17 below) shall be treated for all purposes as if he had been appointed under section 13 of this Act; and the provisions of this Act relating to stipendiary magistrates appointed under section 13 shall have effect in relation to him accordingly.

8. The following provisions of this paragraph shall have effect in relation to any stipendiary magistrate who immediately before the commencement of this Act held office as mentioned in paragraph 7 (*b*) above, that is to say—

(*a*) his salary shall not be less than that payable to him immediately before the beginning of April 1974; and

(*b*) for the purposes of section 14 of this Act the date of his appointment shall be taken to have been that of his appointment to the office held by him immediately before the beginning of that month.

Petty sessional divisions

9. Without prejudice to any power exercisable by virtue of this Act to create or alter petty sessional divisions, the repeal of any enactment by this Act shall not affect the division of any commission area into petty sessional divisions as existing immediately before the commencement of this Act.

Justices' clerks and their staffs

10.—(1) This paragraph applies to any person who immediately before the 1st April 1953 was a justices' clerk and by virtue of section 23 of the Act of 1949 was deemed for the purposes of that Act to have been appointed as such by a magistrates' courts committee.

(2) In so far as, immediately before the commencement of this Act, the salary of any person to whom this paragraph applies was affected by subsection (2) of the said section 23 (which required the salary to be fixed with due regard to any additional duties imposed on him by that Act), the provisions of that subsection shall continue to have effect in relation to him notwithstanding the repeal of that section by this Act.

11.—(1) This paragraph applies to any person who on the 1st April 1953 was transferred to the employment of a magistrates' courts committee by section 23 of the Act of 1949 (which made provision as to persons who immediately before that date were employed by or employed to assist justices' clerks or collecting officers).

(2) In so far as, immediately before the commencement of this Act, the terms and conditions of employment of a person to whom this paragraph applies was affected by subsection (7) of the said section 23 (under which the terms and conditions of the previous employment of persons transferred by that section were made relevant to the terms and conditions of their employment after the transfer), the provisions of that subsection shall continue to have effect in relation to him notwithstanding the repeal of that section by this Act.

(3) In sub-paragraph (2) above any reference to subsection (7) of the said section 23 includes a reference to that subsection as read with subsection (11) of that section (which relates to persons previously employed to assist a justices' clerk).

12.—(1) In this paragraph "transferred officer or employee to whom this paragraph applies means any person who—

(*a*) by virtue of paragraph 10 of Schedule 3 to the Act of 1968 (which related to persons holding office as clerk at either of the justice rooms of the City of London and to their staffs) became a justices' clerk in the City as if appointed by the magistrates' courts committee or was transferred to the employment of the magistrates' courts committee for the City, or

(*b*) by virtue of paragraph 13 (1) or paragraph 13 (3) of that Schedule (which related to persons holding office as clerk to the magistrates under the South Staffordshire Stipendiary Justice Act 1889 or as clerk to the magistrate under the Staffordshire Potteries Stipendiary Justice Acts 1839 to 1895 and to their staffs) was transferred to the employment of a magistrates' courts committee.

(2) In so far as, immediately before the commencement of this Act, the terms and conditions of employment of a transferred officer or employee to whom this paragraph applies were affected by paragraph 15 of Schedule 3 to the Act of 1968 (which made provision for securing that the terms and conditions of employment of any such person after the transfer would be no less favourable than those which he enjoyed immediately before the 10th November 1969), the provisions of that paragraph shall continue to have effect in relation to him notwithstanding the repeal of that paragraph by this Act.

13.—(1) Any regulations made by the Secretary of State under section 42 of the Act of 1949 (which required the Secretary of State to provide for compensation for loss of office or employment, or loss or diminution of emoluments, attributable to Parts II and III of that Act) which were in force immediately before the commencement of this Act (including any such regulations made under that section as extended by section 32 of the Act of 1964) shall continue to have effect notwithstanding the repeal of those sections by this Act and may be revoked or varied accordingly.

(2) Any regulations made by the Secretary of State under paragraph 16 of Schedule 3 to the Act of 1968 (which required the Secretary of State to provide for compensation for loss of office or employment, or loss or diminution of emoluments, attributable to the operation of section 1 of that Act in relation to the City of London and in relation to the Acts relating to Staffordshire mentioned in paragraph 12 (1) (*b*) above) which were in force immediately before the commencement of this Act shall continue to have effect notwithstanding the repeal of the said paragraph 16 by this Act and may be revoked or varied accordingly.

14.—(1) This paragraph applies to any order made before the 1st April 1953 in pursuance of the powers exercisable under section 30 of the Criminal Justice Administration Act 1914 or under section 1 of the Affiliation Orders Act 1914 which directed payments to be made and continues to be in force immediately before the commencement of this Act.

(2) Any such order which by virtue of section 21 (4) of the Act of 1949 had effect immediately before the commencement of this Act as if it required those payments to be made to a justices' clerk in his capacity as collecting officer of a magistrates' court shall, so long as the order remains in force, continue to have the like effect by virtue of this paragraph.

Justices of the Peace Act 1949, *Schedule* 2

15. Where in the preceding paragraphs of this Schedule reference is made to a person's office or employment (whether as justice of the peace, justices' clerk or otherwise) and to any provisions of the enactments repealed by this Act under which he held or was treated as holding that office or employment, the reference to those provisions shall be construed as including a reference to Schedule 2 to the Act of 1949 (provisions consequential on changes in commission of the peace) in so far as any provisions of that Schedule—

(*a*) were relevant to that person's office or employment, and

(*b*) notwithstanding the repeal of that Schedule by Part I of Schedule 5 to the Act of 1973, continued to have effect in accordance with the saving contained in that repeal.

Provisions relating to Part V of Act

16. The provisions of Part V of this Act shall have effect in relation to any act done or omitted to be done, conviction or order made or warrant issued before the

commencement of this Act, and in relation to any proceedings brought before the commencement of this Act, as those provisions would have effect in relation to the like act done or omitted, the like conviction, order or warrant made or issued or the like proceedings brought, as the case may be, after the commencement of this Act.

Saving for superannuation provisions

17. Except as provided by sections 55 to 58 of this Act, nothing in this Act shall affect any pension rights or other superannuation benefits or the person by whom or the manner in which any pension or other superannuation benefit is to be paid or borne.

Savings for Local Government Act 1972, *ss.* 67, 252, 254

18. The provisions of this Act shall have effect without prejudice to the exercise of any power conferred by section 67 of the Act of 1972 (consequential and transitional arrangements relating to Part IV), section 252 of that Act (general power to adapt Acts and instruments) or section 254 of that Act (consequential and supplementary provision); and any such power which, if this Act had not been passed, would have been exercisable in relation to an enactment repealed by this Act shall be exercisable in the like manner and to the like extent in relation to the corresponding provision (if any) of this Act.

Section 71

SCHEDULE 2

Consequential Amendments

Maintenance Orders (Facilities for Enforcement) Act 1920 (*c.* 33)

1. In section 3 (4), in relation to any time after the coming into operation of paragraph 2 of Schedule 2 to the Domestic Proceedings and Magistrates' Courts Act 1978, for "section 1 of the Administration of Justice Act 1973" substitute "the Justices of the Peace Act 1979".

Children and Young Persons Act 1933 (*c.* 12)

2. In section 107 (1), in relation to any time after the coming into operation of paragraph 5 of Schedule 2 to the Domestic Proceedings and Magistrates' Courts Act 1978, for "section 1 of the Administration of Justice Act 1973" substitute "the Justices of the Peace Act 1979".

National Assistance Act 1948 (*c.* 29)

3. In section 43 (4), in relation to any time after the coming into operation of paragraph 6 of Schedule 2 to the Domestic Proceedings and Magistrates' Courts Act 1978, and in section 44 (2), in relation to any time after the coming into operation of paragraph 7 of that Schedule, for "section 1 of the Administration of Justice Act 1973" substitute "the Justices of the Peace Act 1979".

Children Act 1948 (*c.* 43)

4. In section 26, in subsections (1) and (4), in relation to any time after the coming into operation of paragraph 8 of Schedule 2 to the Domestic Proceedings and Magistrates' Courts Act 1978, for "section 1 of the Administration of Justice Act 1973" substitute "the Justices of the Peace Act 1979".

Marriage Act 1949 (*c.* 76)

5. In section 3 (5), in relation to any time after the coming into operation of paragraph 9 of Schedule 2 to the Domestic Proceedings and Magistrates' Courts Act 1978, for "section 1 of the Administration of Justice Act 1973" substitute "the Justices of the Peace Act 1979".

Maintenance Orders Act 1950 (*c.* 37)

6. In section 3 (2), in relation to any time after the coming into operation of paragraph 11 of Schedule 2 to the Domestic Proceedings and Magistrates' Courts Act 1978, for "section 1 of the Administration of Justice Act 1973" substitute "the Justices of the Peace Act 1979".

Magistrates' Courts Act 1952 (*c.* 55)

7. In section 44 for "section 1 of the Administration of Justice Act 1973" substitute "the Justices of the Peace Act 1979".

8. In section 56B (7) for "Administration of Justice Act 1964" substitute "Justices of the Peace Act 1979".

9. In section 114 (1) (*f*), for "section twenty-seven of the Justices of the Peace Act 1949" substitute "section 61 of the Justices of the Peace Act 1979".

Affiliation Proceedings Act 1957 (*c.* 55)

10. In section 3 (1), in relation to any time after the coming into operation of section 49 of the Domestic Proceedings and Magistrates' Courts Act 1978, for "section 1 of the Administration of Justice Act 1973" substitute "the Justices of the Peace Act 1979".

Licensing Act 1964 (*c.* 26)

11. In section 201 (1), in the definition of "the metropolis" (as substituted by paragraph 31 (4) of Schedule 3 to the Administration of Justice Act 1964), for "Administration of Justice Act 1964" substitute "Justices of the Peace Act 1979".

Administration of Justice Act 1964 (*c.* 42)

12. In section 38 (1), in the definition of "London commission areas", "inner London area" and "outer London areas", for "this Act" substitute "the Justices of the Peace Act 1979".

Backing of Warrants (Republic of Ireland) Act 1965 (*c.* 45)

13. In the Schedule, in the proviso to paragraph 2, for the words from "section 121" to "other magistrates" substitute "section 16 (1) of the Justices of the Peace Act 1979 (which exempts stipendiary magistrates from certain restrictions imposed by the Magistrates' Courts Act 1952)" and for "that Act" substitute "the Magistrates' Courts Act 1952".

Criminal Justice Act 1967 (*c.* 80)

14. In section 45 (4), for "Part IV of the Justices of the Peace Act 1949" substitute "Part VI of the Justices of the Peace Act 1979".

Road Traffic Regulation Act 1967 (*c.* 76)

15. In section 80 (5), for "section 27 of the Justices of the Peace Act 1949" substitute "section 61 of the Justices of the Peace Act 1979" and for the words "said section 27", wherever they occur, substitute "said section 61".

Guardianship of Minors Act 1971 (*c.* 3)

16. In section 15, in subsections (1) and (4), in relation to any time after the coming into operation of section 47 (1) of the Domestic Proceedings and Magistrates' Courts Act 1978, for "Administration of Justice Act 1973" substitute "Justices of the Peace Act 1979".

Immigration Act 1971 (*c.* 77)

17. In Schedule 2, in paragraphs 22 (3) and 31 (4), for "Justices of the Peace Act 1949 and, in particular, section 27 thereof" substitute "Justices of the Peace Act 1979 and, in particular, section 61 thereof".

Maintenance Orders (Reciprocal Enforcement) Act 1972 (*c.* 18)

18. In section 27 (2), in relation to any time after the coming into operation of section 56 of the Domestic Proceedings and Magistrates' Courts Act 1978, for "section 1 of the Administration of Justice Act 1973" substitute "the Justices of the Peace Act 1979".

Local Government Act 1972 (*c.* 70)

19. In section 217, for subsection (7) substitute the following:—

"(7) The enactments specified in Part II of Schedule 27 to this Act shall have effect subject to the amendments specified therein".

Criminal Justice Act 1972 (*c.* 71)

20. In section 51, in subsection (4), for "section 5 (1) of the Justices of the Peace Act 1968" substitute "section 28 (1) of the Justices of the Peace Act 1979".

Administration of Justice Act 1973 (*c.* 15)

21. In section 2 (4), after "section" insert "or under section 13 of the Justices of the Peace Act 1979".

22. For section 5 substitute the following:—

"5. Paragraphs 2, 3 and 7 of Schedule 1 to this Act shall have effect; and the enactments specified in paragraphs 10 and 11 of that Schedule shall have effect subject to the amendments specified in those paragraphs".

23. In section 9 (1) (*f*), for "this Act" substitute "section 13 of the Justices of the Peace Act 1979 (or, by virtue of paragraph 7 of Schedule 1 to that Act, treated as so appointed)".

24. In Schedule 1—

(*a*) in paragraph 2 (1), for "paragraph 1 above" substitute "section 14 of the Justices of the Peace Act 1979";

(*b*) in paragraph 7, for "paragraph 6 (2) (*a*) to (*c*) above" substitute "section 10 (2) (*a*) to (*c*) of the Justices of the Peace Act 1979".

Powers of Criminal Courts Act 1973 (*c.* 62)

25. In section 32 (6), for the words from "Justices of the Peace Act 1949" to "magistrates' courts" substitute "Justices of the Peace Act 1979 and, in particular, section 61 thereof (application of fines and fees)".

26. In section 51, after subsection (3) insert—

"(3A) Any sums payable to the Greater London Council under subsection (3) (*a*) above shall be placed to the credit of the special London account out of which expenses of the Council under Schedule 3 to this Act are payable."

Legal Aid Act 1974 (*c.* 4)

27. In section 35—

(*a*) in subsection (6), for "Part IV of the Justices of the Peace Act 1949" substitute "Part VI of the Justices of the Peace Act 1979";

(*b*) in subsection (7), for the words from "section 27" to "fines, fees etc." substitute "section 61 of the Justices of the Peace Act 1979 (application of fines and fees)" and for "subsection (9)" substitute "subsection (4)".

Local Government Act 1974 (*c.* 7)

28. In section 1 (6) (*a*), for "section 27 of the Justices of the Peace Act 1949" substitute "section 59 of the Justices of the Peace Act 1979".

Solicitors Act 1974 (*c.* 47)

29. In section 38—

(*a*) in subsection (3), for "section 1 of the Administration of Justice Act 1973" substitute "section 8 of the Justices of the Peace Act 1979";

(*b*) in subsection (4), for "section 1 (6) of the Administration of Justice Act 1973" substitute "the proviso to section 39 (1) of the Justices of the Peace Act 1979".

Supplementary Benefits Act 1976 (*c.* 71)

30. In section 19 (2), in relation to any time after the coming into operation of paragraph 54 of Schedule 2 to the Domestic Proceedings and Magistrates' Courts Act 1978, for "section 1 of the Administration of Justice Act 1973" substitute "the Justices of the Peace Act 1979".

Domestic Proceedings and Magistrates' Courts Act 1978 (*c.* 22)

31. In section 88 (1), in the definition of "commission area", for "section 1 of the Administration of Justice Act 1973" substitute "the Justices of the Peace Act 1979".

Section 71

SCHEDULE 3

REPEALS

Chapter	Short Title	Extent of Repeal
16 Geo. 2. c. 18.	The Justices Jurisdiction Act 1742.	The whole Act.
11 & 12 Vict. c. 44.	The Justices Protection Act 1848.	The whole Act.
21 & 22 Vict. c. 73.	The Stipendiary Magistrates Act 1858.	The whole Act except sections 7 and 15.
40 & 41 Vict. c. 43.	The Justices' Clerks Act 1877.	The whole Act so far as unrepealed.
51 & 52 Vict. c. 41.	The Local Government Act 1888.	In section 42, subsection (12).
60 & 61 Vict. c. 26.	The Metropolitan Police Courts Act 1897.	Section 1. Section 8.
1 & 2 Geo. 6. c. 63.	The Administration of Justice (Miscellaneous Provisions) Act 1938.	In Schedule 2, the entry relating to the Justices Protection Act 1848.
12, 13 & 14 Geo. 6. c. 101.	The Justices of the Peace Act 1949.	Section 1. Section 3. Section 5. Section 13. In section 15, in subsection (5), the words from the beginning to " with the committee ". Sections 16 to 19. In section 20, subsections (1), (2), (4), (5) and (7). Section 21. Section 23. Sections 25 to 27. Section 42. Section 44. Schedule 4.
15 & 16 Geo. 6 & 1 Eliz. 2. c. 55.	The Magistrates' Courts Act 1952.	In section 116, subsection (1). In section 118, subsection (3) and, in subsection (4), the words from " but " onwards. In section 121, subsection (1).
7 & 8 Eliz. 2. c. 45.	The Metropolitan Magistrates' Courts Act 1959.	Section 2.
1964 c. 42.	The Administration of Justice Act 1964.	Sections 2 and 3. Sections 9 and 10. Sections 13 to 17. Sections 27 and 28. Section 30. Section 32. Section 36. In section 37, subsection (4). In Schedule 3, in paragraph 12, sub-paragraph (1); in paragraph 20, sub-paragraphs (6) and (7).
1965 c. 28.	The Justices of the Peace Act 1965.	The whole Act.
1968 c. 69.	The Justices of the Peace Act 1968.	In section 1, subsections (2) and (3). Section 3. Section 5. Schedule 2. In Schedule 3, paragraphs 2, 3 and 4 (4) and Part III.
1971 c. 23.	The Courts Act 1971.	In section 3, the words from " and commissions of the peace " onwards (but without prejudice to their operation in relation to any commission of the peace issued before the commencement of this Act). In section 53 (1), the words from the beginning to " Schedule 7 to this Act; and ".

SCHEDULE 3—*continued*

Chapter	Short Title	Extent of Repeal
1971 c. 23—*cont.*	The Courts Act 1971—*cont.*	In Schedule 7, paragraphs 1 to 3. In Schedule 8, in paragraph 43, sub-paragraphs (1), (3) and (4).
1972 c. 70.	The Local Government Act 1972.	In section 216, in subsection (2), the words " 217 ". In section 217, subsections (1) to (3), and subsection (5) so far as unrepealed. In Schedule 27, paragraphs 1 to 15, paragraph 17 and paragraph 19.
1972 c. 71.	The Criminal Justice Act 1972.	Sections 61 and 62.
1973 c. 15.	The Administration of Justice Act 1973.	In section 1, subsections (1) to (8). In section 2, subsections (1) to (3) and subsections (5) to (7). Section 3. In section 20, subsections (3) and (4); subsection (5) except, in the proviso to that subsection, the words in paragraph (*b*) from the beginning to " metropolitan stipendiary magistrate "; and in subsection (6), the word " or " where it last occurs in paragraph (*a*) and the words from the beginning of paragraph (*b*) to the end of the subsection. In Schedule 1, paragraphs 1, 4, 5, 6, 8, 9 (1) and 12.
1975 c. 60.	The Social Security Pensions Act 1975.	In Schedule 4, paragraph 5.
1977 c. 38.	The Administration of Justice Act 1977.	Section 21.
1978 c. 22.	The Domestic Proceeding and Magistrates' Courts Act 1978.	In Schedule 2, paragraph 5. Section 86.

Consolidated Fund (No. 2) Act 1979

(1979 c. 56)

An Act to apply certain sums out of the Consolidated Fund to the service of the years ending on 31st March 1980 and 1981.

[20th December 1979]

General Note

This Act authorises the issue of certain moneys out of the consolidated Fund.

The Act received the Royal Assent on December 20, 1979, and came into force on that date.

Issue out of the Consolidated Fund for the year ending 31st March 1980

1. The Treasury may issue out of the Consolidated Fund of the United Kingdom and apply towards making good the supply granted to Her Majesty for the service of the year ending on 31st March 1980 the sum of £2,054,656,000.

Issue out of the Consolidated Fund for the year ending 31st March 1981

2. The Treasury may issue out of the Consolidated Fund of the United Kingdom and apply towards making good the supply granted to Her Majesty for the service of the year ending on 31st March 1981 the sum of £23,238,937,800.

Short title

3. This Act may be cited as the Consolidated Fund (No. 2) Act 1979.

European Communities (Greek Accession) Act 1979

(1979 c. 57)

An Act to extend the meaning in Acts, Measures and subordinate legislation of "the Treaties" and "the Community Treaties" in connection with the accession of the Hellenic Republic to the European Communities. [20th December 1979]

General Note

This Act provides for the accession of the Hellenic Republic to the European Communities.

S. 1 extends the meaning of "the Treaties" and "the Community Treaties" to include the Hellenic Republic; s. 2 contains the short title.

The Act received the Royal Assent on December 20, 1979, and came into force on that date.

Parliamentary debates

Hansard, H.C. Vol. 972, col. 1041; Vol. 973, col. 1366; H.L. Vol. 403, cols. 337, 995, 1538.

Extended meaning of "the Treaties" and "the Community Treaties"

1. In section 1 (2) of the European Communities Act 1972, in the definition of "the Treaties" and "the Community Treaties" there shall be inserted after paragraph (*b*) the words "and

(*c*) the treaty relating to the accession of the Hellenic Republic to the European Economic Community and to the European Atomic Energy Community, signed at Athens on 28th May 1979; and

(*d*) the decision, of 24th May 1979, of the Council relating to the accession of the Hellenic Republic to the European Coal and Steel Community;".

Short title

2. This Act may be cited as the European Communities (Greek Accession) Act 1979.

Isle of Man Act 1979

(1979 c. 58)

ARRANGEMENT OF SECTIONS

An Act to make such amendments of the law relating to customs and excise, value added tax, car tax and the importation and exportation of goods as are required for giving effect to an Agreement between the government of the United Kingdom and the government of the Isle of Man signed on 15th October 1979; to make other amendments as respects the Isle of Man in the law relating to those matters; to provide for the transfer of functions vested in the Lieutenant Governor of the Isle of Man or, as respects that Island, in the Commissioners of Customs and Excise; and for purposes connected with those matters. [20th December 1979]

General Note

This Act amends the law relating to customs and excise, value added tax, car tax and the importation and exportation of goods between the United Kingdom and the Isle of Man.

S. 1 relates to common duties; s. 2 deals with the Isle of Man share of common duties; s. 3 provides for the recovery of common duties chargeable in the Isle of Man; s. 4 makes provision as to the enforcement of Isle of Man judgments for common duties; s. 5 specifies offences relating to common duties, etc.; s. 6 deals with value added tax; s. 7 contains provisions relating to car tax; s. 8 provides for the removal of goods from the Isle of Man to the U.K.; s. 9 deals with the removal of goods from the U.K. to the Isle of Man; s. 10 relates to the exchange of information; s. 11 provides for the transfer of functions to Isle of Man authorities; s. 12 deals with proof of Acts of Tynwald, etc.; s. 13 makes various amendments to customs and excise Acts; s. 14 contains the short title, interpretation, repeals, commencement and extent.

The Act received the Royal Assent on December 30, 1979, and ss. 6, 7, 10 and 11 came into force on that date, the remaining provisions come into force on April 1, 1980.

Parliamentary debates

Hansard, H.C. Vol. 973, col. 1599; H.L. Vol. 403, cols. 495, 1390.

Common duties

1.—(1) Subject to subsection (2) below, in this Act " common duties " means—

(*a*) customs duties chargeable on goods imported into the United Kingdom or the Isle of Man;

(*b*) excise duties chargeable on goods, other than beer, imported into or produced in the United Kingdom or the Isle of Man;

(*c*) pool betting duty chargeable under the law of the United Kingdom or the Isle of Man;

(*d*) value added tax chargeable under the law of the United Kingdom or the Isle of Man except tax chargeable in accordance with section 21 of the Finance (No. 2) Act 1975 (gaming machines);

(*e*) car tax chargeable under the law of the United Kingdom or the Isle of Man.

(2) The Treasury may by order amend subsection (1) above by adding or deleting any duty or tax which is under the care and management of the Commissioners of Customs and Excise (in this Act referred to as " the Commissioners ") or any corresponding duty or tax chargeable under the law of the Isle of Man; and any such order may apply to a duty or tax generally or in such cases or subject to such restrictions as may be specified in the order.

(3) The power to make orders under subsection (2) above shall be exercisable by statutory instrument subject to annulment in pursuance of a resolution of the House of Commons.

Isle of Man share of common duties

2.—(1) Out of the moneys standing to the credit of the General Account of the Commissioners an amount ascertained for each financial year in accordance with subsection (2) below shall be paid by the Commissioners, at such times and in such manner as they may determine, to the Treasurer of the Isle of Man.

(2) There shall be calculated in such manner as the Treasury may direct—

(*a*) the amount of common duties, whether collected in the United Kingdom or the Isle of Man, which is attributable to goods consumed or used in the Island, to services supplied in the Island or (as respects pool betting duty) to bets placed by persons in the Island;

(*b*) the cost incurred by the Commissioners in collecting the amount so attributable together with the amount of any drawback or repayment referable to that amount;

and the amount arrived at by deducting from the amount calculated under paragraph (*a*) above the amount calculated under paragraph (*b*) above shall be known as the net Isle of Man share of common duties; and the amount mentioned in subsection (1) above shall be the excess of the net Isle of Man share of common duties over the common duties collected in the Island.

(3) For the purposes of this section the amount of common duties collected in the Isle of Man and the United Kingdom, or in the Isle of Man, shall be calculated by reference to the amount so collected in respect of such duties after giving effect to any addition or deduction provided for under section 1 of the Excise Duties (Surcharges or Rebates) Act 1979 or any Isle of Man equivalent.

(4) The Commissioners shall for each financial year prepare, in such form and manner as the Treasury may direct, an account showing the payments made by them under this section and shall send it, not later

than the end of November in the following financial year, to the Comptroller and Auditor General, who shall examine and certify the account.

(5) The Comptroller and Auditor General shall send every account examined and certified by him under this section and his report thereon to the Treasury and a copy of every such account and report to the Treasurer of the Isle of Man; and the Treasury shall lay copies of the account and report before Parliament.

Recovery of common duties chargeable in Isle of Man

3.—(1) Any liability to pay an amount on account of a common duty chargeable under the law of the Isle of Man shall, to the extent to which it has not been discharged or enforced there, be enforceable in the United Kingdom as if it were a liability to pay an amount on account of the corresponding common duty chargeable under the law of the United Kingdom.

(2) Any amount recoverable by the Commissioners from any person under subsection (1) above may be set off against any amount recoverable by him from the Commissioners on account of a common duty chargeable under the law of the United Kingdom.

Enforcement of Isle of Man judgments for common duties

4.—(1) Subject to subsection (2) below, the provisions of sections 2 to 5 of the Foreign Judgments (Reciprocal Enforcement) Act 1933 shall have effect in relation to any judgment of order given or made by the High Court of Justice of the Isle of Man under which an amount is payable on account of—

(*a*) a common duty chargeable under the law of the Island; or

(*b*) a fine or penalty imposed in connection with such a duty,

as if the judgment or order were a judgment to which Part I of that Act applied.

(2) Subsection (1) above does not apply to a judgment or order given or made on appeal from a lower court but, except when given or made in criminal proceedings, applies notwithstanding that it is subject to appeal or that an appeal against it is pending.

(3) In their application by virtue of subsection (1) above the provisions there mentioned shall have effect—

(*a*) with the omission of so much of section 2 (1) as imposes a time-limit for applications for registration;

(*b*) with the omission of section 4 (1) (*a*) (v) and (vi); and

(*c*) as if the Commissioners were the judgment creditor and any criminal proceedings in which the judgment or order was given or made were an action.

(4) The reference in subsection (1) above to sections 2 to 5 of the said Act of 1933 includes a reference to so much of sections 11 to 13 of that Act as is relevant to those sections and the definition of " appeal " in section 11 shall apply for the purposes of subsection (2) above.

(5) The reference in subsection (1) above to the High Court of Justice of the Isle of Man includes a reference to the Court of General Gaol Delivery.

Offences relating to common duties etc.

5.—(1) Any summons or other process requiring a person in the Isle of Man to appear before a court in the United Kingdom—

(*a*) to answer a charge that he has committed an offence relating to a common duty chargeable under the law of the United Kingdom or to the importation or exportation of anything into or from the United Kingdom; or (*b*) to give evidence or to produce any document or thing in proceedings for any such offence,

may be served by being sent to him by registered post or the recorded delivery service.

(2) In relation to proceedings for any such offence as is mentioned in subsection (1) above—

(*a*) section 77 of the Magistrates' Courts Act 1952 (summons to witness and warrant for his arrest) shall have effect as if the reference in subsection (1) of that section to a person in England and Wales included a reference to a person in the Isle of Man;

(*b*) in Scotland a warrant for the citation of accused persons and witnesses shall include a warrant to cite accused persons and witnesses in the Isle of Man.

(3) In relation to proceedings for any such offence as is mentioned in subsection (1) above—

(*a*) sections 2 and 9 of the Criminal Justice Act 1967 (admission of written statements) shall apply also to written statements made in the Isle of Man but with the omission of subsections (2) (*b*) and (3A) of section 2 and subsections (2) (*b*) and (3A) of section 9;

(*b*) section 1 of the Criminal Justice (Miscellaneous Provisions) Act (Northern Ireland) 1968 and section 3 of the Criminal Procedure (Committal for Trial) Act (Northern Ireland) 1968 (which contain corresponding provisions) shall apply also to written statements made in the Isle of Man but with the omission of subsection (2) (*b*) of section 1 and subsection (2) (*c*) of section 3.

(4) Subject to subsection (5) below, a warrant issued in the Isle of Man for the arrest of—

(*a*) a person charged with an offence relating to a common duty chargeable under the law of the Isle of Man or to the importation or exportation of anything into or from the Island; or

(*b*) a person required to give evidence or to produce any document or thing in proceedings for any such offence,

may be executed in England and Wales by any constable acting within his police area, in Scotland by any officer of law as defined in section 462 (1) of the Criminal Procedure (Scotland) Act 1975 and in Northern Ireland by any member of the Royal Ulster Constabulary or the Royal Ulster Constabulary Reserve.

(5) A warrant, other than one for the arrest of a person charged with an offence punishable with at least two years' imprisonment, shall not be executed under subsection (4) above unless it has been endorsed for execution under that subsection by a justice of the peace in England, Wales, Scotland or Northern Ireland, as the case may be; and any warrant which purports to have been issued as mentioned in that subsection may be so endorsed without further proof.

(6) A warrant for the arrest of a person charged with an offence may be executed by a constable under subsection (4) above notwithstanding that it is not in his possession at the time; but the warrant shall, on demand of that person, be shown to him as soon as practicable.

(7) Subsections (1) and (4) above are without prejudice to any other enactment enabling any process to be served or executed otherwise than as provided in those subsections.

(8) References in this section to a warrant for the arrest of any person include references to any process for that purpose available under the law of the Isle of Man; and references to an offence relating to a common duty or to importation of exportation include references to any

offence which relates to any of those matters whether or not it is an offence under a provision dealing specifically with that matter.

Value added tax

6.—(1) For the purpose of giving effect to any Agreement between the government of the United Kingdom and the government of the Isle of Man whereby both countries are to be treated as a single area for the purposes of value added tax charged under the Finance Act 1972 and value added tax charged under the corresponding Act of Tynwald, Her Majesty may by Order in Council make provision for securing that tax is charged under the Act of 1972 as if all or any of the references in it to the United Kingdom included both the United Kingdom and the Isle of Man but so that tax is not charged under both Acts in respect of the same transaction.

(2) An Order in Council under this section may make provision—

(*a*) for determining, or enabling the Commissioners to determine, under which Act a person is to be registered and for transferring a person registered under one Act to the register kept under the other;

(*b*) for treating a person who is a taxable person for the purposes of the Act of Tynwald as a taxable person for all or any of the purposes of the Act of 1972;

(*c*) for extending any reference in the Act of 1972 to tax under that Act so as to include tax under the Act of Tynwald;

(*d*) for treating any requirement imposed by or under either Act as a requirement imposed by or under the other;

(*e*) for treating any permission, direction, notice, determination or other thing given, made or done under the Act of Tynwald by the Isle of Man authority corresponding to the Commissioners as given, made or done by the Commissioners under the Act of 1972;

(*f*) for enabling the Commissioners to determine for the purposes of section 21 of the Act of 1972 (groups of companies) which member of a group is to be the representative member in cases where supplies are made both in the United Kingdom and the Isle of Man;

(*g*) for modifying or excluding, as respects goods removed from the Isle of Man to the United Kingdom or from the United Kingdom to the Isle of Man, any provision relating to importation or exportation contained in the Act of 1972 or in the customs and excise Acts as applied by that Act;

(*h*) for any supplementary, incidental or transitional matter.

(3) An Order in Council under this section may make such modifications of any provision contained in or having effect under any Act of Parliament relating to value added tax as appears to Her Majesty to be necessary or expedient for the purposes of the Order.

(4) While an Order in Council under this section is in force and without prejudice to the powers conferred by the foregoing provisions—

(*a*) section 12 (8) of the Act of 1972 (forfeiture of zero-rated goods) shall have effect as if the reference to goods zero-rated under the regulations there mentioned included a reference to goods zero-rated under any corresponding regulations made under the Act of Tynwald;

(*b*) section 37 (3) of the Act of 1972 (search of premises where offence is suspected) shall have effect as if the references to an offence in connection with the tax included references to an offence in connection with the tax charged under the Act of Tynwald;

(*c*) section 38 (3) of the Act of 1972 (course of conduct involving offences) shall have effect as if the reference to offences under the provisions there mentioned included a reference to offences under the corresponding provisions of the Act of Tynwald.

(5) Provision may be made by or under an Act of Tynwald for purposes corresponding to those of this section and of any Order in Council made under it.

Car tax

7.—(1) For the purpose of giving effect to any Agreement between the government of the United Kingdom and the government of the Isle of Man whereby both countries are to be treated as a single area for the purposes of the car tax charged under the Finance Act 1972 and the car tax charged under the corresponding Act of Tynwald, Her Majesty may by Order in Council make provision for securing that tax is charged under the Act of 1972 as if all or any of the references in it to the United Kingdom included both the United Kingdom and the Isle of Man but so that tax is not charged under both Acts in respect of the same vehicle.

(2) An Order in Council under this section may make provision—

(*a*) for determining, or enabling the Commissioners to determine, under which Act a person is to be registered and for transferring a person registered under one Act to the register kept under the other;

(*b*) for treating a person who is registered for the purposes of the Act of Tynwald as registered for all or any of the purposes of the Act of 1972;

(*c*) for extending any reference in the Act of 1972 to tax under that Act so as to include tax under the Act of Tynwald;

(*d*) for treating any requirement imposed by or under either Act as a requirement imposed by or under the other;

(*e*) for treating any permission, direction, notice, determination or other thing given, made or done under the Act of Tynwald by the Isle of Man authority corresponding to the Commissioners as given, made or done by the Commissioners under the Act of 1972;

(*f*) for modifying or excluding, as respects a vehicle removed from the Isle of Man to the United Kingdom or from the United Kingdom to the Isle of Man, any provision of the Act of 1972 which relates to importation or exportation;

(*g*) for any supplementary, incidental or transitional matter.

(3) An Order in Council under this section may make such modifications of any provision contained in or having effect under any Act of Parliament relating to car tax as appears to Her Majesty to be necessary or expedient for the purposes of the Order.

(4) While an Order in Council under this section is in force and without prejudice to the powers conferred by the foregoing provisions—

(*a*) paragraph 21 (3) of Schedule 7 to the Act of 1972 (search of premises where offence is suspected) shall have effect as if the references to an offence in connection with the tax included references to an offence in connection with the tax charged under the Act of Tynwald;

(*b*) paragraph 23 of that Schedule (forfeiture of chargeable vehicle if not registered or tax not paid etc.) shall have effect as if references to chargeable vehicles, the registration of a vehicle and tax included references to a chargeable vehicle, the registration of a vehicle and tax within the meaning of the Act of Tynwald.

(5) Provision may be made by or under an Act of Tynwald for purposes corresponding to those of this section and of any Order in Council made under it.

Removal of goods from Isle of Man to United Kingdom

8.—(1) Except as provided in subsection (2) below, goods removed to the United Kingdom from the Isle of Man shall be deemed for the purposes of the customs and excise Acts not to be imported into the United Kingdom.

(2) Subsection (1) above does not apply to—

(*a*) goods imported into or produced in the Isle of Man which are of a class or description chargeable with customs or excise duty under the law of the United Kingdom and which have not borne a corresponding duty under the law of the Isle of Man;

(*b*) goods which were imported into the Isle of Man in contravention of any prohibition or restriction and which are of a class or description the importation of which into the United Kingdom is for the time being subject to a corresponding prohibition or restriction; or

(*c*) any explosives within the meaning of the Explosives Act 1875 on the unloading or landing of which any restriction is for the time being in force under or by virtue of that Act.

(3) The goods referred to in subsection (2) (*a*) above do not include goods which have been wholly or partly exempted from duty under any Isle of Man equivalent to section 48 of the Customs and Excise Management Act 1979 (relief for goods temporarily imported) or section 13 of the Customs and Excise Duties (General Reliefs) Act 1979 (personal reliefs for imported goods) but where—

(*a*) any such exemption was subject to conditions required to be complied with after importation of the goods into the Isle of Man; and

(*b*) the goods are removed to the United Kingdom,

the customs and excise Acts shall apply to the goods as if they had been imported into the United Kingdom when they were imported into the Isle of Man and as if corresponding conditions had then been imposed under the said section 48 or 13.

(4) For the purposes of subsection (2) (*a*) above goods of any class or description shall be treated as having borne a corresponding duty under the law of the Isle of Man if they have borne duty under that law at a rate not less than that at which duty was then chargeable under the law of the United Kingdom in respect of goods of that class or description; and where goods have borne duty under the law of the Isle of Man at a lower rate, the duty charged on their importation into the United Kingdom shall be reduced by an amount equal to the duty borne under that law.

Removal of goods from United Kingdom to Isle of Man

9.—(1) Except as provided in subsection (2) below, goods removed to the Isle of Man from the United Kingdom shall be deemed for the purposes of the customs and excise Acts not to be exported from the United Kingdom.

(2) Any enactment relating to the allowance of drawback of any excise duty on the exportation from the United Kingdom of any goods shall have effect, subject to such conditions and modifications as the

Commissioners may by regulations prescribe, as if the removal of such goods to the Isle of Man were the exportation of the goods.

(3) The power to make regulations under subsection (2) above shall be exercisable by statutory instrument subject to annulment in pursuance of a resolution of either House of Parliament.

(4) Where goods imported into or produced in the United Kingdom have not borne customs or excise duty and would be chargeable with customs or excise duty if imported into the Isle of Man, the goods shall not be removed from the United Kingdom to the Isle of Man until—

(*a*) they have been cleared for that purpose by the proper officer; and

(*b*) security has been given to the satisfaction of the Commissioners for the due delivery of the goods at some port, airport or place of security in the Isle of Man approved for customs and excise purposes under the law of the Island;

but paragraph (*b*) above shall not apply if the goods are reported on arrival in the United Kingdom for removal to the Isle of Man in the same ship or aircraft and in continuance of the same voyage or flight.

(5) The goods referred to in subsection (4) above do not include passengers' baggage or goods that have been relieved or exempted from duty under any of the provisions of sections 7 to 11 or 13 of the Customs and Excise Duties (General Reliefs) Act 1979.

(6) Any goods removed from the United Kingdom contrary to subsection (4) above shall be liable to forfeiture and any person concerned in the removal of the goods shall be liable on summary conviction to a penalty of £200.

Exchange of information

10. No obligation as to secrecy or other restriction on the disclosure of information imposed by statute or otherwise shall prevent the Commissioners or any officer of the Commissioners from disclosing information to the Isle of Man customs and excise service for the purpose of facilitating the proper administration of common duties and the enforcement of prohibitions or restrictions on importation or exportation into or from the Isle of Man or the United Kingdom.

Transfer of functions to Isle of Man authorities

11.—(1) Her Majesty may by Order in Council make such modifications in any provision contained in or having effect under any Act of Parliament extending to the Isle of Man as appear to Her Majesty to be appropriate for the purpose of transferring to any authority or person constituted by or having functions under the law of the Island—

(*a*) any functions under that provision of the Lieutenant Governor of the Isle of Man (whether referred to by that title or otherwise) or of a deputy governor of the Island;

(*b*) any functions under that provision, so far as exercisable in relation to the Island, of the Commissioners or an office of the Commissioners.

(2) Any statutory instrument made by virtue of this section shall be subject to annulment in pursuance of a resolution of either House of Parliament.

Proof of Acts of Tynwald etc.

12.—(1) Without prejudice to the Evidence (Colonial Statutes) Act 1907, any Act of Tynwald or other instrument forming part of the law of the Isle of Man may, in any proceedings in the United Kingdom relating to a common duty or to importation or exportation into or from the United Kingdom or the Isle of Man, be proved by producing a copy of the Act or instrument authenticated by a certificate purporting to be signed by or on behalf of the Attorney General for the Island.

(2) Any provision contained in or having effect under an Act of Tynwald which—

(*a*) prescribes the mode or burden of proof with respect to any matter in proceedings relating to a common duty chargeable under the law of the Isle of Man; and

(*b*) corresponds to a provision of United Kingdom law for similar purposes,

shall apply to any proceedings in the United Kingdom relating to that duty.

(3) For the purposes of any proceedings in the United Kingdom relating to a common duty an order may be made under the Bankers' Books Evidence Act 1879 in respect of books and persons in the Isle of Man.

Amendments of customs and excise Acts etc.

13. The enactments mentioned in Schedule 1 to this Act shall have effect with the amendments there specified, being amendments which—

(*a*) extend certain references to the United Kingdom in the customs and excise Acts so as to include the Isle of Man; or

(*b*) are otherwise consequential on the provisions of this Act.

Short title, interpretation, repeals, commencement and extent

14.—(1) This Act may be cited as the Isle of Man Act 1979.

(2) In this Act—

"the Commissioners" means the Commissioners of Customs and Excise;

"common duties" has the meaning given in section 1 above and "common duty" shall be construed accordingly;

"customs duty" includes any levy or other charge which is treated as a customs duty by section 6 of the European Communities Act 1972.

(3) Any other expression used in this Act which is also used in the Customs and Excise Management Act 1979 has the same meaning as in that Act.

(4) Without prejudice to section 2 (3) above,—

(*a*) any addition to an excise duty by virtue of section 1 of the Excise Duties (Surcharges or Rebates) Act 1979 or any Isle of Man equivalent; and

(*b*) any sum recoverable as a debt due to the Crown under section 33 (2A) of the Finance Act 1972 (sums shown in invoices as value added tax) or any Isle of Man equivalent,

shall be treated for the purposes of this Act as an amount of excise duty or value added tax chargeable under the law of the United Kingdom or, as the case may be, the Isle of Man.

(5) The enactments mentioned in Schedule 2 to this Act (which include spent provisions) are hereby repealed to the extent specified in the third column of that Schedule.

(6) Subject to subsection (7) below, this Act shall come into force on 1st April 1980.

(7) Sections 6, 7, 10 and 11 above shall come into force on the passing of this Act but no Order in Council shall be made under section 6, 7 or 11, and no provision shall by virtue of section 6 (5) or 7 (5) be made by or under an Act of Tynwald, so as to come into force before 1st April 1980.

(8) Except for sections 6, 7, 11 and this section, this Act does not extend to the Isle of Man as part of the law of the Island.

SCHEDULES

Section 13

SCHEDULE 1

AMENDMENTS OF CUSTOMS AND EXCISE ACTS ETC.

The Finance Act 1972

1. After section 17 (2B) of the Finance Act 1972 there shall be inserted—

" (2C) Sections 8 and 9 of the Isle of Man Act 1979 shall also be excepted from the enactments which are to have effect as mentioned in subsection (1) of this subsection."

The Customs and Excise Management Act 1979

2. In section 1 (1) of the Customs and Excise Management Act 1979, at the end of the definition of " Community transit goods " there shall be inserted the words " and for the purposes of paragraph (*a*) (i) above the Isle of Man shall be treated as if it were part of the United Kingdom ".

3. In section 17 (3) of that Act for the words from " subject, however " onwards there shall be substituted the words " subject, however, to section 2 of the Isle of Man Act 1979 (payments of Isle of Man share of common duties) ".

4. In section 21 of that Act after subsection (7) there shall be inserted—

" (8) References in this section to a place or area outside the United Kingdom do not include references to a place or area in the Isle of Man and in subsection (3) (*b*) above the reference to a place in the United Kingdom includes a reference to a place in the Isle of Man."

5. In section 34 (1) of that Act after the words " outside the United Kingdom " there shall be inserted the words " and the Isle of Man ".

6. In section 35 of that Act after subsection (8) there shall be inserted—

" (9) References in this section to a place, area or destination outside the United Kingdom do not include references to a place, area or destination in the Isle of Man and in subsection (3) (*b*) (i) above the reference to a destination in the United Kingdom includes a reference to a destination in the Isle of Man."

7. In section 36 (1) of that Act after the words " the United Kingdom " there shall be inserted the words " and the Isle of Man ".

8. In section 43 (5) of that Act for the words " after exportation therefrom " there shall be substituted the words " after exportation from the United Kingdom or the Isle of Man ".

9. In section 53 (1) of that Act after the words " the United Kingdom " there shall be inserted the words " and the Isle of Man ".

10. In section 57 of that Act after subsection (12) there shall be inserted—

" (13) References in this section to a destination, place or consignee outside the United Kingdom do not include references to a destination, place or consignee in the Isle of Man."

11. In section 61 of that Act after subsection (8) there shall be inserted—

" (9) References in this section to a destination, place or area outside the United Kingdom do not include references to a destination, place or area in the Isle of Man and subsection (5) above applies whether the goods were shipped in the United Kingdom or the Isle of Man."

12. In section 63 of that Act after subsection (6) there shall be inserted—

" (7) References in this section to a destination or place outside the United Kingdom do not include references to a destination or place in the Isle of Man and in subsections (2) and (4) above references to a place in the United Kingdom and to discharge in the United Kingdom include references to a place in the Isle of Man and to discharge in the Island."

13. In section 64 (1) of that Act after the words " the United Kingdom " there shall be inserted the words " and the Isle of Man ".

14. In section 66 (1) (*a*) and (*d*) of that Act after the words "the United Kingdom" there shall be inserted the words "and the Isle of Man".

15. In section 69 (1) and (3) of that Act after the words "between places in the United Kingdom" there shall be inserted the words "or between a place in the United Kingdom and a place in the Isle of Man".

16. In section 70 of that Act after subsection (4) there shall be inserted—

"(5) References in this section to a place or destination outside the United Kingdom do not include references to a place or destination in the Isle of Man and in subsection (2) above the reference to some other place in the United Kingdom includes a reference to a place in the Isle of Man."

17. In section 74 of that Act after subsection (4) there shall be inserted—

"(5) References in this section to a place outside the United Kingdom do not include references to a place in the Isle of Man."

18. In section 78 of that Act after subsection (1) there shall be inserted—

"(1A) Subsection (1) above does not apply to a person entering the United Kingdom from the Isle of Man as respects anything obtained by him in the Island unless it is chargeable there with duty or value added tax and he has obtained it without payment of the duty or tax."

19. In section 83 (1) (*a*) of that Act after the words "between ports in the United Kingdom" there shall be inserted the words "or between a port in the United Kingdom and a port in the Isle of Man".

20. In section 90 of that Act after the word "port" there shall be inserted the words "in the United Kingdom or the Isle of Man", after the words "the United Kingdom" there shall be inserted the words "or the Isle of Man" and after the word "found" there shall be inserted the words "in the United Kingdom".

21. In section 92 (1) (*c*) and (*d*) of that Act after the words "the United Kingdom" there shall be inserted the words "or the Isle of Man".

22. In section 159 (1) (*c*) of that Act after the words "the United Kingdom" there shall be inserted the words "or the Isle of Man".

23. In paragraph 2 (*c*) of Schedule 3 to that Act after the words "the United Kingdom" there shall be inserted the words "or the Isle of Man".

24. In paragraph 4 (1) of Schedule 3 to that Act after the words "outside the United Kingdom" there shall be inserted the words "and the Isle of Man".

The Customs and Excise Duties (*General Reliefs*) *Act* 1979

25. In section 7 (*b*) of the Customs and Excise Duties (General Reliefs) Act 1979 after the words "the United Kingdom" there shall be inserted the words "or the Isle of Man".

26. In section 8 (*b*) of that Act after the words "the United Kingdom" there shall be inserted the words "or the Isle of Man".

27. In section 10 (1) of that Act after the words "manufactured or produced in the United Kingdom" there shall be inserted the words "or the Isle of Man".

28. In section 11 (1) of that Act after the words "manufactured or produced outside the United Kingdom" there shall be inserted the words "and the Isle of Man".

The Alcoholic Liquor Duties Act 1979

29. In section 22 (2) and (3) (*a*) of the Alcoholic Liquor Duties Act 1979 after the word "exportation" there shall be inserted the words "or removal to the Isle of Man".

30. In section 43 (1) of that Act after the word "exportation", in both places where it occurs, there shall be inserted the words "or removal to the Isle of Man".

31. In section 57 of that Act after the words "whether imported into or produced in the United Kingdom" there shall be inserted the words "or removed to the United Kingdom from the Isle of Man".

32. In section 58 (1) of that Act after the words "whether imported into or produced in the United Kingdom" there shall be inserted the words "or removed to the United Kingdom from the Isle of Man".

33. In section 59 (1) of that Act after the words "imported made-wine" there shall be inserted the words "nor wine or made-wine removed to the United Kingdom from the Isle of Man".

The Matches and Mechanical Lighters Duties Act 1979

34. In section 3 (1) (*d*) of the Matches and Mechanical Lighters Duties Act 1979 after the word " exportation " there shall be inserted the words ", removal to the Isle of Man ".

35. In section 7 (1) (*f*) of that Act the word " exportation ", in both places where it occurs, there shall be inserted the words ", removal to the Isle of Man ".

Section 14 (5)

SCHEDULE 2

REPEALS

Chapter	Short title	Extent of repeal
39 & 40 Vict. c. 36.	The Customs Consolidation Act 1876.	Section 283.
6 & 7 Eliz. 2. c. 11.	The Isle of Man Act 1958.	The whole Act, so far as unrepealed.
9 & 11 Eliz. 2. c. 36.	The Finance Act 1961.	Section 5 (3).
1964 c. 28.	The Agriculture and Horticulture Act 1964.	Section 1 (12).
1972 c. 41.	The Finance Act 1972.	Section 17 (2) (*e*) together with the word " and " immediately preceding it. In section 43 (3) the words " an Order in Council and ". Section 50. In Schedule 7, paragraph 28.
1979 c. 2.	The Customs and Excise Management Act 1979.	Section 174. In Schedule 4 paragraph 2 and in the Table in paragraph 12 the entry relating to the Isle of Man Act 1958.
1979 c. 3.	The Customs and Excise Duties (General Reliefs) Act 1979.	In Schedule 7, paragraph 4. Section 6. Schedule 1.
1979 c. 8.	The Excise Duties (Surcharges or Rebates) Act 1979.	Section 3 (3).

Shipbuilding Act 1979

(1979 c. 59)

An Act to raise the limits imposed by section 11 of the Aircraft and Shipbuilding Industries Act 1977 in relation to the finances of British Shipbuilders and its wholly owned subsidiaries; and to extend the application of section 10 of the Industry Act 1972 to include the alteration of completed and partially constructed ships and mobile offshore installations.

[20th December 1979]

General Note

This Act increases the financial limits of British Shipbuilders.

S. 1 increases the limits on borrowing as imposed by s. 11 (7) of the Aircraft and Shipbuilding Industries Act 1977; s. 2 authorises the Secretary of State to guarantee payment for alterations, as well as constructions which were already covered by s. 10 of the Industry Act 1972; s. 3 gives the short title and extent.

The Act received the Royal Assent on December 20, 1979, and came into force on that day.

Parliamentary debates

Hansard, H.C. Vol. 972, col. 1481; Vol. 973, col. 1408; H.L. Vol. 403, col. 581.

British Shipbuilders: limit on borrowing, etc.

1.—(1) In section 11 (7) of the Aircraft and Shipbuilding Industries Act 1977 (which imposes an overall limit, increased from £200 million to £300 million by the British Shipbuilders Borrowing Powers (Increase of Limit) Order 1979, on certain sums borrowed by British Shipbuilders and its wholly owned subsidiaries and on its public dividend capital) for " £200 million " and " £300 million " there shall be substituted respectively " £500 million " and " £600 million ".

(2) The British Shipbuilders Borrowing Powers (Increase of Limit) Order 1979 is hereby revoked.

Guarantees in respect of alterations of ships, etc.

2. In section 10 of the Industry Act 1972 (which among other things authorises the Secretary of State to guarantee the payment of certain sums payable under arrangements for financing the construction of a ship or mobile offshore installation) in subsection (9) (which provides that in that section " construction " includes the completion of a partially constructed ship or installation) after the word " installation " there shall be inserted the words " and the alteration of a ship or installation and of a partially constructed ship or installation ".

Short title and extent

3.—(1) This Act may be cited as the Shipbuilding Act 1979.

(2) This Act extends to Northern Ireland.

Zimbabwe Act 1979

(1979 c. 60)

ARRANGEMENT OF SECTIONS

General Note

This Act provides for Zimbabwe to attain a fully responsible status as a Republic.

S. 1 grants independence to Southern Rhodesia (from thence to be known as Zimbabwe) on such day as appointed by Order in Council; s. 2 deals with nationality; s. 3 gives amnesty in respect of certain acts done before the date on which the Governor of Southern Rhodesia took up office; s. 4 concerns supplementary provisions relating to independence; s. 5 sets out provisions for Zimbabwe should she wish to become a member of the Commonwealth at any time; s. 6 makes provisions as to existing laws; s. 7 contains the short title and miscellaneous provisions.

The Act received the Royal Assent on December 20, 1979, and came into force on that day.

Parliamentary debates

Hansard, H.C. Vol. 975, cols. 1328, 1415; H.L. Vol. 403, cols. 1368, 1440.

An Act to make provision for, and in connection with, the attainment by Zimbabwe of fully responsible status as a Republic. [20th December 1979]

Independence for Zimbabwe

1.—(1) On such day as Her Majesty may by Order in Council appoint (in this Act referred to as " Independence Day ") Southern Rhodesia shall become an independent Republic under the name of Zimbabwe, and the unexpired provisions of the Southern Rhodesia Act 1965 shall cease to have effect.

(2) On and after Independence Day Her Majesty's Government in the United Kingdom shall have no responsibility for the government of Zimbabwe; and no Act of the Parliament of the United Kingdom passed on or after that day shall extend, or be deemed to extend, to Zimbabwe as part of its law.

(3) An Order in Council under this section shall be laid before Parliament after being made.

Nationality

2.—(1) In section 1 (3) of the British Nationality Act 1948 (which specifies the countries whose citizens are by virtue of that citizenship British subjects) the words " Southern Rhodesia " are hereby repealed as from Independence Day; and accordingly any person who immediately before that day is a British subject by virtue only of his citizenship of Southern Rhodesia shall cease to be a British subject on that day.

(2) The transitional provisions contained in Schedule 1 shall have effect as to applications by citizens of Zimbabwe for registration as citizens of the United Kingdom and Colonies.

Amnesty in respect of certain acts

3.—(1) No criminal proceedings or proceedings in tort or for reparation shall be instituted in any court of law in any part of the United Kingdom in respect of any act to which this section applies done, whether in the United Kingdom or in Southern Rhodesia or elsewhere, before the date on which the Governor appointed by Her Majesty under the Southern Rhodesia Constitution (Interim Provisions) Order 1979 entered upon the duties of his office in the seat of government of Southern Rhodesia.

(2) The acts to which this section applies are—

(*a*) the making with respect to Southern Rhodesia of the purported declaration of independence on 11th November 1965;

(*b*) the purported making of constitutional provision for Southern Rhodesia otherwise than under the authority of the Parliament of the United Kingdom, and in particular the making of any of the instruments styling themselves respectively " the Constitution of Rhodesia 1965 ", " the Constitution of Rhodesia 1969 " and " the Constitution of Zimbabwe Rhodesia 1979 ";

(*c*) any act (including any act by way of conspiracy or incitement) preparatory or incidental to any act falling within paragraph (*a*) or (*b*);

(*d*) any act which would have been lawful if the instruments mentioned in paragraph (*b*) had been lawfully made;

(*e*) any act done on or after 11th November 1965 in the conduct or on the orders of any organisation having the purpose of resisting, frustrating or overthrowing the administration purporting to be the Government of Rhodesia or of Zimbabwe Rhodesia established under any of the instruments mentioned in paragraph (*b*), being an act done in good faith for any of those purposes;

(*f*) any act done in good faith on or after 11th November 1965 for the purpose of resisting or combating any such organisation as is mentioned in paragraph (*e*) or resisting, or securing the apprehension of, any person acting in the conduct or on the orders of any such organisation.

(3) Any criminal proceedings or proceedings in tort or for reparation in respect of any act to which this section applies which are pending in any court in the United Kingdom on the day on which this Act is passed shall be treated as discontinued on that day; and any judgment, order or decree of any court in the United Kingdom given or made before that day in any proceedings in tort or for reparation in respect of any act to which this section applies shall, so far as not enforced before that day, be unenforceable.

(4) In this section " act " includes an omission, and references to the doing of an act shall be construed accordingly.

Powers exercisable in connection with Zimbabwe's becoming independent

4.—(1) Her Majesty may by Order in Council—

(*a*) make such modifications of any enactment of the Parliament of the United Kingdom or of any instrument having effect by virtue of such an enactment as appear to Her to be necessary or expedient in consequence of section 1 or 2 (1);

(*b*) make such provision as appears to Her to be necessary or expedient for regulating the satisfaction of claims against any assets in the United Kingdom owned by, or held by any person on behalf of, the Government of Zimbabwe as the successor in title of the Government of Southern Rhodesia.

(2) An Order in Council under this section may be made at any time after the passing of this Act but, if made before Independence Day, shall not come into force before that day.

(3) Any provision made by Order in Council under this section after Independence Day may be made with retrospective effect as from Independence Day or any later date.

(4) Subject to subsection (5), any provision made by an Order in Council under this section with respect to any such enactment or instrument as is mentioned in subsection (1) (*a*) shall, except in so far as the Order otherwise provides, have effect as part of the law of every place to which the enactment or instrument in question extends.

(5) An Order in Council under this section shall not have effect as part of the law of any associated state or of any country or territory for whose government, at the date on which the Order is made, Her Majesty's Government in the United Kingdom have no responsibility.

(6) The power of modification conferred by subsection (1) (*a*) applies to enactments and instruments whenever passed or made.

(7) No recommendation shall be made to Her Majesty to make an Order in Council under this section unless a draft of the Order has been laid before Parliament and has been approved by resolution of each House of Parliament.

Provision in event of Zimbabwe becoming a member of the Commonwealth

5.—(1) If at any time Zimbabwe becomes a member of the Commonwealth, Her Majesty may by Order in Council make such modifications of any enactment of the Parliament of the United Kingdom or of any instrument having effect by virtue of such an enactment as appear to Her to be necessary or expedient in consequence of that event.

(2) Without prejudice to the generality of subsection (1), an Order in Council under this section—

(*a*) may modify subsection (3) of section 1 of the British Nationality Act 1948 (Commonwealth countries having separate citizenship) so as to add Zimbabwe to the countries mentioned in that subsection; and

(*b*) may repeal or modify any provision contained in Schedule 1 or 2 to this Act.

(3) Any provision made by Order in Council under this section after Zimbabwe becomes a member of the Commonwealth may be made with retrospective effect as from the date of that event or any later date.

(4) No recommendation shall be made to Her Majesty to make an Order in Council under this section unless a draft of the Order has been laid before Parliament and has been approved by resolution of each House of Parliament.

Other provisions as to existing laws

6.—(1) The provisions of Schedule 2 (continuation of certain provisions in relation to Zimbabwe, and savings) shall have effect.

(2) Section 26 (5) of the Prevention of Fraud (Investments) Act 1958 (construction of references to Her Majesty's dominions) shall be amended as from Independence Day by the insertion of the words " and Zimbabwe " after the words " South Africa ".

(3) The enactments and instruments mentioned in Schedule 3 are hereby repealed as from Independence Day to the extent specified in the third column of that Schedule.

Citation, etc.

7.—(1) This Act may be cited as the Zimbabwe Act 1979.

(2) An Order in Council under any provision of this Act may contain such transitional or other incidental and supplementary provisions as appear to Her Majesty to be expedient.

(3) In this Act " modifications " includes additions, omissions and alterations, and related expressions shall be construed accordingly.

SCHEDULES

Section 2

SCHEDULE 1

Transitional Provisions as to Applications for Registration as a Citizen of the United Kingdom and Colonies

1. A person whose application for registration as a citizen of the United Kingdom and Colonies was received but not determined before Independence Day shall be treated for the purposes of his application as if Zimbabwe were a country mentioned in section 1 (3) of the 1948 Act.

2. A person whose application for registration as a citizen of the United Kingdom and Colonies is received on or after Independence Day shall be treated for the purposes of his application as if Zimbabwe were a country mentioned in section 1 (3) of the 1948 Act if the application is made under section 5A (1) of the 1948 Act or section 6 (1) thereof as modified by Schedule 1 to the Immigration Act 1971, and is received before the first anniversary of Independence Day or such later date as the Secretary of State may in the special circumstances of any particular case allow.

3. Notwithstanding the provision in paragraph (*a*) of section 3 (1) of the Britith Nationality Act 1958 that (subject to limited exceptions) no person shall be registered as a citizen of the United Kingdom and Colonies under section 12 (6) of the 1948 Act (as amended by the said section 3 (1)) on an application made after the end of the year 1962, a citizen of Zimbabwe (and any of his minor children) may be so registered—

(*a*) on an application made on or after 18th November 1965 which was received but not determined before Independence Day; or

(*b*) on an application received before the first anniversary of Independence Day or such later date as the Secretary of State may in the special circumstances of any particular case allow.

4. In this Schedule "the 1948 Act" means the British Nationality Act 1948.

Section 6 (1)

SCHEDULE 2

Continuation of certain provisions in relation to Zimbabwe, and Savings

Temporary saving from certain disabilities

1.—(1) Until the end of the period of twelve months beginning with Independence Day, a citizen of Zimbabwe shall not be subject, in respect of any office, place, or employment held by him immediately before that day, or any qualification to act in any capacity in which he was acting immediately before that day, to any disability imposed in the case of aliens by or by virtue of any of the following enactments, that is to say—

(*a*) section 3 of the Act of Settlement;

(*b*) sections 4 to 6 of the Aliens Restriction (Amendment) Act 1919;

(*c*) any Northern Ireland legislation, or any regulations in force under any such legislation.

(2) For the purposes of sub-paragraph (1) a person who immediately before Independence Day was on leave or otherwise temporarily absent from employment in any capacity mentioned in section 5 (1) of the Aliens Restriction (Amendment) Act 1919 (master etc. of British merchant ship) shall be treated as if he were employed in such employment immediately before that day; and where sub-paragraph (1) applies to any person in respect of any office, place or employment held by him immediately before that day, it shall apply to him also in respect of any office, place or employment to or in which he may be appointed thereafter by way of re-engagement or transfer.

(3) If, at the end of the period of twelve months mentioned in sub-paragraph (1), a person to whom that sub-paragraph applies is awaiting determination of an application by him for registration as a citizen of the United Kingdom and Colonies, that sub-paragraph shall apply as if for the period of twelve months there mentioned there were substituted a period ending on the determination of his application.

(4) A person who by virtue of section 2 (1) ceases to be a British subject shall not for that reason be precluded from remaining a member of a local authority until his membership ceases on some other ground.

Colonial probates

2.—(1) The Colonial Probates Act 1892 (which provides for the recognition in the United Kingdom of probates and letters of administration granted in British possessions) shall apply in relation to Zimbabwe as it applies in relation to a British possession, and any Order in Council in force under that Act in relation to Southern Rhodesia immediately before Independence Day shall have effect on and after that day as if any reference to Southern Rhodesia were a reference to Zimbabwe.

(2) Nothing in sub-paragraph (1) shall affect the operation of the said Act of 1892 with respect to probate or letters of administration granted before Independence Day by a court in Southern Rhodesia.

Maintenance orders

3.—(1) The Maintenance Orders (Facilities for Enforcement) Act 1920 (which provides for the enforcement in England, Wales and Northern Ireland of maintenance orders made in parts of Her Majesty's dominions outside the United Kingdom, and vice versa) shall apply in relation to Zimbabwe as it applies in relation to a part of Her Majesty's dominions, and any Order in Council in force under that Act in relation to Southern Rhodesia immediately before Independence Day shall have effect on and after that day as if any reference to Southern Rhodesia were a reference to Zimbabwe.

(2) For the purposes of the application of the said Act of 1920 in accordance with sub-paragraph (1), references in that Act to the governor of a part of Her Majesty's dominions shall, in the case of Zimbabwe, be construed as references to the Minister of Justice.

(3) Nothing in sub-paragraph (1) or (2) shall affect the operation of the said Act of 1920 with respect to any maintenance order made before Independence Day by a court in Southern Rhodesia.

(4) An order under section 49 (2) of the Maintenance Orders (Reciprocal Enforcement) Act 1972 appointing a day for the coming into operation of the repeal by that Act of the Maintenance Orders (Facilities for Enforcement) Act 1920 may include provision, to take effect on that day, for the repeal of the preceding provisions of this paragraph.

Company registers

4. The following provisions, namely—

(*a*) sections 119 to 122 of the Companies Act 1948 and sections 116 to 118 of the Companies Act (Northern Ireland) 1960 (which enable a company registered in Great Britain, or in Northern Ireland, to keep in any other part of Her Majesty's dominions a branch register of its members resident there); and

(*b*) section 123 of the said Act of 1948 (which enables a company registered in another part of Her Majesty's dominions to keep in Great Britain a branch register of its members resident there),

shall apply in relation to Zimbabwe as they apply in relation to a part of Her Majesty's dominions.

Parliamentary and local elections

5.—(1) Where a person by virtue of section 2 (1) ceases to be a British subject—

(*a*) if immediately before Independence Day he was registered in a register of parliamentary electors or local government electors, he shall be treated as remaining a British subject for the purposes of any election at which that register is used;

(*b*) if—

(i) on the qualifying date for a parliamentary or local government election held within the period of twelve months beginning with 16th February in a year to which this paragraph applies he is awaiting determination of an application received before the first anniversary of Independence Day for his registration as a citizen of the United Kingdom and Colonies, and

(ii) where the application was made under section 5A of the British Nationality Act 1948 or section 6 (1) thereof as modified by Schedule 1 to the Immigration Act 1971, he was throughout the relevant period ending with that qualifying date ordinarily resident in the United Kingdom,

he shall be treated as a British subject for the purposes of any election at which a register of parliamentary electors or local government electors published in that year is used.

(2) For the purposes of sub-paragraph (1) (*b*) (ii) " the relevant period " ending as there mentioned—

(*a*) in the case of an application under section 5A of the British Nationality Act 1948, is the period of five years so ending;

(*b*) in the case of an application under section 6 (1) of that Act, is the period beginning with 1st January 1973 and ending as aforesaid.

(3) Paragraph (*b*) of sub-paragraph (1) applies to the year 1980 and any subsequent year, not being later than such year as the Secretary of State may specify in an order (made by statutory instrument subject to annulment in pursuance of a resolution of either House of Parliament) as the final year to which that paragraph is to apply.

(4) The Representation of the People Regulations 1974, the Representation of the People (Northern Ireland) Regulations 1969, the Representation of the People (Scotland) Regulations 1975 and Schedule 3 to the Electoral Law Act (Northern Ireland) 1962 shall each have effect as if the requirements that may be made under regulation 24 (1), regulation 10 (1), regulation 24 (1) and Rule 8 (2) respectively included a requirement that a person who asserts that he is entitled to be registered by virtue of sub-paragraph (1) should make a statutory declaration as to any fact relevant in establishing that entitlement.

Dentists and veterinary surgeons

6. A person who on Independence Day is registered by virtue of a qualification granted in Southern Rhodesia—

(*a*) in the Commonwealth list contained in the dentists register kept under the Dentists Act 1957, or

(*b*) in the Commonwealth list contained in the veterinary surgeons register kept under the Veterinary Surgeons Act 1966,

shall not cease to be so registered by reason of anything contained in this Act or of any decision as to Zimbabwe's membership of the Commonwealth.

Right of abode in the United Kingdom

7.—(1) Until the end of the period of twelve months beginning with Independence Day—

(*a*) subsection (1) (*d*) of section 2 of the Immigration Act 1971 (right of abode) shall have effect in the case of a person who—

(i) is a citizen of Zimbabwe, and

(ii) was immediately before that day a citizen of Southern Rhodesia,

as if he had remained a Commonwealth citizen; and

(*b*) subsection (2) of that section sshall have effect accordingly.

(2) Section 36 of the said Act of 1971 (power to extend provisions to Channel Islands and Isle of Man) shall apply to the provisions of this paragraph as it applies to provisions of that Act.

Liability to deportation

8.—(1) Until the end of the period of twelve months beginning with Independence Day section 7 of the Immigration Act 1971 (which provides that certain Commonwealth citizens ordinarily resident in the United Kingdom are not liable to deportation) shall continue to apply to a person who by virtue of section 2 (1) of this Act ceases to be a Commonwealth citizen on that day.

(2) If when that period expires such a person is awaiting the determination of an application made by him for registration as a citizen of the United Kingdom and Colonies, the said section 7 shall continue to apply to him until that application is determined, subject to sub-paragraph (3).

(3) In the further period provided for by sub-paragraph (2) a recommendation for deportation under section 3 (6) of the said Act of 1971 (recommendation by

court convicting of offence punishable with imprisonment) may be made in respect of a person to whom that sub-paragraph applies, but no effect shall be given to such a recommendation unless and until that person's application for registration as a citizen of the United Kingdom and Colonies is refused.

(4) Section 36 of the said Act of 1971 (power to extend provisions to Channel Islands and Isle of Man) shall apply to the provisions of this paragraph as it applies to provisions of that Act.

Section 6 (3)

SCHEDULE 3

Repeals

Acts

Chapter	Short title	Extent of repeal
15 & 16 Geo. 5. c. xvii.	Imperial Institute Act 1925.	In Schedule 2, in paragraph (1) (*b*), the words " one by the Government of Southern Rhodesia ".
16 & 17 Geo. 5. c. 40.	Indian and Colonial Divorce Jurisdiction Act 1926.	In section 2 (2), the words " the Colony of Southern Rhodesia ".
18 & 19 Geo. 5. c. 35.	Easter Act 1928.	In the Schedule, in Part I, the words " Southern Rhodesia ".
9 & 10 Geo. 6. c. 45.	United Nations Act 1946.	In section 1 (2), the words " Southern Rhodesia ".
12, 13 & 14 Geo. 6. c. 67.	Civil Aviation Act 1949.	Section 66 (2).
9 & 10 Eliz. 2. c. 11.	Diplomatic Immunities (Conferences with Commonwealth Countries and Republic of Ireland) Act 1961.	In section 1 (5), the words " Southern Rhodesia ".
10 & 11 Eliz. 2. c. 2.	Southern Rhodesia (Constitution) Act 1961.	The whole Act.
1964 c. 81.	Diplomatic Privileges Act 1964.	Section 8 (2).
1965 c. 76.	Southern Rhodesia Act 1965.	The whole Act.
1973 c. 45.	Domicile and Matrimonial Proceedings Act 1973.	Section 17 (3).
1978 c. 2.	Commonwealth Development Corporation Act 1978.	In section 17 (1), in the definition of " dependent territory ", the words " excluding Southern Rhodesia ".
1978 c. 33.	State Immunity Act 1978.	In section 4 (5), the words " or a citizen of Southern Rhodesia ".
1979 c. 52.	Southern Rhodesia Act 1979.	Section 3 (4) and (5).

Instruments

Number	Title	Extent of repeal
S.I. 1964/2043.	Diplomatic Privileges (Citizens of the United Kingdom and Colonies) Order 1964.	In Article 2 (2), the words " to Southern Rhodesia ".
S.I. 1965/1125.	Judicial Committee (Southern Rhodesia) Order 1965.	The whole Order.
S.I. 1965/1952.	Southern Rhodesia Constitution Order 1965.	The whole Order.
S.I. 1965/1957.	Southern Rhodesia (British Nationality Act 1948) Order 1965.	The whole Order.

SCHEDULE 3—*continued*

Number	Title	Extent of repeal
S.I. 1970/892.	Southern Rhodesia (Higher Authority for Power) Order 1970.	The whole Order.
S.I. 1970/1540.	Southern Rhodesia (Matrimonial Jurisdiction) Order 1970.	The whole Order.
S.I. 1970/1903.	Consular Relations (Merchant Shipping) (Republic of Austria) Order 1970.	In Article 4 (*a*) (i), the words " a citizen of Southern Rhodesia ".
S.I. 1970/1904.	Consular Relations (Merchant Shipping) (Kingdom of Belgium) Order 1970.	In Article 4 (*a*) (i), the words " a citizen of Southern Rhodesia ".
S.I. 1970/1905.	Consular Relations (Merchant Shipping) (Kingdom of Denmark) Order 1970.	In Article 4 (*a*) (i), the words " a citizen of Southern Rhodesia ".
S.I. 1970/1907.	Consular Relations (Merchant Shipping) (Federal Republic of Germany) Order 1970.	In Article 4 (*a*) (i), the words " a citizen of Southern Rhodesia ".
S.I. 1970/1909.	Consular Relations (Merchant Shipping) (Italian Republic) Order 1970.	In Article 4 (*a*) (i), the words " a citizen of Southern Rhodesia ".
S.I. 1970/1910.	Consular Relations (Merchant Shipping) (Japan) Order 1970.	In Article 4 (*a*) (i), the words " a citizen of Southern Rhodesia ".
S.I. 1970/1911.	Consular Relations (Merchant Shipping) (United States of Mexico) Order 1970.	In Article 3 (*a*), the words " a citizen of Southern Rhodesia ".
S.I. 1970/1913.	Consular Relations (Merchant Shipping) (Spanish State) Order 1970.	In Article 4 (*a*) (i), the words " a citizen of Southern Rhodesia ".
S.I. 1970/1917.	Consular Relations (Merchant Shipping) (Socialist Federal Republic of Yugoslavia) Order 1970.	In Article 4 (*a*) (i), the words " a citizen of Southern Rhodesia ".
S.I. 1972/1718.	Southern Rhodesia (Marriages, Matrimonial Causes and Adoptions) Order 1972.	The whole Order.
S.I. 1979/1374.	Southern Rhodesia (Immunity for Persons attending Meetings and Consultations) (No. 2) Order 1979.	The whole Order.

INDEX

References, e.g. 2/56, are to the Statutes of 1979, Chapter 2, section 56.